North Carolina State Building Code:

Residential Code

(2009 IRC®, IMC®, IFGC®, IPC® and 2011 NEC with North Carolina Amendments)

2012

2012 North Carolina Residential Code

First Printing: March 2012
Second Printing: July 2012

ISBN-978-1-60983-117-2

T022022

PRINTED IN THE U.S.A.

NORTH CAROLINA STATE BUILDING CODE COUNCIL
MARCH 1, 2012
www.ncbuildingcodes.com

NORTH CAROLINA
DEPARTMENT OF INSURANCE

www.ncdoi.com/osfm
919-661-5880

By Statute, the Commissioner of Insurance has general supervision of the administration and enforcement of the North Carolina State Building Code, and the Engineering Division serves as the Staff for the Building Code Council. Officials of the Department of Insurance are:

WAYNE GOODWIN
Commissioner

TIM BRADLEY
Senior Deputy Commissioner

CHRIS NOLES, PE
Deputy Commissioner

BARRY GUPTON, PE
Chief Code Consultant

DAVID CONNER, PE
Residential Code Consultant

COMMITTEES OF THE COUNCIL
MARCH 1, 2012

ADMINISTRATION
Dan Tingen – Chair
Al Bass, PE
Ralph Euchner
John Hitch, AIA
Steve Knight, PE
Lon McSwain
Alan Perdue
Kim Reitterer, PE
David Smith

BUILDING
Lon McSwain – Chair
Cindy Browning, PE
Leah Faile, AIA
John Hitch, AIA
Ed Moore, Sr.
Alan Perdue
Bob Ruffner, Jr.
Paula Strickland

ELECTRICAL
Kim Reitterer, PE – Chair
Al Bass, PE
Cindy Browning, PE
Leah Faile, AIA
John Hitch, AIA
Ed Moore, Sr.
Bob Ruffner, Jr.

ENERGY
Ralph Euchner – Chair
Al Bass, PE
Leah Faile, AIA
Mack Nixon
Mack Paul
Kim Reitterer, PE
Bob Ruffner, Jr.
David Smith
Scott Stevens

FIRE PREVENTION
Alan Perdue – Chair
Ralph Euchner
John Hitch, AIA
Mack Nixon
Mack Paul
Bob Ruffner, Jr.
Scott Stevens

MECHANICAL
Al Bass, PE – Chair
Ralph Euchner
Ed Moore, Sr.
David Smith
Paula Strickland

RESIDENTIAL
David Smith – Chair
Cindy Browning, PE
Ralph Euchner
Steve Knight, PE
Lon McSwain
Mack Nixon
Scott Stevens
Paula Strickland

STRUCTURAL
Steve Knight, PE – Chair
Al Bass, PE
Leah Faile, AIA
John Hitch, AIA
Bob Ruffner, Jr.
Scott Stevens

PREFACE

Introduction

Internationally, code officials recognize the need for a modern, up-to-date residential code addressing the design and construction of one- and two-family dwellings and townhouses. The *International Residential Code®*, in this 2009 edition, is designed to meet these needs through model code regulations that safeguard the public health and safety in all communities, large and small.

This comprehensive, stand-alone residential code establishes minimum regulations for one- and two-family dwellings and townhouses using prescriptive provisions. It is founded on broad-based principles that make possible the use of new materials and new building designs. This 2009 edition is fully compatible with all the *International Codes®* (I-Codes®) published by the International Code Council® (ICC)®, including the *International Building Code®, International Energy Conservation Code®, International Existing Building Code®, International Fire Code®, International Fuel Gas Code®, International Mechanical Code®,* ICC *Performance Code®, International Plumbing Code®, International Private Sewage Disposal Code®, International Property Maintenance Code®, International Wildland-Urban Interface Code™* and *International Zoning Code®.*

The *International Residential Code* provisions provide many benefits, among which is the model code development process that offers an international forum for residential construction professionals to discuss prescriptive code requirements. This forum provides an excellent arena to debate proposed revisions. This model code also encourages international consistency in the application of provisions.

Development

The first edition of the *International Residential Code* (2000) was the culmination of an effort initiated in 1996 by ICC and consisting of representatives from the three statutory members of the International Code Council at the time, including: Building Officials and Code Administrators International, Inc. (BOCA), International Conference of Building Officials (ICBO) and Southern Building Code Congress International (SBCCI), and representatives from the National Association of Home Builders (NAHB). The intent was to draft a stand-alone residential code consistent with and inclusive of the scope of the existing model codes. Technical content of the 1998 *International One- and Two-Family Dwelling Code* and the latest model codes promulgated by BOCA, ICBO, SBCCI and ICC was used as the basis for the development, followed by public hearings in 1998 and 1999 to consider proposed changes. This 2009 edition represents the code as originally issued, with changes reflected in the 2006 edition, and further changes developed through the ICC Code Development Process through 2008. Residential electrical provisions are based on the 2008 *National Electrical Code®* (NFPA 70). A new edition such as this is promulgated every three years.

Fuel gas provisions have been included through an agreement with the American Gas Association (AGA). Electrical provisions have been included through an agreement with the National Fire Protection Association (NFPA).

This code is founded on principles intended to establish provisions consistent with the scope of a residential code that adequately protects public health, safety and welfare; provisions that do not unnecessarily increase construction costs; provisions that do not restrict the use of new materials, products or methods of construction; and provisions that do not give preferential treatment to particular types or classes of materials, products or methods of construction.

Adoption

The *International Residential Code* is available for adoption and use by jurisdictions internationally. Its use within a governmental jurisdiction is intended to be accomplished through adoption by reference in accordance with proceedings establishing the jurisdiction's laws. At the time of adoption, jurisdictions should insert the appropriate information in provisions requiring specific local information, such as the name of the adopting jurisdiction. These locations are shown in bracketed words in small capital letters in the code and in the sample ordinance. The sample adoption ordinance on page xiii addresses several key elements of a code adoption ordinance, including the information required for insertion into the code text.

Maintenance

The *International Residential Code* is kept up-to-date through the review of proposed changes submitted by code enforcing officials, industry representatives, design professionals and other interested parties. Proposed changes are carefully considered through an open code development process in which all interested and affected parties may participate.

The contents of this work are subject to change both through the Code Development Cycles and the governmental body that enacts the code into law. For more information regarding the code development process, contact the Code and Standard Development Department of the International Code Council.

The maintenance process for the fuel gas provisions is based upon the process used to maintain the *International Fuel Gas Code*, in conjunction with the American Gas Association. The maintenance process for the electrical provisions is undertaken by the National Fire Protection Association.

While the development procedure of the *International Residential Code* assures the highest degree of care, ICC, the founding members of ICC, its members and those participating in the development of this code do not accept any liability resulting from compliance or noncompliance with the provisions because ICC and its founding members do not have the power or authority to police or enforce compliance with the contents of this code. Only the governmental body that enacts the code into law has such authority.

Marginal and Text Markings

Solid vertical lines in the margins within the body of the code indicate a technical change from the requirements of the 2006 edition of the *International Building Code*. Deletion indicators in the form of an arrow (➡) are provided in the margin where an entire section, paragraph, exception or table has been deleted or an item in a list of items or a table has been deleted. Underlining within the body of the code indicate a technical change to the 2012 *North Carolina Building Code* from the requirements of the 2009 edition of the *International Building Code*.

Italicized Terms

Selected terms set forth in Chapter 2, Definitions, are italicized where they appear in code text. Such terms are not italicized where the definition set forth in Chapter 2 does not impart the intended meaning in the use of the term. The terms selected have definitions which the user should read carefully to facilitate better understanding of the code.

Effective Use of the International Residential Code

The *International Residential Code®* (IRC®) was created to serve as a complete, comprehensive code regulating the construction of single-family houses, two-family houses (duplexes) and buildings consisting of three or more townhouse units. All buildings within the scope of the IRC are limited to three stories above grade plane. For example, a four-story single-family house would fall within the scope of the *International Building Code®* (IBC®), not the IRC. The benefits of devoting a separate code to residential construction include the fact that the user need not navigate through a multitude of code provisions that do not apply to residential construction in order to locate that which is applicable. A separate code also allows for residential and nonresidential code provisions to be distinct and tailored to the structures that fall within the appropriate code's scopes.

The IRC contains coverage for all components of a house or townhouse, including structural components, fireplaces and chimneys, thermal insulation, mechanical systems, fuel gas systems, plumbing systems and electrical systems.

The IRC is a prescriptive-oriented (specification) code with some examples of performance code language. It has been said that the IRC is the complete cookbook for residential construction. Section R301.1, for example, is written in performance language, but states that the prescriptive requirements of the code will achieve such performance.

It is important to understand that the IRC contains coverage for what is conventional and common in residential construction practice. While the IRC will provide all of the needed coverage for most residential construction, it might not address construction practices and systems that are atypical or rarely encountered in the industry. Sections such as R301.1.3, R301.2.2, R320.1, R322.1, N1101.2, M1301.1, G2401.1, P2601.1 and E3401.2 refer to other codes either as an alternative to the provisions of the IRC or where the IRC lacks coverage for a particular type of structure, design, system, appliance or method of construction. In other words, the IRC is meant to be all inclusive for typical residential construction and it relies on other codes only where alternatives are desired or where the code lacks coverage for the uncommon aspect of residential construction. Of course, the IRC constantly evolves to address new technologies and construction practices that were once uncommon, but now common.

The IRC is unique in that much of it, including Chapters 3 through 9 and Chapters 34 through 43, is presented in an ordered format that is consistent with the normal progression of construction, starting with the design phase and continuing through the final trim-out phase. This is consistent with the "cookbook" philosophy of the IRC.

The IRC is divided into eight main parts, specifically, Part I—Administration, Part II—Definitions, Part III—Building Planning and Construction, Part IV—Energy Conservation, Part V—Mechanical, Part VI—Fuel Gas, Part VII—Plumbing and Part VIII—Electrical.

The following provides a brief description of the content of each chapter and appendix of the IRC:

Chapter 1 Scope and Administration. This chapter contains provisions for the application, enforcement and administration of subsequent requirements of the code. In addition to establishing the scope of the code, Chapter 1 identifies which buildings and structures come under its purview. Chapter 1 is largely concerned with maintaining "due process of law" in enforcing the building criteria contained in the body of the code. Only through careful observation of the administrative provisions can the building official reasonably expect to demonstrate that "equal protection under the law" has been provided.

Chapter 2 Definitions. Terms defined in the code are listed alphabetically in Chapter 2. It is important to note that two chapters have their own definitions sections: Chapter 24 for the defined terms that are unique to fuel gas and Chapter 35 containing terms that are applicable to electrical Chapters 34 through 43. In the case where Chapter 2 and another chapter both define the same term differently, the definition found in Chapter 24 and/or 35 is intended to prevail where the term is used in Chapter 24 and/or 35 and the definition contained in Chapter 2 is intended to prevail where the term is used in all other locations in the code. Except where Chapter 24 or 35 has a definition that will prevail therein, the definitions in Chapter 2 are applicable throughout the code.

Additional definitions regarding skylights that are not listed in Chapter 2 are found in Section R308.6.1.

Where understanding a term's definition is key to or necessary for understanding a particular code provision, the term is shown in italics where it appears in the code. This is true only for those terms that have a meaning that is unique to the code. In other words, the generally understood meaning of a term or phrase might not be sufficient or consistent with the meaning prescribed by the code; therefore, it is essential that the code-defined meaning be known.

Guidance regarding not only tense, gender and plurality of defined terms, but also terms not defined in this code, is provided.

Chapter 3 Building Planning. Chapter 3 provides guidelines for a minimum level of structural integrity, life safety, fire safety and livability for inhabitants of dwelling units regulated by this code. Chapter 3 is a compilation of the code requirements specific to the building planning sector of the design and construction process. This chapter sets forth code requirements dealing with light, ventilation, sanitation, minimum room size, ceiling height and environmental comfort. Chapter 3 establishes life-safety provisions including limitations on glazing used in hazardous areas, specifications on stairways, use of guards at elevated surfaces and rules for means of egress. Snow, wind and seismic design and flood-resistant construction, as well as live and dead loads, are addressed in this chapter.

Chapter 4 Foundations. Chapter 4 provides the requirements for the design and construction of foundation systems for buildings regulated by this code. Provisions for seismic load, flood load and frost protection are contained in this chapter. A foundation system consists of two interdependent components: the foundation structure itself and the supporting soil.

The prescriptive provisions of this chapter provide requirements for constructing footings and walls for foundations of wood, masonry, concrete and precast concrete. In addition to a foundation's ability to support the required design loads, this chapter addresses several other factors that can affect foundation performance. These include controlling surface water and subsurface drainage, requiring soil tests where conditions warrant and evaluating proximity to slopes and minimum depth requirements. The chapter also provides requirements to minimize adverse effects of moisture, decay and pests in basements and crawl spaces.

Chapter 5 Floors. Chapter 5 provides the requirements for the design and construction of floor systems that will be capable of supporting minimum required design loads. This chapter covers four different types: wood floor framing, wood floors on the ground, cold-formed steel floor framing and concrete slabs on the ground. Allowable span tables are provided that greatly simplify the determination of joist, girder and sheathing sizes for raised floor systems of wood framing and cold-formed steel framing. This chapter also contains prescriptive requirements for attaching a deck to the main building.

Chapter 6 Wall Construction. Chapter 6 contains provisions that regulate the design and construction of walls. The wall construction covered in Chapter 6 consists of five different types: wood framed, cold-formed steel framed, masonry, concrete and structural insulated panel (SIP). The primary concern of this chapter is the structural integrity of wall construction and transfer of all imposed loads to the supporting structure. This chapter provides the requirements for the design and construction of wall systems that are capable of supporting the minimum design vertical loads (dead, live and snow loads) and lateral loads (wind or seismic loads). This chapter contains the prescriptive requirements for wall bracing and/or shear walls to resist the imposed lateral loads due to wind and seismic. Chapter 6 also contains requirements for the use of vapor retarders for moisture control in walls.

Chapter 6 also regulates exterior windows and doors installed in walls. The chapter contains criteria for the performance of exterior windows and doors and includes provisions for window sill height, testing and labeling, vehicular access doors, wind-borne debris protection and anchorage details.

Chapter 7 Wall Covering. Chapter 7 contains provisions for the design and construction of interior and exterior wall coverings. This chapter establishes the various types of materials, materials standards and methods of application permitted for use as interior coverings, including interior plaster, gypsum board, ceramic tile, wood veneer paneling, hardboard paneling, wood shakes and wood shingles.

Exterior wall coverings provide the weather-resistant exterior envelope that protects the building's interior from the elements. Chapter 7 provides the requirements for wind resistance and water-resistive barrier for exterior wall coverings. This chapter prescribes the exterior wall coverings as well as the water-resistive barrier required beneath the exterior materials. Exterior wall coverings regulated by this section include aluminum, stone and masonry veneer, wood, hardboard, particleboard, wood structural panel siding, wood shakes and shingles, exterior plaster, steel, vinyl, fiber cement and exterior insulation finish systems.

Chapter 8 Roof-ceiling Construction. Chapter 8 regulates the design and construction of roof-ceiling systems. This chapter contains two roof-ceiling framing systems: wood framing and cold-formed steel framing. Allowable span tables are provided to simplify the selection of rafter and ceiling joist size for wood roof framing and cold-formed steel framing. Chapter 8 also provides requirements for the application of ceiling finishes, the proper ventilation of concealed spaces in roofs (e.g., enclosed attics and rafter spaces), unvented attic assemblies and attic access.

Chapter 9 Roof Assemblies. Chapter 9 regulates the design and construction of roof assemblies. A roof assembly includes the roof deck, vapor retarder, substrate or thermal barrier, insulation, vapor retarder and roof covering. This chapter provides the requirement for wind resistance of roof coverings.

The types of roof covering materials and installation regulated by Chapter 9 are: asphalt shingles, clay and concrete tile, metal roof shingles, mineral-surfaced roll roofing, slate and slate-type shingles, wood shakes and shingles, built-up roofs, metal roof panels, modified bitumen roofing, thermoset and thermoplastic single-ply roofing, sprayed polyurethane foam roofing and liquid applied coatings. Chapter 9 also provides requirements for roof drainage, flashing, above deck thermal insulation and recovering or replacing an existing roof covering.

Chapter 10 Chimneys and Fireplaces. Chapter 10 contains requirements for the safe construction of masonry chimneys and fireplaces and establishes the standards for the use and installation of factory-built chimneys, fireplaces and masonry heaters. Chimneys and fireplaces constructed of masonry rely on prescriptive requirements for the details of their construction; the factory-built type relies on the listing and labeling method of approval. Chapter 10 provides the requirements for seismic reinforcing and anchorage of masonry fireplaces and chimneys.

Chapter 11 Energy Efficiency. Chapter 11 contains the energy-efficiency-related requirements for the design and construction of buildings regulated under this code. The applicable portions of the building must comply with the provisions within this chapter for energy efficiency. This chapter defines requirements for the portions of the building and building systems that impact energy use in new construction and promotes the effective use of energy. The provisions within the chapter promote energy efficiency in the building envelope, the heating and cooling system, the service water heating system and the lighting system of the building. This chapter also provides energy efficiency requirements for snow melt systems and pool heaters.

Chapters 12 through 23 Mechanical. Refer to the North Carolina Mechanical Code for a brief description of the content of each chapter and appendix.

Chapter 24 Fuel Gas. Refer to the North Carolina Fuel Gas Code for a brief description of the content of each chapter and appendix.

Chapters 25 through 33 Plumbing. Refer to the North Carolina Plumbing Code for a brief description of the content of each chapter and appendix.

Chapters 34 through 43 Electrical. Refer to the North Carolina Electrical Code for a brief description of the content of each chapter and appendix.

Chapter 44 Referenced Standards. The code contains numerous references to standards that are used to regulate materials and methods of construction. Chapter 44 contains a comprehensive list of all standards that are referenced in the code. The standards are part of the code to the extent of the reference to the standard. Compliance with the referenced standard is necessary for compliance with this code. By providing specifically adopted standards, the construction and installation requirements necessary for compliance with the code can be readily determined. The basis for code compliance is, therefore, established and available on an equal basis to the code official, contractor, designer and owner.

Chapter 44 is organized in a manner that makes it easy to locate specific standards. It lists all of the referenced standards, alphabetically, by acronym of the promulgating agency of the standard. Each agency's standards are then listed in either alphabetical or numeric order based upon the standard identification. The list also contains the title of the standard; the edition (date) of the standard referenced; any addenda included as part of the ICC adoption; and the section or sections of this code that reference the standard.

Chapter 45. High Wind Zones. This chapter applies to buildings constructed in North Carolina high wind zones. These provisions shall be in addition to or in lieu of the requirements of Chapters 1–8.

Chapter 46. Coastal and Flood Plains Standards. The requirements of this chapter apply to all construction located within areas identified by governmental agency (state and federal) as coastal high hazard area, ocean hazard areas, the regulatory flood plain areas, and all areas designated as 130 miles per hour (57 m/s) wind zone.

Residential Ad Hoc Committee Acknowledgements

David W. Conner, Sr, PE
NC Department of Insurance
1202 Mail Service Center
Raleigh, NC 27699-1202

Jeff Griffin
Mecklenburg County Government
700 North Tryon Street
Charlotte, NC 28202

Steve L. Knight, PE
Structural Engineer
1507 Mt. Vernon Ave
Statesville, NC 28677

Jim Lane
City of Raleigh Inspections Department
P.O. Box 590
Raleigh, NC 27602

Mike Page
NC Department of Insurance
1202 Mail Service Center
Raleigh, NC 27699-1202

Robert Privott
NC Home Builders Association
P.O. Box 99090
Raleigh, NC 27624

Leon Skinner
City of Raleigh Inspections Department
P.O. Box 590
Raleigh, NC 27602

David Smith, Committee Chair
D. Smith, Builder
905 Saltwood Lane
Wilmington, NC 28411

Dan Tingen, President
Tingen Construction Company, Inc.
8411-101 Garvey Drive
Raleigh, NC 27616

Hawley Truax
Z. Smith Reynolds Foundation
147 South Cherry St., #200
Winston-Salem, NC 27101-5287

Thomas P. Turner, FAIA Architect
ADEP, PA
3225 Wickersham Road
Charlotte, NC 28211

Hiram Williams
Action Construction Company
P.O. Box 4270, 51 J.H. Batts Road
Surf City, NC 28445

TABLE OF CONTENTS

Part I—Administrative

CHAPTER 1
SCOPE AND ADMINISTRATION

PART I—SCOPE AND APPLICATION

SECTION R101 GENERAL

R101.1 Title. These provisions shall be known as the North Carolina *Residential Code for One- and Two-family Dwellings* and shall be cited as such and will be referred to herein as "this code." These regulations were adopted by the North Carolina Building Code Council on December 14, 2010, to be effective January 1, 2012. References to the *International Codes* shall mean the North Carolina Codes. The North Carolina amendments to the *International Codes* are underlined.

R101.2 Scope. The provisions of the North Carolina *Residential Code for One- and Two-family Dwellings* shall apply to the construction, *alteration*, movement, enlargement, replacement, repair, equipment, use and occupancy, location, removal and demolition of detached one- and two-family dwellings and townhouses not more than three stories above *grade plane* in height with a separate means of egress and their *accessory* buildings and *structures*.

> **Exception:** Live/work units complying with the requirements of Section 419 of the North Carolina *Building Code* shall be permitted to be built as one- and two-family *dwellings* or townhouses. Fire suppression required by Section 419.5 of the North Carolina *Building Code* when constructed under the North Carolina *Residential Code for One- and Two-family Dwellings* shall conform to Section 903.3.1.3 of the *International Building Code*.

Accessory buildings with any dimension greater than 12 feet must meet the provisions of this code. Accessory buildings may be constructed without a masonry or concrete foundation, except in coastal high hazard or ocean hazard areas, provided all of the following conditions are met:

1. The building shall not exceed 400 sq. ft. or one story in height;
2. The building is supported on a wood foundation of a minimum 2x6 or 3x4 mud sill of approved wood in accordance with Section R317; and
3. The building is anchored to resist overturning and sliding by installing a minimum of one ground anchor at each corner of the building. The total resisting force of the anchors shall be equal to 20 psf times the plan area of the building.

Accessory structures except decks, gazebos, and retaining walls as required by Section R404.4, are not required to meet the provisions of this code. For swimming pools and spas, see Appendix G.

R101.3 Purpose. The purpose of this code is to establish minimum requirements to safeguard the public safety, health and general welfare through affordability, structural strength, means of egress facilities, stability, sanitation, light and ventilation, energy conservation and safety to life and property from fire and other hazards attributed to the built environment.

SECTION R102 APPLICABILITY

R102.1 General. Where there is a conflict between a general requirement and a specific requirement, the specific requirement shall be applicable. Where, in any specific case, different sections of this code specify different materials, methods of construction or other requirements, the most restrictive shall govern.

R102.2 Other laws. The provisions of this code shall not be deemed to nullify any provisions of local, state or federal law.

R102.3 Application of references. References to chapter or section numbers, or to provisions not specifically identified by number, shall be construed to refer to such chapter, section or provision of this code.

R102.4 Referenced codes and standards. The codes and standards referenced in this code shall be considered part of the requirements of this code to the prescribed extent of each such reference. Where differences occur between provisions of this code and referenced codes and standards, the provisions of this code shall apply.

> **Exception:** Where enforcement of a code provision would violate the conditions of the *listing* of the *equipment* or *appliance*, the conditions of the *listing* and manufacturer's instructions shall apply.

R102.5 Appendices. Provisions in the appendices shall not apply unless specifically referenced in the code text.

R102.6 Partial invalidity. In the event any part or provision of this code is held to be illegal or void, this shall not have the effect of making void or illegal any of the other parts or provisions.

R102.7 Existing structures. For requirements of existing structures, refer to the North Carolina Administration and Enforcement Requirements Code.

R102.7.1 Additions, alterations or repairs. *Additions*, *alterations* or repairs to any structure shall conform to the requirements for a new structure without requiring the existing structure to comply with all of the requirements of this code, unless otherwise stated. *Additions*, *alterations* or repairs shall not cause an existing structure to become unsafe or adversely affect the performance of the building.

PART II—ADMINISTRATION AND ENFORCEMENT

SECTION R103 DEPARTMENT OF BUILDING SAFETY

Information concerning the creation and operation of inspections departments may be found in the North Carolina Administrative Code and Policies.

SECTION R104 DUTIES AND POWERS OF THE BUILDING OFFICIAL

Information concerning the duties and powers of the building official may be found in the North Carolina Administrative Code and Policies.

SECTION R105 PERMITS

Information concerning permits may be found in the North Carolina Administrative Code and Policies.

SECTION R106 CONSTRUCTION DOCUMENTS

Information concerning construction documents may be found in the North Carolina Administrative Code and Policies.

SECTION R107 TEMPORARY STRUCTURES AND USES

Deleted

SECTION R108 FEES

Deleted

SECTION R109 INSPECTIONS

Deleted

SECTION R110 CERTIFICATE OF OCCUPANCY

Deleted

SECTION R111 SERVICE UTILITIES

Deleted

SECTION R112 BOARD OF APPEALS

Deleted

SECTION R113 VIOLATIONS

Deleted

SECTION R114 STOP WORK ORDER

Deleted

Part II—Definitions

CHAPTER 2
DEFINITIONS

SECTION R201
GENERAL

R201.1 Scope. Unless otherwise expressly stated, the following words and terms shall, for the purposes of this code, have the meanings indicated in this chapter.

R201.2 Interchangeability. Words used in the present tense include the future; words in the masculine gender include the feminine and neuter; the singular number includes the plural and the plural, the singular.

R201.3 Terms defined in other codes. Where terms are not defined in this code such terms shall have meanings ascribed to them as in other code publications of the North Carolina Building Code Council.

R201.4 Terms not defined. Where terms are not defined through the methods authorized by this section, such terms shall have ordinarily accepted meanings such as the context implies.

SECTION R202
DEFINITIONS

ACCESSIBLE. Signifies access that requires the removal of an access panel or similar removable obstruction. For energy purposes, ACCESSIBLE means admitting close approach as a result of not being guarded by locked doors, elevation or other effective means (see "Readily *accessible*").

ACCESSIBLE, READILY. Signifies access without the necessity for removing a panel or similar obstruction.

ACCESSORY BUILDINGS. In one- and two-family dwellings not more than three stories high with separate means of egress, a building, the use of which is incidental to that of the main building and which is detached and located on the same lot.

ACCESSORY STRUCTURE. Accessory structure is any structure not roofed over and enclosed that is not considered an accessory building located on one- and two-family dwelling sites which is incidental to that of the main building. Examples of accessory structures are, but not limited to; fencing, decks, gazebos, arbors, retaining walls, barbecue pits, detached chimneys, tree houses, playground equipment, yard art, etc. Accessory structures except decks, gazebos, and retaining walls as required by Section R404.4, are not required to meet the provisions of this code.

ACH50. Air Changes per Hour of measured air flow in relation to the building volume while the building is maintained at a pressure difference of 50 Pascals.

ADDITION. An extension or increase in floor area or height of a building or structure. For energy purposes, an extension or increase in the *conditioned space* floor area or height of a building or structure.

ADHERED STONE OR MASONRY VENEER. Stone or masonry veneer secured and supported through the adhesion of an *approved* bonding material applied to an *approved* backing.

AIR ADMITTANCE VALVE. A one-way valve designed to allow air into the plumbing drainage system when a negative pressure develops in the piping. This device shall close by gravity and seal the terminal under conditions of zero differential pressure (no flow conditions) and under positive internal pressure.

AIR BARRIER. Material(s) assembled and joined together to provide a barrier to air leakage through the building envelope. An air barrier may be a single material, or a combination of materials.

AIR BARRIER MATERIAL. Material(s) that have an air permeability not to exceed 0.004 cfm/ft^2 under a pressure differential of 0.3 in. water (1.57 psf) (0.02 L/s.m^2 @ 75 Pa) when tested in accordance with ASTM E 2178.

AIR BARRIER SYSTEM. Material(s) assembled and joined together to provide a barrier to air leakage through the building envelope. An air barrier is a combination of *air barrier materials* and sealants.

AIR BREAK (DRAINAGE SYSTEM). An arrangement in which a discharge pipe from a fixture, *appliance* or device drains indirectly into a receptor below the flood-level rim of the receptor, and above the trap seal.

AIR CIRCULATION, FORCED. A means of providing space conditioning utilizing movement of air through ducts or plenums by mechanical means.

AIR-CONDITIONING SYSTEM. A system that consists of heat exchangers, blowers, filters, supply, exhaust and return-air systems, and shall include any apparatus installed in connection therewith.

AIR GAP, DRAINAGE SYSTEM. The unobstructed vertical distance through free atmosphere between the outlet of a waste pipe and the flood-level rim of the fixture or receptor into which it is discharging.

AIR GAP, WATER-DISTRIBUTION SYSTEM. The unobstructed vertical distance through free atmosphere between the lowest opening from a water supply discharge to the flood-level rim of a plumbing fixture.

AIR-IMPERMEABLE INSULATION. An insulation having an air permanence equal to or less than 0.02 L/s-m^2 at 75 Pa pressure differential tested according to ASTM E 2178 or E 283.

ALTERATION. Any construction or renovation to an existing structure other than repair or addition that requires a *permit*. Also, a change in a mechanical system that involves an extension, addition or change to the arrangement, type or purpose of the original installation that requires a *permit*.

ANCHORED STONE OR MASONRY VENEER. Stone or masonry veneer secured with *approved* mechanical fasteners to an approved backing.

ANCHORS. See "Supports."

ANTISIPHON. A term applied to valves or mechanical devices that eliminate siphonage.

APPLIANCE. A device or apparatus that is manufactured and designed to utilize energy and for which this code provides specific requirements.

APPROVED. Acceptable to the *building official.*

APPROVED AGENCY. An established and recognized agency regularly engaged in conducting tests or furnishing inspection services, when such agency has been *approved* by the *building official.*

ASPECT RATIO. The ratio of longest to shortest perpendicular dimensions, or for wall sections, the ratio of height to length.

ATTIC. The unfinished space between the ceiling assembly of the top *story* and the roof assembly.

ATTIC, HABITABLE. A finished attic area meeting the definition of Habitable Space and complying with all of the following requirements:

1. The occupiable floor area is at least 70 square feet (17 m^2), in accordance with Section R304,
2. The occupiable floor area has a ceiling height in accordance with Section R305, and
3. The occupiable space is enclosed by the roof assembly above, knee walls (if applicable) on the sides and the floor-ceiling assembly below.

ATTIC STORAGE. A floored area, regardless of size, within an attic space that is served by an attic access.

> **Exception:** A floor walkway not less than 24 inches wide or greater than 48 inches wide that serves as an access for the service of utilities or equipment, and a level service space not less than 30 inches deep or greater than 48 inches deep and not less than 30 inches wide or greater than 48 inches wide at the front or service side of the appliance, shall not be considered as attic storage. Such floored area shall be labeled at the attic access opening, "NOT FOR STORAGE." The lettering shall be a minimum of 2 inches in height.

BACKFLOW, DRAINAGE. A reversal of flow in the drainage system.

BACKFLOW PREVENTER. A device or means to prevent backflow.

BACKFLOW PREVENTER, REDUCED-PRESSURE-ZONE TYPE. A backflow-prevention device consisting of two independently acting check valves, internally force loaded to a normally closed position and separated by an intermediate chamber (or zone) in which there is an automatic relief means of venting to atmosphere internally loaded to a normally open position between two tightly closing shutoff valves and with means for testing for tightness of the checks and opening of relief means.

BACKFLOW, WATER DISTRIBUTION. The flow of water or other liquids into the potable water-supply piping from any sources other than its intended source. Backsiphonage is one type of backflow.

BACKPRESSURE. Pressure created by any means in the water distribution system, which by being in excess of the pressure in the water supply mains causes a potential backflow condition.

BACKPRESSURE, LOW HEAD. A pressure less than or equal to 4.33 psi (29.88 kPa) or the pressure exerted by a 10-foot (3048 mm) column of water.

BACKSIPHONAGE. The flowing back of used or contaminated water from piping into a potable water-supply pipe due to a negative pressure in such pipe.

BACKWATER VALVE. A device installed in a drain or pipe to prevent backflow of sewage.

BALCONY, EXTERIOR. An exterior floor projecting from and supported by a structure without additional independent supports.

BASEMENT. That portion of a building that is partly or completely below *grade* (see "*Story above grade*").

BASEMENT WALL. The opaque portion of a wall that encloses one side of a *basement* and has an average below *grade* wall area that is 50 percent or more of the total opaque and non-opaque area of that enclosing side. For energy purposes, a wall 50 percent or more below grade and enclosing conditioned space.

BASIC WIND SPEED. Three-second gust speed at 33 feet (10 058 mm) above the ground in Exposure C (see Section R301.2.1) as given in Figure R301.2(4).

BATHROOM GROUP. A group of fixtures, including or excluding a bidet, consisting of a water closet, lavatory, and bathtub or shower. Such fixtures are located together on the same floor level.

BEDROOM. Sleeping room.

BEND. A drainage fitting, designed to provide a change in direction of a drain pipe of less than the angle specified by the amount necessary to establish the desired slope of the line (see "Elbow" and "Sweep").

BOILER. A self-contained *appliance* from which hot water is circulated for heating purposes and then returned to the boiler, and which operates at water pressures not exceeding 160 pounds per square inch gage (psig) (1102 kPa gauge) and at water temperatures not exceeding 250°F (121°C).

BOND BEAM. A horizontal grouted element within masonry in which reinforcement is embedded.

BPI ENVELOPE PROFESSIONAL. An individual that has successfully passed the Building Performance Institute written and field examination requirements for the Building Envelope certification.

BRACED WALL LINE. A straight line through the building plan that represents the location of the lateral resistance provided by the wall bracing.

BRACED WALL LINE, CONTINUOUSLY SHEATHED. A *braced wall line* with structural sheathing applied to all sheathable surfaces including the areas above and below openings.

BRACED WALL PANEL. A full-height section of wall constructed to resist in-plane shear loads through interaction of framing members, sheathing material and anchors. The panel's length meets the requirements of its particular bracing method, and contributes toward the total amount of bracing required along its *braced wall line* in accordance with Section R602.10.1.

BRANCH. Any part of the piping system other than a riser, main or stack.

BRANCH, FIXTURE. See "Fixture branch, drainage."

BRANCH, HORIZONTAL. See "Horizontal branch, drainage."

BRANCH INTERVAL. A vertical measurement of distance, 8 feet (2438 mm) or more in *developed length*, between the connections of horizontal branches to a drainage stack. Measurements are taken down the stack from the highest horizontal branch connection.

BRANCH, MAIN. A water-distribution pipe that extends horizontally off a main or riser to convey water to branches or fixture groups.

BRANCH, VENT. A vent connecting two or more individual vents with a vent stack or stack vent.

BTU/H. The *listed* maximum capacity of an *appliance*, absorption unit or burner expressed in British thermal units input per hour.

BUILDING. Building shall mean any one- and two-family dwelling or portion thereof, including *townhouses*, that is used, or designed or intended to be used for human habitation, for living, sleeping, cooking or eating purposes, or any combination thereof, and shall include accessory structures thereto.

BUILDING DRAIN. The lowest piping that collects the discharge from all other drainage piping inside the house and extends 30 inches (762 mm) in *developed length* of pipe, beyond the *exterior walls* and conveys the drainage to the *building sewer.*

BUILDING, EXISTING. Existing building is a building erected prior to the adoption of this code, or one for which a legal building *permit* has been issued.

BUILDING LINE. The line established by law, beyond which a building shall not extend, except as specifically provided by law.

BUILDING OFFICIAL. The officer or other designated authority charged with the administration and enforcement of this code.

BUILDING SEWER. That part of the drainage system that extends from the end of the *building drain* and conveys its discharge to a public sewer, private sewer, individual sewage-disposal system or other point of disposal.

BUILDING THERMAL ENVELOPE. The *basement walls*, *exterior walls*, floor, roof and any other building element that enclose *conditioned spaces*. This boundary also includes the boundary between *conditioned space* and any exempt or unconditioned space.

BUILT-UP ROOF COVERING. Two or more layers of felt cemented together and surfaced with a cap sheet, mineral aggregate, smooth coating or similar surfacing material.

CAP PLATE. The top plate of the double top plates used in structural insulated panel (SIP) construction. The cap plate is cut to match the panel thickness such that it overlaps the wood structural panel facing on both sides.

CFM25. Cubic Feet per Minute of measured air flow while the building is maintained at a pressure difference of 25 Pascals (0.1 inches w.p.).

CFM50. Cubic Feet per Minute of measured air flow while the building is maintained at a pressure difference of 50 Pascals (0.2 inches w.p.).

CEILING HEIGHT. The clear vertical distance from the finished floor to the finished ceiling.

CEMENT PLASTER. A mixture of portland or blended cement, portland cement or blended cement and hydrated lime, masonry cement or plastic cement and aggregate and other *approved* materials as specified in this code.

CHIMNEY. A primary vertical structure containing one or more flues, for the purpose of carrying gaseous products of combustion and air from a fuel-burning *appliance* to the outside atmosphere.

CHIMNEY CONNECTOR. A pipe that connects a fuel-burning *appliance* to a chimney.

CHIMNEY TYPES.

Residential-type appliance. An *approved* chimney for removing the products of combustion from fuel-burning, residential-type *appliances* producing combustion gases not in excess of 1,000°F (538°C) under normal operating conditions, but capable of producing combustion gases of 1,400°F (760°C) during intermittent forces firing for periods up to 1 hour. All temperatures shall be measured at the *appliance* flue outlet. Residential-type *appliance* chimneys include masonry and factory-built types.

CIRCUIT VENT. A vent that connects to a horizontal drainage branch and vents two traps to a maximum of eight traps or trapped fixtures connected into a battery.

CLADDING. The exterior materials that cover the surface of the building envelope that is directly loaded by the wind.

CLEANOUT. An accessible opening in the drainage system used for the removal of possible obstruction.

CLOSED CRAWL SPACE. A foundation without wall vents that uses air sealed walls, ground and foundation moisture control, and mechanical drying potential to control crawl space moisture. Insulation may be located at the floor level or at the exterior walls.

CLOSET. A small room or chamber used for storage.

CODE OFFICIAL. The officer or other designated authority charged with the administration and enforcement of this code, or a duly authorized representative.

COMBINATION WASTE AND VENT SYSTEM. A specially designed system of waste piping embodying the horizontal wet venting of one or more sinks or floor drains by means of a common waste and vent pipe adequately sized to provide free movement of air above the flow line of the drain.

COMBUSTIBLE MATERIAL. Any material not defined as noncombustible.

COMBUSTION AIR. The air provided to fuel-burning *equipment* including air for fuel combustion, draft hood dilution and ventilation of the *equipment* enclosure.

COMMON VENT. A single pipe venting two trap arms within the same *branch interval*, either back-to-back or one above the other.

CONDENSATE. The liquid that separates from a gas due to a reduction in temperature, e.g., water that condenses from flue gases and water that condenses from air circulating through the cooling coil in air conditioning *equipment*.

CONDENSING APPLIANCE. An *appliance* that condenses water generated by the burning of fuels.

CONDITIONED AIR. Air treated to control its temperature, relative humidity or quality.

CONDITIONED AREA. That area within a building provided with heating and/or cooling systems or *appliances* capable of maintaining, through design or heat loss/gain, 68°F (20°C) during the heating season and/or 80°F (27°C) during the cooling season, or has a fixed opening directly adjacent to a conditioned area.

CONDITIONED CRAWL SPACE. A conditioned crawl space is a foundation without wall vents that encloses an intentionally heated or cooled space. Insulation is located at the exterior walls.

CONDITIONED FLOOR AREA. The horizontal projection of the floors associated with the *conditioned space*.

CONDITIONED SPACE. An area or room within a building being heated or cooled, containing uninsulated ducts, or with a fixed opening directly into an adjacent conditioned space.

CONSTRUCTION DOCUMENTS. Written, graphic and pictorial documents prepared or assembled for describing the design, location and physical characteristics of the elements of a project necessary for obtaining a building *permit*. Construction drawings shall be drawn to an appropriate scale.

CONTAMINATION. An impairment of the quality of the potable water that creates an actual hazard to the public health through poisoning or through the spread of disease by sewage, industrial fluids or waste.

CONTINUOUS WASTE. A drain from two or more similar adjacent fixtures connected to a single trap.

CONTROL, LIMIT. An automatic control responsive to changes in liquid flow or level, pressure, or temperature for limiting the operation of an *appliance*.

CONTROL, PRIMARY SAFETY. A safety control responsive directly to flame properties that senses the presence or absence of flame and, in event of ignition failure or unintentional flame extinguishment, automatically causes shutdown of mechanical equipment.

CONVECTOR. A system-incorporating heating element in an enclosure in which air enters an opening below the heating element, is heated and leaves the enclosure through an opening located above the heating element.

CORE. The light-weight middle section of the structural insulated panel composed of foam plastic insulation, which provides the link between the two facing shells.

CORROSION RESISTANCE. The ability of a material to withstand deterioration of its surface or its properties when exposed to its environment.

COURT. A space, open and unobstructed to the sky, located at or above *grade* level on a *lot* and bounded on three or more sides by walls or a building.

CRIPPLE WALL. A framed wall extending from the top of the foundation to the underside of the floor framing of the first *story above grade plane*.

CROSS CONNECTION. Any connection between two otherwise separate piping systems whereby there may be a flow from one system to the other.

DALLE GLASS. A decorative composite glazing material made of individual pieces of glass that are embedded in a cast matrix of concrete or epoxy.

DAMPER, VOLUME. A device that will restrict, retard or direct the flow of air in any duct, or the products of combustion of heat-producing *equipment*, vent connector, vent or chimney.

DAMPPROOFING. A coating or the application of coatings applied to retard the penetration of water vapor and moisture through or into walls or into interior spaces.

DEAD END. A branch leading from a DWV system terminating at a *developed length* of 2 feet (610 mm) or more. Dead ends shall be prohibited except as an *approved* part of a rough-in for future connection.

DEAD LOADS. The weight of all materials of construction incorporated into the building, including but not limited to walls, floors, roofs, ceilings, stairways, built-in partitions, finishes, cladding, and other similarly incorporated architectural and structural items, and fixed service *equipment*.

DECK. An exterior floor system supported on at least two opposing sides by an adjoining structure or posts, piers, or other independent supports.

DECORATIVE GLASS. A carved, leaded or Dalle glass or glazing material whose purpose is decorative or artistic, not functional; whose coloring, texture or other design qualities or components cannot be removed without destroying the glazing material; and whose surface, or assembly into which it is incorporated, is divided into segments.

DESIGN PROFESSIONAL. See "*Registered design professional.*"

DEVELOPED LENGTH. The length of a pipeline measured along the center line of the pipe and fittings.

DIAMETER. Unless specifically stated, the term "diameter" is the nominal diameter as designated by the *approved* material standard.

DIAPHRAGM. A horizontal or nearly horizontal system acting to transmit lateral forces to the vertical resisting elements. When the term "*diaphragm*" is used, it includes horizontal bracing systems.

DILUTION AIR. Air that enters a draft hood or draft regulator and mixes with flue gases.

DIRECT-VENT APPLIANCE. A fuel-burning *appliance* with a sealed combustion system that draws all air for combustion from the outside atmosphere and discharges all flue gases to the outside atmosphere.

DRAFT. The pressure difference existing between the *appliance* or any component part and the atmosphere, that causes a continuous flow of air and products of combustion through the gas passages of the *appliance* to the atmosphere.

Induced draft. The pressure difference created by the action of a fan, blower or ejector, that is located between the *appliance* and the chimney or vent termination.

Natural draft. The pressure difference created by a vent or chimney because of its height, and the temperature difference between the flue gases and the atmosphere.

DRAFT HOOD. A device built into an *appliance*, or a part of the vent connector from an *appliance*, which is designed to provide for the ready escape of the flue gases from the *appliance* in the event of no draft, backdraft or stoppage beyond the draft hood; prevent a backdraft from entering the *appliance*; and neutralize the effect of stack action of the chimney or gas vent on the operation of the *appliance*.

DRAFT REGULATOR. A device that functions to maintain a desired draft in the *appliance* by automatically reducing the draft to the desired value.

DRAFT STOP. A material, device or construction installed to restrict the movement of air within open spaces of concealed areas of building components such as crawl spaces, floor-ceiling assemblies, roof-ceiling assemblies and *attics*.

DRAIN. Any pipe that carries soil and water-borne wastes in a building drainage system.

DRAINAGE FITTING. A pipe fitting designed to provide connections in the drainage system that have provisions for establishing the desired slope in the system. These fittings are made from a variety of both metals and plastics. The methods of coupling provide for required slope in the system (see "Durham fitting").

DUCT SYSTEM. A continuous passageway for the transmission of air which, in addition to ducts, includes duct fittings, dampers, plenums, fans and accessory air-handling *equipment* and *appliances*.

DURHAM FITTING. A special type of drainage fitting for use in the durham systems installations in which the joints are made with recessed and tapered threaded fittings, as opposed to bell and spigot lead/oakum or solvent/cemented or soldered joints. The tapping is at an angle (not 90 degrees) to provide for proper slope in otherwise rigid connections.

DURHAM SYSTEM. A term used to describe soil or waste systems where all piping is of threaded pipe, tube or other such rigid construction using recessed drainage fittings to correspond to the types of piping.

DWELLING. Any building that contains one or two *dwelling units* used, intended, or designed to be built, used, rented, leased, let or hired out to be occupied, or that are occupied for living purposes.

DWELLING UNIT. A single unit providing complete independent living facilities for one or more persons, including permanent provisions for living, sleeping, eating, cooking and sanitation.

DWV. Abbreviated term for drain, waste and vent piping as used in common plumbing practice.

EFFECTIVE OPENING. The minimum cross-sectional area at the point of water-supply discharge, measured or expressed in terms of diameter of a circle and if the opening is not circular, the diameter of a circle of equivalent cross-sectional area. (This is applicable to air gap.)

ELBOW. A pressure pipe fitting designed to provide an exact change in direction of a pipe run. An elbow provides a sharp turn in the flow path (see "Bend" and "Sweep").

EMERGENCY ESCAPE AND RESCUE OPENING. An operable exterior window, door or similar device that provides for a means of escape and access for rescue in the event of an emergency.

EQUIPMENT. All piping, ducts, vents, control devices and other components of systems other than *appliances* that are permanently installed and integrated to provide control of environmental conditions for buildings. This definition shall also include other systems specifically regulated in this code.

EQUIVALENT LENGTH. For determining friction losses in a piping system, the effect of a particular fitting equal to the friction loss through a straight piping length of the same nominal diameter.

ESCARPMENT. With respect to topographic wind effects, a cliff or steep slope generally separating two levels or gently sloping areas.

ESSENTIALLY NONTOXIC TRANSFER FLUIDS. Fluids having a Gosselin rating of 1, including propylene glycol; mineral oil; polydimenthyoil oxane; hydrochlorofluorocarbon, chlorofluorocarbon and hydrofluorocarbon refrigerants; and FDA-*approved* boiler water additives for steam boilers.

ESSENTIALLY TOXIC TRANSFER FLUIDS. Soil, water or gray water and fluids having a Gosselin rating of 2 or more including ethylene glycol, hydrocarbon oils, ammonia refrigerants and hydrazine.

EVAPORATIVE COOLER. A device used for reducing air temperature by the process of evaporating water into an airstream.

EXCESS AIR. Air that passes through the combustion chamber and the *appliance* flue in excess of that which is theoretically required for complete combustion.

EXHAUST HOOD, FULL OPENING. An exhaust hood with an opening at least equal to the diameter of the connecting vent.

EXISTING INSTALLATIONS. Any plumbing system regulated by this code that was legally installed prior to the effective date of this code, or for which a *permit* to install has been issued.

EXTERIOR INSULATION AND FINISH SYSTEMS (EIFS). EIFS are nonstructural, nonload-bearing *exterior wall* cladding systems that consist of an insulation board attached either adhesively or mechanically, or both, to the substrate; an integrally reinforced base coat; and a textured protective finish coat.

EXTERIOR INSULATION AND FINISH SYSTEMS (EIFS) WITH DRAINAGE. An EIFS that incorporates a means of drainage applied over a water-resistive barrier.

EXTERIOR WALL. An above-*grade* wall that defines the exterior boundaries of a building. Includes between-floor spandrels, peripheral edges of floors, roof and *basement* knee walls, dormer walls, gable end walls, walls enclosing a mansard roof and *basement walls* with an average below-*grade* wall area that is less than 50 percent of the total opaque and nonopaque area of that enclosing side.

***F*-FACTOR.** The perimeter heat loss factor for slab-on-grade floors (Btu/h × ft × °F) [W/(m × K)].

FACING. The wood structural panel facings that form the two outmost rigid layers of the structural insulated panel.

FACTORY-BUILT CHIMNEY. A *listed* and *labeled* chimney composed of factory-made components assembled in the field in accordance with the manufacturer's instructions and the conditions of the listing.

FAMILY. Family is an individual, two or more persons related by blood, marriage or law, or a group of not more than any five persons living together in a dwelling unit. Servants having common housekeeping facilities with a family consisting of an individual, or more persons related by blood, marriage or law, are a part of the family for this code.

FENESTRATION. Skylights, roof windows, vertical windows (whether fixed or moveable); opaque doors; glazed doors; glass block; and combination opaque/glazed doors.

FIBER-CEMENT SIDING. A manufactured, fiber-reinforcing product made with an inorganic hydraulic or calcium silicate binder formed by chemical reaction and reinforced with discrete organic or inorganic nonasbestos fibers, or both. Additives which enhance manufacturing or product performance are permitted. Fiber-cement siding products have either smooth or textured faces and are intended for *exterior wall* and related applications.

FIREBLOCKING. Building materials or materials *approved* for use as fireblocking, installed to resist the free passage of flame to other areas of the building through concealed spaces.

FIREPLACE. An assembly consisting of a hearth and fire chamber and smoke chamber, beginning at the hearth and ending at the top of the smoke chamber, of noncombustible material and provided with a chimney, for use with solid fuels.

Factory-built fireplace. A *listed* and *labeled* fireplace and chimney system composed of factory-made components, and assembled in the field in accordance with manufacturer's instructions and the conditions of the listing.

Masonry chimney. A field-constructed chimney composed of solid masonry units, bricks, stones or concrete, beginning at the top of the smoke chamber and ending at the flue termination.

Masonry fireplace. A field-constructed fireplace composed of solid masonry units, bricks, stones or concrete, beginning at the hearth and ending at the top of the smoke chamber.

Smoke chamber. That part of a masonry fireplace which extends from the top of the firebox to the start of the chimney flue lining. A smoke chamber shall have a damper and a smoke shelf.

FIREPLACE STOVE. A free-standing, chimney-connected solid-fuel-burning heater designed to be operated with the fire chamber doors in either the open or closed position.

FIREPLACE THROAT. The opening between the top of the firebox and the smoke chamber.

FIRE-RETARDANT-TREATED WOOD. Pressure-treated lumber and plywood that exhibit reduced surface burning characteristics and resist propagation of fire.

Other means during manufacture. A process where the wood raw material is treated with a fire-retardant formulation while undergoing creation as a finished product.

Pressure process. A process for treating wood using an initial vacuum followed by the introduction of pressure above atmospheric.

FIRE SEPARATION DISTANCE. The distance measured from the building face to one of the following:

1. To the closest interior *lot line*;
2. To the centerline of a street, an alley or public way; or
3. To an imaginary line between two buildings on the *lot*.

The distance shall be measured at a right angle from the face of the wall.

FIXTURE. See "Plumbing fixture."

FIXTURE BRANCH, DRAINAGE. A drain serving two or more fixtures that discharges into another portion of the drainage system.

FIXTURE BRANCH, WATER-SUPPLY. A water-supply pipe between the fixture supply and a main water-distribution pipe or fixture group main.

FIXTURE DRAIN. The drain from the trap of a fixture to the junction of that drain with any other drain pipe.

FIXTURE FITTING.

Supply fitting. A fitting that controls the volume and/or directional flow of water and is either attached to or accessible from a fixture or is used with an open or atmospheric discharge.

Waste fitting. A combination of components that conveys the sanitary waste from the outlet of a fixture to the connection of the sanitary drainage system.

FIXTURE GROUP, MAIN. The main water-distribution pipe (or secondary branch) serving a plumbing fixture grouping such as a bath, kitchen or laundry area to which two or more individual fixture branch pipes are connected.

FIXTURE SUPPLY. The water-supply pipe connecting a fixture or fixture fitting to a fixture branch.

FIXTURE UNIT, DRAINAGE (d.f.u.). A measure of probable discharge into the drainage system by various types of plumbing fixtures, used to size DWV piping systems. The drainage fixture-unit value for a particular fixture depends on its volume rate of drainage discharge, on the time duration of a single drainage operation and on the average time between successive operations.

FIXTURE UNIT, WATER-SUPPLY (w.s.f.u.). A measure of the probable hydraulic demand on the water supply by various types of plumbing fixtures used to size water-piping systems. The water-supply fixture-unit value for a particular fixture depends on its volume rate of supply, on the time duration of a single supply operation and on the average time between successive operations.

FLAME SPREAD. The propagation of flame over a surface.

FLAME SPREAD INDEX. A comparative measure, expressed as a dimensionless number, derived from visual measurements of the spread of flame versus time for a material tested in accordance with ASTM E 84.

FLIGHT. A continuous run of rectangular treads or winders or combination thereof from one landing to another.

FLOOD-LEVEL RIM. The edge of the receptor or fixture from which water overflows.

FLOOR DRAIN. A plumbing fixture for recess in the floor having a floor-level strainer intended for the purpose of the collection and disposal of waste water used in cleaning the floor and for the collection and disposal of accidental spillage to the floor.

FLOOR FURNACE. A self-contained furnace suspended from the floor of the space being heated, taking air for combustion from outside such space, and with means for lighting the *appliance* from such space.

FLOW PRESSURE. The static pressure reading in the water-supply pipe near the faucet or water outlet while the faucet or water outlet is open and flowing at capacity.

FLUE. See "Vent."

FLUE, APPLIANCE. The passages within an *appliance* through which combustion products pass from the combustion chamber to the flue collar.

FLUE COLLAR. The portion of a fuel-burning *appliance* designed for the attachment of a draft hood, vent connector or venting system.

FLUE GASES. Products of combustion plus excess air in *appliance* flues or heat exchangers.

FLUSH VALVE. A device located at the bottom of a flush tank that is operated to flush water closets.

FLUSHOMETER TANK. A device integrated within an air accumulator vessel that is designed to discharge a predetermined quantity of water to fixtures for flushing purposes.

FLUSHOMETER VALVE. A flushometer valve is a device that discharges a predetermined quantity of water to fixtures for flushing purposes and is actuated by direct water pressure.

FOAM BACKER BOARD. Foam plastic used in siding applications where the foam plastic is a component of the siding.

FOAM PLASTIC INSULATION. A plastic that is intentionally expanded by the use of a foaming agent to produce a reduced-density plastic containing voids consisting of open or closed cells distributed throughout the plastic for thermal insulating or acoustic purposes and that has a density less than 20 pounds per cubic foot (320 kg/m^3) unless it is used as interior trim.

FOAM PLASTIC INTERIOR TRIM. Exposed foam plastic used as picture molds, chair rails, crown moldings, baseboards, handrails, ceiling beams, door trim and window trim and similar decorative or protective materials used in fixed applications.

FUEL-PIPING SYSTEM. All piping, tubing, valves and fittings used to connect fuel utilization *equipment* to the point of fuel delivery.

FULLWAY VALVE. A valve that in the full open position has an opening cross-sectional area equal to a minimum of 85 percent of the cross-sectional area of the connecting pipe.

FULLY ENCLOSED ATTIC FLOOR SYSTEM. The ceiling insulation is enclosed on all six sides by an air barrier system, such as taped drywall below, solid framing joists on the sides, solid blocking on the ends, and solid sheathing on top which totally enclose the insulation. This system provides for full depth insulation over the exterior walls.

FURNACE. A vented heating *appliance* designed or arranged to discharge heated air into a *conditioned space* or through a duct or ducts.

GLAZING AREA. The interior surface area of all glazed fenestration, including the area of sash, curbing or other framing elements, that enclose *conditioned space*. Includes the area of glazed fenestration assemblies in walls bounding conditioned *basements*.

GRADE. The finished ground level adjoining the building at all *exterior walls*.

GRADE FLOOR OPENING. A window or other opening located such that the sill height of the opening is not more than 44 inches (1118 mm) above or below the finished ground level adjacent to the opening.

GRADE, PIPING. See "Slope."

GRADE PLANE. A reference plane representing the average of the finished ground level adjoining the building at all *exterior walls*. Where the finished ground level slopes away from the *exterior walls*, the reference plane shall be established by the lowest points within the area between the building and the *lot line* or, where the *lot line* is more than 6 ft (1829 mm) from the building between the structure and a point 6 ft (1829 mm) from the building.

GRIDDED WATER DISTRIBUTION SYSTEM. A water distribution system where every water distribution pipe is interconnected so as to provide two or more paths to each fixture supply pipe.

GROSS AREA OF EXTERIOR WALLS. The normal projection of all *exterior walls*, including the area of all windows and doors installed therein.

GROUND-SOURCE HEAT PUMP LOOP SYSTEM. Piping buried in horizontal or vertical excavations or placed in a body of water for the purpose of transporting heat transfer liquid to and from a heat pump. Included in this definition are closed loop systems in which the liquid is recirculated and open loop systems in which the liquid is drawn from a well or other source.

GUARD. A building component or a system of building components located near the open sides of elevated walking surfaces that minimizes the possibility of a fall from the walking surface to the lower level.

HABITABLE SPACE. A space in a building for living, sleeping, eating or cooking. Bathrooms, toilet rooms, closets, halls, storage or utility spaces and similar areas are not considered *habitable spaces*.

HANDRAIL. A horizontal or sloping rail intended for grasping by the hand for guidance or support.

HANGERS. See "Supports."

HAZARDOUS LOCATION. Any location considered to be a fire hazard for flammable vapors, dust, combustible fibers or other highly combustible substances.

HAZARDOUS LOCATION, GLAZING. See Section R308.4.

HEAT PUMP. An *appliance* having heating or heating/cooling capability and that uses refrigerants to extract heat from air, liquid or other sources.

HEAT TRAP. An arrangement of piping and fittings, such as elbows, or a commercially available heat trap that prevents thermosyphoning of hot water during standby periods.

HEATED SLAB. Slab-on-grade construction in which the heating elements, hydronic tubing, or hot air distribution system is in contact with, or placed within or under, the slab.

HEATING DEGREE DAYS (HDD). The sum, on an annual basis, of the difference between 65°F (18°C) and the mean temperature for each day as determined from "NOAA Annual Degree Days to Selected Bases Derived from the 1960-1990 Normals" or other weather data sources acceptable to the code official.

HEIGHT, BUILDING. The vertical distance from *grade plane* to the average height of the highest roof surface.

HEIGHT, STORY. The vertical distance from top to top of two successive tiers of beams or finished floor surfaces; and, for the topmost *story*, from the top of the floor finish to the top of the ceiling joists or, where there is not a ceiling, to the top of the roof rafters.

HERS RATER. An individual that has completed training and been certified by RESNET (Residential Energy Services Network) Accredited Rating Provider.

HIGH-EFFICACY LAMPS. Compact fluorescent lamps, T-8 or smaller diameter linear fluorescent lamps or lamps with a minimum efficacy of:

1. 60 lumens per watt for lamps over 40 watts.
2. 50 lumens per watt for lamps over 15 watts to 40 watts.
3. 40 lumens per watt for lamps 15 watts or less.

HIGH-TEMPERATURE (H.T.) CHIMNEY. A high temperature chimney complying with the requirements of UL 103. A Type H.T. chimney is identifiable by the markings "Type H.T." on each chimney pipe section.

HILL. With respect to topographic wind effects, a land surface characterized by strong relief in any horizontal direction.

HORIZONTAL BRANCH, DRAINAGE. A drain pipe extending laterally from a soil or waste stack or *building drain*, that receives the discharge from one or more *fixture drains*.

HORIZONTAL PIPE. Any pipe or fitting that makes an angle of less than 45 degrees (0.79 rad) with the horizontal.

HOT WATER. Water at a temperature greater than or equal to 110°F (43°C).

HUMIDISTAT. A regulatory device, actuated by changes in humidity, used for automatic control of relative humidity.

HURRICANE-PRONE REGIONS. Areas vulnerable to hurricanes, defined as the U.S. Atlantic Ocean and Gulf of Mexico coasts where the basic wind speed is greater than or equal to 110 miles per hour (145 km/h), and Hawaii, Puerto Rico, Guam, Virgin Islands, and America Samoa.

HYDROGEN GENERATING APPLIANCE. A self-contained package or factory-matched packages of integrated systems for generating gaseous hydrogen. Hydrogen generating *appliances* utilize electrolysis, reformation, chemical, or other processes to generate hydrogen.

IGNITION SOURCE. A flame, spark or hot surface capable of igniting flammable vapors or fumes. Such sources include *appliance* burners, burner ignitions and electrical switching devices.

INDIRECT WASTE PIPE. A waste pipe that discharges into the drainage system through an air gap into a trap, fixture or receptor.

INDIVIDUAL SEWAGE DISPOSAL SYSTEM. A system for disposal of sewage by means of a septic tank or mechanical treatment, designed for use apart from a public sewer to serve a single establishment or building.

INDIVIDUAL VENT. A pipe installed to vent a single-*fixture drain* that connects with the vent system above or terminates independently outside the building.

INDIVIDUAL WATER SUPPLY. A supply other than an *approved* public water supply that serves one or more families.

INFILTRATION. The uncontrolled inward air leakage into a building caused by the pressure effects of wind or the effect of differences in the indoor and outdoor air density or both.

INSULATING CONCRETE FORM (ICF). A concrete forming system using stay-in-place forms of rigid foam plastic insulation, a hybrid of cement and foam insulation, a hybrid of cement and wood chips, or other insulating material for constructing cast-in-place concrete walls.

INSULATING SHEATHING. An insulating board having a minimum thermal resistance of R-2 of the core material.

JURISDICTION. The governmental unit that has adopted this code under due legislative authority.

KITCHEN. Kitchen shall mean an area used, or designated to be used, for the preparation of food.

LABEL. An identification applied on a product by the manufacturer which contains the name of the manufacturer, the function and performance characteristics of the product or material, and the name and identification of an *approved agency* and that indicates that the representative sample of the product or material has been tested and evaluated by an *approved agency.* (See also "Manufacturer's designation" and "Mark.")

LABELED. Appliances, *equipment*, materials or products to which have been affixed a *label*, seal, symbol or other identifying *mark* of a nationally recognized testing laboratory, inspection agency or other organization as approved by the North Carolina Building Code Council concerned with product evaluation that maintains periodic inspection of the production of the above-*labeled* items and whose labeling indicates either that the appliance, *equipment*, material or product meets identified standards or has been tested and found suitable for a specified purpose.

LIGHT-FRAME CONSTRUCTION. A type of construction whose vertical and horizontal structural elements are primarily formed by a system of repetitive wood or cold-formed steel framing members.

LISTED. *Equipment*, materials, products or services included in a list published by an organization acceptable to the code official and concerned with evaluation of products or services that maintains periodic inspection of production of *listed equipment* or materials or periodic evaluation of services and whose listing states either that the *equipment*, material, product or service meets identified standards or has been tested and found suitable for a specified purpose.

LIVE LOADS. Those loads produced by the use and occupancy of the building or other structure and do not include construction or environmental loads such as wind load, snow load, rain load, earthquake load, flood load or dead load.

LIVING SPACE. Space within a *dwelling unit* utilized for living, sleeping, eating, cooking, bathing, washing and sanitation purposes.

LOT. A portion or parcel of land considered as a unit.

LOT LINE. A line dividing one *lot* from another, or from a street or any public place.

MACERATING TOILET SYSTEMS. A system comprised of a sump with macerating pump and with connections for a water closet and other plumbing fixtures, that is designed to accept, grind and pump wastes to an *approved* point of discharge.

MAIN. The principal pipe artery to which branches may be connected.

MAIN SEWER. See "Public sewer."

MANIFOLD WATER DISTRIBUTION SYSTEMS. A fabricated piping arrangement in which a large supply main is fitted with multiple branches in close proximity in which water is distributed separately to fixtures from each branch.

MANUFACTURED HOME. *Manufactured home* means a structure, transportable in one or more sections, which in the traveling mode is 8 body feet (2438 body mm) or more in width or 40 body feet (12 192 body mm) or more in length, or, when erected on site, is 320 square feet (30 m^2) or more, and which is built on a permanent chassis and designed to be used as a *dwelling* with or without a permanent foundation when connected to the required utilities, and includes the plumbing, heating, air-conditioning and electrical systems contained therein; except that such term shall include any structure that meets all the requirements of this paragraph except the size requirements and with respect to which the manufacturer voluntarily files a certification required by the secretary (HUD) and complies with the standards established under this title. For mobile homes built prior to June 15, 1976, a *label* certifying compliance to the Standard for Mobile Homes, NFPA 501, in effect at the time of manufacture is required. For the purpose of these provisions, a mobile home shall be considered a *manufactured home.*

MANUFACTURER'S DESIGNATION. An identification applied on a product by the manufacturer indicating that a product or material complies with a specified standard or set of rules. (See also "*Mark*" and "*Label*.")

MANUFACTURER'S INSTALLATION INSTRUCTIONS. Printed instructions included with *equipment* as part of the conditions of listing and labeling.

MARK. An identification applied on a product by the manufacturer indicating the name of the manufacturer and the function of a product or material. (See also "Manufacturer's designation" and "*Label*.")

MASONRY CHIMNEY. Deleted.

MASONRY HEATER. A masonry heater is a solid fuel burning heating *appliance* constructed predominantly of concrete or solid masonry having a mass of at least 1,100 pounds (500 kg), excluding the chimney and foundation. It is designed to absorb and store a substantial portion of heat from a fire built in the firebox by routing exhaust gases through internal heat exchange channels in which the flow path downstream of the firebox includes at least one 180-degree (3.14-rad) change in flow direction before entering the chimney and which deliver heat by radiation through the masonry surface of the heater.

MASONRY, SOLID. Masonry consisting of solid masonry units laid contiguously with the joints between the units filled with mortar.

MASONRY UNIT. Brick, tile, stone, glass block or concrete block conforming to the requirements specified in Section 2103 of the *North Carolina Building Code.*

Clay. A building unit larger in size than a brick, composed of burned clay, shale, fire clay or mixtures thereof.

Concrete. A building unit or block larger in size than 12 inches by 4 inches by 4 inches (305 mm by 102 mm by 102 mm) made of cement and suitable aggregates.

Glass. Nonload-bearing masonry composed of glass units bonded by mortar.

Hollow. A masonry unit whose net cross-sectional area in any plane parallel to the loadbearing surface is less than 75 percent of its gross cross-sectional area measured in the same plane.

Solid. A masonry unit whose net cross-sectional area in every plane parallel to the loadbearing surface is 75 percent or more of its cross-sectional area measured in the same plane.

MASS WALL. Masonry or concrete walls having a mass greater than or equal to 30 pounds per square foot (146 kg/m^2), solid wood walls having a mass greater than or equal to 20 pounds per square foot (98 kg/m^2), and any other walls having a heat capacity greater than or equal to 6 Btu/ft^2 · °F [266 J/(m^2 · K)].

MEAN ROOF HEIGHT. The average of the roof eave height and the height to the highest point on the roof surface, except that eave height shall be used for roof angle of less than or equal to 10 degrees (0.18 rad).

MECHANICAL DRAFT SYSTEM. A venting system designed to remove flue or vent gases by mechanical means, that consists of an induced draft portion under nonpositive static pressure or a forced draft portion under positive static pressure.

Forced-draft venting system. A portion of a venting system using a fan or other mechanical means to cause the removal of flue or vent gases under positive static pressure.

Induced draft venting system. A portion of a venting system using a fan or other mechanical means to cause the removal of flue or vent gases under nonpositive static vent pressure.

Power venting system. A portion of a venting system using a fan or other mechanical means to cause the removal of flue or vent gases under positive static vent pressure.

MECHANICAL EXHAUST SYSTEM. A system for removing air from a room or space by mechanical means.

MECHANICAL SYSTEM. A system specifically addressed and regulated in this code and composed of components, devices, *appliances* and *equipment*.

METAL ROOF PANEL. An interlocking metal sheet having a minimum installed weather exposure of at least 3 square feet (0.28 m^2) per sheet.

METAL ROOF SHINGLE. An interlocking metal sheet having an installed weather exposure less than 3 square feet (0.28 m^2) per sheet.

MEZZANINE, LOFT. An intermediate level or levels between the floor and ceiling of any *story* with an aggregate floor area of not more than one-third of the area of the room or space in which the level or levels are located.

MODIFIED BITUMEN ROOF COVERING. One or more layers of polymer modified asphalt sheets. The sheet materials shall be fully adhered or mechanically attached to the substrate or held in place with an *approved* ballast layer.

MULTIPLE STATION SMOKE ALARM. Two or more single station alarm devices that are capable of interconnection such that actuation of one causes all integral or separate audible alarms to operate.

NATURAL DRAFT SYSTEM. A venting system designed to remove flue or vent gases under nonpositive static vent pressure entirely by natural draft.

NATURALLY DURABLE WOOD. The heartwood of the following species with the exception that an occasional piece with corner sapwood is permitted if 90 percent or more of the width of each side on which it occurs is heartwood.

Decay resistant. Redwood, cedar, black locust and black walnut.

Termite resistant. Alaska yellow cedar, redwood, Eastern red cedar and Western red cedar including all sapwood of Western red cedar.

NONCOMBUSTIBLE MATERIAL. Materials that pass the test procedure for defining noncombustibility of elementary materials set forth in ASTM E 136.

NONCONDITIONED SPACE. A space that is not a *conditioned space* by insulated walls, floors or ceilings.

NOSING. The leading edge of treads of stairs and of landings at the top of stairway flights.

OCCUPIED SPACE. The total area of all buildings or structures on any *lot* or parcel of ground projected on a horizontal plane, excluding permitted projections as allowed by this code.

OFFSET. A combination of fittings that makes two changes in direction bringing one section of the pipe out of line but into a line parallel with the other section.

OWNER. Any person, agent, firm or corporation having a legal or equitable interest in the property.

PANEL THICKNESS. Thickness of core plus two layers of structural wood panel facings.

PELLET FUEL-BURNING APPLIANCE. A closed combustion, vented *appliance* equipped with a fuel feed mechanism for burning processed pellets of solid fuel of a specified size and composition.

PELLET VENT. A vent *listed* and *labeled* for use with a *listed* pellet fuel-burning *appliance.*

PERMIT. An official document or certificate issued by the authority having *jurisdiction* that authorizes performance of a specified activity.

PERSON. An individual, heirs, executors, administrators or assigns, and also includes a firm, partnership or corporation, its or their successors or assigns, or the agent of any of the aforesaid.

PITCH. See "Slope."

PLANS. Construction documents.

PLATFORM CONSTRUCTION. A method of construction by which floor framing bears on load bearing walls that are not continuous through the *story* levels or floor framing.

PLENUM. A chamber that forms part of an air-circulation system other than the *occupied space* being conditioned.

PLUMBING. For the purpose of this code, plumbing refers to those installations, repairs, maintenance and *alterations* regulated by Chapters25 through 33.

PLUMBING APPLIANCE. An energized household *appliance* with plumbing connections, such as a dishwasher, food-waste grinder, clothes washer or water heater.

PLUMBING APPURTENANCE. A device or assembly that is an adjunct to the basic plumbing system and demands no additional water supply nor adds any discharge load to the system. It is presumed that it performs some useful function in the operation, maintenance, servicing, economy or safety of the plumbing system. Examples include filters, relief valves and aerators.

PLUMBING FIXTURE. A receptor or device that requires both a water-supply connection and a discharge to the drainage system, such as water closets, lavatories, bathtubs and sinks. Plumbing *appliances* as a special class of fixture are further defined.

PLUMBING SYSTEM. Includes the water supply and distribution pipes, plumbing fixtures, supports and appurtenances; soil, waste and vent pipes; sanitary drains and *building sewers* to an *approved* point of disposal.

POLLUTION. An impairment of the quality of the potable water to a degree that does not create a hazard to the public health but that does adversely and unreasonably affect the aesthetic qualities of such potable water for domestic use.

PORTABLE-FUEL-CELL APPLIANCE. A fuel cell generator of electricity, which is not fixed in place. A portable-fuel-cell *appliance* utilizes a cord and plug connection to a grid-isolated load and has an integral fuel supply.

POSITIVE ROOF DRAINAGE. Deleted.

POTABLE WATER. Water free from impurities present in amounts sufficient to cause disease or harmful physiological effects and conforming in bacteriological and chemical quality to the requirements of the public health authority having *jurisdiction.*

PRECAST CONCRETE. A structural concrete element cast elsewhere than its final position in the structure.

PRECAST CONCRETE FOUNDATION WALLS. Preengineered, precast concrete wall panels that are designed to withstand specified stresses and used to build below-*grade* foundations.

PRESSURE-RELIEF VALVE. A pressure-actuated valve held closed by a spring or other means and designed to automatically relieve pressure at the pressure at which it is set.

PUBLIC SEWER. A common sewer directly controlled by public authority.

PUBLIC WATER MAIN. A water-supply pipe for public use controlled by public authority.

PUBLIC WAY. Any street, alley or other parcel of land open to the outside air leading to a public street, which has been deeded, dedicated or otherwise permanently appropriated to the public for public use and that has a clear width and height of not less than 10 feet (3048 mm).

PURGE. To clear of air, gas or other foreign substances.

QUICK-CLOSING VALVE. A valve or faucet that closes automatically when released manually or controlled by mechanical means for fast-action closing.

***R*-VALUE, THERMAL RESISTANCE.** The inverse of the time rate of heat flow through a *building thermal envelope* element from one of its bounding surfaces to the other for a unit temperature difference between the two surfaces, under steady state conditions, per unit area ($h \cdot ft^2 \cdot °F/Btu$) [($m^2 \times K$)/W].

RAMP. A walking surface that has a running slope steeper than 1 unit vertical in 20 units horizontal (5-percent slope).

RECEPTOR. A fixture or device that receives the discharge from indirect waste pipes.

REFRIGERANT. A substance used to produce refrigeration by its expansion or evaporation.

REFRIGERANT COMPRESSOR. A specific machine, with or without accessories, for compressing a given refrigerant vapor.

REFRIGERATING SYSTEM. A combination of interconnected parts forming a closed circuit in which refrigerant is circulated for the purpose of extracting, then rejecting, heat. A direct refrigerating system is one in which the evaporator or condenser of the refrigerating system is in direct contact with the air or other substances to be cooled or heated. An indirect refrigerating system is one in which a secondary coolant cooled or heated by the refrigerating system is circulated to the air or other substance to be cooled or heated.

REGISTERED DESIGN PROFESSIONAL. An individual who is registered or licensed to practice their respective design profession as defined by the statutory requirements of the professional registration laws of the state or *jurisdiction* in which the project is to be constructed. Design by a registered design professional is not required where exempt under the registration or licensure laws.

RELIEF VALVE, VACUUM. A device to prevent excessive buildup of vacuum in a pressure vessel.

REPAIR. The reconstruction or renewal of any part of an existing building for the purpose of its maintenance.

REROOFING. The process of recovering or replacing an existing roof covering. See "Roof recover."

RETURN AIR. Air removed from an *approved conditioned space* or location and recirculated or exhausted.

RIDGE. With respect to topographic wind effects, an elongated crest of a hill characterized by strong relief in two directions.

RISER. A water pipe that extends vertically one full *story* or more to convey water to branches or to a group of fixtures.

ROOF ASSEMBLY. A system designed to provide weather protection and resistance to design loads. The system consists of a roof covering and roof deck or a single component serving as both the roof covering and the roof deck. A roof assembly includes the roof deck, vapor retarder, substrate or thermal barrier, insulation, vapor retarder, and roof covering.

ROOF COVERING. The covering applied to the roof deck for weather resistance, fire classification or appearance.

ROOF COVERING SYSTEM. See "Roof assembly."

ROOF DECK. The flat or sloped surface not including its supporting members or vertical supports.

ROOF RECOVER. The process of installing an additional roof covering over a prepared existing roof covering without removing the existing roof covering.

ROOF REPAIR. Reconstruction or renewal of any part of an existing roof for the purposes of its maintenance.

ROOFTOP STRUCTURE. An enclosed structure on or above the roof of any part of a building.

ROOM HEATER. A freestanding heating *appliance* installed in the space being heated and not connected to ducts.

ROUGH-IN. The installation of all parts of the plumbing system that must be completed prior to the installation of fixtures. This includes DWV, water supply and built-in fixture supports.

RUNNING BOND. The placement of masonry units such that head joints in successive courses are horizontally offset at least one-quarter the unit length.

SANITARY SEWER. A sewer that carries sewage and excludes storm, surface and groundwater.

SCREW LAMP HOLDERS. A lamp base that requires a screw-in-type lamp, such as a compact-fluorescent, incandescent, or tungsten-halogen bulb.

SCUPPER. An opening in a wall or parapet that allows water to drain from a roof.

SEISMIC DESIGN CATEGORY (SDC). A classification assigned to a structure based on its occupancy category and the severity of the design earthquake ground motion at the site.

SEMI-CONDITIONED SPACE. A space indirectly conditioned within the thermal envelope that is not directly heated or cooled. For energy purposes, semi-conditioned spaces are treated as conditioned spaces.

SEPTIC TANK. A water-tight receptor that receives the discharge of a building sanitary drainage system and is constructed so as to separate solids from the liquid, digest organic matter through a period of detention, and allow the liquids to discharge into the soil outside of the tank through a system of open joint or perforated piping or a seepage pit.

SERVICE WATER HEATING. Supply of hot water for purposes other than comfort heating.

SEWAGE. Any liquid waste containing animal matter, vegetable matter or other impurity in suspension or solution.

SEWAGE PUMP. A permanently installed mechanical device for removing sewage or liquid waste from a sump.

SHALL. The term, when used in the code, is construed as mandatory.

SHEAR WALL. A general term for walls that are designed and constructed to resist racking from seismic and wind by use of masonry, concrete, cold-formed steel or wood framing in accordance with Chapter 6 of this code and the associated limitations in Section R301.2 of this code.

SIDE VENT. A vent connecting to the drain pipe through a fitting at an angle less than 45 degrees (0.79 rad) to the horizontal.

SINGLE PLY MEMBRANE. A roofing membrane that is field applied using one layer of membrane material (either homogeneous or composite) rather than multiple layers.

SINGLE STATION SMOKE ALARM. An assembly incorporating the detector, control *equipment* and alarm sounding device in one unit that is operated from a power supply either in the unit or obtained at the point of installation.

SKYLIGHT AND SLOPED GLAZING. See Section R308.6.1.

SKYLIGHT, UNIT. See Section R308.6.1.

SLEEPING ROOM. A room designated as sleeping or bedroom on the plans.

SLIP JOINT. A mechanical-type joint used primarily on fixture traps. The joint tightness is obtained by compressing a friction-type washer such as rubber, nylon, neoprene, lead or special packing material against the pipe by the tightening of a (slip) nut.

SLOPE. The fall (pitch) of a line of pipe in reference to a horizontal plane. In drainage, the slope is expressed as the fall in units vertical per units horizontal (percent) for a length of pipe.

SMOKE-DEVELOPED INDEX. A comparative measure, expressed as a dimensionless number, derived from measurements of smoke obscuration versus time for a material tested in accordance with ASTM E 84.

SOIL STACK OR PIPE. A pipe that conveys sewage containing fecal material.

SOLAR HEAT GAIN COEFFICIENT (SHGC). The ratio of the solar heat gain entering the space through the fenestration assembly to the incident solar radiation. Solar heat gain includes directly transmitted solar heat and absorbed solar radiation which is then reradiated, conducted or convected into the space. This value is related to the Shading Coefficient (SC) by the formula SHGC = 0.87 × SC.

SOLID MASONRY. Load-bearing or nonload-bearing construction using masonry units where the net cross-sectional area of each unit in any plane parallel to the bearing surface is not less than 75 percent of its gross cross-sectional area. Solid masonry units shall conform to ASTM C 55, C 62, C 73, C 145 or C 216.

SPLINE. A strip of wood structural panel cut from the same material used for the panel facings, used to connect two structural insulated panels. The strip (spline) fits into a groove cut into the vertical edges of the two structural insulated panels to be joined. Splines are used behind each facing of the structural insulated panels being connected as shown in Figure R613.8.

STACK. Any main vertical DWV line, including offsets, that extends one or more stories as directly as possible to its vent terminal.

STACK BOND. The placement of masonry units in a bond pattern is such that head joints in successive courses are vertically aligned. For the purpose of this code, requirements for stack bond shall apply to all masonry laid in other than running bond.

STACK VENT. The extension of soil or waste stack above the highest horizontal drain connected.

STACK VENTING. A method of venting a fixture or fixtures through the soil or waste stack without individual fixture vents.

STAIR. A change in elevation, consisting of one or more risers.

STAIRWAY. One or more flights of stairs, either interior or exterior, with the necessary landings and platforms connecting them to form a continuous and uninterrupted passage from one level to another within or attached to a building, porch or deck.

STANDARD TRUSS. Any construction that does not permit the roof/ceiling insulation to achieve the required R-value over the *exterior walls*.

STATIONARY FUEL CELL POWER PLANT. A self-contained package or factory-matched packages which constitute an automatically-operated assembly of integrated systems for generating useful electrical energy and recoverable thermal energy that is permanently connected and fixed in place.

STORM SEWER, DRAIN. A pipe used for conveying rainwater, surface water, subsurface water and similar liquid waste.

STORY. That portion of a building included between the upper surface of a floor and the upper surface of the floor or roof next above. A flood resistant enclosure, designed to break away so as not to cause collapse, shall not be considered as a story when determining height.

STORY, ATTIC. Any story situated wholly or partly in the roof, so designated, arranged or built as to be used for storage or habitation. If an attic which is accessible by a fixed stairway has a 7 foot clear height for greater than 50 percent of the floor area of the story below, then the space shall be considered as a story.

STORY ABOVE GRADE PLANE. Any *story* having its finished floor surface entirely above *grade plane*, except that a *basement* shall be considered as a *story above grade plane* where the finished surface of the floor above the *basement* meets any one of the following:

1. Is more than 6 feet (1829 mm) *above grade plane*.
2. Is more than 6 feet (1829 mm) above the finished ground level for more than 50 percent of the total building perimeter.
3. Is more than 12 feet (3658 mm) above the finished ground level at any point.

STRUCTURAL INSULATED PANEL (SIP). A structural sandwich panel that consists of a light-weight foam plastic core securely laminated between two thin, rigid wood structural panel facings.

STRUCTURE. Deleted.

SUBSOIL DRAIN. A drain that collects subsurface water or seepage water and conveys such water to a place of disposal.

SUMP. A tank or pit that receives sewage or waste, located below the normal *grade* of the gravity system and that must be emptied by mechanical means.

SUMP PUMP. A pump installed to empty a sump. These pumps are used for removing storm water only. The pump is selected for the specific head and volume of the load and is usually operated by level controllers.

SUNROOM ADDITION. A one-story structure added to an existing dwelling with a glazing area in excess of 40 percent of the gross area of the structure's exterior walls and roof.

SUPPLY AIR. Air delivered to a *conditioned space* through ducts or plenums from the heat exchanger of a heating, cooling or ventilating system.

SUPPORTS. Devices for supporting, hanging and securing pipes, fixtures and *equipment*.

SWEEP. A drainage fitting designed to provide a change in direction of a drain pipe of less than the angle specified by the amount necessary to establish the desired slope of the line. Sweeps provide a longer turning radius than bends and a less turbulent flow pattern (see "Bend" and "Elbow").

TEMPERATURE- AND PRESSURE-RELIEF (T AND P) VALVE. A combination relief valve designed to function as both a temperature-relief and pressure-relief valve.

TEMPERATURE-RELIEF VALVE. A temperature-actuated valve designed to discharge automatically at the temperature at which it is set.

TERMITE-RESISTANT MATERIAL. Pressure-preservative treated wood in accordance with the AWPA standards in Section R318.1, naturally durable termite-resistant wood, steel, concrete, masonry or other *approved* material.

THERMAL ISOLATION. Physical and space conditioning separation from *conditioned space(s)* consisting of existing or new walls, doors and/or windows. The *conditioned space(s)* shall be controlled as separate zones for heating and cooling or conditioned by separate *equipment*.

THERMAL RESISTANCE, *R*-VALUE. The inverse of the time rate of heat flow through a body from one of its bounding surfaces to the other for a unit temperature difference between the two surfaces, under steady state conditions, per unit area ($h \cdot ft^2 \cdot °F/Btu$).

THERMAL TRANSMITTANCE, *U*-FACTOR. The coefficient of heat transmission (air to air) through a building envelope component or assembly, equal to the time rate of heat flow per unit area and unit temperature difference between the warm side and cold side air films ($Btu/h \cdot ft^2 \cdot °F$).

TOWNHOUSE. A single-family *dwelling unit* constructed in a row of attached units separated by property lines and with open space on at least two sides.

TRAP. A fitting, either separate or built into a fixture, that provides a liquid seal to prevent the emission of sewer gases without materially affecting the flow of sewage or waste water through it.

TRAP ARM. That portion of a *fixture drain* between a trap weir and the vent fitting.

TRAP PRIMER. A device or system of piping to maintain a water seal in a trap, typically installed where infrequent use of the trap would result in evaporation of the trap seal, such as floor drains.

TRAP SEAL. The trap seal is the maximum vertical depth of liquid that a trap will retain, measured between the crown weir and the top of the dip of the trap.

TRIM. Picture molds, chair rails, baseboards, handrails, door and window frames, and similar decorative or protective materials used in fixed applications.

TRUSS DESIGN DRAWING. The graphic depiction of an individual truss, which describes the design and physical characteristics of the truss.

TYPE L VENT. A *listed* and *labeled* vent conforming to UL 641 for venting oil-burning *appliances listed* for use with Type L vents or with gas *appliances listed* for use with Type B vents.

***U*-FACTOR, THERMAL TRANSMITTANCE.** The coefficient of heat transmission (air to air) through a building envelope component or assembly, equal to the time rate of heat flow per unit area and unit temperature difference between the warm side and cold side air films (Btu/h · ft^2 · °F).

UNDERLAYMENT. One or more layers of felt, sheathing paper, nonbituminous saturated felt, or other *approved* material over which a roof covering, with a slope of 2 to 12 (17-percent slope) or greater, is applied.

VACUUM BREAKERS. A device which prevents backsiphonage of water by admitting atmospheric pressure through ports to the discharge side of the device.

VAPOR PERMEABLE MEMBRANE. A material or covering having a permeance rating of 5 perms ($2.9 \cdot 10^{-10}$ kg/Pa · s · m^2) or greater, when tested in accordance with the desiccant method using Procedure A of ASTM E 96. A vapor permeable material permits the passage of moisture vapor.

VAPOR RETARDER CLASS. A measure of the ability of a material or assembly to limit the amount of moisture that passes through that material or assembly. Vapor retarder class shall be defined using the desiccant method with Procedure A of ASTM E 96 as follows:

Class I: 0.1 perm or less

Class II: 0.1 < perm ≤ 1.0 perm

Class III: 1.0 < perm ≤ 10 perm

VEHICULAR ACCESS DOOR. A door that is used primarily for vehicular traffic at entrances of buildings such as garages and parking lots, and that is not generally used for pedestrian traffic.

VENT. A passageway for conveying flue gases from fuel-fired *appliances*, or their vent connectors, to the outside atmosphere.

VENT COLLAR. See "Flue collar."

VENT CONNECTOR. That portion of a venting system which connects the flue collar or draft hood of an *appliance* to a vent.

VENT DAMPER DEVICE, AUTOMATIC. A device intended for installation in the venting system, in the outlet of an individual, automatically operated fuel burning *appliance* and that is designed to open the venting system automatically when the *appliance* is in operation and to close off the venting system automatically when the *appliance* is in a standby or shutdown condition.

VENT GASES. Products of combustion from fuel-burning *appliances*, plus excess air and dilution air, in the venting system above the draft hood or draft regulator.

VENT STACK. A vertical vent pipe installed to provide circulation of air to and from the drainage system and which extends through one or more stories.

VENT SYSTEM. Piping installed to equalize pneumatic pressure in a drainage system to prevent trap seal loss or blow-back due to siphonage or back pressure.

VENTILATION. The natural or mechanical process of supplying conditioned or unconditioned air to, or removing such air from, any space.

VENTING. Removal of combustion products to the outdoors.

VENTING SYSTEM. A continuous open passageway from the flue collar of an *appliance* to the outside atmosphere for the purpose of removing flue or vent gases. A venting system is usually composed of a vent or a chimney and vent connector, if used, assembled to form the open passageway.

VERTICAL PIPE. Any pipe or fitting that makes an angle of 45 degrees (0.79 rad) or more with the horizontal.

VINYL SIDING. A shaped material, made principally from rigid polyvinyl chloride (PVC), that is used to cover exterior walls of buildings.

WALL, ABOVE-GRADE. A wall more than 50 percent above grade and enclosing *conditioned space*. This includes between-floor spandrels, peripheral edges of floors, roof and basement knee walls, dormer walls, gable end walls, walls enclosing a mansard roof and skylight shafts.

WALL, CRAWLSPACE. The opaque portion of a wall that encloses a crawl space and is partially or totally below grade.

WALL, RETAINING. A wall not laterally supported at the top, that resists lateral soil load and other imposed loads.

WALL VENTED CRAWL SPACE. A foundation that uses foundation wall vents as a primary means to control space moisture. Insulation is located at the floor level.

WALLS. Walls shall be defined as follows:

Load-bearing wall is a wall supporting any vertical load in addition to its own weight.

Nonbearing wall is a wall which does not support vertical loads other than its own weight.

WASTE. Liquid-borne waste that is free of fecal matter.

WASTE PIPE OR STACK. Piping that conveys only liquid sewage not containing fecal material.

WATER-DISTRIBUTION SYSTEM. Piping which conveys water from the service to the plumbing fixtures, *appliances*, appurtenances, *equipment*, devices or other systems served, including fittings and control valves.

WATER HEATER. Any heating *appliance* or *equipment* that heats potable water and supplies such water to the potable hot water distribution system.

WATER MAIN. A water-supply pipe for public use.

WATER OUTLET. A valved discharge opening, including a hose bibb, through which water is removed from the potable water system supplying water to a plumbing fixture or plumbing *appliance* that requires either an air gap or backflow prevention device for protection of the supply system.

WATER-RESISTIVE BARRIER. A material behind an *exterior wall* covering that is intended to resist liquid water that has penetrated behind the exterior covering from further intruding into the *exterior wall* assembly.

WATER-SERVICE PIPE. The outside pipe from the water main or other source of potable water supply to the water-distribution system inside the building, terminating at the service valve.

WATER-SUPPLY SYSTEM. The water-service pipe, the water-distributing pipes and the necessary connecting pipes, fittings, control valves and all appurtenances in or adjacent to the building or premises.

WATERPROOFING. A coating or the application of coatings applied to prevent the penetration of water through or into walls or into interior spaces.

WET VENT. A vent that also receives the discharge of wastes from other fixtures.

WINDER. A tread with nonparallel edges.

WINDOW. See Fenestration.

WIND BORNE DEBRIS REGION. Areas within hurricane prone regions defined as that area east of the Intracoastal waterway from the NC/SC state line north to Beaufort Inlet and from that point to include the barrier islands to the NC/VA state line.

WOOD/PLASTIC COMPOSITE. A composite material made primarily from wood or cellulose-based materials and plastic.

WOOD STRUCTURAL PANEL. A panel manufactured from veneers; or wood strands or wafers; bonded together with waterproof synthetic resins or other suitable bonding systems. Examples of wood structural panels are plywood, OSB or composite panels.

YARD. An open space, other than a court, unobstructed from the ground to the sky, except where specifically provided by this code, on the *lot* on which a building is situated.

ZONE. A space or group of spaces within a building with heating or cooling requirements that are sufficiently similar so that desired conditions can be maintained throughout using a single controlling device.

Part III—Building Planning and Construction

CHAPTER 3
BUILDING PLANNING

SECTION R301
DESIGN CRITERIA

R301.1 Application. Buildings and structures, and all parts thereof, shall be constructed to safely support all loads, including dead loads, live loads, roof loads, flood loads, snow loads, wind loads and seismic loads as prescribed by this code. The construction of buildings and structures in accordance with the provisions of this code shall result in a system that provides a complete load path that meets all requirements for the transfer of all loads from their point of origin through the load-resisting elements to the foundation. Buildings and structures constructed as prescribed by this code are deemed to comply with the requirements of this section.

R301.1.1 Alternative provisions. As an alternative to the requirements in Section R301.1 the following standards are permitted subject to the limitations of this code and the limitations therein. Where engineered design is used in conjunction with these standards, the design shall comply with the *International Building Code*.

1. American Forest and Paper Association (AF&PA) *Wood Frame Construction Manual* (WFCM).
2. American Iron and Steel Institute (AISI) *Standard for Cold-Formed Steel Framing—Prescriptive Method for One- and Two-Family Dwellings* (AISI S230).
3. ICC-400 *Standard on the Design and Construction of Log Structures*.

R301.1.2 Construction systems. The requirements of this code are based on platform and balloon-frame construction for light-frame buildings. The requirements for concrete and masonry buildings are based on a balloon framing system. Other framing systems must have equivalent detailing to ensure force transfer, continuity and compatible deformations.

R301.1.3 Engineered design. When a building of otherwise conventional construction contains structural elements exceeding the limits of Section R301 or otherwise not conforming to this code, these elements shall be designed in accordance with accepted engineering practice. The extent of such design need only demonstrate compliance of nonconventional elements with other applicable provisions and shall be compatible with the performance of the conventional framed system. Engineered design in accordance with the *International Building Code* is permitted for all buildings and structures, and parts thereof, included in the scope of this code.

R301.2 Climatic and geographic design criteria. Buildings shall be constructed in accordance with the provisions of this code as limited by the provisions of this section. Additional criteria shall be established by the local *jurisdiction* and set forth in Table R301.2(1).

R301.2.1 Wind limitations. Buildings and portions thereof shall be limited by wind speed, as defined in Table R301.2(1) and construction methods in accordance with this code. Basic wind speeds shall be determined from Figure R301.2(4). Where different construction methods and structural materials are used for various portions of a building, the applicable requirements of this section for each portion shall apply. Where loads for curtain walls, exterior windows, skylights, garage doors and exterior doors are not otherwise specified, the loads listed in Table R301.2(2) adjusted for height and exposure using Table R301.2(3) shall be used to determine design load performance requirements for curtain walls, exterior windows, skylights, garage doors and exterior doors.

R301.2.1.1 Design criteria. Construction in regions where the basic wind speeds from Figure R301.2(4) equal or exceed 110 miles per hour (49 m/s) shall be designed in accordance with one of the following:

1. American Forest and Paper Association (AF&PA) *Wood Frame Construction Manual for One- and Two-Family Dwellings* (WFCM); or
2. International Code Council (ICC) *Standard for Residential Construction in High Wind Regions* (ICC-600); or
3. *Minimum Design Loads for Buildings and Other Structures* (ASCE-7); or
4. American Iron and Steel Institute (AISI), *Standard for Cold-Formed Steel Framing—Prescriptive Method For One- and Two-Family Dwellings* (AISI S230).
5. Concrete construction shall be designed in accordance with the provisions of this code.
6. Structural insulated panel (SIP) walls shall be designed in accordance with the provisions of this code.
7. High wind Chapters 45 and 46.

TABLE R301.2(1)
CLIMATIC AND GEOGRAPHIC DESIGN CRITERIA

ROOF LOAD	WIND SPEED (mph)	SEISMIC DESIGN CATEGORY	SUBJECT TO DAMAGE FROM			WINTER DESIGN TEMP	ICE BARRIER UNDERLAYMENT REQUIRED	FLOOD HAZARD[b]	AIR FREEZING INDEX	MEAN ANNUAL TEMP
			Weathering[a]	Frost line depth	Termite[c]					
20	Figure 301.2(4)	301.2(2)	Moderate	12″	Moderate-Heavy	Local	Local	Local	Local	Local

For SI: 1 pound per square foot = 0.0479 kN/m^2, 1 mile per hour = 1.609 km/h.

a. Weathering may require a higher strength concrete or grade of masonry than necessary to satisfy the structural requirements of this code. The grade of masonry units shall be determined from ASTM C 34, C 55, C 62, C 73, C 90, C 129, C 145, C 216 or C 652.

b. The Jurisdiction shall fill in this part of the table with (a) the date of the jurisdiction's entry into the National Flood Insurance Program (date of adoptions of the first code or ordinance for management of flood hazard areas), (b) the date(s) of the currently effective FIRM and FBFM, or other flood hazard map adopted by the community, as may be amended.

c. Protection is required in all of North Carolina per Section R318.

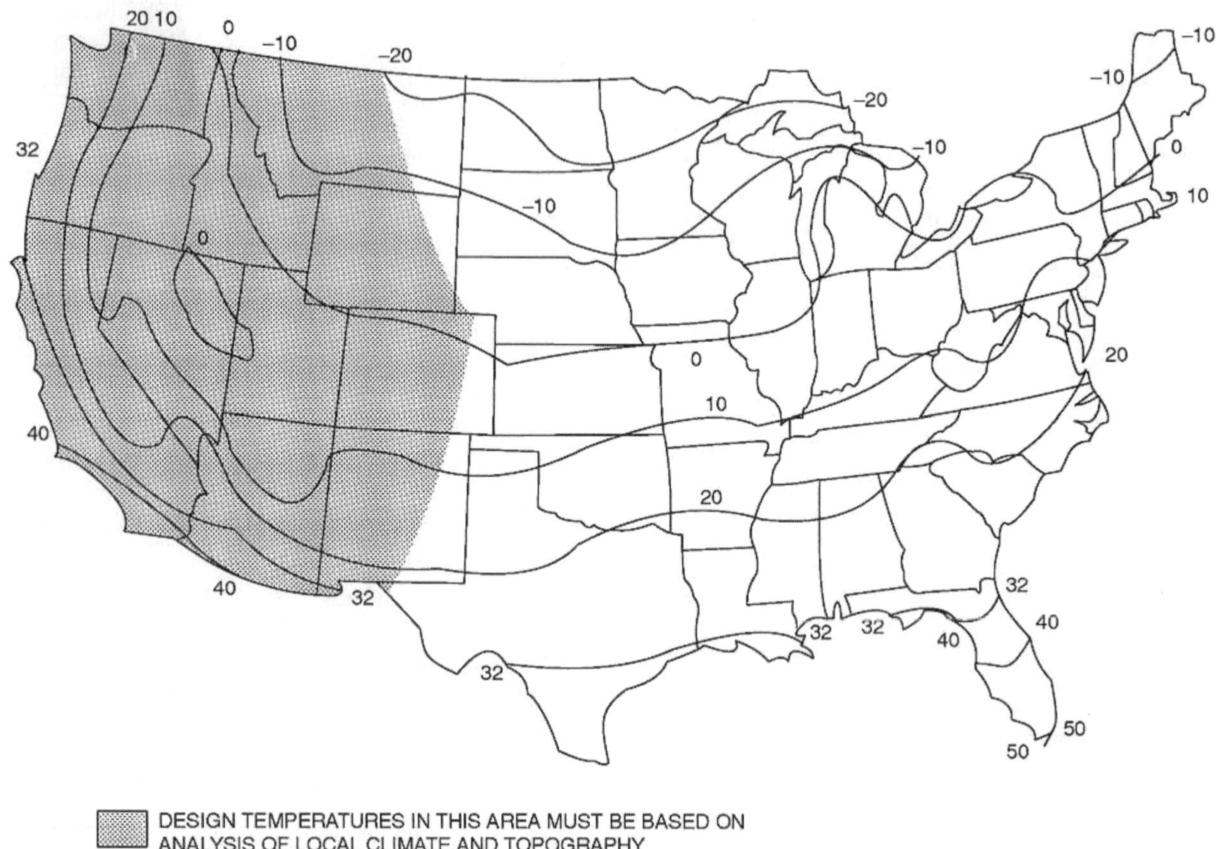

For SI: °C = [(°F)-32]/1.8.

FIGURE R301.2(1)
ISOLINES OF THE 97$^1/_2$ PERCENT WINTER (DECEMBER, JANUARY AND FEBRUARY) DESIGN TEMPERATURES (°F)

TABLE R301.2(2)
COMPONENT AND CLADDING LOADS FOR A BUILDING WITH A MEAN ROOF HEIGHT OF 30 FEET LOCATED IN EXPOSURE B (psf)[a, b, c, d, e]

	ZONE	EFFECTIVE WIND AREA (feet^2)	BASIC WIND SPEED (mph—3-second gust) 85		90		100		105		110		120		125		130		140		145		150		170	
Roof > 0 to 10 degrees	1	10	10.0	-13.0	10.0	-14.6	10.0	-18.0	10.0	-19.8	10.0	-21.8	10.5	-25.9	11.4	-28.1	12.4	-30.4	14.3	-35.3	15.4	-37.8	16.5	-40.5	21.1	-52.0
	1	20	10.0	-12.7	10.0	-14.2	10.0	-17.5	10.0	-19.3	10.0	-21.2	10.0	-25.2	10.7	-27.4	11.6	-29.6	13.4	-34.4	14.4	-36.9	15.4	-39.4	19.8	-50.7
	1	50	10.0	-12.2	10.0	-13.7	10.0	-16.9	10.0	-18.7	10.0	-20.5	10.0	-24.4	10.0	-26.4	10.6	-28.6	12.3	-33.2	13.1	-35.6	14.1	-38.1	18.1	-48.9
	1	100	10.0	-11.9	10.0	-13.3	10.0	-18.5	10.0	-18.2	10.0	-19.9	10.0	-23.7	10.0	-25.7	10.0	-27.8	11.4	-32.3	12.2	-34.6	13.0	-37.0	16.7	-47.6
	2	10	10.0	-21.8	10.0	-24.4	10.0	-30.2	10.0	-33.3	10.0	-36.5	10.5	-43.5	11.4	-47.2	12.4	-51.0	14.3	-59.2	15.4	-63.5	16.5	-67.9	21.1	-87.2
	2	20	10.0	-19.5	10.0	-21.8	10.0	-27.0	10.0	-29.7	10.0	-32.6	10.0	-38.8	10.7	-42.1	11.6	-45.6	13.4	-52.9	14.4	-56.7	15.4	-60.7	19.8	-78.0
	2	50	10.0	-16.4	10.0	-18.4	10.0	-22.7	10.0	-25.1	10.0	-27.5	10.0	-32.7	10.0	-35.5	10.6	-38.4	12.3	-44.5	13.1	-47.8	14.1	-51.1	18.1	-65.7
	2	100	10.0	-14.1	10.0	-15.8	10.0	-19.5	10.0	-21.5	10.0	-23.6	10.0	-28.1	10.0	-30.5	10.0	-33.0	11.4	-38.2	12.2	-41.0	13.0	-43.9	16.7	-56.4
	3	10	10.0	-32.8	10.0	-36.8	10.0	-45.4	10.0	-50.1	10.0	-55.0	10.5	-65.4	11.4	-71.0	12.4	-76.8	14.3	-89.0	15.4	-95.5	16.5	-102.2	21.1	-131.3
	3	20	10.0	-27.2	10.0	-30.5	10.0	-37.6	10.0	-41.5	10.0	-45.5	10.0	-54.2	10.7	-58.8	11.6	-63.6	13.4	-73.8	14.4	-79.1	15.4	-84.7	19.8	-108.7
	3	50	10.0	-19.7	10.0	-22.1	10.0	-27.3	10.0	-30.1	10.0	-33.1	10.0	-39.3	10.0	-42.7	10.6	-46.2	12.3	-53.5	13.1	-57.4	14.1	-61.5	18.1	-78.9
	3	100	10.0	-14.1	10.0	-15.8	10.0	-19.5	10.0	-21.5	10.0	-23.6	10.0	-28.1	10.0	-30.5	10.0	-33.0	11.4	-38.2	12.2	-41.0	13.0	-43.9	16.7	-56.4
Roof > 10 to 30 degrees	1	10	10.0	-11.9	10.0	-13.3	10.4	-16.5	11.4	-18.2	12.5	-19.9	14.9	-23.7	16.2	-25.7	17.5	-27.8	20.3	-32.3	21.8	-34.6	23.3	-37.0	30.0	-47.6
	1	20	10.0	-11.6	10.0	-13.0	10.0	-16.0	10.4	-17.6	11.4	-19.4	13.6	-23.0	14.8	-25.0	16.0	-27.0	18.5	-31.4	19.9	-33.7	21.3	-36.0	27.3	-46.3
	1	50	10.0	-11.1	10.0	-12.5	10.0	-15.4	10.0	-17.0	10.0	-18.6	11.9	-22.2	12.9	-24.1	13.9	-26.0	16.1	-30.2	17.3	-32.4	18.5	-34.6	23.8	-44.5
	1	100	10.0	-10.8	10.0	-12.1	10.0	-14.9	10.0	-16.5	10.0	-18.1	10.5	-21.5	11.4	-23.3	12.4	-25.2	14.3	-29.3	15.4	-31.4	16.5	-33.6	21.1	-43.2
	2	10	10.0	-25.1	10.0	-28.2	10.4	-34.8	11.4	-38.3	12.5	-42.1	14.9	-50.1	16.2	-54.3	17.5	-58.7	20.3	-68.1	21.8	-73.1	23.3	-78.2	30.0	-100.5
	2	20	10.0	-22.8	10.0	-25.6	10.0	-31.5	10.4	-34.8	11.4	-38.2	13.6	-45.4	14.8	-49.3	16.0	-53.3	18.5	-61.8	19.9	-66.3	21.3	-71.0	27.3	-91.2
	2	50	10.0	-19.7	10.0	-22.1	10.0	-27.3	10.0	-30.1	10.0	-33.0	11.9	-39.3	12.9	-42.7	13.9	-46.1	16.1	-53.5	17.3	-57.4	18.5	-61.4	23.8	-78.9
	2	100	10.0	-17.4	10.0	-19.5	10.0	-24.1	10.0	-26.6	10.0	-29.1	10.5	-34.7	11.4	-37.6	12.4	-40.7	14.3	-47.2	15.4	-50.6	16.5	-54.2	21.1	-69.6
	3	10	10.0	-25.1	10.0	-28.2	10.4	-34.8	11.4	-38.3	12.5	-42.1	14.9	-50.1	16.2	-54.3	17.5	-58.7	20.3	-68.1	21.8	-73.1	23.3	-78.2	30.0	-100.5
	3	20	10.0	-22.8	10.0	-25.6	10.0	-31.5	10.4	-34.8	11.4	-38.2	13.6	-45.4	14.8	-49.3	16.0	-53.3	18.5	-61.8	19.9	-66.3	21.3	-71.0	27.3	-91.2
	3	50	10.0	-19.7	10.0	-22.1	10.0	-27.3	10.0	-30.1	10.0	-33.0	11.9	-39.3	12.9	-42.7	13.9	-46.1	16.1	-53.5	17.3	-57.4	18.5	-61.4	23.8	-78.9
	3	100	10.0	-17.4	10.0	-19.5	10.0	-24.1	10.0	-26.6	10.0	-29.1	10.5	-34.7	11.4	-37.6	12.4	-40.7	14.3	-47.2	15.4	-50.6	16.5	-54.2	21.1	-69.6
Roof > 30 to 45 degrees	1	10	11.9	-13.0	13.3	-14.6	16.5	-18.0	18.2	-19.8	19.9	-21.8	23.7	-25.9	25.7	-28.1	27.8	-30.4	32.3	-35.3	34.6	-37.8	37.0	-40.5	47.6	-52.0
	1	20	11.6	-12.3	13.0	-13.8	16.0	-17.1	17.6	-18.8	19.4	-20.7	23.0	-24.6	25.0	-26.7	27.0	-28.9	31.4	-33.5	33.7	-35.9	36.0	-38.4	46.3	-49.3
	1	50	11.1	-11.5	12.5	-12.8	15.4	-15.9	17.0	-17.5	18.6	-19.2	22.2	-22.8	24.1	-24.8	26.0	-25.8	30.2	-31.1	32.4	-33.3	34.6	-35.7	44.5	-45.8
	1	100	10.8	-10.8	12.1	-12.1	14.9	-14.9	16.5	-16.5	18.1	-18.1	21.5	-21.5	23.3	-23.3	25.2	-25.2	29.3	-29.3	31.4	-31.4	33.6	-33.6	43.2	-43.2
	2	10	11.9	-15.2	13.3	-17.0	16.5	-21.0	18.2	-23.2	19.9	-25.5	23.7	-30.3	25.7	-32.9	27.8	-35.6	32.3	-41.2	34.6	-44.2	37.0	-47.3	47.6	-60.8
	2	20	11.6	-14.5	13.0	-16.3	16.0	-20.1	17.6	-22.2	19.4	-24.3	23.0	-29.0	25.0	-31.4	27.0	-34.0	31.4	-39.4	33.7	-42.3	36.0	-45.3	46.3	-58.1
	2	50	11.1	-13.7	12.5	-15.3	15.4	-18.9	17.0	-20.8	18.6	-22.9	22.2	-27.2	24.1	-29.5	26.0	-32.0	30.2	-37.1	32.4	-39.8	34.6	-42.5	44.5	-54.6
	2	100	10.8	-13.0	12.1	-14.6	14.9	-18.0	16.5	-19.8	18.1	-21.8	21.5	-25.9	23.3	-28.1	25.2	-30.4	29.3	-35.3	31.4	-37.8	33.6	-40.5	43.2	-52.0
	3	10	11.9	-15.2	13.3	-17.0	16.5	-21.0	18.2	-23.2	19.9	-25.5	23.7	-30.3	25.7	-32.9	27.8	-35.6	32.3	-41.2	34.6	-44.2	37.0	-47.3	47.6	-60.8
	3	20	11.6	-14.5	13.0	-16.3	16.0	-20.1	17.6	-22.2	19.4	-24.3	23.0	-29.0	25.0	-31.4	27.0	-34.0	31.4	-39.4	33.7	-42.3	36.0	-45.3	46.3	-58.1
	3	50	11.1	-13.7	12.5	-15.3	15.4	-18.9	17.0	-20.8	18.6	-22.9	22.2	-27.2	24.1	-29.5	26.0	-32.0	30.2	-37.1	32.4	-39.8	34.6	-42.5	44.5	-54.5
	3	100	10.8	-13.0	12.1	-14.6	14.9	-18.0	16.5	-19.8	18.1	-21.8	21.5	-25.9	23.3	-28.1	25.2	-30.4	29.3	-35.3	31.4	-37.8	33.6	-40.5	43.2	-52.0
Wall	4	10	13.0	-14.1	14.6	-15.8	18.0	-19.5	19.8	-21.5	21.8	-23.6	25.9	-28.1	28.1	-30.5	30.4	-33.0	35.3	-38.2	37.8	-41.0	40.5	-43.9	52.0	-56.4
	4	20	12.4	-13.5	13.9	-15.1	17.2	-18.7	18.9	-20.6	20.8	-22.6	24.7	-26.9	26.8	-29.2	29.0	-31.6	33.7	-36.7	36.1	-39.3	38.7	-42.1	49.6	-54.1
	4	50	11.6	-12.7	13.0	-14.3	16.1	-17.6	17.8	-19.4	19.5	-21.3	23.2	-25.4	25.2	-27.5	27.2	-29.8	31.6	-34.6	33.9	-37.1	36.2	-39.7	46.6	-51.0
	4	100	11.1	-12.2	12.4	-13.6	15.3	-16.8	16.9	-18.5	18.5	-20.4	22.0	-24.2	23.9	-26.3	25.9	-28.4	30.0	-33.0	32.2	-35.4	34.4	-37.8	44.2	-48.6
	5	10	13.0	-17.4	14.6	-19.5	18.0	-24.1	19.8	-26.6	21.8	-29.1	25.9	-34.7	28.1	-37.6	30.4	-40.7	35.3	-47.2	37.8	-50.6	40.5	-54.2	52.0	-69.6
	5	20	12.4	-16.2	13.9	-18.2	17.2	-22.5	18.9	-24.8	20.8	-27.2	24.7	-32.4	26.8	-35.1	29.0	-38.0	33.7	-44.0	36.1	-47.2	38.7	-50.5	49.6	-64.9
	5	50	11.6	-14.7	13.0	-16.5	16.1	-20.3	17.8	-22.4	19.5	-24.6	23.2	-29.3	25.2	-31.8	27.2	-34.3	31.6	-39.8	33.9	-42.7	36.2	-45.7	46.6	-58.7
	5	100	11.1	-13.5	12.4	-15.1	15.3	-18.7	16.9	-20.6	18.5	-22.6	22.0	-26.9	23.9	-29.2	25.9	-31.6	30.0	-36.7	32.2	-39.3	34.4	-42.1	44.2	-54.1

For SI: 1 foot = 304.8 mm, 1 square foot = 0.0929 m^2, 1 mile per hour = 0.447 m/s, 1 pound per square foot = 0.0479 kPa.

Notes:

a. The effective wind area shall be equal to the span length multiplied by an effective width. This width shall be permitted to be not be less than one-third the span length. For cladding fasteners, the effective wind area shall not be greater than the area that is tributary to an individual fastener.

b. For effective areas between those given above, the load may be interpolated; otherwise, use the load associated with the lower effective area.

c. Table values shall be adjusted for height and exposure by multiplying by the adjustment coefficient in Table R301.2(3).

d. See Figure R301.2(7) for location of zones.

e. Plus and minus signs signify pressures acting toward and away from the building surfaces.

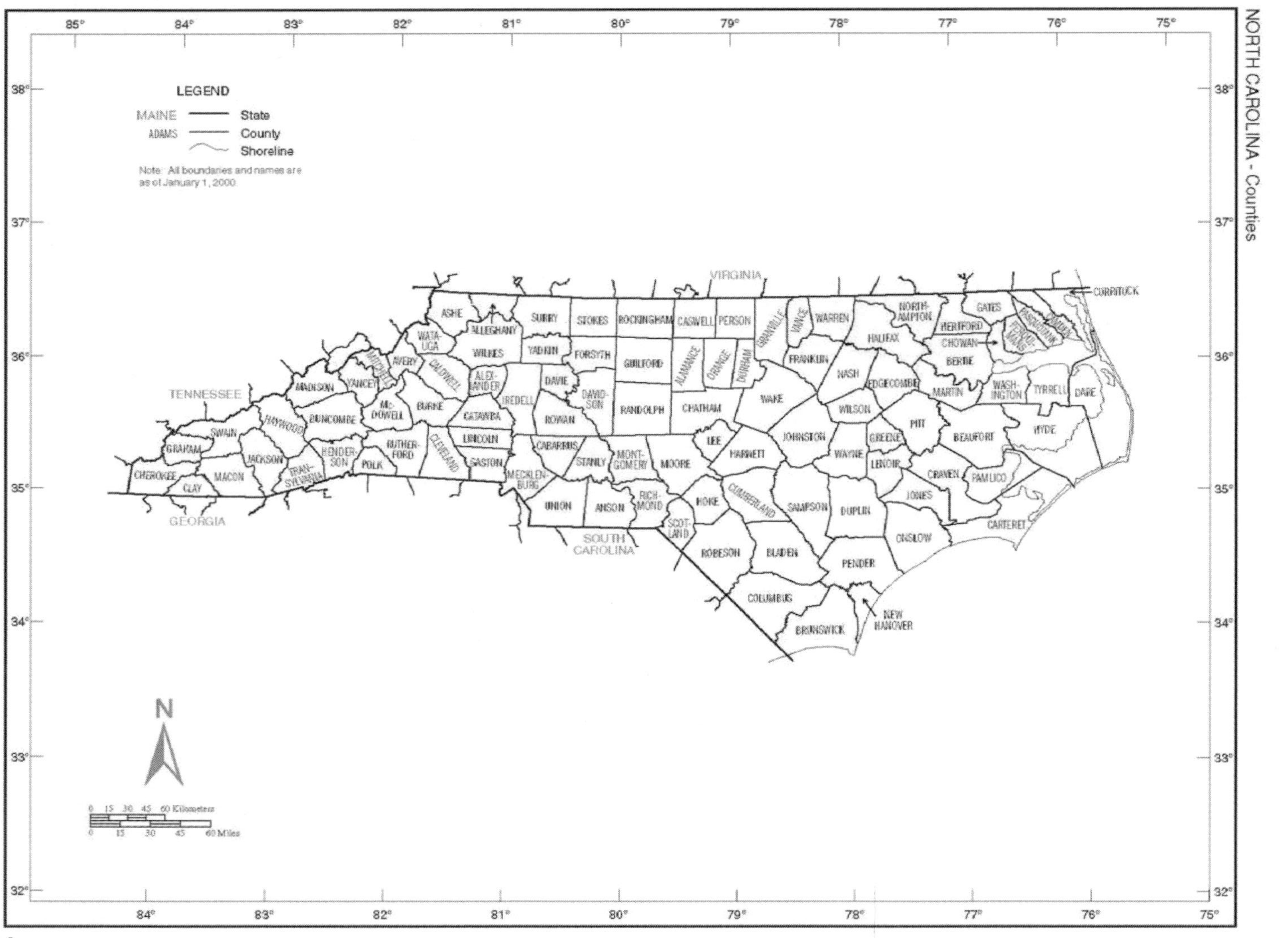

For SI: 1 foot = 304.8 mm.

a. Seismic data is based upon FIGURE R301.2(2) - continued in the *International Residential Code*, as adjusted for North Carolina.

b. The seismic provisions of this code shall apply to buildings constructed in Seismic Design Categories C in accordance with Section R301.2.2.

Exception: Detached one- and two-family dwellings located in Seismic Design Category C are exempt from the seismic requirements of this code.

FIGURE R301.2(2)
INTERNATIONAL RESIDENTIAL CODE - NORTH CAROLINA AMENDMENTS
SEISMIC DESIGN CATEGORIES - SITE CLASS D

(continued)

FIGURE R301.2(2)—continued

COUNTIES IN SEISMIC DESIGN CATEGORY C

Alleghany
Alexander
Anson
Ashe
Avery
Bladen
Brunswick
Buncombe
Burke
Caldwell
Catawba
Cherokee
Clay
Cleveland
Columbus
Gaston
Graham
Haywood
Henderson
Hoke
Iredell
Jackson
Lincoln
Macon
Madison
McDowell
Mecklenburg
Mitchell
Polk
Richmond
Robeson
Rutherford
Scotland
Surry
Swain
Transylvania
Union
Watauga
Wilkes
Yancey

TABLE R301.2(3)
HEIGHT AND EXPOSURE ADJUSTMENT COEFFICIENTS FOR TABLE R301.2(2)

MEAN ROOF HEIGHT	EXPOSURE		
	B	C	D
15	1.00	1.21	1.47
20	1.00	1.29	1.55
25	1.00	1.35	1.61
30	1.00	1.40	1.66
35	1.05	1.45	1.70
40	1.09	1.49	1.74
45	1.12	1.53	1.78
50	1.16	1.56	1.81
55	1.19	1.59	1.84
60	1.22	1.62	1.87

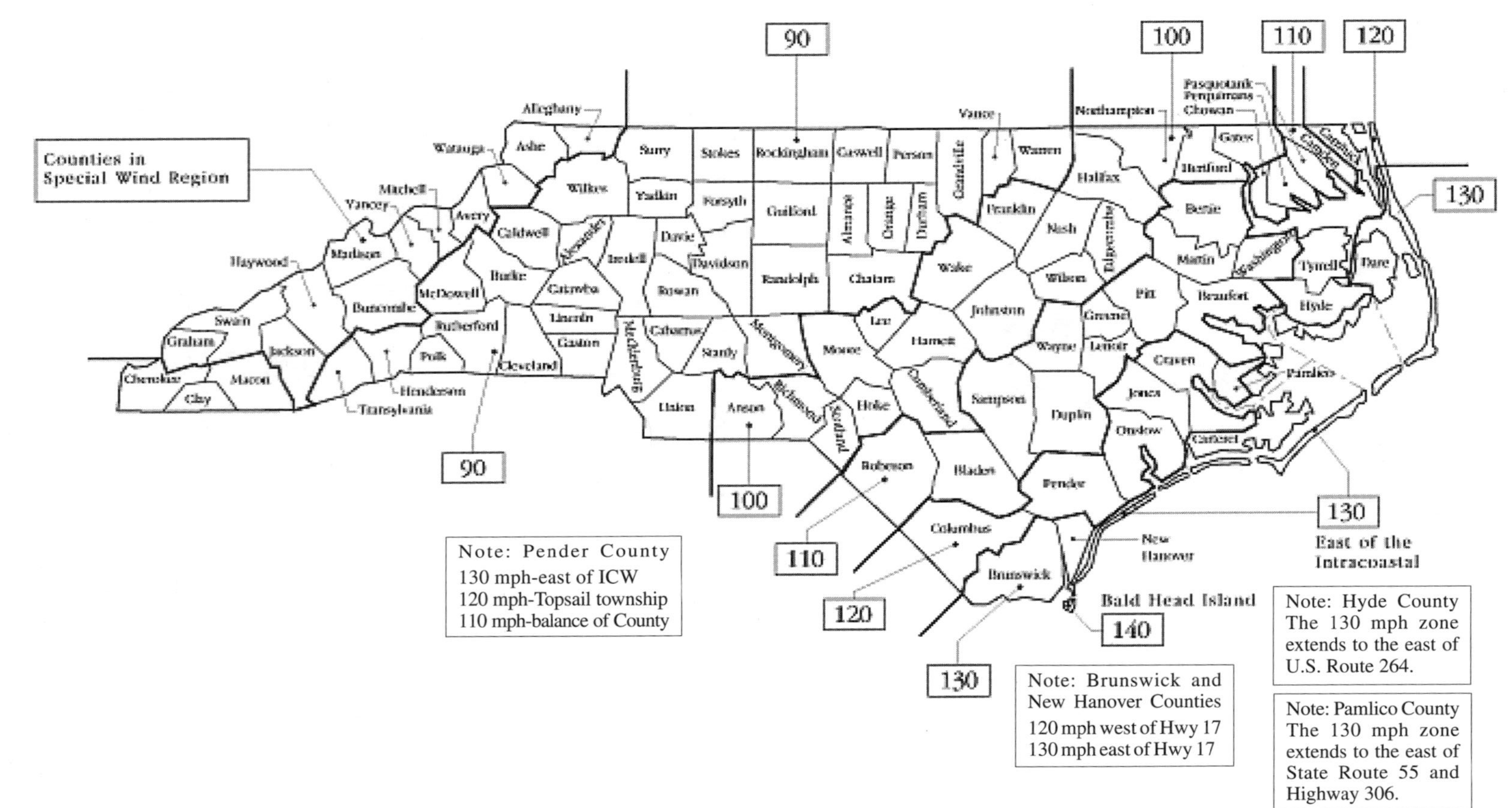

For SI: 1 foot = 304.8 mm, 1 mile per hour = 1.609 km/h..

a. Values are nominal design 3-second gust wind speeds in miles per hour at 33 feet above grade for Exposure C category.

b. Wind speed data is based upon FIGURE R301.2(4)—*continued* in the *International Residential Code*, as adjusted for North Carolina.

c. Mountain terrain, gorges, ocean promontories, and special wind regions shall be examined for unusual wind conditions.

FIGURE R301.2(4)
INTERNATIONAL RESIDENTIAL CODE - NORTH CAROLINA AMENDMENTS
BASIC WIND SPEEDS FOR 50-YEAR MEAN RECURRENCE INTERVAL

(continued)

FIGURE R301.2(4)—continued
BASIC DESIGN WIND SPEEDS FOR 50-YEAR MEAN RECURRENCE INTERVAL

Counties not listed	90		
Anson	100	Lee	100
Alleghany	special mountain region	Lenior	110
Ashe	special mountain region	Madison	special mountain region
Avery	special mountain region	Martin	110
Beaufort	110	Mitchell	special mountain region
Bertie	110	Moore	100
Bladen	110	Nash	100
Brunswick[1]	120/130	New Hanover[3]	120/130
Buncombe	special mountain region	Northampton	100
Camden	110	Onslow	120/130 east of ICW
Carteret	130	Pamlico[5]	120/130
Chowan	110	Pasquotank	110
Columbus	120	Pender[4]	110/120/130
Craven	120	Perquimans	110
Cumberland	100	Pitt	110
Currituck	120	Richmond	100
Dare	130	Robeson	110
Duplin	110	Sampson	110
Edgecombe	100	Scotland	100
Franklin	100	Swain	special mountain region
Gates	100	Tyrell	120
Graham	special mountain region	Wake	100
Greene	110	Washington	110
Halifax	100	Watauga	special mountain region
Harnett	100	Wayne	110
Haywood	special mountain region	Wilson	100
Hertford	100	Yancey	special mountain region
Hoke	100		
Hyde[2]	120/130		
Jackson	special mountain region		
Johnston	100		
Jones	120		

1. Brunswick County - 120 mph zone west of Hwy 17, 130 mph zone east of Hwy 17, 140 mph on Bald Head Island.
2. Hyde County - 120 mph zone west of U.S. Route 264, 130 mph zone east of U.S. Route 264.
3. New Hanover County - 120 mph zone west of Hwy 17, 130 mph zone east of Hwy 17.
4. Pender County - 130 mph zone east of the Intercoastal Waterway, 120 mph zone in the Township of Topsail, and the remainder of the County is the 110 mph zone.
5. Pamilico County - 130 mph zone east of SR 55 and Hwy 306, 120 mph zone west of SR 55 and Hwy 306.

FIGURE R301.2(4)—continued
BASIC DESIGN WIND VELOCITIES FOR MOUNTAIN REGIONS

FIRST FLOOR FINISH ELEVATION IN FEET	DESIGN WIND (MPH)
Less than 2,700	90
2,700 to less than 3,000 feet	100
3,000 to less than 3,500 feet	110
3,500 to less than 4,500 feet	120
4,500 feet or greater	130

For SI: 1 foot = 304.8, 1 mile per hour = 0.44 m/s.

TABLE R301.2(4)—continued
DESIGN PRESSURES FOR DOORS AND WINDOWS [a,b,c,d]
POSITIVE AND NEGATIVE IN PSF

VELOCITY (mph)	MEAN ROOF HEIGHT (ft)		
	15	25	35
90	15	17	19
100	20	23	25

For SI: 1 foot = 304.8, 1 mile per hour = 0.44 m/s.

a. Alternative design pressures may be determined by using *North Carolina State Building Code* – General Construction, ASCE-7, or the 2009 *International Building Code.*

b. If window or door is more than 4 feet (1219 mm) from a corner, the pressure from this table shall be permitted to be multiplied by 0.87. This adjustment does not apply to garage doors.

c. For windows and doors in structures with a roof slope of 10 degrees (0.0745 rad) or less (2:12) from the table may be multiplied by 0.90.

d. Design pressure ratings based on standards listed in Section R613 are adequate documentation of capacity to resist pressures from the table.

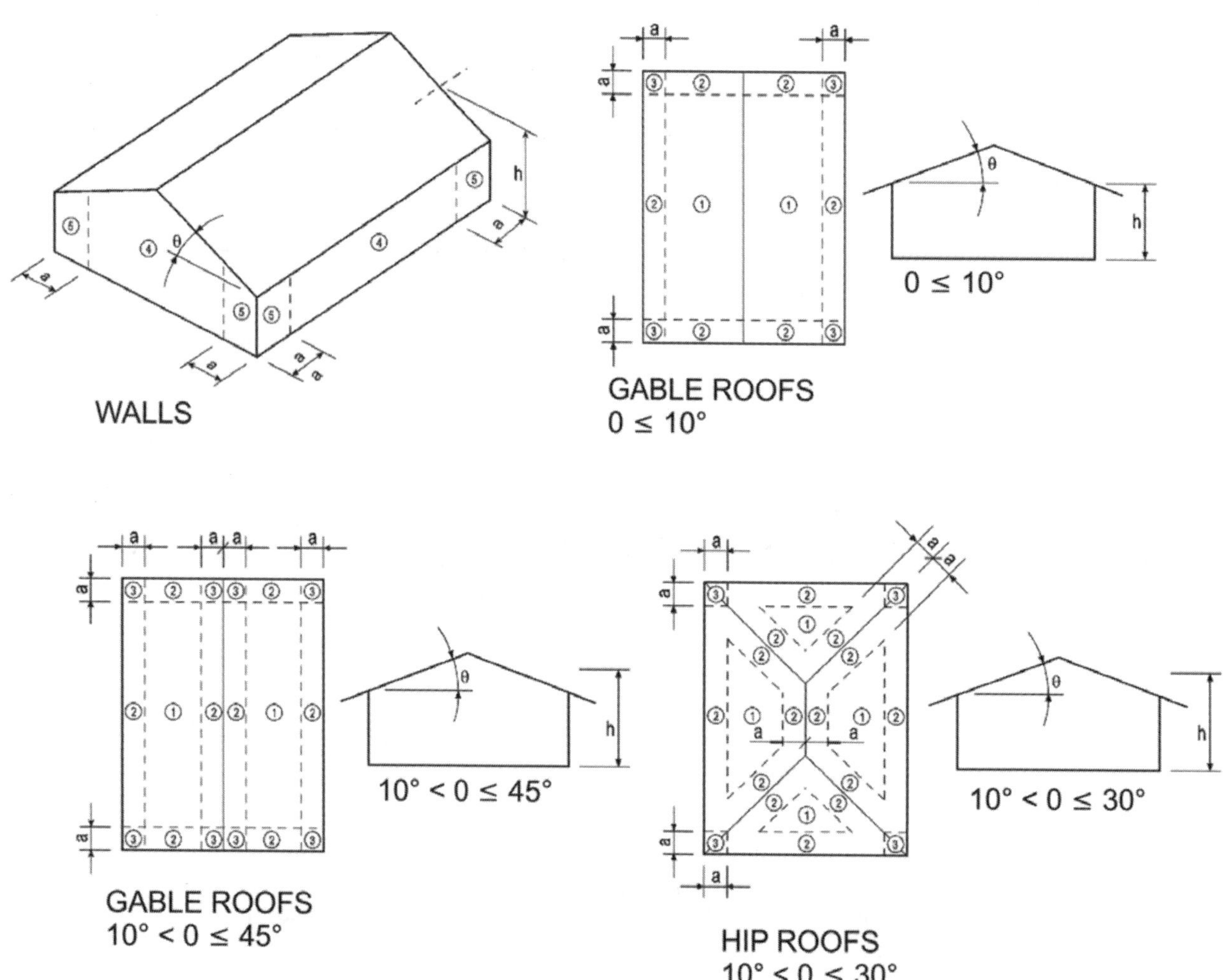

For SI: 1 foot = 304.8 mm, 1 degree = 0.0175 rad.

Note: a = 4 feet in all cases.

FIGURE R301.2(7)
COMPONENT AND CLADDING PRESSURE ZONES

For SI: 1 foot = 304.8 mm, 1 pound per square foot = 0.0479 kPa.

FIGURE R301.2(5)
GROUND SNOW LOADS, P_g, FOR THE UNITED STATES (lb/ft^2)

R301.2.1.2 Protection of openings. Windows in buildings located in windborne debris regions shall have glazed openings protected from windborne debris. Glazed opening protection for windborne debris shall meet the requirements of the Large Missile Test of ASTM E 1996 and ASTM E 1886 referenced therein. Garage door glazed opening protection for windborne debris shall meet the requirements of an *approved* impact resisting standard or ANSI/DASMA 115.

Exception: Wood structural panels with a minimum thickness of $^7/_{16}$ inch (11 mm) and a maximum span of 8 feet (2438 mm) shall be permitted for opening protection in one- and two-story buildings. Panels shall be precut so that they can be attached to the framing surrounding the opening containing the product with the glazed opening. Panels shall be predrilled as required for the anchorage method and shall be secured with the attachment hardware provided. Attachments shall be designed to resist the component and cladding loads determined in accordance with either Table R301.2(2) or ASCE 7, with the permanent corrosion- resistant attachment hardware provided and anchors permanently installed on the building. Attachment in accordance with Table R301.2.1.2 is permitted for buildings with a mean roof height of 33 feet (10 058 mm) or less where windspeeds do not exceed 130 miles per hour (58 m/s).

TABLE R301.2.1.2
WINDBORNE DEBRIS PROTECTION FASTENING SCHEDULE FOR WOOD STRUCTURAL PANELS[a, b, c, d]

FASTENER TYPE	FASTENER SPACING (inches)[a, b]		
	Panel span ≤ 4 feet	4 feet < panel span ≤ 6 feet	6 feet < panel span ≤ 8 feet
No. 8 wood screw based anchor with 2-inch embedment length	16	10	8
No. 10 wood screw based anchor with 2-inch embedment length	16	12	9
$^1/_4$-inch lag screw based anchor with 2-inch embedment length	16	16	16

For SI: 1 inch = 25.4 mm, 1 foot = 304.8 mm, 1 pound = 4.448 N, 1 mile per hour = 0.447 m/s.

a. This table is based on 130 mph wind speeds and a 33-foot mean roof height.

b. Fasteners shall be installed at opposing ends of the wood structural panel. Fasteners shall be located a minimum of 1 inch from the edge of the panel.

c. Anchors shall penetrate through the exterior wall covering with an embedment length of 2 inches minimum into the building frame. Fasteners shall be located a minimum of $2^1/_2$ inches from the edge of concrete block or concrete.

d. Where panels are attached to masonry or masonry/stucco, they shall be attached using vibration-resistant anchors having a minimum ultimate withdrawal capacity of 1500 pounds.

R301.2.1.3 Wind speed conversion. When referenced documents are based on fastest mile wind speeds, the three-second gust basic wind speeds, V_{3s}, of Figure R301.2(4) shall be converted to fastest mile wind speeds, V_{fm}, using Table R301.2.1.3.

R301.2.1.4 Exposure category. For each wind direction considered, an exposure category that adequately reflects the characteristics of ground surface irregularities shall be determined for the site at which the building or structure is to be constructed. For a site located in the transition zone between categories, the category resulting in the largest wind forces shall apply. Account shall be taken of variations in ground surface roughness that arise from natural topography and vegetation as well as from constructed features. For a site where multiple detached one- and two-family dwellings, *townhouses* or other structures are to be constructed as part of a subdivision, master-planned community, or otherwise designated as a developed area by the authority having jurisdiction, the exposure category for an individual structure shall be based upon the site conditions that will exist at the time when all adjacent structures on the site have been constructed, provided their construction is expected to begin within one year of the start of construction for the structure for which the exposure category is determined. For any given wind direction, the exposure in which a specific building or other structure is sited shall be assessed as being one of the following categories:

1. Exposure A. Large city centers with at least 50 percent of the buildings having a height in excess of 70 feet (21 336 mm). Use of this exposure category shall be limited to those areas for which terrain representative of Exposure A prevails in the upwind direction for a distance of at least 0.5 mile (0.8 km) or 10 times the height of the building or other structure, whichever is greater. Possible channeling effects or increased velocity pressures due to the building or structure being located in the wake of adjacent buildings shall be taken into account.

2. Exposure B. Urban and suburban areas, wooded areas, or other terrain with numerous closely spaced obstructions having the size of single-family dwellings or larger. Exposure B shall be assumed unless the site meets the definition of another type exposure.

TABLE R301.2.1.3
EQUIVALENT BASIC WIND SPEEDS[a]

3-second gust, V_{3s}	85	90	100	105	110	120	125	130	140	145	150	160	170
Fastest mile, V_{fm}	71	76	85	90	95	104	109	114	123	128	133	142	152

For SI: 1 mile per hour = 0.447 m/s.

a. Linear interpolation is permitted.

3. Exposure C. Open terrain with scattered obstructions, including surface undulations or other irregularities, having heights generally less than 30 feet (9144 mm) extending more than 1,500 feet (457 m) from the building site in any quadrant. This exposure shall also apply to any building located within Exposure B type terrain where the building is directly adjacent to open areas of Exposure C type terrain in any quadrant for a distance of more than 600 feet (183 m). This category includes flat open country, grasslands and shorelines in hurricane prone regions.
4. Exposure D. Flat, unobstructed areas exposed to wind flowing over open water (excluding shorelines in hurricane prone regions) for a distance of at least 1 mile (1.61 km). Shorelines in Exposure D include inland waterways, the Great Lakes, and coastal areas of California, Oregon, Washington and Alaska. This exposure shall apply only to those buildings and other structures exposed to the wind coming from over the water. Exposure D extends inland from the shoreline a distance of 1500 feet (457 m) or 10 times the height of the building or structure, whichever is greater.

R301.2.2 Seismic provisions. The seismic provisions of this code shall apply to buildings constructed in Seismic Design Categories C, D_0, D_1 and D_2, as determined in accordance with this section.

Exception: Detached one- and two-family *dwellings* located in Seismic Design Category C are exempt from the seismic requirements of this code.

R301.2.2.1 Determination of seismic design category. Buildings shall be assigned a seismic design category in accordance with Figure R301.2(2).

R301.2.2.2 Seismic Design Category C. Townhouse structures assigned to Seismic Design Category C shall conform to the requirements of this section.

R301.2.2.2.1 Weights of materials. Average dead loads shall not exceed 15 pounds per square foot (720 Pa) for the combined roof and ceiling assemblies (on a horizontal projection) or 10 pounds per square foot (480 Pa) for floor assemblies, except as further limited by Section R301.2.2. Dead loads for walls above *grade* shall not exceed:

1. Fifteen pounds per square foot (720 Pa) for exterior light-frame wood walls.
2. Fourteen pounds per square foot (670 Pa) for exterior light-frame cold-formed steel walls.
3. Ten pounds per square foot (480 Pa) for interior light-frame wood walls.
4. Five pounds per square foot (240 Pa) for interior light-frame cold-formed steel walls.
5. Eighty pounds per square foot (3830 Pa) for 8-inch-thick (203 mm) masonry walls.
6. Eighty-five pounds per square foot (4070 Pa) for 6-inch-thick (152 mm) concrete walls.
7. Ten pounds per square foot (480 Pa) for SIP walls.

Exceptions:

1. Roof and ceiling dead loads not exceeding 25 pounds per square foot (1190 Pa) shall be permitted provided the wall bracing amounts in Chapter 6 are increased in accordance with Table R301.2.2.2.1.
2. Light-frame walls with stone or masonry veneer shall be permitted in accordance with the provisions of Sections R702.1 and R703.
3. Fireplaces and chimneys shall be permitted in accordance with Chapter 10.

TABLE R301.2.2.2.1
WALL BRACING ADJUSTMENT FACTORS BY ROOF COVERING DEAD LOAD[a]

WALL SUPPORTING	ROOF/CEILING DEAD LOAD	
	15 psf or less	25 psf
Roof only	1.0	1.2
Roof plus one or two stories	1.0	1.1

For SI: 1 pound per square foot = 0.0479 kPa.
a. Linear interpolation shall be permitted.

R301.2.2.2.2 Stone and masonry veneer. Anchored stone and masonry veneer shall comply with the requirements of Sections R702.1 and R703.

R301.2.2.2.3 Masonry construction. Masonry construction shall comply with the requirements of Section R606.11.2.

R301.2.2.2.4 Concrete construction. *Townhouses* with above-*grade* exterior concrete walls shall comply with the requirements of PCA 100 or shall be designed in accordance with ACI 318.

R301.2.2.2.5 Irregular buildings. Prescriptive construction as regulated by this code shall not be used for irregular structures located in Seismic Design Categories C, D_0, D_1 and D_2. Irregular portions of structures shall be designed in accordance with accepted engineering practice to the extent the irregular features affect the performance of the remaining structural system. When the forces associated with the irregularity are resisted by a structural system designed in accordance with accepted engineering practice, design of the remainder of the building shall be permitted using the provisions of this code. A building or portion of a building shall be considered to be irregular when one or more of the following conditions occur:

1. When exterior shear wall lines or *braced wall panels* are not in one plane vertically from the

foundation to the uppermost *story* in which they are required.

Exception: For wood light-frame construction, floors with cantilevers or setbacks not exceeding four times the nominal depth of the wood floor joists are permitted to support *braced wall panels* that are out of plane with *braced wall panels* below provided that:

1. Floor joists are nominal 2 inches by 10 inches (51 mm by 254 mm) or larger and spaced not more than 16 inches (406 mm) on center.
2. The ratio of the back span to the cantilever is at least 2 to 1.
3. Floor joists at ends of *braced wall panels*are doubled.
4. For wood-frame construction, a continuous rim joist is connected to ends of all cantilever joists. When spliced, the rim joists shall be spliced using a galvanized metal tie not less than 0.058 inch (1.5 mm) (16 gage) and $1^1/_2$ inches (38 mm) wide fastened with six 16d nails on each side of the splice or a block of the same size as the rim joist of sufficient length to fit securely between the joist space at which the splice occurs fastened with eight 16d nails on each side of the splice; and
5. Gravity loads carried at the end of cantilevered joists are limited to uniform wall and roof loads and the reactions from headers having a span of 8 feet (2438 mm) or less.

2. When a section of floor or roof is not laterally supported by shear walls or *braced wall lines* on all edges.

Exception: Portions of floors that do not support shear walls or *braced wall panels* above, or roofs, shall be permitted to extend no more than 6 feet (1829 mm) beyond a shear wall or *braced wall line.*

3. When the end of a *braced wall panel* occurs over an opening in the wall below and ends at a horizontal distance greater than 1 foot (305 mm) from the edge of the opening. This provision is applicable to shear walls and *braced wall panels* offset in plane and to *braced wall panels* offset out of plane as permitted by the exception to Item 1 above.

Exception: For wood light-frame wall construction, one end of a *braced wall panel* shall be permitted to extend more than 1 foot (305 mm) over an opening not more than 8 feet (2438 mm) wide in the wall below provided that the opening includes a header in accordance with the following:

1. The building width, loading condition and framing member species limitations of Table R502.5(1) shall apply; and
2. Not less than one 2 × 12 or two 2 × 10 for an opening not more than 4 feet (1219 mm) wide; or
3. Not less than two 2 × 12 or three 2 × 10 for an opening not more than 6 feet (1829 mm) wide; or
4. Not less than three 2 × 12 or four 2 × 10 for an opening not more than 8 feet (2438 mm) wide; and
5. The entire length of the *braced wall panel* does not occur over an opening in the wall below.

4. When an opening in a floor or roof exceeds the lesser of 12 feet (3658 mm) or 50 percent of the least floor or roof dimension.
5. When portions of a floor level are vertically offset.

Exceptions:

1. Framing supported directly by continuous foundations at the perimeter of the building.
2. For wood light-frame construction, floors shall be permitted to be vertically offset when the floor framing is lapped or tied together as required by Section R502.6.1.

6. When shear walls and *braced wall lines* do not occur in two perpendicular directions.
7. When stories above-*grade* partially or completely braced by wood wall framing in accordance with Section R602 or steel wall framing in accordance with Section R603 include masonry or concrete construction.

Exception: Fireplaces, chimneys and masonry veneer as permitted by this code. When this irregularity applies, the entire *story* shall be designed in accordance with accepted engineering practice.

R301.2.3 Snow loads. Wood framed construction, cold-formed steel framed construction and masonry and concrete construction, and structural insulated panel construction in regions with ground snow loads 70 pounds per square foot (3.35 kPa) or less, shall be in accordance with Chapters 5, 6 and 8. Buildings in regions with ground snow loads greater than 70 pounds per square foot (3.35 kPa) shall be designed in accordance with accepted engineering practice.

R301.2.4 Floodplain construction. Buildings and structures constructed in whole or in part in flood hazard areas (including A or V Zones) as established in Table R301.2(1) shall be designed and constructed in accordance with Section R322.

Exception: Buildings in floodways that are designated on the Flood Insurance Rate Maps (FIRM) or the Flood Boundary and Floodway Maps (FBFM) that are provided by the National Flood Insurance Program shall not be approved under this section; the provisions of the ASCE 24 shall apply.

R301.2.4.1 Alternative provisions. As an alternative to the requirements in Section R322.3 for buildings and structures located in whole or in part in coastal high hazard areas (V Zones), ASCE 24 is permitted subject to the limitations of this code and the limitations therein.

R301.3 Story height. Buildings constructed in accordance with these provisions shall be limited to *story heights* of not more than the following:

1. For wood wall framing, the laterally unsupported bearing wall stud height permitted by Table R602.3(5) plus a height of floor framing not to exceed 16 inches (406 mm).

   Exception: For wood framed wall buildings with bracing in accordance with Tables R602.10.1.2(1) and R602.10.1.2(2), the wall stud clear height used to determine the maximum permitted *story height* may be increased to 12 feet (3658 mm) without requiring an engineered design for the building wind and seismic force resisting systems provided that the length of bracing required by Table R602.10.1.2(1) is increased by multiplying by a factor of 1.10 and the length of bracing required by Table R602.10.1.2(2) is increased by multiplying by a factor of 1.20. Wall studs are still subject to the requirements of this section.

2. For steel wall framing, a stud height of 10 feet (3048 mm), plus a height of floor framing not to exceed 16 inches (406 mm).
3. For masonry walls, a maximum bearing wall clear height of 12 feet (3658 mm) plus a height of floor framing not to exceed 16 inches (406 mm).

   Exception: An additional 8 feet (2438 mm) is permitted for gable end walls.

4. For insulating concrete form walls, the maximum bearing wall height per *story* as permitted by Section R611 tables plus a height of floor framing not to exceed 16 inches (406 mm).
5. For structural insulated panel (SIP) walls, the maximum bearing wall height per *story* as permitted by Section 614 tables shall not exceed 10 feet (3048 mm) plus a height of floor framing not to exceed 16 inches (406 mm).

Individual walls or walls studs shall be permitted to exceed these limits as permitted by Chapter 6 provisions, provided *story heights* are not exceeded. Floor framing height shall be permitted to exceed these limits provided the *story height* does not exceed 11 feet 7 inches (3531 mm). An engineered design shall be provided for the wall or wall framing members when they exceed the limits of Chapter 6. Where the *story height* limits are exceeded, an engineered design shall be provided in accordance with the *International Building Code* for the overall wind and seismic force resisting systems.

R301.4 Dead load. The actual weights of materials and construction shall be used for determining dead load with consideration for the dead load of fixed service *equipment*.

R301.5 Live load. The minimum uniformly distributed live load shall be as provided in Table R301.5.

TABLE R301.5
MINIMUM UNIFORMLY DISTRIBUTED LIVE LOADS
(in pounds per square foot)

USE	LIVE LOAD
Attics without storage[b]	10
Attics with limited storage[b, g]	20
Habitable attics and attics served with fixed stairs	30
Balconies (exterior) and decks[e]	40
Fire escapes	40
Guardrails and handrails[d]	200[h]
Guardrail in-fill components[f]	50[h]
Passenger vehicle garages[a]	50[a]
Rooms other than sleeping room	40
Sleeping rooms	30
Stairs	40[c]

For SI: 1 pound per square foot = 0.0479 kPa, 1 square inch = 645 mm^2, 1 pound = 4.45 N.

a. Elevated garage floors shall be capable of supporting a 2,000-pound load applied over a 20-square-inch area.

b. Attics without storage are those where the maximum clear height between joist and rafter is less than 42 inches, or where there are not two or more adjacent trusses with the same web configuration capable of containing a rectangle 42 inches high by 2 feet wide, or greater, located within the plane of the truss. For attics without storage, this live load need not be assumed to act concurrently with any other live load requirements.

c. Individual stair treads shall be designed for the uniformly distributed live load or a 300-pound concentrated load acting over an area of 4 square inches, whichever produces the greater stresses.

d. A single concentrated load applied in any direction at any point along the top.

e. See Section R502.2.2 for decks attached to exterior walls.

f. Guard in-fill components (all those except the handrail), balusters and panel fillers shall be designed to withstand a horizontally applied normal load of 50 pounds on an area equal to 1 square foot. This load need not be assumed to act concurrently with any other live load requirement.

g. For attics with limited storage and constructed with trusses, this live load need be applied only to those portions of the bottom chord where there are two or more adjacent trusses with the same web configuration capable of containing a rectangle 42 inches high or greater by 2 feet wide or greater, located within the plane of the truss. The rectangle shall fit between the top of the bottom chord and the bottom of any other truss member, provided that each of the following criteria is met.

   1. The attic area is accessible by a pull-down stairway or framed opening in accordance with Section R807.1.
   2. The truss has a bottom chord pitch less than 2:12.
   3. Required insulation depth is less than the bottom chord member depth.

   The bottom chords of trusses meeting the above criteria for limited storage shall be designed for the greater of the actual imposed dead load or 10 psf, uniformly distributed over the entire span.

h. Glazing used in handrail assemblies and guards shall be designed with a safety factor of 4. The safety factor shall be applied to each of the concentrated loads applied to the top of the rail, and to the load on the in-fill components. These loads shall be determined independent of one another, and loads are assumed not to occur with any other live load.

R301.6 Roof load. The roof shall be designed for the live load indicated in Table R301.6 or the snow load indicated in Table R301.2(1), whichever is greater.

R301.7 Deflection. The allowable deflection of any structural member under the live load listed in Sections R301.5 and R301.6 shall not exceed the values in Table R301.7.

R301.8 Nominal sizes. For the purposes of this code, where dimensions of lumber are specified, they shall be deemed to be nominal dimensions unless specifically designated as actual dimensions.

TABLE R301.6
MINIMUM ROOF LIVE LOADS IN POUNDS-FORCE PER SQUARE FOOT OF HORIZONTAL PROJECTION

ROOF SLOPE	TRIBUTARY LOADED AREA IN SQUARE FEET FOR ANY STRUCTURAL MEMBER		
	0 to 200	201 to 600	Over 600
Flat or rise less than 4 inches per foot (1:3)	20	16	12
Rise 4 inches per foot (1:3) to less than 12 inches per foot (1:1)	16	14	12
Rise 12 inches per foot (1:1) and greater	12	12	12

For SI: 1 square foot = 0.0929 m², 1 pound per square foot = 0.0479 kPa, 1 inch per foot = 83.3 mm/m.

TABLE R301.7
ALLOWABLE DEFLECTION OF STRUCTURAL MEMBERS[a, b, c, d, e]

STRUCTURAL MEMBER	ALLOWABLE DEFLECTION
Rafters having slopes greater than 3:12 with no finished ceiling attached to rafters	L/180
Interior walls and partitions	H/180
Floors and plastered ceilings	L/360
All other structural members	L/240
Exterior walls with plaster or stucco finish	H/360
Exterior walls—wind loads[a] with brittle finishes	H/240
Exterior walls—wind loads[a] with flexible finishes	L/120[d]
Lintels supporting masonry veneer walls[e]	L/600

Note: L = span length in inches, H = span height in inches.

a. The wind load shall be permitted to be taken as 0.7 times the Component and Cladding loads for the purpose of the determining deflection limits herein.

b. For cantilever members, *L* shall be taken as twice the length of the cantilever.

c. For aluminum structural members or panels used in roofs or walls of sunroom additions or patio covers, not supporting edge of glass or sandwich panels, the total load deflection shall not exceed L/60. For continuous aluminum structural members supporting edge of glass, the total load deflection shall not exceed L/175 for each glass lite or L/60 for the entire length of the member, whichever is more stringent. For sandwich panels used in roofs or walls of sunroom additions or patio covers, the total load deflection shall not exceed L/120.

d. Deflection for exterior walls with interior gypsum board finish shall be limited to an allowable deflection of H/180.

e. Refer to Section R703.7.2.

f. When floor spans exceed 20 feet, joists, built-up beams and trusses shall not be spaced greater than 24 inches and deflection shall not exceed L/480.

SECTION R302
FIRE-RESISTANT CONSTRUCTION

R302.1 Exterior walls. Construction, projections, openings and penetrations of *exterior walls* of *dwellings* and accessory buildings shall comply with Table R302.1.

Exceptions:

1. Walls, projections, openings or penetrations in walls perpendicular to the line used to determine the *fire separation distance*. Townhouse projections shall comply with R302.2.5.
2. Walls of *dwellings* and *accessory buildings* located on the same *lot*.
3. Detached tool sheds and storage sheds, playhouses and similar structures exempted from permits are not required to provide wall protection based on location on the *lot*. Projections beyond the *exterior wall* shall not extend over the *lot line*.
4. Detached garages accessory to a *dwelling* located within 2 feet (610 mm) of a *lot line* are permitted to have roof eave projections not exceeding 4 inches (102 mm).
5. Foundation vents installed in compliance with this code are permitted.

R302.2 Townhouses. Each *townhouse* shall be considered a separate building and shall be separated by fire-resistance-rated wall assemblies meeting the requirements of Section R302.1 for exterior walls.

Exception: If an automatic residential fire sprinkler is installed, a common 1-hour fire-resistance-rated wall assembly tested in accordance with ASTM E 119 or UL 263 is permitted for townhouses if such walls do not contain plumbing or mechanical equipment, ducts or vents in the cavity of the common wall. The wall shall be rated for fire exposure from both sides and shall extend to and be tight against exterior walls and the underside of the roof sheathing. Electrical installations shall be installed in accordance with Section R302.4.

R302.2.1 Continuity. The fire-resistance-rated wall or assembly separating *townhouses* shall be continuous from the foundation to the underside of the roof sheathing, deck or slab. The fire-resistance rating shall extend the full length of the wall or assembly, including wall extensions through and separating attached enclosed *accessory structures*.

R302.2.2 Parapets. Parapets constructed in accordance with Section R302.2.3 shall be constructed for *townhouses* as an extension of exterior walls or common walls in accordance with the following:

1. Where roof surfaces adjacent to the wall or walls are at the same elevation, the parapet shall extend not less than 30 inches (762 mm) above the roof surfaces.
2. Where roof surfaces adjacent to the wall or walls are at different elevations and the higher roof is not more than 30 inches (762 mm) above the lower roof surface.

Exception: A parapet is not required in the two cases above when the roof is covered with a mini-

TABLE R302.1
EXTERIOR WALLS

EXTERIOR WALL ELEMENT		MINIMUM FIRE-RESISTANCE RATING	MINIMUM FIRE SEPARATION DISTANCE
Walls	(Fire-resistance rated)	1 hour-tested in accordance with ASTM E 119 or UL 263 with exposure from both sides	< 5 feet
	(Not fire-resistance rated)	0 hours	≥ 5 feet
Projections	(Fire-resistance rated)	1 hour on the underside	≥ 2 feet to 5 feet
	(Not fire-resistance rated)	0 hours	5 feet
Openings in walls	Not allowed	N/A	< 3 feet
	25% maximum of wall area	0 hours	3 feet
	Unlimited	0 hours	5 feet
Penetrations	All	Comply with Section R302.4	< 5 feet
		None required	5 feet

For SI: 1 foot = 304.8 mm.
N/A = Not Applicable.

mum class C roof covering, and the roof decking or sheathing is of noncombustible materials or *approved* fire-retardant-treated wood for a distance of 4 feet (1219 mm) on each side of the wall or walls, or one layer of $^5/_8$-*inch* (15.9 mm) Type X gypsum board is installed directly beneath the roof decking or sheathing, supported by a minimum of nominal 2-inch (51 mm) ledgers attached to the sides of the roof framing members, for a minimum distance of 4 feet (1219 mm) on each side of the wall or walls. No openings or penetrations including dormers allowed within this 4 foot (1219 mm) protected area.

3. A parapet is not required where roof surfaces adjacent to the wall or walls are at different elevations and the higher roof is more than 30 inches (762 mm) above the lower roof. The common wall construction from the lower roof to the underside of the higher roof deck shall have not less than a 1-hour fire-resistance rating. The wall shall be rated for exposure from both sides.

R302.2.3 Parapet construction. Parapets shall have the same fire-resistance rating as that required for the supporting wall or walls. On any side adjacent to a roof surface, the parapet shall have noncombustible faces for the uppermost 18 inches (457 mm), to include counterflashing and coping materials. Where the roof slopes toward a parapet at slopes greater than 2 units vertical in 12 units horizontal (16.7-percent slope), the parapet shall extend to the same height as any portion of the roof within a distance of 3 feet (914 mm), but in no case shall the height be less than 30 inches (762 mm).

R302.2.4 Structural independence. Each individual *townhouse* shall be structurally independent.

Exceptions:

1. Foundations supporting *exterior walls* or common walls.
2. Structural roof and wall sheathing from each unit may fasten to the common wall framing.
3. Nonstructural wall and roof coverings.
4. Flashing at termination of roof covering over common wall.
5. *Townhouses* separated by a common 1-hour fire-resistance-rated wall as provided in Section R302.2.

R302.2.5 Townhouse eave protection. In townhouse construction (with three or more attached dwellings) projections extending into the fire separation distance shall have not less than 1 hour fire resistive construction on the underside. Soffit material beyond the fire separation distance shall be securely attached to framing members and shall be constructed using either noncombustible soffit material; fire-retardant-treated soffit material; vinyl soffit installed over $^3/_4$-inch (19 mm) wood sheathing or $^5/_8$-inch (16 mm) gypsum board; or aluminum soffit installed over $^3/_4$-inch (19 mm) wood sheathing or $^5/_8$-inch (16 mm) gypsum board. Venting requirements shall be provided in both soffit and underlayments. Vents shall be either nominal 2-inch (51 mm) continuous or equivalent intermittent and shall not exceed the minimum net free air requirements established in Section R806.2 by more than 50 percent.

Vents in soffit are not allowed within 4 feet (1219 mm) of fire walls or property lines.

R302.2.6 Townhouse eave projections. Overhang projections not exceeding 12 inches (305 mm) shall be allowed to extend beyond the property line in townhouse buildings provided all the following conditions are met:

1. Required fire resistant rated wall assembly is tight to roof deck; and
2. Eaves shall be protected with roof decking and fascia of non-combustible materials or approved fire-retardant-treated wood; and
3. Eaves shall have not less than 1 hour fire-resistive construction on the underside.

R302.2.7 Flame spread. Vinyl Siding and vinyl soffit materials when used in townhouse construction shall have a Flame Spread Index of 25 or less as tested in accordance with ASTM E 84.

R302.2.8 Sound transmission. See Appendix K.

R302.3 Two-family dwellings. *Dwelling units* in two-family dwellings shall be separated from each other by wall and/or floor assemblies having not less than a 1-hour fire-resistance rating when tested in accordance with ASTM E 119 or UL 263. Fire-resistance-rated floor-ceiling and wall assemblies shall extend to and be tight against the *exterior wall*, and wall assemblies shall extend from the foundation to the underside of the roof sheathing.

Exceptions:

1. A fire-resistance rating of $^1/_2$ hour shall be permitted in buildings equipped throughout with an automatic sprinkler system installed in accordance with NFPA 13.
2. Wall assemblies need not extend through *attic* spaces when the ceiling is protected by not less than $^5/_8$-inch (15.9 mm) Type X gypsum board and an *attic* draft stop constructed as specified in Section R302.12.1 is provided above and along the wall assembly separating the *dwellings*. The structural framing supporting the ceiling shall also be protected by not less than $^1/_2$-inch (12.7 mm) gypsum board or equivalent.

R302.3.1 Supporting construction. When floor assemblies are required to be fire-resistance rated by Section R302.3, the supporting construction of such assemblies shall have an equal or greater fire-resistance rating.

R302.4 Dwelling unit rated penetrations. Penetrations of wall or floor/ceiling assemblies required to be fire-resistance rated in accordance with Section R302.2 or R302.3 shall be protected in accordance with this section.

R302.4.1 Through penetrations. Through penetrations of fire-resistance-rated wall or floor assemblies shall comply with Section R302.4.1.1 or R302.4.1.2.

Exception: Where the penetrating items are steel, ferrous or copper pipes, tubes or conduits, the annular space shall be protected as follows:

1. In concrete or masonry wall or floor assemblies, concrete, grout or mortar shall be permitted where installed to the full thickness of the wall or floor assembly or the thickness required to maintain the fire-resistance rating, provided:
   - 1.1. The nominal diameter of the penetrating item is a maximum of 6 inches (152 mm); and
   - 1.2. The area of the opening through the wall does not exceed 144 square inches (92 900 mm^2).
2. The material used to fill the annular space shall prevent the passage of flame and hot gases sufficient to ignite cotton waste where subjected to ASTM E 119 or UL 263 time temperature fire conditions under a minimum positive pressure differential of 0.01 inch of water (3 Pa) at the location of the penetration for the time period equivalent to the fire resistance rating of the construction penetrated.

R302.4.1.1 Fire-resistance-rated assembly. Penetrations shall be installed as tested in the *approved* fire-resistance-rated assembly.

R302.4.1.2 Penetration firestop system. Penetrations shall be protected by an *approved* penetration firestop system installed as tested in accordance with ASTM E 814 or UL 1479, with a minimum positive pressure differential of 0.01 inch of water (3 Pa) and shall have an F rating of not less than the required fire-resistance rating of the wall or floor/ceiling assembly penetrated.

R302.4.2 Membrane penetrations. Membrane penetrations shall comply with Section R302.4.1. Where walls are required to have a fire-resistance rating, recessed fixtures shall be installed so that the required fire-resistance rating will not be reduced.

Exceptions:

1. Membrane penetrations of maximum 2-hour fire-resistance-rated walls and partitions by steel electrical boxes that do not exceed 16 square inches (0.0103 m^2) in area provided the aggregate area of the openings through the membrane does not exceed 100 square inches (0.0645 m^2) in any 100 square feet (9.29 m)^2 of wall area. The annular space between the wall membrane and the box shall not exceed $^1/_8$ inch (3.1 mm). Such boxes on opposite sides of the wall shall be separated by one of the following:
   - 1.1. By a horizontal distance of not less than 24 inches (610 mm) where the wall or partition is constructed with individual noncommunicating stud cavities;
   - 1.2. By a horizontal distance of not less than the depth of the wall cavity when the wall cavity is filled with cellulose loose-fill, rockwool or slag mineral wool insulation;
   - 1.3. By solid fire blocking in accordance with Section R302.11;
   - 1.4. By protecting both boxes with listed putty pads; or
   - 1.5. By other listed materials and methods.
2. Membrane penetrations by listed electrical boxes of any materials provided the boxes have been tested for use in fire-resistance-rated assemblies and are installed in accordance with the instructions included in the listing. The annular space between the wall membrane and the box shall not exceed $^1/_8$ inch (3.1 mm) unless listed otherwise. Such boxes on opposite sides of the wall shall be separated by one of the following:
   - 2.1. By the horizontal distance specified in the listing of the electrical boxes;
   - 2.2. By solid fireblocking in accordance with Section R302.11;

2.3. By protecting both boxes with listed putty pads; or

2.4. By other listed materials and methods.

3. The annular space created by the penetration of a fire sprinkler provided it is covered by a metal escutcheon plate.

R302.5 Dwelling/garage opening/penetration protection. Openings and penetrations through the walls or ceilings separating the *dwelling* from the garage shall be in accordance with Sections R302.5.1 through R302.5.3.

R302.5.1 Opening protection. Openings from a private garage directly into a room used for sleeping purposes shall not be permitted. Other openings between the garage and residence shall be equipped with solid wood doors not less than $1^{3}/_{8}$ inches (35 mm) in thickness, solid or honeycomb core steel doors not less than $1^{3}/_{8}$ inches (35 mm) thick, or 20-minute fire-rated doors.

R302.5.2 Duct penetration. Ducts in the garage and ducts penetrating the walls or ceilings separating the *dwelling* from the garage shall be constructed of a minimum No. 26 gage (0.48 mm) sheet steel or other *approved* material and shall have no openings into the garage.

R302.5.3 Other penetrations. Penetrations through the separation required in Section R302.6 shall be protected as required by Section R302.11, Item 4.

R302.6 Dwelling/garage fire separation. The garage shall be separated as required by Table R302.6. Openings in garage walls shall comply with Section R302.5. This provision does not apply to garage walls that are perpendicular to the adjacent *dwelling unit* wall.

R302.7 Under-stair protection. Enclosed accessible space under stairs shall have walls, under-stair surface and any soffits protected on the enclosed side with $^{1}/_{2}$-inch (12.7 mm) gypsum board.

R302.8 Foam plastics. For requirements for foam plastics see Section R316.

R302.9 Flame spread index and smoke-developed index for wall and ceiling finishes. Flame spread and smoke index for wall and ceiling finishes shall be in accordance with Sections R302.9.1 through R302.9.4.

R302.9.1 Flame spread index. Wall and ceiling finishes shall have a flame spread index of not greater than 200.

Exception: Flame spread index requirements for finishes shall not apply to trim defined as picture molds, chair rails, baseboards and handrails; to doors and windows or their frames; or to materials that are less than $^{1}/_{28}$ inch (0.91 mm) in thickness cemented to the surface of walls or ceilings if these materials exhibit flame spread index values no greater than those of paper of this thickness cemented to a noncombustible backing.

R302.9.2 Smoke-developed index. Wall and ceiling finishes shall have a smoke-developed index of not greater than 450.

R302.9.3 Testing. Tests shall be made in accordance with ASTM E 84 or UL 723.

R302.9.4 Alternate test method. As an alternate to having a flame-spread index of not greater than 200 and a smoke developed index of not greater than 450 when tested in accordance with ASTM E 84 or UL 723, wall and ceiling finishes, other than textiles, shall be permitted to be tested in accordance with NFPA 286. Materials tested in accordance with NFPA 286 shall meet the following criteria:

During the 40 kW exposure, the interior finish shall comply with Item 1. During the 160 kW exposure, the interior finish shall comply with Item 2. During the entire test, the interior finish shall comply with Item 3.

1. During the 40 kW exposure, flames shall not spread to the ceiling.
2. During the 160 kW exposure, the interior finish shall comply with the following:

   2.1. Flame shall not spread to the outer extremity of the sample on any wall or ceiling.

   2.2. Flashover, as defined in NFPA 286, shall not occur.
3. The total smoke released throughout the NFPA 286 test shall not exceed 1,000 m^2.

R302.10 Flame spread index and smoke developed index for insulation. Flame spread and smoke developed index for insulation shall be in accordance with Sections R302.10.1 through R302.10.5.

TABLE R302.6
DWELLING/GARAGE SEPARATION

SEPARATION	MATERIAL
From the residence and attics	Not less than $^{1}/_{2}$-inch gypsum board or equivalent applied to the garage side
From all habitable rooms above the garage	Not less than $^{5}/_{8}$-inch Type X gypsum board or equivalent
Structure(s) supporting floor/ceiling assemblies used for separation required by this section	Not less than $^{1}/_{2}$-inch gypsum board or equivalent
Garages located less than 3 feet from a dwelling unit on the same lot	Not less than $^{1}/_{2}$-inch gypsum board or equivalent applied to the interior side of exterior walls that are within this area

For SI: 1 inch = 25.4 mm, 1 foot = 304.8 mm.

R302.10.1 Insulation. Insulation materials, including facings, such as vapor retarders and vapor-permeable membranes installed within floor-ceiling assemblies, roof-ceiling assemblies, wall assemblies, crawl spaces and *attics* shall have a flame spread index not to exceed 25 with an accompanying smoke-developed index not to exceed 450 when tested in accordance with ASTM E 84 or UL 723.

Exceptions:

1. When such materials are installed in concealed spaces, the flame spread index and smoke-developed index limitations do not apply to the facings, provided that the facing is installed in substantial contact with the unexposed surface of the ceiling, floor or wall finish.
2. Cellulose loose-fill insulation, which is not spray applied, complying with the requirements of Section R302.10.3, shall only be required to meet the smoke-developed index of not more than 450.

R302.10.2 Loose-fill insulation. Loose-fill insulation materials that cannot be mounted in the ASTM E 84 or UL 723 apparatus without a screen or artificial supports shall comply with the flame spread and smoke-developed limits of Section R302.10.1 when tested in accordance with CAN/ULC S102.2.

Exception: Cellulose loose-fill insulation shall not be required to be tested in accordance with CAN/ULC S102.2, provided such insulation complies with the requirements of Section R302.10.1 and Section R302.10.3.

R302.10.3 Cellulose loose-fill insulation. Cellulose loose-fill insulation shall comply with CPSC 16 CFR, Parts 1209 and 1404. Each package of such insulating material shall be clearly *labeled* in accordance with CPSC 16 CFR, Parts 1209 and 1404.

R302.10.4 Exposed attic insulation. All exposed insulation materials installed on *attic* floors shall have a critical radiant flux not less than 0.12 watt per square centimeter.

R302.10.5 Testing. Tests for critical radiant flux shall be made in accordance with ASTM E 970.

R302.11 Fireblocking. In combustible construction, fireblocking shall be provided to cut off all concealed draft openings (both vertical and horizontal) and to form an effective fire barrier between stories, and between a top *story* and the roof space.

Fireblocking shall be provided in wood-frame construction in the following locations:

1. In concealed spaces of stud walls and partitions, including furred spaces and parallel rows of studs or staggered studs, as follows:
   - 1.1. Vertically at the ceiling and floor levels.
   - 1.2. Horizontally at intervals not exceeding 10 feet (3048 mm).
2. At all interconnections between concealed vertical and horizontal spaces such as occur at soffits, drop ceilings and cove ceilings.
3. In concealed spaces between stair stringers at the top and bottom of the run. Enclosed spaces under stairs shall comply with Section R302.7.
4. At openings around vents, pipes, ducts, cables and wires at ceiling and floor level, with an *approved* material to resist the free passage of flame and products of combustion. The material filling this annular space shall not be required to meet the ASTM E 136 requirements.
5. For the fireblocking of chimneys and fireplaces, see Section R1003.19.
6. Fireblocking of cornices of a two-family *dwelling* is required at the line of *dwelling unit* separation.

R302.11.1 Fireblocking materials. Except as provided in Section R302.11, Item 4, fireblocking shall consist of the following materials.

1. Two-inch (51 mm) nominal lumber.
2. Two thicknesses of 1-inch (25.4 mm) nominal lumber with broken lap joints.
3. One thickness of $^{23}/_{32}$-inch (18.3 mm) wood structural panels with joints backed by $^{23}/_{32}$-inch (18.3 mm) wood structural panels.
4. One thickness of $^{3}/_{4}$-inch (19.1 mm) particleboard with joints backed by $^{3}/_{4}$-inch (19.1 mm) particleboard.
5. One-half-inch (12.7 mm) gypsum board.
6. One-quarter-inch (6.4 mm) cement-based millboard.
7. Batts or blankets of mineral wool or glass fiber or other *approved* materials installed in such a manner as to be securely retained in place.

R302.11.1.1 Batts or blankets of mineral or glass fiber. Batts or blankets of mineral or glass fiber or other *approved* nonrigid materials shall be permitted for compliance with the 10-foot (3048 mm) horizontal fireblocking in walls constructed using parallel rows of studs or staggered studs.

R302.11.1.2 Unfaced fiberglass. Unfaced fiberglass batt insulation used as fireblocking shall fill the entire cross section of the wall cavity to a minimum height of 16 inches (406 mm) measured vertically. When piping, conduit or similar obstructions are encountered, the insulation shall be packed tightly around the obstruction.

R302.11.1.3 Loose-fill insulation material. Loose-fill insulation material shall not be used as a fireblock unless specifically tested in the form and manner intended for use to demonstrate its ability to remain in place and to retard the spread of fire and hot gases.

R302.11.2 Fireblocking integrity. The integrity of all fireblocks shall be maintained.

R302.12 Draftstopping. In combustible construction where there is usable space both above and below the concealed space of a floor/ceiling assembly, draftstops shall be installed so that the area of the concealed space does not exceed 1,000 square feet (92.9 m^2). Draftstopping shall divide the concealed space into approximately equal areas. Where the assembly is enclosed by a floor membrane above and a ceiling membrane below, draftstopping shall be provided in floor/ceiling assemblies under the following circumstances:

1. Ceiling is suspended under the floor framing.
2. Floor framing is constructed of truss-type open-web or perforated members.

R302.12.1 Materials. Draftstopping materials shall not be less than $^{1}/_{2}$-inch (12.7 mm) gypsum board, $^{3}/_{8}$-inch (9.5 mm) wood structural panels or other *approved* materials adequately supported. Draftstopping shall be installed parallel to the floor framing members unless otherwise *approved* by the *building official*. The integrity of the draftstops shall be maintained.

R302.13 Combustible insulation clearance. Combustible insulation shall be separated a minimum of 3 inches (76 mm) from recessed luminaires, fan motors and other heat-producing devices.

Exception: Where heat-producing devices are listed for lesser clearances, combustible insulation complying with the listing requirements shall be separated in accordance with the conditions stipulated in the listing.

Recessed luminaires installed in the *building thermal envelope* shall meet the requirements of Section N1102.4.5.

R302.14 Flame spread. Vinyl Siding and vinyl soffit materials when used in townhouse construction shall have a Flame Spread Index of 25 or less as tested in accordance with ASTM E 84.

SECTION R303 LIGHT, VENTILATION AND HEATING

R303.1 Habitable rooms. All habitable rooms shall have an aggregate glazing area of not less than 8 percent of the floor area of such rooms. Natural *ventilation* shall be through windows, doors, louvers or other *approved* openings to the outdoor air. Such openings shall be provided with ready access or shall otherwise be readily controllable by the building occupants. The minimum openable area to the outdoors shall be 4 percent of the floor area being ventilated.

Exceptions:

1. The glazed areas need not be openable where the opening is not required by Section R310 and an *approved* mechanical *ventilation* system capable of producing 0.35 air change per hour in the room is installed or a whole-house mechanical *ventilation* system is installed capable of supplying outdoor *ventilation* air of 15 cubic feet per minute (cfm) (78 L/s) per occupant computed on the basis of two occupants for the first bedroom and one occupant for each additional bedroom.
2. The glazed areas need not be installed in rooms where Exception 1 above is satisfied and artificial light is provided capable of producing an average illumination of 6 footcandles (65 lux) over the area of the room at a height of 30 inches (762 mm) above the floor level.
3. Use of sunroom *additions* and patio covers, as defined in Section R202, shall be permitted for natural *ventilation* if in excess of 40 percent of the exterior sunroom walls are open, or are enclosed only by insect screening.

R303.2 Adjoining rooms. For the purpose of determining light and *ventilation* requirements, any room shall be considered as a portion of an adjoining room when at least one-half of the area of the common wall is open and unobstructed and provides an opening of not less than one-tenth of the floor area of the interior room but not less than 25 square feet (2.3 m^{2}).

Exception: Openings required for light and/or *ventilation* shall be permitted to open into a thermally isolated sunroom *addition* or patio cover, provided that there is an openable area between the adjoining room and the sunroom *addition* or patio cover of not less than one-tenth of the floor area of the interior room but not less than 20 square feet (2 m^{2}). The minimum openable area to the outdoors shall be based upon the total floor area being ventilated.

R303.3 Bathrooms. Bathrooms, water closet compartments and other similar rooms shall be provided with aggregate glazing area in windows of not less than 3 square feet (0.3 m^{2}), one-half of which must be openable.

Exception: The glazed areas shall not be required where artificial light and a mechanical *ventilation* system are provided. The minimum *ventilation* rates shall be 50 cubic feet per minute (24 L/s) for intermittent *ventilation* or 20 cubic feet per minute (10 L/s) for continuous *ventilation*. *Ventilation* air from the space shall be exhausted directly to the outside.

R303.4 Opening location. Outdoor intake and exhaust openings shall be located in accordance with Sections R303.4.1 and R303.4.2.

R303.4.1 Intake openings. Mechanical and gravity outdoor air intake openings shall be located a minimum of 10 feet (3048 mm) from any hazardous or noxious contaminant, such as vents, chimneys, plumbing vents, streets, alleys, parking lots and loading docks, except as otherwise specified in this code. Where a source of contaminant is located within 10 feet (3048 mm) of an intake opening, such opening shall be located a minimum of 2 feet (610 mm) below the contaminant source.

For the purpose of this section, the exhaust from *dwelling* unit toilet rooms, bathrooms and kitchens shall not be considered as hazardous or noxious.

R303.4.2 Exhaust openings. Exhaust air shall not be directed onto walkways.

R303.5 Outside opening protection. Air exhaust and intake openings that terminate outdoors shall be protected with corrosion-resistant screens, louvers or grilles having a minimum opening size of $^{1}/_{4}$ inch (6 mm) and a maximum opening size of $^{1}/_{2}$ inch (13 mm), in any dimension. Openings shall be protected against local weather conditions. Outdoor air exhaust and intake openings shall meet the provisions for *exterior wall* opening protectives in accordance with this code.

R303.6 Stairway illumination. All interior and exterior stairways shall be provided with a means to illuminate the stairs, including the landings and treads. Interior stairways shall be provided with an artificial light source located in the immediate vicinity of each landing of the stairway. For interior stairs the artificial light sources shall be capable of illuminating treads and landings to levels not less than 1 foot-candle (11 lux) measured at the center of treads and landings. Exterior stairways shall be provided with an artificial light source located in the immediate vicinity of the top landing of the stairway. Exterior stairways providing access to a *basement* from the outside *grade* level shall be provided with an artificial light source located in the immediate vicinity of the bottom landing of the stairway.

Exception: An artificial light source is not required at the top and bottom landing, provided an artificial light source is located directly over each stairway section.

R303.6.1 Light activation. Where lighting outlets are installed in interior stairways, there shall be a wall switch at each floor level to control the lighting outlet where the stairway has six or more risers. The illumination of exterior stairways shall be controlled from inside the *dwelling* unit.

Exception: Lights that are continuously illuminated or automatically controlled.

R303.7 Required glazed openings. Required glazed openings shall open directly onto a street or public alley, or a *yard* or court located on the same *lot* as the building.

Exceptions:

1. Required glazed openings may face into a roofed porch where the porch abuts a street, *yard* or court and the longer side of the porch is at least 65 percent unobstructed and the ceiling height is not less than 7 feet (2134 mm).
2. Eave projections shall not be considered as obstructing the clear open space of a *yard* or court.
3. Required glazed openings may face into the area under a deck, balcony, bay or floor cantilever provided a clear vertical space at least 36 inches (914 mm) in height is provided.

R303.7.1 Sunroom additions. Required glazed openings shall be permitted to open into sunroom *additions* or patio covers that abut a street, *yard* or court if in excess of 40 percent of the exterior sunroom walls are open, or are enclosed only by insect screening, and the ceiling height of the sunroom is not less than 7 feet (2134 mm).

R303.8 Required heating. When the winter design temperature in Table R301.2(1) is below 60°F (16°C), every *dwelling unit* shall be provided with heating facilities capable of maintaining a minimum room temperature of 68°F (20°C) at a point 3 feet (914 mm) above the floor and 2 feet (610 mm) from exterior walls in all habitable rooms at the design temperature. The installation of one or more portable space heaters shall not be used to achieve compliance with this section.

SECTION R304
MINIMUM ROOM AREAS

R304.1 Minimum area. Every *dwelling* unit shall have at least one habitable room that shall have not less than 120 square feet (11 m^2) of gross floor area.

R304.2 Other rooms. Other habitable rooms shall have a floor area of not less than 70 square feet (6.5 m^2).

Exception: Kitchens.

R304.3 Minimum dimensions. Habitable rooms shall not be less than 7 feet (2134 mm) in any horizontal dimension.

Exception: Kitchens.

R304.4 Height effect on room area. Portions of a room with a sloping ceiling measuring less than 5 feet (1524 mm) or a furred ceiling measuring less than 7 feet (2134 mm) from the finished floor to the finished ceiling shall not be considered as contributing to the minimum required habitable area for that room.

SECTION R305
CEILING HEIGHT

R305.1 Minimum height. *Habitable space*, hallways, bathrooms, toilet rooms, laundry rooms and portions of *basements* containing these spaces shall have a ceiling height of not less than 7 feet (2134 mm).

Exceptions:

1. For rooms with sloped ceilings, at least 50 percent of the required floor area of the room must have a ceiling height of at least 7 feet (2134 mm) and no portion of the required floor area may have a ceiling height of less than 5 feet (1524 mm).
2. Bathrooms shall have a minimum ceiling height of 6 feet 8 inches (2032 mm) at the center of the front clearance area for fixtures as shown in Figure R307.1. The ceiling height above fixtures shall be such that the fixture is capable of being used for its intended purpose. A shower or tub equipped with a showerhead shall have a minimum ceiling height of 6 feet 8 inches (2032 mm) above a minimum area 30 inches (762 mm) by 30 inches (762 mm) at the showerhead.
3. Beams and girders spaced not less than 4 feet (1219 mm) on center may project not more than 6 inches (152 mm) below the required ceiling height.

R305.1.1 Basements. Portions of *basements* that do not contain *habitable space*, hallways, bathrooms, toilet rooms and laundry rooms shall have a ceiling height of not less than 6 feet 8 inches (2032 mm).

Exception: Beams, girders, ducts or other obstructions may project to within 6 feet 4 inches (1931 mm) of the finished floor.

SECTION R306
SANITATION

R306.1 Toilet facilities. Every *dwelling* unit shall be provided with a water closet, lavatory, and a bathtub or shower.

R306.2 Kitchen. Each *dwelling* unit shall be provided with a kitchen area and every kitchen area shall be provided with a sink.

R306.3 Sewage disposal. All plumbing fixtures shall be connected to a sanitary sewer or to an *approved* private sewage disposal system.

R306.4 Water supply to fixtures. All plumbing fixtures shall be connected to an *approved* water supply. Kitchen sinks, lavatories, bathtubs, showers, bidets, laundry tubs and washing machine outlets shall be provided with hot and cold water.

SECTION R307
TOILET, BATH AND SHOWER SPACES

R307.1 Space required. Fixtures shall be spaced in accordance with Figure R307.1, and in accordance with the requirements of Section P2705.1.

R307.2 Bathtub and shower spaces. Bathtub and shower floors and walls above bathtubs with installed shower heads and in shower compartments shall be finished with a nonabsorbent surface. Such wall surfaces shall extend to a height of not less than 6 feet (1829 mm) above the floor.

SECTION R308
GLAZING

R308.1 Identification. Except as indicated in Section R308.1.1 each pane of glazing installed in hazardous locations as defined in Section R308.4 shall be provided with a manufacturer's designation specifying who applied the designation, designating the type of glass and the safety glazing standard with which it complies, which is visible in the final installation. The designation shall be acid etched, sandblasted, ceramic-fired, laser etched, embossed, or be of a type which once applied cannot be removed without being destroyed.

Exceptions:

1. For other than tempered glass, manufacturer's designations are not required provided the *building official* approves the use of a certificate, affidavit or other evidence confirming compliance with this code.
2. Tempered spandrel glass is permitted to be identified by the manufacturer with a removable paper designation.

R308.1.1 Identification of multiple assemblies. Multipane assemblies having individual panes not exceeding 1 square foot (0.09 m^2) in exposed area shall have at least one pane in the assembly identified in accordance with Section R308.1. All other panes in the assembly shall be *labeled* "CPSC 16 CFR 1201" or "ANSI Z97.1" as appropriate.

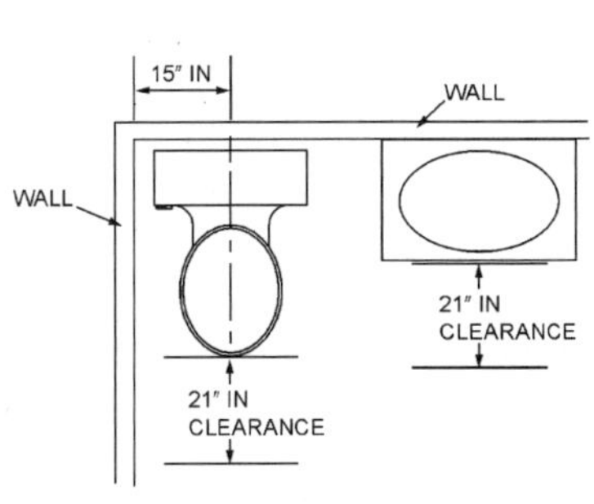

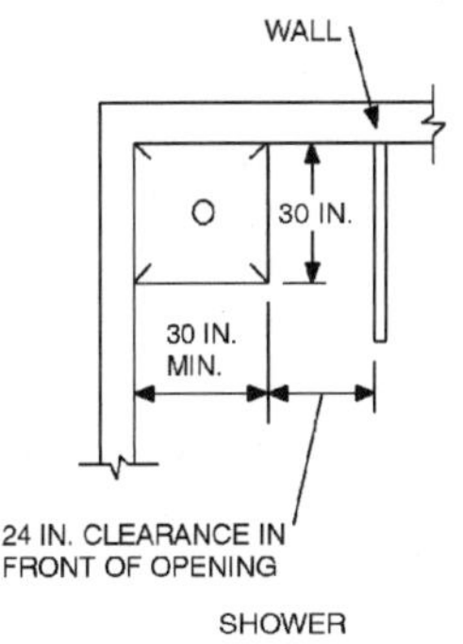

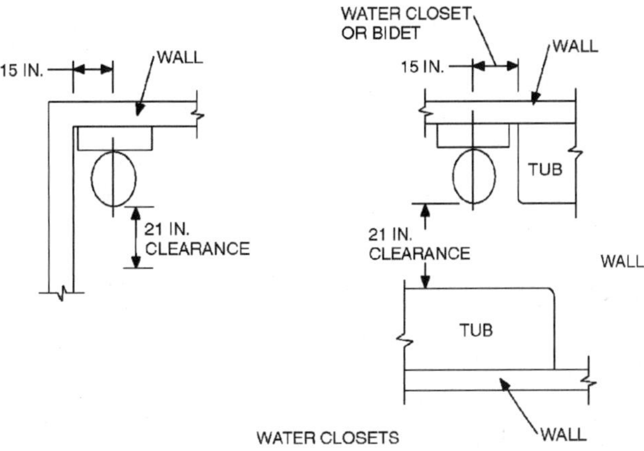

For SI: 1 inch = 25.4 mm.

FIGURE R307.1
MINIMUM FIXTURE CLEARANCES

R308.2 Louvered windows or jalousies. Regular, float, wired or patterned glass in jalousies and louvered windows shall be no thinner than nominal $^{3}/_{16}$ inch (5 mm) and no longer than 48 inches (1219 mm). Exposed glass edges shall be smooth.

R308.2.1 Wired glass prohibited. Wired glass with wire exposed on longitudinal edges shall not be used in jalousies or louvered windows.

R308.3 Human impact loads. Individual glazed areas, including glass mirrors in hazardous locations such as those indicated as defined in Section R308.4, shall pass the test requirements of Section R308.3.1.

Exceptions:

1. Louvered windows and jalousies shall comply with Section R308.2.
2. Mirrors and other glass panels mounted or hung on a surface that provides a continuous backing support.
3. Glass unit masonry complying with Section R610.

R308.3.1 Impact test. Where required by other sections of the code, glazing shall be tested in accordance with CPSC 16 CFR 1201. Glazing shall comply with the test criteria for Category I or II as indicated in Table R308.3.1(1).

Exception: Glazing not in doors or enclosures for hot tubs, whirlpools, saunas, steam rooms, bathtubs and showers shall be permitted to be tested in accordance with ANSI Z97.1. Glazing shall comply with the test criteria for Class A or B as indicated in Table R308.3.1 (2).

R308.4 Hazardous locations. The following shall be considered specific hazardous locations for the purposes of glazing:

1. Glazing in all fixed and operable panels of swinging, sliding and bifold doors.

   Exceptions:

   1. Glazed openings of a size through which a 3-inch diameter (76 mm) sphere is unable to pass.
   2. Decorative glazing.

2. Glazing in an individual fixed or operable panel adjacent to a door where the nearest vertical edge is within 24-inches (610 mm) of the door in a closed position and whose bottom edge is less than 60 inches (1524 mm) above the floor or walking surface.

   Exceptions:

   1. Decorative glazing.
   2. When there is an intervening wall or other permanent barrier between the door and the glazing.
   3. Glazing in walls on the latch side of and perpendicular to the plane of the door in a closed position.
   4. Glazing adjacent to a door where access through the door is to a closet or storage area 3 feet (914 mm) or less in depth.
   5. Glazing that is adjacent to the fixed panel of patio doors.

3. Glazing in an individual fixed or operable panel that meets all of the following conditions:

   3.1. The exposed area of an individual pane is larger than 9 square feet (0.836 m^2); and

TABLE R308.3.1(1)
MINIMUM CATEGORY CLASSIFICATION OF GLAZING USING CPSC 16 CFR 1201

EXPOSED SURFACE AREA OF ONE SIDE OF ONE LITE	GLAZING IN STORM OR COMBINATION DOORS (Category Class)	GLAZING IN DOORS (Category Class)	GLAZED PANELS REGULATED BY ITEM 7 OF SECTION R308.4 (Category Class)	GLAZED PANELS REGULATED BY ITEM 6 OF SECTION R308.4 (Category Class)	GLAZING IN DOORS AND ENCLOSURES REGULATED BY ITEM 5 OF SECTION R308.4 (Category Class)	SLIDING GLASS DOORS PATIO TYPE (Category Class)
9 square feet or less	I	I	NR	I	II	II
More than 9 square feet	II	II	II	II	II	II

For SI: 1 square foot = 0.0929 m^2.
NR means "No Requirement."

TABLE R308.3.1(2)
MINIMUM CATEGORY CLASSIFICATION OF GLAZING USING ANSI Z97.1

EXPOSED SURFACE AREA OF ONE SIDE OF ONE LITE	GLAZED PANELS REGULATED BY ITEM 7 OF SECTION R308.4 (Category Class)	GLAZED PANELS REGULATED BY ITEM 6 OF SECTION R308.4 (Category Class)	DOORS AND ENCLOSURES REGULATED BY ITEM 5 OF SECTION R308.4[a] (Category Class)
9 square feet or less	No requirement	B	A
More than 9 square feet	A	A	A

For SI: 1 square foot = 0.0929 m^2.
a. Use is permitted only by the exception to Section R308.3.1.

3.2. The bottom edge of the glazing is less than 18 inches (457 mm) above the floor; and

3.3. The top edge of the glazing is more than 36 inches (914 mm) above the floor; and

3.4. One or more walking surfaces are within 36 inches (914 mm), measured horizontally and in a straight line, of the glazing.

Exceptions:

1. Decorative glazing.
2. When a horizontal rail is installed on the accessible side(s) of the glazing 34 to 38 inches (864 to 965) above the walking surface. The rail shall be capable of withstanding a horizontal load of 50 pounds per linear foot (730 N/m) without contacting the glass and be a minimum of $1^1/_2$ inches (38 mm) in cross sectional height.
3. Outboard panes in insulating glass units and other multiple glazed panels when the bottom edge of the glass is 25 feet (7620 mm) or more above *grade*, a roof, walking surfaces or other horizontal [within 45 degrees (0.79 rad) of horizontal] surface adjacent to the glass exterior.

4. All glazing in railings regardless of area or height above a walking surface. Included are structural baluster panels and nonstructural infill panels.

5. Glazing in enclosures for or walls facing hot tubs, whirlpools, saunas, steam rooms, bathtubs and showers where the bottom exposed edge of the glazing is less than 60 inches (1524 mm) measured vertically above any standing or walking surface.

   Exception: Glazing that is more than 60 inches (1524 mm), measured horizontally and in a straight line, from the waters edge of a hot tub, whirlpool or bathtub.

6. Glazing in walls and fences adjacent to indoor and outdoor swimming pools, hot tubs and spas where the bottom edge of the glazing is less than 60 inches (1524 mm) above a walking surface and within 60 inches (1524 mm), measured horizontally and in a straight line, of the water's edge. This shall apply to single glazing and all panes in multiple glazing.

7. Glazing adjacent to stairways, landings and ramps within 36 inches (914 mm) horizontally of a walking surface when the exposed surface of the glazing is less than 60 inches (1524 mm) above the plane of the adjacent walking surface.

   Exceptions:

   1. When a rail is installed on the accessible side(s) of the glazing 34 to 38 inches (864 to 965 mm) above the walking surface. The rail shall be capable of withstanding a horizontal load of 50 pounds per linear foot (730 N/m) without contacting the glass and be a minimum of $1^1/_2$ inches (38 mm) in cross sectional height.
   2. The side of the stairway has a guardrail or handrail, including balusters or in-fill panels, complying with Sections R311.7.7 and R312 and the plane of the glazing is more than 18 inches (457 mm) from the railing; or
   3. When a solid wall or panel extends from the plane of the adjacent walking surface to 34 inches (863 mm) to 36 inches (914 mm) above the walking surface and the construction at the top of that wall or panel is capable of withstanding the same horizontal load as a *guard*.

8. Glazing adjacent to stairways within 60 inches (1524 mm) horizontally of the bottom tread of a stairway in any direction when the exposed surface of the glazing is less than 60 inches (1524 mm) above the nose of the tread.

   Exceptions:

   1. The side of the stairway has a guardrail or handrail, including balusters or in-fill panels, complying with Sections R311.7.7 and R312 and the plane of the glass is more than 18 inches (457 mm) from the railing; or
   2. When a solid wall or panel extends from the plane of the adjacent walking surface to 34 inches (864 mm) to 36 inches (914 mm) above the walking surface and the construction at the top of that wall or panel is capable of withstanding the same horizontal load as a *guard*.

R308.5 Site built windows. Site built windows shall comply with Section 2404 of the *International Building Code*.

R308.6 Skylights and sloped glazing. Skylights and sloped glazing shall comply with the following sections.

R308.6.1 Definitions.

SKYLIGHTS AND SLOPED GLAZING. Glass or other transparent or translucent glazing material installed at a slope of 15 degrees (0.26 rad) or more from vertical. Glazing materials in skylights, including unit skylights, solariums, sunrooms, roofs and sloped walls are included in this definition.

UNIT SKYLIGHT. A factory assembled, glazed fenestration unit, containing one panel of glazing material, that allows for natural daylighting through an opening in the roof assembly while preserving the weather-resistant barrier of the roof.

R308.6.2 Permitted materials. The following types of glazing may be used:

1. Laminated glass with a minimum 0.015-inch (0.38 mm) polyvinyl butyral interlayer for glass panes 16 square feet (1.5 m^2) or less in area located such that the highest point of the glass is not more than 12 feet (3658 mm) above a walking surface or other accessible area; for higher or larger sizes, the minimum interlayer thickness shall be 0.030 inch (0.76 mm).
2. Fully tempered glass.
3. Heat-strengthened glass.

4. Wired glass.
5. *Approved* rigid plastics.

R308.6.3 Screens, general. For fully tempered or heat-strengthened glass, a retaining screen meeting the requirements of Section R308.6.7 shall be installed below the glass, except for fully tempered glass that meets either condition listed in Section R308.6.5.

R308.6.4 Screens with multiple glazing. When the inboard pane is fully tempered, heat-strengthened or wired glass, a retaining screen meeting the requirements of Section R308.6.7 shall be installed below the glass, except for either condition listed in Section R308.6.5. All other panes in the multiple glazing may be of any type listed in Section R308.6.2.

R308.6.5 Screens not required. Screens shall not be required when fully tempered glass is used as single glazing or the inboard pane in multiple glazing and either of the following conditions are met:

1. Glass area 16 square feet (1.49 m^2) or less. Highest point of glass not more than 12 feet (3658 mm) above a walking surface or other accessible area, nominal glass thickness not more than $^3/_{16}$ inch (4.8 mm), and (for multiple glazing only) the other pane or panes fully tempered, laminated or wired glass.
2. Glass area greater than 16 square feet (1.49 m^2). Glass sloped 30 degrees (0.52 rad) or less from vertical, and highest point of glass not more than 10 feet (3048 mm) above a walking surface or other accessible area.

R308.6.6 Glass in greenhouses. Any glazing material is permitted to be installed without screening in the sloped areas of greenhouses, provided the greenhouse height at the ridge does not exceed 20 feet (6096 mm) above *grade*.

R308.6.7 Screen characteristics. The screen and its fastenings shall be capable of supporting twice the weight of the glazing, be firmly and substantially fastened to the framing members, and have a mesh opening of no more than 1 inch by 1 inch (25 mm by 25 mm).

R308.6.8 Curbs for skylights. All unit skylights installed in a roof with a pitch flatter than three units vertical in 12 units horizontal (25-percent slope) shall be mounted on a curb extending at least 4 inches (102 mm) above the plane of the roof unless otherwise specified in the manufacturer's installation instructions.

R308.6.9 Testing and labeling. Unit skylights shall be tested by an *approved* independent laboratory, and bear a *label* identifying manufacturer, performance *grade* rating and *approved* inspection agency to indicate compliance with the requirements of AAMA/WDMA/CSA 101/I.S.2/A440.

SECTION R309 GARAGES AND CARPORTS

R309.1 Floor surface. Garage floor surfaces shall be of *approved* noncombustible material.

The area of floor used for parking of automobiles or other vehicles shall be sloped to facilitate the movement of liquids to a drain or toward the main vehicle entry doorway.

R309.2 Carports. Carports shall be open on at least two sides. Carport floor surfaces shall be of *approved* noncombustible material. Carports not open on at least two sides shall be considered a garage and shall comply with the provisions of this section for garages.

Exception: Asphalt surfaces shall be permitted at ground level in carports.

The area of floor used for parking of automobiles or other vehicles shall be sloped to facilitate the movement of liquids to a drain or toward the main vehicle entry doorway.

R309.3 Flood hazard areas. For buildings located in flood hazard areas as established by Table R301.2(1), garage floors shall be:

1. Elevated to or above the design flood elevation as determined in Section R322; or
2. Located below the design flood elevation provided they are at or above *grade* on at least one side, are used solely for parking, building access or storage, meet the requirements of Section R322 and are otherwise constructed in accordance with this code.

R309.4 Automatic garage door openers. Automatic garage door openers, if provided, shall be listed in accordance with UL 325.

SECTION R310 EMERGENCY ESCAPE AND RESCUE OPENINGS

R310.1 Emergency escape and rescue required. *Basements,* habitable attics and every sleeping room shall have at least one operable emergency escape and rescue opening. Where *basements* contain one or more sleeping rooms, emergency egress and rescue openings shall be required in each sleeping room. Where emergency escape and rescue openings are provided they shall have a sill height of not more than 44 inches (1118 mm) above the floor. Where a door opening having a threshold below the adjacent ground elevation serves as an emergency escape and rescue opening and is provided with a bulkhead enclosure, the bulkhead enclosure shall comply with Section R310.3. The net clear opening dimensions required by this section shall be obtained by the normal operation of the emergency escape and rescue opening from the inside. Emergency escape and rescue openings with a finished sill height below the adjacent ground elevation shall be provided with a window well in accordance with Section R310.2. Emergency escape and rescue openings shall open directly into a public way, or to a *yard* or court that opens to a public way.

Exception: *Basements* used only to house mechanical *equipment* and not exceeding total floor area of 200 square feet (18.58 m^2).

R310.1.1 Minimum opening area. All emergency escape and rescue openings shall have a minimum net clear openable area of 4 square feet (0.372 m^2) The minimum net clear opening height shall be 22 inches (558 mm). The minimum net clear opening width shall be 20 inches (508 mm).

Emergency escape and rescue openings must have a minimum total glazing area of not less than 5 square feet (0.465 m^2) in the case of a ground floor level window and not less than 5.7 square feet (0.530 m^2) in the case of an upper story window.

Exception: *Grade* floor openings shall have a minimum net clear opening of 5 square feet (0.465 m^2).

R310.1.2 Minimum opening height. The minimum net clear opening height shall be 22 inches (558 mm).

R310.1.3 Minimum opening width. The minimum net clear opening width shall be 20 inches (508 mm).

R310.1.4 Operational constraints. Emergency escape and rescue openings shall be operational from the inside of the room without the use of keys, tools or special knowledge.

R310.2 Window wells. The minimum horizontal area of the window well shall be 9 square feet (0.9 m^2), with a minimum horizontal projection and width of 36 inches (914 mm). The area of the window well shall allow the emergency escape and rescue opening to be fully opened.

Exception: The ladder or steps required by Section R310.2.1 shall be permitted to encroach a maximum of 6 inches (152 mm) into the required dimensions of the window well.

R310.2.1 Ladder and steps. Window wells with a vertical depth greater than 44 inches (1118 mm) shall be equipped with a permanently affixed ladder or steps usable with the window in the fully open position. Ladders or steps required by this section shall not be required to comply with Sections R311.7 and R311.8. Ladders or rungs shall have an inside width of at least 12 inches (305 mm), shall project at least 3 inches (76 mm) from the wall and shall be spaced not more than 18 inches (457 mm) on center vertically for the full height of the window well.

R310.3 Bulkhead enclosures. Bulkhead enclosures shall provide direct access to the *basement*. The bulkhead enclosure with the door panels in the fully open position shall provide the minimum net clear opening required by Section R310.1.1. Bulkhead enclosures shall also comply with Section R311.7.8.2.

R310.4 Bars, grilles, covers and screens. Bars, grilles, covers, screens or similar devices are permitted to be placed over emergency escape and rescue openings, bulkhead enclosures, or window wells that serve such openings, provided the minimum net clear opening size complies with Sections R310.1.1 to R310.1.3, and such devices shall be releasable or removable from the inside without the use of a key, tool, special knowledge or force greater than that which is required for normal operation of the escape and rescue opening.

R310.5 Emergency escape windows under decks and porches. Emergency escape windows are allowed to be installed under decks and porches provided the location of the deck allows the emergency escape window to be fully opened and provides a path not less than 36 inches (914 mm) in height to a *yard* or court.

SECTION R311
MEANS OF EGRESS

R311.1 Means of egress. All *dwellings* shall be provided with a means of egress as provided in this section. The means of egress shall provide a continuous and unobstructed path of vertical and horizontal egress travel from all portions of the *dwelling* to the exterior of the *dwelling* at the required exterior egress door without requiring travel through a garage.

Exception: Equipment service platforms may be served by ladders constructed per Section R310.2.1.

R311.2 Egress door. At least one exterior egress door shall be provided for each *dwelling* unit. The egress door shall be side-hinged, and shall provide a minimum clear width of 32 inches (813 mm) when measured between the face of the door and the stop, with the door open 90 degrees (1.57 rad). The minimum clear height of the door opening shall not be less than 78 inches (1981 mm) in height measured from the top of the threshold to the bottom of the stop. Other exterior doors shall not be required to comply with these minimum dimensions. All interior egress doors and a minimum of one exterior egress door shall be readily openable from the side from which egress is to be made without the use of a key or special knowledge or effort.

R311.3 Floors and landings at exterior doors. There shall be a landing or floor on each side of each exterior door. The width of each landing shall not be less than the door served. Every landing shall have a minimum dimension of 36 inches (914 mm) measured in the direction of travel. Exterior landings shall be permitted to have a slope not to exceed $^1/_4$ unit vertical in 12 units horizontal (2-percent).

Exception: Exterior balconies less than 60 square feet (5.6 m^2) and only accessible from a door are permitted to have a landing less than 36 inches (914 mm) measured in the direction of travel.

R311.3.1 Floor elevations at the required egress doors. Landings or floors at the required egress door shall not be more than $1^1/_2$ inches (38 mm) lower than the top of the threshold.

Exception: The exterior landing or floor shall not be more than $8^1/_4$ inches (210 mm) below the top of the threshold provided the door does not swing over the landing or floor.

When exterior landings or floors serving the required egress door are not at *grade*, they shall be provided with access to *grade* by means of a ramp in accordance with Section R311.8 or a stairway in accordance with Section R311.7.

R311.3.2 Floor elevations for other exterior doors. Doors other than the required egress door shall be provided with landings or floors not more than $8^1/_4$ inches (210 mm) below the top of the threshold.

Exception: A landing is not required where a stairway is located on the exterior side of the door, provided the door does not swing over the stairway.

R311.3.3 Storm and screen doors. Storm and screen doors shall be permitted to swing over all exterior stairs and landings.

R311.4 Vertical egress. Egress from habitable levels including habitable attics and *basements* not provided with an egress door in accordance with Section R311.2 shall be by a ramp in accordance with Section R311.8 or a stairway in accordance with Section R311.7.

R311.5 Construction. Deleted.

R311.5.1 Attachment. Deleted.

R311.6 Hallways. The minimum width of a hallway shall be not less than 3 feet (914 mm) measured from the finish surface of the walls.

R311.6.1 Interior doors. All doors providing egress from habitable rooms shall have nominal minimum dimensions of 2 feet 6 inches (762 mm) width by 6 feet 8 inches (2032 mm) height.

R311.7 Stairways.

R311.7.1 Width. Stairways shall not be less than 36 inches (914 mm) in clear width at all points above the permitted handrail height and below the required headroom height. Handrails shall not project more than 4.5 inches (114 mm) on either side of the stairway and the minimum clear width of the stairway at and below the handrail height, including treads and landings, shall not be less than $31^1/_2$ inches (787 mm) where a handrail is installed on one side and 27 inches (698 mm) where handrails are provided on both sides.

Exception: The width of spiral stairways shall be in accordance with Section R311.7.9.1.

R311.7.2 Headroom. The minimum headroom in all parts of the stairway shall not be less than 6 feet 8 inches (2032 mm) measured vertically from the sloped line adjoining the tread nosing or from the floor surface of the landing or platform on that portion of the stairway.

Exception: Where the nosings of treads at the side of a flight extend under the edge of a floor opening through which the stair passes, the floor opening shall be allowed to project horizontally into the required headroom a maximum of $4^3/_4$ inches (121 mm).

R311.7.3 Walkline. Deleted.

R311.7.4 Stair treads and risers. Stair treads and risers shall meet the requirements of this section. For the purposes of this section all dimensions and dimensioned surfaces shall be exclusive of carpets, rugs or runners.

R311.7.4.1 Riser height. The maximum riser height shall be $8^1/_4$ inches (210 mm). The riser shall be measured vertically between leading edges of the adjacent treads. The greatest riser height within any flight of stairs shall not exceed the smallest by more than $^3/_8$ inch (9.5 mm). The top and bottom riser of interior stairs shall not exceed the smallest riser within that stair run by more than $^3/_4$ inch (19 mm). The height of the top and bottom riser of the interior stairs shall be measured from the permanent finished surface (carpet excluded). Where the bottom riser of an exterior stair adjoins an exterior walk, porch, driveway, patio, garage floor, or finish grade, the height of the riser may be less than the height of the adjacent risers.

R311.7.4.2 Tread depth. The minimum tread depth shall be 9 inches (229 mm). The tread depth shall be measured horizontally between the vertical planes of the foremost projection of adjacent treads and at a right angle to the tread's leading edge. The greatest tread depth within any flight of stairs shall not exceed the smallest by more than $^3/_8$ inch (9.5 mm). Winder treads shall have a minimum tread depth of 9 inches (229 mm) measured as above at a point 12 inches (305 mm) from the side where the treads are narrower. Winder treads shall have a minimum tread depth of 4 inches (102 mm) at any point. Within any flight of stairs, the greatest winder tread depth at the 12 inch (305 mm) walk line shall not exceed the smallest by more than $^3/_8$ inch (9.5 mm).

R311.7.4.3 Profile. The radius of curvature at the nosing shall be no greater than $^9/_{16}$ inch (14 mm). A nosing not less than $^3/_4$ inch (19 mm) but not more than $1^1/_4$ inches (32 mm) shall be provided on stairways with solid risers. The greatest nosing projection shall not exceed the smallest nosing projection by more than $^3/_8$ inch (9.5 mm) between two stories, including the nosing at the level of floors and landings. Beveling of nosings shall not exceed $^1/_2$ inch (12.7 mm). Risers shall be vertical or sloped under the tread above from the underside of the nosing above at an angle not more than 30 degrees (0.51 rad) from the vertical. Open risers are permitted, provided that the opening between treads does not permit the passage of a 4-inch diameter (102 mm) sphere.

Exceptions:

1. A nosing is not required where the tread depth is a minimum of 11 inches (279 mm).
2. The opening between adjacent treads is not limited on stairs with a total rise of 30 inches (762 mm) or less.

R311.7.4.4 Exterior wood/plastic composite stair treads. Wood/plastic composite stair treads shall comply with the provisions of Section R317.4.

R311.7.5 Landings for stairways. There shall be a floor or landing at the top and bottom of each stairway. A flight of stairs shall not have a vertical rise larger than 12 feet (3658 mm) between floor levels or landings. The width of each landing shall not be less than the width of the stairway served. Every landing shall have a minimum dimension of 36 inches (914 mm) measured in the direction of travel.

Exception: A floor or landing is not required at the top of an interior flight of stairs, including stairs in an enclosed garage, provided a door does not swing over the stairs.

R311.7.6 Stairway walking surface. The walking surface of treads and landings of stairways shall be sloped no steeper than one inch vertical in 48 inches horizontal (2-percent slope).

R311.7.7 Handrails. Handrails shall be provided on at least one side of each continuous run of treads or flight with four or more risers.

R311.7.7.1 Height. Handrail height, measured vertically from the sloped plane adjoining the tread nosing, or finish surface of ramp slope, shall be not less than 34 inches (864 mm) and not more than 38 inches (965 mm).

Exceptions:

1. The use of a volute, turnout or starting easing shall be allowed over the lowest tread.
2. When handrail fittings or bendings are used to provide continuous transition between flights, the transition from handrail to guardrail, or used at the start of a flight, the handrail height at the fittings or bendings shall be permitted to exceed the maximum height.

R311.7.7.2 Continuity. Handrails for stairways shall be continuous for the full length of the flight, from a point directly above the top riser of the flight to a point directly above the lowest riser of the flight. Handrail ends shall be returned or shall terminate in newel posts or safety terminals. Handrails adjacent to a wall shall have a space of not less than $1^1/_2$ inch (38 mm) between the wall and the handrails.

Exceptions:

1. Handrails shall be permitted to be interrupted by a newel post.
2. The use of a volute, turnout, starting easing or starting newel shall be allowed over the lowest tread.
3. Two or more separate rails shall be considered continuous if the termination of the rails occurs within 6 inches (152 mm) of each other. If transitioning between a wall-mounted handrail and a guardrail/handrail, the wall-mounted rail must return into the wall.

R311.7.7.3 Grip-size. All required handrails shall be of one of the following types or provide equivalent graspability.

1. Type I. Handrails with a circular cross section shall have an outside diameter of at least $1^1/_4$ inches (32 mm) and not greater than 2 inches (51 mm). If the handrail is not circular, it shall have a perimeter dimension of at least 4 inches (102 mm) and not greater than $6^1/_4$ inches (160 mm) with a maximum cross section of dimension of 2 $^1/_4$ inches (57 mm). Edges shall have a minimum radius of 0.01 inch (0.25 mm).
2. Type II. Handrails with a perimeter greater than $6^1/_4$ inches (160 mm) shall have a graspable finger recess area on both sides of the profile. The finger recess shall begin within a distance of $^3/_4$ inch (19 mm) measured vertically from the tallest portion of the profile and achieve a depth of at least $^5/_{16}$ inch (8 mm) within $^7/_8$ inch (22 mm) below the widest portion of the profile. This required depth shall continue for at least $^3/_8$ inch (10 mm) to a level that is not less than $1^3/_4$ inches (45 mm) below the tallest portion of the profile. The minimum width of the handrail above the recess shall be $1^1/_4$ inches (32 mm) to a maximum of $2^3/_4$ inches (70 mm). Edges shall have a minimum radius of 0.01 inch (0.25 mm).

 Exception: Exterior handrails (garages and areas exposed to the weather) shall not be more than $3^1/_2$ inches (89 mm) in cross-section dimension.

R311.7.7.4 Exterior wood/plastic composite handrails. Wood/plastic composite handrails shall comply with the provisions of Section R317.4.

R311.7.8 Illumination. All stairs shall be provided with illumination in accordance with Section R303.6.

R311.7.9 Special stairways. Spiral stairways, bulkhead enclosure stairways and bowed tread stairways shall comply with all requirements of Section R311.7 except as specified below.

R311.7.9.1 Spiral stairways. Spiral stairways are permitted, provided the minimum clear width at and below the handrail shall be 26 inches (660 mm) with each tread having a $7^1/_2$-inch (190 mm) minimum tread depth at 12 inches (914 mm) from the narrower edge. All treads shall be identical, and the rise shall be no more than $9^1/_2$ inches (241 mm). A minimum headroom of 6 feet 6 inches (1982 mm) shall be provided.

R311.7.9.2 Bulkhead enclosure stairways. Stairways serving bulkhead enclosures, not part of the required building egress, providing access from the outside *grade* level to the *basement* shall be exempt from the requirements of Sections R311.3 and R311.7 where the maximum height from the *basement* finished floor level to *grade* adjacent to the stairway does not exceed 8 feet (2438 mm) and the *grade* level opening to the stairway is covered by a bulkhead enclosure with hinged doors or other *approved* means.

R311.7.9.3 Bowed tread stairways. Bowed tread stairways are permitted provided they are uniform in bowed tread depth along entire width of tread with not more than $^3/_8$-inch variance from greatest to smallest tread in the stairway flight. At no point shall the tread be less than a minimum of 9 inches with a nosing as listed in Sections R311.7.4.2 and R311.7.4.3 respectively.

R311.7.9.3.1 Standard stairway application. The bottom 3 treads in a standard straight run stairway application as listed under Section R311.7.4.2 are permitted to bow provided at no point along the width of the tread they are less than 9 inches as measured under Section R311.7.4.2 and each bowed tread is uniformed with other bowed treads with no more than $^3/_8$-inch variance from greatest to least. Nosing is required as listed in Section R311.7.4.

R311.7.9.3.2 Bowed tread circular stairways. Bowed treads in a circular stairway are permitted provided they are uniformed as per winder treads as listed in Section R311.7.4.2 measured at a point 12 inches from the side where the treads are narrower. At this walk line, bowed treads must be uniform with other circular stairway treads with the greatest tread not to exceed the smallest by more than $^{3}/_{8}$ inch. Nosing is required as listed in Section R311.7.4.

R311.8 Ramps.

R311.8.1 Maximum slope. Ramps shall have a maximum slope of 1 unit vertical in 12 units horizontal (8.3 percent slope).

Exception: Where it is technically infeasible to comply because of site constraints, ramps may have a maximum slope of one unit vertical in eight horizontal (12.5 percent slope).

R311.8.2 Landings required. A minimum 3-foot-by-3-foot (914 mm by 914 mm) landing shall be provided:

1. At the top and bottom of ramps.
2. Where doors open onto ramps.
3. Where ramps change direction.

R311.8.3 Handrails required. Handrails shall be provided on at least one side of all ramps exceeding a slope of one unit vertical in 12 units horizontal (8.33-percent slope).

R311.8.3.1 Height. Handrail height, measured above the finished surface of the ramp slope, shall be not less than 34 inches (864 mm) and not more than 38 inches (965 mm).

R311.8.3.2 Grip size. Handrails on ramps shall comply with Section R311.7.7.3.

R311.8.3.3 Continuity. Handrails where required on ramps shall be continuous for the full length of the ramp. Handrail ends shall be returned or shall terminate in newel posts or safety terminals. Handrails adjacent to a wall shall have a space of not less than $1^{1}/_{2}$ inches (38 mm) between the wall and the handrails.

SECTION R312 GUARDS

R312.1 Where required. *Guards* shall be located along open-sided walking surfaces, including stairs, ramps and landings, that are located more than 30 inches (762 mm) measured vertically to the floor or *grade* below at any point within 36 inches (914 mm) horizontally to the edge of the open side. Insect screening shall not be considered as a *guard*.

R312.2 Height. Required *guards* at open-sided walking surfaces, including stairs, porches, balconies or landings, shall be not less than 36 inches (914 mm) high measured vertically above the adjacent walking surface, adjacent fixed seating or the line connecting the leading edges of the treads.

Exceptions:

1. *Guards* on the open sides of stairs shall have a height not less than 34 inches (864 mm) measured vertically from a line connecting the leading edges of the treads.
2. Where the top of the *guard* also serves as a handrail on the open sides of stairs, the top of the *guard* shall not be not less than 34 inches (864 mm) and not more than 38 inches (965 mm) measured vertically from a line connecting the leading edges of the treads.

R312.3 Opening limitations. Required *guards* shall not have openings from the walking surface to the required *guard* height which allow passage of a sphere 4 inches (102 mm) in diameter.

Exceptions:

1. The triangular openings at the open side of a stair, formed by the riser, tread and bottom rail of a *guard*, shall not allow passage of a sphere 6 inches (153 mm) in diameter.
2. *Guards* on the open sides of stairs shall not have openings which allow passage of a sphere $4^{3}/_{8}$ inches (111 mm) in diameter.

R312.4 Exterior woodplastic composite guards. Woodplastic composite *guards* shall comply with the provisions of Section R317.4.

SECTION R313 AUTOMATIC FIRE SPRINKLER SYSTEMS

R313.1 Townhouse automatic fire sprinkler systems. An automatic residential fire sprinkler system shall be installed in *townhouses*.

Exceptions:

1. Townhouses constructed with a common 2-hour fire-resistance-rated wall assembly tested in accordance with ASTM E 119 or UL 263 provided such walls do not contain plumbing or mechanical equipment, ducts or vents in the cavity of the common wall. The wall shall be rated for fire exposure from both sides and shall extend to and be tight against exterior walls and the underside of the roof sheathing. Electrical installations shall be installed in accordance with Chapters 34 through 43. Penetrations for electrical outlet boxes shall be in accordance with Section R302.4.
2. An automatic residential fire sprinkler system shall not be required when additions or alterations are made to existing townhouses that do not have an automatic residential fire sprinkler system installed.

R313.1.1 Design and installation. Automatic residential fire sprinkler systems for *townhouses* shall be designed and installed in accordance with Appendix P, Section P2904.

R313.2 One- and two-family dwellings automatic fire systems. Deleted.

R313.2.1 Design and installation. Deleted.

SECTION R314 SMOKE ALARMS

R314.1 Smoke detection and notification. All smoke alarms shall be listed in accordance with UL 217 and installed in accordance with the provisions of this code and the household fire warning *equipment* provisions of NFPA 72.

R314.2 Smoke detection systems. Household fire alarm systems installed in accordance with NFPA 72 that include smoke alarms, or a combination of smoke detector and audible notification device installed as required by this section for smoke alarms, shall be permitted. The household fire alarm system shall provide the same level of smoke detection and alarm as required by this section for smoke alarms. Where a household fire warning system is installed using a combination of smoke detector and audible notification device(s), it shall become a permanent fixture of the occupancy and owned by the homeowner. The system shall be monitored by an *approved* supervising station and be maintained in accordance with NFPA 72.

Exception: Where smoke alarms are provided meeting the requirements of Section R314.4.

R314.3 Location. Smoke alarms shall be installed in the following locations:

1. In each sleeping room.
2. Outside each separate sleeping area in the immediate vicinity of the bedrooms.
3. On each additional *story* of the *dwelling*, including *basements* and habitable attics (finished) but not including crawl spaces, uninhabitable (unfinished) attics and uninhabitable (unfinished) attic-stories. In *dwellings* or *dwelling units* with split levels and without an intervening door between the adjacent levels, a smoke alarm installed on the upper level shall suffice for the adjacent lower level provided that the lower level is less than one full *story* below the upper level.

When more than one smoke alarm is required to be installed within an individual *dwelling* unit the alarm devices shall be interconnected in such a manner that the actuation of one alarm will activate all of the alarms in the individual unit.

R314.3.1 Alterations, repairs and additions. When *alterations*, repairs or *additions* requiring a building *permit* occur, or when one or more sleeping rooms are added or created in existing *dwellings*, the individual *dwelling unit* shall be equipped with smoke alarms located as required for new *dwellings*; the smoke alarms shall be interconnected and hardwired.

Exceptions:

1. Work involving the exterior surfaces of *dwellings*, such as the replacement of roofing or siding, or the *addition* or replacement of windows or doors, or the *addition* of a porch or deck, are exempt from the requirements of this section.
2. Installation, *alteration* or repairs of plumbing or mechanical systems are exempt from the requirements of this section.

R314.4 Power source. Smoke alarms shall receive their primary power from the building wiring when such wiring is served from a commercial source, and when primary power is interrupted, shall receive power from a battery. Wiring shall be permanent and without a disconnecting switch other than those required for overcurrent protection. Smoke alarms shall be interconnected.

Exceptions:

1. Smoke alarms shall be permitted to be battery operated when installed in buildings without commercial power.
2. Interconnection and hard-wiring of smoke alarms in existing areas shall not be required where the *alterations* or repairs do not result in the removal of interior wall or ceiling finishes exposing the structure. Smoke alarm locations are required per Section R314.2, but may be battery powered and shall be designed to emit a recurring signal when batteries are low and need to be replaced.

SECTION R315 CARBON MONOXIDE ALARMS

R315.1 Carbon monoxide alarms. In new construction, one-and two-family dwellings and townhouses within which fuel-fired appliances or fireplaces are installed or that have attached garages shall be provided with an approved carbon monoxide alarm installed outside of each separate sleeping area in the immediate vicinity of the bedroom(s) as directed by the alarm manufacturer.

R315.2 Where required in existing dwellings. For existing dwellings, where interior alterations, repairs, fuel-fired appliance replacements, or additions requiring a building permit occurs, or where one or more sleeping rooms are added or created, or where fuel-fired appliances or fireplaces are added or replaced, carbon monoxide alarms shall be provided in accordance with Section 315.1.

Exception: Work involving the exterior surfaces of dwellings, such as the replacement of roofing or siding, or the addition or replacement of windows or doors, or the addition of a porch or deck, or the installation of a fuel-fired appliance that cannot introduce carbon monoxide to the interior of the dwelling, are exempt from the requirements of this section.

R315.3 Alarm requirements. The required carbon monoxide alarms shall be audible in all bedrooms over background noise levels with all intervening doors closed. Single station carbon monoxide alarms shall be listed as complying with UL 2034 and shall be installed in accordance with this code and the manufacturer's installation instructions. Battery powered, plug-in, or hard-wired alarms are acceptable for use.

SECTION R316 FOAM PLASTIC

R316.1 General. The provisions of this section shall govern the materials, design, application, construction and installation of foam plastic materials.

R316.2 Labeling and identification. Packages and containers of foam plastic insulation and foam plastic insulation components delivered to the job site shall bear the *label* of an *approved agency* showing the manufacturer's name, the product listing, product identification and information sufficient to determine that the end use will comply with the requirements.

R316.3 Surface burning characteristics. Unless otherwise allowed in Section R316.5 or R316.6, all foam plastic or foam plastic cores used as a component in manufactured assemblies used in building construction shall have a flame spread index of not more than 75 and shall have a smoke-developed index of not more than 450 when tested in the maximum thickness intended for use in accordance with ASTM E 84 or UL 723. Loose-fill type foam plastic insulation shall be tested as board stock for the flame spread index and smoke-developed index.

Exception: Foam plastic insulation more than 4 inches (102 mm) thick shall have a maximum flame spread index of 75 and a smoke-developed index of 450 where tested at a minimum thickness of 4 inches (102 mm), provided the end use is *approved* in accordance with Section R316.6 using the thickness and density intended for use.

R316.4 Thermal barrier. Unless otherwise allowed in Section R316.5 or Section R316.6, foam plastic shall be separated from the interior of a building by an *approved* thermal barrier of minimum $^1/_2$ inch (12.7 mm) gypsum wallboard or an *approved* finish material equivalent to a thermal barrier material that will limit the average temperature rise of the unexposed surface to no more than 250°F (139°C) after 15 minutes of fire exposure complying with the ASTM E 119 or UL 263 standard time temperature curve. The thermal barrier shall be installed in such a manner that it will remain in place for 15 minutes based on NFPA 286 with the acceptance criteria of Section R302.9.4, FM 4880, UL 1040 or UL 1715.

R316.5 Specific requirements. The following requirements shall apply to these uses of foam plastic unless specifically *approved* in accordance with Section R316.6 or by other sections of the code or the requirements of Sections R316.2 through R316.4 have been met.

R316.5.1 Masonry or concrete construction. The thermal barrier specified in Section R316.4 is not required in a masonry or concrete wall, floor or roof when the foam plastic insulation is separated from the interior of the building by a minimum 1-inch (25 mm) thickness of masonry or concrete.

R316.5.2 Roofing. The thermal barrier specified in Section R316.4 is not required when the foam plastic in a roof assembly or under a roof covering is installed in accordance with the code and the manufacturer's installation instructions and is separated from the interior of the building by tongue-and-groove wood planks or wood structural panel sheathing in accordance with Section R803, not less than $^{15}/_{32}$ inch (11.9 mm) thick bonded with exterior glue and identified as Exposure 1, with edges supported by blocking or tongue-and-groove joints or an equivalent material. The smoke-developed index for roof applications shall not be limited.

R316.5.3 Attics. The thermal barrier specified in Section R316.4 is not required where all of the following apply:

1. *Attic* access is required by Section R807.1.
2. The space is entered only for purposes of repairs or maintenance.
3. The foam plastic insulation is protected against ignition using one of the following ignition barrier materials:
   - 3.1. $1^1/_2$-inch-thick (38 mm) mineral fiber insulation;
   - 3.2. $^1/_4$-inch-thick (6.4 mm) wood structural panels;
   - 3.3. $^3/_8$-inch (9.5 mm) particleboard;
   - 3.4. $^1/_4$-inch (6.4 mm) hardboard;
   - 3.5. $^3/_8$-inch (9.5 mm) gypsum board; or
   - 3.6. Corrosion-resistant steel having a base metal thickness of 0.016 inch (0.406 mm).

The above ignition barrier is not required where the foam plastic insulation has been tested in accordance with Section R316.6.

R316.5.4 Crawl spaces. The thermal barrier specified in Section R316.4 is not required where all of the following apply:

1. Crawlspace access is required by Section R408.4
2. Entry is made only for purposes of repairs or maintenance.
3. The foam plastic insulation is protected against ignition using one of the following ignition barrier materials:
   - 3.1. $1^1/_2$-inch-thick (38 mm) mineral fiber insulation;
   - 3.2. $^1/_4$-inch-thick (6.4 mm) wood structural panels;
   - 3.3. $^3/_8$-inch (9.5 mm) particleboard;
   - 3.4. $^1/_4$-inch (6.4 mm) hardboard;
   - 3.5. $^3/_8$-inch (9.5 mm) gypsum board; or
   - 3.6. Corrosion-resistant steel having a base metal thickness of 0.016 inch (0.406 mm).

The above ignition barrier is not required where the foam plastic insulation has been tested in accordance with Section R316.6.

R316.5.5 Foam-filled exterior doors. Foam-filled exterior doors are exempt from the requirements of Sections R316.3 and R316.4.

R316.5.6 Foam-filled garage doors. Foam-filled garage doors in attached or detached garages are exempt from the requirements of Sections R316.3 and R316.4.

R316.5.7 Foam backer board. The thermal barrier specified in Section R316.4 is not required where siding backer board foam plastic insulation has a maximum thickness of 0.5 inch (12.7 mm) and a potential heat of not more than 2000 Btu per square foot (22 720 kJ/m^2) when tested in accordance with NFPA 259 provided that:

1. The foam plastic insulation is separated from the interior of the building by not less than 2 inches (51 mm) of mineral fiber insulation or
2. The foam plastic insulation is installed over existing *exterior wall* finish in conjunction with re-siding or
3. The foam plastic insulation has been tested in accordance with Section R316.6.

R316.5.8 Re-siding. The thermal barrier specified in Section R316.4 is not required where the foam plastic insulation is installed over existing *exterior wall* finish in conjunction with re-siding provided the foam plastic has a maximum thickness of 0.5 inch (12.7 mm) and a potential heat of not more than 2000 Btu per square foot (22 720 kJ/m^2) when tested in accordance with NFPA 259.

R316.5.9 Interior trim. The thermal barrier specified in Section R316.4 is not required for exposed foam plastic interior trim, provided all of the following are met:

1. The minimum density is 20 pounds per cubic foot (320 kg/m^3).
2. The maximum thickness of the trim is 0.5 inch (12.7 mm) and the maximum width is 8 inches (204 mm).
3. The interior trim shall not constitute more than 10 percent of the aggregate wall and ceiling area of any room or space.
4. The flame spread index does not exceed 75 when tested per ASTM E 84. The smoke-developed index is not limited.

R316.5.10 Interior finish. Foam plastics shall be permitted as interior finish where *approved* in accordance with Section R316.6 Foam plastics that are used as interior finish shall also meet the flame spread index and smoke-developed index requirements of Sections R302.9.1 and R302.9.2.

R316.5.11 Sill plates and headers. Foam plastic shall be permitted to be spray applied to a sill plate and header without the thermal barrier specified in Section R316.4 subject to all of the following:

1. The maximum thickness of the foam plastic shall be $3^1/_4$ inches (83 mm).
2. The density of the foam plastic shall be in the range of 0.5 to 2.0 pounds per cubic foot (8 to 32 kg/m^3).
3. The foam plastic shall have a flame spread index of 25 or less and an accompanying smoke developed index of 450 or less when tested in accordance with ASTM E 84.

R316.5.12 Sheathing. Foam plastic insulation used as sheathing shall comply with Section R316.3 and Section R316.4. Where the foam plastic sheathing is exposed to the *attic* space at a gable or kneewall, the provisions of Section R316.5.3 shall apply.

R316.6 Specific approval. Foam plastic not meeting the requirements of Sections R316.3 through R316.5 shall be specifically *approved* on the basis of one of the following *approved* tests: NFPA 286 with the acceptance criteria of Section R302.9.4, FM4880, UL 1040 or UL 1715, or fire tests related to actual end-use configurations. The specific approval shall be based on the actual end use configuration and shall be performed on the finished foam plastic assembly in the maximum thickness intended for use. Assemblies tested shall include seams, joints and other typical details used in the installation of the assembly and shall be tested in the manner intended for use.

R316.7 Termite damage. The use of foam plastics in areas of "moderate-heavy" termite infestation probability shall be in accordance with Section R318.4.

SECTION R317 PROTECTION OF WOOD AND WOOD BASED PRODUCTS AGAINST DECAY

R317.1 Location required. Protection of wood and wood based products from decay shall be provided in the following locations by the use of naturally durable wood or wood that is preservative-treated in accordance with AWPA U1 for the species, product, preservative and end use. Preservatives shall be listed in Section 4 of AWPA U1.

1. Wood joists or the bottom of a wood structural floor when closer than 18 inches (457 mm) or wood girders when closer than 12 inches (305 mm) to the exposed ground in crawl spaces or unexcavated area located within the periphery of the building foundation.
2. All exterior sills and plates that rest on concrete or masonry exterior foundation walls.
3. Sills and sleepers on a concrete or masonry slab, unless the slab that is in direct contact with the ground is separated from the ground by an *approved* impervious moisture barrier.
4. The ends of wood girders entering exterior masonry or concrete walls having clearances of less than $^1/_2$ inch (12.7 mm) on tops, sides and ends.
5. Wood siding and sheathing on the exterior of a building having a clearance of less than 6 inches (152 mm) from the ground.
6. Wood structural members supporting moisture-permeable floors or roofs that are exposed to the weather, such as concrete or masonry slabs, unless separated from such floors or roofs by an impervious moisture barrier.
7. Wood furring strips or other wood framing members attached directly to the interior of exterior masonry walls or concrete walls below *grade* except where an *approved* vapor retarder is applied between the wall and the furring strips or framing members.
8. All portions of a porch, screen porch or deck from the bottom of the header down, including posts, guardrails, pickets, steps, and floor structure. Coverings that would prevent moisture or water accumulation on the surface or at joints between members are allowed.

   Exception: Columns complying with Section R317.1.4, Exception #2.

R317.1.1 Field treatment. Deleted.

R317.1.2 Ground contact. All wood in contact with the ground, embedded in concrete in direct contact with the ground or embedded in concrete exposed to the weather that supports permanent structures intended for human occupancy shall be *approved* pressure-preservative-treated wood suitable for ground contact use, except untreated wood may be used where entirely below groundwater level or continuously submerged in fresh water.

R317.1.3 Geographical areas. Deleted.

R317.1.4 Wood columns. Wood columns shall be *approved* wood of natural decay resistance or *approved* pressure-preservative-treated wood.

Exceptions:

1. Columns in *basements* when supported by a concrete floor with an *approved* impervious moisture barrier installed between the slab and earth.
2. Columns exposed to the weather when all of the following conditions are met:
   a. The column is supported by piers or metal pedestals projecting 1 inch (25.4 mm) above a concrete floor or 6 inches (152 mm) above exposed earth and the earth is covered by an approved impervious moisture barrier; and
   b. There is no joints in or between structural members (from the header to the base of the column); and
   c. The column is protected from exposure to surface moisture at the top by a roof, eave, or overhang; and
   d. The exterior surface of the column is fully sealed (paint, sealer, etc..) against moisture intrusion.
3. Columns in enclosed crawl spaces or unexcavated areas located within the periphery of the building when supported by a concrete pier or metal pedestal at a height more than 8 inches (203 mm) from exposed earth and the earth is covered by an impervious moisture barrier.

R317.1.5 Exposed glued-laminated timbers. The portions of glued-laminated timbers that form the structural supports of a building or other structure and are exposed to weather and not properly protected by a roof, eave or similar covering shall be pressure treated with preservative, or be manufactured from naturally durable or preservative-treated wood.

R317.2 Quality mark. Lumber and plywood required to be pressure-preservative-treated in accordance with Section R318.1 shall bear the quality *mark* of an *approved* inspection agency that maintains continuing supervision, testing and inspection over the quality of the product and that has been *approved* by an accreditation body that complies with the requirements of the American Lumber Standard Committee treated wood program.

R317.2.1 Required information. The required quality *mark* on each piece of pressure-preservative-treated lumber or plywood shall contain the following information:

1. Identification of the treating plant.
2. Type of preservative.
3. The minimum preservative retention.
4. End use for which the product was treated.
5. Standard to which the product was treated.
6. Identity of the *approved* inspection agency.
7. The designation "Dry," if applicable.

Exception: Quality *marks* on lumber less than 1 inch (25.4 mm) nominal thickness, or lumber less than nominal 1 inch by 5 inches (25.4 mm by 127 mm) or 2 inches by 4 inches (51 mm by 102 mm) or lumber 36 inches (914 mm) or less in length shall be applied by stamping the faces of exterior pieces or by end labeling not less than 25 percent of the pieces of a bundled unit.

R317.3 Fasteners and connectors in contact with preservative-treated and fire-retardant-treated wood. Fasteners and connectors in contact with preservative-treated wood and fire-retardant-treated wood shall be in accordance with this section. The coating weights for zinc-coated fasteners shall be in accordance with ASTM A 153.

R317.3.1 Fasteners for preservative-treated wood. Fasteners for preservative-treated wood shall be of hot dipped zinc-coated galvanized steel, stainless steel, silicon bronze or copper. Coating types and weights for connectors in contact with preservative-treated wood shall be in accordance with the connector manufacturer's recommendations. In the absence of manufacturer's recommendations, a minimum of ASTM A 653 type G185 zinc-coated galvanized steel, or equivalent, shall be used.

Exceptions:

1. One-half-inch (12.7 mm) diameter or greater steel bolts.
2. Fasteners other than nails and timber rivets shall be permitted to be of mechanically deposited zinc coated steel with coating weights in accordance with ASTM B 695, Class 55 minimum.

R317.3.2 Fastenings for wood foundations. Fastenings for wood foundations shall be as required in AF&PA PWF.

R317.3.3 Fasteners for fire-retardant-treated wood used in exterior applications or wet or damp locations. Fasteners for fire-retardant-treated wood used in exterior applications or wet or damp locations shall be of hot-dipped zinc-coated galvanized steel, stainless steel, silicon bronze or copper. Fasteners other than nails and timber rivets shall be permitted to be of mechanically deposited zinc-coated steel with coating weights in accordance with ASTM B 695, Class 55 minimum.

R317.3.4 Fasteners for fire-retardant-treated wood used in interior applications. Fasteners for fire-retardant-treated wood used in interior locations shall be in accordance with the manufacturer's recommendations. In the absence of the manufacturer's recommendations, Section R317.3.3 shall apply.

R317.4 Wood/plastic composites. Wood/plastic composites used in exterior deck boards, stair treads, handrails and guardrail systems shall bear a *label* indicating the required performance levels and demonstrating compliance with the provisions of ASTM D 7032.

R317.4.1 Wood/plastic composites shall be installed in accordance with the manufacturer's instructions.

SECTION R318
PROTECTION AGAINST SUBTERRANEAN TERMITES

R318.1 Subterranean termite control methods. In areas subject to damage from termites as indicated by Table R301.2(1), methods of protection shall be one of the following methods or a combination of these methods:

1. Chemical termiticide treatment, as provided in Section R318.2.
2. Termite baiting system installed and maintained according to the *label*.
3. Pressure-preservative-treated wood in accordance with the provisions of Section R317.1.
4. Naturally durable termite-resistant wood.
5. Deleted.
6. Cold-formed steel framing in accordance with Sections R505.2.1 and R603.2.1.

R318.1.1 Quality mark. Lumber and plywood required to be pressure-preservative-treated in accordance with Section R318.1 shall bear the quality *mark* of an *approved* inspection agency which maintains continuing supervision, testing and inspection over the quality of the product and which has been *approved* by an accreditation body which complies with the requirements of the American Lumber Standard Committee treated wood program.

R318.1.2 Field treatment. Deleted.

R318.2 Chemical soil treatment. The concentration, rate of application and treatment method of the termiticide shall be consistent with and never less than the termiticide label and applied according to the standards of the North Carolina Department of Agriculture.

R318.3 Barriers. Deleted.

R318.4 Foam plastic protection. This section shall apply to both treated and untreated foam plastic.

R318.4.1 Foundation walls. All foam plastic shall be a minimum of 8 inches (203 mm) above grade. See Appendix 0.

Exception: Foam plastic less than 8 inches (203 mm) above or in contact with grade shall be installed in accordance with Section 318.5.5 and Appendix 0.

R318.4.2 Termite control. When foam plastic is in contact with the ground, subterranean termite control shall be in accordance with Section 318.1.

R318.4.3 Slab on grade (non-structural). Foam plastic shall be installed along the vertical edge and underneath the slab as specified in Section R318.4.5.

R318.4.4 Slab on grade (structural). All slabs which distribute the wall loads to the foundation shall be insulated as specified in this section. Foam plastic shall be installed along the vertical edge and underneath grade as specified in Appendix 0, Figure 0-3.

R318.4.5 Foam plastic in contact with ground.

R318.4.5.1 Inspection and treatment gaps. Foam plastic in contact with the ground shall not be continuous to the bottom of the weather-resistant siding. A clear and unobstructed 2-inch (51 mm) minimum inspection gap shall be maintained from the bottom of the weather-resistant siding to the top of any foam plastic. A minimum 4-inch (102 mm) treatment gap shall be provided beginning not more than 6 inches (152 mm) below grade. The top and bottom edges of the foam plastic installed between the inspection gap and the treatment gap shall be cut at a 45-degree (0.79 rad) angle. See Appendix 0.

Exception: For ICF foundations see Section R404.1.2.3.6.1.

R318.4.5.2 Protection of exposed foam plastic. Exposed foam plastic shall be protected from physical damage. The required inspection gap foam plastic and treatment gap shall be on the exterior with a cementitious coating that extends at least 2 inches (51 mm) below the foam plastic onto the surface of the foundation wall. See Appendix 0.

R318.4.5.3 Waterproofing foam plastic between inspection gap and treatment gap. Waterproofing shall be installed over the required cementitious coating from 6 inches (152 mm) above grade to the treatment gap per manufacturer's installation instructions.

R318.4.5.4 Dampproofing of below grade walls. Any foam plastic applied below the treatment gap shall be installed after required foundation wall dampproofing is in place. See section R406 and Appendix O.

SECTION R319
SITE ADDRESS

R319.1 Address numbers. Buildings shall have *approved* address numbers, building numbers or *approved* building identification placed in a position that is plainly legible and visible from the street or road fronting the property. These numbers shall contrast with their background. Address numbers shall be Arabic numbers or alphabetical letters. Numbers shall be a minimum of 4 inches (102 mm) high with a minimum stroke width of $^1/_2$ inch (12.7 mm). Where access is by means of a private road and the building address cannot be viewed from the public way, a monument, pole or other sign or means shall be used to identify the structure.

SECTION R320
ACCESSIBILITY

R320.1 Scope. Where there are four or more *dwelling* units or sleeping units in a single structure, the provisions of Chapter 11 of the *International Building Code* for Group R-3 shall apply.

SECTION R321
ELEVATORS AND PLATFORM LIFTS

R321.1 Elevators. Where provided elevators shall comply with ASME A17.1.

R321.2 Platform lifts. Where provided, platform lifts shall comply with ASME A18.1.

R321.3 Accessibility. Deleted.

R321.4 Certification. The installer shall certify that the following conditions have been met.

1. The elevator or platform lift has been installed in accordance with the manufacturer's installation instructions.
2. The elevator meets the requirements of ASME A17.1, Part 5, Section 5.3 and other applicable parts.
3. The elevator or platform lift meets the requirements of the *North Carolina Electrical Code*. Before a Certificate of Occupancy is issued, the permit holder shall provide the code enforcement official a letter of certification from the installer, evidencing compliance with the above conditions. Any maintenance requirements required by the manufacturer shall be stated and affixed to the component. When an elevator or platform lift or its components has been serviced, the service provider shall certify to the owner that the elevator continues to meet the above conditions.

SECTION R322
FLOOD-RESISTANT CONSTRUCTION

R322.1 General. Buildings and structures constructed in whole or in part in flood hazard areas (including A or V Zones) as established in Table R301.2(1) shall be designed and constructed in accordance with the provisions contained in this section. See additional provisions of Chapter 46.

Exception: Buildings and structures located in whole or in part in identified floodways shall be designed and constructed in accordance with ASCE 24.

R322.1.1 Alternative provisions. As an alternative to the requirements in Section R322.3 for buildings and structures located in whole or in part in coastal high-hazard areas (V Zones), ASCE 24 is permitted subject to the limitations of this code and the limitations therein.

R322.1.2 Structural systems. All structural systems of all buildings and structures shall be designed, connected and anchored to resist flotation, collapse or permanent lateral movement due to structural loads and stresses from flooding equal to the design flood elevation.

R322.1.3 Flood-resistant construction. All buildings and structures erected in areas prone to flooding shall be constructed by methods and practices that minimize flood damage.

R322.1.4 Establishing the design flood elevation. The design flood elevation shall be used to define areas prone to flooding. At a minimum, the design flood elevation is the higher of:

1. The base flood elevation at the depth of peak elevation of flooding (including wave height) which has a 1 percent (100-year flood) or greater chance of being equaled or exceeded in any given year, or
2. The elevation of the design flood associated with the area designated on a flood hazard map adopted by the community, or otherwise legally designated.

R322.1.4.1 Determination of design flood elevations. If design flood elevations are not specified, the *building official* is authorized to require the applicant to:

1. Obtain and reasonably use data available from a federal, state or other source; or
2. Determine the design flood elevation in accordance with accepted hydrologic and hydraulic engineering practices used to define special flood hazard areas. Determinations shall be undertaken by a registered *design professional* who shall document that the technical methods used reflect currently accepted engineering practice. Studies, analyses and computations shall be submitted in sufficient detail to allow thorough review and approval.

R322.1.4.2 Determination of impacts. In riverine flood hazard areas where design flood elevations are specified but floodways have not been designated, the applicant shall demonstrate that the effect of the proposed buildings and structures on design flood elevations, including fill, when combined with all other existing and anticipated flood hazard area encroachments, will not increase the design flood elevation more than 1 foot (305 mm) at any point within the jurisdiction.

R322.1.5 Lowest floor. The lowest floor shall be the floor of the lowest enclosed area, including *basement*, but excluding any unfinished flood-resistant enclosure that is useable solely for vehicle parking, building access or limited storage provided that such enclosure is not built so as to render the building or structure in violation of this section.

R322.1.6 Protection of mechanical and electrical systems. Electrical systems, *equipment* and components; heating, ventilating, air conditioning; plumbing *appliances* and plumbing fixtures; *duct systems*; and other service *equipment* shall be located at or above the elevation required in Section R322.2 (flood hazard areas including A Zones) or R322.3 (coastal high-hazard areas including V Zones). If replaced as part of a substantial improvement, electrical systems, *equipment* and components; heating, ventilating, air conditioning and plumbing *appliances* and plumbing fixtures; *duct systems*; and other service *equipment* shall meet the requirements of this section. Systems, fixtures, and *equipment* and components shall not be mounted on or penetrate through walls intended to break away under flood loads.

Exception: Locating electrical systems, *equipment* and components; heating, ventilating, air conditioning; plumbing *appliances* and plumbing fixtures; *duct systems*; and other service *equipment* is permitted below the elevation required in Section R322.2 (flood hazard areas including A Zones) or R322.3 (coastal high-hazard areas including V Zones) provided that they are designed and installed to prevent water from entering or accumulating within the components and to resist hydrostatic and hydrodynamic loads and stresses, including the effects of buoyancy, during the occurrence of flooding to the design flood elevation in accordance with ASCE 24. Electrical wiring systems are permitted to be located below the required elevation provided they conform to the provisions of the electrical part of this code for wet locations.

R322.1.7 Protection of water supply and sanitary sewage systems. New and replacement water supply systems shall be designed to minimize or eliminate infiltration of flood waters into the systems in accordance with the plumbing provisions of this code. New and replacement sanitary sewage systems shall be designed to minimize or eliminate infiltration of floodwaters into systems and discharges from systems into floodwaters in accordance with the plumbing provisions of this code and Chapter 3 of the *International Private Sewage Disposal Code.*

R322.1.8 Flood-resistant materials. Building materials used below the elevation required in Section R322.2 (flood hazard areas including A Zones) or R322.3 (coastal high-hazard areas including V Zones) shall comply with the following:

1. All wood, including floor sheathing, shall be pressure-preservative-treated in accordance with AWPA U1 for the species, product, preservative and end use or be the decay-resistant heartwood of redwood, black locust or cedars. Preservatives shall be listed in Section 4 of AWPA U1.
2. Materials and installation methods used for flooring and interior and *exterior walls* and wall coverings shall conform to the provisions of FEMA/FIA-TB-2.

R322.1.9 Manufactured homes. New or replacement *manufactured homes* shall be elevated in accordance with Section R322.2 or Section R322.3 in coastal high-hazard areas (V Zones). The anchor and tie-down requirements of Sections AE604 and AE605 of Appendix E shall apply. The foundation and anchorage of *manufactured homes* to be located in identified floodways shall be designed and constructed in accordance with ASCE 24.

R322.1.10 As-built elevation documentation. A registered *design professional* shall prepare and seal documentation of the elevations specified in Section R322.2 or R322.3.

R322.2 Flood hazard areas (including A Zones). All areas that have been determined to be prone to flooding but not subject to high velocity wave action shall be designated as flood hazard areas. Flood hazard areas that have been delineated as subject to wave heights between $1^1/_2$ feet (457 mm) and 3 feet (914 mm) shall be designated as Coastal A Zones. All building and structures constructed in whole or in part in flood hazard areas shall be designed and constructed in accordance with Sections R322.2.1 through R322.2.3.

R322.2.1 Elevation requirements.

1. Buildings and structures shall have the lowest floors elevated to or above the base flood elevation plus one foot (305 mm), or the design flood elevation, whichever is higher.
2. In areas of shallow flooding (AO Zones), buildings and structures shall have the lowest floor (including basement) elevated at least as high above the highest adjacent grade as the depth number specified in feet (mm) on the FIRM plus one foot (305 mm), or at least 3 feet (915 mm) if a depth number is not specified.
3. Basement floors that are below grade on all sides shall be elevated to or above the base flood elevation plus one foot (305 mm), or the design flood elevation, whichever is higher.

   Exception: Enclosed areas below the design flood elevation, including basements whose floors are not below grade on all sides, shall meet the requirements of Section R322.2.2.

R322.2.2 Enclosed area below design flood elevation. Enclosed areas, including crawl spaces, that are below the design flood elevation shall:

1. Be used solely for parking of vehicles, building access or storage.
2. Be provided with flood openings that meet the following criteria:
   - 2.1. There shall be a minimum of two openings on different sides of each enclosed area; if a building has more than one enclosed area below the design flood elevation, each area shall have openings on exterior walls.
   - 2.2. The total net area of all openings shall be at least 1 square inch (645 mm^2) for each square foot (0.093 m^2) of enclosed area, or the openings shall be designed and the *construction documents* shall include a statement by a registered *design professional* that the design of the openings will provide for equalization of hydrostatic flood forces on exterior walls by allowing for the automatic entry and exit of floodwaters as specified in Section 2.6.2.2 of ASCE 24.
   - 2.3. The bottom of each opening shall be 1 foot (305 mm) or less above the adjacent ground level.
   - 2.4. Openings shall be not less than 3 inches (76 mm) in any direction in the plane of the wall.
   - 2.5. Any louvers, screens or other opening covers shall allow the automatic flow of floodwaters into and out of the enclosed area.
   - 2.6. Openings installed in doors and windows, that meet requirements 2.1 through 2.5, are acceptable; however, doors and windows without installed openings do not meet the requirements of this section.

R322.2.3 Foundation design and construction. Foundation walls for all buildings and structures erected in flood hazard areas shall meet the requirements of Chapter 4.

Exception: Unless designed in accordance with Section R404:

1. The unsupported height of 6-inch (152 mm) plain masonry walls shall be no more than 3 feet (914 mm).
2. The unsupported height of 8-inch (203 mm) plain masonry walls shall be no more than 4 feet (1219 mm).
3. The unsupported height of 8-inch (203 mm) reinforced masonry walls shall be no more than 8 feet (2438 mm).

For the purpose of this exception, unsupported height is the distance from the finished *grade* of the under-floor space and the top of the wall.

R322.3 Coastal high-hazard areas (including V Zones). Areas that have been determined to be subject to wave heights in excess of 3 feet (914 mm) or subject to high-velocity wave action or wave-induced erosion shall be designated as coastal high-hazard areas. Buildings and structures constructed in whole or in part in coastal high-hazard areas shall be designed and constructed in accordance with Sections R322.3.1 through R322.3.6.

R322.3.1 Location and site preparation. Deleted.

R322.3.2 Elevation requirements.

1. All buildings and structures erected within coastal high hazard areas shall be elevated so that the lowest portion of all structural members supporting the lowest floor, with the exception of mat or raft foundations, piling, pile caps, columns, grade beams and bracing, is:
   1.1. Located at or above the design flood elevation, if the lowest horizontal structural member is oriented parallel to the direction of wave approach, where parallel shall mean less than or equal to 20 degrees (0.35 rad) from the direction of approach, or
   1.2. Located at the base flood elevation plus 1 foot (305 mm), or the design flood elevation, whichever is higher, if the lowest horizontal structural member is oriented perpendicular to the direction of wave approach, where perpendicular shall mean greater than 20 degrees (0.35 rad) from the direction of approach.
2. Basement floors that are below *grade*on all sides are prohibited.
3. The use of fill for structural support is prohibited.
4. Minor grading, and the placement of minor quantities of fill, shall be permitted for landscaping and for drainage purposes under and around buildings and for support of parking slabs, pool decks, patios and walkways.

Exception: Walls and partitions enclosing areas below the design flood elevation shall meet the requirements of Sections R322.3.4 and R322.3.5.

R322.3.3 Foundations. Buildings and structures erected in coastal high-hazard areas shall be supported on pilings or columns and shall be adequately anchored to those pilings or columns. Pilings shall have adequate soil penetrations to resist the combined wave and wind loads (lateral and uplift). Water loading values used shall be those associated with the design flood. Wind loading values shall be those required by this code. Pile embedment shall include consideration of decreased resistance capacity caused by scour of soil strata surrounding the piling. Pile systems design and installation shall be certified in accordance with Section R322.3.6. Mat, raft or other foundations that support columns shall not be permitted where soil investigations that are required in accordance with Section R401.4 indicate that soil material under the mat, raft or other foundation is subject to scour or erosion from wave-velocity flow conditions. Slabs, pools, pool decks and walkways shall be located and constructed to be structurally independent of buildings and structures and their foundations to prevent transfer of flood loads to the buildings and structures during conditions of flooding, scour or erosion from wave-velocity flow conditions, unless the buildings and structures and their foundation are designed to resist the additional flood load.

R322.3.4 Walls below design flood elevation. Walls and partitions are permitted below the elevated floor, provided that such walls and partitions are not part of the structural support of the building or structure and:

1. Electrical, mechanical, and plumbing system components are not to be mounted on or penetrate through walls that are designed to break away under flood loads; and
2. Are constructed with insect screening or open lattice; or
3. Are designed to break away or collapse without causing collapse, displacement or other structural damage to the elevated portion of the building or supporting foundation system. Such walls, framing and connections shall have a design safe loading resistance of not less than 10 (479 Pa) and no more than 20 pounds per square foot (958 Pa); or
4. Where wind loading values of this code exceed 20 pounds per square foot (958 Pa), the *construction documents* shall include documentation prepared and sealed by a registered *design professional* that:
   4.1. The walls and partitions below the design flood elevation have been designed to col-

lapse from a water load less than that which would occur during the design flood.

4.2. The elevated portion of the building and supporting foundation system have been designed to withstand the effects of wind and flood loads acting simultaneously on all building components (structural and nonstructural). Water loading values used shall be those associated with the design flood. Wind loading values shall be those required by this code.

R322.3.5 Enclosed areas below design flood elevation. Enclosed areas below the design flood elevation shall be used solely for parking of vehicles, building access or storage.

R322.3.6 Construction documents. The *construction documents* shall include documentation that is prepared and sealed by a registered *design professional* that the design and methods of construction to be used meet the applicable criteria of this section.

SECTION R323
STORM SHELTERS

R323.1 General. This section applies to the construction of storm shelters when constructed as separate detached buildings or when constructed as safe rooms within buildings for the purpose of providing safe refuge from storms that produce high winds, such as tornados and hurricanes. In addition to other applicable requirements in this code, storm shelters shall be constructed in accordance with ICC/NSSA-500.

CHAPTER 4
FOUNDATIONS

SECTION R401
GENERAL

R401.1 Application. The provisions of this chapter shall control the design and construction of the foundation and foundation spaces for all buildings. In addition to the provisions of this chapter, the design and construction of foundations in areas prone to flooding as established by Table R301.2(1) shall meet the provisions of Section R322. Wood foundations shall be designed and installed in accordance with AF&PA PWF.

Exception: The provisions of this chapter shall be permitted to be used for wood foundations only in the following situations:

1. In buildings that have no more than two floors and a roof.
2. When interior *basement* and foundation walls are constructed at intervals not exceeding 50 feet (15 240 mm).

Wood foundations in Seismic Design Category D_0, D_1 or D_2 shall be designed in accordance with accepted engineering practice.

R401.2 Requirements. Foundation construction shall be capable of accommodating all loads according to Section R301 and of transmitting the resulting loads to the supporting soil. Fill soils that support footings and foundations shall be designed, installed and tested in accordance with accepted engineering practice. Gravel fill used as footings for wood and precast concrete foundations shall comply with Section R403.

R401.3 Drainage. Surface drainage shall be diverted to a storm sewer conveyance or other *approved* point of collection that does not create a hazard. *Lots* shall be graded to drain surface water away from foundation walls. The *grade* shall fall a minimum of 6 inches (152 mm) within the first 10 feet (3048 mm).

Exception: Where *lot lines*, walls, slopes or other physical barriers prohibit 6 inches (152 mm) of fall within 10 feet (3048 mm), drains or swales shall be constructed to ensure drainage away from the structure. Impervious surfaces within 10 feet (3048 mm) of the building foundation shall be sloped a minimum of 2 percent away from the building.

R401.4 Soil tests. Where quantifiable data created by accepted soil science methodologies indicate expansive, compressible, shifting or other questionable soil characteristics are likely to be present, the *building official* shall determine whether to require a soil test to determine the soil's characteristics at a particular location. This test shall be done by an *approved agency* using an *approved* method.

R401.4.1 Geotechnical evaluation. The load bearing values greater than 2000 psf in Table R401.4.1 require an engineering evaluation.

TABLE R401.4.1
PRESUMPTIVE LOAD-BEARING VALUES OF FOUNDATION MATERIALS[a]

CLASS OF MATERIAL	LOAD-BEARING PRESSURE (pounds per square foot)
Crystalline bedrock	12,000
Sedimentary and foliated rock	6,000
Sandy gravel and/or gravel (GW and GP)	5,000
Sand, silty sand, clayey sand, silty gravel and clayey gravel (SW, SP, SM, SC, GM and GC)	3,000
Clay, sandy clay, silty clay, clayey silt, silt and sandy silt (CL, ML, MH and CH)	2,000[b]

For SI: 1 pound per square foot = 0.0479 kPa.

a. When soil tests are required by Section R401.4, the allowable bearing capacities of the soil shall be part of the recommendations.

b. Where the building official determines that in-place soils with an allowable bearing capacity of less than 2,000 psf are likely to be present at the site, the allowable bearing capacity shall be determined by a soils investigation.

R401.4.2 Compressible or shifting soil. Instead of a complete geotechnical evaluation, when top or subsoils are compressible or shifting, they shall be removed to a depth and width sufficient to assure stable moisture content in each active zone and shall not be used as fill or stabilized within each active zone by chemical, dewatering or presaturation.

SECTION R402
MATERIALS

R402.1 Wood foundations. Wood foundation systems shall be designed and installed in accordance with the provisions of this code.

R402.1.1 Fasteners. Fasteners used below *grade* to attach plywood to the exterior side of exterior *basement* or crawlspace wall studs, or fasteners used in knee wall construction, shall be of Type 304 or 316 stainless steel. Fasteners used above *grade* to attach plywood and all lumber-to-lumber fasteners except those used in knee wall construction shall be of Type 304 or 316 stainless steel, silicon bronze, copper, hot-dipped galvanized (zinc coated) steel nails, or hot-tumbled galvanized (zinc coated) steel nails. Electrogalvanized steel nails and galvanized (zinc coated) steel staples shall not be permitted.

R402.1.2 Wood treatment. All lumber and plywood shall be pressure-preservative treated and dried after treatment in accordance with AWPA U1 (Commodity Specification A, Use Category 4B and Section 5.2), and shall bear the *label* of an accredited agency. Where lumber and/or plywood is cut or drilled after treatment, the treated surface shall be field treated with copper naphthenate, the concentration of which shall contain a minimum of 2 percent copper metal, by repeated brushing, dipping or soaking until the wood absorbs no more preservative.

R402.2 Concrete. Concrete shall have a minimum specified compressive strength of f'_c, as shown in Table R402.2. Concrete subject to moderate or severe weathering as indicated in Table R301.2(1) shall be air entrained as specified in Table R402.2. The maximum weight of fly ash, other pozzolans, silica fume, slag or blended cements that is included in concrete mixtures for garage floor slabs and for exterior porches, carport slabs and steps that will be exposed to deicing chemicals shall not exceed the percentages of the total weight of cementitious materials specified in Section 4.2.3 of ACI 318. Materials used to produce concrete and testing thereof shall comply with the applicable standards listed in Chapter 3 of ACI 318 or ACI 332.

R402.3 Precast concrete. Precast concrete foundations shall be designed in accordance with Section R404.5 and shall be installed in accordance with the provisions of this code and the manufacturer's installation instructions.

R402.3.1 Precast concrete foundation materials. Materials used to produce precast concrete foundations shall meet the following requirements.

1. All concrete used in the manufacture of precast concrete foundations shall have a minimum compressive strength of 5,000 psi (34 470 kPa) at 28 days. Concrete exposed to a freezing and thawing environment shall be air entrained with a minimum total air content of 5 percent.
2. Structural reinforcing steel shall meet the requirements of ASTM A 615, A 706 or A 996. The minimum yield strength of reinforcing steel shall be 40,000 psi (Grade 40) (276 MPa). Steel reinforcement for precast concrete foundation walls shall have a minimum concrete cover of $^3/_4$ inch (19.1 mm).
3. Panel-to-panel connections shall be made with Grade II steel fasteners.
4. The use of nonstructural fibers shall conform to ASTM C 1116.
5. Grout used for bedding precast foundations placed upon concrete footings shall meet ASTM C 1107.

SECTION R403 FOOTINGS

R403.1 General. All exterior walls shall be supported on continuous solid or fully grouted masonry or concrete footings, crushed stone footings, wood foundations, or other *approved* structural systems which shall be of sufficient design to accommodate all loads according to Section R301 and to transmit the resulting loads to the soil within the limitations as determined from the character of the soil. Footings shall be supported on undisturbed natural soils or engineered fill. Concrete footing shall be designed and constructed in accordance with the provisions of Section R403 or in accordance with ACI 332. Discontinuous footings shall be permitted to be constructed in accordance with ACI 332-04 for concrete foundation walls and Appendix Q for masonry foundation walls.

R403.1.1 Minimum size. Minimum sizes for concrete and masonry footings shall be as set forth in Table R403.1 and Figure R403.1(1). The footing width, W, shall be based on the load-bearing value of the soil in accordance with Table R401.4.1. Spread footings shall be at least 6 inches (152 mm) in thickness, T. Footing projections, P, shall be at least 2 inches (51 mm) and shall not exceed the thickness of the footing. The size of footings supporting piers and columns shall be based on the tributary load and allowable soil pressure in accordance with Table R401.4.1. Footings for wood foundations shall be in accordance with the details set forth in Section R403.2, and Figures R403.1(2) and R403.1(3).

TABLE R402.2
MINIMUM SPECIFIED COMPRESSIVE STRENGTH OF CONCRETE

TYPE OR LOCATION OF CONCRETE CONSTRUCTION	MINIMUM SPECIFIED COMPRESSIVE STRENGTH[a] (f'_c) Weathering Potential[b]		
	Negligible	Moderate	Severe
Basement walls, foundations and other concrete not exposed to the weather	2,500	2,500	2,500[c]
Basement slabs and interior slabs on grade, except garage floor slabs	2,500	2,500	2,500[c]
Basement walls, foundation walls, exterior walls and other vertical concrete work exposed to the weather	2,500	3,000[d]	3,000[d]
Porches, carport slabs and steps exposed to the weather, and garage floor slabs	2,500	3,000[d, e, f]	3,500[d, e, f]

For SI: 1 pound per square inch = 6.895 kPa.
a. Strength at 28 days psi.
b. See Table R301.2(1) for weathering potential.
c. Concrete in these locations that may be subject to freezing and thawing during construction shall be air-entrained concrete in accordance with Footnote d.
d. Concrete shall be air-entrained. Total air content (percent by volume of concrete) shall be not less than 5 percent or more than 7 percent.
e. See Section R402.2 for maximum cementitious materials content.
f. For garage floors with a steel troweled finish, reduction of the total air content (percent by volume of concrete) to not less than 3 percent is permitted if the specified compressive strength of the concrete is increased to not less than 4,000 psi.

TABLE R403.1
MINIMUM WIDTH OF CONCRETE, PRECAST OR MASONRY FOOTINGS (inches)[a]

	LOAD-BEARING VALUE OF SOIL (psf)			
	1,500	2,000	3,000	≥ 4,000
Conventional light-frame construction				
1-story	12	12	12	12
2-story	15[b]	15[b]	12	12
3-story	23	17	12	12
4-inch brick veneer over light frame or 8-inch hollow concrete masonry				
1-story	12	12	12	12
2-story	15[b]	15[b]	12	12
3-story	32	24	16	12
8-inch solid or fully grouted masonry				
1-story	16	16[b]	12	12
2-story	29	21	14	12
3-story	42	32	21	16

For SI: 1 inch = 25.4 mm, 1 pound per square foot = 0.0479 kPa.

a. Where minimum footing width is 12 inches, use of a single wythe of solid or fully grouted 12-inch nominal concrete masonry units is permitted.

b. A minimum footing width of 12 inches is acceptable for monolithic slab foundations.

R403.1.2 Continuous footing in Seismic Design Categories D_0, D_1 and D_2. Deleted.

R403.1.3 Seismic reinforcing. Deleted.

R403.1.3.1 Foundations with stemwalls. Deleted.

R403.1.3.2 Slabs-on-ground with turned-down footings. Deleted.

R403.1.4 Minimum depth. All exterior footings and foundation systems shall extend below the frost line specified in Table R301.2(1). In no case shall the bottom of the exterior footings be less than 12 inches below the undisturbed ground surface or engineered fill.

Exception: Frost protected footings constructed in accordance with Section R403.3 and footings and foundations erected on solid rock shall not be required to extend below the frost line.

R403.1.4.1 Frost protection. Deleted.

R403.1.4.2 Seismic conditions. Deleted.

R403.1.5 Slope. The top surface of footings shall be level ($^1/_2$ inch in 10 feet) or shall be brought level, under the width of the wall, with masonry units with full mortar joints. The bottom surface of footings may have a slope not exceeding one unit vertical in 10 units horizontal (10-percent slope). Footings shall be stepped where it is necessary to change the elevation of the top surface of the footings or where the slope of the bottom surface of the footings will exceed one unit vertical in ten units horizontal (10-percent slope).

TABLE R403.1a
PIER[1] AND FOOTING[2] SIZES FOR SUPPORT OF GIRDERS

	1 (One) STORY		2 (Two) STORY		2-$^1/_2$ (Two & One Half) STORY	
Area[5]	Pier[3,4]	Footing	Pier[3,4]	Footing	Pier[3,4]	Footing
50	8″ × 16″	1′–4″ × 2′–0″ × 8″	8″ × 16″	1′–4″ × 2′–6″ × 8″	8″ × 16″	1′–4″ × 2′–6″ × 8″
100	8″ × 16″	1′–4″ × 2′–0″ × 8″	8″ × 16″	2′–0″ × 2′–0″ × 10″	16″ × 16″	2′–6″ × 2′–6″ × 10″
150	8″ × 16″	2′–0″ × 2′–0″ × 8″	16″ × 16″	2′–8″ × 2′–8″ × 10″	16″ × 16″	3′–0″ × 3′–0″ × 10″
200	8″ × 16″	2′–4″ × 2′–4″ × 10″	16″ × 16″	3′–0″ × 3′–0″ × 10″	16″ × 16″	3′–11″ × 3′–8″ × 1′–0″
250	—	—	16″ × 16″	3′–4″ × 3′–4″ × 1′–0″	16″ × 24″	4′–0″ × 4′–0″ × 1′–0″
300	—	—	16″ × 16″	3′–8″ × 3′–8″ × 1″ –0″	16″ × 24″	4′–6″ × 4′–6″ × 1′–0″

For SI: 1 inch = 25.4 mm, 1 foot = 304.8 mm, 1 pound per square inch = 6.895 kPa, 1 pound per square foot = 0.0479 kPa.

1. Pier sizes are based on hollow CMU capped with 4 inches of solid masonry or concrete for 1 (one) story and 8 inches of solid masonry or concrete for 2 (two) and 2$^1/_2$ (two and one half) story houses or shall have cavities of the top course filled with concrete or grout or other approved methods. Mortar shall be Type S.
2. Footing sizes are based on 2000 psf allowable soil bearing and 2500 psi concrete. This table is based upon the limitations of a tributary area using dimensional framing lumber only.
3. Centers of piers shall bear in the middle one-third of the footings. Girders must have full bearing on piers. Footings shall be full thickness over the entire area of the footing.
4. Pier sizes given are minimum. For height/thickness limitations see Section R606.6.
5. Area at first level supported by pier and footing (square foot).

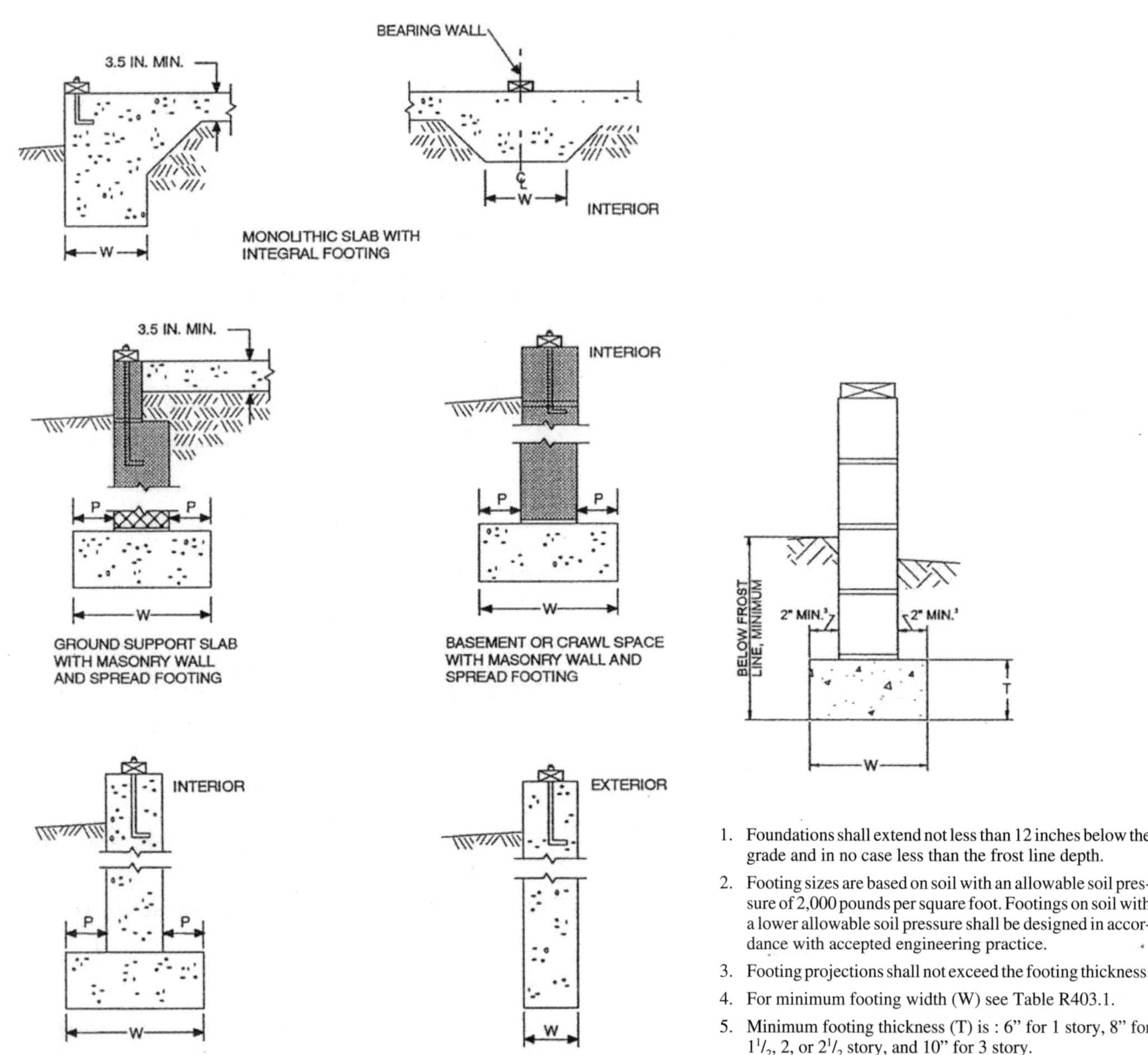

1. Foundations shall extend not less than 12 inches below the grade and in no case less than the frost line depth.
2. Footing sizes are based on soil with an allowable soil pressure of 2,000 pounds per square foot. Footings on soil with a lower allowable soil pressure shall be designed in accordance with accepted engineering practice.
3. Footing projections shall not exceed the footing thickness.
4. For minimum footing width (W) see Table R403.1.
5. Minimum footing thickness (T) is : 6" for 1 story, 8" for $1^1/_2$, 2, or $2^1/_2$ story, and 10" for 3 story.
6. Install anchor bolts per Section R403.1.6.

For SI: 1 inch = 25.4 mm.

FIGURE R403.1(1)
CONCRETE AND MASONRY FOUNDATION DETAILS

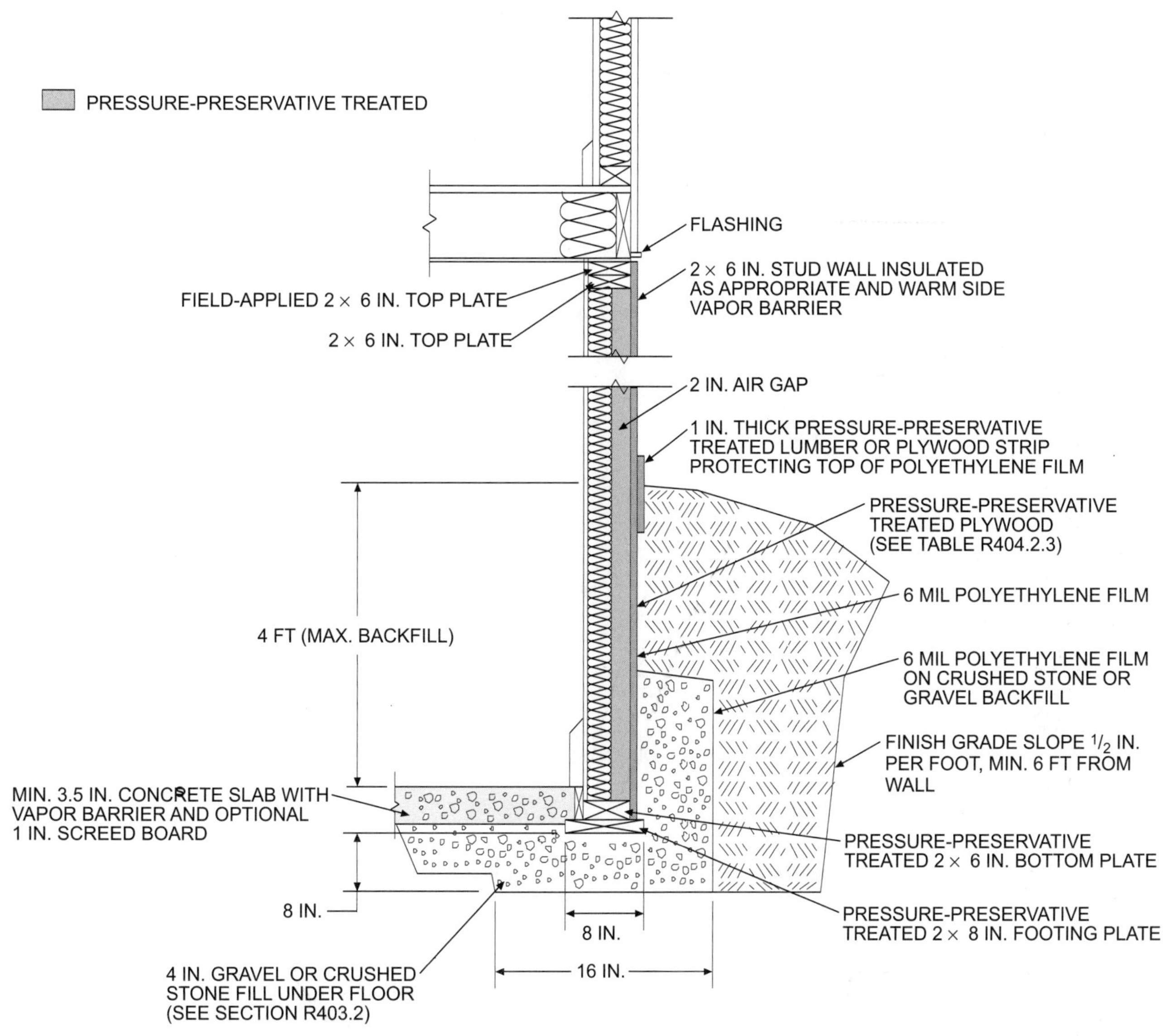

For SI: 1 inch = 25.4 mm, 1 foot = 304.8 mm, 1 mil = 0.0254 mm.

FIGURE R403.1(2)
PERMANENT WOOD FOUNDATION BASEMENT WALL SECTION

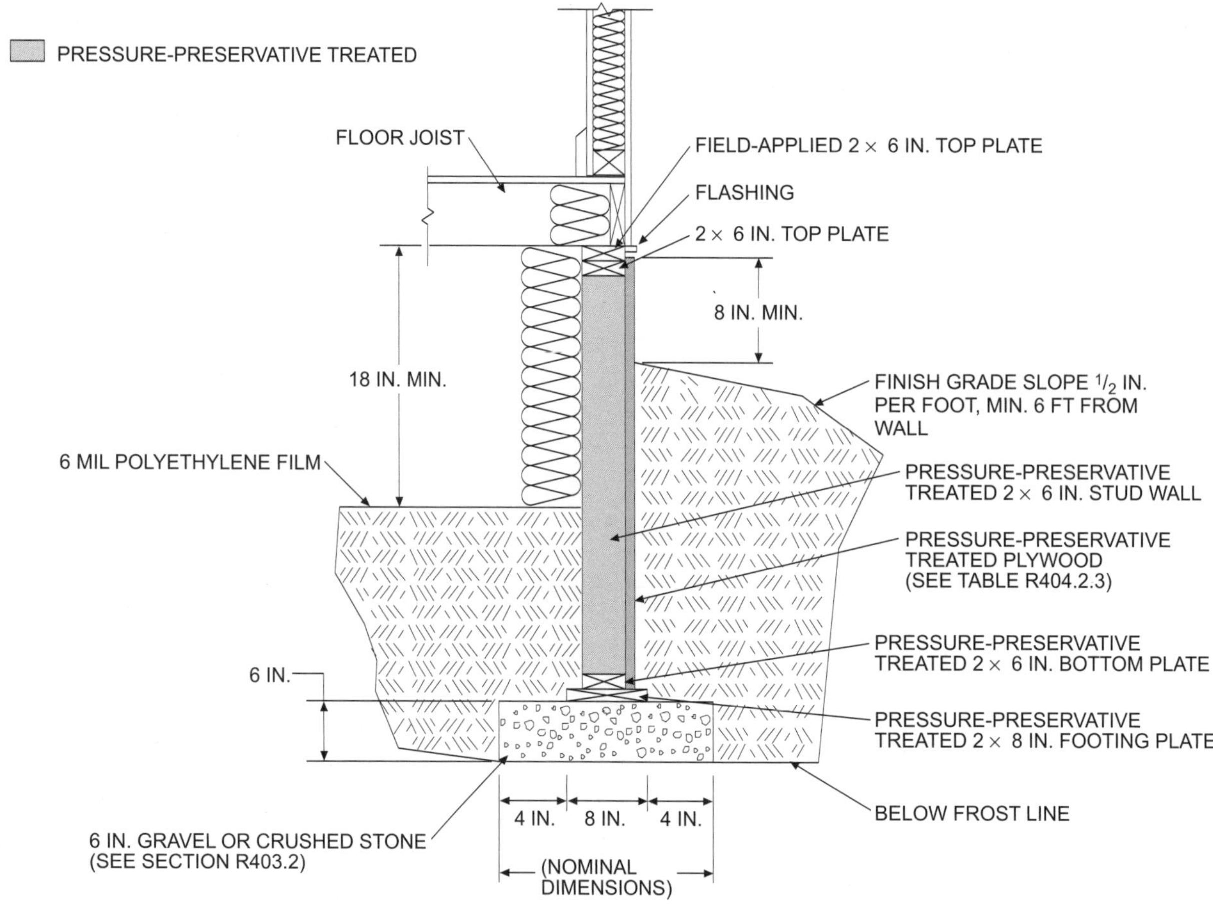

For SI: 1 inch = 25.4 mm, 1 foot = 304.8 mm, 1 mil = 0.0254 mm.

FIGURE R403.1(3)
PERMANENT WOOD FOUNDATION CRAWL SPACE SECTION

R403.1.6 Foundation anchorage. When braced wall panels are supported directly on continuous foundations, the wall wood sill plate or cold-formed steel bottom track shall be anchored to the foundation in accordance with this section.

The wood sole plate at exterior walls on monolithic slabs and wood sill plate shall be anchored to the foundation with anchor bolts spaced a maximum of 6 feet (1829 mm) on center and not more than 12 inches from the corner. There shall be a minimum of two bolts per plate section. In Seismic Design Categories D_1 and D_2, anchor bolts shall also be spaced at 6 feet (1829 mm) on center and located within 12 inches (305 mm) from the ends of each plate section at interior braced wall lines when required by Section R602.10.9 to be supported on a continuous foundation. Bolts shall be at least $^1/_2$ inch (12.7 mm) in diameter and shall extend a minimum of 7 inches (178 mm) into masonry or concrete. Interior bearing wall sole plates on monolithic slab foundations shall be positively anchored with approved fasteners. A nut and washer shall be tightened on each bolt to the plate. Sills and sole plates shall be protected against decay and termites where required by Sections R317 and R318. Cold-formed steel framing systems shall be fastened to the wood sill plates or anchored directly to the foundation as required in Section R505.3.1 or R603.3.1.

Exceptions:

1. Foundation anchorage, spaced as required to provide equivalent anchorage to $^1/_2$-inch-diameter (12.7 mm) anchor bolts.
2. Walls 24 inches (610 mm) total length or shorter connecting offset *braced wall panels* shall be anchored to the foundation with a minimum of one anchor bolt located in the center third of the plate section and shall be attached to adjacent *braced wall panels* at corners as shown in Figure R602.10.4.4(1).
3. Connection of walls 12 inches (305 mm) total length or shorter connecting offset *braced wall panels* to the foundation without anchor bolts shall be permitted. The wall shall be attached to adjacent *braced wall panels* at corners as shown in Figure R602.10.4.4(1).

R403.1.6.1 Foundation anchorage in Seismic Design Categories C, D_0, D_1 and D_2. In addition to the requirements of Section R403.1.6, the following requirements shall apply to wood light-frame structures in Seismic Design Categories D_0, D_1 and D_2 and wood light-frame townhouses in Seismic Design Category C.

1. Plate washers conforming to Section R602.11.1 shall be used on each bolt.
2. Interior braced wall plates shall have anchor bolts spaced at not more than 6 feet (1829 mm) on center and not more than 12 inches (305 mm) from the corner.
3. Interior bearing wall sole plates shall have anchor bolts spaced at not more than 6 feet (1829 mm) on center and not more than 12 inches (305 mm) from the corner.
4. The maximum anchor bolt spacing shall be 4 feet (1219 mm)for buildings over two stories in height.
5. Stepped cripple walls shall conform to Section R602.11.2.
6. Where continuous wood foundations in accordance with Section R404.2 are used, the force transfer shall have a capacity equal to or greater than the connections required by Section R602.11.1 or the *braced wall panel* shall be connected to the wood foundations in accordance with the *braced wall panel*-to-floor fastening requirements of Table R602.3(1).

R403.1.7 Footings on or adjacent to slopes. Deleted.

R403.1.7.1 Building clearances from ascending slopes. Deleted.

R403.1.7.2 Footing setback from descending slope surfaces. Deleted.

R403.1.7.3 Foundation elevation. Deleted.

R403.1.7.4 Alternate setback and clearances. Deleted.

R403.1.8 Foundations on expansive soils. Deleted.

R403.1.8.1 Expansive soils classifications. Deleted.

R403.2 Footings for wood foundations. Footings for wood foundations shall be in accordance with Figures R403.1(2) and R403.1(3). Gravel shall be washed and well graded. The maximum size stone shall not exceed $^3/_4$ inch (19.1 mm). Gravel shall be free from organic, clayey or silty soils. Sand shall be coarse, not smaller than $^1/_{16}$-inch (1.6 mm) grains and shall be free from organic, clayey or silty soils. Crushed stone shall have a maximum size of $^1/_2$ inch (12.7 mm).

R403.3 Frost protected shallow foundations. Deleted.

R403.3.1 Foundations adjoining frost protected shallow foundations. Deleted.

R403.3.1.1 Attachment to unheated slab-on-ground structure. Deleted.

R403.3.1.2 Attachment to heated structure. Where a frost protected shallow foundation abuts a structure that has a monthly mean temperature maintained at a minimum of 64°F (18°C), horizontal insulation and vertical wall insulation shall not be required between the frost protected shallow foundation and the adjoining structure. Where the frost protected shallow foundation abuts the heated structure, the horizontal insulation and vertical wall insulation shall extend along the adjoining foundation in accordance with Figure R403.3(4) a distance of not less than Dimension A in Table R403.3(1).

Exception: Where the frost protected shallow foundation abuts the heated structure to form an inside corner, vertical insulation extending along the adjoining foundation is not required.

R403.3.2 Protection of horizontal insulation below ground. Horizontal insulation placed less than 12 inches (305 mm) below the ground surface or that portion of horizontal insulation extending outward more than 24 inches (610 mm) from the foundation edge shall be protected against damage by use of a concrete slab or asphalt paving on the ground surface directly above the insulation or by cementitious board, plywood rated for below-ground use, or other *approved* materials placed below ground, directly above the top surface of the insulation.

R403.3.3 Drainage. Final *grade* shall be sloped in accordance with Section R401.3. In other than Group I Soils, as detailed in Table R405.1, gravel or crushed stone beneath horizontal insulation below ground shall drain to daylight or into an *approved* sewer system.

R403.3.4 Termite damage. Deleted.

R403.4 Footings for precast concrete foundations. Footings for precast concrete foundations shall comply with Section R403.4.

R403.4.1 Crushed stone footings. Clean crushed stone shall be free from organic, clayey or silty soils. Crushed stone shall be angular in nature and meet ASTM C 33, with the maximum size stone not to exceed $^1/_2$ inch (12.7 mm) and the minimum stone size not to be smaller than $^1/_{16}$-inch (1.6 mm). Crushed stone footings for precast foundations shall be installed in accordance with Figure R403.4(1) and Table R403.4. Crushed stone footings shall be consolidated using a vibratory plate in a maximum of 8-inch lifts. Crushed stone footings shall be limited to Seismic Design Categories A, B and C.

R403.4.2 Concrete footings. Concrete footings shall be installed in accordance with Section R403.1 and Figure R403.4(2).

TABLE R403.4
MINIMUM DEPTH OF CRUSHED STONE FOOTINGS (*D*), (inches)

		LOAD BEARING VALUE OF SOIL (psf)															
		1500				2000				3000				4000			
		MH, CH, CL, ML				SC, GC, SM, GM, SP, SW				GP, GW							
		Wall width (inches)				Wall width (inches)				Wall width (inches)				Wall width (inches)			
		6	8	10	12	6	8	10	12	6	8	10	12	6	8	10	12
Conventional light-frame construction																	
1-story	1100 plf	6	4	4	4	6	4	4	4	6	4	4	4	6	4	4	4
2-story	1800 plf	8	6	4	4	6	4	4	4	6	4	4	4	6	4	4	4
3-story	2900 plf	16	14	12	10	10	8	6	6	6	4	4	4	6	4	4	4
4-inch brick veneer over light-frame or 8-inch hollow concrete masonry																	
1-story	1500 plf	6	4	4	4	6	4	4	4	6	4	4	4	6	4	4	4
2-story	2700 plf	14	12	10	8	10	8	6	4	6	4	4	4	6	4	4	4
3-story	4000 plf	22	22	20	18	16	14	12	10	10	8	6	4	6	4	4	4
8-inch solid or fully grouted masonry																	
1-story	2000 plf	10	8	6	4	6	4	4	4	6	4	4	4	6	4	4	4
2-story	3600 plf	20	18	16	16	14	12	10	8	8	6	4	4	6	4	4	4
3-story	5300 plf	32	30	28	26	22	22	20	18	14	12	10	8	10	8	6	4

For SI: 1 inch = 25.4 mm, 1 pound per square inch = 6.89 kPa.

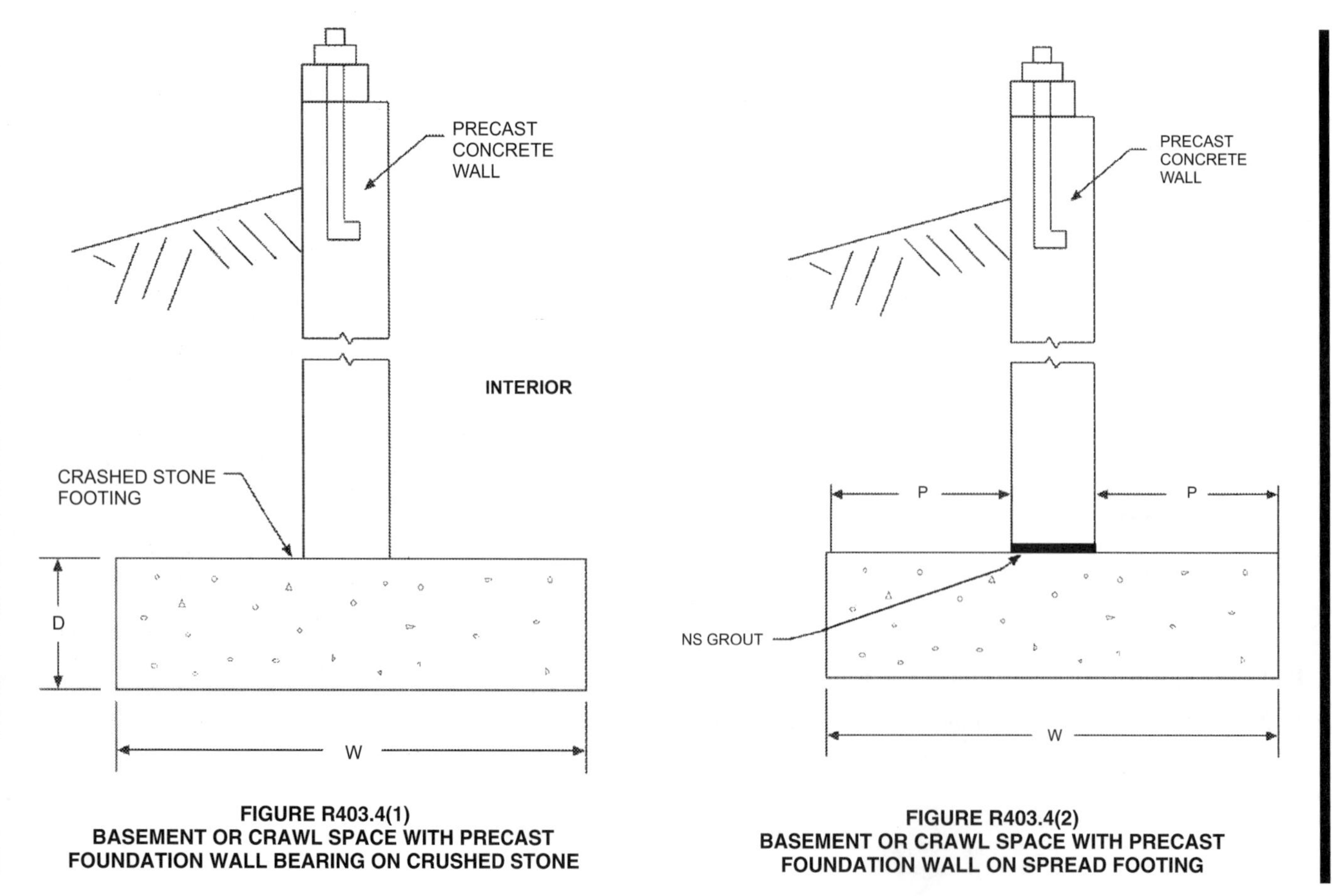

FIGURE R403.4(1)
BASEMENT OR CRAWL SPACE WITH PRECAST FOUNDATION WALL BEARING ON CRUSHED STONE

FIGURE R403.4(2)
BASEMENT OR CRAWL SPACE WITH PRECAST FOUNDATION WALL ON SPREAD FOOTING

SECTION R404
FOUNDATION AND RETAINING WALLS

R404.1 Concrete and masonry foundation walls. Concrete foundation walls shall be selected and constructed in accordance with the provisions of Section R404.1.2. Masonry foundation walls shall be selected and constructed in accordance with the provisions of Section R404.1.1.

R404.1.1 Design of masonry foundation walls. Masonry foundation walls shall be designed and constructed in accordance with the provisions of this section or in accordance with the provisions of TMS 402/ACI 530/ASCE 5 or NCMA TR68-A. When TMS 402/ACI 530/ASCE 5, NCMA TR68-A or the provisions of this section are used to design masonry foundation walls, project drawings, typical details and specifications are not required to bear the seal of the architect or engineer responsible for design, unless otherwise required by the state law of the *jurisdiction* having authority.

R404.1.1.1 Masonry foundation walls. Concrete masonry and clay masonry foundation walls shall be constructed as set forth in Table R404.1.1(1), R404.1.1(2), R404.1.1(3) or R404.1.1(4) and shall also comply with applicable provisions of Sections R606, R607 and R608. In buildings assigned to Seismic Design Categories D_0, D_1 and D_2, concrete masonry and clay masonry foundation walls shall also comply with Section R404.1.4.1. Rubble stone masonry foundation walls shall be constructed in accordance with Sections R404.1.8 and R607.2.2. Rubble stone masonry walls shall not be used in Seismic Design Categories D_0, D_1 and D_2.

R404.1.2 Concrete foundation walls. Concrete foundation walls that support light-frame walls shall be designed and constructed in accordance with the provisions of this section, ACI 318, ACI 332 or PCA 100. Concrete foundation walls that support above-grade concrete walls that are within the applicability limits of Section R611.2 shall be designed and constructed in accordance with the provisions of this section, ACI 318, ACI 332 or PCA 100. Concrete foundation walls that support above-grade concrete walls that are not within the applicability limits of Section R611.2 shall be designed and constructed in accordance with the provisions of ACI 318, ACI 332 or PCA 100. When ACI 318, ACI 332, PCA 100 or the provisions of this section are used to design concrete foundation walls, project drawings, typical details and specifications are not required to bear the seal of the architect or engineer responsible for design, unless otherwise required by the state law of the *jurisdiction* having authority.

R404.1.2.1 Concrete cross-section. Concrete walls constructed in accordance with this code shall comply with the shapes and minimum concrete cross-sectional dimensions required by Table R611.3. Other types of forming systems resulting in concrete walls not in compliance with this section and Table R611.3 shall be designed in accordance with ACI 318.

R404.1.2.2 Reinforcement for foundation walls. Concrete foundation walls shall be laterally supported at the top and bottom. Horizontal reinforcement shall be provided in accordance with Table R404.1.2(1). Vertical reinforcement shall be provided in accordance with Table R404.1.2(2), R404.1.2(3), R404.1.2(4), R404.1.2(5), R404.1.2(6), R404.1.2(7) or R404.1.2(8). Vertical reinforcement for flat *basement* walls retaining 4 feet (1219 mm) or more of unbalanced backfill is permitted to be determined in accordance with Table R404.1.2(9). For *basement* walls supporting above-grade concrete walls, vertical reinforcement shall be the greater of that required by Tables R404.1.2(2) through R404.1.2(8) or by Section R611.6 for the above-grade wall. In buildings assigned to Seismic Design Category D_0, D_1 or D_2, concrete foundation walls shall also comply with Section R404.1.4.2.

R404.1.2.2.1 Concrete foundation stem walls supporting above-grade concrete walls. Foundation stem walls that support above-grade concrete walls shall be designed and constructed in accordance with this section.

1. Stem walls not laterally supported at top. Concrete stem walls that are not monolithic with slabs-on-ground or are not otherwise laterally supported by slabs-on-ground shall comply with this section. Where unbalanced backfill retained by the stem wall is less than or equal to 18 inches (457 mm), the stem wall and above-grade wall it supports shall be provided with vertical reinforcement in accordance with Section R611.6 and Table R611.6(1), R611.6(2) or R611.6(3) for above-grade walls. Where unbalanced backfill retained by the stem wall is greater than 18 inches (457 mm), the stem wall and above-grade wall it supports shall be provided with vertical reinforcement in accordance with Section R611.6 and Table R611.6(4).

2. Stem walls laterally supported at top. Concrete stem walls that are monolithic with slabs-on-ground or are otherwise laterally supported by slabs-on-ground shall be vertically reinforced in accordance with Section R611.6 and Table R611.6(1), R611.6(2) or R611.6(3) for above-grade walls. Where the unbalanced backfill retained by the stem wall is greater than 18 inches (457 mm), the connection between the stem wall and the slab-on-ground, and the portion of the slab-on-ground providing lateral support for the wall shall be designed in accordance with PCA 100 or in accordance with accepted engineering practice. Where the unbalanced backfill retained by the stem wall is greater than 18 inches (457 mm), the minimum nominal thickness of the wall shall be 6 inches (152 mm).

TABLE R404.1.1(1)
PLAIN MASONRY FOUNDATION WALLS

MAXIMUM WALL HEIGHT (feet)	MAXIMUM UNBALANCED BACKFILL HEIGHT[c] (feet)	PLAIN MASONRY[a] MINIMUM NOMINAL WALL THICKNESS (inches)		
		Soil classes[b]		
		GW, GP, SW and SP	GM, GC, SM, SM-SC and ML	SC, MH, ML-CL and inorganic CL
5	4	6 solid[d] or 8	6 solid[d] or 8	6 solid[d] or 8
	5	6 solid[d] or 8	8	10
6	4	6 solid[d] or 8	6 solid[d] or 8	6 solid[d] or 8
	5	6 solid[d] or 8	8	10
	6	8	10	12
7	4	6 solid[d] or 8	8	8
	5	6 solid[d] or 8	10	10
	6	10	12	10 solid[d]
	7	12	10 solid[d]	12 solid[d]
8	4	6 solid[d] or 8	6 solid[d] or 8	8
	5	6 solid[d] or 8	10	12
	6	10	12	12 solid[d]
	7	12	12 solid[d]	Footnote e
	8	10 solid[d]	12 solid[d]	Footnote e
9	4	6 solid[d] or 8	6 solid[d] or 8	8
	5	8	10	12
	6	10	12	12 solid[d]
	7	12	12 solid[d]	Footnote e
	8	12 solid[d]	Footnote e	Footnote e
	9	Footnote e	Footnote e	Footnote e

For SI: 1 inch = 25.4 mm, 1 foot = 304.8 mm, 1 pound per square inch = 6.895 Pa.

a. Mortar shall be Type M or S and masonry shall be laid in running bond. Ungrouted hollow masonry units are permitted except where otherwise indicated.

b. Soil classes are in accordance with the Unified Soil Classification System. Refer to Table R405.1.

c. Unbalanced backfill height is the difference in height between the exterior finish ground level and the lower of the top of the concrete footing that supports the foundation wall or the interior finish ground level. Where an interior concrete slab-on-grade is provided and is in contact with the interior surface of the foundation wall, measurement of the unbalanced backfill height from the exterior finish ground level to the top of the interior concrete slab is permitted.

d. Solid grouted hollow units or solid masonry units.

e. Wall construction shall be in accordance with either Table R404.1.1(2), Table R404.1.1(3), Table R404.1.1(4), or a design shall be provided.

TABLE R404.1.1(2)
8-INCH MASONRY FOUNDATION WALLS WITH REINFORCING WHERE d > 5 INCHES[a, c]

WALL HEIGHT	HEIGHT OF UNBALANCED BACKFILL[e]	MINIMUM VERTICAL REINFORCEMENT AND SPACING (INCHES)[b, c]		
		Soil classes and lateral soil load[d] (psf per foot below grade)		
		GW, GP, SW and SP soils 30	GM, GC, SM, SM-SC and ML soils 45	SC, ML-CL and inorganic CL soils 60
6 feet 8 inches	4 feet (or less)	#4 at 48	#4 at 48	#4 at 48
	5 feet	#4 at 48	#4 at 48	#4 at 48
	6 feet 8 inches	#4 at 48	#5 at 48	#6 at 48
7 feet 4 inches	4 feet (or less)	#4 at 48	#4 at 48	#4 at 48
	5 feet	#4 at 48	#4 at 48	#4 at 48
	6 feet	#4 at 48	#5 at 48	#5 at 48
	7 feet 4 inches	#5 at 48	#6 at 48	#6 at 40
8 feet	4 feet (or less)	#4 at 48	#4 at 48	#4 at 48
	5 feet	#4 at 48	#4 at 48	#4 at 48
	6 feet	#4 at 48	#5 at 48	#5 at 48
	7 feet	#5 at 48	#6 at 48	#6 at 40
	8 feet	#5 at 48	#6 at 48	#6 at 32
8 feet 8 inches	4 feet (or less)	#4 at 48	#4 at 48	#4 at 48
	5 feet	#4 at 48	#4 at 48	#5 at 48
	6 feet	#4 at 48	#5 at 48	#6 at 48
	7 feet	#5 at 48	#6 at 48	#6 at 40
	8 feet 8 inches	#6 at 48	#6 at 32	#6 at 24
9 feet 4 inches	4 feet (or less)	#4 at 48	#4 at 48	#4 at 48
	5 feet	#4 at 48	#4 at 48	#5 at 48
	6 feet	#4 at 48	#5 at 48	#6 at 48
	7 feet	#5 at 48	#6 at 48	#6 at 40
	8 feet	#6 at 48	#6 at 40	#6 at 24
	9 feet 4 inches	#6 at 40	#6 at 24	#6 at 16
10 feet	4 feet (or less)	#4 at 48	#4 at 48	#4 at 48
	5 feet	#4 at 48	#4 at 48	#5 at 48
	6 feet	#4 at 48	#5 at 48	#6 at 48
	7 feet	#5 at 48	#6 at 48	#6 at 32
	8 feet	#6 at 48	#6 at 32	#6 at 24
	9 feet	#6 at 40	#6 at 24	#6 at 16
	10 feet	#6 at 32	#6 at 16	#6 at 16

For SI: 1 inch = 25.4 mm, 1 foot = 304.8 mm, 1 pound per square foot per foot = 0.157 kPa/mm.

a. Mortar shall be Type M or S and masonry shall be laid in running bond.

b. Alternative reinforcing bar sizes and spacings having an equivalent cross-sectional area of reinforcement per lineal foot of wall shall be permitted provided the spacing of the reinforcement does not exceed 72 inches.

c. Vertical reinforcement shall be Grade 60 minimum. The distance, *d*, from the face of the soil side of the wall to the center of vertical reinforcement shall be at least 5 inches.

d. Soil classes are in accordance with the Unified Soil Classification System and design lateral soil loads are for moist conditions without hydrostatic pressure. Refer to Table R405.1.

e. Unbalanced backfill height is the difference in height between the exterior finish ground level and the lower of the top of the concrete footing that supports the foundation wall or the interior finish ground level. Where an interior concrete slab-on-grade is provided and is in contact with the interior surface of the foundation wall, measurement of the unbalanced backfill height from the exterior finish ground level to the top of the interior concrete slab is permitted.

TABLE R404.1.1(3)
10-INCH FOUNDATION WALLS WITH REINFORCING WHERE d > 6.75 INCHES[a, c]

WALL HEIGHT	HEIGHT OF UNBALANCED BACKFILL[e]	MINIMUM VERTICAL REINFORCEMENT AND SPACING (INCHES)[b, c]		
		Soil classes and later soil load[d] (psf per foot below grade)		
		GW, GP, SW and SP soils 30	GM, GC, SM, SM-SC and ML soils 45	SC, ML-CL and inorganic CL soils 60
6 feet 8 inches	4 feet (or less) 5 feet 6 feet 8 inches	#4 at 56 #4 at 56 #4 at 56	#4 at 56 #4 at 56 #5 at 56	#4 at 56 #4 at 56 #5 at 56
7 feet 4 inches	4 feet (or less) 5 feet 6 feet 7 feet 4 inches	#4 at 56 #4 at 56 #4 at 56 #4 at 56	#4 at 56 #4 at 56 #4 at 56 #5 at 56	#4 at 56 #4 at 56 #5 at 56 #6 at 56
8 feet	4 feet (or less) 5 feet 6 feet 7 feet 8 feet	#4 at 56 #4 at 56 #4 at 56 #4 at 56 #5 at 56	#4 at 56 #4 at 56 #4 at 56 #5 at 56 #6 at 56	#4 at 56 #4 at 56 #5 at 56 #6 at 56 #6 at 48
8 feet 8 inches	4 feet (or less) 5 feet 6 feet 7 feet 8 feet 8 inches	#4 at 56 #4 at 56 #4 at 56 #4 at 56 #5 at 56	#4 at 56 #4 at 56 #4 at 56 #5 at 56 #6 at 48	#4 at 56 #4 at 56 #5 at 56 #6 at 56 #6 at 32
9 feet 4 inches	4 feet (or less) 5 feet 6 feet 7 feet 8 feet 9 feet 4 inches	#4 at 56 #4 at 56 #4 at 56 #4 at 56 #5 at 56 #6 at 56	#4 at 56 #4 at 56 #5 at 56 #5 at 56 #6 at 56 #6 at 40	#4 at 56 #4 at 56 #5 at 56 #6 at 56 #6 at 40 #6 at 24
10 feet	4 feet (or less) 5 feet 6 feet 7 feet 8 feet 9 feet 10 feet	#4 at 56 #4 at 56 #4 at 56 #5 at 56 #5 at 56 #6 at 56 #6 at 48	#4 at 56 #4 at 56 #5 at 56 #6 at 56 #6 at 48 #6 at 40 #6 at 32	#4 at 56 #4 at 56 #5 at 56 #6 at 48 #6 at 40 #6 at 24 #6 at 24

For SI: 1 inch = 25.4 mm, 1 foot = 304.8 mm, 1 pound per square foot per foot = 0.157 kPa/mm.

a. Mortar shall be Type M or S and masonry shall be laid in running bond.

b. Alternative reinforcing bar sizes and spacings having an equivalent cross-sectional area of reinforcement per lineal foot of wall shall be permitted provided the spacing of the reinforcement does not exceed 72 inches.

c. Vertical reinforcement shall be Grade 60 minimum. The distance, *d*, from the face of the soil side of the wall to the center of vertical reinforcement shall be at least 6.75 inches.

d. Soil classes are in accordance with the Unified Soil Classification System and design lateral soil loads are for moist conditions without hydrostatic pressure. Refer to Table R405.1.

e. Unbalanced backfill height is the difference in height between the exterior finish ground level and the lower of the top of the concrete footing that supports the foundation wall or the interior finish ground level. Where an interior concrete slab-on-grade is provided and is in contact with the interior surface of the foundation wall, measurement of the unbalanced backfill height from the exterior finish ground level to the top of the interior concrete slab is permitted.

TABLE R404.1.1(4)
12-INCH MASONRY FOUNDATION WALLS WITH REINFORCING WHERE d > 8.75 INCHES[a, c]

WALL HEIGHT	HEIGHT OF UNBALANCED BACKFILL[e]	MINIMUM VERTICAL REINFORCEMENT AND SPACING (INCHES)[b, c]		
		Soil classes and lateral soil load[d] (psf per foot below *grade*)		
		GW, GP, SW and SP soils 30	GM, GC, SM, SM-SC and ML soils 45	SC, ML-CL and inorganic CL soils 60
6 feet 8 inches	4 feet (or less) 5 feet 6 feet 8 inches	#4 at 72 #4 at 72 #4 at 72	#4 at 72 #4 at 72 #4 at 72	#4 at 72 #4 at 72 #5 at 72
7 feet 4 inches	4 feet (or less) 5 feet 6 feet 7 feet 4 inches	#4 at 72 #4 at 72 #4 at 72 #4 at 72	#4 at 72 #4 at 72 #4 at 72 #5 at 72	#4 at 72 #4 at 72 #5 at 72 #6 at 72
8 feet	4 feet (or less) 5 feet 6 feet 7 feet 8 feet	#4 at 72 #4 at 72 #4 at 72 #4 at 72 #5 at 72	#4 at 72 #4 at 72 #4 at 72 #5 at 72 #6 at 72	#4 at 72 #4 at 72 #5 at 72 #6 at 72 #6 at 64
8 feet 8 inches	4 feet (or less) 5 feet 6 feet 7 feet 8 feet 8 inches	#4 at 72 #4 at 72 #4 at 72 #4 at 72 #5 at 72	#4 at 72 #4 at 72 #4 at 72 #5 at 72 #7 at 72	#4 at 72 #4 at 72 #5 at 72 #6 at 72 #6 at 48
9 feet 4 inches	4 feet (or less) 5 feet 6 feet 7 feet 8 feet 9 feet 4 inches	#4 at 72 #4 at 72 #4 at 72 #4 at 72 #5 at 72 #6 at 72	#4 at 72 #4 at 72 #5 at 72 #5 at 72 #6 at 72 #6 at 48	#4 at 72 #4 at 72 #5 at 72 #6 at 72 #6 at 56 #6 at 40
10 feet	4 feet (or less) 5 feet 6 feet 7 feet 8 feet 9 feet 10 feet	#4 at 72 #4 at 72 #4 at 72 #4 at 72 #5 at 72 #6 at 72 #6 at 64	#4 at 72 #4 at 72 #5 at 72 #6 at 72 #6 at 72 #6 at 56 #6 at 40	#4 at 72 #4 at 72 #5 at 72 #6 at 72 #6 at 48 #6 at 40 #6 at 32

For SI: 1 inch = 25.4 mm, 1 foot = 304.8 mm, 1 pound per square foot per foot = 0.157 kPa/mm.

a. Mortar shall be Type M or S and masonry shall be laid in running bond.

b. Alternative reinforcing bar sizes and spacings having an equivalent cross-sectional area of reinforcement per lineal foot of wall shall be permitted provided the spacing of the reinforcement does not exceed 72 inches.

c. Vertical reinforcement shall be Grade 60 minimum. The distance, *d*, from the face of the soil side of the wall to the center of vertical reinforcement shall be at least 8.75 inches.

d. Soil classes are in accordance with the Unified Soil Classification System and design lateral soil loads are for moist conditions without hydrostatic pressure. Refer to Table R405.1.

e. Unbalanced backfill height is the difference in height between the exterior finish ground level and the lower of the top of the concrete footing that supports the foundation wall or the interior finish ground levels. Where an interior concrete slab-on-grade is provided and in contact with the interior surface of the foundation wall, measurement of the unbalanced backfill height is permitted to be measured from the exterior finish ground level to the top of the interior concrete slab is permitted.

TABLE R404.1.2(1)
MINIMUM HORIZONTAL REINFORCEMENT FOR CONCRETE BASEMENT WALLS[a, b]

MAXIMUM UNSUPPORTED HEIGHT OF BASEMENT WALL (feet)	LOCATION OF HORIZONTAL REINFORCEMENT
≤ 8	One No. 4 bar within 12 inches of the top of the wall story and one No. 4 bar near mid-height of the wall story
> 8	One No. 4 bar within 12 inches of the top of the wall story and one No. 4 bar near third points in the wall story

For SI: 1 inch = 25.4 mm, 1 foot = 304.8 mm, 1 pound per square inch = 6.895kPa.

a. Horizontal reinforcement requirements are for reinforcing bars with a minimum yield strength of 40,000 psi and concrete with a minimum concrete compressive strength 2,500 psi.

b. See Section R404.1.2.2 for minimum reinforcement required for foundation walls supporting above-grade concrete walls.

TABLE R404.1.2(2)
MINIMUM VERTICAL REINFORCEMENT FOR 6-INCH NOMINAL FLAT CONCRETE BASEMENT WALLS[b, c, d, e, g, h, i, j]

MAXIMUM UNSUPPORTED WALL HEIGHT (feet)	MAXIMUM UNBALANCED BACKFILL HEIGHT[f] (feet)	MINIMUM VERTICAL REINFORCEMENT—BAR SIZE AND SPACING (inches)		
		Soil classes[a] and design lateral soil (psf per foot of depth)		
		GW, GP, SW, SP 30	GM, GC, SM, SM-SC and ML 45	SC, ML-CL and inorganic CL 60
8	4	NR	NR	NR
	5	NR	6 @ 39	6 @ 48
	6	5 @ 39	6 @ 48	6 @ 35
	7	6 @ 48	6 @ 34	6 @ 25
	8	6 @ 39	6 @ 25	6 @ 18
9	4	NR	NR	NR
	5	NR	5 @ 37	6 @ 48
	6	5 @ 36	6 @ 44	6 @ 32
	7	6 @ 47	6 @ 30	6 @ 22
	8	6 @ 34	6 @ 22	6 @ 16
	9	6 @ 27	6 @ 17	DR
10	4	NR	NR	NR
	5	NR	5 @ 35	6 @ 48
	6	6 @ 48	6 @ 41	6 @ 30
	7	6 @ 43	6 @ 28	6 @ 20
	8	6 @ 31	6 @ 20	DR
	9	6 @ 24	6 @ 15	DR
	10	6 @ 19	DR	DR

For SI:1 foot = 304.8 mm; 1 inch = 25.4 mm; 1 pound per square foot per foot = 0.1571 kPa^2/m, 1 pound per square inch = 6.895 kPa.

a. Soil classes are in accordance with the Unified Soil Classification System. Refer to Table R405.1.

b. Table values are based on reinforcing bars with a minimum yield strength of 60,000 psi concrete with a minimum specified compressive strength of 2,500 psi and vertical reinforcement being located at the centerline of the wall. See Section R404.1.2.3.7.2.

c. Vertical reinforcement with a yield strength of less than 60,000 psi and/or bars of a different size than specified in the table are permitted in accordance with Section R404.1.2.3.7.6 and Table R404.1.2(9).

d. Deflection criterion is *L*/240, where *L* is the height of the basement wall in inches.

e. Interpolation is not permitted.

f. Where walls will retain 4 feet or more of unbalanced backfill, they shall be laterally supported at the top and bottom before backfilling.

g. NR indicates no vertical wall reinforcement is required, except for 6-inch nominal walls formed with stay-in-place forming systems in which case vertical reinforcement shall be No. 4@48 inches on center.

h. See Section R404.1.2.2 for minimum reinforcement required for basement walls supporting above-grade concrete walls.

i. See Table R611.3 for tolerance from nominal thickness permitted for flat walls.

j. DR means design is required in accordance with the applicable building code, or where there is no code, in accordance with ACI 318.

TABLE R404.1.2(3)
MINIMUM VERTICAL REINFORCEMENT FOR 8-INCH (203 mm) NOMINAL FLAT CONCRETE BASEMENT WALLS[b, c, d, e, f, h, i]

MAXIMUM UNSUPPORTED WALL HEIGHT (feet)	MAXIMUM UNBALANCED BACKFILL HEIGHT[g] (feet)	MINIMUM VERTICAL REINFORCEMENT—BAR SIZE AND SPACING (inches)		
		Soil classes[a] and design lateral soil (psf per foot of depth)		
		GW, GP, SW, SP 30	GM, GC, SM, SM-SC and ML 45	SC, ML-CL and inorganic CL 60
8	4	NR	NR	NR
	5	NR	NR	NR
	6	NR	NR	6 @ 37
	7	NR	6 @ 36	6 @ 35
	8	6 @ 41	6 @ 35	6 @ 26
9	4	NR	NR	NR
	5	NR	NR	NR
	6	NR	NR	6 @ 35
	7	NR	6 @ 35	6 @ 32
	8	6 @ 36	6 @ 32	6 @ 23
	9	6 @ 35	6 @ 25	6 @ 18
10	4	NR	NR	NR
	5	NR	NR	NR
	6	NR	NR	6 @ 35
	7	NR	6 @ 35	6 @ 29
	8	6 @ 35	6 @ 29	6 @ 21
	9	6 @ 34	6 @ 22	6 @ 16
	10	6 @ 27	6 @ 17	6 @ 13

For SI:1 foot = 304.8 mm; 1 inch = 25.4 mm; 1 pound per square foot per foot = 0.1571 kPa^2/m, 1 pound per square inch = 6.895 kPa.

a. Soil classes are in accordance with the Unified Soil Classification System. Refer to Table R405.1.

b. Table values are based on reinforcing bars with a minimum yield strength of 60,000 psi (420 MPa), concrete with a minimum specified compressive strength of 2,500 psi and vertical reinforcement being located at the centerline of the wall. See Section R404.1.2.3.7.2.

c. Vertical reinforcement with a yield strength of less than 60,000 psi and/or bars of a different size than specified in the table are permitted in accordance with Section R404.1.2.3.7.6 and Table R404.1.2(9).

d. NR indicates no vertical reinforcement is required.

e. Deflection criterion is *L*/240, where *L* is the height of the basement wall in inches.

f. Interpolation is not permitted.

g. Where walls will retain 4 feet or more of unbalanced backfill, they shall be laterally supported at the top and bottom before backfilling.

h. See Section R404.1.2.2 for minimum reinforcement required for basement walls supporting above-grade concrete walls.

i. See Table R611.3 for tolerance from nominal thickness permitted for flat walls.

TABLE R404.1.2(4)
MINIMUM VERTICAL REINFORCEMENT FOR 10-INCH NOMINAL FLAT CONCRETE BASEMENT WALLS[b, c, d, e, f, h, i]

MAXIMUM UNSUPPORTED WALL HEIGHT (feet)	MAXIMUM UNBALANCED BACKFILL HEIGHT[g] (feet)	MINIMUM VERTICAL REINFORCEMENT—BAR SIZE AND SPACING (inches)		
		Soil classes[a] and design lateral soil (psf per foot of depth)		
		GW, GP, SW, SP 30	GM, GC, SM, SM-SC and ML 45	SC, ML-CL and inorganic CL 60
8	4	NR	NR	NR
	5	NR	NR	NR
	6	NR	NR	NR
	7	NR	NR	NR
	8	6 @ 48	6 @ 35	6 @ 28
9	4	NR	NR	NR
	5	NR	NR	NR
	6	NR	NR	NR
	7	NR	NR	6 @ 31
	8	NR	6 @ 31	6 @ 28
	9	6 @ 37	6 @ 28	6 @ 24
10	4	NR	NR	NR
	5	NR	NR	NR
	6	NR	NR	NR
	7	NR	NR	6 @ 28
	8	NR	6 @ 28	6 @ 28
	9	6 @ 33	6 @ 28	6 @ 21
	10	6 @ 28	6 @ 23	6 @ 17

For SI:1 foot = 304.8 mm; 1 inch = 25.4 mm; 1 pound per square foot per foot = 0.1571 kPa^2/m, 1 pound per square inch = 6.895 kPa.

a. Soil classes are in accordance with the Unified Soil Classification System. Refer to Table R405.1.

b. Table values are based on reinforcing bars with a minimum yield strength of 60,000 psi concrete with a minimum specified compressive strength of 2,500 psi and vertical reinforcement being located at the centerline of the wall. See Section R404.1.2.3.7.2.

c. Vertical reinforcement with a yield strength of less than 60,000 psi and/or bars of a different size than specified in the table are permitted in accordance with Section R404.1.2.3.7.6 and Table R404.1.2(9).

d. NR indicates no vertical reinforcement is required.

e. Deflection criterion is *L*/240, where *L* is the height of the basement wall in inches.

f. Interpolation is not permitted.

g. Where walls will retain 4 feet or more of unbalanced backfill, they shall be laterally supported at the top and bottom before backfilling.

h. See Section R404.1.2.2 for minimum reinforcement required for basement walls supporting above-grade concrete walls.

i. See Table R611.3 for tolerance from nominal thickness permitted for flat walls.

TABLE R404.1.2(5)
MINIMUM VERTICAL WALL REINFORCEMENT FOR 6-INCH WAFFLE-GRID BASEMENT WALLS[b, c, d, e, g, h, i]

MAXIMUM UNSUPPORTED WALL HEIGHT (feet)	MAXIMUM UNBALANCED BACKFILL HEIGHT[f] (feet)	MINIMUM VERTICAL REINFORCEMENT—BAR SIZE AND SPACING (inches)		
		Soil classes[a] and design lateral soil (psf per foot of depth)		
		GW, GP, SW, SP 30	GM, GC, SM, SM-SC and ML 45	SC, ML-CL and inorganic CL 60
8	4	4 @ 48	4 @ 46	6 @ 39
	5	4 @ 45	5 @ 46	6 @ 47
	6	5 @ 45	6 @ 40	DR
	7	6 @ 44	DR	DR
	8	6 @ 32	DR	DR
9	4	4 @ 48	4 @ 46	4 @ 37
	5	4 @ 42	5 @ 43	6 @ 44
	6	5 @ 41	6 @ 37	DR
	7	6 @ 39	DR	DR
	> 8	DR[i]	DR	DR
10	4	4 @ 48	4 @ 46	4 @ 35
	5	4 @ 40	5 @ 40	6 @ 41
	6	5 @ 38	6 @ 34	DR
	7	6 @ 36	DR	DR
	> 8	DR	DR	DR

For SI: 1 foot = 304.8 mm; 1 inch = 25.4 mm; 1 pound per square foot per foot = 0.1571 kPa^2/m, 1 pound per square inch = 6.895 kPa.

a. Soil classes are in accordance with the Unified Soil Classification System. Refer to Table R405.1.

b. Table values are based on reinforcing bars with a minimum yield strength of 60,000 psi concrete with a minimum specified compressive strength of 2,500 psi and vertical reinforcement being located at the centerline of the wall. See Section R404.1.2.3.7.2.

c. Maximum spacings shown are the values calculated for the specified bar size. Where the bar used is Grade 60 and the size specified in the table, the actual spacing in the wall shall not exceed a whole-number multiple of 12 inches (i.e., 12, 24, 36 and 48) that is less than or equal to the tabulated spacing. Vertical reinforcement with a yield strength of less than 60,000 psi and/or bars of a different size than specified in the table are permitted in accordance with Section R404.1.2.3.7.6 and Table R404.1.2(9).

d. Deflection criterion is $L/240$, where L is the height of the basement wall in inches.

e. Interpolation is not permitted.

f. Where walls will retain 4 feet or more of unbalanced backfill, they shall be laterally supported at the top and bottom before backfilling.

g. See Section R404.1.2.2 for minimum reinforcement required for basement walls supporting above-grade concrete walls.

h. See Table R611.3 for thicknesses and dimensions of waffle-grid walls.

i. DR means design is required in accordance with the applicable building code, or where there is no code, in accordance with ACI 318.

TABLE R404.1.2(6)
MINIMUM VERTICAL REINFORCEMENT FOR 8-INCH WAFFLE-GRID BASEMENT WALLS[b, c, d, e, f, h, i, j]

MAXIMUM UNSUPPORTED WALL HEIGHT (feet)	MAXIMUM UNBALANCED BACKFILL HEIGHT[g] (feet)	MINIMUM VERTICAL REINFORCEMENT—BAR SIZE AND SPACING (inches)		
		Soil classes[a] and design lateral soil (psf per foot of depth)		
		GW, GP, SW, SP 30	GM, GC, SM, SM-SC and ML 45	SC, ML-CL and inorganic CL 60
8	4	NR	NR	NR
	5	NR	5 @ 48	5 @ 46
	6	5 @ 48	5 @ 43	6 @ 45
	7	5 @ 46	6 @ 43	6 @ 31
	8	6 @ 48	6 @ 32	6 @ 23
9	4	NR	NR	NR
	5	NR	5 @ 47	5 @ 46
	6	5 @ 46	5 @ 39	6 @ 41
	7	5 @ 42	6 @ 38	6 @ 28
	8	6 @ 44	6 @ 28	6 @ 20
	9	6 @ 34	6 @ 21	DR
10	4	NR	NR	NR
	5	NR	5 @ 46	5 @ 44
	6	5 @ 46	5 @ 37	6 @ 38
	7	5 @ 38	6 @ 35	6 @ 25
	8	6 @ 39	6 @ 25	DR
	9	6 @ 30	DR	DR
	10	6 @ 24	DR	DR

For SI: 1 foot = 304.8 mm; 1 inch = 25.4 mm; 1 pound per square foot per foot = 0.1571 kPa^2/m, 1 pound per square inch = 6.895 kPa.

a. Soil classes are in accordance with the Unified Soil Classification System. Refer to Table R405.1.

b. Table values are based on reinforcing bars with a minimum yield strength of 60,000 psi concrete with a minimum specified compressive strength of 2,500 psi and vertical reinforcement being located at the centerline of the wall. See Section R404.1.2.3.7.2.

c. Maximum spacings shown are the values calculated for the specified bar size. Where the bar used is Grade 60 (420 MPa) and the size specified in the table, the actual spacing in the wall shall not exceed a whole-number multiple of 12 inches (i.e., 12, 24, 36 and 48) that is less than or equal to the tabulated spacing. Vertical reinforcement with a yield strength of less than 60,000 psi and/or bars of a different size than specified in the table are permitted in accordance with Section R404.1.2.3.7.6 and Table R404.1.2(9).

d. NR indicates no vertical reinforcement is required.

e. Deflection criterion is $L/240$, where L is the height of the basement wall in inches.

f. Interpolation shall not be permitted.

g. Where walls will retain 4 feet or more of unbalanced backfill, they shall be laterally supported at the top and bottom before backfilling.

h. See Section R404.1.2.2 for minimum reinforcement required for basement walls supporting above-grade concrete walls.

i. See Table R611.3 for thicknesses and dimensions of waffle-grid walls.

j. DR means design is required in accordance with the applicable building code, or where there is no code, in accordance with ACI 318.

TABLE R404.1.2(7)
MINIMUM VERTICAL REINFORCEMENT FOR 6-INCH (152 mm) SCREEN-GRID BASEMENT WALLS[b, c, d, e, g, h, i]

MAXIMUM UNSUPPORTED WALL HEIGHT (feet)	MAXIMUM UNBALANCED BACKFILL HEIGHT[f] (feet)	MINIMUM VERTICAL REINFORCEMENT—BAR SIZE AND SPACING (inches)		
		Soil classes[a] and design lateral soil (psf per foot of depth)		
		GW, GP, SW, SP 30	GM, GC, SM, SM-SC and ML 45	SC, ML-CL and inorganic CL 60
8	4	4 @ 48	4 @ 48	5 @ 43
	5	4 @ 48	5 @ 48	5 @ 37
	6	5 @ 48	6 @ 45	6 @ 32
	7	6 @ 48	DR	DR
	8	6 @ 36	DR	DR
9	4	4 @ 48	4 @ 48	4 @ 41
	5	4 @ 48	5 @ 48	6 @ 48
	6	5 @ 45	6 @ 41	DR
	7	6 @ 43	DR	DR
	> 8	DR	DR	DR
10	4	4 @ 48	4 @ 48	4 @ 39
	5	4 @ 44	5 @ 44	6 @ 46
	6	5 @ 42	6 @ 38	DR
	7	6 @ 40	DR	DR
	> 8	DR	DR	DR

For SI: 1 foot = 304.8 mm; 1 inch = 25.4 mm; 1 pound per square foot per foot = 0.1571 kPa^2/m, 1 pound per square inch = 6.895 kPa.

a. Soil classes are in accordance with the Unified Soil Classification System. Refer to Table R405.1.

b. Table values are based on reinforcing bars with a minimum yield strength of 60,000 psi (420 MPa), concrete with a minimum specified compressive strength of 2,500 psi and vertical reinforcement being located at the centerline of the wall. See Section R404.1.2.3.7.2.

c. Maximum spacings shown are the values calculated for the specified bar size. Where the bar used is Grade 60 and the size specified in the table, the actual spacing in the wall shall not exceed a whole-number multiple of 12 inches (i.e., 12, 24, 36 and 48) that is less than or equal to the tabulated spacing. Vertical reinforcement with a yield strength of less than 60,000 psi and/or bars of a different size than specified in the table are permitted in accordance with Section R404.1.2.3.7.6 and Table R404.1.2(9).

d. Deflection criterion is $L/240$, where L is the height of the basement wall in inches.

e. Interpolation is not permitted.

f. Where walls will retain 4 feet or more of unbalanced backfill, they shall be laterally supported at the top and bottom before backfilling.

g. See Sections R404.1.2.2 for minimum reinforcement required for basement walls supporting above-grade concrete walls.

h. See Table R611.3 for thicknesses and dimensions of screen-grid walls.

i. DR means design is required in accordance with the applicable building code, or where there is no code, in accordance with ACI 318.

TABLE R404.1.2(8)
MINIMUM VERTICAL REINFORCEMENT FOR 6-, 8-, 10-INCH AND 12-INCH NOMINAL FLAT BASEMENT WALLS[b, c, d, e, f, h, i, k, n]

MAXIMUM WALL HEIGHT (feet)	MAXIMUM UNBALANCED BACKFILL HEIGHT[g] (feet)	MINIMUM VERTICAL REINFORCEMENT—BAR SIZE AND SPACING (inches)											
		Soil classes[a] and design lateral soil (psf per foot of depth)											
		GW, GP, SW, SP 30				GM, GC, SM, SM-SC and ML 45				SC, ML-CL and inorganic CL 60			
		Minimum nominal wall thickness (inches)											
		6	8	10	12	6	8	10	12	6	8	10	12
5	4	NR	NR	NR	NR	NR	NR	NR	NR	NR	NR	NR	NR
	5	NR	NR	NR	NR	NR	NR	NR	NR	NR	NR	NR	NR
6	4	NR	NR	NR	NR	NR	NR	NR	NR	NR	NR	NR	NR
	5	NR	NR	NR	NR	NR	NR[l]	NR	NR	4 @ 35	NR[l]	NR	NR
	6	NR	NR	NR	NR	5 @ 48	NR	NR	NR	5 @ 36	NR	NR	NR
7	4	NR	NR	NR	NR	NR	NR	NR	NR	NR	NR	NR	NR
	5	NR	NR	NR	NR	NR	NR	NR	NR	5 @ 47	NR	NR	NR
	6	NR	NR	NR	NR	5 @ 42	NR	NR	NR	6 @ 43	5 @ 48	NR[l]	NR
	7	5 @ 46	NR	NR	NR	6 @ 42	5 @ 46	NR[l]	NR	6 @ 34	6 @ 48	NR	NR
8	4	NR	NR	NR	NR	NR	NR	NR	NR	NR	NR	NR	NR
	5	NR	NR	NR	NR	4 @ 38	NR[l]	NR	NR	5 @ 43	NR	NR	NR
	6	4 @ 37	NR[l]	NR	NR	5 @ 37	NR	NR	NR	6 @ 37	5 @ 43	NR[l]	NR
	7	5 @ 40	NR	NR	NR	6 @ 37	5 @ 41	NR[l]	NR	6 @ 34	6 @ 43	NR	NR
	8	6 @ 43	5 @ 47	NR[l]	NR	6 @ 34	6 @ 43	NR	NR	6 @ 27	6 @ 32	6 @ 44	NR
9	4	NR	NR	NR	NR	NR	NR	NR	NR	NR	NR	NR	NR
	5	NR	NR	NR	NR	4 @ 35	NR[l]	NR	NR	5 @ 40	NR	NR	NR
	6	4 @ 34	NR[l]	NR	NR	6 @ 48	NR	NR	NR	6 @ 36	6 @ 39	NR[l]	NR
	7	5 @ 36	NR	NR	NR	6 @ 34	5 @ 37	NR	NR	6 @ 33	6 @ 38	5 @ 37	NR[l]
	8	6 @ 38	5 @ 41	NR[l]	NR	6 @ 33	6 @ 38	5 @ 37	NR[l]	6 @ 24	6 @ 29	6 @ 39	4 @ 48[m]
	9	6 @ 34	6 @ 46	NR	NR	6 @ 26	6 @ 30	6 @ 41	NR	6 @ 19	6 @ 23	6 @ 30	6 @ 39
10	4	NR	NR	NR	NR	NR	NR	NR	NR	NR	NR	NR	NR
	5	NR	NR	NR	NR	4 @ 33	NR[l]	NR	NR	5 @ 38	NR	NR	NR
	6	5 @ 48	NR[l]	NR	NR	6 @ 45	NR	NR	NR	6 @ 34	5 @ 37	NR	NR
	7	6 @ 47	NR	NR	NR	6 @ 34	6 @ 48	NR	NR	6 @ 30	6 @ 35	6 @ 48	NR[l]
	8	6 @ 34	5 @ 38	NR	NR	6 @ 30	6 @ 34	6 @ 47	NR[l]	6 @ 22	6 @ 26	6 @ 35	6 @ 45[m]
	9	6 @ 34	6 @ 41	4 @ 48	NR[l]	6 @ 23	6 @ 27	6 @ 35	4 @ 48[m]	DR	6 @ 22	6 @ 27	6 @ 34
	10	6 @ 28	6 @ 33	6 @ 45	NR	DR[j]	6 @ 23	6 @ 29	6 @ 38	DR	6 @ 22	6 @ 22	6 @ 28

For SI: 1 foot = 304.8 mm; 1 inch = 25.4 mm; 1 pound per square foot per foot = 0.1571 kPa^2/m, 1 pound per square inch = 6.895 kPa.

a. Soil classes are in accordance with the Unified Soil Classification System. Refer to Table R405.1.

b. Table values are based on reinforcing bars with a minimum yield strength of 60,000 psi.

c. Vertical reinforcement with a yield strength of less than 60,000 psi and/or bars of a different size than specified in the table are permitted in accordance with Section R404.1.2.3.7.6 and Table R404.1.2(9).

d. NR indicates no vertical wall reinforcement is required, except for 6-inch nominal walls formed with stay-in-place forming systems in which case vertical reinforcement shall be #4@48 inches on center.

e. Allowable deflection criterion is $L/240$, where L is the unsupported height of the basement wall in inches.

f. Interpolation is not permitted.

g. Where walls will retain 4 feet or more of unbalanced backfill, they shall be laterally supported at the top and bottom before backfilling.

h. Vertical reinforcement shall be located to provide a cover of 1.25 inches measured from the inside face of the wall. The center of the steel shall not vary from the specified location by more than the greater of 10 percent of the wall thickness or $^{3}/_{8}$-inch.

i. Concrete cover for reinforcement measured from the inside face of the wall shall not be less than $^{3}/_{4}$-inch. Concrete cover for reinforcement measured from the outside face of the wall shall not be less than $1^{1}/_{2}$ inches for No. 5 bars and smaller, and not less than 2 inches for larger bars.

j. DR means design is required in accordance with the applicable building code, or where there is no code in accordance with ACI 318.

k. Concrete shall have a specified compressive strength, f'_c, of not less than 2,500 psi at 28 days, unless a higher strength is required by footnote l or m.

l. The minimum thickness is permitted to be reduced 2 inches, provided the minimum specified compressive strength of concrete, f'_c, is 4,000 psi.

m. A plain concrete wall with a minimum nominal thickness of 12 inches is permitted, provided minimum specified compressive strength of concrete, f'_c, is 3,500 psi.

n. See Table R611.3 for tolerance from nominal thickness permitted for flat walls.

TABLE R404.1.2(9)
MINIMUM SPACING FOR ALTERNATE BAR SIZE AND/OR ALTERNATE GRADE OF STEEL[a, b, c]

BAR SPACING FROM APPLICABLE TABLE IN SECTION R404.1.2.2 (inches)	BAR SIZE FROM APPLICABLE TABLE IN SECTION R404.1.2.2														
	#4					#5					#6				
	Alternate bar size and/or alternate grade of steel desired														
	Grade 60		Grade 40			Grade 60		Grade 40			Grade 60		Grade 40		
	#5	#6	#4	#5	#6	#4	#6	#4	#5	#6	#4	#5	#4	#5	#6
	Maximum spacing for alternate bar size and/or alternate grade of steel (inches)														
8	12	18	5	8	12	5	11	3	5	8	4	6	2	4	5
9	14	20	6	9	13	6	13	4	6	9	4	6	3	4	6
10	16	22	7	10	15	6	14	4	7	9	5	7	3	5	7
11	17	24	7	11	16	7	16	5	7	10	5	8	3	5	7
12	19	26	8	12	18	8	17	5	8	11	5	8	4	6	8
13	20	29	9	13	19	8	18	6	9	12	6	9	4	6	9
14	22	31	9	14	21	9	20	6	9	13	6	10	4	7	9
15	23	33	10	16	22	10	21	6	10	14	7	11	5	7	10
16	25	35	11	17	23	10	23	7	11	15	7	11	5	8	11
17	26	37	11	18	25	11	24	7	11	16	8	12	5	8	11
18	28	40	12	19	26	12	26	8	12	17	8	13	5	8	12
19	29	42	13	20	28	12	27	8	13	18	9	13	6	9	13
20	31	44	13	21	29	13	28	9	13	19	9	14	6	9	13
21	33	46	14	22	31	14	30	9	14	20	10	15	6	10	14
22	34	48	15	23	32	14	31	9	15	21	10	16	7	10	15
23	36	48	15	24	34	15	33	10	15	22	10	16	7	11	15
24	37	48	16	25	35	15	34	10	16	23	11	17	7	11	16
25	39	48	17	26	37	16	35	11	17	24	11	18	8	12	17
26	40	48	17	27	38	17	37	11	17	25	12	18	8	12	17
27	42	48	18	28	40	17	38	12	18	26	12	19	8	13	18
28	43	48	19	29	41	18	40	12	19	26	13	20	8	13	19
29	45	48	19	30	43	19	41	12	19	27	13	20	9	14	19
30	47	48	20	31	44	19	43	13	20	28	14	21	9	14	20
31	48	48	21	32	45	20	44	13	21	29	14	22	9	15	21
32	48	48	21	33	47	21	45	14	21	30	15	23	10	15	21
33	48	48	22	34	48	21	47	14	22	31	15	23	10	16	22
34	48	48	23	35	48	22	48	15	23	32	15	24	10	16	23
35	48	48	23	36	48	23	48	15	23	33	16	25	11	16	23
36	48	48	24	37	48	23	48	15	24	34	16	25	11	17	24
37	48	48	25	38	48	24	48	16	25	35	17	26	11	17	25
38	48	48	25	39	48	25	48	16	25	36	17	27	12	18	25
39	48	48	26	40	48	25	48	17	26	37	18	27	12	18	26
40	48	48	27	41	48	26	48	17	27	38	18	28	12	19	27
41	48	48	27	42	48	26	48	18	27	39	19	29	12	19	27
42	48	48	28	43	48	27	48	18	28	40	19	30	13	20	28
43	48	48	29	44	48	28	48	18	29	41	20	30	13	20	29
44	48	48	29	45	48	28	48	19	29	42	20	31	13	21	29
45	48	48	30	47	48	29	48	19	30	43	20	32	14	21	30

(continued)

TABLE R404.1.2(9)—continued
MINIMUM SPACING FOR ALTERNATE BAR SIZE AND/OR ALTERNATE GRADE OF STEEL[a, b, c]

BAR SPACING FROM APPLICABLE TABLE IN SECTION R404.1.2.2 (inches)	BAR SIZE FROM APPLICABLE TABLE IN SECTION R404.1.2.2														
	#4					#5					#6				
	Alternate bar size and/or alternate grade of steel desired to be used														
	Grade 60		Grade 40			Grade 60		Grade 40			Grade 60		Grade 40		
	#5	#6	#4	#5	#6	#4	#6	#4	#5	#6	#4	#5	#4	#5	#6
	Maximum spacing for alternate bar size and/or alternate grade of steel (inches)														
46	48	48	31	48	48	30	48	20	31	44	21	32	14	22	31
47	48	48	31	48	48	30	48	20	31	44	21	33	14	22	31
48	48	48	32	48	48	31	48	21	32	45	22	34	15	23	32

For SI: 1 inch = 25.4 mm, 1 pound per square inch = 6.895 kPa.

a. This table is for use with tables in Section R404.1.2.2 that specify the minimum bar size and maximum spacing of vertical wall reinforcement for foundation walls and above-grade walls. Reinforcement specified in tables in Sections R404.1.2.2 is based on Grade 60 steel reinforcement.

b. Bar spacing shall not exceed 48 inches on center and shall not be less than one-half the nominal wall thickness.

c. For Grade 50 steel bars (ASTM A 996, Type R), use spacing for Grade 40 bars or interpolate between Grades 40 and 60.

TABLE R404.2.3
PLYWOOD GRADE AND THICKNESS FOR WOOD FOUNDATION CONSTRUCTION
(30 pcf equivalent-fluid weight soil pressure)

HEIGHT OF FILL (inches)	STUD SPACING (inches)	FACE GRAIN ACROSS STUDS			FACE GRAIN PARALLEL TO STUDS		
		Grade[a]	Minimum thickness (inches)	Span rating	Grade[a]	Minimum thickness (inches)[b, c]	Span rating
24	12	B	$^{15}/_{32}$	32/16	A	$^{15}/_{32}$	32/16
					B	$^{15}/_{32}$[c]	32/16
	16	B	$^{15}/_{32}$	32/16	A	$^{15}/_{32}$[c]	32/16
					B	$^{19}/_{32}$[c] (4, 5 ply)	40/20
36	12	B	$^{15}/_{32}$	32/16	A	$^{15}/_{32}$	32/16
					B	$^{15}/_{32}$[c] (4, 5 ply)	32/16
					B	$^{19}/_{32}$ (4, 5 ply)	40/20
	16	B	$^{15}/_{32}$[c]	32/16	A	$^{19}/_{32}$	40/20
					B	$^{23}/_{32}$	48/24
48	12	B	$^{15}/_{32}$	32/16	A	$^{15}/_{32}$[c]	32/16
					B	$^{19}/_{32}$[c] (4, 5 ply)	40/20
	16	B	$^{19}/_{32}$	40/20	A	$^{19}/_{32}$[c]	40/20
					A	$^{23}/_{32}$	48/24

For SI: 1 inch = 25.4 mm, 1 foot = 304.8 mm, 1 pound per cubic foot = 0.1572 kN/m^3.

a. Plywood shall be of the following minimum grades in accordance with DOC PS 1 or DOC PS 2:

1. DOC PS 1 Plywood grades marked:
   - 1.1. Structural I C-D (Exposure 1)
   - 1.2. C-D (Exposure 1)
2. DOC PS 2 Plywood grades marked:
   - 2.1. Structural I Sheathing (Exposure 1)
   - 2.2. Sheathing (Exposure 1)
3. Where a major portion of the wall is exposed above ground and a better appearance is desired, the following plywood grades marked exterior are suitable:
   - 3.1. Structural I A-C, Structural I B-C or Structural I C-C (Plugged) in accordance with DOC PS 1
   - 3.2. A-C Group 1, B-C Group 1, C-C (Plugged) Group 1 or MDO Group 1 in accordance with DOC PS 1
   - 3.3. Single Floor in accordance with DOC PS 1 or DOC PS 2

b. Minimum thickness $^{15}/_{32}$ inch, except crawl space sheathing may be $^{3}/_{8}$ inch for face grain across studs 16 inches on center and maximum 2-foot depth of unequal fill.

c. For this fill height, thickness and grade combination, panels that are continuous over less than three spans (across less than three stud spacings) require blocking 16 inches above the bottom plate. Offset adjacent blocks and fasten through studs with two 16d corrosion-resistant nails at each end.

R404.1.2.2.2 Concrete foundation stem walls supporting light-frame above-grade walls. Concrete foundation stem walls that support light-frame above-grade walls shall be designed and constructed in accordance with this section.

1. Stem walls not laterally supported at top. Concrete stem walls that are not monolithic with slabs-on-ground or are not otherwise laterally supported by slabs-on-ground and retain 48 inches (1219 mm) or less of unbalanced fill, measured from the top of the wall, shall be constructed in accordance with Section R404.1.2. Foundation stem walls that retain more than 48 inches (1219 mm) of unbalanced fill, measured from the top of the wall, shall be designed in accordance with Sections R404.1.3 and R404.4.
2. Stem walls laterally supported at top. Concrete stem walls that are monolithic with slabs-on-ground or are otherwise laterally supported by slabs-on-ground shall be constructed in accordance with Section R404.1.2. Where the unbalanced backfill retained by the stem wall is greater than 48 inches (1219 mm), the connection between the stem wall and the slab-on- ground, and the portion of the slab-on-ground providing lateral support for the wall shall be designed in accordance with PCA 100 or in accordance with accepted engineering practice.

R404.1.2.3 Concrete, materials for concrete, and forms. Materials used in concrete, the concrete itself and forms shall conform to requirements of this section or ACI 318.

R404.1.2.3.1 Compressive strength. The minimum specified compressive strength of concrete, f'_c, shall comply with Section R402.2 and shall be not less than 2,500 psi (17.2 MPa) at 28 days in buildings assigned to Seismic Design Category A, B or C and 3000 psi (20.5 MPa) in buildings assigned to Seismic Design Category D_0, D_1 or D_2.

R404.1.2.3.2 Concrete mixing and delivery. Mixing and delivery of concrete shall comply with ASTM C 94 or ASTM C 685.

R404.1.2.3.3 Maximum aggregate size. The nominal maximum size of coarse aggregate shall not exceed one-fifth the narrowest distance between sides of forms, or three-fourths the clear spacing between reinforcing bars or between a bar and the side of the form.

Exception: When *approved*, these limitations shall not apply where removable forms are used and workability and methods of consolidation permit concrete to be placed without honeycombs or voids.

R404.1.2.3.4 Proportioning and slump of concrete. Proportions of materials for concrete shall be established to provide workability and consistency to permit concrete to be worked readily into forms and around reinforcement under conditions of placement to be employed, without segregation or excessive bleeding. Slump of concrete placed in removable forms shall not exceed 6 inches (152 mm).

Exception: When *approved*, the slump is permitted to exceed 6 inches (152 mm) for concrete mixtures that are resistant to segregation, and are in accordance with the form manufacturer's recommendations.

Slump of concrete placed in stay-in-place forms shall exceed 6 inches (152 mm). Slump of concrete shall be determined in accordance with ASTM C 143.

R404.1.2.3.5 Consolidation of concrete. Concrete shall be consolidated by suitable means during placement and shall be worked around embedded items and reinforcement and into corners of forms. Where stay-in-place forms are used, concrete shall be consolidated by internal vibration.

Exception: When *approved* for concrete to be placed in stay-in-place forms, self-consolidating concrete mixtures with slumps equal to or greater than 8 inches (203 mm) that are specifically designed for placement without internal vibration need not be internally vibrated.

R404.1.2.3.6 Form materials and form ties. Forms shall be made of wood, steel, aluminum, plastic, a composite of cement and foam insulation, a composite of cement and wood chips, or other *approved* material suitable for supporting and containing concrete. Forms shall provide sufficient strength to contain concrete during the concrete placement operation.

Form ties shall be steel, solid plastic, foam plastic, a composite of cement and wood chips, a composite of cement and foam plastic, or other suitable material capable of resisting the forces created by fluid pressure of fresh concrete.

R404.1.2.3.6.1 Stay-in-place forms. Stay-in-place concrete forms shall comply with this section.

1. Surface burning characteristics. The flame-spread index and smoke-developed index of forming material, other than foam plastic, left exposed on the interior shall comply with Section R302. The surface burning characteristics of foam plastic used in insulating concrete forms shall comply with Section R316.3.
2. Interior covering. Stay-in-place forms constructed of rigid foam plastic shall be protected on the interior of the building as required by Section R316. Where gypsum board is used to protect the foam plastic, it shall be installed with a mechanical fastening system. Use of adhesives in addition to mechanical fasteners is permitted.
3. Exterior wall covering. Stay-in-place forms constructed of rigid foam plastics shall be protected from sunlight and physical damage by the application of an *approved* exte-

rior wall covering complying with this code. Exterior surfaces of other stay-in-place forming systems shall be protected in accordance with this code.

4. Termite hazards. In areas where hazard of termite damage is very heavy in accordance with Figure R301.2(6), foam plastic insulation shall be permitted below *grade* on foundation walls in accordance with one of the following conditions:
   4.1. Where in addition to the requirements in Section R318.1, an *approved* method of protecting the foam plastic and structure from subterranean termite damage is provided.
   4.2. The structural members of walls, floors, ceilings and roofs are entirely of noncombustible materials or pressure-preservative-treated wood.
   4.3. On the interior side of *basement* walls.

R404.1.2.3.7 Reinforcement.

R404.1.2.3.7.1 Steel reinforcement. Steel reinforcement shall comply with the requirements of ASTM A 615, A 706, or A 996. ASTM A 996 bars produced from rail steel shall be Type R. In buildings assigned to Seismic Design Category A, B or C, the minimum yield strength of reinforcing steel shall be 40,000 psi (Grade 40) (276 MPa). In buildings assigned to Seismic Design Category D_0, D_1 or D_2, reinforcing steel shall comply with the requirements of ASTM A 706 for low-alloy steel with a minimum yield strength of 60,000 psi (Grade 60) (414 MPa).

R404.1.2.3.7.2 Location of reinforcement in wall. The center of vertical reinforcement in *basement* walls determined from Tables R404.1.2(2) through R404.1.2(7) shall be located at the centerline of the wall. Vertical reinforcement in *basement* walls determined from Table R404.1.2(8) shall be located to provide a maximum cover of 1.25 inches (32 mm) measured from the inside face of the wall. Regardless of the table used to determine vertical wall reinforcement, the center of the steel shall not vary from the specified location by more than the greater of 10 percent of the wall thickness and $^3/_8$-inch (10 mm). Horizontal and vertical reinforcement shall be located in foundation walls to provide the minimum cover required by Section R404.1.2.3.7.4.

R404.1.2.3.7.3 Wall openings. Vertical wall reinforcement required by Section R404.1.2.2 that is interrupted by wall openings shall have additional vertical reinforcement of the same size placed within 12 inches (305 mm) of each side of the opening.

R404.1.2.3.7.4 Support and cover. Reinforcement shall be secured in the proper location in the forms with tie wire or other bar support system to prevent displacement during the concrete placement operation. Steel reinforcement in concrete cast against the earth shall have a minimum cover of 3 inches (75 mm). Minimum cover for reinforcement in concrete cast in removable forms that will be exposed to the earth or weather shall be $1^1/_2$ inches (38 mm) for No. 5 bars and smaller, and 2 inches (50 mm) for No. 6 bars and larger. For concrete cast in removable forms that will not be exposed to the earth or weather, and for concrete cast in stay-in-place forms, minimum cover shall be $^3/_4$ inch (19 mm). The minus tolerance for cover shall not exceed the smaller of one-third the required cover or $^3/_8$ inch (10 mm).

R404.1.2.3.7.5 Lap splices. Vertical and horizontal wall reinforcement shall be the longest lengths practical. Where splices are necessary in reinforcement, the length of lap splice shall be in accordance with Table R611.5.4.(1) and Figure R611.5.4(1). The maximum gap between noncontact parallel bars at a lap splice shall not exceed the smaller of one-fifth the required lap length and 6 inches (152 mm). See Figure R611.5.4(1).

R404.1.2.3.7.6 Alternate grade of reinforcement and spacing. Where tables in Section R404.1.2.2 specify vertical wall reinforcement based on minimum bar size and maximum spacing, which are based on Grade 60 (414 MPa) steel reinforcement, different size bars and/or bars made from a different grade of steel are permitted provided an equivalent area of steel per linear foot of wall is provided. Use of Table R404.1.2(9) is permitted to determine the maximum bar spacing for different bar sizes than specified in the tables and/or bars made from a different grade of steel. Bars shall not be spaced less than one-half the wall thickness, or more than 48 inches (1219 mm) on center.

R404.1.2.3.7.7 Standard hooks. Where reinforcement is required by this code to terminate with a standard hook, the hook shall comply with Section R611.5.4.5 and Figure R611.5.4(3).

R404.1.2.3.7.8 Construction joint reinforcement. Construction joints in foundation walls shall be made and located to not impair the strength of the wall. Construction joints in plain concrete walls, including walls required to have not less than No. 4 bars at 48 inches (1219 mm) on center by Sections R404.1.2.2 and R404.1.4.2, shall be located at points of lateral support, and a minimum of one No. 4 bar shall extend across the construction joint at a spacing not to exceed 24 inches (610 mm) on center. Construction joint reinforcement shall have a minimum of 12 inches (305 mm) embedment on both sides of the joint. Construction joints in reinforced concrete walls shall be located in the middle third of the span between lateral supports, or located and constructed as required for joints in plain concrete walls.

Exception: Use of vertical wall reinforcement required by this code is permitted in lieu of construction joint reinforcement provided the spacing does not exceed 24 inches (610 mm), or the combination of wall reinforcement and No.4 bars described above does not exceed 24 inches (610 mm).

R404.1.2.3.8 Exterior wall coverings. Requirements for installation of masonry veneer, stucco and other wall coverings on the exterior of concrete walls and other construction details not covered in this section shall comply with the requirements of this code.

R404.1.2.4 Requirements for Seismic Design Category C. Concrete foundation walls supporting above-grade concrete walls in townhouses assigned to Seismic Design Category C shall comply with ACI 318, ACI 332 or PCA 100 (see Section R404.1.2).

R404.1.3 Design required. Concrete or masonry foundation walls shall be designed in accordance with accepted engineering practice when either of the following conditions exists:

1. Walls are subject to hydrostatic pressure from groundwater.
2. Walls supporting more than 48 inches (1219 mm) of unbalanced backfill that do not have permanent lateral support at the top or bottom.

R404.1.4 Seismic Design Category D_0, D_1 or D_2. Deleted.

R404.1.4.1 Masonry foundation walls. Deleted.

R404.1.4.2 Concrete foundation walls. Deleted.

R404.1.5 Foundation wall thickness based on walls supported. The thickness of masonry or concrete foundation walls shall not be less than that required by Section R404.1.5.1 or R404.1.5.2, respectively.

R404.1.5.1 Masonry wall thickness. Masonry foundation walls shall not be less than the thickness of the wall supported, except that masonry foundation walls of at least 8-inch (203 mm) nominal thickness shall be permitted under brick veneered frame walls and under 10-inch-wide (254 mm) cavity walls where the total height of the wall supported, including gables, is not more than 20 feet (6096 mm), provided the requirements of Section R404.1.1 are met.

R404.1.5.2 Concrete wall thickness. The thickness of concrete foundation walls shall be equal to or greater than the thickness of the wall in the *story* above. Concrete foundation walls with corbels, brackets or other projections built into the wall for support of masonry veneer or other purposes are not within the scope of the tables in this section.

Where a concrete foundation wall is reduced in thickness to provide a shelf for the support of masonry veneer, the reduced thickness shall be equal to or greater than the thickness of the wall in the *story* above. Vertical reinforcement for the foundation wall shall be based on Table R404.1.2(8) and located in the wall as required by Section R404.1.2.3.7.2 where that table is used. Vertical reinforcement shall be based on the thickness of the thinner portion of the wall.

Exception: Where the height of the reduced thickness portion measured to the underside of the floor assembly or sill plate above is less than or equal to 24 inches (610 mm) and the reduction in thickness does not exceed 4 inches (102 mm), the vertical reinforcement is permitted to be based on the thicker portion of the wall.

R404.1.5.3 Pier and curtain walls. Curtain walls 4 inch (nominal) minimum thickness between piers and bonded into piers supported on concrete footings poured integrally with pier footings may be used for frame construction and for masonry veneer frame construction not more than 2 stories in height subject to the following limitations:

1. All load-bearing walls shall be placed on continuous concrete footings placed integrally with the exterior wall footings.
2. The minimum actual thickness of a load-bearing masonry wall shall be not less than 4 inches (102 mm) nominal or $3^3/_8$ inches (92 mm) actual thickness, and shall be bonded integrally with piers spaced in accordance with Section R606.9.
3. Piers shall be constructed in accordance with Section R606.6 and Section R606.6.1, and shall be bonded into the load-bearing masonry wall in accordance with Section R608.1.1 or Section R608.1.1.2.
4. The maximum height of a 4-inch (102 mm) load-bearing masonry foundation wall supporting wood-frame walls and floors shall not be more than 6 feet (1829 mm) in height.
5. Anchorage shall be in accordance with Section R403.1.6, Figure R404.1.5(1), or as specified by engineered design accepted by the *building official*.
6. The unbalanced fill for 4-inch (102 mm) foundation walls shall not exceed 24 inches (610 mm) for solid masonry or 16 inches (406 mm) for hollow masonry.
7. Pier size shall be based on Table 403.1(a).
8. See Chapter 45 for special anchorage and reinforcement in high wind zones.

R404.1.5.4 Piers. The unsupported height of masonry piers shall not exceed 10 times their least dimension. When structural clay tile or hollow concrete masonry units are used for isolated piers to support beams and girders, the cellular spaces shall be filled solidly with concrete or Type M or S mortar, except that unfilled hollow piers may be used if their unsupported height is not more than four times their least dimension. When hollow masonry units are solidly filled with concrete or Type M or S mortar, the allowable compressive stress may be increased as provided in Table 606.5.

R404.1.6 Height above finished grade. Concrete and masonry foundation walls shall extend above the finished *grade* adjacent to the foundation at all points a minimum of 4 inches (102 mm) where masonry veneer is used and a minimum of 6 inches (152 mm) elsewhere.

R404.1.7 Backfill placement. Backfill shall not be placed against the wall until the wall has sufficient strength and has been anchored to the floor above, or has been sufficiently braced to prevent damage by the backfill.

Exception: Bracing is not required for walls supporting less than 4 feet (1219 mm) of unbalanced backfill.

R404.1.8 Rubble stone masonry. Rubble stone masonry foundation walls shall have a minimum thickness of 16 inches (406 mm), shall not support an unbalanced backfill exceeding 8 feet (2438 mm) in height, shall not support a soil pressure greater than 30 pounds per square foot per foot (4.71 kPa/m), and shall not be constructed in Seismic Design Categories D_0, D_1, D_2 or townhouses in Seismic Design Category C, as established in Figure R301.2(2).

R404.2 Wood foundation walls. Wood foundation walls shall be constructed in accordance with the provisions of Sections R404.2.1 through R404.2.6 and with the details shown in Figures R403.1(2) and R403.1(3).

R404.2.1 Identification. All load-bearing lumber shall be identified by the grade *mark* of a lumber grading or inspection agency which has been *approved* by an accreditation body that complies with DOC PS 20. In lieu of a grade *mark*, a certificate of inspection issued by a lumber grading or inspection agency meeting the requirements of this section shall be accepted. Wood structural panels shall conform to DOC PS 1 or DOC PS 2 and shall be identified by a grade *mark* or certificate of inspection issued by an *approved agency*.

R404.2.2 Stud size. The studs used in foundation walls shall be 2-inch by 6-inch (51 mm by 152 mm) members. When spaced 16 inches (406 mm) on center, a wood species with an F_b value of not less than 1,250 pounds per square inch (8619 kPa) as listed in AF&PA/NDS shall be used. When spaced 12 inches (305 mm) on center, an F_b of not less than 875 psi (6033 kPa) shall be required.

R404.2.3 Height of backfill. For wood foundations that are not designed and installed in accordance with AF&PA PWF, the height of backfill against a foundation wall shall not exceed 4 feet (1219 mm). When the height of fill is more than 12 inches (305 mm) above the interior *grade* of a crawl space or floor of a *basement*, the thickness of the plywood sheathing shall meet the requirements of Table R404.2.3.

R404.2.4 Backfilling. Wood foundation walls shall not be backfilled until the *basement* floor and first floor have been constructed or the walls have been braced. For crawl space construction, backfill or bracing shall be installed on the interior of the walls prior to placing backfill on the exterior.

R404.2.5 Drainage and dampproofing. Wood foundation basements shall be drained and dampproofed in accordance with Sections R405 and R406, respectively.

R404.2.6 Fastening. Wood structural panel foundation wall sheathing shall be attached to framing in accordance with Table R602.3(1) and Section R402.1.1.

R404.3 Wood sill plates. Wood sill plates shall be a minimum of 2-inch by 4-inch (51 mm by 102 mm) nominal lumber. Sill plate anchorage shall be in accordance with Sections R403.1.6 and R602.11.

R404.4 Retaining walls. Retaining walls that are not laterally supported at the top and that retain in excess of 48 inches of unbalanced fill shall be designed to ensure stability against overturning, sliding, excessive foundation pressure and water uplift. In addition any retaining wall which meets the following:

1. Any retaining wall systems on a residential site that cross over adjacent property lines regardless of vertical height, and
2. Retaining walls that support buildings and their accessory structures.

Retaining walls shall be designed for a safety factor of 1.5 against lateral sliding and overturning.

404.5 Precast concrete foundation walls.

R404.5.1 Design. Precast concrete foundation walls shall be designed in accordance with accepted engineering practice. The design and manufacture of precast concrete foundation wall panels shall comply with the materials requirements of Section R402.3 or ACI 318. The panel design drawings shall be prepared by a registered design professional where required by the statutes of the *jurisdiction* in which the project is to be constructed in accordance with Section R106.1.

R404.5.2 Precast concrete foundation design drawings. Precast concrete foundation wall design drawings shall be submitted to the *building official* and *approved* prior to installation. Drawings shall include, at a minimum, the information specified below:

1. Design loading as applicable;
2. Footing design and material;
3. Concentrated loads and their points of application;
4. Soil bearing capacity;
5. Maximum allowable total uniform load;
6. Seismic design category; and
7. Basic wind speed.

R404.5.3 Identification. Precast concrete foundation wall panels shall be identified by a certificate of inspection *label* issued by an *approved* third party inspection agency.

SECTION R405
FOUNDATION DRAINAGE

R405.1 Concrete or masonry foundations. Drains shall be provided around all concrete or masonry foundations that retain earth and enclose habitable or usable spaces located below *grade*. Drainage tiles, gravel or crushed stone drains, perforated pipe or other *approved* systems or materials shall be installed at or below the area to be protected and shall discharge by gravity or mechanical means into an *approved* drainage system. Gravel or crushed stone drains shall extend at least 1 foot (305 mm) beyond the outside edge of the footing and 6 inches (152 mm) above the top of the footing and be covered with an *approved* filter membrane material. The top of open joints of drain tiles shall be protected with strips of building paper, and the drainage tiles or perforated pipe shall be placed on a minimum of 2 inches (51 mm) of washed gravel or crushed rock at least one sieve size larger than the tile joint opening or perforation and covered with not less than 6 inches (152 mm) of the same material.

Exception: A drainage system is not required when the foundation is installed on well-drained ground or sand-gravel mixture soils according to the Unified Soil Classification System, Group I Soils, as detailed in Table R405.1.

R405.1.1 Precast concrete foundation. Precast concrete walls that retain earth and enclose habitable or useable space located below-grade that rest on crushed stone footings shall have a perforated drainage pipe installed below the base of the wall on either the interior or exterior side of the wall, at least one foot (305 mm) beyond the edge of the wall. If the exterior drainage pipe is used, an *approved* filter membrane material shall cover the pipe. The drainage system shall discharge to daylight.

R405.2 Wood foundations. Wood foundations enclosing habitable or usable spaces located below *grade* shall be adequately drained in accordance with Sections R405.2.1 through R405.2.3.

R405.2.1 Base. A porous layer of gravel, crushed stone or coarse sand shall be placed to a minimum thickness of 4 inches (102 mm) under the *basement* floor. Provision shall be made for automatic draining of this layer and the gravel or crushed stone wall footings.

TABLE R405.1
PROPERTIES OF SOILS CLASSIFIED ACCORDING TO THE UNIFIED SOIL CLASSIFICATION SYSTEM

SOIL GROUP	UNIFIED SOIL CLASSIFICATION SYSTEM SYMBOL	SOIL DESCRIPTION	DRAINAGE CHARACTERISTICS[a]	FROST HEAVE POTENTIAL	VOLUME CHANGE POTENTIAL EXPANSION[b]
Group I	GW	Well-graded gravels, gravel sand mixtures, little or no fines	Good	Low	Low
	GP	Poorly graded gravels or gravel sand mixtures, little or no fines	Good	Low	Low
	SW	Well-graded sands, gravelly sands, little or no fines	Good	Low	Low
	SP	Poorly graded sands or gravelly sands, little or no fines	Good	Low	Low
	GM	Silty gravels, gravel-sand-silt mixtures	Good	Medium	Low
	SM	Silty sand, sand-silt mixtures	Good	Medium	Low
Group II	GC	Clayey gravels, gravel-sand-clay mixtures	Medium	Medium	Low
	SC	Clayey sands, sand-clay mixture	Medium	Medium	Low
	ML	Inorganic silts and very fine sands, rock flour, silty or clayey fine sands or clayey silts with slight plasticity	Medium	High	Low
	CL	Inorganic clays of low to medium plasticity, gravelly clays, sandy clays, silty clays, lean clays	Medium	Medium	Medium to Low
Group III	CH	Inorganic clays of high plasticity, fat clays	Poor	Medium	High
	MH	Inorganic silts, micaceous or diatomaceous fine sandy or silty soils, elastic silts	Poor	High	High
Group IV	OL	Organic silts and organic silty clays of low plasticity	Poor	Medium	Medium
	OH	Organic clays of medium to high plasticity, organic silts	Unsatisfactory	Medium	High
	Pt	Peat and other highly organic soils	Unsatisfactory	Medium	High

For SI: 1 inch = 25.4 mm.

a. The percolation rate for good drainage is over 4 inches per hour, medium drainage is 2 inches to 4 inches per hour, and poor is less than 2 inches per hour.

b. Soils with a low potential expansion typically have a plasticity index (PI) of 0 to 15, soils with a medium potential expansion have a PI of 10 to 35 and soils with a high potential expansion have a PI greater than 20.

R405.2.2 Vapor retarder. A 6-mil-thick (0.15 mm) polyethylene vapor retarder shall be applied over the porous layer with the *basement* floor constructed over the polyethylene.

R405.2.3 Drainage system. In other than Group I soils, a sump shall be provided to drain the porous layer and footings. The sump shall be at least 24 inches (610 mm) in diameter or 20 inches square (0.0129 m^2), shall extend at least 24 inches (610 mm) below the bottom of the *basement* floor and shall be capable of positive gravity or mechanical drainage to remove any accumulated water. The drainage system shall discharge to daylight.

SECTION R406 FOUNDATION WATERPROOFING AND DAMPPROOFING

R406.1 Concrete and masonry foundation dampproofing. Foundation walls where the outside grade is higher than the inside grade shall be dampproofed from the top of the footing to the finished grade. The foundation walls shall be dampproofed with a bituminous coating, 3 pounds per square yard (1.63 kg/m) of acrylic modified cement, or $^1/_8$-inch (3.2 mm) coat of surface bonding mortar complying with ASTM C 887 or any material permitted for waterproofing in Section R406.2. Concrete walls shall be dampproofed by applying any one of the above listed dampproofing materials or any one of the waterproofing materials listed in Section R406.2 to the exterior of the wall.

R406.2 Concrete and masonry foundation waterproofing. In areas where a high water table or other severe soil-water conditions are known to exist, exterior foundation walls that retain earth and enclose interior spaces and floors below *grade* shall be waterproofed from the top of the footing to the finished *grade*. Walls shall be waterproofed in accordance with one of the following:

1. Two-ply hot-mopped felts.
2. Fifty five pound (25 kg) roll roofing.
3. Six-mil (0.15 mm) polyvinyl chloride.
4. Six-mil (0.15 mm) polyethylene.
5. Forty-mil (1 mm) polymer-modified asphalt.
6. Sixty-mil (1.5 mm) flexible polymer cement.
7. One-eighth inch (3 mm) cement-based, fiber-reinforced, waterproof coating.
8. Sixty-mil (0.22 mm) solvent-free liquid-applied synthetic rubber.

Exception: Organic-solvent-based products such as hydrocarbons, chlorinated hydrocarbons, ketones and esters shall not be used for ICF walls with expanded polystyrene form material. Use of plastic roofing cements, acrylic coatings, latex coatings, mortars and pargings to seal ICF walls is permitted. Cold-setting asphalt or hot asphalt shall conform to type C of ASTM D 449. Hot asphalt shall be applied at a temperature of less than 200°F (93°C).

All joints in membrane waterproofing shall be lapped and sealed with an adhesive compatible with the membrane.

R406.3 Dampproofing for wood foundations. Wood foundations enclosing habitable or usable spaces located below *grade* shall be dampproofed in accordance with Sections R406.3.1 through R406.3.4.

R406.3.1 Panel joint sealed. Plywood panel joints in the foundation walls shall be sealed full length with a caulking compound capable of producing a moisture-proof seal under the conditions of temperature and moisture content at which it will be applied and used.

R406.3.2 Below-grade moisture barrier. A 6-mil-thick (0.15 mm) polyethylene film shall be applied over the below-grade portion of exterior foundation walls prior to backfilling. Joints in the polyethylene film shall be lapped 6 inches (152 mm) and sealed with adhesive. The top edge of the polyethylene film shall be bonded to the sheathing to form a seal. Film areas at *grade* level shall be protected from mechanical damage and exposure by a pressure preservatively treated lumber or plywood strip attached to the wall several inches above finish *grade* level and extending approximately 9 inches (229 mm) below *grade*. The joint between the strip and the wall shall be caulked full length prior to fastening the strip to the wall. Other coverings appropriate to the architectural treatment may also be used. The polyethylene film shall extend down to the bottom of the wood footing plate but shall not overlap or extend into the gravel or crushed stone footing.

R406.3.3 Porous fill. The space between the excavation and the foundation wall shall be backfilled with the same material used for footings, up to a height of 1 foot (305 mm) above the footing for well-drained sites, or one-half the total back-fill height for poorly drained sites. The porous fill shall be covered with strips of 30-pound (13.6 kg) asphalt paper or 6-mil (0.15 mm) polyethylene to permit water seepage while avoiding infiltration of fine soils.

R406.3.4 Backfill. The remainder of the excavated area shall be backfilled with the same type of soil as was removed during the excavation.

R406.4 Precast concrete foundation system dampproofing. Except where required by Section R406.2 to be waterproofed, precast concrete foundation walls enclosing habitable or useable spaces located below *grade* shall be dampproofed in accordance with Section R406.1.

R406.4.1 Panel joints sealed. Precast concrete foundation panel joints shall be sealed full height with a sealant meeting ASTM C 920, Type S or M, *Grade* NS, Class 25, Use NT, M or A. Joint sealant shall be installed in accordance with the manufacturer's installation instructions.

SECTION R407 COLUMNS

R407.1 Wood column protection. Wood columns shall be protected against decay as set forth in Section R317.

R407.2 Steel column protection. All surfaces (inside and outside) of steel columns shall be given a shop coat of

Foundation Ventilation

rust-inhibitive paint, except for corrosion-resistant steel and steel treated with coatings to provide corrosion resistance.

R407.3 Structural requirements. The columns shall be restrained to prevent lateral displacement at the top and bottom ends. Wood columns shall not be less in nominal size than 4 inches by 4 inches (102 mm by 102 mm). Steel columns shall not be less than 3-inch-diameter (76 mm) Schedule 40 pipe manufactured in accordance with ASTM A 53 Grade B or *approved* equivalent.

> **Exception:** In Seismic Design Categories A, B and C, columns no more than 48 inches (1219 mm) in height on a pier or footing are exempt from the bottom end lateral displacement requirement within under-floor areas enclosed by a continuous foundation.

SECTION R408
WALL-VENTED CRAWL SPACES

R408.1 Space moisture vapor control. Vented crawl space foundations shall be provided with foundation vent openings through the exterior foundation walls.

R408.1.1 Foundation vent sizing. The minimum net area of ventilation openings shall be not less than 1 square foot (0.0929 m²) for each 150 square feet (13.9 m²) of crawl space ground area.

> **Exception:** The total area of ventilation openings may be reduced to $^1/_{1,500}$ of the under-floor area where the ground surface is treated with an approved vapor retarder material in accordance with Section R408.2 and the required openings are placed so as to provide cross-ventilation of the crawl space. The installation of operable louvers shall not be prohibited.

R408.1.2 Foundation vent location. One foundation vent shall be within 3 feet (914 mm) of each corner of the building. To prevent rainwater entry when the crawlspace is built on a sloped site, the uphill foundation walls may be constructed without wall vent openings. Vent dams shall be provided when the bottom of the foundation vent opening is less than 4 inches above the finished exterior grade.

R408.1.3 Covering material. To prevent rodent entry, foundation vents shall be covered with any of the following materials provided that the ventilation holes through the covering material shall not exceed $^1/_4$ inch (6.4 mm) in any direction:

1. Perforated sheet metal plates not less than 0.070 inch (1.8 mm) thick.
2. Expanded sheet metal plates no less than 0.047 inch (1.2 mm) thick.
3. Cast iron grills or grating.
4. Extruded load-bearing brick vents.
5. Hardware cloth of 0.035 inch (0.89 mm) wire or heavier.
6. Corrosion-resistant mesh, with the least dimension being $^1/_8$ inch (3.2 mm).

R408.1.4 Drains and vent terminations. Drains (including but not limited to pressure relief and drain pans) shall terminate outdoors, to crawl space floor drains or interior pumps, and shall not intentionally discharge water into the crawl space. Crawl space drains shall be separate from roof gutter drain systems and foundation perimeter drains. Dryer vents shall terminate outdoors.

R408.1.5 Space separation. Wall vented crawl spaces shall be separated from adjoining basements, porches and garages by permanent solid wall surfaces with all utility penetrations thru the separating wall sealed. Latched, weather-stripped doors or access panels shall provide access between the crawl space and such adjoining spaces.

R408.2 Ground vapor retarder. A minimum 6-mil (0.15 mm) polyethylene vapor retarder or equivalent shall be installed to nominally cover all exposed earth in the crawl space, with joints lapped not less than 12 inches. Where there is no evidence that the groundwater table can rise to within 6 inches (152 mm) of the floor of the crawl space, it is acceptable to puncture the ground vapor retarder at low spots to prevent water puddles from forming on top of the vapor retarder due to condensation. Install a drain to daylight or sump pump at each low spot. Crawl space drains shall be kept separate from roof gutter drain systems and foundation perimeter drains.

R408.3 Wall damp proofing. Where the outside grade is higher than the inside grade the exterior walls shall be dampproofed from the top of the footing to the finished grade as required by Section R406.1.

R408.4 Site grading. Building site shall be graded to drain water away from the crawl space foundation per the requirements of Section R401.3.

R408.5 Insulation. The thermal insulation in a wall vented crawl space shall be placed in the floor system. Wall insulation is not allowed as the only insulation system in a wall vented crawl space. The required insulation value can be determined from Table N1102.1.

R408.6 Floor air leakage control. All plumbing, electrical, duct, plenum, phone, cable, computer wiring and other penetrations through the subfloor shall be sealed with non-porous materials, caulks, or sealants. The use of rockwool or fiberglass insulation is prohibited as an air sealant.

R408.7 Duct air leakage control. All heating and cooling ductwork located in the crawl space shall be sealed with mastic or other industry approved duct closure systems.

R408.8 Access. A minimum access opening measuring 18 inches by 24 inches (457 mm by 610 mm) shall be provided to the crawl space. See the North Carolina Mechanical Code for access requirements where mechanical equipment is located under floors.

R408.9 Removal of debris. The crawl space floor shall be cleaned of all vegetation and organic material. All wood forms used for placing shall be removed before the building is occupied or used for any purpose. All construction materials shall be removed before the building is occupied or used for any purpose.

R408.10 Finished grade. The finished grade of the crawl space may be located at the bottom of the footings; however, where there is evidence that the groundwater table can rise to within 6 inches (152 mm) of the finished grade of the crawl space at the perimeter or where there is evidence that the surface water does not readily drain from the building site, the grade in the crawl space shall be as high as the outside finished grade, unless an approved drainage system is provided.

R408.11 Flood resistance. For buildings located in areas prone to flooding as established in Table R301.2 (1), the walls enclosing the crawl space shall be provided with flood openings in accordance with Section R323.2.2.

SECTION R409 CLOSED CRAWL SPACES

R409.1 Air sealed walls. Closed crawl spaces shall be built to minimize the entry of outdoor air into the crawl space. Specifically prohibited are foundation wall vents and wall openings to ventilated porch foundations. When outdoor packaged heating and cooling equipment is used, solid blocking and sealants shall be used to seal gaps between the exterior wall opening and the smaller supply and return ducts that pass through the opening.

R409.1.1 Caulking and sealants. Air sealing caulk, gaskets or sealants shall be applied to the foundation wall and floor assemblies that separate the crawl space from outside and other ventilated areas such as joints around access door and frame, between foundation and sill plate, at penetrations for plumbing, mechanical, electrical and gas lines and at duct penetrations.

R409.1.2 Access panel/door. A minimum access opening measuring 18 inches by 24 inches (457 mm by 610 mm) shall be provided to the crawl space. See the North Carolina Mechanical Code for access requirements where mechanical equipment is located under floors. To minimize air entry, provide a tight fitting access panel/door with a latch mechanism. Access panels or doors shall be insulated to a minimum of R-2.

R409.2 Groundwater vapor retarder. Closed crawl spaces shall be protected from water entry by the evaporation of water from the ground surface.

R409.2.1 Ground vapor retarder. A minimum 6-mil (0.15 mm) polyethylene vapor retarder or equivalent shall be installed to nominally cover all exposed earth in the crawl space, with joints lapped not less than 12 inches. Minor pockets or wrinkles that prevent total drainage across the surface of the vapor retarder are allowed. The floor of the crawl space shall be graded so that it drains to one or more low spots. Install a drain to daylight or sump pump at each low spot. Crawl space drains shall be kept separate from roof gutter drain systems and foundation perimeter drains.

R409.2.2 Liner. The ground vapor retarder may be installed as a full interior liner by sealing the edges to the walls and beam columns and sealing the seams. Single piece liner systems are approved. The top edge of the wall liner shall terminate 3 inches below the top edge of the masonry foundation wall. The top edge of the liner shall be brought up the interior columns a minimum of 4 inches above the crawl space floor. The floor of the crawl space shall be graded so that it drains to one or more low spots. Install a drain to daylight or sump pump at each low spot. Crawl space drains shall be separate from roof gutter drain systems and foundation perimeter drains.

R409.2.2.1 Wall liner termite inspection gap. Provide a clear and unobstructed 3 inch minimum inspection gap between the top of the wall liner and the bottom of the wood sill. This inspection gap may be ignored with regards to energy performance and is not intended to create an energy penalty.

R409.2.3 Concrete floor surfacing. The ground vapor retarder may be protected against ripping and displacement by pouring an unreinforced, minimum 2-inch thick, concrete surface directly over the vapor barrier. A base course of gravel or other drainage material under the ground moisture barrier is not required. The floor of the crawl space shall be graded so that the concrete surface drains to one or more low spots. Install a drain to daylight or sump pump at each low spot. Crawl space drains shall be separate from roof gutter drain systems and foundation perimeter drains.

R409.2.4 Drains and vent terminations. Drains (including but not limited to pressure relief and drain pans) shall terminate outdoors, to crawl space floor drains or interior pumps, and shall not intentionally discharge water into the crawl space. Crawl space drains shall be separate from roof gutter drain systems and foundation perimeter drains. Dryer vents shall terminate outdoors.

R409.3 Wall damp proofing. Where the outside grade is higher than the inside grade, the exterior walls shall be dampproofed from the top of the footing to the finished grade as required by Section R406.1.

R409.4 Site grading. Building site shall be graded to drain water away from the crawl space foundation per the requirements of Section R401.3.

R409.5 Space moisture vapor control. Closed crawl spaces shall be provided with a mechanical drying capability to control space moisture levels. The allowed methods are listed below in Sections R409.5.1 through R409.5.5. At least one method shall be provided; however, combination systems shall be allowed.

R409.5.1 Dehumidifier. A permanently installed dehumidifier shall be provided in the crawl space. The minimum rated capacity per day is 15 pints (7.1 Liters). Condensate discharge shall be drained to daylight or interior condensate pump. Permanently installed dehumidifier shall be provided with an electrical outlet.

R409.5.2 Supply air. Supply air from the dwelling air conditioning system shall be ducted into the crawl space at the rate of 1 cubic foot per minute (0.5 L/s) per 30 square feet (4.6 m^2) of crawl space floor area. No return air duct from the crawl space to the dwelling air conditioning system is allowed. The crawl space supply air duct shall be fitted with a backflow damper to prevent the entry of crawl space air into the supply duct system when the system fan is not operating. An air relief vent to the outdoors may be installed.

Crawl spaces with moisture vapor control installed in accordance with this section are not considered plenums.

R409.5.3 House air. House air shall be blown into the crawl space with a fan at the rate of 1 cubic foot per minute (0.5 L/s) per 50 square feet (4.6 m^2) of crawl space floor area. The fan motor shall be rated for continuous duty. No return air duct from the crawl space to the dwelling air conditioning system is allowed. An air relief vent to the outdoors may be installed. Crawl spaces with moisture vapor control installed in accordance with this section are not considered plenums.

R409.5.4 Exhaust fan. Crawl space air shall be exhausted to outside with a fan at the rate of 1 cubic foot per minute (0.5 L/s) per 50 square feet (4.6 m^2) of crawl space floor area. The fan motor shall be rated for continuous duty. There is no requirement for make-up air.

R409.6 Plenums. Closed crawl spaces used as supply or return plenums for distribution of heated or cooled air shall comply with the requirements of the *North Carolina Mechanical Code*. Crawl space plenums shall not contain plumbing cleanouts, gas lines or other prohibited components. Foam plastic insulation located in a crawl space plenum shall be protected against ignition by an approved thermal barrier.

R409.7 Combustion air. The air sealing requirements of a closed crawl space may result in a foundation which can not provide adequate combustion air for fuel-burning appliances; therefore, fuel-burning appliances located in the crawl space such as furnaces and water heaters shall obtain combustion air from outdoors as per the *North Carolina Mechanical Code*.

R409.8 Insulation. The thermal insulation in a crawl space may be located in the floor system or at the exterior walls. The required insulation value can be determined from Table N1102.1.

Exception: Insulation shall be placed at the walls when the following condition exists:

1. The closed crawl space is designed to be intentionally heated or cooled, conditioned space.

R409.8.1 Wall insulation. Where the floor above a crawl space is not insulated, the walls shall be insulated. Wall insulation can be located on any combination of the exterior and interior surfaces and within the structural cavities or materials of the exterior crawl space walls. Wall insulation systems require that the band joist area of the floor frame be insulated. Wall insulation shall begin 3 inches below the top of the masonry foundation wall and shall extend down to 3 inches above the top of the footing or concrete floor, 3 inches above the interior ground surface or 24-inches below the outside finished ground level, whichever is less. No insulation shall be required on masonry walls of 9 inches height or less.

R409.8.1.1 Foam plastic termite inspection gap. For outside walls Section R324 governs applications. When expanded polystyrene, polyisocyanurate, or other foam plastic insulation is installed on the inside surface of the exterior foundation walls, provisions in Sections R409.8.1.1.1 through R409.8.1.1.2 below apply.

R409.8.1.1.1 Earth floored crawl spaces. Provide a clear and unobstructed 3-inch minimum termite inspection gap between the top of the foam plastic wall insulation and the bottom of the wood sill. Because insulation ground contact is not allowed, provide a continuous 3-inch minimum clearance gap between the bottom edge of the foam plastic wall insulation and the earth floor surface. Refer to Section N1102.1.7 to determine maximum allowances for insulation gaps.

R409.8.1.1.2 Concrete floor surfaced crawl spaces. Provide a clear and unobstructed 3-inch minimum termite inspection gap between the top of the foam plastic wall insulation and the bottom of the wood sill. Provide a continuous 3-inch minimum clearance gap between the bottom edge of the foam plastic wall insulation and the earth floor surface. Refer to Section N1102.1.7 to determine maximum allowances for insulation gaps.

R409.8.1.2 Porous insulation material. When fiberglass, rockwool, cellulose or other porous insulation materials are installed on the inside wall surface of a closed crawl space, provide a clear and unobstructed 3-inch minimum termite inspection gap between the top of the porous wall insulation and the bottom of the wood sill.

To reduce wicking potential, porous insulation ground contact is not allowed in earth floored or concrete surfaces crawl spaces. Provide a continuous 3-inch minimum wicking gap between the bottom edge of the porous wall insulation and the earth or concrete floor surface. Refer to Section N1102.1.7 to determine maximum allowances for insulation gaps.

R409.8.2 Foam plastic fire safety. Foam plastic insulation may be intalled inside crawl spaces without a thermal cover when the insulation product has been tested in accordance with ASTM E 84 to have a flame-spread rating of not more than 25 and a smoke developed rating of not more than 450. Foam plastics that have not been tested to meet these ratings shall be protected against ignition by covering them with a thermal barrier. Acceptable thermal barriers include but are not limited to $^1/_2$ inch cement board, metal foil sheets, metal foil tape, steel or aluminum metal sheets or other approved materials installed in such a manner that the foam is not exposed.

Exception: Foam plastic insulation located in closed crawl spaces used as conditioned spaces or plenums shall be protected against ignition by an approved thermal barrier.

R409.9 Floor air leakage control. All plumbing, electrical, duct, plenum, phone, cable, computer wiring and other penetrations through the subfloor shall be sealed with non-porous materials, caulks, or sealants. The use of rockwool or fiberglass insulation is prohibited as an air sealant.

R409.10 Duct air leakage control. All heating and cooling ductwork located in the crawl space shall be sealed with mastic or other industry approved duct closure systems.

R409.11 Access. A minimum access opening measuring 18 inches by 24 inches (457 mm by 610 mm) shall be provided to the crawl space. See the North Carolina Mechanical Code for access requirements where mechanical equipment is located under floors.

R409.12 Removal of debris. The crawl space floor shall be cleaned of all vegetation and organic material. All wood forms used for placing shall be removed before the building is occupied or used for any purpose. All construction materials shall be removed before the building is occupied or used for any purpose.

R409.13 Finished grade. The finished grade of the crawl space may be located at the bottom of the footings; however, where there is evidence that the groundwater table can rise to within 6 inches (152 mm) of the finished grade of the crawl space at the perimeter or where there is evidence that the surface water does not readily drain from the building site, the grade in the crawl space shall be as high as the outside finished grade, unless an approved drainage system is provided.

CHAPTER 5
FLOORS

SECTION R501 GENERAL

R501.1 Application. The provisions of this chapter shall control the design and construction of the floors for all buildings including the floors of *attic* spaces used to house mechanical or plumbing fixtures and *equipment*.

R501.2 Requirements. Floor construction shall be capable of accommodating all loads according to Section R301 and of transmitting the resulting loads to the supporting structural elements.

SECTION R502 WOOD FLOOR FRAMING

R502.1 Identification. Load-bearing dimension lumber for joists, beams and girders shall be identified by a grade *mark* of a lumber grading or inspection agency that has been *approved* by an accreditation body that complies with DOC PS 20. In lieu of a grade *mark*, a certificate of inspection issued by a lumber grading or inspection agency meeting the requirements of this section shall be accepted.

R502.1.1 Preservative-treated lumber. Preservative treated dimension lumber shall also be identified as required by Section R319.1.

R502.1.2 Blocking and subflooring. Blocking shall be a minimum of utility grade lumber. Subflooring may be a minimum of utility grade lumber or No. 4 common grade boards.

R502.1.3 End-jointed lumber. *Approved* end-jointed lumber identified by a grade *mark* conforming to Section R502.1 may be used interchangeably with solid-sawn members of the same species and grade.

R502.1.4 Prefabricated wood I-joists. Structural capacities and design provisions for prefabricated wood I-joists shall be established and monitored in accordance with ASTM D 5055.

R502.1.5 Structural glued laminated timbers. Glued laminated timbers shall be manufactured and identified as required in ANSI/AITC A190.1 and ASTM D 3737.

R502.1.6 Structural log members. Stress grading of structural log members of nonrectangular shape, as typically used in log buildings, shall be in accordance with ASTM D 3957. Such structural log members shall be identified by the grade *mark* of an *approved* lumber grading or inspection agency. In lieu of a grade *mark* on the material, a certificate of inspection as to species and grade issued by a lumber-grading or inspection agency meeting the requirements of this section shall be permitted to be accepted.

R502.1.7 Exterior wood/plastic composite deck boards. Wood/plastic composites used in exterior deck boards shall comply with the provisions of Section R317.4.

R502.2 Design and construction. Floors shall be designed and constructed in accordance with the provisions of this chapter, Figure R502.2 and Sections R317 and R318 or in accordance with AF&PA/NDS.

R502.2.1 Framing at braced wall lines. A load path for lateral forces shall be provided between floor framing and *braced wall panels* located above or below a floor, as specified in Section R602.10.6.

R502.2.2 Decks. Where supported by attachment to an exterior wall, decks shall be positively anchored to the primary structure and designed for both vertical and lateral loads as applicable. Such attachment shall not be accomplished by the use of toenails or nails subject to withdrawal. Where positive connection to the primary building structure cannot be verified during inspection, decks shall be self-supporting. For decks with cantilevered framing members, connections to exterior walls or other framing members, shall be designed and constructed to resist uplift resulting from the full live load specified in Table R301.5 acting on the cantilevered portion of the deck. Exterior decks shall be permitted to be constructed in accordance with Appendix M.

R502.2.2.1 Deck ledger connection to band joist. Deleted.

R502.2.2.1.1 Placement of lag screws or bolts in deck ledgers. Deleted.

R502.2.2.2 Alternate deck ledger connections. Deleted.

R502.2.2.3 Deck lateral load connection. Deleted.

R502.2.2.4 Exterior wood/plastic composite deck boards. Deleted.

R502.3 Allowable joist spans. Spans for floor joists shall be in accordance with Tables R502.3.1(1) and R502.3.1(2). For other grades and species and for other loading conditions, refer to the AF&PA Span Tables for Joists and Rafters.

R502.3.1 Sleeping areas and attic joists. Table R502.3.1(1) shall be used to determine the maximum allowable span of floor joists that support sleeping areas and *attics* that are accessed by means of a fixed stairway in accordance with Section R311.7 provided that the design live load does not exceed 30 pounds per square foot (1.44 kPa) and the design dead load does not exceed 20 pounds per square foot (0.96 kPa). The allowable span of ceiling joists that support *attics* used for limited storage or no storage shall be determined in accordance with Section R802.4.

R502.3.2 Other floor joists. Table R502.3.1(2) shall be used to determine the maximum allowable span of floor joists that support all other areas of the building, other than sleeping rooms and *attics*, provided that the design live load does not exceed 40 pounds per square foot (1.92 kPa) and the design dead load does not exceed 20 pounds per square foot (0.96 kPa).

Floors

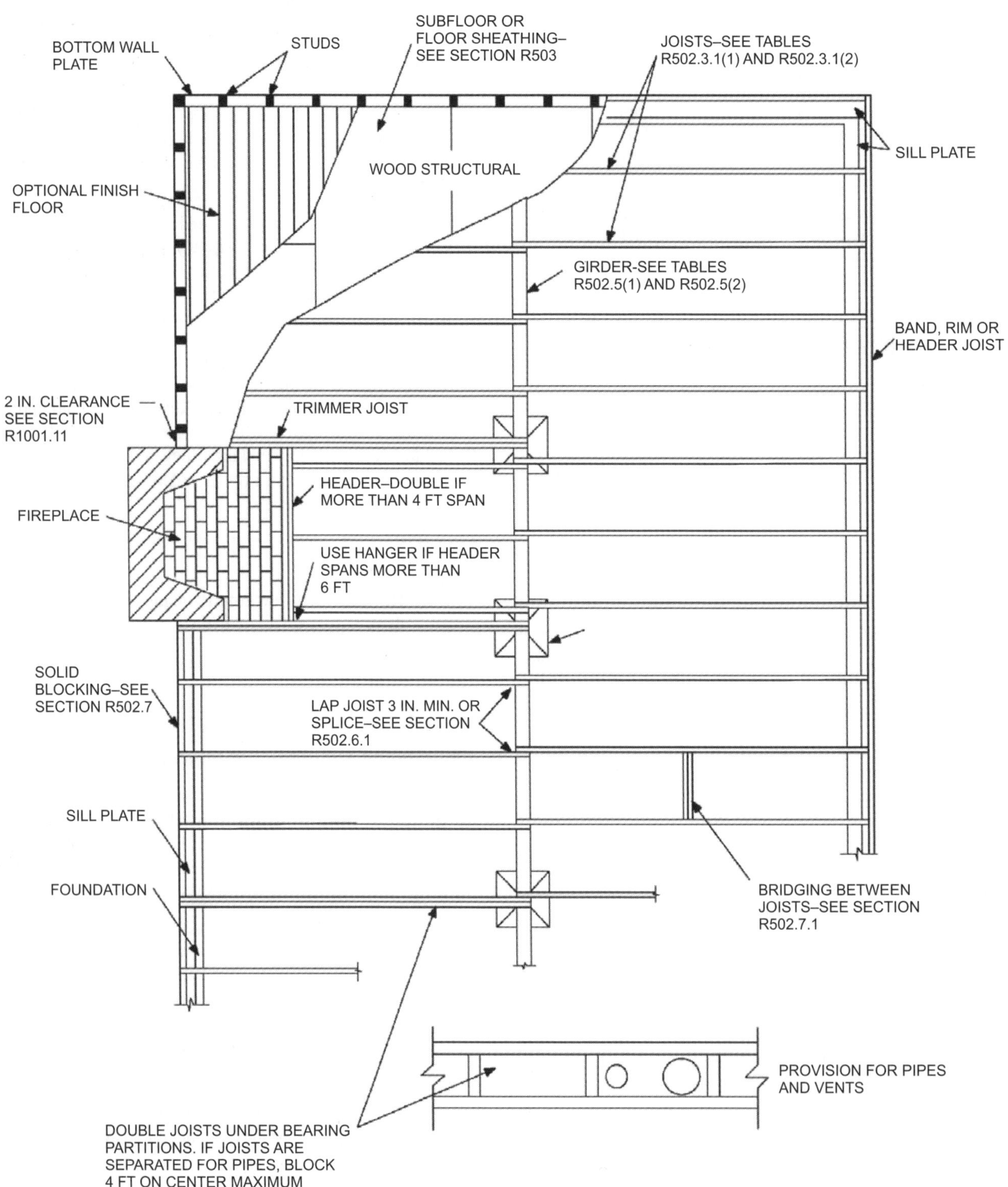

For SI: 1 inch = 25.4 mm, 1 foot = 304.8 mm.

FIGURE R502.2
FLOOR CONSTRUCTION

R502.3.3 Floor cantilevers. Floor cantilever spans shall not exceed the nominal depth of the wood floor joist. Floor cantilevers constructed in accordance with Table R502.3.3(1) shall be permitted when supporting a light-frame bearing wall and roof only. Floor cantilevers supporting an exterior balcony are permitted to be constructed in accordance with Table R502.3.3(2).

R502.4 Joists under bearing partitions. Joists under parallel bearing partitions shall be of adequate size to support the load. Double joists, sized to adequately support the load, that are separated to permit the installation of piping or vents shall be full depth solid blocked with lumber not less than 2 inches (51 mm) in nominal thickness spaced not more than 4 feet (1219 mm) on center. Bearing partitions perpendicular to joists shall not be offset from supporting girders, walls or partitions more than the joist depth unless such joists are of sufficient size to carry the additional load.

R502.5 Allowable girder spans. The allowable spans of girders fabricated of dimension lumber shall not exceed the values set forth in Tables R502.5(1) and R502.5(2).

R502.6 Bearing. The ends of each joist, beam or girder shall have not less than 1.5 inches (38 mm) of bearing on wood or metal and not less than 3 inches (76 mm) on masonry or concrete except where supported on a 1-inch-by-4-inch (25.4 mm by 102 mm) ribbon strip and nailed to the adjacent stud or by the use of *approved* joist hangers.

R502.6.1 Floor systems. Joists framing from opposite sides over a bearing support shall lap a minimum of 3 inches (76 mm) and shall be nailed together with a minimum three 10d face nails. A wood or metal splice with strength equal to or greater than that provided by the nailed lap is permitted.

R502.6.2 Joist framing. Joists framing into the side of a wood girder shall be supported by *approved* framing anchors or on ledger strips not less than nominal 2 inches by 2 inches (51 mm by 51 mm).

R502.7 Lateral restraint at supports. Joists shall be supported laterally at the ends by full-depth solid blocking not less than 2 inches (51 mm) nominal in thickness; or by attachment to a full-depth header, band or rim joist, or to an adjoining stud or shall be otherwise provided with lateral support to prevent rotation.

Exceptions:

1. Trusses, structural composite lumber, structural glued-laminated members and I-joists shall be supported laterally as required by the manufacturer's recommendations.
2. In Seismic Design Categories D_0, D_1 and D_2, lateral restraint shall also be provided at each intermediate support.

R502.7.1 Bridging. Joists exceeding a nominal 2 inches by 12 inches (51 mm by 305 mm) shall be supported laterally by solid blocking, diagonal bridging (wood or metal), or a continuous 1-inch-by-3-inch (25.4 mm by 76 mm) strip nailed across the bottom of joists perpendicular to joists at intervals not exceeding 8 feet (2438 mm).

Exception: Trusses, structural composite lumber, structural glued-laminated members and I-joists shall be supported laterally as required by the manufacturer's recommendations.

R502.8 Drilling and notching. Structural floor members shall not be cut, bored or notched in excess of the limitations specified in this section. See Figure R502.8.

R502.8.1 Sawn lumber. Notches in solid lumber joists, rafters and beams shall not exceed one-sixth of the depth of the member, shall not be longer than one-third of the depth of the member and shall not be located in the middle one-third of the span. Notches at the ends of the member shall not exceed one-fourth the depth of the member. The tension side of members 4 inches (102 mm) or greater in nominal thickness shall not be notched except at the ends of the members. The diameter of holes bored or cut into members shall not exceed one-third the depth of the member. Holes shall not be closer than 2 inches (51 mm) to the top or bottom of the member, or to any other hole located in the member. Where the member is also notched, the hole shall not be closer than 2 inches (51 mm) to the notch.

R502.8.2 Engineered wood products. Cuts, notches and holes bored in trusses, structural composite lumber, structural glue-laminated members or I-joists are prohibited except where permitted by the manufacturer's recommendations or where the effects of such alterations are specifically considered in the design of the member by a *registered design professional*.

R502.9 Fastening. Floor framing shall be nailed in accordance with Table R602.3(1). Where posts and beam or girder construction is used to support floor framing, positive connections shall be provided to ensure against uplift and lateral displacement.

R502.10 Framing of openings. Openings in floor framing shall be framed with a header and trimmer joists. When the header joist span does not exceed 4 feet (1219 mm), the header joist may be a single member the same size as the floor joist. Single trimmer joists may be used to carry a single header joist that is located within 3 feet (914 mm) of the trimmer joist bearing. When the header joist span exceeds 4 feet (1219 mm), the trimmer joists and the header joist shall be doubled and of sufficient cross section to support the floor joists framing into the header. *Approved* hangers shall be used for the header joist to trimmer joist connections when the header joist span exceeds 6 feet (1829 mm). Tail joists over 12 feet (3658 mm) long shall be supported at the header by framing anchors or on ledger strips not less than 2 inches by 2 inches (51 mm by 51 mm).

R502.11 Wood trusses.

R502.11.1 Design. Wood trusses shall be designed in accordance with *approved* engineering practice. The design and manufacture of metal plate connected wood trusses shall comply with ANSI/TPI 1. The truss design drawings shall be prepared by a registered professional where required by the statutes of the *jurisdiction* in which the project is to be constructed in accordance with Section R106.1.

R502.11.2 Bracing. Trusses shall be braced to prevent rotation and provide lateral stability in accordance with the requirements specified in the *construction documents* for the building and on the individual truss design drawings. In the absence of specific bracing requirements, trusses shall be braced in accordance with the Building Component Safety Information (BCSI 1-03) Guide to Good Practice for Handling, Installing & Bracing of Metal Plate Connected Wood Trusses.

R502.11.3 Alterations to trusses. Truss members and components shall not be cut, notched, spliced or otherwise altered in any way without the approval of a registered *design professional. Alterations* resulting in the addition of load (e.g., HVAC *equipment*, water heater, etc.), that exceed the design load for the truss, shall not be permitted without verification that the truss is capable of supporting the additional loading.

R502.11.4 Truss design drawings. Truss design drawings, prepared in compliance with Section R502.11.1, shall be submitted to the *building official* and *approved* prior to installation. Truss design drawings shall be provided with the shipment of trusses delivered to the job site. Truss design drawings shall include, at a minimum, the information specified below:

1. Slope or depth, span and spacing.
2. Location of all joints.
3. Required bearing widths.
4. Design loads as applicable:
   - 4.1. Top chord live load;
   - 4.2. Top chord dead load;
   - 4.3. Bottom chord live load;
   - 4.4. Bottom chord dead load;
   - 4.5. Concentrated loads and their points of application; and
   - 4.6. Controlling wind and earthquake loads.
5. Adjustments to lumber and joint connector design values for conditions of use.
6. Each reaction force and direction.
7. Joint connector type and description, e.g., size, thickness or gauge, and the dimensioned location of each joint connector except where symmetrically located relative to the joint interface.
8. Lumber size, species and grade for each member.
9. Connection requirements for:
   - 9.1. Truss-to-girder-truss;
   - 9.2. Truss ply-to-ply; and
   - 9.3. Field splices.
10. Calculated deflection ratio and/or maximum description for live and total load.
11. Maximum axial compression forces in the truss members to enable the building designer to design the size, connections and anchorage of the permanent continuous lateral bracing. Forces shall be shown on the truss drawing or on supplemental documents.
12. Required permanent truss member bracing location.

R502.12 Draftstopping required. Draftstopping shall be provided in accordance with Section R302.12.

R502.13 Fireblocking required. Fireblocking shall be provided in accordance with Section R302.11.

SECTION R503
FLOOR SHEATHING

R503.1 Lumber sheathing. Maximum allowable spans for lumber used as floor sheathing shall conform to Tables R503.1, R503.2.1.1(1) and R503.2.1.1(2).

R503.1.1 End joints. End joints in lumber used as subflooring shall occur over supports unless end-matched lumber is used, in which case each piece shall bear on at least two joists. Subflooring may be omitted when joist spacing does not exceed 16 inches (406 mm) and a 1-inch (25.4 mm) nominal tongue-and-groove wood strip flooring is applied perpendicular to the joists.

TABLE R503.1
MINIMUM THICKNESS OF LUMBER FLOOR SHEATHING

JOIST OR BEAM SPACING (inches)	MINIMUM NET THICKNESS	
	Perpendicular to joist	Diagonal to joist
24	$^{11}/_{16}$	$^{3}/_{4}$
16	$^{5}/_{8}$	$^{5}/_{8}$
48[a]	$1^{1}/_{2}$ T & G	N/A
54[b]		
60[c]		

For SI: 1 inch = 25.4 mm, 1 pound per square inch = 6.895 kPa.

a. For this support spacing, lumber sheathing shall have a minimum F_b of 675 and minimum E of 1,100,000 (see AF&PA/NDS).

b. For this support spacing, lumber sheathing shall have a minimum F_b of 765 and minimum E of 1,400,000 (see AF&PA/NDS).

c. For this support spacing, lumber sheathing shall have a minimum F_b of 855 and minimum E of 1,700,000 (see AF&PA/NDS).

R503.2 Wood structural panel sheathing.

R503.2.1 Identification and grade. Wood structural panel sheathing used for structural purposes shall conform to DOC PS 1, DOC PS 2 or, when manufactured in Canada, CSA O437 or CSA O325. All panels shall be identified by a grade *mark* of certificate or inspection issued by an *approved agency.*

R503.2.1.1 Subfloor and combined subfloor underlayment. Where used as subflooring or combination subfloor underlayment, wood structural panels shall be of one of the grades specified in Table R503.2.1.1(1). When sanded plywood is used as combination subfloor underlayment, the grade shall be as specified in Table R503.2.1.1(2).

TABLE R502.3.1(1)
FLOOR JOIST SPANS FOR COMMON LUMBER SPECIES
(Residential sleeping areas, live load = 30 psf, L/Δ = 360)[a]

JOIST SPACING (inches)	SPECIES AND *GRADE*		DEAD LOAD = 10 psf				DEAD LOAD = 20 psf			
			2x6	2x8	2x10	2x12	2x6	2x8	2x10	2x12
			Maximum floor joist spans							
			(ft - in.)	(ft - in.)	(ft - in.)	(ft - in.)	(ft - in.)	(ft - in.)	(ft - in.)	(ft - in.)
12	Douglas fir-larch	SS	12-6	16-6	21-0	25-7	12-6	16-6	21-0	25-7
	Douglas fir-larch	#1	12-0	15-10	20-3	24-8	12-0	15-7	19-0	22-0
	Douglas fir-larch	#2	11-10	15-7	19-10	23-0	11-6	14-7	17-9	20-7
	Douglas fir-larch	#3	9-8	12-4	15-0	17-5	8-8	11-0	13-5	15-7
	Hem-fir	SS	11-10	15-7	19-10	24-2	11-10	15-7	19-10	24-2
	Hem-fir	#1	11-7	15-3	19-5	23-7	11-7	15-2	18-6	21-6
	Hem-fir	#2	11-0	14-6	18-6	22-6	11-0	14-4	17-6	20-4
	Hem-fir	#3	9-8	12-4	15-0	17-5	8-8	11-0	13-5	15-7
	Southern pine	SS	12-3	16-2	20-8	25-1	12-3	16-2	20-8	25-1
	Southern pine	#1	12-0	15-10	20-3	24-8	12-0	15-10	20-3	24-8
	Southern pine	#2	11-10	15-7	19-10	24-2	11-10	15-7	18-7	21-9
	Southern pine	#3	10-5	13-3	15-8	18-8	9-4	11-11	14-0	16-8
	Spruce-pine-fir	SS	11-7	15-3	19-5	23-7	11-7	15-3	19-5	23-7
	Spruce-pine-fir	#1	11-3	14-11	19-0	23-0	11-3	14-7	17-9	20-7
	Spruce-pine-fir	#2	11-3	14-11	19-0	23-0	11-3	14-7	17-9	20-7
	Spruce-pine-fir	#3	9-8	12-4	15-0	17-5	8-8	11-0	13-5	15-7
16	Douglas fir-larch	SS	11-4	15-0	19-1	23-3	11-4	15-0	19-1	23-0
	Douglas fir-larch	#1	10-11	14-5	18-5	21-4	10-8	13-6	16-5	19-1
	Douglas fir-larch	#2	10-9	14-1	17-2	19-11	9-11	12-7	15-5	17-10
	Douglas fir-larch	#3	8-5	10-8	13-0	15-1	7-6	9-6	11-8	13-6
	Hem-fir	SS	10-9	14-2	18-0	21-11	10-9	14-2	18-0	21-11
	Hem-fir	#1	10-6	13-10	17-8	20-9	10-4	13-1	16-0	18-7
	Hem-fir	#2	10-0	13-2	16-10	19-8	9-10	12-5	15-2	17-7
	Hem-fir	#3	8-5	10-8	13-0	15-1	7-6	9-6	11-8	13-6
	Southern pine	SS	11-2	14-8	18-9	22-10	11-2	14-8	18-9	22-10
	Southern pine	#1	10-11	14-5	18-5	22-5	10-11	14-5	17-11	21-4
	Southern pine	#2	10-9	14-2	18-0	21-1	10-5	13-6	16-1	18-10
	Southern pine	#3	9-0	11-6	13-7	16-2	8-1	10-3	12-2	14-6
	Spruce-pine-fir	SS	10-6	13-10	17-8	21-6	10-6	13-10	17-8	21-4
	Spruce-pine-fir	#1	10-3	13-6	17-2	19-11	9-11	12-7	15-5	17-10
	Spruce-pine-fir	#2	10-3	13-6	17-2	19-11	9-11	12-7	15-5	17-10
	Spruce-pine-fir	#3	8-5	10-8	13-0	15-1	7-6	9-6	11-8	13-6
19.2	Douglas fir-larch	SS	10-8	14-1	18-0	21-10	10-8	14-1	18-0	21-0
	Douglas fir-larch	#1	10-4	13-7	16-9	19-6	9-8	12-4	15-0	17-5
	Douglas fir-larch	#2	10-1	12-10	15-8	18-3	9-1	11-6	14-1	16-3
	Douglas fir-larch	#3	7-8	9-9	11-10	13-9	6-10	8-8	10-7	12-4
	Hem-fir	SS	10-1	13-4	17-0	20-8	10-1	13-4	17-0	20-7
	Hem-fir	#1	9-10	13-0	16-4	19-0	9-6	12-0	14-8	17-0
	Hem-fir	#2	9-5	12-5	15-6	17-1	8-11	11-4	13-10	16-1
	Hem-fir	#3	7-8	9-9	11-10	13-9	6-10	8-8	10-7	12-4
	Southern pine	SS	10-6	13-10	17-8	21-6	10-6	13-10	17-8	21-6
	Southern pine	#1	10-4	13-7	17-4	21-1	10-4	13-7	16-4	19-6
	Southern pine	#2	10-1	13-4	16-5	19-3	9-6	12-4	14-8	17-2
	Southern pine	#3	8-3	10-6	12-5	14-9	7-4	9-5	11-1	13-2
	Spruce-pine-fir	SS	9-10	13-0	16-7	20-2	9-10	13-0	16-7	19-6
	Spruce-pine-fir	#1	9-8	12-9	15-8	18-3	9-1	11-6	14-1	16-3
	Spruce-pine-fir	#2	9-8	12-9	15-8	18-3	9-1	11-6	14-1	16-3
	Spruce-pine-fir	#3	7-8	9-9	11-10	13-9	6-10	8-8	10-7	12-4
24	Douglas fir-larch	SS	9-11	13-1	16-8	20-3	9-11	13-1	16-2	18-9
	Douglas fir-larch	#1	9-7	12-4	15-0	17-5	8-8	11-0	13-5	15-7
	Douglas fir-larch	#2	9-1	11-6	14-1	16-3	8-1	10-3	12-7	14-7
	Douglas fir-larch	#3	6-10	8-8	10-7	12-4	6-2	7-9	9-6	11-0
	Hem-fir	SS	9-4	12-4	15-9	19-2	9-4	12-4	15-9	18-5
	Hem-fir	#1	9-2	12-0	14-8	17-0	8-6	10-9	13-1	15-2
	Hem-fir	#2	8-9	11-4	13-10	16-1	8-0	10-2	12-5	14-4
	Hem-fir	#3	6-10	8-8	10-7	12-4	6-2	7-9	9-6	11-0
	Southern pine	SS	9-9	12-10	16-5	19-11	9-9	12-10	16-5	19-11
	Southern pine	#1	9-7	12-7	16-1	19-6	9-7	12-4	14-7	17-5
	Southern pine	#2	9-4	12-4	14-8	17-2	8-6	11-0	13-1	15-5
	Southern pine	#3	7-4	9-5	11-1	13-2	6-7	8-5	9-11	11-10
	Spruce-pine-fir	SS	9-2	12-1	15-5	18-9	9-2	12-1	15-0	17-5
	Spruce-pine-fir	#1	8-11	11-6	14-1	16-3	8-1	10-3	12-7	14-7
	Spruce-pine-fir	#2	8-11	11-6	14-1	16-3	8-1	10-3	12-7	14-7
	Spruce-pine-fir	#3	6-10	8-8	10-7	12-4	6-2	7-9	9-6	11-0

For SI: 1 inch = 25.4 mm, 1 foot = 304.8 mm, 1 pound per square foot = 0.0479 kPa.

Note: Check sources for availability of lumber in lengths greater than 20 feet.

a. Dead load limits for townhouses in Seismic Design Category C and all structures in Seismic Design Categories D_0, D_1 and D_2 shall be determined in accordance with Section R301.2.2.2.1.

TABLE R502.3.1(2)
FLOOR JOIST SPANS FOR COMMON LUMBER SPECIES
(Residential living areas, live load = 40 psf, $L/\Delta = 360$)[b]

JOIST SPACING (inches)	SPECIES AND *GRADE*		DEAD LOAD = 10 psf				DEAD LOAD = 20 psf			
			2×6	2×8	2×10	2×12	2×6	2×8	2×10	2×12
			Maximum floor joist spans							
			(ft - in.)	(ft - in.)	(ft - in.)	(ft - in.)	(ft - in.)	(ft - in.)	(ft - in.)	(ft - in.)
12	Douglas fir-larch	SS	11-4	15-0	19-1	23-3	11-4	15-0	19-1	23-3
	Douglas fir-larch	#1	10-11	14-5	18-5	22-0	10-11	14-2	17-4	20-1
	Douglas fir-larch	#2	10-9	14-2	17-9	20-7	10-6	13-3	16-3	18-10
	Douglas fir-larch	#3	8-8	11-0	13-5	15-7	7-11	10-0	12-3	14-3
	Hem-fir	SS	10-9	14-2	18-0	21-11	10-9	14-2	18-0	21-11
	Hem-fir	#1	10-6	13-10	17-8	21-6	10-6	13-10	16-11	19-7
	Hem-fir	#2	10-0	13-2	16-10	20-4	10-0	13-1	16-0	18-6
	Hem-fir	#3	8-8	11-0	13-5	15-7	7-11	10-0	12-3	14-3
	Southern pine	SS	11-2	14-8	18-9	22-10	11-2	14-8	18-9	22-10
	Southern pine	#1	10-11	14-5	18-5	22-5	10-11	14-5	18-5	22-5
	Southern pine	#2	10-9	14-2	18-0	21-9	10-9	14-2	16-11	19-10
	Southern pine	#3	9-4	11-11	14-0	16-8	8-6	10-10	12-10	15-3
	Spruce-pine-fir	SS	10-6	13-10	17-8	21-6	10-6	13-10	17-8	21-6
	Spruce-pine-fir	#1	10-3	13-6	17-3	20-7	10-3	13-3	16-3	18-10
	Spruce-pine-fir	#2	10-3	13-6	17-3	20-7	10-3	13-3	16-3	18-10
	Spruce-pine-fir	#3	8-8	11-0	13-5	15-7	7-11	10-0	12-3	14-3
16	Douglas fir-larch	SS	10-4	13-7	17-4	21-1	10-4	13-7	17-4	21-0
	Douglas fir-larch	#1	9-11	13-1	16-5	19-1	9-8	12-4	15-0	17-5
	Douglas fir-larch	#2	9-9	12-7	15-5	17-10	9-1	11-6	14-1	16-3
	Douglas fir-larch	#3	7-6	9-6	11-8	13-6	6-10	8-8	10-7	12-4
	Hem-fir	SS	9-9	12-10	16-5	19-11	9-9	12-10	16-5	19-11
	Hem-fir	#1	9-6	12-7	16-0	18-7	9-6	12-0	14-8	17-0
	Hem-fir	#2	9-1	12-0	15-2	17-7	8-11	11-4	13-10	16-1
	Hem-fir	#3	7-6	9-6	11-8	13-6	6-10	8-8	10-7	12-4
	Southern pine	SS	10-2	13-4	17-0	20-9	10-2	13-4	17-0	20-9
	Southern pine	#1	9-11	13-1	16-9	20-4	9-11	13-1	16-4	19-6
	Southern pine	#2	9-9	12-10	16-1	18-10	9-6	12-4	14-8	17-2
	Southern pine	#3	8-1	10-3	12-2	14-6	7-4	9-5	11-1	13-2
	Spruce-pine-fir	SS	9-6	12-7	16-0	19-6	9-6	12-7	16-0	19-6
	Spruce-pine-fir	#1	9-4	12-3	15-5	17-10	9-1	11-6	14-1	16-3
	Spruce-pine-fir	#2	9-4	12-3	15-5	17-10	9-1	11-6	14-1	16-3
	Spruce-pine-fir	#3	7-6	9-6	11-8	13-6	6-10	8-8	10-7	12-4
19.2	Douglas fir-larch	SS	9-8	12-10	16-4	19-10	9-8	12-10	16-4	19-2
	Douglas fir-larch	#1	9-4	12-4	15-0	17-5	8-10	11-3	13-8	15-11
	Douglas fir-larch	#2	9-1	11-6	14-1	16-3	8-3	10-6	12-10	14-10
	Douglas fir-larch	#3	6-10	8-8	10-7	12-4	6-3	7-11	9-8	11-3
	Hem-fir	SS	9-2	12-1	15-5	18-9	9-2	12-1	15-5	18-9
	Hem-fir	#1	9-0	11-10	14-8	17-0	8-8	10-11	13-4	15-6
	Hem-fir	#2	8-7	11-3	13-10	16-1	8-2	10-4	12-8	14-8
	Hem-fir	#3	6-10	8-8	10-7	12-4	6-3	7-11	9-8	11-3
	Southern pine	SS	9-6	12-7	16-0	19-6	9-6	12-7	16-0	19-6
	Southern pine	#1	9-4	12-4	15-9	19-2	9-4	12-4	14-11	17-9
	Southern pine	#2	9-2	12-1	14-8	17-2	8-8	11-3	13-5	15-8
	Southern pine	#3	7-4	9-5	11-1	13-2	6-9	8-7	10-1	12-1
	Spruce-pine-fir	SS	9-0	11-10	15-1	18-4	9-0	11-10	15-1	17-9
	Spruce-pine-fir	#	8-9	11-6	14-1	16-3	8-3	10-6	12-10	14-10
	Spruce-pine-fir	#2	8-9	11-6	14-1	16-3	8-3	10-6	12-10	14-10
	Spruce-pine-fir	#3	6-10	8-8	10-7	12-4	6-3	7-11	9-8	11-3
24	Douglas fir-larch	SS	9-0	11-11	15-2	18-5	9-0	11-11	14-9	17-1
	Douglas fir-larch	#1	8-8	11-0	13-5	15-7	7-11	10-0	12-3	14-3
	Douglas fir-larch	#2	8-1	10-3	12-7	14-7	7-5	9-5	11-6	13-4
	Douglas fir-larch	#3	6-2	7-9	9-6	11-0	5-7	7-1	8-8	10-1
	Hem-fir	SS	8-6	11-3	14-4	17-5	8-6	11-3	14-4	16-10[a]
	Hem-fir	#1	8-4	10-9	13-1	15-2	7-9	9-9	11-11	13-10
	Hem-fir	#2	7-11	10-2	12-5	14-4	7-4	9-3	11-4	13-1
	Hem-fir	#3	6-2	7-9	9-6	11-0	5-7	7-1	8-8	10-1
	Southern pine	SS	8-10	11-8	14-11	18-1	8-10	11-8	14-11	18-1
	Southern pine	#1	8-8	11-5	14-7	17-5	8-8	11-3	13-4	15-11
	Southern pine	#2	8-6	11-0	13-1	15-5	7-9	10-0	12-0	14-0
	Southern pine	#3	6-7	8-5	9-11	11-10	6-0	7-8	9-1	10-9
	Spruce-pine-fir	SS	8-4	11-0	14-0	17-0	8-4	11-0	13-8	15-11
	Spruce-pine-fir	#1	8-1	10-3	12-7	14-7	7-5	9-5	11-6	13-4
	Spruce-pine-fir	#2	8-1	10-3	12-7	14-7	7-5	9-5	11-6	13-4
	Spruce-pine-fir	#3	6-2	7-9	9-6	11-0	5-7	7-1	8-8	10-1

For SI: 1 inch = 25.4 mm, 1 foot = 304.8 mm, 1 pound per square foot = 0.0479 kPa.

Note: Check sources for availability of lumber in lengths greater than 20 feet.

a. End bearing length shall be increased to 2 inches.

b. Dead load limits for townhouses in Seismic Design Category C and all structures in Seismic Design Categories D_0, D_1, and D_2 shall be determined in accordance with Section R301.2.2.2.1.

TABLE R502.3.3(1)
CANTILEVER SPANS FOR FLOOR JOISTS SUPPORTING LIGHT-FRAME EXTERIOR BEARING WALL AND ROOF ONLY[a, b, c, f, g, h]
(Floor Live Load ≤ 40 psf, Roof Live Load ≤ 20 psf)

	Maximum Cantilever Span (Uplift Force at Backspan Support in Lbs.)[d, e]											
	Ground Snow Load											
	≤ 20 psf			30 psf			50 psf			70 psf		
	Roof Width			Roof Width			Roof Width			Roof Width		
Member & Spacing	**24 ft**	**32 ft**	**40 ft**	**24 ft**	**32 ft**	**40 ft**	**24 ft**	**32 ft**	**40 ft**	**24 ft**	**32 ft**	**40 ft**
2 × 8 @ 12″	20″ (177)	15″ (227)	—	18″ (209)	—	—	—	—	—	—	—	—
2 × 10 @ 16″	29″ (228)	21″ (297)	16″ (364)	26″ (271)	18″ (354)	—	20″ (375)	—	—	—	—	—
2 × 10 @ 12″	36″ (166)	26″ (219)	20″ (270)	34″ (198)	22″ (263)	16″ (324)	26″ (277)	—	—	19″ (356)	—	—
2 × 12 @ 16″	—	32″ (287)	25″ (356)	36″ (263)	29″ (345)	21″ (428)	29″ (367)	20″ (484)	—	23″ (471)	—	—
2 × 12 @ 12″	—	42″ (209)	31″ (263)	—	37″ (253)	27″ (317)	36″ (271)	27″ (358)	17″ (447)	31″ (348)	19″ (462)	—
2 × 12 @ 8″	—	48″ (136)	45″ (169)	—	48″ (164)	38″ (206)	—	40″ (233)	26″ (294)	36″ (230)	29″ (304)	18″ (379)

For SI: 1 inch = 25.4 mm, 1 foot = 304.8 mm, 1 pound per square foot = 0.0479 kPa.

a. Tabulated values are for clear-span roof supported solely by exterior bearing walls.
b. Spans are based on No. 2 Grade lumber of Douglas fir-larch, hem-fir, southern pine, and spruce-pine-fir for repetitive (3 or more) members.
c. Ratio of backspan to cantilever span shall be at least 3:1.
d. Connections capable of resisting the indicated uplift force shall be provided at the backspan support.
e. Uplift force is for a backspan to cantilever span ratio of 3:1. Tabulated uplift values are permitted to be reduced by multiplying by a factor equal to 3 divided by the actual backspan ratio provided (3/backspan ratio).
f. See Section R301.2.2.2.5, Item 1, for additional limitations on cantilevered floor joists for detached one- and two-family dwellings in Seismic Design Category D_0, D_1, or D_2 and townhouses in Seismic Design Category C, D_0, D_1, or D_2.
g. A full-depth rim joist shall be provided at the cantilever end of the joists. Solid blocking shall be provided at the cantilever support.
h. Linear interpolation shall be permitted for building widths and ground snow loads other than shown.

TABLE R502.3.3(2)
CANTILEVER SPANS FOR FLOOR JOISTS SUPPORTING EXTERIOR BALCONY[a, b, e, f]

		Maximum Cantilever Span (Uplift Force at Backspan Support in lb)[c, d]		
		Ground Snow Load		
Member Size	**Spacing**	**≤ 30 psf**	**50 psf**	**70 psf**
2 × 8	12″	42″ (139)	39″ (156)	34″ (165)
2 × 8	16″	36″ (151)	34″ (171)	29″ (180)
2 × 10	12″	61″ (164)	57″ (189)	49″ (201)
2 × 10	16″	53″ (180)	49″ (208)	42″ (220)
2 × 10	24″	43″ (212)	40″ (241)	34″ (255)
2 × 12	16″	72″ (228)	67″ (260)	57″ (268)
2 × 12	24″	58″ (279)	54″ (319)	47″ (330)

For SI: 1 inch = 25.4 mm, 1 pound per square foot = 0.0479 kPa.

a. Spans are based on No. 2 Grade lumber of Douglas fir-larch, hem-fir, southern pine, and spruce-pine-fir for repetitive (3 or more) members.
b. Ratio of backspan to cantilever span shall be at least 2:1.
c. Connections capable of resisting the indicated uplift force shall be provided at the backspan support.
d. Uplift force is for a backspan to cantilever span ratio of 2:1. Tabulated uplift values are permitted to be reduced by multiplying by a factor equal to 2 divided by the actual backspan ratio provided (2/backspan ratio).
e. A full-depth rim joist shall be provided at the unsupported end of the cantilever joists. Solid blocking shall be provided at the supported end.
f. Linear interpolation shall be permitted for ground snow loads other than shown.

TABLE R502.5(1)
GIRDER SPANS[a] AND HEADER SPANS[a] FOR EXTERIOR BEARING WALLS
(Maximum spans for Douglas fir-larch, hem-fir, southern pine and spruce-pine-fir[b] and required number of jack studs)

GIRDERS AND HEADERS SUPPORTING	SIZE	GROUND SNOW LOAD (psf)[e]																	
		30						50						70					
		Building width[c] (feet)																	
		20		28		36		20		28		36		20		28		36	
		Span	NJ[d]	Span	NJ[d]	Span	NJ[d]	Span	NJ[d]	Span	NJ[d]	Span	NJ[d]	Span	NJ[d]	Span	NJ[d]	Span	NJ[d]
Roof and ceiling	2-2×4	3-6	1	3-2	1	2-10	1	3-2	1	2-9	1	2-6	1	2-10	1	2-6	1	2-3	1
	2-2×6	5-5	1	4-8	1	4-2	1	4-8	1	4-1	1	3-8	2	4-2	1	3-8	2	3-3	2
	2-2×8	6-10	1	5-11	2	5-4	2	5-11	2	5-2	2	4-7	2	5-4	2	4-7	2	4-1	2
	2-2×10	8-5	2	7-3	2	6-6	2	7-3	2	6-3	2	5-7	2	6-6	2	5-7	2	5-0	2
	2-2×12	9-9	2	8-5	2	7-6	2	8-5	2	7-3	2	6-6	2	7-6	2	6-6	2	5-10	3
	3-2×8	8-4	1	7-5	1	6-8	1	7-5	1	6-5	2	5-9	2	6-8	1	5-9	2	5-2	2
	3-2×10	10-6	1	9-1	2	8-2	2	9-1	2	7-10	2	7-0	2	8-2	2	7-0	2	6-4	2
	3-2×12	12-2	2	10-7	2	9-5	2	10-7	2	9-2	2	8-2	2	9-5	2	8-2	2	7-4	2
	4-2×8	9-2	1	8-4	1	7-8	1	8-4	1	7-5	1	6-8	1	7-8	1	6-8	1	5-11	2
	4-2×10	11-8	1	10-6	1	9-5	2	10-6	1	9-1	2	8-2	2	9-5	2	8-2	2	7-3	2
	4-2×12	14-1	1	12-2	2	10-11	2	12-2	2	10-7	2	9-5	2	10-11	2	9-5	2	8-5	2
Roof, ceiling and one center-bearing floor	2-2×4	3-1	1	2-9	1	2-5	1	2-9	1	2-5	1	2-2	1	2-7	1	2-3	1	2-0	1
	2-2×6	4-6	1	4-0	1	3-7	2	4-1	1	3-7	2	3-3	2	3-9	2	3-3	2	2-11	2
	2-2×8	5-9	2	5-0	2	4-6	2	5-2	2	4-6	2	4-1	2	4-9	2	4-2	2	3-9	2
	2-2×10	7-0	2	6-2	2	5-6	2	6-4	2	5-6	2	5-0	2	5-9	2	5-1	2	4-7	3
	2-2×12	8-1	2	7-1	2	6-5	2	7-4	2	6-5	2	5-9	3	6-8	2	5-10	3	5-3	3
	3-2×8	7-2	1	6-3	2	5-8	2	6-5	2	5-8	2	5-1	2	5-11	2	5-2	2	4-8	2
	3-2×10	8-9	2	7-8	2	6-11	2	7-11	2	6-11	2	6-3	2	7-3	2	6-4	2	5-8	2
	3-2×12	10-2	2	8-11	2	8-0	2	9-2	2	8-0	2	7-3	2	8-5	2	7-4	2	6-7	2
	4-2×8	8-1	1	7-3	1	6-7	1	7-5	1	6-6	1	5-11	2	6-10	1	6-0	2	5-5	2
	4-2×10	10-1	1	8-10	2	8-0	2	9-1	2	8-0	2	7-2	2	8-4	2	7-4	2	6-7	2
	4-2×12	11-9	2	10-3	2	9-3	2	10-7	2	9-3	2	8-4	2	9-8	2	8-6	2	7-7	2
Roof, ceiling and one clear span floor	2-2×4	2-8	1	2-4	1	2-1	1	2-7	1	2-3	1	2-0	1	2-5	1	2-1	1	1-10	1
	2-2×6	3-11	1	3-5	2	3-0	2	3-10	2	3-4	2	3-0	2	3-6	2	3-1	2	2-9	2
	2-2×8	5-0	2	4-4	2	3-10	2	4-10	2	4-2	2	3-9	2	4-6	2	3-11	2	3-6	2
	2-2×10	6-1	2	5-3	2	4-8	2	5-11	2	5-1	2	4-7	3	5-6	2	4-9	2	4-3	3
	2-2×12	7-1	2	6-1	3	5-5	3	6-10	2	5-11	3	5-4	3	6-4	2	5-6	3	5-0	3
	3-2×8	6-3	2	5-5	2	4-10	2	6-1	2	5-3	2	4-8	2	5-7	2	4-11	2	4-5	2
	3-2×10	7-7	2	6-7	2	5-11	2	7-5	2	6-5	2	5-9	2	6-10	2	6-0	2	5-4	2
	3-2×12	8-10	2	7-8	2	6-10	2	8-7	2	7-5	2	6-8	2	7-11	2	6-11	2	6-3	2
	4-2×8	7-2	1	6-3	2	5-7	2	7-0	1	6-1	2	5-5	2	6-6	1	5-8	2	5-1	2
	4-2×10	8-9	2	7-7	2	6-10	2	8-7	2	7-5	2	6-7	2	7-11	2	6-11	2	6-2	2
	4-2×12	10-2	2	8-10	2	7-11	2	9-11	2	8-7	2	7-8	2	9-2	2	8-0	2	7-2	2
Roof, ceiling and two center-bearing floors	2-2×4	2-7	1	2-3	1	2-0	1	2-6	1	2-2	1	1-11	1	2-4	1	2-0	1	1-9	1
	2-2×6	3-9	2	3-3	2	2-11	2	3-8	2	3-2	2	2-10	2	3-5	2	3-0	2	2-8	2
	2-2×8	4-9	2	4-2	2	3-9	2	4-7	2	4-0	2	3-8	2	4-4	2	3-9	2	3-5	2
	2-2×10	5-9	2	5-1	2	4-7	3	5-8	2	4-11	2	4-5	3	5-3	2	4-7	3	4-2	3
	2-2×12	6-8	2	5-10	3	5-3	3	6-6	2	5-9	3	5-2	3	6-1	3	5-4	3	4-10	3
	3-2×8	5-11	2	5-2	2	4-8	2	5-9	2	5-1	2	4-7	2	5-5	2	4-9	2	4-3	2
	3-2×10	7-3	2	6-4	2	5-8	2	7-1	2	6-2	2	5-7	2	6-7	2	5-9	2	5-3	2
	3-2×12	8-5	2	7-4	2	6-7	2	8-2	2	7-2	2	6-5	3	7-8	2	6-9	2	6-1	3
	4-2×8	6-10	1	6-0	2	5-5	2	6-8	1	5-10	2	5-3	2	6-3	2	5-6	2	4-11	2
	4-2×10	8-4	2	7-4	2	6-7	2	8-2	2	7-2	2	6-5	2	7-7	2	6-8	2	6-0	2
	4-2×12	9-8	2	8-6	2	7-8	2	9-5	2	8-3	2	7-5	2	8-10	2	7-9	2	7-0	2

(continued)

TABLE R502.5(1)—continued
GIRDER SPANS[a] AND HEADER SPANS[a] FOR EXTERIOR BEARING WALLS
(Maximum spans for Douglas fir-larch, hem-fir, southern pine and spruce-pine-fir[b] and required number of jack studs)

GIRDERS AND HEADERS SUPPORTING	SIZE	GROUND SNOW LOAD (psf)[e]																	
		30						50						70					
		Building width[c] (feet)																	
		20		28		36		20		28		36		20		28		36	
		Span	NJ[d]	Span	NJ[d]	Span	NJ[d]	Span	NJ[d]	Span	NJ[d]	Span	NJ[d]	Span	NJ[d]	Span	NJ[d]	Span	NJ[d]
Roof, ceiling, and two clear span floors	2-2×4	2-1	1	1-8	1	1-6	2	2-0	1	1-8	1	1-5	2	2-0	1	1-8	1	1-5	2
	2-2×6	3-1	2	2-8	2	2-4	2	3-0	2	2-7	2	2-3	2	2-11	2	2-7	2	2-3	2
	2-2×8	3-10	2	3-4	2	3-0	3	3-10	2	3-4	2	2-11	3	3-9	2	3-3	2	2-11	3
	2-2×10	4-9	2	4-1	3	3-8	3	4-8	2	4-0	3	3-7	3	4-7	3	4-0	3	3-6	3
	2-2×12	5-6	3	4-9	3	4-3	3	5-5	3	4-8	3	4-2	3	5-4	3	4-7	3	4-1	4
	3-2×8	4-10	2	4-2	2	3-9	2	4-9	2	4-1	2	3-8	2	4-8	2	4-1	2	3-8	2
	3-2×10	5-11	2	5-1	2	4-7	3	5-10	2	5-0	2	4-6	3	5-9	2	4-11	2	4-5	3
	3-2×12	6-10	2	5-11	3	5-4	3	6-9	2	5-10	3	5-3	3	6-8	2	5-9	3	5-2	3
	4-2×8	5-7	2	4-10	2	4-4	2	5-6	2	4-9	2	4-3	2	5-5	2	4-8	2	4-2	2
	4-2×10	6-10	2	5-11	2	5-3	2	6-9	2	5-10	2	5-2	2	6-7	2	5-9	2	5-1	2
	4-2×12	7-11	2	6-10	2	6-2	3	7-9	2	6-9	2	6-0	3	7-8	2	6-8	2	5-11	3

For SI: 1 inch = 25.4 mm, 1 pound per square foot = 0.0479 kPa.

a. Spans are given in feet and inches.

b. Tabulated values assume #2 grade lumber.

c. Building width is measured perpendicular to the ridge. For widths between those shown, spans are permitted to be interpolated.

d. NJ - Number of jack studs required to support each end. Where the number of required jack studs equals one, the header is permitted to be supported by an approved framing anchor attached to the full-height wall stud and to the header.

e. Use 30 psf ground snow load for cases in which ground snow load is less than 30 psf and the roof live load is equal to or less than 20 psf.

TABLE R502.5(2)
GIRDER SPANS[a] AND HEADER SPANS[a] FOR INTERIOR BEARING WALLS
(Maximum spans for Douglas fir-larch, hem-fir, southern pine and spruce-pine-fir[b] and required number of jack studs)

HEADERS AND GIRDERS SUPPORTING	SIZE	BUILDING WIDTH[c] (feet)					
		20		28		36	
		Span	NJ[d]	Span	NJ[d]	Span	NJ[d]
One floor only	2-2×4	3-1	1	2-8	1	2-5	1
	2-2×6	4-6	1	3-11	1	3-6	1
	2-2×8	5-9	1	5-0	2	4-5	2
	2-2×10	7-0	2	6-1	2	5-5	2
	2-2×12	8-1	2	7-0	2	6-3	2
	3-2×8	7-2	1	6-3	1	5-7	2
	3-2×10	8-9	1	7-7	2	6-9	2
	3-2×12	10-2	2	8-10	2	7-10	2
	4-2×8	9-0	1	7-8	1	6-9	1
	4-2×10	10-1	1	8-9	1	7-10	2
	4-2×12	11-9	1	10-2	2	9-1	2
Two floors	2-2×4	2-2	1	1-10	1	1-7	1
	2-2×6	3-2	2	2-9	2	2-5	2
	2-2×8	4-1	2	3-6	2	3-2	2
	2-2×10	4-11	2	4-3	2	3-10	3
	2-2×12	5-9	2	5-0	3	4-5	3
	3-2×8	5-1	2	4-5	2	3-11	2
	3-2×10	6-2	2	5-4	2	4-10	2
	3-2×12	7-2	2	6-3	2	5-7	3
	4-2×8	6-1	1	5-3	2	4-8	2
	4-2×10	7-2	2	6-2	2	5-6	2
	4-2×12	8-4	2	7-2	2	6-5	2

For SI: 1 inch = 25.4 mm, 1 foot = 304.8 mm.

a. Spans are given in feet and inches.

b. Tabulated values assume #2 grade lumber.

c. Building width is measured perpendicular to the ridge. For widths between those shown, spans are permitted to be interpolated.

d. NJ - Number of jack studs required to support each end. Where the number of required jack studs equals one, the header is permitted to be supported by an approved framing anchor attached to the full-height wall stud and to the header.

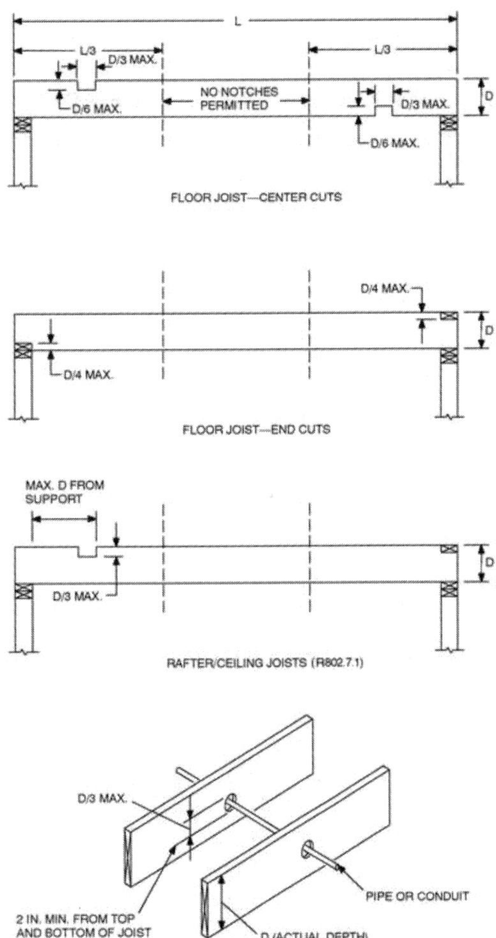

For SI: 1 inch = 25.4 mm.

FIGURE R502.8
CUTTING, NOTCHING AND DRILLING

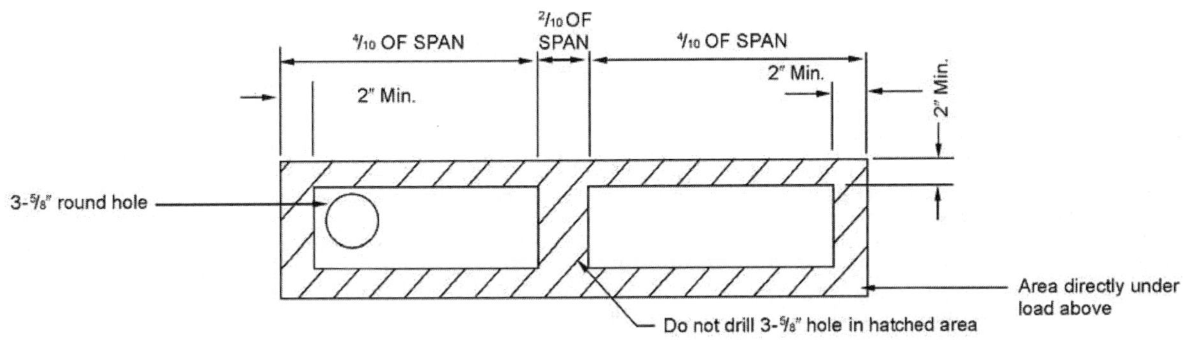

For SI: 1 inch = 24.5 mm, 1 foot = 304.8 mm

1. Do not drill in center 2/10's of joist span.
2. Do not drill directly under load bearing walls at end.
3. Do not drill closer than 2″ to top or bottom edge.
4. Apply 4′ joist width × $^1/_2$″ CDX plywood with face grain running with joist to both sides using 6d nails or $1^1/_2$″ screws 1″ from top and bottom 4″ o.c.
5. Holes shall not be closer that 2′-0″ o.c. within unhatched area only.
6. Plywood shall be attached such that 2′ minimum of plywood is centered on each side of the hole location, except when the hole is located within 2′ of the end of joist.

FIGURE R502.8(a)
ACCEPTABLE LOCATION OF $3^5/_8$-inch DIAMETER HOLE IN 2 x 10 JOIST

TABLE R503.2.1.1(1)
ALLOWABLE SPANS AND LOADS FOR WOOD STRUCTURAL PANELS FOR ROOF AND SUBFLOOR SHEATHING AND COMBINATION SUBFLOOR UNDERLAYMENT[a, b, c]

SPAN RATING ROOF/FLOOR	MINIMUM NOMINAL PANEL THICKNESS (inch)	ALLOWABLE LIVE LOAD (psf)[h, l]		MAXIMUM SPAN (inches)		LOAD (pounds per square foot, at maximum span)		MAXIMUM SPAN (inches)
		SPAN @ 16″ o.c.	SPAN @ 24″ o.c.	With edge support[d]	Without edge support	Total load	Live load	
Sheathing[e]				Roof[f]				Subfloor[j]
16/0	3/8	30	—	16	16	40	30	0
20/0	3/8	50	—	20	20	40	30	0
24/0	3/8	100	30	24	20[g]	40	30	0
24/16	7/16	100	40	24	24	50	40	16
32/16	15/32, 1/2	180	70	32	28	40	30	16[h]
40/20	19/32, 5/8	305	130	40	32	40	30	20[h, i]
48/24	23/32, 3/4	—	175	48	36	45	35	24
60/32	7/8	—	305	60	48	45	35	32
Underlayment, C-C plugged, single floor[e]				Roof[f]				Combination subfloor underlayment[k]
16 o.c.	19/32, 5/8	100	40	24	24	50	40	16[i]
20 o.c.	19/32, 5/8	150	60	32	32	40	30	20[i, j]
24 o.c.	23/32, 3/4	240	100	48	36	35	25	24
32 o.c.	7/8	—	185	48	40	50	40	32
48 o.c.	1 3/32, 1 1/8	—	290	60	48	50	40	48

For SI: 1 inch = 25.4 mm, 1 pound per square foot = 0.0479 kPa.

a. The allowable total loads were determined using a dead load of 10 psf. If the dead load exceeds 10 psf, then the live load shall be reduced accordingly.

b. Panels continuous over two or more spans with long dimension (strength axis) perpendicular to supports. Spans shall be limited to values shown because of possible effect of concentrated loads.

c. Applies to panels 24 inches or wider.

d. Lumber blocking, panel edge clips (one midway between each support, except two equally spaced between supports when span is 48 inches), tongue-and-groove panel edges, or other approved type of edge support.

e. Includes Structural 1 panels in these grades.

f. Uniform load deflection limitation: $^1/_{180}$ of span under live load plus dead load, $^1/_{240}$ of span under live load only.

g. Maximum span 24 inches for $^{15}/_{32}$-and $^1/_2$-inch panels.

h. Maximum span 24 inches where $^3/_4$-inch wood finish flooring is installed at right angles to joists.

i. Maximum span 24 inches where 1.5 inches of lightweight concrete or approved cellular concrete is placed over the subfloor.

j. Unsupported edges shall have tongue-and-groove joints or shall be supported with blocking unless minimum nominal $^1/_4$-inch thick underlayment with end and edge joints offset at least 2 inches or 1.5 inches of lightweight concrete or approved cellular concrete is placed over the subfloor, or $^3/_4$-inch wood finish flooring is installed at right angles to the supports. Allowable uniform live load at maximum span, based on deflection of $^1/_{360}$ of span, is 100 psf.

k. Unsupported edges shall have tongue-and-groove joints or shall be supported by blocking unless nominal $^1/_4$-inch-thick underlayment with end and edge joints offset at least 2 inches or $^3/_4$-inch wood finish flooring is installed at right angles to the supports. Allowable uniform live load at maximum span, based on deflection of $^1/_{360}$ of span, is 100 psf, except panels with a span rating of 48 on center are limited to 65 psf total uniform load at maximum span.

l. Allowable live load values at spans of 16" o.c. and 24" o.c taken from reference standard APA E30, APA Engineered Wood Construction Guide. Refer to reference standard for allowable spans not listed in the table.

TABLE R503.2.1.1(2)
ALLOWABLE SPANS FOR SANDED PLYWOOD COMBINATION SUBFLOOR UNDERLAYMENT[a]

IDENTIFICATION	SPACING OF JOISTS (inches)		
	16	20	24
Species group[b]	—	—	—
1	$^1/_2$	$^5/_8$	$^3/_4$
2, 3	$^5/_8$	$^3/_4$	$^7/_8$
4	$^3/_4$	$^7/_8$	1

For SI: 1 inch = 25.4 mm, 1 pound per square foot = 0.0479 kPa.

a. Plywood continuous over two or more spans and face grain perpendicular to supports. Unsupported edges shall be tongue-and-groove or blocked except where nominal $^1/_4$-inch-thick underlayment or $^3/_4$-inch wood finish floor is used. Allowable uniform live load at maximum span based on deflection of $^1/_{360}$ of span is 100 psf.

b. Applicable to all grades of sanded exterior-type plywood.

R503.2.2 Allowable spans. The maximum allowable span for wood structural panels used as subfloor or combination subfloor underlayment shall be as set forth in Table R503.2.1.1(1), or APA E30. The maximum span for sanded plywood combination subfloor underlayment shall be as set forth in Table R503.2.1.1(2).

R503.2.3 Installation. Wood structural panels used as subfloor or combination subfloor underlayment shall be attached to wood framing in accordance with Table R602.3(1) and shall be attached to cold-formed steel framing in accordance with Table R505.3.1(2).

R503.3 Particleboard.

R503.3.1 Identification and grade. Particleboard shall conform to ANSI A208.1 and shall be so identified by a grade *mark* or certificate of inspection issued by an *approved agency*.

R503.3.2 Floor underlayment. Particleboard floor underlayment shall conform to Type PBU and shall not be less than $^1/_4$ inch (6.4 mm) in thickness.

R503.3.3 Installation. Particleboard underlayment shall be installed in accordance with the recommendations of the manufacturer and attached to framing in accordance with Table R602.3(1).

SECTION R504 PRESSURE PRESERVATIVELY TREATED-WOOD FLOORS (ON GROUND)

R504.1 General. Pressure preservatively treated-wood *basement* floors and floors on ground shall be designed to withstand axial forces and bending moments resulting from lateral soil pressures at the base of the exterior walls and floor live and dead loads. Floor framing shall be designed to meet joist deflection requirements in accordance with Section R301.

R504.1.1 Unbalanced soil loads. Unless special provision is made to resist sliding caused by unbalanced lateral soil loads, wood *basement* floors shall be limited to applications where the differential depth of fill on opposite exterior foundation walls is 2 feet (610 mm) or less.

R504.1.2 Construction. Joists in wood *basement* floors shall bear tightly against the narrow face of studs in the foundation wall or directly against a band joist that bears on the studs. Plywood subfloor shall be continuous over lapped joists or over butt joints between in-line joists. Sufficient blocking shall be provided between joists to transfer lateral forces at the base of the end walls into the floor system.

R504.1.3 Uplift and buckling. Where required, resistance to uplift or restraint against buckling shall be provided by interior bearing walls or properly designed stub walls anchored in the supporting soil below.

R504.2 Site preparation. The area within the foundation walls shall have all vegetation, topsoil and foreign material removed, and any fill material that is added shall be free of vegetation and foreign material. The fill shall be compacted to assure uniform support of the pressure preservatively treated-wood floor sleepers.

R504.2.1 Base. A minimum 4-inch-thick (102 mm) granular base of gravel having a maximum size of $^3/_4$ inch (19.1 mm) or crushed stone having a maximum size of $^1/_2$ inch (12.7 mm) shall be placed over the compacted earth.

R504.2.2 Moisture barrier. Polyethylene sheeting of minimum 6-mil (0.15 mm) thickness shall be placed over the granular base. Joints shall be lapped 6 inches (152 mm) and left unsealed. The polyethylene membrane shall be placed over the pressure preservatively treated-wood sleepers and shall not extend beneath the footing plates of the exterior walls.

R504.3 Materials. All framing materials, including sleepers, joists, blocking and plywood subflooring, shall be pressure-preservative treated and dried after treatment in accordance with AWPA U1 (Commodity Specification A, Use Category 4B and section 5.2), and shall bear the *label* of an accredited agency.

SECTION R505 STEEL FLOOR FRAMING

R505.1 Cold-formed steel floor framing. Elements shall be straight and free of any defects that would significantly affect structural performance. Cold-formed steel floor framing members shall comply with the requirements of this section.

R505.1.1 Applicability limits. The provisions of this section shall control the construction of cold-formed steel floor framing for buildings not greater than 60 feet (18 288 mm) in length perpendicular to the joist span, not greater than 40 feet (12 192 mm) in width parallel to the joist span, and less than or equal to three stories above *grade* plane. Cold-formed steel floor framing constructed in accordance with the provisions of this section shall be limited to sites subjected to a maximum design wind speed of 110 miles per hour (49 m/s), Exposure B or C, and a maximum ground snow load of 70 pounds per square foot (3.35 kPa).

R505.1.2 In-line framing. When supported by cold-formed steel framed walls in accordance with Section R603, cold-formed steel floor framing shall be constructed with floor joists located in-line with load-bearing studs located below the joists in accordance with Figure R505.1.2 and the tolerances specified as follows:

1. The maximum tolerance shall be $^3/_4$ inch (19.1 mm) between the centerline of the horizontal framing member and the centerline of the vertical framing member.
2. Where the centerline of the horizontal framing member and bearing stiffener are located to one side of the centerline of the vertical framing member, the maximum tolerance shall be $^1/_8$ inch (3 mm) between the web of the horizontal framing member and the edge of the vertical framing member.

R505.1.3 Floor trusses. Cold-formed steel trusses shall be designed, braced and installed in accordance with AISI S100, Section D4. Truss members shall not be notched, cut or altered in any manner without an *approved* design.

R505.2 Structural framing. Load-bearing cold-formed steel floor framing members shall comply with Figure R505.2(1) and with the dimensional and minimum thickness requirements specified in Tables R505.2(1) and R505.2(2). Tracks shall comply with Figure R505.2(2) and shall have a minimum flange width of $1^1/_4$ inches (32 mm). The maximum inside bend radius for members shall be the greater of $^3/_{32}$ inch (2.4 mm) minus half the base steel thickness or 1.5 times the base steel thickness.

R505.2.1 Material. Load-bearing cold-formed steel framing members shall be cold-formed to shape from structural quality sheet steel complying with the requirements of one of the following:

1. ASTM A 653: Grades 33 and 50 (Class 1 and 3).
2. ASTM A 792: Grades 33 and 50A.
3. ASTM A 1003: Structural Grades 33 Type H and 50 Type H.

R505.2.2 Identification. Load-bearing cold-formed steel framing members shall have a legible *label*, stencil, stamp or embossment with the following information as a minimum:

1. Manufacturer's identification.
2. Minimum base steel thickness in inches (mm).
3. Minimum coating designation.
4. Minimum yield strength, in kips per square inch (ksi) (MPa).

R505.2.3 Corrosion protection. Load-bearing cold-formed steel framing shall have a metallic coating complying with ASTM A 1003 and one of the following:

1. A minimum of G 60 in accordance with ASTM A 653.
2. A minimum of AZ 50 in accordance with ASTM A 792.

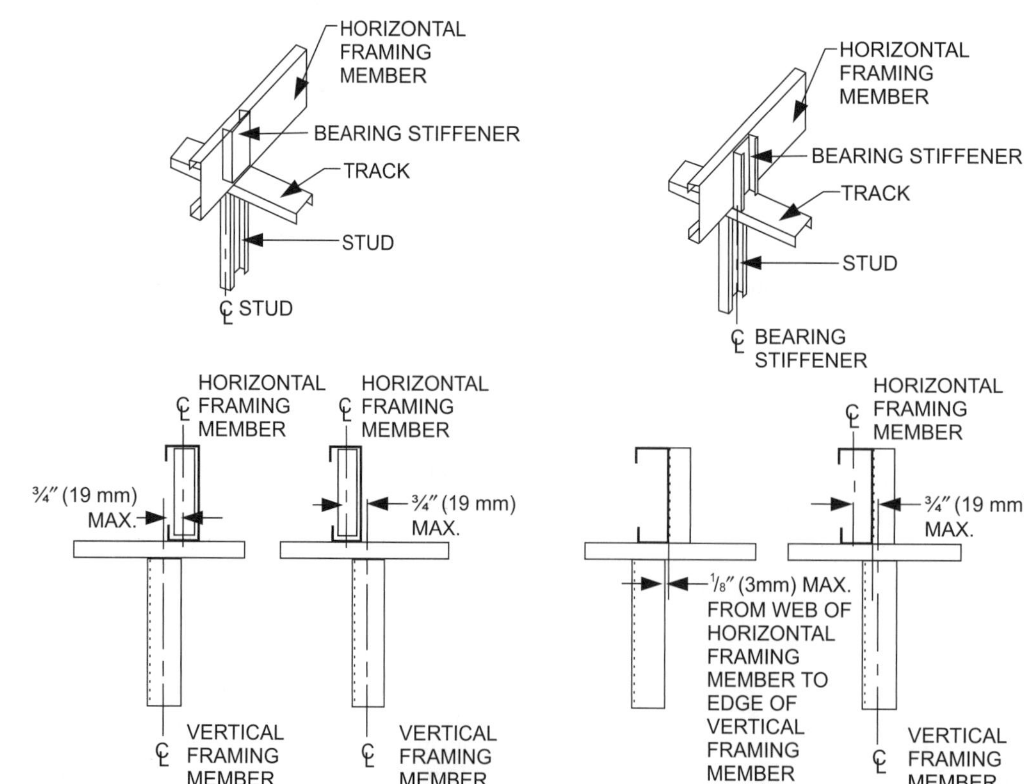

For SI: 1 inch = 25.4 mm.

FIGURE R505.1.2
IN-LINE FRAMING

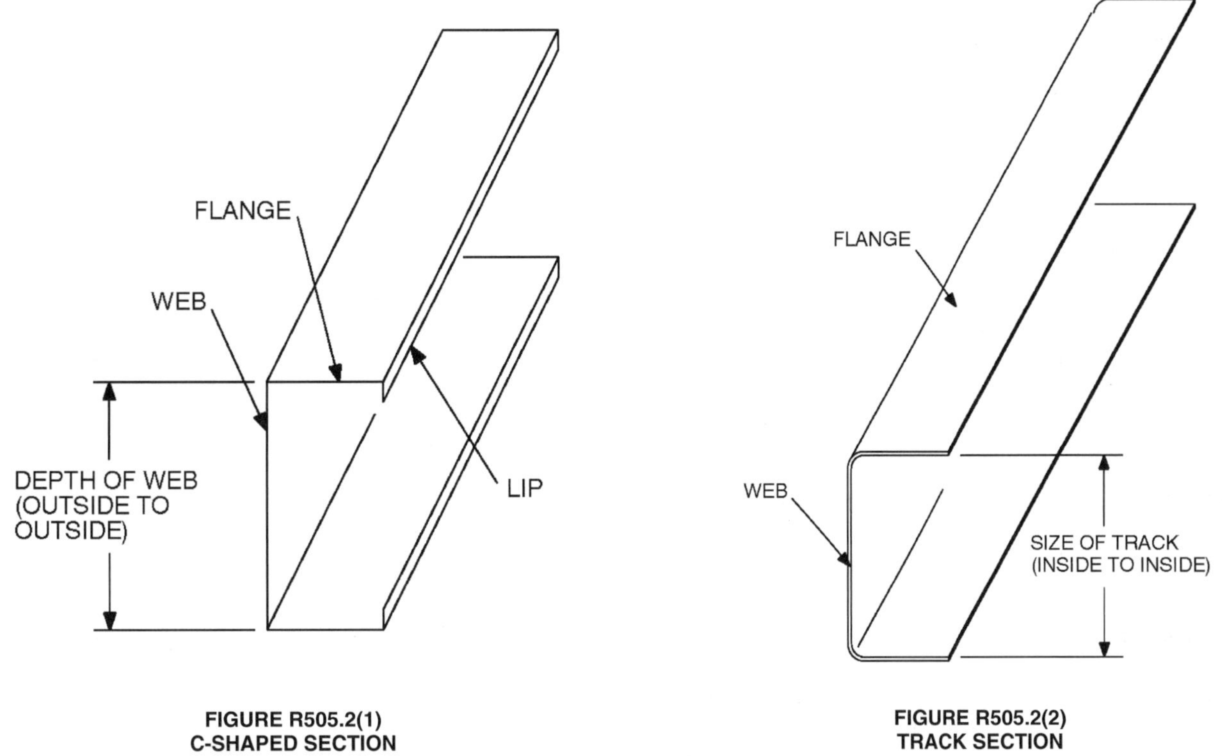

FIGURE R505.2(1)
C-SHAPED SECTION

FIGURE R505.2(2)
TRACK SECTION

TABLE R505.2(1)
COLD-FORMED STEEL JOIST SIZES

MEMBER DESIGNATION[a]	WEB DEPTH (inches)	MINIMUM FLANGE WIDTH (inches)	MAXIMUM FLANGE WIDTH (inches)	MINIMUM LIP SIZE (inches)
550S162-t	5.5	1.625	2	0.5
800S162-t	8	1.625	2	0.5
1000S162-t	10	1.625	2	0.5
1200S162-t	12	1.625	2	0.5

For SI: 1 inch = 25.4 mm, 1 mil = 0.0254 mm.

a. The member designation is defined by the first number representing the member depth in 0.01 inch, the letter "S" representing a stud or joist member, the second number representing the flange width in 0.01 inch, and the letter "t" shall be a number representing the minimum base metal thickness in mils [See Table R505.2(2)].

TABLE R505.2(2)
MINIMUM THICKNESS OF COLD-FORMED STEEL MEMBERS

DESIGNATION THICKNESS (mils)	MINIMUM BASE STEEL THICKNESS (inches)
33	0.0329
43	0.0428
54	0.0538
68	0.0677
97	0.0966

For SI: 1 inch = 25.4 mm, 1 mil = 0.0254 mm.

R505.2.4 Fastening requirements. Screws for steel-to-steel connections shall be installed with a minimum edge distance and center-to-center spacing of $^1/_2$ inch (12.7 mm), shall be self-drilling tapping, and shall conform to ASTM C 1513. Floor sheathing shall be attached to cold-formed steel joists with minimum No. 8 self-drilling tapping screws that conform to ASTM C 1513. Screws attaching floor-sheathing to cold-formed steel joists shall have a minimum head diameter of 0.292 inch (7.4 mm) with countersunk heads and shall be installed with a minimum edge distance of $^3/_8$ inch (9.5 mm). Gypsum board ceilings shall be attached to cold-formed steel joists with minimum No. 6 screws conforming to ASTM C 954 or ASTM C 1513 with a bugle head style and shall be installed in accordance with Section R702. For all connections, screws shall extend through the steel a minimum of three exposed threads. All fasteners shall have rust inhibitive coating suitable for the installation in which they are being used, or be manufactured from material not susceptible to corrosion.

Where No. 8 screws are specified in a steel-to-steel connection, the required number of screws in the connection is permitted to be reduced in accordance with the reduction factors in Table R505.2.4 when larger screws are used or when one of the sheets of steel being connected is thicker than 33 mils (0.84 mm). When applying the reduction factor, the resulting number of screws shall be rounded up.

TABLE R505.2.4
SCREW SUBSTITUTION FACTOR

SCREW SIZE	THINNEST CONNECTED STEEL SHEET (mils)	
	33	43
#8	1.0	0.67
#10	0.93	0.62
#12	0.86	0.56

For SI: 1 mil = 0.0254 mm.

R505.2.5 Web holes, web hole reinforcing and web hole patching. Web holes, web hole reinforcing, and web hole patching shall be in accordance with this section.

R505.2.5.1 Web holes. Web holes in floor joists shall comply with all of the following conditions:

1. Holes shall conform to Figure R505.2.5.1;
2. Holes shall be permitted only along the centerline of the web of the framing member;
3. Holes shall have a center-to-center spacing of not less than 24 inches (610 mm);
4. Holes shall have a web hole width not greater than 0.5 times the member depth, or $2^1/_2$ inches (64.5 mm);
5. Holes shall have a web hole length not exceeding $4^1/_2$ inches (114 mm); and
6. Holes shall have a minimum distance between the edge of the bearing surface and the edge of the web hole of not less than 10 inches (254 mm).

Framing members with web holes not conforming to the above requirements shall be reinforced in accordance with Section R505.2.5.2, patched in accordance with Section R505.2.5.3 or designed in accordance with accepted engineering practices.

R505.2.5.2 Web hole reinforcing. Reinforcement of web holes in floor joists not conforming to the requirements of Section R505.2.5.1 shall be permitted if the hole is located fully within the center 40 percent of the span and the depth and length of the hole does not exceed 65 percent of the flat width of the web. The reinforcing shall be a steel plate or C-shape section with a hole that does not exceed the web hole size limitations of Section R505.2.5.1 for the member being reinforced. The steel reinforcing shall be the same thickness as the receiving member and shall extend at least 1 inch (25.4 mm) beyond all edges of the hole. The steel reinforcing shall be fastened to the web of the receiving member with No.8 screws spaced no more than 1 inch (25.4 mm) center-to-center along the edges of the patch with minimum edge distance of $^1/_2$ inch (12.7 mm).

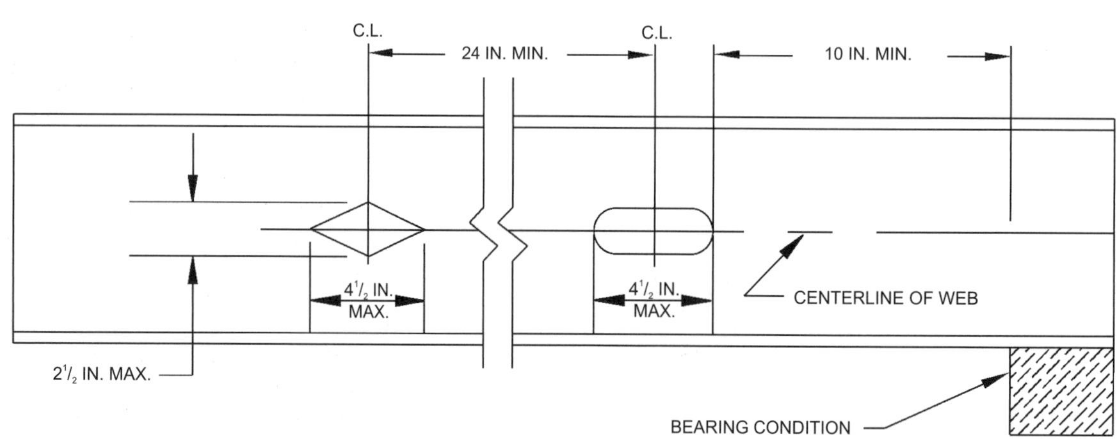

For SI: 1 inch = 25.4 mm.

FIGURE R505.2.5.1
FLOOR JOIST WEB HOLES

R505.2.5.3 Hole patching. Patching of web holes in floor joists not conforming to the requirements in Section R505.2.5.1 shall be permitted in accordance with either of the following methods:

1. Framing members shall be replaced or designed in accordance with accepted engineering practices where web holes exceed the following size limits:
   1.1. The depth of the hole, measured across the web, exceeds 70 percent of the flat width of the web; or
   1.2. The length of the hole measured along the web, exceeds 10 inches (254 mm) or the depth of the web, whichever is greater.
2. Web holes not exceeding the dimensional requirements in Section R505.2.5.3, Item 1, shall be patched with a solid steel plate, stud section, or track section in accordance with Figure R505.2.5.3. The steel patch shall, as a minimum, be of the same thickness as the receiving member and shall extend at least 1 inch (25 mm) beyond all edges of the hole. The steel patch shall be fastened to the web of the receiving member with No.8 screws spaced no more than 1 inch (25 mm) center-to-center along the edges of the patch with minimum edge distance of $^1/_2$ inch (13 mm).

R505.3 Floor construction. Cold-formed steel floors shall be constructed in accordance with this section.

R505.3.1 Floor to foundation or load-bearing wall connections. Cold-formed steel framed floors shall be anchored to foundations, wood sills or load-bearing walls in accordance with Table R505.3.1(1) and Figure R505.3.1(1), R505.3.1(2), R505.3.1(3), R505.3.1(4), R505.3.1(5) or R505.3.1(6). Anchor bolts shall be located not more than 12 inches (305 mm) from corners or the termination of bottom tracks. Continuous cold-formed steel joists supported by interior load-bearing walls shall be constructed in accordance with Figure R505.3.1(7). Lapped cold-formed steel joists shall be constructed in accordance with Figure R505.3.1(8). End floor joists constructed on foundation walls parallel to the joist span shall be doubled unless a C-shaped bearing stiffener, sized in accordance with Section R505.3.4, is installed web-to-web with the floor joist beneath each supported wall stud, as shown in Figure R505.3.1(9). Fastening of cold-formed steel joists to other framing members shall be in accordance with Section R505.2.4 and Table R505.3.1(2).

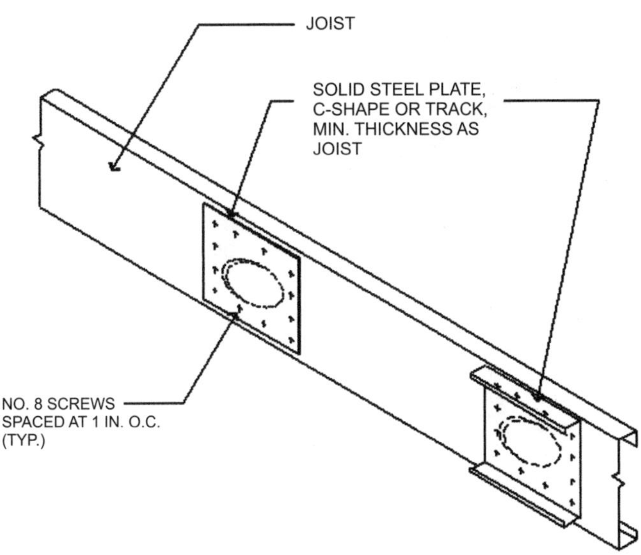

FIGURE R505.2.5.3
WEB HOLE PATCH

R505.3.2 Minimum floor joist sizes. Floor joist size and thickness shall be determined in accordance with the limits set forth in Table R505.3.2(1) for single spans, and Tables R505.3.2(2) and R505.3.2(3) for multiple spans. When continuous joist members are used, the interior bearing supports shall be located within 2 feet (610 mm) of mid-span of the cold-formed steel joists, and the individual spans shall not exceed the spans in Table R505.3.2(2) or R505.3.2(3), as applicable. Floor joists shall have a bearing support length of not less than $1^1/_2$ inches (38 mm) for exterior wall supports and $3^1/_2$ inches (89 mm) for interior wall supports. Tracks shall be a minimum of 33 mils (0.84 mm) thick except when used as part of a floor header or trimmer in accordance with Section R505.3.8. Bearing stiffeners shall be installed in accordance with Section R505.3.4.

R505.3.3 Joist bracing and blocking. Joist bracing and blocking shall be in accordance with this section.

R505.3.3.1 Joist top flange bracing. The top flanges of cold-formed steel joists shall be laterally braced by the application of floor sheathing fastened to the joists in accordance with Section R505.2.4 and Table R505.3.1(2).

R505.3.3.2 Joist bottom flange bracing/blocking. Floor joists with spans that exceed 12 feet (3658 mm) shall have the bottom flanges laterally braced in accordance with one of the following:

1. Gypsum board installed with minimum No. 6 screws in accordance with Section R702.
2. Continuous steel straps installed in accordance with Figure R505.3.3.2(1). Steel straps shall be spaced at a maximum of 12 feet (3658 mm) on center and shall be at least $1^1/_2$ inches (38 mm) in width and 33 mils (0.84 mm) in thickness. Straps shall be fastened to the bottom flange of each joist with one No. 8 screw, fastened to blocking with two No. 8 screws, and fastened at each end (of strap) with two No. 8 screws. Blocking in accordance with Figure R505.3.3.2(1) or Figure R505.3.3.2(2) shall be installed between joists at each end of the continuous strapping and at a maximum spacing of 12 feet (3658 mm) measured along the continuous strapping (perpendicular to the joist run). Blocking shall also be located at the termination of all straps. As an alternative to blocking at the ends, anchoring the strap to a stable building component with two No. 8 screws shall be permitted.

TABLE R505.3.1(1)
FLOOR TO FOUNDATION OR BEARING WALL CONNECTION REQUIREMENTS[a, b]

FRAMING CONDITION	BASIC WIND SPEED (mph) AND EXPOSURE	
	85 mph Exposure C or less than 110 mph Exposure B	Less than 110 mph Exposure C
Floor joist to wall track of exterior wall per Figure R505.3.1(1)	2-No. 8 screws	3-No. 8 screws
Rim track or end joist to load-bearing wall top track per Figure R505.3.1(1)	1-No. 8 screw at 24 inches o.c.	1-No. 8 screw at 24 inches o.c.
Rim track or end joist to wood sill per Figure R505.3.1(2)	Steel plate spaced at 4 feet o.c. with 4-No. 8 screws and 4-10d or 6-8d common nails	Steel plate spaced at 2 feet o.c. with 4-No. 8 screws and 4-10d or 6-8d common nails
Rim track or end joist to foundation per Figure R505.3.1(3)	$^1/_2$ inch minimum diameter anchor bolt and clip angle spaced at 6 feet o.c. with 8-No. 8 screws	$^1/_2$ inch minimum diameter anchor bolt and clip angle spaced at 4 feet o.c. with 8-No. 8 screws
Cantilevered joist to foundation per Figure R505.3.1(4)	$^1/_2$ inch minimum diameter anchor bolt and clip angle spaced at 6 feet o.c. with 8-No. 8 screws	$^1/_2$ inch minimum diameter anchor bolt and clip angle spaced at 4 feet o.c. with 8-No. 8 screws
Cantilevered joist to wood sill per Figure R505.3.1(5)	Steel plate spaced at 4 feet o.c. with 4-No. 8 screws and 4-10d or 6-8d common nails	Steel plate spaced at 2 feet o.c. with 4-No. 8 screws and 4-10d or 6-8d common nails
Cantilevered joist to exterior load-bearing wall track per Figure R505.3.1(6)	2-No. 8 screws	3-No. 8 screws

For SI: 1 inch = 25.4 mm, 1 pound per square foot = 0.0479 kPa, 1 mile per hour = 0.447 m/s, 1 foot = 304.8 mm.

a. Anchor bolts are to be located not more than 12 inches from corners or the termination of bottom tracks (e.g., at door openings or corners). Bolts extend a minimum of 15 inches into masonry or 7 inches into concrete. Anchor bolts connecting cold-formed steel framing to the foundation structure are to be installed so that the distance from the center of the bolt hole to the edge of the connected member is not less than one and one-half bolt diameters.

b. All screw sizes shown are minimum.

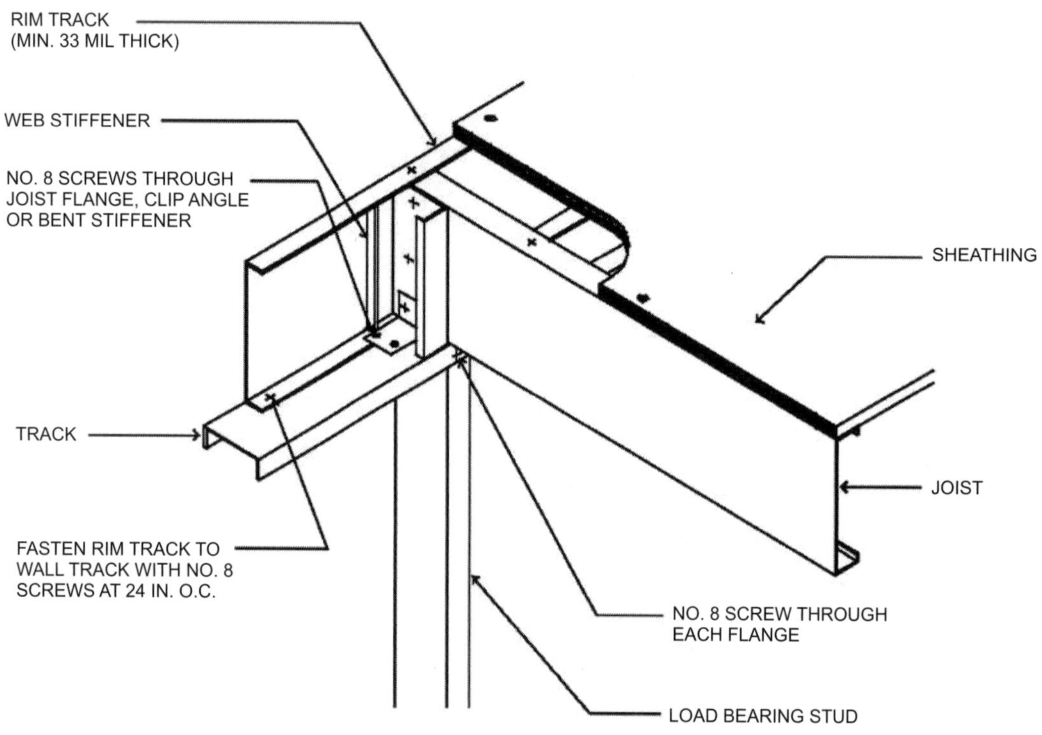

For SI: 1 mil = 0.0254 mm, 1 inch = 25.4 mm.

FIGURE 505.3.1(1)
FLOOR TO EXTERIOR LOAD-BEARING WALL STUD CONNECTION

TABLE R505.3.1(2)
FLOOR FASTENING SCHEDULE[a]

DESCRIPTION OF BUILDING ELEMENTS	NUMBER AND SIZE OF FASTENERS	SPACING OF FASTENERS
Floor joist to track of an interior load-bearing wall per Figures R505.3.1(7) and R505.3.1(8)	2 No. 8 screws	Each joist
Floor joist to track at end of joist	2 No. 8 screws	One per flange or two per bearing stiffener
Subfloor to floor joists	No. 8 screws	6 in. o.c. on edges and 12 in. o.c. at intermediate supports

For SI: 1 inch = 25.4 mm.
a. All screw sizes shown are minimum.

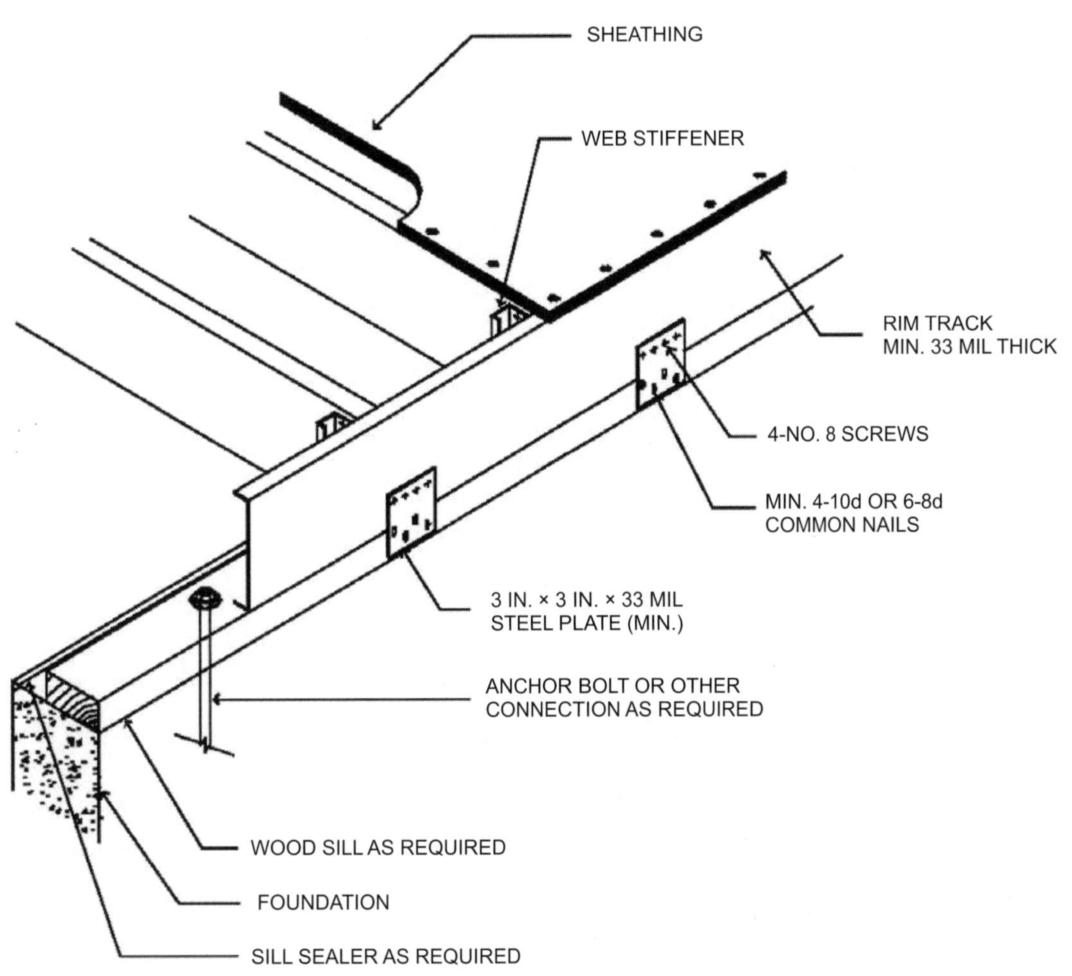

For SI: 1 mil = 0.0254 mm, 1 inch = 25.4 mm.

FIGURE R505.3.1(2)
FLOOR TO WOOD SILL CONNECTION

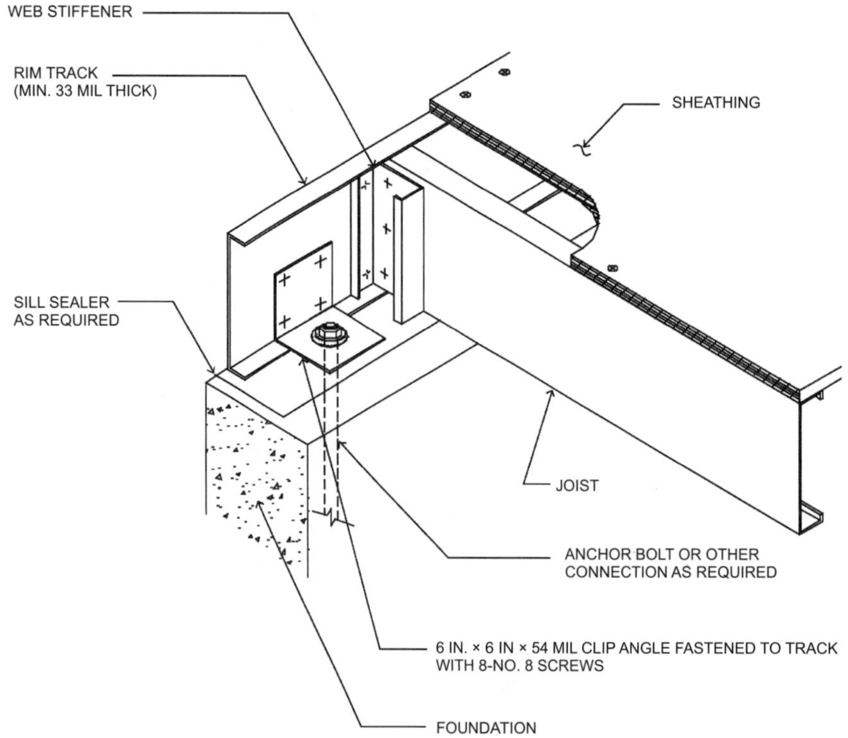

For SI: 1 mil = 0.0254 mm, 1 inch = 25.4 mm.

FIGURE R505.3.1(3)
FLOOR TO FOUNDATION CONNECTION

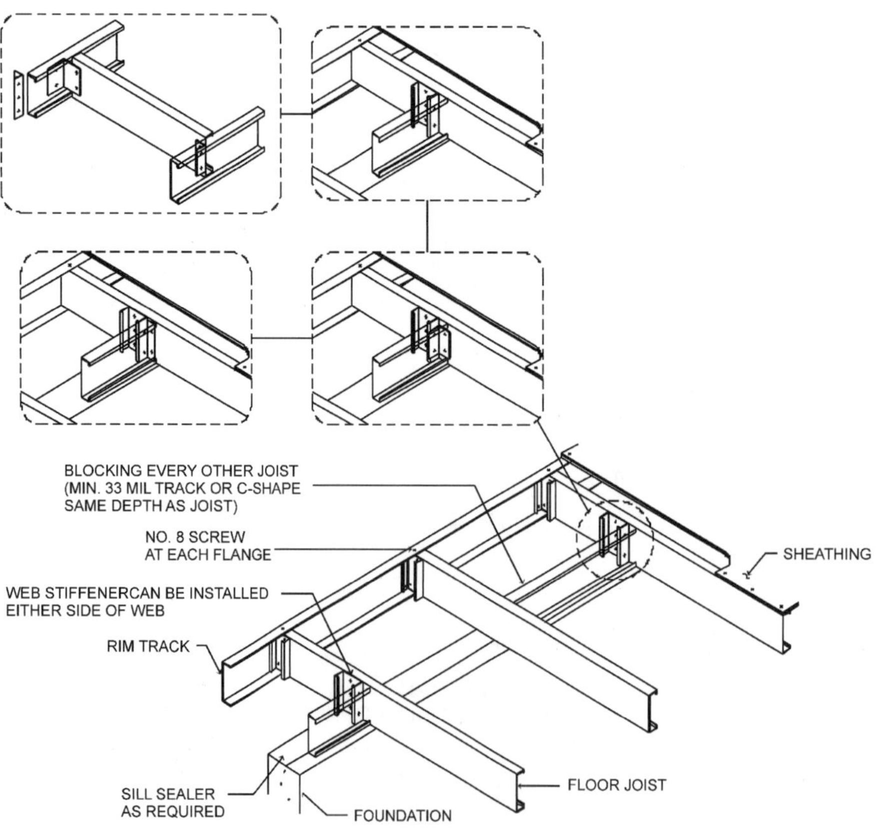

For SI: 1 mil = 0.0254 mm.

FIGURE R505.3.1(4)
CANTILEVERED FLOOR TO FOUNDATION CONNECTION

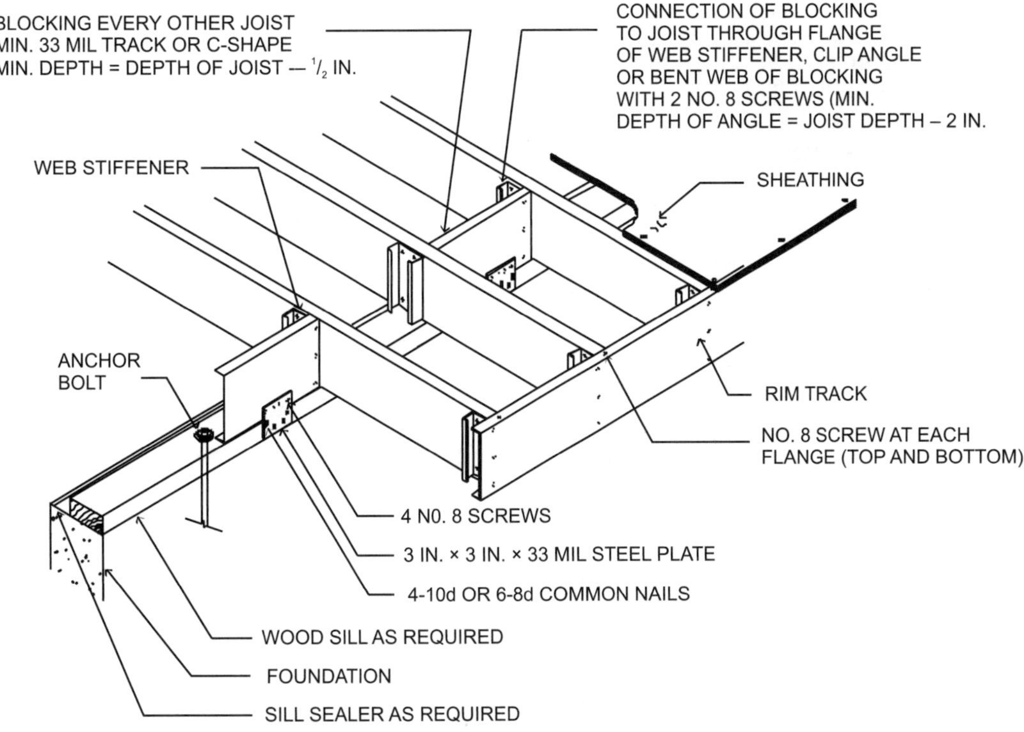

For SI: 1 mil = 0.0254 mm, 1 inch = 25.4 mm.

FIGURE R505.3.1(5)
CANTILEVERED FLOOR TO WOOD SILL CONNECTION

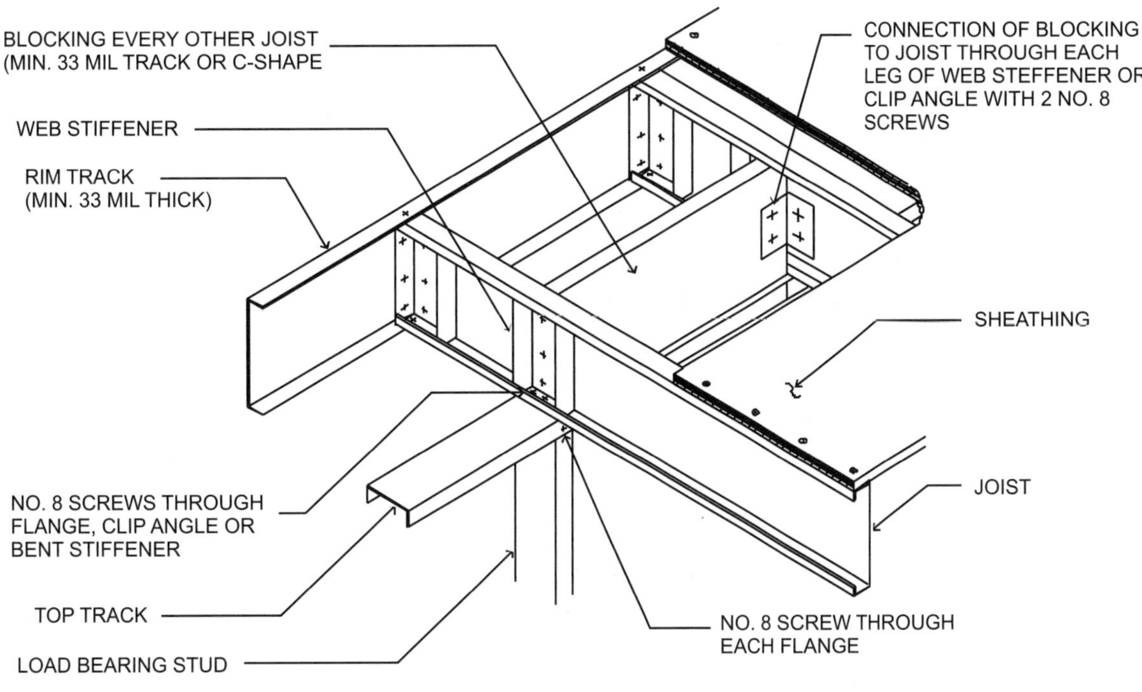

For SI: 1 mil = 0.0254 mm.

FIGURE R505.3.1(6)
CANTILEVERED FLOOR TO EXTERIOR LOAD-BEARING WALL CONNECTION

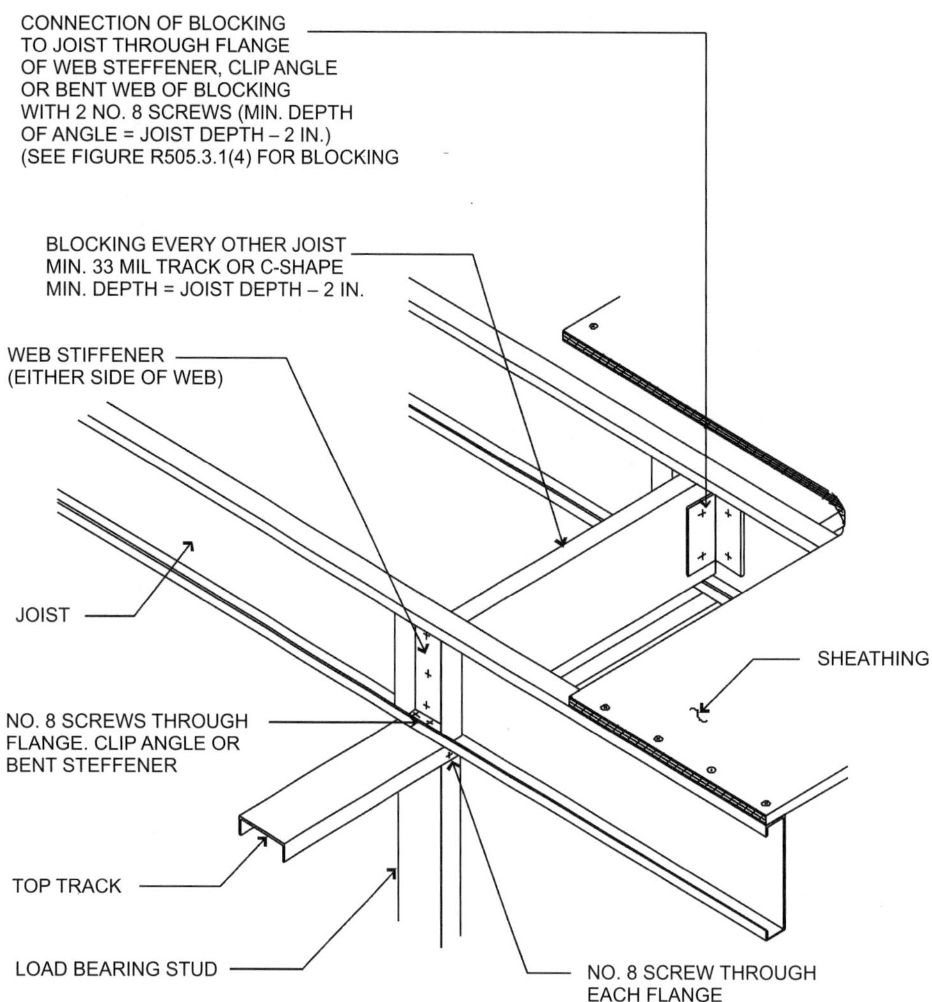

For SI: 1 mil = 0.0254 mm, 1 inch = 25.4 mm.

FIGURE R505.3.1(7)
CONTINUOUS SPAN JOIST SUPPORTED ON INTERIOR LOAD-BEARING WALL

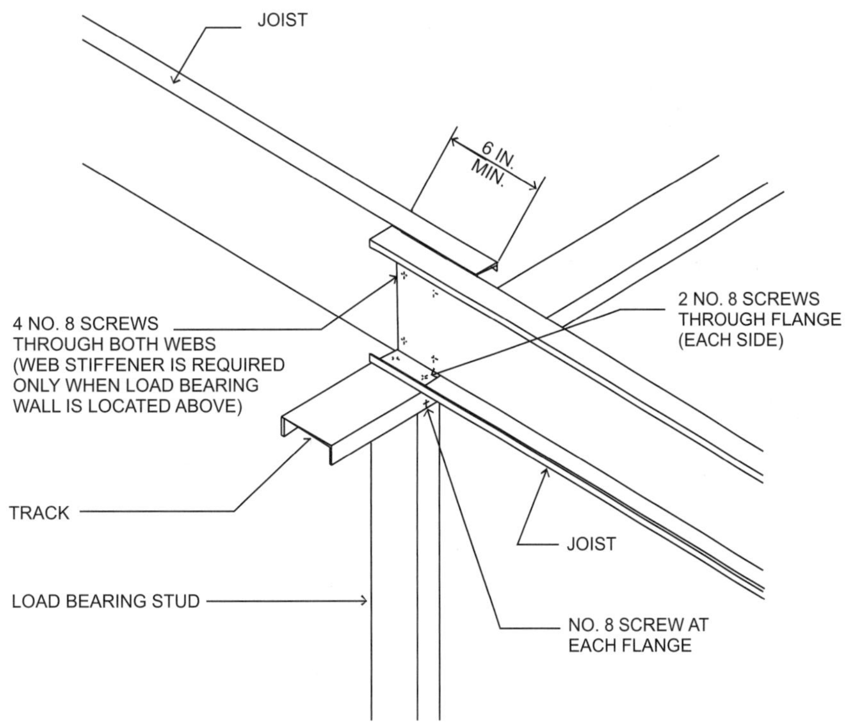

For SI: 1 inch = 25.4 mm.

FIGURE R505.3.1(8)
LAPPED JOISTS SUPPORTED ON INTERIOR LOAD-BEARING WALL

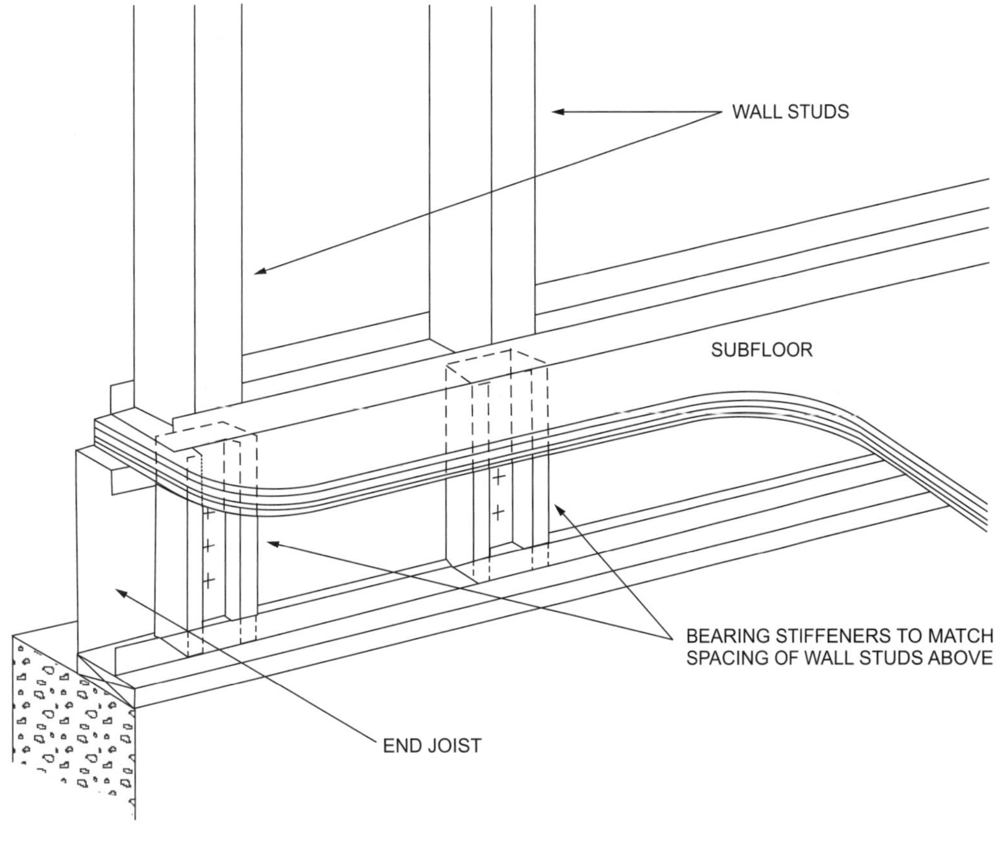

FIGURE R505.3.1(9)
BEARING STIFFENERS FOR END JOISTS

**TABLE R505.3.2(1)
ALLOWABLE SPANS FOR COLD-FORMED STEEL JOISTS—SINGLE SPANS[a, b, c, d] 33 ksi STEEL**

JOIST DESIGNATION	30 PSF LIVE LOAD				40 PSF LIVE LOAD			
	Spacing (inches)				Spacing (inches)			
	12	16	19.2	24	12	16	19.2	24
550S162-33	11′-7″	10′-7″	9′-6″	8′-6″	10′-7″	9′-3″	8′-6″	7′-6″
550S162-43	12′-8″	11′-6″	10′-10″	10′-2″	11′-6″	10′-5″	9′-10″	9′-1″
550S162-54	13′-7″	12′-4″	11′-7″	10′-9″	12′-4″	11′-2″	10′-6″	9′-9″
550S162-68	14′-7″	13′-3″	12′-6″	11′-7″	13′-3″	12′-0″	11′-4″	10′-6″
550S162-97	16′-2″	14′-9″	13′-10″	12′-10″	14′-9″	13′-4″	12′-7″	11′-8″
800S162-33	15′-8″	13′-11″	12′-9″	11′-5″	14′-3″	12′-5″	11′-3″	9′-0″
800S162-43	17′-1″	15′-6″	14′-7″	13′-7″	15′-6″	14′-1″	13′-3″	12′-4″
800S162-54	18′-4″	16′-8″	15′-8″	14′-7″	16′-8″	15′-2″	14′-3″	13′-3″
800S162-68	19′-9″	17′-11″	16′-10″	15′-8″	17′-11″	16′-3″	15′-4″	14′-2″
800S162-97	22′-0″	20′-0″	16′-10″	17′-5″	20′-0″	18′-2″	17′-1″	15′-10″
1000S162-43	20′-6″	18′-8″	17′-6″	15′-8″	18′-8″	16′-11″	15′-6″	13′-11″
1000S162-54	22′-1″	20′-0″	18′-10″	17′-6″	20′-0″	18′-2″	17′-2″	15′-11″
1000S162-68	23′- 9″	21′-7″	20′-3″	18′-10″	21′-7″	19′-7″	18′-5″	17′-1″
1000S162-97	26′-6″	24′-1″	22′-8″	21′-0″	24′-1″	21′-10″	20′-7″	19′-1″
1200S162-43	23′-9″	20′-10″	19′-0″	16′-8″	21′-5″	18′-6″	16′-6″	13′-2″
1200S162-54	25′-9″	23′-4″	22′-0″	20′-1″	23′-4″	21′-3″	20′-0″	17′-10″
1200S162-68	27′-8″	25′-1″	23′-8″	21′-11″	25′-1″	22′-10″	21′-6″	21′-1″
1200S162-97	30′-11″	28′-1″	26′-5″	24′-6″	28′-1″	25′-6″	24′-0″	22′-3″

For SI: 1 inch = 25.4 mm, 1 foot = 304.8 mm, 1 pound per square foot = 0.0479kPa.

a. Deflection criteria: *L*/480 for live loads, *L*/240 for total loads.

b. Floor dead load = 10 psf.

c. Table provides the maximum clear span in feet and inches.

d. Bearing stiffeners are to be installed at all support points and concentrated loads.

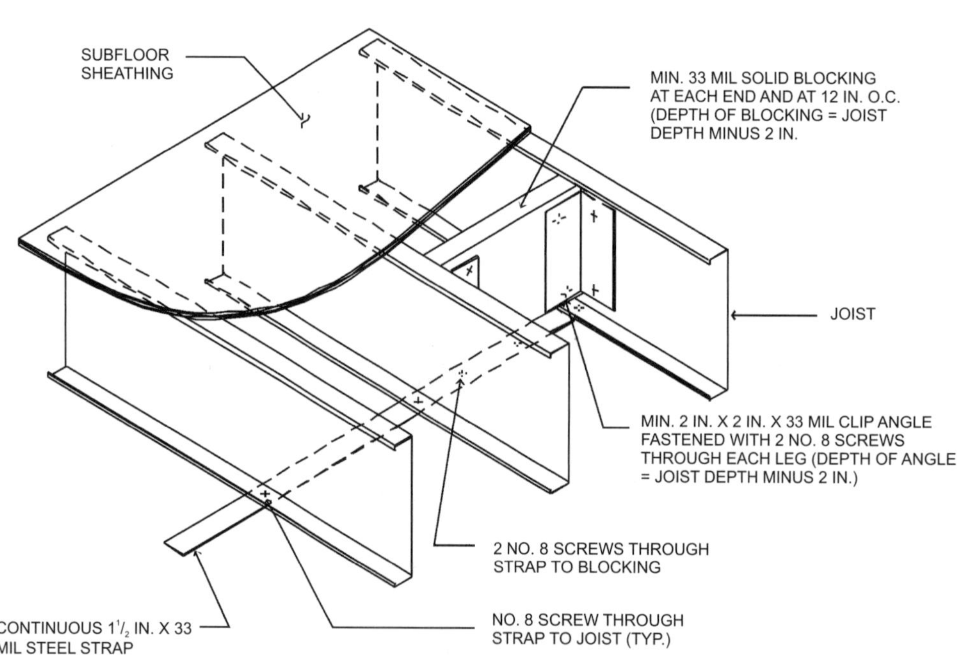

For SI: 1 mil = 0.0254 mm, 1 inch = 25.4 mm.

**FIGURE R505.3.3.2(1)
JOIST BLOCKING (SOLID)**

TABLE R505.3.2(2)
ALLOWABLE SPANS FOR COLD-FORMED STEEL JOISTS—MULTIPLE SPANS[a, b, c, d, e, f] 33 ksi STEEL

JOIST DESIGNATION	30 PSF LIVE LOAD				40 PSF LIVE LOAD			
	Spacing (inches)				Spacing (inches)			
	12	16	19.2	24	12	16	19.2	24
550S162-33	12′-1″	10′-5″	9′-6″	8′-6″	10′-9″	9′-3″	8′-6″	7′-6″
550S162-43	14′-5″	12′-5″	11′-4″	10′-2″	12′-9″	11′-11″	10′-1″	9′-0″
550S162-54	16′-3″	14′-1″	12′-10″	11′-6″	14′-5″	12′-6″	11′-5″	10′-2″
550S162-68	19′-7″	17′-9″	16′-9″	15′-6″	17′-9″	16′-2″	15′-2″	14′-1″
550S162-97	21′-9″	19′-9″	18′-7″	17′-3″	19′-9″	17′-11″	16′-10″	15′-4″
800S162-33	14′-8″	11′-10″	10′-4″	8′-8″	12′-4″	9′-11″	8′-7″	7′-2″
800S162-43	20′-0″	17′-4″	15′-9″	14′-1″	17′-9″	15′-4″	14′-0″	12′-0″
800S162-54	23′-7″	20′-5″	18′-8″	16′-8″	21′-0″	18′-2″	16′-7″	14′-10″
800S162-68	26′-5″	23′-1″	21′-0″	18′-10″	23′-8″	20′-6″	18′-8″	16′-9″
800S162-97	29′-6″	26′-10″	25′-3″	22′-8″	26′-10″	24′-4″	22′-6″	20′-2″
1000S162-43	22′-2″	18′-3″	16′-0″	13′-7″	18′-11″	15′-5″	13′-6″	11′-5″
1000S162-54	26′-2″	22′-8″	20′-8″	18′-6″	23′-3″	20′-2″	18′-5″	16′-5″
1000S162-68	31′- 5″	27′-2″	24′-10″	22′-2″	27′-11″	24′-2″	22′-1″	19′-9″
1000S162-97	35′-6″	32′-3″	29′-11″	26′-9″	32′-3″	29′-2″	26′-7″	23′-9″
1200S162-43	21′-8″	17′-6″	15′-3″	12′-10″	18′-3″	14′-8″	12′-8″	10′-6^{2}
1200S162-54	28′-5″	24′-8″	22′-6″	19′-6″	25′-3″	21′-11″	19′-4″	16′-6″
1200S162-68	33′-7″	29′-1″	26′-6″	23′-9″	29′-10″	25′-10″	23′-7″	21′-1″
1200S162-97	41′-5″	37′-8″	34′-6″	30′-10″	37′-8″	33′-6″	30′-7″	27′-5″

For SI: 1 inch = 25.4 mm, 1 foot = 304.8 mm, 1 pound per square foot = 0.0479kPa.

a. Deflection criteria: *L*/480 for live loads, *L*/240 for total loads.
b. Floor dead load = 10 psf.
c. Table provides the maximum clear span in feet and inches to either side of the interior support.
d. Interior bearing supports for multiple span joists consist of structural (bearing) walls or beams.
e. Bearing stiffeners are to be installed at all support points and concentrated loads.
f. Interior supports shall be located within 2 feet of mid-span provided that each of the resulting spans does not exceed the appropriate maximum span shown in the table above.

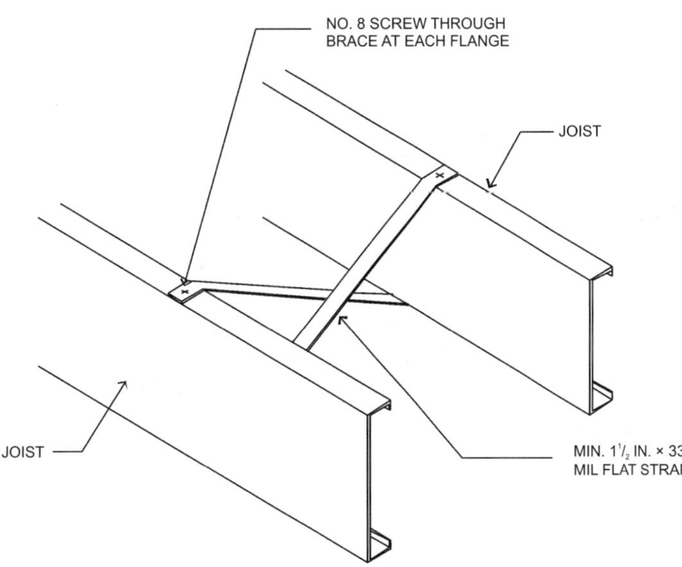

For SI: 1 mil = 0.0254 = 25.4 mm.

FIGURE R505.3.3.2(2)
JOIST BLOCKING (STRAP)

TABLE R505.3.2(3)
ALLOWABLE SPANS FOR COLD-FORMED STEEL JOISTS—MULTIPLE SPANS[a, b, c, d, e, f] 50 ksi STEEL

JOIST DESIGNATION	30 PSF LIVE LOAD				40 PSF LIVE LOAD			
	Spacing (inches)				Spacing (inches)			
	12	16	19.2	24	12	16	19.2	24
550S162-33	13′-11″	12′-0″	11′-0″	9′-3″	12′-3″	10′-8″	9′-7″	8′-4″
550S162-43	16′-3″	14′-1″	12′-10″	11′-6″	14′-6″	12′-6″	11′-5″	10′-3″
550S162-54	18′-2″	16′-6″	15′-4″	13′-8″	16′-6″	14′-11″	13′-7″	12′-2″
550S162-68	19′-6″	17′-9″	16′-8″	15′-6″	17′-9″	16′-1″	15′-2″	14′-0″
550S162-97	21′-9″	19′-9″	18′-6″	17′-2″	19′-8″	17′-10″	16′-8″	15′-8″
800S162-33	15′-6″	12′-6″	10′-10″	9′-1″	13′-0″	10′-5″	8′-11″	6′-9″
800S162-43	22′-0″	19′-1″	17′-5″	15′-0″	19′-7″	16′-11″	14′-10″	12′-8″
800S162-54	24′-6″	22′-4″	20′-6″	17′-11″	22′-5″	19′-9″	17′-11″	15′-10″
800S162-68	26′-6″	24′-1″	22′-8″	21′-0″	24′-1″	21′-10″	20′-7″	19′-2″
800S162-97	29′-9″	26′-8″	25′-2″	23′-5″	26′-8″	24′-3″	22′-11″	21′-4″
1000S162-43	23′-6″	19′-2″	16′-9″	14′-2″	19′-11″	16′-2″	14′-0″	11′-9″
1000S162-54	28′-2″	23′-10″	21′-7″	18′-11″	24′-8″	20′-11″	18′-9″	18′-4″
1000S162-68	31′- 10″	28′-11″	27′-2″	25′-3″	28′-11″	26′-3″	24′-9″	22′-9″
1000S162-97	35′-4″	32′-1″	30′-3″	28′-1″	32′-1″	29′-2″	27′-6″	25′-6″
1200S162-43	22′-11″	18′-5″	16′-0″	13′-4″	19′-2″	15′-4″	13′-2″	10′-6″
1200S162-54	32′-8″	28′-1″	24′-9″	21′-2″	29′-0″	23′-10″	20′-11″	17′-9″
1200S162-68	37′-1″	32′-5″	29′-4″	25′-10″	33′-4″	28′-6″	25′-9″	22′-7″
1200S162-97	41′-2″	37′-6″	35′-3″	32′-9″	37′-6″	34′-1″	32′-1″	29′-9″

For SI: 1 inch = 25.4 mm, 1 foot = 304.8 mm, 1 pound per square foot = 0.0479kPa.

a. Deflection criteria: *L*/480 for live loads, *L*/240 for total loads.

b. Floor dead load = 10 psf.

c. Table provides the maximum clear span in feet and inches to either side of the interior support.

d. Interior bearing supports for multiple span joists consist of structural (bearing) walls or beams.

e. Bearing stiffeners are to be installed at all support points and concentrated loads.

f. Interior supports shall be located within 2 feet of mid-span provided that each of the resulting spans does not exceed the appropriate maximum span shown in the table above.

R505.3.3.3 Blocking at interior bearing supports. Blocking is not required for continuous back-to-back floor joists at bearing supports. Blocking shall be installed between every other joist for single continuous floor joists across bearing supports in accordance with Figure R505.3.1(7). Blocking shall consist of C-shape or track section with a minimum thickness of 33 mils (0.84 mm). Blocking shall be fastened to each adjacent joist through a 33-mil (0.84 mm) clip angle, bent web of blocking or flanges of web stiffeners with two No. 8 screws on each side. The minimum depth of the blocking shall be equal to the depth of the joist minus 2 inches (51 mm). The minimum length of the angle shall be equal to the depth of the joist minus 2 inches (51 mm).

R505.3.3.4 Blocking at cantilevers. Blocking shall be installed between every other joist over cantilever bearing supports in accordance with Figure R505.3.1(4), R505.3.1(5) or R505.3.1(6). Blocking shall consist of C-shape or track section with minimum thickness of 33 mils (0.84 mm). Blocking shall be fastened to each adjacent joist through bent web of blocking, 33 mil clip angle or flange of web stiffener with two No.8 screws at each end. The depth of the blocking shall be equal to the depth of the joist. The minimum length of the angle shall be equal to the depth of the joist minus 2 inches (51 mm). Blocking shall be fastened through the floor sheathing and to the support with three No.8 screws (top and bottom).

R505.3.4 Bearing stiffeners. Bearing stiffeners shall be installed at each joist bearing location in accordance with this section, except for joists lapped over an interior support not carrying a load-bearing wall above. Floor joists supporting jamb studs with multiple members shall have two bearing stiffeners in accordance with Figure R505.3.4(1). Bearing stiffeners shall be fabricated from a C-shaped, track or clip angle member in accordance with the one of following:

1. C-shaped bearing stiffeners:

   1.1. Where the joist is not carrying a load-bearing wall above, the bearing stiffener shall be a minimum 33 mil (0.84 mm) thickness.

1.2. Where the joist is carrying a load-bearing wall above, the bearing stiffener shall be at least the same designation thickness as the wall stud above.

2. Track bearing stiffeners:

   2.1. Where the joist is not carrying a load-bearing wall above, the bearing stiffener shall be a minimum 43 mil (1.09 mm) thickness.

   2.2. Where the joist is carrying a load-bearing wall above, the bearing stiffener shall be at least one designation thickness greater than the wall stud above.

3. Clip angle bearing stiffeners: Where the clip angle bearing stiffener is fastened to both the web of the member it is stiffening and an adjacent rim track using the fastener pattern shown in Figure R505.3.4(2), the bearing stiffener shall be a minimum 2-inch by 2-inch (51 mm by 51 mm) angle sized in accordance with Tables R505.3.4(1),R505.3.4(2),R505.3.4(3), and R505.3.4(4).

The minimum length of a bearing stiffener shall be the depth of member being stiffened minus $^3/_8$ inch (9.5 mm). Each bearing stiffener shall be fastened to the web of the member it is stiffening as shown in Figure R505.3.4(2). Each clip angle bearing stiffener shall also be fastened to the web of the adjacent rim track using the fastener pattern shown in Figure R505.3.4(2). No. 8 screws shall be used for C-shaped and track members of any thickness and for clip angle members with a designation thickness less than or equal to 54. No. 10 screws shall be used for clip angle members with a designation thickness greater than 54.

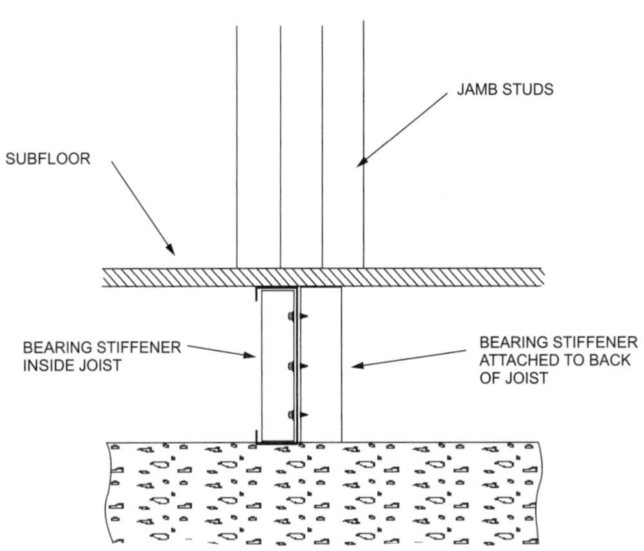

FIGURE R505.3.4(1)
BEARING STIFFENERS UNDER JAMB STUDS

TABLE R505.3.4(1)
CLIP ANGLE BEARING STIFFENERS
(20 psf equivalent snow load)

JOIST DESIGNATION	MINIMUM THICKNESS (mils) OF 2-INCH × 2-INCH (51 mm × 51 mm) CLIP ANGLE											
	Top floor				Bottom floor in 2 story Middle floor in 3 story				Bottom floor in 3 story			
	Joist spacing (inches)				Joist spacing (inches)				Joist spacing (inches)			
	12	16	19.2	24	12	16	19.2	24	12	16	19.2	24
800S162-33	43	43	43	43	43	54	68	68	68	97	97	—
800S162-43	43	43	43	43	54	54	68	68	97	97	97	97
800S162-54	43	43	43	43	43	54	68	68	68	97	97	—
800S162-68	43	43	43	43	43	43	54	68	54	97	97	—
800S162-97	43	43	43	43	43	43	43	43	43	43	54	97
1000S162-43	43	43	43	43	54	68	97	97	97	—	—	—
1000S162-54	43	43	43	43	54	68	68	97	97	97	—	—
1000S162-68	43	43	43	43	54	68	97	97	97	—	—	—
1000S162-97	43	43	43	43	43	43	43	54	43	68	97	—
1200S162-43	43	54	54	54	97	97	97	97	—	—	—	—
1200S162-54	54	54	54	54	97	97	97	97	—	—	—	—
1200S162-68	43	43	54	54	68	97	97	97	—	—	—	—
1200S162-97	43	43	43	43	43	54	68	97	97	—	—	—

For SI: 1 mil = 0.254 mm, 1 inch = 25.4 mm, 1 pound per square foot = 0.0479kPa..

TABLE R505.3.4(2)
CLIP ANGLE BEARING STIFFENERS
(30 psf equivalent snow load)

JOIST DESIGNATION	MINIMUM THICKNESS (mils) OF 2-INCH × 2 INCH (51 mm × 51 mm) CLIP ANGLE											
	Top floor				Bottom floor in 2 story Middle floor in 3 story				Bottom floor in 3 story			
	Joist spacing (inches)				Joist spacing (inches)				Joist spacing (inches)			
	12	16	19.2	24	12	16	19.2	24	12	16	19.2	24
800S162-33	43	43	43	43	54	68	68	97	97	97	97	—
800S162-43	43	43	43	54	68	68	68	97	97	97	97	—
800S162-54	43	43	43	43	54	68	68	97	97	97	—	—
800S162-68	43	43	43	43	43	54	68	97	68	97	97	—
800S162-97	43	43	43	43	43	43	43	43	43	43	68	97
1000S162-43	54	54	54	54	68	97	97	97	97	—	—	—
1000S162-54	54	54	54	54	68	97	97	97	97	—	—	—
1000S162-68	43	43	54	68	68	97	97	—	97	—	—	—
1000S162-97	43	43	43	43	43	43	54	68	54	97	—	—
1200S162-43	54	68	68	68	97	97	97	—	—	—	—	—
1200S162-54	68	68	68	68	97	97	—	—	—	—	—	—
1200S162-68	68	68	68	68	97	97	97	—	—	—	—	—
1200S162-97	43	43	43	43	54	68	97	—	97	—	—	—

For SI: 1 mil = 0.0254 mm, 1 inch = 25.4 mm, 1pound per square foot = 0.0479 kPa.

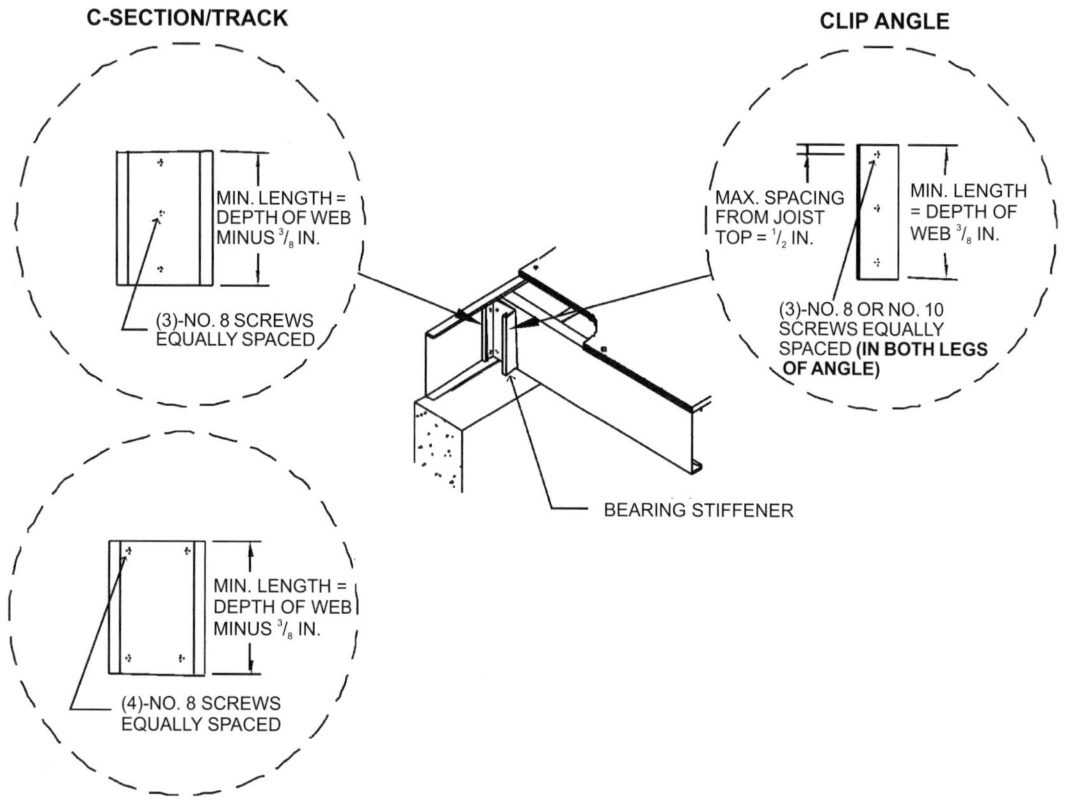

For SI: 1 inch = 25.4 mm.

FIGURE R505.3.4(2)
BEARING STIFFENER

TABLE R505.3.4(3)
CLIP ANGLE BEARING STIFFENERS
(50 psf equivalent snow load)

JOIST DESIGNATION	MINIMUM THICKNESS (mils) OF 2-INCH × 2-INCH (51 mm × 51 mm) CLIP ANGLE											
	Top floor				Bottom floor in 2 story Middle floor in 3 story				Bottom floor in 3 story			
	Joist spacing (inches)				Joist spacing (inches)				Joist spacing (inches)			
	12	16	19.2	24	12	16	19.2	24	12	16	19.2	24
800S162-33	54	54	54	54	68	97	97	97	97	—	—	—
800S162-43	68	68	68	68	97	97	97	97	—	—	—	—
800S162-54	54	68	68	68	97	97	97	97	—	—	—	—
800S162-68	43	43	54	54	68	97	97	97	97	—	—	—
800S162-97	43	43	43	43	43	43	43	54	54	68	97	—
1000S162-43	97	68	68	68	97	97	97	97	—	—	—	—
1000S162-54	97	97	68	68	97	97	97	—	—	—	—	—
1000S162-68	68	97	97	97	97	—	—	—	—	—	—	—
1000S162-97	43	43	43	43	54	68	97	97	—	—	—	—
1200S162-43	97	97	97	97	—	—	—	—	—	—	—	—
1200S162-54	—	97	97	97	—	—	—	—	—	—	—	—
1200S162-68	97	97	97	97	—	—	—	—	—	—	—	—
1200S162-97	54	68	68	97	97	—	—	—	—	—	—	—

For SI: 1 mil = 0.0254 mm, 1 inch = 25.4 mm, 1 pound per square foot = 0.0479kPa.

TABLE R505.3.4(4)
CLIP ANGLE BEARING STIFFENERS
(70 psf equivalent snow load)

JOIST DESIGNATION	MINIMUM THICKNESS (mils) OF 2-INCH × 2-INCH (51 mm × 51 mm) CLIP ANGLE											
	Top floor				Bottom floor in 2 story Middle floor in 3 story				Bottom floor in 3 story			
	Joist spacing (inches)				Joist spacing (inches)				Joist spacing (inches)			
	12	16	19.2	24	12	16	19.2	24	12	16	19.2	24
800S162-33	68	68	68	68	97	97	97	97	—	—	—	—
800S162-43	97	97	97	97	97	97	97	—	—	—	—	—
800S162-54	97	97	97	97	97	—	—	—	—	—	—	—
800S162-68	68	68	68	97	97	97	97	—	—	—	—	—
800S162-97	43	43	43	43	43	54	68	97	97	97	—	—
1000S162-43	97	97	97	97	—	—	—	—	—	—	—	—
1000S162-54	—	97	97	97	—	—	—	—	—	—	—	—
1000S162-68	97	97	—	—	—	—	—	—	—	—	—	—
1000S162-97	68	68	68	68	97	97	—	—	—	—	—	—
1200S162-43	97	97	97	97	—	—	—	—	—	—	—	—
1200S162-54	—	—	—	—	—	—	—	—	—	—	—	—
1200S162-68	—	—	—	—	—	—	—	—	—	—	—	—
1200S162-97	97	97	97	—	—	—	—	—	—	—	—	—

For SI: 1 mil 0.0254 mm, 1 inch = 25.4 mm, 1 pound per square foot = 0.0479kPa.

R505.3.5 Cutting and notching. Flanges and lips of load-bearing cold-formed steel floor framing members shall not be cut or notched.

R505.3.6 Floor cantilevers. Floor cantilevers for the top floor of a two- or three-story building or the first floor of a one-story building shall not exceed 24 inches (610 mm). Cantilevers, not exceeding 24 inches (610 mm) and supporting two stories and roof (i.e., first floor of a two-story building), shall also be permitted provided that all cantilevered joists are doubled (nested or back-to-back). The doubled cantilevered joists shall extend a minimum of 6 feet (1829 mm) toward the inside and shall be fastened with a minimum of two No.8 screws spaced at 24 inches (610 mm) on center through the webs (for back-to-back) or flanges (for nested joists).

R505.3.7 Splicing. Joists and other structural members shall not be spliced. Splicing of tracks shall conform to Figure R505.3.7.

R505.3.8 Framing of floor openings. Openings in floors shall be framed with header and trimmer joists. Header joist spans shall not exceed 6 feet (1829 mm) or 8 feet (2438 mm) in length in accordance with Figure R505.3.8(1) or R505.3.8(2), respectively. Header and trimmer joists shall be fabricated from joist and track members, having a minimum size and thickness at least equivalent to the adjacent floor joists and shall be installed in accordance with Figures R505.3.8(1), R505.3.8(2), R505.3.8(3), and R505.3.8(4). Each header joist shall be connected to trimmer joists with four 2-inch-by-2-inch (51mm by 51 mm) clip angles. Each clip angle shall be fastened to both the header and trimmer joists with four No. 8 screws, evenly spaced, through each leg of the clip angle. The clip angles shall have a thickness not less than that of the floor joist. Each track section for a built-up header or trimmer joist shall extend the full length of the joist (continuous).

SECTION R506
CONCRETE FLOORS (ON GROUND)

R506.1 General. Concrete slab-on-ground floors shall be a minimum 3.5 inches (89 mm) thick (for expansive soils, see Section R403.1.8). The specified compressive strength of concrete shall be as set forth in Section R402.2.

R506.2 Site preparation. The area within the foundation walls shall have all vegetation, top soil and foreign material removed.

R506.2.1 Fill. Fill material shall be free of vegetation and foreign material. The fill shall be compacted to assure uniform support of the slab, and except where *approved*, the fill depths shall not exceed 24 inches (610 mm) for clean sand or gravel and 8 inches (203 mm) for earth.

R506.2.2 Base. A 4-inch-thick (102 mm) base course consisting of clean graded sand, gravel, crushed stone or crushed blast-furnace slag passing a 2-inch (51 mm) sieve shall be placed on the prepared subgrade when the slab is below *grade*.

Exception: A base course is not required when the concrete slab is installed on well-drained or sand-gravel mixture soils classified as Group I according to the United Soil Classification System in accordance with Table R405.1.

R506.2.3 Vapor retarder. A 6 mil (0.006 inch; 152 μm) polyethylene or *approved* vapor retarder with joints lapped not less than 6 inches (152 mm) shall be placed between the concrete floor slab and the base course or the prepared subgrade where no base course exists.

Exception: The vapor retarder may be omitted:

1. From detached garages, utility buildings and other unheated *accessory structures*.
2. For unheated storage rooms having an area of less than 70 square feet (6.5 m²) and carports.
3. From driveways, walks, patios and other flatwork not likely to be enclosed and heated at a later date.
4. Where *approved* by the *building official*, based on local site conditions.

R506.2.4 Reinforcement support. Where provided in slabs on ground, reinforcement shall be supported to remain in place from the center to upper one third of the slab for the duration of the concrete placement.

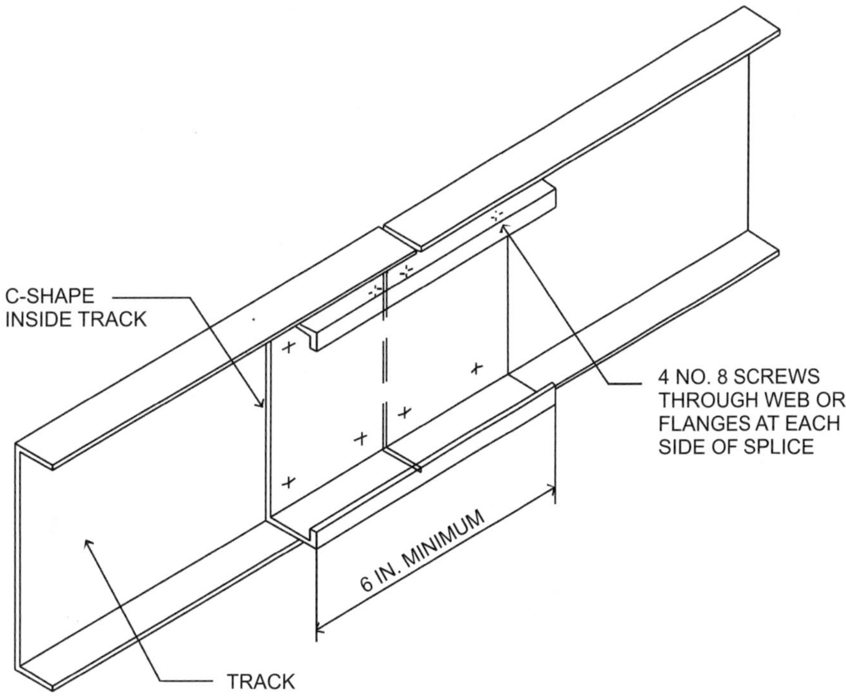

For SI: 1 inch = 25.4 mm.

FIGURE R505.3.7
TRACK SPLICE

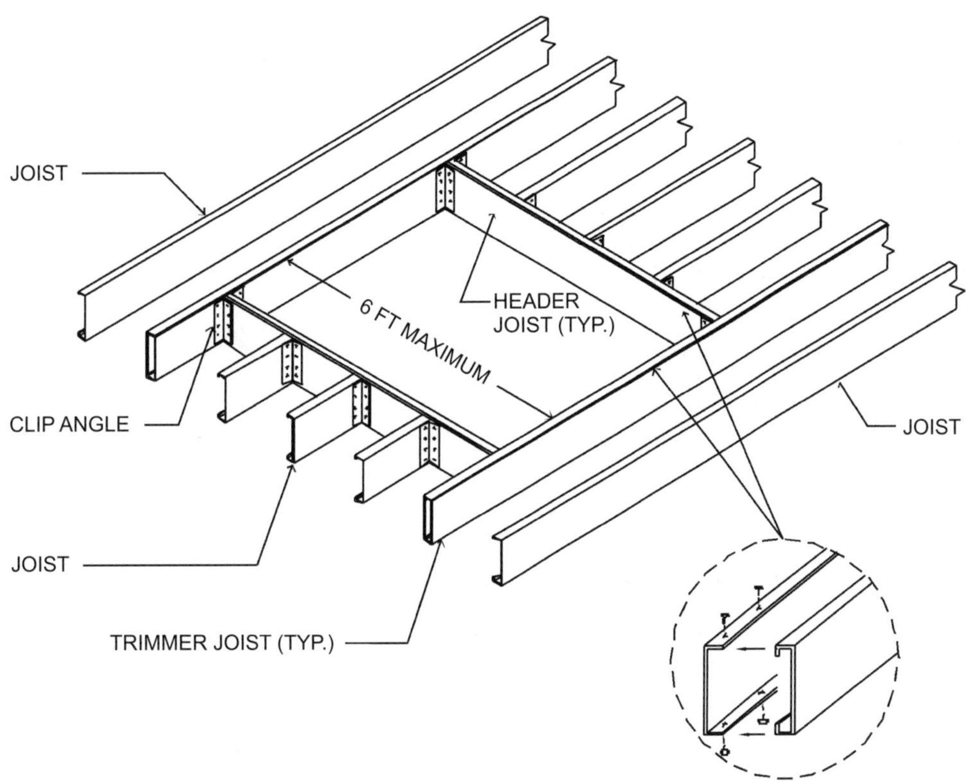

For SI: 1 foot = 304.8 mm.

FIGURE R505.3.8(1)
COLD-FORMED STEEL FLOOR CONSTRUCTION: 6-FOOT FLOOR OPENING

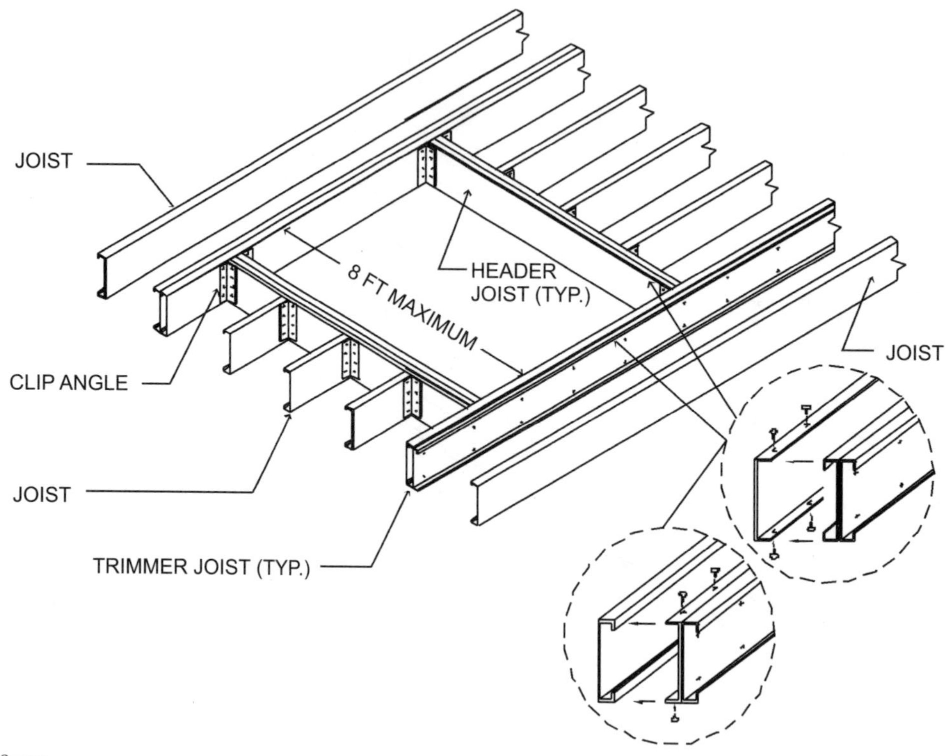

For SI: 1 foot = 304.8 mm.

FIGURE R505.3.8(2)
COLD-FORMED STEEL FLOOR CONSTRUCTION: 8-FOOT FLOOR OPENING

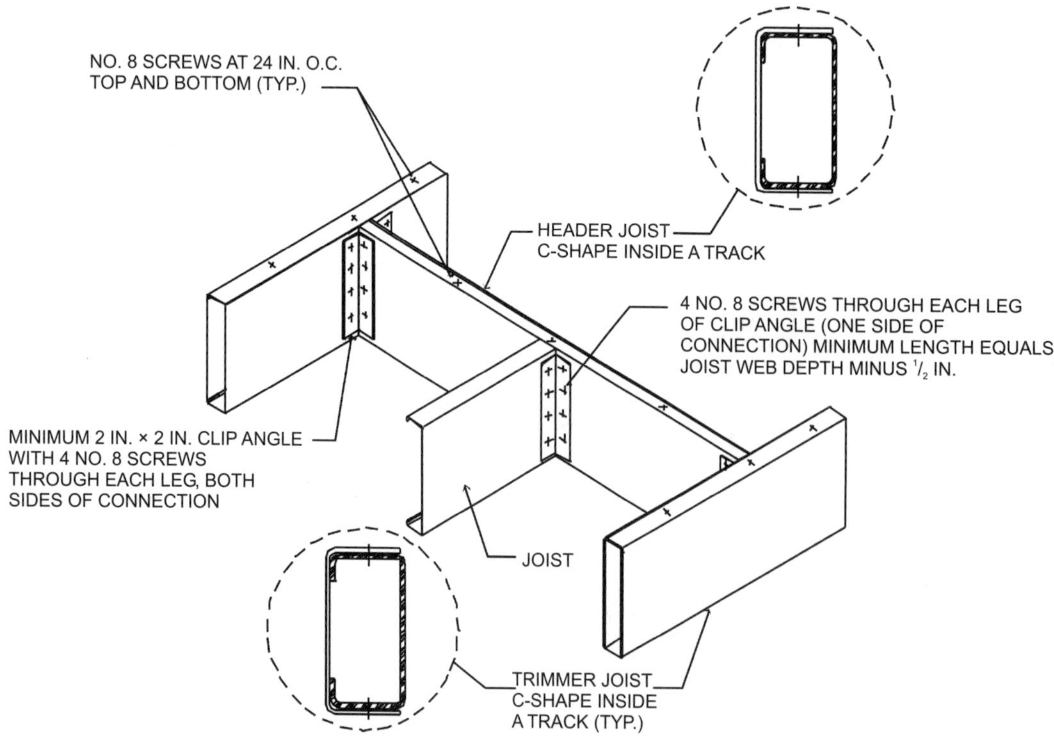

For SI: 1 inch = 25.4 mm.

FIGURE R505.3.8(3)
COLD-FORMED STEEL FLOOR CONSTRUCTION:
FLOOR HEADER TO TRIMMER CONNECTION—6-FOOT OPENING

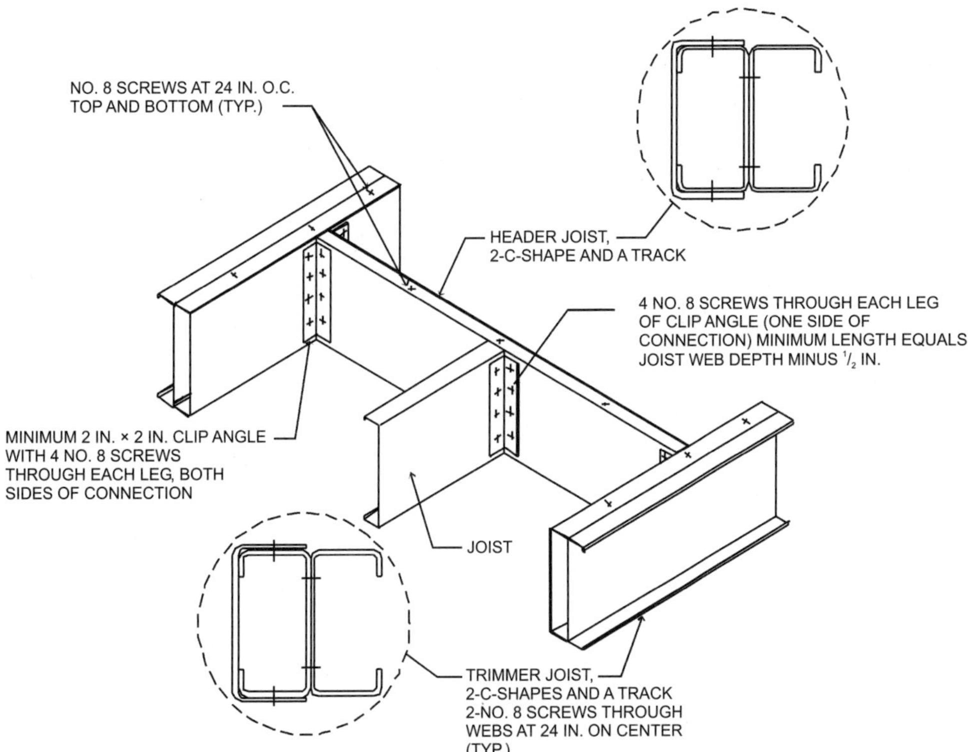

For SI: 1 inch = 25.4 mm.

FIGURE R505.3.8(4)
COLD-FORMED STEEL FLOOR CONSTRUCTION:
FLOOR HEADER TO TRIMMER CONNECTION—8-FOOT OPENING

CHAPTER 6
WALL CONSTRUCTION

SECTION R601
GENERAL

R601.1 Application. The provisions of this chapter shall control the design and construction of all walls and partitions for all buildings.

R601.2 Requirements. Wall construction shall be capable of accommodating all loads imposed according to Section R301 and of transmitting the resulting loads to the supporting structural elements.

R601.2.1 Compressible floor-covering materials. Compressible floor-covering materials that compress more than $^{1}/_{32}$ inch (0.8 mm) when subjected to 50 pounds (23 kg) applied over 1 inch square (645 mm) of material and are greater than $^{1}/_{8}$ inch (3 mm) in thickness in the uncompressed state shall not extend beneath walls, partitions or columns, which are fastened to the floor.

R601.3 Vapor retarders. Class I or II vapor retarders are required on the interior side of frame walls in Zones 5, 6, 7, 8 and Marine 4.

Exceptions:

1. *Basement walls.*
2. Below *grade* portion of any wall.
3. Construction where moisture or its freezing will not damage the materials.

R601.3.1 Class III vapor retarders. Class III vapor retarders shall be permitted where any one of the conditions in Table R601.3.1 is met.

R601.3.2 Material vapor retarder class. The vapor retarder class shall be based on the manufacturer's certified testing or a tested assembly.

The following shall be deemed to meet the class specified:

Class I: Sheet polyethylene, unperforated aluminum foil.

Class II: Kraft-faced fiberglass batts.

Class III: Latex or enamel paint.

R601.3.3 Minimum clear air spaces and vented openings for vented cladding. For the purposes of this section, vented cladding shall include the following minimum clear air spaces. Other openings with the equivalent vent area shall be permitted.

1. Vinyl lap or horizontal aluminum siding applied over a weather resistive barrier as specified in Table R703.4.
2. Brick veneer with a clear airspace as specified in Section R703.7.4.2.
3. Other *approved* vented claddings.

TABLE R601.3.1
CLASS III VAPOR RETARDERS

ZONE	CLASS III VAPOR RETARDERS PERMITTED FOR:[a]
Marine 4	Vented cladding over OSB Vented cladding over plywood Vented cladding over fiberboard Vented cladding over gypsum Insulated sheathing with *R*-value ≥ 2.5 over 2 × 4 wall Insulated sheathing with *R*-value ≥ 3.75 over 2 × 6 wall
5	Vented cladding over OSB Vented cladding over plywood Vented cladding over fiberboard Vented cladding over gypsum Insulated sheathing with *R*-value ≥ 5 over 2 × 4 wall Insulated sheathing with *R*-value ≥ 7.5 over 2 × 6 wall
6	Vented cladding over fiberboard Vented cladding over gypsum Insulated sheathing with *R*-value ≥ 7.5 over 2 × 4 wall Insulated sheathing with *R*-value ≥ 11.25 over 2 × 6 wall
7 and 8	Insulated sheathing with *R*-value ≥ 10 over 2 × 4 wall Insulated sheathing with *R*-value ≥ 15 over 2 × 6 wall

For SI: 1 pound per cubic foot = 16.02 kg/m^3.

a. Spray foam with a minimum density of 2 lb/ft^3 applied to the interior cavity side of OSB, plywood, fiberboard, insulating sheathing or gypsum is deemed to meet the insulating sheathing requirement where the spray foam *R*-value meets or exceeds the specified insulating sheathing *R*-value.

SECTION R602
WOOD WALL FRAMING

R602.1 Identification. Load-bearing dimension lumber for studs, plates and headers shall be identified by a grade mark of a lumber grading or inspection agency that has been *approved* by an accreditation body that complies with DOC PS 20. In lieu of a grade mark, a certification of inspection issued by a lumber grading or inspection agency meeting the requirements of this section shall be accepted.

R602.1.1 End-jointed lumber. *Approved* end-jointed lumber identified by a grade mark conforming to Section R602.1 may be used interchangeably with solid-sawn members of the same species and grade.

R602.1.2 Structural glued laminated timbers. Glued laminated timbers shall be manufactured and identified as required in ANSI/AITC A190.1 and ASTM D 3737.

R602.1.3 Structural log members. Stress grading of structural log members of nonrectangular shape, as typically used in log buildings, shall be in accordance with ASTM D 3957. Such structural log members shall be identified by the grade mark of an *approved* lumber grading or inspection agency. In lieu of a grade mark on the material, a certificate of inspection as to species and grade, issued by a lumber-grading or inspection agency meeting the requirements of this section, shall be permitted to be accepted.

R602.2 Grade. Studs shall be a minimum No. 3, standard or stud grade lumber.

Exception: Bearing studs not supporting floors and nonbearing studs may be utility grade lumber, provided the studs are spaced in accordance with Table R602.3(5).

R602.3 Design and construction. Exterior walls of wood-frame construction shall be designed and constructed in accordance with the provisions of this chapter and Figures R602.3(1) and R602.3.(2) or in accordance with AF&PA's NDS. Components of exterior walls shall be fastened in accordance with Tables R602.3(1) through R602.3(4). Structural wall sheathing shall be fastened directly to structural framing members. Exterior wall coverings shall be capable of resisting the wind pressures listed in Table R301.2(2) adjusted for height and exposure using Table R301.2(3). Wood structural panel sheathing used for exterior walls shall conform to the requirements of Table R602.3(3).

Studs shall be continuous from support at the sole plate to a support at the top plate to resist loads perpendicular to the wall. The support shall be a foundation or floor, ceiling or roof diaphragm or shall be designed in accordance with accepted engineering practice.

Exception: Jack studs, trimmer studs and cripple studs at openings in walls that comply with Tables R502.5(1) and R502.5(2).

R602.3.1 Stud size, height and spacing. The size, height and spacing of studs shall be in accordance with Table R602.3.(5).

Exceptions:

1. Utility grade studs shall not be spaced more than 16 inches (406 mm) on center, shall not support more than a roof and ceiling, and shall not exceed 8 feet (2438 mm) in height for exterior walls and load-bearing walls or 10 feet (3048 mm) for interior nonload-bearing walls.
2. Studs more than 10 feet (3048 mm) in height which are in accordance with Table R602.3.1.

R602.3.2 Top plate. Wood stud walls shall be capped with a double top plate installed to provide overlapping at corners and intersections with bearing partitions. End joints in top plates shall be offset at least 24 inches (610 mm). Joints in plates need not occur over studs. Plates shall be not less than 2-inches (51 mm) nominal thickness and have a width at least equal to the width of the studs.

Exception: A single top plate may be installed in stud walls, provided the plate is adequately tied at joints, corners and intersecting walls by a minimum 3-inch-by-6-inch by a 0.036-inch-thick (76 mm by 152 mm by 0.914 mm) galvanized steel plate that is nailed to each wall or segment of wall by six 8d nails on each side, provided the rafters or joists are centered over the studs with a tolerance of no more than 1 inch (25 mm). The top plate may be omitted over lintels that are adequately tied to adjacent wall sections with steel plates or equivalent as previously described.

R602.3.3 Bearing studs. Where joists, trusses or rafters are spaced more than 16 inches (406 mm) on center and the bearing studs below are spaced 24 inches (610 mm) on center, such members shall bear within 5 inches (127 mm) of the studs beneath.

Exceptions:

1. The top plates are two 2-inch by 6-inch (38 mm by 140 mm) or two 3-inch by 4-inch (64 mm by 89 mm) members.
2. A third top plate is installed.
3. Solid blocking equal in size to the studs is installed to reinforce the double top plate.

R602.3.4 Bottom (sole) plate. Studs shall have full bearing on a nominal 2-by (51 mm) or larger plate or sill having a width at least equal to the width of the studs.

R602.3.5 Fasteners. Nails and staples shall conform to the requirements of ASTM F1667.

R602.3.5.1 Staples.

R602.3.5.1.1 General. Staples shall be manufactured from No. 18 [0.0475 inch (1.21 mm)], No. 16 [0.0625 inch (1.59 mm)], No. 15 [0.072 inch (1.83 mm)] and No. 14 [0.080 inch (2.03 mm)] gage, round, semi-flattened or flattened, plain or zinc-coated steel wire, and driven with power tools. The staples shall be available with outside crown widths varying from $^3/_{16}$ inch to 1 inch (4.8 mm to 25 mm). Leg lengths vary from $^5/_8$ inch to $3^1/_2$ inches (15.9 mm to 89 mm). Staples shall be collated into strips and cohered with polymer coatings. Staples manufactured from aluminum and copper wire are permitted in nonstructural applications only. Staple crown widths and leg lengths specified in Table R602.3(1) are overall dimensions.

R602.3.5.1.2 Staple bending moments (M). For engineered and structural construction, steel staples with the minimum bending moment are required. No. 16 gage staples shall have a minimum average bending moment of 3.6 in.-lbs. (0.41 N-m); No. 15 gage staples shall have a minimum average bending moment 4.0 in.-lbs. (0.45 N-m); and No. 14 gage staples shall have a minimum average bending moment of 4.3 in.-lbs. (0.49 N-m).

R602.3.5.2 Nails.

R602.3.5.2.1 General. Nails shall be manufactured from plain steel wire, galvanized steel wire, aluminum wire, copper wire or stainless steel wire. Aluminum and copper nails are permitted in nonstructural applications only. Nail heads include full round heads or modified round heads such as clipped heads, "D" heads, notched heads, oval heads or T-shaped heads. Nails are supplied with smooth or deformed (threaded) shanks. Deformed shanks may be annularly threaded (ring shank) or helically threaded (screw shank). Nails power driven shall be collated and cohered into strips, clips or coils for loading into a power driving tool. Nails with T-shaped heads are permitted in nonstructural connections only. Table R602.3(1a) lists shank lengths and diameters for nails.

R602.3.5.2.2 Nail bending yield strength (F_{yb}). For engineered and structural construction, steel nails meeting the minimum bending yield strength are required. Nails formed from steel wire having a nominal diameter of 0.135 inch (3.4 mm) or less shall have a minimum average bending yield strength of 100 ksi (689 MPa), and nails with diameters greater than 0.135 inch (3.4 mm) shall have a minimum average bending yield strength of 90 ksi (620 MPa). The 20d common nails described in Table R602.3(1a) shall have a minimum average bending yield strength of 80 ksi (55 MPa).

R602.4 Interior load-bearing walls. Interior load-bearing walls shall be constructed, framed and fireblocked as specified for exterior walls.

R602.5 Interior nonbearing walls. Interior nonbearing walls shall be permitted to be constructed with 2-inch-by-3-inch (51 mm by 76 mm) studs spaced 24 inches (610 mm) on center or, when not part of a *braced wall line*, 2-inch-by-4-inch (51 mm by 102 mm) flat studs spaced at 16 inches (406 mm) on center. Interior nonbearing walls shall be capped with at least a single top plate. Interior nonbearing walls shall be fireblocked in accordance with Section R602.8.

R602.6 Drilling and notching–studs. Drilling and notching of studs shall be in accordance with the following:

1. Notching. Any stud in an exterior wall or bearing partition may be cut or notched to a depth not exceeding 25 percent of its width. Studs in nonbearing partitions may be notched to a depth not to exceed 40 percent of a single stud width. Notching of bearing studs shall be on one edge only and not to exceed one-fourth the height of the stud. Notching shall not occur in the bottom or top 6 inches (152 mm) of bearing studs.
2. Drilling. Any stud may be bored or drilled, provided that the diameter of the resulting hole is no more than 60 percent of the stud width, the edge of the hole is no more than $^5/_8$ inch (16 mm) to the edge of the stud, and the hole shall not be closer than 6 inches (152 mm) from an adjacent hole or notch. Holes not exceeding $^3/_4$ inch (19 mm) diameter can be as close as $1^1/_2$ inches (38.1 mm) on center spacing. Studs located in exterior walls or bearing partitions drilled over 40 percent and up to 60 percent shall also be doubled with no more than two successive doubled studs bored. See Figures R602.6(1) and R602.6(2).

   Exception: Use of *approved* stud shoes is permitted when they are installed in accordance with the manufacturer's recommendations.

3. Cutting and notching of studs may be increased to 65% of the width of the stud in exterior and interior walls and bearing partitions, provided that one of the following conditions are met:

   (a) The wall section is reinforced with $^1/_2$ inch exterior grade plywood or equivalent reinforcement on the notched side of the wall. Plywood, if used, shall reach from the floor to ceiling and at least one stud further on each side of the section that has been notched or cut.

   (b) The exterior walls of a kitchen may be reinforced by placing $^1/_2$ inch plywood or equivalent reinforcement on the notched side of the wall. Plywood, if used, shall reach from the floor to counter-top height and at least one stud further on each side of the section that has been notched or cut.

R602.6.1 Drilling and notching of top plate. When piping or ductwork is placed in or partly in an exterior wall or interior load-bearing wall, necessitating cutting, drilling or notching of the top plate by more than 50 percent of its width, a galvanized metal tie not less than 0.054 inch thick (1.37 mm) (16 ga) and $1^1/_2$ inches (38 mm) wide shall be fastened across and to the plate at each side of the opening with not less than eight 10d (0.148 inch diameter) having a minimum length of $1^1/_2$ inches (38 mm) at each side or equivalent. The metal tie must extend a minimum of 6 inches past the opening. See Figure R602.6.1.

Exception: When the entire side of the wall with the notch or cut is covered by wood structural panel sheathing.

TABLE R602.3(1)
WALL FRAMING[a, e]

CONNECTION[b] (NAIL SIZE ANDPOSITION EXAGGERATED FOR ILLUSTRATIVE PURPOSES)	FASTENER MINIMUM NOMINAL LENGTH IN INCHES X MINIMUM NOMINAL NAIL DIAMETER IN INCHES	QUANTITY PER CONNECTION, OR SPACING BETWEEN FASTENERS (INCHES ON CENTER)[d]
Top or sole plate to stud (face nail)	3 1/2" × 0.162" (16d common)[c]	2
	3" × 0.148" nail (10d common)	3
	3 1/4" × 0.131" nail	
	3" × 0.131" nail	
	3 1/4" × 0.120" nail	4
	3" × 0.120" nail	
Stud to top or sole plate (toe nail)	2 1/2" × 0.131" nail (8d common)[c]	4
	3 1/2" × 0.162" nail (16d common)	3
	3" × 0.148" nail (10d common)	4
	3 1/4" × 0.131" nail	
	3" × 0.131" nail	
	3 1/4" × 0.120" nail	
	3" × 0.120" nail	
	2 3/8" × 0.113" nail	5
	2" × 0.113" nail	
	2 1/4" × 0.105" nail	
	2 1/4" × 0.099" nail	
Cap/top plate laps and intersections	3 1/2" × 0.162" nail (16 common)[c]	2 each side of lap
	3" × 0.148" nail	3 each side of lap
	3 1/4" × 0.131" nail	
	3" × 0.131" nail	
	3 1/4" × 0.120" nail	
	3" × 0.120" nail	
Diagonal bracing	2 1/2" × 0.131" nail (8d common)[c]	2
	3 1/2" × 0.162" nail (16d common)	
	3" × 0.148" nail (10d common)	
	3 1/4" × 0.131" nail	
	3" × 0.131" nail	
	3 1/4" × 0.120" nail	3
	3" × 0.120" nail	
	2 3/8" × 0.113" nail	
	2" × 0.113" nail	4
	2 1/4" × 0.105" nail	
	2 1/4" × 0.099" nail	
Sole plate to joist or blocking at braced panels	3 1/2" × 0.135" nail (16d box)[c]	3 per 16" space
	3 1/2" × 0.162" nail (16d common)	2 per 16" space
	3" × 0.148 nail (10d common)	3 per 16" space
	3 1/4" × 0.131" nail	
	3" × 0.131" nail	4 per 16" space
	3 1/4" × 0.120" nail	
	3" × 0.120" nail	
Sole plate to joist or blocking	3 1/2" × 0.162" nail (16d common)[c]	16" o.c.
	3" × 0.148" nail (10d common)	8" o.c.
	3 1/4" × 0.131" nail	
	3" × 0.131" nail	
	3 1/4" × 0.120" nail	
	3" × 0.120" nail	

(continued)

TABLE R602.3(1)—continued
WALL FRAMING[a, e]

CONNECTION[b] (NAIL SIZE AND POSITION EXAGGERATED FOR ILLUSTRATIVE PURPOSES)	FASTENER MINIMUM NOMINAL LENGTH IN INCHES X MINIMUM NOMINAL NAIL DIAMETER IN INCHES	QUANTITY PER CONNECTION, OR SPACING BETWEEN FASTENERS (INCHES ON CENTER)[d]
Double top plate	3" × 0.148" nail (10d common)[c]	16" o.c.
	3 1/2" × 0.162" nail (16d common)	
	3 1/4" × 0.131" nail	12" o.c.
	3" × 0.131"	
	3 1/4" × 0.120" nail	
	3" × 0.120" nail	
Double Studs	3" × 0.148" nail (10d common)[c]	12" o.c.
	3 1/2" × 0.162" nail (16d common)	
	3 1/4" × 0.131" nail	8" o.c.
	3" × 0.131" nail	
	3 1/4" × 0.120" nail	
	3" × 0.120" nail	
Corner Studs	3 1/2" × 0.162" nail (16d common)[c]	24" o.c.
	3" × 0.148" nail (10d common)	16" o.c.
	3 1/4" × 0.131" nail	
	3" × 0.131" nail	
	3 1/4" × 0.120" nail	12" o.c.
	3" × 0.120" nail	

TABLE R602.3(1)—continued
CEILING AND ROOF FRAMING[a, e]

CONNECTION[b] (NAIL SIZE AND POSITION EXAGGERATED FOR ILLUSTRATIVE PURPOSES)	FASTENER MINIMUM NOMINAL LENGTH IN INCHES X MINIMUM NOMINAL NAIL DIAMETER IN INCHES	QUANTITY PER CONNECTION, OR SPACING BETWEEN FASTENERS (INCHES ON CENTER)[d]
Ceiling joist to plate	3 1/2" × 0.162" nail (16d common)[c]	3
	3" × 0.148" nail (10d common)	4
	3 1/4" × 0.131" nail	5
	3" × 0.131" nail	
	3 1/4" × 0.120" nail	
	3" × 0.120" nail	
	2 3/8" × 0.113" nail	6
Ceiling joists, laps over partitions; Ceiling joist to parallel rafter	3 1/2" × 0.162" nail (16d common)[c]	3
	3" × 0.148" nail (10d common)	4
	3 1/4" × 0.131" nail	
	3" × 0.131" nail	
	3 1/4" × 0.120" nail	
	3" × 0.120" nail	
Collar tie to rafter	3" × 0.148" nail (10d common)[c]	3
	3 1/2" × 0.162" nail (16d common)	
	3 1/4" × 0.131" nail	4
	3" × 0.131" nail	
	3 1/4" × 0.120" nail	
	3" × 0.120" nail	
Jack rafter to hip, toe-nailed	3" × 0.148" nail (10d common)[c]	3
	3 1/2" × 0.162" nail (16d common)	
	3 1/4" × 0.131" nail	4
	3" × 0.131" nail	
	3 1/4" × 0.120" nail	
	3" × 0.120" nail	
Jack rafter to hip, face nailed	3 1/2" × 0.162" nail (16d common)[c]	2
	3" × 0.148" nail (10d common)	3
	3 1/4" × 0.131" nail	
	3" × 0.131" nail	
	3 1/4" × 0.120" nail	4
	3" x 0.120" nail	
Roof rafter to plate (toe-nailed)	2 1/2" × 0.131" nail (8d common)[c]	3
	3 1/2" × 0.162" nail (16d common)	
	3" × 0.148" nail (10d common)	
	3 1/4" × 0.131" nail	
	3" × 0.131" nail	
	3 1/4" × 0.120" nail	4
	3" × 0.120" nail	
	2 3/8" × 0.113" nail	5
	2" × 0.113" nail	
	2 1/4" × 0.105" nail	
	2 1/4" × 0.099" nail	6

(continued)

TABLE R602.3(1)—continued
CEILING AND ROOF FRAMING[a, e]

CONNECTION[b] (NAIL SIZE AND POSITION EXAGGERATED FOR ILLUSTRATIVE PURPOSES)	FASTENER MINIMUM NOMINAL LENGTH IN INCHES X MINIMUM NOMINAL NAIL DIAMETER IN INCHES	QUANTITY PER CONNECTION, OR SPACING BETWEEN FASTENERS (INCHES ON CENTER)[d]
Roof rafter to 2-by ridge beam, face nailed (only the attachment of the top rafter is illustrated	$3^1/_2$" × 0.162" nail (16d common)[c]	2
	3" × 0.148 nail (10d common)	3
	$3^1/_4$" × 0.131" nail	
	3" × 0.131" nail	
	$3^1/_4$" × 0.120" nail	4
	3" × 0.120" nail	
Roof rafter to 2-by ridge beam, toe-nailed	$3^1/_2$" × 0.162" nail (16d common)[c]	2
	3" × 0.148" nail (10d common)	3
	$3^1/_4$" × 0.131" nail	
	3" × 0.131" nail	
	$3^1/_4$" × 0.120" nail	4
	3" x 0.120" nail	

TABLE R602.3(1)—continued
FLOOR FRAMING[a, e]

CONNECTION[b] (NAIL SIZE AND POSITION EXAGGERATED FOR ILLUSTRATIVE PURPOSES)	FASTENER MINIMUM NOMINAL LENGTH IN INCHES X MINIMUM NOMINAL NAIL DIAMETER IN INCHES	QUANTITY PER CONNECTION, OR SPACING BETWEEN FASTENERS[d]
joist to band joist	$3\frac{1}{2}$" × 0.162" nail (16d common)[c]	3
	3" × 0.148" nail (10d common)	5
	$3\frac{1}{4}$" × 0.131" nail	
	3" × 0.131" nail	
	$3\frac{1}{4}$" × 0.120" nail	6
	3" × 0.120" nail	
Ledger strip	$3\frac{1}{2}$" × 0.162" nail (16d common)[c]	3
	3" × 0.148" nail (10d common)	4
	$3\frac{1}{4}$" × 0.131" nail	
	3" × 0.131" nail	
	$3\frac{1}{4}$" × 0.120" nail	
	3" × 0.120" nail	
Joist to sill or girder toe-nailed; Blocking between joist or rafter to top plate (toe-nailed)	$2\frac{1}{2}$" × 0.131" nail (8d common)[c]	3
	3" × 0.148" nail (10d common)	
	$3\frac{1}{4}$" × 0.131" nail	
	3" × 0.131" nail	4
	$3\frac{1}{4}$" × 0.120" nail	
	3" × 0.120" nail	
Bridging to joist (listed number of fasteners at each end	$2\frac{1}{2}$" × 0.131" nail (8d common)[c]	2
	$3\frac{1}{4}$" × 0.120" nail	3
	3" × 0.120" nail	
	$2\frac{3}{8}$" × 0.113" nail	
	2" × 0.113" nail (6d common)	4
	$2\frac{1}{4}$" × 0.105" nail	3
	$2\frac{1}{4}$" × 0.099" nail	4
Rim joist to top plate (toe-nailed)	$2\frac{1}{2}$" × 0.113" (3d box)[c]	6" o.c.
	$3\frac{1}{2}$" × 0162" nail (16d common)	8" o.c.
	3" × 0.148" nail (10d common)	4" o.c.
	$3\frac{1}{4}$" × 0.131" nail	
	3" × 0.131" nail	
	$3\frac{1}{4}$" × 0.120" nail	
	3" × 0.120" nail	4" o.c.
	$2\frac{3}{8}$" × 0.113" nail	4" o.c.
	2" × 0.113" nail (6d common)	3" o.c.
	$2\frac{1}{4}$" × 0.105" nail	
	$2\frac{1}{4}$" x 0.099" nail	

Connection[b] (Nail size and position Exaggerated for Illustrative purposes)	Fastner minimum nominal length in inches × minimum nominal nail diameter in inches	Spacing of fasteners along the top and bottom of beam, staggered on each side of each layer	Number of fasteners at each end and splice for each layer
Built-up girders and beams	4" × 0.192" nail (20d common)[c]	32" o.c.	2
	$3\frac{1}{2}$" × 0.162" nail (16d common)	24" o.c.	3
	3" × 0.148" nail (10d common)		
	$3\frac{1}{4}$" × 0.131" nail		
	3" × 0.131" nail		
	$3\frac{1}{4}$" × 0.120" nail	16" o.c.	3
	3" × 0.120" nail		
	$2\frac{1}{2}$" × 0.131" nail (8d common)	16" o.c.	4

(continued)

TABLE R602.3(1)—continued
FLOOR FRAMING[a, e]

For SI: 1 inch = 25.4 mm, 1 mile per hour = 0.44 m/s, 1 foot = 304.8 mm.

a. This fastening schedule applies to framing members having an actual thickness of $1^1/_2$" (nominal "2-by" lumber).

b. Fastenings listed above may also be used for other connections that are not listed but that have the same configuration and the same code requirement for fastener quantity/spacing and fastener size (pennyweight and style, e.g., 8d common, "8-penny common nail").

c. This fastener, in the quantity or spacing shown in the rightmost column, comprises the most stringent fastening of the connection listed in the International, National, *International One- and Two-family Dwelling*, International Residential, Standard or Uniform Building Codes.

d. Fastening schedule only applies to buildings of conventional wood frame construction where wind or seismic analysis is not required by the applicable code. In areas where wind or seismic analysis is required, required fastening must be determined by structural analysis. The following are conditions for which codes require structural analysis:

   i. For nominal dimensions of nails see Table R602.3(1a)

   ii. *North Carolina Residential Code* – buildings located in areas where the design wind speed equals or exceeds 110 mph (177.1 km/h) (3 second gust) or assigned to seismic design categories C, D1 and D2 (with detached one- and two-family dwellings in category C being exempt).

e. Reprinted by permission of the ICC Evaluation Service, LLC from Evaluation Report ESR-1539.

TABLE R602.3(1)—continued
FASTENER SCHEDULE FOR STRUCTURAL MEMBERS[j]

DESCRIPTION OF BUILDING MATERIALS	DESCRIPTION OF FASTENER[b, c, e]	SPACING OF FASTENERS	
		Edges (inches)[i]	Intermediate supports[c, e] (inches)
Wood structural panels, subfloor, roof and interior wall sheathing to framing and particleboard wall sheathing to framing			
$^3/_8$" - $^1/_2$"	6d common (2" × 0.113") nail (subfloor wall) 8d common ($2^1/_2$" × 0.131") nail (roof)[f]	6	12[g]
$^{19}/_{32}$" - 1"	8d common nail ($2^1/_2$" × 0.131")	6	12[g]
$1^1/_8$" - $1^1/_4$"	10d common (3" × 0.148") nail or 8d ($2^1/_2$" × 0.131") deformed nail	6	12
Other wall sheathing[h]			
$^1/_2$" structural cellulosic fiberboard sheathing	$1^1/_2$" galvanized roofing nail, $^7/_{16}$" crown or 1" crown staple 16 ga., $1^1/_4$" long	3	6
$^{25}/_{32}$" structural cellulosic fiberboard sheathing	$1^3/_4$" galvanized roofing nail, $^7/_{16}$" crown or 1" crown staple 16 ga., $1^1/_2$" long	3	6
$^1/_2$" gypsum sheathing[d]	$1^1/_2$" galvanized roofing nail; staple galvanized, $1^1/_2$" long; $1^1/_4$ screws, Type W or S	7	7
$^5/_8$" gypsum sheathing[d]	$1^3/_4$" glavanized roofing nail; staple galvanized, $1^5/_8$" long; $1^5/_8$" screws, Type W or S	7	7
Wood structural panels, combination subfloor underlayment to framing			
$^3/_4$" and less	6d deformed (2" × 0.120") nail or 8d common ($2^1/_2$" × 0.131") nail	6	12
$^7/_8$" - 1"	8d common ($2^1/_2$" × 0.131") nail or 8d deformed ($2^1/_2$" × 0.120") nail	6	12
$1^1/_8$" - $1^1/_4$"	10d common (3" × 0.148") nail or 8d deformed ($2^1/_2$" × 0.120") nail	6	12

For SI: 1 inch = 25.4 mm, 1 foot = 304.8 mm, 1 mile per hour = 0.447 m/s; 1ksi = 6.895 MPa.

a. Deleted.

b. Staples are 16 gage wire and have a minimum $^7/_{16}$-inch on diameter crown width.

c. Nails shall be spaced at not more than 6 inches on center at all supports where spans are 48 inches or greater.

d. Four-foot-by-8-foot or 4-foot-by-9-foot panels shall be applied vertically.

e. Spacing of fasteners not included in this table shall be based on Table R602.3(2).

f. For regions having basic wind speed of 110 mph or greater, 8d deformed ($2^1/_2$" × 0.120) nails shall be used for attaching plywood and wood structural panel roof sheathing to framing within minimum 48-inch distance from gable end walls, if mean roof height is more than 25 feet, up to 35 feet maximum.

g. For regions having basic wind speed of 100 mph or less, nails for attaching wood structural panel roof sheathing to gable end wall framing shall be spaced 6 inches on center. When basic wind speed is greater than 100 mph, nails for attaching panel roof sheathing to intermediate supports shall be spaced 6 inches on center for minimum 48-inch distance from ridges, eaves and gable end walls; and 4 inches on center to gable end wall framing.

h. Gypsum sheathing shall conform to ASTM C 79 and shall be installed in accordance with GA 253. Fiberboard sheathing shall conform to ASTM C 208.

i. Spacing of fasteners on floor sheathing panel edges applies to panel edges supported by framing members and required blocking and at all floor perimeters only. Spacing of fasteners on roof sheathing panel edges applies to panel edges supported by framing members and required blocking. Blocking of roof or floor sheathing panel edges perpendicular to the framing members need not be provided except as required by other provisions of this code. Floor perimeter shall be supported by framing members or solid blocking. Roof sheathing $^7/_{16}$-inch or greater in thickness does not require perimeter blocking.

j. For nominal dimensions of nails see Table R602.3(1a).

TABLE R602.3(1a)
NOMINAL DIMENSIONS OF NAILS LISTED IN TABLE R602.3.1

NAILS DESCRIBED BY PENNYWEIGHT SYSTEM		
Pennyweight	**Length (inches)**	**Shank diameter (inches)**
	Box	
6d	2	0.099
8d	$2\frac{1}{2}$	0.113
10d	3	0.128
	Casing	
6d	$2\frac{1}{4}$	0.099
8d	$2\frac{1}{2}$	0.113
10d	3	0.128
	Common	
6d	2	0.113
8d	$2\frac{1}{2}$	0.131
10d	3	0.148
16d	$3\frac{1}{2}$	0.162
20d	4	0.192
	Cooler	
5d	$1\frac{5}{8}$	0.086
6d	$1\frac{7}{8}$	0.092
8d	$2\frac{3}{8}$	0.113
	Deformed[a]	
3d	$1\frac{1}{4}$	0.099
4d	$1\frac{1}{2}$	0.099
6d	2	0.120
8d	$2\frac{1}{2}$	0.120
	Finish	
8d	$2\frac{1}{2}$	0.099
10d	3	0.113
	Siding	
6d	$1\frac{7}{8}$	0.106
8d	$2\frac{3}{8}$	0.128
	Additional Recognized Nails	
Smooth shank nails	$2\frac{1}{4}$	0.092
	$2\frac{1}{4}$	0.105
	3	0.120
	$3\frac{1}{4}$	
	$1\frac{1}{2}$	0.131
	3	
	$3\frac{1}{4}$	
	$1\frac{1}{2}$	0.148
	$2\frac{1}{2}$	0.162
Deformed shank nails[a]	$2\frac{1}{4}$	0.099
	2	0.113
	$2\frac{3}{8}$	
	$2\frac{1}{2}$	0.131

For SI: 1 inch = 25.4 mm.
a. A deformed shank nail must have either a helical (screw) shank or an annular (ring) shank.

TABLE R602.3(2)
ALTERNATE ATTACHMENTS

NOMINAL MATERIAL THICKNESS (inches)	DESCRIPTION[a, b] OF FASTENER AND LENGTH (inches)	SPACING[c] OF FASTENERS	
		Edges (inches)	Intermediate supports (inches)
Wood structural panels subfloor, roof and wall sheathing to framing and particleboard wall sheathing to framing[f]			
up to 1/2	Staple 15 ga. 1 3/4	4	8
	0.097 - 0.099 Nail 2 1/4	3	6
	Staple 16 ga. 1 3/4	3	6
19/32 and 5/8	0.113 Nail 2	3	6
	Staple 15 and 16 ga. 2	4	8
	0.097 - 0.099 Nail 2 1/4	4	8
23/32 and 3/4	Staple 14 ga. 2	4	8
	Staple 15 ga. 1 3/4	3	6
	0.097 - 0.099 Nail 2 1/4	4	8
	Staple 16 ga. 2	4	8
1	Staple 14 ga. 2 1/4	4	8
	0.113 Nail 2 1/4	3	6
	Staple 15 ga. 2 1/4	4	8
	0.097 - 0.099 Nail 2 1/2	4	8
NOMINAL MATERIAL THICKNESS (inches)	**DESCRIPTION[a,b] OF FASTENER AND LENGTH (inches)**	**SPACING[c] OF FASTENERS**	
		Edges (inches)	**Body of panel[d] (inches)**
Floor underlayment; plywood-hardboard-particleboard[f]			
Plywood			
1/4 and 5/16	1 1/4 ring or screw shank nail—minimum 12 1/2 ga. (0.099″) shank diameter	3	6
	Staple 18 ga., 7/8, 3/16 crown width	2	5
11/32, 3/8, 15/32, and 1/2	1 1/4 ring or screw shank nail—minimum 12 1/2 ga. (0.099″) shank diameter	6	8[e]
19/32, 5/8, 23/32 and 3/4	1 1/2 ring or screw shank nail—minimum 12 1/2 ga. (0.099″) shank diameter	6	8
	Staple 16 ga. 1 1/2	6	8
Hardboard[f]			
0.200	1 1/2 long ring-grooved underlayment nail	6	6
	4d cement-coated sinker nail	6	6
	Staple 18 ga., 7/8 long (plastic coated)	3	6
Particleboard			
1/4	4d ring-grooved underlayment nail	3	6
	Staple 18 ga., 7/8 long, 3/16 crown	3	6
3/8	6d ring-grooved underlayment nail	6	10
	Staple 16 ga., 1 1/8 long, 3/8 crown	3	6
1/2, 5/8	6d ring-grooved underlayment nail	6	10
	Staple 16 ga., 1 5/8 long, 3/8 crown	3	6

For SI: 1 inch = 25.4 mm.

a. Nail is a general description and may be T-head, modified round head or round head.

b. Staples shall have a minimum crown width of 7/16-inch on diameter except as noted.

c. Nails or staples shall be spaced at not more than 6 inches on center at all supports where spans are 48 inches or greater. Nails or staples shall be spaced at not more than 12 inches on center at intermediate supports for floors.

d. Fasteners shall be placed in a grid pattern throughout the body of the panel.

e. For 5-ply panels, intermediate nails shall be spaced not more than 12 inches on center each way.

f. Hardboard underlayment shall conform to ANSI/AHA A135.4.

TABLE R602.3(3)
REQUIREMENTS FOR WOOD STRUCTURAL PANEL WALL SHEATHING USED TO RESIST WIND PRESSURES[a,b,c]

MINIMUM NAIL		MINIMUM WOOD STRUCTURAL PANEL SPAN RATING	MINIMUM NOMINAL PANEL THICKNESS (inches)	MAXIMUM WALL STUD SPACING (inches)	PANEL NAIL SPACING		MAXIMUM WIND SPEED (mph)		
							Wind exposure category		
Size	Penetration (inches)				Edges (inches o.c.)	Field (inches o.c.)	B	C	D
6d Common (2.0″ × 0.113″)	1.5	24/0	3/8	16	6	12	110	90	85
8d Common (2.5″ × 0.131″)	1.75	24/16	7/16	16	6	12	130	110	105
				24	6	12	110	90	85

For SI: 1 inch = 25.4 mm, 1 mile per hour = 0.447 m/s.

a. Panel strength axis parallel or perpendicular to supports. Three-ply plywood sheathing with studs spaced more than 16 inches on center shall be applied with panel strength axis perpendicular to supports.

b. Table is based on wind pressures acting toward and away from building surfaces per Section R301.2. Lateral bracing requirements shall be in accordance with Section R602.10.

c. Wood Structural Panels with span ratings of Wall-16 or Wall-24 shall be permitted as an alternate to panels with a 24/0 span rating. Plywood siding rated 16 oc or 24 oc shall be permitted as an alternate to panels with a 24/16 span rating. Wall-16 and Plywood siding 16 oc shall be used with studs spaced a maximum of 16 inches on center.

TABLE R602.3(4)
ALLOWABLE SPANS FOR PARTICLEBOARD WALL SHEATHING[a]

THICKNESS (inch)	GRADE	STUD SPACING (inches)	
		When siding is nailed to studs	When siding is nailed to sheathing
$^{3}/_{8}$	M—1 Exterior glue	16	—
$^{1}/_{2}$	M—2 Exterior glue	16	16

For SI: 1 inch = 25.4 mm.

a. Wall sheathing not exposed to the weather. If the panels are applied horizontally, the end joints of the panel shall be offset so that four panels corners will not meet. All panel edges must be supported. Leave a $^{1}/_{16}$-inch gap between panels and nail no closer than $^{3}/_{8}$ inch from panel edges.

TABLE R602.3(5)
SIZE, HEIGHT AND SPACING OF WOOD STUDS[a,d]

STUD SIZE (inches)	BEARING WALLS					NONBEARING WALLS	
	Laterally unsupported stud height[a] (feet)	Maximum spacing when supporting a roof-ceiling assembly or a habitable attic assembly, only (inches)	Maximum spacing when supporting one floor, plus a roof-ceiling assembly or a habitable attic assembly (inches)	Maximum spacing when supporting two floors, plus a roof-ceiling assembly or a habitable attic assembly (inches)	Maximum spacing when supporting one floor height[a] (feet)	Laterally unsupported stud height[a] (feet)	Maximum spacing (inches)
2 × 3[b]	—	—	—	—	—	10	16
2 × 4	10	24[c]	16[c]	—	24	14	24
3 × 4	10	24	24	16	24	14	24
2 × 5	10	24	24	—	24	16	24
2 × 6	10	24	24	16	24	20	24

For SI: 1 inch = 25.4 mm, 1 foot = 304.8 mm, 1 square foot = 0.093 m^2.

a. Listed heights are distances between points of lateral support placed perpendicular to the plane of the wall. Increases in unsupported height are permitted where justified by analysis.

b. Shall not be used in exterior walls.

c. A habitable attic assembly supported by 2 × 4 studs is limited to a roof span of 32 feet. Where the roof span exceeds 32 feet, the wall studs shall be increased to 2 × 6 or the studs shall be designed in accordance with accepted engineering practice.

d. One half of the studs interrupted by a wall opening shall be placed immediately outside the jack studs on each side of the opening as king studs to resist wind loads. King studs shall extend full height from sole plate to top plate of the wall.

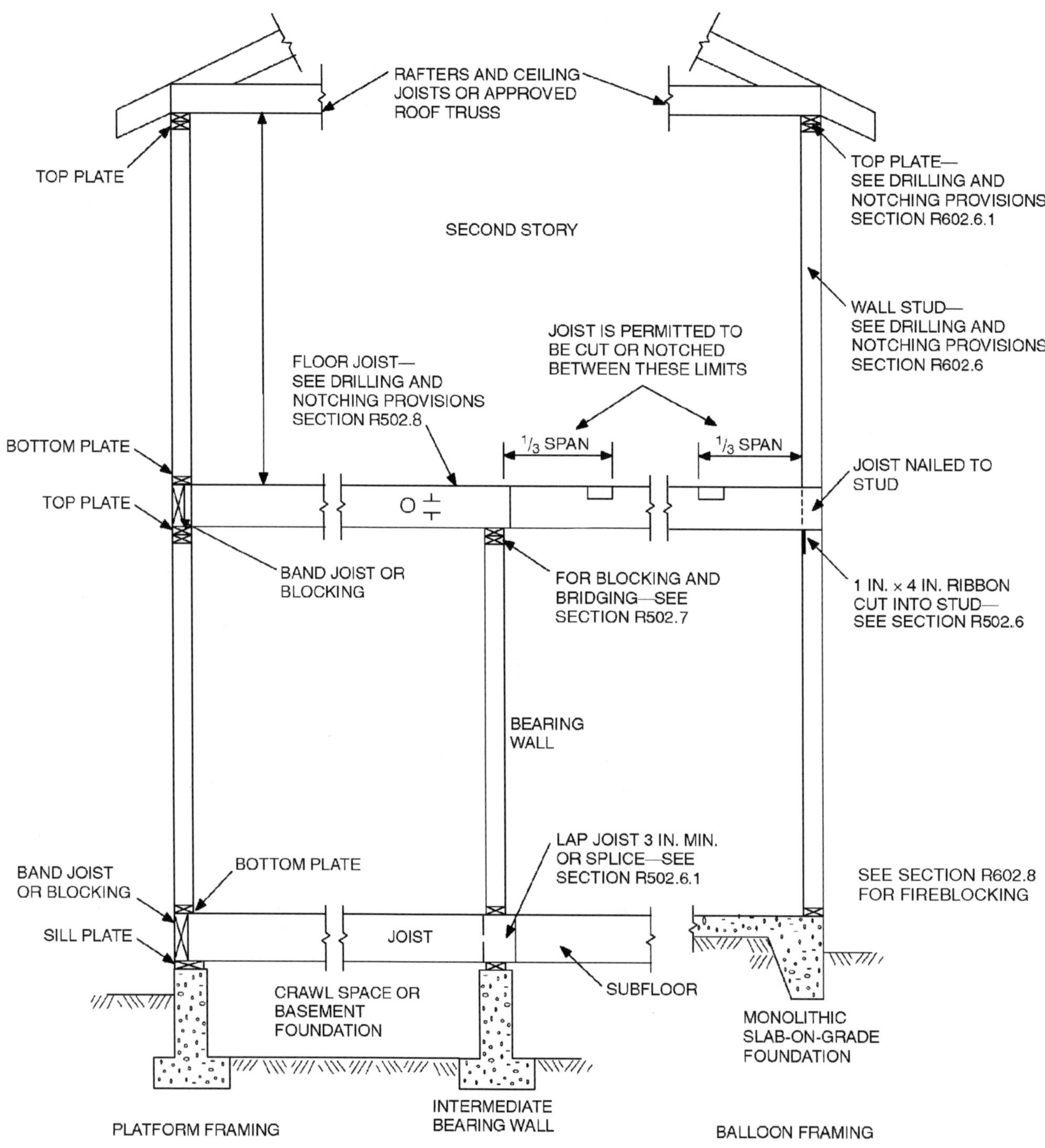

For SI: 1 inch = 25.4 mm.

FIGURE R602.3(1)
TYPICAL WALL, FLOOR AND ROOF FRAMING

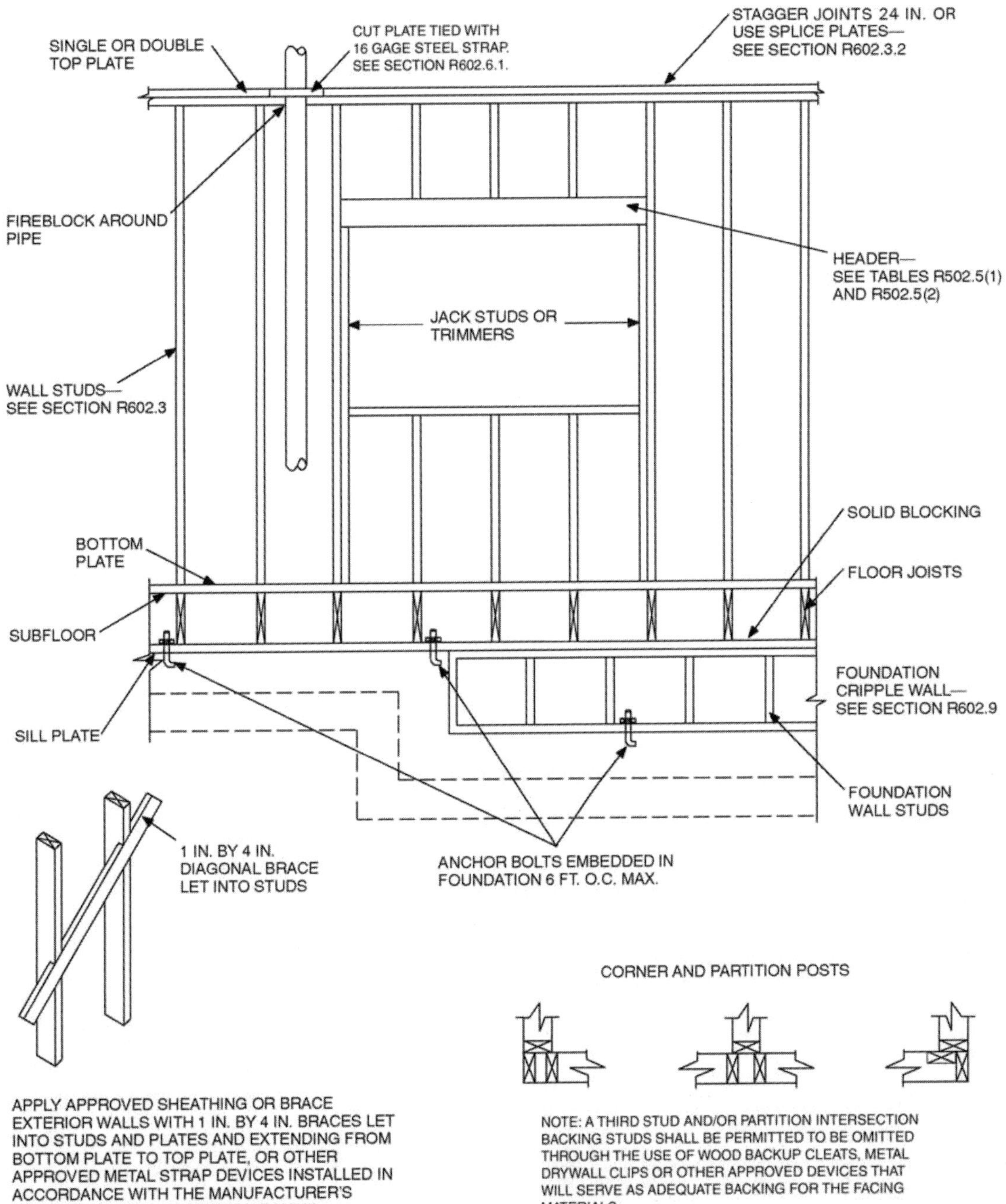

For SI: 1 inch = 25.4 mm, 1 foot = 304.8 mm.

FIGURE R602.3(2)
FRAMING DETAILS

TABLE R602.3.1
MAXIMUM ALLOWABLE LENGTH OF WOOD WALL STUDS EXPOSED TO WIND SPEEDS OF 100 mph OR LESS IN SEISMIC DESIGN CATEGORIES A, B, C, D_0, D_1 and D_2[b, c,d]

HEIGHT (feet)	ON-CENTER SPACING (inches)			
	24	16	12	8
Supporting a roof only				
10	2 × 4	2 × 4	2 × 4	2 × 4
12	2 × 6	2 × 4	2 × 4	2 × 4
14	2 × 6	2 × 6	2 × 6	2 × 4
16	2 × 6	2 × 6	2 × 6	2 × 4
18	NA[a]	2 × 6	2 × 6	2 × 6
20	NA[a]	NA[a]	2 × 6	2 × 6
24	NA[a]	NA[a]	NA[a]	2 × 6
Supporting one floor and a roof				
10	2 × 6	2 × 4	2 × 4	2 × 4
12	2 × 6	2 × 6	2 × 6	2 × 4
14	2 × 6	2 × 6	2 × 6	2 × 6
16	NA[a]	2 × 6	2 × 6	2 × 6
18	NA[a]	2 × 6	2 × 6	2 × 6
20	NA[a]	NA[a]	2 × 6	2 × 6
24	NA[a]	NA[a]	NA[a]	2 × 6
Supporting two floors and a roof				
10	2 × 6	2 × 6	2 × 4	2 × 4
12	2 × 6	2 × 6	2 × 6	2 × 6
14	2 × 6	2 × 6	2 × 6	2 × 6
16	NA[a]	NA[a]	2 × 6	2 × 6
18	NA[a]	NA[a]	2 × 6	2 × 6
20	NA[a]	NA[a]	NA[a]	2 × 6
22	NA[a]	NA[a]	NA[a]	NA[a]
24	NA[a]	NA[a]	NA[a]	NA[a]

For SI: 1 inch = 25.4 mm, 1 foot = 304.8 mm, 1 pound per square foot = 0.0479kPa,
1 pound per square inch = 6.895 kPa, 1 mile per hour = 0.447 m/s.

a. Design required.

b. Applicability of this table assumes the following: Snow load not exceeding 25 psf, f_b not less than 1310 psi determined by multiplying the AF&PA NDS tabular base design value by the repetitive use factor, and by the size factor for all species except southern pine, E not less than 1.6×10^6 psi, tributary dimensions for floors and roofs not exceeding 6 feet, maximum span for floors and roof not exceeding 12 feet, eaves not over 2 feet in dimension and exterior sheathing. Where the conditions are not within these parameters, design is required.

c. Utility, standard, stud and No. 3 grade lumber of any species are not permitted.

d. One half of the studs interrupted by a wall opening shall be placed immediately outside the jack studs on each side of the opening as king studs to resist wind loads. King studs shall extend full height from sole plate to top plate of the wall.

(continued)

TABLE R602.3.1—continued
MAXIMUM ALLOWABLE LENGTH OF WOOD WALL STUDS EXPOSED TO WIND SPEEDS OF 100 mph OR LESS IN SEISMIC DESIGN CATEGORIES A, B, C, D_0, D_1 and D_2

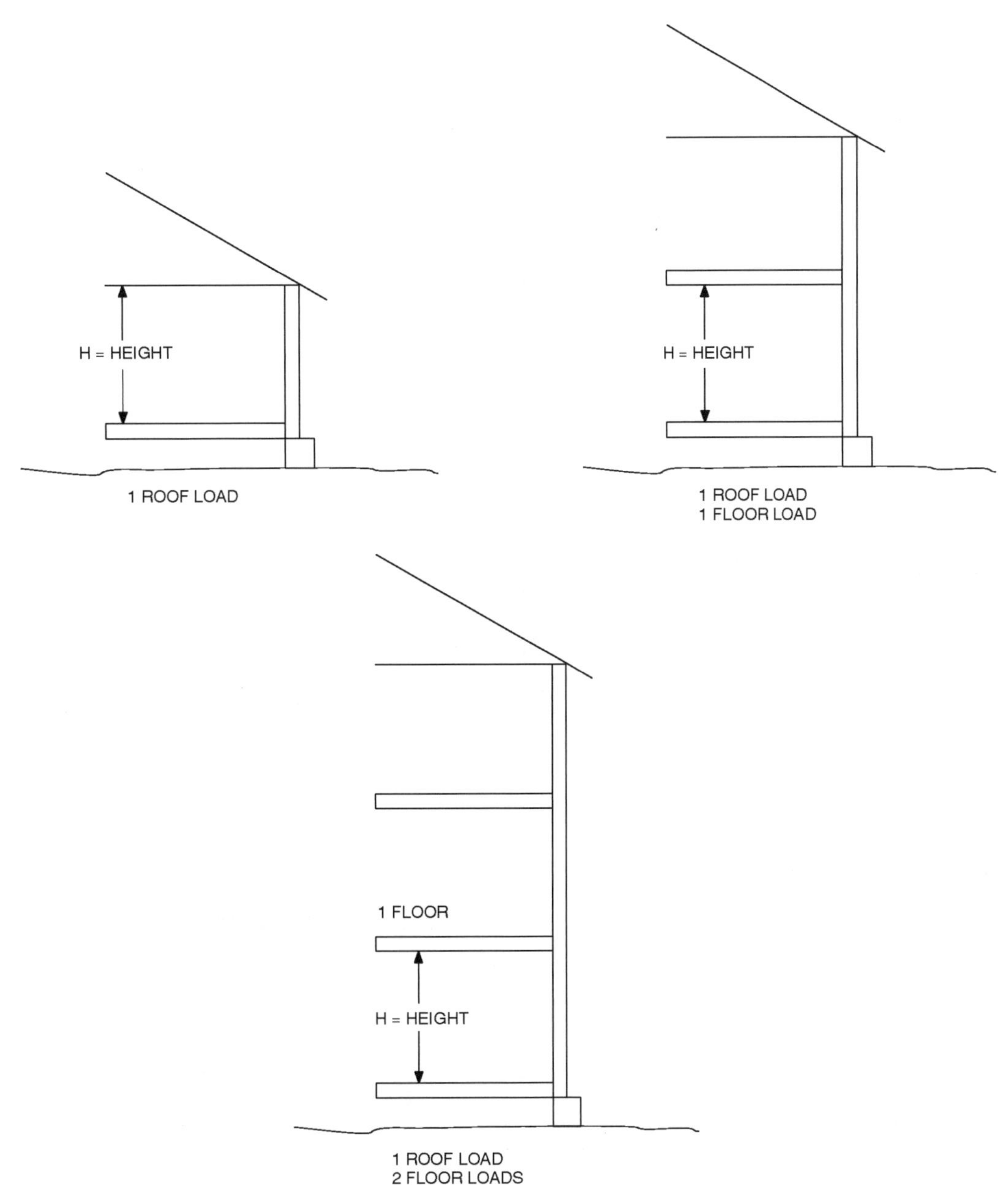

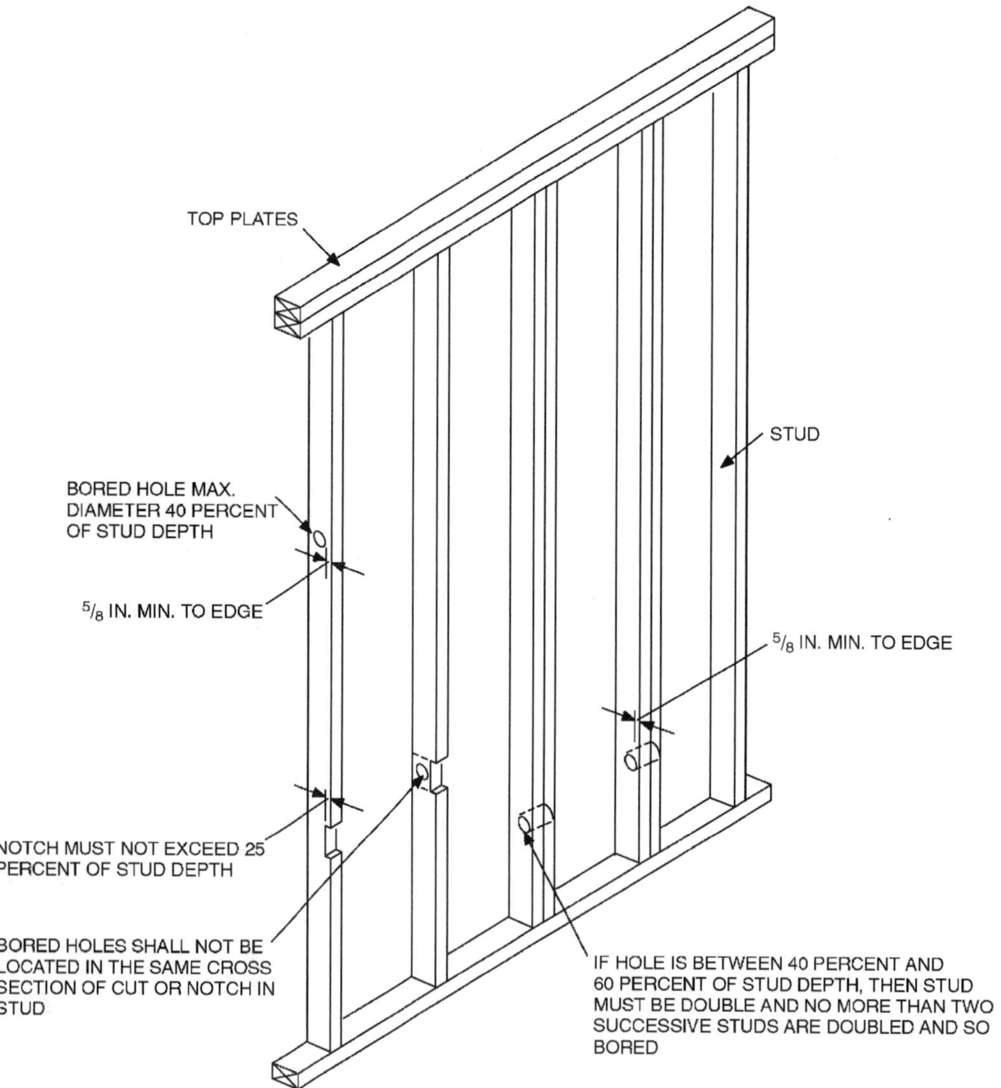

For SI: 1 inch = 25.4 mm.

NOTE: Condition for exterior and bearing walls.

FIGURE R602.6(1)
NOTCHING AND BORED HOLE LIMITATIONS FOR EXTERIOR WALLS AND BEARING WALLS

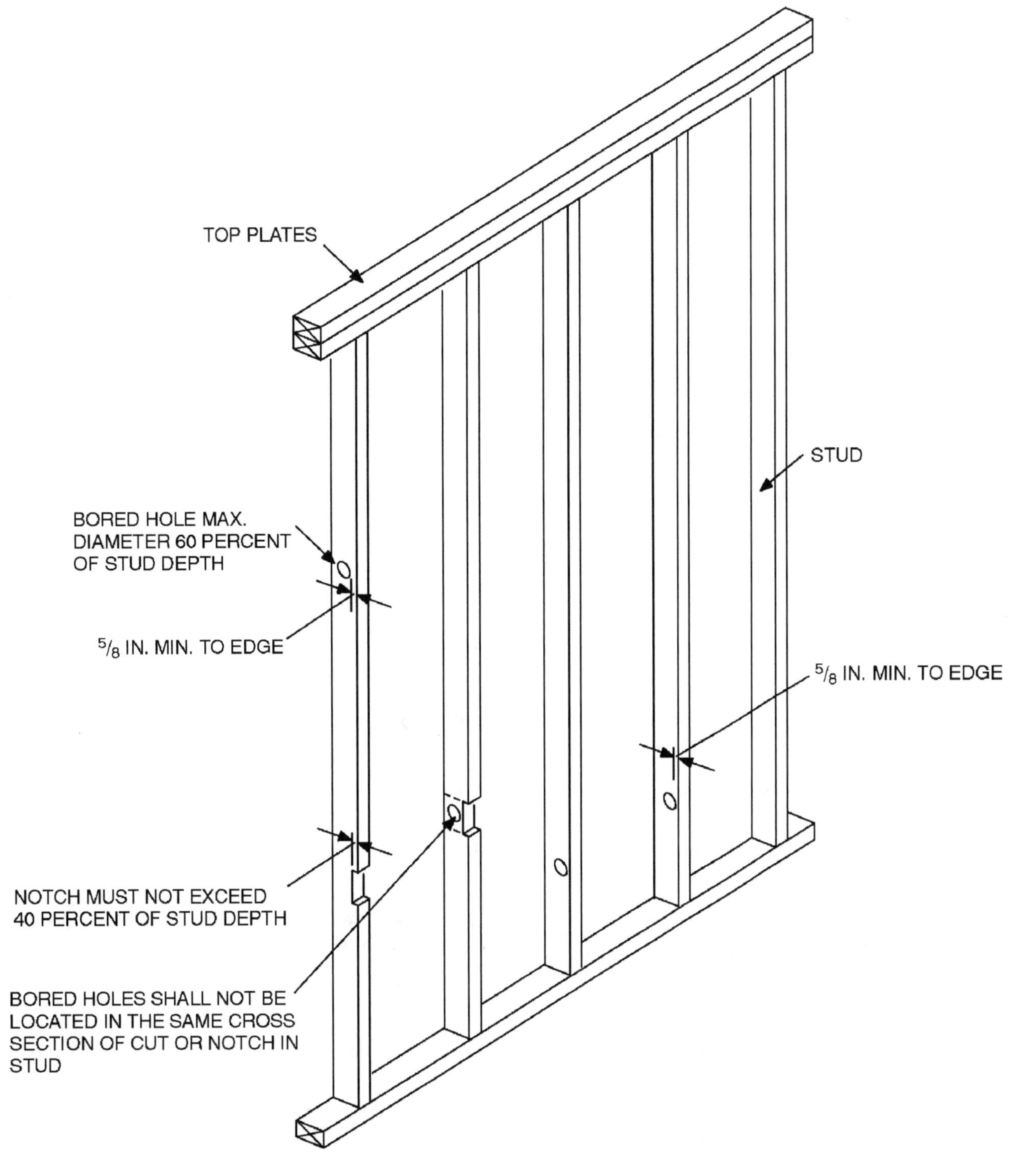

For SI: 1 inch = 25.4 mm.

FIGURE R602.6(2)
NOTCHING AND BORED HOLE LIMITATIONS FOR INTERIOR NONBEARING WALLS

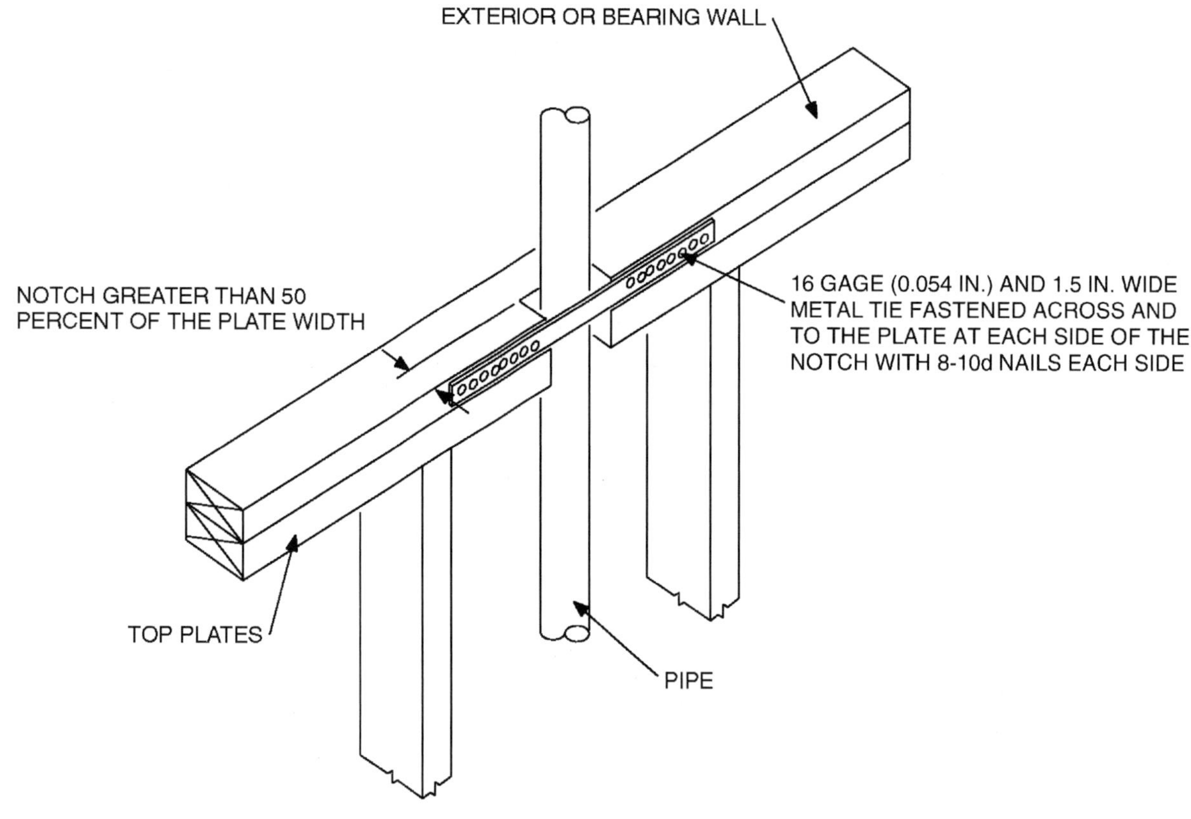

For SI: 1 inch = 25.4 mm.

FIGURE R602.6.1
TOP PLATE FRAMING TO ACCOMMODATE PIPING

R602.7 Headers. For header spans see Tables R502.5(1) and R502.5(2).

R602.7.1 Wood structural panel box headers. Wood structural panel box headers shall be constructed in accordance with Figure R602.7.2 and Table R602.7.2.

R602.7.2 Nonbearing walls. Load-bearing headers are not required in interior or exterior nonbearing walls. A single flat 2-inch-by-4-inch (51 mm by 102 mm) member may be used as a header in interior or exterior nonbearing walls for openings up to 8 feet (2438 mm) in width if the vertical distance to the parallel nailing surface above is not more than 24 inches (610 mm). For such nonbearing headers, no cripples or blocking are required above the header.

R602.8 Fireblocking required. Fireblocking shall be provided in accordance with Section R302.11.

R602.9 Cripple walls. Foundation cripple walls shall be framed of studs not smaller than the studding above. When exceeding 4 feet (1219 mm) in height, such walls shall be framed of studs having the size required for an additional *story*.

Cripple walls with a stud height less than 14 inches (356 mm) shall be sheathed on at least one side with a wood structural panel that is fastened to both the top and bottom plates in accordance with Table R602.3(1), or the cripple walls shall be constructed of solid blocking. Cripple walls shall be supported on continuous foundations.

R602.10 Wall bracing. Buildings shall be braced in accordance with this section. Where a building, or portion thereof, does not comply with one or more of the bracing requirements in this section, those portions shall be designed and constructed in accordance with Section R301.1.

Exception: Detached one- and two-family *dwellings* located in Seismic Design Category C are exempt from the seismic bracing requirements of this section. Wind speed provisions for bracing shall be applicable to detached one- and two-family *dwellings*.

R602.10.1 Braced wall lines. *Braced wall lines* shall be provided in accordance with this section. The length of a *braced wall line* shall be measured as the distance between the ends of the wall line. The end of a *braced wall line* shall be considered to be either:

1. The intersection with perpendicular exterior walls or projection thereof,
2. The intersection with perpendicular *braced wall lines*.

The end of the *braced wall line* shall be chosen such that the maximum length results.

TABLE R602.7.2
MAXIMUM SPANS FOR WOOD STRUCTURAL PANEL BOX HEADERS[a]

HEADER CONSTRUCTION[b]	HEADER DEPTH (inches)	HOUSE DEPTH (feet)				
		24	26	28	30	32
Wood structural panel—one side	9 15	4 5	4 5	3 4	3 3	— 3
Wood structural panel—both sides	9 15	7 8	5 8	5 7	4 7	3 6

For SI: 1 inch = 25.4 mm, 1 foot = 304.8 mm.

a. Spans are based on single story with clear-span trussed roof or two-story with floor and roof supported by interior-bearing walls.

b. See Figure R602.7.2 for construction details.

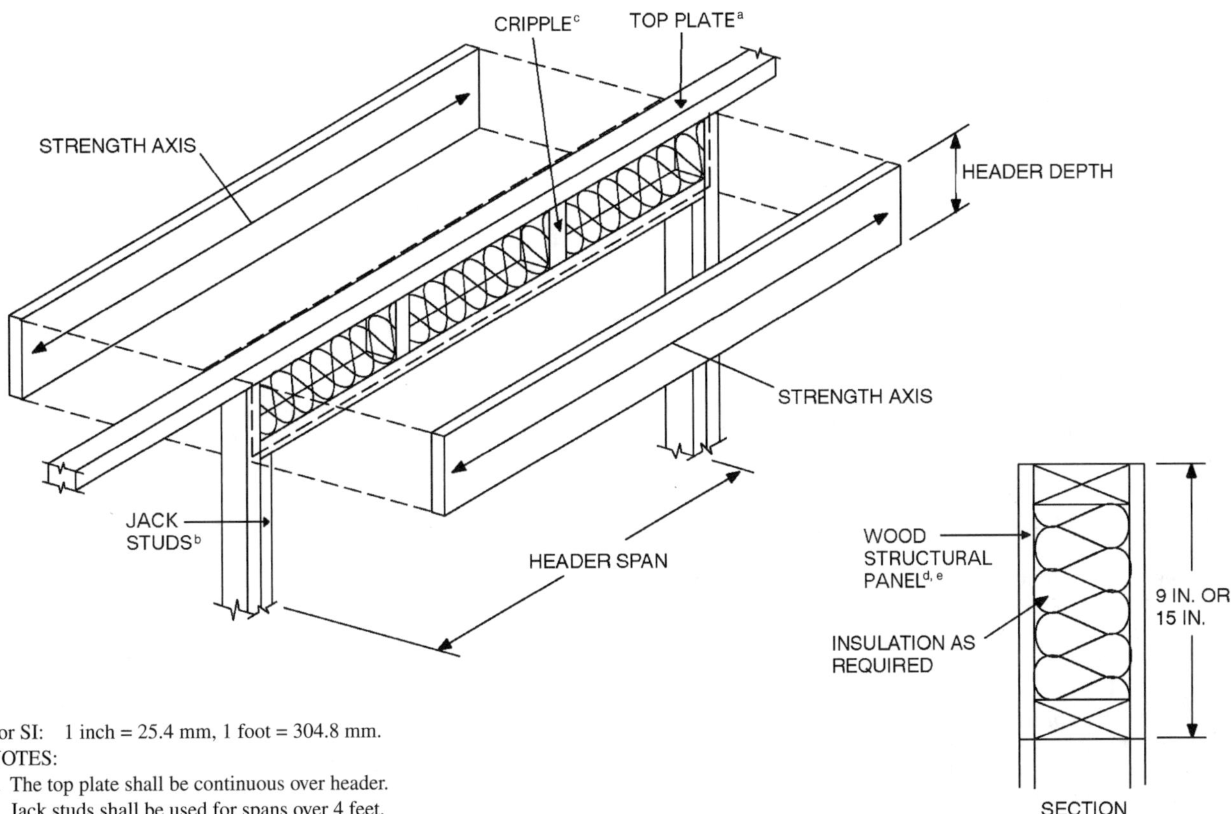

For SI: 1 inch = 25.4 mm, 1 foot = 304.8 mm.

NOTES:

a. The top plate shall be continuous over header.

b. Jack studs shall be used for spans over 4 feet.

c. Cripple spacing shall be the same as for studs.

d. Wood structural panel faces shall be single pieces of $^{15}/_{32}$-inch-thick Exposure 1 (exterior glue) or thicker, installed on the interior or exterior or both sides of the header.

e. Wood structural panel faces shall be nailed to framing and cripples with 8d common or galvanized box nails spaced 3 inches on center, staggering alternate nails $^{1}/_{2}$ inch. Galvanized nails shall be hot-dipped or tumbled.

FIGURE R602.7.2
TYPICAL WOOD STRUCTURAL PANEL BOX HEADER CONSTRUCTION

R602.10.1.1 Braced wall panels. *Braced wall panels* shall be constructed in accordance with the intermittent bracing methods specified in Section R602.10.2, or the continuous sheathing methods specified in Sections R602.10.4 and R602.10.5. Mixing of bracing method shall be permitted as follows:

1. Mixing bracing methods from *story* to *story* is permitted.
2. Mixing bracing methods from *braced wall line* to *braced wall line* within a *story* is permitted, except that continuous sheathing methods shall conform to the additional requirements of Sections R602.10.4 and R602.10.5.
3. Mixing bracing methods within a *braced wall line* is permitted only in Seismic Design Categories A and B, and detached *dwellings* in Seismic Design Category C. The length of required bracing for the *braced wall line* with mixed sheathing types shall have the higher bracing length requirement, in accordance with Tables R602.10.1.2(1) and R602.10.1.2(2), of all types of bracing used.

R602.10.1.2 Length of bracing. The length of bracing along each *braced wall line* shall be the greater of that required by the design wind speed and *braced wall line* spacing in accordance with Table R602.10.1.2(1) as adjusted by the factors in the footnotes or the Seismic Design Category and *braced wall line* length in accordance with Table R602.10.1.2(2) as adjusted by the factors in Table R602.10.1.2(3) or *braced wall panel* location requirements of Section R602.10.1.4. Only walls that are parallel to the *braced wall line* shall be counted toward the bracing requirement of that line, except angled walls shall be counted in accordance with Section R602.10.1.3. In no case shall the minimum total length of bracing in a *braced wall line*, after all adjustments have been taken, be less than 48 inches (1219 mm) total.

R602.10.1.2.1 Braced wall panel uplift load path. *Braced wall panels* located at exterior walls that support roof rafters or trusses (including stories below top *story*) shall have the framing members connected in accordance with one of the following:

1. Fastening in accordance with Table R602.3(1) where:
   - 1.1. The basic wind speed does not exceed 90 mph (40 m/s), the wind exposure category is B, the roof pitch is 5:12 or greater, and the roof span is 32 feet (9754 mm) or less, or
   - 1.2. The net uplift value at the top of a wall does not exceed 100 plf. The net uplift value shall be determined in accordance with Section R802.11 and shall be permitted to be reduced by 60 plf (86 N/mm) for each full wall above.
2. Where the net uplift value at the top of a wall exceeds 100 plf (146 N/mm), installing *approved* uplift framing connectors to provide a continuous load path from the top of the wall to the foundation. The net uplift value shall be as determined in Item 1.2 above.
3. Bracing and fasteners designed in accordance with accepted engineering practice to resist combined uplift and shear forces.

R602.10.1.3 Angled corners. At corners, *braced wall lines* shall be permitted to angle out of plane up to 45 degrees with a maximum diagonal length of 8 feet (2438 mm). When determining the length of bracing required, the length of each *braced wall line* shall be determined as shown in Figure R602.10.1.3. The placement of bracing for the *braced wall lines* shall begin at the point where the *braced wall line*, which contains the angled wall adjoins the adjacent *braced wall line* (Point A as shown in Figure R602.10.1.3). Where an angled corner is constructed at an angle equal to 45 degrees (0.79 rad) and the diagonal length is no more than 8 feet (2438 mm), the angled wall may be considered as part of either of the adjoining *braced wall lines*, but not both. Where the diagonal length is greater than 8 feet (2438 mm), it shall be considered its own *braced wall line* and be braced in accordance with Section R602.10.1 and methods in Section R602.10.2.

R602.10.1.4 Braced wall panel location. *Braced wall panels* shall be located in accordance with Figure R602.10.1.4(1). *Braced wall panels* shall be located not more than 25 feet (7620 mm) on center and shall be permitted to begin no more than 12.5 feet (3810 mm) from the end of a *braced wall line* in accordance with Section R602.10.1 and Figure R602.10.1.4(2). The total combined distance from each end of a *braced wall line* to the outermost *braced wall panel* or panels in the line shall not exceed 12.5 feet (3810 mm). *Braced wall panels* may be offset out-of-plane up to 4 feet (1219 mm) from the designated *braced wall line* provided that the total out-to-out offset of *braced wall panels* in a *braced wall line* is not more than 8 feet (2438 mm) in accordance with Figures R602.10.1.4(3) and R602.10.1.4(4). All *braced wall panels* within a *braced wall line* shall be permitted to be offset from the designated *braced wall line*.

R602.10.1.4.1 Braced wall panel location in Seismic Design Categories D_0, D_1 and D_2. Deleted.

R602.10.1.5 Braced wall line spacing for Seismic Design Categories D_0, D_1 and D_2. Deleted.

R602.10.2 Intermittent braced wall panel construction methods. The construction of intermittent *braced wall panels* shall be in accordance with one of the methods listed in Table R602.10.2.

TABLE R602.10.1.2(1)[a, b, c, d, e]
BRACING REQUIREMENTS BASED ON WIND SPEED
(as a function of braced wall line spacing)

EXPOSURE CATEGORY B, 30 FT MEAN ROOF HEIGHT, 10 FT EAVE TO RIDGE HEIGHT, 10 FT WALL HEIGHT, 2 BRACED WALL LINES			MINIMUM TOTAL LENGTH (feet) OF BRACED WALL PANELS REQUIRED ALONG EACH BRACED WALL LINE			
Basic Wind Speed (mph)	**Story Location**	**Braced Wall Line Spacing (feet)**	**Method LIB[f, h]**	**Method GB (double sided)[g]**	**Methods DWB, WSP, SFB, PBS, PCP, HPS[f, i]**	**Continuous Sheathing**
≤ 85 (mph)		10	3.5	3.5	2.0	1.5
		20	6.0	6.0	3.5	3.0
		30	8.5	8.5	5.0	4.5
		40	11.5	11.5	6.5	5.5
		50	14.0	14.0	8.0	7.0
		60	16.5	16.5	9.5	8.0
		10	6.5	6.5	3.5	3.0
		20	11.5	11.5	6.5	5.5
		30	16.5	16.5	9.5	8.0
		40	21.5	21.5	12.5	10.5
		50	26.5	26.5	15.0	13.0
		60	31.5	31.5	18.0	15.5
		10	NP	9.0	5.5	4.5
		20	NP	17.0	10.0	8.5
		30	NP	24.5	14.0	12.0
		40	NP	32.0	18.0	15.5
		50	NP	39.0	22.5	19.0
		60	NP	46.5	26.5	22.5
≤ 90 (mph)		10	3.5	3.5	2.0	2.0
		20	7.0	7.0	4.0	3.5
		30	9.5	9.5	5.5	5.0
		40	12.5	12.5	7.5	6.0
		50	15.5	15.5	9.0	7.5
		60	18.5	18.5	10.5	9.0
		10	7.0	7.0	4.0	3.5
		20	13.0	13.0	7.5	6.5
		30	18.5	18.5	10.5	9.0
		40	24.0	24.0	14.0	12.0
		50	29.5	29.5	17.0	14.5
		60	35.0	35.0	20.0	17.0
		10	NP	10.5	6.0	5.0
		20	NP	19.0	11.0	9.5
		30	NP	27.5	15.5	13.5
		40	NP	35.5	20.5	17.5
		50	NP	44.0	25.0	21.5
		60	NP	52.0	30.0	25.5

(continued)

TABLE R602.10.1.2(1)[a, b, c, d, e]—continued
BRACING REQUIREMENTS BASED ON WIND SPEED
(as a function of braced wall line spacing)

EXPOSURE CATEGORY B, 30 FT MEAN ROOF HEIGHT, 10 FT EAVE TO RIDGE HEIGHT, 10 FT WALL HEIGHT, 2 BRACED WALL LINES			MINIMUM TOTAL LENGTH (feet) OF BRACED WALL PANELS REQUIRED ALONG EACH BRACED WALL LINE			
Basic Wind Speed (mph)	Story Location	Braced wall Line Spacing (feet)	Method LIB[f, h]	Method GB (doubled sided)[g]	Method DWB, WSP, SFB, PBS, PCP, HPS[f, i]	Continuous Sheathing
≤ 100 (mph)		10	4.5	4.5	2.5	2.5
		20	8.5	8.5	5.0	4.0
		30	12.0	12.0	7.0	6.0
		40	15.5	15.5	9.0	7.5
		50	19.0	19.0	11.0	9.5
		60	22.5	22.5	13.0	11.0
		10	8.5	8.5	5.0	4.5
		20	16.0	16.0	9.0	8.0
		30	23.0	23.0	13.0	11.0
		40	29.5	29.5	17.0	14.5
		50	36.5	36.5	21.0	18.0
		60	43.5	43.5	25.0	21.0
		10	NP	12.5	7.5	6.0
		20	NP	23.5	13.5	11.5
		30	NP	34.0	19.5	16.5
		40	NP	44.0	25.0	21.5
		50	NP	54.0	31.0	26.5
		60	NP	64.0	36.5	31.0
≤ 110 (mph)		10	5.5	5.5	3.0	3.0
		20	10.0	10.0	6.0	5.0
		30	14.5	14.5	8.5	7.0
		40	18.5	18.5	11.0	9.0
		50	23.0	23.0	13.0	11.5
		60	27.5	27.5	15.5	13.5
		10	10.5	10.5	6.0	5.0
		20	19.0	19.0	11.0	9.5
		30	27.5	27.5	16.0	13.5
		40	36.0	36.0	20.5	17.5
		50	44.0	44.0	25.5	21.5
		60	52.5	52.5	30.0	25.5
		10	NP	15.5	9.0	7.5
		20	NP	28.5	16.5	14.0
		30	NP	41.0	23.5	20.0
		40	NP	53.0	30.5	26.0
		50	NP	65.5	37.5	32.0
		60	NP	77.5	44.5	37.5

(continued)

TABLE R602.10.1.2(1)[a, b, c, d, e]—continued
BRACING REQUIREMENTS BASED ON WIND SPEED
(as a function of braced wall line spacing)

For SI: 1 foot = 304.8 mm, 1 inch = 25.4 mm, 1 mile per hour = 0.447 m/s, 1 pound force = 4.448 N.

a. Tabulated bracing lengths are based on Wind Exposure Category B, a 30-ft mean roof height, a 10-ft eave to ridge height, a 10-ft wall height, and two braced wall lines sharing load in a given plan direction on a given story level. Methods of bracing shall be as described in Sections R602.10.2, R602.10.4 and R602.10.5. Interpolation shall be permitted.

b. For other mean roof heights and exposure categories, the required bracing length shall be multiplied by the appropriate factor from the following table:

NUMBER OF STORIES	EXPOSURE/HEIGHT FACTORS		
	Exposure B	Exposure C	Exposure D
1	1.0	1.2	1.5
2	1.0	1.3	1.6
3	1.0	1.4	1.7

c. For other roof-to-eave ridge heights, the required bracing length shall be multiplied by the appropriate factor from the following table: interpolation shall be permitted.

SUPPORT CONDITION	ROOF EAVE-TO-RIDGE HEIGHT			
	5 ft or less	10 ft	15 ft	20 ft
Roof only	0.7	1.0	1.3	1.6
Roof + floor	0.85	1.0	1.15	1.3
Roof + 2 floors	0.9	1.0	1.1	NP

d. For a maximum 9-foot wall height, multiplying the table values by 0.95 shall be permitted. For a maximum 8-foot wall height, multiplying, the table values by 0.90 shall be permitted. For a maximum 12-foot wall height, the table values shall be multiplied by 1.1.

e. For three or more braced wall lines in a given plan direction, the required bracing length on each braced wall line shall be multiplied by the appropriate factor from the following table:

NUMBER OF BRACED WALL LINES	ADJUSTMENT FACTOR
3	1.30
4	1.45
≥ 5	1.60

f. Bracing lengths are based on the application of gypsum board finish (or equivalent) applied to the inside face of a braced wall panel. When gypsum board finish (or equivalent) is not applied to the inside face of braced wall panels, the tabulated lengths shall be multiplied by the appropriate factor from the following table:

BRACING METHOD	ADJUSTMENT FACTOR
Method LIB	1.8
Methods DWB, WSP, SFB, PBS, PCP, HPS	1.4

g. Bracing lengths for Method GB are based on the application of gypsum board on both faces of a braced wall panel. When Method GB is provided on only one side of the wall, the required bracing amounts shall be doubled. When Method GB braced wall panels installed in accordance with Section R602.10.2 are fastened at 4 inches on center at panel edges, including top and bottom plates, and are blocked at all horizontal joints, multiplying the required bracing percentage for wind loading by 0.7 shall be permitted.

h. Method LIB bracing shall have gypsum board attached to at least one side according to the Section R602.10.2 Method GB requirements.

i. Required bracing length for Methods DWB, WSP, SFB, PBS, PCP and HPS in braced wall lines located in one-story buildings and in the top story of two or three story buildings shall be permitted to be multiplied by 0.80 when an approved hold-down device with a minimum uplift design value of 800 pounds is fastened to the end studs of each braced wall panel in the braced wall line and to the foundation or framing below.

TABLE R602.10.1.2(2)[a, b, c]
BRACING REQUIREMENTS BASED ON SEISMIC DESIGN CATEGORY
(AS A FUNCTION OF BRACED WALL LINE LENGTH)

SOIL CLASS D[a] WALL HEIGHT = 10 FT 10 PSF FLOOR DEAD LOAD 15 PSF ROOF/CEILING DEAD LOAD BRACED WALL LINE SPACING ≤ 25 FT			MINIMUM TOTAL LENGTH (feet) OF BRACED WALL PANELS REQUIRED ALONG EACH BRACED WALL LINE			
Seismic Design Category (SDC)	**Story Location**	**Braced Wall Line Length**	**Method LIB**	**Methods DWB, SFB, GB, PBS, PCP, HPS**	**Method WSP**	**Continuous Sheathing**
SDC A and B and Detached Dwellings in C		**Exempt from Seismic Requirements Use Table R602.10.1.2(1) for Bracing Requirements**				
SDC C	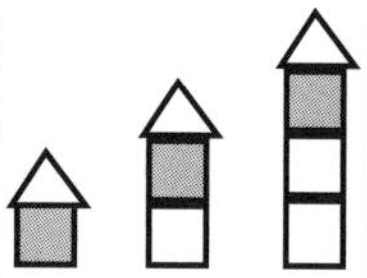	10	2.5	2.5	1.6	1.4
		20	5.0	5.0	3.2	2.7
		30	7.5	7.5	4.8	4.1
		40	10.0	10.0	6.4	5.4
		50	12.5	12.5	8.0	6.8
	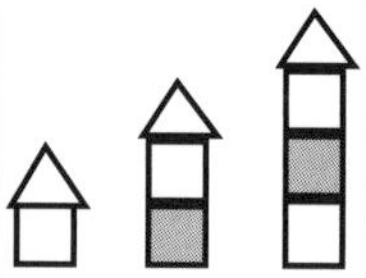	10	NP	4.5	3.0	2.6
		20	NP	9.0	6.0	5.1
		30	NP	13.5	9.0	7.7
		40	NP	18.0	12.0	10.2
		50	NP	22.5	15.0	12.8
	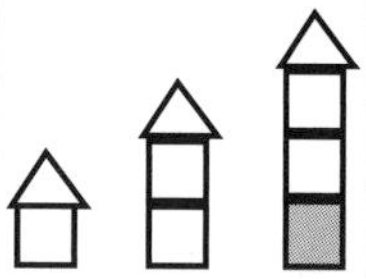	10	NP	6.0	4.5	3.8
		20	NP	12.0	9.0	7.7
		30	NP	18.0	13.5	11.5
		40	NP	24.0	18.0	15.3
		50	NP	30.0	22.5	19.1
SDC D_0 or D_1	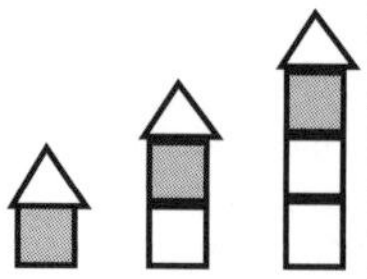	10	NP	3.0	2.0	1.7
		20	NP	6.0	4.0	3.4
		30	NP	9.0	6.0	5.1
		40	NP	12.0	8.0	6.8
		50	NP	15.0	10.0	8.5
	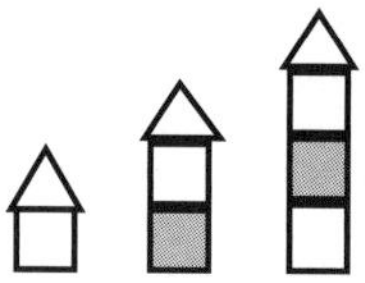	10	NP	6.0	4.5	3.8
		20	NP	12.0	9.0	7.7
		30	NP	18.0	13.5	11.5
		40	NP	24.0	18.0	15.3
		50	NP	30.0	22.5	19.1
	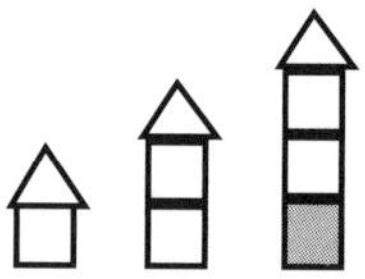	10	NP	8.5	6.0	5.1
		20	NP	17.0	12.0	10.2
		30	NP	25.5	18.0	15.3
		40	NP	34.0	24.0	20.4
		50	NP	42.5	30.0	25.5

(continued)

TABLE R602.10.1.2(2)[a, b, c]—continued
BRACING REQUIREMENTS BASED ON SEISMIC DESIGN CATEGORY
(AS A FUNCTION OF BRACED WALL LINE LENGTH)

SOIL CLASS D[a] WALL HEIGHT = 10 FT 10 PSF FLOOR DEAD LOAD 15 PSF ROOF/CEILING DEAD LOAD BRACED WALL LINE SPACING ≤ 25 FT			MINIMUM TOTAL LENGTH (feet) OF BRACED WALL PANELS REQUIRED ALONG EACH BRACED WALL LINE			
Seismic Design Category (SDC)	**Story Location**	**Braced Wall Line Length**	**Method LIB**	**METHODS DWB, SFB, GB, PBS, PCP, HPS**	**Method WSP**	**Continuous Sheathing**
		10	NP	4.0	2.5	2.1
		20	NP	8.0	5.0	4.3
		30	NP	12.0	7.5	6.4
		40	NP	16.0	10.0	8.5
		50	NP	20.0	12.5	10.6
		10	NP	7.5	5.5	4.7
		20	NP	15.0	11.0	9.4
SDC D_2		30	NP	22.5	16.5	14.0
		40	NP	30.0	22.0	18.7
		50	NP	37.5	27.5	23.4
		10	NP	NP	NP	NP
		20	NP	NP	NP	NP
		30	NP	NP	NP	NP
		40	NP	NP	NP	NP
		50	NP	NP	NP	NP

For SI: 1 foot = 304.8 mm, 1 pound per square foot = 47.89 Pa.

a. Wall bracing lengths are based on a soil site class "D." Interpolation of bracing length between the S_{ds} values associated with the seismic design categories shall be permitted when a site-specific S_{ds} value is determined in accordance with Section 1613.5 of the *International Building Code.*

b. Foundation cripple wall panels shall be braced in accordance with Section R602.10.9.

c. Methods of bracing shall be as described in Sections R602.10.2, R602.10.4 and R602.10.5.

TABLE R602.10.1.2(3)
ADJUSTMENT FACTORS TO THE LENGTH OF REQUIRED SEISMIC WALL BRACING[a]

ADJUSTMENT BASED ON:			MULTIPLY LENGTH OF BRACING PER WALL LINE BY:	APPLIES TO:
Story height[b] (Section R301.3)		≤ 10 ft	1.0	All bracing methods - Sections R602.10.2, R602.10.4 and R602.10.5
		> 10 ≤ 12 ft	1.2	
Braced wall line spacing townhouses in SDC A-C[b,c]		≤ 35 ft	1.0	
		> 35 ≤ 50 ft	1.43	
Wall dead load		> 8 ≤ 15 psf	1.0	
		≤ 8 psf	0.85	
Roof/ceiling dead load for wall supporting[b]	roof only or roof plus one story	≤ 15 psf	1.0	
	roof only	< 15 psf ≤ 25 psf	1.2	
	roof plus one story	< 15 psf ≤ 25 psf	1.1	
Walls with stone or masonry veneer in SDC C-D_2		See Section R703.7		
Cripple walls		See Section R602.10.9		

For SI: 1 foot = 304.8 mm, 1 pound per square foot = 47.89 Pa.

a. The total length of bracing required for a given wall line is the product of all applicable adjustment factors.

b. Linear interpolation shall be permitted.

c. Braced wall line spacing and adjustment to bracing length in SDC D_0, D_1, and D_2 shall comply with Section R602.10.1.5.

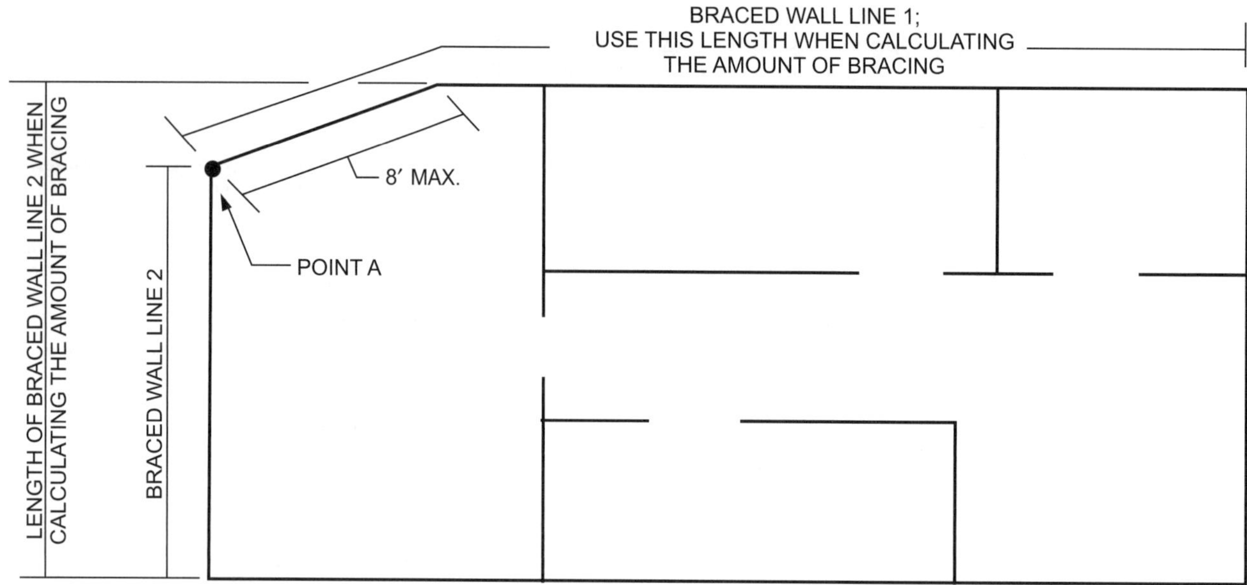

For SI: 1 foot = 304.8 mm.

FIGURE R602.10.1.3
ANGLED CORNERS

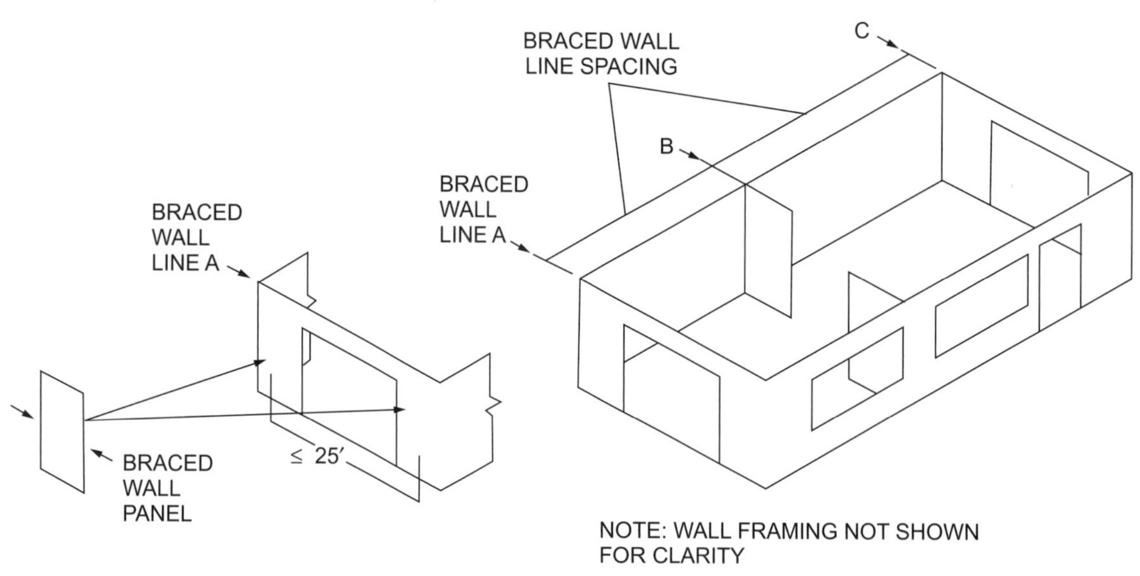

For SI: 1 foot = 304.8 mm.

FIGURE R602.10.1.4(1)
BRACED WALL PANELS AND BRACED WALL LINES

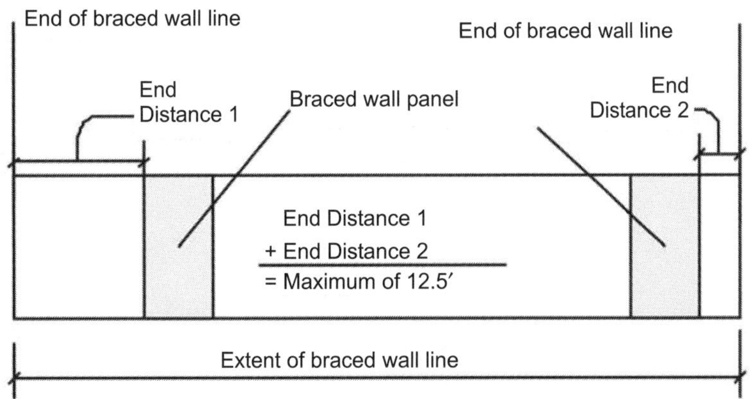

Braced wall panel shall be permitted to be located away from the end of a braced wall line, provided the total end distance from each end to the nearest braced wall panel does not exceed 12.5′. If braced wall panel is located at the end of the braced wall line, then end distance is 0′.

For SI: 1 foot = 304.8 mm.

FIGURE R602.10.1.4(2)
BRACED WALL PANEL END DISTANCE REQUIREMENTS (SDC A, B AND C)

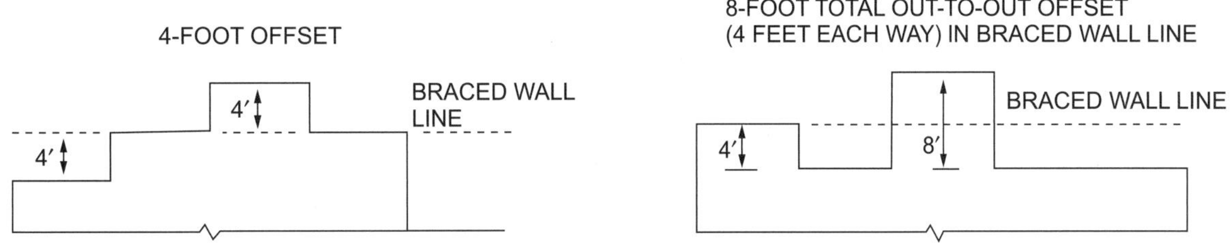

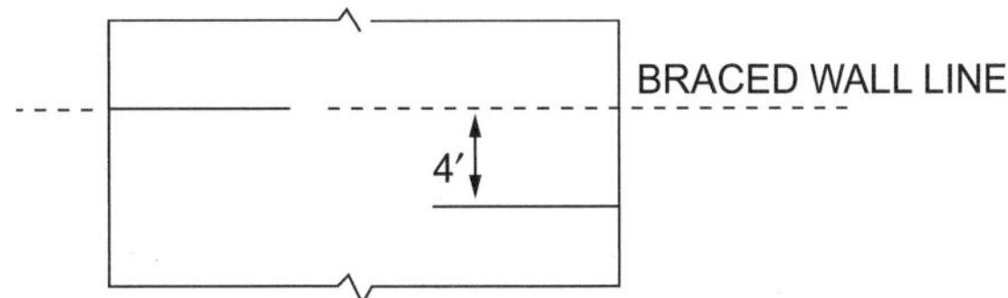

For SI: 1 foot = 304.8 mm.

FIGURE R602.10.1.4(3)
OFFSETS PERMITTED FOR BRACED WALL LINES

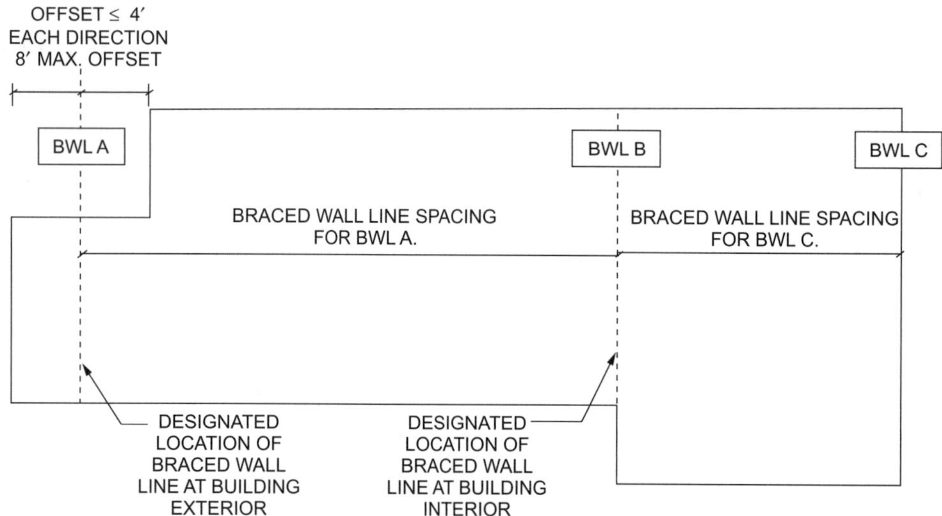

For SI: 1 foot = 304.8 mm.

FIGURE R602.10.1.4(4)
BRACED WALL LINE SPACING

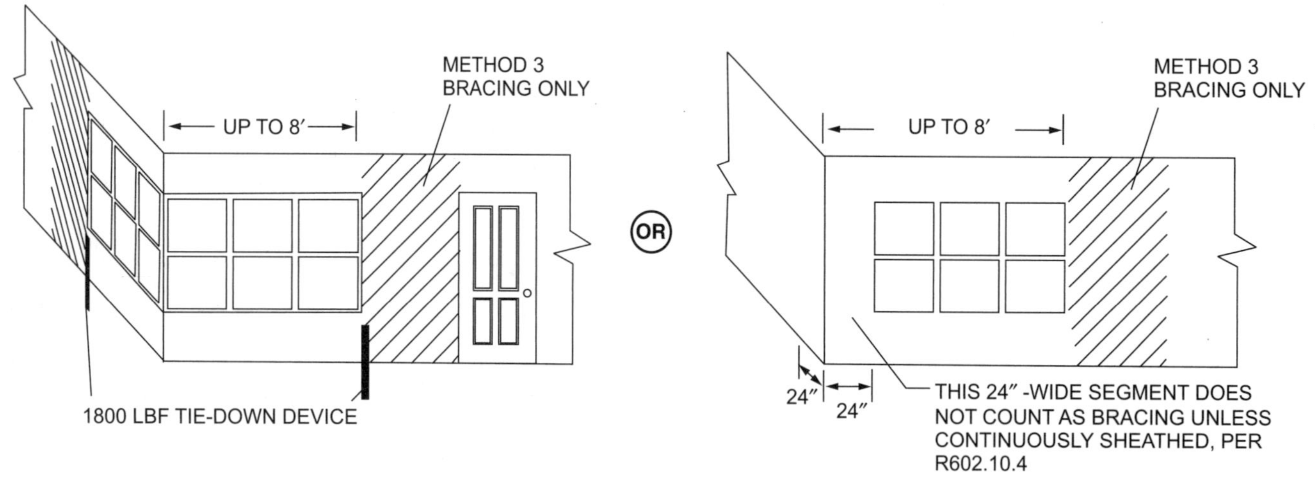

For SI: 1 inch = 25.4 mm, 1 foot = 304.8 mm, 1 pound force = 4,448 N.

FIGURE R602.10.1.4.1
BRACED WALL PANELS AT ENDS OF BRACED WALL LINES IN SEISMIC DESIGN CATEGORIES D_0, D_1 AND D_2

TABLE R602.10.1.5
ADJUSTMENTS OF BRACING LENGTH FOR BRACED WALL LINE SPACING GREATER THAN 25 FEET[a,b]

BRACED WALL LINE SPACING (feet)	MULTIPLY BRACING LENGTH IN TABLE R602.10.1.2(2) BY:
25	1.0
30	1.2
35	1.4

For SI: 1 foot = 304.8 mm.

a. Linear interpolation is permitted.

b. When a braced wall line has a parallel braced wall line on both sides, the larger adjustment factor shall be used.

TABLE R602.10.2
INTERMITTENT BRACING METHODS

METHOD	MATERIAL	MINIMUM THICKNESS	FIGURE	CONNECTION CRITERIA
LIB	Let-in-bracing	1 × 4 wood or approved metal straps at 45° to 60° angles for maximum 16″ stud spacing	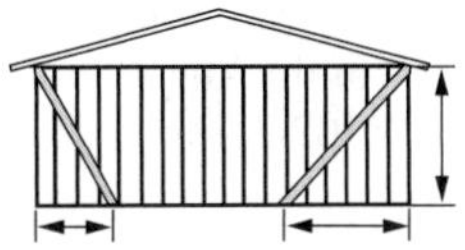	Wood: 2-8d nails per stud including top and bottom plate metal: per manufacturer
DWB	Diagonal wood boards	$^3/_4$″ (1″ nominal) for maximum 24″ stud spacing	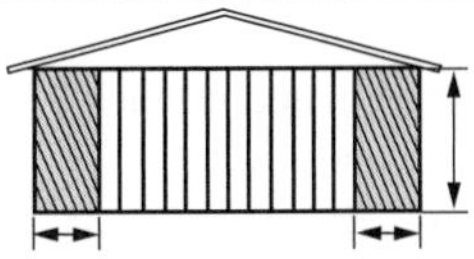	2-8d ($2^1/_2$″ × 0.113″) nails or 2 staples, $1^3/_4$″ per stud
WSP	Wood structural panel (see Section R604)	$^3/_8$″	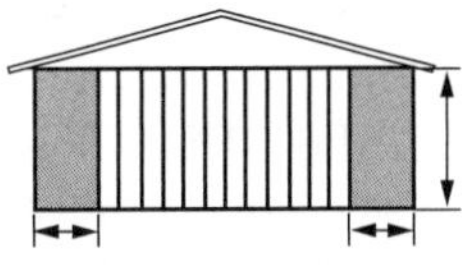	For exterior sheathing see Table R602.3(3) For interior sheathing see Table R602.3(1)
SFB	Structural fiberboard sheathing	$^1/_2$″ or $^{25}/_{32}$″ for maximum 16″ stud spacing		$1^1/_2$″ galvanized roofing nails or 8d common ($2^1/_2$″ × 0.131) nails at 3″ spacing (panel edges) at 6″ spacing (intermediate supports)
GB	Gypsum board	$^1/_2$″	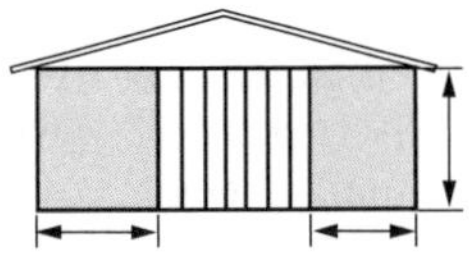	Nails or screws at 7″ spacing at panel edges including top and bottom plates; for all braced wall panel locations for exterior sheathing nail or screw size, see Table R602.3(1); for interior gypsum board nail or screw size, see Table R702.3.5
PBS	Particleboard sheathing (see Section R605)	$^3/_8$″ or $^1/_2$″ for maximum 16″ stud spacing	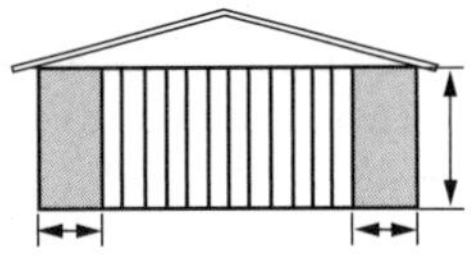	$1^1/_2$″ galvanized roofing nails or 8d common ($2^1/_2$″ × 0.131) nails at 3″ spacing (panel edges) at 6 spacing (intermediate supports)
PCP	Portland cement plaster	See Section R703.6 For maximum 16″ stud spacing	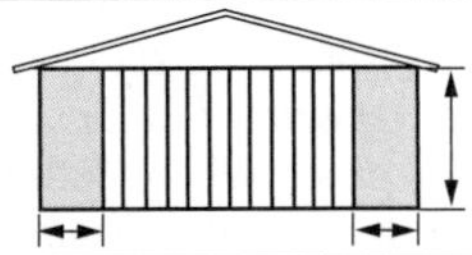	$1^1/_2$″, 11 gage, $^7/_{16}$″ head nails at 6″ spacing or $^7/_8$″, 16 gage staples at 6″ spacing
HPS	Hardboard panel siding	$^7/_{16}$″ For maximum 16″ stud spacing	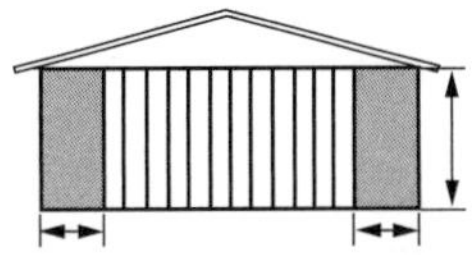	0.092″ dia., 0.225″ head nails with length to accommodate $1^1/_2$″ penetration into studs at 4″ spacing (panel edges), at 8″ spacing (intermediate supports)
ABW	Alternate braced wall	See Section R602.10.3.2	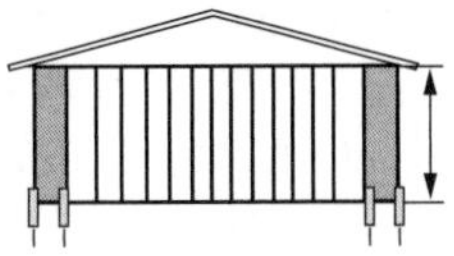	See Section R602.10.3.2
PFH	Intermittent portal frame	See Section R602.10.3.3	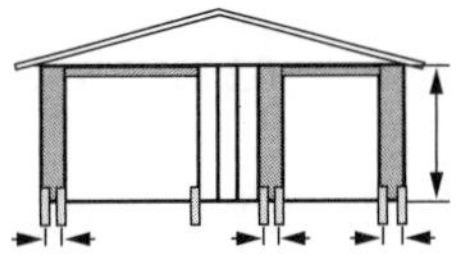	See Section R602.10.3.3
PFG	Intermittent portal frame at garage	See Section R602.10.3.4	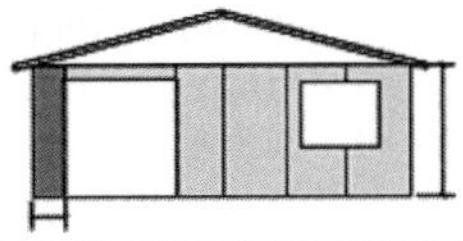	See Section R602.10.3.4

For SI: 1 inch = 25.4 mm, 1 foot = 304.8 mm, 1 degree = 0.0175 rad.

R602.10.2.1 Intermittent braced wall panel interior finish material. Intermittent *braced wall panels* shall have gypsum wall board installed on the side of the wall opposite the bracing material. Gypsum wall board shall be not less than $^1/_2$ inch (12.7 mm) in thickness and be fastened in accordance with Table R702.3.5 for interior gypsum wall board.

Exceptions:

1. Wall panels that are braced in accordance with Methods GB, ABW, PFG and PFH.
2. When an *approved* interior finish material with an in-plane shear resistance equivalent to gypsum board is installed.
3. For Methods DWB, WSP, SFB, PBS, PCP and HPS, omitting gypsum wall board is permitted provided the length of bracing in Tables R602.10.1.2(1) and R602.10.1.2(2) is multiplied by a factor of 1.5.

R602.10.2.2 Adhesive attachment of sheathing in Seismic Design Categories C, D_0, D_1 and D_2. Adhesive attachment of wall sheathing shall not be permitted in Seismic Design Categories C, D_0, D_1 and D_2.

R602.10.3 Minimum length of braced panels. For Methods DWB, WSP, SFB, PBS, PCP and HPS, each *braced wall panel* shall be at least 48 inches (1219 mm) in length, covering a minimum of three stud spaces where studs are spaced 16 inches (406 mm) on center and covering a minimum of two stud spaces where studs are spaced 24 inches (610 mm) on center. For Method GB, each *braced wall panel* and shall be at least 96 inches (2438 mm) in length where applied to one face of a *braced wall panel* and at least 48 inches (1219 mm) where applied to both faces. For Methods DWB, WSP, SFB, PBS, PCP and HPS, for purposes of computing the length of panel bracing required in Tables R602.10.1.2(1) and R602.10.1.2(2), the effective length of the *braced wall panel* shall be equal to the actual length of the panel. When Method GB panels are applied to only one face of a *braced wall panel*, bracing lengths required in Tables R602.10.1.2(1) and R602.10.1.2(2) for Method GB shall be doubled.

Exceptions:

1. Lengths of *braced wall panels* for continuous sheathing methods shall be in accordance with Table R602.10.4.2.
2. Lengths of Method ABW panels shall be in accordance with Sections R602.10.3.2.
3. Length of Methods PFH and PFG panels shall be in accordance with Section R602.10.3.3 and R602.10.3.4 respectively.
4. For Methods DWB, WSP, SFB, PBS, PCP and HPS in Seismic Design Categories A, B, and C: Panels between 36 inches (914 mm)and 48 inches (1219 mm) in length shall be permitted to count towards the required length of bracing in Tables R602.10.1.2(1) and R602.10.1.2(2), and the effective contribution shall comply with Table R602.10.3.

R602.10.3.1 Adjustment of length of braced panels. When *story height* (H), measured in feet, exceeds 10 feet (3048 mm), in accordance with Section R301.3, the minimum length of *braced wall panels* specified in Section R602.10.3 shall be increased by a factor H/10. See Table R602.10.3.1. Interpolation is permitted.

R602.10.3.2 Method ABW: Alternate braced wall panels. Method ABW *braced wall panels* constructed in accordance with one of the following provisions shall be permitted to replace each 4 feet (1219 mm) of *braced wall panel* as required by Section R602.10.3. The maximum height and minimum length and hold-down force of each panel shall be in accordance with Table R602.10.3.2:

1. In one-story buildings, each panel shall be installed in accordance with Figure R602.10.3.2. The hold-down device shall be installed in accordance with the manufacturer's recommendations. The panels shall be supported directly on a foundation or on floor framing supported directly on a foundation which is continuous across the entire length of the *braced wall line*.
2. In the first *story* of two-story buildings, each *braced wall panel* shall be in accordance with Item 1 above, except that the wood structural panel sheathing edge nailing spacing shall not exceed 4 inches (102 mm) on center.

R602.10.3.3 Method PFH: Portal frame with hold-downs. Method PFH *braced wall panels* constructed in accordance with one of the following provisions are also permitted to replace each 4 feet (1219 mm) of *braced wall panel* as required by Section R602.10.3 for use adjacent to a window or door opening with a full-length header:

1. Each panel shall be fabricated in accordance with Figure R602.10.3.3. The wood structural panel sheathing shall extend up over the solid sawn or glued-laminated header and shall be nailed in accordance with Figure R602.10.3.3. A spacer, if used with a built-up header, shall be placed on the side of the built-up beam opposite the wood structural panel sheathing. The header shall extend between the inside faces of the first full-length outer studs of each panel. One anchor bolt not less than $^5/_8$-inch-diameter (16 mm) and installed in accordance with Section R403.1.6 shall be provided in the center of each sill plate. The hold-down devices shall be an embedded-strap type, installed in accordance with the manufacturer's recommendations. The panels shall be supported directly on a foundation which is continuous across the entire length of the braced wall line. The foundation shall be reinforced as shown on Figure R602.10.3.2. This reinforcement shall be lapped not less than 15 inches (381 mm) with the reinforcement required in the continuous foundation located directly under the braced wall line.
2. In the first *story* of two-story buildings, each wall panel shall be braced in accordance with item 1 above, except that each panel shall have a length of not less than 24 inches (610 mm).

TABLE R602.10.3
EFFECTIVE LENGTHS FOR BRACED WALL PANELS LESS THAN 48 INCHES IN ACTUAL LENGTH (BRACE METHODS DWB, WSP, SFB, PBS, PCP AND HPS[a])

ACTUAL LENGTH OF BRACED WALL PANEL (inches)	EFFECTIVE LENGTH OF BRACED WALL PANEL (inches)		
	8-foot Wall Height	9-foot Wall Height	10-foot Wall Height
48	48	48	48
42	36	36	N/A
36	27	N/A	N/A

For SI: 1 inch = 25.4 mm, 1 foot = 304.8 mm.
a. Interpolation shall be permitted.

TABLE R602.10.3.1
MINIMUM LENGTH REQUIREMENTS FOR BRACED WALL PANELS

SEISMIC DESIGN CATEGORY AND WIND SPEED	BRACING METHOD	HEIGHT OF BRACED WALL PANEL				
		8 ft	9 ft	10 ft	11 ft	12 ft
SDC A, B, C, D_0, D_1 and D_2 Wind speed < 110 mph	DWB, WSP, SFB, PBS, PCP, HPS and Method GB when double sided	4′ - 0″	4′ - 0″	4′ - 0″	4′ - 5″	4′ - 10″
	Method GB, single sided	8′ - 0″	8′ - 0″	8′ - 0″	8′ - 10″	9′ - 8″

For SI: 1 inch = 25.4 mm, 1 foot = 304.8 mm.

TABLE R602.10.3.2
MINIMUM LENGTH REQUIREMENTS AND HOLD-DOWN FORCES FOR METHOD ABW BRACED WALL PANELS

SEISMIC DESIGN CATEGORY AND WIND SPEED		HEIGHT OF BRACED WALL PANEL				
		8 ft	9 ft	10 ft	11 ft	12 ft
SDC A, B and C Wind speed < 110 mph	Minimum sheathed length	2′ - 4″	2′ - 8″	2′ - 10″	3′ - 2″	3′ - 6″
	R602.10.3.2, item 1 hold-down force (lb)	1800	1800	1800	2000	2200
	R602.10.3.2, item 2 hold-down force (lb)	3000	3000	3000	3300	3600
SDC D_0, D_1 and D_2 Wind speed < 110 mph	Minimum sheathed length	2′ - 8″	2′ - 8″	2′ - 10″	NP[a]	NP[a]
	R602.10.3.2, item 1 hold-down force (lb)	1800	1800	1800	NP[a]	NP[a]
	R602.10.3.2, item 2 hold-down force (lb)	3000	3000	3000	NP[a]	NP[a]

For SI: 1 inch = 25.4 mm, 1 foot = 305 mm, 1 pound = 4.448 N.
a. NP = Not Permitted. Maximum height of 10 feet.

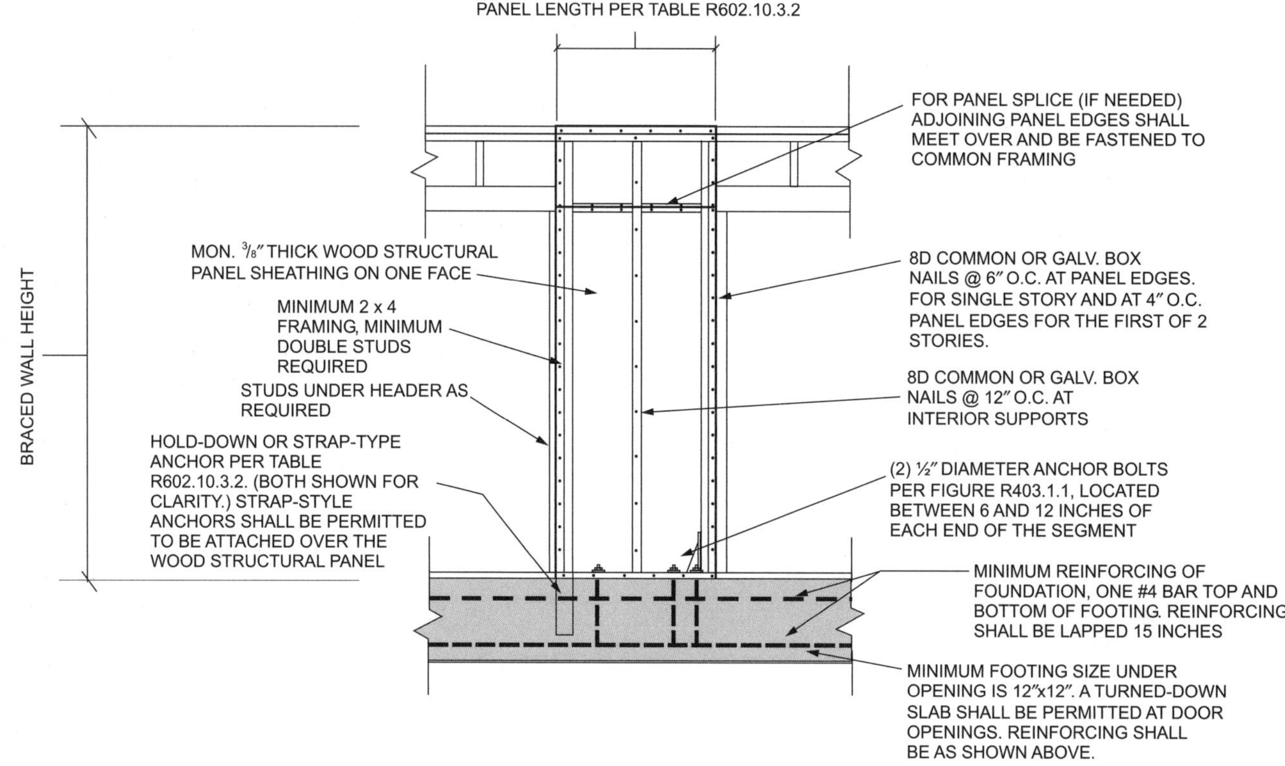

For SI: 1 inch = 25.4 mm.

FIGURE R602.10.3.2
ALTERNATE BRACED WALL PANEL

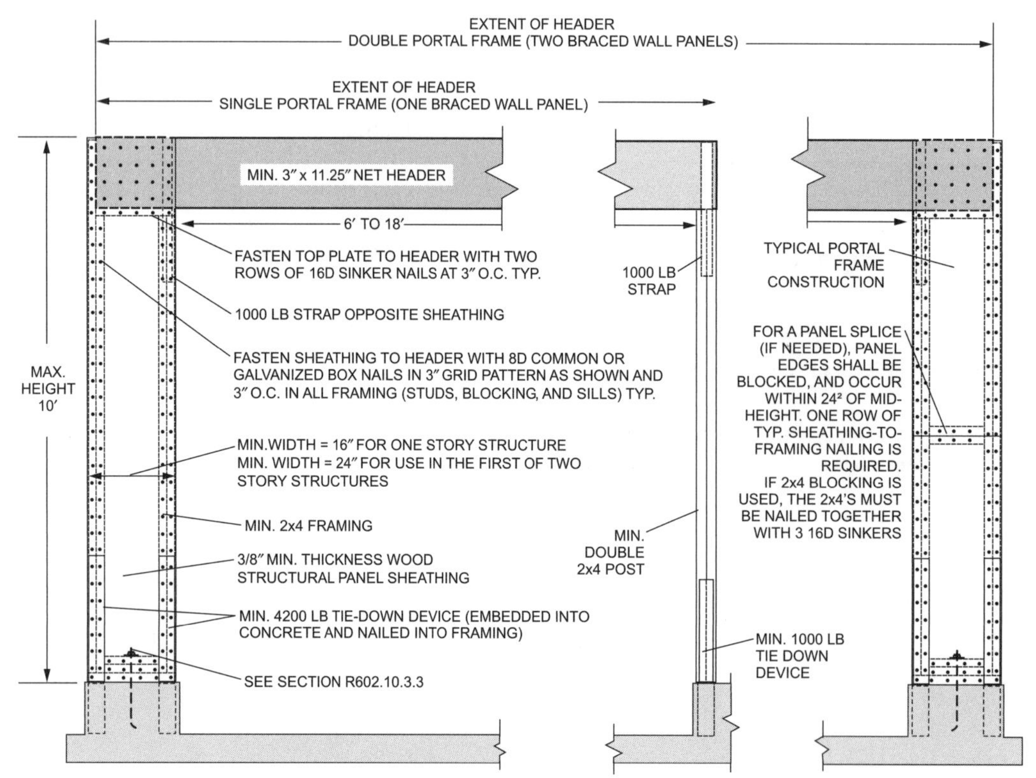

For SI: 1 inch = 25.4 mm, 1 foot = 304.8 mm, 1 pound force = 4.448 N.

FIGURE R602.10.3.3
METHOD PFH: PORTAL FRAME WITH HOLD-DOWNS

R602.10.3.4 Method PFG: at garage door openings in Seismic Design Categories A, B and C. Where supporting a roof or one *story* and a roof, alternate *braced wall panels* constructed in accordance with the following provisions are permitted on either side of garage door openings. For the purpose of calculating wall bracing amounts to satisfy the minimum requirements of Table R602.10.1.2(1), the length of the alternate *braced wall panel* shall be multiplied by a factor of 1.5.

1. *Braced wall panel* length shall be a minimum of 24 inches (610 mm) and *braced wall panel* height shall be a maximum of 10 feet (3048 mm).
2. *Braced wall panel* shall be sheathed on one face with a single layer of $^{7}/_{16}$-inch-minimum (11 mm) thickness wood structural panel sheathing attached to framing with 8d common nails at 3 inches (76 mm) on center in accordance with Figure R602.10.3.4.
3. The wood structural panel sheathing shall extend up over the solid sawn or glued-laminated header and shall be nailed to the header at 3 inches (76 mm) on center grid in accordance with Figure R602.10.3.4.
4. The header shall consist of a minimum of two solid sawn 2×12s (51 by 305 mm) or a 3 inches × 11.25 inch (76 by 286 mm) glued-laminated header. The header shall extend between the inside faces of the first full-length outer studs of each panel in accordance with Figure R602.10.3.4. The clear span of the header between the inner studs of each panel shall be not less than 6 feet (1829 mm) and not more than 18 feet (5486 mm) in length.
5. A strap with an uplift capacity of not less than 1,000 pounds (4448 N) shall fasten the header to the side of the inner studs opposite the sheathing face. Where building is located in Wind Exposure Categories C or D, the strap uplift capacity shall be in accordance with Table R602.10.4.1.1.
6. A minimum of two bolts not less than $^{1}/_{2}$-inch (12.7 mm) diameter shall be installed in accordance with Section R403.1.6. A $^{3}/_{16}$-inch by $2^{1}/_{2}$-inch (4.8 by 63 by 63 mm) by $2^{1}/_{2}$-inch steel plate washer is installed between the bottom plate and the nut of each bolt.
7. *Braced wall panel* shall be installed directly on a foundation.
8. Where an alternate *braced wall panel* is located only on one side of the garage opening, the header shall be connected to a supporting jack stud on the opposite side of the garage opening with a metal strap with an uplift capacity of not less than 1,000 pounds. Where that supporting jack stud is not part of a *braced wall panel* assembly, another 1,000 pounds (4448 N) strap shall be installed to attach the supporting jack stud to the foundation.

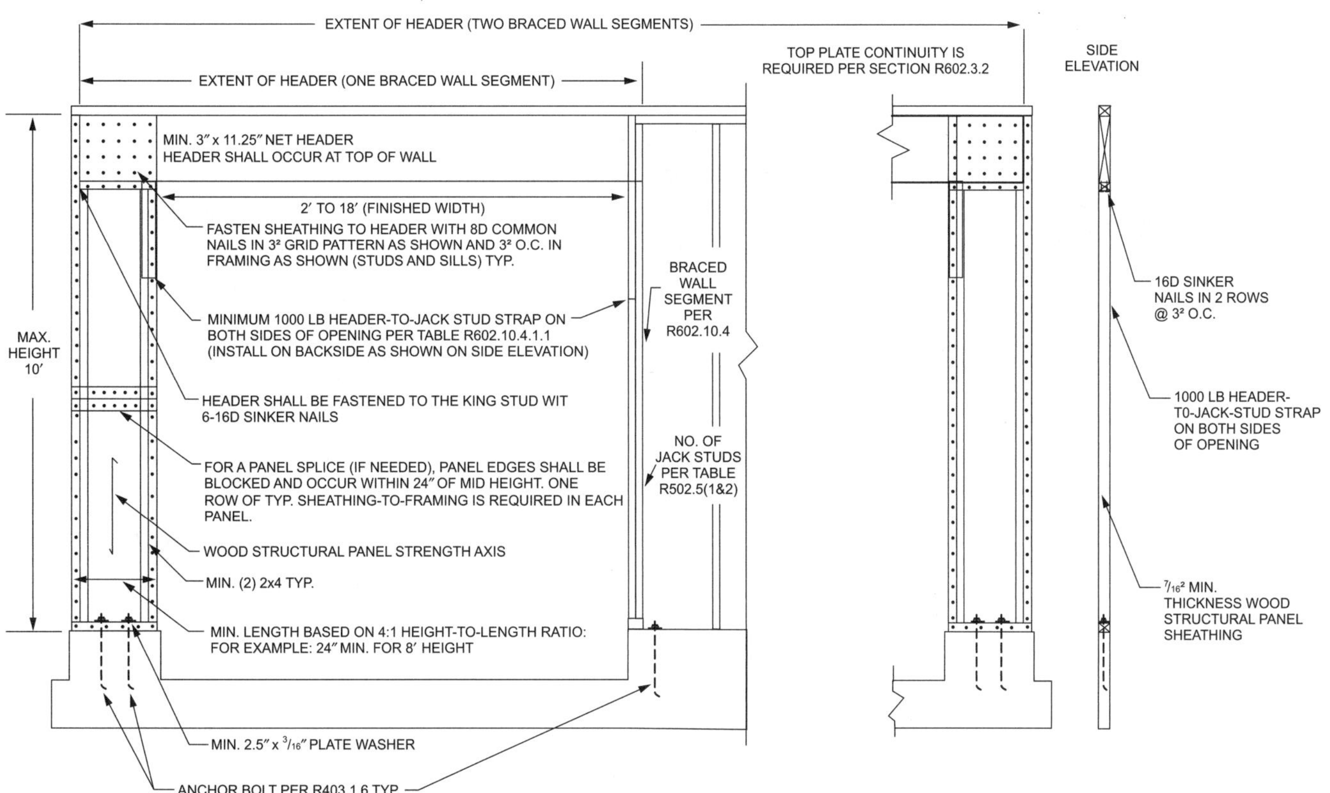

For SI: 1 inch = 25.4 mm, 1 foot = 304.8 mm, 1 pound force = 4.448 N.

FIGURE R602.10.3.4
METHOD PFG PORTAL FRAME AT GARAGE DOOR OPENINGS IN SEISMIC DESIGN CATEGORIES A, B AND C

R602.10.4 Continuous sheathing. *Braced wall lines* with continuous sheathing shall be constructed in accordance with this section. All *braced wall lines* along exterior walls on the same *story* shall be continuously sheathed.

Exception: Within Seismic Design Categories A, B and C or in regions where the basic wind speed is less than or equal to 100 mph (45 m/s), other bracing methods prescribed by this code shall be permitted on other *braced wall lines* on the same *story* level or on any *braced wall line* on different *story* levels of the building.

R602.10.4.1 Continuous sheathing braced wall panels. Continuous sheathing methods require structural panel sheathing to be used on all sheathable surfaces on one side of a *braced wall line* including areas above and below openings and gable end walls. *Braced wall panels* shall be constructed in accordance with one of the methods listed in Table R602.10.4.1. Different bracing methods, other than those listed in Table R602.10.4.1, shall not be permitted along a *braced wall line* with continuous sheathing.

R602.10.4.1.1 Continuous portal frame. Continuous portal frame *braced wall panels* shall be constructed in accordance with Figure R602.10.4.1.1. The number of continuous portal frame panels in a single *braced wall line* shall not exceed four. For purposes of resisting wind pressures acting perpendicular to the wall, the requirements of Figure R602.10.4.1.1 and Table R602.10.4.1.1 shall be met. There shall be a maximum of two braced wall segments per header and header length shall not exceed 22 feet (6706 mm). Tension straps shall be installed in accordance with the manufacturer's recommendations.

R602.10.4.2 Length of braced wall panels with continuous sheathing. *Braced wall panels* along a *braced wall line* with continuous sheathing shall be full-height with a length based on the adjacent clear opening height in accordance with Table R602.10.4.2 and Figure R602.10.4.2. Within a *braced wall line* when a panel has an opening on either side of differing heights, the taller opening height shall be used to determine the panel length from Table R602.10.4.2. For Method CS-PF, wall height shall be measured from the top of the header to the bottom of the bottom plate as shown in Figure R602.10.4.1.1.

R602.10.4.3 Length of bracing for continuous sheathing. *Braced wall lines* with continuous sheathing shall be provided with *braced wall panels* in the length required in Tables R602.10.1.2(1) and R602.10.1.2(2). Only those full-height *braced wall panels* complying with the length requirements of Table R602.10.4.2 shall be permitted to contribute to the minimum required length of bracing.

TABLE R602.10.4.1
CONTINUOUS SHEATHING METHODS

METHOD	MATERIAL	MINIMUM THICKNESS	FIGURE	CONNECTION CRITERIA
CS-WSP	Wood structural panel	$^3/_8''$		6d common (2″ × 0.113″) nails at 6″ spacing (panel edges) and at 12″ spacing (intermediate supports) or 16 ga. × $1^3/_4$ staples at 3″ spacing (panel edges) and 6″ spacing (intermediate supports)
CS-G	Wood structural panel adjacent to garage openings and supporting roof load only[a,b]	$^3/_8''$		See Method CS-WSP
CS-PF	Continuous portal frame	See Section R602.10.4.1.1		See Section R602.10.4.1.1

For SI: 1 inch = 25.4 mm, 1 pound per square foot = 47.89 Pa.

a. Applies to one wall of a garage only.

b. Roof covering dead loads shall be 3 psf or less.

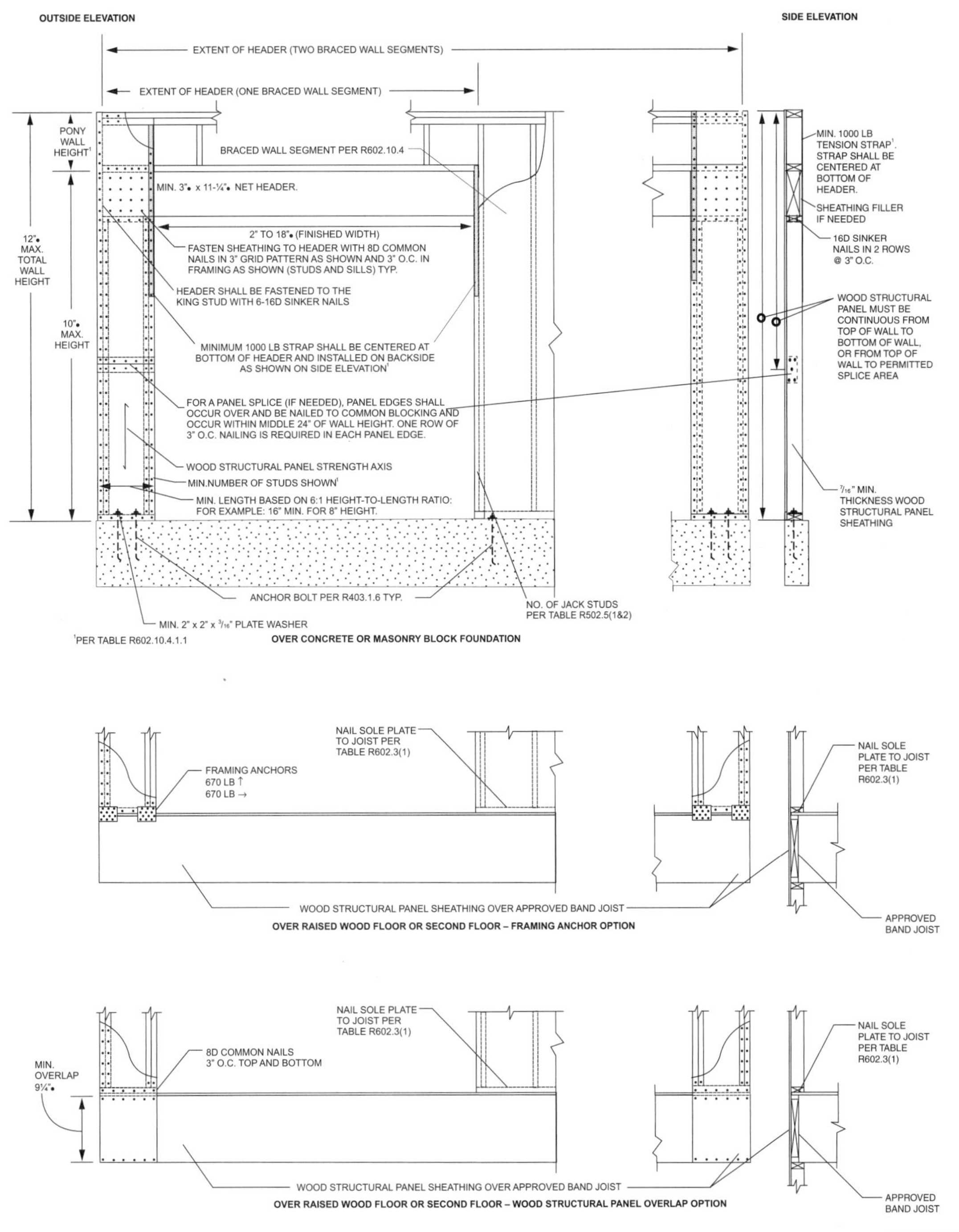

For SI: 1 inch = 25.4 mm, 1 foot = 304.8 mm, 1 pound force = 4.448 N.

FIGURE R602.10.4.1.1
METHOD CS-PF: CONTINUOUS PORTAL FRAME PANEL CONSTRUCTION

TABLE R602.10.4.1.1
TENSION STRAP CAPACITY REQUIRED FOR RESISTING WIND PRESSURES PERPENDICULAR TO 6:1 ASPECT RATIO WALLS[a,b]

MINIMUM WALL STUD FRAMING NOMINAL SIZE AND GRADE	MAXIMUM PONY WALL HEIGHT (feet)	MAXIMUM TOTAL WALL HEIGHT (feet)	MAXIMUM OPENING WIDTH (feet)	BASIC WIND SPEED (mph)					
				85	90	100	85	90	100
				Exposure B			Exposure C		
				Tension strap capacity required (lbf)[a,b]					
2 × 4 No. 2 Grade	0	10	18	1000	1000	1000	1000	1000	1000
	1	10	9	1000	1000	1000	1000	1000	1275
			16	1000	1000	1750	1800	2325	3500
			18	1000	1200	2100	2175	2725	DR
	2	10	9	1000	1000	1025	1075	1550	2500
			16	1525	2025	3125	3200	3900	DR
			18	1875	2400	3575	3700	DR	DR
	2	12	9	1000	1200	2075	2125	2750	4000
			16	2600	3200	DR	DR	DR	DR
			18	3175	3850	DR	DR	DR	DR
	4	12	9	1775	2350	3500	3550	DR	DR
			16	4175	DR	DR	DR	DR	DR
2 × 6 Stud Grade	2	12	9	1000	1000	1325	1375	1750	2550
			16	1650	2050	2925	3000	3550	DR
			18	2025	2450	3425	3500	4100	DR
	4	12	9	1125	1500	2225	2275	2775	3800
			16	2650	3150	DR	DR	DR	DR
			18	3125	3675	DR	DR	DR	DR

For SI: 1 inch = 25.4 mm, 1 foot = 304.8 mm, 1 pound force = 4.448 N.

a. DR = design required.

b. Strap shall be installed in accordance with manufacturer's recommendations.

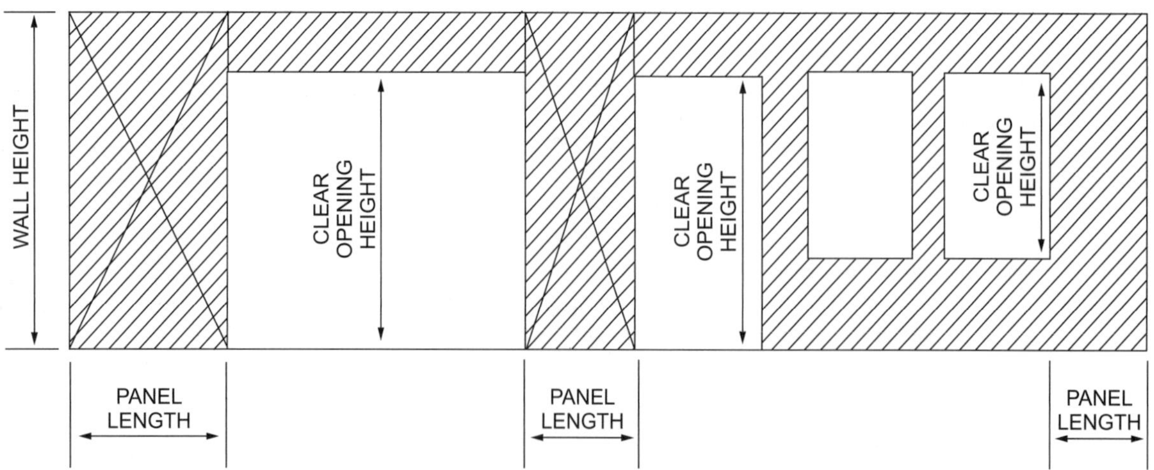

FIGURE R602.10.4.2
BRACED WALL PANELS WITH CONTINUOUS SHEATHING

TABLE R602.10.4.2
LENGTH REQUIREMENTS FOR BRACED WALL PANELS WITH CONTINUOUS SHEATHING[a, b] (inches)

METHOD	ADJACENT CLEAR OPENING HEIGHT (inches)	WALL HEIGHT (feet)				
		8	9	10	11	12
CS-WSP	64	24	27	30	33	36
	68	26	27	30	—	—
	72	28	27	30	—	—
	76	29	30	30	—	—
	80	31	33	30	—	—
	84	35	36	33	—	—
	88	39	39	36	—	—
	92	44	42	39	—	—
	96	48	45	42	—	—
	100	—	48	45	—	—
	104	—	51	48	—	—
	108	—	54	51	—	—
	112	—	—	54	44	—
	116	—	—	57	—	—
	120	—	—	60	—	—
	122	—	—	—	—	48
	132	—	—	—	66	—
	144	—	—	—	—	75
CS-G	≤ 120	24	27	30	—	—
CS-PF	≤ 120	16	18	20	—	—

For SI: 1 inch = 25.4 mm, 1 foot = 304.8 mm.

a. Interpolation shall be permitted.

b. Braced wall panels using wood structural panel (WSP) sheathing on both sides may be used to reduce the panel lengths shown by 50 percent.

R602.10.4.4 Continuously sheathed braced wall panel location and corner construction. For all continuous sheathing methods, full-height *braced wall panels* complying with the length requirements of Table R602.10.4.2 shall be located at each end of a *braced wall line* with continuous sheathing and at least every 25 feet (7620 mm) on center. A minimum 24 inch (610 mm) wood structural panel corner return shall be provided at both ends of a *braced wall line* with continuous sheathing in accordance with Figures R602.10.4.4(1) and R602.10.4.4(2). In lieu of the corner return, a hold-down device with a minimum uplift design value of 800 pounds (3560 N) shall be fastened to the corner stud and to the foundation or framing below in accordance with Figure R602.10.4.4(3).

Exception: The first *braced wall panel* shall be permitted to begin 12.5 feet (3810 mm) from each end of the *braced wall line* in Seismic Design Categories A, B and C and 8 feet (2438 mm) in Seismic Design Categories D_0, D_1 and D_2 provided one of the following is satisfied:

1. A minimum 24 inch (610 mm) long, full-height wood structural panel is provided at both sides of a corner constructed in accordance with Figure R602.10.4.4(1) at the *braced wall line* ends in accordance with Figure R602.10.4.4(4), or
2. The *braced wall panel* closest to the corner shall have a hold-down device with a minimum uplift design value of 800 pounds (3560 N) fastened to the stud at the edge of the *braced wall panel* closest to the corner and to the foundation or framing below in accordance with Figure R602.10.4.4(5).

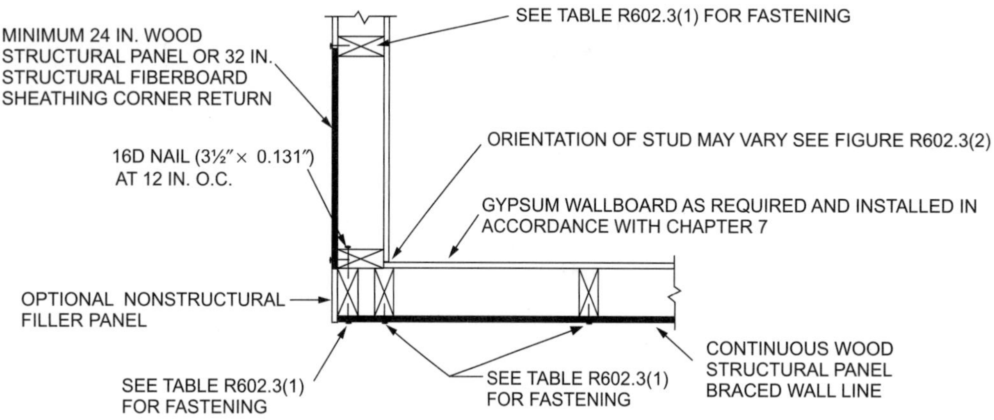

(a) OUTSIDE CORNER DETAIL

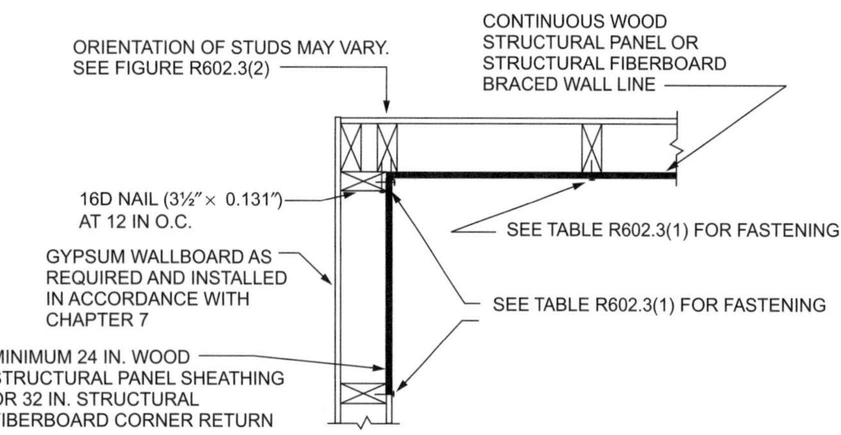

(b) INSIDE CORNER DETAIL

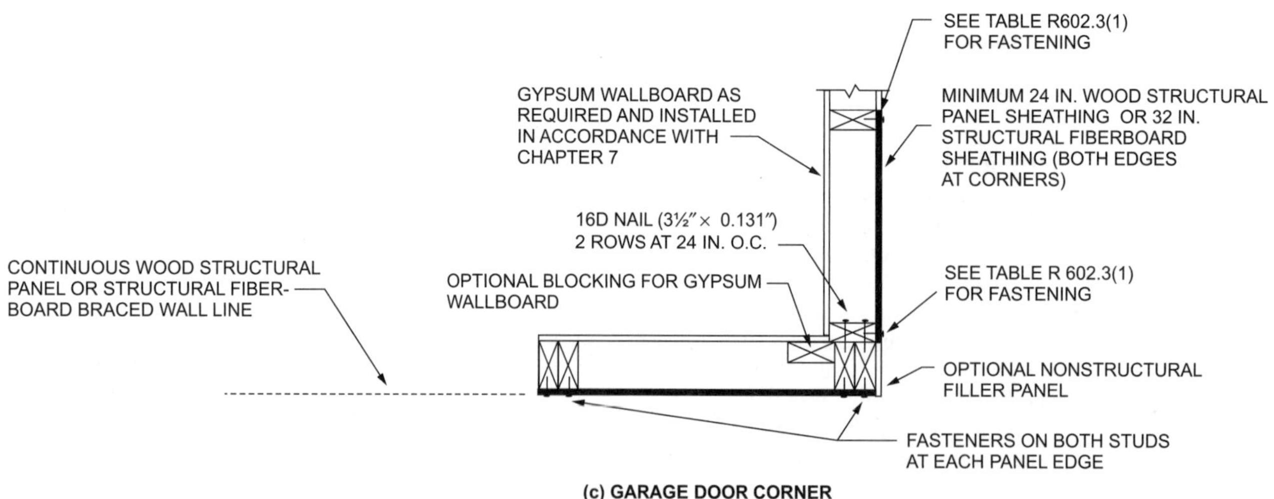

(c) GARAGE DOOR CORNER

For SI: 1 inch = 25.4 mm, 1 foot = 305 mm.

FIGURE R602.10.4.4(1)
TYPICAL EXTERIOR CORNER FRAMING FOR CONTINUOUS SHEATHING

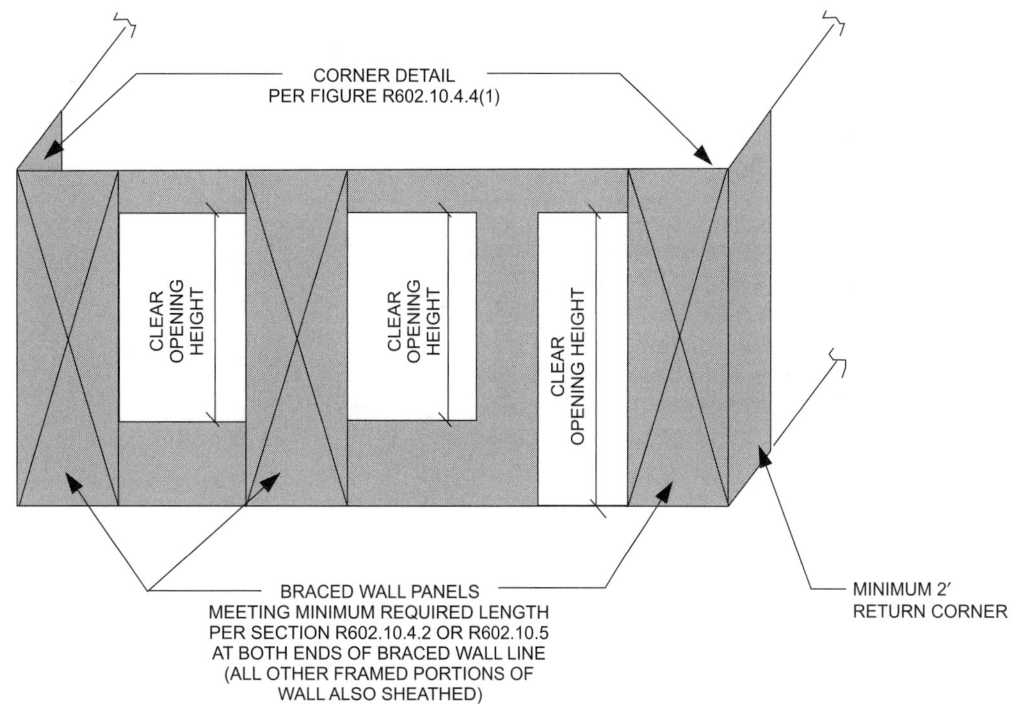

For SI: 1 foot = 304.8 mm.

FIGURE R602.10.4.4(2)
BRACED WALL LINE WITH CONTINUOUS SHEATHING WITH CORNER RETURN PANEL

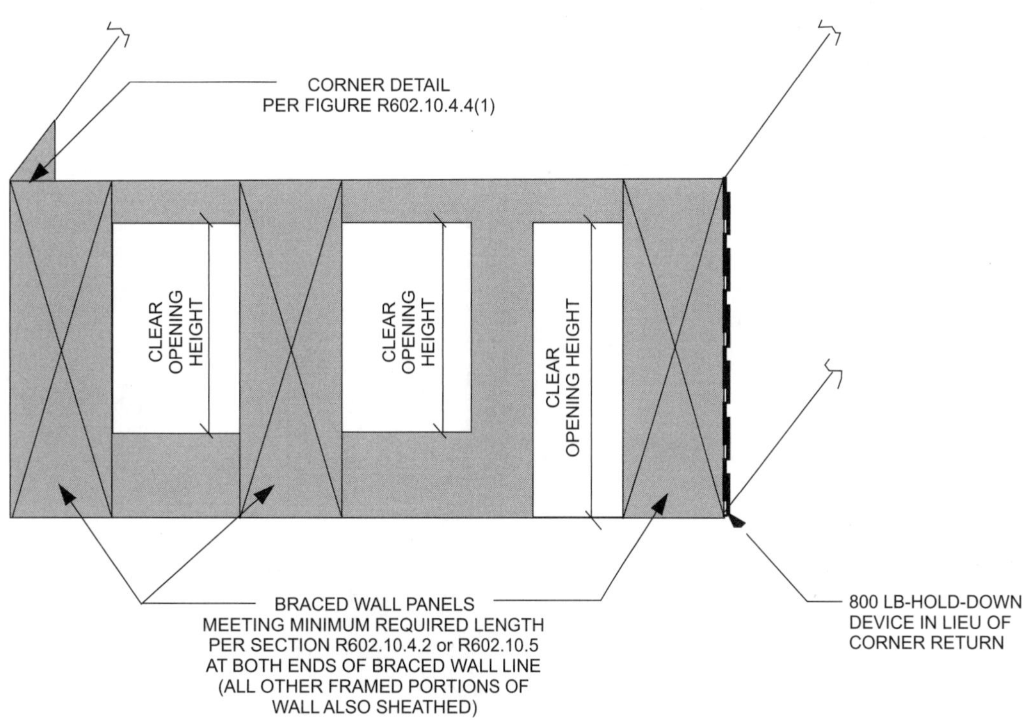

For SI: 1 inch = 25.4 mm, 1 pound = 4.448 N.

FIGURE R602.10.4.4(3)
BRACED WALL LINE WITH CONTINUOUS SHEATHING WITHOUT CORNER RETURN PANEL

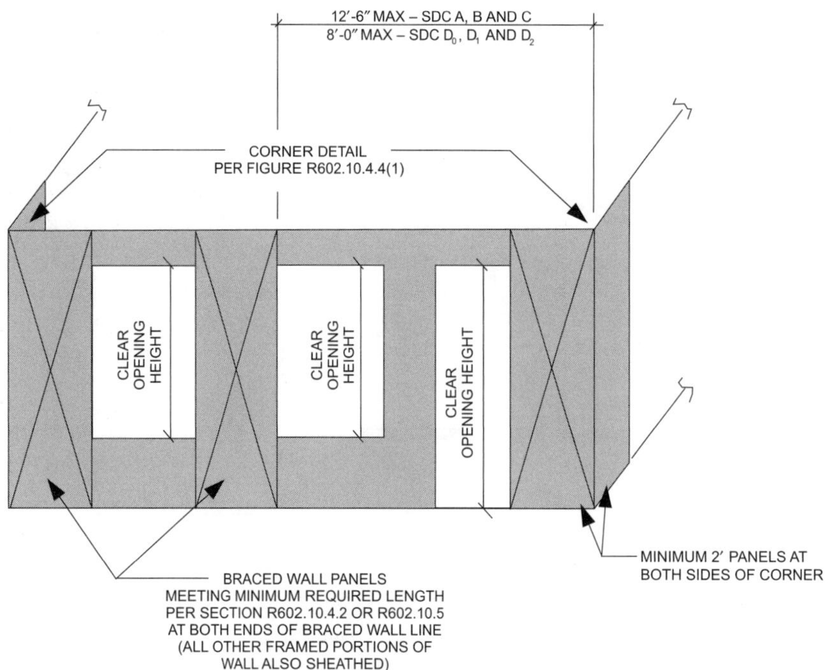

For SI: 1 inch = 25.4 mm.

FIGURE R602.10.4.4(4)
BRACED WALL LINE WITH CONTINUOUS SHEATHING FIRST BRACED WALL PANEL AWAY FROM END OF WALL LINE WITHOUT TIE DOWN

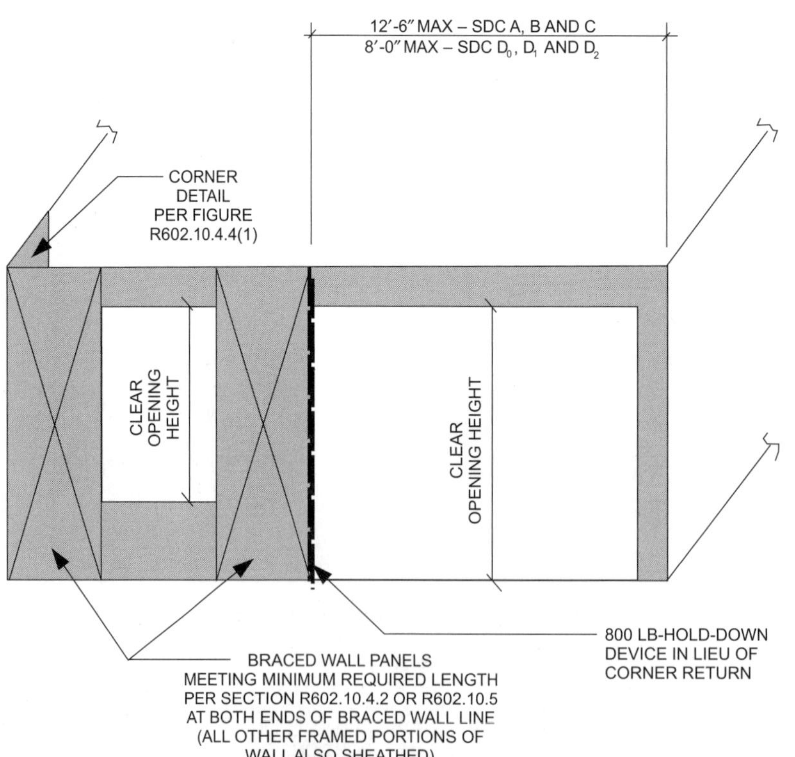

For SI: 1 foot = 305 mm. 1 pound = 4.448 N.

FIGURE R602.10.4.4(5)
BRACED WALL LINE WITH CONTINUOUS SHEATHING—FIRST BRACED WALL PANEL AWAY FROM END OF WALL LINE WITH HOLD-DOWN

R602.10.5 Continuously-sheathed braced wall line using Method CS-SFB (structural fiberboard sheathing). Continuously sheathed *braced wall lines* using structural fiberboard sheathing shall comply with this section. Different bracing methods shall not be permitted within a continuously sheathed *braced wall line*. Other bracing methods prescribed by this code shall be permitted on other *braced wall lines* on the same *story* level or on different *story* levels of the building.

R602.10.5.1 Continuously sheathed braced wall line requirements. Continuously-sheathed *braced wall lines* shall be in accordance with Figure R602.10.4.2 and shall comply with all of the following requirements:

1. Structural fiberboard sheathing shall be applied to all exterior sheathable surfaces of a *braced wall line* including areas above and below openings.
2. Only full-height or blocked *braced wall panels* shall be used for calculating the braced wall length in accordance with Tables R602.10.1.2(1) and R602.10.1.2(2).

R602.10.5.2 Braced wall panel length. In a continuously-sheathed structural fiberboard *braced wall line*, the minimum *braced wall panel* length shall be in accordance with Table R602.10.5.2.

R602.10.5.3 Braced wall panel location and corner construction. A *braced wall panel* shall be located at each end of a continuously-sheathed *braced wall line*. A minimum 32-inch (813 mm) structural fiberboard sheathing panel corner return shall be provided at both ends of a continuously-sheathed *braced wall line* in accordance with Figure R602.10.4.4(1) In lieu of the corner return, a hold-down device with a minimum uplift design value of 800 pounds (3560 N) shall be fastened to the corner stud and to the foundation or framing below in accordance with Figure R602.10.4.4(3).

Exception: The first *braced wall panel* shall be permitted to begin 12 feet 6 inches (3810 mm) from each end of the *braced wall line* in Seismic Design Categories A, B and C provided one of the following is satisfied:

1. A minimum 32-inch-long (813 mm), full-height structural fiberboard sheathing panel is provided at both sides of a corner constructed in accordance with Figure R602.10.4.4(1) at the *braced wall line* ends in accordance with Figure R602.10.4.4(4), or
2. The *braced wall panel* closest to the corner shall have a hold-down device with a minimum uplift design value of 800 pounds (3560 N) fastened to the stud at the edge of the *braced wall panel* closest to the corner and to the foundation or framing below in accordance with Figure R602.10.4.4(5).

R602.10.5.4 Continuously sheathed braced wall lines. Where a continuously-sheathed *braced wall line* is used in Seismic Design Categories D_0, D_1 and D_2 or regions where the basic wind speed exceeds 100 miles per hour (45 m/s), the *braced wall line* shall be designed in accordance with accepted engineering practice and the provisions of the *International Building Code*. Also, all other exterior *braced wall lines* in the same *story* shall be continuously sheathed.

R602.10.6 Braced wall panel connections. *Braced wall panels* shall be connected to floor framing or foundations as follows:

1. Where joists are perpendicular to a *braced wall panel* above or below, a rim joist, band joist or blocking shall be provided along the entire length of the *braced wall panel* in accordance with Figure R602.10.6(1). Fastening of top and bottom wall plates to framing, rim joist, band joist and/or blocking shall be in accordance with Table R602.3(1).
2. Where joists are parallel to a *braced wall panel* above or below, a rim joist, end joist or other parallel framing member shall be provided directly above and below the *braced wall panel* in accordance with Figure R602.10.6(2). Where a parallel framing member cannot be located directly above and below the panel, full-depth blocking at 16 inch (406 mm) spacing shall be provided between the parallel framing members to each side of the *braced wall panel* in accordance with Figure R602.10.6(2). Fastening of blocking and wall plates shall be in accordance with Table R602.3(1) and Figure R602.10.6(2).
3. Connections of *braced wall panels* to concrete or masonry shall be in accordance with Section R403.1.6.

**TABLE R602.10.5.2
MINIMUM LENGTH REQUIREMENTS FOR STRUCTURAL FIBERBOARD BRACED WALL PANELS IN A CONTINUOUSLY-SHEATHED WALL[a]**

MINIMUM LENGTH OF STRUCTURAL FIBERBOARD BRACED WALL PANEL (inches)			MINIMUM OPENING CLEAR HEIGHT NEXT TO THE STRUCTURAL FIBERBOARD BRACED WALL PANEL (% of wall height)
8-foot wall	9-foot wall	10-foot wall	
48	54	60	100
32	36	40	85
24	27	30	67

For SI: 1 inch = 25.4 mm, 1 foot = 304.8 mm.

a. Interpolation is permitted.

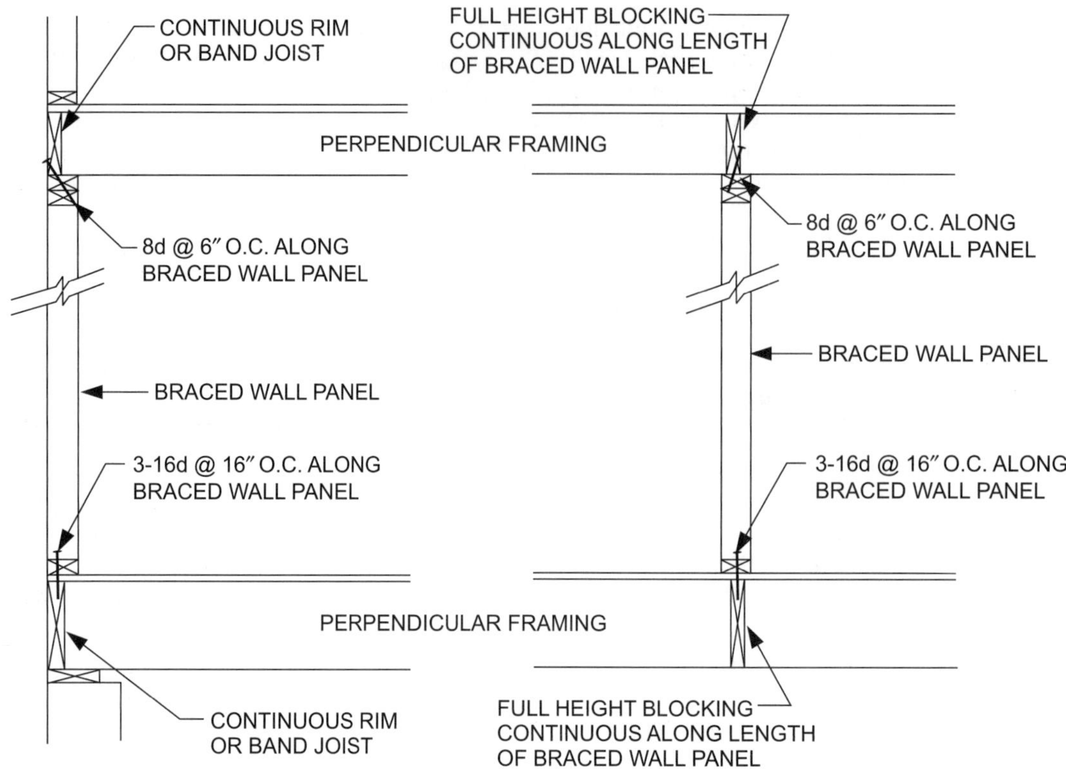

For SI: 1 inch = 25.4 mm.

FIGURE R602.10.6(1)
BRACED WALL PANEL CONNECTION WHEN PERPENDICULAR TO FLOOR/CEILING FRAMING

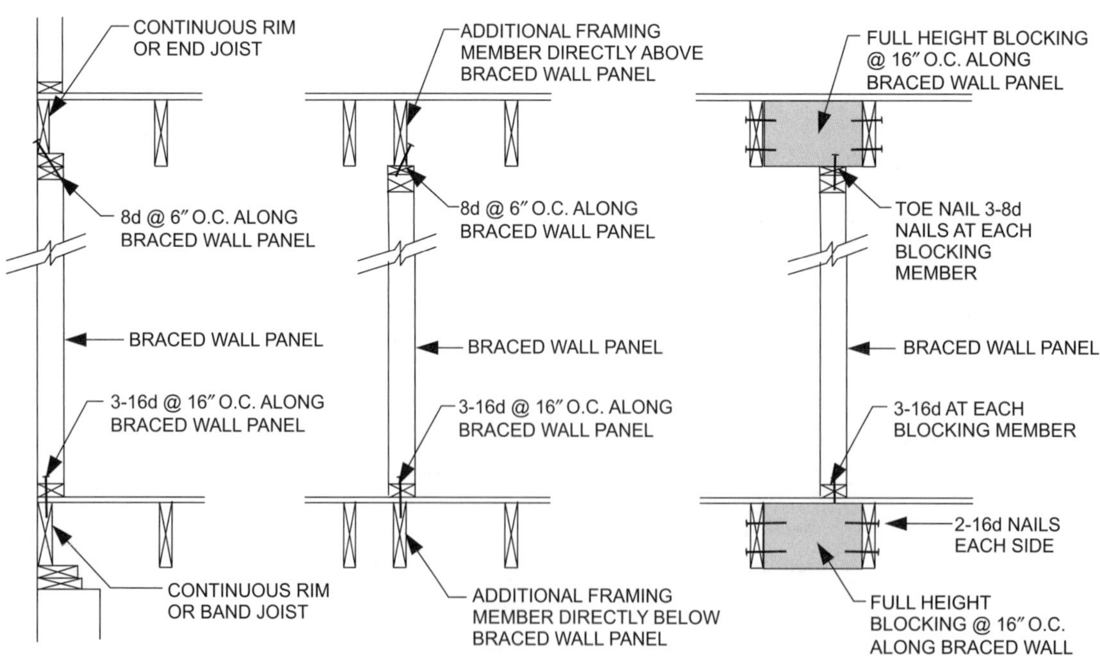

For SI: 1 inch = 25.4 mm.

FIGURE R602.10.6(2)
BRACED WALL PANEL CONNECTION WHEN PARALLEL TO FLOOR/CEILING FRAMING

R602.10.6.1 Braced wall panel connections for Seismic Design Categories D_0, D_1 and D_2. Deleted.

R602.10.6.2 Connections to roof framing. Exterior *braced wall panels* shall be connected to roof framing as follows.

1. Parallel rafters or roof trusses shall be attached to the top plates of *braced wall panels* in accordance with Table R602.3(1).
2. For SDC A, B and C and wind speeds less than 100 miles per hour (45 m/s), where the distance from the top of the rafters or roof trusses and perpendicular top plates is $9^1/_4$ inches (235 mm) or less, the rafters or roof trusses shall be connected to the top plates of *braced wall lines* in accordance with Table R602.3(1) and blocking need not be installed. Where the distance from the top of the rafters and perpendicular top plates is between $9^1/_4$ inches (235 mm) and $15^1/_4$ inches (387 mm) the rafters shall be connected to the top plates of *braced wall panels* with blocking in accordance with Figure R602.10.6.2(1) and attached in accordance with Table R602.3(1). Where the distance from the top of the roof trusses and perpendicular top plates is between $9^1/_4$ inches (235 mm) and $15^1/_4$ inches (387 mm) the roof trusses shall be connected to the top plates of *braced wall panels* with blocking in accordance with Table R602.3(1).
3. For SDC D_0, D_1 and D_2 or wind speeds of 100 miles per hour (45 m/s) or greater, where the distance between the top of rafters or roof trusses and perpendicular top plates is $15^1/_4$ inches (387 mm) or less, rafters or roof trusses shall be connected to the top plates of *braced wall panels* with blocking in accordance with Figure R602.10.6.2(1) and attached in accordance with Table R602.3(1).
4. For all seismic design categories and wind speeds, where the distance between the top of rafters or roof trusses and perpendicular top plates exceeds $15^1/_4$ inches (387 mm), perpendicular rafters or roof trusses shall be connected to the top plates of *braced wall panels* in accordance with one of the following methods:
   4.1. In accordance with Figure R602.10.6.2(2),
   4.2. In accordance with Figure R602.10.6.2(3),
   4.3. With full height engineered blocking panels designed for values listed in American Forest and Paper Association (AF&PA) Wood Frame Construction Manual for One- and Two-Family *Dwellings* (WFCM). Both the roof and floor sheathing shall be attached to the blocking panels in accordance with Table R602.3(1).
   4.4. Designed in accordance with accepted engineering methods.

Lateral support for the rafters and ceiling joists shall be provided in accordance with Section R802.8. Lateral support for trusses shall be provided in accordance with Section R802.10.3. Ventilation shall be provided in accordance with Section R806.1.

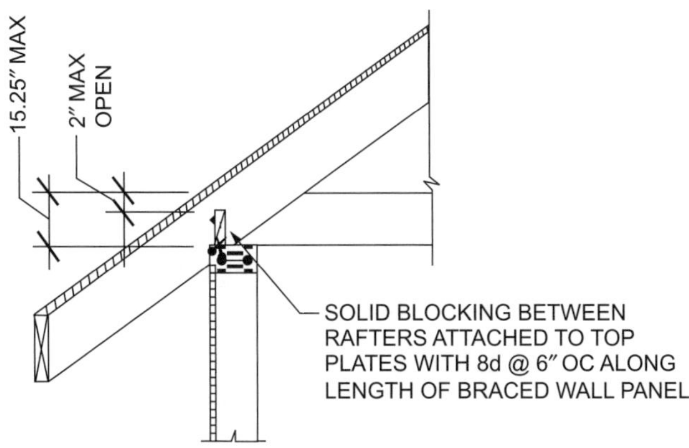

For SI: 1 inch = 25.4 mm.

FIGURE R602.10.6.2(1)
BRACED WALL PANEL CONNECTION TO PERPENDICULAR RAFTERS

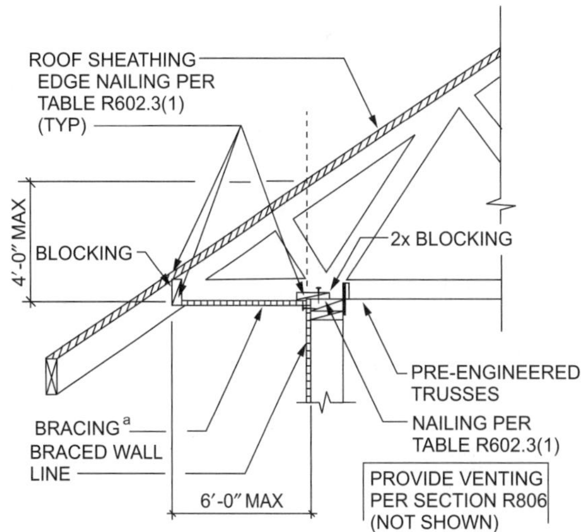

a. METHODS OF BRACING SHALL BE AS DESCRIBED IN SECTION R602.10.2 METHOD DWB, WSP, SFB, GB, PBS, PCP OR HPS

For SI: 1 inch = 25.4 mm.

FIGURE R602.10.6.2(2)
BRACED WALL PANEL CONNECTION OPTION TO PERPENDICULAR RAFTERS OR ROOF TRUSSES

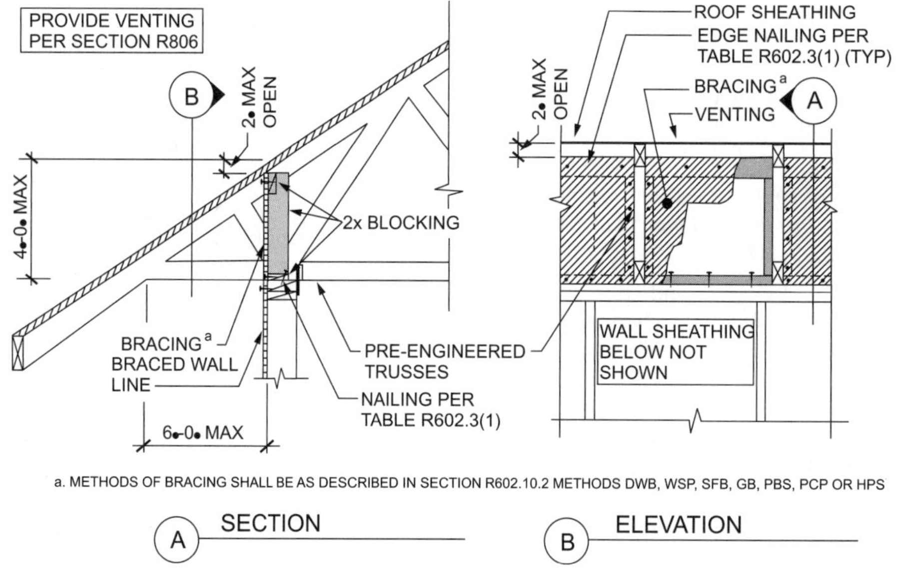

FIGURE R602.10.6.2(3)
BRACED WALL PANEL CONNECTION OPTION TO PERPENDICULAR RAFTERS OR ROOF TRUSSES

R602.10.7 Braced wall panel support. *Braced wall panel* support shall be provided as follows:

1. Cantilevered floor joists, supporting *braced wall lines*, shall comply with Section R502.3.3. Solid blocking shall be provided at the nearest bearing wall location. In Seismic Design Categories A, B and C, where the cantilever is not more than 24 inches (610 mm), a full height rim joist instead of solid blocking shall be provided.
2. Elevated post or pier foundations supporting *braced wall panels* shall be designed in accordance with accepted engineering practice.
3. Masonry stem walls with a length of 48 inches (1220 mm) or less supporting *braced wall panels* shall be reinforced in accordance with Figure R602.10.7. Masonry stem walls with a length greater than 48 inches (1220 mm) supporting *braced wall panels* shall be constructed in accordance with Section R403.1 *Braced wall panels* constructed in accordance with Sections R602.10.3.2 and R602.10.3.3 shall not be attached to masonry stem walls.

R602.10.7.1 Braced wall panel support for Seismic Design Category D_2. Deleted.

R602.10.8 Panel joints. All vertical joints of panel sheathing shall occur over, and be fastened to common studs. Horizontal joints in *braced wall panels* shall occur over, and be fastened to common blocking of a minimum $1^1/_2$ inch (38 mm) thickness.

Exceptions:

1. Blocking at horizontal joints shall not be required in wall segments that are not counted as *braced wall panels*.
2. Where the bracing length provided is at least twice the minimum length required by Tables R602.10.1.2(1) and R602.10.1.2(2) blocking at horizontal joints shall not be required in *braced wall panels* constructed using Methods WSP, SFB, GB, PBS or HPS.
3. When Method GB panels are installed horizontally, blocking of horizontal joints is not required.

R602.10.9 Cripple wall bracing. In Seismic Design Categories other than D_2, cripple walls shall be braced with a length and type of bracing as required for the wall above in accordance with Tables R602.10.1.2(1) and R602.10.1.2(2) with the following modifications for cripple wall bracing:

1. The length of bracing as determined from Tables R602.10.1.2(1) and R602.10.1.2(2) shall be multiplied by a factor of 1.15, and
2. The wall panel spacing shall be decreased to 18 feet (5486 mm) instead of 25 feet (7620 mm).

R602.10.9.1 Cripple wall bracing in Seismic Design Categories D_0, D_1 and D_2. Deleted.

R602.10.9.2 Redesignation of cripple walls. In any Seismic Design Category, cripple walls shall be permitted to be redesignated as the first *story* walls for purposes of determining wall bracing requirements. If the cripple walls are redesignated, the stories above the redesignated *story* shall be counted as the second and third stories, respectively.

R602.11 Wall anchorage. *Braced wall line* sills shall be anchored to concrete or masonry foundations in accordance with Sections R403.1.6 and R602.11.1.

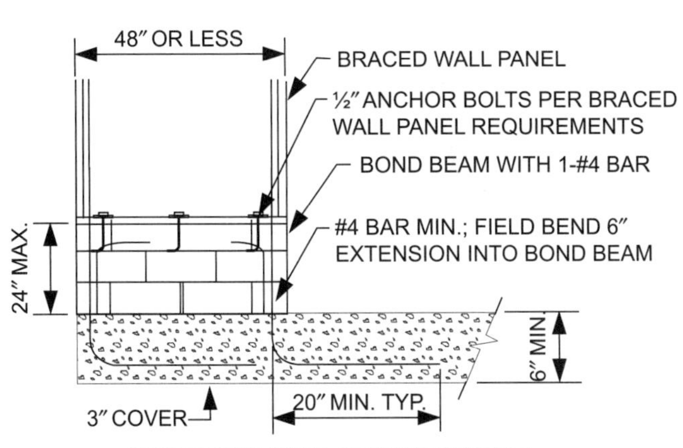

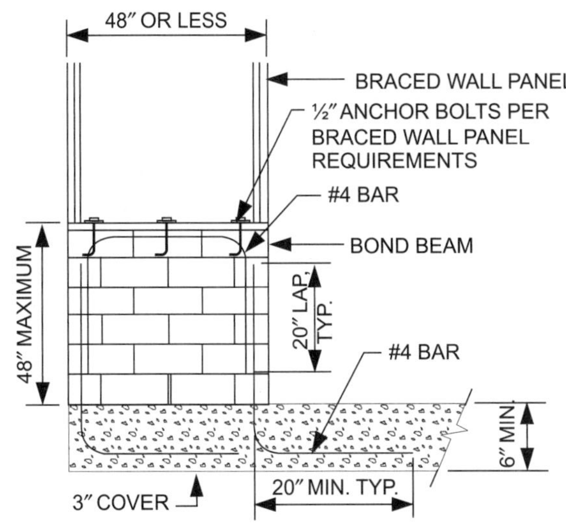

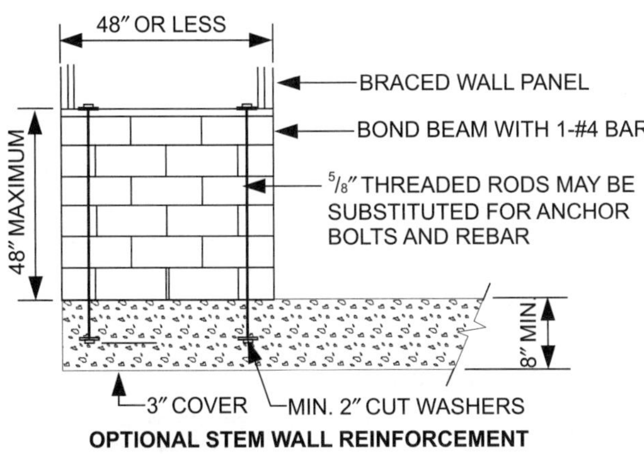

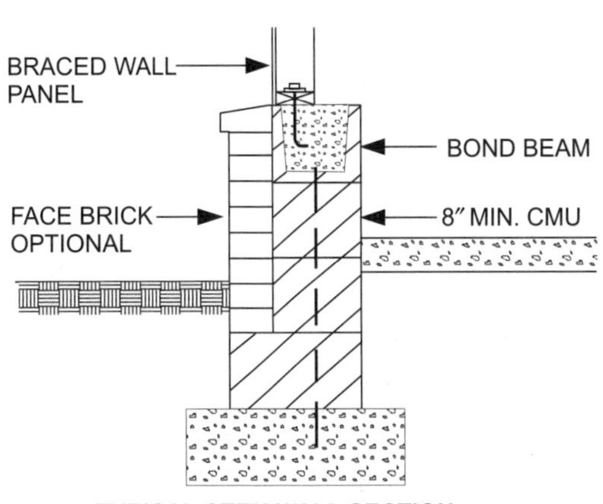

NOTE: GROUT BOND BEAMS AND ALL CELLS WHICH CONTAIN REBAR, THREADED RODS AND ANCHOR BOLTS.

For SI: 1 inch = 25.4 mm.

FIGURE R602.10.7
MASONRY STEM WALLS SUPPORTING BRACED WALL PANELS

602.11.1 Wall anchorage for all buildings in Seismic Design Categories D_0, D_1 and D_2 and townhouses in Seismic Design Category C. Plate washers, a minimum of 0.229 inch by 3 inches by 3 inches (5.8 mm by 76 mm by 76 mm) in size, shall be provided between the foundation sill plate and the nut except where *approved* anchor straps are used. The hole in the plate washer is permitted to be diagonally slotted with a width of up to $^3/_{16}$ inch (5 mm) larger than the bolt diameter and a slot length not to exceed $1^3/_4$ inches (44 mm), provided a standard cut washer is placed between the plate washer and the nut.

R602.11.2 Stepped foundations in Seismic Design Categories D_0, D_1 and D_2. Deleted.

R602.12 Wall bracing and stone and masonry veneer. Where stone and masonry veneer is installed in accordance with Section R703.7, wall bracing shall comply with this section.

For all buildings in Seismic Design Categories A, B and C, wall bracing at exterior and interior *braced wall lines* shall be in accordance with Section R602.10 and the additional requirements of Table R602.12(1).

For detached one- or two-family *dwellings* in Seismic Design Categories D_0, D_1 and D_2, wall bracing and hold downs at exterior and interior *braced wall lines* shall be in accordance with Sections R602.10 and R602.11 and the additional requirements of Section R602.12.1 and Table R602.12(2). In Seismic Design Categories D_0, D_1 and D_2, cripple walls are not permitted, and required interior *braced wall lines* shall be supported on continuous foundations.

R602.12.1 Seismic Design Categories D_0, D_1 and D_2. Deleted.

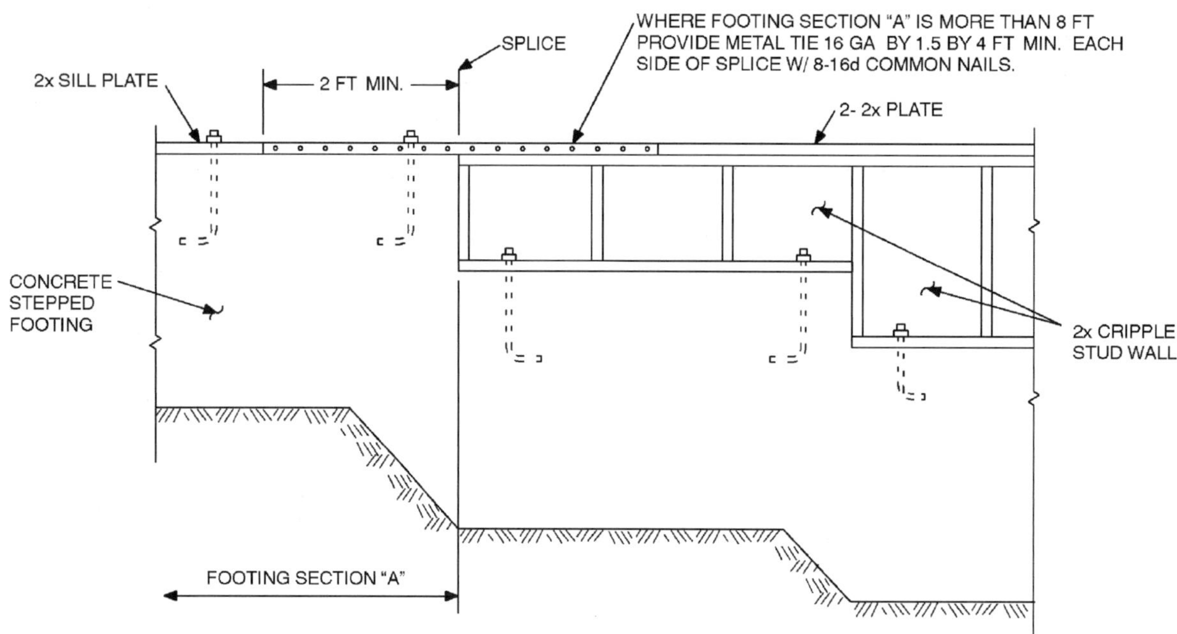

For SI: 1 inch = 25.4 mm, 1 foot = 304.8 mm.

Note: Where footing Section "A" is less than 8 feet long in a 25-foot-long wall, install bracing at cripple stud wall.

FIGURE R602.11.2
STEPPED FOUNDATION CONSTRUCTION

TABLE R602.12(1)
STONE OR MASONRY VENEER WALL BRACING REQUIREMENTS, WOOD OR STEEL FRAMING, SEISMIC DESIGN CATEGORIES A, B and C

SEISMIC DESIGN CATEGORY	NUMBER OF WOOD FRAMED STORIES	WOOD FRAMED STORY	MINIMUM SHEATHING AMOUNT (length of braced wall line length)[a]
A or B	1, 2 or 3	all	Table R602.10.1.2(2)
C	1	1 only	Table R602.10.1.2(2)
	2	top	Table R602.10.1.2(2)
		bottom	1.5 times length required by Table R602.10.1.2(2)
	3	top	Table R602.10.1.2(2)
		middle	1.5 times length required by Table R602.10.1.2(2)
		bottom	1.5 times length required by Table R602.10.1.2(2)

a. Applies to exterior and interior braced wall lines.

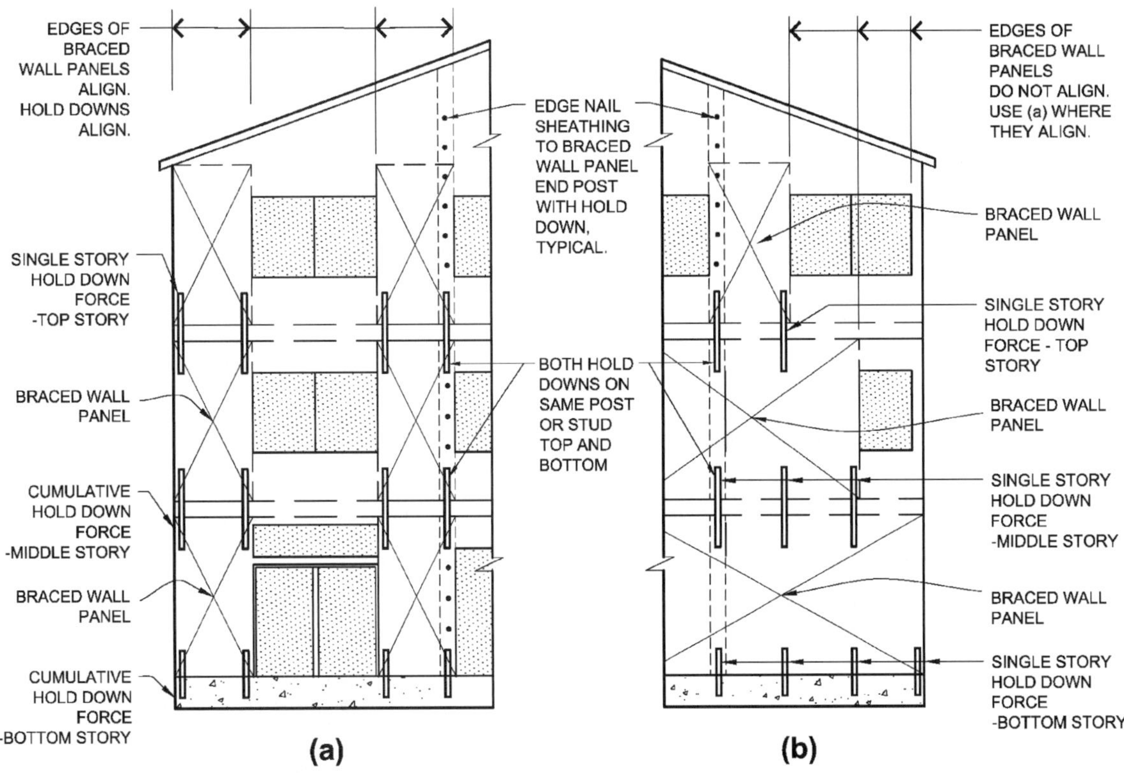

(a) Braced wall panels stacked (aligned story to story). Use cumulative hold down force.
(b) Braced wall panels not stacked. Use single story hold down force.

FIGURE R602.12
HOLD DOWNS AT EXTERIOR AND INTERIOR BRACED WALL PANELS

SECTION R603
STEEL WALL FRAMING

R603.1 General. Elements shall be straight and free of any defects that would significantly affect structural performance. Cold-formed steel wall framing members shall comply with the requirements of this section.

R603.1.1 Applicability limits. The provisions of this section shall control the construction of exterior cold-formed steel wall framing and interior load-bearing cold-formed steel wall framing for buildings not more than 60 feet (18 288 mm) long perpendicular to the joist or truss span, not more than 40 feet (12 192 mm) wide parallel to the joist or truss span, and less than or equal to three stories above *grade plane*. All exterior walls installed in accordance with the provisions of this section shall be considered as load-bearing walls. Cold-formed steel walls constructed in accordance with the provisions of this section shall be limited to sites subjected to a maximum design wind speed of 110 miles per hour (49 m/s) Exposure B or C and a maximum ground snow load of 70 pounds per square foot (3.35 kPa).

R603.1.2 In-line framing. Load-bearing cold-formed steel studs constructed in accordance with Section R603 shall be located in-line with joists, trusses and rafters in accordance with Figure R603.1.2 and the tolerances specified as follows:

1. The maximum tolerance shall be $^3/_4$ inch (19 mm) between the centerline of the horizontal framing member and the centerline of the vertical framing member.
2. Where the centerline of the horizontal framing member and bearing stiffener are located to one side of the centerline of the vertical framing member, the maximum tolerance shall be $^1/_8$ inch (3 mm) between the web of the horizontal framing member and the edge of the vertical framing member.

R603.2 Structural framing. Load-bearing cold-formed steel wall framing members shall comply with Figure R603.2(1) and with the dimensional and minimum thickness requirements specified in Tables R603.2(1) and R603.2(2). Tracks shall comply with Figure R603.2(2) and shall have a minimum flange width of $1^1/_4$ inches (32 mm). The maximum inside bend radius for members shall be the greater of $^3/_{32}$ inch (2.4 mm) minus half the base steel thickness or 1.5 times the base steel thickness.

R603.2.1 Material. Load-bearing cold-formed steel framing members shall be cold-formed to shape from structural quality sheet steel complying with the requirements of one of the following:

1. ASTM A 653: Grades 33, and 50 (Class 1 and 3).
2. ASTM A 792: Grades 33, and 50A.
3. ASTM A 1003: Structural Grades 33 Type H, and 50 Type H.

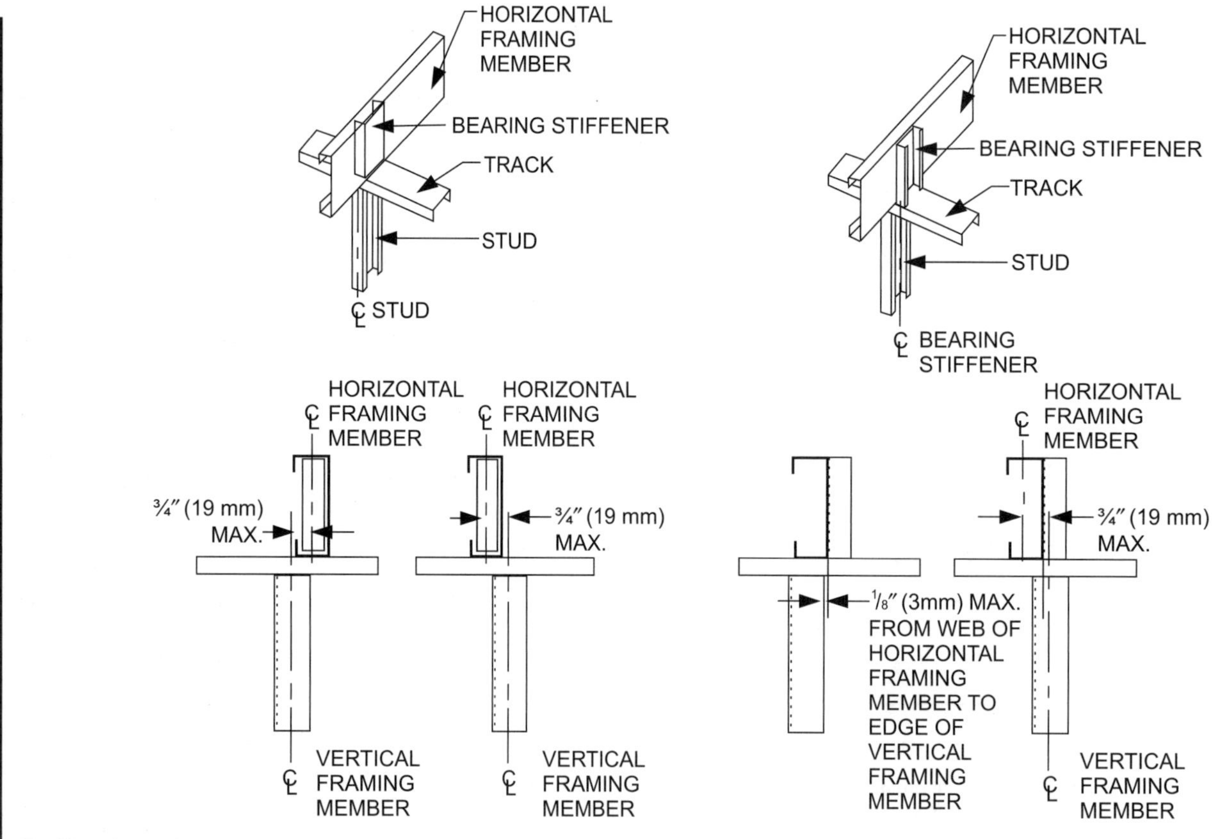

For SI: 1 inch = 25.4 mm,

TABLE R603.2(1)
LOAD-BEARING COLD-FORMED STEEL STUD SIZES

MEMBER DESIGNATION[a]	WEB DEPTH (inches)	MINIMUM FLANGE WIDTH (inches)	MAXIMUM FLANGE WIDTH (inches)	MINIMUM LIP SIZE (inches)
350S162-t	3.5	1.625	2	0.5
550S162-t	5.5	1.625	2	0.5

For SI: 1 inch = 25.4 mm; 1 mil = 0.0254 mm.

a. The member designation is defined by the first number representing the member depth in hundredths of an inch "S" representing a stud or joist member, the second number representing the flange width in hundredths of an inch, and the letter "t" shall be a number representing the minimum base metal thickness in mils [See Table R603.2(2)].

TABLE R603.2(2)
MINIMUM THICKNESS OF COLD-FORMED STEEL MEMBERS

DESIGNATION THICKNESS (mils)	MINIMUM BASE STEEL THICKNESS (inches)
33	0.0329
43	0.0428
54	0.0538
68	0.0677
97	0.0966

For SI: 1 mil = 0.0254 mm, 1 inch = 25.4 mm.

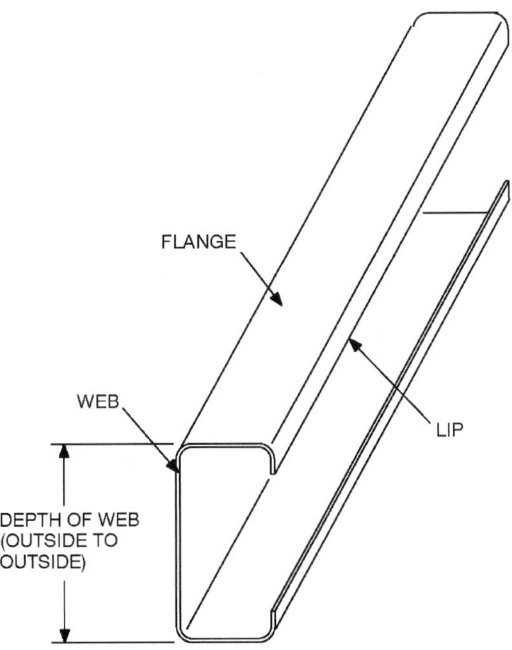

FIGURE R603.2(1)
C-SHAPED SECTION

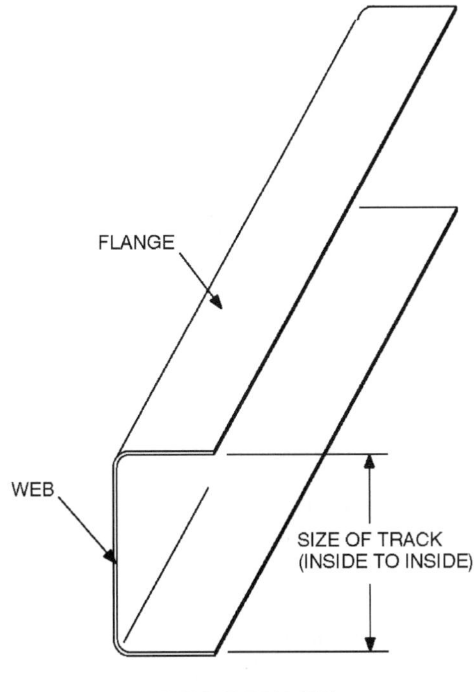

FIGURE R603.2(2)
TRACK SECTION

R603.2.2 Identification. Load-bearing cold-formed steel framing members shall have a legible *label*, stencil, stamp or embossment with the following information as a minimum:

1. Manufacturer's identification.
2. Minimum base steel thickness in inches (mm).
3. Minimum coating designation.
4. Minimum yield strength, in kips per square inch (ksi) (MPa).

R603.2.3 Corrosion protection. Load-bearing cold-formed steel framing shall have a metallic coating complying with ASTM A 1003 and one of the following:

1. A minimum of G 60 in accordance with ASTM A 653.
2. A minimum of AZ 50 in accordance with ASTM A 792.

R603.2.4 Fastening requirements. Screws for steel-to-steel connections shall be installed with a minimum edge distance and center-to-center spacing of $^1/_2$ inch (12.7 mm), shall be self-drilling tapping and shall conform to ASTM C 1513. Structural sheathing shall be attached to cold-formed steel studs with minimum No. 8 self-drilling tapping screws that conform to ASTM C 1513. Screws for attaching structural sheathing to cold-formed steel wall framing shall have a minimum head diameter of 0.292 inch (7.4 mm) with countersunk heads and shall be installed with a minimum edge distance of $^3/_8$ inch (9.5 mm). Gypsum board shall be attached to cold-formed steel wall framing with minimum No. 6 screws conforming to ASTM C 954 or ASTM C 1513 with a bugle head style and shall be installed in accordance with Section R702. For all connections, screws shall extend through the steel a minimum of three exposed threads. All fasteners shall have rust inhibitive coating suitable for the installation in which they are being used, or be manufactured from material not susceptible to corrosion.

Where No. 8 screws are specified in a steel-to-steel connection, the required number of screws in the connection is permitted to be reduced in accordance with the reduction factors in Table R603.2.4, when larger screws are used or when one of the sheets of steel being connected is thicker than 33 mils (0.84 mm). When applying the reduction factor, the resulting number of screws shall be rounded up.

TABLE R603.2.4
SCREW SUBSTITUTION FACTOR

SCREW SIZE	THINNEST CONNECTED STEEL SHEET (mils)	
	33	43
#8	1.0	0.67
#10	0.93	0.62
#12	0.86	0.56

For SI: 1 mil = 0.0254 mm.

R603.2.5 Web holes, web hole reinforcing and web hole patching. Web holes, web hole reinforcing and web hole patching shall be in accordance with this section.

R603.2.5.1 Web holes. Web holes in wall studs and other structural members shall comply with all of the following conditions:

1. Holes shall conform to Figure R603.2.5.1;
2. Holes shall be permitted only along the centerline of the web of the framing member;
3. Holes shall have a center-to-center spacing of not less than 24 inches (610 mm);

4. Holes shall have a web hole width not greater than 0.5 times the member depth, or $1^1/_2$ inches (38 mm);
5. Holes shall have a web hole length not exceeding $4^1/_2$ inches (114 mm); and
6. Holes shall have a minimum distance between the edge of the bearing surface and the edge of the web hole of not less than 10 inches (254 mm).

Framing members with web holes not conforming to the above requirements shall be reinforced in accordance with Section R603.2.5.2, patched in accordance with Section R603.2.5.3 or designed in accordance with accepted engineering practice.

R603.2.5.2 Web hole reinforcing. Web holes in gable endwall studs not conforming to the requirements of Section R603.2.5.1 shall be permitted to be reinforced if the hole is located fully within the center 40 percent of the span and the depth and length of the hole does not exceed 65 percent of the flat width of the web. The reinforcing shall be a steel plate or C-shape section with a hole that does not exceed the web hole size limitations of Section R603.2.5.1 for the member being reinforced. The steel reinforcing shall be the same thickness as the receiving member and shall extend at least 1 inch (25.4 mm) beyond all edges of the hole. The steel reinforcing shall be fastened to the web of the receiving member with No.8 screws spaced no more than 1 inch (25.4 mm) center-to-center along the edges of the patch with minimum edge distance of $^1/_2$ inch (12.7 mm).

R603.2.5.3 Hole patching. Web holes in wall studs and other structural members not conforming to the requirements in Section R603.2.5.1 shall be permitted to be patched in accordance with either of the following methods:

1. Framing members shall be replaced or designed in accordance with accepted engineering practice when web holes exceed the following size limits:
   1.1. The depth of the hole, measured across the web, exceeds 70 percent of the flat width of the web; or
   1.2. The length of the hole measured along the web exceeds 10 inches (254 mm) or the depth of the web, whichever is greater.
2. Web holes not exceeding the dimensional requirements in Section R603.2.5.3, Item 1 shall be patched with a solid steel plate, stud section or track section in accordance with Figure R603.2.5.3. The steel patch shall, as a minimum, be the same thickness as the receiving member and shall extend at least 1 inch (25.4 mm) beyond all edges of the hole. The steel patch shall be fastened to the web of the receiving member with No. 8 screws spaced no more than 1 inch (25.4 mm) center-to-center along the edges of the patch with a minimum edge distance of $^1/_2$ inch (12.7 mm).

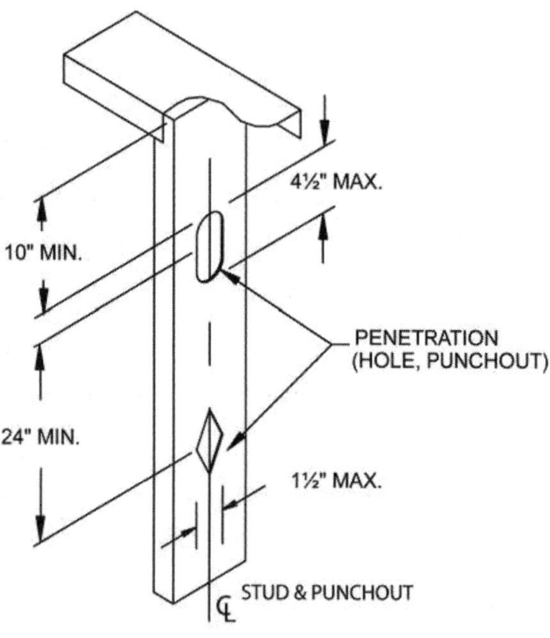

For SI: 1 inch = 25.4 mm.

FIGURE R603.2.5.1
WEB HOLES

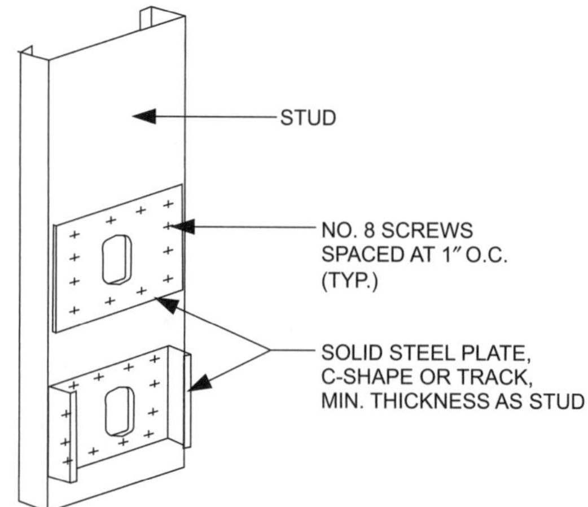

For SI: 1 inch = 25.4 mm.

FIGURE R603.2.5.3
STUD WEB HOLE PATCH

R603.3 Wall construction. All exterior cold-formed steel framed walls and interior load-bearing cold-formed steel framed walls shall be constructed in accordance with the provisions of this section.

R603.3.1 Wall to foundation or floor connection. Cold-formed steel framed walls shall be anchored to foundations or floors in accordance with Table R603.3.1 and Figure R603.3.1(1), R603.3.1(2) or R603.3.1(3). Anchor bolts shall be located not more than 12 inches (305 mm) from corners or the termination of bottom tracks. Anchor bolts shall extend a minimum of 15 inches (381 mm) into masonry or 7 inches (178 mm) into concrete. Foundation anchor straps shall be permitted, in lieu of anchor bolts, if spaced as required to provide equivalent anchorage to the required anchor bolts and installed in accordance with manufacturer's requirements.

R603.3.1.1 Gable endwalls. Gable endwalls with heights greater than 10 feet (3048 mm) shall be anchored to foundations or floors in accordance with Tables R603.3.1.1(1) or R603.3.1.1(2).

R603.3.2 Minimum stud sizes. Cold-formed steel walls shall be constructed in accordance with Figures R603.3.1(1), R603.3.1(2), or R603.3.1(3), as applicable. Exterior wall stud size and thickness shall be determined in accordance with the limits set forth in Tables R603.3.2(2) through R603.3.2(31). Interior load-bearing wall stud size and thickness shall be determined in accordance with the limits set forth in Tables R603.3.2(2) through R603.3.2(31) based upon an 85 miles per hour (38 m/s) Exposure A/B wind value and the building width, stud spacing and snow load, as appropriate. Fastening requirements shall be in accordance with Section R603.2.4 and Table R603.3.2(1). Top and bottom tracks shall have the same minimum thickness as the wall studs.

Exterior wall studs shall be permitted to be reduced to the next thinner size, as shown in Tables R603.3.2(2) through R603.3.2(31), but not less than 33 mils (0.84 mm) ,where both of the following conditions exist:

1. Minimum of $^1/_2$ inch (12.7 mm) gypsum board is installed and fastened in accordance with Section R702 on the interior surface.
2. Wood structural sheathing panels of minimum $^7/_{16}$ inch (11 mm) thick oriented strand board or $^{15}/_{32}$ inch (12 mm) thick plywood is installed and fastened in accordance with Section R603.9.1 and Table R603.3.2(1) on the outside surface.

Interior load-bearing walls shall be permitted to be reduced to the next thinner size, as shown in Tables R603.3.2(2) through R603.3.2(31), but not less than 33 mils (0.84 mm), where a minimum of $^1/_2$ inch (12.7 mm) gypsum board is installed and fastened in accordance with Section R702 on both sides of the wall. The tabulated stud thickness for load-bearing walls shall be used when the *attic* load is 10 pounds per square feet (480 Pa) or less. A limited *attic* storage load of 20 pounds per square feet (960 Pa) shall be permitted provided that the next higher snow load column is used to select the stud size from Tables R603.3.2(2) through R603.3.2(31).

For two-story buildings, the tabulated stud thickness for walls supporting one floor, roof and ceiling shall be used when second floor live load is 30 pounds per square feet (1440 Pa). Second floor live loads of 40 psf (1920 pounds per square feet) shall be permitted provided that the next higher snow load column is used to select the stud size from Tables R603.3.2(2) through R603.3.2(21).

For three-story buildings, the tabulated stud thickness for walls supporting one or two floors, roof and ceiling shall be used when the third floor live load is 30 pounds per square feet (1440 Pa). Third floor live loads of 40 pounds per square feet (1920 Pa) shall be permitted provided that the next higher snow load column is used to select the stud size from Tables R603.3.2(22) through R603.3.2(31).

TABLE R603.3.1
WALL TO FOUNDATION OR FLOOR CONNECTION REQUIREMENTS[a,b]

FRAMING CONDITION	WIND SPEED (mph) AND EXPOSURE					
	85 B	90 B	100 B 85 C	110 B 90 C	100 C	< 110 C
Wall bottom track to floor per Figure R603.3.1(1)	1-No. 8 screw at 12″ o.c.	1-No. 8 screw at 12″ o.c.	1-No. 8 screw at 12″ o.c.	1-No. 8 screw at 12″ o.c.	2-No. 8 screws at 12″ o.c.	2 No. 8 screws at 12″ o.c.
Wall bottom track to foundation per Figure R603.3.1(2)[d]	$^1/_2$″ minimum diameter anchor bolt at 6′ o.c.	$^1/_2$″ minimum diameter anchor bolt at 6′ o.c.	$^1/_2$″ minimum diameter anchor bolt at 4′ o.c.	$^1/_2$″ minimum diameter anchor bolt at 4′ o.c.	$^1/_2$″ minimum diameter anchor bolt at 4′ o.c.	$^1/_2$″ minimum diameter anchor bolt at 4′ o.c.
Wall bottom track to wood sill per Figure R603.3.1(3)	Steel plate spaced at 4′ o.c., with 4-No. 8 screws and 4-10d or 6-8d common nails	Steel plate spaced at 4′ o.c., with 4-No. 8 screws and 4-10d or 6-8d common nails	Steel plate spaced at 3′ o.c., with 4-No. 8 screws and 4-10d or 6-8d common nails	Steel plate spaced at 3′ o.c., with 4-No. 8 screws and 4-10d or 6-8d common nails	Steel plate spaced at 2′ o.c., with 4-No. 8 screws and 4-10d or 6-8d common nails	Steel plate spaced at 2′ o.c., with 4-No. 8 screws and 4-10d or 6-8d common nails
Wind uplift connector strength to 16″ stud spacing[c]	NR	NR	NR	NR	NR	65 lb per foot of wall length
Wind uplift connector strength for 24″ stud spacing[c]	NR	NR	NR	NR	NR	100 lb per foot of wall length

For SI: 1 inch = 25.4 mm, 1 mile per hour = 0.447 m/s, 1 foot = 304.8 mm, 1 lb = 4.45 N.

a. Anchor bolts are to be located not more than 12 inches from corners or the termination of bottom tracks (e.g., at door openings or corners). Bolts are to extend a minimum of 15 inches into masonry or 7 inches into concrete.

b. All screw sizes shown are minimum.

c. NR = uplift connector not required.

d. Foundation anchor straps are permitted in place of anchor bolts, if spaced as required to provide equivalent anchorage to the required anchor bolts and installed in accordance with manufacturer's requirements.

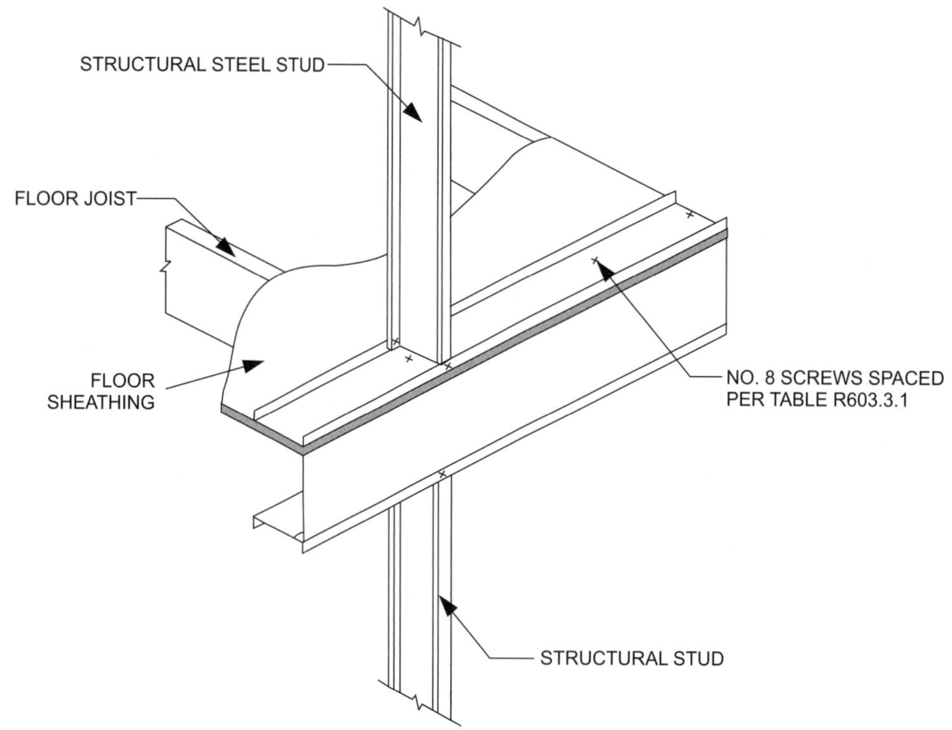

FIGURE R603.3.1(1)
WALL TO FLOOR CONNECTION

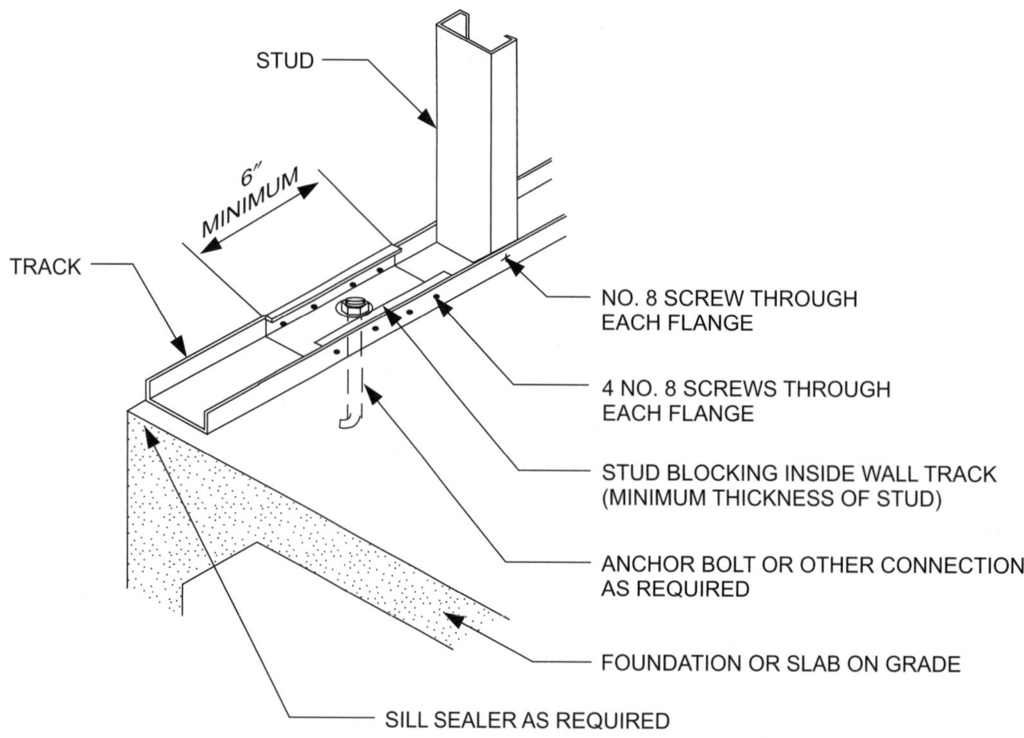

For SI: 1 inch = 25.4 mm.

FIGURE R603.3.1(2)
WALL TO FOUNDATION CONNECTION

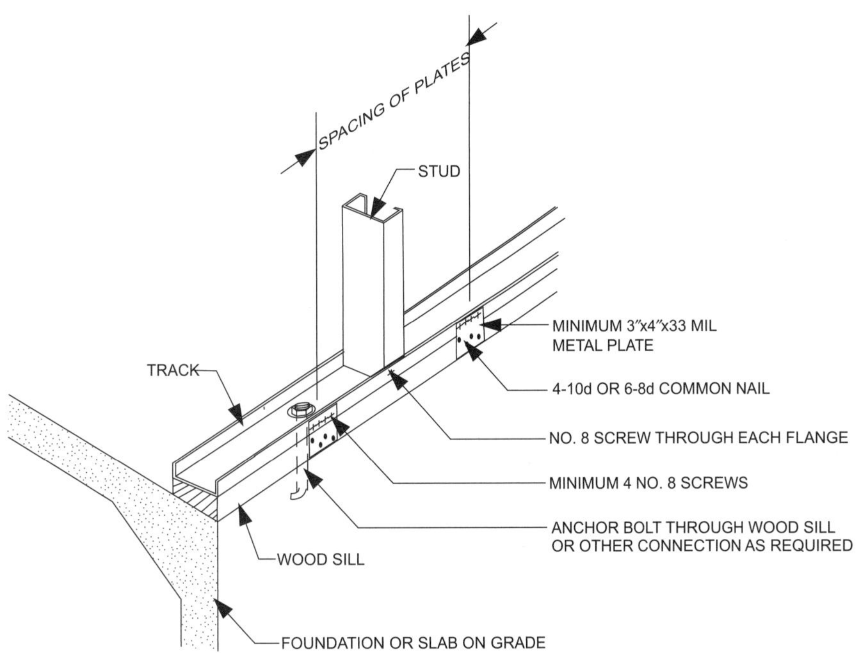

For SI: 1 mil = 0.0254 mm, 1 inch = 25.4 mm.

FIGURE R603.3.1(3)
WALL TO WOOD SILL CONNECTION

TABLE R603.3.1.1(1)
GABLE ENDWALL TO FLOOR CONNECTION REQUIREMENTS[a,b,c]

BASIC WIND SPEED (mph)		WALL BOTTOM TRACK TO FLOOR JOIST OR TRACK CONNECTION		
Exposure		Stud height, h (ft)		
B	C	10 < h ≤ 14	14 < h ≤ 18	18 < h ≤ 22
85	—	1-No. 8 screw @ 12″ o.c.	1-No. 8 screw @ 12″ o.c.	1-No. 8 screw @ 12″ o.c.
90	—	1-No. 8 screw @ 12″ o.c.	1-No. 8 screw @ 12″ o.c.	1-No. 8 screw @ 12″ o.c.
100	85	1-No. 8 screw @ 12″ o.c.	1-No. 8 screw @ 12″ o.c.	1-No. 8 screw @ 12″ o.c.
110	90	1-No. 8 screw @ 12″ o.c.	1-No. 8 screw @ 12″ o.c.	2-No. 8 screws @ 12″ o.c.
—	100	1-No. 8 screw @ 12″ o.c.	2-No. 8 screws @ 12″ o.c.	1-No. 8 screw @ 8″ o.c.
—	110	2-No. 8 screws @ 12″ o.c.	1-No. 8 screw @ 8″ o.c.	2-No. 8 screws @ 8″ o.c.

For SI: 1 inch = 25.4 mm, 1 mile per hour = 0.447 m/s, 1 foot = 304.8 mm.
a. Refer to Table R603.3.1.1(2) for gable endwall bottom track to foundation connections.
b. Where attachment is not given, special design is required.
c. Stud height, *h*, is measured from wall bottom track to wall top track or brace connection height.

TABLE R603.3.1.1(2)
GABLE ENDWALL BOTTOM TRACK TO FOUNDATION CONNECTION REQUIREMENTS[a,b,c]

BASIC WIND SPEED (mph)		MINIMUM SPACING FOR $^1/_2$ IN. DIAMETER ANCHOR BOLTS[d]		
Exposure		Stud height, h (ft)		
B	C	10 < h ≤ 14	14 < h ≤ 18	18 < h ≤ 22
85	—	6′ - 0″ o.c.	6′ - 0″ o.c.	6′ - 0″ o.c.
90	—	6′ - 0″ o.c.	5′ - 7″ o.c.	6′ - 0″ o.c.
100	85	5′ - 10″ o.c.	6′ - 0″ o.c.	6′ - 0″ o.c.
110	90	4′ - 10″ o.c.	5′ - 6″ o.c.	6′ - 0″ o.c.
—	100	4′ - 1″ o.c.	6′ - 0″ o.c.	6′ - 0″ o.c.
—	110	5′ - 1″ o.c.	6′ - 0″ o.c.	5′ - 2″ o.c.

For SI: 1 inch = 25.4 mm, 1 mile per hour = 0.447 m/s, 1 foot = 304.8 mm.
a. Refer to Table R603.3.1.1(1) for gable endwall bottom track to floor joist or track connection connections.
b. Where attachment is not given, special design is required.
c. Stud height, *h*, is measured from wall bottom track to wall top track or brace connection height.
d. Foundation anchor straps are permitted in place of anchor bolts if spaced as required to provide equivalent anchorage to the required anchor bolts and installed in accordance with manufacturer's requirements.

TABLE R603.3.2(1)
WALL FASTENING SCHEDULE[a]

DESCRIPTION OF BUILDING ELEMENT	NUMBER AND SIZE OF FASTENERS[a]	SPACING OF FASTENERS
Floor joist to track of load-bearing wall	2-No. 8 screws	Each joist
Wall stud to top or bottom track	2-No. 8 screws	Each end of stud, one per flange
Structural sheathing to wall studs	No. 8 screws[b]	6″ o.c. on edges and 12″ o.c. at intermediate supports
Roof framing to wall	Approved design or tie down in accordance with Section R802.11	

For SI: 1 inch = 25.4 mm.

a. All screw sizes shown are minimum.

b. Screws for attachment of structural sheathing panels are to be bugle-head, flat-head, or similar head styles with a minimum head diameter of 0.29 inch.

TABLE R603.3.2(2)
24-FOOT-WIDE BUILDING SUPPORTING ROOF AND CEILING ONLY[a, b, c]
33 ksi STEEL

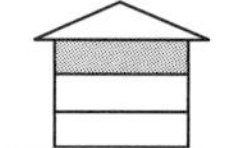

WIND SPEED		MEMBER SIZE	STUD SPACING (inches)	MINIMUM STUD THICKNESS (mils)											
				8-Foot Studs				9-Foot Studs				10-Foot Studs			
				Ground Snow Load (psf)											
Exp. B	Exp. C			20	30	50	70	20	30	50	70	20	30	50	70
85 mph	—	350S162	16	33	33	33	33	33	33	33	33	33	33	33	33
			24	33	33	33	43	33	33	33	43	33	33	43	43
		550S162	16	33	33	33	33	33	33	33	33	33	33	33	33
			24	33	33	33	33	33	33	33	33	33	33	33	33
90 mph	—	350S162	16	33	33	33	33	33	33	33	33	33	33	33	33
			24	33	33	33	43	33	33	33	43	33	33	43	43
		550S162	16	33	33	33	33	33	33	33	33	33	33	33	33
			24	33	33	33	33	33	33	33	33	33	33	33	33
100 mph	85 mph	350S162	16	33	33	33	33	33	33	33	33	33	33	33	33
			24	33	33	33	43	33	33	33	43	43	43	43	43
		550S162	16	33	33	33	33	33	33	33	33	33	33	33	33
			24	33	33	33	43	33	33	33	33	33	33	33	43
110 mph	90 mph	350S162	16	33	33	33	33	33	33	33	33	33	33	33	33
			24	33	33	33	43	43	43	43	43	43	43	43	54
		550S162	16	33	33	33	33	33	33	33	33	33	33	33	33
			24	33	33	33	43	33	33	33	33	43	43	43	43
—	100 mph	350S162	16	33	33	33	33	33	33	33	33	43	43	43	43
			24	43	43	43	43	43	43	43	43	54	54	54	54
		550S162	16	33	33	33	33	33	33	33	33	33	33	33	33
			24	33	33	33	43	43	43	43	43	43	43	43	43
—	110 mph	350S162	16	33	33	33	33	43	43	43	43	43	43	43	43
			24	43	43	43	43	54	54	54	54	68	68	68	68
		550S162	16	33	33	33	33	33	33	33	33	33	33	33	33
			24	33	43	43	43	43	43	43	43	43	43	43	43

For SI: 1 inch = 25.4 mm, 1 foot = 304.8 mm, 1 mil = 0.0254 mm, 1 mile per hour = 0.447 m/s, 1 pound per square foot = 0.0479 kPa, 1 ksi = 1000 psi = 6.895 MPa.

a. Deflection criterion: *L*/240.

b. Design load assumptions:
Second floor dead load is 10 psf.
Second floor live load is 30 psf.
Roof/ceiling dead load is 12 psf.
Attic live load is 10 psf.

c. Building width is in the direction of horizontal framing members supported by the wall studs.

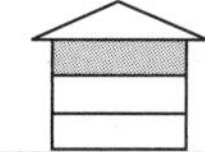

TABLE R603.3.2(3)
24-FOOT-WIDE BUILDING SUPPORTING ROOF AND CEILING ONLY[a,b,c]
50 ksi STEEL

WIND SPEED		MEMBER SIZE	STUD SPACING (inches)	MINIMUM STUD THICKNESS (mils)											
				8-Foot Studs				9-Foot Studs				10-Foot Studs			
				Ground Snow Load (psf)											
Exp. B	Exp. C			20	30	50	70	20	30	50	70	20	30	50	70
85 mph	—	350S162	16	33	33	33	33	33	33	33	33	33	33	33	33
			24	33	33	33	43	33	33	33	33	33	33	33	43
		550S162	16	33	33	33	33	33	33	33	33	33	33	33	33
			24	33	33	33	33	33	33	33	33	33	33	33	33
90 mph	—	350S162	16	33	33	33	33	33	33	33	33	33	33	33	33
			24	33	33	33	43	33	33	33	33	33	33	33	43
		550S162	16	33	33	33	33	33	33	33	33	33	33	33	33
			24	33	33	33	33	33	33	33	33	33	33	33	33
100 mph	85 mph	350S162	16	33	33	33	33	33	33	33	33	33	33	33	33
			24	33	33	33	43	33	33	33	33	33	33	33	43
		550S162	16	33	33	33	33	33	33	33	33	33	33	33	33
			24	33	33	33	33	33	33	33	33	33	33	33	33
110 mph	90 mph	350S162	16	33	33	33	33	33	33	33	33	33	33	33	33
			24	33	33	33	43	33	33	33	43	43	43	43	43
		550S162	16	33	33	33	33	33	33	33	33	33	33	33	33
			24	33	33	33	33	33	33	33	33	33	33	33	33
—	100 mph	350S162	16	33	33	33	33	33	33	33	33	33	33	33	33
			24	33	33	33	43	43	43	43	43	43	43	43	43
		550S162	16	33	33	33	33	33	33	33	33	33	33	33	33
			24	33	33	33	33	33	33	33	33	33	33	33	33
—	110 mph	350S162	16	33	33	33	33	33	33	33	33	33	33	33	33
			24	33	33	33	43	43	43	43	43	54	54	54	54
		550S162	16	33	33	33	33	33	33	33	33	33	33	33	33
			24	33	33	33	33	33	33	33	33	33	33	33	33

For SI: 1 inch = 25.4 mm, 1 foot = 304.8 mm, 1 mil = 0.0254 mm, 1 mile per hour = 0.447 m/s, 1 pound per square foot = 0.0479kPa, 1 ksi = 1000 psi = 6.895 MPa.

a. Deflection criterion: *L*/240.

b. Design load assumptions:
  Second floor dead load is 10 psf.
  Second floor live load is 30 psf.
  Roof/ceiling dead load is 12 psf.
  Attic live load is 10 psf.

c. Building width is in the direction of horizontal framing members supported by the wall studs.

TABLE R603.3.2(4)
28-FOOT-WIDE BUILDING SUPPORTING ROOF AND CEILING ONLY[a,b,c]
33 ksi STEEL

WIND SPEED		MEMBER SIZE	STUD SPACING (inches)	MINIMUM STUD THICKNESS (mils)											
				8-Foot Studs				9-Foot Studs				10-Foot Studs			
				Ground Snow Load (psf)											
Exp. B	Exp. C			20	30	50	70	20	30	50	70	20	30	50	70
85 mph	—	350S162	16	33	33	33	33	33	33	33	33	33	33	33	33
			24	33	33	43	43	33	33	43	43	33	33	43	54
		550S162	16	33	33	33	33	33	33	33	33	33	33	33	33
			24	33	33	33	43	33	33	33	43	33	33	33	43
90 mph	—	350S162	16	33	33	33	33	33	33	33	33	33	33	33	33
			24	33	33	43	43	33	33	43	43	33	33	43	54
		550S162	16	33	33	33	33	33	33	33	33	33	33	33	33
			24	33	33	33	43	33	33	33	43	33	33	33	43
100 mph	85 mph	350S162	16	33	33	33	33	33	33	33	33	33	33	33	33
			24	33	33	43	43	33	33	43	43	43	43	43	54
		550S162	16	33	33	33	33	33	33	33	33	33	33	33	33
			24	33	33	33	43	33	33	33	43	33	33	33	43
110 mph	90 mph	350S162	16	33	33	33	33	33	33	33	33	33	33	33	43
			24	33	33	43	43	43	43	43	43	43	43	43	54
		550S162	16	33	33	33	33	33	33	33	33	33	33	33	33
			24	33	33	33	43	33	33	33	43	33	33	33	43
—	100 mph	350S162	16	33	33	33	33	33	33	33	33	43	43	43	43
			24	43	43	43	54	43	43	43	54	54	54	54	54
		550S162	16	33	33	33	33	33	33	33	33	33	33	33	33
			24	33	33	33	43	33	33	33	43	33	33	33	43
—	110 mph	350S162	16	33	33	33	33	43	43	43	43	43	43	43	43
			24	43	43	43	54	54	54	54	54	68	68	68	68
		550S162	16	33	33	33	33	33	33	33	33	33	33	33	33
			24	33	33	33	43	33	33	33	43	43	43	43	43

For SI: 1 inch = 25.4 mm, 1 foot = 304.8 mm, 1 mil = 0.0254 mm, 1 mile per hour = 0.447 m/s, 1 pound per square foot = 0.0479kPa, 1 ksi = 1000 psi = 6.895 MPa.

a. Deflection criterion: *L*/240.

b. Design load assumptions:
   Second floor dead load is 10 psf.
   Second floor live load is 30 psf.
   Roof/ceiling dead load is 12 psf.
   Attic live load is 10 psf.

c. Building width is in the direction of horizontal framing members supported by the wall studs.

TABLE R603.3.2(5)
28-FOOT-WIDE BUILDING SUPPORTING ROOF AND CEILING ONLY[a,b,c]
50 ksi STEEL

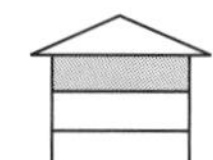

WIND SPEED		MEMBER SIZE	STUD SPACING (inches)	MINIMUM STUD THICKNESS (mils)											
				8-Foot Studs				9-Foot Studs				10-Foot Studs			
				Ground Snow Load (psf)											
Exp. B	Exp. C			20	30	50	70	20	30	50	70	20	30	50	70
85 mph	—	350S162	16	33	33	33	33	33	33	33	33	33	33	33	33
			24	33	33	33	43	33	33	33	43	33	33	33	43
		550S162	16	33	33	33	33	33	33	33	33	33	33	33	33
			24	33	33	33	33	33	33	33	33	33	33	33	33
90 mph	—	350S162	16	33	33	33	33	33	33	33	33	33	33	33	33
			24	33	33	33	43	33	33	33	43	33	33	33	43
		550S162	16	33	33	33	33	33	33	33	33	33	33	33	33
			24	33	33	33	33	33	33	33	33	33	33	33	33
100 mph	85 mph	350S162	16	33	33	33	33	33	33	33	33	33	33	33	33
			24	33	33	33	43	33	33	33	43	33	33	43	43
		550S162	16	33	33	33	33	33	33	33	33	33	33	33	33
			24	33	33	33	33	33	33	33	33	33	33	33	33
110 mph	90 mph	350S162	16	33	33	33	33	33	33	33	33	33	33	33	33
			24	33	33	33	43	33	33	33	43	43	43	43	43
		550S162	16	33	33	33	33	33	33	33	33	33	33	33	33
			24	33	33	33	33	33	33	33	33	33	33	33	33
—	100 mph	350S162	16	33	33	33	33	33	33	33	33	33	33	33	33
			24	33	33	33	43	43	43	43	43	43	43	43	43
		550S162	16	33	33	33	33	33	33	33	33	33	33	33	33
			24	33	33	33	43	33	33	33	33	33	33	33	33
—	110 mph	350S162	16	33	33	33	33	33	33	33	33	33	33	33	33
			24	33	33	43	43	43	43	43	43	54	54	54	54
		550S162	16	33	33	33	33	33	33	33	33	33	33	33	33
			24	33	33	33	33	33	33	33	33	33	33	33	43

For SI: 1 inch = 25.4 mm, 1 foot = 304.8 mm, 1 mil = 0.0254 mm, 1 mile per hour = 0.447 m/s, 1 pound per square foot = 0.0479kPa, 1 ksi = 1000 psi = 6.895 MPa.

a. Deflection criterion: *L*/240.

b. Design load assumptions:
Second floor dead load is 10 psf.
Second floor live load is 30 psf.
Roof/ceiling dead load is 12 psf.
Attic live load is 10 psf.

c. Building width is in the direction of horizontal framing members supported by the wall studs.

TABLE R603.3.2(6)
32-FOOT-WIDE BUILDING SUPPORTING ROOF AND CEILING ONLY[a,b,c]
33 ksi STEEL

WIND SPEED		MEMBER SIZE	STUD SPACING (inches)	MINIMUM STUD THICKNESS (mils)											
				8-Foot Studs				9-Foot Studs				10-Foot Studs			
				Ground Snow Load (psf)											
Exp. B	Exp. C			20	30	50	70	20	30	50	70	20	30	50	70
85 mph	—	350S162	16	33	33	33	33	33	33	33	33	33	33	33	43
			24	33	33	43	54	33	33	43	43	33	33	43	54
		550S162	16	33	33	33	33	33	33	33	33	33	33	33	33
			24	33	33	33	43	33	33	33	43	33	33	33	43
90 mph	—	350S162	16	33	33	33	33	33	33	33	33	33	33	33	43
			24	33	33	43	54	33	33	43	43	33	33	43	54
		550S162	16	33	33	33	33	33	33	33	33	33	33	33	33
			24	33	33	33	43	33	33	33	43	33	33	33	43
100 mph	85 mph	350S162	16	33	33	33	33	33	33	33	33	33	33	33	43
			24	33	33	43	54	33	33	43	54	43	43	43	54
		550S162	16	33	33	33	33	33	33	33	33	33	33	33	33
			24	33	33	33	43	33	33	33	43	33	33	33	43
110 mph	90 mph	350S162	16	33	33	33	43	33	33	33	33	33	33	33	43
			24	33	33	43	54	43	43	43	54	43	43	43	54
		550S162	16	33	33	33	33	33	33	33	33	33	33	33	33
			24	33	33	33	43	33	33	33	43	33	33	43	43
—	100 mph	350S162	16	33	33	33	43	33	33	33	43	43	43	43	43
			24	43	43	43	54	43	43	43	54	54	54	54	54
		550S162	16	33	33	33	33	33	33	33	33	33	33	33	33
			24	33	33	43	43	33	33	33	43	33	33	43	43
—	110 mph	350S162	16	33	33	33	43	43	43	43	43	43	43	43	43
			24	43	43	43	54	54	54	54	54	68	68	68	68
		550S162	16	33	33	33	33	33	33	33	33	33	33	33	33
			24	33	33	43	43	33	33	43	43	43	43	43	43

For SI: 1 inch = 25.4 mm, 1 foot = 304.8 mm, 1 mil = 0.0254 mm, 1 mile per hour = 0.447 m/s, 1 pound per square foot = 0.0479kPa, 1 ksi = 1000 psi = 6.895 MPa.

a. Deflection criterion: *L*/240.

b. Design load assumptions:
   Second floor dead load is 10 psf.
   Second floor live load is 30 psf.
   Roof/ceiling dead load is 12 psf.
   Attic live load is 10 psf.

c. Building width is in the direction of horizontal framing members supported by the wall studs.

TABLE R603.3.2(7)
32-FOOT-WIDE BUILDING SUPPORTING ROOF AND CEILING ONLY[a,b,c]
50 ksi STEEL

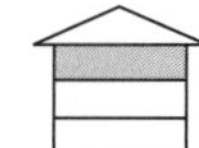

WIND SPEED				MINIMUM STUD THICKNESS (mils)											
				8-Foot Studs				9-Foot Studs				10-Foot Studs			
		MEMBER SIZE	STUD SPACING (inches)	Ground Snow Load (psf)											
Exp. B	Exp. C			20	30	50	70	20	30	50	70	20	30	50	70
85 mph	—	350S162	16	33	33	33	33	33	33	33	33	33	33	33	33
			24	33	33	33	43	33	33	33	43	33	33	43	43
		550S162	16	33	33	33	33	33	33	33	33	33	33	33	33
			24	33	33	33	43	33	33	33	33	33	33	33	43
90 mph	—	350S162	16	33	33	33	33	33	33	33	33	33	33	33	33
			24	33	33	33	43	33	33	33	43	33	33	43	43
		550S162	16	33	33	33	33	33	33	33	33	33	33	33	33
			24	33	33	33	43	33	33	33	33	33	33	33	43
100 mph	85 mph	350S162	16	33	33	33	33	33	33	33	33	33	33	33	33
			24	33	33	43	43	33	33	33	43	33	33	43	43
		550S162	16	33	33	33	33	33	33	33	33	33	33	33	33
			24	33	33	33	43	33	33	33	33	33	33	33	43
110 mph	90 mph	350S162	16	33	33	33	33	33	33	33	33	33	33	33	33
			24	33	33	43	43	33	33	33	43	43	43	43	54
		550S162	16	33	33	33	33	33	33	33	33	33	33	33	33
			24	33	33	33	43	33	33	33	33	33	33	33	43
—	100 mph	350S162	16	33	33	33	33	33	33	33	33	33	33	33	33
			24	33	33	43	43	43	43	43	43	43	43	43	54
		550S162	16	33	33	33	33	33	33	33	33	33	33	33	33
			24	33	33	33	43	33	33	33	43	33	33	33	43
—	110 mph	350S162	16	33	33	33	33	33	33	33	33	33	33	33	43
			24	33	33	43	43	43	43	43	43	54	54	54	54
		550S162	16	33	33	33	33	33	33	33	33	33	33	33	33
			24	33	33	33	43	33	33	33	43	33	33	33	43

For SI: 1 inch = 25.4 mm, 1 foot = 304.8 mm, 1 mil = 0.0254 mm, 1 mile per hour = 0.447 m/s, 1 pound per square foot = 0.0479kPa, 1 ksi = 1000 psi = 6.895 MPa.

a. Deflection criterion: *L*/240.

b. Design load assumptions:
- Second floor dead load is 10 psf.
- Second floor live load is 30 psf.
- Roof/ceiling dead load is 12 psf.
- Attic live load is 10 psf.

c. Building width is in the direction of horizontal framing members supported by the wall studs.

TABLE R603.3.2(8)
36-FOOT-WIDE BUILDING SUPPORTING ROOF AND CEILING ONLY[a,b,c]
33 ksi STEEL

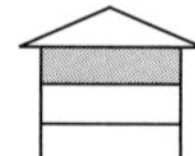

WIND SPEED		MEMBER SIZE	STUD SPACING (inches)	MINIMUM STUD THICKNESS (mils)											
				8-Foot Studs				9-Foot Studs				10-Foot Studs			
				Ground Snow Load (psf)											
Exp. B	Exp. C			20	30	50	70	20	30	50	70	20	30	50	70
85 mph	—	350S162	16	33	33	33	43	33	33	33	43	33	33	33	43
			24	33	33	43	54	33	33	43	54	33	43	43	54
		550S162	16	33	33	33	33	33	33	33	33	33	33	33	33
			24	33	33	43	43	33	33	43	43	33	33	43	43
90 mph	—	350S162	16	33	33	33	43	33	33	33	43	33	33	33	43
			24	33	33	43	54	33	33	43	54	33	43	43	54
		550S162	16	33	33	33	33	33	33	33	33	33	33	33	33
			24	33	33	43	43	33	33	43	43	33	33	43	43
100 mph	85 mph	350S162	16	33	33	33	43	33	33	33	43	33	33	33	43
			24	33	33	43	54	33	33	43	54	43	43	54	54
		550S162	16	33	33	33	33	33	33	33	33	33	33	33	33
			24	33	33	43	43	33	33	43	43	33	33	43	43
110 mph	90 mph	350S162	16	33	33	33	43	33	33	33	33	33	33	33	43
			24	33	33	43	54	43	43	43	43	43	43	54	68
		550S162	16	33	33	33	33	33	33	33	33	33	33	33	33
			24	33	33	43	43	33	33	43	43	33	33	43	43
—	100 mph	350S162	16	33	33	33	43	33	33	33	43	43	43	43	43
			24	43	43	43	54	43	43	43	54	54	54	54	68
		550S162	16	33	33	33	33	33	33	33	33	33	33	33	33
			24	33	33	43	43	33	33	43	43	33	33	43	43
—	110 mph	350S162	16	33	33	33	43	43	43	43	43	43	43	43	43
			24	43	43	54	54	54	54	54	54	68	68	68	68
		550S162	16	33	33	33	33	33	33	33	33	33	33	33	33
			24	33	33	43	54	33	33	43	43	43	43	43	54

For SI: 1 inch = 25.4 mm, 1 foot = 304.8 mm, 1 mil = 0.0254 mm, 1 mile per hour = 0.447 m/s, 1 pound per square foot = 0.0479 kPa, 1 ksi = 1000 psi = 6.895 MPa.

a. Deflection criterion: *L*/240.

b. Design load assumptions:
Second floor dead load is 10 psf.
Second floor live load is 30 psf.
Roof/ceiling dead load is 12 psf.
Attic live load is 10 psf.

c. Building width is in the direction of horizontal framing members supported by the wall studs.

TABLE R603.3.2(9)
36-FOOT-WIDE BUILDING SUPPORTING ROOF AND CEILING ONLY[a,b,c]
50 ksi STEEL

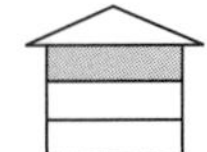

WIND SPEED		MEMBER SIZE	STUD SPACING (inches)	MINIMUM STUD THICKNESS (mils)											
				8-Foot Studs				9-Foot Studs				10-Foot Studs			
				Ground Snow Load (psf)											
Exp. B	Exp. C			20	30	50	70	20	30	50	70	20	30	50	70
85 mph	—	350S162	16	33	33	33	33	33	33	33	33	33	33	33	33
			24	33	33	43	43	33	33	43	43	33	33	43	54
		550S162	16	33	33	33	33	33	33	33	33	33	33	33	33
			24	33	33	33	43	33	33	33	43	33	33	33	43
90 mph	—	350S162	16	33	33	33	33	33	33	33	33	33	33	33	33
			24	33	33	43	43	33	33	43	43	33	33	43	54
		550S162	16	33	33	33	33	33	33	33	33	33	33	33	33
			24	33	33	33	43	33	33	33	43	33	33	33	43
100 mph	85 mph	350S162	16	33	33	33	33	33	33	33	33	33	33	33	33
			24	33	33	43	43	33	33	43	43	33	33	43	54
		550S162	16	33	33	33	33	33	33	33	33	33	33	33	33
			24	33	33	33	43	33	33	33	43	33	33	33	43
110 mph	90 mph	350S162	16	33	33	33	33	33	33	33	33	33	33	33	43
			24	33	33	43	54	33	33	33	43	43	43	43	54
		550S162	16	33	33	33	33	33	33	33	33	33	33	33	33
			24	33	33	33	43	33	33	33	43	33	33	33	43
—	100 mph	350S162	16	33	33	33	33	33	33	33	33	33	33	33	43
			24	33	33	33	54	43	43	43	43	43	43	43	54
		550S162	16	33	33	33	33	33	33	33	33	33	33	33	33
			24	33	33	33	43	33	33	33	43	33	33	33	43
—	110 mph	350S162	16	33	33	33	43	33	33	33	33	33	33	33	43
			24	33	33	43	54	43	43	43	54	54	54	54	54
		550S162	16	33	33	33	33	33	33	33	33	33	33	33	33
			24	33	33	33	43	33	33	33	43	33	33	33	43

For SI: 1 inch = 25.4 mm, 1 foot = 304.8 mm, 1 mil = 0.0254 mm, 1 mile per hour = 0.447 m/s, 1 pound per square foot = 0.0479kPa, 1 ksi = 1000 psi = 6.895 MPa.

a. Deflection criterion: *L*/240.

b. Design load assumptions:
   Second floor dead load is 10 psf.
   Second floor live load is 30 psf.
   Roof/ceiling dead load is 12 psf.
   Attic live load is 10 psf.

c. Building width is in the direction of horizontal framing members supported by the wall studs.

TABLE R603.3.2(10)
40-FOOT-WIDE BUILDING SUPPORTING ROOF AND CEILING ONLY[a,b,c]
33 ksi STEEL

WIND SPEED		MEMBER SIZE	STUD SPACING (inches)	MINIMUM STUD THICKNESS (mils)											
				8-Foot Studs				9-Foot Studs				10-Foot Studs			
				Ground Snow Load (psf)											
Exp. B	Exp. C			20	30	50	70	20	30	50	70	20	30	50	70
85 mph	—	350S162	16	33	33	33	43	33	33	33	43	33	33	33	43
			24	33	33	43	54	33	33	43	54	43	43	54	68
		550S162	16	33	33	33	33	33	33	33	33	33	33	33	33
			24	33	33	43	54	33	33	43	43	33	33	43	54
90 mph	—	350S162	16	33	33	33	43	33	33	33	43	33	33	33	43
			24	33	33	43	54	33	33	43	54	43	43	54	68
		550S162	16	33	33	33	33	33	33	33	33	33	33	33	33
			24	33	33	43	54	33	33	43	43	33	33	43	54
100 mph	85 mph	350S162	16	33	33	33	43	33	33	33	43	33	33	33	43
			24	33	43	43	54	33	43	43	54	43	43	54	68
		550S162	16	33	33	33	43	33	33	33	33	33	33	33	33
			24	33	33	43	54	33	33	43	43	33	33	43	54
110 mph	90 mph	350S162	16	33	33	33	43	33	33	33	43	33	33	43	43
			24	33	43	43	54	43	43	43	54	43	43	54	68
		550S162	16	33	33	33	43	33	33	33	33	33	33	33	43
			24	33	33	43	54	33	33	43	43	33	33	43	54
—	100 mph	350S162	16	33	33	33	43	33	33	33	43	43	43	43	43
			24	43	43	54	68	43	43	54	54	54	54	54	68
		550S162	16	33	33	33	43	33	33	33	33	33	33	33	43
			24	33	33	43	54	33	33	43	54	33	33	43	54
—	110 mph	350S162	16	33	33	43	43	43	43	43	43	43	43	43	54
			24	43	43	54	68	54	54	54	68	68	68	68	68
		550S162	16	33	33	33	43	33	33	33	43	33	33	33	43
			24	33	33	43	54	33	33	43	54	43	43	43	54

For SI: 1 inch = 25.4 mm, 1 foot = 304.8 mm, 1 mil = 0.0254 mm, 1 mile per hour = 0.447 m/s, 1 pound per square foot = 0.0479 kPa, 1 ksi = 1000 psi = 6.895 MPa.

a. Deflection criterion: *L*/240.

b. Design load assumptions:
   Second floor dead load is 10 psf.
   Second floor live load is 30 psf.
   Roof/ceiling dead load is 12 psf.
   Attic live load is 10 psf.

c. Building width is in the direction of horizontal framing members supported by the wall studs.

TABLE R603.3.2(11)
40-FOOT-WIDE BUILDING SUPPORTING ROOF AND CEILING ONLY[a,b,c]
50 ksi STEEL

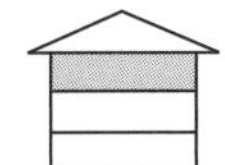

WIND SPEED		MEMBER SIZE	STUD SPACING (inches)	MINIMUM STUD THICKNESS (mils)											
				8-Foot Studs				9-Foot Studs				10-Foot Studs			
				Ground Snow Load (psf)											
Exp. B	Exp. C			20	30	50	70	20	30	50	70	20	30	50	70
85 mph	—	350S162	16	33	33	33	33	33	33	33	33	33	33	33	43
			24	33	33	43	54	33	33	43	43	33	33	43	54
		550S162	16	33	33	33	33	33	33	33	33	33	33	33	33
			24	33	33	33	43	33	33	33	43	33	33	33	43
90 mph	—	350S162	16	33	33	33	33	33	33	33	33	33	33	33	43
			24	33	33	43	54	33	33	43	43	33	33	43	54
		550S162	16	33	33	33	33	33	33	33	33	33	33	33	33
			24	33	33	33	43	33	33	33	43	33	33	33	43
100 mph	85 mph	350S162	16	33	33	33	43	33	33	33	33	33	33	33	43
			24	33	33	43	54	33	33	43	54	33	33	43	54
		550S162	16	33	33	33	33	33	33	33	33	33	33	33	33
			24	33	33	33	43	33	33	33	43	33	33	33	43
110 mph	90 mph	350S162	16	33	33	33	43	33	33	33	33	33	33	33	43
			24	33	33	43	54	33	33	43	54	43	43	43	54
		550S162	16	33	33	33	33	33	33	33	33	33	33	33	33
			24	33	33	33	43	33	33	33	43	33	33	33	43
—	100 mph	350S162	16	33	33	33	43	33	33	33	43	33	33	33	43
			24	33	33	43	54	43	43	43	54	43	43	54	54
		550S162	16	33	33	33	33	33	33	33	33	33	33	33	33
			24	33	33	43	43	33	33	33	43	33	33	43	43
—	110 mph	350S162	16	33	33	33	43	33	33	33	43	33	33	33	43
			24	33	33	43	54	43	43	43	54	54	54	54	68
		550S162	16	33	33	33	33	33	33	33	33	33	33	33	33
			24	33	33	43	43	33	33	33	43	33	33	43	43

For SI: 1 inch = 25.4 mm, 1 foot = 304.8 mm, 1 mil = 0.0254 mm, 1 mile per hour = 0.447 m/s, 1 pound per square foot = 0.0479kPa, 1 ksi = 1000 psi = 6.895 MPa.

a. Deflection criterion: *L*/240.

b. Design load assumptions:
   Second floor dead load is 10 psf.
   Second floor live load is 30 psf.
   Roof/ceiling dead load is 12 psf.
   Attic live load is 10 psf.

c. Building width is in the direction of horizontal framing members supported by the wall studs.

TABLE R603.3.2(12)
24-FOOT-WIDE BUILDING SUPPORTING ONE FLOOR, ROOF AND CEILING[a,b,c]
33 ksi STEEL

WIND SPEED		MEMBER SIZE	STUD SPACING (inches)	MINIMUM STUD THICKNESS (mils)											
				8-Foot Studs				9-Foot Studs				10-Foot Studs			
				Ground Snow Load (psf)											
Exp. B	Exp. C			20	30	50	70	20	30	50	70	20	30	50	70
85 mph	—	350S162	16	33	33	33	33	33	33	33	33	33	33	33	43
			24	33	33	43	43	33	43	43	43	43	43	43	54
		550S162	16	33	33	33	33	33	33	33	33	33	33	33	33
			24	33	33	33	43	33	33	33	43	33	33	33	43
90 mph	—	350S162	16	33	33	33	33	33	33	33	33	33	33	33	43
			24	33	33	43	43	33	43	43	43	43	43	43	54
		550S162	16	33	33	33	33	33	33	33	33	33	33	33	33
			24	33	33	33	43	33	33	33	43	33	33	33	43
100 mph	85 mph	350S162	16	33	33	33	33	33	33	33	33	33	33	33	43
			24	33	43	43	43	43	43	43	43	43	43	43	54
		550S162	16	33	33	33	33	33	33	33	33	33	33	33	33
			24	33	33	33	43	33	33	33	43	33	33	33	43
110 mph	90 mph	350S162	16	33	33	33	43	33	33	33	33	33	33	43	43
			24	43	43	43	43	43	43	43	43	54	54	54	54
		550S162	16	33	33	33	33	33	33	33	33	33	33	33	33
			24	33	33	33	43	33	33	33	43	43	43	43	43
—	100 mph	350S162	16	33	33	33	43	33	33	33	43	43	43	43	43
			24	43	43	43	54	43	43	54	54	54	54	54	54
		550S162	16	33	33	33	33	33	33	33	33	33	33	33	33
			24	33	33	33	43	43	43	43	43	43	43	43	43
—	110 mph	350S162	16	33	33	33	43	43	43	43	43	43	43	43	43
			24	43	43	43	54	54	54	54	54	68	68	68	68
		550S162	16	33	33	33	33	33	33	33	33	33	33	33	33
			24	43	43	43	43	43	43	43	43	43	43	43	43

For SI: 1 inch = 25.4 mm, 1 foot = 304.8 mm, 1 mil = 0.0254 mm, 1 mile per hour = 0.447 m/s, 1 pound per square foot = 0.0479kPa, 1 ksi = 1000 psi = 6.895 MPa.

a. Deflection criterion: *L*/240.

b. Design load assumptions:
   Second floor dead load is 10 psf.
   Second floor live load is 30 psf.
   Roof/ceiling dead load is 12 psf.
   Attic live load is 10 psf.

c. Building width is in the direction of horizontal framing members supported by the wall studs.

TABLE R603.3.2(13)
24-FOOT-WIDE BUILDING SUPPORTING ONE FLOOR, ROOF AND CEILING[a,b,c]
50 ksi STEEL

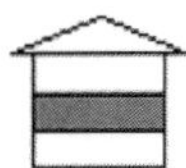

WIND SPEED		MEMBER SIZE	STUD SPACING (inches)	MINIMUM STUD THICKNESS (mils)											
				8-Foot Studs				9-Foot Studs				10-Foot Studs			
				Ground Snow Load (psf)											
Exp. B	Exp. C			20	30	50	70	20	30	50	70	20	30	50	70
85 mph	—	350S162	16	33	33	33	33	33	33	33	33	33	33	33	33
			24	33	33	33	43	33	33	33	43	33	33	43	43
		550S162	16	33	33	33	33	33	33	33	33	33	33	33	33
			24	33	33	33	33	33	33	33	33	33	33	33	33
90 mph	—	350S162	16	33	33	33	33	33	33	33	33	33	33	33	33
			24	33	33	33	43	33	33	33	43	33	33	43	43
		550S162	16	33	33	33	33	33	33	33	33	33	33	33	33
			24	33	33	33	33	33	33	33	33	33	33	33	33
100 mph	85 mph	350S162	16	33	33	33	33	33	33	33	33	33	33	33	33
			24	33	33	33	43	33	33	33	43	43	43	43	43
		550S162	16	33	33	33	33	33	33	33	33	33	33	33	33
			24	33	33	33	33	33	33	33	33	33	33	33	33
110 mph	90 mph	350S162	16	33	33	33	33	33	33	33	33	33	33	33	33
			24	33	33	43	43	33	33	43	43	43	43	43	43
		550S162	16	33	33	33	33	33	33	33	33	33	33	33	33
			24	33	33	33	33	33	33	33	33	33	33	33	33
—	100 mph	350S162	16	33	33	33	33	33	33	33	33	33	33	33	33
			24	33	33	43	43	43	43	43	43	43	43	43	54
		550S162	16	33	33	33	33	33	33	33	33	33	33	33	33
			24	33	33	33	43	33	33	33	33	33	33	33	43
—	110 mph	350S162	16	33	33	33	33	33	33	33	33	33	33	43	43
			24	43	43	43	43	43	43	43	43	54	54	54	54
		550S162	16	33	33	33	33	33	33	33	33	33	33	33	33
			24	33	33	33	43	33	33	33	33	33	33	33	43

For SI: 1 inch = 25.4 mm, 1 foot = 304.8 mm, 1 mil = 0.0254 mm, 1 mile per hour = 0.447 m/s, 1 pound per square foot = 0.0479 kPa, 1 ksi = 1000 psi = 6.895 MPa.

a. Deflection criterion: *L*/240.

b. Design load assumptions:
 Second floor dead load is 10 psf.
 Second floor live load is 30 psf.
 Roof/ceiling dead load is 12 psf.
 Attic live load is 10 psf.

c. Building width is in the direction of horizontal framing members supported by the wall studs.

TABLE R603.3.2(14)
28-FOOT-WIDE BUILDING SUPPORTING ONE FLOOR, ROOF AND CEILING[a,b,c]
33 ksi STEEL

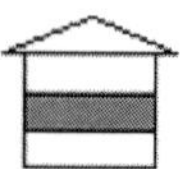

WIND SPEED		MEMBER SIZE	STUD SPACING (inches)	MINIMUM STUD THICKNESS (mils)											
				8-Foot Studs				9-Foot Studs				10-Foot Studs			
				Ground Snow Load (psf)											
Exp. B	Exp. C			20	30	50	70	20	30	50	70	20	30	50	70
85 mph	—	350S162	16	33	33	33	43	33	33	33	43	33	33	33	43
			24	43	43	43	54	43	43	43	54	43	43	43	54
		550S162	16	33	33	33	33	33	33	33	33	33	33	33	33
			24	33	33	43	43	33	33	43	43	33	33	43	43
90 mph	—	350S162	16	33	33	33	43	33	33	33	43	33	33	33	43
			24	43	43	43	54	43	43	43	54	43	43	43	54
		550S162	16	33	33	33	33	33	33	33	33	33	33	33	33
			24	33	33	43	43	33	33	43	43	33	33	43	43
100 mph	85 mph	350S162	16	33	33	33	43	33	33	33	43	33	33	43	43
			24	43	43	43	54	43	43	43	54	43	43	54	54
		550S162	16	33	33	33	33	33	33	33	33	33	33	33	33
			24	33	33	43	43	33	33	43	43	33	33	43	43
110 mph	90 mph	350S162	16	33	33	33	43	33	33	33	43	43	43	43	43
			24	43	43	43	54	43	43	43	54	54	54	54	54
		550S162	16	33	33	33	33	33	33	33	33	33	33	33	33
			24	33	33	43	43	33	33	43	43	43	43	43	43
—	100 mph	350S162	16	33	33	33	43	33	33	43	43	43	43	43	43
			24	43	43	43	54	54	54	54	54	54	54	54	68
		550S162	16	33	33	33	33	33	33	33	33	33	33	33	33
			24	33	33	43	43	43	43	43	43	43	43	43	43
—	110 mph	350S162	16	33	33	43	43	43	43	43	43	43	43	43	54
			24	43	43	54	54	54	54	54	54	68	68	68	68
		550S162	16	33	33	33	33	33	33	33	33	33	33	33	33
			24	43	43	43	43	43	43	43	43	43	43	43	43

For SI: 1 inch = 25.4 mm, 1 foot = 304.8 mm, 1 mil = 0.0254 mm, 1 mile per hour = 0.447 m/s, 1 pound per square foot = 0.0479 kPa, 1 ksi = 1000 psi = 6.895 MPa.

a. Deflection criterion: *L*/240.

b. Design load assumptions:
Second floor dead load is 10 psf.
Second floor live load is 30 psf.
Roof/ceiling dead load is 12 psf.
Attic live load is 10 psf.

c. Building width is in the direction of horizontal framing members supported by the wall studs.

TABLE R603.3.2(15)
28-FOOT-WIDE BUILDING SUPPORTING ONE FLOOR, ROOF AND CEILING[a,b,c]
50 ksi STEEL

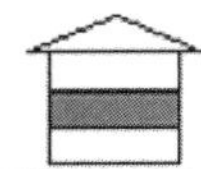

WIND SPEED		MEMBER SIZE	STUD SPACING (inches)	MINIMUM STUD THICKNESS (mils)											
				8-Foot Studs				9-Foot Studs				10-Foot Studs			
				Ground Snow Load (psf)											
Exp. B	Exp. C			20	30	50	70	20	30	50	70	20	30	50	70
85 mph	—	350S162	16	33	33	33	33	33	33	33	33	33	33	33	33
			24	33	33	43	43	33	33	43	43	43	43	43	54
		550S162	16	33	33	33	33	33	33	33	33	33	33	33	33
			24	33	33	33	43	33	33	33	43	33	33	33	43
90 mph	—	350S162	16	33	33	33	33	33	33	33	33	33	33	33	33
			24	33	33	43	43	33	33	43	43	43	43	43	54
		550S162	16	33	33	33	33	33	33	33	33	33	33	33	33
			24	33	33	33	43	33	33	33	43	33	33	33	43
100 mph	85 mph	350S162	16	33	33	33	33	33	33	33	33	33	33	33	43
			24	33	33	43	43	33	33	43	43	43	43	43	54
		550S162	16	33	33	33	33	33	33	33	33	33	33	33	33
			24	33	33	33	43	33	33	33	43	33	33	33	43
110 mph	90 mph	350S162	16	33	33	33	33	33	33	33	33	33	33	33	43
			24	33	33	43	43	43	43	43	43	43	43	43	54
		550S162	16	33	33	33	33	33	33	33	33	33	33	33	33
			24	33	33	33	43	33	33	33	43	33	33	33	43
—	100 mph	350S162	16	33	33	33	33	33	33	33	33	33	33	33	43
			24	43	43	43	54	43	43	43	43	43	43	54	54
		550S162	16	33	33	33	33	33	33	33	33	33	33	33	33
			24	33	33	33	43	33	33	33	43	33	33	33	43
—	110 mph	350S162	16	33	33	33	43	33	33	33	33	43	43	43	43
			24	43	43	43	54	43	43	43	43	54	54	54	54
		550S162	16	33	33	33	33	33	33	33	33	33	33	33	33
			24	33	33	33	43	33	33	33	43	33	33	33	43

For SI: 1 inch = 25.4 mm, 1 foot = 304.8 mm, 1 mil = 0.0254 mm, 1 mile per hour = 0.447 m/s, 1 pound per square foot = 0.0479kPa, 1 ksi = 1000 psi = 6.895 MPa.

a. Deflection criterion: *L*/240.

b. Design load assumptions:
   Second floor dead load is 10 psf.
   Second floor live load is 30 psf.
   Roof/ceiling dead load is 12 psf.
   Attic live load is 10 psf.

c. Building width is in the direction of horizontal framing members supported by the wall studs.

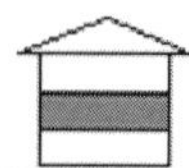

TABLE R603.3.2(16)
32-FOOT-WIDE BUILDING SUPPORTING ONE FLOOR, ROOF AND CEILING[a,b,c]
33 ksi STEEL

WIND SPEED Exp. B	WIND SPEED Exp. C	MEMBER SIZE	STUD SPACING (inches)	MINIMUM STUD THICKNESS (mils) 8-Foot Studs, Ground Snow Load (psf) 20	8-Foot 30	8-Foot 50	8-Foot 70	9-Foot Studs 20	9-Foot 30	9-Foot 50	9-Foot 70	10-Foot Studs 20	10-Foot 30	10-Foot 50	10-Foot 70
85 mph	—	350S162	16	33	33	33	43	33	33	33	43	33	33	43	43
			24	43	43	43	54	43	43	43	54	43	43	54	54
		550S162	16	33	33	33	43	33	33	33	33	33	33	33	43
			24	33	43	43	54	33	33	43	43	33	33	43	43
90 mph	—	350S162	16	33	33	33	43	33	33	33	43	33	33	43	43
			24	43	43	43	54	43	43	43	54	43	43	54	54
		550S162	16	33	33	33	43	33	33	33	33	33	33	33	43
			24	33	43	43	54	33	33	43	43	33	33	43	43
100 mph	85 mph	350S162	16	33	33	33	43	33	33	33	43	33	43	43	43
			24	43	43	43	54	43	43	43	54	54	54	54	68
		550S162	16	33	33	33	43	33	33	33	33	33	33	33	43
			24	33	43	43	54	33	33	43	43	33	33	43	43
110 mph	90 mph	350S162	16	33	33	43	43	33	33	33	43	43	43	43	43
			24	43	43	54	54	43	43	54	54	54	54	54	68
		550S162	16	33	33	33	43	33	33	33	33	33	33	33	43
			24	33	43	43	54	33	33	43	43	43	43	43	54
—	100 mph	350S162	16	33	33	43	43	43	43	43	43	43	43	43	43
			24	43	43	54	54	54	54	54	54	54	54	54	54
		550S162	16	33	33	33	43	33	33	33	33	33	33	33	43
			24	33	43	43	54	43	43	43	43	43	43	43	54
—	110 mph	350S162	16	43	43	43	43	43	43	43	43	43	43	54	54
			24	54	54	54	68	54	54	54	68	68	68	68	68
		550S162	16	33	33	33	43	33	33	33	43	33	33	33	43
			24	43	43	43	54	43	43	43	43	43	43	43	54

For SI: 1 inch = 25.4 mm, 1 foot = 304.8 mm, 1 mil = 0.0254 mm, 1 mile per hour = 0.447 m/s, 1 pound per square foot = 0.0479kPa, 1 ksi = 1000 psi = 6.895 MPa.

a. Deflection criterion: *L*/240.

b. Design load assumptions:
Second floor dead load is 10 psf.
Second floor live load is 30 psf.
Roof/ceiling dead load is 12 psf.
Attic live load is 10 psf.

c. Building width is in the direction of horizontal framing members supported by the wall studs.

TABLE R603.3.2(17)
32-FOOT-WIDE BUILDING SUPPORTING ONE FLOOR, ROOF AND CEILING[a,b,c]
50 ksi STEEL

WIND SPEED		MEMBER SIZE	STUD SPACING (inches)	MINIMUM STUD THICKNESS (mils)											
				8-Foot Studs				9-Foot Studs				10-Foot Studs			
				Ground Snow Load (psf)											
Exp. B	Exp. C			20	30	50	70	20	30	50	70	20	30	50	70
85 mph	—	350S162	16	33	33	33	43	33	33	33	33	33	33	33	43
			24	33	33	43	54	33	33	43	43	43	43	43	54
		550S162	16	33	33	33	33	33	33	33	33	33	33	33	33
			24	33	33	43	43	33	33	33	43	33	33	33	43
90 mph	—	350S162	16	33	33	33	43	33	33	33	33	33	33	33	43
			24	33	33	43	54	33	33	43	43	43	43	43	54
		550S162	16	33	33	33	33	33	33	33	33	33	33	33	33
			24	33	33	43	43	33	33	33	43	33	33	33	43
100 mph	85 mph	350S162	16	33	33	33	43	33	33	33	33	33	33	33	43
			24	33	33	43	54	33	33	43	43	43	43	43	54
		550S162	16	33	33	33	33	33	33	33	33	33	33	33	33
			24	33	33	43	43	33	33	33	43	33	33	33	43
110 mph	90 mph	350S162	16	33	33	33	43	33	33	33	33	33	33	33	43
			24	43	43	43	54	43	43	43	54	43	43	54	54
		550S162	16	33	33	33	33	33	33	33	33	33	33	33	33
			24	33	33	43	43	33	33	33	43	33	33	33	43
—	100 mph	350S162	16	33	33	33	43	33	33	33	43	33	33	43	43
			24	43	43	43	54	43	43	43	54	54	54	54	54
		550S162	16	33	33	33	33	33	33	33	33	33	33	33	33
			24	33	33	43	43	33	33	33	43	33	33	43	43
—	110 mph	350S162	16	33	33	33	43	33	33	33	43	43	43	43	43
			24	43	43	43	54	43	43	43	54	54	54	54	54
		550S162	16	33	33	33	33	33	33	33	33	33	33	33	33
			24	33	33	43	43	33	33	33	43	33	33	43	43

For SI: 1 inch = 25.4 mm, 1 foot = 304.8 mm, 1 mil = 0.0254 mm, 1 mile per hour = 0.447 m/s, 1 pound per square foot = 0.0479 kPa, 1 ksi = 1000 psi = 6.895 MPa.

a. Deflection criterion: *L*/240.

b. Design load assumptions:
   Second floor dead load is 10 psf.
   Second floor live load is 30 psf.
   Roof/ceiling dead load is 12 psf.
   Attic live load is 10 psf.

c. Building width is in the direction of horizontal framing members supported by the wall studs.

TABLE R603.3.2(18)
36-FOOT-WIDE BUILDING SUPPORTING ONE FLOOR, ROOF AND CEILING[a,b,c]
33 ksi STEEL

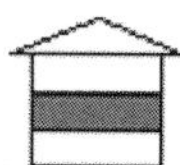

WIND SPEED		MEMBER SIZE	STUD SPACING (inches)	MINIMUM STUD THICKNESS (mils)											
				8-Foot Studs				9-Foot Studs				10-Foot Studs			
				Ground Snow Load (psf)											
Exp. B	Exp. C			20	30	50	70	20	30	50	70	20	30	50	70
85 mph	—	350S162	16	33	33	43	43	33	33	43	43	33	33	43	43
			24	43	43	54	54	43	43	54	54	54	54	54	68
		550S162	16	33	33	33	43	33	33	33	43	33	33	33	43
			24	43	43	43	54	43	43	43	54	43	43	43	54
90 mph	—	350S162	16	33	33	43	43	33	33	43	43	33	33	43	43
			24	43	43	54	54	43	43	54	54	54	54	54	68
		550S162	16	33	33	33	43	33	33	33	43	33	33	33	43
			24	43	43	43	54	43	43	43	54	43	43	43	54
100 mph	85 mph	350S162	16	33	33	43	43	33	33	43	43	43	43	43	43
			24	43	43	54	68	43	43	54	54	54	54	54	68
		550S162	16	33	33	33	43	33	33	33	43	33	33	33	43
			24	43	43	43	54	43	43	43	54	43	43	43	54
110 mph	90 mph	350S162	16	33	33	43	43	33	33	43	43	43	43	43	54
			24	43	43	54	68	54	54	54	54	54	54	54	68
		550S162	16	33	33	33	43	33	33	33	43	33	33	33	43
			24	43	43	43	54	43	43	43	54	43	43	43	54
—	100 mph	350S162	16	33	33	43	43	43	43	43	43	43	43	43	54
			24	54	54	54	68	54	54	54	68	54	68	68	68
		550S162	16	33	33	33	43	33	33	33	43	33	33	33	43
			24	43	43	43	54	43	43	43	54	43	43	43	54
—	110 mph	350S162	16	43	43	43	43	43	43	43	43	43	54	54	54
			24	54	54	54	68	54	54	54	68	68	68	68	68
		550S162	16	33	33	33	43	33	33	33	43	33	33	33	43
			24	43	43	43	54	43	43	43	54	43	43	43	54

For SI: 1 inch = 25.4 mm, 1 foot = 304.8 mm, 1 mil = 0.0254 mm, 1 mile per hour = 0.447 m/s, 1 pound per square foot = 0.0479kPa, 1 ksi = 1000 psi = 6.895 MPa.

a. Deflection criterion: *L*/240.

b. Design load assumptions:
  Second floor dead load is 10 psf.
  Second floor live load is 30 psf.
  Roof/ceiling dead load is 12 psf.
  Attic live load is 10 psf.

c. Building width is in the direction of horizontal framing members supported by the wall studs.

TABLE R603.3.2(19)
36-FOOT-WIDE BUILDING SUPPORTING ONE FLOOR, ROOF AND CEILING[a,b,c]
50 ksi STEEL

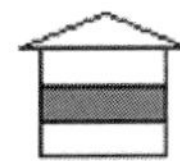

WIND SPEED		MEMBER SIZE	STUD SPACING (inches)	MINIMUM STUD THICKNESS (mils)											
				8-Foot Studs				9-Foot Studs				10-Foot Studs			
				Ground Snow Load (psf)											
Exp. B	Exp. C			20	30	50	70	20	30	50	70	20	30	50	70
85 mph	—	350S162	16	33	33	33	43	33	33	33	43	33	33	33	43
			24	43	43	43	54	33	33	43	54	43	43	43	54
		550S162	16	33	33	33	33	33	33	33	33	33	33	33	33
			24	33	33	43	43	33	33	43	43	33	33	43	43
90 mph	—	350S162	16	33	33	33	43	33	33	33	43	33	33	33	43
			24	43	43	43	54	33	33	43	54	43	43	43	54
		550S162	16	33	33	33	33	33	33	33	33	33	33	33	33
			24	33	33	43	43	33	33	43	43	33	33	43	43
100 mph	85 mph	350S162	16	33	33	33	43	33	33	33	43	33	33	33	43
			24	43	43	43	54	43	43	43	54	43	43	54	54
		550S162	16	33	33	33	33	33	33	33	33	33	33	33	33
			24	33	33	43	43	33	33	43	43	33	33	43	43
110 mph	90 mph	350S162	16	33	33	33	43	33	33	33	43	33	33	43	43
			24	43	43	43	54	43	43	43	54	43	43	54	54
		550S162	16	33	33	33	33	33	33	33	33	33	33	33	33
			24	33	33	43	43	33	33	43	43	33	33	43	43
—	100 mph	350S162	16	33	33	33	43	33	33	33	43	43	43	43	43
			24	43	43	43	54	43	43	43	54	54	54	54	68
		550S162	16	33	33	33	33	33	33	33	33	33	33	33	33
			24	33	33	43	43	33	33	43	43	33	33	43	43
—	110 mph	350S162	16	33	33	43	43	33	33	33	43	43	43	43	43
			24	43	43	54	54	43	43	54	54	54	54	54	68
		550S162	16	33	33	33	33	33	33	33	33	33	33	33	33
			24	33	33	43	43	33	33	43	43	43	43	43	43

For SI: 1 inch = 25.4 mm, 1 foot = 304.8 mm, 1 mil = 0.0254 mm, 1 mile per hour = 0.447 m/s, 1 pound per square foot = 0.0479kPa, 1 ksi = 1000 psi = 6.895 MPa.

a. Deflection criterion: *L*/240.

b. Design load assumptions:
 Second floor dead load is 10 psf.
 Second floor live load is 30 psf.
 Roof/ceiling dead load is 12 psf.
 Attic live load is 10 psf.

c. Building width is in the direction of horizontal framing members supported by the wall studs.

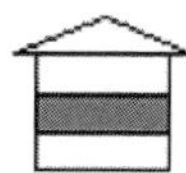

TABLE R603.3.2(20)
40-FOOT-WIDE BUILDING SUPPORTING ONE FLOOR, ROOF AND CEILING[a,b,c]
33 ksi STEEL

WIND SPEED		MEMBER SIZE	STUD SPACING (inches)	MINIMUM STUD THICKNESS (mils)											
				8-Foot Studs				9-Foot Studs				10-Foot Studs			
				Ground Snow Load (psf)											
Exp. B	Exp. C			20	30	50	70	20	30	50	70	20	30	50	70
85 mph	—	350S162	16	33	33	43	43	33	33	43	43	43	43	43	54
			24	43	43	54	68	43	43	54	68	54	54	54	68
		550S162	16	33	33	33	43	33	33	33	43	33	33	33	43
			24	43	43	54	54	43	43	43	54	43	43	43	54
90 mph	—	350S162	16	33	33	43	43	33	33	43	43	43	43	43	54
			24	43	43	54	68	43	43	54	68	54	54	54	68
		550S162	16	33	33	33	43	33	33	33	43	33	33	33	43
			24	43	43	54	54	43	43	43	54	43	43	43	54
100 mph	85 mph	350S162	16	33	33	43	43	33	33	43	43	43	43	43	54
			24	43	43	54	68	43	43	54	68	54	54	54	68
		550S162	16	33	33	33	43	33	33	33	43	33	33	33	43
			24	43	43	54	54	43	43	43	54	43	43	43	54
110 mph	90 mph	350S162	16	33	33	43	43	43	43	43	43	43	43	43	54
			24	43	43	54	68	54	54	54	68	54	54	68	68
		550S162	16	33	33	43	43	33	33	33	43	33	33	33	43
			24	43	43	54	54	43	43	43	54	43	43	43	54
—	100 mph	350S162	16	43	43	43	54	43	43	43	54	43	43	54	54
			24	54	54	54	68	54	54	54	68	68	68	68	97
		550S162	16	33	33	43	43	33	33	33	43	33	33	43	43
			24	43	43	54	54	43	43	43	54	43	43	54	54
—	110 mph	350S162	16	43	43	43	54	43	43	43	54	54	54	54	54
			24	54	54	54	68	54	54	68	68	68	68	68	97
		550S162	16	33	33	43	43	33	33	33	43	33	33	43	43
			24	43	43	54	54	43	43	43	54	43	43	54	54

For SI: 1 inch = 25.4 mm, 1 foot = 304.8 mm, 1 mil = 0.0254 mm, 1 mile per hour = 0.447 m/s, 1 pound per square foot = 0.0479kPa, 1 ksi = 1000 psi = 6.895 MPa.

a. Deflection criterion: *L*/240.

b. Design load assumptions:
  Second floor dead load is 10 psf.
  Second floor live load is 30 psf.
  Roof/ceiling dead load is 12 psf.
  Attic live load is 10 psf.

c. Building width is in the direction of horizontal framing members supported by the wall studs.

TABLE R603.3.2(21)
40-FOOT-WIDE BUILDING SUPPORTING ONE FLOOR, ROOF AND CEILING[a,b,c]
50 ksi STEEL

WIND SPEED		MEMBER SIZE	STUD SPACING (inches)	MINIMUM STUD THICKNESS (mils)											
				8-Foot Studs				9-Foot Studs				10-Foot Studs			
				Ground Snow Load (psf)											
Exp. B	Exp. C			20	30	50	70	20	30	50	70	20	30	50	70
85 mph	—	350S162	16	33	33	33	43	33	33	33	43	33	33	43	43
			24	43	43	43	54	43	43	43	54	43	43	54	54
		550S162	16	33	33	33	43	33	33	33	33	33	33	33	33
			24	33	43	43	54	33	33	43	43	33	33	43	43
90 mph	—	350S162	16	33	33	33	43	33	33	33	43	33	33	43	43
			24	43	43	43	54	43	43	43	54	43	43	54	54
		550S162	16	33	33	33	43	33	33	33	33	33	33	33	33
			24	33	43	43	54	33	33	43	43	33	33	43	43
100 mph	85 mph	350S162	16	33	33	33	43	33	33	33	43	33	33	43	43
			24	43	43	54	54	43	43	43	54	43	43	54	68
		550S162	16	33	33	33	43	33	33	33	33	33	33	33	33
			24	33	43	43	54	33	33	43	43	33	33	43	43
110 mph	90 mph	350S162	16	33	33	43	43	33	33	33	43	33	33	43	43
			24	43	43	54	54	43	43	43	54	54	54	54	68
		550S162	16	33	33	33	43	33	33	33	33	33	33	33	43
			24	33	43	43	54	33	33	43	43	33	33	43	43
—	100 mph	350S162	16	33	33	43	43	33	33	33	43	43	43	43	43
			24	43	43	54	54	43	43	54	54	54	54	54	68
		550S162	16	33	33	33	43	33	33	33	33	33	33	33	43
			24	33	43	43	54	33	33	43	43	33	43	43	43
—	110 mph	350S162	16	33	33	43	43	33	33	43	43	43	43	43	54
			24	43	43	54	68	54	54	54	54	54	54	54	68
		550S162	16	33	33	33	43	33	33	33	33	33	33	33	43
			24	33	43	43	54	33	33	43	43	43	43	43	54

For SI: 1 inch = 25.4 mm, 1 foot = 304.8 mm, 1 mil = 0.0254 mm, 1 mile per hour = 0.447 m/s, 1 pound per square foot = 0.0479 kPa, 1 ksi = 1000 psi = 6.895 MPa.

a. Deflection criterion: *L*/240.

b. Design load assumptions:
Second floor dead load is 10 psf.
Second floor live load is 30 psf.
Roof/ceiling dead load is 12 psf.
Attic live load is 10 psf.

c. Building width is in the direction of horizontal framing members supported by the wall studs.

TABLE R603.3.2(22)
24-FOOT-WIDE BUILDING SUPPORTING TWO FLOORS, ROOF AND CEILING[a,b,c]
33 ksi STEEL

WIND SPEED		MEMBER SIZE	STUD SPACING (inches)	MINIMUM STUD THICKNESS (mils)											
				8-Foot Studs				9-Foot Studs				10-Foot Studs			
				Ground Snow Load (psf)											
Exp. B	Exp. C			20	30	50	70	20	30	50	70	20	30	50	70
85 mph	—	350S162	16	43	43	43	43	33	33	33	43	43	43	43	43
			24	54	54	54	54	43	43	54	54	54	54	54	54
		550S162	16	33	33	43	43	33	33	33	33	33	33	33	43
			24	43	43	54	54	43	43	43	43	43	43	43	54
90 mph	—	350S162	16	43	43	43	43	33	33	33	43	43	43	43	43
			24	54	54	54	54	43	43	54	54	54	54	54	54
		550S162	16	33	33	43	43	33	33	33	33	33	33	33	43
			24	43	43	54	54	43	43	43	43	43	43	43	54
100 mph	85 mph	350S162	16	43	43	43	43	33	33	33	43	43	43	43	43
			24	54	54	54	54	54	54	54	54	54	54	54	68
		550S162	16	33	33	43	43	33	33	33	33	33	33	33	43
			24	43	43	54	54	43	43	43	43	43	43	43	54
110 mph	90 mph	350S162	16	43	43	43	43	43	43	43	43	43	43	43	43
			24	54	54	54	54	54	54	54	54	54	54	68	68
		550S162	16	33	33	43	43	33	33	33	33	33	33	33	43
			24	43	43	54	54	43	43	43	43	43	43	43	54
—	100 mph	350S162	16	43	43	43	43	43	43	43	43	43	43	43	54
			24	54	54	54	54	54	54	54	54	68	68	68	68
		550S162	16	33	33	43	43	33	33	33	33	33	33	33	43
			24	43	43	54	54	43	43	43	43	43	43	43	54
—	110 mph	350S162	16	43	43	43	43	43	43	43	43	54	54	54	54
			24	54	54	54	68	54	54	68	68	68	68	68	97
		550S162	16	33	33	43	43	33	33	33	33	33	33	33	43
			24	43	43	54	54	43	43	43	43	43	43	43	54

For SI: 1 inch = 25.4 mm, 1 foot = 304.8 mm, 1 mil = 0.0254 mm, 1 mile per hour = 0.447 m/s, 1 pound per square foot = 0.0479kPa, 1 ksi = 1000 psi = 6.895 MPa.

a. Deflection criterion: *L*/240.

b. Design load assumptions:
- Top and middle floor dead load is 10 psf.
- Top floor live load is 30 psf.
- Middle floor live load is 40 psf.
- Roof/ceiling dead load is 12 psf.
- Attic live load is 10 psf.

c. Building width is in the direction of horizontal framing members supported by the wall studs.

TABLE R603.3.2(23)
24-FOOT-WIDE BUILDING SUPPORTING TWO FLOORS, ROOF AND CEILING[a,b,c]
50 ksi STEEL

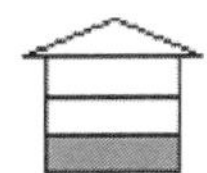

WIND SPEED		MEMBER SIZE	STUD SPACING (inches)	MINIMUM STUD THICKNESS (mils)											
				8-Foot Studs				9-Foot Studs				10-Foot Studs			
				Ground Snow Load (psf)											
Exp. B	Exp. C			20	30	50	70	20	30	50	70	20	30	50	70
85 mph	—	350S162	16	33	33	33	43	33	33	33	33	33	33	33	33
			24	43	43	54	54	43	43	43	43	43	43	43	54
		550S162	16	33	33	33	33	33	33	33	33	33	33	33	33
			24	43	43	43	43	43	43	43	43	43	43	43	43
90 mph	—	350S162	16	33	33	33	43	33	33	33	33	33	33	33	33
			24	43	43	54	54	43	43	43	43	43	43	43	54
		550S162	16	33	33	33	33	33	33	33	33	33	33	33	33
			24	43	43	43	43	43	43	43	43	43	43	43	43
100 mph	85 mph	350S162	16	33	33	33	43	33	33	33	33	33	33	33	33
			24	43	43	54	54	43	43	43	43	43	43	54	54
		550S162	16	33	33	33	33	33	33	33	33	33	33	33	33
			24	43	43	43	43	43	43	43	43	43	43	43	43
110 mph	90 mph	350S162	16	33	33	33	43	33	33	33	33	33	33	43	43
			24	43	43	54	54	43	43	43	43	54	54	54	54
		550S162	16	33	33	33	33	33	33	33	33	33	33	33	33
			24	43	43	43	43	43	43	43	43	43	43	43	43
—	100 mph	350S162	16	33	33	33	43	33	33	33	33	43	43	43	43
			24	43	43	54	54	43	43	54	54	54	54	54	54
		550S162	16	33	33	33	33	33	33	33	33	33	33	33	33
			24	43	43	43	43	43	43	43	43	43	43	43	43
—	110 mph	350S162	16	33	33	33	43	33	33	33	43	43	43	43	43
			24	54	54	54	54	54	54	54	54	54	54	54	68
		550S162	16	33	33	33	33	33	33	33	33	33	33	33	33
			24	43	43	43	43	43	43	43	43	43	43	43	43

For SI: 1 inch = 25.4 mm, 1 foot = 304.8 mm, 1 mil = 0.0254 mm, 1 mile per hour = 0.447 m/s, 1 pound per square foot = 0.0479kPa, 1 ksi = 1000 psi = 6.895 MPa.

a. Deflection criterion: *L*/240.

b. Design load assumptions:
 Top and middle floor dead load is 10 psf.
 Top floor live load is 30 psf.
 Middle floor live load is 40 psf.
 Attic live load is 10 psf.

c. Building width is in the direction of horizontal framing members supported by the wall studs.

TABLE R603.3.2(24)
28-FOOT-WIDE BUILDING SUPPORTING TWO FLOORS, ROOF AND CEILING[a,b,c]
33 ksi STEEL

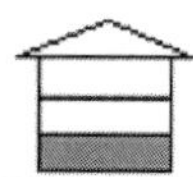

WIND SPEED		MEMBER SIZE	STUD SPACING (inches)	MINIMUM STUD THICKNESS (mils)											
				8-Foot Studs				9-Foot Studs				10-Foot Studs			
				Ground Snow Load (psf)											
Exp. B	Exp. C			20	30	50	70	20	30	50	70	20	30	50	70
85 mph	—	350S162	16	43	43	43	43	43	43	43	43	43	43	43	43
			24	54	54	54	68	54	54	54	54	54	54	54	68
		550S162	16	43	43	43	43	43	43	43	43	43	43	43	43
			24	54	54	54	54	54	54	54	54	54	54	54	54
90 mph	—	350S162	16	43	43	43	43	43	43	43	43	43	43	43	43
			24	54	54	54	68	54	54	54	54	54	54	54	68
		550S162	16	43	43	43	43	43	43	43	43	43	43	43	43
			24	54	54	54	54	54	54	54	54	54	54	54	54
100 mph	85 mph	350S162	16	43	43	43	43	43	43	43	43	43	43	43	43
			24	54	54	54	68	54	54	54	54	54	54	68	68
		550S162	16	43	43	43	43	43	43	43	43	43	43	43	43
			24	54	54	54	54	54	54	54	54	54	54	54	54
110 mph	90 mph	350S162	16	43	43	43	43	43	43	43	43	43	43	43	43
			24	54	54	54	68	54	54	54	54	68	68	68	68
		550S162	16	43	43	43	43	43	43	43	43	43	43	43	43
			24	54	54	54	54	54	54	54	54	54	54	54	54
—	100 mph	350S162	16	43	43	43	43	43	43	43	43	43	43	54	54
			24	54	54	54	68	54	54	68	68	68	68	68	97
		550S162	16	43	43	43	43	43	43	43	43	43	43	43	43
			24	54	54	54	54	54	54	54	54	54	54	54	54
—	110 mph	350S162	16	43	43	43	43	43	43	43	43	54	54	54	54
			24	54	68	68	68	68	68	68	68	68	68	97	97
		550S162	16	43	43	43	43	43	43	43	43	43	43	43	43
			24	54	54	54	54	54	54	54	54	54	54	54	54

For SI: 1 inch = 25.4 mm, 1 foot = 304.8 mm, 1 mil = 0.0254 mm, 1 mile per hour = 0.447 m/s, 1 pound per square foot = 0.0479kPa, 1 ksi = 1000 psi = 6.895 MPa.

a. Deflection criterion: *L*/240.

b. Design load assumptions:
   Top and middle floor dead load is 10 psf.
   Top floor live load is 30 psf.
   Middle floor live load is 40 psf.
   Roof/ceiling dead load is 12 psf.
   Attic live load is 10 psf.

c. Building width is in the direction of horizontal framing members supported by the wall studs.

TABLE R603.3.2(25) 28-FOOT-WIDE BUILDING SUPPORTING TWO FLOORS, ROOF AND CEILING[a,b,c] 50 ksi STEEL

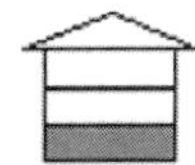

WIND SPEED		MEMBER SIZE	STUD SPACING (inches)	MINIMUM STUD THICKNESS (mils)											
				8-Foot Studs				9-Foot Studs				10-Foot Studs			
				Ground Snow Load (psf)											
Exp. B	Exp. C			20	30	50	70	20	30	50	70	20	30	50	70
85 mph	—	350S162	16	43	43	43	43	33	33	33	43	43	43	43	43
			24	54	54	54	54	43	43	54	54	54	54	54	54
		550S162	16	33	33	33	43	33	33	33	33	33	33	33	33
			24	43	43	43	54	43	43	43	43	43	43	43	43
90 mph	—	350S162	16	43	43	43	43	33	33	33	43	43	43	43	43
			24	54	54	54	54	43	43	54	54	54	54	54	54
		550S162	16	33	33	33	43	33	33	33	33	33	33	33	33
			24	43	43	43	54	43	43	43	43	43	43	43	43
100 mph	85 mph	350S162	16	43	43	43	43	33	33	33	43	43	43	43	43
			24	54	54	54	54	43	43	54	54	54	54	54	54
		550S162	16	33	33	33	43	33	33	33	33	33	33	33	33
			24	43	43	43	54	43	43	43	43	43	43	43	43
110 mph	90 mph	350S162	16	43	43	43	43	33	33	33	43	43	43	43	43
			24	54	54	54	54	43	43	54	54	54	54	54	54
		550S162	16	33	33	33	43	33	33	33	33	33	33	33	33
			24	43	43	43	54	43	43	43	43	43	43	43	43
—	100 mph	350S162	16	43	43	43	43	33	33	33	43	43	43	43	43
			24	54	54	54	54	54	54	54	54	54	54	54	68
		550S162	16	33	33	33	43	33	33	33	33	33	33	33	33
			24	43	43	43	54	43	43	43	43	43	43	43	43
—	110 mph	350S162	16	43	43	43	43	43	43	43	43	43	43	43	43
			24	54	54	54	54	54	54	54	54	68	68	68	68
		550S162	16	33	33	33	43	33	33	33	33	33	33	33	33
			24	43	43	43	54	43	43	43	43	43	43	43	43

For SI: 1 inch = 25.4 mm, 1 foot = 304.8 mm, 1 mil = 0.0254 mm, 1 mile per hour = 0.447 m/s, 1 pound per square foot = 0.0479kPa, 1 ksi = 1000 psi = 6.895 MPa.

a. Deflection criterion: *L*/240.

b. Design load assumptions:
   Top and middle floor dead load is 10 psf.
   Top floor live load is 30 psf.
   Middle floor live load is 40 psf.
   Roof/ceiling dead load is 12 psf.
   Attic live load is 10 psf.

c. Building width is in the direction of horizontal framing members supported by the wall studs.

TABLE R603.3.2(26)
32-FOOT-WIDE BUILDING SUPPORTING TWO FLOORS, ROOF AND CEILING[a,b,c]
33 ksi STEEL

WIND SPEED		MEMBER SIZE	STUD SPACING (inches)	MINIMUM STUD THICKNESS (mils)											
				8-Foot Studs				9-Foot Studs				10-Foot Studs			
				Ground Snow Load (psf)											
Exp. B	Exp. C			20	30	50	70	20	30	50	70	20	30	50	70
85 mph	—	350S162	16	43	43	43	54	43	43	43	43	43	43	43	54
			24	68	68	68	68	54	54	68	68	68	68	68	68
		550S162	16	43	43	43	43	43	43	43	43	43	43	43	43
			24	54	54	54	68	54	54	54	54	54	54	54	54
90 mph	—	350S162	16	43	43	43	54	43	43	43	43	43	43	43	54
			24	68	68	68	68	54	54	68	68	68	68	68	68
		550S162	16	43	43	43	43	43	43	43	43	43	43	43	43
			24	54	54	54	68	54	54	54	54	54	54	54	54
100 mph	85 mph	350S162	16	43	43	43	54	43	43	43	43	43	43	43	54
			24	68	68	68	68	54	54	68	68	68	68	68	68
		550S162	16	43	43	43	43	43	43	43	43	43	43	43	43
			24	54	54	54	68	54	54	54	54	54	54	54	54
110 mph	90 mph	350S162	16	43	43	43	54	43	43	43	43	43	43	54	54
			24	68	68	68	68	54	54	68	68	68	68	68	68
		550S162	16	43	43	43	43	43	43	43	43	43	43	43	43
			24	54	54	54	68	54	54	54	54	54	54	54	54
—	100 mph	350S162	16	43	43	43	54	43	43	43	43	54	54	54	54
			24	68	68	68	68	68	68	68	68	68	68	97	97
		550S162	16	43	43	43	43	43	43	43	43	43	43	43	43
			24	54	54	54	68	54	54	54	54	54	54	54	54
—	110 mph	350S162	16	43	43	43	54	43	43	54	54	54	54	54	54
			24	68	68	68	68	68	68	68	68	97	97	97	97
		550S162	16	43	43	43	43	43	43	43	43	43	43	43	43
			24	54	54	54	68	54	54	54	54	54	54	54	54

For SI: 1 inch = 25.4 mm, 1 foot = 304.8 mm, 1 mil = 0.0254 mm, 1 mile per hour = 0.447 m/s, 1 pound per square foot = 0.0479kPa, 1 ksi = 1000 psi = 6.895 MPa.

a. Deflection criterion: *L*/240.

b. Design load assumptions:
   Top and middle floor dead load is 10 psf.
   Top floor live load is 30 psf.
   Middle floor live load is 40 psf.
   Roof/ceiling dead load is 12 psf.
   Attic live load is 10 psf.

c. Building width is in the direction of horizontal framing members supported by the wall studs.

TABLE R603.3.2(27)
32-FOOT-WIDE BUILDING SUPPORTING TWO FLOORS, ROOF AND CEILING[a,b,c]
50 ksi STEEL

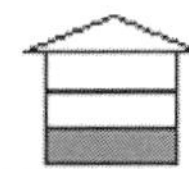

WIND SPEED		MEMBER SIZE	STUD SPACING (inches)	MINIMUM STUD THICKNESS (mils)											
				8-Foot Studs				9-Foot Studs				10-Foot Studs			
				Ground Snow Load (psf)											
Exp. B	Exp. C			20	30	50	70	20	30	50	70	20	30	50	70
85 mph	—	350S162	16	43	43	43	43	43	43	43	43	43	43	43	43
			24	54	54	54	68	54	54	54	54	54	54	54	68
		550S162	16	43	43	43	43	33	33	33	43	33	33	43	43
			24	54	54	54	54	43	43	43	54	43	43	54	54
90 mph	—	350S162	16	43	43	43	43	43	43	43	43	43	43	43	43
			24	54	54	54	68	54	54	54	54	54	54	54	68
		550S162	16	43	43	43	43	33	33	33	43	33	33	43	43
			24	54	54	54	54	43	43	43	54	43	43	54	54
100 mph	85 mph	350S162	16	43	43	43	43	43	43	43	43	43	43	43	43
			24	54	54	54	68	54	54	54	54	54	54	54	68
		550S162	16	43	43	43	43	33	33	33	43	33	33	43	43
			24	54	54	54	54	43	43	43	54	43	43	54	54
110 mph	90 mph	350S162	16	43	43	43	43	43	43	43	43	43	43	43	43
			24	54	54	54	68	54	54	54	54	54	54	54	68
		550S162	16	43	43	43	43	33	33	33	43	33	33	43	43
			24	54	54	54	54	43	43	43	54	43	43	54	54
—	100 mph	350S162	16	43	43	43	43	43	43	43	43	43	43	43	43
			24	54	54	54	68	54	54	54	54	68	68	68	68
		550S162	16	43	43	43	43	33	33	33	43	33	33	43	43
			24	54	54	54	54	43	43	43	54	43	43	54	54
—	110 mph	350S162	16	43	43	43	43	43	43	43	43	43	43	43	54
			24	54	54	54	68	54	54	54	54	68	68	68	68
		550S162	16	43	43	43	43	33	33	33	43	33	33	43	43
			24	54	54	54	54	43	43	43	54	43	43	54	54

For SI: 1 inch = 25.4 mm, 1 foot = 304.8 mm, 1 mil = 0.0254 mm, 1 mile per hour = 0.447 m/s, 1 pound per square foot = 0.0479 kPa, 1 ksi = 1000 psi = 6.895 MPa.

a. Deflection criterion: *L*/240.

b. Design load assumptions:
   Top and middle floor dead load is 10 psf.
   Top floor live load is 30 psf.
   Middle floor live load is 40 psf.
   Roof/ceiling dead load is 12 psf.
   Attic live load is 10 psf.

c. Building width is in the direction of horizontal framing members supported by the wall studs.

TABLE R603.3.2(28)
36-FOOT-WIDE BUILDING SUPPORTING TWO FLOORS, ROOF AND CEILING[a,b,c]
33 ksi STEEL

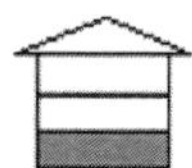

WIND SPEED		MEMBER SIZE	STUD SPACING (inches)	MINIMUM STUD THICKNESS (mils)											
				8-Foot Studs				9-Foot Studs				10-Foot Studs			
				Ground Snow Load (psf)											
Exp. B	Exp. C			20	30	50	70	20	30	50	70	20	30	50	70
85 mph	—	350S162	16	54	54	54	54	43	43	43	54	54	54	54	54
			24	68	68	68	97	68	68	68	68	68	68	68	97
		550S162	16	43	43	43	54	43	43	43	43	43	43	43	43
			24	68	68	68	68	54	54	54	68	54	54	68	68
90 mph	—	350S162	16	54	54	54	54	43	43	43	54	54	54	54	54
			24	68	68	68	97	68	68	68	68	68	68	68	97
		550S162	16	43	43	43	54	43	43	43	43	43	43	43	43
			24	68	68	68	68	54	54	54	68	54	54	68	68
100 mph	85 mph	350S162	16	54	54	54	54	43	43	43	54	54	54	54	54
			24	68	68	68	97	68	68	68	68	68	68	68	97
		550S162	16	43	43	43	54	43	43	43	43	43	43	43	43
			24	68	68	68	68	54	54	54	68	54	54	68	68
110 mph	90 mph	350S162	16	54	54	54	54	43	43	43	54	54	54	54	54
			24	68	68	68	97	68	68	68	68	68	68	97	97
		550S162	16	43	43	43	54	43	43	43	43	43	43	43	43
			24	68	68	68	68	54	54	54	68	54	54	68	68
—	100 mph	350S162	16	54	54	54	54	43	43	54	54	54	54	54	54
			24	68	68	68	97	68	68	68	68	97	97	97	97
		550S162	16	43	43	43	54	43	43	43	43	43	43	43	43
			24	68	68	68	68	54	54	54	68	54	54	68	68
—	110 mph	350S162	16	54	54	54	54	54	54	54	54	54	54	54	68
			24	68	68	68	97	68	68	68	97	97	97	97	97
		550S162	16	43	43	43	54	43	43	43	43	43	43	43	43
			24	68	68	68	68	54	54	54	68	54	54	68	68

For SI: 1 inch = 25.4 mm, 1 foot = 304.8 mm, 1 mil = 0.0254 mm, 1 mile per hour = 0.447 m/s, 1 pound per square foot = 0.0479 kPa, 1 ksi = 1000 psi = 6.895 MPa.

a. Deflection criterion: *L*/240.

b. Design load assumptions:
   Top and middle floor dead load is 10 psf.
   Top floor live load is 30 psf.
   Middle floor live load is 40 psf.
   Roof/ceiling dead load is 12 psf.
   Attic live load is 10 psf.

c. Building width is in the direction of horizontal framing members supported by the wall studs.

TABLE R603.3.2(29)
36-FOOT-WIDE BUILDING SUPPORTING TWO FLOORS, ROOF AND CEILING[a,b,c]
50 ksi STEEL

WIND SPEED		MEMBER SIZE	STUD SPACING (inches)	MINIMUM STUD THICKNESS (mils)											
				8-Foot Studs				9-Foot Studs				10-Foot Studs			
				Ground Snow Load (psf)											
Exp. B	Exp. C			20	30	50	70	20	30	50	70	20	30	50	70
85 mph	—	350S162	16	43	43	43	54	43	43	43	43	43	43	43	43
			24	68	68	68	68	54	54	54	68	68	68	68	68
		550S162	16	43	43	43	43	43	43	43	43	43	43	43	43
			24	54	54	54	54	54	54	54	54	54	54	54	54
90 mph	—	350S162	16	43	43	43	54	43	43	43	43	43	43	43	43
			24	68	68	68	68	54	54	54	68	68	68	68	68
		550S162	16	43	43	43	43	43	43	43	43	43	43	43	43
			24	54	54	54	54	54	54	54	54	54	54	54	54
100 mph	85 mph	350S162	16	43	43	43	54	43	43	43	43	43	43	43	43
			24	68	68	68	68	54	54	54	68	68	68	68	68
		550S162	16	43	43	43	43	43	43	43	43	43	43	43	43
			24	54	54	54	54	54	54	54	54	54	54	54	54
110 mph	90 mph	350S162	16	43	43	43	54	43	43	43	43	43	43	43	43
			24	68	68	68	68	54	54	54	68	68	68	68	68
		550S162	16	43	43	43	43	43	43	43	43	43	43	43	43
			24	54	54	54	54	54	54	54	54	54	54	54	54
—	100 mph	350S162	16	43	43	43	54	43	43	43	43	43	43	43	54
			24	68	68	68	68	54	54	54	68	68	68	68	68
		550S162	16	43	43	43	43	43	43	43	43	43	43	43	43
			24	54	54	54	54	54	54	54	54	54	54	54	54
—	110 mph	350S162	16	43	43	43	54	43	43	43	43	43	54	54	54
			24	68	68	68	68	54	54	68	68	68	68	68	68
		550S162	16	43	43	43	43	43	43	43	43	43	43	43	43
			24	54	54	54	54	54	54	54	54	54	54	54	54

For SI: 1 inch = 25.4 mm, 1 foot = 304.8 mm, 1 mil = 0.0254 mm, 1 mile per hour = 0.447 m/s, 1 pound per square foot = 0.0479kPa, 1 ksi = 1000 psi = 6.895 MPa.

a. Deflection criterion: *L*/240.

b. Design load assumptions:
   Top and middle floor dead load is 10 psf.
   Top floor live load is 30 psf.
   Middle floor live load is 40 psf.
   Roof/ceiling dead load is 12 psf.
   Attic live load is 10 psf.

c. Building width is in the direction of horizontal framing members supported by the wall studs.

TABLE R603.3.2(30)
40-FOOT-WIDE BUILDING SUPPORTING TWO FLOORS, ROOF AND CEILING[a,b,c]
33 ksi STEEL

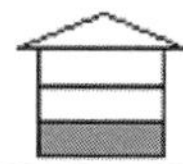

WIND SPEED		MEMBER SIZE	STUD SPACING (inches)	MINIMUM STUD THICKNESS (mils)											
				8-Foot Studs				9-Foot Studs				10-Foot Studs			
				Ground Snow Load (psf)											
Exp. B	Exp. C			20	30	50	70	20	30	50	70	20	30	50	70
85 mph	—	350S162	16	54	54	54	54	54	54	54	54	54	54	54	54
			24	97	97	97	97	68	68	68	97	97	97	97	97
		550S162	16	54	54	54	54	43	43	54	54	43	43	54	54
			24	68	68	68	68	68	68	68	68	68	68	68	68
90 mph	—	350S162	16	54	54	54	54	54	54	54	54	54	54	54	54
			24	97	97	97	97	68	68	68	97	97	97	97	97
		550S162	16	54	54	54	54	43	43	54	54	43	43	54	54
			24	68	68	68	68	68	68	68	68	68	68	68	68
100 mph	85 mph	350S162	16	54	54	54	54	54	54	54	54	54	54	54	54
			24	97	97	97	97	68	68	68	97	97	97	97	97
		550S162	16	54	54	54	54	43	43	54	54	43	43	54	54
			24	68	68	68	68	68	68	68	68	68	68	68	68
110 mph	90 mph	350S162	16	54	54	54	54	54	54	54	54	54	54	54	54
			24	97	97	97	97	68	68	68	97	97	97	97	97
		550S162	16	54	54	54	54	43	43	54	54	43	43	54	54
			24	68	68	68	68	68	68	68	68	68	68	68	68
—	100 mph	350S162	16	54	54	54	54	54	54	54	54	54	54	54	54
			24	97	97	97	97	68	68	68	97	97	97	97	97
		550S162	16	54	54	54	54	43	43	54	54	43	43	54	54
			24	68	68	68	68	68	68	68	68	68	68	68	68
—	110 mph	350S162	16	54	54	54	54	54	54	54	54	54	54	68	68
			24	97	97	97	97	68	68	97	97	97	97	97	97
		550S162	16	54	54	54	54	43	43	54	54	43	43	54	54
			24	68	68	68	68	68	68	68	68	68	68	68	68

For SI: 1 inch = 25.4 mm, 1 foot = 304.8 mm, 1 mil = 0.0254 mm, 1 mile per hour = 0.447 m/s, 1 pound per square foot = 0.0479kPa, 1 ksi = 1000 psi = 6.895 MPa.

a. Deflection criterion: *L*/240.

b. Design load assumptions:
   - Top and middle floor dead load is 10 psf.
   - Top floor live load is 30 psf.
   - Middle floor live load is 40 psf.
   - Roof/ceiling dead load is 12 psf.
   - Attic live load is 10 psf.

c. Building width is in the direction of horizontal framing members supported by the wall studs.

TABLE R603.3.2(31)
40-FOOT-WIDE BUILDING SUPPORTING TWO FLOORS, ROOF AND CEILING[a,b,c]
50 ksi STEEL

WIND SPEED		MEMBER SIZE	STUD SPACING (inches)	MINIMUM STUD THICKNESS (mils)											
				8-Foot Studs				9-Foot Studs				10-Foot Studs			
				Ground Snow Load (psf)											
Exp. B	Exp. C			20	30	50	70	20	30	50	70	20	30	50	70
85 mph	—	350S162	16	54	54	54	54	43	43	43	43	43	54	54	54
			24	68	68	68	68	68	68	68	68	68	68	68	68
		550S162	16	43	43	43	43	43	43	43	43	43	43	43	43
			24	54	54	54	68	54	54	54	54	54	54	54	54
90 mph	—	350S162	16	54	54	54	54	43	43	43	43	43	54	54	54
			24	68	68	68	68	68	68	68	68	68	68	68	68
		550S162	16	43	43	43	43	43	43	43	43	43	43	43	43
			24	54	54	54	68	54	54	54	54	54	54	54	54
100 mph	85 mph	350S162	16	54	54	54	54	43	43	43	43	43	54	54	54
			24	68	68	68	68	68	68	68	68	68	68	68	68
		550S162	16	43	43	43	43	43	43	43	43	43	43	43	43
			24	54	54	54	68	54	54	54	54	54	54	54	54
110 mph	90 mph	350S162	16	54	54	54	54	43	43	43	43	43	54	54	54
			24	68	68	68	68	68	68	68	68	68	68	68	68
		550S162	16	43	43	43	43	43	43	43	43	43	43	43	43
			24	54	54	54	68	54	54	54	54	54	54	54	54
—	100 mph	350S162	16	54	54	54	54	43	43	43	43	43	54	54	54
			24	68	68	68	68	68	68	68	68	68	68	68	68
		550S162	16	43	43	43	43	43	43	43	43	43	43	43	43
			24	54	54	54	68	54	54	54	54	54	54	54	54
—	110 mph	350S162	16	54	54	54	54	43	43	43	43	54	54	54	54
			24	68	68	68	68	68	68	68	68	68	68	68	97
		550S162	16	43	43	43	43	43	43	43	43	43	43	43	43
			24	54	54	54	68	54	54	54	54	54	54	54	54

For SI: 1 inch = 25.4 mm, 1 foot = 304.8 mm, 1 mil = 0.0254 mm, 1 mile per hour = 0.447 m/s, 1 pound per square foot = 0.0479kPa, 1 ksi = 1000 psi = 6.895 MPa.

a. Deflection criterion: *L*/240.

b. Design load assumptions:

Top and middle floor dead load is 10 psf.
Top floor live load is 30 psf.
Middle floor live load is 40 psf.
Roof/ceiling dead load is 12 psf.
Attic live load is 10 psf.

c. Building width is in the direction of horizontal framing members supported by the wall studs.

R603.3.2.1 Gable endwalls. The size and thickness of gable endwall studs with heights less than or equal to 10 feet (3048 mm) shall be permitted in accordance with the limits set forth in Tables R603.3.2.1(1) or R603.3.2.1(2). The size and thickness of gable endwall studs with heights greater than 10 feet (3048 mm) shall be determined in accordance with the limits set forth in Tables R603.3.2.1(3) or R603.3.2.1(4).

R603.3.3 Stud bracing. The flanges of cold-formed steel studs shall be laterally braced in accordance with one of the following:

1. Gypsum board on both sides, structural sheathing on both sides, or gypsum board on one side and structural sheathing on the other side of load-bearing walls with gypsum board installed with minimum No. 6 screws in accordance with Section R702 and structural sheathing installed in accordance with Section R603.9.1 and Table R603.3.2(1).
2. Horizontal steel straps fastened in accordance with Figure R603.3.3(1) on both sides at mid-height for 8-foot (2438 mm) walls, and at one-third points for 9-foot and 10-foot (2743 mm and 3048 mm) walls. Horizontal steel straps shall be at least 1.5 inches in width and 33 mils in thickness (38 mm by 0.84 mm). Straps shall be attached to the flanges of studs with one No. 8 screw. In-line blocking shall be installed between studs at the termination of all straps and at 12 foot (3658 mm) intervals along the strap. Straps shall be fastened to the blocking with two No. 8 screws.
3. Sheathing on one side and strapping on the other side fastened in accordance with Figure R603.3.3(2). Sheathing shall be installed in accordance with Item 1. Steel straps shall be installed in accordance with Item 2.

R603.3.4 Cutting and notching. Flanges and lips of cold-formed steel studs and headers shall not be cut or notched.

R603.3.5 Splicing. Steel studs and other structural members shall not be spliced. Tracks shall be spliced in accordance with Figure R603.3.5.

R603.4 Corner framing. In exterior walls, corner studs and the top tracks shall be installed in accordance with Figure R603.4.

R603.5 Exterior wall covering. The method of attachment of exterior wall covering materials to cold-formed steel stud wall framing shall conform to the manufacturer's installation instructions.

R603.6 Headers. Headers shall be installed above all wall openings in exterior walls and interior load-bearing walls. Box beam headers and back-to-back headers each shall be formed from two equal sized C-shaped members in accordance with Figures R603.6(1) and R603.6(2), respectively, and Tables R603.6(1) through R603.6(24). L-shaped headers shall be permitted to be constructed in accordance with AISI S230. Alternately, headers shall be permitted to be designed and constructed in accordance with AISI S100, Section D4.

R603.6.1 Headers in gable endwalls. Box beam and back-to-back headers in gable endwalls shall be permitted to be constructed in accordance with Section R603.6 or with the header directly above the opening in accordance with Figures R603.6.1(1) and R603.6.1(2) and the following provisions:

1. Two 362S162-33 for openings less than or equal to 4 feet (1219 mm).
2. Two 600S162-43 for openings greater than 4 feet (1219 mm) but less than or equal to 6 feet (1830 mm).
3. Two 800S162-54 for openings greater than 6 feet (1829 mm) but less than or equal to 9 feet (2743 mm).

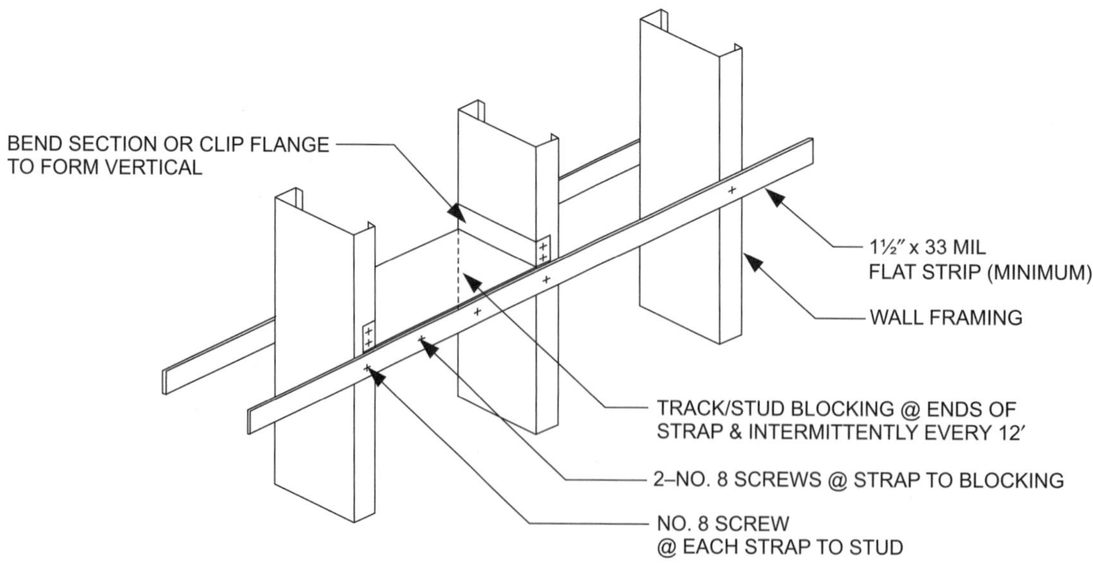

For SI: 1 mil = 0.0254 mm, 1 inch = 25.4 mm.

FIGURE R603.3.3(1)
STUD BRACING WITH STRAPPING ONLY

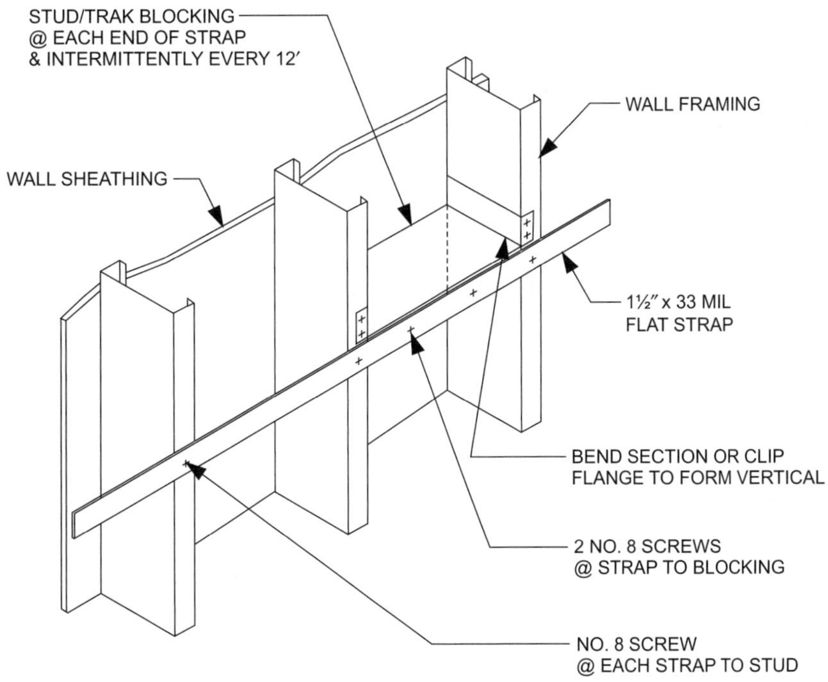

For SI: 1 mil = 0.0254 mm, 1 inch = 25.4 mm.

FIGURE R603.3.3(2)
STUD BRACING WITH STRAPPING AND SHEATHING MATERIAL

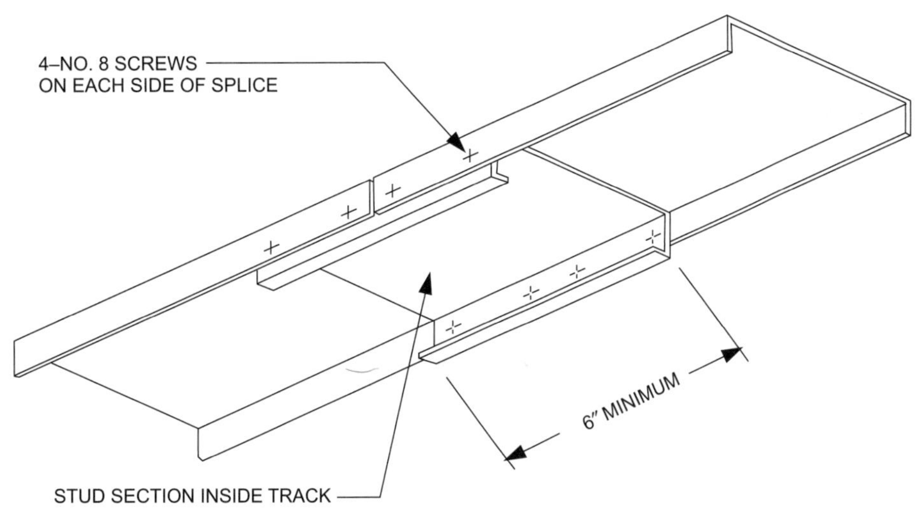

For SI: 1 inch = 25.4 mm.

FIGURE R603.3.5
TRACK SPLICE

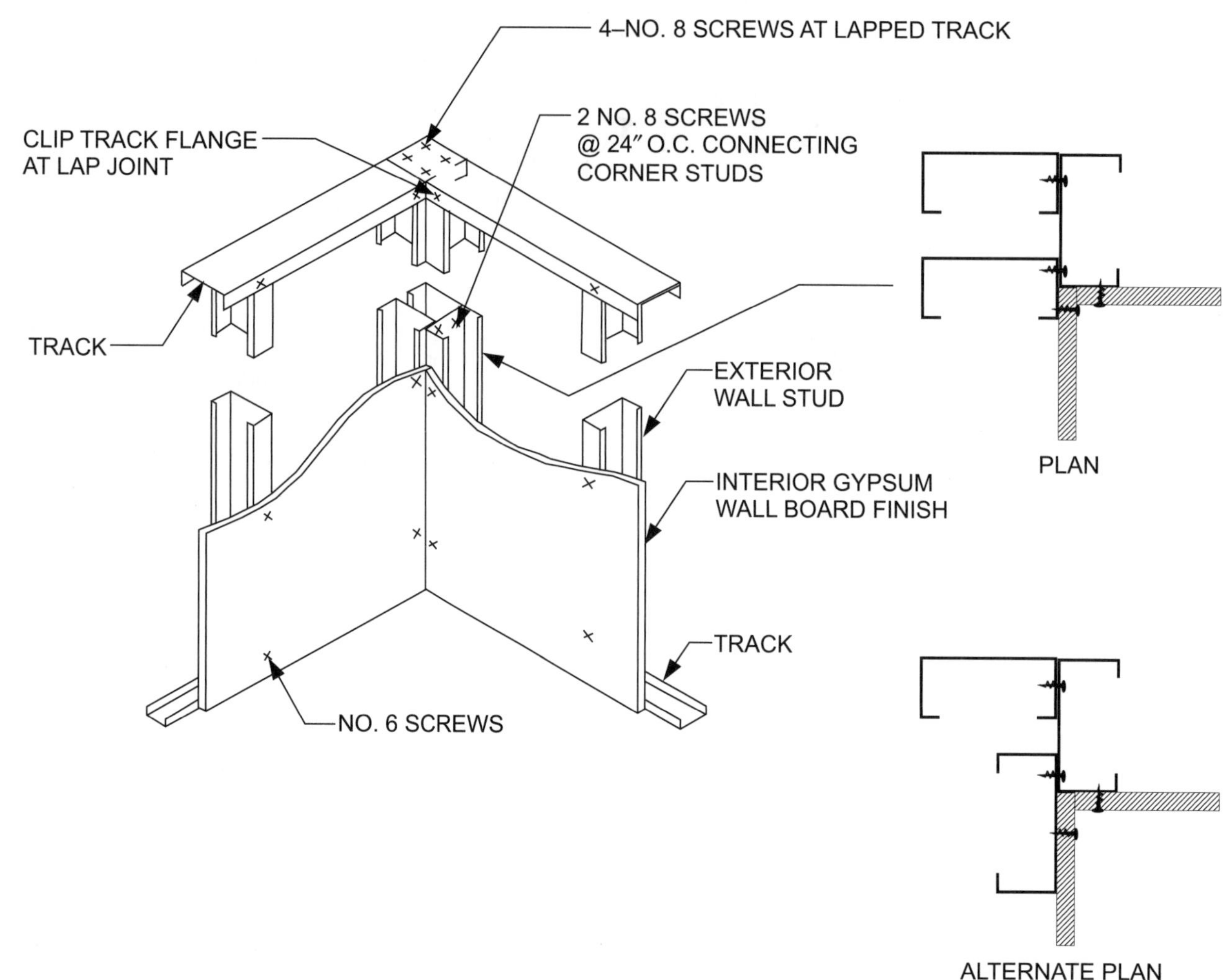

For SI: 1 inch = 25.4 mm.

FIGURE R603.4
CORNER FRAMING

TABLE R603.3.2.1(1)
ALL BUILDING WIDTHS
GABLE ENDWALLS 8, 9 OR 10 FEET IN HEIGHT[a,b,c]
33 ksi STEEL

WIND SPEED		MEMBER SIZE	STUD SPACING (inches)	MINIMUM STUD THICKNESS (Mils)		
Exp. B	Exp. C			8-foot studs	9-foot studs	10-foot studs
85 mph	—	350S162	16	33	33	33
			24	33	33	33
		550S162	16	33	33	33
			24	33	33	33
90 mph	—	350S162	16	33	33	33
			24	33	33	33
		550S162	16	33	33	33
			24	33	33	33
100 mph	85 mph	350S162	16	33	33	33
			24	33	33	43
		550S162	16	33	33	33
			24	33	33	33
110 mph	90 mph	350S162	16	33	33	33
			24	33	33	43
		550S162	16	33	33	33
			24	33	33	33
—	100 mph	350S162	16	33	33	43
			24	43	43	54
		550S162	16	33	33	33
			24	33	33	33
—	110 mph	350S162	16	33	43	43
			24	43	54	54
		550S162	16	33	33	33
			24	33	33	43

For SI: 1 inch = 25.4, 1 foot = 304.8 mm, 1 mil = 0.0254 mm, 1 mile per hour = 0.447 m/s, 1 pound per square foot = 0.0479kPa, 1 ksi = 6.895 MPa.

a. Deflection criterion *L*/240.

b. Design load assumptions:
Ground snow load is 70 psf.
Roof and ceiling dead load is 12 psf.
Floor dead load is 10 psf.
Floor live load is 40 psf.
Attic dead load is 10 psf.

c. Building width is in the direction of horizontal framing members supported by the wall studs.

TABLE R603.3.2.1(2)
ALL BUILDING WIDTHS
GABLE ENDWALLS 8, 9 OR 10 FEET IN HEIGHT[a,b,c]
50 ksi STEEL

WIND SPEED		MEMBER SIZE	STUD SPACING (inches)	MINIMUM STUD THICKNESS (Mils)		
Exp. B	Exp. C			8-foot studs	9-foot studs	10-foot studs
85 mph	—	350S162	16	33	33	33
			24	33	33	33
		550S162	16	33	33	33
			24	33	33	33
90 mph	—	350S162	16	33	33	33
			24	33	33	33
		550S162	16	33	33	33
			24	33	33	33
100 mph	85 mph	350S162	16	33	33	33
			24	33	33	33
		550S162	16	33	33	33
			24	33	33	33
110 mph	90 mph	350S162	16	33	33	33
			24	33	33	43
		550S162	16	33	33	33
			24	33	33	33
—	100 mph	350S162	16	33	33	33
			24	33	33	43
		550S162	16	33	33	33
			24	33	33	33
—	110 mph	350S162	16	33	33	33
			24	33	43	54
		550S162	16	33	33	33
			24	33	33	33

For SI: 1 inch = 25.4, 1 foot = 304.8 mm, 1 mil = 0.0254 mm, 1 mile per hour = 0.447 m/s, 1 pound per square foot = 0.0479kPa, 1 ksi = 6.895 MPa.

a. Deflection criterion *L*/240.

b. Design load assumptions:
Ground snow load is 70 psf.
Roof and ceiling dead load is 12 psf.
Floor dead load is 10 psf.
Floor live load is 40 psf.
Attic dead load is 10 psf.

c. Building width is in the direction of horizontal framing members supported by the wall studs.

TABLE R603.3.2.1(3)
ALL BUILDING WIDTHS
GABLE ENDWALLS OVER 10 FEET IN HEIGHT[a,b,c]
33 ksi STEEL

WIND SPEED		MEMBER SIZE	STUD SPACING (inches)	MINIMUM STUD THICKNESS (Mils)					
				Stud Height, h (feet)					
Exp. B	Exp. C			10 < h ≤ 12	12 < h ≤ 14	14 < h ≤ 16	16 < h ≤ 18	18 < h ≤ 20	20 < h ≤ 22
85 mph	—	350S162	16	33	43	54	97	—	—
			24	43	54	97	—	—	—
		550S162	16	33	33	33	43	43	54
			24	33	33	43	54	68	97
90 mph	—	350S162	16	33	43	68	97	—	—
			24	43	68	97	—	—	—
		550S162	16	33	33	33	43	54	54
			24	33	33	43	54	68	97
100 mph	85 mph	350S162	16	43	54	97	—	—	—
			24	54	97	—	—	—	—
		550S162	16	33	33	43	54	54	68
			24	33	43	54	68	97	97
110 mph	90 mph	350S162	16	43	68	—	—	—	—
			24	68	—	—	—	—	—
		550S162	16	33	43	43	54	68	97
			24	43	54	68	97	97	—
—	100 mph	350S162	16	54	97	—	—	—	—
			24	97	—	—	—	—	—
		550S162	16	33	43	54	68	97	—
			24	43	68	97	97	—	—
—	110 mph	350S162	16	68	97	—	—	—	—
			24	97	—	—	—	—	—
		550S162	16	43	54	68	97	97	—
			24	54	68	97	—	—	—

For SI: 1 inch = 25.4, 1 foot = 304.8 mm, 1 mil = 0.0254 mm, 1 mile per hour = 0.447 m/s, 1 pound per square foot = 0.0479kPa, 1 ksi = 6.895 MPa.

a. Deflection criterion *L*/240.

b. Design load assumptions:
Ground snow load is 70 psf.
Roof and ceiling dead load is 12 psf.
Floor dead load is 10 psf.
Floor live load is 40 psf.
Attic dead load is 10 psf.

c. Building width is in the direction of horizontal framing members supported by the wall studs.

TABLE R603.3.2.1(4)
ALL BUILDING WIDTHS
GABLE ENDWALLS OVER 10 FEET IN HEIGHT[a,b,c]
50 ksi STEEL

WIND SPEED		MEMBER SIZE	STUD SPACING (inches)	MINIMUM STUD THICKNESS (Mils)					
				Stud Height, h (feet)					
Exp. B	Exp. C			10 < h ≤ 12	12 < h ≤ 14	14 < h ≤ 16	16 < h ≤ 18	18 < h ≤ 20	20 < h ≤ 22
85 mph	—	350S162	16	33	43	54	97	—	—
			24	33	54	97	—	—	—
		550S162	16	33	33	33	33	43	54
			24	33	33	33	43	54	97
90 mph	—	350S162	16	33	43	68	97	—	—
			24	43	68	97	—	—	—
		550S162	16	33	33	33	33	43	54
			24	33	33	43	43	68	97
100 mph	85 mph	350S162	16	33	54	97	—	—	—
			24	54	97	—	—	—	—
		550S162	16	33	33	33	43	54	68
			24	33	33	43	54	97	97
110 mph	90 mph	350S162	16	43	68	—	—	—	—
			24	68	—	—	—	—	—
		550S162	16	33	33	43	43	68	97
			24	33	43	54	68	97	—
—	100 mph	350S162	16	54	97	—	—	—	—
			24	97	—	—	—	—	—
		550S162	16	33	33	43	54	97	—
			24	43	54	54	97	—	—
—	110 mph	350S162	16	54	97	—	—	—	—
			24	97	—	—	—	—	—
		550S162	16	33	43	54	68	97	—
			24	43	54	68	97	—	—

For SI: 1 inch = 25.4, 1 foot = 304.8 mm, 1 mil = 0.0254 mm, 1 mile per hour = 0.447 m/s, 1 pound per square foot = 0.0479kPa, 1 ksi = 6.895 MPa.

a. Deflection criterion *L*/240.

b. Design load assumptions:
   Ground snow load is 70 psf.
   Roof and ceiling dead load is 12 psf.
   Floor dead load is 10 psf.
   Floor live load is 40 psf.
   Attic dead load is 10 psf.

c. Building width is in the direction of horizontal framing members supported by the wall studs.

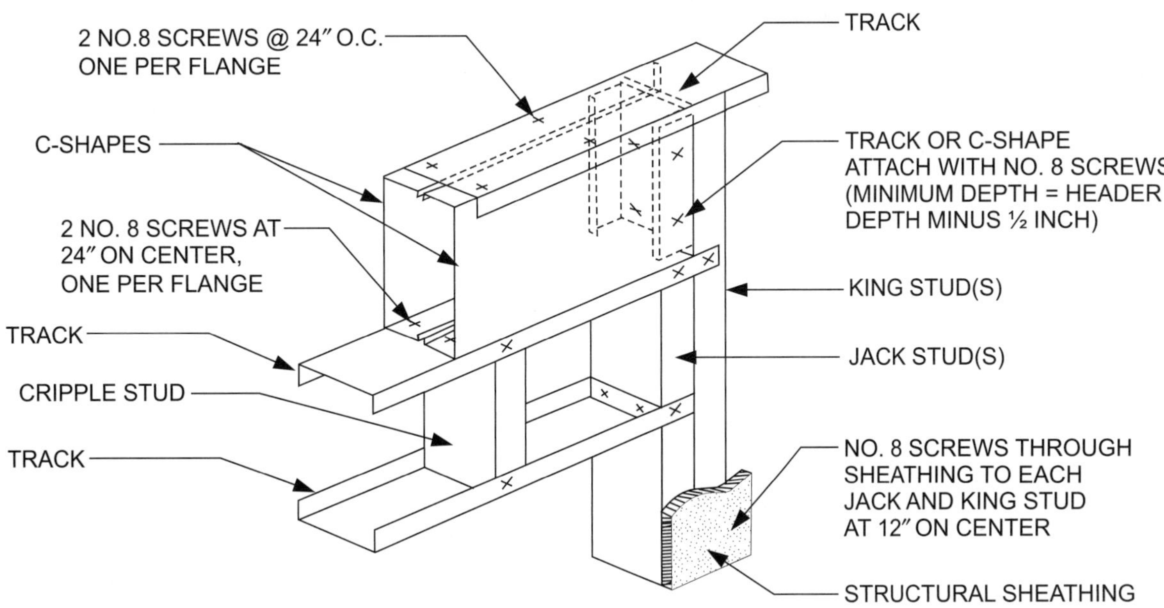

For SI: 1 inch = 25.4 mm.

FIGURE R603.6(1)
BOX BEAM HEADER

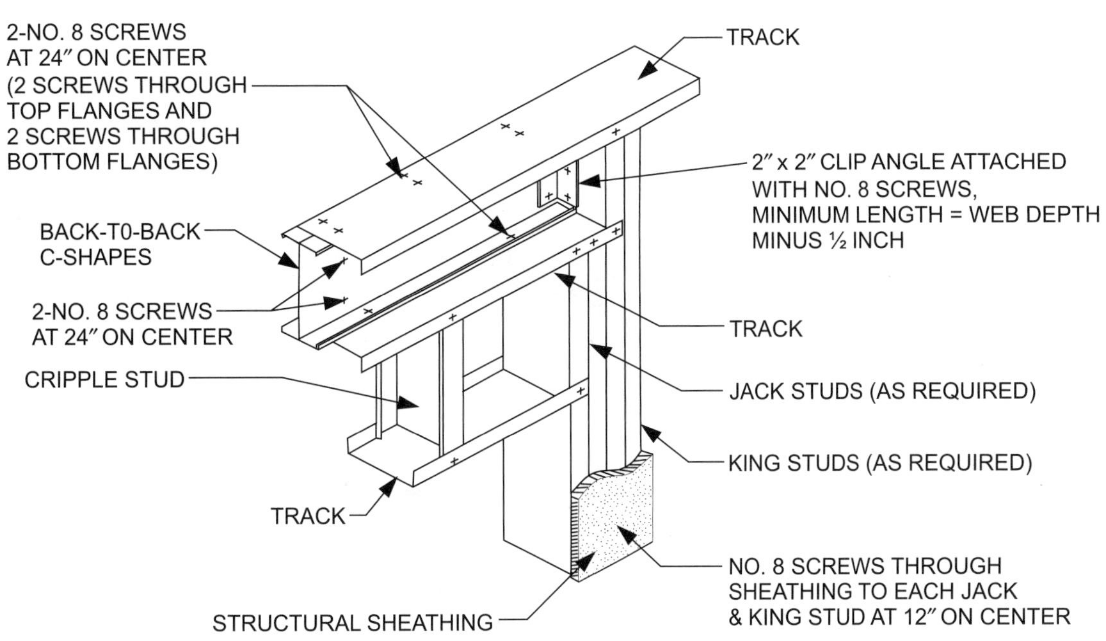

For SI: 1 inch = 25.4 mm.

FIGURE 603.6(2)
BACK-TO-BACK HEADER

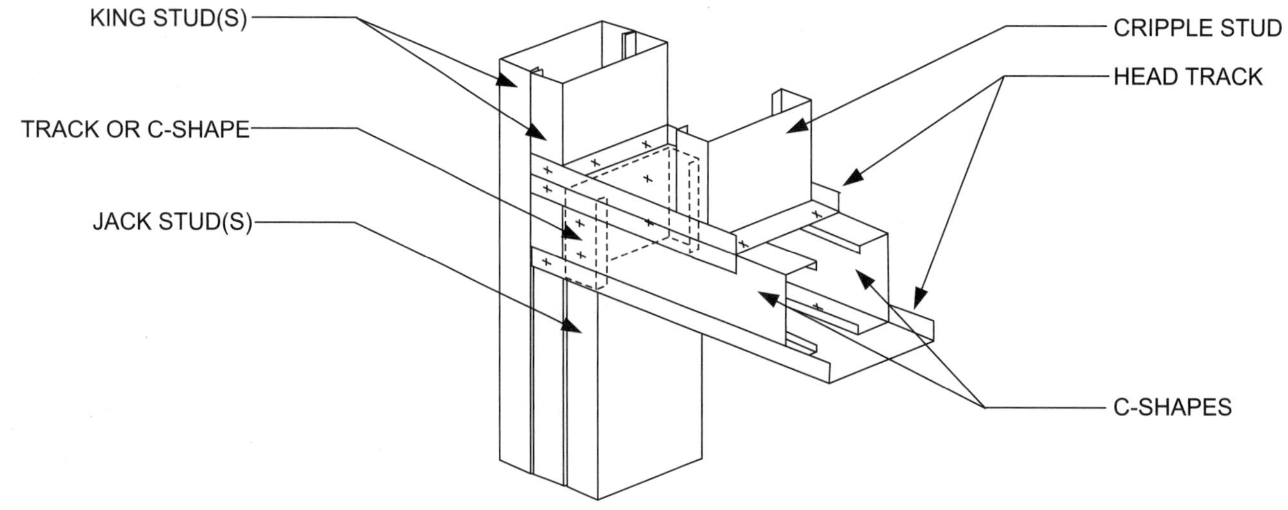

FIGURE R603.6.1(1)
BOX BEAM HEADER IN GABLE ENDWALL

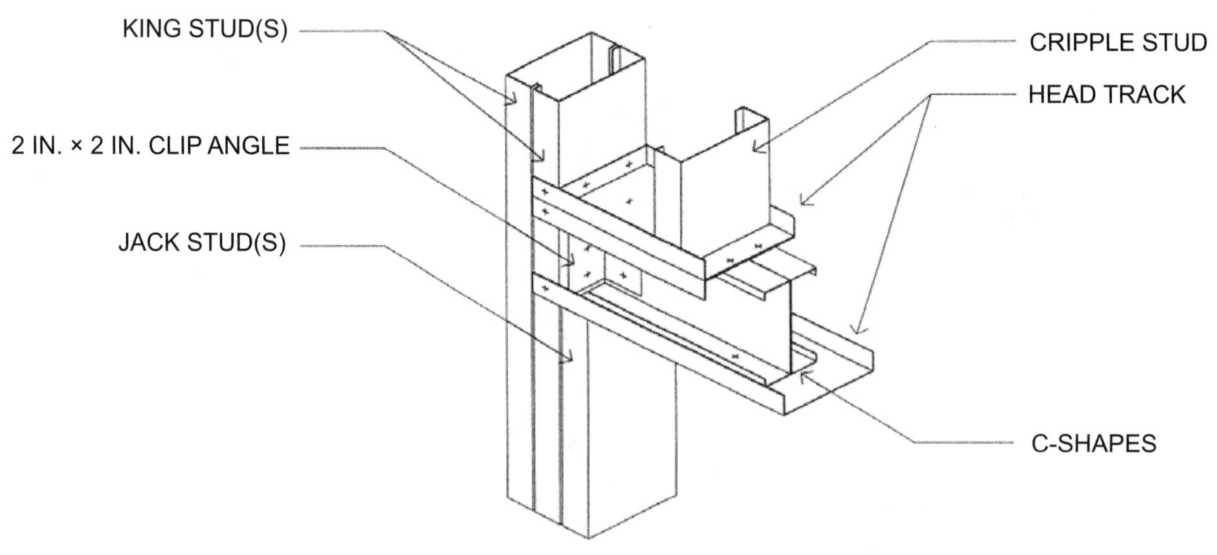

For SI: 1 inch = 25.4 mm.

FIGURE R603.6.1(2)
BACK-TO-BACK HEADER IN GABLE ENDWALL

TABLE R603.6(1)
BOX-BEAM HEADER SPANS
Headers Supporting Roof and Ceiling Only (33 ksi steel)[a, b]

MEMBER DESIGNATION	GROUND SNOW LOAD (20 psf)					GROUND SNOW LOAD (30 psf)				
	Building width[c] (feet)					Building width[c] (feet)				
	24	28	32	36	40	24	28	32	36	40
2-350S162-33	3′-3″	2′-8″	2′-2″	—	—	2′-8″	2′-2″	—	—	—
2-350S162-43	4′-2″	3′-9″	3′-4″	2′-11″	2′-7″	3′-9″	3′-4″	2′-11″	2′-7″	2′-2″
2-350S162-54	5′-0″	4′-6″	4′-1″	3′-8″	3′-4″	4′-6″	4′-1″	3′-8″	3′-3″	3′-0″
2-350S162-68	5′-7″	5′-1″	4′-7″	4′-3″	3′-10″	5′-1″	4′-7″	4′-2″	3′-10″	3′-5″
2-350S162-97	7′-1″	6′-6″	6′-1″	5′-8″	5′-3″	6′-7″	6′-1″	5′-7″	5′-3″	4′-11″
2-550S162-33	4′-8″	4′-0″	3′-6″	3′-0″	2′-6″	4′-1″	3′-6″	3′-0″	2′-6″	—
2-550S162-43	6′-0″	5′-4″	4′-10″	4′-4″	3′-11″	5′-5″	4′-10″	4′-4″	3′-10″	3′-5″
2-550S162-54	7′-0″	6′-4″	5′-9″	5′-4″	4′-10″	6′-5″	5′-9″	5′-3″	4′-10″	4′-5″
2-550S162-68	8′-0″	7′-4″	6′-9″	6′-3″	5′-10″	7′-5″	6′-9″	6′-3″	5′-9″	5′-4″
2-550S162-97	9′-11″	9′-2″	8′-6″	8′-0″	7′-6″	9′-3″	8′-6″	8′-0″	7′-5″	7′-0″
2-800S162-33	4′-5″	3′-11″	3′-5″	3′-1″	2′-10″	3′-11″	3′-6″	3′-1″	2′-9″	2′-3″
2-800S162-43	7′-3″	6′-7″	5′-11″	5′-4″	4′-10″	6′-7″	5′-11″	5′-4″	4′-9″	4′-3″
2-800S162-54	8′-10″	8′-0″	7′-4″	6′-9″	6′-2″	8′-1″	7′-4″	6′-8″	6′-1″	5′-7″
2-800S162-68	10′-5″	9′-7″	8′-10″	8′-2″	7′-7″	9′-8″	8′-10″	8′-1″	7′-6″	7′-0″
2-800S162-97	13′-1″	12′-1″	11′-3″	10′-7″	10′-0″	12′-2″	11′-4″	10′-6″	10′-0″	9′-4″
2-1000S162-43	7′-10″	6′-10″	6′-1″	5′-6″	5′-0″	6′-11″	6′-1″	5′-5″	4′-11″	4′-6″
2-1000S162-54	10′-0″	9′-1″	8′-3″	7′-7″	7′-0″	9′-2″	8′-4″	7′-7″	6′-11″	6′-4″
2-1000S162-68	11′-11″	10′-11″	10′-1″	9′-4″	8′-8″	11′-0″	10′-1″	9′-3″	8′-7″	8′-0″
2-1000S162-97	15′-3″	14′-3″	13′-5″	12′-6″	11′-10″	14′-4″	13′-5″	12′-6″	11′-9″	11′-0″
2-1200S162-54	11′-1″	10′-0″	9′-2″	8′-5″	7′-9″	10′-1″	9′-2″	8′-4″	7′-7″	7′-0″
2-1200S162-68	13′-3″	12′-1″	11′-2″	10′-4″	9′-7″	12′-3″	11′-2″	10′-3″	9′-6″	8′-10″
2-1200S162-97	16′-8″	15′-7″	14′-8″	13′-11″	13′-3″	15′-8″	14′-8″	13′-11″	13′-2″	12′-6″

For SI: 1 inch = 25.4 mm, 1 foot = 304.8 mm, 1 pound per square foot = 0.0479 kPa, 1 pound per square inch = 6.895 kPa.

a. Deflection criterion: $L/360$ for live loads, $L/240$ for total loads.

b. Design load assumptions:
Roof/Ceiling dead load is 12 psf.
Attic dead load is 10 psf.

c. Building width is in the direction of horizontal framing members supported by the header.

TABLE R603.6(2)
BOX-BEAM HEADER SPANS
Headers Supporting Roof and Ceiling Only (50 ksi steel)[a, b]

MEMBER DESIGNATION	GROUND SNOW LOAD (20 psf)					GROUND SNOW LOAD (30 psf)				
	Building width[c] (feet)					Building width[c] (feet)				
	24	28	32	36	40	24	28	32	36	40
2-350S162-33	4′-4″	3′-11″	3′-6″	3′-2″	2′-10″	3′-11″	3′-6″	3′-1″	2′-9″	2′-5″
2-350S162-43	5′-6″	5′-0″	4′-7″	4′-2″	3′-10″	5′-0″	4′-7″	4′-2″	3′-10″	3′-6″
2-350S162-54	6′-2″	5′-10″	5′-8″	5′-3″	4′-10″	5′-11″	5′-8″	5′-2″	4′-10″	4′-6″
2-350S162-68	6′-7″	6′-3″	6′-0″	5′-10″	5′-8″	6′-4″	6′-1″	5′-10″	5′-8″	5′-6″
2-350S162-97	7′-3″	6′-11″	6′-8″	6′-5″	6′-3″	7′-0″	6′-8″	6′-5″	6′-3″	6′-0″
2-550S162-33	6′-2″	5′-6″	5′-0″	4′-7″	4′-2″	5′-7″	5′-0″	4′-6″	4′-1″	3′-8″
2-550S162-43	7′-9″	7′-2″	6′-7″	6′-1″	5′-8″	7′-3″	6′-7″	6′-1″	5′-7″	5′-2″
2-550S162-54	8′-9″	8′-5″	8′-1″	7′-9″	7′-3″	8′-6″	8′-1″	7′-8″	7′-2″	6′-8″
2-550S162-68	9′-5″	9′-0″	8′-8″	8′-4″	8′-1″	9′-1″	8′-8″	8′-4″	8′-1″	7′-10″
2-550S162-97	10′-5″	10′-0″	9′-7″	9′-3″	9′-0″	10′-0″	9′-7″	9′-3″	8′-11″	8′-8″
2-800S162-33	4′-5″	3′-11″	3′-5″	3′-1″	2′-10″	3′-11″	3′-6″	3′-1″	2′-9″	2′-6″
2-800S162-43	9′-1″	8′-5″	7′-8″	6′-11″	6′-3″	8′-6″	7′-8″	6′-10″	6′-2″	5′-8″
2-800S162-54	10′-10″	10′-2″	9′-7″	9′-0″	8′-5″	10′-2″	9′-7″	8′-11″	8′-4″	7′-9″
2-800S162-68	12′-8″	11′-10″	11′-2″	10′-7″	10′-1″	11′-11″	11′-2″	10′-7″	10′-0″	9′-6″
2-800S162-97	14′-2″	13′-6″	13′-0″	12′-7″	12′-2″	13′-8″	13′-1″	12′-7″	12′-2″	11′-9″
2-1000S162-43	7′-10″	6′-10″	6′-1″	5′-6″	5′-0″	6′-11″	6′-1″	5′-5″	4′-11″	4′-6″
2-1000S162-54	12′-3″	11′-5″	10′-9″	10′-2″	9′-6″	11′-6″	10′-9″	10′-1″	9′-5″	8′-9″
2-1000S162-68	14′-5″	13′-5″	12′-8″	12′-0″	11′-6″	13′-6″	12′-8″	12′-0″	11′-5″	10′-10″
2-1000S162-97	17′-1″	16′-4″	15′-8″	14′-11″	14′-3″	16′-5″	15′-9″	14′-10″	14′-1″	13′-6″
2-1200S162-54	12′-11″	11′-3″	10′-0″	9′-0″	8′-2″	11′-5″	10′-0″	9′-0″	8′-1″	7′-4″
2-1200S162-68	15′-11″	14′-10″	14′-0″	13′-4″	12′-8″	15′-0″	14′-0″	13′-3″	12′-7″	11′-11″
2-1200S162-97	19′-11″	18′-7″	17′-6″	16′-8″	15′-10″	18′-9″	17′-7″	16′-7″	15′-9″	15′-0″

For SI: 1 inch = 25.4 mm, 1 foot = 304.8 mm, 1 pound per square foot = 0.0479 kPa, 1 pound per square inch = 6.895 kPa.

a. Deflection criterion: *L*/360 for live loads, *L*/240 for total loads.

b. Design load assumptions:
Roof/Ceiling dead load is 12 psf.
Attic dead load is 10 psf.

c. Building width is in the direction of horizontal framing members supported by the header

TABLE R603.6(3)
BOX-BEAM HEADER SPANS
Headers Supporting Roof and Ceiling Only (33 ksi steel)[a, b]

MEMBER DESIGNATION	GROUND SNOW LOAD (50 psf)					GROUND SNOW LOAD (70 psf)				
	Building width[c] (feet)					Building width[c] (feet)				
	24	28	32	36	40	24	28	32	36	40
2-350S162-33	—	—	—	—	—	—	—	—	—	—
2-350S162-43	2′-4″	—	—	—	—	—	—	—	—	—
2-350S162-54	3′-1″	2′-8″	2′-3″	—	—	2′-1″	—	—	—	—
2-350S162-68	3′-7″	3′-2″	2′-8″	2′-3″	—	2′-6″	—	—	—	—
2-350S162-97	5′-1″	4′-7″	4′-3″	3′-11″	3′-7″	4′-1″	3′-8″	3′-4″	3′-0″	2′-8″
2-550S162-33	2′-2″	—	—	—	—	—	—	—	—	—
2-550S162-43	3′-8″	3′-1″	2′-6″	—	—	2′-3″	—	—	—	—
2-550S162-54	4′-7″	4′-0″	3′-6″	3′-0″	2′-6″	3′-3″	2′-8″	2′-1″	—	—
2-550S162-68	5′-6″	4′-11″	4′-5″	3′-11″	3′-6″	4′-3″	3′-8″	3′-1″	2′-7″	2′-1″
2-550S162-97	7′-3″	6′-7″	6′-1″	5′-8″	5′-3″	5′-11″	5′-4″	4′-11″	4′-6″	4′-1″
2-800S162-33	2′-7″	—	—	—	—	—	—	—	—	—
2-800S162-43	4′-6″	3′-9″	3′-1″	2′-5″	—	2′-10″	—	—	—	—
2-800S162-54	5′-10″	5′-1″	4′-6″	3′-11″	3′-4″	4′-3″	3′-6″	2′-9″	—	—
2-800S162-68	7′-2″	6′-6″	5′-10″	5′-3″	4′-8″	5′-7″	4′-10″	4′-2″	3′-7″	2′-11″
2-800S162-97	9′-7″	8′-9″	8′-2″	7′-7″	7′-0″	7′-11″	7′-2″	6′-7″	6′-0″	5′-7″
2-1000S162-43	4′-8″	4′-1″	3′-6″	2′-9″	—	3′-3″	2′-2″	—	—	—
2-1000S162-54	6′-7″	5′-10″	5′-1″	4′-5″	3′-9″	4′-10″	4′-0″	3′-2″	2′-3″	—
2-1000S162-68	8′-3″	7′-5″	6′-8″	6′-0″	5′-5″	6′-5″	5′-7″	4′-9″	4′-1″	3′-5″
2-1000S162-97	11′-4″	10′-5″	9′-8″	9′-0″	8′-5″	9′-5″	8′-6″	7′-10″	7′-2″	6′-7″
2-1200S162-54	7′-3″	6′-5″	5′-7″	4′-10″	4′-2″	5′-4″	4′-4″	3′-5″	2′-5″	—
2-1200S162-68	9′-2″	8′-2″	7′-5″	6′-8″	6′-0″	7′-1″	6′-2″	5′-4″	4′-6″	3′-9″
2-1200S162-97	12′-10″	11′-9″	10′-11″	10′-2″	9′-6″	10′-7″	9′-8″	8′-10″	8′-2″	7′-6″

For SI: 1 inch = 25.4 mm, 1 foot = 304.8 mm, 1 pound per square foot = 0.0479 kPa, 1 pound per square inch = 6.895 kPa.

a. Deflection criterion: $L/360$ for live loads, $L/240$ for total loads.

b. Design load assumptions:
Roof/Ceiling dead load is 12 psf.
Attic dead load is 10 psf.

c. Building width is in the direction of horizontal framing members supported by the header.

TABLE R603.6(4)
BOX-BEAM HEADER SPANS
Headers Supporting Roof and Ceiling Only (50 ksi steel)[a, b]

MEMBER DESIGNATION	GROUND SNOW LOAD (50 psf)					GROUND SNOW LOAD (70 psf)				
	Building width[c] (feet)					Building width[c] (feet)				
	24	28	32	36	40	24	28	32	36	40
2-350S162-33	2′-7″	2′-2″	—	—	—	—	—	—	—	—
2-350S162-43	3′-8″	3′-3″	2′-10″	2′-6″	2′-1″	2′-8″	2′-3″	—	—	—
2-350S162-54	4′-8″	4′-2″	3′-9″	3′-5″	3′-1″	3′-7″	3′-2″	2′-9″	2′-5″	2′-0″
2-350S162-68	5′-7″	5′-2″	4′-9″	4′-4″	3′-11″	4′-7″	4′-1″	3′-7″	3′-2″	2′-10″
2-350S162-97	6′-2″	5′-11″	5′-8″	5′-6″	5′-4″	5′-8″	5′-5″	5′-3″	4′-11″	4′-7″
2-550S162-33	3′-11″	3′-4″	2′-10″	2′-4″	—	2′-7″	—	—	—	—
2-550S162-43	5′-4″	4′-10″	4′-4″	3′-10″	3′-5″	4′-2″	3′-7″	3′-1″	2′-7″	2′-1″
2-550S162-54	6′-11″	6′-3″	5′-9″	5′-3″	4′-9″	5′-6″	4′-11″	4′-5″	3′-11″	3′-5″
2-550S162-68	8′-0″	7′-6″	6′-11″	6′-5″	5′-11″	6′-9″	6′-1″	5′-6″	5′-0″	4′-7″
2-550S162-97	8′-11″	8′-6″	8′-2″	7′-11″	7′-8″	8′-1″	7′-9″	7′-6″	7′-1″	6′-7″
2-800S162-33	2′-8″	2′-4″	2′-1″	1′-11″	1′-9″	2′-0″	1′-9″	—	—	—
2-800S162-43	5′-10″	5′-2″	4′-7″	4′-2″	3′-10″	4′-5″	3′-11″	3′-6″	3′-0″	2′-6″
2-800S162-54	8′-0″	7′-3″	6′-8″	6′-1″	5′-7″	6′-5″	5′-9″	5′-1″	4′-7″	4′-0″
2-800S162-68	9′-9″	9′-0″	8′-3″	7′-8″	7′-1″	8′-0″	7′-3″	6′-7″	6′-0″	5′-6″
2-800S162-97	12′-1″	11′-7″	11′-2″	10′-8″	10′-2″	11′-0″	10′-4″	9′-9″	9′-2″	8′-7″
2-1000S162-43	4′-8″	4′-1″	3′-8″	3′-4″	3′-0″	3′-6″	3′-1″	2′-9″	2′-6″	2′-3″
2-1000S162-54	9′-1″	8′-2″	7′-3″	6′-7″	6′-0″	7′-0″	6′-2″	5′-6″	5′-0″	4′-6″
2-1000S162-68	11′-1″	10′-2″	9′-5″	8′-8″	8′-1″	9′-1″	8′-3″	7′-6″	6′-10″	6′-3″
2-1000S162-97	13′-9″	12′-11″	12′-2″	11′-7″	11′-1″	11′-11″	11′-3″	10′-7″	9′-11″	9′-4″
2-1200S162-54	7′-8″	6′-9″	6′-1″	5′-6″	5′-0″	5′-10″	5′-1″	4′-7″	4′-1″	3′-9″
2-1200S162-68	12′-3″	11′-3″	10′-4″	9′-7″	8′-11″	10′-1″	9′-1″	8′-3″	7′-6″	6′-10″
2-1200S162-97	15′-4″	14′-5″	13′-7″	12′-11″	12′-4″	13′-4″	12′-6″	11′-10″	11′-1″	10′-5″

For SI: 1 inch = 25.4 mm, 1 foot = 304.8 mm, 1 pound per square foot = 0.0479 kPa, 1 pound per square inch = 6.895 kPa.

a. Deflection criterion: *L*/360 for live loads, *L*/240 for total loads.

b. Design load assumptions:
   Roof/Ceiling dead load is 12 psf.
   Attic dead load is 10 psf.

c. Building width is in the direction of horizontal framing members supported by the header.

TABLE R603.6(5)
BOX-BEAM HEADER SPANS
Headers Supporting One Floor, Roof and Ceiling (33 ksi steel)[a, b]

MEMBER DESIGNATION	GROUND SNOW LOAD (20 psf)					GROUND SNOW LOAD (30 psf)				
	Building width[c] (feet)					Building width[c] (feet)				
	24	28	32	36	40	24	28	32	36	40
2-350S162-33	—	—	—	—	—	—	—	—	—	—
2-350S162-43	2′-2″	—	—	—	—	2′-1″	—	—	—	—
2-350S162-54	2′-11″	2′-5″	—	—	—	2′-10″	2′-4″	—	—	—
2-350S162-68	3′-8″	3′-2″	2′-9″	2′-4″	—	3′-7″	3′-1″	2′-8″	2′-3″	—
2-350S162-97	4′-11″	4′-5″	4′-2″	3′-8″	3′-5″	4′-10″	4′-5″	4′-0″	3′-8″	3′-4″
2-550S162-33	—	—	—	—	—	—	—	—	—	—
2-550S162-43	3′-5″	2′-9″	2′-1″	—	—	3′-3″	2′-7″	—	—	—
2-550S162-54	4′-4″	3′-9″	3′-2″	2′-7″	2′-1″	4′-3″	3′-7″	3′-1″	2′-6″	—
2-550S162-68	5′-3″	4′-8″	4′-1″	3′-7″	3′-2″	5′-2″	4′-7″	4′-0″	3′-6″	3′-1″
2-550S162-97	7′-0″	6′-5″	5′-10″	5′-5″	5′-0″	6′-11″	6′-4″	5′-9″	5′-4″	4′-11″
2-800S162-33	2′-1″	—	—	—	—	—	—	—	—	—
2-800S162-43	4′-2″	3′-4″	2′-7″	—	—	4′-0″	3′-3″	2′-5″	—	—
2-800S162-54	5′-6″	4′-9″	4′-1″	3′-5″	2′-9″	5′-5″	4′-8″	3′-11″	3′-3″	2′-8″
2-800S162-68	6′-11″	6′-2″	5′-5″	4′-10″	4′-3″	6′-9″	6′-0″	5′-4″	4′-8″	4′-1″
2-800S162-97	9′-4″	8′-6″	7′-10″	7′-3″	6′-8″	9′-2″	8′-4″	7′-8″	7′-1″	6′-7″
2-1000S162-43	4′-4″	3′-9″	2′-11″	—	—	4′-3″	3′-8″	2′-9″	—	—
2-1000S162-54	6′-3″	5′-5″	4′-7″	3′-11″	3′-2″	6′-1″	5′-3″	4′-6″	3′-9″	3′-0″
2-1000S162-68	7′-11″	7′-0″	6′-3″	5′-6″	4′-10″	7′-9″	6′-10″	6′-1″	5′-4″	4′-9″
2-1000S162-97	11′-0″	10′-1″	9′-3″	8′-7″	8′-0″	10′-11″	9′-11″	9′-2″	8′-5″	7′-10″
2-1200S162-54	6′-11″	5′-11″	5′-1″	4′-3″	3′-5″	6′-9″	5′-9″	4′-11″	4′-1″	3′-3″
2-1200S162-68	8′-9″	7′-9″	6′-11″	6′-1″	5′-4″	8′-7″	7′-7″	6′-9″	5′-11″	5′-3″
2-1200S162-97	12′-4″	11′-5″	10′-6″	9′-8″	9′-0″	12′-3″	11′-3″	10′-4″	9′-6″	8′-10″

For SI: 1 inch = 25.4 mm, 1 foot = 304.8 mm, 1 pound per square foot = 0.0479 kPa, 1 pound per square inch = 6.895 kPa.

a. Deflection criterion: $L/360$ for live loads, $L/240$ for total loads.

b. Design load assumptions:
   Second floor dead load is 10 psf.
   Roof/Ceiling dead load is 12 psf.
   Second floor live load is 30 psf.
   Attic dead load is 10 psf.

c. Building width is in the direction of horizontal framing members supported by the header

TABLE R603.6(6)
BOX-BEAM HEADER SPANS
Headers Supporting One Floor, Roof and Ceiling (50 ksi steel)[a, b]

MEMBER DESIGNATION	GROUND SNOW LOAD (20 psf)					GROUND SNOW LOAD (30 psf)				
	Building width[c] (feet)					Building width[c] (feet)				
	24	28	32	36	40	24	28	32	36	40
2-350S162-33	2′-4″	—	—	—	—	2′-3″	—	—	—	—
2-350S162-43	3′-4″	2′-11″	2′-6″	2′-1″	—	3′-3″	2′-10″	2′-5″	2′-0″	—
2-350S162-54	4′-4″	3′-10″	3′-5″	3′-1″	2′-9″	4′-3″	2′-9″	3′-4″	3′-0″	2′-8″
2-350S162-68	5′-0″	4′-9″	4′-7″	4′-2″	3′-9″	4′-11″	4′-8″	4′-6″	4′-1″	3′-9″
2-350S162-97	5′-6″	5′-3″	5′-1″	4′-11″	2′-9″	5′-5″	5′-2″	5′-0″	4′-10″	4′-8″
2-550S162-33	3′-6″	2′-11″	2′-4″	—	—	3′-5″	2′-10″	2′-3″	—	—
2-550S162-43	5′-0″	4′-5″	3′-11″	3′-5″	3′-0″	4′-11″	4′-4″	3′-10″	3′-4″	2′-11″
2-550S162-54	6′-6″	5′-10″	5′-3″	4′-9″	4′-4″	6′-4″	5′-9″	5′-2″	4′-8″	4′-3″
2-550S162-68	7′-2″	6′-10″	6′-5″	5′-11″	5′-6″	7′-0″	6′-9″	6′-4″	5′-10″	5′-4″
2-550S162-97	7′-11″	7′-7″	7′-3″	7′-0″	6′-10″	7′-9″	7′-5″	7′-2″	6′-11″	6′-9″
2-800S162-33	2′-5″	2′-2″	1′-11″	1′-9″	—	2′-5″	2′-1″	1′-10″	1′-8″	—
2-800S162-43	5′-5″	4′-9″	4′-3″	3′-9″	3′-5″	5′-3″	4′-8″	4′-1″	3′-9″	3′-5″
2-800S162-54	7′-6″	6′-9″	6′-2″	5′-7″	5′-0″	7′-5″	6′-8″	6′-0″	5′-5″	4′-11″
2-800S162-68	9′-3″	8′-5″	7′-8″	7′-1″	6′-6″	9′-1″	8′-3″	7′-7″	7′-0″	6′-5″
2-800S162-97	10′-9″	10′-3″	9′-11″	9′-7″	9′-3″	10′-7″	10′-1″	9′-9″	9′-5″	9′-1″
2-1000S162-43	4′-4″	3′-9″	3′-4″	3′-0″	2′-9″	4′-3″	3′-8″	3′-3″	2′-11″	2′-8″
2-1000S162-54	8′-6″	7′-6″	6′-8″	6′-0″	5′-5″	8′-4″	7′-4″	6′-6″	5′-10″	5′-4″
2-1000S162-68	10′-6″	9′-7″	8′-9″	8′-0″	7′-5″	10′-4″	9′-5″	8′-7″	7′-11″	7′-3″
2-1000S162-97	12′-11″	12′-4″	11′-8″	11′-1″	10′-6″	12′-9″	12′-2″	11′-6″	10′-11″	10′-5″
2-1200S162-54	7′-1″	6′-2″	5′-6″	5′-0″	4′-6″	6′-11″	6′-1″	5′-5″	4′-10″	4′-5″
2-1200S162-68	11′-7″	10′-7″	9′-8″	8′-11″	8′-2″	11′-5″	10′-5″	9′-6″	8′-9″	8′-0″
2-1200S162-97	14′-9″	13′-9″	13′-0″	12′-4″	11′-9″	14′-7″	13′-8″	12′-10″	12′-3″	11′-8″

For SI: 1 inch = 25.4 mm, 1 foot = 304.8 mm, 1 pound per square foot = 0.0479 kPa, 1 pound per square inch = 6.895 kPa.

a. Deflection criterion: *L*/360 for live loads, *L*/240 for total loads.

b. Design load assumptions:
  Second floor dead load is 10 psf.
  Roof/ceiling dead load is 12 psf.
  Second floor live load is 30 psf.
  Attic live load is 10 psf.

c. Building width is in the direction of horizontal framing members supported by the header.

TABLE R603.6(7)
BOX-BEAM HEADER SPANS
Headers Supporting One Floor, Roof and Ceiling (33 ksi steel)[a, b]

MEMBER DESIGNATION	GROUND SNOW LOAD (50 psf)					GROUND SNOW LOAD (70 psf)				
	Building width[c] (feet)					Building width[c] (feet)				
	24	28	32	36	40	24	28	32	36	40
2-350S162-33	—	—	—	—	—	—	—	—	—	—
2-350S162-43	—	—	—	—	—	—	—	—	—	—
2-350S162-54	—	—	—	—	—	—	—	—	—	—
2-350S162-68	2′-8″	2′-3″	—	—	—	—	—	—	—	—
2-350S162-97	4′-0″	3′-7″	3′-3″	2′-11″	2′-7″	3′-4″	2′-11″	2′-6″	2′-2″	—
2-550S162-33	—	—	—	—	—	—	—	—	—	—
2-550S162-43	2′-0″	—	—	—	—	—	—	—	—	—
2-550S162-54	3′-1″	2′-6″	—	—	—	—	—	—	—	—
2-550S162-68	4′-1″	3′-6″	2′-11″	2′-5″	—	3′-1″	2′-5″	—	—	—
2-550S162-97	5′-10″	5′-3″	4′-10″	4′-5″	4′-0″	4′-11″	4′-5″	3′-11″	3′-6″	3′-2″
2-800S162-33	—	—	—	—	—	—	—	—	—	—
2-800S162-43	2′-6″	—	—	—	—	—	—	—	—	—
2-800S162-54	4′-0″	3′-3″	2′-6″	—	—	2′-8″	—	—	—	—
2-800S162-68	5′-5″	4′-8″	4′-0″	3′-4″	2′-8″	4′-2″	3′-4″	2′-6″	—	—
2-800S162-97	7′-9″	7′-1″	6′-6″	5′-11″	5′-5″	6′-7″	5′-11″	5′-4″	4′-10″	4′-4″
2-1000S162-43	2′-10″	—	—	—	—	—	—	—	—	—
2-1000S162-54	4′-7″	3′-8″	2′-9″	—	—	3′-0″	—	—	—	—
2-1000S162-68	6′-2″	5′-4″	4′-7″	3′-10″	3′-1″	4′-9″	3′-10″	2′-11″	—	—
2-1000S162-97	9′-3″	8′-5″	7′-8″	7′-1″	6′-6″	7′-10″	7′-1″	6′-5″	5′-9″	5′-2″
2-1200S162-54	5′-0″	4′-0″	3′-1″	—	—	3′-4″	—	—	—	—
2-1200S162-68	6′-10″	5′-11″	5′-0″	4′-3″	3′-5″	5′-3″	4′-3″	3′-2″	—	—
2-1200S162-97	10′-5″	9′-6″	8′-8″	8′-0″	7′-4″	8′-10″	8′-0″	7′-3″	6′-6″	5′-10″

For SI: 1 inch = 25.4 mm, 1 foot = 304.8 mm, 1 pound per square foot = 0.0479 kPa, 1 pound per square inch = 6.895 kPa.

a. Deflection criterion: *L*/360 for live loads, *L*/240 for total loads.

b. Design load assumptions:
Second floor dead load is 10 psf.
Roof/ceiling dead load is 12 psf.
Second floor live load is 30 psf.
Attic live load is 10 psf.

c. Building width is in the direction of horizontal framing members supported by the header.

TABLE R603.6(8)
BOX-BEAM HEADER SPANS
Headers Supporting One Floor, Roof and Ceiling (50 ksi steel)[a, b]

MEMBER DESIGNATION	GROUND SNOW LOAD (50 psf)					GROUND SNOW LOAD (70 psf)				
	Building width[c] (feet)					Building width[c] (feet)				
	24	28	32	36	40	24	28	32	36	40
2-350S162-33	—	—	—	—	—	—	—	—	—	—
2-350S162-43	2′-8″	—	—	—	—	—	—	—	—	—
2-350S162-54	3′-5″	3′-0″	2′-7″	2′-2″	—	2′-8″	2′-2″	—	—	—
2-350S162-68	4′-6″	4′-1″	3′-8″	3′-3″	2′-11″	3′-9″	3′-3″	2′-10″	2′-5″	2′-1″
2-350S162-97	5′-1″	4′-10″	4′-8″	4′-6″	4′-5″	4′-10″	4′-7″	4′-4″	4′-0″	3′-8″
2-550S162-33	2′-4″	—	—	—	—	—	—	—	—	—
2-550S162-43	3′-10″	3′-4″	2′-9″	2′-3″	—	2′-11″	2′-3″	—	—	—
2-550S162-54	5′-3″	3′-8″	4′-1″	3′-8″	3′-2″	4′-3″	3′-8″	3′-1″	2′-7″	2′-0″
2-550S162-68	6′-5″	5′-10″	5′-3″	4′-9″	4′-4″	5′-5″	4′-9″	4′-3″	3′-9″	3′-4″
2-550S162-97	7′-4″	7′-0″	6′-9″	6′-6″	6′-4″	6′-11″	6′-8″	6′-3″	5′-10″	5′-5″
2-800S162-33	1′-11″	1′-8″	—	—	—	—	—	—	—	—
2-800S162-43	4′-2″	3′-8″	3′-4″	2′-9″	2′-2″	3′-5″	2′-9″	—	—	—
2-800S162-54	6′-1″	5′-5″	4′-10″	4′-3″	3′-9″	4′-11″	4′-3″	3′-8″	3′-0″	2′-5″
2-800S162-68	7′-8″	6′-11″	6′-3″	5′-9″	5′-2″	6′-5″	5′-9″	5′-1″	4′-6″	4′-0″
2-800S162-97	9′-11″	9′-6″	9′-2″	8′-10″	8′-3″	9′-5″	8′-10″	8′-2″	7′-7″	7′-0″
2-1000S162-43	3′-4″	2′-11″	2′-7″	2′-5″	2′-2″	2′-8″	2′-5″	2′-2″	—	—
2-1000S162-54	6′-7″	5′-10″	5′-3″	4′-9″	4′-3″	5′-4″	4′-9″	4′-1″	3′-5″	2′-9″
2-1000S162-68	8′-8″	7′-10″	7′-2″	6′-6″	5′-11″	7′-4″	6′-6″	5′-9″	5′-1″	4′-6″
2-1000S162-97	11′-7″	10′-11″	10′-3″	9′-7″	9′-0″	10′-5″	9′-7″	8′-10″	8′-2″	7′-8″
2-1200S162-54	5′-6″	4′-10″	4′-4″	3′-11[2]	3′-7″	4′-5″	3′-11″	3′-6″	3′-2″	2′-11″
2-1200S162-68	9′-7″	8′-8″	7′-11″	7′-2″	6′-6″	8′-1″	7′-2″	6′-4″	5′-8″	5′-0″
2-1200S162-97	12′-11″	12′-2″	11′-6″	10′-8″	10′-0″	11′-8″	10′-9″	9′-11″	9′-2″	8′-6″

For SI: 1 inch = 25.4 mm, 1 foot = 304.8 mm, 1 pound per square foot = 0.0479kPa, 1 pound per square inch = 6.895 kPa.

a. Deflection criterion: *L*/360 for live loads, *L*/240 for total loads.

b. Design load assumptions:

Second floor dead load is 10 psf.
Roof/ceiling dead load is 12 psf.
Second floor live load is 30 psf.
Attic live load is 10 psf.

c. Building width is in the direction of horizontal framing members supported by the header.

TABLE R603.6(9)
BOX-BEAM HEADER SPANS
Headers Supporting Two Floors, Roof and Ceiling (33 ksi steel)[a]

MEMBER DESIGNATION	GROUND SNOW LOAD (20 psf)					GROUND SNOW LOAD (30 psf)				
	Building width[c] (feet)					Building width[c] (feet)				
	24	28	32	36	40	24	28	32	36	40
2-350S162-33	—	—	—	—	—	—	—	—	—	—
2-350S162-43	—	—	—	—	—	—	—	—	—	—
2-350S162-54	—	—	—	—	—	—	—	—	—	—
2-350S162-68	—	—	—	—	—	—	—	—	—	—
2-350S162-97	3′-1″	2′-8″	2′-3″	—	—	3′-1″	2′-7″	2′-2″	—	—
2-550S162-33	—	—	—	—	—	—	—	—	—	—
2-550S162-43	—	—	—	—	—	—	—	—	—	—
2-550S162-54	—	—	—	—	—	—	—	—	—	—
2-550S162-68	2′-9″	—	—	—	—	2′-8″	—	—	—	—
2-550S162-97	4′-8″	4′-1″	3′-7″	3′-2″	2′-9″	4′-7″	4′-0″	3′-6″	3′-1″	2′-8″
2-800S162-33	—	—	—	—	—	—	—	—	—	—
2-800S162-43	—	—	—	—	—	—	—	—	—	—
2-800S162-54	2′-1″	—	—	—	—	—	—	—	—	—
2-800S162-68	3′-8″	2′-9″	—	—	—	3′-7″	2′-8″	—	—	—
2-800S162-97	6′-3″	5′-6″	4′-11″	4′-4″	3′-9″	6′-2″	5′-5″	4′-10″	4′-3″	3′-9″
2-1000S162-43	—	—	—	—	—	—	—	—	—	—
2-1000S162-54	2′-5″	—	—	—	—	2′-3″	—	—	—	—
2-1000S162-68	4′-3″	3′-2″	2′-0″	—	—	4′-2″	3′-1″	—	—	—
2-1000S162-97	7′-5″	6′-7″	5′-10″	5′-2″	4′-7″	7′-4″	6′-6″	5′-9″	5′-1″	4′-6″
2-1200S162-54	2′-7″	—	—	—	—	2′-6″	—	—	—	—
2-1200S162-68	4′-8″	3′-6″	2′-2″	—	—	4′-7″	3′-5″	2′-0″	—	—
2-1200S162-97	8′-5″	7′-5″	6′-7″	5′-10″	5′-2″	8′-3″	7′-4″	6′-6″	5′-9″	5′-1″

For SI: 1 inch = 25.4 mm, 1 foot = 304.8 mm, 1 pound per square foot = 0.0479kPa, 1 pound per square inch = 6.895 kPa.

a. Deflection criterion: *L*/360 for live loads, *L*/240 for total loads.

b. Design load assumptions:
   Second floor dead load is 10 psf.
   Roof/ceiling dead load is 12 psf.
   Second floor live load is 40 psf.
   Third floor live load is 30 psf.
   Attic live load is 10 psf.

c. Building width is in the direction of horizontal framing members supported by the header.

TABLE R603.6(10)
BOX-BEAM HEADER SPANS
Headers Supporting Two Floors, Roof and Ceiling (50 ksi steel)[a, b]

MEMBER DESIGNATION	GROUND SNOW LOAD (20 psf)					GROUND SNOW LOAD (30 psf)				
	Building width[c] (feet)					Building width[c] (feet)				
	24	28	32	36	40	24	28	32	36	40
2-350S162-33	—	—	—	—	—	—	—	—	—	—
2-350S162-43	—	—	—	—	—	—	—	—	—	—
2-350S162-54	2′-5″	—	—	—	—	2′-4″	—	—	—	—
2-350S162-68	3′-6″	3′-0″	2′-6″	2′-1″	—	3′-5″	2′-11″	2′-6″	2′-0″	—
2-350S162-97	4′-9″	4′-6″	4′-1″	3′-8″	3′-4″	4′-8″	4′-5″	4′-0″	3′-8″	3′-4″
2-550S162-33	—	—	—	—	—	—	—	—	—	—
2-550S162-43	2′-7″	—	—	—	—	2′-6″	—	—	—	—
2-550S162-54	3′-11″	3′-3″	2′-8″	2′-0″	—	3′-10″	3′-3″	2′-7″	—	—
2-550S162-68	5′-1″	4′-5″	3′-10″	3′-3″	2′-9″	5′-0″	4′-4″	3′-9″	3′-3″	2′-9″
2-550S162-97	6′-10″	6′-5″	5′-10″	5′-5″	4′-11″	6′-9″	6′-4″	5′-10″	5′-4″	4′-11″
2-800S162-33	—	—	—	—	—	—	—	—	—	—
2-800S162-43	3′-1″	2′-3″	—	—	—	3′-0″	2′-2″	—	—	—
2-800S162-54	4′-7″	3′-10″	3′-1″	2′-5″	—	4′-6″	3′-9″	3′-0″	2′-4″	—
2-800S162-68	6′-0″	5′-3″	4′-7″	3′-11″	3′-4″	6′-0″	5′-2″	4′-6″	3′-11″	3′-3″
2-800S162-97	9′-2″	8′-4″	7′-8″	7′-0″	6′-6″	9′-1″	8′-3″	7′-7″	7′-0″	6′-5″
2-1000S162-43	2′-6″	2′-2″	—	—	—	2′-6″	2′-2″	—	—	—
2-1000S162-54	5′-0″	4′-4″	3′-6″	2′-9″	—	4′-11″	4′-3″	3′-5″	2′-7″	—
2-1000S162-68	6′-10″	6′-0″	5′-3″	4′-6″	3′-10″	6′-9″	5′-11″	5′-2″	4′-5″	3′-9″
2-1000S162-97	10′-0″	9′-1″	8′-3″	7′-8″	7′-0″	9′-10″	9′-0″	8′-3″	7′-7″	7′-0″
2-1200S162-54	4′-2″	3′-7″	3′-3″	2′-11″	—	4′-1″	3′-7″	3′-2″	2′-10″	—
2-1200S162-68	7′-7″	6′-7″	5′-9″	5′-0″	4′-2″	7′-6″	6′-6″	5′-8″	4′-10″	4′-1″
2-1200S162-97	11′-2″	10′-1″	9′-3″	8′-6″	7′-10″	11′-0″	10′-0″	9′-2″	9′-2″	7′-9″

For SI: 1 inch = 25.4 mm, 1 foot = 304.8 mm, 1 pound per square foot = 0.0479kPa, 1 pound per square inch = 6.895 kPa.

a. Deflection criterion: *L*/360 for live loads, *L*/240 for total loads.

b. Design load assumptions:
Second floor dead load is 10 psf.
Roof/ceiling dead load is 12 psf.
Second floor live load is 40 psf.
Third floor live load is 30 psf.
Attic live load is 10 psf.

c. Building width is in the direction of horizontal framing members supported by the header.

TABLE R603.6(11)
BOX-BEAM HEADER SPANS
Headers Supporting Two Floors, Roof and Ceiling (33 ksi steel)[a, b]

MEMBER DESIGNATION	GROUND SNOW LOAD (50 psf)					GROUND SNOW LOAD (70 psf)				
	Building width[c] (feet)					Building width[c] (feet)				
	24	28	32	36	40	24	28	32	36	40
2-350S162-33	—	—	—	—	—	—	—	—	—	—
2-350S162-43	—	—	—	—	—	—	—	—	—	—
2-350S162-54	—	—	—	—	—	—	—	—	—	—
2-350S162-68	—	—	—	—	—	—	—	—	—	—
2-350S162-97	2′-11″	2′-5″	2′-0″	—	—	2′-7″	2′-2″	—	—	—
2-550S162-33	—	—	—	—	—	—	—	—	—	—
2-550S162-43	—	—	—	—	—	—	—	—	—	—
2-550S162-54	—	—	—	—	—	—	—	—	—	—
2-550S162-68	2′-5″	—	—	—	—	—	—	—	—	—
2-550S162-97	4′-4″	3′-10″	3′-4″	2′-10″	2′-5″	4′-0″	3′-6″	3′-1″	2′-7″	2′-2″
2-800S162-33	—	—	—	—	—	—	—	—	—	—
2-800S162-43	—	—	—	—	—	—	—	—	—	—
2-800S162-54	—	—	—	—	—	—	—	—	—	—
2-800S162-68	3′-3″	2′-3″	—	—	—	2′-8″	—	—	—	—
2-800S162-97	5′-11″	5′-2″	4′-6″	4′-0″	3′-5″	5′-6″	4′-10″	4′-3″	3′-8″	3′-2″
2-1000S162-43	—	—	—	—	—	—	—	—	—	—
2-1000S162-54	—	—	—	—	—	—	—	—	—	—
2-1000S162-68	3′-9″	2′-7″	—	—	—	3′-1″	—	—	—	—
2-1000S162-97	7′-0″	6′-2″	5′-5″	4′-9″	4′-2″	6′-6″	5′-9″	5′-1″	4′-5″	3′-10″
2-1200S162-54	—	—	—	—	—	—	—	—	—	—
2-1200S162-68	4′-2″	2′-10″	—	—	—	3′-5″	2′-0″	—	—	—
2-1200S162-97	7′-11″	7′-0″	6′-2″	5′-5″	4′-8″	7′-4″	6′-6″	5′-9″	5′-0″	4′-4″

For SI: 1 inch = 25.4 mm, 1 foot = 304.8 mm, 1 pound per square foot = 0.0479kPa, 1 pound per square inch = 6.895 kPa.

a. Deflection criterion: *L*/360 for live loads, *L*/240 for total loads.

b. Design load assumptions:
Second floor dead load is 10 psf.
Roof/ceiling dead load is 12 psf.
Second floor live load is 40 psf.
Third floor live load is 30 psf.
Attic live load is 10 psf.

c. Building width is in the direction of horizontal framing members supported by the header

TABLE R603.6(12)
BOX-BEAM HEADER SPANS[a,b,c]
Headers Supporting Two Floors, Roof and Ceiling (50 ksi steel)[a,b]

MEMBER DESIGNATION	GROUND SNOW LOAD (50 psf)					GROUND SNOW LOAD (70 psf)				
	Building width[c] (feet)					Building width[c] (feet)				
	24	28	32	36	40	24	28	32	36	40
2-350S162-33	—	—	—	—	—	—	—	—	—	—
2-350S162-43	—	—	—	—	—	—	—	—	—	—
2-350S162-54	2′-2″	—	—	—	—	—	—	—	—	—
2-350S162-68	3′-3″	2′-9″	2′-3″	—	—	2′-11″	2′-5″	—	—	—
2-350S162-97	4′-6″	4′-3″	3′-10″	3′-6″	3′-2″	4′-3″	4′-0″	3′-7″	3′-3″	3′-0″
2-550S162-33	—	—	—	—	—	—	—	—	—	—
2-550S162-43	2′-3″	—	—	—	—	—	—	—	—	—
2-550S162-54	3′-7″	2′-11″	2′-3″	—	—	3′-3″	2′-7″	—	—	—
2-550S162-68	4′-9″	2′-1″	3′-6″	3′-0″	2′-5″	4′-4″	3′-9″	3′-2″	2′-8″	2′-1″
2-550S162-97	6′-5″	6′-1″	5′-7″	5′-1″	4′-8″	6′-3″	5′-10″	5′-4″	4′-10″	4′-5″
2-800S162-33	—	—	—	—	—	—	—	—	—	—
2-800S162-43	2′-8″	—	—	—	—	2′-2″	—	—	—	—
2-800S162-54	4′-3″	3′-5″	2′-8″	—	—	3′-9″	3′-0″	2′-3″	—	—
2-800S162-68	5′-8″	4′-11″	4′-2″	3′-7″	2′-11″	5′-3″	4′-6″	3′-10″	3′-3″	2′-7″
2-800S162-97	8′-9″	8′-0″	7′-3″	6′-8″	6′-2″	8′-4″	7′-7″	6′-11″	6′-4″	5′-10″
2-1000S162-43	2′-4″	2′-0″	—	—	—	2′-2″	—	—	—	—
2-1000S162-54	4′-8″	3′-11″	3′-1″	2′-2″	—	4′-3″	3′-5″	2′-7″	—	—
2-1000S162-68	6′-5″	5′-7″	4′-9″	4′-1″	3′-4″	5′-11″	5′-1″	4′-5″	3′-8″	2′-11″
2-1000S162-97	9′-6″	8′-8″	7′-11″	7′-3″	6′-8″	9′-0″	8′-3″	7′-6″	6′-11″	6′-4″
2-1200S162-54	3′-11″	3′-5″	3′-0″	2′-4″	—	3′-7″	3′-2″	2′-10″	—	—
2-1200S162-68	7′-1″	6′-2″	5′-3″	4′-6″	3′-8″	6′-6″	5′-8″	4′-10″	4′-0″	3′-3″
2-1200S162-97	10′-8″	9′-8″	8′-10″	8′-1″	7′-5″	10′-1″	9′-2″	8′-5″	7′-9″	7′-1″

For SI: 1 inch = 25.4 mm, 1 foot = 304.8 mm, 1 pound per square foot = 0.0479kPa, 1 pound per square inch = 6.895 kPa.

a. Deflection criterion: *L*/360 for live loads, *L*/240 for total loads.

b. Design load assumptions:
Second floor dead load is 10 psf.
Roof/ceiling dead load is 12 psf.
Second floor live load is 40 psf.
Third floor live load is 30 psf.
Attic live load is 10 psf.

c. Building width is in the direction of horizontal framing members supported by the header.

TABLE R603.6(13)
BACK-TO-BACK HEADER SPANS
Headers Supporting Roof and Ceiling Only (33 ksi steel)[a,b]

MEMBER DESIGNATION	GROUND SNOW LOAD (20 psf)					GROUND SNOW LOAD (30 psf)				
	Building width[c] (feet)					Building width[c] (feet)				
	24	28	32	36	40	24	28	32	36	40
2-350S162-33	2′-11″	2′-4″	—	—	—	2′-5″	—	—	—	—
2-350S162-43	4′-8″	3′-10″	3′-5″	3′-1″	2′-9″	3′-11″	3′-5″	3′-0″	2′-8″	2′-4″
2-350S162-54	5′-3″	4′-9″	4′-4″	4′-1″	3′-8″	4′-10″	4′-4″	4′-0″	3′-8″	3′-4″
2-350S162-68	6′-1″	5′-7″	5′-2″	4′-10″	4′-6″	5′-8″	5′-3″	4′-10″	4′-6″	4′-2″
2-350S162-97	7′-3″	6′-10″	6′-5″	6′-0″	5′-8″	6′-11″	6′-5″	6′-0″	5′-8″	5′-4″
2-550S162-33	4′-5″	3′-9″	3′-1″	2′-6″	—	3′-9″	3′-2″	2′-6″	—	—
2-550S162-43	6′-2″	5′-7″	5′-0″	4′-7″	4′-2″	5′-7″	5′-0″	4′-6″	4′-1″	3′-8″
2-550S162-54	7′-5″	6′-9″	6′-3″	5′-9″	5′-4″	6′-10″	6′-3″	5′-9″	5′-4″	4′-11″
2-550S162-68	6′-7″	7′-11″	7′-4″	6′-10″	6′-5″	8′-0″	7′-4″	6′-10″	6′-5″	6′-0″
2-550S162-97	10′-5″	9′-8″	9′-0″	8′-6″	8′-0″	9′-9″	9′-0″	8′-6″	8′-0″	7′-7″
2-800S162-33	4′-5″	3′-11″	3′-5″	3′-1″	2′-4″	3′-11″	3′-6″	3′-0″	2′-3″	—
2-800S162-43	7′-7″	6′-10″	6′-2″	5′-8″	5′-2″	6′-11″	6′-2″	5′-7″	5′-1″	4′-7″
2-800S162-54	9′-3″	8′-7″	7′-11″	7′-4″	6′-10″	8′-8″	7′-11″	7′-4″	6′-9″	6′-3″
2-800S162-68	10′-7″	9′-10″	9′-4″	8′-10″	8′-5″	9′-11″	9′-4″	8′-10″	8′-4″	7′-11″
2-800S162-97	13′-9″	12′-9″	12′-0″	11′-3″	10′-8″	12′-10″	12′-0″	11′-3″	10′-7″	10′-0″
2-1000S162-43	7′-10″	6′-10″	6′-1″	5′-6″	5′-0″	6′-11″	6′-1″	5′-5″	4′-11″	4′-6″
2-1000S162-54	10′-5″	9′-9″	9′-0″	8′-4″	7′-9″	9′-10″	9′-0″	8′-4″	7′-9″	7′-2″
2-1000S162-68	12′-1″	11′-3″	10′-8″	10′-1″	9′-7″	11′-4″	10′-8″	10′-1″	9′-7″	9′-1″
2-1000S162-97	15′-3″	14′-3″	13′-5″	12′-9″	12′-2″	14′-4″	13′-5″	12′-8″	12′-1″	11′-6″
2-1200S162-54	11′-6″	10′-9″	10′-0″	9′-0″	8′-2″	10′-10″	10′-0″	9′-0″	8′-1″	7′-4″
2-1200S162-68	13′-4″	12′-6″	11′-9″	11′-2″	10′-8″	12′-7″	11′-10″	11′-2″	10′-7″	10′-1″
2-1200S162-97	16′-8″	15′-7″	14′-8″	13′-11″	13′-3″	15′-8″	14′-8″	13′-11″	13′-2″	12′-7″

For SI: 1 inch = 25.4 mm, 1 foot = 304.8 mm, 1 pound per square foot = 0.0479kPa, 1 pound per square inch = 6.895 kPa.

a. Deflection criterion: *L*/360 for live loads, *L*/240 for total loads.

b. Design load assumptions:
  Second floor dead load is 12 psf.
  Attic live load is 10 psf.

c. Building width is in the direction of horizontal framing members supported by header.

TABLE R603.6(14)
BACK-TO-BACK HEADER SPANS
Headers Supporting Roof and Ceiling Only (50 ksi steel)[a,b]

MEMBER DESIGNATION	GROUND SNOW LOAD (20 psf)					GROUND SNOW LOAD (30 psf)				
	Building width[c] (feet)					Building width[c] (feet)				
	24	28	32	36	40	24	28	32	36	40
2-350S162-33	4′-2″	3′-8″	3′-3″	2′-10″	2′-6″	3′-8″	3′-3″	2′-10″	2′-5″	2′-1″
2-350S162-43	5′-5″	5′-0″	4′-6″	4′-2″	3′-10″	5′-0″	4′-7″	4′-2″	3′-10″	3′-6″
2-350S162-54	6′-2″	5′-10″	5′-8″	5′-4″	5′-0″	5′-11″	5′-8″	5′-4″	5′-0″	4′-8″
2-350S162-68	6′-7″	6′-3″	6′-0″	5′-10″	5′-8″	6′-4″	6′-1″	5′-10″	5′-8″	5′-6″
2-350S162-97	7′-3″	6′-11″	6′-8″	6′-5″	6′-3″	7′-0″	6′-8″	6′-5″	6′-3″	6′-0″
2-550S162-33	5′-10″	5′-3″	4′-8″	4′-3″	3′-9″	5′-3″	4′-9″	4′-2″	3′-9″	3′-3″
2-550S162-43	7′-9″	7′-2″	6′-7″	6′-1″	5′-8″	7′-3″	6′-7″	6′-1″	5′-8″	5′-3″
2-550S162-54	8′-9″	8′-5″	8′-1″	7′-9″	7′-5″	8′-6″	8′-1″	7′-9″	7′-5″	6′-11″
2-550S162-68	9′-5″	9′-0″	8′-8″	8′-4″	8′-1″	9′-1″	8′-8″	8′-4″	8′-1″	7′-10″
2-550S162-97	10′-5″	10′-0″	9′-7″	9′-3″	9′-0″	10′-0″	9′-7″	9′-3″	8′-11″	8′-8″
2-800S162-33	4′-5″	3′-11″	3′-5″	3′-1″	2′-10″	3′-11″	3′-6″	3′-1″	2′-9″	2′-6″
2-800S162-43	9′-1″	8′-5″	7′-8″	6′-11″	6′-3″	8′-6″	7′-8″	6′-10″	6′-2″	5′-8″
2-800S162-54	10′-10″	10′-2″	9′-7″	9′-1″	8′-8″	10′-2″	9′-7″	9′-0″	8′-7″	8′-1″
2-800S162-68	12′-8″	11′-10″	11′-2″	10′-7″	10′-1″	11′-11″	11′-2″	10′-7″	10′-0″	9′-7″
2-800S162-97	14′-2″	13′-6″	13′-0″	12′-7″	12′-2″	13′-8″	13′-1″	12′-7″	12′-2″	11′-9″
2-1000S162-43	7′-10″	6′-10″	6′-1″	5′-6″	5′-0″	6′-11″	6′-1″	5′-5″	4′-11″	4′-6″
2-1000S162-54	12′-3″	11′-5″	10′-9″	10′-3″	9′-9″	11′-6″	10′-9″	10′-2″	9′-8″	8′-11″
2-1000S162-68	14′-5″	13′-5″	12′-8″	12′-0″	11′-6″	13′-6″	12′-8″	12′-0″	11′-5″	10′-11″
2-1000S162-97	17′-1″	16′-4″	15′-8″	14′-11″	14′-3″	16′-5″	15′-9″	14′-10″	14′-1″	13′-6″
2-1200S162-54	12′-11″	11′-3″	10′-0″	9′-0″	8′-2″	11′-5″	10′-0″	9′-0″	8′-1″	7′-4″
2-1200S162-68	15′-11″	14′-10″	14′-0″	13′-4″	12′-8″	15′-0″	14′-0″	13′-3″	12′-7″	12′-0″
2-1200S162-97	19′-11″	18′-7″	17′-6″	16′-8″	15′-10″	18′-9″	17′-7″	16′-7″	15′-9″	15′-0″

For SI: 1 inch = 25.4 mm, 1 foot = 304.8 mm, 1 pound per square foot = 0.0479kPa, 1 pound per square inch = 6.895 kPa.

a. Deflection criterion: *L*/360 for live loads, *L*/240 for total loads.

b. Design load assumptions:
   Roof/ceiling dead load is 12 psf.
   Attic live load is 10 psf.

c. Building width is in the direction of horizontal framing members supported by the header.

TABLE R603.6(15)
BACK-TO-BACK HEADER SPANS
Headers Supporting Roof and Ceiling Only (33 ksi steel)[a, b]

MEMBER DESIGNATION	GROUND SNOW LOAD (50 psf)					GROUND SNOW LOAD (70 psf)				
	Building width[c] (feet)					Building width[c] (feet)				
	24	28	32	36	40	24	28	32	36	40
2-350S162-33	—	—	—	—	—	—	—	—	—	—
2-350S162-43	2′-6″	—	—	—	—	—	—	—	—	—
2-350S162-54	3′-6″	3′-1″	2′-8″	2′-4″	2′-0″	2′-7″	2′-1″	—	—	—
2-350S162-68	4′-4″	3′-11″	3′-7″	3′-3″	2′-11″	3′-5″	3′-0″	2′-8″	2′-4″	2′-1″
2-350S162-97	5′-5″	5′-0″	4′-8″	4′-6″	4′-1″	4′-6″	4′-2″	3′-10″	3′-6″	3′-3″
2-550S162-33	—	—	—	—	—	—	—	—	—	—
2-550S162-43	3′-10″	3′-3″	2′-9″	2′-2″	—	2′-6″	—	—	—	—
2-550S162-54	5′-1″	4′-7″	4′-1″	3′-8″	3′-4″	3′-11″	3′-5″	2′-11″	2′-6″	2′-0″
2-550S162-68	6′-2″	5′-8″	5′-2″	4′-9″	4′-5″	5′-0″	4′-6″	4′-1″	3′-9″	3′-4″
2-550S162-97	7′-9″	7′-2″	6′-8″	6′-3″	5′-11″	6′-6″	6′-0″	5′-7″	5′-2″	4′-10″
2-800S162-33	—	—	—	—	—	—	—	—	—	—
2-800S162-43	4′-10″	4′-1″	3′-6″	2′-11″	2′-3″	3′-3″	2′-5″	—	—	—
2-800S162-54	6′-6″	5′-10″	5′-3″	4′-9″	4′-4″	5′-1″	4′-6″	3′-11″	3′-4″	2′-10″
2-800S162-68	8′-1″	7′-5″	6′-10″	6′-4″	5′-11″	6′-8″	6′-1″	5′-6″	5′-0″	4′-7″
2-800S162-97	10′-3″	9′-7″	8′-11″	8′-5″	7′-11″	8′-8″	8′-0″	7′-6″	7′-0″	6′-7″
2-1000S162-43	4′-8″	4′-1″	3′-8″	3′-4″	2′-8″	3′-6″	2′-10″	—	—	—
2-1000S162-54	7′-5″	6′-8″	6′-1″	5′-6″	5′-0″	5′-10″	5′-1″	4′-6″	3′-11″	3′-4″
2-1000S162-68	9′-4″	8′-7″	7′-11″	7′-4″	6′-10″	7′-8″	7′-0″	6′-4″	5′-10″	5′-4″
2-1000S162-97	11′-9″	11′-0″	10′-5″	9′-11″	9′-5″	10′-3″	9′-7″	8′-11″	8′-4″	7′-10″
2-1200S162-54	7′-8″	6′-9″	6′-1″	5′-6″	5′-0″	5′-10″	5′-1″	4′-7″	4′-1″	3′-9″
2-1200S162-68	10′-4″	9′-6″	8′-10″	8′-2″	7′-7″	8′-7″	7′-9″	7′-1″	6′-6″	6′-0″
2-1200S162-97	12′-10″	12′-1″	11′-5″	10′-10″	10′-4″	11′-2″	10′-6″	9′-11″	9′-5″	9′-0″

For SI: 1 inch = 25.4 mm, 1 foot = 304.8 mm, 1 pound per square foot = 0.0479kPa, 1 pound per square inch = 6.895 kPa.

a. Deflection criterion: *L*/360 for live loads, *L*/240 for total loads.

b. Design load assumptions:
Roof/ceiling dead load is 12 psf.
Attic live load is 10 psf.

c. Building width is in the direction of horizontal framing members supported by the header.

TABLE R603.6(16)
BACK-TO-BACK HEADER SPANS
Headers Supporting Roof and Ceiling Only (50 ksi steel)[a, b]

MEMBER DESIGNATION	GROUND SNOW LOAD (50 psf) Building width[c] (feet) 24	28	32	36	40	GROUND SNOW LOAD (70 psf) Building width[c] (feet) 24	28	32	36	40
2-350S162-33	2′-3″	—	—	—	—	—	—	—	—	—
2-350S162-43	3′-8″	3′-3″	2′-10″	2′-6″	2′-2″	2′-8″	2′-3″	—	—	—
2-350S162-54	4′-9″	4′-4″	4′-0″	3′-8″	3′-8″	3′-10″	3′-5″	3′-1″	2′-9″	2′-5″
2-350S162-68	5′-7″	5′-4″	5′-2″	4′-11″	4′-7″	5′-1″	4′-8″	4′-3″	3′-11″	3′-8″
2-350S162-97	6′-2″	5′-11″	5′-8″	5′-6″	5′-4″	5′-8″	5′-5″	5′-3″	5′-0″	4′-11″
2-550S162-33	3′-6″	2′-10″	2′-3″	—	—	2′-0″	—	—	—	—
2-550S162-43	5′-5″	4′-10″	4′-4″	3′-11″	3′-6″	4′-2″	3′-8″	3′-2″	2′-8″	2′-3″
2-550S162-54	7′-2″	6′-6″	6′-0″	5′-7″	5′-2″	5′-10″	5′-3″	4′-10″	4′-5″	4′-0″
2-550S162-68	8′-0″	7′-8″	7′-3″	6′-11″	6′-6″	7′-2″	6′-7″	6′-1″	5′-8″	5′-4″
2-550S162-97	8′-11″	8′-6″	8′-2″	7′-11″	7′-8″	8′-1″	7′-9″	7′-6″	7′-2″	6′-11″
2-800S162-33	2′-8″	2′-4″	2′-1″	1′-11″	—	2′-0″	—	—	—	—
2-800S162-43	5′-10″	5′-2″	4′-7″	4′-2″	3′-10″	4′-5″	3′-11″	3′-6″	3′-2″	2′-9″
2-800S162-54	8′-4″	7′-8″	7′-1″	6′-7″	6′-1″	6′-10″	6′-3″	5′-8″	5′-2″	4′-9″
2-800S162-68	9′-9″	9′-2″	8′-8″	8′-3″	7′-10″	8′-6″	7′-11″	7′-4″	6′-10″	6′-5″
2-800S162-97	12′-1″	11′-7″	11′-2″	10′-8″	10′-2″	11′-0″	10′-4″	9′-9″	9′-3″	8′-10″
2-1000S162-43	4′-8″	4′-1″	2′-8″	3′-4″	3′-0″	3′-6″	10′-1″	2′-9″	2′-6″	2′-3″
2-1000S162-54	9′-3″	8′-2″	7′-3″	6′-7″	6′-0″	7′-0″	6′-2″	5′-6″	5′-0″	4′-6″
2-1000S162-68	11′-1″	10′-5″	9′-10″	9′-4″	8′-11″	9′-8″	9′-1″	8′-5″	7′-10″	7′-4″
2-1000S162-97	13′-9″	12′-11″	12′-2″	11′-7″	11′-1″	11′-11″	11′-3″	10′-7″	10′-1″	9′-7″
2-1200S162-54	7′-8″	6′-9″	6′-1″	5′-6″	5′-0″	5′-10″	5′-1″	4′-7″	4′-1″	3′-9″
2-1200S162-68	12′-3″	11′-6″	10′-11″	10′-4″	9′-11″	10′-8″	10′-0″	9′-2″	8′-4″	7′-7″
2-1200S162-97	15′-4″	14′-5″	13′-7″	12′-11″	12′-4″	13′-4″	12′-6″	11′-10″	11′-3″	10′-9″

For SI: 1 inch = 25.4 mm, 1 foot = 304.8 mm, 1 pound per square foot = 0.0479kPa, 1 pound per square inch = 6.895 kPa.

a. Deflection criterion: *L*/360 for live loads, *L*/240 for total loads.

b. Design load assumptions:
Roof/ceiling dead load is 12 psf.
Attic live load is 10 psf.

c. Building width is in the direction of horizontal framing members supported by the header

TABLE R603.6(17)
BACK-TO-BACK HEADER SPANS
Headers Supporting One Floor, Roof and Ceiling (33 ksi steel)[a, b]

MEMBER DESIGNATION	GROUND SNOW LOAD (20 psf)					GROUND SNOW LOAD (30 psf)				
	Building width[c] (feet)					Building width[c] (feet)				
	24	28	32	36	40	24	28	32	36	40
2-350S162-33	—	—	—	—	—	—	—	—	—	—
2-350S162-43	2′-2″	—	—	—	—	2′-1″	—	—	—	—
2-350S162-54	3′-3″	2′-9″	2′-5″	2′-0″	—	3′-2″	2′-9″	2′-4″	—	—
2-350S162-68	4′-4″	3′-8″	3′-3″	2′-11″	2′-8″	4′-0″	3′-7″	3′-2″	2′-11″	2′-7″
2-350S162-97	5′-2″	4′-9″	4′-4″	4′-1″	3′-9″	5′-1″	4′-8″	4′-4″	4′-0″	3′-9″
2-550S162-33	—	—	—	—	—	—	—	—	—	—
2-550S162-43	3′-6″	2′-10″	2′-3″	—	—	3′-5″	2′-9″	2′-2″	—	—
2-550S162-54	4′-9″	4′-2″	3′-9″	3′-3″	2′-10″	4′-8″	4′-1″	3′-8″	3′-2″	2′-9″
2-550S162-68	5′-10″	5′-3″	4′-10″	4′-5″	4′-1″	5′-9″	5′-3″	4′-9″	4′-4″	4′-0″
2-550S162-97	7′-4″	6′-9″	6′-4″	5′-11″	5′-6″	7′-3″	6′-9″	6′-3″	5′-10″	5′-5″
2-800S162-33	—	—	—	—	—	—	—	—	—	—
2-800S162-43	4′-4″	3′-8″	2′-11″	2′-3″	—	4′-3″	3′-6″	2′-10″	2′-1″	—
2-800S162-54	6′-1″	5′-5″	4′-10″	4′-4″	3′-10″	6′-0″	5′-4″	4′-9″	4′-3″	3′-9″
2-800S162-68	7′-8″	7′-0″	6′-5″	5′-11″	5′-5″	7′-7″	6′-11″	6′-4″	5′-10″	5′-4″
2-800S162-97	9′-10″	9′-1″	8′-5″	7′-11″	7′-5″	9′-8″	8′-11″	8′-4″	7′-10″	7′-4″
2-1000S162-43	4′-4″	3′-9″	3′-4″	2′-8″	—	4′-3″	3′-8″	3′-3″	2′-6″	—
2-1000S162-54	6′-11″	6′-2″	5′-6″	5′-0″	4′-5″	6′-10″	6′-1″	5′-5″	4′-10″	4′-4″
2-1000S162-68	8′-10″	8′-1″	7′-5″	6′-10″	6′-4″	8′-8″	7′-11″	7′-3″	6′-8″	6′-2″
2-1000S162-97	11′-3″	10′-7″	9′-11″	9′-5″	8′-10″	11′-2″	10′-5″	9′-10″	9′-3″	8′-9″
2-1200S162-54	7′-1″	6′-2″	5′-6″	5′-0″	4′-6″	6′-11″	6′-1″	5′-5″	4′-10″	4′-5″
2-1200S162-68	9′-10″	9′-0″	8′-3″	7′-7″	7′-0″	9′-8″	8′-10″	8′-1^{11}	7′-6″	6′-11″
2-1200S162-97	12′-4″	11′-7″	10′-11″	10′-4″	9′-10″	12′-3″	11′-5″	10′-9″	10′-3″	9′-9″

For SI: 1 inch = 25.4 mm, 1 foot = 304.8 mm, 1 pound per square foot = 0.0479kPa, 1 pound per square inch = 6.895 kPa.

a. Deflection criterion: *L*/360 for live loads, *L*/240 for total loads.

b. Design load assumptions:
   Second floor dead load is 10 psf.
   Roof/ceiling dead load is 12 psf.
   Second floor live load is 30 psf.
   Attic live load is 10 psf.

c. Building width is in the direction of horizontal framing members supported by the header.

TABLE R603.6(18)
BACK-TO-BACK HEADER SPANS
Headers Supporting One Floor, Roof and Ceiling (50 ksi steel)[a, b]

MEMBER DESIGNATION	GROUND SNOW LOAD (20 psf)					GROUND SNOW LOAD (30 psf)				
	Building width[c] (feet)					Building width[c] (feet)				
	24	28	32	36	40	24	28	32	36	40
2-350S162-33	—	—	—	—	—	—	—	—	—	—
2-350S162-43	3′-4″	2′-11″	2′-6″	2′-2″	—	3′-3″	2′-10″	2′-5″	2′-1″	—
2-350S162-54	4′-6″	4′-1″	3′-8″	3′-4″	3′-0″	4′-5″	4′-0″	3′-7″	3′-3″	2′-11″
2-350S162-68	5′-0″	4′-9″	4′-7″	4′-5″	4′-3″	4′-11″	4′-8″	4′-6″	4′-4″	4′-2″
2-350S162-97	5′-6″	5′-3″	5′-1″	4′-11″	4′-9″	5′-5″	5′-2″	5′-0″	4′-10″	4′-8″
2-550S162-33	3′-1″	2′-5″	—	—	—	3′-0″	2′-3″	—	—	—
2-550S162-43	5′-1″	4′-6″	4′-0″	3′-6″	3′-1″	4′-11″	4′-5″	3′-11″	3′-5″	3′-0″
2-550S162-54	6′-8″	6′-2″	5′-7″	5′-2″	4′-9″	6′-6″	6′-0″	5′-6″	5′-1″	4′-8″
2-550S162-68	7′-2″	6′-10″	6′-7″	6′-4″	6′-1″	7′-0″	6′-9″	6′-6″	6′-3″	6′-0″
2-550S162-97	7′-11″	7′-7″	7′-3″	7′-0″	6′-10″	7′-9″	7′-5″	7′-2″	6′-11″	6′-9″
2-800S162-33	2′-5″	2′-2″	1′-11″	—	—	2′-5″	2′-1″	1′-10″	—	—
2-800S162-43	5′-5″	4′-9″	4′-3″	3′-9″	3′-5″	5′-3″	4′-8″	4′-1″	3′-9″	3′-5″
2-800S162-54	7′-11″	7′-2″	6′-7″	6′-1″	5′-7″	7′-9″	7′-1″	6′-6″	6′-0″	5′-6″
2-800S162-68	9′-5″	8′-9″	8′-3″	7′-9″	7′-4″	9′-3″	8′-8″	8′-2″	7′-8″	7′-3″
2-800S162-97	10′-9″	10′-3″	9′-11″	9′-7″	9′-3″	10′-7″	10′-1″	9′-9″	9′-5″	9′-1″
2-1000S162-43	4′-4″	3′-9″	3′-4″	3′-0″	2′-9″	4′-3″	3′-8″	3′-3″	2′-11″	2′-8″
2-1000S162-54	8′-6″	7′-5″	6′-8″	6′-0″	5′-5″	8′-4″	7′-4″	6′-6″	5′-10″	5′-4″
2-1000S162-68	10′-8″	10′-0″	9′-5″	8′-11″	8′-4″	10′-7″	9′-10″	9′-4″	8′-9″	8′-3″
2-1000S162-97	12′-11″	12′-4″	11′-8″	11′-1″	10′-6″	12′-9″	12′-2″	11′-6″	10′-11″	10′-5″
2-1200S162-54	7′-1″	6′-2″	5′-6″	5′-0″	4′-6″	6′-11″	6′-1″	5′-5″	4′-10″	4′-5″
2-1200S162-68	11′-9″	11′-0″	10′-5″	9′-10″	9′-1″	11′-8″	10′-11″	10′-3″	9′-9″	8′-11″
2-1200S162-97	14′-9″	13′-9″	13′-0″	12′-4″	11′-9″	14′-7″	13′-8″	12′-10″	12′-3″	11′-8″

For SI: 1 inch = 25.4 mm, 1 foot = 304.8 mm, 1 pound per square foot = 0.0479kPa, 1 pound per square inch = 6.895 kPa.

a. Deflection criterion: *L*/360 for live loads, *L*/240 for total loads.

b. Design load assumptions:
   Second floor dead load is 10 psf.
   Roof/ceiling dead load is 12 psf.
   Second floor live load is 30 psf.
   Attic live load is 10 psf.

c. Building width is in the direction of horizontal framing members supported by the header

TABLE R603.6(19)
BACK-TO-BACK HEADER SPANS
Headers Supporting One Floor, Roof and Ceiling (33 ksi steel)[a, b]

MEMBER DESIGNATION	GROUND SNOW LOAD (50 psf)					GROUND SNOW LOAD (70 psf)				
	Building width[c] (feet)					Building width[c] (feet)				
	24	28	32	36	40	24	28	32	36	40
2-350S162-33	—	—	—	—	—	—	—	—	—	—
2-350S162-43	—	—	—	—	—	—	—	—	—	—
2-350S162-54	2′-4″	—	—	—	—	—	—	—	—	—
2-350S162-68	3′-3″	2′-10″	2′-6″	2′-2″	—	2′-7″	2′-2″	—	—	—
2-350S162-97	4′-4″	4′-0″	3′-8″	3′-4″	3′-1″	3′-9″	3′-4″	3′-1″	2′-9″	2′-6″
2-550S162-33	—	—	—	—	—	—	—	—	—	—
2-550S162-43	2′-2″	—	—	—	—	—	—	—	—	—
2-550S162-54	3′-8″	3′-2″	2′-8″	2′-3″	—	2′-10″	2′-3″	—	—	—
2-550S162-68	4′-9″	4′-4″	3′-11″	3′-6″	3′-2″	4′-0″	3′-6″	3′-1″	2′-9″	2′-4″
2-550S162-97	6′-3″	5′-9″	5′-4″	5′-0″	4′-8″	5′-6″	5′-0″	4′-7″	4′-3″	3′-11″
2-800S162-33	—	—	—	—	—	—	—	—	—	—
2-800S162-43	2′-11″	2′-0″	—	—	—	—	—	—	—	—
2-800S162-54	4′-9″	4′-2″	3′-7″	3′-1″	2′-7″	3′-9″	3′-1″	2′-5″	—	—
2-800S162-68	6′-4″	5′-9″	5′-3″	4′-9″	4′-4″	5′-4″	4′-9″	4′-3″	3′-10″	3′-4″
2-800S162-97	8′-5″	7′-9″	7′-3″	6′-9″	6′-4″	7′-4″	6′-9″	6′-3″	5′-10″	5′-5″
2-1000S162-43	3′-4″	2′-5″	—	—	—	—	—	—	—	—
2-1000S162-54	5′-6″	4′-10″	4′-2″	3′-7″	3′-0″	4′-4″	3′-7″	2′-11″	2′-2″	—
2-1000S162-68	7′-4″	6′-8″	6′-1″	5′-7″	5′-1″	6′-3″	5′-7″	5′-0″	4′-5″	4′-0″
2-1000S162-97	9′-11″	8′-3″	8′-7″	8′-1″	7′-7″	8′-9″	8′-1″	7′-6″	7′-0″	6′-6″
2-1200S162-54	5′-6″	4′-10″	4′-4″	3′-11″	3′-5″	4′-5″	3′-11″	3′-3″	2′-6″	—
2-1200S162-68	8′-2″	7′-5″	6′-9″	6′-3″	5′-8″	6′-11″	6′-3″	5′-7″	5′-0″	4′-6″
2-1200S162-97	10′-10″	10′-2″	9′-8″	9′-2″	8′-7″	9′-9″	9′-2″	8′-6″	7′-11″	7′-5″

For SI: 1 inch = 25.4 mm, 1 foot = 304.8 mm, 1 pound per square foot = 0.0479kPa, 1 pound per square inch = 6.895 kPa.

a. Deflection criterion: *L*/360 for live loads, *L*/240 for total loads.

b. Design load assumptions:
Second floor dead load is 10 psf.
Roof/ceiling dead load is 12 psf.
Second floor live load is 30 psf.
Attic live load is 10 psf.

c. Building width is in the direction of horizontal framing members supported by the header.

TABLE R603.6(20)
BACK-TO-BACK HEADER SPANS
Headers Supporting One Floor, Roof and Ceiling (50 ksi steel)[a, b]

MEMBER DESIGNATION	GROUND SNOW LOAD (50 psf)					GROUND SNOW LOAD (70 psf)				
	Building width[c] (feet)					Building width[c] (feet)				
	24	28	32	36	40	24	28	32	36	40
2-350S162-33	—	—	—	—	—	—	—	—	—	—
2-350S162-43	2′-6″	2′-0″	—	—	—	—	—	—	—	—
2-350S162-54	3′-8″	3′-3″	2′-11″	2′-7″	2′-3″	3′-0″	2′-7″	2′-2″	—	—
2-350S162-68	4′-7″	4′-5″	4′-1″	3′-9″	3′-6″	4′-2″	3′-9″	3′-5″	3′-1″	2′-10″
2-350S162-97	5′-1″	4′-10″	4′-8″	4′-6″	4′-5″	4′-10″	4′-7″	4′-5″	4′-3″	4′-1″
2-550S162-33	—	—	—	—	—	—	—	—	—	—
2-550S162-43	3′-11″	3′-5″	2′-11″	2′-5″	—	3′-0″	2′-5″	—	—	—
2-550S162-54	5′-7″	5′-0″	4′-7″	4′-2″	3′-9″	4′-8″	4′-2″	3′-8″	3′-3″	2′-11″
2-550S162-68	6′-7″	6′-4″	5′-11″	5′-6″	5′-1″	6′-0″	5′-6″	5′-0″	4′-7″	4′-3″
2-550S162-97	7′-4″	7′-0″	6′-9″	6′-6″	6′-4″	6′-11″	6′-8″	6′-5″	6′-2″	6′-0″
2-800S162-33	1′-11″	—	—	—	—	—	—	—	—	—
2-800S162-43	4′-2″	3′-8″	3′-4″	3′-0″	2′-6″	3′-5″	3′-0″	2′-4″	—	—
2-800S162-54	6′-7″	5′-11″	5′-5″	4′-11″	4′-6″	5′-6″	4′-11″	4′-5″	3′-11″	3′-6″
2-800S162-68	8′-3″	7′-8″	7′-1″	6′-8″	6′-2″	7′-3″	6′-7″	6′-1″	5′-7″	5′-2″
2-800S162-97	9′-11″	9′-6″	9′-2″	8′-10″	8′-7″	9′-5″	9′-0″	8′-7″	8′-2″	7′-9″
2-1000S162-43	3′-4″	2′-11″	2′-7″	2′-5″	2′-2″	2′-8″	2′-5″	2′-2″	1′-11″	—
2-1000S162-54	6′-7″	5′-10″	5′-3″	4′-9″	4′-4″	5′-4″	4′-9″	4′-3″	3′-10″	3′-6″
2-1000S162-68	9′-4″	8′-9″	8′-1″	7′-7″	7′-1″	8′-3″	7′-7″	6′-11″	6′-5″	5′-11″
2-1000S162-97	11′-7″	10′-11″	10′-4″	9′-10″	9′-5″	10′-5″	9′-10″	9′-3″	8′-10″	8′-5″
2-1200S162-54	5′-6″	4′-10″	4′-4″	3′-11″	3′-7″	4′-5″	3′-11″	3′-6″	3′-2″	2′-11″
2-1200S162-68	10′-4″	9′-8″	8′-8″	7′-11″	7′-2″	8′-11″	7′-11″	7′-1″	6′-5″	5′-10″
2-1200S162-97	12′-11″	12′-2″	11′-6″	11′-0″	10′-6″	11′-8″	11′-0″	10′-5″	9′-10″	9′-5″

For SI: 1 inch = 25.4 mm, 1 foot = 304.8 mm, 1 pound per square foot = 0.0479kPa, 1 pound per square inch = 6.895 kPa.

a. Deflection criterion: *L*/360 for live loads, *L*/240 for total loads.

b. Design load assumptions:
Second floor dead load is 10 psf.
Roof/ceiling dead load is 12 psf.
Second floor live load is 30 psf.
Attic live load is 10 psf.

c. Building width is in the direction of horizontal framing members supported by the header.

TABLE R603.6(21)
BACK-TO-BACK HEADER SPANS
Headers Supporting Two Floors, Roof and Ceiling (33 ksi steel)[a, b]

MEMBER DESIGNATION	GROUND SNOW LOAD (20 psf)					GROUND SNOW LOAD (30 psf)				
	Building width[c] (feet)					Building width[c] (feet)				
	24	28	32	36	40	24	28	32	36	40
2-350S162-33	—	—	—	—	—	—	—	—	—	—
2-350S162-43	—	—	—	—	—	—	—	—	—	—
2-350S162-54	—	—	—	—	—	—	—	—	—	—
2-350S162-68	2′-5″	—	—	—	—	2′-4″	—	—	—	—
2-350S162-97	3′-6″	3′-2″	2′-10″	2′-6″	2′-3″	3′-6″	3′-1″	2′-9″	2′-6″	2′-3″
2-550S162-33	—	—	—	—	—	—	—	—	—	—
2-550S162-43	—	—	—	—	—	—	—	—	—	—
2-550S162-54	2′-6″	—	—	—	—	2′-5″	—	—	—	—
2-550S162-68	3′-9″	3′-3″	2′-9″	2′-4″	—	3′-8″	3′-2″	2′-9″	2′-4″	—
2-550S162-97	5′-3″	4′-9″	4′-4″	3′-11″	3′-8″	5′-2″	4′-8″	4′-3″	3′-11″	3′-7″
2-800S162-33	—	—	—	—	—	—	—	—	—	—
2-800S162-43	—	—	—	—	—	—	—	—	—	—
2-800S162-54	3′-5″	2′-8″	—	—	—	3′-4″	2′-7″	—	—	—
2-800S162-68	5′-1″	4′-5″	3′-11″	3′-4″	2′-11″	5′-0″	4′-4″	3′-10″	3′-4″	2′-10″
2-800S162-97	7′-0″	6′-5″	5′-11″	5′-5″	5′-0″	7′-0″	6′-4″	5′-10″	5′-5″	5′-0″
2-1000S162-43	—	—	—	—	—	—	—	—	—	—
2-1000S162-54	3′-11″	3′-1″	2′-3″	—	—	3′-10″	3′-0″	2′-2″	—	—
2-1000S162-68	5′-10″	5′-2″	4′-6″	4′-0″	3′-5″	5′-9″	5′-1″	4′-6″	3′-11″	3′-4″
2-1000S162-97	8′-5″	7′-8″	7′-1″	6′-6″	6′-1″	8′-4″	7′-7″	7′-0″	6′-6″	6′-0″
2-1200S162-54	4′-2″	3′-6″	2′-7″	—	—	4′-1″	3′-5″	2′-6″	—	—
2-1200S162-68	6′-6″	5′-9″	5′-1″	4′-6″	3′-11″	6′-6″	5′-8″	5′-0″	4′-5″	3′-10″
2-1200S162-97	9′-5″	8′-8″	8′-0″	7′-5″	6′-11″	9′-5″	8′-7″	7′-11″	7′-4″	6′-10″

For SI: 1 inch = 25.4 mm, 1 foot = 304.8 mm, 1 pound per square foot = 0.0479kPa, 1 pound per square inch = 6.895 kPa.

a. Deflection criterion: *L*/360 for live loads, *L*/240 for total loads.

b. Design load assumptions:
 Second floor dead load is 10 psf.
 Roof/ceiling dead load is 12 psf.
 Second floor live load is 40 psf.
 Third floor live load is 30 psf.
 Attic live load is 10 psf.

c. Building width is in the direction of horizontal framing members supported by the header.

TABLE R603.6(22)
BACK-TO-BACK HEADER SPANS
Headers Supporting Two Floors, Roof and Ceiling (50 ksi steel)[a, b]

MEMBER DESIGNATION	GROUND SNOW LOAD (20 psf)					GROUND SNOW LOAD (30 psf)				
	Building width[c] (feet)					Building width[c] (feet)				
	24	28	32	36	40	24	28	32	36	40
2-350S162-33	—	—	—	—	—	—	—	—	—	—
2-350S162-43	—	—	—	—	—	—	—	—	—	—
2-350S162-54	2′-9″	2′-3″	—	—	—	2′-8″	2′-3″	—	—	—
2-350S162-68	3′-11″	3′-6″	3′-2″	2′-10″	2′-6″	3′-11″	3′-6″	3′-1″	2′-9″	2′-6″
2-350S162-97	4′-9″	4′-6″	4′-4″	4′-1″	3′-10″	4′-8″	4′-6″	4′-4″	4′-1″	3′-9″
2-550S162-33	—	—	—	—	—	—	—	—	—	—
2-550S162-43	2′-9″	2′-0″	—	—	—	2′-8″	—	—	—	—
2-550S162-54	4′-5″	3′-10″	3′-4″	2′-11″	2′-5″	4′-4″	3′-9″	3′-3″	2′-10″	2′-5″
2-550S162-68	5′-8″	5′-2″	4′-8″	4′-3″	3′-11″	5′-8″	5′-1″	4′-8″	4′-3″	3′-10″
2-550S162-97	6′-10″	6′-6″	6′-3″	6′-0″	5′-7″	6′-9″	6′-5″	6′-3″	5′-11″	5′-6″
2-800S162-33	—	—	—	—	—	—	—	—	—	—
2-800S162-43	3′-2″	2′-7″	—	—	—	3′-1″	2′-6″	—	—	—
2-800S162-54	5′-2″	4′-7″	4′-0″	3′-6″	3′-0″	5′-2″	4′-6″	3′-11″	3′-5″	2′-11″
2-800S162-68	6′-11″	6′-3″	5′-8″	5′-2″	4′-9″	6′-10″	6′-2″	5′-7″	5′-2″	4′-8″
2-800S162-97	9′-3″	8′-8″	8′-3″	7′-9″	7′-4″	9′-2″	8′-8″	8′-2″	7′-9″	7′-4″
2-1000S162-43	2′-6″	2′-2″	2′-0″	—	—	2′-6″	2′-2″	1′-11″	—	—
2-1000S162-54	5′-0″	4′-4″	3′-11″	3′-6″	3′-2″	4′-11″	4′-4″	3′-10″	3′-6″	3′-2″
2-1000S162-68	7′-10″	7′-2″	6′-6″	5′-11″	5′-6″	7′-9″	7′-1″	6′-5″	5′-11″	5′-5″
2-1000S162-97	10′-1″	9′-5″	8′-11″	8′-6″	8′-0″	10′-0″	9′-5″	8′-10″	8′-5″	7′-11″
2-1200S162-54	—	—	—	—	—	—	—	—	—	—
2-1200S162-68	7′-4″	6′-8″	6′-1″	5′-6″	5′-1″	7′-3″	6′-7″	6′-0″	5′-6″	5′-0″
2-1200S162-97	9′-5″	8′-8″	8′-1″	7′-6″	7′-1″	9′-4″	8′-8″	8′-0″	7′-6″	7′-0″

For SI: 1 inch = 25.4 mm, 1 foot = 304.8 mm, 1 pound per square foot = 0.0479kPa, 1 pound per square inch = 6.895 kPa.

a. Deflection criterion: *L*/360 for live loads, *L*/240 for total loads.

b. Design load assumptions:
Second floor dead load is 10 psf.
Roof/ceiling dead load is 12 psf.
Second floor live load is 40 psf.
Third floor live load is 30 psf.
Attic live load is 10 psf.

c. Building width is in the direction of horizontal framing members supported by the header

TABLE R603.6(23)
BACK-TO-BACK HEADER SPANS
Headers Supporting Two Floors, Roof and Ceiling (33 ksi steel)[a, b]

MEMBER DESIGNATION	GROUND SNOW LOAD (50 psf)					GROUND SNOW LOAD (70 psf)				
	Building width[c] (feet)					Building width[c] (feet)				
	24	28	32	36	40	24	28	32	36	40
2-350S162-33	—	—	—	—	—	—	—	—	—	—
2-350S162-43	—	—	—	—	—	—	—	—	—	—
2-350S162-54	—	—	—	—	—	—	—	—	—	—
2-350S162-68	2′-2″	—	—	—	—	—	—	—	—	—
2-350S162-97	3′-3″	3′-0″	2′-8″	2′-4″	2′-1″	3′-1″	2′-9″	2′-6″	2′-2″	—
2-550S162-33	—	—	—	—	—	—	—	—	—	—
2-550S162-43	—	—	—	—	—	—	—	—	—	—
2-550S162-54	2′-2″	—	—	—	—	—	—	—	—	—
2-550S162-68	3′-6″	3′-0″	2′-6″	2′-1″	—	3′-2″	2′-9″	2′-3″	—	—
2-550S162-97	5′-0″	4′-6″	4′-1″	3′-9″	3′-5″	4′-8″	4′-3″	3′-11″	3′-7″	3′-3″
2-800S162-33	—	—	—	—	—	—	—	—	—	—
2-800S162-43	—	—	—	—	—	—	—	—	—	—
2-800S162-54	3′-0″	2′-3″	—	—	—	2′-7″	—	—	—	—
2-800S162-68	4′-9″	4′-2″	3′-7″	3′-1″	2′-7″	4′-5″	3′-10″	3′-3″	2′-9″	2′-3″
2-800S162-97	6′-9″	6′-1″	5′-7″	5′-2″	4′-9″	6′-4″	5′-10″	5′-4″	4′-11″	4′-7″
2-1000S162-43	—	—	—	—	—	—	—	—	—	—
2-1000S162-54	3′-6″	2′-8″	—	—	—	3′-1″	2′-2″	—	—	—
2-1000S162-68	5′-6″	4′-10″	4′-2″	3′-7″	3′-1″	5′-1″	4′-6″	3′-10″	3′-4″	2′-9″
2-1000S162-97	8′-0″	7′-4″	6′-9″	6′-3″	5′-9″	7′-7″	7′-0″	6′-5″	5′-11″	5′-6″
2-1200S162-54	3′-11″	3′-0″	2′-0″	—	—	3′-5″	2′-6″	—	—	—
2-1200S162-68	6′-2″	5′-5″	4′-9″	4′-1″	3′-6″	5′-9″	5′-0″	4′-4″	3′-9″	3′-2″
2-1200S162-97	9′-1″	8′-4″	7′-8″	7′-1″	6′-7″	8′-8″	7′-11″	7′-4″	6′-9″	6′-3″

For SI: 1 inch = 25.4 mm, 1 foot = 304.8 mm, 1 pound per square foot = 0.0479kPa, 1 pound per square inch = 6.895 kPa.

a. Deflection criterion: *L*/360 for live loads, *L*/240 for total loads.

b. Design load assumptions:
 Second floor dead load is 10 psf.
 Roof/ceiling dead load is 12 psf.
 Second floor live load is 40 psf.
 Third floor live load is 30 psf.
 Attic live load is 10 psf.

c. Building width is in the direction of horizontal framing members supported by the header.

TABLE R603.6(24)
BACK-TO-BACK HEADER SPANS
Headers Supporting Two Floors, Roof and Ceiling (50 ksi steel)[a, b]

MEMBER DESIGNATION	GROUND SNOW LOAD (50 psf)					GROUND SNOW LOAD (70 psf)				
	Building width[c] (feet)					Building width[c] (feet)				
	24	28	32	36	40	24	28	32	36	40
2-350S162-33	—	—	—	—	—	—	—	—	—	—
2-350S162-43	—	—	—	—	—	—	—	—	—	—
2-350S162-54	2′-6″	2′-1″	—	—	—	2′-3″	—	—	—	—
2-350S162-68	3′-9″	3′-4″	2′-11″	2′-7″	2′-4″	3′-6″	3′-1″	2′-9″	2′-5″	2′-2″
2-350S162-97	4′-6″	4′-4″	4′-2″	3′-11″	3′-8″	4′-4″	4′-2″	4′-0″	3′-9″	3′-6″
2-550S162-33	—	—	—	—	—	—	—	—	—	—
2-550S162-43	2′-5″	—	—	—	—	—	—	—	—	—
2-550S162-54	4′-1″	3′-7″	3′-1″	2′-7″	2′-2″	3′-10″	3′-3″	2′-10″	2′-4″	—
2-550S162-68	5′-5″	4′-11″	4′-5″	4′-0″	3′-8″	5′-1″	4′-7″	4′-2″	3′-10″	3′-5″
2-550S162-97	6′-5″	6′-2″	5′-11″	5′-9″	5′-4″	6′-3″	6′-0″	5′-9″	5′-6″	5′-2″
2-800S162-33	—	—	—	—	—	—	—	—	—	—
2-800S162-43	2′-11″	2′-2″	—	—	—	2′-6″	—	—	—	—
2-800S162-54	4′-11″	4′-3″	3′-8″	3′-2″	2′-8″	4′-6″	3′-11″	3′-5″	2′-11″	2′-4″
2-800S162-68	6′-7″	5′-11″	5′-4″	4′-11″	4′-6″	6′-2″	5′-7″	5′-1″	4′-8″	4′-3″
2-800S162-97	8′-9″	8′-5″	7′-11″	7′-6″	7′-0″	8′-5″	8′-1″	7′-9″	7′-3″	6′-10″
2-1000S162-43	2′-4″	2′-1″	—	—	—	2′-2″	1′-11″	—	—	—
2-1000S162-54	4′-8″	4′-1″	3′-8″	3′-3″	3′-0″	4′-4″	3′-10″	3′-5″	3′-1″	2′-9″
2-1000S162-68	7′-6″	6′-9″	6′-2″	5′-8″	5′-2″	7′-1″	6′-5″	5′-10″	5′-4″	4′-11″
2-1000S162-97	9′-9″	9′-2″	8′-7″	8′-2″	7′-8″	9′-5″	8′-10″	8′-5″	7′-11″	7′-5″
2-1200S162-54	—	—	—	—	—	—	—	—	—	—
2-1200S162-68	7′-0″	6′-4″	5′-9″	5′-3″	4′-9″	6′-7″	6′-0″	5′-5″	5′-0″	4′-6″
2-1200S162-97	9′-1″	8′-4″	7′-9″	7′-3″	6′-9″	8′-8″	8′-0″	7′-6″	7′-0″	6′-7″

For SI: 1 inch = 25.4 mm, 1 foot = 304.8 mm, 1 pound per square foot = 0.0479kPa, 1 pound per square inch = 6.895 kPa.

a. Deflection criterion: *L*/360 for live loads, *L*/240 for total loads.

b. Design load assumptions:
Second floor dead load is 10 psf.
Roof/ceiling dead load is 12 psf.
Second floor live load is 40 psf.
Third floor live load is 30 psf.
Attic live load is 10 psf.

c. Building width is in the direction of horizontal framing members supported by the header.

R603.7 Jack and king studs. The number of jack and king studs installed on each side of a header shall comply with Table R603.7(1). King, jack and cripple studs shall be of the same dimension and thickness as the adjacent wall studs. Headers shall be connected to king studs in accordance with Table R603.7(2) and the following provisions:

1. For box beam headers, one-half of the total number of required screws shall be applied to the header and one half to the king stud by use of C-shaped or track member in accordance with Figure R603.6(1). The track or C-shape sections shall extend the depth of the header minus $^1/_2$ inch (12.7 mm) and shall have a minimum thickness not less than that of the wall studs.
2. For back-to-back headers, one-half the total number of screws shall be applied to the header and one-half to the king stud by use of a minimum 2-inch-by-2-inch (51 mm × 51 mm) clip angle in accordance with Figure R603.6(2). The clip angle shall extend the depth of the header minus $^1/_2$ inch (12.7 mm) and shall have a minimum thickness not less than that of the wall studs. Jack and king studs shall be interconnected with structural sheathing in accordance with Figures R603.6(1) and R603.6(2).

R603.8 Head and sill track. Head track spans above door and window openings and sill track spans beneath window openings shall comply with Table R603.8. For openings less than 4 feet (1219 mm) in height that have both a head track and a sill track, multiplying the spans by 1.75 shall be permitted in Table R603.8. For openings less than or equal to 6 feet (1829 mm) in height that have both a head track and a sill track, multiplying the spans in Table R603.8 by 1.50 shall be permitted.

R603.9 Structural sheathing. Structural sheathing shall be installed in accordance with Figure R603.9 and this section on all sheathable exterior wall surfaces, including areas above and below openings.

R603.9.1 Sheathing materials. Structural sheathing panels shall consist of minimum $^7/_{16}$-inch (11 mm) thick oriented strand board or $^{15}/_{32}$-inch (12 mm) thick plywood.

R603.9.2 Determination of minimum length of full height sheathing. The minimum length of full height sheathing on each *braced wall line* shall be determined by multiplying the length of the *braced wall line* by the percentage obtained from Table R603.9.2(1) and by the plan aspect-ratio adjustment factors obtained from Table R603.9.2(2). The minimum length of full height sheathing shall not be less than 20 percent of the *braced wall line* length.

To be considered full height sheathing, structural sheathing shall extend from the bottom to the top of the wall without interruption by openings. Only sheathed, full height wall sections, uninterrupted by openings, which are a minimum of 48 inches (1219 mm) wide, shall be counted toward meeting the minimum percentages in Table R603.9.2(1). In addition, structural sheathing shall comply with all of the following requirements:

1. Be installed with the long dimension parallel to the stud framing (i.e. vertical orientation) and shall cover the full vertical height of wall from the bottom of the bottom track to the top of the top track of each *story*. Installing the long dimension perpendicular to the stud framing or using shorter segments shall be permitted provided that the horizontal joint is blocked as described in Item 2 below.
2. Be blocked when the long dimension is installed perpendicular to the stud framing (i.e. horizontal orientation). Blocking shall be a minimum of 33 mil (0.84 mm) thickness. Each horizontal structural sheathing panel shall be fastened with No. 8 screws spaced at 6 inches (152 mm) on center to the blocking at the joint.
3. Be applied to each end (corners) of each of the exterior walls with a minimum 48 inch (1219 mm) wide panel.

R603.9.2.1 The minimum percentage of full-height structural sheathing shall be multiplied by 1.10 for 9 foot (2743 mm) high walls and multiplied by 1.20 for 10 foot (3048 mm) high walls.

TABLE R603.7(1)
TOTAL NUMBER OF JACK AND KING STUDS REQUIRED AT EACH END OF AN OPENING

SIZE OF OPENING (feet-inches)	24″ O.C. STUD SPACING		16″ O.C. STUD SPACING	
	No. of jack studs	No. of king studs	No. of jack studs	No. of king studs
Up to 3′-6″	1	1	1	1
> 3′-6″ to 5′-0″	1	2	1	2
> 5′-0″ to 5′-6″	1	2	2	2
> 5′-6″ to 8′-0″	1	2	2	2
> 8′-0″ to 10′-6″	2	2	2	3
> 10′-6″ to 12′-0″	2	2	3	3
> 12′-0″ to 13′-0″	2	3	3	3
> 13′-0″ to 14′-0″	2	3	3	4
> 14′-0″ to 16′-0″	2	3	3	4
> 16′-0″ to 18′-0″	3	3	4	4

For SI: 1 inch = 25.4 mm, 1 foot = 304.8 mm.

TABLE R603.7(2)
HEADER TO KING STUD CONNECTION REQUIREMENTS[a, b, c, d]

HEADER SPAN (feet)	BASIC WIND SPEED (mph), EXPOSURE		
	85 B or Seismic Design Categories A, B, C, D_0, D_1 and D_2	85 C or less than 110 B	Less than 110 C
≤ 4′	4-No. 8 screws	4-No. 8 screws	6-No. 8 screws
> 4′ to 8′	4-No. 8 screws	4-No. 8 screws	8-No. 8 screws
> 8′ to 12′	4-No. 8 screws	6-No. 8 screws	10-No. 8 screws
> 12′to 16′	4-No. 8 screws	8-No. 8 screws	12-No. 8 screws

For SI: 1 inch = 25.4 mm, 1 foot = 304.8 mm, 1 mile per hour = 0.447 m/s, 1 pound = 4.448 N.

a. All screw sizes shown are minimum.

b. For headers located on the first floor of a two-story building or the first or second floor of a three-story building, the total number of screws is permitted to be reduced by 2 screws, but the total number of screws shall be no less than 4.

c. For roof slopes of 6:12 or greater, the required number of screws may be reduced by half, but the total number of screws shall be no less than four.

d. Screws can be replaced by an uplift connector which has a capacity of the number of screws multiplied by 164 pounds (e.g., 12-No. 8 screws can be replaced by an uplift connector whose capacity exceeds 12 × 164 pounds = 1,968 pounds).

TABLE R603.8
HEAD AND SILL TRACK SPAN
F_y = 33 ksi

BASIC WIND SPEED (mph)		ALLOWABLE HEAD AND SILL TRACK SPAN[a,b,c] (ft-in.)					
EXPOSURE		TRACK DESIGNATION					
B	C	350T125-33	350T125-43	350T125-54	550T125-33	550T125-43	550T125-54
85	—	5′-0″	5′-7″	6′-2″	5′-10″	6′-8″	7′-0″
90	—	4′-10″	5′-5″	6′-0″	5′-8″	6′-3″	6′-10″
100	85	4′-6″	5′-1″	5′-8″	5′-4″	5′-11″	6′-5″
110	90	4′-2″	4′-9″	5′-4″	5′-1″	5′-7″	6′-1″
120	100	3′-11″	4′-6″	5′-0″	4′-10″	5′-4″	5′-10″
130	110	3′-8″	4′-2″	4′-9″	4′-1″	5′-1″	5′-7″
140	120	3′-7″	4′-1″	4′-7″	3′-6″	4′-11″	5′-5″
150	130	3′-5″	3′-10″	4′-4″	2′-11″	4′-7″	5′-2″
—	140	3′-1″	3′-6″	4′-1″	2′-3″	4′-0″	4′-10″
—	150	2′-9″	3′-4″	3′-10″	2′-0″	3′-7″	4′-7″

For SI: 1 inch = 25.4 mm, 1 foot = 304.8 mm, 1 mile per hour = 0.447 m/s.

a. Deflection limit: *L*/240.

b. Head and sill track spans are based on components and cladding wind speeds and 48 inch tributary span.

c. For openings less than 4 feet in height that have both a head track and sill track, the above spans are permitted to be multiplied by 1.75. For openings less than or equal to 6 feet in height that have both a head track and a sill track, the above spans are permitted to be multiplied by a factor of 1.5.

STUD SPACING
WALL HEIGHT
STRUCTURAL SHEATHING PANEL
FIELD FASTENER
EDGE FASTENER

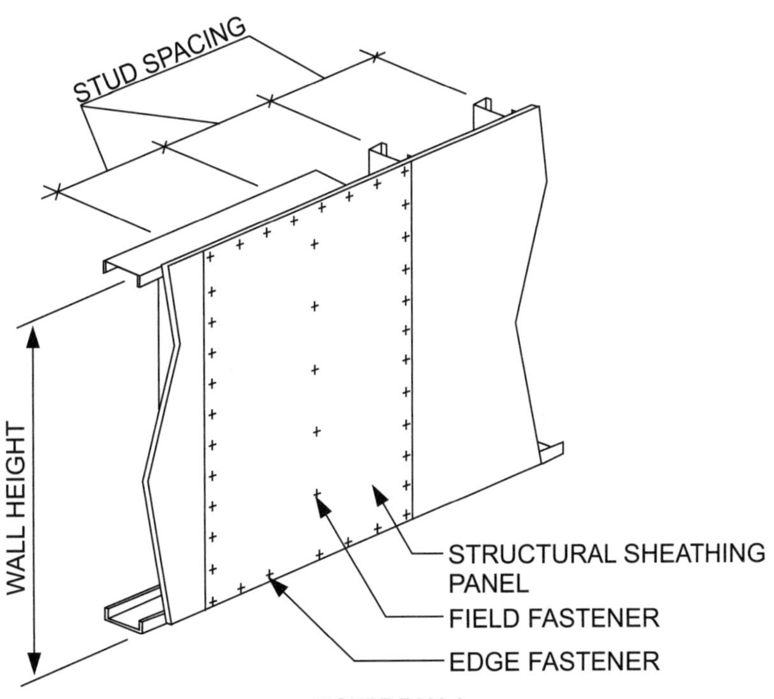

FIGURE R603.9
STRUCTURAL SHEATHING FASTENING PATTERN

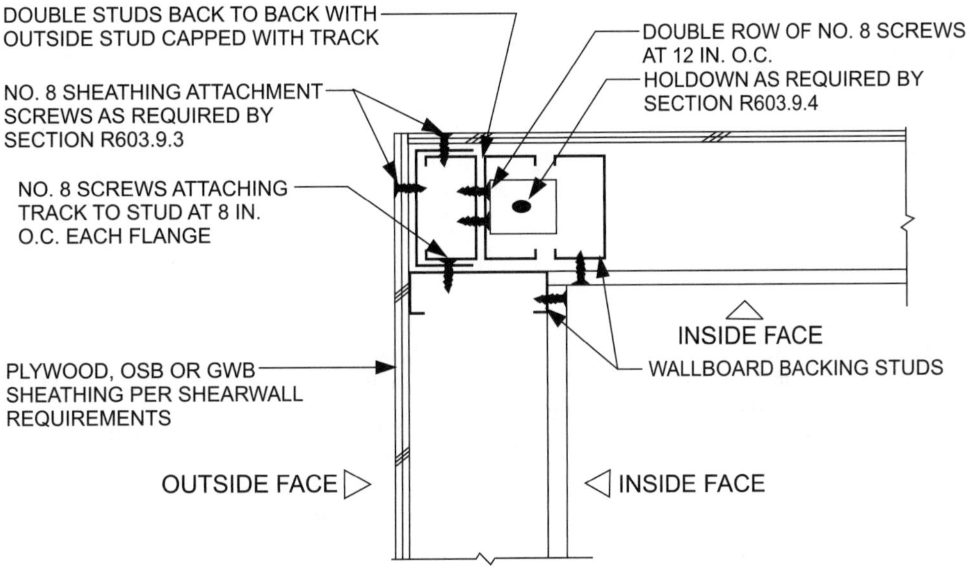

DOUBLE STUDS BACK TO BACK WITH OUTSIDE STUD CAPPED WITH TRACK
NO. 8 SHEATHING ATTACHMENT SCREWS AS REQUIRED BY SECTION R603.9.3
NO. 8 SCREWS ATTACHING TRACK TO STUD AT 8 IN. O.C. EACH FLANGE
PLYWOOD, OSB OR GWB SHEATHING PER SHEARWALL REQUIREMENTS
OUTSIDE FACE
DOUBLE ROW OF NO. 8 SCREWS AT 12 IN. O.C.
HOLDOWN AS REQUIRED BY SECTION R603.9.4
INSIDE FACE
WALLBOARD BACKING STUDS
INSIDE FACE

For SI: 1 inch = 25.4 mm.

FIGURE R603.9.2
CORNER STUD HOLD DOWN DETAIL

**TABLE R603.9.2(1)
MINIMUM PERCENTAGE OF FULL HEIGHT
STRUCTURAL SHEATHING ON EXTERIOR WALLS[a,b]**

WALL SUPPORTING	ROOF SLOPE	BASIC WIND SPEED AND EXPOSURE (mph)					
		85 B	90 B	100 B / 85 C	< 110 B / 90 C	100 C	< 110 C
Roof and ceiling only (One story or top floor of two or three story building)	3:12	8	9	9	12	16	20
	6:12	12	13	15	20	26	35
	9:12	21	23	25	30	50	58
	12:12	30	33	35	40	66	75
One story, roof and ceiling (First floor of a two-story building or second floor of a three story building)	3:12	24	27	30	35	50	66
	6:12	25	28	30	40	58	74
	9:12	35	38	40	55	74	91
	12:12	40	45	50	65	100	115
Two story, roof and ceiling (First floor of a three story building)	3:12	40	45	51	58	84	112
	6:12	38	43	45	60	90	113
	9:12	49	53	55	80	98	124
	12:12	50	57	65	90	134	155

For SI: 1 mile per hour = 0.447 m/s.

a. Linear interpolation is permitted.

b. For hip-roofed homes the minimum percentage of full height sheathing, based upon wind, is permitted to be multiplied by a factor of 0.95 for roof slopes not exceeding 7:12 and a factor of 0.9 for roof slopes greater than 7:12.

**TABLE R603.9.2(2)
FULL HEIGHT SHEATHING LENGTH ADJUSTMENT FACTORS**

PLAN ASPECT RATIO	LENGTH ADJUSTMENT FACTORS	
	Short wall	Long wall
1:1	1.0	1.0
1.5:1	1.5	0.67
2:1	2.0	0.50
3:1	3.0	0.33
4:1	4.0	0.25

R603.9.2.2 For hip roofed homes, the minimum percentages of full height sheathing in Table R603.9.2(1), based upon wind, shall be permitted to be multiplied by a factor of 0.95 for roof slopes not exceeding 7:12 and a factor of 0.9 for roof slopes greater than 7:12.

R603.9.2.3 In the lowest *story* of a *dwelling*, multiplying the percentage of full height sheathing required in Table R603.9.2(1) by 0.6, shall be permitted provided hold down anchors are provided in accordance with Section R603.9.4.2.

R603.9.3 Structural sheathing fastening. All edges and interior areas of structural sheathing panels shall be fastened to framing members and tracks in accordance with Figure R603.9 and Table R603.3.2(1). Screws for attachment of structural sheathing panels shall be bugle-head, flat-head, or similar head style with a minimum head diameter of 0.29 inch (8 mm).

For continuously-sheathed *braced wall lines* using wood structural panels installed with No. 8 screws spaced 4-inches (102 mm) on center at all panel edges and 12 inches (304.8 mm) on center on intermediate framing members, the following shall apply:

1. Multiplying the percentages of full height sheathing in Table R603.9.2(1) by 0.72 shall be permitted.
2. For bottom track attached to foundations or framing below, the bottom track anchor or screw connection spacing in Table R505.3.1(1) and Table R603.3.1 shall be multiplied by 2/3.

R603.9.4 Uplift connection requirements. Uplift connections shall be provided in accordance with this section.

R603.9.4.1 Where wind speeds are in excess of 100 miles per hour (45 m/s), Exposure C, walls shall be provided wind direct uplift connections in accordance with AISI S230, Section E13.3, and AISI S230, Section F7.2, as required for 110 miles per hour (49 m/s), Exposure C.

R603.9.4.2 Where the percentage of full height sheathing is adjusted in accordance with Section R603.9.2.3, a hold-down anchor, with a strength of 4,300 pounds (19 kN), shall be provided at each end of each full-height sheathed wall section used to meet the minimum percent sheathing requirements of Section R603.9.2. Hold down anchors shall be attached to back-to-back studs; structural sheathing panels shall have edge fastening to the studs, in accordance with Section R603.9.3 and AISI S230, Table E11-1.

A single hold down anchor, installed in accordance with Figure R603.9.2, shall be permitted at the corners of buildings.

R603.9.5 Structural sheathing for stone and masonry veneer. In Seismic Design Category C, where stone and masonry veneer is installed in accordance with Section R703.7, the length of structural sheathing for walls supporting one *story*, roof and ceiling shall be the greater of the amount required by Section R603.9.2 or 36 percent, modified by Section R603.9.2 except Section R603.9.2.2 shall not be permitted.

SECTION R604
WOOD STRUCTURAL PANELS

R604.1 Identification and grade. Wood structural panels shall conform to DOC PS 1 or DOC PS 2 or, when manufactured in Canada, CSA O437 or CSA O325. All panels shall be identified by a grade mark or certificate of inspection issued by an *approved* agency.

R604.2 Allowable spans. The maximum allowable spans for wood structural panel wall sheathing shall not exceed the values set forth in Table R602.3(3).

R604.3 Installation. Wood structural panel wall sheathing shall be attached to framing in accordance with Table R602.3(1) or Table R602.3.(3). Wood structural panels marked Exposure 1 or Exterior are considered water-repellent sheathing under the code.

SECTION R605
PARTICLEBOARD

R605.1 Identification and grade. Particleboard shall conform to ANSI A208.1 and shall be so identified by a grade mark or certificate of inspection issued by an *approved* agency. Particleboard shall comply with the grades specified in Table R602.3(4).

SECTION R606
GENERAL MASONRY CONSTRUCTION

R606.1 General. Masonry construction shall be designed and constructed in accordance with the provisions of this section or in accordance with the provisions of TMS 402/ACI 530/ASCE 5.

R606.1.1 Professional registration not required. When the empirical design provisions of ACI 530/ASCE 5/TMS 402 Chapter 5 or the provisions of this section are used to design masonry, project drawings, typical details and specifications are not required to bear the seal of the registered design professional, unless otherwise required by the state law of the *jurisdiction* having authority.

R606.1.2 Used brick. Used materials shall not be used unless such materials conform to these requirements and have been cleaned.

Exception: Used materials may be used for interior nonbearing conditions.

R606.2 Thickness of masonry. The nominal thickness of masonry walls shall conform to the requirements of Sections R606.2.1 through R606.2.4.

R606.2.1 Minimum thickness. The minimum thickness of masonry bearing walls more than one *story* high shall be 8 inches (203 mm). *Solid masonry* walls of one-story *dwellings* and garages shall not be less than 6 inches (152 mm) in thickness when not greater than 9 feet (2743 mm) in height, provided that when gable construction is used, an additional 6 feet (1829 mm) is permitted to the peak of the gable. Masonry walls shall be laterally supported in either the horizontal or vertical direction at intervals as required by Section R606.9.

R606.2.2 Rubble stone masonry wall. The minimum thickness of rough, random or coursed rubble stone masonry walls shall be 16 inches (406 mm).

R606.2.3 Change in thickness. Where walls of masonry of hollow units or masonry-bonded hollow walls are decreased in thickness, a course of *solid masonry* shall be constructed between the wall below and the thinner wall above, or special units or construction shall be used to transmit the loads from face shells or wythes above to those below.

R606.2.4 Parapet walls. Unreinforced *solid masonry* parapet walls shall not be less than 8 inches (203 mm) thick and their height shall not exceed four times their thickness. Unreinforced hollow unit masonry parapet walls shall be not less than 8 inches (203 mm) thick, and their height shall not exceed three times their thickness. Masonry parapet walls in areas subject to wind loads of 30 pounds per square foot (1.44 kPa) located in Seismic Design Category D_0, D_1 or D_2, or on townhouses in Seismic Design Category C shall be reinforced in accordance with Section R606.12.

R606.3 Corbeled masonry. Corbeled masonry shall be in accordance with Sections R606.3.1 through R606.3.3.

R606.3.1 Units. *Solid masonry* units or masonry units filled with mortar or grout shall be used for corbeling.

R606.3.2 Corbel projection. The maximum projection of one unit shall not exceed one-half the height of the unit or

Wall Construction - Masonry

one-third the thickness at right angles to the wall. The maximum corbeled projection beyond the face of the wall shall not exceed:

1. One-half of the wall thickness for multiwythe walls bonded by mortar or grout and wall ties or masonry headers, or
2. One-half the wythe thickness for single wythe walls, masonry-bonded hollow walls, multiwythe walls with open collar joints and veneer walls.

R606.3.3 Corbeled masonry supporting floor or roof-framing members. When corbeled masonry is used to support floor or roof-framing members, the top course of the corbel shall be a header course or the top course bed joint shall have ties to the vertical wall.

R606.4 Support conditions. Bearing and support conditions shall be in accordance with Sections R606.4.1 and R606.4.2.

R606.4.1 Bearing on support. Each masonry wythe shall be supported by at least two-thirds of the wythe thickness.

R606.4.2 Support at foundation. Cavity wall or masonry veneer construction may be supported on an 8-inch (203 mm) foundation wall, provided the 8-inch (203 mm) wall is corbeled to the width of the wall system above with masonry constructed of *solid masonry* units or masonry units filled with mortar or grout. The total horizontal projection of the corbel shall not exceed 2 inches (51 mm) with individual corbels projecting not more than one-third the thickness of the unit or one-half the height of the unit. The hollow space behind the corbeled masonry shall be filled with mortar or grout.

R606.5 Allowable stresses. Allowable compressive stresses in masonry shall not exceed the values prescribed in Table R606.5. In determining the stresses in masonry, the effects of all loads and conditions of loading and the influence of all forces affecting the design and strength of the several parts shall be taken into account.

R606.5.1 Combined units. In walls or other structural members composed of different kinds or grades of units, materials or mortars, the maximum stress shall not exceed the allowable stress for the weakest of the combination of units, materials and mortars of which the member is composed. The net thickness of any facing unit that is used to resist stress shall not be less than 1.5 inches (38 mm).

R606.6 Piers. The unsupported height of masonry piers shall not exceed ten times their least dimension. When structural clay tile or hollow concrete masonry units are used for isolated piers to support beams and girders, the cellular spaces shall be filled solidly with concrete or Type M or S mortar, except that unfilled hollow piers may be used if their unsupported height is not more than four times their least dimension. Where hollow masonry units are solidly filled with concrete or Type M, S or N mortar, the allowable compressive stress shall be permitted to be increased as provided in Table R606.5.

R606.6.1 Pier cap. Hollow piers shall be capped with 4 inches (102 mm) of *solid masonry* or concrete for one story and 8 inches of solid masonry or concrete for two story and two and one-half story or shall have cavities of the top course filled with concrete or grout or other *approved* methods.

TABLE R606.5
ALLOWABLE COMPRESSIVE STRESSES FOR EMPIRICAL DESIGN OF MASONRY

CONSTRUCTION; COMPRESSIVE STRENGTH OF UNIT, GROSS AREA	ALLOWABLE COMPRESSIVE STRESSES[a] GROSS CROSS-SECTIONAL AREA[b]	
	Type M or S mortar	Type N mortar
Solid masonry of brick and other solid units of clay or shale; sand-lime or concrete brick:		
8,000+ psi	350	300
4,500 psi	225	200
2,500 psi	160	140
1,500 psi	115	100
Grouted[c] masonry, of clay or shale; sand-lime or concrete:		
4,500+ psi	225	200
2,500 psi	160	140
1,500 psi	115	100
Solid masonry of solid concrete masonry units:		
3,000+ psi	225	200
2,000 psi	160	140
1,200 psi	115	100
Masonry of hollow load-bearing units:		
2,000+ psi	140	120
1,500 psi	115	100
1,000 psi	75	70
700 psi	60	55
Hollow walls (cavity or masonry bonded[d]) solid units:		
2,500+ psi	160	140
1,500 psi	115	100
Hollow units	75	70
Stone ashlar masonry:		
Granite	720	640
Limestone or marble	450	400
Sandstone or cast stone	360	320
Rubble stone masonry:		
Coarse, rough or random	120	100

For SI: 1 pound per square inch = 6.895 kPa.

a. Linear interpolation shall be used for determining allowable stresses for masonry units having compressive strengths that are intermediate between those given in the table.

b. Gross cross-sectional area shall be calculated on the actual rather than nominal dimensions.

c. See Section R608.

d. Where floor and roof loads are carried upon one wythe, the gross cross-sectional area is that of the wythe under load; if both wythes are loaded, the gross cross-sectional area is that of the wall minus the area of the cavity between the wythes. Walls bonded with metal ties shall be considered as cavity walls unless the collar joints are filled with mortar or grout.

R606.7 Chases. Chases and recesses in masonry walls shall not be deeper than one-third the wall thickness, and the maximum length of a horizontal chase or horizontal projection shall not exceed 4 feet (1219 mm), and shall have at least 8 inches

Wall Construction - Masonry

(203 mm) of masonry in back of the chases and recesses and between adjacent chases or recesses and the jambs of openings. Chases and recesses in masonry walls shall be designed and constructed so as not to reduce the required strength or required fire resistance of the wall and in no case shall a chase or recess be permitted within the required area of a pier. Masonry directly above chases or recesses wider than 12 inches (305 mm) shall be supported on noncombustible lintels.

R606.8 Stack bond. In unreinforced masonry where masonry units are laid in stack bond, longitudinal reinforcement consisting of not less than two continuous wires each with a minimum aggregate cross-sectional area of 0.017 square inch (11 mm^2) shall be provided in horizontal bed joints spaced not more than 16 inches (406 mm) on center vertically.

R606.9 Lateral support. Masonry walls shall be laterally supported in either the horizontal or the vertical direction. The maximum spacing between lateral supports shall not exceed the distances in Table R606.9. Lateral support shall be provided by cross walls, pilasters, buttresses or structural frame members when the limiting distance is taken horizontally, or by floors or roofs when the limiting distance is taken vertically.

TABLE R606.9
SPACING OF LATERAL SUPPORT FOR MASONRY WALLS

CONSTRUCTION	MAXIMUM WALL LENGTH TO THICKNESS OR WALL HEIGHT TO THICKNESS[a,b]
Bearing walls:	
Solid or solid grouted	20
All other	18
Nonbearing walls:	
Exterior	18
Interior	36

For SI: 1 foot = 304.8 mm.

a. Except for cavity walls and cantilevered walls, the thickness of a wall shall be its nominal thickness measured perpendicular to the face of the wall. For cavity walls, the thickness shall be determined as the sum of the nominal thicknesses of the individual wythes. For cantilever walls, except for parapets, the ratio of height to nominal thickness shall not exceed 6 for solid masonry, or 4 for hollow masonry. For parapets, see Section R606.2.4.

b. An additional unsupported height of 6 feet is permitted for gable end walls.

R606.9.1 Horizontal lateral support. Lateral support in the horizontal direction provided by intersecting masonry walls shall be provided by one of the methods in Section R606.9.1.1 or Section R606.9.1.2.

R606.9.1.1 Bonding pattern. Fifty percent of the units at the intersection shall be laid in an overlapping masonry bonding pattern, with alternate units having a bearing of not less than 3 inches (76 mm) on the unit below.

R606.9.1.2 Metal reinforcement. Interior nonloadbearing walls shall be anchored at their intersections, at vertical intervals of not more than 16 inches (406 mm) with joint reinforcement of at least 9 gage [0.148 in. (4mm)], or $^1/_4$ inch (6 mm) galvanized mesh hardware cloth. Intersecting masonry walls, other than interior nonloadbearing walls, shall be anchored at vertical intervals of not more than 8 inches (203 mm) with joint reinforcement of at least 9 gage and shall extend at least 30 inches (762 mm) in each direction at the intersection. Other metal ties, joint reinforcement or anchors, if used, shall be spaced to provide equivalent area of anchorage to that required by this section.

R606.9.2 Vertical lateral support. Vertical lateral support of masonry walls in Seismic Design Category A, B or C shall be provided in accordance with one of the methods in Section R606.9.2.1 or Section R606.9.2.2.

R606.9.2.1 Roof structures. Masonry walls shall be anchored to roof structures with metal strap anchors spaced in accordance with the manufacturer's instructions, $^1/_2$-inch (13 mm) bolts spaced not more than 6 feet (1829 mm) on center, or other *approved* anchors. Anchors shall be embedded at least 16 inches (406 mm) into the masonry, or be hooked or welded to bond beam reinforcement placed not less than 6 inches (152 mm) from the top of the wall.

R606.9.2.2 Floor diaphragms. Masonry walls shall be anchored to floor *diaphragm* framing by metal strap anchors spaced in accordance with the manufacturer's instructions, $^1/_2$-inch-diameter (13 mm) bolts spaced at intervals not to exceed 6 feet (1829 mm) and installed as shown in Figure R606.11(1), or by other *approved* methods.

R606.10 Lintels. Masonry over openings shall be supported by steel lintels, reinforced concrete or masonry lintels or masonry arches, designed to support load imposed.

R606.11 Anchorage. Masonry walls shall be anchored to floor and roof systems in accordance with the details shown in Figure R606.11(1), R606.11(2) or R606.11(3). Footings may be considered as points of lateral support.

R606.12 Seismic requirements. The seismic requirements of this section shall apply to the design of masonry and the construction of masonry building elements located in Seismic Design Category D_0, D_1 or D_2. Townhouses in Seismic Design Category C shall comply with the requirements of Section R606.12.2. These requirements shall not apply to glass unit masonry conforming to Section R610 or masonry veneer conforming to Section R703.7.

R606.12.1 General. Masonry structures and masonry elements shall comply with the requirements of Sections R606.12.2 through R606.12.4 based on the seismic design category established in Table R301.2(1). Masonry structures and masonry elements shall comply with the requirements of Section R606.12 and Figures R606.11(1), R606.11(2) and R606.11(3) or shall be designed in accordance with TMS 402/ACI 530/ASCE 5.

R606.12.1.1 Floor and roof diaphragm construction. Floor and roof *diaphragms* shall be constructed of wood structural panels attached to wood framing in accordance with Table R602.3(1) or to cold-formed steel floor framing in accordance with Table R505.3.1(2) or to cold-formed steel roof framing in accordance with Table R804.3. Additionally, sheathing panel edges perpendicular to framing members shall be backed by blocking, and sheathing shall be connected to the blocking with fasteners at the edge spacing. For Seismic Design Categories C, D_0, D_1 and D_2, where the width-to-thickness dimension of the *diaphragm* exceeds 2-to-1, edge spacing of fasteners shall be 4 inches (102 mm) on center.

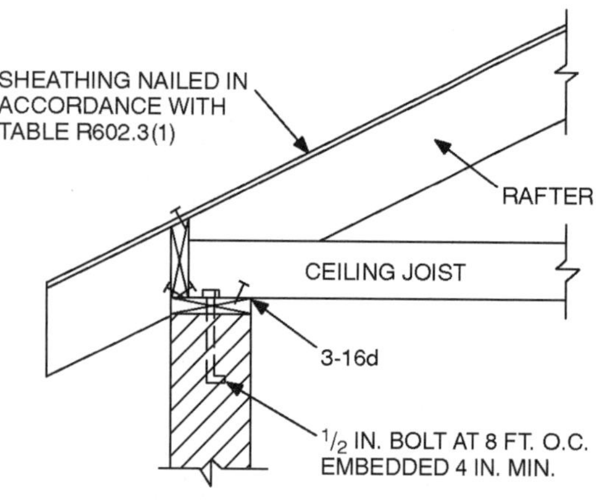

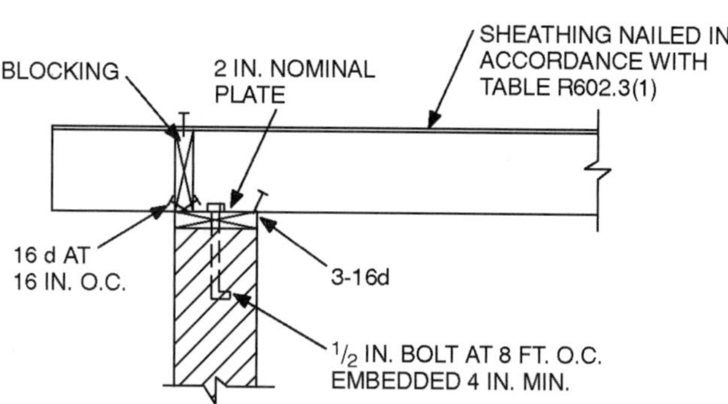

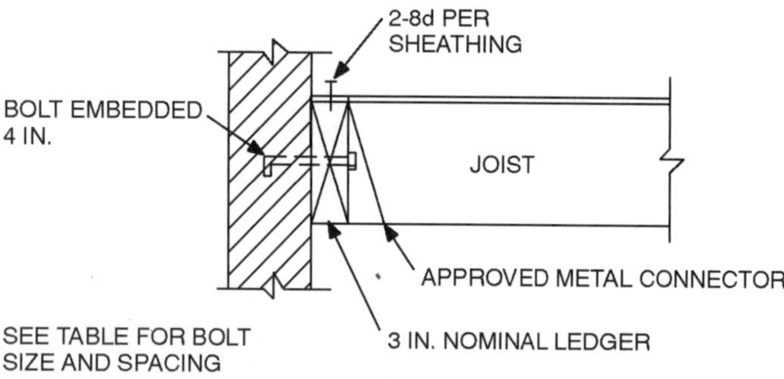

LEDGER BOLT SIZE AND SPACING

JOIST SPAN	BOLT SIZE AND SPACING	
	ROOF	FLOOR
10 FT.	$^{1}/_{2}$ AT 2 FT. 6 IN. $^{7}/_{8}$ AT 3 FT. 6 IN.	$^{1}/_{2}$ AT 2 FT. 0 IN. $^{7}/_{8}$ AT 2 FT. 9 IN.
10–15 FT.	$^{1}/_{2}$ AT 1 FT. 9 IN. $^{7}/_{8}$ AT 2 FT. 6 IN.	$^{1}/_{2}$ AT 1 FT. 4 IN. $^{7}/_{8}$ AT 2 FT. 0 IN.
15-20 FT.	$^{1}/_{2}$ AT 1 FT. 3 IN. $^{7}/_{8}$ AT 2 FT. 0 IN.	$^{1}/_{2}$ AT 1 FT. 0 IN. $^{7}/_{8}$ AT 1 FT. 6 IN.

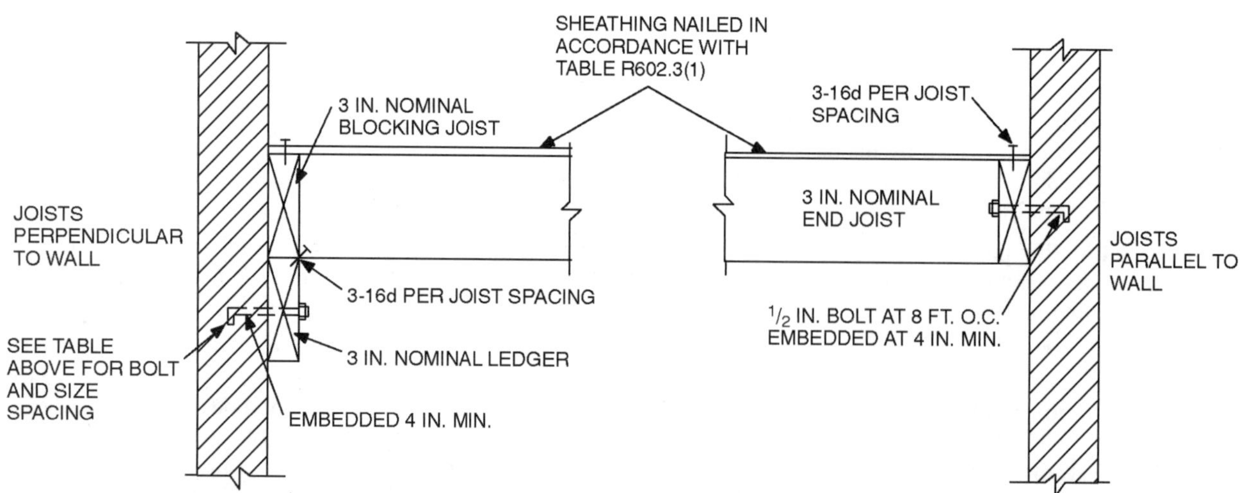

NOTE: Where bolts are located in hollow masonry, the cells in the courses receiving the bolt shall be grouted solid.

For SI: 1 inch = 25.4 mm, 1 foot = 304.8 mm, 1 pound per square foot = 0.0.479kPa.

FIGURE R606.11(1)
ANCHORAGE REQUIREMENTS FOR MASONRY WALLS LOCATED IN SEISMIC DESIGN CATEGORY A, B OR C AND WHERE WIND LOADS ARE LESS THAN 30 PSF

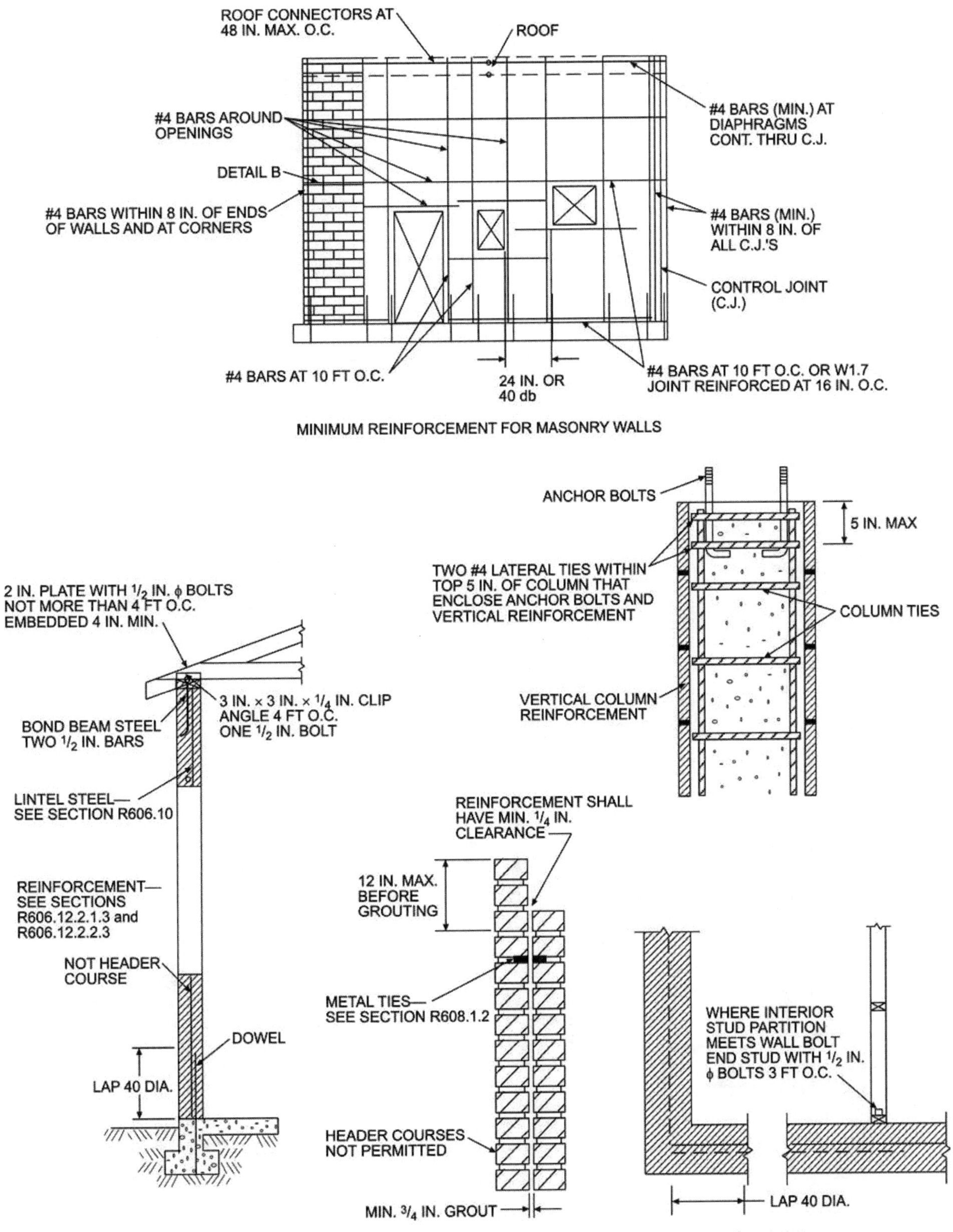

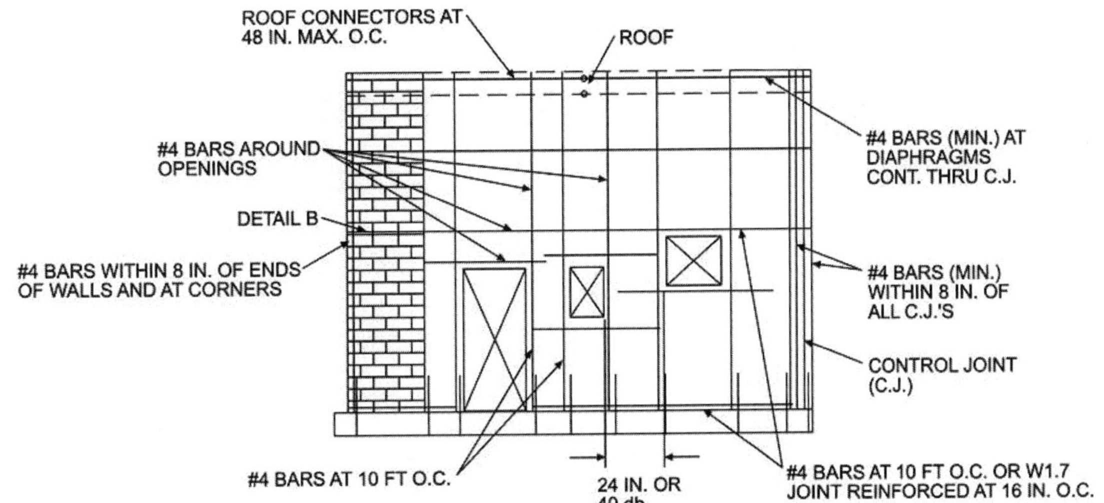

ROOF CONNECTORS AT 48 IN. MAX. O.C.
ROOF
#4 BARS AROUND OPENINGS
DETAIL B
#4 BARS WITHIN 8 IN. OF ENDS OF WALLS AND AT CORNERS
#4 BARS (MIN.) AT DIAPHRAGMS CONT. THRU C.J.
#4 BARS (MIN.) WITHIN 8 IN. OF ALL C.J.'S
CONTROL JOINT (C.J.)
#4 BARS AT 10 FT O.C.
24 IN. OR 40 db
#4 BARS AT 10 FT O.C. OR W1.7 JOINT REINFORCED AT 16 IN. O.C.
MINIMUM REINFORCEMENT FOR MASONRY WALLS
ANCHOR BOLTS
5 IN. MAX
TWO #4 LATERAL TIES WITHIN TOP 5 IN. OF COLUMN THAT ENCLOSE ANCHOR BOLTS AND VERTICAL REINFORCEMENT
COLUMN TIES
VERTICAL COLUMN REINFORCEMENT
2 IN. PLATE WITH 1/2 IN. ϕ BOLTS NOT MORE THAN 4 FT O.C. EMBEDDED 4 IN. MIN.
3 IN. × 3 IN. × 1/4 IN. CLIP ANGLE 4 FT O.C. ONE 1/2 IN. BOLT
BOND BEAM STEEL TWO 1/2 IN. BARS
LINTEL STEEL— SEE SECTION R606.10
REINFORCEMENT— SEE SECTIONS R606.12.2.1.3 and R606.12.2.2.3
NOT HEADER COURSE
DOWEL
LAP 40 DIA.
REINFORCEMENT SHALL HAVE MIN. 1/4 IN. CLEARANCE
12 IN. MAX. BEFORE GROUTING
METAL TIES— SEE SECTION R608.1.2
HEADER COURSES NOT PERMITTED
MIN. 3/4 IN. GROUT
WHERE INTERIOR STUD PARTITION MEETS WALL BOLT END STUD WITH 1/2 IN. ϕ BOLTS 3 FT O.C.
LAP 40 DIA.
SECTION 1

For SI: 1 inch = 25.4 mm, 1 foot = 304.8 mm.

FIGURE R606.11(2)
REQUIREMENTS FOR REINFORCED GROUTED MASONRY CONSTRUCTION IN SEISMIC DESIGN CATEGORY C

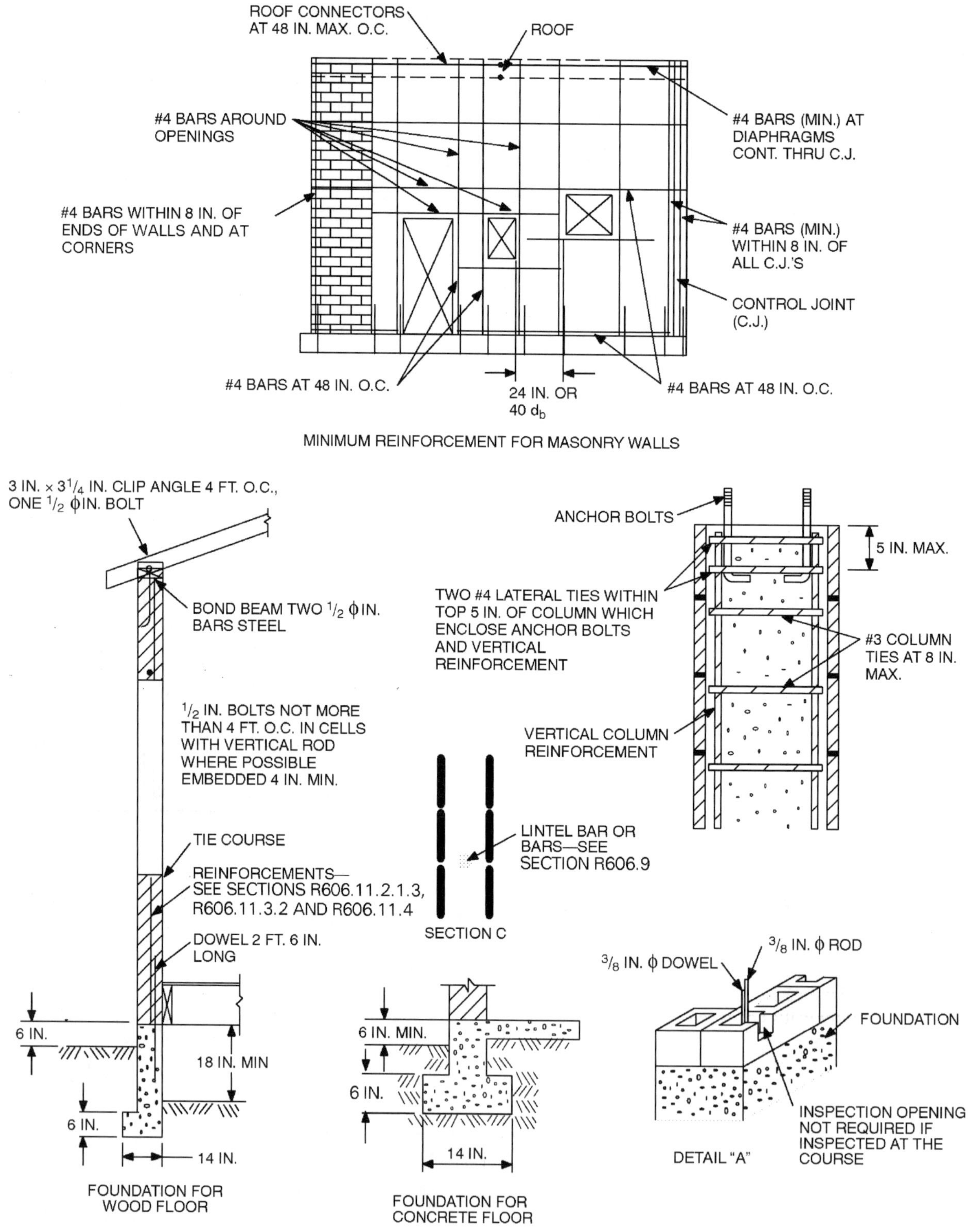

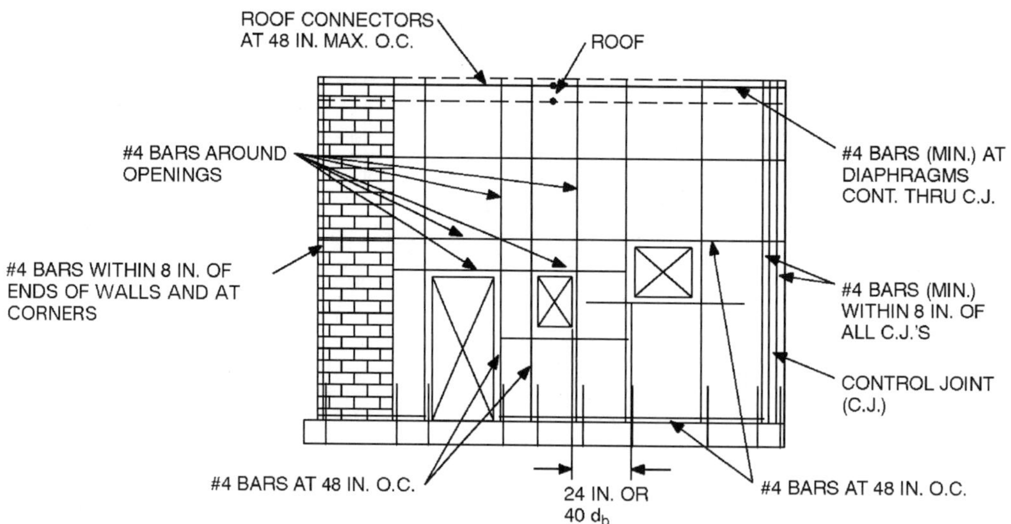

ROOF CONNECTORS AT 48 IN. MAX. O.C.
ROOF
#4 BARS AROUND OPENINGS
#4 BARS (MIN.) AT DIAPHRAGMS CONT. THRU C.J.
#4 BARS WITHIN 8 IN. OF ENDS OF WALLS AND AT CORNERS
#4 BARS (MIN.) WITHIN 8 IN. OF ALL C.J.'S
CONTROL JOINT (C.J.)
#4 BARS AT 48 IN. O.C.
24 IN. OR 40 d_b
#4 BARS AT 48 IN. O.C.
MINIMUM REINFORCEMENT FOR MASONRY WALLS
3 IN. × 3 1/4 IN. CLIP ANGLE 4 FT. O.C., ONE 1/2 ϕ IN. BOLT
BOND BEAM TWO 1/2 ϕ IN. BARS STEEL
1/2 IN. BOLTS NOT MORE THAN 4 FT. O.C. IN CELLS WITH VERTICAL ROD WHERE POSSIBLE EMBEDDED 4 IN. MIN.
TIE COURSE
REINFORCEMENTS—SEE SECTIONS R606.11.2.1.3, R606.11.3.2 AND R606.11.4
DOWEL 2 FT. 6 IN. LONG
6 IN.
18 IN. MIN
6 IN.
14 IN.
FOUNDATION FOR WOOD FLOOR
ANCHOR BOLTS
5 IN. MAX.
TWO #4 LATERAL TIES WITHIN TOP 5 IN. OF COLUMN WHICH ENCLOSE ANCHOR BOLTS AND VERTICAL REINFORCEMENT
#3 COLUMN TIES AT 8 IN. MAX.
VERTICAL COLUMN REINFORCEMENT
LINTEL BAR OR BARS—SEE SECTION R606.9
SECTION C
6 IN. MIN.
6 IN.
14 IN.
FOUNDATION FOR CONCRETE FLOOR
3/8 IN. ϕ DOWEL
3/8 IN. ϕ ROD
FOUNDATION
INSPECTION OPENING NOT REQUIRED IF INSPECTED AT THE COURSE
DETAIL "A"

NOTE: A full bed joint must be provided. All cells containing vertical bars are to be filled to the top of wall and provide inspection opening as shown on detail "A." Horizontal bars are to be laid as shown on detail "B." Lintel bars are to be laid as shown on Section C.

For SI: 1 inch = 25.4 mm, 1 foot = 304.8 mm.

FIGURE R606.11(3)
REQUIREMENTS FOR REINFORCED MASONRY CONSTRUCTION IN SEISMIC DESIGN CATEGORY D_0, D_1, OR D_2

R606.12.2 Seismic Design Category C. Townhouses located in Seismic Design Category C shall comply with the requirements of this section.

R606.12.2.1 Minimum length of wall without openings. Table R606.12.2.1 shall be used to determine the minimum required solid wall length without openings at each masonry exterior wall. The provided percentage of solid wall length shall include only those wall segments that are 3 feet (914 mm) or longer. The maximum clear distance between wall segments included in determining the solid wall length shall not exceed 18 feet (5486 mm). Shear wall segments required to meet the minimum wall length shall be in accordance with Section R606.12.2.2.3.

R606.12.2.2 Design of elements not part of the lateral force-resisting system.

R606.12.2.2.1 Load-bearing frames or columns. Elements not part of the lateral-force-resisting system shall be analyzed to determine their effect on the response of the system. The frames or columns shall be adequate for vertical load carrying capacity and induced moment caused by the design *story* drift.

R606.12.2.2.2 Masonry partition walls. Masonry partition walls, masonry screen walls and other masonry elements that are not designed to resist vertical or lateral loads, other than those induced by their own weight, shall be isolated from the structure so that vertical and lateral forces are not imparted to these elements. Isolation joints and connectors between these elements and the structure shall be designed to accommodate the design *story* drift.

R606.12.2.2.3 Reinforcement requirements for masonry elements. Masonry elements listed in Section R606.12.2.2.2 shall be reinforced in either the horizontal or vertical direction as shown in Figure R606.11(2) and in accordance with the following:

1. Horizontal reinforcement. Horizontal joint reinforcement shall consist of at least two longitudinal W1.7 wires spaced not more than 16 inches (406 mm) for walls greater than 4 inches (102 mm) in width and at least one longitudinal W1.7 wire spaced not more than 16 inches (406 mm) for walls not exceeding 4 inches (102 mm) in width; or at least one No. 4 bar spaced not more than 48 inches (1219 mm). Where two longitudinal wires of joint reinforcement are used, the space between these wires shall be the widest that the mortar joint will accommodate. Horizontal reinforcement shall be provided within 16 inches (406 mm) of the top and bottom of these masonry elements.
2. Vertical reinforcement. Vertical reinforcement shall consist of at least one No. 4 bar spaced not more than 48 inches (1219 mm). Vertical reinforcement shall be located within 16 inches (406 mm) of the ends of masonry walls.

R606.12.2.3 Design of elements part of the lateral-force-resisting system.

R606.12.2.3.1 Connections to masonry shear walls. Connectors shall be provided to transfer forces between masonry walls and horizontal elements in accordance with the requirements of Section 1.7.4 of TMS 402/ACI 530/ASCE 5. Connectors shall be designed to transfer horizontal design forces acting either perpendicular or parallel to the wall, but not less than 200 pounds per linear foot (2919 N/m) of wall. The maximum spacing between connectors shall be 4 feet (1219 mm). Such anchorage mechanisms shall not induce tension stresses perpendicular to grain in ledgers or nailers.

R606.12.2.3.2 Connections to masonry columns. Connectors shall be provided to transfer forces between masonry columns and horizontal elements in accordance with the requirements of Section 1.7.4 of TMS 402/ACI 530/ASCE 5. Where anchor bolts are used to connect horizontal elements to the tops of columns, the bolts shall be placed within lateral ties. Lateral ties shall enclose both the vertical bars in the column and the anchor bolts. There shall be a minimum of two No. 4 lateral ties provided in the top 5 inches (127 mm) of the column.

R606.12.2.3.3 Minimum reinforcement requirements for masonry shear walls. Vertical reinforcement of at least one No. 4 bar shall be provided at corners, within 16 inches (406 mm) of each side of openings, within 8 inches (203 mm) of each side of movement joints, within 8 inches (203 mm) of the ends of walls, and at a maximum spacing of 10 feet (3048 mm).

TABLE R606.12.2.1
MINIMUM SOLID WALL LENGTH ALONG EXTERIOR WALL LINES

SESIMIC DESIGN CATEGORY	MINIMUM SOLID WALL LENGTH (percent)[a]		
	One Story or Top Story of Two Story	Wall Supporting Light-framed Second Story and Roof	Wall Supporting Masonry Second Story and Roof
Townhouses in C	20	25	35
D_0 or D_1	25	NP	NP
D_2	30	NP	NP

NP = Not permitted , except with design in accordance with the *International Building Code.*

a. For all walls, the minimum required length of solid walls shall be based on the table percent multiplied by the dimension, parallel to the wall direction under consideration, of a rectangle inscribing the overall building plan.

Horizontal joint reinforcement shall consist of at least two wires of W1.7 spaced not more than 16 inches (406 mm); or bond beam reinforcement of at least one No. 4 bar spaced not more than 10 feet (3048 mm) shall be provided. Horizontal reinforcement shall also be provided at the bottom and top of wall openings and shall extend not less than 24 inches (610 mm) nor less than 40 bar diameters past the opening; continuously at structurally connected roof and floor levels; and within 16 inches (406 mm) of the top of walls.

R606.12.3 Seismic Design Category D_0 or D_1. Structures in Seismic Design Category D_0 or D_1 shall comply with the requirements of Seismic Design Category C and the additional requirements of this section.

R606.12.3.1 Design requirements. Masonry elements other than those covered by Section R606.12.2.2.2 shall be designed in accordance with the requirements of Chapter 1 and Sections 2.1 and 2.3 of TMS 402/ACI 530/ASCE 5 and shall meet the minimum reinforcement requirements contained in Sections R606.12.3.2 and R606.12.3.2.1.

Exception: Masonry walls limited to one *story* in height and 9 feet (2743 mm) between lateral supports need not be designed provided they comply with the minimum reinforcement requirements of Sections R606.12.3.2 and R606.12.3.2.1.

R606.12.3.2 Minimum reinforcement requirements for masonry walls. Masonry walls other than those covered by Section R606.12.2.2.3 shall be reinforced in both the vertical and horizontal direction. The sum of the cross-sectional area of horizontal and vertical reinforcement shall be at least 0.002 times the gross cross-sectional area of the wall, and the minimum cross-sectional area in each direction shall be not less than 0.0007 times the gross cross-sectional area of the wall. Reinforcement shall be uniformly distributed. Table R606.12.3.2 shows the minimum reinforcing bar sizes required for varying thicknesses of masonry walls. The maximum spacing of reinforcement shall be 48 inches (1219 mm) provided that the walls are solid grouted and constructed of hollow open-end units, hollow units laid with full head joints or two wythes of solid units. The maximum spacing of reinforcement shall be 24 inches (610 mm) for all other masonry.

R606.12.3.2.1 Shear wall reinforcement requirements. The maximum spacing of vertical and horizontal reinforcement shall be the smaller of one-third the length of the shear wall, one-third the height of the shear wall, or 48 inches (1219 mm). The minimum cross-sectional area of vertical reinforcement shall be one-third of the required shear reinforcement. Shear reinforcement shall be anchored around vertical reinforcing bars with a standard hook.

R606.12.3.3 Minimum reinforcement for masonry columns. Lateral ties in masonry columns shall be spaced not more than 8 inches (203 mm) on center and shall be at least $^3/_8$ inch (9.5 mm) diameter. Lateral ties shall be embedded in grout.

R606.12.3.4 Material restrictions. Type N mortar or masonry cement shall not be used as part of the lateral-force-resisting system.

R606.12.3.5 Lateral tie anchorage. Standard hooks for lateral tie anchorage shall be either a 135-degree (2.4 rad) standard hook or a 180-degree (3.2 rad) standard hook.

R606.12.4 Seismic Design Category D_2. All structures in Seismic Design Category D_2 shall comply with the requirements of Seismic Design Category D_1 and to the additional requirements of this section.

R606.12.4.1 Design of elements not part of the lateral-force-resisting system. Stack bond masonry that is not part of the lateral-force-resisting system shall have a horizontal cross-sectional area of reinforcement of at least 0.0015 times the gross cross-sectional area of masonry. Table R606.12.4.1 shows minimum reinforcing bar sizes for masonry walls. The maximum spacing of horizontal reinforcement shall be 24 inches (610 mm). These elements shall be solidly grouted and shall be constructed of hollow open-end units or two wythes of solid units.

TABLE R606.12.3.2
MINIMUM DISTRIBUTED WALL REINFORCEMENT FOR BUILDING ASSIGNED TO SEISMIC DESIGN CATEGORY D_0 or D_1

NOMINAL WALL THICKNESS (inches)	MINIMUM SUM OF THE VERTICAL AND HORIZONTAL REINFORCEMENT AREAS[a] (square inches per foot)	MINIMUM REINFORCEMENT AS DISTRIBUTED IN BOTH HORIZONTAL AND VERTICAL DIRECTIONS[b] (square inches per foot)	MINIMUM BAR SIZE FOR REINFORCEMENT SPACED AT 48 INCHES
6	0.135	0.047	#4
8	0.183	0.064	#5
10	0.231	0.081	#6
12	0.279	0.098	#6

For SI: 1 inch = 25.4 mm, 1 foot = 304.8 mm, 1 square inch per foot = 2064 mm²/m.

a. Based on the minimum reinforcing ratio of 0.002 times the gross cross-sectional area of the wall.

b. Based on the minimum reinforcing ratio each direction of 0.0007 times the gross cross-sectional area of the wall.

R606.12.4.2 Design of elements part of the lateral-force-resisting system. Stack bond masonry that is part of the lateral-force-resisting system shall have a horizontal cross-sectional area of reinforcement of at least 0.0025 times the gross cross-sectional area of masonry. Table R606.12.4.2 shows minimum reinforcing bar sizes for masonry walls. The maximum spacing of horizontal reinforcement shall be 16 inches (406 mm). These elements shall be solidly grouted and shall be constructed of hollow open-end units or two wythes of solid units.

TABLE R606.12.4.1
MINIMUM REINFORCING FOR STACKED BONDED MASONRY WALLS IN SEISMIC DESIGN CATEGORY D_2

NOMINAL WALL THICKNESS (inches)	MINIMUM BAR SIZE SPACED AT 24 INCHES
6	#4
8	#5
10	#5
12	#6

For SI: 1 inch = 25.4 mm.

TABLE R606.12.4.2
MINIMUM REINFORCING FOR STACKED BONDED MASONRY WALLS IN SEISMIC DESIGN CATEGORY D_2

NOMINAL WALL THICKNESS (inches)	MINIMUM BAR SIZE SPACED AT 16 INCHES
6	#4
8	#5
10	#5
12	#6

For SI: 1 inch = 25.4 mm.

R606.13 Protection for reinforcement. Bars shall be completely embedded in mortar or grout. Joint reinforcement embedded in horizontal mortar joints shall not have less than $^5/_8$-inch (15.9 mm) mortar coverage from the exposed face. All other reinforcement shall have a minimum coverage of one bar diameter over all bars, but not less than $^3/_4$ inch (19 mm), except where exposed to weather or soil, in which case the minimum coverage shall be 2 inches (51 mm).

R606.14 Beam supports. Beams, girders or other concentrated loads supported by a wall or column shall have a bearing of at least 3 inches (76 mm) in length measured parallel to the beam upon *solid masonry* not less than 4 inches (102 mm) in thickness, or upon a metal bearing plate of adequate design and dimensions to distribute the load safely, or upon a continuous reinforced masonry member projecting not less than 4 inches (102 mm) from the face of the wall.

R606.14.1 Joist bearing. Joists shall have a bearing of not less than $1^1/_2$ inches (38 mm), except as provided in Section R606.14, and shall be supported in accordance with Figure R606.11(1).

R606.15 Metal accessories. Joint reinforcement, anchors, ties and wire fabric shall conform to the following: ASTM A 82 for wire anchors and ties; ASTM A 36 for plate, headed and bent-bar anchors; ASTM A 510 for corrugated sheet metal anchors and ties; ASTM A 951 for joint reinforcement; ASTM B 227 for copper-clad steel wire ties; or ASTM A 167 for stainless steel hardware.

R606.15.1 Corrosion protection. Minimum corrosion protection of joint reinforcement, anchor ties and wire fabric for use in masonry wall construction shall conform to Table R606.15.1.

TABLE R606.15.1
MINIMUM CORROSION PROTECTION

MASONRY METAL ACCESSORY	STANDARD
Joint reinforcement, interior walls	ASTM A 641, Class 1
Wire ties or anchors in exterior walls completely embedded in mortar or grout	ASTM A 641, Class 3
Wire ties or anchors in exterior walls not completely embedded in mortar or grout	ASTM A 153, Class B-2
Joint reinforcement in exterior walls or interior walls exposed to moist environment	ASTM A 153, Class B-2
Sheet metal ties or anchors exposed to weather	ASTM A 153, Class B-2
Sheet metal ties or anchors completely embedded in mortar or grout	ASTM A 653, Coating Designation G60
Stainless steel hardware for any exposure	ASTM A 167, Type 304

SECTION R607
UNIT MASONRY

R607.1 Mortar. Mortar for use in masonry construction shall comply with ASTM C 270. The type of mortar shall be in accordance with Sections R607.1.1, R607.1.2 and R607.1.3 and shall meet the proportion specifications of Table R607.1 or the property specifications of ASTM C 270.

R607.1.1 Foundation walls. Masonry foundation walls constructed as set forth in Tables R404.1.1(1) through R404.1.1(4) and mortar shall be Type M or S.

R607.1.2 Masonry in Seismic Design Categories A, B and C. Mortar for masonry serving as the lateral-force-resisting system in Seismic Design Categories A, B and C shall be Type M, S or N mortar.

R607.1.3 Masonry in Seismic Design Categories D_0, D_1 and D_2. Mortar for masonry serving as the lateral-force- resisting system in Seismic Design Categories D_0, D_1 and D_2 shall be Type M or S portland cement-lime or mortar cement mortar.

R607.2 Placing mortar and masonry units.

R607.2.1 Bed and head joints. Unless otherwise required or indicated on the project drawings, head and bed joints shall be $^3/_8$ inch (10 mm) thick, except that the thickness of the bed joint of the starting course placed over foundations shall not be less than $^1/_4$ inch (7 mm) and not more than $1^1/_2$ inch (38 mm).

TABLE R607.1
MORTAR PROPORTIONS[a, b]

		PROPORTIONS BY VOLUME (cementitious materials)								
			Mortar cement			Masonry cement				
MORTAR	TYPE	Portland cement or blended cement	M	S	N	M	S	N	Hydrated lime[c] or lime putty	Aggregate ratio (measured in damp, loose conditions)
Cement-lime	M	1	—	—	—	—	—	—	$^{1}/_{4}$	Not less than $2^{1}/_{4}$ and not more than 3 times the sum of separate volumes of lime, if used, and cement
	S	1	—	—	—	—	—	—	over $^{1}/_{4}$ to $^{1}/_{2}$	
	N	1	—	—	—	—	—	—	over $^{1}/_{2}$ to $1^{1}/_{4}$	
	O	1	—	—	—	—	—	—	over $1^{1}/_{4}$ to $2^{1}/_{2}$	
Mortar cement	M	1	—	—	1	—	—	—	—	
	M	—	1	—	—	—	—	—		
	S	$^{1}/_{2}$	—	—	1	—	—	—		
	S	—	—	1	—	—	—	—		
	N	—	—	—	1	—	—	—		
	O	—	—	—	1	—	—	—		
Masonry cement	M	1				—	—	1	—	
	M	—				1	—	—		
	S	$^{1}/_{2}$				—	—	1		
	S	—				—	1	—		
	N	—				—	—	1		
	O	—				—	—	1		

For SI: 1 cubic foot = 0.0283 m^{3}, 1 pound = 0.454 kg.

a. For the purpose of these specifications, the weight of 1 cubic foot of the respective materials shall be considered to be as follows:

Portland Cement	94 pounds	Masonry Cement	Weight printed on bag
Mortar Cement	Weight printed on bag	Hydrated Lime	40 pounds
Lime Putty (Quicklime)	80 pounds	Sand, damp and loose	80 pounds of dry sand

b. Two air-entraining materials shall not be combined in mortar.

c. Hydrated lime conforming to the requirements of ASTM C 270.

R607.2.1.1 Mortar joint thickness tolerance. Mortar joint thickness for load-bearing masonry shall be within the following tolerances from the specified dimensions:

1. Bed joint: + $^{1}/_{8}$ inch (3 mm).
2. Head joint: - $^{1}/_{4}$ inch (7 mm), + $^{3}/_{8}$ inch (10 mm).
3. Collar joints: - $^{1}/_{4}$ inch (7 mm), + $^{3}/_{8}$ inch (10 mm).

R607.2.2 Masonry unit placement. The mortar shall be sufficiently plastic and units shall be placed with sufficient pressure to extrude mortar from the joint and produce a tight joint. Deep furrowing of bed joints that produces voids shall not be permitted. Any units disturbed to the extent that initial bond is broken after initial placement shall be removed and relaid in fresh mortar. Surfaces to be in contact with mortar shall be clean and free of deleterious materials.

R607.2.2.1 Solid masonry. *Solid masonry* units shall be laid with full head and bed joints and all interior vertical joints that are designed to receive mortar shall be filled.

R607.2.2.2 Hollow masonry. For hollow masonry units, head and bed joints shall be filled solidly with mortar for a distance in from the face of the unit not less than the thickness of the face shell.

R607.3 Installation of wall ties. The installation of wall ties shall be as follows:

1. The ends of wall ties shall be embedded in mortar joints. Wall tie ends shall engage outer face shells of hollow units by at least $^{1}/_{2}$ inch (13 mm). Wire wall ties shall be embedded at least $1^{1}/_{2}$ inches (38 mm) into the mortar bed of *solid masonry* units or solid grouted hollow units.
2. Wall ties shall not be bent after being embedded in grout or mortar.

SECTION R608 MULTIPLE WYTHE MASONRY

R608.1 General. The facing and backing of multiple wythe masonry walls shall be bonded in accordance with Section R608.1.1, R608.1.2 or R608.1.3. In cavity walls, neither the facing nor the backing shall be less than 3 inches (76 mm) nominal in thickness and the cavity shall not be more than 4 inches (102 mm) nominal in width. The backing shall be at least as thick as the facing.

Exception: Cavities shall be permitted to exceed the 4-inch (102 mm) nominal dimension provided tie size and tie spacing have been established by calculation.

R608.1.1 Bonding with masonry headers. Bonding with solid or hollow masonry headers shall comply with Sections R608.1.1.1 and R608.1.1.2.

R608.1.1.1 Solid units. Where the facing and backing (adjacent wythes) of *solid masonry* construction are bonded by means of masonry headers, no less than 4 percent of the wall surface of each face shall be composed of headers extending not less than 3 inches (76 mm) into the backing. The distance between adjacent full-length headers shall not exceed 24 inches (610 mm) either vertically or horizontally. In walls in which a single header does not extend through the wall, headers from the opposite sides shall overlap at least 3 inches (76 mm), or headers from opposite sides shall be covered with another header course overlapping the header below at least 3 inches (76 mm).

R608.1.1.2 Hollow units. Where two or more hollow units are used to make up the thickness of a wall, the stretcher courses shall be bonded at vertical intervals not exceeding 34 inches (864 mm) by lapping at least 3 inches (76 mm) over the unit below, or by lapping at vertical intervals not exceeding 17 inches (432 mm) with units that are at least 50 percent thicker than the units below.

R608.1.2 Bonding with wall ties or joint reinforcement. Bonding with wall ties or joint reinforcement shall comply with Sections R608.1.2.1 through R608.1.2.3.

R608.1.2.1 Bonding with wall ties. Bonding with wall ties, except as required by Section R610, where the facing and backing (adjacent wythes) of masonry walls are bonded with $^3/_{16}$-inch-diameter (5 mm) wall ties embedded in the horizontal mortar joints, there shall be at least one metal tie for each 4.5 square feet (0.418 m^2) of wall area. Ties in alternate courses shall be staggered. The maximum vertical distance between ties shall not exceed 24 inches (610 mm), and the maximum horizontal distance shall not exceed 36 inches (914 mm). Rods or ties bent to rectangular shape shall be used with hollow masonry units laid with the cells vertical. In other walls, the ends of ties shall be bent to 90-degree (0.79 rad) angles to provide hooks no less than 2 inches (51 mm) long. Additional bonding ties shall be provided at all openings, spaced not more than 3 feet (914 mm) apart around the perimeter and within 12 inches (305 mm) of the opening.

R608.1.2.2 Bonding with adjustable wall ties. Where the facing and backing (adjacent wythes) of masonry are bonded with adjustable wall ties, there shall be at least one tie for each 2.67 square feet (0.248 m^2) of wall area. Neither the vertical nor the horizontal spacing of the adjustable wall ties shall exceed 24 inches (610 mm). The maximum vertical offset of bed joints from one wythe to the other shall be 1.25 inches (32 mm). The maximum clearance between connecting parts of the ties shall be $^1/_{16}$ inch (2 mm). When pintle legs are used, ties shall have at least two $^3/_{16}$-inch-diameter (5 mm) legs.

R608.1.2.3 Bonding with prefabricated joint reinforcement. Where the facing and backing (adjacent wythes) of masonry are bonded with prefabricated joint reinforcement, there shall be at least one cross wire serving as a tie for each 2.67 square feet (0.248 m^2) of wall area. The vertical spacing of the joint reinforcement shall not exceed 16 inches (406 mm). Cross wires on prefabricated joint reinforcement shall not be smaller than No. 9 gage. The longitudinal wires shall be embedded in the mortar.

TABLE R609.1.1
GROUT PROPORTIONS BY VOLUME FOR MASONRY CONSTRUCTION

TYPE	PORTLAND CEMENT OR BLENDED CEMENT SLAG CEMENT	HYDRATED LIME OR LIME PUTTY	AGGREGATE MEASURED IN A DAMP, LOOSE CONDITION	
			Fine	Coarse
Fine	1	0 to 1/10	$2^1/_4$ to 3 times the sum of the volume of the cementitious materials	—
Coarse	1	0 to 1/10	$2^1/_4$ to 3 times the sum of the volume of the cementitious materials	1 to 2 times the sum of the volumes of the cementitious materials

TABLE R609.1.2
GROUT SPACE DIMENSIONS AND POUR HEIGHTS

GROUT TYPE	GROUT POUR MAXIMUM HEIGHT (feet)	MINIMUM WIDTH OF GROUT SPACES[a,b] (inches)	MINIMUM GROUT[b,c] SPACE DIMENSIONS FOR GROUTING CELLS OF HOLLOW UNITS (inches x inches)
Fine	1	0.75	1.5 × 2
	5	2	2 × 3
	12	2.5	2.5 × 3
	24	3	3 × 3
Coarse	1	1.5	1.5 × 3
	5	2	2.5 × 3
	12	2.5	3 × 3
	24	3	3 × 4

For SI: 1 inch = 25.4 mm, 1 foot = 304.8 mm.

a. For grouting between masonry wythes.

b. Grout space dimension is the clear dimension between any masonry protrusion and shall be increased by the horizontal projection of the diameters of the horizontal bars within the cross section of the grout space.

c. Area of vertical reinforcement shall not exceed 6 percent of the area of the grout space.

R608.1.3 Bonding with natural or cast stone. Bonding with natural and cast stone shall conform to Sections R608.1.3.1 and R608.1.3.2.

R608.1.3.1 Ashlar masonry. In ashlar masonry, bonder units, uniformly distributed, shall be provided to the extent of not less than 10 percent of the wall area. Such bonder units shall extend not less than 4 inches (102 mm) into the backing wall.

R608.1.3.2 Rubble stone masonry. Rubble stone masonry 24 inches (610 mm) or less in thickness shall have bonder units with a maximum spacing of 3 feet (914 mm) vertically and 3 feet (914 mm) horizontally, and if the masonry is of greater thickness than 24 inches (610 mm), shall have one bonder unit for each 6 square feet (0.557 m^2) of wall surface on both sides.

R608.2 Masonry bonding pattern. Masonry laid in running and stack bond shall conform to Sections R608.2.1 and R608.2.2.

R608.2.1 Masonry laid in running bond. In each wythe of masonry laid in running bond, head joints in successive courses shall be offset by not less than one-fourth the unit length, or the masonry walls shall be reinforced longitudinally as required in Section R608.2.2.

R608.2.2 Masonry laid in stack bond. Where unit masonry is laid with less head joint offset than in Section R608.2.1, the minimum area of horizontal reinforcement placed in mortar bed joints or in bond beams spaced not more than 48 inches (1219 mm) apart, shall be 0.0007 times the vertical cross-sectional area of the wall.

SECTION R609
GROUTED MASONRY

R609.1 General. Grouted multiple-wythe masonry is a form of construction in which the space between the wythes is solidly filled with grout. It is not necessary for the cores of masonry units to be filled with grout. Grouted hollow unit masonry is a form of construction in which certain cells of hollow units are continuously filled with grout.

R609.1.1 Grout. Grout shall consist of cementitious material and aggregate in accordance with ASTM C 476 and the proportion specifications of Table R609.1.1. Type M or Type S mortar to which sufficient water has been added to produce pouring consistency can be used as grout.

R609.1.2 Grouting requirements. Maximum pour heights and the minimum dimensions of spaces provided for grout placement shall conform to Table R609.1.2. If the work is stopped for one hour or longer, the horizontal construction joints shall be formed by stopping all tiers at the same elevation and with the grout 1 inch (25 mm) below the top.

R609.1.3 Grout space (cleaning). Provision shall be made for cleaning grout space. Mortar projections that project more than 0.5 inch (13 mm) into grout space and any other foreign matter shall be removed from grout space prior to inspection and grouting.

R609.1.4 Grout placement. Grout shall be a plastic mix suitable for pumping without segregation of the constituents and shall be mixed thoroughly. Grout shall be placed by pumping or by an *approved* alternate method and shall be placed before any initial set occurs and in no case more than $1^1/_2$ hours after water has been added. Grouting shall be done in a continuous pour, in lifts not exceeding 5 feet (1524 mm). It shall be consolidated by puddling or mechanical vibrating during placing and reconsolidated after excess moisture has been absorbed but before plasticity is lost.

R609.1.4.1 Grout pumped through aluminum pipes. Grout shall not be pumped through aluminum pipes.

R609.1.5 Cleanouts. Where required by the *building official*, cleanouts shall be provided as specified in this section. The cleanouts shall be sealed before grouting and after inspection.

R609.1.5.1 Grouted multiple-wythe masonry. Cleanouts shall be provided at the bottom course of the exterior wythe at each pour of grout where such pour exceeds 5 feet (1524 mm) in height.

R609.1.5.2 Grouted hollow unit masonry. Cleanouts shall be provided at the bottom course of each cell to be grouted at each pour of grout, where such pour exceeds 4 feet (1219 mm) in height.

R609.2 Grouted multiple-wythe masonry. Grouted multiple-wythe masonry shall conform to all the requirements specified in Section R609.1 and the requirements of this section.

R609.2.1 Bonding of backup wythe. Where all interior vertical spaces are filled with grout in multiple-wythe construction, masonry headers shall not be permitted. Metal wall ties shall be used in accordance with Section R608.1.2 to prevent spreading of the wythes and to maintain the vertical alignment of the wall. Wall ties shall be installed in accordance with Section R608.1.2 when the backup wythe in multiple-wythe construction is fully grouted.

R609.2.2 Grout spaces. Fine grout shall be used when interior vertical space to receive grout does not exceed 2 inches (51 mm) in thickness. Interior vertical spaces exceeding 2 inches (51 mm) in thickness shall use coarse or fine grout.

R609.2.3 Grout barriers. Vertical grout barriers or dams shall be built of *solid masonry* across the grout space the entire height of the wall to control the flow of the grout horizontally. Grout barriers shall not be more than 25 feet (7620 mm) apart. The grouting of any section of a wall between control barriers shall be completed in one day with no interruptions greater than one hour.

R609.3 Reinforced grouted multiple-wythe masonry. Reinforced grouted multiple-wythe masonry shall conform to all the requirements specified in Sections R609.1 and R609.2 and the requirements of this section.

R609.3.1 Construction. The thickness of grout or mortar between masonry units and reinforcement shall not be less than $^1/_4$ inch (7 mm), except that $^1/_4$-inch (7 mm) bars may be laid in horizontal mortar joints at least $^1/_2$ inch (13 mm) thick, and steel wire reinforcement may be laid in horizontal mortar joints at least twice the thickness of the wire diameter.

R609.4 Reinforced hollow unit masonry. Reinforced hollow unit masonry shall conform to all the requirements of Section R609.1 and the requirements of this section.

R609.4.1 Construction. Requirements for construction shall be as follows:

1. Reinforced hollow-unit masonry shall be built to preserve the unobstructed vertical continuity of the cells to be filled. Walls and cross webs forming cells to be filled shall be full-bedded in mortar to prevent leakage of grout. Head and end joints shall be solidly filled with mortar for a distance in from the face of the wall or unit not less than the thickness of the longitudinal face shells. Bond shall be provided by lapping units in successive vertical courses.
2. Cells to be filled shall have vertical alignment sufficient to maintain a clear, unobstructed continuous vertical cell of dimensions prescribed in Table R609.1.2.
3. Vertical reinforcement shall be held in position at top and bottom and at intervals not exceeding 200 diameters of the reinforcement.
4. Cells containing reinforcement shall be filled solidly with grout. Grout shall be poured in lifts of 8-foot (2438 mm) maximum height. When a total grout pour exceeds 8 feet (2438 mm) in height, the grout shall be placed in lifts not exceeding 5 feet (1524 mm) and special inspection during grouting shall be required.
5. Horizontal steel shall be fully embedded by grout in an uninterrupted pour.

SECTION R610 GLASS UNIT MASONRY

R610.1 General. Panels of glass unit masonry located in load-bearing and nonload-bearing exterior and interior walls shall be constructed in accordance with this section.

R610.2 Materials. Hollow glass units shall be partially evacuated and have a minimum average glass face thickness of $^3/_{16}$ inch (5 mm). The surface of units in contact with mortar shall be treated with a polyvinyl butyral coating or latex-based paint. The use of reclaimed units is prohibited.

R610.3 Units. Hollow or solid glass block units shall be standard or thin units.

R610.3.1 Standard units. The specified thickness of standard units shall be at least $3^7/_8$ inches (98 mm).

R610.3.2 Thin units. The specified thickness of thin units shall be at least $3^1/_8$ inches (79 mm) for hollow units and at least 3 inches (76 mm) for solid units.

R610.4 Isolated panels. Isolated panels of glass unit masonry shall conform to the requirements of this section.

R610.4.1 Exterior standard-unit panels. The maximum area of each individual standard-unit panel shall be 144 square feet (13.4 m^2) when the design wind pressure is 20 psf (958 Pa). The maximum area of such panels subjected to design wind pressures other than 20 psf (958 Pa) shall be in accordance with Figure R610.4.1. The maximum panel dimension between structural supports shall be 25 feet (7620 mm) in width or 20 feet (6096 mm) in height.

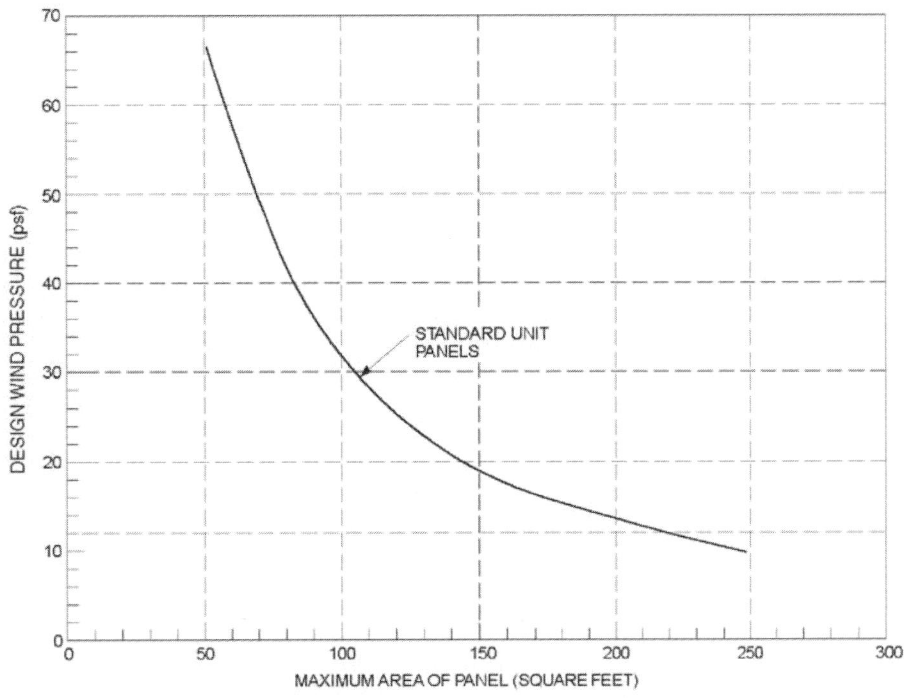

For SI: 1 square foot = 0.0929 m^2, 1 pound per square foot = 0.0479 kPa.

FIGURE R610.4.1
GLASS UNIT MASONRY DESIGN WIND LOAD RESISTANCE

R610.4.2 Exterior thin-unit panels. The maximum area of each individual thin-unit panel shall be 85 square feet (7.9 m^2). The maximum dimension between structural supports shall be 15 feet (4572 mm) in width or 10 feet (3048 mm) in height. Thin units shall not be used in applications where the design wind pressure as stated in Table R301.2(1) exceeds 20 psf (958 Pa).

R610.4.3 Interior panels. The maximum area of each individual standard-unit panel shall be 250 square feet (23.2 m^2). The maximum area of each thin-unit panel shall be 150 square feet (13.9 m^2). The maximum dimension between structural supports shall be 25 feet (7620 mm) in width or 20 feet (6096 mm) in height.

R610.4.4 Curved panels. The width of curved panels shall conform to the requirements of Sections R610.4.1, R610.4.2 and R610.4.3, except additional structural supports shall be provided at locations where a curved section joins a straight section, and at inflection points in multicurved walls.

R610.5 Panel support. Glass unit masonry panels shall conform to the support requirements of this section.

R610.5.1 Deflection. The maximum total deflection of structural members that support glass unit masonry shall not exceed $^1/_{600}$.

R610.5.2 Lateral support. Glass unit masonry panels shall be laterally supported along the top and sides of the panel. Lateral supports for glass unit masonry panels shall be designed to resist a minimum of 200 pounds per lineal feet (2918 N/m) of panel, or the actual applied loads, whichever is greater. Except for single unit panels, lateral support shall be provided by panel anchors along the top and sides spaced a maximum of 16 inches (406 mm) on center or by channel-type restraints. Single unit panels shall be supported by channel-type restraints.

Exceptions:

1. Lateral support is not required at the top of panels that are one unit wide.
2. Lateral support is not required at the sides of panels that are one unit high.

R610.5.2.1 Panel anchor restraints. Panel anchors shall be spaced a maximum of 16 inches (406 mm) on center in both jambs and across the head. Panel anchors shall be embedded a minimum of 12 inches (305 mm) and shall be provided with two fasteners so as to resist the loads specified in Section R610.5.2.

R610.5.2.2 Channel-type restraints. Glass unit masonry panels shall be recessed at least 1 inch (25 mm) within channels and chases. Channel-type restraints shall be oversized to accommodate expansion material in the opening, packing and sealant between the framing restraints, and the glass unit masonry perimeter units.

R610.6 Sills. Before bedding of glass units, the sill area shall be covered with a water base asphaltic emulsion coating. The coating shall be a minimum of $^1/_8$ inch (3 mm) thick.

R610.7 Expansion joints. Glass unit masonry panels shall be provided with expansion joints along the top and sides at all structural supports. Expansion joints shall be a minimum of $^3/_8$ inch (10 mm) in thickness and shall have sufficient thickness to accommodate displacements of the supporting structure. Expansion joints shall be entirely free of mortar and other debris and shall be filled with resilient material.

R610.8 Mortar. Glass unit masonry shall be laid with Type S or N mortar. Mortar shall not be retempered after initial set. Mortar unused within $1^1/_2$ hours after initial mixing shall be discarded.

R610.9 Reinforcement. Glass unit masonry panels shall have horizontal joint reinforcement spaced a maximum of 16 inches (406 mm) on center located in the mortar bed joint. Horizontal joint reinforcement shall extend the entire length of the panel but shall not extend across expansion joints. Longitudinal wires shall be lapped a minimum of 6 inches (152 mm) at splices. Joint reinforcement shall be placed in the bed joint immediately below and above openings in the panel. The reinforcement shall have not less than two parallel longitudinal wires of size W1.7 or greater, and have welded cross wires of size W1.7 or greater.

R610.10 Placement. Glass units shall be placed so head and bed joints are filled solidly. Mortar shall not be furrowed. Head and bed joints of glass unit masonry shall be $^1/_4$ inch (6.4 mm) thick, except that vertical joint thickness of radial panels shall not be less than $^1/_8$ inch (3 mm) or greater than $^5/_8$ inch (16 mm). The bed joint thickness tolerance shall be minus $^1/_{16}$ inch (1.6 mm) and plus $^1/_8$ inch (3 mm). The head joint thickness tolerance shall be plus or minus $^1/_8$ inch (3 mm).

SECTION R611
EXTERIOR CONCRETE WALL CONSTRUCTION

R611.1 General. Insulating concrete form walls shall be designed and constructed in accordance with the provisions of this section or in accordance with the provisions of ACI 318. When ACI 318 or the provisions of this section are used to design concrete walls, project drawings, typical details and specifications are not required to bear the seal of the registered design professional, unless otherwise required by the state law of the jurisdiction having authority.

R611.1.1 Interior construction. These provisions are based on the assumption that interior walls and partitions, both load-bearing and nonload-bearing, floors and roof/ceiling assemblies are constructed of *light-framed construction* complying with the limitations of this code and the additional limitations of Section R611.2. Design and construction of light-framed assemblies shall be in accordance with the applicable provisions of this code. Where second-story exterior walls are of *light-framed construction*, they shall be designed and constructed as required by this code.

Aspects of concrete construction not specifically addressed by this code, including interior concrete walls, shall comply with ACI 318.

R611.1.2 Other concrete walls. Exterior concrete walls constructed in accordance with this code shall comply with the shapes and minimum concrete cross-sectional dimensions of Table R611.3. Other types of forming systems resulting in concrete walls not in compliance with this section shall be designed in accordance with ACI 318.

R611.2 Applicability limits. The provisions of this section shall apply to the construction of exterior concrete walls for buildings not greater than 60 feet (18 288 mm) in plan dimensions, floors with clear spans not greater than 32 feet (9754 mm) and roofs with clear spans not greater than 40 feet (12 192 mm). Buildings shall not exceed 35 feet (10 668 mm) in mean roof height or two stories in height above-grade. Floor/ceiling dead loads shall not exceed 10 pounds per square foot (479 Pa), roof/ceiling dead loads shall not exceed 15 pounds per square foot (718 Pa) and *attic* live loads shall not exceed 20 pounds per square foot (958 Pa). Roof overhangs shall not exceed 2 feet (610 mm) of horizontal projection beyond the exterior wall and the dead load of the overhangs shall not exceed 8 pounds per square foot (383 Pa).

Walls constructed in accordance with the provisions of this section shall be limited to buildings subjected to a maximum design wind speed of 130 miles per hour (58 m/s) Exposure B, 110 miles per hour (49 m/s) Exposure C and 100 miles per hour (45 m/s) Exposure D. Walls constructed in accordance with the provisions of this section shall be limited to detached one- and two-family *dwellings* and townhouses assigned to Seismic Design Category A or B, and detached one- and two-family *dwellings* assigned to Seismic Design Category C.

Buildings that are not within the scope of this section shall be designed in accordance with PCA 100 or ACI 318.

R611.3 Concrete wall systems. Concrete walls constructed in accordance with these provisions shall comply with the shapes and minimum concrete cross-sectional dimensions of Table R611.3.

R611.3.1 Flat wall systems. Flat concrete wall systems shall comply with Table R611.3 and Figure R611.3(1) and have a minimum nominal thickness of 4 inches (102 mm).

R611.3.2 Waffle-grid wall systems. Waffle-grid wall systems shall comply with Table R611.3 and Figure R611.3(2). and shall have a minimum nominal thickness of 6 inches (152 mm) for the horizontal and vertical concrete members (cores). The core and web dimensions shall comply with Table R611. 3. The maximum weight of waffle-grid walls shall comply with Table R611.3.

R611.3.3 Screen-grid wall systems. Screen-grid wall systems shall comply with Table R611.3 and Figure R611.3(3) and shall have a minimum nominal thickness of 6 inches (152 mm) for the horizontal and vertical concrete members (cores). The core dimensions shall comply with Table R611.3. The maximum weight of screen-grid walls shall comply with Table R611.3.

R611.4 Stay-in-place forms. Stay-in-place concrete forms shall comply with this section.

R611.4.1 Surface burning characteristics. The flame spread index and smoke-developed index of forming material, other than foam plastic, left exposed on the interior shall comply with Section R302.9. The surface burning characteristics of foam plastic used in insulating concrete forms shall comply with Section R316.3.

TABLE R611.3
DIMENSIONAL REQUIREMENTS FOR WALLS[a,b]

WALL TYPE AND NOMINAL THICKNESS	MAXIMUM WALL WEIGHT[c] (psf)	MINIMUM WIDTH, W, OF VERTICAL CORES (inches)	MINIMUM THICKNESS, T, OF VERTICAL CORES (inches)	MAXIMUM SPACING OF VERTICAL CORES (inches)	MAXIMUM SPACING OF HORIZONTAL CORES (inches)	MINIMUM WEB THICKNESS (inches)
4″ Flat[d]	50	N/A	N/A	N/A	N/A	N/A
6″ Flat[d]	75	N/A	N/A	N/A	N/A	N/A
8″ Flat[d]	100	N/A	N/A	N/A	N/A	N/A
10″ Flat[d]	125	N/A	N/A	N/A	N/A	N/A
6″ Waffle-grid	56	8[e]	5.5[e]	12	16	2
8″ Waffle-grid	76	8[f]	8[f]	12	16	2
6″ Screen-grid	53	6.25[g]	6.25[g]	12	12	N/A

For SI: 1 inch = 25.4 mm; 1 pound per square foot = 0.0479 kPa, 1 pound per cubic foot = 2402.77 kg/m^3, 1 square inch = 645.16 mm^2.

a. Width "W," thickness "T," spacing and web thickness, refer to Figures R611.3(2) and R611.3(3).

b. N/A indicates not applicable.

c. Wall weight is based on a unit weight of concrete of 150 pcf. For flat walls the weight is based on the nominal thickness. The tabulated values do not include any allowance for interior and exterior finishes.

d. Nominal wall thickness. The actual as-built thickness of a flat wall shall not be more than $^1/_2$-inch less or more than $^1/_4$-inch more than the nominal dimension indicated.

e. Vertical core is assumed to be elliptical-shaped. Another shape core is permitted provided the minimum thickness is 5 inches, the moment of inertia, *I*, about the centerline of the wall (ignoring the web) is not less than 65 in^4, and the area, *A*, is not less than 31.25 in^2. The width used to calculate *A* and *I* shall not exceed 8 inches.

f. Vertical core is assumed to be circular. Another shape core is permitted provided the minimum thickness is 7 inches, the moment of inertia, *I*, about the centerline of the wall (ignoring the web) is not less than 200 in^4, and the area, *A*, is not less than 49 in^2. The width used to calculate *A* and *I* shall not exceed 8 inches.

g. Vertical core is assumed to be circular. Another shape core is permitted provided the minimum thickness is 5.5 inches, the moment of inertia, *I*, about the centerline of the wall is not less than 76 in^4, and the area, *A*, is not less than 30.25 in^2. The width used to calculate *A* and *I* shall not exceed 6.25 inches.

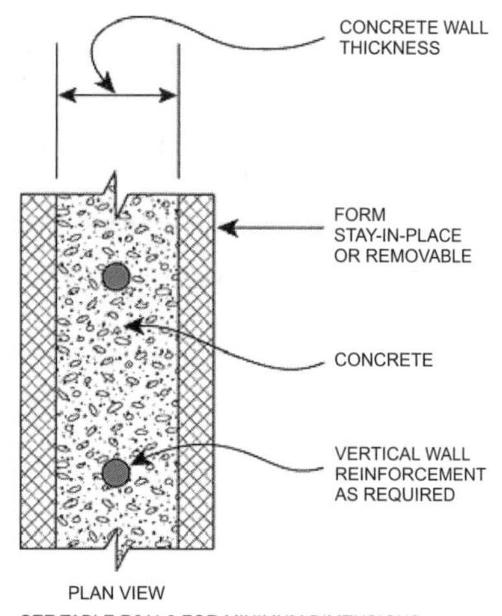

FIGURE R611.3(1)
FLAT WALL SYSTEM

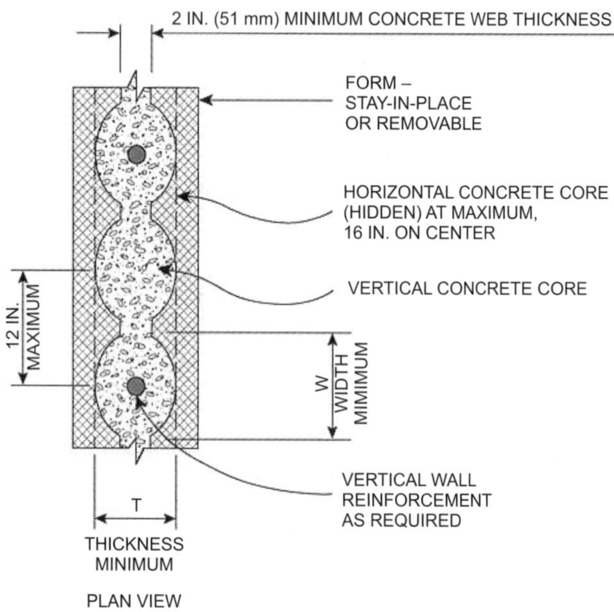

SEE TABLE R611.3 FOR MINIMUM DIMENSIONS

For SI: 1 inch = 25.4 mm.

FIGURE R611.3(2)
WAFFLE-GRID WALL SYSTEM

R611.4.2 Interior covering. Stay-in-place forms constructed of rigid foam plastic shall be protected on the interior of the building as required by Sections R316.4 and R702.3.4. Where gypsum board is used to protect the foam plastic, it shall be installed with a mechanical fastening system. Use of adhesives is permitted in addition to mechanical fasteners.

R611.4.3 Exterior wall covering. Stay-in-place forms constructed of rigid foam plastics shall be protected from sunlight and physical damage by the application of an *approved* exterior wall covering complying with this code. Exterior surfaces of other stay-in-place forming systems shall be protected in accordance with this code.

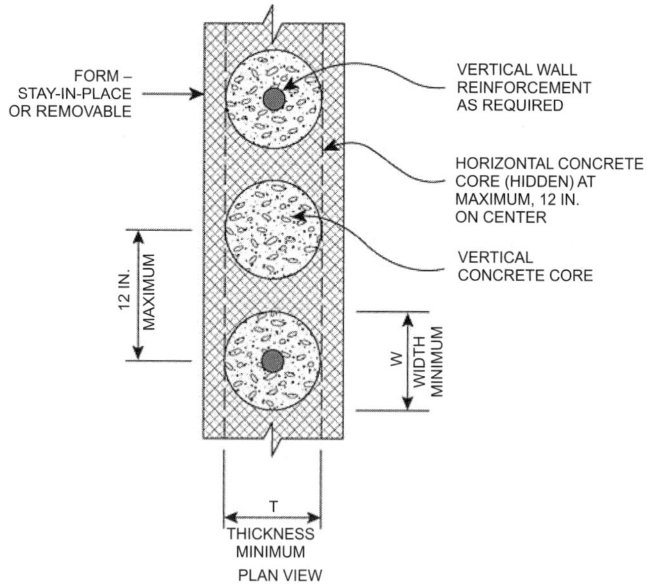

SEE TABLE R611.3 FOR MINIMUM DIMENSIONS.

For SI: 1 inch = 25.4 mm.

FIGURE R611.3(3)
SCREEN-GRID WALL SYSTEM

Requirements for installation of masonry veneer, stucco and other finishes on the exterior of concrete walls and other construction details not covered in this section shall comply with the requirements of this code.

R611.5 Materials. Materials used in the construction of concrete walls shall comply with this section.

R611.5.1 Concrete and materials for concrete. Materials used in concrete, and the concrete itself, shall conform to requirements of this section, or ACI 318.

R611.5.1.1 Concrete mixing and delivery. Mixing and delivery of concrete shall comply with ASTM C 94 or ASTM C 685.

R611.5.1.2 Maximum aggregate size. The nominal maximum size of coarse aggregate shall not exceed one-fifth the narrowest distance between sides of forms, or three-fourths the clear spacing between reinforcing bars or between a bar and the side of the form.

Exception: When *approved*, these limitations shall not apply where removable forms are used and workability and methods of consolidation permit concrete to be placed without honeycombs or voids.

R611.5.1.3 Proportioning and slump of concrete. Proportions of materials for concrete shall be established to provide workability and consistency to permit concrete to be worked readily into forms and around reinforcement under conditions of placement to be employed, without segregation or excessive bleeding. Slump of concrete placed in removable forms shall not exceed 6 inches (152 mm).

Exception: When *approved*, the slump is permitted to exceed 6 inches (152 mm) for concrete mixtures that are resistant to segregation, and are in accordance with the form manufacturer's recommendations.

Slump of concrete placed in stay-in-place forms shall exceed 6 inches (152 mm). Slump of concrete shall be determined in accordance with ASTM C 143.

R611.5.1.4 Compressive strength. The minimum specified compressive strength of concrete, f'_c, shall comply with Section R402.2 and shall be not less than 2,500 pounds per square inch (17.2 MPa) at 28 days.

R611.5.1.5 Consolidation of concrete. Concrete shall be consolidated by suitable means during placement and shall be worked around embedded items and reinforcement and into corners of forms. Where stay-in-place forms are used, concrete shall be consolidated by internal vibration.

Exception: When *approved*, self-consolidating concrete mixtures with slumps equal to or greater than 8 inches (203 mm) that are specifically designed for placement without internal vibration need not be internally vibrated.

R611.5.2 Steel reinforcement and anchor bolts.

R611.5.2.1 Steel reinforcement. Steel reinforcement shall comply with ASTM A 615, A 706, or A 996. ASTM A 996 bars produced from rail steel shall be Type R.

R611.5.2.2 Anchor bolts. Anchor bolts for use with connection details in accordance with Figures R611.9(1) through R611.9(12) shall be bolts with heads complying with ASTM A 307 or ASTM F 1554. ASTM A 307 bolts shall be Grade A (i.e., with heads). ASTM F 1554 bolts shall be Grade 36 minimum. Instead of bolts with heads, it is permissible to use rods with threads on both ends fabricated from steel complying with ASTM A 36. The threaded end of the rod to be embedded in the concrete shall be provided with a hex or square nut.

R611.5.2.3 Sheet steel angles and tension tie straps. Angles and tension tie straps for use with connection details in accordance with Figures R611.9(1) through R611.9(12) shall be fabricated from sheet steel complying with ASTM A 653 SS, ASTM A 792 SS, or ASTM A 875 SS. The steel shall be minimum Grade 33 unless a higher grade is required by the applicable figure.

R611.5.3 Form materials and form ties. Forms shall be made of wood, steel, aluminum, plastic, a composite of cement and foam insulation, a composite of cement and wood chips, or other *approved* material suitable for supporting and containing concrete. Forms shall provide sufficient strength to contain concrete during the concrete placement operation.

Form ties shall be steel, solid plastic, foam plastic, a composite of cement and wood chips, a composite of cement and foam plastic, or other suitable material capable of resisting the forces created by fluid pressure of fresh concrete.

R611.5.4 Reinforcement installation details.

R611.5.4.1 Support and cover. Reinforcement shall be secured in the proper location in the forms with tie wire or other bar support system such that displacement will not occur during the concrete placement operation. Steel reinforcement in concrete cast against the earth shall have a minimum cover of 3 inches (76 mm). Minimum cover for reinforcement in concrete cast in removable forms that will be exposed to the earth or weather shall be $1^1/_2$ inches (38 mm) for No. 5 bars and smaller, and 2 inches (50 mm) for No. 6 bars and larger. For concrete cast in removable forms that will not be exposed to the earth or weather, and for concrete cast in stay-in-place forms, minimum cover shall be $^3/_4$ inch (19 mm). The minus tolerance for cover shall not exceed the smaller of one-third the required cover and $^3/_8$ inch (10 mm). See Section R611.5.4.4 for cover requirements for hooks of bars developed in tension.

R611.5.4.2 Location of reinforcement in walls. For location of reinforcement in foundation walls and above-grade walls, see Sections R404.1.2.3.7.2 and R611.6.5, respectively.

R611.5.4.3 Lap splices. Vertical and horizontal wall reinforcement required by Sections R611.6 and R611.7 shall be the longest lengths practical. Where splices are necessary in reinforcement, the length of lap splices shall be in accordance with Table R611.5.4(1) and Figure R611.5.4 (1). The maximum gap between noncontact parallel bars at a lap splice shall not exceed the smaller of one-fifth the required lap length and 6 inches (152 mm). See Figure R611.5.4(1).

R611.5.4.4 Development of bars in tension. Where bars are required to be developed in tension by other provisions of this code, development lengths and cover for hooks and bar extensions shall comply with Table R611.5.4(1) and Figure R611.5.4 (2). The development lengths shown in Table R611.5.4(1) also apply to bundled bars in lintels installed in accordance with Section R611.8.2.2.

R611.5.4.5 Standard hooks. Where reinforcement is required by this code to terminate with a standard hook, the hook shall comply with Figure R611.5.4(3).

R611.5.4.6 Webs of waffle-grid walls. Reinforcement, including stirrups, shall not be placed in webs of waffle-grid walls, including lintels. Webs are permitted to have form ties.

R611.5.4.7 Alternate grade of reinforcement and spacing. Where tables in Sections R404.1.2 and R611.6 specify vertical wall reinforcement based on minimum bar size and maximum spacing, which are based on Grade 60 (420 MPa) steel reinforcement, different size bars and/or bars made from a different grade of steel are permitted provided an equivalent area of steel per linear foot of wall is provided. Use of Table R611.5.4(2) is permitted to determine the maximum bar spacing for different bar sizes than specified in the tables and/or bars made from a different grade of steel. Bars shall not be spaced less than one-half the wall thickness, or more than 48 inches (1219 mm) on center.

TABLE R611.5.4(1)
LAP SPLICE AND TENSION DEVELOPMENT LENGTHS

	BAR SIZE NO.	YIELD STRENGTH OF STEEL, f_y - psi (MPa) 40,000 (280)	60,000 (420)
		Splice length or tension development length (inches)	
Lap splice length–tension	4	20	30
	5	25	38
	6	30	45
Tension development length for straight bar	4	15	23
	5	19	28
	6	23	34
Tension development length for:	4	6	9
a. 90-degree and 180-degree standard hooks with not less than $2^1/_2$ inches of side cover perpendicular to plane of hook, and	5	7	11
b. 90-degree standard hooks with not less than 2 inches of cover on the bar extension beyond the hook.	6	8	13
Tension development length for bar with 90-degree or 180-degree standard hook having less cover than required above.	4	8	12
	5	10	15
	6	12	18

For SI: 1 inch = 25.4 mm, 1 degree = 0.0175 rad.

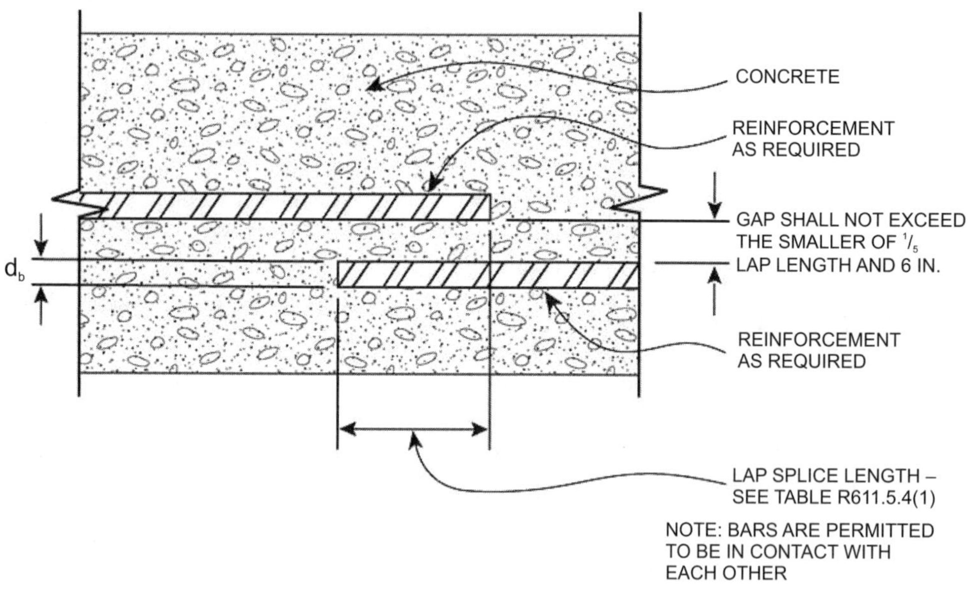

For SI: 1 inch = 25.4 mm.

FIGURE R611.5.4(1)
LAP SPLICES

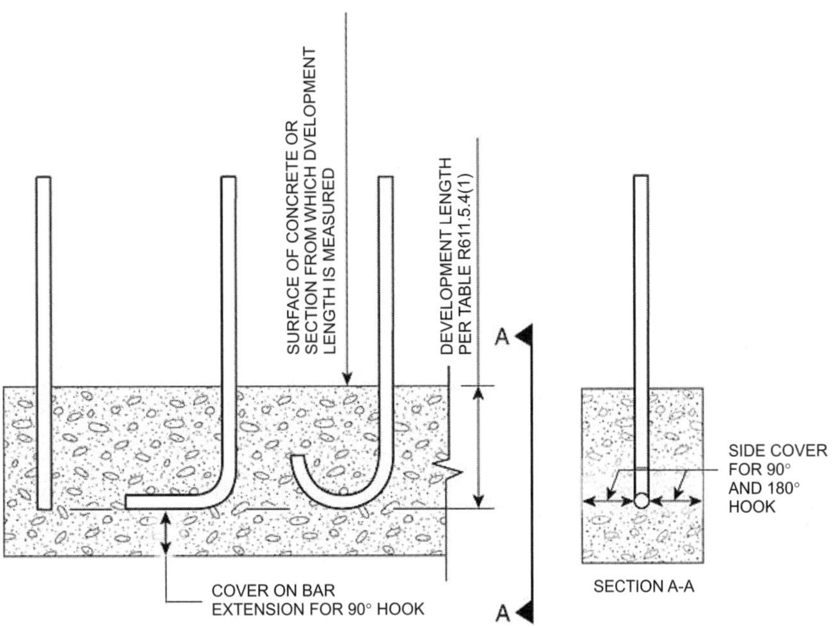

For SI: 1 degree = 0.0175 rad.

FIGURE R611.5.4(2)
DEVELOPMENT LENGTH AND COVER FOR HOOKS AND BAR EXTENSION

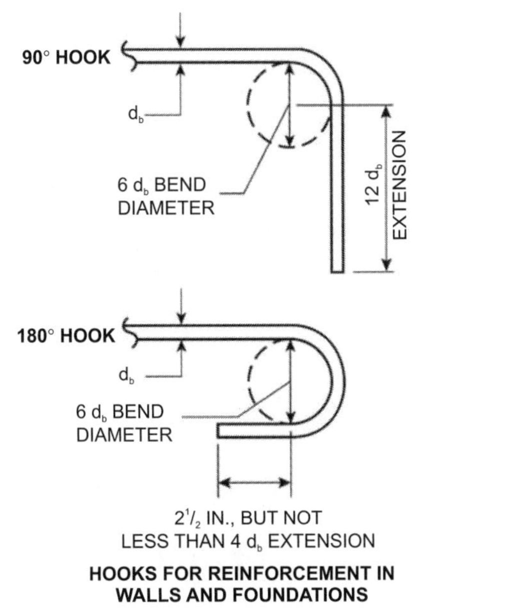

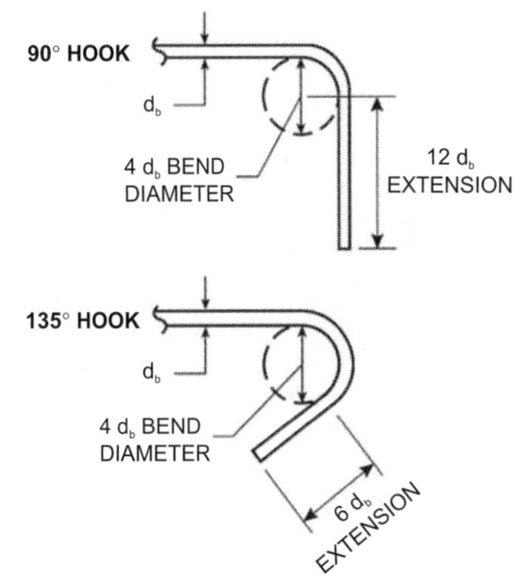

For SI: 1 inch = 25.4 mm, 1 degree = 0.0175 rad.

FIGURE R611.5.4(3)
STANDARD HOOKS

TABLE R611.5.4(2) MAXIMUM SPACING FOR ALTERNATE BAR SIZE AND/OR ALTERNATE GRADE OF STEEL[a, b, c]

BAR SPACING FROM APPLICABLE TABLE IN SECTION R611.6 (inches)	BAR SIZE FROM APPLICABLE TABLE IN SECTION R611.6														
	#4					#5					#6				
	Alternate bar size and/or alternate grade of steel desired														
	Grade 60		Grade 40			Grade 60		Grade 40			Grade 60		Grade 40		
	#5	#6	#4	#5	#6	#4	#6	#4	#5	#6	#4	#5	#4	#5	#6
	Maximum spacing for alternate bar size and/or alternate grade of steel (inches)														
8	12	18	5	8	12	5	11	3	5	8	4	6	2	4	5
9	14	20	6	9	13	6	13	4	6	9	4	6	3	4	6
10	16	22	7	10	15	6	14	4	7	9	5	7	3	5	7
11	17	24	7	11	16	7	16	5	7	10	5	8	3	5	7
12	19	26	8	12	18	8	17	5	8	11	5	8	4	6	8
13	20	29	9	13	19	8	18	6	9	12	6	9	4	6	9
14	22	31	9	14	21	9	20	6	9	13	6	10	4	7	9
15	23	33	10	16	22	10	21	6	10	14	7	11	5	7	10
16	25	35	11	17	23	10	23	7	11	15	7	11	5	8	11
17	26	37	11	18	25	11	24	7	11	16	8	12	5	8	11
18	28	40	12	19	26	12	26	8	12	17	8	13	5	8	12
19	29	42	13	20	28	12	27	8	13	18	9	13	6	9	13
20	31	44	13	21	29	13	28	9	13	19	9	14	6	9	13
21	33	46	14	22	31	14	30	9	14	20	10	15	6	10	14
22	34	48	15	23	32	14	31	9	15	21	10	16	7	10	15
23	36	48	15	24	34	15	33	10	15	22	10	16	7	11	15
24	37	48	16	25	35	15	34	10	16	23	11	17	7	11	16
25	39	48	17	26	37	16	35	11	17	24	11	18	8	12	17
26	40	48	17	27	38	17	37	11	17	25	12	18	8	12	17
27	42	48	18	28	40	17	38	12	18	26	12	19	8	13	18
28	43	48	19	29	41	18	40	12	19	26	13	20	8	13	19
29	45	48	19	30	43	19	41	12	19	27	13	20	9	14	19
30	47	48	20	31	44	19	43	13	20	28	14	21	9	14	20
31	48	48	21	32	45	20	44	13	21	29	14	22	9	15	21
32	48	48	21	33	47	21	45	14	21	30	15	23	10	15	21
33	48	48	22	34	48	21	47	14	22	31	15	23	10	16	22
34	48	48	23	35	48	22	48	15	23	32	15	24	10	16	23
35	48	48	23	36	48	23	48	15	23	33	16	25	11	16	23
36	48	48	24	37	48	23	48	15	24	34	16	25	11	17	24
37	48	48	25	38	48	24	48	16	25	35	17	26	11	17	25
38	48	48	25	39	48	25	48	16	25	36	17	27	12	18	25
39	48	48	26	40	48	25	48	17	26	37	18	27	12	18	26
40	48	48	27	41	48	26	48	17	27	38	18	28	12	19	27
41	48	48	27	42	48	26	48	18	27	39	19	29	12	19	27
42	48	48	28	43	48	27	48	18	28	40	19	30	13	20	28
43	48	48	29	44	48	28	48	18	29	41	20	30	13	20	29
44	48	48	29	45	48	28	48	19	29	42	20	31	13	21	29
45	48	48	30	47	48	29	48	19	30	43	20	32	14	21	30
46	48	48	31	48	48	30	48	20	31	44	21	32	14	22	31
47	48	48	31	48	48	30	48	20	31	44	21	33	14	22	31
48	48	48	32	48	48	31	48	21	32	45	22	34	15	23	32

For SI: 1 inch = 25.4 mm.

a. This table is for use with tables in Section R611.6 that specify the minimum bar size and maximum spacing of vertical wall reinforcement for foundation walls and above-grade walls. Reinforcement specified in tables in Section R611.6 is based on Grade 60 (420 MPa) steel reinforcement.

b. Bar spacing shall not exceed 48 inches on center and shall not be less than one-half the nominal wall thickness.

c. For Grade 50 (350 MPa) steel bars (ASTM A 996, Type R), use spacing for Grade 40 (280 MPa) bars or interpolate between Grade 40 (280 MPa) and Grade 60 (420 MPa).

R611.5.5 Construction joints in walls. Construction joints shall be made and located to not impair the strength of the wall. Construction joints in plain concrete walls, including walls required to have not less than No. 4 bars at 48 inches (1219 mm) on center by Section R611.6, shall be located at points of lateral support, and a minimum of one No. 4 bar shall extend across the construction joint at a spacing not to exceed 24 inches (610 mm) on center. Construction joint reinforcement shall have a minimum of 12 inches (305 mm) embedment on both sides of the joint. Construction joints in reinforced concrete walls shall be located in the middle third of the span between lateral supports, or located and constructed as required for joints in plain concrete walls.

> **Exception:** Vertical wall reinforcement required by this code is permitted to be used in lieu of construction joint reinforcement, provided the spacing does not exceed 24 inches (610 mm), or the combination of wall reinforcement and No. 4 bars described above does not exceed 24 inches (610 mm).

R611.6 Above-grade wall requirements.

R611.6.1 General. The minimum thickness of load-bearing and nonload-bearing above-grade walls and reinforcement shall be as set forth in the appropriate table in this section based on the type of wall form to be used. Where the wall or building is not within the limitations of Section R611.2, design is required by the tables in this section, or the wall is not within the scope of the tables in this section, the wall shall be designed in accordance with ACI 318.

Above-grade concrete walls shall be constructed in accordance with this section and Figure R611.6(1), R611.6(2), R611.6(3), or R611.6(4). Above-grade concrete walls that are continuous with stem walls and not laterally supported by the slab-on-ground shall be designed and constructed in accordance with this section. Concrete walls shall be supported on continuous foundation walls or slabs-on-ground that are monolithic with the footing in accordance with Section R403. The minimum length of solid wall without openings shall be in accordance with Section R611.7. Reinforcement around openings, including lintels, shall be in accordance with Section R611.8. Lateral support for above-grade walls in the out-of-plane direction shall be provided by connections to the floor framing system, if applicable, and to ceiling and roof framing systems in accordance with Section R611.9. The wall thickness shall be equal to or greater than the thickness of the wall in the *story* above.

LIGHT-FRAMED ROOF
SEE SECTION R611.9.3
HORIZONTAL WALL REINFORCEMENT AS REQUIRED
FIRST-STORY UNSUPPORTED WALL HEIGHT 10 FT MAXIMUM
WALL—STAY-IN-PLACE OR REMOVABLE FORM
LIGHT-FRAMED FLOOR (OR CONCRETE SLAB-ON-GROUND)
SEE SECTION R611.9.2
VERTICAL WALL REINFORCEMENT AS REQUIRED
BASEMENT, CRAWLSPACE OR STEM WALL. fOR SLAB-ON-GROUND FOOTING, SEE FIGURE R611.6(4)
SECTION CUT THROUGH FLAT WALL OR VERTICAL CORE OF AWAFFLE—OR SCREEN-GRID WALL

For SI: 1 foot = 304.8 mm.

FIGURE R611.6(1)
ABOVE-GRADE CONCRETE WALL CONSTRUCTION ONE

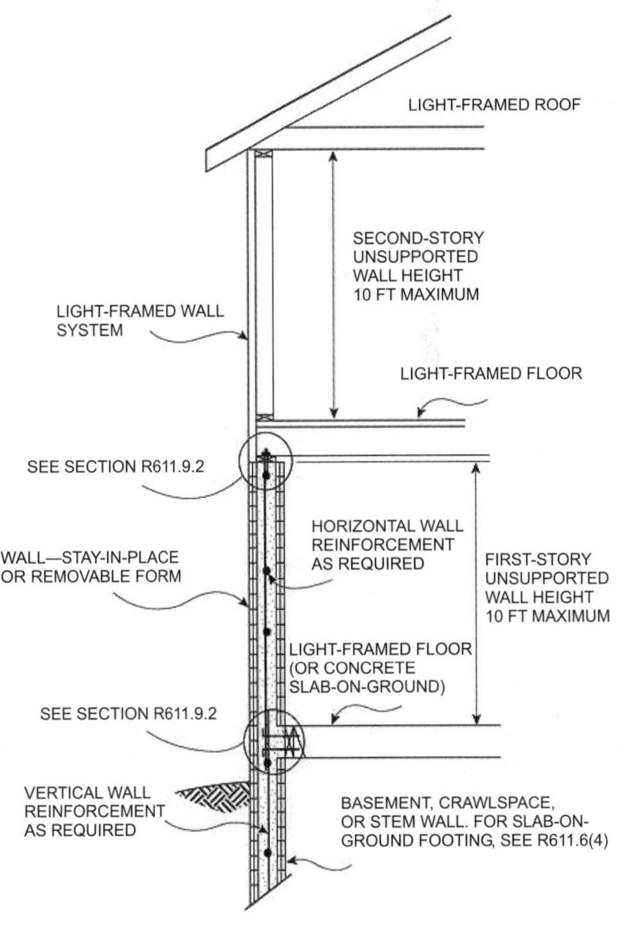

For SI: 1 foot = 304.8 mm.

FIGURE R611.6(2)
ABOVE-GRADE CONCRETE WALL CONSTRUCTION CONCRETE FIRST-STORY AND LIGHT-FRAMED SECOND-STORY

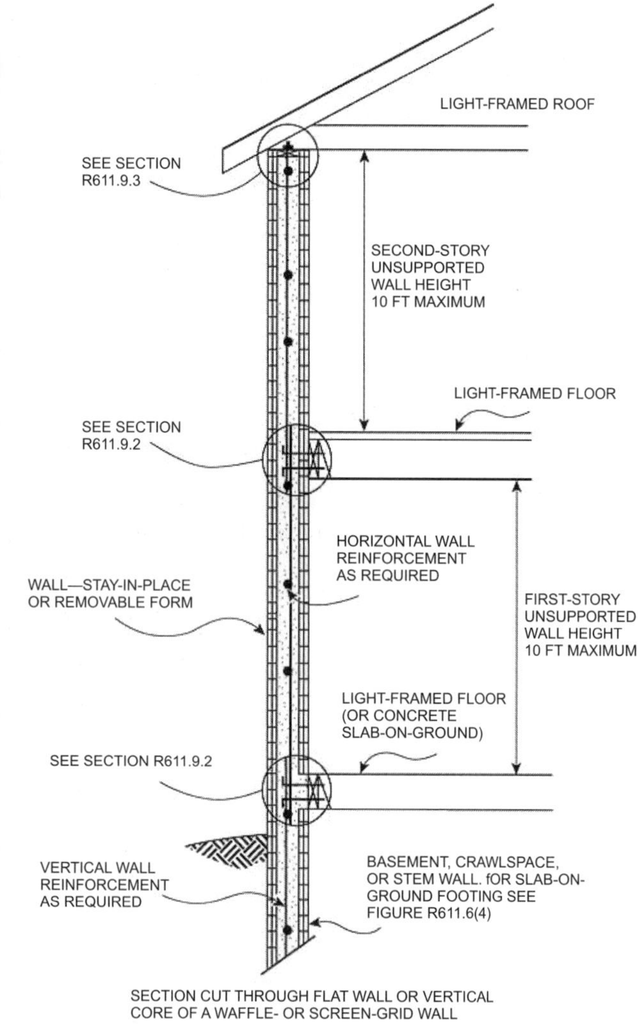

For SI: 1 foot = 304.8 mm.

FIGURE R611.6(3)
ABOVE-GRADE CONCRETE WALL CONSTRUCTION TWO-STORY

R611.6.2 Wall reinforcement for wind. Vertical wall reinforcement for resistance to out-of-plane wind forces shall be determined from Table R611.6(1), R611.6(2), R611.6(3) or R611.6(4). Also, see Sections R611.7.2.2.2 and R611.7.2.2.3. There shall be a vertical bar at all corners of exterior walls. Unless more horizontal reinforcement is required by Section R611.7.2.2.1, the minimum horizontal reinforcement shall be four No. 4 bars [Grade 40 (280 MPa)] placed as follows: top bar within 12 inches (305 mm) of the top of the wall, bottom bar within 12 inches (305 mm) of the finish floor, and one bar each at approximately one-third and two-thirds of the wall height.

R611.6.3 Continuity of wall reinforcement between stories. Vertical reinforcement required by this section shall be continuous between elements providing lateral support for the wall. Reinforcement in the wall of the *story* above shall be continuous with the reinforcement in the wall of the *story* below, or the foundation wall, if applicable. Lap splices, where required, shall comply with Section R611.5.4.3 and

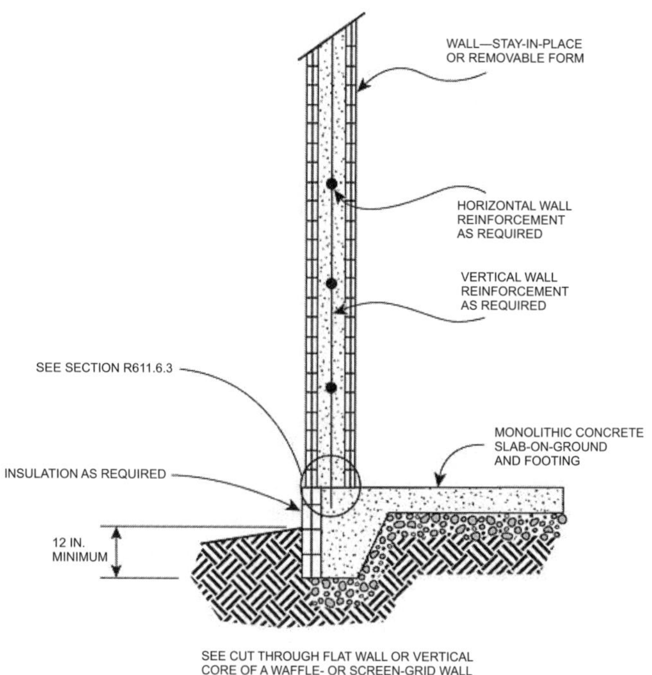

For SI: 1 inch = 25.4 mm.

FIGURE R611.6(4)
ABOVE-GRADE CONCRETE WALL SUPPORTED ON MONOLITHIC SLAB-ON GROUND FOOTING

Figure R611.5.4(1). Where the above-grade wall is supported by a monolithic slab-on-ground and footing, dowel bars with a size and spacing to match the vertical above-grade concrete wall reinforcement shall be embedded in the monolithic slab-on-ground and footing the distance required to develop the dowel bar in tension in accordance with Section R611.5.4.4 and Figure R611.5.4(2) and lap-spliced with the above-grade wall reinforcement in accordance with Section R611.5.4.3 and Figure R611.5.4(1).

Exception: Where reinforcement in the wall above cannot be made continuous with the reinforcement in the wall below, the bottom of the reinforcement in the wall above shall be terminated in accordance with one of the following:

1. Extend below the top of the floor the distance required to develop the bar in tension in accordance with Section R611.5.4.4 and Figure R611.5.4(2).
2. Lap-spliced in accordance with Section R611.5.4.3 and Figure R611.5.4(1) with a dowel bar that extends into the wall below the distance required to develop the bar in tension in accordance with Section R611.5.4.4 and Figure R611.5.4(2).

Where a construction joint in the wall is located below the level of the floor and less than the distance required to develop the bar in tension, the distance required to develop the bar in tension shall be measured from the top of the concrete below the joint. See Section R611.5.5.

TABLE R611.6(1)
MINIMUM VERTICAL REINFORCEMENT FOR FLAT ABOVE-GRADE WALLS[a, b, c, d, e]

MAXIMUM WIND SPEED (mph)			MAXIMUM UNSUPPORTED WALL HEIGHT PER STORY (feet)	MINIMUM VERTICAL REINFORCEMENT—BAR SIZE AND SPACING (inches)[f, g]							
Exposure Category				Nominal[h] wall thickness (inches)							
				4		6		8		10	
B	C	D		Top[i]	Side[i]	Top[i]	Side[i]	Top[i]	Side[i]	Top[i]	Side[i]
85	—	—	8	4@48	4@48	4@48	4@48	4@48	4@48	4@48	4@48
			9	4@48	4@43	4@48	4@48	4@48	4@48	4@48	4@48
			10	4@47	4@36	4@48	4@48	4@48	4@48	4@48	4@48
90	—	—	8	4@48	4@47	4@48	4@48	4@48	4@48	4@48	4@48
			9	4@48	4@39	4@48	4@48	4@48	4@48	4@48	4@48
			10	4@42	4@34	4@48	4@48	4@48	4@48	4@48	4@48
100	85	—	8	4@48	4@40	4@48	4@48	4@48	4@48	4@48	4@48
			9	4@42	4@34	4@48	4@48	4@48	4@48	4@48	4@48
			10	4@34	4@34	4@48	4@48	4@48	4@48	4@48	4@48
110	90	85	8	4@44	4@34	4@48	4@48	4@48	4@48	4@48	4@48
			9	4@34	4@34	4@48	4@48	4@48	4@48	4@48	4@48
			10	4@34	4@31	4@48	4@37	4@48	4@48	4@48	4@48
120	100	90	8	4@36	4@34	4@48	4@48	4@48	4@48	4@48	4@48
			9	4@34	4@32	4@48	4@38	4@48	4@48	4@48	4@48
			10	4@30	4@27	4@48	5@48	4@48	4@48	4@48	4@48
130	110	100	8	4@34	4@34	4@48	4@48	4@48	4@48	4@48	4@48
			9	4@32	4@28	4@48	4@33	4@48	4@48	4@48	4@48
			10	4@26	4@23	4@48	5@43	4@48	4@48	4@48	4@48

For SI:1 inch = 25.4 mm; 1 foot = 304.8 mm; 1 mile per hour = 0.447 m/s, 1 pound per square inch = 1.895kPa.

a. Table is based on ASCE 7 components and cladding wind pressures for an enclosed building using a mean roof height of 35 ft, interior wall area 4, an effective wind area of 10 ft^2, and topographic factor, K_{zt}, and importance factor, I, equal to 1.0.

b. Table is based on concrete with a minimum specified compressive strength of 2,500 psi.

c. See Section R611.6.5 for location of reinforcement in wall.

d. Deflection criterion is $L/240$, where L is the unsupported height of the wall in inches.

e. Interpolation is not permitted.

f. Where No. 4 reinforcing bars at a spacing of 48 inches are specified in the table, use of bars with a minimum yield strength of 40,000 psi or 60,000 psi is permitted.

g. Other than for No. 4 bars spaced at 48 inches on center, table values are based on reinforcing bars with a minimum yield strength of 60,000 psi. Vertical reinforcement with a yield strength of less than 60,000 psi and/or bars of a different size than specified in the table are permitted in accordance with Section R611.5.4.7 and Table R611.5.4(2).

h. See Table R611.3 for tolerances on nominal thicknesses.

i. Top means gravity load from roof and/or floor construction bears on top of wall. Side means gravity load from floor construction is transferred to wall from a wood ledger or cold-formed steel track bolted to side of wall. Where floor framing members span parallel to the wall, use of the top bearing condition is permitted.

TABLE R611.6(2) MINIMUM VERTICAL REINFORCEMENT FOR WAFFLE-GRID ABOVE-GRADE WALLS[a, b, c, d, e]

MAXIMUM WIND SPEED (mph)			MAXIMUM UNSUPPORTED WALL HEIGHT PER STORY (feet)	MINIMUM VERTICAL REINFORCEMENT—BAR SIZE AND SPACING (inches)[f, g]			
				Nominal[h] wall thickness (inches)			
Exposure Category				6		8	
B	C	D		Top[i]	Side[i]	Top[i]	Side[i]
85	—	—	8	4@48	4@36, 5@48	4@48	4@48
			9	4@48	4@30, 5@47	4@48	4@45
			10	4@48	4@26, 5@40	4@48	4@39
90	—	—	8	4@48	4@33, 5@48	4@48	4@48
			9	4@48	4@28, 5@43	4@48	4@42
			10	4@31, 5@48	4@24, 5@37	4@48	4@36
100	85	—	8	4@48	4@28, 5@44	4@48	4@43
			9	4@31, 5@48	4@24, 5@37	4@48	4@36
			10	4@25, 5@39	4@24, 5@37	4@48	4@31, 5@48
110	90	85	8	4@33, 5@48	4@25, 5@38	4@48	4@38
			9	4@26, 5@40	4@24, 5@37	4@48	4@31, 5@48
			10	4@24, 5@37	4@23, 5@35	4@48	4@27, 5@41
120	100	90	8	4@27, 5@42	4@24, 5@37	4@48	4@33, 5@48
			9	4@24, 5@37	4@23, 5@36	4@48	4@27, 5@43
			10	4@23, 5@35	4@19, 5@30	4@48	4@23, 5@36
130	110	100	8	4@24, 5@37	4@24, 5@37	4@48	4@29, 5@45
			9	4@24, 5@37	4@20, 5@32	4@48	4@24, 5@37
			10	4@19, 5@30	4@17, 5@26	4@23, 5@36	4@20, 5@31

For SI: 1 inch = 25.4 mm;1 foot = 304.8 mm; 1 mile per hour = 0.447 m/s, 1 pound per square inch = 6.895kPa.

a. Table is based on ASCE 7 components and cladding wind pressures for an enclosed building using a mean roof height of 35 ft (10 668 mm), interior wall area 4, an effective wind area of 10 ft^2 (0.9 m^2), and topographic factor, K_{zt}, and importance factor, I, equal to 1.0.

b. Table is based on concrete with a minimum specified compressive strength of 2,500 psi (17.2 MPa).

c. See Section R611.6.5 for location of reinforcement in wall.

d. Deflection criterion is $L/240$, where L is the unsupported height of the wall in inches.

e. Interpolation is not permitted.

f. Where No. 4 reinforcing bars at a spacing of 48 inches are specified in the table, use of bars with a minimum yield strength of 40,000 psi or 60,000 psi is permitted.

g. Other than for No. 4 bars spaced at 48 inches on center, table values are based on reinforcing bars with a minimum yield strength of 60,000 psi. Maximum spacings shown are the values calculated for the specified bar size. Where the bar used is Grade 60 (420 MPa) and the size specified in the table, the actual spacing in the wall shall not exceed a whole-number multiple of 12 inches (i.e., 12, 24, 36 and 48) that is less than or equal to the tabulated spacing. Vertical reinforcement with a yield strength of less than 60,000 psi and/or bars of a different size than specified in the table are permitted in accordance with Section R611.5.4.7 and Table R611.5.4(2).

h. See Table R611.3 for minimum core dimensions and maximum spacing of horizontal and vertical cores.

i. Top means gravity load from roof and/or floor construction bears on top of wall. Side means gravity load from floor construction is transferred to wall from a wood ledger or cold-formed steel track bolted to side of wall. Where floor framing members span parallel to the wall, the top bearing condition is permitted to be used.

TABLE R611.6(3)
MINIMUM VERTICAL REINFORCEMENT FOR 6-INCH SCREEN-GRID ABOVE-GRADE WALLS[a, b, c, d, e]

MAXIMUM WIND SPEED (mph)			MAXIMUM UNSUPPORTED WALL HEIGHT PER STORY (feet)	MINIMUM VERTICAL REINFORCEMENT—BAR SIZE AND SPACING (inches)[f, g]	
				Nominal[h] wall thickness (inches)	
Exposure Category				6	
B	C	D		Top[i]	Side[i]
85	—	—	8	4@48	4@34, 5@48
			9	4@48	4@29, 5@45
			10	4@48	4@25, 5@39
90	—	—	8	4@48	4@31, 5@48
			9	4@48	4@27, 5@41
			10	4@30, 5@47	4@23, 5@35
100	85	—	8	4@48	4@27, 5@42
			9	4@30, 5@47	4@23, 5@35
			10	4@24, 5@38	4@22, 5@34
110	90	85	8	4@48	4@24, 5@37
			9	4@25, 5@38	4@22, 5@34
			10	4@22, 5@34	4@22, 5@34
120	100	90	8	4@26, 5@41	4@22, 5@34
			9	4@22, 5@34	4@22, 5@34
			10	4@22, 6@34	4@19, 5@26
130	110	100	8	4@22, 5@35	4@22, 5@34
			9	4@22, 5@34	4@20, 5@30
			10	4@19, 5@29	4@16, 5@25

For SI: 1 inch = 25.4 mm; 1 foot = 304.8 mm; 1 mph = 0.447 m/s, pound per square inch = 6.895kPa.

a. Table is based on ASCE 7 components and cladding wind pressures for an enclosed building using a mean roof height of 35 ft, interior wall area 4, an effective wind area of 10 ft^2, and topographic factor, K_{zt}, and importance factor, I, equal to 1.0.

b. Table is based on concrete with a minimum specified compressive strength of 2,500 psi.

c. See Section R611.6.5 for location of reinforcement in wall.

d. Deflection criterion is $L/240$, where L is the unsupported height of the wall in inches.

e. Interpolation is not permitted.

f. Where No. 4 reinforcing bars at a spacing of 48 inches are specified in the table, use of bars with a minimum yield strength of 40,000 psi or 60,000 psi is permitted.

g. Other than for No. 4 bars spaced at 48 inches on center, table values are based on reinforcing bars with a minimum yield strength of 60,000 psi (420 MPa). Maximum spacings shown are the values calculated for the specified bar size. Where the bar used is Grade 60 and the size specified in the table, the actual spacing in the wall shall not exceed a whole-number multiple of 12 inches (i.e., 12, 24, 36 and 48) that is less than or equal to the tabulated spacing. Vertical reinforcement with a yield strength of less than 60,000 psi and/or bars of a different size than specified in the table are permitted in accordance with Section R611.5.4.7 and Table R611.5.4(2).

h. See Table R611.3 for minimum core dimensions and maximum spacing of horizontal and vertical cores.

i. Top means gravity load from roof and/or floor construction bears on top of wall. Side means gravity load from floor construction is transferred to wall from a wood ledger or cold-formed steel track bolted to side of wall. Where floor framing members span parallel to the wall, use of the top bearing condition is permitted.

TABLE R611.6(4)
MINIMUM VERTICAL REINFORCEMENT FOR FLAT, WAFFLE- AND SCREEN-GRID ABOVE-GRADE WALLS DESIGNED CONTINUOUS WITH FOUNDATION STEM WALLS[a, b, c, d, e, k, l]

MAXIMUM WIND SPEED (mph)			HEIGHT OF STEM WALL[h, i] (feet)	MAXIMUM DESIGN LATERAL SOIL LOAD (psf/ft)	MAXIMUM UNSUPPORTED HEIGHT OF ABOVE-GRADE WALL (feet)	MINIMUM VERTICAL REINFORCEMENT—BAR SIZE AND SPACING (inches)[f, g]						
Exposure Category						Wall type and nominal thickness[j] (inches)						
						Flat				Waffle		Screen
B	C	D				4	6	8	10	6	8	6
85	—	—	3	30	8	4@33	4@39	4@48	4@48	4@24	4@28	4@22
					10	4@26	5@48	4@41	4@48	4@19	4@22	4@18
				60	10	4@21	5@40	5@48	4@44	4@16	4@19	4@15
			6	30	10	DR	5@22	6@35	6@43	DR	4@11	DR
				60	10	DR	DR	6@26	6@28	DR	DR	DR
90	—	—	3	30	8	4@30	4@36	4@48	4@48	4@22	4@26	4@21
					10	4@24	5@44	4@38	4@48	4@17	4@21	4@17
				60	10	4@20	5@37	4@48	4@41	4@15	4@18	4@14
			6	30	10	DR	5@21	6@35	6@41	DR	4@10	DR
				60	10	DR	DR	6@26	6@28	DR	DR	DR
100	85	—	3	30	8	4@26	5@48	4@42	4@48	4@19	4@23	4@18
					10	4@20	5@37	4@33	4@41	4@15	4@18	4@14
			6	60	10	4@17	5@34	5@44	4@36	4@13	4@17	4@12
				30	10	DR	5@20	6@35	6@38	DR	4@9	DR
				60	10	DR	DR	6@24	6@28	DR	DR	DR
110	90	85	3	30	8	4@22	5@42	4@37	4@46	4@16	4@20	4@16
					10	4@17	5@34	5@44	4@35	4@12	4@17	4@12
				60	10	4@15	5@34	5@39	5@48	4@11	4@17	4@11
			6	30	10	DR	5@18	6@35	6@35	DR	4@9	DR
				60	10	DR	DR	6@23	6@28	DR	DR	DR
120	100	90	3	30	8	4@19	5@37	5@48	4@40	4@14	4@17	4@14
					10	4@14	5@34	5@38	5@48	4@11	4@17	4@10
				60	10	4@13	5@33	6@48	5@43	4@10	4@16	4@9
			6	30	10	DR	5@16	6@33	6@32	DR	4@8	DR
				60	10	DR	DR	6@22	6@28	DR	DR	DR
130	110	100	3	30	8	4@17	5@34	5@44	4@36	4@12	4@17	4@10
					10	DR	5@32	6@47	5@42	4@9	4@15	DR
				60	10	DR	5@29	6@43	5@39	DR	4@14	DR
			6	30	10	DR	5@15	6@30	6@29	DR	4@7	DR
				60	10	DR	DR	6@21	6@27	DR	DR	DR

For SI: 1 inch = 25.4 mm; 1 foot = 304.8 mm; 1 mile per hour = 0.447 m/s; 1 pound per square foot per foot = 0.1571kPa/m.

a. Table is based on ASCE 7 components and cladding wind pressures for an enclosed building using a mean roof height of 35 ft (10 668 mm), interior wall area 4, an effective wind area of 10 ft^2, and topographic factor, K_{zt}, and importance factor, I, equal to 1.0.

b. Table is based on concrete with a minimum specified compressive strength of 2,500 psi.

c. See Section R611.6.5 for location of reinforcement in wall.

d. Deflection criterion is $L/240$, where L is the height of the wall in inches from the exterior finish ground level to the top of the above-grade wall.

e. Interpolation is not permitted. For intermediate values of basic wind speed, heights of stem wall and above-grade wall, and design lateral soil load, use next higher value.

f. Where No. 4 reinforcing bars at a spacing of 48 inches are specified in the table, use of bars with a minimum yield strength of 40,000 psi or 60,000 psi is permitted.

g. Other than for No. 4 bars spaced at 48 inches on center, table values are based on reinforcing bars with a minimum yield strength of 60,000 psi. Maximum spacings shown are the values calculated for the specified bar size. In waffle and screen-grid walls where the bar used is Grade 60 and the size specified in the table, the actual spacing in the wall shall not exceed a whole-number multiple of 12 inches (i.e., 12, 24, 36 and 48) that is less than or equal to the tabulated spacing. Vertical reinforcement with a yield strength of less than 60,000 psi and/or bars of a different size than specified in the table are permitted in accordance with Section R611.5.4.7 and Table R611.5.4(2).

h. Height of stem wall is the distance from the exterior finish ground level to the top of the slab-on-ground.

i. Where the distance from the exterior finish ground level to the top of the slab-on-ground is equal to or greater than 4 feet, the stem wall shall be laterally supported at the top and bottom before backfilling. Where the wall is designed and constructed to be continuous with the above-grade wall, temporary supports bracing the top of the stem wall shall remain in place until the above-grade wall is laterally supported at the top by floor or roof construction.

j. See Table R611.3 for tolerances on nominal thicknesses, and minimum core dimensions and maximum spacing of horizontal and vertical cores for waffle- and screen-grid walls.

k. Tabulated values are applicable to construction where gravity loads bear on top of wall, and conditions where gravity loads from floor construction are transferred to wall from a wood ledger or cold-formed steel track bolted to side of wall. See Tables R611.6(1), R611.6(2) and R611.6(3).

l. DR indicates design required.

TABLE R611.7(1A)
UNREDUCED LENGTH, *UR*, OF SOLID WALL REQUIRED IN EACH EXTERIOR ENDWALL FOR WIND PERPENDICULAR TO RIDGE ONE STORY OR TOP STORY OF TWO-STORY[a,c,d,e,f,g]

SIDEWALL LENGTH (feet)	ENDWALL LENGTH (feet)	ROOF SLOPE	UNREDUCED LENGTH, *UR*, OF SOLID WALL REQUIRED IN ENDWALLS FOR WIND PERPENDICULAR TO RIDGE (feet)						
			Basic Wind Speed (mph) Exposure						
			85B	90B	100B	110B	120B	130B	
					85C	90C	100C	110C	
						85D	90D	100D	Minimum[b]
15	15	< 1:12	0.90	1.01	1.25	1.51	1.80	2.11	0.98
		5:12	1.25	1.40	1.73	2.09	2.49	2.92	1.43
		7:12	1.75	1.96	2.43	2.93	3.49	4.10	1.64
		12:12	2.80	3.13	3.87	4.68	5.57	6.54	2.21
	30	< 1:12	0.90	1.01	1.25	1.51	1.80	2.11	1.09
		5:12	1.25	1.40	1.73	2.09	2.49	2.92	2.01
		7:12	2.43	2.73	3.37	4.08	4.85	5.69	2.42
		12:12	4.52	5.07	6.27	7.57	9.01	10.58	3.57
	45	< 1:12	0.90	1.01	1.25	1.51	1.80	2.11	1.21
		5:12	1.25	1.40	1.73	2.09	2.49	2.92	2.59
		7:12	3.12	3.49	4.32	5.22	6.21	7.29	3.21
		12:12	6.25	7.00	8.66	10.47	12.45	14.61	4.93
	60	< 1:12	0.90	1.01	1.25	1.51	1.80	2.11	1.33
		5:12	1.25	1.40	1.73	2.09	2.49	2.92	3.16
		7:12	3.80	4.26	5.26	6.36	7.57	8.89	3.99
		12:12	7.97	8.94	11.05	13.36	15.89	18.65	6.29
30	15	< 1:12	1.61	1.80	2.23	2.70	3.21	3.77	1.93
		5:12	2.24	2.51	3.10	3.74	4.45	5.23	2.75
		7:12	3.15	3.53	4.37	5.28	6.28	7.37	3.12
		12:12	4.90	5.49	6.79	8.21	9.77	11.46	4.14
	30	< 1:12	1.61	1.80	2.23	2.70	3.21	3.77	2.14
		5:12	2.24	2.51	3.10	3.74	4.45	5.23	3.78
		7:12	4.30	4.82	5.96	7.20	8.57	10.05	4.52
		12:12	7.79	8.74	10.80	13.06	15.53	18.23	6.57
	45	< 1:12	1.61	1.80	2.23	2.70	3.21	3.77	2.35
		5:12	2.24	2.51	3.10	3.74	4.45	5.23	4.81
		7:12	5.44	6.10	7.54	9.12	10.85	12.73	5.92
		12:12	10.69	11.98	14.81	17.90	21.30	25.00	9.00
	60	< 1:12	1.61	1.80	2.23	2.70	3.21	3.77	2.56
		5:12	2.24	2.51	3.10	3.74	4.45	5.23	5.84
		7:12	6.59	7.39	9.13	11.04	13.14	15.41	7.32
		12:12	13.58	15.22	18.82	22.75	27.07	31.77	11.43

(continued)

TABLE R611.7(1A)—continued
UNREDUCED LENGTH, *UR*, OF SOLID WALL REQUIRED IN EACH EXTERIOR ENDWALL FOR WIND PERPENDICULAR TO RIDGE ONE STORY OR TOP STORY OF TWO-STORY[a,c,d,e,f,g]

SIDEWALL LENGTH (feet)	ENDWALL LENGTH (feet)	ROOF SLOPE	UNREDUCED LENGTH, *UR*, OF SOLID WALL REQUIRED IN ENDWALLS FOR WIND PERPENDICULAR TO RIDGE (feet)						
			Basic Wind Speed (mph) Exposure						
			85B	90B	100B	110B	120B	130B	Minimum[b]
					85C	90C	100C	110C	
						85D	90D	100D	
60	15	< 1:12	2.99	3.35	4.14	5.00	5.95	6.98	3.83
		5:12	4.15	4.65	5.75	6.95	8.27	9.70	5.37
		7:12	5.91	6.63	8.19	9.90	11.78	13.83	6.07
		12:12	9.05	10.14	12.54	15.16	18.03	21.16	8.00
	30	< 1:12	2.99	3.35	4.14	5.00	5.95	6.98	4.23
		5:12	4.15	4.65	5.75	6.95	8.27	9.70	7.31
		7:12	7.97	8.94	11.05	13.36	15.89	18.65	8.71
		12:12	14.25	15.97	19.74	23.86	28.40	33.32	12.57
	45	< 1:12	3.11	3.48	4.30	5.20	6.19	7.26	4.63
		5:12	4.31	4.84	5.98	7.23	8.60	10.09	9.25
		7:12	10.24	11.47	14.19	17.15	20.40	23.84	11.35
		12:12	19.84	22.24	27.49	33.23	39.54	46.40	17.14
	60	< 1:12	3.22	3.61	4.46	5.39	6.42	7.53	5.03
		5:12	4.47	5.01	6.19	7.49	8.91	10.46	11.19
		7:12	12.57	14.09	17.42	21.05	25.05	29.39	13.99
		12:12	25.61	28.70	35.49	42.90	51.04	59.90	21.71

For SI: 1 inch = 25.4 mm; 1 foot = 304.8 mm; 1 mile per hour = 0.447 m/s, 1 pound-force per linear foot = 0.146kN/m, 1 pound per square foot = 47.88 Pa.

a. Tabulated lengths were derived by calculating design wind pressures in accordance with Figure 6-10 of ASCE 7 for a building with a mean roof height of 35 feet (10 668 mm). For wind perpendicular to the ridge, the effects of a 2-foot overhang on each endwall are included. The design pressures were used to calculate forces to be resisted by solid wall segments in each endwall [Table R611.7(1A) or R611.7(1B) or sidewall (Table R611.7(1C)], as appropriate. The forces to be resisted by each wall line were then divided by the default design strength of 840 pounds per linear foot (12.26 kN/m) of length to determine the required solid wall length. The actual mean roof height of the building shall not exceed the least horizontal dimension of the building.

b. Tabulated lengths in the "minimum" column are based on the requirement of Section 6.1.4.1 of ASCE 7 that the main wind-force resisting system be designed for a minimum service level force of 10 psf multiplied by the area of the building projected onto a vertical plane normal to the assumed wind direction. Tabulated lengths in shaded cells are less than the "minimum" value. Where the minimum controls, it is permitted to be reduced in accordance with Notes c, d and e. See Section R611.7.1.1.

c. For buildings with a mean roof height of less than 35 feet, tabulated lengths are permitted to be reduced by multiplying by the appropriate factor, R_1, from Table R611.7(2). The reduced length shall not be less than the "minimum" value shown in the table.

d. Tabulated lengths for "one story or top story of two-story" are based on a floor-to-ceiling height of 10 feet. Tabulated lengths for "first story of two-story" are based on floor-to-ceiling heights of 10 feet each for the first and second story. For floor-to-ceiling heights less than assumed, use the lengths in Table R611.7(1A), (1B) or (1C), or multiply the value in the table by the reduction factor, R_2, from Table R611.7(3).

e. Tabulated lengths are based on the default design shear strength of 840 pounds per linear foot of solid wall segment. The tabulated lengths are permitted to be reduced by multiplying by the applicable reduction factor for design strength, R_3, from Table R611.7(4).

f. The reduction factors, R_1, R_2, and R_3, in Tables R611.7(2), R611.7(3), and R611.7(4), respectively, are permitted to be compounded, subject to the limitations of Note b. However, the minimum number and minimum length of solid walls segments in each wall line shall comply with Sections R611.7.1 and R611.7.2.1, respectively.

g. For intermediate values of sidewall length, endwall length, roof slope and basic wind speed, use the next higher value, or determine by interpolation.

TABLE R611.7(1B)
UNREDUCED LENGTH, *UR*, OF SOLID WALL REQUIRED IN EACH EXTERIOR ENDWALL FOR WIND PERPENDICULAR TO RIDGE FIRST STORY OF TWO-STORY[a,c,d,e,f,g]

SIDEWALL LENGTH (feet)	ENDWALL LENGTH (feet)	ROOF SLOPE	UNREDUCED LENGTH, *UR*, OF SOLID WALL REQUIRED IN ENDWALLS FOR WIND PERPENDICULAR TO RIDGE (feet)						
			Basic Wind Speed (mph) Exposure						
			85B	90B	100B	110B	120B	130B	
					85C	90C	100C	110C	
						85D	90D	100D	
			Velocity pressure (psf)						
			11.51	12.90	15.95	19.28	22.94	26.92	Minimum[b]
15	15	< 1:12	2.60	2.92	3.61	4.36	5.19	6.09	2.59
		5:12	3.61	4.05	5.00	6.05	7.20	8.45	3.05
		7:12	3.77	4.23	5.23	6.32	7.52	8.82	3.26
		12:12	4.81	5.40	6.67	8.06	9.60	11.26	3.83
	30	< 1:12	2.60	2.92	3.61	4.36	5.19	6.09	2.71
		5:12	3.61	4.05	5.00	6.05	7.20	8.45	3.63
		7:12	4.45	4.99	6.17	7.46	8.88	10.42	4.04
		12:12	6.54	7.33	9.06	10.96	13.04	15.30	5.19
	45	< 1:12	2.60	2.92	3.61	4.36	5.19	6.09	2.83
		5:12	3.61	4.05	5.00	6.05	7.20	8.45	4.20
		7:12	5.14	5.76	7.12	8.60	10.24	12.01	4.83
		12:12	8.27	9.27	11.46	13.85	16.48	19.34	6.55
	60	< 1:12	2.60	2.92	3.61	4.36	5.19	6.09	2.95
		5:12	3.61	4.05	5.00	6.05	7.20	8.45	4.78
		7:12	5.82	6.52	8.06	9.75	11.60	13.61	5.61
		12:12	9.99	11.20	13.85	16.74	19.92	23.37	7.90
30	15	< 1:12	4.65	5.21	6.45	7.79	9.27	10.88	5.16
		5:12	6.46	7.24	8.95	10.82	12.87	15.10	5.98
		7:12	6.94	7.78	9.62	11.62	13.83	16.23	6.35
		12:12	8.69	9.74	12.04	14.55	17.32	20.32	7.38
	30	< 1:12	4.65	5.21	6.45	7.79	9.27	10.88	5.38
		5:12	6.46	7.24	8.95	10.82	12.87	15.10	7.01
		7:12	8.09	9.06	11.21	13.54	16.12	18.91	7.76
		12:12	11.58	12.98	16.05	19.40	23.08	27.09	9.81
	45	< 1:12	4.65	5.21	6.45	7.79	9.27	10.88	5.59
		5:12	6.46	7.24	8.95	10.82	12.87	15.10	8.04
		7:12	9.23	10.35	12.79	15.46	18.40	21.59	9.16
		12:12	14.48	16.22	20.06	24.25	28.85	33.86	12.24
	60	< 1:12	4.65	5.21	6.45	7.79	9.27	10.88	5.80
		5:12	6.46	7.24	8.95	10.82	12.87	15.10	9.08
		7:12	10.38	11.63	14.38	17.38	20.69	24.27	10.56
		12:12	17.37	19.47	24.07	29.10	34.62	40.63	14.67

(continued)

TABLE R611.7(1B)—continued
UNREDUCED LENGTH, *UR*, OF SOLID WALL REQUIRED IN EACH EXTERIOR ENDWALL FOR WIND PERPENDICULAR TO RIDGE FIRST STORY OF TWO-STORY[a,c,d,e,f,g]

SIDEWALL LENGTH (feet)	ENDWALL LENGTH (feet)	ROOF SLOPE	UNREDUCED LENGTH, *UR*, OF SOLID WALL REQUIRED IN ENDWALLS FOR WIND PERPENDICULAR TO RIDGE (feet)						
			Basic Wind Speed (mph) Exposure						
			85B	90B	100B	110B	120B	130B	
					85C	90C	100C	110C	
						85D	90D	100D	
			Velocity Pressure (psf)						
			11.51	12.90	15.95	19.28	22.94	26.92	Minimum[b]
60	15	< 1:12	8.62	9.67	11.95	14.45	17.19	20.17	10.30
		5:12	11.98	13.43	16.61	20.07	23.88	28.03	11.85
		7:12	13.18	14.78	18.27	22.08	26.28	30.83	12.54
		12:12	16.32	18.29	22.62	27.34	32.53	38.17	14.48
	30	< 1:12	8.62	9.67	11.95	14.45	17.19	20.17	10.70
		5:12	11.98	13.43	16.61	20.07	23.88	28.03	13.79
		7:12	15.25	17.09	21.13	25.54	30.38	35.66	15.18
		12:12	21.52	24.12	29.82	36.05	42.89	50.33	19.05
	45	< 1:12	8.97	10.06	12.43	15.03	17.88	20.99	11.10
		5:12	12.46	13.97	17.27	20.88	24.84	29.15	15.73
		7:12	17.67	19.80	24.48	29.59	35.21	41.32	17.82
		12:12	27.27	30.56	37.79	45.68	54.35	63.78	23.62
	60	< 1:12	9.30	10.43	12.89	15.58	18.54	21.76	11.50
		5:12	12.91	14.47	17.90	21.63	25.74	30.20	17.67
		7:12	20.14	22.58	27.91	33.74	40.15	47.11	20.46
		12:12	33.19	37.19	45.99	55.59	66.14	77.62	28.19

For SI: 1 inch = 25.4 mm; 1 foot = 304.8 mm; 1 mile per hour = 0.447 m/s, 1 pound force per linear foot = 0.146kN/m, 1 pound per square foot = 47.88 Pa.

a. Tabulated lengths were derived by calculating design wind pressures in accordance with Figure 6-10 of ASCE 7 for a building with a mean roof height of 35 feet (10 668 mm). For wind perpendicular to the ridge, the effects of a 2-foot (610 mm) overhang on each endwall are included. The design pressures were used to calculate forces to be resisted by solid wall segments in each endwall [Table R611.7(1A) or R611.7(1B)] or sidewall [Table R611.7(1C)], as appropriate. The forces to be resisted by each wall line were then divided by the default design strength of 840 pounds per linear foot (12.26 kN/m) of length to determine the required solid wall length. The actual mean roof height of the building shall not exceed the least horizontal dimension of the building.

b. Tabulated lengths in the "minimum" column are based on the requirement of Section 6.1.4.1 of ASCE 7 that the main wind-force resisting system be designed for a minimum service level force of 10 psf multiplied by the area of the building projected onto a vertical plane normal to the assumed wind direction. Tabulated lengths in shaded cells are less than the "minimum" value. Where the minimum controls, it is permitted to be reduced in accordance with Notes c, d and e. See Section R611.7.1.1.

c. For buildings with a mean roof height of less than 35 feet tabulated lengths are permitted to be reduced by multiplying by the appropriate factor, R_1, from Table R611.7(2). The reduced length shall not be less than the "minimum" value shown in the table.

d. Tabulated lengths for "one story or top story of two-story" are based on a floor-to-ceiling height of 10 feet. Tabulated lengths for "first story of two-story" are based on floor-to-ceiling heights of 10 feet each for the first and second story. For floor-to-ceiling heights less than assumed, use the lengths in Table R611.7(1A), (1B) or (1C), or multiply the value in the table by the reduction factor, R_2, from Table R611.7(3).

e. Tabulated lengths are based on the default design shear strength of 840 pounds per linear foot of solid wall segment. The tabulated lengths are permitted to be reduced by multiplying by the applicable reduction factor for design strength, R_3, from Table R611.7(4).

f. The reduction factors, R_1, R_2, and R_3, in Tables R611.7(2), R611.7(3), and R611.7(4), respectively, are permitted to be compounded, subject to the limitations of Note b. However, the minimum number and minimum length of solid walls segments in each wall line shall comply with Sections R611.7.1 and R611.7.2.1, respectively.

g. For intermediate values of sidewall length, endwall length, roof slope and basic wind speed, use the next higher value, or determine by interpolation.

TABLE R611.7(1C)
UNREDUCED LENGTH, *UR*, OF SOLID WALL REQUIRED IN EACH EXTERIOR SIDEWALL FOR WIND PARALLEL TO RIDGE[a,c,d,e,f,g]

SIDEWALL LENGTH (feet)	ENDWALL LENGTH (feet)	ROOF SLOPE	UNREDUCED LENGTH, *UR*, OF SOLID WALL REQUIRED IN ENDWALLS FOR WIND PERPENDICULAR TO RIDGE (feet)						
			Basic Wind Speed (mph) Exposure						
			85B	90B	100B	110B	120B	130B	
					85C	90C	100C	110C	
						85D	90D	100D	
			One story or top story of two-story						Minimum[b]
< 30	15	< 1:12	0.95	1.06	1.31	1.59	1.89	2.22	0.90
		5:12	1.13	1.26	1.56	1.88	2.24	2.63	1.08
		7:12	1.21	1.35	1.67	2.02	2.40	2.82	1.17
		12:12	1.43	1.60	1.98	2.39	2.85	3.34	1.39
	30	< 1:12	1.77	1.98	2.45	2.96	3.53	4.14	1.90
		5:12	2.38	2.67	3.30	3.99	4.75	5.57	2.62
		7:12	2.66	2.98	3.69	4.46	5.31	6.23	2.95
		12:12	3.43	3.85	4.76	5.75	6.84	8.03	3.86
	45	< 1:12	2.65	2.97	3.67	4.43	5.27	6.19	2.99
		5:12	3.98	4.46	5.51	6.66	7.93	9.31	4.62
		7:12	4.58	5.14	6.35	7.68	9.14	10.72	5.36
		12:12	6.25	7.01	8.67	10.48	12.47	14.63	7.39
	60	< 1:12	3.59	4.03	4.98	6.02	7.16	8.40	4.18
		5:12	5.93	6.65	8.22	9.93	11.82	13.87	7.07
		7:12	6.99	7.83	9.69	11.71	13.93	16.35	8.38
		12:12	9.92	11.12	13.75	16.62	19.77	23.21	12.00
60	45	< 1:12	2.77	3.11	3.84	4.65	5.53	6.49	2.99
		5:12	4.15	4.66	5.76	6.96	8.28	9.72	4.62
		7:12	4.78	5.36	6.63	8.01	9.53	11.18	5.36
		12:12	6.51	7.30	9.03	10.91	12.98	15.23	7.39
	60	< 1:12	3.86	4.32	5.35	6.46	7.69	9.02	4.18
		5:12	6.31	7.08	8.75	10.57	12.58	14.76	7.07
		7:12	7.43	8.32	10.29	12.44	14.80	17.37	8.38
		12:12	10.51	11.78	14.56	17.60	20.94	24.57	12.00
First story of two-story									
< 30	15	< 1:12	2.65	2.97	3.67	4.44	5.28	6.20	2.52
		5:12	2.83	3.17	3.92	4.74	5.64	6.62	2.70
		7:12	2.91	3.26	4.03	4.87	5.80	6.80	2.79
		12:12	3.13	3.51	4.34	5.25	6.24	7.32	3.01
	30	< 1:12	4.81	5.39	6.67	8.06	9.59	11.25	5.14
		5:12	5.42	6.08	7.52	9.09	10.81	12.69	5.86
		7:12	5.70	6.39	7.90	9.55	11.37	13.34	6.19
		12:12	6.47	7.25	8.97	10.84	12.90	15.14	7.10
	45	< 1:12	6.99	7.83	9.69	11.71	13.93	16.35	7.85
		5:12	8.32	9.33	11.53	13.94	16.59	19.47	9.48
		7:12	8.93	10.01	12.37	14.95	17.79	20.88	10.21
		12:12	10.60	11.88	14.69	17.75	21.13	24.79	12.25
	60	< 1:12	9.23	10.35	12.79	15.46	18.40	21.59	10.65
		5:12	11.57	12.97	16.03	19.38	23.06	27.06	13.54
		7:12	12.63	14.15	17.50	21.15	25.17	29.54	14.85
		12:12	15.56	17.44	21.56	26.06	31.01	36.39	18.48

(continued)

TABLE R611.7(1C)—continued
UNREDUCED LENGTH, *UR*, OF SOLID WALL REQUIRED IN EACH EXTERIOR ENDWALL FOR WIND PERPENDICULAR TO RIDGE FIRST STORY OF TWO-STORY[a,c,d,e,f,g]

SIDEWALL LENGTH (feet)	ENDWALL LENGTH (feet)	ROOF SLOPE	UNREDUCED LENGTH, *UR*, OF SOLID WALL REQUIRED IN ENDWALLS FOR WIND PERPENDICULAR TO RIDGE (feet)						
			Basic Wind Speed (mph) Exposure						
			85B	90B	100B	110B	120B	130B	
					85C	90C	100C	110C	
						85D	90D	100D	Minimum[b]
60	45	< 1:12	7.34	8.22	10.17	12.29	14.62	17.16	7.85
		5:12	8.72	9.77	12.08	14.60	17.37	20.39	9.48
		7:12	9.34	10.47	12.95	15.65	18.62	21.85	10.21
		12:12	11.08	12.41	15.35	18.55	22.07	25.90	12.25
	60	< 1:12	9.94	11.14	13.77	16.65	19.81	23.25	10.65
		5:12	12.40	13.89	17.18	20.76	24.70	28.99	13.54
		7:12	13.51	15.14	18.72	22.63	26.92	31.60	14.85
		12:12	16.59	18.59	22.99	27.79	33.06	38.80	18.48

For SI: 1 inch = 25.4 mm, 1 foot = 304.8 mm, 1 mile per hour = 0.447 m/s, 1 pound force per linear foot = 0.146kN/m, 1 pound per square foot = 47.88 Pa.

a. Tabulated lengths were derived by calculating design wind pressures in accordance with Figure 6-10 of ASCE 7 for a building with a mean roof height of 35 feet (10 668 mm). For wind perpendicular to the ridge, the effects of a 2-foot (610 mm) overhang on each endwall are included. The design pressures were used to calculate forces to be resisted by solid wall segments in each endwall [Table R611.7(1A) or R611.7(1B)] or sidewall [(Table R611.7(1C)], as appropriate. The forces to be resisted by each wall line were then divided by the default design strength of 840 pounds per linear foot (12.26 kN/m) of length to determine the required solid wall length. The actual mean roof height of the building shall not exceed the least horizontal dimension of the building.

b. Tabulated lengths in the "minimum" column are based on the requirement of Section 6.1.4.1 of ASCE 7 that the main wind-force resisting system be designed for a minimum service level force of 10 psf multiplied by the area of the building projected onto a vertical plane normal to the assumed wind direction. Tabulated lengths in shaded cells are less than the "minimum" value. Where the minimum controls, it is permitted to be reduced in accordance with Notes c, d and e. See Section R611.7.1.1.

c. For buildings with a mean roof height of less than 35 feet, tabulated lengths are permitted to be reduced by multiplying by the appropriate factor, R_1, from Table R611.7(2). The reduced length shall not be less than the "minimum" value shown in the table.

d. Tabulated lengths for "one story or top story of two-story" are based on a floor-to-ceiling height of 10 feet. Tabulated lengths for "first story of two-story" are based on floor-to-ceiling heights of 10 feet each for the first and second story. For floor-to-ceiling heights less than assumed, use the lengths in Table R611.7(1A), (1B) or (1C), or multiply the value in the table by the reduction factor, R_2, from Table R611.7(3).

e. Tabulated lengths are based on the default design shear strength of 840 pounds per linear foot of solid wall segment. The tabulated lengths are permitted to be reduced by multiplying by the applicable reduction factor for design strength, R_3, from Table R611.7(4).

f. The reduction factors, R_1, R_2, and R_3, in Tables R611.7(2), R611.7(3), and R611.7(4), respectively, are permitted to be compounded, subject to the limitations of Note b. However, the minimum number and minimum length of solid walls segments in each wall line shall comply with Sections R611.7.1 and R611.7.2.1, respectively.

g. For intermediate values of sidewall length, endwall length, roof slope and basic wind speed, use the next higher value, or determine by interpolation.

R611.6.4 Termination of reinforcement. Where indicated in items 1 through 3 below, vertical wall reinforcement in the top-most *story* with concrete walls shall be terminated with a 90-degree (1.57 rad) standard hook complying with Section R611.5.4.5 and Figure R611.5.4(3).

1. Vertical bars adjacent to door and window openings required by Section R611.8.1.2.
2. Vertical bars at the ends of required solid wall segments. See Section R611.7.2.2.2.
3. Vertical bars (other than end bars – see item 2) used as shear reinforcement in required solid wall segments where the reduction factor for design strength, R_3, used is based on the wall having horizontal and vertical shear reinforcement. See Section R611.7.2.2.3.

The bar extension of the hook shall be oriented parallel to the horizontal wall reinforcement and be within 4 inches (102 mm) of the top of the wall.

Horizontal reinforcement shall be continuous around the building corners by bending one of the bars and lap-splicing it with the bar in the other wall in accordance with Section R611.5.4.3 and Figure R611.5.4(1).

Exception: In lieu of bending horizontal reinforcement at corners, separate bent reinforcing bars shall be permitted provided that the bent bar is lap-spliced with the horizontal reinforcement in both walls in accordance with Section R611.5.4.3 and Figure R611.5.4(1).

In required solid wall segments where the reduction factor for design strength, R_3, is based on the wall having horizontal and vertical shear reinforcement in accordance with Section R611.7.2.2.1, horizontal wall reinforcement shall be terminated with a standard hook complying with Section R611.5.4.5 and Figure R611.5.4(3) or in a lap-splice, except at corners where the reinforcement shall be continuous as required above.

R611.6.5 Location of reinforcement in wall. Except for vertical reinforcement at the ends of required solid wall segments, which shall be located as required by Section R611.7.2.2.2, the location of the vertical reinforcement shall not vary from the center of the wall by more than the greater of 10 percent of the wall thickness and $^3/_8$-inch (10 mm). Horizontal and vertical reinforcement shall be located to provide not less than the minimum cover required by Section R611.5.4.1.

R611.7 Solid walls for resistance to lateral forces.

R611.7.1 Length of solid wall. Each exterior wall line in each *story* shall have a total length of solid wall required by Section R611.7.1.1. A solid wall is a section of flat, waffle-grid or screen-grid wall, extending the full *story height* without openings or penetrations, except those permitted by Section R611.7.2. Solid wall segments that contribute to the total length of solid wall shall comply with Section R611.7.2.

R611.7.1.1 Length of solid wall for wind. All buildings shall have solid walls in each exterior endwall line (the side of a building that is parallel to the span of the roof or floor framing) and sidewall line (the side of a building that is perpendicular to the span of the roof or floor framing) to resist lateral in-plane wind forces. The site-appropriate basic wind speed and exposure category shall be used in Tables R611.7(1A) through (1C) to determine the unreduced total length, UR, of solid wall required in each exterior endwall line and sidewall line. For buildings with a mean roof height of less than 35 feet (10 668 mm), the unreduced values determined from Tables R611.7(1A) though (1C) is permitted by multiplying by the applicable factor, R1, from Table R611.7(2); however, reduced values shall not be less than the minimum values in Tables R611.7(1A) through (1C). Where the floor-to-ceiling height of a *story* is less than 10 feet (3048 mm), the unreduced values determined from Tables R611.7(1A) through (C), including minimum values, is permitted to be reduced by multiplying by the applicable factor, R_2, from Table R611.7(3). To account for different design strengths than assumed in determining the values in Tables R611.7(1A) through (1C), the unreduced lengths determined from Tables R611.7(1A) through (1C), including minimum values, are permitted to be reduced by multiplying by the applicable factor, R_3, from Table R611.7(4). The reductions permitted by Tables R611.7(2), R611.7(3) and R611.7(4) are cumulative.

The total length of solid wall segments, *TL*, in a wall line that comply with the minimum length requirements of Section R611.7.2.1 [see Figure R611.7(1)] shall be equal to or greater than the product of the unreduced length of solid wall from Tables R611.7(1A) through (1C), *UR* and the applicable reduction factors, if any, from Tables R611.7(2), R611.7(3) and R611.7(4) as indicated by Equation R611-1.

$$TL \geq R_1 \cdot R_2 \cdot R_3 \cdot UR \quad \textbf{(Equation R611-1)}$$

Where

TL = total length of solid wall segments in a wall line that comply with Section R611.7.2.1 [see Figure R611.7(1)], and

R_1 = 1.0 or reduction factor for mean roof height from Table R611.7(2),

R_2 = 1.0 or reduction factor for floor-to-ceiling wall height from Table R611.7(3),

R_3 = 1.0 or reduction factor for design strength from Table R611.7(4), and

UR = unreduced length of solid wall from Tables R611.7(1A) through (1C).

The total length of solid wall in a wall line, *TL*, shall not be less than that provided by two solid wall segments complying with the minimum length requirements of Section R611.7.2.1.

To facilitate determining the required wall thickness, wall type, number and *grade* of vertical bars at the each end of each solid wall segment, and whether shear reinforcement is required, use of Equation R611-2 is permitted.

$$R_3 \leq \frac{TL}{R_1 \cdot R_2 \cdot UR} \quad \textbf{(Equation R611-2)}$$

After determining the maximum permitted value of the reduction factor for design strength, R_3, in accordance with Equation R611-2, select a wall type from Table R611.7(4) with R_3 less than or equal to the value calculated.

R611.7.2 Solid wall segments. Solid wall segments that contribute to the required length of solid wall shall comply with this section. Reinforcement shall be provided in accordance with Section R611.7.2.2 and Table R611.7(4). Solid wall segments shall extend the full story-height without openings, other than openings for the utilities and other building services passing through the wall. In flat walls and waffle-grid walls, such openings shall have an area of less than 30 square inches (19 355 mm^2) with no dimension exceeding $6^1/_4$ inches (159 mm), and shall not be located within 6 inches (152 mm) of the side edges of the solid wall segment. In screen-grid walls, such openings shall be located in the portion of the solid wall segment between horizontal and vertical cores of concrete and opening size and location are not restricted provided no concrete is removed.

R611.7.2.1 Minimum length of solid wall segment and maximum spacing. Only solid wall segments equal to or greater than 24 inches (610 mm) in length shall be included in the total length of solid wall required by Section R611.7.1. In addition, no more than two solid wall segments equal to or greater than 24 inches (610 mm) in length and less than 48 inches (1219 mm) in length shall be included in the required total length of solid wall. The maximum clear opening width shall be 18 feet (5486 mm). See Figure R611.7(1).

R611.7.2.2 Reinforcement in solid wall segments.

R611.7.2.2.1 Horizontal shear reinforcement. Where reduction factors for design strength, R_3, from Table R611.7(4) based on horizontal and vertical shear reinforcement being provided are used, solid wall segments shall have horizontal reinforcement consisting of minimum No. 4 bars. Horizontal shear reinforcement shall be the same grade of steel required for the vertical reinforcement at the ends of solid wall segments by Section R611.7.2.2.2.

The spacing of horizontal reinforcement shall not exceed the smaller of one-half the length of the solid wall segment, minus 2 inches (51 mm), and 18 inches (457 mm). Horizontal shear reinforcement shall terminate in accordance with Section R611.6.4.

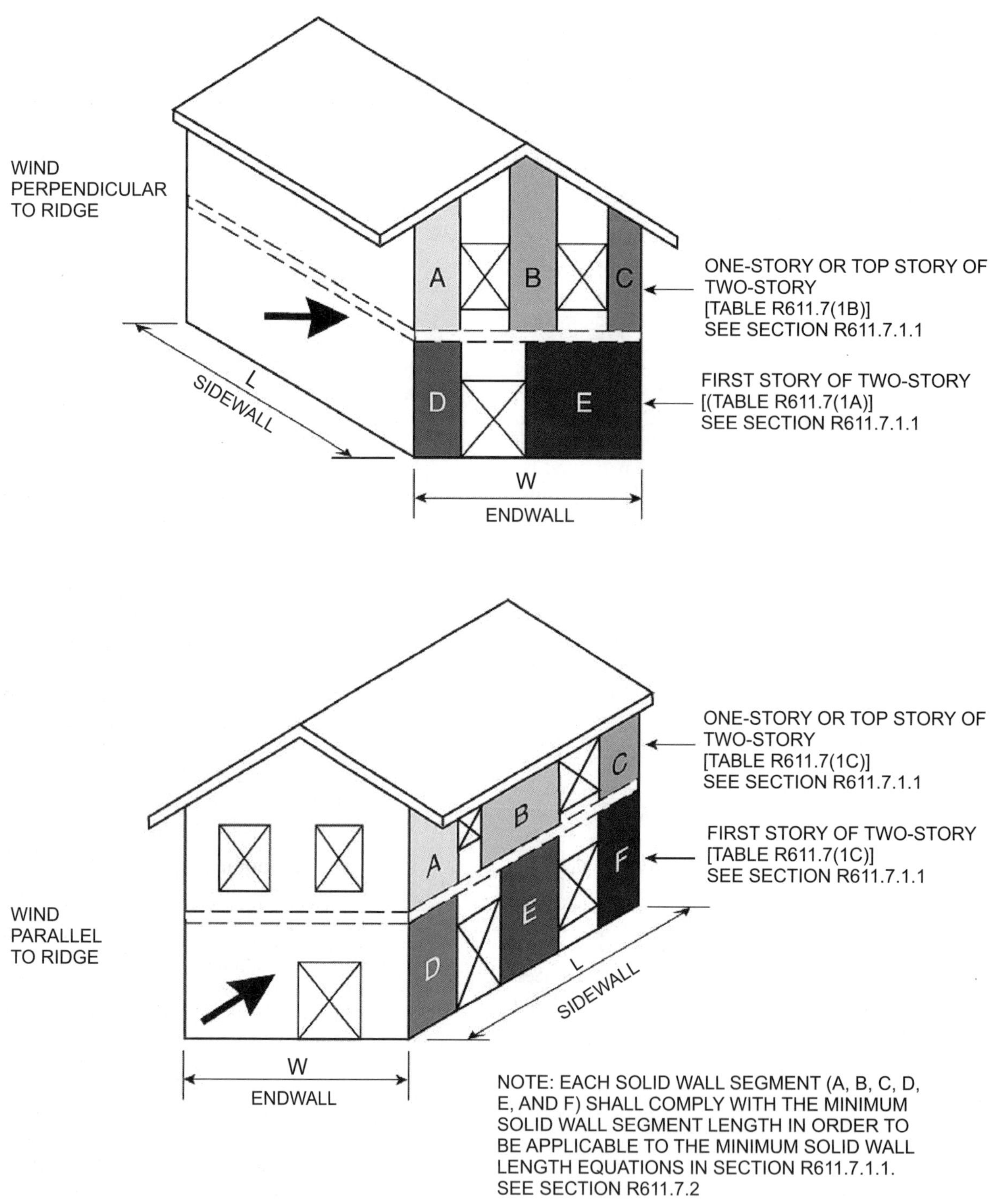

FIGURE R611.7(1)
MINIMUM SOLID WALL LENGTH

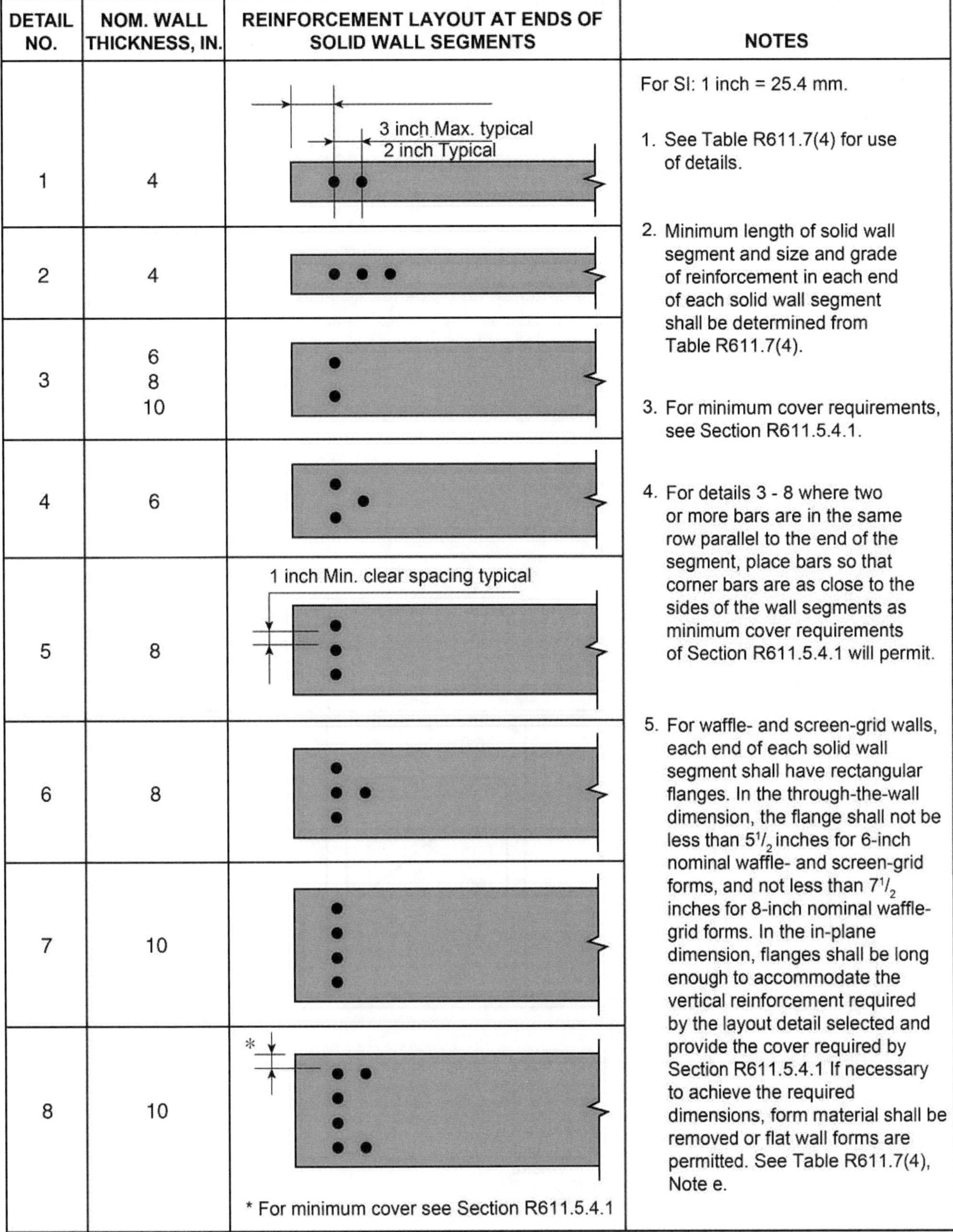

DETAIL NO.	NOM. WALL THICKNESS, IN.	REINFORCEMENT LAYOUT AT ENDS OF SOLID WALL SEGMENTS
1	4	3 inch Max. typical 2 inch Typical
2	4	
3	6 8 10	
4	6	
5	8	1 inch Min. clear spacing typical
6	8	
7	10	
8	10	* For minimum cover see Section R611.5.4.1

NOTES

For SI: 1 inch = 25.4 mm.

1. See Table R611.7(4) for use of details.
2. Minimum length of solid wall segment and size and grade of reinforcement in each end of each solid wall segment shall be determined from Table R611.7(4).
3. For minimum cover requirements, see Section R611.5.4.1.
4. For details 3 - 8 where two or more bars are in the same row parallel to the end of the segment, place bars so that corner bars are as close to the sides of the wall segments as minimum cover requirements of Section R611.5.4.1 will permit.
5. For waffle- and screen-grid walls, each end of each solid wall segment shall have rectangular flanges. In the through-the-wall dimension, the flange shall not be less than $5^1/_2$ inches for 6-inch nominal waffle- and screen-grid forms, and not less than $7^1/_2$ inches for 8-inch nominal waffle-grid forms. In the in-plane dimension, flanges shall be long enough to accommodate the vertical reinforcement required by the layout detail selected and provide the cover required by Section R611.5.4.1 If necessary to achieve the required dimensions, form material shall be removed or flat wall forms are permitted. See Table R611.7(4), Note e.

FIGURE R611.7(2)
VERTICAL REINFORCEMENT LAYOUT DETAIL

TABLE R611.7(2)
REDUCTION FACTOR, R_1, FOR BUILDINGS WITH MEAN ROOF HEIGHT LESS THAN 35 FEET[a]

MEAN ROOF HEIGHT[b,c] (feet)	REDUCTION FACTOR R_1, FOR MEAN ROOF HEIGHT		
	Exposure category		
	B	C	D
< 15	0.96	0.84	0.87
20	0.96	0.89	0.91
25	0.96	0.93	0.94
30	0.96	0.97	0.98
35	1.00	1.00	1.00

For SI: 1 foot = 304.8 mm.

a. See Section R611.7.1.1 and note c to Table R611.7(1A) for application of reduction factors in this table. This reduction is not permitted for "minimum" values.

b. For intermediate values of mean roof height, use the factor for the next greater height, or determine by interpolation.

c. Mean roof height is the average of the roof eave height and height of the highest point on the roof surface, except that for roof slopes of less than or equal to $2^1/_8$:12 (10 degrees), the mean roof height is permitted to be taken as the roof eave height.

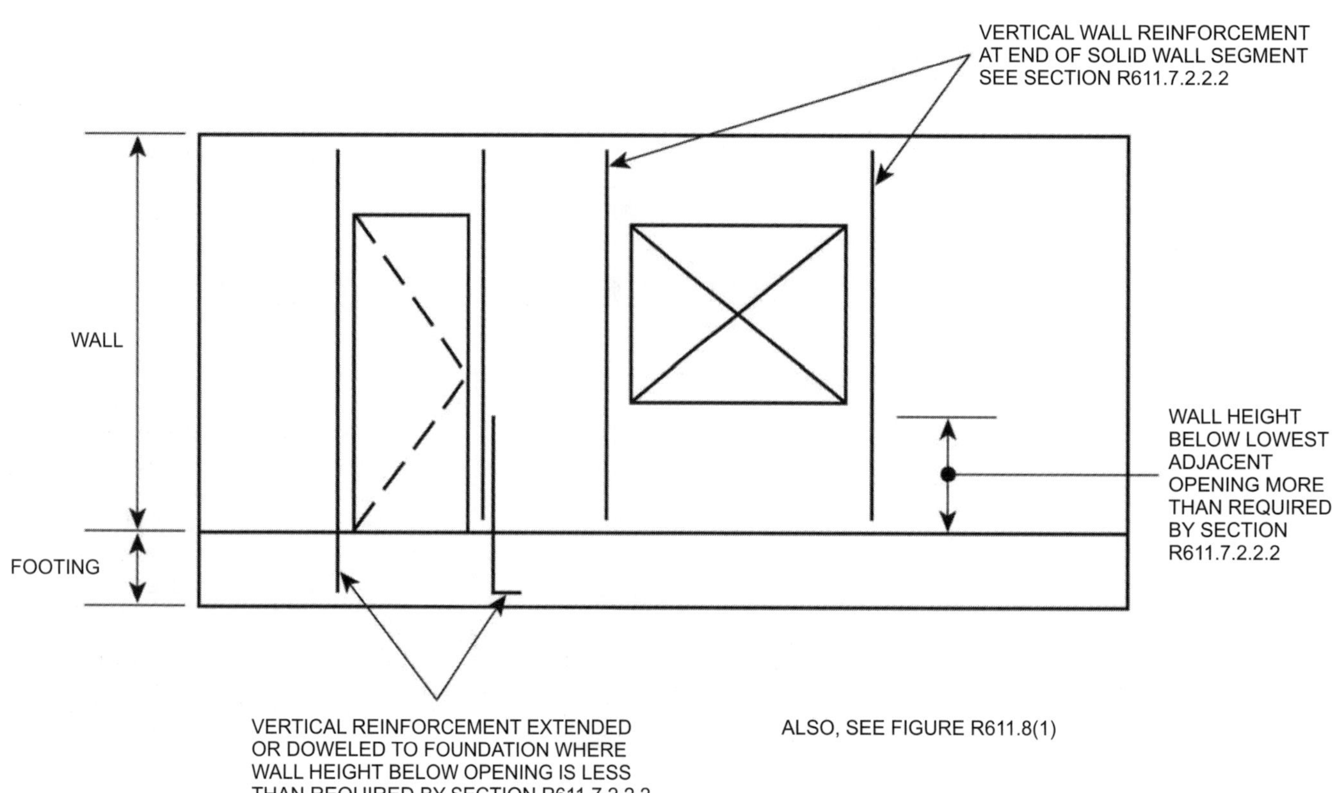

FIGURE R611.7(3)
VERTICAL WALL REINFORCEMENT ADJACENT TO WALL OPENINGS

TABLE R611.7(3) REDUCTION FACTOR, R_2, FOR FLOOR-TO-CEILING WALL HEIGHTS LESS THAN 10 FEET[a,b]

STORY UNDER CONSIDERATION	FLOOR-TO-CEILING HEIGHT[c] (feet)	ENDWALL LENGTH (feet)	ROOF SLOPE	REDUCTION FACTOR, R_2
Endwalls—for wind perpendicular to ridge				
One story or top story of two-story	8	15	< 5:12	0.83
			7:12	0.90
			12:12	0.94
		60	< 5:12	0.83
			7:12	0.95
			12:12	0.98
First story of two-story	16 combined first and second story	15	< 5:12	0.83
			7:12	0.86
			12:12	0.89
		60	< 5:12	0.83
			7:12	0.91
			12:12	0.95
Sidewalls—for wind parallel to ridge				
One story or top story of two-story	8	15	< 1:12	0.84
			5:12	0.87
			7:12	0.88
			12:12	0.89
		60	< 1:12	0.86
			5:12	0.92
			7:12	0.93
			12:12	0.95
First story of two-story	16 combined first and second story	15	< 1:12	0.83
			5:12	0.84
			7:12	0.85
			12:12	0.86
		60	< 1:12	0.84
			5:12	0.87
			7:12	0.88
			12:12	0.90

For SI: 1 foot = 304.8 mm.

a. See Section R611.7.1.1 and Note d to Table R611.7(1A) for application of reduction factors in this table.

b. For intermediate values of endwall length, and/or roof slope, use the next higher value, or determine by interpolation.

c. Tabulated values in Table R611.7(1A) and (1C) for "one story or top story of two-story" are based on a floor-to-ceiling height of 10 feet (3048 mm). Tabulated values in Table R611.7(1B) and (1C) for "first story of two-story" are based on floor-to-ceiling heights of 10 feet each for the first and second story. For floor to ceiling heights between those shown in this table and those assumed in Table R611.7(1A), (1B) or (1C), use the solid wall lengths in Table R611.7(1A), (1B) or (1C), or determine the reduction factor by interpolating between 1.0 and the factor shown in this table.

TABLE R611.7(4)
REDUCTION FACTOR FOR DESIGN STRENGTH, R_3, FOR FLAT, WAFFLE- AND SCREEN-GRID WALLS[a,c]

NOMINAL THICKNESS OF WALL (inches)	VERTICAL BARS AT EACH END OF SOLID WALL SEGMENT		VERTICAL REINFORCEMENT LAYOUT DETAIL [see Figure R611.7(2)]	REDUCTION FACTOR, R_3, FOR LENGTH OF SOLID WALL			
				Horizontal and vertical shear reinforcement provided			
				No		Yes[d]	
	Number of bars	Bar size		40,000[b]	60,000[b]	40,000[b]	60,000[b]
Flat walls							
4	2	4	1	0.74	0.61	0.74	0.50
	3	4	2	0.61	0.61	0.52	0.27
	2	5	1	0.61	0.61	0.48	0.25
	3	5	2	0.61	0.61	0.26	0.18
6	2	4	3	0.70	0.48	0.70	0.48
	3	4	4	0.49	0.38	0.49	0.33
	2	5	3	0.46	0.38	0.46	0.31
	3	5	4	0.38	0.38	0.32	0.16
8	2	4	3	0.70	0.47	0.70	0.47
	3	4	5	0.47	0.32	0.47	0.32
	2	5	3	0.45	0.31	0.45	0.31
	4	4	6	0.36	0.28	0.36	0.25
	3	5	5	0.31	0.28	0.31	0.16
	4	5	6	0.28	0.28	0.24	0.12
10	2	4	3	0.70	0.47	0.70	0.47
	2	5	3	0.45	0.30	0.45	0.30
	4	4	7	0.36	0.25	0.36	0.25
	6	4	8	0.25	0.22	0.25	0.13
	4	5	7	0.24	0.22	0.24	0.12
	6	5	8	0.22	0.22	0.12	0.08
Waffle-grid walls[e]							
6	2	4	3	0.78	0.78	0.70	0.48
	3	4	4	0.78	0.78	0.49	0.25
	2	5	3	0.78	0.78	0.46	0.23
	3	5	4	0.78	0.78	0.24	0.16
8	2	4	3	0.78	0.78	0.70	0.47
	3	4	5	0.78	0.78	0.47	0.24
	2	5	3	0.78	0.78	0.45	0.23
	4	4	6	0.78	0.78	0.36	0.18
	3	5	5	0.78	0.78	0.23	0.16
	4	5	6	0.78	0.78	0.18	0.13
Screen-grid walls[e]							
6	2	4	3	0.93	0.93	0.70	0.48
	3	4	4	0.93	0.93	0.49	0.25
	2	5	3	0.93	0.93	0.46	0.23
	3	5	4	0.93	0.93	0.24	0.16

For SI: 1 inch = 25.4 mm; 1,000 pounds per square inch = 6.895 MPa.

a. See note e to Table R611.7(1A) for application of adjustment factors in this table.

b. Yield strength in pounds per square inch of vertical wall reinforcement at ends of solid wall segments.

c. Values are based on concrete with a specified compressive strength, f'_c, of 2,500 psi. Where concrete with f'_c of not less than 3,000 psi is used, values in shaded cells are permitted to be decreased by multiplying by 0.91.

d. Horizontal and vertical shear reinforcement shall be provided in accordance with Section R611.7.2.2.

e. Each end of each solid wall segment shall have rectangular flanges. In the through-the-wall dimension, the flange shall not be less than $5^1/_2$ inches for 6-inch nominal waffle- and screen-grid walls, and not less than $7^1/_2$ inches for 8-inch nominal waffle-grid walls. In the in-plane dimension, flanges shall be long enough to accommodate the vertical reinforcement required by the layout detail selected from Figure R611.7(2) and provide the cover required by Section R611.5.4.1. If necessary to achieve the required dimensions, form material shall be removed or use of flat wall forms is permitted.

R611.7.2.2.2 Vertical reinforcement. Vertical reinforcement applicable to the reduction factor(s) for design strength, R_3, from Table R611.7(4) that is used, shall be located at each end of each solid wall segment in accordance with the applicable detail in Figure R611.7(2). The No. 4 vertical bar required on each side of an opening by Section R611.8.1.2 is permitted to be used as reinforcement at the ends of solid wall segments where installed in accordance with the applicable detail in Figure R611.7(2). There shall be not less than two No. 4 bars at each end of solid wall segments located as required by the applicable detail in Figure R611.7(2). One of the bars at each end of solid wall segments shall be deemed to meet the requirements for vertical wall reinforcement required by Section R611.6.

The vertical wall reinforcement at each end of each solid wall segment shall be developed below the bottom of the adjacent wall opening [see Figure R611.7(3)] by one of the following methods:

1. Where the wall height below the bottom of the adjacent opening is equal to or greater than 22 inches (559 mm) for No. 4 or 28 inches (711 mm) for No. 5 vertical wall reinforcement, reinforcement around openings in accordance with Section R611.8.1 shall be sufficient, or
2. Where the wall height below the bottom of the adjacent opening is less than required by Item 1 above, the vertical wall reinforcement adjacent to the opening shall extend into the footing far enough to develop the bar in tension in accordance with Section R611.5.4.4 and Figure R611.5.4(2), or shall be lap-spliced with a dowel that is embedded in the footing far enough to develop the dowel-bar in tension.

R611.7.2.2.3 Vertical shear reinforcement. Where reduction factors for design strength, R_3, from Table R611.7(4) based on horizontal and vertical shear reinforcement being provided are used, solid wall segments shall have vertical reinforcement consisting of minimum No. 4 bars. Vertical shear reinforcement shall be the same grade of steel required by Section R611.7.2.2.2 for the vertical reinforcement at the ends of solid wall segments. The spacing of vertical reinforcement throughout the length of the segment shall not exceed the smaller of one third the length of the segment, and 18 inches (457 mm). Vertical shear reinforcement shall be continuous between stories in accordance with Section R611.6.3, and shall terminate in accordance with Section R611.6.4. Vertical shear reinforcement required by this section is permitted to be used for vertical reinforcement required by Table R611.6(1), R611.6(2), R611.6(3) or R611.6(4), whichever is applicable.

R611.7.2.3 Solid wall segments at corners. At all interior and exterior corners of exterior walls, a solid wall segment shall extend the full height of each wall *story*. The segment shall have the length required to develop the horizontal reinforcement above and below the adjacent opening in tension in accordance with Section R611.5.4.4. For an exterior corner, the limiting dimension is measured on the outside of the wall, and for an interior corner the limiting dimension is measured on the inside of the wall. See Section R611.8.1. The length of a segment contributing to the required length of solid wall shall comply with Section R611.7.2.1.

The end of a solid wall segment complying with the minimum length requirements of Section R611.7.2.1 shall be located no more than 6 feet (1829 mm) from each corner.

R611.8 Requirements for lintels and reinforcement around openings.

R611.8.1 Reinforcement around openings. Reinforcement shall be provided around openings in walls equal to or greater than 2 feet (610 mm) in width in accordance with this section and Figure R611.8(1), in addition to the minimum wall reinforcement required by Sections R404.1.2, R611.6 and R611.7. Vertical wall reinforcement required by this section is permitted to be used as reinforcement at the ends of solid wall segments required by Section R611.7.2.2.2 provided it is located in accordance with Section R611.8.1.2. Wall openings shall have a minimum depth of concrete over the width of the opening of 8 inches (203 mm) in flat walls and waffle-grid walls, and 12 inches (305 mm) in screen-grid walls. Wall openings in waffle-grid and screen-grid walls shall be located such that not less than one-half of a vertical core occurs along each side of the opening.

R611.8.1.1 Horizontal reinforcement. Lintels complying with Section R611.8.2 shall be provided above wall openings equal to or greater than 2 feet (610 mm) in width.

Exception: Continuous horizontal wall reinforcement placed within 12 inches (305 mm) of the top of the wall *story* as required in Sections R404.1.2.2 and R611.6.2 is permitted in lieu of top or bottom lintel reinforcement required by Section R611.8.2 provided that the continuous horizontal wall reinforcement meets the location requirements specified in Figures R611.8(2), R611.8(3), and R611.8(4) and the size requirements specified in Tables R611.8(2) through R611.8(10).

Openings equal to or greater than 2 feet (610 mm) in width shall have a minimum of one No. 4 bar placed within 12 inches (305 mm) of the bottom of the opening. See Figure R611.8(1).

Horizontal reinforcement placed above and below an opening shall extend beyond the edges of the opening the dimension required to develop the bar in tension in accordance with Section R611.5.4.4.

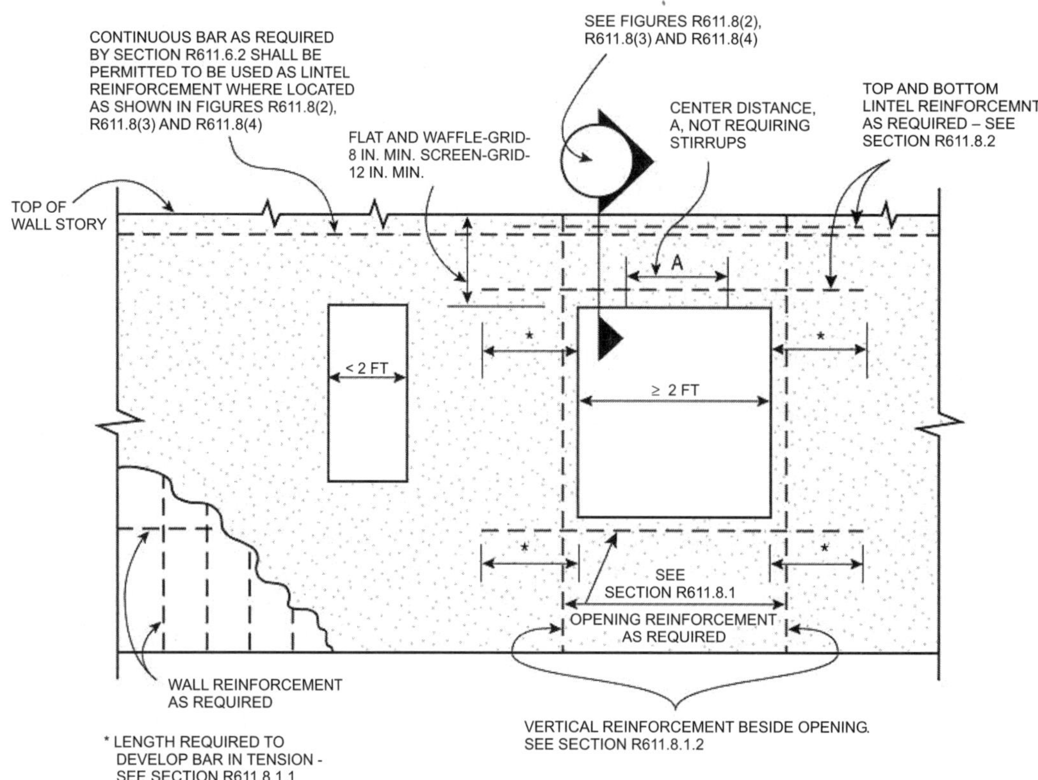

For SI: 1 inch = 25.4 mm, 1 foot = 304.8 mm.

FIGURE R611.8(1)
REINFORCEMENT OF OPENINGS

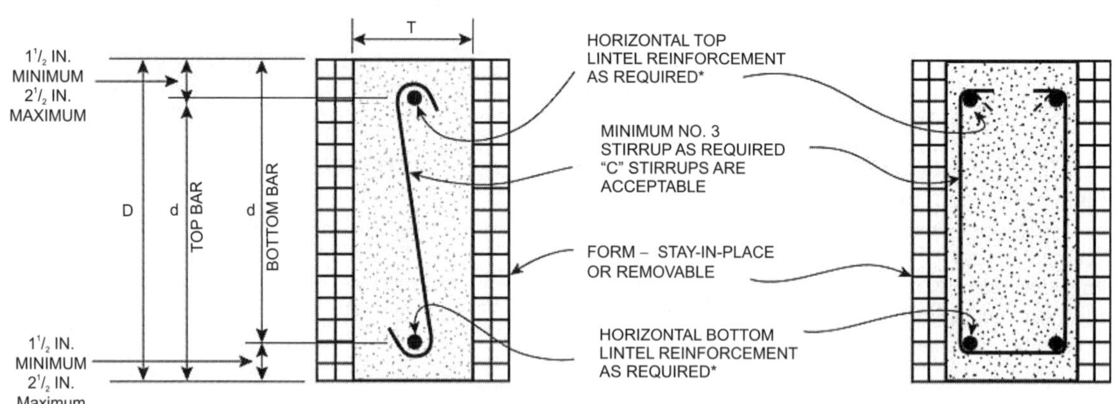

For SI: 1 inch = 25.4 mm.

FIGURE R611.8(2)
LINTEL FOR FLAT WALLS

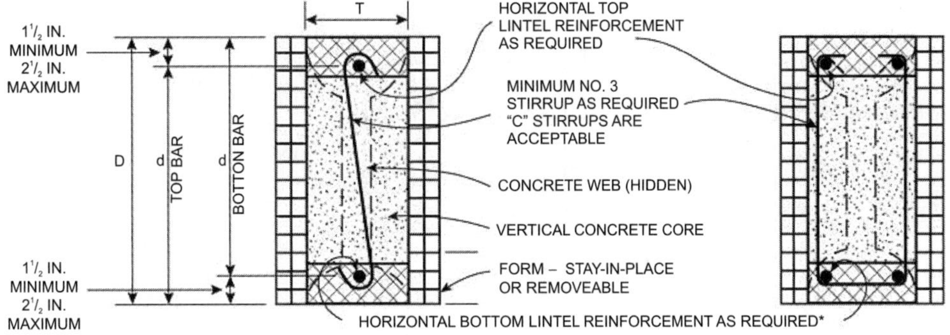

(a) SINGLE FORM HEIGHT SECTION CUT THROUGH VERTICAL CORE OF A WAFFLE-GRID LINTEL

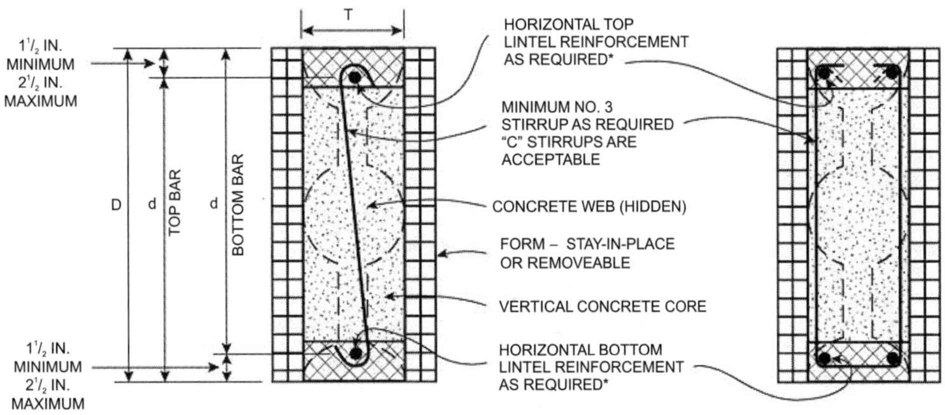

(b) DOUBLE FORM HEIGHT SECTION CUT THROUGH VERTICAL CORE OF A WAFFLE-GRID LINTEL

*FOR BUNDLED BARS, SEE SECTION R611.8.2.2.

NOTE: CROSS-HATCHING REPRESENTS THE AREA IN WHICH FORM MATERIAL SHALL BE REMOVED, IF NECESSARY, TO CREATE FLANGES CONTINUOUS THE LENGTH OF THE LINTEL. FLANGES SHALL HAVE A MINIMUM THICKNESS OF 3 IN., AND A MINIMUM WIDTH OF 5 IN. AND 7 IN. IN 6 IN. NOMINAL AND 8 IN. NOMINAL WAFFLE-GRID WALLS, RESPECTIVELY. SEE NOTE a TO TABLES R611.8(6) AND R611.8(10).

For SI: 1 inch = 25.4 mm.

FIGURE R611.8(3)
LINTELS FOR WAFFLE-GRID WALLS

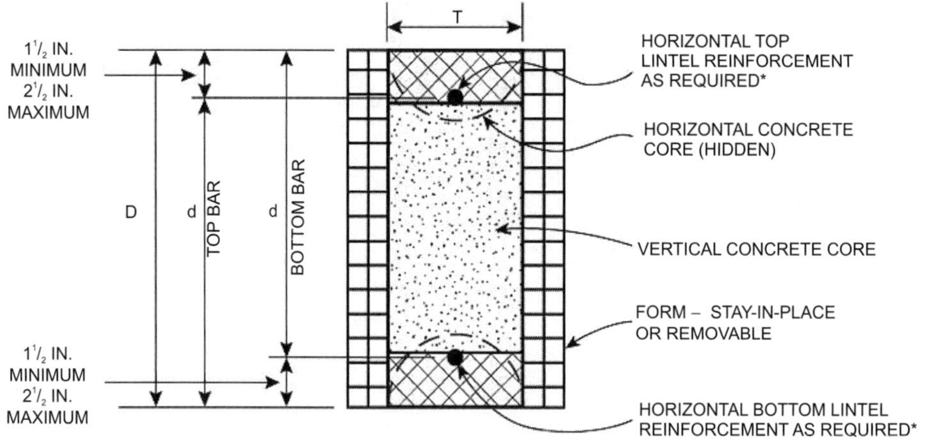

(a) SINGLE FORM HEIGHT SECTION CUT THROUGH VERTICAL CORE OF A SCREEN-GRID LINTEL

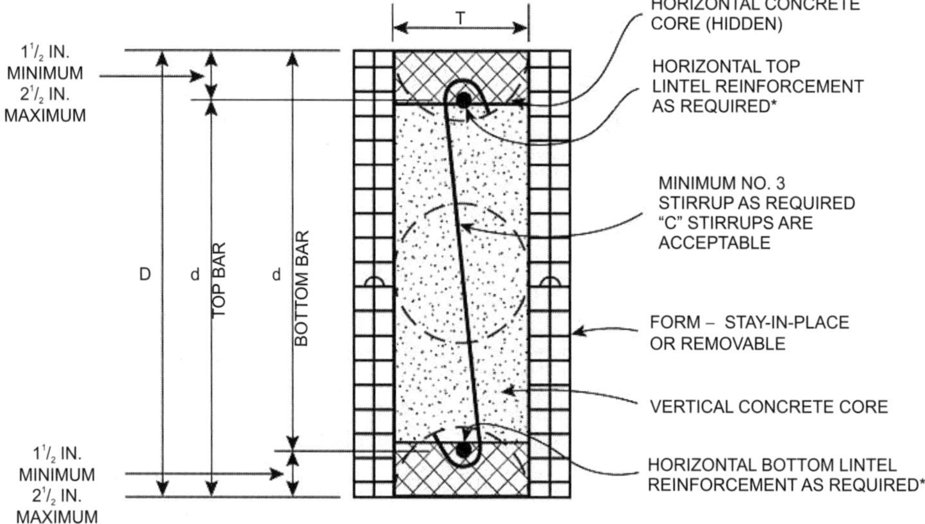

(b) DOUBLE FORM HEIGHT SECTION CUT THROUGH VERTICAL CORE OF A SCREEN-GRID LINTEL

*FOR BUNDLED BARS, SEE SECTION R611.8.2.2.

NOTE: CROSS-HATCHING REPRESENTS THE AREA IN WHICH FORM MATERIAL SHALL BE REMOVED, IF NECESSARY, TO CREATE FLANGES CONTINUOUS THE LENGTH OF THE LINTEL. FLANGES SHALL HAVE A MINIMUM THICKNESS OF 2.5 IN. AND A MINIMUM WIDTH OF 5 IN. SEE NOTE a TO TABLES R611.8(8) AND R611.8(10).

For SI: 1 inch = 25.4 mm.

FIGURE R611.8(4)
LINTELS FOR SCREEN-GRID WALLS

TABLE R611.8(1)
LINTEL DESIGN LOADING CONDITIONS[a, b, d]

<table>
<tr><th colspan="3">DESCRIPTION OF LOADS AND OPENINGS ABOVE INFLUENCING DESIGN OF LINTEL</th><th>DESIGN LOAD CONDITION[c]</th></tr>
<tr><td colspan="4">Opening in wall of top story of two-story building, or first story of one-story building</td></tr>
<tr><td rowspan="2">Wall supporting loads from roof, including attic floor, if applicable, and</td><td colspan="2">Top of lintel equal to or less than W/2 below top of wall</td><td>2</td></tr>
<tr><td colspan="2">Top of lintel greater than W/2 below top of wall</td><td>NLB</td></tr>
<tr><td colspan="3">Wall not supporting loads from roof or attic floor</td><td>NLB</td></tr>
<tr><td colspan="4">Opening in wall of first story of two-story building where wall immediately above is of concrete construction, or opening in basement wall of one-story building where wall immediately above is of concrete construction</td></tr>
<tr><td rowspan="3">LB ledger board mounted to side of wall with bottom of ledger less than or equal to W/2 above top of lintel, and</td><td colspan="2">Top of lintel greater than W/2 below bottom of opening in story above</td><td>1</td></tr>
<tr><td rowspan="2">Top of lintel less than or equal to W/2 below bottom of opening in story above, and</td><td>Opening is entirely within the footprint of the opening in the story above</td><td>1</td></tr>
<tr><td>Opening is partially within the footprint of the opening in the story above</td><td>4</td></tr>
<tr><td colspan="3">LB ledger board mounted to side of wall with bottom of ledger more than W/2 above top of lintel</td><td>NLB</td></tr>
<tr><td rowspan="3">NLB ledger board mounted to side of wall with bottom of ledger less than or equal to W/2 above top of lintel, or no ledger board, and</td><td colspan="2">Top of lintel greater than W/2 below bottom of opening in story above</td><td>NLB</td></tr>
<tr><td rowspan="2">Top of lintel less than or equal to W/2 below bottom of opening in story above, and</td><td>Opening is entirely within the footprint of the opening in the story above</td><td>NLB</td></tr>
<tr><td>Opening is partially within the footprint of the opening in the story above</td><td>1</td></tr>
<tr><td colspan="4">Opening in basement wall of two-story building where walls of two stories above are of concrete construction</td></tr>
<tr><td rowspan="3">LB ledger board mounted to side of wall with bottom of ledger less than or equal to W/2 above top of lintel, and</td><td colspan="2">Top of lintel greater than W/2 below bottom of opening in story above</td><td>1</td></tr>
<tr><td rowspan="2">Top of lintel less than or equal to W/2 below bottom of opening in story above, and</td><td>Opening is entirely within the footprint of the opening in the story above</td><td>1</td></tr>
<tr><td>Opening is partially within the footprint of the opening in the story above</td><td>5</td></tr>
<tr><td colspan="3">LB ledger board mounted to side of wall with bottom of ledger more than W/2 above top of lintel</td><td>NLB</td></tr>
<tr><td rowspan="3">NLB ledger board mounted to side of wall with bottom of ledger less than or equal to W/2 above top of lintel, or no ledger board, and</td><td colspan="2">Top of lintel greater than W/2 below bottom of opening in story above</td><td>NLB</td></tr>
<tr><td rowspan="2">Top of lintel less than or equal to W/2 below bottom of opening in story above, and</td><td>Opening is entirely within the footprint of the opening in the story above</td><td>NLB</td></tr>
<tr><td>Opening is partially within the footprint of the opening in the story above</td><td>1</td></tr>
<tr><td colspan="4">Opening in wall of first story of two-story building where wall immediately above is of light framed construction, or opening in basement wall of one-story building, where wall immediately above is of light framed construction</td></tr>
<tr><td rowspan="2">Wall supporting loads from roof, second floor and top-story wall of light-framed construction, and</td><td colspan="2">Top of lintel equal to or less than W/2 below top of wall</td><td>3</td></tr>
<tr><td colspan="2">Top of lintel greater than W/2 below top of wall</td><td>NLB</td></tr>
<tr><td colspan="3">Wall not supporting loads from roof or second floor</td><td>NLB</td></tr>
</table>

a. LB means load bearing, NLB means nonload-bearing, and W means width of opening.

b. Footprint is the area of the wall below an opening in the story above, bounded by the bottom of the opening and vertical lines extending downward from the edges of the opening.

c. For design loading condition "NLB" see Tables R611.8(9) and R611.8(10). For all other design loading conditions see Tables R611.8(2) through R611.8(8).

d. A NLB ledger board is a ledger attached to a wall that is parallel to the span of the floor, roof or ceiling framing that supports the edge of the floor, ceiling or roof.

TABLE R611.8(2)
MAXIMUM ALLOWABLE CLEAR SPANS FOR 4-INCH NOMINAL THICK FLAT LINTELS IN LOAD-BEARING WALLS[a, b, c, d, e, f, m]
ROOF CLEAR SPAN 40 FEET AND FLOOR CLEAR SPAN 32 FEET

LINTEL DEPTH, D^g (inches)	NUMBER OF BARS AND BAR SIZE IN TOP AND BOTTOM OF LINTEL	STEEL YIELD STRENGTH[h], f_y (psi)	DESIGN LOADING CONDITION DETERMINED FROM TABLE R611.8(1)								
			1	2		3		40		5	
				30	70	30	70	30	70	30	70
			Maximum clear span of lintel (feet - inches)								
8	Span without stirrups[i, j]		3-2	3-4	2-4	2-6	2-2	2-1	2-0	2-0	2-0
	1-#4	40,000	5-2	5-5	4-1	4-3	3-10	3-7	3-4	2-9	2-9
		60,000	6-2	6-5	4-11	5-1	4-6	4-2	3-8	2-11	2-10
	1-#5	40,000	6-3	6-7	5-0	5-2	4-6	4-2	3-8	2-11	2-10
		60,000	DR	DR	DR	DR	DR	DR	DR	DR	DR
	Center distance A[k, l]		1-1	1-2	0-8	0-9	0-7	0-6	0-5	0-4	0-4
12	Span without stirrups[i, j]		3-4	3-7	2-9	2-11	2-8	2-6	2-5	2-2	2-2
	1-#4	40,000	6-7	7-0	5-4	5-7	5-0	4-9	4-4	3-8	3-7
		60,000	7-11	8-6	6-6	6-9	6-0	5-9	5-3	4-5	4-4
	1-#5	40,000	8-1	8-8	6-7	6-10	6-2	5-10	5-4	4-6	4-5
		60,000	9-8	10-4	7-11	8-2	7-4	6-11	6-2	4-10	4-8
	2-#4 1-#6	40,000	9-1	9-8	7-4	7-8	6-10	6-6	6-0	4-10	4-8
		60,000	DR	DR	DR	DR	DR	DR	DR	DR	DR
	Center distance A[k, l]		1-8	1-11	1-1	1-3	1-0	0-11	0-9	0-6	0-6
16	Span without stirrups[i, j]		4-7	5-0	3-11	4-0	3-8	3-7	3-4	3-1	3-0
	1-#4	40,000	6-8	7-3	5-6	5-9	5-2	4-11	4-6	3-10	3-8
		60,000	9-3	10-1	7-9	8-0	7-2	6-10	6-3	5-4	5-2
	1-#4	40,000	9-6	10-4	7-10	8-2	7-4	6-11	6-5	5-5	5-3
		60,000	11-5	12-5	9-6	9-10	8-10	8-4	7-9	6-6	6-4
	2-#4 1-#6	40,000	10-7	11-7	8-10	9-2	8-3	7-9	7-2	6-1	5-11
		60,000	12-9	13-10	10-7	11-0	9-10	9-4	8-7	6-9	6-6
	2-#5	40,000	13-0	14-1	10-9	11-2	9-11	9-2	8-2	6-6	6-3
		60,000	DR	DR	DR	DR	DR	DR	DR	DR	DR
	Center distance[k, l]		2-3	2-8	1-7	1-8	1-4	1-3	1-0	0-9	0-8
20	Span without stirrups[i, j]		5-9	6-5	5-0	5-2	4-9	4-7	4-4	3-11	3-11
	1-#4	40,000	7-5	8-2	6-3	6-6	5-10	5-7	5-1	4-4	4-2
		60,000	9-0	10-0	7-8	7-11	7-1	6-9	6-3	5-3	5-1
	1-#5	40,000	9-2	10-2	7-9	8-1	7-3	6-11	6-4	5-4	5-2
		60,000	12-9	14-2	10-10	11-3	10-1	9-7	8-10	7-5	7-3
	2-#4 1-#6	40,000	11-10	13-2	10-1	10-5	9-4	8-11	8-2	6-11	6-9
		60,000	14-4	15-10	12-1	12-7	11-3	10-9	9-11	8-4	8-1
	2-#5	40,000	14-7	16-2	12-4	12-9	11-4	10-6	9-5	7-7	7-3
		60,000	17-5	19-2	14-9	15-3	13-5	12-4	11-0	8-8	8-4
	2-#6	40,000	16-4	18-11	12-7	13-3	11-4	10-6	9-5	7-7	7-3
		60,000	DR	DR	DR	DR	DR	DR	DR	DR	DR
	Center distance A[k, l]		2-9	3-5	2-0	2-2	1-9	1-7	1-4	0-11	0-11

(continued)

TABLE R611.8(2)—continued
MAXIMUM ALLOWABLE CLEAR SPANS FOR 4-INCH NOMINAL THICK FLAT LINTELS IN LOAD-BEARING WALLS[a, b, c, d, e, f, m]
ROOF CLEAR SPAN 40 FEET AND FLOOR CLEAR SPAN 32 FEET

LINTEL DEPTH, D^g (inches)	NUMBER OF BARS AND BAR SIZE IN TOP AND BOTTOM OF LINTEL		DESIGN LOADING CONDITION DETERMINED FROM TABLE R611.8(1)								
			1	2		3		4		5	
			Maximum ground snow load (psf)								
				30	70	30	70	30	70	30	70
			Maximum clear span of lintel (feet - inches)								
24	Span without stirrups[i, j]		6-11	7-9	6-1	6-3	5-9	5-7	5-3	4-9	4-8
	1-#4	40,000	8-0	9-0	6-11	7-2	6-5	6-2	5-8	4-9	4-8
		60,000	9-9	11-0	8-5	8-9	7-10	7-6	6-11	5-10	5-8
	1-#5	40,000	10-0	11-3	8-7	8-11	8-0	7-7	7-0	5-11	5-9
		60,000	13-11	15-8	12-0	12-5	11-2	10-7	9-10	8-3	8-0
	2-#4 1-#6	40,000	12-11	14-6	11-2	11-6	10-5	9-10	9-1	7-8	7-5
		60,000	15-7	17-7	13-6	13-11	12-7	11-11	11-0	9-3	9-0
	2-#5	40,000	15-11	17-11	13-7	14-3	12-8	11-9	10-8	8-7	8-4
		60,000	19-1	21-6	16-5	17-1	15-1	14-0	12-6	9-11	9-7
	2-#6	40,000	17-7	21-1	14-1	14-10	12-8	11-9	10-8	8-7	8-4
		60,000	DR	DR	DR	DR	DR	DR	DR	DR	DR
	Center distance A[k, l]		3-3	4-1	2-5	2-7	2-1	1-11	1-7	1-2	1-1

For SI: 1 inch = 25.4 mm; 1 foot = 304.8 mm; 1 pound per square foot = 0.0479 kPa; Grade 40 = 280 MPa; Grade 60 = 420 MPa.

a. See Table R611.3 for tolerances permitted from nominal thickness.

b. Table values are based on concrete with a minimum specified compressive strength of 2,500 psi. See note j.

c. Table values are based on uniform loading. See Section R611.8.2 for lintels supporting concentrated loads.

d. Deflection criterion is $L/240$, where L is the clear span of the lintel in inches, or $^1/_2$-inch, whichever is less.

e. Linear interpolation is permitted between ground snow loads and between lintel depths.

f. DR indicates design required.

g. Lintel depth, D, is permitted to include the available height of wall located directly above the lintel, provided that the increased lintel depth spans the entire length of the lintel.

h. Stirrups shall be fabricated from reinforcing bars with the same yield strength as that used for the main longitudinal reinforcement.

i. Allowable clear span without stirrups applicable to all lintels of the same depth, D. Top and bottom reinforcement for lintels without stirrups shall not be less than the least amount of reinforcement required for a lintel of the same depth and loading condition with stirrups. All other spans require stirrups spaced at not more than d/2.

j. Where concrete with a minimum specified compressive strength of 3,000 psi (20.7 MPa) is used, clear spans for lintels without stirrups shall be permitted to be multiplied by 1.05. If the increased span exceeds the allowable clear span for a lintel of the same depth and loading condition with stirrups, the top and bottom reinforcement shall be equal to or greater than that required for a lintel of the same depth and loading condition that has an allowable clear span that is equal to or greater than that of the lintel without stirrups that has been increased.

k. Center distance, A, is the center portion of the clear span where stirrups are not required. This is applicable to all longitudinal bar sizes and steel yield strengths.

l. Where concrete with a minimum specified compressive strength of 3,000 psi is used, center distance, A, shall be permitted to be multiplied by 1.10.

m. The maximum clear opening width between two solid wall segments shall be 18 feet (5486 mm). See Section R611.7.2.1. Lintel clear spans in the table greater than 18 feet are shown for interpolation and information only.

TABLE R611.8(3)
MAXIMUM ALLOWABLE CLEAR SPANS FOR 6-INCH NOMINAL THICK FLAT LINTELS IN LOAD-BEARING WALLS[a, b, c, d, e, f, m]
ROOF CLEAR SPAN 40 FEET AND FLOOR CLEAR SPAN 32 FEET

LINTEL DEPTH, D^g (inches)	NUMBER OF BARS AND BAR SIZE IN TOP AND BOTTOM OF LINTEL	STEEL YIELD STRENGTH[h], f_y (psi)	DESIGN LOADING CONDITION DETERMINED FROM TABLE R611.8(1)								
			1	2		3		4		5	
			Maximum ground snow load (psf)								
				30	70	30	70	30	70	30	70
			Maximum clear span of lintel (feet - inches)								
8	Span without stirrups[i, j]		4-2	4-8	3-1	3-3	2-10	2-6	2-3	2-0	2-0
	1-#4	40,000	5-1	5-5	4-2	4-3	3-10	3-6	3-3	2-8	2-7
		60,000	6-2	6-7	5-0	5-2	4-8	4-2	3-11	3-3	3-2
	1-#5	40,000	6-3	6-8	5-1	5-3	4-9	4-3	4-0	3-3	3-2
		60,000	7-6	8-0	6-1	6-4	5-8	5-1	4-9	3-8	3-6
	2-#4 1-#6	40,000	7-0	7-6	5-8	5-11	5-3	4-9	4-5	3-8	3-6
		60,000	DR	DR	DR	DR	DR	DR	DR	DR	DR
	Center distance A[k, l]		1-7	1-10	1-1	1-2	0-11	0-9	0-8	0-5	0-5
12	Span without stirrups[i, j]		4-2	4-8	3-5	3-6	3-2	2-11	2-9	2-5	2-4
	1-#4	40,000	5-7	6-1	4-8	4-10	4-4	3-11	3-8	3-0	2-11
		60,000	7-9	8-6	6-6	6-9	6-1	5-6	5-1	4-3	4-1
	1-#5	40,000	7-11	8-8	6-8	6-11	6-2	5-7	5-2	4-4	4-2
		60,000	9-7	10-6	8-0	8-4	7-6	6-9	6-3	5-2	5-1
	2-#4 1-#6	40,000	8-11	9-9	7-6	7-9	6-11	6-3	5-10	4-10	4-8
		60,000	10-8	11-9	8-12	9-4	8-4	7-6	7-0	5-10	5-8
	2-#5	40,000	10-11	12-0	9-2	9-6	8-6	7-8	7-2	5-6	5-3
		60,000	12-11	14-3	10-10	11-3	10-1	9-0	8-1	6-1	5-10
	2-#6	40,000	12-9	14-0	10-8	11-1	9-7	8-1	7-3	5-6	5-3
		60,000	DR	DR	DR	DR	DR	DR	DR	DR	DR
	Center distance A[k, l]		2-6	3-0	1-9	1-10	1-6	1-3	1-1	0-9	0-8
16	Span without stirrups[i, j]		5-7	6-5	4-9	4-11	4-5	4-0	3-10	3-4	3-4
	1-#4	40,000	6-5	7-2	5-6	5-9	5-2	4-8	4-4	3-7	3-6
		60,000	7-10	8-9	6-9	7-0	6-3	5-8	5-3	4-4	4-3
	1-#5	40,000	7-11	8-11	6-10	7-1	6-5	5-9	5-4	4-5	4-4
		60,000	11-1	12-6	9-7	9-11	8-11	8-0	7-6	6-2	6-0
	2-#4 1-#6	40,000	10-3	11-7	8-10	9-2	8-3	7-6	6-11	5-9	5-7
		60,000	12-5	14-0	10-9	11-1	10-0	9-0	8-5	7-0	6-9
	2-#5	40,000	12-8	14-3	10-11	11-4	10-2	9-2	8-7	6-9	6-6
		60,000	15-2	17-1	13-1	13-7	12-3	11-0	10-3	7-11	7-7
	2-#6	40,000	14-11	16-9	12-8	13-4	11-4	9-8	8-8	6-9	6-6
		60,000	DR	DR	DR	DR	DR	DR	DR	DR	DR
	Center distance A[k, l]		3-3	4-1	2-5	2-7	2-1	1-9	1-6	1-0	1-0

(continued)

TABLE R611.8(3)—continued
MAXIMUM ALLOWABLE CLEAR SPANS FOR 6-INCH NOMINAL THICK FLAT LINTELS IN LOAD-BEARING WALLS[a, b, c, d, e, f, m]
ROOF CLEAR SPAN 40 FEET AND FLOOR CLEAR SPAN 32 FEET

LINTEL DEPTH, D[g] (inches)	NUMBER OF BARS AND BAR SIZE IN TOP AND BOTTOM OF LINTEL	STEEL YIELD STRENGTH[h], f_y (psi)	DESIGN LOADING CONDITION DETERMINED FROM TABLE R611.8(1)								
			1	2		3		4		5	
			Maximum ground snow load (psf)								
				30	70	30	70	30	70	30	70
			Maximum clear span of lintel (feet - inches)								
20	Span without stirrups[i, j]		6-11	8-2	6-1	6-3	5-8	5-2	4-11	4-4	4-3
	1-#5	40,000	8-9	10-1	7-9	8-0	7-3	6-6	6-1	5-1	4-11
		60,000	10-8	12-3	9-5	9-9	8-10	8-0	7-5	6-2	6-0
	2-#4 1-#6	40,000	9-11	11-4	8-9	9-1	8-2	7-4	6-10	5-8	5-7
		60,000	13-9	15-10	12-2	12-8	11-5	10-3	9-7	7-11	7-9
	2-#5	40,000	14-0	16-2	12-5	12-11	11-7	10-6	9-9	7-11	7-8
		60,000	16-11	19-6	15-0	15-6	14-0	12-7	11-9	9-1	8-9
	2-#6	40,000	16-7	19-1	14-7	15-3	13-1	11-3	10-2	7-11	7-8
		60,000	19-11	22-10	17-4	18-3	15-6	13-2	11-10	9-1	8-9
	Center distance A[k, l]		3-11	5-2	3-1	3-3	2-8	2-2	1-11	1-4	1-3
24	Span without stirrups[i, j]		8-2	9-10	7-4	7-8	6-11	6-4	5-11	5-3	5-2
	1-#5	40,000	9-5	11-1	8-7	8-10	8-0	7-3	6-9	5-7	5-5
		60,000	11-6	13-6	10-5	10-9	9-9	8-9	8-2	6-10	6-8
	2-#4 1-#6	40,000	10-8	12-6	9-8	10-0	9-0	8-2	7-7	6-4	6-2
		60,000	12-11	15-2	11-9	12-2	11-0	9-11	9-3	7-8	7-6
	2-#5	40,000	15-2	17-9	13-9	14-3	12-10	11-7	10-10	9-0	8-9
		60,000	18-4	21-6	16-7	17-3	15-6	14-0	13-1	10-4	10-0
	2-#6	40,000	18-0	21-1	16-4	16-11	14-10	12-9	11-8	9-2	8-11
		60,000	21-7	25-4	19-2	20-4	17-2	14-9	13-4	10-4	10-0
	Center distance A[k, l]		4-6	6-2	3-8	4-0	3-3	2-8	2-3	1-7	1-6

For SI: 1 inch = 25.4 mm; 1 foot = 304.8 mm; 1 psf = 0.0479 kPa; Grade 40 = 280 MPa; Grade 60 = 420 MPa.

a. See Table R611.3 for tolerances permitted from nominal thickness.

b. Table values are based on concrete with a minimum specified compressive strength of 2,500 psi. See Note j.

c. Table values are based on uniform loading. See Section R611.8.2 for lintels supporting concentrated loads.

d. Deflection criterion is *L*/240, where *L* is the clear span of the lintel in inches, or $^1/_2$-inch, whichever is less.

e. Linear interpolation is permitted between ground snow loads and between lintel depths.

f. DR indicates design required.

g. Lintel depth, *D*, is permitted to include the available height of wall located directly above the lintel, provided that the increased lintel depth spans the entire length of the lintel.

h. Stirrups shall be fabricated from reinforcing bars with the same yield strength as that used for the main longitudinal reinforcement.

i. Allowable clear span without stirrups applicable to all lintels of the same depth, *D*. Top and bottom reinforcement for lintels without stirrups shall not be less than the least amount of reinforcement required for a lintel of the same depth and loading condition with stirrups. All other spans require stirrups spaced at not more than d/2.

j. Where concrete with a minimum specified compressive strength of 3,000 psi is used, clear spans for lintels without stirrups shall be permitted to be multiplied by 1.05. If the increased span exceeds the allowable clear span for a lintel of the same depth and loading condition with stirrups, the top and bottom reinforcement shall be equal to or greater than that required for a lintel of the same depth and loading condition that has an allowable clear span that is equal to or greater than that of the lintel without stirrups that has been increased.

k. Center distance, *A*, is the center portion of the clear span where stirrups are not required. This is applicable to all longitudinal bar sizes and steel yield strengths.

l. Where concrete with a minimum specified compressive strength of 3,000 psi is used, center distance, A, shall be permitted to be multiplied by 1.10.

m. The maximum clear opening width between two solid wall segments shall be 18 feet (5486 mm). See Section R611.7.2.1. Lintel clear spans in the table greater than 18 feet are shown for interpolation and information only.

TABLE R611.8(4)
MAXIMUM ALLOWABLE CLEAR SPANS FOR 8-INCH NOMINAL THICK FLAT LINTELS IN LOAD-BEARING WALLS[a, b, c, d, e, f, m]
ROOF CLEAR SPAN 40 FEET AND FLOOR CLEAR SPAN 32 FEET

LINTEL DEPTH, D^g (inches)	NUMBER OF BARS AND BAR SIZE IN TOP AND BOTTOM OF LINTEL	STEEL YIELD STRENGTH[h], f_y (psi)	DESIGN LOADING CONDITION DETERMINED FROM TABLE R611.8(1)								
			1	2		3		4		5	
			Maximum ground snow load (psf)								
				30	70	30	70	30	70	30	70
			Maximum clear span of lintel (feet - inches)								
8	Span without stirrups[i, j]		4-4	4-9	3-7	3-9	3-4	2-10	2-7	2-1	2-0
	1-#4	40,000	4-4	4-9	3-7	3-9	3-4	2-11	2-9	2-3	2-2
		60,000	6-1	6-7	5-0	5-3	4-8	4-0	3-9	3-1	3-0
	1-#5	40,000	6-2	6-9	5-2	5-4	4-9	4-1	3-10	3-2	3-1
		60,000	7-5	8-1	6-2	6-5	5-9	4-11	4-7	3-9	3-8
	2-#4 1-#6	40,000	6-11	7-6	5-9	6-0	5-4	4-7	4-4	3-6	3-5
		60,000	8-3	9-0	6-11	7-2	6-5	5-6	5-2	4-2	4-1
	2-#5	40,000	8-5	9-2	7-0	7-3	6-6	5-7	5-3	4-2	4-0
		60,000	DR	DR	DR	DR	DR	DR	DR	DR	DR
	Center distance A[k, l]		2-1	2-6	1-5	1-6	1-3	0-11	0-10	0-6	0-6
12	Span without stirrups[i, j]		4-10	5-8	4-0	4-2	3-9	3-2	3-0	2-7	2-6
	1-#4	40,000	5-5	6-1	4-8	4-10	4-4	3-9	3-6	2-10	2-10
		60,000	6-7	7-5	5-8	5-11	5-4	4-7	4-3	3-6	3-5
	1-#5	40,000	6-9	7-7	5-9	6-0	5-5	4-8	4-4	3-7	3-6
		60,000	9-4	10-6	8-1	8-4	7-6	6-6	6-1	5-0	4-10
	2-#4 1-#6	40,000	8-8	9-9	7-6	7-9	7-0	6-0	5-8	4-7	4-6
		60,000	10-6	11-9	9-1	9-5	8-5	7-3	6-10	5-7	5-5
	2-#5	40,000	10-8	12-0	9-3	9-7	8-7	7-5	6-11	5-6	5-4
		60,000	12-10	14-5	11-1	11-6	10-4	8-11	8-4	6-7	6-4
	2-#6	40,000	12-7	14-2	10-10	11-3	10-2	8-3	7-6	5-6	5-4
		60,000	DR	DR	DR	DR	DR	DR	DR	DR	DR
	Center distance A[k, l]		3-2	4-0	2-4	2-6	2-0	1-6	1-4	0-11	0-10
16	Span without stirrups[i, j]		6-5	7-9	5-7	5-10	5-2	4-5	4-2	3-7	3-6
	1-#4	40,000	6-2	7-1	5-6	5-8	5-1	4-5	4-2	3-5	3-4
		60,000	7-6	8-8	6-8	6-11	6-3	5-5	5-1	4-2	4-0
	1-#5	40,000	7-8	8-10	6-10	7-1	6-4	5-6	5-2	4-3	4-1
		60,000	9-4	10-9	8-4	8-7	7-9	6-8	6-3	5-2	5-0
	2-#4 1-#6	40,000	8-8	10-0	7-8	8-0	7-2	6-2	5-10	4-9	4-8
		60,000	12-0	13-11	10-9	11-2	10-0	8-8	8-1	6-8	6-6
	2-#5	40,000	12-3	14-2	11-0	11-4	10-3	8-10	8-3	6-9	6-7
		60,000	14-10	17-2	13-3	13-8	12-4	10-8	10-0	7-11	7-8
	2-#6	40,000	14-6	16-10	13-0	13-5	12-1	10-1	9-2	6-11	6-8
		60,000	17-5	20-2	15-7	16-1	14-6	11-10	10-8	7-11	7-8
	Center distance[k, l]		4-1	5-5	3-3	3-6	2-10	2-1	1-10	1-3	1-2

(continued)

TABLE R611.8(4)—continued
MAXIMUM ALLOWABLE CLEAR SPANS FOR 8-INCH NOMINAL THICK FLAT LINTELS IN LOAD-BEARING WALLS[a, b, c, d, e, f, m]
ROOF CLEAR SPAN 40 FEET AND FLOOR CLEAR SPAN 32 FEET

LINTEL DEPTH, D^g (inches)	NUMBER OF BARS AND BAR SIZE IN TOP AND BOTTOM OF LINTEL	STEEL YIELD STRENGTH[h], f_y (psi)	DESIGN LOADING CONDITION DETERMINED FROM TABLE R611.8(1)								
			1	2		3		4		5	
			Maximum ground snow load (psf)								
				30	70	30	70	30	70	30	70
			Maximum clear span of lintel (feet - inches)								
20	Span without stirrups[i, j]		7-10	9-10	7-1	7-5	6-7	5-8	5-4	4-7	4-6
	1-#5	40,000	8-4	9-11	7-8	8-0	7-2	6-3	5-10	4-9	4-8
		60,000	10-2	12-1	9-5	9-9	8-9	7-7	7-1	5-10	5-8
	2-#4 1-#6	40,000	9-5	11-3	8-8	9-0	8-1	7-0	6-7	5-5	5-3
		60,000	11-6	13-8	10-7	11-0	9-11	8-7	8-0	6-7	6-5
	2-#5	40,000	11-9	13-11	10-10	11-2	10-1	8-9	8-2	6-8	6-7
		60,000	16-4	19-5	15-0	15-7	14-0	12-2	11-4	9-3	9-0
	2-#6	40,000	16-0	19-0	14-9	15-3	13-9	11-10	10-10	8-3	8-0
		60,000	19-3	22-11	17-9	18-5	16-7	13-7	12-4	9-3	9-0
	Center distance A[k, l]		4-10	6-10	4-1	4-5	3-7	2-8	2-4	1-7	1-6
24	Span without stirrups[i, j]		9-2	11-9	8-7	8-11	8-0	6-11	6-6	5-7	5-6
	1-#5	40,000	8-11	10-10	8-6	8-9	7-11	6-10	6-5	5-3	5-2
		60,000	10-11	13-3	10-4	10-8	9-8	8-4	7-10	6-5	6-3
	2-#4 1-#6	40,000	10-1	12-3	9-7	9-11	8-11	7-9	7-3	6-0	5-10
		60,000	12-3	15-0	11-8	12-1	10-11	9-5	8-10	7-3	7-1
	2-#5	40,000	12-6	15-3	11-11	12-4	11-1	9-7	9-0	7-5	7-3
		60,000	17-6	21-3	16-7	17-2	15-6	13-5	12-7	10-4	10-1
	2-#6	40,000	17-2	20-11	16-3	16-10	15-3	13-2	12-4	9-7	9-4
		60,000	20-9	25-3	19-8	20-4	18-5	15-4	14-0	10-7	10-3
	Center distance A[k, l]		5-6	8-1	4-11	5-3	4-4	3-3	2-10	1-11	1-10

For SI: 1 inch = 25.4 mm; 1 foot = 304.8 mm; 1 psf = 0.0479 kPa; Grade 40 = 280 MPa; Grade 60 = 420 MPa.

Note: Top and bottom reinforcement for lintels without stirrups shown in shaded cells shall be equal to or greater than that required for lintel of the same depth and loading condition that has an allowable clear span that is equal to or greater than that of the lintel without stirrups.

a. See Table R611.3 for tolerances permitted from nominal thickness.

b. Table values are based on concrete with a minimum specified compressive strength of 2,500 psi. See Note j.

c. Table values are based on uniform loading. See Section R611.8.2 for lintels supporting concentrated loads.

d. Deflection criterion is *L*/240, where *L* is the clear span of the lintel in inches, or $^1/_2$-inch, whichever is less.

e. Linear interpolation is permitted between ground snow loads and between lintel depths.

f. DR indicates design required.

g. Lintel depth, *D*, is permitted to include the available height of wall located directly above the lintel, provided that the increased lintel depth spans the entire length of the lintel.

h. Stirrups shall be fabricated from reinforcing bars with the same yield strength as that used for the main longitudinal reinforcement.

i. Allowable clear span without stirrups applicable to all lintels of the same depth, *D*. Top and bottom reinforcement for lintels without stirrups shall not be less than the least amount of reinforcement required for a lintel of the same depth and loading condition with stirrups. All other spans require stirrups spaced at not more than d/2.

j. Where concrete with a minimum specified compressive strength of 3,000 psi is used, clear spans for lintels without stirrups shall be permitted to be multiplied by 1.05. If the increased span exceeds the allowable clear span for a lintel of the same depth and loading condition with stirrups, the top and bottom reinforcement shall be equal to or greater than that required for a lintel of the same depth and loading condition that has an allowable clear span that is equal to or greater than that of the lintel without stirrups that has been increased.

k. Center distance, *A*, is the center portion of the clear span where stirrups are not required. This is applicable to all longitudinal bar sizes and steel yield strengths.

l. Where concrete with a minimum specified compressive strength of 3,000 psi is used, center distance, *A*, shall be permitted to be multiplied by 1.10.

m. The maximum clear opening width between two solid wall segments shall be 18 feet. See Section R611.7.2.1. Lintel clear spans in the table greater than 18 feet are shown for interpolation and information only.

TABLE R611.8(5)
MAXIMUM ALLOWABLE CLEAR SPANS FOR 10-INCH NOMINAL THICK FLAT LINTELS IN LOAD-BEARING WALLS[a, b, c, d, e, f, m]
ROOF CLEAR SPAN 40 FEET AND FLOOR CLEAR SPAN 32 FEET

LINTEL DEPTH, D^g (inches)	NUMBER OF BARS AND BAR SIZE IN TOP AND BOTTOM OF LINTEL	STEEL YIELD STRENGTH[h], f_y (psi)	DESIGN LOADING CONDITION DETERMINED FROM TABLE R611.8(1)								
			1	2		3		4		5	
			Maximum ground snow load (psf)								
				30	70	30	70	30	70	30	70
			Maximum clear span of lintel (feet - inches)								
8	Span without stirrups[i, j]		6-0	7-2	4-7	4-10	4-1	3-1	2-11	2-3	2-2
	1-#4	40,000	4-3	4-9	3-7	3-9	3-4	2-9	2-7	2-1	2-1
		60,000	5-11	6-7	5-0	5-3	4-8	3-10	3-8	2-11	2-11
	1-#5	40,000	6-1	6-9	5-2	5-4	4-9	3-11	3-9	3-0	2-11
		60,000	7-4	8-1	6-3	6-5	5-9	4-9	4-6	3-7	3-7
	2-#4 1-#6	40,000	6-10	7-6	5-9	6-0	5-5	4-5	4-2	3-4	3-4
		60,000	8-2	9-1	6-11	7-2	6-6	5-4	5-0	4-1	4-0
	2-#5	40,000	8-4	9-3	7-1	7-4	6-7	5-5	5-1	4-1	4-0
		60,000	9-11	11-0	8-5	8-9	7-10	6-6	6-1	4-8	4-6
	2-#6	40,000	9-9	10-10	8-3	8-7	7-9	6-4	5-10	4-1	4-0
		60,000	DR	DR	DR	DR	DR	DR	DR	DR	DR
	Center distance A[k, l]		2-6	3-1	1-10	1-11	1-7	1-1	0-11	0-7	0-7
12	Span without stirrups[i, j]		5-5	6-7	4-7	4-10	4-3	3-5	3-3	2-8	2-8
	1-#4	40,000	5-3	6-0	4-8	4-10	4-4	3-7	3-4	2-9	2-8
		60,000	6-5	7-4	5-8	5-10	5-3	4-4	4-1	3-4	3-3
	1-#5	40,000	6-6	7-6	5-9	6-0	5-5	4-5	4-2	3-5	3-4
		60,000	7-11	9-1	7-0	7-3	6-7	5-5	5-1	4-2	4-0
	2-#4 1-#6	40,000	7-4	8-5	6-6	6-9	6-1	5-0	4-9	3-10	3-9
		60,000	10-3	11-9	9-1	9-5	8-6	7-0	6-7	5-4	5-3
	2-#5	40,000	10-5	12-0	9-3	9-7	8-8	7-2	6-9	5-5	5-4
		60,000	12-7	14-5	11-2	11-6	10-5	8-7	8-1	6-6	6-4
	2-#6	40,000	12-4	14-2	10-11	11-4	10-2	8-5	7-8	5-7	5-5
		60,000	14-9	17-0	13-1	13-6	12-2	10-0	9-1	6-6	6-4
	Center distance A[k, l]		3-9	4-11	2-11	3-2	2-7	1-9	1-7	1-0	1-0
16	Span without stirrups[i, j]		7-1	9-0	6-4	6-8	5-10	4-9	4-6	3-9	3-8
	1-#4	40,000	5-11	7-0	5-5	5-8	5-1	4-3	4-0	3-3	3-2
		60,000	7-3	8-7	6-8	6-11	6-3	5-2	4-10	3-11	3-10
	1-#5	40,000	7-4	8-9	6-9	7-0	6-4	5-3	4-11	4-0	3-11
		60,000	9-0	10-8	8-3	8-7	7-9	6-5	6-0	4-11	4-9
	2-#4 1-#6	40,000	8-4	9-11	7-8	7-11	7-2	5-11	5-7	4-6	4-5
		60,000	10-2	12-0	9-4	9-8	8-9	7-3	6-10	5-6	5-5
	2-#5	40,000	10-4	12-3	9-6	9-10	8-11	7-4	6-11	5-8	5-6
		60,000	14-4	17-1	13-3	13-8	12-4	10-3	9-8	7-10	7-8
	2-#6	40,000	14-1	16-9	13-0	13-5	12-2	10-1	9-6	7-0	6-10
		60,000	17-0	20-2	15-8	16-2	14-7	12-0	10-11	8-0	7-9
	Center distance[k, l]		4-9	6-8	4-0	4-4	3-6	2-5	2-2	1-5	1-4

(continued)

TABLE R611.8(5)—continued
MAXIMUM ALLOWABLE CLEAR SPANS FOR 10-INCH NOMINAL THICK FLAT LINTELS IN LOAD-BEARING WALLS[a, b, c, d, e, f, m]
ROOF CLEAR SPAN 40 FEET AND FLOOR CLEAR SPAN 32 FEET

LINTEL DEPTH, D^g (inches)	NUMBER OF BARS AND BAR SIZE IN TOP AND BOTTOM OF LINTEL	STEEL YIELD STRENGTH[h], f_y (psi)	DESIGN LOADING CONDITION DETERMINED FROM TABLE R611.8(1)								
			1	2		3		4		5	
			Maximum ground snow load (psf)								
				30	70	30	70	30	70	30	70
			Maximum clear span of lintel (feet - inches)								
20	Span without stirrups[i, j]		8-7	11-4	8-1	8-5	7-5	6-1	5-9	4-10	4-9
	1-#4	40,000	6-5	7-10	6-2	6-4	5-9	4-9	4-6	3-8	3-7
		60,000	7-10	9-7	7-6	7-9	7-0	5-10	5-6	4-5	4-4
	1-#5	40,000	8-0	9-9	7-8	7-11	7-2	5-11	5-7	4-6	4-5
		60,000	9-9	11-11	9-4	9-8	8-9	7-3	6-10	5-6	5-5
	2-#4 1-#6	40,000	9-0	11-1	8-8	8-11	8-1	6-9	6-4	5-2	5-0
		60,000	11-0	13-6	10-6	10-11	9-10	8-2	7-9	6-3	6-2
	2-#5	40,000	11-3	13-9	10-9	11-1	10-0	8-4	7-10	6-5	6-3
		60,000	15-8	19-2	15-0	15-6	14-0	11-8	11-0	8-11	8-9
	2-#6	40,000	15-5	18-10	14-8	15-2	13-9	11-5	10-9	8-6	8-3
		60,000	18-7	22-9	17-9	18-5	16-7	13-10	12-9	9-5	9-2
	Center distance A[k, l]		5-7	8-4	5-1	5-5	4-5	3-1	2-9	1-10	1-9
24	Span without stirrups[i, j]		9-11	13-7	9-9	10-2	9-0	7-5	7-0	5-10	5-9
	1-#5	40,000	8-6	10-8	8-5	8-8	7-10	6-6	6-2	5-0	4-11
		60,000	10-5	13-0	10-3	10-7	9-7	8-0	7-6	6-1	6-0
	2-#4 1-#6	40,000	9-7	12-1	9-6	9-9	8-10	7-5	7-0	5-8	5-6
		60,000	11-9	14-9	11-7	11-11	10-10	9-0	8-6	6-11	6-9
	2-#5	40,000	12-0	15-0	11-9	12-2	11-0	9-2	8-8	7-1	6-11
		60,000	14-7	18-3	14-4	14-10	13-5	11-2	10-7	8-7	8-5
	2-#6	40,000	14-3	17-11	14-1	14-7	13-2	11-0	10-4	8-5	8-3
		60,000	19-11	25-0	19-7	20-3	18-4	15-3	14-5	10-10	10-7
	Center distance A[k, l]		6-3	9-11	6-1	6-6	5-4	3-9	3-4	2-2	2-1

For SI: 1 inch = 25.4 mm; 1 foot = 304.8 mm; 1 pound per square foot = 0.0479kPa; Grade 40 = 280 MPa; Grade 60 = 420 MPa.

Note: Top and bottom reinforcement for lintels without stirrups shown in shaded cells shall be equal to or greater than that required for lintel of the same depth and loading condition that has an allowable clear span that is equal to or greater than that of the lintel without stirrups.

a. See Table R611.3 for tolerances permitted from nominal thickness.
b. Table values are based on concrete with a minimum specified compressive strength of 2,500 psi. See Note j.
c. Table values are based on uniform loading. See Section R611.8.2 for lintels supporting concentrated loads.
d. Deflection criterion is $L/240$, where L is the clear span of the lintel in inches, or $^1/_2$-inch, whichever is less.
e. Linear interpolation is permitted between ground snow loads and between lintel depths.
f. DR indicates design required.
g. Lintel depth, D, is permitted to include the available height of wall located directly above the lintel, provided that the increased lintel depth spans the entire length of the lintel.
h. Stirrups shall be fabricated from reinforcing bars with the same yield strength as that used for the main longitudinal reinforcement.
i. Allowable clear span without stirrups applicable to all lintels of the same depth, D. Top and bottom reinforcement for lintels without stirrups shall not be less than the least amount of reinforcement required for a lintel of the same depth and loading condition with stirrups. All other spans require stirrups spaced at not more than d/2.
j. Where concrete with a minimum specified compressive strength of 3,000 psi is used, clear spans for lintels without stirrups shall be permitted to be multiplied by 1.05. If the increased span exceeds the allowable clear span for a lintel of the same depth and loading condition with stirrups, the top and bottom reinforcement shall be equal to or greater than that required for a lintel of the same depth and loading condition that has an allowable clear span that is equal to or greater than that of the lintel without stirrups that has been increased.
k. Center distance, A, is the center portion of the clear span where stirrups are not required. This is applicable to all longitudinal bar sizes and steel yield strengths.
l. Where concrete with a minimum specified compressive strength of 3,000 psi is used, center distance, A, shall be permitted to be multiplied by 1.10.
m. The maximum clear opening width between two solid wall segments shall be 18 feet (5486 mm). See Section R611.7.2.1. Lintel clear spans in the table greater than 18 feet are shown for interpolation and information only.

TABLE R611.8(6)
MAXIMUM ALLOWABLE CLEAR SPANS FOR 6-INCH THICK WAFFLE-GRID LINTELS IN LOAD-BEARING WALLS[a, b, c, d, e, f, o]
MAXIMUM ROOF CLEAR SPAN 40 FEET AND MAXIMUM FLOOR SPAN 32 FEET

LINTEL DEPTH, D^g (inches)	NUMBER OF BARS AND BAR SIZE IN TOP AND BOTTOM OF LINTEL	STEEL YIELD STRENGTH[h], f_y (psi)	DESIGN LOADING CONDITION DETERMINED FROM TABLE R611.8(1)								
			1	2		3		4		5	
			Maximum ground snow load (psf)								
				30	70	30	70	30	70	30	70
			Maximum clear span of lintel (feet - inches)								
8[i]	Span without stirrups[k, l]		2-7	2-9	2-0	2-1	2-0	2-0	2-0	2-0	2-0
	1-#4	40,000	5-2	5-5	4-0	4-3	3-7	3-3	2-11	2-4	2-3
		60,000	5-9	6-3	4-0	4-3	3-7	3-3	2-11	2-4	2-3
	1-#5	40,000	5-9	6-3	4-0	4-3	3-7	3-3	2-11	2-4	2-3
		60,000	5-9	6-3	4-0	4-3	3-7	3-3	2-11	2-4	2-3
	2-#4 1-#6	40,000	5-9	6-3	4-0	4-3	3-7	3-3	2-11	2-4	2-3
		60,000	DR	DR	DR	DR	DR	DR	DR	DR	DR
	Center distance A[m, n]		0-9	0-10	0-6	0-6	0-5	0-5	0-4	STL	STL
12[i]	Span without stirrups[k, l]		2-11	3-1	2-6	2-7	2-5	2-4	2-3	2-1	2-0
	1-#4	40,000	5-9	6-2	4-8	4-10	4-4	4-1	3-9	3-2	3-1
		60,000	8-0	8-7	6-6	6-9	6-0	5-5	4-11	3-11	3-10
	1-#5	40,000	8-1	8-9	6-8	6-11	6-0	5-5	4-11	3-11	3-10
		60,000	9-1	10-3	6-8	7-0	6-0	5-5	4-11	3-11	3-10
	2-#4 1-#6	40,000	9-1	9-9	6-8	7-0	6-0	5-5	4-11	3-11	3-10
	Center distance A[m, n]		1-3	1-5	0-10	0-11	0-9	0-8	0-6	STL	STL
16[i]	Span without stirrups[k, l]		4-0	4-4	3-6	3-7	3-4	3-3	3-1	2-10	2-10
	1-#4	40,000	6-7	7-3	5-6	5-9	5-2	4-10	4-6	3-9	3-8
		60,000	8-0	8-10	6-9	7-0	6-3	5-11	5-5	4-7	4-5
	1-#5	40,000	8-2	9-0	6-11	7-2	6-5	6-0	5-7	4-8	4-6
		60,000	11-5	12-6	9-3	9-9	8-4	7-7	6-10	5-6	5-4
	2-#4 1-#6	40,000	10-7	11-7	8-11	9-3	8-3	7-7	6-10	5-6	5-4
		60,000	12-2	14-0	9-3	9-9	8-4	7-7	6-10	5-6	5-4
	2-#5	40,000	12-2	14-2	9-3	9-9	8-4	7-7	6-10	5-6	5-4
		60,000	DR	DR	DR	DR	DR	DR	DR	DR	DR
	Center distance A[m, n]		1-8	2-0	1-2	1-3	1-0	0-11	0-9	STL	STL
20[i]	Span without stirrups[k, l]		5-0	5-6	4-6	4-7	4-3	4-1	4-0	3-8	3-8
	1-#4	40,000	7-2	8-2	6-3	6-6	5-10	5-6	5-1	4-3	4-2
		60,000	8-11	9-11	7-8	7-11	7-1	6-8	6-2	5-2	5-0
	1-#5	40,000	9-1	10-2	7-9	8-1	7-3	6-10	6-4	5-4	5-2
		60,000	12-8	14-2	10-11	11-3	10-2	9-6	8-9	7-1	6-10
	2-#4 1-#6	40,000	10-3	11-5	8-9	9-1	8-2	7-8	7-1	6-0	5-10
		60,000	14-3	15-11	11-9	12-5	10-8	9-9	8-9	7-1	6-10
	2-#5	40,000	14-6	16-3	11-6	12-1	10-4	9-6	8-6	6-11	6-8
		60,000	DR	DR	DR	DR	DR	DR	DR	DR	DR
	Center distance A[m, n]		2-0	2-6	1-6	1-7	1-3	1-1	1-0	STL	STL

(continued)

TABLE R611.8(6)—continued
MAXIMUM ALLOWABLE CLEAR SPANS FOR 6-INCH THICK WAFFLE-GRID LINTELS IN LOAD-BEARING WALLS[a, b, c, d, e, f, o]
MAXIMUM ROOF CLEAR SPAN 40 FEET AND MAXIMUM FLOOR SPAN 32 FEET

LINTEL DEPTH, D^g (inches)	NUMBER OF BARS AND BAR SIZE IN TOP AND BOTTOM OF LINTEL	STEEL YIELD STRENGTH[h], f_y (psi)	DESIGN LOADING CONDITION DETERMINED FROM TABLE R611.8(1)								
			1	2		3		4		5	
			Maximum ground snow load (psf)								
				30	70	30	70	30	70	30	70
			Maximum clear span of lintel (feet - inches)								
24w[j]	Span without stirrups[k, l]		6-0	6-8	5-5	5-7	5-3	5-0	4-10	4-6	4-5
	1-#4	40,000	7-11	9-0	6-11	7-2	6-5	6-0	5-7	4-8	4-7
		60,000	9-8	10-11	8-5	8-9	7-10	7-4	6-10	5-9	5-7
	1-#5	40,000	9-10	11-2	8-7	8-11	8-0	7-6	7-0	5-10	5-8
		60,000	12-0	13-7	10-6	10-10	9-9	9-2	8-6	7-2	6-11
	2-#4 1-#6	40,000	11-1	12-7	9-8	10-1	9-1	8-6	7-10	6-7	6-5
		60,000	15-6	17-7	13-6	14-0	12-8	11-10	10-8	8-7	8-4
	2-#5	40,000	15-6	17-11	12-8	13-4	11-6	10-7	9-7	7-10	7-7
		60,000	DR	DR	DR	DR	DR	DR	DR	DR	DR
	Center distance A[m, n]		2-4	3-0	1-9	1-11	1-6	1-4	1-2	STL	STL

For SI: 1 inch = 25.4 mm; 1 pound per square foot = 0.0479 kPa; 1 foot = 304.8 mm; Grade 40 = 280 MPa; Grade 60 = 420 MPa.

a. Where lintels are formed with waffle-grid forms, form material shall be removed, if necessary, to create top and bottom flanges of the lintel that are not less than 3 inches in depth (in the vertical direction), are not less than 5 inches (127 mm) in width for 6-inch nominal waffle-grid forms and not less than 7 inches in width for 8-inch nominal waffle-grid forms. See Figure R611.8(3). Flat form lintels shall be permitted in place of waffle-grid lintels. See Tables R611.8(2) through R611.8(5).

b. See Table R611.3 for tolerances permitted from nominal thicknesses and minimum dimensions and spacing of cores.

c. Table values are based on concrete with a minimum specified compressive strength of 2,500 psi (17.2 MPa). See Notes l and n. Table values are based on uniform loading. See Section R611.8.2 for lintels supporting concentrated loads.

d. Deflection criterion is $L/240$, where L is the clear span of the lintel in inches, or $^1/_2$-inch, whichever is less.

e. Linear interpolation is permitted between ground snow loads.

f. DR indicates design required. STL – stirrups required throughout lintel.

g. Lintel depth, D, is permitted to include the available height of wall located directly above the lintel, provided that the increased lintel depth spans the entire length of the lintel.

h. Stirrups shall be fabricated from reinforcing bars with the same yield strength as that used for the main longitudinal reinforcement.

i. Lintels less than 24 inches in depth with stirrups shall be formed from flat-walls forms [see Tables R611.8(2) through R611.8(5)], or, if necessary, form material shall be removed from waffle-grid forms so as to provide the required cover for stirrups. Allowable spans for lintels formed with flat-wall forms shall be determined from Tables R611.8(2) through R611.8(5).

j. Where stirrups are required for 24-inch (610 mm) deep lintels, the spacing shall not exceed 12 inches (305 mm) on center.

k. Allowable clear span without stirrups applicable to all lintels of the same depth, D. Top and bottom reinforcement for lintels without stirrups shall not be less than the least amount of reinforcement required for a lintel of the same depth and loading condition with stirrups. All other spans require stirrups spaced at not more than $d/2$.

l. Where concrete with a minimum specified compressive strength of 3,000 psi is used, clear spans for lintels without stirrups shall be permitted to be multiplied by 1.05. If the increased span exceeds the allowable clear span for a lintel of the same depth and loading condition with stirrups, the top and bottom reinforcement shall be equal to or greater than that required for a lintel of the same depth and loading condition that has an allowable clear span that is equal to or greater than that of the lintel without stirrups that has been increased.

m. Center distance, A, is the center portion of the span where stirrups are not required. This is applicable to all longitudinal bar sizes and steel yield strengths.

n. Where concrete with a minimum specified compressive strength of 3,000 psi is used, center distance, A, shall be permitted to be multiplied by 1.10.

o. The maximum clear opening width between two solid wall segments shall be 18 feet. See Section R611.7.2.1. Lintel spans in the table greater than 18 feet are shown for interpolation and information only.

TABLE R611.8(7)
MAXIMUM ALLOWABLE CLEAR SPANS FOR 8-INCH THICK WAFFLE-GRID LINTELS IN LOAD-BEARING WALLS[a, b, c, d, e, f, o]
MAXIMUM ROOF CLEAR SPAN 40 FEET AND MAXIMUM FLOOR CLEAR SPAN 32 FEET

LINTEL DEPTH, D^g (inches)	NUMBER OF BARS AND BAR SIZE IN TOP AND BOTTOM OF LINTEL	STEEL YIELD STRENGTH[h], f_y (psi)	DESIGN LOADING CONDITION DETERMINED FROM TABLE R611.8(1)								
			1	2		3		4		5	
				Maximum ground snow load (psf)							
				30	70	30	70	30	70	30	70
			Maximum clear span of lintel (feet - inches)								
8[i]	Span with stirrups[k, l]		2-6	2-9	2-0	2-1	2-0	2-0	2-0	2-0	2-0
	1-#4	40,000	4-5	4-9	3-7	3-9	3-4	3-0	2-10	2-3	2-2
		60,000	5-6	6-2	4-0	4-3	3-7	3-1	2-10	2-3	2-2
	1-#5	40,000	5-6	6-2	4-0	4-3	3-7	3-1	2-10	2-3	2-2
	Center distance A[m, n]		0-9	0-10	0-6	0-6	0-5	0-4	0-4	STL	STL
12[i]	Span without stirrups[k, l]		2-10	3-1	2-6	2-7	2-5	2-3	2-2	2-0	2-0
	1-#4	40,000	5-7	6-1	4-8	4-10	4-4	3-11	3-8	3-0	2-11
		60,000	6-9	7-5	5-8	5-11	5-4	4-9	4-5	3-8	3-7
	1-#5	40,000	6-11	7-7	5-10	6-0	5-5	4-10	4-6	3-9	3-7
		60,000	8-8	10-1	6-7	7-0	5-11	5-2	4-8	3-9	3-7
	2-#4	40,000	8-8	9-10	6-7	7-0	5-11	5-2	4-8	3-9	3-7
	1-#6	60,000	8-8	10-1	6-7	7-0	5-11	5-2	4-8	3-9	3-7
	Center distance A[m, n]		1-2	1-5	0-10	0-11	0-9	0-7	0-6	STL	STL
16[i]	Span without stirrups[k, l]		3-10	4-3	3-6	3-7	3-4	3-2	3-0	2-10	2-9
	1-#4	40,000	6-5	7-2	5-6	5-9	5-2	4-8	4-4	3-7	3-6
		60,000	7-9	8-9	6-9	7-0	6-3	5-8	5-3	4-4	4-3
	1-#5	40,000	7-11	8-11	6-10	7-1	6-5	5-9	5-4	4-5	4-4
		60,000	9-8	10-11	8-4	8-8	7-10	7-0	6-6	5-2	5-1
	2-#4	40,000	9-0	10-1	7-9	8-0	7-3	6-6	6-1	5-0	4-11
	1-#6	60,000	11-5	13-10	9-2	9-8	8-3	7-2	6-6	5-2	5-1
	Center distance A[m, n]		1-6	1-11	1-2	1-3	1-0	0-10	0-8	STL	STL
20[i]	Span without stirrups[k, l]		4-10	5-5	4-5	4-7	4-3	4-0	3-11	3-7	3-7
	1-#4	40,000	7-0	8-1	6-3	6-5	5-10	5-3	4-11	4-1	3-11
		60,000	8-7	9-10	7-7	7-10	7-1	6-5	6-0	4-11	4-10
	1-#5	40,000	8-9	10-1	7-9	8-0	7-3	6-6	6-1	5-1	4-11
		60,000	10-8	12-3	9-6	9-10	8-10	8-0	7-5	6-2	6-0
	2-#4	40,000	9-10	11-4	8-9	9-1	8-2	7-4	6-10	5-8	5-7
	1-#6	60,000	12-0	13-10	10-8	11-0	9-11	9-0	8-4	6-8	6-6
	2-#5	40,000	12-3	14-1	10-10	11-3	10-2	8-11	8-1	6-6	6-4
		60,000	14-0	17-6	11-8	12-3	10-6	9-1	8-4	6-8	6-6
	Center distance A[m, n]		1-10	2-5	1-5	1-7	1-3	1-0	0-11	STL	STL
24[j]	Span without stirrups[k, l]		5-9	6-7	5-5	5-6	5-2	4-11	4-9	4-5	4-4
	1-#4	40,000	7-6	8-10	6-10	7-1	6-5	5-9	5-5	4-6	4-4
		60,000	9-2	10-9	8-4	8-8	7-10	7-1	6-7	5-6	5-4
	1-#5	40,000	9-5	11-0	8-6	8-10	8-0	7-2	6-8	5-7	5-5
		60,000	11-5	13-5	10-5	10-9	9-9	8-9	8-2	6-10	6-8
	2-#4	40,000	10-7	12-5	9-8	10-0	9-0	8-1	7-7	6-3	6-2
	1-#6	60,000	12-11	15-2	11-9	12-2	11-0	9-11	9-3	7-8	7-6
	2-#5	40,000	13-2	15-6	12-0	12-5	11-2	9-11	9-2	7-5	7-3
		60,000	16-3	21-0	14-1	14-10	12-9	11-1	10-1	8-1	7-11
	2-#6	40,000	14-4	18-5	12-6	13-2	11-5	9-11	9-2	7-5	7-3
	Center distance A[m, n]		2-1	2-11	1-9	1-10	1-6	1-3	1-1	STL	STL

(continued)

TABLE R611.8(7)—continued
MAXIMUM ALLOWABLE CLEAR SPANS FOR 8-INCH THICK WAFFLE-GRID LINTELS IN LOAD-BEARING WALLS[a, b, c, d, e, f, o]
MAXIMUM ROOF CLEAR SPAN 40 FEET AND MAXIMUM FLOOR CLEAR SPAN 32 FEET

For SI: 1 inch = 25.4 mm; 1 pound per square foot = 0.0479 kPa; 1 foot = 304.8 mm; Grade 40 = 280 MPa; Grade 60 = 420 MPa.

a. Where lintels are formed with waffle-grid forms, form material shall be removed, if necessary, to create top and bottom flanges of the lintel that are not less than 3 inches in depth (in the vertical direction), are not less than 5 inches in width for 6-inch nominal waffle-grid forms and not less than 7 inches in width for 8-inch nominal waffle-grid forms. See Figure R611.8(3). Flat form lintels shall be permitted in lieu of waffle-grid lintels. See Tables R611.8(2) through R611.8(5).

b. See Table R611.3 for tolerances permitted from nominal thicknesses and minimum dimensions and spacing of cores.

c. Table values are based on concrete with a minimum specified compressive strength of 2,500 psi (17.2 MPa). See Notes l and n. Table values are based on uniform loading. See Section R611.8.2 for lintels supporting concentrated loads.

d. Deflection criterion is *L*/240, where *L* is the clear span of the lintel in inches, or $^1/_2$-inch, whichever is less.

e. Linear interpolation is permitted between ground snow loads.

f. DR indicates design required. STL – stirrups required throughout lintel.

g. Lintel depth, *D*, is permitted to include the available height of wall located directly above the lintel, provided that the increased lintel depth spans the entire length of the lintel.

h. Stirrups shall be fabricated from reinforcing bars with the same yield strength as that used for the main longitudinal reinforcement.

i. Lintels less than 24 inches in depth with stirrups shall be formed from flat-walls forms [see Tables R611.8(2) through R611.8(5)], or, if necessary, form material shall be removed from waffle-grid forms so as to provide the required cover for stirrups. Allowable spans for lintels formed with flat-wall forms shall be determined from Tables R611.8(2) through R611.8(5).

j. Where stirrups are required for 24-inch (610 mm) deep lintels, the spacing shall not exceed 12 inches on center.

k. Allowable clear span without stirrups applicable to all lintels of the same depth, *D*. Top and bottom reinforcement for lintels without stirrups shall not be less than the least amount of reinforcement required for a lintel of the same depth and loading condition with stirrups. All other spans require stirrups spaced at not more than *d*/2.

l. Where concrete with a minimum specified compressive strength of 3,000 psi is used, clear spans for lintels without stirrups shall be permitted to be multiplied by 1.05. If the increased span exceeds the allowable clear span for a lintel of the same depth and loading condition with stirrups, the top and bottom reinforcement shall be equal to or greater than that required for a lintel of the same depth and loading condition that has an allowable clear span that is equal to or greater than that of the lintel without stirrups that has been increased.

m. Center distance, *A*, is the center portion of the span where stirrups are not required. This is applicable to all longitudinal bar sizes and steel yield strengths.

n. Where concrete with a minimum specified compressive strength of 3,000 psi is used, center distance, A, shall be permitted to be multiplied by 1.10.

o. The maximum clear opening width between two solid wall segments shall be 18 feet. See Section R611.7.2.1. Lintel spans in the table greater than 18 feet are shown for interpolation and information only.

TABLE R611.8(8)
MAXIMUM ALLOWABLE CLEAR SPANS FOR 6-INCH THICK SCREEN-GRID LINTELS IN LOAD-BEARING WALLS[a, b, c, d, e, f, p]
ROOF CLEAR SPAN 40 FEET AND FLOOR CLEAR SPAN 32 FEET

LINTEL DEPTH, D^g (inches)	NUMBER OF BARS AND BAR SIZE IN TOP AND BOTTOM OF LINTEL	STEEL YIELD STRENGTH[h], f_y (psi)	DESIGN LOADING CONDITION DETERMINED FROM TABLE R611.8(1)								
			1	2		3		4		5	
				Maximum ground snow load (psf)							
				30	70	30	70	30	70	30	70
			Maximum clear span of lintel (feet - inches)								
12[i,j]	Span without stirrups		2-9	2-11	2-4	2-5	2-3	2-3	2-2	2-0	2-0
16[i,j]	Span without stirrups		3-9	4-0	3-4	3-5	3-2	3-1	3-0	2-9	2-9
20[i,j]	Span without stirrups		4-9	5-1	4-3	4-4	4-1	4-0	3-10	3-7	3-7
24[k]	Span without stirrups[l, m]		5-8	6-3	5-2	5-3	5-0	4-10	4-8	4-4	4-4
	1-#4	40,000	7-11	9-0	6-11	7-2	6-5	6-1	5-8	4-9	4-7
		60,000	9-9	11-0	8-5	8-9	7-10	7-5	6-10	5-9	5-7
	1-#5	40,000	9-11	11-2	8-7	8-11	8-0	7-7	7-0	5-11	5-9
		60,000	12-1	13-8	10-6	10-10	9-9	9-3	8-6	7-2	7-0
	2-#4	40,000	11-2	12-8	9-9	10-1	9-1	8-7	7-11	6-8	6-6
	1-#6	60,000	15-7	17-7	12-8	13-4	11-6	10-8	9-8	7-11	7-8
	2-#5	40,000	14-11	18-0	12-2	12-10	11-1	10-3	9-4	7-8	7-5
		60,000	DR	DR	DR	DR	DR	DR	DR	DR	DR
	Center distance A[n, o]		2-0	2-6	1-6	1-7	1-4	1-2	1-0	STL	STL

For SI: 1 inch = 25.4 mm; 1 pound per square foot = 0.0479 kPa; 1 foot = 304.8 mm; Grade 40 = 280 MPa; Grade 60 = 420 MPa.

a. Where lintels are formed with screen-grid forms, form material shall be removed if necessary to create top and bottom flanges of the lintel that are not less than 5 inches in width and not less than 2.5 inches in depth (in the vertical direction). See Figure R611.8(4). Flat form lintels shall be permitted in lieu of screen-grid lintels. See Tables R611.8(2) through R611.8(5).

b. See Table R611.3 for tolerances permitted from nominal thickness and minimum dimensions and spacings of cores.

c. Table values are based on concrete with a minimum specified compressive strength of 2,500 psi. See Notes m and o. Table values are based on uniform loading. See Section R611.7.2.1 for lintels supporting concentrated loads.

d. Deflection criterion is *L*/240, where *L* is the clear span of the lintel in inches, or $^1/_2$-inch, whichever is less.

e. Linear interpolation is permitted between ground snow loads.

f. DR indicates design required. STL indicates stirrups required throughout lintel.

g. Lintel depth, *D*, is permitted to include the available height of wall located directly above the lintel, provided that the increased lintel depth spans the entire length of the lintel.

h. Stirrups shall be fabricated from reinforcing bars with the same yield strength as that used for the main longitudinal reinforcement.

i. Stirrups are not required for lintels less than 24 inches in depth fabricated from screen-grid forms. Top and bottom reinforcement shall consist of a No. 4 bar having a yield strength of 40,000 psi or 60,000 psi.

j. Lintels between 12 and 24 inches in depth with stirrups shall be formed from flat-wall forms [see Tables R611.8(2) through R611.8(5)], or form material shall be removed from screen-grid forms to provide a concrete section comparable to that required for a flat wall. Allowable spans for flat lintels with stirrups shall be determined from Tables R611.8(2) through R6111.8(5).

k. Where stirrups are required for 24-inch deep lintels, the spacing shall not exceed 12 inches on center.

l. Allowable clear span without stirrups applicable to all lintels of the same depth, *D*. Top and bottom reinforcement for lintels without stirrups shall not be less than the least amount of reinforcement required for a lintel of the same depth and loading condition with stirrups. All other spans require stirrups spaced at not more than 12 inches.

m. Where concrete with a minimum specified compressive strength of 3,000 psi is used, clear spans for lintels without stirrups shall be permitted to be multiplied by 1.05. If the increased span exceeds the allowable clear span for a lintel of the same depth and loading condition with stirrups, the top and bottom reinforcement shall be equal to or greater than that required for a lintel of the same depth and loading condition that has an allowable clear span that is equal to or greater than that of the lintel without stirrups that has been increased.

n. Center distance, *A*, is the center portion of the span where stirrups are not required. This is applicable to all longitudinal bar sizes and steel yield strengths.

o. Where concrete with a minimum specified compressive strength of 3,000 psi is used, center distance, *A*, shall be permitted to be multiplied by 1.10.

p. The maximum clear opening width between two solid wall segments shall be 18 feet (5486 mm). See Section R611.7.2.1. Lintel spans in the table greater than 18 feet are shown for interpolation and information only.

TABLE R611.8(9)
MAXIMUM ALLOWABLE CLEAR SPANS FOR FLAT LINTELS WITHOUT STIRRUPS IN NONLOAD-BEARING WALLS[a, b, c, d, e, g, h]

LINTEL DEPTH, D[d] (inches)	NUMBER OF BARS AND BAR SIZE	STEEL YIELD STRENGTH, f_y (psi)	NOMINAL WALL THICKNESS (inches)							
			4		6		8		10	
			Lintel Supporting							
			Concrete Wall	Light-framed Gable	Concrete Wall	Light-framed Gable	Concrete Wall	Light-framed Gable	Concrete Wall	Light-framed Gable
			Maximum Clear Span of Lintel (feet - inches)							
8	1-#4	40,000	10-11	11-5	9-7	11-2	7-10	9-5	7-3	9-2
		60,000	12-5	11-7	10-11	13-5	9-11	13-2	9-3	12-10
	1-#5	40,000	12-7	11-7	11-1	13-8	10-1	13-5	9-4	13-1
		60,000	DR	DR	12-7	16-4	11-6	14-7	10-9	14-6
	2-#4 1-#6	40,000	DR	DR	12-0	15-3	10-11	15-0	10-2	14-8
		60,000	DR	DR	DR	DR	12-2	15-3	11-7	15-3
	2-#5	40,000	DR	DR	DR	DR	12-7	16-7	11-9	16-7
		60,000	DR	DR	DR	DR	DR	DR	13-3	16-7
	2-#6	40,000	DR	DR	DR	DR	DR	DR	13-2	17-8
		60,000	DR	DR	DR	DR	DR	DR	DR	DR
12	1-#4	40,000	11-5	9-10	10-6	12-0	9-6	11-6	8-9	11-1
		60,000	11-5	9-10	11-8	13-3	10-11	14-0	10-1	13-6
	1-#5	40,000	11-5	9-10	11-8	13-3	11-1	14-4	10-3	13-9
		60,000	11-5	9-10	11-8	13-3	11-10	16-0	11-9	16-9
	2-#4 1-#6	40,000	DR	DR	11-8	13-3	11-10	16-0	11-2	15-6
		60,000	DR	DR	11-8	13-3	11-10	16-0	11-11	18-4
	2-#5	40,000	DR	DR	11-8	13-3	11-10	16-0	11-11	18-4
		60,000	DR	DR	11-8	13-3	11-10	16-0	11-11	18-4
16	1-#4	40,000	13-6	13-0	11-10	13-8	10-7	12-11	9-11	12-4
		60,000	13-6	13-0	13-8	16-7	12-4	15-9	11-5	15-0
	1-#5	40,000	13-6	13-0	13-10	17-0	12-6	16-1	11-7	15-4
		60,000	13-6	13-0	13-10	17-1	14-0	19-7	13-4	18-8
	2-#4 1-#6	40,000	13-6	13-0	13-10	17-1	13-8	18-2	12-8	17-4
		60,000	13-6	13-0	13-10	17-1	14-0	20-3	14-1	—
	2-#5	40,000	13-6	13-0	13-10	17-1	14-0	20-3	14-1	—
		60,000	DR	DR	13-10	17-1	14-0	20-3	14-1	—
20	1-#4	40,000	14-11	15-10	13-0	14-10	11-9	13-11	10-10	13-2
		60,000	15-3	15-10	14-11	18-1	13-6	17-0	12-6	16-2
	1-#5	40,000	15-3	15-10	15-2	18-6	13-9	17-5	12-8	16-6
		60,000	15-3	15-10	15-8	20-5	15-9	—	14-7	20-1
	2-#4 1-#6	40,000	15-3	15-10	15-8	20-5	14-11	—	13-10	—
		60,000	15-3	15-10	15-8	20-5	15-10	—	15-11	—
	2-#5	40,000	15-3	15-10	15-8	20-5	15-10	—	15-11	—
		60,000	15-3	15-10	15-8	20-5	15-10	—	15-11	—
24	1-#4	40,000	16-1	17-1	13-11	15-10	12-7	14-9	11-8	13-10
		60,000	16-11	18-5	16-1	19-3	14-6	18-0	13-5	17-0
	1-#5	40,000	16-11	18-5	16-3	19-8	14-9	18-5	13-8	17-4
		60,000	16-11	18-5	17-4	—	17-0	—	15-8	—
	2-#4 1-#6	40,000	16-11	18-5	17-4	—	16-1	—	14-10	—
		60,000	16-11	18-5	17-4	—	17-6	—	17-1	—
	2-#5	40,000	16-11	18-5	17-4	—	17-6	—	17-4	—
		60,000	16-11	18-5	17-4	—	17-6	—	17-8	—

(continued)

TABLE R611.8(9)—continued
MAXIMUM ALLOWABLE CLEAR SPANS FOR FLAT LINTELS WITHOUT STIRRUPS IN NONLOAD-BEARING WALLS[a, b, c, d, e, g, h]
ROOF CLEAR SPAN 40 FEET AND FLOOR CLEAR SPAN 32 FEET

For SI: 1 inch = 25.4 mm; 1 foot = 304.8 mm; Grade 40 = 280 MPa; Grade 60 = 420 MPa.

a. See Table R611.3 for tolerances permitted from nominal thickness.
b. Table values are based on concrete with a minimum specified compressive strength of 2,500 psi. See Note e.
c. Deflection criterion is *L*/240, where *L* is the clear span of the lintel in inches, or $^1/_2$-inch, whichever is less.
d. Linear interpolation between lintels depths, *D*, is permitted provided the two cells being used to interpolate are shaded.
e. Where concrete with a minimum specified compressive strength of 3,000 psi is used, spans in cells that are shaded shall be permitted to be multiplied by 1.05.
f. Lintel depth, *D*, is permitted to include the available height of wall located directly above the lintel, provided that the increased lintel depth spans the entire length of the lintel.
g. DR indicates design required.
h. The maximum clear opening width between two solid wall segments shall be 18 feet (5486 mm). See Section R611.7.2.1. Lintel spans in the table greater than 18 feet are shown for interpolation and information purposes only.

TABLE R611.8(10)
MAXIMUM ALLOWABLE CLEAR SPANS FOR WAFFLE-GRID AND SCREEN GRID LINTELS WITHOUT STIRRUPS IN NONLOAD-BEARING WALLS[c, d, e, f, g]

LINTEL DEPTH[h], *D* (inches)	FORM TYPE AND NOMINAL WALL THICKNESS (inches)					
	6-inch Waffle-grid[a]		8-inch Waffle-grid[a]		6-inch Screen-grid[b]	
	Lintel supporting					
	Concrete Wall	Light-framed Gable	Concrete Wall	Light-framed Gable	Concrete Wall	Light-framed Gable
	Maximum Clear Span of Lintel (feet - inches)					
8	10-3	8-8	8-8	8-3	—	—
12	9-2	7-6	7-10	7-1	8-8	6-9
16	10-11	10-0	9-4	9-3	—	—
20	12-5	12-2	10-7	11-2	—	—
24	13-9	14-2	11-10	12-11	13-0	12-9

For SI: 1 inch = 25.4 mm; 1 foot = 304.8 mm; Grade 40 = 280 MPa; Grade 60 = 420 MPa

a. Where lintels are formed with waffle-grid forms, form material shall be removed, if necessary, to create top and bottom flanges of the lintel that are not less than 3 inches in depth (in the vertical direction), are not less than 5 inches in width for 6-inch waffle-grid forms and not less than 7 inches in width for 8-inch waffle-grid forms. See Figure R611.8(3). Flat form lintels shall be permitted in lieu of waffle-grid lintels. See Tables R611.8(2) through R611.8(5).
b. Where lintels are formed with screen-grid forms, form material shall be removed if necessary to create top and bottom flanges of the lintel that are not less than 5 inches in width and not less than 2.5 inches in depth (in the vertical direction). See Figure R611.8(4). Flat form lintels shall be permitted in lieu of screen-grid lintels. See Tables R611.8(2) through R611.8(5).
c. See Table R611.3 for tolerances permitted from nominal thickness and minimum dimensions and spacing of cores.
d. Table values are based on concrete with a minimum specified compressive strength of 2,500 psi. See Note g.
e. Deflection criterion is *L*/240, where *L* is the clear span of the lintel in inches, or $^1/_2$-inch, whichever is less.
f. Top and bottom reinforcement shall consist of a No. 4 bar having a minimum yield strength of 40,000 psi.
g. Where concrete with a minimum specified compressive strength of 3,000 psi is used, spans in shaded cells shall be permitted to be multiplied by 1.05.
h. Lintel depth, *D*, is permitted to include the available height of wall located directly above the lintel, provided that the increased lintel depth spans the entire length of the lintel.

R611.8.1.2 Vertical reinforcement. Not less than one No. 4 bar [Grade 40 (280 MPa)] shall be provided on each side of openings equal to or greater than 2 feet (610 mm) in width. The vertical reinforcement required by this section shall extend the full height of the wall *story* and shall be located within 12 inches (305 mm) of each side of the opening. The vertical reinforcement required on each side of an opening by this section is permitted to serve as reinforcement at the ends of solid wall segments in accordance with Section R611.7.2.2.2, provided it is located as required by the applicable detail in Figure R611.7(2). Where the vertical reinforcement required by this section is used to satisfy the requirements of Section R611.7.2.2.2 in waffle- and screen-grid walls, a concrete flange shall be created at the ends of the solid wall segments in accordance with Table R611.7(4), note e. In the top-most *story*, the reinforcement shall terminate in accordance with Section R611.6.4.

R611.8.2 Lintels. Lintels shall be provided over all openings equal to or greater than 2 feet (610 mm) in width. Lintels with uniform loading shall conform to Sections R611.8.2.1, and R611.8.2.2, or Section R611.8.2.3. Lintels supporting concentrated loads, such as from roof or floor beams or girders, shall be designed in accordance with ACI 318.

R611.8.2.1 Lintels designed for gravity load-bearing conditions. Where a lintel will be subjected to gravity load condition 1 through 5 of Table R611.8(1), the clear span of the lintel shall not exceed that permitted by Tables R611.8(2) through R611.8(8). The maximum clear span of lintels with and without stirrups in flat walls shall be determined in accordance with Tables R611.8(2) through R611.8(5), and constructed in accordance with Figure R611.8(2). The maximum clear span of lintels with and without stirrups in waffle-grid walls shall be determined in accordance with Tables R611.8(6) and R611.8(7), and constructed in accordance with Figure R611.8(3). The maximum clear span of lintels with and without stirrups in screen-grid walls shall be determined in accordance with Table R611.8(8), and constructed in accordance with Figure R611.8(4).

Where required by the applicable table, No. 3 stirrups shall be installed in lintels at a maximum spacing of *d*/2 where d equals the depth of the lintel, *D*, less the cover of the concrete as shown in Figures R611.8(2) through R611.8(4). The smaller value of *d* computed for the top and bottom bar shall be used to determine the maximum stirrup spacing. Where stirrups are required in a lintel with a single bar or two bundled bars in the top and bottom, they shall be fabricated like the letter "c" or "s" with 135-degree (2.36 rad) standard hooks at each end that comply with Section R611.5.4.5 and Figure R611.5.4(3) and installed as shown in Figures R611.8(2) through R611.8(4). Where two bars are required in the top and bottom of the lintel and the bars are not bundled, the bars shall be separated by a minimum of 1 inch (25 mm). The free end of the stirrups shall be fabricated with 90- or 135-degree (1.57 or 2.36 rad) standard hooks that comply with Section R611.5.4.5 and Figure R611.5.4(3) and installed as shown in Figures R611.8(2) and R611.8(3). For flat, waffle-grid and screen-grid lintels, stirrups are not required in the center distance, A, portion of spans in accordance with Figure R611.8(1) and Tables R611.8(2) through R611.8(8). See Section R611.8.2.2, item 5, for requirement for stirrups throughout lintels with bundled bars.

R611.8.2.2 Bundled bars in lintels. It is permitted to bundle two bars in contact with each other in lintels if all of the following are observed:

1. Bars no larger than No. 6 are bundled.
2. Where the wall thickness is not sufficient to provide not less than 3 inches (76 mm) of clear space beside bars (total on both sides) oriented horizontally in a bundle, the bundled bars shall be oriented in a vertical plane.
3. Where vertically oriented bundled bars terminate with standard hooks to develop the bars in tension beyond the support (see Section R611.5.4.4), the hook extensions shall be staggered to provide a minimum of one inch (25 mm) clear spacing between the extensions.
4. Bundled bars shall not be lap spliced within the lintel span and the length on each end of the lintel that is required to develop the bars in tension.
5. Bundled bars shall be enclosed within stirrups throughout the length of the lintel. Stirrups and the installation thereof shall comply with Section R611.8.2.1.

R611.8.2.3 Lintels without stirrups designed for nonload-bearing conditions. The maximum clear span of lintels without stirrups designed for nonload-bearing conditions of Table R611.8(1).1 shall be determined in accordance with this section. The maximum clear span of lintels without stirrups in flat walls shall be determined in accordance with Table R611.8(9), and the maximum clear span of lintels without stirrups in walls of waffle-grid or screen-grid construction shall be determined in accordance with Table R611.8(10).

R611.9 Requirements for connections–general. Concrete walls shall be connected to footings, floors, ceilings and roofs in accordance with this section.

R611.9.1 Connections between concrete walls and light-framed floor, ceiling and roof systems. Connections between concrete walls and light-framed floor, ceiling and roof systems using the prescriptive details of Figures R611.9(1) through R611.9(12) shall comply with this section and Sections R611.9.2 and R611.9.3.

R611.9.1.1 Anchor bolts. Anchor bolts used to connect light-framed floor, ceiling and roof systems to concrete walls in accordance with Figures R611.9(1) through R611.9(12) shall have heads, or shall be rods with threads on both ends with a hex or square nut on the end embedded in the concrete. Bolts and threaded rods shall comply with Section R611.5.2.2. Anchor bolts with J- or L-hooks shall not be used where the connection details in these figures are used.

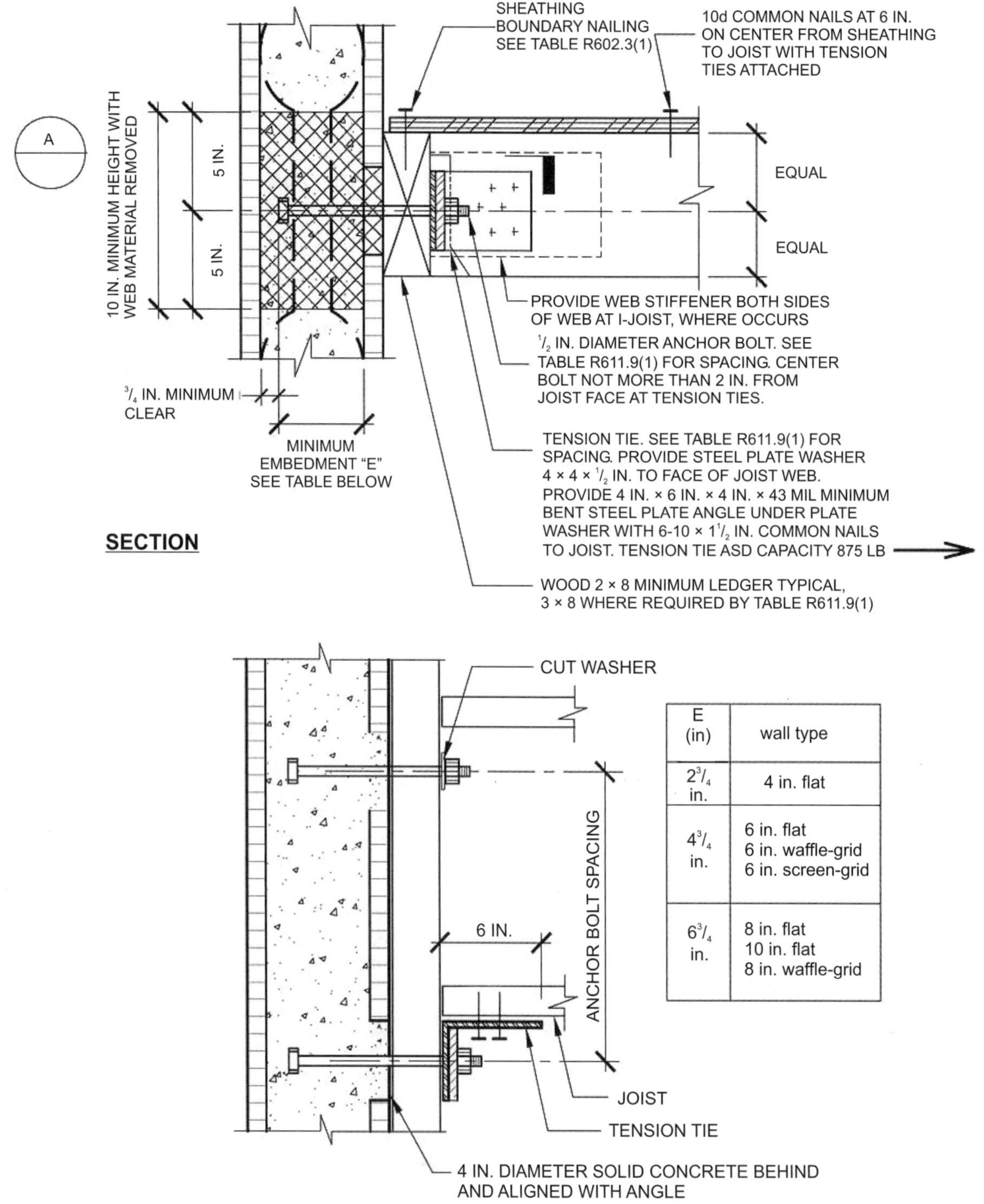

E (in)	wall type
$2^3/_4$ in.	4 in. flat
$4^3/_4$ in.	6 in. flat 6 in. waffle-grid 6 in. screen-grid
$6^3/_4$ in.	8 in. flat 10 in. flat 8 in. waffle-grid

For SI: 1 mil = 0.0254 mm, 1 inch = 25.4 mm, 1 pound-force = 4.448 N.

FIGURE R611.9(1)
WOOD FRAMED FLOOR TO SIDE OF CONCRETE WALL, FRAMING PERPENDICULAR

TABLE R611.9(1)
WOOD FRAMED FLOOR TO SIDE OF CONCRETE WALL, FRAMING PERPENDICULAR[a, b, c]

ANCHOR BOLT SPACING (inches)	TENSION TIE SPACING (inches)	BASIC WIND SPEED (mph)					
		85B	90B	100B	110B	120B	130B
				85C	90C	100C	110C
					85D	90D	100D
12	12						
12	24						
12	36						
12	48						
16	16					A	A
16	32						
16	48						
19.2	19.2	A	A	A	A	A	
19.2	38.4	A	A	A			

For SI: 1 inch = 25.4 mm; 1 mile per hour = 0.447 m/s.

a. This table is for use with the detail in Figure R611.9(1). Use of this detail is permitted where a cell is not shaded and prohibited where shaded.

b. Wall design per other provisions of Section R611 is required.

c. Letter "A" indicates that a minimum nominal 3 × 8 ledger is required.

TABLE R611.9(2)
WOOD FRAMED FLOOR TO SIDE OF CONCRETE WALL, FRAMING PARALLEL[a, b]

ANCHOR BOLT SPACING (inches)	TENSION TIE SPACING (inches)	BASIC WIND SPEED (mph) AND WIND EXPOSURE CATEGORY					
		85b	90B	100B	110B	120B	130B
				85C	90C	100C	110C
					85D	90D	100D
12	12						
12	24						
12	36						
12	48						
16	16						
16	32						
16	48						
19.2	19.2						
19.2	38.4						
24	24						
24	48						

For SI: 1 inch = 25.4 mm; 1 mph = 0.447 m/s.

a. This table is for use with the detail in Figure R611.9(2). Use of this detail is permitted where a cell is not shaded and prohibited where shaded.

b. Wall design per other provisions of Section R611 is required.

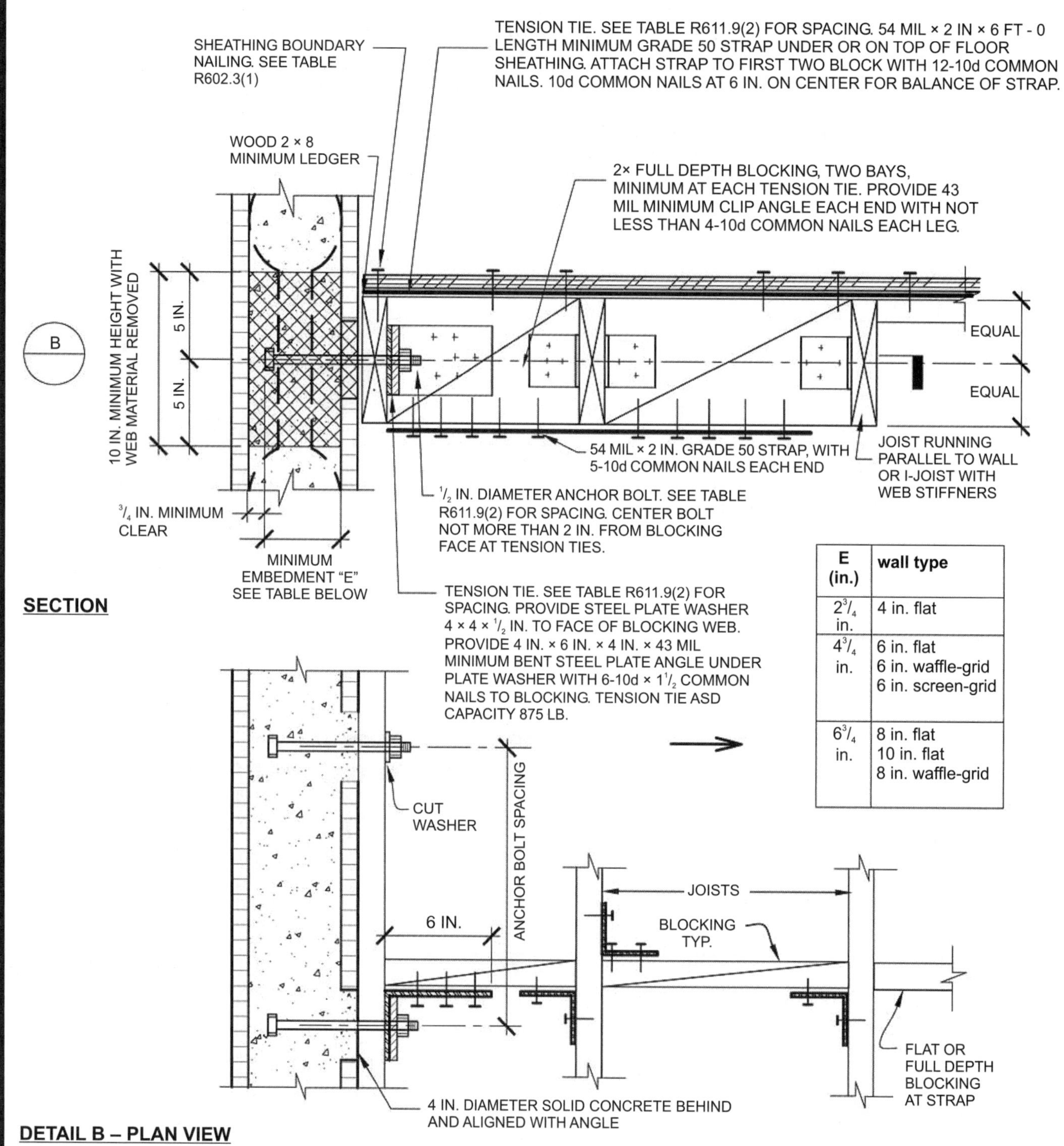

E (in.)	wall type
$2^3/_4$ in.	4 in. flat
$4^3/_4$ in.	6 in. flat 6 in. waffle-grid 6 in. screen-grid
$6^3/_4$ in.	8 in. flat 10 in. flat 8 in. waffle-grid

For SI: 1 mil = 0.0254 mm, 1 inch = 25.4 mm, 1 foot = 304.8 mm, 1 pound-force = 4.448 N.

FIGURE R611.9(2)
WOOD FRAMED FLOOR TO SIDE OF CONCRETE WALL FRAMING PARALLEL

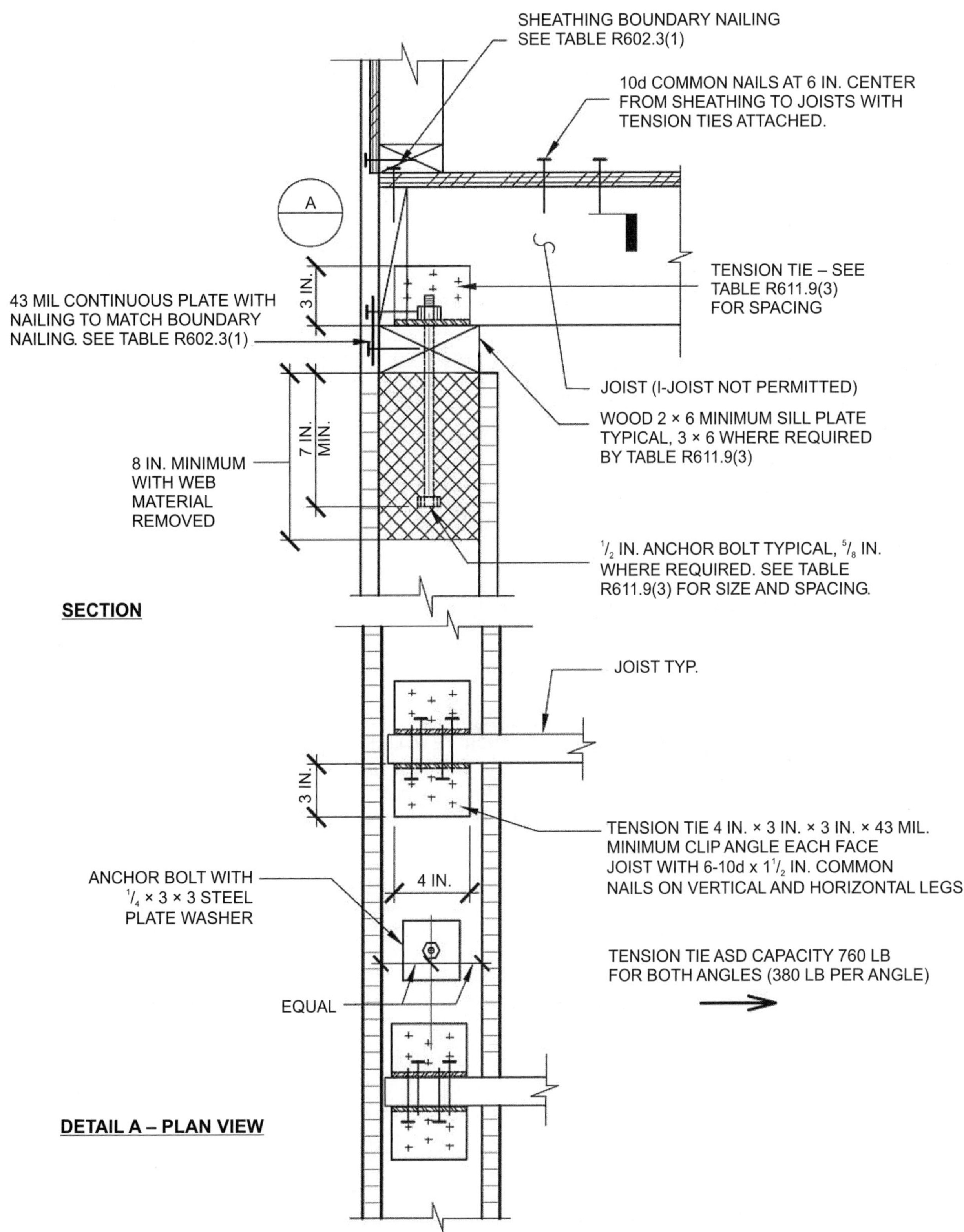

For SI: 1 mil = 0.0254 mm, 1 inch = 25.4 mm, 1 pound-force = 4.448 N.

FIGURE R611.9(3)
WOOD FRAMED FLOOR TO TOP OF CONCRETE WALL FRAMING PERPENDICULAR

TABLE R611.9(3)
WOOD FRAMED FLOOR TO TOP OF CONCRETE WALL, FRAMING PERPENDICULAR[a, b, c, d, e]

ANCHOR BOLT SPACING (inches)	TENSION TIE SPACING (inches)	BASIC WIND SPEED (mph) AND WIND EXPOSURE CATEGORY					
		85B	90B	100B	110B	120B	130B
				85C	90C	100C	110C
					85D	90D	100D
12	12						
12	24						
12	36						
12	48						
16	16					6 A	6 B
16	32					6 A	6 B
16	48						
19.2	19.2				6 A	6 A	6 B
19.2	38.4				6 A	6 A	
24	24			6 A	6 B	6 A	
24	48			6 A			

For SI: 1 inch = 25.4 mm; 1 mile per hour = 0.447 m/s.

a. This table is for use with the detail in Figure R611.9(3). Use of this detail is permitted where cell is not shaded, prohibited where shaded.

b. Wall design per other provisions in Section R611 is required.

c. For wind design, minimum 4-inch nominal wall is permitted in unshaded cells with no number.

d. Number 6 indicates minimum permitted nominal wall thickness in inches necessary to develop required strength (capacity) of connection. As a minimum, this nominal thickness shall occur in the portion of the wall indicated by the cross-hatching in Figure R611.9(3). For the remainder of the wall, see Note b.

e. Letter "A" indicates that a minimum nominal 3 × 6 sill plate is required. Letter "B" indicates that a $^5/_8$ inch (16 mm) diameter anchor bolt and a minimal nominal 3 × 6 sill plate are required.

TABLE R611.9(4)
WOOD FRAMED FLOOR TO TOP OF CONCRETE WALL, FRAMING PARALLEL[a, b, c, d, e]

ANCHOR BOLT SPACING (inches)	TENSION TIE SPACING (inches)	BASIC WIND SPEED (mph) AND WIND EXPOSURE CATEGORY					
		85B	90B	100B	110B	120B	130B
				85C	90C	100C	110C
					85D	90D	100D
	12						
12	24						
12	36						
12	48						
16	16					6 A	6 B
16	32					6 A	6 B
16	48						
19.2	19.2				6 A	6 A	6 B
19.2	38.4				6 A	6 A	
24	24			6 A	6 B	6 B	
24	48			6 A			

For SI: 1 inch = 25.4 mm; 1 mile per hour = 0.447 m/s.

a. This table is for use with the detail in Figure R611.9(4). Use of this detail is permitted where a cell is not shaded, prohibited where shaded.

b. Wall design per other provisions of Section R611 is required.

c. For wind design, minimum 4-inch nominal wall is permitted in unshaded cells with no number.

d. Number 6 indicates minimum permitted nominal wall thickness in inches necessary to develop required strength (capacity) of connection. As a minimum, this nominal thickness shall occur in the portion of the wall indicated by the cross-hatching in Figure R611.9(4). For the remainder of the wall, see Note b.

e. Letter "A" indicates that a minimum nominal 3 × 6 sill plate is required. Letter "B" indicates that a $^5/_8$ inch diameter anchor bolt and a minimal nominal 3 × 6 sill plate are required.

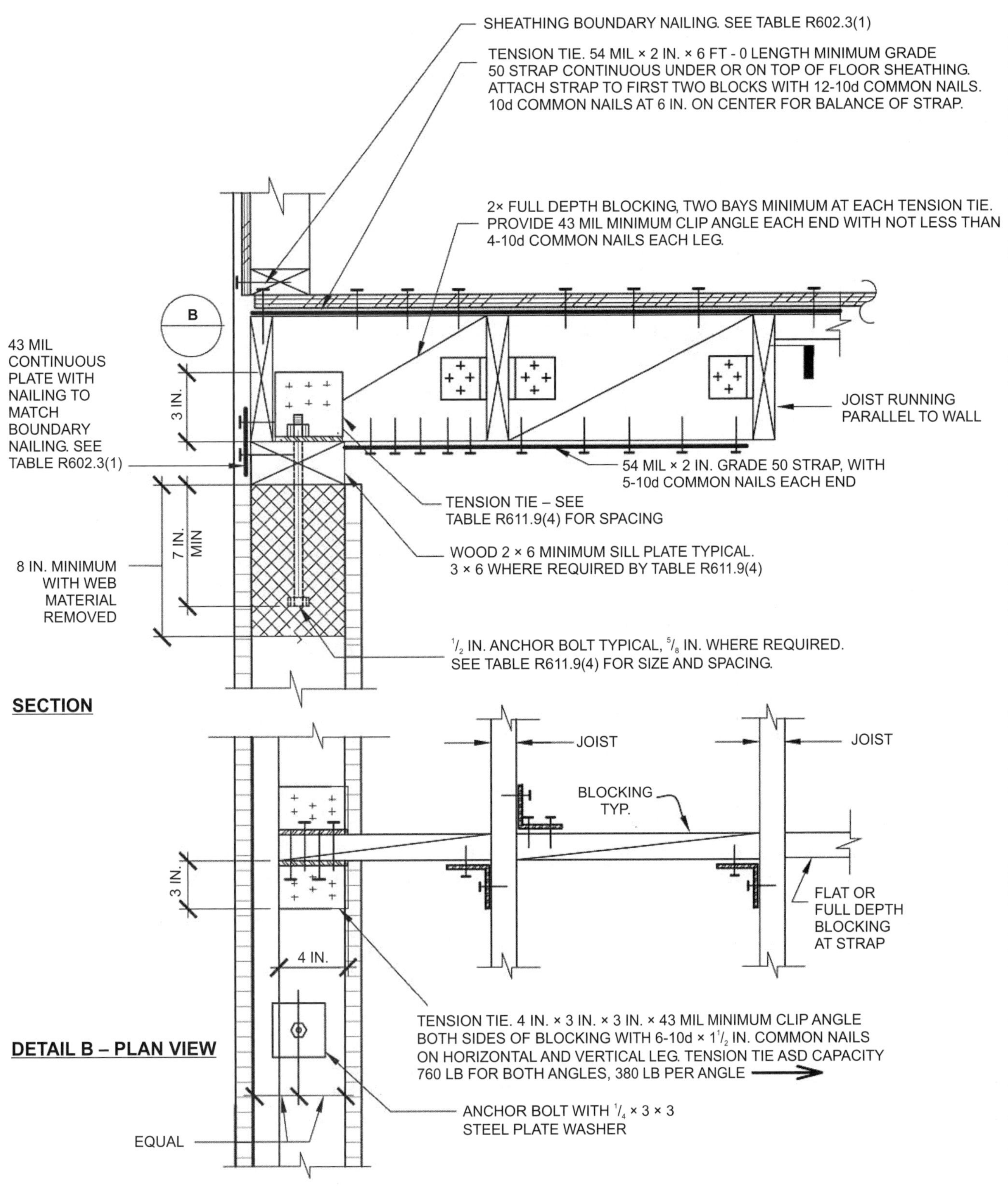

For SI: 1 mil = 0.0254 mm, 1 inch = 25.4 mm, 1 foot = 304.8 mm, 1 pound-force = 4.448 N.

FIGURE R611.9(4)
WOOD FRAMED FLOOR TO TOP OF CONCRETE WALL FRAMING PARALLEL

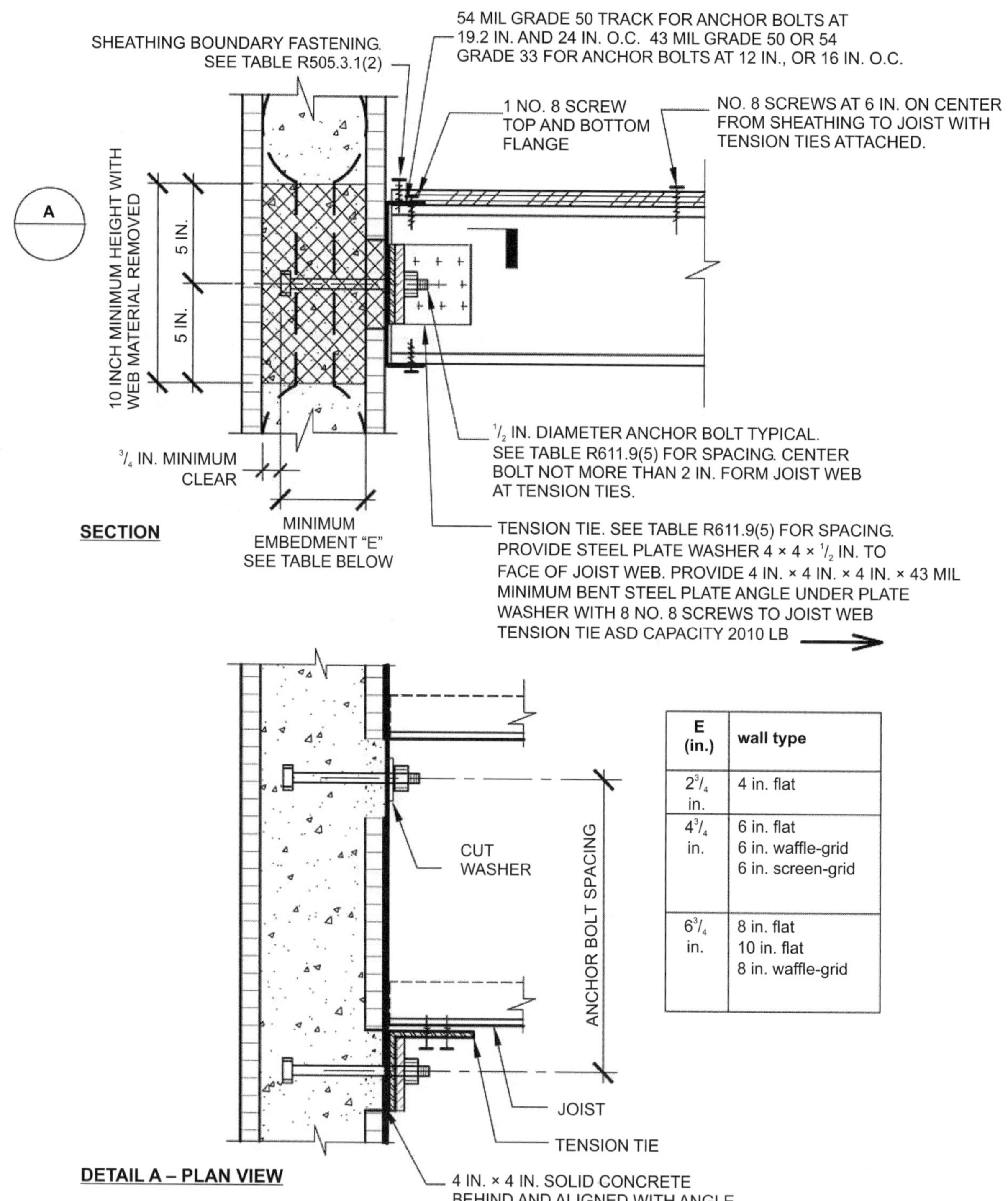

E (in.)	wall type
2 3/4 in.	4 in. flat
4 3/4 in.	6 in. flat 6 in. waffle-grid 6 in. screen-grid
6 3/4 in.	8 in. flat 10 in. flat 8 in. waffle-grid

For SI: 1 mil = 0.0254 mm, 1 inch = 25.4 mm, 1 pound-force = 4.448 N.

FIGURE R611.9(5)
COLD-FORMED STEEL FLOOR TO SIDE OF CONCRETE WALL, FRAMING PERPENDICULAR

TABLE R611.9(5)
COLD-FORMED STEEL FRAMED FLOOR TO SIDE OF CONCRETE WALL, FRAMING PERPENDICULAR[a, b, c, d]

ANCHOR BOLT SPACING (inches)	TENSION TIE SPACING (inches)	BASIC WIND SPEED (mph) AND WIND EXPOSURE CATEGORY					
		85B	90B	100B	110B	120B	130B
				85C	90C	100C	110C
					85D	90D	100D
12	12						
12	24						
12	36						6
12	48					6	6
16	16						
16	32						
16	48					6	6
19.2	19.2						
19.2	38.4						6
24	24						
24	48					6	6

For SI: 1 inch = 25.4 mm; 1 mile per hour = 0.4470 m/s.

a. This table is for use with the detail in Figure R611.9(5). Use of this detail is permitted where a cell is not shaded.

b. Wall design per other provisions of Section R611 is required.

c. For wind design, minimum 4-inch nominal wall is permitted in unshaded cells with no number.

d. Number 6 indicates minimum permitted nominal wall thickness in inches necessary to develop required strength (capacity) of connection. As a minimum, this nominal thickness shall occur in the portion of the wall indicated by the cross-hatching in Figure R611.9(5). For the remainder of the wall, see Note b.

TABLE R611.9(6)
COLD-FORMED STEEL FRAMED FLOOR TO SIDE OF CONCRETE WALL, FRAMING PARALLEL[a, b, c, d]

ANCHOR BOLT SPACING (inches)	TENSION TIE SPACING (inches)	BASIC WIND SPEED (mph) AND WIND EXPOSURE CATEGORY					
		85B	90B	100B	110B	120B	130B
				85C	90C	100C	110C
					85D	90D	100D
12	12						
12	24						
12	36						6
12	48					6	6
16	16						
16	32						
16	48					6	6
19.2	19.2						
19.2	38.4						6
24	24						
24	48					6	6

For SI: 1 inch = 25.4 mm; 1 mile per hour = 0.447 m/s.

a. This table is for use with the detail in Figure R611.9(6). Use of this detail is permitted where a cell is not shaded.

b. Wall design per other provisions of Section R611 is required.

c. For wind design, minimum 4-inch nominal wall is permitted in unshaded cells with no number.

d. Number 6 indicates minimum permitted nominal wall thickness in inches necessary to develop required strength (capacity) of connection. As a minimum, this nominal thickness shall occur in the portion of the wall indicated by the cross-hatching in Figure R611.9(6). For the remainder of the wall, see Note b.

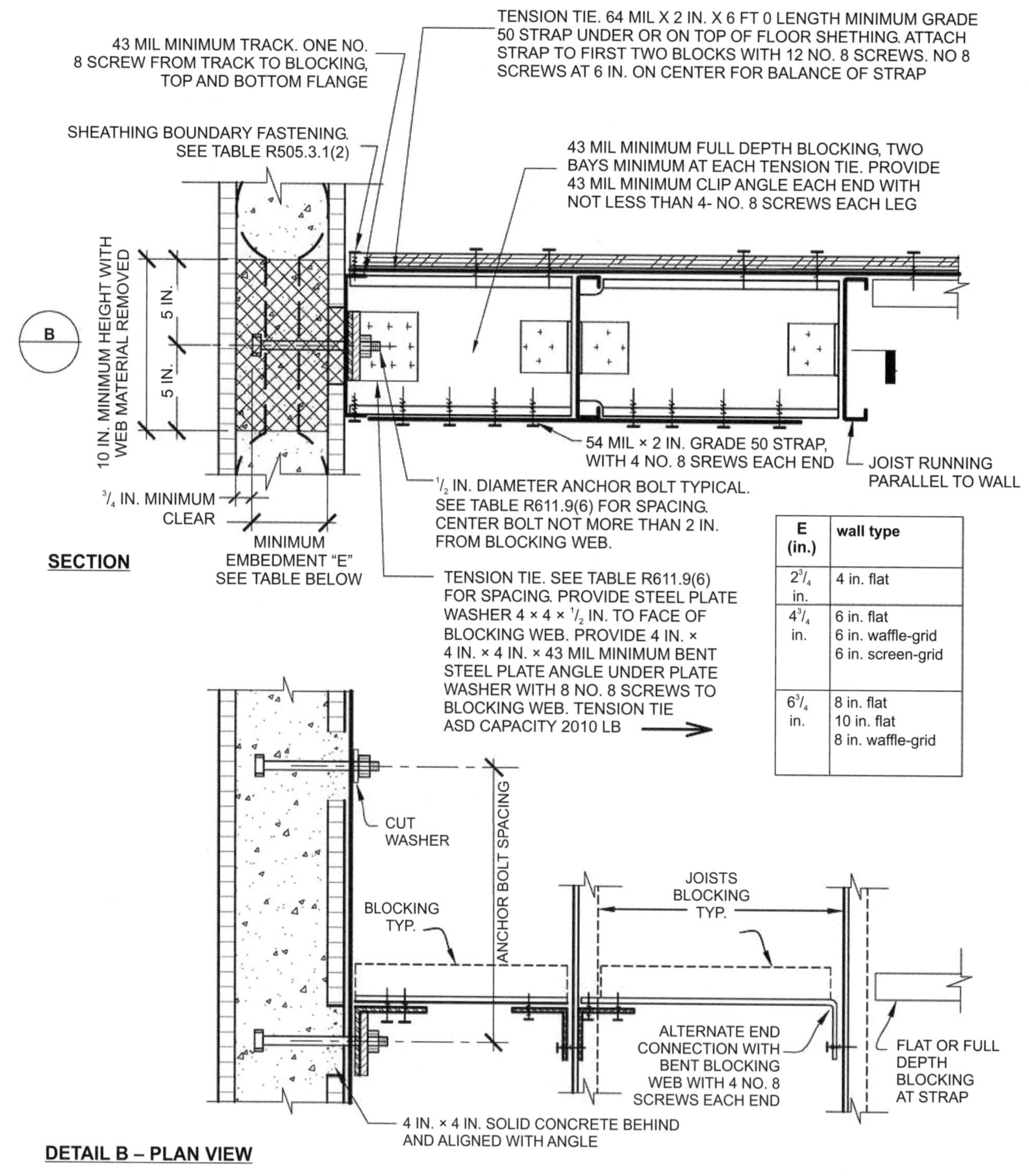

E (in.)	wall type
$2^3/_4$ in.	4 in. flat
$4^3/_4$ in.	6 in. flat 6 in. waffle-grid 6 in. screen-grid
$6^3/_4$ in.	8 in. flat 10 in. flat 8 in. waffle-grid

For SI: 1 mil = 0.0254 mm, 1 inch = 25.4 mm, 1 pound-force = 4.448 N.

FIGURE R611.9(6)
COLD-FORMED STEEL FLOOR TO SIDE OF CONCRETE WALL, FRAMING PARALLEL

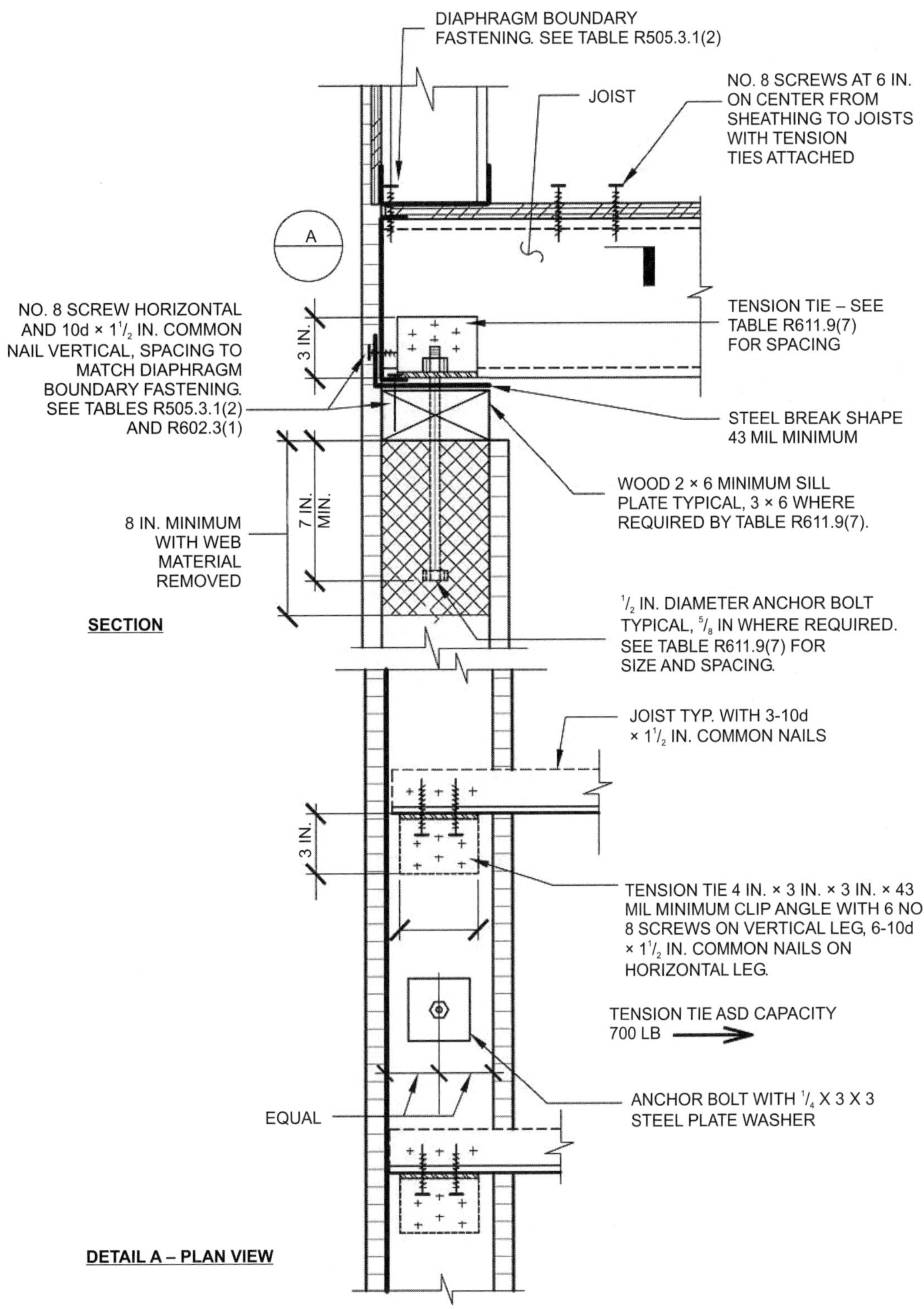

For SI: 1 mil = 0.0254 mm, 1 inch = 25.4 mm, 1 pound-force = 4.448 N.

FIGURE R611.9(7)
COLD-FORMED STEEL FLOOR TO TOP OF CONCRETE WALL FRAMING PERPENDICULAR

TABLE R611.9(7)
COLD-FORMED STEEL FRAMED FLOOR TO TOP OF CONCRETE WALL, FRAMING PERPENDICULAR[a, b, c, d, e]

ANCHOR BOLT SPACING (inches)	TENSION TIE SPACING (inches)	BASIC WIND SPEED (mph) AND WIND EXPOSURE CATEGORY					
		85B	90B	100B	110B	120B	130B
				858C	90C	100C	110C
					85D	90D	100D
12	12						
12	24						
16	16					6 A	6 B
16	32					6 A	6 B
19.2	19.2				6 A	8 B	8 B
19.2	38.4				6 A	8 B	8 B
24	24			6 A	8 B	8 B	

For SI: 1 inch = 25.4 mm; 1 mph = 0.447 m/s.

a. This table is for use with the detail in Figure R611.9(7). Use of this detail is permitted where a cell is not shaded, prohibited where shaded.
b. Wall design per other provisions of Section R611 is required.
c. For wind design, minimum 4-inch nominal wall is permitted in unshaded cells with no number.
d. Numbers 6 and 8 indicate minimum permitted nominal wall thickness in inches necessary to develop required strength (capacity) of connection. As a minimum, this nominal thickness shall occur in the portion of the wall indicated by the cross-hatching in Figure R611.9(7). For the remainder of the wall, see Note b.
e. Letter "A" indicates that a minimum nominal 3 × 6 sill plate is required. Letter "B" indicates that a $^5/_8$ inch diameter anchor bolt and a minimum nominal 3 × 6 sill plate are required.

TABLE R611.9(8)
COLD-FORMED STEEL FRAMED FLOOR TO TOP OF CONCRETE WALL, FRAMING PARALLEL[a, b, c, d, e]

ANCHOR BOLT SPACING (inches)	TENSION TIE SPACING (inches)	BASIC WIND SPEED (mph) AND WIND EXPOSURE CATEGORY					
		85B	90B	100B	110B	120B	130B
				85C	90C	100C	110C
					85D	90D	100D
12	12						
12	24						
16	16					6 A	6 B
16	32					6 A	6 B
19.2	19.2				6 A	8 B	8 B
19.2	38.4				6 A	8 B	8 B
24	24			6 A	8 B	8 B	

For SI: 1 inch = 25.4 mm; 1 mph = 0.447 m/s.

a. This table is for use with the detail in Figure R611.9(8). Use of this detail is permitted where a cell is not shaded, prohibited where shaded.
b. Wall design per other provisions of Section R611 is required.
c. For wind design, minimum 4-inch nominal wall is permitted in unshaded cells with no number.
d. Numbers 6 and 8 indicate minimum permitted nominal wall thickness in inches necessary to develop required strength (capacity) of connection. As a minimum, this nominal thickness shall occur in the portion of the wall indicated by the cross-hatching in Figure R611.9(8). For the remainder of the wall, see Note b.
e. Letter "A" indicates that a minimum nominal 3 × 6 sill plate is required. Letter "B" indicates that a $^5/_8$ inch diameter anchor bolt and a minimum nominal 3 × 6 sill plate are required.

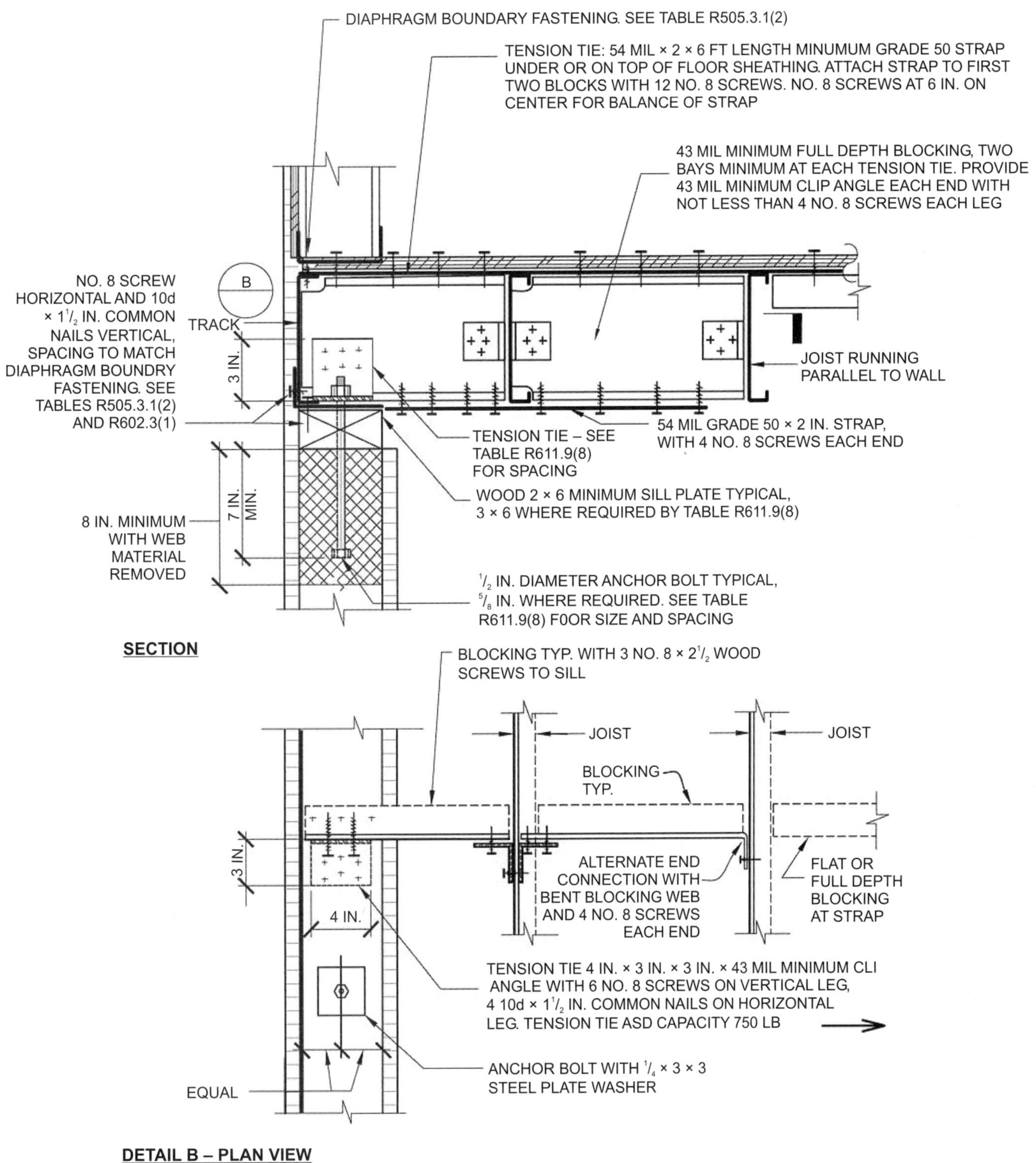

For SI: 1 mil = 0.0254 mm, 1 inch = 25.4 mm, 1 pound-force = 4.448 N.

FIGURE R611.9(8)
COLD-FORMED STEEL FLOOR TO TOP OF CONCRETE WALL, FRAMING PARALLEL

TABLE R611.9(9)
WOOD FRAMED ROOF TO TOP OF CONCRETE WALL, FRAMING PERPENDICULAR[a, b, c, d, e]

ANCHOR BOLT SPACING (inches)	TENSION TIE SPACING (inches)	BASIC WIND SPEED (mph) AND WIND EXPOSURE CATEGORY					
		85B	90B	100B	110B	120B	130B
				85C	90C	100C	110C
					85D	90D	100D
12	12						
12	24						
12	36						
12	48						
16	16						6
16	32						6
16	48						
19.2	19.2					6	6 A
19.2	38.4					6	
24	24				6 A	6 A	6 B
24	48						

For SI: 1 inch = 25.4 mm; 1 mph = 0.447 m/s.

a. This table is for use with the detail in Figure R611.9(9). Use of this detail is permitted where cell a is not shaded, prohibited where shaded.
b. Wall design per other provisions of Section R611 is required.
c. For wind design, minimum 4-inch nominal wall is permitted in unshaded cells with no number.
d. Number 6 indicates minimum permitted nominal wall thickness in inches necessary to develop required strength (capacity) of connection. As a minimum, this nominal thickness shall occur in the portion of the wall indicated by the cross-hatching in Figure R611.9(9). For the remainder of the wall, see Note b.
e. Letter "A" indicates that a minimum nominal 3 × 6 sill plate is required. Letter "B" indicates that a $^5/_8$ inch diameter anchor bolt and a minimum nominal 3 × 6 sill plate are required.

TABLE R611.9(10)
WOOD FRAMED ROOF TO TOP OF CONCRETE WALL, FRAMING PARALLEL[a, b, c, d, e]

ANCHOR BOLT SPACING (inches)	TENSION TIE SPACING (inches)	BASIC WIND SPEED (mph) AND WIND EXPOSURE CATEGORY					
		85B	90B	100B	110B	120B	130B
				85C	90C	100C	110C
					85D	90D	100D
12	12						
12	24						
12	36						
12	48						
16	16					6	6
16	32					6	6
16	48					6	6
19.2	19.2				6	6	6 A
19.2	38.4				6	6	6 A
24	24			6	6 A	6 A	6 B
24	48			6	6 A	6 B	6 B

For SI: 1 inch = 25.4 mm; I mph = 0.447 m/s.

a. This table is for use with the detail in Figure R611.9(10). Use of this detail is permitted where a cell is not shaded.
b. Wall design per other provisions of Section R611 is required.
c. For wind design, minimum 4-inch nominal wall is permitted in cells with no number.
d. Number 6 indicates minimum permitted nominal wall thickness in inches necessary to develop required strength (capacity) of connection. As a minimum, this nominal thickness shall occur in the portion of the wall indicated by the cross-hatching in Figure R611.9(10). For the remainder of the wall, see Note b.
e. Letter "A" indicates that a minimum nominal 3 × 6 sill plate is required. Letter "B" indicates that a $5/_8$ inch diameter anchor bolt and a minimum nominal 3 × 6 sill plate are required.

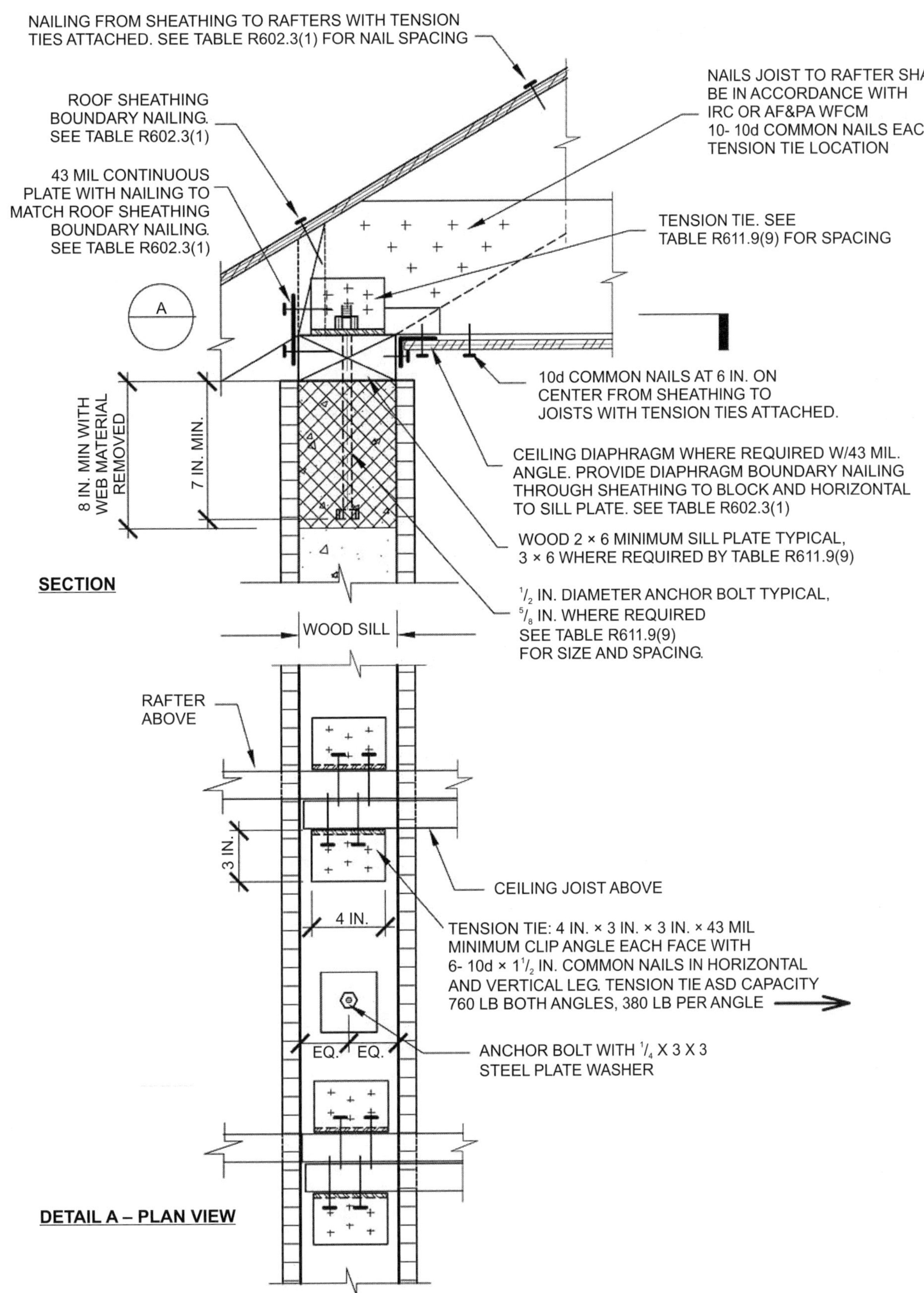

For SI: 1 mil = 0.0254 mm, 1 inch = 25.4 mm, 1 pound-force = 4.448 N.

FIGURE R611.9(9)
WOOD FRAMED ROOF TO TOP OF CONCRETE WALL, FRAMING PERPENDICULAR

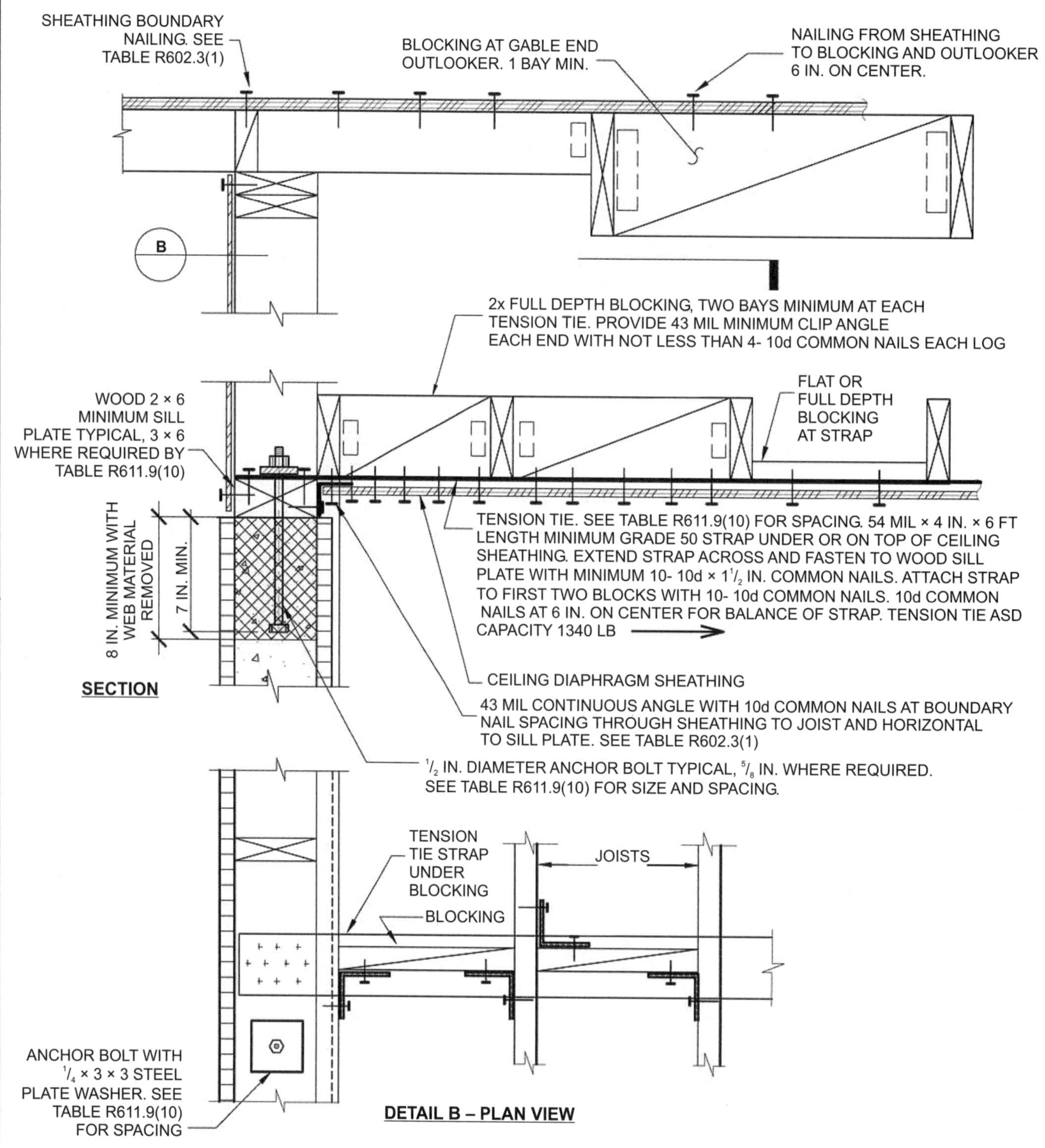

For SI: 1 mil = 0.0254 mm, 1 inch = 25.4 mm, 1 foot = 304.8 mm, 1 pound-force = 4.448 N.

FIGURE R611.9(10)
WOOD FRAMED ROOF TO TOP OF CONCRETE WALL FRAMING PARALLEL

TABLE R611.9(11)
COLD-FORMED STEEL ROOF TO TOP OF CONCRETE WALL, FRAMING PERPENDICULAR[a, b, c, d, e]

ANCHOR BOLT SPACING (inches)	TENSION TIE SPACING (inches)	BASIC WIND SPEED (mph) AND WIND EXPOSURE CATEGORY					
		85B	90B	100B	110B	120B	130B
				85C	90C	100C	110C
					85D	90D	100D
12	12						
12	24						
16	16					6	6
16	32					6	6
19.2	19.2				6	6	8 B
19.2	38.4				6	6	8 B
24	24			6	6	8 B	

For SI: 1 inch = 25.4 mm; 1 mile per hour = 0.447 m/s.

a. This table is for use with the detail in Figure R611.9(11). Use of this detail is permitted where a cell is not shaded, prohibited where shaded.

b. Wall design per other provisions of Section R611 is required.

c. For wind design, minimum 4-inch nominal wall is permitted in unshaded cells with no number.

d. Numbers 6 and 8 indicate minimum permitted nominal wall thickness in inches necessary to develop required strength (capacity) of connection. As a minimum, this nominal thickness shall occur in the portion of the wall indicated by the cross-hatching in Figure R611.9(11). For the remainder of the wall, see Note b.

e. Letter "B" indicates that a $^5/_8$ inch diameter anchor bolt and a minimum nominal 3 × 6 sill plate are required.

TABLE R611.9(12)
COLD-FORMED STEEL ROOF TO TOP OF CONCRETE WALL, FRAMING PARALLEL[a, b, c, d, e]

ANCHOR BOLT SPACING (inches)	TENSION TIE SPACING (inches)	BASIC WIND SPEED (mph) AND WIND EXPOSURE CATEGORY					
		85B	90B	100B	110B	120B	130B
				85C	90C	100C	110C
					85D	90D	100D
12	12						
12	24						
16	16						
16	32						
19.2	19.2					6	6
19.2	38.4					6	6
24	24			6	6	8 B	8 B

For SI: 1 inch = 25.4 mm; 1 mile per hour = 0.447 m/s.

a. This table is for use with the detail in Figure R611.9(12). Use of this detail is permitted where a cell is not shaded.

b. Wall design per other provisions of Section R611 is required.

c. For wind design, minimum 4-inch nominal wall is permitted in cells with no number.

d. Numbers 6 and 8 indicate minimum permitted nominal wall thickness in inches necessary to develop required strength (capacity) of connection. As a minimum, this nominal thickness shall occur in the portion of the wall indicated by the cross-hatching in Figure R611.9(12). For the remainder of the wall, see Note b.

e. Letter"B" indicates that a $^5/_8$ inch diameter anchor bolt is required.

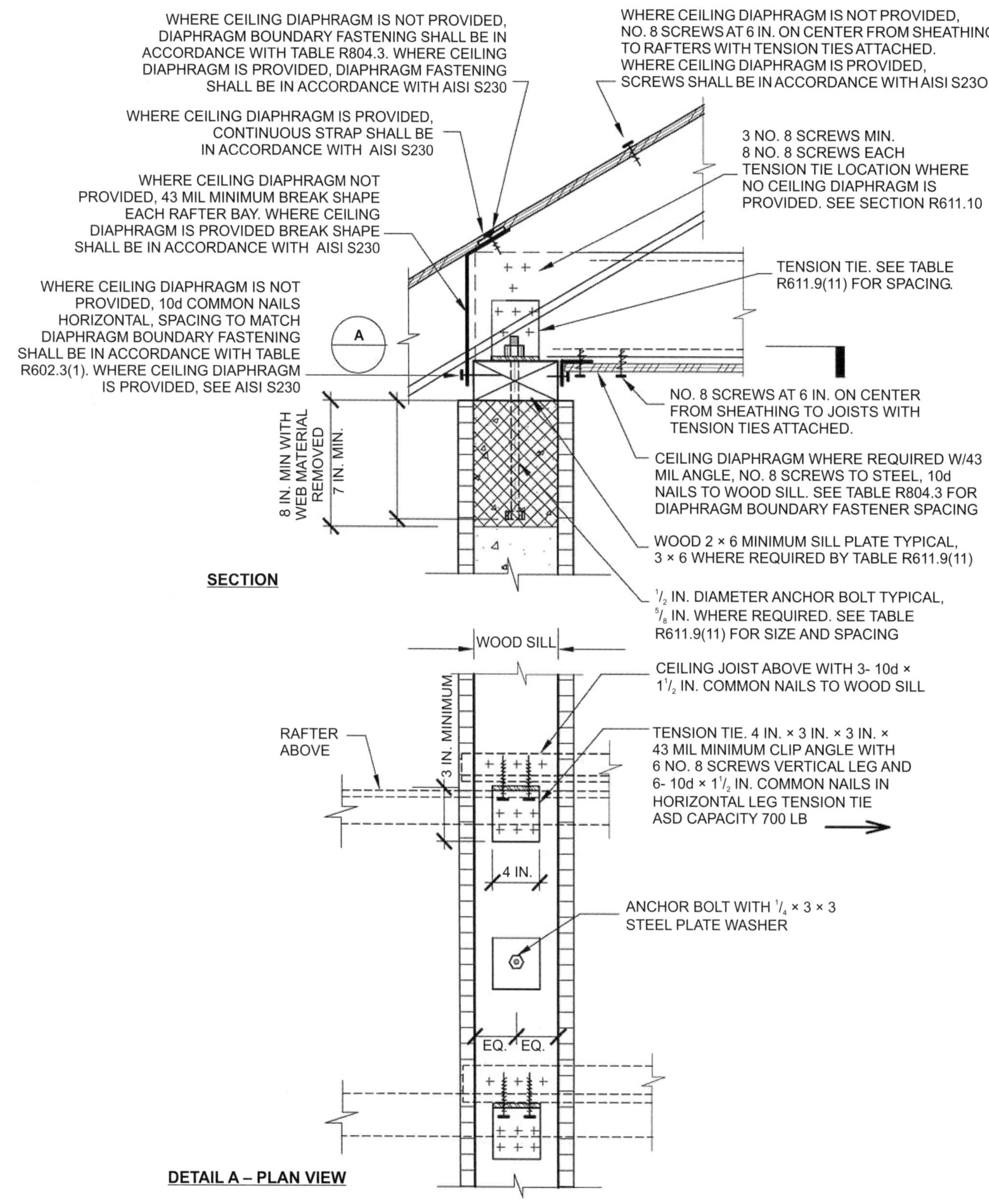

For SI: 1 mil = 0.0254 mm, 1 inch = 25.4 mm, 1 pound-force = 4.448 N.

FIGURE R611.9(11)
COLD-FORMED STEEL ROOF TO TOP OF CONCRETE WALL, FRAMING PERPENDICULAR

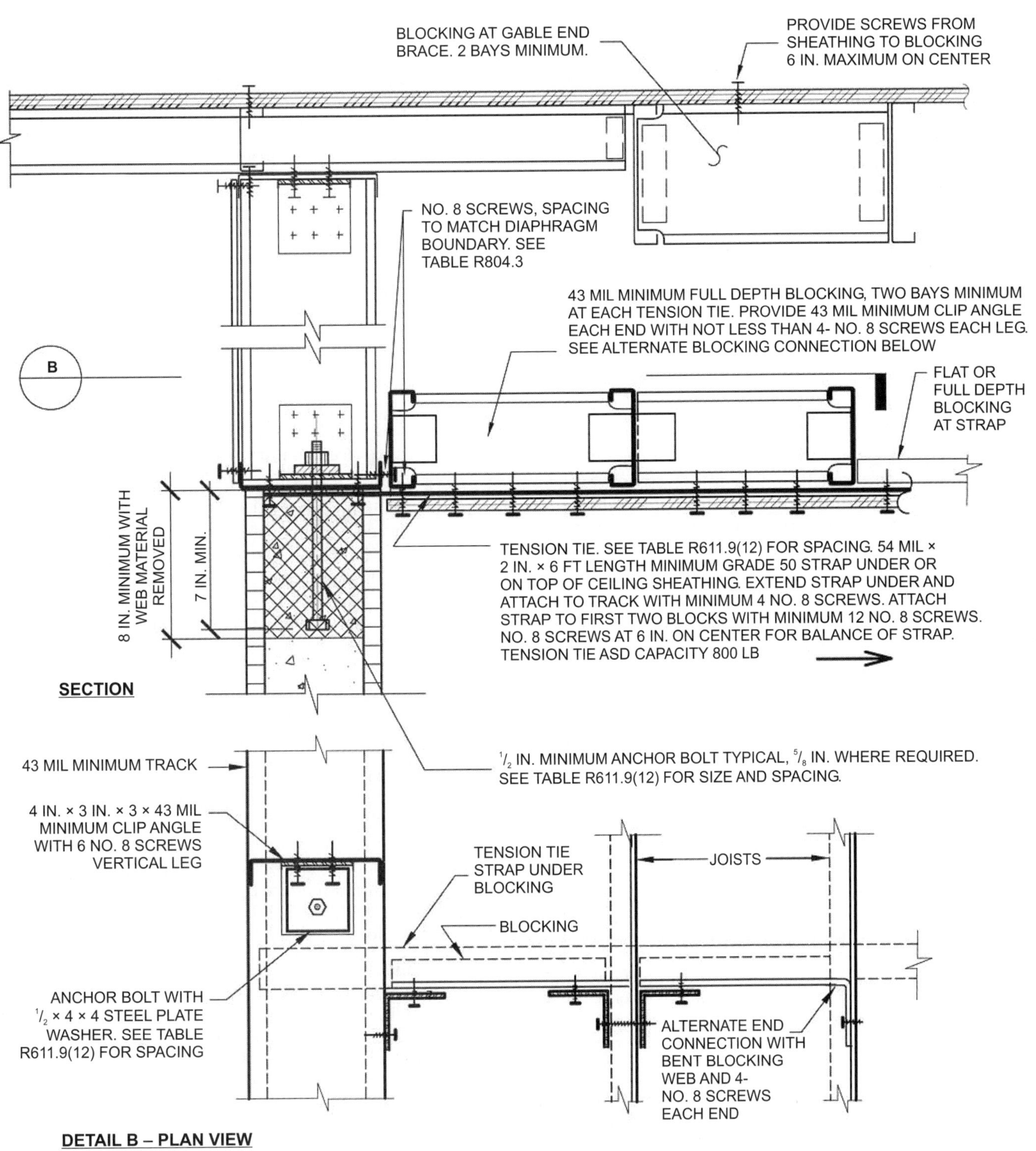

For SI: 1 mil = 0.0254 mm, 1 inch = 25.4 mm, 1 foot = 304.8 mm, 1 pound-force = 4.448 N.

FIGURE R611.9(12)
COLD-FORMED STEEL ROOF TO TOP OF CONCRETE WALL, FRAMING PARALLEL

R611.9.1.2 Removal of stay-in-place form material at bolts. Holes in stay-in-place forms for installing bolts for attaching face-mounted wood ledger boards to the wall shall be a minimum of 4 inches (102 mm) in diameter for forms not greater than $1^1/_2$ inches (38 mm) in thickness, and increased 1 inch (25 mm) in diameter for each $^1/_2$-inch (13 mm) increase in form thickness. Holes in stay-in-place forms for installing bolts for attaching face-mounted cold-formed steel tracks to the wall shall be a minimum of 4 inches (102 mm) square. The wood ledger board or steel track shall be in direct contact with the concrete at each bolt location.

Exception: A vapor retarder or other material less than or equal to $^1/_{16}$-inch (1.6 mm) in thickness is permitted to be installed between the wood ledger or cold-formed track and the concrete.

R611.9.2 Connections between concrete walls and light-framed floor systems. Connections between concrete walls and light-framed floor systems shall be in accordance with one of the following:

1. For floor systems of wood frame construction, the provisions of Section R611.9.1 and the prescriptive details of Figures R611.9(1) through R611.9(4), where permitted by the tables accompanying those figures. Portions of connections of wood-framed floor systems not noted in the figures shall be in accordance with Section R502, or AF&PA/WFCM, if applicable.
2. For floor systems of cold-formed steel construction, the provisions of Section R611.9.1 and the prescriptive details of Figures R611.9(5) through R611.9(8), where permitted by the tables accompanying those figures. Portions of connections of cold-formed-steel framed floor systems not noted in the figures shall be in accordance with Section R505, or AISI S230, if applicable.
3. Proprietary connectors selected to resist loads and load combinations in accordance with Appendix A (ASD) or Appendix B (LRFD) of PCA 100.
4. An engineered design using loads and load combinations in accordance with Appendix A (ASD) or Appendix B (LRFD) of PCA 100.
5. An engineered design using loads and material design provisions in accordance with this code, or in accordance with ASCE 7, ACI 318, and AF&PA/NDS for wood frame construction or AISI S100 for cold-formed steel frame construction.

R611.9.3 Connections between concrete walls and light-framed ceiling and roof systems. Connections between concrete walls and light-framed ceiling and roof systems shall be in accordance with one of the following:

1. For ceiling and roof systems of wood frame construction, the provisions of Section R611.9.1 and the prescriptive details of Figures R611.9(9) and R611.9(10), where permitted by the tables accompanying those figures. Portions of connections of wood-framed ceiling and roof systems not noted in the figures shall be in accordance with Section R802, or AF&PA/WFCM, if applicable.
2. For ceiling and roof systems of cold-formed-steel construction, the provisions of Section R611.9.1 and the prescriptive details of Figures R611.9(11) and R611.9(12), where permitted by the tables accompanying those figures. Portions of connections of cold-formed-steel framed ceiling and roof systems not noted in the figures shall be in accordance with Section R804, or AISI S230, if applicable.
3. Proprietary connectors selected to resist loads and load combinations in accordance with Appendix A (ASD) or Appendix B (LRFD) of PCA 100.
4. An engineered design using loads and load combinations in accordance with Appendix A (ASD) or Appendix B (LRFD) of PCA 100.
5. An engineered design using loads and material design provisions in accordance with this code, or in accordance with ASCE 7, ACI 318, and AF&PA/NDS for wood-frame construction or AISI S100 for cold-formed-steel frame construction.

R611.10 Floor, roof and ceiling diaphragms. Floors and roofs in all buildings with exterior walls of concrete shall be designed and constructed as *diaphragms*. Where gable-end walls occur, ceilings shall also be designed and constructed as *diaphragms*. The design and construction of floors, roofs and ceilings of wood framing or cold-formed-steel framing serving as *diaphragms* shall comply with the applicable requirements of this code, or AF&PA/WFCM or AISI S230, if applicable.

SECTION R612
EXTERIOR WINDOWS AND DOORS

R612.1 General. This section prescribes performance and construction requirements for exterior windows and doors installed in walls. Windows and doors shall be installed and flashed in accordance with the fenestration manufacturer's written installation instructions. Window and door openings shall be flashed in accordance with Section R703.8. Written installation instructions shall be provided by the fenestration manufacturer for each window or door.

R612.2 Window sills. In *dwelling* units, where the opening of an operable window is located more than 72 inches (1829 mm) above the finished *grade* or surface below, the lowest part of the clear opening of the window shall be a minimum of 24 inches (610 mm) above the finished floor of the room in which the window is located. Operable sections of windows shall not permit openings that allow passage of a 4 inch (102 mm) diameter sphere where such openings are located within 24 inches (610 mm) of the finished floor.

Exceptions:

1. Windows whose openings will not allow a 4-inch-diameter (102 mm) sphere to pass through the opening when the opening is in its largest opened position.
2. Openings that are provided with window fall prevention devices that comply with Section R612.3.

3. Openings that are provided with fall prevention devices that comply with ASTM F 2090.
4. Windows that are provided with opening limiting devices that comply with Section R612.4.

R612.3 Window fall prevention devices. Window fall prevention devices and window guards, where provided, shall comply with the requirements of ASTM F 2090.

R612.4 Window opening limiting devices. When required elsewhere in this code, window opening limiting devices shall comply with the provisions of this section.

R612.4.1 General requirements. Window opening limiting devices shall be self acting and shall be positioned to prohibit the free passage of a 4-in. (102-mm) diameter rigid sphere through the window opening when the window opening limiting device is installed in accordance with the manufacturer's instructions.

R612.4.2 Operation for emergency escape. Window opening limiting devices shall be designed with release mechanisms to allow for emergency escape through the window opening without the need for keys, tools or special knowledge. Window opening limiting devices shall comply with all of the following:

1. Release of the window opening-limiting device shall require no more than 15 pounds (66 N) of force.
2. The window opening limiting device release mechanism shall operate properly in all types of weather.
3. Window opening limiting devices shall have their release mechanisms clearly identified for proper use in an emergency.
4. The window opening limiting device shall not reduce the minimum net clear opening area of the window unit below what is required by Section R310.1.1 of the code.

R612.5 Performance. Exterior windows and doors shall be designed to resist the design wind loads specified in Table R301.2(2) adjusted for height and exposure per Table R301.2(3).

R612.6 Testing and labeling. Exterior windows and sliding doors shall be tested by an *approved* independent laboratory, and bear a *label* identifying manufacturer, performance characteristics and *approved* inspection agency to indicate compliance with AAMA/WDMA/CSA 101/I.S.2/A440. Exterior side-hinged doors shall be tested and *labeled* as conforming to AAMA/WDMA/CSA 101/I.S.2/A440 or comply with Section R612.8.

Exception: Decorative glazed openings.

R612.6.1 Comparative analysis. Structural wind load design pressures for window and door units smaller than the size tested in accordance with Section R612.6 shall be permitted to be higher than the design value of the tested unit provided such higher pressures are determined by accepted engineering analysis. All components of the small unit shall be the same as those of the tested unit. Where such calculated design pressures are used, they shall be validated by an additional test of the window or door unit having the highest allowable design pressure.

R612.7 Vehicular access doors. Vehicular access doors shall be tested in accordance with either ASTM E 330 or ANSI/DASMA 108, and shall meet the acceptance criteria of ANSI/DASMA 108.

R612.8 Other exterior window and door assemblies. Exterior windows and door assemblies not included within the scope of Section R612.6 or Section R612.7 shall be tested in accordance with ASTM E 330. Glass in assemblies covered by this exception shall comply with Section R308.5.

R612.9 Wind-borne debris protection. Protection of exterior windows and glass doors in buildings located in wind-borne debris regions shall be in accordance with Section R301.2.1.2.

R612.9.1 Fenestration testing and labeling. Fenestration shall be tested by an *approved* independent laboratory, listed by an *approved* entity, and bear a *label* identifying manufacturer, performance characteristics, and *approved* inspection agency to indicate compliance with the requirements of the following specification:

1. ASTM E 1886 and ASTM E 1996; or
2. AAMA 506.

R612.10 Anchorage methods. The methods cited in this section apply only to anchorage of window and glass door assemblies to the main force-resisting system.

R612.10.1 Anchoring requirements. Window and glass door assemblies shall be anchored in accordance with the published manufacturer's recommendations to achieve the design pressure specified. Substitute anchoring systems used for substrates not specified by the fenestration manufacturer shall provide equal or greater anchoring performance as demonstrated by accepted engineering practice.

R612.10.2 Anchorage details. Products shall be anchored in accordance with the minimum requirements illustrated in Figures R612.8(1), R612.8(2), R612.8(3), R612.8(4), R612.8(5), R612.8(6), R612.8(7) and R612.8(8).

R612.10.2.1 Masonry, concrete or other structural substrate. Where the wood shim or buck thickness is less than $1^1/_2$ inches (38 mm), window and glass door assemblies shall be anchored through the jamb, or by jamb clip and anchors shall be embedded directly into the masonry, concrete or other substantial substrate material. Anchors shall adequately transfer load from the window or door frame into the rough opening substrate [see Figures R612.8(1) and R612.8(2).]

Where the wood shim or buck thickness is $1^1/_2$ inches (38 mm) or more, the buck is securely fastened to the masonry, concrete or other substantial substrate, and the buck extends beyond the interior face of the window or door frame, window and glass door assemblies shall be anchored through the jamb, or by jamb clip, or through the flange to the secured wood buck. Anchors shall be embedded into the secured wood buck to adequately transfer load from the window or door frame assembly [Figures R612.8(3), R612.8(4) and R612.8(5)].

R612.10.2.2 Wood or other approved framing material. Where the framing material is wood or other *approved* framing material, window and glass door assemblies shall be anchored through the frame, or by frame clip, or through the flange. Anchors shall be embedded into the frame construction to adequately transfer load [Figures R612.8(6), R612.8(7) and R612.8(8)].

R612.11 Mullions. Mullions shall be tested by an *approved* testing laboratory in accordance with AAMA 450, or be engineered in accordance with accepted engineering practice. Mullions tested as stand-alone units or qualified by engineering shall use performance criteria cited in Sections R612.11.1, R612.11.2 and R612.11.3. Mullions qualified by an actual test of an entire assembly shall comply with Sections R612.11.1 and R612.11.3.

R612.11.1 Load transfer. Mullions shall be designed to transfer the design pressure loads applied by the window and door assemblies to the rough opening substrate.

R612.11.2 Deflection. Mullions shall be capable of resisting the design pressure loads applied by the window and door assemblies to be supported without deflecting more than *L*/175, where *L* is the span of the mullion in inches.

R612.11.3 Structural safety factor. Mullions shall be capable of resisting a load of 1.5 times the design pressure loads applied by the window and door assemblies to be supported without exceeding the appropriate material stress levels. If tested by an *approved* laboratory, the 1.5 times the design pressure load shall be sustained for 10 seconds, and the permanent deformation shall not exceed 0.4 percent of the mullion span after the 1.5 times design pressure load is removed.

SECTION R613 STRUCTURAL INSULATED PANEL WALL CONSTRUCTION

R613.1 General. Structural insulated panel (SIP) walls shall be designed in accordance with the provisions of this section. When the provisions of this section are used to design structural insulated panel walls, project drawings, typical details and specifications are not required to bear the seal of the architect or engineer responsible for design, unless otherwise required by the state law of the *jurisdiction* having authority.

R613.2 Applicability limits. The provisions of this section shall control the construction of exterior structural insulated panel walls and interior load-bearing structural insulated panel walls for buildings not greater than 60 feet (18 288 mm) in length perpendicular to the joist or truss span, not greater than 40 feet (12 192 mm) in width parallel to the joist or truss span and not greater than two stories in height with each wall not greater than 10 feet (3048 mm) high. All exterior walls installed in accordance with the provisions of this section shall be considered as load-bearing walls. Structural insulated panel walls constructed in accordance with the provisions of this section shall be limited to sites subjected to a maximum design wind speed of 130 miles per hour (58 m/s), Exposure A, B or C, and a maximum ground snow load of 70 pounds per foot (3.35 kPa), and Seismic Design Categories A, B, and C.

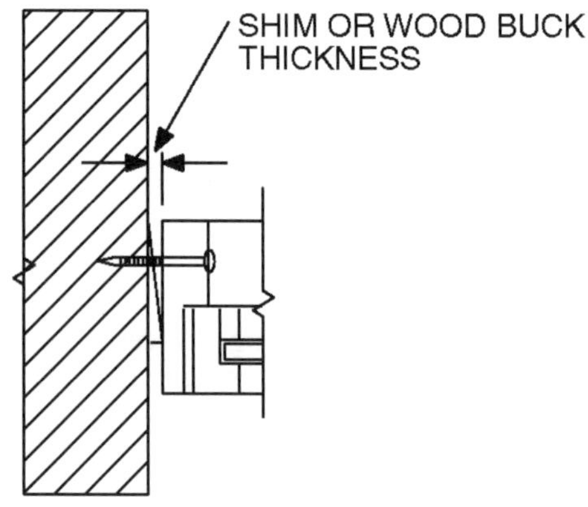

FIGURE R612.8(1)
THROUGH THE FRAME

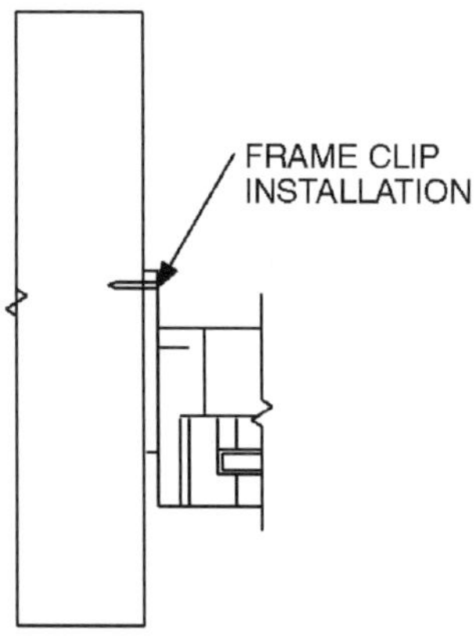

APPLY FRAME CLIP TO WINDOW OR DOOR IN ACCORDANCE WITH PUBLISHED MANUFACTURER'S RECOMMENDATIONS.

FIGURE R612.8(2)
FRAME CLIP

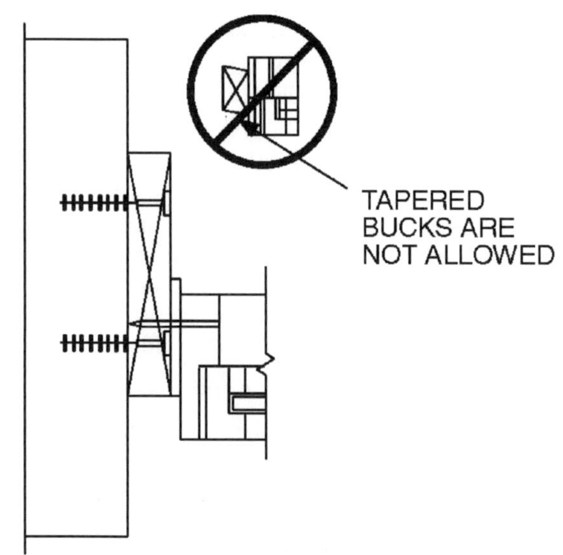

THROUGH THE FRAME ANCHORING METHOD. ANCHORS SHALL BE PROVIDED TO TRANSFER LOAD FROM THE WINDOW OR DOOR FRAME INTO THE ROUGH OPENING SUBSTRATE.

FIGURE R612.8(3)
THROUGH THE FRAME

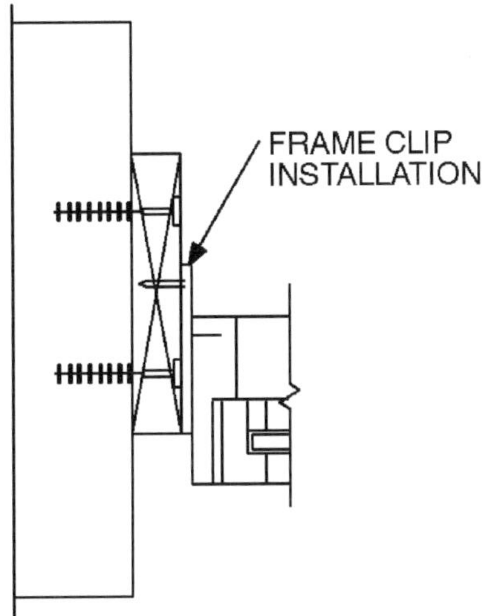

APPLY FRAME CLIP TO WINDOW OR DOOR FRAME IN ACCORDANCE WITH PUBLISHED MANUFACTURER'S RECOMMENDATIONS. ANCHORS SHALL BE PROVIDED TO TRANSFER LOAD FROM THE FRAME CLIP INTO THE ROUGH OPENING SUBSTRATE.

FIGURE R612.8(4)
FRAME CLIP

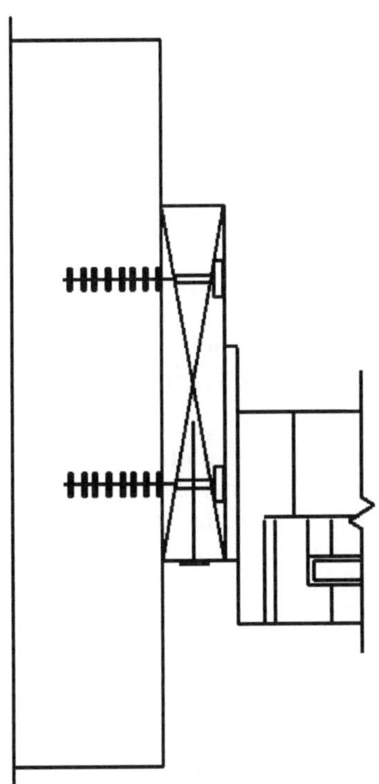

APPLY ANCHORS THROUGH FLANGE IN ACCORDANCE WITH PUBLISHED MANUFACTURER'S RECOMMENDATIONS.

FIGURE R612.8(5)
THROUGH THE FLANGE

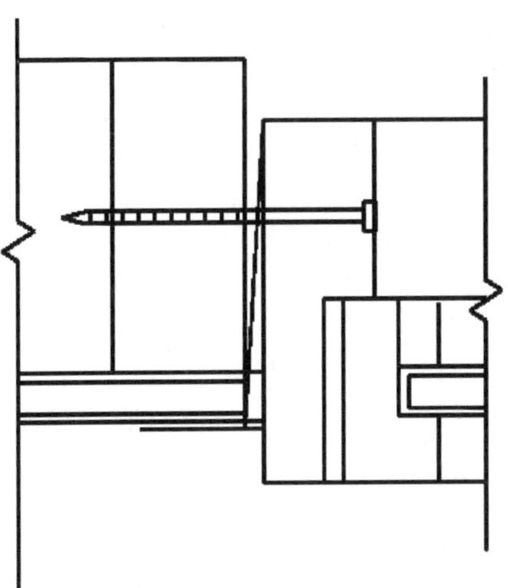

FIGURE R612.8(6)
THROUGH THE FLANGE

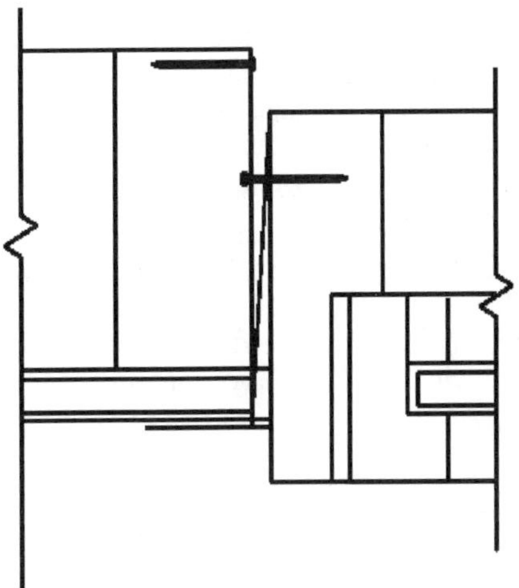

FIGURE R612.8(7)
FRAME CLIP

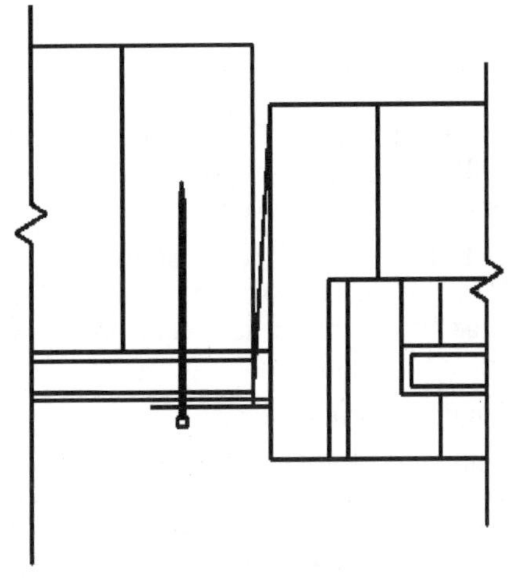

FIGURE R612.8(8)
THROUGH THE FLANGE

R613.3 Materials. SIPs shall comply with the following criteria:

R613.3.1 Core. The core material shall be composed of foam plastic insulation meeting one of the following requirements:

1. ASTM C 578 and have a minimum density of 0.90 pounds per cubic feet (14.4 kg/m^3); or
2. Polyurethane meeting the physical properties shown in Table R613.3.1, or;
3. An *approved* alternative.

All cores shall meet the requirements of Section R316.

R613.3.2 Facing. Facing materials for SIPs shall be wood structural panels conforming to DOC PS 1 or DOC PS 2, each having a minimum nominal thickness of $^7/_{16}$ inch (11 mm) and shall meet the additional minimum properties specified in Table R613.3.2. Facing shall be identified by a grade mark or certificate of inspection issued by an *approved* agency.

R613.3.3 Adhesive. Adhesives used to structurally laminate the foam plastic insulation core material to the structural wood facers shall conform to ASTM D 2559 or *approved* alternative specifically intended for use as an adhesive used in the lamination of structural insulated panels. Each container of adhesive shall bear a *label* with the adhesive manufacturer's name, adhesive name and type and the name of the quality assurance agency.

R613.3.4 Lumber. The minimum lumber framing material used for SIPs prescribed in this document is NLGA graded No. 2 Spruce-pine-fir. Substitution of other wood species/grades that meet or exceed the mechanical properties and specific gravity of No. 2 Spruce-pine-fir shall be permitted.

R613.3.5 SIP screws. Screws used for the erection of SIPs as specified in Section R613.5 shall be fabricated from steel, shall be provided by the SIPs manufacturer and shall be sized to penetrate the wood member to which the assembly is being attached by a minimum of 1 inch (25 mm). The screws shall be corrosion resistant and have a minimum shank diameter of 0.188 inch (4.7 mm) and a minimum head diameter of 0.620 inch (15.5 mm).

R613.3.6 Nails. Nails specified in Section R613 shall be common or galvanized box unless otherwise stated.

R613.4 SIP wall panels. SIPs shall comply with Figure R613.4 and shall have minimum panel thickness in accordance with Tables R613.5(1) and R613.5(2) for above-grade walls. All SIPs shall be identified by grade mark or certificate of inspection issued by an *approved* agency.

R613.4.1 Labeling. All panels shall be identified by grade mark or certificate of inspection issued by an *approved* agency. Each (SIP) shall bear a stamp or *label* with the following minimum information:

1. Manufacturer name/logo.
2. Identification of the assembly.
3. Quality assurance agency.

R613.5 Wall construction. Exterior walls of SIP construction shall be designed and constructed in accordance with the provisions of this section and Tables R613.5(1) and R613.5(2) and Figures R613.5(1) through R613.5(5). SIP walls shall be fastened to other wood building components in accordance with Tables R602.3(1) through R602.3(4).

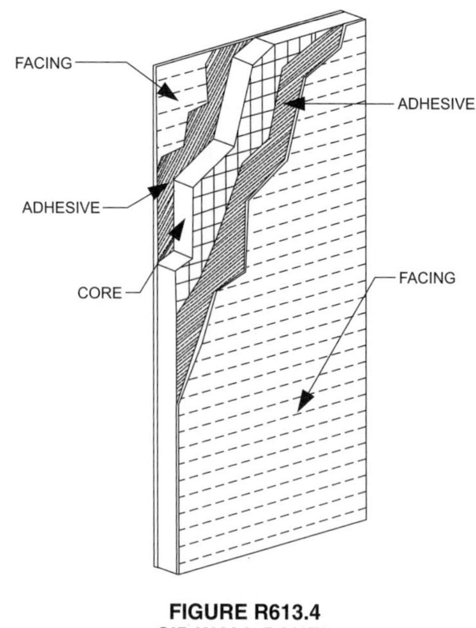

**FIGURE R613.4
SIP WALL PANEL**

Framing shall be attached in accordance with Table R602.3(1) unless otherwise provided for in Section R613.

R613.5.1 Top plate connection. SIP walls shall be capped with a double top plate installed to provide overlapping at corner, intersections and splines in accordance with Figure R613.5.1. The double top plates shall be made up of a single 2 by top plate having a width equal to the width of the panel core, and shall be recessed into the SIP below. Over this top plate a cap plate shall be placed. The cap plate width shall match the SIP thickness and overlap the facers on both sides of the panel. End joints in top plates shall be offset at least 24 inches (610 mm).

R613.5.2 Bottom (sole) plate connection. SIP walls shall have full bearing on a sole plate having a width equal to the nominal width of the foam core. When SIP walls are supported directly on continuous foundations, the wall wood sill plate shall be anchored to the foundation in accordance with Figure R613.5.2 and Section R403.1.

R613.5.3 Wall bracing. SIP walls shall be braced in accordance with Section R602.10. SIP walls shall be considered continuous wood structural panel sheathing for purposes of computing required bracing. SIP walls shall meet the requirements of Section R602.10.4 except that SIPs corners shall be fabricated as shown in Figure R613.9. When SIP walls are used for wall bracing, the SIP bottom plate shall be attached to wood framing below in accordance with Table R602.3(1).

R613.6 Interior load-bearing walls. Interior load-bearing walls shall be constructed as specified for exterior walls.

R613.7 Drilling and notching. The maximum vertical chase penetration in SIPs shall have a maximum side dimension of 2 inches (51 mm) centered in the panel core. Vertical chases shall have a minimum spacing of 24-inches (610 mm) on center. Maximum of two horizontal chases shall be permitted in each wall panel, one at 14 inches (360 mm) from the bottom of the panel and one at mid-height of the wall panel. The maximum allowable penetration size in a wall panel shall be circular or rectangular with a maximum dimension of 12 inches (305 mm). Overcutting of holes in facing panels shall not be permitted.

R613.8 Connection. SIPs shall be connected at vertical in-plane joints in accordance with Figure R613.8 or by other *approved* methods.

R613.9 Corner framing. Corner framing of SIP walls shall be constructed in accordance with Figure R613.9.

R613.10 Headers. SIP headers shall be designed and constructed in accordance with Table R613.10 and Figure R613.5.1. SIPs headers shall be continuous sections without splines. Headers shall be at least $11^7/_8$ inches (302 mm) deep. Headers longer than 4 feet (1219 mm) shall be constructed in accordance with Section R602.7.

R613.10.1 Wood structural panel box headers. Wood structural panel box headers shall be allowed where SIP headers are not applicable. Wood structural panel box headers shall be constructed in accordance with Figure R602.7.2 and Table R602.7.2.

TABLE R613.3.1
MINIMUM PROPERTIES FOR POLYURETHANE INSULATION USED AS SIPS CORE

PHYSICAL PROPERTY	POLYURETHANE
Density, core nominal. (ASTM D 1622)	2.2 lb/ft^3
Compressive resistance at yield or 10% deformation, whichever occurs first. (ASTM D 1621)	19 psi (perpendicular to rise)
Flexural strength, min. (ASTM C 203)	30 psi
Tensile strength, min. (ASTM D 1623)	35 psi
Shear strength, min. (ASTM C 273)	25 psi
Substrate adhesion, min. (ASTM D 1623)	22 psi
Water vapor permeance of 1.00-in. thickness, max. (ASTM E 96)	2.3 perm
Water absorption by total immersion, max. (ASTM C 272)	4.3% (volume)
Dimensional stability (change in dimensions), max. [ASTM D2126 (7 days at 158°F/100% humidity and 7 days at -20°F)]	2%

For SI: 1 pound per cubic foot = 16.02 kg/m^3, 1 pound per square inch = 6.895 kPa, °C = [(°F) - 32]1.8.

TABLE R613.3.2
MINIMUM PROPERTIES[a] FOR WOOD STRUCTURAL PANEL FACING MATERIAL USED IN SIP WALLS

THICKNESS (inch)	PRODUCT	FLATWISE STIFFNESS[b] (lbf-in^2/ft)		FLATWISE STRENGTH[c] (lbf-in/ft)		TENSION[c] (lbf/ft)		DENSITY[b, d] (pcf)
		Along	Across	Along	Across	Along	Across	
$^7/_{16}$	Sheathing	54,700	27,100	950	870	6,800	6,500	35

For SI: 1 inch = 25.4 mm, 1 lbf-in^2/ft = 9.415 × 10^{-6} kPa/m, 1 lbf-in/ft = 3.707 × 10^{-4} kN/m, 1 lbf/ft = 0.0146 N/mm, 1 pound per cubic foot = 16.018 kg/m^3.

a. Values listed in Table R613.3.2 are qualification test values and are not to be used for design purposes.

b. Mean test value shall be in accordance with Section 7.6 of DOC PS 2.

c. Characteristic test value (5th percent with 75% confidence).

d. Density shall be based on oven-dry weight and oven-dry volume.

TABLE R613.5(1)
MINIMUM THICKNESS FOR SIP WALL SUPPORTING SIP LIGHT-FRAME ROOF ONLY (inches)

WIND SPEED (3-second gust)			BUILDING WIDTH (feet)														
			24			28			32			36			40		
			Wall Height (ft)			Wall Height (ft)			Wall Height (ft)			Wall Height (ft)			Wall Height (ft)		
Exp. A/B	Exp. C	SNOW LOAD (psf)	8	9	10	8	9	10	8	9	10	8	9	10	8	9	10
85	—	20	4.5	4.5	4.5	4.5	4.5	4.5	4.5	4.5	4.5	4.5	4.5	4.5	4.5	4.5	4.5
		30	4.5	4.5	4.5	4.5	4.5	4.5	4.5	4.5	4.5	4.5	4.5	4.5	4.5	4.5	4.5
		50	4.5	4.5	4.5	4.5	4.5	4.5	4.5	4.5	4.5	4.5	4.5	4.5	4.5	4.5	4.5
		70	4.5	4.5	4.5	4.5	4.5	4.5	4.5	4.5	4.5	4.5	4.5	4.5	4.5	4.5	4.5
100	85	20	4.5	4.5	4.5	4.5	4.5	4.5	4.5	4.5	4.5	4.5	4.5	4.5	4.5	4.5	4.5
		30	4.5	4.5	4.5	4.5	4.5	4.5	4.5	4.5	4.5	4.5	4.5	4.5	4.5	4.5	4.5
		50	4.5	4.5	4.5	4.5	4.5	4.5	4.5	4.5	4.5	4.5	4.5	4.5	4.5	4.5	4.5
		70	4.5	4.5	4.5	4.5	4.5	4.5	4.5	4.5	4.5	4.5	4.5	4.5	4.5	4.5	4.5
110	100	20	4.5	4.5	4.5	4.5	4.5	4.5	4.5	4.5	4.5	4.5	4.5	4.5	4.5	4.5	4.5
		30	4.5	4.5	4.5	4.5	4.5	4.5	4.5	4.5	4.5	4.5	4.5	4.5	4.5	4.5	4.5
		50	4.5	4.5	4.5	4.5	4.5	4.5	4.5	4.5	4.5	4.5	4.5	4.5	4.5	4.5	4.5
		70	4.5	4.5	4.5	4.5	4.5	4.5	4.5	4.5	4.5	4.5	4.5	4.5	4.5	4.5	4.5
120	110	20	4.5	4.5	4.5	4.5	4.5	4.5	4.5	4.5	4.5	4.5	4.5	4.5	4.5	4.5	4.5
		30	4.5	4.5	4.5	4.5	4.5	4.5	4.5	4.5	4.5	4.5	4.5	4.5	4.5	4.5	4.5
		50	4.5	4.5	4.5	4.5	4.5	4.5	4.5	4.5	4.5	4.5	4.5	4.5	4.5	4.5	4.5
		70	4.5	4.5	4.5	4.5	4.5	4.5	4.5	4.5	4.5	4.5	4.5	6.5	4.5	4.5	6.5
130	120	20	4.5	4.5	4.5	4.5	4.5	4.5	4.5	4.5	4.5	4.5	4.5	4.5	4.5	4.5	4.5
		30	4.5	4.5	4.5	4.5	4.5	4.5	4.5	4.5	4.5	4.5	4.5	4.5	4.5	4.5	4.5
		50	4.5	4.5	4.5	4.5	4.5	4.5	4.5	4.5	6.5	4.5	4.5	6.5	4.5	4.5	6.5
		70	4.5	4.5	4.5	4.5	4.5	6.5	4.5	4.5	6.5	4.5	6.5	N/A	4.5	6.5	N/A
—	130	20	4.5	4.5	6.5	4.5	4.5	N/A	4.5	4.5	N/A	4.5	4.5	N/A	4.5	6.5	N/A
		30	4.5	4.5	N/A	4.5	4.5	N/A	4.5	4.5	N/A	4.5	6.5	N/A	4.5	6.5	N/A
		50	4.5	6.5	N/A	4.5	6.5	N/A	4.5	N/A	N/A	6.5	N/A	N/A	6.5	N/A	N/A
		70	4.5	N/A	N/A	6.5	N/A	N/A	6.5	N/A	N/A	N/A	N/A	N/A	N/A	N/A	N/A

For SI: 1 inch = 25.4 mm; 1 foot = 304.8 mm; 1 pound per square foot = 0.0479 kPa.
Maximum deflection criterion: *L*/240.
Maximum roof dead load: 10 psf.
Maximum roof live load: 70 psf.
Maximum ceiling dead load: 5 psf.
Maximum ceiling live load: 20 psf.
Wind loads based on Table R301.2 (2).
N/A indicates not applicable.

TABLE R613.5(2)
MINIMUM THICKNESS FOR SIP WALLS SUPPORTING SIP OR LIGHT-FRAME ONE STORY AND ROOF (inches)

WIND SPEED (3-second gust)		SNOW LOAD (psf)	BUILDING WIDTH (feet)														
			24			28			32			36			40		
Exp. A/B	Exp. C		Wall Height (feet)			Wall Height (feet)			Wall Height (feet)			Wall Height (feet)			Wall Height (feet)		
			8	9	10	8	9	10	8	9	10	8	9	10	8	9	10
85	—	20	4.5	4.5	4.5	4.5	4.5	4.5	4.5	4.5	4.5	4.5	4.5	4.5	4.5	4.5	4.5
		30	4.5	4.5	4.5	4.5	4.5	4.5	4.5	4.5	4.5	4.5	4.5	4.5	4.5	4.5	4.5
		50	4.5	4.5	4.5	4.5	4.5	4.5	4.5	4.5	4.5	4.5	4.5	4.5	4.5	4.5	4.5
		70	4.5	4.5	4.5	4.5	4.5	4.5	4.5	4.5	4.5	4.5	4.5	6.5	6.5	6.5	6.5
100	85	20	4.5	4.5	4.5	4.5	4.5	4.5	4.5	4.5	4.5	4.5	4.5	4.5	4.5	4.5	4.5
		30	4.5	4.5	4.5	4.5	4.5	4.5	4.5	4.5	4.5	4.5	4.5	4.5	4.5	4.5	6.5
		50	4.5	4.5	4.5	4.5	4.5	4.5	4.5	4.5	4.5	4.5	4.5	6.5	4.5	6.5	6.5
		70	4.5	4.5	4.5	4.5	4.5	4.5	4.5	4.5	6.5	6.5	6.5	6.5	6.5	N/A	N/A
110	100	20	4.5	4.5	4.5	4.5	4.5	4.5	4.5	4.5	4.5	4.5	4.5	4.5	4.5	4.5	6.5
		30	4.5	4.5	4.5	4.5	4.5	4.5	4.5	4.5	4.5	4.5	4.5	6.5	4.5	6.5	6.5
		50	4.5	4.5	4.5	4.5	4.5	4.5	4.5	4.5	6.5	4.5	6.5	6.5	6.5	6.5	N/A
		70	4.5	4.5	4.5	4.5	4.5	6.5	6.5	6.5	N/A	6.5	N/A	N/A	N/A	N/A	N/A
120	110	20	4.5	4.5	4.5	4.5	4.5	4.5	4.5	4.5	6.5	4.5	4.5	6.5	4.5	6.5	N/A
		30	4.5	4.5	4.5	4.5	4.5	6.5	4.5	4.5	6.5	4.5	6.5	N/A	6.5	6.5	N/A
		50	4.5	4.5	6.5	4.5	4.5	6.5	4.5	6.5	N/A	6.5	N/A	N/A	N/A	N/A	N/A
		70	4.5	4.5	6.5	4.5	6.5	N/A	6.5	N/A	N/A	N/A	N/A	N/A	N/A	N/A	N/A
130	120	20	4.5	4.5	6.5	4.5	4.5	6.5	4.5	6.5	N/A	4.5	6.5	N/A	6.5	N/A	N/A
		30	4.5	4.5	6.5	4.5	4.5	N/A	4.5	6.5	N/A	6.5	N/A	N/A	6.5	N/A	N/A
		50	4.5	6.5	N/A	4.5	6.5	N/A	6.5	N/A	N/A	N/A	N/A	N/A	N/A	N/A	N/A
		70	4.5	6.5	N/A	6.5	N/A	N/A	N/A	N/A	N/A	N/A	N/A	N/A	N/A	N/A	N/A
—	130	20	6.5	N/A	N/A	6.5	N/A	N/A	N/A	N/A	N/A	N/A	N/A	N/A	N/A	N/A	N/A
		30	6.5	N/A	N/A	N/A	N/A	N/A	N/A	N/A	N/A	N/A	N/A	N/A	N/A	N/A	N/A
		50	N/A	N/A	N/A	N/A	N/A	N/A	N/A	N/A	N/A	N/A	N/A	N/A	N/A	N/A	N/A
		70	N/A	N/A	N/A	N/A	N/A	N/A	N/A	N/A	N/A	N/A	N/A	N/A	N/A	N/A	N/A

For SI: 1 inch = 25.4 mm; 1 foot = 304.8 mm; 1 pound per square foot = 0.0479 kPa.
Maximum deflection criterion: *L*/240.
Maximum roof dead load: 10 psf.
Maximum roof live load: 70 psf.
Maximum ceiling dead load: 5 psf.
Maximum ceiling live load: 20 psf.
Maximum second floor live load: 30 psf.
Maximum second floor dead load: 10 psf.
Maximum second floor dead load from walls: 10 psf.
Maximum first floor live load: 40 psf.
Maximum first floor dead load: 10 psf.
Wind loads based on Table R301.2 (2).
N/A indicates not applicable.

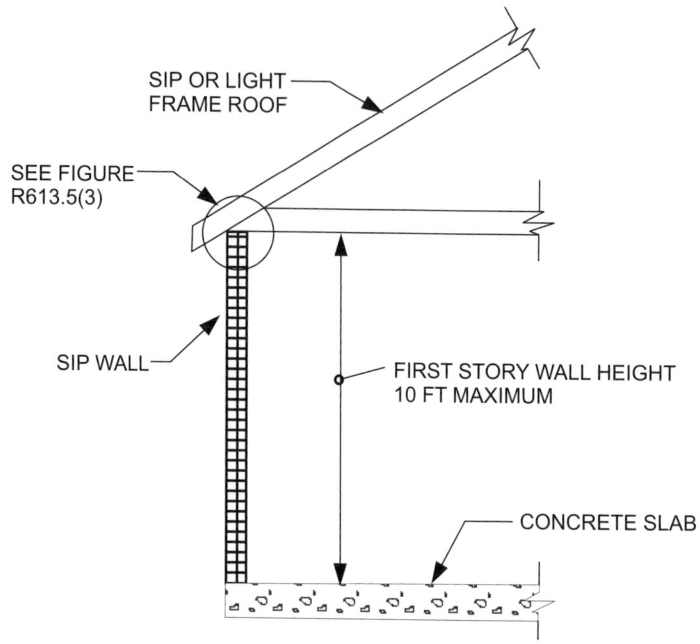

For SI: 1 foot = 304.8 mm.

FIGURE R613.5(1)
MAXIMUM ALLOWABLE HEIGHT OF SIP WALLS

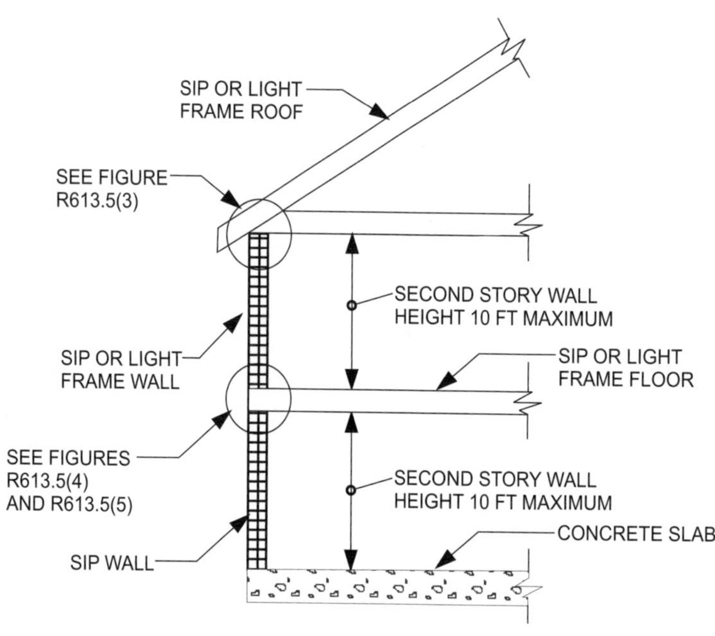

For SI: 1 foot = 304.8 mm.

FIGURE R613.5(2)
MAXIMUM ALLOWABLE HEIGHT OF SIP WALLS

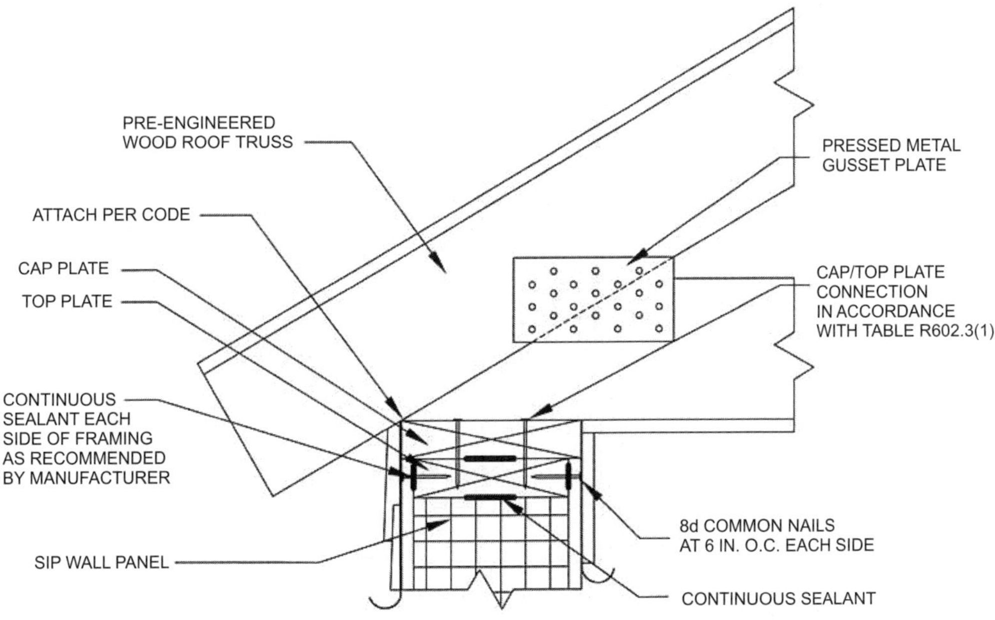

For SI: 1 inch = 25.4 mm.

FIGURE R613.5(3)
TRUSSED ROOF TO TOP PLATE CONNECTION

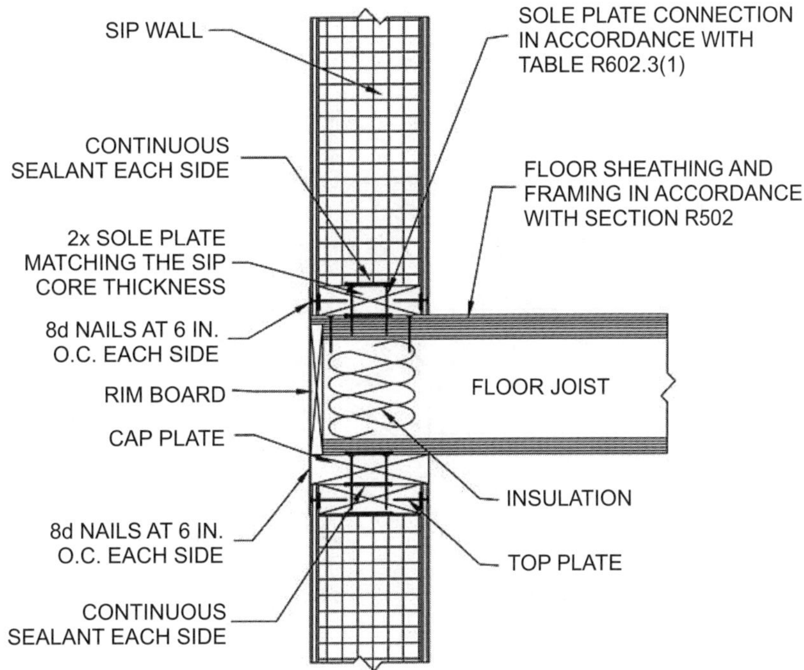

For SI: 1 inch = 25.4 mm.

Note: Figures illustrate SIP-specific attachment requirements. Other connections shall be made in accordance with Table R602.3(1) and (2) as appropriate.

FIGURE R613.5(4)
SIP WALL TO WALL PLATFORM FRAME CONNECTION

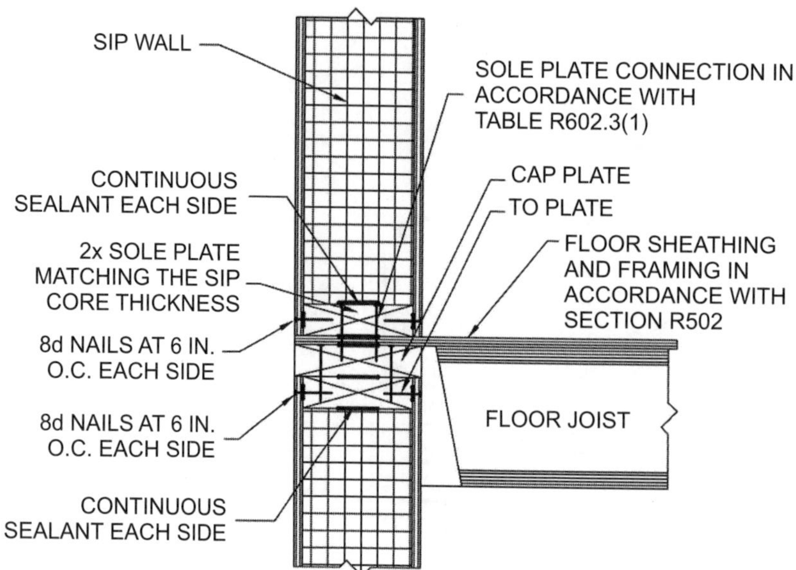

For SI: 1 inch = 25.4 mm.

Note: Figures illustrate SIP-specific attachment requirements. Other connections shall be made in accordance with Tables R602.3(1) and (2), as appropriate.

FIGURE R613.5(5)
SIP WALL TO WALL BALLOON FRAME CONNECTION
(I-Joist floor shown for Illustration only)

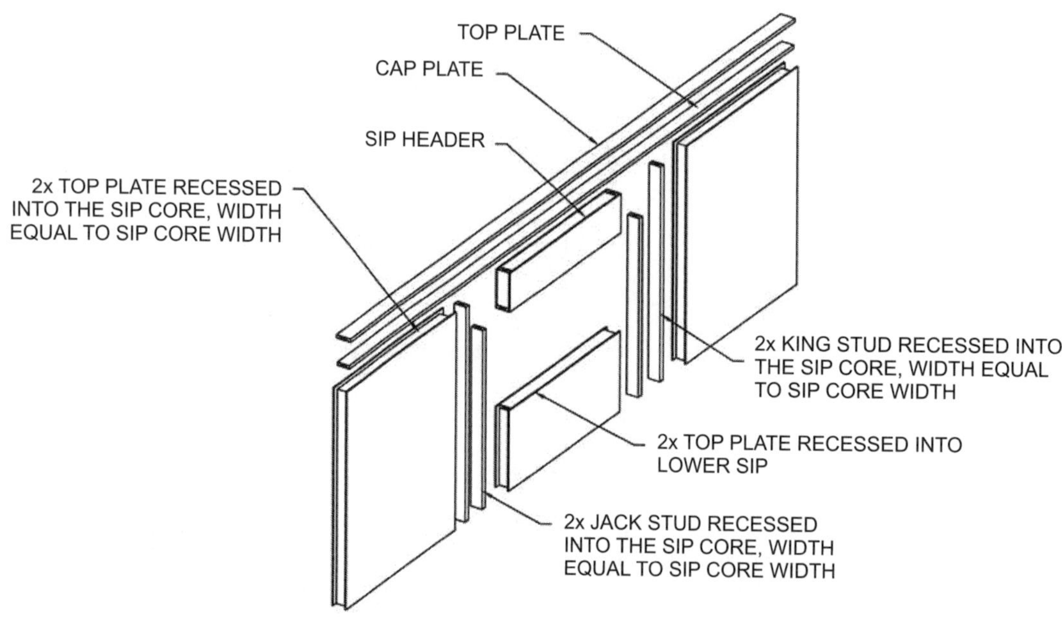

For SI: 1 inch = 25.4 mm.

Notes:

1. Top plates shall be continuous over header.
2. Lower 2x top plate shall have a width equal to the SIP core width and shall be recessed into the top edge of the panel. Cap plate shall be placed over the recessed top plate and shall have a width equal to the SIPs width.
3. SIP facing surfaces shall be nailed to framing and cripples with 8d common or galvanized box nails spaced 6 inches on center.
4. Galvanized nails shall be hot-dipped or tumbled. Framing shall be attached in accordance to Section R602.3(1) unless otherwise provide for in Section R613.

FIGURE R613.5.1
SIP WALL FRAMING CONFIGURATION

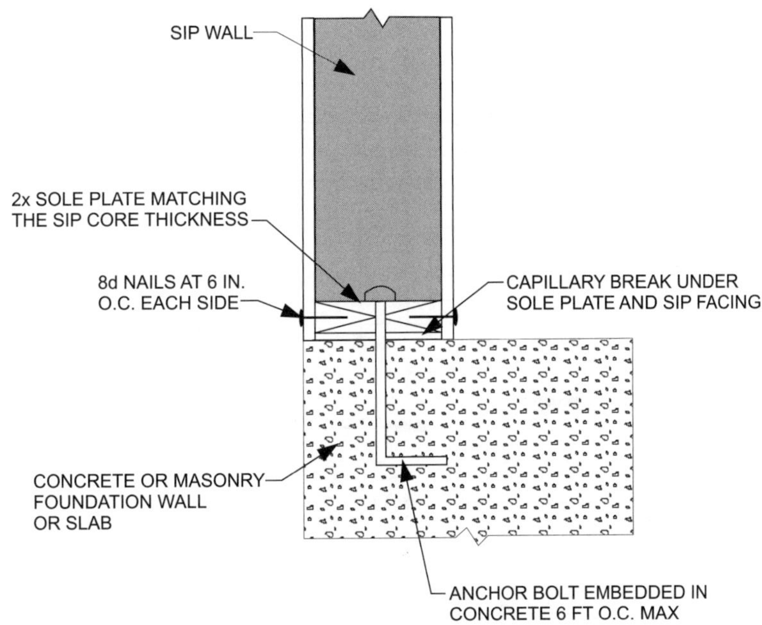

For SI: 1 inch = 25.4 mm, 1 foot = 304.8 mm.

FIGURE R613.5.2
SIP WALL TO CONCRETE SLAB FOR FOUNDATION WALL ATTACHMENT

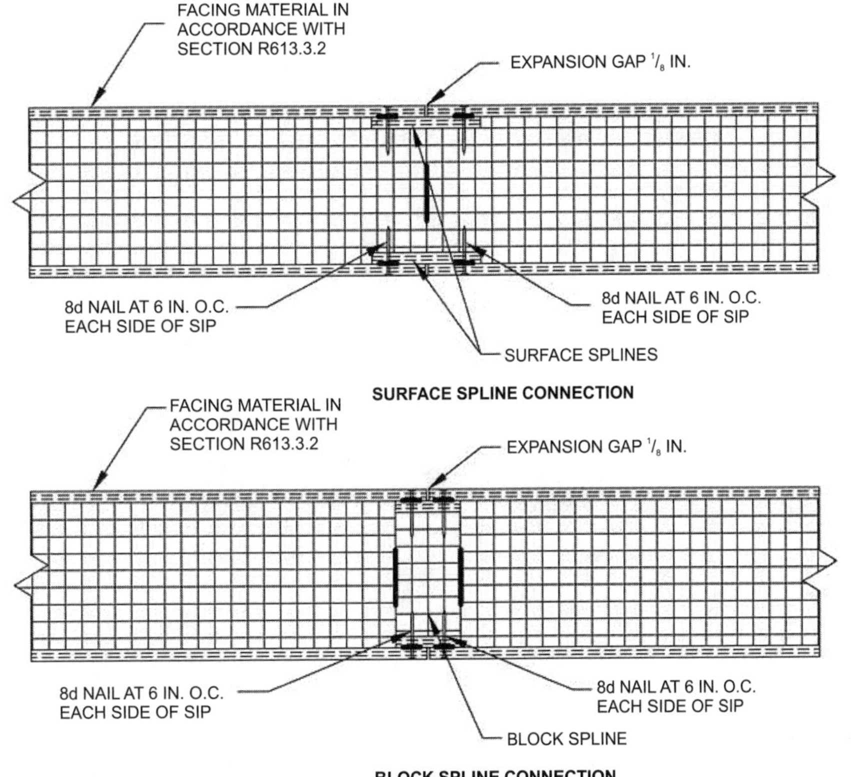

For SI: 1 inch = 25.4 mm.

FIGURE R613.8
TYPICAL SIP CONNECTION DETAILS FOR VERTICAL IN-PLANE JOINTS

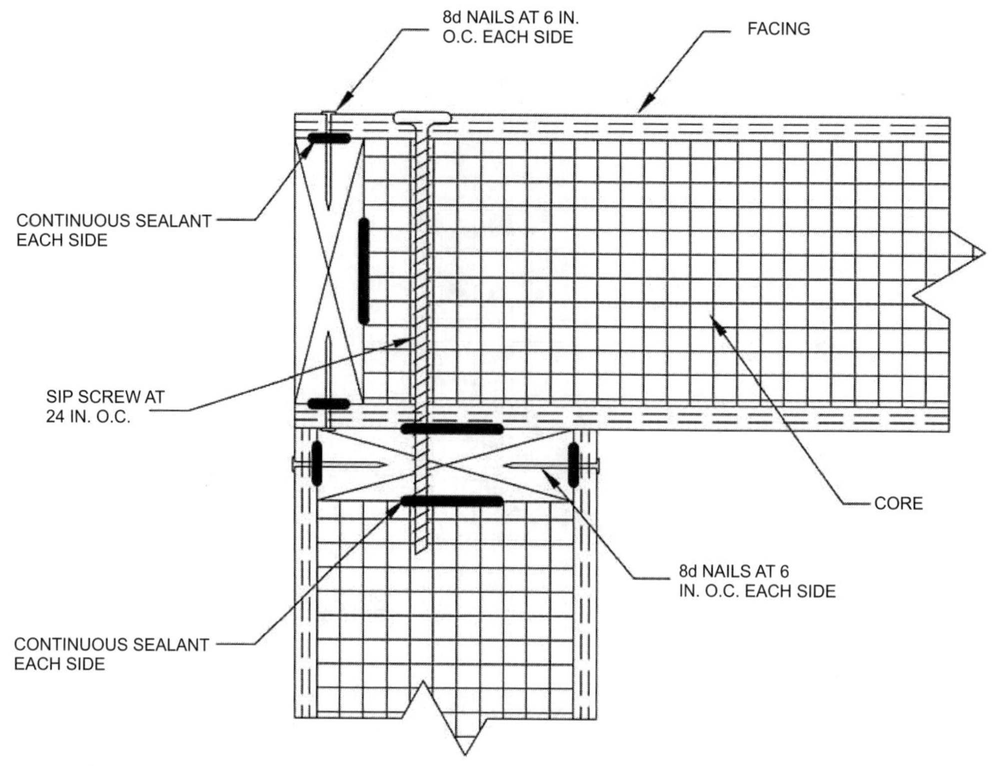

For SI: 1 inch = 25.4 mm.

FIGURE R613.9
SIP CORNER FRAMING DETAIL

TABLE R613.10
MAXIMUM SPANS FOR 11$^7/_8$ INCH DEEP SIP HEADERS (feet)

LOAD CONDITION	SNOW LOAD (psf)	BUILDING WIDTH (feet)				
		24	28	32	36	40
Supporting roof only	20	4	4	4	4	2
	30	4	4	4	2	2
	50	2	2	2	2	2
	70	2	2	2	N/A	N/A
Supporting roof and one-story	20	2	2	N/A	N/A	N/A
	30	2	2	N/A	N/A	N/A
	50	2	N/A	N/A	N/A	N/A
	70	N/A	N/A	N/A	N/A	N/A

For SI: 1 inch = 25.4 mm, 1 foot = 304.8 mm.
Maximum deflection criterion: *L*/360.
Maximum roof dead load: 10 psf.
Maximum ceiling load: 5 psf.
Maximum second floor live load: 30 psf.
Maximum second floor dead load: 10 psf.
Maximum second floor dead load from walls: 10 psf.
N/A indicates not applicable.

CHAPTER 7

WALL COVERING

SECTION R701 GENERAL

R701.1 Application. The provisions of this chapter shall control the design and construction of the interior and exterior wall covering for all buildings.

R701.2 Installation. Products sensitive to adverse weather shall not be installed until adequate weather protection for the installation is provided. Exterior sheathing shall be dry before applying exterior cover.

SECTION R702 INTERIOR COVERING

R702.1 General. Interior coverings or wall finishes shall be installed in accordance with this chapter and Table R702.1(1), Table R702.1(2), Table R702.1(3) and Table R702.3.5. Interior masonry veneer shall comply with the requirements of Section R703.7.1 for support and Section R703.7.4 for anchorage, except an air space is not required. Interior finishes and materials shall conform to the flame spread and smoke-development requirements of Section R302.9.

TABLE R702.1(1) THICKNESS OF PLASTER

PLASTER BASE	FINISHED THICKNESS OF PLASTER FROM FACE OF LATH, MASONRY, CONCRETE (inches)	
	Gypsum Plaster	Cement Plaster
Expanded metal lath	$^5/_8$, minimum[a]	$^5/_8$, minimum[a]
Wire lath	$^5/_8$, minimum[a]	$^3/_4$, minimum (interior)[b] $^7/_8$, minimum (exterior)[b]
Gypsum lath[g]	$^1/_2$, minimum	$^3/_4$, minimum (interior)[b]
Masonry walls[c]	$^1/_2$, minimum	$^1/_2$, minimum
Monolithic concrete walls[c, d]	$^5/_8$, maximum	$^7/_8$, maximum
Monolithic concrete ceilings[c, d]	$^3/_8$, maximum[e]	$^1/_2$, maximum
Gypsum veneer base[f, g]	$^1/_{16}$, minimum	$^3/_4$, minimum (interior)[b]
Gypsum sheathing[g]	—	$^3/_4$, minimum (interior)[b] $^7/_8$, minimum (exterior)[b]

For SI: 1 inch = 25.4 mm.

a. When measured from back plane of expanded metal lath, exclusive of ribs, or self-furring lath, plaster thickness shall be $^3/_4$ inch minimum.

b. When measured from face of support or backing.

c. Because masonry and concrete surfaces may vary in plane, thickness of plaster need not be uniform.

d. When applied over a liquid bonding agent, finish coat may be applied directly to concrete surface.

e. Approved acoustical plaster may be applied directly to concrete or over base coat plaster, beyond the maximum plaster thickness shown.

f. Attachment shall be in accordance with Table R702.3.5.

g. Where gypsum board is used as a base for cement plaster, a water-resistive barrier complying with Section R703.2 shall be provided.

TABLE R702.1(2) GYPSUM PLASTER PROPORTIONS[a]

NUMBER	COAT	PLASTER BASE OR LATH	MAXIMUM VOLUME AGGREGATE PER 100 POUNDS NEAT PLASTER[b] (cubic feet)	
			Damp Loose Sand[a]	Perlite or Vermiculite[c]
Two-coat work	Base coat	Gypsum lath	2.5	2
	Base coat	Masonry	3	3
Three-coat work	First coat	Lath	2[d]	2
	Second coat	Lath	3[d]	2[e]
	First and second coats	Masonry	3	3

For SI: 1 inch = 25.4 mm, 1 cubic foot = 0.0283 m^3, 1 pound = 0.454 kg.

a. Wood-fibered gypsum plaster may be mixed in the proportions of 100 pounds of gypsum to not more than 1 cubic foot of sand where applied on masonry or concrete.

b. When determining the amount of aggregate in set plaster, a tolerance of 10 percent shall be allowed.

c. Combinations of sand and lightweight aggregate may be used, provided the volume and weight relationship of the combined aggregate to gypsum plaster is maintained.

d. If used for both first and second coats, the volume of aggregate may be 2.5 cubic feet.

e. Where plaster is 1 inch or more in total thickness, the proportions for the second coat may be increased to 3 cubic feet.

TABLE R702.1(3)
CEMENT PLASTER PROPORTIONS, PARTS BY VOLUME

COAT	CEMENT PLASTER TYPE	CEMENTITIOUS MATERIALS				VOLUME OF AGGREGATE PER SUM OF SEPARATE VOLUMES OF CEMENTITIOUS MATERIALS[b]
		Portland Cement Type I, II or III or Blended Cement Type IP, I (PM), IS or I (SM)	Plastic Cement	Masonry Cement Type M, S or N	Lime	
First	Portland or blended	1			$^{3}/_{4}$ - $1^{1}/_{2}$[a]	$2^{1}/_{2}$ - 4
	Masonry				1	$2^{1}/_{2}$ - 4
	Plastic		1			$2^{1}/_{2}$ - 4
Second	Portland or blended	1			$^{3}/_{4}$ - $1^{1}/_{2}$	3 - 5
	Masonry			1		3 - 5
	Plastic		1			3 - 5
Finish	Portland or blended	1			$^{3}/_{4}$ - 2	$1^{1}/_{2}$ - 3
	Masonry			1		$1^{1}/_{2}$ - 3
	Plastic		1			$1^{1}/_{2}$ - 3

For SI: 1 inch = 25.4 mm, 1 pound = 0.545 kg.

a. Lime by volume of 0 to $^{3}/_{4}$ shall be used when the plaster will be placed over low-absorption surfaces such as dense clay tile or brick.

b. The same or greater sand proportion shall be used in the second coat than used in the first coat.

TABLE R702.3.5
MINIMUM THICKNESS AND APPLICATION OF GYPSUM BOARD

THICKNESS OF GYPSUM BOARD (inches)	APPLICATION	ORIENTATION OF GYPSUM BOARD TO FRAMING	MAXIMUM SPACING OF FRAMING MEMBERS (inches o.c.)	MAXIMUM SPACING OF FASTENERS (inches)		SIZE OF NAILS FOR APPLICATION TO WOOD FRAMING[c]
				Nails[a]	Screws[b]	
Application without adhesive						
$^{3}/_{8}$	Ceiling[d]	Perpendicular	16	7	12	13 gage, $1^{1}/_{4}''$ long, $^{19}/_{64}''$ head; 0.098″ diameter, $1^{1}/_{4}''$ long, annular-ringed; or 4d cooler nail, 0.080″ diameter, $1^{3}/_{8}''$ long, $^{7}/_{32}''$ head.
	Wall	Either direction	16	8	16	
$^{1}/_{2}$	Ceiling	Either direction	16	7	12	13 gage, $1^{3}/_{8}''$ long, $^{19}/_{64}''$ head; 0.098″ diameter, $1^{1}/_{4}''$ long, annular-ringed; 5d cooler nail, 0.086″ diameter, $1^{5}/_{8}''$ long, $^{15}/_{64}''$ head; or gypsum board nail, 0.086″ diameter, $1^{5}/_{8}''$ long, $^{9}/_{32}''$ head.
	Ceiling[d]	Perpendicular	24	7	12	
	Wall	Either direction	24	8	12	
	Wall	Either direction	16	8	16	
$^{5}/_{8}$	Ceiling	Either direction	16	7	12	13 gage, $1^{5}/_{8}''$ long, $^{19}/_{64}''$ head; 0.098″ diameter, $1^{3}/_{8}''$ long, annular-ringed; 6d cooler nail, 0.092″ diameter, $1^{7}/_{8}''$ long, $^{1}/_{4}''$ head; or gypsum board nail, 0.0915″ diameter, $1^{7}/_{8}''$ long, $^{19}/_{64}''$ head.
	Ceiling[e]	Perpendicular	24	7	12	
	Wall	Either direction	24	8	12	
	Wall	Either direction	16	8	16	
Application with adhesive						
$^{3}/_{8}$	Ceiling[d]	Perpendicular	16	16	16	Same as above for $^{3}/_{8}''$ gypsum board
	Wall	Either direction	16	16	24	
$^{1}/_{2}$ or $^{5}/_{8}$	Ceiling	Either direction	16	16	16	Same as above for $^{1}/_{2}''$ and $^{5}/_{8}''$ gypsum board, respectively
	Ceiling[d]	Perpendicular	24	12	16	
	Wall	Either direction	24	16	24	
Two $^{3}/_{8}$ layers	Ceiling	Perpendicular	16	16	16	Base ply nailed as above for $^{1}/_{2}''$ gypsum board; face ply installed with adhesive
	Wall	Either direction	24	24	24	

For SI: 1 inch = 25.4 mm.

a. For application without adhesive, a pair of nails spaced not less than 2 inches apart or more than $2^{1}/_{2}$ inches apart may be used with the pair of nails spaced 12 inches on center.

b. Screws shall be in accordance with Section R702.3.6. Screws for attaching gypsum board to structural insulated panels shall penetrate the wood structural panel facing not less than $^{7}/_{16}$ inch.

c. Where cold-formed steel framing is used with a clinching design to receive nails by two edges of metal, the nails shall be not less than $^{5}/_{8}$ inch longer than the gypsum board thickness and shall have ringed shanks. Where the cold-formed steel framing has a nailing groove formed to receive the nails, the nails shall have barbed shanks or be 5d, $13^{1}/_{2}$ gage, $^{15}/_{8}$ inches long, $^{15}/_{64}$-inch head for $^{1}/_{2}$-inch gypsum board; and 6d, 13 gage, $1^{7}/_{8}$ inches long, $^{15}/_{64}$-inch head for $^{5}/_{8}$-inch gypsum board.

d. Three-eighths-inch-thick single-ply gypsum board shall not be used on a ceiling where a water-based textured finish is to be applied, or where it will be required to support insulation above a ceiling. On ceiling applications to receive a water-based texture material, either hand or spray applied, the gypsum board shall be applied perpendicular to framing. When applying a water-based texture material, the minimum gypsum board thickness shall be increased from $^{3}/_{8}$ inch to $^{1}/_{2}$ inch for 16-inch on center framing, and from $^{1}/_{2}$ inch to $^{5}/_{8}$ inch for 24-inch on center framing or $^{1}/_{2}$-inch sag-resistant gypsum ceiling board shall be used.

e. Type X gypsum board for garage ceilings beneath habitable rooms shall be installed perpendicular to the ceiling framing and shall be fastened at maximum 6 inches o.c. by minimum $1^{7}/_{8}$ inches 6d coated nails or equivalent drywall screws.

R702.2 Interior plaster.

R702.2.1 Gypsum plaster. Gypsum plaster materials shall conform to ASTM C 5, C 28, C 35, C 37, C 59, C 61, C 587, C 588, C 631, C 847, C 933, C 1032 and C 1047, and shall be installed or applied in conformance with ASTM C 843 and C 844. Plaster shall not be less than three coats when applied over metal lath and not less than two coats when applied over other bases permitted by this section, except that veneer plaster may be applied in one coat not to exceed $^{3}/_{16}$ inch (4.76 mm) thickness, provided the total thickness is in accordance with Table R702.1(1).

R702.2.2 Cement plaster. Cement plaster materials shall conform to ASTM C 37, C 91 (Type M, S or N), C 150 (Type I, II and III), C 588, C 595 [Type IP, I (PM), IS and I (SM), C 847, C 897, C 926, C 933, C 1032, C 1047 and C 1328, and shall be installed or applied in conformance with ASTM C 1063. Plaster shall not be less than three coats when applied over metal lath and not less than two coats when applied over other bases permitted by this section, except that veneer plaster may be applied in one coat not to exceed $^{3}/_{16}$ inch (4.76 mm) thickness, provided the total thickness is in accordance with Table R702.1(1).

R702.2.2.1 Application. Each coat shall be kept in a moist condition for at least 24 hours prior to application of the next coat.

Exception: Applications installed in accordance with ASTM C 926.

R702.2.2.2 Curing. The finish coat for two-coat cement plaster shall not be applied sooner than 48 hours after application of the first coat. For three coat cement plaster the second coat shall not be applied sooner than 24 hours after application of the first coat. The finish coat for three-coat cement plaster shall not be applied sooner than 48 hours after application of the second coat.

R702.2.3 Support. Support spacing for gypsum or metal lath on walls or ceilings shall not exceed 16 inches (406 mm) for $^{3}/_{8}$ inch thick (9.5 mm) or 24 inches (610 mm) for $^{1}/_{2}$-inch-thick (12.7 mm) plain gypsum lath. Gypsum lath shall be installed at right angles to support framing with end joints in adjacent courses staggered by at least one framing space.

R702.3 Gypsum board.

R702.3.1 Materials. All gypsum board materials and accessories shall conform to ASTM C 36, C 79, C 475, C 514, C 630, C 931, C 960, C 1002, C 1047, C 1177, C 1178, C 1278, C 1395, C 1396 or C 1658 and shall be installed in accordance with the provisions of this section. Adhesives for the installation of gypsum board shall conform to ASTM C 557.

R702.3.2 Wood framing. Wood framing supporting gypsum board shall not be less than 2 inches (51 mm) nominal thickness in the least dimension except that wood furring strips not less than 1-inch-by-2 inch (25 mm by 51 mm) nominal dimension may be used over solid backing or framing spaced not more than 24 inches (610 mm) on center.

R702.3.3 Cold-formed steel framing. Cold-formed steel framing supporting gypsum board shall not be less than $1^{1}/_{4}$ inches (32 mm) wide in the least dimension. Nonload-bearing cold-formed steel framing shall comply with ASTM C 645. Load-bearing cold-formed steel framing and all cold-formed steel framing from 0.033 inch to 0.112 inch (1 mm to 3 mm) thick shall comply with ASTM C 955.

R702.3.4 Insulating concrete form walls. Foam plastics for insulating concrete form walls constructed in accordance with Sections R404.1.2 and R611 on the interior of *habitable spaces* shall be protected in accordance with Section R316.4. Use of adhesives in conjunction with mechanical fasteners is permitted. Adhesives used for interior and exterior finishes shall be compatible with the insulating form materials.

R702.3.5 Application. Maximum spacing of supports and the size and spacing of fasteners used to attach gypsum board shall comply with Table R702.3.5. Gypsum sheathing shall be attached to exterior walls in accordance with Table R602.3(1). Gypsum board shall be applied at right angles or parallel to framing members. All edges and ends of gypsum board shall occur on the framing members, except those edges and ends that are perpendicular to the framing members. Interior gypsum board shall not be installed where it is directly exposed to the weather or to water.

R702.3.6 Fastening. Screws for attaching gypsum board to wood framing shall be Type W or Type S in accordance with ASTM C 1002 and shall penetrate the wood not less than $^{5}/_{8}$ inch (16 mm). Gypsum board shall be attached to cold-formed steel framing with minimum No. 6 screws. Screws for attaching gypsum board to cold-formed steel framing less than 0.033 inch (1 mm) thick shall be Type S in accordance with ASTM C 1002 or bugle head style in accordance with ASTM C1513 and shall penetrate the steel not less than $^{3}/_{8}$ inch (9.5 mm). Screws for attaching gypsum board to cold-formed steel framing 0.033 inch to 0.112 inch (1 mm to 3 mm) thick shall be in accordance with ASTM C 954 or bugle head style in accordance with ASTM C1513. Screws for attaching gypsum board to structural insulated panels shall penetrate the wood structural panel facing not less than $^{7}/_{16}$ inch (11 mm).

R702.3.7 Horizontal gypsum board diaphragm ceilings. Use of gypsum board shall be permitted on wood joists to create a horizontal *diaphragm* in accordance with Table R702.3.7. Gypsum board shall be installed perpendicular to ceiling framing members. End joints of adjacent courses of board shall not occur on the same joist. The maximum allowable *diaphragm* proportions shall be $1^{1}/_{2}$:1 between shear resisting elements. Rotation or cantilever conditions shall not be permitted. Gypsum board shall not be used in *diaphragm* ceilings to resist lateral forces imposed by masonry or concrete construction. All perimeter edges shall be blocked using wood members not less than 2-inch (51 mm) by 6-inch (152 mm) nominal dimension. Blocking material shall be installed flat over the top plate of the wall to provide a nailing surface not less than 2 inches (51 mm) in width for the attachment of the gypsum board.

TABLE R702.3.7
SHEAR CAPACITY FOR HORIZONTAL WOOD-FRAMED GYPSUM BOARD DIAPHRAGM CEILING ASSEMBLIES

MATERIAL	THICKNESS OF MATERIAL (min.) (in.)	SPACING OF FRAMING MEMBERS (max.) (in.)	SHEAR VALUE[a, b] (plf of ceiling)	MINIMUM FASTENER SIZE[c, d]
Gypsum board	$^1/_2$	16 o.c.	90	5d cooler or wallboard nail; $1^5/_8$-inch long; 0.086- inch shank; $^{15}/_{64}$-inch head
Gypsum board	$^1/_2$	24 o.c.	70	5d cooler or wallboard nail; $1^5/_8$-inch long; 0.086- inch shank; $^{15}/_{64}$-inch head

For SI: 1 inch = 25.4 mm, 1 pound per linear foot = 1.488 kg/m.

a. Values are not cumulative with other horizontal diaphragm values and are for short-term loading caused by wind or seismic loading. Values shall be reduced 25 percent for normal loading.

b. Values shall be reduced 50 percent in Seismic Design Categories D_0, D_1, D_2 and E.

c. $1^1/_4$", #6 Type S or W screws may be substituted for the listed nails.

d. Fasteners shall be spaced not more than 7 inches on center at all supports, including perimeter blocking, and not less than $^3/_8$ inch from the edges and ends of the gypsum board.

R702.3.8 Water-resistant gypsum backing board. Gypsum board used as the base or backer for adhesive application of ceramic tile or other required nonabsorbent finish material shall conform to ASTM C 1396, C 1178 or C1278. Use of water-resistant gypsum backing board shall be permitted on ceilings where framing spacing does not exceed 12 inches (305 mm) on center for $^1/_2$-inch-thick (12.7 mm) or 16 inches (406 mm) for $^5/_8$-inch-thick (16 mm) gypsum board. Water-resistant gypsum board shall not be installed over a Class I or II vapor retarder in a shower or tub compartment. Cut or exposed edges, including those at wall intersections, shall be sealed as recommended by the manufacturer.

R702.3.8.1 Limitations. Water resistant gypsum backing board shall not be used where there will be direct exposure to water, or in areas subject to continuous high humidity.

R702.4 Ceramic tile.

R702.4.1 General. Ceramic tile surfaces shall be installed in accordance with ANSI A108.1, A108.4, A108.5, A108.6, A108.11, A118.1, A118.3, A136.1 and A137.1.

R702.4.2 Fiber-cement, fiber-mat reinforced cement, glass mat gypsum backers and fiber-reinforced gypsum backers. Fiber-cement, fiber-mat reinforced cement, glass mat gypsum backers or fiber-reinforced gypsum backers in compliance with ASTM C 1288, C 1325, C 1178 or C 1278, respectively, and installed in accordance with manufacturers' recommendations shall be used as backers for wall tile in tub and shower areas and wall panels in shower areas.

R702.5 Other finishes. Wood veneer paneling and hardboard paneling shall be placed on wood or cold-formed steel framing spaced not more than 16 inches (406 mm) on center. Wood veneer and hard board paneling less than $^1/_4$ inch (6 mm) nominal thickness shall not have less than a $^3/_8$-inch (10 mm) gypsum board backer. Wood veneer paneling not less than $^1/_4$-inch (6 mm) nominal thickness shall conform to ANSI/HPVA HP-1. Hardboard paneling shall conform to CPA/ANSI A135.5.

R702.6 Wood shakes and shingles. Wood shakes and shingles shall conform to CSSB *Grading Rules for Wood Shakes and Shingles* and shall be permitted to be installed directly to the studs with maximum 24 inches (610 mm) on-center spacing.

R702.6.1 Attachment. Nails, staples or glue are permitted for attaching shakes or shingles to the wall, and attachment of the shakes or shingles directly to the surface shall be permitted provided the fasteners are appropriate for the type of wall surface material. When nails or staples are used, two fasteners shall be provided and shall be placed so that they are covered by the course above.

R702.6.2 Furring strips. Where furring strips are used, they shall be 1 inch by 2 inches or 1 inch by 3 inches (25 mm by 51 mm or 25 mm by 76 mm), spaced a distance on center equal to the desired exposure, and shall be attached to the wall by nailing through other wall material into the studs.

SECTION R703 EXTERIOR COVERING

R703.1 General. Exterior walls shall provide the building with a weather-resistant exterior wall envelope. The exterior wall envelope shall include flashing as described in Section R703.8.

R703.1.1 Water resistance. The exterior wall envelope shall be designed and constructed in a manner that prevents the accumulation of water within the wall assembly by providing a water-resistant barrier behind the exterior veneer as required by Section R703.2 and a means of draining to the exterior water that enters the assembly. Protection against condensation in the exterior wall assembly shall be provided in accordance with Section R601.3 of this code.

Exceptions:

1. A weather-resistant exterior wall envelope shall not be required over concrete or masonry walls

designed in accordance with Chapter 6 and flashed according to Section R703.7 or R703.8.

2. Compliance with the requirements for a means of drainage, and the requirements of Section R703.2 and Section R703.8, shall not be required for an exterior wall envelope that has been demonstrated to resist wind-driven rain through testing of the exterior wall envelope, including joints, penetrations and intersections with dissimilar materials, in accordance with ASTM E 331 under the following conditions:

   2.1. Exterior wall envelope test assemblies shall include at least one opening, one control joint, one wall/eave interface and one wall sill. All tested openings and penetrations shall be representative of the intended end-use configuration.

   2.2. Exterior wall envelope test assemblies shall be at least 4 feet (1219 mm) by 8 feet (2438 mm) in size.

   2.3. Exterior wall assemblies shall be tested at a minimum differential pressure of 6.24 pounds per square foot (299 Pa).

   2.4. Exterior wall envelope assemblies shall be subjected to the minimum test exposure for a minimum of 2 hours.

   The exterior wall envelope design shall be considered to resist wind-driven rain where the results of testing indicate that water did not penetrate control joints in the exterior wall envelope, joints at the perimeter of openings penetration or intersections of terminations with dissimilar materials.

703.1.2 Wind resistance. Wall coverings, backing materials and their attachments shall be capable of resisting wind loads in accordance with Tables R301.2(2) and R301.2(3). Wind-pressure resistance of the siding and backing materials shall be determined by ASTM E 330 or other applicable standard test methods. Where wind-pressure resistance is determined by design analysis, data from approved design standards and analysis conforming to generally accepted engineering practice shall be used to evaluate the siding and backing material and its fastening. All applicable failure modes including bending rupture of siding, fastener withdrawal and fastener head pull-through shall be considered in the testing or design analysis. Where the wall covering and the backing material resist wind load as an assembly, use of the design capacity of the assembly shall be permitted.

R703.2 Water-resistive barrier. One layer of No. 15 asphalt felt, free from holes and breaks, complying with ASTM D 226 for Type 1 felt or other approved water-resistive barrier shall be applied over studs or sheathing of all exterior walls. Such felt or material shall be applied horizontally, with the upper layer lapped over the lower layer not less than 2 inches (51 mm). Where joints occur, felt shall be lapped not less than 6 inches (152 mm). The felt or other approved material shall be continuous to the top of walls and terminated at penetrations and building appendages in a manner to meet the requirements of the exterior wall envelope as described in Section R703.1.

Exception: Omission of the water-resistive barrier is permitted in the following situations:

1. In detached accessory buildings.
2. Under exterior wall finish materials as permitted in Table R703.4.
3. Under paperbacked stucco lath when the paper backing is an approved water-resistive barrier.

R703.3 Wood, hardboard and wood structural panel siding.

R703.3.1 Panel siding. Joints in wood, hardboard or wood structural panel siding shall be made as follows unless otherwise approved. Vertical joints in panel siding shall occur over framing members, unless wood or wood structural panel sheathing is used, and shall be shiplapped or covered with a batten. Horizontal joints in panel siding shall be lapped a minimum of 1 inch (25 mm) or shall be shiplapped or shall be flashed with Z-flashing and occur over solid blocking, wood or wood structural panel sheathing.

R703.3.2 Horizontal siding. Horizontal lap siding shall be installed in accordance with the manufacturer's recommendations. Where there are no recommendations the siding shall be lapped a minimum of 1 inch (25 mm), or $^1/_2$ inch (13 mm) if rabbeted, and shall have the ends caulked, covered with a batten or sealed and installed over a strip of flashing.

R703.4 Attachments. Unless specified otherwise, all wall coverings shall be securely fastened in accordance with Table R703.4 or with other *approved* aluminum, stainless steel, zinc-coated or other *approved* corrosion-resistive fasteners. Where the basic wind speed per Figure R301.2(4) is 110 miles per hour (49 m/s) or higher, the attachment of wall coverings shall be designed to resist the component and cladding loads specified in Table R301.2(2), adjusted for height and exposure in accordance with Table R301.2(3).

R703.5 Wood shakes and shingles. Wood shakes and shingles shall conform to CSSB *Grading Rules for Wood Shakes and Shingles*.

R703.5.1 Application. Wood shakes or shingles shall be applied either single-course or double-course over nominal $^1/_2$-inch (13 mm) wood-based sheathing or to furring strips over $^1/_2$-inch (13 mm) nominal nonwood sheathing . A permeable water-resistive barrier shall be provided over all sheathing, with horizontal overlaps in the membrane of not less than 2 inches (51mm) and vertical overlaps of not less than 6 inches (152 mm). Where furring strips are used, they shall be 1 inch by 3 inches or 1 inch by 4 inches (25 mm by 76 mm or 25 mm by 102 mm) and shall be fastened horizontally to the studs with 7d or 8d box nails and shall be spaced a distance on center equal to the actual weather exposure of the shakes or shingles, not to exceed the maximum exposure specified in Table R703.5.2. The spacing between adjacent shingles to allow for expansion shall not exceed $^1/_4$ inch (6 mm), and between adjacent shakes, it shall not exceed $^1/_2$ inch (13 mm). The offset spacing between joints in adjacent courses shall be a minimum of $1^1/_2$ inches (38 mm).

TABLE R703.4
WEATHER–RESISTANT SIDING ATTACHMENT AND MINIMUM THICKNESS

SIDING MATERIAL		NOMINAL THICKNESS[a] (inches)	JOINT TREATMENT	WATER-RESISTIVE BARRIER REQUIRED	TYPE OF SUPPORTS FOR THE SIDING MATERIAL AND FASTENERS[b, c, d]					
					Wood or wood structural panel sheathing	Fiberboard sheathing into stud	Gypsum sheathing into stud	Foam plastic sheathing into stud	Direct to studs	Number or spacing of fasteners
Horizontal aluminum[e]	Without insulation	0.019[f]	Lap	Yes	0.120 nail 1 1/2″ long	0.120 nail 2″ long	0.120 nail 2″ long	0.120 nail[y]	Not allowed	Same as stud spacing
		0.024	Lap	Yes	0.120 nail 1 1/2″ long	0.120 nail 2″ long	0.120 nail 2″ long	0.120 nail[y]	Not allowed	
	With insulation	0.019	Lap	Yes	0.120 nail 1 1/2″ long	0.120 nail 2 1/2″ long	0.120 nail 2 1/2″ long	0.120 nail[y]	0.120 nail 1 1/2″ long	
Anchored veneer: brick, concrete, masonry or stone		2	Section R703	Yes	See Section R703 and Figure R703.7[g]					
Adhered veneer: concrete, stone or masonry[w]		—	Section R703	Yes Note w	See Section R703.6.1[g] or in accordance with the manufacturer's instructions.					
Hardboard[k] Panel siding-vertical		7/16	—	Yes	Note m	Note m	Note m	Note m	Note m	6″ panel edges 12″ inter. sup.[n]
Hardboard[k] Lap-siding-horizontal		7/16	Note p	Yes	Note o	Note o	Note o	Note o	Note o	Same as stud spacing 2 per bearing
Steel[h]		29 ga.	Lap	Yes	0.113 nail 1 3/4″ Staple–1 3/4″	0.113 nail 2 3/4″ Staple–2 1/2″	0.113 nail 2 1/2″ Staple–2 1/4″	0.113 nail[v] Staple[v]	Not allowed	Same as stud spacing
Particleboard panels		3/8 – 1/2	—	Yes	6d box nail (2″ × 0.099″)	6d box nail (2″ × 0.099″)	6d box nail (2″ × 0.099″)	box nail[v]	6d box nail (2″ × 0.099″), 3/8 not allowed	6″ panel edge, 12″ inter. sup.
		5/8	—	Yes	6d box nail (2″ × 0.099″)	8d box nail (2 1/2″ × 0.113″)	8d box nail (2 1/2″ × 0.113″)	box nail[v]	6d box nail (2″ × 0.099″)	
Wood structural panel siding[i] (exterior grade)		3/8 – 1/2	Note p	Yes	0.099 nail–2″	0.113 nail–2 1/2″	0.113 nail–2 1/2″	0.113 nail[v]	0.099 nail–2″	6″ panel edges, 12″ inter. sup.
Wood structural panel lapsiding		3/8 – 1/2	Note p Note x	Yes	0.099 nail–2″	0.113 nail–2 1/2″	0.113 nail–2 1/2″	0.113 nail[x]	0.099 nail–2″	8″ along bottom edge
Vinyl siding[l]		0.035	Lap	Yes	0.120 nail (shank) with a 0.313 head or 16 gauge staple with 3/8 to 1/2-inch crown[y, z]	0.120 nail (shank) with a 0.313 head or 16 gage staple with 3/8 to 1/2-inch crown[y]	0.120 nail (shank) with a 0.313 head or 16 gage staple with 3/8 to 1/2-inch crown[y]	0.120 nail (shank) with a 0.313 head per Section R703.11.2	Not allowed	16 inches on center or specified by the manufacturer instructions or test report
Wood[j] rustic, drop		3/8 Min	Lap	Yes	Fastener penetration into stud–1″				0.113 nail–2 1/2″ Staple–2″	Face nailing up to 6″ widths, 1 nail per bearing; 8″ widths and over, 2 nails per bearing
Shiplap		19/32 Average	Lap	Yes						
Bevel		7/16								
Butt tip		3/16	Lap	Yes						
Fiber cement panel siding[q]		5/16	Note q	Yes Note u	6d common corrosion-resistant nail[r]	6d common corrosion-resistant nail[r]	6d common corrosion-resistant nail[r]	6d common corrosion-resistant nail[r, v]	4d common corrosion-resistant nail[r]	6″ o.c. on edges, 12″ o.c. on intermed. studs
Fiber cement lap siding[s]		5/16	Note s	Yes Note u	6d common corrosion-resistant nail[r]	6d common corrosion-resistant nail[r]	6d common corrosion-resistant nail[r]	6d common corrosion-resistant nail[r, v]	6d common corrosion-resistant nail or 11 gage roofing nail[r]	Note t

For SI: 1 inch = 25.4 mm.

a. Based on stud spacing of 16 inches on center where studs are spaced 24 inches, siding shall be applied to sheathing approved for that spacing.

b. Nail is a general description and shall be T-head, modified round head, or round head with smooth or deformed shanks.

c. Staples shall have a minimum crown width of 7/16-inch outside diameter and be manufactured of minimum 16 gage wire.

d. Nails or staples shall be aluminum, galvanized, or rust-preventative coated and shall be driven into the studs for fiberboard or gypsum backing.

e. Aluminum nails shall be used to attach aluminum siding.

f. Aluminum (0.019 inch) shall be unbacked only when the maximum panel width is 10 inches and the maximum flat area is 8 inches. The tolerance for aluminum siding shall be +0.002 inch of the nominal dimension.

g. All attachments shall be coated with a corrosion-resistant coating.

h. Shall be of approved type.

i. Three-eighths-inch plywood shall not be applied directly to studs spaced more than 16 inches on center when long dimension is parallel to studs. Plywood 1/2-inch or thinner shall not be applied directly to studs spaced more than 24 inches on center. The stud spacing shall not exceed the panel span rating provided by the manufacturer unless the panels are installed with the face grain perpendicular to the studs or over sheathing approved for that stud spacing.

j. Wood board sidings applied vertically shall be nailed to horizontal nailing strips or blocking set 24 inches on center. Nails shall penetrate 1 1/2 inches into studs, studs and wood sheathing combined or blocking.

(continued)

TABLE R703.4—continued
WEATHER–RESISTANT SIDING ATTACHMENT AND MINIMUM THICKNESS

k. Hardboard siding shall comply with CPA/ANSI A135.6.
l. Vinyl siding shall comply with ASTM D 3679.
m. Minimum shank diameter of 0.092 inch, minimum head diameter of 0.225 inch, and nail length must accommodate sheathing and penetrate framing $1^1/_2$ inches.
n. When used to resist shear forces, the spacing must be 4 inches at panel edges and 8 inches on interior supports.
o. Minimum shank diameter of 0.099 inch, minimum head diameter of 0.240 inch, and nail length must accommodate sheathing and penetrate framing $1^1/_2$ inches.
p. Vertical end joints shall occur at studs and shall be covered with a joint cover or shall be caulked.
q. See Section R703.10.1.
r. Fasteners shall comply with the nominal dimensions in ASTM F 1667.
s. See Section R703.10.2.
t. Face nailing: one 6d common nail through the overlapping planks at each stud. Concealed nailing: one 11 gage $1^1/_2$ inch long galv. roofing nail through the top edge of each plank at each stud.
u. See Section R703.2 exceptions.
v. Minimum nail length must accommodate sheathing and penetrate framing $1^1/_2$ inches.
w. Adhered masonry veneer shall comply with the requirements of Section R703.6.3 and shall comply with the requirements in Sections 6.1 and 6.3 of TMS 402/ACI 530/ASCE 5.
x. Vertical joints, if staggered shall be permitted to be away from studs if applied over wood structural panel sheathing.
y. Minimum fastener length must accommodate sheathing and penetrate framing .75 inches or in accordance with the manufacturer's installation instructions.
z. Where approved by the manufacturer's instructions or test report siding shall be permitted to be installed with fasteners penetrating not less than .75 inches through wood or wood structural sheathing with or without penetration into the framing.

R703.5.2 Weather exposure. The maximum weather exposure for shakes and shingles shall not exceed that specified in Table R703.5.2.

R703.5.3 Attachment. Each shake or shingle shall be held in place by two hot-dipped zinc-coated, stainless steel, or aluminum nails or staples. The fasteners shall be long enough to penetrate the sheathing or furring strips by a minimum of $^1/_2$ inch (13 mm) and shall not be overdriven.

R703.5.3.1 Staple attachment. Staples shall not be less than16 gage and shall have a crown width of not less than $^7/_{16}$ inch (11 mm), and the crown of the staples shall be parallel with the butt of the shake or shingle. In single-course application, the fasteners shall be concealed by the course above and shall be driven approximately 1 inch (25 mm) above the butt line of the succeeding course and $^3/_4$ inch (19 mm) from the edge. In double-course applications, the exposed shake or shingle shall be face-nailed with two casing nails, driven approximately 2 inches (51 mm) above the butt line and $^3/_4$ inch (19 mm) from each edge. In all applications, staples shall be concealed by the course above. With shingles wider than 8 inches (203 mm) two additional nails shall be required and shall be nailed approximately 1 inch (25 mm) apart near the center of the shingle.

R703.5.4 Bottom courses. The bottom courses shall be doubled.

R703.6 Exterior plaster. Installation of these materials shall be in compliance with ASTM C 926 and ASTM C 1063 and the provisions of this code.

R703.6.1 Lath. All lath and lath attachments shall be of corrosion-resistant materials. Expanded metal or woven wire lath shall be attached with $1^1/_2$-inch-long (38 mm), 11 gage nails having a $^7/_{16}$-inch (11.1 mm) head, or $^7/_8$-inch-long (22.2 mm), 16 gage staples, spaced at no more than 6 inches (152 mm), or as otherwise *approved*.

R703.6.2 Plaster. Plastering with portland cement plaster shall be not less than three coats when applied over metal lath or wire lath and shall be not less than two coats when applied over masonry, concrete, pressure-preservative treated wood or decay-resistant wood as specified in Section R317.1 or gypsum backing. If the plaster surface is completely covered by veneer or other facing material or is completely concealed, plaster application need be only two coats, provided the total thickness is as set forth in Table R702.1(1).

On wood-frame construction with an on-grade floor slab system, exterior plaster shall be applied to cover, but not extend below, lath, paper and screed.

The proportion of aggregate to cementitious materials shall be as set forth in Table R702.1(3).

TABLE R703.5.2
MAXIMUM WEATHER EXPOSURE FOR WOOD SHAKES AND SHINGLES ON EXTERIOR WALLS[a, b, c]
(Dimensions are in inches)

LENGTH	EXPOSURE FOR SINGLE COURSE	EXPOSURE FOR DOUBLE COURSE
Shingles[a]		
16	$7^1/_2$	12[b]
18	$8^1/_2$	14[c]
24	$11^1/_2$	16
Shakes[a]		
18	$8^1/_2$	14
24	$11^1/_2$	18

For SI: 1 inch = 25.4 mm.
a. Dimensions given are for No. 1 grade.
b. A maximum 10-inch exposure is permitted for No. 2 grade.
c. A maximum 11-inch exposure is permitted for No. 2 grade.

R703.6.2.1 Weep screeds. A minimum 0.019-inch (0.5 mm) (No. 26 galvanized sheet gage), corrosion-resistant weep screed or plastic weep screed, with a minimum vertical attachment flange of $3^1/_2$ inches (89 mm) shall be provided at or below the foundation plate line on exterior stud walls in accordance with ASTM C 926. The weep screed shall be placed a minimum of 4 inches (102 mm) above the earth or 2 inches (51 mm) above paved areas and shall be of a type that will allow trapped water to drain to the exterior of the building. The weather-resistant barrier shall lap the attachment flange. The exterior lath shall cover and terminate on the attachment flange of the weep screed.

R703.6.3 Water-resistive barriers. Water-resistive barriers shall be installed as required in Section R703.2 and, where applied over wood-based sheathing, shall include a water-resistive vapor-permeable barrier with a performance at least equivalent to two layers of Grade D paper.

Exception: Where the water-resistive barrier that is applied over wood-based sheathing has a water resistance equal to or greater than that of 60 minute Grade D paper and is separated from the stucco by an intervening, substantially nonwater-absorbing layer or designed drainage space.

R703.6.4 Application. Each coat shall be kept in a moist condition for at least 48 hours prior to application of the next coat.

Exception: Applications installed in accordance with ASTM C 926.

R703.6.5 Curing. The finish coat for two-coat cement plaster shall not be applied sooner than seven days after application of the first coat. For three-coat cement plaster, the second coat shall not be applied sooner than 48 hours after application of the first coat. The finish coat for three-coat cement plaster shall not be applied sooner than seven days after application of the second coat.

R703.7 Stone and masonry veneer, general. Stone and masonry veneer shall be installed in accordance with this chapter, Table R703.4 and Figure R703.7. These veneers installed over a backing of wood or cold-formed steel shall be limited to the first *story* above-grade and shall not exceed 5 inches (127 mm) in thickness. See Section R602.12 for wall bracing requirements for masonry veneer for wood framed construction and Section R603.9.5 for wall bracing requirements for masonry veneer for cold-formed steel construction.

Exceptions:

1. For all buildings in Seismic Design Categories A, B and C, exterior stone or masonry veneer, as specified in Table R703.7(1), with a backing of wood or steel framing shall be permitted to the height specified in Table R703.7(1) above a noncombustible foundation.
2. Deleted.

R703.7.1 Interior veneer support. Veneers used as interior wall finishes shall be permitted to be supported on wood or cold-formed steel floors that are designed to support the loads imposed.

R703.7.2 Exterior veneer support. Except in Seismic Design Categories D_0, D_1 and D_2, exterior masonry veneers having an installed weight of 40 pounds per square foot (195 kg/m^2) or less shall be permitted to be supported on wood or cold-formed steel construction. When masonry veneer supported by wood or cold-formed steel construction adjoins masonry veneer supported by the foundation, there shall be a movement joint between the veneer supported by the wood or cold-formed steel construction and the veneer supported by the foundation. The wood or cold-formed steel construction supporting the masonry veneer shall be designed to limit the deflection to $^1/_{600}$ of the span for the supporting members. The design of the wood or cold-formed steel construction shall consider the weight of the veneer and any other loads.

R703.7.2.1 Support by steel angle. A minimum 6 inches by 4 inches by $^5/_{16}$ inch (152 mm by 102 mm by 8 mm) steel angle, with the long leg placed vertically, shall be anchored to double 2 inches by 4 inches (51 mm by 102 mm) wood studs at a maximum on-center spacing of 16

TABLE R703.7(1)
STONE OR MASONRY VENEER LIMITATIONS AND REQUIREMENTS, WOOD OR STEEL FRAMING, SEISMIC DESIGN CATEGORIES A, B AND C

SEISMIC DESIGN CATEGORY	NUMBER OF WOOD OR STEEL FRAMED STORIES	MAXIMUM HEIGHT OF VENEER ABOVE NONCOMBUSTIBLE FOUNDATION[a] (feet)	MAXIMUM NOMINAL THICKNESS OF VENEER (inches)	MAXIMUM WEIGHT OF VENEER (psf)[b]	WOOD OR STEEL FRAMED STORY
A or B	Steel: 1 or 2 Wood: 1, 2 or 3	30	5	50	all
C	1	30	5	50	1 only
	2	30	5	50	top
					bottom
	Wood only: 3	30	5	50	top
					middle
					bottom

For SI: 1 inch = 25.4 mm, 1 foot = 304.8 mm, 1 pound per square foot = 0.479 kPa.

a. An Additional 8 feet is permitted for gable end walls. See also story height limitations of Section R301.3.

b. Maximum weight is installed weight and includes weight of mortar, grout, lath and other materials used for installation. Where veneer is placed on both faces of a wall, the combined weight shall not exceed that specified in this table.

inches (406 mm) or shall be anchored to solid double 2x blocking firmly attached between single 2-inch by 4-inch (51 mm by 102 mm) wood studs at a maximum on center spacing of 16 inches (406 mm). Anchorage of the steel angle at every double stud spacing shall be a minimum of two $^{7}/_{16}$ inch (11 mm) diameter by 4 inch (102 mm) lag screws at every double stud or shall be a minimum of two $^{7}/_{16}$-inch diameter (11.1 mm) by 4 inches (102 mm) lag screws into solid double blocking with each pair of lag screws spaced at horizontal intervals not to exceed 16 inches (406 mm). The steel angle shall have a minimum clearance to underlying construction of $^{1}/_{16}$ inch (2 mm). A minimum of two-thirds the width of the masonry veneer thickness shall bear on the steel angle. Flashing and weep holes shall be located in the masonry veneer wythe in accordance with Figure R703.7.2.1. The maximum height of masonry veneer above the steel angle support shall be 12 feet, 8 inches (3861 mm). The air space separating the masonry veneer from the wood backing shall be in accordance with Sections R703.7.4 and R703.7.4.2. The method of support for the masonry veneer on steel angle shall be constructed in accordance with Figure R703.7.2.1.

The maximum slope of the roof construction without stops shall be 7:12. Roof construction with slopes greater than 7:12 but not more than 12:12 shall have stops of a minimum 3 inch × 3 inch × $^{1}/_{4}$ inch (76 mm × 76 mm × 6 mm) steel plate welded to the angle at 24 inches (610 mm) on center along the angle or as *approved* by the *building official*.

R703.7.2.2 Support by roof construction. Veneer may be vertically supported on sloping surfaces as shown in Figure R703.7.2.2 and as described in the following provisions:

1. Surface slope shall not exceed 12:12.
2. Member supporting veneer loading shall have three times the capacity of similar beams, joist or rafters supporting the sloped surface.
3. Minimum of 4 inch × 3 $^{1}/_{2}$ inch × $^{1}/_{4}$ inch (102 mm × 89 mm × 6 mm) steel angle shall be attached to the sloping surface. Attachment shall be made by drilling $^{3}/_{16}$-inch (5 mm) diameter holes in the 4-inch (102 mm) leg of the angle at 12 inches (305 mm) o.c. and using 16d nails penetrating the triple members. When the slope exceeds 7:12, minimum 3 inch × 3 inch × $^{1}/_{4}$ inch (76 mm × 76 mm × 6 mm) plates shall be welded at 24 inches (610 mm) o.c. along the steel angle as stops to prevent the veneer from sliding down the slope. Minimum of 1-inch (25 mm) air space shall be maintained between the wall and veneer.
4. Flashing shall be installed over steel angle and a minimum of 6 inches (152 mm) under the wall sheathing.
5. Maximum height of 12 feet 8 inches (386 mm) above steel angle or as approved by a registered design professional.

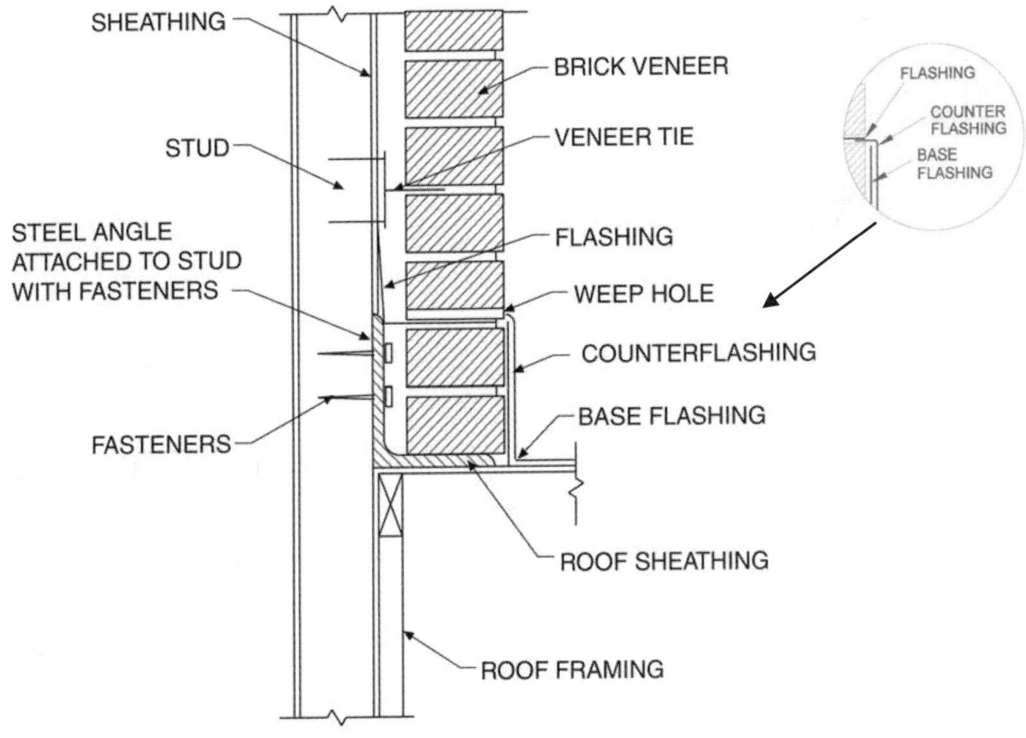

FIGURE R703.7.2.1
EXTERIOR MASONRY VENEER SUPPORT BY STEEL ANGLES

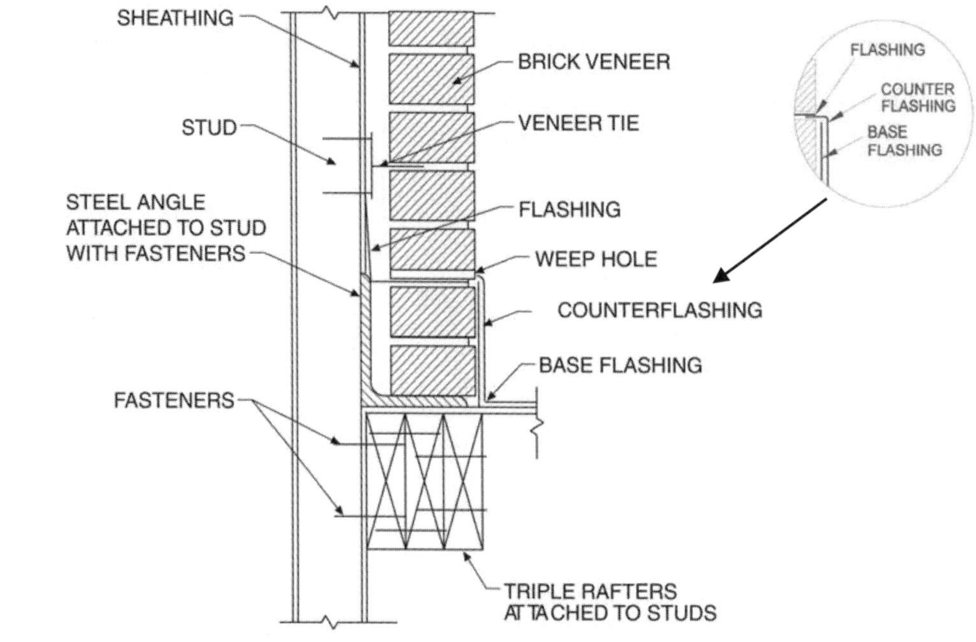

FIGURE R703.7.2.2
EXTERIOR MASONRY VENEER SUPPORT BY ROOF MEMBERS

R703.7.3 Lintels. Masonry veneer shall not support any vertical load other than the dead load of the veneer above. Veneer above openings shall be supported on lintels of noncombustible materials. The lintels shall have a length of bearing not less than 4 inches (102 mm). Steel lintels shall be shop coated with a rust-inhibitive paint, except for lintels made of corrosion-resistant steel or steel treated with coatings to provide corrosion resistance. Construction of openings shall comply with either Section R703.7.3.1 or 703.7.3.2.

TABLE R703.7.3
ALLOWABLE SPANS FOR LINTELS SUPPORTING MASONRY VENEER

SIZE OF STEEL ANGLE[a, c] (inches)	MAXIMUM SPAN[b,d]
$3^1/_2 \times 3^1/_2 \times {}^1/_4$	6′-0″
$5 \times 3^1/_2 \times {}^5/_{16}$	10′-0″

For SI: 1 inch = 25.4 mm, 1 foot =304.8 mm.

a. Long leg of the angle shall be placed in a vertical position.

b. Spans over 4 feet shall be shored up until cured.

c. Steel members indicated are adequate typical examples; other steel members including light-gage steel meeting structural design requirements may be used.

d. Spans over 10 feet shall be designed in accordance with approved standard.

R703.7.3.1 The allowable span shall not exceed the values set forth in Table R703.7.3.1.

R703.7.3.2 The allowable span shall not exceed 18 feet 3 inches (5562 mm) and shall be constructed to comply with Figure R703.7.3.2 and the following:

1. Provide a minimum length of 18 inches (457 mm) of masonry veneer on each side of opening as shown in Figure R703.7.3.2.
2. Provide a minimum 5 inch by $3^1/_2$ inch by $^5/_{16}$ inch (127 mm by 89 mm by 7.9 mm) steel angle above the opening and shore for a minimum of 7 days after installation.
3. Provide double-wire joint reinforcement extending 12 inches (305 mm) beyond each side of the opening. Lap splices of joint reinforcement a minimum of 12 inches (305 mm). Comply with one of the following:

   3.1. Double-wire joint reinforcement shall be $^3/_{16}$ inch (4.8 mm) diameter and shall be placed in the first two bed joints above the opening.

   3.2. Double-wire joint reinforcement shall be 9 gauge (0.144 inch or 3.66 mm diameter) and shall be placed in the first three bed joints above the opening.

R703.7.4 Anchorage. Masonry veneer shall be anchored to the supporting wall with corrosion-resistant metal ties embedded in mortar or grout and extending into the veneer a minimum of $1^1/_2$ inches (38 mm), with not less than $^5/_8$ inch (15.9 mm) mortar or grout cover to outside face. Where veneer is anchored to wood backings by corrugated sheet metal ties, the distance separating the veneer from the sheathing material shall be a maximum of a nominal 1 inch (25 mm). Where the veneer is anchored to wood backings using metal strand wire ties, the distance separating the veneer from the sheathing material shall be a maximum of $4^1/_2$ inches (114 mm). Where the veneer is anchored to cold-formed steel backings, adjustable metal strand wire ties shall be used. Where veneer is anchored to cold-formed steel backings, the distance separating the veneer from the sheathing material shall be a maximum of $4^1/_2$ inches (114 mm).

R703.7.4.1 Size and spacing. Veneer ties, if strand wire, shall not be less in thickness than No. 9 U.S. gage [(0.148 in.) (4 mm)] wire and shall have a hook embedded in the mortar joint, or if sheet metal, shall be not less than No. 22 U.S. gage by [(0.0299 in.)(0.76 mm)] $^7/_8$ inch (22 mm) corrugated. Each tie shall be spaced not more than 24 inches (610 mm) on center horizontally and vertically and shall support not more than 2.67 square feet (0.25 m^2) of wall area.

Exception: In Seismic Design Category D_0, D_1 or D_2 or townhouses in Seismic Design Category C or in wind areas of more than 30 pounds per square foot pressure (1.44 kPa), each tie shall support not more than 2 square feet (0.2 m^2) of wall area.

R703.7.4.1.1 Veneer ties around wall openings. Veneer ties around wall openings. Additional metal ties shall be provided around all wall openings greater than 16 inches (406 mm) in either dimension. Metal ties around the perimeter of openings shall be spaced not more than 3 feet (9144 mm) on center and placed within 12 inches (305 mm) of the wall opening.

R703.7.4.2 Air space. The veneer shall be separated from the sheathing by an air space of a minimum of a nominal 1 inch (25 mm) but not more than $4^1/_2$ inches (114 mm).

R703.7.4. 3 Mortar or grout fill. As an alternate to the air space required by Section R703.7.4.2, mortar or grout shall be permitted to fill the air space .When the air space is filled with mortar, a water-resistive barrier is required over studs or sheathing. When filling the air space, replacing the sheathing and water-resistive barrier with a wire mesh and *approved* water-resistive barrier or an *approved* water-resistive barrier-backed reinforcement attached directly to the studs is permitted.

R703.7.5 Flashing. Flashing of 6 mil (0.152 mm) poly or other corrosion-resistive material shall be located beneath the first course of masonry above finished ground level above the foundation wall or slab and at other points of support, including structural floors, shelf angles and lintels when masonry veneers are designed in accordance with Section R703.7. Top of base flashing shall be installed with a minimum 2-inch (51 mm) lap behind building paper or water-repellent sheathing. See Section R703.8 for additional requirements.

R703.7.6 Weepholes. Weepholes shall be provided in the outside wythe of masonry walls at a maximum spacing of 33 inches (838 mm) on center. Weepholes shall not be less than $^3/_{16}$ inch (5 mm) in diameter. Weepholes shall be located immediately above the flashing.

R703.8 Flashing. *Approved* corrosion-resistant flashing shall be applied shingle-fashion in a manner to prevent entry of water into the wall cavity or penetration of water to the building structural framing components. Install flashing in accordance with ASTM E 2112 Standard Practice for Installation of Exterior Windows, Doors and Skylights, or the manufacturer's supplied written instructions. Aluminum flashing may not be used in contact with cementitious material, except at counter flashing. Self-adhered membranes used as flashing shall comply with AAMA 711. The flashing shall extend to the surface of the exterior wall finish. *Approved* corrosion-resistant flashings shall be installed at all of the following locations:

1. Exterior window and door openings. Flashing at exterior window and door openings shall extend to the surface of the exterior wall finish or to the water-resistive barrier for subsequent drainage.
2. At the intersection of chimneys or other masonry construction with frame or stucco walls, with projecting lips on both sides under stucco copings.
3. Under and at the ends of masonry, wood or metal copings and sills.
4. Continuously above all projecting wood trim.
5. Where exterior porches, decks or stairs attach to a wall or floor assembly of wood-frame construction.
6. At wall and roof intersections.
7. At built-in gutters.

R703.9 Exterior insulation and finish system (EIFS)/EIFS with drainage. Exterior Insulation and Finish System (EIFS) with drainage shall comply with this chapter and Sections R703.9.2, R703.9.3 and R703.9.4.

R703.9.1 Exterior insulation and finish system (EIFS). Non-drainable EIFS shall not be permitted.

R703.9.2 Exterior insulation and finish system (EIFS) with drainage. EIFS with drainage shall comply with ASTM E 2568 and shall have an average minimum drainage efficiency of 90 percent when tested in accordance with ASTM E 2273.

R703.9.2.1 Water-resistive barrier. The water-resistive barrier shall comply with Section R703.2 or ASTM E 2570.

R703.9.2.2 Installation. The water-resistive barrier shall be applied between the EIFS and the wall sheathing.

R703.9.3 Flashing, general. Flashing of EIFS shall be provided in accordance with the requirements of Section R703.8.

R703.9.4 EIFS with drainage installation. All EIFS shall be installed in accordance with the manufacturer's installation instructions and the requirements of this section.

R703.9.4.1 Terminations. The EIFS shall terminate not less than 6 inches (152 mm) above the finished ground level.

R703.9.4.2 Decorative trim. Decorative trim shall not be face nailed though the EIFS.

R703.10 Fiber cement siding.

R703.10.1 Panel siding. Fiber-cement panels shall comply with the requirements of ASTM C1186, Type A, minimum Grade II. Panels shall be installed with the long dimension either parallel or perpendicular to framing. Vertical and horizontal joints shall occur over framing members and shall be sealed with caulking, covered with battens or shall be designed to comply with Section R703.1. Panel siding shall be installed with fasteners according to Table R703.4 or *approved* manufacturer's installation instructions.

R703.10.2 Lap siding. Fiber-cement lap siding having a maximum width of 12 inches shall comply with the requirements of ASTM C1186, Type A, minimum Grade II. Lap siding shall be lapped a minimum of $1^1/_4$ inches (32 mm) and lap siding not having tongue-and-groove end joints shall have the ends sealed with caulking, installed with an H-section joint cover, located over a strip of flashing or shall be designed to comply with Section R703.1. Lap siding courses may be installed with the fastener heads exposed or concealed, according to Table R703.4 or *approved* manufacturers' installation instructions.

R703.11 Vinyl siding. Vinyl siding shall be certified and *labeled* as conforming to the requirements of ASTM D 3679 by an *approved* quality control agency.

R703.11.1 Installation. Vinyl siding, soffit and accessories shall be installed in accordance with the manufacturer's installation instructions.

R703.11.1.1 Soffit panels shall be individually fastened to a supporting component such as a nailing strip, fascia or subfascia component or as specified by the manufacturer's instructions.

R703.11.2 Foam plastic sheathing. Vinyl siding used with foam plastic sheathing shall be installed in accordance with Section R703.11.2.1, R703.11.2.2, or R703.11.2.3.

Exception: Where the foam plastic sheathing is applied directly over wood structural panels, fiberboard, gypsum sheathing or other *approved* backing capable of independently resisting the design wind pressure, the vinyl siding shall be installed in accordance with Section R703.11.1.

R703.11.2.1 Basic wind speed not exceeding 90 miles per hour and Exposure Category B. Where the basic wind speed does not exceed 90 miles per hour (40 m/s), the Exposure Category is B and gypsum wall board or equivalent is installed on the side of the wall opposite the foam plastic sheathing, the minimum siding fastener penetration into wood framing shall be $1^1/_4$ inches (32 mm) using minimum 0.120-inch diameter nail (shank) with a minimum 0.313-inch diameter head, 16 inches on center. The foam plastic sheathing shall be minimum $^1/_2$-inch-thick (12.7 mm) (nominal) extruded polystyrene per ASTM C578, $^1/_2$-inch-thick (12.7 mm) (nominal) polyisocyanurate per ASTM C1289, or 1-inch-thick (25 mm) (nominal) expanded polystyrene per ASTM C 578.

R703.11.2.2 Basic wind speed exceeding 90 miles per hour or Exposure Categories C and D. Where the basic wind speed exceeds 90 miles per hour (40 m/s) or the Exposure Category is C or D, or all conditions of Section R703.11.2.1 are not met, the adjusted design pressure rating for the assembly shall meet or exceed the loads listed in Tables R301.2(2) adjusted for height and exposure using Table R301.2(3). The design wind pressure rating of the vinyl siding for installation over solid sheathing as provided in the vinyl siding manufacturer's product specifications shall be adjusted for the following wall assembly conditions:

1. For wall assemblies with foam plastic sheathing on the exterior side and gypsum wall board or equivalent on the interior side of the wall, the vinyl siding's design wind pressure rating shall be multiplied by 0.39.
2. For wall assemblies with foam plastic sheathing on the exterior side and no gypsum wall board or equivalent on the interior side of wall, the vinyl siding's design wind pressure rating shall be multiplied by 0.27.

R703.11.2.3 Manufacturer specification. Where the vinyl siding manufacturer's product specifications provide an *approved* design wind pressure rating for installation over foam plastic sheathing, use of this design wind pressure rating shall be permitted and the siding shall be installed in accordance with the manufacturer's installation instructions.

R703.11.3 Soffit. In one- and two-family dwelling construction using vinyl or aluminum as a soffit material, the soffit material shall be securely attached to framing members and use an underlayment material of either fire retardant treated wood, $^{23}/_{32}$ inch wood sheathing or $^5/_8$ inch gypsum board. Venting requirements apply to both soffit and underlayment and shall be per Section R806 of the *North Carolina Residential Code*. Where the property line is 10 feet or more from the building face, the provisions of this code section do not apply.

R703.11.4 Flame Spread. Vinyl siding and vinyl soffit materials when used in one- and two-family dwelling construction shall have a flame spread index of 25 or less as tested in accordance with ASTM E 84.

R703.12 Adhered masonry veneer installation. Adhered masonry veneer shall be installed in accordance with the manufacturer's instructions.

CHAPTER 8
ROOF-CEILING CONSTRUCTION

SECTION R801
GENERAL

R801.1 Application. The provisions of this chapter shall control the design and construction of the roof-ceiling system for all buildings.

R801.2 Requirements. Roof and ceiling construction shall be capable of accommodating all loads imposed according to Section R301 and of transmitting the resulting loads to the supporting structural elements.

R801.3 Roof drainage. In areas where expansive or collapsible soils are known to exist, all *dwellings* shall have a controlled method of water disposal from roofs that will collect and discharge roof drainage to the ground surface at least 5 feet (1524 mm) from foundation walls or to an *approved* drainage system.

SECTION R802
WOOD ROOF FRAMING

R802.1 Identification. Load-bearing dimension lumber for rafters, trusses and ceiling joists shall be identified by a grade mark of a lumber grading or inspection agency that has been approved by an accreditation body that complies with DOC PS 20. In lieu of a grade mark, a certificate of inspection issued by a lumber grading or inspection agency meeting the requirements of this section shall be accepted.

R802.1.1 Blocking. Blocking shall be a minimum of utility *grade* lumber.

R802.1.2 End-jointed lumber. *Approved* end-jointed lumber identified by a grade mark conforming to Section R802.1 may be used interchangeably with solid-sawn members of the same species and grade.

R802.1.3 Fire-retardant-treated wood. Fire-retardant-treated wood (FRTW) is any wood product which, when impregnated with chemicals by a pressure process or other means during manufacture, shall have, when tested in accordance with ASTM E 84, a listed flame spread index of 25 or less and shows no evidence of significant progressive combustion when the test is continued for an additional 20-minute period. In addition, the flame front shall not progress more than 10.5 feet (3200 mm) beyond the center line of the burners at any time during the test.

R802.1.3.1 Pressure process. For wood products impregnated with chemicals by a pressure process, the process shall be performed in closed vessels under pressures not less than 50 pounds per square inch gauge (psig) (344.7 kPa).

R802.1.3.2 Other means during manufacture. For wood products produced by other means during manufacture the treatment shall be an integral part of the manufacturing process of the wood product. The treatment shall provide permanent protection to all surfaces of the wood product.

R802.1.3.3 Testing. For wood products produced by other means during manufacture, other than a pressure process, all sides of the wood product shall be tested in accordance with and produce the results required in Section R802.1.3. Testing of only the front and back faces of wood structural panels shall be permitted.

R802.1.3.4 Labeling. Fire-retardant-treated lumber and wood structural panels shall be *labeled*. The *label* shall contain:

1. The identification *mark* of an *approved agency* in accordance with Section 1703.5 of the *International Building Code*.
2. Identification of the treating manufacturer.
3. The name of the fire-retardant treatment.
4. The species of wood treated.
5. Flame spread index and smoke-developed index.
6. Method of drying after treatment.
7. Conformance to applicable standards in accordance with Sections R802.1.3.5 through R802.1.3.8.
8. For FRTW exposed to weather, or a damp or wet location, the words "No increase in the listed classification when subjected to the Standard Rain Test" (ASTM D 2898).

R802.1.3.5 Strength adjustments. Design values for untreated lumber and wood structural panels as specified in Section R802.1 shall be adjusted for fire-retardant-treated wood. Adjustments to design values shall be based upon an *approved* method of investigation which takes into consideration the effects of the anticipated temperature and humidity to which the fire-retardant-treated wood will be subjected, the type of treatment and redrying procedures.

R802.1.3.5.1 Wood structural panels. The effect of treatment and the method of redrying after treatment, and exposure to high temperatures and high humidities on the flexure properties of fire-retardant-treated softwood plywood shall be determined in accordance with ASTM D 5516. The test data developed by ASTM D 5516 shall be used to develop adjustment factors, maximum loads and spans, or both for untreated plywood design values in accordance with ASTM D 6305. Each manufacturer shall publish the allowable maximum loads and spans for service as floor and roof sheathing for their treatment.

R802.1.3.5.2 Lumber. For each species of wood treated, the effect of the treatment and the method of redrying after treatment and exposure to high temperatures and high humidities on the allowable design properties of fire-retardant-treated lumber shall be determined in accordance with ASTM D 5664. The test data developed by ASTM D 5664 shall be used to develop modification factors for use at or near room temperature and at elevated temperatures and humidity in accordance with ASTM D 6841. Each manufacturer shall publish the modification factors for service at temperatures of not less than 80°F (27°C) and for roof framing. The roof framing modification factors shall take into consideration the climatological location.

R802.1.3.6 Exposure to weather. Where fire-retardant-treated wood is exposed to weather or damp or wet locations, it shall be identified as "Exterior" to indicate there is no increase in the listed flame spread index as defined in Section R802.1.3 when subjected to ASTM D 2898.

R802.1.3.7 Interior applications. Interior fire-retardant-treated wood shall have a moisture content of not over 28 percent when tested in accordance with ASTM D 3201 procedures at 92 percent relative humidity. Interior fire-retardant-treated wood shall be tested in accordance with Section R802.1.3.5.1 or R802.1.3.5.2. Interior fire-retardant-treated wood designated as Type A shall be tested in accordance with the provisions of this section.

R802.1.3.8 Moisture content. Fire-retardant-treated wood shall be dried to a moisture content of 19 percent or less for lumber and 15 percent or less for wood structural panels before use. For wood kiln dried after treatment (KDAT) the kiln temperatures shall not exceed those used in kiln drying the lumber and plywood submitted for the tests described in Section R802.1.3.5.1 for plywood and R802.1.3.5.2 for lumber.

R802.1.4 Structural glued laminated timbers. Glued laminated timbers shall be manufactured and identified as required in ANSI/AITC A190.1 and ASTM D 3737.

R802.1.5 Structural log members. Stress grading of structural log members of nonrectangular shape, as typically used in log buildings, shall be in accordance with ASTM D 3957. Such structural log members shall be identified by the grade mark of an *approved* lumber grading or inspection agency. In lieu of a grade mark on the material, a certificate of inspection as to species and grade issued by a lumber-grading or inspection agency meeting the requirements of this section shall be permitted to be accepted.

R802.2 Design and construction. The framing details required in Section R802 apply to roofs having a minimum slope of three units vertical in 12 units horizontal (25-percent slope) or greater. Roof-ceilings shall be designed and constructed in accordance with the provisions of this chapter and Figures R606.11(1), R606.11(2) and R606.11(3) or in accordance with AFPA/NDS. Components of roof-ceilings shall be fastened in accordance with Table R602.3(1).

R802.3 Framing details. Rafters shall be framed to ridge board or to each other with a gusset plate as a tie. Ridge board shall be at least 1-inch (25 mm) nominal thickness and not less in depth than the cut end of the rafter. Opposing rafters at the ridge must align within the thickness of the ridge member. Regularly spaced hip and valley rafters need not align. At all valleys and hips there shall be a valley or hip rafter not less than 2-inch (51 mm) nominal thickness and not less in depth than the cut end of the rafter. Hip and valley rafters shall be supported at the ridge by a brace to a bearing partition or be designed to carry and distribute the specific load at that point. Where the roof pitch is less than three units vertical in 12 units horizontal (25-percent slope), structural members that support rafters and ceiling joists, such as ridge beams, hips and valleys, shall be designed as beams.

R802.3.1 Ceiling joist and rafter connections. Ceiling joists and rafters shall be nailed to each other in accordance with Table R802.5.1(9), and the rafter shall be nailed to the top wall plate in accordance with Table R602.3(1). Ceiling joists shall be continuous or securely joined in accordance with Table R802.5.1(9) where they meet over interior partitions and are nailed to adjacent rafters to provide a continuous tie across the building when such joists are parallel to the rafters.

Where ceiling joists are not connected to the rafters at the top wall plate, joists connected higher in the *attic* shall be installed as rafter ties, or rafter ties shall be installed to provide a continuous tie. Where ceiling joists are not parallel to rafters, subflooring or metal straps attached to the ends of the rafters shall be installed in a manner to provide a continuous tie across the building. Rafter ties shall be a minimum of 2-inch by 4-inch (51 mm by 102 mm) (nominal), installed in accordance with the connection requirements in Table R802.5.1(9), or connections of equivalent capacities shall be provided. Where ceiling joists or rafter ties are not provided, the ridge formed by these rafters shall be supported by a wall or girder designed in accordance with accepted engineering practice.

Rafter ties shall be spaced not more than 4 feet (1219 mm) on center.

Collar ties or ridge straps to resist wind uplift shall be connected in the upper third of the *attic* space in accordance with Table R602.3(1).

Collar ties shall be a minimum of 1-inch by 4-inch (25 mm by 102 mm) (nominal), spaced not more than 4 feet (1219 mm) on center.

R802.3.2 Ceiling joists lapped. Ends of ceiling joists shall be lapped a minimum of 3 inches (76 mm) or butted over bearing partitions or beams and toenailed to the bearing member. When ceiling joists are used to provide resistance to rafter thrust, lapped joists shall be nailed together in accordance with Table R802.5.1(9) and butted joists shall be tied together in a manner to resist such thrust.

R802.4 Allowable ceiling joist spans. Spans for ceiling joists shall be in accordance with Tables R802.4(1) and R802.4(2). For other grades and species and for other loading conditions, refer to the AF&PA Span Tables for Joists and Rafters.

R802.5 Allowable rafter spans. Spans for rafters shall be in accordance with Tables R802.5.1(1) through R802.5.1(8). For other grades and species and for other loading conditions, refer to the AF&PA Span Tables for Joists and Rafters. The span of each rafter shall be measured along the horizontal projection of the rafter.

R802.5.1 Purlins. Installation of purlins to reduce the span of rafters is permitted as shown in Figure R802.5.1. Purlins shall be sized no less than the required size of the rafters that they support. Purlins shall be continuous and shall be supported by 2-inch by 4-inch (51 mm by 102 mm) braces installed to bearing walls at a slope not less than 45 degrees from the horizontal. The braces shall be spaced not more than 4 feet (1219 mm) on center and the unbraced length of braces shall not exceed 8 feet (2438 mm).

R802.6 Bearing. The ends of each rafter or ceiling joist shall have not less than $1^1/_2$ inches (38 mm) of bearing on wood or metal and not less than 3 inches (76 mm) on masonry or concrete.

R802.6.1 Finished ceiling material. If the finished ceiling material is installed on the ceiling prior to the attachment of the ceiling to the walls, such as in construction at a factory, a compression strip of the same thickness as the finish ceiling material shall be installed directly above the top plate of bearing walls if the compressive strength of the finish ceiling material is less than the loads it will be required to withstand. The compression strip shall cover the entire length of such top plate and shall be at least one-half the width of the top plate. It shall be of material capable of transmitting the loads transferred through it.

R802.7 Cutting and notching. Structural roof members shall not be cut, bored or notched in excess of the limitations specified in this section.

R802.7.1 Sawn lumber. Notches in solid lumber joists, rafters, blocking and beams shall not exceed one-sixth of the depth of the member, shall not be longer than one-third of the depth of the member and shall not be located in the middle one-third of the span. Notches at the ends of the member shall not exceed one-fourth the depth of the member. The tension side of members 4 inches (102 mm) or greater in nominal thickness shall not be notched except at the ends of the members. The diameter of the holes bored or cut into members shall not exceed one-third the depth of the member. Holes shall not be closer than 2 inches (51 mm) to the top or bottom of the member, or to any other hole located in the member. Where the member is also notched, the hole shall not be closer than 2 inches (51 mm) to the notch.

Exception: Notches on cantilevered portions of rafters are permitted provided the dimension of the remaining portion of the rafter is not less than 4-inch nominal (102 mm) and the length of the cantilever does not exceed 24 inches (610 mm).

R802.7.2 Engineered wood products. Cuts, notches and holes bored in trusses, structural composite lumber, structural glue-laminated members or I-joists are prohibited except where permitted by the manufacturer's recommendations or where the effects of such *alterations* are specifically considered in the design of the member by a registered *design professional*.

R802.8 Lateral support. Roof framing members and ceiling joists having a depth-to-thickness ratio exceeding 5 to 1 based on nominal dimensions shall be provided with lateral support at points of bearing to prevent rotation. For roof rafters with ceiling joists attached per Table R602.3(1), the depth-thickness ratio for the total assembly shall be determined using the combined thickness of the rafter plus the attached ceiling joist.

Exception: Roof trusses shall be braced in accordance with Section R802.10.3.

R802.8.1 Bridging. Rafters and ceiling joists having a depth-to-thickness ratio exceeding 6 to 1 based on nominal dimensions shall be supported laterally by solid blocking, diagonal bridging (wood or metal) or a continuous 1-inch by 3-inch (25 mm by 76 mm) wood strip nailed across the rafters or ceiling joists at intervals not exceeding 8 feet (2438 mm).

R802.9 Framing of openings. Openings in roof and ceiling framing shall be framed with header and trimmer joists. When the header joist span does not exceed 4 feet (1219 mm), the header joist may be a single member the same size as the ceiling joist or rafter. Single trimmer joists may be used to carry a single header joist that is located within 3 feet (914 mm) of the trimmer joist bearing. When the header joist span exceeds 4 feet (1219 mm), the trimmer joists and the header joist shall be doubled and of sufficient cross section to support the ceiling joists or rafter framing into the header. *Approved* hangers shall be used for the header joist to trimmer joist connections when the header joist span exceeds 6 feet (1829 mm). Tail joists over 12 feet (3658 mm) long shall be supported at the header by framing anchors or on ledger strips not less than 2 inches by 2 inches (51 mm by 51 mm).

R802.10 Wood trusses.

R802.10.1 Truss design drawings. Truss design drawings, prepared in conformance to Section R802.10.1, shall be provided to the *building official* and *approved* prior to installation. Truss design drawings shall include, at a minimum, the information specified below. Truss design drawing shall be provided with the shipment of trusses delivered to the jobsite.

1. Slope or depth, span and spacing.
2. Location of all joints.
3. Required bearing widths.
4. Design loads as applicable.
   - 4.1. Top chord live load (as determined from Section R301.6).
   - 4.2. Top chord dead load.
   - 4.3. Bottom chord live load.
   - 4.4. Bottom chord dead load.
   - 4.5. Concentrated loads and their points of application.
   - 4.6. Controlling wind and earthquake loads.
5. Adjustments to lumber and joint connector design values for conditions of use.
6. Each reaction force and direction.
7. Joint connector type and description (e.g., size, thickness or gage) and the dimensioned location of each joint connector except where symmetrically located relative to the joint interface.
8. Lumber size, species and *grade for each member.*
9. Connection requirements for:
   - 9.1. Truss to girder-truss.
   - 9.2. Truss ply to ply.

9.3. Field splices.

10. Calculated deflection ratio and/or maximum description for live and total load.

11. Maximum axial compression forces in the truss members to enable the building designer to design the size, connections and anchorage of the permanent continuous lateral bracing. Forces shall be shown on the truss design drawing or on supplemental documents.

12. Required permanent truss member bracing location.

R802.10.2 Design. Wood trusses shall be designed in accordance with accepted engineering practice. The design and manufacture of metal-plate-connected wood trusses shall comply with ANSI/TPI 1. The truss design drawings shall be prepared by a registered professional where required by the statutes of the *jurisdiction* in which the project is to be constructed in accordance with Section R106.1.

R802.10.2.1 Applicability limits. The provisions of this section shall control the design of truss roof framing when snow controls for buildings not greater than 60 feet (18 288 mm) in length perpendicular to the joist, rafter or truss span, not greater than 36 feet (10 973 mm) in width parallel to the joist, rafter or truss span, not greater than two stories in height with each *story* not greater than 10 feet (3048 mm) high, and roof slopes not smaller than 3:12 (25-percent slope) or greater than 12:12 (100-percent slope). Truss roof framing constructed in accordance with the provisions of this section shall be limited to sites subjected to a maximum design wind speed of 110 miles per hour (49 m/s), Exposure A, B or C, and a maximum ground snow load of 70 psf (3352 Pa). For consistent loading of all truss types, roof snow load is to be computed as: 0.7 p_g.

R802.10.3 Bracing. Trusses shall be braced to prevent rotation and provide lateral stability in accordance with the requirements specified in the *construction documents* for the building and on the individual truss design drawings. In the absence of specific bracing requirements, trusses shall be braced in accordance with the Building Component Safety Information (BCSI 1-03) Guide to Good Practice for Handling, Installing & Bracing of Metal Plate Connected Wood Trusses.

R802.10.4 Alterations to trusses. Truss members shall not be cut, notched, drilled, spliced or otherwise altered in any way without the approval of a registered *design professional*. Alterations resulting in the addition of load (e.g., HVAC equipment, water heater) that exceeds the design load for the truss shall not be permitted without verification that the truss is capable of supporting such additional loading.

R802.10.5 Truss to wall connection. Trusses shall be connected to wall plates by the use of *approved* connectors having a resistance to uplift of not less than 175 pounds (779 N) and shall be installed in accordance with the manufacturer's specifications. For roof assemblies subject to wind uplift pressures of 20 pounds per square foot (960 Pa) or greater, as established in Table R301.2(2), adjusted for height and exposure per Table R301.2(3), see section R802.11.

R802.11 Roof tie-down.

R802.11.1 Uplift resistance. Roof assemblies which are subject to wind uplift pressures of 20 pounds per square foot (960 Pa) or greater shall have roof rafters or trusses attached to their supporting wall assemblies by connections capable of providing the resistance required in Table R802.11. Wind uplift pressures shall be determined using an effective wind area of 100 square feet (9.3 m^2) and Zone 1 in Table R301.2(2), as adjusted for height and exposure per Table R301.2(3).

A continuous load path shall be designed to transmit the uplift forces from the rafter or truss ties to the foundation.

TABLE R802.4(1)
CEILING JOIST SPANS FOR COMMON LUMBER SPECIES
(Uninhabitable attics without storage, live load = 10 psf, L/Δ = 240)

CEILING JOIST SPACING (inches)	SPECIES AND GRADE		DEAD LOAD = 5 psf			
			2 × 4	2 × 6	2 × 8	2 × 10
			Maximum ceiling joist spans			
			(feet - inches)	(feet - inches)	(feet - inches)	(feet - inches)
12	Douglas fir-larch	SS	13-2	20-8	Note a	Note a
	Douglas fir-larch	#1	12-8	19-11	Note a	Note a
	Douglas fir-larch	#2	12-5	19-6	25-8	Note a
	Douglas fir-larch	#3	10-10	15-10	20-1	24-6
	Hem-fir	SS	12-5	19-6	25-8	Note a
	Hem-fir	#1	12-2	19-1	25-2	Note a
	Hem-fir	#2	11-7	18-2	24-0	Note a
	Hem-fir	#3	10-10	15-10	20-1	24-6
	Southern pine	SS	12-11	20-3	Note a	Note a
	Southern pine	#1	12-8	19-11	Note a	Note a
	Southern pine	#2	12-5	19-6	25-8	Note a
	Southern pine	#3	11-6	17-0	21-8	25-7
	Spruce-pine-fir	SS	12-2	19-1	25-2	Note a
	Spruce-pine-fir	#1	11-10	18-8	24-7	Note a
	Spruce-pine-fir	#2	11-10	18-8	24-7	Note a
	Spruce-pine-fir	#3	10-10	15-10	20-1	24-6
16	Douglas fir-larch	SS	11-11	18-9	24-8	Note a
	Douglas fir-larch	#1	11-6	18-1	23-10	Note a
	Douglas fir-larch	#2	11-3	17-8	23-0	Note a
	Douglas fir-larch	#3	9-5	13-9	17-5	21-3
	Hem-fir	SS	11-3	17-8	23-4	Note a
	Hem-fir	#1	11-0	17-4	22-10	Note a
	Hem-fir	#2	10-6	16-6	21-9	Note a
	Hem-fir	#3	9-5	13-9	17-5	21-3
	Southern pine	SS	11-9	18-5	24-3	Note a
	Southern pine	#1	11-6	18-1	23-1	Note a
	Southern pine	#2	11-3	17-8	23-4	Note a
	Southern pine	#3	10-0	14-9	18-9	22-2
	Spruce-pine-fir	SS	11-0	17-4	22-10	Note a
	Spruce-pine-fir	#1	10-9	16-11	22-4	Note a
	Spruce-pine-fir	#2	10-9	16-11	22-4	Note a
	Spruce-pine-fir	#3	9-5	13-9	17-5	21-3
19.2	Douglas fir-larch	SS	11-3	17-8	23-3	Note a
	Douglas fir-larch	#1	10-10	17-0	22-5	Note a
	Douglas fir-larch	#2	10-7	16-7	21-0	25-8
	Douglas fir-larch	#3	8-7	12-6	15-10	19-5
	Hem-fir	SS	10-7	16-8	21-11	Note a
	Hem-fir	#1	10-4	16-4	21-6	Note a
	Hem-fir	#2	9-11	15-7	20-6	25-3
	Hem-fir	#3	8-7	12-6	15-10	19-5
	Southern -pine	SS	11-0	17-4	22-10	Note a
	Southern pine	#1	10-10	17-0	22-5	Note a
	Southern pine	#2	10-7	16-8	21-11	Note a
	Southern pine	#3	9-1	13-6	17-2	20-3
	Spruce-pine-fir	SS	10-4	16-4	21-6	Note a
	Spruce-pine-fir	#1	10-2	15-11	21-0	25-8
	Spruce-pine-fir	#2	10-2	15-11	21-0	25-8
	Spruce-pine-fir	#3	8-7	12-6	15-10	19-5

(continued)

TABLE R802.4(1)—continued
CEILING JOIST SPANS FOR COMMON LUMBER SPECIES
(Uninhabitable attics without storage, live load = 10 psf, L/Δ = 240)

CEILING JOIST SPACING (inches)	SPECIES AND GRADE		DEAD LOAD = 5 psf			
			2 × 4	2 × 6	2 × 8	2 × 10
			Maximum ceiling joist spans			
			(feet - inches)	(feet - inches)	(feet - inches)	(feet - inches)
24	Douglas fir-larch	SS	10-5	16-4	21-7	Note a
	Douglas fir-larch	#1	10-0	15-9	20-1	24-6
	Douglas fir-larch	#2	9-10	14-10	18-9	22-11
	Douglas fir-larch	#3	7-8	11-2	14-2	17-4
	Hem-fir	SS	9-10	15-6	20-5	Note a
	Hem-fir	#1	9-8	15-2	19-7	23-11
	Hem-fir	#2	9-2	14-5	18-6	22-7
	Hem-fir	#3	7-8	11-2	14-2	17-4
	Southern pine	SS	10-3	16-1	21-2	Note a
	Southern pine	#1	10-0	15-9	20-10	Note a
	Southern pine	#2	9-10	15-6	20-1	23-11
	Southern pine	#3	8-2	12-0	15-4	18-1
	Spruce-pine-fir	SS	9-8	15-2	19-11	25-5
	Spruce-pine-fir	#1	9-5	14-9	18-9	22-11
	Spruce-pine-fir	#2	9-5	14-9	18-9	22-11
	Spruce-pine-fir	#3	7-8	11-2	14-2	17-4

Check sources for availability of lumber in lengths greater than 20 feet.

For SI: 1 inch = 25.4 mm, 1 foot = 304.8 mm, 1 pound per square foot = 0.0479kPa.

a. Span exceeds 26 feet in length.

TABLE R802.4(2)
CEILING JOIST SPANS FOR COMMON LUMBER SPECIES
(Uninhabitable attics with limited storage, live load = 20 psf, L/Δ = 240)

CEILING JOIST SPACING (inches)	SPECIES AND GRADE		DEAD LOAD = 10 psf			
			2 × 4	2 × 6	2 × 8	2 × 10
			Maximum ceiling joist spans			
			(feet - inches)	(feet - inches)	(feet - inches)	(feet - inches)
12	Douglas fir-larch	SS	10-5	16-4	21-7	Note a
	Douglas fir-larch	#1	10-0	15-9	20-1	24-6
	Douglas fir-larch	#2	9-10	14-10	18-9	22-11
	Douglas fir-larch	#3	7-8	11-2	14-2	17-4
	Hem-fir	SS	9-10	15-6	20-5	Note a
	Hem-fir	#1	9-8	15-2	19-7	23-11
	Hem-fir	#2	9-2	14-5	18-6	22-7
	Hem-fir	#3	7-8	11-2	14-2	17-4
	Southern pine	SS	10-3	16-1	21-2	Note a
	Southern pine	#1	10-0	15-9	20-10	Note a
	Southern pine	#2	9-10	15-6	20-1	23-11
	Southern pine	#3	8-2	12-0	15-4	18-1
	Spruce-pine-fir	SS	9-8	15-2	19-11	25-5
	Spruce-pine-fir	#1	9-5	14-9	18-9	22-11
	Spruce-pine-fir	#2	9-5	14-9	18-9	22-11
	Spruce-pine-fir	#3	7-8	11-2	14-2	17-4
16	Douglas fir-larch	SS	9-6	14-11	19-7	25-0
	Douglas fir-larch	#1	9-1	13-9	17-5	21-3
	Douglas fir-larch	#2	8-9	12-10	16-3	19-10
	Douglas fir-larch	#3	6-8	9-8	12-4	15-0
	Hem-fir	SS	8-11	14-1	18-6	23-8
	Hem-fir	#1	8-9	13-5	16-10	20-8
	Hem-fir	#2	8-4	12-8	16-0	19-7
	Hem-fir	#3	6-8	9-8	12-4	15-0
	Southern pine	SS	9-4	14-7	19-3	24-7
	Southern pine	#1	9-1	14-4	18-11	23-1
	Southern pine	#2	8-11	13-6	17-5	20-9
	Southern pine	#3	7-1	10-5	13-3	15-8
	Spruce-pine-fir	SS	8-9	13-9	18-1	23-1
	Spruce-pine-fir	#1	8-7	12-10	16-3	19-10
	Spruce-pine-fir	#2	8-7	12-10	16-3	19-10
	Spruce-pine-fir	#3	6-8	9-8	12-4	15-0
19.2	Douglas fir-larch	SS	8-11	14-0	18-5	23-4
	Douglas fir-larch	#1	8-7	12-6	15-10	19-5
	Douglas fir-larch	#2	8-0	11-9	14-10	18-2
	Douglas fir-larch	#3	6-1	8-10	11-3	13-8
	Hem-fir	SS	8-5	13-3	17-5	22-3
	Hem-fir	#1	8-3	12-3	15-6	18-11
	Hem-fir	#2	7-10	11-7	14-8	17-10
	Hem-fir	#3	6-1	8-10	11-3	13-8
	Southern pine	SS	8-9	13-9	18-1	23-1
	Southern pine	#1	8-7	13-6	17-9	21-1
	Southern pine	#2	8-5	12-3	15-10	18-11
	Southern pine	#3	6-5	9-6	12-1	14-4
	Spruce-pine-fir	SS	8-3	12-11	17-1	21-8
	Spruce-pine-fir	#1	8-0	11-9	14-10	18-2
	Spruce-pine-fir	#2	8-0	11-9	14-10	18-2
	Spruce-pine-fir	#3	6-1	8-10	11-3	13-8

(continued)

TABLE R802.4(2)—continued
CEILING JOIST SPANS FOR COMMON LUMBER SPECIES
(Uninhabitable attics with limited storage, live load = 20 psf, L/Δ = 240)

CEILING JOIST SPACING (inches)	SPECIES AND GRADE		DEAD LOAD = 10 psf			
			2 × 4	2 × 6	2 × 8	2 × 10
			Maximum ceiling joist spans			
			(feet - inches)	(feet - inches)	(feet - inches)	(feet - inches)
24	Douglas fir-larch	SS	8-3	13-0	17-1	20-11
	Douglas fir-larch	#1	7-8	11-2	14-2	17-4
	Douglas fir-larch	#2	7-2	10-6	13-3	16-3
	Douglas fir-larch	#3	5-5	7-11	10-0	12-3
	Hem-fir	SS	7-10	12-3	16-2	20-6
	Hem-fir	#1	7-6	10-11	13-10	16-11
	Hem-fir	#2	7-1	10-4	13-1	16-0
	Hem-fir	#3	5-5	7-11	10-0	12-3
	Southern pine	SS	8-1	12-9	16-10	21-6
	Southern pine	#1	8-0	12-6	15-10	18-10
	Southern pine	#2	7-8	11-0	14-2	16-11
	Southern pine	#3	5-9	8-6	10-10	12-10
	Spruce-pine-fir	SS	7-8	12-0	15-10	19-5
	Spruce-pine-fir	#1	7-2	10-6	13-3	16-3
	Spruce-pine-fir	#2	7-2	10-6	13-3	16-3
	Spruce-pine-fir	#3	5-5	7-11	10-0	12-3

Check sources for availability of lumber in lengths greater than 20 feet.

For SI: 1 inch = 25.4 mm, 1 foot = 304.8 mm, 1 pound per square foot = 0.0479kPa.

a. Span exceeds 26 feet in length.

TABLE R802.5.1(1)
RAFTER SPANS FOR COMMON LUMBER SPECIES
(Roof live load=20 psf, ceiling not attached to rafters, L/Δ = 180)

RAFTER SPACING (inches)	SPECIES AND GRADE		DEAD LOAD = 10 psf					DEAD LOAD = 20 psf				
			2 × 4	2 × 6	2 × 8	2 × 10	2 × 12	2 × 4	2 × 6	2 × 8	2 × 10	2 × 12
			Maximum rafter spans[a]									
			(feet - inches)	(feet - inches)	(feet - inches)	(feet - inches)	(feet - inches)	(feet - inches)	(feet - inches)	(feet - inches)	(feet - inches)	(feet - inches)
12	Douglas fir-larch	SS	11-6	18-0	23-9	Note b	Note b	11-6	18-0	23-5	Note b	Note b
	Douglas fir-larch	#1	11-1	17-4	22-5	Note b	Note b	10-6	15-4	19-5	23-9	Note b
	Douglas fir-larch	#2	10-10	16-7	21-0	25-8	Note b	9-10	14-4	18-2	22-3	25-9
	Douglas fir-larch	#3	8-7	12-6	15-10	19-5	22-6	7-5	10-10	13-9	16-9	19-6
	Hem-fir	SS	10-10	17-0	22-5	Note b	Note b	10-10	17-0	22-5	Note b	Note b
	Hem-fir	#1	10 -7	16-8	21-10	Note b	Note b	10-3	14-11	18-11	23-2	Note b
	Hem-fir	#2	10-1	15-11	20-8	25-3	Note b	9-8	14-2	17-11	21-11	25-5
	Hem-fir	#3	8-7	12-6	15-10	19-5	22-6	7-5	10-10	13-9	16-9	19-6
	Southern pine	SS	11-3	17-8	23-4	Note b	Note b	11-3	17-8	23-4	Note b	Note b
	Southern pine	#1	11-1	17-4	22-11	Note b	Note b	11-1	17-3	21-9	25-10	Note b
	Southern pine	#2	10-10	17-0	22-5	Note b	Note b	10-6	15-1	19-5	23-2	Note b
	Southern pine	#3	9-1	13-6	17-2	20-3	24-1	7-11	11-8	14-10	17-6	20-11
	Spruce-pine-fir	SS	10-7	16-8	21-11	Note b	Note b	10-7	16-8	21-9	Note b	Note b
	Spruce-pine-fir	#1	10-4	16-3	21-0	25-8	Note b	9-10	14-4	18-2	22-3	25-9
	Spruce-pine-fir	#2	10-4	16-3	21-0	25-8	Note b	9-10	14-4	18-2	22-3	25-9
	Spruce-pine-fir	#3	8-7	12-6	15-10	19-5	22-6	7-5	10-10	13-9	16-9	19-6
16	Douglas fir-larch	SS	10-5	16-4	21-7	Note b	Note b	10-5	16-0	20-3	24-9	Note b
	Douglas fir-larch	#1	10-0	15-4	19-5	23-9	Note b	9-1	13-3	16-10	20-7	23-10
	Douglas fir-larch	#2	9-10	14-4	18-2	22-3	25-9	8-6	12-5	15-9	19-3	22-4
	Douglas fir-larch	#3	7-5	10-10	13-9	16-9	19-6	6-5	9-5	11-11	14-6	16-10
	Hem-fir	SS	9-10	15-6	20-5	Note b	Note b	9-10	15-6	19-11	24-4	Note b
	Hem-fir	#1	9-8	14-11	18-11	23-2	Note b	8-10	12-11	16-5	20-0	23-3
	Hem-fir	#2	9-2	14-2	17-11	21-11	25-5	8-5	12-3	15-6	18-11	22-0
	Hem-fir	#3	7-5	10-10	13-9	16-9	19-6	6-5	9-5	11-11	14-6	16-10
	Southern pine	SS	10-3	16-1	21-2	Note b	Note b	10-3	16-1	21-2	Note b	Note b
	Southern pine	#1	10-0	15-9	20-10	25-10	Note b	10-0	15-0	18-10	22-4	Note b
	Southern pine	#2	9-10	15-1	19-5	23-2	Note b	9-1	13-0	16-10	20-1	23-7
	Southern pine	#3	7-11	11-8	14-10	17-6	20-11	6-10	10-1	12-10	15-2	18-1
	Spruce-pine-fir	SS	9-8	15-2	19-11	25-5	Note b	9-8	14-10	18-10	23-0	Note b
	Spruce-pine-fir	#1	9-5	14-4	18-2	22-3	25-9	8-6	12-5	15-9	19-3	22-4
	Spruce-pine-fir	#2	9-5	14-4	18-2	22-3	25-9	8-6	12-5	15-9	19-3	22-4
	Spruce-pine-fir	#3	7-5	10-10	13-9	16-9	19-6	6-5	9-5	11-11	14-6	16-10
19.2	Douglas fir-larch	SS	9-10	15-5	20-4	25-11	Note b	9-10	14-7	18-6	22-7	Note b
	Douglas fir-larch	#1	9-5	14-0	17-9	21-8	25-2	8-4	12-2	15-4	18-9	21-9
	Douglas fir-larch	#2	8-11	13-1	16-7	20-3	23-6	7-9	11-4	14-4	17-7	20-4
	Douglas fir-larch	#3	6-9	9-11	12-7	15-4	17-9	5-10	8-7	10-10	13-3	15-5
	Hem-fir	SS	9-3	14-7	19-2	24-6	Note b	9-3	14-4	18-2	22-3	25-9
	Hem-fir	#1	9-1	13-8	17-4	21-1	24-6	8-1	11-10	15-0	18-4	21-3
	Hem-fir	#2	8-8	12-11	16-4	20-0	23-2	7-8	11-2	14-2	17-4	20-1
	Hem-fir	#3	6-9	9-11	12-7	15-4	17-9	5-10	8-7	10-10	13-3	15-5
	Southern pine	SS	9-8	15-2	19-11	25-5	Note b	9-8	15-2	19-11	25-5	Note b
	Southern pine	#1	9-5	14-10	19-7	23-7	Note b	9-3	13-8	17-2	20-5	24-4
	Southern pine	#2	9-3	13-9	17-9	21-2	24-10	8-4	11-11	15-4	18-4	21-6
	Southern pine	#3	7-3	10-8	13-7	16-0	19-1	6-3	9-3	11-9	13-10	16-6
	Spruce-pine-fir	SS	9-1	14-3	18-9	23-11	Note b	9-1	13-7	17-2	21-0	24-4
	Spruce-pine-fir	#1	8-10	13-1	16-7	20-3	23-6	7-9	11-4	14-4	17-7	20-4
	Spruce-pine-fir	#2	8-10	13-1	16-7	20-3	23-6	7-9	11-4	14-4	17-7	20-4
	Spruce-pine-fir	#3	6-9	9-11	12-7	15-4	17-9	5-10	8-7	10-10	13-3	15-5

(continued)

TABLE R802.5.1(1)—continued
RAFTER SPANS FOR COMMON LUMBER SPECIES
(Roof live load=20 psf, ceiling not attached to rafters, L/Δ = 180)

RAFTER SPACING (inches)	SPECIES AND GRADE		DEAD LOAD = 10 psf					DEAD LOAD = 20 psf				
			2 × 4	2 × 6	2 × 8	2 × 10	2 × 12	2 × 4	2 × 6	2 × 8	2 × 10	2 × 12
			Maximum rafter spans[a]									
			(feet - inches)	(feet - inches)	(feet - inches)	(feet - inches)	(feet - inches)	(feet - inches)	(feet - inches)	(feet - inches)	(feet - inches)	(feet - inches)
24	Douglas fir-larch	SS	9-1	14-4	18-10	23-4	Note b	8-11	13-1	16-7	20-3	23-5
	Douglas fir-larch	#1	8-7	12-6	15-10	19-5	22-6	7-5	10-10	13-9	16-9	19-6
	Douglas fir-larch	#2	8-0	11-9	14-10	18-2	21-0	6-11	10-2	12-10	15-8	18-3
	Douglas fir-larch	#3	6-1	8-10	11-3	13-8	15-11	5-3	7-8	9-9	11-10	13-9
	Hem-fir	SS	8-7	13-6	17-10	22-9	Note b	8-7	12-10	16-3	19-10	23-0
	Hem-fir	#1	8-4	12-3	15-6	18-11	21-11	7-3	10-7	13-5	16-4	19-0
	Hem-fir	#2	7-11	11-7	14-8	17-10	20-9	6-10	10-0	12-8	15-6	17-11
	Hem-fir	#3	6-1	8-10	11-3	13-8	15-11	5-3	7-8	9-9	11-10	13-9
	Southern pine	SS	8-11	14-1	18-6	23-8	Note b	8-11	14-1	18-6	22-11	Note b
	Southern pine	#1	8-9	13-9	17-9	21-1	25-2	8-3	12-3	15-4	18-3	21-9
	Southern pine	#2	8-7	12-3	15-10	18-11	22-2	7-5	10-8	13-9	16-5	19-3
	Southern pine	#3	6-5	9-6	12-1	14-4	17-1	5-7	8-3	10-6	12-5	14-9
	Spruce-pine-fir	SS	8-5	13-3	17-5	21-8	25-2	8-4	12-2	15-4	18-9	21-9
	Spruce-pine-fir	#1	8-0	11-9	14-10	18-2	21-0	6-11	10-2	12-10	15-8	18-3
	Spruce-pine-fir	#2	8-0	11-9	14-10	18-2	21-0	6-11	10-2	12-10	15-8	18-3
	Spruce-pine-fir	#3	6-1	8-10	11-3	13-8	15-11	5-3	7-8	9-9	11-10	13-9

Check sources for availability of lumber in lengths greater than 20 feet.

For SI: 1 inch = 25.4 mm, 1 foot = 304.8 mm, 1 pound per square foot = 0.0479kPa.

a. The tabulated rafter spans assume that ceiling joists are located at the bottom of the attic space or that some other method of resisting the outward push of the rafters on the bearing walls, such as rafter ties, is provided at that location. When ceiling joists or rafter ties are located higher in the attic space, the rafter spans shall be multiplied by the factors given below:

H_C/H_R	Rafter Span Adjustment Factor
1/3	0.67
1/4	0.76
1/5	0.83
1/6	0.90
1/7.5 or less	1.00

where:

H_C = Height of ceiling joists or rafter ties measured vertically above the top of the rafter support walls.

H_R = Height of roof ridge measured vertically above the top of the rafter support walls.

b. Span exceeds 26 feet in length.

TABLE R802.5.1(2)
RAFTER SPANS FOR COMMON LUMBER SPECIES
(Roof live load=20 psf, ceiling attached to rafters, L/Δ = 240)

RAFTER SPACING (inches)	SPECIES AND GRADE		DEAD LOAD = 10 psf					DEAD LOAD = 20 psf				
			2 × 4	2 × 6	2 × 8	2 × 10	2 × 12	2 × 4	2 × 6	2 × 8	2 × 10	2 × 12
			Maximum rafter spans[a]									
			(feet - inches)	(feet - inches)	(feet - inches)	(feet - inches)	(feet - inches)	(feet - inches)	(feet - inches)	(feet - inches)	(feet - inches)	(feet - inches)
12	Douglas fir-larch	SS	10-5	16-4	21-7	Note b	Note b	10-5	16-4	21-7	Note b	Note b
	Douglas fir-larch	#1	10-0	15-9	20-10	Note b	Note b	10-0	15-4	19-5	23-9	Note b
	Douglas fir-larch	#2	9-10	15-6	20-5	25-8	Note b	9-10	14-4	18-2	22-3	25-9
	Douglas fir-larch	#3	8-7	12-6	15-10	19-5	22-6	7-5	10-10	13-9	16-9	19-6
	Hem-fir	SS	9-10	15-6	20-5	Note b	Note b	9-10	15-6	20-5	Note b	Note b
	Hem-fir	#1	9-8	15-2	19-11	25-5	Note b	9-8	14-11	18-11	23-2	Note b
	Hem-fir	#2	9-2	14-5	19-0	24-3	Note b	9-2	14-2	17-11	21-11	25-5
	Hem-fir	#3	8-7	12-6	15-10	19-5	22-6	7-5	10-10	13-9	16-9	19-6
	Southern pine	SS	10-3	16-1	21-2	Note b	Note b	10-3	16-1	21-2	Note b	Note b
	Southern pine	#1	10-0	15-9	20-10	Note b	Note b	10-0	15-9	20-10	25-10	Note b
	Southern pine	#2	9-10	15-6	20-5	Note b	Note b	9-10	15-1	19-5	23-2	Note b
	Southern pine	#3	9-1	13-6	17-2	20-3	24-1	7-11	11-8	14-10	17-6	20-11
	Spruce-pine-fir	SS	9-8	15-2	19-11	25-5	Note b	9-8	15-2	19-11	25-5	Note b
	Spruce-pine-fir	#1	9-5	14-9	19-6	24-10	Note b	9-5	14-4	18-2	22-3	25-9
	Spruce-pine-fir	#2	9-5	14-9	19-6	24-10	Note b	9-5	14-4	18-2	22-3	25-9
	Spruce-pine-fir	#3	8-7	12-6	15-10	19-5	22-6	7-5	10-10	13-9	16-9	19-6
16	Douglas fir-larch	SS	9-6	14-11	19-7	25-0	Note b	9-6	14-11	19-7	24-9	Note b
	Douglas fir-larch	#1	9-1	14-4	18-11	23-9	Note b	9-1	13-3	16-10	20-7	23-10
	Douglas fir-larch	#2	8-11	14-1	18-2	22-3	25-9	8-6	12-5	15-9	19-3	22-4
	Douglas fir-larch	#3	7-5	10-10	13-9	16-9	19-6	6-5	9-5	11-11	14-6	16-10
	Hem-fir	SS	8-11	14-1	18-6	23-8	Note b	8-11	14-1	18-6	23-8	Note b
	Hem-fir	#1	8-9	13-9	18-1	23-1	Note b	8-9	12-11	16-5	20-0	23-3
	Hem-fir	#2	8-4	13-1	17-3	21-11	25-5	8-4	12-3	15-6	18-11	22-0
	Hem-fir	#3	7-5	10-10	13-9	16-9	19-6	6-5	9-5	11-11	14-6	16-10
	Southern pine	SS	9-4	14-7	19-3	24-7	Note b	9-4	14-7	19-3	24-7	Note b
	Southern pine	#1	9-1	14-4	18-11	24-1	Note b	9-1	14-4	18-10	22-4	Note b
	Southern pine	#2	8-11	14-1	18-6	23-2	Note b	8-11	13-0	16-10	20-1	23-7
	Southern pine	#3	7-11	11-8	14-10	17-6	20-11	6-10	10-1	12-10	15-2	18-1
	Spruce-pine-fir	SS	8-9	13-9	18-1	23-1	Note b	8-9	13-9	18-1	23-0	Note b
	Spruce-pine-fir	#1	8-7	13-5	17-9	22-3	25-9	8-6	12-5	15-9	19-3	22-4
	Spruce-pine-fir	#2	8-7	13-5	17-9	22-3	25-9	8-6	12-5	15-9	19-3	22-4
	Spruce-pine-fir	#3	7-5	10-10	13-9	16-9	19-6	6-5	9-5	11-11	14-6	16-10
19.2	Douglas fir-larch	SS	8-11	14-0	18-5	23-7	Note b	8-11	14-0	18-5	22-7	Note b
	Douglas fir-larch	#1	8-7	13-6	17-9	21-8	25-2	8-4	12-2	15-4	18-9	21-9
	Douglas fir-larch	#2	8-5	13-1	16-7	20-3	23-6	7-9	11-4	14-4	17-7	20-4
	Douglas fir-larch	#3	6-9	9-11	12-7	15-4	17-9	5-10	8-7	10-10	13-3	15-5
	Hem-fir	SS	8-5	13-3	17-5	22-3	Note b	8-5	13-3	17-5	22-3	25-9
	Hem-fir	#1	8-3	12-11	17-1	21-1	24-6	8-1	11-10	15-0	18-4	21-3
	Hem-fir	#2	7-10	12-4	16-3	20-0	23-2	7-8	11-2	14-2	17-4	20-1
	Hem-fir	#3	6-9	9-11	12-7	15-4	17-9	5-10	8-7	10-10	13-3	15-5
	Southern pine	SS	8-9	13-9	18-1	23-1	Note b	8-9	13-9	18-1	23-1	Note b
	Southern pine	#1	8-7	13-6	17-9	22-8	Note b	8-7	13-6	17-2	20-5	24-4
	Southern pine	#2	8-5	13-3	17-5	21-2	24-10	8-4	11-11	15-4	18-4	21-6
	Southern pine	#3	7-3	10-8	13-7	16-0	19-1	6-3	9-3	11-9	13-10	16-6
	Spruce-pine-fir	SS	8-3	12-11	17-1	21-9	Note b	8-3	12-11	17-1	21-0	24-4
	Spruce-pine-fir	#1	8-1	12-8	16-7	20-3	23-6	7-9	11-4	14-4	17-7	20-4
	Spruce-pine-fir	#2	8-1	12-8	16-7	20-3	23-6	7-9	11-4	14-4	17-7	20-4
	Spruce-pine-fir	#3	6-9	9-11	12-7	15-4	17-9	5-10	8-7	10-10	13-3	15-5

(continued)

TABLE R802.5.1(2)—continued
RAFTER SPANS FOR COMMON LUMBER SPECIES
(Roof live load=20 psf, ceiling attached to rafters, L/Δ = 240)

RAFTER SPACING (inches)	SPECIES AND GRADE		DEAD LOAD = 10 psf					DEAD LOAD = 20 psf				
			2 × 4	2 × 6	2 × 8	2 × 10	2 × 12	2 × 4	2 × 6	2 × 8	2 × 10	2 × 12
			Maximum rafter spans[a]									
			(feet - inches)	(feet - inches)	(feet - inches)	(feet - inches)	(feet - inches)	(feet - inches)	(feet - inches)	(feet - inches)	(feet - inches)	(feet - inches)
24	Douglas fir-larch	SS	8-3	13-0	17-2	21-10	Note b	8-3	13-0	16-7	20-3	23-5
	Douglas fir-larch	#1	8-0	12-6	15-10	19-5	22-6	7-5	10-10	13-9	16-9	19-6
	Douglas fir-larch	#2	7-10	11-9	14-10	18-2	21-0	6-11	10-2	12-10	15-8	18-3
	Douglas fir-larch	#3	6-1	8-10	11-3	13-8	15-11	5-3	7-8	9-9	11-10	13-9
	Hem-fir	SS	7-10	12-3	16-2	20-8	25-1	7-10	12-3	16-2	19-10	23-0
	Hem-fir	#1	7-8	12-0	15-6	18-11	21-11	7-3	10-7	13-5	16-4	19-0
	Hem-fir	#2	7-3	11-5	14-8	17-10	20-9	6-10	10-0	12-8	15-6	17-11
	Hem-fir	#3	6-1	8-10	11-3	13-8	15-11	5-3	7-8	9-9	11-10	13-9
	Southern pine	SS	8-1	12-9	16-10	21-6	Note b	8-1	12-9	16-10	21-6	Note b
	Southern pine	#1	8-0	12-6	16-6	21-1	25-2	8-0	12-3	15-4	18-3	21-9
	Southern pine	#2	7-10	12-3	15-10	18-11	22-2	7-5	10-8	13-9	16-5	19-3
	Southern pine	#3	6-5	9-6	12-1	14-4	17-1	5-7	8-3	10-6	12-5	14-9
	Spruce-pine-fir	SS	7-8	12-0	15-10	20-2	24-7	7-8	12-0	15-4	18-9	21-9
	Spruce-pine-fir	#1	7-6	11-9	14-10	18-2	21-0	6-11	10-2	12-10	15-8	18-3
	Spruce-pine-fir	#2	7-6	11-9	14-10	18-2	21-0	6-11	10-2	12-10	15-8	18-3
	Spruce-pine-fir	#3	6-1	8-10	11-3	13-8	15-11	5-3	7-8	9-9	11-10	13-9

Check sources for availability of lumber in lengths greater than 20 feet.

For SI: 1 inch = 25.4 mm, 1 foot = 304.8 mm, 1 pound per square foot = 0.0479kPa.

a. The tabulated rafter spans assume that ceiling joists are located at the bottom of the attic space or that some other method of resisting the outward push of the rafters on the bearing walls, such as rafter ties, is provided at that location. When ceiling joists or rafter ties are located higher in the attic space, the rafter spans shall be multiplied by the factors given below:

H_C/H_R	Rafter Span Adjustment Factor
1/3	0.67
1/4	0.76
1/5	0.83
1/6	0.90
1/7.5 or less	1.00

where:

H_C = Height of ceiling joists or rafter ties measured vertically above the top of the rafter support walls.

H_R = Height of roof ridge measured vertically above the top of the rafter support walls.

b. Span exceeds 26 feet in length.

TABLE R802.5.1(3)
RAFTER SPANS FOR COMMON LUMBER SPECIES
(Ground snow load=30 psf, ceiling not attached to rafters, L/Δ = 180)

RAFTER SPACING (inches)	SPECIES AND GRADE		DEAD LOAD = 10 psf					DEAD LOAD = 20 psf				
			2 × 4	2 × 6	2 × 8	2 × 10	2 × 12	2 × 4	2 × 6	2 × 8	2 × 10	2 × 12
			Maximum rafter spans[a]									
			(feet - inches)	(feet - inches)	(feet - inches)	(feet - inches)	(feet - inches)	(feet - inches)	(feet - inches)	(feet - inches)	(feet - inches)	(feet - inches)
12	Douglas fir-larch	SS	10-0	15-9	20-9	Note b	Note b	10-0	15-9	20-1	24-6	Note b
	Douglas fir-larch	#1	9-8	14-9	18-8	22-9	Note b	9-0	13-2	16-8	20-4	23-7
	Douglas fir-larch	#2	9-5	13-9	17-5	21-4	24-8	8-5	12-4	15-7	19-1	22-1
	Douglas fir-larch	#3	7-1	10-5	13-2	16-1	18-8	6-4	9-4	11-9	14-5	16-8
	Hem-fir	SS	9-6	14-10	19-7	25-0	Note b	9-6	14-10	19-7	24-1	Note b
	Hem-fir	#1	9-3	14-4	18-2	22-2	25-9	8-9	12-10	16-3	19-10	23-0
	Hem-fir	#2	8-10	13-7	17-2	21-0	24-4	8-4	12-2	15-4	18-9	21-9
	Hem-fir	#3	7-1	10-5	13-2	16-1	18-8	6-4	9-4	11-9	14-5	16-8
	Southern pine	SS	9-10	15-6	20-5	Note b	Note b	9-10	15-6	20-5	Note b	Note b
	Southern pine	#1	9-8	15-2	20-0	24-9	Note b	9-8	14-10	18-8	22-2	Note b
	Southern pine	#2	9-6	14-5	18-8	22-3	Note b	9-0	12-11	16-8	19-11	23-4
	Southern pine	#3	7-7	11-2	14-3	16-10	20-0	6-9	10-0	12-9	15-1	17-11
	Spruce-pine-fir	SS	9-3	14-7	19-2	24-6	Note b	9-3	14-7	18-8	22-9	Note b
	Spruce-pine-fir	#1	9-1	13-9	17-5	21-4	24-8	8-5	12-4	15-7	19-1	22-1
	Spruce-pine-fir	#2	9-1	13-9	17-5	21-4	24-8	8-5	12-4	15-7	19-1	22-1
	Spruce-pine-fir	#3	7-1	10-5	13-2	16-1	18-8	6-4	9-4	11-9	14-5	16-8
16	Douglas fir-larch	SS	9-1	14-4	18-10	23-9	Note b	9-1	13-9	17-5	21-3	24-8
	Douglas fir-larch	#1	8-9	12-9	16-2	19-9	22-10	7-10	11-5	14-5	17-8	20-5
	Douglas fir-larch	#2	8-2	11-11	15-1	18-5	21-5	7-3	10-8	13-6	16-6	19-2
	Douglas fir-larch	#3	6-2	9-0	11-5	13-11	16-2	5-6	8-1	10-3	12-6	14-6
	Hem-fir	SS	8-7	13-6	17-10	22-9	Note b	8-7	13-6	17-1	20-10	24-2
	Hem-fir	#1	8-5	12-5	15-9	19-3	22-3	7-7	11-1	14-1	17-2	19-11
	Hem-fir	#2	8-0	11-9	14-11	18-2	21-1	7-2	10-6	13-4	16-3	18-10
	Hem-fir	#3	6-2	9-0	11-5	13-11	16-2	5-6	8-1	10-3	12-6	14-6
	Southern pine	SS	8-11	14-1	18-6	23-8	Note b	8-11	14-1	18-6	23-8	Note b
	Southern pine	#1	8-9	13-9	18-1	21-5	25-7	8-8	12-10	16-2	19-2	22-10
	Southern pine	#2	8-7	12-6	16-2	19-3	22-7	7-10	11-2	14-5	17-3	20-2
	Southern pine	#3	6-7	9-8	12-4	14-7	17-4	5-10	8-8	11-0	13-0	15-6
	Spruce-pine-fir	SS	8-5	13-3	17-5	22-1	25-7	8-5	12-9	16-2	19-9	22-10
	Spruce-pine-fir	#1	8-2	11-11	15-1	18-5	21-5	7-3	10-8	13-6	16-6	19-2
	Spruce-pine-fir	#2	8-2	11-11	15-1	18-5	21-5	7-3	10-8	13-6	16-6	19-2
	Spruce-pine-fir	#3	6-2	9-0	11-5	13-11	16-2	5-6	8-1	10-3	12-6	14-6
19.2	Douglas fir-larch	SS	8-7	13-6	17-9	21-8	25-2	8-7	12-6	15-10	19-5	22-6
	Douglas fir-larch	#1	7-11	11-8	14-9	18-0	20-11	7-1	10-5	13-2	16-1	18-8
	Douglas fir-larch	#2	7-5	10-11	13-9	16-10	19-6	6-8	9-9	12-4	15-1	17-6
	Douglas fir-larch	#3	5-7	8-3	10-5	12-9	14-9	5-0	7-4	9-4	11-5	13-2
	Hem-fir	SS	8-1	12-9	16-9	21-4	24-8	8-1	12-4	15-7	19-1	22-1
	Hem-fir	#1	7-9	11-4	14-4	17-7	20-4	6-11	10-2	12-10	15-8	18-2
	Hem-fir	#2	7-4	10-9	13-7	16-7	19-3	6-7	9-7	12-2	14-10	17-3
	Hem-fir	#3	5-7	8-3	10-5	12-9	14-9	5-0	7-4	9-4	11-5	13-2
	Southern pine	SS	8-5	13-3	17-5	22-3	Note b	8-5	13-3	17-5	22-0	25-9
	Southern pine	#1	8-3	13-0	16-6	19-7	23-4	7-11	11-9	14-9	17-6	20-11
	Southern pine	#2	7-11	11-5	14-9	17-7	20-7	7-1	10-2	13-2	15-9	18-5
	Southern pine	#3	6-0	8-10	11-3	13-4	15-10	5-4	7-11	10-1	11-11	14-2
	Spruce-pine-fir	SS	7-11	12-5	16-5	20-2	23-4	7-11	11-8	14-9	18-0	20-11
	Spruce-pine-fir	#1	7-5	10-11	13-9	16-10	19-6	6-8	9-9	12-4	15-1	17-6
	Spruce-pine-fir	#2	7-5	10-11	13-9	16-10	19-6	6-8	9-9	12-4	15-1	17-6
	Spruce-pine-fir	#3	5-7	8-3	10-5	12-9	14-9	5-0	7-4	9-4	11-5	13-2

(continued)

TABLE R802.5.1(3)—continued
RAFTER SPANS FOR COMMON LUMBER SPECIES
(Ground snow load=30 psf, ceiling not attached to rafters, L/Δ = 180)

RAFTER SPACING (inches)	SPECIES AND GRADE		DEAD LOAD = 10 psf					DEAD LOAD = 20 psf				
			2 x 4	2 x 6	2 x 8	2 x 10	2 x 12	2 x 4	2 x 6	2 x 8	2 x 10	2 x 12
			Maximum rafter spans[a]									
			(feet - inches)	(feet - inches)	(feet - inches)	(feet - inches)	(feet - inches)	(feet - inches)	(feet - inches)	(feet - inches)	(feet - inches)	(feet - inches)
24	Douglas fir-larch	SS	7-11	12-6	15-10	19-5	22-6	7-8	11-3	14-2	17-4	20-1
	Douglas fir-larch	#1	7-1	10-5	13-2	16-1	18-8	6-4	9-4	11-9	14-5	16-8
	Douglas fir-larch	#2	6-8	9-9	12-4	15-1	17-6	5-11	8-8	11-0	13-6	15-7
	Douglas fir-larch	#3	5-0	7-4	9-4	11-5	13-2	4-6	6-7	8-4	10-2	11-10
	Hem-fir	SS	7-6	11-10	15-7	19-1	22-1	7-6	11-0	13-11	17-0	19-9
	Hem-fir	#1	6-11	10-2	12-10	15-8	18-2	6-2	9-1	11-6	14-0	16-3
	Hem-fir	#2	6-7	9-7	12-2	14-10	17-3	5-10	8-7	10-10	13-3	15-5
	Hem-fir	#3	5-0	7-4	9-4	11-5	13-2	4-6	6-7	8-4	10-2	11-10
	Southern pine	SS	7-10	12-3	16-2	20-8	25-1	7-10	12-3	16-2	19-8	23-0
	Southern pine	#1	7-8	11-9	14-9	17-6	20-11	7-1	10-6	13-2	15-8	18-8
	Southern pine	#2	7-1	10-2	13-2	15-9	18-5	6-4	9-2	11-9	14-1	16-6
	Southern pine	#3	5-4	7-11	10-1	11-11	14-2	4-9	7-1	9-0	10-8	12-8
	Spruce-pine-fir	SS	7-4	11-7	14-9	18-0	20-11	7-1	10-5	13-2	16-1	18-8
	Spruce-pine-fir	#1	6-8	9-9	12-4	15-1	17-6	5-11	8-8	11-0	13-6	15-7
	Spruce-pine-fir	#2	6-8	9-9	12-4	15-1	17-6	5-11	8-8	11-0	13-6	15-7
	Spruce-pine-fir	#3	5-0	7-4	9-4	11-5	13-2	4-6	6-7	8-4	10-2	11-10

Check sources for availability of lumber in lengths greater than 20 feet.

For SI: 1 inch = 25.4 mm, 1 foot = 304.8 mm, 1 pound per square foot = 0.0479kPa.

a. The tabulated rafter spans assume that ceiling joists are located at the bottom of the attic space or that some other method of resisting the outward push of the rafters on the bearing walls, such as rafter ties, is provided at that location. When ceiling joists or rafter ties are located higher in the attic space, the rafter spans shall be multiplied by the factors given below:

H_C/H_R	Rafter Span Adjustment Factor
1/3	0.67
1/4	0.76
1/5	0.83
1/6	0.90
1/7.5 or less	1.00

where:

H_C = Height of ceiling joists or rafter ties measured vertically above the top of the rafter support walls.

H_R = Height of roof ridge measured vertically above the top of the rafter support walls.

b. Span exceeds 26 feet in length.

TABLE R802.5.1(4)
RAFTER SPANS FOR COMMON LUMBER SPECIES
(Ground snow load=50 psf, ceiling not attached to rafters, L/Δ = 180)

RAFTER SPACING (inches)	SPECIES AND GRADE		DEAD LOAD = 10 psf					DEAD LOAD = 20 psf				
			2 × 4	2 × 6	2 × 8	2 × 10	2 × 12	2 × 4	2 × 6	2 × 8	2 × 10	2 × 12
			Maximum rafter spans[a]									
			(feet - inches)	(feet - inches)	(feet - inches)	(feet - inches)	(feet - inches)	(feet - inches)	(feet - inches)	(feet - inches)	(feet - inches)	(feet - inches)
12	Douglas fir-larch	SS	8-5	13-3	17-6	22-4	26-0	8-5	13-3	17-0	20-9	24-0
	Douglas fir-larch	#1	8-2	12-0	15-3	18-7	21-7	7-7	11-2	14-1	17-3	20-0
	Douglas fir-larch	#2	7-8	11-3	14-3	17-5	20-2	7-1	10-5	13-2	16-1	18-8
	Douglas fir-larch	#3	5-10	8-6	10-9	13-2	15-3	5-5	7-10	10-0	12-2	14-1
	Hem-fir	SS	8-0	12-6	16-6	21-1	25-6	8-0	12-6	16-6	20-4	23-7
	Hem-fir	#1	7-10	11-9	14-10	18-1	21-0	7-5	10-10	13-9	16-9	19-5
	Hem-fir	#2	7-5	11-1	14-0	17-2	19-11	7-0	10-3	13-0	15-10	18-5
	Hem-fir	#3	5-10	8-6	10-9	13-2	15-3	5-5	7-10	10-0	12-2	14-1
	Southern pine	SS	8-4	13-0	17-2	21-11	Note b	8-4	13-0	17-2	21-11	Note b
	Southern pine	#1	8-2	12-10	16-10	20-3	24-1	8-2	12-6	15-9	18-9	22-4
	Southern pine	#2	8-0	11-9	15-3	18-2	21-3	7-7	10-11	14-1	16-10	19-9
	Southern pine	#3	6-2	9-2	11-8	13-9	16-4	5-9	8-5	10-9	12-9	15-2
	Spruce-pine-fir	SS	7-10	12-3	16-2	20-8	24-1	7-10	12-3	15-9	19-3	22-4
	Spruce-pine-fir	#1	7-8	11-3	14-3	17-5	20-2	7-1	10-5	13-2	16-1	18-8
	Spruce-pine-fir	#2	7-8	11-3	14-3	17-5	20-2	7-1	10-5	13-2	16-1	18-8
	Spruce-pine-fir	#3	5-10	8-6	10-9	13-2	15-3	5-5	7-10	10-0	12-2	14-1
16	Douglas fir-larch	SS	7-8	12-1	15-10	19-5	22-6	7-8	11-7	14-8	17-11	20-10
	Douglas fir-larch	#1	7-1	10-5	13-2	16-1	18-8	6-7	9-8	12-2	14-11	17-3
	Douglas fir-larch	#2	6-8	9-9	12-4	15-1	17-6	6-2	9-0	11-5	13-11	16-2
	Douglas fir-larch	#3	5-0	7-4	9-4	11-5	13-2	4-8	6-10	8-8	10-6	12-3
	Hem-fir	SS	7-3	11-5	15-0	19-1	22-1	7-3	11-5	14-5	17-8	20-5
	Hem-fir	#1	6-11	10-2	12-10	15-8	18-2	6-5	9-5	11-11	14-6	16-10
	Hem-fir	#2	6-7	9-7	12-2	14-10	17-3	6-1	8-11	11-3	13-9	15-11
	Hem-fir	#3	5-0	7-4	9-4	11-5	13-2	4-8	6-10	8-8	10-6	12-3
	Southern pine	SS	7-6	11-10	15-7	19-11	24-3	7-6	11-10	15-7	19-11	23-10
	Southern pine	#1	7-5	11-7	14-9	17-6	20-11	7-4	10-10	13-8	16-2	19-4
	Southern pine	#2	7-1	10-2	13-2	15-9	18-5	6-7	9-5	12-2	14-7	17-1
	Southern pine	#3	5-4	7-11	10-1	11-11	14-2	4-11	7-4	9-4	11-0	13-1
	Spruce-pine-fir	SS	7-1	11-2	14-8	18-0	20-11	7-1	10-9	13-8	15-11	19-4
	Spruce-pine-fir	#1	6-8	9-9	12-4	15-1	17-6	6-2	9-0	11-5	13-11	16-2
	Spruce-pine-fir	#2	6-8	9-9	12-4	15-1	17-6	6-2	9-0	11-5	13-11	16-2
	Spruce-pine-fir	#3	5-0	7-4	9-4	11-5	13-2	4-8	6-10	8-8	10-6	12-3
19.2	Douglas fir-larch	SS	7-3	11-4	14-6	17-8	20-6	7-3	10-7	13-5	16-5	19-0
	Douglas fir-larch	#1	6-6	9-6	12-0	14-8	17-1	6-0	8-10	11-2	13-7	15-9
	Douglas fir-larch	#2	6-1	8-11	11-3	13-9	15-11	5-7	8-3	10-5	12-9	14-9
	Douglas fir-larch	#3	4-7	6-9	8-6	10-5	12-1	4-3	6-3	7-11	9-7	11-2
	Hem-fir	SS	6-10	10-9	14-2	17-5	20-2	6-10	10-5	13-2	16-1	18-8
	Hem-fir	#1	6-4	9-3	11-9	14-4	16-7	5-10	8-7	10-10	13-3	15-5
	Hem-fir	#2	6-0	8-9	11-1	13-7	15-9	5-7	8-1	10-3	12-7	14-7
	Hem-fir	#3	4-7	6-9	8-6	10-5	12-1	4-3	6-3	7-11	9-7	11-2
	Southern pine	SS	7-1	11-2	14-8	18-9	22-10	7-1	11-2	14-8	18 7	21-9
	Southern pine	#1	7-0	10-8	13-5	16-0	19-1	6-8	9-11	12-5	14-10	17-8
	Southern pine	#2	6-6	9-4	12-0	14-4	16-10	6-0	8-8	11-2	13-4	15-7
	Southern pine	#3	4-11	7-3	9-2	10-10	12-11	4-6	6-8	8-6	10-1	12-0
	Spruce-pine-fir	SS	6-8	10-6	13-5	16-5	19-1	6-8	9-10	12-5	15-3	17-8
	Spruce-pine-fir	#1	6-1	8-11	11-3	13-9	15-11	5-7	8-3	10-5	12-9	14-9
	Spruce-pine-fir	#2	6-1	8-11	11-3	13-9	15-11	5-7	8-3	10-5	12-9	14-9
	Spruce-pine-fir	#3	4-7	6-9	8-6	10-5	12-1	4-3	6-3	7-11	9-7	11-2

(continued)

TABLE R802.5.1(4)—continued
RAFTER SPANS FOR COMMON LUMBER SPECIES
(Ground snow load=50 psf, ceiling not attached to rafters, L/Δ = 180)

RAFTER SPACING (inches)	SPECIES AND GRADE		DEAD LOAD = 10 psf					DEAD LOAD = 20 psf				
			2 × 4	2 × 6	2 × 8	2 × 10	2 × 12	2 × 4	2 × 6	2 × 8	2 × 10	2 × 12
			Maximum rafter spans[a]									
			(feet - inches)	(feet - inches)	(feet - inches)	(feet - inches)	(feet - inches)	(feet - inches)	(feet - inches)	(feet - inches)	(feet - inches)	(feet - inches)
24	Douglas fir-larch	SS	6-8	10-	13-0	15-10	18-4	6-6	9-6	12-0	14-8	17-0
	Douglas fir-larch	#1	5-10	8-6	10-9	13-2	15-3	5-5	7-10	10-0	12-2	14-1
	Douglas fir-larch	#2	5-5	7-11	10-1	12-4	14-3	5-0	7-4	9-4	11-5	13-2
	Douglas fir-larch	#3	4-1	6-0	7-7	9-4	10-9	3-10	5-7	7-1	8-7	10-0
	Hem-fir	SS	6-4	9-11	12-9	15-7	18-0	6-4	9-4	11-9	14-5	16-8
	Hem-fir	#1	5-8	8-3	10-6	12-10	14-10	5-3	7-8	9-9	11-10	13-9
	Hem-fir	#2	5-4	7-10	9-11	12-1	14-1	4-11	7-3	9-2	11-3	13-0
	Hem-fir	#3	4-1	6-0	7-7	9-4	10-9	3-10	5-7	7-1	8-7	10-0
	Southern pine	SS	6-7	10-4	13-8	17-5	21-0	6-7	10-4	13-8	16-7	19-5
	Southern pine	#1	6-5	9-7	12-0	14-4	17-1	6-0	8-10	11-2	13-3	15-9
	Southern pine	#2	5-10	8-4	10-9	12-10	15-1	5-5	7-9	10-0	11-11	13-11
	Southern pine	#3	4-4	6-5	8-3	9-9	11-7	4-1	6-0	7-7	9-0	10-8
	Spruce-pine-fir	SS	6-2	9-6	12-0	14-8	17-1	6-0	8-10	11-2	13-7	15-9
	Spruce-pine-fir	#1	5-5	7-11	10-1	12-4	14-3	5-0	7-4	9-4	11-5	13-2
	Spruce-pine-fir	#2	5-5	7-11	10-1	12-4	14-3	5-0	7-4	9-4	11-5	13-2
	Spruce-pine-fir	#3	4-1	6-0	7-7	9-4	10-9	3-10	5-7	7-1	8-7	10-0

Check sources for availability of lumber in lengths greater than 20 feet.

For SI: 1 inch = 25.4 mm, 1 foot = 304.8 mm, 1 pound per square foot = 0.0479kPa.

a. The tabulated rafter spans assume that ceiling joists are located at the bottom of the attic space or that some other method of resisting the outward push of the rafters on the bearing walls, such as rafter ties, is provided at that location. When ceiling joists or rafter ties are located higher in the attic space, the rafter spans shall be multiplied by the factors given below:

H_C/H_R	Rafter Span Adjustment Factor
1/3	0.67
1/4	0.76
1/5	0.83
1/6	0.90
1/7.5 or less	1.00

where:

H_C = Height of ceiling joists or rafter ties measured vertically above the top of the rafter support walls.

H_R = Height of roof ridge measured vertically above the top of the rafter support walls.

b. Span exceeds 26 feet in length.

**TABLE R802.5.1(5)
RAFTER SPANS FOR COMMON LUMBER SPECIES
(Ground snow load=30 psf, ceiling attached to rafters, L/Δ = 240)**

RAFTER SPACING (inches)	SPECIES AND GRADE		DEAD LOAD = 10 psf					DEAD LOAD = 20 psf				
			2 × 4	2 × 6	2 × 8	2 × 10	2 × 12	2 × 4	2 × 6	2 × 8	2 × 10	2 × 12
			Maximum rafter spans[a]									
			(feet - inches)	(feet - inches)	(feet - inches)	(feet - inches)	(feet - inches)	(feet - inches)	(feet - inches)	(feet - inches)	(feet - inches)	(feet - inches)
12	Douglas fir-larch	SS	9-1	14-4	18-10	24-1	Note b	9-1	14-4	18-10	24-1	Note b
	Douglas fir-larch	#1	8-9	13-9	18-2	22-9	Note b	8-9	13-2	16-8	20-4	23-7
	Douglas fir-larch	#2	8-7	13-6	17-5	21-4	24-8	8-5	12-4	15-7	19-1	22-1
	Douglas fir-larch	#3	7-1	10-5	13-2	16-1	18-8	6-4	9-4	11-9	14-5	16-8
	Hem-fir	SS	8-7	13-6	17-10	22-9	Note b	8-7	13-6	17-10	22-9	Note b
	Hem-fir	#1	8-5	13-3	17-5	22-2	25-9	8-5	12-10	16-3	19-10	23-0
	Hem-fir	#2	8-0	12-7	16-7	21-0	24-4	8-0	12-2	15-4	18-9	21-9
	Hem-fir	#3	7-1	10-5	13-2	16-1	18-8	6-4	9-4	11-9	14-5	16-8
	Southern pine	SS	8-11	14-1	18-6	23-8	Note b	8-11	14-1	18-6	23-8	Note b
	Southern pine	#1	8-9	13-9	18-2	23-2	Note b	8-9	13-9	18-2	22-2	Note b
	Southern pine	#2	8-7	13-6	17-10	22-3	Note b	8-7	12-11	16-8	19-11	23-4
	Southern pine	#3	7-7	11-2	14-3	16-10	20-0	6-9	10-0	12-9	15-1	17-11
	Spruce-pine-fir	SS	8-5	13-3	17-5	22-3	Note b	8-5	13-3	17-5	22-3	Note b
	Spruce-pine-fir	#1	8-3	12-11	17-0	21-4	24-8	8-3	12-4	15-7	19-1	22-1
	Spruce-pine-fir	#2	8-3	12-11	17-0	21-4	24-8	8-3	12-4	15-7	19-1	22-1
	Spruce-pine-fir	#3	7-1	10-5	13-2	16-1	18-8	6-4	9-4	11-9	14-5	16-8
16	Douglas fir-larch	SS	8-3	13-0	17-2	21-10	Note b	8-3	13-0	17-2	21-3	24-8
	Douglas fir-larch	#1	8-0	12-6	16-2	19-9	22-10	7-10	11-5	14-5	17-8	20-5
	Douglas fir-larch	#2	7-10	11-11	15-1	18-5	21-5	7-3	10-8	13-6	16-6	19-2
	Douglas fir-larch	#3	6-2	9-0	11-5	13-11	16-2	5-6	8-1	10-3	12-6	14-6
	Hem-fir	SS	7-10	12-3	16-2	20-8	25-1	7-10	12-3	16-2	20-8	24-2
	Hem-fir	#1	7-8	12-0	15-9	19-3	22-3	7-7	11-1	14-1	17-2	19-11
	Hem-fir	#2	7-3	11-5	14-11	18-2	21-1	7-2	10-6	13-4	16-3	18-10
	Hem-fir	#3	6-2	9-0	11-5	13-11	16-2	5-6	8-1	10-3	12-6	14-6
	Southern pine	SS	8-1	12-9	16-10	21-6	Note b	8-1	12-9	16-10	21-6	Note b
	Southern pine	#1	8-0	12-6	16-6	21-1	25-7	8-0	12-6	16-2	19-2	22-10
	Southern pine	#2	7-10	12-3	16-2	19-3	22-7	7-10	11-2	14-5	17-3	20-2
	Southern pine	#3	6-7	9-8	12-4	14-7	17-4	5-10	8-8	11-0	13-0	15-6
	Spruce-pine-fir	SS	7-8	12-0	15-10	20-2	24-7	7-8	12-0	15-10	19-9	22-10
	Spruce-pine-fir	#1	7-6	11-9	15-1	18-5	21-5	7-3	10-8	13-6	16-6	19-2
	Spruce-pine-fir	#2	7-6	11-9	15-1	18-5	21-5	7-3	10-8	13-6	16-6	19-2
	Spruce-pine-fir	#3	6-2	9-0	11-5	13-11	16-2	5-6	8-1	10-3	12-6	14-6
19.2	Douglas fir-larch	SS	7-9	12-3	16-1	20-7	25-0	7-9	12-3	15-10	19-5	22-6
	Douglas fir-larch	#1	7-6	11-8	14-9	18-0	20-11	7-1	10-5	13-2	16-1	18-8
	Douglas fir-larch	#2	7-4	10-11	13-9	16-10	19-6	6-8	9-9	12-4	15-1	17-6
	Douglas fir-larch	#3	5-7	8-3	10-5	12-9	14-9	5-0	7-4	9-4	11-5	13-2
	Hem-fir	SS	7-4	11-7	15-3	19-5	23-7	7-4	11-7	15-3	19-1	22-1
	Hem-fir	#1	7-2	11-4	14-4	17-7	20-4	6-11	10-2	12-10	15-8	18-2
	Hem-fir	#2	6-10	10-9	13-7	16-7	19-3	6-7	9-7	12-2	14-10	17-3
	Hem-fir	#3	5-7	8-3	10-5	12-9	14-9	5-0	7-4	9-4	11-5	13-2
	Southern pine	SS	7-8	12-0	15-10	20-2	24-7	7-8	12-0	15-10	20-2	24-7
	Southern pine	#1	7-6	11-9	15-6	19-7	23-4	7-6	11-9	14-9	17-6	20-11
	Southern pine	#2	7-4	11-5	14-9	17-7	20-7	7-1	10-2	13-2	15-9	18-5
	Southern pine	#3	6-0	8-10	11-3	13-4	15-10	5-4	7-11	10-1	11-11	14-2
	Spruce-pine-fir	SS	7-2	11-4	14-11	19-0	23-1	7-2	11-4	14-9	18-0	20-11
	Spruce-pine-fir	#1	7-0	10-11	13-9	16-10	19-6	6-8	9-9	12-4	15-1	17-6
	Spruce-pine-fir	#2	7-0	10-11	13-9	16-10	19-6	6-8	9-9	12-4	15-1	17-6
	Spruce-pine-fir	#3	5-7	8-3	10-5	12-9	14-9	5-0	7-4	9-4	11-5	13-2

(continued)

TABLE R802.5.1(5)—continued
RAFTER SPANS FOR COMMON LUMBER SPECIES
(Ground snow load=30 psf, ceiling attached to rafters, L/Δ = 240)

RAFTER SPACING (inches)	SPECIES AND GRADE		DEAD LOAD = 10 psf					DEAD LOAD = 20 psf				
			2 × 4	2 × 6	2 × 8	2 × 10	2 × 12	2 × 4	2 × 6	2 × 8	2 × 10	2 × 12
			Maximum rafter spans[a]									
			(feet-inches)	(feet-inches)	(feet-inches)	(feet-inches)	(feet-inches)	(feet-inches)	(feet-inches)	(feet-inches)	(feet-inches)	(feet-inches)
24	Douglas fir-larch	SS	7-3	11-4	15-0	19-1	22-6	7-3	11-3	14-2	17-4	20-1
	Douglas fir-larch	#1	7-0	10-5	13-2	16-1	18-8	6-4	9-4	11-9	14-5	16-8
	Douglas fir-larch	#2	6-8	9-9	12-4	15-1	17-6	5-11	8-8	11-0	13-6	15-7
	Douglas fir-larch	#3	5-0	7-4	9-4	11-5	13-2	4-6	6-7	8-4	10-2	11-10
	Hem-fir	SS	6-10	10-9	14-2	18-0	21-11	6-10	10-9	13-11	17-0	19-9
	Hem-fir	#1	6-8	10-2	12-10	15-8	18-2	6-2	9-1	11-6	14-0	16-3
	Hem-fir	#2	6-4	9-7	12-2	14-10	17-3	5-10	8-7	10-10	13-3	15-5
	Hem-fir	#3	5-0	7-4	9-4	11-5	13-2	4-6	6-7	8-4	10-2	11-10
	Southern pine	SS	7-1	11-2	14-8	18-9	22-10	7-1	11-2	14-8	18-9	22-10
	Southern pine	#1	7-0	10-11	14-5	17-6	20-11	7-0	10-6	13-2	15-8	18-8
	Southern pine	#2	6-10	10-2	13-2	15-9	18-5	6-4	9-2	11-9	14-1	16-6
	Southern pine	#3	5-4	7-11	10-1	11-11	14-2	4-9	7-1	9-0	10-8	12-8
	Spruce-pine-fir	SS	6-8	10-6	13-10	17-8	20-11	6-8	10-5	13-2	16-1	18-8
	Spruce-pine-fir	#1	6-6	9-9	12-4	15-1	17-6	5-11	8-8	11-0	13-6	15-7
	Spruce-pine-fir	#2	6-6	9-9	12-4	15-1	17-6	5-11	8-8	11-0	13-6	15-7
	Spruce-pine-fir	#3	5-0	7-4	9-4	11-5	13-2	4-6	6-7	8-4	10-2	11-10

Check sources for availability of lumber in lengths greater than 20 feet.

For SI: 1 inch = 25.4 mm, 1 foot = 304.8 mm, 1 pound per square foot = 0.0479kPa.

a. The tabulated rafter spans assume that ceiling joists are located at the bottom of the attic space or that some other method of resisting the outward push of the rafters on the bearing walls, such as rafter ties, is provided at that location. When ceiling joists or rafter ties are located higher in the attic space, the rafter spans shall be multiplied by the factors given below:

H_C/H_R	Rafter Span Adjustment Factor
1/3	0.67
1/4	0.76
1/5	0.83
1/6	0.90
1/7.5 or less	1.00

where:

H_C = Height of ceiling joists or rafter ties measured vertically above the top of the rafter support walls.

H_R = Height of roof ridge measured vertically above the top of the rafter support walls.

b. Span exceeds 26 feet in length.

TABLE R802.5.1(6)
RAFTER SPANS FOR COMMON LUMBER SPECIES
(Ground snow load=50 psf, ceiling attached to rafters, L/Δ = 240)

RAFTER SPACING (inches)	SPECIES AND GRADE		DEAD LOAD = 10 psf					DEAD LOAD = 20 psf				
			2 × 4	2 × 6	2 × 8	2 × 10	2 × 12	2 × 4	2 × 6	2 × 8	2 × 10	2 × 12
			Maximum rafter spans[a]									
			(feet-inches)	(feet-inches)	(feet-inches)	(feet-inches)	(feet-inches)	(feet-inches)	(feet-inches)	(feet-inches)	(feet-inches)	(feet-inches)
12	Douglas fir-larch	SS	7-8	12-1	15-11	20-3	24-8	7-8	12-1	15-11	20-3	24-0
	Douglas fir-larch	#1	7-5	11-7	15-3	18-7	21-7	7-5	11-2	14-1	17-3	20-0
	Douglas fir-larch	#2	7-3	11-3	14-3	17-5	20-2	7-1	10-5	13-2	16-1	18-8
	Douglas fir-larch	#3	5-10	8-6	10-9	13-2	15-3	5-5	7-10	10-0	12-2	14-1
	Hem-fir	SS	7-3	11-5	15-0	19-2	23-4	7-3	11-5	15-0	19-2	23-4
	Hem-fir	#1	7-1	11-2	14-8	18-1	21-0	7-1	10-10	13-9	16-9	19-5
	Hem-fir	#2	6-9	10-8	14-0	17-2	19-11	6-9	10-3	13-0	15-10	18-5
	Hem-fir	#3	5-10	8-6	10-9	13-2	15-3	5-5	7-10	10-0	12-2	14-1
	Southern pine	SS	7-6	11-10	15-7	19-11	24-3	7-6	11-10	15-7	19-11	24-3
	Southern pine	#1	7-5	11-7	15-4	19-7	23-9	7-5	11-7	15-4	18-9	22-4
	Southern pine	#2	7-3	11-5	15-0	18-2	21-3	7-3	10-11	14-1	16-10	19-9
	Southern pine	#3	6-2	9-2	11-8	13-9	16-4	5-9	8-5	10-9	12-9	15-2
	Spruce-pine-fir	SS	7-1	11-2	14-8	18-9	22-10	7-1	11-2	14-8	18-9	22-4
	Spruce-pine-fir	#1	6-11	10-11	14-3	17-5	20-2	6-11	10-5	13-2	16-1	18-8
	Spruce-pine-fir	#2	6-11	10-11	14-3	17-5	20-2	6-11	10-5	13-2	16-1	18-8
	Spruce-pine-fir	#3	5-10	8-6	10-9	13-2	15-3	5-5	7-10	10-0	12-2	14-1
16	Douglas fir-larch	SS	7-0	11-0	14-5	18-5	22-5	7-0	11-0	14-5	17-11	20-10
	Douglas fir-larch	#1	6-9	10-5	13-2	16-1	18-8	6-7	9-8	12-2	14-11	17-3
	Douglas fir-larch	#2	6-7	9-9	12-4	15-1	17-6	6-2	9-0	11-5	13-11	16-2
	Douglas fir-larch	#3	5-0	7-4	9-4	11-5	13-2	4-8	6-10	8-8	10-6	12-3
	Hem-fir	SS	6-7	10-4	13-8	17-5	21-2	6-7	10-4	13-8	17-5	20-5
	Hem-fir	#1	6-5	10-2	12-10	15-8	18-2	6-5	9-5	11-11	14-6	16-10
	Hem-fir	#2	6-2	9-7	12-2	14-10	17-3	6-1	8-11	11-3	13-9	15-11
	Hem-fir	#3	5-0	7-4	9-4	11-5	13-2	4-8	6-10	8-8	10-6	12-3
	Southern pine	SS	6-10	10-9	14-2	18-1	22-0	6-10	10-9	14-2	18-1	22-0
	Southern pine	#1	6-9	10-7	13-11	17-6	20-11	6-9	10-7	13-8	16-2	19-4
	Southern pine	#2	6-7	10-2	13-2	15-9	18-5	6-7	9-5	12-2	14-7	17-1
	Southern pine	#3	5-4	7-11	10-1	11-11	14-2	4-11	7-4	9-4	11-0	13-1
	Spruce-pine-fir	SS	6-5	10-2	13-4	17-0	20-9	6-5	10-2	13-4	16-8	19-4
	Spruce-pine-fir	#1	6-4	9-9	12-4	15-1	17-6	6-2	9-0	11-5	13-11	16-2
	Spruce-pine-fir	#2	6-4	9-9	12-4	15-1	17-6	6-2	9-0	11-5	13-11	16-2
	Spruce-pine-fir	#3	5-0	7-4	9-4	11-5	13-2	4-8	6-10	8-8	10-6	12-3
19.2	Douglas fir-larch	SS	6-7	10-4	13-7	17-4	20-6	6-7	10-4	13-5	16-5	19-0
	Douglas fir-larch	#1	6-4	9-6	12-0	14-8	17-1	6-0	8-10	11-2	13-7	15-9
	Douglas fir-larch	#2	6-1	8-11	11-3	13-9	15-11	5-7	8-3	10-5	12-9	14-9
	Douglas fir-larch	#3	4-7	6-9	8-6	10-5	12-1	4-3	6-3	7-11	9-7	11-2
	Hem-fir	SS	6-2	9-9	12-10	16-5	19-11	6-2	9-9	12-10	16-1	18-8
	Hem-fir	#1	6-1	9-3	11-9	14-4	16-7	5-10	8-7	10-10	13-3	15-5
	Hem-fir	#2	5-9	8-9	11-1	13-7	15-9	5-7	8-1	10-3	12-7	14-7
	Hem-fir	#3	4-7	6-9	8-6	10-5	12-1	4-3	6-3	7-11	9-7	11-2
	Southern pine	SS	6-5	10-2	13-4	17-0	20-9	6-5	10-2	13-4	17-0	20-9
	Southern pine	#1	6-4	9-11	13-1	16-0	19-1	6-4	9-11	12-5	14-10	17-8
	Southern pine	#2	6-2	9-4	12-0	14-4	16-10	6-0	8-8	11-2	13-4	15-7
	Southern pine	#3	4-11	7-3	9-2	10-10	12-11	4-6	6-8	8-6	10-1	12-0
	Spruce-pine-fir	SS	6-1	9-6	12-7	16-0	19-1	6-1	9-6	12-5	15-3	17-8
	Spruce-pine-fir	#1	5-11	8-11	11-3	13-9	15-11	5-7	8-3	10-5	12-9	14-9
	Spruce-pine-fir	#2	5-11	8-11	11-3	13-9	15-11	5-7	8-3	10-5	12-9	14-9
	Spruce-pine-fir	#3	4-7	6-9	8-6	10-5	12-1	4-3	6-3	7-11	9-7	11-2

(continued)

TABLE R802.5.1(6)—continued
RAFTER SPANS FOR COMMON LUMBER SPECIES
(Ground snow load=50 psf, ceiling attached to rafters, L/Δ = 240)

RAFTER SPACING (inches)	SPECIES AND GRADE		DEAD LOAD = 10 psf					DEAD LOAD = 20 psf				
			2 × 4	2 × 6	2 × 8	2 × 10	2 × 12	2 × 4	2 × 6	2 × 8	2 × 10	2 × 12
			Maximum rafter spans[a]									
			(feet-inches)	(feet-inches)	(feet-inches)	(feet-inches)	(feet-inches)	(feet-inches)	(feet-inches)	(feet-inches)	(feet-inches)	(feet-inches)
24	Douglas fir-larch	SS	6-1	9-7	12-7	15-10	18-4	6-1	9-6	12-0	14-8	17-0
	Douglas fir-larch	#1	5-10	8-6	10-9	13-2	15-3	5-5	7-10	10-0	12-2	14-1
	Douglas fir-larch	#2	5-5	7-11	10-1	12-4	14-3	5-0	7-4	9-4	11-5	13-2
	Douglas fir-larch	#3	4-1	6-0	7-7	9-4	10-9	3-10	5-7	7-1	8-7	10-0
	Hem-fir	SS	5-9	9-1	11-11	15-2	18-0	5-9	9-1	11-9	14-5	15-11
	Hem-fir	#1	5-8	8-3	10-6	12-10	14-10	5-3	7-8	9-9	11-10	13-9
	Hem-fir	#2	5-4	7-10	9-11	12-1	14-1	4-11	7-3	9-2	11-3	13-0
	Hem-fir	#3	4-1	6-0	7-7	9-4	10-9	3-10	5-7	7-1	8-7	10-0
	Southern pine	SS	6-0	9-5	12-5	15-10	19-3	6-0	9-5	12-5	15-10	19-3
	Southern pine	#1	5-10	9-3	12-0	14-4	17-1	5-10	8-10	11-2	13-3	15-9
	Southern pine	#2	5-9	8-4	10-9	12-10	15-1	5-5	7-9	10-0	11-11	13-11
	Southern pine	#3	4-4	6-5	8-3	9-9	11-7	4-1	6-0	7-7	9-0	10-8
	Spruce-pine-fir	SS	5-8	8-10	11-8	14-8	17-1	5-8	8-10	11-2	13-7	15-9
	Spruce-pine-fir	#1	5-5	7-11	10-1	12-4	14-3	5-0	7-4	9-4	11-5	13-2
	Spruce-pine-fir	#2	5-5	7-11	10-1	12-4	14-3	5-0	7-4	9-4	11-5	13-2
	Spruce-pine-fir	#3	4-1	6-0	7-7	9-4	10-9	3-10	5-7	7-1	8-7	10-0

Check sources for availability of lumber in lengths greater than 20 feet.

For SI: 1 inch = 25.4 mm, 1 foot = 304.8 mm, 1 pound per square foot = 0.0479kPa.

a. The tabulated rafter spans assume that ceiling joists are located at the bottom of the attic space or that some other method of resisting the outward push of the rafters on the bearing walls, such as rafter ties, is provided at that location. When ceiling joists or rafter ties are located higher in the attic space, the rafter spans shall be multiplied by the factors given below:

H_C/H_R	Rafter Span Adjustment Factor
1/3	0.67
1/4	0.76
1/5	0.83
1/6	0.90
1/7.5 or less	1.00

where:

H_C = Height of ceiling joists or rafter ties measured vertically above the top of the rafter support walls.

H_R = Height of roof ridge measured vertically above the top of the rafter support walls.

TABLE R802.5.1(7)
RAFTER SPANS FOR 70 PSF GROUND SNOW LOAD
(Ceiling not attached to rafters, L/Δ = 180)

RAFTER SPACING (inches)	SPECIES AND GRADE		DEAD LOAD = 10 psf					DEAD LOAD = 20 psf				
			2 × 4	2 × 6	2 × 8	2 × 10	2 × 12	2 × 4	2 × 6	2 × 8	2 × 10	2 × 12
			Maximum Rafter Spans[a]									
			(feet-inches)	(feet-inches)	(feet-inches)	(feet-inches)	(feet-inches)	(feet-inches)	(feet-inches)	(feet-inches)	(feet-inches)	(feet-inches)
12	Douglas fir-larch	SS	7-7	11-10	15-8	19-5	22-6	7-7	11-10	15-0	18-3	21-2
	Douglas fir-larch	#1	7-1	10-5	13-2	16-1	18-8	6-8	9-10	12-5	15-2	17-7
	Douglas fir-larch	#2	6-8	9-9	12-4	15-1	17-6	6-3	9-2	11-8	14-2	16-6
	Douglas fir-larch	#3	5-0	7-4	9-4	11-5	13-2	4-9	6-11	8-9	10-9	12-5
	Hem-fir	SS	7-2	11-3	14-9	18-10	22-1	7-2	11-3	14-8	18-0	20-10
	Hem-fir	#1	6-11	10-2	12-10	15-8	18-2	6-6	9-7	12-1	14-10	17-2
	Hem-fir	#2	6-7	9-7	12-2	14-10	17-3	6-2	9-1	11-5	14-0	16-3
	Hem-fir	#3	5-0	7-4	9-4	11-5	13-2	4-9	6-11	8-9	10-9	12-5
	Southern pine	SS	7-5	11-8	15-4	19-7	23-10	7-5	11-8	15-4	19-7	23-10
	Southern pine	#1	7-3	11-5	14-9	17-6	20-11	7-3	11-1	13-11	16-6	19-8
	Southern pine	#2	7-1	10-2	13-2	15-9	18-5	6-8	9-7	12-5	14-10	17-5
	Southern pine	#3	5-4	7-11	10-1	11-11	14-2	5-1	7-5	9-6	11-3	13-4
	Spruce-pine-fir	SS	7-0	11-0	14-6	18-0	20-11	7-0	11-0	13-11	17-0	19-8
	Spruce-pine-fir	#1	6-8	9-9	12-4	15-1	17-6	6-3	9-2	11-8	14-2	16-6
	Spruce-pine-fir	#2	6-8	9-9	12-4	15-1	17-6	6-3	9-2	11-8	14-2	16-6
	Spruce-pine-fir	#3	5-0	7-4	9-4	11-5	13-2	4-9	6-11	8-9	10-9	12-5
16	Douglas fir-larch	SS	6-10	10-9	13-9	16-10	19-6	6-10	10-3	13-0	15-10	18-4
	Douglas fir-larch	#1	6-2	9-0	11-5	13-11	16-2	5-10	8-6	10-9	13-2	15-3
	Douglas fir-larch	#2	5-9	8-5	10-8	13-1	15-2	5-5	7-11	10-1	12-4	14-3
	Douglas fir-larch	#3	4-4	6-4	8-1	9-10	11-5	4-1	6-0	7-7	9-4	10-9
	Hem-fir	SS	6-6	10-2	13-5	16-6	19-2	6-6	10-1	12-9	15-7	18-0
	Hem-fir	#1	6-0	8-9	11-2	13-7	15-9	5-8	8-3	10-6	12-10	14-10
	Hem-fir	#2	5-8	8-4	10-6	12-10	14-11	5-4	7-10	9-11	12-1	14-1
	Hem-fir	#3	4-4	6-4	8-1	9-10	11-5	4-1	6-0	7-7	9-4	10-9
	Southern pine	SS	6-9	10-7	14-0	17-10	21-8	6-9	10-7	14-0	17-10	21-0
	Southern pine	#1	6-7	10-2	12-9	15-2	18-1	6-5	9-7	12-0	14-4	17-1
	Southern pine	#2	6-2	8-10	11-5	13-7	16-0	5-10	8-4	10-9	12-10	15-1
	Southern pine	#3	4-8	6-10	8-9	10-4	12-3	4-4	6-5	8-3	9-9	11-7
	Spruce-pine-fir	SS	6-4	10-0	12-9	15-7	18-1	6-4	9-6	12-0	14-8	17-1
	Spruce-pine-fir	#1	5-9	8-5	10-8	13-1	15-2	5-5	7-11	10-1	12-4	14-3
	Spruce-pine-fir	#2	5-9	8-5	10-8	13-1	15-2	5-5	7-11	10-1	12-4	14-3
	Spruce-pine-fir	#3	4-4	6-4	8-1	9-10	11-5	4-1	6-0	7-7	9-4	10-9
19.2	Douglas fir-larch	SS	6-5	9-11	12-7	15-4	17-9	6-5	9-4	11-10	14-5	16-9
	Douglas fir-larch	#1	5-7	8-3	10-5	12-9	14-9	5-4	7-9	9-10	12-0	13-11
	Douglas fir-larch	#2	5-3	7-8	9-9	11-11	13-10	5-0	7-3	9-2	11-3	13-0
	Douglas fir-larch	#3	4-0	5-10	7-4	9-0	10-5	3-9	5-6	6-11	8-6	9-10
	Hem-fir	SS	6-1	9-7	12-4	15-1	17-4	6-1	9-2	11-8	14-2	15-5
	Hem-fir	#1	5-6	8-0	10-2	12-5	14-5	5-2	7-7	9-7	11-8	13-7
	Hem-fir	#2	5-2	7-7	9-7	11-9	13-7	4-11	7-2	9-1	11-1	12-10
	Hem-fir	#3	4-0	5-10	7-4	9-0	10-5	3-9	5-6	6-11	8-6	9-10
	Southern pine	SS	6-4	10-0	13-2	16-9	20-4	6-4	10-0	13-2	16-5	19-2
	Southern pine	#1	6-3	9-3	11-8	13-10	16-6	5-11	8-9	11-0	13-1	15-7
	Southern pine	#2	5-7	8-1	10-5	12-5	14-7	5-4	7-7	9-10	11-9	13-9
	Southern pine	#3	4-3	6-3	8-0	9-5	11-2	4-0	5-11	7-6	8-10	10-7
	Spruce-pine-fir	SS	6-0	9-2	11-8	14-3	16-6	5-11	8-8	11-0	13-5	15-7
	Spruce-pine-fir	#1	5-3	7-8	9-9	11-11	13-10	5-0	7-3	9-2	11-3	13-0
	Spruce-pine-fir	#2	5-3	7-8	9-9	11-11	13-10	5-0	7-3	9-2	11-3	13-0
	Spruce-pine-fir	#3	4-0	5-10	7-4	9-0	10-5	3-9	5-6	6-11	8-6	9-10

(continued)

TABLE R802.5.1(7)—continued
RAFTER SPANS FOR 70 PSF GROUND SNOW LOAD
(Ceiling not attached to rafters, L/Δ = 180)

RAFTER SPACING (inches)	SPECIES AND GRADE		DEAD LOAD = 10 psf					DEAD LOAD = 20 psf				
			2 × 4	2 × 6	2 × 8	2 × 10	2 × 12	2 × 4	2 × 6	2 × 8	2 × 10	2 × 12
			Maximum rafter spans[a]									
			(feet-inches)	(feet - inches)	(feet - inches)	(feet - inches)	(feet - inches)	(feet - inches)	(feet - inches)	(feet - inches)	(feet - inches)	(feet - inches)
24	Douglas fir-larch	SS	6-0	8-10	11-3	13-9	15-11	5-9	8-4	10-7	12-11	15-0
	Douglas fir-larch	#1	5-0	7-4	9-4	11-5	13-2	4-9	6-11	8-9	10-9	12-5
	Douglas fir-larch	#2	4-8	6-11	8-9	10-8	12-4	4-5	6-6	8-3	10-0	11-8
	Douglas fir-larch	#3	3-7	5-2	6-7	8-1	9-4	3-4	4-11	6-3	7-7	8-10
	Hem-fir	SS	5-8	8-8	11-0	13-6	13-11	5-7	8-3	10-5	12-4	12-4
	Hem-fir	#1	4-11	7-2	9-1	11-1	12-10	4-7	6-9	8-7	10-6	12-2
	Hem-fir	#2	4-8	6-9	8-7	10-6	12-2	4-4	6-5	8-1	9-11	11-6
	Hem-fir	#3	3-7	5-2	6-7	8-1	9-4	3-4	4-11	6-3	7-7	8-10
	Southern pine	SS	5-11	9-3	12-2	15-7	18-2	5-11	9-3	12-2	14-8	17-2
	Southern pine	#1	5-7	8-3	10-5	12-5	14-9	5-3	7-10	9-10	11-8	13-11
	Southern pine	#2	5-0	7-3	9-4	11-1	13-0	4-9	6-10	8-9	10-6	12-4
	Southern pine	#3	3-9	5-7	7-1	8-5	10-0	3-7	5-3	6-9	7-11	9-5
	Spruce-pine-fir	SS	5-6	8-3	10-5	12-9	14-9	5-4	7-9	9-10	12-0	12-11
	Spruce-pine-fir	#1	4-8	6-11	8-9	10-8	12-4	4-5	6-6	8-3	10-0	11-8
	Spruce-pine-fir	#2	4-8	6-11	8-9	10-8	12-4	4-5	6-6	8-3	10-0	11-8
	Spruce-pine-fir	#3	3-7	5-2	6-7	8-1	9-4	3-4	4-11	6-3	7-7	8-10

Check sources for availability of lumber in lengths greater than 20 feet.

For SI: 1 inch = 25.4 mm, 1 foot = 304.8 mm, 1 pound per square foot = 0.0479kPa.

a. The tabulated rafter spans assume that ceiling joists are located at the bottom of the attic space or that some other method of resisting the outward push of the rafters on the bearing walls, such as rafter ties, is provided at that location. When ceiling joists or rafter ties are located higher in the attic space, the rafter spans shall be multiplied by the factors given below:

H_C/H_R	Rafter Span Adjustment Factor
1/3	0.67
1/4	0.76
1/5	0.83
1/6	0.90
1/7.5 or less	1.00

where:

H_C = Height of ceiling joists or rafter ties measured vertically above the top of the rafter support walls.

H_R = Height of roof ridge measured vertically above the top of the rafter support walls.

TABLE R802.5.1(8)
RAFTER SPANS FOR 70 PSF GROUND SNOW LOAD
(Ceiling attached to rafters, L/Δ = 240)

RAFTER SPACING (inches)	SPECIES AND GRADE		DEAD LOAD = 10 psf					DEAD LOAD = 20 psf				
			2 × 4	2 × 6	2 × 8	2 × 10	2 × 12	2 × 4	2 × 6	2 × 8	2 × 10	2 × 12
			Maximum rafter spans[a]									
			(feet - inches)	(feet - inches)	(feet - inches)	(feet - inches)	(feet - inches)	(feet - inches)	(feet - inches)	(feet - inches)	(feet - inches)	(feet - inches)
12	Douglas fir-larch	SS	6-10	10-9	14-3	18-2	22-1	6-10	10-9	14-3	18-2	21-2
	Douglas fir-larch	#1	6-7	10-5	13-2	16-1	18-8	6-7	9-10	12-5	15-2	17-7
	Douglas fir-larch	#2	6-6	9-9	12-4	15-1	17-6	6-3	9-2	11-8	14-2	16-6
	Douglas fir-larch	#3	5-0	7-4	9-4	11-5	13-2	4-9	6-11	8-9	10-9	12-5
	Hem-fir	SS	6-6	10-2	13-5	17-2	20-10	6-6	10-2	13-5	17-2	20-10
	Hem-fir	#1	6-4	10-0	12-10	15-8	18-2	6-4	9-7	12-1	14-10	17-2
	Hem-fir	#2	6-1	9-6	12-2	14-10	17-3	6-1	9-1	11-5	14-0	16-3
	Hem-fir	#3	5-0	7-4	9-4	11-5	13-2	4-9	6-11	8-9	10-9	12-5
	Southern pine	SS	6-9	10-7	14-0	17-10	21-8	6-9	10-7	14-0	17-10	21-8
	Southern pine	#1	6-7	10-5	13-8	17-6	20-11	6-7	10-5	13-8	16-6	19-8
	Southern pine	#2	6-6	10-2	13-2	15-9	18-5	6-6	9-7	12-5	14-10	17-5
	Southern pine	#3	5-4	7-11	10-1	11-11	14-2	5-1	7-5	9-6	11-3	13-4
	Spruce-pine-fir	SS	6-4	10-0	13-2	16-9	20-5	6-4	10-0	13-2	16-9	19-8
	Spruce-pine-fir	#1	6-2	9-9	12-4	15-1	17-6	6-2	9-2	11-8	14-2	16-6
	Spruce-pine-fir	#2	6-2	9-9	12-4	15-1	17-6	6-2	9-2	11-8	14-2	16-6
	Spruce-pine-fir	#3	5-0	7-4	9-4	11-5	13-2	4-9	6-11	8-9	10-9	12-5
16	Douglas fir-larch	SS	6-3	9-10	12-11	16-6	19-6	6-3	9-10	12-11	15-10	18-4
	Douglas fir-larch	#1	6-0	9-0	11-5	13-11	16-2	5-10	8-6	10-9	13-2	15-3
	Douglas fir-larch	#2	5-9	8-5	10-8	13-1	15-2	5-5	7-11	10-1	12-4	14-3
	Douglas fir-larch	#3	4-4	6-4	8-1	9-10	11-5	4-1	6-0	7-7	9-4	10-9
	Hem-fir	SS	5-11	9-3	12-2	15-7	18-11	5-11	9-3	12-2	15-7	18-0
	Hem-fir	#1	5-9	8-9	11-2	13-7	15-9	5-8	8-3	10-6	12-10	14-10
	Hem-fir	#2	5-6	8-4	10-6	12-10	14-11	5-4	7-10	9-11	12-1	14-1
	Hem-fir	#3	4-4	6-4	8-1	9-10	11-5	4-1	6-0	7-7	9-4	10-9
	Southern pine	SS	6-1	9-7	12-8	16-2	19-8	6-1	9-7	12-8	16-2	19-8
	Southern pine	#1	6-0	9-5	12-5	15-2	18-1	6-0	9-5	12-0	14-4	17-1
	Southern pine	#2	5-11	8-10	11-5	13-7	16-0	5-10	8-4	10-9	12-10	15-1
	Southern pine	#3	4-8	6-10	8-9	10-4	12-3	4-4	6-5	8-3	9-9	11-7
	Spruce-pine-fir	SS	5-9	9-1	11-11	15-3	18-1	5-9	9-1	11-11	14-8	17-1
	Spruce-pine-fir	#1	5-8	8-5	10-8	13-1	15-2	5-5	7-11	10-1	12-4	14-3
	Spruce-pine-fir	#2	5-8	8-5	10-8	13-1	15-2	5-5	7-11	10-1	12-4	14-3
	Spruce-pine-fir	#3	4-4	6-4	8-1	9-10	11-5	4-1	6-0	7-7	9-4	10-9
19.2	Douglas fir-larch	SS	5-10	9-3	12-2	15-4	17-9	5-10	9-3	11-10	14-5	16-9
	Douglas fir-larch	#1	5-7	8-3	10-5	12-9	14-9	5-4	7-9	9-10	12-0	13-11
	Douglas fir-larch	#2	5-3	7-8	9-9	11-11	13-10	5-0	7-3	9-2	11-3	13-0
	Douglas fir-larch	#3	4-0	5-10	7-4	9-0	10-5	3-9	5-6	6-11	8-6	9-10
	Hem-fir	SS	5-6	8-8	11-6	14-8	17-4	5-6	8-8	11-6	14-2	15-5
	Hem-fir	#1	5-5	8-0	10-2	12-5	14-5	5-2	7-7	9-7	11-8	13-7
	Hem-fir	#2	5-2	7-7	9-7	11-9	13-7	4-11	7-2	9-1	11-1	12-10
	Hem-fir	#3	4-0	5-10	7-4	9-0	10-5	3-9	5-6	6-11	8-6	9-10
	Southern pine	SS	5-9	9-1	11-11	15-3	18-6	5-9	9-1	11-11	15-3	18-6
	Southern pine	#1	5-8	8-11	11-8	13-10	16-6	5-8	8-9	11-0	13-1	15-7
	Southern pine	#2	5-6	8-1	10-5	12-5	14-7	5-4	7-7	9-10	11-9	13-9
	Southern pine	#3	4-3	6-3	8-0	9-5	11-2	4-0	5-11	7-6	8-10	10-7
	Spruce-pine-fir	SS	5-5	8-6	11-3	14-3	16-6	5-5	8-6	11-0	13-5	15-7
	Spruce-pine-fir	#1	5-3	7-8	9-9	11-11	13-10	5-0	7-3	9-2	11-3	13-0
	Spruce-pine-fir	#2	5-3	7-8	9-9	11-11	13-10	5-0	7-3	9-2	11-3	13-0
	Spruce-pine-fir	#3	4-0	5-10	7-4	9-0	10-5	3-9	5-6	6-11	8-6	9-10

(continued)

TABLE R802.5.1(8)—continued
RAFTER SPANS FOR 70 PSF GROUND SNOW LOAD[a]
(Ceiling attached to rafters, L/Δ = 240)

RAFTER SPACING (inches)	SPECIES AND GRADE		DEAD LOAD = 10 psf					DEAD LOAD = 20 psf				
			2 × 4	2 × 6	2 × 8	2 × 10	2 × 12	2 × 4	2 × 6	2 × 8	2 × 10	2 × 12
			Maximum rafter spans[a]									
			(feet - inches)	(feet - inches)	(feet - inches)	(feet - inches)	(feet - inches)	(feet - inches)	(feet - inches)	(feet - inches)	(feet - inches)	(feet - inches)
24	Douglas fir-larch	SS	5-5	8-7	11-3	13-9	15-11	5-5	8-4	10-7	12-11	15-0
	Douglas fir-larch	#1	5-0	7-4	9-4	11-5	13-2	4-9	6-11	8-9	10-9	12-5
	Douglas fir-larch	#2	4-8	6-11	8-9	10-8	12-4	4-5	6-6	8-3	10-0	11-8
	Douglas fir-larch	#3	3-7	5-2	6-7	8-1	9-4	3-4	4-11	6-3	7-7	8-10
	Hem-fir	SS	5-2	8-1	10-8	13-6	13-11	5-2	8-1	10-5	12-4	12-4
	Hem-fir	#1	4-11	7-2	9-1	11-1	12-10	4-7	6-9	8-7	10-6	12-2
	Hem-fir	#2	4-8	6-9	8-7	10-6	12-2	4-4	6-5	8-1	9-11	11-6
	Hem-fir	#3	3-7	5-2	6-7	8-1	9-4	3-4	4-11	6-3	7-7	8-10
	Southern pine	SS	5-4	8-5	11-1	14-2	17-2	5-4	8-5	11-1	14-2	17-2
	Southern pine	#1	5-3	8-3	10-5	12-5	14-9	5-3	7-10	9-10	11-8	13-11
	Southern pine	#2	5-0	7-3	9-4	11-1	13-0	4-9	6-10	8-9	10-6	12-4
	Southern pine	#3	3-9	5-7	7-1	8-5	10-0	3-7	5-3	6-9	7-11	9-5
	Spruce-pine-fir	SS	5-0	7-11	10-5	12-9	14-9	5-0	7-9	9-10	12-0	12-11
	Spruce-pine-fir	#1	4-8	6-11	8-9	10-8	12-4	4-5	6-6	8-3	10-0	11-8
	Spruce-pine-fir	#2	4-8	6-11	8-9	10-8	12-4	4-5	6-6	8-3	10-0	11-8
	Spruce-pine-fir	#3	3-7	5-2	6-7	8-1	9-4	3-4	4-11	6-3	7-7	8-10

Check sources for availability of lumber in lengths greater than 20 feet.

For SI: 1 inch = 25.4 mm, 1 foot = 304.8 mm, 1 pound per square foot = 0.0479kPa.

a. The tabulated rafter spans assume that ceiling joists are located at the bottom of the attic space or that some other method of resisting the outward push of the rafters on the bearing walls, such as rafter ties, is provided at that location. When ceiling joists or rafter ties are located higher in the attic space, the rafter spans shall be multiplied by the factors given below:

H_C/H_R	Rafter Span Adjustment Factor
1/3	0.67
1/4	0.76
1/5	0.83
1/6	0.90
1/7.5 or less	1.00

where:

H_C = Height of ceiling joists or rafter ties measured vertically above the top of the rafter support walls.

H_R = Height of roof ridge measured vertically above the top of the rafter support walls.

TABLE R802.5.1(9) RAFTER/CEILING JOIST HEEL JOINT CONNECTIONS[a, b, c, d, e, f, h]

RAFTER SLOPE	RAFTER SPACING (inches)	GROUND SNOW LOAD (psf)															
		20[g]				30				50				70			
		Roof span (feet)															
		12	20	28	36	12	20	28	36	12	20	28	36	12	20	28	36
		Required number of 16d common nails[a, b] per heel joint splices[c, d, e, f]															
3:12	12	4	6	8	10	4	6	8	11	5	8	12	15	6	11	15	20
	16	5	8	10	13	5	8	11	14	6	11	15	20	8	14	20	26
	24	7	11	15	19	7	11	16	21	9	16	23	30	12	21	30	39
4:12	12	3	5	6	8	3	5	6	8	4	6	9	11	5	8	12	15
	16	4	6	8	10	4	6	8	11	5	8	12	15	6	11	15	20
	24	5	8	12	15	5	9	12	16	7	12	17	22	9	16	23	29
5:12	12	3	4	5	6	3	4	5	7	3	5	7	9	4	7	9	12
	16	3	5	6	8	3	5	7	9	4	7	9	12	5	9	12	16
	24	4	7	9	12	4	7	10	13	6	10	14	18	7	13	18	23
7:12	12	3	4	4	5	3	3	4	5	3	4	5	7	3	5	7	9
	16	3	4	5	6	3	4	5	6	3	5	7	9	4	6	9	11
	24	3	5	7	9	3	5	7	9	4	7	10	13	5	9	13	17
9:12	12	3	3	4	4	3	3	3	4	3	3	4	5	3	4	5	7
	16	3	4	4	5	3	3	4	5	3	4	5	7	3	5	7	9
	24	3	4	6	7	3	4	6	7	3	6	8	10	4	7	10	13
12:12	12	3	3	3	3	3	3	3	3	3	3	3	4	3	3	4	5
	16	3	3	4	4	3	3	3	4	3	3	4	5	3	4	5	7
	24	3	4	4	5	3	3	4	6	3	4	6	8	3	6	8	10

For SI: 1 inch = 25.4 mm, 1 foot = 304.8 mm, 1 pound per square foot = 0.0479kPa.

a. 40d box nails shall be permitted to be substituted for 16d common nails.

b. Nailing requirements shall be permitted to be reduced 25 percent if nails are clinched.

c. Heel joint connections are not required when the ridge is supported by a load-bearing wall, header or ridge beam.

d. When intermediate support of the rafter is provided by vertical struts or purlins to a loadbearing wall, the tabulated heel joint connection requirements shall be permitted to be reduced proportionally to the reduction in span.

e. Equivalent nailing patterns are required for ceiling joist to ceiling joist lap splices.

f. When rafter ties are substituted for ceiling joists, the heel joint connection requirement shall be taken as the tabulated heel joint connection requirement for two-thirds of the actual rafter-slope.

g. Applies to roof live load of 20 psf or less.

h. Tabulated heel joint connection requirements assume that ceiling joists or rafter ties are located at the bottom of the attic space. When ceiling joists or rafter ties are located higher in the attic, heel joint connection requirements shall be increased by the following factors:

H_C/H_R	Heel Joint Connection Adjustment Factor
1/3	1.5
1/4	1.33
1/5	1.25
1/6	1.2
1/10 or less	1.11

where:

H_C = Height of ceiling joists or rafter ties measured vertically above the top of the rafter support walls.

H_R = Height of roof ridge measured vertically above the top of the rafter support walls.

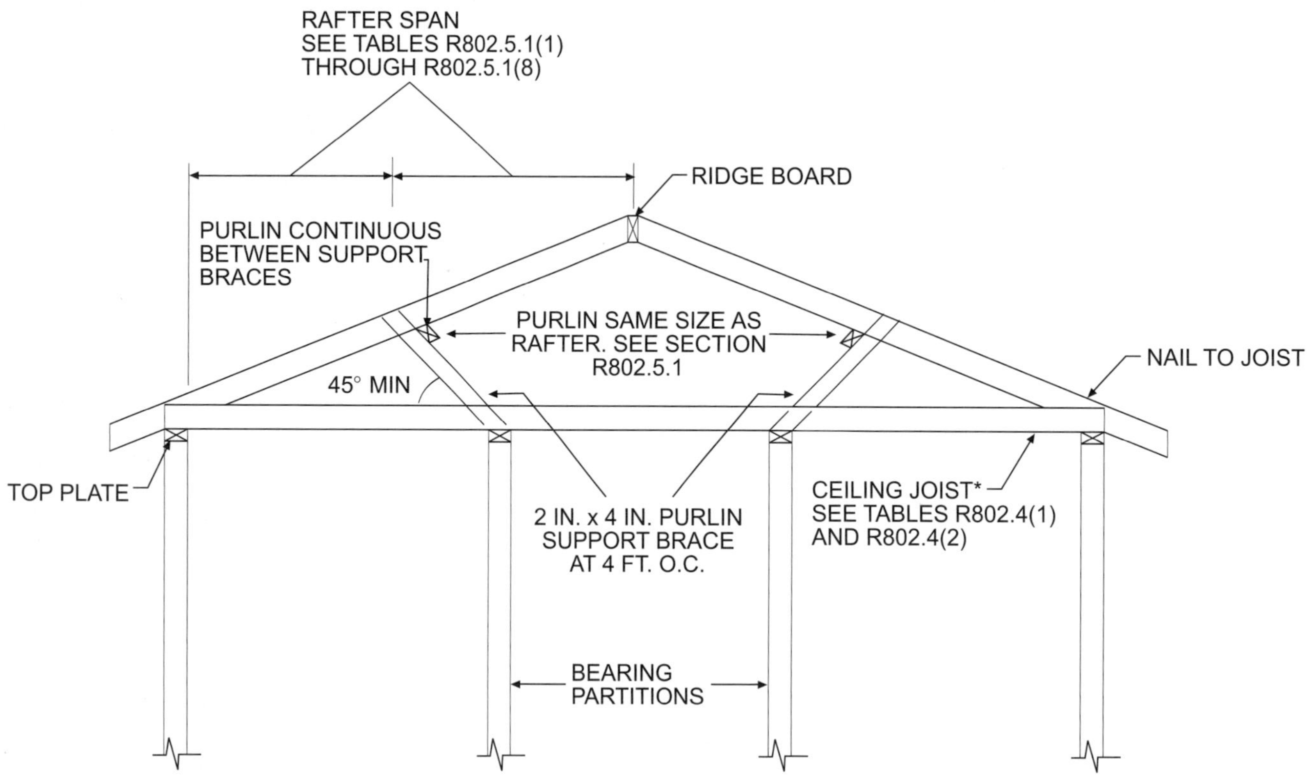

For SI: 1 inch = 25.4 mm, 1 foot = 305 mm, 1 degree = 0.018 rad.

Note: Where ceiling joists run perpendicular to the rafters, rafter ties shall be nailed to the rafter near the plate line and spaced not more than 4 feet on center .

FIGURE R802.5.1
BRACED RAFTER CONSTRUCTION

TABLE R802.11
REQUIRED STRENGTH OF TRUSS OR RAFTER CONNECTIONS TO RESIST WIND UPLIFT FORCES OF 20 PSF OR GREATER[a, b, c, e, f]
(Pounds per connection)

BASIC WIND SPEED (mph) (3–second gust)	ROOF SPAN (feet)							OVERHANGS[d] (pounds/foot)
	12	20	24	28	32	36	40	
85	-72	-120	-145	-169	-193	-217	-241	-38.55
90	-91	-151	-181	-212	-242	-272	-302	-43.22
100	-131	-218	-262	-305	-349	-393	-436	-53.36
110	-175	-292	-351	-409	-467	-526	-584	-64.56

For SI: 1 inch = 25.4 mm, 1 foot = 305 mm, 1 mph = 0.447 m/s, 1 pound/foot = 14.5939 N/m, 1 pound = 0.454 kg.

a. The uplift connection requirements are based on a 30 foot mean roof height located in Exposure B. For Exposures C and D and for other mean roof heights, multiply the above loads by the Adjustment Coefficients in Table R301.2(3).

b. The uplift connection requirements are based on the framing being spaced 24 inches on center. Multiply by 0.67 for framing spaced 16 inches on center and multiply by 0.5 for framing spaced 12 inches on center.

c. The uplift connection requirements include an allowance for 10 pounds of dead load.

d. The uplift connection requirements do not account for the effects of overhangs. The magnitude of the above loads shall be increased by adding the overhang loads found in the table. The overhang loads are also based on framing spaced 24 inches on center. The overhang loads given shall be multiplied by the overhang projection and added to the roof uplift value in the table.

e. The uplift connection requirements are based on wind loading on end zones as defined in Figure 6-2 of ASCE 7. Connection loads for connections located a distance of 20% of the least horizontal dimension of the building from the corner of the building are permitted to be reduced by multiplying the table connection value by 0.7 and multiplying the overhang load by 0.8.

f. For wall-to-wall and wall-to-foundation connections, the capacity of the uplift connector is permitted to be reduced by 100 pounds for each full wall above. (For example, if a 600-pound rated connector is used on the roof framing, a 500-pound rated connector is permitted at the next floor level down).

SECTION R803
ROOF SHEATHING

R803.1 Lumber sheathing. Allowable spans for lumber used as roof sheathing shall conform to Table R803.1. Spaced lumber sheathing for wood shingle and shake roofing shall conform to the requirements of Sections R905.7 and R905.8. Spaced lumber sheathing is not allowed in Seismic Design Category D_2.

TABLE R803.1
MINIMUM THICKNESS OF LUMBER ROOF SHEATHING

RAFTER OR BEAM SPACING (inches)	MINIMUM NET THICKNESS (inches)
24	$^5/_8$
48[a]	$1^1/_2$ T & G
60[b]	
72[c]	

For SI: 1 inch = 25.4 mm.
a. Minimum 270 F_b, 340,000 *E*.
b. Minimum 420 F_b, 660,000 *E*.
c. Minimum 600 F_b, 1,150,000 *E*.

R803.2 Wood structural panel sheathing.

R803.2.1 Identification and grade. Wood structural panels shall conform to DOC PS 1, DOC PS 2 or, when manufactured in Canada, CSA 0437 or CSA 0325, and shall be identified by a grade mark or certificate of inspection issued by an *approved* agency. Wood structural panels shall comply with the grades specified in Table R503.2.1.1(1).

R803.2.1.1 Exposure durability. All wood structural panels, when designed to be permanently exposed in outdoor applications, shall be of an exterior exposure durability. Wood structural panel roof sheathing exposed to the underside may be of interior type bonded with exterior glue, identified as Exposure 1.

R803.2.1.2 Fire-retardant-treated plywood. The allowable unit stresses for fire-retardant-treated plywood, including fastener values, shall be developed from an *approved* method of investigation that considers the effects of anticipated temperature and humidity to which the fire-retardant-treated plywood will be subjected, the type of treatment and redrying process. The fire-retardant- treated plywood shall be graded by an *approved agency.*

R803.2.2 Allowable spans. The maximum allowable spans for wood structural panel roof sheathing shall not exceed the values set forth in Table R503.2.1.1(1), or APA E30.

R803.2.3 Installation. Wood structural panel used as roof sheathing shall be installed with joints staggered or not staggered in accordance with Table R602.3(1), or APA E30 for wood roof framing or with Table R804.3 for steel roof framing.

SECTION R804
STEEL ROOF FRAMING

R804.1 General. Elements shall be straight and free of any defects that would significantly affect their structural performance. Cold-formed steel roof framing members shall comply with the requirements of this section.

R804.1.1 Applicability limits. The provisions of this section shall control the construction of cold-formed steel roof framing for buildings not greater than 60 feet (18 288 mm) perpendicular to the joist, rafter or truss span, not greater than 40 feet (12 192 mm) in width parallel to the joist span or truss, less than or equal to three stories above *grade* plane and with roof slopes not less than 3:12 (25-percent slope) or greater than 12:12 (100 percent slope). Cold-formed steel roof framing constructed in accordance with the provisions of this section shall be limited to sites subjected to a maximum design wind speed of 110 miles per hour (49 m/s), Exposure B or C, and a maximum ground snow load of 70 pounds per square foot (3350 Pa).

R804.1.2 In-line framing. Cold-formed steel roof framing constructed in accordance with Section R804 shall be located in line with load-bearing studs in accordance with Figure R804.1.2 and the tolerances specified as follows:

1. The maximum tolerance shall be $^3/_4$ inch (19.1 mm) between the centerline of the horizontal framing member and the centerline of the vertical framing member.
2. Where the centerline of the horizontal framing member and bearing stiffener are located to one side of the center line of the vertical framing member, the maximum tolerance shall be $^1/_8$ inch (3 mm) between the web of the horizontal framing member and the edge of the vertical framing member.

R804.2 Structural framing. Load-bearing cold-formed steel roof framing members shall comply with Figure R804.2(1) and with the dimensional and minimum thickness requirements specified in Tables R804.2(1) and R804.2(2). Tracks shall comply with Figure R804.2(2) and shall have a minimum flange width of $1^1/_4$ inches (32 mm). The maximum inside bend radius for members shall be the greater of $^3/_{32}$ inch (2.4 mm) minus half the base steel thickness or 1.5 times the base steel thickness.

R804.2.1 Material. Load-bearing cold-formed steel framing members shall be cold-formed to shape from structural quality sheet steel complying with the requirements of one of the following:

1. ASTM A 653: *Grades* 33 and 50 (Class 1 and 3).
2. ASTM A 792: *Grades* 33 and 50A.
3. ASTM A 1003: Structural *Grades* 33 Type H and 50 Type H.

R804.2.2 Identification. Load-bearing cold-formed steel framing members shall have a legible *label*, stencil, stamp or embossment with the following information as a minimum:

1. Manufacturer's identification.
2. Minimum base steel thickness in inches (mm).
3. Minimum coating designation.
4. Minimum yield strength, in kips per square inch (ksi) (MPa).

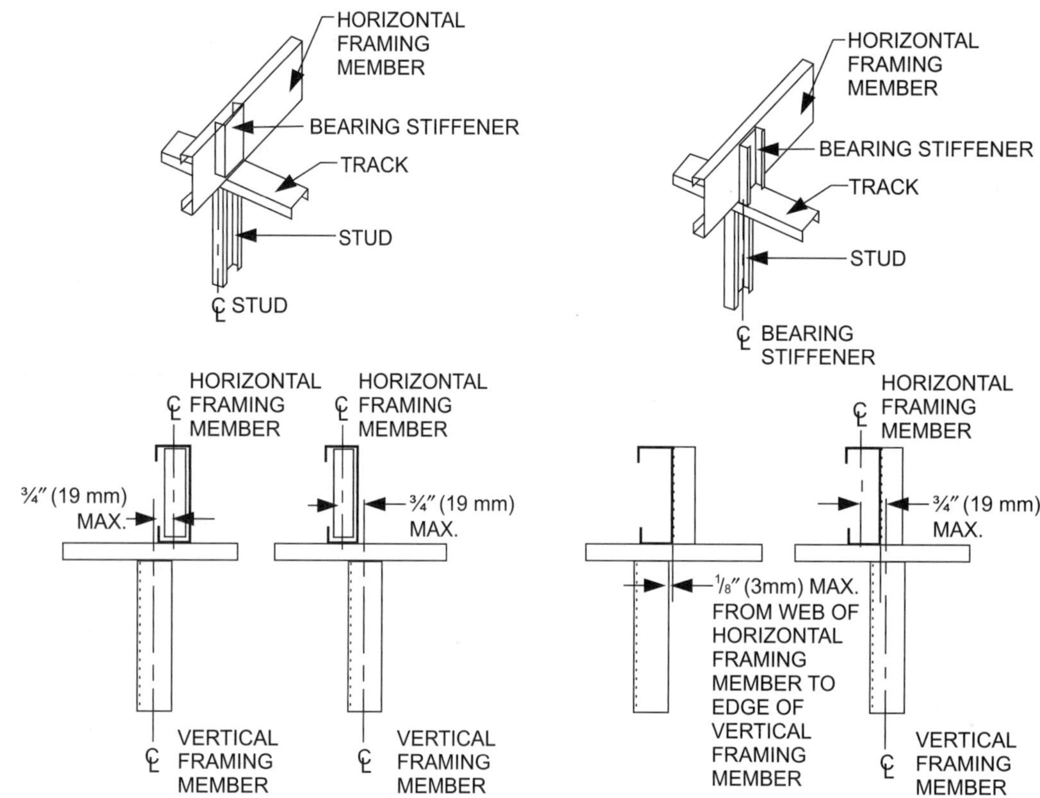

For SI: 1 inch = 25.4 mm.

FIGURE R804.1.2
IN-LINE FRAMING

TABLE R804.2(1)
LOAD-BEARING COLD-FORMED STEEL MEMBER SIZES

NOMINAL MEMBER SIZE MEMBER DESIGNATION[a]	WEB DEPTH (inches)	MINIMUM FLANGE WIDTH (inches)	MAXIMUM FLANGE WIDTH (inches)	MINIMUM LIP SIZE (inches)
350S162-t	3.5	1.625	2	0.5
550S162-t	5.5	1.625	2	0.5
800S162-t	8	1.625	2	0.5
1000S162-t	10	1.625	2	0.5
1200S162-t	12	1.625	2	0.5

For SI: 1 inch = 25.4 mm.

a. The member designation is defined by the first number representing the member depth in hundredths of an inch, the letter "s" representing a stud or joist member, the second number representing the flange width in hundredths of an inch, and the letter "t" shall be a number representing the minimum base metal thickness in mils [see Table R804.2(2)].

TABLE R804.2(2)
MINIMUM THICKNESS OF COLD-FORMED STEEL MEMBERS

DESIGNATION THICKNESS (mils)	MINIMUM BASE STEEL THICKNESS (inches)
33	0.0329
43	0.0428
54	0.0538
68	0.0677
97	0.0966

For SI: 1 inch = 25.4 mm, 1 mil = 0.0254 mm.

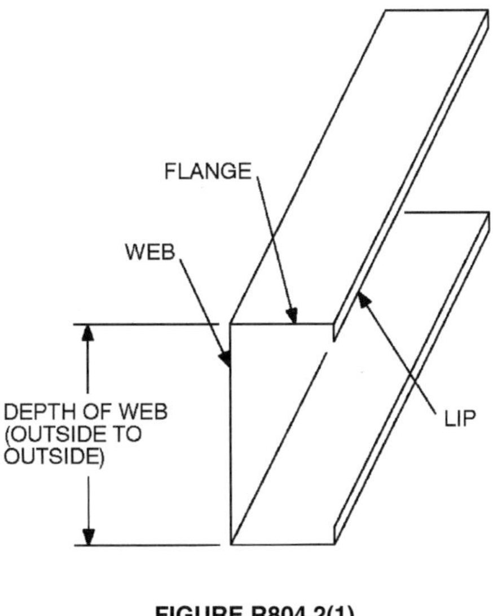

FIGURE R804.2(1)
C-SHAPED SECTION

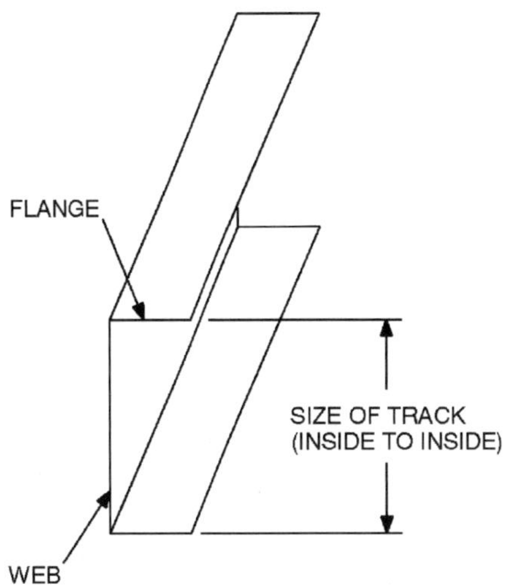

FIGURE R804.2(2)
TRACK SECTION

R804.2.3 Corrosion protection. Load-bearing cold-formed steel framing shall have a metallic coating complying with ASTM A 1003 and one of the following:

1. A minimum of G 60 in accordance with ASTM A 653.
2. A minimum of AZ 50 in accordance with ASTM A 792.

R804.2.4 Fastening requirements. Screws for steel-to-steel connections shall be installed with a minimum edge distance and center-to-center spacing of $^1/_2$ inch (13 mm), shall be self-drilling tapping, and shall conform to ASTM C 1513. Structural sheathing shall be attached to cold-formed steel roof rafters with minimum No. 8 self-drilling tapping screws that conform to ASTM C 1513. Screws for attaching structural sheathing to cold-formed steel roof framing shall have a minimum head diameter of 0.292 inch (7.4 mm) with countersunk heads and shall be installed with a minimum edge distance of $^3/_8$ inch (10 mm). Gypsum board ceilings shall be attached to cold-formed steel joists with minimum No. 6 screws conforming to ASTM C 954 or ASTM C 1513 with a bugle head style and shall be installed in accordance with Section R805. For all connections, screws shall extend through the steel a minimum of three exposed threads. All fasteners shall have rust inhibitive coating suitable for the installation in which they are being used, or be manufactured from material not susceptible to corrosion.

Where No. 8 screws are specified in a steel-to-steel connection, reduction of the required number of screws in the connection is permitted in accordance with the reduction factors in Table R804.2.4 when larger screws are used or when one of the sheets of steel being connected is thicker than 33 mils (0.84 mm). When applying the reduction factor, the resulting number of screws shall be rounded up.

TABLE R804.2.4
SCREW SUBSTITUTION FACTOR

SCREW SIZE	THINNEST CONNECTED STEEL SHEET (mils)	
	33	43
#8	1.0	0.67
#10	0.93	0.62
#12	0.86	0.56

For SI: 1 mil = 0.0254 mm.

R804.2.5 Web holes, web hole reinforcing and web hole patching. Web holes, web hole reinforcing, and web hole patching shall be in accordance with this section.

R804.2.5.1 Web holes. Web holes in roof framing members shall comply with all of the following conditions:

1. Holes shall conform to Figure R804.2.5.1;
2. Holes shall be permitted only along the centerline of the web of the framing member;
3. Center-to-center spacing of holes shall not be less than 24 inches (610 mm);
4. The web hole width shall not be greater than one-half the member depth, or $2^1/_2$ inches (64.5 mm);
5. Holes shall have a web hole length not exceeding $4^1/_2$ inches (114 mm); and
6. The minimum distance between the edge of the bearing surface and the edge of the web hole shall not be less than 10 inches (254 mm).

Framing members with web holes not conforming to the above requirements shall be reinforced in accordance with Section R804.2.5.2, patched in accordance with

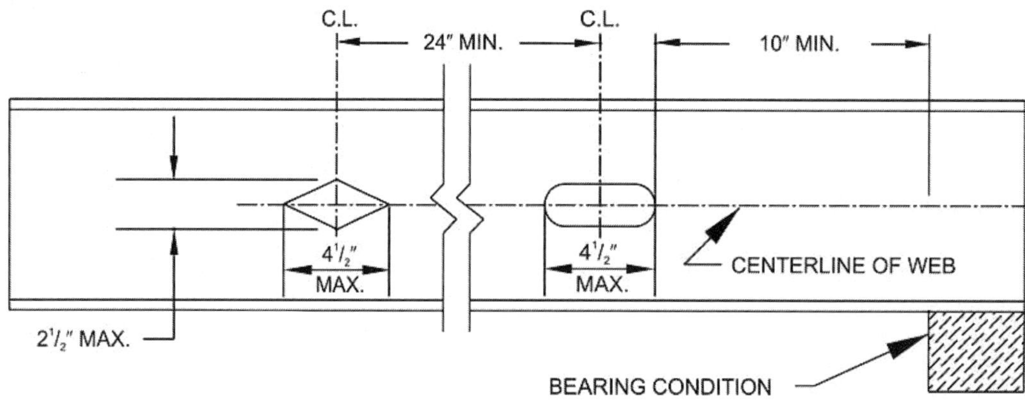

For SI: 1 inch = 25.4 mm.

**FIGURE R804.2.5.1
WEB HOLES**

Section R804.2.5.3 or designed in accordance with accepted engineering practices.

R804.2.5.2 Web hole reinforcing. Reinforcement of web holes in ceiling joists not conforming to the requirements of Section R804.2.5.1 shall be permitted if the hole is located fully within the center 40 percent of the span and the depth and length of the hole does not exceed 65 percent of the flat width of the web. The reinforcing shall be a steel plate or C-shape section with a hole that does not exceed the web hole size limitations of Section R804.2.5.1 for the member being reinforced. The steel reinforcing shall be the same thickness as the receiving member and shall extend at least 1 inch (25.4 mm) beyond all edges of the hole. The steel reinforcing shall be fastened to the web of the receiving member with No.8 screws spaced no greater than 1 inch (25.4 mm) center-to-center along the edges of the patch with minimum edge distance of $^1/_2$ inch (13 mm).

R804.2.5.3 Hole patching. Patching of web holes in roof framing members not conforming to the requirements in Section R804.2.5.1 shall be permitted in accordance with either of the following methods:

1. Framing members shall be replaced or designed in accordance with accepted engineering practices where web holes exceed the following size limits:
   1.1. The depth of the hole, measured across the web, exceeds 70 percent of the flat width of the web; or
   1.2. The length of the hole measured along the web, exceeds 10 inches (254 mm) or the depth of the web, whichever is greater.
2. Web holes not exceeding the dimensional requirements in Section R804.2.5.3, Item 1, shall be patched with a solid steel plate, stud section or track section in accordance with Figure R804.2.5.3. The steel patch shall, as a minimum, be the same thickness as the receiving member and shall extend at least 1 inch (25 mm) beyond all edges of the hole. The steel patch shall be fastened to the web of the receiving member with No.8 screws spaced no greater than 1 inch (25 mm) center-to-center along the edges of the patch with minimum edge distance of $^1/_2$ inch (13 mm).

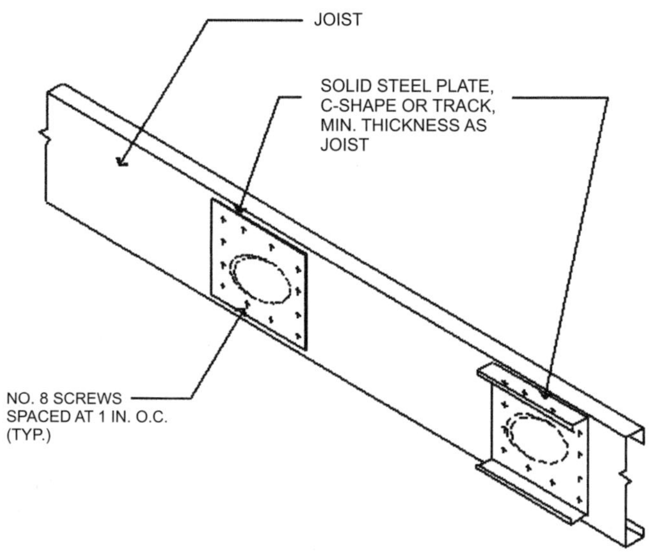

For SI: 1 inch = 25.4 mm.

**FIGURE R804.2.5.3
WEB HOLE PATCH**

R804.3 Roof construction. Cold-formed steel roof systems constructed in accordance with the provisions of this section shall consist of both ceiling joists and rafters in accordance with Figure R804.3 and fastened in accordance with Table R804.3, and hip framing in accordance with Section R804.3.3.

R804.3.1 Ceiling joists. Cold-formed steel ceiling joists shall be in accordance with this section.

R804.3.1.1 Minimum ceiling joist size. Ceiling joist size and thickness shall be determined in accordance with the limits set forth in Tables R804.3.1.1(1) through R804.3.1.1(8). When determining the size of ceiling joists, the lateral support of the top flange shall be classified as unbraced, braced at mid-span or braced at third points in accordance with Section R804.3.1.4. Where sheathing material is attached to the top flange of ceiling joists or where the bracing is spaced closer than third point of the joists, the "third point" values from Tables R804.3.1.1(1) through R804.3.1.1(8) shall be used.

Ceiling joists shall have a bearing support length of not less than 1$^1/_2$ inches (38 mm) and shall be connected to roof rafters (heel joint) with No. 10 screws in accordance with Figures R804.3.1.1(1) and R804.3.1.1(2) and Table 804.3.1.1(9).

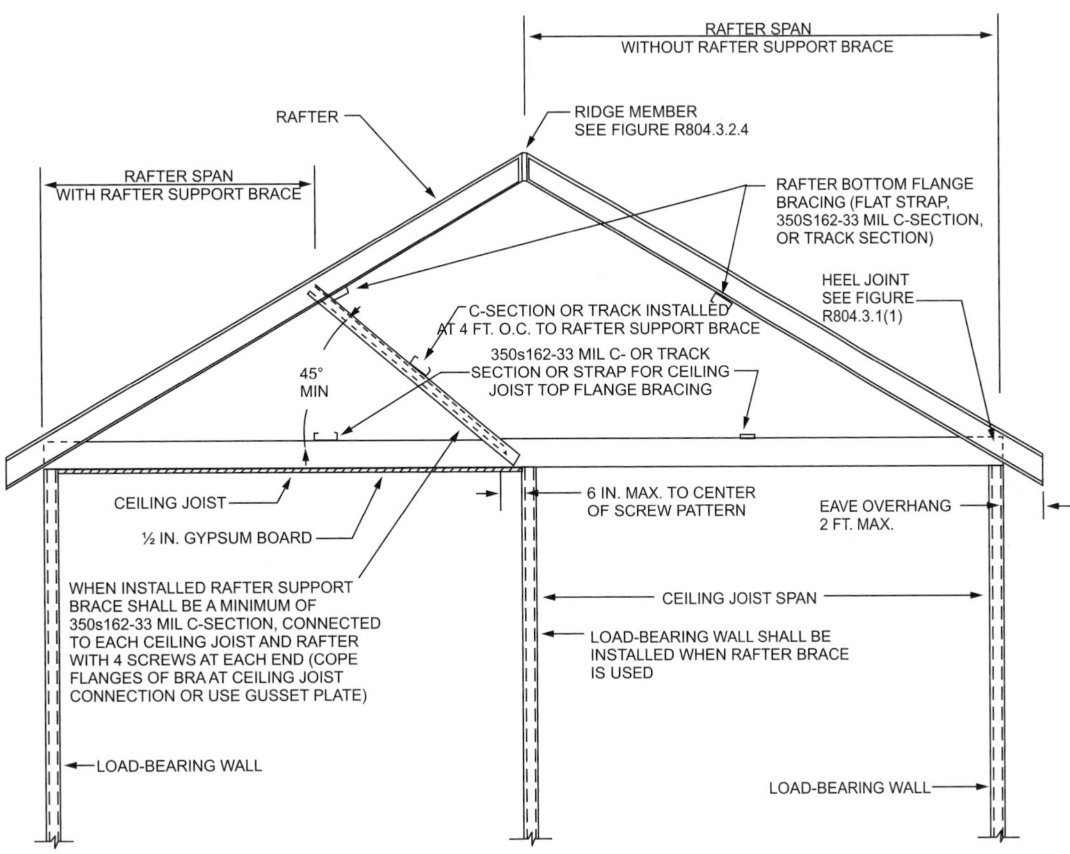

For SI: 1 inch = 25.4 mm, 1 foot = 304.8 mm, 1 mil = 0.0254 mm.

FIGURE R804.3
STEEL ROOF CONSTRUCTION

TABLE R804.3
ROOF FRAMING FASTENING SCHEDULE[a, b]

DESCRIPTION OF BUILDING ELEMENTS	NUMBER AND SIZE OF FASTENERS	SPACING OF FASTENERS
Ceiling joist to top track of load-bearing wall	2 No. 10 screws	Each joist
Roof sheathing (oriented strand board or plywood) to rafters	No. 8 screws	6″ o.c. on edges and 12″ o.c. at interior supports. 6″ o.c. at gable end truss
Truss to bearing wall[a]	2 No. 10 screws	Each truss
Gable end truss to endwall top track	No. 10 screws	12″ o.c.
Rafter to ceiling joist	Minimum No. 10 screws, per Table R804.3.1.1(9)	Evenly spaced, not less than $^1/_2$″ from all edges.

For SI: 1 inch = 25.4 mm, 1 foot = 304.8 mm, 1 pound per square foot = 0.0479 kPa, 1 mil = 0.0254 mm.

a. Screws shall be applied through the flanges of the truss or ceiling joist or a 54 mil clip angle shall be used with two No. 10 screws in each leg. See Section R804.3.9 for additional requirements to resist uplift forces.

b. Spacing of fasteners on roof sheathing panel edges applies to panel edges supported by framing members and at all roof plane perimeters. Blocking of roof sheathing panel edges perpendicular to the framing members shall not be required except at the intersection of adjacent roof planes. Roof perimeter shall be supported by framing members or cold-formed blocking of the same depth and gage as the floor members.

When continuous joists are framed across interior bearing supports, the interior bearing supports shall be located within 24 inches (610 mm) of midspan of the ceiling joist, and the individual spans shall not exceed the applicable spans in Tables R804.3.1.1(2), R804.3.1.1(4), R804.3.1.1(6) and R804.3.1.1(8).

When the *attic* is to be used as an *occupied space*, the ceiling joists shall be designed in accordance with Section R505.

R804.3.1.2 Ceiling joist bearing stiffeners. Where required in Tables R804.3.1.1(1) through R804.3.1.1(8), bearing stiffeners shall be installed at each bearing support in accordance with Figure R804.3.1.1(2). Bearing stiffeners shall be fabricated from a C-shaped or track member in accordance with the one of following:

1. C-shaped bearing stiffeners shall be a minimum 33 mils (0.84 mm) thick.
2. Track bearing stiffener shall be a minimum 43 mils (1.09 mm) thick.

The minimum length of a bearing stiffener shall be the depth of member being stiffened minus $^3/_8$ inch (9.5 mm). Each stiffener shall be fastened to the web of the ceiling joist with a minimum of four No. 8 screws equally spaced as shown in Figure R804.3.1.1(2). Installation of stiffeners shall be permitted on either side of the web.

R804.3.1.3 Ceiling joist bottom flange bracing. The bottom flanges of ceiling joists shall be laterally braced by the application of gypsum board or continuous steel straps installed perpendicular to the joist run in accordance with one of the following:

1. Gypsum board shall be fastened with No. 6 screws in accordance with Section R702.
2. Steel straps with a minimum size of $1^1/_2$ inches × 33 mils (38 mm × 0.84 mm) shall be installed at a maximum spacing of 4 feet (1219 mm). Straps shall be fastened to the bottom flange at each joist with one No.8 screw and shall be fastened to blocking with two No.8 screws. Blocking shall be installed between joists at a maximum spacing of 12 feet (3658 mm) measured along a line of continuous strapping (perpendicular to the joist run). Blocking shall also be located at the termination of all straps.

R804.3.1.4 Ceiling joist top flange bracing. The top flanges of ceiling joists shall be laterally braced as required by Tables R804.3.1.1(1) through R804.3.1.1(8), in accordance with one of the following:

1. Minimum 33-mil (0.84 mm) C-shaped member in accordance with Figure R804.3.1.4(1).
2. Minimum 33-mil (0.84 mm) track section in accordance with Figure R804.3.1.4(1).
3. Minimum 33-mil (0.84 mm) hat section in accordance with Figure R804.3.1.4(1).
4. Minimum 54-mil (1.37 mm) $1^1/_2$ inch cold-rolled channel section in accordance with Figure R804.3.1.4(1).
5. Minimum $1^1/_2$ inch by 33 mil (38 mm by 0.84 mm) continuous steel strap in accordance with Figure R804.3.1.4(2).

Lateral bracing shall be installed perpendicular to the ceiling joists and shall be fastened to the top flange of each joist with one No. 8 screw. Blocking shall be installed between joists in line with bracing at a maximum spacing of 12 feet (3658 mm) measured perpendicular to the joists. Ends of lateral bracing shall be attached to blocking or anchored to a stable building component with two No. 8 screws.

R804.3.1.5 Ceiling joist splicing. Splices in ceiling joists shall be permitted, if ceiling joist splices are supported at interior bearing points and are constructed in accordance with Figure R804.3.1.5. The number of screws on each side of the splice shall be the same as required for the heel joint connection in Table R804.3.1.1(9).

R804.3.2 Roof rafters. Cold-formed steel roof rafters shall be in accordance with this section.

R804.3.2.1 Minimum roof rafter sizes. Roof rafter size and thickness shall be determined in accordance with the limits set forth in Tables R804.3.2.1(1) and R804.3.2.1(2) based on the horizontal projection of the roof rafter span. For determination of roof rafter sizes, reduction of roof spans shall be permitted when a roof rafter support brace is installed in accordance with Section R804.3.2.2. The reduced roof rafter span shall be taken as the larger of the distance from the roof rafter support brace to the ridge or to the heel measured horizontally.

For the purpose of determining roof rafter sizes in Tables R804.3.2.1(1) and R804.3.2.1(2), wind speeds shall be converted to equivalent ground snow loads in accordance with Table R804.3.2.1(3). Roof rafter sizes shall be based on the higher of the ground snow load or the equivalent snow load converted from the wind speed.

R804.3.2.1.1 Eave overhang. Eave overhangs shall not exceed 24 inches (610 mm) measured horizontally.

R804.3.2.1.2 Rake overhangs. Rake overhangs shall not exceed 12 inches (305 mm) measured horizontally. Outlookers at gable endwalls shall be installed in accordance with Figure R804.3.2.1.2.

R804.3.2.2 Roof rafter support brace. When used to reduce roof rafter spans in determining roof rafter sizes, a roof rafter support brace shall meet all of the following conditions:

1. Minimum 350S162-33 C-shaped brace member with maximum length of 8 feet (2438 mm).
2. Minimum brace member slope of 45 degrees (0.785 rad) to the horizontal.

3. Minimum connection of brace to a roof rafter and ceiling joist with four No.10 screws at each end.
4. Maximum 6 inches (152 mm) between brace/ceiling joist connection and load-bearing wall below.
5. Each roof rafter support brace greater than 4 feet (1219 mm) in length, shall be braced with a supplemental brace having a minimum size of 350S162-33 or 350T162-33 such that the maximum unsupported length of the roof rafter support brace is 4 feet (1219 mm). The supplemental brace shall be continuous and shall be connected to each roof rafter support brace using two No.8 screws.

R804.3.2.3 Roof rafter splice. Roof rafters shall not be spliced.

R804.3.2.4 Roof rafter to ceiling joist and ridge member connection. Roof rafters shall be connected to a parallel ceiling joist to form a continuous tie between exterior walls in accordance with Figures R804.3.1.1(1) or R804.3.1.1(2) and Table R804.3.1.1(9). Ceiling joists shall be connected to the top track of the load-bearing wall in accordance with Table R804.3, either with two No.10 screws applied through the flange of the ceiling joist or by using a 54 mil (1.37 mm) clip angle with two No.10 screws in each leg. Roof rafters shall be connected to a ridge member with a minimum 2-inch by 2-inch (51 mm by 51 mm) clip angle fastened with No. 10 screws to the ridge member in accordance with Figure R804.3.2.4 and Table R804.3.2.4. The clip angle shall have a steel thickness equivalent to or greater than the roof rafter thickness and shall extend the depth of the roof rafter member to the extent possible. The ridge member shall be fabricated from a C-shaped member and a track section, which shall have a minimum size and steel thickness equivalent to or greater than that of adjacent roof rafters and shall be installed in accordance with Figure R804.3.2.4.The ridge member shall extend the full depth of the sloped roof rafter cut.

R804.3.2.5 Roof rafter bottom flange bracing. The bottom flanges of roof rafters shall be continuously braced, at a maximum spacing of 8 feet (2440 mm) as measured parallel to the roof rafters, with one of the following members:

1. Minimum 33-mil (0.84 mm) C-shaped member.
2. Minimum 33-mil (0.84 mm) track section.
3. Minimum $1^{1}/_{2}$-inch by 33-mil (38 mm by 0.84 mm) steel strap.

The bracing element shall be fastened to the bottom flange of each roof rafter with one No.8 screw and shall be fastened to blocking with two No.8 screws. Blocking shall be installed between roof rafters in-line with the continuous bracing at a maximum spacing of 12 feet (3658 mm) measured perpendicular to the roof rafters. The ends of continuous bracing shall be fastened to blocking or anchored to a stable building component with two No.8 screws.

R804.3.3 Hip framing. Hip framing shall consist of jack-rafters, hip members, hip support columns and connections in accordance with this section, or shall be in accordance with an *approved* design. The provisions of this section for hip members and hip support columns shall apply only where the jack rafter slope is greater than or equal to the roof slope. For the purposes of determining member sizes in this section, wind speeds shall be converted to equivalent ground snow load in accordance with Table R804.3.2.1(3).

R804.3.3.1 Jack rafters. Jack rafters shall meet the requirements for roof rafters in accordance with Section R804.3.2, except that the requirements in Section R804.3.2.4 shall not apply.

R804.3.3.2 Hip members. Hip members shall be fabricated from C-shape members and track section, which shall have minimum sizes determined in accordance with Table R804.3.3.2. The C-shape member and track section shall be connected at a maximum spacing of 24 inches (610 mm) using No. 10 screws through top and bottom flanges in accordance with Figure R804.3.2.4. The depth of the hip member shall match that of the roof rafters and jack rafters, or shall be based on an *approved* design for a beam pocket at the corner of the supporting wall.

R804.3.3.3 Hip support columns. Hip support columns shall be used to support hip members at the ridge. A hip support column shall consist of a pair of C-shape members, with a minimum size determined in accordance with Table R804.3.3.3. The C-shape members shall be connected at a maximum spacing of 24 inches (610 mm) on center to form a box using minimum 3-inch (76 mm) × 33-mil (0.84 mm) strap connected to each of the flanges of the C-shape members with three-No. 10 screws. Hip support columns shall have a continuous load path to the foundation and shall be supported at the ceiling line by an interior wall or by an *approved* design for a supporting element.

TABLE R804.3.1.1(1)
CEILING JOIST SPANS
SINGLE SPANS WITH BEARING STIFFENERS
10 lb per sq ft LIVE LOAD (NO ATTIC STORAGE)[a, b, c] 33 ksi STEEL

MEMBER DESIGNATION	ALLOWABLE SPAN (feet-inches)					
	Lateral Support of Top (Compression) Flange					
	Unbraced		Mid-Span Bracing		Third-Point Bracing	
	Ceiling Joist Spacing (inches)					
	16	24	16	24	16	24
350S162-33	9′-5″	8′-6″	12′-2″	10′-4″	12′-2″	10′-7″
350S162-43	10′-3″	9′-2″	12′-10″	11′-2″	12′-10″	11′-2″
350S162-54	11′-1″	9′-11″	13′-9″	12′-0″	13′-9″	12′-0″
350S162-68	12′-1″	10′-9″	14′-8″	12′-10″	14′-8″	12′-10″
350S162-97	14′-4″	12′-7″	16′-4″	14′-3″	16′-4″	14′-3″
550S162-33	10′-7″	9′-6″	14′-10″	12′-10″	15′-11″	13′-4″
550S162-43	11′-8″	10′-6″	16′-4″	14′-3″	17′-10″	15′-3″
550S162-54	12′-6″	11′-2″	17′-7″	15′-7″	19′-5″	16′-10″
550S162-68	13′-6″	12′-1″	19′-2″	17′-1″	21′-0″	18′-4″
550S162-97	15′-9″	13′-11″	21′-8″	19′-3″	23′-5″	20′-5″
800S162-33	12′-2″	10′-11″	17′-8″	15′-10″	19′-10″	17′-1″
800S162-43	13′-0″	11′-9″	18′-10″	17′-0″	21′-6″	19′-1″
800S162-54	13′-10″	12′-5″	20′-0″	18′-0″	22′-9″	20′-4″
800S162-68	14′-11″	13′-4″	21′-3″	19′-1″	24′-1″	21′-8″
800S162-97	17′-1″	15′-2″	23′-10″	21′-3″	26′-7″	23′-10″
1000S162-43	13′-11″	12′-6″	20′-2″	18′-3″	23′-1″	20′-9″
1000S162-54	14′-9″	13′-3″	21′-4″	19′-3″	24′-4″	22′-0″
1000S162-68	15′-10″	14′-2″	22′-8″	20′-5″	25′-9″	23′-2″
1000S162-97	18′-0″	16′-0″	25′-3″	22′-7″	28′-3″	25′-4″
1200S162-43	14′-8″	13′-3″	21′-4″	19′-3″	24′-5″	21′-8″
1200S162-54	15′-7″	14′-0″	22′-6″	20′-4″	25′-9″	23′-2″
1200S162-68	16′-8″	14′-11″	23′-11″	21′-6″	27′-2″	24′-6″
1000S162-97	18′-9″	16′-9″	26′-6″	23′-8″	29′-9″	26′-9″

For SI: 1 inch = 25.4 mm, 1 foot = 304.8 mm, 1 pound per square foot = 0.0479 kPa.

a. Deflection criterion: $L/240$ for total loads.

b. Ceiling dead load = 5 psf.

c. Bearing stiffeners are required at all bearing points and concentrated load locations.

TABLE R804.3.1.1(2)
CEILING JOIST SPANS
TWO EQUAL SPANS WITH BEARING STIFFENERS
10 lb per sq ft LIVE LOAD (NO ATTIC STORAGE)[a, b, c] 33 ksi STEEL

MEMBER DESIGNATION	ALLOWABLE SPAN (feet-inches)					
	Lateral Support of Top (Compression) Flange					
	Unbraced		Mid-Span Bracing		Third-Point Bracing	
	Ceiling Joist Spacing (inches)					
	16	24	16	24	16	24
350S162-33	12′-11″	10′-11″	13′-5″	10′-11″	13′-5″	10′-11″
350S162-43	14′-2″	12′-8″	15′-10″	12′-11″	15′-10″	12′-11″
350S162-54	15′-6″	13′-10″	17′-1″	14′-6″	17′-9″	14′-6″
350S162-68	17′-3″	15′-3″	18′-6″	16′-1″	19′-8″	16′-1″
350S162-97	20′-10″	18′-4″	21′-5″	18′-10″	21′-11″	18′-10″
550S162-33	14′-4″	12′-11″	16′-7″	14′-1″	17′-3″	14′-1″
550S162-43	16′-0″	14′-1″	17′-11″	16′-1″	20′-7″	16′-10″
550S162-54	17′-4″	15′-6″	19′-5″	17′-6″	23′-2″	19′-0″
550S162-68	19′-1″	16′-11″	20′-10″	18′-8″	25′-2″	21′-5″
550S162-97	22′-8″	19′-9″	23′-6″	20′-11″	27′-11″	25′-1″
800S162-33	16′-5″	14′-10″	19′-2″	17′-3″	23′-1″	18′-3″
800S162-43	17′-9″	15′-11″	20′-6″	18′-5″	25′-0″	22′-6″
800S162-54	19′-1″	17′-1″	21′-8″	19′-6″	26′-4″	23′-9″
800S162-68	20′-9″	18′-6″	23′-1″	20′-9″	28′-0″	25′-2″
800S162-97	24′-5″	21′-6″	26′-0″	23′-2″	31′-1″	27′-9″
1000S162-43	18′-11″	17′-0″	21′-11″	19′-9″	26′-8″	24′-1″
1000S162-54	20′-3″	18′-2″	23′-2″	20′-10″	28′-2″	25′-5″
1000S162-68	21′-11″	19′-7″	24′-7″	22′-2″	29′-10″	26′-11″
1000S162-97	25′-7″	22′-7″	27′-6″	24′-6″	33′-0″	29′-7″
1200S162-43	19′-11″	17′-11″	23′-1″	20′-10″	28′-3″	25′-6″
1200S162-54	21′-3″	19′-1″	24′-5″	22′-0″	29′-9″	26′-10″
1200S162-68	23′-0″	20′-7″	25′-11″	23′-4″	31′-6″	28′-4″
1000S162-97	26′-7″	23′-6″	28′-9″	25′-10″	34′-8″	31′-1″

For SI: 1 inch = 25.4 mm, 1 foot = 304.8 mm, 1 pound per square foot = 0.0479 kPa.

a. Deflection criterion: *L*/240 for total loads.

b. Ceiling dead load = 5 psf.

c. Bearing stiffeners are required at all bearing points and concentrated load locations.

TABLE R804.3.1.1(3)
CEILING JOIST SPANS
SINGLE SPANS WITH BEARING STIFFENERS
20 lb per sq ft LIVE LOAD (LIMITED ATTIC STORAGE)[a, b, c] 33 ksi STEEL

MEMBER DESIGNATION	ALLOWABLE SPAN (feet-inches)					
	Lateral Support of Top (Compression) Flange					
	Unbraced		Mid-Span Bracing		Third-Point Bracing	
	Ceiling Joist Spacing (inches)					
	16	24	16	24	16	24
350S162-33	8′-2″	7′-2″	9′-9″	8′-1″	9′-11″	8′-1″
350S162-43	8′-10″	7′-10″	11′-0″	9′-5″	11′-0″	9′-7″
350S162-54	9′-6″	8′-6″	11′-9″	10′-3″	11′-9″	10′-3″
350S162-68	10′-4″	9′-2″	12′-7″	11′-0″	12′-7″	11′-0″
350S162-97	12′-1″	10′-8″	14′-0″	12′-0″	14′-0″	12′-0″
550S162-33	9′-2″	8′-3″	12′-2″	10′-2″	12′-6″	10′-5″
550S162-43	10′-1″	9′-1″	13′-7″	11′-7″	14′-5″	12′-2″
550S162-54	10′-9″	9′-8″	14′-10″	12′-10″	15′-11″	13′-6″
550S162-68	11′-7″	10′-4″	16′-4″	14′-0″	17′-5″	14′-11″
550S162-97	13′-4″	11′-10″	18′-5″	16′-2″	20′-1″	17′-1″
800S162-33	10′-7″	9′-6″	15′-1″	13′-0″	16′-2″	13′-7″
800S162-43	11′-4″	10′-2″	16′-5″	14′-6″	18′-2″	15′-9″
800S162-54	12′-0″	10′-9″	17′-4″	15′-6″	19′-6″	17′-0″
800S162-68	12′-10″	11′-6″	18′-5″	16′-6″	20′-10″	18′-3″
800S162-97	14′-7″	12′-11″	20′-5″	18′-3″	22′-11″	20′-5″
1000S162-43	12′-1″	10′-11″	17′-7″	15′-10″	19′-11″	17′-3″
1000S162-54	12′-10″	11′-6″	18′-7″	16′-9″	21′-2″	18′-10″
1000S162-68	13′-8″	12′-3″	19′-8″	17′-8″	22′-4″	20′-1″
1000S162-97	15′-4″	13′-8″	21′-8″	19′-5″	24′-5″	21′-11″
1200S162-43	12′-9″	11′-6″	18′-7″	16′-6″	20′-9″	18′-2″
1200S162-54	13′-6″	12′-2″	19′-7″	17′-8″	22′-5″	20′-2″
1200S162-68	14′-4″	12′-11″	20′-9″	18′-8″	23′-7″	21′-3″
1000S162-97	16′-1″	14′-4″	22′-10″	20′-6″	25′-9″	23′-2″

For SI: 1 inch = 25.4 mm, 1 foot = 304.8 mm, 1 pound per square foot = 0.0479 kPa.

a. Deflection criterion: *L*/240 for total loads.

b. Ceiling dead load = 5 psf.

c. Bearing stiffeners are required at all bearing points and concentrated load locations.

TABLE R804.3.1.1(4)
CEILING JOIST SPANS
TWO EQUAL SPANS WITH BEARING STIFFENERS
20 lb per sq ft LIVE LOAD (LIMITED ATTIC STORAGE)[a, b, c] 33 ksi STEEL

MEMBER DESIGNATION	ALLOWABLE SPAN (feet-inches)					
	Lateral Support of Top (Compression) Flange					
	Unbraced		Mid-Span Bracing		Third-Point Bracing	
	Ceiling Joist Spacing (inches)					
	16	24	16	24	16	24
350S162-33	10′-2″	8′-4″	10′-2″	8′-4″	10′-2″	8′-4″
350S162-43	12′-1″	9′-10″	12′-1″	9′-10″	12′-1″	9′-10″
350S162-54	13′-3″	11′-0″	13′-6″	11′-0″	13′-6″	11′-0″
350S162-68	14′-7″	12′-3″	15′-0″	12′-3″	15′-0″	12′-3″
350S162-97	17′-6″	14′-3″	17′-6″	14′-3″	17′-6″	14′-3″
550S162-33	12′-5″	10′-9″	13′-2″	10′-9″	13′-2″	10′-9″
550S162-43	13′-7″	12′-1″	15′-6″	12′-9″	15′-8″	12′-9″
550S162-54	14′-11″	13′-4″	16′-10″	14′-5″	17′-9″	14′-5″
550S162-68	16′-3″	14′-5″	18′-0″	16′-1″	20′-0″	16′-4″
550S162-97	19′-1″	16′-10″	20′-3″	18′-0″	23′-10″	19′-5″
800S162-33	14′-3″	12′-4″	16′-7″	12′-4″	16′-7″	12′-4″
800S162-43	15′-4″	13′-10″	17′-9″	16′-0″	21′-8″	17′-9″
800S162-54	16′-5″	14′-9″	18′-10″	16′-11″	22′-11″	20′-6″
800S162-68	17′-9″	15′-11″	20′-0″	18′-0″	24′-3″	21′-10″
800S162-97	20′-8″	18′-3″	22′-3″	19′-11″	26′-9″	24′-0″
1000S162-43	16′-5″	14′-9″	19′-0″	17′-2″	23′-3″	18′-11″
1000S162-54	17′-6″	15′-8″	20′-1″	18′-1″	24′-6″	22′-1″
1000S162-68	18′-10″	16′-10″	21′-4″	19′-2″	25′-11″	23′-4″
1000S162-97	21′-8″	19′-3″	23′-7″	21′-2″	28′-5″	25′-6″
1200S162-43	17′-3″	15′-7″	20′-1″	18′-2″	24′-6″	18′-3″
1200S162-54	18′-5″	16′-6″	21′-3″	19′-2″	25′-11″	23′-5″
1200S162-68	19′-9″	17′-8″	22′-6″	20′-3″	27′-4″	24′-8″
1000S162-97	22′-7″	20′-1″	24′-10″	22′-3″	29′-11″	26′-11″

For SI: 1 inch = 25.4 mm, 1 foot = 304.8 mm, 1 pound per square foot = 0.0479 kPa.

a. Deflection criterion: *L*/240 for total loads.

b. Ceiling dead load = 5 psf.

c. Bearing stiffeners are required at all bearing points and concentrated load locations.

TABLE R804.3.1.1(5)
CEILING JOIST SPANS
SINGLE SPANS WITHOUT BEARING STIFFENERS
10 lb per sq ft LIVE LOAD (NO ATTIC STORAGE)[a, b] 33 ksi STEEL

MEMBER DESIGNATION	ALLOWABLE SPAN (feet-inches)					
	Lateral Support of Top (Compression) Flange					
	Unbraced		Mid-Span Bracing		Third-Point Bracing	
	Ceiling Joist Spacing (inches)					
	16	24	16	24	16	24
350S162-33	9′-5″	8′-6″	12′-2″	10′-4″	12′-2″	10′-7″
350S162-43	10′-3″	9′-12″	13′-2″	11′-6″	13′-2″	11′-6″
350S162-54	11′-1″	9′-11″	13′-9″	12′-0″	13′-9″	12′-0″
350S162-68	12′-1″	10′-9″	14′-8″	12′-10″	14′-8″	12′-10″
350S162-97	14′-4″	12′-7″	16′-10″	14′-3″	16′-4″	14′-3″
550S162-33	10′-7″	9′-6″	14′-10″	12′-10″	15′-11″	13′-4″
550S162-43	11′-8″	10′-6″	16′-4″	14′-3″	17′-10″	15′-3″
550S162-54	12′-6″	11′-2″	17′-7″	15′-7″	19′-5″	16′-10″
550S162-68	13′-6″	12′-1″	19′-2″	17′-0″	21′-0″	18′-4″
550S162-97	15′-9″	13′-11″	21′-8″	19′-3″	23′-5″	20′-5″
800S162-33	—	—	—	—	—	—
800S162-43	13′-0″	11′-9″	18′-10″	17′-0″	21′-6″	19′-0″
800S162-54	13′-10″	12′-5″	20′-0″	18′-0″	22′-9″	20′-4″
800S162-68	14′-11″	13′-4″	21′-3″	19′-1″	24′-1″	21′-8″
800S162-97	17′-1″	15′-2″	23′-10″	21′-3″	26′-7″	23′-10″
1000S162-43	—	—	—	—	—	—
1000S162-54	14′-9″	13′-3″	21′-4″	19′-3″	24′-4″	22′-0″
1000S162-68	15′-10″	14′-2″	22′-8″	20′-5″	25′-9″	23′-2″
1000S162-97	18′-0″	16′-0″	25′-3″	22′-7″	28′-3″	25′-4″
1200S162-43	—	—	—	—	—	—
1200S162-54	—	—	—	—	—	—
1200S162-68	16′-8″	14′-11″	23′-11″	21′-6″	27′-2″	24′-6″
1000S162-97	18′-9″	16′-9″	26′-6″	23′-8″	29′-9″	26′-9″

For SI: 1 inch = 25.4 mm, 1 foot = 304.8 mm, 1 pound per square foot = 0.0479 kPa.

a. Deflection criterion: *L*/240 for total loads.

b. Ceiling dead load = 5 psf.

TABLE R804.3.1.1(6)
CEILING JOIST SPANS
TWO EQUAL SPANS WITHOUT BEARING STIFFENERS
10 lb per sq ft LIVE LOAD (NO ATTIC STORAGE)[a, b] 33 ksi STEEL

MEMBER DESIGNATION	ALLOWABLE SPAN (feet-inches)					
	Lateral Support of Top (Compression) Flange					
	Unbraced		Mid-Span Bracing		Third-Point Bracing	
	Ceiling Joist Spacing (inches)					
	16	24	16	24	16	24
350S162-33	11′-9″	8′-11″	11′-9″	8′-11″	11′-9″	8′-11″
350S162-43	14′-2″	11′-7″	14′-11″	11′-7″	14′-11″	11′-7″
350S162-54	15′-6″	13′-10″	17′-1″	13′-10″	17′-7″	13′-10″
350S162-68	17′-3″	15′-3″	18′-6″	16′-1″	19′-8″	16′-1″
350S162-97	20′-10″	18′-4″	21′-5″	18′-9″	21′-11″	18′-9″
550S162-33	13′-4″	9′-11″	13′-4″	9′-11″	13′-4″	9′-11″
550S162-43	16′-0″	13′-6″	17′-9″	13′-6″	17′-9″	13′-6″
550S162-54	17′-4″	15′-6″	19′-5″	16′-10″	21′-9″	16′-10″
550S162-68	19′-1″	16′-11″	20′-10″	18′-8″	24′-11″	20′-6″
550S162-97	22′-8″	20′-0″	23′-9″	21′-1″	28′-2″	25′-1″
800S162-33	—	—	—	—	—	—
800S162-43	17′-9″	15′-7″	20′-6″	15′-7″	21′-0″	15′-7″
800S162-54	19′-1″	17′-1″	21′-8″	19′-6″	26′-4″	23′-10″
800S162-68	20′-9″	18′-6″	23′-1″	20′-9″	28′-0″	25′-2″
800S162-97	24′-5″	21′-6″	26′-0″	23′-2″	31′-1″	27′-9″
1000S162-43	—	—	—	—	—	—
1000S162-54	20′-3″	18′-2″	23′-2″	20′-10″	28′-2″	21′-2″
1000S162-68	21′-11″	19′-7″	24′-7″	22′-2″	29′-10″	26′-11″
1000S162-97	25′-7″	22′-7″	27′-6″	24′-6″	33′-0″	29′-7″
1200S162-43	—	—	—	—	—	—
1200S162-54	—	—	—	—	—	—
1200S162-68	23′-0″	20′-7″	25′-11″	23′-4″	31′-6″	28′-4″
1000S162-97	26′-7″	23′-6″	28′-9″	25′-10″	34′-8″	31′-1″

For SI: 1 inch = 25.4 mm, 1 foot = 304.8 mm, 1 pound per square foot = 0.0479 kPa.

a. Deflection criterion: *L*/240 for total loads.

b. Ceiling dead load = 5 psf.

TABLE R804.3.1.1(7)
CEILING JOIST SPANS
SINGLE SPANS WITHOUT BEARING STIFFENERS
20 lb per sq ft LIVE LOAD (LIMITED ATTIC STORAGE)[a, b] 33 ksi STEEL

MEMBER DESIGNATION	ALLOWABLE SPAN (feet-inches)					
	Lateral Support of Top (Compression) Flange					
	Unbraced		Mid-Span Bracing		Third-Point Bracing	
	Ceiling Joist Spacing (inches)					
	16	24	16	24	16	24
350S162-33	8′-2″	6′-10″	9′-9″	6′-10″	9′-11″	6′-10″
350S162-43	8′-10″	7′-10″	11′-0″	9′-5″	11′-0″	9′-7″
350S162-54	9′-6″	8′-6″	11′-9″	10′-3″	11′-9″	10′-3″
350S162-68	10′-4″	9′-2″	12′-7″	11′-0″	12′-7″	11′-0″
350S162-97	12′-10″	10′-8″	13′-9″	12′-0″	13′-9″	12′-0″
550S162-33	9′-2″	8′-3″	12′-2″	8′-5″	12′-6″	8′-5″
550S162-43	10′-1″	9′-1″	13′-7″	11′-8″	14′-5″	12′-2″
550S162-54	10′-9″	9′-8″	14′-10″	12′-10″	15′-11″	13′-6″
550S162-68	11′-7″	10′-4″	16′-4″	14′-0″	17′-5″	14′-11″
550S162-97	13′-4″	11′-10″	18′-5″	16′-2″	20′-1″	17′-4″
800S162-33	—	—	—	—	—	—
800S162-43	11′-4″	10′-1″	16′-5″	13′-6″	18′-1″	13′-6″
800S162-54	20′-0″	10′-9″	17′-4″	15′-6″	19′-6″	27′-0″
800S162-68	12′-10″	11′-6″	18′-5″	16′-6″	20′-10″	18′-3″
800S162-97	14′-7″	12′-11″	20′-5″	18′-3″	22′-11″	20′-5″
1000S162-43	—	—	—	—	—	—
1000S162-54	12′-10″	11′-6″	18′-7″	16′-9″	21′-2″	15′-5″
1000S162-68	13′-8″	12′-3″	19′-8″	17′-8″	22′-4″	20′-1″
1000S162-97	15′-4″	13′-8″	21′-8″	19′-5″	24′-5″	21′-11″
1200S162-43	—	—	—	—	—	—
1200S162-54	—	—	—	—	—	—
1200S162-68	14′-4″	12′-11″	20′-9″	18′-8″	23′-7″	21′-3″
1000S162-97	16′-1″	14′-4″	22′-10″	20′-6″	25′-9″	23′-2″

For SI: 1 inch = 25.4 mm, 1 foot = 304.8 mm, 1 pound per square foot = 0.0479 kPa.

a. Deflection criterion: *L*/240 for total loads.

b. Ceiling dead load = 5 psf.

**TABLE R804.3.1.1(8)
CEILING JOIST SPANS
TWO EQUAL SPANS WITHOUT BEARING STIFFENERS
20 lb per sq ft LIVE LOAD (LIMITED ATTIC STORAGE)[a, b] 33 ksi STEEL**

MEMBER DESIGNATION	ALLOWABLE SPAN (feet-inches)					
	Lateral Support of Top (Compression) Flange					
	Unbraced		Mid-Span Bracing		Third-Point Bracing	
	Ceiling Joist Spacing (inches)					
	16	24	16	24	16	24
350S162-33	8′-1″	6′-1″	8′-1″	6′-1″	8′-1″	6′-1″
350S162-43	10′-7″	8′-1″	10′-7″	8′-1″	10′-7″	8′-1″
350S162-54	12′-8″	9′-10″	12′-8″	9′-10″	12′-8″	9′-10″
350S162-68	14′-7″	11′-10″	14′-11″	11′-10″	14′-11″	11′-10″
350S162-97	17′-6″	14′-3″	17′-6″	14′-3″	17′-6″	14′-3″
550S162-33	8′-11″	6′-8″	8′-11″	6′-8″	8′-11″	6′-8″
550S162-43	12′-3″	9′-2″	12′-3″	9′-2″	12′-3″	9′-2″
550S162-54	14′-11″	11′-8″	15′-4″	11′-8″	15′-4″	11′-8″
550S162-68	16′-3″	14′-5″	18′-0″	15′-8″	18′-10″	14′-7″
550S162-97	19′-1″	16′-10″	20′-3″	18′-0″	23′-9″	19′-5″
800S162-33	—	—	—	—	—	—
800S162-43	13′-11″	9′-10″	13′-11″	9′-10″	13′-11″	9′-10″
800S162-54	16′-5″	13′-9″	18′-8″	13′-9″	18′-8″	13′-9″
800S162-68	17′-9″	15′-11″	20′-0″	18′-0″	24′-1″	18′-3″
800S162-97	20′-8″	18′-3″	22′-3″	19′-11″	26′-9″	24′-0″
1000S162-43	—	—	—	—	—	—
1000S162-54	17′-6″	13′-11″	19′-1″	13′-11″	19′-1″	13′-11″
1000S162-68	18′-10″	16′-10″	21′-4″	19′-2″	25′-11″	19′-7″
1000S162-97	21′-8″	19′-3″	23′-7″	21′-2″	28′-5″	25′-6″
1200S162-43	—	—	—	—	—	—
1200S162-54	—	—	—	—	—	—
1200S162-68	19′-9″	17′-8″	22′-6″	19′-8″	26′-8″	19′-8″
1000S162-97	22′-7″	20′-1″	24′-10″	22′-3″	29′-11″	26′-11″

For SI: 1 inch = 25.4 mm, 1 foot = 304.8 mm, 1 pound per square foot = 0.0479 kPa.

a. Deflection criterion: *L*/240 for total loads.

b. Ceiling dead load = 5 psf.

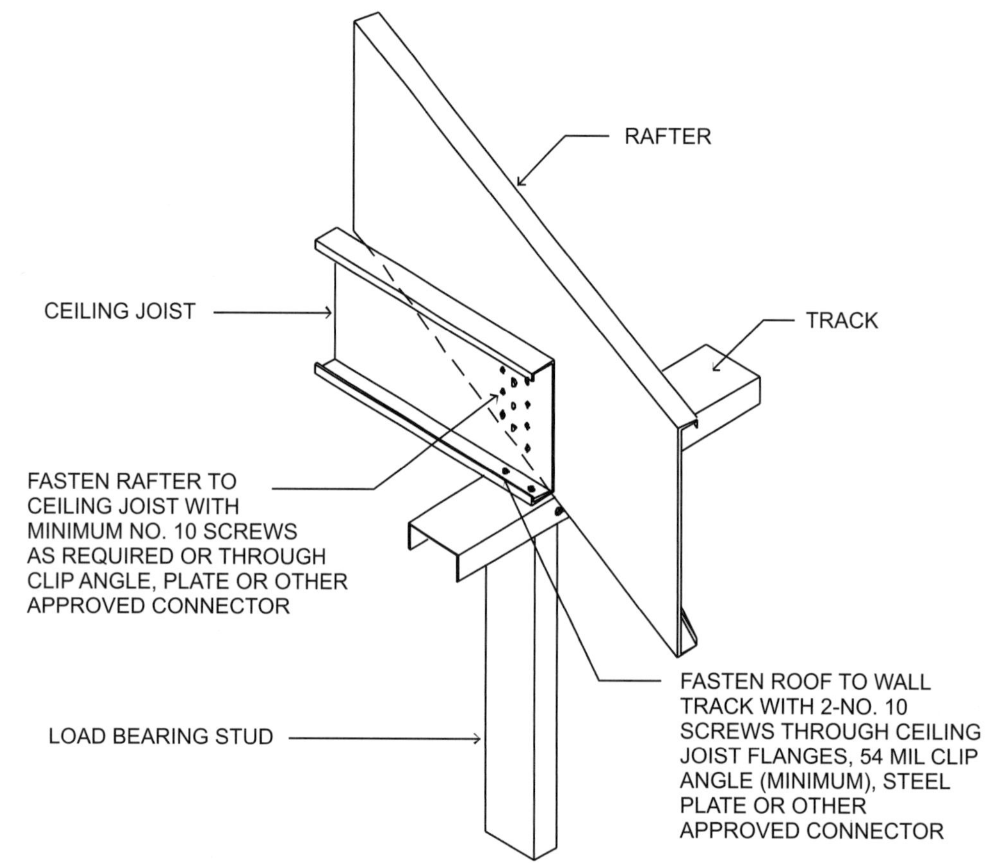

For SI: 1 mil = 0.0254 mm.

FIGURE R804.3.1.1(1)
JOIST TO RAFTER CONNECTION

TABLE R804.3.1.1(9)
NUMBER OF SCREWS REQUIRED FOR CEILING JOIST TO ROOF RAFTER CONNECTION[a]

ROOF SLOPE	NUMBER OF SCREWS																			
	Building width (feet)																			
	24				28				32				36				40			
	Ground snow load (psf)																			
	20	30	50	70	20	30	50	70	20	30	50	70	20	30	50	70	20	30	50	70
3/12	5	6	9	11	5	7	10	13	6	8	11	15	7	8	13	17	8	9	14	19
4/12	4	5	7	9	4	5	8	10	5	6	9	12	5	7	10	13	6	7	11	14
5/12	3	4	6	7	4	4	6	8	4	5	7	10	5	5	8	11	5	6	9	12
6/12	3	3	5	6	3	4	6	7	4	4	6	8	4	5	7	9	4	5	8	10
7/12	3	3	4	6	3	3	5	7	3	4	6	7	4	4	6	8	4	5	7	9
8/12	2	3	4	5	3	3	5	6	3	4	5	7	3	4	6	8	4	4	6	8
9/12	2	3	4	5	3	3	4	6	3	3	5	6	3	4	5	7	3	4	6	8
10/12	2	2	4	5	2	3	4	5	3	3	5	6	3	3	5	7	3	4	6	7
11/12	2	2	3	4	2	3	4	5	3	3	4	6	3	3	5	6	3	4	5	7
12/12	2	2	3	4	2	3	4	5	2	3	4	5	3	3	5	6	3	4	5	7

For SI: 1 inch = 25.4 mm, 1 foot = 304.8 mm, 1 pound per square foot = 0.0479 kPa.

a. Screws shall be No. 10.

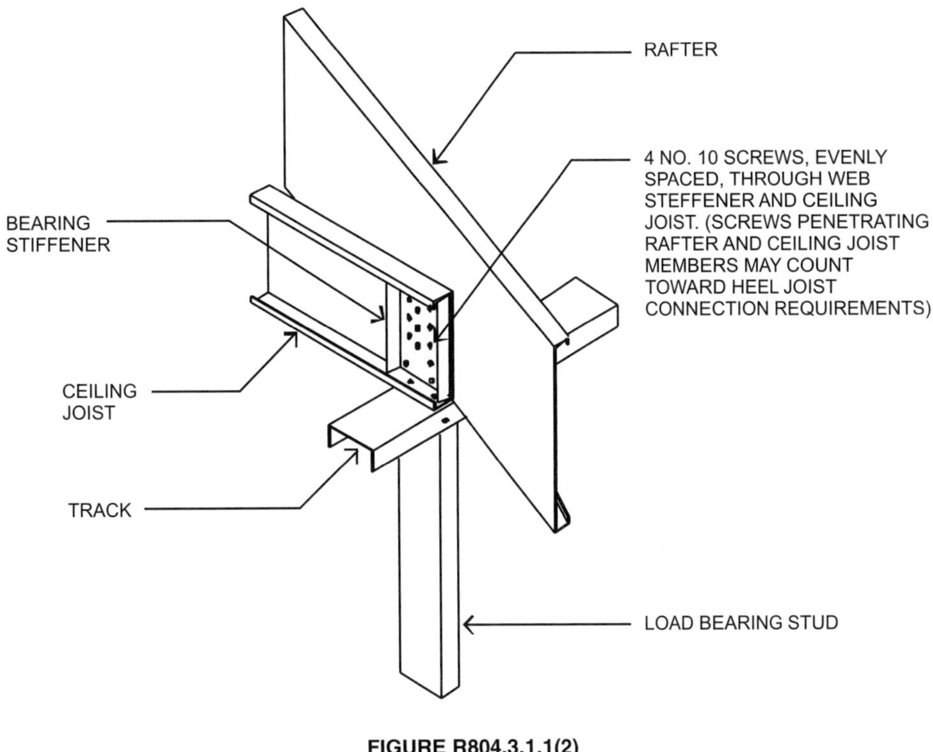

FIGURE R804.3.1.1(2)
BEARING STIFFENER

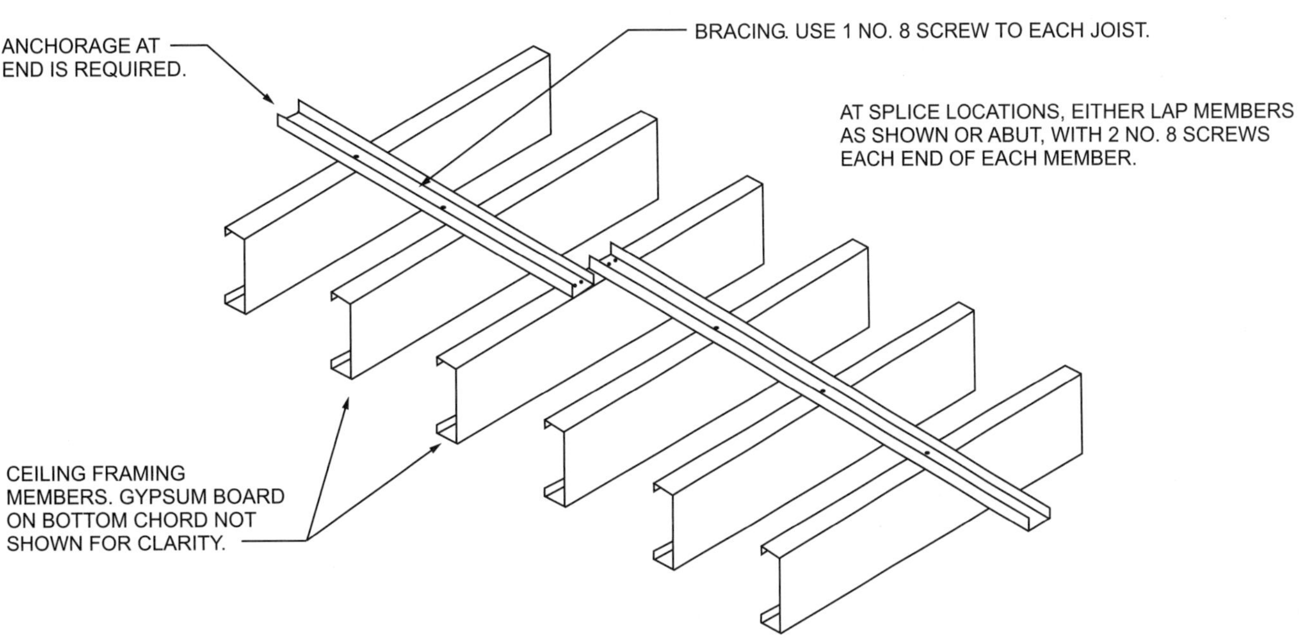

FIGURE R804.3.1.4(1)
CEILING JOIST TOP FLANGE BRACING WITH C-SHAPE, TRACK OR COLD-ROLLED CHANNEL

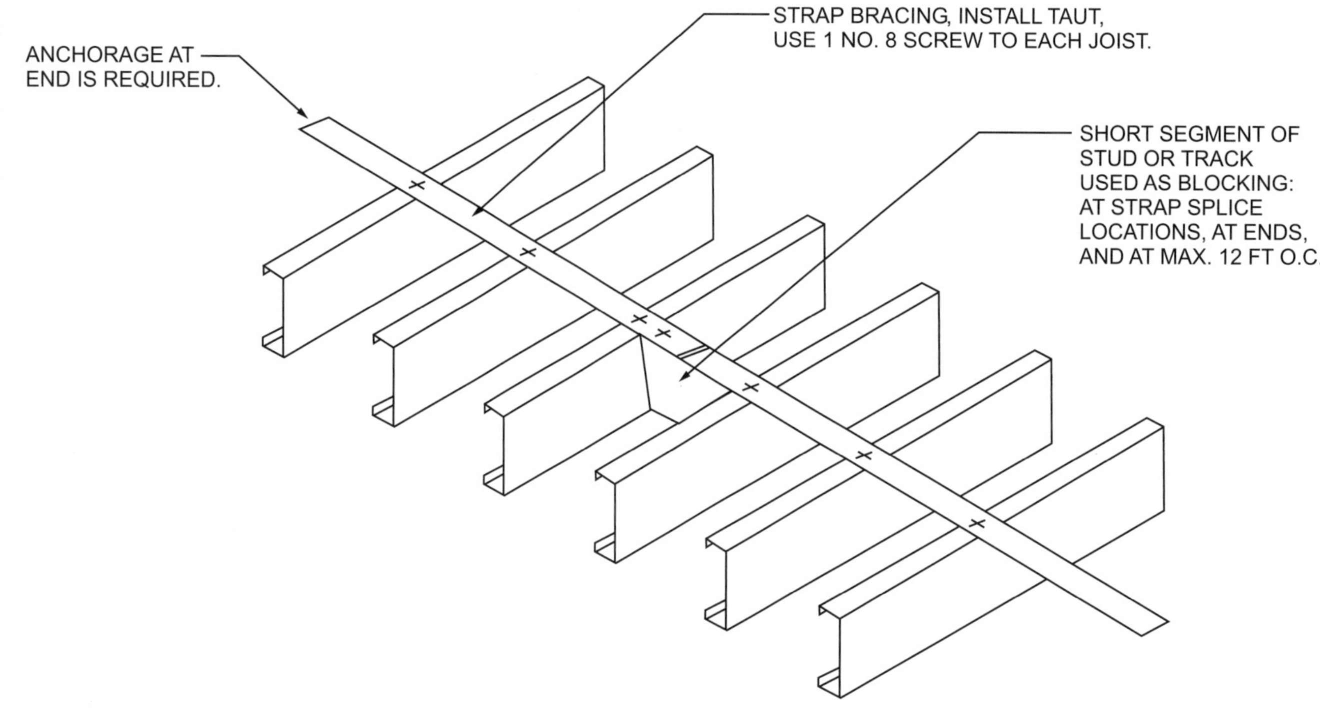

For SI: 1 foot = 304.8 mm.

FIGURE R804.3.1.4(2)
CEILING JOIST TOP FLANGE BRACING WITH CONTINUOUS STEEL STRAP AND BLOCKING

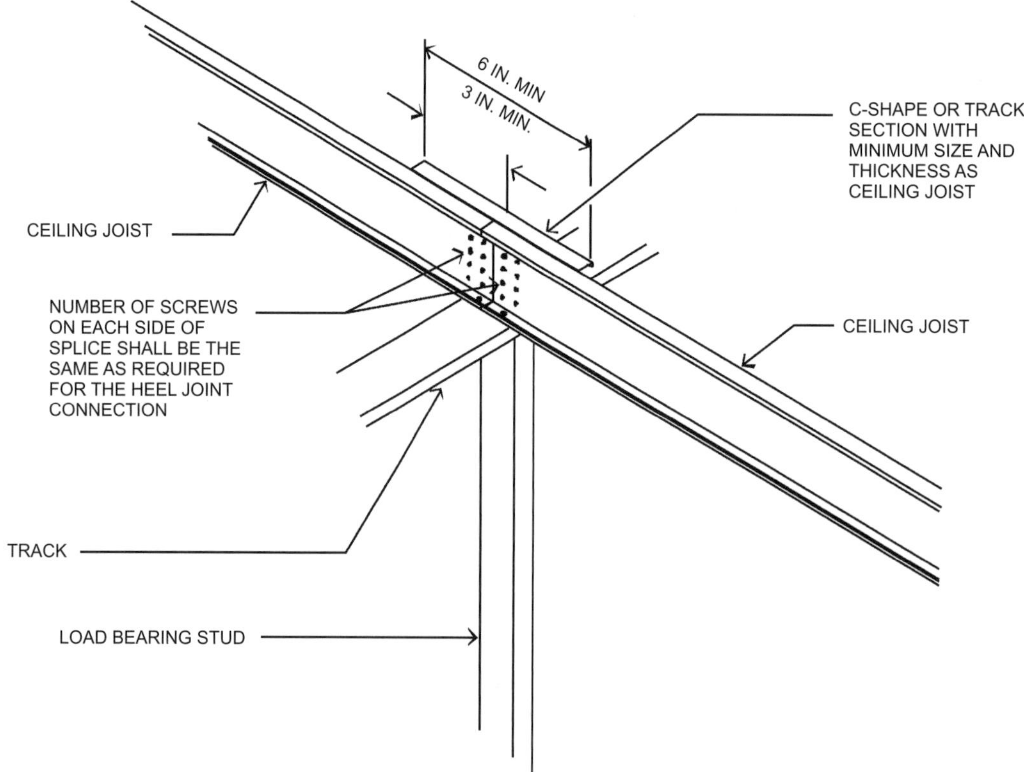

For SI: 1 inch = 25.4 mm.

FIGURE R804.3.1.5
SPLICED CEILING JOISTS

TABLE R804.3.2.1(1)
ROOF RAFTER SPANS[a, b, c]
33 ksi STEEL

MEMBER DESIGNATION	ALLOWABLE SPAN MEASURED HORIZONTALLY (feet-inches)							
	Ground snow load (psf)							
	20		30		50		70	
	Rafter spacing (inches)							
	16	24	16	24	16	24	16	24
550S162-33	14′-0″	11′-6″	11′-11″	9′-7″	9′-6″	7′-9″	8′-2″	6′-8″
550S162-43	16′-8″	13′-11″	14′-5″	11′-9″	11′-6″	9′-5″	9′-10″	8′-0″
550S162-54	17′-11″	15′-7″	15′-7″	13′-3″	12′-11″	10′-7″	11′-1″	9′-1″
550S162-68	19′-2″	16′-9″	16′-9″	14′-7″	14′-1″	11′-10″	12′-6″	10′-2″
550S162-97	21′-3″	18′-6″	18′-6″	16′-2″	15′-8″	13′-8″	14′-0″	12′-2″
800S162-33	16′-5″	13′-5″	13′-11″	11′-4″	11′-1″	8′-2″	9′-0″	6′-0″
800S162-43	19′-9″	16′-1″	16′-8″	13′-7″	13′-4″	10′-10″	11′-5″	9′-4″
800S162-54	22′-8″	18′-6″	19′-2″	15′-8″	15′-4″	12′-6″	13′-1″	10′-8″
800S162-68	25′-10″	21′-2″	21′-11″	17′-10″	17′-6″	14′-4″	15′-0″	12′-3″
800S162-97	21′-3″	18′-6″	18′-6″	16′-2″	15′-8″	13′-8″	14′-0″	12′-2″
1000S162-43	22′-3″	18′-2″	18′-9″	15′-8″	15′-0″	12′-3″	12′-10″	10′-6″
1000S162-54	25′-8″	20′-11″	21′-8″	17′-9″	17′-4″	14′-2″	14′-10″	12′-1″
1000S162-68	29′-7″	24′-2″	25′-0″	20′-5″	20′-0″	16′-4″	17′-2″	14′-0″
1000S162-97	34′-8″	30′-4″	30′-4″	25′-10″	25′-3″	20′-8″	21′-8″	17′-8″
1200S162-54	28′-3″	23′-1″	23′-11″	19′-7″	19′-2″	15′-7″	16′-5″	13′-5″
1200S162-68	32′-10″	26′-10″	27′-9″	22′-8″	22′-2″	18′-1″	19′-0″	15′-6″
1200S162-97	40′-6″	33′-5″	34′-6″	28′-3″	27′-7″	22′-7″	23′-8″	19′-4″

For SI: 1 inch = 25.4 mm, 1 foot = 304.8 mm, 1 pound per square foot = 0.0479kPa.

a. Table provides maximum horizontal rafter spans in feet and inches for slopes between 3:12 and 12:12.

b. Deflection criterion: *L*/240 for live loads and *L*/180 for total loads.

c. Roof dead load = 12 psf.

TABLE R804.3.2.1(2)
ROOF RAFTER SPANS[a, b, c]
50 ksi STEEL

MEMBER DESIGNATION	ALLOWABLE SPAN MEASURED HORIZONTALLY (feet-inches)							
	Equivalent ground snow load (psf)							
	20		30		50		70	
	Rafter spacing (inches)							
	16	24	16	24	16	24	16	24
550S162-33	15′-4″	12′-11″	13′-4″	10′′-11″	10′-9″	8′-9″	9′-2″	7′-6″
550S162-43	16′-8″	14′-7″	14′-7″	12′-9″	12′-3″	10′-6″	11′-0″	9′-0″
550S162-54	17′-11″	15′-7″	15′-7″	13′-8″	13′-2″	11′-6″	11′-9″	10′-3″
550S162-68	19′-2″	16′-9″	16′-9″	14′-7″	14′-1″	12′-4″	12′-7″	11′-0″
550S162-97	21′-3″	18′-6″	18′-6″	16′-2″	15′-8″	13′-8″	14′-0″	12′-3″
800S162-33	18′-10″	15′-5″	15′-11″	12′-9″	12′-3″	8′-2″	9′-0″	6′-0″
800S162-43	22′-3″	18′-2″	18′-10″	15′-5″	15′-1″	12′-3″	12′-11″	10′-6″
800S162-54	24′-2″	21′-2″	21′-1″	18′-5″	17′-10″	14′-8″	15′-5″	12′-7″
800S162-68	25′-11″	22′-8″	22′-8″	19′-9″	19′-1″	16′-8″	17′-1″	14′-9″
800S162-97	28′-10″	25′-2″	25′-2″	22′-0″	21′-2″	18′-6″	19′-0″	16′-7″
1000S162-43	25′-2″	20′-7″	21′-4″	17′-5″	17′-0″	13′-11″	14′-7″	10′ – 7″
1000S162-54	29′-0″	24′-6″	25′-4″	20′-9″	20′-3″	16′-7″	17′-5″	14′-2″
1000S162-68	31′-2″	27′-3″	27′-3″	23′-9″	20′-0″	19′-6″	20′-6″	16′-8″
1000S162-97	34′-8″	30′-4″	30′-4″	26′-5″	25′-7″	22′-4″	22′-10″	20′-0″
1200S162-54	33′-2″	27′-1″	28′-1″	22′-11″	22′-5″	18′-4″	19′-3″	15′-8″
1200S162-68	36′- 4″	31′-9″	31′-9″	27′-0″	26′-5″	21′-6″	22′-6″	18′-6″
1200S162-97	40′-6″	35′-4″	35′-4″	30′-11″	29′-10″	26′-1″	26′-8″	23′-1″

For SI: 1 inch = 25.4 mm, 1 foot = 304.8 mm, 1 pound per square foot = 0.0479 kPa.

a. Table provides maximum horizontal rafter spans in feet and inches for slopes between 3:12 and 12:12.

b. Deflection criterion: *L*/240 for live loads and *L*/180 for total loads.

c. Roof dead load = 12 psf.

TABLE R804.3.2.1(3)
BASIC WIND SPEED TO EQUIVALENT SNOW LOAD CONVERSION

BASIC WIND SPEED AND EXPOSURE		EQUIVALENT GROUND SNOW LOAD (psf)									
		Roof slope									
Exp. B	Exp. C	3:12	4:12	5:12	6:12	7:12	8:12	9:12	10:12	11:12	12:12
85 mph	—	20	20	20	20	20	20	30	30	30	30
100 mph	85 mph	20	20	20	20	30	30	30	30	50	50
110 mph	100 mph	20	20	20	20	30	50	50	50	50	50
—	110 mph	30	30	30	50	50	50	70	70	70	—

For SI: 1 mile per hour = 0.447 m/s, 1 pound per square foot = 0.0479 kPa.

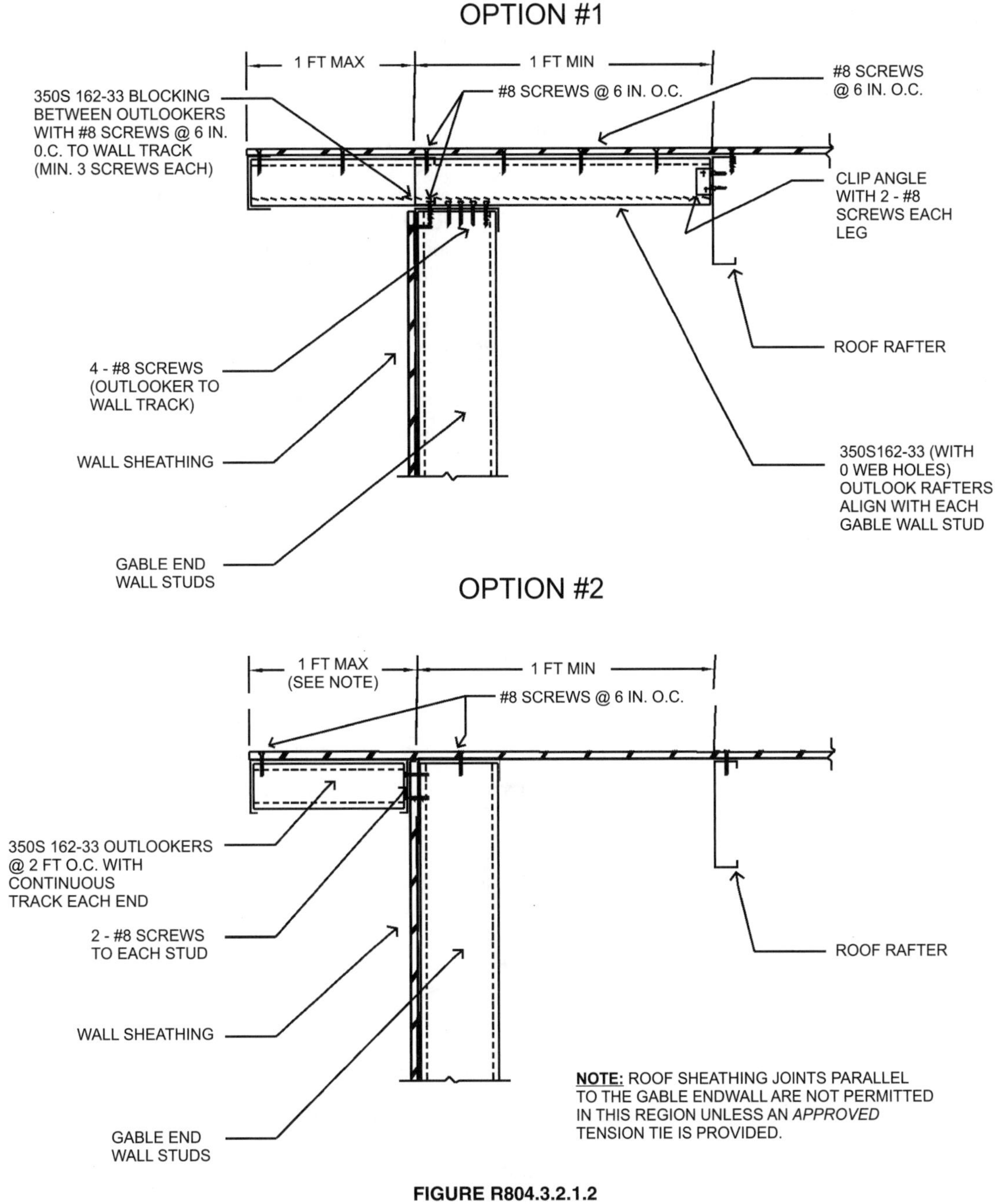

FIGURE R804.3.2.1.2
GABLE ENDWALL OVERHANG DETAILS

R804.3.3.4 Hip framing connections. Hip rafter framing connections shall be installed in accordance with the following:

1. Jack rafters shall be connected at the eave to a parallel C-shape blocking member in accordance with Figure R804.3.3.4(1). The C-shape blocking member shall be attached to the supporting wall track with minimum two No. 10 screws.
2. Jack rafters shall be connected to a hip member with a minimum 2 inch × 2 inch (51 mm × 51 mm) clip angle fastened with No. 10 screws to the hip member in accordance with Figure R804.3.2.4 and Table R804.3.2.4. The clip angle shall have a steel thickness equivalent to or greater than the jack rafter thickness and shall extend the depth of the jack rafter member to the extent possible.
3. The connection of the hip support columns at the ceiling line shall be in accordance with Figure R804.3.3.4(2), with an uplift strap sized in accordance with Table R804.3.3.4(1).
4. The connection of hip support members, ridge members and hip support columns at the ridge shall be in accordance with Figures R804.3.3.4(3) and R804.3.3.4(4) and Table R804.3.3.4(2).
5. The connection of hip members to the wall corner shall be in accordance with Figure R804.3.3.4(5) and Table R804.3.3.4(3).

R804.3.4 Cutting and notching. Flanges and lips of load-bearing cold-formed steel roof framing members shall not be cut or notched.

R804.3.5 Headers. Roof-ceiling framing above wall openings shall be supported on headers. The allowable spans for headers in load-bearing walls shall not exceed the values set forth in Section R603.6 and Tables R603.6(1) through R603.6(24).

R804.3.6 Framing of openings in roofs and ceilings. Openings in roofs and ceilings shall be framed with header and trimmer joists. Header joist spans shall not exceed 4 feet (1219 mm) in length. Header and trimmer joists shall be fabricated from joist and track members having a minimum size and thickness at least equivalent to the adjacent ceiling joists or roof rafters and shall be installed in accordance with Figures R804.3.6(1) and R804.3.6(2). Each header joist shall be connected to trimmer joists with a minimum of four 2-inch by 2-inch (51 by 51 mm) clip angles. Each clip angle shall be fastened to both the header

TABLE R804.3.2.4
SCREWS REQUIRED AT EACH LEG OF CLIP ANGLE FOR HIP RAFTER TO HIP MEMBER OR ROOF RAFTER TO RIDGE MEMBER CONNECTION[a]

BUILDING WIDTH (feet)	NUMBER OF SCREWS			
	Ground snow load (psf)			
	0 to 20	21 to 30	31 to 50	51 to 70
24	2	2	3	4
28	2	3	4	5
32	2	3	4	5
36	3	3	5	6
40	3	4	5	7

For SI: 1 inch = 25.4 mm, 1 foot = 304.8 mm, 1 pound per square foot = 0.0479 kPa.

a. Screws shall be No. 10 minimum.

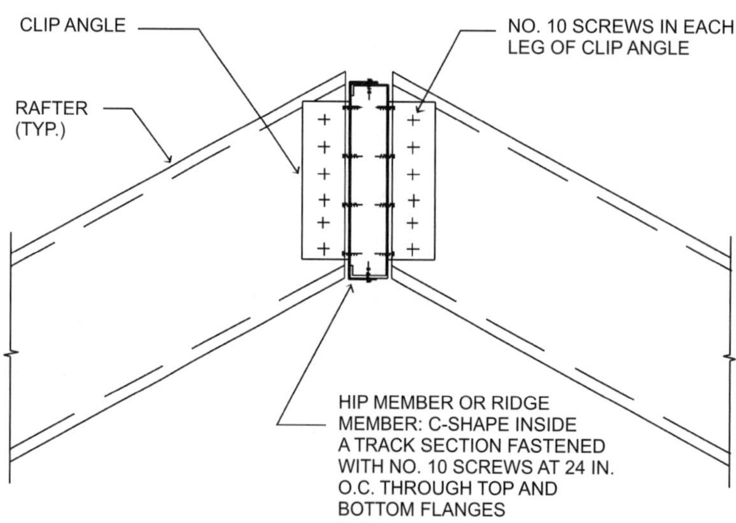

FIGURE R804.3.2.4
HIP MEMBER OR RIDGE MEMBER CONNECTION

and trimmer joists with four No. 8 screws, evenly spaced, through each leg of the clip angle. The steel thickness of the clip angles shall be not less than that of the ceiling joist or roof rafter. Each track section for a built-up header or trimmer joist shall extend the full length of the joist (continuous).

R804.3.7 Roof trusses. Cold-formed steel trusses shall be designed and installed in accordance with AISI S100, Section D4. Trusses shall be connected to the top track of the load-bearing wall in accordance with Table R804.3, either with two No.10 screws applied through the flange of the truss or by using a 54 mil (1.37 mm) clip angle with two No.10 screws in each leg.

R804.3.8 Ceiling and roof diaphragms. Ceiling and roof diaphragms shall be in accordance with this section.

R804.3.8.1 Ceiling diaphragm. At gable endwalls a ceiling *diaphragm* shall be provided by attaching a minimum $^{1}/_{2}$-inch (12.7 mm) gypsum board in accordance with Tables R804.3.8(1) and R804.3.8(2) or a minimum $^{3}/_{8}$-inch (9.5 mm) wood structural panel sheathing, which complies with Section R803, in accordance with Table R804.3.8(3) to the bottom of ceiling joists or roof trusses and connected to wall framing in accordance with Figures R804.3.8(1) and R804.3.8(2), unless studs are designed as full height without bracing at the ceiling. Flat blocking shall consist of C-shape or track section with a minimum thickness of 33 mils (0.84 mm).

The ceiling *diaphragm* shall be secured with screws spaced at a maximum 6 inches (152 mm) o.c. at panel edges and a maximum 12 inches (305 mm) o.c. in the field. Multiplying the required lengths in Tables R804.3.8(1) and R804.3.8(2) for gypsum board sheathed ceiling diaphragms shall be permitted to be multiplied by 0.35 shall be permitted if all panel edges are blocked. Multiplying the required lengths in Tables R804.3.8(1) and R804.3.8(2) for gypsum board sheathed ceiling diaphragms by 0.9 shall be permitted if all panel edges are secured with screws spaced at 4 inches (102 mm) o.c.

R804.3.8.2 Roof diaphragm. A roof *diaphragm* shall be provided by attaching a minimum of $^{3}/_{8}$ inch (9.5 mm) wood structural panel which complies with Section R803 to roof rafters or truss top chords in accordance with Table R804.3. Buildings with 3:1 or larger plan *aspect ratio* and with roof rafter slope (pitch) of 9:12 or larger shall have the roof rafters and ceiling joists blocked in accordance with Figure R804.3.8(3).

R804.3.9 Roof tie-down. Roof assemblies subject to wind uplift pressures of 20 pounds per square foot (0.96 kPa) or greater, as established in Table R301.2(2), shall have rafter-to-bearing wall ties provided in accordance with Table R802.11.

TABLE R804.3.3.2
HIP MEMBER SIZES, 33 ksi STEEL

BUILDING WIDTH (feet)	HIP MEMBER DESIGNATION[a]			
	Equivalent ground snow load (psf)			
	0 to 20	21 to 30	31 to 50	51 to 70
24	800S162-68 800T150-68	800S162-68 800T150-68	800S162-97 800T150-97	1000S162-97 1000T150-97
28	1000S162-68 1000T150-68	1000S162-68 1000T150-68	1000S162-97 1000T150-97	1200S162-97 1200T150-97
32	1000S162-97 1000T150-97	1000S162-97 1000T150-97	1200S162-97 1200T150-97	—
36	1200S162-97 1200T150-97	—	—	—
40	—	—	—	—

For SI: 1 foot = 304.8 mm, 1 pound per square foot = 0.0479 kPa.

a. The web depth of the roof rafters and jack rafters is to match at the hip or they shall be installed in accordance with an approved design.

TABLE R804.3.3.3
HIP SUPPORT COLUMN SIZES

BUILDING WIDTH (feet)	HIP SUPPORT COLUMN DESIGNATION[a, b]			
	Equivalent ground snow load (psf)			
	0 to 20	21 to 30	31 to 50	51 to 70
24	2-350S162-33	2-350S162-33	2-350S162-43	2-350S162-54
28	2-350S162-54	2-550S162-54	2-550S162-68	2-550S162-68
32	2-550S162-68	2-550S162-68	2-550S162-97	—
36	2-550S162-97	—	—	—
40	—	—	—	—

For SI: 1 foot = 304,8 mm, 1 pound per square foot = 0.0479 kPa.

a. Box shape column only in accordance with Figure R804.3.3.4(2).

b. 33 ksi steel for 33 and 43 mil material; 50 ksi steel for thicker material.

**TABLE R804.3.3.4(1)
UPLIFT STRAP CONNECTION REQUIREMENTS
HIP SUPPORT COLUMN AT CEILING LINE**

BUILDING WIDTH (feet)	BASIC WIND SPEED (mph) EXPOSURE B				
	85	100	110	—	—
	BASIC WIND SPEED (mph) EXPOSURE C				
	—	85	—	100	110
	Number of No. 10 screws in each end of each 3 inch by 54-mil steel strap[a, b, c]				
24	3	4	4	6	7
28	4	6	6	8	10
32	5	8	8	11	13
36	7	10	11	14	17
40	—	—	—	—	—

For SI: 1 foot = 304.8 mm, 1 pound per square foot = 0.0479 kPa, 1 mil = 0.0254 mm.

a. Two straps are required, one each side of the column.

b. Space screws at $^3/_4$ inch on-center and provide $^3/_4$ inch end distance.

c. 50 ksi steel strap.

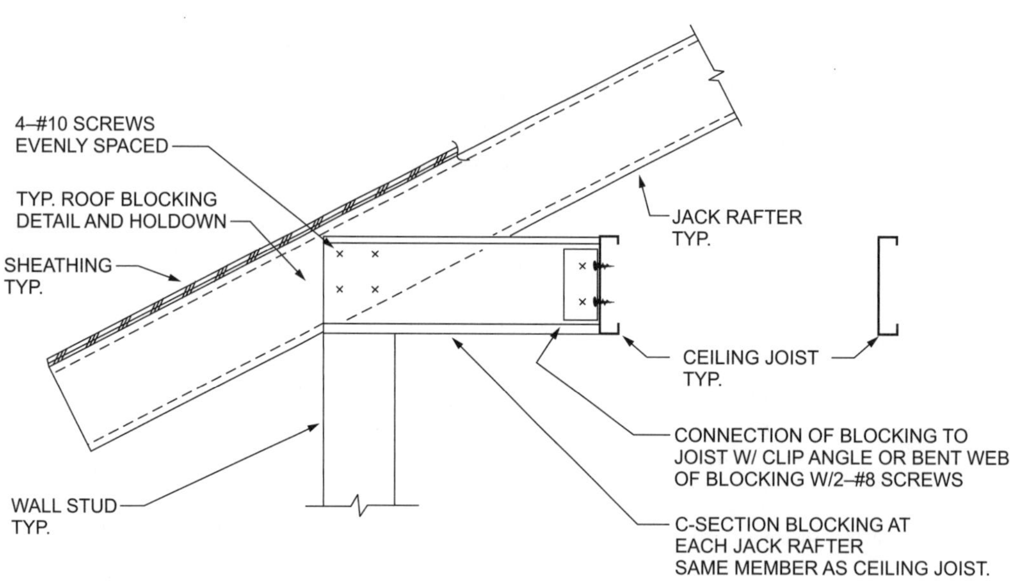

**FIGURE R804.3.3.4(1)
JACK RAFTER CONNECTION AT EAVE**

TABLE R804.3.3.4(2)
CONNECTION REQUIREMENTS
HIP MEMBER TO HIP SUPPORT COLUMN

BUILDING WIDTH (feet)	NUMBER OF NO. 10 SCREWS IN EACH FRAMING ANGLE[a, b, c]			
	Equivalent ground snow load (psf)			
	0 to 20	21 to 30	31 to 50	51 to 70
24	10	10	10	12
28	10	10	14	18
32	10	12	—	—
36	14	—	—	—
40	—	—	—	—

For SI: 1 foot = 304.8 mm, 1 pound per square foot = 0.0479 kPa.

a. Screws to be divided equally between the connection to the hip member and the column. Refer to Figures R804.3.3.4(3) and R804.3.3.4(4).

b. The number of screws required in each framing angle is not to be less than shown in Table R804.3.3.4(1).

c. 50 ksi steel from the framing angle.

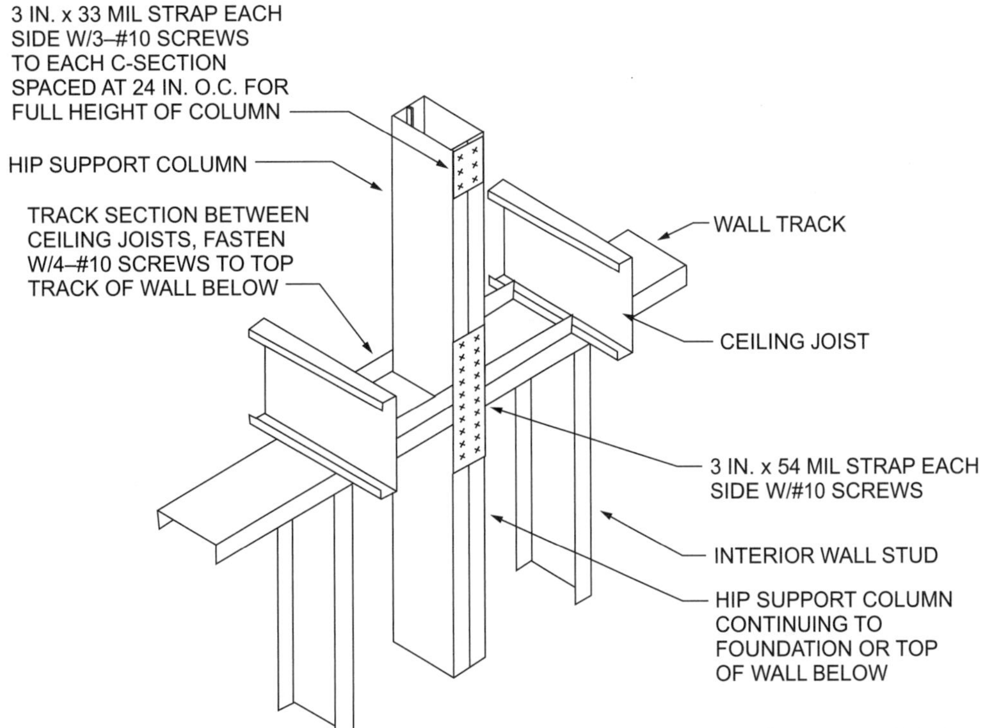

For SI: 1 inch = 25.4 mm, 1 mil = 0.0254 mm.

FIGURE R804.3.3.4(2)
HIP SUPPORT COLUMN

TABLE R804.3.3.4(3)
UPLIFT STRAP CONNECTION REQUIREMENTS
HIP MEMBER TO WALL

BUILDING WIDTH (feet)	BASIC WIND SPEED (mph) EXPOSURE B				
	85	100	110	—	—
	BASIC WIND SPEED (mph) EXPOSURE C				
	—	85	—	100	110
	Number of No. 10 screws in each end of each 3 inch by 54-mil Steel strap[a, b, c]				
24	2	2	3	3	4
28	2	3	3	4	5
32	3	4	4	6	7
36	3	5	5	7	8
40	—	—	—	—	—

For SI: 1 foot = 304.8 mm, 1 pound per square foot = 0.0479 kPa.

a. Two straps are required, one each side of the column.

b. Space screws at $^{3}/_{4}$ inches on-center and provide $^{3}/_{4}$ inch end distance.

c. 50 ksi steel strap.

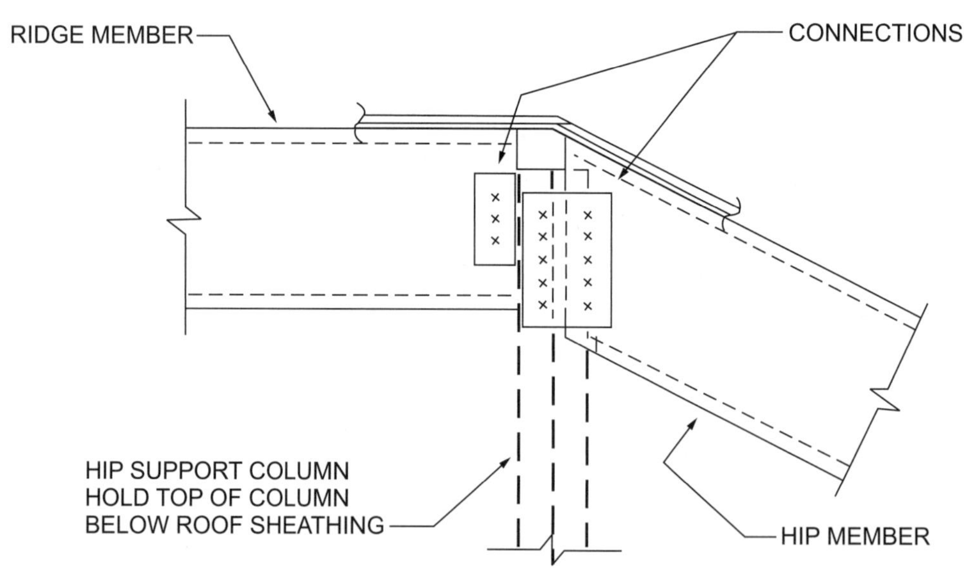

FIGURE R804.3.3.4(3)
HIP CONNECTIONS AT RIDGE

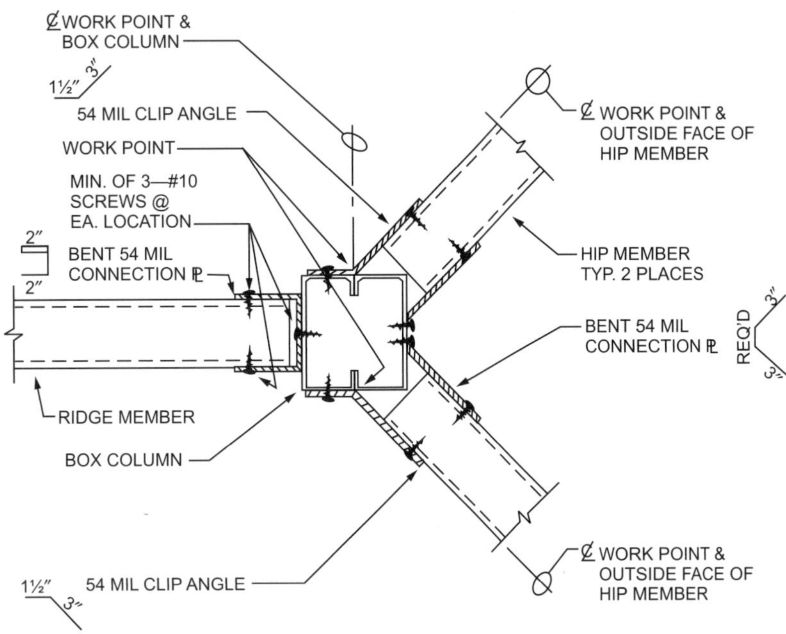

CONNECTION @ 3½″ BOX COLUMN

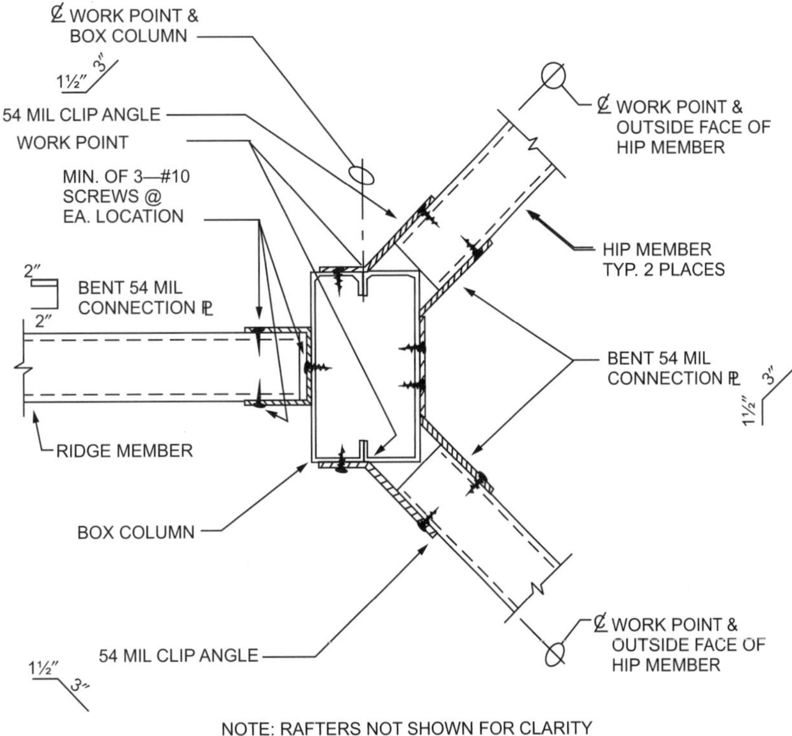

CONNECTION @ 5½″ BOX COLUMN

For SI: 1 inch = 25.4 mm, 1 mil = 0.0254 mm.

FIGURE R804.3.3.4(4)
HIP CONNECTIONS AT RIDGE AND BOX COLUMN

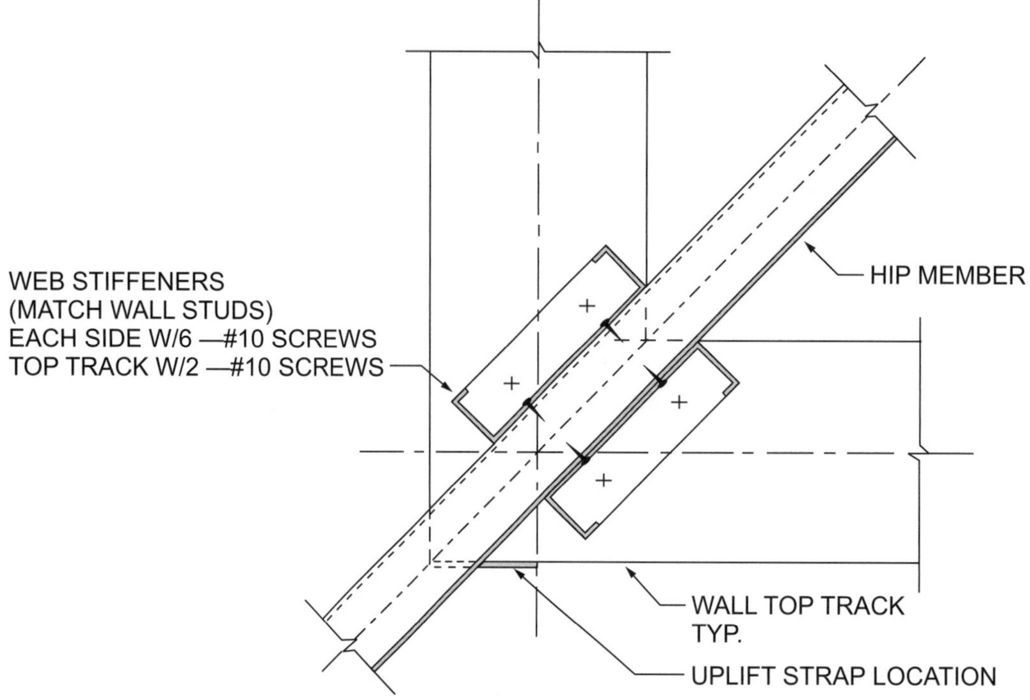

FIGURE R804.3.3.4(5)
HIP MEMBER CONNECTION AT WALL CORNER

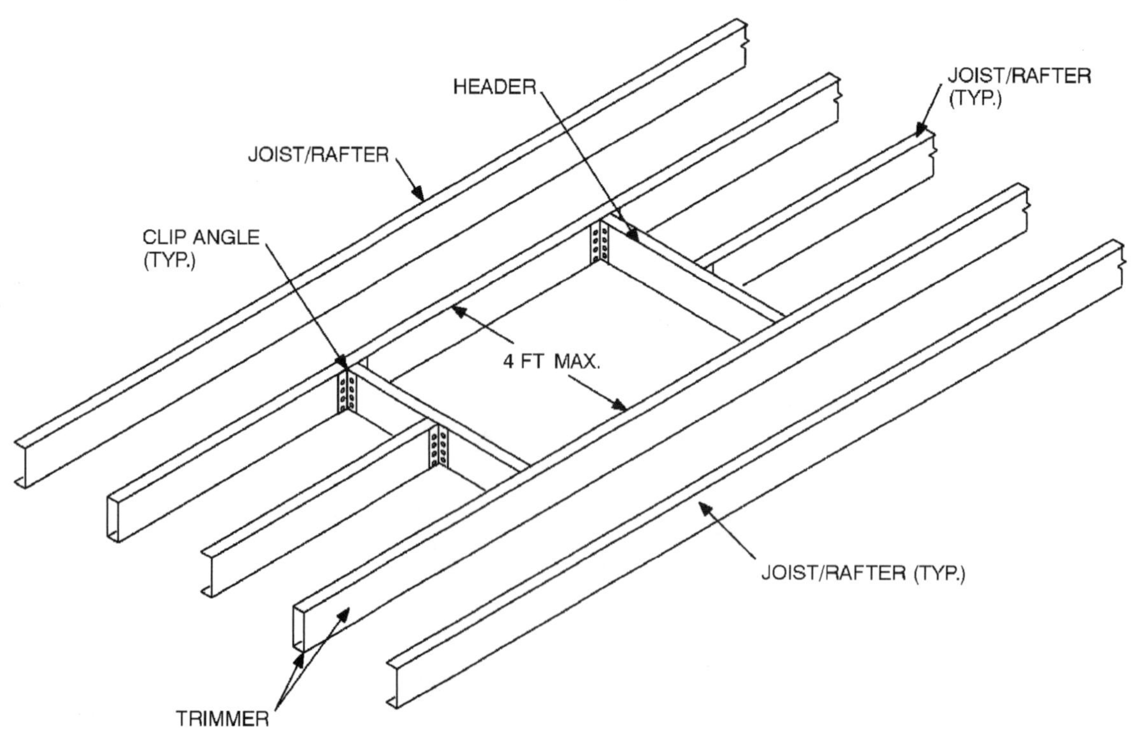

For SI: 1 foot = 304.8 mm.

FIGURE R804.3.6(1)
ROOF OR CEILING OPENING

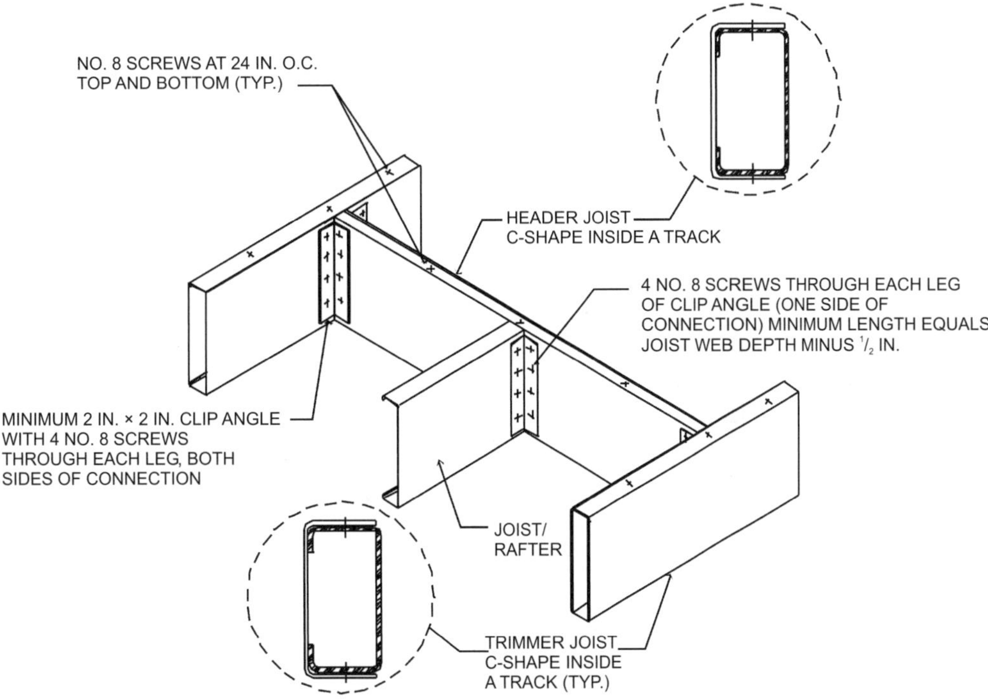

For SI: 1 inch = 25.4 mm.

FIGURE R804.3.6(2)
HEADER TO TRIMMER CONNECTION

TABLE R804.3.8(1)
REQUIRED LENGTHS FOR CEILING DIAPHRAGMS AT GABLE ENDWALLS
GYPSUM BOARD SHEATHED, CEILING HEIGHT = 8 FT [a, b, c, d, e, f]

		BASIC WIND SPEED (mph)				
	Exposure B	85	100	110	—	—
	Exposure C	—	85	—	100	110
Roof pitch	Building endwall width (feet)	Minimum diaphragm length (feet)				
3:12 to 6:12	24 - 28	14	20	22	28	32
	28 - 32	16	22	28	32	38
	32 - 36	20	26	32	38	44
	36 - 40	22	30	36	44	50
6:12 to 9:12	24 - 28	16	22	26	32	36
	28 - 32	20	26	32	38	44
	32 - 36	22	32	38	44	52
	36 - 40	26	36	44	52	60
9:12 to 12:12	24 - 28	18	26	30	36	42
	28 - 32	22	30	36	42	50
	32 - 36	26	36	42	50	60
	36 - 40	30	42	50	60	70

For SI: 1 inch = 25.4 mm, 1 pound per square foot = 0.0479 kPa, 1 mile per hour = 0.447 m/s, 1 foot = 304.8 mm, 1 mil = 0.0254 mm.

a. Ceiling diaphragm is composed of $^1/_2$ inch gypsum board (min. thickness) secured with screws spaced at 6 inches o.c. at panel edges and 12 inches o.c. in field. Use No. 8 screws (min.) when framing members have a designation thickness of 54 mils or less and No. 10 screws (min.) when framing members have a designation thickness greater than 54 mils.

b. Maximum aspect ratio (length/width) of diaphragms is 2:1.

c. Building width is in the direction of horizontal framing members supported by the wall studs.

d. Required diaphragm lengths are to be provided at each end of the structure.

e. Multiplying required diaphragm lengths by 0.35 is permitted if all panel edges are blocked.

f. Multiplying required diaphragm lengths by 0.9 is permitted if all panel edges are secured with screws spaced at 4 inches o.c.

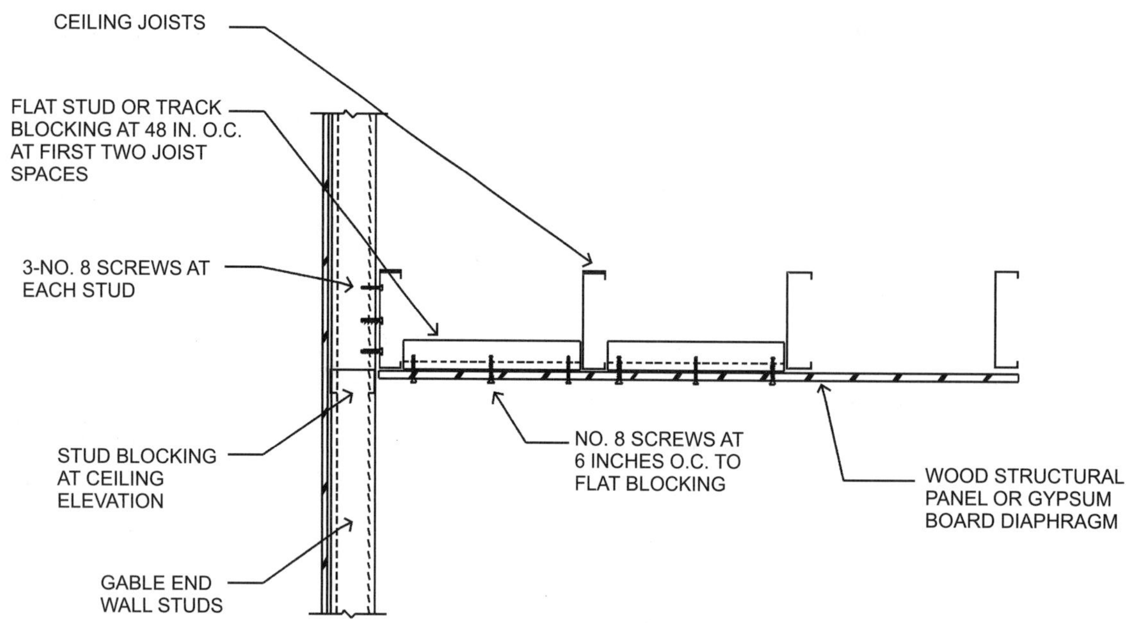

For SI: 1 inch = 25.4 mm.

FIGURE R804.3.8(1)
CEILING DIAPHRAGM TO GABLE ENDWALL DETAIL

TABLE R804.3.8(2)
REQUIRED LENGTHS FOR CEILING DIAPHRAGMS AT GABLE ENDWALLS
GYPSUM BOARD SHEATHED
CEILING HEIGHT = 9 OR 10 FT[a, b, c, d, e, f]

		BASIC WIND SPEED (mph)				
	Exposure B	85	100	110	—	—
	Exposure C	—	85	—	100	110
Roof pitch	Building endwall width (feet)	Minimum diaphragm length (feet)				
3:12 to 6:12	24 - 28	16	22	26	32	38
	28 - 32	20	26	32	38	44
	32 - 36	22	30	36	44	50
	36 - 40	26	36	42	50	58
6:12 to 9:12	24 - 28	18	26	30	36	42
	28 - 32	22	30	36	42	50
	32 - 36	26	36	42	50	58
	36 - 40	30	42	48	58	68
9:12 to 12:12	24 - 28	20	28	34	40	46
	28 - 32	24	34	40	48	56
	32 - 36	28	40	48	56	66
	36 - 40	34	46	56	66	78

For SI: 1 inch = 25.4 mm, 1 pound per square foot = 0.0479 kPa, 1 mph = 0.447 m/s, 1 foot = 304.8 mm, 1 mil = 0.0254 mm.

a. Ceiling diaphragm is composed of $^1/_2$ inch gypsum board (min. thickness) secured with screws spaced at 6 inches o.c. at panel edges and 12 inches o.c. in field. Use No. 8 screws (min.) when framing members have a designation thickness of 54 mils or less and No. 10 screws (min.) when framing members have a designation thickness greater than 54 mils.

b. Maximum aspect ratio (length/width) of diaphragms is 2:1.

c. Building width is in the direction of horizontal framing members supported by the wall studs.

d. Required diaphragm lengths are to be provided at each end of the structure.

e. Required diaphragm lengths are permitted to be multiplied by 0.35 if all panel edges are blocked.

f. Required diaphragm lengths are permitted to be multiplied by 0.9 if all panel edges are secured with screws spaced at 4 inches o.c.

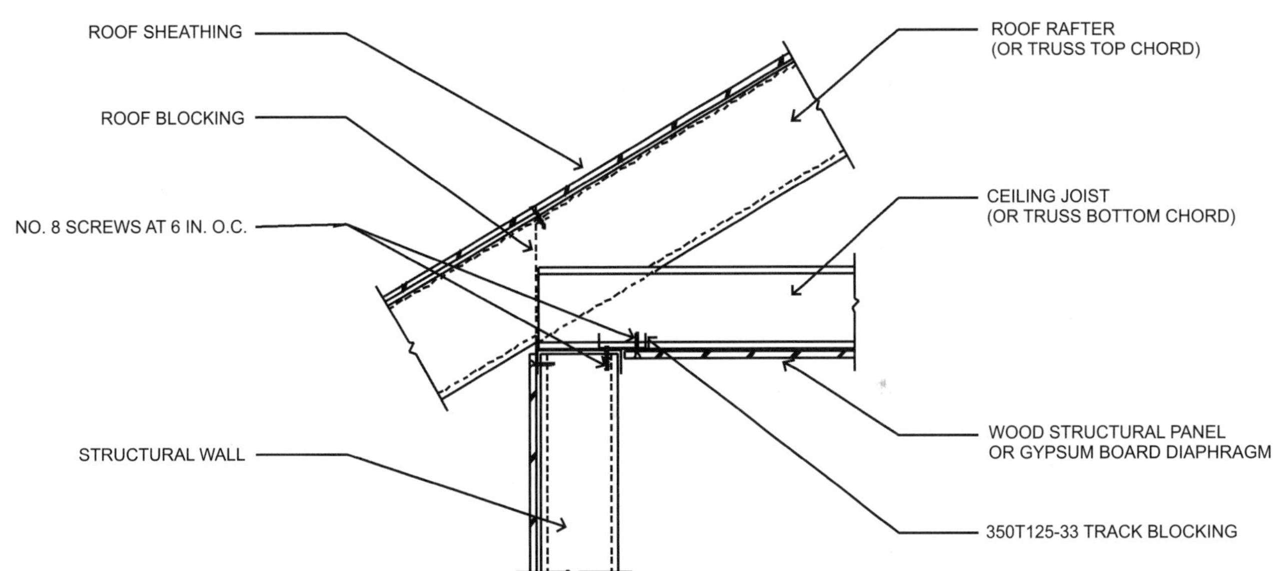

For SI: 1 inch = 25.4 mm.

FIGURE R804.3.8(2)
CEILING DIAPHRAGM TO SIDEWALL DETAIL

TABLE R804.3.8(3)
REQUIRED LENGTHS FOR CEILING DIAPHRAGMS AT GABLE ENDWALLS
WOOD STRUCTURAL PANEL SHEATHED
CEILING HEIGHT = 8, 9 OR 10 FT[a, b, c, d]

		BASIC WIND SPEED (mph)				
	Exposure B	85	100	110	—	—
	Exposure C	—	85	—	100	110
Roof pitch	Building endwall width (feet)	Minimum diaphragm length (feet)				
3:12 to 6:12	24 - 28	10	10	10	10	10
	28 - 32	12	12	12	12	12
	32 - 36	12	12	12	12	12
	36 - 40	14	14	14	14	14
6:12 to 9:12	24 - 28	10	10	10	10	10
	28 - 32	12	12	12	12	12
	32 - 36	12	12	12	12	12
	36 - 40	14	14	14	14	14
9:12 to 12:12	24 - 28	10	10	10	10	10
	28 - 32	12	12	12	12	12
	32 - 36	12	12	12	12	12
	36 - 40	14	14	14	14	14

For SI: 1 inch = 25.4 mm, 1 pound per square foot = 0.0479 kPa, 1 mile per hour = 0.447 m/s, 1 foot = 304.8 mm, 1 mil = 0.0254 mm.

a. Ceiling diaphragm is composed of $^3/_8$ inch wood structural panel sheathing (min. thickness) secured with screws spaced at 6 inches o.c. at panel edges and in field. Use No. 8 screws (min.) when framing members have a designation thickness of 54 mils or less and No. 10 screws (min.) when framing members have a designation thickness greater than 54 mils.

b. Maximum aspect ratio (length/width) of diaphragms is 3:1.

c. Building width is in the direction of horizontal framing members supported by the wall studs.

d. Required diaphragm lengths are to be provided at each end of the structure.

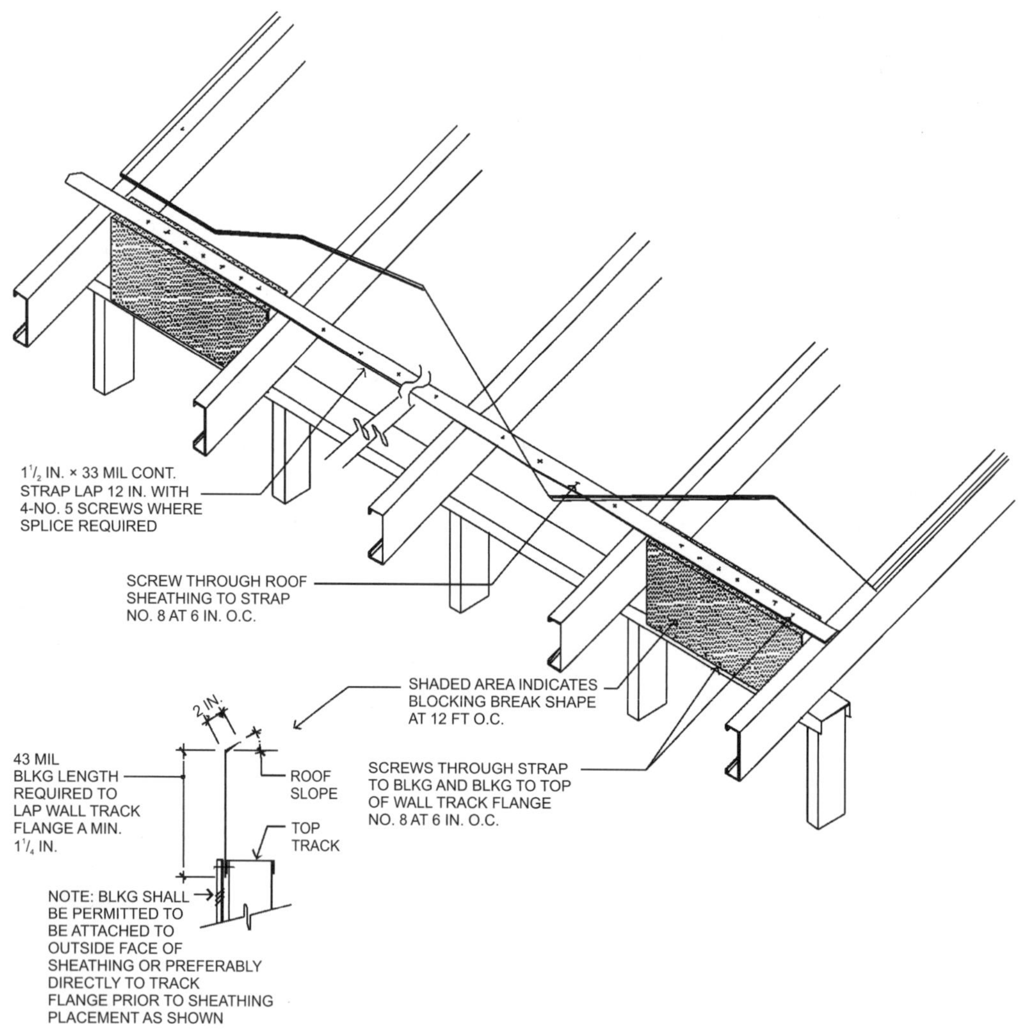

For SI: 1 mil = 0.0254 mm, 1 inch = 25.4 mm.

FIGURE R804.3.8(3)
ROOF BLOCKING DETAIL

SECTION R805
CEILING FINISHES

R805.1 Ceiling installation. Ceilings shall be installed in accordance with the requirements for interior wall finishes as provided in Section R702.

SECTION R806
ROOF VENTILATION

R806.1 Ventilation required. Enclosed *attics* and enclosed rafter spaces formed where ceilings are applied directly to the underside of roof rafters shall have cross ventilation for each separate space by ventilating openings protected against the entrance of rain or snow. Ventilation openings shall have a least dimension of $^1/_{16}$ inch (1.6 mm) minimum and $^1/_4$ inch (6.4 mm) maximum. Ventilation openings having a least dimension larger than $^1/_4$ inch (6.4 mm) shall be provided with corrosion-resistant wire cloth screening, hardware cloth, or similar material with openings having a least dimension of $^1/_{16}$ inch (1.6 mm) minimum and $^1/_4$ inch (6.4 mm) maximum. Openings in roof framing members shall conform to the requirements of Section R802.7.

R806.2 Minimum area. The total net free ventilating area shall not be less than $^1/_{150}$ of the area of the space ventilated except that reduction of the total area to $^1/_{300}$ is permitted provided that at least 50 percent and not more than 80 percent of the required ventilating area is provided by ventilators located in the upper portion of the space to be ventilated at least 3 feet (914 mm) above the eave or cornice vents with the balance of the required ventilation provided by eave or cornice vents. As an alternative, the net free cross-ventilation area may be reduced to $^1/_{300}$ when a Class I or II vapor retarder is installed on the warm-in-winter side of the ceiling.

Exceptions:

1. Enclosed attic/rafter spaces requiring less than 1 square foot (0.0929 m^2) of ventilation may be vented with continuous soffit ventilation only.
2. Enclosed attic/rafter spaces over unconditioned space may be vented with continuous soffit vent only.

R806.3 Vent and insulation clearance. Where eave or cornice vents are installed, insulation shall not block the free flow of air. A minimum of a 1-inch (25 mm) space shall be provided between the insulation and the roof sheathing and at the location of the vent.

R806.4 Unvented attic assemblies. Unvented *attic* assemblies (spaces between the ceiling joists of the top *story* and the roof rafters) shall be permitted if all the following conditions are met:

1. The unvented *attic* space is completely contained within the *building thermal envelope*.
2. No interior vapor retarders are installed on the ceiling side (*attic* floor) of the unvented *attic* assembly.
3. Where wood shingles or shakes are used, a minimum $^1/_4$ inch (6 mm) vented air space separates the shingles or shakes and the roofing underlayment above the structural sheathing.
4. In climate zones 5, 6, 7 and 8, any *air-impermeable insulation* shall be a vapor retarder, or shall have a vapor retarder coating or covering in direct contact with the underside of the insulation.
5. Either Items 5.1, 5.2 or 5.3 shall be met, depending on the air permeability of the insulation directly under the structural roof sheathing.
   - 5.1. *Air-impermeable insulation* only. Insulation shall be applied in direct contact with the underside of the structural roof sheathing.
   - 5.2. Air-permeable insulation only. In addition to the air-permeable installed directly below the structural sheathing, rigid board or sheet insulation shall be installed directly above the structural roof sheathing as specified in Table R806.4 for condensation control.
   - 5.3. Air-impermeable and air-permeable insulation. The *air-impermeable insulation* shall be applied in direct contact with the underside of the structural roof sheathing as specified in Table R806.4 for condensation control. The air-permeable insulation shall be installed directly under the *air-impermeable insulation*.

SECTION R807
ATTIC ACCESS

R807.1 Attic access. An attic access opening shall be provided to attic areas that exceed 400 square feet (37.16 m^2) and have a vertical height of 60 inches (1524 mm) or greater. The net clear opening shall not be less than 20 inches by 30 inches (508 mm by 762 mm) and shall be located in a hallway or other readily accessible location. A 30-inch (762 mm) minimum unobstructed headroom in the attic space shall be provided at some point above the access opening. See Section M1305.1.3 for access requirements where mechanical equipment is located in attics.

Exceptions:

1. Concealed areas not located over the main structure including porches, areas behind knee walls, dormers, bay windows, etc. are not required to have access.
2. Pull down stair treads, stringers, handrails, and hardware may protrude into the net clear opening.

TABLE R806.4
INSULATION FOR CONDENSATION CONTROL

CLIMATE ZONE	MINIMUM RIGID BOARD ON AIR-IMPERMEABLE INSULATION *R*-VALUE[a]
2B and 3B tile roof only	0 (none required)
1, 2A, 2B, 3A, 3B, 3C	R-5
4C	R-10
4A, 4B	R-15
5	R-20
6	R-25
7	R-30
8	R-35

a. Contributes to but does not supersede Chapter 11 energy requirements.

CHAPTER 9
ROOF ASSEMBLIES

SECTION R901
GENERAL

R901.1 Scope. The provisions of this chapter shall govern the design, materials, construction and quality of roof assemblies.

SECTION R902
ROOF CLASSIFICATION

R902.1 Roofing covering materials. Roofs shall be covered with materials as set forth in Sections R904 and R905. Class A, B or C roofing shall be installed in areas designated by law as requiring their use or when the edge of the roof is less than 3 feet (914 mm) from a property line. Classes A, B and C roofing required by this section to be listed shall be tested in accordance with UL 790 or ASTM E 108.

Exceptions:

1. Class A roof assemblies include those with coverings of brick, masonry and exposed concrete roof deck.
2. Class A roof assemblies also include ferrous or copper shingles or sheets, metal sheets and shingles, clay or concrete roof tile, or slate installed on noncombustible decks.

R902.2 Fire-retardant-treated shingles and shakes. Fire-retardant-treated wood shakes and shingles shall be treated by impregnation with chemicals by the full-cell vacuum-pressure process, in accordance with AWPA C1. Each bundle shall be marked to identify the manufactured unit and the manufacturer, and shall also be *labeled* to identify the classification of the material in accordance with the testing required in Section R902.1, the treating company and the quality control agency.

SECTION R903
WEATHER PROTECTION

R903.1 General. Roof decks shall be covered with *approved* roof coverings secured to the building or structure in accordance with the provisions of this chapter. Roof assemblies shall be designed and installed in accordance with this code and the *approved* manufacturer's installation instructions such that the roof assembly shall serve to protect the building or structure.

R903.2 Flashing. Flashings shall be installed in a manner that prevents moisture from entering the wall and roof through joints in copings, through moisture permeable materials and at intersections with parapet walls and other penetrations through the roof plane.

R903.2.1 Locations. Flashings shall be installed at wall and roof intersections, wherever there is a change in roof slope or direction and around roof openings. Where flashing is of metal, the metal shall be corrosion resistant with a thickness of not less than 0.019 inch (0.5 mm) (No. 26 galvanized sheet).

R903.2.2 Crickets and saddles. A cricket or saddle shall be installed on the ridge side of any chimney or penetration more than 30 inches (762 mm) wide as measured perpendicular to the slope. Cricket or saddle coverings shall be sheet metal or of the same material as the roof covering.

R903.3 Coping. Parapet walls shall be properly coped with noncombustible, weatherproof materials of a width no less than the thickness of the parapet wall. Parapet coping shall extend 2 inches minimum down the faces of the parapet.

R903.4 Roof drainage. Unless roofs are sloped to drain over roof edges, roof drains shall be installed at each low point of the roof. Where required for roof drainage, scuppers shall be placed level with the roof surface in a wall or parapet. The scupper shall be located as determined by the roof slope and contributing roof area.

R903.4.1 Overflow drains and scuppers. Where roof drains are required, overflow drains having the same size as the roof drains shall be installed with the inlet flow line located 2 inches (51 mm) above the low point of the roof, or overflow scuppers having three times the size of the roof drains and having a minimum opening height of 4 inches (102 mm) shall be installed in the adjacent parapet walls with the inlet flow located 2 inches (51 mm) above the low point of the roof served. The installation and sizing of overflow drains, leaders and conductors shall comply with the North Carolina *Plumbing Code*.

Overflow drains shall discharge to an *approved* location and shall not be connected to roof drain lines.

R903.5 Hail exposure. Deleted.

R903.5.1 Moderate hail exposure. Deleted.

R903.5.2 Severe hail exposure. Deleted.

SECTION R904
MATERIALS

R904.1 Scope. The requirements set forth in this section shall apply to the application of roof covering materials specified herein. Roof assemblies shall be applied in accordance with this chapter and the manufacturer's installation instructions. Installation of roof assemblies shall comply with the applicable provisions of Section R905.

R904.2 Compatibility of materials. Roof assemblies shall be of materials that are compatible with each other and with the building or structure to which the materials are applied.

R904.3 Material specifications and physical characteristics. Roof covering materials shall conform to the applicable standards listed in this chapter. In the absence of applicable standards or where materials are of questionable suitability, testing by an *approved* testing agency shall be required by the *building official* to determine the character, quality and limitations of application of the materials.

R904.4 Product identification. Roof covering materials shall be delivered in packages bearing the manufacturer's identifying marks and *approved* testing agency *labels* when required. Bulk shipments of materials shall be accompanied by the same information issued in the form of a certificate or on a bill of lading by the manufacturer.

SECTION R905
REQUIREMENTS FOR ROOF COVERINGS

R905.1 Roof covering application. Roof coverings shall be applied in accordance with the applicable provisions of this section and the manufacturer's installation instructions. Unless otherwise specified in this section, roof coverings shall be installed to resist the component and cladding loads specified in Table R301.2(2), adjusted for height and exposure in accordance with Table R301.2(3).

R905.2 Asphalt shingles. The installation of asphalt shingles shall comply with the provisions of this section.

R905.2.1 Sheathing requirements. Asphalt shingles shall be fastened to solidly sheathed decks.

R905.2.2 Slope. Asphalt shingles shall be used only on roof slopes of two units vertical in 12 units horizontal (2:12) or greater. For roof slopes from two units vertical in 12 units horizontal (2:12) up to four units vertical in 12 units horizontal (4:12), double underlayment application is required in accordance with Section R905.2.7.

R905.2.3 Underlayment. Unless otherwise noted, required underlayment shall conform to ASTM D 226 Type I, ASTM D 4869 Type I, or ASTM D 6757.

Self-adhering polymer modified bitumen sheet shall comply with ASTM D 1970.

R905.2.4 Asphalt shingles. Asphalt shingles shall comply with ASTM D 225 or D 3462.

R905.2.4.1 Wind resistance of asphalt shingles. Asphalt shingles shall be tested in accordance with ASTM D 7158. Asphalt shingles shall meet the classification requirements of Table R905.2.4.1(1) for the appropriate maximum basic wind speed. Asphalt shingle packaging shall bear a *label* to indicate compliance with ASTM D 7158 and the required classification in Table R905.2.4.1(1).

Exception: Asphalt shingles not included in the scope of ASTM D 7158 shall be tested and *labeled* to indicate compliance with ASTM D 3161 and the required classification in Table R905.2.4.1(2).

R905.2.5 Fasteners. Fasteners for asphalt shingles shall be galvanized steel, stainless steel, aluminum or copper roofing nails, minimum 12 gage [0.105 inch (3 mm)] shank with a minimum $^3/_8$-inch (10 mm) diameter head, ASTM F 1667, of a length to penetrate through the roofing materials and a minimum of $^3/_4$ inch (19 mm) into the roof sheathing. Where the roof sheathing is less than $^3/_4$ inch (19 mm) thick, the fasteners shall penetrate through the sheathing. Fasteners shall comply with ASTM F 1667.

**TABLE R905.2.4.1(1)
CLASSIFICATION OF ASPHALT ROOF SHINGLES PER ASTM D 7158**

MAXIMUM BASIC WIND SPEED FROM FIGURE 301.2(4) (mph)	CLASSIFICATION REQUIREMENT
85	D, G or H
90	D, G or H
100	G or H
110	G or H
120	G or H
130	H
140	H
150	H

For SI: 1 mile per hour = 0.447 m/s.

**TABLE R905.2.4.1(2)
CLASSIFICATION OF ASPHALT SHINGLES PER ASTM D 3161**

MAXIMUM BASIC WIND SPEED FROM FIGURE 301.2(4) (mph)	CLASSIFICATION REQUIREMENT
85	A, D or F
90	A, D or F
100	A, D or F
110	F
120	F
130	F
140	F
150	F

For SI: 1 mile per hour = 0.447 m/s.

R905.2.6 Attachment. Asphalt shingles shall have the minimum number of fasteners required by the manufacturer, but not less than four fasteners per strip shingle or two fasteners per individual shingle. Where the roof slope exceeds 21 units vertical in 12 units horizontal (21:12, 175 percent slope), shingles shall be installed as required by the manufacturer.

R905.2.7 Underlayment application. For roof slopes from two units vertical in 12 units horizontal (17-percent slope), up to four units vertical in 12 units horizontal (33-percent slope), underlayment shall be two layers applied in the following manner. Apply a 19-inch (483 mm) strip of underlayment felt parallel to and starting at the eaves, fastened sufficiently to hold in place. Starting at the eave, apply 36-inch-wide (914 mm) sheets of underlayment, overlapping successive sheets 19 inches (483 mm), and fastened sufficiently to hold in place. Distortions in the underlayment shall not interfere with the ability of the shingles to seal. For roof slopes of four units vertical in 12 units horizontal (33-percent slope) or greater, underlayment shall be one layer applied in the following manner. Underlayment shall be applied shingle fashion, parallel to and starting from the eave and lapped 2 inches (51 mm), fastened sufficiently to hold in place. Distortions in the underlayment shall not interfere with the ability of the shingles to seal. End laps shall be offset by 6 feet (1829 mm).

R905.2.7.1 Ice barrier. In areas where the average daily temperature in January is 25°F (-4°C) or less or when Table R301.2(1) criteria so designates, an ice barrier that consists of a least two layers of underlayment cemented together or of a self-adhering polymer modified bitumen sheet, shall be used in lieu of normal underlayment and extend from the lowest edges of all roof surfaces to a point at least 24 inches (610 mm) inside the exterior wall line of the building.

Exception: Detached *accessory structures* that contain no *conditioned floor area*.

R905.2.7.2 Underlayment and high wind. Underlayment applied in areas subject to high winds [above 110 mph (49 m/s) per Figure R301.2(4)] shall be applied with corrosion-resistant fasteners in accordance with manufacturer's installation instructions. Fasteners are to be applied along the overlap not farther apart than 36 inches (914 mm) on center.

R905.2.8 Flashing. Flashing for asphalt shingles shall comply with this section.

R905.2.8.1 Base and cap flashing. Base and cap flashing shall be installed in accordance with manufacturer's installation instructions. Base flashing shall be of either corrosion-resistant metal of minimum nominal 0.019-inch (0.5 mm) thickness or mineral surface roll roofing weighing a minimum of 77 pounds per 100 square feet (4 kg/m^2). Cap flashing shall be corrosion-resistant metal of minimum nominal 0.019-inch (0.5 mm) thickness.

R905.2.8.2 Valleys. Valley linings shall be installed in accordance with the manufacturer's installation instructions before applying shingles. Valley linings of the following types shall be permitted:

1. For open valleys (valley lining exposed) lined with metal, the valley lining shall be at least 24 inches (610 mm) wide and of any of the corrosion-resistant metals in Table R905.2.8.2.
2. For open valleys, valley lining of two plies of mineral surfaced roll roofing, complying with ASTM D 3909 or ASTM D 6380 Class M, shall be permitted. The bottom layer shall be 18 inches (457 mm) and the top layer a minimum of 36 inches (914 mm) wide.
3. For closed valleys (valley covered with shingles), valley lining of one ply of smooth roll roofing complying with ASTM D 6380 and at least 36 inches wide (914 mm) or valley lining as described in Item 1 or 2 above shall be permitted. Self-adhering polymer modified bitumen underlayment complying with ASTM D 1970 shall be permitted in lieu of the lining material.

R905.2.8.3 Sidewall flashing. Flashing against a vertical sidewall shall be by the step-flashing method. The flashing shall be a minimum of 4 inches (102 mm) high and 4 inches (102 mm) wide. At the end of the vertical sidewall the step flashing shall be turned out in a manner that directs water away from the wall and onto the roof and/or gutter.

R905.2.8.4 Other flashing. Flashing against a vertical front wall, as well as soil stack, vent pipe and chimney flashing, shall be applied according to the asphalt shingle manufacturer's printed instructions.

TABLE R905.2.8.2
VALLEY LINING MATERIAL

MATERIAL	MINIMUM THICKNESS (inches)	GAGE	WEIGHT (pounds)
Cold-rolled copper	0.0216 nominal	—	ASTM B 370, 16 oz. per square foot
Lead-coated copper	0.0216 nominal	—	ASTM B 101, 16 oz. per square foot
High-yield copper	0.0162 nominal	—	ASTM B 370, 12 oz. per square foot
Lead-coated high-yield copper	0.0162 nominal	—	ASTM B 101, 12 oz. per square foot
Aluminum	0.024	—	—
Stainless steel	—	28	—
Galvanized steel	0.0179	26 (zinc coated G90)	—
Zinc alloy	0.027	—	—
Lead	—	—	$2^1/_2$
Painted terne	—	—	20

For SI: 1 inch = 25.4 mm, 1 pound = 0.454 kg.

R905.3 Clay and concrete tile. The installation of clay and concrete tile shall comply with the provisions of this section.

R905.3.1 Deck requirements. Concrete and clay tile shall be installed only over solid sheathing or spaced structural sheathing boards.

R905.3.2 Deck slope. Clay and concrete roof tile shall be installed on roof slopes of two and one-half units vertical in 12 units horizontal ($2^1/_2$:12) or greater. For roof slopes from two and one-half units vertical in 12 units horizontal ($2^1/_2$:12) to four units vertical in 12 units horizontal (4:12), double underlayment application is required in accordance with Section R905.3.3.

R905.3.3 Underlayment. Unless otherwise noted, required underlayment shall conform to ASTM D 226 Type II; ASTM D 2626 Type I; or ASTM D 6380 Class M mineral surfaced roll roofing.

R905.3.3.1 Low slope roofs. For roof slopes from two and one-half units vertical in 12 units horizontal ($2^1/_2$:12), up to four units vertical in 12 units horizontal (4:12), underlayment shall be a minimum of two layers underlayment applied as follows:

1. Starting at the eave, a 19-inch (483 mm) strip of underlayment shall be applied parallel with the eave and fastened sufficiently in place.
2. Starting at the eave, 36-inch-wide (914 mm) strips of underlayment felt shall be applied, overlapping successive sheets 19 inches (483 mm), and fastened sufficiently in place.

R905.3.3.2 High slope roofs. For roof slopes of four units vertical in 12 units horizontal (4:12) or greater, underlayment shall be a minimum of one layer of underlayment felt applied shingle fashion, parallel to and starting from the eaves and lapped 2 inches (51 mm), fastened sufficiently in place.

R905.3.3.3 Underlayment and high wind. Underlayment applied in areas subject to high wind [over 110 miles per hour (49 m/s) per Figure R301.2(4)] shall be applied with corrosion-resistant fasteners in accordance with manufacturer's installation instructions. Fasteners are to be applied along the overlap not farther apart than 36 inches (914 mm) on center.

R905.3.4 Clay tile. Clay roof tile shall comply with ASTM C 1167.

R905.3.5 Concrete tile. Concrete roof tile shall comply with ASTM C 1492.

R905.3.6 Fasteners. Nails shall be corrosion resistant and not less than 11 gage, $^5/_{16}$-inch (11 mm) head, and of sufficient length to penetrate the deck a minimum of $^3/_4$ inch (19 mm) or through the thickness of the deck, whichever is less. Attaching wire for clay or concrete tile shall not be smaller than 0.083 inch (2 mm). Perimeter fastening areas include three tile courses but not less than 36 inches (914 mm) from either side of hips or ridges and edges of eaves and gable rakes.

R905.3.7 Application. Tile shall be applied in accordance with this chapter and the manufacturer's installation instructions, based on the following:

1. Climatic conditions.
2. Roof slope.
3. Underlayment system.
4. Type of tile being installed.

Clay and concrete roof tiles shall be fastened in accordance with this section and the manufacturer's installation instructions. Perimeter tiles shall be fastened with a minimum of one fastener per tile. Tiles with installed weight less than 9 pounds per square foot (0.4 kg/m^2) require a minimum of one fastener per tile regardless of roof slope. Clay and concrete roof tile attachment shall be in accordance with the manufacturer's installation instructions where applied in areas where the wind speed exceeds 100 miles per hour (45 m/s) and on buildings where the roof is located more than 40 feet (12 192 mm) above *grade*. In areas subject to snow, a minimum of two fasteners per tile is required. In all other areas, clay and concrete roof tiles shall be attached in accordance with Table R905.3.7.

TABLE R905.3.7
CLAY AND CONCRETE TILE ATTACHMENT

SHEATHING	ROOF SLOPE	NUMBER OF FASTENERS
Solid without battens	All	One per tile
Spaced or solid with battens and slope < 5:12	Fasteners not required	—
Spaced sheathing without battens	5:12 ≤ slope < 12:12	One per tile/every other row
	12:12 ≤ slope < 24:12	One per tile

R905.3.8 Flashing. At the juncture of roof vertical surfaces, flashing and counterflashing shall be provided in accordance with this chapter and the manufacturer's installation instructions and, where of metal, shall not be less than 0.019 inch (0.5 mm) (No. 26 galvanized sheet gage) corrosion-resistant metal. The valley flashing shall extend at least 11 inches (279 mm) from the centerline each way and have a splash diverter rib not less than 1 inch (25 mm) high at the flow line formed as part of the flashing. Sections of flashing shall have an end lap of not less than 4 inches (102 mm). For roof slopes of three units vertical in 12 units horizontal (25-percent slope) and greater, valley flashing shall have a 36-inch-wide (914 mm) underlayment of one layer of Type I underlayment running the full length of the valley, in addition to other required underlayment. In areas where the average daily temperature in January is 25°F (-4°C) or less, metal valley flashing underlayment shall be solid-cemented to the roofing underlayment for slopes less than seven units vertical in 12 units horizontal (58-percent slope) or be of self-adhering polymer modified bitumen sheet.

R905.4 Metal roof shingles. The installation of metal roof shingles shall comply with the provisions of this section.

R905.4.1 Deck requirements. Metal roof shingles shall be applied to a solid or closely fitted deck, except where the roof covering is specifically designed to be applied to spaced sheathing.

R905.4.2 Deck slope. Metal roof shingles shall not be installed on roof slopes below three units vertical in 12 units horizontal (25-percent slope).

R905.4.3 Underlayment. Underlayment shall comply with ASTM D 226, Type I or Type II, ASTM D 4869, Type I or Type II, or ASTM D 1970. Underlayment shall be installed in accordance with the manufacturer's installation instructions.

R905.4.3.1 Ice barrier. In areas where the average daily temperature in January is 25°F (-4°C) or less or when Table R301.2(1) criteria so designates, an ice barrier that consists of a least two layers of underlayment cemented together or of a self-adhering polymer modified bitumen sheet, shall be used in lieu of normal underlayment and extend from the eave's edge to a point at least 24 inches (610 mm) inside the exterior wall line of the building.

Exception: Detached *accessory structures* that contain no *conditioned floor area*.

R905.4.4 Material standards. Metal roof shingle roof coverings shall comply with Table R905.10.3(1). The materials used for metal roof shingle roof coverings shall be naturally corrosion resistant or be made corrosion resistant in accordance with the standards and minimum thicknesses listed in Table R905.10.3(2).

R905.4.5 Application. Metal roof shingles shall be secured to the roof in accordance with this chapter and the *approved* manufacturer's installation instructions.

R905.4.6 Flashing. Roof valley flashing shall be of corrosion-resistant metal of the same material as the roof covering or shall comply with the standards in Table R905.10.3(1). The valley flashing shall extend at least 8 inches (203 mm) from the center line each way and shall have a splash diverter rib not less than $^{3}/_{4}$ inch (19 mm) high at the flow line formed as part of the flashing. Sections of flashing shall have an end lap of not less than 4 inches (102 mm). The metal valley flashing shall have a 36-inch-wide (914 mm) underlayment directly under it consisting of one layer of underlayment running the full length of the valley, in addition to underlayment required for metal roof shingles. In areas where the average daily temperature in January is 25°F (-4°C) or less, the metal valley flashing underlayment shall be solid cemented to the roofing underlayment for roof slopes under seven units vertical in 12 units horizontal (58-percent slope) or self-adhering polymer modified bitumen sheet.

R905.5 Mineral-surfaced roll roofing. The installation of mineral-surfaced roll roofing shall comply with this section.

R905.5.1 Deck requirements. Mineral-surfaced roll roofing shall be fastened to solidly sheathed roofs.

R905.5.2 Deck slope. Mineral-surfaced roll roofing shall not be applied on roof slopes below one unit vertical in 12 units horizontal (8-percent slope).

R905.5.3 Underlayment. Underlayment shall comply with ASTM D 226, Type I or ASTM D 4869, Type I or II.

R905.5.3.1 Ice barrier. In areas where the average daily temperature in January is 25°F (-4°C) or less or when Table R301.2(1) criteria so designates, an ice barrier that consists of a least two layers of underlayment cemented together or of a self-adhering polymer modified bitumen sheet, shall be used in lieu of normal underlayment and extend from the eave's edge to a point at least 24 inches (610 mm) inside the exterior wall line of the building.

Exception: Detached *accessory structures* that contain no *conditioned floor area*.

R905.5.4 Material standards. Mineral-surfaced roll roofing shall conform to ASTM D 3909 or ASTM D 6380, Class M.

R905.5.5 Application. Mineral-surfaced roll roofing shall be installed in accordance with this chapter and the manufacturer's installation instructions.

R905.6 Slate and slate-type shingles. The installation of slate and slate-type shingles shall comply with the provisions of this section.

R905.6.1 Deck requirements. Slate shingles shall be fastened to solidly sheathed roofs.

R905.6.2 Deck slope. Slate shingles shall be used only on slopes of four units vertical in 12 units horizontal (33-percent slope) or greater.

R905.6.3 Underlayment. Underlayment shall comply with ASTM D 226, Type I, or ASTM D 4869, Type I or II. Underlayment shall be installed in accordance with the manufacturer's installation instructions.

R905.6.3.1 Ice barrier. In areas where the average daily temperature in January is 25°F (-4°C) or less or when Table R301.2(1) criteria so designates, an ice barrier that consists of a least two layers of underlayment cemented together or of a self-adhering polymer modified bitumen sheet, shall be used in lieu of normal underlayment and extend from the eave's edge to a point at least 24 inches (610 mm) inside the exterior wall line of the building.

Exception: Detached *accessory structures* that contain no *conditioned floor area*.

R905.6.4 Material standards. Slate shingles shall comply with ASTM C 406.

R905.6.5 Application. Minimum headlap for slate shingles shall be in accordance with Table R905.6.5. Slate shingles shall be secured to the roof with two fasteners per slate. Slate shingles shall be installed in accordance with this chapter and the manufacturer's installation instructions.

TABLE R905.6.5
SLATE SHINGLE HEADLAP

SLOPE	HEADLAP (inches)
4:12 ≤ slope < 8:12	4
8:12 ≤ slope < 20:12	3
Slope ≤ 20:12	2

For SI: 1 inch = 25.4 mm.

R905.6.6 Flashing. Flashing and counterflashing shall be made with sheet metal. Valley flashing shall be a minimum of 15 inches (381 mm) wide. Valley and flashing metal shall be a minimum uncoated thickness of 0.0179-inch (0.5 mm) zinc coated G90. Chimneys, stucco or brick walls shall have a minimum of two plies of felt for a cap flashing consisting of a 4-inch-wide (102 mm) strip of felt set in plastic cement and extending 1 inch (25 mm) above the first felt and a top coating of plastic cement. The felt shall extend over the base flashing 2 inches (51 mm).

R905.7 Wood shingles. The installation of wood shingles shall comply with the provisions of this section.

R905.7.1 Deck requirements. Wood shingles shall be installed on solid or spaced sheathing. Where spaced sheathing is used, sheathing boards shall not be less than 1-inch by 4-inch (25.4 mm by 102 mm) nominal dimensions and shall be spaced on centers equal to the weather exposure to coincide with the placement of fasteners.

R905.7.1.1 Solid sheathing required. In areas where the average daily temperature in January is 25°F (-4°C) or less, solid sheathing is required on that portion of the roof requiring the application of an ice barrier.

R905.7.2 Deck slope. Wood shingles shall be installed on slopes of three units vertical in 12 units horizontal (25-percent slope) or greater.

R905.7.3 Underlayment. Underlayment shall comply with ASTM D 226, Type I or ASTM D 4869, Type I or II.

R905.7.3.1 Ice barrier. In areas where the average daily temperature in January is 25°F (-4°C) or less or when Table R301.2(1) criteria so designates, an ice barrier that consists of a least two layers of underlayment cemented together or of a self-adhering polymer modified bitumen sheet, shall be used in lieu of normal underlayment and extend from the eave's edge to a point at least 24 inches (610 mm) inside the exterior wall line of the building.

Exception: Detached *accessory structures* that contain no *conditioned floor area*.

R905.7.4 Material standards. Wood shingles shall be of naturally durable wood and comply with the requirements of Table R905.7.4.

TABLE R905.7.4
WOOD SHINGLE MATERIAL REQUIREMENTS

MATERIAL	MINIMUM GRADES	APPLICABLE GRADING RULES
Wood shingles of naturally durable wood	1, 2 or 3	Cedar Shake and Shingle Bureau

R905.7.5 Application. Wood shingles shall be installed according to this chapter and the manufacturer's installation instructions. Wood shingles shall be laid with a side lap not less than $1^{1}/_{2}$ inches (38 mm) between joints in courses, and no two joints in any three adjacent courses shall be in direct alignment. Spacing between shingles shall not be less than $^{1}/_{4}$ inch to $^{3}/_{8}$ inch (6 mm to 10 mm). Weather exposure for wood shingles shall not exceed those set in Table R905.7.5. Fasteners for wood shingles shall be corrosion resistant with a minimum penetration of $^{1}/_{2}$ inch (13 mm) into the sheathing. For sheathing less than $^{1}/_{2}$ inch (13 mm) in thickness, the fasteners shall extend through the sheathing. Wood shingles shall be attached to the roof with two fasteners per shingle, positioned no more than $^{3}/_{4}$ inch (19 mm) from each edge and no more than 1 inch (25 mm) above the exposure line.

TABLE R905.7.5
WOOD SHINGLE WEATHER EXPOSURE AND ROOF SLOPE

ROOFING MATERIAL	LENGTH (inches)	GRADE	EXPOSURE (inches)	
			3:12 pitch to < 4:12	4:12 pitch or steeper
Shingles of naturally durable wood	16	No. 1	$3^{3}/_{4}$	5
		No. 2	$3^{1}/_{2}$	4
		No. 3	3	$3^{1}/_{2}$
	18	No. 1	$4^{1}/_{4}$	$5^{1}/_{2}$
		No. 2	4	$4^{1}/_{2}$
		No. 3	$3^{1}/_{2}$	4
	24	No. 1	$5^{3}/_{4}$	$7^{1}/_{2}$
		No. 2	$5^{1}/_{2}$	$6^{1}/_{2}$
		No. 3	5	$5^{1}/_{2}$

For SI: 1 inch = 25.4 mm.

R905.7.6 Valley flashing. Roof flashing shall be not less than No. 26 gage [0.019 inches (0.5 mm)] corrosion-resistant sheet metal and shall extend 10 inches (254 mm) from the centerline each way for roofs having slopes less than 12 units vertical in 12 units horizontal (100-percent slope), and 7 inches (178 mm) from the centerline each way for slopes of 12 units vertical in 12 units horizontal and greater. Sections of flashing shall have an end lap of not less than 4 inches (102 mm).

R905.7.7 Label required. Each bundle of shingles shall be identified by a *label* of an *approved* grading or inspection bureau or agency.

R905.8 Wood shakes. The installation of wood shakes shall comply with the provisions of this section.

R905.8.1 Deck requirements. Wood shakes shall be used only on solid or spaced sheathing. Where spaced sheathing is used, sheathing boards shall not be less than 1-inch by 4-inch (25 mm by 102 mm) nominal dimensions and shall be spaced on centers equal to the weather exposure to coincide with the placement of fasteners. Where 1-inch by 4-inch (25 mm by 102 mm) spaced sheathing is installed at 10 inches (254 mm) on center, additional 1-inch by 4-inch (25 mm by 102 mm) boards shall be installed between the sheathing boards.

R905.8.1.1 Solid sheathing required. In areas where the average daily temperature in January is 25°F (-4°C) or less, solid sheathing is required on that portion of the roof requiring an ice barrier.

R905.8.2 Deck slope. Wood shakes shall only be used on slopes of three units vertical in 12 units horizontal (25-percent slope) or greater.

R905.8.3 Underlayment. Underlayment shall comply with ASTM D 226, Type I or ASTM D 4869, Type I or II.

R905.8.3.1 Ice barrier. In areas where the average daily temperature in January is 25°F (-4°C) or less or when Table R301.2(1) criteria so designates, an ice barrier that consists of a least two layers of underlayment cemented together or of a self-adhering polymer modified bitumen sheet, shall be used in lieu of normal underlayment and extend from the eave's edge to a point at least 24 inches (610 mm) inside the exterior wall line of the building.

Exception: Detached *accessory structures* that contain no *conditioned floor area*.

R905.8.4 Interlayment. Interlayment shall comply with ASTM D 226, Type I.

R905.8.5 Material standards. Wood shakes shall comply with the requirements of Table R905.8.5.

TABLE R905.8.5
WOOD SHAKE MATERIAL REQUIREMENTS

MATERIAL	MINIMUM GRADES	APPLICABLE GRADING RULES
Wood shakes of naturally durable wood	1	Cedar Shake and Shingle Bureau
Taper sawn shakes of naturally durable wood	1 or 2	Cedar Shake and Shingle Bureau
Preservative-treated shakes and shingles of naturally durable wood	1	Cedar Shake and Shingle Bureau
Fire-retardant-treated shakes and shingles of naturally durable wood	1	Cedar Shake and Shingle Bureau

R905.8.6 Application. Wood shakes shall be installed according to this chapter and the manufacturer's installation instructions. Wood shakes shall be laid with a side lap not less than $1^1/_2$ inches (38 mm) between joints in adjacent courses. Spacing between shakes in the same course shall be $^3/_8$ inch to $^5/_8$ inch (9.5 mm to 15.9 mm) for shakes and tapersawn shakes of naturally durable wood and shall be $^3/_8$ inch to $^5/_8$ inch (9.5 mm to 15.9 mm) for preservative-treated taper sawn shakes. Weather exposure for wood shakes shall not exceed those set forth in Table R905.8.6. Fasteners for wood shakes shall be corrosion-resistant, with a minimum penetration of $^1/_2$ inch (12.7 mm) into the sheathing. For sheathing less than $^1/_2$ inch (12.7 mm) thick, the fasteners shall extend through the sheathing. Wood shakes shall be attached to the roof with two fasteners per shake, positioned no more than 1 inch (25 mm) from each edge and no more than 2 inches (51 mm) above the exposure line.

R905.8.7 Shake placement. The starter course at the eaves shall be doubled and the bottom layer shall be either 15-inch (381 mm), 18-inch (457 mm) or 24-inch (610 mm) wood shakes or wood shingles. Fifteen-inch (381 mm) or 18-inch (457 mm) wood shakes may be used for the final course at the ridge. Shakes shall be interlaid with 18-inch-wide (457 mm) strips of not less than No. 30 felt shingled between each course in such a manner that no felt is exposed to the weather by positioning the lower edge of each felt strip above the butt end of the shake it covers a distance equal to twice the weather exposure.

TABLE R905.8.6
WOOD SHAKE WEATHER EXPOSURE AND ROOF SLOPE

ROOFING MATERIAL	LENGTH (inches)	GRADE	EXPOSURE (inches) 4:12 pitch or steeper
Shakes of naturally durable wood	18	No. 1	$7^1/_2$
	24	No. 1	10[a]
Preservative-treated taper sawn shakes of Southern Yellow Pine	18	No. 1	$7^1/_2$
	24	No. 1	10
	18	No. 2	$5^1/_2$
	24	No. 2	$7^1/_2$
Taper-sawn shakes of naturally durable wood	18	No. 1	$7^1/_2$
	24	No. 1	10
	18	No. 2	$5^1/_2$
	24	No. 2	$7^1/_2$

For SI: 1 inch = 25.4 mm.

a. For 24-inch by $^3/_8$-inch handsplit shakes, the maximum exposure is $7^1/_2$ inches.

R905.8.8 Valley flashing. Roof valley flashing shall not be less than No. 26 gage [0.019 inch (0.5 mm)] corrosion-resistant sheet metal and shall extend at least 11 inches (279 mm) from the centerline each way. Sections of flashing shall have an end lap of not less than 4 inches (102 mm).

R905.8.9 Label required. Each bundle of shakes shall be identified by a *label* of an *approved* grading or inspection bureau or agency.

R905.9 Built-up roofs. The installation of built-up roofs shall comply with the provisions of this section.

R905.9.1 Slope. Built-up roofs shall have a design slope of a minimum of one-fourth unit vertical in 12 units horizontal (2-percent slope) for drainage, except for coal-tar built-up roofs, which shall have a design slope of a minimum one-eighth unit vertical in 12 units horizontal (1-percent slope).

R905.9.2 Material standards. Built-up roof covering materials shall comply with the standards in Table R905.9.2.

R905.9.3 Application. Built-up roofs shall be installed according to this chapter and the manufacturer's installation instructions.

R905.10 Metal roof panels. The installation of metal roof panels shall comply with the provisions of this section.

R905.10.1 Deck requirements. Metal roof panel roof coverings shall be applied to solid or spaced sheathing, except where the roof covering is specifically designed to be applied to spaced supports.

R905.10.2 Slope. Minimum slopes for metal roof panels shall comply with the following:

1. The minimum slope for lapped, nonsoldered-seam metal roofs without applied lap sealant shall be three units vertical in 12 units horizontal (25-percent slope).
2. The minimum slope for lapped, nonsoldered-seam metal roofs with applied lap sealant shall be one-half vertical unit in 12 units horizontal (4-percent slope). Lap sealants shall be applied in accordance with the *approved* manufacturer's installation instructions.
3. The minimum slope for standing-seam roof systems shall be one-quarter unit vertical in 12 units horizontal (2-percent slope).

R905.10.3 Material standards. Metal-sheet roof covering systems that incorporate supporting structural members shall be designed in accordance with the *International Building Code*. Metal-sheet roof coverings installed over structural decking shall comply with Table R905.10.3(1). The materials used for metal-sheet roof coverings shall be naturally corrosion resistant or provided with corrosion resistance in accordance with the standards and minimum thicknesses shown in Table R905.10.3(2).

TABLE R905.10.3(2)
MINIMUM CORROSION RESISTANCE

55% aluminum-zinc alloy coated steel	ASTM A 792 AZ 50
5% aluminum alloy-coated steel	ASTM A 875 GF60
Aluminum-coated steel	ASTM A 463 T2 65
Galvanized steel	ASTM A 653 G-90
Prepainted steel	ASTM A 755[a]

a. Paint systems in accordance with ASTM A 755 shall be applied over steel products with corrosion-resistant coatings complying with ASTM A 792, ASTM A 875, ASTM A 463, or ASTM A 653.

R905.10.4 Attachment. Metal roof panels shall be secured to the supports in accordance with this chapter and the manufacturer's installation instructions. In the absence of manufacturer's installation instructions, the following fasteners shall be used:

1. Galvanized fasteners shall be used for steel roofs.

Wood Shakes

2. Copper, brass, bronze, copper alloy and Three hundred series stainless steel fasteners shall be used for copper roofs.
3. Stainless steel fasteners are acceptable for metal roofs.

R905.10.5 Underlayment. Underlayment shall be installed in accordance with the manufacturer's installation instructions.

R905.11 Modified bitumen roofing. The installation of modified bitumen roofing shall comply with the provisions of this section.

TABLE R905.9.2
BUILT-UP ROOFING MATERIAL STANDARDS

MATERIAL STANDARD	STANDARD
Acrylic coatings used in roofing	ASTM D 6083
Aggregate surfacing	ASTM D 1863
Asphalt adhesive used in roofing	ASTM D 3747
Asphalt cements used in roofing	ASTM D 3019; D 2822; D 4586
Asphalt-coated glass fiber base sheet	ASTM D 4601
Asphalt coatings used in roofing	ASTM D 1227; D 2823; D 2824; D 4479
Asphalt glass felt	ASTM D 2178
Asphalt primer used in roofing	ASTM D 41
Asphalt-saturated and asphalt-coated organic felt base sheet	ASTM D 2626
Asphalt-saturated organic felt (perforated)	ASTM D 226
Asphalt used in roofing	ASTM D 312
Coal-tar cements used in roofing	ASTM D 4022; D 5643
Coal-tar primer used in roofing, dampproofing and waterproofing	ASTM D 43
Coal-tar saturated organic felt	ASTM D 227
Coal-tar used in roofing	ASTM D 450, Types I or II
Glass mat, coal tar	ASTM D 4990
Glass mat, venting type	ASTM D 4897
Mineral-surfaced inorganic cap sheet	ASTM D 3909
Thermoplastic fabrics used in roofing	ASTM D 5665; D 5726

TABLE R905.10.3(1)
METAL ROOF COVERINGS STANDARDS

ROOF COVERING TYPE	STANDARD APPLICATION RATE/THICKNESS
Galvanized steel	ASTM A 653 G90 Zinc coated
Stainless steel	ASTM A 240, 300 Series alloys
Steel	ASTM A 924
Lead-coated copper	ASTM B 101
Cold rolled copper	ASTM B 370 minimum 16 oz/square ft and 12 oz/square ft high yield copper for metal-sheet roof-covering systems; 12 oz/square ft for preformed metal shingle systems.
Hard lead	2 lb/sq ft
Soft lead	3 lb/sq ft
Aluminum	ASTM B 209, 0.024 minimum thickness for rollformed panels and 0.019 inch minimum thickness for pressformed shingles.
Terne (tin) and terne-coated stainless	Terne coating of 40 lb per double base box, field painted where applicable in accordance with manufacturer's installation instructions.
Zinc	0.027 inch minimum thickness: 99.995% electrolytic high grade zinc with alloy additives of copper (0.08 - 0.20%), titanium (0.07% - 0.12%) and aluminum (0.015%).

For SI: 1 ounce per square foot = 0.305 kg/m^2, 1 pound per square foot = 4.214 kg/m^2, 1 inch = 25.4 mm, 1 pound = 0.454 kg.

R905.11.1 Slope. Modified bitumen membrane roofs shall have a design slope of a minimum of one-fourth unit vertical in 12 units horizontal (2-percent slope) for drainage.

R905.11.2 Material standards. Modified bitumen roof coverings shall comply with the standards in Table R905.11.2.

TABLE R905.11.2
MODIFIED BITUMEN ROOFING MATERIAL STANDARDS

MATERIAL	STANDARD
Acrylic coating	ASTM D 6083
Asphalt adhesive	ASTM D 3747
Asphalt cement	ASTM D 3019
Asphalt coating	ASTM D 1227; D 2824
Asphalt primer	ASTM D 41
Modified bitumen roof membrane	ASTM D 6162; D 6163; D 6164; D 6222; D 6223; D 6298; CGSB 37–GP–56M

R905.11.3 Application. Modified bitumen roofs shall be installed according to this chapter and the manufacturer's installation instructions.

R905.12 Thermoset single-ply roofing. The installation of thermoset single-ply roofing shall comply with the provisions of this section.

R905.12.1 Slope. Thermoset single-ply membrane roofs shall have a design slope of a minimum of one-fourth unit vertical in 12 units horizontal (2-percent slope) for drainage.

R905.12.2 Material standards. Thermoset single-ply roof coverings shall comply with ASTM D 4637, ASTM D 5019 or CGSB 37-GP-52M.

R905.12.3 Application. Thermoset single-ply roofs shall be installed according to this chapter and the manufacturer's installation instructions.

R905.13 Thermoplastic single-ply roofing. The installation of thermoplastic single-ply roofing shall comply with the provisions of this section.

R905.13.1 Slope. Thermoplastic single-ply membrane roofs shall have a design slope of a minimum of one-fourth unit vertical in 12 units horizontal (2-percent slope).

R905.13.2 Material standards. Thermoplastic single-ply roof coverings shall comply with ASTM D 4434, ASTM D 6754, ASTM D 6878, or CGSB CAN/CGSB 37.54.

R905.13.3 Application. Thermoplastic single-ply roofs shall be installed according to this chapter and the manufacturer's installation instructions.

R905.14 Sprayed polyurethane foam roofing. The installation of sprayed polyurethane foam roofing shall comply with the provisions of this section.

R905.14.1 Slope. Sprayed polyurethane foam roofs shall have a design slope of a minimum of one-fourth unit vertical in 12 units horizontal (2-percent slope) for drainage.

R905.14.2 Material standards. Spray-applied polyurethane foam insulation shall comply with ASTM C 1029, Type III or IV.

R905.14.3 Application. Foamed-in-place roof insulation shall be installed in accordance with this chapter and the manufacturer's installation instructions. A liquid-applied protective coating that complies with Section R905.15 shall be applied no less– than 2 hours nor more than 72 hours following the application of the foam.

R905.14.4 Foam plastics. Foam plastic materials and installation shall comply with Section R316.

R905.15 Liquid-applied coatings. The installation of liquid-applied coatings shall comply with the provisions of this section.

R905.15.1 Slope. Liquid-applied roofs shall have a design slope of a minimum of one-fourth unit vertical in 12 units horizontal (2-percent slope).

R905.15.2 Material standards. Liquid-applied roof coatings shall comply with ASTM C 836, C 957, D 1227, D 3468, D 6083, D 6694 or D 6947.

R905.15.3 Application. Liquid-applied roof coatings shall be installed according to this chapter and the manufacturer's installation instructions.

SECTION R906
ROOF INSULATION

R906.1 General. The use of above-deck thermal insulation shall be permitted provided such insulation is covered with an *approved* roof covering and passes FM 4450 or UL 1256.

R906.2 Material standards. Above-deck thermal insulation board shall comply with the standards in Table R906.2.

TABLE R906.2
MATERIAL STANDARDS FOR ROOF INSULATION

Cellular glass board	ASTM C 552
Composite boards	ASTM C 1289, Type III, IV, V or VI
Expanded polystyrene	ASTM C 578
Extruded polystyrene board	ASTM C 578
Perlite board	ASTM C 728
Polyisocyanurate board	ASTM C 1289, Type I or Type II
Wood fiberboard	ASTM C 208

SECTION R907
REROOFING

R907.1 General. Materials and methods of application used for re-covering or replacing an existing roof covering shall comply with the requirements of Chapter 9.

Exception: Reroofing shall not be required to meet the minimum design slope requirement of one-quarter unit vertical in 12 units horizontal (2-percent slope) in Section R905 for roofs that provide positive roof drainage.

R907.2 Structural and construction loads. The structural roof components shall be capable of supporting the roof covering system and the material and equipment loads that will be encountered during installation of the roof covering system.

R907.3 Recovering versus replacement. New roof coverings shall not be installed without first removing all existing layers of roof coverings where any of the following conditions exist:

1. Where the existing roof or roof covering is water-soaked or has deteriorated to the point that the existing roof or roof covering is not adequate as a base for additional roofing.
2. Where the existing roof covering is wood shake, slate, clay, cement or asbestos-cement tile.
3. Where the existing roof has two or more applications of any type of roof covering.
4. Deleted.

Exceptions:

1. Complete and separate roofing systems, such as standing-seam metal roof systems, that are designed to transmit the roof loads directly to the building's structural system and that do not rely on existing roofs and roof coverings for support, shall not require the removal of existing roof coverings.
2. Installation of metal panel, metal shingle and concrete and clay tile roof coverings over existing wood shake roofs shall be permitted when the application is in accordance with Section R907.4.
3. The application of new protective coating over existing spray polyurethane foam roofing systems shall be permitted without tear-off of existing roof coverings.

R907.4 Roof recovering. Where the application of a new roof covering over wood shingle or shake roofs creates a combustible concealed space, the entire existing surface shall be covered with gypsum board, mineral fiber, glass fiber or other *approved* materials securely fastened in place.

R907.5 Reinstallation of materials. Existing slate, clay or cement tile shall be permitted for reinstallation, except that damaged, cracked or broken slate or tile shall not be reinstalled. Existing vent flashing, metal edgings, drain outlets, collars and metal counterflashings shall not be reinstalled where rusted, damaged or deteriorated. Aggregate surfacing materials shall not be reinstalled.

R907.6 Flashings. Flashings shall be reconstructed in accordance with *approved* manufacturer's installation instructions. Metal flashing to which bituminous materials are to be adhered shall be primed prior to installation.

CHAPTER 10

CHIMNEYS AND FIREPLACES

SECTION R1001
MASONRY FIREPLACES

R1001.1 General. Masonry fireplaces shall be constructed in accordance with this section and the applicable provisions of Chapters 3 and 4.

R1001.2 Footings and foundations. Footings for masonry fireplaces and their chimneys shall be constructed of concrete or *solid masonry* at least 12 inches (305 mm) thick and shall extend at least 12 inches (305 mm) beyond the face of the fireplace or foundation wall on all sides. Footings shall be founded on natural, undisturbed earth or engineered fill below frost depth. In areas not subjected to freezing, footings shall be at least 12 inches (305 mm) below finished *grade*.

R1001.2.1 Ash dump cleanout. Cleanout openings located within foundation walls below fireboxes, when provided, shall be equipped with ferrous metal or masonry doors and frames constructed to remain tightly closed except when in use. Cleanouts shall be accessible and located so that ash removal will not create a hazard to combustible materials.

R1001.3 Seismic reinforcing. Masonry or concrete chimneys in Seismic Design Category D_0, D_1 or D_2 shall be reinforced. Reinforcing shall conform to the requirements set forth in Table R1001.1 and Section R609, Grouted Masonry.

R1001.3.1 Vertical reinforcing. For chimneys up to 40 inches (1016 mm) wide, four No. 4 continuous vertical bars shall be placed between wythes of *solid masonry* or within the cells of hollow unit masonry and grouted in accordance with Section R609. Grout shall be prevented from bonding with the flue liner so that the flue liner is free to move with thermal expansion. For chimneys more than 40 inches (1016 mm) wide, two additional No. 4 vertical bars shall be provided for each additional flue incorporated into the chimney or for each additional 40 inches (1016 mm) in width or fraction thereof.

R1001.3.2 Horizontal reinforcing. Vertical reinforcement shall be placed within $^1/_4$-inch (6 mm) ties, or other reinforcing of equivalent net cross-sectional area, placed in the bed joints according to Section R607 at a minimum of every 18 inches (457 mm) of vertical height. Two such ties shall be installed at each bend in the vertical bars.

R1001.4 Seismic anchorage. Masonry or concrete chimneys in Seismic Design Categories D_0, D_1 or D_2 shall be anchored at each floor, ceiling or roof line more than 6 feet (1829 mm) above *grade*, except where constructed completely within the exterior walls. Anchorage shall conform to the requirements of Section R1001.4.1.

R1001.4.1 Anchorage. Two $^3/_{16}$-inch by 1-inch (5 mm by 25 mm) straps shall be embedded a minimum of 12 inches (305 mm) into the chimney. Straps shall be hooked around the outer bars and extend 6 inches (152 mm) beyond the bend. Each strap shall be fastened to a minimum of four floor ceiling or floor joists or rafters with two $^1/_2$-inch (13 mm) bolts.

R1001.5 Firebox walls. Masonry fireboxes shall be constructed of *solid masonry* units, hollow masonry units grouted solid, stone or concrete. When a lining of firebrick at least 2 inches (51 mm) thick or other *approved* lining is provided, the minimum thickness of back and side walls shall each be 8 inches (203 mm) of *solid masonry*, including the lining. The width of joints between firebricks shall not be greater than $^1/_4$ inch (6 mm). When no lining is provided, the total minimum thickness of back and side walls shall be 10 inches (254 mm) of *solid masonry*. Firebrick shall conform to ASTM C 27 or C 1261 and shall be laid with medium duty refractory mortar conforming to ASTM C 199.

R1001.5.1 Steel fireplace units. Installation of steel fireplace units with *solid masonry* to form a masonry fireplace is permitted when installed either according to the requirements of their listing or according to the requirements of this section. Steel fireplace units incorporating a steel firebox lining, shall be constructed with steel not less than $^1/_4$ inch (6 mm) thick, and an air circulating chamber which is ducted to the interior of the building. The firebox lining shall be encased with *solid masonry* to provide a total thickness at the back and sides of not less than 8 inches (203 mm), of which not less than 4 inches (102 mm) shall be of *solid masonry* or concrete. Circulating air ducts used with steel fireplace units shall be constructed of metal or masonry.

R1001.6 Firebox dimensions. The firebox of a concrete or masonry fireplace shall have a minimum depth of 20 inches (508 mm). The throat shall not be less than 8 inches (203 mm) above the fireplace opening. The throat opening shall not be less than 4 inches (102 mm) deep. The cross-sectional area of the passageway above the firebox, including the throat, damper and smoke chamber, shall not be less than the cross-sectional area of the flue.

Exception: Rumford fireplaces shall be permitted provided that the depth of the fireplace is at least 12 inches (305 mm) and at least one-third of the width of the fireplace opening, that the throat is at least 12 inches (305 mm) above the lintel and is at least $^1/_{20}$ the cross-sectional area of the fireplace opening.

R1001.7 Lintel and throat. Masonry over a fireplace opening shall be supported by a lintel of noncombustible material. The minimum required bearing length on each end of the fireplace opening shall be 4 inches (102 mm). The fireplace throat or damper shall be located a minimum of 8 inches (203 mm) above the lintel.

R1001.7.1 Damper. Masonry fireplaces shall be equipped with a ferrous metal damper located at least 8 inches (203 mm) above the top of the fireplace opening. Dampers shall be installed in the fireplace or the chimney venting the fireplace, and shall be operable from the room containing the fireplace.

TABLE R1001.1
SUMMARY OF REQUIREMENTS FOR MASONRY FIREPLACES AND CHIMNEYS

ITEM	LETTER[a]	REQUIREMENTS
Hearth slab thickness	A	4″
Hearth extension (each side of opening)	B	8″ fireplace opening < 6 square foot. 12″ fireplace opening ≥ 6 square foot.
Hearth extension (front of opening)	C	16″ fireplace opening < 6 square foot. 20″ fireplace opening ≥ 6 square foot.
Hearth reinforcing	D	Reinforced to carry its own weight and all imposed loads.
Thickness of wall of firebox	E	10″ solid brick or 8″ where a firebrick lining is used. Joints in firebrick $^1/_4$″ maximum.
Distance from top of opening to throat	F	8″
Smoke chamber wall thickness	G	6″
Chimney Vertical reinforcing[b]	H	Four No. 4 full-length bars for chimney up to 40″ wide. Add two No. 4 bars for each additional 40″ or fraction of width or each additional flue.
Horizontal reinforcing[b]	J	$^1/_4$″ ties at 18″ and two ties at each bend in vertical steel.
Bond beams[b]	K	No specified requirements.
Fireplace lintel	L	Noncombustible material.
Chimney walls with flue lining	M	Solid masonry units or hollow masonry units grouted solid with at least 4 inch nominal thickness.
Distances between adjacent flues	—	See Section R1003.13.
Effective flue area (based on area of fireplace opening)	P	See Section R1003.15.
Clearances: Combustible material Mantel and trim Above roof	R	 See Sections R1001.11 and R1003.18. See Section R1001.11, Exception 4. 2′ at roofline and 2′ at 10′.
Anchorage[b] Strap Number Embedment into chimney Fasten to Bolts	S	 $^3/_{16}$″ × 1″ Two 12″ hooked around outer bar with 6″ extension. 4 joists Three $^1/_2$″ diameter.
Footing Thickness Width	T	 12″ min. 12″ each side of fireplace wall.

For SI: 1 inch = 25.4 mm, 1 foot = 304.8 mm, 1 square foot = 0.0929 m^2.

NOTE: This table provides a summary of major requirements for the construction of masonry chimneys and fireplaces. Letter references are to Figure R1001.1, which shows examples of typical construction. This table does not cover all requirements, nor does it cover all aspects of the indicated requirements. For the actual mandatory requirements of the code, see the indicated section of text.

a. The letters refer to Figure R1001.1.

b. Not required in Seismic Design Category A, B or C.

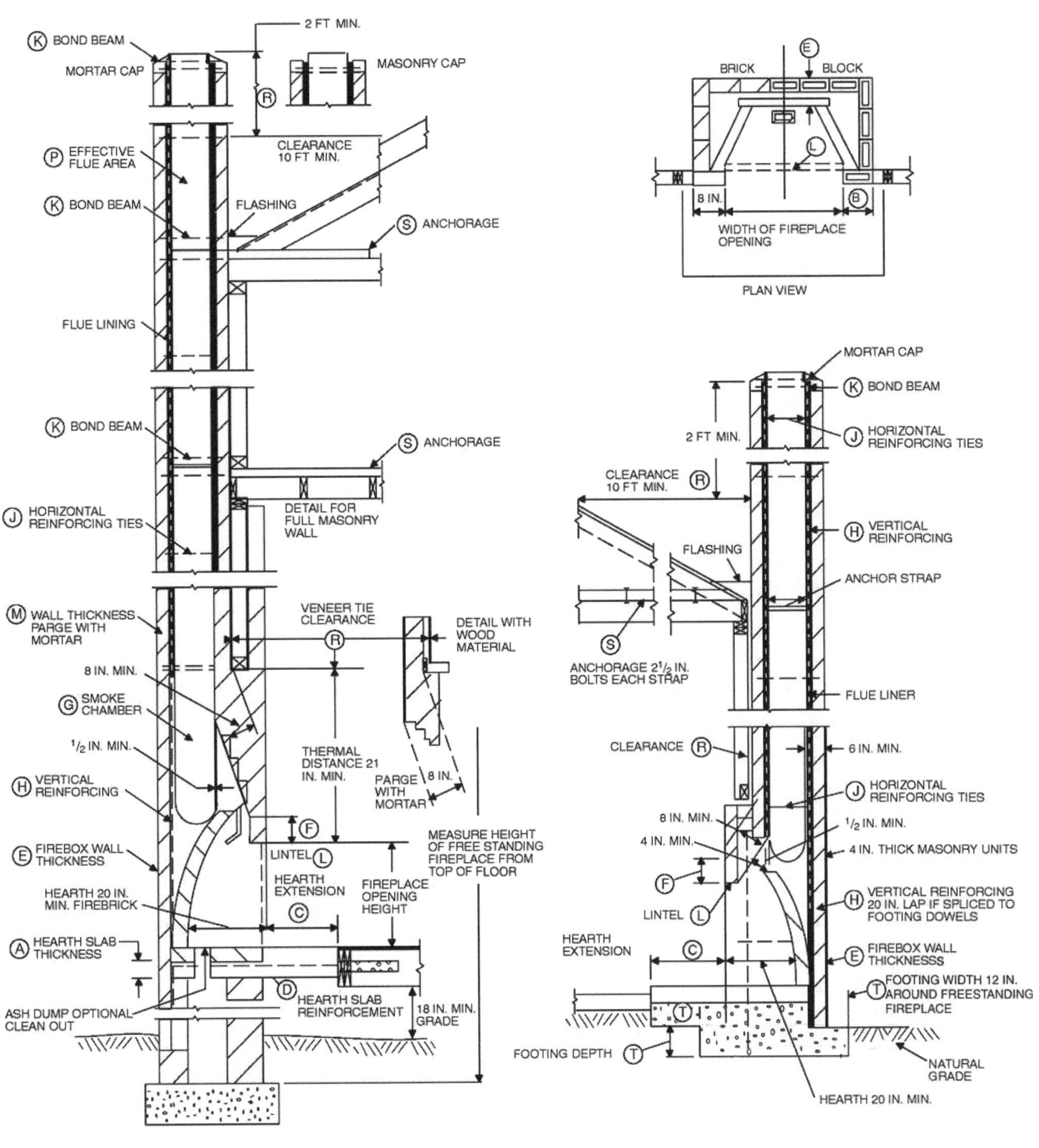

For SI: 1 inch = 25.4 mm, 1 foot = 304.8 mm.

FIGURE R1001.1
FIREPLACE AND CHIMNEY DETAILS

R1001.8 Smoke chamber. Smoke chamber walls shall be constructed of *solid masonry* units, hollow masonry units grouted solid, stone or concrete. The total minimum thickness of front, back and side walls shall be 8 inches (203 mm) of *solid masonry*. The inside surface shall be parged smooth with refractory mortar conforming to ASTM C 199. When a lining of firebrick at least 2 inches (51 mm) thick, or a lining of vitrified clay at least $^5/_8$ inch (16 mm) thick, is provided, the total minimum thickness of front, back and side walls shall be 6 inches (152 mm) of *solid masonry*, including the lining. Firebrick shall conform to ASTM C 1261 and shall be laid with medium duty refractory mortar conforming to ASTM C 199. Vitrified clay linings shall conform to ASTM C 315.

R1001.8.1 Smoke chamber dimensions. The inside height of the smoke chamber from the fireplace throat to the beginning of the flue shall not be greater than the inside width of the fireplace opening. The inside surface of the smoke chamber shall not be inclined more than 45 degrees (0.79 rad) from vertical when prefabricated smoke chamber linings are used or when the smoke chamber walls are rolled or sloped rather than corbeled. When the inside surface of the smoke chamber is formed by corbeled masonry, the walls shall not be corbeled more than 30 degrees (0.52 rad) from vertical.

R1001.9 Hearth and hearth extension. Masonry fireplace hearths and hearth extensions shall be constructed of concrete or masonry, supported by noncombustible materials, and reinforced to carry their own weight and all imposed loads. No combustible material shall remain against the underside of hearths and hearth extensions after construction.

R1001.9.1 Hearth thickness. The minimum thickness of fireplace hearths shall be 4 inches (102 mm).

R1001.9.2 Hearth extension thickness. The minimum thickness of hearth extensions shall be 2 inches (51 mm).

Exception: When the bottom of the firebox opening is raised at least 8 inches (203 mm) above the top of the hearth extension, a hearth extension of not less than $^3/_8$-inch-thick (10 mm) brick, concrete, stone, tile or other *approved* noncombustible material is permitted.

R1001.10 Hearth extension dimensions. Hearth extensions shall extend at least 16 inches (406 mm) in front of and at least 8 inches (203 mm) beyond each side of the fireplace opening. Where the fireplace opening is 6 square feet (0.6 m^2) or larger, the hearth extension shall extend at least 20 inches (508 mm) in front of and at least 12 inches (305 mm) beyond each side of the fireplace opening.

R1001.11 Fireplace clearance. All wood beams, joists, studs and other combustible material shall have a clearance of not less than 2 inches (51 mm) from the front faces and sides of masonry fireplaces and not less than 4 inches (102 mm) from the back faces of masonry fireplaces. The air space shall not be filled, except to provide fire blocking in accordance with Section R1001.12.

Exceptions:

1. Masonry fireplaces *listed* and *labeled* for use in contact with combustibles in accordance with UL 127 and installed in accordance with the manufacturer's installation instructions are permitted to have combustible material in contact with their exterior surfaces.
2. When masonry fireplaces are part of masonry or concrete walls, combustible materials shall not be in contact with the masonry or concrete walls less than 12 inches (306 mm) from the inside surface of the nearest firebox lining.
3. Exposed combustible trim and the edges of sheathing materials such as wood siding, flooring and drywall shall be permitted to abut the masonry fireplace side walls and hearth extension in accordance with Figure R1001.11, provided such combustible trim or sheathing is a minimum of 12 inches (305 mm) from the inside surface of the nearest firebox lining.
4. Exposed combustible mantels or trim may be placed directly on the masonry fireplace front surrounding the fireplace opening providing such combustible materials are not placed within 6 inches (152 mm) of a fireplace opening. Combustible material within 12 inches (306 mm) of the fireplace opening shall not project more than $^1/_8$ inch (3 mm) for each 1-inch (25 mm) distance from such an opening.

R1001.12 Fireplace fireblocking. Fireplace fireblocking shall comply with the provisions of Section R602.8.

SECTION R1002 MASONRY HEATERS

R1002.1 Definition. A masonry heater is a heating *appliance* constructed of concrete or *solid masonry*, hereinafter referred to as masonry, which is designed to absorb and store heat from a solid-fuel fire built in the firebox by routing the exhaust gases through internal heat exchange channels in which the flow path downstream of the firebox may include flow in a horizontal or downward direction before entering the chimney and which delivers heat by radiation from the masonry surface of the heater.

R1002.2 Installation. Masonry heaters shall be installed in accordance with this section and comply with one of the following:

1. Masonry heaters shall comply with the requirements of ASTM E 1602; or
2. Masonry heaters shall be *listed* and *labeled* in accordance with UL 1482 and installed in accordance with the manufacturer's installation instructions.

R1002.3 Footings and foundation. The firebox floor of a masonry heater shall be a minimum thickness of 4 inches (102 mm) of noncombustible material and be supported on a noncombustible footing and foundation in accordance with Section R1003.2.

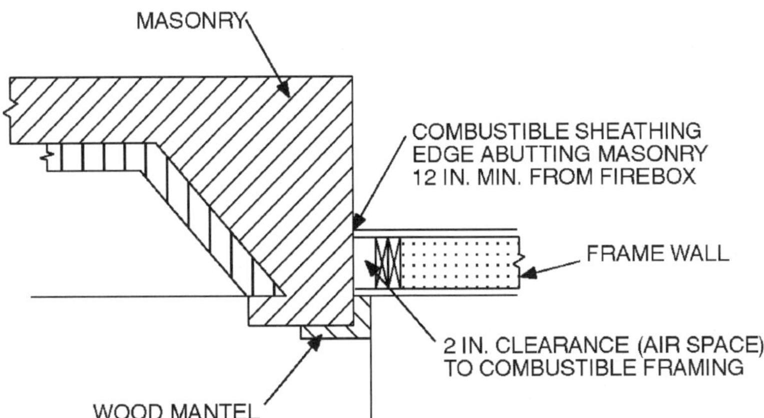

For SI: 1 inch = 25.4 mm.

FIGURE R1001.11
CLEARANCE FROM COMBUSTIBLES

R1002.4 Seismic reinforcing. In Seismic Design Categories D_0, D_1 and D_2, masonry heaters shall be anchored to the masonry foundation in accordance with Section R1003.3. Seismic reinforcing shall not be required within the body of a masonry heater whose height is equal to or less than 3.5 times it's body width and where the masonry chimney serving the heater is not supported by the body of the heater. Where the masonry chimney shares a common wall with the facing of the masonry heater, the chimney portion of the structure shall be reinforced in accordance with Section R1003.

R1002.5 Masonry heater clearance. Combustible materials shall not be placed within 36 inches (914 mm) of the outside surface of a masonry heater in accordance with NFPA 211 Section 8-7 (clearances for solid-fuel-burning *appliances*), and the required space between the heater and combustible material shall be fully vented to permit the free flow of air around all heater surfaces.

Exceptions:

1. When the masonry heater wall is at least 8 inches (203 mm) thick of *solid masonry* and the wall of the heat exchange channels is at least 5 inches (127 mm) thick of *solid masonry*, combustible materials shall not be placed within 4 inches (102 mm) of the outside surface of a masonry heater. A clearance of at least 8 inches (203 mm) shall be provided between the gas-tight capping slab of the heater and a combustible ceiling.
2. Masonry heaters tested and listed by an American National Standards Association (ANSI)-accredited laboratory to the requirements of UL1482 may be installed in accordance with the listing specifications and the manufacturer's written instructions.

SECTION R1003
MASONRY CHIMNEYS

R1003.1 Definition. A masonry chimney is a chimney constructed of *solid masonry* units, hollow masonry units grouted solid, stone or concrete, hereinafter referred to as masonry. Masonry chimneys shall be constructed, anchored, supported and reinforced as required in this chapter.

R1003.2 Footings and foundations. Footings for masonry chimneys shall be constructed of concrete or *solid masonry* at least 12 inches (305 mm) thick and shall extend at least 12 inches (305 mm) beyond the face of the foundation or support wall on all sides. Footings shall be founded on natural undisturbed earth or engineered fill below frost depth. In areas not subjected to freezing, footings shall be at least 12 inches (305 mm) below finished *grade*.

R1003.3 Seismic reinforcing. Masonry or concrete chimneys shall be constructed, anchored, supported and reinforced as required in this chapter. In Seismic Design Category D_0, D_1 or D_2 masonry and concrete chimneys shall be reinforced and anchored as detailed in Section R1003.3.1, R1003.3.2 and R1003.4. In Seismic Design Category A, B or C, reinforcement and seismic anchorage is not required.

R1003.3.1 Vertical reinforcing. For chimneys up to 40 inches (1016 mm) wide, four No. 4 continuous vertical bars, anchored in the foundation, shall be placed in the concrete, or between wythes of *solid masonry*, or within the cells of hollow unit masonry, and grouted in accordance with Section R609.1.1. Grout shall be prevented from bonding with the flue liner so that the flue liner is free to move with thermal expansion. For chimneys more than 40 inches (1016 mm) wide, two additional No. 4 vertical bars shall be installed for each additional 40 inches (1016 mm) in width or fraction thereof.

R1003.3.2 Horizontal reinforcing. Vertical reinforcement shall be placed enclosed within $^1/_4$-inch (6 mm) ties, or other reinforcing of equivalent net cross-sectional area, spaced not to exceed 18 inches (457 mm) on center in concrete, or placed in the bed joints of unit masonry, at a minimum of every 18 inches (457 mm) of vertical height. Two such ties shall be installed at each bend in the vertical bars.

R1003.4 Seismic anchorage. Masonry and concrete chimneys and foundations in Seismic Design Category D_0, D_1 or D_2 shall be anchored at each floor, ceiling or roof line more than 6 feet (1829 mm) above *grade*, except where constructed completely within the exterior walls. Anchorage shall conform to the requirements in Section R1003.4.1.

R1003.4.1 Anchorage. Two $^{3}/_{16}$-inch by 1-inch (5 mm by 25 mm) straps shall be embedded a minimum of 12 inches (305 mm) into the chimney. Straps shall be hooked around the outer bars and extend 6 inches (152 mm) beyond the bend. Each strap shall be fastened to a minimum of four floor joists with two $^{1}/_{2}$-inch (13 mm) bolts.

R1003.5 Corbeling. Masonry chimneys shall not be corbeled more than one-half of the chimney's wall thickness from a wall or foundation, nor shall a chimney be corbeled from a wall or foundation that is less than 12 inches (305 mm) thick unless it projects equally on each side of the wall, except that on the second *story* of a two-story *dwelling*, corbeling of chimneys on the exterior of the enclosing walls may equal the wall thickness. The projection of a single course shall not exceed one-half the unit height or one-third of the unit bed depth, whichever is less.

R1003.6 Changes in dimension. The chimney wall or chimney flue lining shall not change in size or shape within 6 inches (152 mm) above or below where the chimney passes through floor components, ceiling components or roof components.

R1003.7 Offsets. Where a masonry chimney is constructed with a fireclay flue liner surrounded by one wythe of masonry, the maximum offset shall be such that the centerline of the flue above the offset does not extend beyond the center of the chimney wall below the offset. Where the chimney offset is supported by masonry below the offset in an *approved* manner, the maximum offset limitations shall not apply. Each individual corbeled masonry course of the offset shall not exceed the projection limitations specified in Section R1003.5.

R1003.8 Additional load. Chimneys shall not support loads other than their own weight unless they are designed and constructed to support the additional load. Construction of masonry chimneys as part of the masonry walls or reinforced concrete walls of the building shall be permitted.

R1003.9 Termination. Chimneys shall extend at least 2 feet (610 mm) higher than any portion of a building within 10 feet (3048 mm), but shall not be less than 3 feet (914 mm) above the highest point where the chimney passes through the roof.

R1003.9.1 Spark arrestors. Where a spark arrestor is installed on a masonry chimney, the spark arrestor shall meet all of the following requirements:

1. The net free area of the arrestor shall not be less than four times the net free area of the outlet of the chimney flue it serves.
2. The arrestor screen shall have heat and corrosion resistance equivalent to 19-gage galvanized steel or 24-gage stainless steel.
3. Openings shall not permit the passage of spheres having a diameter greater than $^{1}/_{2}$ inch (13 mm) nor block the passage of spheres having a diameter less than $^{3}/_{8}$ inch (10 mm).
4. The spark arrestor shall be accessible for cleaning and the screen or chimney cap shall be removable to allow for cleaning of the chimney flue.

R1003.10 Wall thickness. Masonry chimney walls shall be constructed of *solid masonry* units or hollow masonry units grouted solid with not less than a 4-inch (102 mm) nominal thickness.

R1003.10.1 Masonry veneer chimneys. Where masonry is used to veneer a frame chimney, through-flashing and weep holes shall be installed as required by Section R703.

R1003.11 Flue lining (material). Masonry chimneys shall be lined. The lining material shall be appropriate for the type of *appliance* connected, according to the terms of the *appliance* listing and manufacturer's instructions.

R1003.11.1 Residential-type appliances (general). Flue lining systems shall comply with one of the following:

1. Clay flue lining complying with the requirements of ASTM C 315.
2. Listed chimney lining systems complying with UL 1777.
3. Factory-built chimneys or chimney units listed for installation within masonry chimneys.
4. Other *approved* materials that will resist corrosion, erosion, softening or cracking from flue gases and condensate at temperatures up to 1,800°F (982°C).

R1003.11.2 Flue linings for specific appliances. Flue linings other than these covered in Section R1003.11.1, intended for use with specific types of *appliances*, shall comply with Sections R1003.11.3 through R1003.11.6.

R1003.11.3 Gas appliances. Flue lining systems for gas *appliances* shall be in accordance with Chapter 24.

R1003.11.4 Pellet fuel-burning appliances. Flue lining and vent systems for use in masonry chimneys with pellet fuel-burning *appliances* shall be limited to the following:

1. Flue lining systems complying with Section R1003.11.1.
2. Pellet vents listed for installation within masonry chimneys. (See Section R1003.11.6 for marking.)

R1003.11.5 Oil-fired appliances approved for use with Type L vent. Flue lining and vent systems for use in masonry chimneys with oil-fired *appliances approved* for use with Type L vent shall be limited to the following:

1. Flue lining systems complying with Section R1003.11.1.
2. Listed chimney liners complying with UL 641. (See Section R1003.11.6 for marking.)

R1003.11.6 Notice of usage. When a flue is relined with a material not complying with Section R1003.11.1, the chimney shall be plainly and permanently identified by a *label* attached to a wall, ceiling or other conspicuous location adjacent to where the connector enters the chimney. The *label* shall include the following message or equivalent language:

THIS CHIMNEY FLUE IS FOR USE ONLY WITH [TYPE OR CATEGORY OF *APPLIANCE*] *APPLIANCES* THAT BURN [TYPE OF FUEL]. DO NOT CONNECT OTHER TYPES OF *APPLIANCES*.

R1003.12 Clay flue lining (installation). Clay flue liners shall be installed in accordance with ASTM C 1283 and extend from a point not less than 8 inches (203 mm) below the lowest inlet or, in the case of fireplaces, from the top of the smoke chamber to a point above the enclosing walls. The lining shall be carried up vertically, with a maximum slope no greater than 30 degrees (0.52 rad) from the vertical.

Clay flue liners shall be laid in medium-duty water insoluble refractory mortar conforming to ASTM C 199 (Types M and S) with tight mortar joints left smooth on the inside and installed to maintain an air space or insulation not to exceed the thickness of the flue liner separating the flue liners from the interior face of the chimney masonry walls. Flue liners shall be supported on all sides. Only enough mortar shall be placed to make the joint and hold the liners in position.

R1003.12.1 Listed materials. *Listed* materials used as flue linings shall be installed in accordance with the terms of their listings and manufacturer's instructions.

R1003.12.2 Space around lining. The space surrounding a chimney lining system or vent installed within a masonry chimney shall not be used to vent any other *appliance*.

Exception: This shall not prevent the installation of a separate flue lining in accordance with the manufacturer's installation instructions.

R1003.13 Multiple flues. When two or more flues are located in the same chimney, masonry wythes shall be built between adjacent flue linings. The masonry wythes shall be at least 4 inches (102 mm) thick and bonded into the walls of the chimney.

Exception: When venting only one *appliance*, two flues may adjoin each other in the same chimney with only the flue lining separation between them. The joints of the adjacent flue linings shall be staggered at least 4 inches (102 mm).

R1003.14 Flue area (appliance). Chimney flues shall not be smaller in area than that of the area of the connector from the *appliance* [see Tables R1003.14(1) and R1003.14(2)]. The sizing of a chimney flue to which multiple *appliance* venting systems are connected shall be in accordance with Section M1805.3.

R1003.15 Flue area (masonry fireplace). Flue sizing for chimneys serving fireplaces shall be in accordance with Section R1003.15.1 or Section R1003.15.2.

R1003.15.1 Option 1. Round chimney flues shall have a minimum net cross-sectional area of at least $^1/_{12}$ of the fireplace opening. Square chimney flues shall have a minimum net cross-sectional area of $^1/_{10}$ of the fireplace opening. Rectangular chimney flues with an *aspect ratio* less than 2 to 1 shall have a minimum net cross-sectional area of $^1/_{10}$ of the fireplace opening. Rectangular chimney flues with an *aspect ratio* of 2 to 1 or more shall have a minimum net cross-sectional area of $^1/_8$ of the fireplace opening. Cross-sectional areas of clay flue linings are shown in Tables R1003.14(1) and R1003.14(2) or as provided by the manufacturer or as measured in the field.

R1003.15.2 Option 2. The minimum net cross-sectional area of the chimney flue shall be determined in accordance with Figure R1003.15.2. A flue size providing at least the equivalent net cross-sectional area shall be used. Cross-sectional areas of clay flue linings are shown in Tables R1003.14(1) and R1003.14(2) or as provided by the manufacturer or as measured in the field. The height of the chimney shall be measured from the firebox floor to the top of the chimney flue.

TABLE R1003.14(1)
NET CROSS–SECTIONAL AREA OF ROUND FLUE SIZES[a]

FLUE SIZE, INSIDE DIAMETER (inches)	CROSS–SECTIONAL AREA (square inches)
6	28
7	38
8	50
10	78
$10^3/_4$	90
12	113
15	176
18	254

For SI: 1 inch = 25.4 mm, 1 square inch = 645.16 mm^2.

a. Flue sizes are based on ASTM C 315.

TABLE R1003.14(2)
NET CROSS–SECTIONAL AREA OF SQUARE AND RECTANGULAR FLUE SIZES

FLUE SIZE, OUTSIDE NOMINAL DIMENSIONS (inches)	CROSS–SECTIONAL AREA (square inches)
4.5 × 8.5	23
4.5 × 13	34
8 × 8	42
8.5 × 8.5	49
8 × 12	67
8.5 × 13	76
12 × 12	102
8.5 × 18	101
13 × 13	127
12 × 16	131
13 × 18	173
16 × 16	181
16 × 20	222
18 × 18	233
20 × 20	298
20 × 24	335
24 × 24	431

For SI: 1 inch = 25.4 mm, 1 square inch = 645.16 mm^2.

R1003.16 Inlet. Inlets to masonry chimneys shall enter from the side. Inlets shall have a thimble of fireclay, rigid refractory material or metal that will prevent the connector from pulling out of the inlet or from extending beyond the wall of the liner.

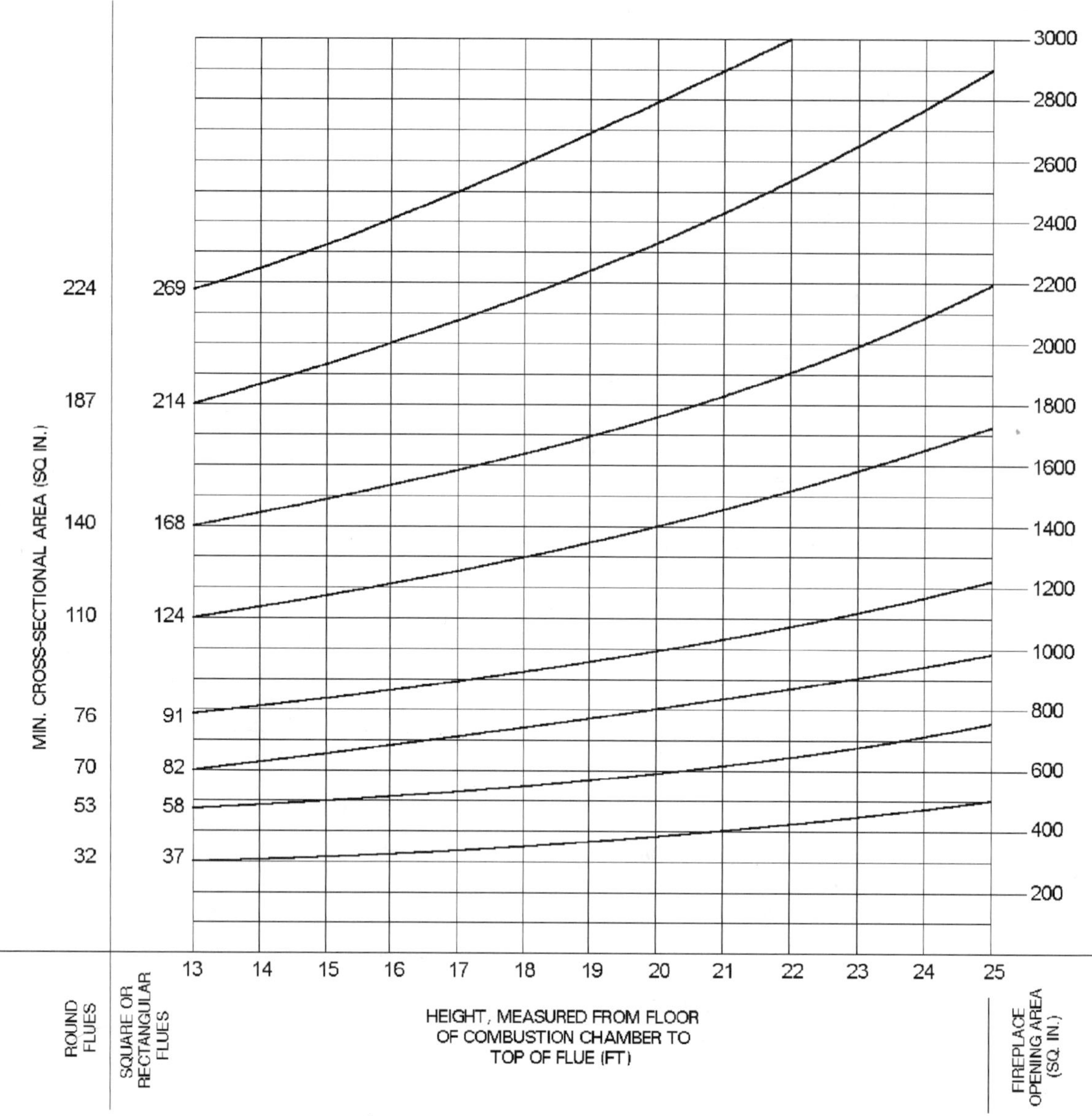

For SI: 1 foot = 304.8 mm, 1 square inch = 645.16 mm².

FIGURE R1003.15.2
FLUE SIZES FOR MASONRY CHIMNEYS

R1003.17 Masonry chimney cleanout openings. Cleanout openings shall be provided within 6 inches (152 mm) of the base of each flue within every masonry chimney. The upper edge of the cleanout shall be located at least 6 inches (152 mm) below the lowest chimney inlet opening. The height of the opening shall be at least 6 inches (152 mm). The cleanout shall be provided with a noncombustible cover.

Exception: Chimney flues serving masonry fireplaces where cleaning is possible through the fireplace opening.

R1003.18 Chimney clearances. Any portion of a masonry chimney located in the interior of the building or within the exterior wall of the building shall have a minimum air space clearance to combustibles of 2 inches (51 mm). Chimneys located entirely outside the exterior walls of the building, including chimneys that pass through the soffit or cornice, shall have a minimum air space clearance of 1 inch (25 mm). The air space shall not be filled, except to provide fire blocking in accordance with Section R1003.19.

Exceptions:

1. Masonry chimneys equipped with a chimney lining system listed and *labeled* for use in chimneys in contact with combustibles in accordance with UL 1777 and installed in accordance with the manufacturer's installation instructions are permitted to have combustible material in contact with their exterior surfaces.

2. When masonry chimneys are constructed as part of masonry or concrete walls, combustible materials shall not be in contact with the masonry or concrete

wall less than 12 inches (305 mm) from the inside surface of the nearest flue lining.

3. Exposed combustible trim and the edges of sheathing materials, such as wood siding and flooring, shall be permitted to abut the masonry chimney side walls, in accordance with Figure R1003.18, provided such combustible trim or sheathing is a minimum of 12 inches (305 mm) from the inside surface of the nearest flue lining. Combustible material and trim shall not overlap the corners of the chimney by more than 1 inch (25 mm).

R1003.19 Chimney fireblocking. All spaces between chimneys and floors and ceilings through which chimneys pass shall be fireblocked with noncombustible material securely fastened in place. The fireblocking of spaces between chimneys and wood joists, beams or headers shall be self-supporting or be placed on strips of metal or metal lath laid across the spaces between combustible material and the chimney.

R1003.20 Chimney crickets. Chimneys shall be provided with crickets when the dimension parallel to the ridgeline is greater than 30 inches (762 mm) and does not intersect the ridgeline. The intersection of the cricket and the chimney shall be flashed and counterflashed in the same manner as normal roof-chimney intersections. Crickets shall be constructed in compliance with Figure R1003.20 and Table R1003.20.

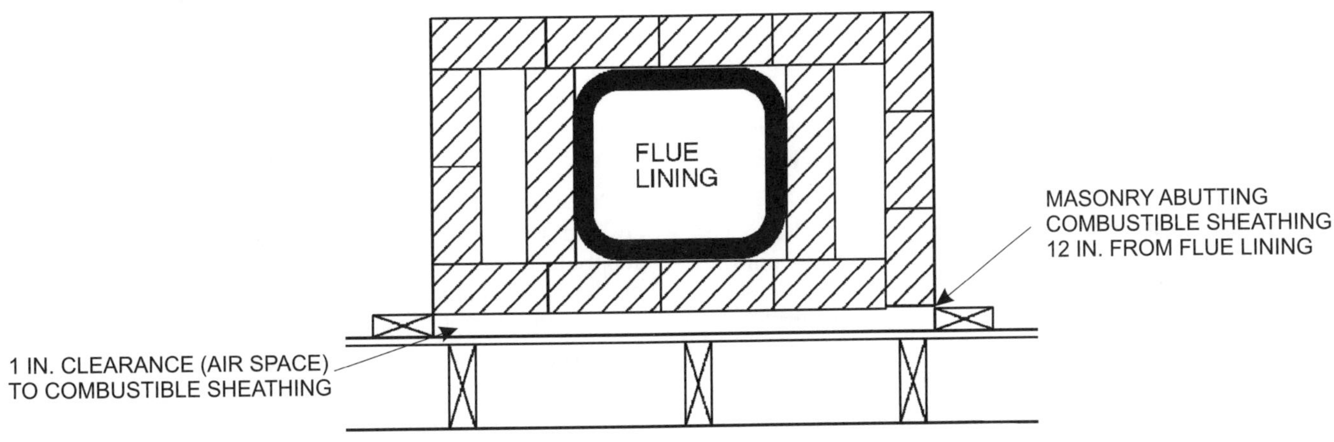

For SI: 1 inch = 25.4 mm.

FIGURE R1003.18
CLEARANCE FROM COMBUSTIBLES

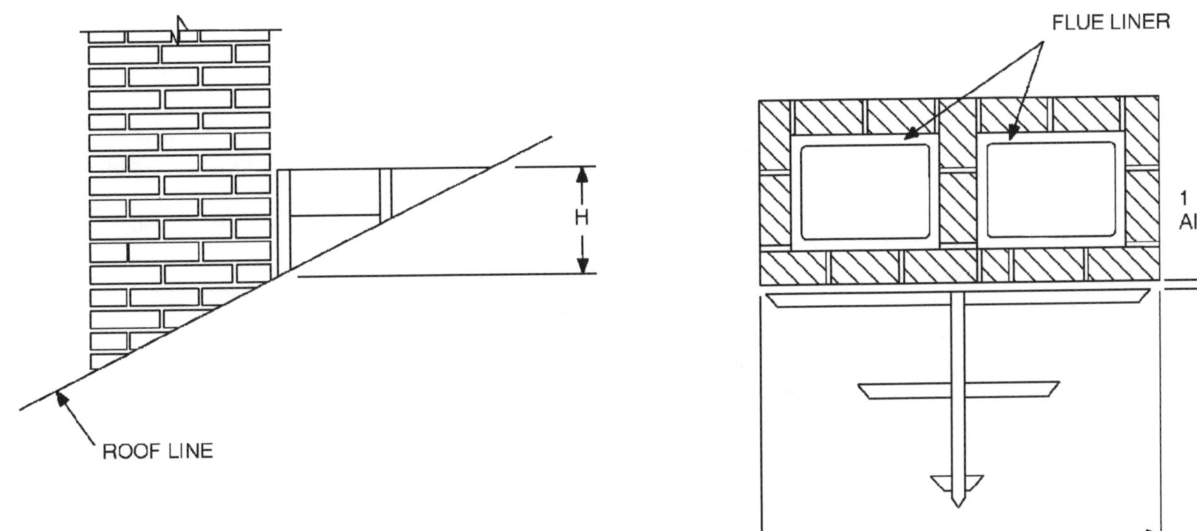

For SI: 1 inch = 25.4 mm.

FIGURE R1003.20
CHIMNEY CRICKET

TABLE R1003.20
CRICKET DIMENSIONS

ROOF SLOPE	H
12 - 12	$^{1}/_{2}$ of W
8 - 12	$^{1}/_{3}$ of W
6 - 12	$^{1}/_{4}$ of W
4 - 12	$^{1}/_{6}$ of W
3 - 12	$^{1}/_{8}$ of W

SECTION R1004 FACTORY-BUILT FIREPLACES

R1004.1 General. Factory-built fireplaces shall be *listed* and *labeled* and shall be installed in accordance with the conditions of the *listing*. Factory-built fireplaces shall be tested in accordance with UL 127.

R1004.2 Hearth extensions. Hearth extensions of *approved* factory-built fireplaces shall be installed in accordance with the *listing* of the fireplace. The hearth extension shall be readily distinguishable from the surrounding floor area.

R1004.3 Decorative shrouds. Decorative shrouds shall not be installed at the termination of chimneys for factory-built fireplaces except where the shrouds are listed and *labeled* for use with the specific factory-built fireplace system and installed in accordance with the manufacturer's installation instructions.

R1004.4 Unvented gas log heaters. An unvented gas log heater shall not be installed in a factory-built fireplace unless the fireplace system has been specifically tested, *listed* and *labeled* for such use in accordance with UL 127.

SECTION R1005 FACTORY-BUILT CHIMNEYS

R1005.1 General. Factory-built fireplace stoves, consisting of a freestanding fire chamber assembly, that have been tested and are listed by a nationally recognized testing laboratory, shall be installed in accordance with the requirements of said listing and the manufacturer's instructions. The supporting structure for a hearth extension shall be at the same level as the supporting structure for the fireplace unit of the firebox opening on or near the floor. The inlet shall be closable and designed to prevent burning material from dropping into concealed combustible spaces.

R1005.2 Decorative shrouds. Decorative shrouds shall not be installed at the termination of factory-built chimneys except where the shrouds are *listed* and *labeled* for use with the specific factory-built chimney system and installed in accordance with the manufacturer's installation instructions.

R1005.3 Solid-fuel appliances. Factory-built chimneys installed in *dwelling units* with solid-fuel-burning *appliances* shall comply with the Type HT requirements of UL 103 and shall be marked "Type HT and "Residential Type and Building Heating *Appliance* Chimney."

Exception: Chimneys for use with open combustion chamber fireplaces shall comply with the requirements of UL 103 and shall be marked "Residential Type and Building Heating *Appliance* Chimney."

Chimneys for use with open combustion chamber *appliances* installed in buildings other than *dwelling units* shall comply with the requirements of UL 103 and shall be marked "Building Heating *Appliance* Chimney" or "Residential Type and Building Heating *Appliance* Chimney."

R1005.4 Factory-built fireplaces. Chimneys for use with factory-built fireplaces shall comply with the requirements of UL 127.

R1005.5 Support. Where factory-built chimneys are supported by structural members, such as joists and rafters, those members shall be designed to support the additional load.

R1005.6 Medium-heat *appliances*. Factory-built chimneys for medium-heat *appliances* producing flue gases having a temperature above 1,000°F (538°C), measured at the entrance to the chimney shall comply with UL 959.

SECTION R1006 EXTERIOR AIR SUPPLY

R1006.1 Exterior air. Factory-built or masonry fireplaces covered in this chapter shall be equipped with an exterior air supply to assure proper fuel combustion unless the room is mechanically ventilated and controlled so that the indoor pressure is neutral or positive.

R1006.1.1 Factory-built fireplaces. Exterior *combustion air* ducts for factory-built fireplaces shall be a *listed* component of the fireplace and shall be installed according to the fireplace manufacturer's instructions.

R1006.1.2 Masonry fireplaces. *Listed combustion air* ducts for masonry fireplaces shall be installed according to the terms of their *listing* and the manufacturer's instructions.

R1006.2 Exterior air intake. The exterior air intake shall be capable of supplying all *combustion air* from the exterior of the *dwelling* or from spaces within the *dwelling* ventilated with outside air such as nonmechanically ventilated crawl or *attic* spaces. The exterior air intake shall not be located within the garage or *basement* of the *dwelling* nor shall the air intake be located at an elevation higher than the firebox. The exterior air intake shall be covered with a corrosion-resistant screen of $^{1}/_{4}$-inch (6 mm) mesh.

R1006.3 Clearance. Unlisted *combustion air* ducts shall be installed with a minimum 1-inch (25 mm) clearance to combustibles for all parts of the duct within 5 feet (1524 mm) of the duct outlet.

R1006.4 Passageway. The *combustion air* passageway shall be a minimum of 6 square inches (3870 mm^2) and not more than 55 square inches (0.035 m^2), except that *combustion air* systems for listed fireplaces shall be constructed according to the fireplace manufacturer's instructions.

R1006.5 Outlet. Locating the exterior air outlet in the back or sides of the firebox chamber or within 24 inches (610 mm) of the firebox opening on or near the floor is permitted. The outlet shall be closable and designed to prevent burning material from dropping into concealed combustible spaces.

Part IV — Energy Conservation

CHAPTER 11

ENERGY EFFICIENCY

This chapter has been revised in its entirety; there will be no marginal markings or underlines.

SECTION N1101 SCOPE, GENERAL REQUIREMENTS, AND ADDITIONAL DEFINITIONS

N1101.1 Scope. This chapter shall regulate the design and construction of buildings for the effective use of energy. This code is intended to provide flexibility to permit the use of innovative approaches and techniques to achieve the effective use of energy. This code is not intended to prevent the use of any material, method of construction, design or insulating system not specifically prescribed herein, provided that such construction, design or insulating system has been *approved* by the *code official* as meeting the intent of this code.

Exception: Portions of the building envelope that do not enclose conditioned space.

N1101.1.2 Existing buildings. Except as specified in this chapter, this code shall not be used to require the removal, *alteration* or abandonment of, nor prevent the continued use and maintenance of, an existing building or building system lawfully in existence at the time of adoption of this code.

N1101.1.3 Additions, alterations, renovations or repairs. Additions, alterations, renovations or repairs to an existing building, building system or portion thereof shall conform to the provisions of this code as they relate to new construction without requiring the unaltered portion(s) of the existing building or building system to comply with this code. Additions, alterations, renovations or repairs shall not create an unsafe or hazardous condition or overload existing building systems. An addition shall be deemed to comply with this code if the addition alone complies or if the existing building and addition comply with this code as a single building.

Exception:

1. The following need not comply provided the energy use of the building is not increased:
   a. Storm windows installed over existing fenestration.
   b. Incidental repairs requiring a new sash or new glazing.
   c. Existing ceiling, wall or floor cavities exposed during construction provided that these cavities are filled with insulation.
   d. Construction where the existing roof, wall or floor cavity is not exposed.
2. Converting unconditioned attic space to conditioned attic space. Ceilings shall be insulated to a minimum of R-30, walls shall be insulated to the exterior wall requirements in Table N1102.1 and follow backing requirements in Section N1102.2.12.

N1101.2 Compliance. Compliance shall be demonstrated by either meeting the requirements of the *North Carolina Energy Conservation Code* or meeting the requirements of this chapter. Climate zones from Figures N1101.2(1), Figure N1101.2(2) or Table N1101.2 shall be used in determining the applicable requirements from this chapter. Projects shall comply with Sections N1101, N1102.4, N1102.5, and N1103.1, N1103.2.2, N1103.2.3, and N1103.3 through N1103.9 and either:

1. Sections N1102.1 through N1102.3, N1103.2.1 and N1104.1; or
2. North Carolina specific REScheck shall be permitted to demonstrate compliance with this code. Envelope requirements may not be traded off against the use of high efficiency heating and/or cooling equipment. No trade-off calculations are needed for required termite inspection and treatment gaps.

N1101.2.1 Warm humid counties. Warm humid counties are identified in Table N1101.2 by an asterisk.

N1101.2.2 Change in space conditioning. Any nonconditioned space that is altered to become *conditioned space* shall be required to be brought into full compliance with this code.

Exception:

1. Existing enclosed ceiling, wall or floor cavities comply provided that these cavities are filled with insulation.
2. See N1101.1.3, Exception 2.

N1101.3 Identification. Materials, systems and *equipment* shall be identified in a manner that will allow a determination of compliance with the applicable provisions of this chapter.

N1101.4 Building thermal envelope insulation. An *R*-value identification mark shall be applied by the manufacturer to each piece of *building thermal envelope* insulation 12 inches (305 mm) or greater in width. Alternately, the insulation installers shall provide a certification listing the type, manufacturer and *R*-value of insulation installed in each element of the *building thermal envelope*. For blown or sprayed insulation (fiberglass and cellulose), the initial installed thickness, settled thickness, settled *R*-value, installed density, coverage area and number of bags installed shall be *listed* on the certification. For

Energy

sprayed polyurethane foam (SPF) insulation, the installed thickness of the areas covered and *R*-value of installed thickness shall be *listed* on the certification. The insulation installer shall sign, date and post the certification in a conspicuous location on the job site.

N1101.4.1 Blown or sprayed roof/ceiling insulation. The thickness of blown-in or sprayed roof/ceiling insulation (fiberglass or cellulose) shall be written in inches (mm) on markers that are installed at least one for every 300 square feet (28 m^2) throughout the attic space. The markers shall be affixed to the trusses or joists and marked with the minimum initial installed thickness with numbers a minimum of 1 inch (25 mm) in height. Each polyurethane foam thickness and installed *R*-value shall be *listed* on certification provided by the insulation installer.

N1101.4.2 Insulation mark installation. Insulating materials shall be installed such that the manufacturer's *R*-value mark is readily observable upon inspection.

N1101.5 Fenestration product rating. *U*-factors of fenestration products (windows, doors and skylights) shall be determined in accordance with NFRC 100 by an accredited, independent laboratory, and labeled and certified by the manufacturer. Products lacking such a labeled *U*-factor shall be assigned a default *U*-factor from Tables N1101.5(1) or N1101.5(2). The solar heat gain coefficient (SHGC) of glazed fenestration products (windows, glazed doors and skylights) shall be determined in accordance with NFRC 200 by an accredited, independent laboratory, and labeled and certified by the manufacturer. Products lacking such a labeled SHGC shall be assigned a default SHGC from Table N1101.5(3).

N1101.6 Insulation product rating. The thermal resistance (*R*-value) of insulation shall be determined in accordance with the U.S. Federal Trade Commission *R*-value rule (CFR Title 16, Part 460, May 31, 2005) in units of $h \times ft^2 \times °F/Btu$ at a mean temperature of 75°F (24°C).

N1101.7 Installation. All materials, systems and equipment shall be installed in accordance with the manufacturer's installation instructions and this code.

N1101.7.1 Protection of exposed foundation insulation. Insulation applied to the exterior of basement walls, crawlspace walls and the perimeter of slab-on-grade floors shall have a rigid, opaque and weather-resistant protective covering to prevent the degradation of the insulation's thermal performance. The protective covering shall cover the exposed exterior insulation and extend a minimum of 6 inches (153 mm) below grade.

N1101.8 Above code programs. Deleted.

N1101.9 Certificate. A permanent certificate shall be posted on or in the electrical distribution panel, in the attic next to the attic insulation card, or inside a kitchen cabinet or other approved location. The certificate shall not cover or obstruct the visibility of the circuit directory label, service disconnect label or other required labels. The builder, permit holder, or registered design professional shall be responsible for completing the certificate. The certificate shall list the predominant *R*-values of insulation installed in or on ceiling/roof, walls, foundation (slab, *basement wall,* crawlspace wall and floor) and ducts outside conditioned spaces; *U*-factors for fenestration and the solar heat gain coefficient (SHGC) of fenestration.

Where there is more than one value for each component, the certificate shall list the value covering the largest area. The certificate shall indicate whether the building air leakage was visually inspected as required in Section N1102.4.2.1 or provide results of the air leakage testing required in Section N1102.4.2.2 The certificate shall provide results of duct leakage test required in Section N1102.4.2.2. Appendix E-1 contains a sample certificate.

N1101.10 Additional Voluntary Criteria for Increasing Residential Energy Efficiency. Appendix E-4 contains additional voluntary measures for increasing residential energy efficiency beyond code minimums. Implementation of the increased energy efficiency measures is strictly voluntary at the option of the permit holder. The sole purpose of the appendix is to provide guidance for achieving additional residential energy efficiency improvements that have been evaluated to be those that are most cost effective for achieving an additional 15-20 percent improvement in energy efficiency beyond code minimums.

TABLE N1101.2
NORTH CAROLINA CLIMATE ZONES, MOISTURE REGIMES, AND WARM-HUMID DESIGNATIONS BY COUNTY
Key: A – Moist, B – Dry, C – Marine. Absence of moisture designation indicates moisture regime is irrelevant. Asterisk (*) indicates a warm-humid location.

NORTH CAROLINA

4A Alamance
4A Alexander
5A Alleghany
3A Anson
5A Ashe
5A Avery
3A Beaufort
4A Bertie
3A Bladen
3A Brunswick*
4A Buncombe
4A Burke
3A Cabarrus
4A Caldwell
3A Camden
3A Carteret*
4A Caswell
4A Catawba
4A Chatham
4A Cherokee
3A Chowan
4A Clay
4A Cleveland
3A Columbus*
3A Craven
3A Cumberland
3A Currituck
3A Dare
3A Davidson
4A Davie
3A Duplin
4A Durham
3A Edgecombe
4A Forsyth
4A Franklin
3A Gaston
4A Gates
4A Graham
4A Granville
3A Greene
4A Guilford
4A Halifax
4A Harnett
4A Haywood
4A Henderson
4A Hertford
3A Hoke
3A Hyde
4A Iredell
4A Jackson
3A Johnston
3A Jones
4A Lee
3A Lenoir
4A Lincoln
4A Macon
4A Madison
3A Martin
4A McDowell
3A Mecklenburg
5A Mitchell
3A Montgomery
3A Moore
4A Nash
3A New Hanover*
4A Northampton
3A Onslow*
4A Orange
3A Pamlico
3A Pasquotank
3A Pender*
3A Perquimans
4A Person
3A Pitt
4A Polk
3A Randolph
3A Richmond
3A Robeson
4A Rockingham
3A Rowan
4A Rutherford
3A Sampson
3A Scotland
3A Stanly
4A Stokes
4A Surry
4A Swain
4A Transylvania
3A Tyrrell
3A Union
4A Vance
4A Wake
4A Warren
3A Washington
5A Watauga
3A Wayne
4A Wilkes
3A Wilson
4A Yadkin
5A Yancey

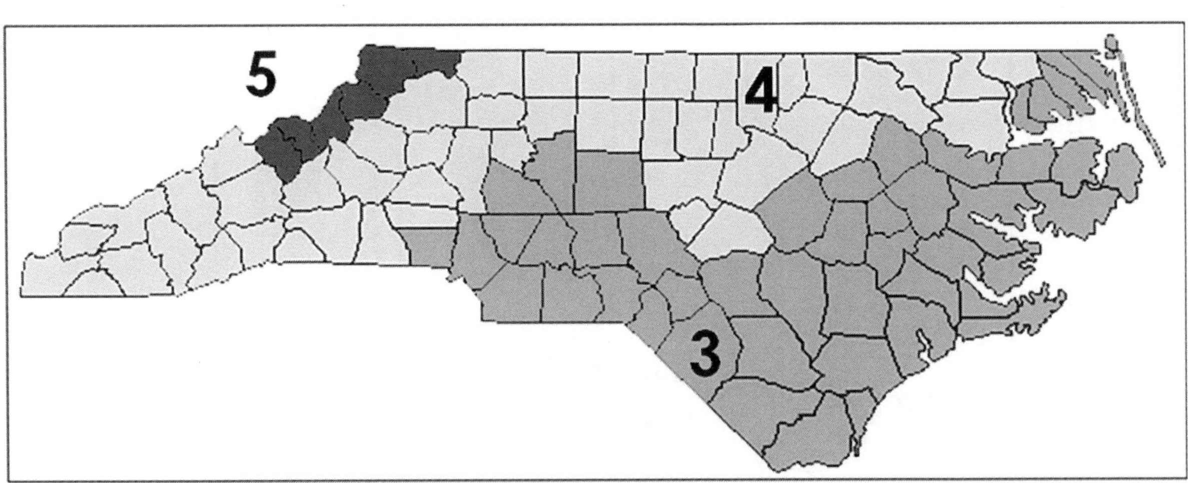

FIGURE N1101.2(1)
NORTH CAROLINA CLIMATE ZONES

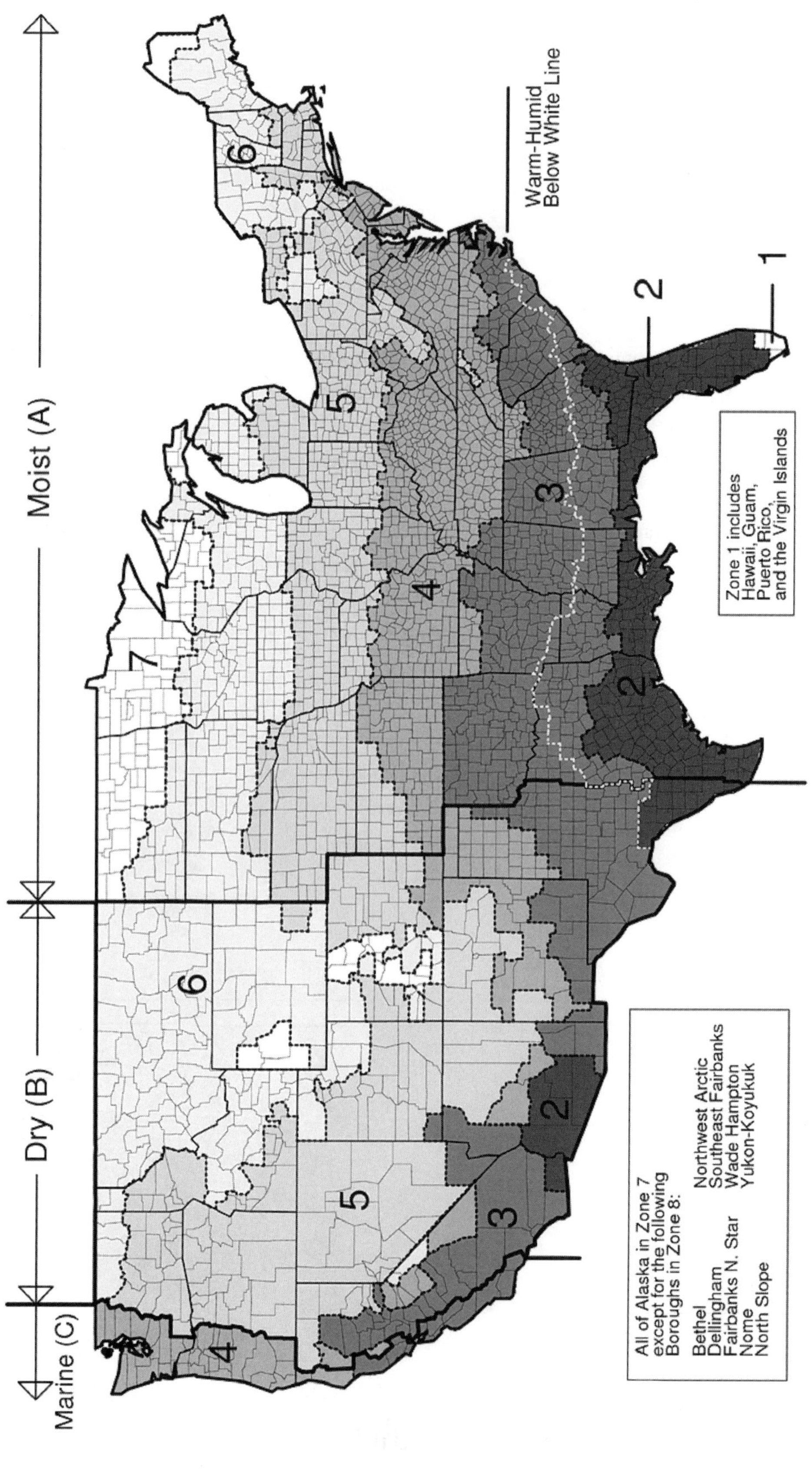
Marine (C)
Dry (B)
Moist (A)
Warm-Humid
Below White Line
1
2
3
4
5
6
7
Zone 1 includes
Hawaii, Guam,
Puerto Rico,
and the Virgin Islands
All of Alaska in Zone 7
except for the following
Boroughs in Zone 8:
Bethel
Dellingham
Fairbanks N. Star
Nome
North Slope
Northwest Arctic
Southeast Fairbanks
Wade Hampton
Yukon-Koyukuk

**FIGURE N1101.2(2)
CLIMATE ZONES**

TABLE N1101.5(1)
DEFAULT GLAZED FENESTRATION *U*-FACTORS

FRAME TYPE	SINGLE PANE	DOUBLE PANE	SKYLIGHT	
			Single	Double
Metal	1.2	0.8	2	1.3
Metal with thermal break	1.1	0.65	1.9	1.1
Nonmetal or metal clad	0.95	0.55	1.75	1.05
Glazed block	0.6			

TABLE N1101.5(2)
DEFAULT DOOR *U*-FACTORS

DOOR TYPE	*U*-FACTOR
Uninsulated metal	1.2
Insulated metal	0.6
Wood	0.5
Insulated, nonmetal edge, max 45% glazing, any glazing double pane	0.35

TABLE N1101.5(3)
DEFAULT GLAZED FENESTRATION SHGC

SINGLE GLAZED		DOUBLE GLAZED		GLAZED BLOCK
Clear	Tinted	Clear	Tinted	
0.8	0.7	0.7	0.6	0.6

SECTION N1102
BUILDING THERMAL ENVELOPE

N1102.1 Insulation and fenestration criteria. The *building thermal envelope* shall meet the requirements of Table N1102.1 based on the climate *zone* specified in Table N1101.2.

N1102.1.1 *R*-value computation. Insulation material used in layers, such as framing cavity insulation and insulating sheathing, shall be summed to compute the component *R*-value. The manufacturer's settled *R*-value shall be used for blown insulation.

Computed *R*-values shall not include an *R*-value for other building materials or air films.

N1102.1.2 *U*-factor alternative. An assembly with a *U*-factor equal to or less than that specified in Table N1102.1.2 shall be permitted as an alternative to the *R*-value in Table N1102.1.

N1102.1.3 Total UA alternative. If the total *building thermal envelope* UA (sum of *U*-factor times assembly area) is less than or equal to the total UA resulting from using the *U*-factors in Table N1102.1.2 (multiplied by the same assembly area as in the proposed building), the building shall be considered in compliance with Table N1102.1. The UA calculation shall be done using a method consistent with the ASHRAE *Handbook of Fundamentals* and shall include the thermal bridging effects of framing materials. The SHGC requirements shall be met in addition to UA compliance.

N1102.2 Specific insulation requirements.

N1102.2.1 Ceilings with attic spaces. Ceilings with attic spaces over conditioned space shall meet the insulation requirements in Table N1102.1.

Exceptions:

1. When insulation is installed in a *fully enclosed attic floor system,* as described in Appendix E 2.1, R-30 shall be deemed compliant.
2. In roof edge and other details such as bay windows, dormers, and similar areas where the space is limited, the insulation must fill the space up to the air baffle.

N1102.2.2 Ceilings without attic spaces. Where the design of the roof/ceiling assembly, including cathedral ceilings, bay windows and other similar areas, does not allow sufficient space for the required insulation, the minimum required insulation for such roof/ceiling assemblies shall be R-30. This reduction of insulation from the requirements of Section N1102.1 shall be limited to 500 square feet (46 m^2) of ceiling surface area. This reduction shall not apply to the *U*-factor alternative approach in Section N1102.1.2 and the total UA alternative in Section N1102.1.3.

TABLE N1102.1
INSULATION AND FENESTRATION REQUIREMENTS BY COMPONENT[a]

CLIMATE ZONE	FENESTRATION U-FACTOR	SKYLIGHT[b] U-FACTOR	GLAZED FENESTRATION SHGC[b, e]	CEILING R-VALUE[k]	WOOD FRAME WALL R-VALUE[e]	MASS WALL R-VALUE[i]	FLOOR R-VALUE	BASEMENT[c] WALL R-VALUE	SLAB[d] R-VALUE AND DEPTH	CRAWL SPACE[c] WALL R-VALUE
3	0.35	0.65	0.30	30	13	5/10	19	10/13[f]	0	5/13
4	0.35	0.60	0.30	38 or 30 cont.[j]	15 13 + 2.5[h]	5/10	19	10/13	10[d]	10/13
5	0.35	0.60	NR	38 or 30 cont.[j]	15, 13 + 5, or 15 + 3[e,h]	13/17	30[g]	10/13	10[d]	10/13

For SI: 1 foot = 304.8 mm.

a. *R*-values are minimums. *U*-factors and SHGC are maximums.

b. The fenestration *U*-factor column excludes skylights. The SHGC column applies to all glazed fenestration.

c. "10/13" means R-10 continuous insulated sheathing on the interior or exterior of the home or R-13 cavity insulation at the interior of the basement wall or crawl space wall.

d. For monolithic slabs, insulation shall be applied from the inspection gap downward to the bottom of the footing or a maximum of 18 inches below grade whichever is less. For floating slabs, insulation shall extend to the bottom of the foundation wall or 24 inches, whichever is less. (See Appendix O) R-5 shall be added to the required slab edge *R*-values for heated slabs.

e. R-19 fiberglass batts compressed and installed in a nominal 2 × 6 framing cavity is deemed to comply. Fiberglass batts rated R-19 or higher compressed and installed in a 2 × 4 wall is not deemed to comply.

f. Basement wall insulation is not required in warm-humid locations as defined by Figure N1101.2(1) and (2) and Table N1101.2.

g. Or insulation sufficient to fill the framing cavity, R-19 minimum.

h. "13+5" means R-13 cavity insulation plus R-5 insulated sheathing. 15+3 means R-15 cavity insulation plus R-3 insulated sheathing. If structural sheathing covers 25 percent or less of the exterior, insulating sheathing is not required where structural sheathing is used. If structural sheathing covers more than 25 percent of exterior, structural sheathing shall be supplemented with insulated sheathing of at least R-2. 13+2.5 means R-13 cavity insulation plus R-2.5 sheathing.

i. For Mass Walls, the second *R*-value applies when more than half the insulation is on the interior of the mass wall.

j. R-30 shall be deemed to satisfy the ceiling insulation requirement wherever the full height of uncompressed R-30 insulation extends over the wall top plate at the eaves. Otherwise R-38 insulation is required where adequate clearance exists or insulation must extend to either the insulation baffle or within 1" of the attic roof deck.

k. Table value required except for roof edge where the space is limited by the pitch of the roof, there the insulation must fill the space up to the air baffle.

N1102.2.3 Access hatches and doors. Horizontal access doors from conditioned spaces to unconditioned spaces (e.g., attics and crawl spaces) shall be weatherstripped and insulated to an R-10 minimum value, and vertical doors to such spaces shall be weatherstripped and insulated to R-5. Access shall be provided to all equipment that prevents damaging or compressing the insulation. A wood framed or equivalent baffle or retainer is required to be provided when loose fill insulation is installed, the purpose of which is to prevent the loose fill insulation from spilling into the living space when the attic access is opened, and to provide a permanent means of maintaining the installed *R*-value of the loose fill insulation.

Exceptions:

1. Pull down stair systems shall be weatherstripped and insulated with a minimum of R-5 insulation. The insulation shall not interfere with proper operation of the stair. Non-rigid insulation materials are not allowed. Additional insulation systems that enclose the stair system from above are allowed. Exposed foam plastic must meet the provisions of the *North Carolina Residential Code.*
2. Full size doors that are part of the building thermal envelope and provide a passageway to unconditioned spaces shall meet the requirements of exterior doors in Section N1102.3.4.

N1102.2.4 Mass walls. Mass walls for the purposes of this chapter shall be considered above-grade walls of concrete block, concrete, insulated concrete form (ICF), masonry cavity, brick (other than brick veneer), earth (adobe, compressed earth block, rammed earth) and solid timber/logs.

N1102.2.5 Steel-frame ceilings, walls, and floors. Steel-frame ceilings, walls and floors shall meet the insulation requirements of Table N1102.2.5 or shall meet the *U*-factor requirements in Table N1102.1.2. The calculation of the *U*-factor for a steel-frame envelope assembly shall use a series-parallel path calculation method.

N1102.2.6 Floors. Floor insulation shall be installed to maintain permanent contact with the underside of the subfloor decking. The distance between tension support wires or other devices that hold the floor insulation in place against the subfloor shall be no more than 18 inches. In addition, supports shall be located no further than 6 inches from each end of the insulation.

Exception: Enclosed floor cavity such as garage ceilings, cantilevers or buildings on pilings with enclosed floor cavity with the insulation fully in contact with the lower air barrier. In this case, the band boards shall be fully insulated to maintain thermal envelope continuity.

N1102.2.7 Basement walls. Walls associated with conditioned basements shall be insulated from the top of the *basement wall* down to 10 feet (3048 mm) below *grade* or to the basement floor, whichever is less. Walls associated with unconditioned basements shall meet this requirement unless the floor overhead is insulated in accordance with Sections N1102.1 and N1102.2.6.

TABLE N1102.1.2
EQUIVALENT *U*-FACTORS[a]

CLIMATE ZONE	FENESTRATION *U*-FACTOR	SKYLIGHT *U*-FACTOR	CEILING *U*-FACTOR	FRAME WALL *U*-FACTOR	MASS WALL *U*-FACTOR[b]	FLOOR *U*-FACTOR	BASEMENT WALL *U*-FACTOR[d]	CRAWL SPACE WALL *U*-FACTOR[c]
3	0.35	0.65	0.035	0.082	0.141	0.047	0.059	0.136
4	0.35	0.60	0.030	0.077	0.141	0.047	0.059	0.065
5	0.35	0.60	0.030	0.061	0.082	0.033	0.059	0.065

a. Nonfenestration *U*-factors shall be obtained from measurement, calculation or an approved source.

b. When more than half the insulation is on the interior, the mass wall *U*-factors shall be a maximum 0.12 in Zone 3, 0.10 in Zone 4, and the same as the frame wall *U*-factor in Zone 5.

c. Basement wall *U*-factor of 0.360 in warm-humid locations as defined by Figures N1101.2(1), N1101.2(2) and Table N1101.2.

d. Foundation *U*-factor requirements shown in Table N1102.1.2 include wall construction and interior air films but exclude soil conductivity and exterior air films. *U*-factors for determining code compliance in accordance with Section N1102.1.3 (total UA alternative) shall be modified to include soil conductivity and exterior air films.

TABLE N1102.2.5
STEEL-FRAME CEILING, WALL AND FLOOR INSULATION (*R*-VALUE)

WOOD FRAME *R*-VALUE REQUIREMENT	COLD-FORMED STEEL EQUIVALENT *R*-VALUE[a]
Steel Truss Ceilings[a]	
R-30	R-38 or R-30 + 3 or R-26 + 5
R-38	R-49 or R-38 + 3
R-49	R-38 + 5
Steel Joist Ceilings[b]	
R-30	R-38 in 2 × 4 or 2 × 6 or 2 × 8 R-49 in any framing
R-38	R-49 in 2 × 4 or 2 × 6 or 2 × 8 or 2 × 10
Steel Framed Wall	
R-13	R-13 + 5 or R-15 + 4 or R-21 + 3
R-19	R-13 + 9 or R-19 + 8 or R-25 + 7
R-21	R-13 +10 or R-19 + 9 or R-25 + 8
Steel Joist Floor	
R-13	R-19 in 2 × 6 R-19 + R-6 in 2 × 8 or 2 ×10
R-19	R-19 + R-6 in 2 × 6 R-19 + R-12 in 2 × 8 or 2 × 10

a. Cavity insulation *R*-value is listed first, followed by continuous insulation *R*-value.

b. Insulation exceeding the height of the framing shall cover the framing.

N1102.2.8 Slab-on-grade floors. Slab-on-grade floors with a floor surface less than 12 inches (305 mm) below grade shall be insulated in accordance with Table N1102.1. The top edge of the insulation installed between the *exterior wall* and the edge of the interior slab shall be permitted to be cut at a 45-degree (0.79 rad) angle away from the *exterior wall*. Slab edge insulation shall have 2 inch termite inspection gap consistent with Appendix O of this code.

N1102.2.9 Closed crawl space walls. Where the floor above a closed crawl space is not insulated, the exterior crawlspace walls shall be insulated in accordance with table 1102.1.

Wall insulation may be located in any combination of the outside and inside wall surfaces and within the structural cavities or materials of the wall system.

Wall insulation requires that the exterior wall band joist area of the floor frame be insulated. Wall insulation shall begin 3 inches (76.2 mm) below the top of the masonry foundation wall and shall extend down to 3 inches (76.2 mm) above the top of the footing or concrete floor, 3 inches (76.2 mm) above the interior ground surface or 24 inches (609.6 mm) below the outside finished ground level, whichever is less. (See Appendix E-2.2 details.)

Termite inspection, clearance, and wicking gaps are allowed in wall insulation systems. Insulation may be omitted in the gap area without energy penalty. The allowable insulation gap widths are listed in Table N1102.2.9. If gap width exceeds the allowances, one of the following energy compliance options shall be met:

1. Wall insulation is not allowed and the required insulation value shall be provided in the floor system.
2. Compliance shall be demonstrated with energy trade-off methods provided by a North Carolina-specific version of RESCHECK.

TABLE N1102.2.9
WALL INSULATION ALLOWANCES FOR TERMITE TREATMENT AND INSULATION GAPS

MAXIMUM GAP WIDTH (inches)	INSULATION LOCATION	GAP DESCRIPTION
3	Outside	Above grade inspection between top of insulation and bottom of siding
6	Outside	Below grade treatment
4[a]	Inside	Wall inspection between top of insulation and bottom of sill
		Clearance/wicking space between bottom of insulation and top of ground surface, footing, or concrete floor.

For SI: 1 inch = 25.4 mm.

a. No insulation shall be required on masonry wall of 9 inches in height or less.

N1102.2.10 Masonry veneer. Insulation shall not be required on the horizontal portion of the foundation that supports a masonry veneer.

N1102.2.11 Thermally isolated conditioned sunroom insulation. The minimum ceiling insulation *R*-values shall be R-19 in Zones 3 and 4, and R-24 in Zone 5. The minimum wall *R*-value shall be R-13. New wall(s) separating a sunroom from *conditioned space* shall meet the *building thermal envelope* requirements. Floor and slab insulation shall comply with values in Table N1102.1.

N1102.2.12 Framed cavity walls. The exterior thermal envelope wall insulation shall be installed in substantial contact and continuous alignment with the building envelope air barrier. Insulation shall be substantially free from installation gaps, voids, or compression. For framed walls, the cavity insulation shall be enclosed on all sides with a rigid material or an air barrier material. Wall insulation shall be enclosed at the following locations when installed on exterior walls prior to being covered by subsequent construction, consistent with Appendix E-2.3 of this code:

1. Tubs
2. Showers
3. Stairs
4. Fireplace units

Enclosure of wall cavity insulation also applies to walls that adjoin attic spaces by placing a rigid material or air barrier material on the attic space side of the wall on the attic space side of the wall.

N1102.3 Fenestration.

N1102.3.1 *U*-factor. An area-weighted average of fenestration products shall be permitted to satisfy the *U*-factor requirements.

N1102.3.2 Glazed fenestration SHGC. An area-weighted average of fenestration products more than 50 percent glazed shall be permitted to satisfy the SHGC requirements.

N1102.3.3 Glazed fenestration exemption. Up to 15 square feet (1.4 m^2) of glazed fenestration per dwelling unit shall be permitted to be exempt from *U*-factor and SHGC requirements in Section N1102.1. This exemption shall not apply to the *U*-factor alternative approach in Section N1102.1.2 and the Total UA alternative in Section N1102.1.3.

N1102.3.4 Opaque door. Opaque doors separating conditioned and unconditioned space shall have a maximum *U*-factor of 0.35.

Exception: One side-hinged opaque door assembly up to 24 square feet (2.22 m^2) in area is exempted from the *U*-factor requirement in Section N1102.1. This exemption shall not apply to the *U*-factor alternative approach in Section N1102.1.2 and the Total UA alternative in Section N1102.1.3.

N1102.3.5 Thermally isolated conditioned sunroom *U*-factor and SHGC. The maximum fenestration *U*-factor shall be 0.40 and the maximum skylight *U*-factor shall be 0.75. Sunrooms with cooling systems shall have a maximum fenestration SHGC of 0.40 for all glazing.

New windows and doors separating the sunroom from conditioned space shall meet the building thermal envelope requirements. Sunroom additions shall maintain thermal isolation; and shall be served by a separate heating or cooling system, or be thermostatically controlled as a separate zone of the existing system.

N1102.3.6 Replacement fenestration. Where an entire existing fenestration unit is replaced with a new fenestration product, including frame, sash and glazing, the replacement fenestration unit shall meet the applicable requirements for *U*-factor and SHGC in Table N1102.1.

N1102.4 Air leakage control.

N1102.4.1 Building thermal envelope. The *building thermal envelope* shall be durably sealed with an air barrier system to limit infiltration. The sealing methods between dissimilar materials shall allow for differential expansion and contraction. For all homes, where present, the following shall be caulked, gasketed, weatherstripped or otherwise sealed with an air barrier material or solid material consistent with Appendix E-2.4 of this code:

1. Blocking and sealing floor/ceiling systems and under knee walls open to unconditioned or exterior space.
2. Capping and sealing shafts or chases, including flue shafts.
3. Capping and sealing soffit or dropped ceiling areas.

N1102.4.2 Air sealing. Building envelope air tightness shall be demonstrated by Section N1102.4.2.1 or N1102.4.2.2. Appendix E-3 contains optional sample worksheets for visual inspection or testing for the permit holder's use only.

N1102.4.2.1 Visual inspection option. Building envelope tightness shall be considered acceptable when items providing insulation enclosure in Section N1102.2.12 and air sealing in Section N1102.4.1 are addressed and when the items listed in Table N1102.4.2, applicable to the method of construction, are certified by the builder, permit holder or registered design professional via the certificate in Appendix E-1.

N1102.4.2.2 Testing option. Building envelope tightness shall be considered acceptable when items providing insulation enclosure in Section N1102.2.12 and air sealing in Section N1102.4.1 are addressed and when tested air leakage is less than or equal to one of the two following performance measurements:

1. 0.30 CFM50/square foot of surface area (SFSA) or
2. Five (5) air changes per hour (ACH50)

when tested with a blower door fan assembly, at a pressure of 33.5 psf (50 Pa). A single point depressurization, not temperature corrected, test is sufficient to comply with this provision, provided that the blower door fan assembly has been certified by the manufacturer to be capable of conducting tests in accordance with ASTM E 779-03. Testing shall occur after rough in and after installation of penetrations of the building envelope, including penetrations for utilities, plumbing, electrical, ventilation and combustion appliances. Testing shall be reported by the permit holder, a NC licensed general contractor, a NC licensed HVAC contractor, a NC licensed Home Inspector, a registered design professional, a *certified BPI Envelope Professional or a certified HERS rater.*

During testing:

1. Exterior windows and doors, fireplace and stove doors shall be closed, but not sealed;
2. Dampers shall be closed, but not sealed, including exhaust, backdraft, and flue dampers;
3. Interior doors shall be open;
4. Exterior openings for continuous ventilation systems, air intake ducted to the return side of the conditioning system, and energy or heat recovery ventilators shall be closed and sealed;
5. Heating and cooling system(s) shall be turned off; and
6. Supply and return registers shall not be sealed.

The air leakage information, including building air leakage result, tester name, date, and contact information, shall be included on the certificate described in Section N1101.9.

TABLE N1102.4.2
AIR BARRIER INSPECTION

COMPONENT	CRITERIA
Ceiling/attic	Sealants or gaskets provide a continuous air barrier system joining the top plate of framed walls with either the ceiling drywall or the top edge of wall drywall to prevent air leakage. Top plate penetrations are sealed. For ceiling finishes that are not air barrier systems such as tongue-and-groove planks, air barrier systems,(for example, taped house wrap), shall be used above the finish **Note:** It is acceptable that sealants or gaskets applied as part of the application of the drywall will not be observable by the code official.
Walls	Sill plate is gasketed or sealed to subfloor or slab.
Windows and doors	Space between window and exterior door jambs and framing is sealed.
Floors (including above garage and cantilevered floors)	Air barrier system is installed at any exposed edge of insulation.
Penetrations	Utility penetrations through the building thermal envelope, including those for plumbing, electrical wiring, ductwork, security and fire alarm wiring, and control wiring, shall be sealed.
Garage separation	Air sealing is provided between the garage and conditioned spaces. An air barrier system shall be installed between the ceiling system above the garage and the ceiling system of interior spaces.
Duct boots	Sealing HVAC register boots and return boxes to subfloor or drywall.
Recessed lighting	Recessed light fixtures are airtight, IC rated and sealed to drywall. **Exception**—fixtures in conditioned space.

For Test Criteria 1 above, the report shall be produced in the following manner: perform the blower door test and record the *CFM50*. Calculate the total square feet of surface area for the building thermal envelope (all floors, ceilings, and walls, including windows and doors, bounding conditioned space) and record the area. Divide *CFM50* by the total square feet and record the result. If the result is less than or equal to 0.30 CFM50/SFSA the envelope tightness is acceptable; or

For Test Criteria 2 above, the report shall be produced in the following manner: perform a blower door test and record the *CFM50*. Multiply the *CFM50* by 60 minutes to create CFHour50 and record. Then calculate the total conditioned volume of the home and record. Divide the *CFH50* by the total volume and record the result. If the result is less than or equal to 5 ACH50 the envelope tightness is acceptable.

N1102.4.3 Fireplaces. Site-built masonry fireplaces shall have doors and comply with Section R1006 of the *North Carolina Residential Code* for combustion air.

N1102.4.4 Fenestration air leakage. Windows, skylights and sliding glass doors shall have an air infiltration rate of no more than 0.3 cfm per square foot (1.5 L/s/m^2), and swinging doors no more than 0.5 cfm per square foot (2.6 L/s/m^2), when tested according to NFRC 400 or AAMA/WDMA/CSA 101/I.S.2/A440 by an accredited, independent laboratory and *listed* and *labeled* by the manufacturer.

Exception: Site-built windows, skylights and doors.

N1102.4.5 Recessed lighting. Recessed luminaires installed in the *building thermal envelope* shall be sealed to limit air leakage between conditioned and unconditioned spaces. All recessed luminaires shall be IC-rated and *labeled* as meeting ASTM E 283 when tested at 1.57 psf (75 Pa) pressure differential with no more than 2.0 cfm (0.944 L/s) of air movement from the *conditioned space* to the ceiling cavity. All recessed luminaires shall be sealed with a gasket or caulk between the housing and the interior wall or ceiling covering.

N1102.5 Maximum fenestration *U*-factor and SHGC. The area-weighted average maximum fenestration *U*-factor permitted using trade-offs from Section 1102.1.3 shall be 0.40. Maximum skylight *U*-factors shall be 0.65 in zones 4 and 5 and 0.60 in zone 3.

SECTION N1103
SYSTEMS

N1103.1 Controls. At least one thermostat shall be provided for each separate heating and cooling system.

N1103.1.1 Programmable thermostat. Where the primary heating system is a forced-air furnace, at least one thermostat per dwelling unit shall be capable of controlling the heating and cooling system on a daily schedule to maintain different temperature set points at different times of the day. This thermostat shall include the capability to set back or temporarily operate the system to maintain zone temperatures down to 55°F (13°C) or up to 85°F (29°C).

N1103.1.2 Heat pump supplementary heat. Heat pumps having supplementary electric-resistance heat shall have controls that, except during defrost, prevent supplemental heat operation when the heat pump compressor can meet the heating load.

A heat strip outdoor temperature lockout shall be provided to prevent supplemental heat operation in response to the thermostat being changed to a warmer setting. The lockout shall be set no lower than 35°F and no higher than 40°F.

1103.1.3 Maintenance information. Maintenance instructions shall be furnished for equipment and systems that require preventive maintenance.

N1103.2 Ducts.

N1103.2.1 Insulation. Supply and return ducts in unconditioned space and outdoors shall be insulated to R-8. Supply ducts inside semiconditioned space shall be insulated to R-4; return ducts inside conditioned and semi-conditioned space are not required to be insulated. Ducts located inside conditioned space are not required to be insulated other than as may be necessary for preventing the formation of condensation on the exterior of cooling ducts.

N1103.2.2 Sealing. All ducts, air handlers, filter boxes and building cavities used as ducts shall be sealed. Joints and seams shall comply with Part V—Mechanical, Section 603.9 of the *North Carolina Residential Code.*

Duct tightness shall be verified as follows:

Total duct leakage less than or equal to 6 CFM (18 L/min) per 100 ft^2 (9.29 m^2) of *conditioned floor area* served by that system when tested at a pressure differential of 0.1 inches w.g. (25 Pa) across the entire system, including the manufacturer's air handler enclosure.

During testing:

1. Block, if present, the ventilation air duct connected to the conditioning system.
2. The duct air leakage testing equipment shall be attached to the largest return in the system or to the air handler.
3. The filter shall be removed and the air handler power shall be turned off.
4. Supply boots or registers and return boxes or grilles shall be taped, plugged, or otherwise sealed air tight.
5. The hose for measuring the 25 Pascals of pressure differential shall be inserted into the boot of the supply that is nominally closest to the air handler.
6. Specific instructions from the duct testing equipment manufacturer shall be followed to reach duct test pressure and measure duct air leakage.

Testing shall be performed and reported by the permit holder, a North Carolina licensed general contractor, a North Carolina licensed HVAC contractor, a North Carolina licensed Home Inspector, a registered design professional, a certified BPI Envelope Professional or a certified HERS rater.

A single point depressurization, not temperature corrected, test is sufficient to comply with this provision, provided that the duct testing fan assembly has been certified by the manufacturer to be capable of conducting tests in accordance with ASTM E 1554-07.

The duct leakage information, including duct leakage result, tester name, date, and contact information, shall be included on the certificate described in Section N1101.9.

For the Test Criteria, the report shall be produced in the following manner: perform the HVAC system air leakage test and record the CFM25. Calculate the total square feet of Conditioned Floor Area (CFA) served by that system. Multiply the CFM25 by 100, then divide by the Conditioned Floor Area to find the CFM25/100SF and record the result. If the result is less than or equal to 6CFM25/100 SF the HVAC system air tightness is acceptable. Appendix E-3C contains optional sample worksheets for duct testing for the permit holder's use only.

Exceptions to testing requirements:

1. Duct systems or portions thereof inside the building thermal envelope shall not be required to be leak tested.
2. Installation of a partial system as part of replacement, renovation or addition does not require a duct leakage test.

N1103.2.3 Building cavities. Building framing cavities shall not be used as supply ducts.

N1103.3 Mechanical system piping insulation. Mechanical system piping capable of carrying fluids above 105°F (41°C) or below 55°F (13°C) shall be insulated to a minimum of R-3.

N1103.4 Circulating hot water systems. All circulating service hot water piping shall be insulated to at least R-2. Circulating hot water systems shall include an automatic or readily *accessible* manual switch that can turn off the hot water circulating pump when the system is not in use.

N1103.5 Mechanical ventilation. Exhausts shall have automatic or gravity dampers that close when the ventilation system is not operating.

N1103.6 Equipment sizing and efficiency.

N1103.6.1 Equipment sizing. Heating and cooling equipment shall be sized in accordance with the mechanical section of the *North Carolina Residential Code.*

N1103.6.2 Equipment Efficiencies. Equipment efficiencies shall comply with the current NAECA minimum standards.

N1103.7 Snow melt system controls. Snow- and ice-melting systems, supplied through energy service to the building, shall include automatic controls capable of shutting off the system when the pavement temperature is above 50°F, and no precipitation is falling and an automatic or manual control that will allow shutoff when the outdoor temperature is above 40°F.

N1103.8 Pools, inground permanently installed spas (Mandatory). Pools and inground permanently installed spas shall comply with Sections N1103.8.1 through N1103.8.3.

N1103.8.1 Heaters. All heaters shall be equipped with a readily accessible on-off switch that is mounted outside of the heater to allow shutting off the heater without adjusting the thermostat setting. Gas-fired heaters shall not be equipped with constant burning pilot lights.

N1103.8.2 Time switches. Time switches or other control method that can automatically turn off and on heaters and pumps according to a preset schedule shall be installed on all heaters and pumps. Heaters, pumps and motors that have built-in timers shall be deemed in compliance with this requirement.

Exceptions:

1. Where public health standards require 24-hour pump operation.
2. Where pumps are required to operate solar- and waste-heat-recovery pool heating systems.

N1103.8.3 Covers. Heated pools and inground permanently installed spas shall be provided with a vapor-retardant pool cover.

Exception: Pools deriving over 70 percent of the energy for heating from site-recovered energy, such as a heat pump or solar energy source computed over an operating season.

SECTION N1104
LIGHTING SYSTEMS

N1104.1 Lighting equipment. A minimum of 75 percent of the *lamps* in permanently installed lighting fixtures shall be *high-efficacy lamps.*

Part V — Mechanical

CHAPTERS 12 THROUGH 23

Deleted

The following text is extracted from the 2012 *North Carolina Mechanical Code* and has been modified where necessary to conform to the scope of application of the 2012 *North Carolina Residential Code for One-and Two-Family Dwellings*. The section numbers appearing in Part V are the section numbers of the corresponding text in the *North Carolina Mechanical Code*. Where differences occur between the provisions of this abridged text and the *North Carolina Mechanical Code*, the provisions of the *North Carolina Mechanical Code* shall apply. Requirements not specifically covered by this text shall conform to the *North Carolina Mechanical Code*.

Part V
North Carolina State Building Code:
Mechanical Code
Abridged for Residential Code

(2009 IMC® with North Carolina Amendments)

Abridged Residential Code Edition

2012

TABLE OF CONTENTS

CHAPTER 9 SPECIFIC APPLIANCES, FIREPLACES AND SOLID FUEL-BURNING EQUIPMENT 487

Section

CHAPTER 10 BOILERS, WATER HEATERS AND PRESSURE VESSELS 493

Section

CHAPTER 11 REFRIGERATION 497

Section

CHAPTER 12 HYDRONIC PIPING 499

Section

CHAPTER 13 FUEL OIL PIPING AND STORAGE 505

Section

CHAPTER 1
SCOPE AND ADMINISTRATION

PART I—SCOPE AND APPLICATION

SECTION 101
GENERAL

101.1 Title. These regulations shall be known as the *North Carolina Mechanical Code* as adopted by the North Carolina Building Code Council on September 14, 2010, to be effective September 1, 2011. References to the *International Codes* shall mean the North Carolina Codes. The North Carolina amendments to the *International Codes* are underlined.

101.2 Scope. This code shall regulate the design, installation, maintenance, *alteration* and inspection of mechanical systems that are permanently installed and utilized to provide control of environmental conditions and related processes within buildings. This code shall also regulate those mechanical systems, system components, *equipment* and appliances specifically addressed herein. The installation of fuel gas distribution piping and *equipment*, fuel gas-fired appliances and fuel gas-fired *appliance* venting systems shall be regulated by the *International Fuel Gas Code.*

> **Exception:** Detached one- and two-family dwellings and multiple single-family dwellings (townhouses) not more than three stories high with separate means of egress and their accessory structures shall comply with the *International Residential Code.*

101.2.1 Appendices. Provisions in the appendices shall not apply unless specifically adopted or referenced in this code.

101.3 Intent. The purpose of this code is to provide minimum standards to safeguard life or limb, health, property and public welfare by regulating and controlling the design, construction, installation, quality of materials, location, operation and maintenance or use of mechanical systems.

101.4 Severability. If a section, subsection, sentence, clause or phrase of this code is, for any reason, held to be unconstitutional, such decision shall not affect the validity of the remaining portions of this code.

101.5 Requirements of other State agencies, occupational licensing boards or commissions. The North Carolina State Building Codes do not include all additional requirements for buildings and structures that may be imposed by other State agencies, occupational licensing boards and commissions. It shall be the responsibility of a permit holder, registered design professional, contractor or occupational license holder to determine whether any additional requirements exist.

SECTION 102
APPLICABILITY

102.1 General. Where there is a conflict between a general requirement and a specific requirement, the specific requirement shall govern. Where, in a specific case, different sections of this code specify different materials, methods of construction or other requirements, the most restrictive shall govern.

102.2 Existing installations. Except as otherwise provided for in this chapter, a provision in this code shall not require the removal, *alteration* or abandonment of, nor prevent the continued utilization and maintenance of, a mechanical system lawfully in existence at the time of the adoption of this code.

102.3 Maintenance. Mechanical systems, both existing and new, and parts thereof shall be maintained in proper operating condition in accordance with the original design and in a safe and sanitary condition. Devices or safeguards which are required by this code shall be maintained in compliance with the code edition under which they were installed. The owner or the owner's designated agent shall be responsible for maintenance of mechanical systems. To determine compliance with this provision, the code official shall have the authority to require a mechanical system to be reinspected.

102.4 Additions, alterations or repairs. Additions, alterations, renovations or repairs to a mechanical system shall conform to that required for a new mechanical system without requiring the existing mechanical system to comply with all of the requirements of this code. Additions, alterations or repairs shall not cause an existing mechanical system to become unsafe, hazardous or overloaded.

Minor additions, alterations, renovations and repairs to existing mechanical systems shall meet the provisions for new construction, unless such work is done in the same manner and arrangement as was in the existing system, is not hazardous and is *approved.*

102.5 Change in occupancy. It shall be unlawful to make a change in the *occupancy* of any structure which will subject the structure to any special provision of this code applicable to the new *occupancy* without approval. The code official shall certify that such structure meets the intent of the provisions of law governing building construction for the proposed new *occupancy* and that such change of *occupancy* does not result in any hazard to the public health, safety or welfare.

102.6 Historic buildings. The provisions of this code relating to the construction, *alteration*, repair, enlargement, restoration, relocation or moving of buildings or structures shall not be mandatory for existing buildings or structures identified and classified by the state or local jurisdiction as historic buildings when such buildings or structures are judged by the code official to be safe and in the public interest of health, safety and welfare regarding any proposed construction, *alteration*, repair, enlargement, restoration, relocation or moving of buildings.

102.7 Moved buildings. Except as determined by Section 102.2, mechanical systems that are a part of buildings or structures moved into or within the jurisdiction shall comply with the provisions of this code for new installations.

102.8 Referenced codes and standards. The codes and standards referenced herein shall be those that are listed in Chapter 15 and such codes and standards shall be considered as part of the requirements of this code to the prescribed extent of each such reference. Where differences occur between provisions of this code and the referenced standards, the provisions of this code shall apply.

Exception: Where enforcement of a code provision would violate the conditions of the listing of the *equipment* or *appliance*, the conditions of the listing and the manufacturer's installation instructions shall apply.

102.9 Requirements not covered by this code. Requirements necessary for the strength, stability or proper operation of an existing or proposed mechanical system, or for the public safety, health and general welfare, not specifically covered by this code, shall be determined by the code official.

102.10 Other laws. The provisions of this code shall not be deemed to nullify any provisions of local, state or federal law.

102.11 Application of references. Reference to chapter section numbers, or to provisions not specifically identified by number, shall be construed to refer to such chapter, section or provision of this code.

PART 2—ADMINISTRATION AND ENFORCEMENT

SECTION 103 DEPARTMENT OF MECHANICAL INSPECTION

Deleted. See the North Carolina Administrative Code and Policies.

SECTION 104 DUTIES AND POWERS OF THE CODE OFFICIAL

Deleted. See the North Carolina Administrative Code and Policies.

SECTION 105 APPROVAL

105.1 Modifications. Whenever there are practical difficulties involved in carrying out the provisions of this code, the code official shall have the authority to grant modifications for individual cases upon application of the owner or owner's representative, provided that the code official shall first find that special individual reason makes the strict letter of this code impractical and the modification is in compliance with the intent and purpose of this code and does not lessen health, life and fire safety requirements. The details of action granting modifications shall be recorded and entered in the files of the mechanical inspection department.

105.2 Alternative materials, methods, equipment and appliances. The provisions of this code are not intended to prevent the installation of any material or to prohibit any method of construction not specifically prescribed by this code, provided that any such alternative has been *approved*. An alternative material or method of construction shall be *approved* where the code official finds that the proposed design is satisfactory and complies with the intent of the provisions of this code, and that the material, method or work offered is, for the purpose intended, at least the equivalent of that prescribed in this code in quality, strength, effectiveness, fire resistance, durability and safety.

105.2.1 Research reports. Supporting data, where necessary to assist in the approval of materials or assemblies not specifically provided for in this code, shall consist of valid research reports from *approved* sources.

105.3 Required testing. Whenever there is insufficient evidence of compliance with the provisions of this code, or evidence that a material or method does not conform to the requirements of this code, or in order to substantiate claims for alternative materials or methods, the code official shall have the authority to require tests as evidence of compliance to be made at no expense to the jurisdiction.

105.3.1 Test methods. Test methods shall be as specified in this code or by other recognized test standards. In the absence of recognized and accepted test methods, the code official shall approve the testing procedures.

105.3.2 Testing agency. All tests shall be performed by an *approved* agency.

105.3.3 Test reports. Reports of tests shall be retained by the code official for the period required for retention of public records.

105.4 Approved materials and equipment. Materials, *equipment* and devices *approved* by the code official shall be constructed and installed in accordance with such approval.

105.5 Material, equipment and appliance reuse. Materials, *equipment*, appliances and devices shall not be reused unless such elements have been reconditioned, tested and placed in good and proper working condition and *approved*.

SECTION 106 PERMITS

Deleted. See the North Carolina Administrative Code and Policies.

SECTION 107 INSPECTIONS AND TESTING

Deleted. See the North Carolina Administrative Code and Policies.

SECTION 108 VIOLATIONS

Deleted. See the North Carolina Administrative Code and Policies.

SECTION 109 MEANS OF APPEAL

Deleted. See the North Carolina Administrative Code and Policies.

SECTION 110
TEMPORARY EQUIPMENT, SYSTEMS AND USES

110.1 General. The code official is authorized to issue a permit for temporary *equipment*, systems and uses. Such permits shall be limited as to time of service, but shall not be permitted for more than 180 days. The code official is authorized to grant extensions for demonstrated cause.

110.2 Conformance. Temporary *equipment*, systems and uses shall conform to the structural strength, fire safety, means of egress, accessibility, light, ventilation and sanitary requirements of this code as necessary to ensure the public health, safety and general welfare.

110.3 Temporary utilities. The code official is authorized to give permission to temporarily supply utilities before an installation has been fully completed and the final certificate of completion has been issued. The part covered by the temporary certificate shall comply with the requirements specified for temporary lighting, heat or power in the code.

110.4 Termination of approval. The code official is authorized to terminate such permit for temporary *equipment*, systems or uses and to order the temporary *equipment*, systems or uses to be discontinued.

CHAPTER 2
DEFINITIONS

SECTION 201
GENERAL

201.1 Scope. Unless otherwise expressly stated, the following words and terms shall, for the purposes of this code, have the meanings indicated in this chapter.

201.2 Interchangeability. Words used in the present tense include the future; words in the masculine gender include the feminine and neuter; the singular number includes the plural and the plural, the singular.

201.3 Terms defined in other codes. Where terms are not defined in this code and are defined in the *International Building Code, International Fire Code, International Fuel Gas Code* or the *International Plumbing Code*, such terms shall have meanings ascribed to them as in those codes.

201.4 Terms not defined. Where terms are not defined through the methods authorized by this section, such terms shall have ordinarily accepted meanings such as the context implies.

SECTION 202
GENERAL DEFINITIONS

ABRASIVE MATERIALS. Deleted.

ABSORPTION SYSTEM. Deleted.

ACCESS (TO). That which enables a device, *appliance* or *equipment* to be reached by ready access or by a means that first requires the removal or movement of a panel, door or similar obstruction [see also "Ready access (to)"].

AIR. All air supplied to mechanical *equipment* and appliances for *combustion*, ventilation, cooling, etc. Standard air is air at standard temperature and pressure, namely, 70°F (21°C) and 29.92 inches of mercury (101.3 kPa).

AIR CONDITIONING. The treatment of air so as to control simultaneously the temperature, humidity, cleanness and distribution of the air to meet the requirements of a conditioned space.

AIR-CONDITIONING SYSTEM. A system that consists of heat exchangers, blowers, filters, supply, exhaust and return ducts, and shall include any apparatus installed in connection therewith.

AIR DISPERSION SYSTEM. Deleted.

AIR DISTRIBUTION SYSTEM. Any system of ducts, plenums and air-handling *equipment* that circulates air within a space or spaces and includes systems made up of one or more air-handling units.

AIR, EXHAUST. Air being removed from any space, *appliance* or piece of *equipment* and conveyed directly to the atmosphere by means of openings or ducts.

AIR-HANDLING UNIT. A blower or fan used for the purpose of distributing supply air to a room, space or area.

AIR, MAKEUP. Air that is provided to replace air being exhausted.

ALTERATION. A change in a mechanical system that involves an extension, addition or change to the arrangement, type or purpose of the original installation.

APPLIANCE. A device or apparatus that is manufactured and designed to utilize energy and for which this code provides specific requirements.

APPLIANCE, EXISTING. Any *appliance* regulated by this code which was legally installed prior to the effective date of this code, or for which a permit to install has been issued.

APPLIANCE TYPE.

High-heat appliance. Deleted.

Low-heat appliance (residential appliance). Any *appliance* in which the products of *combustion* at the point of entrance to the flue under normal operating conditions have a temperature of 1,000°F (538°C) or less.

Medium-heat appliance. Deleted.

APPLIANCE, VENTED. An *appliance* designed and installed in such a manner that all of the products of *combustion* are conveyed directly from the *appliance* to the outdoor atmosphere through an *approved chimney* or vent system.

APPROVED. Acceptable to the code official for compliance with the provisions of the applicable code or referenced standard.

APPROVED AGENCY. An established and recognized agency that is *approved* by the code official and regularly engaged in conducting tests or furnishing inspection services.

AUTOMATIC BOILER. Any class of boiler that is equipped with the controls and limit devices specified in Chapter 10.

BATHROOM. A room containing a bathtub, shower, spa or similar bathing fixture.

BOILER. A closed heating *appliance* intended to supply hot water or steam for space heating, processing or power purposes. Low-pressure boilers operate at pressures less than or equal to 15 pounds per square inch (psi) (103 kPa) for steam and 160 psi (1103 kPa) for water. High-pressure boilers operate at pressures exceeding those pressures.

BOILER ROOM. A room primarily utilized for the installation of a boiler.

BRAZED JOINT. A gas-tight joint obtained by the joining of metal parts with metallic mixtures or alloys which melt at a temperature above 1,000°F (538°C), but lower than the melting temperature of the parts to be joined.

BRAZING. A metal joining process wherein coalescence is produced by the use of a nonferrous filler metal having a melting point above 1,000°F (538°C), but lower than that of the base metal being joined. The filler material is distributed between the closely fitted surfaces of the joint by capillary attraction.

BREATHING ZONE. The region within an occupied space between planes 3 and 72 inches (76 and 1829 mm) above the floor and more than 2 feet (610 mm) from the walls of the space or from fixed air-conditioning *equipment*.

BTU. Abbreviation for British thermal unit, which is the quantity of heat required to raise the temperature of 1 pound (454 g) of water 1°F (0.56°C) (1 Btu = 1055 J).

BUILDING. Any structure occupied or intended for supporting or sheltering any *occupancy*.

CEILING RADIATION DAMPER. Deleted.

CHIMNEY. A primarily vertical structure containing one or more flues, for the purpose of carrying gaseous products of *combustion* and air from a fuel-burning *appliance* to the outdoor atmosphere.

Factory-built chimney. A *listed* and *labeled chimney* composed of factory-made components, assembled in the field in accordance with manufacturer's instructions and the conditions of the listing.

Masonry chimney. A field-constructed *chimney* composed of solid masonry units, bricks, stones or concrete.

Metal chimney. A field-constructed *chimney* of metal.

CHIMNEY CONNECTOR. A pipe that connects a fuel-burning *appliance* to a *chimney*.

CLEARANCE. The minimum distance through air measured between the heat-producing surface of the mechanical *appliance*, device or *equipment* and the surface of the combustible material or assembly.

CLOSED COMBUSTION SOLID-FUEL-BURNING APPLIANCE. A heat-producing *appliance* that employs a *combustion* chamber that has no openings other than the flue collar, fuel charging door and adjustable openings provided to control the amount of *combustion air* that enters the *combustion* chamber.

CLOSET. An enclosed or recessed area used to store clothing, linens or other household items.

CLOTHES DRYER. An *appliance* used to dry wet laundry by means of heat. Dryer classifications are as follows:

Type 1. Factory-built package, multiple production. Primarily used in family living environment. Usually the smallest unit physically and in function output.

Type 2. Deleted.

CODE. These regulations, subsequent amendments thereto, or any emergency rule or regulation that the administrative authority having jurisdiction has lawfully adopted.

CODE OFFICIAL. The officer or other designated authority charged with the administration and enforcement of this code, or a duly authorized representative.

COMBINATION FIRE/SMOKE DAMPER. Deleted.

COMBUSTIBLE ASSEMBLY. Wall, floor, ceiling or other assembly constructed of one or more component materials that are not defined as noncombustible.

COMBUSTIBLE LIQUIDS. Deleted.

COMBUSTIBLE MATERIAL. Any material not defined as noncombustible.

COMBUSTION. In the context of this code, refers to the rapid oxidation of fuel accompanied by the production of heat or heat and light.

COMBUSTION AIR. Air necessary for complete *combustion* of a fuel, including *theoretical air* and excess air.

COMBUSTION CHAMBER. The portion of an *appliance* within which *combustion* occurs.

COMBUSTION PRODUCTS. Constituents resulting from the *combustion* of a fuel with the oxygen of the air, including the inert gases, but excluding excess air.

COMMERCIAL COOKING APPLIANCES. Appliances used in a commercial food service establishment for heating or cooking food and which produce grease vapors, steam, fumes, smoke or odors that are required to be removed through a local exhaust ventilation system. Such appliances include deep fat fryers; upright broilers; griddles; broilers; steam-jacketed kettles; hot-top ranges; under-fired broilers (charbroilers); ovens; barbecues; rotisseries; and similar appliances. For the purpose of this definition, a food service establishment shall include any building or a portion thereof used for the preparation and serving of food.

COMMERCIAL COOKING RECIRCULATING SYSTEM. Deleted.

COMMERCIAL KITCHEN HOODS. Deleted.

COMPENSATING HOODS. Deleted.

COMPRESSOR. Deleted.

COMPRESSOR, POSITIVE DISPLACEMENT. Deleted.

COMPRESSOR UNIT. Deleted.

CONCEALED LOCATION. A location that cannot be accessed without damaging permanent parts of the building structure or finish surface. Spaces above, below or behind readily removable panels or doors shall not be considered as concealed.

CONDENSATE. The liquid that condenses from a gas (including flue gas) caused by a reduction in temperature.

CONDENSER. Deleted.

CONDENSING UNIT. A specific refrigerating machine combination for a given refrigerant, consisting of one or more power-driven compressors, condensers, liquid receivers (when required) and the regularly furnished accessories.

CONDITIONED SPACE. An area, room or space being heated or cooled by any *equipment* or *appliance*.

CONSTRUCTION DOCUMENTS. All of the written, graphic and pictorial documents prepared or assembled for describing the design, location and physical characteristics of the elements of the project necessary for obtaining a building permit. The construction drawings shall be drawn to an appropriate scale.

CONTROL. A manual or automatic device designed to regulate the gas, air, water or electrical supply to, or operation of, a mechanical system.

CONVERSION BURNER. A burner designed to supply gaseous fuel to an *appliance* originally designed to utilize another fuel.

COOKING APPLIANCE. See "*Commercial cooking appliances*."

DAMPER. A manually or automatically controlled device to regulate draft or the rate of flow of air or *combustion* gases.

Volume damper. A device that, when installed, will restrict, retard or direct the flow of air in a duct, or the products of *combustion* in a heat-producing *appliance*, its vent connector, vent or *chimney* therefrom.

DESIGN FLOOD ELEVATION. The elevation of the "design flood," including wave height, relative to the datum specified on the community's legally designated flood hazard area map.

DESIGN WORKING PRESSURE. The maximum allowable working pressure for which a specific part of a system is designed.

DIRECT REFRIGERATION SYSTEM. Deleted.

DIRECT-VENT APPLIANCES. Appliances that are constructed and installed so that all air for *combustion* is derived from the outdoor atmosphere and all flue gases are discharged to the outdoor atmosphere.

DRAFT. The pressure difference existing between the *appliance* or any component part and the atmosphere, that causes a continuous flow of air and products of *combustion* through the gas passages of the *appliance* to the atmosphere.

Induced draft. The pressure difference created by the action of a fan, blower or ejector, that is located between the *appliance* and the *chimney* or vent termination.

Natural draft. The pressure difference created by a vent or *chimney* because of its height, and the temperature difference between the flue gases and the atmosphere.

DRIP. The container placed at a low point in a system of piping to collect condensate and from which the condensate is removable.

DRY CLEANING SYSTEMS. Deleted.

DUCT. A tube or conduit utilized for conveying air. The air passages of self-contained systems are not to be construed as air ducts.

DUCT FURNACE. Deleted.

DUCT SYSTEM. A continuous passageway for the transmission of air that, in addition to ducts, includes duct fittings, dampers, plenums, fans and accessory air-handling *equipment* and appliances.

DWELLING. A building or portion thereof that contains not more than two *dwelling* units.

DWELLING UNIT. A single unit providing complete, independent living facilities for one or more persons, including permanent provisions for living, sleeping, eating, cooking and sanitation.

ELECTRIC HEATING APPLIANCE. An *appliance* that produces heat energy to create a warm environment by the application of electric power to resistance elements, refrigerant compressors or dissimilar material junctions.

ENERGY RECOVERY VENTILATION SYSTEM. Systems that employ air-to-air heat exchangers to recover energy from or reject energy to *exhaust air* for the purpose of pre-heating, pre-cooling, humidifying or dehumidifying outdoor *ventilation air* prior to supplying such air to a space, either directly or as part of an HVAC system.

ENVIRONMENTAL AIR. Air that is conveyed to or from occupied areas through ducts which are not part of the heating or air-conditioning system, such as ventilation for human usage, domestic kitchen range exhaust, bathroom exhaust and domestic clothes dryer exhaust.

EQUIPMENT. All piping, ducts, vents, control devices and other components of systems other than appliances which are permanently installed and integrated to provide control of environmental conditions for buildings. This definition shall also include other systems specifically regulated in this code.

EQUIPMENT, EXISTING. Any *equipment* regulated by this code which was legally installed prior to the effective date of this code, or for which a permit to install has been issued.

EVAPORATIVE COOLER. Deleted.

EVAPORATIVE COOLING SYSTEM. Deleted.

EVAPORATOR. Deleted.

EXCESS AIR. The amount of air provided in addition to *theoretical air* to achieve complete *combustion* of a fuel, thereby preventing the formation of dangerous products of *combustion*.

EXHAUST SYSTEM. An assembly of connected ducts, plenums, fittings, registers, grilles and hoods through which air is conducted from the space or spaces and exhausted to the outdoor atmosphere.

EXTRA-HEAVY-DUTY COOKING APPLIANCE. Deleted.

FIRE DAMPER. Deleted.

FIREPLACE. An assembly consisting of a hearth and fire chamber of noncombustible material and provided with a *chimney*, for use with solid fuels.

Factory-built fireplace. A *listed* and *labeled* fireplace and *chimney* system composed of factory-made components, and assembled in the field in accordance with manufacturer's instructions and the conditions of the listing.

Masonry fireplace. A field-constructed fireplace composed of solid masonry units, bricks, stones or concrete.

FIREPLACE STOVE. A free-standing chimney-connected solid-fuel-burning heater, designed to be operated with the fire chamber doors in either the open or closed position.

FLAME SAFEGUARD. A device that will automatically shut off the fuel supply to a main burner or group of burners when the means of ignition of such burners becomes inoperative, and when flame failure occurs on the burner or group of burners.

FLAME SPREAD INDEX. The numerical value assigned to a material tested in accordance with ASTM E 84 or UL 723.

FLAMMABILITY CLASSIFICATION. Deleted.

FLAMMABLE LIQUIDS. Deleted.

FLAMMABLE VAPOR OR FUMES. Deleted.

FLASH POINT. Deleted.

FLOOR AREA, NET. Deleted.

FLOOR FURNACE. A completely self-contained furnace suspended from the floor of the space being heated, taking air for *combustion* from outside such space and with means for observing flames and lighting the *appliance* from such space.

FLUE. A passageway within a *chimney* or vent through which gaseous *combustion* products pass.

FLUE CONNECTION (BREECHING). A passage for conducting the products of *combustion* from a fuel-fired *appliance* to the vent or *chimney* (see also "*Chimney* connector" and "Vent connector").

FLUE GASES. Products of *combustion* and excess air.

FLUE LINER (LINING). A system or material used to form the inside surface of a flue in a *chimney* or vent, for the purpose of protecting the surrounding structure from the effects of *combustion* products and conveying *combustion* products without leakage to the atmosphere.

FUEL GAS. A natural gas, manufactured gas, liquefied petroleum gas or a mixture of these.

FUEL OIL. Kerosene or any hydrocarbon oil having a flash point not less than 100°F (38°C).

FUEL-OIL PIPING SYSTEM. A closed piping system that connects a combustible liquid from a source of supply to a fuel-oil-burning *appliance*.

FURNACE. A completely self-contained heating unit that is designed to supply heated air to spaces remote from or adjacent to the *appliance* location.

FURNACE ROOM. A room primarily utilized for the installation of fuel-burning, space-heating and water-heating appliances other than boilers (see also "Boiler room").

FUSIBLE PLUG. A device arranged to relieve pressure by operation of a fusible member at a predetermined temperature.

GROUND SOURCE HEAT PUMP LOOP SYSTEM. Piping buried in horizontal or vertical excavations or placed in a body of water for the purpose of transporting heat transfer liquid to and from a heat pump. Included in this definition are closed loop systems in which the liquid is recirculated and open loop systems in which the liquid is drawn from a well or other source.

HAZARDOUS LOCATION. Deleted.

HEAT EXCHANGER. A device that transfers heat from one medium to another.

HEAT PUMP. A refrigeration system that extracts heat from one substance and transfers it to another portion of the same substance or to a second substance at a higher temperature for a beneficial purpose.

HEAT TRANSFER LIQUID. The operating or thermal storage liquid in a mechanical system, including water or other liquid base, and additives at the concentration present under operating conditions used to move heat from one location to another. Refrigerants are not included as heat transfer liquids.

HEAVY-DUTY COOKING APPLIANCE. Deleted.

HIGH-PROBABILITY SYSTEMS. Deleted.

HIGH-SIDE PRESSURE. Deleted.

HOOD. An air intake device used to capture by entrapment, impingement, adhesion or similar means, grease, moisture, heat and similar contaminants before they enter a duct system.

Type I. Deleted.

Type II. Deleted.

HYDROGEN GENERATING APPLIANCE. A self-contained package or factory-matched packages of integrated systems for generating gaseous hydrogen. Hydrogen generating appliances utilize electrolysis, reformation, chemical, or other processes to generate hydrogen.

IGNITION SOURCE. A flame, spark or hot surface capable of igniting flammable vapors or fumes. Such sources include *appliance* burners, burner ignitors and electrical switching devices.

IMMEDIATELY DANGEROUS TO LIFE OR HEALTH (IDLH). Deleted.

INDIRECT REFRIGERATION SYSTEM. Deleted.

INTERLOCK. A device actuated by another device with which it is directly associated, to govern succeeding operations of the same or allied devices. A circuit in which a given action cannot occur until after one or more other actions have taken place.

JOINT, FLANGED. A joint made by bolting together a pair of flanged ends.

JOINT, FLARED. A metal-to-metal compression joint in which a conical spread is made on the end of a tube that is compressed by a flare nut against a mating flare.

JOINT, MECHANICAL. A general form of gas-tight joints obtained by the joining of metal parts through a positive-holding mechanical construction, such as flanged joint, screwed joint or flared joint. These joints include both the press-type and push-fit joining systems.

JOINT, PLASTIC ADHESIVE. A joint made in thermoset plastic piping by the use of an adhesive substance which forms a continuous bond between the mating surfaces without dissolving either one of them.

JOINT, PLASTIC HEAT FUSION. A joint made in thermoplastic piping by heating the parts sufficiently to permit fusion of the materials when the parts are pressed together.

JOINT, PLASTIC SOLVENT CEMENT. A joint made in thermoplastic piping by the use of a solvent or solvent cement which forms a continuous bond between the mating surfaces.

JOINT, SOLDERED. A gas-tight joint obtained by the joining of metal parts with metallic mixtures of alloys which melt at temperatures between 400°F (204°C) and 1,000°F (538°C).

JOINT, WELDED. A gas-tight joint obtained by the joining of metal parts in molten state.

LABELED. *Appliances*, *equipment*, materials or products to which have been affixed a label, seal, symbol or other identifying mark of a nationally recognized testing laboratory, inspection agency or other organization concerned with product evaluation that maintains periodic inspection of the production of the above-labeled items and whose labeling indicates either that the *appliance*, *equipment*, material or product meets identified standards or has been tested and found suitable for a specified purpose. (Laboratories, agencies or organizations that have been identified by approval and accreditation bodies, such as ANSI, IAS, ICC or OSHA, are acceptable.)

LIGHT-DUTY COOKING APPLIANCE. Deleted.

LIMIT CONTROL. A device responsive to changes in pressure, temperature or level for turning on, shutting off or throttling the gas supply to an *appliance*.

LIMITED CHARGE SYSTEM. Deleted.

LISTED. *Appliances*, *Equipment*, materials, products or services included in a list published by an organization acceptable to the code official and concerned with evaluation of products or services that maintains periodic inspection of production of *listed equipment* or materials or periodic evaluation of services and whose listing states either that the *appliance*, *equipment*, material, product or service meets identified standards or has been tested and found suitable for a specified purpose.

LIVING SPACE. Space within a *dwelling unit* utilized for living, sleeping, eating, cooking, bathing, washing and sanitation purposes.

LOWER EXPLOSIVE LIMIT (LEL). Deleted.

LOWER FLAMMABLE LIMIT (LFL). Deleted.

LOW-PRESSURE HOT-WATER-HEATING BOILER. A boiler furnishing hot water at pressures not exceeding 160 psi (1103 kPa) and at temperatures not exceeding 250°F (121°C).

LOW-PRESSURE STEAM-HEATING BOILER. A boiler furnishing steam at pressures not exceeding 15 psi (103 kPa).

LOW-PROBABILITY SYSTEMS. Deleted.

LOW-SIDE PRESSURE. The parts of a refrigerating system subject to evaporator pressure.

MACHINERY ROOM. Deleted.

MECHANICAL DRAFT SYSTEM. A venting system designed to remove flue or vent gases by mechanical means, that consists of an induced-draft portion under nonpositive static pressure or a forced-draft portion under positive static pressure.

Forced-draft venting system. A portion of a venting system using a fan or other mechanical means to cause the removal of flue or vent gases under positive static pressure.

Induced-draft venting system. A portion of a venting system using a fan or other mechanical means to cause the removal of flue or vent gases under nonpositive static vent pressure.

Power venting system. A portion of a venting system using a fan or other mechanical means to cause the removal of flue or vent gases under positive static vent pressure.

MECHANICAL EQUIPMENT/APPLIANCE ROOM. A room or space in which nonfuel-fired mechanical *equipment* and *appliances* are located.

MECHANICAL EXHAUST SYSTEM. A system for removing air from a room or space by mechanical means.

MECHANICAL JOINT. Deleted.

MECHANICAL SYSTEM. A system specifically addressed and regulated in this code and composed of components, devices, *appliances* and *equipment*.

MEDIUM-DUTY COOKING APPLIANCE. Deleted.

MODULAR BOILER. Deleted.

NATURAL DRAFT SYSTEM. A venting system designed to remove flue or vent gases under nonpositive static vent pressure entirely by natural draft.

NATURAL VENTILATION. The movement of air into and out of a space through intentionally provided openings, such as windows and doors, or through nonpowered ventilators.

NET OCCUPIABLE FLOOR AREA. Deleted.

NONABRASIVE/ABRASIVE MATERIALS.

NONCOMBUSTIBLE MATERIALS. Deleted.

OCCUPANCY. Deleted.

OCCUPIABLE SPACE. An enclosed space intended for human activities, excluding those spaces intended primarily for other purposes, such as storage rooms and *equipment* rooms, that are only intended to be occupied occasionally and for short periods of time.

OFFSET (VENT). A combination of *approved* bends that make two changes in direction bringing one section of the vent out of line but into a line parallel with the other section.

OUTDOOR AIR. Air taken from the outdoors, and therefore not previously circulated through the system.

OUTDOOR OPENING. A door, window, louver or skylight openable to the outdoor atmosphere.

OUTLET. Deleted.

PANEL HEATING. A method of radiant space heating in which heat is supplied by large heated areas of room surfaces. The heating element usually consists of warm water piping, warm air ducts, or electrical resistance elements embedded in or located behind ceiling, wall or floor surfaces.

PELLET FUEL-BURNING APPLIANCE. A closed-combustion, vented *appliance* equipped with a fuel-feed mechanism for burning processed pellets of solid fuel of a specified size and composition.

PIPING. Where used in this code, "piping" refers to either pipe or tubing, or both.

Pipe. A rigid conduit of iron, steel, copper, brass or plastic.

Tubing. Semirigid conduit of copper, aluminum, plastic or steel.

PLASTIC, THERMOPLASTIC. Deleted.

PLASTIC, THERMOSETTING. A plastic that is capable of being changed into a substantially infusible or insoluble product when cured under application of heat or chemical means.

PLENUM. An enclosed portion of the building structure, other than an *occupiable space* being conditioned, that is designed to allow air movement, and thereby serve as part of an air distribution system.

PORTABLE FUEL CELL APPLIANCE. A fuel cell generator of electricity, which is not fixed in place. A portable fuel cell *appliance* utilizes a cord and plug connection to a grid-isolated load and has an integral fuel supply.

POWER BOILER. See "Boiler."

PREMISES. Deleted.

PRESSURE, FIELD TEST. A test performed in the field to prove system tightness.

PRESSURE-LIMITING DEVICE. A pressure-responsive mechanism designed to stop automatically the operation of the pressure-imposing element at a predetermined pressure.

PRESSURE RELIEF DEVICE. A pressure-actuated valve or rupture member designed to relieve excessive pressure automatically.

PRESSURE RELIEF VALVE. A pressure-actuated valve held closed by a spring or other means and designed to relieve pressure automatically in excess of the device's setting.

PRESSURE VESSELS. Closed containers, tanks or vessels that are designed to contain liquids or gases, or both, under pressure.

PRESSURE VESSELS—REFRIGERANT. Deleted.

PROTECTIVE ASSEMBLY (REDUCED CLEARANCE). Any noncombustible assembly that is *labeled* or constructed in accordance with Table 308.6 and is placed between combustible materials or assemblies and mechanical appliances, devices or *equipment*, for the purpose of reducing required airspace clearances. Protective assemblies attached directly to a combustible assembly shall not be considered as part of that combustible assembly.

PURGE. To clear of air, water or other foreign substances.

PUSH-FIT JOINTS. A type of mechanical joint consisting of elastomeric seals and corrosion-resistant tube grippers. Such joints are permanent or removable depending on the design.

QUICK-OPENING VALVE. A valve that opens completely by fast action, either manually or automatically controlled. A valve requiring one-quarter round turn or less is considered to be quick opening.

RADIANT HEATER. A heater designed to transfer heat primarily by direct radiation.

READY ACCESS (TO). That which enables a device, *appliance* or *equipment* to be directly reached, without requiring the removal or movement of any panel, door or similar obstruction [see "Access (to)"].

RECEIVER, LIQUID. Deleted.

RECIRCULATED AIR. Air removed from a conditioned space and intended for reuse as supply air.

RECLAIMED REFRIGERANTS. Deleted.

RECOVERED REFRIGERANTS. Deleted.

RECYCLED REFRIGERANTS. Deleted.

REFRIGERANT. A substance utilized to produce refrigeration by its expansion or vaporization.

REFRIGERANT SAFETY CLASSIFICATIONS. Deleted.

REFRIGERATED ROOM OR SPACE. Deleted.

REFRIGERATING SYSTEM. Deleted.

REFRIGERATION CAPACITY RATING. Deleted.

REFRIGERATION MACHINERY ROOM. Deleted.

REFRIGERATION SYSTEM, ABSORPTION. Deleted.

REFRIGERATION SYSTEM CLASSIFICATION. Deleted.

REFRIGERATION SYSTEM, MECHANICAL. Deleted.

REFRIGERATION SYSTEM, SELF-CONTAINED. Deleted.

REGISTERED DESIGN PROFESSIONAL. Deleted.

RETURN AIR. Air removed from an *approved* conditioned space or location and recirculated or exhausted.

RETURN AIR SYSTEM. An assembly of connected ducts, plenums, fittings, registers and grilles through which air from the space or spaces to be heated or cooled is conducted back to the supply unit (see also "Supply air system").

ROOM HEATER VENTED. A free-standing heating unit burning solid or liquid fuel for direct heating of the space in and adjacent to that in which the unit is located.

SAFETY VALVE. A valve that relieves pressure in a steam boiler by opening fully at the rated discharge pressure. The valve is of the spring-pop type.

SELF-CONTAINED EQUIPMENT. Complete, factory-assembled and tested, heating, air-conditioning or refrigeration *equipment* installed as a single unit, and having all working parts, complete with motive power, in an enclosed unit of said machinery.

SHAFT. Deleted.

SHAFT ENCLOSURE. Deleted.

SLEEPING UNIT. Deleted.

SMOKE DAMPER. Deleted.

SMOKE-DEVELOPED INDEX. A numerical value assigned to a material tested in accordance with ASTM E 84.

SOLID FUEL (COOKING APPLICATIONS). Deleted.

SOURCE CAPTURE SYSTEM. Deleted.

STATIONARY FUEL CELL POWER PLANT. Deleted.

STEAM-HEATING BOILER. A boiler operated at pressures not exceeding 15 psi (103 kPa) for steam.

STOP VALVE. A shutoff valve for controlling the flow of liquid or gases.

STORY. Deleted.

STRENGTH, ULTIMATE. Deleted.

SUPPLY AIR. That air delivered to each or any space supplied by the air distribution system or the total air delivered to all spaces supplied by the air distribution system, which is provided for ventilating, heating, cooling, humidification, dehumidification and other similar purposes.

SUPPLY AIR SYSTEM. An assembly of connected ducts, plenums, fittings, registers and grilles through which air, heated or cooled, is conducted from the supply unit to the space or spaces to be heated or cooled (see also "Return air system").

THEORETICAL AIR. The exact amount of air required to supply oxygen for complete *combustion* of a given quantity of a specific fuel.

THERMAL RESISTANCE (*R*). A measure of the ability to retard the flow of heat. The *R*-value is the reciprocal of thermal conductance.

TLV-TWA (THRESHOLD LIMIT VALUE-TIME-WEIGHTED AVERAGE). Deleted.

TOILET ROOM. Deleted.

TOXICITY CLASSIFICATION. Deleted.

TRANSITION FITTINGS, PLASTIC TO STEEL. Deleted.

UNIT HEATER. Deleted.

VENT. A pipe or other conduit composed of factory-made components, containing a passageway for conveying *combustion* products and air to the atmosphere, *listed* and *labeled* for use with a specific type or class of *appliance*.

Pellet vent. A vent *listed* and *labeled* for use with *listed* pellet-fuel-burning appliances.

Type L vent. A vent *listed* and *labeled* for use with the following:

1. Oil-burning appliances that are *listed* for use with Type L vents.
2. Gas-fired appliances that are *listed* for use with Type B vents.

VENT CONNECTOR. The pipe that connects an *approved* fuel-fired *appliance* to a vent.

VENT DAMPER DEVICE, AUTOMATIC. A device intended for installation in the venting system, in the outlet of an individual automatically operated fuel-burning *appliance* that is designed to open the venting system automatically when the *appliance* is in operation and to close off the venting system automatically when the *appliance* is in a standby or shutdown condition.

VENTILATION. The natural or mechanical process of supplying conditioned or unconditioned air to, or removing such air from, any space.

VENTILATION AIR. That portion of supply air that comes from the outside (outdoors), plus any recirculated air that has been treated to maintain the desired quality of air within a designated space.

VENTING SYSTEM. A continuous open passageway from the flue collar of an *appliance* to the outside atmosphere for the purpose of removing flue or vent gases. A venting system is usually composed of a vent or a *chimney* and vent connector, if used, assembled to form the open passageway.

WATER HEATER. Any heating *appliance* or *equipment* that heats potable water and supplies such water to the potable hot water distribution system.

ZONE. One *occupiable space* or several occupiable spaces with similar *occupancy* classification (see Table 403.3), occupant density, zone air distribution effectiveness and zone primary airflow rate per unit area.

CHAPTER 3
GENERAL REGULATIONS

SECTION 301
GENERAL

301.1 Scope. This chapter shall govern the approval and installation of all *equipment* and appliances that comprise parts of the building mechanical systems regulated by this code in accordance with Section 101.2.

301.2 Energy utilization. Heating, ventilating and air-conditioning systems of all structures shall be designed and installed for efficient utilization of energy in accordance with the *International Energy Conservation Code*.

301.3 Fuel gas appliances and equipment. The approval and installation of fuel gas distribution piping and *equipment*, fuel gas-fired appliances and fuel gas-fired *appliance* venting systems shall be in accordance with the *International Fuel Gas Code*.

301.4 Listed and labeled. Appliances regulated by this code shall be *listed* and *labeled* for the application in which they are installed and used, unless otherwise *approved* in accordance with Section 105.

Exception: Deleted.

301.4.1 Foundation and exterior wall sealing. Annular spaces around pipes, electric cables, conduits or other openings in the walls shall be protected against the passage of rodents by closing such opening with cement mortar, concrete masonry, silicone caulking or noncorrosive metal.

301.5 Labeling. Labeling shall be in accordance with the procedures set forth in Sections 301.5.1 through 301.5.2.3.

301.5.1 Testing. An *approved* agency shall test a representative sample of the mechanical *equipment* and appliances being *labeled* to the relevant standard or standards. The *approved* agency shall maintain a record of all of the tests performed. The record shall provide sufficient detail to verify compliance with the test standard.

301.5.2 Inspection and identification. The *approved* agency shall periodically perform an inspection, which shall be in-plant if necessary, of the mechanical *equipment* and appliances to be *labeled*. The inspection shall verify that the *labeled* mechanical *equipment* and appliances are representative of the mechanical *equipment* and appliances tested.

301.5.2.1 Independent. The agency to be *approved* shall be objective and competent. To confirm its objectivity, the agency shall disclose all possible conflicts of interest.

301.5.2.2 Equipment. An *approved* agency shall have adequate *equipment* to perform all required tests. The *equipment* shall be periodically calibrated.

301.5.2.3 Personnel. An *approved* agency shall employ experienced personnel educated in conducting, supervising and evaluating tests.

301.6 Label information. A permanent factory-applied nameplate(s) shall be affixed to appliances on which shall appear in legible lettering, the manufacturer's name or trademark, the model number, serial number and the seal or mark of the *approved* agency. A label shall also include the following:

1. Electrical *equipment* and appliances: Electrical rating in volts, amperes and motor phase; identification of individual electrical components in volts, amperes or watts, motor phase; Btu/h (W) output; and required clearances.
2. Deleted.
3. Fuel-burning units: Hourly rating in Btu/h (W); type of fuel *approved* for use with the *appliance*; and required clearances.
4. Electric comfort heating appliances: Name and trademark of the manufacturer; the model number or equivalent; the electric rating in volts, ampacity and phase; Btu/h (W) output rating; individual marking for each electrical component in amperes or watts, volts and phase; required clearances from combustibles; and a seal indicating approval of the *appliance* by an *approved* agency.

301.7 Electrical. Electrical wiring, controls and connections to *equipment* and appliances regulated by this code shall be in accordance with NFPA 70.

301.8 Plumbing connections. Potable water supply and building drainage system connections to *equipment* and appliances regulated by this code shall be in accordance with the *International Plumbing Code*.

301.9 Fuel types. Fuel-fired appliances shall be designed for use with the type of fuel to which they will be connected and the altitude at which they are installed. Appliances that comprise parts of the building mechanical system shall not be converted for the usage of a different fuel, except where *approved* and converted in accordance with the manufacturer's instructions. The fuel input rate shall not be increased or decreased beyond the limit rating for the altitude at which the *appliance* is installed.

301.10 Vibration isolation. Deleted.

301.11 Repair. Defective material or parts shall be replaced or repaired in such a manner so as to preserve the original approval or listing.

301.12 Wind resistance. Mechanical *equipment*, appliances and supports that are exposed to wind shall be designed and installed to resist the wind pressures determined in accordance with the *International Building Code*.

[B] 301.13 Flood hazard. For structures located in flood hazard areas, mechanical systems, *equipment* and appliances shall be located at or above the *design flood elevation*.

Exception: Mechanical systems, *equipment* and appliances are permitted to be located below the *design flood elevation* provided that they are designed and installed to prevent water from entering or accumulating within the components and to resist hydrostatic and hydrodynamic loads and stresses, including the effects of buoyancy, during the occurrence of flooding to the *design flood elevation* in compliance with the flood-resistant construction requirements of the *International Building Code*.

[B] 301.13.1 High-velocity wave action. In flood hazard areas subject to high-velocity wave action, mechanical systems and *equipment* shall not be mounted on or penetrate walls intended to break away under flood loads.

301.14 Rodentproofing. Buildings or structures and the walls enclosing habitable or occupiable rooms and spaces in which persons live, sleep or work, or in which feed, food or foodstuffs are stored, prepared, processed, served or sold, shall be constructed to protect against the entrance of rodents in accordance with the *International Building Code*.

301.15 Seismic resistance. Deleted.

SECTION 302 PROTECTION OF STRUCTURE

302.1 Structural safety. The building or structure shall not be weakened by the installation of mechanical systems. Where floors, walls, ceilings or any other portion of the building or structure are required to be altered or replaced in the process of installing or repairing any system, the building or structure shall be left in a safe structural condition in accordance with the *International Building Code*.

302.2 Penetrations of floor/ceiling assemblies and fire-resistance-rated assemblies. Deleted.

[B] 302.3 Cutting, notching and boring in wood framing. The cutting, notching and boring of wood framing members shall comply with Sections 302.3.1 through 302.3.4.

[B] 302.3.1 Joist notching. Notches on the ends of joists shall not exceed one-fourth the joist depth. Holes bored in joists shall not be within 2 inches (51 mm) of the top or bottom of the joist, and the diameter of any such hole shall not exceed one-third the depth of the joist. Notches in the top or bottom of joists shall not exceed one-sixth the depth and shall not be located in the middle third of the span.

[B] 302.3.2 Stud cutting and notching. In exterior walls and bearing partitions, any wood stud is permitted to be cut or notched not to exceed 25 percent of its depth. Cutting or notching of studs not greater than 40 percent of their depth is permitted in nonbearing partitions supporting no loads other than the weight of the partition.

[B] 302.3.3 Bored holes. A hole not greater in diameter than 40 percent of the stud depth is permitted to be bored in any wood stud. Bored holes not greater than 60 percent of the depth of the stud are permitted in nonbearing partitions or in any wall where each bored stud is doubled, provided not more than two such successive doubled studs are so bored. In no case shall the edge of the bored hole be nearer than 0.625 inch (15.9 mm) to the edge of the stud. Bored holes shall not be located at the same section of stud as a cut or notch.

[B] 302.3.4 Engineered wood products. Cuts, notches and holes bored in trusses, structural composite veneer lumber, structural glue-laminated members and I-joists are prohibited except where permitted by the manufacturer's recommendations or where the effects of such alterations are specifically considered in the design of the member.

[B] 302.4 Alterations to trusses. Truss members and components shall not be cut, drilled, notched, spliced or otherwise altered in any way without written concurrence and approval of a *registered design professional*. Alterations resulting in the addition of loads to any member (e.g., HVAC *equipment*, water heaters) shall not be permitted without verification that the truss is capable of supporting such additional loading.

[B] 302.5 Cutting, notching and boring in steel framing. Deleted.

[B] 302.5.1 Cutting, notching and boring holes in structural steel framing. Deleted.

[B] 302.5.2 Cutting, notching and boring holes in cold-formed steel framing. Deleted.

[B] 302.5.3 Cutting, notching and boring holes in nonstructural cold-formed steel wall framing. Deleted.

SECTION 303 EQUIPMENT AND APPLIANCE LOCATION

303.1 General. *Equipment* and appliances shall be located as required by this section, specific requirements elsewhere in this code and the conditions of the *equipment* and *appliance* listing.

303.2 Hazardous locations. Appliances shall not be located in a *hazardous location* unless *listed* and *approved* for the specific installation.

303.3 Prohibited locations. Fuel-fired appliances shall not be located in, or obtain *combustion* air from, any of the following rooms or spaces:

1. Sleeping rooms.
2. Bathrooms.
3. Deleted.
4. Storage closets.
5. Deleted.

Exception: This section shall not apply to the following appliances:

1. *Direct-vent appliances* that obtain all *combustion air* directly from the outdoors.
2. Solid fuel-fired appliances, provided that the room is not a confined space and the building is not of unusually tight construction.
3. Appliances installed in a dedicated enclosure in which all *combustion* air is taken directly from the outdoors, in accordance with Chapter 7. *Access to* such enclosure shall be through a solid door, weather-stripped in accordance with the exterior door air leakage requirements of the *International Energy Conservation Code* and equipped with an *approved* self-closing device.

303.4 Protection from damage. Appliances shall not be installed in a location where subject to mechanical damage unless protected by *approved* barriers.

303.5 Indoor locations for fuel-fired appliances. Fuel-fired furnaces, fuel-fired water heaters and fuel-fired boilers installed in closets and alcoves shall be *listed* for such installation. For purposes of this section, a closet or alcove shall be defined as a room or space having a volume less than 12 times the total volume of fuel-fired appliances other than boilers and less than 16 times the total volume of boilers. Room volume shall be computed using the gross floor area and the actual ceiling height up to a maximum computation height of 8 feet (2438 mm).

303.6 Outdoor locations. Appliances installed in other than indoor locations shall be *listed* and *labeled* for outdoor installation.

303.7 Pit locations. Appliances installed in pits or excavations shall not come in direct contact with the surrounding soil. The sides of the pit or excavation shall be held back a minimum of 12 inches (305 mm) from the *appliance*. Where the depth exceeds 12 inches (305 mm) below adjoining grade, the walls of the pit or excavation shall be lined with concrete or masonry. Such concrete or masonry shall extend a minimum of 4 inches (102 mm) above adjoining grade and shall have sufficient lateral load-bearing capacity to resist collapse. The *appliance* shall be protected from flooding in an *approved* manner.

[B] 303.8 Elevator shafts. Deleted.

SECTION 304 INSTALLATION

304.1 General. *Equipment* and appliances shall be installed as required by the terms of their approval, in accordance with the conditions of the listing, the manufacturer's installation instructions and this code. Manufacturer's installation instructions shall be available on the job site at the time of inspection.

304.2 Conflicts. Deleted.

304.3 Elevation of ignition source. Equipment and appliances having an *ignition source* and located in hazardous locations and public garages, private garages, repair garages, automotive motor fuel-dispensing facilities and parking garages shall be elevated such that the source of ignition is not less than 18 inches (457 mm) above the floor surface on which the *equipment* or *appliance* rests. For the purpose of this section, rooms or spaces that are not part of the living space of a *dwelling unit* and that communicate directly with a private garage through openings shall be considered to be part of the private garage.

304.3.1 Parking garages. Connection of a parking garage with any room in which there is a fuel-fired *appliance* shall be by means of a vestibule providing a two-doorway separation, except that a single door is permitted where the sources of ignition in the *appliance* are elevated in accordance with Section 304.3.

Exceptions:

1. This section shall not apply to *appliance* installations complying with Section 304.6.
2. This does not apply to one- and two-family dwellings and townhouses.

304.4 Prohibited equipment and appliance location. Deleted.

[FG] 304.5 Hydrogen-generating and refueling operations. Deleted.

304.6 Public garages. Deleted.

304.7 Private garages. Appliances located in private garages and carports shall be installed with a minimum clearance of 6 feet (1829 mm) above the floor.

Exception: The requirements of this section shall not apply where the appliances are protected from motor vehicle impact and installed in accordance with Section 304.3.

304.8 Construction and protection. Deleted.

304.9 Clearances to combustible construction. Heat-producing *equipment* and *appliances* shall be installed to maintain the required *clearances* to combustible construction as specified in the listing and manufacturer's instructions. *Clearances* to combustibles shall include such considerations as door swing, drawer pull, overhead projections or shelving and window swing, shutters, coverings and drapes. Devices such as doorstops or limits, closers, drapery ties or guards shall not be used to provide the required *clearances*.

304.10 Under-floor and exterior grade installations.

304.10.1 Exterior grade installations. Equipment and appliances installed above grade level shall be supported on a solid base or approved material a minimum of 2 inches (51 mm) thick.

304.10.2 Under-floor installation. Suspended equipment shall be a minimum of 6 inches (152 mm) above the adjoining grade.

304.10.3 Crawl space supports. A support shall be provided at each corner of the unit not less than 8 inches by 8 inches (203.2 mm by 203.2 mm). The unit shall be supported a minimum of 2 inches (51 mm) above grade. When constructed of brick, the bricks shall be mortared together. All units stacked shall be mortared together. Fabricated units, formed concrete, or other approved materials shall be permitted.

304.10.4 Drainage. Below-grade installations shall be provided with a natural drain or an automatic lift or sump pump. For pit requirements, see Section 303.7.

[B] 304.11 Guards. Deleted.

304.12 Area served. Deleted.

SECTION 305
PIPING SUPPORT

305.1 General. All mechanical system piping shall be supported in accordance with this section.

305.2 Materials. Pipe hangers and supports shall have sufficient strength to withstand all anticipated static and specified dynamic loading conditions associated with the intended use. Pipe hangers and supports that are in direct contact with piping shall be of *approved* materials that are compatible with the piping and that will not promote galvanic action.

305.3 Structural attachment. Hangers and anchors shall be attached to the building construction in an *approved* manner.

305.4 Interval of support. Piping shall be supported at distances not exceeding the spacing specified in Table 305.4, or in accordance with MSS SP-69.

TABLE 305.4
PIPING SUPPORT SPACING[a]

PIPING MATERIAL	MAXIMUM HORIZONTAL SPACING (feet)	MAXIMUM VERTICAL SPACING (feet)
ABS pipe	4	10[c]
Aluminum pipe and tubing	10	15
Brass pipe	10	10
Brass tubing, $1^1/_4$-inch diameter and smaller	6	10
Brass tubing, $1^1/_2$-inch diameter and larger	10	10
Cast-iron pipe[b]	5	15
Copper or copper-alloy pipe	12	10
Copper or copper-alloy tubing, $1^1/_4$-inch diameter and smaller	6	10
Copper or copper-alloy tubing, $1^1/_2$-inch diameter and larger	10	10
CPVC pipe or tubing, 1 inch and smaller	3	10[c]
CPVC pipe or tubing, $1^1/_4$-inch and larger	4	10[c]
Lead pipe	Continuous	4
PB pipe or tubing	$2^2/_3$ (32 inches)	4
PEX tubing	$2^2/_3$ (32 inches)	10[c]
Polypropylene (PP) pipe or tubing, 1 inch or smaller	$2^2/_3$ (32 inches)	10[c]
Polypropylene (PP) pipe or tubing, $1^1/_4$ inches or larger	4	10[c]
PVC pipe	4	10[c]
Steel tubing	8	10
Steel pipe	12	15

For SI: 1 inch = 25.4 mm, 1 foot = 304.8 mm.

a. See Section 301.15.

b. The maximum horizontal spacing of cast-iron pipe hangers shall be increased to 10 feet where 10-foot lengths of pipe are installed.

c. Mid-story guide.

305.5 Protection against physical damage. In concealed locations where piping, other than cast-iron or steel, is installed through holes or notches in studs, joists, rafters or similar members less than $1^1/_2$ inches (38 mm) from the nearest edge of the member, the pipe shall be protected by shield plates. Protective steel shield plates having a minimum thickness of 0.0575 inch (1.463 mm) (No. 16 gage) shall cover the area of the pipe where the member is notched or bored, and shall extend a minimum of 2 inches (51 mm) above sole plates and below top plates.

SECTION 306
ACCESS AND SERVICE SPACE

306.1 Access for maintenance and replacement. Appliances shall be accessible for inspection, service, repair and replacement without disabling the function of a fire-resistance-rated assembly or removing permanent construction, other appliances, venting systems or any other piping or ducts not connected to the *appliance* being inspected, serviced, repaired or replaced. A level working space at least 30 inches deep and 30 inches wide (762 mm by 762 mm) shall be provided in front of the control side to service an *appliance*.

306.1.1 Central furnaces. Deleted.

306.2 Appliances in rooms. Appliances installed in a compartment, alcove, basement or similar space shall be accessed by an opening or door and an unobstructed passageway measuring not less than 24 inches (610 mm) wide and large enough to allow removal of the largest *appliance* in the space, provided that a level service space of not less than 30 inches (762 mm) deep and the height of the *appliance*, but not less than 30 inches (762 mm), is present at the front or service side of the *appliance* with the door open.

306.3 Appliances in attics. Attics containing appliances shall be provided with an opening and unobstructed passageway large enough to allow removal of the largest *appliance*. The passageway shall not be less than 30 inches (762 mm) high and 22 inches (559 mm) wide and not more than 20 feet (6096 mm) in length measured along the centerline of the passageway from the opening to the *appliance*. The passageway shall have continuous solid flooring not less than 24 inches (610 mm) wide. A level service space not less than 30 inches (762 mm) deep and 30 inches (762 mm) wide shall be present at the front or service side of the *appliance*. The clear access opening dimensions shall be a minimum of 20 inches by 30 inches (508 mm by 762 mm), and large enough to allow removal of the largest *appliance*.

Exceptions:

1. The passageway and level service space are not required where the *appliance* is capable of being serviced and removed through the required opening.
2. Where the passageway is not less than 6 feet (1829 mm) high for its entire length, the passageway shall not be limited in length.

306.3.1 Electrical requirements. Deleted.

306.4 Appliances under floors. Underfloor spaces containing appliances shall be provided with an access opening and unobstructed passageway large enough to remove the largest *appli-*

ance. The passageway shall not be less than 22 inches (559 mm) high and 36 inches (914 mm) wide, nor more than 20 feet (6096 mm) in length measured along the centerline of the passageway from the opening to the *appliance*. A level service space not less than 30 inches (762 mm) deep and 30 inches (762 mm) wide shall be present at the front or service side of the *appliance*. If the depth of the passageway or the service space exceeds 12 inches (305 mm) below the adjoining grade, the walls of the passageway shall be lined with concrete or masonry. Such concrete or masonry shall extend a minimum of 4 inches (102 mm) above the adjoining grade and shall have sufficient lateral-bearing capacity to resist collapse. The clear access opening dimensions shall be a minimum of 22 inches high by 30 inches wide (559 mm by 762 mm), and large enough to allow removal of the largest *appliance*.

Exceptions:

1. The passageway is not required where the level service space is present when the access is open and the *appliance* is capable of being serviced and removed through the required opening.
2. Where the passageway is not less than 6 feet (1829 mm) high unobstructed and not less than 6 feet high (1929 mm) for its entire length, the passageway shall not be limited in length.

306.4.1 Electrical requirements. Deleted.

306.5 Equipment and appliances on roofs or elevated structures. Deleted.

306.5.1 Sloped roofs. Deleted.

306.5.2 Electrical requirements. Deleted.

SECTION 307
CONDENSATE DISPOSAL

307.1 Fuel-burning appliances. Liquid *combustion* by-products of condensing appliances shall be collected and discharged to an *approved* plumbing fixture or disposal area in accordance with the manufacturer's installation instructions. Condensate piping shall be of *approved* corrosion-resistant material and shall not be smaller than the drain connection on the appliance. Such piping shall maintain a minimum horizontal slope in the direction of discharge of not less than one-eighth unit vertical in 12 units horizontal (1-percent slope).

307.2 Evaporators, condensing furnaces and cooling coils. Condensate drain systems shall be provided for *equipment* and appliances containing evaporators, cooling coils or condensing furnaces. Condensate drain systems shall be designed, constructed and installed in accordance with Sections 307.2.1 through 307.2.4.

307.2.1 Condensate disposal. Condensate from all condensing furnaces, cooling coils and evaporators shall be conveyed from the drain pan outlet to an *approved* place of disposal. Such piping shall maintain a minimum horizontal slope in the direction of discharge of not less than one-eighth unit vertical in 12 units horizontal (1-percent slope). When unable to drain by gravity a condensate pump may be used. Where pumps are used, they shall be installed with a factory-equipped auxiliary high-level switch and shall shut off equipment served upon activation of the auxiliary high-level switch. Where damage to any building components will occur as a result of overflow from the pump, the pump shall also be located in the auxiliary drain pan or in a separate drain pan equipped with a separate drain line or water-level detection device. Condensate shall not discharge into a street, alley or other areas so as to cause a nuisance.

307.2.2 Drain pipe materials and sizes. Components of the condensate disposal system shall be cast iron, galvanized steel, copper, cross-linked polyethylene, polybutylene, polyethylene, ABS, CPVC or PVC pipe or tubing. All components shall be selected for the pressure and temperature rating of the installation. Joints and connections shall be made in accordance with the applicable provisions of Chapter 7 of the *International Plumbing Code* relative to the material type.

TABLE 307.2.2
CONDENSATE DRAIN SIZING

Deleted.

307.2.3 Auxiliary and secondary drain systems. In addition to the requirements of Section 307.2.1, where damage to any building components could occur as a result of overflow from the *equipment* primary condensate removal system, one of the following auxiliary protection methods shall be provided for each cooling coil or fuel-fired *appliance* that produces condensate:

1. An auxiliary drain pan with a separate drain shall be provided under the coils on which condensation will occur. The auxiliary pan drain shall discharge to a conspicuous point of disposal to alert occupants in the event of a stoppage of the primary drain. The pan shall have a minimum depth of $1^1/_2$ inches (38 mm), shall not be less than 3 inches (76 mm) larger than the unit or the coil dimensions in width and length and shall be constructed of corrosion-resistant material. Galvanized sheet steel pans shall have a minimum thickness of not less than 0.0236 inch (0.6010 mm) (No. 24 gage). Nonmetallic pans shall have a minimum thickness of not less than 0.0625 inch (1.6 mm).
2. A separate overflow drain line shall be connected to the drain pan provided with the *equipment*. Such overflow drain shall discharge to a conspicuous point of disposal to alert occupants in the event of a stoppage of the primary drain. The overflow drain line shall connect to the drain pan at a higher level than the primary drain connection.
3. An auxiliary drain pan without a separate drain line shall be provided under the coils on which condensate will occur. Such pan shall be equipped with a water-level detection device conforming to UL 508 that will shut off the *equipment* served prior to overflow of the pan. The auxiliary drain pan shall be constructed in accordance with Item 1 of this section.
4. A water-level detection device conforming to UL 508 shall be provided that will shut off the *equipment* served in the event that the primary drain is blocked. The device shall be installed in the primary drain line,

upstream of the primary drain line trap, the overflow drain line, or in the equipment-supplied drain pan, located at a point higher than the primary drain line connection and below the overflow rim of such pan.

Exception: Fuel-fired appliances that automatically shut down operation in the event of a stoppage in the condensate drainage system.

307.2.3.1 Water-level monitoring devices. On downflow units and all other coils that do not have a secondary drain or provisions to install a secondary or auxiliary drain pan, a water-level monitoring device shall be installed inside the primary drain pan. This device shall shut off the *equipment* served in the event that the primary drain becomes restricted. Devices installed in the drain line shall not be permitted.

307.2.3.2 Appliance, equipment and insulation in pans. Where appliances, *equipment* or insulation are subject to water damage when auxiliary drain pans fill, that portion of the *appliance*, *equipment* and insulation shall be installed above the rim of the pan. Supports located inside of the pan to support the *appliance* or *equipment* shall be water resistant and *approved*.

307.2.4 Traps. Condensate drains shall be trapped as required by the *equipment* or *appliance* manufacturer.

SECTION 308 CLEARANCE REDUCTION FOR UNLISTED EQUIPMENT AND UNLISTED APPLIANCES

308.1 Scope. This section shall govern the reduction in required *clearances* to combustible materials and combustible assemblies for *chimneys,* vents, kitchen exhaust equipment, mechanical appliances, and mechanical devices and *equipment*.

308.2 Listed appliances and equipment. Deleted.

308.3 Protective assembly construction and installation. Reduced *clearance* protective assemblies, including structural and support elements, shall be constructed of noncombustible materials. Spacers utilized to maintain an airspace between the protective assembly and the protected material or assembly shall be noncombustible. Where a space between the protective assembly and protected combustible material or assembly is specified, the same space shall be provided around the edges of the protective assembly and the spacers shall be placed so as to allow air circulation by convection in such space. Protective assemblies shall not be placed less than 1 inch (25 mm) from the mechanical appliances, devices or *equipment*, regardless of the allowable reduced *clearance*.

308.4 Allowable reduction. The reduction of required *clearances* to combustible assemblies or combustible materials shall be based on the utilization of a reduced *clearance* protective assembly in accordance with Section 308.5 or 308.6.

308.5 Labeled assemblies. The allowable *clearance* reduction shall be based on an *approved* reduced *clearance* protective assembly that has been tested and bears the label of an *approved* agency.

308.6 Reduction table. The allowable *clearance* reduction shall be based on one of the methods specified in Table 308.6. Where required *clearances* are not listed in Table 308.6, the reduced *clearances* shall be determined by linear interpolation between the distances listed in the table. Reduced *clearances* shall not be derived by extrapolation below the range of the table.

308.7 Solid fuel-burning appliances. The *clearance* reduction methods specified in Table 308.6 shall not be utilized to reduce the *clearance* required for solid fuel-burning appliances that are *labeled* for installation with clearances.

308.8 Masonry chimneys. The *clearance* reduction methods specified in Table 308.6 shall not be utilized to reduce the *clearances* required for masonry *chimneys* as specified in Chapter 8 and the *International Building Code*.

308.9 Chimney connector pass-throughs. The *clearance* reduction methods specified in Table 308.6 shall not be utilized to reduce the *clearances* required for *chimney* connector pass-throughs as specified in Section 803.10.4.

308.10 Masonry fireplaces. The *clearance* reduction methods specified in Table 308.6 shall not be utilized to reduce the *clearances* required for masonry fireplaces as specified in Chapter 8 and the *International Building Code*.

308.11 Kitchen exhaust ducts. Deleted.

[B] SECTION 309 TEMPERATURE CONTROL

[B] 309.1 Space-heating systems. Interior spaces intended for human occupancy shall be provided with active or passive space-heating systems capable of maintaining a minimum indoor temperature of 68°F (20°C) at a point 3 feet (914 mm) above floor on the design heating day. The installation of portable space heaters shall not be used to achieve compliance with this section.

Exception: Interior spaces where the primary purpose is not associated with human comfort.

[F] SECTION 310 EXPLOSION CONTROL

Deleted

[F] SECTION 311 SMOKE AND HEAT VENTS

Deleted

SECTION 312 HEATING AND COOLING LOAD CALCULATIONS

312.1 Load calculations. Heating and cooling system design loads for the purpose of sizing systems, appliances and *equipment* shall be determined in accordance with the procedures described in the ASHRAE/ACCA Standard 183. Alternatively, design loads shall be determined by an *approved* equivalent computation procedure, using the design parameters specified in Chapter 3 of the *International Energy Conservation Code*.

For one- and two-family dwellings and townhouses, heating and cooling equipment shall be sized in accordance with ACCA Manual S based on building loads calculated in accordance with ACCA Manual J, or other approved heating and cooling calculation methodologies.

TABLE 308.6
CLEARANCE REDUCTION METHODS[b] FOR UNLISTED EQUIPMENT

TYPE OF PROTECTIVE ASSEMBLY[a]	REDUCED CLEARANCE WITH PROTECTION (inches)[a]							
	Horizontal combustible assemblies located above the heat source				Horizontal combustible assemblies located beneath the heat source and all vertical combustible assemblies			
	Required clearance to combustibles without protection (inches)[a]				Required clearance to combustibles without protection (inches)			
	36	18	9	6	36	18	9	6
Galvanized sheet steel, having a minimum thickness of 0.0236 inch (0.6010 mm) (No. 24 gage), mounted on 1-inch glass fiber or mineral wool batt reinforced with wire on the back, 1 inch off the combustible assembly	18	9	5	3	12	6	3	3
Galvanized sheet steel, having a minimum thickness of 0.0236 inch (0.6010 mm) (No. 24 gage), spaced 1 inch off the combustible assembly	18	9	5	3	12	6	3	3
Two layers of galvanized sheet steel, having a minimum thickness of 0.0236 inch (0.6010 mm) (No. 24 gage), having a 1-inch airspace between layers, spaced 1 inch off the combustible assembly	18	9	5	3	12	6	3	3
Two layers of galvanized sheet steel, having a minimum thickness of 0.0236 inch (0.6010 mm) (No. 24 gage), having 1 inch of fiberglass insulation between layers, spaced 1 inch off the combustible assembly	18	9	5	3	12	6	3	3
0.5-inch inorganic insulating board, over 1 inch of fiberglass or mineral wool batt, against the combustible assembly	24	12	6	4	18	9	5	3
$3^1/_2$-inch brick wall, spaced 1 inch off the combustible wall	—	—	—	—	12	6	6	6
$3^1/_2$-inch brick wall, against the combustible wall	—	—	—	—	24	12	6	5

For SI: 1 inch = 25.4 mm, °C = [(°F)-32]/1.8, 1 pound per cubic foot = 16.02 kg/m^3, 1.0 Btu · in/ft^2 · h · °F = 0.144 W/m^2 · K.

a. Mineral wool and glass fiber batts (blanket or board) shall have a minimum density of 8 pounds per cubic foot and a minimum melting point of 1,500°F. Insulation material utilized as part of a clearance reduction system shall have a thermal conductivity of 1.0 Btu · in/(ft^2 · h · °F) or less. Insulation board shall be formed of noncombustible material.

b. For limitations on clearance reduction for solid fuel-burning appliances, masonry chimneys, connector pass-throughs, masonry fireplaces and kitchen ducts, see Sections 308.7 through 308.11.

CHAPTER 4
VENTILATION

SECTION 401
GENERAL

401.1 Scope. This chapter shall govern the ventilation of spaces within a building intended to be occupied. Mechanical exhaust systems, including exhaust systems serving clothes dryers and cooking appliances shall comply with Chapter 5.

401.2 Ventilation required. Every occupied space shall be ventilated by natural means in accordance with Section 402 or by mechanical means in accordance with Section 403.

401.3 When required. Deleted.

401.4 Intake opening location. Air intake openings shall comply with all of the following:

1. Intake openings shall be located a minimum of 10 feet (3048 mm) from lot lines or buildings on the same lot. Where openings front on a street or public way, the distance shall be measured to the centerline of the street or public way.
2. Mechanical and gravity outdoor air intake openings shall be located not less than 10 feet (3048 mm) horizontally from any hazardous or noxious contaminant source, such as vents, streets, alleys, parking lots and loading docks, except as specified in Item 3 or Section 501.2.1.
3. Intake openings shall be located not less than 3 feet (914 mm) below contaminant sources where such sources are located within 10 feet (3048 mm) of the opening.
4. Intake openings on structures in flood hazard areas shall be at or above the design flood level.

401.5 Intake opening protection. Air intake openings that terminate outdoors shall be protected with corrosion-resistant screens, louvers or grilles. Openings in louvers, grilles and screens shall be sized in accordance with Table 401.5, and shall be protected against local weather conditions. Outdoor air intake openings located in exterior walls shall meet the provisions for exterior wall opening protectives in accordance with the *International Building Code.*

TABLE 401.5
OPENING SIZES IN LOUVERS, GRILLES AND SCREENS PROTECTING AIR INTAKE OPENINGS

OUTDOOR OPENING TYPE	MINIMUM AND MAXIMUM OPENING SIZES IN LOUVERS, GRILLES AND SCREENS MEASURED IN ANY DIRECTION
Intake openings in residential occupancies	Not < $^1/_4$ inch and not > $^1/_2$ inch

For SI: 1 inch = 25.4 mm.

401.6 Contaminant sources. Stationary local sources producing airborne particulates, heat, odors, fumes, spray, vapors, smoke or gases in such quantities as to be irritating or injurious to health shall be provided with an exhaust system in accordance with Chapter 5 or a means of collection and removal of the contaminants. Such exhaust shall discharge directly to an *approved* location at the exterior of the building.

SECTION 402
NATURAL VENTILATION

[B] 402.1 Natural ventilation. *Natural ventilation* of an occupied space shall be through windows, doors, louvers or other openings to the outdoors. The operating mechanism for such openings shall be provided with ready access so that the openings are readily controllable by the building occupants.

[B] 402.2 Ventilation area required. The minimum openable area to the outdoors shall be 4 percent of the floor area being ventilated.

[B] 402.3 Adjoining spaces. Where rooms and spaces without openings to the outdoors are ventilated through an adjoining room, the opening to the adjoining rooms shall be unobstructed and shall have an area not less than 8 percent of the floor area of the interior room or space, but not less than 25 square feet (2.3 m^2). The minimum openable area to the outdoors shall be based on the total floor area being ventilated.

> **Exception:** Exterior openings required for ventilation shall be permitted to open into a thermally isolated sunroom addition or patio cover, provided that the openable area between the sunroom addition or patio cover and the interior room has an area of not less than 8 percent of the floor area of the interior room or space, but not less than 20 square feet (1.86 m^2). The minimum openable area to the outdoors shall be based on the total floor area being ventilated.

[B] 402.4 Openings below grade. Where openings below grade provide required *natural ventilation*, the outside horizontal clear space measured perpendicular to the opening shall be one and one-half times the depth of the opening. The depth of the opening shall be measured from the average adjoining ground level to the bottom of the opening.

SECTION 403
MECHANICAL VENTILATION

403.1 Ventilation system. Mechanical ventilation shall be provided by a method of supply air and return or *exhaust air.* The amount of supply air shall be approximately equal to the amount of return and *exhaust air.* The system shall not be prohibited from producing negative or positive pressure. The system to convey *ventilation air* shall be designed and installed in accordance with Chapter 6.

403.2 Outdoor air required. The minimum outdoor airflow rate shall be determined in accordance with Section 403.3. Ventilation supply systems shall be designed to deliver the required rate of outdoor airflow to the *breathing zone* within each *occupiable space*.

> **Exception:** Where the *registered design professional* demonstrates that an engineered ventilation system design will prevent the maximum concentration of contaminants from exceeding that obtainable by the rate of outdoor air ventilation determined in accordance with Section 403.3, the mini-

mum required rate of outdoor air shall be reduced in accordance with such engineered system design.

403.2.1 Recirculation of air. The air required by Section 403.3 shall not be recirculated. Air in excess of that required by Section 403.3 shall not be prohibited from being recirculated as a component of supply air to building spaces, except that:

1. Ventilation air shall not be recirculated from one *dwelling* to another.
2. Deleted.
3. Where mechanical exhaust is required by Note b in Table 403.3, recirculation of air from such spaces shall be prohibited. All air supplied to such spaces shall be exhausted, including any air in excess of that required by Table 403.3.
4. Where mechanical exhaust is required by Note g in Table 403.3, mechanical exhaust is required and recirculation to other spaces is prohibited where 10 percent or more of the resulting supply airstream consists of air recirculated from these spaces.

403.2.2 Transfer air. Deleted.

403.3 Outdoor airflow rate. Ventilation systems shall be designed to have the capacity to supply the minimum outdoor airflow rate determined in accordance with this section. The occupant load utilized for design of the ventilation system shall not be less than the number determined from the estimated maximum occupant load rate indicated in Table 403.3.

403.3.1 Zone outdoor airflow. Deleted.

403.3.2 System outdoor airflow. Deleted.

403.4 Exhaust ventilation. Exhaust airflow rate shall be provided in accordance with the requirements in Table 403.3.

403.5 System operation. Deleted.

403.6 Variable air volume system control. Deleted.

403.7 Balancing. The *ventilation air* distribution system shall be provided with means to adjust the system to achieve at least the minimum ventilation airflow rate as required by Sections 403.3 and 403.4. Ventilation systems shall be balanced by an *approved* method. Such balancing shall verify that the ventilation system is capable of supplying and exhausting the airflow rates required by Sections 403.3 and 403.4.

SECTION 404 ENCLOSED PARKING GARAGES
Deleted

SECTION 405 SYSTEMS CONTROL
Deleted

SECTION 406 VENTILATION OF UNINHABITED SPACES
Deleted

TABLE 403.3
MINIMUM VENTILATION RATES

OCCUPANCY CLASSIFICATION	PEOPLE OUTDOOR AIRFLOW RATE IN BREATHING ZONE, R_p CFM/PERSON	AREA OUTDOOR AIRFLOW RATE IN BREATHING ZONE, R_a CFM/FT² [a]	DEFAULT OCCUPANT DENSITY #/1000 FT² [a]	EXHAUST AIRFLOW RATE CFM/FT² [a]
Private dwellings, single and multiple				
Garages, common for multiple units[b]	—	—	—	0.75
Kitchens[b]	—	—	—	25/100[f]
Living areas[c]	0.35 ACH but not less than 15 cfm/person	—	Based upon number of bedrooms. First bedroom, 2; each additional bedroom, 1	—
Toilet rooms and bathrooms[g]	—	—	—	20/50[f]

For SI: 1 cubic foot per minute = 0.0004719 m³/s, 1 ton = 908 kg, 1 cubic foot per minute per square foot = 0.00508 m³/(s · m²), C = [(F) -32]/1.8, 1 square foot = 0.0929 m².

a. Based upon net occupiable floor area.

b. Where mechanical exhaust is required and the recirculation of air to other spaces is prohibited (see Section 403.2.1, Item 3).

c. Spaces unheated or maintained below 50°F are not covered by these requirements unless the occupancy is continuous.

d. Ventilation systems in enclosed parking garages shall comply with Section 404.

e. Rates are per water closet or urinal. The higher rate shall be provided where periods of heavy use are expected to occur, such as toilets in theaters, schools and sports facilities. The lower rate shall be permitted where periods of heavy use are not expected.

f. Rates are per room unless otherwise indicated. The higher rate shall be provided where the exhaust system is designed to operate intermittently. The lower rate shall be permitted where the exhaust system is designed to operate continuously during normal hours of use.

g. Where mechanical exhaust is required and recirculation to other spaces is prohibited except that recirculation shall be permitted where the resulting supply airstream consists of not more than 10 percent air recirculated from these spaces (see Section 403.2.1, Items 2 and 4).

h. For nail salons, the required exhaust shall include ventilation tables or other systems that capture the contaminants and odors at their source and are capable of exhausting a minimum of 50 cfm per station.

i. **Exception:** Each school classroom's ventilation may be reduced to a minimum of 7.5 cfm/person in accordance with ASHRAE 62, Section 6.1.3.4. Additional ventilation or exhaust systems shall be provided as required for conditions to generate unusual odors or sensory irritating contaminants. Outside air intake components (louvers, fresh air ducts) shall be sized to provide 15 cfm/person temporarily for special ventilation needs.

CHAPTER 5
EXHAUST SYSTEMS

SECTION 501
GENERAL

501.1 Scope. This chapter shall govern the design, construction and installation of mechanical exhaust systems, including exhaust systems serving clothes dryers and cooking appliances.

501.2 Exhaust discharge. The air removed by every mechanical exhaust system shall be discharged outdoors at a point where it will not cause a nuisance and not less than the distances specified in Section 501.2.1. The air shall be discharged to a location from which it cannot again be readily drawn in by a ventilating system. Air shall not be exhausted into an attic or crawl space.

Exceptions:

1. Whole-house ventilation-type attic fans shall be permitted to discharge into the attic space of *dwelling units* having private attics.
2. Deleted.

501.2.1 Location of exhaust outlets. The termination point of exhaust outlets and ducts discharging to the outdoors shall be located with the following minimum distances:

1. Deleted.
2. Deleted.
3. For all *environmental air* exhaust: 3 feet (914 mm) from property lines; 3 feet (914 mm) from operable openings into buildings for all occupancies other than Group U, and 10 feet (3048 mm) from mechanical air intakes. Such exhaust shall not be considered hazardous or noxious.
4. Exhaust outlets serving structures in flood hazard areas shall be installed at or above the design flood level.
5. For specific systems see the following sections:
   - 5.1. Clothes dryer exhaust, Section 504.4.
   - 5.2. Deleted.
   - 5.3. Deleted.
   - 5.4. Deleted.
   - 5.5. Deleted.
   - 5.6. Deleted.
   - 5.7. Deleted.

501.2.1.1 Exhaust discharge. Deleted.

501.2.2 Exhaust opening protection. Exhaust openings that terminate outdoors shall be protected with corrosion-resistant screens, louvers or grilles. Openings in screens, louvers and grilles shall be sized not less than $^1/_4$ inch (6 mm) and not larger than $^1/_2$ inch (13 mm). Openings shall be protected against local weather conditions. Outdoor openings located in exterior walls shall meet the provisions for exterior wall opening protectives in accordance with the *International Building Code*.

501.3 Pressure equalization. Mechanical exhaust systems shall be sized to remove the quantity of air required by this chapter to be exhausted. The system shall operate when air is required to be exhausted.

Exception: Domestic exhaust systems in residential occupancies and similar uses (domestic clothes dryer, domestic range hood, domestic bathroom exhaust).

501.4 Ducts. Where exhaust duct construction is not specified in this chapter, such construction shall comply with Chapter 6.

SECTION 502
REQUIRED SYSTEMS

502.1 General. An exhaust system shall be provided, maintained and operated as specifically required by this section.

502.1.1 Exhaust location. The inlet to an exhaust system shall be located in the area of heaviest concentration of contaminants.

[F] 502.1.2 Fuel-dispensing areas. Deleted.

502.1.3 Equipment, appliance and service rooms. Deleted.

[F] 502.1.4 Hazardous exhaust. Deleted.

[F] 502.2 Aircraft fueling and defueling. Deleted.

[F] 502.3 Battery-charging areas for powered industrial trucks and equipment. Deleted.

[F] 502.4 Stationary storage battery systems. Deleted.

[F] 502.5 Valve-regulated lead-acid batteries in cabinets. Deleted.

[F] 502.6 Dry cleaning plants. Deleted.

[F] 502.7 Application of flammable finishes. Deleted.

[F] 502.8 Hazardous materials—general requirements. Deleted.

[F] 502.9 Hazardous materials—requirements for specific materials. Deleted.

[F] 502.10 Hazardous production materials (HPM). Deleted.

502.11 Motion picture projectors. Deleted.

[F] 502.12 Organic coating processes. Deleted.

502.13 Public garages. Deleted.

502.14 Motor vehicle operation. Deleted.

[F] 502.15 Repair garages. Deleted.

[F] 502.16 Repair garages for natural gas- and hydrogen-fueled vehicles. Deleted.

502.17 Tire rebuilding or recapping. Deleted.

502.18 Specific rooms. Deleted.

502.19 Indoor firing ranges. Deleted.

SECTION 503 MOTORS AND FANS Deleted

SECTION 504 CLOTHES DRYER EXHAUST

504.1 Installation. Clothes dryers shall be exhausted in accordance with the manufacturer's instructions. Dryer exhaust systems shall be independent of all other systems and shall convey the moisture and any products of *combustion* to the outside of the building.

Exception: This section shall not apply to *listed* and *labeled* condensing (ductless) clothes dryers.

504.2 Exhaust penetrations. Where a clothes dryer exhaust duct penetrates a wall or ceiling membrane, the annular space shall be sealed with noncombustible material, *approved* fire caulking or a noncombustible dryer exhaust duct wall receptacle. Ducts that exhaust clothes dryers shall not penetrate or be located within any fireblocking, draftstopping or any wall, floor/ceiling or other assembly required by the *International Building Code* to be fire-resistance rated, unless such duct is constructed of galvanized steel or aluminum of the thickness specified in Section 603.4 and the fire-resistance rating is maintained in accordance with the *International Building Code*. Fire dampers, combination fire/smoke dampers and any similar devices that will obstruct the exhaust flow shall be prohibited in clothes dryer exhaust ducts.

504.3 Cleanout. Each vertical riser shall be provided with a means for cleanout.

504.4 Exhaust installation. Dryer exhaust ducts for clothes dryers shall terminate on the outside of the building and shall be equipped with a backdraft damper. Screens shall not be installed at the duct termination. Ducts shall not be connected or installed with sheet metal screws or other fasteners that will obstruct the exhaust flow. Clothes dryer exhaust ducts shall not be connected to a vent connector, vent or *chimney*. Clothes dryer exhaust ducts shall not extend into or through ducts or plenums.

504.5 Makeup air. Where a closet is designed for the installation of a clothes dryer, an opening having an area of not less than 100 square inches (0.0645 m^2) shall be provided in the closet enclosure or *makeup air* shall be provided by other *approved* means.

504.6 Domestic clothes dryer ducts. Exhaust ducts for domestic clothes dryers shall conform to the requirements of Sections 504.6.1 through 504.6.7.

504.6.1 Material and size. Exhaust ducts shall have a smooth interior finish and shall be constructed of metal a minimum 0.016 inch (0.4 mm) thick. With the exception of the transition duct, flexible ducts are prohibited. The exhaust duct size shall be 4 inches (102 mm) nominal in diameter.

504.6.2 Duct installation. Exhaust ducts shall be supported at 4-foot (1219 mm) intervals and secured in place and shall terminate not less than 12 inches (305 mm) above finished grade. The insert end of the duct shall extend into the adjoining duct or fitting in the direction of airflow. Ducts shall not be joined with screws or similar fasteners that protrude into the inside of the duct.

Exception: Where the duct termination is less than 12 inches (305 mm) above finished grade, an areaway shall be provided with a cross-sectional area not less than 200 square inches (1290 cm^2). The bottom of the duct termination shall be no less than 12 inches (305 mm) above the areaway bottom.

504.6.3 Transition ducts. Transition ducts used to connect the dryer to the exhaust duct system shall be a single length that is *listed* and *labeled* in accordance with UL 2158A. Transition ducts shall be a maximum of 8 feet (2438 mm) in length, shall not be concealed within construction, and must remain entirely within the room in which the appliance is installed.

504.6.4 Duct length. The maximum allowable exhaust duct length shall be determined by one of the methods specified in Section 504.6.4.1 or 504.6.4.2.

504.6.4.1 Specified length. The maximum length of the exhaust duct shall be 35 feet (10 668 mm) from the connection to the transition duct from the dryer to the outlet terminal. Where fittings are used, the maximum length of the exhaust duct shall be reduced in accordance with Table 504.6.4.1.

TABLE 504.6.4.1
DRYER EXHAUST DUCT FITTING EQUIVALENT LENGTH

DRYER EXHAUST DUCT FITTING TYPE	EQUIVALENT LENGTH
4″ radius mitered 45-degree elbow	2 feet 6 inches
4″ radius mitered 90-degree elbow	5 feet
6″ radius smooth 45-degree elbow	1 foot
6″ radius smooth 90-degree elbow	1 foot 9 inches
8″ radius smooth 45-degree elbow	1 foot
8″ radius smooth 90-degree elbow	1 foot 7 inches
10″ radius smooth 45-degree elbow	9 inches
10″ radius smooth 90-degree elbow	1 foot 6 inches

For SI: 1 inch = 25.4 mm, 1 foot = 304.8 mm, 1 degree = 0.0175 rad.

504.6.4.2 Manufacturer's instructions. The maximum length of the exhaust duct shall be determined by the dryer manufacturer's installation instructions. The code official shall be provided with a copy of the installation instructions for the make and model of the dryer. Where the exhaust duct is to be concealed, the installation instructions shall be provided to the code official prior to the concealment inspection. In the absence of fitting equivalent length calculations from the clothes dryer manufacturer, Table 504.6.4.1 shall be used.

504.6.5 Length identification. The equivalent length of the exhaust duct shall be identified on a permanent label or tag. The label or tag shall be located within 6 feet (1829 mm) of the exhaust duct connection.

504.6.6 Exhaust duct required. Where space for a clothes dryer is provided, an exhaust duct system shall be installed.

Exception: Where a *listed* condensing clothes dryer is installed prior to occupancy of structure.

504.6.7 Protection required. Protective shield plates shall be placed where nails or screws from finish or other work are likely to penetrate the clothes dryer exhaust duct. Shield plates shall be placed on the finished face of all framing members where there is less than $1^1/_4$ inches (32 mm) between the duct and the finished face of the framing member. Protective shield plates shall be constructed of steel, have a thickness of 0.062 inch (1.6 mm) and extend a minimum of 2 inches (51 mm) above sole plates and below top plates.

504.7 Commercial clothes dryers. Deleted.

504.8 Common exhaust systems for clothes dryers located in multistory structures. Deleted.

SECTION 505
DOMESTIC KITCHEN EXHAUST EQUIPMENT

505.1 Domestic systems. Where domestic range hoods and domestic appliances equipped with downdraft exhaust are located within dwelling units, such hoods and appliances shall discharge to the outdoors through sheet metal ducts constructed of galvanized steel, stainless steel, aluminum or copper. Such ducts shall have smooth inner walls and shall be air tight and equipped with a backdraft damper.

Exceptions:

1. Where installed in accordance with the manufacturer's installation instructions and where mechanical or *natural ventilation* is otherwise provided in accordance with Chapter 4, *listed* and *labeled* ductless range hoods shall not be required to discharge to the outdoors.
2. Ducts for domestic kitchen cooking appliances equipped with downdraft exhaust systems shall be permitted to be constructed of Schedule 40 PVC pipe and fittings provided that the installation complies with all of the following:
   - 2.1. The duct shall be installed under a concrete slab poured on grade.
   - 2.2. The underfloor trench in which the duct is installed shall be completely backfilled with sand or gravel.
   - 2.3. The PVC duct shall extend not more than 2 inches (50 mm) above the indoor concrete floor surface.
   - 2.4. The PVC duct shall extend not more than 2 inches (50 mm) above grade outside of the building.
   - 2.5. The PVC ducts shall be solvent cemented.

505.2 Makeup air required. Exhaust hood systems capable of exhausting in excess of 400 cfm (0.19 m^3/s) shall be provided with *makeup air* at a rate approximately equal to the *exhaust air* rate. Such *makeup air* systems shall be equipped with a means of closure and shall be automatically controlled to start and operate simultaneously with the exhaust system.

SECTION 506
COMMERCIAL KITCHEN HOOD VENTILATION SYSTEM DUCTS AND EXHAUST EQUIPMENT
Deleted

SECTION 507
COMMERCIAL KITCHEN HOODS
Deleted

SECTION 508
COMMERCIAL KITCHEN MAKEUP AIR
Deleted

SECTION 509
FIRE SUPPRESSION SYSTEMS
Deleted

SECTION 510
HAZARDOUS EXHAUST SYSTEMS
Deleted

SECTION 511
DUST, STOCK AND REFUSE CONVEYING SYSTEMS
Deleted

SECTION 512
SUBSLAB SOIL EXHAUST SYSTEMS
Deleted

SECTION 513
SMOKE CONTROL SYSTEMS
Deleted

SECTION 514
ENERGY RECOVERY VENTILATION SYSTEMS
Deleted

CHAPTER 6
DUCT SYSTEMS

SECTION 601
GENERAL

601.1 Scope. Duct systems used for the movement of air in air-conditioning, heating, ventilating and exhaust systems shall conform to the provisions of this chapter except as otherwise specified in Chapters 5 and 7.

> **Exception:** Ducts discharging combustible material directly into any *combustion* chamber shall conform to the requirements of NFPA 82.

[B] 601.2 Air movement in egress elements. Deleted.

[B] 601.3 Exits. Deleted.

601.4 Contamination prevention. Exhaust ducts under positive pressure, chimneys and vents shall not extend into or pass through ducts or plenums.

> **Exception:** Exhaust systems located in ceiling return air plenums over spaces that are permitted to have 10 percent recirculation in accordance with Section 403.2.1, Item 4. The exhaust duct joints, seams and connections shall comply with Section 603.9.

SECTION 602
PLENUMS

602.1 General. Supply, return, exhaust, relief and *ventilation air* plenums shall be limited to uninhabited crawl spaces, areas above a ceiling or below the floor, attic spaces and mechanical *equipment* rooms. Plenums shall be limited to one fire area. Fuel-fired appliances shall not be installed within a *plenum*.

602.2 Construction. *Plenum* enclosures shall be constructed of materials permitted for the type of construction classification of the building.

The use of gypsum boards to form plenums shall be limited to systems where the air temperatures do not exceed 125°F (52°C) and the building and mechanical system design conditions are such that the gypsum board surface temperature will be maintained above the airstream dew-point temperature. Air plenums formed by gypsum boards shall not be incorporated in air-handling systems utilizing evaporative coolers.

602.2.1 Materials within plenums. Deleted.

602.2.1.1 Wiring. Deleted.

602.2.1.2 Fire sprinkler piping. Deleted.

602.2.1.3 Pneumatic tubing. Deleted.

602.2.1.4 Electrical equipment in plenums. Deleted.

602.2.1.5 Foam plastic insulation. Foam plastic insulation used as wall or ceiling finish in plenums shall exhibit a flame spread index of 75 or less and a smoke-developed index of 450 or less when tested in accordance with ASTM E 84 or UL 723 and shall also comply with Section 602.2.1.5.1, 602.2.1.5.2 or 602.2.1.5.3.

602.2.1.5.1 Separation required. The foam plastic insulation shall be separated from the *plenum* by a thermal barrier complying with Section 2603.4 of the *International Building Code*.

602.2.1.5.2 Approval. The foam plastic insulation shall be *approved* based on tests conducted in accordance with Section 2603.9 of the *International Building Code*.

602.2.1.5.3 Covering. The foam plastic insulation shall be covered by corrosion-resistant steel having a base metal thickness of not less than 0.0160 inch (0.4 mm).

602.2.1.6 Semiconductor fabrication areas. Deleted.

602.3 Stud cavity and joist space plenums. Stud wall cavities and the spaces between solid floor joists to be utilized as air plenums shall comply with the following conditions:

1. Such cavities or spaces shall not be utilized as a *plenum* for supply air.
2. Such cavities or spaces shall not be part of a required fire-resistance-rated assembly.
3. Stud wall cavities shall not convey air from more than one floor level.
4. Deleted.
5. Stud wall cavities and joist space plenums shall be isolated from adjacent concealed spaces by *approved* fireblocking as required in the *Residential Building Code*.

[B] 602.4 Flood hazard. For structures located in flood hazard areas, *plenum* spaces shall be located above the *design flood elevation* or shall be designed and constructed to prevent water from entering or accumulating within the *plenum* spaces during floods up to the *design flood elevation*. If the *plenum* spaces are located below the *design flood elevation*, they shall be capable of resisting hydrostatic and hydrodynamic loads and stresses, including the effects of buoyancy, during the occurrence of flooding to the *design flood elevation*.

SECTION 603
DUCT CONSTRUCTION AND INSTALLATION

603.1 General. An air distribution system shall be designed and installed to supply the required distribution of air. Ducts shall be constructed, braced, reinforced and installed to provide structural strength and durability.

603.1.1 Nothing in this section shall be deemed to preclude the use, within a conditioned space, of a fabric air distribution device that combines the function of air transport and air diffusion, provided that the materials used shall have a flame spread/smoke-developed rating not greater that 25/50.

603.2 Duct sizing. Ducts installed within a single *dwelling unit* shall be sized in accordance with ACCA Manual D or other *approved* methods.

603.3 Duct classification. Deleted.

603.4 Metallic ducts. All metallic ducts shall have a minimum thickness as specified in Table 603.4.

603.4.1 Minimum fasteners. Round metallic ducts shall be mechanically fastened by means of at least three sheet metal screws or rivets spaced equally around the joint.

Exception: Where a duct connection is made that is partially inaccessible, three screws or rivets shall be equally spaced on the exposed portion so as to prevent a hinge effect.

603.5 Nonmetallic ducts. Nonmetallic ducts shall be constructed with Class 0 or Class 1 duct material in accordance with UL 181. Fibrous duct construction shall conform to the SMACNA *Fibrous Glass Duct Construction Standards* or NAIMA *Fibrous Glass Duct Construction Standards.* The maximum air temperature within nonmetallic ducts shall not exceed 250°F (121°C).

603.5.1 Gypsum ducts. The use of gypsum boards to form air shafts (ducts) shall be limited to return air systems where the air temperatures do not exceed 125°F (52°C) and the gypsum board surface temperature is maintained above the airstream dew-point temperature. Air ducts formed by gypsum boards shall not be incorporated in air-handling systems utilizing evaporative coolers.

603.6 Flexible air ducts and flexible air connectors. Flexible air ducts, both metallic and nonmetallic, shall comply with Sections 603.6.1, 603.6.1.1, 603.6.3 and 603.6.4. Flexible air connectors, both metallic and nonmetallic, shall comply with Sections 603.6.2 through 603.6.4.

603.6.1 Flexible air ducts. Flexible air ducts, both metallic and nonmetallic, shall be tested in accordance with UL 181. Such ducts shall be *listed* and *labeled* as Class 0 or Class 1 flexible air ducts and shall be installed in accordance with Section 304.1.

603.6.1.1 Duct length. Flexible air ducts shall not be limited in length.

603.6.2 Flexible air connectors. Flexible air connectors, both metallic and nonmetallic, shall be tested in accordance with UL 181. Such connectors shall be *listed* and *labeled* as Class 0 or Class 1 flexible air connectors and shall be installed in accordance with Section 304.1.

603.6.2.1 Connector length. Flexible air connectors shall be limited in length to 14 feet (4267 mm).

603.6.2.2 Connector penetration limitations. Flexible air connectors shall not pass through any wall, floor or ceiling.

603.6.3 Air temperature. The design temperature of air to be conveyed in flexible air ducts and flexible air connectors shall be less than 250°F (121°C).

603.6.4 Flexible air duct and air connector clearance. Flexible air ducts and air connectors shall be installed with a minimum *clearance* to an *appliance* as specified in the *appliance* manufacturer's installation instructions.

603.7 Rigid duct penetrations. Ducts in a private garage and ducts penetrating the walls or ceilings separating a *dwelling* from a private garage shall be continuous and constructed of a minimum 26 gage [0.0187 inch (0.4712 mm)] galvanized sheet metal or other approved noncombustible material and shall not have openings into the garage. Fire and smoke dampers are not required in such ducts passing through the wall or ceiling separating a *dwelling* from a private garage.

603.8 Underground ducts. Ducts shall be *approved* for underground installation. Metallic ducts not having an *approved* protective coating shall be completely encased in a minimum of 2 inches (51 mm) of concrete.

603.8.1 Slope. Ducts shall have a minimum slope of $^1/_8$ inch per foot (10.4 mm/m) to allow drainage to a point provided with access.

603.8.2 Sealing. Ducts shall be sealed and secured prior to pouring the concrete encasement.

603.8.3 Plastic ducts and fittings. Plastic ducts shall be constructed of PVC having a minimum pipe stiffness of 8 psi (55 kPa) at 5-percent deflection when tested in accordance with ASTM D 2412. Plastic duct fittings shall be constructed of either PVC or high-density polyethylene. Plastic duct and fittings shall be utilized in underground installations only. The maximum design temperature for systems utilizing plastic duct and fittings shall be 150°F (66°C).

603.9 Joints, seams and connections. All longitudinal and transverse joints, seams and connections in metallic and nonmetallic ducts shall be constructed as specified in SMACNA *HVAC Duct Construction Standards—Metal and Flexible* and NAIMA *Fibrous Glass Duct Construction Standards.* All joints, longitudinal and transverse seams and connections in ductwork shall be securely fastened and sealed with welds, gaskets, mastics (adhesives), mastic-plus-embedded-fabric systems, liquid sealants or tapes. Closure systems used to seal ductwork *listed* and *labeled* in accordance with UL 181A shall be marked "181A-P" for pressure-sensitive tape, "181 A-M" for mastic or "181 A-H" for heat-sensitive tape. Closure systems used to seal flexible air ducts and flexible air connectors shall comply with UL 181B and shall be marked "181B-FX" for pressure-sensitive tape or "181B-M" for mastic. Duct connections to flanges of air distribution system *equipment* shall be sealed and mechanically fastened. Mechanical fasteners for use with flexible nonmetallic air ducts shall comply with UL 181B and shall be marked "181B-C." Closure systems used to seal metal ductwork shall be installed in accordance with the manufacturer's installation instructions. Unlisted duct tape is not permitted as a sealant on any metal ducts.

Exceptions:

1. Continuously welded joints and seams in ducts.
2. Ducts exposed within the conditioned space the ducts serve shall not be required to be sealed.

603.10 Supports. Ducts shall be supported with *approved* hangers at intervals not exceeding 10 feet (3048 mm) or by other *approved* duct support systems designed in accordance with the *International Building Code*. Flexible and other factory-made ducts shall be supported in accordance with the manufacturer's installation instructions.

603.10.1 For one- and two-family dwellings and townhouses. Metal ducts shall be securely supported. Where hung or suspended, metal straps a minimum of 1 inch (25 mm) in width and equivalent to or heavier gage than the duct being supported shall be used. Straps, when used, shall be at maximum 64-inch (1626 mm) intervals and shall be securely attached to the building structure. Straps shall be attached to the duct at a minimum of two points with screws or rivets. Hanger systems shall comply with this section or other approved means. Nonmetallic or listed duct systems shall be supported in accordance with the manufacturer's installation instructions. All equipment shall be supported independently of the duct system except when the duct is used as a support base. When used as a support base, the duct shall be of sufficient strength and designed to support the weight of the unit. Listed bases shall be installed in accordance with the manufacturer's installation instructions.

603.11 Furnace connections. Ducts connecting to a furnace shall have a *clearance* to combustibles in accordance with the furnace manufacturer's installation instructions.

603.12 Condensation. Provisions shall be made to prevent the formation of condensation on the exterior of new duct. Ducts installed in attics, crawl spaces or outdoors, insulated in accordance with Section 403.2.1, or Section 503.2.7 of the *North Carolina Energy Code* shall be deemed to meet the intent of this section.

[B] 603.13 Flood hazard areas. For structures in flood hazard areas, ducts shall be located above the *design flood elevation* or shall be designed and constructed to prevent water from entering or accumulating within the ducts during floods up to the *design flood elevation*. If the ducts are located below the *design flood elevation*, the ducts shall be capable of resisting hydrostatic and hydrodynamic loads and stresses, including the effects of buoyancy, during the occurrence of flooding to the *design flood elevation*.

603.14 Location. Ducts shall not be installed in or within 4 inches (102 mm) of the earth, except where such ducts comply with Section 603.8.

603.15 Mechanical protection. Ducts installed in locations where they are exposed to mechanical damage by vehicles or from other causes shall be protected by *approved* barriers.

603.16 Weather protection. All ducts including linings, coverings and vibration isolation connectors installed on the exterior of the building shall be protected against the elements.

603.17 Registers, grilles and diffusers. Duct registers, grilles and diffusers shall be installed in accordance with the manufacturer's installation instructions. Volume dampers or other means of supply air adjustment shall be provided in the branch ducts or at each individual duct register, grille or diffuser. Each volume damper or other means of supply air adjustment used in balancing shall be provided with access.

603.17.1 Floor registers. Floor registers shall resist, without structural failure, a 200-pound (90.8 kg) concentrated load on a 2-inch-diameter (51 mm) disc applied to the most critical area of the exposed face.

603.17.2 Prohibited locations. Deleted.

603.18 Return-air intake (nonengineered systems). If only one central return-air grille is installed, it shall be of a size sufficient to return a volume of air compatible with the CFM requirements and the temperature rise limitations specified by the equipment manufacturer. The face velocity of return air grilles shall not exceed 450 feet per minute (fpm) (2.3 m/s). At least one separate return shall be installed on each level of a multilevel structure. For split-level and split-foyer structures, one return may serve more than one level if located within the split area and the total area of the levels does not exceed 1,600 square feet (148.6 m^2). Return-air grilles shall not be located in bathrooms. The return air from one residential living unit shall not be mixed with the return air from other living units.

In dwellings with 1,600 square feet (148.6 m^2) or less of conditioned area, a central return is permitted. When the dwelling contains more than 1,600 square feet (148.6 m^2) of conditioned area, additional returns shall be provided. Each return shall serve not more than 1,600 square feet (148.6 m^2) of area and shall be located in the area it serves. Return air may travel through the living space to the return-air intake if there are no restrictions, such as solid doors, to the air movement. When panned joists are used for return air, the structural integrity

TABLE 603.4
DUCT CONSTRUCTION MINIMUM SHEET METAL THICKNESSES FOR SINGLE DWELLING UNITS

DUCT SIZE	GALVANIZED		ALUMINUM MINIMUM THICKNESS (in.)
	Minimum thickness (in.)	Equivalent galvanized gage no.	
Round ducts and enclosed rectangular ducts			
14 inches or less	0.0157	28	0.0175
16 and 18 inches	0.0187	26	0.018
20 inches and over	0.0236	24	0.023
Exposed rectangular ducts			
14 inches or less	0.0157	28	0.0175
Over 14 inches[a]	0.0187	26	0.018

For SI: 1 inch = 25.4 mm, 1 inch water gage = 249 Pa.

a. For duct gages and reinforcement requirements at static pressures of $^1/_2$-inch, 1-inch and 2-inch w.g., SMACNA *HVAC Duct Construction Standards*, Tables 2-1, 2-2 and 2-3, shall apply.

shall be maintained. Air capacity for joists 16 inches (406 mm) on center shall be a maximum of 375 cubic feet per minute (0.177 m^3/s) for 8-inch (203 mm) joists and 525 cubic feet per minute (0.248 m^3/s) for 10-inch (254 mm) joists. Wiring located in spaces used for return-air ducts shall comply with the *North Carolina Electrical Code.*

603.19 Under-floor furnace plenums. Under-floor furnace plenums shall be prohibited in new structures. Modification or repairs to existing under-floor furnace plenums in existing structures shall conform to the requirements of this section.

603.19.1 General. The space shall be cleaned of loose combustible materials and scrap, and shall be tightly enclosed. The ground surface of the space shall be covered with a moisture barrier having a minimum thickness of 4 mils (0.1 mm). Plumbing waste cleanouts shall not be located within the space.

603.19.2 Materials. The under-floor space, including the sidewall insulation, shall be formed by materials having flame spread ratings not greater than 200 when tested in accordance with ASTM E 84.

603.19.3 Furnace connections. A duct shall extend from the furnace supply outlet to not less than 6 inches (152 mm) below the combustible framing. This duct shall comply with the provisions of Section 603. A noncombustible receptacle shall be installed below any floor opening into the plenum in accordance with the following requirements:

1. The receptacle shall be securely suspended from the floor members and shall not be more than 18 inches (457 mm) below the floor opening.
2. The area of the receptacle shall extend 3 inches (76 mm) beyond the opening on all sides.
3. The perimeter of the receptacle shall have a vertical lip at least 1 inch (25 mm) high at the open sides.

603.19.4 Access. Access to an under-floor furnace plenum shall be provided through an opening in the floor with minimum dimensions of 18 inches by 24 inches (457 mm by 610 mm).

603.19.5 Furnace controls. The furnace shall be equipped with an automatic control that will start the air-circulating fan when the air in the furnace bonnet reaches a temperature not higher than 150°F (66°C). The furnace shall additionally be equipped with an approved automatic control that limits the outlet air temperature to 200°F (93°C).

SECTION 604
INSULATION

604.1 General. Duct insulation shall conform to the requirements of Part IV of the *North Carolina Residntial Code.* Replacement or addition of cooling equipment to existing ductwork located in an attic shall require the ductwork to be insulated. Replacement of heating or the addition of cooling equipment in a crawl space shall not require the existing ductwork to be insulated.

604.2 Surface temperature. Ducts that operate at temperatures exceeding 120°F (49°C) shall have sufficient thermal insulation to limit the exposed surface temperature to 120°F (49°C).

604.3 Coverings and linings. Coverings and linings, including adhesives when used, shall have a flame spread index not more than 25 and a smoke-developed index not more than 50, when tested in accordance with ASTM E 84 or UL 723, using the specimen preparation and mounting procedures of ASTM E 2231. Duct coverings and linings shall not flame, glow, smolder or smoke when tested in accordance with ASTM C 411 at the temperature to which they are exposed in service. The test temperature shall not fall below 250°F (121°C).

604.4 Foam plastic insulation. Foam plastic used as duct coverings and linings shall conform to the requirements of Section 604.

604.5 Appliance insulation. *Listed* and *labeled* appliances that are internally insulated shall be considered as conforming to the requirements of Section 604.

604.6 Penetration of assemblies. Deleted.

604.7 Identification. External duct insulation, except spray polyurethane foam, and factory-insulated flexible duct shall be legibly printed or identified at intervals not greater than 36 inches (914 mm) with the name of the manufacturer, the thermal resistance *R*-value at the specified installed thickness and the flame spread and smoke-developed indexes of the composite materials. All duct insulation product *R*-values shall be based on insulation only, excluding air films, vapor retarders or other duct components, and shall be based on tested *C*-values at 75°F (24°C) mean temperature at the installed thickness, in accordance with recognized industry procedures. The installed thickness of duct insulation used to determine its *R*-value shall be determined as follows:

1. For duct board, duct liner and factory-made rigid ducts not normally subjected to compression, the nominal insulation thickness shall be used.
2. For duct wrap, the installed thickness shall be assumed to be 75 percent (25 percent compression) of nominal thickness.
3. For factory-made flexible air ducts, the installed thickness shall be determined by dividing the difference between the actual outside diameter and nominal inside diameter by two.
4. For spray polyurethane foam, the aged *R*-value per inch, measured in accordance with recognized industry standards, shall be provided to the customer in writing at the time of foam application.

604.8 Lining installation. Linings shall be interrupted at the area of operation of a fire damper and at a minimum of 6 inches (152 mm) upstream of and 6 inches (152 mm) downstream of electric-resistance and fuel-burning heaters in a duct system. Metal nosings or sleeves shall be installed over exposed duct liner edges that face opposite the direction of airflow.

604.9 Thermal continuity. Where a duct liner has been interrupted, a duct covering of equal thermal performance shall be installed.

Exception: See Section 604.6.

604.10 Service openings. Deleted.

604.11 Vapor retarders. Where ducts used for cooling are externally insulated, the insulation shall be covered with a vapor retarder having a maximum permeance of 0.05 perm [2.87 ng/(Pa • s • m^2)] or aluminum foil having a minimum thickness of 2 mils (0.051 mm). Insulations having a permeance of 0.05 perm [2.87 ng/(Pa • s • m^2)] or less shall not be required to be covered. All joints and seams shall be sealed to maintain the continuity of the vapor retarder.

604.12 Weatherproof barriers. Insulated exterior ducts shall be protected with an *approved* weatherproof barrier.

604.13 Internal insulation. Materials used as internal insulation and exposed to the airstream in ducts shall be shown to be durable when tested in accordance with UL 181. Exposed internal insulation that is not impermeable to water shall not be used to line ducts or plenums from the exit of a cooling coil to the downstream end of the drain pan.

SECTION 605
AIR FILTERS

605.1 General. Heating and air-conditioning systems of the central type shall be provided with *approved* air filters. Filters shall be installed in the return air system, upstream from any heat exchanger or coil, in an *approved* convenient location. Liquid adhesive coatings used on filters shall have a flash point not lower than 325°F (163°C).

605.2 Approval. Media-type and electrostatic-type air filters shall be *listed* and *labeled.* Media-type air filters shall comply with UL 900. High efficiency particulate air filters shall comply with UL 586. Electrostatic-type air filters shall comply with UL 867. Air filters utilized within *dwelling units* shall be designed for the intended application and shall not be required to be *listed* and *labeled.*

605.3 Airflow over the filter. Ducts shall be constructed to allow an even distribution of air over the entire filter.

SECTION 606
SMOKE DETECTION SYSTEMS CONTROL
Deleted

[B] SECTION 607
DUCT AND TRANSFER OPENINGS
Deleted

CHAPTER 7
COMBUSTION AIR

SECTION 701
GENERAL

701.1 Scope. Solid fuel-burning *appliances* shall be provided with *combustion air* in accordance with the appliance manufacturer's installation instructions. Oil-fired *appliances* shall be provided with *combustion air* in accordance with NFPA 31. The methods of providing *combustion air* in this chapter do not apply to fireplaces, fireplace stoves and direct-vent *appliances*. The requirements for combustion and dilution air for gas-fired *appliances* shall be in accordance with the *International Fuel Gas Code*.

CHAPTER 8
CHIMNEYS AND VENTS

SECTION 801
GENERAL

801.1 Scope. This chapter shall govern the installation, maintenance, repair and approval of factory-built chimneys, *chimney* liners, vents and connectors. This chapter shall also govern the utilization of masonry chimneys. Gas-fired *appliances* shall be vented in accordance with the *International Fuel Gas Code.*

801.2 General. Every fuel-burning *appliance* shall discharge the products of *combustion* to a vent, factory-built *chimney* or masonry *chimney*, except for *appliances* vented in accordance with Section 804. The *chimney* or vent shall be designed for the type of *appliance* being vented.

Exception: Deleted.

801.2.1 Oil-fired appliances. Oil-fired *appliances* shall be vented in accordance with this code and NFPA 31.

801.3 Masonry chimneys. Masonry *chimneys* shall be constructed in accordance with the *International Building Code*.

801.4 Positive flow. Venting systems shall be designed and constructed so as to develop a positive flow adequate to convey all *combustion* products to the outside atmosphere.

801.5 Design. Venting systems shall be designed in accordance with this chapter or shall be *approved* engineered systems.

801.6 Minimum size of chimney or vent. Except as otherwise provided for in this chapter, the size of the *chimney* or vent, serving a single *appliance*, except engineered systems, shall have a minimum area equal to the area of the *appliance* connection.

801.7 Solid fuel appliance flues. The cross-sectional area of a flue serving a solid-fuel-burning *appliance* shall be not greater than three times the cross-sectional area of the *appliance* flue collar or flue outlet.

801.8 Abandoned inlet openings. Abandoned inlet openings in chimneys and vents shall be closed by an *approved* method.

801.9 Positive pressure. Where an *appliance* equipped with a forced or induced draft system creates a positive pressure in the venting system, the venting system shall be designed and *listed* for positive pressure applications.

801.10 Connection to fireplace. Connection of *appliances* to *chimney* flues serving fireplaces shall be in accordance with Sections 801.10.1 through 801.10.3.

801.10.1 Closure and access. A noncombustible seal shall be provided below the point of connection to prevent entry of room air into the flue. Means shall be provided for *access* to the flue for inspection and cleaning.

801.10.2 Connection to factory-built fireplace flue. An *appliance* shall not be connected to a flue serving a factory-built fireplace unless the *appliance* is specifically *listed* for such installation. The connection shall be made in accordance with the *appliance* manufacturer's installation instructions.

801.10.3 Connection to masonry fireplace flue. A connector shall extend from the *appliance* to the flue serving a masonry fireplace such that the flue gases are exhausted directly into the flue. The connector shall be provided with access or shall be removable for inspection and cleaning of both the connector and the flue. *Listed* direct connection devices shall be installed in accordance with their listing.

801.11 Multiple solid fuel prohibited. A solid fuel-burning *appliance* or fireplace shall not connect to a *chimney* passageway venting another *appliance*.

801.12 Chimney entrance. Connectors shall connect to a *chimney* flue at a point not less than 12 inches (305 mm) above the lowest portion of the interior of the *chimney* flue.

801.13 Cleanouts. Masonry *chimney* flues shall be provided with a cleanout opening having a minimum height of 6 inches (152 mm). The upper edge of the opening shall be located not less than 6 inches (152 mm) below the lowest *chimney* inlet opening. The cleanout shall be provided with a tight-fitting, noncombustible cover.

Exception: Cleanouts shall not be required for *chimney* flues serving masonry fireplaces, if such flues are provided with access through the fireplace opening.

801.14 Connections to exhauster. All *appliance* connections to a *chimney* or vent equipped with a power exhauster shall be made on the inlet side of the exhauster. All joints and piping on the positive pressure side of the exhauster shall be *listed* for positive pressure applications as specified by the manufacturer's installation instructions for the exhauster.

801.15 Fuel-fired appliances. Masonry chimneys utilized to vent fuel-fired *appliances* shall be located, constructed and sized as specified in the manufacturer's installation instructions for the *appliances* being vented.

801.16 Flue lining. Masonry chimneys shall be lined. The lining material shall be compatible with the type of *appliance* connected, in accordance with the *appliance* listing and manufacturer's installation instructions. *Listed* materials used as flue linings shall be installed in accordance with their listings and the manufacturer's installation instructions.

801.16.1 Residential and low-heat appliances (general). Flue lining systems for use with residential-type and low-heat appliances shall be limited to the following:

1. Clay flue lining complying with the requirements of ASTM C 315 or equivalent. Clay flue lining shall be installed in accordance with the *International Building Code*.

2. *Listed chimney* lining systems complying with UL 1777.
3. Other *approved* materials that will resist, without cracking, softening or corrosion, flue gases and condensate at temperatures up to 1,800°F (982°C).

801.17 Space around lining. The space surrounding a flue lining system or other vent installed within a masonry *chimney* shall not be used to vent any other *appliance*. This shall not prevent the installation of a separate flue lining in accordance with the manufacturer's installation instructions and this code.

801.18 Existing chimneys and vents. Where an *appliance* is permanently disconnected from an existing *chimney* or vent, or where an *appliance* is connected to an existing *chimney* or vent during the process of a new installation, the *chimney* or vent shall comply with Sections 801.18.1 through 801.18.4.

801.18.1 Size. The *chimney* or vent shall be resized as necessary to control flue gas condensation in the interior of the *chimney* or vent and to provide the *appliance* or *appliances* served with the required draft. For the venting of oil-fired *appliances* to masonry chimneys, the resizing shall be in accordance with NFPA 31.

801.18.2 Flue passageways. The flue gas passageway shall be free of obstructions and combustible deposits and shall be cleaned if previously used for venting a solid or liquid fuel-burning *appliance* or fireplace. The flue liner, *chimney* inner wall or vent inner wall shall be continuous and shall be free of cracks, gaps, perforations or other damage or deterioration which would allow the escape of *combustion* products, including gases, moisture and creosote. Where an oil-fired *appliance* is connected to an existing masonry *chimney*, such *chimney* flue shall be repaired or relined in accordance with NFPA 31.

801.18.3 Cleanout. Masonry chimneys shall be provided with a cleanout opening complying with Section 801.13.

801.18.4 Clearances. Chimneys and vents shall have air-space *clearance* to combustibles in accordance with the *International Building Code* and the *chimney* or vent manufacturer's installation instructions.

Exception: Masonry chimneys without the required air-space *clearances* shall be permitted to be used if lined or relined with a *chimney* lining system *listed* for use in chimneys with reduced *clearances* in accordance with UL 1777. The *chimney clearance* shall be not less than permitted by the terms of the *chimney* liner listing and the manufacturer's instructions.

801.18.4.1 Fireblocking. Noncombustible fireblocking shall be provided in accordance with the *International Building Code.*

801.19 Multistory prohibited. Common venting systems for appliances located on more than one floor level shall be prohibited, except where all of the appliances served by the common vent are located in rooms or spaces that are accessed only from the outdoors. The *appliance* enclosures shall not communicate with the occupiable areas of the building.

801.20 Plastic vent joints. Plastic pipe and fittings used to vent appliances shall be installed in accordance with the pipe manufacturer's installation instructions and the appliance manufacturer's installation instructions. Solvent cement joints between ABS pipe and fittings shall be cleaned. Solvent cement joints between CPVC pipe and fittings or PVC pipe and fittings shall be primed. The primer shall be a contrasting color.

SECTION 802
VENTS

802.1 General. All vent systems shall be *listed* and *labeled.* Type L vents and pellet vents shall be tested in accordance with UL 641.

802.2 Vent application. The application of vents shall be in accordance with Table 802.2.

TABLE 802.2
VENT APPLICATION

VENT TYPES	APPLIANCE TYPES
Type L oil vents	Oil-burning appliances listed and labeled for venting with Type L vents; gas appliances listed and labeled for venting with Type B vents.
Pellet vents	Pellet fuel-burning appliances listed and labeled for venting with pellet vents.

802.3 Installation. Vent systems shall be sized, installed and terminated in accordance with the vent and *appliance* manufacturer's installation instructions.

802.4 Vent termination caps required. Type L vents shall terminate with a *listed* and *labeled* cap in accordance with the vent manufacturer's installation instructions.

802.5 Type L vent terminations. Type L vents shall terminate not less than 2 feet (610 mm) above the highest point of the roof penetration and not less than 2 feet (610 mm) higher than any portion of a building within 10 feet (3048 mm).

802.6 Minimum vent heights. Vents shall terminate not less than 5 feet (1524 mm) in vertical height above the highest connected *appliance* flue collar.

Exceptions:

1. Venting systems of direct vent *appliances* shall be installed in accordance with the *appliance* and the vent manufacturer's instructions.
2. Appliances *listed* for outdoor installations incorporating integral venting means shall be installed in accordance with their listings and the manufacturer's installation instructions.
3. Pellet vents shall be installed in accordance with the *appliance* and the vent manufacturer's installation instructions.

802.7 Support of vents. All portions of vents shall be adequately supported for the design and weight of the materials employed.

802.8 Insulation shield. Where vents pass through insulated assemblies, an insulation shield constructed of not less than No. 26 gage sheet metal shall be installed to provide *clearance* between the vent and the insulation material. The *clearance* shall be not less than the *clearance* to combustibles specified by the vent manufacturer's installation instructions. Where vents pass through attic space, the shield shall terminate not less than 2 inches (51 mm) above the insulation materials and shall be secured in place to prevent displacement. Insulation shields provided as part of a *listed* vent system shall be installed in accordance with the manufacturer's installation instructions.

SECTION 803
CONNECTORS

803.1 Connectors required. Connectors shall be used to connect *appliances* to the vertical *chimney* or vent, except where the *chimney* or vent is attached directly to the *appliance*.

803.2 Location. Connectors shall be located entirely within the room in which the connecting *appliance* is located, except as provided for in Section 803.10.4. Where passing through an unheated space, a connector shall not be constructed of single-wall pipe.

803.3 Size. The connector shall not be smaller than the size of the flue collar supplied by the manufacturer of the *appliance*. Where the *appliance* has more than one flue outlet, and in the absence of the manufacturer's specific instructions, the connector area shall be not less than the combined area of the flue outlets for which it acts as a common connector.

803.4 Branch connections. All branch connections to the vent connector shall be made in accordance with the vent manufacturer's instructions.

803.5 Manual dampers. Manual dampers shall not be installed in connectors except in *chimney* connectors serving solid fuel-burning *appliances*.

803.6 Automatic dampers. Automatic dampers shall be *listed* and *labeled* in accordance with UL 17 for oil-fired heating appliances. The dampers shall be installed in accordance with the manufacturer's installation instructions. An automatic vent damper device shall not be installed on an existing *appliance* unless the *appliance* is *listed* and *labeled* and the device is installed in accordance with the terms of its listing. The name of the installer and date of installation shall be marked on a label affixed to the damper device.

803.7 Connectors serving two or more appliances. Where two or more connectors enter a common vent or *chimney*, the smaller connector shall enter at the highest level consistent with available headroom or *clearance* to combustible material.

803.8 Vent connector construction. Vent connectors shall be constructed of metal. The minimum thickness of the connector shall be 0.0136 inch (0.345 mm) (No. 28 gage) for galvanized steel, 0.022 inch (0.6 mm) (No. 26 B & S gage) for copper, and 0.020 inch (0.5 mm) (No. 24 B & S gage) for aluminum.

803.9 Chimney connector construction. *Chimney* connectors for low-heat *appliances* shall be of sheet steel pipe having resistance to corrosion and heat not less than that of galvanized steel specified in Table 803.9(1).

TABLE 803.9(1)
MINIMUM CHIMNEY CONNECTOR THICKNESS FOR LOW-HEAT APPLIANCES

DIAMETER OF CONNECTOR (inches)	MINIMUM NOMINAL THICKNESS (galvanized) (inches)
5 and smaller	0.022 (No. 26 gage)
Larger than 5 and up to 10	0.028 (No. 24 gage)
Larger than 10 and up to 16	0.034 (No. 22 gage)
Larger than 16	0.064 (No. 16 gage)

For SI: 1 inch = 25.4 mm.

803.10 Installation. Connectors shall be installed in accordance with Sections 803.10.1 through 803.10.6.

803.10.1 Supports and joints. Connectors shall be supported in an *approved* manner, and joints shall be fastened with sheet metal screws, rivets or other *approved* means.

803.10.2 Length. The maximum horizontal length of a single-wall connector shall be 75 percent of the height of the *chimney* or vent.

803.10.3 Connection. The connector shall extend to the inner face of the *chimney* or vent liner, but not beyond. A connector entering a masonry *chimney* shall be cemented to masonry in an *approved* manner. Where thimbles are installed to facilitate removal of the connector from the masonry *chimney*, the thimble shall be permanently cemented in place with high-temperature cement.

803.10.4 Connector pass-through. *Chimney* connectors shall not pass through any floor or ceiling, nor through a fire-resistance-rated wall assembly. *Chimney* connectors for domestic-type *appliances* shall not pass through walls or partitions constructed of combustible material to reach a masonry *chimney* unless:

1. The connector is *labeled* for wall pass-through and is installed in accordance with the manufacturer's instructions;
2. The connector is put through a device *labeled* for wall pass-through; or
3. The connector has a diameter not larger than 10 inches (254 mm) and is installed in accordance with one of the methods in Table 803.10.4. Concealed metal parts of the pass-through system in contact with flue gases shall be of stainless steel or equivalent material that resists corrosion, softening or cracking up to 1,800°F (980°C).

TABLE 803.10.4
CHIMNEY CONNECTOR SYSTEMS AND CLEARANCES TO COMBUSTIBLE WALL MATERIALS FOR DOMESTIC HEATING APPLIANCES[a, b, c, d]
(FOR CHIMNEY CONNECTOR SYSTEM DETAILS, SEE APPENDIX A)

System A (12-inch clearance)	A 3.5-inch-thick brick wall shall be framed into the combustible wall. An 0.625-inch-thick fire-clay liner (ASTM C 315 or equivalent)[e] shall be firmly cemented in the center of the brick wall maintaining a 12-inch clearance to combustibles. The clay liner shall run from the outer surface of the bricks to the inner surface of the chimney liner.
System B (9-inch clearance)	A labeled solid-insulated factory-built chimney section (1-inch insulation) the same inside diameter as the connector shall be utilized. Sheet steel supports cut to maintain a 9-inch clearance to combustibles shall be fastened to the wall surface and to the chimney section. Fasteners shall not penetrate the chimney flue liner. The chimney length shall be flush with the masonry chimney liner and sealed to the masonry with water-insoluble refractory cement. Chimney manufacturers' parts shall be utilized to securely fasten the chimney connector to the chimney section.
System C (6-inch clearance)	A steel ventilated thimble having a minimum thickness of 0.0236 inch (No. 24 gage) having two 1-inch air channels shall be installed with a steel chimney connector. Steel supports shall be cut to maintain a 6-inch clearance between the thimble and combustibles. The chimney connector and steel supports shall have a minimum thickness of 0.0236 inch (No. 24 gage). One side of the support shall be fastened to the wall on all sides. Glass-fiber insulation shall fill the 6-inch space between the thimble and the supports.
System D (2-inch clearance)	A labeled solid-insulated factory-built chimney section (1-inch insulation) with a diameter 2 inches larger than the chimney connector shall be installed with a steel chimney connector having a minimum thickness of 0.0236 inch (24 gage). Sheet steel supports shall be positioned to maintain a 2-inch clearance to combustibles and to hold the chimney connector to ensure that a 1-inch airspace surrounds the chimney connector through the chimney section. The steel support shall be fastened to the wall on all sides and the chimney section shall be fastened to the supports. Fasteners shall not penetrate the liner of the chimney section.

For SI: 1 inch = 25.4 mm, 1.0 Btu × in/ft^2 · h · °F = 0.144 W/m^2 · K.

a. Insulation material that is part of the wall pass-through system shall be noncombustible and shall have a thermal conductivity of 1.0 Btu × in/ft^2 · h · °F or less.

b. All clearances and thicknesses are minimums.

c. Materials utilized to seal penetrations for the connector shall be noncombustible.

d. Connectors for all systems except System B shall extend through the wall pass-through system to the inner face of the flue liner.

e. ASTM C 315.

803.10.5 Pitch. Connectors shall rise vertically to the *chimney* or vent with a minimum pitch equal to one-fourth unit vertical in 12 units horizontal (2-percent slope).

803.10.6 Clearances. Connectors shall have a minimum *clearance* to combustibles in accordance with Table 803.10.6. The clearances specified in Table 803.10.6 apply, except where the listing and labeling of an *appliance* specifies a different *clearance*, in which case the *labeled clearance* shall apply. The *clearance* to combustibles for connectors shall be reduced only in accordance with Section 308.

TABLE 803.10.6
CONNECTOR CLEARANCES TO COMBUSTIBLES

TYPE OF APPLIANCE	MINIMUM CLEARANCE (inches)
Domestic-type appliances	
Chimney and vent connectors	
Electric and oil incinerators	18
Oil and solid-fuel appliances	18
Oil appliances labeled for venting	9
with Type L vents	9

For SI: 1 inch = 25.4 mm.

SECTION 804
DIRECT-VENT, INTEGRAL VENT AND MECHANICAL DRAFT SYSTEMS

804.1 Direct-vent terminations. Vent terminals for *direct-vent appliances* shall be installed in accordance with the manufacturer's installation instructions

804.2 Appliances with integral vents. *Appliances* incorporating integral venting means shall be installed in accordance with their listings and the manufacturer's installation instructions.

804.2.1 Terminal clearances. *Appliances* designed for natural draft venting and incorporating integral venting means shall be located so that a minimum *clearance* of 9 inches (229 mm) is maintained between vent terminals and from any openings through which *combustion* products enter the building. *Appliances* using forced draft venting shall be located so that a minimum clearance of 12 inches (305 mm) is maintained between vent terminals and from any openings through which *combustion* products enter the building.

804.3 Mechanical draft systems. Mechanical draft systems of either forced or induced draft design shall comply with Sections 804.3.1 through 804.3.7.

804.3.1 Forced draft systems. Forced draft systems and all portions of induced draft systems under positive pressure during operation shall be designed and installed so as to be gas tight to prevent leakage of *combustion* products into a building.

804.3.2 Automatic shutoff. Power exhausters serving automatically fired *appliances* shall be electrically connected to each *appliance* to prevent operation of the *appliance* when the power exhauster is not in operation.

804.3.3 Termination. The termination of *chimneys* or vents equipped with power exhausters shall be located a minimum of 10 feet (3048 mm) from the lot line or from adjacent buildings. The exhaust shall be directed away from the building.

804.3.4 Horizontal terminations. Horizontal terminations shall comply with the following requirements:

1. Where located adjacent to walkways, the termination of mechanical draft systems shall be not less than 7 feet (2134 mm) above the level of the walkway.
2. Vents shall terminate at least 3 feet (914 mm) above any forced air inlet located within 10 feet (3048 mm).
3. The vent system shall terminate at least 4 feet (1219 mm) below, 4 feet (1219 mm) horizontally from or 1 foot (305 mm) above any door, window or gravity air inlet into the building.
4. The vent termination point shall not be located closer than 3 feet (914 mm) to an interior corner formed by two walls perpendicular to each other.
5. The vent termination shall not be mounted directly above or within 3 feet (914 mm) horizontally from an oil tank vent or gas meter.
6. The bottom of the vent termination shall be located at least 12 inches (305 mm) above finished grade.

804.3.5 Vertical terminations. Vertical terminations shall comply with the following requirements:

1. Where located adjacent to walkways, the termination of mechanical draft systems shall be not less than 7 feet (2134 mm) above the level of the walkway.
2. Vents shall terminate at least 3 feet (914 mm) above any forced air inlet located within 10 feet (3048 mm) horizontally.
3. Where the vent termination is located below an adjacent roof structure, the termination point shall be located at least 3 feet (914 mm) from such structure.
4. The vent shall terminate at least 4 feet (1219 mm) below, 4 feet (1219 mm) horizontally from or 1 foot (305 mm) above any door, window or gravity air inlet for the building.
5. A vent cap shall be installed to prevent rain from entering the vent system.
6. The vent termination shall be located at least 3 feet (914 mm) horizontally from any portion of the roof structure.

804.3.6 Exhauster connections. An *appliance* vented by natural draft shall not be connected into a vent, *chimney* or vent connector on the discharge side of a mechanical flue exhauster.

804.3.7 Exhauster sizing. Mechanical flue exhausters and the vent system served shall be sized and installed in accordance with the manufacturer's installation instructions.

804.3.8 Mechanical draft systems for manually fired appliances and fireplaces. Deleted.

SECTION 805 FACTORY-BUILT CHIMNEYS

805.1 Listing. Factory-built *chimneys* shall be *listed* and *labeled* and shall be installed and terminated in accordance with the manufacturer's installation instructions.

805.2 Solid fuel appliances. Factory-built *chimneys* installed in *dwelling units* with solid fuel-burning appliances shall comply with the Type HT requirements of UL 103 and shall be marked "Type HT" and "Residential Type and Building Heating *Appliance Chimney*."

> **Exception:** *Chimneys* for use with open *combustion* chamber fireplaces shall comply with the requirements of UL 103 and shall be marked "Residential Type and Building Heating *Appliance Chimney*."

Chimneys for use with open *combustion* chamber appliances installed in buildings other than *dwelling units* shall comply with the requirements of UL 103 and shall be marked "Building Heating *Appliance Chimney*" or "Residential Type and Building Heating *Appliance Chimney*."

805.3 Factory-built fireplaces. *Chimneys* for use with factory-built fireplaces shall comply with the requirements of UL 127.

805.4 Support. Where factory-built *chimneys* are supported by structural members, such as joists and rafters, such members shall be designed to support the additional load.

805.5 Medium-heat appliances. Deleted.

805.6 Decorative shrouds. Decorative shrouds shall not be installed at the termination of factory-built *chimneys* except where such shrouds are *listed* and *labeled* for use with the specific factory-built *chimney* system and are installed in accordance with Section 304.1.

SECTION 806 METAL CHIMNEYS

Deleted

CHAPTER 9

SPECIFIC APPLIANCES, FIREPLACES AND SOLID FUEL-BURNING EQUIPMENT

SECTION 901 GENERAL

901.1 Scope. This chapter shall govern the approval, design, installation, construction, maintenance, *alteration* and repair of the appliances and *equipment* specifically identified herein and factory-built fireplaces. The approval, design, installation, construction, maintenance, *alteration* and repair of gas-fired appliances shall be regulated by the *International Fuel Gas Code.*

901.2 General. The requirements of this chapter shall apply to the mechanical *equipment* and appliances regulated by this chapter, in addition to the other requirements of this code.

901.3 Hazardous locations. Fireplaces and solid fuel-burning appliances shall not be installed in hazardous locations.

901.4 Fireplace accessories. *Listed* fireplace accessories shall be installed in accordance with the conditions of the listing and the manufacturer's installation instructions.

SECTION 902 MASONRY FIREPLACES

902.1 General. Masonry fireplaces shall be constructed in accordance with the *International Building Code.*

SECTION 903 FACTORY-BUILT FIREPLACES

903.1 General. Factory-built fireplaces shall be *listed* and *labeled* and shall be installed in accordance with the conditions of the listing. Factory-built fireplaces shall be tested in accordance with UL 127.

903.2 Hearth extensions. Hearth extensions of *approved* factory-built fireplaces and fireplace stoves shall be installed in accordance with the listing of the fireplace. The hearth extension shall be readily distinguishable from the surrounding floor area.

903.3 Unvented gas log heaters. An unvented gas log heater shall not be installed in a factory-built fireplace unless the fireplace system has been specifically tested, *listed* and *labeled* for such use in accordance with UL 127.

SECTION 904 PELLET FUEL-BURNING APPLIANCES

904.1 General. Pellet fuel-burning appliances shall be *listed* and *labeled* in accordance with ASTM E 1509 and shall be installed in accordance with the terms of the listing.

SECTION 905 FIREPLACE STOVES AND ROOM HEATERS

905.1 General. Fireplace stoves and solid-fuel-type room heaters shall be *listed* and *labeled* and shall be installed in accordance with the conditions of the listing. Fireplace stoves shall be tested in accordance with UL 737. Solid-fuel-type room heaters shall be tested in accordance with UL 1482. Fireplace inserts intended for installation in fireplaces shall be *listed* and *labeled* in accordance with the requirements of UL 1482 and shall be installed in accordance with the manufacturer's installation instructions.

905.2 Connection to fireplace. The connection of solid fuel appliances to *chimney* flues serving fireplaces shall comply with Sections 801.7 and 801.10.

SECTION 906 FACTORY-BUILT BARBECUE APPLIANCES

906.1 General. Factory-built barbecue appliances shall be of an *approved* type and shall be installed in accordance with the manufacturer's installation instructions, this chapter and Chapters 3, 5, 7, 8 and the *International Fuel Gas Code.*

SECTION 907 INCINERATORS AND CREMATORIES

Deleted

SECTION 908 COOLING TOWERS, EVAPORATIVE CONDENSERS AND FLUID COOLERS

Deleted

SECTION 909 VENTED WALL FURNACES

909.1 General. Vented wall furnaces shall be installed in accordance with their listing and the manufacturer's installation instructions. Oil-fired furnaces shall be tested in accordance with UL 730.

909.2 Location. Vented wall furnaces shall be located so as not to cause a fire hazard to walls, floors, combustible furnishings or doors. Vented wall furnaces installed between bathrooms and adjoining rooms shall not circulate air from bathrooms to other parts of the building.

909.3 Door swing. Vented wall furnaces shall be located so that a door cannot swing within 12 inches (305 mm) of an air inlet or air outlet of such furnace measured at right angles to the opening. Doorstops or door closers shall not be installed to obtain this *clearance.*

909.4 Ducts prohibited. Ducts shall not be attached to wall furnaces. Casing extension boots shall not be installed unless *listed* as part of the *appliance*.

909.5 Manual shutoff valve. A manual shutoff valve shall be installed ahead of all controls.

909.6 Access. Vented wall furnaces shall be provided with access for cleaning of heating surfaces, removal of burners, replacement of sections, motors, controls, filters and other working parts, and for adjustments and lubrication of parts requiring such attention. Panels, grilles and access doors that must be removed for normal servicing operations shall not be attached to the building construction.

SECTION 910
FLOOR FURNACES

910.1 General. Floor furnaces shall be installed in accordance with their listing and the manufacturer's installation instructions. Oil-fired furnaces shall be tested in accordance with UL 729.

910.2 Placement. Floor furnaces shall not be installed in the floor of any aisle or passageway of any auditorium, public hall, place of assembly, or in any egress element from any such room or space.

With the exception of wall register models, a floor furnace shall not be placed closer than 6 inches (152 mm) to the nearest wall, and wall register models shall not be placed closer than 6 inches (152 mm) to a corner.

The furnace shall be placed such that a drapery or similar combustible object will not be nearer than 12 inches (305 mm) to any portion of the register of the furnace. Floor furnaces shall not be installed in concrete floor construction built on grade. The controlling thermostat for a floor furnace shall be located within the same room or space as the floor furnace or shall be located in an adjacent room or space that is permanently open to the room or space containing the floor furnace.

910.3 Bracing. The floor around the furnace shall be braced and headed with a support framework design in accordance with the *International Building Code*.

910.4 Clearance. The lowest portion of the floor furnace shall have not less than a 6-inch (152 mm) clearance from the grade level; except where the lower 6-inch (152 mm) portion of the floor furnace is sealed by the manufacturer to prevent entrance of water, the minimum clearance shall be reduced to not less than 2 inches (51 mm). Where these clearances are not present, the ground below and to the sides shall be excavated to form a pit under the furnace so that the required clearance is provided beneath the lowest portion of the furnace. A 12-inch (305 mm) minimum clearance shall be provided on all sides except the control side, which shall have an 18-inch (457 mm) minimum clearance.

SECTION 911
DUCT FURNACES
Deleted

SECTION 912
INFRARED RADIANT HEATERS
Deleted

SECTION 913
CLOTHES DRYERS

913.1 General. Clothes dryers shall be installed in accordance with the manufacturer's installation instructions. Electric residential clothes dryers shall be tested in accordance with UL 2158.

913.2 Exhaust required. Clothes dryers shall be exhausted in accordance with Section 504.

913.3 Clearances. Deleted.

SECTION 914
SAUNA HEATERS

914.1 Location and protection. Sauna heaters shall be located so as to minimize the possibility of accidental contact by a person in the room.

914.1.1 Guards. Sauna heaters shall be protected from accidental contact by an *approved* guard or barrier of material having a low coefficient of thermal conductivity. The guard shall not substantially affect the transfer of heat from the heater to the room.

914.2 Installation. Sauna heaters shall be *listed* and *labeled* in accordance with UL 875 and shall be installed in accordance with their listing and the manufacturer's installation instructions.

914.3 Access. Panels, grilles and access doors that are required to be removed for normal servicing operations shall not be attached to the building.

914.4 Heat and time controls. Sauna heaters shall be equipped with a thermostat that will limit room temperature to 194°F (90°C). If the thermostat is not an integral part of the sauna heater, the heat-sensing element shall be located within 6 inches (152 mm) of the ceiling. If the heat-sensing element is a capillary tube and bulb, the assembly shall be attached to the wall or other support, and shall be protected against physical damage.

914.4.1 Timers. A timer, if provided to control main burner operation, shall have a maximum operating time of 1 hour. The control for the timer shall be located outside the sauna room.

914.5 Sauna room. A ventilation opening into the sauna room shall be provided. The opening shall be not less than 4 inches by 8 inches (102 mm by 203 mm) located near the top of the door into the sauna room.

914.5.1 Warning notice. Deleted.

SECTION 915 ENGINE AND GAS TURBINE-POWERED EQUIPMENT AND APPLIANCES Deleted

SECTION 916 POOL AND SPA HEATERS

916.1 General. Pool and spa heaters shall be installed in accordance with the manufacturer's installation instructions. Oil-fired pool and spa heaters shall be tested in accordance with UL 726. Electric pool and spa heaters shall be tested in accordance with UL 1261.

SECTION 917 COOKING APPLIANCES

917.1 Cooking appliances. Cooking appliances that are designed for permanent installation, including ranges, ovens, stoves, broilers, grills, fryers, griddles and barbecues, shall be *listed*, *labeled* and installed in accordance with the manufacturer's installation instructions. Household electric ranges shall be *listed* and *labeled* in accordance with UL 858. Microwave cooking appliances shall be *listed* and *labeled* in accordance with UL 923. Oil-burning stoves shall be *listed* and *labeled* in accordance with UL 896. Solid-fuel-fired ovens shall be *listed* and *labeled* in accordance with UL 2162.

917.2 Prohibited location. Cooking appliances designed, tested, *listed* and *labeled* for use in commercial occupancies shall not be installed within *dwelling units* or within any area where domestic cooking operations occur.

917.3 Domestic appliances. Cooking appliances installed within *dwelling units* and within areas where domestic cooking operations occur shall be *listed* and *labeled* as household-type appliances for domestic use.

917.4 Installation of microwave oven over a cooking appliance. The installation of a listed and labeled cooking appliance or microwave oven over a listed and labeled cooking appliance shall conform to the terms of the upper appliance's listing and label and the manufacturer's installation instructions.

SECTION 918 FORCED-AIR WARM-AIR FURNACES

918.1 Forced-air furnaces. Oil-fired furnaces shall be tested in accordance with UL 727. Electric furnaces shall be tested in accordance with UL 1995. Solid fuel furnaces shall be tested in accordance with UL 391. Forced-air furnaces shall be installed in accordance with the listings and the manufacturer's installation instructions.

918.2 Minimum duct sizes. The minimum unobstructed total area of the outdoor and return air ducts or openings to a forced-air warm-air furnace shall be not less than 2 square inches per 1,000 Btu/h (4402 mm^2/kW) output rating capacity of the furnace and not less than that specified in the furnace manufacturer's installation instructions. The minimum unobstructed total area of supply ducts from a forced-air warm-air furnace shall not be less than 2 square inches for each 1,000 Btu/h (4402 mm^2/kW) output rating capacity of the furnace and not less than that specified in the furnace manufacturer's installation instructions.

> **Exception:** The total area of the supply air ducts and outdoor and return air ducts shall not be required to be larger than the minimum size required by the furnace manufacturer's installation instructions. With the addition of a cooling coil the sizing criteria shall be based on 6 square inches (3871 mm^2) for each 1,000 Btu/h (13 208 mm^2/kW) output.

918.3 Heat pumps. The minimum unobstructed total area of the outdoor and return air ducts or openings to a heat pump shall be not less than 6 square inches per 1,000 Btu/h (13 208 mm^2/kW) output rating or as indicated by the conditions of listing of the heat pump. Electric heat pumps shall be tested in accordance with UL 1995.

918.4 Dampers. Volume dampers shall not be placed in the air inlet to a furnace in a manner that will reduce the required air to the furnace.

918.5 Circulating air ducts for forced-air warm-air furnaces. Circulating air for fuel-burning, forced-air-type, warm-air furnaces shall be conducted into the blower housing from outside the furnace enclosure by continuous air-tight ducts.

918.6 Prohibited sources. Outdoor or return air for a forced-air heating system shall not be taken from the following locations:

1. Less than 10 feet (3048 mm) from an *appliance* vent outlet, a vent opening from a plumbing drainage system or the discharge outlet of an exhaust fan, unless the outlet is 3 feet (914 mm) above the outdoor air inlet.
2. Where there is the presence of objectionable odors, fumes or flammable vapors; or where located less than 10 feet (3048 mm) above the surface of any abutting public way or driveway; or where located at grade level by a sidewalk, street, alley or driveway.
3. Deleted.
4. A room or space, the volume of which is less than 25 percent of the entire volume served by such system. Where connected by a permanent opening having an area sized in accordance with Sections 918.2 and 918.3, adjoining rooms or spaces shall be considered as a single room or space for the purpose of determining the volume of such rooms or spaces.

   Exception: The minimum volume requirement shall not apply where the amount of return air taken from a room or space is less than or equal to the amount of supply air delivered to such room or space.
5. A closet, bathroom, toilet room, kitchen, garage, mechanical room, boiler room, furnace room or unconditioned attic.

   Exception: Where return air intakes are located not less than 10 feet (3048 mm) from cooking appliances, and serve the kitchen area only, taking return air from a kitchen shall not be prohibited.

6. An unconditioned crawl space by means of direct connection to the return side of a forced air system.
7. A room or space containing a fuel-burning *appliance* or fireplace where such room or space serves as the sole source of return air.

Exceptions:

7.1. This shall not apply where the fuel-burning *appliance* is a direct-vent *appliance*.

7.2. This shall not apply where the room or space complies with the following requirements:

7.2.1. The return air shall be taken from a room or space having a volume exceeding 1 cubic foot for each 10 Btu/h (9.6 L/W) of combined input rating of all fuel-burning appliances therein.

7.2.2. The volume of supply air discharged back into the same space shall be approximately equal to the volume of return air taken from the space.

7.2.3. Return-air inlets shall not be located within 10 feet (3048 mm)of any *appliance* firebox or draft hood in the same room or space.

7.3. This shall not apply to rooms or spaces containing solid-fuel-burning appliances, provided that return-air inlets are located not less than 10 feet (3048 mm) from the firebox of the appliances.

7.4. This shall not apply to rooms and spaces containing a fireplace provided that return air inlets are located not less than 10 feet (3048 mm) from the fireplace opening.

918.7 Outside opening protection. Outdoor air intake openings shall be protected in accordance with Section 401.5.

918.8 Return-air limitation. Return air from one *dwelling unit* shall not be discharged into another *dwelling unit.*

918.9 Refrigeration coils in warm-air furnaces. When a cooling coil is located in the supply plenum of a warm-air furnace, the furnace blower shall be rated at not less than 0.5-inch water column (124 Pa) static pressure unless the furnace is listed and labeled for use with a cooling coil. Cooling coils shall not be located upstream from heat exchangers unless listed and labeled for such use. Conversion of existing furnaces for use with cooling coils shall be permitted provided the furnace will operate within the temperature rise specified for the furnace.

SECTION 919 CONVERSION BURNERS

919.1 Conversion burners. The installation of conversion burners shall conform to ANSI Z21.8.

SECTION 920 UNIT HEATERS

Deleted

SECTION 921 VENTED ROOM HEATERS

921.1 General. Vented room heaters shall be *listed* and *labeled* and shall be installed in accordance with the conditions of the listing and the manufacturer's instructions.

SECTION 922 KEROSENE AND OIL-FIRED STOVES

922.1 General. Kerosene and oil-fired stoves shall be *listed* and *labeled* and shall be installed in accordance with the conditions of the listing and the manufacturer's installation instructions. Kerosene and oil-fired stoves shall comply with NFPA 31. Oil-fired stoves shall be tested in accordance with UL 896.

SECTION 923 SMALL CERAMIC KILNS

Deleted

SECTION 924 STATIONARY FUEL CELL POWER SYSTEMS

Deleted

SECTION 925 MASONRY HEATERS

Deleted

SECTION 926 GASEOUS HYDROGEN SYSTEMS

Deleted

SECTION 927 HEAT RECOVERY VENTILATORS

Deleted

SECTION 928 RADIANT HEATING SYSTEMS

928.1 General. Electric radiant heating systems shall be installed in accordance with the manufacturer's installation instructions and the *North Carolina Electrical Code.*

928.2 Clearances. Clearances for radiant heating panels or elements to any wiring, outlet boxes and junction boxes used for installing electrical devices or mounting light fixtures shall comply with the *North Carolina Electrical Code.*

928.3 Installation of radiant panels. Radiant panels installed on wood framing shall conform to the following requirements:

1. Heating panels shall be installed parallel to framing members and secured to the surface of framing members or mounted between framing members.
2. Panels shall be nailed or stapled only through the unheated portions provided for this purpose and shall not be fastened at any point closer than $^1/_4$ inch (6.4 mm) from an element.
3. Unless listed and labeled for field cutting, heating panels shall be installed as complete units.

928.4 Installation in concrete or masonry. Radiant heating systems installed in concrete or masonry shall conform to the following requirements:

1. Radiant heating systems shall be identified as being suitable for the installation, and shall be secured in place, as specified in the manufacturer's installation instructions.
2. Radiant heating panels or radiant heating panel sets shall not be installed where they bridge expansion joints unless protected from expansion and contraction.

928.5 Gypsum panels. Where radiant heating systems are used on gypsum assemblies, operating temperatures shall not exceed 125°F (52°C).

928.6 Finish surfaces. Finish materials installed over radiant heating panels or systems shall be installed in accordance with the manufacturer's installation instructions. Surfaces shall be secured so that nails or other fastenings do not pierce the radiant heating elements.

SECTION 929 BASEBOARD CONVECTORS

929.1 Baseboard convectors. Electric baseboard convectors shall be installed in accordance with the manufacturer's installation instructions and the *North Carolina Electrical Code.*

SECTION 930 DUCT HEATERS

930.1 General. Electric duct heaters shall be installed in accordance with the manufacturer's installation instructions and the *North Carolina Electrical Code*. Electric furnaces shall be tested in accordance with UL 1996.

930.2 Installation. Electric duct heaters shall be installed so they will not create a fire hazard. Class I ducts, duct coverings and linings shall be interrupted at each heater to provide the clearances specified in the manufacturer's installation instructions. Such interruptions are not required for duct heaters listed and labeled for zero clearance to combustible materials. Insulation installed in the immediate area of each heater shall be classified for the maximum temperature produced on the duct surface.

930.3 Installation with heat pumps and air conditioners. Duct heaters located within 4 feet (1219 mm) of a heat pump or air conditioner shall be listed and labeled for such installations. The heat pump or air conditioner shall additionally be listed and labeled for such duct heater installations.

930.4 Access. Duct heaters shall be accessible for servicing, and clearance shall be maintained to permit adjustment, servicing and replacement of controls and heating elements.

930.5 Fan interlock. The fan circuit shall be provided with an interlock to prevent heater operation when the fan is not operating.

CHAPTER 10

BOILERS, WATER HEATERS AND PRESSURE VESSELS

SECTION 1001 GENERAL

1001.1 Scope. This chapter shall govern the installation, *alteration* and repair of boilers, water heaters and pressure vessels.

Exceptions:

1. Pressure vessels used for unheated water supply.
2. Portable unfired pressure vessels and Interstate Commerce Commission containers.
3. Containers for bulk oxygen and medical gas.
4. Unfired pressure vessels having a volume of 5 cubic feet (0.14 m^3) or less operating at pressures not exceeding 250 pounds per square inch (psi) (1724 kPa) and located within occupancies of Groups B, F, H, M, R, S and U.
5. Pressure vessels used in refrigeration systems that are regulated by Chapter 11 of this code.
6. Pressure tanks used in conjunction with coaxial cables, telephone cables, power cables and other similar humidity control systems.
7. Boilers that exceed one of the following (in other than one- and two-family dwellings and apartment houses of less than six families) are under the jurisdiction of the North Carolina Department of Labor in accordance with General Statute Chapter 95, Article 7A, Section 95-69.10:
   - 7.1. A heat input capacity of 200,000 Btu/h (58.6 kW).
   - 7.2. A water temperature of 200°F (93.3°C).
   - 7.3. A nominal water capacity of 120 gallons (454 L).

SECTION 1002 WATER HEATERS

1002.1 General. Potable water heaters and hot water storage tanks shall be *listed* and *labeled* and installed in accordance with the manufacturer's installation instructions, the *International Plumbing Code* and this code. All water heaters shall be capable of being removed without first removing a permanent portion of the building structure. The potable water connections and relief valves for all water heaters shall conform to the requirements of the *International Plumbing Code*. Domestic electric water heaters shall comply with UL 174 or UL 1453. Commercial electric water heaters shall comply with UL 1453. Oil-fired water heaters shall comply with UL 732.

1002.2 Water heaters utilized for space heating. Water heaters utilized both to supply potable hot water and provide hot water for space-heating applications shall be *listed* and *labeled* for such applications by the manufacturer and shall be installed in accordance with the manufacturer's installation instructions and the *International Plumbing Code*.

1002.2.1 Sizing. Water heaters utilized for both potable water heating and space-heating applications shall be sized to prevent the space-heating load from diminishing the required potable water-heating capacity.

1002.2.2 Temperature limitation. Where a combination potable water-heating and space-heating system requires water for space heating at temperatures higher than 140°F (60°C), a temperature actuated mixing valve that conforms to ASSE 1017 shall be provided to temper the water supplied to the potable hot water distribution system to a temperature of 140°F (60°C) or less.

1002.3 Supplemental water-heating devices. Potable water-heating devices that utilize refrigerant-to-water heat exchangers shall be *approved* and installed in accordance with the *International Plumbing Code* and the manufacturer's installation instructions.

SECTION 1003 PRESSURE VESSELS

1003.1 General. All pressure vessels shall be in accordance with the ASME *Boiler and Pressure Vessel Code,* shall bear the label of an *approved* agency and shall be installed in accordance with the manufacturer's installation instructions.

1003.2 Piping. All piping materials, fittings, joints, connections and devices associated with systems utilized in conjunction with pressure vessels shall be designed for the specific application and shall be *approved.*

1003.3 Welding. Welding on pressure vessels shall be performed by *approved* welders in compliance with nationally recognized standards.

SECTION 1004 BOILERS

1004.1 Standards. Oil-fired boilers and their control systems shall be *listed* and *labeled* in accordance with UL 726. Electric boilers and their control systems shall be *listed* and *labeled* in accordance with UL 834. Boilers shall be designed and constructed in accordance with the requirements of ASME CSD-1 and as applicable, the ASME *Boiler and Pressure Vessel Code*, Sections I or IV; NFPA 8501; NFPA 8502 or NFPA 8504.

1004.2 Installation. In addition to the requirements of this code, the installation of boilers shall conform to the manufacturer's instructions. Operating instructions of a permanent type shall be attached to the boiler. Boilers shall have all controls set, adjusted and tested by the installer. The manufacturer's rating data and the nameplate shall be attached to the boiler.

1004.3 Working clearance. Deleted.

1004.4 Mounting. *Equipment* shall be set or mounted on a level base capable of supporting and distributing the weight contained thereon. Boilers, tanks and *equipment* shall be secured in accordance with the manufacturer's installation instructions.

1004.5 Floors. Boilers shall be mounted on floors of noncombustible construction, unless *listed* for mounting on combustible flooring.

1004.6 Boiler rooms and enclosures. Boiler rooms shall be equipped with a floor drain or other *approved* means for disposing of liquid waste.

1004.7 Operating adjustments and instructions. Hot water and steam boilers shall have all operating and safety controls set and operationally tested by the installing contractor. A complete control diagram and boiler operating instructions shall be furnished by the installer for each installation.

SECTION 1005
BOILER CONNECTIONS

1005.1 Valves. Every boiler or modular boiler shall have a shutoff valve in the supply and return piping. For multiple boiler or multiple modular boiler installations, each boiler or modular boiler shall have individual shutoff valves in the supply and return piping.

Exception: Deleted.

1005.2 Potable water supply. The water supply to all boilers shall be connected in accordance with the *International Plumbing Code*.

SECTION 1006
SAFETY AND PRESSURE RELIEF VALVES AND CONTROLS

1006.1 Safety valves for steam boilers. All steam boilers shall be protected with a safety valve.

1006.2 Safety relief valves for hot water boilers. Hot water boilers shall be protected with a safety relief valve.

1006.3 Pressure relief for pressure vessels. All pressure vessels shall be protected with a pressure relief valve or pressure-limiting device as required by the manufacturer's installation instructions for the pressure vessel.

1006.4 Approval of safety and safety relief valves. Safety and safety relief valves shall be *listed* and *labeled*, and shall have a minimum rated capacity for the *equipment* or appliances served. Safety and safety relief valves shall be set at a maximum of the nameplate pressure rating of the boiler or pressure vessel.

1006.5 Installation. Safety or relief valves shall be installed directly into the safety or relief valve opening on the boiler or pressure vessel. Valves shall not be located on either side of a safety or relief valve connection. The relief valve shall discharge by gravity.

1006.6 Safety and relief valve discharge. Safety and relief valve discharge pipes shall be of rigid pipe that is *approved* for the temperature of the system. The discharge pipe shall be the same diameter as the safety or relief valve outlet. Safety and relief valves shall not discharge so as to be a hazard, a potential cause of damage or otherwise a nuisance. High-pressure-steam safety valves shall be vented to the outside of the structure. Where a low-pressure safety valve or a relief valve discharges to the drainage system, the installation shall conform to the *International Plumbing Code*.

1006.7 Boiler safety devices. Boilers shall be equipped with controls and limit devices as required by the manufacturer's installation instructions and the conditions of the listing.

1006.8 Electrical requirements. The power supply to the electrical control system shall be from a two-wire branch circuit that has a grounded conductor, or from an isolation transformer with a two-wire secondary. Where an isolation transformer is provided, one conductor of the secondary winding shall be grounded. Control voltage shall not exceed 150 volts nominal, line to line. Control and limit devices shall interrupt the ungrounded side of the circuit. A means of manually disconnecting the control circuit shall be provided and controls shall be arranged so that when deenergized, the burner shall be inoperative. Such disconnecting means shall be capable of being locked in the off position and shall be provided with ready access.

SECTION 1007
BOILER LOW-WATER CUTOFF

1007.1 General. All steam and hot water boilers shall be protected with a low-water cutoff control.

1007.2 Operation. The low-water cutoff shall automatically stop the *combustion* operation of the *appliance* when the water level drops below the lowest safe water level as established by the manufacturer.

SECTION 1008
STEAM BLOWOFF VALVE

1008.1 General. Every steam boiler shall be equipped with a quick-opening blowoff valve. The valve shall be installed in the opening provided on the boiler. The minimum size of the valve shall be the size specified by the boiler manufacturer or the size of the boiler blowoff-valve opening.

1008.2 Discharge. Blowoff valves shall discharge to a safe place of disposal. Where discharging to the drainage system, the installation shall conform to the *International Plumbing Code*.

SECTION 1009
HOT WATER BOILER EXPANSION TANK

1009.1 Where required. An expansion tank shall be installed in every hot water system. For multiple boiler installations, a minimum of one expansion tank is required. Expansion tanks shall be of the closed or open type. Tanks shall be rated for the pressure of the hot water system.

1009.2 Closed-type expansion tanks. Closed-type expansion tanks shall be installed in accordance with the manufacturer's instructions. The size of the tank shall be based on the capacity of the hot-water-heating system. The minimum size of the tank shall be determined in accordance with the following equation:

$$V_t = \frac{(0.00041T - 0.0466)V_s}{\left(\frac{P_a}{P_f}\right) - \left(\frac{P_a}{P_o}\right)}$$ **(Equation 10-1)**

For SI:

$$V_t = \frac{(0.000738T - 0.03348)V_s}{\left(\frac{P_a}{P_f}\right) - \left(\frac{P_a}{P_o}\right)}$$

where:

V_t = Minimum volume of tanks (gallons) (L).

V_s = Volume of system, not including expansion tanks (gallons) (L).

T = Average operating temperature (°F) (°C).

P_a = Atmospheric pressure (psi) (kPa).

P_f = Fill pressure (psi) (kPa).

P_o = Maximum operating pressure (psi) (kPa).

1009.3 Open-type expansion tanks. Open-type expansion tanks shall be located a minimum of 4 feet (1219 mm) above the highest heating element. The tank shall be adequately sized for the hot water system. An overflow with a minimum diameter of 1 inch (25 mm) shall be installed at the top of the tank. The overflow shall discharge to the drainage system in accordance with the *International Plumbing Code*.

SECTION 1010 GAUGES

1010.1 Hot water boiler gauges. Every hot water boiler shall have a pressure gauge and a temperature gauge, or a combination pressure and temperature gauge. The gauges shall indicate the temperature and pressure within the normal range of the system's operation.

1010.2 Steam boiler gauges. Every steam boiler shall have a water-gauge glass and a pressure gauge. The pressure gauge shall indicate the pressure within the normal range of the system's operation.

1010.2.1 Water-gauge glass. The gauge glass shall be installed so that the midpoint is at the normal boiler water level.

SECTION 1011 TESTS Deleted

CHAPTER 11
REFRIGERATION

SECTION 1101
GENERAL

1101.1 Scope. This chapter shall govern the design, installation, construction and repair of refrigeration systems that vaporize and liquefy a fluid during the refrigerating cycle. Refrigerant piping design and installation, including pressure vessels and pressure relief devices, shall conform to this code. Permanently installed refrigerant storage systems and other components shall be considered as part of the refrigeration system to which they are attached.

1101.2 Factory-built equipment and appliances. Deleted.

1101.3 Protection. Any portion of a refrigeration system that is subject to physical damage shall be protected in an *approved* manner.

1101.4 Water connection. Deleted.

1101.5 Fuel gas connection. Deleted.

1101.6 General. Deleted.

1101.7 Maintenance. Deleted.

1101.8 Change in refrigerant type. Deleted.

[F] 1101.9 Refrigerant discharge. Deleted.

1101.10 Locking access port caps. Deleted.

SECTION 1102
SYSTEM REQUIREMENTS

1102.1 General. Deleted.

1102.2 Refrigerants. The refrigerant shall be that which the *equipment* or *appliance* was designed to utilize or converted to utilize. Refrigerants not identified in Table 1103.1 shall be *approved* before use.

1102.2.1 Mixing. Refrigerants, including refrigerant blends, with different designations in ASHRAE 34 shall not be mixed in a system.

Exception: Addition of a second refrigerant is allowed where permitted by the *equipment* or *appliance* manufacturer to improve oil return at low temperatures. The refrigerant and amount added shall be in accordance with the manufacturer's instructions.

1102.2.2 Purity. Refrigerants used in refrigeration systems shall be new, recovered or *reclaimed refrigerants* in accordance with Section 1102.2.2.1, 1102.2.2.2 or 1102.2.2.3. Where required by the *equipment* or *appliance* owner or the code official, the installer shall furnish a signed declaration that the refrigerant used meets the requirements of Section 1102.2.2.1, 1102.2.2.2 or 1102.2.2.3.

Exception: The refrigerant used shall meet the purity specifications set by the manufacturer of the *equipment* or *appliance* in which such refrigerant is used where such specifications are different from that specified in Sections 1102.2.2.1, 1102.2.2.2 and 1102.2.2.3.

1102.2.2.1 New refrigerants. Refrigerants shall be of a purity level specified by the *equipment* or *appliance* manufacturer.

1102.2.2.2 Recovered refrigerants. Refrigerants that are recovered from refrigeration and air-conditioning systems shall not be reused in other than the system from which they were recovered and in other systems of the same owner. *Recovered refrigerants* shall be filtered and dried before reuse. *Recovered refrigerants* that show clear signs of contamination shall not be reused unless reclaimed in accordance with Section 1102.2.2.3.

1102.2.2.3 Reclaimed refrigerants. Used refrigerants shall not be reused in a different owner's *equipment* or appliances unless tested and found to meet the purity requirements of ARI 700. Contaminated refrigerants shall not be used unless reclaimed and found to meet the purity requirements of ARI 700.

SECTION 1103
REFRIGERATION SYSTEM CLASSIFICATION
Deleted

SECTION 1104
SYSTEM APPLICATION REQUIREMENTS
Deleted

SECTION 1105
MACHINERY ROOM, GENERAL REQUIREMENTS
Deleted

SECTION 1106
MACHINERY ROOM, SPECIAL REQUIREMENTS
Deleted

SECTION 1107
REFRIGERANT PIPING

1107.1 General. All refrigerant piping shall be installed, tested and placed in operation in accordance with this chapter.

1107.2 Piping location. Refrigerant piping that crosses an open space that affords passageway in any building shall be not less than 7 feet 3 inches (2210 mm) above the floor unless the piping is located against the ceiling of such space.

1107.2.1 Piping in concrete floors. Refrigerant piping installed in concrete floors shall be encased in pipe ducts. The piping shall be isolated and supported to prevent damaging vibration, stress and corrosion.

1107.2.2 Refrigerant penetrations. Deleted.

1107.3 Pipe enclosures. Deleted.

1107.4 Condensation. All refrigerating piping and fittings, brine piping and fittings that, during normal operation, will reach a surface temperature below the dew point of the surrounding air, and are located in spaces or areas where condensation will cause a safety hazard to the building occupants, structure, electrical *equipment* or any other *equipment* or appliances, shall be protected in an *approved* manner to prevent such damage.

1107.5 Materials for refrigerant pipe and tubing. Deleted.

1107.6 Joints and refrigerant-containing parts in air ducts. Deleted.

1107.7 Exposure of refrigerant pipe joints. Deleted.

1107.8 Stop valves. Deleted.

SECTION 1108 FIELD TEST Deleted

[F] SECTION 1109 PERIODIC TESTING Deleted

CHAPTER 12
HYDRONIC PIPING

SECTION 1201
GENERAL

1201.1 Scope. The provisions of this chapter shall govern the construction, installation, *alteration* and repair of hydronic piping systems. This chapter shall apply to hydronic piping systems that are part of heating, ventilation and air-conditioning systems. Such piping systems shall include steam, hot water, chilled water, steam condensate and ground source heat pump loop systems. Potable cold and hot water distribution systems shall be installed in accordance with the *International Plumbing Code*.

1201.2 Sizing. Piping and piping system components for hydronic systems shall be sized for the demand of the system.

1201.3 Standards. As an alternative to the provisions of Sections 1202 and 1203, piping shall be designed, installed, inspected and tested in accordance with ASME B31.9.

SECTION 1202
MATERIAL

1202.1 Piping. Piping material shall conform to the standards cited in this section.

Exception: Embedded piping regulated by Section 1209.

1202.2 Used materials. Reused pipe, fittings, valves or other materials shall be clean and free of foreign materials and shall be *approved* by the code official for reuse.

1202.3 Material rating. Materials shall be rated for the operating temperature and pressure of the hydronic system. Materials shall be suitable for the type of fluid in the hydronic system.

1202.4 Piping materials standards. Hydronic pipe shall conform to the standards listed in Table 1202.4. The exterior of the pipe shall be protected from corrosion and degradation.

TABLE 1202.4
HYDRONIC PIPE

MATERIAL	STANDARD (see Chapter 15)
Acrylonitrile butadiene styrene (ABS) plastic pipe	ASTM D 1527; ASTM D 2282
Brass pipe	ASTM B 43
Brass tubing	ASTM B 135
Copper or copper-alloy pipe	ASTM B 42; ASTM B 302
Copper or copper-alloy tube (Type K, L or M)	ASTM B 75; ASTM B 88; ASTM B 251
Chlorinated polyvinyl chloride (CPVC) plastic pipe	ASTM D 2846; ASTM F 441; ASTM F 442
Cross-linked polyethylene/ aluminum/cross-linked polyethylene (PEX-AL-PEX) pressure pipe	ASTM F 1281; CSA CAN/CSA-B-137.10
Cross-linked polyethylene (PEX) tubing	ASTM F 876; ASTM F 877
Ductile iron pipe	AWWA C151/A21.51; AWWA C115/A21.15
Lead pipe	FS WW-P-325B
Polybutylene (PB) plastic pipe and tubing	ASTM D 3309
Polyethylene/aluminum/polyethylen (PE-AL-PE) pressure pipe	ASTM F 1282; CSA B137.9
Polyethylene (PE) pipe, tubing and fittings (for ground source heat pump loop systems)	ASTM D 2513; ASTM D 3035; ASTM D 2447; ASTM D 2683; ASTM F 1055; ASTM D 2837; ASTM D 3350; ASTM D 1693
Polypropylene (PP) plastic pipe	ASTM F 2389
Polyvinyl chloride (PVC) plastic pipe	ASTM D 1785; ASTM D 2241
Raised temperature polyethylene (PE-RT)	ASTM F 2623
Steel pipe	ASTM A 53; ASTM A 106
Steel tubing	ASTM A 254

1202.5 Pipe fittings. Hydronic pipe fittings shall be *approved* for installation with the piping materials to be installed, and shall conform to the respective pipe standards or to the standards listed in Table 1202.5.

TABLE 1202.5
HYDRONIC PIPE FITTINGS

MATERIAL	STANDARD (see Chapter 15)
Brass	ASTM F 1974
Bronze	ASME B16.24
Copper and copper alloys	ASME B16.15; ASME B16.18; ASME B16.22; ASME B16.23; ASME B16.26; ASME B16.29
Ductile iron and gray iron	ANSI/AWWA C110/A21.10
Ductile iron	ANSI/AWWA C153/A21.53
Gray iron	ASTM A 126
Malleable iron	ASME B16.3
Plastic	ASTM D 2466; ASTM D 2467; ASTM D 2468; ASTM F 438; ASTM F 439; ASTM F 877; ASTM F 2389
Steel	ASME B16.5; ASME B16.9; ASME B16.11; ASME B16.28; ASTM A 420

1202.6 Valves. Valves shall be constructed of materials that are compatible with the type of piping material and fluids in the system. Valves shall be rated for the temperatures and pressures of the systems in which the valves are installed.

1202.7 Flexible connectors, expansion and vibration compensators. Flexible connectors, expansion and vibration control devices and fittings shall be of an *approved* type.

SECTION 1203
JOINTS AND CONNECTIONS

1203.1 Approval. Joints and connections shall be of an *approved* type. Joints and connections shall be tight for the pressure of the hydronic system.

1203.1.1 Joints between different piping materials. Joints between different piping materials shall be made with *approved* adapter fittings. Joints between different metallic piping materials shall be made with *approved* dielectric fittings or brass converter fittings.

1203.2 Preparation of pipe ends. Pipe shall be cut square, reamed and chamfered, and shall be free of burrs and obstructions. Pipe ends shall have full-bore openings and shall not be undercut.

1203.3 Joint preparation and installation. When required by Sections 1203.4 through 1203.14, the preparation and installation of brazed, mechanical, soldered, solvent-cemented, threaded and welded joints shall comply with Sections 1203.3.1 through 1203.3.7.

1203.3.1 Brazed joints. Joint surfaces shall be cleaned. An *approved* flux shall be applied where required. The joint shall be brazed with a filler metal conforming to AWS A5.8.

1203.3.2 Mechanical joints. Mechanical joints shall be installed in accordance with the manufacturer's instructions.

1203.3.3 Soldered joints. Joint surfaces shall be cleaned. A flux conforming to ASTM B 813 shall be applied. The joint shall be soldered with a solder conforming to ASTM B 32.

1203.3.4 Solvent-cemented joints. Joint surfaces shall be clean and free of moisture. An *approved* primer shall be applied to CPVC and PVC pipe-joint surfaces. Joints shall be made while the cement is wet. Solvent cement conforming to the following standards shall be applied to all joint surfaces:

1. ASTM D 2235 for ABS joints.
2. ASTM F 493 for CPVC joints.
3. ASTM D 2564 for PVC joints.

CPVC joints shall be made in accordance with ASTM D 2846.

1203.3.5 Threaded joints. Threads shall conform to ASME B1.20.1. Schedule 80 or heavier plastic pipe shall be threaded with dies specifically designed for plastic pipe. Thread lubricant, pipe-joint compound or tape shall be applied on the male threads only and shall be *approved* for application on the piping material.

1203.3.6 Welded joints. Joint surfaces shall be cleaned by an *approved* procedure. Joints shall be welded with an *approved* filler metal.

1203.3.7 Grooved and shouldered mechanical joints. Grooved and shouldered mechanical joints shall conform to the requirements of ASTM F 1476 and shall be installed in accordance with the manufacturer's installation instructions.

1203.3.8 Mechanically formed tee fittings. Mechanically extracted outlets shall have a height not less than three times the thickness of the branch tube wall.

1203.3.8.1 Full flow assurance. Branch tubes shall not restrict the flow in the run tube. A dimple/depth stop shall be formed in the branch tube to ensure that penetration into the outlet is of the correct depth. For inspection purposes, a second dimple shall be placed $^1/_4$ inch (6.4 mm) above the first dimple. Dimples shall be aligned with the tube run.

1203.3.8.2 Brazed joints. Mechanically formed tee fittings shall be brazed in accordance with Section 1203.3.1.

1203.4 ABS plastic pipe. Joints between ABS plastic pipe or fittings shall be solvent-cemented or threaded joints conforming to Section 1203.3.

1203.5 Brass pipe. Joints between brass pipe or fittings shall be brazed, mechanical, threaded or welded joints conforming to Section 1203.3.

1203.6 Brass tubing. Joints between brass tubing or fittings shall be brazed, mechanical or soldered joints conforming to Section 1203.3.

1203.7 Copper or copper-alloy pipe. Joints between copper or copper-alloy pipe or fittings shall be brazed, mechanical, soldered, threaded or welded joints conforming to Section 1203.3.

1203.8 Copper or copper-alloy tubing. Joints between copper or copper-alloy tubing or fittings shall be brazed, mechanical or soldered joints conforming to Section 1203.3, flared joints conforming to Section 1203.8.1 or push-fit joints conforming to Section 1203.8.2.

1203.8.1 Flared joints. Flared joints shall be made by a tool designed for that operation.

1203.8.2 Push-fit joints. Push-fit joints shall be installed in accordance with the manufacturer's instructions.

1203.9 CPVC plastic pipe. Joints between CPVC plastic pipe or fittings shall be solvent-cemented or threaded joints conforming to Section 1203.3.

1203.10 Polybutylene plastic pipe and tubing. Joints between polybutylene plastic pipe and tubing or fittings shall be mechanical joints conforming to Section 1203.3 or heat-fusion joints conforming to Section 1203.10.1.

1203.10.1 Heat-fusion joints. Joints shall be of the socket-fusion or butt-fusion type. Joint surfaces shall be clean and free of moisture. Joint surfaces shall be heated to melt temperatures and joined. The joint shall be undisturbed until cool. Joints shall be made in accordance with ASTM D 3309.

1203.11 Cross-linked polyethylene (PEX) plastic tubing. Joints between cross-linked polyethylene plastic tubing and fittings shall conform to Sections 1203.11.1 and 1203.11.2. Mechanical joints shall conform to Section 1203.3.

1203.11.1 Compression-type fittings. When compression-type fittings include inserts and ferrules or O-rings, the fittings shall be installed without omitting the inserts and ferrules or O-rings.

1203.11.2 Plastic-to-metal connections. Soldering on the metal portion of the system shall be performed at least 18 inches (457 mm) from a plastic-to-metal adapter in the same water line.

1203.12 PVC plastic pipe. Joints between PVC plastic pipe and fittings shall be solvent-cemented or threaded joints conforming to Section 1203.3.

1203.13 Steel pipe. Joints between steel pipe or fittings shall be mechanical joints that are made with an *approved* elastomeric seal, or shall be threaded or welded joints conforming to Section 1203.3.

1203.14 Steel tubing. Joints between steel tubing or fittings shall be mechanical or welded joints conforming to Section 1203.3.

1203.15 Polyethylene plastic pipe and tubing for ground source heat pump loop systems. Joints between polyethylene plastic pipe and tubing or fittings for ground source heat pump loop systems shall be heat fusion joints conforming to Section 1203.15.1, electrofusion joints conforming to Section 1203.15.2, or stab-type insertion joints conforming to Section 1203.15.3.

1203.15.1 Heat-fusion joints. Joints shall be of the socket-fusion, saddle-fusion or butt-fusion type, joined in accordance with ASTM D 2657. Joint surfaces shall be clean and free of moisture. Joint surfaces shall be heated to melt temperatures and joined. The joint shall be undisturbed until cool. Fittings shall be manufactured in accordance with ASTM D 2683 or ASTM D 3261.

1203.15.2 Electrofusion joints. Joints shall be of the electrofusion type. Joint surfaces shall be clean and free of moisture, and scoured to expose virgin resin. Joint surfaces shall be heated to melt temperatures for the period of time specified by the manufacturer. The joint shall be undisturbed until cool. Fittings shall be manufactured in accordance with ASTM F 1055.

1203.15.3 Stab-type insert fittings. Joint surfaces shall be clean and free of moisture. Pipe ends shall be chamfered and inserted into the fittings to full depth. Fittings shall be manufactured in accordance with ASTM F 1924.

1203.16 Polypropylene (PP) plastic. Joints between PP plastic pipe and fittings shall comply with Sections 1203.16.1 and 1203.16.2.

1203.16.1 Heat-fusion joints. Heat-fusion joints for polypropylene (PP) pipe and tubing joints shall be installed with socket-type heat-fused polypropylene fittings, electrofusion polypropylene fittings or by butt fusion. Joint surfaces shall be clean and free from moisture. The joint shall be undisturbed until cool. Joints shall be made in accordance with ASTM F 2389.

1203.16.2 Mechanical and compression sleeve joints. Mechanical and compression sleeve joints shall be installed in accordance with the manufacturer's instructions.

1203.17 Raised temperature polyethylene (PE-RT) plastic tubing. Joints between raised temperature polyethylene tubing and fittings shall conform to Sections 1203.17.1 and 1203.17.2. Mechanical joints shall conform to Section 1203.3.

1203.17.1 Compression-type fittings. Where compression-type fittings include inserts and ferrules or O-rings, the fittings shall be installed without omitting the inserts and ferrules or O-rings.

1203.17.2 PE-RT-to-metal connections. Solder joints in a metal pipe shall not occur within 18 inches (457 mm) of a transition from such metal pipe to PE-RT pipe.

1203.18 Polyethylene/aluminum/polyethylene (PE-AL-PE) pressure pipe. Joints between polyethylene/aluminum/polyethylene pressure pipe and fittings shall conform to Sections 1203.18.1 and 1203.18.2. Mechanical joints shall comply with Section 1203.3.

1203.18.1 Compression-type fittings. Where compression-type fittings include inserts and ferrules or O-rings, the fittings shall be installed without omitting the inserts and ferrules or O-rings.

1203.18.2 PE-AL-PE-to-metal connections. Solder joints in a metal pipe shall not occur within 18 inches (457 mm) of a transition from such metal pipe to PE-AL-PE pipe.

1203.19 Cross-linked polyethylene/aluminum/cross-linked polyethylene (PEX-AL-PEX) pressure pipe. Joints between cross-linked polyethylene/aluminum/cross-linked polyethylene pressure pipe and fittings shall conform to Sections 1203.19.1 and 1203.19.2. Mechanical joints shall comply with Section 1203.3.

1203.19.1 Compression-type fittings. Where compression-type fittings include inserts and ferrules or O-rings, the fittings shall be installed without omitting the inserts and ferrules or O-rings.

1203.19.2 PEX-AL-PEX-to-metal connections. Solder joints in a metal pipe shall not occur within 18 inches (457 mm) of a transition from such metal pipe to PEX-AL-PEX pipe.

SECTION 1204 PIPE INSULATION

1204.1 Insulation characteristics. Pipe insulation installed in buildings shall conform to the requirements of the *International Energy Conservation Code*; shall be tested in accordance with ASTM E 84 or UL 723, using the specimen preparation and mounting procedures of ASTM E 2231; and shall have a maximum flame spread index of 25 and a smoke-developed index not exceeding 450. Insulation installed in an air *plenum* shall comply with Section 602.2.1.

Exception: The maximum flame spread index and smoke-developed index shall not apply to one- and two-family dwellings.

1204.2 Required thickness. Hydronic piping shall be insulated to the thickness required by the *International Energy Conservation Code.*

SECTION 1205 VALVES

1205.1 Where required. Shutoff valves shall be installed in hydronic piping systems in the locations indicated in Sections 1205.1.1 through 1205.1.6.

1205.1.1 Heat exchangers. Shutoff valves shall be installed on the supply and return side of a heat exchanger.

Exception: Shutoff valves shall not be required when heat exchangers are integral with a boiler; or are a component of a manufacturer's boiler and heat exchanger packaged unit and are capable of being isolated from the hydronic system by the supply and return valves required by Section 1005.1.

1205.1.2 Central systems. Shutoff valves shall be installed on the building supply and return of a central utility system.

1205.1.3 Pressure vessels. Shutoff valves shall be installed on the connection to any pressure vessel.

1205.1.4 Pressure-reducing valves. Shutoff valves shall be installed on both sides of a pressure-reducing valve.

1205.1.5 Equipment and appliances. Shutoff valves shall be installed on connections to mechanical *equipment* and appliances. This requirement does not apply to components of a hydronic system such as pumps, air separators, metering devices and similar *equipment.*

1205.1.6 Expansion tanks. Shutoff valves shall be installed at connections to nondiaphragm-type expansion tanks.

1205.2 Reduced pressure. A pressure relief valve shall be installed on the low-pressure side of a hydronic piping system that has been reduced in pressure. The relief valve shall be set at the maximum pressure of the system design. The valve shall be installed in accordance with Section 1006.

SECTION 1206 PIPING INSTALLATION

1206.1 General. Piping, valves, fittings and connections shall be installed in accordance with the conditions of approval.

1206.2 System drain down. Hydronic piping systems shall be designed and installed to permit the system to be drained. Where the system drains to the plumbing drainage system, the installation shall conform to the requirements of the *International Plumbing Code.*

Exception: The buried portions of systems embedded underground or under floors.

1206.3 Protection of potable water. The potable water system shall be protected from backflow in accordance with the *International Plumbing Code.*

1206.4 Pipe penetrations. Openings for pipe penetrations in walls, floors or ceilings shall be larger than the penetrating pipe. Openings through concrete or masonry building elements shall be sleeved. The annular space surrounding pipe penetrations shall be protected in accordance with the *International Building Code.*

1206.5 Clearance to combustibles. A pipe in a hydronic piping system in which the exterior temperature exceeds 250°F (121°C) shall have a minimum *clearance* of 1 inch (25 mm) to combustible materials.

1206.6 Contact with building material. A hydronic piping system shall not be in direct contact with building materials that cause the piping material to degrade or corrode, or that interfere with the operation of the system.

1206.7 Water hammer. The flow velocity of the hydronic piping system shall be controlled to reduce the possibility of water hammer. Where a quick-closing valve creates water hammer, an *approved* water-hammer arrestor shall be installed. The arrestor shall be located within a range as specified by the manufacturer of the quick-closing valve.

1206.8 Steam piping pitch. Steam piping shall be installed to drain to the boiler or the steam trap. Steam systems shall not have drip pockets that reduce the capacity of the steam piping.

1206.9 Strains and stresses. Piping shall be installed so as to prevent detrimental strains and stresses in the pipe. Provisions shall be made to protect piping from damage resulting from expansion, contraction and structural settlement. Piping shall be installed so as to avoid structural stresses or strains within building components.

1206.9.1 Flood hazard. Piping located in a flood hazard area shall be capable of resisting hydrostatic and hydrodynamic loads and stresses, including the effects of buoyancy, during the occurrence of flooding to the *design flood elevation.*

1206.10 Pipe support. Pipe shall be supported in accordance with Section 305.

1206.11 Condensation. Provisions shall be made to prevent the formation of condensation on the exterior of piping.

SECTION 1207 TRANSFER FLUID Deleted

SECTION 1208 TESTS

1208.1 General. Hydronic piping systems other than ground-source heat pump loop systems shall be tested hydrostatically at one and one half times the maximum system design pressure, but not less than 100 psi (689 kPa). The duration of each test shall be not less than 15 minutes. Ground-source heat pump loop systems shall be tested in accordance with Section 1208.1.1.

1208.1.1 Ground source heat pump loop systems. Before connection (header) trenches are backfilled, the assembled loop system shall be pressure tested with water at 100 psi (689 kPa) for 30 minutes with no observed leaks. Flow and pressure loss testing shall be performed and the actual flow rates and pressure drops shall be compared to the calculated design values. If actual flow rate or pressure drop values differ from calculated design values by more than 10 percent, the problem shall be identified and corrected.

SECTION 1209 EMBEDDED PIPING

1209.1 Materials. Piping for heating panels shall be standard-weight steel pipe, Type L copper tubing, polybutylene or other *approved* plastic pipe or tubing rated at 100 psi (689 kPa) at 180°F (82°C).

1209.2 Pressurizing during installation. Piping to be embedded in concrete shall be pressure tested prior to pouring concrete. During pouring, the pipe shall be maintained at the proposed operating pressure.

1209.3 Embedded joints. Joints of pipe or tubing that are embedded in a portion of the building, such as concrete or plaster, shall be in accordance with the requirements of Sections 1209.3.1 through 1209.3.3.

1209.3.1 Steel pipe joints. Steel pipe shall be welded by electrical arc or oxygen/acetylene method.

1209.3.2 Copper tubing joints. Copper tubing shall be joined by brazing with filler metals having a melting point of not less than 1,000°F (538°C).

1209.3.3 Polybutylene joints. Polybutylene pipe and tubing shall be installed in continuous lengths or shall be joined by heat fusion in accordance with Section 1203.10.1.

1209.4 Not embedded related piping. Joints of other piping in cavities or running exposed shall be joined by *approved* methods in accordance with manufacturer's installation instructions and related sections of this code.

1209.5 Thermal barrier required. Radiant floor heating systems shall be provided with a thermal barrier in accordance with Sections 1209.5.1 through 1209.5.4.

Exception: Insulation shall not be required in engineered systems where it can be demonstrated that the insulation will decrease the efficiency or have a negative effect on the installation.

1209.5.1 Slab-on-grade installation. Radiant piping utilized in slab-on-grade applications shall be provided with insulating materials installed beneath the piping having a minimum *R*-value of 5.

1209.5.2 Suspended floor installation. In suspended floor applications, insulation shall be installed in the joist bay cavity serving the heating space above and shall consist of materials having a minimum *R*-value of 11.

1209.5.3 Thermal break required. A thermal break shall be provided consisting of asphalt expansion joint materials or similar insulating materials at a point where a heated slab meets a foundation wall or other conductive slab.

1209.5.4 Thermal barrier material marking. Insulating materials utilized in thermal barriers shall be installed such that the manufacturer's *R*-value mark is readily observable upon inspection.

CHAPTER 13
FUEL OIL PIPING AND STORAGE

SECTION 1301
GENERAL

1301.1 Scope. This chapter shall govern the design, installation, construction and repair of fuel-oil storage and piping systems. The storage of fuel oil and flammable and combustible liquids shall be in accordance with Chapters 6 and 34 of the *International Fire Code*.

1301.2 Storage and piping systems. Fuel-oil storage systems shall comply with Section 603.3 of the *International Fire Code*. Fuel-oil piping systems shall comply with the requirements of this code.

Exception: Fuel-oil storage tanks for one- and two-family dwellings and townhouses shall comply with Section 1309.

1301.3 Fuel type. See Section 301.9.

1301.4 Fuel tanks, piping and valves. The tank, piping and valves for appliances burning oil shall be installed in accordance with the requirements of this chapter. When an oil burner is served by a tank, any part of which is above the level of the burner inlet connection and where the fuel supply line is taken from the top of the tank, an *approved* antisiphon valve or other siphon-breaking device shall be installed in lieu of the shutoff valve.

1301.5 Tanks abandoned or removed. All exterior above-grade fill piping shall be removed when tanks are abandoned or removed. Tank abandonment and removal shall be in accordance with Section 3404.2.13 of the *International Fire Code*.

SECTION 1302
MATERIAL

1302.1 General. Piping materials shall conform to the standards cited in this section.

1302.2 Rated for system. All materials shall be rated for the operating temperatures and pressures of the system, and shall be compatible with the type of liquid.

1302.3 Pipe standards. Fuel oil pipe shall comply with one of the standards listed in Table 1302.3.

1302.4 Nonmetallic pipe. All nonmetallic pipe shall be *listed* and *labeled* as being acceptable for the intended application for flammable and combustible liquids. Nonmetallic pipe shall be installed only outside, underground.

1302.5 Fittings and valves. Fittings and valves shall be *approved* for the piping systems, and shall be compatible with, or shall be of the same material as, the pipe or tubing.

1302.6 Bending of pipe. Pipe shall be *approved* for bending. Pipe bends shall be made with *approved equipment*. The bend shall not exceed the structural limitations of the pipe.

TABLE 1302.3
FUEL OIL PIPING

MATERIAL	STANDARD (see Chapter 15)
Brass pipe	ASTM B 43
Brass tubing	ASTM B 135
Copper or copper-alloy pipe	ASTM B 42; ASTM B 302
Copper or copper-alloy tubing (Type K, L or M)	ASTM B 75; ASTM B 88; ASTM B 280
Labeled pipe	(See Section 1302.4)
Nonmetallic pipe	ASTM D 2996
Steel pipe	ASTM A 53; ASTM A 106
Steel tubing	ASTM A 254; ASTM A 539

1302.7 Pumps. Pumps that are not part of an *appliance* shall be of a positive-displacement type. The pump shall automatically shut off the supply when not in operation. Pumps shall be *listed* and *labeled* in accordance with UL 343.

1302.8 Flexible connectors and hoses. Flexible connectors and hoses shall be *listed* and *labeled* in accordance with UL 536.

SECTION 1303
JOINTS AND CONNECTIONS

1303.1 Approval. Joints and connections shall be *approved* and of a type *approved* for fuel-oil piping systems. All threaded joints and connections shall be made tight with suitable lubricant or pipe compound. Unions requiring gaskets or packings, right or left couplings, and sweat fittings employing solder having a melting point of less than 1,000°F (538°C) shall not be used in oil lines. Cast-iron fittings shall not be used. Joints and connections shall be tight for the pressure required by test.

1303.1.1 Joints between different piping materials. Joints between different piping materials shall be made with *approved* adapter fittings. Joints between different metallic piping materials shall be made with *approved* dielectric fittings or brass converter fittings.

1303.2 Preparation of pipe ends. All pipe shall be cut square, reamed and chamfered and be free of all burrs and obstructions. Pipe ends shall have full-bore openings and shall not be undercut.

1303.3 Joint preparation and installation. Where required by Sections 1303.4 through 1303.10, the preparation and installation of brazed, mechanical, threaded and welded joints shall comply with Sections 1303.3.1 through 1303.3.4.

1303.3.1 Brazed joints. All joint surfaces shall be cleaned. An *approved* flux shall be applied where required. The joints shall be brazed with a filler metal conforming to AWS A5.8.

1303.3.2 Mechanical joints. Mechanical joints shall be installed in accordance with the manufacturer's instructions.

1303.3.3 Threaded joints. Threads shall conform to ASME B1.20.1. Pipe-joint compound or tape shall be applied on the male threads only.

1303.3.4 Welded joints. All joint surfaces shall be cleaned by an *approved* procedure. The joint shall be welded with an *approved* filler metal.

1303.4 Brass pipe. Joints between brass pipe or fittings shall be brazed, mechanical, threaded or welded joints complying with Section 1303.3.

1303.5 Brass tubing. Joints between brass tubing or fittings shall be brazed or mechanical joints complying with Section 1303.3.

1303.6 Copper or copper-alloy pipe. Joints between copper or copper-alloy pipe or fittings shall be brazed, mechanical, threaded or welded joints complying with Section 1303.3.

1303.7 Copper or copper-alloy tubing. Joints between copper or copper-alloy tubing or fittings shall be brazed or mechanical joints complying with Section 1303.3 or flared joints. Flared joints shall be made by a tool designed for that operation.

1303.8 Nonmetallic pipe. Joints between nonmetallic pipe or fittings shall be installed in accordance with the manufacturer's instructions for the *labeled* pipe and fittings.

1303.9 Steel pipe. Joints between steel pipe or fittings shall be threaded or welded joints complying with Section 1303.3 or mechanical joints complying with Section 1303.9.1.

1303.9.1 Mechanical joints. Joints shall be made with an *approved* elastomeric seal. Mechanical joints shall be installed in accordance with the manufacturer's instructions. Mechanical joints shall be installed outside, underground, unless otherwise *approved.*

1303.10 Steel tubing. Joints between steel tubing or fittings shall be mechanical or welded joints complying with Section 1303.3.

1303.11 Piping protection. Proper allowance shall be made for expansion, contraction, jarring and vibration. Piping other than tubing, connected to underground tanks, except straight fill lines and test wells, shall be provided with flexible connectors, or otherwise arranged to permit the tanks to settle without impairing the tightness of the piping connections.

SECTION 1304
PIPING SUPPORT

1304.1 General. Pipe supports shall be in accordance with Section 305.

SECTION 1305
FUEL OIL SYSTEM INSTALLATION

1305.1 Size. The fuel oil system shall be sized for the maximum capacity of fuel oil required. The minimum size of a supply line shall be $^3/_8$-inch (9.5 mm) inside diameter nominal pipe or $^3/_8$-inch (9.5 mm) od tubing. The minimum size of a return line shall be $^1/_4$-inch (6.4 mm) inside diameter nominal pipe or $^5/_{16}$-inch (7.9 mm) outside diameter tubing. Copper tubing shall have 0.035-inch (0.9 mm) nominal and 0.032-inch (0.8 mm) minimum wall thickness.

1305.2 Protection of pipe, equipment and appliances. All fuel oil pipe, *equipment* and appliances shall be protected from physical damage.

1305.2.1 Flood hazard. All fuel oil pipe, *equipment* and appliances located in flood hazard areas shall be located above the *design flood elevation* or shall be capable of resisting hydrostatic and hydrodynamic loads and stresses, including the effects of buoyancy, during the occurrence of flooding to the *design flood elevation.*

1305.3 Supply piping. Supply piping shall connect to the top of the fuel oil tank. Fuel oil shall be supplied by a transfer pump or automatic pump or by other *approved* means.

Exception: This section shall not apply to inside or above-ground fuel oil tanks.

1305.4 Return piping. Return piping shall connect to the top of the fuel oil tank. Valves shall not be installed on return piping.

1305.5 System pressure. The system shall be designed for the maximum pressure required by the fuel-oil-burning *appliance.* Air or other gases shall not be used to pressurize tanks.

1305.6 Fill piping. A fill pipe shall terminate outside of a building at a point at least 2 feet (610 mm) from any building opening at the same or lower level. A fill pipe shall terminate in a manner designed to minimize spilling when the filling hose is disconnected. Fill opening shall be equipped with a tight metal cover designed to discourage tampering.

1305.7 Vent piping. Liquid fuel vent pipes shall terminate outside of buildings at a point not less than 2 feet (610 mm) measured vertically or horizontally from any building opening. Outer ends of vent pipes shall terminate in a weatherproof vent cap or fitting or be provided with a weatherproof hood. All vent caps shall have a minimum free open area equal to the cross-sectional area of the vent pipe and shall not employ screens finer than No. 4 mesh. Vent pipes shall terminate sufficiently above the ground to avoid being obstructed with snow or ice. Vent pipes from tanks containing heaters shall be extended to a location where oil vapors discharging from the vent will be readily diffused. If the static head with a vent pipe filled with oil exceeds 10 pounds per square inch (psi) (69 kPa), the tank shall be designed for the maximum static head that will be imposed.

Liquid fuel vent pipes shall not be cross connected with fill pipes, lines from burners or overflow lines from auxiliary tanks.

SECTION 1306
OIL GAUGING

1306.1 Level indication. All tanks in which a constant oil level is not maintained by an automatic pump shall be equipped with a method of determining the oil level.

1306.2 Test wells. Test wells shall not be installed inside buildings. For outside service, test wells shall be equipped with a tight metal cover designed to discourage tampering.

1306.3 Inside tanks. The gauging of inside tanks by means of measuring sticks shall not be permitted. An inside tank provided with fill and vent pipes shall be provided with a device to indicate either visually or audibly at the fill point when the oil in the tank has reached a predetermined safe level.

1306.4 Gauging devices. Gauging devices such as liquid level indicators or signals shall be designed and installed so that oil vapor will not be discharged into a building from the liquid fuel supply system.

1306.5 Gauge glass. A tank used in connection with any oil burner shall not be equipped with a glass gauge or any gauge which, when broken, will permit the escape of oil from the tank.

SECTION 1307
FUEL OIL VALVES

1307.1 Building shutoff. A shutoff valve shall be installed on the fuel-oil supply line at the entrance to the building. Inside or above-ground tanks are permitted to have valves installed at the tank. The valve shall be capable of stopping the flow of fuel oil to the building or to the *appliance* served where the valve is installed at a tank inside the building.

1307.2 Appliance shutoff. A shutoff valve shall be installed at the connection to each *appliance* where more than one fuel-oil-burning *appliance* is installed.

1307.3 Pump relief valve. A relief valve shall be installed on the pump discharge line where a valve is located downstream of the pump and the pump is capable of exceeding the pressure limitations of the fuel oil system.

1307.4 Fuel-oil heater relief valve. A relief valve shall be installed on the discharge line of fuel-oil-heating appliances.

1307.5 Relief valve operation. The relief valve shall discharge fuel oil when the pressure exceeds the limitations of the system. The discharge line shall connect to the fuel oil tank.

SECTION 1308
TESTING

1308.1 Testing required. Fuel oil piping shall be tested in accordance with NFPA 31.

SECTION 1309
OIL TANKS FOR ONE- AND TWO-FAMILY DWELLINGS AND TOWNHOUSES

1309.1 Materials. Supply tanks shall be listed and labeled and shall conform to UL 142 for above-ground tanks, UL 58 for underground tanks, and UL 80 for inside tanks.

1309.2 Above-ground tanks. The maximum amount of fuel oil stored above ground or inside of a building shall be 660 gallons (2498 L). The supply tank shall be supported on rigid noncombustible supports to prevent settling or shifting.

1309.2.1 Tanks with buildings. Supply tanks for use inside of buildings shall be of such size and shape to permit installation and removal from dwellings as whole units. Supply tanks larger than 10 gallons (38 L) shall be placed not less than 5 feet (1524 mm) from any fire or flame either within or external to any fuel-burning appliance.

1309.2.2 Outside above-ground tanks. Tanks installed outside above ground shall be a minimum of 5 feet (1524 mm) from an adjoining property line. Such tanks shall be protected from the weather and from physical damage.

1309.3 Underground tanks. Excavations for underground tanks shall not undermine the foundations of existing structures. The clearance from the tank to the nearest wall of a basement, pit or property line shall not be less than 1 foot (305 mm). Tanks shall be set on and surrounded with noncorrosive inert materials such as clean earth, sand or gravel well tamped in place. Tanks shall be covered with not less than1 foot (305 mm) of earth. Corrosion protection shall be provided in accordance with Section 1309.8.

1309.4 Multiple tanks. Cross connection of two supply tanks shall be permitted in accordance with Section 1309.7.

1309.5 Oil gauges. Inside tanks shall be provided with a device to indicate when the oil in the tank has reached a predetermined safe level. Glass gauges or a gauge subject to breakage that could result in the escape of oil from the tank shall not be used.

1309.6 Flood-resistant installation. In areas prone to flooding as established by Table R301.2(1) of the *International Residential Code*, tanks shall be installed at or above the design flood elevation established in Section R324 of the *International Residential Code* or shall be anchored to prevent flotation, collapse and lateral movement under conditions of the design flood.

1309.7 Cross connection of tanks. Cross connection of supply tanks, not exceeding 660 gallons (2498 L) of aggregate capacity, with gravity flow from one tank to another, shall be acceptable provided that the two tanks are on the same horizontal plane.

1309.8 Corrosion protection. Underground tanks and buried piping shall be protected by corrosion-resistant coatings or alloys or fiberglass-reinforced plastic.

CHAPTER 14
SOLAR SYSTEMS

SECTION 1401 GENERAL

1401.1 Scope. This chapter shall govern the design, construction, installation, *alteration* and repair of systems, *equipment* and appliances intended to utilize solar energy for space heating or cooling, domestic hot water heating, swimming pool heating or process heating.

1401.2 Potable water supply. Potable water supplies to solar systems shall be protected against contamination in accordance with the *International Plumbing Code*.

> **Exception:** Where all solar system piping is a part of the potable water distribution system, in accordance with the requirements of the *International Plumbing Code*, and all components of the piping system are *listed* for potable water use, cross-connection protection measures shall not be required.

1401.3 Heat exchangers. Heat exchangers used in domestic water-heating systems shall be *approved* for the intended use. The system shall have adequate protection to ensure that the potability of the water supply and distribution system is properly safeguarded.

1401.4 Solar energy equipment and appliances. Solar energy *equipment* and appliances shall conform to the requirements of this chapter and shall be installed in accordance with the manufacturer's installation instructions.

1401.5 Ducts. Ducts utilized in solar heating and cooling systems shall be constructed and installed in accordance with Chapter 6 of this code.

SECTION 1402 INSTALLATION

1402.1 Access. Access shall be provided to solar energy *equipment* and appliances for maintenance. Solar systems and appurtenances shall not obstruct or interfere with the operation of any doors, windows or other building components requiring operation or access.

1402.2 Protection of equipment. Solar *equipment* exposed to vehicular traffic shall be installed not less than 6 feet (1829 mm) above the finished floor.

> **Exception:** This section shall not apply where the *equipment* is protected from motor vehicle impact.

1402.3 Controlling condensation. Where attics or structural spaces are part of a passive solar system, ventilation of such spaces, as required by Section 406, is not required where other *approved* means of controlling condensation are provided.

1402.4 Roof-mounted collectors. Roof-mounted solar collectors that also serve as a roof covering shall conform to the requirements for roof coverings in accordance with the *International Building Code*.

> **Exception:** The use of plastic solar collector covers shall be limited to those *approved* plastics meeting the requirements for plastic roof panels in the *International Building Code*.

1402.4.1 Collectors mounted above the roof. When mounted on or above the roof covering, the collector array and supporting construction shall be constructed of noncombustible materials or fire-retardant-treated wood conforming to the *International Building Code* to the extent required for the type of roof construction of the building to which the collectors are accessory.

> **Exception:** The use of plastic solar collector covers shall be limited to those *approved* plastics meeting the requirements for plastic roof panels in the *International Building Code*.

1402.5 Equipment. The solar energy system shall be equipped in accordance with the requirements of Sections 1402.5.1 through 1402.5.4.

1402.5.1 Pressure and temperature. Solar energy system components containing pressurized fluids shall be protected against pressures and temperatures exceeding design limitations with a pressure and temperature relief valve. Each section of the system in which excessive pressures are capable of developing shall have a relief device located so that a section cannot be valved off or otherwise isolated from a relief device. Relief valves shall comply with the requirements of Section 1006.4 and discharge in accordance with Section 1006.6.

1402.5.2 Vacuum. The solar energy system components that are subjected to a vacuum while in operation or during shutdown shall be designed to withstand such vacuum or shall be protected with vacuum relief valves.

1402.5.3 Protection from freezing. System components shall be protected from damage by freezing of heat transfer liquids at the lowest ambient temperatures that will be encountered during the operation of the system.

1402.5.4 Expansion tanks. Liquid single-phase solar energy systems shall be equipped with expansion tanks sized in accordance with Section 1009.

1402.6 Penetrations. Roof and wall penetrations shall be flashed and sealed to prevent entry of water, rodents and insects.

1402.7 Filtering. Air transported to occupied spaces through rock or dust-producing materials by means other than natural convection shall be filtered at the outlet from the heat storage system.

SECTION 1403
HEAT TRANSFER FLUIDS

1403.1 Flash point. The flash point of the actual heat transfer fluid utilized in a solar system shall be not less than 50°F (28°C) above the design maximum nonoperating (no-flow) temperature of the fluid attained in the collector.

1403.2 Flammable gases and liquids. A flammable liquid or gas shall not be utilized as a heat transfer fluid. The flash point of liquids used in occupancies classified in Group H or F shall not be lower unless *approved*.

SECTION 1404
MATERIALS

1404.1 Collectors. Factory-built collectors shall be *listed* and *labeled*, and bear a label showing the manufacturer's name and address, model number, collector dry weight, collector maximum allowable operating and nonoperating temperatures and pressures, minimum allowable temperatures and the types of heat transfer fluids that are compatible with the collector. The label shall clarify that these specifications apply only to the collector.

1404.2 Thermal storage units. Pressurized thermal storage units shall be *listed* and *labeled*, and bear a label showing the manufacturer's name and address, model number, serial number, storage unit maximum and minimum allowable operating temperatures, storage unit maximum and minimum allowable operating pressures and the types of heat transfer fluids compatible with the storage unit. The label shall clarify that these specifications apply only to the thermal storage unit.

CHAPTER 15

REFERENCED STANDARDS

This chapter lists the standards that are referenced in various sections of this document. The standards are listed herein by the promulgating agency of the standard, the standard identification, the effective date and title, and the section or sections of this document that reference the standard. The application of the referenced standards shall be as specified in Section 102.8.

ACCA

Air Conditioning Contractors of America
2800 Shirlington Road, Suite 300
Arlington, VA 22206

Standard Reference Number	Title	Referenced in code section number
Manual D—95	Residential Duct Systems	603.2
Manual J—02	Residential Load Calculations, Eighth Edition	312
Manual S—04	Residential Equipment Selection	312
183—2007	Peak Cooling and Heating Load Calculations in Buildings Except Low-Rise Residential Buildings	312.1

AHRI

Air-Conditioning, Heating and Refrigeration Institute
4100 North Fairfax Drive, Suite 200
Arlington, VA 22203

Standard Reference Number	Title	Referenced in code section number
700—99	Purity Specifications for Fluorocarbon and Other Refrigerants	1102.2.2.3

ANSI

American National Standards Institute
11 West 42nd Street
New York, NY 10036

Standard Reference Number	Title	Referenced in code section number
Z21.8—1994 (R2002)	Installation of Domestic Gas Conversion Burners	919.1

ASHRAE

American Society of Heating, Refrigerating
and Air-Conditioning Engineers, Inc.
1791 Tullie Circle, NE
Atlanta, GA 30329

Standard Reference Number	Title	Referenced in code section number
ASHRAE—2005	ASHRAE Fundamentals Handbook—2005	603.2
15—2004	Safety Standard for Refrigeration Systems	1101.6, 1105.8, 1108.1
34—2004	Designation and Safety Classification of Refrigerants	202, 1102.2.1, 1103.1
62.1—2004	Ventilation for Acceptable Indoor Air Quality	403.3.2.3.2

ASME

American Society of Mechanical Engineers
Three Park Avenue
New York, NY 10016-5990

Standard Reference Number	Title	Referenced in code section number
B1.20.1—1983 (R2006)	Pipe Threads, General Purpose (Inch)	1203.3.5, 1303.3.3
B16.3—2006	Malleable Iron Threaded Fittings, Classes 150 & 300	Table 1202.5
B16.5—2003	Pipe Flanges and Flanged Fittings NPS $^1/_2$ through NPS 24—	Table 1202.5
B16.9—2003	Factory Made Wrought Steel Buttwelding Fittings	Table 1202.5
B16.11—2005	Forged Fittings, Socket-welding and Threaded	Table 1202.5
B16.15—2006	Cast Bronze Threaded Fittings	Table 1202.5

ASME—continued

B16.18—2001 (Reaffirmed 2005)	Cast Copper Alloy Solder Joint Pressure Fittings	513.13.1, Table 1202.5
B16.22—2001 (Reaffirmed 2005)	Wrought Copper and Copper Alloy Solder Joint Pressure Fittings	513.13.1, Table 1202.5
B16.23—2002 (Reaffirmed 2006)	Cast Copper Alloy Solder Joint Drainage Fittings DWV	Table 1202.5
B16.24—2001	Cast Copper Alloy Pipe Flanges and Flanged Fittings: Class 150, 300, 400, 600, 900, 1500 and 2500	Table 1202.5
B16.26—2006	Cast Copper Alloy Fittings for Flared Copper Tubes	Table 1202.5
B16.28—1994	Wrought Steel Buttwelding Short Radius Elbows and Returns	Table 1202.5
B16.29—2001	Wrought Copper and Wrought Copper Alloy Solder Joint Drainage Fittings-DWV	Table 1202.5
B31.9—04	Building Services Piping	1201.3
BPVC—2004	Boiler & Pressure Vessel Code	1004.1, 1011.1
CSD-1—2004	Controls and Safety Devices for Automatically Fired Boilers	1004.1

ASSE

American Society of Sanitary Engineering
901 Canterbury, Suite A
Westlake, OH 44145

Standard Reference Number	Title	Referenced in code section number
1017—03	Performance Requirements for Temperature Actuated Mixing Values for Hot Water Distribution Systems	1002.2.2

ASTM

ASTM International
100 Barr Harbor Drive
West Conshohocken, PA 19428

Standard Reference Number	Title	Referenced in code section number
A 53/A 53M—06a	Specification for Pipe, Steel, Black and Hot-dipped, Zinc-coated Welded and Seamless	Table 1202.4, Table 1302.3
A 106/A106M—06a	Specification for Seamless Carbon Steel Pipe for High-Temperature Service	Table 1202.4, Table 1302.3
A 126—04	Specification for Gray Iron Castings for Valves, Flanges and Pipe Fittings	Table 1202.5
A 254—97 (2002)	Specification for Copper Brazed Steel Tubing	Table 1202.4, Table 1302.3
A 420/A 420M—07	Specification for Piping Fittings of Wrought Carbon Steel and Alloy Steel for Low-Temperature Service	Table 1202.5
A 539—99	Specification for Electric-Resistance-Welded Coiled Steel Tubing for Gas and Fuel Oil Lines	Table 1302.3
B 32—04	Specification for Solder Metal	1203.3.3
B 42—02e01	Specification for Seamless Copper Pipe, Standard Sizes	513.13.1, 1107.5.2, Table 1202.4, Table 1302.3
B 43—98(2004)	Specification for Seamless Red Brass Pipe, Standard Sizes	513.13.1, 1107.5.2, Table 1202.4, Table 1302.3
B 68—02	Specification for Seamless Copper Tube, Bright Annealed	513.13.1
B 75—02	Specification for Seamless Copper Tube	Table 1202.4, Table 1302.3
B 88—03	Specification for Seamless Copper Water Tube	513.13.1, 1107.5.3, Table 1202.4, Table 1302.3
B 135—02	Specification for Seamless Brass Tube	Table 1202.4, Table 1302.3
B 251—02e01	Specification for General Requirements for Wrought Seamless Copper and Copper-alloy Tube	513.13.1, Table 1202.4
B 280—03	Specification for Seamless Copper Tube for Air Conditioning and Refrigeration Field Service	513.13.1, 1107.4.3, Table 1302.3
B 302—02	Specification for Threadless Copper Pipe, Standard Sizes	Table 1202.4, Table 1302.3
B 813—00e01	Specification for Liquid and Paste Fluxes for Soldering of Copper and Copper Alloy Tube	1203.3.3
C 315—07	Specification for Clay Flue Liners and Chimney Pots	801.16.1, Table 803.10.4
C 411—05	Test Method for Hot-surface Performance of High-temperature Thermal Insulation	604.3
D 56—05	Test Method for Flash Point by Tag Closed Tester	202
D 93—07	Test Method for Flash Point of Pensky-Martens Closed Cup Tester	202
D 1527—99(2005)	Specification for Acrylonitrile-Butadiene-Styrene (ABS) Plastic Pipe, Schedules 40 and 80	Table 1202.4
D 1693—07	Test Method for Environmental Stress-Cracking of Ethylene Plastics	Table 1202.4
D 1785—06	Specification for Poly (Vinyl Chloride)(PVC) Plastic Pipe, Schedules 40, 80 and 120	Table 1202.4
D 2235—04	Specifications for Solvent Cement for Acrylonitrile-Butadiene-Styrene (ABS) Plastic Pipe and Fittings	1203.3.4
D 2241—05	Specification for Poly (Vinyl Chloride)(PVC) Pressure-rated Pipe (SDR-Series)	Table 1202.4
D 2282—99(2005)	Specification for Acrylonitrile-Butadiene-Styrene (ABS) Plastic Pipe (SDR-PR)	Table 1202.4
D 2412—02	Test Method for Determination of External Loading Characteristics of Plastic Pipe by Parallel-plate Loading	603.8.3
D 2447—03	Specification for Polyethylene (PE) Plastic Pipe, Schedules 40 and 80, Based on Outside Diameter	Table 1202.4

ASTM—continued

D 2466—06	Specification for Poly (Vinyl Chloride)(PVC) Plastic Pipe Fittings, Schedule 40	Table 1202.5
D 2467—06	Specification for Poly (Vinyl Chloride)(PVC) Plastic Pipe Fittings, Schedule 80	Table 1202.5
D 2468—96a	Specification for Acrylonitrile-Butadiene-Styrene (ABS) Plastic Pipe Fittings, Schedule 40	Table 1202.5
D 2513—07a	Specification for Thermoplastic Gas Pressure Pipe, Tubing, and Fittings	Table 1202.4
D 2564—04e01	Specification for Solvent Cements for Poly (Vinyl Chloride) (PVC) Plastic Piping Systems	1203.3.4
D 2657—07	Standard Practice for Heat Fusion Joining of Polyolefin Pipe and Fittings	1203.15.1
D 2683—04	Specification for Socket-type Polyethylene Fittings for Outside Diameter-controlled Polyethylene Pipe and Tubing	Table 1202.4, 1203.15.1
D 2837—04e01	Test Method for Obtaining Hydrostatic Design Basis for Thermoplastic Pipe Materials or Pressure Design Basis for Thermoplastic Pipe Products	Table 1202.4
D 2846/D 2846M—06	Specification for Chlorinated Poly (Vinyl Chloride) (CPVC) Plastic Hot and Cold Water Distribution Systems	Table 1202.4, 1203.3.4
D 2996—01(2007)e01	Specification for Filament-wound Fiberglass (Glass Fiber Reinforced Thermosetting Resin) Pipe	Table 1302.3
D 3035—06	Specification for Polyethylene (PE) Plastic Pipe (DR-PR) Based on Controlled Outside Diameter	Table 1202.4
D 3278—96(2004)e01	Test Methods for Flash Point of Liquids by Small Scale Closed-cup Apparatus	202
D 3261—03	Standard Specification for Butt Heat Fusion Polyethylene (PE) Plastic Fittings for Polyethylene (PE) Plastic Pipe and Tubing	1203.15.1
D 3309—96a(2002)	Specification for Polybutylene (PB) Plastic Hot and Cold Water Distribution Systems	Table 1202.4, 1203.10.1
D 3350—06	Specification for Polyethylene Plastics Pipe and Fittings Materials	Table 1202.4
E 84—07	Test Method for Surface Burning Characteristics of Building Materials	202, 510.8, 602.2.1, 602.2.1.5, 604.3, 1204.1
E 119—07	Test Method for Fire Tests of Building Construction and Materials	607.5.2, 607.5.5, 607.6.1, 607.2.1
E 136—04	Test Method for Behavior of Materials in a Vertical Tube Furnace at 750 Degrees C	202
E 814—06	Test Method for Fire Tests of Through-penetration Fire Stops	506.3.10.2, 506.3.10.3
E 1509—04	Specification for Room Heaters, Pellet Fuel-burning Type	904.1
E 2231—04	Standard Practice For Specimen Preparation and Mounting of Pipe and Duct Insulation Materials to Assess Surface Burning Characteristics	604.3, 1204.1
E 2336-04	Standard Test Methods for Fire Resistive Grease Duct Enclosure Systems	506.3.6, 506.3.10.2
F 438—04	Specification for Socket Type Chlorinated Poly (Vinyl Chloride) (CPVC) Plastic Pipe Fittings, Schedule 40	Table 1202.5
F 439—06	Specification for Socket Type Chlorinated Poly (Vinyl Chloride) (CPVC) Plastic Pipe Fittings, Schedule 80	Table 1202.5
F 441/F 441M—02	Specification for Chlorinated Poly (Vinyl Chloride) (CPVC) Plastic Pipe, Schedules 40 and 80	Table 1202.4
F 442/F 442M—99(2005)	Specification for Chlorinated Poly (Vinyl Chloride) (CPVC) Plastic Pipe (SDR-PR)	Table 1202.4
F 493—04	Specification for Solvent Cements for Chlorinated Poly (Vinyl Chloride) (CPVC) Plastic Pipe and Fittings	1203.3.4
F 876—06	Specification for Crosslinked Polyethylene (PEX) Tubing	Table 1202.4
F 877—07	Specification for Crosslinked Polyethylene (PEX) Plastic Hot and Cold Water Distribution Systems	Table 1202.4, Table 1202.5
F 1055—98(2006)	Specification for Electrofusion Type Polyethylene Fittings for Outside Diameter Controlled Polyethylene Pipe and Fittings	Table 1202.4, 1203.15.2
F 1281—07	Specification for Crosslinked Polyethylene/Aluminum/Crosslinked Polyethylene (PEX-AL-PEX) Pressure Pipe	Table 1202.4
F 1282—06	Standard Specification for Polyethylene/Aluminum/Polyethylene (PE-AL-PE) Composite Pressure Pipe	Table 1202.4
F 1476—(2006)	Specification for Performance of Gasketed Mechanical Couplings for Use in Piping Applications	1203.3.7
F 1924—05	Standard Specification for Plastic Mechanical Fittings for Use on Outside Diameter Controlled Polyethylene Gas Distribution Pipe and Tubing	1203.15.3
F 1974—04	Standard Specification for Metal Insert Fittings for Polyethylene/Aluminum/Polyethylene and Crosslinked Polyethylene/Aluminum/Crosslinked Polyethylene Composite Pressure Pipe	Table 1202.5
F 2389—06	Specification for Pressure-Rated Polypropylene Piping Systems	Table 1202.4, Table 1202.5
F 2623—07	Standard Specification for Polyethylene of Raised Temperature (PE-RT) SDR 9 Tubing1	Table 1202.4

AWS

American Welding Society
550 N.W. LeJeune Road
P.O. Box 351040
Miami, FL 33135

Standard Reference Number	Title	Referenced in code section number
A5.8—2004	Specifications for Filler Metals for Brazing and Braze Welding	1203.3.1, 1303.3.1

AWWA

American Water Work Association
6666 West Quincy Avenue
Denver, CO 80235

Standard Reference Number	Title	Referenced in code section number
C110/A21.10—03	Standard for Ductile Iron & Gray Iron Fittings, 2 inches Through 48 inches for Water	Table 1202.5
C115/A21.15—99	Standard for Flanged Ductile-iron Pipe with Ductile Iron or Grey-iron Threaded Flanges	Table 1202.4
C151/A21.51—02	Standard for Ductile-Iron Pipe, Centrifugally Cast for Water	Table 1202.4
C153/A21.53—00	Standard for Ductile-Iron Compact Fittings for Water Service	Table 1202.5

CSA

Canadian Standards Association
5060 Spectrum Way
Mississauga, Ontario, Canada L4W 5N6

Standard Reference Number	Title	Referenced in code section number
B137.9-M91 CAN/CSA	Polyethylene/Aluminum/Polyethylene (PE-AL-PE) Composite Pressure-Pipe Systems	Table 1202.4
B137.10—02	Cross-linked Polyethylene/Aluminum/Cross-linked Polyethylene Composite Pressure-Pipe Systems	Table 1202.4
ANSI CSA America FC1-03	Stationary Fuel Cell Power Systems	924.1

DOL

Department of Labor
Occupational Safety and Health Administration
c/o Superintendent of Documents
US Government Printing Office
Washington, DC 20402-9325

Standard Reference Number	Title	Referenced in code section number
29 CFR Part 1910.1000 (1974)	Air Contaminants	502.6
29 CFR Part 1910. 1025	Toxic and Hazardous Substances	502.19

FS

Federal Specifications*
General Services Administration
7th & D Streets
Specification Section, Room 6039
Washington, DC 20407

Standard Reference Number	Title	Referenced in code section number
WW-P-325B (1976)	Pipe, Bends, Traps, Caps and Plugs; Lead (for Industrial Pressure and Soil and Waste Applications	Table 1202.4

*Standards are available from the Supt. of Documents, U.S. Government Printing Office, Washington, DC 20402-9325.

ICC

International Code Council, Inc.
500 New Jersey Ave, NW
6th Floor
Washington, DC 20001

Standard Reference Number	Title	Referenced in code section number
IBC—09	International Building Code®	201.3, 202, 301.12, 301.12, 301.14, 301.15, 302.1, 302.2, 304.7, 304.10, 308.8, 308.10, 401.4, 401.6, 406.1, 502.10, 502.10.1, 504.2, 506.3.3, 506.3.10, 506.3.12.2, 506.4.1, 509.1, 510.6, 510.6.3, 510.6.2, 510.7, 511.1.5, 513.1, 513.2, 513.3, 513.4.3, 513.5, 513.5.2, 513.5.2.1, 513.6.2, 513.10.5, 513.12, 513.12.2, 513.20, 602.2.1.5.1, 602.2.1.5.2, 602.3, 603.1, 603.10, 604.5.4, 607.1.1, 607.3.2.1, 607.5.1, 607.5.2, 607.5.3, 607.5.4, 607.5.4.1, 607.5.5, 607.5.5.1, 607.6, 607.6.2, 701.4.1, 701.4.2, 801.3, 801.16.1, 801.18.4, 902.1, 908.3, 908.4, 910.3, 925.1, 1004.6, 1105.1, 1206.4, 1402.4, 1402.4.1
IEBC—09	International Existing Building Code®	101.2
IECC—09	International Energy Conservation Code®	202, 301.2, 303.3, 312.1, 603.9, 604.1, 1204.1, 1204.2

ICC—continued

IFC—09	International Fire Code®	201.3, 310.1, 311.1, 502.4, 502.5, 502.7.2, 502.8.1, 502.9.5, 502.9.5.2, 502.9.5.3, 502.9.8.2, 502.9.8.3, 502.9.8.5, 502.9.8.6, 502.10, 502.10.3, 502.16.2, 509.1, 510.2.1, 510.2.2, 510.4, 511.1.1 513.12.3, 513.15, 513.16, 513.17, 513.18, 513.19, 513.20.2, 513.20.3, 606.2.1, 908.7, 1101.9, 1105.3, 1105.9, 1106.5, 1106.6, 1301.1, 1301.2
IFGC—09	International Fuel Gas Code®	101.2, 201.3, 301.3, 701.1, 801.1, 901.1, 906.1, 1101.5
IPC—09	International Plumbing Code®	201.3, 301.8, 512.2, 908.5, 1002.1, 1002.2, 1002.3, 1005.2, 1006.6, 1008.2, 1009.3, 1101.4, 1201.1, 1206.2, 1206.3, 1401.2
IRC—09	International Residential Code®	101.2

IIAR

International Institute of Ammonia Refrigeration
1110 North Glebe Road
Arlington, VA 22201

Standard Reference Number	Title	Referenced in code section number
2—99 (with Addendum A-2005)	Addendum A to Equipment, Design, and Installation of Ammonia Mechanical Refrigerating Systems	1101.6

MSS

Manufacturers Standardization Society of the Valve & Fittings Industry, Inc.
127 Park Street, N.E.
Vienna, VA 22180

Standard Reference Number	Title	Referenced in code section number
SP-69—2002	Pipe Hangers and Supports—Selection and Application	305.4

NAIMA

North American Insulation Manufacturers Association
44 Canal Center Plaza, Suite 310
Alexandria, VA 22314

Standard Reference Number	Title	Referenced in code section number
AH116—02	Fibrous Glass Duct Construction Standards	603.5, 603.9

NFPA

National Fire Protection Association
1 Batterymarch Park
Quincy, MA 02169-7471

Standard Reference Number	Title	Referenced in code section number
30A—08	Code for Motor Fuel-dispensing Facilities and Repair Garages	304.6
31—06	Installation of Oil-burning Equipment	801.2.1, 801.18.1, 801.18.2, 920.2, 922.1, 1308.1
37—06	Stationary Combustion Engines and Gas Turbines	915.1, 915.2
58—08	Liquefied Petroleum Gas Code	502.9.10
69—08	Explosion Prevention Systems	510.8.3
70—08	National Electrical Code	301.7, 306.3.1, 306.4.1, 511.1.1, 513.11, 513.12.1, 602.2.1.1, 1106.3, 1106.4
72—07	National Fire Alarm Code	606.3
82—04	Incinerators and Waste and Linen Handling Systems and Equipment	601.1
91—04	Exhaust Systems for Air Conveying of Vapors, Gases, and Noncombustible Particulate Solids	502.9.5.1, 502.17
92B—05	Smoke Management Systems in Malls, Atria and Large Spaces	513.8
211—06	Chimneys, Fireplaces, Vents and Solid Fuel-burning Appliances	806.1
262—07	Standard Method of Test for Flame Travel and Smoke of Wires and Cables for Use in Air-handling Spaces	602.2.1.1
704—07	Identification of the Hazards of Materials for Emergency Response	502.8.4, Table 1103.1, 510.1
853—07	Installation of Stationary Fuel Power Plants	924.1
8501—97	Single Burner Boiler Operation	1004.1
8502—99	Prevention of Furnace Explosions/Implosions in Multiple Burner Boiler-furnaces	1004.1
8504—96	Atmospheric Fluidized-bed Boiler Operation	1004.1

SMACNA

Sheet Metal & Air Conditioning Contractors National Assoc., Inc.
4201 Lafayette Center Drive
Chantilly, VA 20151-1209

Standard Reference Number	Title	Referenced in code section number
SMACNA/ANSI—2005	HVAC Duct Construction Standards—Metal and Flexible (2005)	603.4, 603.9
SMACNA—03	Fibrous Glass Duct Construction Standards	603.5, 603.9

UL

Underwriters Laboratories, Inc.
333 Pfingsten Road
Northbrook, IL 60062-2096

Standard Reference Number	Title	Referenced in code section number
17—94	Vent or Chimney Connector Dampers for Oil-fired Appliances—with Revisions through September 1999	803.6
58—96	Standard for Steel Underground Tanks for Flammable and Combustible Liquids	1309
80—09	Standard for Steel Tanks for Oil-burner Fuels and Other Combustible Liquids	1309
103—01	Factory-built Chimneys, Residential Type and Building Heating Appliance—with Revisions through June 2006	805.2
127—96	Factory-built Fireplaces—with Revisions through November 2006	805.3, 903.1, 903.3
142—2010	Standard for Steel Above ground Tanks for Flammable and Combustible Liquids	1309
174—04	Household Electric Storage Tank Water Heaters—with Revisions through May 2006	1002.1
181—05	Factory-made Air Ducts and Air Connectors—with Revisions through December 1998	512.2, 603.5, 603.6.1, 603.6.2, 604.13
181A—05	Closure Systems for Use with Rigid Air Ducts and Air Connectors—with Revisions through December 1998	603.9
181B—05	Closure Systems for Use with Flexible Air Ducts and Air Connectors—with Revisions through December 1998	603.9
207—01	Refrigerant-containing Components and Accessories, Nonelectrical—with Revisions through November 2004	1101.2
263—03	Standard for Fire Test of Building Construction and Materials	607.5.2, 607.5.5, 607.6.1
268—06	Smoke Detectors for Fire Prevention Signaling Systems—with Revisions through October 2003	606.1
268A—98	Smoke Detectors for Duct Applications—with Revisions through April 2006	606.1
343—97	Pumps for Oil-Burning Appliances—with Revisions through May 2006	1302.7
391—2006	Solid-fuel and Combination-fuel Central and Supplementary Furnaces	918.1
412—04	Refrigeration Unit Coolers—with Revisions through February 2007	1101.2
471—06	Commercial Refrigerators and Freezers—with Revisions through March 2006	1101.2
508—99	Industrial Control Equipment—with Revisions through July 2005	307.2.3
536—97	Flexible Metallic Hose—with Revisions through June 2003	1302.8
555—06	Fire Dampers—with Revisions through January 2002	607.3
555C—06	Ceiling Dampers	607.3.1
555S—99	Smoke Dampers—with Revisions through July 2006	607.3.1
586—96	High-efficiency, Particulate, Air Filter Units—with Revisions through August 2004	605.2
641—95	Type L Low-temperature Venting Systems—with Revisions through August 2005	802.1
710—95	Exhaust Hoods for Commercial Cooking Equipment—with Revisions through February 2007	507.1
710B—04	Recirculating Systems	507.1
723—03	Standard for Test for Surface Burning Characteristics of Building Materials—with Revisions through May 2005	510.8, 602.2.1, 602.2.1.5, 604.3, 1204.1
726—95	Oil-fired Boiler Assemblies—with Revisions through March 2006	916.1, 1004.1
727—06	Oil-fired Central Furnaces	918.1
729—03	Oil-fired Floor Furnaces—with Revisions through January 1999	910.1
730—03	Oil-fired Wall Furnaces—with Revisions through January 1999	909.1
731—95	Oil-fired Unit Heaters—with Revisions through February 2006	920.1
732—95	Oil-fired Storage Tank Water Heaters—with Revisions through February 2005	1002.1
737—96	Fireplace Stoves—with Revisions through January 2000	905.1
762—03	Outline of Investigation for Power Ventilators for Restaurant Exhaust Appliances	506.5.1
791—06	Residential Incinerators	907.1
834—04	Heating, Water Supply and Power Boilers Electric—with Revisions through March 2006	1004.1
858—05	Household Electric Ranges—with Revisions through April 2006	917.1
867—00	Electrostatic Air Cleaners—with Revisions through May 2004	605.2
875—04	Electric Dry Bath Heater—with Revisions through March 2006	914.2
896—93	Oil-burning Stoves—with Revisions through May 2004	917.1, 922.1
900—04	Air Filter Units	605.2
923—02	Microwave Cooking Appliances—with Revisions through February 2006	914.2

UL—continued

959—01	Medium Heat Appliance Factory-built Chimneys—with Revisions through September 2006	805.5
1240—05	Electric Commercial Clothes	913.1
1261—01	Electric Water Heaters for Pools and Tubs—with Revisions through June 2004.	916.1
1453—04	Electric Booster and Commercial Storage Tank Water Heaters—with Revisions through May 2006.	1002.1
1479—03	Fire Tests of Through-penetration Firestops—with Revisions through April 2007	506.3.10.2, 506.3.10.3
1482—96	Solid-fuel Type Room Heaters—with Revisions through November 2006	905.1
1777—04	Chimney Liners	801.16.1, 801.18.4
1812—05	Standard for Ducted Heat Recovery Ventilators—with Revisions through January 2006.	927.1
1815—01	Standard for Nonducted Heat Recovery Ventilators—with Revisions through January 2006.	927.2
1820—04	Fire Test of Pneumatic Tubing for Flame and Smoke Characteristics	602.2.1.3
1887—04	Fire Tests of Plastic Sprinkler Pipe for Visible Flame and Smoke Characteristics	602.2.1.2
1978—95	Grease Ducts	506.3.2
1995—05	Heating and Cooling Equipment	911.1, 918.1, 918.3, 1101.2
2043—08	Fire Test for Heat and Visible Smoke Release for Discrete Products and their Accessories Installed in Air-handling Spaces	602.2.1.4.2
2158—97	Electric Clothes Dryers—with Revisions through May 2004	504.6.3, 913.1
2158A—2006	Outline of Investigation for Clothes Dryer Transition Duct	504.6.3
2162—01	Outline of Investigation for Commercial Wood-fired Baking Ovens—Refractory Type	917.1
2200—04	Stationery Engine Generator Assemblies	915.1
2221—01	Tests of Fire Resistive Grease Duct Enclosure Assemblies	506.3.10.3

APPENDIX A

COMBUSTION AIR OPENINGS AND CHIMNEY CONNECTOR PASS-THROUGHS

The provisions contained in this appendix are adopted as part of this code.

FIGURE A-1
ALL AIR FROM INSIDE THE BUILDING

Deleted.

FIGURE A-2
ALL AIR FROM OUTDOORS—INLET AIR FROM VENTILATED CRAWL SPACE AND OUTLET AIR TO VENTILATED ATTIC

Deleted.

FIGURE A-3
ALL AIR FROM OUTDOORS THROUGH VENTILATED ATTIC

Deleted.

FIGURE A-4
ALL AIR FROM OUTDOORS THROUGH HORIZONTAL DUCTS OR DIRECT OPENINGS

Deleted.

SYSTEM A

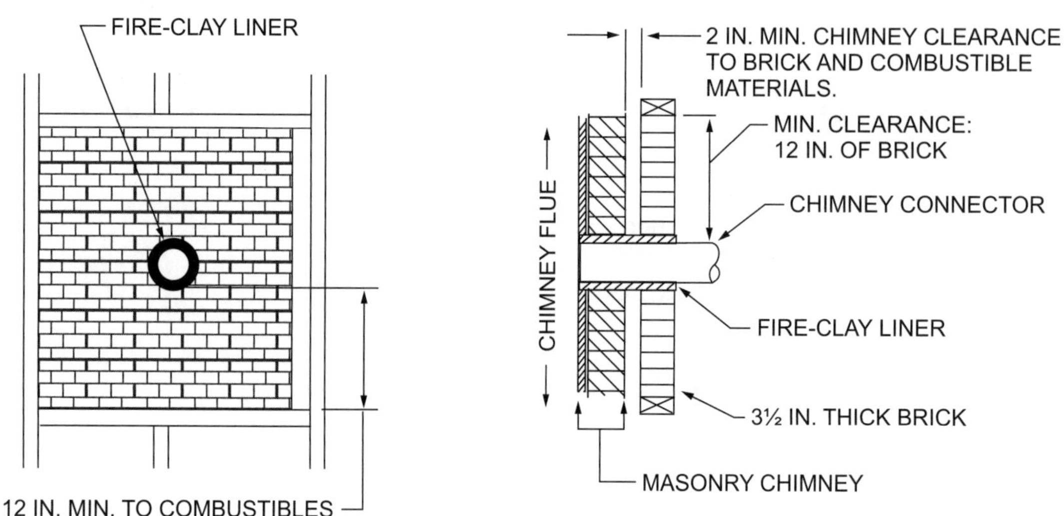

SYSTEM B

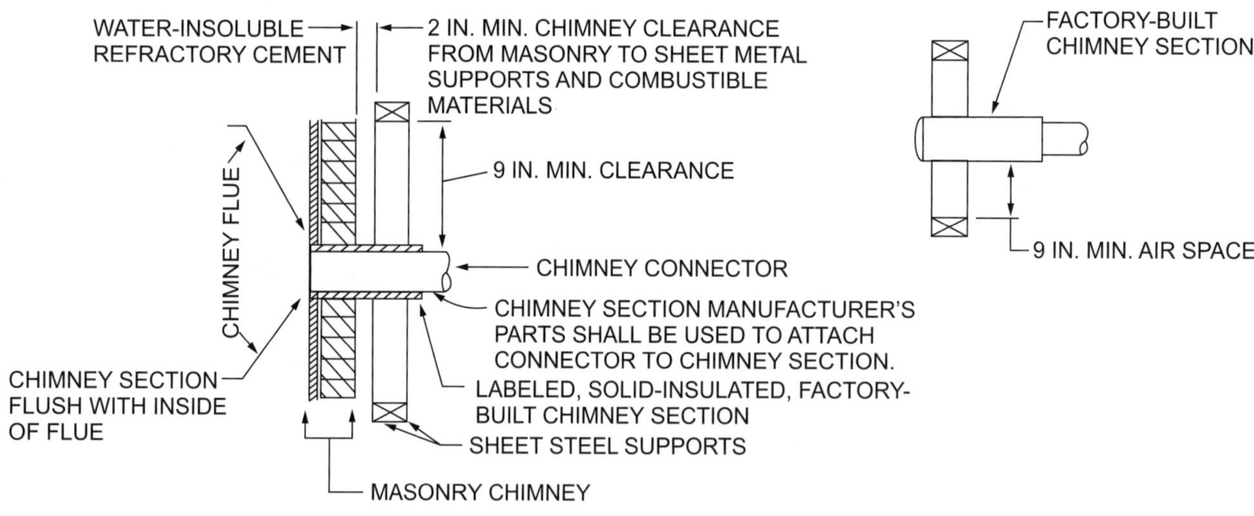

For SI: 1 inch = 25.4 mm.

FIGURE A-5
CHIMNEY CONNECTOR SYSTEMS

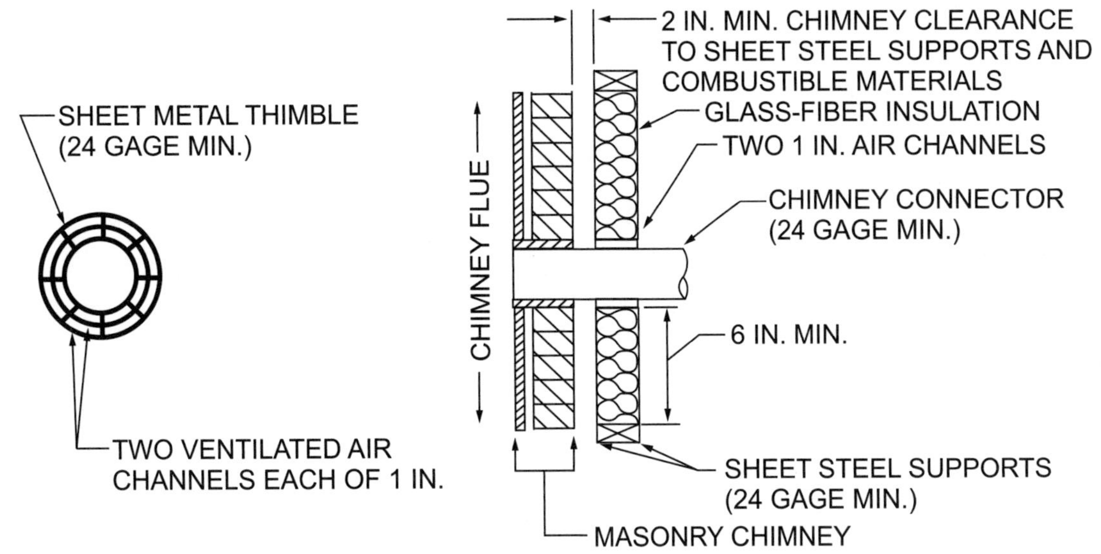

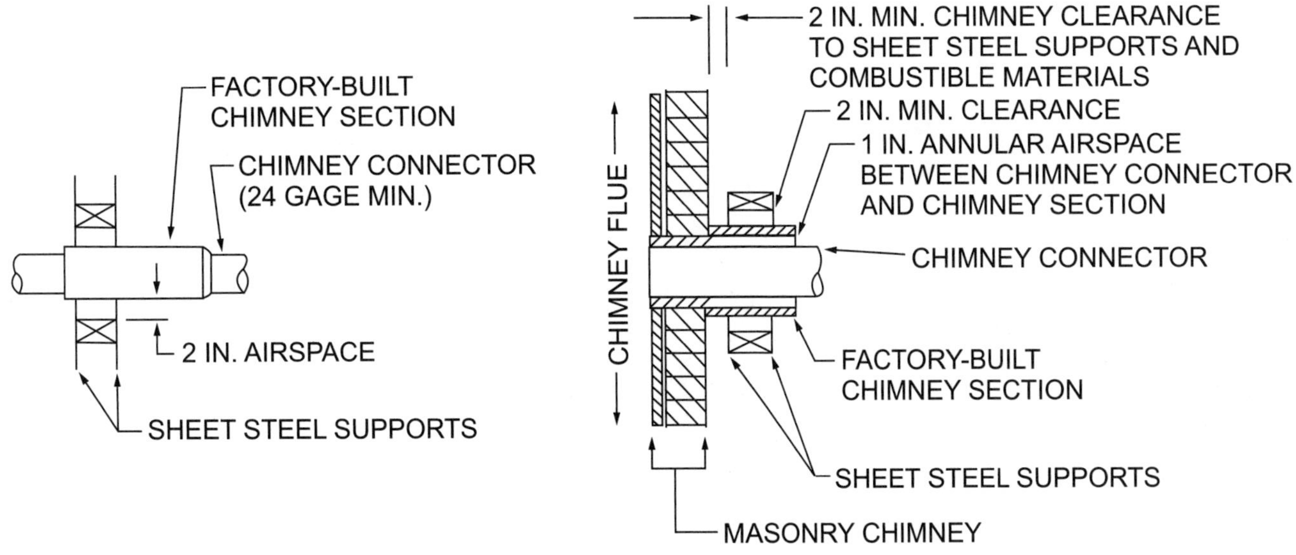

For SI: 1 inch = 25.4 mm.

FIGURE A-5—continued
CHIMNEY CONNECTOR SYSTEMS

APPENDIX B

RECOMMENDED PERMIT FEE SCHEDULE

Deleted

Part VI — Fuel Gas

CHAPTER 24

Deleted

The following text is extracted from the 2012 *North Carolina Fuel Gas Code* and has been modified where necessary to conform to the scope of application of the 2012 *North Carolina Residential Code for One-and Two-Family Dwellings*. The section numbers appearing in Part VI are the section numbers of the corresponding text in the *North Carolina Fuel Gas Code*. Where differences occur between the provisions of this abridged text and the *North Carolina Fuel Gas Code*, the provisions of the *North Carolina Fuel Gas Code* shall apply. Requirements not specifically covered by this text shall conform to the *North Carolina Fuel Gas Code*.

Part VI North Carolina State Building Code: Fuel Gas Code

Abridged for Residential Code

(2009 IFGC® with North Carolina Amendments)

Abridged Residential Code Edition

2012

TABLE OF CONTENTS

CHAPTER 1

SCOPE AND ADMINISTRATION

PART 1—SCOPE AND APPLICATION

SECTION 101 (IFGC) GENERAL

101.1 Title. These regulations shall be known as the *North Carolina Fuel Gas Code* as adopted by the North Carolina Building Code Council on September 14, 2010, to be effective September 1, 2011. References to the *International Codes* shall mean the North Carolina Codes. The North Carolina amendments to the *International Codes* are underlined.

101.2 Scope. This code shall apply to the installation of fuel-gas *piping* systems, fuel gas appliances, gaseous hydrogen systems and related accessories in accordance with Sections 101.2.1 through 101.2.5.

Exception: Detached one- and two-family dwellings and multiple single-family dwellings (townhouses) not more than three stories high with separate means of egress and their accessory structures shall comply with the *International Residential Code*.

101.2.1 Gaseous hydrogen systems. Gaseous hydrogen systems shall be regulated by Chapter 7.

101.2.2 Piping systems. These regulations cover *piping* systems for natural gas with an operating pressure of 125 pounds per square inch gauge (psig) (862 kPa gauge) or less, and for LP-gas with an operating pressure of 20 psig (140 kPa gauge) or less, except as provided in Section 402.6. Coverage shall extend from the *point of delivery* to the outlet of the *appliance* shutoff valves. *Piping* system requirements shall include design, materials, components, fabrication, assembly, installation, testing, inspection, operation and maintenance.

101.2.3 Gas appliances. Requirements for gas appliances and related accessories shall include installation, combustion and ventilation air and venting and connections to *piping* systems.

101.2.4 Systems, appliances and equipment outside the scope. This code shall not apply to the following:

1. Portable LP-gas appliances and *equipment* of all types that is not connected to a fixed fuel *piping* system.
2. Installation of farm appliances and *equipment* such as brooders, dehydrators, dryers and irrigation *equipment*.
3. Raw material (feedstock) applications except for *piping* to special atmosphere generators.
4. Oxygen-fuel gas cutting and welding systems.
5. Industrial gas applications using gases such as acetylene and acetylenic compounds, hydrogen, ammonia, carbon monoxide, oxygen and nitrogen.
6. Petroleum refineries, pipeline compressor or pumping stations, loading terminals, compounding plants, refinery tank farms and natural gas processing plants.
7. Integrated chemical plants or portions of such plants where flammable or combustible liquids or gases are produced by, or used in, chemical reactions.
8. LP-gas installations at utility gas plants.
9. Liquefied natural gas (LNG) installations.
10. Fuel gas *piping* in power and atomic energy plants.
11. Proprietary items of *equipment*, apparatus or instruments such as gas-generating sets, compressors and calorimeters.
12. LP-gas *equipment* for vaporization, gas mixing and gas manufacturing.
13. Temporary LP-gas *piping* for buildings under construction or renovation that is not to become part of the permanent *piping* system.
14. Installation of LP-gas systems for railroad switch heating.
15. Installation of hydrogen gas, LP-gas and compressed natural gas (CNG) systems on vehicles.
16. Except as provided in Section 401.1.1, gas *piping*, meters, gas pressure regulators and other appurtenances used by the serving gas supplier in the distribution of gas, other than undiluted LP-gas.
17. Building design and construction, except as specified herein.
18. *Piping* systems for mixtures of gas and air within the flammable range with an operating pressure greater than 10 psig (69 kPa gauge).
19. Portable fuel cell appliances that are neither connected to a fixed *piping* system nor interconnected to a power grid.

101.2.5 Other fuels. The requirements for the design, installation, maintenance, *alteration* and inspection of mechanical systems operating with fuels other than fuel gas shall be regulated by the *International Mechanical Code*.

101.3 Appendices. Provisions in the appendices shall not apply unless specifically adopted or referenced in this code.

101.4 Intent. The purpose of this code is to provide minimum standards to safeguard life or limb, health, property and public welfare by regulating and controlling the design, construction, installation, quality of materials, location, operation and maintenance or use of fuel gas systems.

101.5 Severability. If a section, subsection, sentence, clause or phrase of this code is, for any reason, held to be unconstitutional, such decision shall not affect the validity of the remaining portions of this code.

101.6 Requirements of other State agencies, occupational licensing board or commissions. The North Carolina State Building Codes do not include all additional requirements for buildings and structures that may be imposed by other State agencies, occupational licensing boards and commissions. It shall be the responsibility of a permit holder, registered design professional, contractor or occupational license holder to determine whether any additional requirements exist.

SECTION 102 (IFGC) APPLICABILITY

102.1 General. Where there is a conflict between a general requirement and a specific requirement, the specific requirement shall govern. Where, in a specific case, different sections of this code specify different materials, methods of construction or other requirements, the most restrictive shall govern.

102.2 Existing installations. Except as otherwise provided for in this chapter, a provision in this code shall not require the removal, *alteration* or abandonment of, nor prevent the continued utilization and maintenance of, existing installations lawfully in existence at the time of the adoption of this code.

[EB] 102.2.1 Existing buildings. Additions, alterations, renovations or repairs related to building or structural issues shall be regulated by the *International Building Code*.

102.3 Maintenance. Installations, both existing and new, and parts thereof shall be maintained in proper operating condition in accordance with the original design and in a safe condition. Devices or safeguards which are required by this code shall be maintained in compliance with the code edition under which they were installed. The owner or the owner's designated agent shall be responsible for maintenance of installations. To determine compliance with this provision, the code official shall have the authority to require an installation to be reinspected.

102.4 Additions, alterations or repairs. Additions, alterations, renovations or repairs to installations shall conform to that required for new installations without requiring the existing installation to comply with all of the requirements of this code. Additions, alterations or repairs shall not cause an existing installation to become unsafe, hazardous or overloaded.

Minor additions, alterations, renovations and repairs to existing installations shall meet the provisions for new construction, unless such work is done in the same manner and arrangement as was in the existing system, is not hazardous and is *approved*.

102.5 Change in occupancy. It shall be unlawful to make a change in the *occupancy* of a structure which will subject the structure to the special provisions of this code applicable to the new *occupancy* without approval. The code official shall certify that such structure meets the intent of the provisions of law governing building construction for the proposed new *occupancy* and that such change of *occupancy* does not result in any hazard to the public health, safety or welfare.

102.6 Historic buildings. The provisions of this code relating to the construction, *alteration*, repair, enlargement, restoration, relocation or moving of buildings or structures shall not be mandatory for existing buildings or structures identified and classified by the state or local jurisdiction as historic buildings when such buildings or structures are judged by the code official to be safe and in the public interest of health, safety and welfare regarding any proposed construction, *alteration*, repair, enlargement, restoration, relocation or moving of buildings.

102.7 Moved buildings. Except as determined by Section 102.2, installations that are a part of buildings or structures moved into or within the jurisdiction shall comply with the provisions of this code for new installations.

102.8 Referenced codes and standards. The codes and standards referenced in this code shall be those that are *listed* in Chapter 8 and such codes and standards shall be considered part of the requirements of this code to the prescribed extent of each such reference. Where differences occur between provisions of this code and the referenced standards, the provisions of this code shall apply.

Exception: Where enforcement of a code provision would violate the conditions of the listing of the *equipment* or *appliance*, the conditions of the listing and the manufacturer's installation instructions shall apply.

102.9 Requirements not covered by code. Requirements necessary for the strength, stability or proper operation of an existing or proposed installation, or for the public safety, health and general welfare, not specifically covered by this code, shall be determined by the code official.

102.10 Other laws. The provisions of this code shall not be deemed to nullify any provisions of local, state or federal law.

102.11 Application of references. Reference to chapter section numbers, or to provisions not specifically identified by number, shall be construed to refer to such chapter, section or provision of this code.

SECTION 103 (IFGC) DEPARTMENT OF INSPECTION

Deleted. See the North Carolina Administrative Code and Policies.

SECTION 104 (IFGC) DUTIES AND POWERS OF THE CODE OFFICIAL

Deleted. See the North Carolina Administrative Code and Policies.

SECTION 105 (IFGC) APPROVAL

105.1 Modifications. Whenever there are practical difficulties involved in carrying out the provisions of this code, the code official shall have the authority to grant modifications for individual cases, upon application of the owner or owner's representative, provided that the code official shall first find that special individual reason makes the strict letter of this code impractical and that such modification is in compliance with the intent and purpose of this code and does not lessen health, life and fire safety requirements. The details of action granting modifications shall be recorded and entered in the files of the Department of Inspection.

105.2 Alternative materials, methods, appliances and equipment. The provisions of this code are not intended to prevent the installation of any material or to prohibit any method of construction not specifically prescribed by this code, provided that any such alternative has been *approved*. An alternative material or method of construction shall be *approved* where the code official finds that the proposed design is satisfactory and complies with the intent of the provisions of this code, and that the material, method or work offered is, for the purpose intended, at least the equivalent of that prescribed in this code in quality, strength, effectiveness, fire resistance, durability and safety.

105.2.1 Research reports. Supporting data, where necessary to assist in the approval of materials or assemblies not specifically provided for in this code, shall consist of valid research reports from *approved* sources.

105.3 Required testing. Whenever there is insufficient evidence of compliance with the provisions of this code, evidence that a material or method does not conform to the requirements of this code, or in order to substantiate claims for alternative materials or methods, the code official shall have the authority to require tests as evidence of compliance to be made at no expense to the jurisdiction.

105.3.1 Test methods. Test methods shall be as specified in this code or by other recognized test standards. In the absence of recognized and accepted test methods, the code official shall approve the testing procedures.

105.3.2 Testing agency. All tests shall be performed by an *approved* agency.

105.3.3 Test reports. Reports of tests shall be retained by the code official for the period required for retention of public records.

105.4 Used material, appliances and equipment. The use of used materials which meet the requirements of this code for new materials is permitted. Used appliances, *equipment* and devices shall not be reused unless such elements have been reconditioned, tested and placed in good and proper working condition, and *approved* by the code official.

105.5 Approved materials and equipment. Materials, *equipment* and devices *approved* by the code official shall be constructed and installed in accordance with such approval.

SECTION 106 (IFGC) PERMITS

106.1 Where required. An owner, authorized agent or contractor who desires to erect, install, enlarge, alter, repair, remove, convert or replace an installation regulated by this code, or to cause such work to be done, shall first make application to the code official and obtain the required permit for the work.

Exception: Where *appliance* and *equipment* replacements and repairs are required to be performed in an emergency situation, the permit application shall be submitted within the next working business day of the Department of Inspection.

106.2 Permits not required. Permits shall not be required for the following:

1. Any portable heating *appliance*.
2. Replacement of any minor component of an *appliance* or *equipment* that does not alter approval of such *appliance* or *equipment* or make such *appliance* or *equipment* unsafe.

Exemption from the permit requirements of this code shall not be deemed to grant authorization for work to be done in violation of the provisions of this code or of other laws or ordinances of this jurisdiction.

Remainder of Section 106 deleted. See the North Carolina Administrative Code and Policies.

SECTION 107 (IFGC) INSPECTIONS AND TESTING

Deleted. See the North Carolina Administrative Code and Policies.

SECTION 108 (IFGC) VIOLATIONS

Deleted. See the North Carolina Administrative Code and Policies.

SECTION 109 (IFGC) MEANS OF APPEAL

Deleted. See the North Carolina Administrative Code and Policies.

SECTION 110 (IFGC) TEMPORARY EQUIPMENT, SYSTEMS AND USES

110.1 General. The code official is authorized to issue a permit for temporary *equipment*, systems and uses. Such permits shall be limited as to time of service, but shall not be permitted for more than 180 days. The code official is authorized to grant extensions for demonstrated cause.

110.2 Conformance. Temporary *equipment*, systems and uses shall conform to the structural strength, fire safety, means of egress, accessibility, light, ventilation and sanitary requirements of this code as necessary to ensure the public health, safety and general welfare.

110.3 Temporary utilities. The code official is authorized to give permission to temporarily supply utilities before an installation has been fully completed and the final certificate of completion has been issued. The part covered by the temporary certificate shall comply with the requirements specified for temporary lighting, heat or power in the code.

110.4 Termination of approval. The code official is authorized to terminate such permit for a temporary structure or use and to order the temporary structure or use to be discontinued.

CHAPTER 2
DEFINITIONS

SECTION 201 (IFGC) GENERAL

201.1 Scope. Unless otherwise expressly stated, the following words and terms shall, for the purposes of this code and standard, have the meanings indicated in this chapter.

201.2 Interchangeability. Words used in the present tense include the future; words in the masculine gender include the feminine and neuter; the singular number includes the plural and the plural, the singular.

201.3 Terms defined in other codes. Where terms are not defined in this code and are defined in the *International Building Code*, *International Fire Code*, *International Mechanical Code* or *International Plumbing Code*, such terms shall have meanings ascribed to them as in those codes.

201.4 Terms not defined. Where terms are not defined through the methods authorized by this section, such terms shall have ordinarily accepted meanings such as the context implies.

SECTION 202 (IFGC) GENERAL DEFINITIONS

ACCESS (TO). That which enables a device, *appliance* or *equipment* to be reached by ready *access* or by a means that first requires the removal or movement of a panel, door or similar obstruction (see also "Ready *access*").

AIR CONDITIONER, GAS-FIRED. Deleted.

AIR CONDITIONING. The treatment of air so as to control simultaneously the temperature, humidity, cleanness and distribution of the air to meet the requirements of a conditioned space.

AIR, EXHAUST. Air being removed from any space or piece of *equipment* or *appliance* and conveyed directly to the atmosphere by means of openings or ducts.

AIR-HANDLING UNIT. A blower or fan used for the purpose of distributing supply air to a room, space or area.

AIR, MAKEUP. Air that is provided to replace air being exhausted.

ALTERATION. A change in a system that involves an extension, addition or change to the arrangement, type or purpose of the original installation.

ANODELESS RISER. A transition assembly in which plastic *piping* is installed and terminated above ground outside of a building.

APPLIANCE. Any apparatus or device that utilizes gas as a fuel or raw material to produce light, heat, power, refrigeration or *air conditioning*.

APPLIANCE, AUTOMATICALLY CONTROLLED. Appliances equipped with an automatic burner ignition and safety shutoff device and other automatic devices which accomplish complete turn-on and shutoff of the gas to the main burner or burners, and graduate the gas supply to the burner or burners, but do not affect complete shutoff of the gas.

APPLIANCE, FAN-ASSISTED COMBUSTION. An *appliance* equipped with an integral mechanical means to either draw or force products of combustion through the combustion chamber or heat exchanger.

APPLIANCE TYPE.

Low-heat appliance (residential appliance). Any *appliance* in which the products of combustion at the point of entrance to the flue under normal operating conditions have a temperature of 1,000°F (538°C) or less.

Medium-heat appliance. Deleted.

APPLIANCE, UNVENTED. An *appliance* designed or installed in such a manner that the products of combustion are not conveyed by a vent or chimney directly to the outside atmosphere.

APPLIANCE, VENTED. An *appliance* designed and installed in such a manner that all of the products of combustion are conveyed directly from the *appliance* to the outside atmosphere through an *approved* chimney or vent system.

APPROVED. Acceptable to the code official or other authority having jurisdiction for compliance with the provisions of the applicable code or referenced standard.

APPROVED AGENCY. An established and recognized agency that is *approved* by the code official and regularly engaged in conducting tests or furnishing inspection services.

ATMOSPHERIC PRESSURE. The pressure of the weight of air and water vapor on the surface of the earth, approximately 14.7 pounds per square inch (psi) (101 kPa absolute) at sea level.

AUTOMATIC IGNITION. Ignition of gas at the burner(s) when the gas controlling device is turned on, including reignition if the flames on the burner(s) have been extinguished by means other than by the closing of the gas controlling device.

BAFFLE. An object placed in an *appliance* to change the direction of or retard the flow of air, air-gas mixtures or flue gases.

BAROMETRIC DRAFT REGULATOR. A balanced damper device attached to a chimney, vent connector, breeching or flue gas manifold to protect combustion appliances by controlling chimney draft. A double-acting barometric draft regulator is one whose balancing damper is free to move in either direction to protect combustion appliances from both excessive draft and backdraft.

BOILER, LOW-PRESSURE. A self-contained *appliance* for supplying steam or hot water.

Hot water heating boiler. A boiler in which no steam is generated, from which hot water is circulated for heating purposes and then returned to the boiler, and that operates at water pressures not exceeding 160 pounds per square inch gauge (psig) (1100 kPa gauge) and at water temperatures not exceeding 250°F (121°C) at or near the boiler *outlet*.

Hot water supply boiler. A boiler, completely filled with water, which furnishes hot water to be used externally to itself, and that operates at water pressures not exceeding 160 psig (1100 kPa gauge) and at water temperatures not exceeding 250°F (121°C) at or near the boiler *outlet*.

Steam heating boiler. A boiler in which steam is generated and that operates at a steam pressure not exceeding 15 psig (100 kPa gauge).

BONDING JUMPER. A conductor installed to electrically connect metallic gas *piping* to the grounding electrode system.

BRAZING. A metal-joining process wherein coalescence is produced by the use of a nonferrous filler metal having a melting point above 1,000°F (538°C), but lower than that of the base metal being joined. The filler material is distributed between the closely fitted surfaces of the joint by capillary action.

BROILER. A general term including salamanders, barbecues and other appliances cooking primarily by radiated heat, excepting toasters.

BTU. Abbreviation for British thermal unit, which is the quantity of heat required to raise the temperature of 1 pound (454 g) of water 1°F (0.56°C) (1 Btu = 1055 J).

BURNER. A device for the final conveyance of the gas, or a mixture of gas and air, to the combustion zone.

Induced-draft. A burner that depends on draft induced by a fan that is an integral part of the *appliance* and is located downstream from the burner.

Power. A burner in which gas, air or both are supplied at pressures exceeding, for gas, the line pressure, and for air, atmospheric pressure, with this added pressure being applied at the burner.

CHIMNEY. A primarily vertical structure containing one or more flues, for the purpose of carrying gaseous products of combustion and air from an *appliance* to the outside atmosphere.

Factory-built chimney. A *listed* and *labeled* chimney composed of factory-made components, assembled in the field in accordance with manufacturer's instructions and the conditions of the listing.

Masonry chimney. A field-constructed chimney composed of solid masonry units, bricks, stones or concrete.

Metal chimney. A field-constructed chimney of metal.

CLEARANCE. The minimum distance through air measured between the heat-producing surface of the mechanical *appliance*, device or *equipment* and the surface of the combustible material or assembly.

CLOSET. An enclosed or recessed area used to store clothing, linens or other household items.

CLOTHES DRYER. An *appliance* used to dry wet laundry by means of heated air. Dryer classifications are as follows:

Type 1. Factory-built package, multiple production. Primarily used in family living environment. Usually the smallest unit physically and in function output.

Type 2. Deleted.

CODE. These regulations, subsequent amendments thereto or any emergency rule or regulation that the administrative authority having jurisdiction has lawfully adopted.

CODE OFFICIAL. The officer or other designated authority charged with the administration and enforcement of this code, or a duly authorized representative.

COMBUSTION. In the context of this code, refers to the rapid oxidation of fuel accompanied by the production of heat or heat and light.

COMBUSTION AIR. Air necessary for complete combustion of a fuel, including theoretical air and excess air.

COMBUSTION CHAMBER. The portion of an *appliance* within which combustion occurs.

COMBUSTION PRODUCTS. Constituents resulting from the combustion of a fuel with the oxygen of the air, including inert gases, but excluding excess air.

CONCEALED LOCATION. A location that cannot be accessed without damaging permanent parts of the building structure or finish surface. Spaces above, below or behind readily removable panels or doors shall not be considered as concealed. Buried underground piping shall not be considered concealed.

CONCEALED PIPING. *Piping* that is located in a *concealed location* (see "*Concealed location*").

CONDENSATE. The liquid that condenses from a gas (including flue gas) caused by a reduction in temperature or increase in pressure.

CONNECTOR, APPLIANCE (Fuel). Rigid metallic pipe and fittings, semirigid metallic tubing and fittings or a *listed* and *labeled* device that connects an *appliance* to the gas *piping* system.

CONNECTOR, CHIMNEY OR VENT. The pipe that connects an *appliance* to a chimney or vent.

CONSTRUCTION DOCUMENTS. Deleted.

CONTROL. A manual or automatic device designed to regulate the gas, air, water or electrical supply to, or operation of, a mechanical system.

CONVERSION BURNER. A unit consisting of a burner and its controls for installation in an *appliance* originally utilizing another fuel.

COUNTER APPLIANCES. Deleted.

CUBIC FOOT. The amount of gas that occupies 1 cubic foot (0.02832 m^3) when at a temperature of 60°F (16°C), saturated with water vapor and under a pressure equivalent to that of 30 inches of mercury (101 kPa).

DAMPER. A manually or automatically controlled device to regulate draft or the rate of flow of air or combustion gases.

DECORATIVE APPLIANCE, VENTED. A vented *appliance* wherein the primary function lies in the aesthetic effect of the flames.

DECORATIVE APPLIANCES FOR INSTALLATION IN VENTED FIREPLACES. A vented *appliance* designed for installation within the fire chamber of a vented *fireplace*, wherein the primary function lies in the aesthetic effect of the flames.

DEMAND. The maximum amount of gas input required per unit of time, usually expressed in cubic feet per hour, or Btu/h (1 Btu/h = 0.2931 W).

DESIGN FLOOD ELEVATION. The elevation of the "design flood," including wave height, relative to the datum specified on the community's legally designated flood hazard map.

DILUTION AIR. Air that is introduced into a draft hood and is mixed with the flue gases.

DIRECT-VENT APPLIANCES. Appliances that are constructed and installed so that all air for combustion is derived directly from the outside atmosphere and all flue gases are discharged directly to the outside atmosphere.

DRAFT. The pressure difference existing between the *appliance* or any component part and the atmosphere, that causes a continuous flow of air and products of combustion through the gas passages of the *appliance* to the atmosphere.

Mechanical or induced draft. The pressure difference created by the action of a fan, blower or ejector that is located between the *appliance* and the chimney or vent termination.

Natural draft. The pressure difference created by a vent or chimney because of its height, and the temperature difference between the flue gases and the atmosphere.

DRAFT HOOD. A nonadjustable device built into an *appliance*, or made as part of the vent connector from an *appliance*, that is designed to (1) provide for ready escape of the flue gases from the *appliance* in the event of no draft, backdraft or stoppage beyond the draft hood, (2) prevent a backdraft from entering the *appliance*, and (3) neutralize the effect of stack action of the chimney or gas vent upon operation of the *appliance*.

DRAFT REGULATOR. A device that functions to maintain a desired draft in the *appliance* by automatically reducing the draft to the desired value.

DRIP. The container placed at a low point in a system of *piping* to collect condensate and from which the condensate is removable.

DRY GAS. A gas having a moisture and hydrocarbon dew point below any normal temperature to which the gas *piping* is exposed.

DUCT FURNACE. A warm-air furnace normally installed in an air distribution duct to supply warm air for heating. This definition shall apply only to a warm-air heating *appliance* that depends for air circulation on a blower not furnished as part of the furnace.

DUCT SYSTEM. A continuous passageway for the transmission of air that, in addition to ducts, includes duct fittings, dampers, plenums, fans and accessory air-handling *equipment*.

DWELLING UNIT. A single unit providing complete, independent living facilities for one or more persons, including permanent provisions for living, sleeping, eating, cooking and sanitation.

EQUIPMENT. Apparatus and devices other than appliances.

EXTERIOR MASONRY CHIMNEYS. Masonry chimneys exposed to the outdoors on one or more sides below the roof line.

FIREPLACE. A fire chamber and hearth constructed of noncombustible material for use with solid fuels and provided with a chimney.

Factory-built fireplace. A *fireplace* composed of *listed* factory-built components assembled in accordance with the terms of listing to form the completed *fireplace*.

Masonry fireplace. A hearth and fire chamber of solid masonry units such as bricks, stones, *listed* masonry units or reinforced concrete, provided with a suitable chimney.

FIRING VALVE. Deleted.

FLAME SAFEGUARD. A device that will automatically shut off the fuel supply to a main burner or group of burners when the means of ignition of such burners becomes inoperative, and when flame failure occurs on the burner or group of burners.

FLOOD HAZARD AREA. The greater of the following two areas:

1. The area within a floodplain subject to a 1 percent or greater chance of flooding in any given year.
2. This area designated as a *flood hazard area* on a community's flood hazard map, or otherwise legally designated.

FLOOR FURNACE. A completely self-contained furnace suspended from the floor of the space being heated, taking air for combustion from outside such space and with means for observing flames and lighting the *appliance* from such space.

Fan type. A floor furnace equipped with a fan which provides the primary means for circulating air.

Gravity type. A floor furnace depending primarily upon circulation of air by gravity. This classification shall also include floor furnaces equipped with booster-type fans which do not materially restrict free circulation of air by gravity flow when such fans are not in operation.

FLUE, APPLIANCE. The passage(s) within an *appliance* through which combustion products pass from the combustion chamber of the *appliance* to the draft hood inlet opening on an *appliance* equipped with a draft hood or to the *outlet* of the *appliance* on an *appliance* not equipped with a draft hood.

FLUE COLLAR. That portion of an *appliance* designed for the attachment of a draft hood, vent connector or venting system.

FLUE GASES. Products of combustion plus excess air in *appliance* flues or heat exchangers.

FLUE LINER (LINING). A system or material used to form the inside surface of a flue in a chimney or vent, for the purpose of protecting the surrounding structure from the effects of combustion products and for conveying combustion products without leakage to the atmosphere.

FUEL GAS. A natural gas, manufactured gas, liquefied petroleum gas or mixtures of these gases.

FUEL GAS UTILIZATION EQUIPMENT. See "*Appliance*."

FURNACE. A completely self-contained heating unit that is designed to supply heated air to spaces remote from or adjacent to the *appliance* location.

FURNACE, CENTRAL. A self-contained *appliance* for heating air by transfer of heat of combustion through metal to the air, and designed to supply heated air through ducts to spaces remote from or adjacent to the *appliance* location.

Downflow furnace. A furnace designed with airflow discharge vertically downward at or near the bottom of the furnace.

Forced air furnace with cooling unit. A single-package unit, consisting of a gas-fired forced-air furnace of one of the types listed below combined with an electrically or fuel gas-powered summer air-conditioning system, contained in a common casing.

Forced-air type. A central furnace equipped with a fan or blower which provides the primary means for circulation of air.

Gravity furnace with booster fan. A furnace equipped with a booster fan that does not materially restrict free circulation of air by gravity flow when the fan is not in operation.

Gravity type. A central furnace depending primarily on circulation of air by gravity.

Horizontal forced-air type. A furnace with airflow through the *appliance* essentially in a horizontal path.

Multiple-position furnace. A furnace designed so that it can be installed with the airflow discharge in the upflow, horizontal or downflow direction.

Upflow furnace. A furnace designed with airflow discharge vertically upward at or near the top of the furnace. This classification includes "highboy" furnaces with the blower mounted below the heating element and "lowboy" furnaces with the blower mounted beside the heating element.

FURNACE, ENCLOSED. A specific heating, or heating and ventilating, furnace incorporating an integral total enclosure and using only outside air for combustion.

FURNACE PLENUM. An air compartment or chamber to which one or more ducts are connected and which forms part of an air distribution system.

GAS CONVENIENCE OUTLET. A permanently mounted, manually operated device that provides the means for connecting an *appliance* to, and disconnecting an *appliance* from, the supply *piping*. The device includes an integral, manually operated valve with a nondisplaceable valve member and is designed so that disconnection of an *appliance* only occurs when the manually operated valve is in the closed position.

GAS PIPING. An installation of pipe, valves or fittings installed on a premises or in a building and utilized to convey fuel gas.

GASEOUS HYDROGEN SYSTEM. Deleted.

HAZARDOUS LOCATION. Any location considered to be a fire hazard for flammable vapors, dust, combustible fibers or other highly combustible substances. The location is not necessarily categorized in the building code as a high-hazard group classification.

HOUSE PIPING. See "*Piping* system."

HYDROGEN CUT-OFF ROOM. Deleted.

HYDROGEN GENERATING APPLIANCE. Deleted.

IGNITION PILOT. A pilot that operates during the lighting cycle and discontinues during main burner operation.

IGNITION SOURCE. A flame, spark or hot surface capable of igniting flammable vapors or fumes. Such sources include *appliance* burners, burner ignitors and electrical switching devices.

INCINERATOR. Deleted.

INDUSTRIAL AIR HEATERS, DIRECT-FIRED NONRECIRCULATING. Deleted.

INDUSTRIAL AIR HEATERS, DIRECT-FIRED RECIRCULATING. Deleted.

INFRARED RADIANT HEATER. A heater that directs a substantial amount of its energy output in the form of infrared radiant energy into the area to be heated. Such heaters are of either the vented or unvented type.

JOINT, FLANGED. Deleted.

JOINT, FLARED. A metal-to-metal compression joint in which a conical spread is made on the end of a tube that is compressed by a flare nut against a mating flare.

JOINT, MECHANICAL. A general form of gas-tight joints obtained by the joining of metal parts through a positive-holding mechanical construction, such as flanged joint, threaded joint, flared joint or compression joint.

JOINT, PLASTIC ADHESIVE. A joint made in thermoset plastic *piping* by the use of an adhesive substance which forms a continuous bond between the mating surfaces without dissolving either one of them.

JOINT, PLASTIC HEAT FUSION. A joint made in thermoplastic *piping* by heating the parts sufficiently to permit fusion of the materials when the parts are pressed together.

JOINT, WELDED. Deleted.

LABELED. *Appliances*, equipment, materials or products to which have been affixed a label, seal, symbol or other identifying mark of a nationally recognized testing laboratory, inspection agency or other organization concerned with product evaluation that maintains periodic inspection of the production of the above-labeled items and whose labeling indicates either that the *appliance*, *equipment*, material or product meets identified standards or has been tested and found suitable for a specified purpose. (Laboratories, agencies or organizations that have been identified by approval and accreditation bodies, such as ANSI, IAS, ICC or OSHA, are acceptable.)

LEAK CHECK. An operation performed on a gas *piping* system to verify that the system does not leak.

LIMIT CONTROL. A device responsive to changes in pressure, temperature or level for turning on, shutting off or throttling the gas supply to an *appliance*.

LIQUEFIED PETROLEUM GAS or LPG (LP-GAS). Liquefied petroleum gas composed predominately of propane, propylene, butanes or butylenes, or mixtures thereof that is gaseous under normal atmospheric conditions, but is capable of being liquefied under moderate pressure at normal temperatures.

LISTED. *Appliances*, equipment, materials, products or services included in a list published by an organization acceptable to the code official and concerned with evaluation of products or services that maintains periodic inspection of production of *listed equipment* or materials or periodic evaluation of services and whose listing states either that the *appliance*, *equipment*, material, product or service meets identified standards or has been tested and found suitable for a specified purpose.

LIVING SPACE. Space within a *dwelling unit* utilized for living, sleeping, eating, cooking, bathing, washing and sanitation purposes.

LOG LIGHTER. A manually operated solid fuel ignition *appliance* for installation in a vented solid fuel-burning *fireplace*.

LUBRICATED PLUG-TYPE VALVE. Deleted.

MAIN BURNER. A device or group of devices essentially forming an integral unit for the final conveyance of gas or a mixture of gas and air to the combustion zone, and on which combustion takes place to accomplish the function for which the *appliance* is designed.

METER. The instrument installed to measure the volume of gas delivered through it.

MODULATING. Modulating or throttling is the action of a control from its maximum to minimum position in either predetermined steps or increments of movement as caused by its actuating medium.

OCCUPANCY. The purpose for which a building, or portion thereof, is utilized or occupied.

OFFSET(VENT). A combination of *approved* bends that makes two changes in direction bringing one section of the vent out of line but into a line parallel with the other section.

ORIFICE. The opening in a cap, spud or other device whereby the flow of gas is limited and through which the gas is discharged to the burner.

OUTLET. The point at which a gas-fired *appliance* connects to the gas *piping* system.

OXYGEN DEPLETION SAFETY SHUTOFF SYSTEM (ODS). A system designed to act to shut off the gas supply to the main and pilot burners if the oxygen in the surrounding atmosphere is reduced below a predetermined level.

PILOT. A small flame that is utilized to ignite the gas at the main burner or burners.

PIPING. Where used in this code, "*piping*" refers to either pipe or tubing, or both.

Pipe. A rigid conduit of iron, steel, copper, brass or plastic.

Tubing. Semirigid conduit of copper, aluminum, plastic or steel.

PIPING SYSTEM. All fuel *piping*, valves and fittings from the outlet of the *point of delivery* to the outlets of the *appliance* shutoff valves.

PLASTIC, THERMOPLASTIC. A plastic that is capable of being repeatedly softened by increase of temperature and hardened by decrease of temperature.

POINT OF DELIVERY. For natural gas systems, the *point of delivery* is the outlet of the service meter assembly or the outlet of the service regulator or service shutoff valve where a meter is not provided. Where a valve is provided at the outlet of the service meter assembly, such valve shall be considered to be downstream of the *point of delivery*. For undiluted liquefied petroleum gas systems, the *point of delivery* shall be considered to be the outlet of the first regulator that reduces pressure.

PORTABLE FUEL CELL APPLIANCE. Deleted.

PRESSURE DROP. The loss in pressure due to friction or obstruction in pipes, valves, fittings, regulators and burners.

PRESSURE TEST. An operation performed to verify the gas-tight integrity of gas *piping* following its installation or modification.

PURGE. To free a gas conduit of air or gas, or a mixture of gas and air.

QUICK-DISCONNECT DEVICE. A hand-operated device that provides a means for connecting and disconnecting an *appliance* or an *appliance* connector to a gas supply and that is equipped with an automatic means to shut off the gas supply when the device is disconnected.

READY ACCESS (TO). That which enables a device, *appliance* or *equipment* to be directly reached, without requiring the removal or movement of any panel, door or similar obstruction (see "*Access*").

REGISTERED DESIGN PROFESSIONAL. An individual who is registered or licensed to practice their respective design profession as defined by the statutory requirements of the professional registration laws of the state or jurisdiction in which the project is to be constructed. Design by a registered design professional is not required where exempt under the registration or licensure laws.

REGULATOR. A device for controlling and maintaining a uniform supply pressure, either pounds-to-inches water column (MP regulator) or inches-to-inches water column (*appliance* regulator).

REGULATOR, GAS APPLIANCE. A pressure regulator for controlling pressure to the manifold of the *appliance*. Types of *appliance* regulators are as follows:

Adjustable.

1. Spring type, limited adjustment. A regulator in which the regulating force acting upon the diaphragm is derived principally from a spring, the loading of which is adjustable over a range of not more than 15 percent of the outlet pressure at the midpoint of the adjustment range.
2. Spring type, standard adjustment. A regulator in which the regulating force acting upon the diaphragm is derived principally from a spring, the loading of which is adjustable. The adjustment means shall be concealed.

Multistage. A regulator for use with a single gas whose adjustment means is capable of being positioned manually or automatically to two or more predetermined outlet pressure settings. Each of these settings shall be adjustable or nonadjustable. The regulator may modulate outlet pressures automatically between its maximum and minimum predetermined outlet pressure settings.

Nonadjustable.

1. Spring type, nonadjustable. A regulator in which the regulating force acting upon the diaphragm is derived principally from a spring, the loading of which is not field adjustable.
2. Weight type. A regulator in which the regulating force acting upon the diaphragm is derived from a weight or combination of weights.

REGULATOR, LINE GAS PRESSURE. A device placed in a gas line between the service pressure regulator and the *appliance* for controlling, maintaining or reducing the pressure in that portion of the *piping* system downstream of the device.

REGULATOR, MEDIUM-PRESSURE (MP Regulator). A line pressure regulator that reduces gas pressure from the range of greater than 0.5 psig (3.4 kPa) and less than or equal to 5 psig (34.5 kPa) to a lower pressure.

REGULATOR, PRESSURE. A device placed in a gas line for reducing, controlling and maintaining the pressure in that portion of the *piping* system downstream of the device.

REGULATOR, SERVICE PRESSURE. A device installed by the serving gas supplier to reduce and limit the service line pressure to delivery pressure.

RELIEF OPENING. The opening provided in a draft hood to permit the ready escape to the atmosphere of the flue products from the draft hood in the event of no draft, back draft or stoppage beyond the draft hood, and to permit air into the draft hood in the event of a strong chimney updraft.

RELIEF VALVE (DEVICE). A safety valve designed to forestall the development of a dangerous condition by relieving either pressure, temperature or vacuum in the hot water supply system.

RELIEF VALVE, PRESSURE. An automatic valve that opens and closes a relief vent, depending on whether the pressure is above or below a predetermined value.

RELIEF VALVE, TEMPERATURE.

Manual reset type. A valve that automatically opens a relief vent at a predetermined temperature and that must be manually returned to the closed position.

Reseating or self-closing type. An automatic valve that opens and closes a relief vent, depending on whether the temperature is above or below a predetermined value.

RELIEF VALVE, VACUUM. A valve that automatically opens and closes a vent for relieving a vacuum within the hot water supply system, depending on whether the vacuum is above or below a predetermined value.

RISER, GAS. A vertical pipe supplying fuel gas.

ROOM HEATER, UNVENTED. See "Unvented room heater."

ROOM HEATER, VENTED. A free-standing heating unit used for direct heating of the space in and adjacent to that in which the unit is located (see also "Vented room heater").

ROOM LARGE IN COMPARISON WITH SIZE OF THE APPLIANCE. Rooms having a volume equal to at least 12 times the total volume of a furnace, water heater or air-conditioning *appliance* and at least 16 times the total volume of a boiler. Total volume of the *appliance* is determined from exterior dimensions and is to include fan compartments and burner vestibules, when used. When the actual ceiling height of a room is greater than 8 feet (2438 mm), the volume of the room is figured on the basis of a ceiling height of 8 feet (2438 mm).

SAFETY SHUTOFF DEVICE. See "Flame safeguard."

SHAFT. An enclosed space extending through one or more stories of a building, connecting vertical openings in successive floors, or floors and the roof.

SLEEPING UNIT. A room or space in which people sleep, which can also include permanent provisions for living, eating and either sanitation or kitchen facilities, but not both. Such rooms and spaces that are also part of a *dwelling unit* are not sleeping units.

SPECIFIC GRAVITY. As applied to gas, specific gravity is the ratio of the weight of a given volume to that of the same volume of air, both measured under the same condition.

STATIONARY FUEL CELL POWER PLANT. Deleted.

THERMOSTAT.

Electric switch type. A device that senses changes in temperature and controls electrically, by means of separate components, the flow of gas to the burner(s) to maintain selected temperatures.

Integral gas valve type. An automatic device, actuated by temperature changes, designed to control the gas supply to the burner(s) in order to maintain temperatures between predetermined limits, and in which the thermal actuating element is an integral part of the device.

1. Graduating thermostat. A thermostat in which the motion of the valve is approximately in direct proportion to the effective motion of the thermal element induced by temperature change.
2. Snap-acting thermostat. A thermostat in which the thermostatic valve travels instantly from the closed to the open position, and vice versa.

TRANSITION FITTINGS, PLASTIC TO STEEL. An adapter for joining plastic pipe to steel pipe. The purpose of this fitting is to provide a permanent, pressure-tight connection between two materials which cannot be joined directly one to another.

UNIT HEATER. Deleted.

UNLISTED BOILER. Deleted.

UNVENTED ROOM HEATER. An unvented heating *appliance* designed for stationary installation and utilized to provide comfort heating. Such appliances provide radiant heat or convection heat by gravity or fan circulation directly from the heater and do not utilize ducts.

VALVE. A device used in *piping* to control the gas supply to any section of a system of *piping* or to an *appliance*.

Appliance shutoff. A valve located in the *piping* system, used to isolate individual appliances for purposes such as service or replacement.

Automatic. An automatic or semiautomatic device consisting essentially of a valve and operator that control the gas supply to the burner(s) during operation of an *appliance*. The operator shall be actuated by application of gas pressure on a flexible diaphragm, by electrical means, by mechanical means, or by other *approved* means.

Automatic gas shutoff. A valve used in conjunction with an automatic gas shutoff device to shut off the gas supply to a water-heating system. It shall be constructed integrally with the gas shutoff device or shall be a separate assembly.

Individual main burner. A valve that controls the gas supply to an individual main burner.

Main burner control. A valve that controls the gas supply to the main burner manifold.

Manual main gas-control. A manually operated valve in the gas line for the purpose of completely turning on or shutting off the gas supply to the *appliance*, except to pilot or pilots that are provided with independent shutoff.

Manual reset. An automatic shutoff valve installed in the gas supply *piping* and set to shut off when unsafe conditions occur. The device remains closed until manually reopened.

Service shutoff. A valve, installed by the serving gas supplier between the service meter or source of supply and the customer *piping* system, to shut off the entire *piping* system.

VENT. A pipe or other conduit composed of factory-made components, containing a passageway for conveying combustion products and air to the atmosphere, *listed* and *labeled* for use with a specific type or class of *appliance*.

Special gas vent. A vent *listed* and *labeled* for use with *listed* Category II, III and IV appliances.

Type B vent. A vent *listed* and *labeled* for use with appliances with draft hoods and other Category I appliances that are *listed* for use with Type B vents.

Type BW vent. A vent *listed* and *labeled* for use with wall furnaces.

Type L vent. A vent *listed* and *labeled* for use with appliances that are *listed* for use with Type L or Type B vents.

VENT CONNECTOR. See "Connector."

VENT GASES. Products of combustion from appliances plus excess air plus dilution air in the vent connector, gas vent or chimney above the draft hood or draft regulator.

VENT PIPING.

Breather. *Piping* run from a pressure-regulating device to the outdoors, designed to provide a reference to atmospheric pressure. If the device incorporates an integral pressure relief mechanism, a breather vent can also serve as a relief vent.

Relief. *Piping* run from a pressure-regulating or pressure-limiting device to the outdoors, designed to provide for the safe venting of gas in the event of excessive pressure in the gas *piping* system.

VENTED APPLIANCE CATEGORIES. Appliances that are categorized for the purpose of vent selection are classified into the following four categories:

Category I. An *appliance* that operates with a nonpositive vent static pressure and with a vent gas temperature that avoids excessive condensate production in the vent.

Category II. An *appliance* that operates with a nonpositive vent static pressure and with a vent gas temperature that is capable of causing excessive condensate production in the vent.

Category III. An *appliance* that operates with a positive vent static pressure and with a vent gas temperature that avoids excessive condensate production in the vent.

Category IV. An *appliance* that operates with a positive vent static pressure and with a vent gas temperature that is capable of causing excessive condensate production in the vent.

VENTED ROOM HEATER. A vented self-contained, free-standing, nonrecessed *appliance* for furnishing warm air to the space in which it is installed, directly from the heater without duct connections.

VENTED WALL FURNACE. A self-contained vented *appliance* complete with grilles or equivalent, designed for incorporation in or permanent attachment to the structure of a building, mobile home or travel trailer, and furnishing heated air circulated by gravity or by a fan directly into the space to be heated through openings in the casing. This definition shall exclude floor furnaces, unit heaters and central furnaces as herein defined.

VENTING SYSTEM. A continuous open passageway from the flue collar or draft hood of an *appliance* to the outside atmosphere for the purpose of removing flue or vent gases. A venting system is usually composed of a vent or a chimney and vent connector, if used, assembled to form the open passageway.

Forced-draft venting system. A portion of a venting system using a fan or other mechanical means to cause the removal of flue or vent gases under positive static vent pressure.

Induced draft venting system. A portion of a venting system using a fan or other mechanical means to cause the removal of flue or vent gases under nonpositive static vent pressure.

Mechanical draft venting system. A venting system designed to remove flue or vent gases by mechanical means, that consists of an induced draft portion under nonpositive static pressure or a forced draft portion under positive static pressure.

Natural draft venting system. A venting system designed to remove flue or vent gases under nonpositive static vent pressure entirely by natural draft.

WALL HEATER, UNVENTED-TYPE. A room heater of the type designed for insertion in or attachment to a wall or partition. Such heater does not incorporate concealed venting arrangements in its construction and discharges all products of combustion through the front into the room being heated.

WATER HEATER. Any heating *appliance* or *equipment* that heats potable water and supplies such water to the potable hot water distribution system.

CHAPTER 3
GENERAL REGULATIONS

SECTION 301 (IFGC) GENERAL

301.1 Scope. This chapter shall govern the approval and installation of all *equipment* and appliances that comprise parts of the installations regulated by this code in accordance with Section 101.2.

301.1.1 Other fuels. The requirements for combustion and dilution air for gas-fired appliances shall be governed by Section 304. The requirements for combustion and dilution air for appliances operating with fuels other than fuel gas shall be regulated by the *International Mechanical Code*.

301.2 Energy utilization. Heating, ventilating and air-conditioning systems of all structures shall be designed and installed for efficient utilization of energy in accordance with the *International Energy Conservation Code*.

301.3 Listed and labeled. Appliances regulated by this code shall be *listed* and *labeled* for the application in which they are used unless otherwise *approved* in accordance with Section 105. The approval of unlisted appliances in accordance with Section 105 shall be based upon *approved* engineering evaluation.

301.4 Labeling. Labeling shall be in accordance with the procedures set forth in Sections 301.4.1 through 301.4.2.3.

301.4.1 Testing. An *approved* agency shall test a representative sample of the appliances being *labeled* to the relevant standard or standards. The *approved* agency shall maintain a record of all of the tests performed. The record shall provide sufficient detail to verify compliance with the test standard.

301.4.2 Inspection and identification. The *approved* agency shall periodically perform an inspection, which shall be in-plant if necessary, of the appliances to be *labeled*. The inspection shall verify that the *labeled* appliances are representative of the appliances tested.

301.4.2.1 Independent. The agency to be *approved* shall be objective and competent. To confirm its objectivity, the agency shall disclose all possible conflicts of interest.

301.4.2.2 Equipment. An *approved* agency shall have adequate *equipment* to perform all required tests. The *equipment* shall be periodically calibrated.

301.4.2.3 Personnel. An *approved* agency shall employ experienced personnel educated in conducting, supervising and evaluating tests.

301.5 Label information. A permanent factory-applied nameplate(s) shall be affixed to appliances on which shall appear in legible lettering, the manufacturer's name or trademark, the model number, serial number and, for *listed* appliances, the seal or mark of the testing agency. A label shall also include the hourly rating in British thermal units per hour (Btu/h) (W); the type of fuel *approved* for use with the *appliance*; and the minimum *clearance* requirements.

301.6 Plumbing connections. Potable water supply and building drainage system connections to appliances regulated by this code shall be in accordance with the *International Plumbing Code*.

301.7 Fuel types. Appliances shall be designed for use with the type of fuel gas that will be supplied to them.

301.7.1 Appliance fuel conversion. Appliances shall not be converted to utilize a different fuel gas except where complete instructions for such conversion are provided in the installation instructions, by the serving gas supplier or by the *appliance* manufacturer.

301.8 Vibration isolation. Where means for isolation of vibration of an *appliance* is installed, an *approved* means for support and restraint of that *appliance* shall be provided.

301.9 Repair. Defective material or parts shall be replaced or repaired in such a manner so as to preserve the original approval or listing.

301.10 Wind resistance. Appliances and supports that are exposed to wind shall be designed and installed to resist the wind pressures determined in accordance with the *International Building Code*.

301.11 Flood hazard. For structures located in flood hazard areas, the *appliance, equipment* and system installations regulated by this code shall be located at or above the *design flood elevation* and shall comply with the flood-resistant construction requirements of the *International Building Code*.

Exception: The *appliance, equipment* and system installations regulated by this code are permitted to be located below the *design flood elevation* provided that they are designed and installed to prevent water from entering or accumulating within the components and to resist hydrostatic and hydrodynamic loads and stresses, including the effects of buoyancy, during the occurrence of flooding to the *design flood elevation* and shall comply with the flood-resistant construction requirements of the *International Building Code*.

301.12 Seismic resistance. When earthquake loads are applicable in accordance with the *International Building Code*, the supports shall be designed and installed for the seismic forces in accordance with that code.

301.13 Ducts. All ducts required for the installation of systems regulated by this code shall be designed and installed in accordance with the *International Mechanical Code*.

301.14 Rodentproofing. Buildings or structures and the walls enclosing habitable or occupiable rooms and spaces in which persons live, sleep or work, or in which feed, food or foodstuffs are stored, prepared, processed, served or sold, shall be constructed to protect against rodents in accordance with the *International Building Code*.

301.14.1 Foundation and exterior wall sealing. Annular spaces around pipes, electric cables, conduits or other openings in the walls shall be protected against the passage of rodents by closing such opening with cement mortar, concrete masonry, silicone caulking or noncorrosive metal.

301.15 Prohibited location. The appliances, *equipment* and systems regulated by this code shall not be located in an elevator shaft.

SECTION 302 (IFGC) STRUCTURAL SAFETY

[B] 302.1 Structural safety. The building shall not be weakened by the installation of any gas *piping*. In the process of installing or repairing any gas *piping*, the finished floors, walls, ceilings, tile work or any other part of the building or premises which is required to be changed or replaced shall be left in a safe structural condition in accordance with the requirements of the *International Building Code*.

[B] 302.2 Penetrations of floor/ceiling assemblies and fire-resistance-rated assemblies. Penetrations of floor/ceiling assemblies and assemblies required to have a fire-resistance rating shall be protected in accordance with the *International Building Code*.

[B] 302.3 Cutting, notching and boring in wood members. The cutting, notching and boring of wood members shall comply with Sections 302.3.1 through 302.3.4.

[B] 302.3.1 Engineered wood products. Cuts, notches and holes bored in trusses, structural composite lumber, structural glued-laminated members and I-joists are prohibited except where permitted by the manufacturer's recommendations or where the effects of such alterations are specifically considered in the design of the member by a registered design professional.

[B] 302.3.2 Joist notching and boring. Notching at the ends of joists shall not exceed one-fourth the joist depth. Holes bored in joists shall not be within 2 inches (51 mm) of the top and bottom of the joist and their diameter shall not exceed one-third the depth of the member. Notches in the top or bottom of the joist shall not exceed one-sixth the depth and shall not be located in the middle one-third of the span.

[B] 302.3.3 Stud cutting and notching. In exterior walls and bearing partitions, any wood stud is permitted to be cut or notched to a depth not exceeding 25 percent of its width. Cutting or notching of studs to a depth not greater than 40 percent of the width of the stud is permitted in nonload-bearing partitions supporting no loads other than the weight of the partition.

[B] 302.3.4 Bored holes. A hole not greater in diameter than 40 percent of the stud depth is permitted to be bored in any wood stud. Bored holes not greater than 60 percent of the depth of the stud are permitted in nonload-bearing partitions or in any wall where each bored stud is doubled, provided not more than two such successive doubled studs are so bored. In no case shall the edge of the bored hole be nearer than $^5/_8$ inch (15.9 mm) to the edge of the stud. Bored holes shall not be located at the same section of a stud as a cut or notch.

[B] 302.4 Alterations to trusses. Truss members and components shall not be cut, drilled, notched, spliced or otherwise altered in any way without the written concurrence and approval of a registered design professional. Alterations resulting in the addition of loads to any member (e.g., HVAC *equipment*, water heaters) shall not be permitted without verification that the truss is capable of supporting such additional loading.

[B] 302.5 Cutting, notching and boring holes in structural steel framing. The cutting, notching and boring of holes in structural steel framing members shall be as prescribed by the registered design professional.

[B] 302.6 Cutting, notching and boring holes in cold-formed steel framing. Flanges and lips of load-bearing, cold-formed steel framing members shall not be cut or notched. Holes in webs of load-bearing, cold-formed steel framing members shall be permitted along the centerline of the web of the framing member and shall not exceed the dimensional limitations, penetration spacing or minimum hole edge distance as prescribed by the registered design professional. Cutting, notching and boring holes of steel floor/roof decking shall be as prescribed by the registered design professional.

[B] 302.7 Cutting, notching and boring holes in nonstructural cold-formed steel wall framing. Flanges and lips of nonstructural cold-formed steel wall studs shall be permitted along the centerline of the web of the framing member, shall not exceed $1^1/_2$ inches (38 mm) in width or 4 inches (102 mm) in length, and the holes shall not be spaced less than 24 inches (610 mm) center to center from another hole or less than 10 inches (254 mm) from the bearing end.

SECTION 303 (IFGC) APPLIANCE LOCATION

303.1 General. Appliances shall be located as required by this section, specific requirements elsewhere in this code and the conditions of the *equipment* and *appliance* listing.

303.2 Hazardous locations. Appliances shall not be located in a *hazardous location* unless *listed* and *approved* for the specific installation.

303.3 Prohibited locations. Appliances shall not be located in sleeping rooms, bathrooms, toilet rooms, closets used for storage or surgical rooms, or in a space that opens only into such rooms or spaces, except where the installation complies with one of the following:

1. The *appliance* is a direct-vent *appliance* installed in accordance with the conditions of the listing and the manufacturer's instructions.
2. Vented room heaters, wall furnaces, vented decorative appliances, vented gas fireplaces, vented gas fireplace heaters and decorative appliances for installation in vented solid fuel-burning fireplaces are installed in rooms that meet the required volume criteria of Section 304.5.

3. A single wall-mounted unvented room heater is installed in a bathroom and such unvented room heater is equipped as specified in Section 621.6 and has an input rating not greater than 6,000 Btu/h (1.76 kW). The bathroom shall meet the required volume criteria of Section 304.5.
4. Deleted.
5. The *appliance* is installed in a room or space that opens only into a bedroom or bathroom, and such room or space is used for no other purpose and is provided with a solid weather-stripped door equipped with an *approved* self-closing device. All *combustion air* shall be taken directly from the outdoors in accordance with Section 304.6.

303.4 Protection from vehicle impact damage. Appliances shall not be installed in a location subject to vehicle impact damage except where protected by an *approved* means. Protection is not required for appliances located out of the vehicle's normal travel path.

303.5 Indoor locations. Furnaces and boilers installed in closets and alcoves shall be *listed* for such installation.

303.6 Outdoor locations. Appliances installed in outdoor locations shall be either *listed* for outdoor installation or provided with protection from outdoor environmental factors that influence the operability, durability and safety of the appliances.

303.7 Pit locations. Appliances installed in pits or excavations shall not come in direct contact with the surrounding soil. The sides of the pit or excavation shall be held back a minimum of 12 inches (305 mm) from the *appliance*. Where the depth exceeds 12 inches (305 mm) below adjoining grade, the walls of the pit or excavation shall be lined with concrete or masonry, such concrete or masonry shall extend a minimum of 4 inches (102 mm) above adjoining grade and shall have sufficient lateral load-bearing capacity to resist collapse.

303.8 Drainage. Below-grade installations shall be provided with a natural drain or an automatic lift or sump pump.

SECTION 304 (IFGS) COMBUSTION, VENTILATION AND DILUTION AIR

304.1 General. Air for combustion, ventilation and dilution of flue gases for appliances installed in buildings shall be provided by application of one of the methods prescribed in Sections 304.5 through 304.9. Where the requirements of Section 304.5 are not met, outdoor air shall be introduced in accordance with one of the methods prescribed in Sections 304.6 through 304.9. *Direct-vent appliances*, gas appliances of other than natural draft design and vented gas appliances other than Category I shall be provided with combustion, ventilation and dilution air in accordance with the *appliance* manufacturer's instructions.

Exception: Type 1 clothes dryers that are provided with makeup air in accordance with Section 614.5.

304.2 Appliance location. Appliances shall be located so as not to interfere with proper circulation of combustion, ventilation and dilution air.

304.3 Draft hood/regulator location. Where used, a draft hood or a barometric draft regulator shall be installed in the same room or enclosure as the *appliance* served so as to prevent any difference in pressure between the hood or regulator and the *combustion air* supply.

304.4 Makeup air provisions. Where exhaust fans, clothes dryers and kitchen ventilation systems interfere with the operation of appliances and fireplaces, makeup air shall be provided.

304.5 Indoor combustion air. The required volume of indoor air shall be determined in accordance with Section 304.5.1 or 304.5.2, except that where the air infiltration rate is known to be less than 0.40 air changes per hour (ACH), Section 304.5.2 shall be used. The total required volume shall be the sum of the required volume calculated for all appliances located within the space. Rooms communicating directly with the space in which the appliances are installed through openings not furnished with doors, and through *combustion air* openings sized and located in accordance with Section 304.5.3, are considered to be part of the required volume.

304.5.1 Standard method. The minimum required volume shall be 50 cubic feet per 1,000 Btu/h (4.8 m^3/kW) of the *appliance* input rating.

304.5.2 Known air-infiltration-rate method. Where the air infiltration rate of a structure is known, the minimum required volume shall be determined as follows:

For appliances other than fan-assisted, calculate volume using Equation 3-1.

$$Required\ Volume_{other} \geq \frac{21\ \text{ft}^3}{ACH}\left(\frac{I_{other}}{1{,}000\ \text{Btu / hr}}\right)$$

(Equation 3-1)

For fan-assisted appliances, calculate volume using Equation 3-2.

$$Required\ Volume_{fan} \geq \frac{15\ \text{ft}^3}{ACH}\left(\frac{I_{fan}}{1{,}000\ \text{Btu / hr}}\right)$$

(Equation 3-2)

where:

I_{other} = All appliances other than fan assisted (input in Btu/h).

I_{fan} = Fan-assisted *appliance* (input in Btu/h).

ACH = Air change per hour (percent of volume of space exchanged per hour, expressed as a decimal).

For purposes of this calculation, an infiltration rate greater than 0.60 ACH shall not be used in Equations 3-1 and 3-2.

304.5.3 Indoor opening size and location. Openings used to connect indoor spaces shall be sized and located in accordance with Sections 304.5.3.1 and 304.5.3.2 (see Figure 304.5.3).

304.5.3.1 Combining spaces on the same story. Each opening shall have a minimum free area of 1 square inch per 1,000 Btu/h (2,200 mm^2/kW) of the total input rating of all appliances in the space, but not less than 100 square inches (0.06 m^2). One opening shall commence within 12 inches (305 mm) of the top and one opening shall commence within 12 inches (305 mm) of the bottom of the enclosure. The minimum dimension of air openings shall be not less than 3 inches (76 mm).

304.5.3.2 Combining spaces in different stories. The volumes of spaces in different stories shall be considered as communicating spaces where such spaces are connected by one or more openings in doors or floors having a total minimum free area of 2 square inches per 1,000 Btu/h (4402 mm²/kW) of total input rating of all appliances.

304.6 Outdoor combustion air. Outdoor *combustion air* shall be provided through opening(s) to the outdoors in accordance with Section 304.6.1 or 304.6.2. The minimum dimension of air openings shall be not less than 3 inches (76 mm). Penetration of the thermal envelope shall comply with the *North Carolina Energy Conservation Code*.

304.6.1 Two-permanent-openings method. Two permanent openings, one commencing within 12 inches (305 mm) of the top and one commencing within 12 inches (305 mm) of the bottom of the enclosure, shall be provided. The openings shall communicate directly, or by ducts, with the outdoors or spaces that freely communicate with the outdoors.

Where directly communicating with the outdoors, or where communicating with the outdoors through vertical ducts, each opening shall have a minimum free area of 1 square inch per 4,000 Btu/h (550 mm²/kW) of total input rating of all appliances in the enclosure [see Figures 304.6.1(1) and 304.6.1(2)].

Where communicating with the outdoors through horizontal ducts, each opening shall have a minimum free area of not less than 1 square inch per 2,000 Btu/h (1,100 mm²/kW) of total input rating of all appliances in the enclosure [see Figure 304.6.1(3)].

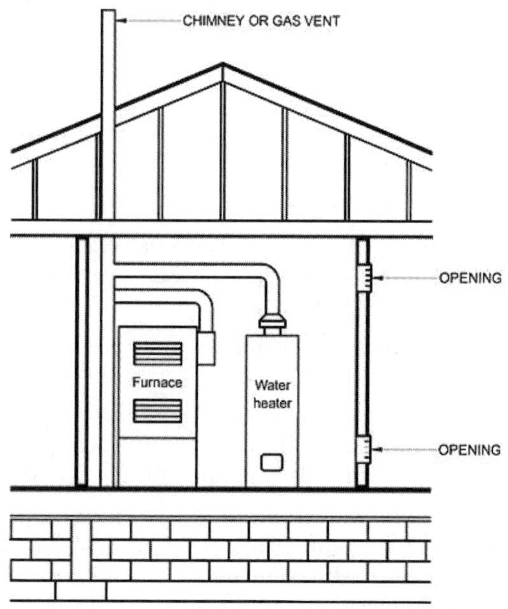

FIGURE 304.5.3
ALL AIR FROM INSIDE THE BUILDING
(see Section 304.5.3)

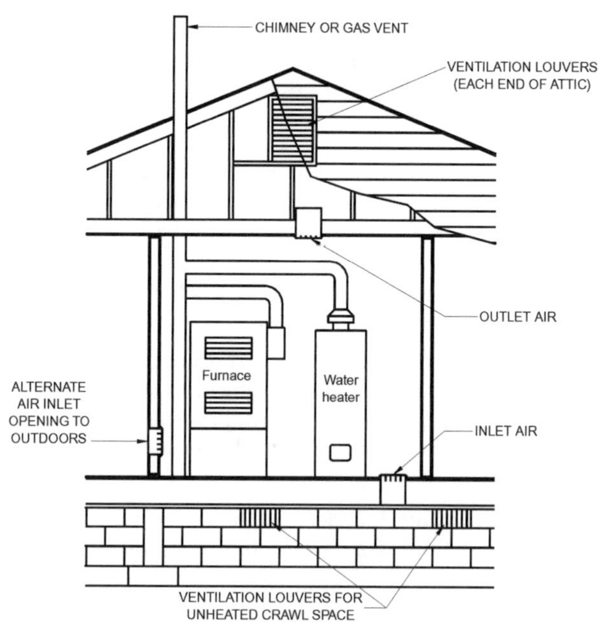

FIGURE 304.6.1(1)
ALL AIR FROM OUTDOORS—INLET AIR FROM VENTILATED CRAWL SPACE AND OUTLET AIR TO VENTILATED ATTIC
(see Section 304.6.1)

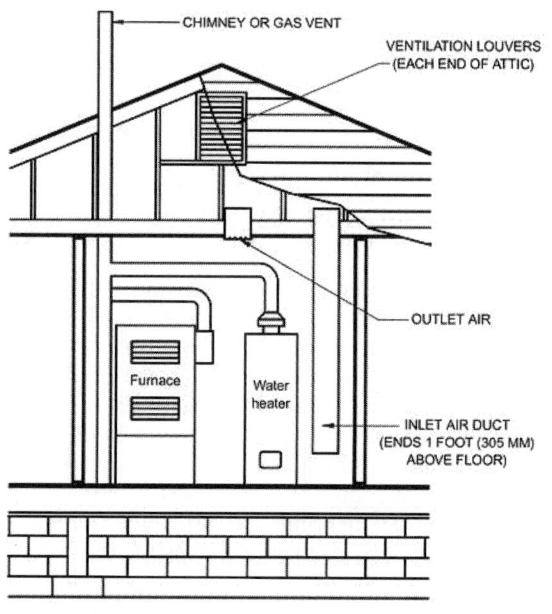

For SI: 1 foot = 304.8 mm.

FIGURE 304.6.1(2)
ALL AIR FROM OUTDOORS THROUGH VENTILATED ATTIC
(see Section 304.6.1)

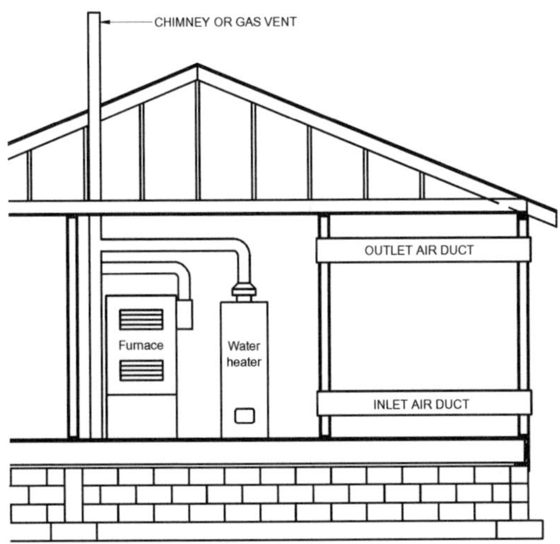

FIGURE 304.6.1(3)
ALL AIR FROM OUTDOORS
(see Section 304.6.1)

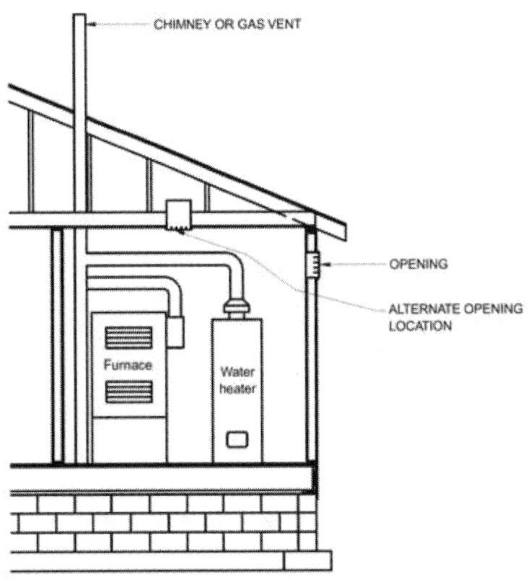

FIGURE 304.6.2
SINGLE COMBUSTION AIR OPENING,
ALL AIR FROM THE OUTDOORS
(see Section 304.6.2)

304.6.2 One-permanent-opening method. One permanent opening, commencing within 12 inches (305 mm) of the top of the enclosure, shall be provided. The *appliance* shall have clearances of at least 1 inch (25 mm) from the sides and back and 6 inches (152 mm) from the front of the *appliance*. The opening shall directly communicate with the outdoors or through a vertical or horizontal duct to the outdoors, or spaces that freely communicate with the outdoors (see Figure 304.6.2) and shall have a minimum free area of 1 square inch per 3,000 Btu/h (734 mm^2/kW) of the total input rating of all appliances located in the enclosure and not less than the sum of the areas of all vent connectors in the space.

304.7 Combination indoor and outdoor combustion air. The use of a combination of indoor and outdoor *combustion air* shall be in accordance with Sections 304.7.1 through 304.7.3.

304.7.1 Indoor openings. Where used, openings connecting the interior spaces shall comply with Section 304.5.3.

304.7.2 Outdoor opening location. Outdoor opening(s) shall be located in accordance with Section 304.6.

304.7.3 Outdoor opening(s) size. The outdoor opening(s) size shall be calculated in accordance with the following:

1. The ratio of interior spaces shall be the available volume of all communicating spaces divided by the required volume.
2. The outdoor size reduction factor shall be one minus the ratio of interior spaces.
3. The minimum size of outdoor opening(s) shall be the full size of outdoor opening(s) calculated in accordance with Section 304.6, multiplied by the reduction factor. The minimum dimension of air openings shall be not less than 3 inches (76 mm).

304.8 Engineered installations. Engineered *combustion air* installations shall provide an adequate supply of combustion, ventilation and dilution air and shall be *approved*.

304.9 Mechanical combustion air supply. Where all *combustion air* is provided by a mechanical air supply system, the *combustion air* shall be supplied from the outdoors at a rate not less than 0.35 cubic feet per minute per 1,000 Btu/h (0.034 m^3/min per kW) of total input rating of all appliances located within the space.

304.9.1 Makeup air. Where exhaust fans are installed, makeup air shall be provided to replace the exhausted air.

304.9.2 Appliance interlock. Each of the appliances served shall be interlocked with the mechanical air supply system to prevent main burner operation when the mechanical air supply system is not in operation.

304.9.3 Combined combustion air and ventilation air system. Where *combustion air* is provided by the building's mechanical ventilation system, the system shall provide the specified *combustion air* rate in addition to the required ventilation air.

304.10 Louvers and grilles. The required size of openings for combustion, ventilation and dilution air shall be based on the net free area of each opening. Where the free area through a design of louver, grille or screen is known, it shall be used in calculating the size opening required to provide the free area specified. Where the design and free area of louvers and grilles are not known, it shall be assumed that wood louvers will have 25-percent free area and metal louvers and grilles will have 75-percent free area. Screens shall have a mesh size not smaller than $^1/_4$ inch (6.4 mm). Nonmotorized louvers and grilles shall be fixed in the open position. Motorized louvers shall be interlocked with the *appliance* so that they are proven to be in the full open position prior to main burner ignition and during main burner operation. Means shall be provided to prevent the main burner from igniting if the louvers fail to open during burner start-up and to shut down the main burner if the louvers close during operation.

304.11 Combustion air ducts. *Combustion air* ducts shall comply with all of the following:

1. Ducts shall be constructed of galvanized steel complying with Chapter 6 of the *International Mechanical Code* or of a material having equivalent corrosion resistance, strength and rigidity.

   Exception: Within dwellings units, unobstructed stud and joist spaces shall not be prohibited from conveying *combustion air*, provided that not more than one required fireblock is removed.

2. Ducts shall terminate in an unobstructed space allowing free movement of *combustion air* to the appliances.
3. Ducts shall serve a single enclosure.
4. Ducts shall not serve both upper and lower *combustion air* openings where both such openings are used. The separation between ducts serving upper and lower *combustion air* openings shall be maintained to the source of *combustion air*.
5. Ducts shall not be screened where terminating in an attic space.
6. Horizontal upper *combustion air*ducts shall not slope downward toward the source of *combustion air*.
7. The remaining space surrounding a chimney liner, gas vent, special gas vent or plastic *piping* installed within a masonry, metal or factory-built chimney shall not be used to supply *combustion air*.

   Exception: Direct-vent gas-fired appliances designed for installation in a solid fuel-burning *fireplace* where installed in accordance with the manufacturer's instructions.

8. *Combustion air* intake openings located on the exterior of a building shall have the lowest side of such openings located not less than 12 inches (305 mm) vertically from the adjoining finished ground level.

304.12 Protection from fumes and gases. Where corrosive or flammable process fumes or gases, other than products of combustion, are present, means for the disposal of such fumes or gases shall be provided. Such fumes or gases include carbon monoxide, hydrogen sulfide, ammonia, chlorine and halogenated hydrocarbons.

In barbershops, beauty shops and other facilities where chemicals that generate corrosive or flammable products, such as aerosol sprays, are routinely used, nondirect vent-type appliances shall be located in a mechanical room separated or partitioned off from other areas with provisions for *combustion air* and dilution air from the outdoors. *Direct-vent appliances* shall be installed in accordance with the *appliance* manufacturer's installation instructions.

SECTION 305 (IFGC) INSTALLATION

305.1 General. *Equipment* and appliances shall be installed as required by the terms of their approval, in accordance with the conditions of listing, the manufacturer's instructions and this code. Manufacturers' installation instructions shall be available on the job site at the time of inspection. Where a code provision is less restrictive than the conditions of the listing of the *equipment* or *appliance* or the manufacturer's installation instructions, the conditions of the listing and the manufacturer's installation instructions shall apply.

Unlisted appliances *approved* in accordance with Section 301.3 shall be limited to uses recommended by the manufacturer and shall be installed in accordance with the manufacturer's instructions, the provisions of this code and the requirements determined by the code official.

305.2 Hazardous area. *Equipment* and appliances having an *ignition source* shall not be installed in Group H occupancies or control areas where open use, handling or dispensing of combustible, flammable or explosive materials occurs.

305.3 Elevation of ignition source. *Equipment* and appliances having an *ignition source* shall be elevated such that the source of ignition is not less than 18 inches (457 mm) above the floor in hazardous locations and public garages, private garages, repair garages, motor fuel-dispensing facilities and parking garages. For the purpose of this section, rooms or spaces that are not part of the *living space* of a *dwelling unit* and that communicate directly with a private garage through openings shall be considered to be part of the private garage.

Exception: Elevation of the *ignition source* is not required for appliances that are *listed* as flammable vapor ignition resistant.

305.3.1 (IFGS) Installation in residential garages. In residential garages where appliances are installed in a separate, enclosed space having *access* only from outside of the garage, such appliances shall be permitted to be installed at floor level, provided that the required *combustion air* is taken from the exterior of the garage.

305.3.2 Parking garages. Deleted.

305.4 Public garages. Deleted.

305.5 Private garages. Appliances located in private garages shall be installed with a minimum *clearance* of 6 feet (1829 mm) above the floor.

Exception: The requirements of this section shall not apply where the appliances are protected from motor vehicle impact and installed in accordance with Section 303.4 and NFPA 30A.

305.6 Construction and protection. Boiler rooms and furnace rooms shall be protected as required by the *International Building Code*.

305.7 Under-floor and exterior grade installations.

305.7.1 Exterior grade installations. Equipment and appliances installed above grade level shall be supported on a solid base or on approved material that is a minimum of 2 inches (51 mm) thick.

305.7.2 Under-floor installation. Suspended equipment shall be a minimum of 6 inches (152 mm) above the adjoining grade.

305.7.3 Crawl space supports. A support shall be provided at each corner of the unit not less than 8 inches by 8 inches (204 mm by 204 mm). The unit shall be supported a minimum of 2 inches (51 mm) above grade. When constructed of brick, the bricks shall be mortared together. All units stacked shall be mortared together. Fabricated units, formed concrete, or other approved materials shall be permitted.

305.7.4 Drainage. Below-grade installations shall be provided with a natural drain or an automatic lift or sump pump. For pit requirements, see Section 303.7.

305.8 Clearances to combustible construction. Heat-producing *equipment* and appliances shall be installed to maintain the required clearances to combustible construction as specified in the listing and manufacturer's instructions. Such clearances shall be reduced only in accordance with Section 308. Clearances to combustibles shall include such considerations as door swing, drawer pull, overhead projections or shelving and window swing. Devices, such as door stops or limits and closers, shall not be used to provide the required clearances.

305.9 (IFGS) Parking structures. Deleted.

305.10 (IFGS) Repair garages. Deleted.

305.11 (IFGS) Installation in aircraft hangars. Deleted.

305.12 (IFGS) Avoid strain on gas *piping*. Appliances shall be supported and connected to the *piping* so as not to exert undue strain on the connections.

SECTION 306 (IFGC) ACCESS AND SERVICE SPACE

[M] 306.1 Access for maintenance and replacement. Appliances shall be accessible for inspection, service, repair and replacement without disabling the function of a fire-resistance-rated assembly or removing permanent construction, other appliances, or any other *piping* or ducts not connected to the *appliance* being inspected, serviced, repaired or replaced. A level working space at least 30 inches deep and 30 inches wide (762 mm by 762 mm) shall be provided in front of the control side to service an *appliance.*

[M] 306.2 Appliances in rooms. Rooms containing appliances shall be provided with a door and an unobstructed passageway measuring not less than 36 inches (914 mm) wide and 80 inches (2032 mm) high.

Exception: Within a *dwelling unit*, appliances installed in a compartment, alcove, basement or similar space shall be provided with *access* by an opening or door and an unobstructed passageway measuring not less than 24 inches (610 mm) wide and large enough to allow removal of the largest *appliance* in the space, provided that a level service space of not less than 30 inches (762 mm) deep and the height of the *appliance*, but not less than 30 inches (762 mm), is present at the front or service side of the *appliance* with the door open.

[M] 306.3 Appliances in attics. Attics containing appliances shall be provided with an opening and unobstructed passageway large enough to allow removal of the largest *appliance.* The passageway shall not be less than 30 inches (762 mm) high and 22 inches (559 mm) wide and not more than 20 feet (6096 mm) in length measured along the centerline of the passageway from the opening to the *appliance.* The passageway shall have continuous solid flooring not less than 24 inches (610 mm) wide. A level service space not less than 30 inches (762 mm) deep and 30 inches (762 mm) wide shall be present at the front or service side of the *appliance.* The clear *access* opening dimensions shall be a minimum of 20 inches by 30 inches (508 mm by 762 mm), and large enough to allow removal of the largest *appliance.*

Exceptions:

1. The passageway and level service space are not required where the *appliance* is capable of being serviced and removed through the required opening.
2. Where the passageway is not less than 6 feet (1829 mm) high for its entire length, the passageway shall not be limited in length.

[M] 306.3.1 Electrical requirements. Deleted.

[M] 306.4 Appliances under floors. Under-floor spaces containing appliances shall be provided with an *access* opening and unobstructed passageway large enough to remove the largest *appliance.* The passageway shall not be less than 22 inches (559 mm) high and 36 inches (914 mm) wide, nor more than 20 feet (6096 mm) in length measured along the centerline of the passageway from the opening to the *appliance.* A level service space not less than 30 inches (762 mm) deep and 30 inches (762 mm) wide shall be present at the front or service side of the *appliance.* If the depth of the passageway or the service space exceeds 12 inches (305 mm) below the adjoining grade, the walls of the passageway shall be lined with concrete or masonry extending 4 inches (102 mm) above the adjoining grade and having sufficient lateral-bearing capacity to resist collapse. The clear *access* opening dimensions shall be a minimum of 22 inches high by 30 inches wide (559 mm by 762 mm), and large enough to allow removal of the largest *appliance.*

Exceptions:

1. The passageway is not required where the level service space is present when the *access* is open and the *appliance* is capable of being serviced and removed through the required opening.
2. Where the passageway is not less than 6 feet (1829 mm) high for its entire length, the passageway shall not be limited in length.

[M] 306.4.1 Electrical requirements. Deleted.

[M] 306.5 Appliances on roofs or elevated structures. Deleted.

[M] 306.5.1 Sloped roofs. Where appliances, *equipment*, fans or other components that require periodic maintenance are installed on a roof having a slope of 3 units vertical in 12 units horizontal (25-percent slope) or greater and having an edge more than 30 inches (762 mm) above grade at such edge, a level platform shall be provided on each side of the *appliance* or *equipment* to which *access* is required for service, repair or maintenance. The platform shall be not less than 30 inches (762 mm) in any dimension and shall be provided with guards. The guards shall extend not less than 42 inches (1067 mm) above the platform, shall be constructed so as to prevent the passage of a 21-inch-diameter (533 mm) sphere and shall comply with the loading requirements for guards specified in the *International Building Code. Access* shall not require walking on roofs having a slope greater than 4 units vertical in 12 units horizontal (33-percent slope). Where *access* involves obstructions greater than 30 inches (762 mm) in height, such obstructions shall be provided with ladders installed in accordance with Section 306.5 or stairs installed in accordance with the requirements specified in the *International Building Code* in the path of travel to and from appliances, fans or *equipment* requiring service.

[M] 306.5.2 Electrical requirements. Deleted.

[M] 306.6 Guards. Guards shall be provided where appliances or other components that require service and roof hatch openings are located within 6 feet (1829 mm) of a roof edge or open side of a walking surface and such edge or open side is located more than 30 inches (762 mm) above the floor, roof or grade below. The guard shall extend not less than 30 inches (762 mm) beyond each end of such appliances, components and roof hatch openings and the top of the guard shall be located not less than 42 inches (1067 mm) above the elevated surface adjacent to the guard. The guard shall be constructed so as to prevent the passage of a 21-inch-diameter (533 mm) sphere and shall comply with the loading requirements for guards specified in the *International Building Code.*

SECTION 307 (IFGC) CONDENSATE DISPOSAL

307.1 Evaporators and cooling coils. Condensate drainage systems shall be provided for *equipment* and appliances containing evaporators and cooling coils in accordance with the *International Mechanical Code.*

307.2 Fuel-burning appliances. Liquid combustion by-products of condensing appliances shall be collected and discharged to an *approved* plumbing fixture or disposal area in accordance with the manufacturer's installation instructions. Condensate *piping* shall be of *approved* corrosion-resistant material and shall not be smaller than the drain connection on the *appliance.* Such *piping* shall maintain a minimum slope in the direction of discharge of not less than one-eighth unit vertical in 12 units horizontal (1-percent slope).

[M] 307.3 Drain pipe materials and sizes. Components of the condensate disposal system shall be cast iron, galvanized steel, copper, polybutylene, polyethylene, ABS, CPVC or PVC pipe or tubing. All components shall be selected for the pressure and temperature rating of the installation. Condensate waste and drain line size shall be not less than $^3/_4$-inch internal diameter (19 mm) and shall not decrease in size from the drain connection to the place of condensate disposal. Where the drain pipes from more than one unit are manifolded together for condensate drainage, the pipe or tubing shall be sized in accordance with an approved method. All horizontal sections of drain piping shall be installed in uniform alignment at a uniform slope.

307.4 Traps. Condensate drains shall be trapped as required by the *equipment* or *appliance* manufacturer.

307.5 Auxiliary drain pan. Category IV condensing appliances shall be provided with an auxiliary drain pan where damage to any building component will occur as a result of stoppage in the condensate drainage system. Such pan shall be installed in accordance with the applicable provisions of Section 307 of the *International Mechanical Code.*

> **Exception:** An auxiliary drain pan shall not be required for appliances that automatically shut down operation in the event of a stoppage in the condensate drainage system.

SECTION 308 (IFGS) CLEARANCE REDUCTION FOR UNLISTED EQUIPMENT

308.1 Scope. This section shall govern the reduction in required clearances to combustible materials and combustible assemblies for chimneys, vents, appliances, devices and *equipment. Clearance* requirements for air-conditioning *equipment* and central heating boilers and furnaces shall comply with Sections 308.3 and 308.4.

308.2 Reduction table. The allowable *clearance* reduction shall be based on one of the methods specified in Table 308.2 or shall utilize an assembly *listed* for such application. Where required clearances are not listed in Table 308.2, the reduced clearances shall be determined by linear interpolation between the distances listed in the table. Reduced clearances shall not be derived by extrapolation below the range of the table. The reduction of the required clearances to combustibles for *listed* and *labeled* appliances and *equipment* shall be in accordance with the manufacturer's equipment listing and installation instructions.

308.3 Clearances for indoor air-conditioning appliances. *Clearance* requirements for indoor air-conditioning appliances shall comply with Sections 308.3.1 through 308.3.5.

308.3.1 Appliances installed in rooms that are large in comparison with the size of the appliance. Air-conditioning appliances installed in rooms that are large in comparison with the size of the *appliance* shall be installed with clearances in accordance with the manufacturer's instructions.

308.3.2 Appliances installed in rooms that are not large in comparison with the size of the appliance. Air-conditioning appliances installed in rooms that are not large in comparison with the size of the *appliance*, such as alcoves and closets, shall be *listed* for such installations and installed in accordance with the manufacturer's instructions. *Listed* clearances shall not be reduced by the protection methods described in Table 308.2, regardless of whether the enclosure is of combustible or noncombustible material.

308.3.3 Clearance reduction. Deleted.

308.3.4 Plenum clearances. Where the *furnace plenum* is adjacent to plaster on metal lath or noncombustible material attached to combustible material, the *clearance* shall be measured to the surface of the plaster or other noncombustible finish where the *clearance* specified is 2 inches (51 mm) or less.

308.3.5 Clearance from supply ducts. Air-conditioning appliances shall have the *clearance* from supply ducts within 3 feet (914 mm) of the *furnace plenum* be not less than that specified from the *furnace plenum. Clearance* is not necessary beyond this distance.

308.4 Central-heating boilers and furnaces. *Clearance* requirements for central-heating boilers and furnaces shall comply with Sections 308.4.1 through 308.4.6. The *clearance* to these appliances shall not interfere with *combustion air*; draft hood *clearance* and relief; and accessibility for servicing.

308.4.1 Appliances installed in rooms that are large in comparison with the size of the appliance. Central-heating furnaces and low-pressure boilers installed in rooms large in comparison with the size of the *appliance* shall be installed with clearances in accordance with the manufacturer's instructions.

308.4.2 Appliances installed in rooms that are not large in comparison with the size of the appliance. Central-heating furnaces and low-pressure boilers installed in rooms that are not large in comparison with the size of the *appliance*, such as alcoves and closets, shall be *listed* for such installations. *Listed* clearances shall not be reduced by the protection methods described in Table 308.2 and illustrated in Figures 308.2(1) through 308.2(3), regardless of whether the enclosure is of combustible or noncombustible material.

308.4.3 Clearance reduction. Deleted.

308.4.4 Clearance for servicing appliances. Front *clearance* shall be sufficient for servicing the burner and the furnace or boiler.

308.4.5 Plenum clearances. Where the *furnace plenum* is adjacent to plaster on metal lath or noncombustible material attached to combustible material, the *clearance* shall be measured to the surface of the plaster or other noncombustible finish where the *clearance* specified is 2 inches (51 mm) or less.

308.4.6 Clearance from supply ducts. Central-heating furnaces shall have the *clearance* from supply ducts within 3 feet (914 mm) of the *furnace plenum* be not less than that specified from the *furnace plenum*. No *clearance* is necessary beyond this distance.

SECTION 309 (IFGC) ELECTRICAL

309.1 Grounding. Gas *piping* shall not be used as a grounding electrode.

309.2 Connections. Electrical connections between appliances and the building wiring, including the grounding of the appliances, shall conform to NFPA 70.

SECTION 310 (IFGS) ELECTRICAL BONDING

310.1 Pipe and tubing other than CSST. Each above-ground portion of a gas *piping* system other than corrugated stainless steel tubing (CSST) that is likely to become energized shall be electrically continuous and bonded to an effective ground-fault current path. Gas *piping* other than CSST shall be considered to be bonded where it is connected to appliances that are connected to the *equipment* grounding conductor of the circuit supplying that *appliance*.

310.1.1 CSST. Corrugated stainless steel tubing (CSST) gas *piping* systems shall be bonded to the electrical service grounding electrode system at the point where the gas service enters the building. The bonding jumper shall be not smaller than 6 AWG copper wire or equivalent.

TABLE 308.2[a through k]
REDUCTION OF CLEARANCES WITH SPECIFIED FORMS OF PROTECTION

TYPE OF PROTECTION APPLIED TO AND COVERING ALL SURFACES OF COMBUSTIBLE MATERIAL WITHIN THE DISTANCE SPECIFIED AS THE REQUIRED CLEARANCE WITH NO PROTECTION [see Figures 308.2(1), 308.2(2), and 308.2(3)]	WHERE THE REQUIRED CLEARANCE WITH NO PROTECTION FROM APPLIANCE, VENT CONNECTOR, OR SINGLE-WALL METAL PIPE IS: (inches)									
	36		18		12		9		6	
	Allowable clearances with specified protection (inches)									
	Use Column 1 for clearances above appliance or horizontal connector. Use Column 2 for clearances from appliance, vertical connector and single-wall metal pipe.									
	Above Col. 1	Sides and rear Col. 2	Above Col. 1	Sides and rear Col. 2	Above Col. 1	Sides and rear Col. 2	Above Col. 1	Sides and rear Col. 2	Above Col. 1	Sides and rear Col. 2
1. 3$^1/_2$-inch-thick masonry wall without ventilated airspace	—	24	—	12	—	9	—	6	—	5
2. $^1/_2$-inch insulation board over 1-inch glass fiber or mineral wool batts	24	18	12	9	9	6	6	5	4	3
3. 0.024-inch (nominal 24 gage) sheet metal over 1-inch glass fiber or mineral wool batts reinforced with wire on rear face with ventilated airspace	18	12	9	6	6	4	5	3	3	3
4. 3$^1/_2$-inch-thick masonry wall with ventilated airspace	—	12	—	6	—	6	—	6	—	6
5. 0.024-inch (nominal 24 gage) sheet metal with ventilated airspace	18	12	9	6	6	4	5	3	3	3
6. $^1/_2$-inch-thick insulation board with ventilated airspace	18	12	9	6	6	4	5	3	3	3
7. 0.024-inch (nominal 24 gage) sheet metal with ventilated airspace over 0.024-inch (nominal 24 gage) sheet metal with ventilated airspace	18	12	9	6	6	4	5	3	3	3
8. 1-inch glass fiber or mineral wool batts sandwiched between two sheets 0.024-inch (nominal 24 gage) sheet metal with ventilated airspace	18	12	9	6	6	4	5	3	3	3

For SI: 1 inch = 25.4 mm, °C = [(°F - 32)/1.8], 1 pound per cubic foot = 16.02 kg/m^3, 1 Btu per inch per square foot per hour per °F = 0.144 W/m^2 · K.

a. Reduction of clearances from combustible materials shall not interfere with combustion air, draft hood clearance and relief, and accessibility of servicing.

b. All clearances shall be measured from the outer surface of the combustible material to the nearest point on the surface of the appliance, disregarding any intervening protection applied to the combustible material.

c. Spacers and ties shall be of noncombustible material. No spacer or tie shall be used directly opposite an appliance or connector.

d. For all clearance reduction systems using a ventilated airspace, adequate provision for air circulation shall be provided as described [see Figures 308.2(2) and 308.2(3)].

e. There shall be at least 1 inch between clearance reduction systems and combustible walls and ceilings for reduction systems using ventilated airspace.

f. Where a wall protector is mounted on a single flat wall away from corners, it shall have a minimum 1-inch air gap. To provide air circulation, the bottom and top edges, or only the side and top edges, or all edges shall be left open.

g. Mineral wool batts (blanket or board) shall have a minimum density of 8 pounds per cubic foot and a minimum melting point of 1500°F.

h. Insulation material used as part of a clearance reduction system shall have a thermal conductivity of 1.0 Btu per inch per square foot per hour per °F or less.

i. There shall be at least 1 inch between the appliance and the protector. In no case shall the clearance between the appliance and the combustible surface be reduced below that allowed in this table.

j. All clearances and thicknesses are minimum; larger clearances and thicknesses are acceptable.

k. Listed single-wall connectors shall be installed in accordance with the manufacturer's installation instructions.

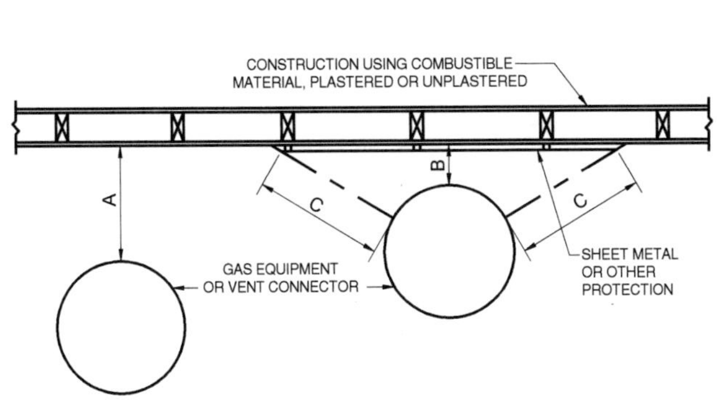

"A" equals the clearance with no protection.

"B" equals the reduced clearance permitted in accordance with Table 308.2. The protection applied to the construction using combustible material shall extend far enough in each direction to make "C" equal to "A."

FIGURE 308.2(1)
EXTENT OF PROTECTION NECESSARY TO REDUCE CLEARANCES FROM APPLIANCE OR VENT CONNECTIONS

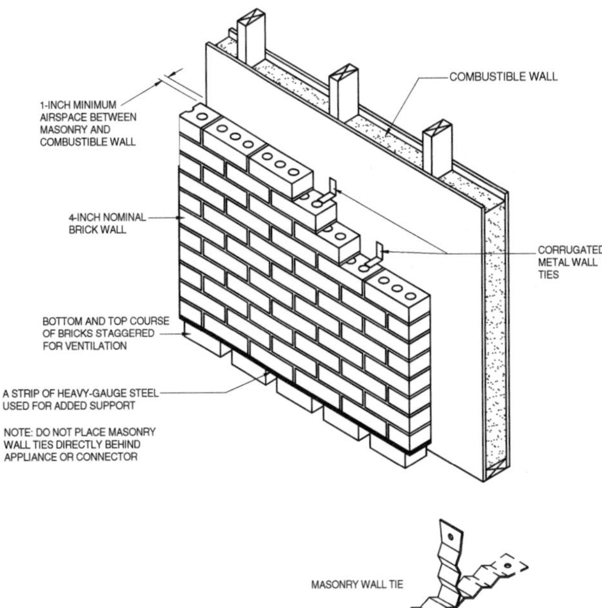

For SI: 1 inch = 25.4 mm.

FIGURE 308.2(3)
MASONRY CLEARANCE REDUCTION SYSTEM

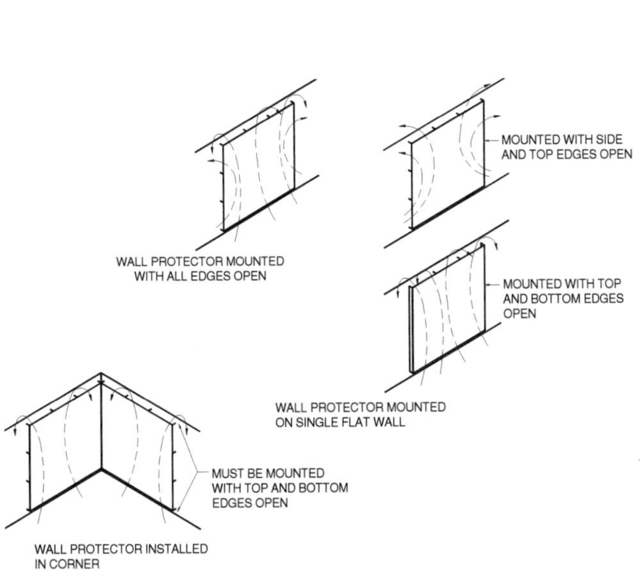

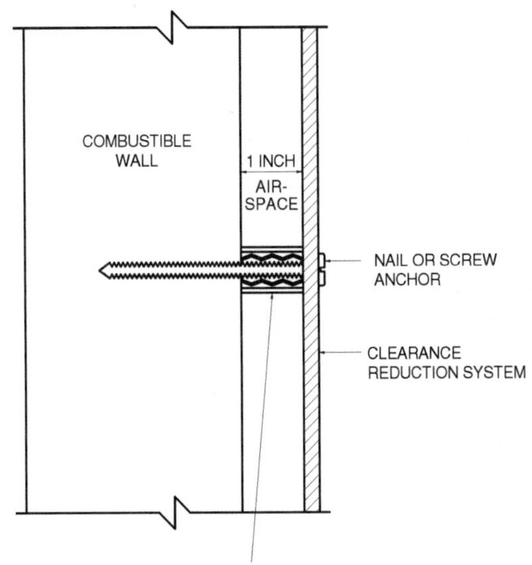

1-INCH NONCOMBUSTIBLE SPACER SUCH AS STACKED WASHERS, SMALL-DIAMETER PIPE, TUBING OR ELECTRICAL CONDUIT.

MASONRY WALLS CAN BE ATTACHED TO COMBUSTIBLE WALLS USING WALL TIES.

DO NOT USE SPACERS DIRECTLY BEHIND APPLIANCE OR CONNECTOR.

For SI: 1 inch = 25.4 mm.

FIGURE 308.2(2)
WALL PROTECTOR CLEARANCE REDUCTION SYSTEM

CHAPTER 4
GAS PIPING INSTALLATIONS

SECTION 401 (IFGC) GENERAL

401.1 Scope. This chapter and Appendix A shall govern the design, installation, modification and maintenance of *piping* systems. The applicability of this code to *piping* systems extends from the *point of delivery* to the connections with the appliances and includes the design, materials, components, fabrication, assembly, installation, testing, inspection, operation and maintenance of such *piping* systems.

401.1.1 Utility piping systems located within buildings. Utility service *piping* located within buildings shall be installed in accordance with the structural safety and fire protection provisions of the *International Building Code.*

401.2 Liquefied petroleum gas storage. The enforcement of the location of undiluted liquefied petroleum gas containers shall be the responsibility of the North Carolina Department of Agriculture and Consumer Services in accordance with Article 5 of Chapter 119 of the General Statutes.

401.3 Modifications to existing systems. In modifying or adding to existing *piping* systems, sizes shall be maintained in accordance with this chapter.

401.4 Additional appliances. Where an additional *appliance* is to be served, the existing *piping* shall be checked to determine if it has adequate capacity for all appliances served. If inadequate, the existing system shall be enlarged as required or separate *piping* of adequate capacity shall be provided.

401.5 Identification. Exposed *piping* shall be identified by a yellow label marked "Gas" in black letters. The marking shall be spaced at intervals not exceeding 5 feet (1524 mm). All piping and tubing systems, greater than 0.5-pounds per square inch (3.45 kPa) service pressure, shall be identified by a yellow label with black letters indicating the piping system pressure. The system shall be marked at the beginning, all ends and at intervals not exceeding 5 feet (1524 mm) along its exposed length.

Exceptions:

1. Gas lines extending from the undiluted liquefied petroleum gas storage tanks to the building are not required to be labeled.
2. Black steel piping, 0.5-pounds per square inch (3.45 kPa) or less, located at dwelling units shall not be required to be labeled.

401.6 Interconnections. Where two or more meters are installed on the same premises but supply separate consumers, the *piping* systems shall not be interconnected on the *outlet* side of the meters.

401.7 Piping meter identification. *Piping* from multiple meter installations shall be marked with an *approved* permanent identification by the installer so that the *piping* system supplied by each meter is readily identifiable.

401.8 Minimum sizes. All pipe utilized for the installation, extension and *alteration* of any *piping* system shall be sized to supply the full number of *outlets* for the intended purpose and shall be sized in accordance with Section 402.

401.9 Meter location. When required, a meter shall be provided for the building or residence to be served. The location shall be such that the meter can be read, serviced or changed. The location, space requirements, dimensions and proper clearances shall be acceptable to the local gas company.

SECTION 402 (IFGS) PIPE SIZING

402.1 General considerations. Piping systems shall be of such size and so installed as to provide a supply of gas sufficient to meet the maximum demand and supply gas to each *appliance* inlet at not less than the minimum supply pressure required by the *appliance.*

402.2 Maximum gas demand. The volume of gas to be provided, in cubic feet per hour, shall be determined directly from the manufacturer's input ratings of the appliances served. Where an input rating is not indicated, the gas supplier, *appliance* manufacturer or a qualified agency shall be contacted, or the rating from Table 402.2 shall be used for estimating the volume of gas to be supplied.

The total connected hourly load shall be used as the basis for pipe sizing, assuming that all appliances could be operating at full capacity simultaneously. Where a diversity of load can be established, pipe sizing shall be permitted to be based on such loads.

402.3 Sizing. Gas *piping* shall be sized in accordance with one of the following:

1. Pipe sizing tables or sizing equations in accordance with Section 402.4.
2. The sizing tables included in a *listed piping* system's manufacturer's installation instructions.
3. Other *approved* engineering methods.

402.4 Sizing tables and equations. Where Tables 402.4(1) through 402.4(35) are used to size *piping* or tubing, the pipe length shall be determined in accordance with Section 402.4.1, 402.4.2 or 402.4.3.

Where Equations 4-1 and 4-2 are used to size *piping* or tubing, the pipe or tubing shall have smooth inside walls and the pipe length shall be determined in accordance with Section 402.4.1, 402.4.2 or 402.4.3.

1. Low-pressure gas equation [Less than $1^1/_2$ pounds per square inch (psi) (10.3 kPa)]:

$$D = \frac{Q^{0.381}}{19.17\left(\frac{\Delta H}{C_r \times L}\right)^{0.206}} \quad \textbf{(Equation 4-1)}$$

2. High-pressure gas equation [$1^1/_2$ psi (10.3 kPa) and above]:

$$D = \frac{Q^{0.381}}{18.93 \left[\frac{\left(P_1^2 - P_2^2\right) \times Y}{C_r \times L} \right]^{0.206}} \quad \textbf{(Equation 4-2)}$$

where:

D = Inside diameter of pipe, inches (mm).

Q = Input rate *appliance*(s), cubic feet per hour at 60°F (16°C) and 30-inch mercury column.

P_1 = Upstream pressure, psia (P_1 + 14.7).

P_2 = Downstream pressure, psia (P_2 + 14.7).

L = Equivalent length of pipe, feet.

ΔH = Pressure drop, inch water column (27.7 inch water column = 1 psi).

TABLE 402.2
APPROXIMATE GAS INPUT FOR TYPICAL APPLIANCES

APPLIANCE	INPUT BTU/H (Approx.)
Space Heating Units	
Hydronic boiler	
Single family	100,000
Multifamily, per unit	60,000
Warm-air furnace	
Single family	100,000
Multifamily, per unit	60,000
Space and Water Heating Units	
Hydronic boiler	
Single family	120,000
Multifamily, per unit	75,000
Water Heating Appliances	
Water heater, automatic instantaneous	
Capacity at 2 gal./minute	142,800
Capacity at 4 gal./minute	285,000
Capacity at 6 gal./minute	428,400
Water heater, automatic storage, 30- to 40-gal. tank	35,000
Water heater, automatic storage, 50-gal. tank	50,000
Water heater, domestic, circulating or side-arm	35,000
Cooking Appliances	
Built-in oven or broiler unit, domestic	25,000
Built-in top unit, domestic	40,000
Range, free-standing, domestic	65,000
Other Appliances	
Barbecue	40,000
Clothes dryer, Type 1 (domestic)	35,000
Gas fireplace, direct-vent	40,000
Gas light	2,500
Gas log	80,000
Refrigerator	3,000

For SI: 1 British thermal unit per hour = 0.293 W, 1 gallon = 3.785 L, 1 gallon per minute = 3.785 L/m.

TABLE 402.4
C_r AND Y VALUES FOR NATURAL GAS AND UNDILUTED PROPANE AT STANDARD CONDITIONS

GAS	EQUATION FACTORS	
	C_r	Y
Natural gas	0.6094	0.9992
Undiluted propane	1.2462	0.9910

For SI: 1 cubic foot = 0.028 m³, 1 foot = 305 mm, 1-inch water column = 0.2488 kPa, 1 pound per square inch = 6.895 kPa, 1 British thermal unit per hour = 0.293 W.

TABLE 402.4(1)
SCHEDULE 40 METALLIC PIPE
Deleted

TABLE 402.4(4)
SCHEDULE 40 METALLIC PIPE
Deleted

TABLE 402.4(6)
SEMIRIGID COPPER TUBING
Deleted

TABLE 402.4(9)
SEMIRIGID COPPER TUBING
Deleted

TABLE 402.4(11)
SEMIRIGID COPPER TUBING
Deleted

TABLE 402.4(14)
CORRUGATED STAINLESS STEEL TUBING (CSST)
Deleted

TABLE 402.4(15)
CORRUGATED STAINLESS STEEL TUBING (CSST)
Deleted

TABLE 402.4(18)
POLYETHYLENE PLASTIC PIPE
Deleted

TABLE 402.4(21)
POLYETHYLENE PLASTIC TUBING
Deleted

402.4.1 Longest length method. The pipe size of each section of gas *piping* shall be determined using the longest length of *piping* from the *point of delivery* to the most remote *outlet* and the load of the section.

402.4.2 Branch length method. Pipe shall be sized as follows:

1. Pipe size of each section of the longest pipe run from the *point of delivery* to the most remote *outlet* shall be determined using the longest run of *piping* and the load of the section.
2. The pipe size of each section of branch *piping* not previously sized shall be determined using the length of *piping* from the *point of delivery* to the most remote *outlet* in each branch and the load of the section.

402.4.3 Hybrid pressure. The pipe size for each section of higher pressure gas *piping* shall be determined using the longest length of *piping* from the *point of delivery* to the most remote line pressure regulator. The pipe size from the line pressure regulator to each *outlet* shall be determined using the length of *piping* from the regulator to the most remote *outlet* served by the regulator.

Gas	Natural
Inlet Pressure	Less than 2 psi
Pressure Drop	0.5 in. w.c.
Specific Gravity	0.60

TABLE 402.4(2)
SCHEDULE 40 METALLIC PIPE

	PIPE SIZE (inch)													
Nominal	1/2	3/4	1	1 1/4	1 1/2	2	2 1/2	3	4	5	6	8	10	12
Actual ID	0.622	0.824	1.049	1.380	1.610	2.067	2.469	3.068	4.026	5.047	6.065	7.981	10.020	11.938
Length (ft)	Capacity in Cubic Feet of Gas Per Hour													
10	172	360	678	1,390	2,090	4,020	6,400	11,300	23,100	41,800	67,600	139,000	252,000	399,000
20	118	247	466	957	1,430	2,760	4,400	7,780	15,900	28,700	46,500	95,500	173,000	275,000
30	95	199	374	768	1,150	2,220	3,530	6,250	12,700	23,000	37,300	76,700	139,000	220,000
40	81	170	320	657	985	1,900	3,020	5,350	10,900	19,700	31,900	65,600	119,000	189,000
50	72	151	284	583	873	1,680	2,680	4,740	9,660	17,500	28,300	58,200	106,000	167,000
60	65	137	257	528	791	1,520	2,430	4,290	8,760	15,800	25,600	52,700	95,700	152,000
70	60	126	237	486	728	1,400	2,230	3,950	8,050	14,600	23,600	48,500	88,100	139,000
80	56	117	220	452	677	1,300	2,080	3,670	7,490	13,600	22,000	45,100	81,900	130,000
90	52	110	207	424	635	1,220	1,950	3,450	7,030	12,700	20,600	42,300	76,900	122,000
100	50	104	195	400	600	1,160	1,840	3,260	6,640	12,000	19,500	40,000	72,600	115,000
125	44	92	173	355	532	1,020	1,630	2,890	5,890	10,600	17,200	35,400	64,300	102,000
150	40	83	157	322	482	928	1,480	2,610	5,330	9,650	15,600	32,100	58,300	92,300
175	37	77	144	296	443	854	1,360	2,410	4,910	8,880	14,400	29,500	53,600	84,900
200	34	71	134	275	412	794	1,270	2,240	4,560	8,260	13,400	27,500	49,900	79,000
250	30	63	119	244	366	704	1,120	1,980	4,050	7,320	11,900	24,300	44,200	70,000
300	27	57	108	221	331	638	1,020	1,800	3,670	6,630	10,700	22,100	40,100	63,400
350	25	53	99	203	305	587	935	1,650	3,370	6,100	9,880	20,300	36,900	58,400
400	23	49	92	189	283	546	870	1,540	3,140	5,680	9,190	18,900	34,300	54,300
450	22	46	86	177	266	512	816	1,440	2,940	5,330	8,620	17,700	32,200	50,900
500	21	43	82	168	251	484	771	1,360	2,780	5,030	8,150	16,700	30,400	48,100
550	20	41	78	159	239	459	732	1,290	2,640	4,780	7,740	15,900	28,900	45,700
600	19	39	74	152	228	438	699	1,240	2,520	4,560	7,380	15,200	27,500	43,600
650	18	38	71	145	218	420	669	1,180	2,410	4,360	7,070	14,500	26,400	41,800
700	17	36	68	140	209	403	643	1,140	2,320	4,190	6,790	14,000	25,300	40,100
750	17	35	66	135	202	389	619	1,090	2,230	4,040	6,540	13,400	24,400	38,600
800	16	34	63	130	195	375	598	1,060	2,160	3,900	6,320	13,000	23,600	37,300
850	16	33	61	126	189	363	579	1,020	2,090	3,780	6,110	12,600	22,800	36,100
900	15	32	59	122	183	352	561	992	2,020	3,660	5,930	12,200	22,100	35,000
950	15	31	58	118	178	342	545	963	1,960	3,550	5,760	11,800	21,500	34,000
1,000	14	30	56	115	173	333	530	937	1,910	3,460	5,600	11,500	20,900	33,100
1,100	14	28	53	109	164	316	503	890	1,810	3,280	5,320	10,900	19,800	31,400
1,200	13	27	51	104	156	301	480	849	1,730	3,130	5,070	10,400	18,900	30,000
1,300	12	26	49	100	150	289	460	813	1,660	3,000	4,860	9,980	18,100	28,700
1,400	12	25	47	96	144	277	442	781	1,590	2,880	4,670	9,590	17,400	27,600
1,500	11	24	45	93	139	267	426	752	1,530	2,780	4,500	9,240	16,800	26,600
1,600	11	23	44	89	134	258	411	727	1,480	2,680	4,340	8,920	16,200	25,600
1,700	11	22	42	86	130	250	398	703	1,430	2,590	4,200	8,630	15,700	24,800
1,800	10	22	41	84	126	242	386	682	1,390	2,520	4,070	8,370	15,200	24,100
1,900	10	21	40	81	122	235	375	662	1,350	2,440	3,960	8,130	14,800	23,400
2,000	NA	20	39	79	119	229	364	644	1,310	2,380	3,850	7,910	14,400	22,700

For SI: 1 inch = 25.4 mm, 1 foot = 304.8 mm, 1 pound per square inch = 6.895 kPa, 1-inch water column = 0.2488 kPa, 1 British thermal unit per hour = 0.2931 W, 1 cubic foot per hour = 0.0283 m^3/h, 1 degree = 0.01745 rad.

Notes:

1. NA means a flow of less than 10 cfh.
2. All table entries have been rounded to three significant digits.

Gas	Natural
Inlet Pressure	2.0 psi
Pressure Drop	1.0 psi
Specific Gravity	0.60

TABLE 402.4(3)
SCHEDULE 40 METALLIC PIPE

	PIPE SIZE (inch)								
Nominal	$^1/_2$	$^3/_4$	1	$1^1/_4$	$1^1/_2$	2	$2^1/_2$	3	4
Actual ID	0.622	0.824	1.049	1.380	1.610	2.067	2.469	3.068	4.026
Length (ft)	Capacity in Cubic Feet of Gas Per Hour								
10	1,510	3,040	5,560	11,400	17,100	32,900	52,500	92,800	189,000
20	1,070	2,150	3,930	8,070	12,100	23,300	37,100	65,600	134,000
30	869	1,760	3,210	6,590	9,880	19,000	30,300	53,600	109,000
40	753	1,520	2,780	5,710	8,550	16,500	26,300	46,400	94,700
50	673	1,360	2,490	5,110	7,650	14,700	23,500	41,500	84,700
60	615	1,240	2,270	4,660	6,980	13,500	21,400	37,900	77,300
70	569	1,150	2,100	4,320	6,470	12,500	19,900	35,100	71,600
80	532	1,080	1,970	4,040	6,050	11,700	18,600	32,800	67,000
90	502	1,010	1,850	3,810	5,700	11,000	17,500	30,900	63,100
100	462	934	1,710	3,510	5,260	10,100	16,100	28,500	58,200
125	414	836	1,530	3,140	4,700	9,060	14,400	25,500	52,100
150	372	751	1,370	2,820	4,220	8,130	13,000	22,900	46,700
175	344	695	1,270	2,601	3,910	7,530	12,000	21,200	43,300
200	318	642	1,170	2,410	3,610	6,960	11,100	19,600	40,000
250	279	583	1,040	2,140	3,210	6,180	9,850	17,400	35,500
300	253	528	945	1,940	2,910	5,600	8,920	15,800	32,200
350	232	486	869	1,790	2,670	5,150	8,210	14,500	29,600
400	216	452	809	1,660	2,490	4,790	7,640	13,500	27,500
450	203	424	759	1,560	2,330	4,500	7,170	12,700	25,800
500	192	401	717	1,470	2,210	4,250	6,770	12,000	24,400
550	182	381	681	1,400	2,090	4,030	6,430	11,400	23,200
600	174	363	650	1,330	2,000	3,850	6,130	10,800	22,100
650	166	348	622	1,280	1,910	3,680	5,870	10,400	21,200
700	160	334	598	1,230	1,840	3,540	5,640	9,970	20,300
750	154	322	576	1,180	1,770	3,410	5,440	9,610	19,600
800	149	311	556	1,140	1,710	3,290	5,250	9,280	18,900
850	144	301	538	1,100	1,650	3,190	5,080	8,980	18,300
900	139	292	522	1,070	1,600	3,090	4,930	8,710	17,800
950	135	283	507	1,040	1,560	3,000	4,780	8,460	17,200
1,000	132	275	493	1,010	1,520	2,920	4,650	8,220	16,800
1,100	125	262	468	960	1,440	2,770	4,420	7,810	15,900
1,200	119	250	446	917	1,370	2,640	4,220	7,450	15,200
1,300	114	239	427	878	1,320	2,530	4,040	7,140	14,600
1,400	110	230	411	843	1,260	2,430	3,880	6,860	14,000
1,500	106	221	396	812	1,220	2,340	3,740	6,600	13,500
1,600	102	214	382	784	1,180	2,260	3,610	6,380	13,000
1,700	99	207	370	759	1,140	2,190	3,490	6,170	12,600
1,800	96	200	358	736	1,100	2,120	3,390	5,980	12,200
1,900	93	195	348	715	1,070	2,060	3,290	5,810	11,900
2,000	91	189	339	695	1,040	2,010	3,200	5,650	11,500

For SI: 1 inch = 25.4 mm, 1 foot = 304.8 mm, 1 pound per square inch = 6.895 kPa, 1-inch water column = 0.2488 kPa, 1 British thermal unit per hour = 0.2931 W, 1 cubic foot per hour = 0.0283 m^3/h, 1 degree = 0.01745 rad.

Note: All table entries have been rounded to three significant digits.

Gas	Natural
Inlet Pressure	5.0 psi
Pressure Drop	3.5 psi
Specific Gravity	0.60

TABLE 402.4(5)
SCHEDULE 40 METALLIC PIPE

	PIPE SIZE (inch)								
Nominal	$^1/_2$	$^3/_4$	1	$1^1/_4$	$1^1/_2$	2	$2^1/_2$	3	4
Actual ID	0.622	0.824	1.049	1.380	1.610	2.067	2.469	3.068	4.026
Length (ft)	**Capacity in Cubic Feet of Gas Per Hour**								
10	3,190	6,430	11,800	24,200	36,200	69,700	111,000	196,000	401,000
20	2,250	4,550	8,320	17,100	25,600	49,300	78,600	139,000	283,000
30	1,840	3,720	6,790	14,000	20,900	40,300	64,200	113,000	231,000
40	1,590	3,220	5,880	12,100	18,100	34,900	55,600	98,200	200,000
50	1,430	2,880	5,260	10,800	16,200	31,200	49,700	87,900	179,000
60	1,300	2,630	4,800	9,860	14,800	28,500	45,400	80,200	164,000
70	1,200	2,430	4,450	9,130	13,700	26,400	42,000	74,300	151,000
80	1,150	2,330	4,260	8,540	12,800	24,700	39,300	69,500	142,000
90	1,060	2,150	3,920	8,050	12,100	23,200	37,000	65,500	134,000
100	979	1,980	3,620	7,430	11,100	21,400	34,200	60,400	123,000
125	876	1,770	3,240	6,640	9,950	19,200	30,600	54,000	110,000
150	786	1,590	2,910	5,960	8,940	17,200	27,400	48,500	98,900
175	728	1,470	2,690	5,520	8,270	15,900	25,400	44,900	91,600
200	673	1,360	2,490	5,100	7,650	14,700	23,500	41,500	84,700
250	558	1,170	2,200	4,510	6,760	13,000	20,800	36,700	74,900
300	506	1,060	1,990	4,090	6,130	11,800	18,800	33,300	67,800
350	465	973	1,830	3,760	5,640	10,900	17,300	30,600	62,400
400	433	905	1,710	3,500	5,250	10,100	16,100	28,500	58,100
450	406	849	1,600	3,290	4,920	9,480	15,100	26,700	54,500
500	384	802	1,510	3,100	4,650	8,950	14,300	25,200	51,500
550	364	762	1,440	2,950	4,420	8,500	13,600	24,000	48,900
600	348	727	1,370	2,810	4,210	8,110	12,900	22,900	46,600
650	333	696	1,310	2,690	4,030	7,770	12,400	21,900	44,600
700	320	669	1,260	2,590	3,880	7,460	11,900	21,000	42,900
750	308	644	1,210	2,490	3,730	7,190	11,500	20,300	41,300
800	298	622	1,170	2,410	3,610	6,940	11,100	19,600	39,900
850	288	602	1,130	2,330	3,490	6,720	10,700	18,900	38,600
900	279	584	1,100	2,260	3,380	6,520	10,400	18,400	37,400
950	271	567	1,070	2,190	3,290	6,330	10,100	17,800	36,400
1,000	264	551	1,040	2,130	3,200	6,150	9,810	17,300	35,400
1,100	250	524	987	2,030	3,030	5,840	9,320	16,500	33,600
1,200	239	500	941	1,930	2,900	5,580	8,890	15,700	32,000
1,300	229	478	901	1,850	2,770	5,340	8,510	15,000	30,700
1,400	220	460	866	1,780	2,660	5,130	8,180	14,500	29,500
1,500	212	443	834	1,710	2,570	4,940	7,880	13,900	28,400
1,600	205	428	806	1,650	2,480	4,770	7,610	13,400	27,400
1,700	198	414	780	1,600	2,400	4,620	7,360	13,000	26,500
1,800	192	401	756	1,550	2,330	4,480	7,140	12,600	25,700
1,900	186	390	734	1,510	2,260	4,350	6,930	12,300	25,000
2,000	181	379	714	1,470	2,200	4,230	6,740	11,900	24,300

For SI: 1 inch = 25.4 mm, 1 foot = 304.8 mm, 1 pound per square inch = 6.895 kPa, 1-inch water column = 0.2488 kPa, 1 British thermal unit per hour = 0.2931 W, 1 cubic foot per hour = 0.0283 m^3/h, 1 degree = 0.01745 rad.

Note: All table entries have been rounded to three significant digits.

TABLE 402.4(7)
SEMIRIGID COPPER TUBING

Gas	Natural
Inlet Pressure	Less than 2 psi
Pressure Drop	0.5 in. w.c.
Specific Gravity	0.60

		TUBE SIZE (inch)								
Nominal	K & L	1/4	3/8	1/2	5/8	3/4	1	1 1/4	1 1/2	2
	ACR	3/8	1/2	5/8	3/4	7/8	1 1/8	1 3/8	—	—
Outside		0.375	0.500	0.625	0.750	0.875	1.125	1.375	1.625	2.125
Inside		0.305	0.402	0.527	0.652	0.745	0.995	1.245	1.481	1.959
Length (ft)		Capacity in Cubic Feet of Gas Per Hour								
10		27	55	111	195	276	590	1,060	1,680	3,490
20		18	38	77	134	190	406	730	1,150	2,400
30		15	30	61	107	152	326	586	925	1,930
40		13	26	53	92	131	279	502	791	1,650
50		11	23	47	82	116	247	445	701	1,460
60		10	21	42	74	105	224	403	635	1,320
70		NA	19	39	68	96	206	371	585	1,220
80		NA	18	36	63	90	192	345	544	1,130
90		NA	17	34	59	84	180	324	510	1,060
100		NA	16	32	56	79	170	306	482	1,000
125		NA	14	28	50	70	151	271	427	890
150		NA	13	26	45	64	136	245	387	806
175		NA	12	24	41	59	125	226	356	742
200		NA	11	22	39	55	117	210	331	690
250		NA	NA	20	34	48	103	186	294	612
300		NA	NA	18	31	44	94	169	266	554
350		NA	NA	16	28	40	86	155	245	510
400		NA	NA	15	26	38	80	144	228	474
450		NA	NA	14	25	35	75	135	214	445
500		NA	NA	13	23	33	71	128	202	420
550		NA	NA	13	22	32	68	122	192	399
600		NA	NA	12	21	30	64	116	183	381
650		NA	NA	12	20	29	62	111	175	365
700		NA	NA	11	20	28	59	107	168	350
750		NA	NA	11	19	27	57	103	162	338
800		NA	NA	10	18	26	55	99	156	326
850		NA	NA	10	18	25	53	96	151	315
900		NA	NA	NA	17	24	52	93	147	306
950		NA	NA	NA	17	24	50	90	143	297
1,000		NA	NA	NA	16	23	49	88	139	289
1,100		NA	NA	NA	15	22	46	84	132	274
1,200		NA	NA	NA	15	21	44	80	126	262
1,300		NA	NA	NA	14	20	42	76	120	251
1,400		NA	NA	NA	13	19	41	73	116	241
1,500		NA	NA	NA	13	18	39	71	111	232
1,600		NA	NA	NA	13	18	38	68	108	224
1,700		NA	NA	NA	12	17	37	66	104	217
1,800		NA	NA	NA	12	17	36	64	101	210
1,900		NA	NA	NA	11	16	35	62	98	204
2,000		NA	NA	NA	11	16	34	60	95	199

For SI: 1 inch = 25.4 mm, 1 foot = 304.8 mm, 1 pound per square inch = 6.895kPa, 1-inch water column = 0.2488 kPa, 1 British thermal unit per hour = 0.2931 W, 1 cubic foot per hour = 0.0283 m^3/h, 1 degree = 0.01745 rad.

Notes:

1. Table capacities are based on Type K copper tubing inside diameter (shown), which has the smallest inside diameter of the copper tubing products.
2. NA means a flow of less than 10 cfh.
3. All table entries have been rounded to three significant digits.

Gas	Natural
Inlet Pressure	Less than 2 psi
Pressure Drop	1.0 in. w.c.
Specific Gravity	0.60

TABLE 402.4(8)
SEMIRIGID COPPER TUBING

INTENDED USE: SIZING BETWEEN HOUSE LINE REGULATOR AND THE APPLIANCE										
		TUBE SIZE (inch)								
Nominal	K & L	1/4	3/8	1/2	5/8	3/4	1	1 1/4	1 1/2	2
	ACR	3/8	1/2	5/8	3/4	7/8	1 1/8	1 3/8	—	—
Outside		0.375	0.500	0.625	0.750	0.875	1.125	1.375	1.625	2.125
Inside		0.305	0.402	0.527	0.652	0.745	0.995	1.245	1.481	1.959
Length (ft)		Capacity in Cubic Feet of Gas Per Hour								
10		39	80	162	283	402	859	1,550	2,440	5,080
20		27	55	111	195	276	590	1,060	1,680	3,490
30		21	44	89	156	222	474	853	1,350	2,800
40		18	38	77	134	190	406	730	1,150	2,400
50		16	33	68	119	168	359	647	1,020	2,130
60		15	30	61	107	152	326	586	925	1,930
70		13	28	57	99	140	300	539	851	1,770
80		13	26	53	92	131	279	502	791	1,650
90		12	24	49	86	122	262	471	742	1,550
100		11	23	47	82	116	247	445	701	1,460
125		NA	20	41	72	103	219	394	622	1,290
150		NA	18	37	65	93	198	357	563	1,170
175		NA	17	34	60	85	183	329	518	1,080
200		NA	16	32	56	79	170	306	482	1,000
250		NA	14	28	50	70	151	271	427	890
300		NA	13	26	45	64	136	245	387	806
350		NA	12	24	41	59	125	226	356	742
400		NA	11	22	39	55	117	210	331	690
450		NA	10	21	36	51	110	197	311	647
500		NA	NA	20	34	48	103	186	294	612
550		NA	NA	19	32	46	98	177	279	581
600		NA	NA	18	31	44	94	169	266	554
650		NA	NA	17	30	42	90	162	255	531
700		NA	NA	16	28	40	86	155	245	510
750		NA	NA	16	27	39	83	150	236	491
800		NA	NA	15	26	38	80	144	228	474
850		NA	NA	15	26	36	78	140	220	459
900		NA	NA	14	25	35	75	135	214	445
950		NA	NA	14	24	34	73	132	207	432
1,000		NA	NA	13	23	33	71	128	202	420
1,100		NA	NA	13	22	32	68	122	192	399
1,200		NA	NA	12	21	30	64	116	183	381
1,300		NA	NA	12	20	29	62	111	175	365
1,400		NA	NA	11	20	28	59	107	168	350
1,500		NA	NA	11	19	27	57	103	162	338
1,600		NA	NA	10	18	26	55	99	156	326
1,700		NA	NA	10	18	25	53	96	151	315
1,800		NA	NA	NA	17	24	52	93	147	306
1,900		NA	NA	NA	17	24	50	90	143	297
2,000		NA	NA	NA	16	23	49	88	139	289

For SI: 1 inch = 25.4 mm, 1 foot = 304.8 mm, 1 pound per square inch = 6.895 kPa, 1-inch water column = 0.2488 kPa, 1 British thermal unit per hour = 0.2931 W, 1 cubic foot per hour = 0.0283 m^3/h, 1 degree = 0.01745 rad.

Notes:

1. Table capacities are based on Type K copper tubing inside diameter (shown), which has the smallest inside diameter of the copper tubing products.
2. NA means a flow of less than 10 cfh.
3. All table entries have been rounded to three significant digits.

Gas	Natural
Inlet Pressure	2.0 psi
Pressure Drop	1.0 psi
Specific Gravity	0.60

TABLE 402.4(10)
SEMIRIGID COPPER TUBING

		TUBE SIZE (inch)								
Nominal	K & L	1/4	3/8	1/2	5/8	3/4	1	1 1/4	1 1/2	2
	ACR	3/8	1/2	5/8	3/4	7/8	1 1/8	1 3/8	—	—
Outside		0.375	0.500	0.625	0.750	0.875	1.125	1.375	1.625	2.125
Inside		0.305	0.402	0.527	0.652	0.745	0.995	1.245	1.481	1.959
Length (ft)		Capacity in Cubic Feet of Gas Per Hour								
10		245	506	1,030	1,800	2,550	5,450	9,820	15,500	32,200
20		169	348	708	1,240	1,760	3,750	6,750	10,600	22,200
30		135	279	568	993	1,410	3,010	5,420	8,550	17,800
40		116	239	486	850	1,210	2,580	4,640	7,310	15,200
50		103	212	431	754	1,070	2,280	4,110	6,480	13,500
60		93	192	391	683	969	2,070	3,730	5,870	12,200
70		86	177	359	628	891	1,900	3,430	5,400	11,300
80		80	164	334	584	829	1,770	3,190	5,030	10,500
90		75	154	314	548	778	1,660	2,990	4,720	9,820
100		71	146	296	518	735	1,570	2,830	4,450	9,280
125		63	129	263	459	651	1,390	2,500	3,950	8,220
150		57	117	238	416	590	1,260	2,270	3,580	7,450
175		52	108	219	383	543	1,160	2,090	3,290	6,850
200		49	100	204	356	505	1,080	1,940	3,060	6,380
250		43	89	181	315	448	956	1,720	2,710	5,650
300		39	80	164	286	406	866	1,560	2,460	5,120
350		36	74	150	263	373	797	1,430	2,260	4,710
400		33	69	140	245	347	741	1,330	2,100	4,380
450		31	65	131	230	326	696	1,250	1,970	4,110
500		30	61	124	217	308	657	1,180	1,870	3,880
550		28	58	118	206	292	624	1,120	1,770	3,690
600		27	55	112	196	279	595	1,070	1,690	3,520
650		26	53	108	188	267	570	1,030	1,620	3,370
700		25	51	103	181	256	548	986	1,550	3,240
750		24	49	100	174	247	528	950	1,500	3,120
800		23	47	96	168	239	510	917	1,450	3,010
850		22	46	93	163	231	493	888	1,400	2,920
900		22	44	90	158	224	478	861	1,360	2,830
950		21	43	88	153	217	464	836	1,320	2,740
1,000		20	42	85	149	211	452	813	1,280	2,670
1,100		19	40	81	142	201	429	772	1,220	2,540
1,200		18	38	77	135	192	409	737	1,160	2,420
1,300		18	36	74	129	183	392	705	1,110	2,320
1,400		17	35	71	124	176	376	678	1,070	2,230
1,500		16	34	68	120	170	363	653	1,030	2,140
1,600		16	33	66	116	164	350	630	994	2,070
1,700		15	31	64	112	159	339	610	962	2,000
1,800		15	30	62	108	154	329	592	933	1,940
1,900		14	30	60	105	149	319	575	906	1,890
2,000		14	29	59	102	145	310	559	881	1,830

For SI: 1 inch = 25.4 mm, 1 foot = 304.8 mm, 1 pound per square inch = 6.895kPa, 1-inch water column = 0.2488 kPa, 1 British thermal unit per hour = 0.2931 W, 1 cubic foot per hour = 0.0283 m^3/h, 1 degree = 0.01745 rad.

Notes:

1. Table capacities are based on Type K copper tubing inside diameter (shown), which has the smallest inside diameter of the copper tubing products.
2. All table entries have been rounded to three significant digits.

TABLE 402.4(12) SEMIRIGID COPPER TUBING

Gas	Natural
Inlet Pressure	5.0 psi
Pressure Drop	3.5 psi
Specific Gravity	0.60

		TUBE SIZE (inch)								
Nominal	K & L	1/4	3/8	1/2	5/8	3/4	1	1 1/4	1 1/2	2
	ACR	3/8	1/2	5/8	3/4	7/8	1 1/8	1 3/8	—	—
Outside		0.375	0.500	0.625	0.750	0.875	1.125	1.375	1.625	2.125
Inside		0.305	0.402	0.527	0.652	0.745	0.995	1.245	1.481	1.959
Length (ft)		Capacity in Cubic Feet of Gas Per Hour								
10		511	1,050	2,140	3,750	5,320	11,400	20,400	32,200	67,100
20		351	724	1,470	2,580	3,650	7,800	14,000	22,200	46,100
30		282	582	1,180	2,070	2,930	6,270	11,300	17,800	37,000
40		241	498	1,010	1,770	2,510	5,360	9,660	15,200	31,700
50		214	441	898	1,570	2,230	4,750	8,560	13,500	28,100
60		194	400	813	1,420	2,020	4,310	7,750	12,200	25,500
70		178	368	748	1,310	1,860	3,960	7,130	11,200	23,400
80		166	342	696	1,220	1,730	3,690	6,640	10,500	21,800
90		156	321	653	1,140	1,620	3,460	6,230	9,820	20,400
100		147	303	617	1,080	1,530	3,270	5,880	9,270	19,300
125		130	269	547	955	1,360	2,900	5,210	8,220	17,100
150		118	243	495	866	1,230	2,620	4,720	7,450	15,500
175		109	224	456	796	1,130	2,410	4,350	6,850	14,300
200		101	208	424	741	1,050	2,250	4,040	6,370	13,300
250		90	185	376	657	932	1,990	3,580	5,650	11,800
300		81	167	340	595	844	1,800	3,250	5,120	10,700
350		75	154	313	547	777	1,660	2,990	4,710	9,810
400		69	143	291	509	722	1,540	2,780	4,380	9,120
450		65	134	273	478	678	1,450	2,610	4,110	8,560
500		62	127	258	451	640	1,370	2,460	3,880	8,090
550		58	121	245	429	608	1,300	2,340	3,690	7,680
600		56	115	234	409	580	1,240	2,230	3,520	7,330
650		53	110	224	392	556	1,190	2,140	3,370	7,020
700		51	106	215	376	534	1,140	2,050	3,240	6,740
750		49	102	207	362	514	1,100	1,980	3,120	6,490
800		48	98	200	350	497	1,060	1,910	3,010	6,270
850		46	95	194	339	481	1,030	1,850	2,910	6,070
900		45	92	188	328	466	1,000	1,790	2,820	5,880
950		43	90	182	319	452	967	1,740	2,740	5,710
1,000		42	87	177	310	440	940	1,690	2,670	5,560
1,100		40	83	169	295	418	893	1,610	2,530	5,280
1,200		38	79	161	281	399	852	1,530	2,420	5,040
1,300		37	76	154	269	382	816	1,470	2,320	4,820
1,400		35	73	148	259	367	784	1,410	2,220	4,630
1,500		34	70	143	249	353	755	1,360	2,140	4,460
1,600		33	68	138	241	341	729	1,310	2,070	4,310
1,700		32	65	133	233	330	705	1,270	2,000	4,170
1,800		31	63	129	226	320	684	1,230	1,940	4,040
1,900		30	62	125	219	311	664	1,200	1,890	3,930
2,000		29	60	122	213	302	646	1,160	1,830	3,820

For SI: 1 inch = 25.4 mm, 1 foot = 304.8 mm, 1 pound per square inch = 6.895 kPa, 1-inch water column = 0.2488 kPa, 1 British thermal unit per hour = 0.2931 W, 1 cubic foot per hour = 0.0283 m^3/h, 1 degree = 0.01745 rad.

Notes:

1. Table capacities are based on Type K copper tubing inside diameter (shown), which has the smallest inside diameter of the copper tubing products.
2. All table entries have been rounded to three significant digits.

Gas	Natural
Inlet Pressure	Less than 2 psi
Pressure Drop	0.5 in. w.c.
Specific Gravity	0.60

TABLE 402.4(13)
CORRUGATED STAINLESS STEEL TUBING (CSST)

	TUBE SIZE (EHD)													
Flow Designation	13	15	18	19	23	25	30	31	37	39	46	48	60	62
Length (ft)	Capacity in Cubic Feet of Gas Per Hour													
5	46	63	115	134	225	270	471	546	895	1,037	1,790	2,070	3,660	4,140
10	32	44	82	95	161	192	330	383	639	746	1,260	1,470	2,600	2,930
15	25	35	66	77	132	157	267	310	524	615	1,030	1,200	2,140	2,400
20	22	31	58	67	116	137	231	269	456	536	888	1,050	1,850	2,080
25	19	27	52	60	104	122	206	240	409	482	793	936	1,660	1,860
30	18	25	47	55	96	112	188	218	374	442	723	856	1,520	1,700
40	15	21	41	47	83	97	162	188	325	386	625	742	1,320	1,470
50	13	19	37	42	75	87	144	168	292	347	559	665	1,180	1,320
60	12	17	34	38	68	80	131	153	267	318	509	608	1,080	1,200
70	11	16	31	36	63	74	121	141	248	295	471	563	1,000	1,110
80	10	15	29	33	60	69	113	132	232	277	440	527	940	1,040
90	10	14	28	32	57	65	107	125	219	262	415	498	887	983
100	9	13	26	30	54	62	101	118	208	249	393	472	843	933
150	7	10	20	23	42	48	78	91	171	205	320	387	691	762
200	6	9	18	21	38	44	71	82	148	179	277	336	600	661
250	5	8	16	19	34	39	63	74	133	161	247	301	538	591
300	5	7	15	17	32	36	57	67	95	148	226	275	492	540

For SI: 1 inch = 25.4 mm, 1 foot = 304.8 mm, 1 pound per square inch = 6.895kPa, 1-inch water column = 0.2488 kPa, 1 British thermal unit per hour = 0.2931 W, 1 cubic foot per hour = 0.0283 m^3/h, 1 degree = 0.01745 rad.

Notes:

1. Table includes losses for four 90-degree bends and two end fittings. Tubing runs with larger numbers of bends and/or fittings shall be increased by an equivalent length of tubing to the following equation: $L = 1.3n$, where L is additional length (feet) of tubing and n is the number of additional fittings and/or bends.
2. EHD—Equivalent Hydraulic Diameter, which is a measure of the relative hydraulic efficiency between different tubing sizes. The greater the value of EHD, the greater the gas capacity of the tubing.
3. All table entries have been rounded to three significant digits.

TABLE 402.4(16)
CORRUGATED STAINLESS STEEL TUBING (CSST)

Gas	Natural
Inlet Pressure	2.0 psi
Pressure Drop	1.0 psi
Specific Gravity	0.60

	TUBE SIZE (EHD)													
Flow Designation	13	15	18	19	23	25	30	31	37	39	46	48	60	62
Length (ft)	Capacity in Cubic Feet of Gas Per Hour													
10	270	353	587	700	1,100	1,370	2,590	2,990	4,510	5,037	9,600	10,700	18,600	21,600
25	166	220	374	444	709	876	1,620	1,870	2,890	3,258	6,040	6,780	11,900	13,700
30	151	200	342	405	650	801	1,480	1,700	2,640	2,987	5,510	6,200	10,900	12,500
40	129	172	297	351	567	696	1,270	1,470	2,300	2,605	4,760	5,380	9,440	10,900
50	115	154	266	314	510	624	1,140	1,310	2,060	2,343	4,260	4,820	8,470	9,720
75	93	124	218	257	420	512	922	1,070	1,690	1,932	3,470	3,950	6,940	7,940
80	89	120	211	249	407	496	892	1,030	1,640	1,874	3,360	3,820	6,730	7,690
100	79	107	189	222	366	445	795	920	1,470	1,685	3,000	3,420	6,030	6,880
150	64	87	155	182	302	364	646	748	1,210	1,389	2,440	2,800	4,940	5,620
200	55	75	135	157	263	317	557	645	1,050	1,212	2,110	2,430	4,290	4,870
250	49	67	121	141	236	284	497	576	941	1,090	1,890	2,180	3,850	4,360
300	44	61	110	129	217	260	453	525	862	999	1,720	1,990	3,520	3,980
400	38	52	96	111	189	225	390	453	749	871	1,490	1,730	3,060	3,450
500	34	46	86	100	170	202	348	404	552	783	1,330	1,550	2,740	3,090

For SI: 1 inch = 25.4 mm, 1 foot = 304.8 mm, 1 pound per square inch = 6.895 kPa, 1-inch water column = 0.2488 kPa, 1 British thermal unit per hour = 0.2931 W, 1 cubic foot per hour = 0.0283 m^3/h, 1 degree = 0.01745 rad.

Notes:

1. Table does not include effect of pressure drop across the line regulator. Where regulator loss exceeds $^3/_4$ psi, DO NOT USE THIS TABLE. Consult with the regulator manufacturer for pressure drops and capacity factors. Pressure drops across a regulator may vary with flow rate.
2. CAUTION: Capacities shown in the table might exceed maximum capacity for a selected regulator. Consult with the regulator or tubing manufacturer for guidance.
3. Table includes losses for four 90-degree bends and two end fittings. Tubing runs with larger numbers of bends and/or fittings shall be increased by an equivalent length of tubing to the following equation: $L = 1.3n$ where L is additional length (feet) of tubing and n is the number of additional fittings and/or bends.
4. EHD—Equivalent Hydraulic Diameter, which is a measure of the relative hydraulic efficiency between different tubing sizes. The greater the value of EHD, the greater the gas capacity of the tubing.
5. All table entries have been rounded to three significant digits.

Gas	Natural
Inlet Pressure	5.0 psi
Pressure Drop	3.5 psi
Specific Gravity	0.60

TABLE 402.4(17)
CORRUGATED STAINLESS STEEL TUBING (CSST)

	TUBE SIZE (EHD)													
Flow Designation	13	15	18	19	23	25	30	31	37	39	46	48	60	62
Length (ft)	**Capacity in Cubic Feet of Gas Per Hour**													
10	523	674	1,080	1,300	2,000	2,530	4,920	5,660	8,300	9,140	18,100	19,800	34,400	40,400
25	322	420	691	827	1,290	1,620	3,080	3,540	5,310	5,911	11,400	12,600	22,000	25,600
30	292	382	632	755	1,180	1,480	2,800	3,230	4,860	5,420	10,400	11,500	20,100	23,400
40	251	329	549	654	1,030	1,280	2,420	2,790	4,230	4,727	8,970	10,000	17,400	20,200
50	223	293	492	586	926	1,150	2,160	2,490	3,790	4,251	8,020	8,930	15,600	18,100
75	180	238	403	479	763	944	1,750	2,020	3,110	3,506	6,530	7,320	12,800	14,800
80	174	230	391	463	740	915	1,690	1,960	3,020	3,400	6,320	7,090	12,400	14,300
100	154	205	350	415	665	820	1,510	1,740	2,710	3,057	5,650	6,350	11,100	12,800
150	124	166	287	339	548	672	1,230	1,420	2,220	2,521	4,600	5,200	9,130	10,500
200	107	143	249	294	478	584	1,060	1,220	1,930	2,199	3,980	4,510	7,930	9,090
250	95	128	223	263	430	524	945	1,090	1,730	1,977	3,550	4,040	7,110	8,140
300	86	116	204	240	394	479	860	995	1,590	1,813	3,240	3,690	6,500	7,430
400	74	100	177	208	343	416	742	858	1,380	1,581	2,800	3,210	5,650	6,440
500	66	89	159	186	309	373	662	766	1,040	1,422	2,500	2,870	5,060	5,760

For SI: 1 inch = 25.4 mm, 1 foot = 304.8 mm, 1 pound per square inch = 6.895 kPa, 1-inch water column = 0.2488 kPa, 1 British thermal unit per hour = 0.2931 W, 1 cubic foot per hour = 0.0283 m^3/h, 1 degree = 0.01745 rad.

Notes:

1. Table does not include effect of pressure drop across the line regulator. Where regulator loss exceeds $^3/_4$ psi, DO NOT USE THIS TABLE. Consult with the regulator manufacturer for pressure drops and capacity factors. Pressure drops across a regulator may vary with flow rate.
2. CAUTION: Capacities shown in the table might exceed maximum capacity for a selected regulator. Consult with the regulator or tubing manufacturer for guidance.
3. Table includes losses for four 90-degree bends and two end fittings. Tubing runs with larger numbers of bends and/or fittings shall be increased by an equivalent length of tubing to the following equation: $L = 1.3n$ where L is additional length (feet) of tubing and n is the number of additional fittings and/or bends.
4. EHD—Equivalent Hydraulic Diameter, which is a measure of the relative hydraulic efficiency between different tubing sizes. The greater the value of EHD, the greater the gas capacity of the tubing.
5. All table entries have been rounded to three significant digits.

TABLE 402.4(19)
POLYETHYLENE PLASTIC PIPE

Gas	Natural
Inlet Pressure	Less than 2 psi
Pressure Drop	0.5 in. w.c.
Specific Gravity	0.60

	PIPE SIZE (inch)					
Nominal OD	$^1/_2$	$^3/_4$	1	$1^1/_4$	$1^1/_2$	2
Designation	SDR 9.33	SDR 11.0	SDR 11.00	SDR 10.00	SDR 11.00	SDR 11.00
Actual ID	0.660	0.860	1.077	1.328	1.554	1.943
Length (ft)	**Capacity in Cubic Feet of Gas per Hour**					
10	201	403	726	1,260	1,900	3,410
20	138	277	499	865	1,310	2,350
30	111	222	401	695	1,050	1,880
40	95	190	343	594	898	1,610
50	84	169	304	527	796	1,430
60	76	153	276	477	721	1,300
70	70	140	254	439	663	1,190
80	65	131	236	409	617	1,110
90	61	123	221	383	579	1,040
100	58	116	209	362	547	983
125	51	103	185	321	485	871
150	46	93	168	291	439	789
175	43	86	154	268	404	726
200	40	80	144	249	376	675
250	35	71	127	221	333	598
300	32	64	115	200	302	542
350	29	59	106	184	278	499
400	27	55	99	171	258	464
450	26	51	93	160	242	435
500	24	48	88	152	229	411

For SI: 1 inch = 25.4 mm, 1 foot = 304.8 mm, 1 pound per square inch = 6.895kPa, 1-inch water column = 0.2488 kPa, 1 British thermal unit per hour = 0.2931 W, 1 cubic foot per hour = 0.0283 m^3/h, 1 degree = 0.01745 rad.

Note: All table entries have been rounded to three significant digits.

Gas	Natural
Inlet Pressure	2.0 psi
Pressure Drop	1.0 psi
Specific Gravity	0.60

TABLE 402.4(20)
POLYETHYLENE PLASTIC PIPE

	PIPE SIZE (inch)					
Nominal OD	$^{1}/_{2}$	$^{3}/_{4}$	1	$1^{1}/_{4}$	$1^{1}/_{2}$	2
Designation	SDR 9.33	SDR 11.0	SDR 11.00	SDR 10.00	SDR 11.00	SDR 11.00
Actual ID	0.660	0.860	1.077	1.328	1.554	1.943
Length (ft)	**Capacity in Cubic Feet of Gas per Hour**					
10	1,860	3,720	6,710	11,600	17,600	31,600
20	1,280	2,560	4,610	7,990	12,100	21,700
30	1,030	2,050	3,710	6,420	9,690	17,400
40	878	1,760	3,170	5,490	8,300	14,900
50	778	1,560	2,810	4,870	7,350	13,200
60	705	1,410	2,550	4,410	6,660	12,000
70	649	1,300	2,340	4,060	6,130	11,000
80	603	1,210	2,180	3,780	5,700	10,200
90	566	1,130	2,050	3,540	5,350	9,610
100	535	1,070	1,930	3,350	5,050	9,080
125	474	949	1,710	2,970	4,480	8,050
150	429	860	1,550	2,690	4,060	7,290
175	395	791	1,430	2,470	3,730	6,710
200	368	736	1,330	2,300	3,470	6,240
250	326	652	1,180	2,040	3,080	5,530
300	295	591	1,070	1,850	2,790	5,010
350	272	544	981	1,700	2,570	4,610
400	253	506	913	1,580	2,390	4,290
450	237	475	856	1,480	2,240	4,020
500	224	448	809	1,400	2,120	3,800
550	213	426	768	1,330	2,010	3,610
600	203	406	733	1,270	1,920	3,440
650	194	389	702	1,220	1,840	3,300
700	187	374	674	1,170	1,760	3,170
750	180	360	649	1,130	1,700	3,050
800	174	348	627	1,090	1,640	2,950
850	168	336	607	1,050	1,590	2,850
900	163	326	588	1,020	1,540	2,770
950	158	317	572	990	1,500	2,690
1,000	154	308	556	963	1,450	2,610
1,100	146	293	528	915	1,380	2,480
1,200	139	279	504	873	1,320	2,370
1,300	134	267	482	836	1,260	2,270
1,400	128	257	463	803	1,210	2,180
1,500	124	247	446	773	1,170	2,100
1,600	119	239	431	747	1,130	2,030
1,700	115	231	417	723	1,090	1,960
1,800	112	224	404	701	1,060	1,900
1,900	109	218	393	680	1,030	1,850
2,000	106	212	382	662	1,000	1,800

For SI: 1 inch = 25.4 mm, 1 foot = 304.8 mm, 1 pound per square inch = 6.895 kPa, 1-inch water column = 0.2488 kPa, 1 British thermal unit per hour = 0.2931 W, 1 cubic foot per hour = 0.0283 m^3/h, 1 degree = 0.01745 rad.

Note: All table entries have been rounded to three significant digits.

Gas	Natural
Inlet Pressure	Less than 2.0 psi
Pressure Drop	0.5 in. w.c.
Specific Gravity	0.60

TABLE 402.4(22)
POLYETHYLENE PLASTIC TUBING

	PLASTIC TUBING SIZE (CTS) (inch)	
Nominal OD	$^1/_2$	$^3/_4$
Designation	SDR 7.00	SDR 11.00
Actual ID	0.445	0.927
Length (ft)	Capacity in Cubic Feet of Gas per Hour	
10	72	490
20	49	337
30	39	271
40	34	232
50	30	205
60	27	186
70	25	171
80	23	159
90	22	149
100	21	141
125	18	125
150	17	113
175	15	104
200	14	97
225	13	91
250	12	86
275	11	82
300	11	78
350	10	72
400	NA	67
450	NA	63
500	NA	59

For SI: 1 inch = 25.4 mm, 1 foot = 304.8 mm,
1 pound per square inch = 6.895 kPa,
1-inch water column = 0.2488 kPa,
1 British thermal unit per hour = 0.2931 W,
1 cubic foot per hour = 0.0283 m^3/h, 1 degree = 0.01745 rad.

Notes:

1. NA means a flow of less than 10 cfh.
2. All table entries have been rounded to three significant digits.

Gas	Undiluted Propane
Inlet Pressure	10.0 psi
Pressure Drop	1.0 psi
Specific Gravity	1.50

TABLE 402.4(23)
SCHEDULE 40 METALLIC PIPE

INTENDED USE	Pipe sizing between first stage (high-pressure regulator) and second stage (low-pressure regulator).								
	PIPE SIZE (inch)								
Nominal	$^1/_2$	$^3/_4$	1	$1^1/_4$	$1^1/_2$	2	$2^1/_2$	3	4
Actual ID	0.622	0.824	1.049	1.380	1.610	2.067	2.469	3.068	4.026
Length (ft)	Capacity in Thousands of Btu per Hour								
10	3,320	6,950	13,100	26,900	40,300	77,600	124,000	219,000	446,000
20	2,280	4,780	9,000	18,500	27,700	53,300	85,000	150,000	306,000
30	1,830	3,840	7,220	14,800	22,200	42,800	68,200	121,000	246,000
40	1,570	3,280	6,180	12,700	19,000	36,600	58,400	103,000	211,000
50	1,390	2,910	5,480	11,300	16,900	32,500	51,700	91,500	187,000
60	1,260	2,640	4,970	10,200	15,300	29,400	46,900	82,900	169,000
70	1,160	2,430	4,570	9,380	14,100	27,100	43,100	76,300	156,000
80	1,080	2,260	4,250	8,730	13,100	25,200	40,100	70,900	145,000
90	1,010	2,120	3,990	8,190	12,300	23,600	37,700	66,600	136,000
100	956	2,000	3,770	7,730	11,600	22,300	35,600	62,900	128,000
125	848	1,770	3,340	6,850	10,300	19,800	31,500	55,700	114,000
150	768	1,610	3,020	6,210	9,300	17,900	28,600	50,500	103,000
175	706	1,480	2,780	5,710	8,560	16,500	26,300	46,500	94,700
200	657	1,370	2,590	5,320	7,960	15,300	24,400	43,200	88,100
250	582	1,220	2,290	4,710	7,060	13,600	21,700	38,300	78,100
300	528	1,100	2,080	4,270	6,400	12,300	19,600	34,700	70,800
350	486	1,020	1,910	3,930	5,880	11,300	18,100	31,900	65,100
400	452	945	1,780	3,650	5,470	10,500	16,800	29,700	60,600
450	424	886	1,670	3,430	5,140	9,890	15,800	27,900	56,800
500	400	837	1,580	3,240	4,850	9,340	14,900	26,300	53,700
550	380	795	1,500	3,070	4,610	8,870	14,100	25,000	51,000
600	363	759	1,430	2,930	4,400	8,460	13,500	23,900	48,600
650	347	726	1,370	2,810	4,210	8,110	12,900	22,800	46,600
700	334	698	1,310	2,700	4,040	7,790	12,400	21,900	44,800
750	321	672	1,270	2,600	3,900	7,500	12,000	21,100	43,100
800	310	649	1,220	2,510	3,760	7,240	11,500	20,400	41,600
850	300	628	1,180	2,430	3,640	7,010	11,200	19,800	40,300
900	291	609	1,150	2,360	3,530	6,800	10,800	19,200	39,100
950	283	592	1,110	2,290	3,430	6,600	10,500	18,600	37,900
1,000	275	575	1,080	2,230	3,330	6,420	10,200	18,100	36,900
1,100	261	546	1,030	2,110	3,170	6,100	9,720	17,200	35,000
1,200	249	521	982	2,020	3,020	5,820	9,270	16,400	33,400
1,300	239	499	940	1,930	2,890	5,570	8,880	15,700	32,000
1,400	229	480	903	1,850	2,780	5,350	8,530	15,100	30,800
1,500	221	462	870	1,790	2,680	5,160	8,220	14,500	29,600
1,600	213	446	840	1,730	2,590	4,980	7,940	14,000	28,600
1,700	206	432	813	1,670	2,500	4,820	7,680	13,600	27,700
1,800	200	419	789	1,620	2,430	4,670	7,450	13,200	26,900
1,900	194	407	766	1,570	2,360	4,540	7,230	12,800	26,100
2,000	189	395	745	1,530	2,290	4,410	7,030	12,400	25,400

For SI: 1 inch = 25.4 mm, 1 foot = 304.8 mm, 1 pound per square inch = 6.895 kPa, 1-inch water column = 0.2488 kPa, 1 British thermal unit per hour = 0.2931 W, 1 cubic foot per hour = 0.0283 m^3/h, 1 degree = 0.01745 rad.

Note: All table entries have been rounded to three significant digits.

TABLE 402.4(24) SCHEDULE 40 METALLIC PIPE

Gas	Undiluted Propane
Inlet Pressure	10.0 psi
Pressure Drop	3.0 psi
Specific Gravity	1.50

INTENDED USE	Pipe sizing between first stage (high-pressure regulator) and second stage (low-pressure regulator).								
	PIPE SIZE (inch)								
Nominal	$^1/_2$	$^3/_4$	1	$1^1/_4$	$1^1/_2$	2	$2^1/_2$	3	4
Actual ID	0.622	0.824	1.049	1.380	1.610	2.067	2.469	3.068	4.026
Length (ft)	**Capacity in Thousands of Btu per Hour**								
10	5,890	12,300	23,200	47,600	71,300	137,000	219,000	387,000	789,000
20	4,050	8,460	15,900	32,700	49,000	94,400	150,000	266,000	543,000
30	3,250	6,790	12,800	26,300	39,400	75,800	121,000	214,000	436,000
40	2,780	5,810	11,000	22,500	33,700	64,900	103,000	183,000	373,000
50	2,460	5,150	9,710	19,900	29,900	57,500	91,600	162,000	330,000
60	2,230	4,670	8,790	18,100	27,100	52,100	83,000	147,000	299,000
70	2,050	4,300	8,090	16,600	24,900	47,900	76,400	135,000	275,000
80	1,910	4,000	7,530	15,500	23,200	44,600	71,100	126,000	256,000
90	1,790	3,750	7,060	14,500	21,700	41,800	66,700	118,000	240,000
100	1,690	3,540	6,670	13,700	20,500	39,500	63,000	111,000	227,000
125	1,500	3,140	5,910	12,100	18,200	35,000	55,800	98,700	201,000
150	1,360	2,840	5,360	11,000	16,500	31,700	50,600	89,400	182,000
175	1,250	2,620	4,930	10,100	15,200	29,200	46,500	82,300	167,800
200	1,160	2,430	4,580	9,410	14,100	27,200	43,300	76,500	156,100
250	1,030	2,160	4,060	8,340	12,500	24,100	38,400	67,800	138,400
300	935	1,950	3,680	7,560	11,300	21,800	34,800	61,500	125,400
350	860	1,800	3,390	6,950	10,400	20,100	32,000	56,500	115,300
400	800	1,670	3,150	6,470	9,690	18,700	29,800	52,600	107,300
450	751	1,570	2,960	6,070	9,090	17,500	27,900	49,400	100,700
500	709	1,480	2,790	5,730	8,590	16,500	26,400	46,600	95,100
550	673	1,410	2,650	5,450	8,160	15,700	25,000	44,300	90,300
600	642	1,340	2,530	5,200	7,780	15,000	23,900	42,200	86,200
650	615	1,290	2,420	4,980	7,450	14,400	22,900	40,500	82,500
700	591	1,240	2,330	4,780	7,160	13,800	22,000	38,900	79,300
750	569	1,190	2,240	4,600	6,900	13,300	21,200	37,400	76,400
800	550	1,150	2,170	4,450	6,660	12,800	20,500	36,200	73,700
850	532	1,110	2,100	4,300	6,450	12,400	19,800	35,000	71,400
900	516	1,080	2,030	4,170	6,250	12,000	19,200	33,900	69,200
950	501	1,050	1,970	4,050	6,070	11,700	18,600	32,900	67,200
1,000	487	1,020	1,920	3,940	5,900	11,400	18,100	32,000	65,400
1,100	463	968	1,820	3,740	5,610	10,800	17,200	30,400	62,100
1,200	442	923	1,740	3,570	5,350	10,300	16,400	29,000	59,200
1,300	423	884	1,670	3,420	5,120	9,870	15,700	27,800	56,700
1,400	406	849	1,600	3,280	4,920	9,480	15,100	26,700	54,500
1,500	391	818	1,540	3,160	4,740	9,130	14,600	25,700	52,500
1,600	378	790	1,490	3,060	4,580	8,820	14,100	24,800	50,700
1,700	366	765	1,440	2,960	4,430	8,530	13,600	24,000	49,000
1,800	355	741	1,400	2,870	4,300	8,270	13,200	23,300	47,600
1,900	344	720	1,360	2,780	4,170	8,040	12,800	22,600	46,200
2,000	335	700	1,320	2,710	4,060	7,820	12,500	22,000	44,900

For SI: 1 inch = 25.4 mm, 1 foot = 304.8 mm, 1 pound per square inch = 6.895 kPa, 1-inch water column = 0.2488 kPa, 1 British thermal unit per hour = 0.2931 W, 1 cubic foot per hour = 0.0283 m^3/h, 1 degree = 0.01745 rad.

Note: All table entries have been rounded to three significant digits.

Gas	Undiluted Propane
Inlet Pressure	2.0 psi
Pressure Drop	1.0 psi
Specific Gravity	1.50

TABLE 402.4(25)
SCHEDULE 40 METALLIC PIPE

INTENDED USE	Pipe sizing between 2 psig service and line pressure regulator.								
	PIPE SIZE (inch)								
Nominal	$^1/_2$	$^3/_4$	1	$1^1/_4$	$1^1/_2$	2	$2^1/_2$	3	4
Actual ID	0.622	0.824	1.049	1.380	1.610	2.067	2.469	3.068	4.026
Length (ft)	Capacity in Thousands of Btu per Hour								
10	2,680	5,590	10,500	21,600	32,400	62,400	99,500	176,000	359,000
20	1,840	3,850	7,240	14,900	22,300	42,900	68,400	121,000	247,000
30	1,480	3,090	5,820	11,900	17,900	34,500	54,900	97,100	198,000
40	1,260	2,640	4,980	10,200	15,300	29,500	47,000	83,100	170,000
50	1,120	2,340	4,410	9,060	13,600	26,100	41,700	73,700	150,000
60	1,010	2,120	4,000	8,210	12,300	23,700	37,700	66,700	136,000
70	934	1,950	3,680	7,550	11,300	21,800	34,700	61,400	125,000
80	869	1,820	3,420	7,020	10,500	20,300	32,300	57,100	116,000
90	815	1,700	3,210	6,590	9,880	19,000	30,300	53,600	109,000
100	770	1,610	3,030	6,230	9,330	18,000	28,600	50,600	103,000
125	682	1,430	2,690	5,520	8,270	15,900	25,400	44,900	91,500
150	618	1,290	2,440	5,000	7,490	14,400	23,000	40,700	82,900
175	569	1,190	2,240	4,600	6,890	13,300	21,200	37,400	76,300
200	529	1,110	2,080	4,280	6,410	12,300	19,700	34,800	71,000
250	469	981	1,850	3,790	5,680	10,900	17,400	30,800	62,900
300	425	889	1,670	3,440	5,150	9,920	15,800	27,900	57,000
350	391	817	1,540	3,160	4,740	9,120	14,500	25,700	52,400
400	364	760	1,430	2,940	4,410	8,490	13,500	23,900	48,800
450	341	714	1,340	2,760	4,130	7,960	12,700	22,400	45,800
500	322	674	1,270	2,610	3,910	7,520	12,000	21,200	43,200
550	306	640	1,210	2,480	3,710	7,140	11,400	20,100	41,100
600	292	611	1,150	2,360	3,540	6,820	10,900	19,200	39,200
650	280	585	1,100	2,260	3,390	6,530	10,400	18,400	37,500
700	269	562	1,060	2,170	3,260	6,270	9,990	17,700	36,000
750	259	541	1,020	2,090	3,140	6,040	9,630	17,000	34,700
800	250	523	985	2,020	3,030	5,830	9,300	16,400	33,500
850	242	506	953	1,960	2,930	5,640	9,000	15,900	32,400
900	235	490	924	1,900	2,840	5,470	8,720	15,400	31,500
950	228	476	897	1,840	2,760	5,310	8,470	15,000	30,500
1,000	222	463	873	1,790	2,680	5,170	8,240	14,600	29,700
1,100	210	440	829	1,700	2,550	4,910	7,830	13,800	28,200
1,200	201	420	791	1,620	2,430	4,680	7,470	13,200	26,900
1,300	192	402	757	1,550	2,330	4,490	7,150	12,600	25,800
1,400	185	386	727	1,490	2,240	4,310	6,870	12,100	24,800
1,500	178	372	701	1,440	2,160	4,150	6,620	11,700	23,900
1,600	172	359	677	1,390	2,080	4,010	6,390	11,300	23,000
1,700	166	348	655	1,340	2,010	3,880	6,180	10,900	22,300
1,800	161	337	635	1,300	1,950	3,760	6,000	10,600	21,600
1,900	157	327	617	1,270	1,900	3,650	5,820	10,300	21,000
2,000	152	318	600	1,230	1,840	3,550	5,660	10,000	20,400

For SI: 1 inch = 25.4 mm, 1 foot = 304.8 mm, 1 pound per square inch = 6.895kPa, 1-inch water column = 0.2488 kPa,
1 British thermal unit per hour = 0.2931 W, 1 cubic foot per hour = 0.0283 m^3/h, 1 degree = 0.01745 rad.

Note: All table entries have been rounded to three significant digits.

Gas	Undiluted Propane
Inlet Pressure	11.0 in. w.c.
Pressure Drop	0.5 in. w.c.
Specific Gravity	1.50

TABLE 402.4(26)
SCHEDULE 40 METALLIC PIPE

INTENDED USE	Pipe sizing between single- or second-stage (low pressure) regulator and appliance.								
	PIPE SIZE (inch)								
Nominal	$^1/_2$	$^3/_4$	1	$1^1/_4$	$1^1/_2$	2	$2^1/_2$	3	4
Actual ID	0.622	0.824	1.049	1.380	1.610	2.067	2.469	3.068	4.026
Length (ft)	Capacity in Thousands of Btu per Hour								
10	291	608	1,150	2,350	3,520	6,790	10,800	19,100	39,000
20	200	418	787	1,620	2,420	4,660	7,430	13,100	26,800
30	160	336	632	1,300	1,940	3,750	5,970	10,600	21,500
40	137	287	541	1,110	1,660	3,210	5,110	9,030	18,400
50	122	255	480	985	1,480	2,840	4,530	8,000	16,300
60	110	231	434	892	1,340	2,570	4,100	7,250	14,800
80	101	212	400	821	1,230	2,370	3,770	6,670	13,600
100	94	197	372	763	1,140	2,200	3,510	6,210	12,700
125	89	185	349	716	1,070	2,070	3,290	5,820	11,900
150	84	175	330	677	1,010	1,950	3,110	5,500	11,200
175	74	155	292	600	899	1,730	2,760	4,880	9,950
200	67	140	265	543	814	1,570	2,500	4,420	9,010
250	62	129	243	500	749	1,440	2,300	4,060	8,290
300	58	120	227	465	697	1,340	2,140	3,780	7,710
350	51	107	201	412	618	1,190	1,900	3,350	6,840
400	46	97	182	373	560	1,080	1,720	3,040	6,190
450	42	89	167	344	515	991	1,580	2,790	5,700
500	40	83	156	320	479	922	1,470	2,600	5,300
550	37	78	146	300	449	865	1,380	2,440	4,970
600	35	73	138	283	424	817	1,300	2,300	4,700
650	33	70	131	269	403	776	1,240	2,190	4,460
700	32	66	125	257	385	741	1,180	2,090	4,260
750	30	64	120	246	368	709	1,130	2,000	4,080
800	29	61	115	236	354	681	1,090	1,920	3,920
850	28	59	111	227	341	656	1,050	1,850	3,770
900	27	57	107	220	329	634	1,010	1,790	3,640
950	26	55	104	213	319	613	978	1,730	3,530
1,000	25	53	100	206	309	595	948	1,680	3,420
1,100	25	52	97	200	300	578	921	1,630	3,320
1,200	24	50	95	195	292	562	895	1,580	3,230
1,300	23	48	90	185	277	534	850	1,500	3,070
1,400	22	46	86	176	264	509	811	1,430	2,930
1,500	21	44	82	169	253	487	777	1,370	2,800
1,600	20	42	79	162	243	468	746	1,320	2,690
1,700	19	40	76	156	234	451	719	1,270	2,590
1,800	19	39	74	151	226	436	694	1,230	2,500
1,900	18	38	71	146	219	422	672	1,190	2,420
2,000	18	37	69	142	212	409	652	1,150	2,350

For SI: 1 inch = 25.4 mm, 1 foot = 304.8 mm, 1 pound per square inch = 6.895 kPa, 1-inch water column = 0.2488 kPa, 1 British thermal unit per hour = 0.2931 W, 1 cubic foot per hour = 0.0283 m^3/h, 1 degree = 0.01745 rad.

Note: All table entries have been rounded to three significant digits.

Gas	Undiluted Propane
Inlet Pressure	10.0 psi
Pressure Drop	1.0 psi
Specific Gravity	1.50

TABLE 402.4(27)
SEMIRIGID COPPER TUBING

INTENDED USE		Sizing between first stage (high-pressure regulator) and second stage (low-pressure regulator).								
		TUBE SIZE (in.)								
Nominal	K & L	1/4	3/8	1/2	5/8	3/4	1	1 1/4	1 1/2	2
	ACR	3/8	1/2	5/8	3/4	7/8	1 1/8	1 3/8	—	—
Outside		0.375	0.500	0.625	0.750	0.875	1.125	1.375	1.625	2.125
Inside		0.305	0.402	0.527	0.652	0.745	0.995	1.245	1.481	1.959
Length (ft)		Capacity in Thousands of Btu per Hour								
10		513	1,060	2,150	3,760	5,330	11,400	20,500	32,300	67,400
20		352	727	1,480	2,580	3,670	7,830	14,100	22,200	46,300
30		283	584	1,190	2,080	2,940	6,290	11,300	17,900	37,200
40		242	500	1,020	1,780	2,520	5,380	9,690	15,300	31,800
50		215	443	901	1,570	2,230	4,770	8,590	13,500	28,200
60		194	401	816	1,430	2,020	4,320	7,780	12,300	25,600
70		179	369	751	1,310	1,860	3,980	7,160	11,300	23,500
80		166	343	699	1,220	1,730	3,700	6,660	10,500	21,900
90		156	322	655	1,150	1,630	3,470	6,250	9,850	20,500
100		147	304	619	1,080	1,540	3,280	5,900	9,310	19,400
125		131	270	549	959	1,360	2,910	5,230	8,250	17,200
150		118	244	497	869	1,230	2,630	4,740	7,470	15,600
175		109	225	457	799	1,130	2,420	4,360	6,880	14,300
200		101	209	426	744	1,060	2,250	4,060	6,400	13,300
250		90	185	377	659	935	2,000	3,600	5,670	11,800
300		81	168	342	597	847	1,810	3,260	5,140	10,700
350		75	155	314	549	779	1,660	3,000	4,730	9,840
400		70	144	292	511	725	1,550	2,790	4,400	9,160
450		65	135	274	480	680	1,450	2,620	4,130	8,590
500		62	127	259	453	643	1,370	2,470	3,900	8,120
550		59	121	246	430	610	1,300	2,350	3,700	7,710
600		56	115	235	410	582	1,240	2,240	3,530	7,350
650		54	111	225	393	558	1,190	2,140	3,380	7,040
700		51	106	216	378	536	1,140	2,060	3,250	6,770
750		50	102	208	364	516	1,100	1,980	3,130	6,520
800		48	99	201	351	498	1,060	1,920	3,020	6,290
850		46	96	195	340	482	1,030	1,850	2,920	6,090
900		45	93	189	330	468	1,000	1,800	2,840	5,910
950		44	90	183	320	454	970	1,750	2,750	5,730
1,000		42	88	178	311	442	944	1,700	2,680	5,580
1,100		40	83	169	296	420	896	1,610	2,540	5,300
1,200		38	79	161	282	400	855	1,540	2,430	5,050
1,300		37	76	155	270	383	819	1,470	2,320	4,840
1,400		35	73	148	260	368	787	1,420	2,230	4,650
1,500		34	70	143	250	355	758	1,360	2,150	4,480
1,600		33	68	138	241	343	732	1,320	2,080	4,330
1,700		32	66	134	234	331	708	1,270	2,010	4,190
1,800		31	64	130	227	321	687	1,240	1,950	4,060
1,900		30	62	126	220	312	667	1,200	1,890	3,940
2,000		29	60	122	214	304	648	1,170	1,840	3,830

For SI: 1 inch = 25.4 mm, 1 foot = 304.8 mm, 1 pound per square inch = 6.895kPa, 1-inch water column = 0.2488 kPa, 1 British thermal unit per hour = 0.2931 W, 1 cubic foot per hour = 0.0283 m^3/h, 1 degree = 0.01745 rad.

Notes:

1. Table capacities are based on Type K copper tubing inside diameter (shown), which has the smallest inside diameter of the copper tubing products.
2. All table entries have been rounded to three significant digits.

Gas	Undiluted Propane
Inlet Pressure	11.0 in. w.c.
Pressure Drop	0.5 in. w.c.
Specific Gravity	1.50

TABLE 402.4(28) SEMIRIGID COPPER TUBING

INTENDED USE		Sizing between single or second stage (low-pressure regulator) and appliance.								
TUBE SIZE (inch)										
Nominal	K & L	$^1/_4$	$^3/_8$	$^1/_2$	$^5/_8$	$^3/_4$	1	$1^1/_4$	$1^1/_2$	2
	ACR	$^3/_8$	$^1/_2$	$^5/_8$	$^3/_4$	$^7/_8$	$1^1/_8$	$1^3/_8$	—	—
Outside		0.375	0.500	0.625	0.750	0.875	1.125	1.375	1.625	2.125
Inside		0.305	0.402	0.527	0.652	0.745	0.995	1.245	1.481	1.959
Length (ft)		Capacity in Thousands of Btu per Hour								
10		45	93	188	329	467	997	1,800	2,830	5,890
20		31	64	129	226	321	685	1,230	1,950	4,050
30		25	51	104	182	258	550	991	1,560	3,250
40		21	44	89	155	220	471	848	1,340	2,780
50		19	39	79	138	195	417	752	1,180	2,470
60		17	35	71	125	177	378	681	1,070	2,240
70		16	32	66	115	163	348	626	988	2,060
80		15	30	61	107	152	324	583	919	1,910
90		14	28	57	100	142	304	547	862	1,800
100		13	27	54	95	134	287	517	814	1,700
125		11	24	48	84	119	254	458	722	1,500
150		10	21	44	76	108	230	415	654	1,360
175		NA	20	40	70	99	212	382	602	1,250
200		NA	18	37	65	92	197	355	560	1,170
250		NA	16	33	58	82	175	315	496	1,030
300		NA	15	30	52	74	158	285	449	936
350		NA	14	28	48	68	146	262	414	861
400		NA	13	26	45	63	136	244	385	801
450		NA	12	24	42	60	127	229	361	752
500		NA	11	23	40	56	120	216	341	710
550		NA	11	22	38	53	114	205	324	674
600		NA	10	21	36	51	109	196	309	643
650		NA	NA	20	34	49	104	188	296	616
700		NA	NA	19	33	47	100	180	284	592
750		NA	NA	18	32	45	96	174	274	570
800		NA	NA	18	31	44	93	168	264	551
850		NA	NA	17	30	42	90	162	256	533
900		NA	NA	17	29	41	87	157	248	517
950		NA	NA	16	28	40	85	153	241	502
1,000		NA	NA	16	27	39	83	149	234	488
1,100		NA	NA	15	26	37	78	141	223	464
1,200		NA	NA	14	25	35	75	135	212	442
1,300		NA	NA	14	24	34	72	129	203	423
1,400		NA	NA	13	23	32	69	124	195	407
1,500		NA	NA	13	22	31	66	119	188	392
1,600		NA	NA	12	21	30	64	115	182	378
1,700		NA	NA	12	20	29	62	112	176	366
1,800		NA	NA	11	20	28	60	108	170	355
1,900		NA	NA	11	19	27	58	105	166	345
2,000		NA	NA	11	19	27	57	102	161	335

For SI: 1 inch = 25.4 mm, 1 foot = 304.8 mm, 1 pound per square inch = 6.895 kPa, 1-inch water column = 0.2488 kPa,
1 British thermal unit per hour = 0.2931 W, 1 cubic foot per hour = 0.0283 m^3/h, 1 degree = 0.01745 rad.

Notes:

1. Table capacities are based on Type K copper tubing inside diameter (shown), which has the smallest inside diameter of the copper tubing products.
2. NA means a flow of less than 10,000 Btu/hr.
3. All table entries have been rounded to three significant digits.

TABLE 402.4(29)
SEMIRIGID COPPER TUBING

Gas	Undiluted Propane
Inlet Pressure	2.0 psi
Pressure Drop	1.0 psi
Specific Gravity	1.50

INTENDED USE		Tube sizing between 2 psig service and line pressure regulator.								
		TUBE SIZE (inch)								
Nominal	K & L	1/4	3/8	1/2	5/8	3/4	1	1 1/4	1 1/2	2
	ACR	3/8	1/2	5/8	3/4	7/8	1 1/8	1 3/8	—	—
Outside		0.375	0.500	0.625	0.750	0.875	1.125	1.375	1.625	2.125
Inside		0.305	0.402	0.527	0.652	0.745	0.995	1.245	1.481	1.959
Length (ft)		Capacity in Thousands of Btu per Hour								
10		413	852	1,730	3,030	4,300	9,170	16,500	26,000	54,200
20		284	585	1,190	2,080	2,950	6,310	11,400	17,900	37,300
30		228	470	956	1,670	2,370	5,060	9,120	14,400	29,900
40		195	402	818	1,430	2,030	4,330	7,800	12,300	25,600
50		173	356	725	1,270	1,800	3,840	6,920	10,900	22,700
60		157	323	657	1,150	1,630	3,480	6,270	9,880	20,600
70		144	297	605	1,060	1,500	3,200	5,760	9,090	18,900
80		134	276	562	983	1,390	2,980	5,360	8,450	17,600
90		126	259	528	922	1,310	2,790	5,030	7,930	16,500
100		119	245	498	871	1,240	2,640	4,750	7,490	15,600
125		105	217	442	772	1,100	2,340	4,210	6,640	13,800
150		95	197	400	700	992	2,120	3,820	6,020	12,500
175		88	181	368	644	913	1,950	3,510	5,540	11,500
200		82	168	343	599	849	1,810	3,270	5,150	10,700
250		72	149	304	531	753	1,610	2,900	4,560	9,510
300		66	135	275	481	682	1,460	2,620	4,140	8,610
350		60	124	253	442	628	1,340	2,410	3,800	7,920
400		56	116	235	411	584	1,250	2,250	3,540	7,370
450		53	109	221	386	548	1,170	2,110	3,320	6,920
500		50	103	209	365	517	1,110	1,990	3,140	6,530
550		47	97	198	346	491	1,050	1,890	2,980	6,210
600		45	93	189	330	469	1,000	1,800	2,840	5,920
650		43	89	181	316	449	959	1,730	2,720	5,670
700		41	86	174	304	431	921	1,660	2,620	5,450
750		40	82	168	293	415	888	1,600	2,520	5,250
800		39	80	162	283	401	857	1,540	2,430	5,070
850		37	77	157	274	388	829	1,490	2,350	4,900
900		36	75	152	265	376	804	1,450	2,280	4,750
950		35	72	147	258	366	781	1,410	2,220	4,620
1,000		34	71	143	251	356	760	1,370	2,160	4,490
1,100		32	67	136	238	338	721	1,300	2,050	4,270
1,200		31	64	130	227	322	688	1,240	1,950	4,070
1,300		30	61	124	217	309	659	1,190	1,870	3,900
1,400		28	59	120	209	296	633	1,140	1,800	3,740
1,500		27	57	115	201	286	610	1,100	1,730	3,610
1,600		26	55	111	194	276	589	1,060	1,670	3,480
1,700		26	53	108	188	267	570	1,030	1,620	3,370
1,800		25	51	104	182	259	553	1,000	1,570	3,270
1,900		24	50	101	177	251	537	966	1,520	3,170
2,000		23	48	99	172	244	522	940	1,480	3,090

For SI: 1 inch = 25.4 mm, 1 foot = 304.8 mm, 1 pound per square inch = 6.895kPa, 1-inch water column = 0.2488 kPa, 1 British thermal unit per hour = 0.2931 W, 1 cubic foot per hour = 0.0283 m^3/h, 1 degree = 0.01745 rad.

Notes:

1. Table capacities are based on Type K copper tubing inside diameter (shown), which has the smallest inside diameter of the copper tubing products.
2. All table entries have been rounded to three significant digits.

TABLE 402.4(30)
CORRUGATED STAINLESS STEEL TUBING (CSST)

Gas	Undiluted Propane
Inlet Pressure	11.0 in. w.c.
Pressure Drop	0.5 in. w.c.
Specific Gravity	1.50

INTENDED USE: SIZING BETWEEN SINGLE OR SECOND STAGE (Low Pressure) REGULATOR AND THE APPLIANCE SHUTOFF VALVE														
	TUBE SIZE (EHD)													
Flow Designation	13	15	18	19	23	25	30	31	37	39	46	48	60	62
Length (ft)	Capacity in Thousands of Btu per Hour													
5	72	99	181	211	355	426	744	863	1,420	1,638	2,830	3,270	5,780	6,550
10	50	69	129	150	254	303	521	605	971	1,179	1,990	2,320	4,110	4,640
15	39	55	104	121	208	248	422	490	775	972	1,620	1,900	3,370	3,790
20	34	49	91	106	183	216	365	425	661	847	1,400	1,650	2,930	3,290
25	30	42	82	94	164	192	325	379	583	762	1,250	1,480	2,630	2,940
30	28	39	74	87	151	177	297	344	528	698	1,140	1,350	2,400	2,680
40	23	33	64	74	131	153	256	297	449	610	988	1,170	2,090	2,330
50	20	30	58	66	118	137	227	265	397	548	884	1,050	1,870	2,080
60	19	26	53	60	107	126	207	241	359	502	805	961	1,710	1,900
70	17	25	49	57	99	117	191	222	330	466	745	890	1,590	1,760
80	15	23	45	52	94	109	178	208	307	438	696	833	1,490	1,650
90	15	22	44	50	90	102	169	197	286	414	656	787	1,400	1,550
100	14	20	41	47	85	98	159	186	270	393	621	746	1,330	1,480
150	11	15	31	36	66	75	123	143	217	324	506	611	1,090	1,210
200	9	14	28	33	60	69	112	129	183	283	438	531	948	1,050
250	8	12	25	30	53	61	99	117	163	254	390	476	850	934
300	8	11	23	26	50	57	90	107	147	234	357	434	777	854

For SI: 1 inch = 25.4 mm, 1 foot = 304.8 mm, 1 pound per square inch = 6.895kPa, 1-inch water column = 0.2488 kPa, 1 British thermal unit per hour = 0.2931 W, 1 cubic foot per hour = 0.0283 m^3/h, 1 degree = 0.01745 rad.

Notes:

1. Table includes losses for four 90-degree bends and two end fittings. Tubing runs with larger numbers of bends and/or fittings shall be increased by an equivalent length of tubing to the following equation: $L = 1.3n$ where L is additional length (feet) of tubing and n is the number of additional fittings and/or bends.
2. EHD—Equivalent Hydraulic Diameter, which is a measure of the relative hydraulic efficiency between different tubing sizes. The greater the value of EHD, the greater the gas capacity of the tubing.
3. All table entries have been rounded to three significant digits.

Gas	Undiluted Propane
Inlet Pressure	2.0 psi
Pressure Drop	1.0 psi
Specific Gravity	1.50

TABLE 402.4(31) CORRUGATED STAINLESS STEEL TUBING (CSST)

INTENDED USE: SIZING BETWEEN 2 PSI SERVICE AND THE LINE PRESSURE REGULATOR														
	TUBE SIZE (EHD)													
Flow Designation	13	15	18	19	23	25	30	31	37	39	46	48	60	62
Length (ft)	Capacity in Thousands of Btu per Hour													
10	426	558	927	1,110	1,740	2,170	4,100	4,720	7,130	7,958	15,200	16,800	29,400	34,200
25	262	347	591	701	1,120	1,380	2,560	2,950	4,560	5,147	9,550	10,700	18,800	21,700
30	238	316	540	640	1,030	1,270	2,330	2,690	4,180	4,719	8,710	9,790	17,200	19,800
40	203	271	469	554	896	1,100	2,010	2,320	3,630	4,116	7,530	8,500	14,900	17,200
50	181	243	420	496	806	986	1,790	2,070	3,260	3,702	6,730	7,610	13,400	15,400
75	147	196	344	406	663	809	1,460	1,690	2,680	3,053	5,480	6,230	11,000	12,600
80	140	189	333	393	643	768	1,410	1,630	2,590	2,961	5,300	6,040	10,600	12,200
100	124	169	298	350	578	703	1,260	1,450	2,330	2,662	4,740	5,410	9,530	10,900
150	101	137	245	287	477	575	1,020	1,180	1,910	2,195	3,860	4,430	7,810	8,890
200	86	118	213	248	415	501	880	1,020	1,660	1,915	3,340	3,840	6,780	7,710
250	77	105	191	222	373	448	785	910	1,490	1,722	2,980	3,440	6,080	6,900
300	69	96	173	203	343	411	716	829	1,360	1,578	2,720	3,150	5,560	6,300
400	60	82	151	175	298	355	616	716	1,160	1,376	2,350	2,730	4,830	5,460
500	53	72	135	158	268	319	550	638	1,030	1,237	2,100	2,450	4,330	4,880

For SI: 1 inch = 25.4 mm, 1 foot = 304.8 mm, 1 pound per square inch = 6.895kPa, 1-inch water column = 0.2488 kPa, 1 British thermal unit per hour = 0.2931 W, 1 cubic foot per hour = 0.0283 m^3/h, 1 degree = 0.01745 rad.

Notes:

1. Table does not include effect of pressure drop across the line regulator. Where regulator loss exceeds $^1/_2$ psi (based on 13 in. w.c. outlet pressure), DO NOT USE THIS TABLE. Consult with the regulator manufacturer for pressure drops and capacity factors. Pressure drops across a regulator may vary with flow rate.
2. CAUTION: Capacities shown in the table might exceed maximum capacity for a selected regulator. Consult with the regulator or tubing manufacturer for guidance.
3. Table includes losses for four 90-degree bends and two end fittings. Tubing runs with larger numbers of bends and/or fittings shall be increased by an equivalent length of tubing to the following equation: $L = 1.3n$ where L is additional length (feet) of tubing and n is the number of additional fittings and/or bends.
4. EHD—Equivalent Hydraulic Diameter, which is a measure of the relative hydraulic efficiency between different tubing sizes. The greater the value of EHD, the greater the gas capacity of the tubing.
5. All table entries have been rounded to three significant digits.

Gas	Undiluted Propane
Inlet Pressure	5.0 psi
Pressure Drop	3.5 psi
Specific Gravity	1.50

TABLE 402.4(32)
CORRUGATED STAINLESS STEEL TUBING (CSST)

	TUBE SIZE (EHD)													
Flow Designation	13	15	18	19	23	25	30	31	37	39	46	48	60	62
Length (ft)	Capacity in Thousands of Btu per Hour													
10	826	1,070	1,710	2,060	3,150	4,000	7,830	8,950	13,100	14,441	28,600	31,200	54,400	63,800
25	509	664	1,090	1,310	2,040	2,550	4,860	5,600	8,400	9,339	18,000	19,900	34,700	40,400
30	461	603	999	1,190	1,870	2,340	4,430	5,100	7,680	8,564	16,400	18,200	31,700	36,900
40	396	520	867	1,030	1,630	2,030	3,820	4,400	6,680	7,469	14,200	15,800	27,600	32,000
50	352	463	777	926	1,460	1,820	3,410	3,930	5,990	6,717	12,700	14,100	24,700	28,600
75	284	376	637	757	1,210	1,490	2,770	3,190	4,920	5,539	10,300	11,600	20,300	23,400
80	275	363	618	731	1,170	1,450	2,680	3,090	4,770	5,372	9,990	11,200	19,600	22,700
100	243	324	553	656	1,050	1,300	2,390	2,760	4,280	4,830	8,930	10,000	17,600	20,300
150	196	262	453	535	866	1,060	1,940	2,240	3,510	3,983	7,270	8,210	14,400	16,600
200	169	226	393	464	755	923	1,680	1,930	3,050	3,474	6,290	7,130	12,500	14,400
250	150	202	352	415	679	828	1,490	1,730	2,740	3,124	5,620	6,390	11,200	12,900
300	136	183	322	379	622	757	1,360	1,570	2,510	2,865	5,120	5,840	10,300	11,700
400	117	158	279	328	542	657	1,170	1,360	2,180	2,498	4,430	5,070	8,920	10,200
500	104	140	251	294	488	589	1,050	1,210	1,950	2,247	3,960	4,540	8,000	9,110

For SI: 1 inch = 25.4 mm, 1 foot = 304.8 mm, 1 pound per square inch = 6.895kPa, 1-inch water column = 0.2488 kPa, 1 British thermal unit per hour = 0.2931 W, 1 cubic foot per hour = 0.0283 m^3/h, 1 degree = 0.01745 rad.

Notes:

1. Table does not include effect of pressure drop across line regulator. Where regulator loss exceeds1 psi, DO NOT USE THIS TABLE. Consult with the regulator manufacturer for pressure drops and capacity factors. Pressure drop across regulator may vary with the flow rate.
2. CAUTION: Capacities shown in the table might exceed maximum capacity of selected regulator. Consult with the tubing manufacturer for guidance.
3. Table includes losses for four 90-degree bends and two end fittings. Tubing runs with larger numbers of bends and/or fittings shall be increased by an equivalent length of tubing to the following equation: $L = 1.3n$ where L is additional length (feet) of tubing and n is the number of additional fittings and/or bends.
4. EHD— Equivalent Hydraulic Diameter, which is a measure of the relative hydraulic efficiency between different tubing sizes. The greater the value of EHD, the greater the gas capacity of the tubing.
5. All table entries have been rounded to three significant digits.

Gas	Undiluted Propane
Inlet Pressure	11.0 in. w.c.
Pressure Drop	0.5 in. w.c.
Specific Gravity	1.50

TABLE 402.4(33) POLYETHYLENE PLASTIC PIPE

INTENDED USE	PE pipe sizing between integral two-stage regulator at tank or second stage (low-pressure regulator) and building.					
	PIPE SIZE (inch)					
Nominal OD	$^1/_2$	$^3/_4$	1	$1^1/_4$	$1^1/_2$	2
Designation	SDR 9.33	SDR 11.0	SDR 11.00	SDR 10.00	SDR 11.00	SDR 11.00
Actual ID	0.660	0.860	1.077	1.328	1.554	1.943
Length (ft)	Capacity in Thousands of Btu per Hour					
10	340	680	1,230	2,130	3,210	5,770
20	233	468	844	1,460	2,210	3,970
30	187	375	677	1,170	1,770	3,180
40	160	321	580	1,000	1,520	2,730
50	142	285	514	890	1,340	2,420
60	129	258	466	807	1,220	2,190
70	119	237	428	742	1,120	2,010
80	110	221	398	690	1,040	1,870
90	103	207	374	648	978	1,760
100	98	196	353	612	924	1,660
125	87	173	313	542	819	1,470
150	78	157	284	491	742	1,330
175	72	145	261	452	683	1,230
200	67	135	243	420	635	1,140
250	60	119	215	373	563	1,010
300	54	108	195	338	510	916
350	50	99	179	311	469	843
400	46	92	167	289	436	784
450	43	87	157	271	409	736
500	41	82	148	256	387	695

For SI: 1 inch = 25.4 mm, 1 foot = 304.8 mm, 1 pound per square inch = 6.895kPa, 1-inch water column = 0.2488 kPa, 1 British thermal unit per hour = 0.2931 W, 1 cubic foot per hour = 0.0283 m^3/h, 1 degree = 0.01745 rad.

Note: All table entries have been rounded to three significant digits.

Gas	Undiluted Propane
Inlet Pressure	2.0 psi
Pressure Drop	1.0 psi
Specific Gravity	1.50

TABLE 402.4(34)
POLYETHYLENE PLASTIC PIPE

INTENDED USE	PE pipe sizing between 2 psig service regulator and line pressure regulator.					
	PIPE SIZE (inch)					
Nominal OD	1/2	3/4	1	1 1/4	1 1/2	2
Designation	SDR 9.33	SDR 11.0	SDR 11.00	SDR 10.00	SDR 11.00	SDR 11.00
Actual ID	0.660	0.860	1.077	1.328	1.554	1.943
Length (ft)	Capacity in Thousands of Btu per Hour					
10	3,130	6,260	11,300	19,600	29,500	53,100
20	2,150	4,300	7,760	13,400	20,300	36,500
30	1,730	3,450	6,230	10,800	16,300	29,300
40	1,480	2,960	5,330	9,240	14,000	25,100
50	1,310	2,620	4,730	8,190	12,400	22,200
60	1,190	2,370	4,280	7,420	11,200	20,100
70	1,090	2,180	3,940	6,830	10,300	18,500
80	1,010	2,030	3,670	6,350	9,590	17,200
90	952	1,910	3,440	5,960	9,000	16,200
100	899	1,800	3,250	5,630	8,500	15,300
125	797	1,600	2,880	4,990	7,530	13,500
150	722	1,450	2,610	4,520	6,830	12,300
175	664	1,330	2,400	4,160	6,280	11,300
200	618	1,240	2,230	3,870	5,840	10,500
250	548	1,100	1,980	3,430	5,180	9,300
300	496	994	1,790	3,110	4,690	8,430
350	457	914	1,650	2,860	4,320	7,760
400	425	851	1,530	2,660	4,020	7,220
450	399	798	1,440	2,500	3,770	6,770
500	377	754	1,360	2,360	3,560	6,390
550	358	716	1,290	2,240	3,380	6,070
600	341	683	1,230	2,140	3,220	5,790
650	327	654	1,180	2,040	3,090	5,550
700	314	628	1,130	1,960	2,970	5,330
750	302	605	1,090	1,890	2,860	5,140
800	292	585	1,050	1,830	2,760	4,960
850	283	566	1,020	1,770	2,670	4,800
900	274	549	990	1,710	2,590	4,650
950	266	533	961	1,670	2,520	4,520
1,000	259	518	935	1,620	2,450	4,400
1,100	246	492	888	1,540	2,320	4,170
1,200	234	470	847	1,470	2,220	3,980
1,300	225	450	811	1,410	2,120	3,810
1,400	216	432	779	1,350	2,040	3,660
1,500	208	416	751	1,300	1,960	3,530
1,600	201	402	725	1,260	1,900	3,410
1,700	194	389	702	1,220	1,840	3,300
1,800	188	377	680	1,180	1,780	3,200
1,900	183	366	661	1,140	1,730	3,110
2,000	178	356	643	1,110	1,680	3,020

For SI: 1 inch = 25.4 mm, 1 foot = 304.8 mm, 1 pound per square inch = 6.895 kPa, 1-inch water column = 0.2488 kPa, 1 British thermal unit per hour = 0.2931 W, 1 cubic foot per hour = 0.0283 m^3/h, 1 degree = 0.01745 rad.

Note: All table entries have been rounded to three significant digits.

Gas	Undiluted Propane
Inlet Pressure	11.0 in. w.c.
Pressure Drop	0.5 in. w.c.
Specific Gravity	1.50

TABLE 402.4(35)
POLYETHYLENE PLASTIC TUBING

INTENDED USE	PE pipe sizing between integral two-stage regulator at tank or second stage (low-pressure regulator) and building.	
Plastic Tubing Size (CTS) (inch)		
Nominal OD	$^1/_2$	1
Designation	SDR 7.00	SDR 11.00
Actual ID	0.445	0.927
Length (ft)	Capacity in Cubic Feet of Gas per Hour	
10	121	828
20	83	569
30	67	457
40	57	391
50	51	347
60	46	314
70	42	289
80	39	269
90	37	252
100	35	238
125	31	211
150	28	191
175	26	176
200	24	164
225	22	154
250	21	145
275	20	138
300	19	132
350	18	121
400	16	113
450	15	106
500	15	100

For SI: 1 inch = 25.4 mm, 1 foot = 304.8 mm,
1 pound per square inch = 6.895 kPa,
1-inch water column = 0.2488 kPa,
1 British thermal unit per hour = 0.2931 W,
1 cubic foot per hour = 0.0283 m^3/h, 1 degree = 0.01745 rad.

Note: All table entries have been rounded to three significant digits.

TABLE 402.4(36)
POLYETHYLENE PLASTIC PIPE SIZING
BETWEEN FIRST STAGE AND SECOND STAGE REGULATOR

Maximum undiluted propane capacities listed are based on 10 psi first stage and 1 psi pressure drop. Capacities in 1000 Btu/hr

PLASTIC PIPE LENGTH (feet)	PLASTIC PIPE NOMINAL OUTSIDE DIAMETER (IPS) (dimensions in parenthesis are inside diameter)					
	1/2 in. SDR 9.33 (0.660)	3/4 in. SDR 11.0 (0.860)	1 in. SDR 11.00 (1.077)	1 1/4 in. SDR 10.00 (1.328)	1 1/2 in. SDR 11.00 (1.554)	2. in. SDR 11.00 (1.943)
30	2143	4292	7744	13416	20260	36402
40	1835	3673	6628	11482	17340	31155
50	1626	3256	5874	10176	15368	27612
60	1473	2950	5322	9220	13924	25019
70	1355	2714	4896	8483	12810	23017
80	1261	2525	4555	7891	11918	21413
90	1183	2369	4274	7404	11182	20091
100	1117	2238	4037	6994	10562	18978
125	990	1983	3578	6199	9361	16820
150	897	1797	3242	5616	8482	15240
175	826	1653	2983	5167	7803	14020
200	678	1539	2775	4807	7259	13043
225	721	1443	2603	4510	6811	12238
250	681	1363	2459	4260	6434	11560
275	646	1294	2336	4046	6111	10979
300	617	1235	2228	3860	5830	10474
350	567	1136	2050	3551	5363	9636
400	528	1057	1907	3304	4989	8965
450	495	992	1789	3100	4681	8411
500	468	937	1690	2928	4422	7945
600	424	849	1531	2653	4007	7199
700	390	781	1409	2441	3686	6623
800	363	726	1311	2271	3429	6161
900	340	682	1230	2131	3217	5781
1000	322	644	1162	2012	3039	5461
1500	258	517	933	1616	2441	4385
2000	221	443	798	1383	2089	3753

For SI: 1 inch = 25.4 mm, 304.8 mm, 1 foot = 304.8 mm, 1 pound per square inch - 6.895 kPa, 1 British thermal unit per hour = 0.2931 W.

TABLE 402.4(37)
POLYETHYLENE PLASTIC TUBE SIZING

Sizing between first stage and second stage regulator maximum undiluted propane capacities listed are based on 10 psi first stage setting and 1 psi pressure drop Capacities in 1000 Btu/hr

PLASTIC TUBING LENGTH (feet)	PLASTIC TUBING SIZE (CTS) (dimensions in parenthesis are inside diameter)	
	$^1/_2$ in. CTS SDR 7.00 (0.445)	1 in. CTS SDR 11.00 (0.927)
30	762	5225
40	653	4472
50	578	3964
60	524	3591
70	482	3304
80	448	3074
90	421	2884
100	397	2724
125	352	2414
150	319	2188
175	294	2013
200	273	1872
225	256	1757
250	242	1659
275	230	1576
300	219	1503
350	202	1383
400	188	1287
450	176	1207
500	166	1140
600	151	1033
700	139	951
800	129	884
900	121	830
1000	114	784
1500	92	629
2000	79	539

For SI: 1 inch = 25.4 mm, 304.8 mm, 1 foot = 304.8 mm, 1 pound per square inch - 6.895 kPa, 1 British thermal unit per hour = 0.2931 W.

402.5 Allowable pressure drop. The design pressure loss in any *piping* system under maximum probable flow conditions, from the *point of delivery* to the inlet connection of the *appliance*, shall be such that the supply pressure at the *appliance* is greater than or equal to the minimum pressure required by the *appliance*.

402.6 Maximum design operating pressure. The maximum design operating pressure for *piping* systems located inside buildings shall not exceed 5 pounds per square inch gauge (psig) (34 kPa gauge).

402.6.1 Liquefied petroleum gas systems. LP-gas systems designed to operate below -5°F (-21°C) or with butane or a propane-butane mix shall be designed to either accommodate liquid LP-gas or prevent LP-gas vapor from condensing into a liquid.

SECTION 403 (IFGS) PIPING MATERIALS

403.1 General. Materials used for *piping* systems shall comply with the requirements of this chapter or shall be *approved*.

403.2 Used materials. Pipe, fittings, valves and other materials shall not be used again except where they are free of foreign materials and have been ascertained to be adequate for the service intended.

403.3 Other materials. Material not covered by the standards specifications listed herein shall be investigated and tested to determine that it is safe and suitable for the proposed service, and, in addition, shall be recommended for that service by the manufacturer and shall be *approved* by the code official.

403.4 Metallic pipe. Metallic pipe shall comply with Sections 403.4.1 through 403.4.4.

403.4.1 Cast iron. Cast-iron pipe shall not be used.

403.4.2 Steel. Steel and wrought-iron pipe shall be at least of standard weight (Schedule 40) and shall comply with one of the following standards:

1. ASME B 36.10, 10M;
2. ASTM A 53/A53M; or
3. ASTM A 106.

403.4.3 Copper and brass. Copper and brass pipe shall not be used if the gas contains more than an average of 0.3 grains of hydrogen sulfide per 100 standard cubic feet of gas (0.7 milligrams per 100 liters). Threaded copper, brass and aluminum-alloy pipe shall not be used with gases corrosive to such materials.

403.4.4 Aluminum. Aluminum-alloy pipe shall comply with ASTM B 241 (except that the use of alloy 5456 is prohibited), and shall be marked at each end of each length indicating compliance. Aluminum-alloy pipe shall be coated to protect against external corrosion where it is in contact with masonry, plaster or insulation, or is subject to repeated wettings by such liquids as water, detergents or sewage. Aluminum-alloy pipe shall not be used in exterior locations or underground.

403.5 Metallic tubing. Seamless copper, aluminum alloy and steel tubing shall not be used with gases corrosive to such materials.

403.5.1 Steel tubing. Steel tubing shall comply with ASTM A 254.

403.5.2 Copper and brass tubing. Copper tubing shall comply with Standard Type K or L of ASTM B 88 or ASTM B 280.

Copper and brass tubing shall not be used if the gas contains more than an average of 0.3 grains of hydrogen sulfide per 100 standard cubic feet of gas (0.7 milligrams per 100 liters).

403.5.3 Aluminum tubing. Aluminum-alloy tubing shall comply with ASTM B 210 or ASTM B 241. Aluminum-alloy tubing shall be coated to protect against external corrosion where it is in contact with masonry, plaster or insulation, or is subject to repeated wettings by such liquids as water, detergent or sewage.

Aluminum-alloy tubing shall not be used in exterior locations or underground.

403.5.4 Corrugated stainless steel tubing. Corrugated stainless steel tubing shall be *listed* in accordance with ANSI LC 1/CSA 6.26.

403.6 Plastic pipe, tubing and fittings. Plastic pipe, tubing and fittings used to supply fuel gas shall conform to ASTM D 2513. Pipe shall be marked "Gas" and "ASTM D 2513."

403.6.1 Anodeless risers. Plastic pipe, tubing and anodeless risers shall comply with the following:

1. Factory-assembled anodeless risers shall be recommended by the manufacturer for the gas used and shall be leak tested by the manufacturer in accordance with written procedures.
2. Service head adapters and field-assembled anodeless risers incorporating service head adapters shall be recommended by the manufacturer for the gas used, and shall be designed and certified to meet the requirements of Category I of ASTM D 2513, and U.S. Department of Transportation, Code of Federal Regulations, Title 49, Part 192.281(e). The manufacturer shall provide the user with qualified installation instructions as prescribed by the U.S. Department of Transportation, Code of Federal Regulations, Title 49, Part 192.283(b).

403.6.2 LP-gas systems. The use of plastic pipe, tubing and fittings in undiluted liquefied petroleum gas *piping* systems shall be in accordance with NFPA 58.

403.6.3 Regulator vent piping. Plastic pipe, tubing and fittings used to connect regulator vents to remote vent terminations shall be PVC conforming to ANSI/UL 651. PVC vent *piping* shall not be installed indoors.

403.7 Workmanship and defects. Pipe, tubing and fittings shall be clear and free from cutting burrs and defects in structure or threading, and shall be thoroughly brushed, and chip and scale blown.

Defects in pipe, tubing and fittings shall not be repaired. Defective pipe, tubing and fittings shall be replaced (see Section 406.1.2).

403.8 Protective coating. Where in contact with material or atmosphere exerting a corrosive action, metallic *piping* and fittings coated with a corrosion-resistant material shall be used. External or internal coatings or linings used on *piping* or components shall not be considered as adding strength.

403.9 Metallic pipe threads. Metallic pipe and fitting threads shall be taper pipe threads and shall comply with ASME B1.20.1.

403.9.1 Damaged threads. Pipe with threads that are stripped, chipped, corroded or otherwise damaged shall not be used. Where a weld opens during the operation of cutting or threading, that portion of the pipe shall not be used.

403.9.2 Number of threads. Field threading of metallic pipe shall be in accordance with Table 403.9.2.

TABLE 403.9.2
SPECIFICATIONS FOR THREADING METALLIC PIPE

IRON PIPE SIZE (inches)	APPROXIMATE LENGTH OF THREADED PORTION (inches)	APPROXIMATE NUMBER OF THREADS TO BE CUT
$^1/_2$	$^3/_4$	10
$^3/_4$	$^3/_4$	10
1	$^7/_8$	10
$1^1/_4$	1	11
$1^1/_2$	1	11
2	1	11
$2^1/_2$	$1^1/_2$	12
3	$1^1/_2$	12
4	$1^5/_8$	13

For SI: 1 inch = 25.4 mm.

403.9.3 Thread compounds. Thread (joint) compounds (pipe dope) shall be resistant to the action of liquefied petroleum gas or to any other chemical constituents of the gases to be conducted through the piping.

403.10 Metallic piping joints and fittings. The type of *piping* joint used shall be suitable for the pressure-temperature conditions and shall be selected giving consideration to joint tightness and mechanical strength under the service conditions. The joint shall be able to sustain the maximum end force caused by the internal pressure and any additional forces caused by temperature expansion or contraction, vibration, fatigue or the weight of the pipe and its contents.

403.10.1 Pipe joints. Pipe joints shall be threaded, flanged, brazed or welded. Where nonferrous pipe is brazed, the brazing materials shall have a melting point in excess of 1,000°F (538°C). Brazing alloys shall not contain more than 0.05-percent phosphorus.

403.10.2 Tubing joints. Tubing joints shall be made with *approved* gas tubing fittings, brazed with a material having a melting point in excess of 1,000°F (538°C) or made with press-connect fittings complying with ANSI LC-4. Brazing alloys shall not contain more than 0.05-percent phosphorus.

403.10.3 Flared joints. Flared joints shall be used only in systems constructed from nonferrous pipe and tubing where experience or tests have demonstrated that the joint is suitable for the conditions and where provisions are made in the design to prevent separation of the joints.

403.10.4 Metallic fittings. Metallic fittings shall comply with the following:

1. Threaded fittings in sizes larger than 4 inches (102 mm) shall not be used except where *approved.*
2. Fittings used with steel or wrought-iron pipe shall be steel, brass, bronze, malleable iron or cast iron.
3. Fittings used with copper or brass pipe shall be copper, brass or bronze.
4. Fittings used with aluminum-alloy pipe shall be of aluminum alloy.
5. Cast-iron fittings:
   - 5.1. Flanges shall be permitted.
   - 5.2. Bushings shall not be used.
   - 5.3. Fittings shall not be used in systems containing flammable gas-air mixtures.
   - 5.4. Fittings in sizes 4 inches (102 mm) and larger shall not be used indoors except where *approved.*
   - 5.5. Fittings in sizes 6 inches (152 mm) and larger shall not be used except where *approved.*
6. Aluminum-alloy fittings. Threads shall not form the joint seal.
7. Zinc aluminum-alloy fittings. Fittings shall not be used in systems containing flammable gas-air mixtures.
8. Special fittings. Fittings such as couplings, proprietary-type joints, saddle tees, gland-type compression fittings, and flared, flareless or compression-type tubing fittings shall be: used within the fitting manufacturer's pressure-temperature recommendations; used within the service conditions anticipated with respect to vibration, fatigue, thermal expansion or contraction; installed or braced to prevent separation of the joint by gas pressure or external physical damage; and shall be *approved.*

403.11 Plastic pipe, joints and fittings. Plastic pipe, tubing and fittings shall be joined in accordance with the manufacturer's instructions. Such joint shall comply with the following:

1. The joint shall be designed and installed so that the longitudinal pull-out resistance of the joint will be at least equal to the tensile strength of the plastic *piping* material.
2. Heat-fusion joints shall be made in accordance with qualified procedures that have been established and proven by test to produce gas-tight joints at least as strong as the pipe or tubing being joined. Joints shall be made with the joining method recommended by the pipe manufacturer. Heat fusion fittings shall be marked "ASTM D 2513."
3. Where compression-type mechanical joints are used, the gasket material in the fitting shall be compatible with the plastic *piping* and with the gas distributed by the system.

An internal tubular rigid stiffener shall be used in conjunction with the fitting. The stiffener shall be flush with the end of the pipe or tubing and shall extend at least to the outside end of the compression fitting when installed. The stiffener shall be free of rough or sharp edges and shall not be a force fit in the plastic. Split tubular stiffeners shall not be used.

4. Plastic *piping* joints and fittings for use in liquefied petroleum gas *piping* systems shall be in accordance with NFPA 58.

403.12 Flanges. Deleted.

403.13 Flange gaskets. Deleted.

SECTION 404 (IFGC) PIPING SYSTEM INSTALLATION

404.1 Prohibited locations. *Piping* shall not be installed in or through a ducted supply, return or exhaust, or a clothes chute, chimney or gas vent, dumbwaiter or elevator shaft. *Piping* installed downstream of the *point of delivery* shall not extend through any townhouse unit other than the unit served by such *piping*.

404.2 Piping in solid partitions and walls. *Concealed piping* shall not be located in solid partitions and solid walls, unless installed in a chase or casing.

404.3 Piping in concealed locations. Portions of a *piping* system installed in concealed locations shall not have unions, tubing fittings, right and left couplings, bushings, compression couplings and swing joints made by combinations of fittings.

Exceptions:

1. Tubing joined by brazing.
2. Fittings *listed* for use in concealed locations.

404.4 Piping through foundation wall. Underground piping, where installed below grade through the outer foundation or basement wall of a building, shall be encased in a protective pipe sleeve, or shall be protected by an approved device or method. The annular space between the gas piping and the sleeve and between the sleeve and the wall shall be sealed.

404.5 Protection against physical damage. In concealed locations, where *piping* other than black or galvanized steel is installed through holes or notches in wood studs, joists, rafters or similar members less than $1^1/_2$ inches (38 mm) from the nearest edge of the member, the pipe shall be protected by shield plates. Protective steel shield plates having a minimum thickness of 0.0575 inch (1.463 mm) (No. 16 gage) shall cover the area of the pipe where the member is notched or bored and shall extend a minimum of 4 inches (102 mm) above sole plates, below top plates and to each side of a stud, joist or rafter.

404.6 Piping in solid floors. *Piping* in solid floors shall be laid in channels in the floor and covered in a manner that will allow *access* to the *piping* with a minimum amount of damage to the building. Where such *piping* is subject to exposure to excessive moisture or corrosive substances, the *piping* shall be protected in an *approved* manner. As an alternative to installation in channels, the piping shall be installed in a conduit of Schedule 40 steel, wrought iron, PVC or ABS pipe in accordance with Section 404.6.1 or 404.6.2.

404.6.1 Conduit with one end terminating outdoors. The conduit shall extend into an occupiable portion of the building and, at the point where the conduit terminates in the building, the space between the conduit and the gas *piping* shall be sealed to prevent the possible entrance of any gas leakage. The conduit shall extend not less than 2 inches (51 mm) beyond the point where the pipe emerges from the floor. If the end sealing is capable of withstanding the full pressure of the gas pipe, the conduit shall be designed for the same pressure as the pipe. Such conduit shall extend not less than 4 inches (102 mm) outside the building, shall be vented above grade to the outdoors and shall be installed so as prevent the entrance of water and insects.

404.6.2 Conduit with both ends terminating indoors. Where the conduit originates and terminates within the same building, the conduit shall originate and terminate in an accessible portion of the building and shall not be sealed. The conduit shall extend not less than 2 inches (51 mm) beyond the point where the pipe emerges from the floor.

404.7 Above-ground outdoor piping. All *piping* installed outdoors shall be elevated not less than $3^1/_2$ inches (152 mm) above ground and where installed across roof surfaces, shall be elevated not less than $3^1/_2$ inches (152 mm) above the roof surface. *Piping* installed above ground, outdoors, and installed across the surface of roofs shall be securely supported and located where it will be protected from physical damage. Where passing through an outside wall, the *piping* shall also be protected against corrosion by coating or wrapping with an inert material. Where *piping* is encased in a protective pipe sleeve, the annular space between the *piping* and the sleeve shall be sealed. Ferrous metal exposed in exterior locations shall be protected from corrosion with one coat of exterior paint. Zinc coatings (galvanized) shall be deemed adequate protection for gas piping above ground.

404.8 Isolation. Metallic *piping* and metallic tubing that conveys fuel gas from an LP-gas storage container shall be provided with an *approved* dielectric fitting to electrically isolate the underground portion of the pipe or tube from the above ground portion that enters a building. Such dielectric fitting shall be installed above ground, outdoors.

404.9 Protection against corrosion underground. Metallic pipe or tubing exposed to corrosive action, such as soil condition or moisture, shall be protected in an *approved* manner. Zinc coatings (galvanizing) shall not be deemed adequate protection for gas *piping* underground. Where dissimilar metals are joined underground, an insulating coupling or fitting shall be used. *Piping* shall not be laid in contact with cinders.

404.9.1 Prohibited use. Uncoated threaded or socket welded joints shall not be used in *piping* in contact with soil or where internal or external crevice corrosion is known to occur.

404.9.2 Protective coatings and wrapping. Pipe protective coatings and wrappings shall be *approved* for the application and shall be factory applied.

Exception: Where installed in accordance with the manufacturer's installation instructions, field application of coatings and wrappings shall be permitted.

404.10 Minimum burial depth. Underground *piping* systems shall be installed a minimum depth of 12 inches (305 mm) below grade, except as provided for in Section 404.10.1.

404.10.1 Individual outside appliances. Individual lines to outside lights, grills or other appliances shall be installed a minimum of 8 inches (203 mm) below finished grade, provided that such installation is *approved* and is installed in locations not susceptible to physical damage.

404.11 Trenches. The trench shall be graded so that the pipe has a firm, substantially continuous bearing on the bottom of the trench.

404.12 Piping underground beneath buildings. *Piping* installed underground beneath buildings is prohibited except where the *piping* is encased in a conduit of wrought iron, plastic pipe, steel pipe or other *approved* conduit material designed to withstand the superimposed loads. The conduit shall be protected from corrosion in accordance with Section 404.9 and shall be installed in accordance with Section 404.12.1 or 404.12.2.

404.12.1 Conduit with one end terminating outdoors. The conduit shall extend into an occupiable portion of the building and, at the point where the conduit terminates in the building, the space between the conduit and the gas *piping* shall be sealed to prevent the possible entrance of any gas leakage. The conduit shall extend not less than 2 inches (51 mm) beyond the point where the pipe emerges from the floor. Where the end sealing is capable of withstanding the full pressure of the gas pipe, the conduit shall be designed for the same pressure as the pipe. Such conduit shall extend not less than 4 inches (102 mm) outside of the building, shall be vented above grade to the outdoors and shall be installed so as to prevent the entrance of water and insects.

404.12.2 Conduit with both ends terminating indoors. Where the conduit originates and terminates within the same building, the conduit shall originate and terminate in an accessible portion of the building and shall not be sealed. The conduit shall extend not less than 2 inches (51 mm) beyond the point where the pipe emerges from the floor.

404.13 Outlet closures. Gas *outlets* that do not connect to appliances shall be capped gas tight.

Exception: *Listed* and *labeled*flush-mounted-type quick-disconnect devices and *listed* and *labeled* gas convenience *outlets* shall be installed in accordance with the manufacturer's installation instructions.

404.14 Location of outlets. The unthreaded portion of *piping outlets* shall extend not less than 1 inch (25 mm) through finished ceilings and walls and where extending through floors or outdoor patios and slabs, shall not be less than 2 inches (51 mm) above them. The *outlet* fitting or *piping* shall be securely supported. *Outlets* shall not be placed behind doors. *Outlets* shall be located in the room or space where the *appliance* is installed.

Exception: *Listed* and *labeled* flush-mounted-type quick-disconnect devices and *listed* and *labeled* gas convenience *outlets* shall be installed in accordance with the manufacturer's installation instructions.

404.15 Plastic pipe. The installation of plastic pipe shall comply with Sections 404.15.1 through 404.15.3.

404.15.1 Limitations. Plastic pipe shall be installed outdoors underground only. Plastic pipe shall not be used within or under any building or slab or be operated at pressures greater than 100 psig (689 kPa) for natural gas or 30 psig (207 kPa) for LP-gas.

Exceptions:

1. Plastic pipe shall be permitted to terminate above ground outside of buildings where installed in premanufactured anodeless risers or service head adapter risers that are installed in accordance with the manufacturer's installation instructions.
2. Plastic pipe shall be permitted to terminate with a wall head adapter within buildings where the plastic pipe is inserted in a *piping* material for fuel gas use in buildings.
3. Plastic pipe shall be permitted under outdoor patio, walkway and driveway slabs provided that the burial depth complies with Section 404.10.

404.15.2 Connections. Connections made outdoors and underground between metallic and plastic *piping* shall be made only with transition fittings conforming with ASTM D 2513 Category I or ASTM F 1973.

404.15.3 Tracer. A yellow insulated copper tracer wire or other *approved* conductor shall be installed adjacent to underground nonmetallic *piping*. *Access* shall be provided to the tracer wire or the tracer wire shall terminate above ground at each end of the nonmetallic *piping*. The tracer wire size shall not be less than 18 AWG and the insulation type shall be suitable for direct burial.

404.16 Prohibited devices. A device shall not be placed inside the *piping* or fittings that will reduce the cross-sectional area or otherwise obstruct the free flow of gas.

Exception: *Approved* gas filters.

404.17 Testing of piping. Before any system of *piping* is put in service or concealed, it shall be tested to ensure that it is gas tight. Testing, inspection and purging of *piping* systems shall comply with Section 406.

SECTION 405 (IFGS)
PIPING BENDS AND CHANGES IN DIRECTION

405.1 General. Changes in direction of pipe shall be permitted to be made by the use of fittings, factory bends or field bends.

405.2 Metallic pipe. Metallic pipe bends shall comply with the following:

1. Bends shall be made only with bending tools and procedures intended for that purpose.

2. All bends shall be smooth and free from buckling, cracks or other evidence of mechanical damage.
3. The longitudinal weld of the pipe shall be near the neutral axis of the bend.
4. Pipe shall not be bent through an arc of more than 90 degrees (1.6 rad).
5. The inside radius of a bend shall be not less than six times the outside diameter of the pipe.

405.3 Plastic pipe. Plastic pipe bends shall comply with the following:

1. The pipe shall not be damaged and the internal diameter of the pipe shall not be effectively reduced.
2. Joints shall not be located in pipe bends.
3. The radius of the inner curve of such bends shall not be less than 25 times the inside diameter of the pipe.
4. Where the *piping* manufacturer specifies the use of special bending tools or procedures, such tools or procedures shall be used.

405.4 Elbows. Deleted.

SECTION 406 (IFGS) INSPECTION, TESTING AND PURGING

406.1 General. Prior to acceptance and initial operation, all *piping* installations shall be inspected and pressure tested to determine that the materials, design, fabrication and installation practices comply with the requirements of this code.

406.1.1 Inspections. Inspection shall consist of visual examination, during or after manufacture, fabrication, assembly or pressure tests as appropriate. Supplementary types of nondestructive inspection techniques, such as magnetic-particle, radiographic, ultrasonic, etc., shall not be required unless specifically *listed* herein or in the engineering design.

406.1.2 Repairs and additions. In the event repairs or additions are made after the pressure test, the affected *piping* shall be tested.

Minor repairs and additions are not required to be pressure tested provided that the work is inspected and connections are tested with a noncorrosive leak-detecting fluid or other *approved* leak-detecting methods.

406.1.3 New branches. Where new branches are installed to new appliances, only the newly installed branches shall be required to be pressure tested. Connections between the new *piping* and the existing *piping* shall be tested with a noncorrosive leak-detecting fluid or other *approved* leak-detecting methods.

406.1.4 Section testing. A *piping* system shall be permitted to be tested as a complete unit or in sections. Under no circumstances shall a valve in a line be used as a bulkhead between gas in one section of the *piping* system and test medium in an adjacent section, unless two valves are installed in series with a valved "telltale" located between these valves. A valve shall not be subjected to the test pressure unless it can be determined that the valve, including the valve-closing mechanism, is designed to safely withstand the test pressure.

406.1.5 Regulators and valve assemblies. Regulator and valve assemblies fabricated independently of the *piping* system in which they are to be installed shall be permitted to be tested with inert gas or air at the time of fabrication.

406.2 Test medium. The test medium shall be air, nitrogen, carbon dioxide or an inert gas. Oxygen shall not be used.

406.3 Test preparation. Pipe joints, including welds, shall be left exposed for examination during the test.

Exception: Covered or concealed pipe end joints that have been previously tested in accordance with this code.

406.3.1 Expansion joints. Deleted.

406.3.2 Appliance and equipment isolation. Appliances and *equipment* that are not to be included in the test shall be either disconnected from the *piping* or isolated by blanks, blind flanges or caps. Flanged joints at which blinds are inserted to blank off other *equipment* during the test shall not be required to be tested.

406.3.3 Appliance and equipment disconnection. Where the *piping* system is connected to appliances or *equipment* designed for operating pressures of less than the test pressure, such appliances or *equipment* shall be isolated from the *piping* system by disconnecting them and capping the *outlet*(s).

406.3.4 Valve isolation. Where the *piping* system is connected to appliances or *equipment* designed for operating pressures equal to or greater than the test pressure, such appliances or *equipment* shall be isolated from the *piping* system by closing the individual *appliance* or *equipment* shutoff valve(s).

406.3.5 Testing precautions. All testing of *piping* systems shall be done with due regard for the safety of employees and the public during the test. Bulkheads, anchorage, and bracing suitably designed to resist test pressures shall be installed if necessary. Prior to testing, the interior of the pipe shall be cleared of all foreign material.

406.4 Test pressure measurement. Test pressure shall be measured with a manometer or with a pressure-measuring device designed and calibrated to read, record or indicate a pressure loss caused by leakage during the pressure test period. The source of pressure shall be isolated before the pressure tests are made. Mechanical gauges used to measure test pressures shall have a range such that the highest end of the scale is not greater than five times the test pressure.

406.4.1 Test pressure. The test pressure to be used shall be no less than $1^1/_2$ times the proposed maximum working pressure, but not less than 3 psig (20 kPa gauge), irrespective of design pressure. Where the test pressure exceeds 125 psig (862 kPa gauge), the test pressure shall not exceed a value that produces a hoop stress in the piping greater than 50 percent of the specified minimum yield strength of the pipe.

406.4.2 Test duration. Test duration shall be not less than $^1/_2$ hour for each 500 cubic feet (14 m^3) of pipe volume or fraction thereof. When testing a system having a volume less than 10 cubic feet (0.28 m^3) or a system in a single-family dwelling, the test duration shall be not less than 10 minutes. The duration of the test shall not be required to exceed 24 hours.

406.5 Detection of leaks and defects. The *piping* system shall withstand the test pressure specified without showing any evidence of leakage or other defects.

Any reduction of test pressures as indicated by pressure gauges shall be deemed to indicate the presence of a leak unless such reduction can be readily attributed to some other cause.

406.5.1 Detection methods. The leakage shall be located by means of an *approved* gas detector, a noncorrosive leak detection fluid or other *approved* leak detection methods. Matches, candles, open flames or other methods that could provide a source of ignition shall not be used.

406.5.2 Corrections. Where leakage or other defects are located, the affected portion of the *piping* system shall be repaired or replaced and retested.

406.6 Piping system and equipment leakage check. Leakage checking of systems and *equipment* shall be in accordance with Sections 406.6.1 through 406.6.4.

406.6.1 Test gases. Leak checks using fuel gas shall be permitted in *piping* systems that have been pressure tested in accordance with Section 406.

406.6.2 Before turning gas on. During the process of turning gas on into a system of new gas *piping*, the entire system shall be inspected to determine that there are no open fittings or ends and that all valves at unused outlets are closed and plugged or capped.

406.6.3 Leak check. Immediately after the gas is turned on into a new system or into a system that has been initially restored after an interruption of service, the *piping* system shall be checked for leakage. Where leakage is indicated, the gas supply shall be shut off until the necessary repairs have been made.

406.6.4 Placing appliances and equipment in operation. Appliances and *equipment* shall not be placed in operation until after the *piping* system has been checked for leakage in accordance with Section 406.6.3 and determined to be free of leakage and purged in accordance with Section 406.7.2.

406.7 Purging. Purging of piping shall shall comply with Sections 406.7.1 through 406.7.4.

Exception: Purging is not required for low pressure gas piping 2 inches nominal pipe size or less and length not exceeding 200 feet. The open end of piping systems being purged shall not discharge into confined spaces or areas where there are sources of ignition unless precautions are taken to perform this operation in a safe manner by ventilation of the space, control of purging rate and elimination of hazardous conditions.

406.7.1 Removal from service. Where gas *piping* is to be opened for servicing, addition or modification, the section to be worked on shall be turned off from the gas supply at the nearest convenient point, and the line pressure vented to the outdoors.

Exception: If the line pressure cannot be vented to the outdoors; the building an all effected spaces shall be evacuated of personnel not involved with purging the gas lines, quantities of flammable gas shall not exceed 25 percent of the lower explosive limit (1.0-percent fuel/air mixture for natural gas or 0.6-percent fuel/air mixture for LP-gas) as measured by a combustible gas detector, all ignition sources shall be eliminated, and adequate ventiliation to prevent accumulation of flammable gases shall be provided.

Table 406.7.1 Size and Length of Piping Requiring Purging with Inert Gas for Servicing or Modification. Deleted.

406.7.2 Placing in operation. Where *piping* full of air is placed in operation, the air in the *piping* shall be displaced with fuel gas. The air can be safely displaced with fuel gas provided that a moderately rapid and continuous flow of fuel gas is introduced at one end of the line and air is vented out at the other end. The fuel gas flow shall be continued without interruption until the vented gas is free of air. The point of discharge shall not be left unattended during purging. After purging, the vent shall then be closed.

Table 406.7.2 Size and Length of Piping Requiring Purging with Inert Gas Before Placing in Operation. Deleted.

406.7.3 Discharge of purged gases. The open end of *piping* systems being purged shall not discharge into confined spaces or areas where there are sources of ignition unless precautions are taken to perform this operation in a safe manner. All potential sources of ignition shall be identified and eliminated or controlled. Precautions shall be taken to maintain the concentration of the flammable gas below 25-percent of the lower explosive limits (1.0-percent fuel/air mixture for natural gas or 0.6-percent fuel/air mixture for LP gas) such as adequate ventilation and control of purging rate. The point of discharge shall not be left unattended during purging.

406.7.4 Placing appliances and equipment in operation. After the *piping* system has been placed in operation, all appliances and *equipment* shall be purged and then placed in operation, as necessary.

406.7.5 Personnel training. Personnel performing purging operation shall be trained according to the hazards associated with purging and shall not rely on odor when monitoring the concentration of combustible gas.

SECTION 407 (IFGC)
PIPING SUPPORT

407.1 General. *Piping* shall be provided with support in accordance with Section 407.2.

407.2 Design and installation. *Piping* shall be supported with metal pipe hooks, metal pipe straps, metal bands, metal brackets, metal hangers or building structural components, suitable for the size of *piping*, of adequate strength and quality, and located at intervals so as to prevent or damp out excessive vibration. *Piping* shall be anchored to prevent undue strains on connected appliances and shall not be supported by other *piping*. Pipe hangers and supports shall conform to the requirements of MSS SP-58 and shall be spaced in accordance with

Section 415. Supports, hangers and anchors shall be installed so as not to interfere with the free expansion and contraction of the *piping* between anchors. All parts of the supporting *equipment* shall be designed and installed so they will not be disengaged by movement of the supported *piping*.

SECTION 408 (IFGC) DRIPS AND SLOPED PIPING

408.1 Slopes. Deleted.

408.2 Drips. Deleted.

408.3 Location of drips. Deleted.

408.4 Sediment trap. Where a sediment trap is not incorporated as part of the *appliance*, a sediment trap shall be installed downstream of the *appliance* shutoff valve as close to the inlet of the *appliance* as practical. The sediment trap shall be either a tee fitting having a capped nipple of any length installed vertically in the bottommost opening of the tee or other device *approved* as an effective sediment trap. Illuminating appliances, ranges, clothes dryers, gas logs, log lighters and outdoor grills need not be so equipped.

SECTION 409 (IFGC) SHUTOFF VALVES

409.1 General. *Piping* systems shall be provided with shutoff valves in accordance with this section.

409.1.1 Valve approval. Shutoff valves shall be of an *approved* type; shall be constructed of materials compatible with the *piping*; and shall comply with the standard that is applicable for the pressure and application, in accordance with Table 409.1.1.

409.1.2 Prohibited locations. Shutoff valves shall be prohibited in concealed locations and *furnace plenums.*

409.1.3 Access to shutoff valves. Shutoff valves shall be located in places so as to provide *access* for operation and shall be installed so as to be protected from damage.

409.2 Meter valve. Deleted.

409.3 Shutoff valves for multiple-house line systems. Where a single meter is used to supply gas to more than one building or tenant, a separate shutoff valve shall be provided for each building.

409.3.1 Multiple tenant buildings. Deleted.

409.3.2 Individual buildings. In a common system serving more than one building, shutoff valves shall be installed outdoors at each building.

409.3.3 Identification of shutoff valves. Each house line shutoff valve shall be plainly marked with an identification tag attached by the installer so that the *piping* systems supplied by such valves are readily identified.

409.4 MP regulator valves. A *listed* shutoff valve shall be installed immediately ahead of each MP regulator.

409.5 Appliance shutoff valve. Each *appliance* shall be provided with a shutoff valve in accordance with Section 409.5.1, 409.5.2 or 409.5.3.

409.5.1 Located within same room. The shutoff valve shall be located in the same room as the *appliance*. The shutoff valve shall be within 6 feet (1829 mm) of the *appliance*, and shall be installed upstream of the union, connector or quick disconnect device it serves. Such shutoff valves shall be provided with *access. Appliance* shutoff valves located in the firebox of a *fireplace* shall be installed in accordance with the *appliance* manufacturer's instructions. This section shall not prohibit the use or the installation of gas shutoff valves in the firebox of fireplaces serving listed gas appliances.

409.5.2 Vented decorative appliances and room heaters. Shutoff valves for vented decorative appliances, room heaters and decorative appliances for installation in vented *fireplaces* shall be permitted to be installed in an area remote from the appliances where such valves are provided with ready *access*. Such valves shall be permanently identified and shall serve no other *appliance*. The *piping* from the shutoff valve to within 6 feet (1829 mm) of the *appliance* shall be designed, sized and installed in accordance with Sections 401 through 408.

409.5.3 Located at manifold. Deleted.

409.6 Shutoff valve for laboratories. Deleted.

SECTION 410 (IFGC) FLOW CONTROLS

410.1 Pressure regulators. A line pressure regulator shall be installed where the *appliance* is designed to operate at a lower

TABLE 409.1.1 MANUAL GAS VALVE STANDARDS

VALVE STANDARDS	APPLIANCE SHUTOFF VALVE APPLICATION UP TO $^1/_2$ psig PRESSURE	OTHER VALVE APPLICATIONS			
		UP TO $^1/_2$ psig PRESSURE	UP TO 2 psig PRESSURE	UP TO 5 psig PRESSURE	UP TO 125 psig PRESSURE
ANSI Z21.15	X	—	—	—	—
CSA Requirement 3-88	X	X	X[a]	X[b]	—
ASME B16.44	X	X	X[a]	X[b]	—
ASME B16.33	X	X	X	X	X

For SI: 1 pound per square inch gauge = 6.895 kPa.

a. If labeled 2G.

b. If labeled 5G.

pressure than the supply pressure. Line gas pressure regulators shall be *listed* as complying with ANSI Z21.80. *Access* shall be provided to pressure regulators. Pressure regulators shall be protected from physical damage. Regulators installed on the exterior of the building shall be *approved* for outdoor installation.

410.2 MP regulators. MP pressure regulators shall comply with the following:

1. The MP regulator shall be *approved* and shall be suitable for the inlet and outlet gas pressures for the application.
2. The MP regulator shall maintain a reduced outlet pressure under lockup (no-flow) conditions.
3. The capacity of the MP regulator, determined by published ratings of its manufacturer, shall be adequate to supply the appliances served.
4. The MP pressure regulator shall be provided with *access*. Where located indoors, the regulator shall be vented to the outdoors or shall be equipped with a leak-limiting device, in either case complying with Section 410.3.
5. A tee fitting with one opening capped or plugged shall be installed between the MP regulator and its upstream shutoff valve. Such tee fitting shall be positioned to allow connection of a pressure-measuring instrument and to serve as a sediment trap.
6. A means to test pressure shall be installed not less than 10 pipe diameters downstream of the MP regulator outlet. Such fitting shall be positioned to allow connection of a pressure-measuring instrument.

410.3 Venting of regulators. Pressure regulators that require a vent shall be vented directly to the outdoors. The vent shall be designed to prevent the entry of insects, water and foreign objects.

Exception: A vent to the outdoors is not required for regulators equipped with and *labeled* for utilization with an *approved* vent-limiting device installed in accordance with the manufacturer's instructions.

410.3.1 Vent piping. Vent *piping* for relief vents and breather vents shall be constructed of materials allowed for gas *piping* in accordance with Section 403. Vent *piping* shall be not smaller than the vent connection on the pressure regulating device. Vent *piping* serving relief vents and combination relief and breather vents shall be run independently to the outdoors and shall serve only a single device vent. Vent *piping* serving only breather vents is permitted to be connected in a manifold arrangement where sized in accordance with an *approved* design that minimizes back pressure in the event of diaphragm rupture. Regulator vent *piping* shall not exceed the length specified in the regulator manufacturer's installation instructions.

SECTION 411 (IFGC) APPLIANCE AND MANUFACTURED HOME CONNECTIONS

411.1 Connecting appliances. Except as required by Section 411.1.1, appliances shall be connected to the piping system by one of the following:

1. Rigid metallic pipe and fittings.
2. Corrugated stainless steel tubing (CSST) where installed in accordance with the manufacturer's instructions.
3. Semirigid metallic tubing and metallic fittings. Lengths shall not exceed 6 feet (1829 mm) and shall be located entirely in the same room as the appliance. Semirigid metallic tubing shall not enter a motor-operated appliance through an unprotected knockout opening.
4. Listed and labeled appliance connectors in compliance with ANSI Z21.24 and installed in accordance with the manufacturer's instructions and located entirely in the same room as the appliance.
5. Listed and labeled quick-disconnect devices used in conjunction with listed and labeled appliance connectors.
6. Listed and labeled convenience outlets used in conjunction with listed and labeled appliance connectors.
7. Listed and labeled outdoor appliance connectors in compliance with ANSI Z21.75/CSA 6.27 and installed in accordance with the manufacturer's instructions.

411.1.1 Commercial cooking appliances. Deleted.

411.1.2 Protection against damage. Connectors and tubing shall be installed so as to be protected against physical damage.

411.1.3 Connector installation. *Appliance* fuel connectors shall be installed in accordance with the manufacturer's instructions and Sections 411.1.3.1 through 411.1.3.4.

411.1.3.1 Maximum length. Connectors shall have an overall length not to exceed 6 feet (1829 mm). Measurement shall be made along the centerline of the connector. Only one connector shall be used for each *appliance*.

Exception: Rigid metallic *piping* used to connect an *appliance* to the *piping* system shall be permitted to have a total length greater than 6 feet (1829 mm), provided that the connecting pipe is sized as part of the *piping* system in accordance with Section 402 and the location of the *appliance* shutoff valve complies with Section 409.5.

411.1.3.2 Minimum size. Connectors shall have the capacity for the total demand of the connected *appliance*.

411.1.3.3 Prohibited locations and penetrations. Connectors shall not be concealed within, or extended through, walls, floors, partitions, ceilings or *appliance* housings.

Exceptions:

1. Connectors constructed of materials allowed for *piping* systems in accordance with Section 403 shall be permitted to pass through walls, floors, partitions and ceilings where installed in accordance with Section 409.5.2.
2. Rigid steel pipe connectors shall be permitted to extend through openings in *appliance* housings.
3. *Fireplace* inserts that are factory equipped with grommets, sleeves or other means of protection in accordance with the listing of the *appliance*.
4. Semirigid tubing and *listed* connectors shall be permitted to extend through an opening in an *appliance* housing, cabinet or casing where the tubing or connector is protected against damage.

411.1.3.4 Shutoff valve. A shutoff valve not less than the nominal size of the connector shall be installed ahead of the connector in accordance with Section 409.5.

411.1.4 Movable appliances. Where appliances are equipped with casters or are otherwise subject to periodic movement or relocation for purposes such as routine cleaning and maintenance, such appliances shall be connected to the supply system *piping* by means of an *approved* flexible connector designed and *labeled* for the application. Such flexible connectors shall be installed and protected against physical damage in accordance with the manufacturer's installation instructions.

411.1.5 (IFGS) Connection of gas engine-powered air conditioners. Internal combustion engines shall not be rigidly connected to the gas supply *piping*.

411.1.6 Unions. A union fitting shall be provided for appliances connected by rigid metallic pipe. Such unions shall be accessible and located within 6 feet (1829 mm) of the *appliance*.

411.2 Manufactured home connections. Manufactured homes shall be connected to the distribution *piping* system by one of the following materials:

1. Metallic pipe in accordance with Section 403.4.
2. Metallic tubing in accordance with Section 403.5.
3. *Listed* and *labeled* connectors in compliance with ANSI Z21.75/CSA 6.27 and installed in accordance with the manufacturer's installation instructions.

411.3 Suspended low-intensity infrared tube heaters. Suspended low-intensity infrared tube heaters shall be connected to the building *piping* system with a connector *listed* for the application complying with ANSI Z21.24/CGA 6.10. The connector shall be installed as specified by the tube heater manufacturer's instructions.

SECTION 412 (IFGC) LIQUEFIED PETROLEUM GAS MOTOR VEHICLE FUEL-DISPENSING FACILITIES

Deleted

SECTION 413 (IFGC) COMPRESSED NATURAL GAS MOTOR VEHICLE FUEL-DISPENSING FACILITIES

Deleted

SECTION 414 (IFGC) SUPPLEMENTAL AND STANDBY GAS SUPPLY

Deleted

SECTION 415 (IFGS) PIPING SUPPORT INTERVALS

415.1 Interval of support. *Piping* shall be supported at intervals not exceeding the spacing specified in Table 415.1. Spacing of supports for CSST shall be in accordance with the CSST manufacturer's instructions.

TABLE 415.1 SUPPORT OF PIPING

STEEL PIPE, NOMINAL SIZE OF PIPE (inches)	SPACING OF SUPPORTS (feet)	NOMINAL SIZE OF TUBING (SMOOTH-WALL) (inch O.D.)	SPACING OF SUPPORTS (feet)
$^1/_2$	6	$^1/_2$	4
$^3/_4$ or 1	8	$^5/_8$ or $^3/_4$	6
$1^1/_4$ or larger (horizontal)	10	$^7/_8$ or 1 (horizontal)	8
$1^1/_4$ or larger (vertical)	Every floor level	1 or larger (vertical)	Every floor level

For SI: 1 inch = 25.4 mm, 1 foot = 304.8 mm.

SECTION 416 (IFGS) OVERPRESSURE PROTECTION DEVICES

416.1 General. Overpressure protection devices shall be provided in accordance with this section to prevent the pressure in the *piping* system from exceeding the pressure that would cause unsafe operation of any connected and properly adjusted appliances.

416.2 Protection methods. The requirements of this section shall be considered to be met and a *piping* system deemed to have overpressure protection where a service or line pressure regulator plus one other device are installed such that the following occur:

1. Each device limits the pressure to a value that does not exceed the maximum working pressure of the downstream system.
2. The individual failure of either device does not result in the overpressurization of the downstream system.

416.3 Device maintenance. The pressure regulating, limiting and relieving devices shall be properly maintained; and inspection procedures shall be devised or suitable instrumentation installed to detect failures or malfunctions of such devices; and replacements or repairs shall be promptly made.

416.4 Where required. A pressure-relieving or pressure-limiting device shall not be required where: (1) the gas does not contain materials that could seriously interfere with the operation of the service or line pressure regulator; (2) the operating pressure of the gas source is 60 psi (414 kPa) or less; and (3) the service or line pressure regulator has all of the following design features or characteristics:

1. Pipe connections to the service or line regulator do not exceed 2 inches (51 mm) nominal diameter.
2. The regulator is self-contained with no external static or control *piping*.
3. The regulator has a single port valve with an orifice diameter not greater than that recommended by the manufacturer for the maximum gas pressure at the regulator inlet.
4. The valve seat is made of resilient material designed to withstand abrasion of the gas, impurities in the gas and cutting by the valve, and to resist permanent deformation where it is pressed against the valve port.
5. The regulator is capable, under normal operating conditions, of regulating the downstream pressure within the necessary limits of accuracy and of limiting the discharge pressure under no-flow conditions to not more than 150 percent of the discharge pressure maintained under flow conditions.

416.5 Devices. Pressure-relieving or pressure-limiting devices shall be one of the following:

1. Spring-loaded relief device.
2. Pilot-loaded back pressure regulator used as a relief valve and designed so that failure of the pilot system or external control *piping* will cause the regulator relief valve to open.
3. A monitoring regulator installed in series with the service or line pressure regulator.
4. A series regulator installed upstream from the service or line regulator and set to continuously limit the pressure on the inlet of the service or line regulator to the maximum working pressure of the downstream *piping* system.
5. An automatic shutoff device installed in series with the service or line pressure regulator and set to shut off when the pressure on the downstream *piping* system reaches the maximum working pressure or some other predetermined pressure less than the maximum working pressure. This device shall be designed so that it will remain closed until manually reset.
6. A liquid seal relief device that can be set to open accurately and consistently at the desired pressure.

The devices shall be installed either as an integral part of the service or line pressure regulator or as separate units. Where separate pressure-relieving or pressure-limiting devices are installed, they shall comply with Sections 416.5.1 through 416.5.6.

416.5.1 Construction and installation. Pressure relieving and pressure-limiting devices shall be constructed of materials so that the operation of the devices will not be impaired by corrosion of external parts by the atmosphere or of internal parts by the gas. Pressure-relieving and pressure-limiting devices shall be designed and installed so that they can be operated to determine whether the valve is free. The devices shall also be designed and installed so that they can be tested to determine the pressure at which they will operate and examined for leakage when in the closed position.

416.5.2 External control piping. External control *piping* shall be protected from falling objects, excavations and other causes of damage and shall be designed and installed so that damage to any control *piping* will not render both the regulator and the overpressure protective device inoperative.

416.5.3 Setting. Each pressure-relieving or pressure-limiting device shall be set so that the pressure does not exceed a safe level beyond the maximum allowable working pressure for the connected *piping* and appliances.

416.5.4 Unauthorized operation. Precautions shall be taken to prevent unauthorized operation of any shutoff valve that will make a pressure-relieving valve or pressure-limiting device inoperative. The following are acceptable methods for complying with this provision:

1. The valve shall be locked in the open position. Authorized personnel shall be instructed in the importance of leaving the shutoff valve open and of being present while the shutoff valve is closed so that it can be locked in the open position before leaving the premises.
2. Duplicate relief valves shall be installed, each having adequate capacity to protect the system, and the isolating valves and three-way valves shall be arranged so that only one safety device can be rendered inoperative at a time.

416.5.5 Vents. The discharge stacks, vents and outlet parts of all pressure-relieving and pressure-limiting devices shall be located so that gas is safely discharged to the outdoors. Discharge stacks and vents shall be designed to prevent the entry of water, insects and other foreign material that could cause blockage. The discharge stack or vent line shall be at least the same size as the outlet of the pressure-relieving device.

416.5.6 Size of fittings, pipe and openings. The fittings, pipe and openings located between the system to be protected and the pressure-relieving device shall be sized to prevent hammering of the valve and to prevent impairment of relief capacity.

CHAPTER 5
CHIMNEYS AND VENTS

SECTION 501 (IFGC) GENERAL

501.1 Scope. This chapter, and Appendices B and C shall govern the installation, maintenance, repair and approval of factory-built chimneys, chimney liners, vents and connectors and the utilization of masonry chimneys serving gas-fired appliances. The requirements for the installation, maintenance, repair and approval of factory-built chimneys, chimney liners, vents and connectors serving appliances burning fuels other than fuel gas shall be regulated by the *International Mechanical Code*. The construction, repair, maintenance and approval of masonry chimneys shall be regulated by the *International Building Code*.

501.2 General. Every *appliance* shall discharge the products of combustion to the outdoors, except for appliances exempted by Section 501.8.

501.3 Masonry chimneys. Masonry chimneys shall be constructed in accordance with Section 503.5.3 and the *International Building Code*.

501.4 Minimum size of chimney or vent. Chimneys and vents shall be sized in accordance with Sections 503 and 504.

501.5 Abandoned inlet openings. Abandoned inlet openings in chimneys and vents shall be closed by an *approved* method.

501.6 Positive pressure. Where an *appliance* equipped with a mechanical forced draft system creates a positive pressure in the venting system, the venting system shall be designed for positive pressure applications.

501.7 Connection to fireplace. Connection of appliances to chimney flues serving fireplaces shall be in accordance with Sections 501.7.1 through 501.7.3.

501.7.1 Closure and access. A noncombustible seal shall be provided below the point of connection to prevent entry of room air into the flue. Means shall be provided for *access* to the flue for inspection and cleaning.

501.7.2 Connection to factory-built fireplace flue. An *appliance* shall not be connected to a flue serving a factory-built *fireplace* unless the *appliance* is specifically *listed* for such installation. The connection shall be made in accordance with the *appliance* manufacturer's installation instructions.

501.7.3 Connection to masonry fireplace flue. A connector shall extend from the *appliance* to the flue serving a masonry *fireplace* such that the flue gases are exhausted directly into the flue. The connector shall be accessible or removable for inspection and cleaning of both the connector and the flue. *Listed* direct connection devices shall be installed in accordance with their listing.

501.8 Appliances not required to be vented. The following appliances shall not be required to be vented.

1. Ranges.
2. Built-in domestic cooking units *listed* and marked for optional venting.
3. Hot plates and laundry stoves.
4. Type 1 clothes dryers (Type 1 clothes dryers shall be exhausted in accordance with the requirements of Section 614).
5. A single booster-type automatic instantaneous water heater, where designed and used solely for the sanitizing rinse requirements of a dishwashing machine, provided that the heater is installed in a commercial kitchen having a mechanical exhaust system. Where installed in this manner, the draft hood, if required, shall be in place and unaltered and the draft hood *outlet* shall be not less than 36 inches (914 mm) vertically and 6 inches (152 mm) horizontally from any surface other than the heater.
6. Refrigerators.
7. Counter appliances.
8. Room heaters *listed* for unvented use.
9. Direct-fired makeup air heaters.
10. Other appliances *listed* for unvented use and not provided with flue collars.
11. Specialized appliances of limited input such as laboratory burners and gas lights.

Where the appliances listed in Items 5 through 11 above are installed so that the aggregate input rating exceeds 20 British thermal units (Btu) per hour per cubic feet (207 watts per m^3) of volume of the room or space in which such appliances are installed, one or more shall be provided with venting systems or other *approved* means for conveying the vent gases to the outdoor atmosphere so that the aggregate input rating of the remaining unvented appliances does not exceed 20 Btu per hour per cubic foot (207 watts per m^3). Where the room or space in which the *appliance* is installed is directly connected to another room or space by a doorway, archway or other opening of comparable size that cannot be closed, the volume of such adjacent room or space shall be permitted to be included in the calculations.

501.9 Chimney entrance. Connectors shall connect to a masonry chimney flue at a point not less than 12 inches (305 mm) above the lowest portion of the interior of the chimney flue.

501.10 Connections to exhauster. *Appliance* connections to a chimney or vent equipped with a power exhauster shall be made on the inlet side of the exhauster. Joints on the positive pressure side of the exhauster shall be sealed to prevent flue-gas leakage as specified by the manufacturer's installation instructions for the exhauster.

501.11 Masonry chimneys. Masonry chimneys utilized to vent appliances shall be located, constructed and sized as specified in the manufacturer's installation instructions for the appliances being vented and Section 503.

501.12 Residential and low-heat appliances flue lining systems. Flue lining systems for use with residential-type and low-heat appliances shall be limited to the following:

1. Clay flue lining complying with the requirements of ASTM C 315 or equivalent. Clay flue lining shall be installed in accordance with the *International Building Code*.
2. *Listed* chimney lining systems complying with UL 1777.
3. Other *approved* materials that will resist, without cracking, softening or corrosion, flue gases and condensate at temperatures up to 1,800°F (982°C).

501.13 Category I appliance flue lining systems. Flue lining systems for use with Category I appliances shall be limited to the following:

1. Flue lining systems complying with Section 501.12.
2. Chimney lining systems *listed* and *labeled* for use with gas appliances with draft hoods and other Category I gas appliances *listed* and *labeled* for use with Type B vents.

501.14 Category II, III and IV appliance venting systems. The design, sizing and installation of vents for Category II, III and IV appliances shall be in accordance with the *appliance* manufacturer's installation instructions.

501.15 Existing chimneys and vents. Where an *appliance* is permanently disconnected from an existing chimney or vent, or where an *appliance* is connected to an existing chimney or vent during the process of a new installation, the chimney or vent shall comply with Sections 501.15.1 through 501.15.4.

501.15.1 Size. The chimney or vent shall be resized as necessary to control flue gas condensation in the interior of the chimney or vent and to provide the *appliance* or appliances served with the required draft. For Category I appliances, the resizing shall be in accordance with Section 502.

501.15.2 Flue passageways. The flue gas passageway shall be free of obstructions and combustible deposits and shall be cleaned if previously used for venting a solid or liquid fuel-burning *appliance* or *fireplace*. The flue liner, chimney inner wall or vent inner wall shall be continuous and shall be free of cracks, gaps, perforations or other damage or deterioration which would allow the escape of combustion products, including gases, moisture and creosote.

501.15.3 Cleanout. Masonry chimney flues shall be provided with a cleanout opening having a minimum height of 6 inches (152 mm). The upper edge of the opening shall be located not less than 6 inches (152 mm) below the lowest chimney inlet opening. The cleanout shall be provided with a tight-fitting, noncombustible cover.

501.15.4 Clearances. Chimneys and vents shall have airspace *clearance* to combustibles in accordance with the *International Building Code* and the chimney or vent manufacturer's installation instructions.

Exception: Masonry chimneys without the required airspace clearances shall be permitted to be used if lined or relined with a chimney lining system *listed* for use in chimneys with reduced clearances in accordance with UL 1777. The chimney *clearance* shall be not less than permitted by the terms of the chimney liner listing and the manufacturer's instructions.

501.15.4.1 Fireblocking. Noncombustible fireblocking shall be provided in accordance with the *International Building Code*.

SECTION 502 (IFGC) VENTS

502.1 General. All vents, except as provided in Section 503.7, shall be *listed* and *labeled*. Type B and BW vents shall be tested in accordance with UL 441. Type L vents shall be tested in accordance with UL 641. Vents for Category II and III appliances shall be tested in accordance with UL 1738. Plastic vents for Category IV appliances shall not be required to be *listed* and *labeled* where such vents are as specified by the *appliance* manufacturer and are installed in accordance with the *appliance* manufacturer's installation instructions.

502.2 Connectors required. Connectors shall be used to connect appliances to the vertical chimney or vent, except where the chimney or vent is attached directly to the *appliance*. Vent connector size, material, construction and installation shall be in accordance with Section 503.

502.3 Vent application. The application of vents shall be in accordance with Table 503.4.

502.4 Insulation shield. Where vents pass through insulated assemblies, an insulation shield constructed of steel having a minimum thickness of 0.0187 inch (0.4712 mm) (No. 26 gage) shall be installed to provide *clearance* between the vent and the insulation material. The *clearance* shall not be less than the *clearance* to combustibles specified by the vent manufacturer's installation instructions. Where vents pass through attic space, the shield shall terminate not less than 2 inches (51 mm) above the insulation materials and shall be secured in place to prevent displacement. Insulation shields provided as part of a *listed* vent system shall be installed in accordance with the manufacturer's installation instructions.

502.5 Installation. Vent systems shall be sized, installed and terminated in accordance with the vent and *appliance* manufacturer's installation instructions and Section 503.

502.6 Support of vents. All portions of vents shall be adequately supported for the design and weight of the materials employed.

502.7 Protection against physical damage. In concealed locations, where a vent is installed through holes or notches in studs, joists, rafters or similar members less than $1^1/_2$ inches (38 mm) from the nearest edge of the member, the vent shall be protected by shield plates. Protective steel shield plates having a minimum thickness of 0.0575 inch (1.463 mm) (No. 16 gage) shall cover the area of the vent where the member is notched or bored and shall extend a minimum of 4 inches (102 mm) above sole plates, below top plates and to each side of a stud, joist or rafter.

SECTION 503 (IFGS) VENTING OF APPLIANCES

503.1 General. This section recognizes that the choice of venting materials and the methods of installation of venting systems are dependent on the operating characteristics of the *appliance* being vented. The operating characteristics of vented appliances can be categorized with respect to: (1) positive or negative pressure within the venting system; and (2) whether or not the *appliance* generates flue or vent gases that might condense in the venting system. See Section 202 for the definitions of these *vented appliance categories*.

503.2 Venting systems required. Except as permitted in Sections 503.2.1 through 503.2.4 and 501.8, all appliances shall be connected to venting systems.

503.2.1 Ventilating hoods. Deleted.

503.2.2 Well-ventilated spaces. Deleted.

503.2.3 Direct-vent appliances. *Listed direct-vent appliances* shall be installed in accordance with the manufacturer's instructions and Section 503.8, Item 3.

503.2.4 Appliances with integral vents. Appliances incorporating integral venting means shall be considered properly vented where installed in accordance with the manufacturer's instructions and Section 503.8, Items 1 and 2.

503.3 Design and construction. A venting system shall be designed and constructed so as to develop a positive flow adequate to convey flue or vent gases to the outdoors.

503.3.1 Appliance draft requirements. A venting system shall satisfy the draft requirements of the *appliance* in accordance with the manufacturer's instructions.

503.3.2 Design and construction. Appliances required to be vented shall be connected to a venting system designed and installed in accordance with the provisions of Sections 503.4 through 503.16.

503.3.3 Mechanical draft systems. Mechanical draft systems shall comply with the following:

1. Mechanical draft systems shall be *listed* and shall be installed in accordance with the manufacturer's installation instructions for both the *appliance* and the mechanical draft system.
2. Appliances, except incinerators, requiring venting shall be permitted to be vented by means of mechanical draft systems of either forced or induced draft design.
3. Forced draft systems and all portions of induced draft systems under positive pressure during operation shall be designed and installed so as to prevent leakage of flue or vent gases into a building.
4. Vent connectors serving appliances vented by natural draft shall not be connected into any portion of mechanical draft systems operating under positive pressure.
5. Where a mechanical draft system is employed, provisions shall be made to prevent the flow of gas to the main burners when the draft system is not performing so as to satisfy the operating requirements of the *appliance* for safe performance.
6. The exit terminals of mechanical draft systems shall be not less than 7 feet (2134 mm) above finished ground level where located adjacent to public walkways and shall be located as specified in Section 503.8, Items 1 and 2.

503.3.4 Ventilating hoods and exhaust systems. Deleted.

503.3.5 Air ducts and furnace plenums. Venting systems shall not extend into or pass through any fabricated air duct or *furnace plenum*.

503.3.6 Above-ceiling air-handling spaces. Deleted.

503.4 Type of venting system to be used. The type of venting system to be used shall be in accordance with Table 503.4.

503.4.1 Plastic piping. Plastic *piping* used for venting appliances *listed* for use with such venting materials shall be *approved*.

503.4.1.1 Plastic vent joints. Plastic pipe and fittings used to vent appliances shall be installed in accordance with the *appliance* manufacturer's installation instructions. Where a primer is required, it shall be of a contrasting color.

503.4.2 Special gas vent. Special gas vent shall be *listed* and installed in accordance with the special gas vent manufacturer's installation instructions.

503.5 Masonry, metal and factory-built chimneys. Masonry, metal and factory-built chimneys shall comply with Sections 503.5.1 through 503.5.10.

503.5.1 Factory-built chimneys. Factory-built chimneys shall be installed in accordance with the manufacturer's installation instructions. Factory-built chimneys used to vent appliances that operate at a positive vent pressure shall be *listed* for such application.

503.5.2 Metal chimneys. Metal chimneys shall be built and installed in accordance with NFPA 211.

503.5.3 Masonry chimneys. Masonry chimneys shall be built and installed in accordance with NFPA 211 and shall be lined with *approved* clay flue lining, a *listed* chimney lining system or other *approved* material that will resist corrosion, erosion, softening or cracking from vent gases at temperatures up to 1,800°F (982°C).

Exception: Masonry chimney flues serving *listed* gas appliances with draft hoods, Category I appliances and other gas appliances *listed* for use with Type B vents shall be permitted to be lined with a chimney lining system specifically *listed* for use only with such appliances. The liner shall be installed in accordance with the liner manufacturer's installation instructions. A permanent identifying label shall be attached at the point where the connection is to be made to the liner. The label shall read: "This chimney liner is for appliances that burn gas only. Do not connect to solid or liquid fuel-burning appliances or incinerators."

For installation of gas vents in existing masonry chimneys, see Section 503.6.3.

TABLE 503.4
TYPE OF VENTING SYSTEM TO BE USED

APPLIANCES	TYPE OF VENTING SYSTEM
Listed Category I appliances Listed appliances equipped with draft hood Appliances listed for use with Type B gas vent	Type B gas vent (Section 503.6) Chimney (Section 503.5) Single-wall metal pipe (Section 503.7) Listed chimney lining system for gas venting (Section 503.5.3) Special gas vent listed for these appliances (Section 503.4.2)
Listed vented wall furnaces	Type B-W gas vent (Sections 503.6, 608)
Category II appliances	As specified or furnished by manufacturers of listed appliances (Sections 503.4.1, 503.4.2)
Category III appliances	As specified or furnished by manufacturers of listed appliances (Sections 503.4.1, 503.4.2)
Category IV appliances	As specified or furnished by manufacturers of listed appliances (Sections 503.4.1, 503.4.2)
Incinerators, indoors	Chimney (Section 503.5)
Incinerators, outdoors	Single-wall metal pipe (Sections 503.7, 503.7.6)
Appliances that can be converted for use with solid fuel	Chimney (Section 503.5)
Unlisted combination gas and oil-burning appliances	Chimney (Section 503.5)
Listed combination gas and oil-burning appliances	Type L vent (Section 503.6) or chimney (Section 503.5)
Combination gas and solid fuel-burning appliances	Chimney (Section 503.5)
Appliances listed for use with chimneys only	Chimney (Section 503.5)
Unlisted appliances	Chimney (Section 503.5)
Decorative appliances in vented fireplaces	Chimney
Gas-fired toilets	Single-wall metal pipe (Section 626)
Direct-vent appliances	See Section 503.2.3
Appliances with integral vent	See Section 503.2.4

503.5.4 Chimney termination. Chimneys for residential-type or low-heat appliances shall extend at least 3 feet (914 mm) above the highest point where they pass through a roof of a building and at least 2 feet (610 mm) higher than any portion of a building within a horizontal distance of 10 feet (3048 mm) (see Figure 503.5.4). Chimneys for medium-heat appliances shall extend at least 10 feet (3048 mm) higher than any portion of any building within 25 feet (7620 mm). Chimneys shall extend at least 5 feet (1524 mm) above the highest connected *appliance* draft hood outlet or flue collar. Decorative shrouds shall not be installed at the termination of factory-built chimneys except where such shrouds are *listed* and *labeled* for use with the specific factory-built chimney system and are installed in accordance with the manufacturer's installation instructions.

503.5.5 Size of chimneys. The effective area of a chimney venting system serving *listed* appliances with draft hoods, Category I appliances and other appliances *listed* for use with Type B vents shall be determined in accordance with one of the following methods:

1. The provisions of Section 504.
2. For sizing an individual chimney venting system for a single *appliance* with a draft hood, the effective areas of the vent connector and chimney flue shall be not less than the area of the *appliance* flue collar or draft hood outlet, nor greater than seven times the draft hood outlet area.
3. For sizing a chimney venting system connected to two appliances with draft hoods, the effective area of the chimney flue shall be not less than the area of the larger draft hood outlet plus 50 percent of the area of the smaller draft hood outlet, nor greater than seven times the smallest draft hood outlet area.
4. Chimney venting systems using mechanical draft shall be sized in accordance with *approved* engineering methods.
5. Other *approved* engineering methods.

503.5.6 Inspection of chimneys. Before replacing an existing *appliance* or connecting a vent connector to a chimney, the chimney passageway shall be examined to ascertain that it is clear and free of obstructions and it shall be cleaned if previously used for venting solid or liquid fuel-burning appliances or fireplaces.

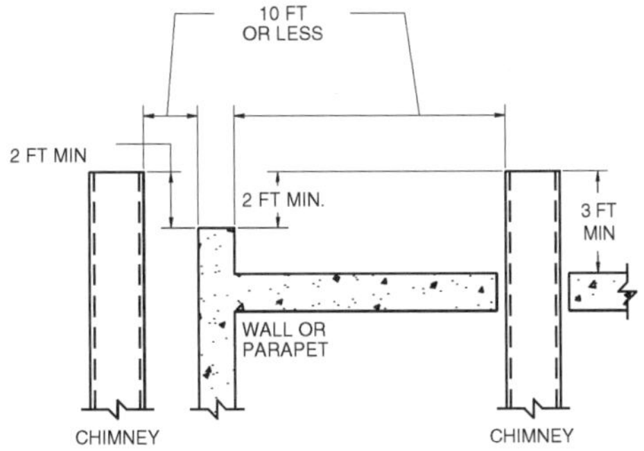

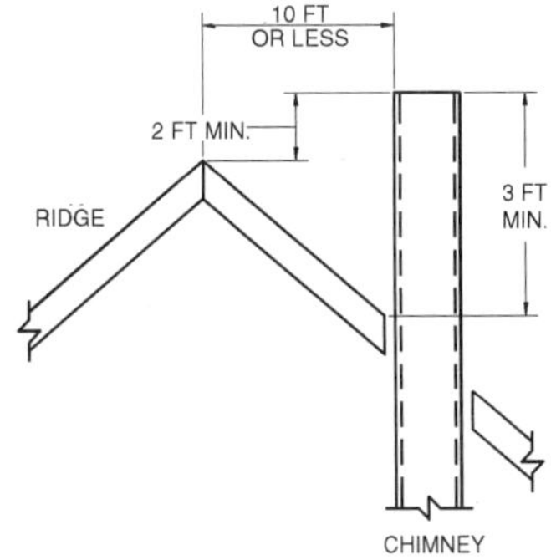

A. TERMINATION 10 FT OR LESS FROM RIDGE, WALL, OR PARAPET

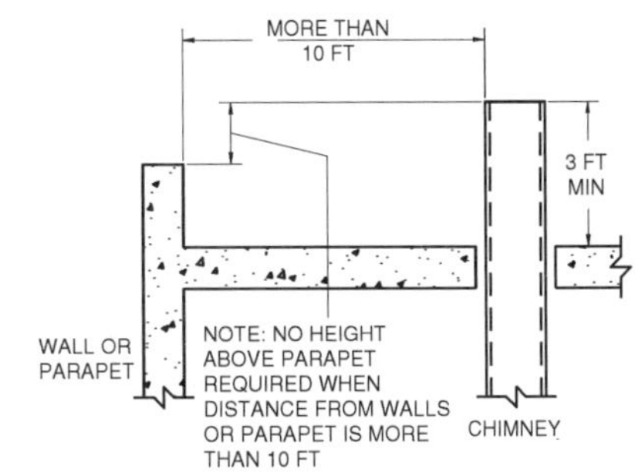

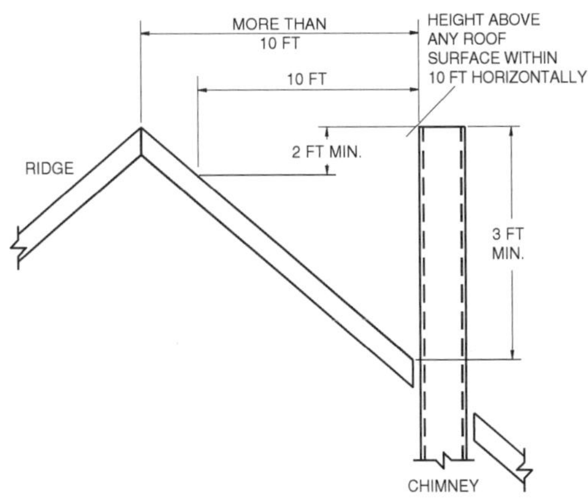

B. TERMINATION MORE THAN 10 FT FROM RIDGE, WALL, OR PARAPET

For SI: 1 inch = 25.4 mm, 1 foot = 304.8 mm.

FIGURE 503.5.4
TYPICAL TERMINATION LOCATIONS FOR CHIMNEYS AND SINGLE-WALL METAL PIPES SERVING RESIDENTIAL-TYPE AND LOW-HEAT APPLIANCES

503.5.6.1 Chimney lining. Chimneys shall be lined in accordance with NFPA 211.

Exception: Where an existing chimney complies with Sections 503.5.6 through 503.5.6.3 and its sizing is in accordance with Section 503.5.5, its continued use shall be allowed where the *appliance* vented by such chimney is replaced by an *appliance* of similar type, input rating and efficiency.

503.5.6.2 Cleanouts. Cleanouts shall be examined to determine if they will remain tightly closed when not in use.

503.5.6.3 Unsafe chimneys. Where inspection reveals that an existing chimney is not safe for the intended application, it shall be repaired, rebuilt, lined, relined or replaced with a vent or chimney to conform to NFPA 211 and it shall be suitable for the appliances to be vented.

503.5.7 Chimneys serving appliances burning other fuels. Chimneys serving *appliances* burning other fuels shall comply with Sections 503.5.7.1 through 503.5.7.4.

503.5.7.1 Solid fuel-burning appliances. An *appliance* shall not be connected to a chimney flue serving a separate *appliance* designed to burn solid fuel.

503.5.7.2 Liquid fuel-burning appliances. Where one chimney flue serves gas appliances and liquid fuel-burning appliances, the appliances shall be connected through separate openings or shall be connected through a single opening where joined by a suitable fitting located as close as practical to the chimney. Where two or more openings are provided into one chimney flue, they shall be at different levels. Where the appliances are automatically controlled, they shall be equipped with safety shutoff devices.

503.5.7.3 Combination gas and solid fuel-burning appliances. A combination gas- and solid fuel-burning *appliance* shall be permitted to be connected to a single chimney flue where equipped with a manual reset device to shut off gas to the main burner in the event of sustained backdraft or flue gas spillage. The chimney flue shall be sized to properly vent the *appliance*.

503.5.7.4 Combination gas- and oil fuel-burning appliances. A *listed* combination gas- and oil fuel-burning *appliance* shall be permitted to be connected to a single chimney flue. The chimney flue shall be sized to properly vent the *appliance*.

503.5.8 Support of chimneys. All portions of chimneys shall be supported for the design and weight of the materials employed. Factory-built chimneys shall be supported and spaced in accordance with the manufacturer's installation instructions.

503.5.9 Cleanouts. Where a chimney that formerly carried flue products from liquid or solid fuel-burning appliances is used with an *appliance* using fuel gas, an accessible cleanout shall be provided. The cleanout shall have a tight-fitting cover and shall be installed so its upper edge is at least 6 inches (152 mm) below the lower edge of the lowest chimney inlet opening.

503.5.10 Space surrounding lining or vent. The remaining space surrounding a chimney liner, gas vent, special gas vent or plastic *piping* installed within a masonry chimney flue shall not be used to vent another *appliance*. The insertion of another liner or vent within the chimney as provided in this code and the liner or vent manufacturer's instructions shall not be prohibited.

The remaining space surrounding a chimney liner, gas vent, special gas vent or plastic *piping* installed within a masonry, metal or factory-built chimney shall not be used to supply *combustion air*. Such space shall not be prohibited from supplying *combustion air* to *direct-vent appliances* designed for installation in a solid fuel-burning *fireplace* and installed in accordance with the manufacturer's installation instructions.

503.6 Gas vents. Gas vents shall comply with Sections 503.6.1 through 503.6.13 (see Section 202, Definitions).

503.6.1 Installation, general. Gas vents shall be installed in accordance with the manufacturer's installation instructions.

503.6.2 Type B-W vent capacity. A Type B-W gas vent shall have a *listed* capacity not less than that of the *listed* vented wall furnace to which it is connected.

503.6.3 Gas vents installed within masonry chimneys. Gas vents installed within masonry chimneys shall be installed in accordance with the manufacturer's installation instructions. Gas vents installed within masonry chimneys shall be identified with a permanent label installed at the point where the vent enters the chimney. The label shall contain the following language: "This gas vent is for appliances that burn gas. Do not connect to solid or liquid fuel-burning appliances or incinerators."

503.6.4 Gas vent terminations. A gas vent shall terminate in accordance with one of the following:

1. Gas vents that are 12 inches (305 mm) or less in size and located not less than 8 feet (2438 mm) from a vertical wall or similar obstruction shall terminate above the roof in accordance with Figure 503.6.4.
2. Gas vents that are over 12 inches (305 mm) in size or are located less than 8 feet (2438 mm) from a vertical wall or similar obstruction shall terminate not less than 2 feet (610 mm) above the highest point where they pass through the roof and not less than 2 feet (610 mm) above any portion of a building within 10 feet (3048 mm) horizontally.
3. As provided for industrial appliances in Section 503.2.2.
4. As provided for direct-vent systems in Section 503.2.3.
5. As provided for appliances with integral vents in Section 503.2.4.
6. As provided for mechanical draft systems in Section 503.3.3.
7. As provided for ventilating hoods and exhaust systems in Section 503.3.4.

503.6.4.1 Decorative shrouds. Decorative shrouds shall not be installed at the termination of gas vents except where such shrouds are *listed* for use with the specific gas venting system and are installed in accordance with manufacturer's installation instructions.

503.6.5 Minimum height. A Type B or L gas vent shall terminate at least 5 feet (1524 mm) in vertical height above the highest connected *appliance* draft hood or flue collar. A Type B-W gas vent shall terminate at least 12 feet (3658 mm) in vertical height above the bottom of the wall furnace.

503.6.6 Roof terminations. Gas vents shall extend through the roof flashing, roof jack or roof thimble and terminate with a *listed* cap or *listed* roof assembly.

503.6.7 Forced air inlets. Gas vents shall terminate not less than 3 feet (914 mm) above any forced air inlet located within 10 feet (3048 mm).

503.6.8 Exterior wall penetrations. A gas vent extending through an exterior wall shall not terminate adjacent to the wall or below eaves or parapets, except as provided in Sections 503.2.3 and 503.3.3.

503.6.9 Size of gas vents. Venting systems shall be sized and constructed in accordance with Section 504 or other *approved* engineering methods and the gas vent and *appliance* manufacturer's installation instructions.

503.6.9.1 Category I appliances. The sizing of natural draft venting systems serving one or more *listed* appliances equipped with a draft hood or appliances *listed* for use with Type B gas vent, installed in a single story of a building, shall be in accordance with one of the following methods:

1. The provisions of Section 504.
2. For sizing an individual gas vent for a single, draft-hood-equipped *appliance*, the effective area of the vent connector and the gas vent shall be not less than the area of the *appliance* draft hood outlet, nor greater than seven times the draft hood outlet area.
3. For sizing a gas vent connected to two appliances with draft hoods, the effective area of the vent shall be not less than the area of the larger draft hood outlet plus 50 percent of the area of the smaller draft hood outlet, nor greater than seven times the smaller draft hood outlet area.
4. *Approved* engineering practices.

503.6.9.2 Vent offsets. Type B and L vents sized in accordance with Item 2 or 3 of Section 503.6.9.1 shall extend in a generally vertical direction with offsets not exceeding 45 degrees (0.79 rad), except that a vent system having not more than one 60-degree (1.04 rad) *offset* shall be permitted. Any angle greater than 45 degrees (0.79 rad) from the vertical is considered horizontal. The total horizontal distance of a vent plus the horizontal vent connector serving draft hood-equipped appliances shall be not greater than 75 percent of the vertical height of the vent.

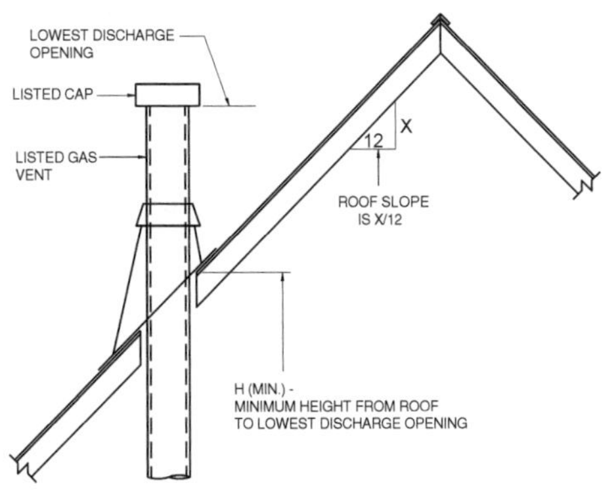

ROOF SLOPE	H (min) ft
Flat to 6/12	1.0
Over 6/12 to 7/12	1.25
Over 7/12 to 8/12	1.5
Over 8/12 to 9/12	2.0
Over 9/12 to 10/12	2.5
Over 10/12 to 11/12	3.25
Over 11/12 to 12/12	4.0
Over 12/12 to 14/12	5.0
Over 14/12 to 16/12	6.0
Over 16/12 to 18/12	7.0
Over 18/12 to 20/12	7.5
Over 20/12 to 21/12	8.0

For SI: 1 inch = 25.4 mm, 1 foot = 304.8 mm.

FIGURE 503.6.4
TERMINATION LOCATIONS FOR GAS VENTS WITH LISTED CAPS 12 INCHES OR LESS IN SIZE AT LEAST 8 FEET FROM A VERTICAL WALL

503.6.9.3 Category II, III and IV appliances. The sizing of gas vents for Category II, III and IV appliances shall be in accordance with the *appliance* manufacturer's instructions.

503.6.9.4 Mechanical draft. Chimney venting systems using mechanical draft shall be sized in accordance with *approved* engineering methods.

503.6.10 Gas vents serving appliances on more than one floor. A common gas vent shall be permitted in multistory installations to vent Category I appliances located on more than one floor level, provided that the venting system is designed and installed in accordance with *approved* engineering methods. For the purpose of this section, crawl spaces, basements and attics shall be considered as floor levels.

503.6.10.1 Appliance separation. Deleted.

Figure 503.6.10.1 Plan View of Practical Separation Method for Multistory Gas Venting. Deleted.

503.6.10.2 Sizing. The size of the connectors and common segments of multistory venting systems for appliances *listed* for use with Type B double-wall gas vents shall be in accordance with Table 504.3(1), provided that:

1. The available total height (*H*) for each segment of a multistory venting system is the vertical distance between the level of the highest draft hood outlet or flue collar on that floor and the centerline of the next highest interconnection tee (see Figure B-13).
2. The size of the connector for a segment is determined from the *appliance* input rating and available connector rise, and shall not be smaller than the draft hood outlet or flue collar size.
3. The size of the common vertical segment, and of the interconnection tee at the base of that segment, shall be based on the total *appliance* input rating entering that segment and its available total height.

503.6.11 Support of gas vents. Gas vents shall be supported and spaced in accordance with the manufacturer's installation instructions.

503.6.12 Marking. In those localities where solid and liquid fuels are used extensively, gas vents shall be permanently identified by a label attached to the wall or ceiling at a point where the vent connector enters the gas vent. The determination of where such localities exist shall be made by the code official. The label shall read:

"This gas vent is for appliances that burn gas. Do not connect to solid or liquid fuel-burning appliances or incinerators."

503.6.13 Fastener penetrations. Screws, rivets and other fasteners shall not penetrate the inner wall of double-wall gas vents, except at the transition from an *appliance* draft hood outlet, a flue collar or a single-wall metal connector to a double-wall vent.

503.7 Single-wall metal pipe. Single-wall metal pipe vents shall comply with Sections 503.7.1 through 503.7.13.

503.7.1 Construction. Single-wall metal pipe shall be constructed of galvanized sheet steel not less than 0.0304 inch (0.7 mm) thick, or other *approved*, noncombustible, corrosion-resistant material.

503.7.2 Cold climate. Uninsulated single-wall metal pipe shall not be used outdoors for venting appliances in regions where the 99-percent winter design temperature is below 32°F (0°C).

503.7.3 Termination. Single-wall metal pipe shall terminate at least 5 feet (1524 mm) in vertical height above the highest connected *appliance* draft hood *outlet* or flue collar. Single-wall metal pipe shall extend at least 2 feet (610 mm) above the highest point where it passes through a roof of a building and at least 2 feet (610 mm) higher than any portion of a building within a horizontal distance of 10 feet (3048 mm) (see Figure 503.5.4). An *approved* cap or roof assembly shall be attached to the terminus of a single-wall metal pipe (see also Section 503.7.9, Item 3).

503.7.4 Limitations of use. Single-wall metal pipe shall be used only for runs directly from the space in which the *appliance* is located through the roof or exterior wall to the outdoor atmosphere.

503.7.5 Roof penetrations. A pipe passing through a roof shall extend without interruption through the roof flashing, roof jack or roof thimble. Where a single-wall metal pipe passes through a roof constructed of combustible material, a noncombustible, nonventilating thimble shall be used at the point of passage. The thimble shall extend at least 18 inches (457 mm) above and 6 inches (152 mm) below the roof with the annular space open at the bottom and closed only at the top. The thimble shall be sized in accordance with Section 503.7.7.

503.7.6 Installation. Single-wall metal pipe shall not originate in any unoccupied attic or concealed space and shall not pass through any attic, inside wall, concealed space or floor. The installation of a single-wall metal pipe through an exterior combustible wall shall comply with Section 503.7.7. Single-wall metal pipe used for venting an incinerator shall be exposed and readily examinable for its full length and shall have suitable clearances maintained.

503.7.7 Single-wall penetrations of combustible walls. A single-wall metal pipe shall not pass through a combustible exterior wall unless guarded at the point of passage by a ventilated metal thimble not smaller than the following:

1. For *listed* appliances equipped with draft hoods and appliances *listed* for use with Type B gas vents, the thimble shall be not less than 4 inches (102 mm) larger in diameter than the metal pipe. Where there is a run of not less than 6 feet (1829 mm) of metal pipe in the open between the draft hood outlet and the thimble, the thimble shall be permitted to be not less than 2 inches (51 mm) larger in diameter than the metal pipe.
2. For unlisted appliances having draft hoods, the thimble shall be not less than 6 inches (152 mm) larger in diameter than the metal pipe.
3. For residential and low-heat appliances, the thimble shall be not less than 12 inches (305 mm) larger in diameter than the metal pipe.

Exception: In lieu of thimble protection, all combustible material in the wall shall be removed a sufficient distance from the metal pipe to provide the specified *clearance* from such metal pipe to combustible material. Any material used to close up such opening shall be noncombustible.

503.7.8 Clearances. Minimum clearances from single-wall metal pipe to combustible material shall be in accordance with Table 503.10.5. The *clearance* from single-wall metal pipe to combustible material shall be permitted to be reduced where the combustible material is protected as specified for vent connectors in Table 308.2.

503.7.9 Size of single-wall metal pipe. A venting system constructed of single-wall metal pipe shall be sized in accordance with one of the following methods and the appliance manufacturer's instructions:

1. For a draft-hood-equipped *appliance*, in accordance with Section 504.
2. For a venting system for a single *appliance* with a draft hood, the areas of the connector and the pipe each shall be not less than the area of the *appliance* flue collar or draft hood outlet, whichever is smaller. The vent area shall not be greater than seven times the draft hood outlet area.
3. Other *approved* engineering methods.

503.7.10 Pipe geometry. Any shaped single-wall metal pipe shall be permitted to be used, provided that its equivalent effective area is equal to the effective area of the round pipe for which it is substituted, and provided that the minimum internal dimension of the pipe is not less than 2 inches (51 mm).

503.7.11 Termination capacity. The vent cap or a roof assembly shall have a venting capacity not less than that of the pipe to which it is attached.

503.7.12 Support of single-wall metal pipe. All portions of single-wall metal pipe shall be supported for the design and weight of the material employed.

503.7.13 Marking. Single-wall metal pipe shall comply with the marking provisions of Section 503.6.12.

503.8 Venting system termination location. The location of venting system terminations shall comply with the following (see Appendix C):

1. A mechanical draft venting system shall terminate at least 3 feet (914 mm) above any forced-air inlet located within 10 feet (3048 mm).

   Exceptions:

   1. This provision shall not apply to the *combustion air* intake of a direct-vent *appliance*.
   2. This provision shall not apply to the separation of the integral outdoor air inlet and flue gas discharge of *listed* outdoor appliances.

2. A mechanical draft venting system, excluding *direct-vent appliances*, shall terminate at least 4 feet (1219 mm) below, 4 feet (1219 mm) horizontally from, or 1 foot (305 mm) above any door, operable window or gravity air inlet into any building. The bottom of the vent terminal shall be located at least 12 inches (305 mm) above finished ground level.
3. The vent terminal of a direct-vent *appliance* with an input of 10,000 Btu per hour (3 kW) or less shall be located at least 6 inches (152 mm) from any air opening into a building, and such an *appliance* with an input over 10,000 Btu per hour (3 kW) but not over 50,000 Btu per hour (14.7 kW) shall be installed with a 9-inch (230 mm) vent termination *clearance*, and an *appliance* with an input over 50,000 Btu/h (14.7 kW) shall have at least a 12-inch (305 mm) vent termination *clearance*. The bottom of the vent terminal and the air intake shall be located at least 12 inches (305 mm) above finished ground level.

4. Through-the-wall vents for Category II and IV appliances and noncategorized condensing appliances shall not terminate over public walkways or over an area where condensate or vapor could create a nuisance or hazard or could be detrimental to the operation of regulators, relief valves or other *equipment*. Where local experience indicates that condensate is a problem with Category I and III appliances, this provision shall also apply. Drains for condensate shall be installed in accordance with the manufacturer's installation instructions.

503.9 Condensation drainage. Provisions shall be made to collect and dispose of condensate from venting systems serving Category II and IV appliances and noncategorized condensing appliances in accordance with Section 503.8, Item 4. Where local experience indicates that condensation is a problem, provision shall be made to drain off and dispose of condensate from venting systems serving Category I and III appliances in accordance with Section 503.8, Item 4.

503.10 Vent connectors for Category I appliances. Vent connectors for Category I *appliances* shall comply with Sections 503.10.1 through 503.10.15.

503.10.1 Where required. A vent connector shall be used to connect an *appliance* to a gas vent, chimney or single-wall metal pipe, except where the gas vent, chimney or single-wall metal pipe is directly connected to the *appliance*.

503.10.2 Materials. Vent connectors shall be constructed in accordance with Sections 503.10.2.1 through 503.10.2.5.

503.10.2.1 General. A vent connector shall be made of noncombustible corrosion-resistant material capable of withstanding the vent gas temperature produced by the *appliance* and of sufficient thickness to withstand physical damage.

503.10.2.2 Vent connectors located in unconditioned areas. Where the vent connector used for an *appliance* having a draft hood or a Category I *appliance* is located in or passes through attics, crawl spaces or other unconditioned spaces, that portion of the vent connector shall be *listed* Type B, Type L or *listed* vent material having equivalent insulation properties.

Exception: Single-wall metal pipe located within the exterior walls of the building in areas having a local 99-percent winter design temperature of 5°F (-15°C) or higher shall be permitted to be used in unconditioned spaces other than attics and crawl spaces.

503.10.2.3 Residential-type appliance connectors. Where vent connectors for residential-type appliances are not installed in attics or other unconditioned spaces, connectors for *listed* appliances having draft hoods, appliances having draft hoods and equipped with *listed* conversion burners and Category I appliances shall be one of the following:

1. Type B or L vent material;
2. Galvanized sheet steel not less than 0.018 inch (0.46 mm) thick;
3. Aluminum (1100 or 3003 alloy or equivalent) sheet not less than 0.027 inch (0.69 mm) thick;
4. Stainless steel sheet not less than 0.012 inch (0.31 mm) thick;
5. Smooth interior wall metal pipe having resistance to heat and corrosion equal to or greater than that of Item 2, 3 or 4 above; or
6. A *listed* vent connector.

Vent connectors shall not be covered with insulation.

Exception: *Listed* insulated vent connectors shall be installed in accordance with the manufacturer's installation instructions.

503.10.2.4 Low-heat equipment. A vent connector for a nonresidential, low-heat *appliance* shall be a factory-built chimney section or steel pipe having resistance to heat and corrosion equivalent to that for the appropriate galvanized pipe as specified in Table 503.10.2.4. Factory-built chimney sections shall be joined together in accordance with the chimney manufacturer's instructions.

TABLE 503.10.2.4
MINIMUM THICKNESS FOR GALVANIZED STEEL VENT CONNECTORS FOR LOW-HEAT APPLIANCES

DIAMETER OF CONNECTOR (inches)	MINIMUM THICKNESS (inch)
Less than 6	0.019
6 to less than 10	0.023
10 to 12 inclusive	0.029
14 to 16 inclusive	0.034
Over 16	0.056

For SI: 1 inch = 25.4 mm.

503.10.2.5 Medium-heat appliances. Deleted.

Table 503.10.2.5 Minimum Thickness for Steel Vent Connectors for Medium-heat Appliances and Commercial and Industrial Incinerators Vent Connector Size. Deleted.

503.10.3 Size of vent connector. Vent connectors shall be sized in accordance with Sections 503.10.3.1 through 503.10.3.5.

503.10.3.1 Single draft hood and fan-assisted. A vent connector for an *appliance* with a single draft hood or for a Category I fan-assisted combustion system *appliance* shall be sized and installed in accordance with Section 504 or other *approved* engineering methods.

503.10.3.2 Multiple draft hood. For a single *appliance* having more than one draft hood outlet or flue collar, the manifold shall be constructed according to the instructions of the *appliance* manufacturer. Where there are no instructions, the manifold shall be designed and constructed in accordance with *approved* engineering practices. As an alternate method, the effective area of the manifold shall equal the combined area of the flue collars or draft hood outlets and the vent connectors shall have a minimum 1-foot (305 mm) rise.

503.10.3.3 Multiple appliances. Where two or more appliances are connected to a common vent or chimney, each vent connector shall be sized in accordance with Section 504 or other *approved* engineering methods.

As an alternative method applicable only when all of the appliances are draft hood equipped, each vent connector shall have an effective area not less than the area of the draft hood outlet of the *appliance* to which it is connected.

503.10.3.4 Common connector/manifold. Where two or more appliances are vented through a common vent connector or vent manifold, the common vent connector or vent manifold shall be located at the highest level consistent with available headroom and the required *clearance* to combustible materials and shall be sized in accordance with Section 504 or other *approved* engineering methods.

As an alternate method applicable only where there are two draft hood-equipped appliances, the effective area of the common vent connector or vent manifold and all junction fittings shall be not less than the area of the larger vent connector plus 50 percent of the area of the smaller flue collar outlet.

503.10.3.5 Size increase. Where the size of a vent connector is increased to overcome installation limitations and obtain connector capacity equal to the *appliance* input, the size increase shall be made at the *appliance* draft hood outlet.

503.10.4 Two or more appliances connected to a single vent or chimney. Where two or more vent connectors enter a common gas vent, chimney flue or single-wall metal pipe, the smaller connector shall enter at the highest level consistent with the available headroom or *clearance* to combustible material. Vent connectors serving Category I appliances shall not be connected to any portion of a mechanical draft system operating under positive static pressure, such as those serving Category III or IV appliances.

503.10.4.1 Two or more openings. Where two or more openings are provided into one chimney flue or vent, the openings shall be at different levels, or the connectors shall be attached to the vertical portion of the chimney or vent at an angle of 45 degrees (0.79 rad) or less relative to the vertical.

503.10.5 Clearance. Minimum clearances from vent connectors to combustible material shall be in accordance with Table 503.10.5.

Exception: The *clearance* between a vent connector and combustible material shall be permitted to be reduced where the combustible material is protected as specified for vent connectors in Table 308.2.

503.10.6 Flow resistance. A vent connector shall be installed so as to avoid turns or other construction features that create excessive resistance to flow of vent gases.

503.10.7 Joints. Joints between sections of connector *piping* and connections to flue collars and draft hood outlets shall be fastened by one of the following methods:

1. Sheet metal screws.
2. Vent connectors of *listed* vent material assembled and connected to flue collars or draft hood outlets in accordance with the manufacturers' instructions.
3. Other *approved* means.

503.10.8 Slope. A vent connector shall be installed without dips or sags and shall slope upward toward the vent or chimney at least $^1/_4$ inch per foot (21 mm/m).

Exception: Vent connectors attached to a mechanical draft system installed in accordance with the *appliance* and draft system manufacturers' instructions.

TABLE 503.10.5[a]
CLEARANCES FOR CONNECTORS

APPLIANCE	MINIMUM DISTANCE FROM COMBUSTIBLE MATERIAL			
	Listed Type B gas vent material	Listed Type L vent material	Single-wall metal pipe	Factory-built chimney sections
Listed appliances with draft hoods and appliances listed for use with Type B gas vents	As listed	As listed	6 inches	As listed
Residential boilers and furnaces with listed gas conversion burner and with draft hood	6 inches	6 inches	9 inches	As listed
Residential appliances listed for use with Type L vents	Not permitted	As listed	9 inches	As listed
Listed gas-fired toilets	Not permitted	As listed	As listed	As listed
Unlisted residential appliances with draft hood	Not permitted	6 inches	9 inches	As listed
Residential and low-heat appliances other than above	Not permitted	9 inches	18 inches	As listed
Medium-heat appliances	Not permitted	Not permitted	36 inches	As listed

For SI: 1 inch = 25.4 mm.

a. These clearances shall apply unless the manufacturer's installation instructions for a listed appliance or connector specify different clearances, in which case the listed clearances shall apply.

503.10.9 Length of vent connector. A vent connector shall be as short as practical and the *appliance* located as close as practical to the chimney or vent. The maximum horizontal length of a single-wall connector shall be 75 percent of the height of the chimney or vent except for engineered systems. The maximum horizontal length of a Type B double-wall connector shall be 100 percent of the height of the chimney or vent except for engineered systems.

503.10.10 Support. A vent connector shall be supported for the design and weight of the material employed to maintain clearances and prevent physical damage and separation of joints.

503.10.11 Chimney connection. Where entering a flue in a masonry or metal chimney, the vent connector shall be installed above the extreme bottom to avoid stoppage. Where a thimble or slip joint is used to facilitate removal of the connector, the connector shall be firmly attached to or inserted into the thimble or slip joint to prevent the connector from falling out. Means shall be employed to prevent the connector from entering so far as to restrict the space between its end and the opposite wall of the chimney flue (see Section 501.9).

503.10.12 Inspection. The entire length of a vent connector shall be provided with ready *access* for inspection, cleaning and replacement.

503.10.13 Fireplaces. A vent connector shall not be connected to a chimney flue serving a *fireplace* unless the *fireplace* flue opening is permanently sealed.

503.10.14 Passage through ceilings, floors or walls. Single-wall metal pipe connectors shall not pass through any wall, floor or ceiling except as permitted by Section 503.7.4.

➡ **503.10.15 Medium-heat connectors.** Deleted.

503.11 Vent connectors for Category II, III and IV appliances. Vent connectors for Category II, III and IV appliances shall be as specified for the venting systems in accordance with Section 503.4.

503.12 Draft hoods and draft controls. The installation of draft hoods and draft controls shall comply with Sections 503.12.1 through 503.12.7.

503.12.1 Appliances requiring draft hoods. Vented appliances shall be installed with draft hoods.

Exception: Dual oven-type combination ranges; incinerators; *direct-vent appliances*; fan-assisted combustion system appliances; appliances requiring chimney draft for operation; single firebox boilers equipped with conversion burners with inputs greater than 400,000 Btu per hour (117 kW); appliances equipped with blast, power or pressure burners that are not *listed* for use with draft hoods; and appliances designed for forced venting.

503.12.2 Installation. A draft hood supplied with or forming a part of a *listed* vented *appliance* shall be installed without *alteration*, exactly as furnished and specified by the *appliance* manufacturer.

503.12.2.1 Draft hood required. If a draft hood is not supplied by the *appliance* manufacturer where one is required, a draft hood shall be installed, shall be of a *listed* or *approved* type and, in the absence of other instructions, shall be of the same size as the *appliance* flue collar. Where a draft hood is required with a conversion burner, it shall be of a *listed* or *approved* type.

503.12.2.2 Special design draft hood. Where it is determined that a draft hood of special design is needed or preferable for a particular installation, the installation shall be in accordance with the recommendations of the *appliance* manufacturer and shall be *approved.*

503.12.3 Draft control devices. Where a draft control device is part of the *appliance* or is supplied by the *appliance* manufacturer, it shall be installed in accordance with the manufacturer's instructions. In the absence of manufacturer's instructions, the device shall be attached to the flue collar of the *appliance* or as near to the *appliance* as practical.

503.12.4 Additional devices. Appliances (except incinerators) requiring a controlled chimney draft shall be permitted to be equipped with a *listed* double-acting barometric-draft regulator installed and adjusted in accordance with the manufacturer's instructions.

503.12.5 Location. Draft hoods and barometric draft regulators shall be installed in the same room or enclosure as the *appliance* in such a manner as to prevent any difference in pressure between the hood or regulator and the *combustion air* supply.

503.12.6 Positioning. Draft hoods and draft regulators shall be installed in the position for which they were designed with reference to the horizontal and vertical planes and shall be located so that the relief opening is not obstructed by any part of the *appliance* or adjacent construction. The *appliance* and its draft hood shall be located so that the relief opening is accessible for checking vent operation.

503.12.7 Clearance. A draft hood shall be located so its relief opening is not less than 6 inches (152 mm) from any surface except that of the *appliance* it serves and the venting system to which the draft hood is connected. Where a greater or lesser *clearance* is indicated on the *appliance* label, the *clearance* shall be not less than that specified on the label. Such clearances shall not be reduced.

503.13 Manually operated dampers. A manually operated damper shall not be placed in the vent connector for any *appliance*. Fixed baffles shall not be classified as manually operated dampers.

503.14 Automatically operated vent dampers. An automatically operated vent damper shall be of a *listed* type.

503.15 Obstructions. Devices that retard the flow of vent gases shall not be installed in a vent connector, chimney or vent. The following shall not be considered as obstructions:

1. Draft regulators and safety controls specifically *listed* for installation in venting systems and installed in accordance with the manufacturer's installation instructions.
2. *Approved* draft regulators and safety controls that are designed and installed in accordance with *approved* engineering methods.

3. *Listed* heat reclaimers and automatically operated vent dampers installed in accordance with the manufacturer's installation instructions.
4. *Approved* economizers, heat reclaimers and recuperators installed in venting systems of appliances not required to be equipped with draft hoods, provided that the *appliance* manufacturer's instructions cover the installation of such a device in the venting system and performance in accordance with Sections 503.3 and 503.3.1 is obtained.
5. Vent dampers serving *listed* appliances installed in accordance with Sections 504.2.1 and 504.3.1 or other *approved* engineering methods.

503.16 Outside wall penetrations. Where vents, including those for *direct-vent appliances*, penetrate outside walls of buildings, the annular spaces around such penetrations shall be permanently sealed using *approved* materials to prevent entry of combustion products into the building.

SECTION 504 (IFGS) SIZING OF CATEGORY I APPLIANCE VENTING SYSTEMS

504.1 Definitions. The following definitions apply to the tables in this section.

APPLIANCE CATEGORIZED VENT DIAMETER/AREA. The minimum vent area/diameter permissible for Category I appliances to maintain a nonpositive vent static pressure when tested in accordance with nationally recognized standards.

FAN-ASSISTED COMBUSTION SYSTEM. An *appliance* equipped with an integral mechanical means to either draw or force products of combustion through the combustion chamber or heat exchanger.

FAN Min. The minimum input rating of a Category I fan-assisted *appliance* attached to a vent or connector.

FAN Max. The maximum input rating of a Category I fan-assisted *appliance* attached to a vent or connector.

NAT Max. The maximum input rating of a Category I draft-hood-equipped *appliance* attached to a vent or connector.

FAN + FAN. The maximum combined *appliance* input rating of two or more Category I fan-assisted appliances attached to the common vent.

FAN + NAT. The maximum combined *appliance* input rating of one or more Category I fan-assisted appliances and one or more Category I draft-hood-equipped appliances attached to the common vent.

NA. Vent configuration is not allowed due to potential for condensate formation or pressurization of the venting system, or not applicable due to physical or geometric restraints.

NAT + NAT. The maximum combined *appliance* input rating of two or more Category I draft-hood-equipped appliances attached to the common vent.

504.2 Application of single-appliance vent Tables 504.2(1) through 504.2(6). The application of Tables 504.2(1) through 504.2(6) shall be subject to the requirements of Sections 504.2.1 through 504.2.16.

504.2.1 Vent obstructions. These venting tables shall not be used where obstructions, as described in Section 503.15, are installed in the venting system. The installation of vents serving *listed* appliances with vent dampers shall be in accordance with the *appliance* manufacturer's instructions or in accordance with the following:

1. The maximum capacity of the vent system shall be determined using the "NAT Max" column.
2. The minimum capacity shall be determined as if the *appliance* were a fan-assisted *appliance*, using the "FAN Min" column to determine the minimum capacity of the vent system. Where the corresponding "FAN Min" is "NA," the vent configuration shall not be permitted and an alternative venting configuration shall be utilized.

504.2.2 Minimum size. Where the vent size determined from the tables is smaller than the *appliance* draft hood *outlet* or flue collar, the smaller size shall be permitted to be used provided that all of the following requirements are met:

1. The total vent height (*H*) is at least 10 feet (3048 mm).
2. Vents for *appliance* draft hood outlets or flue collars 12 inches (305 mm) in diameter or smaller are not reduced more than one table size.
3. Vents for *appliance* draft hood outlets or flue collars larger than 12 inches (305 mm) in diameter are not reduced more than two table sizes.
4. The maximum capacity listed in the tables for a fan-assisted *appliance* is reduced by 10 percent (0.90 × maximum table capacity).
5. The draft hood outlet is greater than 4 inches (102 mm) in diameter. Do not connect a 3-inch-diameter (76 mm) vent to a 4-inch-diameter (102 mm) draft hood *outlet*. This provision shall not apply to fan-assisted appliances.

504.2.3 Vent offsets. Single-appliance venting configurations with zero (0) lateral lengths in Tables 504.2(1), 504.2(2) and 504.2(5) shall not have elbows in the venting system. Single-appliance venting configurations with lateral lengths include two 90-degree (1.57 rad) elbows. For each additional elbow up to and including 45 degrees (0.79 rad), the maximum capacity listed in the venting tables shall be reduced by 5 percent. For each additional elbow greater than 45 degrees (0.79 rad) up to and including 90 degrees (1.57 rad), the maximum capacity listed in the venting tables shall be reduced by 10 percent. Where multiple offsets occur in a vent, the total lateral length of all offsets combined shall not exceed that specified in Tables 504.2(1) through 504.2(5).

504.2.4 Zero lateral. Zero (0) lateral (*L*) shall apply only to a straight vertical vent attached to a top outlet draft hood or flue collar.

504.2.5 High-altitude installations. Sea-level input ratings shall be used when determining maximum capacity for high altitude installation. Actual input (derated for altitude) shall be used for determining minimum capacity for high altitude installation.

504.2.6 Multiple input rate appliances. For appliances with more than one input rate, the minimum vent capacity (FAN Min) determined from the tables shall be less than the lowest *appliance* input rating, and the maximum vent capacity (FAN Max/NAT Max) determined from the tables shall be greater than the highest *appliance* rating input.

504.2.7 Liner system sizing and connections. *Listed* corrugated metallic chimney liner systems in masonry chimneys shall be sized by using Table 504.2(1) or 504.2(2) for Type B vents with the maximum capacity reduced by 20 percent (0.80 × maximum capacity) and the minimum capacity as shown in Table 504.2(1) or 504.2(2). Corrugated metallic liner systems installed with bends or offsets shall have their maximum capacity further reduced in accordance with Section 504.2.3. The 20-percent reduction for corrugated metallic chimney liner systems includes an allowance for one long-radius 90-degree (1.57 rad) turn at the bottom of the liner.

Connections between chimney liners and *listed* double-wall connectors shall be made with *listed* adapters designed for such purpose.

504.2.8 Vent area and diameter. Where the vertical vent has a larger diameter than the vent connector, the vertical vent diameter shall be used to determine the minimum vent capacity, and the connector diameter shall be used to determine the maximum vent capacity. The flow area of the vertical vent shall not exceed seven times the flow area of the listed appliance categorized vent area, flue collar area or draft hood outlet area unless designed in accordance with *approved* engineering methods.

504.2.9 Chimney and vent locations. Tables 504.2(1), 504.2(2), 504.2(3), 504.2(4) and 504.2(5) shall be used only for chimneys and vents not exposed to the outdoors below the roof line. A Type B vent or listed chimney lining system passing through an unused masonry chimney flue shall not be considered to be exposed to the outdoors. A Type B vent shall not be considered to be exposed to the outdoors where it passes through an unventilated enclosure or chase insulated to a value of not less than R8.

Table 504.2(3) in combination with Table 504.2(6) shall be used for clay-tile-lined *exterior masonry chimneys*, provided that all of the following are met:

1. Vent connector is a Type B double wall.
2. Vent connector length is limited to $1^1/_2$ feet for each inch (18 mm per mm) of vent connector diameter.
3. The appliance is draft hood equipped.
4. The input rating is less than the maximum capacity given by Table 504.2(3).
5. For a water heater, the outdoor design temperature is not less than 5°F (-15°C).
6. For a space-heating appliance, the input rating is greater than the minimum capacity given by Table 504.2(6).

Exception: The installation of vents serving listed appliances shall be permitted to be in accordance with the appliance manufacturer's installation instructions.

504.2.10 Corrugated vent connector size. Corrugated vent connectors shall be not smaller than the listed appliance categorized vent diameter, flue collar diameter or draft hood outlet diameter.

504.2.11 Vent connector size limitation. Vent connectors shall not be increased in size more than two sizes greater than the listed appliance categorized vent diameter, flue collar diameter or draft hood outlet diameter.

504.2.12 Component commingling. In a single run of vent or vent connector, different diameters and types of vent and connector components shall be permitted to be used, provided that all such sizes and types are permitted by the tables.

504.2.13 Draft hood conversion accessories. Draft hood conversion accessories for use with masonry chimneys venting listed Category I fan-assisted appliances shall be listed and installed in accordance with the manufacturer's installation instructions for such listed accessories.

504.2.14 Table interpolation. Interpolation shall be permitted in calculating capacities for vent dimensions that fall between the table entries (see Example 3, Appendix B).

504.2.15 Extrapolation prohibited. Extrapolation beyond the table entries shall not be permitted.

504.2.16 Engineering calculations. For vent heights less than 6 feet (1829 mm) and greater than shown in the tables, engineering methods shall be used to calculate vent capacities.

Number of Appliances	Single
Appliance Type	Category I
Appliance Vent Connection	Connected directly to vent

TABLE 504.2(1)
TYPE B DOUBLE-WALL GAS VENT

HEIGHT (H) (feet)	LATERAL (L) (feet)	VENT DIAMETER—(D) inches																				
		3			4			5			6			7			8			9		
		APPLIANCE INPUT RATING IN THOUSANDS OF BTU/H																				
		FAN		NAT	FAN		NAT	FAN		NAT	FAN		NAT	FAN		NAT	FAN		NAT	FAN		NAT
		Min	Max	Max	Min	Max	Max	Min	Max	Max	Min	Max	Max	Min	Max	Max	Min	Max	Max	Min	Max	Max
6	0	0	78	46	0	152	86	0	251	141	0	375	205	0	524	285	0	698	370	0	897	470
	2	13	51	36	18	97	67	27	157	105	32	232	157	44	321	217	53	425	285	63	543	370
	4	21	49	34	30	94	64	39	153	103	50	227	153	66	316	211	79	419	279	93	536	362
	6	25	46	32	36	91	61	47	149	100	59	223	149	78	310	205	93	413	273	110	530	354
8	0	0	84	50	0	165	94	0	276	155	0	415	235	0	583	320	0	780	415	0	1,006	537
	2	12	57	40	16	109	75	25	178	120	28	263	180	42	365	247	50	483	322	60	619	418
	5	23	53	38	32	103	71	42	171	115	53	255	173	70	356	237	83	473	313	99	607	407
	8	28	49	35	39	98	66	51	164	109	64	247	165	84	347	227	99	463	303	117	596	396
10	0	0	88	53	0	175	100	0	295	166	0	447	255	0	631	345	0	847	450	0	1,096	585
	2	12	61	42	17	118	81	23	194	129	26	289	195	40	402	273	48	533	355	57	684	457
	5	23	57	40	32	113	77	41	187	124	52	280	188	68	392	263	81	522	346	95	671	446
	10	30	51	36	41	104	70	54	176	115	67	267	175	88	376	245	104	504	330	122	651	427
15	0	0	94	58	0	191	112	0	327	187	0	502	285	0	716	390	0	970	525	0	1,263	682
	2	11	69	48	15	136	93	20	226	150	22	339	225	38	475	316	45	633	414	53	815	544
	5	22	65	45	30	130	87	39	219	142	49	330	217	64	463	300	76	620	403	90	800	529
	10	29	59	41	40	121	82	51	206	135	64	315	208	84	445	288	99	600	386	116	777	507
	15	35	53	37	48	112	76	61	195	128	76	301	198	98	429	275	115	580	373	134	755	491
20	0	0	97	61	0	202	119	0	349	202	0	540	307	0	776	430	0	1,057	575	0	1,384	752
	2	10	75	51	14	149	100	18	250	166	20	377	249	33	531	346	41	711	470	50	917	612
	5	21	71	48	29	143	96	38	242	160	47	367	241	62	519	337	73	697	460	86	902	599
	10	28	64	44	38	133	89	50	229	150	62	351	228	81	499	321	95	675	443	112	877	576
	15	34	58	40	46	124	84	59	217	142	73	337	217	94	481	308	111	654	427	129	853	557
	20	48	52	35	55	116	78	69	206	134	84	322	206	107	464	295	125	634	410	145	830	537

(continued)

TABLE 504.2(1)—continued
TYPE B DOUBLE-WALL GAS VENT

Number of Appliances	Single
Appliance Type	Category I
Appliance Vent Connection	Connected directly to vent

HEIGHT (*H*) (feet)	LATERAL (*L*) (feet)	VENT DIAMETER—(*D*) inches																				
		3			4			5			6			7			8			9		
		APPLIANCE INPUT RATING IN THOUSANDS OF BTU/H																				
		FAN		NAT	FAN		NAT	FAN		NAT	FAN		NAT	FAN		NAT	FAN		NAT	FAN		NAT
		Min	Max	Max	Min	Max	Max	Min	Max	Max	Min	Max	Max	Min	Max	Max	Min	Max	Max	Min	Max	Max
30	0	0	100	64	0	213	128	0	374	220	0	587	336	0	853	475	0	1,173	650	0	1,548	855
	2	9	81	56	13	166	112	14	283	185	18	432	280	27	613	394	33	826	535	42	1,072	700
	5	21	77	54	28	160	108	36	275	176	45	421	273	58	600	385	69	811	524	82	1,055	688
	10	27	70	50	37	150	102	48	262	171	59	405	261	77	580	371	91	788	507	107	1,028	668
	15	33	64	NA	44	141	96	57	249	163	70	389	249	90	560	357	105	765	490	124	1,002	648
	20	56	58	NA	53	132	90	66	237	154	80	374	237	102	542	343	119	743	473	139	977	628
	30	NA	NA	NA	73	113	NA	88	214	NA	104	346	219	131	507	321	149	702	444	171	929	594
50	0	0	101	67	0	216	134	0	397	232	0	633	363	0	932	518	0	1,297	708	0	1,730	952
	2	8	86	61	11	183	122	14	320	206	15	497	314	22	715	445	26	975	615	33	1,276	813
	5	20	82	NA	27	177	119	35	312	200	43	487	308	55	702	438	65	960	605	77	1,259	798
	10	26	76	NA	35	168	114	45	299	190	56	471	298	73	681	426	86	935	589	101	1,230	773
	15	59	70	NA	42	158	NA	54	287	180	66	455	288	85	662	413	100	911	572	117	1,203	747
	20	NA	NA	NA	50	149	NA	63	275	169	76	440	278	97	642	401	113	888	556	131	1,176	722
	30	NA	NA	NA	69	131	NA	84	250	NA	99	410	259	123	605	376	141	844	522	161	1,125	670
100	0	NA	NA	NA	0	218	NA	0	407	NA	0	665	400	0	997	560	0	1,411	770	0	1,908	1,040
	2	NA	NA	NA	10	194	NA	12	354	NA	13	566	375	18	831	510	21	1,155	700	25	1,536	935
	5	NA	NA	NA	26	189	NA	33	347	NA	40	557	369	52	820	504	60	1,141	692	71	1,519	926
	10	NA	NA	NA	33	182	NA	43	335	NA	53	542	361	68	801	493	80	1,118	679	94	1,492	910
	15	NA	NA	NA	40	174	NA	50	321	NA	62	528	353	80	782	482	93	1,095	666	109	1,465	895
	20	NA	NA	NA	47	166	NA	59	311	NA	71	513	344	90	763	471	105	1,073	653	122	1,438	880
	30	NA	NA	NA	NA	NA	NA	78	290	NA	92	483	NA	115	726	449	131	1,029	627	149	1,387	849
	50	NA	NA	NA	NA	NA	NA	NA	NA	NA	147	428	NA	180	651	405	197	944	575	217	1,288	787

(continued)

Number of Appliances	Single
Appliance Type	Category I
Appliance Vent Connection	Connected directly to vent

TABLE 504.2(1)—continued
TYPE B DOUBLE-WALL GAS VENT

HEIGHT (*H*) (feet)	LATERAL (*L*) (feet)	VENT DIAMETER—(*D*) inches																							
		10			12			14			16			18			20			22			24		
		APPLIANCE INPUT RATING IN THOUSANDS OF BTU/H																							
		FAN		NAT	FAN		NAT	FAN		NAT	FAN		NAT	FAN		NAT	FAN		NAT	FAN		NAT	FAN		NAT
		Min	Max	Max	Min	Max	Max	Min	Max	Max	Min	Max	Max	Min	Max	Max	Min	Max	Max	Min	Max	Max	Min	Max	Max
6	0	0	1,121	570	0	1,645	850	0	2,267	1,170	0	2,983	1,530	0	3,802	1,960	0	4,721	2,430	0	5,737	2,950	0	6,853	3,520
	2	75	675	455	103	982	650	138	1,346	890	178	1,769	1,170	225	2,250	1,480	296	2,782	1,850	360	3,377	2,220	426	4,030	2,670
	4	110	668	445	147	975	640	191	1,338	880	242	1,761	1,160	300	2,242	1,475	390	2,774	1,835	469	3,370	2,215	555	4,023	2,660
	6	128	661	435	171	967	630	219	1,330	870	276	1,753	1,150	341	2,235	1,470	437	2,767	1,820	523	3,363	2,210	618	4,017	2,650
8	0	0	1,261	660	0	1,858	970	0	2,571	1,320	0	3,399	1,740	0	4,333	2,220	0	5,387	2,750	0	6,555	3,360	0	7,838	4,010
	2	71	770	515	98	1,124	745	130	1,543	1,020	168	2,030	1,340	212	2,584	1,700	278	3,196	2,110	336	3,882	2,560	401	4,634	3,050
	5	115	758	503	154	1,110	733	199	1,528	1,010	251	2,013	1,330	311	2,563	1,685	398	3,180	2,090	476	3,863	2,545	562	4,612	3,040
	8	137	746	490	180	1,097	720	231	1,514	1,000	289	2,000	1,320	354	2,552	1,670	450	3,163	2,070	537	3,850	2,530	630	4,602	3,030
10	0	0	1,377	720	0	2,036	1,060	0	2,825	1,450	0	3,742	1,925	0	4,782	2,450	0	5,955	3,050	0	7,254	3,710	0	8,682	4,450
	2	68	852	560	93	1,244	850	124	1,713	1,130	161	2,256	1,480	202	2,868	1,890	264	3,556	2,340	319	4,322	2,840	378	5,153	3,390
	5	112	839	547	149	1,229	829	192	1,696	1,105	243	2,238	1,461	300	2,849	1,871	382	3,536	2,318	458	4,301	2,818	540	5,132	3,371
	10	142	817	525	187	1,204	795	238	1,669	1,080	298	2,209	1,430	364	2,818	1,840	459	3,504	2,280	546	4,268	2,780	641	5,099	3,340
15	0	0	1,596	840	0	2,380	1,240	0	3,323	1,720	0	4,423	2,270	0	5,678	2,900	0	7,099	3,620	0	8,665	4,410	0	10,393	5,300
	2	63	1,019	675	86	1,495	985	114	2,062	1,350	147	2,719	1,770	186	3,467	2,260	239	4,304	2,800	290	5,232	3,410	346	6,251	4,080
	5	105	1,003	660	140	1,476	967	182	2,041	1,327	229	2,696	1,748	283	3,442	2,235	355	4,278	2,777	426	5,204	3,385	501	6,222	4,057
	10	135	977	635	177	1,446	936	227	2,009	1,289	283	2,659	1,712	346	3,402	2,193	432	4,234	2,739	510	5,159	3,343	599	6,175	4,019
	15	155	953	610	202	1,418	905	257	1,976	1,250	318	2,623	1,675	385	3,363	2,150	479	4,192	2,700	564	5,115	3,300	665	6,129	3,980
20	0	0	1,756	930	0	2,637	1,350	0	3,701	1,900	0	4,948	2,520	0	6,376	3,250	0	7,988	4,060	0	9,785	4,980	0	11,753	6,000
	2	59	1,150	755	81	1,694	1,100	107	2,343	1,520	139	3,097	2,000	175	3,955	2,570	220	4,916	3,200	269	5,983	3,910	321	7,154	4,700
	5	101	1,133	738	135	1,674	1,079	174	2,320	1,498	219	3,071	1,978	270	3,926	2,544	337	4,885	3,174	403	5,950	3,880	475	7,119	4,662
	10	130	1,105	710	172	1,641	1,045	220	2,282	1,460	273	3,029	1,940	334	3,880	2,500	413	4,835	3,130	489	5,896	3,830	573	7,063	4,600
	15	150	1,078	688	195	1,609	1,018	248	2,245	1,425	306	2,988	1,910	372	3,835	2,465	459	4,786	3,090	541	5,844	3,795	631	7,007	4,575
	20	167	1,052	665	217	1,578	990	273	2,210	1,390	335	2,948	1,880	404	3,791	2,430	495	4,737	3,050	585	5,792	3,760	689	6,953	4,550

(continued)

Number of Appliances	Single
Appliance Type	Category I
Appliance Vent Connection	Connected directly to vent

TABLE 504.2(1)—continued TYPE B DOUBLE-WALL GAS VENT

HEIGHT (H) (feet)	LATERAL (L) (feet)	VENT DIAMETER—(D) inches																							
		10			12			14			16			18			20			22			24		
		APPLIANCE INPUT RATING IN THOUSANDS OF BTU/H																							
		FAN		NAT	FAN		NAT	FAN		NAT	FAN		NAT	FAN		NAT	FAN		NAT	FAN		NAT	FAN		NAT
		Min	Max	Max	Min	Max	Max	Min	Max	Max	Min	Max	Max	Min	Max	Max	Min	Max	Max	Min	Max	Max	Min	Max	Max
30	0	0	1,977	1,060	0	3,004	1,550	0	4,252	2,170	0	5,725	2,920	0	7,420	3,770	0	9,341	4,750	0	11,483	5,850	0	13,848	7,060
	2	54	1,351	865	74	2,004	1,310	98	2,786	1,800	127	3,696	2,380	159	4,734	3,050	199	5,900	3,810	241	7,194	4,650	285	8,617	5,600
	5	96	1,332	851	127	1,981	1,289	164	2,759	1,775	206	3,666	2,350	252	4,701	3,020	312	5,863	3,783	373	7,155	4,622	439	8,574	5,552
	10	125	1,301	829	164	1,944	1,254	209	2,716	1,733	259	3,617	2,300	316	4,647	2,970	386	5,803	3,739	456	7,090	4,574	535	8,505	5,471
	15	143	1,272	807	187	1,908	1,220	237	2,674	1,692	292	3,570	2,250	354	4,594	2,920	431	5,744	3,695	507	7,026	4,527	590	8,437	5,391
	20	160	1,243	784	207	1,873	1,185	260	2,633	1,650	319	3,523	2,200	384	4,542	2,870	467	5,686	3,650	548	6,964	4,480	639	8,370	5,310
	30	195	1,189	745	246	1,807	1,130	305	2,555	1,585	369	3,433	2,130	440	4,442	2,785	540	5,574	3,565	635	6,842	4,375	739	8,239	5,225
50	0	0	2,231	1,195	0	3,441	1,825	0	4,934	2,550	0	6,711	3,440	0	8,774	4,460	0	11,129	5,635	0	13,767	6,940	0	16,694	8,430
	2	41	1,620	1,010	66	2,431	1,513	86	3,409	2,125	113	4,554	2,840	141	5,864	3,670	171	7,339	4,630	209	8,980	5,695	251	10,788	6,860
	5	90	1,600	996	118	2,406	1,495	151	3,380	2,102	191	4,520	2,813	234	5,826	3,639	283	7,295	4,597	336	8,933	5,654	394	10,737	6,818
	10	118	1,567	972	154	2,366	1,466	196	3,332	2,064	243	4,464	2,767	295	5,763	3,585	355	7,224	4,542	419	8,855	5,585	491	10,652	6,749
	15	136	1,536	948	177	2,327	1,437	222	3,285	2,026	274	4,409	2,721	330	5,701	3,534	396	7,155	4,511	465	8,779	5,546	542	10,570	6,710
	20	151	1,505	924	195	2,288	1,408	244	3,239	1,987	300	4,356	2,675	361	5,641	3,481	433	7,086	4,479	506	8,704	5,506	586	10,488	6,670
	30	183	1,446	876	232	2,214	1,349	287	3,150	1,910	347	4,253	2,631	412	5,523	3,431	494	6,953	4,421	577	8,557	5,444	672	10,328	6,603
100	0	0	2,491	1,310	0	3,925	2,050	0	5,729	2,950	0	7,914	4,050	0	10,485	5,300	0	13,454	6,700	0	16,817	8,600	0	20,578	10,300
	2	30	1,975	1,170	44	3,027	1,820	72	4,313	2,550	95	5,834	3,500	120	7,591	4,600	138	9,577	5,800	169	11,803	7,200	204	14,264	8,800
	5	82	1,955	1,159	107	3,002	1,803	136	4,282	2,531	172	5,797	3,475	208	7,548	4,566	245	9,528	5,769	293	11,748	7,162	341	14,204	8,756
	10	108	1,923	1,142	142	2,961	1,775	180	4,231	2,500	223	5,737	3,434	268	7,478	4,509	318	9,447	5,717	374	11,658	7,100	436	14,105	8,683
	15	126	1,892	1,124	163	2,920	1,747	206	4,182	2,469	252	5,678	3,392	304	7,409	4,451	358	9,367	5,665	418	11,569	7,037	487	14,007	8,610
	20	141	1,861	1,107	181	2,880	1,719	226	4,133	2,438	277	5,619	3,351	330	7,341	4,394	387	9,289	5,613	452	11,482	6,975	523	13,910	8,537
	30	170	1,802	1,071	215	2,803	1,663	265	4,037	2,375	319	5,505	3,267	378	7,209	4,279	446	9,136	5,509	514	11,310	6,850	592	13,720	8,391
	50	241	1,688	1,000	292	2,657	1,550	350	3,856	2,250	415	5,289	3,100	486	6,956	4,050	572	8,841	5,300	659	10,979	6,600	752	13,354	8,100

For SI: 1 inch = 25.4 mm, 1 foot = 304.8 mm, 1 British thermal unit per hour = 0.2931 W.

Number of Appliances	Single
Appliance Type	Category I
Appliance Vent Connection	Single-wall metal connector

TABLE 504.2(2)
TYPE B DOUBLE-WALL GAS VENT

HEIGHT (H) (feet)	LATERAL (L) (feet)	VENT DIAMETER—(D) inches																										
		3			4			5			6			7			8			9			10			12		
		APPLIANCE INPUT RATING IN THOUSANDS OF BTU/H																										
		FAN		NAT	FAN		NAT	FAN		NAT	FAN		NAT	FAN		NAT	FAN		NAT	FAN		NAT	FAN		NAT	FAN		NAT
		Min	Max	Max	Min	Max	Max	Min	Max	Max	Min	Max	Max	Min	Max	Max	Min	Max	Max	Min	Max	Max	Min	Max	Max	Min	Max	Max
6	0	38	77	45	59	151	85	85	249	140	126	373	204	165	522	284	211	695	369	267	894	469	371	1,118	569	537	1,639	849
	2	39	51	36	60	96	66	85	156	104	123	231	156	159	320	213	201	423	284	251	541	368	347	673	453	498	979	648
	4	NA	NA	33	74	92	63	102	152	102	146	225	152	187	313	208	237	416	277	295	533	360	409	664	443	584	971	638
	6	NA	NA	31	83	89	60	114	147	99	163	220	148	207	307	203	263	409	271	327	526	352	449	656	433	638	962	627
8	0	37	83	50	58	164	93	83	273	154	123	412	234	161	580	319	206	777	414	258	1,002	536	360	1,257	658	521	1,852	967
	2	39	56	39	59	108	75	83	176	119	121	261	179	155	363	246	197	482	321	246	617	417	339	768	513	486	1,120	743
	5	NA	NA	37	77	102	69	107	168	114	151	252	171	193	352	235	245	470	311	305	604	404	418	754	500	598	1,104	730
	8	NA	NA	33	90	95	64	122	161	107	175	243	163	223	342	225	280	458	300	344	591	392	470	740	486	665	1,089	715
10	0	37	87	53	57	174	99	82	293	165	120	444	254	158	628	344	202	844	449	253	1,093	584	351	1,373	718	507	2,031	1,057
	2	39	61	41	59	117	80	82	193	128	119	287	194	153	400	272	193	531	354	242	681	456	332	849	559	475	1,242	848
	5	52	56	39	76	111	76	105	185	122	148	277	186	190	388	261	241	518	344	299	667	443	409	834	544	584	1,224	825
	10	NA	NA	34	97	100	68	132	171	112	188	261	171	237	369	241	296	497	325	363	643	423	492	808	520	688	1,194	788
15	0	36	93	57	56	190	111	80	325	186	116	499	283	153	713	388	195	966	523	244	1,259	681	336	1,591	838	488	2,374	1,237
	2	38	69	47	57	136	93	80	225	149	115	337	224	148	473	314	187	631	413	232	812	543	319	1,015	673	457	1,491	983
	5	51	63	44	75	128	86	102	216	140	144	326	217	182	459	298	231	616	400	287	795	526	392	997	657	562	1,469	963
	10	NA	NA	39	95	116	79	128	201	131	182	308	203	228	438	284	284	592	381	349	768	501	470	966	628	664	1,433	928
	15	NA	NA	NA	NA	NA	72	158	186	124	220	290	192	272	418	269	334	568	367	404	742	484	540	937	601	750	1,399	894
20	0	35	96	60	54	200	118	78	346	201	114	537	306	149	772	428	190	1,053	573	238	1,379	750	326	1,751	927	473	2,631	1,346
	2	37	74	50	56	148	99	78	248	165	113	375	248	144	528	344	182	708	468	227	914	611	309	1,146	754	443	1,689	1,098
	5	50	68	47	73	140	94	100	239	158	141	363	239	178	514	334	224	692	457	279	896	596	381	1,126	734	547	1,665	1,074
	10	NA	NA	41	93	129	86	125	223	146	177	344	224	222	491	316	277	666	437	339	866	570	457	1,092	702	646	1,626	1,037
	15	NA	NA	NA	NA	NA	80	155	208	136	216	325	210	264	469	301	325	640	419	393	838	549	526	1,060	677	730	1,587	1,005
	20	NA	NA	NA	NA	NA	NA	186	192	126	254	306	196	309	448	285	374	616	400	448	810	526	592	1,028	651	808	1,550	973

(continued)

Number of Appliances	Single
Appliance Type	Category I
Appliance Vent Connection	Single-wall metal connector

TABLE 504.2(2)—continued
TYPE B DOUBLE-WALL GAS VENT

HEIGHT (*H*) (feet)	LATERAL (*L*) (feet)	VENT DIAMETER—(*D*) inches																										
		3			4			5			6			7			8			9			10			12		
		APPLIANCE INPUT RATING IN THOUSANDS OF BTU/H																										
		FAN		NAT	FAN		NAT	FAN		NAT	FAN		NAT	FAN		NAT	FAN		NAT	FAN		NAT	FAN		NAT	FAN		NAT
		Min	Max	Max	Min	Max	Max	Min	Max	Max	Min	Max	Max	Min	Max	Max	Min	Max	Max	Min	Max	Max	Min	Max	Max	Min	Max	Max
30	0	34	99	63	53	211	127	76	372	219	110	584	334	144	849	472	184	1,168	647	229	1,542	852	312	1,971	1,056	454	2,996	1,545
	2	37	80	56	55	164	111	76	281	183	109	429	279	139	610	392	175	823	533	219	1,069	698	296	1,346	863	424	1,999	1,308
	5	49	74	52	72	157	106	98	271	173	136	417	271	171	595	382	215	806	521	269	1,049	684	366	1,324	846	524	1,971	1,283
	10	NA	NA	NA	91	144	98	122	255	168	171	397	257	213	570	367	265	777	501	327	1,017	662	440	1,287	821	620	1,927	1,234
	15	NA	NA	NA	115	131	NA	151	239	157	208	377	242	255	547	349	312	750	481	379	985	638	507	1,251	794	702	1,884	1,205
	20	NA	NA	NA	NA	NA	NA	181	223	NA	246	357	228	298	524	333	360	723	461	433	955	615	570	1,216	768	780	1,841	1,166
	30	NA	NA	NA	NA	NA	NA	NA	NA	NA	NA	NA	NA	389	477	305	461	670	426	541	895	574	704	1,147	720	937	1,759	1,101
50	0	33	99	66	51	213	133	73	394	230	105	629	361	138	928	515	176	1,292	704	220	1,724	948	295	2,223	1,189	428	3,432	1,818
	2	36	84	61	53	181	121	73	318	205	104	495	312	133	712	443	168	971	613	209	1,273	811	280	1,615	1,007	401	2,426	1,509
	5	48	80	NA	70	174	117	94	308	198	131	482	305	164	696	435	204	953	602	257	1,252	795	347	1,591	991	496	2,396	1,490
	10	NA	NA	NA	89	160	NA	118	292	186	162	461	292	203	671	420	253	923	583	313	1,217	765	418	1,551	963	589	2,347	1,455
	15	NA	NA	NA	112	148	NA	145	275	174	199	441	280	244	646	405	299	894	562	363	1,183	736	481	1,512	934	668	2,299	1,421
	20	NA	NA	NA	NA	NA	NA	176	257	NA	236	420	267	285	622	389	345	866	543	415	1,150	708	544	1,473	906	741	2,251	1,387
	30	NA	NA	NA	NA	NA	NA	NA	NA	NA	315	376	NA	373	573	NA	442	809	502	521	1,086	649	674	1,399	848	892	2,159	1,318
100	0	NA	NA	NA	49	214	NA	69	403	NA	100	659	395	131	991	555	166	1,404	765	207	1,900	1,033	273	2,479	1,300	395	3,912	2,042
	2	NA	NA	NA	51	192	NA	70	351	NA	98	563	373	125	828	508	158	1,152	698	196	1,532	933	259	1,970	1,168	371	3,021	1,817
	5	NA	NA	NA	67	186	NA	90	342	NA	125	551	366	156	813	501	194	1,134	688	240	1,511	921	322	1,945	1,153	460	2,990	1,796
	10	NA	NA	NA	85	175	NA	113	324	NA	153	532	354	191	789	486	238	1,104	672	293	1,477	902	389	1,905	1,133	547	2,938	1,763
	15	NA	NA	NA	132	162	NA	138	310	NA	188	511	343	230	764	473	281	1,075	656	342	1,443	884	447	1,865	1,110	618	2,888	1,730
	20	NA	NA	NA	NA	NA	NA	168	295	NA	224	487	NA	270	739	458	325	1,046	639	391	1,410	864	507	1,825	1,087	690	2,838	1,696
	30	NA	NA	NA	NA	NA	NA	231	264	NA	301	448	NA	355	685	NA	418	988	NA	491	1,343	824	631	1,747	1,041	834	2,739	1,627
	50	NA	NA	NA	NA	NA	NA	NA	NA	NA	NA	NA	NA	540	584	NA	617	866	NA	711	1,205	NA	895	1,591	NA	1,138	2,547	1,489

For SI: 1 inch = 25.4 mm, 1 foot = 304.8 mm, 1 British thermal unit per hour = 0.2931 W.

TABLE 504.2(3) MASONRY CHIMNEY

Number of Appliances	Single
Appliance Type	Category I
Appliance Vent Connection	Type B double-wall connector

HEIGHT (*H*) (feet)	LATERAL (*L*) (feet)	TYPE B DOUBLE-WALL CONNECTOR DIAMETER—(*D*) inches to be used with chimney areas within the size limits at bottom																										
		3			4			5			6			7			8			9			10			12		
		APPLIANCE INPUT RATING IN THOUSANDS OF BTU/H																										
		FAN		NAT	FAN		NAT	FAN		NAT	FAN		NAT	FAN		NAT	FAN		NAT	FAN		NAT	FAN		NAT	FAN		NAT
		Min	Max	Max	Min	Max	Max	Min	Max	Max	Min	Max	Max	Min	Max	Max	Min	Max	Max	Min	Max	Max	Min	Max	Max	Min	Max	Max
6	2	NA	NA	28	NA	NA	52	NA	NA	86	NA	NA	130	NA	NA	180	NA	NA	247	NA	NA	320	NA	NA	401	NA	NA	581
	5	NA	NA	25	NA	NA	49	NA	NA	82	NA	NA	117	NA	NA	165	NA	NA	231	NA	NA	298	NA	NA	376	NA	NA	561
8	2	NA	NA	29	NA	NA	55	NA	NA	93	NA	NA	145	NA	NA	198	NA	NA	266	84	590	350	100	728	446	139	1,024	651
	5	NA	NA	26	NA	NA	52	NA	NA	88	NA	NA	134	NA	NA	183	NA	NA	247	NA	NA	328	149	711	423	201	1,007	640
	8	NA	NA	24	NA	NA	48	NA	NA	83	NA	NA	127	NA	NA	175	NA	NA	239	NA	NA	318	173	695	410	231	990	623
10	2	NA	NA	31	NA	NA	61	NA	NA	103	NA	NA	162	NA	NA	221	68	519	298	82	655	388	98	810	491	136	1,144	724
	5	NA	NA	28	NA	NA	57	NA	NA	96	NA	NA	148	NA	NA	204	NA	NA	277	124	638	365	146	791	466	196	1,124	712
	10	NA	NA	25	NA	NA	50	NA	NA	87	NA	NA	139	NA	NA	191	NA	NA	263	155	610	347	182	762	444	240	1,093	668
15	2	NA	NA	35	NA	NA	67	NA	NA	114	NA	NA	179	53	475	250	64	613	336	77	779	441	92	968	562	127	1,376	841
	5	NA	NA	35	NA	NA	62	NA	NA	107	NA	NA	164	NA	NA	231	99	594	313	118	759	416	139	946	533	186	1,352	828
	10	NA	NA	28	NA	NA	55	NA	NA	97	NA	NA	153	NA	NA	216	126	565	296	148	727	394	173	912	567	229	1,315	777
	15	NA	NA	NA	NA	NA	48	NA	NA	89	NA	NA	141	NA	NA	201	NA	NA	281	171	698	375	198	880	485	259	1,280	742
20	2	NA	NA	38	NA	NA	74	NA	NA	124	NA	NA	201	51	522	274	61	678	375	73	867	491	87	1,083	627	121	1,548	953
	5	NA	NA	36	NA	NA	68	NA	NA	116	NA	NA	184	80	503	254	95	658	350	113	845	463	133	1,059	597	179	1,523	933
	10	NA	NA	NA	NA	NA	60	NA	NA	107	NA	NA	172	NA	NA	237	122	627	332	143	811	440	167	1,022	566	221	1,482	879
	15	NA	NA	NA	NA	NA	NA	NA	NA	97	NA	NA	159	NA	NA	220	NA	NA	314	165	780	418	191	987	541	251	1,443	840
	20	NA	NA	NA	NA	NA	NA	NA	NA	83	NA	NA	148	NA	NA	206	NA	NA	296	186	750	397	214	955	513	277	1,406	807

(continued)

TABLE 504.2(3)—continued
MASONRY CHIMNEY

Number of Appliances	Single
Appliance Type	Category I
Appliance Vent Connection	Type B double-wall connector

TYPE B DOUBLE-WALL CONNECTOR DIAMETER—(*D*) inches to be used with chimney areas within the size limits at bottom

APPLIANCE INPUT RATING IN THOUSANDS OF BTU/H

HEIGHT (*H*) (feet)	LATERAL (*L*) (feet)	3			4			5			6			7			8			9			10			12		
		FAN		NAT	FAN		NAT	FAN		NAT	FAN		NAT	FAN		NAT	FAN		NAT	FAN		NAT	FAN		NAT	FAN		NAT
		Min	Max	Max	Min	Max	Max	Min	Max	Max	Min	Max	Max	Min	Max	Max	Min	Max	Max	Min	Max	Max	Min	Max	Max	Min	Max	Max
30	2	NA	NA	41	NA	NA	82	NA	NA	137	NA	NA	216	47	581	303	57	762	421	68	985	558	81	1,240	717	111	1,793	1,112
	5	NA	NA	NA	NA	NA	76	NA	NA	128	NA	NA	198	75	561	281	90	741	393	106	962	526	125	1,216	683	169	1,766	1,094
	10	NA	NA	NA	NA	NA	67	NA	NA	115	NA	NA	184	NA	NA	263	115	709	373	135	927	500	158	1,176	648	210	1,721	1,025
	15	NA	NA	NA	NA	NA	NA	NA	NA	107	NA	NA	171	NA	NA	243	NA	NA	353	156	893	476	181	1,139	621	239	1,679	981
	20	NA	NA	NA	NA	NA	NA	NA	NA	91	NA	NA	159	NA	NA	227	NA	NA	332	176	860	450	203	1,103	592	264	1,638	940
	30	NA	NA	NA	NA	NA	NA	NA	NA	NA	NA	NA	NA	NA	NA	188	NA	NA	288	NA	NA	416	249	1,035	555	318	1,560	877
50	2	NA	NA	NA	NA	NA	92	NA	NA	161	NA	NA	251	NA	NA	351	51	840	477	61	1,106	633	72	1,413	812	99	2,080	1,243
	5	NA	NA	NA	NA	NA	NA	NA	NA	151	NA	NA	230	NA	NA	323	83	819	445	98	1,083	596	116	1,387	774	155	2,052	1,225
	10	NA	NA	NA	NA	NA	NA	NA	NA	138	NA	NA	215	NA	NA	304	NA	NA	424	126	1,047	567	147	1,347	733	195	2,006	1,147
	15	NA	NA	NA	NA	NA	NA	NA	NA	127	NA	NA	199	NA	NA	282	NA	NA	400	146	1,010	539	170	1,307	702	222	1,961	1,099
	20	NA	NA	NA	NA	NA	NA	NA	NA	NA	NA	NA	185	NA	NA	264	NA	NA	376	165	977	511	190	1,269	669	246	1,916	1,050
	30	NA	NA	NA	NA	NA	NA	NA	NA	NA	NA	NA	NA	NA	NA	NA	NA	NA	327	NA	NA	468	233	1,196	623	295	1,832	984
Minimum Internal Area of Chimney (square inches)		12			19			28			38			50			63			78			95			132		
Maximum Internal Area of Chimney (square inches)		Seven times the listed appliance categorized vent area, flue collar area or draft hood outlet area.																										

For SI: 1 inch = 25.4 mm, 1 square inch = 645.16 mm^2, 1 foot = 304.8 mm, 1 British thermal unit per hour = 0.2931 W.

TABLE 504.2(4)
MASONRY CHIMNEY

Number of Appliances	Single
Appliance Type	Category I
Appliance Vent Connection	Single-wall metal connector

HEIGHT (*H*) (feet)	LATERAL (*L*) (feet)	SINGLE-WALL METAL CONNECTOR DIAMETER—(*D*) inches to be used with chimney areas within the size limits at bottom																									
		3			4			5			6			7			8			9			10			12	
		APPLIANCE INPUT RATING IN THOUSANDS OF BTU/H																									
		FAN		NAT	FAN		NAT	FAN		NAT	FAN		NAT	FAN		NAT	FAN		NAT	FAN		NAT	FAN		NAT	FAN		NAT
		Min	Max	Max	Min	Max	Max	Min	Max	Max	Min	Max	Max	Min	Max	Max	Min	Max	Max	Min	Max	Max	Min	Max	Max	Min	Max	Max
6	2	NA	NA	28	NA	NA	52	NA	NA	86	NA	NA	130	NA	NA	180	NA	NA	247	NA	NA	319	NA	NA	400	NA	NA	580
	5	NA	NA	25	NA	NA	48	NA	NA	81	NA	NA	116	NA	NA	164	NA	NA	230	NA	NA	297	NA	NA	375	NA	NA	560
8	2	NA	NA	29	NA	NA	55	NA	NA	93	NA	NA	145	NA	NA	197	NA	NA	265	NA	NA	349	382	725	445	549	1,021	650
	5	NA	NA	26	NA	NA	51	NA	NA	87	NA	NA	133	NA	NA	182	NA	NA	246	NA	NA	327	NA	NA	422	673	1,003	638
	8	NA	NA	23	NA	NA	47	NA	NA	82	NA	NA	126	NA	NA	174	NA	NA	237	NA	NA	317	NA	NA	408	747	985	621
10	2	NA	NA	31	NA	NA	61	NA	NA	102	NA	NA	161	NA	NA	220	216	518	297	271	654	387	373	808	490	536	1,142	722
	5	NA	NA	28	NA	NA	56	NA	NA	95	NA	NA	147	NA	NA	203	NA	NA	276	334	635	364	459	789	465	657	1,121	710
	10	NA	NA	24	NA	NA	49	NA	NA	86	NA	NA	137	NA	NA	189	NA	NA	261	NA	NA	345	547	758	441	771	1,088	665
15	2	NA	NA	35	NA	NA	67	NA	NA	113	NA	NA	178	166	473	249	211	611	335	264	776	440	362	965	560	520	1,373	840
	5	NA	NA	32	NA	NA	61	NA	NA	106	NA	NA	163	NA	NA	230	261	591	312	325	775	414	444	942	531	637	1,348	825
	10	NA	NA	27	NA	NA	54	NA	NA	96	NA	NA	151	NA	NA	214	NA	NA	294	392	722	392	531	907	504	749	1,309	774
	15	NA	NA	NA	NA	NA	46	NA	NA	87	NA	NA	138	NA	NA	198	NA	NA	278	452	692	372	606	873	481	841	1,272	738
20	2	NA	NA	38	NA	NA	73	NA	NA	123	NA	NA	200	163	520	273	206	675	374	258	864	490	252	1,079	625	508	1,544	950
	5	NA	NA	35	NA	NA	67	NA	NA	115	NA	NA	183	80	NA	252	255	655	348	317	842	461	433	1,055	594	623	1,518	930
	10	NA	NA	NA	NA	NA	59	NA	NA	105	NA	NA	170	NA	NA	235	312	622	330	382	806	437	517	1,016	562	733	1,475	875
	15	NA	NA	NA	NA	NA	NA	NA	NA	95	NA	NA	156	NA	NA	217	NA	NA	311	442	773	414	591	979	539	823	1,434	835
	20	NA	NA	NA	NA	NA	NA	NA	NA	80	NA	NA	144	NA	NA	202	NA	NA	292	NA	NA	392	663	944	510	911	1,394	800

(continued)

Number of Appliances	Single
Appliance Type	Category I
Appliance Vent Connection	Single-wall metal connector

TABLE 504.2(4)—continued MASONRY CHIMNEY

HEIGHT (*H*) (feet)	LATERAL (*L*) (feet)	SINGLE-WALL METAL CONNECTOR DIAMETER—(*D*) inches to be used with chimney areas within the size limits at bottom																										
		3			4			5			6			7			8			9			10			12		
		APPLIANCE INPUT RATING IN THOUSANDS OF BTU/H																										
		FAN		NAT	FAN		NAT	FAN		NAT	FAN		NAT	FAN		NAT	FAN		NAT	FAN		NAT	FAN		NAT	FAN		NAT
		Min	Max	Max	Min	Max	Max	Min	Max	Max	Min	Max	Max	Min	Max	Max	Min	Max	Max	Min	Max	Max	Min	Max	Max	Min	Max	Max
30	2	NA	NA	41	NA	NA	81	NA	NA	136	NA	NA	215	158	578	302	200	759	420	249	982	556	340	1,237	715	489	1,789	1,110
	5	NA	NA	NA	NA	NA	75	NA	NA	127	NA	NA	196	NA	NA	279	245	737	391	306	958	524	417	1,210	680	600	1,760	1,090
	10	NA	NA	NA	NA	NA	66	NA	NA	113	NA	NA	182	NA	NA	260	300	703	370	370	920	496	500	1,168	644	708	1,713	1,020
	15	NA	NA	NA	NA	NA	NA	NA	NA	105	NA	NA	168	NA	NA	240	NA	NA	349	428	884	471	572	1,128	615	798	1,668	975
	20	NA	NA	NA	NA	NA	NA	NA	NA	88	NA	NA	155	NA	NA	223	NA	NA	327	NA	NA	445	643	1,089	585	883	1,624	932
	30	NA	NA	NA	NA	NA	NA	NA	NA	NA	NA	NA	NA	NA	NA	182	NA	NA	281	NA	NA	408	NA	NA	544	1,055	1,539	865
50	2	NA	NA	NA	NA	NA	91	NA	NA	160	NA	NA	250	NA	NA	350	191	837	475	238	1,103	631	323	1,408	810	463	2,076	1,240
	5	NA	NA	NA	NA	NA	NA	NA	NA	149	NA	NA	228	NA	NA	321	NA	NA	442	293	1,078	593	398	1,381	770	571	2,044	1,220
	10	NA	NA	NA	NA	NA	NA	NA	NA	136	NA	NA	212	NA	NA	301	NA	NA	420	355	1,038	562	447	1,337	728	674	1,994	1,140
	15	NA	NA	NA	NA	NA	NA	NA	NA	124	NA	NA	195	NA	NA	278	NA	NA	395	NA	NA	533	546	1,294	695	761	1,945	1,090
	20	NA	NA	NA	NA	NA	NA	NA	NA	NA	NA	NA	180	NA	NA	258	NA	NA	370	NA	NA	504	616	1,251	660	844	1,898	1,040
	30	NA	NA	NA	NA	NA	48	NA	NA	NA	NA	NA	NA	NA	NA	NA	NA	NA	318	NA	NA	458	NA	NA	610	1,009	1,805	970
Minimum Internal Area of Chimney (square inches)		12			19			28			38			50			63			78			95			132		
Maximum Internal Area of Chimney (square inches)		Seven times the listed appliance categorized vent area, flue collar area or draft hood outlet area.																										

For SI: 1 inch = 25.4 mm, 1 square inch = 645.16 mm^2, 1 foot = 304.8 mm, 1 British thermal unit per hour = 0.2931 W.

Number of Appliances	Single
Appliance Type	Draft hood equipped
Appliance Vent Connection	Connected directly to pipe or vent

TABLE 504.2(5) SINGLE-WALL METAL PIPE OR TYPE B ASBESTOS CEMENT VENT

HEIGHT (*H*) (feet)	LATERAL (*L*) (feet)	VENT DIAMETER—(*D*) inches							
		3	4	5	6	7	8	10	12
		MAXIMUM APPLIANCE INPUT RATING IN THOUSANDS OF BTU/H							
6	0	39	70	116	170	232	312	500	750
	2	31	55	94	141	194	260	415	620
	5	28	51	88	128	177	242	390	600
8	0	42	76	126	185	252	340	542	815
	2	32	61	102	154	210	284	451	680
	5	29	56	95	141	194	264	430	648
	10	24	49	86	131	180	250	406	625
10	0	45	84	138	202	279	372	606	912
	2	35	67	111	168	233	311	505	760
	5	32	61	104	153	215	289	480	724
	10	27	54	94	143	200	274	455	700
	15	NA	46	84	130	186	258	432	666
15	0	49	91	151	223	312	420	684	1,040
	2	39	72	122	186	260	350	570	865
	5	35	67	110	170	240	325	540	825
	10	30	58	103	158	223	308	514	795
	15	NA	50	93	144	207	291	488	760
	20	NA	NA	82	132	195	273	466	726
20	0	53	101	163	252	342	470	770	1,190
	2	42	80	136	210	286	392	641	990
	5	38	74	123	192	264	364	610	945
	10	32	65	115	178	246	345	571	910
	15	NA	55	104	163	228	326	550	870
	20	NA	NA	91	149	214	306	525	832
30	0	56	108	183	276	384	529	878	1,370
	2	44	84	148	230	320	441	730	1,140
	5	NA	78	137	210	296	410	694	1,080
	10	NA	68	125	196	274	388	656	1,050
	15	NA	NA	113	177	258	366	625	1,000
	20	NA	NA	99	163	240	344	596	960
	30	NA	NA	NA	NA	192	295	540	890
50	0	NA	120	210	310	443	590	980	1,550
	2	NA	95	171	260	370	492	820	1,290
	5	NA	NA	159	234	342	474	780	1,230
	10	NA	NA	146	221	318	456	730	1,190
	15	NA	NA	NA	200	292	407	705	1,130
	20	NA	NA	NA	185	276	384	670	1,080
	30	NA	NA	NA	NA	222	330	605	1,010

For SI: 1 inch = 25.4 mm, 1 foot = 304.8 mm, 1 British thermal unit per hour = 0.2931 W.

Number of Appliances	Single
Appliance Type	NAT
Appliance Vent Connection	Type B double-wall connector

TABLE 504.2(6)
EXTERIOR MASONRY CHIMNEY

VENT HEIGHT (feet)	MINIMUM ALLOWABLE INPUT RATING OF SPACE-HEATING APPLIANCE IN THOUSANDS OF BTU PER HOUR							
	Internal area of chimney (square inches)							
	12	19	28	38	50	63	78	113
37°F or Greater	Local 99% Winter Design Temperature: 37°F or Greater							
6	0	0	0	0	0	0	0	0
8	0	0	0	0	0	0	0	0
10	0	0	0	0	0	0	0	0
15	NA	0	0	0	0	0	0	0
20	NA	NA	123	190	249	184	0	0
30	NA	NA	NA	NA	NA	393	334	0
50	NA	NA	NA	NA	NA	NA	NA	579
27 to 36°F	Local 99% Winter Design Temperature: 27 to 36°F							
6	0	0	68	116	156	180	212	266
8	0	0	82	127	167	187	214	263
10	0	51	97	141	183	201	225	265
15	NA	NA	NA	NA	233	253	274	305
20	NA	NA	NA	NA	NA	307	330	362
30	NA	NA	NA	NA	NA	419	445	485
50	NA	NA	NA	NA	NA	NA	NA	763
17 to 26°F	Local 99% Winter Design Temperature: 17 to 26°F							
6	NA	NA	NA	NA	NA	215	259	349
8	NA	NA	NA	NA	197	226	264	352
10	NA	NA	NA	NA	214	245	278	358
15	NA	NA	NA	NA	NA	296	331	398
20	NA	NA	NA	NA	NA	352	387	457
30	NA	NA	NA	NA	NA	NA	507	581
50	NA	NA	NA	NA	NA	NA	NA	NA
5 to 16°F	Local 99% Winter Design Temperature: 5 to 16°F							
6	NA	NA	NA	NA	NA	NA	NA	416
8	NA	NA	NA	NA	NA	NA	312	423
10	NA	NA	NA	NA	NA	289	331	430
15	NA	NA	NA	NA	NA	NA	393	485
20	NA	NA	NA	NA	NA	NA	450	547
30	NA	NA	NA	NA	NA	NA	NA	682
50	NA	NA	NA	NA	NA	NA	NA	972
-10 to 4°F	Local 99% Winter Design Temperature: -10 to 4°F							
6	NA	NA	NA	NA	NA	NA	NA	484
8	NA	NA	NA	NA	NA	NA	NA	494
10	NA	NA	NA	NA	NA	NA	NA	513
15	NA	NA	NA	NA	NA	NA	NA	586
20	NA	NA	NA	NA	NA	NA	NA	650
30	NA	NA	NA	NA	NA	NA	NA	805
50	NA	NA	NA	NA	NA	NA	NA	1,003
-11°F or Lower	Local 99% Winter Design Temperature: -11°F or Lower							
	Not recommended for any vent configurations							

For SI: °C = (°F - 32)/1.8, 1 inch = 25.4 mm, 1 foot = 304.8 mm, 1 British thermal unit per hour = 0.2931 W.

Note: See Figure B-19 in Appendix B for a map showing local 99 percent winter design temperatures in the United States.

504.3 Application of multiple appliance vent Tables 504.3(1) through 504.3(7). The application of Tables 504.3(1) through 504.3(7) shall be subject to the requirements of Sections 504.3.1 through 504.3.27.

504.3.1 Vent obstructions. These venting tables shall not be used where obstructions, as described in Section 503.15, are installed in the venting system. The installation of vents serving listed appliances with vent dampers shall be in accordance with the appliance manufacturer's instructions or in accordance with the following:

1. The maximum capacity of the vent connector shall be determined using the NAT Max column.
2. The maximum capacity of the vertical vent or chimney shall be determined using the FAN+NAT column when the second appliance is a fan-assisted appliance, or the NAT+NAT column when the second appliance is equipped with a draft hood.
3. The minimum capacity shall be determined as if the appliance were a fan-assisted appliance.
   3.1. The minimum capacity of the vent connector shall be determined using the FAN Min column.
   3.2. The FAN+FAN column shall be used where the second appliance is a fan-assisted appliance, and the FAN+NAT column shall be used where the second appliance is equipped with a draft hood, to determine whether the vertical vent or chimney configuration is not permitted (NA). Where the vent configuration is NA, the vent configuration shall not be permitted and an alternative venting configuration shall be utilized.

504.3.2 Connector length limit. The vent connector shall be routed to the vent utilizing the shortest possible route. Except as provided in Section 504.3.3, the maximum vent connector horizontal length shall be $1^1/_2$ feet for each inch (18 mm per mm) of connector diameter as shown in Table 504.3.2.

504.3.3 Connectors with longer lengths. Connectors with longer horizontal lengths than those listed in Section 504.3.2 are permitted under the following conditions:

1. The maximum capacity (FAN Max or NAT Max) of the vent connector shall be reduced 10 percent for each additional multiple of the length allowed by Section 504.3.2. For example, the maximum length listed in Table 504.3.2 for a 4-inch (102 mm) connector is 6 feet (1829 mm). With a connector length greater than 6 feet (1829 mm) but not exceeding 12 feet (3658 mm), the maximum capacity must be reduced by 10 percent (0.90 × maximum vent connector capacity). With a connector length greater than 12 feet (3658 mm) but not exceeding 18 feet (5486 mm), the maximum capacity must be reduced by 20 percent (0.80 × maximum vent capacity).
2. For a connector serving a fan-assisted appliance, the minimum capacity (FAN Min) of the connector shall be determined by referring to the corresponding single appliance table. For Type B double-wall connectors, Table 504.2(1) shall be used. For single-wall connectors, Table 504.2(2) shall be used. The height (*H*) and lateral (*L*) shall be measured according to the procedures for a single-appliance vent, as if the other appliances were not present.

TABLE 504.3.2
MAXIMUM VENT CONNECTOR LENGTH

CONNECTOR DIAMETER (inches)	CONNECTOR MAXIMUM HORIZONTAL LENGTH (feet)
3	$4^1/_2$
4	6
5	$7^1/_2$
6	9
7	$10^1/_2$
8	12
9	$13^1/_2$
10	15
12	18
14	21
16	24
18	27
20	30
22	33
24	36

For SI: 1 inch = 25.4 mm, 1 foot = 304.8 mm.

504.3.4 Vent connector manifold. Where the vent connectors are combined prior to entering the vertical portion of the common vent to form a common vent manifold, the size of the common vent manifold and the common vent shall be determined by applying a 10-percent reduction (0.90 × maximum common vent capacity) to the common vent capacity part of the common vent tables. The length of the common vent connector manifold (L_m) shall not exceed $1^1/_2$ feet for each inch (18 mm per mm) of common vent connector manifold diameter (*D*) (see Figure B-11).

504.3.5 Common vertical vent offset. Where the common vertical vent is *offset*, the maximum capacity of the common vent shall be reduced in accordance with Section 504.3.6. The horizontal length of the common vent *offset* (L_o) shall not exceed $1^1/_2$ feet for each inch (18 mm per mm) of common vent diameter *(D)*. Where multiple offsets occur in a common vent, the total horizontal length of all offsets combined shall not exceed $1^1/_2$ feet for each inch (18 mm per mm) of common vent diameter *(D)*.

504.3.6 Elbows in vents. For each elbow up to and including 45 degrees (0.79 rad) in the common vent, the maximum common vent capacity listed in the venting tables shall be reduced by 5 percent. For each elbow greater than 45 degrees (0.79 rad) up to and including 90 degrees (1.57 rad), the maximum common vent capacity listed in the venting tables shall be reduced by 10 percent.

504.3.7 Elbows in connectors. The vent connector capacities listed in the common vent sizing tables include allowance for two 90-degree (1.57 rad) elbows. For each additional elbow up to and including 45 degrees (0.79 rad), the maximum vent connector capacity listed in the venting tables shall be reduced by 5 percent. For each elbow greater than 45 degrees (0.79 rad) up to and including 90 degrees (1.57 rad), the maximum vent connector capacity listed in the venting tables shall be reduced by 10 percent.

504.3.8 Common vent minimum size. The cross-sectional area of the common vent shall be equal to or greater than the cross-sectional area of the largest connector.

504.3.9 Common vent fittings. At the point where tee or wye fittings connect to a common vent, the opening size of the fitting shall be equal to the size of the common vent. Such fittings shall not be prohibited from having reduced-size openings at the point of connection of appliance vent connectors.

504.3.9.1 Tee and wye fittings. Tee and wye fittings connected to a common gas vent shall be considered as part of the common gas vent and shall be constructed of materials consistent with that of the common gas vent.

504.3.10 High-altitude installations. Sea-level input ratings shall be used when determining maximum capacity for high-altitude installation. Actual input (derated for altitude) shall be used for determining minimum capacity for high-altitude installation.

504.3.11 Connector rise measurement. Connector rise (*R*) for each appliance connector shall be measured from the draft hood outlet or flue collar to the centerline where the vent gas streams come together.

504.3.12 Vent height measurement. For multiple appliances all located on one floor, available total height (*H*) shall be measured from the highest draft hood outlet or flue collar up to the level of the outlet of the common vent.

504.3.13 Multistory height measurement. For multistory installations, available total height (*H*) for each segment of the system shall be the vertical distance between the highest draft hood outlet or flue collar entering that segment and the centerline of the next higher interconnection tee (see Figure B-13).

504.3.14 Multistory lowest portion sizing. The size of the lowest connector and of the vertical vent leading to the lowest interconnection of a multistory system shall be in accordance with Table 504.2(1) or 504.2(2) for available total height (*H*) up to the lowest interconnection (see Figure B-14).

504.3.15 Multistory common vents. Where used in multistory systems, vertical common vents shall be Type B double wall and shall be installed with a listed vent cap.

504.3.16 Multistory common vent offsets. *Offsets* in multistory common vent systems shall be limited to a single *offset* in each system, and systems with an *offset* shall comply with all of the following:

1. The *offset* angle shall not exceed 45 degrees (0.79 rad) from vertical.
2. The horizontal length of the *offset* shall not exceed $1^1/_2$ feet for each inch (18 mm per mm) of common vent diameter of the segment in which the *offset* is located.
3. For the segment of the common vertical vent containing the *offset*, the common vent capacity listed in the common venting tables shall be reduced by 20 percent (0.80 × maximum common vent capacity).
4. A multistory common vent shall not be reduced in size above the *offset*.

504.3.17 Vertical vent maximum size. Where two or more appliances are connected to a vertical vent or chimney, the flow area of the largest section of vertical vent or chimney shall not exceed seven times the smallest listed appliance categorized vent areas, flue collar area or draft hood outlet area unless designed in accordance with *approved* engineering methods.

504.3.18 Multiple input rate appliances. For appliances with more than one input rate, the minimum vent connector capacity (FAN Min) determined from the tables shall be less than the lowest appliance input rating, and the maximum vent connector capacity (FAN Max or NAT Max) determined from the tables shall be greater than the highest appliance input rating.

504.3.19 Liner system sizing and connections. Listed, corrugated metallic chimney liner systems in masonry chimneys shall be sized by using Table 504.3(1) or 504.3(2) for Type B vents, with the maximum capacity reduced by 20 percent (0.80 × maximum capacity) and the minimum capacity as shown in Table 504.3(1) or 504.3(2). Corrugated metallic liner systems installed with bends or offsets shall have their maximum capacity further reduced in accordance with Sections 504.3.5 and 504.3.6. The 20-percent reduction for corrugated metallic chimney liner systems includes an allowance for one long-radius 90-degree (1.57 rad) turn at the bottom of the liner. Where double-wall connectors are required, tee and wye fittings used to connect to the common vent chimney liner shall be listed double-wall fittings. Connections between chimney liners and listed double-wall fittings shall be made with listed adapter fittings designed for such purpose.

504.3.20 Chimney and vent location. Tables 504.3(1), 504.3(2), 504.3(3), 504.3(4) and 504.3(5) shall be used only for chimneys and vents not exposed to the outdoors below the roof line. A Type B vent or listed chimney lining system passing through an unused masonry chimney flue shall not be considered to be exposed to the outdoors. A Type B vent shall not be considered to be exposed to the outdoors where it passes through an unventilated enclosure or chase insulated to a value of not less than R8.

Tables 504.3(6a), 504.3(6b), 504.3(7a) and 504.3(7b) shall be used for clay-tile-lined *exterior masonry chimneys*, provided that all of the following conditions are met:

1. Vent connector is Type B double wall.
2. At least one appliance is draft hood equipped.

3. The combined appliance input rating is less than the maximum capacity given by Table 504.3(6a) for NAT+NAT or Table 504.3(7a) for FAN+NAT.
4. The input rating of each space-heating appliance is greater than the minimum input rating given by Table 504.3(6b) for NAT+NAT or Table 504.3(7b) for FAN+NAT.
5. The vent connector sizing is in accordance with Table 504.3(3).

Exception: Vents serving listed appliances installed in accordance with the appliance manufacturer's installation instructions.

504.3.21 Connector maximum and minimum size. Vent connectors shall not be increased in size more than two sizes greater than the listed appliance categorized vent diameter, flue collar diameter or draft hood outlet diameter. Vent connectors for draft hood-equipped appliances shall not be smaller than the draft hood outlet diameter. Where a vent connector size(s) determined from the tables for a fan-assisted appliance(s) is smaller than the flue collar diameter, the use of the smaller size(s) shall be permitted provided that the installation complies with all of the following conditions:

1. Vent connectors for fan-assisted appliance flue collars 12 inches (305 mm) in diameter or smaller are not reduced by more than one table size [e.g., 12 inches to 10 inches (305 mm to 254 mm) is a one-size reduction] and those larger than 12 inches (305 mm) in diameter are not reduced more than two table sizes [e.g., 24 inches to 20 inches (610 mm to 508 mm) is a two-size reduction].
2. The fan-assisted appliance(s) is common vented with a draft-hood-equipped appliances(s).
3. The vent connector has a smooth interior wall.

504.3.22 Component commingling. All combinations of pipe sizes, single-wall and double-wall metal pipe shall be allowed within any connector run(s) or within the common vent, provided that all of the appropriate tables permit all of the desired sizes and types of pipe, as if they were used for the entire length of the subject connector or vent. Where single-wall and Type B double-wall metal pipes are used for vent connectors within the same venting system, the common vent must be sized using Table 504.3(2) or 504.3(4), as appropriate.

504.3.23 Draft hood conversion accessories. Draft hood conversion accessories for use with masonry chimneys venting listed Category I fan-assisted appliances shall be listed and installed in accordance with the manufacturer's installation instructions for such listed accessories.

504.3.24 Multiple sizes permitted. Where a table permits more than one diameter of pipe to be used for a connector or vent, all the permitted sizes shall be permitted to be used.

504.3.25 Table interpolation. Interpolation shall be permitted in calculating capacities for vent dimensions that fall between table entries (see Appendix B, Example 3).

504.3.26 Extrapolation prohibited. Extrapolation beyond the table entries shall not be permitted.

504.3.27 Engineering calculations. For vent heights less than 6 feet (1829 mm) and greater than shown in the tables, engineering methods shall be used to calculate vent capacities.

SECTION 505 (IFGC) DIRECT-VENT, INTEGRAL VENT, MECHANICAL VENT AND VENTILATION/EXHAUST HOOD VENTING

505.1 General. The installation of direct-vent and integral vent appliances shall be in accordance with Section 503. Mechanical venting systems and exhaust hood venting systems shall be designed and installed in accordance with Section 503.

505.1.1 Commercial cooking appliances vented by exhaust hoods. Deleted.

SECTION 506 (IFGC) FACTORY-BUILT CHIMNEYS

506.1 Building heating appliances. Factory-built chimneys for building heating appliances producing flue gases having a temperature not greater than 1,000°F (538°C), measured at the entrance to the chimney, shall be listed and *labeled* in accordance with UL 103 and shall be installed and terminated in accordance with the manufacturer's installation instructions.

506.2 Support. Where factory-built chimneys are supported by structural members, such as joists and rafters, such members shall be designed to support the additional load.

506.3 Medium-heat appliances. Deleted.

Number of Appliances	Two or more
Appliance Type	Category I
Appliance Vent Connection	Type B double-wall connector

TABLE 504.3(1) TYPE B DOUBLE-WALL VENT

VENT CONNECTOR CAPACITY

VENT HEIGHT (H) (feet)	CONNECTOR RISE (R) (feet)	TYPE B DOUBLE-WALL VENT AND CONNECTOR DIAMETER—(D) inches																							
		3			4			5			6			7			8			9			10		
		APPLIANCE INPUT RATING LIMITS IN THOUSANDS OF BTU/H																							
		FAN		NAT	FAN		NAT	FAN		NAT	FAN		NAT	FAN		NAT	FAN		NAT	FAN		NAT	FAN		NAT
		Min	Max	Max	Min	Max	Max	Min	Max	Max	Min	Max	Max	Min	Max	Max	Min	Max	Max	Min	Max	Max	Min	Max	Max
6	1	22	37	26	35	66	46	46	106	72	58	164	104	77	225	142	92	296	185	109	376	237	128	466	289
	2	23	41	31	37	75	55	48	121	86	60	183	124	79	253	168	95	333	220	112	424	282	131	526	345
	3	24	44	35	38	81	62	49	132	96	62	199	139	82	275	189	97	363	248	114	463	317	134	575	386
8	1	22	40	27	35	72	48	49	114	76	64	176	109	84	243	148	100	320	194	118	408	248	138	507	303
	2	23	44	32	36	80	57	51	128	90	66	195	129	86	269	175	103	356	230	121	454	294	141	564	358
	3	24	47	36	37	87	64	53	139	101	67	210	145	88	290	198	105	384	258	123	492	330	143	612	402
10	1	22	43	28	34	78	50	49	123	78	65	189	113	89	257	154	106	341	200	125	436	257	146	542	314
	2	23	47	33	36	86	59	51	136	93	67	206	134	91	282	182	109	374	238	128	479	305	149	596	372
	3	24	50	37	37	92	67	52	146	104	69	220	150	94	303	205	111	402	268	131	515	342	152	642	417
15	1	21	50	30	33	89	53	47	142	83	64	220	120	88	298	163	110	389	214	134	493	273	162	609	333
	2	22	53	35	35	96	63	49	153	99	66	235	142	91	320	193	112	419	253	137	532	323	165	658	394
	3	24	55	40	36	102	71	51	163	111	68	248	160	93	339	218	115	445	286	140	565	365	167	700	444
20	1	21	54	31	33	99	56	46	157	87	62	246	125	86	334	171	107	436	224	131	552	285	158	681	347
	2	22	57	37	34	105	66	48	167	104	64	259	149	89	354	202	110	463	265	134	587	339	161	725	414
	3	23	60	42	35	110	74	50	176	116	66	271	168	91	371	228	113	486	300	137	618	383	164	764	466
30	1	20	62	33	31	113	59	45	181	93	60	288	134	83	391	182	103	512	238	125	649	305	151	802	372
	2	21	64	39	33	118	70	47	190	110	62	299	158	85	408	215	105	535	282	129	679	360	155	840	439
	3	22	66	44	34	123	79	48	198	124	64	309	178	88	423	242	108	555	317	132	706	405	158	874	494
50	1	19	71	36	30	133	64	43	216	101	57	349	145	78	477	197	97	627	257	120	797	330	144	984	403
	2	21	73	43	32	137	76	45	223	119	59	358	172	81	490	234	100	645	306	123	820	392	148	1,014	478
	3	22	75	48	33	141	86	46	229	134	61	366	194	83	502	263	103	661	343	126	842	441	151	1,043	538
100	1	18	82	37	28	158	66	40	262	104	53	442	150	73	611	204	91	810	266	112	1,038	341	135	1,285	417
	2	19	83	44	30	161	79	42	267	123	55	447	178	75	619	242	94	822	316	115	1,054	405	139	1,306	494
	3	20	84	50	31	163	89	44	272	138	57	452	109	78	627	272	97	834	355	118	1,069	455	142	1,327	555

COMMON VENT CAPACITY

VENT HEIGHT (H) (feet)	TYPE B DOUBLE-WALL COMMON VENT DIAMETER—(D) inches																				
	4			5			6			7			8			9			10		
	COMBINED APPLIANCE INPUT RATING IN THOUSANDS OF BTU/H																				
	FAN +FAN	FAN +NAT	NAT +NAT	FAN +FAN	FAN +NAT	NAT +NAT	FAN +FAN	FAN +NAT	NAT +NAT	FAN +FAN	FAN +NAT	NAT +NAT	FAN +FAN	FAN +NAT	NAT +NAT	FAN +FAN	FAN +NAT	NAT +NAT	FAN +FAN	FAN +NAT	NAT +NAT
6	92	81	65	140	116	103	204	161	147	309	248	200	404	314	260	547	434	335	672	520	410
8	101	90	73	155	129	114	224	178	163	339	275	223	444	348	290	602	480	378	740	577	465
10	110	97	79	169	141	124	243	194	178	367	299	242	477	377	315	649	522	405	800	627	495
15	125	112	91	195	164	144	283	228	206	427	352	280	556	444	365	753	612	465	924	733	565
20	136	123	102	215	183	160	314	255	229	475	394	310	621	499	405	842	688	523	1,035	826	640
30	152	138	118	244	210	185	361	297	266	547	459	360	720	585	470	979	808	605	1,209	975	740
50	167	153	134	279	244	214	421	353	310	641	547	423	854	706	550	1,164	977	705	1,451	1,188	860
100	175	163	NA	311	277	NA	489	421	NA	751	658	479	1,025	873	625	1,408	1,215	800	1,784	1,502	975

(continued)

Number of Appliances	Two or more
Appliance Type	Category I
Appliance Vent Connection	Type B double-wall connector

TABLE 504.3(1)—continued
TYPE B DOUBLE-WALL VENT

VENT CONNECTOR CAPACITY

VENT HEIGHT (*H*) (feet)	CONNECTOR RISE (*R*) (feet)	TYPE B DOUBLE-WALL VENT AND DIAMETER—(*D*) inches																				
		12			14			16			18			20			22			24		
		APPLIANCE INPUT RATING LIMITS IN THOUSANDS OF BTU/H																				
		FAN		NAT	FAN		NAT	FAN		NAT	FAN		NAT	FAN		NAT	FAN		NAT	FAN		NAT
		Min	Max	Max	Min	Max	Max	Min	Max	Max	Min	Max	Max	Min	Max	Max	Min	Max	Max	Min	Max	Max
6	2	174	764	496	223	1,046	653	281	1,371	853	346	1,772	1,080	NA	NA	NA	NA	NA	NA	NA	NA	NA
	4	180	897	616	230	1,231	827	287	1,617	1,081	352	2,069	1,370	NA	NA	NA	NA	NA	NA	NA	NA	NA
	6	NA	NA	NA	NA	NA	NA	NA	NA	NA	NA	NA	NA	NA	NA	NA	NA	NA	NA	NA	NA	NA
8	2	186	822	516	238	1,126	696	298	1,478	910	365	1,920	1,150	NA	NA	NA	NA	NA	NA	NA	NA	NA
	4	192	952	644	244	1,307	884	305	1,719	1,150	372	2,211	1,460	471	2,737	1,800	560	3,319	2,180	662	3,957	2,590
	6	198	1,050	772	252	1,445	1,072	313	1,902	1,390	380	2,434	1,770	478	3,018	2,180	568	3,665	2,640	669	4,373	3,130
10	2	196	870	536	249	1,195	730	311	1,570	955	379	2,049	1,205	NA	NA	NA	NA	NA	NA	NA	NA	NA
	4	201	997	664	256	1,371	924	318	1,804	1,205	387	2,332	1,535	486	2,887	1,890	581	3,502	2,280	686	4,175	2,710
	6	207	1,095	792	263	1,509	1,118	325	1,989	1,455	395	2,556	1,865	494	3,169	2,290	589	3,849	2,760	694	4,593	3,270
15	2	214	967	568	272	1,334	790	336	1,760	1,030	408	2,317	1,305	NA	NA	NA	NA	NA	NA	NA	NA	NA
	4	221	1,085	712	279	1,499	1,006	344	1,978	1,320	416	2,579	1,665	523	3,197	2,060	624	3,881	2,490	734	4,631	2,960
	6	228	1,181	856	286	1,632	1,222	351	2,157	1,610	424	2,796	2,025	533	3,470	2,510	634	4,216	3,030	743	5,035	3,600
20	2	223	1,051	596	291	1,443	840	357	1,911	1,095	430	2,533	1,385	NA	NA	NA	NA	NA	NA	NA	NA	NA
	4	230	1,162	748	298	1,597	1,064	365	2,116	1,395	438	2,778	1,765	554	3,447	2,180	661	4,190	2,630	772	5,005	3,130
	6	237	1,253	900	307	1,726	1,288	373	2,287	1,695	450	2,984	2,145	567	3,708	2,650	671	4,511	3,190	785	5,392	3,790
30	2	216	1,217	632	286	1,664	910	367	2,183	1,190	461	2,891	1,540	NA	NA	NA	NA	NA	NA	NA	NA	NA
	4	223	1,316	792	294	1,802	1,160	376	2,366	1,510	474	3,110	1,920	619	3,840	2,365	728	4,861	2,860	847	5,606	3,410
	6	231	1,400	952	303	1,920	1,410	384	2,524	1,830	485	3,299	2,340	632	4,080	2,875	741	4,976	3,480	860	5,961	4,150
50	2	206	1,479	689	273	2,023	1,007	350	2,659	1,315	435	3,548	1,665	NA	NA	NA	NA	NA	NA	NA	NA	NA
	4	213	1,561	860	281	2,139	1,291	359	2,814	1,685	447	3,730	2,135	580	4,601	2,633	709	5,569	3,185	851	6,633	3,790
	6	221	1,631	1,031	290	2,242	1,575	369	2,951	2,055	461	3,893	2,605	594	4,808	3,208	724	5,826	3,885	867	6,943	4,620
100	2	192	1,923	712	254	2,644	1,050	326	3,490	1,370	402	4,707	1,740	NA	NA	NA	NA	NA	NA	NA	NA	NA
	4	200	1,984	888	263	2,731	1,346	336	3,606	1,760	414	4,842	2,220	523	5,982	2,750	639	7,254	3,330	769	8,650	3,950
	6	208	2,035	1,064	272	2,811	1,642	346	3,714	2,150	426	4,968	2,700	539	6,143	3,350	654	7,453	4,070	786	8,892	4,810

COMMON VENT CAPACITY

VENT HEIGHT (*H*) (feet)	TYPE B DOUBLE-WALL COMMON VENT DIAMETER—(*D*) inches																				
	12			14			16			18			20			22			24		
	COMBINED APPLIANCE INPUT RATING IN THOUSANDS OF BTU/H																				
	FAN +FAN	FAN +NAT	NAT +NAT	FAN +FAN	FAN +NAT	NAT +NAT	FAN +FAN	FAN +NAT	NAT +NAT	FAN +FAN	FAN +NAT	NAT +NAT	FAN +FAN	FAN +NAT	NAT +NAT	FAN +FAN	FAN +NAT	NAT +NAT	FAN +FAN	FAN +NAT	NAT +NAT
6	900	696	588	1,284	990	815	1,735	1,336	1,065	2,253	1,732	1,345	2,838	2,180	1,660	3,488	2,677	1970	4,206	3,226	2,390
8	994	773	652	1,423	1,103	912	1,927	1,491	1,190	2,507	1,936	1,510	3,162	2,439	1,860	3,890	2,998	2,200	4,695	3,616	2,680
10	1,076	841	712	1,542	1,200	995	2,093	1,625	1,300	2,727	2,113	1645	3,444	2,665	2,030	4,241	3,278	2,400	5,123	3,957	2,920
15	1,247	986	825	1,794	1,410	1,158	2,440	1,910	1,510	3,184	2,484	1,910	4,026	3,133	2,360	4,971	3,862	2,790	6,016	4,670	3,400
20	1,405	1,116	916	2,006	1,588	1,290	2,722	2,147	1,690	3,561	2,798	2,140	4,548	3,552	2,640	5,573	4,352	3,120	6,749	5,261	3,800
30	1,658	1,327	1,025	2,373	1,892	1,525	3,220	2,558	1,990	4,197	3,326	2,520	5,303	4,193	3,110	6,539	5,157	3,680	7,940	6,247	4,480
50	2,024	1,640	1,280	2,911	2,347	1,863	3,964	3,183	2,430	5,184	4,149	3,075	6,567	5,240	3,800	8,116	6,458	4,500	9,837	7,813	5,475
100	2,569	2,131	1,670	3,732	3,076	2,450	5,125	4,202	3,200	6,749	5,509	4,050	8,597	6,986	5,000	10,681	8,648	5,920	13,004	10,499	7,200

For SI: 1 inch = 25.4 mm, 1 foot = 304.8 mm, 1 British thermal unit per hour = 0.2931 W.

Number of Appliances	Two or more
Appliance Type	Category I
Appliance Vent Connection	Single-wall metal connector

TABLE 504.3(2)
TYPE B DOUBLE-WALL VENT

VENT CONNECTOR CAPACITY

VENT HEIGHT (*H*) (feet)	CONNECTOR RISE (*R*) (feet)	SINGLE-WALL METAL VENT CONNECTOR DIAMETER—(*D*) inches																							
		3			4			5			6			7			8			9			10		
		APPLIANCE INPUT RATING LIMITS IN THOUSANDS OF BTU/H																							
		FAN		NAT	FAN		NAT	FAN		NAT	FAN		NAT	FAN		NAT	FAN		NAT	FAN		NAT	FAN		NAT
		Min	Max	Max	Min	Max	Max	Min	Max	Max	Min	Max	Max	Min	Max	Max	Min	Max	Max	Min	Max	Max	Min	Max	Max
	1	NA	NA	26	NA	NA	46	NA	NA	71	NA	NA	102	207	223	140	262	293	183	325	373	234	447	463	286
6	2	NA	NA	31	NA	NA	55	NA	NA	85	168	182	123	215	251	167	271	331	219	334	422	281	458	524	344
	3	NA	NA	34	NA	NA	62	121	131	95	175	198	138	222	273	188	279	361	247	344	462	316	468	574	385
	1	NA	NA	27	NA	NA	48	NA	NA	75	NA	NA	106	226	240	145	285	316	191	352	403	244	481	502	299
8	2	NA	NA	32	NA	NA	57	125	126	89	184	193	127	234	266	173	293	353	228	360	450	292	492	560	355
	3	NA	NA	35	NA	NA	64	130	138	100	191	208	144	241	287	197	302	381	256	370	489	328	501	609	400
	1	NA	NA	28	NA	NA	50	119	121	77	182	186	110	240	253	150	302	335	196	372	429	252	506	534	308
10	2	NA	NA	33	84	85	59	124	134	91	189	203	132	248	278	183	311	369	235	381	473	302	517	589	368
	3	NA	NA	36	89	91	67	129	144	102	197	217	148	257	299	203	320	398	265	391	511	339	528	637	413
	1	NA	NA	29	79	87	52	116	138	81	177	214	116	238	291	158	312	380	208	397	482	266	556	596	324
15	2	NA	NA	34	83	94	62	121	150	97	185	230	138	246	314	189	321	411	248	407	522	317	568	646	387
	3	NA	NA	39	87	100	70	127	160	109	193	243	157	255	333	215	331	438	281	418	557	360	579	690	437
	1	49	56	30	78	97	54	115	152	84	175	238	120	233	325	165	306	425	217	390	538	276	546	664	336
20	2	52	59	36	82	103	64	120	163	101	182	252	144	243	346	197	317	453	259	400	574	331	558	709	403
	3	55	62	40	87	107	72	125	172	113	190	264	164	252	363	223	326	476	294	412	607	375	570	750	457
	1	47	60	31	77	110	57	112	175	89	169	278	129	226	380	175	296	497	230	378	630	294	528	779	358
30	2	51	62	37	81	115	67	117	185	106	177	290	152	236	397	208	307	521	274	389	662	349	541	819	425
	3	54	64	42	85	119	76	122	193	120	185	300	172	244	412	235	316	542	309	400	690	394	555	855	482
	1	46	69	34	75	128	60	109	207	96	162	336	137	217	460	188	284	604	245	364	768	314	507	951	384
50	2	49	71	40	79	132	72	114	215	113	170	345	164	226	473	223	294	623	293	376	793	375	520	983	458
	3	52	72	45	83	136	82	119	221	123	178	353	186	235	486	252	304	640	331	387	816	423	535	1,013	518
	1	45	79	34	71	150	61	104	249	98	153	424	140	205	585	192	269	774	249	345	993	321	476	1,236	393
100	2	48	80	41	75	153	73	110	255	115	160	428	167	212	593	228	279	788	299	358	1,011	383	490	1,259	469
	3	51	81	46	79	157	85	114	260	129	168	433	190	222	603	256	289	801	339	368	1,027	431	506	1,280	527

COMMON VENT CAPACITY

VENT HEIGHT (*H*) (feet)	TYPE B DOUBLE-WALL COMMON VENT DIAMETER—(*D*) inches																				
	4			5			6			7			8			9			10		
	COMBINED APPLIANCE INPUT RATING IN THOUSANDS OF BTU/H																				
	FAN +FAN	FAN +NAT	NAT +NAT	FAN +FAN	FAN +NAT	NAT +NAT	FAN +FAN	FAN +NAT	NAT +NAT	FAN +FAN	FAN +NAT	NAT +NAT	FAN +FAN	FAN +NAT	NAT +NAT	FAN +FAN	FAN +NAT	NAT +NAT	FAN +FAN	FAN +NAT	NAT +NAT
6	NA	78	64	NA	113	99	200	158	144	304	244	196	398	310	257	541	429	332	665	515	407
8	NA	87	71	NA	126	111	218	173	159	331	269	218	436	342	285	592	473	373	730	569	460
10	NA	94	76	163	137	120	237	189	174	357	292	236	467	369	309	638	512	398	787	617	487
15	121	108	88	189	159	140	275	221	200	416	343	274	544	434	357	738	599	456	905	718	553
20	131	118	98	208	177	156	305	247	223	463	383	302	606	487	395	824	673	512	1,013	808	626
30	145	132	113	236	202	180	350	286	257	533	446	349	703	570	459	958	790	593	1,183	952	723
50	159	145	128	268	233	208	406	337	296	622	529	410	833	686	535	1,139	954	689	1,418	1,157	838
100	166	153	NA	297	263	NA	469	398	NA	726	633	464	999	846	606	1,378	1,185	780	1,741	1,459	948

For SI: 1 inch = 25.4 mm, 1 foot = 304.8 mm, 1 British thermal unit per hour = 0.2931 W.

TABLE 504.3(3)
MASONRY CHIMNEY

Number of Appliances	Two or more
Appliance Type	Category I
Appliance Vent Connection	Type B double-wall connector

VENT CONNECTOR CAPACITY

VENT HEIGHT (*H*) (feet)	CONNECTOR RISE (*R*) (feet)	TYPE B DOUBLE-WALL VENT CONNECTOR DIAMETER—(*D*) inches																							
		3			4			5			6			7			8			9			10		
		APPLIANCE INPUT RATING LIMITS IN THOUSANDS OF BTU/H																							
		FAN		NAT	FAN		NAT	FAN		NAT	FAN		NAT	FAN		NAT	FAN		NAT	FAN		NAT	FAN		NAT
		Min	Max	Max	Min	Max	Max	Min	Max	Max	Min	Max	Max	Min	Max	Max	Min	Max	Max	Min	Max	Max	Min	Max	Max
6	1	24	33	21	39	62	40	52	106	67	65	194	101	87	274	141	104	370	201	124	479	253	145	599	319
	2	26	43	28	41	79	52	53	133	85	67	230	124	89	324	173	107	436	232	127	562	300	148	694	378
	3	27	49	34	42	92	61	55	155	97	69	262	143	91	369	203	109	491	270	129	633	349	151	795	439
8	1	24	39	22	39	72	41	55	117	69	71	213	105	94	304	148	113	414	210	134	539	267	156	682	335
	2	26	47	29	40	87	53	57	140	86	73	246	127	97	350	179	116	473	240	137	615	311	160	776	394
	3	27	52	34	42	97	62	59	159	98	75	269	145	99	383	206	119	517	276	139	672	358	163	848	452
10	1	24	42	22	38	80	42	55	130	71	74	232	108	101	324	153	120	444	216	142	582	277	165	739	348
	2	26	50	29	40	93	54	57	153	87	76	261	129	103	366	184	123	498	247	145	652	321	168	825	407
	3	27	55	35	41	105	63	58	170	100	78	284	148	106	397	209	126	540	281	147	705	366	171	893	463
15	1	24	48	23	38	93	44	54	154	74	72	277	114	100	384	164	125	511	229	153	658	297	184	824	375
	2	25	55	31	39	105	55	56	174	89	74	299	134	103	419	192	128	558	260	156	718	339	187	900	432
	3	26	59	35	41	115	64	57	189	102	76	319	153	105	448	215	131	597	292	159	760	382	190	960	486
20	1	24	52	24	37	102	46	53	172	77	71	313	119	98	437	173	123	584	239	150	752	312	180	943	397
	2	25	58	31	39	114	56	55	190	91	73	335	138	101	467	199	126	625	270	153	805	354	184	1,011	452
	3	26	63	35	40	123	65	57	204	104	75	353	157	104	493	222	129	661	301	156	851	396	187	1,067	505
30	1	24	54	25	37	111	48	52	192	82	69	357	127	96	504	187	119	680	255	145	883	337	175	1,115	432
	2	25	60	32	38	122	58	54	208	95	72	376	145	99	531	209	122	715	287	149	928	378	179	1,171	484
	3	26	64	36	40	131	66	56	221	107	74	392	163	101	554	233	125	746	317	152	968	418	182	1,220	535
50	1	23	51	25	36	116	51	51	209	89	67	405	143	92	582	213	115	798	294	140	1,049	392	168	1,334	506
	2	24	59	32	37	127	61	53	225	102	70	421	161	95	604	235	118	827	326	143	1,085	433	172	1,379	558
	3	26	64	36	39	135	69	55	237	115	72	435	80	98	624	260	121	854	357	147	1,118	474	176	1,421	611
100	1	23	46	24	35	108	50	49	208	92	65	428	155	88	640	237	109	907	334	134	1,222	454	161	1,589	596
	2	24	53	31	37	120	60	51	224	105	67	444	174	92	660	260	113	933	368	138	1,253	497	165	1,626	651
	3	25	59	35	38	130	68	53	237	118	69	458	193	94	679	285	116	956	399	141	1,282	540	169	1,661	705

COMMON VENT CAPACITY

VENT HEIGHT (*H*) (feet)	MINIMUM INTERNAL AREA OF MASONRY CHIMNEY FLUE (square inches)																							
	12			19			28			38			50			63			78			113		
	COMBINED APPLIANCE INPUT RATING IN THOUSANDS OF BTU/H																							
	FAN +FAN	FAN +NAT	NAT +NAT	FAN +FAN	FAN +NAT	NAT +NAT	FAN +FAN	FAN +NAT	NAT +NAT	FAN +FAN	FAN +NAT	NAT +NAT	FAN +FAN	FAN +NAT	NAT +NAT	FAN +FAN	FAN +NAT	NAT +NAT	FAN +FAN	FAN +NAT	NAT +NAT	FAN +FAN	FAN +NAT	NAT +NAT
6	NA	74	25	NA	119	46	NA	178	71	NA	257	103	NA	351	143	NA	458	188	NA	582	246	1,041	853	NA
8	NA	80	28	NA	130	53	NA	193	82	NA	279	119	NA	384	163	NA	501	218	724	636	278	1,144	937	408
10	NA	84	31	NA	138	56	NA	207	90	NA	299	131	NA	409	177	606	538	236	776	686	302	1,226	1,010	454
15	NA	NA	36	NA	152	67	NA	233	106	NA	334	152	523	467	212	682	611	283	874	781	365	1,374	1,156	546
20	NA	NA	41	NA	NA	75	NA	250	122	NA	368	172	565	508	243	742	668	325	955	858	419	1,513	1,286	648
30	NA	NA	NA	NA	NA	NA	NA	270	137	NA	404	198	615	564	278	816	747	381	1,062	969	496	1,702	1,473	749
50	NA	NA	NA	NA	NA	NA	NA	NA	NA	NA	NA	NA	NA	620	328	879	831	461	1,165	1,089	606	1,905	1,692	922
100	NA	NA	NA	NA	NA	NA	NA	NA	NA	NA	NA	NA	NA	NA	348	NA	NA	499	NA	NA	669	2,053	1,921	1,058

For SI: 1 inch = 25.4 mm, 1 square inch = 645.16 mm^2, 1 foot = 304.8 mm, 1 British thermal unit per hour = 0.2931 W.

Number of Appliances	Two or more
Appliance Type	Category I
Appliance Vent Connection	Single-wall metal connector

TABLE 504.3(4)
MASONRY CHIMNEY

VENT CONNECTOR CAPACITY

VENT HEIGHT (*H*) (feet)	CONNECTOR RISE (*R*) (feet)	SINGLE-WALL METAL VENT CONNECTOR DIAMETER—(*D*) inches																							
		3			4			5			6			7			8			9			10		
		APPLIANCE INPUT RATING LIMITS IN THOUSANDS OF BTU/H																							
		FAN		NAT	FAN		NAT	FAN		NAT	FAN		NAT	FAN		NAT	FAN		NAT	FAN		NAT	FAN		NAT
		Min	Max	Max	Min	Max	Max	Min	Max	Max	Min	Max	Max	Min	Max	Max	Min	Max	Max	Min	Max	Max	Min	Max	Max
6	1	NA	NA	21	NA	NA	39	NA	NA	66	179	191	100	231	271	140	292	366	200	362	474	252	499	594	316
	2	NA	NA	28	NA	NA	52	NA	NA	84	186	227	123	239	321	172	301	432	231	373	557	299	509	696	376
	3	NA	NA	34	NA	NA	61	134	153	97	193	258	142	247	365	202	309	491	269	381	634	348	519	793	437
8	1	NA	NA	21	NA	NA	40	NA	NA	68	195	208	103	250	298	146	313	407	207	387	530	263	529	672	331
	2	NA	NA	28	NA	NA	52	137	139	85	202	240	125	258	343	177	323	465	238	397	607	309	540	766	391
	3	NA	NA	34	NA	NA	62	143	156	98	210	264	145	266	376	205	332	509	274	407	663	356	551	838	450
10	1	NA	NA	22	NA	NA	41	130	151	70	202	225	106	267	316	151	333	434	213	410	571	273	558	727	343
	2	NA	NA	29	NA	NA	53	136	150	86	210	255	128	276	358	181	343	489	244	420	640	317	569	813	403
	3	NA	NA	34	97	102	62	143	166	99	217	277	147	284	389	207	352	530	279	430	694	363	580	880	459
15	1	NA	NA	23	NA	NA	43	129	151	73	199	271	112	268	376	161	349	502	225	445	646	291	623	808	366
	2	NA	NA	30	92	103	54	135	170	88	207	295	132	277	411	189	359	548	256	456	706	334	634	884	424
	3	NA	NA	34	96	112	63	141	185	101	215	315	151	286	439	213	368	586	289	466	755	378	646	945	479
20	1	NA	NA	23	87	99	45	128	167	76	197	303	117	265	425	169	345	569	235	439	734	306	614	921	347
	2	NA	NA	30	91	111	55	134	185	90	205	325	136	274	455	195	355	610	266	450	787	348	627	986	443
	3	NA	NA	35	96	119	64	140	199	103	213	343	154	282	481	219	365	644	298	461	831	391	639	1,042	496
30	1	NA	NA	24	86	108	47	126	187	80	193	347	124	259	492	183	338	665	250	430	864	330	600	1,089	421
	2	NA	NA	31	91	119	57	132	203	93	201	366	142	269	518	205	348	699	282	442	908	372	613	1,145	473
	3	NA	NA	35	95	127	65	138	216	105	209	381	160	277	540	229	358	729	312	452	946	412	626	1,193	524
50	1	NA	NA	24	85	113	50	124	204	87	188	392	139	252	567	208	328	778	287	417	1,022	383	582	1,302	492
	2	NA	NA	31	89	123	60	130	218	100	196	408	158	262	588	230	339	806	320	429	1,058	425	596	1,346	545
	3	NA	NA	35	94	131	68	136	231	112	205	422	176	271	607	255	349	831	351	440	1,090	466	610	1,386	597
100	1	NA	NA	23	84	104	49	122	200	89	182	410	151	243	617	232	315	875	328	402	1,181	444	560	1,537	580
	2	NA	NA	30	88	115	59	127	215	102	190	425	169	253	636	254	326	899	361	415	1,210	488	575	1,570	634
	3	NA	NA	34	93	124	67	133	228	115	199	438	188	262	654	279	337	921	392	427	1,238	529	589	1,604	687

COMMON VENT CAPACITY

VENT HEIGHT (*H*) (feet)	MINIMUM INTERNAL AREA OF MASONRY CHIMNEY FLUE (square inches)																							
	12			19			28			38			50			63			78			113		
	COMBINED APPLIANCE INPUT RATING IN THOUSANDS OF BTU/H																							
	FAN +FAN	FAN +NAT	NAT +NAT	FAN +FAN	FAN +NAT	NAT +NAT	FAN +FAN	FAN +NAT	NAT +NAT	FAN +FAN	FAN +NAT	NAT +NAT	FAN +FAN	FAN +NAT	NAT +NAT	FAN +FAN	FAN +NAT	NAT +NAT	FAN +FAN	FAN +NAT	NAT +NAT	FAN +FAN	FAN +NAT	NAT +NAT
6	NA	NA	25	NA	118	45	NA	176	71	NA	255	102	NA	348	142	NA	455	187	NA	579	245	NA	846	NA
8	NA	NA	28	NA	128	52	NA	190	81	NA	276	118	NA	380	162	NA	497	217	NA	633	277	1,136	928	405
10	NA	NA	31	NA	136	56	NA	205	89	NA	295	129	NA	405	175	NA	532	234	171	680	300	1,216	1,000	450
15	NA	NA	36	NA	NA	66	NA	230	105	NA	335	150	NA	400	210	677	602	280	866	772	360	1,359	1,139	540
20	NA	NA	NA	NA	NA	74	NA	247	120	NA	362	170	NA	503	240	765	661	321	947	849	415	1,495	1,264	640
30	NA	NA	NA	NA	NA	NA	NA	NA	135	NA	398	195	NA	558	275	808	739	377	1,052	957	490	1,682	1,447	740
50	NA	NA	NA	NA	NA	NA	NA	NA	NA	NA	NA	NA	NA	612	325	NA	821	456	1,152	1,076	600	1,879	1,672	910
100	NA	NA	NA	NA	NA	NA	NA	NA	NA	NA	NA	NA	NA	NA	NA	NA	NA	494	NA	NA	663	2,006	1,885	1,046

For SI: 1 inch = 25.4 mm, 1 square inch = 645.16 mm^2, 1 foot = 304.8 mm, 1 British thermal unit per hour = 0.2931 W.

Number of Appliances	Two or more
Appliance Type	Draft hood-equipped
Appliance Vent Connection	Direct to pipe or vent

TABLE 504.3(5)
SINGLE-WALL METAL PIPE OR TYPE ASBESTOS CEMENT VENT

VENT CONNECTOR CAPACITY

TOTAL VENT HEIGHT (*H*) (feet)	CONNECTOR RISE (*R*) (feet)	VENT CONNECTOR DIAMETER—(*D*) inches					
		3	4	5	6	7	8
		MAXIMUM APPLIANCE INPUT RATING IN THOUSANDS OF BTU/H					
6-8	1	21	40	68	102	146	205
	2	28	53	86	124	178	235
	3	34	61	98	147	204	275
15	1	23	44	77	117	179	240
	2	30	56	92	134	194	265
	3	35	64	102	155	216	298
30 and up	1	25	49	84	129	190	270
	2	31	58	97	145	211	295
	3	36	68	107	164	232	321

COMMON VENT CAPACITY

TOTAL VENT HEIGHT (*H*) (feet)	COMMON VENT DIAMETER—(*D*) inches						
	4	5	6	7	8	10	12
	COMBINED APPLIANCE INPUT RATING IN THOUSANDS OF BTU/H						
6	48	78	111	155	205	320	NA
8	55	89	128	175	234	365	505
10	59	95	136	190	250	395	560
15	71	115	168	228	305	480	690
20	80	129	186	260	340	550	790
30	NA	147	215	300	400	650	940
50	NA	NA	NA	360	490	810	1,190

For SI: 1 inch = 25.4 mm, 1 foot = 304.8 mm, 1 British thermal unit per hour = 0.2931 W.

TABLE 504.3(6a)
EXTERIOR MASONRY CHIMNEY

Number of Appliances	Two or more
Appliance Type	NAT + NAT
Appliance Vent Connection	Type B double-wall connector

Combined Appliance Maximum Input Rating in Thousands of Btu per Hour

VENT HEIGHT (feet)	INTERNAL AREA OF CHIMNEY (square inches)							
	12	19	28	38	50	63	78	113
6	25	46	71	103	143	188	246	NA
8	28	53	82	119	163	218	278	408
10	31	56	90	131	177	236	302	454
15	NA	67	106	152	212	283	365	546
20	NA	NA	NA	NA	NA	325	419	648
30	NA	NA	NA	NA	NA	NA	496	749
50	NA	NA	NA	NA	NA	NA	NA	922
100	NA	NA	NA	NA	NA	NA	NA	NA

TABLE 504.3(6b)
EXTERIOR MASONRY CHIMNEY

Number of Appliances	Two or more
Appliance Type	NAT + NAT
Appliance Vent Connection	Type B double-wall connector

Minimum Allowable Input Rating of Space-heating Appliance in Thousands of Btu per Hour

VENT HEIGHT (feet)	INTERNAL AREA OF CHIMNEY (square inches)							
	12	19	28	38	50	63	78	113
37°F or Greater	Local 99% Winter Design Temperature: 37°F or Greater							
6	0	0	0	0	0	0	0	NA
8	0	0	0	0	0	0	0	0
10	0	0	0	0	0	0	0	0
15	NA	0	0	0	0	0	0	0
20	NA	NA	NA	NA	NA	184	0	0
30	NA	NA	NA	NA	NA	393	334	0
50	NA	NA	NA	NA	NA	NA	NA	579
100	NA	NA	NA	NA	NA	NA	NA	NA
27 to 36°F	Local 99% Winter Design Temperature: 27 to 36°F							
6	0	0	68	NA	NA	180	212	NA
8	0	0	82	NA	NA	187	214	263
10	0	51	NA	NA	NA	201	225	265
15	NA	NA	NA	NA	NA	253	274	305
20	NA	NA	NA	NA	NA	307	330	362
30	NA	NA	NA	NA	NA	NA	445	485
50	NA	NA	NA	NA	NA	NA	NA	763
100	NA	NA	NA	NA	NA	NA	NA	NA

TABLE 504.3(6b)
EXTERIOR MASONRY CHIMNEY—continued

Minimum Allowable Input Rating of Space-heating Appliance in Thousands of Btu per Hour

VENT HEIGHT (feet)	INTERNAL AREA OF CHIMNEY (square inches)							
	12	19	28	38	50	63	78	113
17 to 26°F	Local 99% Winter Design Temperature: 17 to 26°F							
6	NA	NA	NA	NA	NA	NA	NA	NA
8	NA	NA	NA	NA	NA	NA	264	352
10	NA	NA	NA	NA	NA	NA	278	358
15	NA	NA	NA	NA	NA	NA	331	398
20	NA	NA	NA	NA	NA	NA	387	457
30	NA	NA	NA	NA	NA	NA	NA	581
50	NA	NA	NA	NA	NA	NA	NA	862
100	NA	NA	NA	NA	NA	NA	NA	NA
5 to 16°F	Local 99% Winter Design Temperature: 5 to 16°F							
6	NA	NA	NA	NA	NA	NA	NA	NA
8	NA	NA	NA	NA	NA	NA	NA	NA
10	NA	NA	NA	NA	NA	NA	NA	430
15	NA	NA	NA	NA	NA	NA	NA	485
20	NA	NA	NA	NA	NA	NA	NA	547
30	NA	NA	NA	NA	NA	NA	NA	682
50	NA	NA	NA	NA	NA	NA	NA	NA
100	NA	NA	NA	NA	NA	NA	NA	NA
4°F or Lower	Local 99% Winter Design Temperature: 4°F or Lower							
Not recommended for any vent configurations								

For SI: °C = (°F - 32)/1.8, 1 inch = 25.4 mm, 1 square inch = 645.16 mm^2, 1 foot = 304.8 mm, 1 British thermal unit per hour = 0.2931 W.

Note: See Figure B-19 in Appendix B for a map showing local 99 percent winter design temperatures in the United States.

TABLE 504.3(7a)
EXTERIOR MASONRY CHIMNEY

Number of Appliances	Two or more
Appliance Type	FAN + NAT
Appliance Vent Connection	Type B double-wall connector

Combined Appliance Maximum Input Rating in Thousands of Btu per Hour

VENT HEIGHT (feet)	INTERNAL AREA OF CHIMNEY (square inches)							
	12	19	28	38	50	63	78	113
6	74	119	178	257	351	458	582	853
8	80	130	193	279	384	501	636	937
10	84	138	207	299	409	538	686	1,010
15	NA	152	233	334	467	611	781	1,156
20	NA	NA	250	368	508	668	858	1,286
30	NA	NA	NA	404	564	747	969	1,473
50	NA	NA	NA	NA	NA	831	1,089	1,692
100	NA	NA	NA	NA	NA	NA	NA	1,921

TABLE 504.3(7b)
EXTERIOR MASONRY CHIMNEY

Number of Appliances	Two or more
Appliance Type	FAN + NAT
Appliance Vent Connection	Type B double-wall connector

Minimum Allowable Input Rating of Space-heating Appliance in Thousands of Btu per Hour

VENT HEIGHT (feet)	INTERNAL AREA OF CHIMNEY (square inches)							
	12	19	28	38	50	63	78	113
37°F or Greater	Local 99% Winter Design Temperature: 37°F or Greater							
6	0	0	0	0	0	0	0	0
8	0	0	0	0	0	0	0	0
10	0	0	0	0	0	0	0	0
15	NA	0	0	0	0	0	0	0
20	NA	NA	123	190	249	184	0	0
30	NA	NA	NA	334	398	393	334	0
50	NA	NA	NA	NA	NA	714	707	579
100	NA	NA	NA	NA	NA	NA	NA	1,600
27 to 36°F	Local 99% Winter Design Temperature: 27 to 36°F							
6	0	0	68	116	156	180	212	266
8	0	0	82	127	167	187	214	263
10	0	51	97	141	183	210	225	265
15	NA	111	142	183	233	253	274	305
20	NA	NA	187	230	284	307	330	362
30	NA	NA	NA	330	319	419	445	485
50	NA	NA	NA	NA	NA	672	705	763
100	NA	NA	NA	NA	NA	NA	NA	1,554

TABLE 504.3(7b)
EXTERIOR MASONRY CHIMNEY—continued

Minimum Allowable Input Rating of Space-heating Appliance in Thousands of Btu per Hour

VENT HEIGHT (feet)	INTERNAL AREA OF CHIMNEY (square inches)							
	12	19	28	38	50	63	78	113
17 to 26°F	Local 99% Winter Design Temperature: 17 to 26°F							
6	0	55	99	141	182	215	259	349
8	52	74	111	154	197	226	264	352
10	NA	90	125	169	214	245	278	358
15	NA	NA	167	212	263	296	331	398
20	NA	NA	212	258	316	352	387	457
30	NA	NA	NA	362	429	470	507	581
50	NA	NA	NA	NA	NA	723	766	862
100	NA	NA	NA	NA	NA	NA	NA	1,669
5 to 16°F	Local 99% Winter Design Temperature: 5 to 16°F							
6	NA	78	121	166	214	252	301	416
8	NA	94	135	182	230	269	312	423
10	NA	111	149	198	250	289	331	430
15	NA	NA	193	247	305	346	393	485
20	NA	NA	NA	293	360	408	450	547
30	NA	NA	NA	377	450	531	580	682
50	NA	NA	NA	NA	NA	797	853	972
100	NA	NA	NA	NA	NA	NA	NA	1,833
-10 to 4°F	Local 99% Winter Design Temperature: -10 to 4°F							
6	NA	NA	145	196	249	296	349	484
8	NA	NA	159	213	269	320	371	494
10	NA	NA	175	231	292	339	397	513
15	NA	NA	NA	283	351	404	457	586
20	NA	NA	NA	333	408	468	528	650
30	NA	NA	NA	NA	NA	603	667	805
50	NA	NA	NA	NA	NA	NA	955	1,003
100	NA	NA	NA	NA	NA	NA	NA	NA
-11°F or Lower	Local 99% Winter Design Temperature: -11°F or Lower							
	Not recommended for any vent configurations							

For SI: °C = (°F - 32)/1.8, 1 inch = 25.4 mm, 1 square inch = 645.16 mm², 1 foot = 304.8 mm, 1 British thermal unit per hour = 0.2931 W.

Note: See Figure B-19 in Appendix B for a map showing local 99 percent winter design temperatures in the United States.

CHAPTER 6
SPECIFIC APPLIANCES

SECTION 601 (IFGC) GENERAL

601.1 Scope. This chapter shall govern the approval, design, installation, construction, maintenance, *alteration* and repair of the appliances and *equipment* specifically identified herein.

SECTION 602 (IFGC) DECORATIVE APPLIANCES FOR INSTALLATION IN FIREPLACES

602.1 General. Decorative appliances for installation in *approved* solid fuel-burning fireplaces shall be tested in accordance with ANSI Z21.60 and shall be installed in accordance with the manufacturer's installation instructions. Manually lighted natural gas decorative appliances shall be tested in accordance with ANSI Z21.84.

602.2 Flame safeguard device. Decorative appliances for installation in *approved* solid fuel-burning fireplaces, with the exception of those tested in accordance with ANSI Z21.84, shall utilize a direct ignition device, an ignitor or a pilot flame to ignite the fuel at the main burner, and shall be equipped with a flame safeguard device. The flame safeguard device shall automatically shut off the fuel supply to a main burner or group of burners when the means of ignition of such burners becomes inoperative.

602.3 Prohibited installations. Decorative appliances for installation in fireplaces shall not be installed where prohibited by Section 303.3.

SECTION 603 (IFGC) LOG LIGHTERS

603.1 General. Log lighters shall be tested in accordance with CSA 8 and installed in accordance with the manufacturer's installation instructions.

SECTION 604 (IFGC) VENTED GAS FIREPLACES (DECORATIVE APPLIANCES)

604.1 General. Vented gas fireplaces shall be tested in accordance with ANSI Z21.50, shall be installed in accordance with the manufacturer's installation instructions and shall be designed and equipped as specified in Section 602.2.

604.2 Access. Panels, grilles and *access* doors that are required to be removed for normal servicing operations shall not be attached to the building.

SECTION 605 (IFGC) VENTED GAS FIREPLACE HEATERS

605.1 General. Vented gas fireplace heaters shall be installed in accordance with the manufacturer's installation instructions, shall be tested in accordance with ANSI Z21.88 and shall be designed and equipped as specified in Section 602.2.

SECTION 606 (IFGC) INCINERATORS AND CREMATORIES

Deleted

SECTION 607 (IFGC) COMMERCIAL-INDUSTRIAL INCINERATORS

Deleted

SECTION 608 (IFGC) VENTED WALL FURNACES

608.1 General. Vented wall furnaces shall be tested in accordance with ANSI Z21.86/CSA 2.32 and shall be installed in accordance with the manufacturer's installation instructions.

608.2 Venting. Vented wall furnaces shall be vented in accordance with Section 503.

608.3 Location. Vented wall furnaces shall be located so as not to cause a fire hazard to walls, floors, combustible furnishings or doors. Vented wall furnaces installed between bathrooms and adjoining rooms shall not circulate air from bathrooms to other parts of the building.

608.4 Door swing. Vented wall furnaces shall be located so that a door cannot swing within 12 inches (305 mm) of an air inlet or air outlet of such furnace measured at right angles to the opening. Doorstops or door closers shall not be installed to obtain this *clearance*.

608.5 Ducts prohibited. Ducts shall not be attached to wall furnaces. Casing extension boots shall not be installed unless *listed* as part of the *appliance*.

608.6 Access. Vented wall furnaces shall be provided with *access* for cleaning of heating surfaces, removal of burners, replacement of sections, motors, controls, filters and other working parts, and for adjustments and lubrication of parts requiring such attention. Panels, grilles and *access* doors that are required to be removed for normal servicing operations shall not be attached to the building construction.

SECTION 609 (IFGC) FLOOR FURNACES

609.1 General. Floor furnaces shall be tested in accordance with ANSI Z21.86/CSA 2.32 and shall be installed in accordance with the manufacturer's installation instructions.

609.2 Placement. The following provisions apply to floor furnaces:

1. Floors. Floor furnaces shall not be installed in the floor of any doorway, stairway landing, aisle or passageway of any enclosure, public or private, or in an exitway from any such room or space.
2. Walls and corners. The register of a floor furnace with a horizontal warm-air outlet shall not be placed closer than 6 inches (152 mm) to the nearest wall. A distance of at least 18 inches (457 mm) from two adjoining sides of the floor furnace register to walls shall be provided to eliminate the necessity of occupants walking over the warm-air discharge. The remaining sides shall be permitted to be placed not closer than 6 inches (152 mm) to a wall. Wall-register models shall not be placed closer than 6 inches (152 mm) to a corner.
3. Draperies. The furnace shall be placed so that a door, drapery or similar object cannot be nearer than 12 inches (305 mm) to any portion of the register of the furnace.
4. Floor construction. Floor furnaces shall not be installed in concrete floor construction built on grade.
5. Thermostat. The controlling thermostat for a floor furnace shall be located within the same room or space as the floor furnace or shall be located in an adjacent room or space that is permanently open to the room or space containing the floor furnace.

609.3 Bracing. The floor around the furnace shall be braced and headed with a support framework designed in accordance with the *International Building Code*.

609.4 Clearance. The lowest portion of the floor furnace shall have not less than a 6-inch (152 mm) *clearance* from the grade level; except where the lower 6-inch (152 mm) portion of the floor furnace is sealed by the manufacturer to prevent entrance of water, the minimum *clearance* shall be not less than 2 inches (51 mm). Where such clearances cannot be provided, the ground below and to the sides shall be excavated to form a pit under the furnace so that the required *clearance* is provided beneath the lowest portion of the furnace. A 12-inch (305 mm) minimum *clearance* shall be provided on all sides except the control side, which shall have an 18-inch (457 mm) minimum *clearance*.

609.5 First floor installation. Where the basement story level below the floor in which a floor furnace is installed is utilized as habitable space, such floor furnaces shall be enclosed as specified in Section 609.6 and shall project into a nonhabitable space.

609.6 Upper floor installations. Floor furnaces installed in upper stories of buildings shall project below into nonhabitable space and shall be separated from the nonhabitable space by an enclosure constructed of noncombustible materials. The floor furnace shall be provided with *access*, *clearance* to all sides and bottom of not less than 6 inches (152 mm) and *combustion air* in accordance with Section 304.

SECTION 610 (IFGC) DUCT FURNACES

610.1 General. Duct furnaces shall be tested in accordance with ANSI Z83.8 or UL 795 and shall be installed in accordance with the manufacturer's installation instructions.

610.2 Access panels. Ducts connected to duct furnaces shall have removable *access* panels on both the upstream and downstream sides of the furnace.

610.3 Location of draft hood and controls. The controls, *combustion air* inlets and draft hoods for duct furnaces shall be located outside of the ducts. The draft hood shall be located in the same enclosure from which *combustion air* is taken.

610. 4 Circulating air. Where a duct furnace is installed so that supply ducts convey air to areas outside the space containing the furnace, the return air shall also be conveyed by a duct(s) sealed to the furnace casing and terminating outside the space containing the furnace.

The duct furnace shall be installed on the positive pressure side of the circulating air blower.

SECTION 611 (IFGC) NONRECIRCULATING DIRECT-FIRED INDUSTRIAL AIR HEATERS

Deleted

SECTION 612 (IFGC) RECIRCULATING DIRECT-FIRED INDUSTRIAL AIR HEATERS

Deleted

SECTION 613 (IFGC) CLOTHES DRYERS

613.1 General. Clothes dryers shall be tested in accordance with ANSI Z21.5.1 or ANSI Z21.5.2 and shall be installed in accordance with the manufacturer's installation instructions.

SECTION 614 (IFGC) CLOTHES DRYER EXHAUST

[M] 614.1 Installation. Clothes dryers shall be exhausted in accordance with the manufacturer's instructions. Dryer exhaust systems shall be independent of all other systems, shall convey the moisture and any products of combustion to the outside of the building.

[M] 614.2 Duct penetrations. Ducts that exhaust clothes dryers shall not penetrate or be located within any fireblocking, draftstopping or any wall, floor/ceiling or other assembly required by the *International Building Code* to be fire-resistance rated, unless such duct is constructed of galvanized steel or aluminum of the thickness specified in Table 603.4 of the *International Mechanical Code* and the fire-resistance rating is maintained in accordance with the *International Building Code*. Fire dampers shall not be installed in clothes dryer exhaust duct systems.

[M] 614.3 Cleaning access. Each vertical duct riser for dryers *listed* to ANSI Z21.5.2 shall be provided with a cleanout or other means for cleaning the interior of the duct.

[M] 614.4 Exhaust installation. Exhaust ducts for clothes dryers shall terminate on the outside of the building and shall be equipped with a backdraft damper. Screens shall not be installed at the duct termination. Ducts shall not be connected or installed with sheet metal screws or other fasteners that will obstruct the flow. Clothes dryer exhaust ducts shall not be connected to a vent connector, vent or chimney. Clothes dryer exhaust ducts shall not extend into or through ducts or plenums.

[M] 614.5 Makeup air. Installations exhausting more than 200 cfm (0.09 m^3/s) shall be provided with makeup air. Where a closet is designed for the installation of a clothes dryer, an opening having an area of not less than 100 square inches (645 mm^2) for makeup air shall be provided in the closet enclosure, or makeup air shall be provided by other *approved* means.

[M] 614.6 Domestic clothes dryer exhaust ducts. Exhaust ducts for domestic clothes dryers shall conform to the requirements of Sections 614.6.1 through 614.6.7.

[M] 614.6.1 Material and size. Exhaust ducts shall have a smooth interior finish and shall be constructed of metal a minimum 0.016-inch (0.4 mm) thick. With the exception of the transition duct, flexible ducts are prohibited. The exhaust duct size shall be 4 inches (102 mm) nominal in diameter.

[M] 614.6.2 Duct installation. Exhaust ducts shall be supported at 4-foot (1219 mm) intervals and secured in place and shall terminate not less than 12 inches (305 mm) above finished grade. The insert end of the duct shall extend into the adjoining duct or fitting in the direction of airflow. Ducts shall not be joined with screws or similar fasteners that protrude into the inside of the duct.

Exception: Where the duct termination is less than 12 inches (305 mm) above finished grade an areaway shall be provided with a cross-sectional area not less than 200 square inches (1290 cm^2). The bottom of the duct termination shall be no less than 12 inches (305 mm) above the areaway bottom.

614.6.3 Protection required. Protective shield plates shall be placed where nails or screws from finish or other work are likely to penetrate the clothes dryer exhaust duct. Shield plates shall be placed on the finished face of all framing members where there is less than $1^1/_4$ inches (32 mm) between the duct and the finished face of the framing member. Protective shield plates shall be constructed of steel, shall have a minimum thickness of 0.062 inch (1.6 mm) and shall extend a minimum of 2 inches (51 mm) above sole plates and below top plates.

[M] 614.6.4 Transition ducts. Transition ducts used to connect the dryer to the exhaust duct system shall be a single length that is *listed* and *labeled* in accordance with UL 2158A. Transition ducts shall be a maximum of 8 feet (2438 mm) in length, shall not be concealed within construction, and must remain entirely within the room in which the appliance is installed.

[M] 614.6.5 Duct length. The maximum allowable exhaust duct length shall be determined by one of the methods specified in Section 614.6.5.1 or 614.6.5.2.

[M] 614.6.5.1 Specified length. The maximum length of the exhaust duct shall be 35 feet (10 668 mm) from the connection to the transition duct from the dryer to the outlet terminal. Where fittings are utilized, the maximum length of the exhaust duct shall be reduced in accordance with Table 614.6.5.1.

[M] 614.6.5.2 Manufacturer's instructions. The maximum length of the exhaust duct shall be determined by the dryer manufacturer's installation instructions. The code official shall be provided with a copy of the installation instructions for the make and model of the dryer. Where the exhaust duct is to be concealed, the installation instructions shall be provided to the code official prior to the concealment inspection. In the absence of fitting equivalent length calculations from the clothes dryer manufacturer, Table 614.6.5.1 shall be utilized.

[M] 614.6.6 Length identification. The equivalent length of the exhaust duct shall be identified on a permanent label or tag. The label or tag shall be located within 6 feet (1829 mm) of the exhaust duct connection.

[M] 614.6.7 Exhaust duct required. Where space for a clothes dryer is provided, an exhaust duct system shall be installed.

Where the clothes dryer is not installed at the time of occupancy, the exhaust duct shall be capped at the location of the future dryer.

Exception: Where a *listed* condensing clothes dryer is installed prior to occupancy of the structure.

[M] 614.7 Commercial clothes dryers. Deleted.

[M] 614.8 Common exhaust systems for clothes dryers located in multistory structures. Deleted.

SECTION 615 (IFGC) SAUNA HEATERS

615.1 General. Sauna heaters shall be installed in accordance with the manufacturer's installation instructions.

615.2 Location and protection. Sauna heaters shall be located so as to minimize the possibility of accidental contact by a person in the room.

615.2.1 Guards. Sauna heaters shall be protected from accidental contact by an *approved* guard or barrier of material having a low coefficient of thermal conductivity. The guard shall not substantially affect the transfer of heat from the heater to the room.

615.3 Access. Panels, grilles and *access* doors that are required to be removed for normal servicing operations shall not be attached to the building.

615.4 Combustion and dilution air intakes. Sauna heaters of other than the direct-vent type shall be installed with the draft hood and *combustion air* intake located outside the sauna room. Where the *combustion air* inlet and the draft hood are in a dressing room adjacent to the sauna room, there shall be provisions to prevent physically blocking the *combustion air* inlet and the draft hood inlet, and to prevent physical contact with the draft hood and vent assembly, or warning notices shall be posted to avoid such contact. Any warning notice shall be easily readable, shall contrast with its background and the wording shall be in letters not less than $^1/_4$ inch (6.4 mm) high.

615.5 Combustion and ventilation air. *Combustion air* shall not be taken from inside the sauna room. Combustion and ventilation air for a sauna heater not of the direct-vent type shall be provided to the area in which the *combustion air* inlet and draft hood are located in accordance with Section 304.

615.6 Heat and time controls. Sauna heaters shall be equipped with a thermostat which will limit room temperature to 194°F (90°C). If the thermostat is not an integral part of the sauna heater, the heat-sensing element shall be located within 6 inches (152 mm) of the ceiling. If the heat-sensing element is a capillary tube and bulb, the assembly shall be attached to the wall or other support, and shall be protected against physical damage.

615.6.1 Timers. A timer, if provided to control main burner operation, shall have a maximum operating time of 1 hour. The control for the timer shall be located outside the sauna room.

615.7 Sauna room. A ventilation opening into the sauna room shall be provided. The opening shall be not less than 4 inches by 8 inches (102 mm by 203 mm) located near the top of the door into the sauna room.

615.7.1 Warning notice. Deleted.

SECTION 616 (IFGC) ENGINE AND GAS TURBINE-POWERED EQUIPMENT

616.1 Powered equipment. Permanently installed *equipment* powered by internal combustion engines and turbines shall be installed in accordance with the manufacturer's installation instructions and NFPA 37. Stationary engine generator assemblies shall meet the requirements of UL 2200.

616.2 Gas supply connection. *Equipment* powered by internal combustion engines and turbines shall not be rigidly connected to the gas supply *piping*.

SECTION 617 (IFGC) POOL AND SPA HEATERS

617.1 General. Pool and spa heaters shall be tested in accordance with ANSI Z21.56 and shall be installed in accordance with the manufacturer's installation instructions.

SECTION 618 (IFGC) FORCED-AIR WARM-AIR FURNACES

618.1 General. Forced-air warm-air furnaces shall be tested in accordance with ANSI Z21.47 or UL 795 and shall be installed in accordance with the manufacturer's installation instructions.

618.2 Forced-air furnaces. The minimum unobstructed total area of the outside and return air ducts or openings to a forced-air warm-air furnace shall be not less than 2 square inches (1290 mm^2) for each 1,000 Btu/h (4402 mm^2/W) output rating capacity of the furnace and not less than that specified in the furnace manufacturer's installation instructions. The minimum unobstructed total area of supply ducts from a forced-air warm-air furnace shall be not less than 2 square inches (1290 mm^2) for each 1,000 Btu/h (4402 mm^2/W) output rating capacity of the furnace and not less than that specified in the furnace manufacturer's installation instructions. With the addition of a cooling coil, the sizing criteria shall be based on 6 square inches (3870 mm^2) for each 1,000 Btu/h (13 206 mm^2/W) output.

Exception: The total area of the supply air ducts and outside and return air ducts shall not be required to be larger than the minimum size required by the furnace manufacturer's installation instructions.

618.3 Dampers. Volume dampers shall not be placed in the air inlet to a furnace in a manner that will reduce the required air to the furnace.

618.4 Circulating air ducts for forced-air warm-air furnaces. Circulating air for fuel-burning, forced-air-type, warm-air fur-

**[M] TABLE 614.6.5.1
DRYER EXHAUST DUCT FITTING EQUIVALENT LENGTH**

DRYER EXHAUST DUCT FITTING TYPE	EQUIVALENT LENGTH
4 inch radius mitered 45-degree elbow	2 feet, 6 inches
4 inch radius mitered 90-degree elbow	5 feet
6 inch radius smooth 45-degree elbow	1 foot
6 inch radius smooth 90-degree elbow	1 foot, 9 inches
8 inch radius smooth 45-degree elbow	1 foot
8 inch radius smooth 90-degree elbow	1 foot, 7 inches
10 inch radius smooth 45-degree elbow	9 inches
10 inch radius smooth 90-degree elbow	1 foot, 6 inches

For SI: 1 inch = 25.4 mm, 1 foot = 304.8 mm, 1 degree = 0.01745 rad.

naces shall be conducted into the blower housing from outside the furnace enclosure by continuous air-tight ducts.

618.5 Prohibited sources. Outside or return air for a forced-air heating system shall not be taken from the following locations:

1. Closer than 10 feet (3048 mm) from an *appliance* vent outlet, a vent opening from a plumbing drainage system or the discharge outlet of an exhaust fan, unless the outlet is 3 feet (914 mm) above the outside air inlet.
2. Where there is the presence of objectionable odors, fumes or flammable vapors; or where located less than 10 feet (3048 mm) above the surface of any abutting public way or driveway; or where located at grade level by a sidewalk, street, alley or driveway.
3. Deleted.
4. A room or space, the volume of which is less than 25 percent of the entire volume served by such system. Where connected by a permanent opening having an area sized in accordance with Section 618.2, adjoining rooms or spaces shall be considered as a single room or space for the purpose of determining the volume of such rooms or spaces.

   Exception: The minimum volume requirement shall not apply where the amount of return air taken from a room or space is less than or equal to the amount of supply air delivered to such room or space.

5. A room or space containing a fuel-burning appliance or fireplace where such a room or space serves as a source of return air.

   Exception: This shall not apply where:

   1. The *appliance* is a direct-vent *appliance* or an *appliance* not requiring a vent in accordance with Section 501.8.
   2. The room or space complies with the following requirements:

      2.1. The return air shall be taken from a room or space having a volume exceeding 1 cubic foot for each 10 Btu/h (9.6 L/W) of combined input rating of all fuel-burning appliances therein.

      2.2. The volume of supply air discharged back into the same space shall be approximately equal to the volume of return air taken from the space.

      2.3. Return-air inlets shall not be located within 10 feet (3048 mm) of any *appliance* firebox or draft hood in the same room or space.

   3. Rooms or spaces containing solid fuel-burning appliances, provided that return-air inlets are located not less than 10 feet (3048 mm) from the firebox of such appliances.

6. A closet, bathroom, toilet room, kitchen, garage, mechanical room, boiler room, furnace room or attic.

   Exception: Where return air intakes are located not less than 10 feet (3048 mm) from cooking appliances and serve only the kitchen area, taking return air from a kitchen area shall not be prohibited.

7. A nonconditioned crawl space by means of direct connection to the return side of a forced air system.

618.6 Screen. Required outdoor air inlets for residential portions of a building shall be covered with a screen having $^1/_4$-inch (6.4 mm) openings. Required outdoor air inlets serving a nonresidential portion of a building shall be covered with screen having openings larger than $^1/_4$ inch (6.4 mm) and not larger than 1 inch (25 mm).

618.7 Return-air limitation. Return air from one *dwelling unit* shall not be discharged into another *dwelling unit.*

618.8 (IFGS) Furnace plenums and air ducts. Where a furnace is installed so that supply ducts carry air circulated by the furnace to areas outside of the space containing the furnace, the return air shall also be handled by a duct(s) sealed to the furnace casing and terminating outside of the space containing the furnace.

618.9 Refrigeration coils in warm-air furnaces. When a cooling coil is located in the supply plenum of a warm-air furnace, the furnace blower shall be rated at not less than 0.5-inch water column (124 Pa) static pressure unless the furnace is listed and labeled for use with a cooling coil. Cooling coils shall not be located upstream from heat exchangers unless listed and labeled for such use. Conversion of existing furnaces for use with cooling coils shall be permitted, provided the furnace will operate within the temperature rise specified for the furnace.

618.10 Return-air intake (nonengineered systems). If only one central return-air grille is installed, it shall be of a size sufficient to return a volume of air compatible with the cubic foot per minute requirements and the temperature rise limitations specified by the equipment manufacturer. The face velocity of return air grilles shall not exceed 450 feet per minute (fpm) (2.3 m/s). At least one separate return shall be installed on each level of a multilevel structure. For split-level and split-foyer structures, one return may serve more than one level if located within the split area and the total area of the levels does not exceed 1,600 square feet (148.6 m^2). Return-air grilles shall not be located in bathrooms. The return air from one residential living unit shall not be mixed with the return air from other living units.

In dwellings with 1,600 square feet (148.6 m^2) or less of conditioned area, a central return is permitted. When the dwelling contains more than 1,600 square feet (148.6 m^2) of conditioned area, additional returns shall be provided. Each return shall serve not more than 1,600 square feet (148.6 m^2) of area and shall be located in the area it serves. Return air may travel through the living space to the return-air intake if there are no restrictions, such as solid doors, to the air movement. When panned joists are used for return air, the structural integrity shall be maintained. Air capacity for joists 16 inches (406 mm) on center shall be a maximum of 375 cubic foot per minute (0.177 m^3/s) for 8-inch (203 mm) joists and 525 cubic foot per minute (0.248 m^3/s) for 10-inch (254 mm) joists. Wiring located in spaces used for return-air ducts shall comply with the *North Carolina Electrical Code.*

SECTION 619 (IFGC) CONVERSION BURNERS

619.1 Conversion burners. The installation of conversion burners shall conform to ANSI Z21.8.

SECTION 620 (IFGC) UNIT HEATERS Deleted

SECTION 621 (IFGC) UNVENTED ROOM HEATERS

621.1 General. Unvented room heaters shall be tested in accordance with ANSI Z21.11.2 and shall be installed in accordance with the conditions of the listing and the manufacturer's installation instructions. Unvented room heaters utilizing fuels other than fuel gas shall be regulated by the *International Mechanical Code.*

621.2 Prohibited use. One or more unvented room heaters shall not be used as the sole source of comfort heating in a *dwelling unit.*

621.3 Input rating. Unvented room heaters shall not have an input rating in excess of 40,000 Btu/h (11.7 kW).

621.4 Prohibited locations. Unvented room heaters shall not be installed within occupancies in Groups A, E and I. The location of unvented room heaters shall also comply with Section 303.3.

621.5 Room or space volume. The aggregate input rating of all unvented appliances installed in a room or space shall not exceed 20 Btu/h per cubic foot (207 W/m^3) of volume of such room or space. Where the room or space in which the appliances are installed is directly connected to another room or space by a doorway, archway or other opening of comparable size that cannot be closed, the volume of such adjacent room or space shall be permitted to be included in the calculations.

621.6 Oxygen-depletion safety system. Unvented room heaters shall be equipped with an oxygen-depletion-sensitive safety shutoff system. The system shall shut off the gas supply to the main and pilot burners when the oxygen in the surrounding atmosphere is depleted to the percent concentration specified by the manufacturer, but not lower than 18 percent. The system shall not incorporate field adjustment means capable of changing the set point at which the system acts to shut off the gas supply to the room heater.

621.7 Unvented log heaters. An unvented log heater shall not be installed in a factory-built *fireplace* unless the *fireplace* system has been specifically tested, *listed* and *labeled* for such use in accordance with UL 127.

621.7.1 Ventless firebox enclosures. Ventless firebox enclosures used with unvented log heaters shall be *listed* as complying with ANSI Z21.91.

SECTION 622 (IFGC) VENTED ROOM HEATERS

622.1 General. Vented room heaters shall be tested in accordance with ANSI Z21.86/CSA 2.32, shall be designed and equipped as specified in Section 602.2 and shall be installed in accordance with the manufacturer's installation instructions.

SECTION 623 (IFGC) COOKING APPLIANCES

623.1 Cooking appliances. Cooking appliances that are designed for permanent installation, including ranges, ovens, stoves, broilers, grills, fryers, griddles, hot plates and barbecues, shall be tested in accordance with ANSI Z21.1, ANSI Z21.58 or ANSI Z83.11 and shall be installed in accordance with the manufacturer's installation instructions.

623.2 Prohibited location. Cooking appliances designed, tested, *listed* and *labeled* for use in commercial occupancies shall not be installed within dwelling units or within any area where domestic cooking operations occur.

623.3 Domestic appliances. Cooking appliances installed within dwelling units and within areas where domestic cooking operations occur shall be *listed* and *labeled* as household-type appliances for domestic use.

623.4 Domestic range installation. Domestic ranges installed on combustible floors shall be set on their own bases or legs and shall be installed with clearances of not less than that shown on the label.

623.5 Open-top broiler unit hoods. A ventilating hood shall be provided above a domestic open-top broiler unit, unless otherwise *listed* for forced down draft ventilation.

623.5.1 Clearances. A minimum *clearance* of 24 inches (610 mm) shall be maintained between the cooking top and combustible material above the hood. The hood shall be at least as wide as the open-top broiler unit and be centered over the unit.

623.6 Commercial cooking appliance venting. Deleted.

623.7 (IFGS) Vertical clearance above cooking top. Household cooking appliances shall have a vertical *clearance* above the cooking top of not less than 30 inches (760 mm) to combustible material and metal cabinets. A minimum *clearance* of 24 inches (610 mm) is permitted where one of the following is installed:

1. The underside of the combustible material or metal cabinet above the cooking top is protected with not less than $^1/_4$-inch (6 mm) insulating millboard covered with sheet metal not less than 0.0122 inch (0.3 mm) thick.
2. A metal ventilating hood constructed of sheet metal not less than 0.0122 inch (0.3 mm) thick is installed above the cooking top with a *clearance* of not less than $^1/_4$ inch (6.4 mm) between the hood and the underside of the

combustible material or metal cabinet. The hood shall have a width not less than the width of the *appliance* and shall be centered over the *appliance*.

3. A *listed* cooking *appliance* or microwave oven is installed over a *listed* cooking *appliance* and in compliance with the terms of the manufacturer's installation instructions for the upper appliance.

SECTION 624 (IFGC) WATER HEATERS

624.1 General. Water heaters shall be tested in accordance with ANSI Z 21.10.1 and ANSI Z 21.10.3 and shall be installed in accordance with the manufacturer's installation instructions. Water heaters utilizing fuels other than fuel gas shall be regulated by the *International Mechanical Code*.

624.1.1 Installation requirements. The requirements for water heaters relative to sizing, relief valves, drain pans and scald protection shall be in accordance with the *International Plumbing Code*.

624.2 Water heaters utilized for space heating. Water heaters utilized both to supply potable hot water and provide hot water for space-heating applications shall be *listed* and *labeled* for such applications by the manufacturer and shall be installed in accordance with the manufacturer's installation instructions and the *International Plumbing Code*.

SECTION 625 (IFGC) REFRIGERATORS

Deleted

SECTION 626 (IFGC) GAS-FIRED TOILETS

Deleted

SECTION 627 (IFGC) AIR-CONDITIONING APPLIANCES

627.1 General. Gas-fired air-conditioning appliances shall be tested in accordance with ANSI Z21.40.1 or ANSI Z21.40.2 and shall be installed in accordance with the manufacturer's installation instructions.

627.2 Independent piping. Deleted.

627.3 Connection of gas engine-powered air conditioners. Deleted.

627.4 Clearances for indoor installation. Deleted.

627.5 Alcove and closet installation. Deleted.

627.6 Installation. Deleted.

627.7 Plenums and air ducts. Deleted.

627.8 Refrigeration coils. A refrigeration coil shall not be installed in conjunction with a forced-air furnace where circulation of cooled air is provided by the furnace blower, unless the blower has sufficient capacity to overcome the external static resistance imposed by the duct system and cooling coil at the air throughput necessary for heating or cooling, whichever is greater. Furnaces shall not be located upstream from cooling units, unless the cooling unit is designed or equipped so as not to develop excessive temperature or pressure. Refrigeration coils shall be installed in parallel with or on the downstream side of central furnaces to avoid condensation in the heating element, unless the furnace has been specifically *listed* for downstream installation. With a parallel flow arrangement, the dampers or other means used to control flow of air shall be sufficiently tight to prevent any circulation of cooled air through the furnace.

Means shall be provided for disposal of condensate and to prevent dripping of condensate onto the heating element.

627.9 Cooling units used with heating boilers. Deleted.

627.10 Switches in electrical supply line. Deleted.

SECTION 628 (IFGC) ILLUMINATING APPLIANCES

628.1 General. Illuminating appliances shall be tested in accordance with ANSI Z21.42 and shall be installed in accordance with the manufacturer's installation instructions.

628.2 Mounting on buildings. Illuminating appliances designed for wall or ceiling mounting shall be securely attached to substantial structures in such a manner that they are not dependent on the gas *piping* for support.

628.3 Mounting on posts. Illuminating appliances designed for post mounting shall be securely and rigidly attached to a post. Posts shall be rigidly mounted. The strength and rigidity of posts greater than 3 feet (914 mm) in height shall be at least equivalent to that of a $2^1/_2$-inch-diameter (64 mm) post constructed of 0.064-inch-thick (1.6-mm) steel or a 1-inch (25.4 mm) Schedule 40 steel pipe. Posts 3 feet (914 mm) or less in height shall not be smaller than a $^3/_4$-inch (19.1 mm) Schedule 40 steel pipe. Drain openings shall be provided near the base of posts where there is a possibility of water collecting inside them.

628.4 Appliance pressure regulators. Where an *appliance* pressure regulator is not supplied with an illuminating *appliance* and the service line is not equipped with a service pressure regulator, an *appliance* pressure regulator shall be installed in the line to the illuminating *appliance*. For multiple installations, one regulator of adequate capacity shall be permitted to serve more than one illuminating *appliance*.

SECTION 629 (IFGC) SMALL CERAMIC KILNS

629.1 General. Ceramic kilns with a maximum interior volume of 20 cubic feet (0.566 m^3) and used for hobby and noncommercial purposes shall be installed in accordance with the manufacturer's installation instructions and the provisions of this code.

SECTION 630 (IFGC) INFRARED RADIANT HEATERS

630.1 General. Infrared radiant heaters shall be tested in accordance with ANSI Z83.6 and shall be installed in accordance with the manufacturer's installation instructions.

630.2 Support. Infrared radiant heaters shall be fixed in a position independent of gas and electric supply lines. Hangers and brackets shall be of noncombustible material.

630.3 (IFGS) Combustion and ventilation air. Where unvented infrared heaters are installed, natural or mechanical means shall provide outdoor ventilation air at a rate of not less than 4 cfm per 1,000 Btu/h (0.38 m^3/min/kW) of the aggregate input rating of all such heaters installed in the space. Exhaust openings for removing flue products shall be above the level of the heaters.

630.4 (IFGS) Installation in commercial garages and aircraft hangars. Deleted.

SECTION 631 (IFGC) BOILERS

631.1 Standards. Boilers shall be *listed* in accordance with the requirements of ANSI Z21.13 or UL 795. If applicable, the boiler shall be designed and constructed in accordance with the requirements of ASME CSD-1 and as applicable, the ASME *Boiler and Pressure Vessel Code*, Sections I, II, IV, V and IX and NFPA 85.

631.2 Installation. In addition to the requirements of this code, the installation of boilers shall be in accordance with the manufacturer's instructions and the *International Mechanical Code*. Operating instructions of a permanent type shall be attached to the boiler. Boilers shall have all conrols set, adjusted and tested by the installer. A complete control diagram together with complete boiler operating instructions shall be furnished by the installer. The manufacturer's rating data and the nameplate shall be attached to the boiler.

631.3 Clearance to combustible materials. Clearances to combustible materials shall be in accordance with Section 308.4.

SECTION 632 (IFGC) EQUIPMENT INSTALLED IN EXISTING UNLISTED BOILERS

Deleted

SECTION 633 (IFGC) STATIONARY FUEL-CELL POWER SYSTEMS

Deleted

SECTION 634 (IFGS) CHIMNEY DAMPER OPENING AREA

Deleted

SECTION 635 (IFGC) GASEOUS HYDROGEN SYSTEMS

Deleted

CHAPTER 7
GASEOUS HYDROGEN SYSTEMS

Deleted

IFGC/IFGS CHAPTER 8

REFERENCED STANDARDS

This chapter lists the standards that are referenced in various sections of this document. The standards are listed herein by the promulgating agency of the standard, the standard identification, the effective date and title, and the section or sections of this document that reference the standard. The application of the referenced standards shall be as specified in Section 102.8.

ANSI

American National Standards Institute
25 West 43rd Street
Fourth Floor
New York, NY 10036

Standard reference number	Title	Referenced in code section number
ANSI A13.1-96	Scheme for the Identification of Piping Systems	704.1.2.2
ANSI CSA-America FC 1-03	Stationery Fuel Cell Power Systems	633.1
LC 1—97	Interior Gas Piping Systems Using Corrugated Stainless Steel Tubing—with Addenda LC1a-1999 and LC1b-2001	403.5.4
ANSI LC-4—07	Press-connect Copper and Copper Alloy Fittings for Use In Fuel Gas Distribution Systems	403.10.2
Z21.1—03	Household Cooking Gas Appliances—with Addenda Z21.1a-2003 and Z21.1b-2003	623.1
Z21.5.1—02	Gas Clothes Dryers—Volume I—Type 1 Clothes Dryers—with Addenda Z21.5.1a-2003	613.1
Z21.5.2—01	Gas Clothes Dryers—Volume II—Type 2 Clothes Dryers—with Addenda Z21.5.2a-2003 and Z21.5.2b-2003	613.1, 614.3
Z21.8—94 (R2002)	Installation of Domestic Gas Conversion Burners	619.1
Z21.10.1—04	Gas Water Heaters—Volume I—Storage, Water Heaters with Input Ratings of 75,000 Btu per Hour or Less	624.1
Z21.10.3—01	Gas Water Heaters—Volume III—Storage, Water Heaters with Input Ratings Above 75,000 Btu per hour, Circulating and Instantaneous—with Addenda Z21.10.3a-2003 and Z21.10.3b-2004	624.1
Z21.11.2—02	Gas-fired Room Heaters—Volume II—Unvented Room Heaters—with Addenda Z21.11.2a-2003	621.1
Z21.13—04	Gas-fired Low-pressure Steam and Hot Water Boilers	631.1
Z21.15—97 (R2003)	Manually Operated Gas Valves for Appliances, Appliance Connector Valves and Hose End Valves—with Addenda Z21.15a-2001(R2003)	409.1.1
Z21.19—02	Refrigerators Using Gas (R1999) Fuel	625.1
Z21.24—97	Connectors for Gas Appliances	411.1
Z21.40.1—96 (R2002)	Gas-fired Heat Activated Air Conditioning and Heat Pump Appliances—with Addendum Z21.40.1a-1997 (R2002)	627.1
Z21.40.2—96 (R2002)	Gas-fired Work Activated Air Conditioning and Heat Pump Appliances (Internal Combustion)—with Addendum Z21.40.2a-1997 (R2002)	627.1
Z21.42—93 (R2002)	Gas-fired Illuminating Appliances	628.1
Z21.47—03	Gas-fired Central Furnaces	618.1
Z21.50—03	Vented Gas Fireplaces—with Addenda Z21.50a-2003	604.1
Z21.56—01	Gas-fired Pool Heaters—with Addenda Z21.56a-2004 and Z21.56b-2004	617.1
Z21.58—95 (R2002)	Outdoor Cooking Gas Appliances—with Addendum Z21.58a-1998 (R2002) and Z21.58b-2002	623.1
Z21.60—03	Decorative Gas Appliances for Installation in Solid-fuel Burning Fireplaces—with Addenda Z21.60a-2003	602.1
Z21.61—83 (R1996)	Toilets, Gas-fired	626.1
Z21.69—02	Connectors for Movable Gas Appliances—with Addenda Z21.69a-2003	411.1.1
Z21.75/CSA 6.27—01	Connectors for Outdoor Gas Appliances and Manufactured Homes	411.1, 411.2
Z21.80—03	Line Pressure Regulators	410.1
Z21.84—02	Manually-lighted, Natural Gas Decorative Gas Appliances for Installation in Solid Fuel Burning Fireplaces—with Addenda Z21.84a-2003	602.1, 602.2
Z21.86—04	Gas-fired Vented Space Heating Appliances	608.1, 609.1, 622.1
Z21.88—02	Vented Gas Fireplace Heaters—with Addenda Z21.88a-2003 and Z21.88b-2004	605.1
Z21.91—01	Ventless Firebox Enclosures for Gas-fired Unvented Decorative Room Heaters	621.7.1
Z83.4—03	Nonrecirculating Direct-gas-fired Industrial Air Heaters	611.1
Z83.6—90 (R1998)	Gas-fired Infrared Heaters	630.1
Z83.8—02	Gas Unit Heaters and Gas-fired Duct Furnaces	620.1
Z83.11—02	Gas Food Service Equipment—with Addenda Z83.11a-2004	623.1
Z83.18—00	Recirculating Direct Gas-fired Industrial Air Heaters—with Addenda Z83.18a-2001 and Z83.18b-2003	612.1

ASME

American Society of Mechanical Engineers
Three Park Avenue
New York, NY 10016-5990

Standard reference number	Title	Referenced in code section number
B1.20.1—83 (Reaffirmed 2006)	Pipe Threads, General Purpose (inch)	403.9
B16.1—2005 (Reaffirmed 2004)	Cast-iron Pipe Flanges and Flanged Fittings, Class 25, 125 and 250	403.12
B16.20—98	Metallic Gaskets for Pipe Flanges Ring-joint, Spiral-wound and Jacketed	403.12
B16.33—02	Manually Operated Metallic Gas Valves for Use in Gas Piping Systems up to 125 psig (Sizes $^1/_2$ through 2)	409.1.1
B16.44—2002	Manually Operated Metallic Gas Valves for Use in Aboveground Piping Systems Up to 5 psi	409.1.1
B31.3—04	Process Piping	704.1.2, 704.1.2.4, 705.2, 705.3
B36.10M—2004	Welded and Seamless Wrought-steel Pipe	403.4.2
BPVC—04	ASME Boiler & Pressure Vessel Code (2001 Edition)	631.1, 703.2.2, 703.3.3, 703.3.4
CSD-1—2004	Controls and Safety Devices for Automatically Fired Boilers	631.1

ASTM

ASTM International
100 Barr Harbor Drive
West Conshohocken, PA 19428-2959

Standard reference number	Title	Referenced in code section number
A 53/A 53M—06a	Specification for Pipe, Steel, Black and Hot Dipped Zinc-coated Welded and Seamless	403.4.2
A 106/A 106M—06a	Specification for Seamless Carbon Steel Pipe for High-temperature Service	403.4.2
A 254—97 (2002)	Specification for Copper Brazed Steel Tubing	403.5.1
B 88—03	Specification for Seamless Copper Water Tube	403.5.2
B 210—02	Specification for Aluminum and Aluminum-alloy Drawn Seamless Tubes	403.5.3
B 241/B 241M—02	Specification for Aluminum and Aluminum-alloy, Seamless Pipe and Seamless Extruded Tube	403.4.4, 403.5.3
C 315—07	Specification for Clay Flue Liners and Chimney Pots	501.12
D 2513—07a	Specification for Thermoplastic Gas Pressure Pipe, Tubing and Fittings	403.6, 403.6.1, 403.11, 404.15.2
F 1973—05	Standard Specification for Factory Assembled Anodeless Risers and Transition Fittings in Polyethylene (PE) and Polyamide 11 (PA11) Fuel Gas Distribution Systems	404.15.2

CGA

Compressed Gas Association
1725 Jefferson Davis Highway, 5th Floor
Arlington, VA 22202-4102

Standard reference number	Title	Referenced in code section number
S-1.1—(2002)	Pressure Relief Device Standards—Part 1—Cylinders for Compressed Gases	703.3
S-1.2—(1995)	Pressure Relief Device Standards—Part 2—Cargo and Portable Tanks for Compressed Gases	703.3
S-1.3—(1995)	Pressure Relief Device Standards—Part 3—Stationary Storage Containers for Compressed Gases	703.3

CSA

CSA America Inc.
8501 E. Pleasant Valley Rd.
Cleveland, OH USA 44131-5575

Standard reference number	Title	Referenced in code section number
ANSI CSA America FC1-03	Stationary Fuel Cell Power Systems	633.1
CSA Requirement 3-88	Manually Operated Gas Valves for Use in House Piping Systems	409.1.1
CSA 8—93	Requirements for Gas-fired Log Lighters for Wood Burning Fireplaces—with Revisions through January 1999	603.1

DOTn

Department of Transportation
400 Seventh St. SW.
Washington, DC 20590

Standard reference number	Title	Referenced in code section number
49 CFR, Parts 192.281(e) & 192.283 (b)	Transportation of Natural and Other Gas by Pipeline: Minimum Federal Safety Standards	403.6.1
49 CFR Parts 100-180	Hazardous Materials Regulations	703.2.2, 703.3.3, 703.3.4

ICC

International Code Council, Inc.
500 New Jersey Ave, NW
6th Floor
Washington, DC 20001

Standard reference number	Title	Referenced in code section number
IBC—09	International Building Code®	102.2.1, 201.3, 301.10, 301.11, 301.12, 301.14, 302.1, 302.2, 305.6, 306.6, 401.1.1, 412.6, 413.3, 413.3.1, 501.1, 501.3, 501.12, 501.15.4, 609.3, 614.2, 706.2, 706.3
IECC—09	International Energy Conservation Code®	301.2
IFC—09	International Fire Code®	201.3, 401.2, 412.1, 412.6, 412.7, 412.7.3, 412.8, 413.1, 413.3, 413.3.1, 413.5, 413.9.2.5, 701.1, 701.2, 703.2, 703.2.2, 703.3.8, 703.4, 703.5, 704.1.2, 704.3, 704.4, 706.2, 706.3, 707.1, 707.2, 708.1
IMC—09	International Mechanical Code®	101.2.5, 201.3, 301.1.1, 301.13, 304.11, 501.1, 614.2, 618.5, 621.1, 624.1, 631.2, 632.1, 703.1.2
IPC—09	International Plumbing Code®	201.3, 301.6, 624.1.1, 624.2
IRC—09	International Residential Code®	703.2.1

MSS

Manufacturers Standardization Society of
the Valve and Fittings Industry
127 Park Street, Northeast
Vienna, VA 22180

Standard reference number	Title	Referenced in code section number
SP-6—01	Standard Finishes for Contact Faces of Pipe Flanges and Connecting-end Flanges of Valves and Fittings	403.12
SP-58—93	Pipe Hangers and Supports—Materials, Design and Manufacture	407.2

NFPA

National Fire Protection Association
1 Batterymarch Park
Quincy, MA 02269-9101

Standard reference number	Title	Referenced in code section number
30A—03	Code for Motor Fuel Dispensing Facilities and Repair Garages	305.4
37—06	Installation and Use of Stationary Combustion Engines and Gas Turbines	616.1
51—02	Design and Installation of Oxygen-fuel Gas Systems for Welding, Cutting and Allied Processes	414.1
58—08	Liquefied Petroleum Gas Code	401.2, 402.6, 403.11
70—08	National Electrical Code	306.3.1, 306.4.1, 306.5.2, 309.2, 413.9.2.4, 703.6
82—04	Incinerators, Waste and Linen Handling Systems and Equipment	607.1
85—07	Boiler and Combustion Systems Hazards Code	631.1
88A—02	Parking Structures	305.9
211—06	Chimneys, Fireplaces, Vents and Solid Fuel-burning Appliances	503.5.2, 503.5.3, 503.5.6.1, 503.5.6.3
409—01	Aircraft Hangars	305.11
853—07	Installation of Stationary Fuel Cell Power Systems	633.1

UL

Underwriters Laboratories Inc.
333 Pfingsten Road
Northbrook, IL 60062

Standard reference number	Title	Referenced in code section number
103—2001	Factory-built Chimneys, Residential Type and Building Heating Appliances—with Revisions through June 2006	506.1
127—96	Factory-built Fireplaces—with Revisions through 2006	621.7
441—96	Gas Vents—with Revisions through August 2006	502.1
641—95	Type L Low-temperature Venting Systems—with Revisions through April 1999	502.1
651—05	Schedule 40 and 80 Rigid PVC Conduit and Fittings	403.6.3
795—2006	Commercial-industrial Gas Heating Equipment	610.1, 618.1, 631.1
959—01	Medium Heat Appliance Factory-built Chimneys—with Revisions through September 2006	506.3
1738—06	Venting Systems for Gas Burning Appliances, Categories II, III and IV	502.1
1777—04	Standard for Chimney Liners	501.12, 501.15.4
2200—04	Stationary Engine Generator Assemblies	616.1

APPENDIX A (IFGS)

SIZING AND CAPACITIES OF GAS PIPING

(This appendix is informative and is not part of the code.)

A.1 General piping considerations. The first goal of determining the pipe sizing for a fuel gas *piping* system is to make sure that there is sufficient gas pressure at the inlet to each *appliance*. The majority of systems are residential and the appliances will all have the same, or nearly the same, requirement for minimum gas pressure at the *appliance* inlet. This pressure will be about 5-inch water column (w.c.) (1.25 kPa), which is enough for proper operation of the *appliance* regulator to deliver about 3.5-inches water column (w.c.) (875 kPa) to the burner itself. The pressure drop in the *piping* is subtracted from the source delivery pressure to verify that the minimum is available at the *appliance*.

There are other systems, however, where the required inlet pressure to the different appliances may be quite varied. In such cases, the greatest inlet pressure required must be satisfied, as well as the farthest *appliance*, which is almost always the critical *appliance* in small systems.

There is an additional requirement to be observed besides the capacity of the system at 100-percent flow. That requirement is that at minimum flow, the pressure at the inlet to any *appliance* does not exceed the pressure rating of the *appliance* regulator. This would seldom be of concern in small systems if the source pressure is $^1/_2$ psi (14-inch w.c.) (3.5 kPa) or less but it should be verified for systems with greater gas pressure at the point of supply.

To determine the size of *piping* used in a gas *piping* system, the following factors must be considered:

(1) Allowable loss in pressure from *point of delivery* to *appliance*.

(2) Maximum gas demand.

(3) Length of *piping* and number of fittings.

(4) Specific gravity of the gas.

(5) Diversity factor.

For any gas *piping* system, or special *appliance*, or for conditions other than those covered by the tables provided in this code, such as longer runs, greater gas demands or greater pressure drops, the size of each gas *piping* system should be determined by standard engineering practices acceptable to the code official.

A.2 Description of tables.

A.2.1 General. The quantity of gas to be provided at each *outlet* should be determined, whenever possible, directly from the manufacturer's gas input Btu/h rating of the *appliance* that will be installed. In case the ratings of the appliances to be installed are not known, Table 402.2 shows the approximate consumption (in Btu per hour) of certain types of typical household appliances.

To obtain the cubic feet per hour of gas required, divide the total Btu/h input of all appliances by the average Btu heating value per cubic feet of the gas. The average Btu per cubic feet of the gas in the area of the installation can be obtained from the serving gas supplier.

A.2.2 Low pressure natural gas tables. Capacities for gas at low pressure [less than 2.0 psig (13.8 kPa gauge)] in cubic feet per hour of 0.60 specific gravity gas for different sizes and lengths are shown in Tables 402.4(1) and 402.4(2) for iron pipe or equivalent rigid pipe; in Tables 402.4(6) through 402.4(9) for smooth wall semirigid tubing; and in Tables 402.4(13) through 402.4(15) for corrugated stainless steel tubing. Tables 402.4(1) and 402.4(6) are based upon a pressure drop of 0.3-inch w.c. (75 Pa), whereas Tables 402.4(2), 402.4(7) and 402.4(13) are based upon a pressure drop of 0.5-inch w.c. (125 Pa). Tables 402.4(8), 402.4(9), 402.4(14) and 402.4(15) are special low-pressure applications based upon pressure drops greater than 0.5-inch w.c. (125 Pa). In using these tables, an allowance (in equivalent length of pipe) should be considered for any *piping* run with four or more fittings (see Table A.2.2).

A.2.3 Undiluted liquefied petroleum tables. Capacities in thousands of Btu per hour of undiluted liquefied petroleum gases based on a pressure drop of 0.5-inch w.c. (125 Pa) for different sizes and lengths are shown in Table 402.4(26) for iron pipe or equivalent rigid pipe, in Table 402.4(28) for smooth wall semi-rigid tubing, in Table 402.4(30) for corrugated stainless steel tubing, and in Tables 402.4(33) and 402.4(35) for polyethylene plastic pipe and tubing. Tables 402.4(31) and 402.4(32) for corrugated stainless steel tubing and Table 402.4(34) for polyethylene plastic pipe are based on operating pressures greater than $1^1/_2$ pounds per square inch (psi) (3.5 kPa) and pressure drops greater than 0.5-inch w.c. (125 Pa). In using these tables, an allowance (in equivalent length of pipe) should be considered for any *piping* run with four or more fittings [see Table A.2.2].

A.2.4 Natural gas specific gravity. Gas *piping* systems that are to be supplied with gas of a specific gravity of 0.70 or less can be sized directly from the tables provided in this code, unless the code official specifies that a gravity factor be applied. Where the specific gravity of the gas is greater than 0.70, the gravity factor should be applied.

Application of the gravity factor converts the figures given in the tables provided in this code to capacities for another gas of different specific gravity. Such application is accomplished by multiplying the capacities given in the tables by the multipliers shown in Table A.2.4. In case the exact specific gravity does not appear in the table, choose the next higher value specific gravity shown.

TABLE A.2.2
EQUIVALENT LENGTHS OF PIPE FITTINGS AND VALVES

		SCREWED FITTINGS[1]				90° WELDING ELBOWS AND SMOOTH BENDS[2]					
		45°/Ell	90°/Ell	180° close return bends	Tee	*R/d* = 1	*R/d* = 1 1/3	*R/d* = 2	*R/d* = 4	*R/d* = 6	*R/d* = 8
k factor =		0.42	0.90	2.00	1.80	0.48	0.36	0.27	0.21	0.27	0.36
L/d′ ratio[4] *n* =		14	30	67	60	16	12	9	7	9	12
Nominal pipe size, inches	Inside diameter *d*, inches, Schedule 40[6]	*L* = Equivalent Length In Feet of Schedule 40 (Standard-weight) Straight Pipe[6]									
1/2	0.622	0.73	1.55	3.47	3.10	0.83	0.62	0.47	0.36	0.47	0.62
3/4	0.824	0.96	2.06	4.60	4.12	1.10	0.82	0.62	0.48	0.62	0.82
1	1.049	1.22	2.62	5.82	5.24	1.40	1.05	0.79	0.61	0.79	1.05
1 1/4	1.380	1.61	3.45	7.66	6.90	1.84	1.38	1.03	0.81	1.03	1.38
1 1/2	1.610	1.88	4.02	8.95	8.04	2.14	1.61	1.21	0.94	1.21	1.61
2	2.067	2.41	5.17	11.5	10.3	2.76	2.07	1.55	1.21	1.55	2.07
2 1/2	2.469	2.88	6.16	13.7	12.3	3.29	2.47	1.85	1.44	1.85	2.47
3	3.068	3.58	7.67	17.1	15.3	4.09	3.07	2.30	1.79	2.30	3.07
4	4.026	4.70	10.1	22.4	20.2	5.37	4.03	3.02	2.35	3.02	4.03
5	5.047	5.88	12.6	28.0	25.2	6.72	5.05	3.78	2.94	3.78	5.05
6	6.065	7.07	15.2	33.8	30.4	8.09	6.07	4.55	3.54	4.55	6.07
8	7.981	9.31	20.0	44.6	40.0	10.6	7.98	5.98	4.65	5.98	7.98
10	10.02	11.7	25.0	55.7	50.0	13.3	10.0	7.51	5.85	7.51	10.0
12	11.94	13.9	29.8	66.3	59.6	15.9	11.9	8.95	6.96	8.95	11.9
14	13.13	15.3	32.8	73.0	65.6	17.5	13.1	9.85	7.65	9.85	13.1
16	15.00	17.5	37.5	83.5	75.0	20.0	15.0	11.2	8.75	11.2	15.0
18	16.88	19.7	42.1	93.8	84.2	22.5	16.9	12.7	9.85	12.7	16.9
20	18.81	22.0	47.0	105.0	94.0	25.1	18.8	14.1	11.0	14.1	18.8
24	22.63	26.4	56.6	126.0	113.0	30.2	22.6	17.0	13.2	17.0	22.6

continued

TABLE A.2.2—continued
EQUIVALENT LENGTHS OF PIPE FITTINGS AND VALVES

		MITER ELBOWS[3] (No. of miters)					WELDING TEES		VALVES (screwed, flanged, or welded)			
		1-45°	1-60°	1-90°	2-90°[5]	3-90°[5]	Forged	Miter[3]	Gate	Globe	Angle	Swing Check
k factor =		0.45	0.90	1.80	0.60	0.45	1.35	1.80	0.21	10	5.0	2.5
L/d' ratio[4] *n* =		15	30	60	20	15	45	60	7	333	167	83
Nominal pipe size, inches	Inside diameter *d*, inches, Schedule 40[6]	*L* = Equivalent Length In Feet of Schedule 40 (Standard-weight) Straight Pipe[6]										
$^{1}/_{2}$	0.622	0.78	1.55	3.10	1.04	0.78	2.33	3.10	0.36	17.3	8.65	4.32
$^{3}/_{4}$	0.824	1.03	2.06	4.12	1.37	1.03	3.09	4.12	0.48	22.9	11.4	5.72
1	1.049	1.31	2.62	5.24	1.75	1.31	3.93	5.24	0.61	29.1	14.6	7.27
$1^{1}/_{4}$	1.380	1.72	3.45	6.90	2.30	1.72	5.17	6.90	0.81	38.3	19.1	9.58
$1^{1}/_{2}$	1.610	2.01	4.02	8.04	2.68	2.01	6.04	8.04	0.94	44.7	22.4	11.2
2	2.067	2.58	5.17	10.3	3.45	2.58	7.75	10.3	1.21	57.4	28.7	14.4
$2^{1}/_{2}$	2.469	3.08	6.16	12.3	4.11	3.08	9.25	12.3	1.44	68.5	34.3	17.1
3	3.068	3.84	7.67	15.3	5.11	3.84	11.5	15.3	1.79	85.2	42.6	21.3
4	4.026	5.04	10.1	20.2	6.71	5.04	15.1	20.2	2.35	112.0	56.0	28.0
5	5.047	6.30	12.6	25.2	8.40	6.30	18.9	25.2	2.94	140.0	70.0	35.0
6	6.065	7.58	15.2	30.4	10.1	7.58	22.8	30.4	3.54	168.0	84.1	42.1
8	7.981	9.97	20.0	40.0	13.3	9.97	29.9	40.0	4.65	22.0	111.0	55.5
10	10.02	12.5	25.0	50.0	16.7	12.5	37.6	50.0	5.85	278.0	139.0	69.5
12	11.94	14.9	29.8	59.6	19.9	14.9	44.8	59.6	6.96	332.0	166.0	83.0
14	13.13	16.4	32.8	65.6	21.9	16.4	49.2	65.6	7.65	364.0	182.0	91.0
16	15.00	18.8	37.5	75.0	25.0	18.8	56.2	75.0	8.75	417.0	208.0	104.0
18	16.88	21.1	42.1	84.2	28.1	21.1	63.2	84.2	9.85	469.0	234.0	117.0
20	18.81	23.5	47.0	94.0	31.4	23.5	70.6	94.0	11.0	522.0	261.0	131.0
24	22.63	28.3	56.6	113.0	37.8	28.3	85.0	113.0	13.2	629.0	314.0	157.0

For SI: 1 foot = 305 mm, 1 degree = 0.01745 rad.

Note: Values for welded fittings are for conditions where bore is not obstructed by weld spatter or backing rings. If appreciably obstructed, use values for "Screwed Fittings."

1. Flanged fittings have three-fourths the resistance of screwed elbows and tees.
2. Tabular figures give the extra resistance due to curvature alone to which should be added the full length of travel.
3. Small size socket-welding fittings are equivalent to miter elbows and miter tees.
4. Equivalent resistance in number of diameters of straight pipe computed for a value of (f - 0.0075) from the *relation* (n - $k/4f$).
5. For condition of minimum resistance where the centerline length of each miter is between d and $2^{1}/_{2}d$.
6. For pipe having other inside diameters, the equivalent resistance may be computed from the above n values.

Source: Crocker, S. *Piping Handbook*, 4th ed., Table XIV, pp. 100-101. Copyright 1945 by McGraw-Hill, Inc. Used by permission of McGraw-Hill Book Company.

TABLE A.2.4
MULTIPLIERS TO BE USED WITH TABLES 402.4(1) THROUGH 402.4(22) WHERE THE SPECIFIC GRAVITY OF THE GAS IS OTHER THAN 0.60

SPECIFIC GRAVITY	MULTIPLIER	SPECIFIC GRAVITY	MULTIPLIER
0.35	1.31	1.00	0.78
0.40	1.23	1.10	0.74
0.45	1.16	1.20	0.71
0.50	1.10	1.30	0.68
0.55	1.04	1.40	0.66
0.60	1.00	1.50	0.63
0.65	0.96	1.60	0.61
0.70	0.93	1.70	0.59
0.75	0.90	1.80	0.58
0.80	0.87	1.90	0.56
0.85	0.84	2.00	0.55
0.90	0.82	2.10	0.54

A.2.5 Higher pressure natural gas tables. Capacities for gas at pressures 2.0 psig (13.8 kPa) or greater in cubic feet per hour of 0.60 specific gravity gas for different sizes and lengths are shown in Tables 402.4(3) through 402.4(5) for iron pipe or equivalent rigid pipe; Tables 402.4(10) to 402.4(12) for semirigid tubing; Tables 402.4(16) and 402.4(17) for corrugated stainless steel tubing; and Table 402.4(20) for polyethylene plastic pipe.

A.3 Use of capacity tables.

A.3.1 Longest length method. This sizing method is conservative in its approach by applying the maximum operating conditions in the system as the norm for the system and by setting the length of pipe used to size any given part of the *piping* system to the maximum value.

To determine the size of each section of gas *piping* in a system within the range of the capacity tables, proceed as follows (also see sample calculations included in this Appendix):

(1) Divide the *piping* system into appropriate segments consistent with the presence of tees, branch lines and main runs. For each segment, determine the gas load (assuming all appliances operate simultaneously) and its overall length. An allowance (in equivalent length of pipe) as determined from Table A.2.2 shall be considered for *piping* segments that include four or more fittings.

(2) Determine the gas demand of each *appliance* to be attached to the *piping* system. Where Tables 402.4(1) through 402.4(22) are to be used to select the *piping* size, calculate the gas demand in terms of cubic feet per hour for each *piping* system *outlet*. Where Tables 402.4(23) through 402.4(35) are to be used to select the *piping* size, calculate the gas demand in terms of thousands of Btu per hour for each *piping* system *outlet*.

(3) Where the *piping* system is for use with other than undiluted liquefied petroleum gases, determine the design system pressure, the allowable loss in pressure (pressure drop), and specific gravity of the gas to be used in the *piping* system.

(4) Determine the length of *piping* from the *point of delivery* to the most remote *outlet* in the building/*piping* system.

(5) In the appropriate capacity table, select the row showing the measured length or the next longer length if the table does not give the exact length. This is the only length used in determining the size of any section of gas *piping*. If the gravity factor is to be applied, the values in the selected row of the table are multiplied by the appropriate multiplier from Table A.2.4.

(6) Use this horizontal row to locate ALL gas demand figures for this particular system of *piping*.

(7) Starting at the most remote *outlet*, find the gas demand for that *outlet* in the horizontal row just selected. If the exact figure of demand is not shown, choose the next larger figure left in the row.

(8) Opposite this demand figure, in the first row at the top, the correct size of gas *piping* will be found.

(9) Proceed in a similar manner for each *outlet* and each section of gas *piping*. For each section of *piping*, determine the total gas demand supplied by that section.

When a large number of *piping* components (such as elbows, tees and valves) are installed in a pipe run, additional pressure loss can be accounted for by the use of equivalent lengths. Pressure loss across any *piping* component can be equated to the pressure drop through a length of pipe. The equivalent length of a combination of only four elbows/tees can result in a jump to the next larger length row, resulting in a significant reduction in capacity. The equivalent lengths in feet shown in Table A.2.2 have been computed on a basis that the inside diameter corresponds to that of Schedule 40 (standard-weight) steel pipe, which is close enough for most purposes involving other schedules of pipe. Where a more specific solution for equivalent length is desired, this may be made by multiplying the actual inside diameter of the pipe in inches by $n/12$, or the actual inside diameter in feet by n (n can be read from the table heading). The equivalent length values can be used with reasonable accuracy for copper or brass fittings and bends although the resistance per foot of copper or brass pipe is less than that of steel. For copper or brass valves, however, the equivalent length of pipe should be taken as 45 percent longer than the values in the table, which are for steel pipe.

A.3.2 Branch length method. This sizing method reduces the amount of conservatism built into the traditional Longest Length Method. The longest length as measured from the meter to the furthest remote *appliance* is only used to size the initial parts of the overall *piping* system. The Branch Length Method is applied in the following manner:

(1) Determine the gas load for each of the connected appliances.

(2) Starting from the meter, divide the *piping* system into a number of connected segments, and determine the length and amount of gas that each segment would carry assuming that all appliances were operated simul-

taneously. An allowance (in equivalent length of pipe) as determined from Table A.2.2 should be considered for piping segments that include four or more fittings.

(3) Determine the distance from the *outlet* of the gas meter to the *appliance* furthest removed from the meter.

(4) Using the longest distance (found in Step 3), size each *piping* segment from the meter to the most remote *appliance outlet*.

(5) For each of these *piping* segments, use the longest length and the calculated gas load for all of the connected appliances for the segment and begin the sizing process in Steps 6 through 8.

(6) Referring to the appropriate sizing table (based on operating conditions and *piping* material), find the longest length distance in the first column or the next larger distance if the exact distance is not listed. The use of alternative operating pressures and/or pressure drops will require the use of a different sizing table, but will not alter the sizing methodology. In many cases, the use of alternative operating pressures and/or pressure drops will require the approval of both the code official and the local gas serving utility.

(7) Trace across this row until the gas load is found or the closest larger capacity if the exact capacity is not listed.

(8) Read up the table column and select the appropriate pipe size in the top row. Repeat Steps 6, 7 and 8 for each pipe segment in the longest run.

(9) Size each remaining section of branch *piping* not previously sized by measuring the distance from the gas meter location to the most remote *outlet* in that branch, using the gas load of attached appliances and following the procedures of Steps 2 through 8.

A.3.3 Hybrid pressure method. The sizing of a 2 psi (13.8 kPa) gas *piping* system is performed using the traditional Longest Length Method but with modifications. The 2 psi (13.8 kPa) system consists of two independent pressure zones, and each zone is sized separately. The Hybrid Pressure Method is applied as follows:

The sizing of the 2 psi (13.8 kPa) section (from the meter to the line regulator) is as follows:

(1) Calculate the gas load (by adding up the name plate ratings) from all connected appliances. (In certain circumstances the installed gas load may be increased up to 50 percent to accommodate future addition of appliances.) Ensure that the line regulator capacity is adequate for the calculated gas load and that the required pressure drop (across the regulator) for that capacity does not exceed $^3/_4$ psi (5.2 kPa) for a 2 psi (13.8 kPa) system. If the pressure drop across the regulator is too high (for the connected gas load), select a larger regulator.

(2) Measure the distance from the meter to the line regulator located inside the building.

(3) If there are multiple line regulators, measure the distance from the meter to the regulator furthest removed from the meter.

(4) The maximum allowable pressure drop for the 2 psi (13.8 kPa) section is 1 psi (6.9 kPa).

(5) Referring to the appropriate sizing table (based on *piping* material) for 2 psi (13.8 kPa) systems with a 1 psi (6.9 kPa) pressure drop, find this distance in the first column, or the closest larger distance if the exact distance is not listed.

(6) Trace across this row until the gas load is found or the closest larger capacity if the exact capacity is not listed.

(7) Read up the table column to the top row and select the appropriate pipe size.

(8) If there are multiple regulators in this portion of the *piping* system, each line segment must be sized for its actual gas load, but using the longest length previously determined above.

The low pressure section (all *piping* downstream of the line regulator) is sized as follows:

(1) Determine the gas load for each of the connected appliances.

(2) Starting from the line regulator, divide the *piping* system into a number of connected segments and/or independent parallel *piping* segments, and determine the amount of gas that each segment would carry assuming that all appliances were operated simultaneously. An allowance (in equivalent length of pipe) as determined from Table A.2.2 should be considered for *piping* segments that include four or more fittings.

(3) For each *piping* segment, use the actual length or longest length (if there are sub-branchlines) and the calculated gas load for that segment and begin the sizing process as follows:

   (a) Referring to the appropriate sizing table (based on operating pressure and *piping* material), find the longest length distance in the first column or the closest larger distance if the exact distance is not listed. The use of alternative operating pressures and/or pressure drops will require the use of a different sizing table, but will not alter the sizing methodology. In many cases, the use of alternative operating pressures and/or pressure drops may require the approval of the code official.

   (b) Trace across this row until the *appliance* gas load is found or the closest larger capacity if the exact capacity is not listed.

   (c) Read up the table column to the top row and select the appropriate pipe size.

   (d) Repeat this process for each segment of the *piping* system.

A.3.4 Pressure drop per 100 feet method. This sizing method is less conservative than the others, but it allows the designer to immediately see where the largest pressure drop occurs in the system. With this information, modifications can be made to bring the total drop to the critical *appliance* within the limitations that are presented to the designer.

Follow the procedures described in the Longest Length Method for Steps (1) through (4) and (9).

For each *piping* segment, calculate the pressure drop based on pipe size, length as a percentage of 100 feet (30 480 mm) and gas flow. Table A.3.4 shows pressure drop per 100 feet (30 480 mm) for pipe sizes from $^1/_2$ inch (12.7 mm) through 2 inches (51 mm). The sum of pressure drops to the critical *appliance* is subtracted from the supply pressure to verify that sufficient pressure will be available. If not, the layout can be examined to find the high drop section(s) and sizing selections modified.

Note: Other values can be obtained by using the following equation:

$$\text{Desired Value} = MBH \times \sqrt{\frac{\text{Desired Drop}}{\text{Table Drop}}}$$

For example, if it is desired to get flow through $^3/_4$-inch (19.1 mm) pipe at 2 inches/100 feet, multiply the capacity of $^3/_4$-inch pipe at 1 inch/100 feet by the square root of the pressure ratio:

$$147\,MBH \times \sqrt{\frac{2''\,w.c.}{1''\,w.c.}} = 147 \times 1.414 = 208\,MBH$$

$(MBH = 1000$ Btu/h$)$

A.4 Use of sizing equations. Capacities of smooth wall pipe or tubing can also be determined by using the following formulae:

(1) High Pressure [1.5 psi (10.3 kPa) and above]:

$$Q = 181.6\sqrt{\frac{D^5 \cdot (P_1^2 - P_2^2) \cdot Y}{C_r \cdot fba \cdot L}}$$

$$= 2237\,D^{2.623}\left[\frac{(P_1^2 - P_2^2) \cdot Y}{C_r \cdot L}\right]^{0.541}$$

(2) Low Pressure [Less than 1.5 psi (10.3 kPa)]:

$$Q = 187.3\sqrt{\frac{D^5 \cdot \Delta H}{C_r \cdot fba \cdot L}}$$

$$= 2313\,D^{2.623}\left(\frac{\Delta H}{C_r \cdot L}\right)^{0.541}$$

where:

Q = Rate, cubic feet per hour at 60°F and 30-inch mercury column

D = Inside diameter of pipe, in.

P_1 = Upstream pressure, psia

P_2 = Downstream pressure, psia

Y = Superexpansibility factor = 1/supercompressibility factor

C_r = Factor for viscosity, density and temperature*

$$= 0.00354\,ST\left(\frac{Z}{S}\right)^{0.152}$$

Note: See Table 402.4 for Y and C_r for natural gas and propane.

S = Specific gravity of gas at 60°F and 30-inch mercury column (0.60 for natural gas, 1.50 for propane), or = 1488μ

T = Absolute temperature, °F or = $t + 460$

t = Temperature, °F

Z = Viscosity of gas, centipoise (0.012 for natural gas, 0.008 for propane), or = 1488μ

fba = Base friction factor for air at 60°F (CF = 1)

L = Length of pipe, ft

ΔH = Pressure drop, in. w.c. (27.7 in. H_2O = 1 psi)

(For SI, see Section 402.4)

TABLE A.3.4
THOUSANDS OF BTU/H (MBH) OF NATURAL GAS PER 100 FEET OF PIPE AT VARIOUS PRESSURE DROPS AND PIPE DIAMETERS

PRESSURE DROP PER 100 FEET IN INCHES W.C.	PIPE SIZES (inch)					
	$^1/_2$	$^3/_4$	1	$1^1/_4$	$1^1/_2$	2
0.2	31	64	121	248	372	716
0.3	38	79	148	304	455	877
0.5	50	104	195	400	600	1160
1.0	71	147	276	566	848	1640

For SI: 1 inch = 25.4 mm, 1 foot = 304.8 mm.

A.5 Pipe and tube diameters. Where the internal diameter is determined by the formulas in Section 402.4, Tables A.5.1 and A.5.2 can be used to select the nominal or standard pipe size based on the calculated internal diameter.

TABLE A.5.1
SCHEDULE 40 STEEL PIPE STANDARD SIZES

NOMINAL SIZE (inch)	INTERNAL DIAMETER (inch)	NOMINAL SIZE (inch)	INTERNAL DIAMETER (inch)
1/4	0.364	1 1/2	1.610
3/8	0.493	2	2.067
1/2	0.622	2 1/2	2.469
3/4	0.824	3	3.068
1	1.049	3 1/2	3.548
1 1/4	1.380	4	4.026

For SI: 1 inch = 25.4 mm.

A.6 Use of sizing charts. A third method of sizing gas *piping* is detailed below as an option that is useful when large quantities of *piping* are involved in a job (e.g., an apartment house) and material costs are of concern. If the user is not completely familiar with this method, the resulting pipe sizing should be checked by a knowledgeable gas engineer. The sizing charts are applied as follows:

(1) With the layout developed according to Section 106.3.1 of the code, indicate in each section the design gas flow under maximum operation conditions. For many layouts, the maximum design flow will be the sum of all connected loads; however, in some cases, certain combinations of appliances will not occur simultaneously (e.g., gas heating and *air conditioning*). For these cases, the design flow is the greatest gas flow that can occur at any one time.

(2) Determine the inlet gas pressure for the system being designed. In most cases, the point of inlet will be the gas meter or service regulator, but in the case of a system addition, it could be the point of connection to the existing system.

(3) Determine the minimum pressure required at the inlet to the critical *appliance*. Usually, the critical item will be the *appliance* with the highest required pressure for satisfactory operation. If several items have the same required pressure, it will be the one with the greatest length of *piping* from the system inlet.

(4) The difference between the inlet pressure and critical item pressure is the allowable system pressure drop. Figures A.6(a) and A.6(b) show the relationship between gas flow, pipe size and pipe length for natural gas with 0.60 specific gravity.

(5) To use Figure A.6(a) (low pressure applications), calculate the *piping* length from the inlet to the critical *appliance*. Increase this length by 50 percent to allow for fittings. Divide the allowable pressure drop by the equivalent length (in hundreds of feet) to determine the allowable pressure drop per 100 feet (30 480 mm). Select the pipe size from Figure A.6(a) for the required volume of flow.

(6) To use Figure A.6(b) (high pressure applications), calculate the equivalent length as above. Calculate the index number for Figure A.6(b) by dividing the difference between the squares of the absolute values of inlet and *outlet* pressures by the equivalent length (in hundreds of feet). Select the pipe size from Figure A.6(b) for the gas volume required.

TABLE A.5.2
COPPER TUBE STANDARD SIZES

TUBE TYPE	NOMINAL OR STANDARD SIZE (inches)	INTERNAL DIAMETER (inches)
K	1/4	0.305
L	1/4	0.315
ACR (D)	3/8	0.315
ACR (A)	3/8	0.311
K	3/8	0.402
L	3/8	0.430
ACR (D)	1/2	0.430
ACR (A)	1/2	0.436
K	1/2	0.527
L	1/2	0.545
ACR (D)	5/8	0.545
ACR (A)	5/8	0.555
K	5/8	0.652
L	5/8	0.666
ACR (D)	3/4	0.666
ACR (A)	3/4	0.680
K	3/4	0.745
L	3/4	0.785
ACR	7/8	0.785
K	1	0.995
L	1	1.025
ACR	1 1/8	1.025
K	1 1/4	1.245
L	1 1/4	1.265
ACR	1 3/8	1.265
K	1 1/2	1.481
L	1 1/2	1.505
ACR	1 5/8	1.505
K	2	1.959
L	2	1.985
ACR	2 1/8	1.985
K	2 1/2	2.435
L	2 1/2	2.465
ACR	2 5/8	2.465
K	3	2.907
L	3	2.945
ACR	3 1/8	2.945

For SI: 1 inch = 25.4 mm.

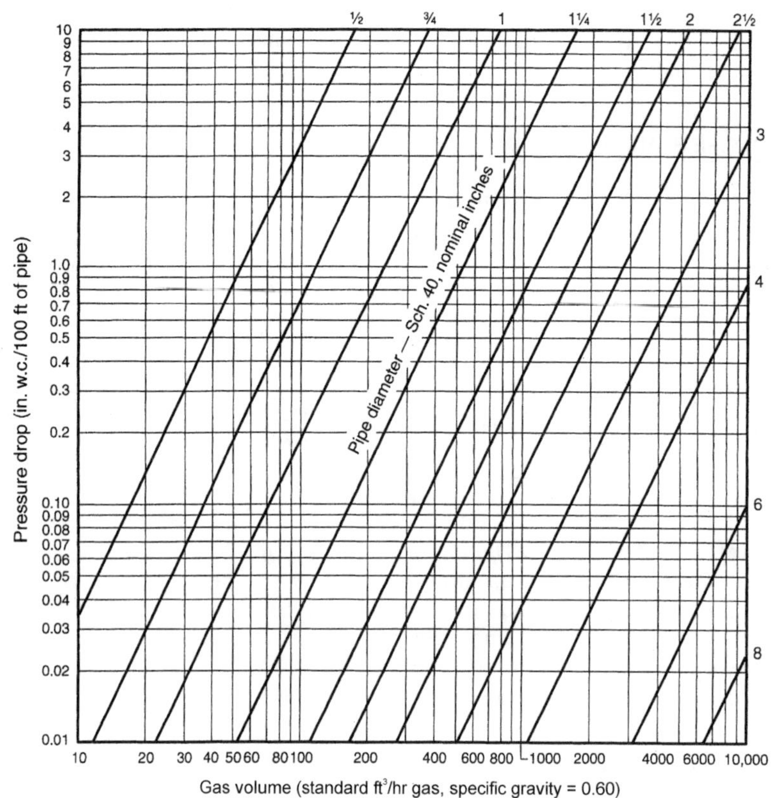

FIGURE A.6 (a)
CAPACITY OF NATURAL GAS PIPING, LOW PRESSURE (0.60 WC)

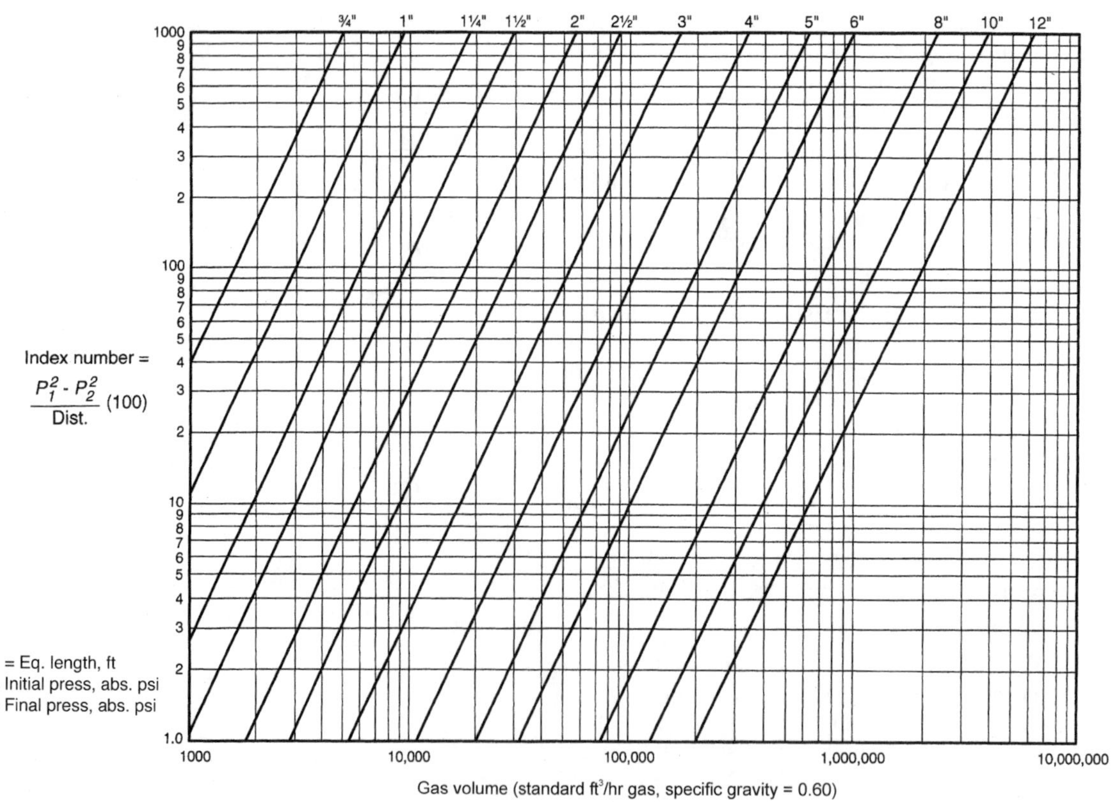

FIGURE A.6 (b)
CAPACITY OF NATURAL GAS PIPING, HIGH PRESSURE (1.5 psi and above)

A.7 Examples of piping system design and sizing.

A.7.1 Example 1: Longest length method. Determine the required pipe size of each section and *outlet* of the *piping* system shown in Figure A.7.1, with a designated pressure drop of 0.5-inch w.c. (125 Pa) using the Longest Length Method. The gas to be used has 0.60 specific gravity and a heating value of 1,000 Btu/ft^3 (37.5 MJ/m^3).

Solution:

(1) Maximum gas demand for *Outlet* A:

$$\frac{\text{Consumption (rating plate input, or Table 402.2 if necessary)}}{\text{Btu of gas}} =$$

$$\frac{\text{35,000 Btu per hour rating}}{\text{1,000 Btu per cubic foot}} = \text{35 cubic feet per hour} = \text{35 cfh}$$

Maximum gas demand for *Outlet* B:

$$\frac{\text{Consumption}}{\text{Btu of gas}} = \frac{75{,}000}{1{,}000} = \text{75 cfh}$$

Maximum gas demand for *Outlet* C:

$$\frac{\text{Consumption}}{\text{Btu of gas}} = \frac{35{,}000}{1{,}000} = \text{35 cfh}$$

Maximum gas demand for *Outlet* D:

$$\frac{\text{Consumption}}{\text{Btu of gas}} = \frac{100{,}000}{1{,}000} = \text{100 cfh}$$

(2) The length of pipe from the *point of delivery* to the most remote *outlet* (A) is 60 feet (18 288 mm). This is the only distance used.

(3) Using the row marked 60 feet (18 288 mm) in Table 402.4(2):

(a) *Outlet* A, supplying 35 cfh (0.99 m^3/hr), requires $^1/_2$-inch pipe.

(b) *Outlet* B, supplying 75 cfh (2.12 m^3/hr), requires $^3/_4$-inch pipe.

(c) Section 1, supplying *Outlets* A and B, or 110 cfh (3.11 m^3/hr), requires $^3/_4$-inch pipe.

(d) Section 2, supplying *Outlets* C and D, or 135 cfh (3.82 m^3/hr), requires $^3/_4$-inch pipe.

(e) Section 3, supplying *Outlets* A, B, C and D, or 245 cfh (6.94 m^3/hr), requires 1-inch pipe.

(4) If a different gravity factor is applied to this example, the values in the row marked 60 feet (18 288 mm) of Table 402.4(2) would be multiplied by the appropriate multiplier from Table A.2.4 and the resulting cubic feet per hour values would be used to size the *piping*.

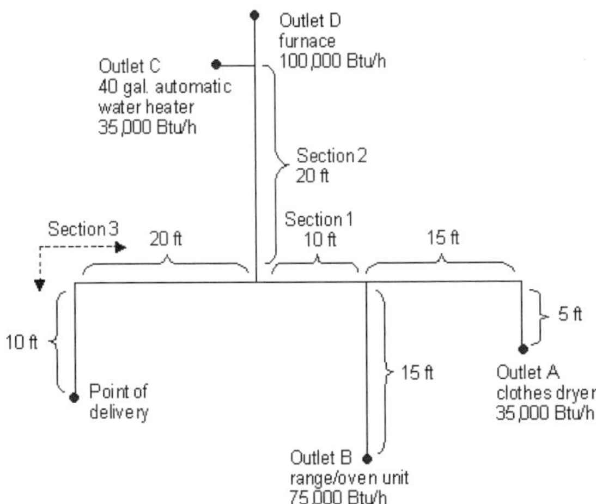

FIGURE A.7.1
PIPING PLAN SHOWING A STEEL PIPING SYSTEM

A.7.2 Example 2: Hybrid or dual pressure systems. Determine the required CSST size of each section of the *piping* system shown in Figure A.7.2, with a designated pressure drop of 1 psi (6.9 kPa) for the 2 psi (13.8 kPa) section and 3-inch w.c. (0.75 kPa) pressure drop for the 13-inch w.c. (2.49 kPa) section. The gas to be used has 0.60 specific gravity and a heating value of 1,000 Btu/ft^3 (37.5 MJ/ m^3).

Solution:

(1) Size 2 psi (13.8 kPa) line using Table 402.4(16).

(2) Size 10-inch w.c. (2.5 kPa) lines using Table 402.4(14).

(3) Using the following, determine if sizing tables can be used.

(a) Total gas load shown in Figure A.7.2 equals 110 cfh (3.11 m^3/hr).

(b) Determine pressure drop across regulator [see notes in Table 402.4 (16)].

(c) If pressure drop across regulator exceeds $^3/_4$ psig (5.2 kPa), Table 402.4 (16) cannot be used. Note: If pressure drop exceeds $^3/_4$ psi (5.2 kPa), then a larger regulator must be selected or an alternative sizing method must be used.

(d) Pressure drop across the line regulator [for 110 cfh (3.11 m^3/hr)] is 4-inch w.c. (0.99 kPa) based on manufacturer's performance data.

(e) Assume the CSST manufacturer has tubing sizes or EHDs of 13, 18, 23 and 30.

(4) Section A [2 psi (13.8 kPa) zone]

(a) Distance from meter to regulator = 100 feet (30 480 mm).

(b) Total load supplied by A = 110 cfh (3.11 m^3/hr) (furnace + water heater + dryer).

(c) Table 402.4 (16) shows that EHD size 18 should be used.

Note: It is not unusual to oversize the supply line by 25 to 50 percent of the as-installed load. EHD size 18 has a capacity of 189 cfh (5.35 m^3/hr).

(5) Section B (low pressure zone)

(a) Distance from regulator to furnace is 15 feet (4572 mm).

(b) Load is 60 cfh (1.70 m^3/hr).

(c) Table 402.4 (14) shows that EHD size 13 should be used.

(6) Section C (low pressure zone)

(a) Distance from regulator to water heater is 10 feet (3048 mm).

(b) Load is 30 cfh (0.85 m^3/hr).

(c) Table 402.4 (14) shows that EHD size 13 should be used.

(7) Section D (low pressure zone)

(a) Distance from regulator to dryer is 25 feet (7620 mm).

(b) Load is 20 cfh (0.57 m^3/hr).

(c) Table 402.4(14) shows that EHD size 13 should be used.

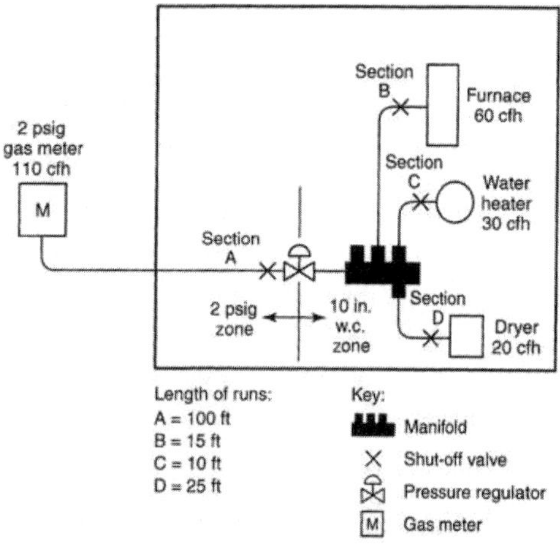

FIGURE A.7.2
PIPING PLAN SHOWING A CSST SYSTEM

A.7.3 Example 3: Branch length method. Determine the required semirigid copper tubing size of each section of the *piping* system shown in Figure A.7.3, with a designated pressure drop of 1-inch w.c. (250 Pa) (using the Branch Length Method). The gas to be used has 0.60 specific gravity and a heating value of 1,000 Btu/ft^3 (37.5 MJ/m^3).

Solution:

(1) Section A

(a) The length of tubing from the *point of delivery* to the most remote *appliance* is 50 feet (15 240 mm), A + C.

(b) Use this longest length to size Sections A and C.

(c) Using the row marked 50 feet (15 240 mm) in Table 402.4(8), Section A, supplying 220 cfh (6.2 m^3/hr) for four appliances requires 1-inch tubing.

(2) Section B

(a) The length of tubing from the *point of delivery* to the range/oven at the end of Section B is 30 feet (9144 mm), A + B.

(b) Use this branch length to size Section B only.

(c) Using the row marked 30 feet (9144 mm) in Table 402.4(8), Section B, supplying 75 cfh (2.12 m^3/hr) for the range/oven requires $^1/_2$-inch tubing.

(3) Section C

(a) The length of tubing from the *point of delivery* to the dryer at the end of Section C is 50 feet (15 240 mm), A + C.

(b) Use this branch length (which is also the longest length) to size Section C.

(c) Using the row marked 50 feet (15 240 mm) in Table 402.4(8), Section C, supplying 30 cfh (0.85 m^3/hr) for the dryer requires $^3/_8$-inch tubing.

(4) Section D

(a) The length of tubing from the *point of delivery* to the water heater at the end of Section D is 30 feet (9144 mm), A + D.

(b) Use this branch length to size Section D only.

(c) Using the row marked 30 feet (9144 mm) in Table 402.4(8), Section D, supplying 35 cfh (0.99 m^3/hr) for the water heater requires $^3/_8$-inch tubing.

(5) Section E

(a) The length of tubing from the *point of delivery* to the furnace at the end of Section E is 30 feet (9144 mm), A + E.

(b) Use this branch length to size Section E only.

(c) Using the row marked 30 feet (9144 mm) in Table 402.4(8), Section E, supplying 80 cfh (2.26 m^3/hr) for the furnace requires $^1/_2$-inch tubing.

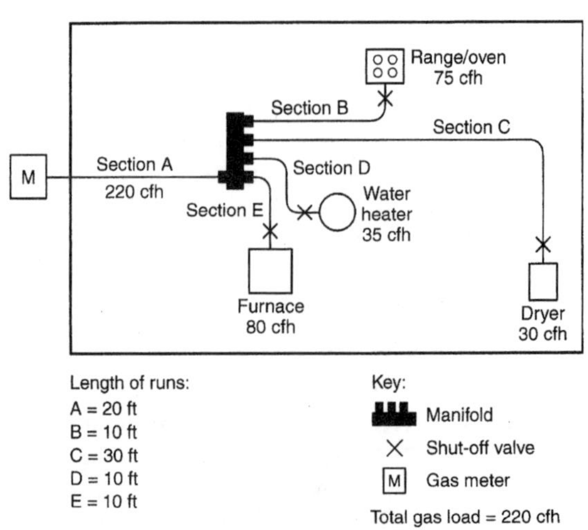

FIGURE A.7.3
PIPING PLAN SHOWING A COPPER TUBING SYSTEM

A.7.4 Example 4: Modification to existing piping system. Determine the required CSST size for Section G (retrofit application) of the *piping* system shown in Figure A.7.4, with a designated pressure drop of 0.5-inch w.c. (125 Pa) using the branch length method. The gas to be used has 0.60 specific gravity and a heating value of 1,000 Btu/ft^3 (37.5 MJ/m^3).

Solution:

(1) The length of pipe and CSST from the *point of delivery* to the retrofit *appliance* (barbecue) at the end of Section G is 40 feet (12 192 mm), A + B + G.

(2) Use this branch length to size Section G.

(3) Assume the CSST manufacturer has tubing sizes or EHDs of 13, 18, 23 and 30.

(4) Using the row marked 40 feet (12 192 mm) in Table 402.4(13), Section G, supplying 40 cfh (1.13 m^3/hr) for the barbecue requires EHD 18 CSST.

(5) The sizing of Sections A, B, F and E must be checked to ensure adequate gas carrying capacity since an *appliance* has been added to the *piping* system (see A.7.1 for details).

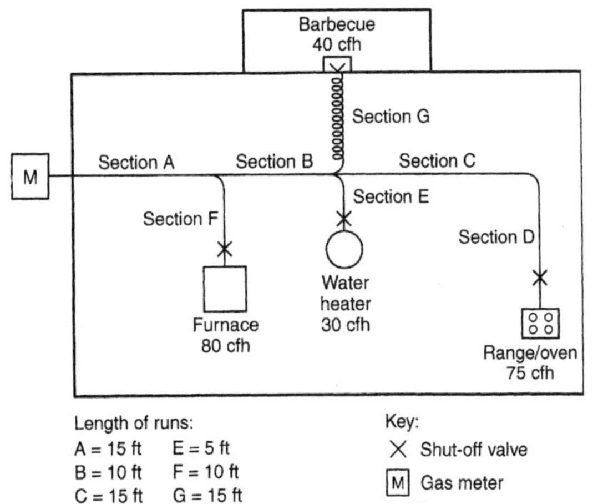

FIGURE A.7.4
PIPING PLAN SHOWING A MODIFICATION TO EXISTING PIPING SYSTEM

A.7.5 Example 5: Calculating pressure drops due to temperature changes. A test *piping* system is installed on a warm autumn afternoon when the temperature is 70°F (21°C). In accordance with local custom, the new *piping* system is subjected to an air pressure test at 20 psig (138 kPa). Overnight, the temperature drops and when the inspector shows up first thing in the morning the temperature is 40°F (4°C).

If the volume of the *piping* system is unchanged, then the formula based on Boyle's and Charles' law for determining the new pressure at a reduced temperature is as follows:

$$\frac{T_1}{T_2} = \frac{P_1}{P_2}$$

where:

T_1 = Initial temperature, absolute (T_1 + 459)

T_2 = Final temperature, absolute (T_2 + 459)

P_1 = Initial pressure, psia (P_1 + 14.7)

P_2 = Final pressure, psia (P_2 + 14.7)

$$\frac{(70+459)}{(40+459)} = \frac{(20+14.7)}{(P_2+14.7)}$$

$$\frac{529}{499} = \frac{34.7}{(P_2+14.7)}$$

$$(P_2+14.7) \times \frac{529}{499} = 34.7$$

$$(P_2+14.7) = \frac{34.7}{1.060}$$

$$P_2 = 32.7 - 14.7$$

$$P_2 = 18\,psig$$

Therefore, the gauge could be expected to register 18 psig (124 kPa) when the ambient temperature is 40°F (4°C)≈

A7.6 Example 6: Pressure drop per 100 feet of pipe method. Using the layout shown in Figure A.7.1 and ΔH = pressure drop, in w.c. (27.7 in. H_2O = 1 psi), proceed as follows:

(1) Length to A = 20 feet, with 35,000 Btu/hr.

For $^1/_2$-inch pipe, $\Delta H = {}^{20\text{ feet}}/_{100\text{ feet}} \times 0.3$ inch w.c. = 0.06 in w.c.

(2) Length to B = 15 feet, with 75,000 Btu/hr.

For $^3/_4$-inch pipe, $\Delta H = {}^{15\text{ feet}}/_{100\text{ feet}} \times 0.3$ inch w.c. = 0.045 in w.c.

(3) Section 1 = 10 feet, with 110,000 Btu/hr. Here there is a choice:

For 1 inch pipe: $\Delta H = {}^{10\text{ feet}}/_{100\text{ feet}} \times 0.2$ inch w.c. = 0.02 in w.c.

For $^3/_4$-inch pipe: $\Delta H = {}^{10\text{ feet}}/_{100\text{ feet}} \times$ [0.5 inch w.c. + ${}^{(110{,}000\text{ Btu/hr}-104{,}000\text{ Btu/hr})}/_{(147{,}000\text{ Btu/hr}-104{,}000\text{ Btu/hr})} \times$ (1.0 inches w.c. - 0.5 inch w.c.)] = 0.1 × 0.57 inch w.c.≈ 0.06 inch w.c.

Note that the pressure drop between 104,000 Btu/hr and 147,000 Btu/hr has been interpolated as 110,000 Btu/hr.

(4) Section 2 = 20 feet, with 135,000 Btu/hr. Here there is a choice:

For 1-inch pipe: $\Delta H = {}^{20\text{ feet}}/_{100\text{ feet}} \times$ [0.2 inch w.c. + ${}^{(14{,}000\text{ Btu/hr})}/_{(27{,}000\text{ Btu/hr})} \times 0.1$ inch w.c.)] = 0.05 inch w.c.)]

For $^3/_4$-inch pipe: $\Delta H = {}^{20\text{ feet}}/_{100\text{ feet}} \times 1.0$ inch w.c. = 0.2 inch w.c.)

Note that the pressure drop between 121,000 Btu/hr and 148,000 Btu/hr has been interpolated as 135,000 Btu/hr, but interpolation for the ¾-inch pipe (trivial for 104,000 Btu/hr to 147,000 Btu/hr) was not used.

(5) Section 3 = 30 feet, with 245,000 Btu/hr. Here there is a choice:

For 1-inch pipe: $\Delta H = {}^{30\text{ feet}}/_{100\text{ feet}} \times 1.0$ inches w.c. = 0.3 inch w.c.

For $1^1/_4$-inch pipe: $\Delta H = {}^{30\text{ feet}}/_{100\text{ feet}} \times 0.2$ inch w.c. = 0.06 inch w.c.

Note that interpolation for these options is ignored since the table values are close to the 245,000 Btu/hr carried by that section.

(6) The total pressure drop is the sum of the section approaching A, Sections 1 and 3, or either of the following, depending on whether an absolute minimum is needed or the larger drop can be accommodated.

Minimum pressure drop to farthest *appliance*:

ΔH = 0.06 inch w.c. + 0.02 inch w.c. + 0.06 inch w.c. = 0.14 inch w.c.

Larger pressure drop to the farthest *appliance*:

ΔH = 0.06 inch w.c. + 0.06 inch w.c. + 0.3 inch w.c. = 0.42 inch w.c.

Notice that Section 2 and the run to B do not enter into this calculation, provided that the appliances have similar input pressure requirements.

For SI units: 1 Btu/hr = 0.293 W, 1 cubic foot = 0.028 m^3, 1 foot = 0.305 m, 1 inch w.c. = 249 Pa.

APPENDIX B (IFGS)

SIZING OF VENTING SYSTEMS SERVING APPLIANCES EQUIPPED WITH DRAFT HOODS, CATEGORY I APPLIANCES, AND APPLIANCES LISTED FOR USE WITH TYPE B VENTS

(This appendix is informative and is not part of the code.)

EXAMPLES USING SINGLE APPLIANCE VENTING TABLES

Example 1: Single draft-hood-equipped appliance.

An installer has a 120,000 British thermal unit (Btu) per hour input *appliance* with a 5-inch-diameter draft hood outlet that needs to be vented into a 10-foot-high Type B vent system. What size vent should be used assuming (a) a 5-foot lateral single-wall metal vent connector is used with two 90-degree elbows, or (b) a 5-foot lateral single-wall metal vent connector is used with three 90-degree elbows in the vent system?

Solution:

Table 504.2(2) should be used to solve this problem, because single-wall metal vent connectors are being used with a Type B vent.

(a) Read down the first column in Table 504.2(2) until the row associated with a 10-foot height and 5-foot lateral is found. Read across this row until a vent capacity greater than 120,000 Btu per hour is located in the shaded columns *labeled* "NAT Max" for draft-hood-equipped appliances. In this case, a 5-inch-diameter vent has a capacity of 122,000 Btu per hour and may be used for this application.

(b) If three 90-degree elbows are used in the vent system, then the maximum vent capacity listed in the tables must be reduced by 10 percent (see Section 504.2.3 for single *appliance* vents). This implies that the 5-inch-diameter vent has an adjusted capacity of only 110,000 Btu per hour. In this case, the vent system must be increased to 6 inches in diameter (see calculations below).

122,000 (.90) = 110,000 for 5-inch vent
From Table 504.2(2), Select 6-inch vent
186,000 (.90) = 167,000; This is greater than the required 120,000. Therefore, use a 6-inch vent and connector where three elbows are used.

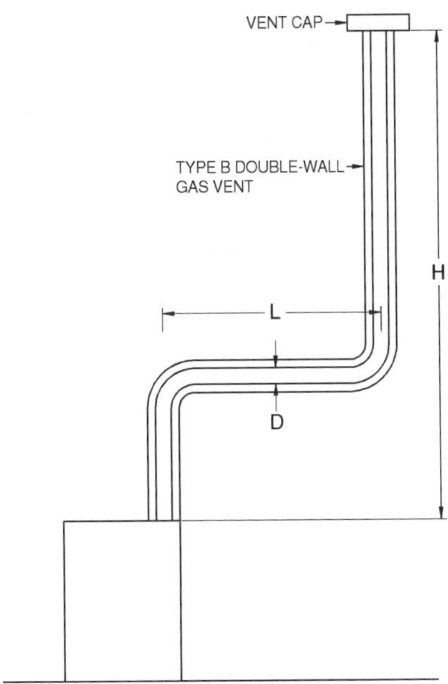

For SI: 1 foot = 304.8 mm, 1 British thermal unit per hour = 0.2931 W.

Table 504.2(1) is used when sizing Type B double-wall gas vent connected directly to the appliance.

Note: The appliance may be either Category I draft hood equipped or fan-assisted type.

FIGURE B-1
TYPE B DOUBLE-WALL VENT SYSTEM SERVING A SINGLE APPLIANCE WITH A TYPE B DOUBLE-WALL VENT

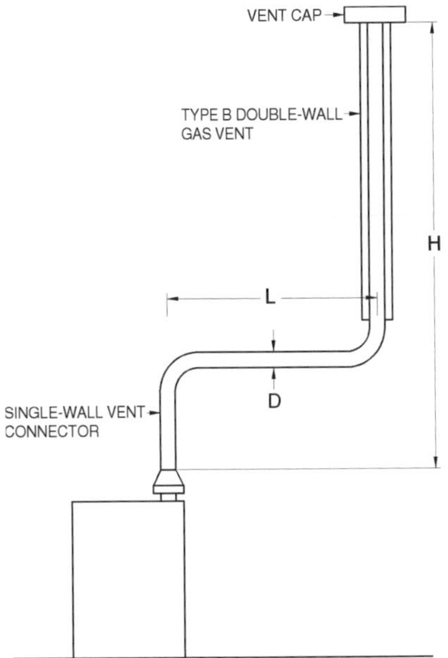

For SI: 1 foot = 304.8 mm, 1 British thermal unit per hour = 0.2931W.

Table 504.2(2) is used when sizing a single-wall metal vent connector attached to a Type B double-wall gas vent.

Note: The appliance may be either Category I draft hood equipped or fan-assisted type.

FIGURE B-2
TYPE B DOUBLE-WALL VENT SYSTEM SERVING A SINGLE APPLIANCE WITH A SINGLE-WALL METAL VENT CONNECTOR

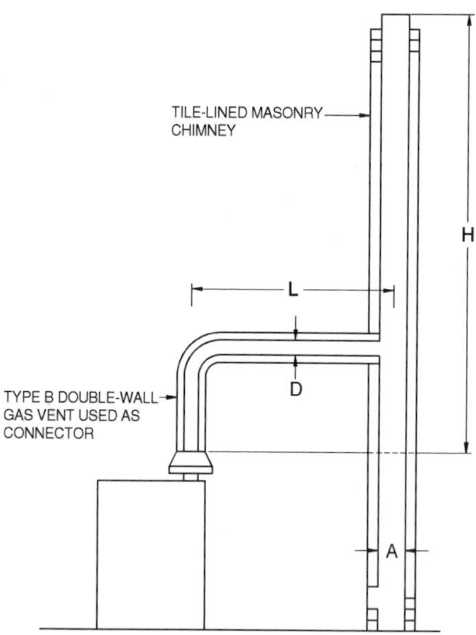

Table 504.2(3) is used when sizing a Type B double-wall gas vent connector attached to a tile-lined masonry chimney.

Note: "A" is the equivalent cross-sectional area of the tile liner.

Note: The appliance may be either Category I draft hood equipped or fan-assisted type.

FIGURE B-3
VENT SYSTEM SERVING A SINGLE APPLIANCE WITH A MASONRY CHIMNEY OF TYPE B DOUBLE-WALL VENT CONNECTOR

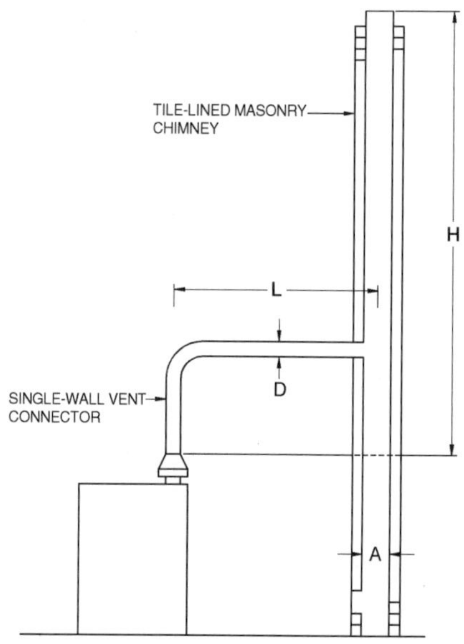

Table 504.2(4) is used when sizing a single-wall vent connector attached to a tile-lined masonry chimney.

Note: "A" is the equivalent cross-sectional area of the tile liner.

Note: The appliance may be either Category I draft hood equipped or fan-assisted type.

FIGURE B-4
VENT SYSTEM SERVING A SINGLE APPLIANCE USING A MASONRY CHIMNEY AND A SINGLE-WALL METAL VENT CONNECTOR

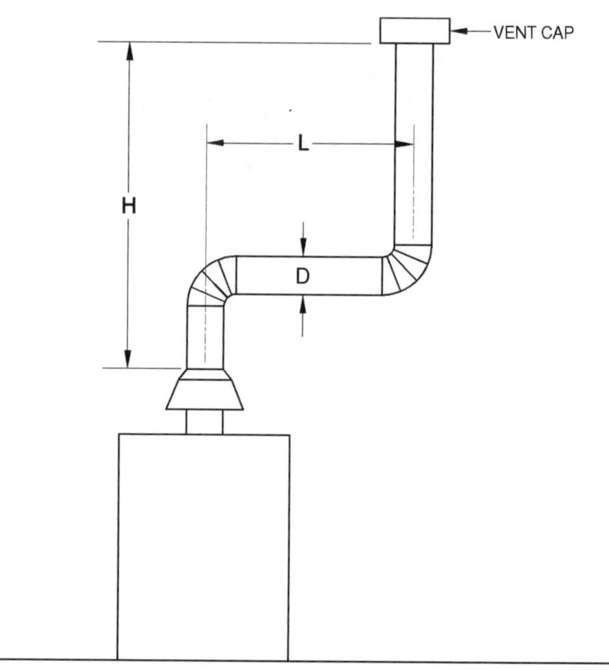

Asbestos cement Type B or single-wall metal vent serving a single draft-hood-equipped appliance [see Table 504.2(5)].

FIGURE B-5
ASBESTOS CEMENT TYPE B OR SINGLE-WALL METAL VENT SYSTEM SERVING A SINGLE DRAFT-HOOD-EQUIPPED APPLIANCE

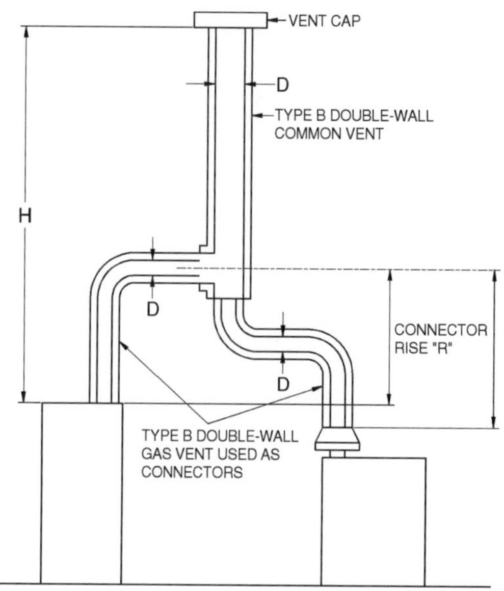

Table 504.3(1) is used when sizing Type B double-wall vent connectors attached to a Type B double-wall common vent.

Note: Each appliance may be either Category I draft hood equipped or fan-assisted type.

FIGURE B-6
VENT SYSTEM SERVING TWO OR MORE APPLIANCES WITH TYPE B DOUBLE-WALL VENT AND TYPE B DOUBLE-WALL VENT CONNECTOR

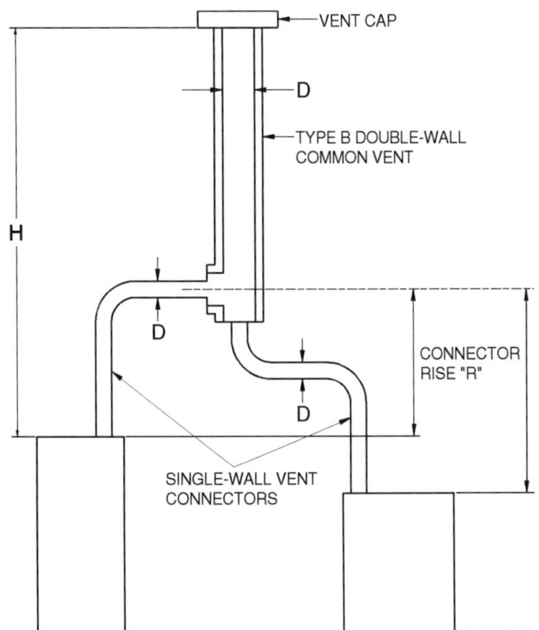

Table 504.3(2) is used when sizing single-wall vent connectors attached to a Type B double-wall common vent.

Note: Each appliance may be either Category I draft hood equipped or fan-assisted type.

FIGURE B-7
VENT SYSTEM SERVING TWO OR MORE APPLIANCES WITH TYPE B DOUBLE-WALL VENT AND SINGLE-WALL METAL VENT CONNECTORS

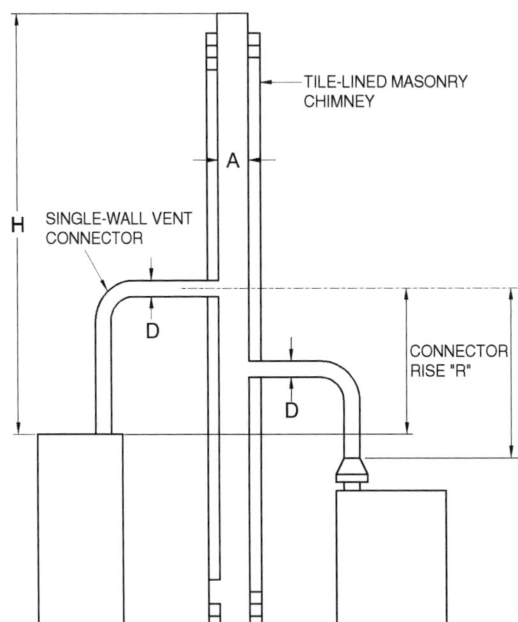

Table 504.3(4) is used when sizing single-wall metal vent connectors attached to a tile-lined masonry chimney.

Note: "A" is the equivalent cross-sectional area of the tile liner.

Note: Each appliance may be either Category I draft hood equipped or fan-assisted type.

FIGURE B-9
MASONRY CHIMNEY SERVING TWO OR MORE APPLIANCES WITH SINGLE-WALL METAL VENT CONNECTORS

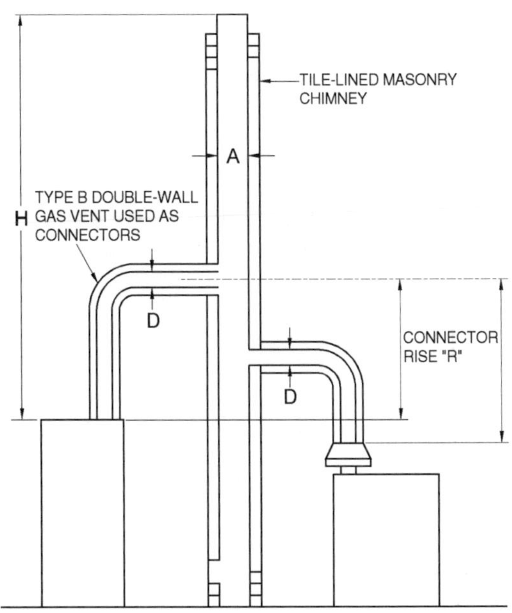

Table 504.3(3) is used when sizing Type B double-wall vent connectors attached to a tile-lined masonry chimney.

Note: "A" is the equivalent cross-sectional area of the tile liner.

Note: Each appliance may be either Category I draft hood equipped or fan-assisted type.

FIGURE B-8
MASONRY CHIMNEY SERVING TWO OR MORE APPLIANCES WITH TYPE B DOUBLE-WALL VENT CONNECTOR

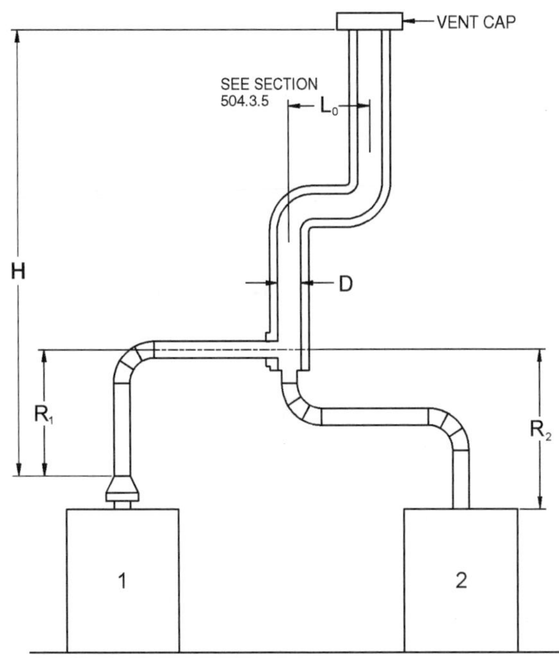

Asbestos cement Type B or single-wall metal pipe vent serving two or more draft-hood-equipped appliances [see Table 504.3(5)].

FIGURE B-10
ASBESTOS CEMENT TYPE B OR SINGLE-WALL METAL VENT SYSTEM SERVING TWO OR MORE DRAFT-HOOD-EQUIPPED APPLIANCES

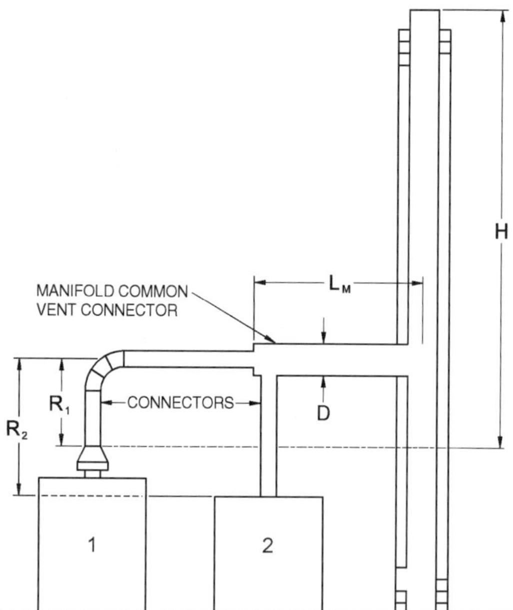

Example: Manifolded Common Vent Connector L_M shall be no greater than 18 times the common vent connector manifold inside diameter; i.e., a 4-inch (102 mm) inside diameter common vent connector manifold shall not exceed 72 inches (1829 mm) in length (see Section 504.3.4).

Note: This is an illustration of a typical manifolded vent connector. Different appliance, vent connector, or common vent types are possible. Consult Section 502.3.

FIGURE B-11
USE OF MANIFOLD COMMON VENT CONNECTOR

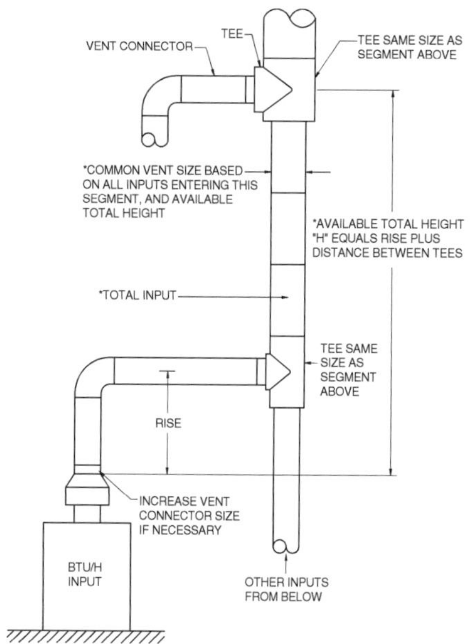

Vent connector size depends on:

- Input
- Rise
- Available total height "*H*"
- Table 504.3(1) connectors

Common vent size depends on:

- Combined inputs
- Available total height "*H*"
- Table 504.3(1) common vent

FIGURE B-13
MULTISTORY GAS VENT DESIGN PROCEDURE FOR EACH SEGMENT OF SYSTEM

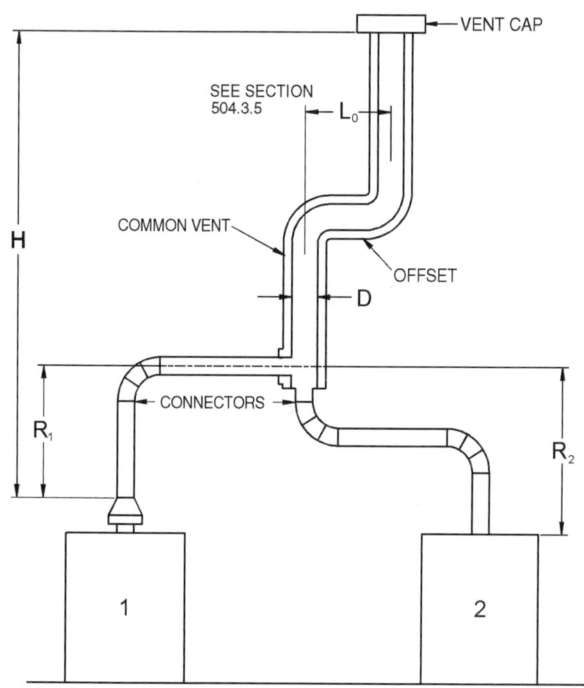

Example: Offset Common Vent

Note: This is an illustration of a typical offset vent. Different appliance, vent connector, or vent types are possible. Consult Sections 504.2 and 504.3.

FIGURE B-12
USE OF OFFSET COMMON VENT

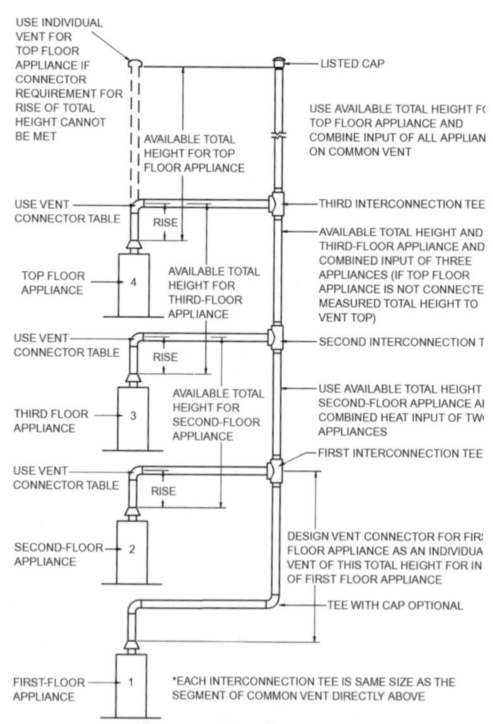

Principles of design of multistory vents using vent connector and common vent design tables (see Sections 504.3.11 through 504.3.17).

FIGURE B-14
MULTISTORY VENT SYSTEMS

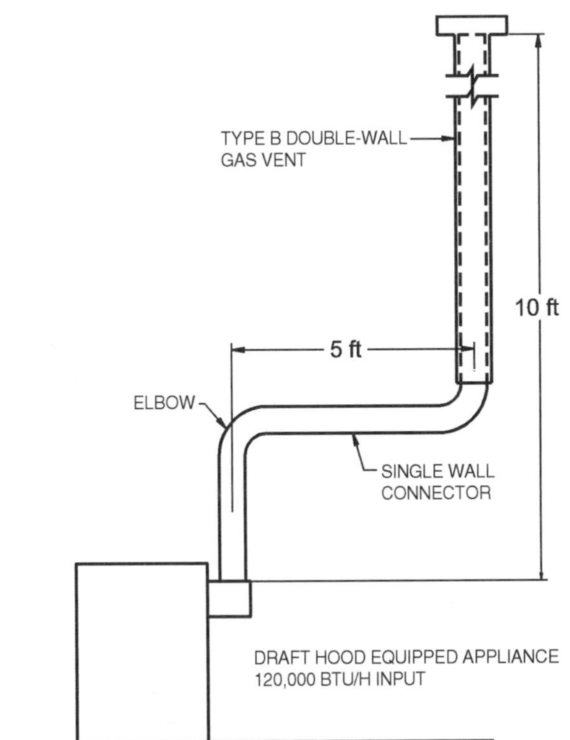

For SI: 1 foot = 304.8 mm, 1 British thermal unit per hour = 0.2931 W.

FIGURE B-15 (EXAMPLE 1)
SINGLE DRAFT-HOOD-EQUIPPED APPLIANCE

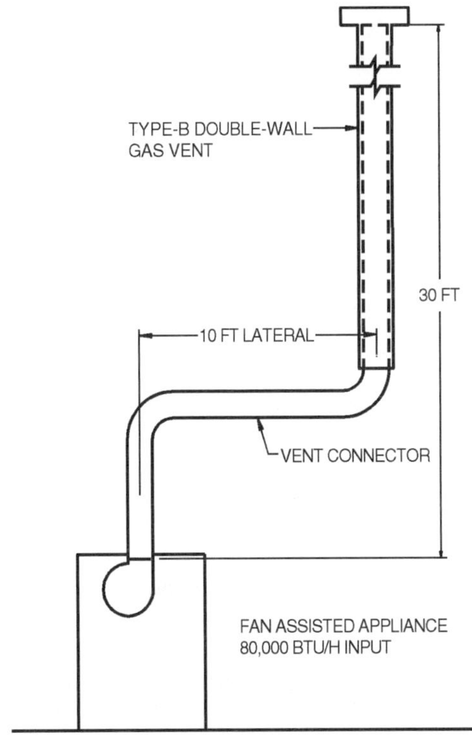

For SI: 1 foot = 304.8 mm, 1 British thermal unit per hour = 0.2931 W.

FIGURE B-16 (EXAMPLE 2)
SINGLE FAN-ASSISTED APPLIANCE

Example 2: Single fan-assisted appliance.

An installer has an 80,000 Btu per hour input fan-assisted *appliance* that must be installed using 10 feet of lateral connector attached to a 30-foot-high Type B vent. Two 90-degree elbows are needed for the installation. Can a single-wall metal vent connector be used for this application?

Solution:

Table 504.2(2) refers to the use of single-wall metal vent connectors with Type B vent. In the first column find the row associated with a 30-foot height and a 10-foot lateral. Read across this row, looking at the FAN Min and FAN Max columns, to find that a 3-inch-diameter single-wall metal vent connector is not recommended. Moving to the next larger size single wall connector (4 inches), note that a 4-inch-diameter single-wall metal connector has a recommended minimum vent capacity of 91,000 Btu per hour and a recommended maximum vent capacity of 144,000 Btu per hour. The 80,000 Btu per hour fan-assisted *appliance* is outside this range, so the conclusion is that a single-wall metal vent connector cannot be used to vent this *appliance* using 10 feet of lateral for the connector.

However, if the 80,000 Btu per hour input *appliance* could be moved to within 5 feet of the vertical vent, then a 4-inch single-wall metal connector could be used to vent the *appliance*. Table 504.2(2) shows the acceptable range of vent capacities for a 4-inch vent with 5 feet of lateral to be between 72,000 Btu per hour and 157,000 Btu per hour.

If the *appliance* cannot be moved closer to the vertical vent, then Type B vent could be used as the connector material. In this case, Table 504.2(1) shows that for a 30-foot-high vent with 10 feet of lateral, the acceptable range of vent capacities for a 4-inch-diameter vent attached to a fan-assisted *appliance* is between 37,000 Btu per hour and 150,000 Btu per hour.

Example 3: Interpolating between table values.

An installer has an 80,000 Btu per hour input *appliance* with a 4-inch-diameter draft hood outlet that needs to be vented into a 12-foot-high Type B vent. The vent connector has a 5-foot lateral length and is also Type B. Can this *appliance* be vented using a 4-inch-diameter vent?

Solution:

Table 504.2(1) is used in the case of an all Type B vent system. However, since there is no entry in Table 504.2(1) for a height of 12 feet, interpolation must be used. Read down the 4-inch diameter NAT Max column to the row associated with 10-foot height and 5-foot lateral to find the capacity value of 77,000 Btu per hour. Read further down to the 15-foot height, 5-foot lateral row to find the capacity value of 87,000 Btu per hour. The difference between the 15-foot height capacity value and the 10-foot height capacity value is 10,000 Btu per hour. The capacity for a vent system with a 12-foot height is equal to the capacity for a 10-foot height plus $^2/_5$ of the difference between the 10-foot and 15-foot height values, or $77,000 + ^2/_5(10,000) = 81,000$ Btu per hour. Therefore, a 4-inch-diameter vent may be used in the installation.

EXAMPLES USING COMMON VENTING TABLES

Example 4: Common venting two draft-hood-equipped appliances.

A 35,000 Btu per hour water heater is to be common vented with a 150,000 Btu per hour furnace using a common vent with a total height of 30 feet. The connector rise is 2 feet for the water heater with a horizontal length of 4 feet. The connector rise for the furnace is 3 feet with a horizontal length of 8 feet. Assume single-wall metal connectors will be used with Type B vent. What size connectors and combined vent should be used in this installation?

Solution:

Table 504.3(2) should be used to size single-wall metal vent connectors attached to Type B vertical vents. In the vent connector capacity portion of Table 504.3(2), find the row associated with a 30-foot vent height. For a 2-foot rise on the vent connector for the water heater, read the shaded columns for draft-hood-equipped appliances to find that a 3-inch-diameter vent connector has a capacity of 37,000 Btu per hour. Therefore, a 3-inch single-wall metal vent connector may be used with the water heater. For a draft-hood-equipped furnace with a 3-foot rise, read across the appropriate row to find that a 5-inch-diameter vent connector has a maximum capacity of 120,000 Btu per hour (which is too small for the furnace) and a 6-inch-diameter vent connector has a maximum vent capacity of 172,000 Btu per hour. Therefore, a 6-inch-diameter vent connector should be used with the 150,000 Btu per hour furnace. Since both vent connector horizontal lengths are less than the maximum lengths *listed* in Section 504.3.2, the table values may be used without adjustments.

In the common vent capacity portion of Table 504.3(2), find the row associated with a 30-foot vent height and read over to the NAT + NAT portion of the 6-inch-diameter column to find a maximum combined capacity of 257,000 Btu per hour. Since the two appliances total only 185,000 Btu per hour, a 6-inch common vent may be used.

Example 5a: Common venting a draft-hood-equipped water heater with a fan-assisted furnace into a Type B vent.

In this case, a 35,000 Btu per hour input draft-hood-equipped water heater with a 4-inch-diameter draft hood *outlet*, 2 feet of connector rise, and 4 feet of horizontal length is to be common vented with a 100,000 Btu per hour fan-assisted furnace with a 4-inch-diameter flue collar, 3 feet of connector rise, and 6 feet of horizontal length. The common vent consists of a 30-foot height of Type B vent. What are the recommended vent diameters for each connector and the common vent? The installer would like to use a single-wall metal vent connector.

Solution: - [Table 504.3(2)]

Water Heater Vent Connector Diameter. Since the water heater vent connector horizontal length of 4 feet is less than the maximum value listed in Section 504.3.2, the venting table values may be used without adjustments. Using the Vent Connector Capacity portion of Table 504.3(2), read down the Total Vent Height (*H*) column to 30 feet and read across the 2-foot Connector Rise (*R*) row to the first Btu per hour rating in the NAT Max column that is equal to or greater than the water heater input rating. The table shows that a 3-inch vent connector has a maximum input rating of 37,000 Btu per hour. Although this is greater than the water heater input rating, a 3-inch vent connector is prohibited by Section 504.3.21. A 4-inch vent connector

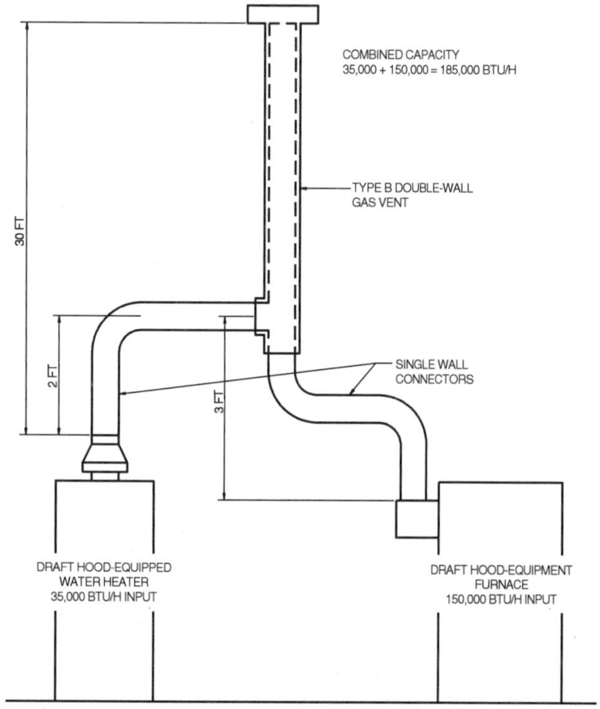

COMBINED CAPACITY
35,000 + 150,000 = 185,000 BTU/H
TYPE B DOUBLE-WALL GAS VENT
30 FT
2 FT
3 FT
SINGLE WALL CONNECTORS
DRAFT HOOD-EQUIPPED WATER HEATER 35,000 BTU/H INPUT
DRAFT HOOD-EQUIPMENT FURNACE 150,000 BTU/H INPUT

**FIGURE B-17 (EXAMPLE 4)
COMMON VENTING TWO DRAFT-HOOD-EQUIPPED APPLIANCES**

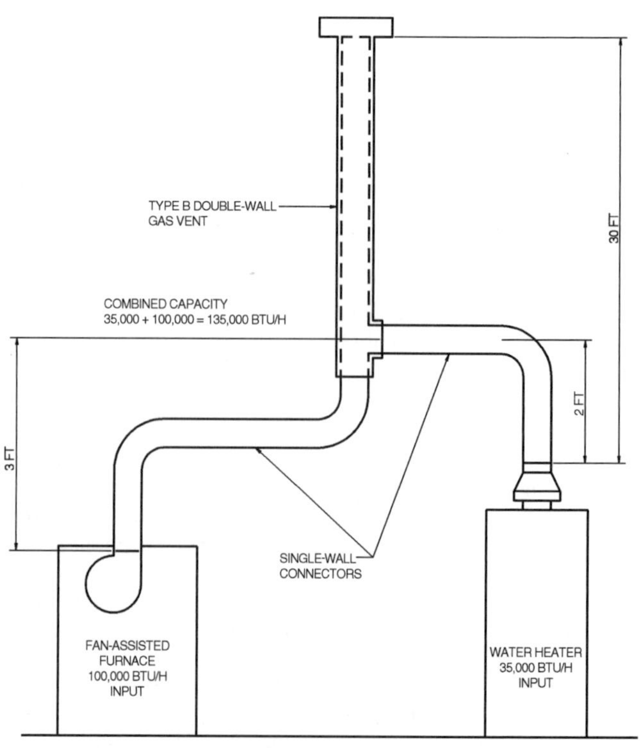

**FIGURE B-18 (EXAMPLE 5A)
COMMON VENTING A DRAFT HOOD WITH A FAN-ASSISTED FURNACE INTO A TYPE B DOUBLE-WALL COMMON VENT**

has a maximum input rating of 67,000 Btu per hour and is equal to the draft hood *outlet* diameter. A 4-inch vent connector is selected. Since the water heater is equipped with a draft hood, there are no minimum input rating restrictions.

Furnace Vent Connector Diameter. Using the Vent Connector Capacity portion of Table 504.3(2), read down the Total Vent Height (*H*) column to 30 feet and across the 3-foot Connector Rise (*R*) row. Since the furnace has a fan-assisted combustion system, find the first FAN Max column with a Btu per hour rating greater than the furnace input rating. The 4-inch vent connector has a maximum input rating of 119,000 Btu per hour and a minimum input rating of 85,000 Btu per hour. The 100,000 Btu per hour furnace in this example falls within this range, so a 4-inch connector is adequate. Since the furnace vent connector horizontal length of 6 feet does not exceed the maximum value listed in Section 504.3.2, the venting table values may be used without adjustment. If the furnace had an input rating of 80,000 Btu per hour, then a Type B vent connector [see Table 504.3(1)] would be needed in order to meet the minimum capacity limit.

Common Vent Diameter. The total input to the common vent is 135,000 Btu per hour. Using the Common Vent Capacity portion of Table 504.3(2), read down the Total Vent Height (*H*) column to 30 feet and across this row to find the smallest vent diameter in the FAN + NAT column that has a Btu per hour rating equal to or greater than 135,000 Btu per hour. The 4-inch common vent has a capacity of 132,000 Btu per hour and the 5-inch common vent has a capacity of 202,000 Btu per hour. Therefore, the 5-inch common vent should be used in this example.

Summary. In this example, the installer may use a 4-inch-diameter, single-wall metal vent connector for the water heater and a 4-inch-diameter, single-wall metal vent connector for the furnace. The common vent should be a 5-inch-diameter Type B vent.

Example 5b: Common venting into a masonry chimney.

In this case, the water heater and fan-assisted furnace of Example 5a are to be common vented into a clay tile-lined masonry chimney with a 30-foot height. The chimney is not exposed to the outdoors below the roof line. The internal dimensions of the clay tile liner are nominally 8 inches by 12 inches. Assuming the same vent connector heights, laterals, and materials found in Example 5a, what are the recommended vent connector diameters, and is this an acceptable installation?

Solution:

Table 504.3(4) is used to size common venting installations involving single-wall connectors into masonry chimneys.

Water Heater Vent Connector Diameter. Using Table 504.3(4), Vent Connector Capacity, read down the Total Vent Height (*H*) column to 30 feet, and read across the 2-foot Connector Rise (*R*) row to the first Btu per hour rating in the NAT Max column that is equal to or greater than the water heater input rating. The table shows that a 3-inch vent connector has a maximum input of only 31,000 Btu per hour while a 4-inch vent connector has a maximum input of 57,000 Btu per hour. A 4-inch vent connector must therefore be used.

Furnace Vent Connector Diameter. Using the Vent Connector Capacity portion of Table 504.3(4), read down the Total Vent Height (*H*) column to 30 feet and across the 3-foot Connector Rise (*R*) row. Since the furnace has a fan-assisted combustion system, find the first FAN Max column with a Btu per hour rating greater than the furnace input rating. The 4-inch vent connector has a maximum input rating of 127,000 Btu per hour and a minimum input rating of 95,000 Btu per hour. The 100,000 Btu per hour furnace in this example falls within this range, so a 4-inch connector is adequate.

Masonry Chimney. From Table B-1, the equivalent area for a nominal liner size of 8 inches by 12 inches is 63.6 square inches. Using Table 504.3(4), Common Vent Capacity, read down the FAN + NAT column under the Minimum Internal Area of Chimney value of 63 to the row for 30-foot height to find a capacity value of 739,000 Btu per hour. The combined input rating of the furnace and water heater, 135,000 Btu per hour, is less than the table value, so this is an acceptable installation.

Section 504.3.17 requires the common vent area to be no greater than seven times the smallest *listed appliance* categorized vent area, flue collar area, or draft hood outlet area. Both appliances in this installation have 4-inch-diameter outlets. From Table B-1, the equivalent area for an inside diameter of 4 inches is 12.2 square inches. Seven times 12.2 equals 85.4, which is greater than 63.6, so this configuration is acceptable.

Example 5c: Common venting into an exterior masonry chimney.

In this case, the water heater and fan-assisted furnace of Examples 5a and 5b are to be common vented into an exterior masonry chimney. The chimney height, clay tile liner dimensions, and vent connector heights and laterals are the same as in Example 5b. This system is being installed in Charlotte, North Carolina. Does this exterior masonry chimney need to be relined? If so, what corrugated metallic liner size is recommended? What vent connector diameters are recommended?

Solution:

According to Section 504.3.20, Type B vent connectors are required to be used with exterior masonry chimneys. Use Table 504.3(7) to size FAN+NAT common venting installations involving Type-B double wall connectors into exterior masonry chimneys.

The local 99-percent winter design temperature needed to use Table 504.3(7) can be found in the ASHRAE *Handbook of Fundamentals*. For Charlotte, North Carolina, this design temperature is 19°F.

Chimney Liner Requirement. As in Example 5b, use the 63 square inch Internal Area columns for this size clay tile liner. Read down the 63 square inch column of Table 504.3(7a) to the 30-foot height row to find that the combined *appliance* maximum input is 747,000 Btu per hour. The combined input rating of the appliances in this installation, 135,000 Btu per hour, is less than the maximum value, so this criterion is satisfied. Table 504.3(7b), at a 19°F design temperature, and at the same vent height and internal area used above, shows that the minimum allowable input rating of a space-heating appliance is 470,000 Btu per hour. The furnace input rating of 100,000 Btu per hour is less than this minimum value. So this criterion is not satisfied, and an alternative venting design needs to be used, such as a Type B vent shown in Example 5a or a *listed* chimney liner system shown in the remainder of the example.

According to Section 504.3.19, Table 504.3(1) or 504.3(2) is used for sizing corrugated metallic liners in masonry chimneys, with the maximum common vent capacities reduced by 20 percent. This example will be continued assuming Type B vent connectors.

Water Heater Vent Connector Diameter. Using Table 504.3(1), Vent Connector Capacity, read down the Total Vent Height (H) column to 30 feet, and read across the 2-foot Connector Rise (R) row to the first Btu/h rating in the NAT Max column that is equal to or greater than the water heater input rating. The table shows that a 3-inch vent connector has a maximum capacity of 39,000 Btu/h. Although this rating is greater than the water heater input rating, a 3-inch vent connector is prohibited by Section 504.3.21. A 4-inch vent connector has a maximum input rating of 70,000 Btu/h and is equal to the draft hood outlet diameter. A 4-inch vent connector is selected.

Furnace Vent Connector Diameter. Using Table 504.3(1), Vent Connector Capacity, read down the Vent Height (H) column to 30 feet, and read across the 3-foot Connector Rise (R) row to the first Btu per hour rating in the FAN Max column that is equal to or greater than the furnace input rating. The 100,000 Btu per hour furnace in this example falls within this range, so a 4-inch connector is adequate.

Chimney Liner Diameter. The total input to the common vent is 135,000 Btu per hour. Using the Common Vent Capacity Portion of Table 504.3(1), read down the Vent Height (H) column to 30 feet and across this row to find the smallest vent diameter in the FAN+NAT column that has a Btu per hour rating greater than 135,000 Btu per hour. The 4-inch common vent has a capacity of 138,000 Btu per hour. Reducing the maximum capacity by 20 percent (Section 504.3.19) results in a maximum capacity for a 4-inch corrugated liner of 110,000 Btu per hour, less than the total input of 135,000 Btu per hour. So a larger liner is needed. The 5-inch common vent capacity *listed* in Table 504.3(1) is 210,000 Btu per hour, and after reducing by 20 percent is 168,000 Btu per hour. Therefore, a 5-inch corrugated metal liner should be used in this example.

Single-Wall Connectors. Once it has been established that relining the chimney is necessary, Type B double-wall vent connectors are not specifically required. This example could be redone using Table 504.3(2) for single-wall vent connectors. For this case, the vent connector and liner diameters would be the same as found above with Type B double-wall connectors.

TABLE B-1
MASONRY CHIMNEY LINER DIMENSIONS WITH CIRCULAR EQUIVALENTS[a]

NOMINAL LINER SIZE (inches)	INSIDE DIMENSIONS OF LINER (inches)	INSIDE DIAMETER OR EQUIVALENT DIAMETER (inches)	EQUIVALENT AREA (square inches)
4 × 8	$2\,^{1}/_{2} \times 6\,^{1}/_{2}$	4	12.2
		5	19.6
		6	28.3
		7	38.3
8 × 8	$6\,^{3}/_{4} \times 6\,^{3}/_{4}$	7.4	42.7
		8	50.3
8 × 12	$6^{1}/_{2} \times 10^{1}/_{2}$	9	63.6
		10	78.5
12 × 12	$9\,^{3}/_{4} \times 9\,^{3}/_{4}$	10.4	83.3
		11	95
12 × 16	$9^{1}/_{2} \times 13^{1}/_{2}$	11.8	107.5
		12	113.0
		14	153.9
16 × 16	$13^{1}/_{4} \times 13^{1}/_{4}$	14.5	162.9
		15	176.7
16 × 20	13 × 17	16.2	206.1
		18	254.4
20 × 20	$16^{3}/_{4} \times 16^{3}/_{4}$	18.2	260.2
		20	314.1
20 × 24	$16^{1}/_{2} \times 20^{1}/_{2}$	20.1	314.2
		22	380.1
24 × 24	$20^{1}/_{4} \times 20^{1}/_{4}$	22.1	380.1
		24	452.3
24 × 28	$20^{1}/_{4} \times 20^{1}/_{4}$	24.1	456.2
28 × 28	$24^{1}/_{4} \times 24^{1}/_{4}$	26.4	543.3
		27	572.5
30 × 30	$25^{1}/_{2} \times 25^{1}/_{2}$	27.9	607
		30	706.8
30 × 36	$25^{1}/_{2} \times 31^{1}/_{2}$	30.9	749.9
		33	855.3
36 × 36	$31^{1}/_{2} \times 31^{1}/_{2}$	34.4	929.4
		36	1017.9

For SI: 1 inch = 25.4 mm, 1 square inch = 645.16 m^2.

a. Where liner sizes differ dimensionally from those shown in Table B-1, equivalent diameters may be determined from published tables for square and rectangular ducts of equivalent carrying capacity or by other engineering methods.

5°F
(-15°C)
-10°F
(-23°C)
17°F
(-8°C)
27°F
(-3°C)
37°F
(3°C)
-10°F
(-23°C)
-10°F
(-23°C)
5°F
(-15°C)
17°F
(-8°C)
27°F
(-3°C)
37°F
(3°C)

FIGURE B-19

APPENDIX C (IFGS)

EXIT TERMINALS OF MECHANICAL DRAFT AND DIRECT-VENT VENTING SYSTEMS

(This appendix is informative and is not part of the code.)

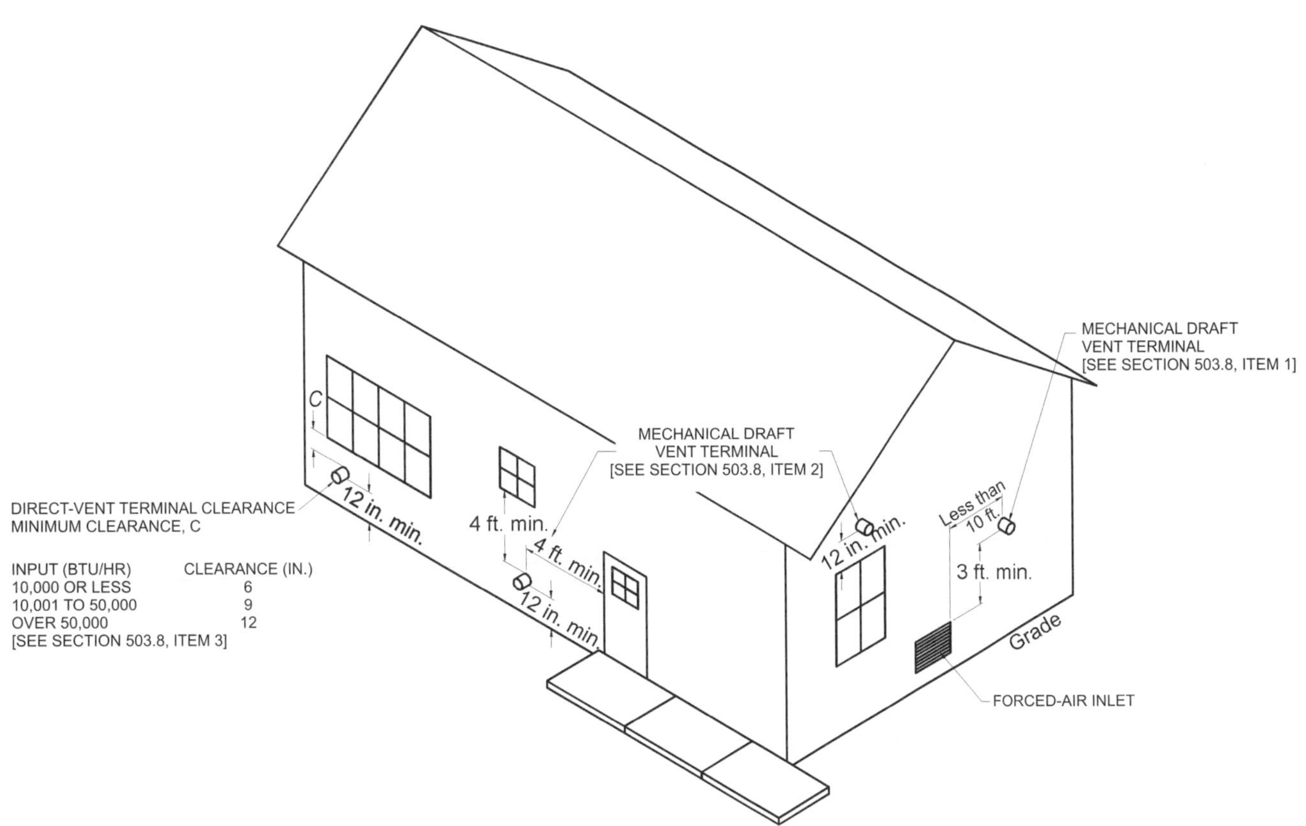

For SI: 1 inch = 25.4 mm, 1 foot = 304.8 mm, 1 British thermal unit per hour = 0.2931 W.

APPENDIX C
EXIT TERMINALS OF MECHANICAL DRAFT AND DIRECT-VENT VENTING SYSTEMS

APPENDIX D (IFGS)

RECOMMENDED PROCEDURE FOR SAFETY INSPECTION OF AN EXISTING APPLIANCE INSTALLATION

(This appendix is informative and is not part of the code.)

The following procedure is intended as a guide to aid in determining that an *appliance* is properly installed and is in a safe condition for continuing use.

This procedure is intended for cental furnace and boiler installations and may not be applicable to all installations.

(a) This procedure should be performed prior to any attempt at modification of the *appliance* or of the installation.

(b) If it is determined that there is a condition that could result in unsafe operation, shut off the *appliance* and advise the owner of the unsafe condition. The following steps should be followed in making the safety inspection:

1. Conduct a check for gas leakage. (See Section 406.6)
2. Visually inspect the venting system for proper size and horizontal pitch and determine there is no blockage or restriction, leakage, corrosion and other deficiencies that could cause an unsafe condition.
3. Shut off all gas to the *appliance* and shut off any other fuel-gas-burning *appliance* within the same room. **Use the shutoff valve in the supply line to each appliance.**
4. Inspect burners and crossovers for blockage and corrosion.
5. **Furnace installations:** Inspect the heat exchanger for cracks, openings or excessive corrosion.
6. **Boiler installations:** Inspect for evidence of water or combustion product leaks.
7. Close all building doors and windows and all doors between the space in which the *appliance* is located and other spaces of the building that can be closed. Turn on any clothes dryers. Turn on any exhaust fans, such as range hoods and bathroom exhausts, so they will operate at maximum speed. Do not operate a summer exhaust fan. Close *fireplace* dampers. If, after completing Steps 8 through 13, it is believed sufficient *combustion air* is not available, refer to Section 304 of this code.
8. Place the *appliance* being inspected in operation. **Follow the lighting instructions.** Adjust the thermostat so *appliance* will operate continuously.
9. Determine that the pilot, where provided, is burning properly and that the main burner ignition is satisfactory by interrupting and reestablishing the electrical supply to the *appliance* in any convenient manner. If the *appliance* is equipped with a continuous pilot, test all pilot safety devices to determine if they are operating properly by extinguishing the pilot when the main burner is off and determining, after 3 minutes, that the main burner gas does not flow upon a call for heat. If the *appliance* is not provided with a pilot, test for proper operation of the ignition system in accordance with the *appliance* manufacturer's lighting and operating instructions.
10. Visually determine that the main burner gas is burning properly (i.e., no floating, lifting or flashback). Adjust the primary air shutters as required. If the *appliance* is equipped with high and low flame controlling or flame modulation, check for proper main burner operation at low flame.
11. Test for spillage at the draft hood relief opening after 5 minutes of main burner operation. Use the flame of a match or candle or smoke.
12. Turn on all other fuel-gas-burning appliances within the same room so they will operate at their full inputs. **Follow lighting instructions for each appliance.**
13. Repeat Steps 10 and 11 on the *appliance* being inspected.
14. Return doors, windows, exhaust fans, *fireplace* dampers and any other fuel-gas-burning *appliance* to their previous conditions of use.
15. **Furnace installations:** Check both the limit control and the fan control for proper operation. Limit control operation can be checked by blocking the circulating air inlet or temporarily disconnecting the electrical supply to the blower motor and determining that the limit control acts to shut off the main burner gas.
16. **Boiler installations:** Verify that the water pumps are in operating condition. Test low water cutoffs, automatic feed controls, pressure and temperature limit controls and relief valves in accordance with the manufacturer's recommendations to determine that they are in operating condition.

Part VII — Plumbing

CHAPTERS 25 THROUGH 33

Deleted

The following text is extracted from the 2012 *North Carolina Plumbing Code* and has been modified where necessary to conform to the scope of application of the 2012 *North Carolina Residential Code for One-and Two-Family Dwellings*. The section numbers appearing in Part VII are the section numbers of the corresponding text in the *North Carolina Plumbing Code*. Where differences occur between the provisions of this abridged text and the *North Carolina Plumbing Code*, the provisions of the *North Carolina Plumbing Code* shall apply. Requirements not specifically covered by this text shall conform to the *North Carolina Plumbing Code*.

Part VII
North Carolina State Building Code:
Plumbing Code
Abridged for Residential Code

(2009 IPC® with North Carolina Amendments)

Abridged Residential Code Edition

2012

TABLE OF CONTENTS

CHAPTER 1

SCOPE AND ADMINISTRATION

PART 1—SCOPE AND APPLICATION

SECTION 101
GENERAL

101.1 Title. These regulations shall be known as the *North Carolina Plumbing Code* as adopted by the North Carolina Building Code Council on September 14, 2010, to be effective September 1, 2011. References to the *International Codes* shall mean the North Carolina Codes. The North Carolina amendments to the *International Codes* are underlined.

101.2 Scope. The provisions of this code shall apply to the erection, installation, alteration, repairs, relocation, replacement, addition to, use or maintenance of plumbing systems within this jurisdiction. This code shall also regulate nonflammable medical gas, inhalation anesthetic, vacuum piping, nonmedical oxygen systems and sanitary and condensate vacuum collection systems. The installation of fuel gas distribution piping and equipment, fuel-gas-fired water heaters and water heater venting systems shall be regulated by the *International Fuel Gas Code*. Provisions in the appendices shall not apply unless specifically adopted.

> **Exception:** Detached one- and two-family dwellings and multiple single-family dwellings (townhouses) not more than three stories high with separate means of egress and their accessory structures shall comply with the *International Residential Code*.

101.3 Intent. The purpose of this code is to provide minimum standards to safeguard life or limb, health, property and public welfare by regulating and controlling the design, construction, installation, quality of materials, location, operation and maintenance or use of plumbing equipment and systems.

101.4 Severability. If any section, subsection, sentence, clause or phrase of this code is for any reason held to be unconstitutional, such decision shall not affect the validity of the remaining portions of this code.

101.5 Appendices. Provisions in the appendices shall not apply unless specifically adopted or referenced in this code.

101.6 Requirements of other State agencies, occupational licensing board or commissions. The North Carolina State Building Codes do not include all additional requirements for buildings and structures that may be imposed by other State agencies, occupational licensing boards and commissions. It shall be the responsibility of a permit holder, design professional, contractor or occupational license holder to determine whether any additional requirements exist.

SECTION 102
APPLICABILITY

102.1 General. Where there is a conflict between a general requirement and a specific requirement, the specific requirement shall govern. Where, in any specific case, different sections of this code specify different materials, methods of construction or other requirements, the most restrictive shall govern.

102.2 Existing installations. Plumbing systems lawfully in existence at the time of the adoption of this code shall be permitted to have their use and maintenance continued if the use, maintenance or repair is in accordance with the original design and no hazard to life, health or property is created by such plumbing system.

102.3 Maintenance. All plumbing systems, materials and appurtenances, both existing and new, and all parts thereof, shall be maintained in proper operating condition in accordance with the original design in a safe and sanitary condition. All devices or safeguards required by this code shall be maintained in compliance with the code edition under which they were installed.

The owner or the owner's designated agent shall be responsible for maintenance of plumbing systems. To determine compliance with this provision, the code official shall have the authority to require any plumbing system to be reinspected.

102.4 Additions, alterations or repairs. Additions, alterations, renovations or repairs to any plumbing system shall conform to that required for a new plumbing system without requiring the existing plumbing system to comply with all the requirements of this code. Additions, alterations or repairs shall not cause an existing system to become unsafe, insanitary or overloaded.

Minor additions, alterations, renovations and repairs to existing plumbing systems shall meet the provisions for new construction, unless such work is done in the same manner and arrangement as was in the existing system, is not hazardous and is *approved*.

102.5 Change in occupancy. It shall be unlawful to make any change in the *occupancy* of any structure that will subject the structure to any special provision of this code applicable to the new *occupancy* without approval of the code official. The code official shall certify that such structure meets the intent of the provisions of law governing building construction for the proposed new *occupancy* and that such change of *occupancy* does not result in any hazard to the public health, safety or welfare.

102.6 Historic buildings. The provisions of this code relating to the construction, alteration, repair, enlargement, restoration, relocation or moving of buildings or structures shall not be mandatory for existing buildings or structures identified and classified by the state or local jurisdiction as historic buildings when such buildings or structures are judged by the code official to be safe and in the public interest of health, safety and welfare regarding any proposed construction, alteration, repair, enlargement, restoration, relocation or moving of buildings.

102.7 Moved buildings. Except as determined by Section 102.2, plumbing systems that are a part of buildings or structures moved into or within the jurisdiction shall comply with the provisions of this code for new installations.

102.8 Referenced codes and standards. The codes and standards referenced in this code shall be those that are listed in Chapter 13 and such codes and standards shall be considered as part of the requirements of this code to the prescribed extent of each such reference. Where differences occur between provisions of this code and the referenced standards, the provisions of this code shall be the minimum requirements.

102.9 Requirements not covered by code. Any requirements necessary for the strength, stability or proper operation of an existing or proposed plumbing system, or for the public safety, health and general welfare, not specifically covered by this code shall be determined by the code official.

102.10 Other laws. The provisions of this code shall not be deemed to nullify any provisions of local, state or federal law.

102.11 Application of references. Reference to chapter section numbers, or to provisions not specifically identified by number, shall be construed to refer to such chapter, section or provision of this code.

SECTION 103
DEPARTMENT OF PLUMBING INSPECTION

Deleted. See the North Carolina Administrative Code and Policies.

SECTION 104
DUTIES AND POWERS OF THE CODE OFFICIAL

Deleted. See the North Carolina Administrative Code and Policies.

SECTION 105
APPROVAL

105.1 Modifications. Whenever there are practical difficulties involved in carrying out the provisions of this code, the code official shall have the authority to grant modifications for individual cases, upon application of the owner or owner's representative, provided the code official shall first find that special individual reason makes the strict letter of this code impractical and the modification conforms to the intent and purpose of this code and that such modification does not lessen health, life and fire safety requirements. The details of action granting modifications shall be recorded and entered in the files of the plumbing inspection department.

105.2 Alternative materials, methods and equipment. The provisions of this code are not intended to prevent the installation of any material or to prohibit any method of construction not specifically prescribed by this code, provided that any such alternative has been *approved*. An alternative material or method of construction shall be *approved* where the code official finds that the proposed alternative material, method or equipment complies with the intent of the provisions of this code and is at least the equivalent of that prescribed in this code.

105.2.1 Research reports. Supporting data, where necessary to assist in the approval of materials or assemblies not specifically provided for in this code, shall consist of valid research reports from *approved* sources.

105.3 Required testing. Whenever there is insufficient evidence of compliance with the provisions of this code, or evidence that a material or method does not conform to the requirements of this code, or in order to substantiate claims for alternate materials or methods, the code official shall have the authority to require tests as evidence of compliance to be made at no expense to the jurisdiction.

105.3.1 Test methods. Test methods shall be as specified in this code or by other recognized test standards. In the absence of recognized and accepted test methods, the code official shall approve the testing procedures.

105.3.2 Testing agency. All tests shall be performed by an *approved* agency.

105.3.3 Test reports. Reports of tests shall be retained by the code official for the period required for retention of public records.

105.4 Alternative engineered design. The design, documentation, inspection, testing and approval of an *alternative engineered design* plumbing system shall comply with Sections 105.4.1 through 105.4.6.

105.4.1 Design criteria. An *alternative engineered design* shall conform to the intent of the provisions of this code and shall provide an equivalent level of quality, strength, effectiveness, fire resistance, durability and safety. Material, equipment or components shall be designed and installed in accordance with the manufacturer's installation instructions.

105.4.2 Submittal. The registered design professional shall indicate on the permit application that the plumbing system is an *alternative engineered design*. The permit and permanent permit records shall indicate that an *alternative engineered design* was part of the *approved* installation.

105.4.3 Technical data. The registered design professional shall submit sufficient technical data to substantiate the proposed *alternative engineered design* and to prove that the performance meets the intent of this code.

105.4.4 Construction documents. The registered design professional shall submit to the code official two complete sets of signed and sealed construction documents for the *alternative engineered design*. The construction documents shall include floor plans and a riser diagram of the work. Where appropriate, the construction documents shall indicate the direction of flow, all pipe sizes, grade of horizontal piping, loading, and location of fixtures and appliances.

105.4.5 Design approval. Where the code official determines that the *alternative engineered design* conforms to the intent of this code, the plumbing system shall be *approved*. If the *alternative engineered design* is not *approved*, the code official shall notify the registered design professional in writing, stating the reasons thereof.

105.4.6 Inspection and testing. The *alternative engineered design* shall be tested and inspected in accordance with the requirements of Sections 107 and 312.

105.5 Approved materials and equipment. Materials, equipment and devices *approved* by the code official shall be constructed and installed in accordance with such approval.

105.5.1 Material and equipment reuse. Materials, equipment and devices shall not be reused unless such elements have been reconditioned, tested, placed in good and proper working condition and *approved*.

SECTION 106 PERMITS

Deleted. See the North Carolina Administrative Code and Policies.

SECTION 107 INSPECTIONS AND TESTING

Deleted. See the North Carolina Administrative Code and Policies.

SECTION 108 VIOLATIONS

Deleted. See the North Carolina Administrative Code and Policies.

SECTION 109 MEANS OF APPEAL

Deleted. See the North Carolina Administrative Code and Policies.

SECTION 110 TEMPORARY EQUIPMENT, SYSTEMS AND USES

110.1 General. The code official is authorized to issue a permit for temporary equipment, systems and uses. Such permits shall be limited as to time of service, but shall not be permitted for more than 180 days. The code official is authorized to grant extensions for demonstrated cause.

110.2 Conformance. Temporary equipment, systems and uses shall conform to the structural strength, fire safety, means of egress, accessibility, light, ventilation and sanitary requirements of this code as necessary to ensure the public health, safety and general welfare.

110.3 Temporary utilities. The code official is authorized to give permission to temporarily supply utilities before an installation has been fully completed and the final certificate of completion has been issued. The part covered by the temporary certificate shall comply with the requirements specified for temporary lighting, heat or power in the code.

110.4 Termination of approval. The code official is authorized to terminate such permit for temporary equipment, systems or uses and to order the temporary equipment, systems or uses to be discontinued.

CHAPTER 2
DEFINITIONS

SECTION 201
GENERAL

201.1 Scope. Unless otherwise expressly stated, the following words and terms shall, for the purposes of this code, have the meanings shown in this chapter.

201.2 Interchangeability. Words stated in the present tense include the future; words stated in the masculine gender include the feminine and neuter; the singular number includes the plural and the plural the singular.

201.3 Terms defined in other codes. Where terms are not defined in this code and are defined in the *International Building Code*, *International Fire Code*, *International Fuel Gas Code* or the *International Mechanical Code*, such terms shall have the meanings ascribed to them as in those codes.

201.4 Terms not defined. Where terms are not defined through the methods authorized by this section, such terms shall have ordinarily accepted meanings such as the context implies.

SECTION 202
GENERAL DEFINITIONS

ACCEPTED ENGINEERING PRACTICE. That which conforms to accepted principles, tests or standards of nationally recognized technical or scientific authorities.

ACCESS (TO). That which enables a fixture, appliance or equipment to be reached by ready *access* or by a means that first requires the removal or movement of a panel, door or similar obstruction (see "Ready *access*").

ACCESS COVER. A removable plate, usually secured by bolts or screws, to permit *access* to a pipe or pipe fitting for the purposes of inspection, repair or cleaning.

ADAPTER FITTING. An *approved* connecting device that suitably and properly joins or adjusts pipes and fittings which do not otherwise fit together.

AIR ADMITTANCE VALVE. One-way valve designed to allow air to enter the plumbing drainage system when negative pressures develop in the piping system. The device shall close by gravity and seal the vent terminal at zero differential pressure (no flow conditions) and under positive internal pressures. The purpose of an air admittance valve is to provide a method of allowing air to enter the plumbing drainage system without the use of a vent extended to open air and to prevent *sewer* gases from escaping into a building.

AIR BREAK (Drainage System). A piping arrangement in which a drain from a fixture, appliance or device discharges indirectly into another fixture, receptacle or interceptor at a point below the *flood level rim* and above the trap seal.

AIR GAP (Drainage System). The unobstructed vertical distance through the free atmosphere between the outlet of the waste pipe and the *flood level rim* of the receptacle into which the waste pipe is discharging.

AIR GAP (Water Distribution System). The unobstructed vertical distance through the free atmosphere between the lowest opening from any pipe or faucet supplying water to a tank, plumbing fixture or other device and the *flood level rim* of the receptacle.

ALTERNATIVE ENGINEERED DESIGN. A plumbing system that performs in accordance with the intent of Chapters 3 through 12 and provides an equivalent level of performance for the protection of public health, safety and welfare. The system design is not specifically regulated by Chapters 3 through 12.

ANCHORS. See "Supports."

ANTISIPHON. A term applied to valves or mechanical devices that eliminate siphonage.

APPROVED. Acceptable to the code official or other authority having jurisdiction.

APPROVED AGENCY. An established and recognized agency approved by the code official and that is regularly engaged in conducting tests or furnishing inspection services.

AREA DRAIN. A receptacle designed to collect surface or storm water from an open area.

ASPIRATOR. A fitting or device supplied with water or other fluid under positive pressure that passes through an integral orifice or constriction, causing a vacuum. Aspirators are also referred to as suction apparatus, and are similar in operation to an ejector.

BACKFLOW. Pressure created by any means in the water distribution system, which by being in excess of the pressure in the water supply mains causes a potential backflow condition.

Backpressure, low head. A pressure less than or equal to 4.33 psi (29.88 kPa) or the pressure exerted by a 10-foot (3048 mm) column of water.

Backsiphonage. The backflow of potentially contaminated water into the potable water system as a result of the pressure in the potable water system falling below atmospheric pressure of the plumbing fixtures, pools, tanks or vats connected to the potable water distribution piping.

Drainage. A reversal of flow in the drainage system.

Water supply system. The flow of water or other liquids, mixtures or substances into the distribution pipes of a potable water supply from any source except the intended source.

BACKFLOW CONNECTION. Any arrangement whereby backflow is possible.

BACKFLOW PREVENTER. A device or means to prevent backflow.

BACKWATER VALVE. A device or valve installed in the *building drain* or *sewer* pipe where a *sewer* is subject to backflow, and which prevents drainage or waste from backing up into a lower level or fixtures and causing a flooding condition.

BASE FLOOD ELEVATION. A reference point, determined in accordance with the building code, based on the depth or peak elevation of flooding, including wave height, which has a 1 percent (100-year flood) or greater chance of occurring in any given year.

BATHROOM GROUP. A group of fixtures consisting of a water closet, lavatory, bathtub or shower, including or excluding a bidet, an *emergency floor drain* or both. Such fixtures are located together on the same floor level.

BATTERY OF FIXTURES. Any group of two or more similar adjacent fixtures that discharge into a common horizontal waste or soil branch.

BEDPAN STEAMER OR BOILER. A fixture utilized for scalding bedpans or urinals by direct application of steam or boiling water.

BEDPAN WASHER AND STERILIZER. A fixture designed to wash bedpans and to flush the contents into the sanitary drainage system. Included are fixtures of this type that provide for disinfecting utensils by scalding with steam or *hot water.*

BEDPAN WASHER HOSE. A device supplied with hot and cold water and located adjacent to a water closet or clinical sink to be utilized for cleansing bedpans.

BRANCH. Any part of the piping system except a riser, main or *stack*.

BRANCH INTERVAL. A distance along a soil or waste stack corresponding, in general, to a story height, but not less than 8 feet (2438 mm) within which the horizontal branches from one floor or story of a structure are connected to the stack.

BRANCH VENT. A vent connecting one or more individual vents with a vent *stack* or *stack* vent.

BUILDING. Any structure occupied or intended for supporting or sheltering any *occupancy*.

BUILDING DRAIN. That part of the lowest piping of a drainage system that receives the discharge from soil, waste and other drainage pipes inside and that extends to 10 feet (3048 mm) beyond the walls of the building and conveys the drainage to the *building sewer.*

Combined. A *building drain* that conveys both sewage and storm water or other drainage.

Sanitary. A *building drain* that conveys sewage only.

Storm. A *building drain* that conveys storm water or other drainage, but not sewage.

BUILDING SEWER. That part of the drainage system that extends from the end of the *building drain* and conveys the discharge to a *public sewer, private sewer,* individual sewage disposal system or other point of disposal.

Combined. A *building sewer* that conveys both sewage and storm water or other drainage.

Sanitary. A *building sewer* that conveys sewage only.

Storm. A *building sewer* that conveys storm water or other drainage, but not sewage.

BUILDING SUBDRAIN. That portion of a drainage system that does not drain by gravity into the *building sewer.*

BUILDING TRAP. A device, fitting or assembly of fittings installed in the *building drain* to prevent circulation of air between the drainage system of the building and the *building sewer.*

CIRCUIT VENT. A vent that connects to a horizontal drainage *branch* and vents two traps to a maximum of eight traps or trapped fixtures connected into a battery.

CISTERN. A small covered tank for storing water for a home or farm. Generally, this tank stores rainwater to be utilized for purposes other than in the potable water supply, and such tank is placed underground in most cases.

CLEANOUT. An *access* opening in the drainage system utilized for the removal of obstructions. Types of cleanouts include a removable plug or cap, and a removable fixture or fixture trap.

CLOSET. An enclosed or recessed area used to store clothing, linens or other household items.

CODE. These regulations, subsequent amendments thereto, or any emergency rule or regulation that the administrative authority having jurisdiction has lawfully adopted.

CODE OFFICIAL. The officer or other designated authority charged with the administration and enforcement of this code, or a duly authorized representative.

COMBINATION FIXTURE. A fixture combining one sink and laundry tray or a two- or three-compartment sink or laundry tray in one unit.

COMBINATION WASTE AND VENT SYSTEM. A specially designed system of waste piping embodying the horizontal wet venting of one or more sinks or floor drains by means of a common waste and vent pipe adequately sized to provide free movement of air above the flow line of the drain.

COMBINED BUILDING DRAIN. See "*Building drain,* combined."

COMBINED BUILDING SEWER. See "*Building sewer,* combined."

COMMON VENT. A vent connecting at the junction of two fixture drains or to a fixture *branch* and serving as a vent for both fixtures.

CONCEALED FOULING SURFACE. Any surface of a plumbing fixture which is not readily visible and is not scoured or cleansed with each fixture operation.

CONDUCTOR. A pipe inside the building that conveys storm water from the roof to a storm or combined *building drain.*

CONSTRUCTION DOCUMENTS. All of the written, graphic and pictorial documents prepared or assembled for describing the design, location and physical characteristics of the elements of the project necessary for obtaining a building permit. The construction drawings shall be drawn to an appropriate scale.

CONTAMINATION. An impairment of the quality of the potable water that creates an actual hazard to the public health through poisoning or through the spread of disease by sewage, industrial fluids or waste.

CRITICAL LEVEL (C-L). An elevation (height) reference point that determines the minimum height at which a backflow preventer or vacuum breaker is installed above the *flood level rim* of the fixture or receptor served by the device. The critical level is the elevation level below which there is a potential for backflow to occur. If the critical level marking is not indicated on the device, the bottom of the device shall constitute the critical level.

CROSS CONNECTION. Any physical connection or arrangement between two otherwise separate piping systems, one of which contains potable water and the other either water of unknown or questionable safety or steam, gas or chemical, whereby there exists the possibility for flow from one system to the other, with the direction of flow depending on the pressure differential between the two systems (see "Backflow").

DEAD END. A *branch* leading from a soil, waste or vent pipe; a *building drain*; or a *building sewer*, and terminating at a *developed length* of 2 feet (610 mm) or more by means of a plug, cap or other closed fitting.

DEPTH OF TRAP SEAL. The depth of liquid that would have to be removed from a full trap before air could pass through the trap.

DESIGN FLOOD ELEVATION. The elevation of the "design flood," including wave height, relative to the datum specified on the community's legally designated flood hazard map.

DEVELOPED LENGTH. The length of a pipeline measured along the centerline of the pipe and fittings.

DISCHARGE PIPE. A pipe that conveys the discharges from plumbing fixtures or appliances.

DRAIN. Any pipe that carries wastewater or water-borne wastes in a building drainage system.

DRAINAGE FITTINGS. Type of fitting or fittings utilized in the drainage system. Drainage fittings are similar to cast-iron fittings, except that instead of having a bell and spigot, drainage fittings are recessed and tapped to eliminate ridges on the inside of the installed pipe.

DRAINAGE FIXTURE UNIT

Drainage (dfu). A measure of the probable discharge into the drainage system by various types of plumbing fixtures. The drainage fixture-unit value for a particular fixture depends on its volume rate of drainage discharge, on the time duration of a single drainage operation and on the average time between successive operations.

DRAINAGE SYSTEM. Piping within a *public* or *private* premise that conveys sewage, rainwater or other liquid wastes to a point of disposal. A drainage system does not include the mains of a *public sewer* system or a private or public sewage treatment or disposal plant.

Building gravity. A drainage system that drains by gravity into the *building sewer.*

Sanitary. A drainage system that carries sewage and excludes storm, surface and ground water.

Storm. A drainage system that carries rainwater, surface water, subsurface water and similar liquid wastes.

EFFECTIVE OPENING. The minimum cross-sectional area at the point of water supply discharge, measured or expressed in terms of the diameter of a circle or, if the opening is not circular, the diameter of a circle of equivalent cross-sectional area. For faucets and similar fittings, the *effective opening* shall be measured at the smallest orifice in the fitting body or in the supply piping to the fitting.

EMERGENCY FLOOR DRAIN. A floor drain that does not receive the discharge of any drain or indirect waste pipe, and that protects against damage from accidental spills, fixture overflows and leakage.

ESSENTIALLY NONTOXIC TRANSFER FLUIDS. Fluids having a Gosselin rating of 1, including propylene glycol; mineral oil; polydimethylsiloxane; hydrochlorofluorocarbon, chlorofluorocarbon and carbon refrigerants; and FDA-approved boiler water additives for steam boilers.

ESSENTIALLY TOXIC TRANSFER FLUIDS. Soil, waste or gray water and fluids having a Gosselin rating of 2 or more including ethylene glycol, hydrocarbon oils, ammonia refrigerants and hydrazine.

EXISTING INSTALLATIONS. Any plumbing system regulated by this code that was legally installed prior to the effective date of this code, or for which a permit to install has been issued.

FAUCET. A valve end of a water pipe through which water is drawn from or held within the pipe.

FILL VALVE. A water supply valve, opened or closed by means of a float or similar device, utilized to supply water to a tank. An antisiphon fill valve contains an antisiphon device in the form of an *approved air gap* or vacuum breaker that is an integral part of the fill valve unit and that is positioned on the discharge side of the water supply control valve.

FIXTURE. See "Plumbing fixture."

FIXTURE BRANCH. A drain serving two or more fixtures that discharges to another drain or to a *stack.*

FIXTURE DRAIN. The drain from the trap of a fixture to a junction with any other drain pipe.

FIXTURE FITTING

Supply fitting. A fitting that controls the volume and/or directional flow of water and is either attached to or accessible from a fixture, or is used with an open or atmospheric discharge.

Waste fitting. A combination of components that conveys the sanitary waste from the outlet of a fixture to the connection to the sanitary drainage system.

FIXTURE SUPPLY. The water supply pipe connecting a fixture to a *branch* water supply pipe or directly to a main water supply pipe.

FLOOD HAZARD AREA. The greater of the following two areas:

1. The area within a flood plain subject to a 1-percent or greater chance of flooding in any given year.
2. The area designated as a *flood hazard area* on a community's flood hazard map or as otherwise legally designated.

FLOOD LEVEL RIM. The edge of the receptacle from which water overflows.

FLOW CONTROL (Vented). A device installed upstream from the interceptor having an orifice that controls the rate of flow through the interceptor and an air intake (vent) downstream from the orifice that allows air to be drawn into the flow stream.

FLOW PRESSURE. The pressure in the water supply pipe near the faucet or water outlet while the faucet or water outlet is wide open and flowing.

FLUSH TANK. A tank designed with a fill valve and flush valve to flush the contents of the bowl or usable portion of the fixture.

FLUSHOMETER TANK. A device integrated within an air accumulator vessel that is designed to discharge a predetermined quantity of water to fixtures for flushing purposes.

FLUSHOMETER VALVE. A valve attached to a pressurized water supply pipe and so designed that when activated it opens the line for direct flow into the fixture at a rate and quantity to operate the fixture properly, and then gradually closes to reseal fixture traps and avoid water hammer.

GREASE INTERCEPTOR. A plumbing appurtenance that is installed in a sanitary drainage system to intercept oily and greasy wastes from a wastewater discharge. Such device has the ability to intercept free-floating fats and oils.

GREASE-LADEN WASTE. Effluent discharge that is produced from food processing, food preparation or other sources where grease, fats and oils enter automatic dishwater prerinse stations, sinks or other appurtenances.

GREASE REMOVAL DEVICE, AUTOMATIC (GRD). A plumbing appurtenance that is installed in the sanitary drainage system to intercept free-floating fats, oils and grease from wastewater discharge. Such a device operates on a time- or event-controlled basis and has the ability to remove free-floating fats, oils and grease automatically without intervention from the user except for maintenance.

GRIDDED WATER DISTRIBUTION SYSTEM. A water distribution system where every water distribution pipe is interconnected so as to provide two or more paths to each fixture supply pipe.

HANGERS. See "Supports."

HORIZONTAL BRANCH DRAIN. A drainage *branch* pipe extending laterally from a soil or waste *stack* or *building drain*, with or without vertical sections or branches, that receives the discharge from two or more fixture drains or branches and conducts the discharge to the soil or waste *stack* or to the *building drain*.

HORIZONTAL PIPE. Any pipe or fitting that makes an angle of less than 45 degrees (0.79 rad) with the horizontal.

HOT WATER. Water at a temperature greater than or equal to 110°F (43°C).

HOUSE TRAP. See "Building trap."

INDIRECT WASTE PIPE. A waste pipe that does not connect directly with the drainage system, but that discharges into the drainage system through an *air break* or *air gap* into a trap, fixture, receptor or interceptor.

INDIRECT WASTE RECEPTOR. A plumbing fixture designed to collect and dispose of liquid waste from other plumbing fixtures, plumbing equipment or appliances that are required to discharge to the drainage system through an air gap. The following types of fixtures fall within the classification of indirect liquid waste receptors: floor sinks, mop receptors, service sinks and standpipe drains with integral air gaps.

INDIVIDUAL SEWAGE DISPOSAL SYSTEM. A system for disposal of domestic sewage by means of a septic tank, cesspool or mechanical treatment, designed for utilization apart from a public *sewer* to serve a single establishment or building.

INDIVIDUAL VENT. A pipe installed to vent a fixture trap and that connects with the vent system above the fixture served or terminates in the open air.

INDIVIDUAL WATER SUPPLY. A water supply that serves one or more families, and that is not an *approved* public water supply.

INTERCEPTOR. A device designed and installed to separate and retain for removal, by automatic or manual means, deleterious, hazardous or undesirable matter from normal wastes, while permitting normal sewage or wastes to discharge into the drainage system by gravity.

JOINT

Expansion. A loop, return bend or return offset that provides for the expansion and contraction in a piping system and is utilized in tall buildings or where there is a rapid change of temperature, as in power plants, steam rooms and similar occupancies.

Flexible. Any joint between two pipes that permits one pipe to be deflected or moved without movement or deflection of the other pipe.

Mechanical. See "Mechanical joint."

Slip. A type of joint made by means of a washer or a special type of packing compound in which one pipe is slipped into the end of an adjacent pipe.

LABELED. Equipment, devices, fixtures or materials bearing the label of an approved agency.

LEAD-FREE PIPE AND FITTINGS. Containing not more than 8.0-percent lead.

LEAD-FREE SOLDER AND FLUX. Containing not more than 0.2-percent lead.

LEADER. An exterior drainage pipe for conveying storm water from roof or gutter drains to an *approved* means of disposal.

LOCAL VENT STACK. A vertical pipe to which connections are made from the fixture side of traps and through which vapor or foul air is removed from the fixture or device utilized on bedpan washers.

MACERATING TOILET SYSTEMS. An assembly consisting of a water closet and sump with a macerating pump that is designed to collect, grind and pump wastes from the water closet and up to two other fixtures connected to the sump.

MAIN. The principal pipe artery to which branches are connected.

MANIFOLD. See "Plumbing appurtenance."

MECHANICAL JOINT. A connection between pipes, fittings, or pipes and fittings that is not screwed, caulked, threaded, soldered, solvent cemented, brazed or welded. A joint in which compression is applied along the centerline of the pieces being joined. In some applications, the joint is part of a coupling, fitting or adapter.

MEDICAL GAS SYSTEM. The complete system to convey medical gases for direct patient application from central supply systems (bulk tanks, manifolds and medical air compressors), with pressure and operating controls, alarm warning systems, related components and piping networks extending to station outlet valves at patient use points.

MEDICAL VACUUM SYSTEMS. A system consisting of central-vacuum-producing equipment with pressure and operating controls, shutoff valves, alarm-warning systems, gauges and a network of piping extending to and terminating with suitable station inlets at locations where patient suction may be required.

NONPOTABLE WATER. Water not safe for drinking, personal or culinary utilization.

NUISANCE. Public nuisance as known in common law or in equity jurisprudence; whatever is dangerous to human life or detrimental to health; whatever structure or premises is not sufficiently ventilated, sewered, drained, cleaned or lighted, with respect to its intended *occupancy*; and whatever renders the air, or human food, drink or water supply unwholesome.

OCCUPANCY. The purpose for which a building or portion thereof is utilized or occupied.

OFFSET. A combination of *approved* bends that makes two changes in direction bringing one section of the pipe out of line but into a line parallel with the other section.

OPEN AIR. Outside the structure.

PIPE SIZES. For the purposes of determining the minimum size of pipe required, cross-sectional areas are the essential characteristic, not the pipe diameter. When the Code instructs to "increase by one pipe size," some pipe sizes may not be commercially available. The following pipe sizes are presumed to be commercially available: $\frac{1}{2}$, $\frac{3}{4}$, 1, $1\frac{1}{4}$, $1\frac{1}{2}$, 2, $2\frac{1}{2}$, 3, $3\frac{1}{2}$, 4, $4\frac{1}{2}$, 5, 6, 7, 8, 9, 10.

PLUMBING. The practice, materials and fixtures utilized in the installation, maintenance, extension and alteration of all piping, fixtures, plumbing appliances and plumbing appurtenances, within or adjacent to any structure, in connection with sanitary drainage or storm drainage facilities; venting systems; and public or private water supply systems.

PLUMBING APPLIANCE. Any one of a special class of plumbing fixtures intended to perform a special function. Included are fixtures having the operation or control dependent on one or more energized components, such as motors, controls, heating elements, or pressure- or temperature-sensing elements.

Such fixtures are manually adjusted or controlled by the owner or operator, or are operated automatically through one or more of the following actions: a time cycle, a temperature range, a pressure range, a measured volume or weight.

PLUMBING APPURTENANCE. A manufactured device, prefabricated assembly or an on-the-job assembly of component parts that is an adjunct to the basic piping system and plumbing fixtures. An appurtenance demands no additional water supply and does not add any discharge load to a fixture or to the drainage system.

PLUMBING FIXTURE. A receptacle or device that is either permanently or temporarily connected to the water distribution system of the premises and demands a supply of water therefrom; discharges wastewater, liquid-borne waste materials or sewage either directly or indirectly to the drainage system of the premises; or requires both a water supply connection and a discharge to the drainage system of the premises.

PLUMBING SYSTEM. Includes the water supply and distribution pipes; plumbing fixtures and traps; water-treating or water-using equipment; soil, waste and vent pipes; and sanitary and storm sewers and building drains; in addition to their respective connections, devices and appurtenances within a structure or premises.

POLLUTION. An impairment of the quality of the potable water to a degree that does not create a hazard to the public health but that does adversely and unreasonably affect the aesthetic qualities of such potable water for domestic use.

POTABLE WATER. Water free from impurities present in amounts sufficient to cause disease or harmful physiological effects and conforming to the bacteriological and chemical quality requirements of the Public Health Service Drinking Water Standards or the regulations of the public health authority having jurisdiction.

PRIVATE. In the classification of plumbing fixtures, "*private*" applies to fixtures in residences and apartments, and to fixtures in nonpublic toilet rooms of hotels and motels and similar installations in buildings where the plumbing fixtures are intended for utilization by a family or an individual.

PUBLIC OR PUBLIC UTILIZATION. In the classification of plumbing fixtures, "*public*" applies to fixtures in general toilet rooms of schools, gymnasiums, hotels, airports, bus and railroad stations, public buildings, bars, public comfort stations, office buildings, stadiums, stores, restaurants and other installations where a number of fixtures are installed so that their utilization is similarly unrestricted.

PUBLIC WATER MAIN. A water supply pipe for public utilization controlled by public authority.

QUICK-CLOSING VALVE. A valve or faucet that closes automatically when released manually or that is controlled by a mechanical means for fast-action closing.

READY ACCESS. That which enables a fixture, appliance or equipment to be directly reached without requiring the removal or movement of any panel, door or similar obstruction and without the use of a portable ladder, step stool or similar device.

REDUCED PRESSURE PRINCIPLE BACKFLOW PREVENTER. A backflow prevention device consisting of two independently acting check valves, internally force-loaded to a normally closed position and separated by an intermediate chamber (or zone) in which there is an automatic relief means of venting to the atmosphere, internally loaded to a normally open position between two tightly closing shutoff valves and with a means for testing for tightness of the checks and opening of the relief means.

REGISTERED DESIGN PROFESSIONAL. An individual who is registered or licensed to practice professional architecture or engineering as defined by the statutory requirements of the professional registration laws of the state or jurisdiction in which the project is to be constructed. Design by a registered design professional is not required where exempt under the registration or licensure laws.

RELIEF VALVE

Pressure relief valve. A pressure-actuated valve held closed by a spring or other means and designed to relieve pressure automatically at the pressure at which such valve is set.

Temperature and pressure relief (T&P) valve. A combination relief valve designed to function as both a temperature relief and a pressure relief valve.

Temperature relief valve. A temperature-actuated valve designed to discharge automatically at the temperature at which such valve is set.

RELIEF VENT. A vent whose primary function is to provide circulation of air between drainage and vent systems.

RIM. An unobstructed open edge of a fixture.

RISER. See "Water pipe, riser."

ROOF DRAIN. A drain installed to receive water collecting on the surface of a roof and to discharge such water into a leader or a conductor.

ROUGH-IN. Parts of the plumbing system that are installed prior to the installation of fixtures. This includes drainage, water supply, vent piping and the necessary fixture supports and any fixtures that are built into the structure.

SCUPPER. An opening in a wall or parapet that allows water to drain from a roof.

SELF-CLOSING FAUCET. A faucet containing a valve that automatically closes upon deactivation of the opening means.

SEPARATOR. See "Interceptor."

SEWAGE. Any liquid waste containing animal or vegetable matter in suspension or solution, including liquids containing chemicals in solution.

SEWAGE EJECTORS. A device for lifting sewage by entraining the sewage in a high-velocity jet of steam, air or water.

SEWER

Building sewer. See "Building sewer."

Public sewer. A common *sewer* directly controlled by public authority.

Sanitary sewer. A *sewer* that carries sewage and excludes storm, surface and ground water.

Storm sewer. A *sewer* that conveys rainwater, surface water, subsurface water and similar liquid wastes.

SLOPE. The fall (pitch) of a line of pipe in reference to a horizontal plane. In drainage, the slope is expressed as the fall in units vertical per units horizontal (percent) for a length of pipe.

SOIL PIPE. A pipe that conveys sewage containing fecal matter to the *building drain* or *building sewer.*

SPILLPROOF VACUUM BREAKER. An assembly consisting of one check valve force-loaded closed and an air-inlet vent valve force-loaded open to atmosphere, positioned downstream of the check valve, and located between and including two tightly closing shutoff valves and a test cock.

STACK. A general term for any vertical line of soil, waste, vent or inside conductor piping that extends through at least one story with or without offsets.

STACK VENT. The extension of a soil or waste *stack* above the highest horizontal drain connected to the *stack.*

STACK VENTING. A method of venting a fixture or fixtures through the soil or waste *stack.*

STERILIZER

Boiling type. A boiling-type sterilizer is a fixture of a nonpressure type utilized for boiling instruments, utensils or other equipment for disinfection. These devices are portable or are connected to the plumbing system.

Instrument. A device for the sterilization of various instruments.

Pressure (autoclave). A pressure vessel fixture designed to utilize steam under pressure for sterilizing.

Pressure instrument washer sterilizer. A pressure instrument washer sterilizer is a pressure vessel fixture designed to both wash and sterilize instruments during the operating cycle of the fixture.

Utensil. A device for the sterilization of utensils as utilized in health care services.

Water. A water sterilizer is a device for sterilizing water and storing sterile water.

STERILIZER VENT. A separate pipe or *stack*, indirectly connected to the building drainage system at the lower terminal, that receives the vapors from nonpressure sterilizers, or the exhaust vapors from pressure sterilizers, and conducts the vapors directly to the open air. Also called vapor, steam, atmospheric or exhaust vent.

STORM DRAIN. See "Drainage system, storm."

STRUCTURE. That which is built or constructed or a portion thereof.

SUBSOIL DRAIN. A drain that collects subsurface water or seepage water and conveys such water to a place of disposal.

SUMP. A tank or pit that receives sewage or liquid waste, located below the normal grade of the gravity system and that must be emptied by mechanical means.

SUMP PUMP. An automatic water pump powered by an electric motor for the removal of drainage, except raw sewage, from a sump, pit or low point.

SUMP VENT. A vent from pneumatic sewage ejectors, or similar equipment, that terminates separately to the open air.

SUPPORTS. Devices for supporting and securing pipe, fixtures and equipment.

SWIMMING POOL. Any structure, basin, chamber or tank containing an artificial body of water for swimming, diving or recreational bathing having a depth of 2 feet (610 mm) or more at any point.

TEMPERED WATER. Water having a temperature range between 85°F (29°C) and 110°F (43°C).

THIRD-PARTY CERTIFICATION AGENCY. An *approved* agency operating a product or material certification sytem that incorporates initial product testing, assessment and surveillance of a manufacturer's quality control system.

THIRD-PARTY CERTIFIED. Certification obtained by the manufacturer indicating that the function and performance characteristics of a product or material have been determined by testing and ongoing surveillance by an *approved third-party certification agency*. Assertion of certification is in the form of identification in accordance with the requirements of the *third-party certification agency*.

THIRD-PARTY TESTED. Procedure by which an *approved* testing laboratory provides documentation that a product, material or system conforms to specified requirements.

TOILET. Water closet and frequently a lavatory, but not a bathtub, shower, spa or similar bathing fixture.

TOILET ROOM. A room containing a water closet and frequently a lavatory, but not a bathtub, shower, spa or similar bathing fixture.

TRAP. A fitting or device that provides a liquid seal to prevent the emission of *sewer* gases without materially affecting the flow of sewage or wastewater through the trap.

TRAP SEAL. The vertical distance between the weir and the top of the dip of the trap.

UNSTABLE GROUND. Earth that does not provide a uniform bearing for the barrel of the *sewer* pipe between the joints at the bottom of the pipe trench.

VACUUM. Any pressure less than that exerted by the atmosphere.

VACUUM BREAKER. A type of backflow preventer installed on openings subject to normal atmospheric pressure that prevents backflow by admitting atmospheric pressure through ports to the discharge side of the device.

VENT PIPE. See "Vent system."

VENT STACK. A vertical vent pipe installed primarily for the purpose of providing circulation of air to and from any part of the drainage system.

VENT SYSTEM. A pipe or pipes installed to provide a flow of air to or from a drainage system, or to provide a circulation of air within such system to protect trap seals from siphonage and backpressure.

VERTICAL PIPE. Any pipe or fitting that makes an angle of 45 degrees (0.79 rad) or more with the horizontal.

WALL-HUNG WATER CLOSET. A wall-mounted water closet installed in such a way that the fixture does not touch the floor.

WASTE. The discharge from any fixture, appliance, area or appurtenance that does not contain fecal matter.

WASTE PIPE. A pipe that conveys only waste.

WATER-HAMMER ARRESTOR. A device utilized to absorb the pressure surge (water hammer) that occurs when water flow is suddenly stopped in a water supply system.

WATER HEATER. Any heating appliance or equipment that heats potable water and supplies such water to the potable *hot water* distribution system.

WATER MAIN. A water supply pipe or system of pipes, installed and maintained by a city, township, county, public utility company or other public entity, on public property, in the street or in an *approved* dedicated easement of public or community use.

WATER OUTLET. A discharge opening through which water is supplied to a fixture, into the atmosphere (except into an open tank that is part of the water supply system), to a boiler or heating system, or to any devices or equipment requiring water to operate but which are not part of the plumbing system.

WATER PIPE

Riser. A water supply pipe that extends one full story or more to convey water to branches or to a group of fixtures.

Water distribution pipe. A pipe within the structure or on the premises that conveys water from the water service pipe, or from the meter when the meter is at the structure, to the points of utilization.

Water service pipe. The pipe from the water main or other source of potable water supply, or from the meter when the meter is at the public right of way, to the water distribution system of the building served. Water service pipe shall terminate 5 feet (1524 mm) outside the foundation wall.

WATER SUPPLY SYSTEM. The water service pipe, water distribution pipes, and the necessary connecting pipes, fittings, control valves and all appurtenances in or adjacent to the structure or premises.

WELL

Bored. A well constructed by boring a hole in the ground with an auger and installing a casing.

Drilled. A well constructed by making a hole in the ground with a drilling machine of any type and installing casing and screen.

Driven. A well constructed by driving a pipe in the ground. The drive pipe is usually fitted with a well point and screen.

Dug. A well constructed by excavating a large-diameter shaft and installing a casing.

WHIRLPOOL BATHTUB. A plumbing appliance consisting of a bathtub fixture that is equipped and fitted with a circulating piping system designed to accept, circulate and discharge bathtub water upon each use.

YOKE VENT. A pipe connecting upward from a soil or waste *stack* to a vent *stack* for the purpose of preventing pressure changes in the stacks.

CHAPTER 3
GENERAL REGULATIONS

SECTION 301 GENERAL

301.1 Scope. The provisions of this chapter shall govern the general regulations regarding the installation of plumbing not specific to other chapters.

301.2 System installation. Plumbing shall be installed with due regard to preservation of the strength of structural members and prevention of damage to walls and other surfaces through fixture usage.

301.3 Connections to the sanitary drainage system. All plumbing fixtures, drains, appurtenances and appliances used to receive or discharge liquid wastes or sewage shall be directly connected to the sanitary drainage system of the building or premises, in accordance with the requirements of this code. This section shall not be construed to prevent the indirect waste systems required by Chapter 8. All drain, waste and vent piping associated with gray water or rain water recycling systems shall be installed in compliance with this code.

301.4 Connections to water supply. Every plumbing fixture, device or appliance requiring or using water for its proper operation shall be directly or indirectly connected to the water supply system in accordance with the provisions of this code.

301.5 Pipe, tube and fitting sizes. See Chapter 2, Definitions, "Pipe sizes."

301.6 Prohibited locations. Plumbing systems shall not be located in an elevator shaft or in an elevator equipment room.

> **Exception:** Floor drains, sumps and sump pumps shall be permitted at the base of the shaft, provided that they are indirectly connected to the plumbing system and comply with Section 1003.4.

301.7 Conflicts. Where conflicts between this code and the conditions of the listing or the manufacturer's installation instructions occur, the provisions of this code apply.

> **Exception:** Where a code provision is less restrictive than the conditions of the listing of the equipment or appliance or the manufacturer's installation instructions, the conditions of the listing and manufacturer's installation instructions shall apply.

SECTION 302 EXCLUSION OF MATERIALS DETRIMENTAL TO THE SEWER SYSTEM

302.1 Detrimental or dangerous materials. *Note: The following text is provided for informational purposes only.*

Ashes, cinders or rags; flammable, poisonous or explosive liquids or gases; oil, grease or any other insoluble material capable of obstructing, damaging or overloading the building drainage or *sewer* system, or capable of interfering with the normal operation of the sewage treatment processes or private disposal system, should not be deposited, into such systems.

302.2 Industrial wastes. Waste products from manufacturing or industrial operations shall not be introduced into the *public sewer* until it has been determined by the code official or other authority having jurisdiction that the introduction thereof will not damage the *public sewer* system or interfere with the functioning of the sewage treatment plant.

SECTION 303 MATERIALS

303.1 Identification. Each length of pipe and each pipe fitting, trap, fixture, material and device utilized in a plumbing system shall bear the identification of the manufacturer, and the applicable standard to which it was manufactured.

303.2 Installation of materials. All materials used shall be installed in strict accordance with the standards under which the materials are accepted and *approved*. In the absence of such installation procedures, the manufacturer's installation instructions shall be followed. Where the requirements of referenced standards or manufacturer's installation instructions do not conform to minimum provisions of this code, the provisions of this code shall apply.

303.3 Plastic pipe, fittings and components. All plastic pipe, fittings and components shall be third-party certified as conforming to NSF 14.

303.4 Third-party testing and certification. All plumbing products and materials shall comply with the referenced standards, specifications and performance criteria of this code and shall be identified in accordance with Section 303.1. When required by Table 303.4, plumbing products and materials shall either be tested by an *approved* third-party testing agency or certified by an *approved third-party certification agency.*

SECTION 304 RODENTPROOFING

304.1 General. Plumbing systems shall be designed and installed in accordance with Sections 304.2 through 304.4 and the *North Carolina Building Code*, Appendix H, to prevent rodents from entering structures.

304.2 Strainer plates. All strainer plates on drain inlets shall be designed and installed so that all openings are not greater than $^1/_2$ inch (12.7 mm) in least dimension.

304.3 Meter boxes. Deleted.

304.4 Openings for pipes. In or on structures where openings have been made in walls, floors or ceilings for the passage of pipes, such openings shall be closed and protected by the installation of *approved* metal collars or other aproved materials that are securely fastened to the adjoining structure.

SECTION 305 PROTECTION OF PIPES AND PLUMBING SYSTEM COMPONENTS

305.1 Corrosion. Pipes passing through concrete or cinder walls and floors or other corrosive material shall be protected against external corrosion by a protective sheathing or wrapping or other means that will withstand any reaction from the lime and acid of concrete, cinder or other corrosive material. Sheathing or wrapping shall allow for movement including expansion and contraction of piping. Minimum wall thickness of material shall be 0.025 inch (0.64 mm).

305.2 Breakage. Pipes passing through or under walls shall be protected from breakage.

305.3 Stress and strain. Piping in a plumbing system shall be installed so as to prevent strains and stresses that exceed the structural strength of the pipe. Where necessary, provisions shall be made to protect piping from damage resulting from expansion, contraction and structural settlement.

305.4 Sleeves. Annular spaces between sleeves and pipes shall be filled or tightly caulked in an *approved* manner. Annular spaces between sleeves and pipes in fire-resistance-rated assemblies shall be filled or tightly caulked in accordance with the *International Building Code*.

305.5 Pipes through or under footings or foundation walls. Any pipe that passes within 12 inches (305 mm) under a footing or through a foundation wall shall be provided with a relieving arch, or a pipe sleeve pipe shall be built into the foundation wall. The sleeve shall be two pipe sizes greater than the pipe passing through the wall. Piping shall not be run under pier footing (refer to Section 307).

305.6 Freezing. The top of water pipes, installed below grade outside the building, shall be below the frost line or a minimum of 12 inches (305 mm) below finished grade, whichever is greater. Water pipes installed in a wall exposed to the exterior shall be located on the heated side of the wall insulation. Water piping installed in an unconditioned attic or unconditioned utility room shall have insulation with a minimum *R*-factor of 6.5 determined at 75°F (24°C) in accordance with ASTM C177.

Note: These provisions are minimum requirements, which have been found suitable for normal weather conditions. Abnormally low temperatures for extended periods may require additional provisions to prevent freezing.

305.6.1 Frost protection. No traps of soil or waste pipe shall be installed or permitted outside of a building, or concealed in outside walls or in any place where they may be subjected to freezing temperatures, unless adequate provision is made to protect them from freezing. Waste and soil piping leaving the building shall have a minimum cover of 3 inches (76.2 mm).

305.7 Waterproofing of openings. Joints at the roof and around vent pipes, shall be made water-tight by the use of lead, copper, galvanized steel, aluminum, plastic or other *approved* flashings or flashing material. Exterior wall openings shall be made water-tight.

305.8 Protection against physical damage. In concealed locations where piping, other than cast-iron or galvanized steel, is installed through holes or notches in studs, joists, rafters or similar members less than $1^1/_2$ inches (38 mm) from the nearest edge of the member, the pipe shall be protected by steel shield plates. Such shield plates shall have a thickness of not less than 0.0575 inch (1.463 mm) (No. 16 gage). Such plates shall cover the area of the pipe where the member is notched or bored, and shall extend a minimum of 2 inches (51 mm) above sole plates and below top plates.

305.9 Protection of components of plumbing system. Components of a plumbing system installed along alleyways, driveways, parking garages or other locations exposed to damage shall be recessed into the wall or otherwise protected in an *approved* manner.

Exception: One- and two-family dwellings and townhouses.

TABLE 303.4
PRODUCTS AND MATERIALS REQUIRING THIRD-PARTY TESTING AND THIRD-PARTY CERTIFICATION

PRODUCT OR MATERIAL	THIRD-PARTY CERTIFIED	THIRD-PARTY TESTED
Potable water supply system components and potable water fixture fittings	Required	—
Sanitary drainage and vent system components	Plastic pipe, fittings and pipe-related components	All others
Waste fixture fittings	Plastic pipe, fittings and pipe-related components	All others
Storm drainage system components	Plastic pipe, fittings and pipe-related components	All others
Plumbing fixtures	—	Required
Plumbing appliances	Required	—
Backflow prevention devices	Required	—
Water distribution system safety devices	Required	—
Special waste system components	—	Required
Subsoil drainage system components	—	Required

SECTION 306
TRENCHING, EXCAVATION AND BACKFILL

306.1 Support of piping. Buried piping shall be supported throughout its entire length.

306.2 Trenching and bedding. Where trenches are excavated such that the bottom of the trench forms the bed for the pipe, solid and continuous load-bearing support shall be provided between joints. Bell holes, hub holes and coupling holes shall be provided at points where the pipe is joined. Such pipe shall not be supported on blocks to grade. In instances where the materials manufacturer's installation instructions are more restrictive than those prescribed by the code, the material shall be installed in accordance with the more restrictive requirement.

306.2.1 Overexcavation. Where trenches are excavated below the installation level of the pipe such that the bottom of the trench does not form the bed for the pipe, the trench shall be backfilled to the installation level of the bottom of the pipe with sand or fine gravel placed in layers of 6 inches (152 mm) maximum depth and such backfill shall be compacted after each placement.

306.2.2 Rock removal. Where rock is encountered in trenching, the rock shall be removed to a minimum of 3 inches (76 mm) below the installation level of the bottom of the pipe, and the trench shall be backfilled to the installation level of the bottom of the pipe with sand tamped in place so as to provide uniform load-bearing support for the pipe between joints. The pipe, including the joints, shall not rest on rock at any point.

306.2.3 Soft load-bearing materials. If soft materials of poor load-bearing quality are found at the bottom of the trench, stabilization shall be achieved by overexcavating a minimum of two pipe diameters and backfilling to the installation level of the bottom of the pipe with fine gravel, crushed stone or a concrete foundation. The concrete foundation shall be bedded with sand tamped into place so as to provide uniform load-bearing support for the pipe between joints.

306.3 Backfilling. Backfill shall be free from discarded construction material and debris. Loose earth free from rocks, broken concrete and frozen chunks shall be placed in the trench in 6-inch (152 mm) layers and tamped in place until the crown of the pipe is covered by 12 inches (305 mm) of tamped earth. The backfill under and beside the pipe shall be compacted for pipe support. Backfill shall be brought up evenly on both sides of the pipe so that the pipe remains aligned. In instances where the manufacturer's installation instructions for materials are more restrictive than those prescribed by the code, the material shall be installed in accordance with the more restrictive requirement.

306.4 Tunneling. Where pipe is to be installed by tunneling, jacking or a combination of both, the pipe shall be protected from damage during installation and from subsequent uneven loading. Where earth tunnels are used, adequate supporting structures shall be provided to prevent future settling or caving.

SECTION 307
STRUCTURAL SAFETY

307.1 General. In the process of installing or repairing any part of a plumbing and drainage installation, the finished floors, walls, ceilings, tile work or any other part of the building or premises that must be changed or replaced shall be left in a safe structural condition in accordance with the requirements of the *International Building Code*.

307.2 Cutting, notching or bored holes. A framing member shall not be cut, notched or bored in excess of limitations specified in the *International Building Code* or Appendix F in this code.

307.3 Penetrations of floor/ceiling assemblies and fire-resistance-rated assemblies. Deleted.

[B] 307.4 Alterations to trusses. Truss members and components shall not be cut, drilled, notched, spliced or otherwise altered in any way without written concurrence and approval of a registered design professional. Alterations resulting in the addition of loads to any member (e.g., HVAC equipment, water heater) shall not be permitted without verification that the truss is capable of supporting such additional loading.

307.5 Trench location. Trenches installed parallel to footings shall not extend below the 45-degree (0.79 rad) bearing plane of the footing or wall.

307.6 Piping materials exposed within plenums. All piping materials exposed within plenums shall comply with the provisions of the *International Mechanical Code*.

SECTION 308
PIPING SUPPORT

308.1 General. All plumbing piping shall be supported in accordance with this section.

308.2 Piping seismic supports. Deleted.

308.3 Materials. Hangers, anchors and supports shall support the piping and the contents of the piping. Hangers and strapping material shall be of *approved* material that will not promote galvanic action.

308.4 Structural attachment. Hangers and anchors shall be attached to the building construction in an *approved* manner.

308.5 Interval of support. Pipe shall be supported in accordance with Table 308.5.

Exception: The interval of support for piping systems designed to provide for expansion/contraction shall conform to the engineered design in accordance with Section 105.4.

TABLE 308.5
HANGER SPACING

PIPING MATERIAL	MAXIMUM HORIZONTAL SPACING (feet)	MAXIMUM VERTICAL SPACING (feet)
ABS pipe	4	10[b]
Aluminum tubing	10	15
Brass pipe	10	10
Cast-iron pipe	5[a]	15
Copper or copper-alloy pipe	12	10
Copper or copper-alloy tubing, $1^1/_4$-inch diameter and smaller	6	10
Copper or copper-alloy tubing, $1^1/_2$-inch diameter and larger	10	10
Cross-linked polyethylene (PEX) pipe	2.67 (32 inches)	10[b]
Cross-linked polyethylene/ aluminum/cross-linked polyethylene (PEX-AL-PEX) pipe	2.67 (32 inches)	4
CPVC pipe or tubing, 1 inch and smaller	3	10[b]
CPVC pipe or tubing, $1^1/_4$ inches and larger	4	10[b]
Steel pipe	12	15
Lead pipe	Continuous	4
Polyethylene/aluminum/ polyethylene (PE-AL-PE) pipe	2.67 (32 inches)	4
Polypropylene (PP) pipe or tubing 1 inch and smaller	2.67 (32 inches)	10[b]
Polypropylene (PP) pipe or tubing, $1^1/_4$ inches and larger	4	10[b]
PVC pipe	4	10[b]
Stainless steel drainage systems	10	10[b]

For SI: 1 inch = 25.4 mm, 1 foot = 304.8 mm.

a. The maximum horizontal spacing of cast-iron pipe hangers shall be increased to 10 feet where 10-foot lengths of pipe are installed.

b. Midstory guide for sizes 2 inches and smaller.

308.6 Sway bracing. Rigid support sway bracing shall be provided at changes in direction greater than 45 degrees (0.79 rad) for pipe sizes 4 inches (102 mm) and larger.

308.7 Anchorage. Anchorage shall be provided to restrain drainage piping from axial movement.

308.7.1 Location. For plastic pipe sizes greater than 6 inches (152 mm), and other pipe sizes greater than 4 inches (102 mm), restraints shall be provided for drain pipes at all changes in direction and at all changes in diameter greater than two pipe sizes. Braces, blocks, rodding, backfill and other methods specified as suitable by the coupling manufacturer shall be utilized.

308.8 Expansion joint fittings. Expansion joint fittings shall be used only where necessary to provide for expansion and contraction of the pipes. Expansion joint fittings shall be of the typical material suitable for use with the type of piping in which such fittings are installed.

308.9 Parallel water distribution systems. Piping bundles for manifold systems shall be supported in accordance with Table 308.5. Support at changes in direction shall be in accordance with the manufacturer's installation instructions. Hot and cold water piping shall not be grouped in the same bundle.

308.10 Stacks. Bases of stacks shall be supported by the building structure, virgin or compacted earth, or other material suitable to support the weight of the piping.

SECTION 309
FLOOD HAZARD RESISTANCE

309.1 General. Plumbing systems and equipment in structures erected in flood hazard areas shall be constructed in accordance with the requirements of this section and the *International Building Code*.

[B] 309.2 Flood hazard. For structures located in flood hazard areas, the following systems and equipment shall be located at or above the *design flood elevation*.

Exception: The following systems are permitted to be located below the *design flood elevation* provided that the systems are designed and installed to prevent water from entering or accumulating within their components and the systems are constructed to resist hydrostatic and hydrodynamic loads and stresses, including the effects of buoyancy, during the occurrence of flooding to the *design flood elevation*.

1. All water service pipes.
2. Deleted.
3. Deleted.
4. All sanitary drainage piping.
5. All storm drainage piping.
6. Manhole covers shall be sealed, except where elevated to or above the *design flood elevation*.
7. All other plumbing fixtures, faucets, fixture fittings, piping systems and equipment.
8. Water heaters.
9. Vents and vent systems.

[B] 309.3 Flood hazard areas subject to high-velocity wave action. Structures located in flood hazard areas subject to high-velocity wave action shall meet the requirements of Section 309.2. The plumbing systems, pipes and fixtures shall not be mounted on or penetrate through walls intended to break away under flood loads.

SECTION 310
WASHROOM AND TOILET ROOM REQUIREMENTS
Deleted

SECTION 311
TOILET FACILITIES FOR WORKERS

311.1 Temporary toilet facilities at construction sites. Toilet facilities shall be provided and maintained in a sanitary condition during construction. An adequate number of facilities must be provided for the number of employees at the construction site according to the following:

NUMBER OF EMPLOYEES	MINIMUM NUMBER OF FACILITIES
Less than 20	1 toilet
20 to 200	1 toilet & 1 urinal per 40 workers
More than 200	1 toilet & 1 urinal per 50 workers

There shall be at least one facility for every two contiguous construction sites. Such facilities may be portable, enclosed, chemically treated, tank-tight units. Portable toilets shall be enclosed, screened and weatherproofed with internal latches.

Temporary toilet facilities need not be provided on site for crews on a job site for no more than one working day and having transportation readily available to toilet facilities.

SECTION 312
TESTS AND INSPECTIONS

312.1 Required tests. The permit holder shall make the applicable tests prescribed in Sections 312.2 through 312.10 to determine compliance with the provisions of this code. The permit holder shall give reasonable advance notice to the code official when the plumbing work is ready for tests. The equipment, material, power and labor necessary for the inspection and test shall be furnished by the permit holder and the permit holder shall be responsible for determining that the work will withstand the test pressure prescribed in the following tests. All plumbing system piping shall be tested with either water or air. After the plumbing fixtures have been set and their traps filled with water, the entire drainage system shall be submitted to final tests. The code official shall require the removal of any cleanouts if necessary to ascertain whether the pressure has reached all parts of the system.

312.1.1 Test gauges. Gauges used for testing shall be as follows:

1. Tests requiring a pressure of 10 pounds per square inch (psi) (69 kPa) or less shall utilize a testing gauge having increments of 0.10 psi (0.69 kPa) or less.
2. Tests requiring a pressure of greater than 10 psi (69 kPa) but less than or equal to 100 psi (689 kPa) shall utilize a testing gauge having increments of 1 psi (6.9 kPa) or less.
3. Tests requiring a pressure of greater than 100 psi (689 kPa) shall utilize a testing gauge having increments of 2 psi (14 kPa) or less.

312.2 Drainage and vent water test. A water test shall be applied to the drainage system within the building either in its entirety or in sections. If applied to the entire system, all openings in the piping shall be tightly closed, except the highest opening, and the system shall be filled with water to the point of overflow. If the system is tested in sections, each opening shall be tightly plugged except the highest openings of the section under test, and each section shall be filled with water, but no section shall be tested with less than a 10-foot (3048 mm) head of water. In testing successive sections, at least the upper 10 feet (3048 mm) of the next preceding section shall be tested so that no joint or pipe in the building, except the uppermost 10 feet (3048 mm) of the system, shall have been submitted to a test of less than a 10-foot (3048 mm) head of water. This pressure shall be held for at least 15 minutes. The system shall then be tight at all points.

Exception: Rough plumbing testing for one- and two-family dwellings shall be as specified above except the water level shall be a minimum of 3 feet (914 mm) above the highest drainage fitting.

312.3 Drainage and vent air test. An air test shall be made by forcing air into the system until there is a uniform gauge pressure of 5 psi (34.5 kPa) or sufficient to balance a 10-inch (254 mm) column of mercury. This pressure shall be held for a test period of at least 15 minutes. Any adjustments to the test pressure required because of changes in ambient temperature or the seating of gaskets shall be made prior to the beginning of the test period.

312.4 Drainage and vent final test. The final test of the completed drainage and vent systems shall be visual and in sufficient detail to determine compliance with the provisions of this code. Where a smoke test is utilized, it shall be made by filling all traps with water and then introducing into the entire system a pungent, thick smoke produced by one or more smoke machines. When the smoke appears at *stack* openings on the roof, the *stack* openings shall be closed and a pressure equivalent to a 1-inch water column (248.8 Pa) shall be held for a test period of not less than 15 minutes.

312.5 Water supply system test. Upon completion of a section of or the entire water supply system, the system, or portion completed, shall be tested and proved tight under a water pressure not less than the working pressure of the system; or an air test of not less than 100 psi (688 kPa). This pressure shall be held for at least 15 minutes. The water utilized for tests shall be obtained from a potable source of supply. The required tests shall be performed in accordance with this section and Section 107.

312.6 Gravity sewer test. Deleted.

312.7 Forced sewer test. Deleted.

312.8 Storm drainage system test. *Storm drain* systems within a building shall be tested by water or air in accordance with Section 312.2 or 312.3.

312.9 Shower liner test. Where shower floors and receptors are made water-tight by the application of materials required by Section 417.5.2, the completed liner installation shall be tested. The pipe from the shower drain shall be plugged water tight for the test. The floor and receptor area shall be filled with potable water to a depth of not less than 2 inches (51 mm) measured at the threshold. Where a threshold of at least 2 inches (51 mm) high does not exist, a temporary threshold shall be constructed to retain the test water in the lined floor or receptor area to a level not less than 2 inches (51 mm) deep measured at the threshold. The water shall be retained for a test period of not less than 15 minutes, and there shall not be evidence of leakage.

312.10 Inspection and testing of backflow prevention assemblies. Deleted.

312.10.1 Inspections. Deleted.

312.10.2 Testing. Deleted.

SECTION 313 EQUIPMENT EFFICIENCIES

313.1 General. Equipment efficiencies shall be in accordance with the *International Energy Conservation Code*.

SECTION 314 CONDENSATE DISPOSAL

[M] 314.1 Approved location. Approved location shall be in accordance with the *North Carolina Mechanical Code*.

[M] 314.2 Evaporators and cooling coils. Deleted.

[M] 314.2.1 Condensate disposal. Deleted.

[M] 314.2.2 Drain pipe materials and sizes. Deleted.

[M] 314.2.3 Auxiliary and secondary drain systems. Deleted.

[M] 314.2.3.1 Water-level monitoring devices. Deleted.

[M] 314.2.3.2 Appliance, equipment and insulation in pans. Deleted.

[M] 314.2.4 Traps. Deleted.

CHAPTER 4
FIXTURES, FAUCETS AND FIXTURE FITTINGS

SECTION 401
GENERAL

401.1 Scope. This chapter shall govern the materials, design and installation of plumbing fixtures, faucets and fixture fittings in accordance with the type of *occupancy*, and shall provide for the minimum number of fixtures for various types of occupancies.

401.2 Prohibited fixtures and connections. Water closets having a concealed trap seal or an unventilated space or having walls that are not thoroughly washed at each discharge in accordance with ASME A112.19.2M shall be prohibited. Any water closet that permits siphonage of the contents of the bowl back into the tank shall be prohibited. Trough urinals shall be prohibited.

401.3 Water conservation. The maximum water flow rates and flush volume for plumbing fixtures and fixture fittings shall comply with Section 604.4.

SECTION 402
FIXTURE MATERIALS

402.1 Quality of fixtures. Plumbing fixtures shall be constructed of *approved* materials, with smooth, impervious surfaces, free from defects and concealed fouling surfaces, and shall conform to standards cited in this code. All porcelain enameled surfaces on plumbing fixtures shall be acid resistant.

402.2 Materials for specialty fixtures. Materials for specialty fixtures not otherwise covered in this code shall be of stainless steel, soapstone, chemical stoneware or plastic, or shall be lined with lead, copper-base alloy, nickel-copper alloy, corrosion-resistant steel or other material especially suited to the application for which the fixture is intended.

402.3 Sheet copper. Sheet copper for general applications shall conform to ASTM B 152 and shall not weigh less than 12 ounces per square foot (3.7 kg/m^2).

402.4 Sheet lead. Sheet lead for pans shall not weigh less than 4 pounds per square foot (19.5 kg/m^2) coated with an asphalt paint or other *approved* coating.

SECTION 403
MINIMUM PLUMBING FACILITIES

403.1 Minimum number of fixtures. In new construction or building additions and in changes of occupancy as defined in the *North Carolina Building Code*, plumbing fixtures shall be provided for the type of occupancy and in the minimum number shown in Table 403.1. Types of occupancies not shown in Table 403.1 shall be considered individually by the code official. The number of occupants shall be determined by the *International Building Code*. Occupancy classification shall be determined in accordance with the *International Building Code*.

403.1.1 Fixture calculations. Deleted.

403.1.2 Family or assisted-use toilet and bath fixtures. Deleted.

403.2 Separate facilities. Deleted.

403.3 Adjustments in occupant content. Deleted.

403.4 Location of employee toilet facilities in occupancies other than assembly or mercantile. Deleted.

403.5 Location of employee toilet facilities in mercantile and assembly occupancies. Deleted.

403.6 Public facilities. Deleted.

403.7 Signage. Deleted.

403.8 Multiplex theaters. Deleted.

403.9 Plumbing fixtures for public schools. Deleted.

SECTION 404
ACCESSIBLE PLUMBING FACILITIES
Deleted

SECTION 405
INSTALLATION OF FIXTURES

405.1 Water supply protection. The supply lines and fittings for every plumbing fixture shall be installed so as to prevent backflow.

TABLE 403.1
MINIMUM NUMBER OF REQUIRED PLUMBING FIXTURES[a]
(See Sections 403.2 and 403.3)

CLASSIFICATION	OCCUPANCY	DESCRIPTION	WATER CLOSETS (URINALS SEE SECTION 419.2) MALE	WATER CLOSETS FEMALE	LAVATORIES MALE	LAVATORIES FEMALE	BATHTUBS/ SHOWERS	DRINKING FOUNTAIN (SEE SECTION 410.1)	OTHER
Residential	R-3	One- and two-family dwellings	1 per dwelling unit		1 per dwelling unit		1 per dwelling unit	—	1 kitchen sink per dwelling unit

a. The fixtures shown are based on one fixture being the minimum required for the number of persons indicated or any fraction of the number of persons indicated. The number of occupants shall be determined by the *International Building Code*.

405.2 Access for cleaning. Plumbing fixtures shall be installed so as to afford easy *access* for cleaning both the fixture and the area around the fixture.

405.3 Setting. Fixtures shall be set level and in proper alignment with reference to adjacent walls.

405.3.1 Water closets, urinals, lavatories and bidets. A water closet, urinal, lavatory or bidet shall not be set closer than 15 inches (381 mm) from its center to any side wall, partition, vanity or other obstruction, or closer than 30 inches (762 mm) center-to-center between adjacent fixtures. There shall be at least a 21-inch (533 mm) clearance in front of the water closet, urinal, lavatory or bidet to any wall, fixture or door. Water closet compartments shall not be less than 30 inches (762 mm) wide and 60 inches (1524 mm) deep.

Exception: For one- and two-family dwellings and townhouses, see the *North Carolina Residential Code*.

405.3.2 Public lavatories. Deleted.

405.4 Floor and wall drainage connections. Connections between the drain and floor outlet plumbing fixtures shall be made with a floor flange. The flange shall be attached to the drain and anchored to the structure. Connections between the drain and wall-hung water closets shall be made with an *approved* extension nipple or horn adaptor. The water closet shall be bolted to the hanger with corrosion-resistant bolts or screws. Joints shall be sealed with an *approved* elastomeric gasket, flange-to-fixture connection complying with ASME A112.4.3 or an *approved* setting compound.

405.4.1 Floor flanges. Floor flanges for water closets or similar fixtures shall not be less than 0.125 inch (3.2 mm) thick for brass, 0.25 inch (6.4 mm) thick for plastic, and 0.25 inch (6.4 mm) thick and not less than a 2-inch (51 mm) caulking depth for cast-iron or galvanized malleable iron.

Floor flanges of hard lead shall weigh not less than 1 pound, 9 ounces (0.7 kg) and shall be composed of lead alloy with not less than 7.75-percent antimony by weight. Flanges shall be secured to the building structure with corrosion-resistant screws or bolts.

405.4.2 Securing floor outlet fixtures. Floor outlet fixtures shall be secured to the floor or floor flanges by screws or bolts of corrosion-resistant material.

405.4.3 Securing wall-hung water closet bowls. Wall-hung water closet bowls shall be supported by a concealed metal carrier that is attached to the building structural members so that strain is not transmitted to the closet connector or any other part of the plumbing system. The carrier shall conform to ASME A112.6.1M or ASME A112.6.2.

405.5 Water-tight joints. Joints formed where fixtures come in contact with walls or floors shall be sealed.

405.6 Plumbing in mental health centers. Deleted.

405.7 Design of overflows. Where any fixture is provided with an overflow, the waste shall be designed and installed so that standing water in the fixture will not rise in the overflow when the stopper is closed, and no water will remain in the overflow when the fixture is empty.

405.7.1 Connection of overflows. The overflow from any fixture shall discharge into the drainage system on the inlet or fixture side of the trap.

Exception: The overflow from a flush tank serving a water closet or urinal shall discharge into the fixture served.

405.8 Slip joint connections. Slip joints shall be made with an *approved* elastomeric gasket and shall only be installed on the trap outlet, trap inlet and within the trap seal. Fixtures with concealed slip-joint connections shall be provided with an *access* panel or utility space at least 12 inches (305 mm) in its smallest dimension or other *approved* arrangement so as to provide *access* to the slip joint connections for inspection and repair. Where such access cannot be provided, access doors shall not be required, provided that all joints are soldered, solvent cemented or screwed to form a solid connection.

405.9 Design and installation of plumbing fixtures. Integral fixture fitting mounting surfaces on manufactured plumbing fixtures or plumbing fixtures constructed on site, shall meet the design requirements of ASME A112.19.2M or ASME A112.19.3M.

SECTION 406 AUTOMATIC CLOTHES WASHERS

406.1 Approval. Domestic automatic clothes washers shall conform to ASSE 1007.

406.2 Water connection. The water supply to an automatic clothes washer shall be protected against backflow by an *air gap* installed integrally within the machine conforming to ASSE 1007 or with the installation of a backflow preventer in accordance with Section 608.

406.3 Waste connection. The waste from an automatic clothes washer shall connect to a vertical drain of not less than 2 inches (51 mm) in diameter, or a horizontal drain of not less than 3 inches (76 mm) in diameter. The 2-inch (51 mm) trap in the waste connection may be used as a cleanout for both the 2-inch (51 mm) and the 3-inch (76 mm). Automatic clothes washers that discharge by gravity shall be permitted to drain to a waste receptor or an approved trench drain.

SECTION 407 BATHTUBS

407.1 Approval. Bathtubs shall conform to ANSI Z124.1, ASME A112.19.1M, ASME A112.19.4M, ASME A112.19.9M, CSA B45.2, CSA B45.3 or CSA B45.5.

407.2 Bathtub waste outlets. Bathtubs shall have waste outlets a minimum of $1^1/_2$ inches (38 mm) in diameter. The waste outlet shall be equipped with an *approved* stopper.

407.3 Glazing. Windows and doors within a bathtub enclosure shall conform to the safety glazing requirements of the *International Building Code*.

407.4 Bathtub enclosure. Doors within a bathtub enclosure shall conform to ASME A112.19.15.

SECTION 408 BIDETS

408.1 Approval. Bidets shall conform to ASME A112.19.2M, ASME A112.19.9M or CSA B45.1.

408.2 Water connection. The water supply to a bidet shall be protected against backflow by an *air gap* or backflow preventer in accordance with Section 608.13.1, 608.13.2, 608.13.3, 608.13.5, 608.13.6 or 608.13.8.

408.3 Bidet water temperature. Deleted.

SECTION 409 DISHWASHING MACHINES

409.1 Approval. Domestic dishwashing machines shall conform to ASSE 1006. Commercial dishwashing machines shall conform to ASSE 1004 and NSF 3.

409.2 Water connection. The water supply to a dishwashing machine shall be protected against backflow by an *air gap* or backflow preventer in accordance with Section 608.

409.3 Waste connection. The waste connection of a dishwashing machine shall comply with Section 802.1.6 or 802.1.7, as applicable.

SECTION 410 DRINKING FOUNTAINS

410.1 Approval. Drinking fountains shall conform to ASME A112.19.1M, ASME A112.19.2M or ASME A112.19.9M and water coolers shall conform to ARI 1010. Drinking fountains and water coolers shall conform to NSF 61, Section 9. Where water is served in restaurants, night clubs, taverns, or bars, drinking fountains shall not be required. In other occupancies, where drinking fountains are required, water coolers or bottled water dispensers shall be permitted to be substituted for not more than 50 percent of the required drinking fountains.

410.2 Prohibited location. Drinking fountains, water coolers and bottled water dispensers shall not be installed in *public* restrooms.

SECTION 411 EMERGENCY SHOWERS AND EYEWASH STATIONS Deleted

SECTION 412 FLOOR AND TRENCH DRAINS

412.1 Approval. Floor drains shall conform to ASME A112.3.1, ASME A112.6.3 or CSA B79. Trench drains shall comply with ASME A112.6.3.

412.2 Floor drains. Floor drains shall have removeable strainers. The floor drain shall be constructed so that the drain is capable of being cleaned. *Access* shall be provided to the drain inlet. Ready *access* shall be provided to floor drains.

> **Exception:** Floor drains serving refrigerated display cases shall be provided with *access*.

412.3 Size of floor drains. Floor drains shall have a minimum 2-inch-diameter (51 mm) drain outlet.

412.4 Public laundries and central washing facilities. Deleted.

412.5 Location. Floor drains shall be located to drain the entire floor area.

412.6 Trap primers. The water seal of floor drain traps shall be maintained in conformance to Section 1002.4, Trap seals, or another method acceptable to the authority having jurisdiction.

> **Exception:** Hose bibbs located in rooms with nonabsorbent floors may be used in lieu of an automatic trap primer.

SECTION 413 FOOD WASTE GRINDER UNITS

413.1 Approval. Domestic food waste grinders shall conform to ASSE 1008. Commercial food waste grinders shall conform to ASSE 1009. Food waste grinders shall not increase the *drainage fixture unit* load on the sanitary drainage system.

413.2 Domestic food waste grinder waste outlets. Domestic food waste grinders shall be connected to a drain of not less than $1^1/_2$ inches (38 mm) in diameter.

413.3 Commercial food waste grinder waste outlets. Deleted.

413.4 Water supply required. All food waste grinders shall be provided with a supply of cold water. The water supply shall be protected against backflow by an *air gap* or backflow preventer in accordance with Section 608.

SECTION 414 GARBAGE CAN WASHERS Deleted

SECTION 415 LAUNDRY TRAYS

415.1 Approval. Laundry trays shall conform to ANSI Z124.6, ASME A112.19.1M, ASME A112.19.3M, ASME A112.19.9M, CSA B45.2 or CSA B45.4.

415.2 Waste outlet. Each compartment of a laundry tray shall be provided with a waste outlet a minimum of $1^1/_2$ inches (38 mm) in diameter and a strainer or crossbar to restrict the clear opening of the waste outlet.

SECTION 416
LAVATORIES

416.1 Approval. Lavatories shall conform to ANSI Z124.3, ASME A112.19.1M, ASME A112.19.2M, ASME A112.19.3M, ASME A112.19.4M, ASME A112.19.9M, CSA B45.1, CSA B45.2, CSA B45.3 or CSA B45.4. Group wash-up equipment shall conform to the requirements of Section 402. Every 20 inches (508 mm) of rim space shall be considered as one lavatory.

416.2 Cultured marble lavatories. Cultured marble vanity tops with an integral lavatory shall conform to ANSI Z124.3 or CSA B45.5.

416.3 Lavatory waste outlets. Lavatories shall have waste outlets not less than 1$^{1}/_{4}$ inches (32 mm) in diameter. A strainer, pop-up stopper, crossbar or other device shall be provided to restrict the clear opening of the waste outlet.

416.4 Moveable lavatory systems. Deleted.

416.5 Tempered water for public hand-washing facilities. Deleted.

SECTION 417
SHOWERS

417.1 Approval. Prefabricated showers and shower compartments shall conform to ANSI Z124.2, ASME A112.19.9M or CSA B45.5. Shower valves for individual showers shall conform to the requirements of Section 424.3.

417.2 Water supply riser. Water supply risers from the shower valve to the shower head outlet, whether exposed or concealed, shall be attached to the structure. The attachment to the structure shall be made by the use of support devices designed for use with the specific piping material or by fittings anchored with screws.

417.3 Shower waste outlet. Waste outlets serving showers shall be at least 2 inches (51 mm) in diameter and, for other than waste outlets in bathtubs, shall have removable strainers not less than 3 inches (76 mm) in diameter with strainer openings not less than $^{1}/_{4}$ inch (6.4 mm) in minimum dimension. Where each shower space is not provided with an individual waste outlet, the waste outlet shall be located and the floor pitched so that waste from one shower does not flow over the floor area serving another shower. Waste outlets shall be fastened to the waste pipe in an *approved* manner.

Exception: Retaining pre-existing 1$^{1}/_{2}$ inch (12.3 mm) in diameter waste outlets shall be permitted when removing an existing bathtub and installing in its place a shower.

417.4 Shower compartments. Shower compartments shall conform to Table 417.4 and shall have approved shower pan material or the equivalent thereof as determined by the plumbing official. The pan shall turn up on three sides at least 2 inches (51 mm) above the finished curb level. The remaining side shall wrap over the curb. Shower drains shall be constructed with a clamping device so that the pan may be securely fastened to the shower drain thereby making a water-tight joint. Shower drains shall have an approved weephole device system to ensure constant drainage of water from the shower pan to the sanitary drainage system. There shall be a water-tight joint between the shower and drain and trap. Shower receptacle waste outlets shall be not less than 2 inches (51mm)and shall have a removable strainer.

Exception: Shower compartments with prefabricated receptors conforming to the standards listed in Table 417.4.

TABLE 417.4
PREFABRICATED SHOWER
RECEPTOR STANDARDS MATERIALS STANDARDS

Plastic shower receptors and shower stalls	ANSI Z124.2
Shower pans, nonmetallic	ASTM D 4551, See Section 303.8

417.4.1 Wall area. The wall area above built-in tubs with installed shower heads and in shower compartments shall be constructed of smooth, noncorrosive and nonabsorbent waterproof materials to a height not less than 6 feet (1829 mm) above the room floor level, and not less than 70 inches (1778 mm) where measured from the compartment floor at the drain. Such walls shall form a water-tight joint with each other and with either the tub, receptor or shower floor.

417.4.2 Access. Deleted.

417.5 Shower floors or receptors. Floor surfaces shall be constructed of impervious, noncorrosive, nonabsorbent and waterproof materials.

417.5.1 Support. Floors or receptors under shower compartments shall be laid on, and supported by, a smooth and structurally sound base.

417.5.2 Shower lining. Floors under shower compartments, except where prefabricated receptors have been provided, shall be lined and made water tight utilizing material complying with Sections 417.5.2.1 through 417.5.2.5. Such liners shall turn up on all sides at least 2 inches (51 mm) above the finished threshold level. Liners shall be recessed and fastened to an *approved* backing so as not to occupy the space required for wall covering, and shall not be nailed or perforated at any point less than 1 inch (25 mm) above the finished threshold. Liners shall be securely fastened to the waste outlet at the seepage entrance, making a water-tight joint between the liner and the outlet. Liners shall be installed in accordance with manufacturer's instructions.

Exceptions:

1. Floor surfaces under shower heads provided for rinsing laid directly on the ground are not required to comply with this section.
2. Where a sheet-applied, load-bearing, bonded, waterproof membrane is installed as the shower lining, the membrane shall not be required to be recessed.

417.5.2.1 PVC sheets. Plasticized polyvinyl chloride (PVC) sheets shall be a minimum of 0.040 inch (1.02 mm) thick, and shall meet the requirements of ASTM D 4551. Sheets shall be joined by solvent welding in accordance with the manufacturer's installation instructions.

417.5.2.2 Chlorinated polyethylene (CPE) sheets. Nonplasticized chlorinated polyethylene sheet shall be a minimum 0.040 inch (1.02 mm) thick, and shall meet the requirements of ASTM D 4068. The liner shall be joined in accordance with the manufacturer's installation instructions.

417.5.2.3 Sheet lead. Sheet lead shall not weigh less than 4 pounds per square foot (19.5 kg/m^2) coated with an asphalt paint or other *approved* coating. The lead sheet shall be insulated from conducting substances other than the connecting drain by 15-pound (6.80 kg) asphalt felt or its equivalent. Sheet lead shall be joined by burning.

417.5.2.4 Sheet copper. Sheet copper shall conform to ASTM B 152 and shall not weigh less than 12 ounces per square foot (3.7 kg/m^2). The copper sheet shall be insulated from conducting substances other than the connecting drain by 15-pound (6.80 kg) asphalt felt or its equivalent. Sheet copper shall be joined by brazing or soldering.

417.5.2.5 Sheet-applied, load-bearing, bonded, waterproof membranes. Sheet-applied, load-bearing, bonded, waterproof membranes shall meet requirements of ANSI A118.10 and shall be applied in accordance with the manufacturer's installation instructions.

417.6 Glazing. Windows and doors within a shower enclosure shall conform to the safety glazing requirements of the *International Building Code*.

SECTION 418 SINKS

418.1 Approval. Sinks shall conform to ANSI Z124.6, ASME A112.19.1M, ASME A112.19.2M, ASME A112.19.3M, ASME A112.19.4M, ASME A112.19.9M, CSA B45.1, CSA B45.2, CSA B45.3 or CSA B45.4.

418.2 Sink waste outlets. Sinks shall be provided with waste outlets a minimum of 1$^1/_2$ inches (38 mm) in diameter. A strainer or crossbar shall be provided to restrict the clear opening of the waste outlet.

418.3 Moveable sink systems. Moveable sink systems shall comply with ASME A112.19.12.

SECTION 419 URINALS Deleted

SECTION 420 WATER CLOSETS

420.1 Approval. Water closets shall conform to the water consumption requirements of Section 604.4 and shall conform to ANSI Z124.4, ASME A112.19.2M, CSA B45.1, CSA B45.4 or CSA B45.5. Water closets shall conform to the hydraulic performance requirements of ASME A112.19.6. Water closet tanks shall conform to ANSI Z124.4, ASME A112.19.2, ASME A112.19.9M, CSA B45.1, CSA B45.4 or CSA B45.5. Electro-hydraulic water closets shall comply with ASME A112.19.13.

420.2 Water closets for public or employee toilet facilities. Deleted.

420.3 Water closet seats. Water closets shall be equipped with seats of smooth, nonabsorbent material. Water closet seats shall be sized for the water closet bowl type.

420.4 Water closet connections. A 4-inch by 3-inch (102 mm by 76 mm) closet bend shall be acceptable. Where a 3-inch (76 mm) bend is utilized on water closets, a 4-inch by 3-inch (102 mm by 76 mm) flange shall be installed to receive the fixture horn.

SECTION 421 WHIRLPOOL BATHTUBS

421.1 Approval. Whirlpool bathtubs shall comply with ASME A112.19.7M or with CSA B45.5 and CSA B45 (Supplement 1).

421.2 Installation. Whirlpool bathtubs shall be installed and tested in accordance with the manufacturer's installation instructions. The pump shall be located above the weir of the fixture trap.

421.3 Drain. The pump drain and circulation piping shall be sloped to drain the water in the volute and the circulation piping when the whirlpool bathtub is empty.

421.4 Suction fittings. Suction fittings for whirlpool bathtubs shall comply with ASME A112.19.8M.

421.5 Access to pump. *Access* shall be provided to circulation pumps in accordance with the fixture or pump manufacturer's installation instructions. Where the manufacturer's instructions do not specify the location and minimum size of field-fabricated *access* openings, a 12-inch by 12-inch (305 mm by 305 mm) minimum sized opening shall be installed to provide *access* to the circulation pump. Where pumps are located more than 2 feet (609 mm) from the *access* opening, an 18-inch by 18-inch (457 mm by 457 mm) minimum sized opening shall be installed. A door or panel shall be permitted to close the opening. In all cases, the *access* opening shall be unobstructed and of the size necessary to permit the removal and replacement of the circulation pump. A minimum clearance of 21 inches (514.5 mm) is required in front of the access door.

421.6 Whirlpool enclosure. Doors within a whirlpool enclosure shall conform to ASME A112.19.15.

SECTION 422 HEALTH CARE FIXTURES AND EQUIPMENT Deleted

SECTION 423 SPECIALTY PLUMBING FIXTURES

423.1 Water connections. Baptisteries, ornamental and lily pools, aquariums, ornamental fountain basins, swimming pools, and similar constructions, where provided with water supplies, shall be protected against backflow in accordance with Section 608.

423.2 Approval. Specialties requiring water and waste connections shall be submitted for approval.

SECTION 424
FAUCETS AND OTHER FIXTURE FITTINGS

424.1 Approval. Faucets and fixture fittings shall conform to ASME A112.18.1/CSA B125.1. Faucets and fixture fittings that supply drinking water for human ingestion shall conform to the requirements of NSF 61, Section 9. Flexible water connectors exposed to continuous pressure shall conform to the requirements of Section 605.6.

424.1.1 Faucets and supply fittings. Faucets and supply fittings shall conform to the water consumption requirements of Section 604.4.

424.1.2 Waste fittings. Waste fittings shall conform to ASME A112.18.2/CSA B125.2, ASTM F 409 or to one of the standards listed in Tables 702.1 and 702.4 for aboveground drainage and vent pipe and fittings.

424.2 Hand showers. Hand-held showers shall conform to ASME A112.18.1 or CSA B125.1. Hand-held showers shall provide backflow protection in accordance with ASME A112.18.1 or CSA B125.1 or shall be protected against backflow by a device complying with ASME A112.18.3.

424.3 Individual shower valves. Individual shower and tub-shower combination valves shall be balanced-pressure, thermostatic or combination balanced-pressure/thermostatic valves that conform to the requirements of ASSE 1016 or ASME A112.18.1/CSA B125.1 and shall be installed at the point of use. Shower and tub-shower combination valves required by this section shall be equipped with a means to limit the maximum setting of the valve to 120°F (49°C), which shall be field adjusted in accordance with the manufacturer's instructions. In-line thermostatic valves shall not be utilized for compliance with this section. Scald preventative valves are not required in dwelling units with individual water heaters set at 120°F (49°C).

424.4 Multiple (gang) showers. Deleted.

424.5 Bathtub and whirlpool bathtub valves. The *hot water* supplied to bathtubs and whirlpool bathtubs shall be limited to a maximum temperature of 120°F (49°C) by a water-temperature limiting device that conforms to ASSE 1070 or CSA B125.3, except where such protection is otherwise provided by a combination tub/shower valve in accordance with Section 424.3. Scald preventative valves are not required in dwelling units with individual water heaters set at 120°F (49°C).

424.6 Hose-connected outlets. Faucets and fixture fittings with hose-connected outlets shall conform to ASME A112.18.3M or CSA B125.

424.7 Temperature-actuated, flow reduction valves for individual fixture fittings. Temperature-actuated, flow reduction devices, where installed for individual fixture fittings, shall conform to ASSE 1062. Such valves shall not be used alone as a substitute for the balanced pressure, thermostatic or combination shower valves required in Section 424.3.

424.8 Transfer valves. Deck-mounted bath/shower transfer valves containing an integral atmospheric vacuum breaker shall conform to the requirements of ASME A112.18.7.

SECTION 425
FLUSHING DEVICES FOR WATER CLOSETS AND URINALS

425.1 Flushing devices required. Each water closet, urinal, clinical sink and any plumbing fixture that depends on trap siphonage to discharge the fixture contents to the drainage system shall be provided with a flushometer valve, flushometer tank or a flush tank designed and installed to supply water in quantity and rate of flow to flush the contents of the fixture, cleanse the fixture and refill the fixture trap.

A flushometer valve, flush tank or similar device shall not be required for urinal fixtures that comply with the waterless test requirements of ANSI Z124.9 and that:

1. Provide a barrier liquid sealant contained in a removable trap to maintain the trap seal;
2. Permit the uninhibited flow of water through the trap to the sanitary drainage system;
3. Comply with ANSI Z124.9 and ASME 112.19.2, as applicable.

425.1.1 Separate for each fixture. A flushing device shall not serve more than one fixture.

425.2 Flushometer valves and tanks. Flushometer valves and tanks shall comply with ASSE 1037. Vacuum breakers on flushometer valves shall conform to the performance requirements of ASSE 1001 or CAN/CSA B64.1.1. *Access* shall be provided to vacuum breakers. Flushometer valves shall be of the water-conservation type and shall not be utilized where the water pressure is lower than the minimum required for normal operation. When operated, the valve shall automatically complete the cycle of operation, opening fully and closing positively under the water supply pressure. Each flushometer valve shall be provided with a means for regulating the flow through the valve. The trap seal to the fixture shall be automatically refilled after each valve flushing cycle.

425.3 Flush tanks. Flush tanks equipped for manual flushing shall be controlled by a device designed to refill the tank after each discharge and to shut off completely the water flow to the tank when the tank is filled to operational capacity. The trap seal to the fixture shall be automatically refilled after each flushing. The water supply to flush tanks equipped for automatic flushing shall be controlled with a timing device or sensor control devices.

425.3.1 Fill valves. All flush tanks shall be equipped with an antisiphon fill valve conforming to ASSE 1002 or CSA B125.3. The fill valve backflow preventer shall be located at least 1 inch (25 mm) above the full opening of the overflow pipe.

425.3.2 Overflows in flush tanks. Flush tanks shall be provided with overflows discharging to the water closet or urinal connected thereto and shall be sized to prevent flooding the tank at the maximum rate at which the tanks are supplied with water according to the manufacturer's design conditions. The opening of the overflow pipe shall be located above the flood level rim of the water closet or urinal or above a secondary overflow in the flush tank.

425.3.3 Sheet copper. Sheet copper utilized for flush tank linings shall conform to ASTM B 152 and shall not weigh less than 10 ounces per square foot (0.03 kg/m^2).

425.3.4 Access required. All parts in a flush tank shall be accessible for repair and replacement.

425.4 Flush pipes and fittings. Flush pipes and fittings shall be of nonferrous material and shall conform to ASME A112.19.5 or CSA B125.

SECTION 426
MANUAL FOOD AND BEVERAGE DISPENSING EQUIPMENT
Deleted

SECTION 427
FLOOR SINKS
Deleted

CHAPTER 5

WATER HEATERS

SECTION 501 GENERAL

501.1 Scope. The provisions of this chapter shall govern the materials, design and installation of water heaters and the related safety devices and appurtenances.

501.2 Water heater as space heater. Where a combination potable water heating and space heating system requires water for space heating at temperatures higher than 140°F (60°C), a master thermostatic mixing valve complying with ASSE 1017 shall be provided to limit the water supplied to the potable *hot water* distribution system to a temperature of 140°F (60°C) or less. The potability of the water shall be maintained throughout the system.

501.3 Drain valves. Drain valves for emptying shall be installed at the bottom of each tank-type water heater and *hot water* storage tank. Drain valves shall conform to ASSE 1005.

501.4 Location. Water heaters and storage tanks shall be located and connected so as to provide *access* for observation, maintenance, servicing and replacement.

501.5 Water heater labeling. All water heaters shall be third-party certified.

501.6 Water temperature control in piping from tankless heaters. The temperature of water from tankless water heaters shall be a maximum of 140°F (60°C) when intended for domestic uses. This provision shall not supersede the requirement for protective shower valves in accordance with Section 424.3.

501.7 Pressure marking of storage tanks. Storage tanks and water heaters installed for domestic hot water shall have the maximum allowable working pressure clearly and indelibly stamped in the metal or marked on a plate welded thereto or otherwise permanently attached. Such markings shall be in an accessible position outside of the tank so as to make inspection or reinspection readily possible.

501.8 Temperature controls. All hot water supply systems shall be equipped with automatic temperature controls capable of adjustments from the lowest to the highest acceptable temperature settings for the intended temperature operating range. In a water heating system where temperatures exceed 140°F (60°C), a means such as a mixing valve shall be installed to temper the water for domestic uses.

501.9 Installation by manufacturer. The following is a reprint of GS 66-27.1, "Safety Features of HotWater Heaters."

(a) No individual, firm, corporation or business shall install, sell or offer for sale any automatic hot water tank or heater of 120-gallon (454 L) capacity or less, except for a tankless water heater, which does not have installed thereon by the manufacturer of the tank or heater an American Society of Mechanical Engineers and National Board of Boiler and Pressure Vessel Inspectors approved type pressure-temperature relief valve set at or below the safe working pressure of the tank as indicated, and so labeled by the manufacturer's identification stamped or cast upon the tank or heater or upon a plate secured to it.

(b) No individual, firm, corporation or business shall install, sell or offer for sale any relief valve, whether it be pressure type, temperature type or pressure-temperature type, which does not carry the stamp of approval of the American Society of Mechanical Engineers and the National Board of Boiler and Pressure Vessel Inspectors.

The following is a reprint of GS 66-27.1A, "Water heater thermostat settings."

(a) The thermostat of any new residential water heater offered for sale or lease for use in a single-family or multifamily dwelling in the State shall be preset by the manufacturer or installer no higher than approximately 120°F (49°C). A water heater reservoir temperature may be set higher if it is supplying space heaters that require higher temperatures. For purposes of this section, a water heater shall mean the primary source of hot water for any single-family or multifamily residential dwelling including, but not limited to any solar or other hot water heating systems.

(b) Nothing in this section shall prohibit the occupant of a single-family or multiunit residential dwelling with an individual water heater from resetting or having reset the thermostat on the water heater. Any such resetting shall relieve the manufacturer or installer of the water heater and, in the case of a residential dwelling that is leased or rented, also the unit's owner, from liability for damages attributed to the resetting.

(c) A warning tag or sticker shall be placed on or near the operating thermostat control of any residential water heater. This tag or sticker shall state that the thermostat settings above the preset temperature may cause severe burns. This tag or sticker may carry such other appropriate warnings as may be agreed upon by manufacturers, installers and other interested parties.

501.10 Fossil fuel equipment installation. The installation of the following equipment and systems shall comply with the *North Carolina Fuel Gas Code*:

1. Fuel piping for any fossil fuel-burning equipment.
2. Venting systems for fossil fuel-burning equipment which is part of the plumbing system.

SECTION 502
INSTALLATION

502.1 General. Water heaters shall be installed in accordance with the manufacturer's installation instructions. Oil-fired water heaters shall conform to the requirements of this code and the *International Mechanical Code*. Electric water heaters shall conform to the requirements of this code and provisions of NFPA 70. Gas-fired water heaters shall conform to the requirements of the *International Fuel Gas Code*.

502.1.1 Elevation and protection. Elevation of water heater ignition sources and mechanical damage protection requirements for water heaters shall be in accordance with the *International Mechanical Code* and the *International Fuel Gas Code*.

502.2 Rooms used as a plenum. Water heaters using solid, liquid or gas fuel shall not be installed in a room containing air-handling machinery when such room is used as a plenum.

502.3 Water heaters installed in attics. Attics containing a water heater shall be provided with an opening and unobstructed passageway large enough to allow removal of the water heater. The passageway shall not be less than 30 inches (762 mm) high and 22 inches (559 mm) wide and not more than 20 feet (6096 mm) in length when measured along the centerline of the passageway from the opening to the water heater. If 6 feet (1829 mm) of headroom is provided along the centerline of the passageway from the opening to the water heater, the length of the passageway is permitted to exceed 20 feet (6096 mm) in length. The passageway shall have continuous solid flooring not less than 24 inches (610 mm) wide. A level service space at least 30 inches (762 mm) deep and 30 inches (762 mm) wide shall be present at the front or service side of the water heater. The clear *access* opening dimensions shall be a minimum of 20 inches by 30 inches (508 mm by 762 mm) where such dimensions are large enough to allow removal of the water heater.

502.4 Seismic supports. Deleted.

502.5 Water heaters installed in garages. Water heaters having an ignition source shall be elevated such that the source of ignition is not less than 18 inches (457 mm) above the garage floor. Appliances shall be located or protected so that they are not subject to physical damage by a moving vehicle.

Exception: Elevation of the ignition source is not required for appliances that are listed as flammable vapor ignition resistant.

502.6 Installation in crawl spaces. Under-floor spaces containing appliances requiring access shall be provided with an access opening and unobstructed passageway large enough to remove the largest component of the appliance. The passageway shall not be less than 22 inches (559 mm) high and 36 inches (914 mm) wide, nor more than 20 feet (6096 mm) in length when measured along the centerline of the passageway from the opening to the equipment. A level service space not less than 30 inches (762 mm) deep and 30 inches (762 mm) wide shall be present at the front or service side of the appliance. If the depth of the passageway or the service space exceeds 12 inches (305mm) below the adjoining grade, the walls of the passageway shall be lined with concrete or masonry extending 4 inches (102 mm) above the adjoining grade and having sufficient lateral-bearing capacity to resist collapse.

The clear access opening dimensions shall be a minimum of 22 inches by 30 inches (559 mm by 762 mm), where such dimensions are large enough to allow removal of the largest component of the appliance.

Exceptions:

1. The passageway is not required where the level service space is present when the access is open and the appliance is capable of being serviced and removed through the required opening.
2. Where the passageway is not less than 6 feet high (1829 mm) for its entire length, the passageway shall not be limited in length.

502.7 Under-floor and exterior-grade installation.

502.7.1 Exterior-grade installations. Equipment and appliances installed above grade level shall be supported on a solid base or approved material a minimum of 2 inches (51 mm) thick.

502.7.2 Under-floor installation. Suspended equipment shall be a minimum of 6 inches (152 mm) above the adjoining grade.

502.7.3 Crawl space supports. The support shall be a minimum of a 2-inch (51 mm) thick solid base, 2-inch (51 mm) thick formed concrete, or stacked masonry units held in place by mortar or other approved method. The water heater shall be supported not less than 2 inches (51 mm) above grade.

502.7.4 Drainage. Below-grade installations shall be provided with a natural drain or an automatic lift or sump pump. Existing installation that can be terminated outdoors must terminate outdoors. Where the installation is such that outdoor termination is impossible, indoor termination is allowable.

502.8 Prohibited installations. Water heaters, (using solid, liquid or gas fuel) with the exception of those having direct vent systems, shall not be installed in bathrooms and bedrooms or in a closet with access only through a bedroom or bathroom. However, water heaters of the automatic storage type may be installed as replacement in a bathroom, when approved by the plumbing official, provided they are vented and supplied with adequate combustion air.

Exception: When a closet, having a weather-stripped solid door with an approved closing device, has been designed exclusively for the water heater and where all air for combustion and ventilation is supplied from outdoors.

SECTION 503
CONNECTIONS

503.1 Cold water line valve. The cold water *branch* line from the main water supply line to each hot water storage tank or water heater shall be provided with a valve, located within 3 feet (914 mm) of the equipment and serving only the hot water storage tank or water heater. The valve shall not interfere or cause a disruption of the cold water supply to the remainder of the cold water system. The valve shall be provided with *access* on the same floor level as the water heater served.

503.2 Water circulation. The method of connecting a circulating water heater to the tank shall provide circulation of water through the water heater. The pipe or tubes required for the installation of appliances that will draw from the water heater or storage tank shall comply with the provisions of this code for material and installation. Installation shall comply with the manufacturer's instructions.

SECTION 504 SAFETY DEVICES

504.1 Antisiphon devices. An *approved* means, such as a cold water "dip" tube with a hole at the top or a vacuum relief valve installed in the cold water supply line above the top of the heater or tank, shall be provided to prevent siphoning of any storage water heater or tank.

504.2 Vacuum relief valve. Bottom fed water heaters and bottom fed tanks connected to water heaters shall have a vacuum relief valve installed. The vacuum relief valve shall comply with ANSI Z21.22.

504.3 Shutdown. A means for disconnecting an electric hot water supply system from its energy supply shall be provided in accordance with NFPA 70. A separate valve shall be provided to shut off the energy fuel supply to all other types of hot water supply systems.

504.4 Relief valve. All storage water heaters operating above atmospheric pressure shall be provided with an *approved*, self-closing (levered) pressure relief valve and temperature relief valve or combination thereof. The relief valve shall conform to ANSI Z21.22. The relief valve shall not be used as a means of controlling thermal expansion.

504.4.1 Installation. Such valves shall be installed in the shell of the water heater tank. Temperature relief valves shall be so located in the tank as to be actuated by the water in the top 6 inches (152 mm) of the tank served. For installations with separate storage tanks, the valves shall be installed on the tank and there shall not be any type of valve installed between the water heater and the storage tank. There shall not be a check valve or shutoff valve between a relief valve and the heater or tank served.

504.5 Relief valve approval. Temperature and pressure relief valves, or combinations thereof, and energy cutoff devices shall bear the label of an *approved* agency and shall have a temperature setting of not more than 210°F (99°C) and a pressure setting not exceeding the tank or water heater manufacturer's rated working pressure or 150 psi (1035 kPa), whichever is less. The relieving capacity of each pressure relief valve and each temperature relief valve shall equal or exceed the heat input to the water heater or storage tank.

504.6 Requirements for discharge piping. The discharge piping serving a pressure relief valve, temperature relief valve or combination thereof shall:

1. Not be directly connected to the drainage system.
2. Discharge through an *air gap* located in the same room as the water heater, either on the floor, into an indirect waste receptor or outdoors.
3. Not be smaller than the diameter of the outlet of the valve served and shall discharge full size to the *air gap*.
4. Serve a single relief device and shall not connect to piping serving any other relief device or equipment.
5. Discharge to the floor, to the pan serving the water heater or storage tank, to a waste receptor or to the outdoors.
6. Discharge in a manner that does not cause personal injury or structural damage.
7. Discharge to a termination point that is readily observable by the building occupants.
8. Not be trapped.
9. Be installed so as to flow by gravity.
10. Not terminate more than 6 inches (152 mm) above the floor or waste receptor.
11. Not have a threaded connection at the end of such piping.
12. Not have valves or tee fittings.
13. Be constructed of those materials listed in Section 605.4 or materials tested, rated and *approved* for such use in accordance with ASME A112.4.1.

504.7 Required pan. Where water heaters or hot water storage tanks are installed in: (a) remote locations such as a suspended ceiling, (b) attics, (c) above occupied spaces, or (d) unventilated crawl spaces, the tank or water heater shall be installed in a galvanized steel pan having a material thickness of not less than 0.0236 inch (0.6010 mm) (No. 24 gage), or other pans approved for such use.

Exceptions:

1. Electric water heaters may rest in a high-impact plastic pan of at least $^{1}/_{16}$ inch (1.6 mm) thickness.
2. Water heater mounted on concrete floor for floor drains.

504.7.1 Pan size and drain. The pan drain shall not be less than $1^{1}/_{2}$ inches (38 mm) deep and shall not be obstructed by the appliance. The pan shall be drained by an indirect waste pipe having a minimum diameter of 1 inch (25.4 mm). Piping for safety pan drains shall be of those materials listed in Table 605.4.

504.7.2 Pan drain termination. The pan drain shall extend full-size and terminate over a suitably located indirect waste receptor or floor drain or extend to the exterior of the building and terminate not less than 6 inches (152 mm) and not more than 24 inches (610 mm) above the adjacent ground surface.

SECTION 505 INSULATION

[E] 505.1 Unfired vessel insulation. Unfired hot water storage tanks shall be insulated to R-12.5 (h · ft^2 · °F)/Btu (R-2.2 m^2 · K/W).

CHAPTER 6
WATER SUPPLY AND DISTRIBUTION

SECTION 601
GENERAL

601.1 Scope. This chapter shall govern the materials, design and installation of water supply systems, both hot and cold, for utilization in connection with human occupancy and habitation and shall govern the installation of individual water supply systems.

601.2 Solar energy utilization. Solar energy systems used for heating potable water or using an independent medium for heating potable water shall comply with the applicable requirements of this code. The use of solar energy shall not compromise the requirements for cross connection or protection of the potable water supply system required by this code.

601.3 Existing piping used for grounding. Existing metallic water service piping used for electrical grounding shall not be replaced with nonmetallic pipe or tubing until other *approved* means of grounding is provided.

601.4 Tests. The potable water distribution system shall be tested in accordance with Section 312.5.

SECTION 602
WATER REQUIRED

602.1 General. Every structure equipped with plumbing fixtures and utilized for human occupancy or habitation shall be provided with a potable supply of water in the amounts and at the pressures specified in this chapter.

602.2 Potable water required. Only potable water shall be supplied to plumbing fixtures that provide water for drinking, bathing or culinary purposes, or for the processing of food, medical or pharmaceutical products. Unless otherwise provided in this code, potable water shall be supplied to all plumbing fixtures.

602.3 Individual water supply. Where a potable public water supply is not available, individual sources of potable water supply shall be utilized.

602.3.1 Sources. Deleted.

602.3.2 Minimum quantity. Deleted.

602.3.3 Water quality. Deleted.

602.3.4 Disinfection of system. Deleted.

602.3.5 Pumps. Deleted.

602.3.5.1 Pump enclosure. Deleted.

SECTION 603
WATER SERVICE

603.1 Size of water service pipe. The water service pipe shall be sized to supply water to the structure in the quantities and at the pressures required in this code. The minimum diameter of water service pipe shall be $^3/_4$ inch (19.1 mm).

603.2 Separation of water service and building sewer. Water service pipe and the *building sewer* shall be separated by 5 feet (1524 mm) of undisturbed or compacted earth.

Exceptions:

1. The required separation distance shall not apply where the bottom of the water service pipe within 5 feet (1524 mm) of the *sewer* is a minimum of 12 inches (305 mm) above the top of the highest point of the *sewer* and the pipe materials conform to Table 702.3.
2. Water service pipe is permitted to be located in the same trench with a *building sewer*, provided such *sewer* is constructed of materials listed in Table 702.2.
3. The required separation distance shall not apply where a water service pipe crosses a *sewer* pipe, provided the water service pipe is sleeved to at least 5 feet (1524 mm) horizontally from the *sewer* pipe centerline on both sides of such crossing with pipe materials listed in Table 605.3, 702.2 or 702.3.

603.2.1 Water service near sources of pollution. Potable water service pipes shall not be located in, under or above cesspools, septic tanks, septic tank drainage fields or seepage pits (see Section 605.1 for soil and groundwater conditions).

SECTION 604
DESIGN OF BUILDING WATER DISTRIBUTION SYSTEM

604.1 General. The design of the water distribution system shall conform to *accepted engineering practice*. Methods utilized to determine pipe sizes shall be *approved*.

604.2 System interconnection. At the points of interconnection between the hot and cold water supply piping systems and the individual fixtures, appliances or devices, provisions shall be made to prevent flow between such piping systems.

604.3 Water distribution system design criteria. The water distribution system shall be designed, and pipe sizes shall be selected such that under conditions of peak demand, the capacities at the fixture supply pipe outlets shall not be less than shown in Table 604.3. The minimum flow rate and flow pressure provided to fixtures and appliances not listed in Table 604.3 shall be in accordance with the manufacturer's installation instructions.

604.4 Maximum flow and water consumption. The maximum water consumption flow rates and quantities for all plumbing fixtures and fixture fittings shall be in accordance with Table 604.4.

Exceptions:

1. Blowout design water closets having a maximum water consumption of $3^1/_2$ gallons (13 L) per flushing cycle.
2. Vegetable sprays.

3. Clinical sinks having a maximum water consumption of $4^1/_2$ gallons (17 L) per flushing cycle.
4. Service sinks.
5. Emergency showers.

**TABLE 604.3
WATER DISTRIBUTION SYSTEM DESIGN CRITERIA
REQUIRED CAPACITY AT FIXTURE SUPPLY PIPE OUTLETS**

FIXTURE SUPPLY OUTLET SERVING	FLOW RATE[a] (gpm)	FLOW PRESSURE (psi)
Bathtub, balanced-pressure, thermostatic or combination balanced-pressure/thermostatic mixing valve	4	20
Bidet, thermostatic mixing valve	2	20
Combination fixture	4	8
Dishwasher, residential	2.75	8
Drinking fountain	0.75	8
Laundry tray	4	8
Lavatory	2	8
Shower	3	8
Shower, balanced-pressure, thermostatic or combination balanced-pressure/thermostatic mixing valve	3	20
Sillcock, hose bibb	5	8
Sink, residential	2.5	8
Sink, service	3	8
Urinal, valve	12	25
Water closet, blow out, flushometer valve	25	45
Water closet, flushometer tank	1.6	20
Water closet, siphonic, flushometer valve	25	35
Water closet, tank, close coupled	3	20
Water closet, tank, one piece	6	20

For SI: 1 pound per square inch = 6.895 kPa, 1 gallon per minute = 3.785 L/m.
a. For additional requirements for flow rates and quantities, see Section 604.4.

604.4.1 Lavatory faucets. Deleted.

604.5 Size of fixture supply. The minimum size of a fixture supply pipe shall be as shown in Table 604.5. The fixture supply pipe shall not terminate more than 30 inches (762 mm) from the point of connection to the fixture. A reduced-size flexible water connector installed between the supply pipe and the fixture shall be of an *approved* type. The supply pipe shall extend to the floor or wall adjacent to the fixture. The minimum size of individual distribution lines utilized in gridded or parallel water distribution systems shall be as shown in Table 604.5.

Exception: The length of restriction shall not apply to residential dishwashers or ice makers.

604.6 Variable street pressures. Where street water main pressures fluctuate, the building water distribution system shall be designed for the minimum pressure available.

604.7 Inadequate water pressure. Wherever water pressure from the street main or other source of supply is insufficient to provide flow pressures at fixture outlets as required under Table 604.3, a water pressure booster system conforming to Section 606.5 shall be installed on the building water supply system.

**TABLE 604.4
MAXIMUM FLOW RATES AND CONSUMPTION FOR
PLUMBING FIXTURES AND FIXTURE FITTINGS**

PLUMBING FIXTURE OR FIXTURE FITTING	MAXIMUM FLOW RATE OR QUANTITY[b]
Lavatory, private	2.2 gpm at 60 psi
Lavatory, public (metering)	0.25 gallon per metering cycle
Lavatory, public (other than metering)	0.5 gpm at 60 psi
Shower head[a]	2.5 gpm at 80 psi
Sink faucet	2.2 gpm at 60 psi
Urinal	1.0 gallon per flushing cycle
Water closet	1.6 gallons per flushing cycle

For SI: 1 gallon = 3.785 L, 1 gallon per minute = 3.785 L/m,
1 pound per square inch = 6.895 kPa.
a. A hand-held shower spray is a shower head.
b. Consumption tolerances shall be determined from referenced standards.

**TABLE 604.5
MINIMUM SIZES OF FIXTURE WATER SUPPLY PIPES**

FIXTURE	MINIMUM PIPE SIZE (inch)
Bathtubs[a] (60″ × 32″ and smaller)	$^1/_2$
Bathtubs[a] (larger than 60″ × 32″)	$^1/_2$
Bidet	$^3/_8$
Combination sink and tray	$^1/_2$
Dishwasher, domestic[a]	$^1/_2$
Drinking fountain	$^3/_8$
Hose bibbs	$^1/_2$
Kitchen sink[a]	$^1/_2$
Laundry, 1, 2 or 3 compartments[a]	$^1/_2$
Lavatory	$^3/_8$
Shower, single head[a]	$^1/_2$
Sinks, flushing rim	$^3/_4$
Sinks, service	$^1/_2$
Urinal, flush tank	$^1/_2$
Urinal, flush valve	$^3/_4$
Wall hydrant	$^1/_2$
Water closet, flush tank	$^3/_8$
Water closet, flush valve	1
Water closet, flushometer tank	$^3/_8$
Water closet, one piece[a]	$^1/_2$

For SI: 1 inch = 25.4 mm, 1 foot = 304.8 mm,
1 pound per square inch = 6.895 kPa.
a. Where the developed length of the distribution line is 60 feet or less, and the available pressure at the meter is a minimum of 35 psi, the minimum size of an individual distribution line supplied from a manifold and installed as part of a parallel water distribution system shall be one nominal tube size smaller than the sizes indicated.

604.8 Water-pressure reducing valve or regulator. Where water pressure within a building exceeds 80 psi (552 kPa) static, an *approved* water-pressure reducing valve conforming to ASSE 1003 with strainer shall be installed to reduce the pressure in the building water distribution piping to 80 psi (552 kPa) static or less.

Exception: Service lines to sill cocks and outside hydrants, and main supply risers where pressure from the mains is reduced to 80 psi (552 kPa) or less at individual fixtures.

604.8.1 Valve design. The pressure-reducing valve shall be designed to remain open to permit uninterrupted water flow in case of valve failure.

604.8.2 Repair and removal. All water-pressure reducing valves, regulators and strainers shall be so constructed and installed as to permit repair or removal of parts without breaking a pipeline or removing the valve and strainer from the pipeline.

604.9 Water hammer. The flow velocity of the water distribution system shall be controlled to reduce the possibility of water hammer. A water-hammer arrestor shall be installed where quick-closing valves (example: clothes washers, dishwashers, ice makers) and metallic piping is used. The water-hammer arrestor shall not be required on any valves where plastic pipe is used for water distribution piping. Water-hammer arrestors shall be installed in accordance with the manufacturer's specifications. Water-hammer arrestors shall conform to ASSE 1010.

604.10 Gridded and parallel water distribution system manifolds. Hot water and cold water manifolds installed with gridded or parallel connected individual distribution lines to each fixture or fixture fitting shall be designed in accordance with Sections 604.10.1 through 604.10.3.

604.10.1 Manifold sizing. Hot water and cold water manifolds shall be sized in accordance with Table 604.10.1. The total gallons per minute is the demand of all outlets supplied.

TABLE 604.10.1
MANIFOLD SIZING

NOMINAL SIZE INTERNAL DIAMETER (inches)	MAXIMUM DEMAND (gpm)	
	Velocity at 4 feet per second	Velocity at 8 feet per second
$^1/_2$	2	5
$^3/_4$	6	11
1	10	20
$1^1/_4$	15	31
$1^1/_2$	22	44

For SI: 1 inch = 25.4 mm, 1 gallon per minute = 3.785 L/m, 1 foot per second = 0.305 m/s.

604.10.2 Valves. Individual fixture shutoff valves installed at the manifold shall be identified as to the fixture being supplied.

604.10.3 Access. *Access* shall be provided to manifolds.

604.11 Individual pressure balancing in-line valves for individual fixture fittings. Where individual pressure balancing in-line valves for individual fixture fittings are installed, such valves shall comply with ASSE 1066. Such valves shall be installed in an accessible location and shall not be utilized alone as a substitute for the balanced pressure, thermostatic or combination shower valves required in Section 424.3.

SECTION 605
MATERIALS, JOINTS AND CONNECTIONS

605.1 Soil and ground water. The installation of a water service or water distribution pipe shall be prohibited in soil and ground water contaminated with solvents, fuels, organic compounds or other detrimental materials causing permeation, corrosion, degradation or structural failure of the piping material. Where detrimental conditions are suspected, a chemical analysis of the soil and ground water conditions shall be required to ascertain the acceptability of the water service or water distribution piping material for the specific installation. Where detrimental conditions exist, *approved* alternative materials or routing shall be required.

605.2 Lead content of water supply pipe and fittings. Pipe and pipe fittings, including valves and faucets, utilized in the water supply system shall have a maximum of 8-percent lead content.

605.3 Water service pipe. Water service pipe shall conform to NSF 61 and shall conform to one of the standards listed in Table 605.3. All water service pipe or tubing, installed underground and outside of the structure, shall have a minimum working pressure rating of 160 psi (1100 kPa) at 73.4°F (23°C). Where the water pressure exceeds 160 psi (1100 kPa), piping material shall have a minimum rated working pressure equal to the highest available pressure. Water service piping materials not third-party certified for water distribution shall terminate 5 feet (1524 mm) outside the building. All ductile iron water service piping shall be cement mortar lined in accordance with AWWA C104.

605.3.1 Dual check-valve-type backflow preventer. Where a dual check-valve backflow preventer is installed on the water supply system, it shall comply with ASSE 1024 or CSA B64.6.

605.4 Water distribution pipe. Water distribution pipe shall conform to NSF 61 and shall conform to one of the standards listed in Table 605.4. All water distribution pipe and tubing shall have a minimum pressure rating of 100 psi (690 kPa) at 180°F (82°C).

605.5 Fittings. Pipe fittings shall be *approved* for installation with the piping material installed and shall conform to the respective pipe standards or one of the standards listed in Table 605.5. All pipe fittings utilized in water supply systems shall also comply with NSF 61. The fittings shall not have ledges, shoulders or reductions capable of retarding or obstructing flow in the piping. Ductile and gray iron pipe fittings shall be cement mortar lined in accordance with AWWA C104.

TABLE 605.3
WATER SERVICE PIPE

MATERIAL	STANDARD
Acrylonitrile butadiene styrene (ABS) plastic pipe	ASTM D 1527; ASTM D 2282
Asbestos-cement pipe	ASTM C 296
Brass pipe	ASTM B 43
Chlorinated polyvinyl chloride (CPVC) plastic pipe	ASTM D 2846; ASTM F 441; ASTM F 442; CSA B137.6
Copper or copper-alloy pipe	ASTM B 42; ASTM B 302
Copper or copper-alloy tubing (Type K, WK, L, WL)	ASTM B 75; ASTM B 88; ASTM B 251; ASTM B 447
Cross-linked polyethylene (PEX) plastic tubing	ASTM F 876; ASTM F 877; CSA B137.5
Cross-linked polyethylene/aluminum/cross-linked polyethylene (PEX-AL-PEX) pipe	ASTM F 1281; ASTM F 2262; CAN/CSA B137.10M
Cross-linked polyethylene/aluminum/high-density polyethylene (PEX-AL-HDPE)	ASTM F 1986
Ductile iron water pipe	AWWA C151; AWWA C115
Galvanized steel pipe	ASTM A 53
Polyethylene (PE) plastic pipe	ASTM D 2239; ASTM D 3035; CSA B137.1
Polyethylene (PE) plastic tubing	ASTM D 2737; CSA B137.1
Polyethylene/aluminum/polethylene (PE-AL-PE) pipe	ASTM F 1282; CAN/CSA B137.9
Polypropylene (PP) plastic pipe or tubing	ASTM F 2389; CSA B137.11
Polyvinyl chloride (PVC) plastic pipe	ASTM D 1785; ASTM D 2241; ASTM D 2672; CSA B137.3
Stainless steel pipe (Type 304/304L)	ASTM A 312; ASTM A 778
Stainless steel pipe (Type 316/316L)	ASTM A 312; ASTM A 778

TABLE 605.4
WATER DISTRIBUTION PIPE

MATERIAL	STANDARD
Brass pipe	ASTM B 43
Chlorinated polyvinyl chloride (CPVC) plastic pipe and tubing	ASTM D 2846; ASTM F 441; ASTM F 442; CSA B137.6
Copper or copper-alloy pipe	ASTM B 42; ASTM B 302
Copper or copper-alloy tubing (Type K, WK, L, WL, M or WM)[a]	ASTM B 75; ASTM B 88; ASTM B 251; ASTM B 447
Cross-linked polyethylene (PEX) plastic tubing	ASTM F 876; ASTM F 877; CSA B137.5
Cross-linked polyethylene/aluminum/cross-linked polyethylene (PEX-AL-PEX) pipe	ASTM F 1281; ASTM F 2262; CAN/CSA B137.10M
Cross-linked polyethylene/aluminum/high-density polyethylene (PEX-AL-HDPE)	ASTM F 1986
Ductile iron pipe	AWWA C151/A21.51; AWWA C115/A21.15
Galvanized steel pipe	ASTM A 53
Polyethylene/aluminum/polyethylene (PE-AL-PE) composite pipe	ASTM F 1282
Polypropylene (PP) plastic pipe or tubing	ASTM F 2389; CSA B137.11
Stainless steel pipe (Type 304/304L)	ASTM A 312; ASTM A 778
Stainless steel pipe (Type 316/316L)	ASTM A 312; ASTM A 778

a. Below grade Type K, WK, L, WL

605.5.1 Mechanically formed tee fittings. Mechanically extracted outlets shall have a height not less than three times the thickness of the branch tube wall.

605.5.1.1 Full flow assurance. Branch tubes shall not restrict the flow in the run tube. A dimple/depth stop shall be formed in the branch tube to ensure that penetration into the collar is of the correct depth. For inspection purposes, a second dimple shall be placed $^1/_4$ inch (6.4 mm) above the first dimple. Dimples shall be aligned with the tube run.

605.5.1.2 Brazed joints. Mechanically formed tee fittings shall be brazed in accordance with Section 605.14.1.

605.6 Flexible water connectors. Flexible water connectors exposed to continuous pressure shall conform to ASME A112.18.6. *Access* shall be provided to all flexible water connectors.

605.7 Valves. All valves shall be of an *approved* type and compatible with the type of piping material installed in the system. Ball valves, gate valves, globe valves and plug valves intended to supply drinking water shall meet the requirements of NSF 61.

605.8 Manufactured pipe nipples. Manufactured pipe nipples shall conform to one of the standards listed in Table 605.8.

TABLE 605.8
MANUFACTURED PIPE NIPPLES

MATERIAL	STANDARD
Brass-, copper-, chromium-plated	ASTM B 687
Steel	ASTM A 733

605.9 Prohibited joints and connections. The following types of joints and connections shall be prohibited:

1. Cement or concrete joints.
2. Joints made with fittings not *approved* for the specific installation.
3. Solvent-cement joints between different types of plastic pipe.
4. Saddle-type fittings.

605.10 ABS plastic. Joints between ABS plastic pipe or fittings shall comply with Sections 605.10.1 through 605.10.3.

605.10.1 Mechanical joints. Mechanical joints on water pipes shall be made with an elastomeric seal conforming to ASTM D 3139. Mechanical joints shall only be installed in underground systems, unless otherwise *approved*. Joints shall be installed only in accordance with the manufacturer's instructions.

605.10.2 Solvent cementing. Joint surfaces shall be clean and free from moisture. Solvent cement that conforms to ASTM D 2235 shall be applied to all joint surfaces. The joint shall be made while the cement is wet. Joints shall be made in accordance with ASTM D 2235. Solvent-cement joints shall be permitted above or below ground.

605.10.3 Threaded joints. Threads shall conform to ASME B1.20.1. Schedule 80 or heavier pipe shall be permitted to be threaded with dies specifically designed for plastic pipe. *Approved* thread lubricant or tape shall be applied on the male threads only.

TABLE 605.5
PIPE FITTINGS

MATERIAL	STANDARD
Acrylonitrile butadiene styrene (ABS) plastic	ASTM D 2468
Cast-iron	ASME B16.4; ASME B16.12
Chlorinated polyvinyl chloride (CPVC) plastic	ASSE 1061; ASTM D 2846; ASTM F 437; ASTM F 438; ASTM F 439; CSA B137.6
Copper or copper alloy	ASSE 1061; ASME B16.15; ASME B16.18; ASME B16.22; ASME B16.23; ASME B16.26; ASME B16.29
Cross-linked polyethylene/aluminum/high-density polyethylene (PEX-AL-HDPE)	ASTM F 1986
Fittings for cross-linked polyethylene (PEX) plastic tubing	ASSE 1061; ASTM F 877; ASTM F 1807; ASTM F 1960; ASTM F 2080; ASTM F 2098; ASTM F 2159; ASTM F 2434; CSA B137.5
Gray iron and ductile iron	AWWA C110; AWWA C153
Insert fittings for polyethylene/aluminum/polyethylene (PE-AL-PE) and cross-linked polyethylene/aluminum/cross-linked polyethylene (PEX-AL-PEX)	ASTM F 1974; ASTM F1281; ASTM F1282; CAN/CSA B137.9; CAN/CSA B137.10
Malleable iron	ASME B16.3
Metal (brass) insert fittings for polyethylene/aluminum/polyethylene (PE-AL-PE) and cross-linked polyethylene/aluminum/cross-linked polyethylene (PEX-AL-PEX)	ASTM F 1974
Polybutylene (PB) plastic	ASSE 1061; CSA B137.8
Polyethylene (PE) plastic pipe	ASTM D 2609; ASTM D 2683; ASTM D 3261; ASTM F 1055; CSA B137.1
Polypropylene (PP) plastic pipe or tubing	ASTM F 2389; CSA B137.11
Polyvinyl chloride (PVC) plastic	ASTM D 2464; ASTM D 2466; ASTM D 2467; CSA B137.2; CSA B137.3
Stainless steel (Type 304/304L)	ASTM A 312; ASTM A 778
Stainless steel (Type 316/316L)	ASTM A 312; ASTM A 778
Steel	ASME B16.9; ASME B16.11; ASME B16.28

605.11 Asbestos-cement. Joints between asbestos-cement pipe or fittings shall be made with a sleeve coupling of the same composition as the pipe, sealed with an elastomeric ring conforming to ASTM D 1869.

605.12 Brass. Joints between brass pipe or fittings shall comply with Sections 605.12.1 through 605.12.4.

605.12.1 Brazed joints. All joint surfaces shall be cleaned. An *approved* flux shall be applied where required. The joint shall be brazed with a filler metal conforming to AWS A5.8.

605.12.2 Mechanical joints. Mechanical joints shall be installed in accordance with the manufacturer's instructions.

605.12.3 Threaded joints. Threads shall conform to ASME B1.20.1. Pipe-joint compound or tape shall be applied on the male threads only.

605.12.4 Welded joints. All joint surfaces shall be cleaned. The joint shall be welded with an *approved* filler metal.

605.13 Gray iron and ductile iron joints. Joints for gray and ductile iron pipe and fittings shall comply with AWWA C111 and shall be installed in accordance with the manufacturer's installation instructions.

605.14 Copper pipe. Joints between copper or copper-alloy pipe or fittings shall comply with Sections 605.14.1 through 605.14.5.

605.14.1 Brazed joints. All joint surfaces shall be cleaned. An *approved* flux shall be applied where required. The joint shall be brazed with a filler metal conforming to AWS A5.8.

605.14.2 Mechanical joints. Mechanical joints shall be installed in accordance with the manufacturer's instructions.

605.14.3 Soldered joints. Solder joints shall be made in accordance with the methods of ASTM B 828. All cut tube ends shall be reamed to the full inside diameter of the tube end. All joint surfaces shall be cleaned. A flux conforming to ASTM B 813 shall be applied. The joint shall be soldered with a solder conforming to ASTM B 32. The joining of water supply piping shall be made with lead-free solder and fluxes. "Lead free" shall mean a chemical composition equal to or less than 0.2-percent lead.

605.14.4 Threaded joints. Threads shall conform to ASME B1.20.1. Pipe-joint compound or tape shall be applied on the male threads only.

605.14.5 Welded joints. All joint surfaces shall be cleaned. The joint shall be welded with an *approved* filler metal.

605.15 Copper tubing. Joints between copper or copper-alloy tubing or fittings shall comply with Sections 605.15.1 through 605.15.4.

605.15.1 Brazed joints. All joint surfaces shall be cleaned. An *approved* flux shall be applied where required. The joint shall be brazed with a filler metal conforming to AWS A5.8.

605.15.2 Flared joints. Flared joints for water pipe shall be made by a tool designed for that operation.

605.15.3 Mechanical joints. Mechanical joints shall be installed in accordance with the manufacturer's instructions.

605.15.4 Soldered joints. Solder joints shall be made in accordance with the methods of ASTM B 828. All cut tube ends shall be reamed to the full inside diameter of the tube end. All joint surfaces shall be cleaned. A flux conforming to ASTM B 813 shall be applied. The joint shall be soldered with a solder conforming to ASTM B 32. The joining of water supply piping shall be made with lead-free solders and fluxes. "Lead free" shall mean a chemical composition equal to or less than 0.2-percent lead.

605.16 CPVC plastic. Joints between CPVC plastic pipe or fittings shall comply with Sections 605.16.1 through 605.16.3.

605.16.1 Mechanical joints. Mechanical joints shall be installed in accordance with the manufacturer's instructions.

605.16.2 Solvent cementing. Joint surfaces shall be clean and free from moisture, and an *approved* primer shall be applied. Solvent cement, orange in color and conforming to ASTM F 493, shall be applied to all joint surfaces. The joint shall be made while the cement is wet, and in accordance with ASTM D 2846 or ASTM F 493. Solvent-cement joints shall be permitted above or below ground.

Exception: A primer is not required where all of the following conditions apply:

1. The solvent cement used is third-party certified as conforming to ASTM F 493.
2. The solvent cement used is yellow in color.
3. The solvent cement is used only for joining $^1/_2$ inch (12.7 mm) through 2 inch (51 mm) diameter CPVC pipe and fittings.
4. The CPVC pipe and fittings are manufactured in accordance with ASTM D 2846.

605.16.3 Threaded joints. Threads shall conform to ASME B1.20.1. Schedule 80 or heavier pipe shall be permitted to be threaded with dies specifically designed for plastic pipe, but the pressure rating of the pipe shall be reduced by 50 percent. Thread by socket molded fittings shall be permitted. *Approved* thread lubricant or tape shall be applied on the male threads only.

605.17 Cross-linked polyethylene plastic. Joints between cross-linked polyethylene plastic tubing or fittings shall comply with Sections 605.17.1 and 605.17.2.

605.17.1 Flared joints. Flared pipe ends shall be made by a tool designed for that operation.

605.17.2 Mechanical joints. Mechanical joints shall be installed in accordance with the manufacturer's instructions. Fittings for cross-linked polyethylene (PEX) plastic tubing shall comply with the applicable standards listed in Table 605.5 and shall be installed in accordance with the manufacturer's instructions. PEX tubing shall be factory marked with the appropriate standards for the fittings that the PEX manufacturer specifies for use with the tubing.

605.18 Steel. Joints between galvanized steel pipe or fittings shall comply with Sections 605.18.1 and 605.18.2.

605.18.1 Threaded joints. Threads shall conform to ASME B1.20.1. Pipe-joint compound or tape shall be applied on the male threads only.

605.18.2 Mechanical joints. Joints shall be made with an *approved* elastomeric seal. Mechanical joints shall be installed in accordance with the manufacturer's instructions.

605.19 Polyethylene plastic. Joints between polyethylene plastic pipe and tubing or fittings shall comply with Sections 605.19.1 through 605.19.4.

605.19.1 Flared joints. Flared joints shall be permitted where so indicated by the pipe manufacturer. Flared joints shall be made by a tool designed for that operation.

605.19.2 Heat-fusion joints. Joint surfaces shall be clean and free from moisture. All joint surfaces shall be heated to melt temperature and joined. The joint shall be undisturbed until cool. Joints shall be made in accordance with ASTM D 2657.

605.19.3 Mechanical joints. Mechanical joints shall be installed in accordance with the manufacturer's instructions.

605.19.4 Installation. Polyethylene pipe shall be cut square, with a cutter designed for plastic pipe. Except where joined by heat fusion, pipe ends shall be chamfered to remove sharp edges. Kinked pipe shall not be installed. The minimum pipe bending radius shall not be less than 30 pipe diameters, or the minimum coil radius, whichever is greater. Piping shall not be bent beyond straightening of the curvature of the coil. Bends shall not be permitted within 10 pipe diameters of any fitting or valve. Stiffener inserts installed with compression-type couplings and fittings shall not extend beyond the clamp or nut of the coupling or fitting.

605.20 Polypropylene (PP) plastic. Joints between PP plastic pipe and fittings shall comply with Section 605.20.1 or 605.20.2.

605.20.1 Heat-fusion joints. Heat-fusion joints for polypropylene pipe and tubing joints shall be installed with socket-type heat-fused polypropylene fittings, butt-fusion polypropylene fittings or electrofusion polypropylene fittings. Joint surfaces shall be clean and free from moisture. The joint shall be undisturbed until cool. Joints shall be made in accordance with ASTM F 2389.

605.20.2 Mechanical and compression sleeve joints. Mechanical and compression sleeve joints shall be installed in accordance with the manufacturer's instructions.

605.21 Polyethylene/aluminum/polyethylene (PE-AL-PE) and cross-linked polyethylene/aluminum/cross-linked polyethylene (PEX-AL-PEX). Joints between PE-AL-PE and PEX-AL-PEX pipe and fittings shall comply with Section 605.21.1.

605.21.1 Mechanical joints. Mechanical joints shall be installed in accordance with the manufacturer's instructions. Fittings for PE-AL-PE and PEX-AL-PEX as described in ASTM F 1974, ASTM F 1281, ASTM F 1282, CAN/CSA B137.9 and CAN/CSA B137.10 shall be installed in accordance with the manufacturer's instructions.

605.22 PVC plastic. Joints between PVC plastic pipe or fittings shall comply with Sections 605.22.1 through 605.22.3.

605.22.1 Mechanical joints. Mechanical joints on water pipe shall be made with an elastomeric seal conforming to ASTM D 3139. Mechanical joints shall not be installed in above-ground systems unless otherwise *approved.* Joints shall be installed in accordance with the manufacturer's instructions.

605.22.2 Solvent cementing. Joint surfaces shall be clean and free from moisture. A purple primer or an ultraviolet purple primer that conforms to ASTM F 656 shall be applied. When an ultraviolet primer is used, the installer shall provide an ultraviolet light to the inspector to be used during the inspection. Solvent cement not purple in color and conforming to ASTM D 2564 or CSA-B137.3 shall be applied to all joint surfaces. The joint shall be made while the cement is wet and shall be in accordance with ASTM D 2855. Solvent-cement joints shall be permitted above or below ground.

605.22.3 Threaded joints. Threads shall conform to ASME B1.20.1. Schedule 80 or heavier pipe shall be permitted to be threaded with dies specifically designed for plastic pipe, but the pressure rating of the pipe shall be reduced by 50 percent. Thread by socket molded fittings shall be permitted. *Approved* thread lubricant or tape shall be applied on the male threads only.

605.23 Stainless steel. Joints between stainless steel pipe and fittings shall comply with Sections 605.23.1 and 605.23.2.

605.23.1 Mechanical joints. Mechanical joints shall be installed in accordance with the manufacturer's instructions.

605.23.2 Welded joints. All joint surfaces shall be cleaned. The joint shall be welded autogenously or with an *approved* filler metal as referenced in ASTM A 312.

605.24 Joints between different materials. Joints between different piping materials shall be made with a mechanical joint of the compression or mechanical-sealing type, or as permitted in Sections 605.24.1, 605.24.2 and 605.24.3. Connectors or adapters shall have an elastomeric seal conforming to ASTM D 1869 or ASTM F 477. Joints shall be installed in accordance with the manufacturer's instructions.

605.24.1 Copper or copper-alloy tubing to galvanized steel pipe. Joints between copper or copper-alloy tubing and galvanized steel pipe shall be made with a brass fitting or dielectric fitting or a dielectric union conforming to ASSE 1079. The copper tubing shall be soldered to the fitting in an *approved* manner, and the fitting shall be screwed to the threaded pipe.

605.24.2 Plastic pipe or tubing to other piping material. Joints between different grades of plastic pipe or between plastic pipe and other piping material shall be made with an *approved* adapter fitting.

605.24.3 Stainless steel. Joints between stainless steel and different piping materials shall be made with a mechanical joint of the compression or mechanical sealing type or a dielectric fitting or a dielectric union conforming to ASSE 1079.

605.25 Polybutylene plastic. Joints between polybutylene plastic pipe and tubing or fittings shall comply with Sections 605.25.1 through 605.25.3.

605.25.1 Flared joints. Flared pipe ends shall be made by a tool designed for that operation.

605.25.2 Heat-fusion joints. Joints shall be of the socket-fusion or butt-fusion type. Joint surfaces shall be clean and free from moisture. All joint surfaces shall be heated to the melting temperature and joined. The joint shall be undisturbed until cool. Joints shall be made in accordance with ASTM D 2657, ASTM D 3309 or CAN3-B137.8M.

605.25.3 Mechanical joints. Mechanical joints shall be installed in accordance with the manufacturer's installation instructions.

SECTION 606
INSTALLATION OF THE BUILDING WATER DISTRIBUTION SYSTEM

606.1 Location of full-open valves. Full-open valves shall be installed in the following locations:

1. Deleted.
2. A full-open valve shall be located either outside the building within 5 feet (1524 mm) of the foundation wall in a readily accessible valve box, in the crawl space within 3 feet (914 mm) of the crawl space access door or

within the building in a location where it may be accessed without the use of a ladder or a tool.

3. Deleted.
4. Deleted.
5. Deleted.
6. On the entrance to every water supply pipe to a dwelling unit, except where supplying a single fixture equipped with individual stops.
7. On the water supply pipe to a gravity or pressurized water tank.
8. On the water supply pipe to every water heater.

606.2 Location of shutoff valves. Shutoff valves shall be installed in the following locations:

1. On the fixture supply to each plumbing fixture other than bathtubs and showers.
2. Deleted.
3. On the water supply pipe to each appliance or mechanical equipment.

606.2.1 Buildings other than dwellings or dwelling units. Each supply branch line serving more than one fixture shall have a shut-off valve installed so as to isolate all fixtures and all pieces of equipment supplied by the branch line. The shut-off valve shall be labeled and located as close to the connection to the supply main and riser as practical.

606.3 Access to valves. *Access* shall be provided to all full-open valves and shutoff valves.

606.4 Valve identification. Service valves shall be identified. All other valves installed in locations that are not adjacent to the fixture or appliance shall be identified, indicating the fixture or appliance served.

606.5 Water pressure booster systems. Water pressure booster systems shall be provided as required by Sections 606.5.1 through 606.5.10.

606.5.1 Water pressure booster systems required. Where the water pressure in the public water main or individual water supply system is insufficient to supply the minimum pressures and quantities specified in this code, the supply shall be supplemented by an elevated water tank, a hydropneumatic pressure booster system or a water pressure booster pump installed in accordance with Section 606.5.5.

606.5.2 Support. All water supply tanks shall be supported in accordance with the *International Building Code*.

606.5.3 Covers. All water supply tanks shall be covered to keep out unauthorized persons, dirt and vermin. The covers of gravity tanks shall be vented with a return bend vent pipe with an area not less than the area of the down-feed riser pipe, and the vent shall be screened with a corrosion-resistant screen of not less than 16 by 20 mesh per inch (630 by 787 mesh per m).

606.5.4 Overflows for water supply tanks. Each gravity or suction water supply tank shall be provided with an overflow with a diameter not less than that shown in Table 606.5.4. The overflow outlet shall discharge at a point not less than 6 inches (152 mm) above the roof or roof drain; floor or floor drain; or over an open water-supplied fixture. The overflow outlet shall be covered with a corrosion-resistant screen of not less than 16 by 20 mesh per inch (630 by 787 mesh per m) and by $^{1}/_{4}$-inch (6.4 mm) hardware cloth or shall terminate in a horizontal angle seat check valve. Drainage from overflow pipes shall be directed so as not to freeze on roof walks.

TABLE 606.5.4
SIZES FOR OVERFLOW PIPES FOR WATER SUPPLY TANKS

MAXIMUM CAPACITY OF WATER SUPPLY LINE TO TANK (gpm)	DIAMETER OF OVERFLOW PIPE (inches)
0 – 50	2
51 – 150	$2^{1}/_{2}$
151 – 200	3
201 – 400	4
401 – 700	5
701 – 1,000	6
Over 1,000	8

For SI: 1 inch = 25.4 mm, 1 gallon per minute = 3.785 L/m.

606.5.5 Low-pressure cutoff required on booster pumps. A low-pressure cutoff shall be installed on all booster pumps in a water pressure booster system to prevent creation of a vacuum or negative pressure on the suction side of the pump when a positive pressure of 10 psi (68.94 kPa) or less occurs on the suction side of the pump.

606.5.6 Potable water inlet control and location. Potable water inlets to gravity tanks shall be controlled by a fill valve or other automatic supply valve installed so as to prevent the tank from overflowing. The inlet shall be terminated so as to provide an *air gap* not less than 4 inches (102 mm) above the overflow.

606.5.7 Tank drain pipes. A valved pipe shall be provided at the lowest point of each tank to permit emptying of the tank. The tank drain pipe shall discharge as required for overflow pipes and shall not be smaller in size than specified in Table 606.5.7.

TABLE 606.5.7
SIZE OF DRAIN PIPES FOR WATER TANKS

TANK CAPACITY (gallons)	DRAIN PIPE (inches)
Up to 750	1
751 to 1,500	$1^{1}/_{2}$
1,501 to 3,000	2
3,001 to 5,000	$2^{1}/_{2}$
5,001 to 7,500	3
Over 7,500	4

For SI: 1 inch = 25.4 mm, 1 gallon = 3.785 L.

606.5.8 Prohibited location of potable supply tanks. Potable water gravity tanks or manholes of potable water pressure tanks shall not be located directly under any soil or waste piping or any source of contamination.

606.5.9 Pressure tanks, vacuum relief. All water pressure tanks shall be provided with a vacuum relief valve at the top of the tank that will operate up to a maximum water pressure of 200 psi (1380 kPa) and up to a maximum temperature of 200°F (93°C). The minimum size of such vacuum relief valve shall be $^1/_2$ inch (12.7 mm).

Exception: This section shall not apply to pressurized captive air diaphragm/bladder tanks.

606.5.10 Pressure relief for tanks. Every pressure tank in a hydropneumatic pressure booster system shall be protected with a pressure relief valve. The pressure relief valve shall be set at a maximum pressure equal to the rating of the tank. The relief valve shall be installed on the supply pipe to the tank or on the tank. The relief valve shall discharge by gravity to a safe place of disposal.

606.6 Water supply system test. Upon completion of a section of or the entire water supply system, the system, or portion completed, shall be tested in accordance with Section 312.

SECTION 607
HOT WATER SUPPLY SYSTEM

607.1 Where required. Each dwelling unit shall be provided with a source of hot water for each family unit in accordance with Appendix E. Central water heating facilities shall be accessible for emergency maintenance without entering any individual apartment or living unit when supplying hot water to that unit. In other occupied structures, hot water may be supplied to all plumbing fixtures and equipment utilized for bathing, washing, culinary purposes, cleansing, laundry or building maintenance.

607.2 Hot water supply temperature maintenance. Deleted.

607.2.1 Piping insulation. Circulating hot water system piping shall be insulated in accordance with the *International Energy Conservation Code.*

[E] 607.2.2 Hot water system controls. Automatic circulating hot water system pumps or heat trace shall be arranged to be conveniently turned off, automatically or manually, when the hot water system is not in operation.

607.2.3 Recirculating pump. Deleted.

607.3 Thermal expansion control. A means of controlling increased pressure caused by thermal expansion shall be provided where required in accordance with Sections 607.3.1 and 607.3.2.

607.3.1 Pressure-reducing valve. For water service system sizes up to and including 2 inches (51 mm), a device for controlling pressure shall be installed where, because of thermal expansion, the pressure on the downstream side of a pressure-reducing valve exceeds the pressure-reducing valve setting.

607.3.2 Backflow prevention device or check valve. Where a backflow prevention device, check valve or other device is installed on a water supply system utilizing storage water heating equipment such that thermal expansion causes an increase in pressure, a device for controlling pressure shall be installed.

607.4 Flow of hot water to fixtures. Fixture fittings, faucets and diverters shall be installed and adjusted so that the flow of hot water from the fittings corresponds to the left-hand side of the fixture fitting.

Exception: Shower and tub/shower mixing valves conforming to ASSE 1016 or ASME A112.18.1/CSA B125.1, where the flow of hot water corresponds to the markings on the device.

SECTION 608
PROTECTION OF POTABLE WATER SUPPLY

608.1 General. A potable water supply system shall be designed, installed and maintained in such a manner so as to prevent contamination from nonpotable liquids, solids or gases being introduced into the potable water supply through cross-connections or any other piping connections to the system. Backflow preventer applications shall conform to Table 608.1, except as specifically stated in Sections 608.2 through 608.16.10.

608.2 Plumbing fixtures. The supply lines and fittings for every plumbing fixture shall be installed so as to prevent backflow. Plumbing fixture fittings shall provide backflow protection in accordance with ASME A112.18.1.

608.3 Devices, appurtenances, appliances and apparatus. All devices, appurtenances, appliances and apparatus intended to serve some special function, such as sterilization, distillation, processing, cooling, or storage of ice or foods, and that connect to the water supply system, shall be provided with protection against backflow and contamination of the water supply system. Water pumps, filters, softeners, tanks and all other appliances and devices that handle or treat potable water shall be protected against contamination.

608.3.1 Special equipment, water supply protection. Deleted.

608.4 Water service piping. Water service piping shall be protected in accordance with Sections 603.2 and 603.2.1.

608.5 Chemicals and other substances. Chemicals and other substances that produce either toxic conditions, taste, odor or discoloration in a potable water system shall not be introduced into, or utilized in, such systems.

608.6 Cross-connection control. Cross connections shall be prohibited, except where *approved* protective devices are installed.

TABLE 608.1
APPLICATION OF BACKFLOW PREVENTERS

DEVICE	DEGREE OF HAZARD[a]	APPLICATION[b]	APPLICABLE STANDARDS
Air gap	High or low hazard	Backsiphonage or backpressure	ASME A112.1.2
Air gap fittings for use with plumbing fixtures, appliances and appurtenances	High or low hazard	Backsiphonage or backpressure	ASME A112.1.3
Antisiphon-type fill valves for gravity water closet flush tanks	High hazard	Backsiphonage only	ASSE 1002, CSA B125.3
Backflow preventer for carbonated beverage machines	Low hazard	Backpressure or backsiphonage Sizes $^1/_4$″- $^3/_8$″	ASSE 1022
Backflow preventer with intermediate atmospheric vents	Low hazard	Backpressure or backsiphonage Sizes $^1/_4$″ - $^3/_4$″	ASSE 1012, CAN/CSA B64.3
Barometric loop	High or low hazard	Backsiphonage only	(See Section 608.13.4)
Double check backflow prevention assembly and double check fire protection backflow prevention assembly	Low hazard	Backpressure or backsiphonage Sizes $^3/_8$″ - 16″	ASSE 1015, AWWA C510, CSA B64.5, CSA B64.5.1
Double check detector fire protection backflow prevention assemblies	Low hazard	Backpressure or backsiphonage (Fire sprinkler systems) Sizes 2″ - 16″	ASSE 1048
Dual-check-valve-type backflow preventer	Low hazard	Backpressure or backsiphonage Sizes $^1/_4$″ - 1″	ASSE 1024, CSA B64.6
Hose connection backflow preventer	High or low hazard	Low head backpressure, rated working pressure, backpressure or backsiphonage Sizes $^1/_2$″-1″	ASSE 1052, CSA B64.2.1.1
Hose connection vacuum breaker	High or low hazard	Low head backpressure or backsiphonage Sizes $^1/_2$″, $^3/_4$″, 1″	ASSE 1011, CAN/CSA B64.2, CSA B64.2.1
Laboratory faucet backflow preventer	High or low hazard	Low head backpressure and backsiphonage	ASSE 1035, CSA B64.7
Pipe-applied atmospheric-type vacuum breaker	High or low hazard	Backsiphonage only Sizes $^1/_4$″ - 4″	ASSE 1001, CAN/CSA B64.1.1
Pressure vacuum breaker assembly	High or low hazard	Backsiphonage only Sizes $^1/_2$″ - 2″	ASSE 1020, CSA B64.1.2
Reduced pressure principle backflow preventer and reduced pressure principle fire protection backflow preventer	High or low hazard	Backpressure or backsiphonage Sizes $^3/_8$″- 16″	ASSE 1013, AWWA C511, CAN/CSA B64.4, CSA B64.4.1
Reduced pressure detector fire protection backflow prevention assemblies	High or low hazard	Backsiphonage or backpressure (Fire sprinkler systems)	ASSE 1047
Spillproof vacuum breaker	High or low hazard	Backsiphonage only Sizes $^1/_4$″-2″	ASSE 1056
Vacuum breaker wall hydrants, frost-resistant, automatic draining type	High or low hazard	Low head backpressure or backsiphonage Sizes $^3/_4$″, 1″	ASSE 1019, CAN/CSA B64.2.2

For SI: 1 inch = 25.4 mm.

a. Low hazard–See Pollution (Section 202).
High hazard–See Contamination (Section 202).

b. See Backpressure (Section 202).
See Backpressure, low head (Section 202).
See Backsiphonage (Section 202).

608.6.1 Private water supplies. Cross connections between a private water supply and a potable public supply shall be prohibited.

608.7 Valves and outlets prohibited below grade. Potable water outlets and combination stop-and-waste valves shall not be installed underground or below grade. Freezeproof yard hydrants that drain the riser into the ground are considered to be stop-and-waste valves.

Exception: Freezeproof yard hydrants that drain the riser into the ground shall be permitted to be installed, provided that the potable water supply to such hydrants is protected upstream of the hydrants in accordance with Section 608 and the hydrants are permanently identified as nonpotable outlets by *approved* signage that reads as follows: "Caution, Nonpotable Water. Do Not Drink."

608.8 Identification of nonpotable water. In buildings where nonpotable water systems are installed, the piping conveying the nonpotable water shall be identified either by color marking or metal tags in accordance with Sections 608.8.1 through 608.8.3. All nonpotable water outlets such as hose connections, open ended pipes, and faucets shall be identified at the point of use for each outlet with the words, "Nonpotable—not safe for drinking." The words shall be indelibly printed on a tag or sign constructed of corrosion-resistant waterproof material or shall be indelibly printed on the fixture. The letters of the words shall be not less than 0.5 inches in height and color in contrast to the background on which they are applied.

608.8.1 Information. Pipe identification shall include the contents of the piping system and an arrow indicating the direction of flow. Hazardous piping systems shall also contain information addressing the nature of the hazard. Pipe identification shall be repeated at maximum intervals of 25 feet (7620 mm) and at each point where the piping passes through a wall, floor or roof. Lettering shall be readily observable within the room or space where the piping is located.

608.8.2 Color. The color of the pipe identification shall be discernable and consistent throughout the building. The color purple shall be used to identify reclaimed, rain and gray water distribution systems.

608.8.3 Size. The size of the background color field and lettering shall comply with Table 608.8.3.

TABLE 608.8.3
SIZE OF PIPE IDENTIFICATION

PIPE DIAMETER (inches)	LENGTH BACKGROUND COLOR FIELD (inches)	SIZE OF LETTERS (inches)
$^3/_8$ to $1^1/_4$	8	0.5
$1^1/_2$ to 2	8	0.75
$2^1/_2$ to 6	12	1.25
8 to 10	24	2.5
over 10	32	3.5

For SI: 1 inch = 25.4 mm.

608.9 Reutilization prohibited. Water utilized for the cooling of equipment or other processes shall not be returned to the potable water system. Such water shall be discharged into a drainage system through an *air gap* or shall be utilized for nonpotable purposes.

608.10 Reuse of piping. Piping that has been utilized for any purpose other than conveying potable water shall not be utilized for conveying potable water.

608.11 Painting of water tanks. The interior surface of a potable water tank shall not be lined, painted or repaired with any material that changes the taste, odor, color or potability of the water supply when the tank is placed in, or returned to, service.

608.12 Pumps and other appliances. Water pumps, filters, softeners, tanks and all other devices that handle or treat potable water shall be protected against contamination.

608.13 Backflow protection. Means of protection against backflow shall be provided in accordance with Sections 608.13.1 through 608.13.9.

608.13.1 Air gap. The minimum required *air gap* shall be measured vertically from the lowest end of a potable water outlet to the *flood level rim* of the fixture or receptacle into which such potable water outlet discharges. Air gaps shall comply with ASME A112.1.2 and *air gap* fittings shall comply with ASME A112.1.3.

608.13.2 Reduced pressure principle backflow preventers. Reduced pressure principle backflow preventers shall conform to ASSE 1013, AWWA C511, CAN/CSA B64.4 or CSA B64.4.1. Reduced pressure detector assembly backflow preventers shall conform to ASSE 1047. These devices shall be permitted to be installed where subject to continuous pressure conditions. The relief opening shall discharge by *air gap* and shall be prevented from being submerged.

608.13.3 Backflow preventer with intermediate atmospheric vent. Backflow preventers with intermediate atmospheric vents shall conform to ASSE 1012 or CAN/CSA B64.3. These devices shall be permitted to be installed where subject to continuous pressure conditions. The relief opening shall discharge by *air gap* and shall be prevented from being submerged.

608.13.4 Barometric loop. Barometric loops shall precede the point of connection and shall extend vertically to a height of 35 feet (10 668 mm). A barometric loop shall only be utilized as an atmospheric-type or pressure-type vacuum breaker.

608.13.5 Pressure-type vacuum breakers. Pressure-type vacuum breakers shall conform to ASSE 1020 or CSA B64.1.2 and spillproof vacuum breakers shall comply with ASSE 1056. These devices are designed for installation under continuous pressure conditions when the critical level is installed at the required height. Pressure-type vacuum breakers shall not be installed in locations where spillage could cause damage to the structure.

608.13.6 Atmospheric-type vacuum breakers. Pipe-applied atmospheric-type vacuum breakers shall conform to ASSE 1001 or CAN/CSA B64.1.1. Hose-connection vacuum breakers shall conform to ASSE 1011, ASSE 1019, ASSE 1035, ASSE 1052, CAN/CSA B64.2, CSA B64.2.1, CSA B64.2.1.1, CAN/CSA B64.2.2 or CSA B64.7. These devices shall operate under normal atmospheric pressure when the critical level is installed at the required height.

608.13.7 Double check-valve assemblies. Double check-valve assemblies shall conform to ASSE 1015, CSA B64.5, CSA B64.5.1 or AWWA C510. Double-detector check-valve assemblies shall conform to ASSE 1048. These devices shall be capable of operating under continuous pressure conditions.

608.13.8 Spillproof vacuum breakers. Spillproof vacuum breakers (SVB) shall conform to ASSE 1056. These devices are designed for installation under continuous-pressure conditions when the critical level is installed at the required height.

608.13.9 Chemical dispenser backflow devices. Deleted.

608.14 Location of backflow preventers. *Access* shall be provided to backflow preventers as specified by the installation instructions of the *approved* manufacturer.

608.14.1 Outdoor enclosures for backflow prevention devices. Outdoor enclosures for backflow prevention devices shall comply with ASSE 1060.

608.14.2 Protection of backflow preventers. Backflow preventers shall not be located in areas subject to freezing except where they can be removed by means of unions or are protected from freezing by heat, insulation or both.

608.14.2.1 Relief port piping. The termination of the piping from the relief port or *air gap* fitting of a backflow preventer shall discharge to an *approved* indirect waste receptor or to the outdoors where it will not cause damage or create a nuisance.

608.15 Protection of potable water outlets. All potable water openings and outlets shall be protected against backflow in accordance with Section 608.15.1, 608.15.2, 608.15.3, 608.15.4, 608.15.4.1 or 608.15.4.2.

608.15.1 Protection by air gap. Openings and outlets shall be protected by an *air gap* between the opening and the fixture *flood level rim* as specified in Table 608.15.1. Openings and outlets equipped for hose connection shall be protected by means other than an *air gap*.

608.15.2 Protection by a reduced pressure principle backflow preventer. Openings and outlets shall be protected by a reduced pressure principle backflow preventer.

608.15.3 Protection by a backflow preventer with intermediate atmospheric vent. Openings and outlets shall be protected by a backflow preventer with an intermediate atmospheric vent.

608.15.4 Protection by a vacuum breaker. Openings and outlets shall be protected by atmospheric-type or pressure-type vacuum breakers. The critical level of the vacuum breaker shall be set a minimum of 6 inches (152 mm) above the *flood level rim* of the fixture or device. Fill valves shall be set in accordance with Section 425.3.1. Vacuum breakers shall not be installed under exhaust hoods or similar locations that will contain toxic fumes or vapors. Pipe-applied vacuum breakers shall be installed not less than 6 inches (152 mm) above the *flood level rim* of the fixture, receptor or device served.

608.15.4.1 Deck-mounted and integral vacuum breakers. *Approved* deck-mounted or equipment-mounted vacuum breakers and faucets with integral atmospheric or spillproof vacuum breakers shall be installed in accordance with the manufacturer's instructions and the requirements for labeling with the critical level not less than 1 inch (25 mm) above the *flood level rim*.

TABLE 608.15.1
MINIMUM REQUIRED AIR GAPS

FIXTURE	MINIMUM AIR GAP	
	Away from a wall[a] (inches)	Close to a wall (inches)
Lavatories and other fixtures with effective opening not greater than $^1/_2$ inch in diameter	1	$1^1/_2$
Sink, laundry trays, gooseneck back faucets and other fixtures with effective openings not greater than $^3/_4$ inch in diameter	$1^1/_2$	$2^1/_2$
Over-rim bath fillers and other fixtures with effective openings not greater than 1 inch in diameter	2	3
Drinking water fountains, single orifice not greater than $^7/_{16}$ inch in diameter or multiple orifices with a total area of 0.150 square inch (area of circle $^7/_{16}$ inch in diameter)	1	$1^1/_2$
Effective openings greater than 1 inch	Two times the diameter of the effective opening	Three times the diameter of the effective opening

For SI: 1 inch = 25.4 mm.

a. Applicable where walls or obstructions are spaced from the nearest inside-edge of the spout opening a distance greater than three times the diameter of the effective opening for a single wall, or a distance greater than four times the diameter of the effective opening for two intersecting walls.

608.15.4.2 Hose connections. Sillcocks, hose bibbs, wall hydrants and other openings with a hose connection shall be protected by an atmospheric-type or pressure-type vacuum breaker or a permanently attached hose connection vacuum breaker.

Exceptions:

1. This section shall not apply to water heater and boiler drain valves that are provided with hose connection threads and that are intended only for tank or vessel draining.
2. This section shall not apply to water supply valves intended for connection of clothes washing machines where backflow prevention is otherwise provided or is integral with the machine.

608.16 Connections to the potable water system. Connections to the potable water system shall conform to Sections 608.16.1 through 608.16.10.

608.16.1 Beverage dispensers. Deleted.

608.16.2 Connections to boilers. The potable supply to the boiler shall be equipped with a backflow preventer with an intermediate atmospheric vent complying with ASSE 1012 or CAN/CSA B64.3. Where conditioning chemicals are introduced into the system, the potable water connection shall be protected by an *air gap* or a reduced pressure principle backflow preventer, complying with ASSE 1013, CAN/CSA B64.4 or AWWA C511.

608.16.3 Heat exchangers. Heat exchangers utilizing an essentially toxic transfer fluid shall be separated from the potable water by double-wall construction. An *air gap* open to the atmosphere shall be provided between the two walls. Heat exchangers utilizing an essentially nontoxic transfer fluid shall be permitted to be of single-wall construction.

608.16.4 Connections to automatic fire sprinkler systems and standpipe systems. The potable water supply to automatic fire sprinkler and standpipe systems shall be protected against backflow by a double check-valve assembly or a reduced pressure principle backflow preventer.

Exceptions:

1. Where systems are installed as a portion of the water distribution system in accordance with the requirements of this code and are not provided with a fire department connection, isolation of the water supply system shall not be required.
2. Isolation of the water distribution system is not required for deluge, preaction or dry pipe systems.

608.16.4.1 Additives or nonpotable source. Where systems under continuous pressure contain chemical additives or antifreeze, or where systems are connected to a nonpotable secondary water supply, the potable water supply shall be protected against backflow by a reduced pressure principle backflow preventer. Where chemical additives or antifreeze are added to only a portion of an automatic fire sprinkler or standpipe system, the reduced pressure principle backflow preventer shall be permitted to be located so as to isolate that portion of the system. Where systems are not under continuous pressure, the potable water supply shall be protected against backflow by an *air gap* or a pipe applied atmospheric vacuum breaker conforming to ASSE 1001 or CAN/CSA B64.1.1.

608.16.5 Connections to lawn irrigation systems. The potable water supply to lawn irrigation systems shall be protected against backflow by an atmospheric-type vacuum breaker, a pressure-type vacuum breaker or a reduced pressure principle backflow preventer. A valve shall not be installed downstream from an atmospheric vacuum breaker. Where chemicals are introduced into the system, the potable water supply shall be protected against backflow by a reduced pressure principle backflow preventer.

608.16.6 Connections subject to backpressure. Where a potable water connection is made to a nonpotable line, fixture, tank, vat, pump or other equipment subject to backpressure, the potable water connection shall be protected by a reduced pressure principle backflow preventer.

608.16.7 Chemical dispensers. Where chemical dispensers connect to the potable water distribution system, the water supply system shall be protected against backflow in accordance with Section 608.13.1, 608.13.2, 608.13.5, 608.13.6, 608.13.8 or 608.13.9.

608.16.8 Portable cleaning equipment. Where the portable cleaning equipment connects to the water distribution system, the water supply system shall be protected against backflow in accordance with Section 608.13.1, 608.13.2, 608.13.3, 608.13.7 or 608.13.8.

608.16.9 Dental pump equipment. Deleted.

608.16.10 Coffee machines and noncarbonated beverage dispensers. Deleted.

608.17 Protection of individual water supplies. Deleted.

Table 608.17.1 Distance from Contamination to Private Water Supplies and Pump Suction Lines. Deleted.

SECTION 609
HEALTH CARE PLUMBING
Deleted

SECTION 610
DISINFECTION OF POTABLE WATER SYSTEM

610.1 General. Permitted new or repaired potable water systems shall be purged of deleterious matter prior to utilization.

SECTION 611
DRINKING WATER TREATMENT UNITS

611.1 Design. Drinking water treatment units shall meet the requirements of NSF 42, NSF 44, NSF 53 or NSF 62.

611.2 Reverse osmosis systems. The discharge from a reverse osmosis drinking water treatment unit shall enter the drainage system through an *air gap* or an *air gap* device that meets the requirements of NSF 58.

611.3 Connection tubing. The tubing to and from drinking water treatment units shall be of a size and material as recommended by the manufacturer. The tubing shall comply with NSF 14, NSF 42, NSF 44, NSF 53, NSF 58 or NSF 61.

SECTION 612
SOLAR SYSTEMS

612.1 Solar systems. The construction, installation, alterations and repair of systems, equipment and appliances intended to utilize solar energy for space heating or cooling, domestic hot water heating, swimming pool heating or process heating shall be in accordance with the *International Mechanical Code*.

SECTION 613
TEMPERATURE CONTROL DEVICES AND VALVES

613.1 Temperature-actuated mixing valves. Temperature-actuated mixing valves, which are installed to reduce water temperatures to defined limits, shall comply with ASSE 1016 or ASSE 1017.

SECTION 614
PARTIAL FIRE SPRINKLER PROTECTION IN ONE- AND TWO-FAMILY DWELLINGS

614.1 Partial fire protection. Nothing in this section shall be deemed to prohibit the connection to the domestic water distribution system of a system of one or more fire suppression sprinkler heads in one or more rooms of a one- or two-family dwelling, nor shall such installation impose additional requirements on the domestic water distribution system with regard to pipe size, water pressure, meter size, monitoring or alarm, provided that:

1. The sprinkler heads used are residential fast-response type.
2. Each branch feeding one or more sprinkler heads shall be provided with an isolation valve which shall be readily accessible and the function thereof shall be marked.
3. Each isolation valve shall be identified as to function with a tag or other device which shall indicate that the system does not meet the requirements of NFPA 13D.
4. The piping installation and material shall comply with the requirements of the *North Carolina Plumbing Code*.

SECTION 615
FULL FIRE SPRINKLER PROTECTION IN ONE- AND TWO-FAMILY DWELLINGS

615.1 Full fire protection. Where a full fire sprinkler system is installed, it shall comply with NFPA 13D.

CHAPTER 7
SANITARY DRAINAGE

SECTION 701
GENERAL

701.1 Scope. The provisions of this chapter shall govern the materials, design, construction and installation of sanitary drainage systems.

701.2 Sewer required. Every building in which plumbing fixtures are installed and all premises having drainage piping shall be connected to a *public sewer*, where available, or an *approved private* sewage disposal system.

701.3 Separate sewer connection. Every building having plumbing fixtures installed and intended for human habitation, occupancy or use on premises abutting on a street, alley or easement in which there is a *public sewer* shall have a separate connection with the *sewer*. Where located on the same lot, multiple buildings shall not be prohibited from connecting to a common *building sewer* that connects to the *public sewer*.

701.4 Sewage treatment. *Note: The following text is provided for informational purposes only.*

Sewage or other waste from a plumbing system that is deleterious to surface or subsurface waters shall not be discharged into the ground or into any waterway unless it has first been rendered innocuous through treatment aproved by the authority having jurisdiction.

701.5 Damage to drainage system or public sewer. Wastes detrimental to the *public sewer* system or detrimental to the functioning of the private sewage system shall be treated and disposed of in accordance with Section 1003.

701.6 Tests. The sanitary drainage system shall be tested in accordance with Section 312.

701.7 Connections. Direct connection of a steam exhaust, blowoff or drip pipe shall not be made with the building drainage system. Wastewater when discharged into the building drainage system shall be at a temperature not higher than 140°F (60°C). When higher temperatures exist, *approved* cooling methods shall be provided.

701.8 Engineered systems. Deleted.

701.9 Drainage piping in food service areas. Exposed soil or waste piping shall not be installed above any working, storage or eating surfaces in food service establishments.

SECTION 702
MATERIALS

702.1 Above-ground sanitary drainage and vent pipe. Above-ground soil, waste and vent pipe shall conform to one of the standards listed in Table 702.1.

> **Exception:** Plastic pipe shall not be used for drain, waste and vents in buildings in which the top occupied floor exceeds 75 feet (23 m) in height.

TABLE 702.1
ABOVE-GROUND DRAINAGE AND VENT PIPE

MATERIAL	STANDARD
Acrylonitrile butadiene styrene (ABS) plastic pipe in IPS diameters, including Schedule 40, DR 22 (PS 200) and DR 24 (PS 140); with a solid, cellular core or composite wall	ASTM D 2661; ASTM F 628; ASTM F 1488; CSA B181.1
Brass pipe	ASTM B 43
Cast-iron pipe	ASTM A 74; ASTM A 888; CISPI 301
Copper or copper-alloy pipe	ASTM B 42; ASTM B 302
Copper or copper-alloy tubing (Type K, L, M or DWV)	ASTM B 75; ASTM B 88; ASTM B 251; ASTM B 306
Galvanized steel pipe	ASTM A 53
Glass pipe	ASTM C 1053
Polyolefin pipe	ASTM F 1412; CAN/CSA B181.3
Polyvinyl chloride (PVC) plastic pipe in IPS diameters, including schedule 40, DR 22 (PS 200), and DR 24 (PS 140); with a solid, cellular core or composite wall	ASTM D 2665; ASTM F 891; ASTM F 1488; CSA B181.2
Polyvinyl chloride (PVC) plastic pipe with a 3.25-inch O.D. and a solid, cellular core or composite wall	ASTM D 2949, ASTM F 1488
Polyvinylidene fluoride (PVDF) plastic pipe	ASTM F 1673; CAN/CSA B181.3
Stainless steel drainage systems, Types 304 and 316L	ASME A112.3.1

702.2 Underground building sanitary drainage and vent pipe. Underground building sanitary drainage and vent pipe shall conform to one of the standards listed in Table 702.2.

702.3 Building sewer pipe. *Building sewer* pipe shall conform to one of the standards listed in Table 702.3.

702.4 Fittings. Pipe fittings shall be *approved* for installation with the piping material installed and shall comply with the applicable standards listed in Table 702.4.

> **Exception:** Plastic pipe shall not be used for drain, waste and vents in buildings in which the top occupied floor exceeds 75 feet (23 m) in height.

702.5 Chemical waste system. Deleted.

702.6 Lead bends and traps. Lead bends and traps shall not be less than $^1/_8$ inch (3.2 mm) wall thickness.

TABLE 702.2
UNDERGROUND BUILDING DRAINAGE AND VENT PIPE

MATERIAL	STANDARD
Acrylonitrile butadiene styrene (ABS) plastic pipe in IPS diameters, including schedule 40, DR 22 (PS 200) and DR 24 (PS 140); with a solid, cellular core, or composite wall	ASTM D 2661; ASTM F 628; ASTM F 1488; CSA B181.1
Asbestos-cement pipe	ASTM C 428
Cast-iron pipe	ASTM A 74; ASTM A 888; CISPI 301
Copper or copper-alloy tubing (Type K or L)	ASTM B 75; ASTM B 88; ASTM B 251; ASTM B 306
Polyolefin pipe	ASTM F 1412; CAN/CSA B181.3
Polyvinyl chloride (PVC) plastic pipe in IPS diameters, including schedule 40, DR 22 (PS 200) and DR 24 (PS 140); with a solid, cellular core, or composite wall	ASTM D 2665; ASTM F 891; ASTM F 1488; CSA B181.2
Polyvinyl chloride (PVC) plastic pipe with a 3.25-inch O.D. and a solid, cellular core, or composite wall	ASTM D 2949, ASTM F 1488
Polyvinylidene fluoride (PVDF) plastic pipe	ASTM F 1673; CAN/CSA B181.3
Stainless steel drainage systems, Type 316L	ASME A 112.3.1

TABLE 702.3
BUILDING SEWER PIPE

MATERIAL	STANDARD
Acrylonitrile butadiene styrene (ABS) plastic pipe in IPS diameters, including schedule 40, DR 22 (PS 200) and DR 24 (PS 140); with a solid, cellular core or composite wall	ASTM D 2661; ASTM F 628; ASTM F 1488; CSA B181.1
Acrylonitrile butadiene styrene (ABS) plastic pipe in sewer and drain diameters, including SDR 42 (PS 20), PS 35, SDR 35 (PS 45), PS 50, PS 100, PS 140, SDR 23.5 (PS 150) and PS 200; with a solid, cellular core or composite wall	ASTM F 1488; ASTM D 2751
Asbestos-cement pipe	ASTM C 428
Cast-iron pipe	ASTM A 74; ASTM A 888; CISPI 301
Concrete pipe	ASTM C14; ASTM C76; CAN/CSA A257.1M; CAN/CSA A257.2M
Copper or copper-alloy tubing (Type K or L)	ASTM B 75; ASTM B 88; ASTM B 251
Polyethylene (PE) plastic pipe (SDR-PR)	ASTM F 714
Polyvinyl chloride (PVC) plastic pipe in IPS diameters, including schedule 40, DR 22 (PS 200) and DR 24 (PS 140); with a solid, cellular core or composite wall	ASTM D 2665; ASTM F 891; ASTM F 1488
Polyvinyl chloride (PVC) plastic pipe in sewer and drain diameters, including PS 25, SDR 41 (PS 28), PS 35, SDR 35 (PS 46), PS 50, PS 100, SDR 26 (PS 115), PS 140 and PS 200; with a solid, cellular core or composite wall	ASTM F 891; ASTM F 1488; ASTM D 3034; CSA B182.2; CSA B182.4
Polyvinyl chloride (PVC) plastic pipe with a 3.25-inch O.D. and a solid, cellular core or composite wall.	ASTM D 2949, ASTM F 1488
Polyvinylidene fluoride (PVDF) plastic pipe	ASTM F 1673; CAN/CSA B181.3
Stainless steel drainage systems, Types 304 and 316L	ASME A112.3.1
Vitrified clay pipe	ASTM C 4; ASTM C 700

TABLE 702.4
PIPE FITTINGS

MATERIAL	STANDARD
Acrylonitrile butadiene styrene (ABS) plastic pipe in IPS diameters	ASTM D 2661; ASTM F 628; CSA B181.1
Acrylonotrile butadiene styrene (ABS) plastic pipe in sewer and drain diameters	ASTM D 2751
Asbestos cement	ASTM C 428
Cast iron	ASME B 16.4; ASME B 16.12; ASTM A 74; ASTM A 888; CISPI 301
Copper or copper alloy	ASME B 16.15; ASME B 16.18; ASME B 16.22; ASME B 16.23; ASME B 16.26; ASME B 16.29
Glass	ASTM C 1053
Gray iron and ductile iron	AWWA C 110
Malleable iron	ASME B 16.3
Polyolefin	ASTM F 1412; CAN/CSA B181.3
Polyvinyl chloride (PVC) plastic in IPS diameters	ASTM D 2665; ASTM F 1866 (10 inches diameter and larger)
Polyvinyl chloride (PVC) plastic pipe in sewer and drain diameters	ASTM D 3034
Polyvinyl chloride (PVC) plastic pipe with a 3.25-inch O.D.	ASTM D 2949
Polyvinylidene fluoride (PVDF) plastic pipe	ASTM F 1673; CAN/CSA B181.3
Stainless steel drainage systems, Types 304 and 316L	ASME A 112.3.1
Steel	ASME B 16.9; ASME B 16.11; ASME B 16.28
Vitrified clay	ASTM C 700

SECTION 703 BUILDING SEWER

703.1 Building sewer pipe near the water service. Where the *building sewer* is installed within 5 feet (1524 mm) of the water service, the installation shall comply with the provisions of Section 603.2.

703.2 Drainage pipe in filled ground. Where a *building sewer* or *building drain* is installed in unstable fill or unstable ground shall be of cast-iron pipe, except that nonmetallic drains may be laid upon an approved continuous supporting system if installed in accordance with the manufacturer's installation instructions.

703.3 Sanitary and storm sewers. Where separate systems of sanitary drainage and storm drainage are installed in the same property, the sanitary and storm building sewers or drains shall be permitted to be laid side by side in one trench.

703.4 Existing building sewers and drains. Existing building sewers and drains shall connect with new *building sewer* and drainage systems only where found by examination and test to conform to the new system in quality of material. The code official shall notify the owner to make the changes necessary to conform to this code.

703.5 Cleanouts on building sewers. Cleanouts on building sewers shall be located as set forth in Section 708.

SECTION 704 DRAINAGE PIPING INSTALLATION

704.1 Slope of horizontal drainage piping. Horizontal drainage piping shall be installed in uniform alignment at uniform slopes. The minimum slope of a horizontal drainage pipe shall be in accordance with Table 704.1.

TABLE 704.1
SLOPE OF HORIZONTAL DRAINAGE PIPE

SIZE (inches)	MINIMUM SLOPE (inch per foot)
$2^1/_2$ or less	$^1/_4$
3 to 6	$^1/_8$
8 or larger	$^1/_{16}$

For SI: 1 inch = 25.4 mm, 1 inch per foot = 83.3 mm/m.

704.2 Change in size. The size of the drainage piping shall not be reduced in size in the direction of the flow. A 4-inch by 3-inch (102 mm by 76 mm) water closet connection shall not be considered as a reduction in size.

704.3 Connections to offsets and bases of stacks. Horizontal branches shall connect to the bases of stacks at a point located not less than 10 times the diameter of the drainage *stack* downstream from the *stack*. Except as prohibited by Section 711.2, horizontal branches shall connect to horizontal *stack* offsets at a point located not less than 10 times the diameter of the drainage *stack* downstream from the upper *stack*.

704.4 Future fixtures. Drainage piping for future fixtures shall terminate with an *approved* cap or plug.

704.5 Dead ends. In the installation or removal of any part of a drainage system, dead ends shall be prohibited. Cleanout extensions and approved future fixture drainage piping shall not be considered as dead ends.

SECTION 705 JOINTS

705.1 General. This section contains provisions applicable to joints specific to sanitary drainage piping.

705.2 ABS plastic. Joints between ABS plastic pipe or fittings shall comply with Sections 705.2.1 through 705.2.3.

705.2.1 Mechanical joints. Mechanical joints on drainage pipes shall be made with an elastomeric seal conforming to ASTM C 1173, ASTM D 3212 or CSA B602. Mechanical joints shall be installed only in underground systems unless otherwise *approved.* Joints shall be installed in accordance with the manufacturer's instructions.

705.2.2 Solvent cementing. Joint surfaces shall be clean and free from moisture. Solvent cement that conforms to ASTM D 2235 or CSA B181.1 shall be applied to all joint surfaces. The joint shall be made while the cement is wet. Joints shall be made in accordance with ASTM D 2235, ASTM D 2661, ASTM F 628 or CSA B181.1. Solvent-cement joints shall be permitted above or below ground.

705.2.3 Threaded joints. Threads shall conform to ASME B1.20.1. Schedule 80 or heavier pipe shall be permitted to be threaded with dies specifically designed for plastic pipe. *Approved* thread lubricant or tape shall be applied on the male threads only.

705.3 Asbestos cement. Joints between asbestos-cement pipe or fittings shall be made with a sleeve coupling of the same composition as the pipe, sealed with an elastomeric ring conforming to ASTM D 1869.

705.4 Brass. Joints between brass pipe or fittings shall comply with Sections 705.4.1 through 705.4.4.

705.4.1 Brazed joints. All joint surfaces shall be cleaned. An *approved* flux shall be applied where required. The joint shall be brazed with a filler metal conforming to AWS A5.8.

705.4.2 Mechanical joints. Mechanical joints shall be installed in accordance with the manufacturer's instructions.

705.4.3 Threaded joints. Threads shall conform to ASME B1.20.1. Pipe-joint compound or tape shall be applied on the male threads only.

705.4.4 Welded joints. All joint surfaces shall be cleaned. The joint shall be welded with an *approved* filler metal.

705.5 Cast iron. Joints between cast-iron pipe or fittings shall comply with Sections 705.5.1 through 705.5.3.

705.5.1 Caulked joints. Joints for hub and spigot pipe shall be firmly packed with oakum or hemp. Molten lead shall be poured in one operation to a depth of not less than 1 inch (25 mm). The lead shall not recede more than $^{1}/_{8}$ inch (3.2 mm) below the rim of the hub and shall be caulked tight. Paint, varnish or other coatings shall not be permitted on the jointing material until after the joint has been tested and *approved.* Lead shall be run in one pouring and shall be caulked tight. Acid-resistant rope and acidproof cement shall be permitted.

705.5.2 Compression gasket joints. Compression gaskets for hub and spigot pipe and fittings shall conform to ASTM C 564 and shall be tested to ASTM C 1563. Gaskets shall be compressed when the pipe is fully inserted.

705.5.3 Mechanical joint coupling. Mechanical joint couplings for hubless pipe and fittings shall comply with CISPI 310, ASTM C 1277 or ASTM C 1540. The elastomeric sealing sleeve shall conform to ASTM C 564 or CAN/CSA B602 and shall be provided with a center stop. Mechanical joint couplings shall be installed in accordance with the manufacturer's installation instructions.

705.6 Concrete joints. Joints between concrete pipe and fittings shall be made with an elastomeric seal conforming to ASTM C 443, ASTM C 1173, CAN/CSA A257.3M or CAN/CSA B602.

705.7 Coextruded composite ABS pipe, joints. Joints between coextruded composite pipe with an ABS outer layer or ABS fittings shall comply with Sections 705.7.1 and 705.7.2.

705.7.1 Mechanical joints. Mechanical joints on drainage pipe shall be made with an elastomeric seal conforming to ASTM C1173, ASTM D 3212 or CSA B602. Mechanical joints shall not be installed in above-ground systems, unless otherwise *approved.* Joints shall be installed in accordance with the manufacturer's instructions.

705.7.2 Solvent cementing. Joint surfaces shall be clean and free from moisture. Solvent cement that conforms to ASTM D 2235 or CSA B181.1 shall be applied to all joint surfaces. The joint shall be made while the cement is wet. Joints shall be made in accordance with ASTM D 2235, ASTM D 2661, ASTM F 628 or CSA B181.1. Solvent-cement joints shall be permitted above or below ground.

705.8 Coextruded composite PVC pipe. Joints between coextruded composite pipe with a PVC outer layer or PVC fittings shall comply with Sections 705.8.1 and 705.8.2.

705.8.1 Mechanical joints. Mechanical joints on drainage pipe shall be made with an elastomeric seal conforming to ASTM D 3212. Mechanical joints shall not be installed in above-ground systems, unless otherwise *approved.* Joints shall be installed in accordance with the manufacturer's instructions.

705.8.2 Solvent cementing. Joint surfaces shall be clean and free from moisture. A purple primer or an ultraviolet purple primer that conforms to ASTM F 656 shall be applied. When an ultraviolet primer is used, the installer shall provide an ultraviolet light to the inspector to be used during the inspection. Solvent cement not purple in color and conforming to ASTM D 2564, CSA-B137.3, CSA B181.2 or CSA B182.1 shall be applied to all joint surfaces. The joint shall be made while the cement is wet and shall be in accordance with ASTM D 2855. Solvent-cement joints shall be permitted above or below ground.

705.9 Copper pipe. Joints between copper or copper-alloy pipe or fittings shall comply with Sections 705.9.1 through 705.9.5.

705.9.1 Brazed joints. All joint surfaces shall be cleaned. An *approved* flux shall be applied where required. The joint shall be brazed with a filler metal conforming to AWS A5.8.

705.9.2 Mechanical joints. Mechanical joints shall be installed in accordance with the manufacturer's instructions.

705.9.3 Soldered joints. Solder joints shall be made in accordance with the methods of ASTM B 828. All cut tube ends shall be reamed to the full inside diameter of the tube end. All joint surfaces shall be cleaned. A flux conforming to ASTM B 813 shall be applied. The joint shall be soldered with a solder conforming to ASTM B 32.

705.9.4 Threaded joints. Threads shall conform to ASME B1.20.1. Pipe-joint compound or tape shall be applied on the male threads only.

705.9.5 Welded joints. All joint surfaces shall be cleaned. The joint shall be welded with an *approved* filler metal.

705.10 Copper tubing. Joints between copper or copper-alloy tubing or fittings shall comply with Sections 705.10.1 through 705.10.3.

705.10.1 Brazed joints. All joint surfaces shall be cleaned. An *approved* flux shall be applied where required. The joint shall be brazed with a filler metal conforming to AWS A5.8.

705.10.2 Mechanical joints. Mechanical joints shall be installed in accordance with the manufacturer's instructions.

705.10.3 Soldered joints. Solder joints shall be made in accordance with the methods of ASTM B 828. All cut tube ends shall be reamed to the full inside diameter of the tube end. All joint surfaces shall be cleaned. A flux conforming to ASTM B 813 shall be applied. The joint shall be soldered with a solder conforming to ASTM B 32.

705.11 Borosilicate glass joints. Deleted.

705.11.1 Caulked joints. Every lead-caulked joint for hub and spigot soil pipe shall be firmly packed with oakum or hemp and filled with molten lead not less than 1 inch (25 mm) deep and not to extend more than $^1/_8$ inch (3.2 mm) below the rim of the hub. Paint, varnish or other coatings shall not be permitted on the jointing material until after the joint has been tested and *approved.* Lead shall be run in one pouring and shall be caulked tight. Acid-resistant rope and acidproof cement shall be permitted.

705.12 Steel. Joints between galvanized steel pipe or fittings shall comply with Sections 705.12.1 and 705.12.2.

705.12.1 Threaded joints. Threads shall conform to ASME B1.20.1. Pipe-joint compound or tape shall be applied on the male threads only.

705.12.2 Mechanical joints. Joints shall be made with an *approved* elastomeric seal. Mechanical joints shall be installed in accordance with the manufacturer's instructions.

705.13 Lead. Joints between lead pipe or fittings shall comply with Sections 705.13.1 and 705.13.2.

705.13.1 Burned. Burned joints shall be uniformly fused together into one continuous piece. The thickness of the joint shall be at least as thick as the lead being joined. The filler metal shall be of the same material as the pipe.

705.13.2 Wiped. Joints shall be fully wiped, with an exposed surface on each side of the joint not less than $^3/_4$ inch (19.1 mm). The joint shall be at least 0.325 inch (9.5 mm) thick at the thickest point.

705.14 PVC plastic. Joints between PVC plastic pipe or fittings shall comply with Sections 705.14.1 through 705.14.3.

705.14.1 Mechanical joints. Mechanical joints on drainage pipe shall be made with an elastomeric seal conforming to ASTM C 1173, ASTM D 3212 or CAN/CSA B602. Mechanical joints shall not be installed in above-ground systems, unless otherwise *approved.* Joints shall be installed in accordance with the manufacturer's instructions.

705.14.2 Solvent cementing. Joint surfaces shall be clean and free from moisture. A purple primer or an ultraviolet purple primer that conforms to ASTM F 656 shall be applied. When an ultraviolet primer is used, the installer shall provide an ultraviolet light to the inspector to be used during the inspection. Solvent cement not purple in color and conforming to ASTM D 2564, CSA-B137.3, CSA B181.2 or CSA B182.1 shall be applied to all joint surfaces. The joint shall be made while the cement is wet and shall be in accordance with ASTM D 2855. Solvent-cement joints shall be permitted above or below ground.

705.14.3 Threaded joints. Threads shall conform to ASME B1.20.1. Schedule 80 or heavier pipe shall be permitted to be threaded with dies specifically designed for plastic pipe. *Approved* thread lubricant or tape shall be applied on the male threads only.

705.15 Vitrified clay. Joints between vitrified clay pipe or fittings shall be made with an elastomeric seal conforming to ASTM C 425, ASTM C 1173 or CAN/CSA B602.

705.16 Polyethylene plastic pipe. Joints between polyethylene plastic pipe and fittings shall be underground and shall comply with Section 705.16.1 or 705.16.2.

705.16.1 Heat-fusion joints. Joint surfaces shall be clean and free from moisture. All joint surfaces shall be cut, heated to melting temperature and joined using tools specifically designed for the operation. Joints shall be undisturbed until cool. Joints shall be made in accordance with ASTM D 2657 and the manufacturer's instructions.

705.16.2 Mechanical joints. Mechanical joints in drainage piping shall be made with an elastomeric seal conforming to ASTM C 1173, ASTM D 3212 or CAN/CSA B602. Mechanical joints shall be installed in accordance with the manufacturer's instructions.

705.17 Polyolefin plastic. Joints between polyolefin plastic pipe and fittings shall comply with Sections 705.17.1 and 705.17.2.

705.17.1 Heat-fusion joints. Heat-fusion joints for polyolefin pipe and tubing joints shall be installed with socket-type heat-fused polyolefin fittings or electrofusion polyolefin fittings. Joint surfaces shall be clean and free from moisture. The joint shall be undisturbed until cool. Joints shall be made in accordance with ASTM F 1412 or CAN/CSA B181.3.

705.17.2 Mechanical and compression sleeve joints. Mechanical and compression sleeve joints shall be installed in accordance with the manufacturer's instructions.

705.18 Polyvinylidene fluoride plastic. Joints between polyvinylidene plastic pipe and fittings shall comply with Sections 705.18.1 and 705.18.2.

705.18.1 Heat-fusion joints. Heat-fusion joints for polyvinylidene fluoride pipe and tubing joints shall be installed with socket-type heat-fused polyvinylidene fluoride fittings or electrofusion polyvinylidene fittings and couplings. Joint surfaces shall be clean and free from moisture. The joint shall be undisturbed until cool. Joints shall be made in accordance with ASTM F 1673.

705.18.2 Mechanical and compression sleeve joints. Mechanical and compression sleeve joints shall be installed in accordance with the manufacturer's instructions.

705.19 Joints between different materials. Joints between different piping materials shall be made with a mechanical joint of the compression or mechanical-sealing type conforming to ASTM C 1173, ASTM C 1460 or ASTM C 1461. Connectors and adapters shall be *approved* for the application and such joints shall have an elastomeric seal conforming to ASTM C 425, ASTM C 443, ASTM C 564, ASTM C 1440, ASTM D 1869, ASTM F 477, CAN/CSA A257.3M or CAN/CSA B602, or as required in Sections 705.19.1 through 705.19.7. Joints between glass pipe and other types of materials shall be made with adapters having a TFE seal. Joints shall be installed in accordance with the manufacturer's instructions.

705.19.1 Copper or copper-alloy tubing to cast-iron hub pipe. Joints between copper or copper-alloy tubing and cast-iron hub pipe shall be made with a brass ferrule or compression joint. The copper or copper-alloy tubing shall be soldered to the ferrule in an *approved* manner, and the ferrule shall be joined to the cast-iron hub by a caulked joint or a mechanical compression joint.

705.19.2 Copper or copper-alloy tubing to galvanized steel pipe. Joints between copper or copper-alloy tubing and galvanized steel pipe shall be made with a brass converter fitting or dielectric fitting. The copper tubing shall be soldered to the fitting in an *approved* manner, and the fitting shall be screwed to the threaded pipe.

705.19.3 Cast-iron pipe to galvanized steel or brass pipe. Joints between cast-iron and galvanized steel or brass pipe shall be made by either caulked or threaded joints or with an *approved* adapter fitting.

705.19.4 Plastic pipe or tubing to other piping material. Joints between different types of plastic pipe or between plastic pipe and other piping material shall be made with an *approved* adapter fitting. Joints between plastic pipe and cast-iron hub pipe shall be made by a caulked joint or a mechanical compression joint.

705.19.5 Lead pipe to other piping material. Joints between lead pipe and other piping material shall be made by a wiped joint to a caulking ferrule, soldering nipple, or bushing or shall be made with an *approved* adapter fitting.

705.19.6 Borosilicate glass to other materials. Deleted.

705.19.7 Stainless steel drainage systems to other materials. Deleted.

705.20 Drainage slip joints. Slip joints shall comply with Section 405.8.

705.21 Caulking ferrules. Ferrules shall be of red brass and shall be in accordance with Table 705.21.

TABLE 705.21
CAULKING FERRULE SPECIFICATIONS

PIPE SIZES (inches)	INSIDE DIAMETER (inches)	LENGTH (inches)	MINIMUM WEIGHT EACH
2	$2^1/_4$	$4^1/_2$	1 pound
3	$3^1/_4$	$4^1/_2$	1 pound 12 ounces
4	$4^1/_4$	$4^1/_2$	2 pounds 8 ounces

For SI: 1 inch = 25.4 mm, 1 ounce = 28.35 g, 1 pound = 0.454 kg.

705.22 Soldering bushings. Soldering bushings shall be of red brass and shall be in accordance with Table 705.22.

TABLE 705.22
SOLDERING BUSHING SPECIFICATIONS

PIPE SIZES (inches)	MINIMUM WEIGHT EACH
$1^1/_4$	6 ounces
$1^1/_2$	8 ounces
2	14 ounces
$2^1/_2$	1 pound 6 ounces
3	2 pounds
4	3 pounds 8 ounces

For SI: 1 inch = 25.4 mm, 1 ounce = 28.35 g, 1 pound = 0.454 kg.

705.23 Stainless steel drainage systems. O-ring joints for stainless steel drainage systems shall be made with an *approved* elastomeric seal.

SECTION 706
CONNECTIONS BETWEEN DRAINAGE PIPING AND FITTINGS

706.1 Connections and changes in direction. All connections and changes in direction of the sanitary drainage system shall be made with *approved* drainage fittings. Connections between drainage piping and fixtures shall conform to Section 405.

706.2 Obstructions. The fittings shall not have ledges, shoulders or reductions capable of retarding or obstructing flow in the piping. Threaded drainage pipe fittings shall be of the recessed drainage type.

706.3 Installation of fittings. Fittings shall be installed to guide sewage and waste in the direction of flow. Change in direction shall be made by fittings installed in accordance with Table 706.3. Change in direction by combination fittings, side inlets or increasers shall be installed in accordance with Table 706.3 based on the pattern of flow created by the fitting. Double sanitary tee patterns shall not receive the discharge of back-to-back appliances with pumping action discharge.

Exception: Deleted.

TABLE 706.3
FITTINGS FOR CHANGE IN DIRECTION

TYPE OF FITTING PATTERN	CHANGE IN DIRECTION		
	Horizontal to vertical	Vertical to horizontal	Horizontal to horizontal
Sixteenth bend	X	X	X
Eighth bend	X	X	X
Sixth bend	X	X	X
Quarter bend	X	X[d,f]	X[e]
Short sweep	X	X[b]	X[a]
Long sweep	X	X	X
Sanitary tee	X[c]	—	—
Wye	X	X	X
Combination wye and eighth bend	X	X	X

For SI: 1 inch = 25.4 mm.

a. The fittings shall only be permitted for a 2-inch or smaller sink or lavatory fixture drain.

b. Two inches or larger.

c. For a limitation on double sanitary tees, see Section 706.3.

d. May be used only within 12 inches below water closet flange measured to centerline of the quarter bend.

e. This fitting shall only be permitted to be used as the first fitting directly behind the fixture for drains 2 inches and smaller, except clothes washers.

f. The heel inlet connection of a quarter bend may be used as a wet or dry vent if the heel inlet connection of the quarter bend is located in the vertical position. The heel or side inlet connectionmay be used as a wet vent if the quarter bend is located directly below a water closet or other fixture with one integral trap.

706.4 Heel- or side-inlet quarter bends. Heel-inlet quarter bends shall be an acceptable means of connection, except where the quarter bend serves a water closet. A low-heel inlet shall not be used as a wet-vented connection. Side-inlet quarter bends shall be an acceptable means of connection for drainage, wet venting and *stack* venting arrangements.

SECTION 707
PROHIBITED JOINTS AND CONNECTIONS

707.1 Prohibited joints. The following types of joints and connections shall be prohibited:

1. Cement or concrete joints.
2. Mastic or hot-pour bituminous joints.
3. Joints made with fittings not *approved* for the specific installation.
4. Joints between different diameter pipes made with elastomeric rolling O-rings.
5. Solvent-cement joints between different types of plastic pipe.
6. Saddle-type fittings.

SECTION 708
CLEANOUTS

708.1 Scope. This section shall govern the size, location, installation and maintenance of gravity drainage pipe cleanouts.

708.2 Cleanout plugs. Cleanout plugs shall be brass or plastic, or other *approved* materials. Brass cleanout plugs shall be utilized with metallic drain, waste and vent piping only, and shall conform to ASTM A 74, ASME A112.3.1 or ASME A112.36.2M. Cleanouts with plate-style *access* covers shall be fitted with corrosion-resisting fasteners. Plastic cleanout plugs shall conform to the requirements of Section 702.4. Plugs shall have raised square or countersunk square heads. Countersunk heads shall be installed where raised heads are a trip hazard. Cleanout plugs with borosilicate glass systems shall be of borosilicate glass.

708.3 Where required. Cleanouts shall be located in accordance with Sections 708.3.1 through 708.3.6.

708.3.1 Horizontal drains within buildings. All horizontal drains shall be provided with cleanouts located not more than 100 feet (30 480 mm) apart.

708.3.2 Gravity building sewers. Building sewers shall be provided with cleanouts located not more than 100 feet (30 480 mm) apart measured from the upstream entrance of the cleanout. For building sewers 8 inches (203 mm) and larger, manholes shall be provided and located not more than 200 feet (60 960 mm) from the junction of the *building drain* and *building sewer*, at each change in direction and at intervals of not more than 400 feet (122 m) apart. Manholes and manhole covers shall be of an *approved* type.

708.3.3 Changes of direction. One cleanout shall be required for every four horizontal 45-degree (0.79 rad) changes located in series [a long sweep is equivalent to two 45-degree (0.79 rad) bends].

708.3.4 Base of stack. A cleanout shall be provided at the base of each waste or soil *stack*.

708.3.5 Building drain and building sewer junction. There shall be a cleanout at the junction of the *building drain* and the *building sewer*. The cleanout shall be outside the building wall and shall be brought up to the finished ground level. An *approved* two-way cleanout is allowed to be used at this location to serve as a required cleanout for both the *building drain* and *building sewer*. The cleanout at the junction of the *building drain* and *building sewer* shall not be required if the cleanout on a 3-inch (76 mm) or larger diameter soil *stack* is located within a *developed length* of not more than 15 feet (4572 mm) from of the *building drain* and *building sewer* connection and is extended to the outside of the building. The minimum size of the cleanout at the junction of the *building drain* and *building sewer* shall comply with Section 708.7.

708.3.6 Manholes. Manholes serving a *building drain* shall have secured gas-tight covers and shall be located in accordance with Section 708.3.2.

708.4 Concealed piping. Cleanouts on concealed piping or piping under a floor slab or in a crawl space of less than 24 inches (610 mm) in height or a plenum shall be extended through and terminate flush with the finished wall, floor or ground surface or shall be extended to the outside of the building. Cleanout plugs shall not be covered with cement, plaster or any other permanent finish material. Where it is necessary to conceal a cleanout or to terminate a cleanout in an area subject to vehicular traffic, the covering plate, *access* door or cleanout shall be of an *approved* type designed and installed for this purpose.

708.5 Opening direction. Every cleanout shall be installed to open to allow cleaning in the direction of the flow of the drainage pipe or at right angles thereto.

708.6 Prohibited installation. Cleanout openings shall not be utilized for the installation of new fixtures, except where *approved* and where another cleanout of equal *access* and capacity is provided.

708.7 Minimum size. Cleanouts shall be the same nominal size as the pipe they serve up to 4 inches (102 mm). For pipes larger than 4 inches (102 mm) nominal size, the minimum size of the cleanout shall be 4 inches (102 mm).

Exceptions: Deleted.

708.8 Clearances. Cleanouts on 6-inch (153 mm) and smaller pipes shall be provided with a clearance of not less than 18 inches (457 mm) for rodding. Cleanouts on 8-inch (203 mm) and larger pipes shall be provided with a clearance of not less than 36 inches (914 mm) for rodding.

708.9 Access. *Access* shall be provided to all cleanouts.

708.10 Location. Each horizontal drainage pipe shall be provided with a cleanout at the upstream end of the pipe.

Exceptions: The following plumbing arrangements are acceptable in lieu of the upstream cleanout.

1. "P" traps connected to the drainage piping with slip joints or ground joint connections.
2. "P" traps into which floor drains, shower drains or tub drains with removable strainers discharge.
3. "P" traps into which the straight-through type waste and overflow discharge with the overflow connecting to the top of the tee.
4. "P" traps into which residential washing machines discharge.
5. Test tees or cleanouts in a vertical pipe.
6. Cleanout near the junction of the building drain and the building sewer which may be rodded bothways.
7. Water closets for the water closet fixture drain only.
8. Cast-iron cleanout sizing shall be in accordance with referenced standards in Table 702.4, ASTM A 74 for hub and spigot fittings or ASTM A 888 or CISPI 301 for hubless fittings.

SECTION 709 FIXTURE UNITS

709.1 Values for fixtures. *Drainage fixture unit* values as given in Table 709.1 designate the relative load weight of different kinds of fixtures that shall be employed in estimating the total load carried by a soil or waste pipe, and shall be used in connection with Tables 710.1(1) and 710.1(2) of sizes for soil, waste and vent pipes for which the permissible load is given in terms of fixture units.

709.2 Fixtures not listed in Table 709.1. Fixtures not listed in Table 709.1 shall have a *drainage fixture unit* load based on the outlet size of the fixture in accordance with Table 709.2. The minimum trap size for unlisted fixtures shall be the size of the drainage outlet but not less than $1^1/_4$ inches (32 mm).

TABLE 709.2
DRAINAGE FIXTURE UNITS FOR FIXTURE DRAINS OR TRAPS

FIXTURE DRAIN OR TRAP SIZE (inches)	DRAINAGE FIXTURE UNIT VALUE
$1^1/_4$	1
$1^1/_2$	2
2	3
$2^1/_2$	4
3	5
4	6

For SI: 1 inch = 25.4 mm.

709.3 Values for continuous and semicontinuous flow. *Drainage fixture unit* values for continuous and semicontinuous flow into a drainage system shall be computed on the basis that 1 gpm (0.06 L/s) of flow is equivalent to two fixture units.

709.4 Values for indirect waste receptor. The *drainage fixture unit* load of an indirect waste receptor receiving the discharge of indirectly connected fixtures shall be the sum of the *drainage fixture unit* values of the fixtures that discharge to the receptor, but not less than the *drainage fixture unit* value given for the indirect waste receptor in Table 709.1 or 709.2.

709.4.1 Clear-water waste receptors. Where waste receptors such as floor drains, floor sinks and hub drains receive only clear-water waste from display cases, refrigerated display cases, ice bins, coolers and freezers, such receptors shall have a *drainage fixture unit* value of one-half.

SECTION 710 DRAINAGE SYSTEM SIZING

710.1 Maximum fixture unit load. The maximum number of drainage fixture units connected to a given size of *building sewer, building drain* or horizontal *branch* of the *building drain* shall be determined using Table 710.1(1). The maximum number of drainage fixture units connected to a given size of horizontal *branch* or vertical soil or waste *stack* shall be determined using Table 710.1(2).

710.1.1 Horizontal stack offsets. Deleted.

710.1.2 Vertical stack offsets. Deleted.

710.2 Future fixtures. Where provision is made for the future installation of fixtures, those provided for shall be considered in determining the required sizes of drain pipes.

TABLE 709.1
DRAINAGE FIXTURE UNITS FOR FIXTURES AND GROUPS

FIXTURE TYPE	DRAINAGE FIXTURE UNIT VALUE AS LOAD FACTORS	MINIMUM SIZE OF TRAP (inches)
Automatic clothes washers, commercial[a,g]	3	2
Automatic clothes washers, residential[g]	2	2
Bathroom group as defined in Section 202 (1.6 gpf water closet)[f,j]	5	—
Bathroom group as defined in Section 202 (water closet flushing greater than 1.6 gpf)[f]	6	—
Bathtub[b] (with or without overhead shower or whirpool attachments)	2	$1^1/_2$
Bidet	1	$1^1/_4$
Combination sink and tray	2	$1^1/_2$
Dental lavatory	1	$1^1/_4$
Dental unit or cuspidor	1	$1^1/_4$
Dishwashing machine,[c] domestic	2	$1^1/_2$
Drinking fountain	$^1/_2$	$1^1/_4$
Emergency floor drain	0	2
Floor drains[h]	2[h]	2
Floor sinks	Note h	2
Kitchen sink, domestic	2	$1^1/_2$
Kitchen sink, domestic with food waste grinder and/or dishwasher[i]	2	$1^1/_2$
Laundry tray (1 or 2 compartments)	2	$1^1/_2$
Lavatory	1	$1^1/_4$
Shower (based on the total flow rate through showerheads and body sprays) Flow rate: 5.7 gpm or less Greater than 5.7 gpm to 12.3 gpm Greater than 12.3 gpm to 25.8 gpm Greater than 25.8 gpm to 55.6 gpm	 2 3 5 6	 $1^1/_2$ 2 3 4
Service sink	2	$1^1/_2$
Sink	2	$1^1/_2$
Urinal	4	Note d
Urinal, 1 gallon per flush or less	2[e]	Note d
Urinal, nonwater supplied	$^1/_2$	Note d
Wash sink (circular or multiple) each set of faucets	2	$1^1/_2$
Water closet, flushometer tank, public or private	4[e]	Note d
Water closet, private (1.6 gpf)	3[e]	Note d
Water closet, private (flushing greater than 1.6 gpf)	4[e]	Note d
Water closet, public (1.6 gpf)	4[e]	Note d
Water closet, public (flushing greater than 1.6 gpf)	6[e]	Note d

For SI: 1 inch = 25.4 mm, 1 gallon = 3.785 L, gpf = gallon per flushing cycle, gpm = gallon per minute.

a. For traps larger than 3 inches, use Table 709.2.

b. A showerhead over a bathtub or whirlpool bathtub attachment does not increase the drainage fixture unit value.

c. See Sections 709.2 through 709.4.1 for methods of computing unit value of fixtures not listed in this table or for rating of devices with intermittent flows.

d. Trap size shall be consistent with the fixture outlet size.

e. For the purpose of computing loads on building drains and sewers, water closets and urinals shall not be rated at a lower drainage fixture unit unless the lower values are confirmed by testing.

f. For fixtures added to a dwelling unit bathroom group, add the dfu value of those additional fixtures to the bathroom group fixture count.

g. See Section 406.3 for sizing requirements for fixture drain, branch drain, and drainage stack for an automatic clothes washer standpipe.

h. See Sections 709.4 and 709.4.1.

i. Fixture arm and trap shall be $1^1/_2$-inch minimum; vertical drain shall be 2-inch minimum.

j. For one- and two-family dwelling units, add 2 DFU for each additional full bath.

TABLE 710.1(1)
BUILDING DRAINS AND SEWERS

DIAMETER OF PIPE (inches)	MAXIMUM NUMBER OF DRAINAGE FIXTURE UNITS CONNECTED TO ANY PORTION OF THE BUILDING DRAIN OR THE BUILDING SEWER, INCLUDING BRANCHES OF THE BUILDING DRAIN[a, b, d]			
	Slope per foot			
	$^1/_{16}$ inch	$^1/_8$ inch	$^1/_4$ inch	$^1/_2$ inch
$1^1/_4$	—	—	1	1
$1^1/_2$	—	—	3	3
2	—	—	21	26
$2^1/_2$	—	—	24	31
3[c]	—	36	42	50
4	—	180	216	250
5	—	390	480	575
6	—	700	840	1,000
8	1,400	1,600	1,920	2,300
10	2,500	2,900	3,500	4,200
12	3,900	4,600	5,600	6,700
15	7,000	8,300	10,000	12,000

For SI: 1 inch = 25.4 mm, 1 inch per foot = 83.3 mm/m.

a. The minimum size of any building drain serving a water closet shall be 3 inches.

b. No building sewer shall be less than 4 inches in size.

c. No more than three water closets.

d. Minimum 2-inch diameter.

TABLE 710.1(2)
HORIZONTAL FIXTURE BRANCHES AND STACKS[a, f]

DIAMETER OF PIPE (inches)	MAXIMUM NUMBER OF DRAINAGE FIXTURE UNITS (dfu)			
		Stacks[b]		
	Total for horizontal branch[e]	Total discharge into one branch interval	Total for stack of three branch Intervals or less	Total for stack greater than three branch intervals
$1^1/_2$	3	2	4	8
2	6	6	10	24
$2^1/_2$	12	9	20	42
3[g]	20[d]	20[d]	48	72
4	160	90	240	500
5	360	200	540	1,100
6	620	350	960	1,900
8	1,400	600	2,200	3,600
10	2,500	1,000	3,800	5,600
12	3,900	1,500	6,000	8,400
15	7,000	Note c	Note c	Note c

For SI: 1 inch = 25.4 mm.

a. Does not include branches of the building drain. Refer to Table 710.1(1).

b. Stacks shall be sized based on the total accumulated connected load at each story or branch interval. As the total accumulated connected load decreases, stacks are permitted to be reduced in size. Stack diameters shall not be reduced to less than one-half of the diameter of the lagest stack size required.

c. Sizing load based on design criteria.

d. No more than three water closets.

e. 50 percent less for circuit-vented fixture branches.

f. Minimum of 2-inch diameter underground.

g. The minimum size of any branches serving a water closet shall be 3 inches.

SECTION 711 OFFSETS IN DRAINAGE PIPING IN BUILDINGS OF FIVE STORIES OR MORE Deleted

SECTION 712 SUMPS AND EJECTORS

712.1 Building subdrains. Building subdrains that cannot be discharged to the *sewer* by gravity flow shall be discharged into a tightly covered and vented sump from which the liquid shall be lifted and discharged into the building gravity drainage system by automatic pumping equipment or other *approved* method. In other than existing structures, the sump shall not receive drainage from any piping within the building capable of being discharged by gravity to the *building sewer.*

712.2 Fittings required. A check valve and a full open valve, and cleanout located on the discharge side of the check valve shall be installed in the pump or ejector discharge piping between the pump or ejector and the gravity drainage system. *Access* shall be provided to such valves. Such valves shall be located above the sump cover required by Section 712.1 or, where the discharge pipe from the ejector is below grade, the valves shall be accessibly located outside the sump below grade in an *access* pit with a removable *access* cover.

712.3 Sump design. The sump pump, pit and discharge piping shall conform to the requirements of Sections 712.3.1 through 712.3.5.

712.3.1 Sump pump. The sump pump capacity and head shall be appropriate to anticipated use requirements.

712.3.2 Sump pit. The sump pit shall be not less than 18 inches (457 mm) in diameter and 24 inches (610 mm) deep, unless otherwise *approved.* The pit shall be accessible and located such that all drainage flows into the pit by gravity. The sump pit shall be constructed of tile, concrete, steel, plastic or other *approved* materials. The pit bottom shall be solid and provide permanent support for the pump. The sump pit shall be fitted with a gas-tight removable cover adequate to support anticipated loads in the area of use. The sump pit shall be vented in accordance with Chapter 9.

712.3.3 Discharge piping. Discharge piping and fittings shall be constructed of *approved* pressure rated materials.

712.3.4 Maximum effluent level. The effluent level control shall be adjusted and maintained to at all times prevent the effluent in the sump from rising to within 2 inches (51 mm) of the invert of the gravity drain inlet into the sump.

712.3.4.1 Sump alarms. Sumps that discharge by means of automatic pumping equipment shall be provided with an approved, electrically operated high-water indicating alarm. A remote sensor shall activate the alarm when the fluid level exceeds a preset level that is less than the maximum capacity of the sump. The alarm shall function to provide an audiovisual signal to occupants within the dwelling. Electrical power for the alarm shall be supplied through a branch circuit separate from that supplying the pump motor.

712.3.5 Ejector connection to the drainage system. Pumps connected to the drainage system shall connect to the *building sewer* or shall connect to a wye fitting in the *building drain* a minimum of 10 feet (3048 mm) from the base of any soil *stack*, waste *stack* or *fixture drain*. Where the discharge line connects into horizontal drainage piping, the connector shall be made through a wye fitting into the top of the drainage piping.

712.4 Sewage pumps and sewage ejectors. A sewage pump or ejector pump discharge pipe shall not discharge directly into a septic tank. The pumped line shall discharge laterally into a 4-inch (102 mm) gravity line not less than 10 feet (3048 mm) from the connection to the tank through a lateral wye branch.

712.4.1 Macerating toilet systems. Macerating toilet systems shall comply with CSA B45.9 or ASME A112.3.4 and shall be installed in accordance with the manufacturer's installation instructions.

712.4.2 Capacity. A sewage pump or sewage ejector shall have the capacity and head for the application requirements. Pumps or ejectors that receive the discharge of water closets shall be capable of handling spherical solids with a diameter of up to and including 2 inches (51 mm). Other pumps or ejectors shall be capable of handling spherical solids with a diameter of up to and including 1 inch (25.4 mm). The minimum capacity of a pump or ejector based on the diameter of the discharge pipe shall be in accordance with Table 712.4.2.

Exceptions:

1. Grinder pumps or grinder ejectors that receive the discharge of water closets shall have a minimum discharge opening of $1^1/_4$ inches (32 mm).
2. Macerating toilet assemblies that serve single water closets shall have a minimum discharge opening of $^3/_4$ inch (19 mm).

TABLE 712.4.2 MINIMUM CAPACITY OF SEWAGE PUMP OR SEWAGE EJECTOR

DIAMETER OF THE DISCHARGE PIPE (inches)	CAPACITY OF PUMP OR EJECTOR (gpm)
2	21
$2^1/_2$	30
3	46

For SI: 1 inch = 25.4 mm, 1 gallon per minute = 3.785 L/m.

SECTION 713 HEALTH CARE PLUMBING Deleted

SECTION 714 COMPUTERIZED DRAINAGE DESIGN Deleted

SECTION 715
BACKWATER VALVES

715.1 Sewage backflow. Where the flood level rims of plumbing fixtures are below the elevation of the manhole cover of the next upstream manhole in the *public sewer*, such fixtures shall be protected by a backwater valve installed in the *building drain*, *branch* of the *building drain* or horizontal *branch* serving such fixtures. Plumbing fixtures having flood level rims above the elevation of the manhole cover of the next upstream manhole in the *public sewer* shall not discharge through a backwater valve.

715.2 Material. All bearing parts of backwater valves shall be of corrosion-resistant material. Backwater valves shall comply with ASME A112.14.1, CSA B181.1 or CSA B181.2.

715.3 Seal. Backwater valves shall be so constructed as to provide a mechanical seal against backflow.

715.4 Diameter. Backwater valves, when fully opened, shall have a capacity not less than that of the pipes in which they are installed.

715.5 Location. Backwater valves shall be installed so that *access* is provided to the working parts for service and repair.

CHAPTER 8
INDIRECT/SPECIAL WASTE

SECTION 801
GENERAL
Deleted

SECTION 802
INDIRECT WASTES

802.1 Where required. Deleted.

802.1.1 Food handling. Deleted.

802.1.2 Floor drains in food storage areas. Deleted

802.1.3 Potable clear-water waste. Deleted.

802.1.4 Swimming pools. Deleted.

802.1.5 Nonpotable clear-water waste. Deleted.

802.1.6 Domestic dishwashing machines. Domestic dishwashing machines shall discharge indirectly through an *air gap* or *air break* into a standpipe or waste receptor in accordance with Section 802.2, or discharge into a wye-branch fitting on the tailpiece of the kitchen sink or the dishwasher connection of a food waste grinder. The waste line of a domestic dishwashing machine discharging into a kitchen sink tailpiece or food waste grinder shall connect to a deck-mounted *air gap* or the waste line shall rise and be securely fastened to the underside of the sink rim or counter.

802.1.7 Commercial dishwashing machines. Deleted.

802.1.8 Food utensils, dishes, pots and pans sinks. Deleted.

802.2 Installation. Deleted.

802.3 Waste receptors. Deleted.

802.4 Standpipes. Standpipes shall be 2 inches (51 mm) in diameter and not less than 18 inches (762 mm) or more than 48 inches (1219 mm) in height as measured from the crown weir. The standpipe shall extend 34 inches (864 mm) minimum above the base of the clothes washer unless recommended otherwise by the manufacturer. The connection of a laundry tray waste line may be made into a standpipe for the automatic clothes-washer drain. The outlet of the laundry tray shall be a maximum horizontal distance of 30 inches (762 mm) from the standpipe trap.

SECTION 803
SPECIAL WASTES
Deleted

SECTION 804
MATERIALS, JOINTS AND CONNECTIONS
Deleted

CHAPTER 9
VENTS

SECTION 901
GENERAL

901.1 Scope. The provisions of this chapter shall govern the materials, design, construction and installation of vent systems.

901.2 Trap seal protection. The plumbing system shall be provided with a system of vent piping that will permit the admission or emission of air so that the seal of any fixture trap shall not be subjected to a pneumatic pressure differential of more than 1 inch of water column (249 Pa).

901.2.1 Venting required. Every trap and trapped fixture shall be vented in accordance with one of the venting methods specified in this chapter. All fixtures discharging downstream from a water closet shall be individually vented except as provided in Section 911.

901.3 Chemical waste vent system. Deleted.

901.4 Use limitations. The plumbing vent system shall not be utilized for purposes other than the venting of the plumbing system.

901.5 Tests. The vent system shall be tested in accordance with Section 312.

901.6 Engineered systems. Deleted.

SECTION 902
MATERIALS

902.1 Vents. The materials and methods utilized for the construction and installation of venting systems shall comply with the applicable provisions of Section 702.

902.2 Sheet copper. Sheet copper for vent pipe flashings shall conform to ASTM B 152 and shall weigh not less than 8 ounces per square foot (2.5 kg/m^2).

902.3 Sheet lead. Sheet lead for vent pipe flashings shall weigh not less than 3 pounds per square foot (15 kg/m^2) for field-constructed flashings and not less than $2^1/_2$ pounds per square foot (12 kg/m^2) for prefabricated flashings.

SECTION 903
OUTDOOR VENT EXTENSION

903.1 Stack required. Every building in which plumbing is installed shall have at least one stack the size of which is not less than one-half of the required diameter of the building drain, and not less than 2 inches (51 mm) in diameter. Such stack shall run undiminished in size and as directly as possible from the building drain through to the open air or to a vent header that extends to the open air.

903.1.1 Connection to drainage system. A vent stack shall connect to the building drain or to the base of a drainage stack in accordance with Section 903.4. A stack vent shall be an extension of the drainage stack. For townhouses and one- and two-family dwellings, the main vent shall connect to the building drain, building stack or branch thereof not less than 3 inches (76 mm) in size.

903.1.2 Size. Deleted.

903.2 Vent stack required. Deleted.

903.3 Vent termination. Vent stacks or stack vents shall extend outdoors and terminate open air.

903.4 Vent connection at base. Every vent *stack* shall connect to the base of the drainage *stack*. The vent *stack* shall connect at or below the lowest horizontal *branch*. Where the vent *stack* connects to the *building drain*, the connection shall be located downstream of the drainage *stack* and within a distance of 10 times the diameter of the drainage *stack*.

903.5 Vent headers. Deleted.

SECTION 904
VENT TERMINALS

904.1 Roof extension. All open vent pipes that extend through a roof shall be terminated at least 6 inches (152 mm) above the roof, except that where a roof is used by the public or tenants for any purpose, the vent extensions shall be run at least 7 feet (2134 mm) above the roof.

904.2 Frost closure. Where the 97.5-percent value for outside design temperature is 0°F (-18°C) or less, every vent extension through a roof or wall shall be a minimum of 3 inches (76 mm) in diameter. Any increase in the size of the vent shall be made inside the structure a minimum of 1 foot (305 mm) below the roof or inside the wall.

904.3 Flashings. The juncture of each vent pipe with the roof line shall be made water-tight by an *approved* flashing.

904.4 Prohibited use. Vent terminals shall not be used as a flag pole or to support flag poles, television aerials or similar items, except when the piping has been anchored in an *approved* manner.

904.5 Location of vent terminal. An open vent terminal from a drainage system shall not be located directly beneath any door, openable window, or other air intake opening of the building or of an adjacent building or property line, and any such vent terminal shall not be within 10 feet (3048 mm) horizontally of such an opening unless it is at least 2 feet (610 mm) above the top of such opening.

904.6 Extension through the wall. Vent terminals extending through the wall shall terminate a minimum of 10 feet (3048 mm) from the lot line and 10 feet (3048 mm) above average ground level. Vent terminals shall not terminate under the overhang of a structure with soffit vents. Side wall vent terminals shall not terminate horizontally to prevent birds or rodents from entering or blocking the vent opening.

904.7 Extension outside a structure. In climates where the 97.5-percent value for outside design temperature is less than 0°F (-18°C), vent pipes installed on the exterior of the structure shall be protected against freezing by insulation, heat or both.

SECTION 905
VENT CONNECTIONS AND GRADES

905.1 Connection. All individual, *branch* and circuit vents shall connect to a vent *stack*, *stack vent*, air admittance valve or extend to the open air.

905.2 Grade. All vent and *branch* vent pipes shall be so graded and connected as to drain back to the drainage pipe by gravity.

905.3 Vent connection to drainage system. Every dry vent connecting to a horizontal drain shall connect above the centerline of the horizontal drain pipe.

905.4 Vertical rise of vent. Every dry vent shall rise vertically to a minimum of 6 inches (152 mm) above the *flood level rim* of the highest trap or trapped fixture being vented.

Exception: When vents for interceptors and isolated floor drains are not located near an adjacent wall, the vent must rise 6 inches (152 mm) vertically before turning horizontally and continuing to the nearest wall. For cleaning purposes, a cleanout the same size as the vent shall be installed.

905.5 Height above fixtures. A connection between a vent pipe and a vent *stack* or *stack vent* shall be made at least 6 inches (152 mm) above the *flood level rim* of the highest fixture served by the vent. Horizontal vent pipes forming *branch* vents, relief vents or loop vents shall be at least 6 inches (152 mm) above the *flood level rim* of the highest fixture served.

905.6 Vent for future fixtures. Where the drainage piping has been roughed-in for future fixtures, a rough-in connection for a vent shall be installed. The vent size shall be not less than one-half the diameter of the rough-in drain to be served. The vent rough-in shall connect to the vent system, or shall be vented by other means as provided for in this chapter. The connection shall be identified to indicate that it is a vent.

SECTION 906
FIXTURE VENTS

906.1 Distance of trap from vent. Each fixture trap shall have a protecting vent located so that the slope and the *developed length* in the *fixture drain* from the trap weir to the vent fitting are within the requirements set forth in Table 906.1.

Exception: Deleted.

906.2 Venting of fixture drains. The total fall in a *fixture drain* due to pipe slope shall not exceed the diameter of the *fixture drain*, nor shall the vent connection to a *fixture drain*, except for water closets, be below the weir of the trap.

906.3 Crown vent. A vent shall not be installed within two pipe diameters of the trap weir.

TABLE 906.1
MAXIMUM DISTANCE OF FIXTURE TRAP FROM VENT

SIZE OF TRAP (inches)	SLOPE (inch per foot)	DISTANCE FROM TRAP (feet)
$1^1/_4$	$^1/_4$	5
$1^1/_2$	$^1/_4$	6
2	$^1/_4$	8
3	$^1/_8$	12
4	$^1/_8$	16

For SI: 1 inch = 25.4 mm, 1 foot = 304.8 mm, 1 inch per foot = 83.3 mm/m.

SECTION 907
INDIVIDUAL VENT

907.1 Individual vent permitted. Each trap and trapped fixture is permitted to be provided with an individual vent. The individual vent shall connect to the *fixture drain* of the trap or trapped fixture being vented.

SECTION 908
COMMON VENT

908.1 Individual vent as common vent. An individual vent is permitted to vent two traps or trapped fixtures as a common vent. The traps or trapped fixtures being common vented shall be located on the same floor level.

908.2 Connection at the same level. Where the fixture drains being common vented connect at the same level, the vent connection shall be at the interconnection of the fixture drains or downstream of the interconnection.

908.3 Connection at different levels. Where the fixture drains connect at different levels, the vent shall connect as a vertical extension of the vertical drain. The vertical drain pipe connecting the two fixture drains shall be considered the vent for the lower *fixture drain*, and shall be sized in accordance with Table 908.3. The upper fixture shall not be a water closet or clothes washer.

TABLE 908.3
COMMON VENT SIZES

PIPE SIZE (inches)	MAXIMUM DISCHARGE FROM UPPER FIXTURE DRAIN (dfu)
$1^1/_2$	1
2	4
$2^1/_2$ to 3	6

For SI: 1 inch = 25.4 mm.

SECTION 909
WET VENTING

909.1 Wet vent permitted. Any combination of fixtures within two bathroom groups located on the same floor level is permitted to be vented by a horizontal wet vent. The wet vent shall be considered the vent for the fixtures and shall extend from the connection of the dry vent along the direction of the flow in the drain pipe to the most downstream *fixture drain* connection to the *horizontal branch drain*. Each wet-vented *fixture drain* shall connect independently to the horizontal wet vent. Only the fixtures within the bathroom groups shall connect to the wet-vented *horizontal branch* drain. A residential clothes washer drain line shall not be used as a wet vent.

909.1.1 Vertical wet vent permitted. Any combination of fixtures located on the same floor level is permitted to be vented by a vertical wet vent. The vertical wet vent shall be considered the vent for the fixtures and shall extend from the connection of the dry vent down to the lowest *fixture drain* connection. Each fixture shall connect independently to the vertical wet vent. Water closet drains shall connect at the same elevation. Other fixture drains shall connect above or at the same elevation as the water closet fixture drains. The dry- vent connection to the vertical wet vent shall be an individual or common vent serving one or two fixtures.

909.2 Vent connection. The dry-vent connection to the wet vent shall be an individual vent or common vent. The dry vent shall be sized based on the largest required diameter of pipe within the wet vent system served by the dry vent.

909.2.1 Horizontal wet vent. Deleted.

909.2.2 Vertical wet vent. Deleted.

909.3 Size. The wet vent serving the wet vent shall be sized based on the largest required diameter of pipe within the wet-vent system served by the dry vent. The wet vent shall be of a minimum size as specified in Table 909.3, based on the fixture unit discharge to the wet vent.

TABLE 909.3
WET VENT SIZE

WET VENT PIPE SIZE (inches)	DRAINAGE FIXTURE UNIT LOAD (dfu)
$1^1/_2$	1
2	4
$2^1/_2$	6
3	12

For SI: 1 inch = 25.4 mm.

909.4 Multistory bathroom groups. On the lower floors of a multistory building, the waste pipe from one or two lavatories may be used as a wet vent for one or two bathtubs or showers provided that:

1. The wet vent and its extension to the vent stack is not less than 2-inch (51 mm) diameter;
2. Each water closet below the top floor is individually back vented; and
3. The vent stack is sized in accordance with Table 909.4.

Exception: In multistory bathroom groups (does not apply to one- and two-family dwellings), wet vented in accordance with Section 909.4, the water closets below the top floor need not be individually vented if a 2-inch (51 mm) wet vent connects downstream of the water closet.

TABLE 909.4
SIZE OF VENT STACK

NUMBER OF WET VENTED FIXTURES	DIAMETER OF VENT STACKS (in.)
1 or 2 bathtubs or showers	2
3 to 5 bathtubs or showers	$2^1/_2$
6 to 9 bathtubs or showers	3
10 to 16 bathtubs or showers	4

For SI: 1 inch = 25.4 mm.

SECTION 910
WASTE STACK VENT

910.1 Waste stack vent permitted. A waste *stack* shall be considered a vent for all of the fixtures discharging to the *stack* where installed in accordance with the requirements of this section.

910.2 Stack installation. The waste *stack* shall be vertical, and both horizontal and vertical offsets shall be prohibited between the lowest *fixture drain* connection and the highest *fixture drain* connection. Every *fixture drain* shall connect separately to the waste *stack*. The *stack* shall not receive the discharge of water closets or urinals.

910.3 Stack vent. A *stack vent* shall be provided for the waste *stack*. The size of the *stack vent* shall be not less than the size of the waste *stack*. Offsets shall be permitted in the *stack vent*, shall be located at least 6 inches (152 mm) above the flood level of the highest fixture and shall be in accordance with Section 905.2. The *stack vent* shall be permitted to connect with other *stack vents* and vent stacks in accordance with Section 903.5.

910.4 Waste stack size. The waste *stack* shall be sized based on the total discharge to the *stack* and the discharge within a *branch* interval in accordance with Table 910.4. The waste *stack* shall be the same size throughout its length.

TABLE 910.4
WASTE STACK VENT SIZE

STACK SIZE (inches)	MAXIMUM NUMBER OF DRAINAGE FIXTURE UNITS (dfu)	
	Total discharge into one branch interval	Total discharge for stack
$1^1/_2$	1	2
2	2	4
$2^1/_2$	No limit	8
3	No limit	24
4	No limit	50
5	No limit	75
6	No limit	100

For SI: 1 inch = 25.4 mm.

SECTION 911
CIRCUIT VENTING

911.1 Circuit vent permitted. A maximum of eight fixtures connected to a horizontal *branch* drain shall be permitted to be circuit vented. Each *fixture drain* shall connect horizontally to the horizontal *branch* being circuit vented. The horizontal *branch* drain shall be classified as a vent from the most downstream *fixture drain* connection to the most upstream *fixture drain* connection to the horizontal *branch*.

911.1.1 Multiple circuit-vented branches. Circuit-vented horizontal *branch* drains are permitted to be connected together. Each group of a maximum of eight fixtures shall be considered a separate circuit vent and shall conform to the requirements of this section.

911.2 Vent connection. The circuit vent connection shall be located between the two most upstream fixture drains. The vent shall connect to the horizontal *branch* and shall be installed in accordance with Section 905. The circuit vent pipe shall not receive the discharge of any soil or waste.

911.3 Slope and size of horizontal branch. The maximum slope of the vent section of the *horizontal branch drain* shall be one unit vertical in 12 units horizontal (8-percent slope). The entire length of the vent section of the *horizontal branch drain* shall be sized for the total drainage discharge to the *branch*.

911.3.1 Size of multiple circuit vent. Each separate circuit-vented horizontal *branch* that is interconnected shall be sized independently in accordance with Section 911.3. The downstream circuit-vented horizontal *branch* shall be sized for the total discharge into the *branch*, including the upstream branches and the fixtures within the *branch*.

911.4 Relief vent. A relief vent shall be provided for circuit-vented horizontal branches receiving the discharge of four or more water closets and connecting to a drainage *stack* that receives the discharge of soil or waste from upper horizontal branches.

911.4.1 Connection and installation. The relief vent shall connect to the horizontal *branch* drain between the *stack* and the most downstream *fixture drain* of the circuit vent. The relief vent shall be installed in accordance with Section 905.

911.4.2 Fixture drain or branch. The relief vent is permitted to be a *fixture drain* or fixture *branch* for fixtures located within the same *branch interval* as the circuit-vented horizontal *branch*. The maximum discharge to a relief vent shall be four fixture units.

911.5 Additional fixtures. Fixtures, other than the circuit-vented fixtures, are permitted to discharge to the horizontal *branch* drain. Such fixtures shall be located on the same floor as the circuit-vented fixtures and shall be either individually or common vented.

SECTION 912
COMBINATION WASTE DRAIN AND VENT SYSTEM
Deleted

SECTION 913
ISLAND FIXTURE VENTING

913.1 Limitation. Island fixture venting shall not be permitted for fixtures other than sinks and lavatories. Residential kitchen sinks with a dishwasher waste connection, a food waste grinder, or both, in combination with the kitchen sink waste, shall be permitted to be vented in accordance with this section.

913.2 Vent connection. The island fixture vent shall connect to the *fixture drain* as required for an individual or common vent. The vent shall rise vertically to above the drainage outlet of the fixture being vented before offsetting horizontally or vertically downward. For multiple island fixture vents, the vent or branch vent shall extend to a minimum of 6 inches (152 mm) above the highest island fixture being vented before connecting to the outside vent terminal.

913.3 Vent installation below the fixture flood level rim. The vent located below the *flood level rim* of the fixture being vented shall be installed as required for drainage piping in accordance with Chapter 7, except for sizing. The vent shall be sized in accordance with Section 916.2. The lowest point of the island fixture vent shall connect full size to the drainage system. The connection shall be to a vertical drain pipe or to the top half of a horizontal drain pipe. Cleanouts shall be provided in the island fixture vent to permit rodding of all vent piping located below the *flood level rim* of the fixtures. Rodding in both directions shall be permitted through a cleanout.

SECTION 914
RELIEF VENTS—STACKS OF MORE THAN 10 BRANCH INTERVALS
Deleted

SECTION 915
VENTS FOR STACK OFFSETS
Deleted

SECTION 916
VENT PIPE SIZING

916.1 Size of stack vents and vent stacks. Deleted.

Table 916.1 Size and Developed Length of Stack Vents and Vent Stacks. Deleted.

916.2 Vents other than stack vents or vent stacks. The diameter of individual vents, *branch* vents, circuit vents and relief vents shall be at least one-half the required diameter of the drain served. The required size of the drain shall be determined in accordance with Table 710.1(2). Vent pipes shall not be less than $1^1/_4$ inches (32 mm) in diameter. Vents exceeding 40 feet (12 192 mm) in *developed length* shall be increased by one nominal pipe size for the entire *developed length* of the vent pipe. Relief vents for soil and waste stacks in buildings having more than 10 *branch intervals* shall be sized in accordance with Section 914.2.

916.3 Developed length. The *developed length* of individual, *branch*, circuit and relief vents shall be measured from the farthest point of vent connection to the drainage system to the point of connection to the vent *stack*, *stack vent* or termination outside of the building.

916.4 Multiple branch vents. Where multiple *branch* vents are connected to a common *branch* vent, the common *branch* vent shall be sized in accordance with this section based on the size of the common horizontal drainage *branch* that is or would be required to serve the total *drainage fixture unit* (*dfu*) load being vented.

916.4.1 Branch vents exceeding 40 feet in developed length. *Branch* vents exceeding 40 feet (12 192 mm) in *developed length* shall be increased by one nominal size for the entire *developed length* of the vent pipe.

916.5 Sump vents. Sump vent sizes shall be determined in accordance with Sections 916.5.1 and 916.5.2.

916.5.1 Sewage pumps and sewage ejectors other than pneumatic. Drainage piping below *sewer* level shall be vented in a similar manner to that of a gravity system. Building sump vent sizes for sumps with sewage pumps or sewage ejectors, other than pneumatic, shall be determined in accordance with Table 916.5.1. An open vent terminal from a drainage system shall not be located directly beneath any door, openable window, or other air intake opening of the building or of an adjacent building or property line, and any such vent terminal shall not be within 10 feet (3048 mm) horizontally of such an opening unless it is at least 2 feet (610 mm) above the top of such opening.

916.5.2 Pneumatic sewage ejectors. The air pressure relief pipe from a pneumatic sewage ejector shall be connected to an independent vent *stack* terminating as required for vent extensions through the roof. The relief pipe shall be sized to relieve air pressure inside the ejector to atmospheric pressure, but shall not be less than $1^1/_4$ inches (32 mm) in size.

SECTION 917 AIR ADMITTANCE VALVES

Deleted

SECTION 918 ENGINEERED VENT SYSTEMS

Deleted

SECTION 919 COMPUTERIZED VENT DESIGN

Deleted

SECTION 920 SINGLE STACK PLUMBING SYSTEMS (SOVENT)

920.1 Design and installation shall be in accordance with design criteria contained in the Copper Development Association (CDA) Handbook No. 802. Materials shall meet standards and specifications listed in Tables 702.1 and 702.4 for drain, waste and vent pipe and fittings.

TABLE 916.5.1
SIZE AND LENGTH OF SUMP VENTS

DISCHARGE CAPACITY OF PUMP (gpm)	MAXIMUM DEVELOPED LENGTH OF VENT (feet)[a]					
	Diameter of vent (inches)					
	$1^1/_4$	$1^1/_2$	2	$2^1/_2$	3	4
10	No limit[b]	No limit	No limit	No limit	No limit	No limit
20	270	No limit	No limit	No limit	No limit	No limit
40	72	160	No limit	No limit	No limit	No limit
60	31	75	270	No limit	No limit	No limit
80	16	41	150	380	No limit	No limit
100	10[c]	25	97	250	No limit	No limit
150	Not permitted	10[c]	44	110	370	No limit
200	Not permitted	Not permitted	20	60	210	No limit
250	Not permitted	Not permitted	10	36	132	No limit
300	Not permitted	Not permitted	10[c]	22	88	380
400	Not permitted	Not permitted	Not permitted	10[c]	44	210
500	Not permitted	Not permitted	Not permitted	Not permitted	24	130

For SI: 1 inch = 25.4 mm, 1 foot = 304.8 mm, 1 gallon per minute = 3.785 L/m.

a. Developed length plus an appropriate allowance for entrance losses and friction due to fittings, changes in direction and diameter. Suggested allowances shall be obtained from NSB Monograph 31 or other approved sources. An allowance of 50 percent of the developed length shall be assumed if a more precise value is not available.

b. Actual values greater than 500 feet.

c. Less than 10 feet.

CHAPTER 10

TRAPS, INTERCEPTORS AND SEPARATORS

SECTION 1001 GENERAL

1001.1 Scope. This chapter shall govern the material and installation of traps, interceptors and separators.

SECTION 1002 TRAP REQUIREMENTS

1002.1 Fixture traps. Each plumbing fixture shall be separately trapped by a liquid-seal trap, except as otherwise permitted by this code. The vertical distance from the fixture outlet to the trap weir shall not exceed 24 inches (610 mm), and the horizontal distance shall not exceed 30 inches (610 mm) measured from the centerline of the fixture outlet to the centerline of the inlet of the trap. The height of a clothes washer standpipe above a trap shall conform to Section 802.4. A fixture shall not be double trapped.

Exceptions:

1. This section shall not apply to fixtures with integral traps.
2. A combination plumbing fixture or up to three similar fixtures is permitted to be installed on one trap, provided that one compartment is not more than 6 inches (152 mm) deeper than the other compartment and the waste outlets are not more than 30 inches (762 mm) apart.
3. A grease interceptor intended to serve as a fixture trap in accordance with the manufacturer's installation instructions shall be permitted to serve as the trap for a single fixture or a combination sink of not more than three compartments where the vertical distance from the fixture outlet to the inlet of the interceptor does not exceed 30 inches (762 mm) and the *developed length* of the waste pipe from the most upstream fixture outlet to the inlet of the interceptor does not exceed 60 inches (1524 mm).
4. The connection of a laundry tray complying with Section 802.4.

1002.2 Design of traps. Fixture traps shall be self-scouring. Fixture traps shall not have interior partitions, except where such traps are integral with the fixture or where such traps are constructed of an *approved* material that is resistant to corrosion and degradation. Slip joints shall be made with an *approved* elastomeric gasket and shall be installed only on the trap inlet, trap outlet and within the trap seal.

1002.3 Prohibited traps. The following types of traps are prohibited:

1. Traps that depend on moving parts to maintain the seal.
2. Bell traps.
3. Crown-vented traps.
4. Traps not integral with a fixture and that depend on interior partitions for the seal, except those traps constructed of an *approved* material that is resistant to corrosion and degradation.
5. "S" traps.
6. Drum traps.

Exception: Drum traps used as solids interceptors and drum traps serving chemical waste systems shall not be prohibited.

1002.4 Trap seals. Each fixture trap shall have a liquid seal of not less than 2 inches (51 mm) and not more than 4 inches (102 mm), or deeper for special designs relating to accessible fixtures. Where a trap seal is subject to loss by evaporation, a trap seal primer valve shall be installed. Trap seal primer valves shall connect to the trap at a point above the level of the trap seal. A trap seal primer valve shall conform to ASSE 1018 or ASSE 1044.

1002.5 Size of fixture traps. Fixture trap size shall be sufficient to drain the fixture rapidly and not less than the size indicated in Table 709.1. A trap shall not be larger than the drainage pipe into which the trap discharges.

1002.6 Building traps. Deleted.

1002.7 Trap setting and protection. Traps shall be set level with respect to the trap seal and, where necessary, shall be protected from freezing.

1002.8 Recess for trap connection. Deleted.

1002.9 Acid-resisting traps. Deleted.

1002.10 Plumbing in mental health centers. Deleted.

SECTION 1003 INTERCEPTORS AND SEPARATORS Deleted

SECTION 1004 MATERIALS, JOINTS AND CONNECTIONS

1004.1 General. The materials and methods utilized for the construction and installation of traps, interceptors and separators shall comply with this chapter and the applicable provisions of Chapters 4 and 7. The fittings shall not have ledges, shoulders or reductions capable of retarding or obstructing flow of the piping.

CHAPTER 11
STORM DRAINAGE

Deleted

CHAPTER 12

SPECIAL PIPING AND STORAGE SYSTEMS

Deleted

CHAPTER 13
REFERENCED STANDARDS

This chapter lists the standards that are referenced in various sections of this document. The standards are listed herein by the promulgating agency of the standard, the standard identification, the effective date and title, and the section or sections of this document that reference the standard. The application of the referenced standards shall be as specified in Section 102.8.

ANSI

American National Standards Institute
25 West 43rd Street, Fourth Floor
New York, NY 10036

Standard Reference Number	Title	Referenced in code section number
A118.10—99	Specifications for Load Bearing, Bonded, Waterproof Membranes for Thin Set Ceramic Tile and Dimension Stone Installation	417.5.2.5
Z4.3—95	Minimum Requirements for Nonsewered Waste-disposal Systems	311.1
Z21.22—99 (R2003)	Relief Valves for Hot Water Supply Systems with Addenda Z21.22a-2000 (R2003) and Z21.22b-2001 (R2003)	504.2, 504.4
Z124.1—95	Plastic Bathtub Units	407.1
Z124.2—95	Plastic Shower Receptors and Shower Stalls	417.1
Z124.3—95	Plastic Lavatories	416.1, 416.2, 417.1
Z124.4—96	Plastic Water Closet Bowls and Tanks	420.1
Z124.6—97	Plastic Sinks	415.1, 418.1
Z124.9—94	Plastic Urinal Fixtures	419.1

AHRI

Air-Conditioning, Heating, & Refrigeration Institute
4100 North Fairfax Drive, Suite 200
Arlington, VA 22203

Standard Reference Number	Title	Referenced in code section number
1010—02	Self-contained, Mechanically Refrigerated Drinking-Water Coolers	410.1

ASME

American Society of Mechanical Engineers
Three Park Avenue
New York, NY 10016-5990

Standard Reference Number	Title	Referenced in code section number
A112.1.2—2004	Air Gaps in Plumbing Systems	Table 608.1, 608.13.1
A112.1.3—2000 Reaffirmed 2005	Air Gap Fittings for Use with Plumbing Fixtures, Appliances and Appurtenances	Table 608.1, 608.13.1
A112.3.1—2007	Stainless Steel Drainage Systems for Sanitary, DWV, Storm and Vacuum Applications Above and Below Ground	412.1, Table 702.1, Table 702.2, Table 702.3, Table 702.4, 708.2, Table 1102.4, Table 1102.5, 1102.6, Table 1102.7
A112.3.4—2000 (Reaffirmed 2004)	Macerating Toilet Systems and Related Components	712.4.1
A112.4.1—1993 (R2002)	Water Heater Relief Valve Drain Tubes	504.6
A112.4.3—1999 (Reaffirmed 2004)	Plastic Fittings for Connecting Water Closets to the Sanitary Drainage System	405.4
A112.6.1M—1997 (R2002)	Floor-affixed Supports for Off-the-floor Plumbing Fixtures for Public Use	405.4.3
A112.6.2—2000 (Reaffirmed 2004)	Framing-affixed Supports for Off-the-floor Water Closets with Concealed Tanks	405.4.3
A112.6.3—2001 (Reaffirmed 2007)	2001 Floor and Trench Drains	412.1
A112.6.7—2001 (Reaffirmed 2007)	Enameled and Epoxy-coated Cast-iron and PVC Plastic Sanitary Floor Sinks	427.1

ASME—continued

A112.14.1—2003	Backwater Valves	715.2
A112.14.3—2000	Grease Interceptors	1003.3.4
A112.14.4—2001 (Reaffirmed 2007)	Grease Removal Devices	1003.3.4
A112.18.1-2005/ CSA B125.1-2005	Plumbing Supply Fittings	424.1, 424.2, 424.3, 607.4, 608.2
A112.18.2-2005/ CSA B125.2-2005	Plumbing Waste Fittings	424.1.2
A112.18.3—2002	Performance Requirements for Backflow Protection Devices and Systems in Plumbing Fixture Fittings	424.2, 424.6
A112.18.6—2003	Flexible Water Connectors	605.6
A112.18.7—1999 (Reaffirmed 2004)	Deck mounted Bath/Shower Transfer Valves with Integral Backflow Protection	424.8
A112.19.1M—2004 (Reaffirmed 2004)	Enameled Cast Iron Plumbing Fixtures	407.1, 410.1, 415.1, 416.1, 418.1
A112.19.2—2003	Vitreous China Plumbing Fixtures and Hydraulic Requirements for Water Closets and Urinals	401.2, 405.9, 408.1, 410.1, 416.1, 418.1, 419.1, 420.1
A112.19.3M—2000 (Reaffirmed 2007)	Stainless Steel Plumbing Fixtures (Designed for Residential Use)	405.9, 415.1, 416.1, 418.1
A112.19.4M—1994 (Reaffirmed 2004)	Porcelain Enameled Formed Steel Plumbing Fixtures	407.1, 416.1, 418.1
A112.19.5—2005	Trim for Water-closet Bowls, Tanks and Urinals	425.4
A112.19.6—1995	Hydraulic Performance Requirements for Water Closets and Urinals	419.1, 420.1
A112.19.7M—2006	Hydromassage Bathtub Appliances	421.1
A112.19.8M—2007	Suction Fittings for Use in Swimming Pools, Wading Pools, Spas, Hot Tubs	421.4
A112.19.9M—1991(R2002)	Nonvitreous Ceramic Plumbing Fixtures with 2002 Supplement	407.1, 408.1, 410.1, 415.1, 416.1, 417.1, 418.1, 420.1
A112.19.12—2006	Wall Mounted and Pedestal Mounted, Adjustable, Elevating, Tilting and Pivoting Lavatory, Sink and Shampoo Bowl Carrier Systems and Drain Systems	416.4, 418.3
A112.19.13—2001 (Reaffirmed 2007)	Electrohydraulic Water Closets	420.1
A112.19.15— 2005	Bathtub/Whirlpool Bathtubs with Pressure Sealed Doors	407.4, 421.5
A112.19.19—2006	Vitreous China Nonwater Urinals	419.1
A112.21.2M—1983	Roof Drains	1102.6
A112.36.2M—1991(R2002)	Cleanouts	708.2
B1.20.1—1983(R2006)	Pipe Threads, General Purpose (inch)	605.10.3, 605.12.3, 605.14.4, 605.16.3, 605.18.1, 705.2.3, 705.4.3, 705.9.4, 705.12.1, 705.14.3
B16.3—2006	Malleable Iron Threaded Fittings Classes 150 and 300	Table 605.5, Table 702.4, Table 1102.7
B16.4—2006	Gray Iron Threaded Fittings Classes 125 and 250.	Table 605.5, Table 702.4, Table 1102.7
B16.9—2003	Factory-made Wrought Steel Buttwelding Fittings	Table 605.5, Table 702.4, Table 1102.7
B16.11—2005	Forged Fittings, Socket-welding and Threaded	Table 605.5, Table 702.4, Table 1102.7
B16.12—1998 (Reaffirmed 2006)	Cast-iron Threaded Drainage Fittings	Table 605.5, Table 702.4, Table 1102.7
B16.15—2006	Cast Bronze Threaded Fittings	Table 605.5, Table 702.4, Table 1102.7
B16.18—2001 (Reaffirmed 2005)	Cast Copper Alloy Solder Joint Pressure Fittings	Table 605.5, Table 702.4, Table 1102.7
B16.22—2001 (Reaffirmed 2005)	Wrought Copper and Copper Alloy Solder Joint Pressure Fittings	Table 605.5, Table 702.4, Table 1102.7
B16.23—2002 (Reaffirmed 2006)	Cast Copper Alloy Solder Joint Drainage Fittings DWV	Table 605.5, Table 702.4, Table 1102.7
B16.26—2006	Cast Copper Alloy Fittings for Flared Copper Tubes	Table 605.5, Table 702.4, Table 1102.7
B16.28—1994	Wrought Steel Buttwelding Short Radius Elbows and Returns	Table 605.5, Table 702.4, Table 1102.7
B16.29—2001	Wrought Copper and Wrought Copper Alloy Solder Joint Drainage Fittings (DWV)	Table 605.5, Table 702.4, Table 1102.7

ASSE

American Society of Sanitary Engineering
901 Canterbury Road, Suite A
Westlake, OH 44145

Standard Reference Number	Title	Referenced in code section number
1001—02	Performance Requirements for Atmospheric Type Vacuum Breakers	425.2, Table 608.1, 608.13.6, 608.16.4.1
1002—99	Performance Requirements for Antisiphon Fill Valves (Ballcocks) for Gravity Water Closet Flush Tanks	425.3.1, Table 608.1

ASSE—continued

1003—01	Performance Requirements for Water Pressure Reducing Valves	604.8
1004—90	Performance Requirements for Backflow Prevention Requirements for Commercial Dishwashing Machines	409.1
1005—99	Performance Requirements for Water Heater Drain Valves	501.3
1006—89	Performance Requirements for Residential Use Dishwashers	409.1
1007—92	Performance Requirements for Home Laundry Equipment	406.1, 406.2
1008—89	Performance Requirements for Household Food Waste Disposer Units	413.1
1009—90	Performance Requirements for Commercial Food Waste Grinder Units	413.1
1010—04	Performance Requirements for Water Hammer Arresters	604.9
1011—04	Performance Requirements for Hose Connection Vacuum Breakers	Table 608.1, 608.13.6
1012—02	Performance Requirements for Backflow Preventers with Intermediate Atmospheric Vent	Table 608.1, 608.13.3, 608.16.2
1013—05	Performance Requirements for Reduced Pressure Principle Backflow Preventers and Reduced Pressure Fire Protection Principle Backflow Preventers	Table 608.1, 608.13.2, 608.16.2
1015—05	Performance Requirements for Double Check Backflow Prevention Assemblies and Double Check Fire Protection Backflow Prevention Assemblies	Table 608.1, 608.13.7
1016—96	Performance Requirements for Individual Thermostatic, Pressure Balancing and Combination Control Valves for Individual Fixture Fittings	424.3, 424.4, 607.4
1017—03	Performance Requirements for Temperature Actuated Mixing Valves for Hot Water Distribution Systems	501.2, 613.1
1018—01	Performance Requirements for Trap Seal Primer Valves; Potable Water Supplied	1002.4
1019—04	Performance Requirements for Vacuum Breaker Wall Hydrants, Freeze Resistant, Automatic Draining Type	Table 608.1, 608.13.6
1020—04	Performance Requirements for Pressure Vacuum Breaker Assembly	Table 608.1, 608.13.5
1022—03	Performance Requirements for Backflow Preventer for Beverage Dispensing Equipment	Table 608.1, 608.16.1, 608.16.10
1024—04	Performance Requirements for Dual Check Valve Type Backflow Preventers (for Residential Supply Service or Individual Outlets)	605.3.1, Table 608.1
1035—02	Performance Requirements for Laboratory Faucet Backflow Preventers	Table 608.1, 608.13.6
1037—90	Performance Requirements for Pressurized Flushing Devices for Plumbing Fixtures	425.2
1044—01	Performance Requirements for Trap Seal Primer Devices Drainage Types and Electronic Design Types	1002.4
1047—05	Performance Requirements for Reduced Pressure Detector Fire Protection Backflow Prevention Assemblies	Table 608.1, 608.13.2
1048—05	Performance Requirements for Double Check Detector Fire Protection Backflow Prevention Assemblies	Table 608.1, 608.13.7
1050—02	Performance Requirements for Stack Air Admittance Valves for Sanitary Drainage Systems	917.1
1051—02	Performance Requirements for Individual and Branch Type Air Admittance Valves for Sanitary Drainage Systems-fixture and Branch Devices	917.1
1052—04	Performance Requirements for Hose Connection Backflow Preventers	Table 608.1, 608.13.6
1055—97	Performance Requirements for Chemical Dispensing Systems	608.13.9
1056—01	Performance Requirements for Spill Resistant Vacuum Breaker	Table 608.1, 608.13.5, 608.13.8
1060—96	Performance Requirements for Outdoor Enclosures for Backflow Prevention Assemblies	608.14.1
1061—06	Performance Requirements for Removable and Nonremovable Push Fit Fittings	Table 605.5
1062—97	Performance Requirements for Temperature Actuated, Flow Reduction Valves to Individual Fixture Fittings	424.7
1066—97	Performance Requirements for Individual Pressure Balancing In-line Valves for Individual Fixture Fittings	604.11
1069—05	Performance Requirements for Automatic Temperature Control Mixing Valves	424.4
1070—04	Performance Requirements for Water-temperature Limiting Devices	408.3, 416.5, 424.5, 607.1
1079—2005	Dielectric Pipe Unions	605.24.1, 605.24.3
5013—98	Performance Requirements for Testing Reduced Pressure Principle Backflow Prevention Assembly (RPA) and Reduced Pressure Fire Protection Principle Backflow Preventers (RFP)	312.10.2
5015—98	Performance Requirements for Testing Double Check Valve Backflow Prevention Assembly (DCVA)	312.10.2
5020—98	Performance Requirements for Testing Pressure Vacuum Breaker Assembly (PVBA)	312.10.2
5047—98	Performance Requirements for Testing Reduced Pressure Detector Fire Protection Backflow Prevention Assemblies (RPDA)	312.10.2
5048—98	Performance Requirements for Testing Double Check Valve Detector Assembly (DCDA)	312.10.2
5052—98	Performance Requirements for Testing Hose Connection Backflow Preventers	312.10.2
5056—98	Performance Requirements for Testing Spill Resistant Vacuum Breaker	312.10.2

ASTM

ASTM International
100 Barr Harbor Drive
West Conshohocken, PA 19428-2959

Standard Reference Number	Title	Referenced in code section number
A 53/A 53M—06a	Specification for Pipe, Steel, Black and Hot-dipped, Zinc-coated Welded and Seamless	Table 605.3, Table 605.4, Table 702.1
A 74—06	Specification for Cast-iron Soil Pipe and Fittings	Table 702.1, Table 702.2, Table 702.3, Table 702.4, 708.2, 708.7, Table 1102.4, Table 1102.5, Table 1102.7
A 312/A 312M—06	Specification for Seamless and Welded Austenitic Stainless Steel Pipes	Table 605.3, Table 605.4, Table 605.5, 605.23.2
A 733—03	Specification for Welded and Seamless Carbon Steel and Austenitic Stainless Steel Pipe Nipples	Table 605.8
A 778—01	Specification for Welded Unannealed Austenitic Stainless Steel Tubular Products	Table 605.3, Table 605.4, Table 605.5
A 888—07a	Specification for Hubless Cast-iron Soil Pipe and Fittings for Sanitary and Storm Drain, Waste, and Vent Piping Application	Table 702.1, Table 702.2, Table 702.3, Table 702.4, 708.7, Table 1102.4, Table 1102.5, Table 1102.7
B 32—04	Specification for Solder Metal	605.14.3, 605.15.4, 705.9.3, 705.10.3
B 42—02e01	Specification for Seamless Copper Pipe, Standard Sizes	Table 605.3, Table 605.4, Table 702.1
B 43—98(2004)	Specification for Seamless Red Brass Pipe, Standard Sizes	Table 605.3, Table 605.4, Table 702.1
B 75—02	Specification for Seamless Copper Tube	Table 605.3, Table 605.4, Table 702.1, Table 702.2, Table 702.3, Table 1102.4
B 88—03	Specification for Seamless Copper Water Tube	Table 605.3, Table 605.4, Table 702.1, Table 702.2, Table 702.3, Table 1102.4
B 152/B 152M—06a	Specification for Copper Sheet, Strip Plate and Rolled Bar	402.3, , 417.5.2.4, 425.3.3, 902.2
B 251—02e01	Specification for General Requirements for Wrought Seamless Copper and Copper-alloy Tube	Table 605.3, Table 605.4, Table 702.1, Table 702.2, Table 702.3, Table 1102.4
B 302—02	Specification for Threadless Copper Pipe, Standard Sizes	Table 605.3, Table 605.4, Table 702.1
B 306—02	Specification for Copper Drainage Tube (DWV)	Table 702.1, Table 702.2, Table 1102.4
B 447—07	Specification for Welded Copper Tube	Table 605.3, Table 605.4
B 687—99(2005)e01	Specification for Brass, Copper and Chromium-plated Pipe Nipples	Table 605.8
B 813—00e01	Specification for Liquid and Paste Fluxes for Soldering of Copper and Copper Alloy Tube	605.14.3, 605.15.4, 705.9.3, 705.10.3
B 828—02	Practice for Making Capillary Joints by Soldering of Copper and Copper Alloy Tube and Fittings	605.14.3, 605.15.4, 705.9.3, 705.10.3
C 4—04e01	Specification for Clay Drain Tile and Perforated Clay Drain Tile	Table 702.3, Table 1102.4, Table 1102.5
C 14—07	Specification for Nonreinforced Concrete Sewer, Storm Drain and Culvert Pipe	Table 702.3, Table 1102.4
C 76—07	Specification for Reinforced Concrete Culvert, Storm Drain and Sewer Pipe	Table 702.3, Table 1102.4
C 296—(2004)e01	Specification for Asbestos-cement Pressure Pipe	Table 605.3
C 425—04	Specification for Compression Joints for Vitrified Clay Pipe and Fittings	705.15, 705.19
C 428—97(2006)	Specification for Asbestos-cement Nonpressure Sewer Pipe	Table 702.2, Table 702.3, Table 702.4, Table 1102.4
C 443—05a	Specification for Joints for Concrete Pipe and Manholes, Using Rubber Gaskets	705.6, 705.19
C 508—00(2004)	Specification for Asbestos-cement Underdrain Pipe	Table 1102.5
C 564—04a	Specification for Rubber Gaskets for Cast-iron Soil Pipe and Fittings	705.5.2, 705.5.3, 705.19, Table 1102.4
C 700—07	Specification for Vitrified Clay Pipe, Extra Strength, Standard Strength, and Perforated	Table 702.3, 702.4, Table 1102.4, Table 1102.5
C 1053—00(2005)	Specification for Borosilicate Glass Pipe and Fittings for Drain, Waste, and Vent (DWV) Applications	Table 702.1, Table 702.4
C 1173—06	Specification for Flexible Transition Couplings for Underground Piping System	705.2.1, 705.7.1, 705.14.1, 705.15, 705.16.1, 705.19
C 1277—06	Specification for Shielded Coupling Joining Hubless Cast-iron Soil Pipe and Fittings	705.5.3
C 1440—03	Specification for Thermoplastic Elastomeric (TPE) Gasket Materials for Drain, Waste,and Vent (DWV), Sewer, Sanitary and Storm Plumbing Systems	705.19
C 1460—04	Specification for Shielded Transition Couplings for Use with Dissimilar DWV Pipe and Fittings Above Ground	705.19
C 1461—06	Specification for Mechanical Couplings Using Thermoplastic Elastomeric (TPE) Gaskets for Joining Drain, Waste and Vent (DWV) Sewer, Sanitary and Storm Plumbing Systems for Above and Below Ground Use	705.19
C 1540—04	Specification for Heavy Duty Shielded Couplings Joining Hubless Cast-iron Soil Pipe and Fittings	705.5.3
C 1563—04	Standard Test Method for Gaskets for Use in Connection with Hub and Spigot Cast Iron Soil Pipe and Fittings for Sanitary Drain, Waste, Vent and Storm Piping Applications.	705.5.2

ASTM—continued

D 1527—99(2005)	Specification for Acrylonitrile-Butadiene-Styrene (ABS) Plastic Pipe, Schedules 40 and 80	Table 605.3
D 1785—06	Specification for Poly (Vinyl Chloride) (PVC) Plastic Pipe, Schedules 40, 80 and 120	Table 605.3
D 1869—95(2005)	Specification for Rubber Rings for Asbestos-cement Pipe	605.11, 605.24, 705.3, 705.19
D 2235—04	Specification for Solvent Cement for Acrylonitrile-Butadiene-Styrene (ABS) Plastic Pipe and Fittings	605.10.2, 705.2.2, 705.7.2
D 2239—03	Specification for Polyethylene (PE) Plastic Pipe (SIDR-PR) Based on Controlled Inside Diameter	Table 605.3
D 2241—05	Specification for Poly (Vinyl Chloride) (PVC) Pressure-rated Pipe (SDR-Series)	Table 605.3
D 2282—(2005)99e01	Specification for Acrylonitrile-Butadiene-Styrene (ABS) Plastic Pipe (SDR-PR)	Table 605.3
D 2464—06	Specification for Threaded Poly (Vinyl Chloride) (PVC) Plastic Pipe Fittings, Schedule 80	Table 605.5, Table 1102.7
D 2466—06	Specification for Poly (Vinyl Chloride) (PVC) Plastic Pipe Fittings, Schedule 40	Table 605.5, Table 1102.7
D 2467—06	Specification for Poly (Vinyl Chloride) (PVC) Plastic Pipe Fittings, Schedule 80	Table 605.5, Table 1102.7
D 2468—96a	Specification for Acrylonitrile-Butadiene-Styrene (ABS) Plastic Pipe Fittings, Schedule 40	Table 605.5, Table 1102.7
D 2564—04e01	Specification for Solvent Cements for Poly (Vinyl Chloride) (PVC) Plastic Piping Systems	605.21.2, 705.8.2, 705.14.2
D 2609—02	Specification for Plastic Insert Fittings for Polyethylene (PE) Plastic Pipe	Table 605.5, Table 1102.7
D 2657—07	Practice for Heat Fusion-joining of Polyolefin Pipe and Fitting	605.19.2, 705.16.1
D 2661—06	Specification for Acrylonitrile-Butadiene-Styrene (ABS) Schedule 40 Plastic Drain, Waste, and Vent Pipe and Fittings	Table 702.1, Table 702.2, Table 702.3, Table 702.4, 705.2.2, 705.7.2, Table 1102.4, Table 1102.7
D 2665—07	Specification for Poly (Vinyl Chloride) (PVC) Plastic Drain, Waste, and Vent Pipe and Fittings	Table 702.1, Table 702.2, Table 702.3, Table 702.4, Table 1102.4, Table 1102.7
D 2672—96a(2003)	Specification for Joints for IPS PVC Pipe Using Solvent Cement	Table 605.3
D 2683—04	Standard Specification for Socket-type Polyethylene fittings for Outside Diameter-controlled Polyethylene Pipe and Tubing	Table 605.5
D 2729—04e01	Specification for Poly (Vinyl Chloride) (PVC) Sewer Pipe and Fittings	Table 1102.5
D 2737—03	Specification for Polyethylene (PE) Plastic Tubing	Table 605.3
D 2751—05	Specification for Acrylonitrile-Butadiene-Styrene (ABS) Sewer Pipe and Fittings	Table 702.3, Table 702.4, Table 1102.7
D 2846/D 2846M—06	Specification for Chlorinated Poly (Vinyl Chloride) (CPVC) Plastic Hot and Cold Water Distribution Systems	Table 605.3, Table 605.4, Table 605.5, 605.16.2
D 2855—96(2002)	Standard Practice for Making Solvent-cemented Joints with Poly (Vinyl Chloride) (PVC) Pipe and Fittings	605.22.2, 705.8.2, 705.14.2
D 2949—01ae01	Specification for 3.25-in Outside Diameter Poly (Vinyl Chloride) (PVC) Plastic Drain, Waste, and Vent Pipe and Fittings	Table 702.1, Table 702.2, Table 702.3, Table 702.4
D 3034—06	Specification for Type PSM Poly (Vinyl Chloride) (PVC) Sewer Pipe and Fittings	Table 702.3, Table 702.4, Table 1102.7, Table 1102.4
D 3035-03	Standard Specification for Polyethylene (PE) Plastic Pipe (DR-PR) Based on Controlled Outside Diameter	Table 605.3
D 3139—98(2005)	Specification for Joints for Plastic Pressure Pipes Using Flexible Elastomeric Seals	605.10.1, 605.22.1
D 3212—96a(2003)e01	Specification for Joints for Drain and Sewer Plastic Pipes Using Flexible Elastomeric Seals	705.2.1, 705.8.1, 705.14.1, 705.16.2
D 3261—03	Standard Specification for Butt Heat Fusion Polyethylene (PE) Plastic fittings for Polyethylene (PE) Plastic Pipe and Tubing	Table 605.5
D 3311—06a	Specification for Drain, Waste and Vent (DWV) Plastic Fittings Patterns	Table 1102.7
D 4068—01	Specification for Chlorinated Polyethlene (CPE) Sheeting for Concealed Water-containment Membrane	417.5.2.2
D 4551—96(2001)	Specification for Poly (Vinyl Chloride) (PVC) Plastic Flexible Concealed Water-containment Membrane	417.5.2.1
F 405—05	Specification for Corrugated Polyethylene (PE) Tubing and Fittings	Table 1102.5
F 409—02	Specification for Thermoplastic Accessible and Replaceable Plastic Tube and Tubular Fittings	424.1.2, Table 1102.7
F 437—06	Specification for Threaded Chlorinated Poly (Vinyl Chloride) (CPVC) Plastic Pipe Fittings, Schedule 80	Table 605.5
F 438—04	Specification for Socket-type Chlorinated Poly (Vinyl Chloride) (CPVC) Plastic Pipe Fittings, Schedule 40	Table 605.5
F 439—06	Standard Specification for Chlorinated Poly (Vinyl Chloride) (CPVC) Plastic Pipe Fittings, Schedule 80	Table 605.5
F 441/F 441M—02	Specification for Chlorinated Poly (Vinyl Chloride) (CPVC) Plastic Pipe, Schedules 40 and 80	Table 605.3, Table 605.4
F 442/F 442M—99(2005)	Specification for Chlorinated Poly (Vinyl Chloride) (CPVC) Plastic Pipe (SDR-PR)	Table 605.3, Table 605.4
F 477—07	Specification for Elastomeric Seals (Gaskets) for Joining Plastic Pipe	605.24, 705.19
F 493—04	Specification for Solvent Cements for Chlorinated Poly (Vinyl Chloride) (CPVC) Plastic Pipe and Fittings	605.16.2
F 628—06e01	Specification for Acrylonitrile-Butadiene-Styrene (ABS) Schedule 40 Plastic Drain, Waste, and Vent Pipe with a Cellular Core	Table 702.1, Table 702.2, Table 702.3, Table 702.4, 705.2.2, 705.7.2, Table 1102.4, Table 1102.7

ASTM—continued

F 656—02	Specification for Primers for Use in Solvent Cement Joints of Poly (Vinyl Chloride) (PVC) Plastic Pipe and Fittings	605.22.2, 705.8.2, 705.14.2
F 714—06a	Specification for Polyethylene (PE) Plastic Pipe (SDR-PR) Based on Outside Diameter	Table 702.3
F 876—06	Specification for Cross-linked Polyethylene (PEX) Tubing	Table 605.3, Table 605.4
F 877—07	Specification for Cross-linked Polyethylene (PEX) Plastic Hot and Cold Water Distribution Systems	Table 605.3, Table 605.4, Table 605.5
F 891—04	Specification for Coextruded Poly (Vinyl Chloride) (PVC) Plastic Pipe with a Cellular Core	Table 702.1 Table 702.2, Table 702.3, Table 1102.4, Table 1102.5, Table 1102.7
F 1055—98(2006)	Standard Specification for Electrofusion Type Polyethylene Fittings for Outside Diameter Controlled Polyethylene Pipe and Tubing	Table 605.5
F 1281—07	Specification for Cross-linked Polyethylene/Aluminum/ Cross-linked Polyethylene (PEX-AL-PEX) Pressure Pipe	Table 605.3, Table 605.4, Table 605.5, 605.21.1
F 1282—06	Specification for Polyethylene/Aluminum/Polyethylene (PE-AL-PE) Composite Pressure Pipe	Table 605.3, Table 605.4, Table 605.5, 605.21.1
F 1412—01e01	Specification for Polyolefin Pipe and Fittings for Corrosive Waste Drainage	Table 702.1, Table 702.2, Table 702.4, 705.17.1
F 1488—03	Specification for Coextruded Composite Pipe	Table 702.1, Table 702.2, Table 702.3
F 1673—04	Polyvinylidene Fluoride (PVDF) Corrosive Waste Drainage Systems	Table 702.1, Table 702.2, Table 702.3, Table 702.4, 705.18.1
F 1807—07	Specification for Metal Insert Fittings Utilizing a Copper Crimp Ring for SDR9 Cross-linked Polyethylene (PEX) Tubing	Table 605.5
F 1866—07	Specification for Poly (Vinyl Chloride) (PVC) Plastic Schedule 40 Drainage and DWV Fabricated Fittings	Table 702.4, Table 1102.7
F 1960—07	Specification for Cold Expansion Fittings with PEX Reinforcing Rings for use with Cross-linked Polyethylene (PEX) Tubing	Table 605.5
F 1974—04	Specification for Metal Insert Fittings for Polyethylene/Aluminum/Polyethylene and Cross-linked Polyethylene/Aluminum/Cross-linked Polyethylene Composite Pressure Pipe	Table 605.5, 605.21.1
F 1986—01(2006)	Specification for Multilayer Pipe, Type 2, Compression Fittings and Compression Joints for Hot and Cold Drinking Water Systems	Table 605.3, Table 605.4, Table 605.5
F 2080—05	Specifications for Cold-expansion Fittings with Metal Compression-sleeves for Cross-linked Polyethylene (PEX) Pipe	Table 605.5
F 2098—04e01	Standard specification for Stainless Steel Clamps for Securing SDR9 Cross-linked Polyethylene (PEX) Tubing to Metal Insert Fittings	Table 605.5
F 2159—05	Specification for Plastic Insert Fittings Utilizing a Copper Crimp Ring for SDR9 Cross-linked Polyethylene (PEX) Tubing	Table 605.5
F 2262—05	Specification for Cross-linked Polyethylene/Aluminum/Cross-linked Polyethylene Tubing OD Controlled SDR9	Table 605.3, Table 605.4
F 2306/F 2306M-05	12" to 60" Annular Corrugated Profile-wall Polyethylene (PE) Pipe and Fittings for Gravity Flow Storm Sewer and Subsurface Drainage Applications	Table 1102.4, Table 1102.7
F 2389—06	Specification for Pressure-rated Polypropylene (PP) Piping Systems	Table 605.3, Table 605.4, Table 605.5, 605.20.1
F 2434—05	Standard Specification for Metal Insert Fittings Utilizing a Copper Crimp Ring for SDR9 Cross-linked Polyethylene (PEX) Tubing and SDR9 Cross-linked Polyethylene/ Aluminum/Cross-linked Polyethylene (PEX AL-PEX) Tubing	Table 605.5

AWS

American Welding Society
550 N.W. LeJeune Road
Miami, FL 33126

Standard Reference Number	Title	Referenced in code section number
A5.8—04	Specifications for Filler Metals for Brazing and Braze Welding	605.12.1, 605.14.1, 605.15.1, 705.4.1, 705.9.1, 705.10.1

AWWA

American Water Works Association
6666 West Quincy Avenue
Denver, CO 80235

Standard Reference Number	Title	Referenced in code section number
C104—98	Standard for Cement-mortar Lining for Ductile-iron Pipe and Fittings for Water	605.3, 605.5
C110—/A21.10—03	Standard for Ductile-iron and Gray-iron Fittings, 3 Inches through 48 Inches, for Water	Table 605.5, Table 702.4, Table 1102.7
C111—00	Standard for Rubber-gasket Joints for Ductile-iron Pressure Pipe and Fittings	605.13

AWWA—continued

C115/A21.15—99	Standard for Flanged Ductile-iron Pipe with Ductile-iron or Gray-iron Threaded Flanges	Table 605.3, Table 605.4
C151/A21.51—02	Standard for Ductile-iron Pipe, Centrifugally Cast for Water	Table 605.3, Table 605.4
C153—00/A21.53—00	Standard for Ductile-iron Compact Fittings for Water Service	Table 605.5
C510—00	Double Check Valve Backflow Prevention Assembly	Table 608.1, 608.13.7
C511—00	Reduced-pressure Principle Backflow Prevention Assembly	Table 608.1, 608.13.2, 608.16.2
C651—99	Disinfecting Water Mains	610.1
C652—02	Disinfection of Water-storage Facilities	610.1

CISPI

Cast Iron Soil Pipe Institute
5959 Shallowford Road, Suite 419
Chattanooga, TN 37421

Standard Reference Number	Title	Referenced in code section number
301—04a	Specification for Hubless Cast-iron Soil Pipe and Fittings for Sanitary and Storm Drain, Waste and Vent Piping Applications	Table 702.1, Table 702.2, Table 702.3, Table 702.4, 708.7, Table 1102.4, Table 1102.5, Table 1102.7
310—04	Specification for Coupling for Use in Connection with Hubless Cast-iron Soil Pipe and Fittings for Sanitary and Storm Drain, Waste and Vent Piping Applications	705.5.3

CSA

Canadian Standards Association
5060 Spectrum Way.
Mississauga, Ontario, Canada L4W 5N6

Standard Reference Number	Title	Referenced in code section number
B45.1—02	Ceramic Plumbing Fixtures	408.1, 416.1, 418.1, 419.1, 420.1
B45.2—02	Enameled Cast-iron Plumbing Fixtures	407.1, 415.1, 416.1, 418.1
B45.3—02	Porcelain Enameled Steel Plumbing Fixtures	407.1, 416.1, 418.1
B45.4—02	Stainless-steel Plumbing Fixtures	415.1, 416.1, 418.1, 420.1
B45.5—02	Plastic Plumbing Fixtures	407.1, 416.2, 417.1, 419.1, 420.1, 421.1
B45.9—99	Macerating Systems and Related Components	712.4.1
B64.1.2—01	Vacuum Breakers, Pressure Type (PVB)	Table 608.1, 608.13.5
B64.2.1—01	Vacuum Breakers, Hose Connection Type (HCVB) with Manual Draining Feature	Table 608.1, 608.13.6
B64.2.1.1—01	Vacuum Breakers, Hose Connection Dual Check Type (HCDVB)	Table 608.1, 608.13.6
B64.4.1—01	Backflow Preventers, Reduced Pressure Principle Type for Fire Sprinklers (RPF)	Table 608.1, 608.13.2
B64.5—01	Backflow Preventers, Double Check Type (DCVA)	Table 608.1, 608.13.7
B64.5.1—01	Backflow Preventers, Double Check Type for Fire Systems (DCVAF)	Table 608.1 608.13.7
B64.6—01	Backflow Preventers, Dual Check Valve Type (DuC)	605.3.1, Table 608.1
B64.7—94	Vacuum Breakers, Laboratory Faucet Type (LFVB	Table 608.1, 608.13.6
B64.10/B64.10.1—01	Manual for the Selection and Installation of Backflow Prevention Devices/Manual for the Maintenance and Field Testing of Backflow Prevention Devices	312.10.2
B79—94(2000)	Floor, Area and Shower Drains, and Cleanouts for Residential Construction	412.1
B125—01	Plumbing Fittings	424.4, 424.6, 425.4
B125.1/ASME A112.18.1—05	Plumbing Supply Fittings	424.1, 424.2, 424.3, 607.4, 608.2
B125.2/ASME A112.18.2—05	Plumbing Waste Fittings	424.1.2
B125.3—2005	Plumbing Fittings	416.5, 424.5, 425.3.1, Table 608.1
B137.1—02	Polyethylene Pipe, Tubing and Fittings for Cold Water Pressure Services	Table 605.3
B137.2—02	PVC Injection-moulded Gasketed Fittings for Pressure Applications	Table 605.5, Table 1102.7
B137.3—02	Rigid Poly (Vinyl Chloride) (PVC) Pipe for Pressure Applications	Table 605.3, Table 605.4, Table 605.5, 605.22.2, 705.8.2, 705.14.2
B137.5—02	Cross-linked Polyethylene (PEX) Tubing Systems for Pressure Applications—with Revisions through September 1992	Table 605.3, Table 605.4, Table 605.5
B137.6—02	CPVC Pipe, Tubing and Fittings for Hot and Cold Water Distribution Systems—with Revisions through May 1986	Table 605.3, Table 605.4
B137.11—02	Polypropylene (PP-R) Pipe and Fittings for Pressure Applications	Table 605.3, Table 605.4, Table 605.5
B181.1—02	ABS Drain, Waste and Vent Pipe and Pipe Fittings	Table 702.1, Table 702.2, Table 702.3, Table 702.4, 705.2.2, 705.7.2, 715.2, Table 1102.4, Table 1102.7
B181.2—02	PVC Drain, Waste, and Vent Pipe and Pipe Fittings—with Revisions through December 1993	Table 702.1 Table 702.2, 705.8.2, 705.14.2, 715.2
B182.1—02	Plastic Drain and Sewer Pipe and Pipe Fittings	705.8.2, 705.14.2, Table 1102.4
B182.2—02	PVC Sewer Pipe and Fittings (PSM Type)	Table 702.3, Table 1102.4, Table 1102.5

CSA—continued

B182.4—02	Profile PVC Sewer Pipe and Fittings	Table 702.3, Table 1102.4, Table 1102.5
B182.6—02	Profile Polyethylene Sewer Pipe and Fittings for Leak-proof Sewer Applications	Table 1102.5
B182.8—02	Profile Polyethylene Storm Sewer and Drainage Pipe and Fittings	Table 1102.5
CAN/CSA-A257.1M—92	Circular Concrete Culvert, Storm Drain, Sewer Pipe and Fittings	Table 702.3, Table 1102.4
CAN/CSA-A257.2M—92	Reinforced Circular Concrete Culvert, Storm Drain, Sewer Pipe and Fittings	Table 702.3, Table 1102.4
CAN/CSA-A257.3M—92	Joints for Circular Concrete Sewer and Culvert Pipe, Manhole Sections and Fittings Using Rubber Gaskets	705.6, 705.19
CAN/CSA-B64.1.1—01	Vacuum Breakers, Atmospheric Type (AVB)	425.2, Table 608.1, 608.13.6
CAN/CSA-B64.2—01	Vacuum Breakers, Hose Connection Type (HCVB)	Table 608.1, 608.13.6
CAN/CSA-B64.2.2—01	Vacuum Breakers, Hose Connection Type (HCVB) with Automatic Draining Feature	Table 608.1, 608.13.6
CAN/CSA-B64.3—01	Backflow Preventers, Dual Check Valve Type with Atmospheric Port (DCAP)	Table 608.1, 608.13.3, 608.16.2
CAN/CSA-B64.4—01	Backflow Preventers, Reduced Pressure Principle Type (RP)	Table 608.1, 608.13.2, 608.16.2
CAN/CSA-B64.10—01	Manual for the Selection, Installation, Maintenance and Field Testing of Backflow Prevention Devices	312.10.2
CAN/CSA-B137.9—02	Polyethylene/Aluminum/Polyethylene Composite Pressure Pipe Systems	Table 605.3, Table 605.5, 605.21.1
CAN/CSA-B137.10M—02	Cross-linked Polyethylene/Aluminum/Polyethylene Composite Pressure Pipe Systems	Table 605.3, Table 605.4, Table 605.5, 605.21.1
CAN/CSA-B181.3—02	Polyolefin Laboratory Drainage Systems	Table 702.1, Table 702.2, Table 702.4, 705.17.1
CAN/CSA-B182.4—02	Profile PVC Sewer Pipe and Fittings	Table 702.3, Table 1102.4, Table 1102.5
CAN/CSA-B602—02	Mechanical Couplings for Drain, Waste and Vent Pipe and Sewer Pipe	705.2.1, 705.5.3, 705.6, 705.7.1, 705.14.1, 705.15, 705.16.2, 705.19

ICC

International Code Council, Inc.
500 New Jersey Ave, NW
6th Floor
Washington, DC 20001

Standard Reference Number	Title	Referenced in code section number
IBC—09	International Building Code®	201.3, 305.4, 307.1, 307.2, 307.3, 308.2, 309.1,310.1, 310.3, 403.1, Table 403.1, 404.1, 407.3, 417.6, 502.6, 606.5.2, 1106.5
IEBC—09	International Existing Building Code	101.2
IECC—09	International Energy Conservation Code	313.1, 607.2, 607.2.1
IFC—09	International Fire Code®	201.3, 1201.1
IFGC—09	International Fuel Gas Code®	101.2, 201.3, 502.1
IMC—09	International Mechanical Code®	201.3, 307.6, 310.1, 422.9, 502.1, 612.1, 1202.1
IPSDC—09	International Private Sewage Disposal Code®	701.2
IRC—09	International Residential Code	101.2

ISEA

International Safety Equipment Association
1901 N. Moore Street, Suite 808
Arlington, VA 22209

Standard Reference Number	Title	Referenced in code section number
Z358.1—98	Emergency Eyewash and Shower Equipment	411.1

NFPA

National Fire Protection Association
1 Batterymarch Park
Quincy, MA 02169-7471

Standard Reference Number	Title	Referenced in code section number
13D—07	Installation of Sprinkler Systems in One- and Two-family Dwellings and Manufactured Homes	614, 615
50—01	Bulk Oxygen Systems at Consumer Sites	1203.1
51—07	Design and Installation of Oxygen-fuel Gas Systems for Welding, Cutting and Allied Processes	1203.1
70—08	National Electric Code	502.1, 504.3, 1113.1.3
99C—05	Gas and Vacuum Systems	1202.1

NSF

NSF International
789 Dixboro Road
Ann Arbor, MI 48105

Standard Reference Number	Title	Referenced in code section number
3—2007	Commercial Warewashing Equipment	409.1
14—2007	Plastic Piping System Components and Related Materials	303.3, 611.3
18—2007	Manual Food and Beverage Dispensing Equipment	426.1
42—2007e	Drinking Water Treatment Units—Aesthetic Effects	611.1, 611.3
44—2004	Residential Cation Exchange Water Softeners	611.1, 611.3
53—2007	Drinking Water Treatment Units—Health Effects	611.1, 611.3
58—2006	Reverse Osmosis Drinking Water Treatment Systems	611.2
61—2007a	Drinking Water System Components—Health Effects	410.1, 424.1, 605.3, 605.4, 605.5, 605.7, 611.3, 611.3
62—2004	Drinking Water Distillation Systems	611.1

PDI

Plumbing and Drainage Institute
800 Turnpike Street, Suite 300
North Andover, MA 01845

Standard Reference Number	Title	Referenced in code section number
G101(2003)	Testing and Rating Procedure for Grease Interceptors with Appendix of Sizing and Installation Data	1003.3.4

UL

Underwriters Laboratories, Inc.
333 Pfingsten Road
Northbrook, IL 60062-2096

Standard Reference Number	Title	Referenced in code section number
UL508—99	Industrial Control Equipment with Revision through July 2005	314.2.3

APPENDIX A
PLUMBING PERMIT FEE SCHEDULE

The provisions contained in this appendix are deleted.

APPENDIX B

RATES OF RAINFALL FOR VARIOUS CITIES

<u>*The provisions contained in this appendix are adopted as part of this code.*</u>

Rainfall rates, in inches per hour, are based on a storm of 1-hour duration and a 100-year return period. The rainfall rates shown in the appendix are derived from Figure 1106.1.

Alabama:
- Birmingham . . . 3.8
- Huntsville . . . 3.6
- Mobile . . . 4.6
- Montgomery . . . 4.2

Alaska:
- Fairbanks . . . 1.0
- Juneau . . . 0.6

Arizona:
- Flagstaff . . . 2.4
- Nogales . . . 3.1
- Phoenix . . . 2.5
- Yuma . . . 1.6

Arkansas:
- Fort Smith . . . 3.6
- Little Rock . . . 3.7
- Texarkana . . . 3.8

California:
- Barstow . . . 1.4
- Crescent City . . . 1.5
- Fresno . . . 1.1
- Los Angeles . . . 2.1
- Needles . . . 1.6
- Placerville . . . 1.5
- San Fernando . . . 2.3
- San Francisco . . . 1.5
- Yreka . . . 1.4

Colorado:
- Craig . . . 1.5
- Denver . . . 2.4
- Durango . . . 1.8
- Grand Junction . . . 1.7
- Lamar . . . 3.0
- Pueblo . . . 2.5

Connecticut:
- Hartford . . . 2.7
- New Haven . . . 2.8
- Putnam . . . 2.6

Delaware:
- Georgetown . . . 3.0
- Wilmington . . . 3.1

District of Columbia:
- Washington . . . 3.2

Florida:
- Jacksonville . . . 4.3
- Key West . . . 4.3
- Miami . . . 4.7
- Pensacola . . . 4.6
- Tampa . . . 4.5

Georgia:
- Atlanta . . . 3.7
- Dalton . . . 3.4
- Macon . . . 3.9
- Savannah . . . 4.3
- Thomasville . . . 4.3

Hawaii:
- Hilo . . . 6.2
- Honolulu . . . 3.0
- Wailuku . . . 3.0

Idaho:
- Boise . . . 0.9
- Lewiston . . . 1.1
- Pocatello . . . 1.2

Illinois:
- Cairo . . . 3.3
- Chicago . . . 3.0
- Peoria . . . 3.3
- Rockford . . . 3.2
- Springfield . . . 3.3

Indiana:
- Evansville . . . 3.2
- Fort Wayne . . . 2.9
- Indianapolis . . . 3.1

Iowa:
- Davenport . . . 3.3
- Des Moines . . . 3.4
- Dubuque . . . 3.3
- Sioux City . . . 3.6

Kansas:
- Atwood . . . 3.3
- Dodge City . . . 3.3
- Topeka . . . 3.7
- Wichita . . . 3.7

Kentucky:
- Ashland . . . 3.0
- Lexington . . . 3.1
- Louisville . . . 3.2
- Middlesboro . . . 3.2
- Paducah . . . 3.3

Louisiana:
- Alexandria . . . 4.2
- Lake Providence . . . 4.0
- New Orleans . . . 4.8
- Shreveport . . . 3.9

Maine:
- Bangor . . . 2.2
- Houlton . . . 2.1
- Portland . . . 2.4

Maryland:
- Baltimore . . . 3.2
- Hagerstown . . . 2.8
- Oakland . . . 2.7
- Salisbury . . . 3.1

Massachusetts:
- Boston . . . 2.5
- Pittsfield . . . 2.8
- Worcester . . . 2.7

Michigan:
- Alpena . . . 2.5
- Detroit . . . 2.7
- Grand Rapids . . . 2.6
- Lansing . . . 2.8
- Marquette . . . 2.4
- Sault Ste. Marie . . . 2.2

Minnesota:
- Duluth . . . 2.8
- Grand Marais . . . 2.3
- Minneapolis . . . 3.1
- Moorhead . . . 3.2
- Worthington . . . 3.5

Mississippi:
- Biloxi . . . 4.7
- Columbus . . . 3.9
- Corinth . . . 3.6
- Natchez . . . 4.4
- Vicksburg . . . 4.1

Missouri:
- Columbia . . . 3.2
- Kansas City . . . 3.6
- Springfield . . . 3.4
- St. Louis . . . 3.2

Montana:
- Ekalaka . . . 2.5
- Havre . . . 1.6
- Helena . . . 1.5
- Kalispell . . . 1.2
- Missoula . . . 1.3

Nebraska:
- North Platte . . . 3.3
- Omaha . . . 3.8
- Scottsbluff . . . 3.1
- Valentine . . . 3.2

Nevada:
- Elko . . . 1.0
- Ely . . . 1.1
- Las Vegas . . . 1.4
- Reno . . . 1.1

New Hampshire:
- Berlin . . . 2.5
- Concord . . . 2.5
- Keene . . . 2.4

New Jersey:
- Atlantic City . . . 2.9
- Newark . . . 3.1
- Trenton . . . 3.1

New Mexico:
- Albuquerque . . . 2.0
- Hobbs . . . 3.0
- Raton . . . 2.5
- Roswell . . . 2.6
- Silver City . . . 1.9

New York:
- Albany . . . 2.5
- Binghamton . . . 2.3
- Buffalo . . . 2.3
- Kingston . . . 2.7
- New York . . . 3.0
- Rochester . . . 2.2

North Carolina:
- Asheville . . . 4.1
- Charlotte . . . 3.7
- Greensboro . . . 3.4

Wilmington 4.2

North Dakota:
Bismarck 2.8
Devils Lake 2.9
Fargo 3.1
Williston. 2.6

Ohio:
Cincinnati. 2.9
Cleveland 2.6
Columbus. 2.8
Toledo 2.8

Oklahoma:
Altus. 3.7
Boise City. 3.3
Durant 3.8
Oklahoma City 3.8

Oregon:
Baker 0.9
Coos Bay 1.5
Eugene 1.3
Portland 1.2

Pennsylvania:
Erie. 2.6
Harrisburg 2.8
Philadelphia 3.1
Pittsburgh. 2.6
Scranton 2.7

Rhode Island:
Block Island 2.75
Providence 2.6

South Carolina:
Charleston 4.3
Columbia 4.0
Greenville. 4.1

South Dakota:
Buffalo 2.8
Huron 3.3
Pierre 3.1
Rapid City 2.9
Yankton 3.6

Tennessee:
Chattanooga 3.5
Knoxville 3.2
Memphis 3.7
Nashville 3.3

Texas:
Abilene. 3.6
Amarillo. 3.5
Brownsville 4.5
Dallas. 4.0
Del Rio 4.0
El Paso 2.3
Houston 4.6
Lubbock. 3.3
Odessa 3.2
Pecos 3.0
San Antonio 4.2

Utah:
Brigham City 1.2
Roosevelt 1.3
Salt Lake City 1.3
St. George. 1.7

Vermont:
Barre 2.3
Bratteboro 2.7
Burlington 2.1
Rutland. 2.5

Virginia:
Bristol 2.7
Charlottesville 2.8
Lynchburg 3.2
Norfolk. 3.4
Richmond. 3.3

Washington:
Omak 1.1
Port Angeles. 1.1
Seattle 1.4
Spokane 1.0
Yakima. 1.1

West Virginia:
Charleston 2.8
Morgantown. 2.7

Wisconsin:
Ashland 2.5
Eau Claire. 2.9
Green Bay 2.6
La Crosse 3.1
Madison 3.0
Milwaukee 3.0

Wyoming:
Cheyenne 2.2
Fort Bridger 1.3
Lander 1.5
New Castle 2.5
Sheridan 1.7
Yellowstone Park 1.4

APPENDIX C
GRAY WATER RECYCLING SYSTEMS

The provisions contained in this appendix are adopted as part of this code.

Note: *Section 301.3 of this code requires all plumbing fixtures that receive water or waste to discharge to the sanitary drainage system of the structure. In order to allow for the utilization of a gray water system, Section 301.3 should be revised to read as follows:*

301.3 Connections to drainage system. All plumbing fixtures, drains, appurtenances and appliances used to receive or discharge liquid wastes or sewage shall be directly connected to the sanitary drainage system of the building or premises, in accordance with the requirements of this code. This section shall not be construed to prevent indirect waste systems required by Chapter 8.

> **Exception:** Bathtubs, showers, lavatories, clothes washers and laundry trays shall not be required to discharge to the sanitary drainage system where such fixtures discharge to an *approved* gray water system for flushing of water closets and urinals or for subsurface landscape irrigation.

SECTION C101 GENERAL

C101.1 Scope. The provisions of this appendix shall govern the materials, design, construction and installation of gray water systems for flushing of water closets and urinals and for subsurface landscape irrigation (see Figures 1 and 2).

C101.2 Definition. The following term shall have the meaning shown herein.

GRAY WATER. Waste discharged from lavatories, bathtubs, showers, clothes washers and laundry trays.

RAIN WATER. Water collected from roof areas and other approved areas.

C101.3 Permits. Permits shall be required in accordance with Section 106.

C101.4 Installation. In addition to the provisions of Section C101, systems for flushing of water closets and urinals shall comply with Section C102 and systems for subsurface landscape irrigation shall comply with Section C103. Except as provided for in Appendix C, all systems shall comply with the provisions of the *International Plumbing Code*.

C101.5 Materials. Above-ground drain, waste and vent piping for gray water systems shall conform to one of the standards listed in Table 702.1. Gray water underground building drainage and vent pipe shall conform to one of the standards listed in Table 702.2.

C101.6 Tests. Drain, waste and vent piping for gray water systems shall be tested in accordance with Section 312.

C101.7 Inspections. Gray water systems shall be inspected in accordance with Section 107.

C101.8 Potable water connections. Only connections in accordance with Section C102.3 shall be made between a gray water recycling system and a potable water system.

C101.9 Waste water connections. Gray water recycling systems shall receive only the waste discharge of bathtubs, showers, lavatories, clothes washers or laundry trays.

C101.10 Collection reservoir. Gray water shall be collected in an *approved* reservoir constructed of durable, nonabsorbent and corrosion-resistant materials. The reservoir shall be a closed and gas-tight vessel. *Access* openings shall be provided to allow inspection and cleaning of the reservoir interior.

> **Exception:** Does not need to be closed and gas tight for rainwater.

C101.11 Filtration. Gray water entering the reservoir shall pass through an *approved* filter such as a media, sand or diatomaceous earth filter.

> **Exception:** Filters may be placed on discharge from the reservoir.

> **C101.11.1 Required valve.** A full-open valve shall be installed downstream of the last fixture connection to the gray water discharge pipe before entering the required filter.

C101.12 Overflow. The collection reservoir shall be equipped with an overflow pipe having the same or larger diameter as the influent pipe for the gray water. The overflow pipe shall be trapped and shall be indirectly connected to the sanitary drainage system.

C101.13 Drain. A drain shall be located at the lowest point of the collection reservoir and shall be indirectly connected to the sanitary drainage system. The drain shall be the same diameter as the overflow pipe required in Section C101.12.

C101.14 Vent required. The reservoir shall be provided with a vent sized in accordance with Chapter 9 and based on the diameter of the reservoir influent pipe.

SECTION C102 SYSTEMS FOR FLUSHING WATER CLOSETS AND URINALS

C102.1 Collection reservoir. The holding capacity of the reservoir shall be a minimum of twice the volume of water required to meet the daily flushing requirements of the fixtures supplied with gray water, but not less than 50 gallons (189 L).

C102.2 Disinfection. Gray water shall be disinfected by an *approved* method that employs one or more disinfectants such as chlorine, iodine or ozone that are recommended for use with the pipes, fittings and equipment by the manufacturer of the pipes, fittings and equipment.

C102.3 Makeup water. Potable water shall be supplied as a source of makeup water for the gray water system. The potable water supply shall be protected against backflow in accordance with Section 608. There shall be a full-open valve located on the makeup water supply line to the collection reservoir.

C102.4 Coloring. The gray water shall be dyed blue or green with a food grade vegetable dye before such water is supplied to the fixtures.

C102.5 Materials. Distribution piping shall conform to one of the standards listed in Table 605.3.

C102.6 Identification. Distribution piping and reservoirs shall be identified as containing nonpotable water. Piping identification shall be in accordance with Section 608.8.

SECTION C103 SUBSURFACE LANDSCAPE IRRIGATION SYSTEMS

Note: Not applicable for rain water systems.

Deleted

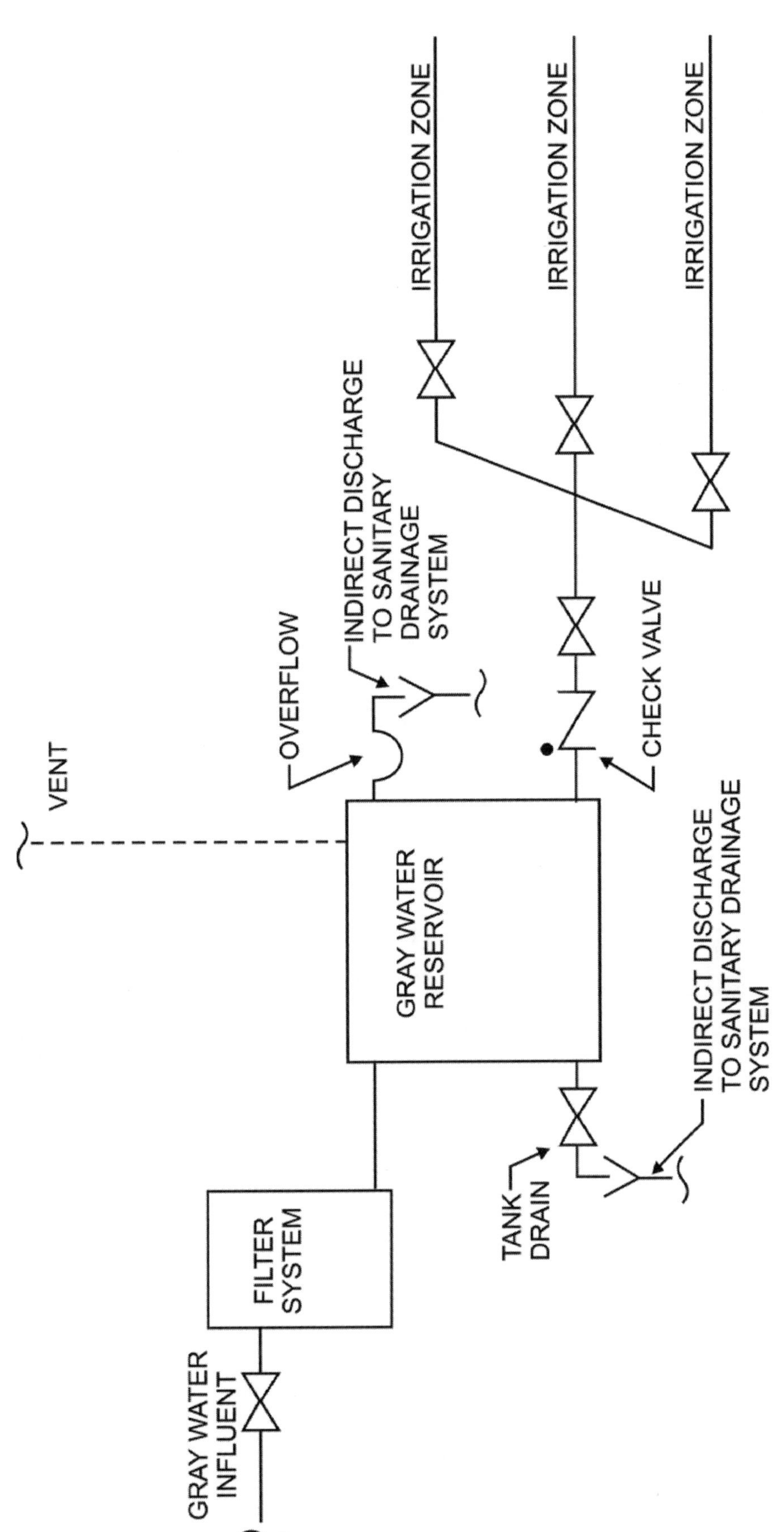

FIGURE 1
GRAY WATER RECYCLING SYSTEM FOR SUBSURFACE LANDSCAPE IRRIGATION

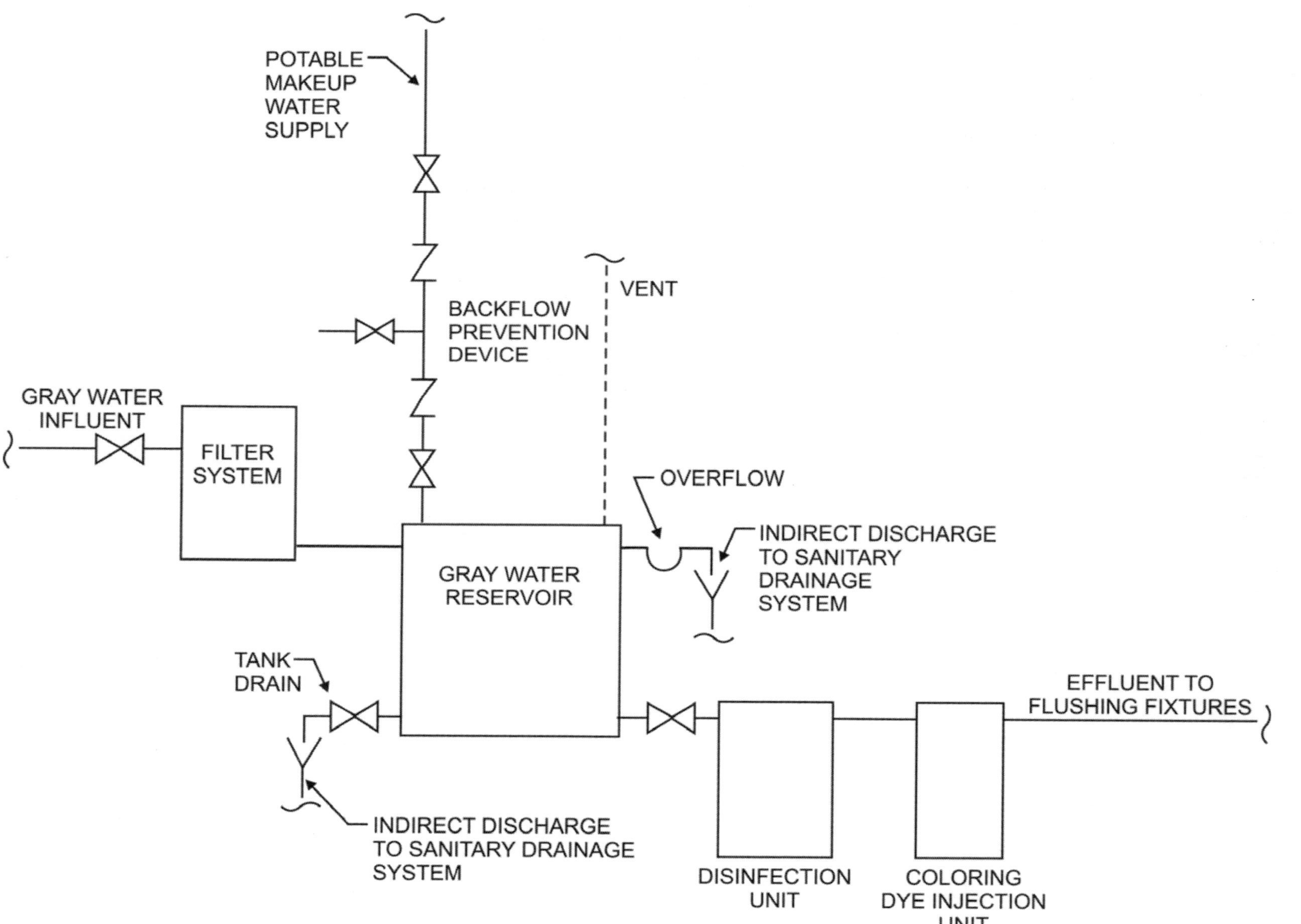

FIGURE 2
GRAY WATER RECYCLING SYSTEM FOR FLUSHING WATER CLOSETS AND URINALS

APPENDIX C1

RAIN WATER RECYCLING SYSTEMS

The provisions contained in this appendix are adopted as part of this code.
***Note:** See Section 301.3 for connections to drainage system.*

SECTION C1-101
GENERAL

C1-101.1 Scope. The provisions of this appendix shall govern the materials, design, construction and installation of rain water systems for flushing of water closets and urinals.

C1-101.2 Definitions. The following terms shall have the meaning shown herein.

GRAY WATER. Waste discharged from lavatories, bathtubs, showers, clothes washers and laundry trays.

RAIN WATER. Water collected from the roof of a building or other catchment surface during a rainfall event and stored in a reservoir for nonpotable use.

C1-101.3 Permits. Permits shall be required in accordance with the *North Carolina Administrative Code and Policies.*

C1-101.4 Installation. In addition to the provisions of Section C1-101, systems for flushing of water closets and urinals shall comply with Section C1-102. Except as provided for in Appendix C1, all systems shall comply with the provisions of the *International Plumbing Code.*

C1-101.5 Materials. Above-ground drain, waste and vent piping for rain water systems shall conform to one of the standards listed in Table 702.1. Rain water underground building drainage and vent pipe shall conform to one of the standards listed in Table 702.2.

C1-101.6 Tests. Drain, waste and vent piping for rain water systems shall be tested in accordance with Section 312.

C1-101.7 Inspections. Rain water systems shall be inspected in accordance with the *North Carolina Administrative Code and Policies.*

C1-101.8 Potable water connections. Only connections in accordance with Section C1-102.3 shall be made between rain water recycling system and a potable water system.

C1-101.9 Rain water connections. Rain water recycling systems shall receive only the water discharge from the roof of buildings or other catchments.

C1-101.10 Collection reservoir. Rain water shall be collected in an approved reservoir constructed of durable, nonabsorbent and corrosion-resistant materials. Access openings shall be provided to allow inspecting and cleaning of the reservoir interior.

C1-101.11 Filtration. Rain water entering the reservoir shall pass through an approved filter strainer, disinfected and colored blue or green.

C1-101.12 Overflow. The collection reservoir shall be equipped with an overflow pipe having the same or larger diameter as the influent pipe for the rain water. The overflow pipe shall discharge to the storm drainage system or to daylight.

SECTION C1-102
SYSTEMS FOR FLUSHING WATER CLOSETS AND URINALS

C1-102.1 Collection reservoir. The holding capacity of the reservoir is not limited.

C1-102.2 Makeup water. An alternative water supply shall be provided as a source of makeup water for the rain water system. An alternative water supply shall be protected against backflow in accordance with Section 608. The alternative water source may be a potable water system or an irrigation well.

C1-102.3 Materials. Distribution piping shall conform to one of the standards listed in Table 605.4. This does not apply to the irrigation portion of the system.

C1-102.4 Identification. Distribution piping (not including irrigation piping) and reservoirs shall be identified as containing nonpotable water. Piping identification shall be in accordance with Section 608.8.

APPENDIX D

DEGREE DAY AND DESIGN TEMPERATURES

The provisions contained in this appendix are deleted.

APPENDIX E

SIZING OF WATER PIPING SYSTEM

The provisions contained in this appendix are adopted as part of this code.

SECTION E101 GENERAL

E101.1 Scope.

E101.1.1 This appendix outlines two procedures for sizing a water piping system (see Sections E103.3 and E201.1). The design procedures are based on the minimum static pressure available from the supply source, the head changes in the system caused by friction and elevation, and the rates of flow necessary for operation of various fixtures.

E101.1.2 Because of the variable conditions encountered in hydraulic design, it is impractical to specify definite and detailed rules for sizing of the water piping system. Accordingly, other sizing or design methods conforming to good engineering practice standards are acceptable alternatives to those presented herein.

SECTION E102 INFORMATION REQUIRED

E102.1 Preliminary. Obtain the necessary information regarding the minimum daily static service pressure in the area where the building is to be located. If the building supply is to be metered, obtain information regarding friction loss relative to the rate of flow for meters in the range of sizes likely to be used. Friction loss data can be obtained from most manufacturers of water meters.

E102.2 Demand load.

E102.2.1 Estimate the supply demand of the building main and the principal branches and risers of the system by totaling the corresponding demand from the applicable part of Table E103.3(3).

E102.2.2 Estimate continuous supply demands in gallons per minute (L/m) for lawn sprinklers, air conditioners, etc., and add the sum to the total demand for fixtures. The result is the estimated supply demand for the building supply.

SECTION E103 SELECTION OF PIPE SIZE

E103.1 General. Decide from Table 604.3 what is the desirable minimum residual pressure that should be maintained at the highest fixture in the supply system. If the highest group of fixtures contains flush valves, the pressure for the group should not be less than 15 pounds per square inch (psi) (103.4 kPa) flowing. For flush tank supplies, the available pressure should not be less than 8 psi (55.2 kPa) flowing, except blowout action fixtures must not be less than 25 psi (172.4 kPa) flowing.

E103.2 Pipe sizing.

E103.2.1 Pipe sizes can be selected according to the following procedure or by other design methods conforming to acceptable engineering practice and *approved* by the administrative authority. The sizes selected must not be less than the minimum required by this code.

E103.2.2 Water pipe sizing procedures are based on a system of pressure requirements and losses, the sum of which must not exceed the minimum pressure available at the supply source. These pressures are as follows:

1. Pressure required at fixture to produce required flow. See Sections 604.3 and 604.5.
2. Static pressure loss or gain (due to head) is computed at 0.433 psi per foot (9.8 kPa/m) of elevation change.

   Example: Assume that the highest fixture supply outlet is 20 feet (6096 mm) above or below the supply source. This produces a static pressure differential of 20 feet by 0.433 psi/foot (2096 mm by 9.8 kPa/m) and an 8.66 psi (59.8 kPa) loss.
3. Loss through water meter. The friction or pressure loss can be obtained from meter manufacturers.
4. Loss through taps in water main.
5. Losses through special devices such as filters, softeners, backflow prevention devices and pressure regulators. These values must be obtained from the manufacturers.
6. Loss through valves and fittings. Losses for these items are calculated by converting to equivalent length of piping and adding to the total pipe length.
7. Loss due to pipe friction can be calculated when the pipe size, the pipe length and the flow through the pipe are known. With these three items, the friction loss can be determined. For piping flow charts not included, use manufacturers' tables and velocity recommendations.

   Note: For the purposes of all examples, the following metric conversions are applicable:

   1 cubic foot per minute = 0.4719 L/s

   1 square foot = 0.0929 m^2

   1 degree = 0.0175 rad

   1 pound per square inch = 6.895 kPa

   1 inch = 25.4 mm

   1 foot = 304.8 mm

   1 gallon per minute = 3.785 L/m

E103.3 Segmented loss method. The size of water service mains, *branch* mains and risers by the segmented loss method, must be determined according to water supply demand [gpm (L/m)], available water pressure [psi (kPa)] and friction loss caused by the water meter and *developed length* of pipe [feet (m)], including equivalent length of fittings. This design procedure is based on the following parameters:

- Calculates the friction loss through each length of the pipe.
- Based on a system of pressure losses, the sum of which must not exceed the minimum pressure available at the street main or other source of supply.
- Pipe sizing based on estimated peak demand, total pressure losses caused by difference in elevation, equipment, *developed length* and pressure required at most remote fixture, loss through taps in water main, losses through fittings, filters, backflow prevention devices, valves and pipe friction.

Because of the variable conditions encountered in hydraulic design, it is impractical to specify definite and detailed rules for sizing of the water piping system. Current sizing methods do not address the differences in the probability of use and flow characteristics of fixtures between types of occupancies. Creating an exact model of predicting the demand for a building is impossible and final studies assessing the impact of water conservation on demand are not yet complete. The following steps are necessary for the segmented loss method.

1. **Preliminary.** Obtain the necessary information regarding the minimum daily static service pressure in the area where the building is to be located. If the building supply is to be metered, obtain information regarding friction loss relative to the rate of flow for meters in the range of sizes to be used. Friction loss data can be obtained from manufacturers of water meters. It is essential that enough pressure be available to overcome all system losses caused by friction and elevation so that plumbing fixtures operate properly. Section 604.6 requires the water distribution system to be designed for the minimum pressure available taking into consideration pressure fluctuations. The lowest pressure must be selected to guarantee a continuous, adequate supply of water. The lowest pressure in the public main usually occurs in the summer because of lawn sprinkling and supplying water for air-conditioning cooling towers. Future demands placed on the public main as a result of large growth or expansion should also be considered. The available pressure will decrease as additional loads are placed on the public system.

2. **Demand load.** Estimate the supply demand of the building main and the principal branches and risers of the system by totaling the corresponding demand from the applicable part of Table E103.3(3). When estimating peak demand sizing methods typically use water supply fixture units (w.s.f.u.) [see Table E103.3(2)]. This numerical factor measures the load-producing effect of a single plumbing fixture of a given kind. The use of such fixture units can be applied to a single basic probability curve (or table), found in the various sizing methods [Table E103.3(3)]. The fixture units are then converted into gallons per minute (L/m) flow rate for estimating demand.

   2.1. Estimate continuous supply demand in gallons per minute (L/m) for lawn sprinklers, air conditioners, etc., and add the sum to the total demand for fixtures. The result is the estimated supply demand for the building supply. Fixture units cannot be applied to constant use fixtures such as hose bibbs, lawn sprinklers and air conditioners. These types of fixtures must be assigned the gallon per minute (L/m) value.

3. **Selection of pipe size.** This water pipe sizing procedure is based on a system of pressure requirements and losses, the sum of which must not exceed the minimum pressure available at the supply source. These pressures are as follows:

   3.1. Pressure required at the fixture to produce required flow. See Section 604.3 and Section 604.5.

   3.2. Static pressure loss or gain (because of head) is computed at 0.433 psi per foot (9.8 kPa/m) of elevation change.

   3.3. Loss through a water meter. The friction or pressure loss can be obtained from the manufacturer.

   3.4. Loss through taps in water main [see Table E103.3(4)].

   3.5. Losses through special devices such as filters, softeners, backflow prevention devices and pressure regulators. These values must be obtained from the manufacturers.

   3.6. Loss through valves and fittings [see Tables E103.3(5) and E103.3(6)]. Losses for these items are calculated by converting to equivalent length of piping and adding to the total pipe length.

   3.7. Loss caused by pipe friction can be calculated when the pipe size, the pipe length and the flow through the pipe are known. With these three items, the friction loss can be determined using Figures E103.3(2) through E103.3(7). When using charts, use pipe inside diameters. For piping flow charts not included, use manufacturers' tables and velocity recommendations. Before attempting to size any water supply system, it is necessary to gather preliminary information which includes available pressure, piping material, select design velocity, elevation differences and *developed length* to most remote fixture. The water supply system is divided into sections at major changes in elevation or where branches lead to fixture groups. The peak demand must be determined in each part of the hot and cold water supply system which includes the corresponding water supply fixture unit and conversion to gallons per minute (L/m) flow rate to be expected through each section. Sizing methods require the determination of the "most hydraulically remote" fixture to compute the pressure loss caused by pipe and fittings. The hydraulically remote fixture represents the most downstream fixture along the circuit of piping requiring the most available pressure to operate properly. Consideration must be given to all pressure demands and losses, such as friction caused by pipe, fittings and equipment, elevation and the residual pressure required by Table 604.3. The two most common and frequent complaints about the water supply system operation are lack of adequate pressure and noise.

Problem: What size Type L copper water pipe, service and distribution will be required to serve a two-story factory building having on each floor, back-to-back, two toilet rooms each equipped with hot and cold water? The highest fixture is 21 feet (6401 mm) above the street main, which is tapped with a 2-inch (51 mm) corporation cock at which point the minimum pressure is 55 psi (379.2 kPa). In the building basement, a 2-inch (51 mm) meter with a maximum pressure drop of 11 psi (75.8 kPa) and 3-inch (76 mm) reduced pressure principle backflow preventer with a maximum pressure drop of 9 psi (621 kPa) are to be installed. The system is shown by Figure E103.3(1). To be determined are the pipe sizes for the service main and the cold and hot water distribution pipes.

Solution: A tabular arrangement such as shown in Table E103.3(1) should first be constructed. The steps to be followed are indicated by the tabular arrangement itself as they are in sequence, columns 1 through 10 and lines A through L.

Step 1

Columns 1 and 2: Divide the system into sections breaking at major changes in elevation or where branches lead to fixture groups. After point B [see Figure E103.3(1)], separate consideration will be given to the hot and cold water piping. Enter the sections to be considered in the service and cold water piping in Column 1 of the tabular arrangement. Column 1 of Table E103.3(1) provides a line-by-line recommended tabular arrangement for use in solving pipe sizing.

The objective in designing the water supply system is to ensure an adequate water supply and pressure to all fixtures and equipment. Column 2 provides the pounds per square inch (psi) to be considered separately from the minimum pressure available at the main. Losses to take into consideration are the following: the differences in elevations between the water supply source and the highest water supply outlet, meter pressure losses, the tap in main loss, special fixture devices such as water softeners and backflow prevention devices and the pressure required at the most remote fixture outlet. The difference in elevation can result in an increase or decrease in available pressure at the main. Where the water supply outlet is located above the source, this results in a loss in the available pressure and is subtracted from the pressure at the water source. Where the highest water supply outlet is located below the water supply source, there will be an increase in pressure that is added to the available pressure of the water source.

Column 3: According to Table E103.3(3), determine the gpm (L/m) of flow to be expected in each section of the system. These flows range from 28.6 to 108 gpm. Load values for fixtures must be determined as water supply fixture units and then converted to a gallon-per-minute (gpm) rating to determine peak demand. When calculating peak demands, the water supply fixture units are added and then converted to the gallon-per-minute rating. For continuous flow fixtures such as hose bibbs and lawn sprinkler systems, add the gallon-per-minute demand to the intermittent demand of fixtures. For example, a total of 120 water supply fixture units is converted to a demand of 48 gallons per minute. Two hose bibbs × 5 gpm demand = 10 gpm. Total gpm rating = 48.0 gpm + 10 gpm = 58.0 gpm demand.

Step 2

Line A: Enter the minimum pressure available at the main source of supply in Column 2. This is 55 psi (379.2 kPa). The local water authorities generally keep records of pressures at different times of day and year. The available pressure can also be checked from nearby buildings or from fire department hydrant checks.

Line B: Determine from Table 604.3 the highest pressure required for the fixtures on the system, which is 15 psi (103.4 kPa), to operate a flushometer valve. The most remote fixture outlet is necessary to compute the pressure loss caused by pipe and fittings, and represents the most downstream fixture along the circuit of piping requiring the available pressure to operate properly as indicated by Table 604.3.

Line C: Determine the pressure loss for the meter size given or assumed. The total water flow from the main through the service as determined in Step 1 will serve to aid in the meter selected. There are three common types of water meters; the pressure losses are determined by the American Water Works Association Standards for displacement type, compound type and turbine type. The maximum pressure loss of such devices takes into consideration the meter size, safe operating capacity (gpm) and maximum rates for continuous operations (gpm). Typically, equipment imparts greater pressure losses than piping.

Line D: Select from Table E103.3(4) and enter the pressure loss for the tap size given or assumed. The loss of pressure through taps and tees in pounds per square inch (psi) are based on the total gallon-per-minute flow rate and size of the tap.

Line E: Determine the difference in elevation between the main and source of supply and the highest fixture on the system. Multiply this figure, expressed in feet, by 0.43 psi (2.9 kPa). Enter the resulting psi loss on Line E. The difference in elevation between the water supply source and the highest water supply outlet has a significant impact on the sizing of the water supply system. The difference in elevation usually results in a loss in the available pressure because the water supply outlet is generally located above the water supply source. The loss is caused by the pressure required to lift the water to the outlet. The pressure loss is subtracted from the pressure at the water source. Where the highest water supply outlet is located below the water source, there will be an increase in pressure which is added to the available pressure of the water source.

Lines F, G and H: The pressure losses through filters, backflow prevention devices or other special fixtures must be obtained from the manufacturer or estimated and entered on these lines. Equipment such as backflow prevention devices, check valves, water softeners, instantaneous or tankless water heaters, filters and strainers can impart a much greater pressure loss than the piping. The pressure losses can range from 8 psi to 30 psi.

Step 3

Line I: The sum of the pressure requirements and losses that affect the overall system (Lines B through H) is entered on this line. Summarizing the steps, all of the system losses are subtracted from the minimum water pressure. The remainder is the pressure available for friction, defined as the energy available to push the water through the pipes to each fixture. This force can be used as an average pressure loss, as long as the pressure available for friction is not exceeded. Saving a certain amount for available water supply pressures as an area incurs growth, or because of aging of the pipe or equipment added to the system is recommended.

Step 4

Line J: Subtract Line I from Line A. This gives the pressure that remains available from overcoming friction losses in the system. This figure is a guide to the pipe size that is chosen for each section, incorporating the total friction losses to the most remote outlet (measured length is called *developed length*).

> **Exception:** When the main is above the highest fixture, the resulting psi must be considered a pressure gain (static head gain) and omitted from the sums of Lines B through H and added to Line J.

The maximum friction head loss that can be tolerated in the system during peak demand is the difference between the static pressure at the highest and most remote outlet at no-flow conditions and the minimum flow pressure required at that outlet. If the losses are within the required limits, then every run of pipe will also be within the required friction head loss. Static pressure loss is the most remote outlet in feet × 0.433 = loss in psi caused by elevation differences.

Step 5

Column 4: Enter the length of each section from the main to the most remote outlet (at Point E). Divide the water supply system into sections breaking at major changes in elevation or where branches lead to fixture groups.

Step 6

Column 5: When selecting a trial pipe size, the length from the water service or meter to the most remote fixture outlet must be measured to determine the *developed length*. However, in systems having a flush valve or temperature controlled shower at the topmost floors the *developed length* would be from the water meter to the most remote flush valve on the system. A rule of thumb is that size will become progressively smaller as the system extends farther from the main source of supply. Trial pipe size may be arrived at by the following formula:

Line J: (Pressure available to overcome pipe friction) × 100/equivalent length of run total *developed length* to most remote fixture × percentage factor of 1.5 (note: a percentage factor is used only as an estimate for friction losses imposed for fittings for initial trial pipe size) = psi (average pressure drops per 100 feet of pipe).

For trial pipe size see Figure E 103.3(3) (Type L copper) based on 2.77 psi and a 108 gpm = $2^1/_2$ inches. To determine the equivalent length of run to the most remote outlet, the *developed length* is determined and added to the friction losses for fittings and valves. The developed lengths of the designated pipe sections are as follows:

A - B	54 ft
B - C	8 ft
C - D	13 ft
D - E	150 ft

Total developed length = 225 ft

The equivalent length of the friction loss in fittings and valves must be added to the *developed length* (most remote outlet). Where the size of fittings and valves is not known, the added friction loss should be approximated. A general rule that has been used is to add 50 percent of the *developed length* to allow for fittings and valves. For example, the equivalent length of run equals the *developed length* of run (225 ft × 1.5 = 338 ft). The total equivalent length of run for determining a trial pipe size is 338 feet.

> **Example:** 9.36 (pressure available to overcome pipe friction) × 100/ 338 (equivalent length of run = 225 × 1.5) = 2.77 psi (average pressure drop per 100 feet of pipe).

Step 7

Column 6: Select from Table E103.3(6) the equivalent lengths for the trial pipe size of fittings and valves on each pipe section. Enter the sum for each section in Column 6. (The number of fittings to be used in this example must be an estimate.) The equivalent length of piping is the *developed length* plus the equivalent lengths of pipe corresponding to friction head losses for fittings and valves. Where the size of fittings and valves is not known, the added friction head losses must be approximated. An estimate for this example is found in Table E.1.

Step 8

Column 7: Add the figures from Column 4 and Column 6, and enter in Column 7. Express the sum in hundreds of feet.

TABLE E.1

COLD WATER PIPE SECTION	FITTINGS/VALVES	PRESSURE LOSS EXPRESSED AS EQUIVALENT LENGTH OF TUBE (feet)	HOT WATER PIPE SECTION	FITTINGS/VALVES	PRESSURE LOSS EXPRESSED AS EQUIVALENT OF TUBE (feet)
A-B	3-2 $^{1}/_{2}$″ Gate valves	3	A-B	3-2 $^{1}/_{2}$″ Gate valves	3
	1-2 $^{1}/_{2}$″ Side branch tee	12		1-2 $^{1}/_{2}$″ Side branch tee	12
B-C	1-2 $^{1}/_{2}$″ Straight run tee	0.5	B-C	1-2″ Straight run tee	7
				1-2″ 90-degree ell	0.5
C-F	1-2 $^{1}/_{2}$″ Side branch tee	12	C-F	1-1 $^{1}/_{2}$″ Side branch tee	7
C-D	1-2 $^{1}/_{2}$″ 90-degree ell	7	C-D	1- $^{1}/_{2}$″ 90-degree ell	4
D-E	1-2 $^{1}/_{2}$″ Side branch tee	12	D-E	1-1 $^{1}/_{2}$″ Side branch tee	7

Step 9

Column 8: Select from Figure E103.3(3) the friction loss per 100 feet (30 480 mm) of pipe for the gallon-per-minute flow in a section (Column 3) and trial pipe size (Column 5). Maximum friction head loss per 100 feet is determined on the basis of total pressure available for friction head loss and the longest equivalent length of run. The selection is based on the gallon-per-minute demand, the uniform friction head loss, and the maximum design velocity. Where the size indicated by hydraulic table indicates a velocity in excess of the selected velocity, a size must be selected which produces the required velocity.

Step 10

Column 9: Multiply the figures in Columns 7 and 8 for each section and enter in Column 9.

Total friction loss is determined by multiplying the friction loss per 100 feet (30 480 mm) for each pipe section in the total *developed length* by the pressure loss in fittings expressed as equivalent length in feet. Note: Section C-F should be considered in the total pipe friction losses only if greater loss occurs in Section C-F than in pipe section D-E. Section C-F is not considered in the total *developed length.* Total friction loss in equivalent length is determined in Table E.2.

Step 11

Line K: Enter the sum of the values in Column 9. The value is the total friction loss in equivalent length for each designated pipe section.

Step 12

Line L: Subtract Line J from Line K and enter in Column 10.

The result should always be a positive or plus figure. If it is not, repeat the operation using Columns 5, 6, 8 and 9 until a balance or near balance is obtained. If the difference between Lines J and K is a high positive number, it is an indication that the pipe sizes are too large and should be reduced, thus saving materials. In such a case, the operations using Columns 5, 6, 8 and 9 should again be repeated.

The total friction losses are determined and subtracted from the pressure available to overcome pipe friction for trial pipe size. This number is critical as it provides a guide to whether the pipe size selected is too large and the process should be repeated to obtain an economically designed system.

Answer: The final figures entered in Column 5 become the design pipe size for the respective sections. Repeating this operation a second time using the same sketch but considering the demand for hot water, it is possible to size the hot water distribution piping. This has been worked up as a part of the overall problem in the tabular arrangement used for sizing the service and water distribution piping. Note that consideration must be given to the pressure losses from the street main to the water heater (Section A-B) in determining the hot water pipe sizes.

TABLE E.2

PIPE SECTIONS	FRICTION LOSS EQUIVALENT LENGTH (feet)	
	Cold Water	Hot Water
A-B	$0.69 \times 3.2 = 2.21$	$0.69 \times 3.2 = 2.21$
B-C	$0.085 \times 3.1 = 0.26$	$0.16 \times 1.4 = 0.22$
C-D	$0.20 \times 1.9 = 0.38$	$0.17 \times 3.2 = 0.54$
D-E	$1.62 \times 1.9 = 3.08$	$1.57 \times 3.2 = 5.02$
Total pipe friction losses (Line K)	5.93	7.99

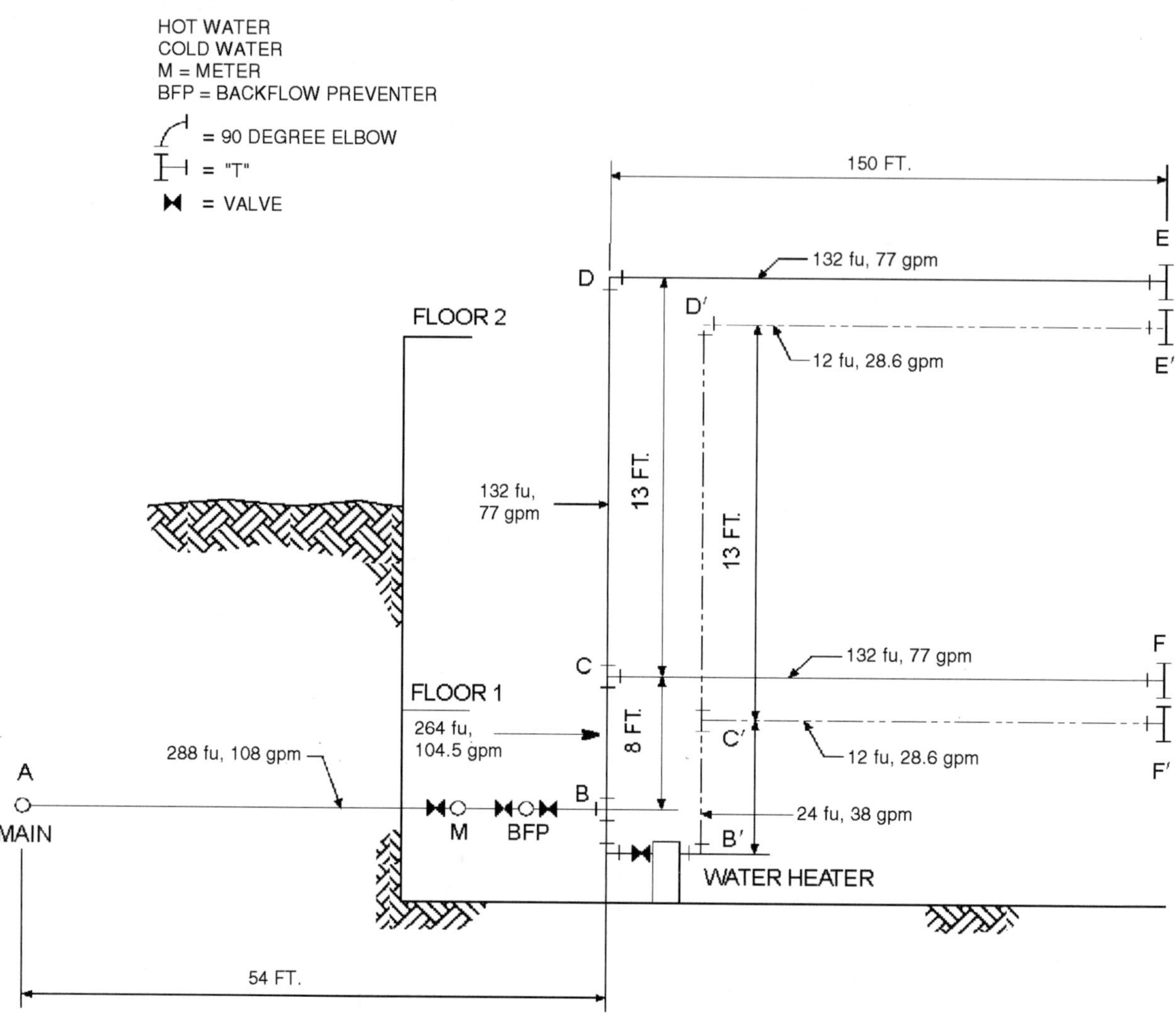

For SI: 1 foot = 304.8 mm, 1 gpm = 3.785 L/m.

FIGURE E103.3(1)
EXAMPLE-SIZING

TABLE E103.3(1)
RECOMMENDED TABULAR ARRANGEMENT FOR USE IN SOLVING PIPE SIZING PROBLEMS

COLUMN	1	2	3	4	5	6	7	8	9	10
Line	Description	Lb per square inch (psi)	Gal. per min through section	Length of section (feet)	Trial pipe size (inches)	Equivalent length of fittings and valves (feet)	Total equivalent length col. 4 and col. 6 (100 feet)	Friction loss per 100 feet of trial size pipe (psi)	Friction loss in equivalent length col. 8 x col. 7 (psi)	Excess pressure over friction losses (psi)
A	Service and cold water distribution piping[a]: Minimum pressure available at main	55.00								
B	Highest pressure required at a fixture (Table 604.3)	15.00								
C	Meter loss 2″ meter	11.00								
D	Tap in main loss 2″ tap (Table E103A)	1.61								
E	Static head loss 21 × 43 psi	9.03								
F	Special fixture loss backflow preventer	9.00								
G	Special fixture loss—Filter	0.00								
H	Special fixture loss—Other	0.00								
I	Total overall losses and requirements (Sum of Lines B through H)	45.64								
J	Pressure available to overcome pipe friction (Line A minus Lines B to H)	9.36								
	DESIGNATION Pipe section (from diagram) Cold water Distribution piping	FU								
	AB	288	108.0	54	$2\frac{1}{2}$	15.00	0.69	3.2	2.21	—
	BC	264	104.5	8	$2\frac{1}{2}$	0.5	0.85	3.1	0.26	—
	CD	132	77.0	13	$2\frac{1}{2}$	7.00	0.20	1.9	0.38	—
	CF[b]	132	77.0	150	$2\frac{1}{2}$	12.00	1.62	1.9	3.08	—
	DE[b]	132	77.0	150	$2\frac{1}{2}$	12.00	1.62	1.9	3.08	—
K	Total pipe friction losses (cold)		—	—	—	—	—	—	5.93	—
L	Difference (Line J minus Line K)		—	—	—	—	—	—	—	3.43
	Pipe section (from diagram) Diagram Hot water Distribution Piping: A′B′	288	108.0	54	$2\frac{1}{2}$	12.00	0.69	3.3	2.21	—
	B′C′	24	38.0	8	2	7.5	0.16	1.4	0.22	—
	C′D′	12	28.6	13	$1\frac{1}{2}$	4.0	0.17	3.2	0.54	—
	C′F′[b]	12	28.6	150	$1\frac{1}{2}$	7.00	1.57	3.2	5.02	—
	D′E′[b]	12	28.6	150	$1\frac{1}{2}$	7.00	1.57	3.2	5.02	—
K	Total pipe friction losses (hot)		—	—	—	—	—	—	7.99	—
L	Difference (Line J minus Line K)		—	—	—	—	—	—	—	1.37

For SI: 1 inch = 25.4 mm, 1 foot = 304.8 mm, 1 psi = 6.895 kPa, 1 gpm = 3.785 L/m.

a. To be considered as pressure gain for fixtures below main (to consider separately, omit from "I" and add to "J").

b. To consider separately, in K use C-F only if greater loss than above.

TABLE E103.3(2)
LOAD VALUES ASSIGNED TO FIXTURES[a]

FIXTURE	OCCUPANCY	TYPE OF SUPPLY CONTROL	LOAD VALUES, IN WATER SUPPLY FIXTURE UNITS (wsfu)		
			Cold	Hot	Total
Bathroom group	Private	Flush tank	2.7	1.5	3.6
Bathroom group	Private	Flush valve	6.0	3.0	8.0
Bathtub	Private	Faucet	1.0	1.0	1.4
Bathtub	Public	Faucet	3.0	3.0	4.0
Bidet	Private	Faucet	1.5	1.5	2.0
Combination fixture	Private	Faucet	2.25	2.25	3.0
Dishwashing machine	Private	Automatic	—	1.4	1.4
Drinking fountain	Offices, etc.	$^{3}/_{8}''$ valve	0.25	—	0.25
Kitchen sink	Private	Faucet	1.0	1.0	1.4
Kitchen sink	Hotel, restaurant	Faucet	3.0	3.0	4.0
Laundry trays (1 to 3)	Private	Faucet	1.0	1.0	1.4
Lavatory	Private	Faucet	0.5	0.5	0.7
Lavatory	Public	Faucet	1.5	1.5	2.0
Service sink	Offices, etc.	Faucet	2.25	2.25	3.0
Shower head	Public	Mixing valve	3.0	3.0	4.0
Shower head	Private	Mixing valve	1.0	1.0	1.4
Urinal	Public	1″ flush valve	10.0	—	10.0
Urinal	Public	$^{3}/_{4}''$ flush valve	5.0	—	5.0
Urinal	Public	Flush tank	3.0	—	3.0
Washing machine (8 lb)	Private	Automatic	1.0	1.0	1.4
Washing machine (8 lb)	Public	Automatic	2.25	2.25	3.0
Washing machine (15 lb)	Public	Automatic	3.0	3.0	4.0
Water closet	Private	Flush valve	6.0	—	6.0
Water closet	Private	Flush tank	2.2	—	2.2
Water closet	Public	Flush valve	10.0	—	10.0
Water closet	Public	Flush tank	5.0	—	5.0
Water closet	Public or private	Flushometer tank	2.0	—	2.0

For SI: 1 inch = 25.4 mm, 1 pound = 0.454 kg.

a. For fixtures not listed , loads should be assumed by comparing the fixture to one listed using water in similar quantities and at similar rates. The assigned loads for fixtures with both hot and cold water supplies are given for separate hot and cold water loads and for total load. The separate hot and cold water loads being three-fourths of the total load for the fixture in each case.

TABLE E103.3(3)
TABLE FOR ESTIMATING DEMAND

SUPPLY SYSTEMS PREDOMINANTLY FOR FLUSH TANKS			SUPPLY SYSTEMS PREDOMINANTLY FOR FLUSH VALVES		
Load	Demand		Load	Demand	
(Water supply fixture units)	(Gallons per minute)	(Cubic feet per minute)	(Water supply fixture units)	(Gallons per minute)	(Cubic feet per minute)
1	3.0	0.04104	—	—	—
2	5.0	0.0684	—	—	—
3	6.5	0.86892	—	—	—
4	8.0	1.06944	—	—	—
5	9.4	1.256592	5	15.0	2.0052
6	10.7	1.430376	6	17.4	2.326032
7	11.8	1.577424	7	19.8	2.646364
8	12.8	1.711104	8	22.2	2.967696
9	13.7	1.831416	9	24.6	3.288528
10	14.6	1.951728	10	27.0	3.60936
11	15.4	2.058672	11	27.8	3.716304
12	16.0	2.13888	12	28.6	3.823248
13	16.5	2.20572	13	29.4	3.930192
14	17.0	2.27256	14	30.2	4.037136
15	17.5	2.3394	15	31.0	4.14408
16	18.0	2.90624	16	31.8	4.241024
17	18.4	2.459712	17	32.6	4.357968
18	18.8	2.513184	18	33.4	4.464912
19	19.2	2.566656	19	34.2	4.571856
20	19.6	2.620128	20	35.0	4.6788
25	21.5	2.87412	25	38.0	5.07984
30	23.3	3.114744	30	42.0	5.61356
35	24.9	3.328632	35	44.0	5.88192
40	26.3	3.515784	40	46.0	6.14928
45	27.7	3.702936	45	48.0	6.41664
50	29.1	3.890088	50	50.0	6.684
60	32.0	4.27776	60	54.0	7.21872
70	35.0	4.6788	70	58.0	7.75344
80	38.0	5.07984	80	61.2	8.181216
90	41.0	5.48088	90	64.3	8.595624
100	43.5	5.81508	100	67.5	9.0234
120	48.0	6.41664	120	73.0	9.75864
140	52.5	7.0182	140	77.0	10.29336
160	57.0	7.61976	160	81.0	10.82808
180	61.0	8.15448	180	85.5	11.42964
200	65.0	8.6892	200	90.0	12.0312
225	70.0	9.3576	225	95.5	12.76644
250	75.0	10.026	250	101.0	13.50168

(continued)

TABLE E103.3(3)—continued
TABLE FOR ESTIMATING DEMAND

SUPPLY SYSTEMS PREDOMINANTLY FOR FLUSH TANKS			SUPPLY SYSTEMS PREDOMINANTLY FOR FLUSH VALVES		
Load	Demand		Load	Demand	
(Water supply fixture units)	(Gallons per minute)	(Cubic feet per minute)	(Water supply fixture units)	(Gallons per minute)	(Cubic feet per minute)
275	80.0	10.6944	275	104.5	13.96956
300	85.0	11.3628	300	108.0	14.43744
400	105.0	14.0364	400	127.0	16.97736
500	124.0	16.57632	500	143.0	19.11624
750	170.0	22.7256	750	177.0	23.66136
1,000	208.0	27.80544	1,000	208.0	27.80544
1,250	239.0	31.94952	1,250	239.0	31.94952
1,500	269.0	35.95992	1,500	269.0	35.95992
1,750	297.0	39.70296	1,750	297.0	39.70296
2,000	325.0	43.446	2,000	325.0	43.446
2,500	380.0	50.7984	2,500	380.0	50.7984
3,000	433.0	57.88344	3,000	433.0	57.88344
4,000	525.0	70.182	4,000	525.0	70.182
5,000	593.0	79.27224	5,000	593.0	79.27224

TABLE E103.3(4)
LOSS OF PRESSURE THROUGH TAPS AND TEES IN POUNDS PER SQUARE INCH (psi)

GALLONS PER MINUTE	SIZE OF TAP OR TEE (inches)						
	$^5/_8$	$^3/_4$	1	$1^1/_4$	$1^1/_2$	2	3
10	1.35	0.64	0.18	0.08	—	—	—
20	5.38	2.54	0.77	0.31	0.14	—	—
30	12.10	5.72	1.62	0.69	0.33	0.10	—
40	—	10.20	3.07	1.23	0.58	0.18	—
50	—	15.90	4.49	1.92	0.91	0.28	—
60	—	—	6.46	2.76	1.31	0.40	—
70	—	—	8.79	3.76	1.78	0.55	0.10
80	—	—	11.50	4.90	2.32	0.72	0.13
90	—	—	14.50	6.21	2.94	0.91	0.16
100	—	—	17.94	7.67	3.63	1.12	0.21
120	—	—	25.80	11.00	5.23	1.61	0.30
140	—	—	35.20	15.00	7.12	2.20	0.41
150	—	—	—	17.20	8.16	2.52	0.47
160	—	—	—	19.60	9.30	2.92	0.54
180	—	—	—	24.80	11.80	3.62	0.68
200	—	—	—	30.70	14.50	4.48	0.84
225	—	—	—	38.80	18.40	5.60	1.06
250	—	—	—	47.90	22.70	7.00	1.31
275	—	—	—	—	27.40	7.70	1.59
300	—	—	—	—	32.60	10.10	1.88

For SI: 1 inch = 25.4 mm, 1 pound per square inch = 6.895 kpa, 1 gallon per minute = 3.785 L/m.

TABLE E103.3(5)
ALLOWANCE IN EQUIVALENT LENGTHS OF PIPE FOR FRICTION LOSS IN VALVES AND THREADED FITTINGS (feet)

FITTING OR VALVE	PIPE SIZE (inches)							
	1/2	3/4	1	1 1/4	1 1/2	2	2 1/2	3
45-degree elbow	1.2	1.5	1.8	2.4	3.0	4.0	5.0	6.0
90-degree elbow	2.0	2.5	3.0	4.0	5.0	7.0	8.0	10.0
Tee, run	0.6	0.8	0.9	1.2	1.5	2.0	2.5	3.0
Tee, branch	3.0	4.0	5.0	6.0	7.0	10.0	12.0	15.0
Gate valve	0.4	0.5	0.6	0.8	1.0	1.3	1.6	2.0
Balancing valve	0.8	1.1	1.5	1.9	2.2	3.0	3.7	4.5
Plug-type cock	0.8	1.1	1.5	1.9	2.2	3.0	3.7	4.5
Check valve, swing	5.6	8.4	11.2	14.0	16.8	22.4	28.0	33.6
Globe valve	15.0	20.0	25.0	35.0	45.0	55.0	65.0	80.0
Angle valve	8.0	12.0	15.0	18.0	22.0	28.0	34.0	40.0

For SI: 1 inch = 25.4 mm, 1 foot = 304.8 mm, 1 degree = 0.0175 rad.

TABLE E103.3(6)
PRESSURE LOSS IN FITTINGS AND VALVES EXPRESSED AS EQUIVALENT LENGTH OF TUBE[a] (feet)

NOMINAL OR STANDARD SIZE (inches)	FITTINGS					VALVES			
	Standard Ell		90-Degree Tee						
	90 Degree	45 Degree	Side Branch	Straight Run	Coupling	Ball	Gate	Butterfly	Check
3/8	0.5	—	1.5	—	—	—	—	—	1.5
1/2	1	0.5	2	—	—	—	—	—	2
5/8	1.5	0.5	2	—	—	—	—	—	2.5
3/4	2	0.5	3	—	—	—	—	—	3
1	2.5	1	4.5	—	—	0.5	—	—	4.5
1 1/4	3	1	5.5	0.5	0.5	0.5	—	—	5.5
1 1/2	4	1.5	7	0.5	0.5	0.5	—	—	6.5
2	5.5	2	9	0.5	0.5	0.5	0.5	7.5	9
2 1/2	7	2.5	12	0.5	0.5	—	1	10	11.5
3	9	3.5	15	1	1	—	1.5	15.5	14.5
3 1/2	9	3.5	14	1	1	—	2	—	12.5
4	12.5	5	21	1	1	—	2	16	18.5
5	16	6	27	1.5	1.5	—	3	11.5	23.5
6	19	7	34	2	2	—	3.5	13.5	26.5
8	29	11	50	3	3	—	5	12.5	39

For SI: 1 inch = 25.4 mm, 1 foot = 304.8 mm, 1 degree = 0.01745 rad.

a. Allowances are for streamlined soldered fittings and recessed threaded fittings. For threaded fittings, double the allowances shown in the table. The equivalent lengths presented above are based on a C factor of 150 in the Hazen-Williams friction loss formula. The lengths shown are rounded to the nearest half-foot.

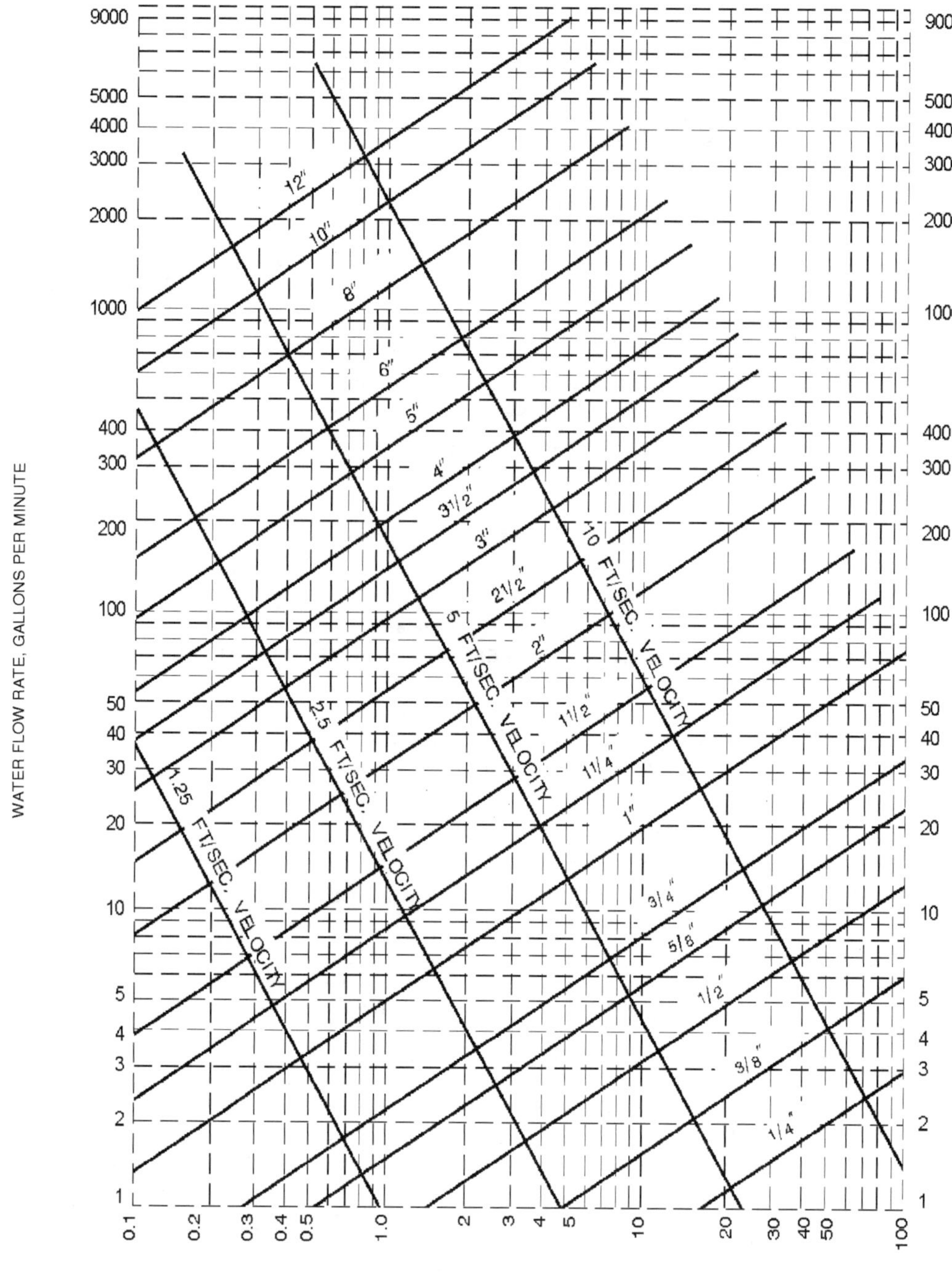

Note: Fluid velocities in excess of 5 to 8 feet/second are not usually recommended.

FIGURE E103.3(2)
FRICTION LOSS IN SMOOTH PIPE[a] (TYPE K, ASTM B 88 COPPER TUBING)

For SI: 1 inch = 25.4 mm, 1 foot = 304.8 mm, 1 gpm = 3.785 L/m, 1 psi = 6.895 kPa,
1 foot per second = 0.305 m/s.

a. This chart applies to smooth new copper tubing with recessed (streamline) soldered joints and to the actual sizes of types indicated on the diagram.

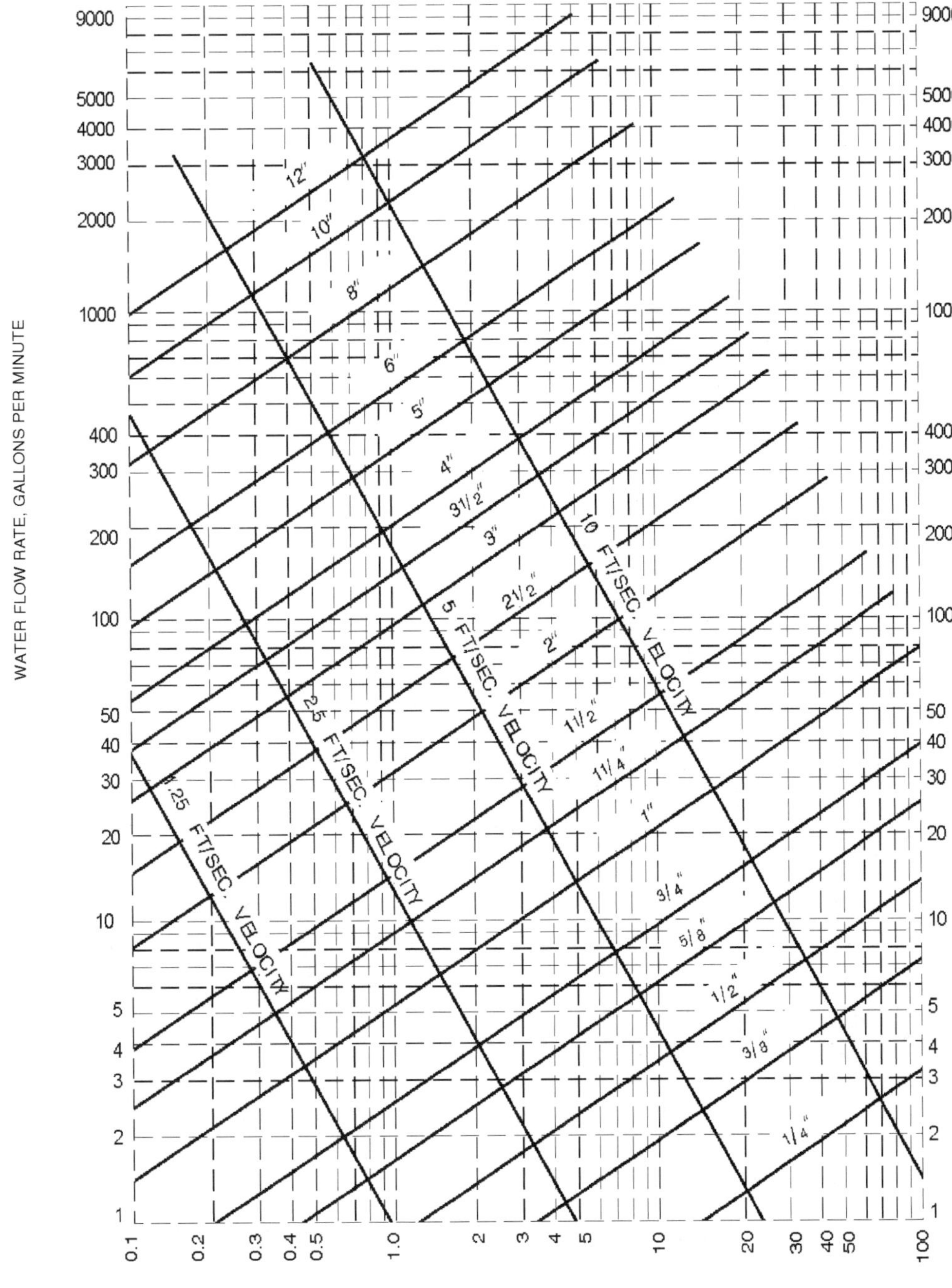

Note: Fluid velocities in excess of 5 to 8 feet/second are not usually recommended.

FIGURE E103.3(3)
FRICTION LOSS IN SMOOTH PIPE[a] (TYPE L, ASTM B 88 COPPER TUBING)

For SI: 1 inch = 25.4 mm, 1 foot = 304.8 mm, 1 gpm = 3.785 L/m, 1 psi = 6.895 kPa,
1 foot per second = 0.305 m/s.

a. This chart applies to smooth new copper tubing with recessed (streamline) soldered joints and to the actual sizes of types indicated on the diagram.

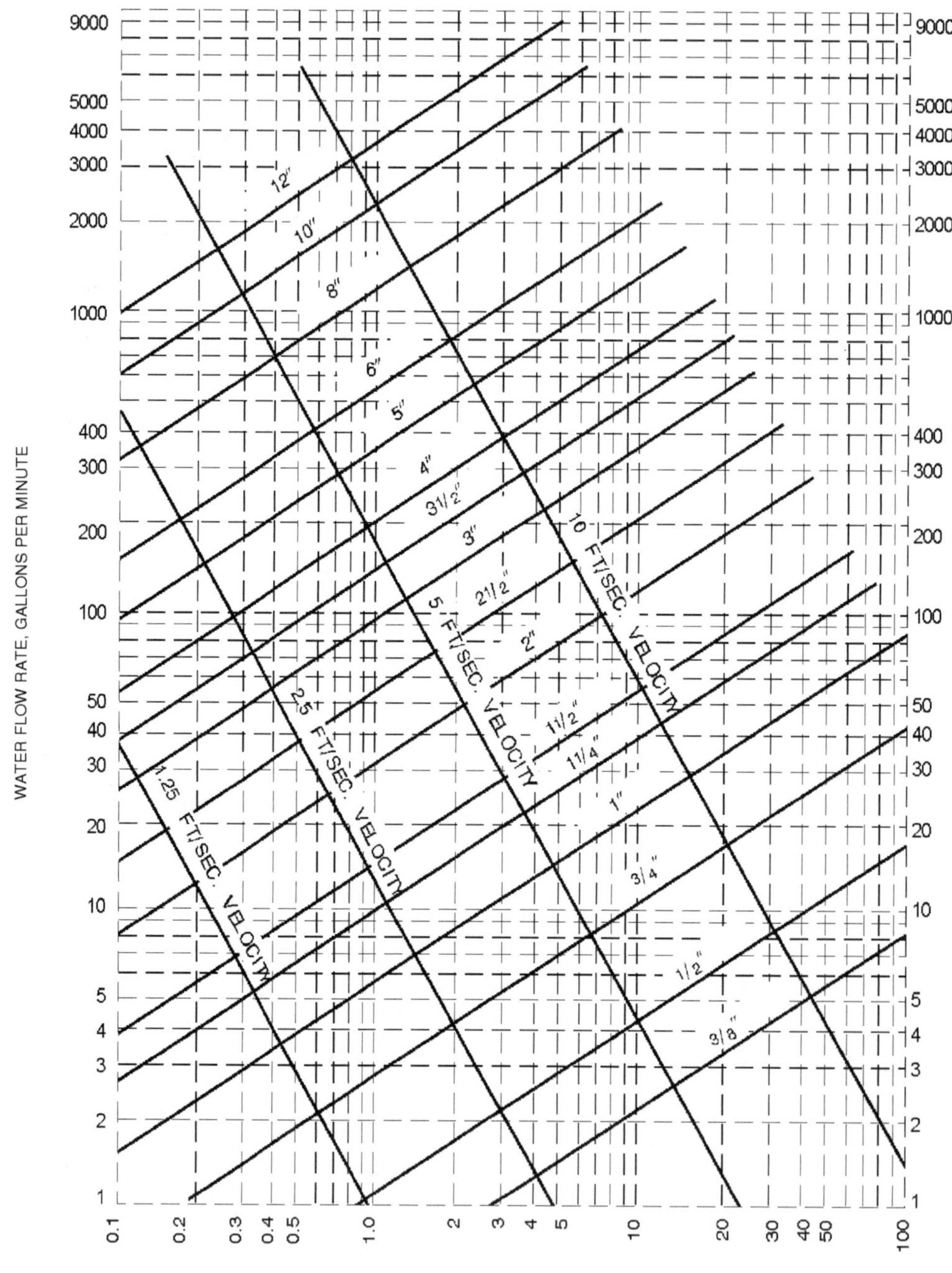

Note: Fluid velocities in excess of 5 to 8 feet/second are not usually recommended.

FIGURE E103.3(4)
FRICTION LOSS IN SMOOTH PIPE[a] (TYPE M, ASTM B 88 COPPER TUBING)

For SI: 1 inch = 25.4 mm, 1 foot = 304.8 mm, 1 gpm = 3.785 L/m, 1 psi = 6.895 kPa,
1 foot per second = 0.305 m/s.

a. This chart applies to smooth new copper tubing with recessed (streamline) soldered joints and to the actual sizes of types indicated on the diagram.

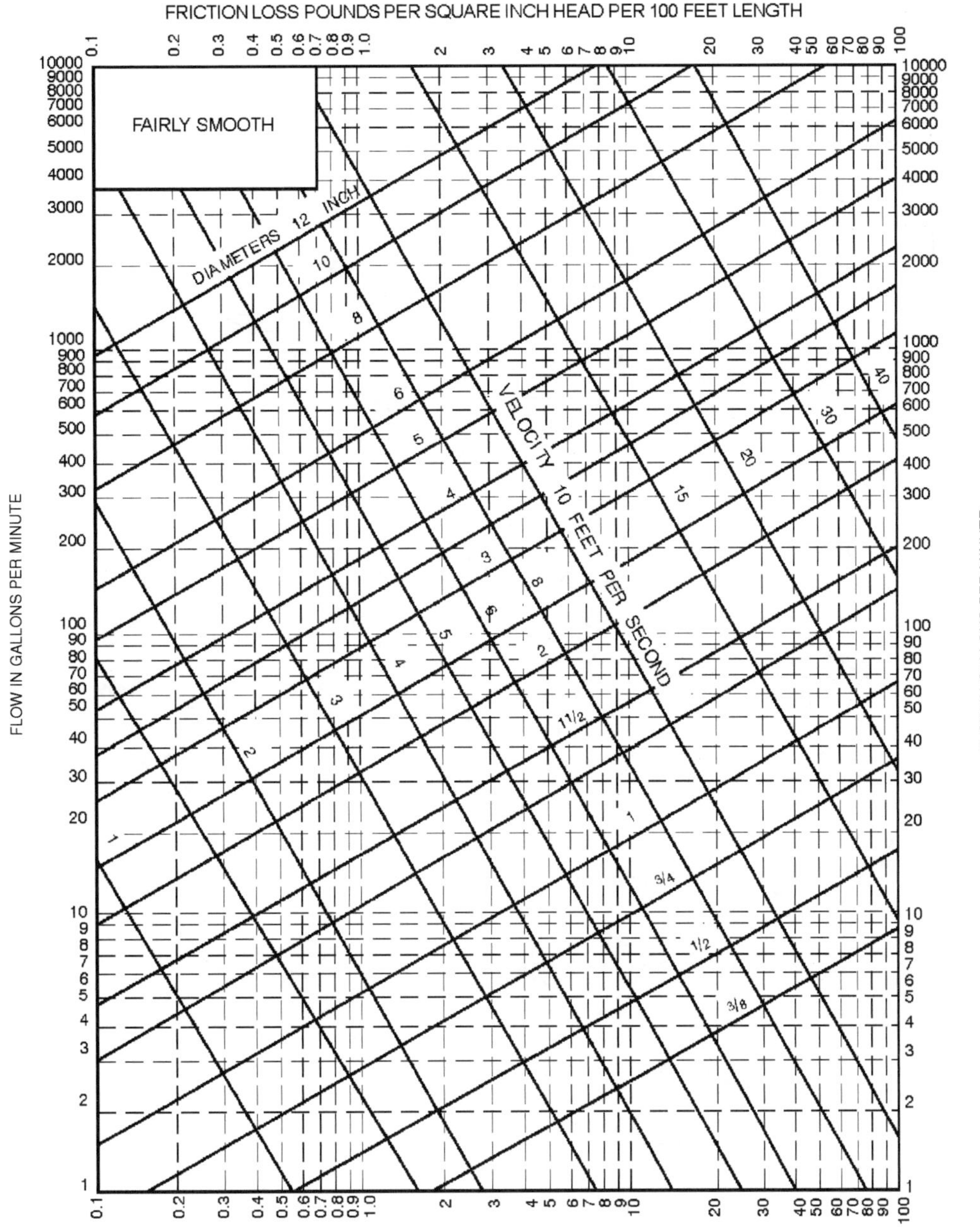

FIGURE E103.3(5)
FRICTION LOSS IN FAIRLY SMOOTH PIPE[a]

For SI: 1 inch = 25.4 mm, 1 foot = 304.8 mm, 1 gpm = 3.785 L/m, 1 psi = 6.895 kPa, 1 foot per second = 0.305 m/s.

a. This chart applies to smooth new steel (fairly smooth) pipe and to actual diameters of standard-weight pipe.

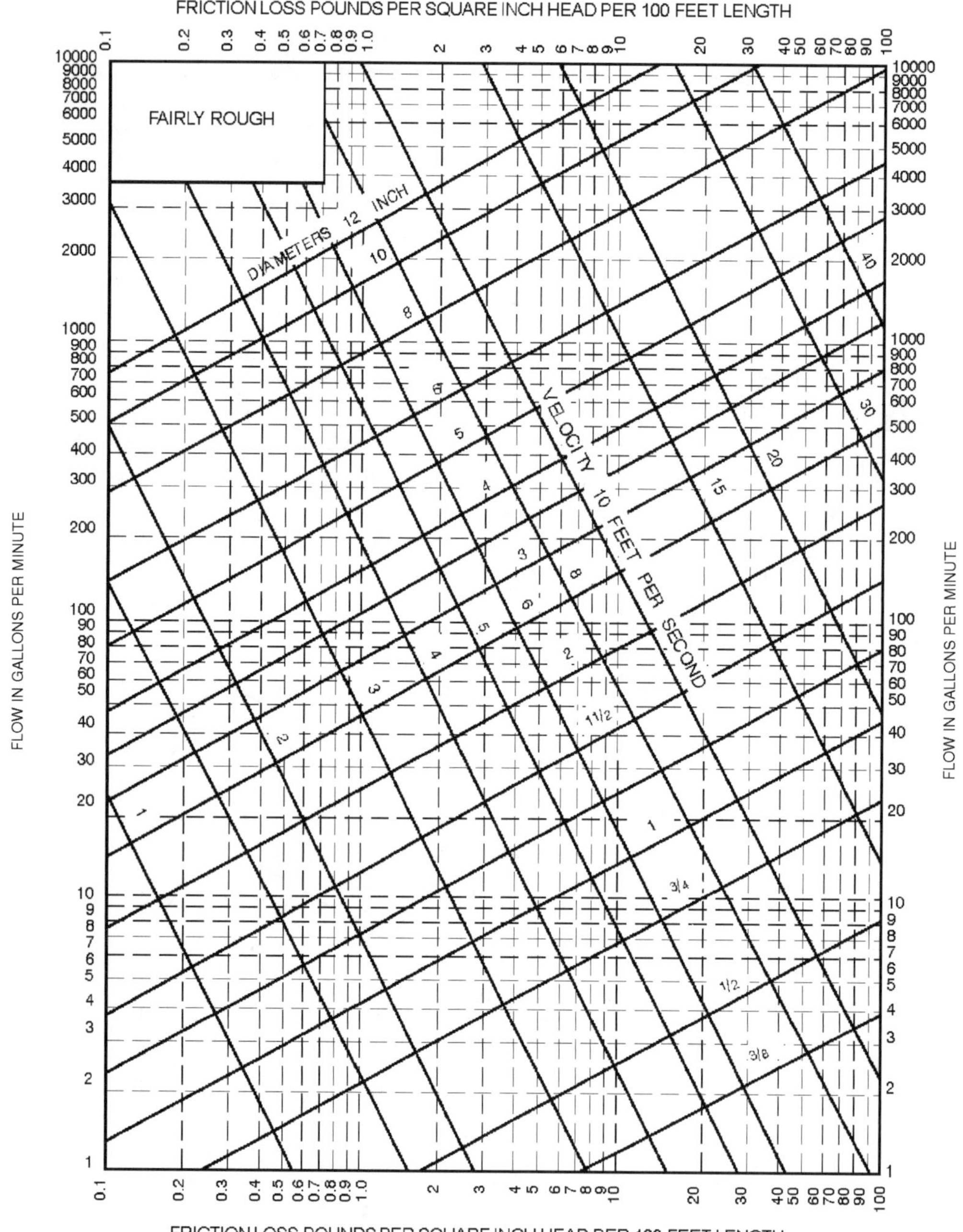

FIGURE E103.3(6)
FRICTION LOSS IN FAIRLY ROUGH PIPE[a]

For SI: 1 inch = 25.4 mm, 1 foot = 304.8 mm, 1 gpm = 3.785 L/m, 1 psi = 6.895 kPa,
1 foot per second = 0.305 m/s.

a. This chart applies to fairly rough pipe and to actual diameters which in general will be less than the actual diameters of the new pipe of the same kind.

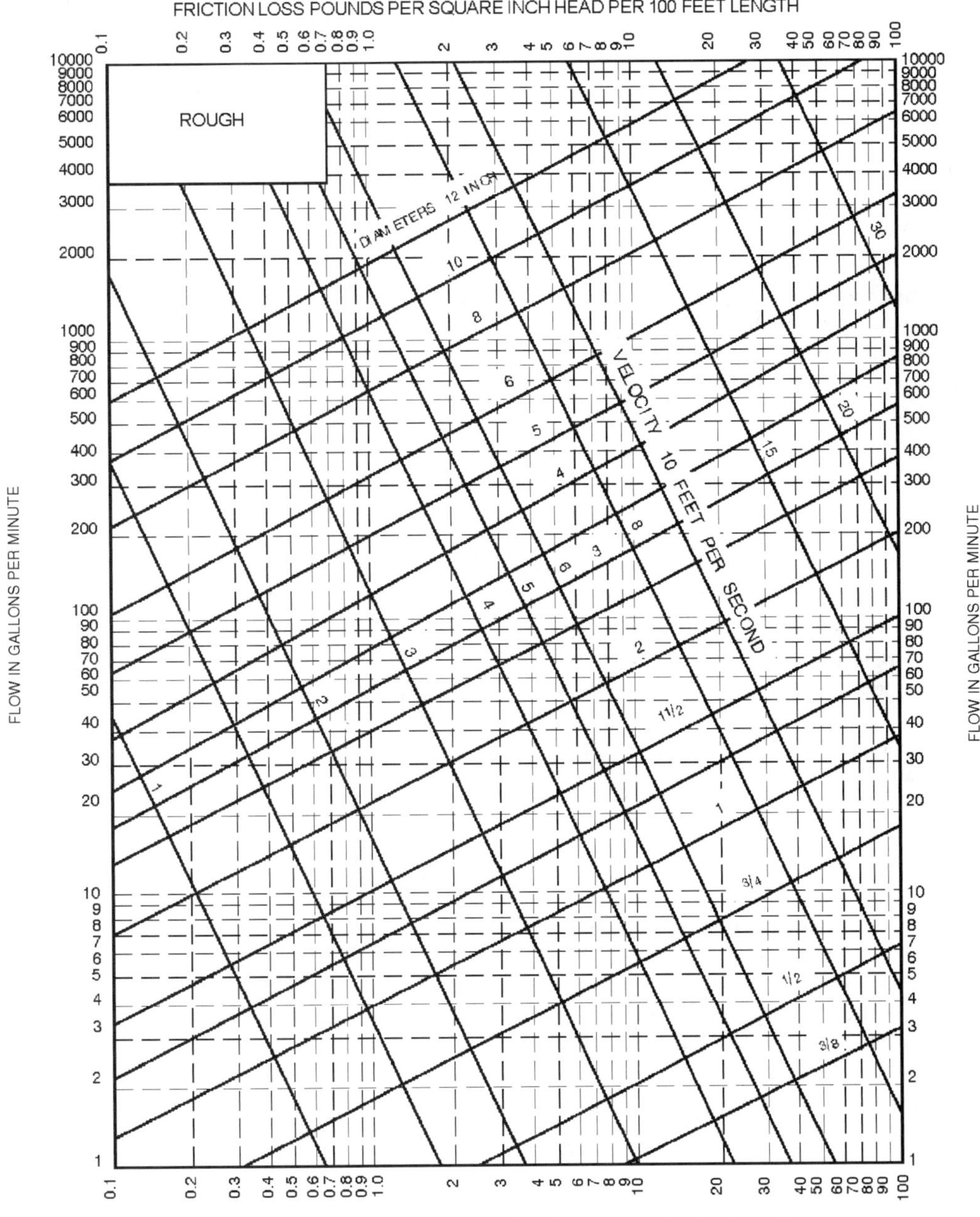

FIGURE E103.3(7)
FRICTION LOSS IN FAIRLY ROUGH PIPE[a]

For SI: 1 inch = 25.4 mm, 1 foot = 304.8 mm, 1 gpm = 3.785 L/m, 1 psi = 6.895 kPa,
1 foot per second = 0.305 m/s.

a. This chart applies to very rough pipe and existing pipe and to their actual diameters.

SECTION E201
SELECTION OF PIPE SIZE

E201.1 Size of water-service mains, branch mains and risers. The minimum size water service pipe shall be $^3/_4$ inch (19.1 mm). The size of water service mains, *branch* mains and risers shall be determined according to water supply demand [gpm (L/m)], available water pressure [psi (kPa)] and friction loss due to the water meter and *developed length* of pipe [feet (m)], including equivalent length of fittings. The size of each water distribution system shall be determined according to the procedure outlined in this section or by other design methods conforming to acceptable engineering practice and *approved* by the code official:

1. Supply load in the building water-distribution system shall be determined by total load on the pipe being sized, in terms of water-supply fixture units (w.s.f.u.), as shown in Table E103.3(2). For fixtures not listed, choose a w.s.f.u. value of a fixture with similar flow characteristics.
2. Obtain the minimum daily static service pressure [psi (kPa)] available (as determined by the local water authority) at the water meter or other source of supply at the installation location. Adjust this minimum daily static pressure [psi (kPa)] for the following conditions:
   2.1. Determine the difference in elevation between the source of supply and the highest water supply outlet. Where the highest water supply outlet is located above the source of supply, deduct 0.5 psi (3.4 kPa) for each foot (0.3 m) of difference in elevation. Where the highest water supply outlet is located below the source of supply, add 0.5 psi (3.4 kPa) for each foot (0.3 m) of difference in elevation.

   2.2. Where a water pressure reducing valve is installed in the water distribution system, the minimum daily static water pressure available is 80 percent of the minimum daily static water pressure at the source of supply or the set pressure downstream of the pressure reducing valve, whichever is smaller.

   2.3. Deduct all pressure losses due to special equipment such as a backflow preventer, water filter and water softener. Pressure loss data for each piece of equipment shall be obtained through the manufacturer of such devices.

   2.4. Deduct the pressure in excess of 8 psi (55 kPa) due to installation of the special plumbing fixture, such as temperature controlled shower and flushometer tank water closet.

   Using the resulting minimum available pressure, find the corresponding pressure range in Table E201.1.
3. The maximum *developed length* for water piping is the actual length of pipe between the source of supply and the most remote fixture, including either hot (through the water heater) or cold water branches multiplied by a factor of 1.2 to compensate for pressure loss through fittings.

   Select the appropriate column in Table E201.1 equal to or greater than the calculated maximum *developed length*.
4. To determine the size of water service pipe, meter and main distribution pipe to the building using the appropriate table, follow down the selected "maximum *developed length*" column to a fixture unit equal to, or greater than the total installation demand calculated by using the "combined" water supply fixture unit column of Table E103.3(2). Read the water service pipe and meter sizes in the first left-hand column and the main distribution pipe to the building in the second left-hand column on the same row.
5. To determine the size of each water distribution pipe, start at the most remote outlet on each *branch* (either hot or cold *branch*) and, working back toward the main distribution pipe to the building, add up the water supply fixture unit demand passing through each segment of the distribution system using the related hot or cold column of Table E103.3(2). Knowing demand, the size of each segment shall be read from the second left-hand column of the same table and maximum *developed length* column selected in Steps 1 and 2, under the same or next smaller size meter row. In no case does the size of any *branch* or main need to be larger that the size of the main distribution pipe to the building established in Step 4.

SECTION E202
DETERMINATION OF PIPE VOLUMES

E202.1 Determining volume of piping systems. Where required for engineering design purposes, Table E202.1 shall be used to determine the approximate internal volume of water distribution piping.

TABLE E201.1
MINIMUM SIZE OF WATER METERS, MAINS AND DISTRIBUTION PIPING BASED ON WATER SUPPLY FIXTURE UNIT VALUES (w.s.f.u.)

METER AND SERVICE PIPE (inches)	DISTRIBUTION PIPE (inches)	MAXIMUM DEVELOPMENT LENGTH (feet)									
Pressure Range 30 to 39 psi		40	60	80	100	150	200	250	300	400	500
3/4	1/2[a]	2.5	2	1.5	1.5	1	1	0.5	0.5	0	0
3/4	3/4	9.5	7.5	6	5.5	4	3.5	3	2.5	2	1.5
3/4	1	32	25	20	16.5	11	9	7.8	6.5	5.5	4.5
1	1	32	32	27	21	13.5	10	8	7	5.5	5
3/4	1 1/4	32	32	32	32	30	24	20	17	13	10.5
1	1 1/4	80	80	70	61	45	34	27	22	16	12
1 1/2	1 1/4	80	80	80	75	54	40	31	25	17.5	13
1	1 1/2	87	87	87	87	84	73	64	56	45	36
1 1/2	1 1/2	151	151	151	151	117	92	79	69	54	43
2	1 1/2	151	151	151	151	128	99	83	72	56	45
1	2	87	87	87	87	87	87	87	87	87	86
1 1/2	2	275	275	275	275	258	223	196	174	144	122
2	2	365	365	365	365	318	266	229	201	160	134
2	2 1/2	533	533	533	533	533	495	448	409	353	311

METER AND SERVICE PIPE (inches)	DISTRIBUTION PIPE (inches)	MAXIMUM DEVELOPMENT LENGTH (feet)									
Pressure Range 40 to 49 psi		40	60	80	100	150	200	250	300	400	500
3/4	1/2[a]	3	2.5	2	1.5	1.5	1	1	0.5	0.5	0.5
3/4	3/4	9.5	9.5	8.5	7	5.5	4.5	3.5	3	2.5	2
3/4	1	32	32	32	26	18	13.5	10.5	9	7.5	6
1	1	32	32	32	32	21	15	11.5	9.5	7.5	6.5
3/4	1 1/4	32	32	32	32	32	32	32	27	21	16.5
1	1 1/4	80	80	80	80	65	52	42	35	26	20
1 1/2	1 1/4	80	80	80	80	75	59	48	39	28	21
1	1 1/2	87	87	87	87	87	87	87	78	65	55
1 1/2	1 1/2	151	151	151	151	151	130	109	93	75	63
2	1 1/2	151	151	151	151	151	139	115	98	77	64
1	2	87	87	87	87	87	87	87	87	87	87
1 1/2	2	275	275	275	275	275	275	264	238	198	169
2	2	365	365	365	365	365	349	304	270	220	185
2	2 1/2	533	533	533	533	533	533	533	528	456	403

(continued)

TABLE E201.1—continued
MINIMUM SIZE OF WATER METERS, MAINS AND DISTRIBUTION PIPING BASED ON WATER SUPPLY FIXTURE UNIT VALUES (w.s.f.u.)

METER AND SERVICE PIPE (inches)	DISTRIBUTION PIPE (inches)	MAXIMUM DEVELOPMENT LENGTH (feet)									
Pressure Range 50 to 60 psi		40	60	80	100	150	200	250	300	400	500
$^3/_4$	$^1/_2$[a]	3	3	2.5	2	1.5	1	1	1	0.5	0.5
$^3/_4$	$^3/_4$	9.5	9.5	9.5	8.5	6.5	5	4.5	4	3	2.5
$^3/_4$	1	32	32	32	32	25	18.5	14.5	12	9.5	8
1	1	32	32	32	32	30	22	16.5	13	10	8
$^3/_4$	$1^1/_4$	32	32	32	32	32	32	32	32	29	24
1	$1^1/_4$	80	80	80	80	80	68	57	48	35	28
$1^1/_2$	$1^1/_4$	80	80	80	80	80	75	63	53	39	29
1	$1^1/_2$	87	87	87	87	87	87	87	87	82	70
$1^1/_2$	$1^1/_2$	151	151	151	151	151	151	139	120	94	79
2	$1^1/_2$	151	151	151	151	151	151	146	126	97	81
1	2	87	87	87	87	87	87	87	87	87	87
$1^1/_2$	2	275	275	275	275	275	275	275	275	247	213
2	2	365	365	365	365	365	365	365	329	272	232
2	$2^1/_2$	533	533	533	533	533	533	533	533	533	486

METER AND SERVICE PIPE (inches)	DISTRIBUTION PIPE (inches)	MAXIMUM DEVELOPMENT LENGTH (feet)									
Pressure Range Over 60		40	60	80	100	150	200	250	300	400	500
$^3/_4$	$^1/_2$[a]	3	3	3	2.5	2	1.5	1.5	1	1	0.5
$^3/_4$	$^3/_4$	9.5	9.5	9.5	9.5	7.5	6	5	4.5	3.5	3
$^3/_4$	1	32	32	32	32	32	24	19.5	15.5	11.5	9.5
1	1	32	32	32	32	32	28	28	17	12	9.5
$^3/_4$	$1^1/_4$	32	32	32	32	32	32	32	32	32	30
1	$1^1/_4$	80	80	80	80	80	80	69	60	46	36
$1^1/_2$	$1^1/_4$	80	80	80	80	80	80	76	65	50	38
1	$1^1/_2$	87	87	87	87	87	87	87	87	87	84
$1^1/_2$	$1^1/_2$	151	151	151	151	151	151	151	144	114	94
2	$1^1/_2$	151	151	151	151	151	151	151	151	118	97
1	2	87	87	87	87	87	87	87	87	87	87
$1^1/_2$	2	275	275	275	275	275	275	275	275	275	252
2	2	365	368	368	368	368	368	368	368	318	273
2	$2^1/_2$	533	533	533	533	533	533	533	533	533	533

For SI: 1 inch = 25.4, 1 foot = 304.8 mm.
a. Minimum size for building supply is $^3/_4$-inch pipe.

TABLE E202.1
INTERNAL VOLUME OF VARIOUS WATER DISTRIBUTION TUBING

	OUNCES OF WATER PER FOOT OF TUBE						
Size Nominal, Inch	Copper Type M	Copper Type L	Copper Type K	CPVC CTS SDR 11	CPVC SCH 40	Composite ASTM F 1281	PEX CTS SDR 9
3/8	1.06	0.97	0.84	N/A	1.17	0.63	0.64
1/2	1.69	1.55	1.45	1.25	1.89	1.31	1.18
3/4	3.43	3.22	2.90	2.67	3.38	3.39	2.35
1	5.81	5.49	5.17	4.43	5.53	5.56	3.91
1 1/4	8.70	8.36	8.09	6.61	9.66	8.49	5.81
1 1/2	12.18	11.83	11.45	9.22	13.20	13.88	8.09
2	21.08	20.58	20.04	15.79	21.88	21.48	13.86

For SI: 1 ounce = 0.030 liter.

APPENDIX F
STRUCTURAL SAFETY

The provisions contained in this appendix are adopted as part of this code.

SECTION F101 CUTTING, NOTCHING AND BORING IN WOOD MEMBERS

[B] F101.1 Joist notching. Notches on the ends of joists shall not exceed one-fourth the joist depth. Holes bored in joists shall not be within 2 inches (51 mm) of the top or bottom of the joist, and the diameter of any such hole shall not exceed one-third the depth of the joist. Notches in the top or bottom of joists shall not exceed one sixth the depth and shall not be located in the middle third of the span.

[B] F101.2 Stud cutting and notching. In exterior walls and bearing partitions, any wood stud is permitted to be cut or notched to a depth not exceeding 25 percent of its width. Cutting or notching of studs to a depth not greater than 40 percent of the width of the stud is permitted in nonbearing partitions supporting no loads other than the weight of the partition.

[B] F101.3 Bored holes. A hole not greater in diameter than 40 percent of the stud width is permitted to be bored in any wood stud. Bored holes not greater than 60 percent of the width of the stud are permitted in nonbearing partitions or in any wall where each bored stud is doubled, provided not more than two such successive doubled studs are so bored. In no case shall the edge of the bored hole be nearer than 0.625 inch (15.9 mm) to the edge of the stud. Bored holes shall not be located at the same section of stud as a cut or notch.

[B] F101.4 Cutting, notching and boring holes in structural steel framing. The cutting, notching and boring of holes in structural steel framing members shall be as prescribed by the registered design professional.

[B] F101.5 Cutting, notching and boring holes in cold-formed steel framing. Flanges and lips of load-bearing cold-formed steel framing members shall not be cut or notched. Holes in webs of load-bearing cold-formed steel framing members shall be permitted along the centerline of the web of the framing member and shall not exceed the dimensional limitations, penetration spacing or minimum hole edge distance as prescribed by the registered design professional. Cutting, notching and boring holes of steel floor/roof decking shall be as prescribed by the registered design professional.

[B] F101.6 Cutting, notching and boring holes in nonstructural cold-formed steel wall framing. Flanges and lips of nonstructural cold-formed steel wall studs shall not be cut or notched. Holes in webs of nonstructural cold-formed steel wall studs shall be permitted along the centerline of the web of the framing member, shall not exceed $1^1/_2$ inches (38 mm) in width or 4 inches (102 mm) in length, and the holes shall not be spaced less than 24 inches (610 mm) center to center from another hole or less than 10 inches (254 mm) from the bearing end.

APPENDIX G

VACUUM DRAINAGE SYSTEM

The provisions contained in this appendix are adopted as part of this code.

SECTION G101
VACUUM DRAINAGE SYSTEM

G101.1 Scope. This appendix provides general guidelines for the requirements for vacuum drainage systems.

G101.2 General requirements.

G101.2.1 System design. Vacuum drainage systems shall be designed in accordance with manufacturer's recommendations. The system layout, including piping layout, tank assemblies, vacuum pump assembly and other components/designs necessary for proper function of the system shall be per manufacturer's recommendations. Plans, specifications and other data for such systems shall be submitted to the local administrative authority for review and approval prior to installation.

G101.2.2 Fixtures. Gravity-type fixtures used in vacuum drainage systems shall comply with Chapter 4 of this code.

G101.2.3 Drainage fixture units. Fixture units for gravity drainage systems which discharge into or receive discharge from vacuum drainage systems shall be based on values in Chapter 7 of this code.

G101.2.4 Water supply fixture units. Water supply fixture units shall be based on values in Chapter 6 of this code with the addition that the fixture unit of a vacuum-type water closet shall be "1."

G101.2.5 Traps and cleanouts. Gravity-type fixtures shall be provided with traps and cleanouts in accordance with Chapters 7 and 10 of this code.

G101.2.6 Materials. Vacuum drainage pipe, fitting and valve materials shall be as recommended by the vacuum drainage system manufacturer and as permitted by this code.

G101.3 Testing and demonstrations. After completion of the entire system installation, the system shall be subjected to a vacuum test of 19 inches (483 mm) of mercury and shall be operated to function as required by the administrative authority and the manufacturer. Recorded proof of all tests shall be submitted to the administrative authority.

G101.4 Written instructions. Written instructions for the operations, maintenance, safety and emergency procedures shall be provided by the building owner as verified by the administrative authority.

APPENDIX H

RODENTPROOFING

The provisions contained in this appendix are adopted as part of this code.

H304.1 General. Buildings or structures and the walls enclosing habitable or occupiable rooms and spaces in which persons live, sleep or work, or in which feed, food or foodstuffs are stored, prepared, processed, served or sold, shall be constructed in accordance with the provisions of this section.

H304.2 Foundation wall ventilation openings. Foundation wall ventilator openings shall be covered for their height and width with perforated sheet metal plates no less than 0.070-inch (1.8 mm) thick, expanded sheet metal plates not less than 0.047-inch (1.2 mm) thick, cast iron grills or grating, extruded aluminum load-bearing vents or with hardware cloth of 0.035-inch (0.89 mm) wire or heavier. The openings therein shall not exceed $^{1}/_{4}$ inch (6.4 mm).

H304.3 Foundation and exterior wall sealing. Annular spaces around pipes, electric cables, conduits, or other openings in the walls shall be protected against the passage of rodents by closing such openings with cement mortar, concrete masonry, silicone caulking or noncorrosive metal.

Part VIII — Electrical

CHAPTERS 34 THROUGH 43

Deleted

Refer to the *North Carolina Electrical Code* for requirements.

Part VIII – Electrical (Abridged for Residential)
CHAPTERS 34 THROUGH 43 DELETED

Note: *The Rules Review Commission received 10-written requests for Legislative review of this rule (2011 NC Electrical Code). The rule becomes* ***effective on the thirty-first legislative day of the 2012 session*** *of the General Assembly unless a bill that specifically disapproves this rule is introduced. The rule becomes* ***effective on day of adjournment of the 2012 session*** *of the General Assembly if a bill is introduced and not ratified.*

The following text is extracted from the 2011 *North Carolina Electrical Code* and has been modified where necessary to conform to the scope of application of the 2012 *North Carolina Residential Code for One- and Two-Family Dwellings.* The article numbers appearing in Part VIII are the article numbers of the corresponding text in the *North Carolina Electrical Code.* Where differences occur between the provisions of this abridged text and the *North Carolina Electrical Code*, the provisions of the *North Carolina Electrical Code* shall apply. Requirements not specifically covered by this text shall conform to the *North Carolina Electrical Code.*

Part VIII
North Carolina State Building Code:
Electrical Code

Abridged for Residential Code

(2011 NEC® with North Carolina Amendments)

Abridged Residential Code Edition

2011

TABLE OF CONTENTS

Amend Table of Contents

CHAPTER 4 EQUIPMENT FOR GENERAL USE

Article

CHAPTER 5 SPECIAL OCCUPANCIES

Article

CHAPTER 6 SPECIAL EQUIPMENT

Article

CHAPTER 7 SPECIAL CONDITIONS

Article

CHAPTER 8 COMMUNICATIONS SYSTEMS

Article

Article 10 - ADMINISTRATIVE SECTION

10.1 TITLE

These Administrative Regulations along with the requirements included in the 2011 Edition of the National Electrical Code (NFiPA-70 - 2011) as approved by the North Carolina Building Code Council on June 14, 2011, to be effective September 1, 2011, with the following amendments:

(1) 210.8(a)(3) (Exception No. 2)
(2) 250.50
(3) 334.15 Exposed Work

shall be known as the North Carolina Electrical Code, and may be cited as such or as the State Electrical Code; and will be referred to herein as "the code" or "this code".

10.2 SCOPE

Article 80 Administration and Enforcement of the code is hereby not adopted and does not apply for this code. For Scope and Exceptions to Applicability of Technical Codes, refer to the North Carolina Administrative Code and Policies.

10.3 PURPOSE

The purpose of the code is to provide minimum standards, provisions and requirements of safe and stable design, methods of construction and uses of materials in buildings or structures hereafter erected, constructed, enlarged, altered, repaired, moved, converted to other uses of demolished and to regulate the electrical systems, equipment, maintenance, use and occupancy of all buildings or structures. All regulations contained in this code have a reasonable and substantial connection with the public health, safety, morals, or general welfare, and their provisions shall be construed liberally to those ends.

10.4 ADMINISTRATION

For administrative regulations pertaining to inspection (rough-ins and finals), permits and Certificates of Electrical Compliance, see local ordinances and the North Carolina Administrative Code and Policies. When the provisions of other codes are determined to be contrary to the requirements of this code, this code shall prevail.

10.5 DEFINITION

Unless the context indicates otherwise, whenever the word "building" is used in this chapter, it shall be deemed to include the word "structure" and all installations such as plumbing systems, heating systems, cooling systems, electrical systems, elevators and other installations which are parts of, or permanently affixed to, the building or structure.

10.6 APPLICATION OF CODE TO EXISTING BUILDINGS

For requirements of existing structures, refer to the North Carolina Administrative Code and Policies.

10.7 SERVICE UTILITIES

10.7.1 Connection of Service Utilities. No person shall make connections from a utility, source of energy, fuel or power to any building or system which is regulated by the technical codes until approved by the Inspection Department and a Certificate of Compliance is issued (General Statute 143-143.2).

10.7.2 Authority to disconnect Service Utilities. The Inspection Department shall have the authority to require disconnecting a utility service to the building, structure or system regulated by the technical codes, in case of emergency or where necessary to eliminate an imminent hazard to life or property. The Inspection Department shall have the authority to disconnect a utility service when a building has been occupied prior to Certificate of Compliance, or entry into the building for purposes of making inspections cannot be readily granted. The Inspection Department shall notify the serving utility, and whenever possible the owner or occupant of the building, structure or service system, of the decision to disconnect prior to taking such action. If not notified prior to disconnecting, the owner or occupant shall be notified in writing within eight (8) working hours (General Statutes 143-143.2, 153A-365, 153A-366, 160A-425 and 160A-426).

10.8 TEMPORARY POWER

10.8.1 Scope. The provisions of this section apply to the utilization of portions of the wiring system within a building to facilitate construction.

10.8.2 Provisions for Temporary Power. The Code enforcement official shall give permission and issue a permit to energize the electrical service when the provisions of 10.8 and the following requirements have been met:

1) The service wiring and equipment, including the meter socket enclosure, shall be installed, the service wiring terminated, and the service equipment covers installed.

2) The portions of the electrical system that are to be energized shall be complete and physically protected.

3) The grounding electrode system shall be complete.

4) The grounding and the grounded conductors shall be terminated in the service equipment.

5) At least one receptacle outlet with ground fault circuit interrupter protection for personnel shall be installed with the circuit wiring terminated.

6) The applicable requirements of the North Carolina Electrical Code apply.

10.8.3 Uses Prohibited. In no case shall any portion of the permanent wiring be energized until the portions have been inspected and approved by an electrical Code Enforcement Official. Failure to comply with this section may result in disconnection of power or revocation of permit.

10.8.4 Application for Temporary Power. Application for temporary power shall be made by and in the name of the applicant. The application shall explicitly state the portions of the energized electrical system, mechanical system, or plumbing system for which application is made, its intended use and duration.

10.8.5 Security and Notification. The applicant shall maintain the energized electrical system or that portion of the building containing the energized electrical system in a secured and locked manner or under constant supervision to exclude unauthorized personnel. The applicant shall alert personnel working in the vicinity of the energized electrical system to its presence.

10.9 REQUIREMENTS OF OTHER STATE AGENCIES, OCCUPATIONAL LICENSING BOARDS, OR COMMISSIONS. The North Carolina State Building Codes do not include all additional requirements for buildings and structures that may be imposed by other State agencies, occupational licensing boards, and commissions. It shall be the responsibility of a permit holder, design professional, contractor, or occupational license holder to determine whether any additional requirements exist.

AMENDMENT 210.8(A)(3)

Amend NEC 2011:

(3) Outdoors

Exception No. 1 to (3): Receptacles that are not readily accessible and are supplied by a branch circuit dedicated to electric snow-melting, deicing, or pipeline and vessel heating equipment shall be permitted to be installed in accordance with Article 426.28 or 427.22, as applicable.

Exception No. 2 to (3): A single outlet receptacle supplied by dedicated branch circuit which is located and identified for specific use by a sewage lift pump.

AMENDMENT 250.50

Amend NEC 2011:

250.50 Grounding Electrode System. All grounding electrodes as described in 250.52(A)(1) through (A)(7) that are available at each building or structure served shall be bonded together to form the grounding electrode system. Where none of these grounding electrodes exist, one or more of the grounding electrodes specified in 250.52(A)(4) through (A)(8) shall be installed and used.

AMENDMENT 334.15(C)

Amend NEC 2011:

(C) In Unfinished Basements: Where cable is run at angles with joist in unfinished basements it shall be permissible to secure cables not smaller than two 6 AWG or three 8 AWG conductors directly to the lower edges of the joists. Smaller cables shall be run either through bored holes in joists or on running boards. Nonmetallic-sheathed cable installed on the wall of an unfinished basement shall be permitted to be installed in a listed conduit or tubing or shall be protected in accordance with 300.4. Conduit or tubing shall be provided with an insulating bushing or adapter at the point the cable enters the raceway. The sheath of the nonmetallic-sheathed cable sheath shall extend through the conduit or tubing and into the outlet or device box not less than 6 mm ($^1/_4$ in.). The cable shall be secured within 300 mm (12 in.) of the point where the cable enters the conduit or tubing. Metal conduit, tubing, and metal outlet boxes shall be connected to an equipment grounding conductor complying with the provisions of 250.86 and 250.148.

Part IX—Referenced Standards

CHAPTER 44
REFERENCED STANDARDS

This chapter lists the standards that are referenced in various sections of this document. The standards are listed herein by the promulgating agency of the standard, the standard identification, the effective date and title, and the section or sections of this document that reference the standard. The application of the referenced standards shall be as specified in Section R102.4.

AAMA

American Architectural Manufacturers Association
1827 Walden Office Square, Suite 550
Schaumburg, IL 60173

Standard reference number	Title	Referenced in code section number
AAMA/WDMA/CSA 101/I.S.2/A440—08	North American Fenestration Standards/Specifications for Windows, Doors and Skylights	N1102.4.4, R308.6.9, R613.6
450—06	Voluntary Performance Rating Method for Mulled Fenestration Assemblies	R612.11.1
506—06	Voluntary Specifications for Hurricane Impact and Cycle Testing of Fenestration Products	R612.9.1
711—07	Voluntary Specification for Self Adhering Flashing Used for Installation of Exterior Wall Fenestration Products	R703.8

ACI

American Concrete Institute
38800 Country Club Drive
Farmington Hills, MI 48331

Standard reference number	Title	Referenced in code section number
318—08	Building Code Requirements for Structural Concrete	R301.2.2.2.4, R301.2.2.3.4, R402.2, R404.1.2, Table R404.1.2(5), Table R404.1.2(6), Table R404.1.2(7), Table R404.1.2(8), Table R404.1.2(9), R404.1.2.1, R404.1.2.3, R404.1.2.4, R404.1.4.2, R404.5.1, R611.1, R611.1.1, R611.1.2, R611.2, R611.5.1, R611.8.2, R611.9.2, R611.9.3
332—08	Code Requirements for Residential Concrete Construction	R402.2, R403.1, R404.1.2, R404.1.2.4, R404.1.4.2
530—08	Building Code Requirements for Masonry Structures	R404.1.1, R606.1, R606.1.1, R606.12.1, R606.12.2.3.1, R606.12.2.3.2, R606.12.3.1, Table R703.4
530.1—08	Specification for Masonry Structures	R404.1.1, R606.1, R606.1.1, R606.12.1, R606.12.2.3.1, R606.12.2.3.2, R606.12.3.1, Table R703.4

ACCA

Air Conditioning Contractors of America
2800 Shirlington Road, Suite 300
Arlington, VA 22206

Standard reference number	Title	Referenced in code section number
Manual D—95	Residential Duct Systems	M1601.1, M1602.2
Manual J—02	Residential Load Calculation—Eighth Edition	M1401.3
Manual S—04	Residential Equipment Selection	M1401.3

AFPA

American Forest and Paper Association
1111 19th Street, NW, Suite 800
Washington, DC 20036

Standard reference number	Title	Referenced in code section number
NDS—05	National Design Specification (NDS) for Wood Construction—with 2005 Supplement	R404.2.2, R502.2, Table R503.1, R602.3, Table R602.3.1 R611.9.2, R611.9.3, R802.2,
WFCM—01	Wood Frame Construction Manual for One- and Two-family Dwellings	R301.1.1, R301.2.1.1, R602.10.6.2, R611.9.2, R611.9.3, R611.10
AFPA—93	Span Tables for Joists and Rafters	R502.3, R802.4, R802.5
PWF—07	Permanent Wood Foundation Design Specification	R317.3.2, R401.1, R404.2.3

AISI

American Iron and Steel Institute
1140 Connecticut Ave, Suite 705
Washington, DC 20036

Standard reference number	Title	Referenced in code section number
AISI S100—07	North American Specification for the Design of Cold-formed Steel Structural Members	R505.1.3, R603.6, R611.9.2, R611.9.3, R804.3.7
AISI S230—07	Standard for Cold-formed Steel Framing-prescriptive Method for One- and Two-family Dwellings	R301.1.1, R301.2.1.1, R301.2.2.3.1, R301.2.2.3.5, R603.6, R611.9.2, R611.9.3, R611.10

AITC

American Institute of Timber Construction
7012 S. Revere Parkway, Suite 140
Centennial, CO 80112

Standard reference number	Title	Referenced in code section number
ANSI/AITC A 190.1—07	Structural Glued Laminated Timber	R502.1.5, R602.1.2, R802.1.4

ANSI

American National Standards Institute
25 West 43rd Street, Fourth Floor
New York, NY 10036

Standard reference number	Title	Referenced in code section number
A108.1A—99	Installation of Ceramic Tile in the Wet-set Method, with Portland Cement Mortar	R702.4.1
A108.1B—99	Installation of Ceramic Tile, Quarry Tile on a Cured Portland Cement Mortar Setting Bed with Dry-set or Latex-Portland Mortar	R702.4.1
A108.4—99	Installation of Ceramic Tile with Organic Adhesives or Water Cleanable Tile-setting Epoxy Adhesive	R702.4.1
A108.5—99	Installation of Ceramic Tile with Dry-set Portland Cement Mortar or Latex-Portland Cement Mortar	R702.4.1
A108.6—99	Installation of Ceramic Tile with Chemical-resistant, Water-cleanable Tile-setting and -grouting Epoxy	R702.4.1
A108.11—99	Interior Installation of Cementitious Backer Units	R702.4.1
A118.1—99	American National Standard Specifications for Dry-set Portland Cement Mortar	R702.4.1
A118.3—99	American National Standard Specifications for Chemical-resistant, Water-cleanable Tile-setting and Grouting Epoxy and Water-cleanable Tile-setting Epoxy Adhesive	R702.4.1
A118.10—99	Specification for Load Bearing, Bonded, Waterproof Membranes for Thin-set Ceramic Tile and Dimension Stone Installation	P2709.2
A136.1—99	American National Standard Specifications for Organic Adhesives for Installation of Ceramic Tile	R702.4.1
A137.1—88	American National Standard Specifications for Ceramic Tile	R702.4.1
A208.1—99	Particleboard	R503.3.1, R605.1
LC1—97	Interior Fuel Gas Piping Systems Using Corrugated Stainless Steel Tubing —with Addenda LC 1a-1999 and LC 1b-2001	G2414.5.3
LC4—07	Press-connect Copper and Copper Alloy Fittings for use in Fuel Gas Distribution Systems	G2414.10.2
Z21.1—03	Household Cooking Gas Appliances—with Addenda Z21.1a-2003 and Z21.1b-2003	G2447.1
Z21.5.1—02	Gas Clothes Dryers—Volume I—Type I Clothes Dryers—with Addenda Z21.5.1a-2003	G2438.1
Z21.8—94 (R2002)	Installation of Domestic Gas Conversion Burners	G2443.1

ANSI—continued

Z21.10.1—04	Gas Water Heaters—Volume I—Storage Water Heaters with Input Ratings of 75,000 Btu per hour or Less	G2448.1
Z21.10.3—01	Gas Water Heaters—Volume III—Storage Water Heaters with Input Ratings above 75,000 Btu per hour, Circulating and Instantaneous Water Heaters—with Addenda Z21.10.3a-2003 and Z21.10.3b-2004	G2448.1
Z21.11.2—02	Gas-fired Room Heaters—Volume II—Unvented Room Heaters—with Addenda Z21.11.2a-2003	G2445.1
Z21.13—04	Gas-fired Low-Pressure Steam and Hot Water Boilers	G2452.1
Z21.15—97 (R2003)	Manually Operated Gas Valves for Appliances, Appliance Connector Valves and Hose End Valves—with Addenda Z21.15a-2001 (R2003)	Table G2420.1.1
Z21.22—99 (R2003)	Relief Valves for Hot Water Supply Systems—with Addenda Z21.22a-2000 (R2003) and 21.22b-2001 (R2003)	P2803.2, P2803.7
Z21.24-97	Connectors for Gas Appliances	G2422.1
Z21.40.1—96 (R2002)	Gas-fired, Heat-activated Air Conditioning and Heat Pump Appliances—with Z21.40.1a-97 (R2002)	G2449.1
Z21.40.2—96 (R2002)	Gas-fired, Work-activated Air Conditioning and Heat Pump Appliances (Internal Combustion)—with Z21.40.2a-1997 (R2002)	G2449.1
Z21.42—93 (R2002)	Gas-fired Illuminating Appliances	G2450.1
Z21.47—03	Gas-fired Central Furnaces	G2442.1
Z21.50—03	Vented Gas Fireplaces—with Addenda Z21.50a-2003	G2434.1
Z21.56—01	Gas-fired Pool Heaters—with Addenda Z21.56a-2004 and Z21.56b—2004	G2441.1
Z21.58—95 (R2002)	Outdoor Cooking Gas Appliances—with Addenda Z21.58a-1998 (R2002) and Z21.58b-2002	G2447.1
Z21.60—03	Decorative Gas Appliances for Installation in Solid Fuel Burning Fireplaces—with Addenda Z21.60a-2003	G2432.1
Z21.75/CSA 6.27—01	Connectors for Outdoor Gas Appliances	G2422.1
Z21.80—03	Line Pressure Regulators	G2421.1
Z21.83—98	Fuel Cell Power Plants	M1903.1
Z21.84—02	Manually Listed, Natural Gas Decorative Gas Appliances for Installation in Solid Fuel-burning Fireplaces—with Addenda Z21.84a -2003	G2432.1, G2432.2
Z21.86—04	Gas-fired Vented Space Heating Appliances	G2436.1, G2437.1, G2446.1
Z21.88—02	Vented Gas Fireplace Heaters—with Addenda A21.88a-2003 and Z21.88b—2004	G2435.1
Z21.91—01	Ventless Firebox Enclosures for Gas-fired Unvented Decorative Room Heaters	G2445.7.1
Z83.6—90 (R1998)	Gas-fired Infrared Heaters	G2451.1
Z83.8—02	Gas-fired Unit Heaters and Gas-fired Duct Furnaces—with Addenda Z83.8a-2003	G2444.1
Z97.1—04	Safety Glazing Materials Used in Buildings—Safety Performance Specifications and Methods of Test	R308.1.1, R308.3.1
Z124.1—95	Plastic Bathtub Units	Table P2701.1
Z124.2—95	Plastic Shower Receptors and Shower Stalls	Table P2701.1
Z124.3—95	Plastic Lavatories	Table P2701.1, P2711.1, P2711.2
Z124.4—96	Plastic Water Closet Bowls and Tanks	Table P2701.1, P2712.1
Z124.6—97	Plastic Sinks	Table P2701.1

APA

APA–The Engineered Wood Association
7011 South 19th
Tacoma, WA 98466

Standard reference number	Title	Referenced in code section number
APA E30—03	Engineered Wood Construction Guide	Table R503.2.1.1(1), R503.2.2, R803.2.2, R803.2.3

APSP

The Association of Pool & Spa Professionals
2111 Eisenhower Avenue
Alexandria, VA 22314

Standard reference number	Title	Referenced in code section number
ANSI/APSP 7—06	Standard for Suction Entrapment Avoidance in Swimming Pools Wading Pools, Spas, Hot Tubs and Catch Basins	AG106.1
ANSI/NSPI 3—99	Standard for Permanently Installed Residential Spas	AG104.1
ANSI/NSPI 4—99	Standard for Above-ground/On-ground Residential Swimming Pools	AG103.2

APSP—continued

ANSI/NSPI-5—2003	Standard for Residential In-ground Swimming Pools	AG103.1
ANSI/NSPI 6—99	Standard for Residential Portable Spas	AG104.2

ASCE/SEI

American Society of Civil Engineers
Structural Engineering Institute
1801 Alexander Bell Drive
Reston, VA 20191

Standard reference number	Title	Referenced in code section number
5—08	Building Code Requirements for Masonry Structures	R404.1.1, R606.1, R606.1.1, R606.12.1, R606.12.2.3.1, R606.12.2.3.2, R606.12.3.1, Table R703.4
6—08	Specification for Masonry Structures	R404.1.1, R606.1, R606.1.1, R606.12.1, R606.12.2.3.1, R606.12.2.3.2, R606.12.3.1, Table R703.4
7—05	Minimum Design Loads for Buildings and Other Structures	R301.2.1.1, R301.2.1.2, R301.2.1.5, R301.2.1.5.1, R301.2.4.1, Table R611.6(1), Table R611.6(2), Table R611.6(3), Table R611.6(4), Table R611.7(1A), R611.9.2, R611.9.3, Table R802.11, AH107.4.3
24—05	Flood-resistant Design and Construction	R301.2.4, R301.2.4.1, R322.1, R322.1.1, R322.1.6, R322.1.9, R322.2.2, AG103.3
32—01	Design and Construction of Frost-protected Shallow Foundations	R403.1.4.1

ASHRAE

American Society of Heating, Refrigerating
and Air-Conditioning Engineers, Inc.
1791 Tullie Circle, NE
Atlanta, GA 30329-2305

Standard reference number	Title	Referenced in code section number
34—2004	Designation and Safety Classification of Refrigerants	M1411.1
ASHRAE—2005	ASHRAE Handbook of Fundamentals	N1102.1.3

ASME

American Society of Mechanical Engineers
Three Park Avenue
New York, NY 10016-5990

Standard reference number	Title	Referenced in code section number
A17.1/CSA B44—2007	Safety Code for Elevators and Escalators	R321.1
A18.1—2005	Safety Standard for Platforms and Stairway Chair Lifts	R321.2
A112.1.2—2004	Air Gaps in Plumbing Systems	Table P2902.3, P2902.3.1
A112.1.3—2000 (Reaffirmed 2005)	Air Gap Fittings for Use with Plumbing Fixtures, Appliances and Appurtenances	Table P2701.1, P2902.3.1
A112.3.1—2007	Stainless Steel Drainage Systems for Sanitary, DWV, Storm and Vacuum Applications Above and Below Ground	Table P3002.1(1), Table P3002.1(2), Table P3002.2, Table P3002.3, Table P3302.1
A112.3.4—2000 (R2004)	Macerating Toilet Systems and Related Components	Table P2701.1, P3007.5
A112.4.1—1993 (R2002)	Water Heater Relief Valve Drain Tubes	P2803.6.2
A112.4.3—1999 (R2004)	Plastic Fittings for Connecting Water Closets to the Sanitary Drainage System	P3003.19
A112.6.1M—1997 (R2002)	Floor Affixed Supports for Off-the-floor Plumbing Fixtures for Public Use	Table P2701.1, P2702.4
A112.6.2—2000 (R2004)	Framing-affixed Supports for Off-the-floor Water Closets with Concealed Tanks	Table P2701.1, P2702.4
A112.6.3—2001 (R2007)	Floor and Trench Drains	Table P2701.1
A112.14.1—03	Backwater Valves	P3008.2
A112.18.1—2005/ CSA B125.1-2005	Plumbing Supply Fittings	Table P2701.1, P2708.4, P2722.1, P2902.2
A112.18.2—2005/ CSA B125.2-2005	Plumbing Waste Fittings	Table P2701.1, P2702.2

ASME—continued

A112.18.3—2002	Performance Requirements for Backflow Protection Devices and Systems in Plumbing Fixture Fittings	P2708.4, P2722.3
A112.18.6—2003	Flexible Water Connectors	P2905.7
A112.19.1M—1994 (R2004)	Enameled Cast Iron Plumbing Fixtures—with 1998 and 2000 Supplements	Table P2701.1, P2711.1
A112.19.2—2003	Vitreous China Plumbing Fixtures—and Hydraulic Requirements for Water Closets and Urinals	Table P2701.1, P2705.1, P2711.1, P2712.1, P2712.2
A112.19.3M—2000 (R2007)	Stainless Steel Plumbing Fixtures (Designed for Residential Use)—with 2002 Supplement	Table P2701.1, P2705.1, P2711.1
A112.19.4M—1994 (R2004)	Porcelain Enameled Formed Steel Plumbing Fixtures—with 1998 and 2000 Supplements	Table P2701.1, P2711.1
A112.19.5—2005	Trim for Water-closet Bowls, Tanks and Urinals	Table P2701.1
A112.19.6—1995	Hydraulic Performance Requirements for Water Closets and Urinals	P2712.1, P2712.2
A112.19.7M—2006	Hydromassage Bathtub Appliances	Table P2701.1
A112.19.8M—1987 (R1996)	Suction Fittings for Use in Swimming Pools, Wading Pools, Spas, Hot Tubs and Whirlpool Bathtub Appliances	Table P2701.1
A112.19.9M—1991 (R2002)	Nonvitreous Ceramic Plumbing Fixtures—with 2002 Supplement	Table P2701.1, P27.11.1, P2712.1
A112.19.12—2006	Wall-mounted and Pedestal-mounted, Adjustable and Pivoting Lavatory and Sink Carrier Systems	Table P2701.1, P2711.4, P2714.2
A112.19.13—2001 (R2007)	Electrohydraulic Water Closets	P2712.9
A112.19.15—2005	Bathtub/Whirlpool Bathtubs with Pressure Sealed Doors	Table P2701.1, P2713.2
B1.20.1—1983 (R2006)	Pipe Threads, General Purpose (Inch)	G2414.9, P3003.3.3, P3003.5.3, P3003.10.4, P3003.12.1, P3003.14.3
B16.3—2006	Malleable-iron-threaded Fittings Classes 150 and 300	Table P2905.6
B16.4—2006	Gray-iron-threaded Fittings Classes 125 and 250	Table P2905.6, Table P3002.3
B16.9—2003	Factory-made Wrought Steel Buttwelding Fittings	Table P2905.6
B16.11—2005	Forged Fittings, Socket-welding and Threaded	Table P2905.6
B16.12—1998	Cast-iron-threaded Drainage Fittings	Table P2905.6, Table P3002.3 (R2006)
B16.15—2006	Cast-bronze-threaded Fittings	Table P2905.6, Table P3002.3
B16.18—2001 (R2005)	Cast Copper Alloy Solder Joint Pressure Fittings	Table P2905.6, Table P3002.3
B16.22—2001(R2005)	Wrought Copper and Copper Alloy Solder Joint Pressure Fittings	Table P2905.6, Table P3002.3
B16.23—2002 (R2006)	Cast Copper Alloy Solder Joint Drainage Fittings (DWV)	Table P2905.6, Table P3002.3
B16.26—2006	Cast Copper Alloy Fittings for Flared Copper Tubes	Table P2905.6, Table P3002.3
B16.28—1994	Wrought Steel Buttwelding Short Radius Elbows and Returns	Table P2905.6
B16.29—2001	Wrought Copper and Wrought Copper Alloy Solder Joint Drainage Fittings (DWV)	Table P2905.6, Table P3002.3
B16.33—2002 (R2006)	Manually Operated Metallic Gas Valves for Use in Gas Piping Systems up to 125 psig (Sizes $^1/_2$ through 2)	Table G2420.1.1
B16.44—02	Manually Operated Metallic Gas Valves For Use in Above-ground Piping Systems up to 5 psi	Table G2420.1.1
B36.10M—2004	Welded and Seamless Wrought-steel Pipe	G2414.4.2
BPVC—2004	ASME Boiler and Pressure Vessel Code	G2452.1, M2001.1.1
CSD-1—2004	Controls and Safety Devices for Automatically Fired Boilers	G2452.1, M2001.1.1

ASSE

American Society of Sanitary Engineering
901 Canterbury, Suite A
Westlake, OH 44145

Standard reference number	Title	Referenced in code section number
1001—02	Performance Requirements for Atmospheric-type Vacuum Breakers	Table P2902.3, P2902.3.2
1002—99	Performance Requirements for Antisiphon Fill Valves (Ballcocks) for Gravity Water Closet Flush Tank	Table P2701.1, Table P2902.3, P2902.4.1
1003—01	Performance Requirements for Water-pressure-reducing Valves	P2903.3.1
1006—89	Performance Requirements for Residential Use Dishwashers	Table P2701.1
1007—92	Performance Requirements for Home Laundry Equipment	Table P2701.1
1008—89	Performance Requirements for Household Food Waste Disposer Units	Table P2701.1
1010—04	Performance Requirements for Water Hammer Arresters	P2903.5

ASSE—continued

1011—04	Performance Requirements for Hose Connection Vacuum Breakers	Table P2902.3, P2902.3.2
1012—02	Performance Requirements for Backflow Preventers with Intermediate Atmospheric Vent	Table P2902.3, P2902.3.3, P2902.5.1, P2902.5.5
1013—05	Performance Requirements for Reduced Pressure Principle Backflow Preventers and Reduced Pressure Fire Protection Principle Backflow Preventers	Table P2902.3, P2902.3.5, P2902.5.1, P2902.5.5
1015—05	Performance Requirements For Double Check Backflow Prevention Assemblies and Double Check Fire Protection Backflow Prevention Assemblies	Table P2902.3, P2902.3.6
1016—96	Performance Requirements for Automatic Compensating Valves for Individual Showers and Tub/Shower Combinations	Table P2701.1, P2708.3, P2722.2
1017—03	Performance Requirements for Temperature Actuated Mixing Valves for Hot Water Distribution Systems	P2802.2
1019—04	Performance Requirements for Wall Hydrants, Freeze Resistant, Automatic Draining Types	Table P2701.1, P2902.3
1020—04	Performance Requirements for Pressure Vacuum Breaker Assembly	Table P2902.3, P2902.3.4
1023—79	Performance Requirements for Hot Water Dispensers Household Storage Type-electrical	Table P2701.1
1024—04	Performance Requirements for Dual Check Backflow Preventers	Table P2902.3
1025—78	Performance Requirements for Diverters for Plumbing Faucets with Hose Spray, Anti-siphon Type, Residential Applications	Table P2701.1
1035—02	Performance Requirements for Laboratory Faucet Backflow Preventers	Table P2902.3, P2902.3.2
1037—90	Performance Requirements for Pressurized Flushing Devices (Flushometer) for Plumbing Fixtures	Table P2701.1
1047—05	Performance Requirements for Reduced Pressure Detector Fire Protection Backflow Prevention Assemblies	Table P2902.3, P2902.3.5
1048—05	Performance Requirements for Double Check Detector Fire Protection Backflow Prevention Assemblies	Table P2902.3, P2902.3.6
1050—02	Performance Requirements for Stack Air Admittance Valves for Sanitary Drainage Systems	P3114.1
1051—02	Performance Requirements for Individual and Branch Type Air Admittance Valves for Plumbing Drainage Systems	P3114.1
1052—04	Performance Requirements for Hose Connection Backflow Preventers	Table P2701.1, Table P2902.3, P2902.3.2
1056—01	Performance Requirements for Spill Resistant Vacuum Breakers	Table P2902.3, P2902.3.4
1060—96	Performance Requirements for Outdoor Enclosures for Fluid Conveying Components	P2902.6.1
1061—06	Performance Requirements for Removable and Nonremovable Push Fit Fittings	Table P2905.6
1062—97	Performance Requirements for Temperature Actuated, Flow Reduction (TAFR) Valves for Individual Supply Fittings	Table P2701.1, P2724.1
1066—97	Performance Requirements for Individual Pressure Balancing In-line Valves for Individual Fixture Fittings	Table P2701.1, P2722.4
1070—04	Performance Requirements for Water Temperature Limiting Devices	P2713.3, P2721.2

ASTM

ASTM International
100 Barr Harbor Drive
West Conshohocken, PA 19428-2859

Standard reference number	Title	Referenced in code section number
A 36/A 36M—05	Specification for Carbon Structural Steel	R606.15, R611.5.2.2
A 53/A 53M—06a	Specification for Pipe, Steel, Black and Hot-dipped, Zinc-coated Welded and Seamless	G2414.4.2, Table M2101.1, Table P2905.4, Table P2905.5, Table P3002.1(1)
A 74—06	Specification for Cast Iron Soil Pipe and Fittings	Table P3002.1(1), Table P3002.1(2), Table P3002.2 Table P3002.3, P3005.2.9, Table P3302.1
A 82/A 82M—05a	Specification for Steel Wire, Plain, for Concrete Reinforcement	R606.15
A 106/A 106M—06a	Specification for Seamless Carbon Steel Pipe for High Temperature Service	G2414.4.2, Table M2101.1
A 153/A 153M—05	Specification for Zinc Coating (Hot Dip) on Iron and Steel Hardware	R317.3, Table R606.15.1
A 167—99(2004)	Specification for Stainless and Heat-resisting Chromium-nickel Steel Plate, Sheet and Strip	R606.15, Table R606.15.1
A 240/A 240M—07	Standard Specification for Chromium and Chromium-nickel Stainless Steel Plate, Sheet and Strip for Pressure Vessels and for General Applications	Table R905.10.3(1)
A 254—97(2002)	Specification for Copper Brazed Steel Tubing	G2414.5.1, Table M2101.1
A 307—04e01	Specification for Carbon Steel Bolts and Studs, 6000 psi Tensile Strength	R611.5.2.2
A 312/A 312M—06	Specification for Seamless and Welded Austenitic Stainless Steel Pipes	Table P2905.4, Table P2905.5, Table P2905.6, P2905.12.2

ASTM—continued

Standard	Title	Referenced in code section number
A 463/A 463M—05	Standard Specification for Steel Sheet, Aluminum-coated by the Hot-dip Process	Table R905.10.3(2)
A 510—06	Specification for General Requirements for Wire Rods and Coarse Round Wire, Carbon Steel	R606.15
A 539—99	Specification for Electric-resistance-welded Coiled Steel Tubing for Gas and Fuel Oil Lines	M2202.1
A 615/A 615M—04a	Specification for Deformed and Plain Billet-steel Bars for Concrete Reinforcement	R402.3.1, R404.1.2.3.7.1, R611.5.2.1
A 641/A 641M—03	Specification for Zinc-coated (Galvanized) Carbon Steel Wire	Table R606.15.1
A 653/A 653M—07	Specification for Steel Sheet, Zinc-coated (Galvanized) or Zinc-iron Alloy-coated (Galvanized) by the Hot-dip Process	M1601.1.1, R317.3.1, R505.2.1, R505.2.3, R603.2.1, R603.2.3, Table R606.15.1, R611.5.2.3, R804.2.1, R804.2.3, Table R905.10.3(1), Table R905.10.3(2)
A 706/A 706/M—05a	Specification for Low-alloy Steel Deformed and Plain Bars for Concrete Reinforcement	R402.3.1, R404.1.2.3.7.1, R611.5.2.1
A 755/A 755M—07	Specification for Steel Sheet, Metallic Coated by the Hot-dip Process and Prepainted by the Coil-coating Process for Exterior Exposed Building Products	Table R905.10.3(2)
A 778—01	Specification for Welded Unannealed Austenitic Stainless Steel Tubular Products	Table P2905.4, Table P2905.5, Table P2905.6
A 792/A 792M—06a	Specification for Steel Sheet, 55% Aluminum-zinc Alloy-coated by the Hot-dip Process	R505.2.1, R505.2.3, R603.2.1, R603.2.3, R611.5.2.3, R804.2.1, R804.2.3, Table 905.10.3 (2)
A 875/A 875M—06	Specification for Steel Sheet, Zinc-5%, Aluminum Alloy-coated by the Hot-dip Process	R611.5.3.2, Table R905.10.3 (2)
A 888—07a	Specification for Hubless Cast Iron Soil Pipe and Fittings for Sanitary and Storm Drain, Waste and Vent Piping Application	Table P3002.1(1), Table P3002.1(2), Table P3002.2, Table P3002.3, P3005.2.9, Table P3302.1
A 924/A 924M—07	Standard Specification for General Requirements for Steel Sheet, Metallic-coated by the Hot-Dip Process	Table R905.10.3(1)
A 951—06	Specification for Steel Wire Masonry Joint Reinforcement	R606.15
A 996/A 996M—06a	Specifications for Rail-steel and Axel-steel Deformed Bars for Concrete Reinforcement	R404.1.2.3.7, R404.1.2.3.7.1, R611.5.2.1, Table R611.5.4(2)
A 1003/A 1003M—05	Standard Specification for Steel Sheet, Carbon, Metallic and Nonmetallic-coated for Cold-formed Framing Members	R505.2.1, R505.2.3, R603.2.1, R603.2.3, R804.2.1, R804.2.3
B 32—04	Specification for Solder Metal	P3003.10.3, P3003.11.3
B 42—02e01	Specification for Seamless Copper Pipe, Standard Sizes	Table M2101.1, Table P2905.4, Table P2905.5, Table P3002.1(1)
B 43—98 (2004)	Specification for Seamless Red Brass Pipe, Standard Sizes	G2413.5.2, Table M2101.1, Table P2905.4, Table P3002.1(1)
B 75—02	Specification for Seamless Copper Tube	Table M2101.1, Table P2905.4, Table P2905.5, Table P3002.1(1), Table P3002.1(2), Table P3002.2
B 88—03	Specification for Seamless Copper Water Tube	G2414.5.2, Table M2101.1, Table, P2905.4, Table P2905.5, Table P3002.1(1), Table P3002.1(2), Table P3002.2
B 101—02	Specification for Lead-coated Copper Sheet and Strip for Building Construction	Table R905.2.8.2, Table R905.10.3(1)
B 135—02	Specification for Seamless Brass Tube	Table M2101.1
B 209—06	Specification for Aluminum and Aluminum-alloy Sheet and Plate	Table 905.10.3(1)
B 227—04	Specification for Hard-drawn Copper-clad Steel Wire	R606.15
B 251—02e01	Specification for General Requirements for Wrought Seamless Copper and Copper-alloy Tube	Table M2101.1, Table P2905.4, Table P2905.5 Table P3002.1(1), Table P3002.1(2), Table P3002.2
B 302—02	Specification for Threadless Copper Pipe, Standard Sizes	Table M2101.1, Table P2905.4, Table P2905.5,Table P3002.1(1)
B 306—02	Specification for Copper Drainage Tube (DWV)	Table M2101.1, Table P3002.1(1), Table P3002.1(2), Table P3002.2
B 370—03	Specification for Copper Sheet and Strip for Building Construction	Table P2701.1, Table R905.2.8.2, Table R905.10.3(1)
B 447—07	Specification for Welded Copper Tube	Table P2904.4, Table P2905.5
B 695—04	Standard Specification for Coatings of Zinc Mechanically Deposited on Iron and Steel	R317.3.1, R317.3.3
B 813—00e01	Specification for Liquid and Paste Fluxes for Soldering Applications of Copper and Copper Alloy Tube	Table M2101.1, P2905.14, P3003.10.3, P3003.11.3
B 828—02	Practice for Making Capillary Joints by Soldering of Copper and Copper Alloy Tube and Fittings	P2905.14, P3003.10.3, P3003.11.3
C 4—04e01	Specification for Clay Drain Tile and Perforated Clay Drain Tile	Table P3302.1
C 5—03	Specification for Quicklime for Structural Purposes	R702.2.1
C 14—07	Specification for Concrete Sewer, Storm Drain and Culvert Pipe	Table P3002.2

ASTM—continued

C 27—98 (2002)	Specification for Standard Classification of Fireclay and High-alumina Refractory Brick	R1001.5, R1001.8
C 28/C 28M—00(2005)	Specification for Gypsum Plasters	R702.2.1
C 33—03	Specification for Concrete Aggregates	R403.4.1
C 34—03	Specification for Structural Clay Load-bearing Wall Tile	Table R301.2(1)
C 35—01(2005)	Specification for Inorganic Aggregates for Use in Gypsum Plaster	R702.2.1
C 36/C 36M—03	Specification for Gypsum Wallboard	R702.3.1
C 37/C 37M—01	Specification for Gypsum Lath	R702.2.1, R702.2.2
C 55—06e01	Specification for Concrete Building Brick	R202, Table R301.2(1)
C 59/C 59M—00 (2006)	Specification for Gypsum Casting and Molding Plaster	R702.2
C 61/C 61M—00 (2006)	Specification for Gypsum Keene's Cement	R702.2.1
C 62—05	Specification for Building Brick (Solid Masonry Units Made from Clay or Shale)	R202, Table R301.2(1)
C 73—05	Specification for Calcium Silicate Face Brick (Sand Lime Brick)	R202, Table R301.2(1)
C 76—07	Specification for Reinforced Concrete Culvert, Storm Drain and Sewer Pipe	Table P3002.2
C 79—04a	Specification for Treated Core and Nontreated Core Gypsum Sheathing Board	R702.3.1
C 90—06b	Specification for Load-bearing Concrete Masonry Units	Table R301.2(1)
C 91—05	Specification for Masonry Cement	R702.2.2
C 94/C 94M—07	Specification for Ready-mixed Concrete	R404.1.2.3.2, R611.5.1.1
C 129—06	Specification for Nonload-bearing Concrete Masonry Units	Table R301.2(1)
C 143/C 143M—05a	Test Method for Slump or Hydraulic Cement Concrete	R404.1.2.3.4, R611.5.1.3, R611.6.1
C 145—85	Specification for Solid Load-bearing Concrete Masonry Units	R202, Table R301.2(1)
C 150—07	Specification for Portland Cement	R702.2.2
C 199—84 (2005)	Test Method for Pier Test for Refractory Mortar	R1001.5, R1001.8, R1003.12
C 203—05a	Standard Test Methods for Breaking Load and Flexural Properties of Block-type Thermal Insulation	Table R613.3.1
C 207—06	Specification for Hydrated Lime for Masonry Purposes	Table R607.1
C 208—95 (2001)	Specification for Cellulosic Fiber Insulating Board	Table R602.3(1)
C 216—07	Specification for Facing Brick (Solid Masonry Units Made from Clay or Shale)	R202, Table R301.2(1)
C 270—07	Specification for Mortar for Unit Masonry	R607.1, AE602
C 272—01	Standard Test Method for Water Absorption of Core Materials for Structural Sandwich Constructions	Table R613.3.1
C 273—00e1	Standard Test Method for Shear Properties of Sandwich Core Materials	Table R613.3.1
C 296—(2004)e01	Specification for Asbestos Cement Pressure Pipe	Table P2905.4
C 315—07	Specification for Clay Flue Liners and Chimney Pots	G2425.12, R1001.8, R1003.11.1, Table R1003.14(1)
C 406—06e01	Specifications for Roofing Slate	R905.6.4
C 411—05	Test Method for Hot-surface Performance of High-temperature Thermal Insulation	M1601.3
C 425—04	Specification for Compression Joints for Vitrified Clay Pipe and Fittings	Table P3002.2, P3003.15, P3003.18
C 428—97 (2006)	Specification for Asbestos-cement Nonpressure Sewer Pipe	Table P3002.2
C 443—05a	Specification for Joints for Concrete Pipe and Manholes, Using Rubber Gaskets	P3003.7, P3003.18
C 475/C 475—05	Specification for Joint Compound and Joint Tape for Finishing Gypsum Wallboard	R702.3.1
C 476—02	Specification for Grout for Masonry	R609.1.1
C 508—04	Specification for Asbestos-cement Underdrain Pipe	Table P3302.1
C 514—04	Specification for Nails for the Application of Gypsum Wallboard	R702.3.1
C 552—03	Standard Specification for Cellular Glass Thermal Insulation	Table R906.2
C 557—03e01	Specification for Adhesives for Fastening Gypsum Wallboard to Wood Framing	R702.3.1
C 564—03a	Specification for Rubber Gaskets for Cast Iron Soil Pipe and Fittings	P3003.6.2, P3003.6.3, P3003.18
C 578—07	Specification for Rigid, Cellular Polystyrene Thermal Insulation	R403.3, R613.3.1, R703.11.2.1, Table R906.2
C 587—04	Specification for Gypsum Veneer Plaster	R702.2.1
C 588/C 588M—01	Specification for Gypsum Base for Veneer Plasters	R702.2.1, R702.2.2
C 595—07	Specification for Blended Hydraulic Cements	R702.2.2
C 630/C 630M—03	Specification for Water-resistant Gypsum Backing Board	R702.3.1
C 631—95a (2004)	Specification for Bonding Compounds for Interior Gypsum Plastering	R702.2.1
C 645—07	Specification for Nonstructural Steel Framing Members	R702.3.3
C 652—05a	Specification for Hollow Brick (Hollow Masonry Units Made from Clay or Shale)	R202, Table R301.2(1)
C 685—01	Specification for Concrete Made by Volumetric Batching and Continuous Mixing	R404.1.2.3.2, R611.5.1.1
C 700—07	Specification for Vitrified Clay Pipe, Extra Strength, Standard Strength and Perforated	Table P3002.2, Table P3002.3, Table P3302.1
C 728—05	Standard Specification for Perlite Thermal Insulation Board	Table R906.2

ASTM—continued

C 836—06	Specification for High Solids Content, Cold Liquid-applied Elastomeric Waterproofing Membrane for Use with Separate Wearing Course. . . . R905.15.2
C 843—99 (2006)	Specification for Application of Gypsum Veneer Plaster R702.2.1
C 844—04	Specification for Application of Gypsum Base to Receive Gypsum Veneer Plaster R702.2.1
C 847—06	Specification for Metal Lath. . . . R702.2.1, R702.2.2
C 887—05	Specification for Packaged, Dry, Combined Materials for Surface Bonding Mortar R406.1
C 897—05	Specification for Aggregate for Job-mixed Portland Cement-based Plasters. . . . R702.2.2
C 920—05	Standard Specification for Elastomeric Joint Sealants R406.4.1
C 926—98a (2005)	Specification for Application of Portland Cement-based Plaster. . . . R702.2.2, R703.6, R703.6.2, R703.6.4
C 931/C 931M—04	Specification for Exterior Gypsum Soffit Board. . . . R702.3.1
C 933—05	Specification for Welded Wire Lath R702.2.1, R702.2.2
C 954—04	Specification for Steel Drill Screws for the Application of Gypsum Panel Products or Metal Plaster Bases to Steel Studs from 0.033 in. (0.84 mm) to 0.112 in. (2.84 mm) in Thickness R505.2.4, R603.2.4, R702.3.6, R804.2.4
C 955—06	Specification for Load-bearing (Transverse and Axial) Steel Studs, Runners (Tracks), and Bracing or Bridging for Screw Application of Gypsum Panel Products and Metal Plaster Bases. . . . R702.3.3
C 957—06	Specification for High-solids Content, Cold Liquid-applied Elastomeric Waterproofing Membrane for Use with Integral Wearing Surface R905.15.2
C 960—04	Specification for Predecorated Gypsum Board. . . . R702.3.1
C 1002—04	Specification for Steel Drill Screws for the Application of Gypsum Panel Products or Metal Plaster Bases R702.3.1, R702.3.6
C 1029—05a	Specification for Spray-applied Rigid Cellular Polyurethane Thermal Insulation. . . . R905.14.2
C 1032—06	Specification for Woven Wire Plaster Base R702.2.1, R702.2.2
C 1047—05	Specification for Accessories for Gypsum Wallboard and Gypsum Veneer Base R702.2.1, R702.2.2, R702.3.1
C 1063—06	Specification for Installation of Lathing and Furring to Receive Interior and Exterior Portland Cement-based Plaster. . . . R702.2.2, R703.6
C 1107—07	Standard Specification for Packaged Dry, Hydraulic-cement Grout (Nonshrink) R402.3.1
C 1116—06	Standard Specification for Fiber-reinforced Concrete and Shotcrete R402.3.1
C 1167—03	Specification for Clay Roof Tiles R905.3.4
C 1173—06	Specification for Flexible Transition Couplings for Underground Piping Systems. . . . P3003.3, P3003.7, P3003.8.1, P3003.14.1, P3003.15, P3003.17.2, P3003.18
C 1177/C 1177M—06	Specification for Glass Mat Gypsum Substrate for Use as Sheathing R702.3.1
C 1178/C 1178M—06	Specification for Glass Mat Water-resistant Gypsum Backing Panel R702.3.1, R702.3.8, R702.4.2
C 1186—07	Specification for Flat Nonasbestos Fiber Cement Sheets. . . . R703.10.1, R703.10.2
C 1261—07	Specification for Firebox Brick for Residential Fireplaces R1001.5, R1001.8
C 1277—06	Specification for Shielded Couplings Joining Hubless Cast Iron Soil Pipe and Fittings P3003.6.3
C 1278/C 1278M—06	Specification for Fiber-reinforced Gypsum Panels R702.3.1, R702.3.8, R702.4.2
C 1283—07	Practice for Installing Clay Flue Lining. . . . R1003.12
C 1288—99(2004)	Standard Specification for Discrete Nonasbestos Fiber-cement Interior Substrate Sheets. . . . R702.4.2
C 1289—07	Standard Specification for Faced Rigid Cellular Polyisocyanurate Thermal Insulation Board . . . . R703.11.2.1, Table R906.2
C 1325—04	Standard Specification for Nonasbestos Fiber-mat Reinforced Cement Interior Substrate Sheets. . . . R702.4.2
C 1328—05	Specification for Plastic (Stucco) Cement. . . . R702.2.2
C 1395/C 1395M—06a	Specification for Gypsum Ceiling Board R702.3.1
C 1396/C 1396M—06a	Specification for Gypsum Board . . . . Table R602.3(1), R702.3.1, R702.3.8
C 1440—03	Specification for Thermoplastic Elastomeric (TPE) Gasket Materials for Drain, Waste and Vent (DWV), Sewer, Sanitary and Storm Plumbing Systems P3003.18
C 1460—04	Specification for Shielded Transition Couplings for Use with Dissimilar DWV Pipe and Fittings Above Ground P3003.18
C 1461—06	Specification for Mechanical Couplings Using Thermoplastic Elastomeric (TPE) Gaskets for Joining Drain, Waste and Vent (DWV) Sewer, Sanitary and Storm Plumbing Systems for Above and Below Ground Use P3003.18
C 1492—03	Specification for Concrete Roof Tile. . . . R905.3.5
C 1513—04	Standard Specification for Steel Tapping Screws for Cold-formed Steel Framing Connections R505.2.4, R603.2.4, R702.3.6, R804.2.4
C 1658/C 1658M—06	Standard Specification for Glass Mat Gypsum Panels R702.3.1
D 41—05	Specification for Asphalt Primer Used in Roofing, Dampproofing and Waterproofing . . . . Table R905.9.2, Table R905.11.2
D 43—00(2006)	Specification for Coal Tar Primer Used in Roofing, Dampproofing and Waterproofing . . . . Table R905.9.2

ASTM—continued

D 225—04	Specification for Asphalt Shingles (Organic Felt) Surfaced with Mineral Granules	R905.2.4
D 226—06	Specification for Asphalt-saturated (Organic Felt) Used in Roofing and Waterproofing	R703.2, R905.2.3, R905.3.3, R905.4.3, R905.5.3, R905.6.3, R905.7.3, R905.8.3, R905.8.4, Table R905.9.2
D 227—03	Specification for Coal Tar Saturated (Organic Felt) Used in Roofing and Waterproofing	Table R905.9.2
D 312—00(2006)	Specification for Asphalt Used in Roofing	Table R905.9.2
D 422—63(2002)e01	Test Method for Particle-size Analysis of Soils	R403.1.8.1
D 449—03	Specification for Asphalt Used in Dampproofing and Waterproofing	R406.2
D 450—07	Specification for Coal-tar Pitch Used in Roofing, Dampproofing and Waterproofing	Table R905.9.2
D 1227—95(2007)	Specification for Emulsified Asphalt Used as a Protective Coating for Roofing	Table R905.9.2, Table R905.11.2, R905.15.2
D 1248—05	Specification for Polyethylene Plastics Extrusion Materials for Wire and Cable	M1601.1.2
D 1527—99(2005)	Specification for Acrylonite-butadiene-styrene (ABS) Plastic Pipe, Schedules 40 and 80	Table P2905.4
D 1621—04a	Standard Test Method for Compressive Properties of Rigid Cellular Plastics	Table R613.3.1
D 1622—03	Standard Test Method for Apparent Density of Rigid Cellular Plastics	Table R613.3.1
D 1623—78(1995)	Standard Test Method for Tensile and Tensile Adhesion Properties of Rigid Cellular Plastics	Table R613.3.1
D 1693—07	Test Method for Environmental Stress-cracking of Ethylene Plastics	Table M2101.1
D 1784—06a	Standard Specification for Rigid Poly (Vinyl Chloride) (PVC) Compounds and Chlorinated Poly (Vinyl Chloride) (CPVC) Compounds	M1601.1.2
D 1785—06	Specification for Poly (Vinyl Chloride) (PVC) Plastic Pipe, Schedules 40, 80 and 120	Table P2905.4
D 1863—05	Specification for Mineral Aggregate Used in Built-up Roofs	Table R905.9.2
D 1869—95(2005)	Specification for Rubber Rings for Asbestos-cement Pipe	P2904.17, P3003.4, P3003.18
D 1970—01	Specification for Self-adhering Polymer Modified Bitumen Sheet Materials Used as Steep Roofing Underlayment for Ice Dam Protection	R905.2.3, R905.2.8, R905.4.3
D 2104—03	Specification for Polyethylene (PE) Plastic Pipe, Schedule 40	Table P2905.4
D 2126—04	Standard Test Method for Response of Rigid Cellular Plastics to Thermal and Humid Aging	Table R613.3.1
D 2178—04	Specification for Asphalt Glass Felt Used in Roofing and Waterproofing	Table R905.9.2
D 2235—04	Specification for Solvent Cement for Acrylonitrile-butadiene-styrene (ABS) Plastic Pipe and Fittings	P2905.9.1.1, P3003.3.2, P3003.8.2
D 2239—03	Specification for Polyethylene (PE) Plastic Pipe (SIDR-PR) Based on Controlled Inside Diameter	Table P2905.4
D 2241—05	Specification for Poly (Vinyl Chloride) (PVC) Pressure-rated Pipe (SDR-Series)	Table P2905.4
D 2282—05	Specification for Acrylonitrile-butadiene-styrene (ABS) Plastic Pipe (SDR-PR)	Table P2905.4
D 2412—02	Test Method for Determination of External Loading Characteristics of Plastic Pipe by Parallel-plate Loading	M1601.1.2
D 2447—03	Specification for Polyethylene (PE) Plastic Pipe Schedules 40 and 80, Based on Outside Diameter	Table M2101.1
D 2464—06	Specification for Threaded Poly (Vinyl Chloride) (PVC) Plastic Pipe Fittings, Schedule 80	Table P2905.6
D 2466—06	Specification for Poly (Vinyl Chloride) (PVC) Plastic Pipe Fittings, Schedule 40	Table P2905.6
D 2467—06	Specification for Poly (Vinyl Chloride) (PVC) Plastic Pipe Fittings, Schedule 80	Table P2905.6
D 2468—96a	Specification for Acrylonitrile-butadiene-styrene (ABS) Plastic Pipe Fittings, Schedule 40	Table P2905.6
D 2513—07a	Specification for Thermoplastic Gas Pressure Pipe, Tubing and Fittings	G2414.6, G2414.6.1, G2414.11, G2415.15.2, Table M2101.1, M2104.2.1.3
D 2559—04	Standard Specification for Adhesives for Structural Laminated Wood Products for Use Under Exterior (West Use) Exposure Conditions	R613.3.3
D 2564—04e01	Specification for Solvent Cements for Poly (Vinyl Chloride) (PVC) Plastic Piping Systems	P2905.9.1.3, Table P3002.2, P3003.9.2, P3003.14.2
D 2609—02	Specification for Plastic Insert Fittings for Polyethylene (PE) Plastic Pipe	Table P2905.6
D 2626—04	Specification for Asphalt-saturated and Coated Organic Felt Base Sheet Used in Roofing	R905.3.3, Table R905.9.2
D 2657—07	Standard Practice for Heat Fusion-joining of Polyolefin Pipe Fittings	P2905.3.1, P3003.17.1
D 2661—06	Specification for Acrylonitrile-butadiene-styrene (ABS) Schedule 40 Plastic Drain, Waste, and Vent Pipe and Fittings	Table P3002.1(1), Table P3002.1(2), Table P3002.2, Table P3002.3, P3003.3.2, P3003.8.2
D 2665—07	Specification for Poly (Vinyl Chloride) (PVC) Plastic Drain, Waste and Vent Pipe and Fittings	Table P3002.1(1), Table P3002.1(2), Table P3002.2, Table P3002.3
D 2672—96a(2003)	Specification for Joints for IPS PVC Pipe Using Solvent Cement	Table P2905.4
D 2683—04	Specification for Socket-type Polyethylene Fittings for Outside Diameter-controlled Polyethylene Pipe and Tubing	Table M2101.1, M2104.2.1.1
D 2729—04e01	Specification for Poly (Vinyl Chloride) (PVC) Sewer Pipe and Fittings	P3302.1, Table P3302.1, Table AO103.10
D 2737—03	Specification for Polyethylene (PE) Plastic Tubing	Table P2905.4

ASTM—continued

D 2751—05	Specification for Acrylonitrile-butadiene-styrene (ABS) Sewer Pipe and Fittings	Table P3002.2, Table P3002.3
D 2822—05	Specification for Asphalt Roof Cement	Table R905.9.2
D 2823—05	Specification for Asphalt Roof Coatings	Table R905.9.2
D 2824—06	Specification for Aluminum-pigmented Asphalt Roof Coatings, Nonfibered, Asbestos Fibered and Fibered without Asbestos	Table R905.9.2, Table R905.11.2
D 2837—04e01	Test Method for Obtaining Hydrostatic Design Basis for Thermoplastic Pipe Materials or Pressure Design Basis for Thermoplastic Pipe Products	Table M2101.1
D 2846/D 2846M—06	Specification for Chlorinated Poly (Vinyl Chloride) (CPVC) Plastic Hot- and Cold-water Distribution Systems	Table M2101.1, P2904.9.1.2, Table P2905.4, Table P2905.5, Table P2905.6
D 2855-96 (2002)	Standard Practice for Making Solvent-cemented Joints with Poly (Vinyl Chloride) (PVC) Pipe and Fittings	P3003.9.2, P3003.14.2
D 2898—04	Test Methods for Accelerated Weathering of Fire-retardant-treated Wood for Fire Testing	R802.1.3.4, R802.1.3.6
D 2949—01ae01	Specification for 3.25-in. Outside Diameter Poly (Vinyl Chloride) (PVC) Plastic Drain, Waste and Vent Pipe and Fittings	Table P3002.1(1), Table P3002.1(2), Table P3002.2, Table P3002.3
D 3019—94 (2007)	Specification for Lap Cement Used with Asphalt Roll Roofing, Nonfibered, Asbestos Fibered and Nonasbestos Fibered	Table R905.9.2, Table R905.11.2
D 3034—06	Specification for Type PSM Poly (Vinyl Chloride) (PVC) Sewer Pipe and Fittings	Table P3002.2, Table P3002.3
D 3035—06	Specification for Polyethylene (PE) Plastic Pipe (DR-PR) Based On Controlled Outside Diameter	Table M2101.1
D 3161—06	Test Method for Wind Resistance of Asphalt Shingles (Fan Induced Method)	R905.2.4.1, Table R905.2.4.1(2)
D 3201—07	Test Method for Hygroscopic Properties of Fire-retardant Wood and Wood-base Products	R802.1.3.7
D 3212—96a (2003)e01	Specification for Joints for Drain and Sewer Plastic Pipes Using Flexible Elastomeric Seals	P3003.3.1 P3003.8.1, P3003.9.1, P3003.14.1, P3003.17.2
D 3309—96a (2002)	Specification for Polybutylene (PB) Plastic Hot- and Code-water Distribution System	Table M2101.1
D 3311—06a	Specification for Drain, Waste and Vent (DWV) Plastic Fittings Patters	P3002.3
D 3350—06	Specification for Polyethylene Plastic Pipe and Fitting Materials	Table M2101.1
D 3462—07	Specification for Asphalt Shingles Made From Glass Felt and Surfaced with Mineral Granules	R905.2.4
D 3468—99 (2006)e01	Specification for Liquid-applied Neoprene and Chlorosulfanated Polyethylene Used in Roofing and Waterproofing	R905.15.2
D 3679—06a	Specification for Rigid Poly (Vinyl Chloride) (PVC) Siding	Table R703.4, R703.11
D 3737—07	Practice for Establishing Allowable Properties for Structural Glued Laminated Timber (Glulam)	R502.1.5, R602.1.2, R802.1.4
D 3747—79 (2007)	Specification for Emulsified Asphalt Adhesive for Adhering Roof Insulation	Table R905.9.2, Table R905.11.2
D 3909—97b (2004)e01	Specification for Asphalt Roll Roofing (Glass Felt) Surfaced with Mineral Granules	R905.2.8.2, R905.5.4, Table R905.9.2
D 3957—06	Standard Practices for Establishing Stress Grades for Structural Members Used in Log Buildings	R502.1.6, R602.1.3, R802.1.5
D 4022—07	Specification for Coal Tar Roof Cement, Asbestos Containing	Table R905.9.2
D 4068—01	Specification for Chlorinated Polyethylene (CPE) Sheeting for Concealed Water Containment Membrane	P2709.2, P2709.2.2
D 4318—05	Test Methods for Liquid Limit, Plastic Limit and Plasticity Index of Soils	R403.1.8.1
D 4434—06	Specification for Poly (Vinyl Chloride) Sheet Roofing	R905.13.2
D 4479—07	Specification for Asphalt Roof Coatings-asbestos-free	Table R905.9.2
D 4551—96 (2001)	Specification for Poly (Vinyl) Chloride (PVC) Plastic Flexible Concealed Water-containment Membrane	P2709.2, P2709.2.1
D 4586—00	Specification for Asphalt Roof Cement-asbestos-free	Table R905.9.2
D 4601—04	Specification for Asphalt-coated Glass Fiber Base Sheet Used in Roofing	Table R905.9.2
D 4637—04	Specification for EPDM Sheet Used in Single-ply Roof Membrane	R905.12.2
D 4829—07	Test Method for Expansion Index of Soils	R403.1.8.1
D 4869—05e01	Specification for Asphalt-saturated (Organic Felt) Underlayment Used in Steep Slope Roofing	R905.2.3, R905.4.3, R905.5.3, R905.6.3, R905.7.3, R905.8.3
D 4897—01	Specification for Asphalt Coated Glass-fiber Venting Base Sheet Used in Roofing	Table R905.9.2
D 4990—97a (2005)e01	Specification for Coal Tar Glass Felt Used in Roofing and Waterproofing	Table R905.9.2
D 5019—07	Specification for Reinforced Nonvulcanized Polymeric Sheet Used in Roofing Membrane	R905.12.2
D 5055—05	Specification for Establishing and Monitoring Structural Capacities of Prefabricated Wood I-joists	R502.1.4
D 5516—03	Test Method for Evaluating the Flexural Properties of Fire-retardant-treated Softwood Plywood Exposed to the Elevated Temperatures	R802.1.3.5.1
D 5643—06	Specification for Coal Tar Roof Cement Asbestos-free	Table R905.9.2

ASTM—continued

Standard reference number	Title	Referenced in code section number
D 5664—02	Test Methods For Evaluating the Effects of Fire-retardant Treatments and Elevated Temperatures on Strength Properties of Fire-retardant-treated Lumber	R802.1.3.5.2
D 5665—99a(2006)	Specification for Thermoplastic Fabrics Used in Cold-applied Roofing and Waterproofing	Table R905.9.2
D 5726—98(2005)	Specification for Thermoplastic Fabrics Used in Hot-applied Roofing and Waterproofing	Table R905.9.2
D 6083—05e01	Specification for Liquid-applied Acrylic Coating Used in Roofing	Table R905.9.2, Table R905.11.2, R905.15.2
D 6162—00a	Specification for Styrene Butadiene Styrene (SBS) Modified Bituminous Sheet Materials Using a Combination of Polyester and Glass Fiber Reinforcements	Table R905.11.2
D 6163—00e01	Specification for Styrene Butadiene Styrene (SBS) Modified Bituminous Sheet Materials Using Glass Fiber Reinforcements	Table R905.11.2
D 6164—05	Specification for Styrene Butadiene Styrene (SBS) Modified Bituminous Sheet Materials Using Polyester Reinforcements	Table R905.11.2
D 6222—02e01	Specification for Atactic Polypropelene (APP) Modified Bituminous Sheet Materials Using Polyester Reinforcement	Table R905.11.2
D 6223—02e01	Specification for Atactic Polypropelene (APP) Modified Bituminous Sheet Materials Using a Combination of Polyester and Glass Fiber Reinforcement	Table R905.11.2
D 6298—05	Specification for Fiberglass-reinforced Styrene Butadiene Styrene (SBS) Modified Bituminous Sheets with a Factory Applied Metal Surface	Table R905.11.2
D 6305—02e01	Practice for Calculating Bending Strength Design Adjustment Factors for Fire-retardant-treated Plywood Roof Sheathing	R802.1.3.5.1
D 6380—03	Standard Specification for Asphalt Roll Roofing (Organic Felt)	R905.2.8.2, R905.3.3, R905.5.4
D 6694—07	Standard Specification Liquid-applied Silicone Coating Used in Spray Polurethane Foam Roofing	R905.15.2
D 6754—02	Standard Specification for Ketone-ethylene-ester-based Sheet Roofing	R905.13.2
D 6757—07	Standard Specification for Inorganic Underlayment for Use with Steep Slope Roofing Products	R905.2.3
D 6841—03	Standard Practice for Calculating Design Value Treatment Adjustment Factors for Fire-retardant-treated Lumber	R802.1.3.5.2
D 6878—06a	Standard Specification for Thermoplastic-polyolefin-based Sheet Roofing	R905.13.2
D 6947—07	Standard Specification for Liquid Applied Moisture Cured Polyurethane Coating Used in Spray Polyurethane Foam Roofing System	R905.15.2
D 7032—07	Standard Specification for Establishing Perfomance Ratings for Wood-plastic Composite Deck Boards and Guardrail Systems (Guards or Handrails)	R317.4
D 7158—07	Standard Test Method for Wind Resistance of Sealed Asphalt Shingles (Uplift Force/ Uplift Resistance Method)	R905.2.4.1, Table R905.2.4.1(1)
E 84—07	Test Method for Surface Burning Characteristics of Building Materials	M1601.3, M1601.5.2, R202, R302.9.3, R302.9.4, R302.10.1, R302.10.2, R316.3, R316.5.9, R316.5.11, R802.1.3
E 90—04	Test Method for Laboratory Measurement of Airborne Sound Transmission Loss of Building Partitions and Elements	AK102, AK102,1.1
E 96/E 96M—05	Test Method for Water Vapor Transmission of Materials	M1411.5, M1601.4.5, R202, Table R613.3.1
E 108—07a	Test Methods for Fire Tests of Roof Coverings	R902.1
E 119—07	Test Methods for Fire Tests of Building Construction and Materials	Table R302.1, R302.2, R302.3, R302.4.1, R316.4
E 136—04	Test Method for Behavior of Materials in a Vertical Tube Furnace at 750°C	R202, R302.11
E 283—04	Test Method for Determining the Rate of Air Leakage through Exterior Windows, Curtain Walls and Doors Under Specified Pressure Differences Across the Specimen	N1102.4.5
E 330—02	Test Method for Structural Performance of Exterior Windows, Curtain Walls and Doors by Uniform Static Air Pressure Difference	R612.7, R612.8, R703.1.2
E 331—00	Test Method for Water Penetration of Exterior Windows, Skylights, Doors and Curtain Walls by Uniform Static Air Pressure Difference	R703.1.1
E 492—04	Specification for Laboratory Measurement of Impact Sound Transmission through Floor-ceiling Assemblies Using the Tapping Machine	AK103
E 814—06	Test Method for Fire Tests of Through-penetration Firestops	R302.4.1.2
E 970—00	Test Method for Critical Radiant Flux of Exposed Attic Floor Insulation Using a Radiant Heat Energy Source	R302.10.5
E 1509—04	Standard Specification for Room Heaters, Pellet Fuel-burning Type	M1410.1
E 1602—03	Guide for Construction of Solid Fuel Burning Masonry Heaters	R1002.2
E 1886—06	Test Method for Performance of Exterior Windows, Curtain Walls, Doors and Storm Shutters Impacted by Missles and Exposed to Cyclic Pressure Differentials	R301.2.1.2, R612.9.1
E 1996—06	Standard Specification for Performance of Exterior Windows, Curtain Walls, Doors and Impact Protective Systems Impacted by Windborne Debris in Hurricanes	R301.2.1.2, R612.9.1
E 2178—03	Standard Test Method for Air Permeance of Building Materials	R202
E 2231—04	Standard Practice for Specimen Preparation and Mounting of Pipe and Duct Insulation Materials to Assess Surface Burning Characteristics	M1601.3
E 2273—03	Standard Test Method for Determining the Drainage Efficiency of Exterior Insulation and Finish Systems (EIFS) Clad Wall Assemblies	R703.9.2
E 2568—07	Standard Specification for PB Exterior Insulation and Finish Systems (EIFS)	R703.9.1, R703.9.2

ASTM—continued

E 2570—07	Standard Test Methods for Evaluating Water-resistive Barrier (WRB) Coatings Used Under Exterior Insulation and Finish Systems (EIFS) or EIFS with Drainage	R703.9.2.1
F 405—05	Specification for Corrugated Polyethylene (PE) Tubing and Fittings	Table P3302.1, Table AO103.10
F 409—02	Specification for Thermoplastic Accessible and Replaceable Plastic Tube and Tubular Fittings	Table P2701.1, P2702.2, P2702.3
F 437—06	Specification for Threaded Chlorinated Poly (Vinyl Chloride) (CPVC) Plastic Pipe Fittings, Schedule 80	Table P2905.6
F 438—04	Specification for Socket-type Chlorinated Poly (Vinyl Chloride) (CPVC) Plastic Pipe Fittings, Schedule 40	Table P2905.6
F 439—06	Specification for Socket-type Chlorinated Poly (Vinyl Chloride) (CPVC) Plastic Pipe Fittings, Schedule 80	Table P2905.6
F 441/F 441M—02	Specification for Chlorinated Poly (Vinyl Chloride) (CPVC) Plastic Pipe, Schedules 40 and 80	Table P2905.4, Table P2905.5
F 442/F 442M—99(2005)	Specification for Chlorinated Poly (Vinyl Chloride) (CPVC) Plastic Pipe (SDR-PR)	Table P2905.4, Table P2905.5
F 477—07	Specification for Elastomeric Seals (Gaskets) for Joining Plastic Pipe	P2905.17, P3003.18
F 493—04	Specification for Solvent Cements for Chlorinated Poly (Vinyl Chloride) (CPVC) Plastic Pipe and Fittings	P2905.9.1.2
F 628—06e01	Specification for Acrylonitrile-butadiene-styrene (ABS) Schedule 40 Plastic Drain, Waste and Vent Pipe with a Cellular Core	Table P3002.1(1), Table P3002.1(2), Table P3002.2, Table P3002.3, P3003.3.2, P3003.8.2
F 656—02	Specification for Primers for Use in Solvent Cement Joints of Poly (Vinyl Chloride) (PVC) Plastic Pipe and Fittings	P2905.9.1.3, P3003.9.2, P3003.14.2
F 714—06a	Specification for Polyethylene (PE) Plastic Pipe (SDR-PR) Based on Outside Diameter	Table P3002.2
F 876—06	Specification for Cross-linked Polyethylene (PEX) Tubing	Table M2101.1, Table P2905.4, Table P2905.5
F 877—07	Specification for Cross-linked Polyethylene (PEX) Plastic Hot- and Cold-water Distribution Systems	Table M2101.1, Table P2905.4, Table P2905.5, Table P2905.6
F 891—04	Specification for Coextruded Poly (Vinyl Chloride) (PVC) Plastic Pipe with a Cellular Core	P2905.6, Table P3002.1(1), Table P3002.1(2), Table P3002.2, Table P3302.1
F 1055—98(2006)	Specification for Electrofusion Type Polyethylene Fittings for Outside Diameter Controlled Polyethylene Pipe and Fittings	Table M2101.1, M2104.2.1.2
F 1281—07	Specification for Cross-linked Polyethylene/Aluminum/Cross-linked Polyethylene (PEX-AL-PEX) Pressure Pipe	Table M2101.1, Table P2905.4, Table P2905.5, Table P2905.6, P2905.11.1
F 1282—06	Specification for Polyethylene/Aluminum/Polyethylene (PE-AL-PE) Composite Pressure Pipe	Table M2101.1, Table P2905.4, Table P2905.5, Table P2905.6, P2905.11.1
F 1346—91(2003)	Performance Specification for Safety Covers and Labeling Requirements for All Covers for Swimming Pools, Spas and Hot Tubs	AG105.2, AG105.5
F 1412—01e01	Specification for Polyolefin Pipe and Fittings for Corrosive Waste Drainage	Table P3002.1(2), Table P3002.2, Table P3002.3, P3003.16.1
F 1488—03	Specification for Coextruded Composite Pipe	Table P3002.1(1), Table P3002.1(2) Table P3002.2, Table AO103.10
F 1554—04e1	Specification for Anchor Bolts, Steel, 36, 55 and 105-ksi Yield Strength	R611.5.2.2
F 1667—05	Specification for Driven Fasteners, Nails, Spikes and Staples	Table R703.4, R905.2.5
F 1807—07	Specification for Metal Insert Fittings Utilizing a Copper Crimp Ring for SDR9 Cross-linked Polyethylene (PEX) Tubing	Table M2101.1, Table P2905.6
F 1866—07	Specification for Poly (Vinyl Chloride) (PVC) Plastic Schedule 40 Drainage and DWV Fabricated Fittings	Table P3002.3
F 1960—07	Specification for Cold Expansion Fittings with PEX Reinforcing Rings for Use with Cross-linked Polyethylene (PEX) Tubing	Table M2101.1, Table P2905.6
F 1973—05	Standard Specification for Factory Assembled Anodeless Risers and Transition Fittings in Polyethylene (PE) and Polyamide 11 (PA 11) Fuel Gas Distribution Systems	G2415.15.2
F 1974—04	Specification for Metal Insert Fittings for Polyethylene/Aluminum/Polyethylene and Cross-linked Polyethylene/Aluminum/Cross-linked Polyethylene Composite Pressure Pipe	P2505.11.1, Table P2905.6
F 1986—01(2006)	Multilayer Pipe Type 2, Compression Joints for Hot and Cold Drinking Water Systems	Table P2905.4, Table P2905.5, Table P2905.6
F 2080—05	Specification for Cold-expansion Fittings with Metal Compression-sleeves for Cross-linked Polyethylene (PEX) Pipe	P2905.6
F 2090—01A(2007)	Specification for Window Fall Prevention Devices—with Emergency Escape (Egress) Release Mechanisms	R612.2, R612.3
F 2098—04e1	Standard Specification for Stainless Steel Clamps for SDR9 PEX Tubing to Metal Insert Fittings	Table M2101.1, Table P2905.6

ASTM—continued

F 2159—05	Standard Specification for Plastic Insert Fittings Utilizing a Copper Crimp Ring for SDR9 Cross-linked Polyethylene (PEX) Tubing	P2905.6
F 2262—05	Standard Specification for Cross-linked Polyethylene /Aluminum/Cross-linked Polyethylene Tubing OD Controlled SDR9	Table P2905.4, Table P2905.5
F 2389—06	Standard for Pressure-rated Polypropylene (PP) Piping Systems	Table M2101.1, Table P2905.4, Table P2905.5,Table P2905.6, P2905.10.1
F 2434—05	Standard Specification for Metal Insert Fittings Utilizing a Copper Crimp Ring for Polyethylene/Aluminum/Cross-linked Polyethylene (PEX-AL-PEX) Tubing	Table P2905.6
F 2623—07	Standard Specification for Polyethylene of Raised Temperature (PE-RT) SDRG Tubing	Table M2101.1

AWPA

American Wood Protection Association
P.O. Box 361784
Birmingham, AL 35236-1784

Standard reference number	Title	Referenced in code section number
C1—03	All Timber Products—Preservative Treatment by Pressure Processes	R902.2
M4—06	Standard for the Care of Preservative-treated Wood Products	R317.1.1, R318.1.2
U1—07	USE CATEGORY SYSTEM: User Specification for Treated Wood Except Section 6 Commodity Specification H	R317.1, R322.1.8, R402.1.2, R504.3, Table R905.8.5, R4603.7

AWS

American Welding Society
550 N. W. LeJeune Road
Miami, FL 33126

Standard reference number	Title	Referenced in code section number
A5.8—04	Specifications for Filler Metals for Brazing and Braze Welding	P3003.5.1, P3003.10.1, P3003.11.1

AWWA

American Water Works Association
6666 West Quincy Avenue
Denver, CO 80235

Standard reference number	Title	Referenced in code section number
C104—98	Standard for Cement-mortar Lining for Ductile-iron Pipe and Fittings for Water	P2905.4
C110/A21.10—03	Standard for Ductile-iron and Gray-iron Fittings, 3 Inches through 48 Inches, for Water	Table P2905.6, Table P3002.3
C115/A21.15—99	Standard for Flanged Ductile-iron Pipe with Ductile-iron or Gray-iron Threaded Flanges	Table P2905.4
C151/A21.51—02	Standard for Ductile-iron Pipe, Centrifugally Cast, for Water	Table P2905.4
C153/A21.53—00	Standard for Ductile-iron Compact Fittings for Water Service	Table P2905.6
C510—00	Double Check Valve Backflow Prevention Assembly	Table P2902.3, P2902.3.6
C511—00	Reduced-pressure Principle Backflow Prevention Assembly	Table P2902.3, P2902.3.5, P2902.5.1

CGSB

Canadian General Standards Board
Place du Portage 111, 6B1
11 Laurier Street
Gatineau, Quebec, Canada KIA 1G6

Standard reference number	Title	Referenced in code section number
37-GP—52M—(1984)	Roofing and Waterproofing Membrane, Sheet Applied, Elastomeric	R905.12.2
37-GP—56M—(1980)	Membrane, Modified Bituminous, Prefabricated and Reinforced for Roofing —with December 1985 Amendment	Table R905.11.2
CAN/CGSB-37.54—95	Polyvinyl Chloride Roofing and Waterproofing Membrane	R905.13.2

CISPI

Cast Iron Soil Pipe Institute
5959 Shallowford Road, Suite 419
Chattanooga, TN 37421

Standard reference number	Title	Referenced in code section number
301—04a	Standard Specification for Hubless Cast Iron Soil Pipe and Fittings for Sanitary and Storm Drain, Waste and Vent Piping Applications	Table P3002.1(1), Table P3002.1(2), Table P3002.2, Table P3002.3, P3005.2.9, Table P3302.1
310—04	Standard Specification for Coupling for Use in Connection with Hubless Cast Iron Soil Pipe and Fittings for Sanitary and Storm Drain, Waste and Vent Piping Applications	P3003.6.3

CPA

Composite Panel Association
19465 Deerfield Avenue, Suite 306
Leesburg, VA 20176

Standard reference number	Title	Referenced in code section number
ANSI A135.4—04	Basic Hardboard	Table R602.3(2)
ANSI A135.5—04	Prefinished Hardboard Paneling	R702.5
ANSI A135.6—98	Hardboard Siding	Table R703.4

CPSC

Consumer Product Safety Commission
4330 East West Highway
Bethesda, MD 20814-4408

Standard reference number	Title	Referenced in code section number
16 CFR Part 1201—(1977)	Safety Standard for Architectural Glazing	R308.1.1, R308.3.1
16 CFR Part 1209—(1979)	Interim Safety Standard for Cellulose Insulation	R302.10.3
16 CFR Part 1404—(1979)	Cellulose Insulation	R302.10.3

CSA

Canadian Standards Association
5060 Spectrum Way
Mississauga, Ontario, Canada L4N 5N6

Standard reference number	Title	Referenced in code section number
CSA Requirement 3—88	Manually Operated Gas Valves for Use in House Piping Systems	Table G2420.1.1
CSA 8-93	Requirements for Gas Fired Log Lighters for Wood Burning Fireplaces —with Revisions through January 1999	G2433.1
O325—07	Construction Sheathing	R503.2.1
O437-Series—93	Standards on OSB and Waferboard (Reaffirmed 2006)	R503.2.1, R803.2.1
CAN/CSA A 257.1M—92	Circular Concrete Culvert, Storm Drain, Sewer Pipe and Fittings	Table P3002.2
CAN/CSA A 257.2M—92	Reinforced Circular Concrete Culvert, Storm Drain, Sewer Pipe and Fittings	Table P3002.2
CAN/CSA A 257.3M—92	Joints for Circular Concrete Sewer and Culvert Pipe, Manhole Sections and Fittings Using Rubber Gaskets	P3003.7, P3003.18
101/I.S.2/A440—08	Specifications for Windows, Doors and Unit Skylights	N1102.4.4
B45.1—02	Ceramic Plumbing Fixtures	Table P2701.1, P2711.1, P2712.1
B45.2—02	Enameled Cast Iron Plumbing Fixtures	Table 2701.1, P2711.1
B45.3—02	Porcelain Enameled Steel Plumbing Fixtures	Table P2701.1, P2711.1
B45.4—02	Stainless Steel Plumbing Fixtures	Table P2701.1, P2711.1, P2712.1
B45.5—02	Plastic Plumbing Fixtures	Table P2701.1, P2711.2, P2712.1
B45.9—02	Macerating Systems and Related Components	P3007.1, P3007.2.1, P3007.5
B64.1.2—01	Vacuum Breakers, Pressure Type (PVB)	Table P2902.2, P2902.3.4
B64.2.1—01	Vacuum Breakers, Hose Connection Type (HCVB) with Manual Draining Feature	Table P2902.2, P2902.3.2
B64.2.1.1—01	Vacuum Breakers, Hose Connection Dual Check Type (HCDVB)	Table P2902.2, P2902.3.2
B64.3—01	Backflow Preventers, Dual Check ValDrain, Wasteve Type with Atmospheric Port (DCAP)	Table P2902.2

CSA—continued

B64.4.1—01	Backflow Preventers, Reduced Pressure Principle Type for Fire Systems (RPF)	Table P2902.2
B64.5—01	Backflow Preventers, Double Check Valve Type (DCVA)	Table P2902.2, P2902.3.6
B64.5.1—01	Backflow Preventers, Double Check Valve Type for Fire Systems (DCVAF)	Table P2902.2, P2902.3.6
B64.6—01	Backflow Preventers, Dual Check Valve Type (DuC)	Table P2902.3
B64.7—94	Vacuum Breakers, Laboratory Faucet Type (LFVB)	Table P2902.2, P2902.3.2
B125.1—2005/ ASME A112.18.1—2005	Plumbing Supply Fittings	Table P2701.1, P2708.4, P2722.1
B125.1—01	Plumbing Fittings	Table P2701.1, P2708.3, P2722.2, P2722.3
B125.2—2005	Plumbing Waste Fittings	Table P2701.1, P2702.2
B125.3—2005	Plumbing Fittings	Table 2701.1
B137.1—02	Polyethylene Pipe, Tubing and Fittings for Cold Water Pressure Services	Table P2905.4, Table P2905.6
B137.2—02	PVC Injection-moulded Gasketed Fittings for Pressure Applications	Table P2905.6
B137.3—02	Rigid Poly (Vinyl Chloride) (PVC) Pipe for Pressure Applications	Table P2905.4, P3003.9.2, P3003.14.2
B137.5—02	Cross-linked Polyethylene (PEX) Tubing Systems for Pressure Applications	Table P2905.4, Table P2905.5, Table P2905.6
B137.6—02	CPVC Pipe, Tubing and Fittings For Hot- and Cold-water Distribution Systems	Table P2905.4, Table P2905.5, Table 2905.6
B137.11—02	Polypropylene (PP-R) Pipe and Fittings for Pressure Applications	Table P2905.4.1, Table 2905.4, Table P2905.6
B181.1—02	ABS Drain, Waste and Vent Pipe and Pipe Fittings	Table P3002.1(1), Table P3002.1(2), Table P3002.2, Table P3002.3, P3003.3.2, P3003.8.2
B181.2—02	PVC Drain, Waste and Vent Pipe and Pipe Fittings	Table P3002.1(1), Table P3002.1(2), Table P3002.2, Table P3002.3, P3003.9.2, P3003.14.2, P3008.2, Table P3302.1
B181.3—02	Polyolefin Laboratory Drainage Systems	Table P3002.1(1), Table P3002.1(2), Table P3002.2, Table P3002.3, P3003.16.1
B182.2—02	PVC Sewer Pipe and Fittings (PSM Type)	Table P3002.1(1), Table P3002.1(2), Table P3002.2, Table P3002.3, Table P3302.1
B182.4—02	Profile PVC Sewer Pipe & Fittings	Table P3002.2, Table P3002.3, Table P3302.1
B182.6—02	Profile Polyethylene Sewer Pipe and Fittings for Leak-proof Sewer Applications	Table P3302.1
B182.8—02	Profile Polyethylene Storm Sewer and Drainage Pipe and Fittings	Table P3302.1
B602—02	Mechanical Couplings for Drain, Waste and Vent Pipe and Sewer Pipe	P3003.3.1, P3003.6.3, P3003.7, P3003.8.1, P3003.14.1, P3003.15, P3003.17.2
LC3—00	Appliance Stands and Drain Pans	P2801.5
CAN/CSA B64.1.1—01	Vacuum Breakers, Atmospheric Type (AVB)	Table P2902.2, P2902.3.2
CAN/CSA B64.2—01	Vacuum Breakers, Hose Connection Type (HCVP)	Table P2902.2, P2902.3.2
CAN/CSA B64.2.2—01	Vacuum Breakers, Hose Connection Type (HCVP) with Automatic Draining Feature	Table P2902.2, P2902.3.2
CAN/CSA B64.3—01	Backflow Preventers, Dual Check Valve Type with Atmospheric Port (DCAP)	Table P2902.2, P2902.3.3
CAN/CSA B64.4—01	Backflow Preventers, Reduced Pressure Principle Type (RP)	Table P2902.3, P2902.3.5, P2902.5.1,.
CAN/CSA B137.9—02	Polyethylene/Aluminum/Polyethylene Composite Pressure Pipe Systems	P2505.11.1, Table P2905.4
CAN/CSA B137.10M—02	Cross-linked Polyethylene/Aluminum/Polyethylene Composite Pressure Pipe Systems	Table M2101.1, P2505.11.1, Table P2905.4, Table P2905.5

CSSB

Cedar Shake & Shingle Bureau
P. O. Box 1178
Sumas, WA 98295-1178

Standard reference number	Title	Referenced in code section number
CSSB—97	Grading and Packing Rules for Western Red Cedar Shakes and Western Red Shingles of the Cedar Shake and Shingle Bureau	R702.6, R703.5, Table R905.7.4, Table R905.8.5

DASMA

Door and Access Systems Manufacturers
Association International
1300 Summer Avenue
Cleveland, OH 44115-2851

Standard reference number	Title	Referenced in code section number
108—05	Standard Method for Testing Garage Doors: Determination of Structural Performance Under Uniform Static Air Pressure Difference	R612.7

DASMA—continued

115—05	Standard Method for Testing Garage Doors: Determination of Structural Performance Under Missile Impact and Cyclic Wind Pressure	R301.2.1.2

DOC

United States Department of Commerce
1401 Constitution Avenue, NW
Washington, DC 20230

Standard reference number	Title	Referenced in code section number
PS 1—07	Structural Plywood	R404.2.1, Table R404.2.3, R503.2.1, R604.1, R613.3.2, R803.2.1
PS 2—04	Performance Standard for Wood-based Structural-use Panels	R404.2.1, Table R404.2.3, R503.2.1, R604.1, R613.3.2, Table 613.3.2, R803.2.1
PS 20—05	American Softwood Lumber Standard	R404.2.1, R502.1, R602.1, R802.1

DOTn

Department of Transportation
1200 New Jersey Avenue SE
East Building, 2nd floor
Washington, DC 20590

Standard reference number	Title	Referenced in code section number
49 CFR, Parts 192.281(e) & 192.283 (b)	Transportation of Natural and Other Gas by Pipeline: Minimum Federal Safety Standards	G2414.6.1

FEMA

Federal Emergency Management Agency
500 C Street, SW
Washington, DC 20472

Standard reference number	Title	Referenced in code section number
TB-2—93	Flood-resistant Materials Requirements	R322.1.8
FIA-TB-11—01	Crawlspace Construction for Buildings Located in Special Flood Hazard Area	R408.7

FM

Factory Mutual Global Research
Standards Laboratories Department
1301 Atwood Avenue, P. O. Box 7500
Johnson, RI 02919

Standard reference number	Title	Referenced in code section number
4450—(1989)	Approval Standard for Class 1 Insulated Steel Deck Roofs—with Supplements through July 1992	R906.1
4880—(2005)	American National Standard for Evaluating Insulated Wall or Wall and Roof/Ceiling Assemblies, Plastic Interior Finish Materials, Plastic Exterior Building Panels, Wall/Ceiling Coating Systems, Interior or Exterior Finish Systems	R316.4, R316.6

GA

Gypsum Association
810 First Street, Northeast, Suite 510
Washington, DC 20002-4268

Standard reference number	Title	Referenced in code section number
GA-253—07	Application of Gypsum Sheathing	Table R602.3(1)

HPVA

Hardwood Plywood & Veneer Association
1825 Michael Faraday Drive
Reston, Virginia 20190-5350

Standard reference number	Title	Referenced in code section number
HP-1—2004	The American National Standard for Hardwood and Decorative Plywood	R702.5

ICC

International Code Council, Inc.
500 New Jersey Avenue, NW
6th Floor
Washington, DC 20001

Standard reference number	Title	Referenced in code section number
IBC—09	International Building Code®	G2402.3, R101.2, R110.2, R301.1, R301.1.3, R301.2.2.1.1, R301.2.2.1.2,R301.2.2.4, R301.3, R308.5, R320.1, R321.3, R322.1, R403.1.8, R802.1.3.4, R905.10.3, Table AH107.4(1), AH107.4.3
ICC/ANSI A117.1—03	Accessible and Usable Buildings and Facilities	R321.3
ICC 400—06	Standard on the Design and Construction of Log Structures	R301.1.1
ICC 500—08	ICC/NSSA Standard on the Design and Construction of Storm Shelters	R323.1
ICC 600—08	Standard for Residential Construction in High Wind Regions	R301.2.1.1
IECC—09	International Energy Conservation Code®	N1101.2
IFC—09	International Fire Code®	G2402.3, G2412.2, G2423.1, M2201.7, R102.7
IFGC—09	International Fuel Gas Code®	G2401.1, G2423.1
IMC—09	International Mechanical Code®	G2402.3
IPC—09	International Plumbing Code®	G2402.3, Table R301.2(1), R903.4.1, AO102.6
IPMC—09	International Property Maintenance Code®	R102.7
IPSDC—09	International Private Sewage Disposal Code®	R322.1.7, AI101.1
IRC—09	International Residential Code®	N1102.2.3, N1103.6

ISO

International Organization for Standardization
1, ch. de la Voie - Creuse
Case postale 56
CH-1211 Geneva 20, Switzerland

Standard reference number	Title	Referenced in code section number
15874—2002	Polypropylene Plastic Piping Systems for Hot and Cold Water Installations	Table M2101.1

MSS

Manufacturers Standardization Society of the Valve and Fittings Industry
127 Park Street, Northeast
Vienna, VA 22180

Standard reference number	Title	Referenced in code section number
SP-58—93	Pipe Hangers and Supports—Materials, Design and Manufacture	G2418.2

NAIMA

North American Insulation Manufacturers Association
44 Canal Center Plaza, Suite 310
Alexandria, VA 22314

Standard reference number	Title	Referenced in code section number
AH 116—02	Fibrous Glass Duct Construction Standards, Fifth Edition	M1601.1.1

NCMA

National Concrete Masonry Association
13750 Sunrise Valley Drive
Herndon, VA 20171-4662

Standard reference number	Title	Referenced in code section number
TR 68-A—75	Design and Construction of Plain and Reinforced Concrete Masonry and Basement and Foundation Walls	R404.1.1

NFPA

National Fire Protection Association
1 Batterymarch Park
Quincy, MA 02269

Standard reference number	Title	Referenced in code section number
13—07	Installation of Sprinkler Systems	R302.3
13D—07	Standard for the Installation of Sprinkler Systems in One- and Two-family Dwellings and Manufactured Homes	P2904.1, P2904.2, P2904.6.1, R313.2.1
31—06	Installation of Oil-burning Equipment	M1801.3.1, M1805.3
58—08	Liquefied Petroleum Gas Code	G2412.2, G2414.6.2
70—08	National Electrical Code	E3401.1, E3401.2, E4301.1, Table E4303.2, E4304.3, E4304.4
72—07	National Fire Alarm Code	R314.1, R314.2
85—07	Boiler and Construction Systems Hazards Code	G2452.1
211—06	Chimneys, Fireplaces, Vents and Solid Fuel Burning Appliances	G2427.5.5.1, R1002.5
259—03	Test Method for Potential Heat of Building Materials	R316.5.7, 316.5.8
286—06	Standard Methods of Fire Tests for Evaluating Contribution of Wall and Ceiling Interior Finish to Room Fire Growth	R302.9.4, R316.4, R316.5.8, R316.6
501—05	Standard on Manufactured Housing	R202, AE201
853—07	Standard for the Installation of Stationary Fuel Cell Power Systems	M1903.1

NFRC

National Fenestration Rating Council Inc.
8484 Georgia Avenue, Suite 320
Silver Spring, MD 20910

Standard reference number	Title	Referenced section number
100—2004	Procedure for Determining Fenestration Product *U*-factors	N1101.5
200—2004	Procedure for Determining Fenestration Product Solar Heat Gain Coefficients and Visible Transmittance at Normal Incidence	N1101.5
400—2004	Procedure for Determining Fenestration Product Air Leakage	N1102.4.4

NSF

NSF International
789 N. Dixboro
Ann Arbor, MI 48105

Standard reference number	Title	Referenced in code section number
14—2007	Plastic Piping System Components and Related Materials	P2608.3, P2908.3
42—2007e	Drinking Water Treatment Units—Anesthetic Effects	P2908.1, P2908.3
44—2004	Residential Cation Exchange Water Softeners	P2908.1, P2908.3
53—2007	Drinking Water Treatment Units—Health Effects	P2908.1, P2908.3
58—2006	Reverse Osmosis Drinking Water Treatment Systems	P2908.2, P2908.3
61—2007a	Drinking Water System Components—Health Effects	P2608.5, P2722.1, P2903.9.4, P2905.4, P2905.5, P2905.6, P2907.3

PCA

Portland Cement Association
5420 Old Orchard Road
Skokie, IL 60077

Standard reference number	Title	Referenced in code section number
100—07	Prescriptive Design of Exterior Concrete Walls for One- and Two-family Dwellings (Pub. No. EB241)	R404.1.2, R404.1.2.2.1, R404.1.2.2.2, R404.1.2.4, R404.1.4.2, R611.1, R611.2, R611.9.2, R611.9.3

SMACNA

Sheet Metal & Air Conditioning Contractors National Assoc. Inc.
4021 Lafayette Center Road
Chantilly, VA 22021

Standard reference number	Title	Referenced in code section number
SMACNA—03	Fibrous Glass Duct Construction Standards (2003)	M1601.1.1

TMS

The Masonry Society
3970 Broadway, Suite 201-D
Boulder, CO 80304

Standard reference number	Title	Referenced in code section number
302—07	Standard Method for Determining the Sound Transmission Class Rating for Masonry Walls	AK102.1.1
402—08	Building Code Requirements for Masonry Structures	R404.1.1, R606.1, R606.1.1, R606.11.2.2.2, R606.12.1, R606.12.2.3.1, R606.12.2.3.2, R606.12.3.1, Table R703.4
602—08	Specification for Masonry Structures	R404.1.1, R606.1, R606.1.1, R606.12.1, R606.12.2.3.1, R606.12.2.3.2, R606.12.3.1, Table R703.4

TPI

Truss Plate Institute
583 D'Onofrio Drive, Suite 200
Madison, WI 53719

Standard reference number	Title	Referenced in code section number
TPI 1—2007	National Design Standard for Metal-plate-connected Wood Truss Construction	R502.11.1, R802.10.2

UL

Underwriters Laboratories, Inc.
333 Pfingsten Road
Northbrook, IL 60062

Standard reference number	Title	Referenced in code section number
17—94	Vent or Chimney Connector Dampers for Oil-fired Appliances—with Revisions through September 1999	M1802.2.2
58—96	Steel Underground Tanks for Flammable and Combustible Liquids—with Revisions through July 1998	M2201.1
80—04	Steel Tanks for Oil-burner Fuel	M2201.1
103—01	Factory-built Chimneys for Residential Type and Building Heating Appliances—with Revisions through June 2006	G2430.1, R202, R1005.3
127—96	Factory-built Fireplaces—with Revisions through November 2006	G2445.7, R1001.11, R1004.1, R1004.4, R1005.4
174—04	Household Electric Storage Tank Water Heaters—with Revisions through November 2005	M2005.1
181—05	Factory-made Air Ducts and Air Connectors—with Revisions through May 2003	M1601.2, M1601.4.1
181A—05	Closure Systems for Use with Rigid Air Ducts and Air Connectors—with Revisions through December 1998	M1601.2, M1601.4.1
181B—05	Closure Systems for Use with Flexible Air Ducts and Air Connectors—with Revisions through August 2003	M1601.2, M1601.4.1

UL—continued

217—06	Single- and Multiple-station Smoke Alarms—with Revisions through January 2004	R313.1
263—03	Standards for Fire Test of Building Construction and Materials	R302.2, R302.4.1, R316.4
325—02	Standard for Door, Drapery, Gate, Louver and Window Operations and Systems —with Revisions through February 2006	R309.4
343—97	Pumps for Oil-burning Appliances—with Revisions through May 2002	M2204.1
441—96	Gas Vents—with Revisions through August 2006	G2426.1
508—99	Industrial Control Equipment—with Revisions through July 2005	M1411.3.1
536—97	Flexible Metallic Hose—with Revisions through June 2003	M2202.3
641—95	Type L, Low-temperature Venting Systems—with Revisions through August 2005	G2426.1, M1804.2.4, R202, R1003.11.5
651—05	Schedule 40 and Schedule 80 Rigid PVC Conduit and Fittings	G2414.6.3
723—03	Standard for Test for Surface Burning Characteristics of Building Materials—with Revisions through May 2005	M1601.3, R302.9.3, R302.10.1, R302.10.2, R316.3, R316.6
726—95	Oil-fired Boiler Assemblies—with Revisions through March 2006	M2001.1.1, M2006.1
727—06	Oil-fired Central Furnaces	M1402.1
729—03	Oil-fired Floor Furnaces	M1408.1
730—03	Oil-fired Wall Furnaces	M1409.1
732—95	Oil-fired Storage Tank Water Heaters—with Revisions through February 2005	M2005.1
737—96	Fireplaces Stoves—with Revisions through January 2000	M1414.1
790—04	Standard Test Methods for Fire Tests of Roof Coverings	R902.1
795—06	Commercial-industrial Gas Heating Equipment	G2442.1, G2452.1
834—04	Heating, Water Supply and Power Boilers-Electric	M2001.1.1
896—93	Oil-burning Stoves—with Revisions through May 2004	M1410.1
923—02	Microwave Cooking Appliances—with Revisions through February 2006	M1504.1
959—01	Medium Heat Appliance Factory-built Chimneys—with Revisions through September 2006	R1005.6
1040—96	Fire Test of Insulated Wall Construction—with Revisions through June 2001	R316.4, R316.6
1256—02	Fire Test of Roof Deck Construction	R906.1
1261—01	Electric Water Heaters for Pools and Tubs—with Revisions through June 2004	M2006.1
1453—04	Electronic Booster and Commercial Storage Tank Water Heaters	M2005.1
1479—03	Fire Tests of Through-penetration Firestops	R302.4.1.2
1482—98	Solid-fuel-type Room Heaters—with Revisions through January 2000	M1410.1, R1002.2, R1002.5
1715—97	Fire Test of Interior Finish Material—with Revisions through March 2004	R316.4
1738—06	Venting Systems for Gas-burning Appliances, Categories II, III and IV	G2426.1
1777—04	Standard for Chimney Liners	G2425.12, G2425.15.4, M1801.3.4, R1003.11.1, R1003.18
1995—05	Heating and Cooling Equipment	M1402.1, M1403.1, M1407.1
2017—2000	Standard for General-purpose Signaling Devices and Systems—with Revisions through June 2004	AG105.2
2034—2008	Standard for Single- and Multiple-station Carbon Monoxide Alarms	R315.3
2158A—2006	Outline of Investigation for Clothes Dryer Transition Duct	M1502.4.3

ULC

Underwriters' Laboratories of Canada
7 Underwriters Road
Toronto, Ontario, Canada M1R 3B4

Standard reference number	Title	Referenced in code section number
CAN/ULC S 102—1988	Standard Methods for Test for Surface Burning Characteristics of Building Materials and Assemblies—with 2000 Revisions	R302.10.2

US-FTC

United States - Federal Trade Commission
600 Pennsylvania Avenue NW
Washington, DC 20580

Standard reference number	Title	Referenced in code section number
CFR Title 16	*R*-value Rule	N1101.6

Window & Door Manufacturers Association
1400 East Touhy Avenue, Suite 470
Des Plaines, IL 60018

Standard reference number	Title	Referenced in code section number
AAMA/WDMA/CSA 101/I.S2/A440—08	Specifications for Windows, Doors and Skylights	N1102.4.4, R308.6.9, R613.6

CHAPTER 45
HIGH WIND ZONES

This chapter is a North Carolina addition to the 2009 International Residential Code. There will be no underlined text.

SECTION R4501 GENERAL

R4501.1 General. The provisions of this chapter shall be applicable to buildings constructed in high wind zones as noted by the text. These provisions shall be in addition to or in lieu of previous chapters.

R4501.2 Alternate construction. In lieu of specific code requirements for structures in the 110, 120, and 130 miles per hour wind (48 m/s, 53 *m/s* and 57m/*s)* zones, compliance with International Code Council *ICC 600-2008 Standard for Residential Construction in High-Wind Regions* or AF&PA *Wood Frame Construction Manual for One- and Two-Family Dwellings* is acceptable.

SECTION R4502 DESIGN PRESSURE FOR DOORS AND WINDOWS

TABLE R4502(a)
DESIGN PRESSURES FOR DOORS AND WINDOWS[a, b, c, d]
POSITIVE AND NEGATIVE IN PSF

VELOCITY (mph)	MEAN ROOF HEIGHT (ft)		
	15	25	35[e]
110	25	29	32
120	31	35	39
130	37	43	47

For SI: 1 foot = 304.8 mm, 1 mile per hour = 0.R45 m/s, 1 degree = 0.01745 rad.

a. Alternate pressures may be determined by using the *North Carolina Building Code*, ASCE-7, or the *International Building Code.*

b. If window or door is more than 4 feet from a corner, the pressure from this table shall be permitted to be multiplied by 0.87. This adjustment does not apply to garage doors.

c. For windows or doors in structures with a roof slope of 10 degrees (2:12) or less from the horizontal, the pressure from this table may be multiplied by 0.90.

d. Design pressure ratings based on the standards listed in Section R613 are adequate documentation of capacity to resist pressures from the table.

e. Where the mean roof height exceeds this table, values shall be determined by a design professional.

TABLE R4502(b)
DESIGN PRESSURES (IN PSF) GARAGE DOORS[a, b, c, d, e]

VELOCITY (mph)	MEAN ROOF HEIGHT (ft)		
	15	25	35[f]
110	20	23	26
120	25	29	32
130	30	35	39

For SI: 1 foot = 304.8 mm, 1 mile per hour = 0.R45 m/s, 1 degree = 0.01745 rad.

a. The pressures in this table are for garage doors at least 9 feet by 7 feet and at least 2 feet from the corner.

b. Alternate design pressures may be determined by using the *North Carolina Building Code*, ASCE-7, or the *International Building Code.*

c. For doors in a structure with a roof slope of 10 degrees (2:12) or less from the horizontal the pressures from this table may be multiplied by 0.90.

d. Design pressure ratings based on tests done according to ASTM E330 are adequate documentation.

e. Garage doors on the ground level of a structure in a flood zone do not have to meet the above design pressures provided all of the following conditions are met:

1. Structure is anchored to the girders and top of the piling to resist the forces given in Chapter R45.
2. The garage door occurs below the top of the piling.
3. Provide openings at the garage level that comply with either of the following options:
   i. Design all exterior walls at the garage level to break away at 20 psf or less or;
   ii. Provide openings (in walls at the garage level without the garage level without the garage door) equal to at least 20 percent of the total wall area from the ground to the roof.

f. Where the mean roof height exceeds this table, values shall be determined by a design professional.

SECTION R4503 FOOTINGS

R4503.1 Foundation wall footings. Foundation wall footings in the 120 and 130 mph (53 m/s and 57 m/s) wind zones shall be a minimum of 8 inches by 24 inches (203 mm by 610 mm) for houses $2^1/_2$ stories and less. The footing for a three-story building shall be 10 inches by 24 inches (254 mm by 610 mm). Footings shall be reinforced with three #4 (or two #5 bars) at 3 inches (76 mm) above the bottom of the footing. The bars shall be continuous or lapped 25 inches (635 mm) at all splices.

R4503.2 Pier and curtain wall footings.

R4503.2.1 Enlarged footings at piers. The curtain wall footing must meet the minimum projection requirements in Figure R403.1(1) and footing dimensions for the pier footings shall comply with Table R4503.2.1.

TABLE R4503.2.1
FOOTINGS TO RESIST UPLIFT FROM PIERS IN 120 AND 130 MPH WIND ZONES SUPPORTING GIRDERS IN EXTERIOR WALLS

VELOCITY (mph)	FOOTING SIZE GIRDER SPAN		
	4′-0″	6′-0″	8′-0″
120	2′-0″ × 2′-0″ × 10″	2′-4″ × 2′-4″ × 10″	2′-8″ × 2′-8″ × 10″
130	3′-0″ × 3′-0″ × 10″	3′-4″ × 3′-4″ × 12″	3′-8″ × 3′-8″ × 12″

For SI: 1 inch = 25.4 mm, 1 foot = 304.8 mm, 1 mile per hour = 0.R45 m/s.
Note: See Table R403.1a for 110 mph.

R4503.2.2 Continuous width footings. Uniform continuous width footings for pier and curtain wall foundations shall be a minimum of 8 inches (203 mm) thick and 24 inches (60 mm) wide. Footings shall be reinforced with three #4 bars (or two #5 bars) at 3 inches (76 mm) above the bottom of the footing. The bars shall be continuous or lapped 25 inches (635 mm) at all splices.

R4503.3 Footing dowels. All footings shall have dowels to match reinforcing in the foundation wall or pier above (see Sections R4504.1.1 and R4504.3). Dowels shall have a standard hook length of 12 times the bar diameter embedded in the footing and shall lap the wall or pier reinforcing at least 25 inches (635 mm).

SECTION R4504 WALL AND FOUNDATION ANCHORAGE

R4504.1 Anchorage. Exterior walls of structures in the 120 and 130 mph (53 m/s and 57 m/s) wind zones shall be anchored to the footing to resist the forces specified in Section R4508.2, by the prescriptive requirements of this section, or as allowed by Section R4508.4 and Figures R4504.3(a) through R4504.3(d). Exterior walls of structures in the 110 mph (53 m/s) wind zone shall be anchored to the foundation wall, pier/curtain wall, or slab on grade with $^1/_2$-inch (13 mm) anchor bolts, 4 feet (1219 mm) on center extended 15 inches (381 mm) into masonry and 7 inches (178 mm) into concrete and are exempt from the requirements of this section.

TABLE R4504.1 STRUCTURAL ANCHORAGE[a]

WIND SPEED (mph)	120	130
MAXIMUM SPACING (inches)	21	18

For SI: 1 inch = 25.4 mm, 1 mile per hour = 0.R45 m/s.

a. Required spacing of $^1/_2$-inch anchor bolts where a bond beam is required and for slab on grade with a single sole plate. [See Figure R403.1(1) for 110 mph or less.]

R4504.1.1 Exterior foundation walls. Vertical reinforcement shall be installed not more than 2 feet (51 mm) from each corner at intervals not to exceed Table R4504.1.1 with all reinforced cells grouted and shall either terminate in a bond beam or connect to the wall above.

TABLES R4504.1.1 WALL REINFORCEMENT OR CONTINUOUS ANCHORAGE[a, b, c, d]

BAR/BOLT SIZE (inches)	$^5/_8$	$^1/_2$	$^3/_8$
MAXIMUM SPACING (inches)	96	72	42

For SI: 1 inch = 25.4 mm.

a. Applies to 120 and 130 mph wind zones.

b. Continuous anchorage from footing to girder or wall framing.

c. Applies to footing dowel bars, vertical reinforcement and anchor bolts.

d. Spacing may exceed the tabulated values by up to 8 inches provided the total number of required bars is installed.

R4504.1.2. An 8 inch × 8 inch (203 × 203 mm) concrete or CMU bond beam with one #5 bar shall be used at the floor level. The bar shall be continuous or lapped 25 inches (635 mm) at all splices.

Exception: The bond beam may be eliminated where the uplift connectors are continuous from the footing to the exterior wall framing and the rim band is continuous (doubled or adequately spliced).

R4504.2 Sill plates. A minimum 2 × 6 sill plate shall be installed.

Exception: Where the uplift connectors are continuous from the footing to the exterior wall framing.

R4504.2.1. Sill plates shall be anchored with $^1/_2$-inch (13 mm) anchor bolts with 2 × 2 × $^1/_8$ inch (51 × 51 × 3 mm) washers at intervals not to exceed Table R4504.1. Where the vertical reinforcement bars/bolts terminate at the sill plate with a connector capable of developing the bar/bolt capacity, approved strap anchors from the sill plate to the wall framing shall be installed (Note: Cable clamps have no rated capacity when used with reinforcing steel or bolts).

Exception: Where the uplift connectors are continuous from the footing to the exterior wall framing, the spacing of the continuous anchorage may be increased in accordance with Table R4504.1.1.

R4504.3 Exterior foundation piers. Vertical reinforcement shall be installed not more than 2 feet (51 mm) from each corner at intervals not to exceed Table R4504.1.1 with all reinforced cells grouted and shall connect to all sill plates, to the exterior girder, or to the wall above [see Figures R4504.3(a) through R4504.3(d)].

R4504.3.1. Where the vertical reinforcement bars terminate at the sill plate, a minimum 2 × 6 sill plate and approved strap anchors from the sill plate to the wall framing shall be installed.

R4504.3.2. Two #4 footing dowel bars shall be embedded into the footing and grouted to the top of each pier. If the vertical reinforcement bars are placed inside the piers (not between the pier/curtain wall), then one footing dowel bar may be omitted from each pier.

R4504.4 Exterior concrete slab-on-grade footings. Vertical reinforcement shall be installed at intervals not to exceed Table R4504.1.1 and shall terminate in a double sole plate.

Exception: Vertical reinforcement (anchorage) shall be installed at intervals not to exceed Table R4504.1 where the bars terminate in a single sole plate. Approved strap anchors or wood structural panels shall be installed to provide a continuous load-path from the single sole plate to the wall.

SECTION R4505 WALL CONSTRUCTION

R4505.1 Construction. Exterior walls of wood frame construction shall be in accordance with Figures R602.3(1) and R602.3(2). Components of exterior walls shall be fastened in accordance with Table R602.3(1). Walls of wood frame construction shall be designed and constructed in accordance with AF&PA "National Design Specifications for Wood Construction," listed in Chapter 44.

Exterior walls subject to wind pressures of 110 mph (48 m/s) or greater as established in Table R301.2(1) shall be designed in accordance with accepted engineering practice [such as Tables R4505(a) and R4505(b)].

In bearing walls, studs which are not more than 10 feet (3048 mm) in length shall be spaced not more than is specified in Tables R4505(a) and R4505(b) for the corresponding stud size.

TABLE R4505(a)
STUDS IN 110, 120, AND 130 MPH ZONES

Requirements for Wood Stud In: Exterior Walls Supporting One Floor, Roof and Ceiling or Less/ Exterior Nonloadbearing Walls in Two Story Structure or Less/Interior Walls Supporting One Floor, Roof and Ceiling or Less

		110 MPH		110 MPH		120 MPH		130 MPH	
STUD LENGTH	STUD SPACING	2x4	2x6	2x4	2x6	2x4	2x6	2x4	2x6
8	16	Species: Spruce Pine Fir (South) without Structural Sheathing		Species: Spruce Pine Fir (South) with $^3/_8''$ Wood Structural Sheathing					
		#2	Stud	Stud	Stud	Stud	Stud	#2	Stud
8	24	#2	Stud	#2	Stud	#2	Stud	#2	Stud
10	16	#2	Stud	#2	Stud	#2	Stud	#2	Stud
10	24	Design	#2	Design	#2	Design	#2	Design	#2
		Species: Spruce Pine Fir without Structural Sheathing		Species: Spruce Pine Fir (South) with $^3/_8''$ Wood Structural Sheathing					
8	16	Stud	Stud	Stand	Stud	Stud	Stud	#3	Stud
8	24	#2	Stud	#3	Stud	#2	Stud	#2	Stud
10	16	#2	Stud	#2	Stud	#2	Stud	#2	Stud
10	24	Design	Stud	#2	Stud	Design	Stud	Design	Stud
		Species: Southern Pine without Structural Sheathing		Species: Southern Pine with $^3/_8''$ Wood Structural Sheathing					
8	16	Stud	Stud	Stand	Stud	Stud	Stud	Stud	Stud
8	24	#2	Stud	Stud	Stud	#2	Stud	#2	Stud
10	16	#2	Stud	Stud	Stud	#2	Stud	#2	Stud
10	24	Design	Stud	#2	Stud	#2	Stud	Design	Stud

For SI: 1 inch = 25.4 mm, 1 mile per hour = 0.R45 m/s.

Explanation of Table Entries:

Design – Studs with this entry shall be in accordance with accepted engineering practice.

#2 – #2 Grade construction

#3 – #3 Grade

Stud – Stud grade

Standard – Standard grade

Utility – Utility grade

$^3/_8''$ wood structural sheathing shall be attached with 8 D nails at 6″ at perimeter and 12″ at intermediate supports. When a grade is specified in the table any grade above it in this list may be used.

TABLE R4505(b)

EXTERIOR BEARING WALLS[a,b,c,d,e] FIRST FLOOR OF THREE STORY				
	SPF		SP	
WIND ZONE (mph)	2x4 @ 12″ oc Structural Sheathing	3x4 or 2x6 @ 16″ oc Structural Sheathing	2x4 @ 12″ oc Structural Sheathing	3x4 or 2x6 @ 16″ oc Structural Sheathing
110	#2	Any grade	Any grade	Any grade
120	#2	Any grade	#2, #3, Stud	Any grade
130	#2	Any grade	#2, #3, Stud	Any grade

Exterior Nonbearing Walls[a, b, c, d, e, f] First Floor of Three Story						
WIND ZONE (mph)	2x4 @ 12″ oc Blocking	2x4 @ 16″ oc Blocking	3x4 or 2x6 @ 16″ oc Blocking	2x4 @ 12″ oc Blocking	2x4 @ 16″ oc Blocking	3x4 or 2x6 @ 16″ oc Blocking
110	#2, Stud	#2	Any grade	Any grade	#2, #3, Stud	Any grade
120	#2, Stud	NP	Any grade	#2, #3, Stud	#2, #3 Stud	Any grade
130	#2	NP	Any grade	#2, #3, Stud	#2	Any grade

For SI: 1 inch = 25.4 mm, 1 foot = 304.8 mm.

a. Any grade = any grade except standard, utility and economy.

b. Corner bracing is REQUIRED where "Blocking" is specified.

c. 2 – 2x4s at 16 inches or 1 – 2x4 at 8 inches may be used where 3x4 at 16 inches is specified.

d. Refer to Sections R4506 and R4508.4 for sheathing requirements.

e. Bearing stud height is limited to 10 feet.

f. 2x full depth blocking at mid-height.

SECTION R4506
STRUCTURAL BRACING

R4506.1 Structural bracing in 110 mph wind zone.

1. When the wall studs are engineered and do not require structural sheathing, for one story or top story – brace each corner and at 25-foot (7620 mm) intervals with 1 × 4 let-in bracing or 4 foot × 8 foot (1219 × 2438 mm) wood structural panels.
2. All other stories – wood structural sheathing panels.
3. See also Section R602.10.

R4506.2 Structural bracing in 120 and 130 mph wind zones. All stories – wood structural sheathing panels. Blocking shall be installed if less than 50 percent of the wall length is sheathed. Where blocking is required, all panels shall be fastened at 3 inches (76 mm) on center along the edges and 6 inches (152 mm) on center at intermediate framing. If a wall is sheathed less than 25 percent of its length, then that wall shall be designed in accordance with approved engineering practice. See also Section R602.10.

R4506.3 Gable endwalls. Gable endwalls in the 110, 120 and 130 mph (48 m/s, 53 m/s and 57 m/s) wind zones shall either be supported by lateral bracing at the ceiling or have continuous studs from the floor to the roof. 2 × 4 studs at 16 inches (406 mm) on center are limited to 10 feet (3048 mm) in length between supports. Nonbearing 2 × 6 SPF#2 studs at 16 inches (406 mm) on center with $^3/_8$-inch (9 mm) wood structural panel sheathing are limited to unsupported lengths of 18 feet (5486 mm) in 110 mph (48 m/s), 16 feet (4877 mm) in 120 mph (53 m/s) and 14 feet (4267 mm) in 130 mph (57 m/s) wind zones. Wood structural panel sheathing shall extend 12 inches (305 mm) beyond horizontal construction joints except where the horizontal joint occurs over minimum 1 inch (25 mm) thick OSB or plywood rimboard with a minimum 1-$^1/_2$ inch (38 mm) overlap.

R4506.4 Lateral support at ceiling. Where studs are not continuous, the ceiling must be used to support the endwall. 2 × 4 lateral bracing shall be installed on the top of ceiling joists or truss bottom chords at 8 feet (2438 mm) on center and extend 8 feet (2438 mm) inward from the gable endwall. See Figure R4506.7(a).

R4506.5 Full height studs. Full height studs may be sized using the bracing at the ceiling to limit the stud length. See Figure R4506.5.

R4506.6 Cathedral endwalls. Studs shall be continuous from the uppermost floor to either the ceiling or the roof.

R4506.7 Overhang at endwalls. The overhang is limited to 12 inches (305 mm) where a laddered soffit is installed. The overhang may be increased to 24 inches (610 mm) where outlookers are framed over a dropped endwall into the first rafter or truss. See Figure R4506.7(a) and R4506.7(b). If the overhang exceeds 24 inches (610 mm), then the overhang shall be designed in accordance with approved engineering practice.

R4506.8 Roof sheathing attachment. The roof sheathing panel edges shall be blocked and nailed at the end two rafter or truss spaces. See Figure R4506.8.

> **Exception:** The panel edges need not be blocked where 2 × 4 diagonal braces are framed from the top of the endwall to the lateral bracing at the ceiling.

SECTION R4507
MASONRY WALL CONSTRUCTION

R4507.1 Reinforcement. Masonry walls subject to wind loads of 120 mph (53 m/s) or greater, as established in Table R301.2(1), shall be constructed in accordance with Table R4507.1a or R4507.1b or the requirements of Figures R4507.1(a) and R4507.1(b) and this section. Additionally, the minimum area of reinforcement shall not be less than 0.002 times the gross cross-sectional area wall, not more than two-thirds of which may be used in either direction. No required vertical reinforcement shall be less than $^3/_8$ inch (9.5 mm) in diameter. Principal wall reinforcement shall have a maximum spacing of 4 feet (1219 mm) on center.

> **Note:** For 110 mph (48 m/s) wind zones, see Figure 606.11(1) and Table 606.9.

TABLE R4507.1a
H/T LATERAL SUPPORT RATIOS FOR UNREINFORCED EXTERIOR MASONRY WALLS[a,b,d,e]

	OTHER THAN ENCLOSED BUILDINGS[3] DESIGN WIND SPEED, MPH	
Wall construction	120	130
Solid masonry units	13	11
Hollow concrete masonry units or masonry bonded hollow walls	9	8
Cavity walls identical wythes	The H/t ratio shall be 0.70 of the H/t ratio for single wythe walls. The *t*-value shall be the sum of the nominal thickness of the individual wythes.	
Cavity walls with wythes of different types or size masonry	The wall shall be designed based on ACI-530 or the H/t ratio may be 0.70 of the H/t ratio of a single wythe hollow wall. The *t*-value shall be the sum of the nominal thickness of the individual wythes.	

a. *H* = clear height or length between lateral supports.
t = nominal wall thickness.

b. All masonry units shall be laid in Type M, S or N mortar. Where Type N mortar is used and the wall spans in the vertical direction, the ratios shall be reduced by 10 percent.

c. Design based on partially enclosed building.

d. These values are based on using masonry cement mortar. If nonair-entrained Portland cement/lime mortar is used the values in the table may be increased by 1.25. Larger H/t ratios may be used if the design is done in accordance with ACI-530.

e. Larger H/t ratios may be used if the design is done in accordance with ACI-530.

TABLE R4507.1b
H/T LATERAL SUPPORT RATIOS FOR UNREINFORCED EXTERIOR MASONRY WALLS[a,b,d,e]

	ENCLOSED BUILDING[c] DESIGN WIND SPEED, MPH	
Wall construction	120	130
Solid masonry units	15	13
Hollow concrete masonry units or masonry bonded hollow walls	10	9
Cavity walls identical wythes	The H/t ratio shall be 0.70 of the H/t ratio for single wythe walls. The *t*-value shall be the sum of the nominal thickness of the individual wythes.	
Cavity walls with wythes of different types or size masonry	The wall shall be designed based on ACI-530 or the H/t ratio may be 0.70 of the H/t ratio of a single wythe hollow wall. The *t*-value shall be the sum of the nominal thickness of the individual wythes.	

a. *H* = clear height or length between lateral supports.
t = nominal wall thickness.
b. All masonry units shall be laid in Type M, S or N mortar. Where Type N mortar is used and the wall spans in the vertical direction, the ratio shall be reduced by 10 percent.
c. Enclosed buildings are buildings in which the openings in any wall do not exceed the sum of the percentages of openings in the remaining walls and roof surfaces by 5 percent. Buildings in which the 5 percent limit is exceeded by one wall may still be considered enclosed if the percentage of openings in no other wall exceeds 20 percent.
d. These values are based on using masonry cement mortar. If nonair-entrained Portland cement/lime mortar is used the values in the table may be increased 1.2.
e. Larger H/t ratios may be used if the design is done in accordance with ACI-530.

SECTION R4508 ROOF TIE DOWN

R4508.1 Roof tie down. Roof assemblies in the 110, 120 and 130 mph (48 m/s, 53 m/s and 57 m/s) wind zones as established in Table 301.2(1) shall have rafter or truss ties provided in accordance with either Table R4508.2 or the prescriptive requirements of this Section R4508. Anchorage in the 110 mph (48 m/s) wind zone shall be continuous from the roof to the foundation wall or pier. Anchorage in the 120 and 130 mph (53 m/s and 57 m/s) wind zones shall be continuous from the roof to the footing (see Section R4504.1).

R4508.2 Considerations. For trusses, the nailing requirements from Table R4508.2 shall include the nailing requirements for both rafters and ceiling joists. As an alternative to the anchorage requirements of Tables 602.3(1) and R4508.2, the anchorage for roof members may be based on a designed connection taking into account all horizontal and vertical forces. Forces for alternative anchorage design may result from wind uplift; wind lateral on roof; wind lateral on walls to be transferred to the top plate of the wall; roof/ceiling loads; and other loads depending on the specific building design. If roof members align with the studs, the connection may be made from the roof member directly to the studs. If the connection is from the roof member to the top plate, a double top plate is required and both connections must meet the requirements of Table R4508.2. Where ceiling joists are not parallel with and connect to the roof members, the anchorage requirements for each roof member shall be increased by 110 pound (50 kg). Hip end walls and hip rafters shall be anchored in accordance with this section.

TABLE R4508.2
ROOF TIE DOWN REQUIREMENTS ALONG EXTERIOR WALLS (plf)[a,b,c,d]

WIND SPEED (mph)	STRUCTURE WIDTH	
	24 feet	36 feet
110	240	345
120	330	470
130	430	615

For SI: 1 foot = 304.8 mm, 1 mile per hour = 0.R45 m/s.
a. Alternate to the requirements of this table or roof not covered by this table shall be designed in accordance with the *North Carolina State Building Code* or SSTD10, "Standard for Hurricane Resistant Residential Construction."
b. See Section 4505 for material requirements in Coastal High Hazard Areas and Ocean Hazard Areas and Ocean Hazard Areas.
c. Roof slope 2:12 to 12:12.
d. The uplift load requirements may be interpolated for intermediate structure widths.

R4508.3 Anchorage from roof to wall. One and one-half inch (38 mm) by 18 gage fabricated metal ties at 24 inches (610 mm) on center with five 8d nails at each end may be used to resist the uplift loads from the roof to the double top plate. Install one tie at each end of each rafter in 110 mph (48 m/s) and two ties at each end of each rafter in 120 mph (53 m/s) and 130 mph (57 m/s) wind zones. Truss anchorage shall be per designed specifications.

R4508.4 Anchorage using wood structural panels. Wood structural panel sheathing may be used to resist both lateral load and uplift simultaneously. Panels shall be installed as follows:

1. Panels may be installed with face grain parallel or perpendicular to studs.
2. Panels shall be $^3/_8$-inch (10 mm) minimum thickness.
3. Nail spacing shall be 8d at 6 inches (152 mm) on center along vertical edges of panel and 12 inches (305 mm) at intermediate vertical framing.
4. Horizontal nail spacing at double row of 8d staggered at 3 inches (76 mm) on center.
5. Panel shall extend 12 inches (305 mm) beyond horizontal construction joints and shall overlap girders their full depth except where the horizontal joint occurs over minimum 1 inch (25 mm) thick OSB or plywood rimboard with a minimum 1-$^1/_2$ inch (38 mm) overlap.
6. Panel attachment to framing shall be as illustrated in Figure R4508.4.
7. Blocking shall be required at all joints if sheathing is used to resist uplift.

TABLE R4508.4
UPLIFT CAPACITY OF WOOD STRUCTURAL PANEL SHEATHING USED TO RESIST BOTH LATERAL LOAD AND UPLIFT[a]

VERTICAL NAIL SPACING	8D @ 6″ EDGE AND 12″ INTERMEDIATE		
Alternate nail spacing at top and bottom edges	6″	4″	3″
Uplift capacity (plf) nails – double row	240	474	710

For SI: 1 inch = 25.4 mm.
a. Tabulated values are for Spruce-Pine-Fir framing. For Southern Pine framing the uplift values listed may be divided by 0.82.

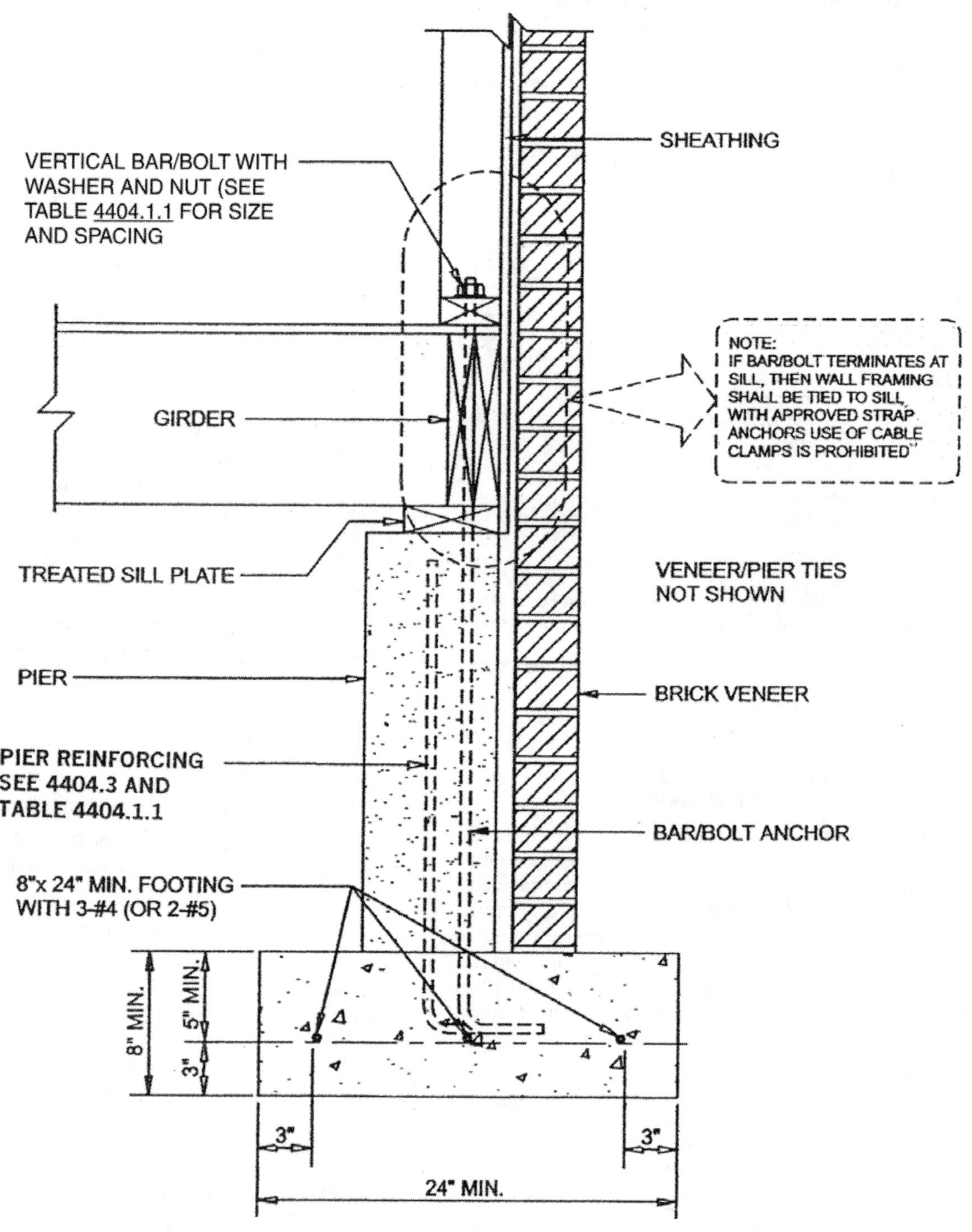

For SI: 1 inch = 25.4 mm.

FIGURE R4504.3(a)
CONTINUOUS VENEER PIER/CURTAIN WALL

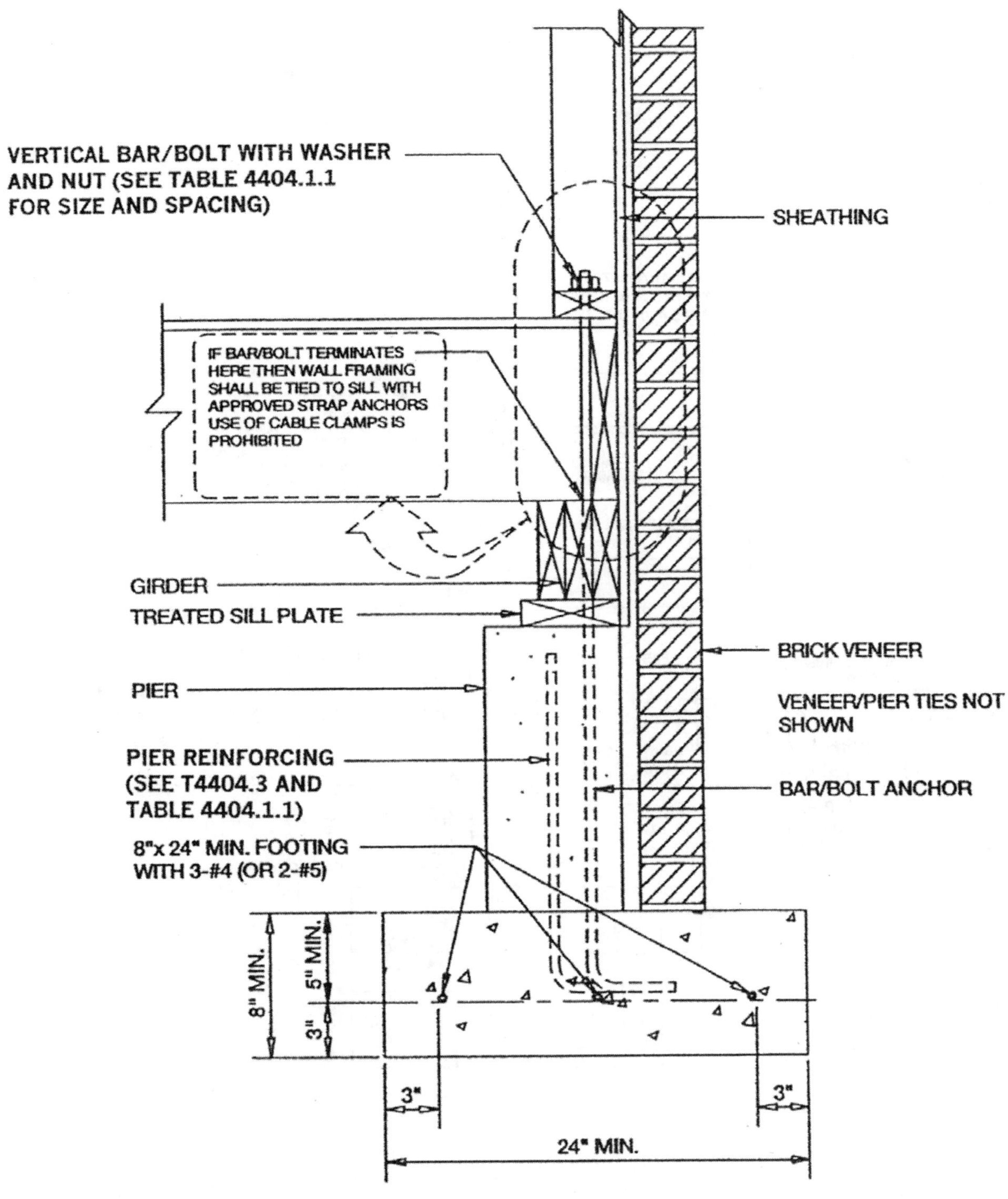

For SI: 1 inch = 25.4 mm.

FIGURE R4504.3(b)
CONTINUOUS VENEER PIER/CURTAIN WALL

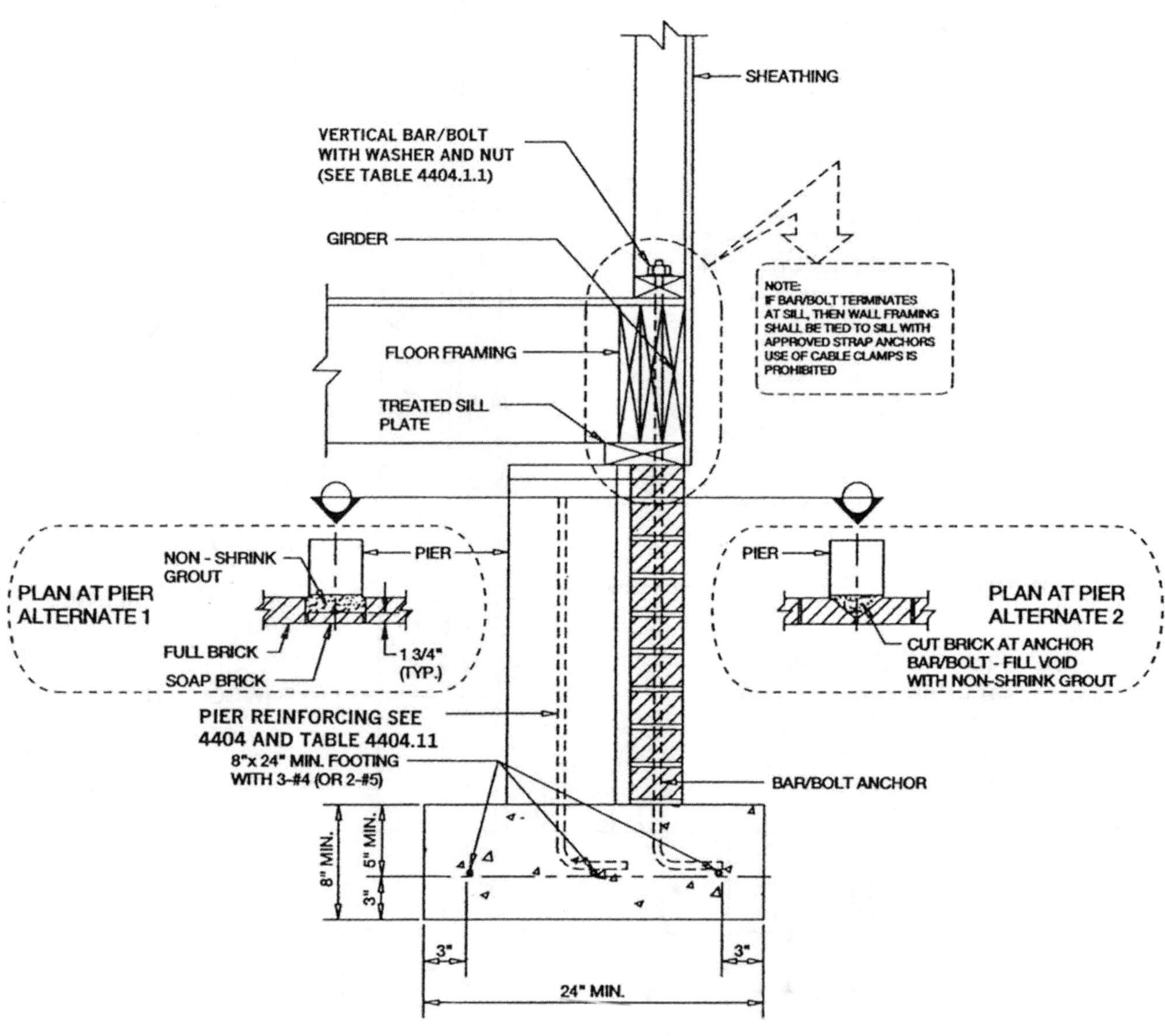

For SI: 1 inch = 25.4 mm.

FIGURE R4504.3(c)
VENEER SHIRT WALL
PIER/CURTAIN WALL

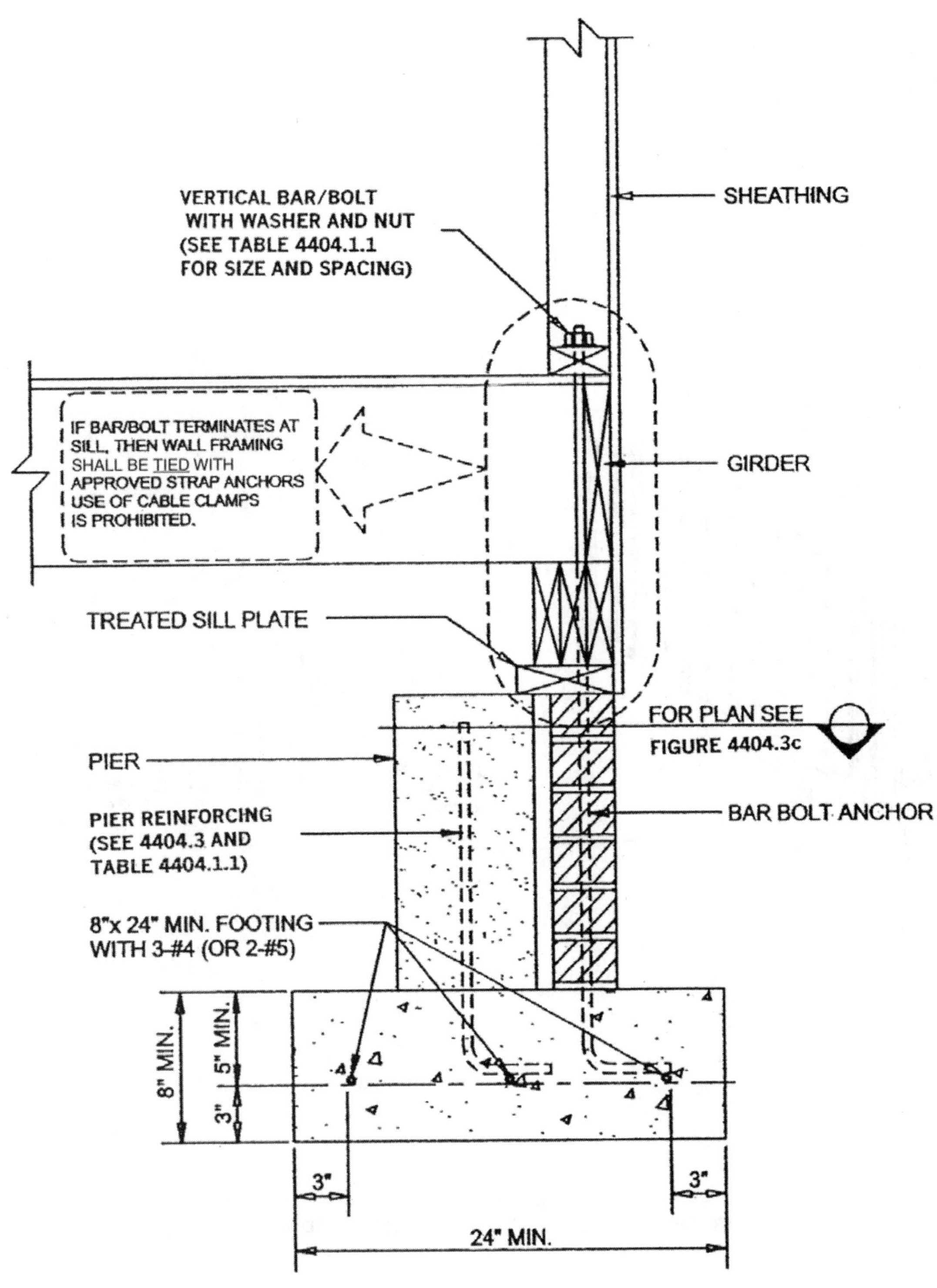

For SI: 1 inch = 25.4 mm.

FIGURE R4504.3(d)
VENEER SHIRT WALL PIER/CURTAIN WALL

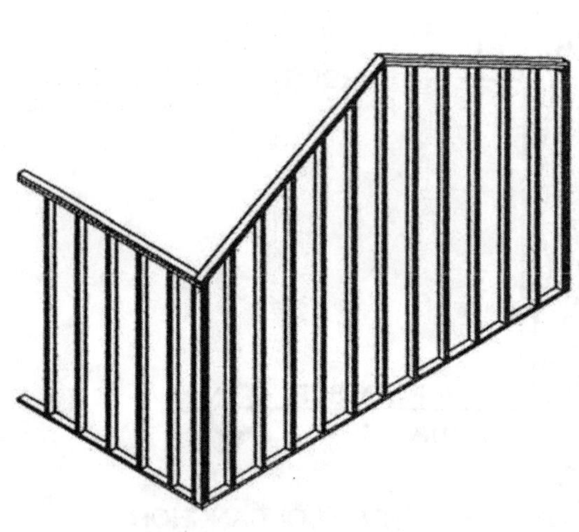

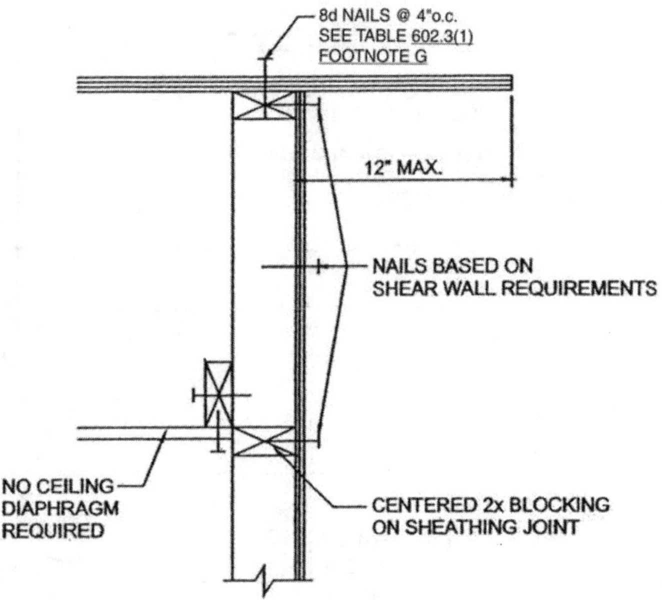

For SI: 1 inch = 25.4 mm.

FIGURE R4506.5
GABLE ENDWALL BALLOON FRAMING PREFERRED METHOD

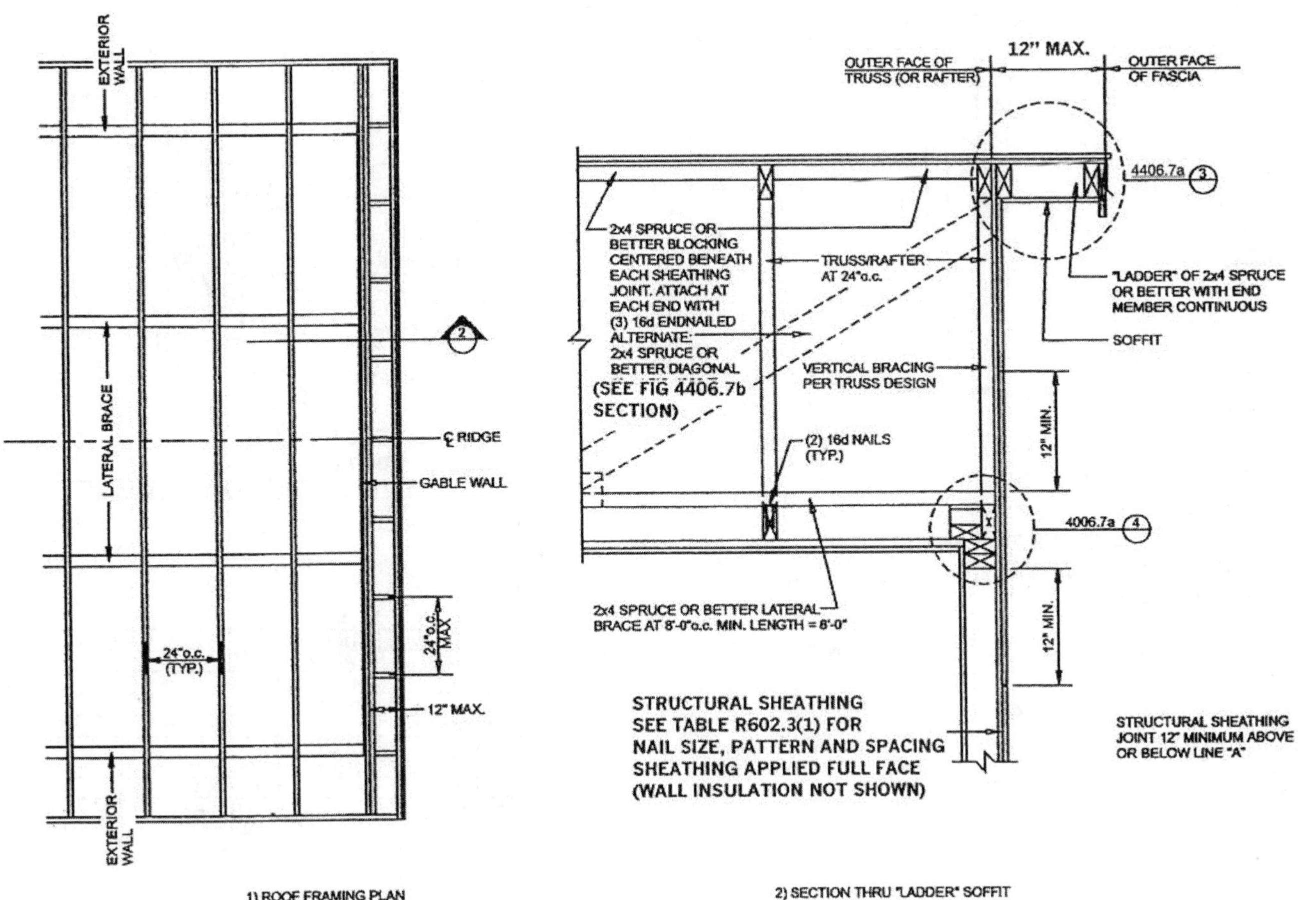

For SI: 1 inch = 25.4 mm.

**FIGURE R4506.7(a)
OVERHANG AT ENDWALLS**

(continued)

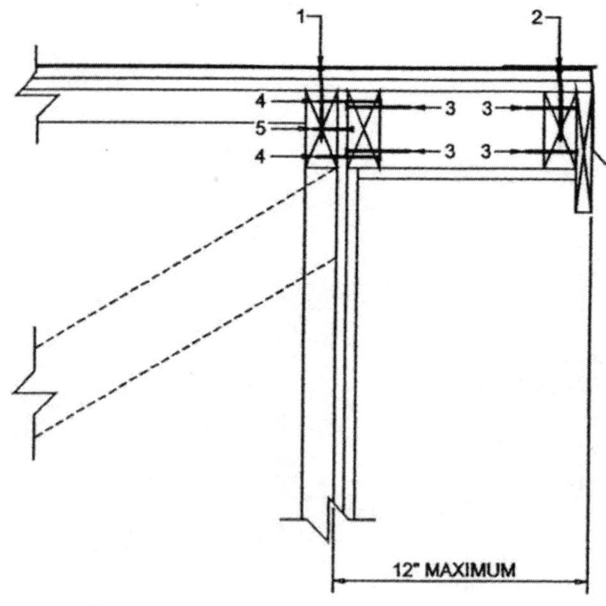

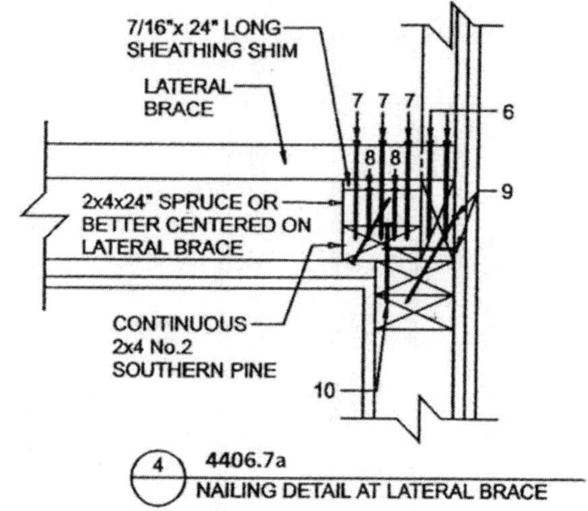

NAIL SCHEDULE			
MARK	No. & SIZE	SPACING	REMARKS
1	8d	4"o.c.	
2	8d	6"o.c.	
3	(2) 16d		EACH SIDE
4	(2) 16d	24"o.c.	
5	8d	6"o.c.	
6	(2) 16d		EACH TRUSS
7	(5) 16d		TYPICAL
8	(6) 16d (* TO 2x4 BELOW)		ALTERNATE: (8) 8d
9	16d	8"o.c.	ALTERNATE TOENAIL & ENDNAIL
10	16d	8"o.c.	

For SI: 1 inch = 25.4 mm.

FIGURE R4506.7a—continued
OVERHANG AT ENDWALLS

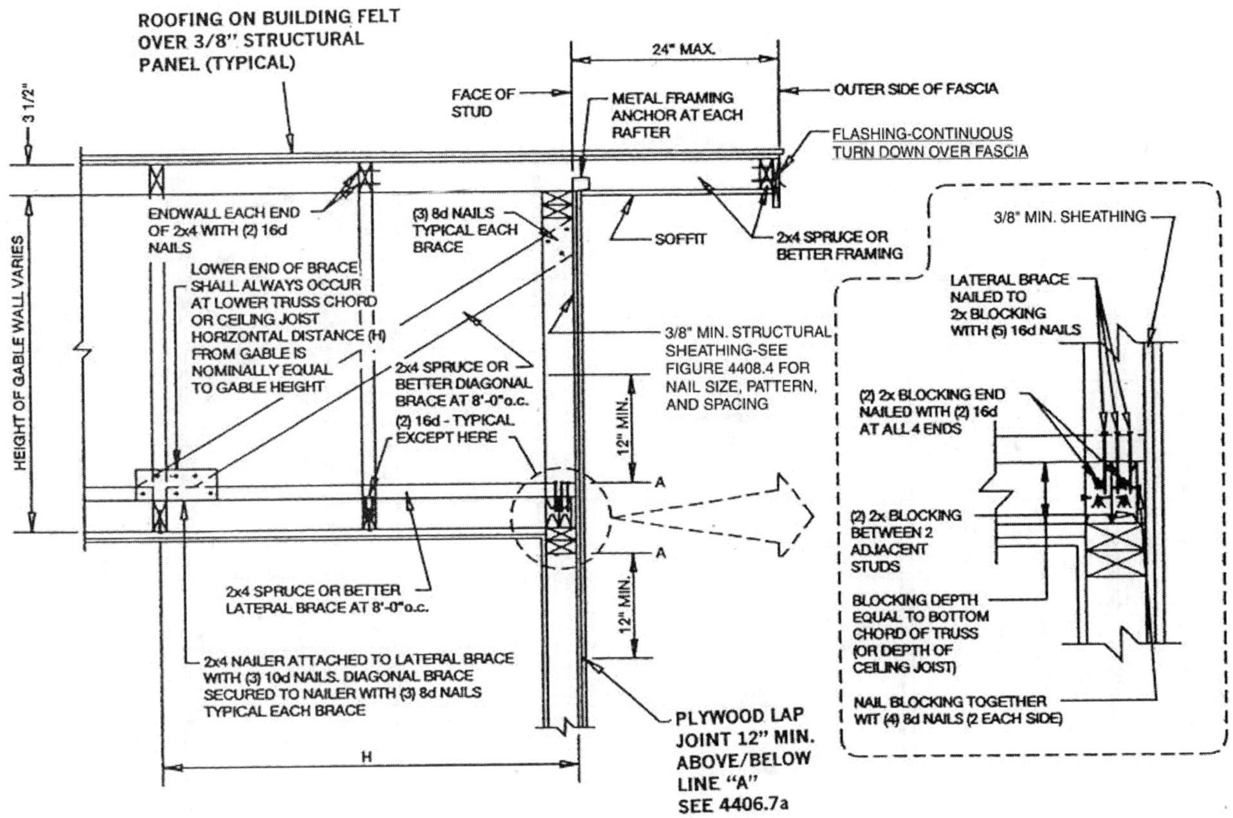

For SI: 1 inch = 25.4 mm.

FIGURE R4506.7b
GABLE END OVERHANG

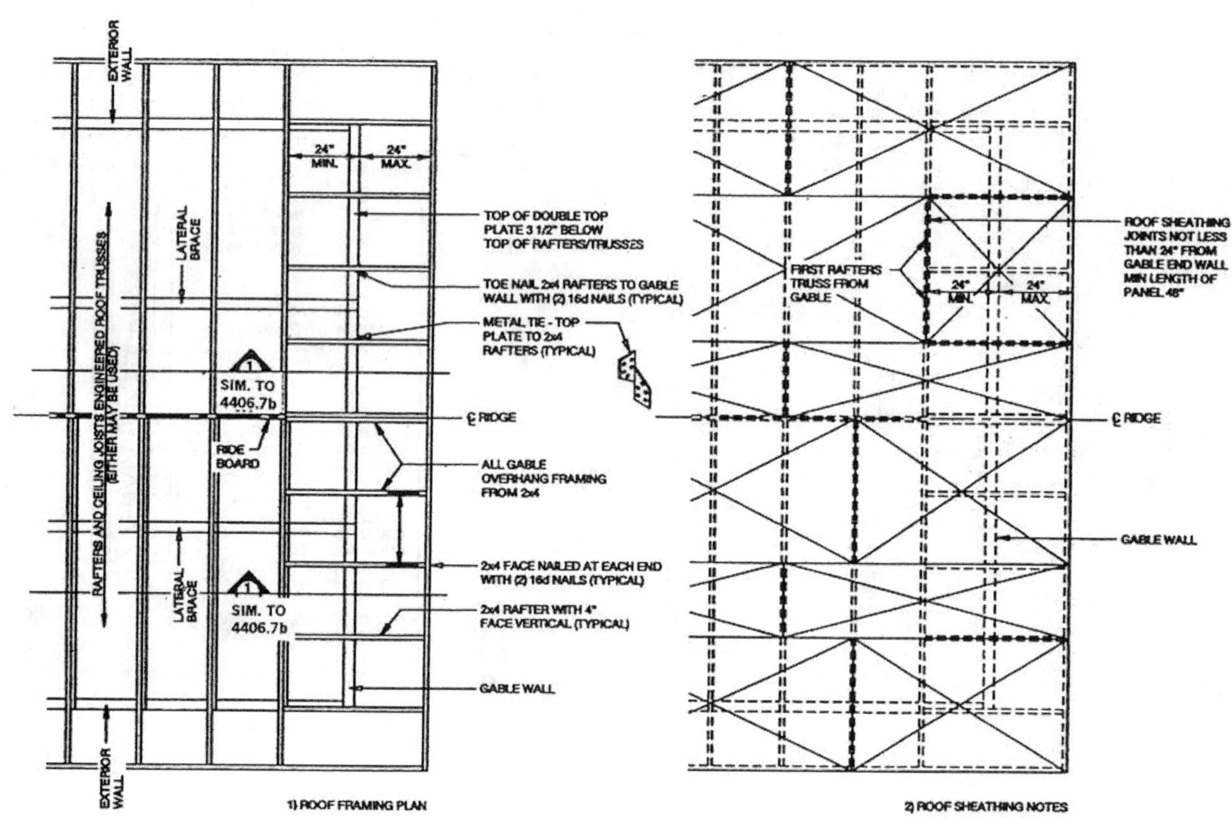

FIGURE R4506.7(c)
GABLE END OVERHANG

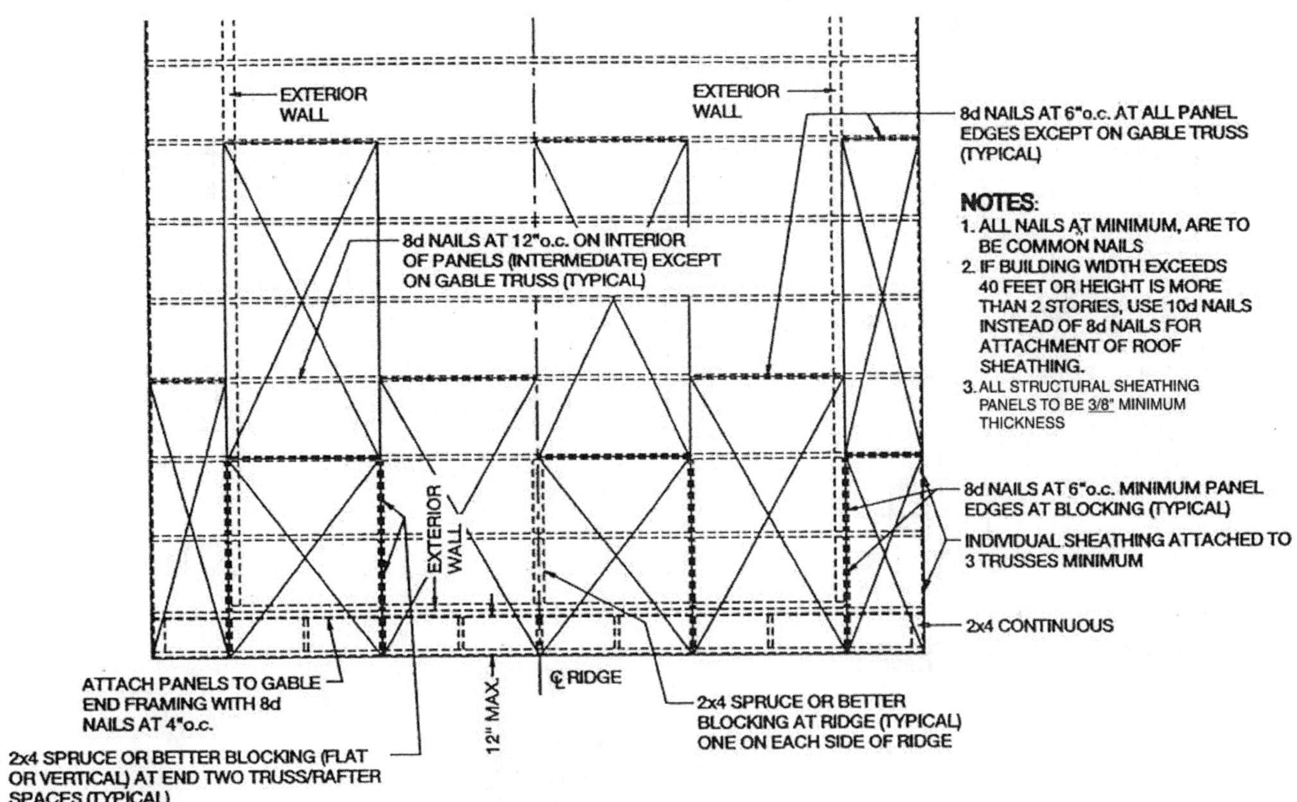

FIGURE R4506.8
ROOF SHEATHING ATTACHMENT PLAN

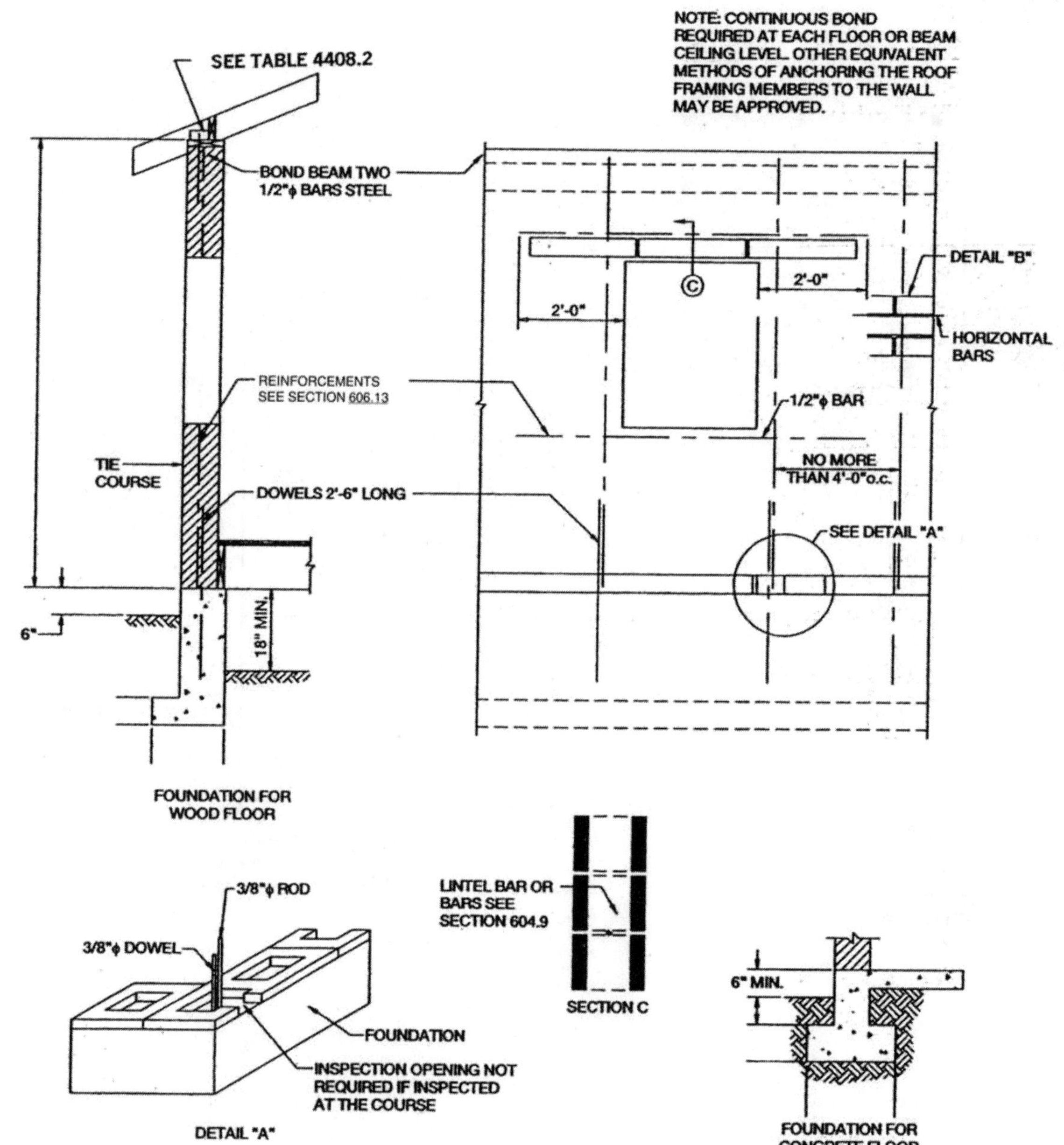

A FULL BED JOINT MUST BE PROVIDED. ALL CELLS CONTAINING VERTICAL BARS ARE TO BE FILLED TO TOP OF WALL. PROVIDE INSPECTION OPENING AS SHOWN ON DETAIL "A". HORIZONTAL BARS ARE TO BE LAID AS SHOWN ON DETAIL "B". LINTEL BARS ARE TO BE LAID AS SHOWN ON SECTION "C".

For SI: 1 inch = 25.4 mm, 1 foot = 304.8 mm, 1 psf = 0.0479 kN/m^2.

FIGURE R4507.1(a)
REQUIREMENTS FOR REINFORCED GROUTED MASONRY CONSTRUCTION WHERE WIND ZONES ARE 120 MPH OR GREATER

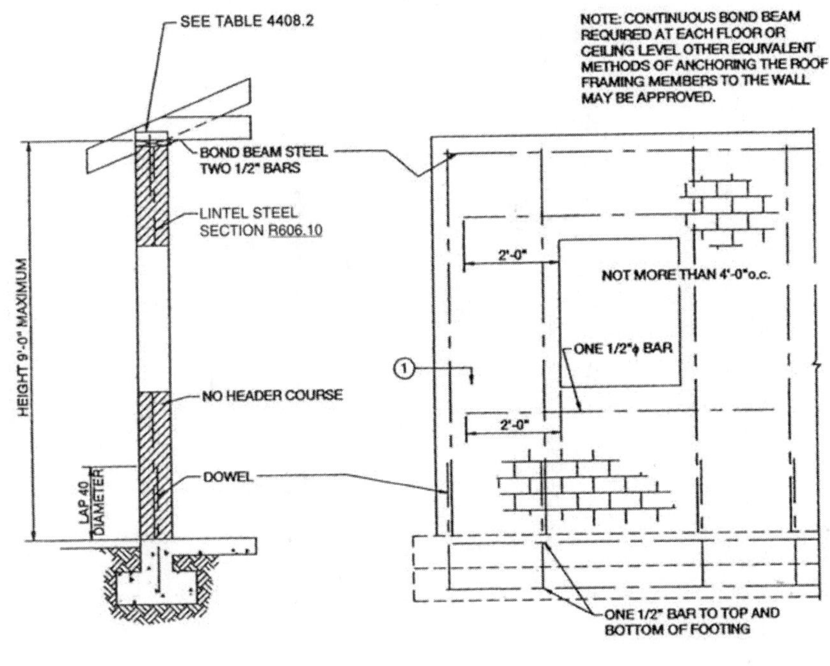

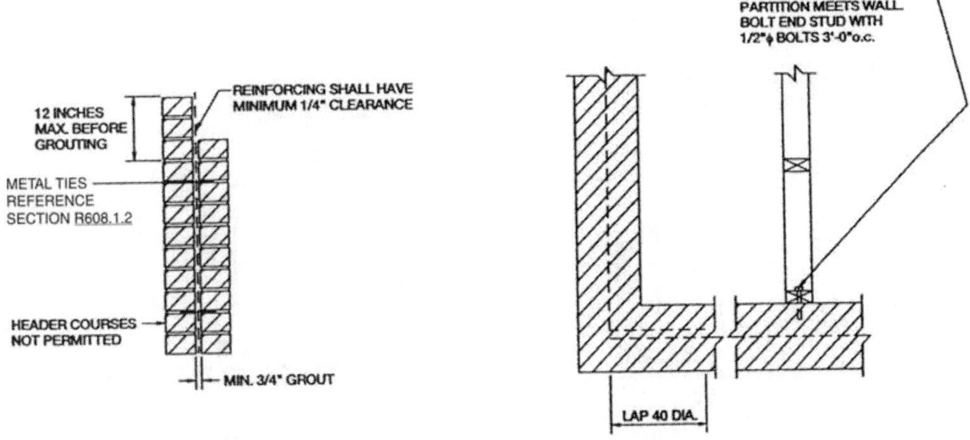

For SI: 1 inch = 25.4 mm, 1 foot = 304.8 mm, 1 psf = 0.0479 kN/m^2.

FIGURE R4507.1(b)
REQUIREMENTS FOR REINFORCED HOLLOW-UNIT MASONRY CONSTRUCTION WHERE WIND ZONES ARE 120 MPH OR GREATER

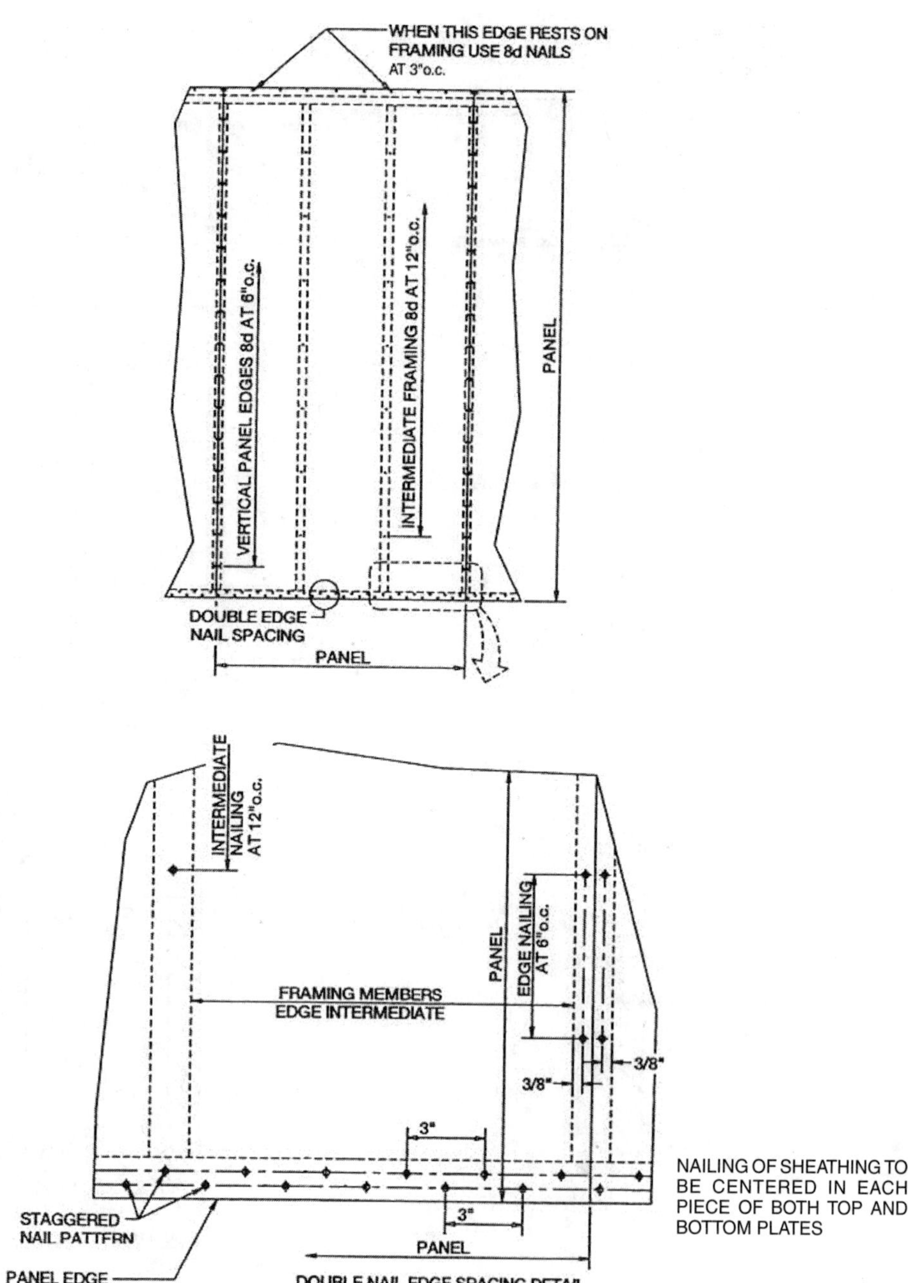

FIGURE R4508.4
PANEL ATTACHMENT TO COUNTER UPLIFT HORIZONTAL OR VERTICAL

CHAPTER 46

COASTAL AND FLOOD PLAIN CONSTRUCTION STANDARDS

This chapter is a North Carolina addition to the 2009 International Residential Code. There will be no underlined text.

SECTION R4601 PURPOSE, APPLICATION AND SCOPE

R4601.1. The requirements set forth in this section shall apply to all construction located within areas identified by governmental agency (state and federal) as coastal high hazard areas, ocean hazard areas, the regulatory flood plain areas, and all areas designated as 130 mph (57 m/s) wind zone. See Table R301.2(1).

SECTION R4602 DEFINITIONS

BASE FLOOD ELEVATION. The peak water elevation in relation to MSL expected to be reached during a design flood which is established by the North Carolina Building Code Council as a flood having a 1 percent chance of being equaled or exceeded in any given year.

COASTAL HIGH HAZARD AREA. An area subject to coastal flooding and high velocity waters including storm wave wash, as shown by Federal Emergency Management Agency Maps and subject to the approval of the Building Code Council.

FLOOD PLAIN. Land below base flood elevation, which of record has in the past been flooded by storm water-surface runoffs, or tidal influx, and as defined by the Corps of Engineers' maps, the Federal Emergency Management Agency maps or as approved by the Building Code Council.

LOWEST FLOOR. The lowest floor of the lowest enclosed area (including basement). An unfinished or flood-resistant enclosure, usable solely for parking of vehicles, building access or storage in an area other than a basement area is not considered a building's lowest floor: provided

1. That the walls are substantially impermeable to the passage of water and the structural components have the capability of resisting hydrostatic and hydrodynamic loads and effects of buoyancy, or
2. Construction shall be designed to automatically equalize hydrostatic flood forces on exterior walls by allowing the entry and exit of flood waters.

MSL. Mean Sea Level as defined by National Geodetic Vertical Datum.

OCEAN HAZARD AREA. An area, as identified by the North Carolina Coastal Resources Commission, and subject to approval by the Building Code Council, near the shoreline of the Atlantic Ocean which has been identified as subject to at least one of the following hazards: (A) Historical or predicted future trends of long-term erosion, (B) erosion expected to occur during a coastal storm reaching the base flood elevation, or (C) shoreline fluctuations due to tidal inlets.

SECTION R4603 PILING STANDARDS

R4603.1. All one- and two-family dwellings in areas identified as coastal high hazard areas or ocean hazard areas shall be constructed on a pile foundation of wood or concrete.

R4603.2 Concrete piles. Concrete piles may be used if made and installed in accordance with the *North Carolina Building Code*, Chapter 18.

R4603.3 Size of wood piles. Round timber piles shall not be less than 8 inches (203 mm) in diameter at building level and have a minimum tip diameter of 6 inches (152 mm). Square timber piles shall not be less than 8 inches square (0.005 m^2), nominal. Piles supporting uncovered stairs, uncovered walkways and uncovered decks shall be 6 inches × 6 inches (153 mm × 153 mm) minimum, or if round, have a minimum tip diameter of 6 inches (153 mm). Piles supporting uncovered stairs, uncovered walkways and uncovered decks less than 5 feet (1524 mm) above grade may be 4 inches × 4 inches (102 mm × 102 mm) minimum.

R4603.4 Required depth of piles. Pile tip shall extend to a depth of not less than 8 feet (2438 mm) below the natural grade or finished grade of the lot, whichever is lower. All pilings within the Ocean Hazard Area shall have a tip penetration of at least 5 feet (1524 mm) below mean sea level or 16 feet (4877 mm) below average original grade, whichever is least. Structures within Ocean Hazard Areas which are placed upon the site behind a line 60 times the annual erosion rate away from the most seaward line of stable natural vegetation are exempt from this additional tip penetration requirement.

R4603.5 Spacing of wood piles. The maximum center-to-center spacing of wood piles shall not be more than 8 feet (2438 mm) on center under load-bearing sills, beams, or girders. However, for dwellings having more than two stories above piles or where the piling spacing exceeds 8 feet (2438 mm) on center, the pile foundation shall be designed by a professional engineer or architect. Pile spacing in the nonload-bearing direction may be 12 feet (305 mm).

R4603.6 Tieing and bracing of wood piles. If sills, beams or girders are attached to the piling, a minimum of two $^5/_8$-inch (16 mm) galvanized steel bolts per beam member shall be through bolted at each piling connection. Piling shall not be notched so that the cross-section is reduced below 50 percent. Sills, beams or girders may be attached using $^3/_{16}$ × 4 × 18-inch (5 × 102 × R467 mm) hot dip galvanized straps, one each side, bolted with two $^1/_2$-inch (12.7mm) galvanized through bolts [see Figure R4603.6(a)]. Bracing of pile foundations is required where the clear height from ground to sill, beam or girder exceeds 10 feet (3048 mm) or the dwelling is more than one story above piles. A line of X-bracing is defined as a row of piles with X-bracing provided in at least two bays. A line of X-bracing shall be provided at all exterior pile lines. Where the perimeter lines of X-bracing exceed 40 feet (12 192 mm), an additional line of

Coastal/Flood Plain

X-bracing shall be provided near the center of the building [see Figure R4603.6(b)]. X-bracing shall be with 2 × 10s through bolted with two $^{3}/_{4}$-inch (19.1 mm) bolts at each end. The building inspector may accept alternate bracing designs if they bear the seal of a professional engineer or architect.

R4603.7. The minimum net retention of preservatives shall be in accordance with AWPA U1.

R4603.8 Piling may be placed by auger, jetting or drop hammer. Piling shall receive a final set by drop hammer or other approved methods, acceptable to the building inspector to ensure compaction of material at end bearing.

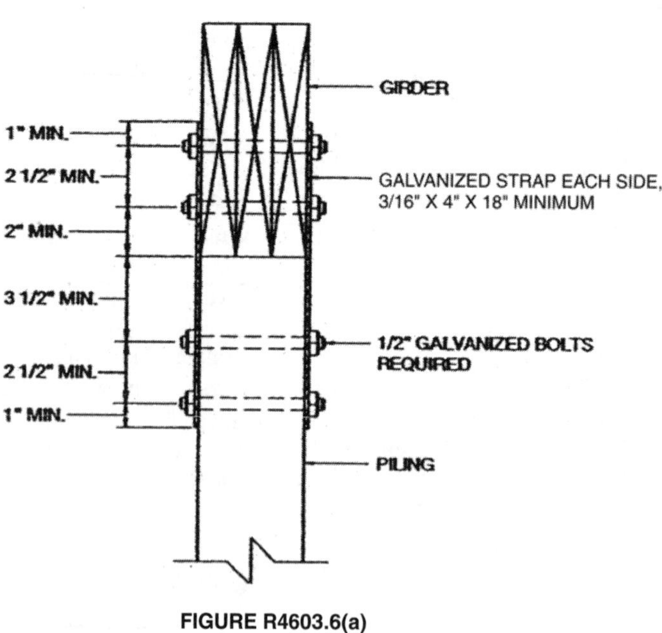

FIGURE R4603.6(a)

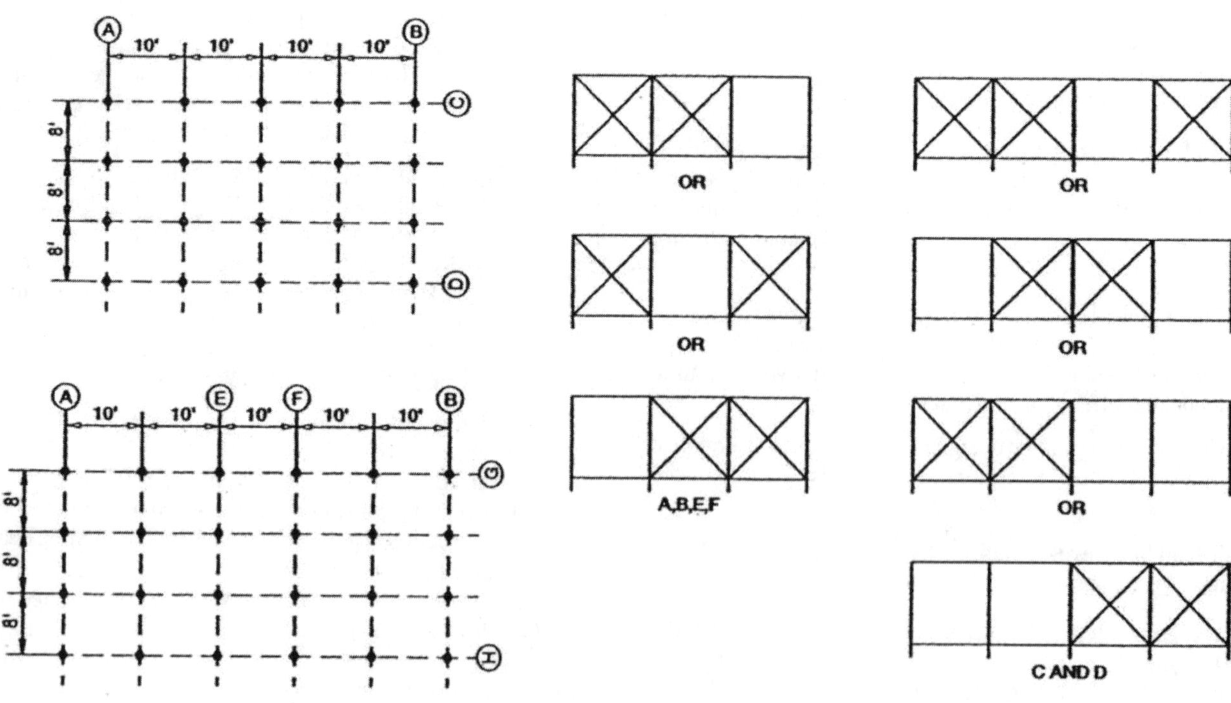

FIGURE R4603.6(b)

ELEVATIONS
(SHOWING POSSIBLE ARRANGEMENT OF X-BRACING IN LINE) (G AND H SIMILAR)

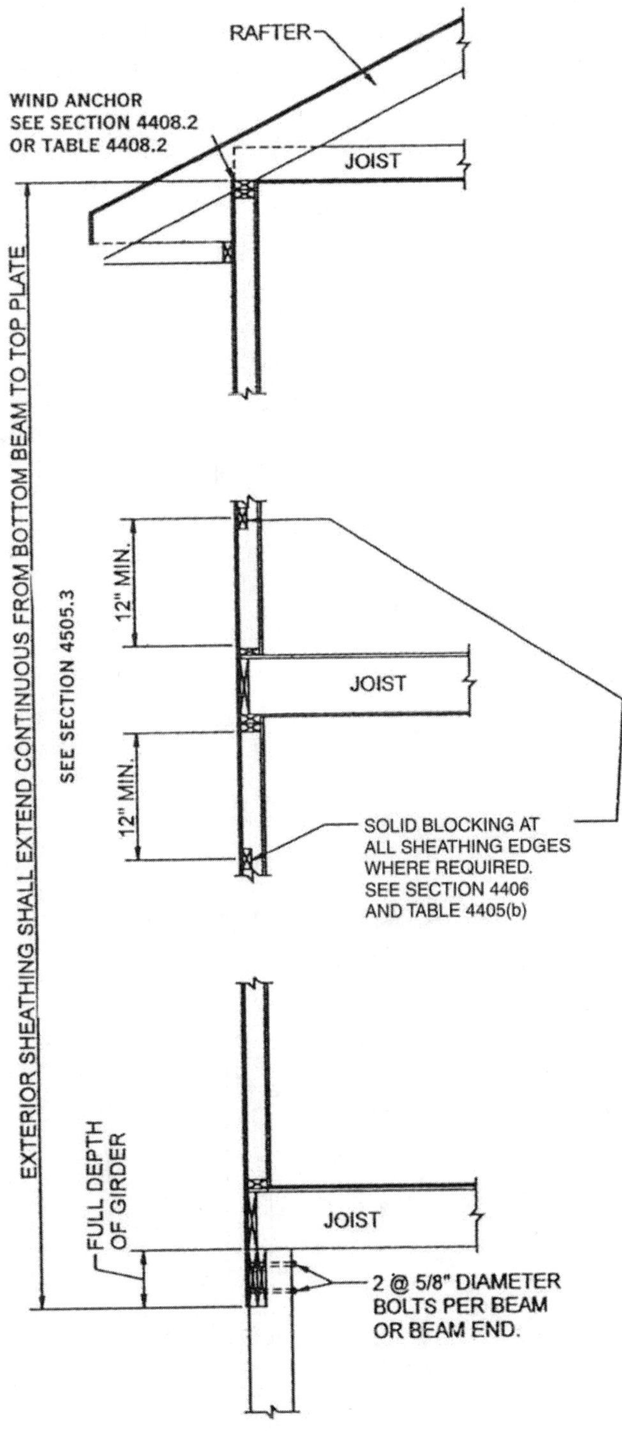

For SI: 1 inch = 25.4 mm.

FIGURE R4605.3(a)
TWO-STORY WALL SECTION (TYPICAL)

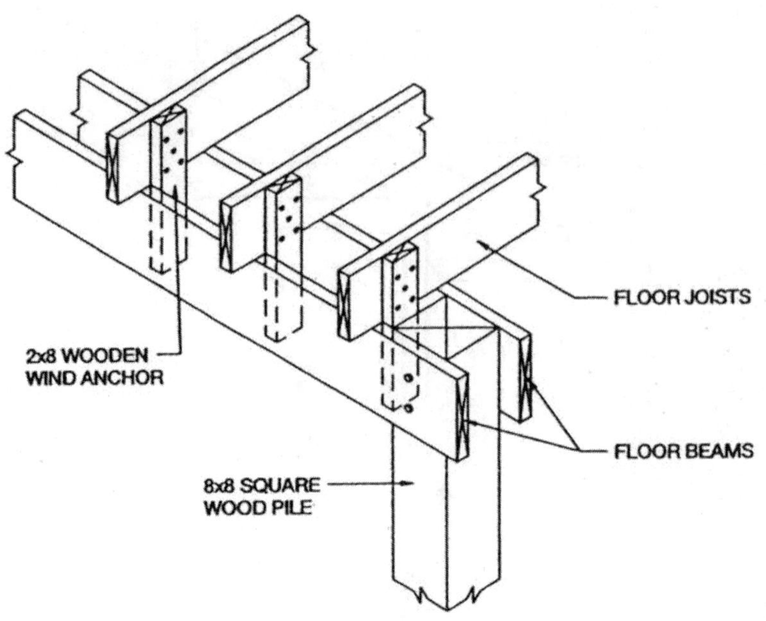

SPACED BEAM TIE DETAILS

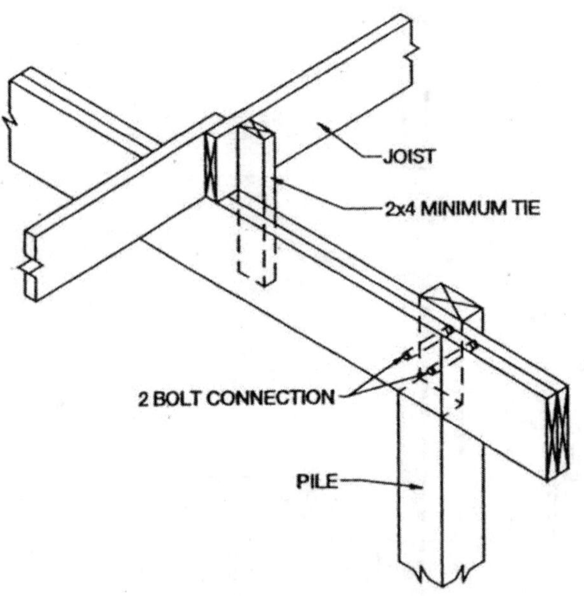

SOLID BEAM TIE DETAIL

FIGURE R4605.3(b)

SECTION R4604 ELEVATION STANDARDS

R4604.1. The lowest structural member, excluding pilings and bracing supporting the lowest habitable floor in the coastal high hazard area and ocean hazard area, shall be elevated above the base flood elevation.

R4604.2. The elevation of the first habitable floor of all structures in the regulatory flood plain except in the coastal high hazard areas shall be above the base flood elevation.

> **Exception:** This requirement does not apply to the addition, renovation or reconstruction to any building which was constructed prior to the initial Flood Insurance Study for that area if the addition, renovation or reconstruction does not exceed 50 percent of the present market value of the structure.

R4604.3. Where walls are constructed below flood elevation in coastal high hazard area and ocean hazard area, they shall be constructed in a manner to eliminate wave forces on the piling.

SECTION R4605 CONSTRUCTION MATERIALS AND METHODS STANDARDS

R4605.1. The requirements of Sections R4605.2 through R4605.9 are applicable in the coastal high-hazard area, the ocean hazard area, and all areas defined as 130 mph (57 m/s) wind zone.

R4605.2. Every rafter or roof truss shall be anchored to the bearing wall as required by Section 4408. At the ridges, rafters shall have a minimum 1 × 6 or 2 × 4 collar or wind beam. Every third rafter not to exceed 4 feet (1219 mm) on center shall be anchored vertically with minimum 1 × 6 or 2 × 4 from its midpoint to ceiling joists below.

R4605.3 Wood frame wall construction. Maximum stud spacing shall be 16 inches o.c. (406 mm) for 2 × 4s and 24 inches (610 mm) for 2 × 6s. See Section 4405 for wall construction requirements. See Section 4408 for uplift anchorage requirements. Wood structural panel sheathing, including endwall sheathing, shall extend 12 inches (305 mm) beyond construction joints and shall overlap girders their full depth. Panels may be installed with face grain either parallel or perpendicular to stud.

R4605.4. Equal or better methods of tying structures together and to foundations designed for a specific building by a registered design professional shall be accepted by the building inspector.

R4605.5. In the coastal hazard area and the ocean hazard area, all metal connectors and fasteners outside of conditioned spaces shall be hot-dip galvanized steel after fabrication and meet ASTM A 153. Exposed metal connectors, such as tie-down straps on porches, decks, and areas under the structure, shall be a minimum $^{3}/_{16}$-inch (5 mm) thick, and shall be hot-dip galvanized after fabrication and meet ASTM A 123 or ASTM A 153. Stainless steel light-gage metal connectors shall be permitted in exposed or partially exposed locations. Metal connectors of approved equivalent corrosion-resistant material may be accepted. See Table R4605.5.

R4605.6 Building anchorage.

1. For masonry buildings, the roof structure, including rafters and joists, shall be anchored to the wall in accordance with Section R606.9.2.1. All mortar used for masonry walls shall be Type M or S.
2. For masonry or wood frame buildings, all sills, beams or girders which resist uplift (including interior sills, beams, girders, and joists where the perimeter is unenclosed) shall be anchored to the footing in accordance with Section 4404. Footing dowel bars shall have an 8-inch (203 mm) hook.
3. Where wood partitions and masonry walls join, the stud abutting the masonry shall be double and bolted to the masonry with three $^{1}/_{2}$-inch (13 mm) galvanized bolts.
4. Steel and wooden columns and posts, including porch columns, shall be anchored with metal ties and bolts to their foundations and to the members that they support.

R4605.7 Roof coverings. Deleted.

R4605.8 Insulation. Insulation installed in floors in buildings elevated on pilings shall be held in place with plywood with exterior glue or other material approved by the building inspector.

R4605.9 Accessory structures. Detached accessory structures and out buildings shall be bolted to their foundation or otherwise constructed so as to prevent overturning during high winds.

TABLE R4605.5[a]
CORROSION RESISTANCE
(Applies only to Structure Located in Coastal High-Hazard Areas and Ocean Hazard Areas)

	OPEN (exterior, porches, under house)	EXPOSURE LEVEL VENTED/ENCLOSED (attic, floor trusses, enclosed crawl spaces and stud cavity)	CONDITIONED (heated/cooled living areas)
Nails, staples, screws	Hot-dip galvanized	Hot-dip galvanized	—
Nuts, bolts, washers, tie rods	Hot-dip galvanized	Hot-dip galvanized	—
Steel connection plates & straps ($^3/_{16}''$ minimum thickness)	Hot-dip galvanized after fabrication	Hot-dip galvanized	—
Sheet metal connectors, wind anchors, joists hangers, steel joists and beams	Stainless steel or hot-dipped galvanized after fabrication	Hot-dip galvanized after plate fabrication	Hot-dip galvanized
Truss plates	Stainless steel or hot-dipped galvanized after fabrication	Hot-dip galvanized after fabrication or stainless steel within 6′-0″ of a gable louver or soffit vent. Otherwise in accordance with TPI-1 of the Truss Plate Institute.	Standard galvanized

a. Applies only to structures located in Coastal High-Hazard Area and Ocean High Hazard Area.

APPENDIX A

SIZING AND CAPACITIES OF GAS PIPING

<u>Deleted</u>

APPENDIX B

SIZING OF VENTING SYSTEMS SERVING APPLIANCES EQUIPPED WITH DRAFT HOODS, CATEGORY I APPLIANCES, AND APPLIANCES LISTED FOR USE WITH TYPE B VENTS

Deleted

APPENDIX C

EXIT TERMINALS OF MECHANICAL DRAFT AND DIRECT-VENT VENTING SYSTEMS

Deleted

APPENDIX D

RECOMMENDED PROCEDURE FOR SAFETY INSPECTION OF AN EXISTING APPLIANCE INSTALLATION

Deleted

APPENDICES E-1 THROUGH E-4

RESIDENTIAL REQUIREMENTS

(The provisions contained in this appendix are adopted as part of this Code.)

APPENDIX E-1
ENERGY EFFICIENCY CERTIFICATE (Section N1101.9)

ENERGY EFFICIENCY CERTIFICATE N1101.9	
Builder, Permit Holder or Registered Design Professional Print Name: Signature:	
Property Address:	
Date:	
Insulation Rating - List the value covering largest area to all that apply	***R*-Value**
Ceiling/roof:	R-
Wall:	R-
Floor:	R-
Closed Crawl Space Wall:	R-
Closed Crawl Space Floor:	R-
Slab:	R-
Basement Wall:	R-
Fenestration:	
U-Factor	
Solar Heat Gain Coefficient(SHGC)	
Building Air Leakage	
❑ Visually inspected according to N1102.4.2.1 OR	
❑ Building Air Leakage Test Results (Sec. N1102.4.2.2) ACH50 [Target: 5.0] or CFM50/SFSA [Target: 0.30]	
Name of Tester / Company: Date: Phone:	
Ducts:	
Insulation	R-
Total Duct Leakage Test Result (Sect. N1103.2.2) (CFM25 Total/100SF) [Target: 6]	
Name of Tester or Company: Date: Phone:	
Certificate to be displayed permanently	

APPENDIX E-2
INSULATION AND AIR SEALING DETAILS

APPENDIX E-2.1

N1102.2.1 Ceilings with attic spaces: Exception for fully enclosed attic floor systems.

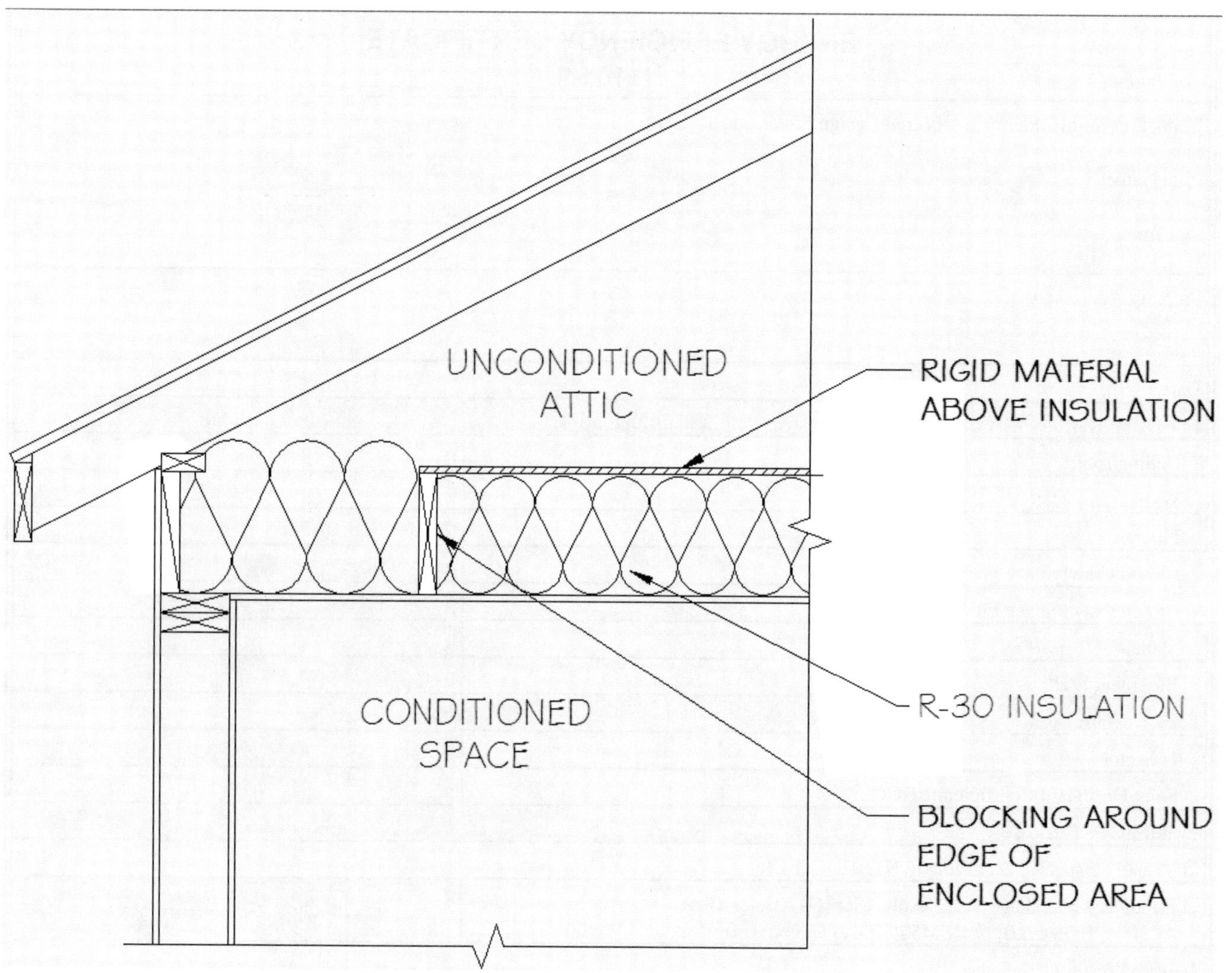

SECTION VIEW OF CEILING WITH ATTIC SPACE

APPENDIX E-2.2

N1102.2.9 Closed crawl space walls. Insulation illustrations.

Foam or porous insulation has 3" top inspection gap and extends down 3" above top of wall footing or concrete floor

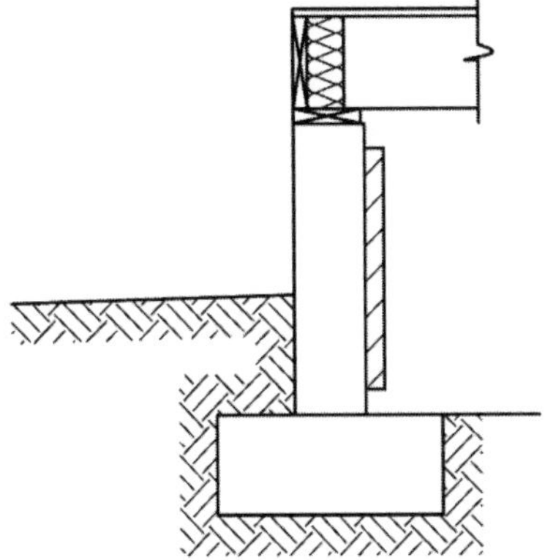

Foam or porous insulation has 3" top inspection gap and extends down 3" above interior ground surface

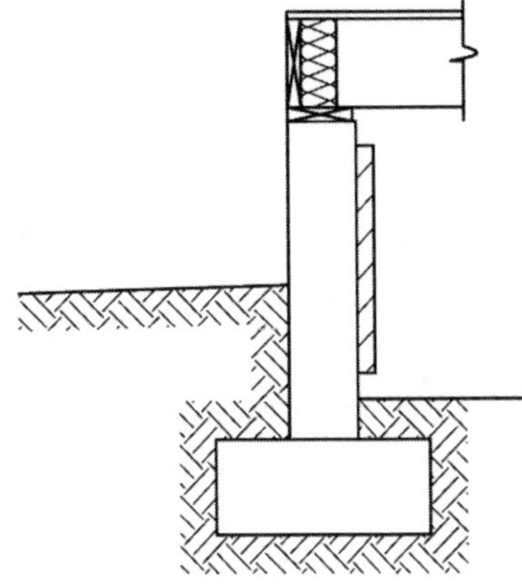

Foam or porous insulation has 3" top inspection gap and extends down 24" below grade

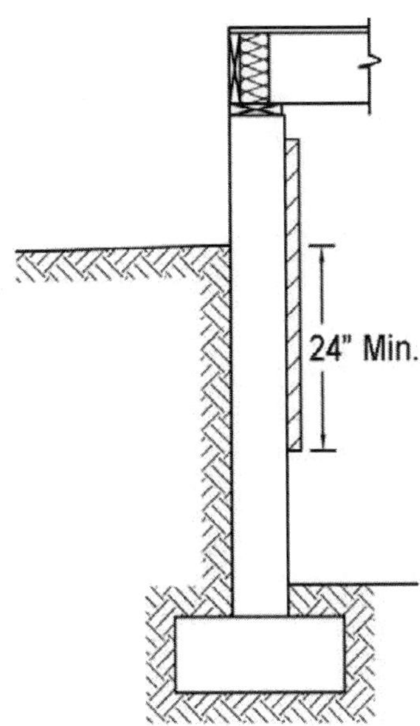

APPENDIX E-2.3

N1102.2.12 Framed cavity walls. Insulation enclosure – 1. Tubs

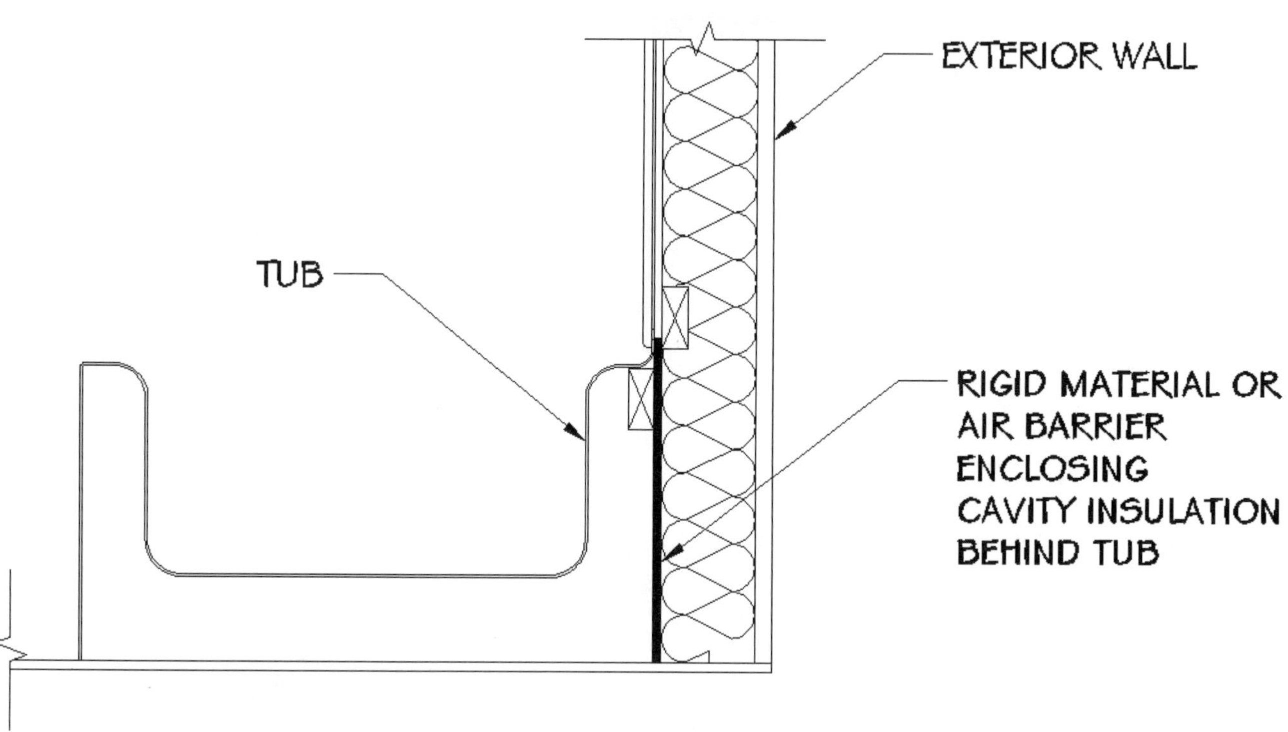

SECTION VIEW OF BATH TUB ON EXTERIOR WALL

N1102.2.12 Framed cavity walls. Insulation enclosure – 2. Showers

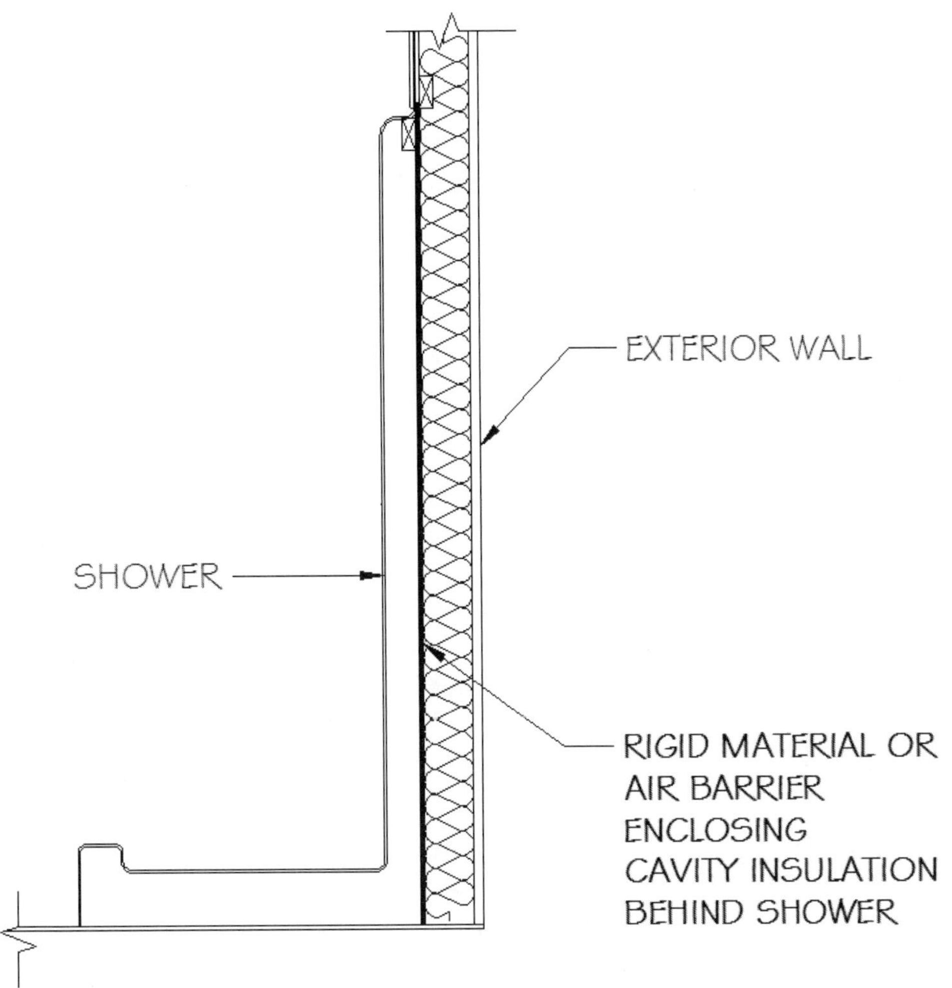

SECTION VIEW OF SHOWER ON EXTERIOR WALL

N1102.2.12 Framed cavity walls. Insulation enclosure – 3. Stairs

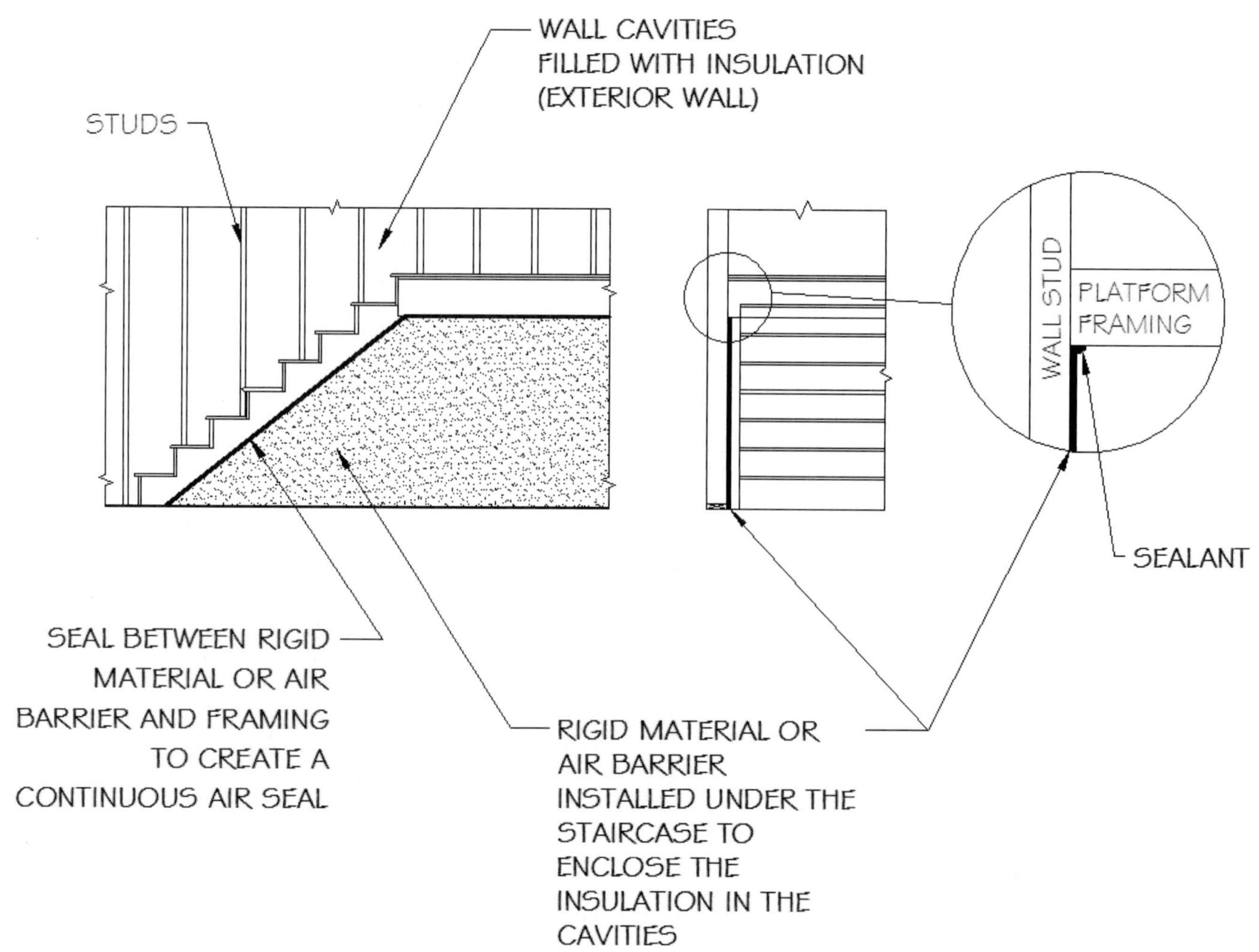

SECTION VIEW OF INTERIOR STAIRCASE ON EXTERIOR WALL (OPTION 1)

N1102.2.12 Framed cavity walls. Insulation enclosure – 3. Stairs

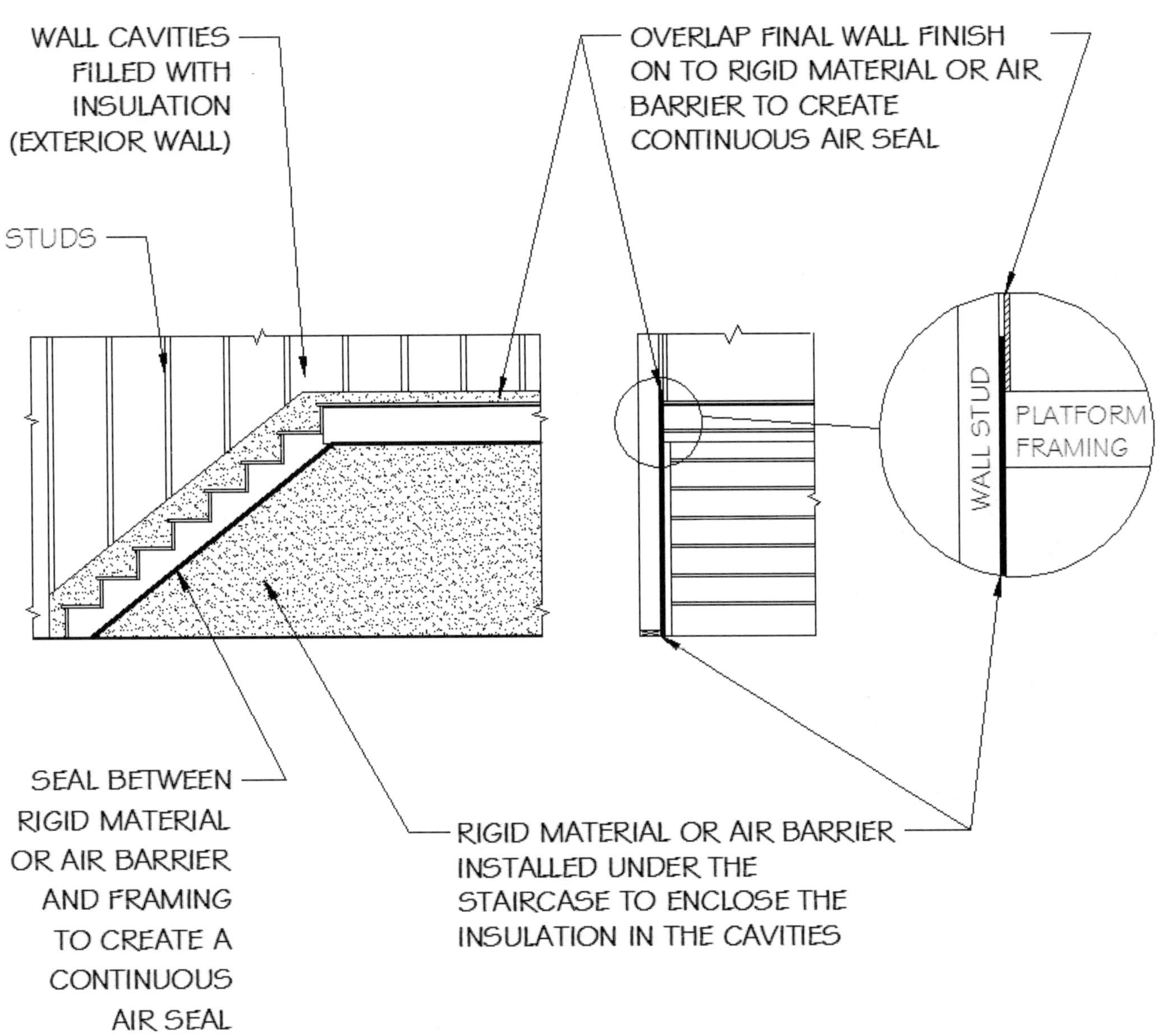

SECTION VIEW OF INTERIOR STAIRCASE ON EXTERIOR WALL (OPTION 2)

N1102.2.12 Framed cavity wall. Insulation enclosure – 4. Direct vent gas fireplace

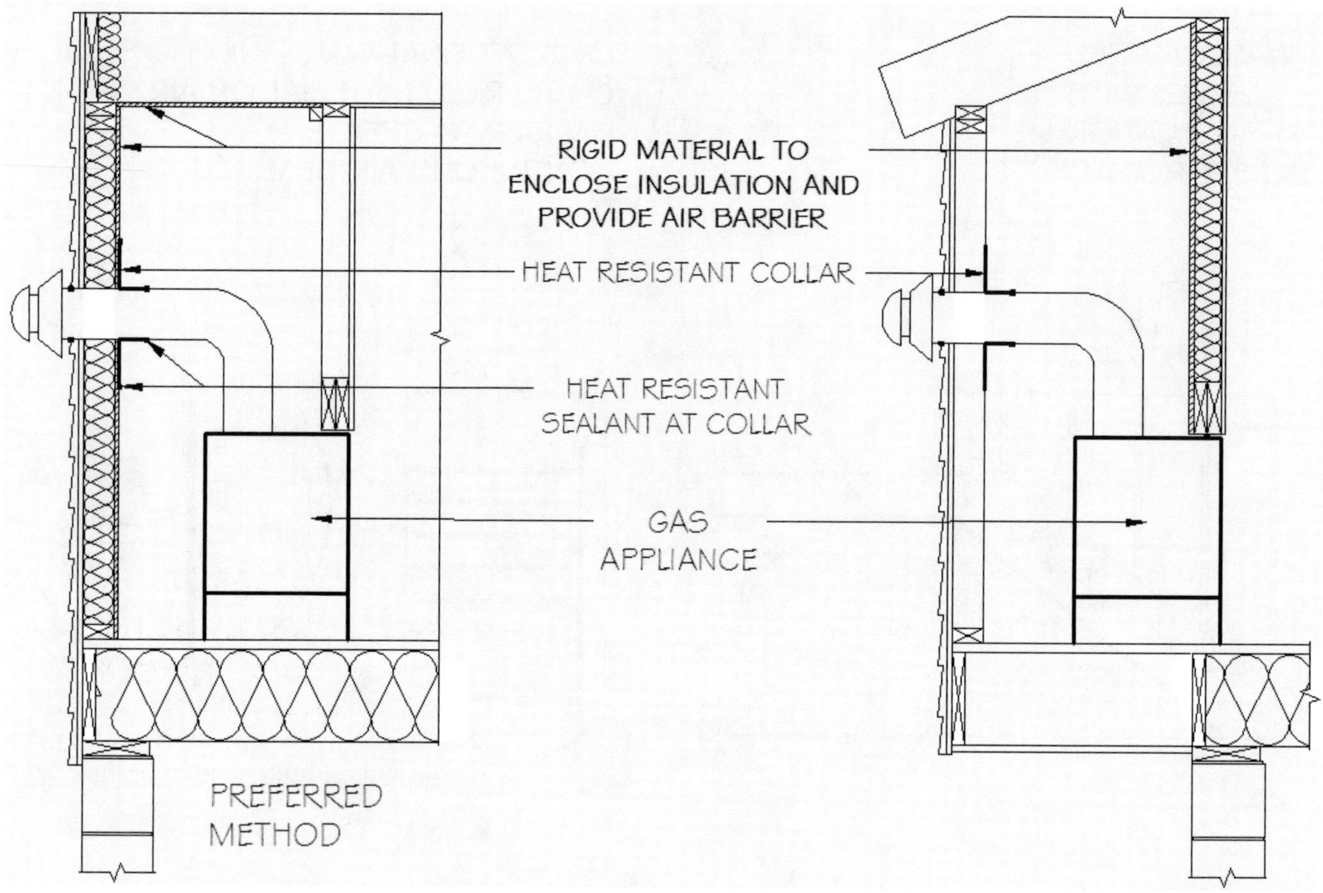

SECTION VIEW OF DIRECT VENT GAS FIREPLACE

N1102.2.12 Framed cavity walls. Insulation enclosure – 5. Walls that adjoin attic spaces

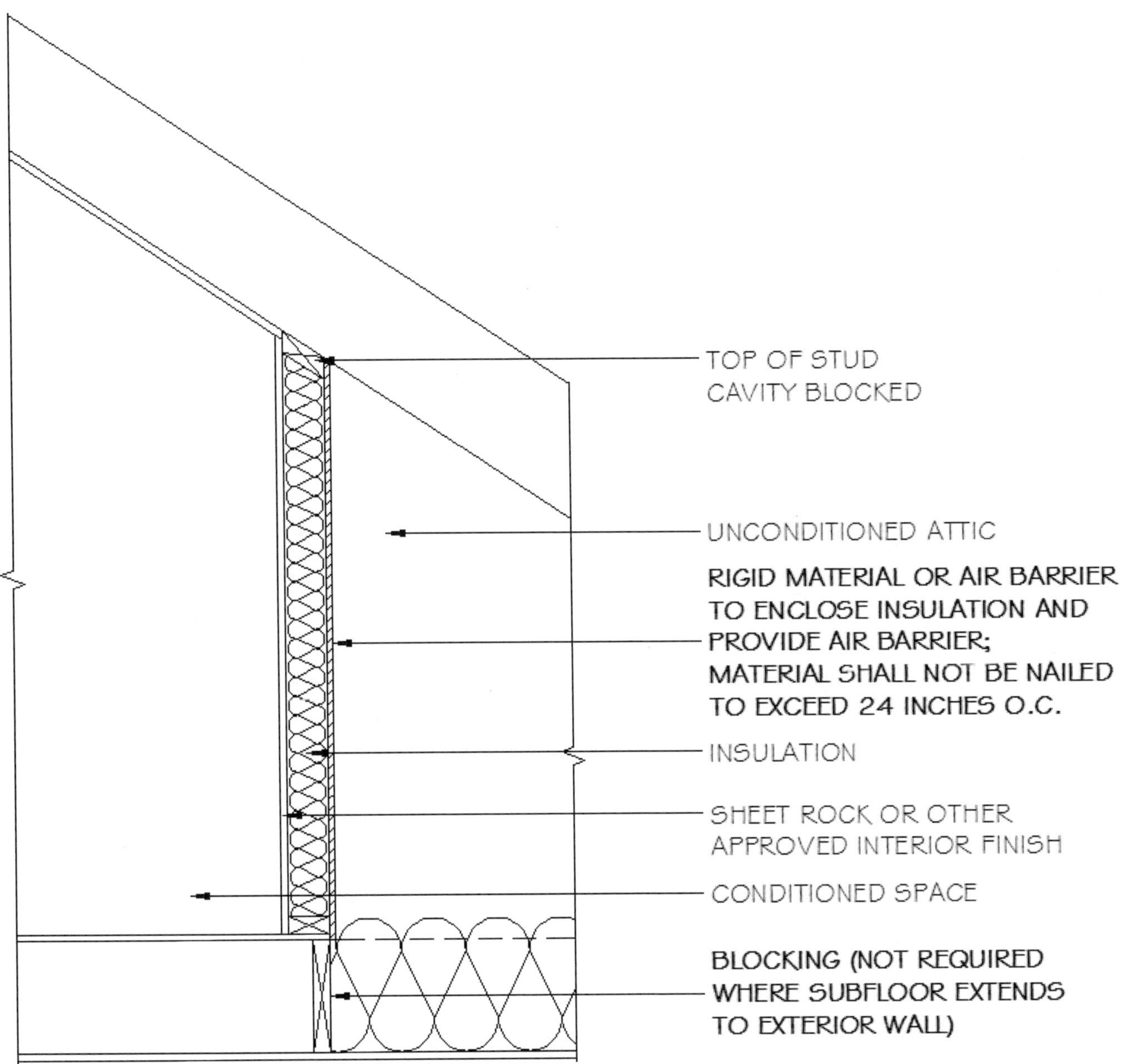

SECTION VIEW OF WALL ADJOINING ATTIC SPACE

N1102.2.12 Framed cavity walls. Insulation enclosure – 5. Walls that adjoin attic spaces

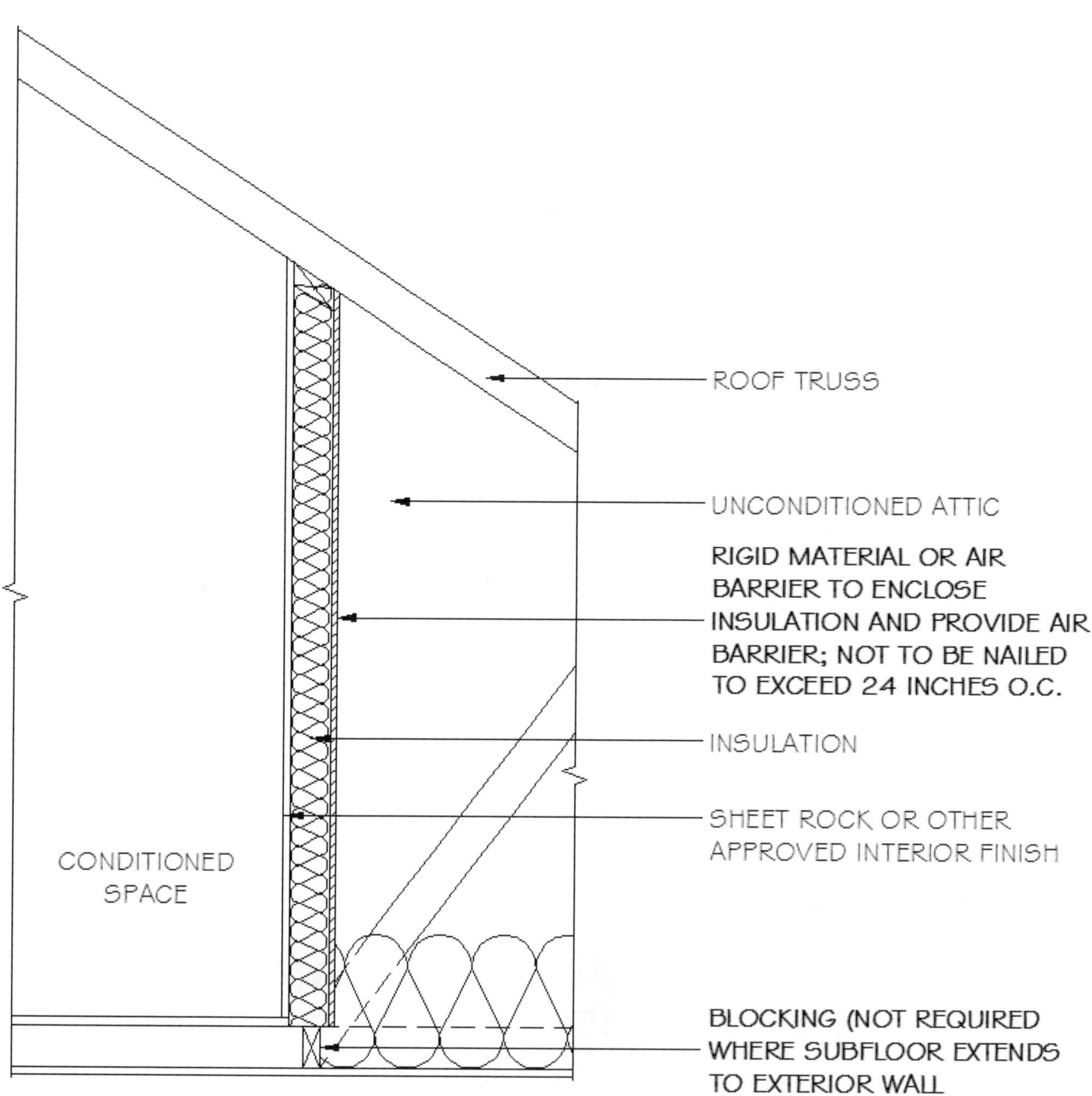

SECTION VIEW OF WALL ADJOINING ATTIC SPACE

APPENDIX E-2.4

N1102.4.1 Building thermal envelope. – 1. Block and seal floor/ceiling systems

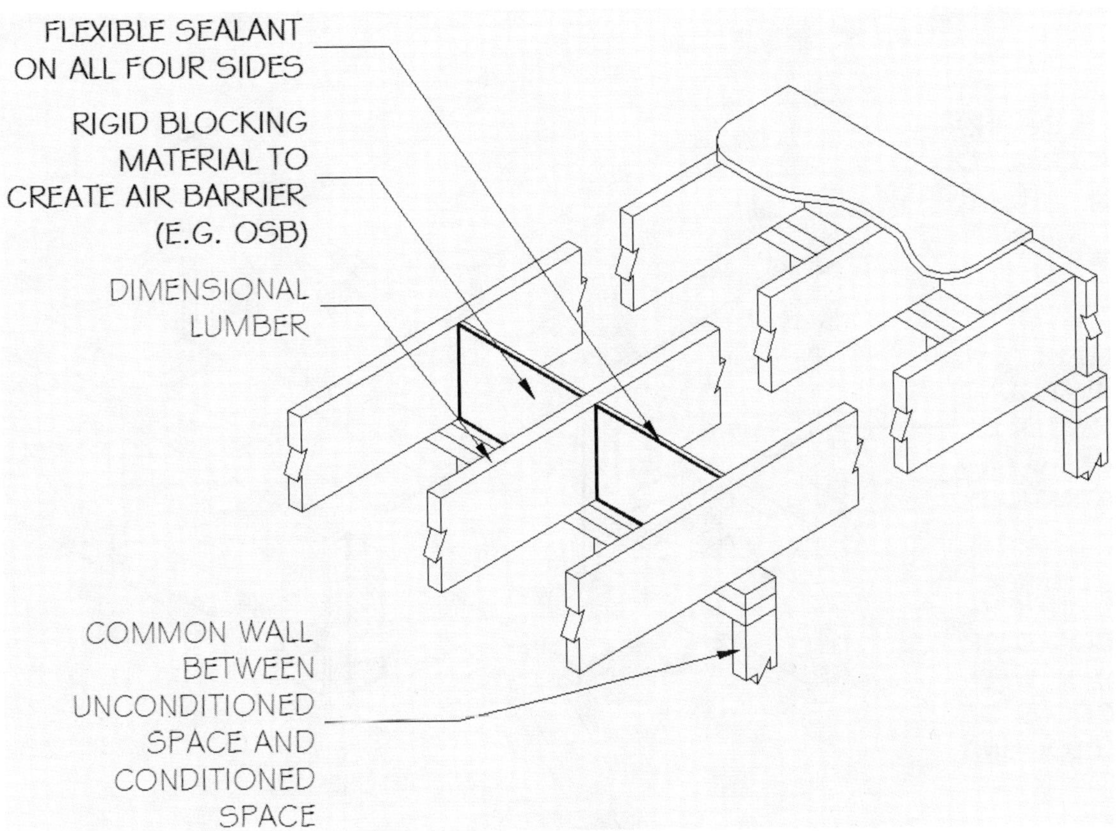

ISOMETRIC VIEW OF DIMENSIONAL LUMBER FLOOR/CEILING SYSTEM
ABOVE COMMON WALL BETWEEN UNCONDITIONED AND CONDITIONED SPACE

N1102.4.1 Building thermal envelope. – 1. Block and seal floor/ceiling systems

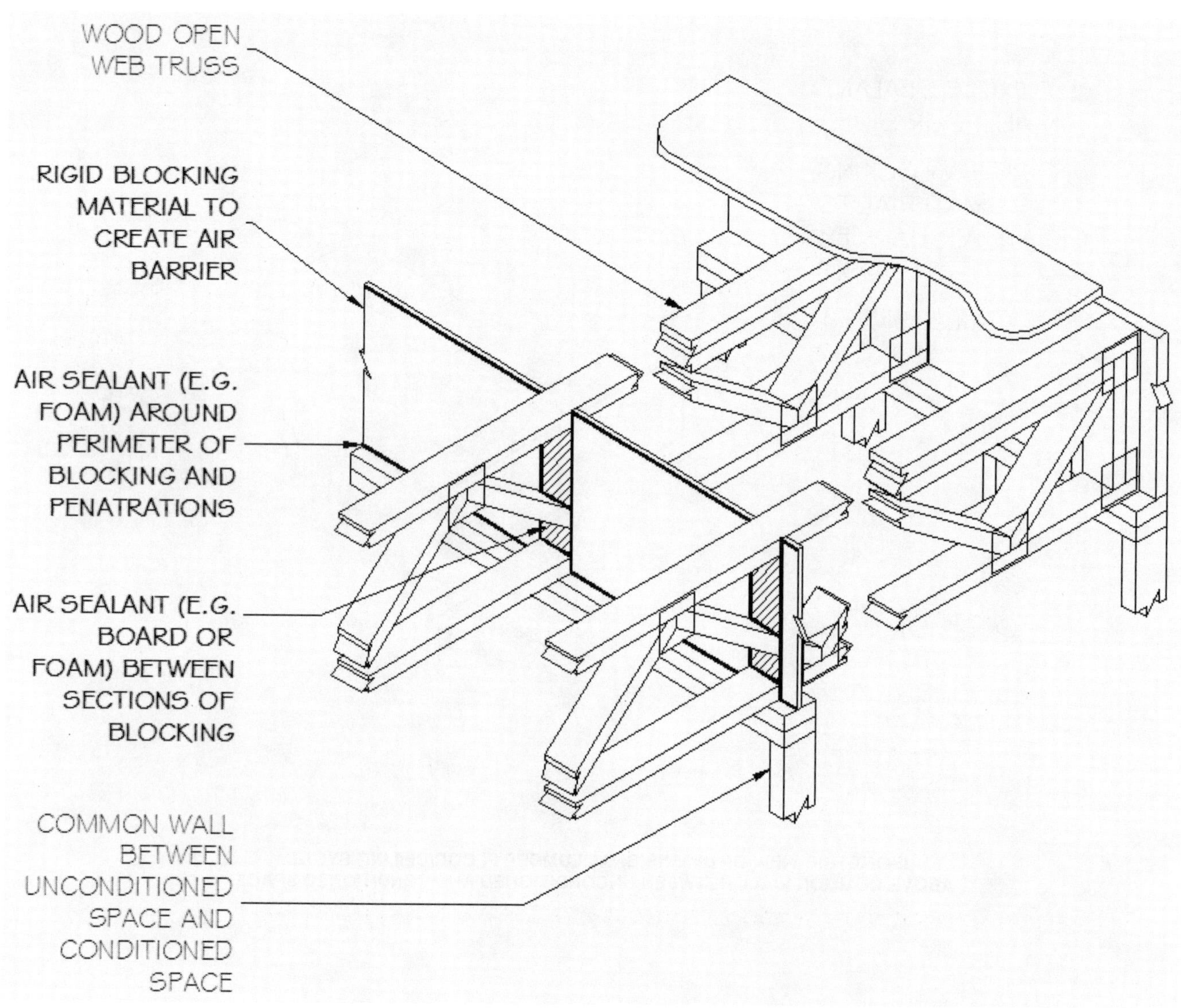

ISOMETRIC VIEW OF WOOD TRUSS FLOOR/CEILING SYSTEM
ABOVE COMMON WALL BETWEEN UNCONDITIONED AND CONDITIONED SPACE

N1102.4.1 Building thermal envelope. – 1. Block and seal floor/ceiling systems

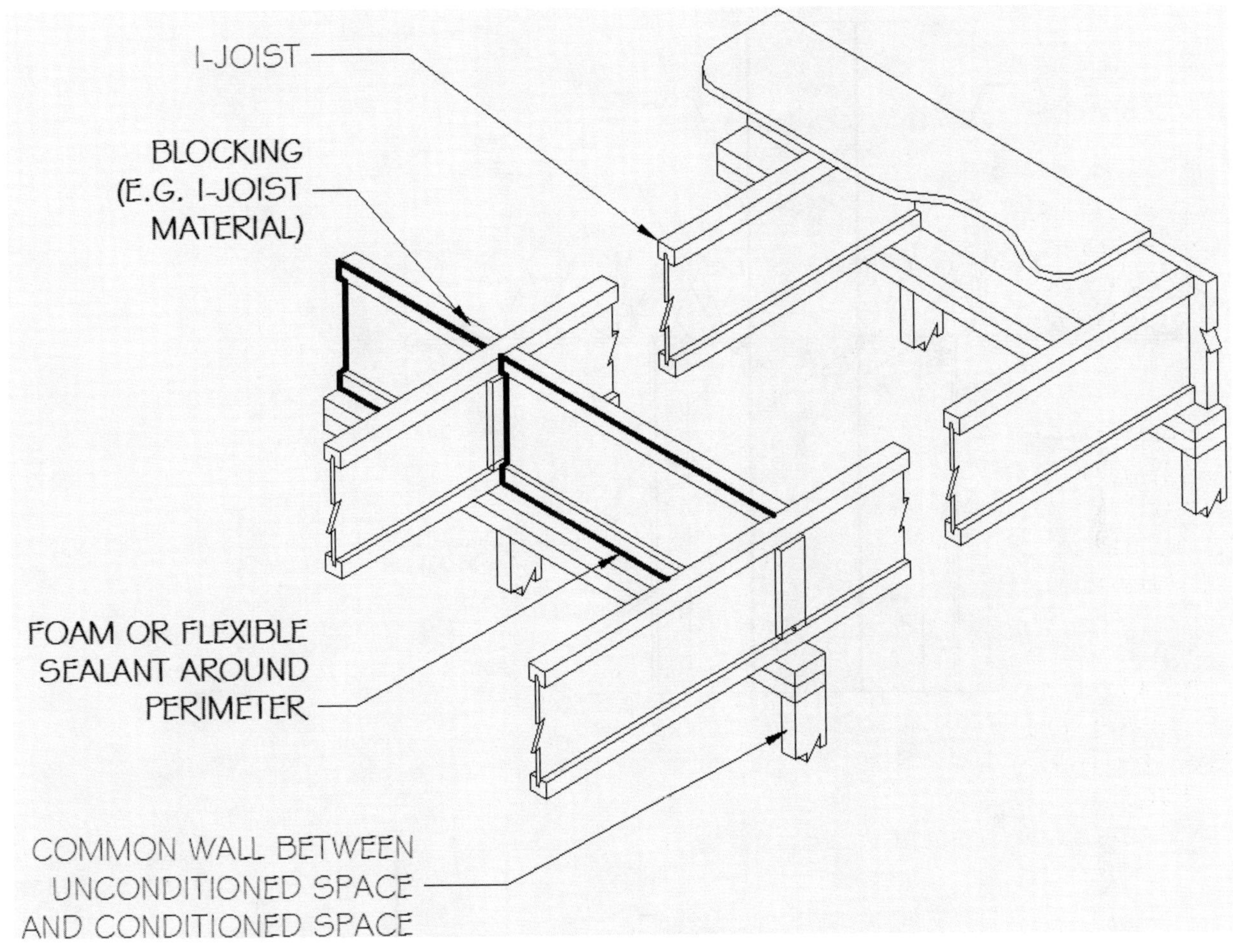

ISOMETRIC VIEW OF I-JOIST FLOOR/CEILING SYSTEM ABOVE COMMON WALL BETWEEN UNCONDITIONED AND CONDITIONED SPACE

N1102.4.1 Building thermal envelope – 2. Cap and seal shafts and chases

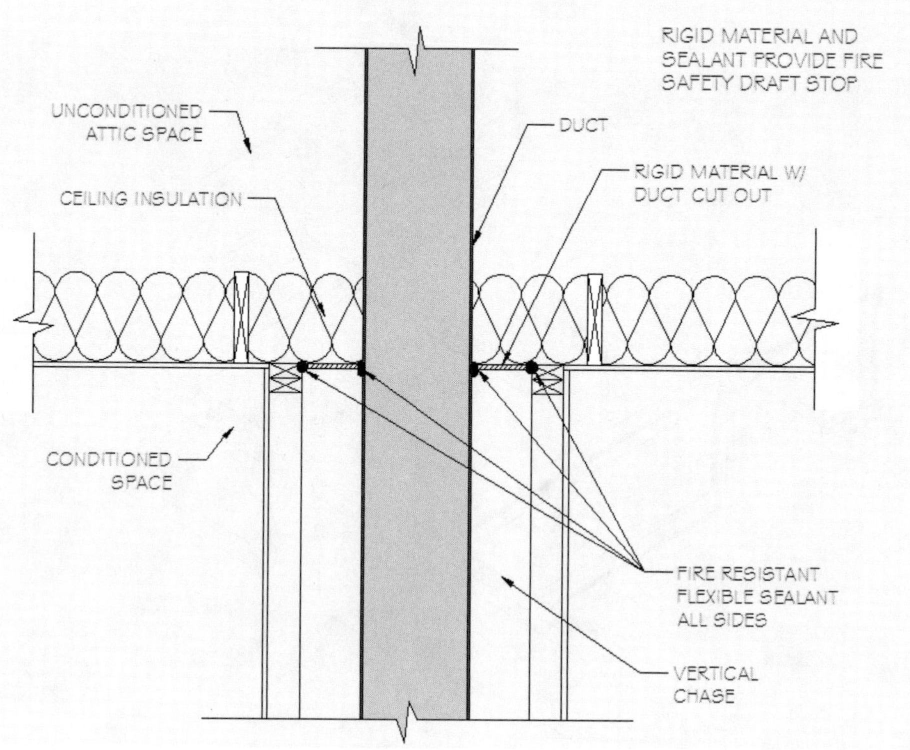

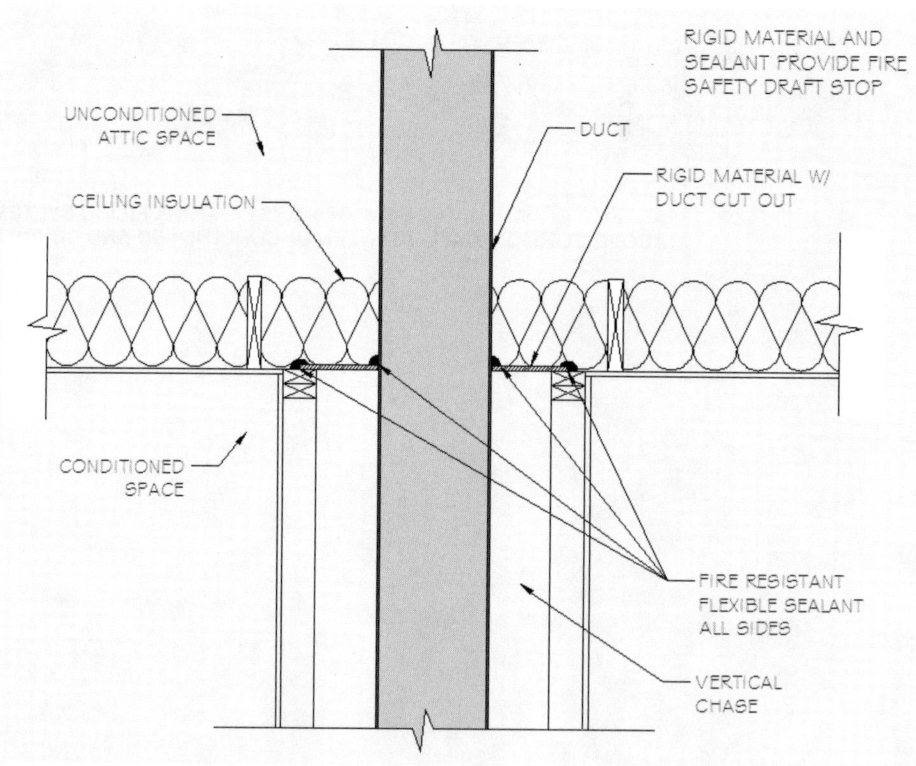

SECTION VIEWS OF DUCT PENETRATING INTO ATTIC

N1102.4.1 Building thermal envelope. – 3. Cap and seal soffit or dropped ceiling

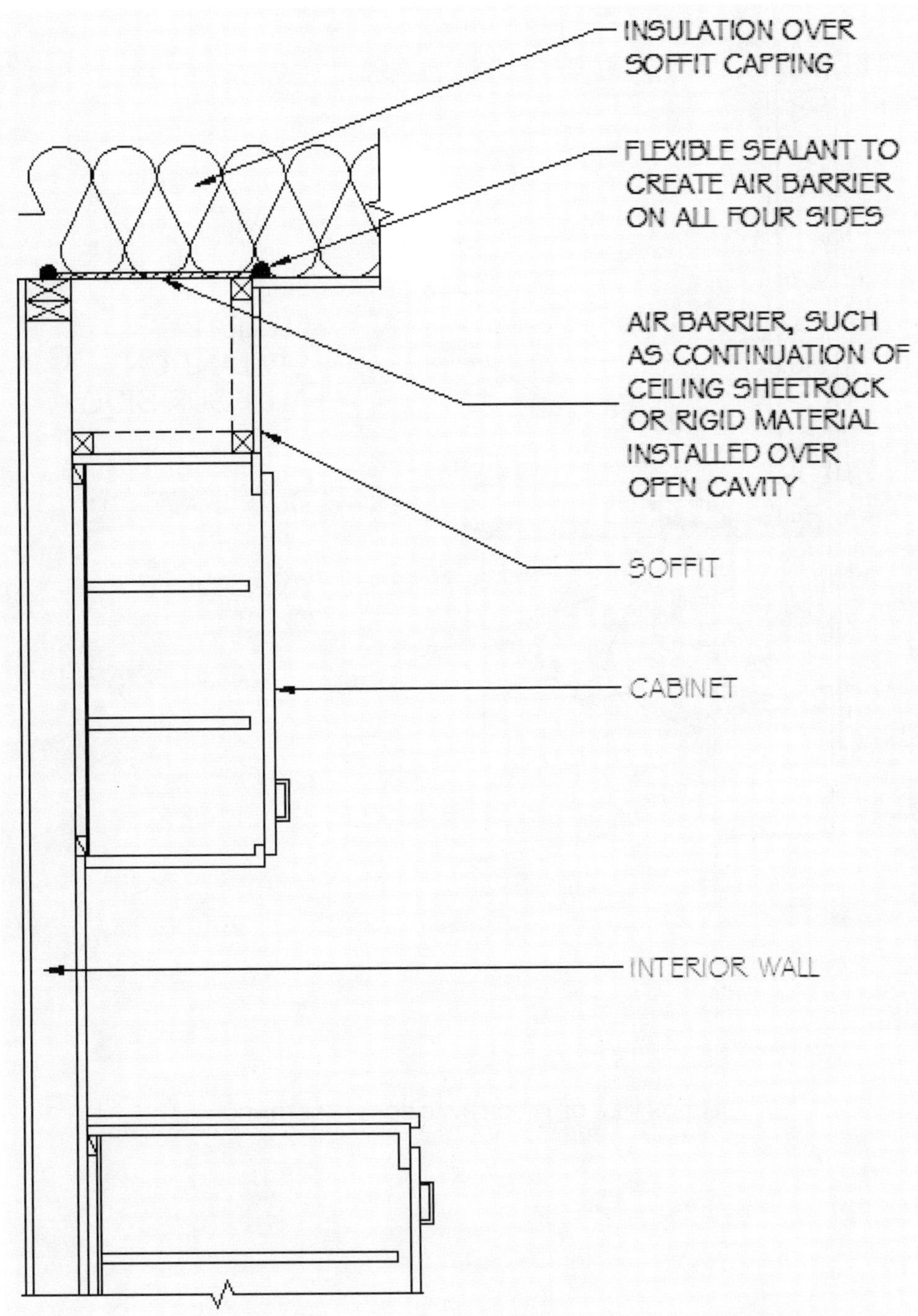

SECTION VIEW OF SOFFIT OVER CABINET

N1102.4.1 Building thermal envelope. – 4. Seal HVAC boot penetration – floor

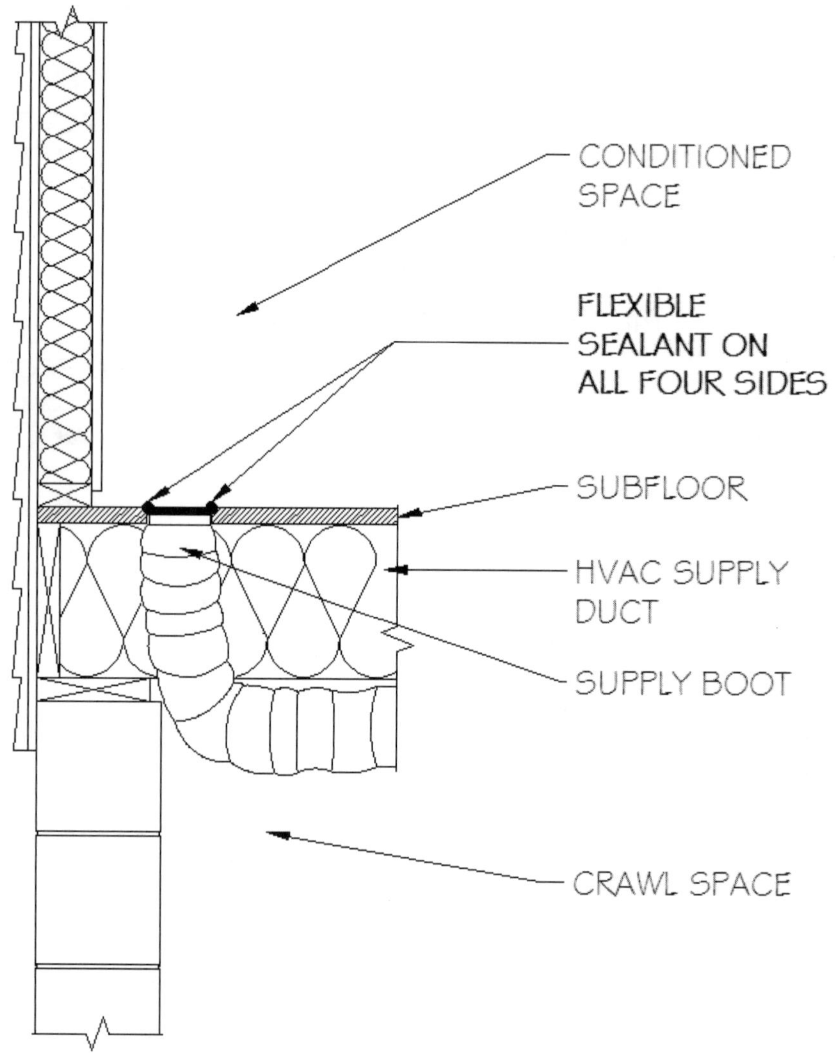

SECTION VIEW OF FLOOR HVAC BOOT PENETRATION

N1102.4.1 Building thermal envelope. – 4. Seal HVAC boot penetration – ceiling

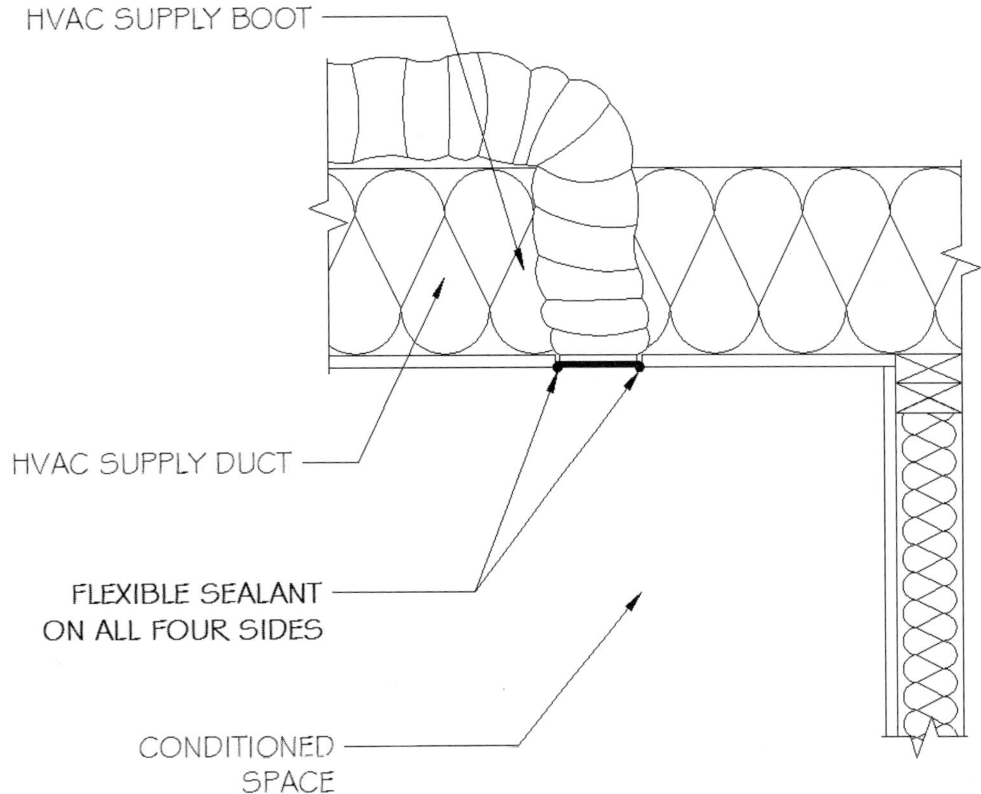

SECTION VIEW OF CEILING HVAC BOOT PENETRATION

APPENDIX E-3:
SAMPLE WORKSHEETS FOR RESIDENTIAL AIR AND DUCT LEAKAGE TESTING

APPENDIX E-3A: Air sealing: Visual inspection option (Section N1102.4.2.1)

Sample Worksheet

N1102.4.2 Air sealing. Building envelope air tightness shall be demonstrated by Section N1102.4.2.1 or N1102.4.2.2.

N1102.4.2.1 Visual inspection option. Building envelope tightness shall be considered acceptable when items providing insulation enclosure in Section N1102.2.12 and air sealing in Section N1102.4.1 are addressed and when the items listed in Table N1102.4.2, applicable to the method of construction, are certified by the builder, permit holder or registered design professional via the certificate in Appendix E-1.

TABLE N1102.4.2
AIR BARRIER INSPECTION

COMPONENT	CRITERIA
Ceiling/attic	Sealants or gaskets provide a continuous air barrier system joining the top plate of framed walls with either the ceiling drywall or the top edge of wall drywall to prevent air leakage. Top plate penetrations are sealed. For ceiling finishes that are not air barrier systems such as tongue-and-groove planks, air barrier systems,(for example, taped house wrap), shall be used above the finish. **Note:** It is acceptable that sealants or gaskets applied as part of the application of the drywall will not be observable by the code official.
Walls	Sill plate is gasketed or sealed to subfloor or slab.
Windows and doors	Space between window and exterior door jambs and framing is sealed.
Floors (including above-garage and cantilevered floors)	Air barrier system is installed at any exposed edge of insulation.
Penetrations	Utility penetrations through the building thermal envelope, including those for plumbing, electrical wiring, ductwork, security and fire alarm wiring, and control wiring, shall be sealed.
Garage separation	Air sealing is provided between the garage and conditioned spaces. An air barrier system shall be installed between the ceiling system above the garage and the ceiling system of interior spaces.
Duct boots	Sealing HVAC register boots and return boxes to subfloor or drywall.
Recessed lighting	Recessed light fixtures are air tight, IC rated, and sealed to drywall. **Exception**—fixtures not penetrating the building envelope.

Property Address:

____

N1102.4.2.1 Visual Inspection Option

The inspection information including tester name, date, and contact shall be included on the certificate described in Section N1101.9.

______________________________ ______________________

Signature Date

APPENDIX E-3B
Air sealing: Testing option (Section N1102.4.2.2)

Sample Worksheet

N1102.4.2 Air sealing. Building envelope air tightness shall be demonstrated by Section N1102.4.2.1 or N1102.4.2.2:

N1102.4.2.2 Testing option. Building envelope tightness shall be considered acceptable when items providing insulation enclosure in Section N1102.2.12 and air sealing in Section N1102.4.1 are addressed and when tested air leakage is less than or equal to one of the two following performance measurements:

1. 0.30 CFM50/Square Foot of Surface Area (SFSA) or
2. Five (5) air changes per hour (ACH50)

When tested with a blower door fan assembly, at a pressure of 33.5 psf (50 Pa). A single point depressurization, not temperature corrected, test is sufficient to comply with this provision, provided that the blower door fan assembly has been certified by the manufacturer to be capable of conducting tests in accordance with ASTM E 779-03. Testing shall occur after rough in and after installation of penetrations of the building envelope, including penetrations for utilities, plumbing, electrical, ventilation and combustion appliances. Testing shall be reported by the permit holder, a North Carolina licensed general contractor, a North Carolina licensed HVAC contractor, a North Carolina licensed Home Inspector, a registered design professional, a *certified BPI Envelope Professional* or a *certified HERS rater.*

During testing:

1. Exterior windows and doors, fireplace and stove doors shall be closed, but not sealed;
2. Dampers shall be closed, but not sealed, including exhaust, backdraft, and flue dampers;
3. Interior doors shall be open;
4. Exterior openings for continuous ventilation systems, air intake ducted to the return side of the conditioning system, and energy or heat recovery ventilators shall be closed and sealed;
5. Heating and cooling system(s) shall be turned off; and
6. Supply and return registers shall not be sealed.

The air leakage information, including building air leakage result, tester name, date, and contact information, shall be included on the certificate described in Section N1101.9.

For Test Criteria 1 above, the report shall be produced in the following manner: Perform the blower door test and record the *CFM50*___________. Calculate the total square feet of surface area for the building thermal envelope, all floors, ceilings, and walls (this includes windows and doors) and record the area______________. Divide *CFM50* by the total square feet and record the result below. If the result is less than or equal to **[0.30 CFM50/SFSA]** the envelope tightness is acceptable; or

For Test Criteria 2 above, the report shall be produced in the following manner: Perform a blower door test and record the *CFM50*___________. Multiply the *CFM50* by 60 minutes to create CFHour50 and record ______________. Then calculate the total conditioned volume of the home and record_________________. Divide the CFH50 by the total volume and record the result below. If the result is less than or equal to **[5 ACH50]** the envelope tightness is acceptable.

Property Address:____

Company Name:____

Contact Information:____

____

______________________________ ______________

Signature of Tester Date

Permit Holder, North Carolina Licensed General Contractor, North Carolina Licensed HVAC Contractor, North Carolina Licensed Home Inspector, Registered Design Professional, Certified BPI Envelope Professional, or Certified HERS Rater **(circle one)**

APPENDIX E-3C
Duct sealing. Duct air leakage test (Section N1103.2.2)

Sample Worksheet

N1103.2.2 Sealing. All ducts, air handlers, filter boxes and building cavities used as ducts shall be sealed. Joints and seams shall comply with Part V – Mechanical, Section 603.9 of the *North Carolina Residential Code.*

Duct tightness shall be verified as follows:

Total duct leakage less than or equal to 6 CFM (18 L/min) per 100 ft^2 (9.29 m^2) of conditioned floor area served by that system when tested at a pressure differential of 0.1 inches w.g. (25 Pa) across the entire system, including the manufacturer's air handler enclosure.

During testing:

1. Block, if present, the ventilation air duct connected to the conditioning system.
2. The duct air leakage testing equipment shall be attached to the largest return in the system or to the air handler.
3. The filter shall be removed and the air handler power shall be turned off.
4. Supply boots or registers and return boxes or grilles shall be taped, plugged, or otherwise sealed air tight.
5. The hose for measuring the 25 Pascals of pressure differential shall be inserted into the boot of the supply that is nominally closest to the air handler.
6. Specific instructions from the duct testing equipment manufacturer shall be followed to reach duct test pressure and measure duct air leakage.

Testing shall be performed and reported by the permit holder, a North Carolina licensed general contractor, a North Carolina licensed HVAC contractor, a North Carolina licensed Home Inspector, a registered design professional, a certified BPI Envelope Professional or a certified HERS rater. A single point depressurization, not temperature corrected, test is sufficient to comply with this provision, provided that the duct testing fan assembly has been certified by the manufacturer to be capable of conducting tests in accordance with ASTM E1554-07.

The duct leakage information, including duct leakage result, tester name, date, company and contact information, shall be included on the certificate described in Section N1101.9.

For the Test Criteria, the report shall be produced in the following manner: perform the HVAC system air leakage test and record the CFM25. Calculate the total square feet of Conditioned Floor Area (CFA) served by that system. Multiply CFM25 by 100, divide the result by the CFA and record the result. If the result is less than or equal to [6 CFM25/100 SF] the HVAC system air tightness is acceptable.

Complete one duct leakage report for each HVAC system serving the home:

Property Address: ____

HVAC System Number: __________________ Describe area of home served: ______________________________

CFM25 Total _________. Conditioned Floor Area (CFA) served by system: __________ s.f.

CFM25 × 100 divided by CFA = ____ CFM25/100SF (e.g. 100 CFM25 × 100/2,000 CFA = 5 CFM25/100SF)

Fan attachment location __________________

Company Name ____

Contact Information: ____

____

______________________________ ____________________

Signature of Tester Date

Permit Holder, North Carolina Licensed General Contractor, North Carolina Licensed HVAC Contractor, North Carolina Licensed Home Inspector, Registered Design Professional, Certified BPI Envelope Professional, or Certified HERS Rater **(circle one)**

APPENDIX E-4

ADDITIONAL VOLUNTARY CRITERIA FOR INCREASING ENERGY EFFICIENCY (High Efficiency Residential Option)

1. **Introduction.** The increased energy efficiency measures identified in this appendix are strictly voluntary at the option of the permit holder and have been evaluated to be the most cost effective measures for achieving an additional 15-20 percent energy efficiency beyond the code minimums.
2. **Requirements.** Follow all sections of the Chapter 11 of the *North Carolina Residential Energy Code*, except the following:
   a. Instead of using Table N1102.1 in Section N1102.1, use Table E-4A shown below.

TABLE E-4A
OPTIONAL INSULATION AND FENESTRATION REQUIREMENTS BY COMPONENT[a]

CLIMATE ZONE	FENESTRATION *U*-FACTOR[b]	SKYLIGHT[b] *U*-FACTOR	GLAZED FENESTRATION SHGC[b, e]	CEILING *R*-VALUE[k]	WOOD FRAME WALL *R*-VALUE[e]	MASS WALL *R*-VALUE[i]	FLOOR *R*-VALUE	BASEMENT[c] WALL *R*-VALUE	SLAB[d] *R*-VALUE	CRAWL SPACE[c] WALL *R*-VALUE
3	0.32	0.65	0.25	38	19, 13+5, or 15+3[eh]	5/10	19	10/13f	5	10/13
4	0.32	0.60	0.25	38	19, 13+5, or 15+3[eh]	5/10	19	10/13	10	10/13
5	0.32	0.60	(NR)	38	19, 13+5, or 15+3[eh]	13/17	30g	10/13	10	15/19

For SI: 1 foot = 304.8 mm.

a. *R*-values are minimums. *U*-factors and SHGC are maximums.

b. The fenestration *U*-factor column excludes skylights. The SHGC column applies to all glazed fenestration.

c. "10/13" means R-10 continuous insulated sheathing on the interior or exterior of the home or R-13 cavity insulation at the interior of the basement wall or crawl space wall.

d. For monolithic slabs, insulation shall be applied from the inspection gap downward to the bottom of the footing or a maximum of 18 inches below grade. For floating slabs, insulation shall extend to the bottom of the foundation wall or 24 inches, whichever is less. (See Appendix O) R-5 shall be added to the required slab edge *R*-values for heated slabs.

e. R -19 fiberglass batts compressed and installed in a nominal 2 × 6 framing cavity is deemed to comply. Fiberglass batts rated R-19 or higher compressed and installed in a 2x4 wall is not deemed to comply.

f. Basement wall insulation is not required in warm-humid locations as defined by Figure N1101.2(1 and 2) and Table N1101.2.

g. Or insulation sufficient to fill the framing cavity, R-19 minimum.

h. "13+5" means R-13 cavity insulation plus R-5 insulated sheathing. 15+3 means R-15 cavity insulation plus R-3 insulated sheathing. If structural sheathing covers 25 percent or less of the exterior, insulating sheathing is not required where structural sheathing is used. If structural sheathing covers more than 25 percent of exterior, structural sheathing shall be supplemented with insulated sheathing of at least R-2. 13+2.5 means R-13 cavity insulation plus R-2.5 sheathing.

i. For Mass Walls, the second *R*-value applies when more than half the insulation is on the interior of the mass wall.

j. R-30 shall be deemed to satisfy the ceiling insulation requirement wherever the full height of uncompressed R-30 insulation extends over the wall top plate at the eaves. Otherwise R-38 insulation is required where adequate clearance exists or insulation must extend to either the insulation baffle or within 1" of the attic roof deck.

k. Table value required except for roof edge where the space is limited by the pitch of the roof, there the insulation must fill the space up to the air baffle.

   b. Instead of using Table N1102.2 in Section N1102.2, use Table E-4B to find the maximum *U*-factors for building components.

3. TABLE E-4B
EQUIVALENT *U*-FACTORS[a]

CLIMATE ZONE	FENESTRATION *U*-FACTOR	SKYLIGHT *U*-FACTOR	CEILING *U*-FACTOR	FRAME WALL *U*-FACTOR	MASS WALL *U*-FACTOR[b]	FLOOR *U*-FACTOR	BASEMENT WALL *U*-FACTOR[d]	CRAWL SPACE WALL *U*-FACTOR[c]
3	0.32	0.65	0.030	0.061	0.141	0.047	0.059	0.065
4	0.32	0.60	0.030	0.061	0.141	0.047	0.059	0.065
5	0.32	0.60	0.030	0.061	0.082	0.033	0.059	0.055

a. Nonfenestration *U*-factors shall be obtained from measurement, calculation or an approved source.

b. When more than half the insulation is on the interior, the mass wall *U*-factors shall be a maximum 0.12 in Zone 3, 0.10 in Zone 4, and the same as the frame wall *U*-factor in Zone 5.

c. Basement wall *U*-factor of 0.360 in warm-humid locations as defined by Figures N1101.2(1), N1101.2(2) and Table N1101.2.

d. Foundation *U*-factor requirements shown in Table E-4B include wall construction and interior air films but exclude soil conductivity and exterior air films. *U*-factors for determining code compliance in accordance with Section N1102.1.3 (total UA alternative) shall be modified to include soil conductivity and exterior air films.

c. Instead of using the air leakage value for maximum leakage shown in Section N1102.4.2.2, use the following:

i. 0.24 CFM50/Square Foot of Surface Area (SFSA) or

ii. Four (4) air changes per hour (ACH50)

d. Instead of using the duct leakage value for maximum leakage shown in Section N1103.2.2 use the following:

Total duct leakage less than or equal to 4 CFM (12 L/min) per 100 ft^2 (9.29 m^2) of *conditioned floor area* served by that system when tested at a pressure differential of 0.1 inches w.g. (25 Pa) across

TABLE E-4C:
Sample Confirmation Form for ADDITIONAL VOLUNTARY CRITERIA FOR INCREASING ENERGY EFFICIENCY
(High Efficiency Residential Option)

INSULATION AND FENESTRATION VALUES				PROPOSED PROJECT VALUES
Climate Zone	3	4	5	
Fenestration *U*-Factor	0.32[j]	0.32[j]	0.32[j]	
Skylight *U*-Factor	0.65	0.6	0.6	
Glazed Fenestration SHGC[b,e]	0.25	0.25	(NR)	
Ceiling *R*-value	38	38	38	
Wood Frame Wall *R*-value[e]	19, 13+5, or 15+3[e,h]	19, 13+5, or 15+3[e,h]	19, 13+5, or 15+3[e,h]	
Mass Wall *R*-value[j]	5/10	5/10	13/17	
Floor *R*-value	19	19	30g	
Basement Wall *R*-value[c]	10/13[f]	10/13[f]	10/13[f]	
Slab *R*-value and Depth[d]	5, 2 ft	10, 2 ft	10, 2 ft	
Crawl Space Wall *R*-value[c]	10/13	10/13	15/19	
Building Air Leakage				
Visually inspected according to N1102.4.2.1 (check box) OR				
Building Air Leakage Test according to N1102.4.2.2 (check box). Show test value:				
ACH550 [Target: 4.0], or				
CFM50/SFSA [Target: 0.24]				
Name of Tester/Company:				
Date:				
Duct Insulation and Sealing				
Insulation value	*R*-			
Duct Leakage Test Result (Section N1103.2.2)				
(CFM25 Total/100SF) [Target: 4]				
Name of Tester/Company:				
Date:				

For SI: 1 foot = 304.8 mm.

a. *R*-values are minimums. *U*-factors and SHGC are maximums.

b. The fenestration *U*-factor column excludes skylights. The SHGC column applies to all glazed fenestration.

c. "10/13" means R-10 continuous insulated sheathing on the interior or exterior of the home or R-13 cavity insulation at the interior of the basement wall or crawl space wall.

d. For monolithic slabs, insulation shall be applied from the inspection gap downward to the bottom of the footing or a maximum of 18 inches below grade. For floating slabs, insulation shall extend to the bottom of the foundation wall or 24 inches, whichever is less. (See Appendix O) R-5 shall be added to the required slab edge *R*-values for heated slabs.

e. R -19 fiberglass batts compressed and installed in a nominal 2 × 6 framing cavity is deemed to comply. Fiberglass batts rated R-19 or higher compressed and installed in a 2x4 wall is not deemed to comply.

f. Basement wall insulation is not required in warm-humid locations as defined by Figure N1101.2(1 and 2) and Table N1101.2.

g. Or insulation sufficient to fill the framing cavity, R-19 minimum.

h. "13+5" means R-13 cavity insulation plus R-5 insulated sheathing. 15+3 means R-15 cavity insulation plus R-3 insulated sheathing. If structural sheathing covers 25 percent or less of the exterior, insulating sheathing is not required where structural sheathing is used. If structural sheathing covers more than 25 percent of exterior, structural sheathing shall be supplemented with insulated sheathing of at least R-2. 13+2.5 means R-13 cavity insulation plus R-2.5 sheathing.

i. For Mass Walls, the second *R*-value applies when more than half the insulation is on the interior of the mass wall.

j. R-30 shall be deemed to satisfy the ceiling insulation requirement wherever the full height of uncompressed R-30 insulation extends over the wall top plate at the eaves. Otherwise R-38 insulation is required where adequate clearance exists or insulation must extend to either the insulation baffle or within 1" of the attic roof deck.

k. Table value required except for roof edge where the space is limited by the pitch of the roof, there the insulation must fill the space up to the air baffle.

E-4D: SAMPLE WORKSHEETS FOR RESIDENTIAL AIR AND DUCT LEAKAGE TESTING
E-4D.1
Air sealing: Visual inspection option (Section N1102.4.2.1)
Sample Worksheet for Alternative Residential Energy Code for Higher Efficiency

N1102.4.2 Air sealing. Building envelope air tightness shall be demonstrated by Section N1102.4.2.1 or N1102.4.2.2.

N1102.4.2.1 Visual inspection option. Building envelope tightness shall be considered acceptable when items providing insulation enclosure in Section N1102.2.12 and air sealing in Section N1102.4.1 are addressed and when the items listed in Table N1102.4.2, applicable to the method of construction, are certified by the by the builder, permit holder or registered design professional via the certificate in Appendix E-1.

TABLE N1102.4.2
AIR BARRIER INSPECTION

COMPONENT	CRITERIA
Ceiling/attic	Sealants or gaskets provide a continuous air barrier system joining the top plate of framed walls with either the ceiling drywall or the top edge of wall drywall to prevent air leakage. Top plate penetrations are sealed. For ceiling finishes that are not air barrier systems such as tongue-and-groove planks, air barrier systems,(for example, taped house wrap), shall be used above the finish **Note:** It is acceptable that sealants or gaskets applied as part of the application of the drywall will not be observable by the code official.
Walls	Sill plate is gasketed or sealed to subfloor or slab.
Windows and doors	Space between window and exterior door jambs and framing is sealed.
Floors (including above garage and cantilevered floors)	Air barrier system is installed at any exposed edge of insulation.
Penetrations	Utility penetrations through the building thermal envelope, including those for plumbing, electrical wiring, ductwork, security and fire alarm wiring, and control wiring, shall be sealed.
Garage separation	Air sealing is provided between the garage and conditioned spaces. An air barrier system shall be installed between the ceiling system above the garage and the ceiling system of interior spaces.
Duct boots	Sealing HVAC register boots and return boxes to subfloor or drywall.
Recessed lighting	Recessed light fixtures are airtight, IC rated and sealed to drywall. **Exception**—fixtures in conditioned space.

Property Address:

____

N1102.4.2.1 Visual Inspection Option
The inspection information including tester name, date, and contact shall be included on the certificate described in Section N1101.9.

______________________________ ______________

Signature Date

E-4D.2
Air sealing: Testing option (Section N1102.4.2.2)
Sample Worksheet for Alternative Residential Energy Code for Higher Efficiency

N1102.4.2 Air sealing. Building envelope air tightness shall be demonstrated by Section N1102.4.2.1 or N1102.4.2.2:

N1102.4.2.2 Testing option. Building envelope tightness shall be considered acceptable when items providing insulation enclosure in Section N1102.2.12 and air sealing in Section N1102.4.1 are addressed and when tested air leakage is less than or equal to one of the two following performance measurements:

1. 0.24 CFM50/Square Foot of Surface Area (SFSA) or
2. Four (4) air changes per hour (ACH50)

When tested with a blower door fan assembly, at a pressure of 33.5 psf (50 Pa). A single point depressurization, not temperature corrected, test is sufficient to comply with this provision, provided that the blower door fan assembly has been certified by the manufacturer to be capable of conducting tests in accordance with ASTM E 779-03. Testing shall occur after rough in and after installation of penetrations of the building envelope, including penetrations for utilities, plumbing, electrical, ventilation and combustion appliances. Testing shall be reported by the permit holder, a North Carolina licensed general contractor, a North Carolina licensed HVAC contractor, a North Carolina licensed Home Inspector, a registered design professional, a *certified BPI Envelope Professional* or a *certified HERS rater.*

During testing:

1. Exterior windows and doors, fireplace and stove doors shall be closed, but not sealed;
2. Dampers shall be closed, but not sealed, including exhaust, backdraft, and flue dampers;
3. Interior doors shall be open;
4. Exterior openings for continuous ventilation systems, air intake ducted to the return side of the conditioning system, and energy or heat recovery ventilators shall be closed and sealed;
5. Heating and cooling system(s) shall be turned off; and
6. Supply and return registers shall not be sealed.

The air leakage information, including building air leakage result, tester name, date, and contact information, shall be included on the certificate described in Section N1101.9.

For Test Criteria 1 above, the report shall be produced in the following manner: Perform the blower door test and record the *CFM50*___________. Calculate the total square feet of surface area for the building thermal envelope, all floors, ceilings, and walls (this includes windows and doors) and record the area______________. Divide *CFM50* by the total square feet and record the result below. If the result is less than or equal to **[0.24 CFM50/SFSA]** the envelope tightness is acceptable; or

For Test Criteria 2 above, the report shall be produced in the following manner: Perform a blower door test and record the *CFM50*___________. Multiply the *CFM50* by 60 minutes to create CFHour50 and record ______________. Then calculate the total conditioned volume of the home and record________________. Divide the CFH50 by the total volume and record the result below. If the result is less than or equal to **[4 ACH50]** the envelope tightness is acceptable.

Property Address:____

Company Name:____

Contact Information:____

____

____ ______________________

Signature of Tester Date

Permit Holder, North Carolina Licensed General Contractor, North Carolina Licensed HVAC Contractor, North Carolina Licensed Home Inspector, Registered Design Professional, Certified BPI Envelope Professional, or Certified HERS Rater **(circle one)**

E-4D.3
Duct sealing. Duct air leakage test (Section N1103.2.2)
Sample Worksheet for Alternative Residential Energy Code for Higher Efficiency

N1103.2.2 Sealing. All ducts, air handlers, filter boxes and building cavities used as ducts shall be sealed. Joints and seams shall comply with Part V – Mechanical, Section 603.9 of the *North Carolina Residential Code.*

Duct tightness shall be verified as follows:

Total duct leakage less than or equal to 6 CFM (18 L/min) per 100 ft^2 (9.29 m^2) of *conditioned floor area* served by that system when tested at a pressure differential of 0.1 inches w.g. (25 Pa) across the entire system, including the manufacturer's air handler enclosure.

During testing:

1. Block, if present, the ventilation air duct connected to the conditioning system.
2. The duct air leakage testing equipment shall be attached to the largest return in the system or to the air handler.
3. The filter shall be removed and the air handler power shall be turned off.
4. Supply boots or registers and return boxes or grilles shall be taped, plugged, or otherwise sealed air tight.
5. The hose for measuring the 25 Pascals of pressure differential shall be inserted into the boot of the supply that is nominally closest to the air handler.
6. Specific instructions from the duct testing equipment manufacturer shall be followed to reach duct test pressure and measure duct air leakage.

Testing shall be performed and reported by the permit holder, a North Carolina licensed general contractor, a North Carolina licensed HVAC contractor, a North Carolina licensed Home Inspector, a registered design professional, a certified BPI Envelope Professional or a certified HERS rater. A single point depressurization, not temperature corrected, test is sufficient to comply with this provision, provided that the duct testing fan assembly has been certified by the manufacturer to be capable of conducting tests in accordance with ASTM E1554-07.

The duct leakage information, including duct leakage result, tester name, date, company and contact information, shall be included on the certificate described in Section N1101.9.

For the Test Criteria, the report shall be produced in the following manner: perform the HVAC system air leakage test and record the CFM25. Calculate the total square feet of Conditioned Floor Area (CFA) served by that system. Multiply CFM25 by 100, divide the result by the CFA and record the result. If the result is less than or equal to [6 CFM25/100 SF] the HVAC system air tightness is acceptable.

Complete one duct leakage report for each HVAC system serving the home:

Property Address: ______________________________

HVAC System Number: ______________ Describe area of home served: ______________________________

CFM25 Total ________. Conditioned Floor Area (CFA) served by system: __________ s.f.

CFM25 × 100 divided by CFA = ____ CFM25/100SF (e.g. 70 CFM25 × 100/2,000 CFA = 3.5 CFM25/100SF)

Fan attachment location ______________

Company Name ______________________________

Contact Information: ______________________________

____

______________________________ ______________

Signature of Tester Date

Permit Holder, North Carolina Licensed General Contractor, North Carolina Licensed HVAC Contractor, North Carolina Licensed Home Inspector, Registered Design Professional, Certified BPI Envelope Professional, or Certified HERS Rater **(circle one)**

APPENDIX F

RADON CONTROL METHODS

Deleted

APPENDIX G

SWIMMING POOLS, SPAS AND HOT TUBS

(The provisions contained in this appendix are adopted as part of this code.)

SECTION AG101
GENERAL

AG101.1 General. The provisions of this appendix shall control the design and construction of swimming pools, spas and hot tubs installed in or on the *lot* of a one- or two-family dwelling.

AG101.2 Pools in flood hazard areas. Pools that are located in flood hazard areas established by Table R301.2(1), including above-ground pools, on-ground pools and in-ground pools that involve placement of fill, shall comply with Sections AG101.2.1 or AG101.2.2.

Exception: Pools located in riverine flood hazard areas which are outside of designated floodways.

AG101.2.1 Pools located in designated floodways. Where pools are located in designated floodways, documentation shall be submitted to the *building official*, which demonstrates that the construction of the pool will not increase the design flood elevation at any point within the *jurisdiction*.

AG101.2.2 Pools located where floodways have not been designated. Where pools are located where design flood elevations are specified but floodways have not been designated, the applicant shall provide a floodway analysis that demonstrates that the proposed pool will not increase the design flood elevation more than 1 foot (305 mm) at any point within the *jurisdiction*.

SECTION AG102
DEFINITIONS

AG102.1 General. For the purposes of these requirements, the terms used shall be defined as follows and as set forth in Chapter 2.

ABOVE-GROUND/ON-GROUND POOL. See "Swimming pool."

BARRIER. A fence, wall, building wall or combination thereof which completely surrounds the swimming pool and obstructs access to the swimming pool.

HOT TUB. See "Swimming pool."

IN-GROUND POOL. See "Swimming pool."

RESIDENTIAL. That which is situated on the premises of a detached one- or two-family dwelling or a one-family *townhouse* not more than three stories in height.

SPA, NONPORTABLE. See "Swimming pool."

SPA, PORTABLE. A nonpermanent structure intended for recreational bathing, in which all controls, water-heating and water-circulating *equipment* are an integral part of the product.

SWIMMING POOL. Any structure intended for swimming or recreational bathing that contains water over 24 inches (610 mm) deep. This includes in-ground, above-ground and on-ground swimming pools, hot tubs and spas.

SWIMMING POOL, INDOOR. A swimming pool which is totally contained within a structure and surrounded on all four sides by the walls of the enclosing structure.

SWIMMING POOL, OUTDOOR. Any swimming pool which is not an indoor pool.

SECTION AG103
SWIMMING POOLS

AG103.1 In-ground pools. In-ground pools shall be designed and constructed in conformance with ANSI/NSPI-5 as listed in Section AG108.

AG103.2 Above-ground and on-ground pools. Above-ground and on-ground pools shall be designed and constructed in conformance with ANSI/NSPI-4 as listed in Section AG108.

AG103.3 Pools in flood hazard areas. In flood hazard areas established by Table R301.2(1), pools in coastal high hazard areas shall be designed and constructed in conformance with ASCE 24.

SECTION AG104
SPAS AND HOT TUBS

AG104.1 Permanently installed spas and hot tubs. Permanently installed spas and hot tubs shall be designed and constructed in conformance with ANSI/NSPI-3 as listed in Section AG108.

AG104.2 Portable spas and hot tubs. Portable spas and hot tubs shall be designed and constructed in conformance with ANSI/NSPI-6 as listed in Section AG108.

SECTION AG105
BARRIER REQUIREMENTS

AG105.1 Application. The provisions of this chapter shall control the design of barriers for residential swimming pools, spas and hot tubs. These design controls are intended to provide protection against potential drownings and near-drownings by restricting access to swimming pools, spas and hot tubs.

AG105.2 Outdoor swimming pool. An outdoor swimming pool, including an in-ground, above-ground or on-ground pool, hot tub or spa shall be surrounded by a barrier which shall comply with the following:

1. The top of the barrier shall be at least 48 inches (1219 mm) above *grade* measured on the side of the barrier which faces away from the swimming pool. The maximum vertical clearance between grade and the bottom of

the barrier shall be 2 inches (51 mm) measured on the side of the barrier which faces away from the swimming pool. Where the top of the pool structure is above grade, such as an above-ground pool, the barrier may be at ground level, such as the pool structure, or mounted on top of the pool structure. Where the barrier is mounted on top of the pool structure, the maximum vertical clearance between the top of the pool structure and the bottom of the barrier shall be 4 inches (102 mm).

2. Openings in the barrier shall not allow passage of a 4-inch-diameter (102 mm) sphere.
3. Solid barriers which do not have openings, such as a masonry or stone wall, shall not contain indentations or protrusions except for normal construction tolerances and tooled masonry joints.
4. Where the barrier is composed of horizontal and vertical members and the distance between the tops of the horizontal members is less than 45 inches (1143 mm), the horizontal members shall be located on the swimming pool side of the fence. Spacing between vertical members shall not exceed $1^3/_4$ inches (44 mm) in width. Where there are decorative cutouts within vertical members, spacing within the cutouts shall not exceed $1^3/_4$ inches (44 mm) in width.
5. Where the barrier is composed of horizontal and vertical members and the distance between the tops of the horizontal members is 45 inches (1143 mm) or more, spacing between vertical members shall not exceed 4 inches (102 mm). Where there are decorative cutouts within vertical members, spacing within the cutouts shall not exceed $1^3/_4$ inches (44 mm) in width.
6. Maximum mesh size for chain link fences shall be a $2^1/_4$-inch (57 mm) square unless the fence has slats fastened at the top or the bottom which reduce the openings to not more than $1^3/_4$ inches (44 mm).
7. Where the barrier is composed of diagonal members, such as a lattice fence, the maximum opening formed by the diagonal members shall not be more than $1^3/_4$ inches (44 mm).
8. Access gates shall comply with the requirements of Section AG105.2, Items 1 through 7, and shall be equipped to accommodate a locking device. Pedestrian access gates shall open outward away from the pool and shall be self-closing and have a self-latching device. Gates other than pedestrian access gates shall have a self-latching device. Where the release mechanism of the self-latching device is located less than 54 inches (1372 mm) from the bottom of the gate, the release mechanism and openings shall comply with the following:
   8.1. The release mechanism shall be located on the pool side of the gate at least 3 inches (76 mm) below the top of the gate; and
   8.2. The gate and barrier shall have no opening larger than $^1/_2$ inch (12.7 mm) within 18 inches (457 mm) of the release mechanism.
9. Where a wall of a *dwelling* serves as part of the barrier, one of the following conditions shall be met:
   9.1. The pool shall be equipped with a powered safety cover in compliance with ASTM F 1346; or
   9.2. Doors with direct access to the pool through that wall shall be equipped with an alarm which produces an audible warning when the door and/or its screen, if present, are opened. The alarm shall be listed and *labeled* in accordance with UL 2017. The deactivation switch(es) shall be located at least 54 inches (1372 mm) above the threshold of the door; or
   9.3. Other means of protection, such as self-closing doors with self-latching devices, which are *approved* by the governing body, shall be acceptable as long as the degree of protection afforded is not less than the protection afforded by Item 9.1 or 9.2 described above.
10. Where an above-ground pool structure is used as a barrier or where the barrier is mounted on top of the pool structure, and the means of access is a ladder or steps:
   10.1. The ladder or steps shall be capable of being secured, locked or removed to prevent access; or
   10.2. The ladder or steps shall be surrounded by a barrier which meets the requirements of Section AG105.2, Items 1 through 9. When the ladder or steps are secured, locked or removed, any opening created shall not allow the passage of a 4-inch-diameter (102 mm) sphere.

AG105.3 Indoor swimming pool. Walls surrounding an indoor swimming pool shall comply with Section AG105.2, Item 9.

AG105.4 Prohibited locations. Barriers shall be located to prohibit permanent structures, *equipment* or similar objects from being used to climb them.

AG105.5 Barrier exceptions. Spas or hot tubs with a safety cover which complies with ASTM F 1346, as listed in Section AG107, shall be exempt from the provisions of this appendix.

SECTION AG106 ENTRAPMENT PROTECTION FOR SWIMMING POOL AND SPA SUCTION OUTLETS

AG106.1 General. Suction outlets shall be designed and installed in accordance with ANSI/APSP-7.

SECTION AG107 ABBREVIATIONS

AG107.1 General.

ANSI—American National Standards Institute
11 West 42nd Street
New York, NY 10036

APSP—Association of Pool and Spa Professionals
NSPI—National Spa and Pool Institute
2111 Eisenhower Avenue
Alexandria, VA 22314

ASCE—American Society of Civil Engineers
1801 Alexander Bell Drive
Reston, VA 98411-0700

ASTM—ASTM International
100 Barr Harbor Drive,
West Conshohocken, PA 19428

UL—Underwriters Laboratories, Inc.
333 Pfingsten Road
Northbrook, IL 60062-2096

SECTION AG108 STANDARDS

AG108.1 General.

ANSI/NSPI

ANSI/NSPI-3-99 Standard for Permanently Installed Residential Spas AG104.1

ANSI/NSPI-4-07 Standard for Above-ground/ On-ground Residential Swimming Pools. AG103.2

ANSI/NSPI-5-2003 Standard for Residential In-ground Swimming Pools. AG103.1

ANSI/NSPI-6-99 Standard for Residential Portable Spas AG104.2

ANSI/APSP

ANSI/APSP-7-06 Standard for Suction Entrapment avoidance in Swimming Pools, Wading Pools, Spas, Hot Tubs and Catch Basins. AG106.1

ASCE

ASCE/SEI-24-05 Flood Resistant Design and Construction. AG103.3

ASTM

ASTM F 1346-91 (2003) Performance Specification for Safety Covers and Labeling Requirements for All Covers for Swimming Pools, Spas and Hot Tubs AG105.2, AG105.5

UL

UL 2017-2000 Standard for General-purpose Signaling Devices and Systems—with Revisions through June 2004. . . . . AG105.2

APPENDIX H

PATIO COVERS

Deleted

APPENDIX I

PRIVATE SEWAGE DISPOSAL

Deleted

[EB] APPENDIX J

EXISTING BUILDINGS AND STRUCTURES

Deleted

APPENDIX K

SOUND TRANSMISSION

(The provisions contained in this appendix are adopted as part of this code.)

SECTION AK101 GENERAL

AK101.1 General. Wall and floor-ceiling assemblies separating *dwelling units* including those separating adjacent *townhouse* units shall provide air-borne sound insulation for walls, and both air-borne and impact sound insulation for floor-ceiling assemblies.

SECTION AK102 AIR-BORNE SOUND

AK102.1 General. Air-borne sound insulation for wall and floor-ceiling assemblies shall meet a Sound Transmission Class (STC) rating of 45 when tested in accordance with ASTM E 90. Penetrations or openings in construction assemblies for piping; electrical devices; recessed cabinets; bathtubs; soffits; or heating, ventilating or exhaust ducts shall be sealed, lined, insulated or otherwise treated to maintain the required ratings. *Dwelling unit* entrance doors, which share a common space, shall be tight fitting to the frame and sill.

AK102.1.1 Masonry. The sound transmission class of concrete masonry and clay masonry assemblies shall be calculated in accordance with TMS 0302 or determined through testing in accordance with ASTM E 90.

SECTION AK103 STRUCTURAL-BORNE SOUND

AK103.1 General. Floor/ceiling assemblies between *dwelling units* or between a *dwelling unit* and a public or service area within a structure shall have an Impact Insulation Class (IIC) rating of not less than 45 when tested in accordance with ASTM E 492.

SECTION AK104 REFERENCED STANDARDS

ASTM E 90-04 Test Method for Laboratory Measurement of Airborne Sound Transmission Loss of Building Partitions and Elements AK102

ASTM E 492-04 Specification for Laboratory Measurement of Impact Sound Transmission through Floor-ceiling Assemblies Using the Tapping Machine AK103

The Masonry Society

TMS 0302-07 Standard for Determining the Sound Transmission Class Rating for Masonry Walls. AK102.1.1

APPENDIX L

PERMIT FEES

Deleted

APPENDIX M

WOOD DECKS

This appendix is a North Carolina addition to the 2009 International Residential Code. There will be no underlined text. (The provisions contained in this appendix are adopted as part of this code.)

SECTION AM101
GENERAL

AM101.1 General. A deck is an exposed exterior wood floor structure which may be attached to the structure or freestanding. Roofed porches (open or screened-in) may be constructed using these provisions.

AM101.2 Deck design. Computer deck design programs may be accepted by the code enforcement official.

SECTION AM102
FOOTERS

AM102.1 Footers. Support post shall be supported by a minimum footing per Figure AM102 and Table AM102.1. Minimum footing depth shall be 12-inches below finished grade per Section R403.1.4. Tributary area is calculated per Figure AM102.1.

SECTION AM103
FLASHING

AM103.1 Flashing. When attached to a structure, the structure to which attached shall have a treated wood band for the length of the deck, or corrosion-resistant flashing shall be used to prevent moisture from coming in contact with the untreated framing of the structure. Aluminum flashing shall not be used in conjunction with deck construction. The deck band and the structure band shall be constructed in contact with each other except on brick veneer structures and where plywood sheathing is required and properly flashed. Siding shall not be installed between the structure and the deck band. If attached to a brick structure, neither the flashing nor a treated band for brick structure is required. In addition, the treated deckband shall be constructed in contact with the brick veneer. Flashing shall be installed per Figure AM103.

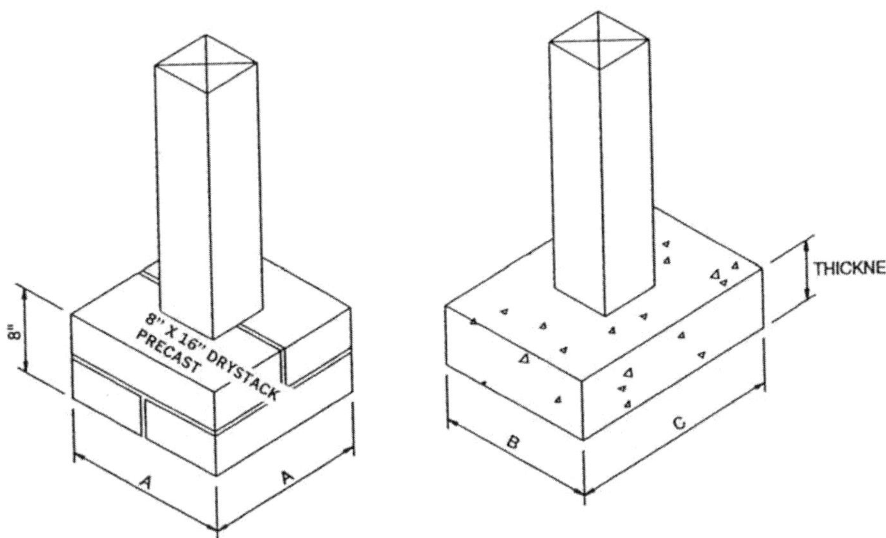

FIGURE AM102

TABLE AM102.1
FOOTING TABLE[a,b,c]

SIZE (inches)		TRIBUTARY AREA	THICKNESS (inches)	
A x A	B x C	(sq. ft.)	Precast	Cast-in-Place
8 × 16	8 × 16	36	4	6
12 × 12	12 × 12	40	4	6
16 × 16	16 × 16	70	8	8
—	16 × 24	100	—	8
—	24 × 24	150	—	8

For SI: 1 inch = 25.4 mm, 1 square foot = 0.0929 m^2.

a. Footing values are based on single floor and roof loads

b. Support post must rest in center $^1/_3$ of footer

c. Top of footer shall be level for full bearing support of post

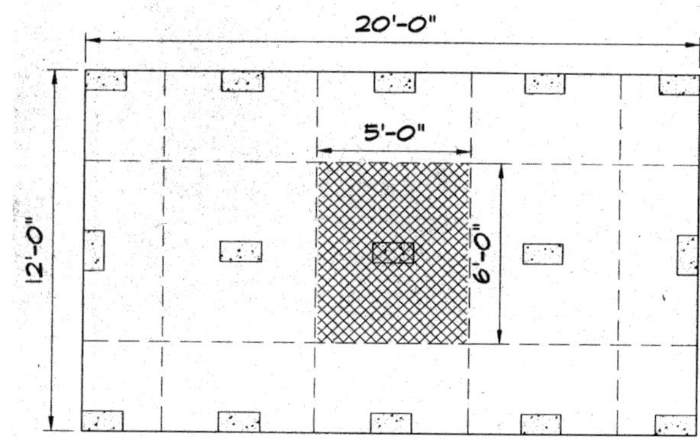

Note: Tributary area of shaded section on free standing deck shown is 5′ × 6′ = 30 sq. ft. Code will require a minimum footer of 8″ × 16″ per Table AM102.1.

FIGURE AM102.1

SECTION AM104 DECK ATTACHMENT

AM104.1 Deck attachment. When a deck is supported at the structure by attaching the deck to the structure, the following attachment schedules shall apply for attaching the deck band to the structure.

AM104.1.1 All structures except brick veneer structures.

FASTENERS	8′ MAX JOIST SPAN[a]	16′ MAX JOIST SPAN[a]
$^5/_8$″ Hot dipped galv. bolts with nut and washer[b]	1 @ 3′-6″ o.c.	1 @ 1′-8″ o.c.
and	and	and
12d Common hot dipped galv. nails[c]	2 @ 8″ o.c.	3 @ 6″ o.c.

a. Attachment interpolation between 8 foot and 16 foot joists span is allowed.
b. Minimum edge distance for bolts is $2^1/_2$ inches.
c. Nails must penetrate the supporting structure band a minimum of $1^1/_2$ inches.

AM104.1.2 Brick veneer structures.

FASTENERS	8′ MAX JOIST SPAN[a]	16′ MAX JOIST SPAN[a]
$^5/_8$″ Hot dipped galv. bolts with nut and washer[b]	1@ 2′-4″ o.c.	1@ 1′-4″ o.c.

a. Attachment interpolation between 8 foot and 16 foot joist span is allowed.
b. Minimum edge distance for bolts is $2^1/_2$ inches.

AM104.1.3 Masonry ledge support. If the deck band is supported by a minimum of $^1/_2$ inch masonry ledge along the foundation wall, $^5/_8$ inch hot dipped galvanized bolts with washers spaced at 48 inches o.c. may be used for support.

AM104.1.4 Other means of support. Joist hangers or other means of attachment may be connected to house band and shall be properly flashed.

SECTION AM105 GIRDER SUPPORT AND SPAN

AM105.1 Girder support and span. Girders shall bear directly on support post with post attached at top to prevent lateral displacement or be connected to the side of posts with two $^5/_8$ inch hot dipped galvanized bolts with nut and washer. Girder spans are per Tables R502.5(1) and (2). Girder support may be installed per Figure AM105 for top mount; Figure AM105.1 for side mount and Figure AM105.2 for split girder detail. Girders may also be cantilevered off ends of support post no more than 1 joist spacing or 16 inches, whichever is greater per Figure AM105.3.

SECTION AM106 JOIST SPANS AND CANTILEVERS

AM106.1 Joist spans and cantilevers. Joists spans shall be based upon Table R502.3.1(2) with 40 lbs per sq. ft. live load and 10 lbs per sq. ft. dead load. Floor joists for exterior decks may be cantilevered per Table R502.3.3 (1).

SPACING	2 x 6	2 x 8	2 x 10	2 x 12
12 inches	10-9	14-2	18-0	21-9
16 inches	9-9	12-10	16-1	18-10
19.2 inches	9-2	12-1	14-8	17-2
24 inches	8-6	11-0	13-1	15-5

Partial reprint of Table R502.3.1(2), #2 SYP only joist spans (ft-in)

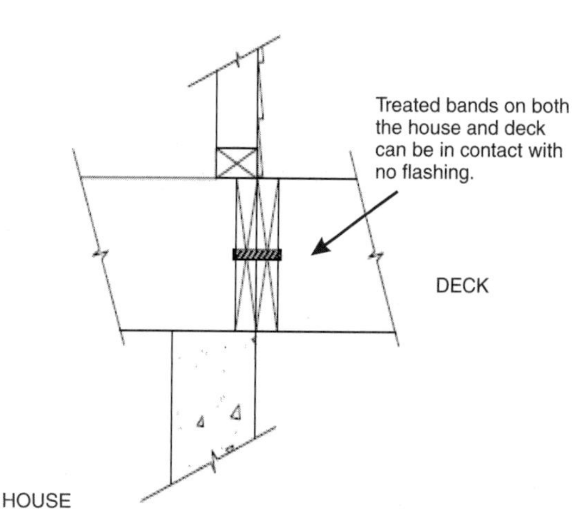

NO FLASHING-TREATED

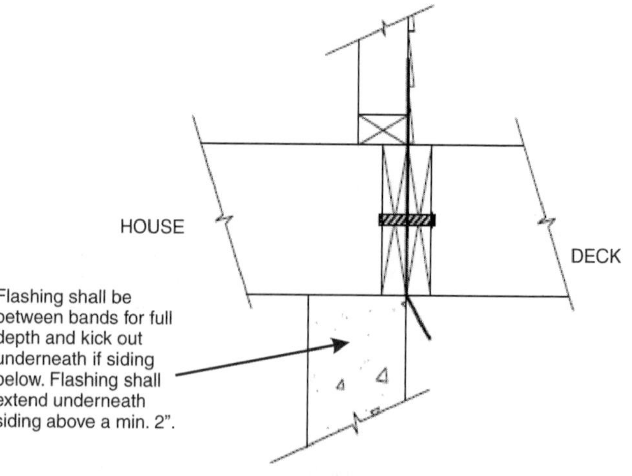

FLASHING BETWEEN

FIGURE AM103

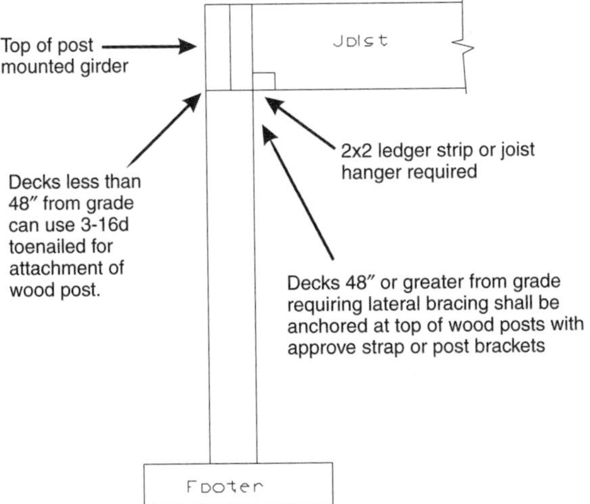

TOP MOUNT/FLUSH
FIGURE AM105

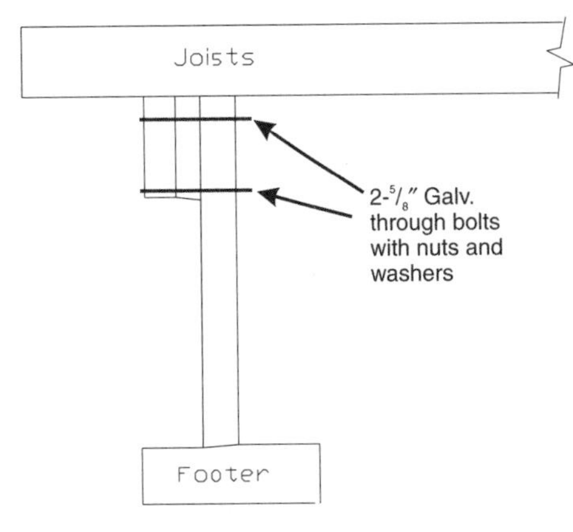

SIDE MOUNT DROPPED GIRDER
FIGURE AM105.1

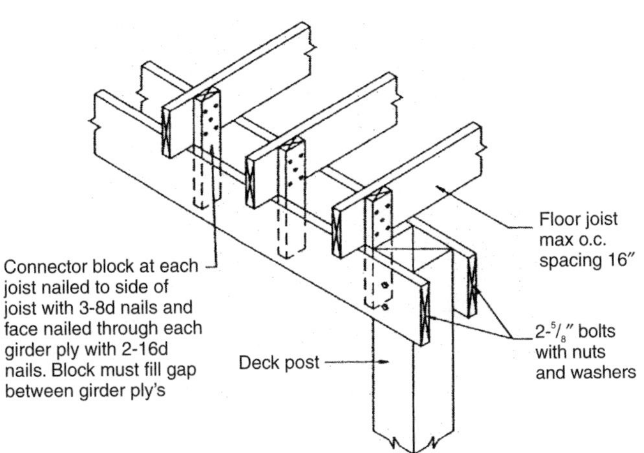

SPLIT GIRDER DETAIL
FIGURE AM105.2

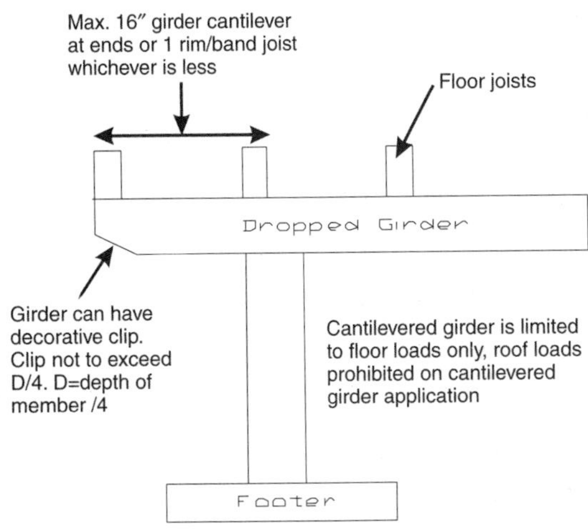

CANTILEVERED DROPPED GIRDER DETAIL
FIGURE AM105.3

SECTION AM107 FLOOR DECKING

AM107.1 Floor decking. Floor decking shall be No. 2 grade treated Southern Pine or equivalent. The minimum floor decking thickness shall be as follows:

SPACING	DECKING (nominal)
12" o.c	1" S4S
16" o.c.	1" T&G
19.2" o.c.	1$^1/_4$" S4S
24"-36" o.c.	2" S4S

SECTION AM108 POST HEIGHT

AM108.1 Post height. Maximum height of deck support posts as follows:

Post size[a]	Max. Post Height[b,c]
4x4 6x6	8'-0" 20'-0"

a. This table is based on No. 2 Southern Pine posts.
b. From top of footing to bottom of girder.
c. Decks with post heights exceeding these requirements shall be designed by a registered design professional.

SECTION AM109
DECK BRACING

AM109.1 Deck bracing. Decks shall be braced to provide lateral stability. The following are acceptable means to provide lateral stability.

AM109.1.1. When the deck floor height is less than 4′-0″ above finished grade per Figure AM109 and the deck is attached to the structure in accordance with Section AM104, lateral bracing is not required.

AM109.1.2. 4x4 wood knee braces may be provided on each column in both directions. The knee braces shall attach to each post at a point not less than $^1/_3$ of the post length from the top of the post, and the braces shall be angled between 45 degrees and 60 degrees from the horizontal. Knee braces shall be bolted to the post and the girder/double band with one $^5/_8$ inch hot dipped galvanized bolt with nut and washer at both ends of the brace per Figure AM109.1

AM109.1.3. For freestanding decks without knee braces or diagonal bracing, lateral stability may be provided by embedding the post in accordance with Figure AM109.2 and the following:

POST SIZE	MAXIMUM TRIBUTARY AREA	MAXIMUM POST HEIGHT	EMBEDMENT DEPTH	CONCRETE DIAMETER
4x4	48 SF	4'-0"	2'-6"	1'-0"
6x6	120 SF	6'-0"	3'-6"	1'-8"

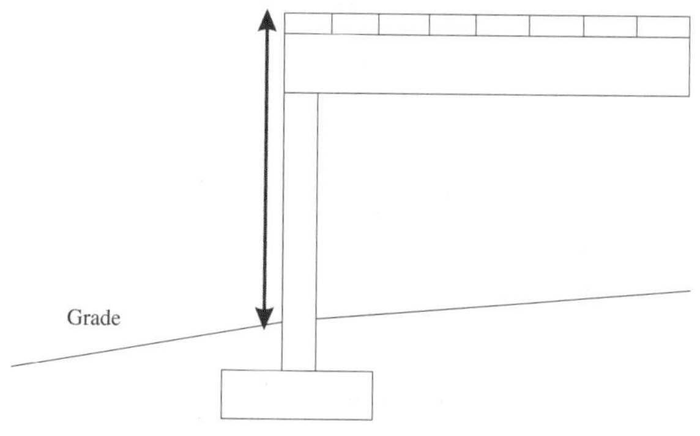

FIGURE AM109

AM109.1.4. 2x6 diagonal vertical cross bracing may be provided in two perpendicular directions for freestanding decks or parallel to the structure at the exterior column line for attached decks. The 2x6's shall be attached to the posts with one $^5/_8$ inch hot dipped galvanized bolt with nut and washer at each end of each bracing member per Figure AM109.3.

AM109.1.5. For embedment of piles in Coastal Regions, see Chapter 45.

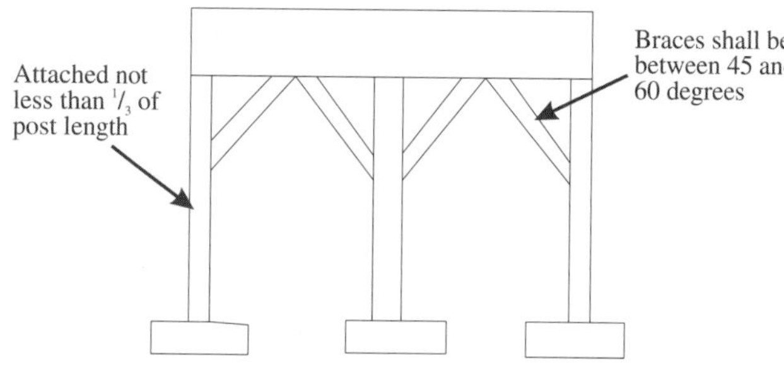

FIGURE AM109.1

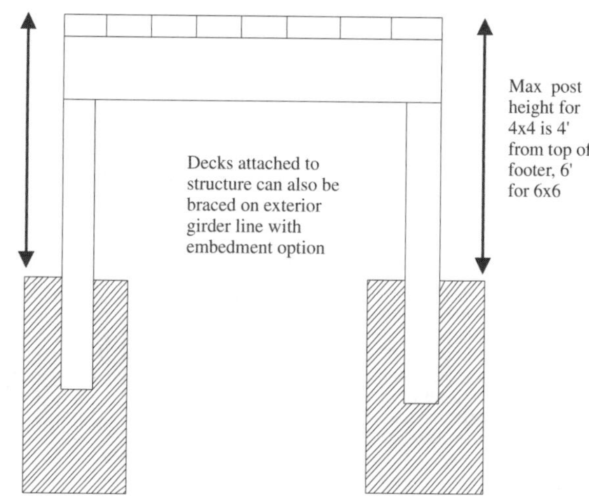

FIGURE AM109.2

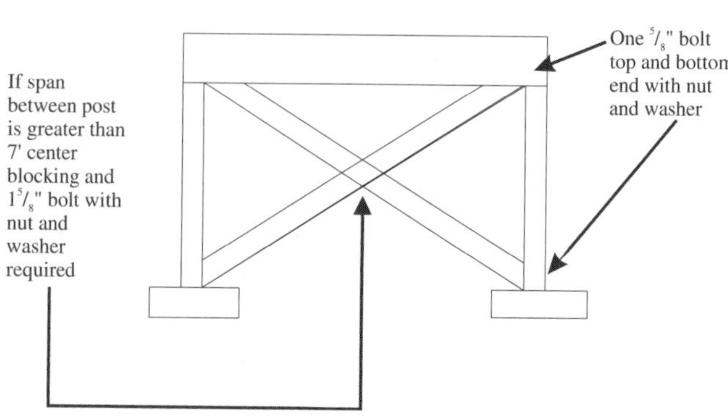

FIGURE AM109.3

SECTION AM110 STAIRS

AM110.1 Stairs shall be constructed per Figure AM110. Stringer spans shall be no greater than 7 foot span between supports. Spacing between stringers shall be based upon decking material used per AM107.1. Each Stringer shall have minimum $3^1/_2$ inches between step cut and back of stringer. If used, suspended headers shall shall be attached with $^3/_8$ inch galvinized bolts with nuts and washers to securely support stringers at the top.

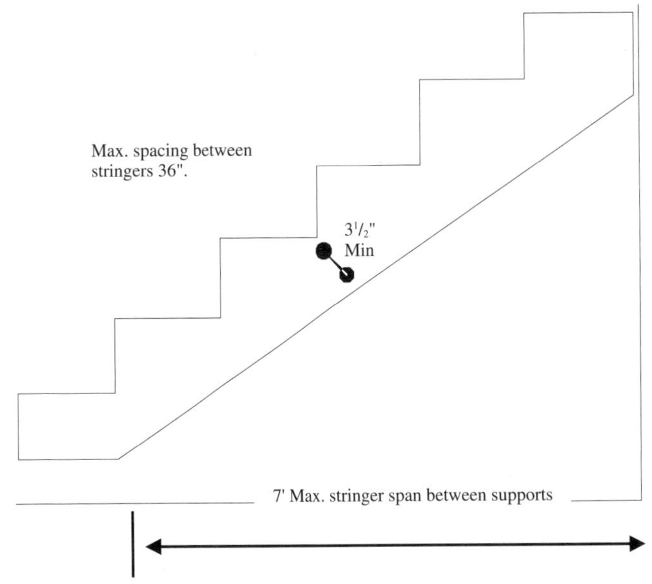

SECTION AM111 HANDRAILS, GUARDS AND GENERAL

AM111.1 Handrails, guards and general. Deck handrails, guards and general construction shall be per Figure AM111.

Max. spacing between stringers 36".
3 1/2" Min
7' Max. stringer span between supports

FIGURE AM110

Guards at a Minimum 36" required per R312.1 with 30" drop and opening limits per R312.2 & R312.3 (4" on vertical pickets, 6" on horizontal and ornamental guard rails), top rail and post to support 200 lbs with infill to meet 50 lbs per Table R301.5 and footnotes.
Attachment to structure based upon all cladding types but brick veneer per AM104.1.1, Brick veneer per AM104.1.2, Masonry ledge per AM104.1.3 or other per AM104.1.4.
4" MAX.
Rail posts cannot exceed 8' o.c. spacing and shall be attached with 2 3/8" Galv bolts with nut & washer to outer bands.
Decking per AM107 for #2 SYP and attached with 2-8d galv nails at each joist or approved screws. Other materials per mfg installation based upon joists o.c. spacing. Alternate material attached per mfg installation instructions.
Stair handrail/Guard. Height between 34"-38" per R311.7.1 & R312.2. Openings on side of stairs requiring guards shall not allow a sphere 4 3/8" to pass per R312.3 exception #2.
Deck post per AM108
Footers per Table AM102.1. Minimum base of footers 12" below grade.
Stairs treads and risers per R311.7.4.1 (8 1/4" Max riser) & R311.7.4.2 (9" minimum tread depth). Stairways min 36" width per R311.5.1 (rail projections allowed).
Riser openings. Stairs with a 30" or more vertical rise must have solid risers or opening restricted to prevent a 4" sphere from passing per R311.7.4.3.
Lateral Bracing per AM 109. AM109.1.1 height required; AM109.1.2 knee bracing; AM109.1.3 freestanding embedment; AM109.1.4 diagonal bracing; AM109.1.5 Coastal embedment.
Floor joist cantilevers allowed per Table R502.3.3(1)

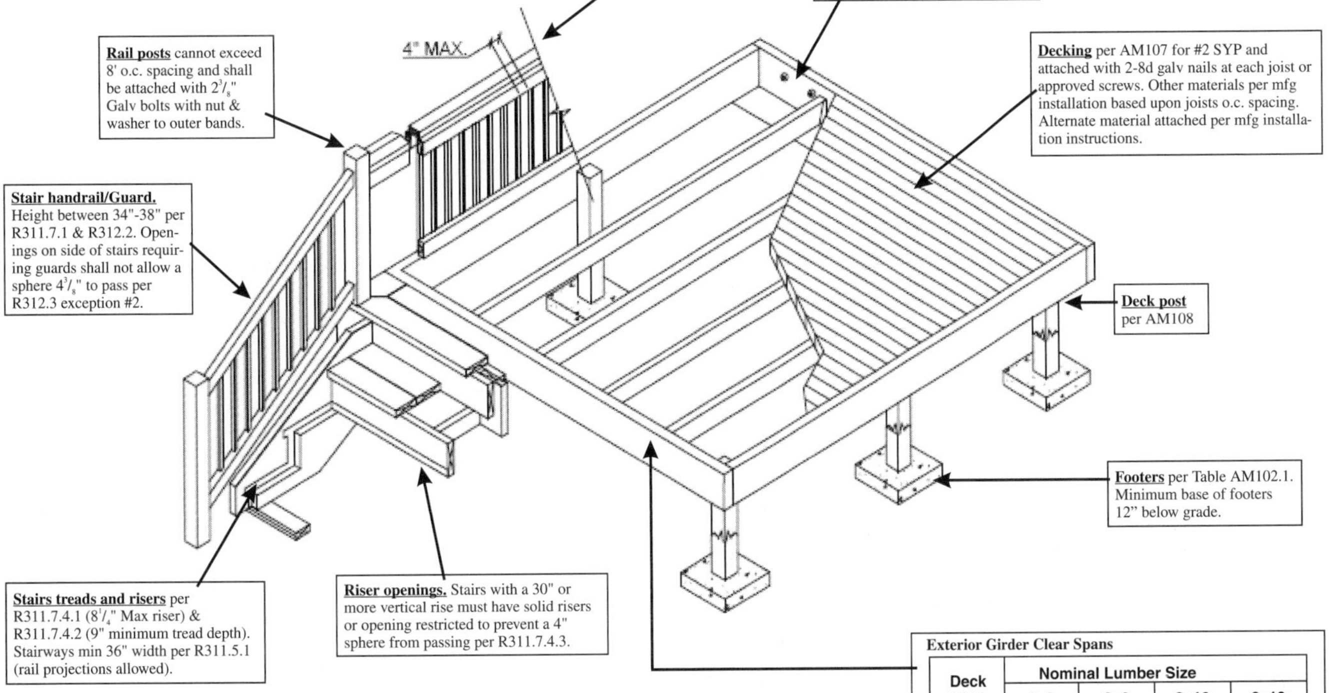

Exterior Girder Clear Spans

Deck Width	Nominal Lumber Size 2x6	2x8	2x10	2x12
20' (2ply)	3-11	5-0	6-1	7-1
20' (3ply)	—	6-3	7-7	8-10
20' (4ply)	—	—	8-9	10-2

*Partial reproduction of Table R502.5(1) at 30 ground snow load and roof ceiling and 1 clear span floor. Deck width is 20' or less measured in the direction of joists span. Splices in plys must break over bearing supports.

FIGURE AM111

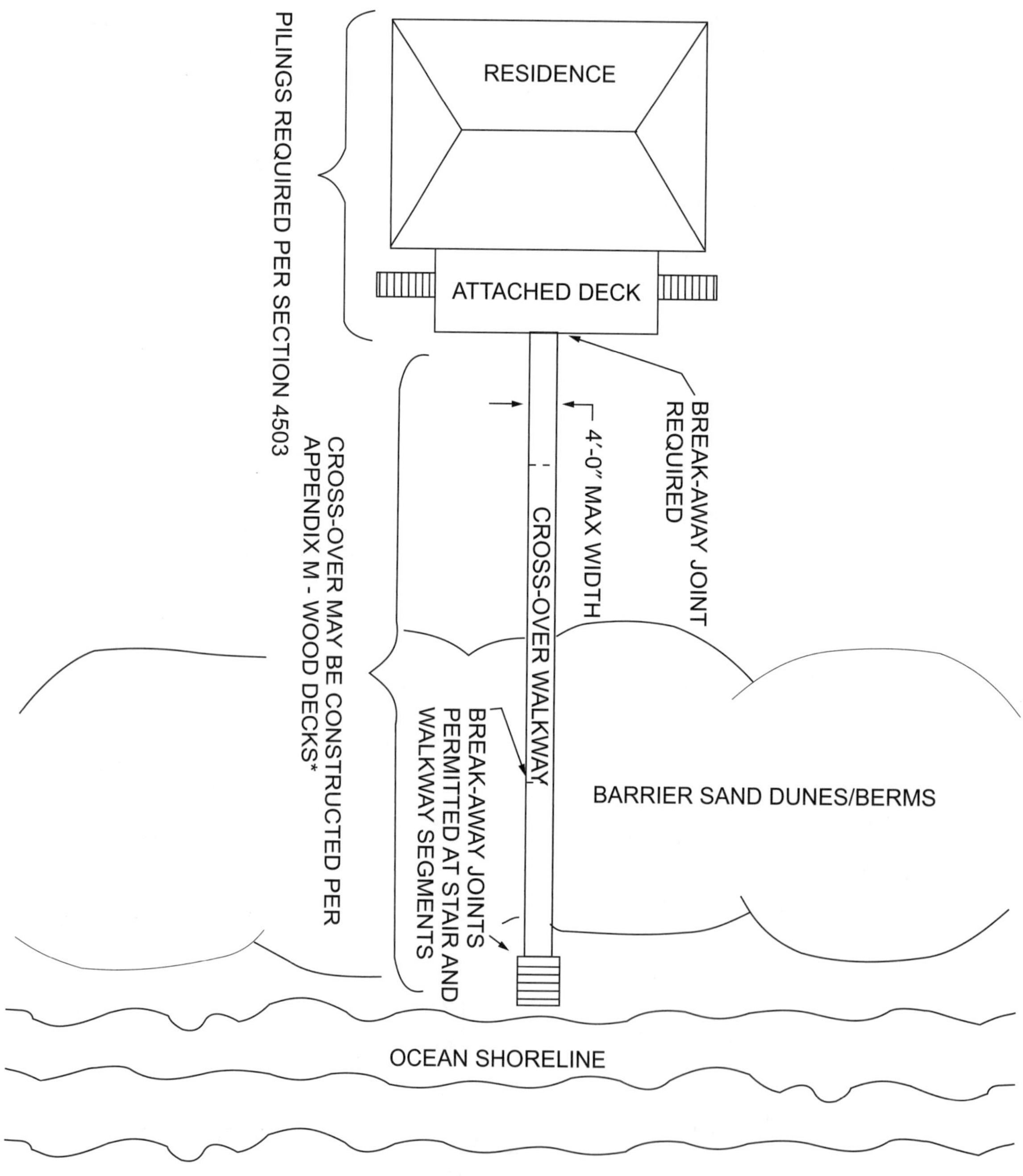

FIGURE AM112
WALKWAYS OVER DUNES OR BERMS IN OCEAN HAZARD AREAS

For SI: 1 inch = 25.4, 1 foot = 304.8 mm.

* Posts for walkways over dunes or berms shall be embedded a minimum depth of 4′ - 0″ and post heights shall be limited to 5′- 0″ above grade for 4 × 4 and 10′ - 0″ above grade for 6 × 6. Walkways or portions of walkways over 4′ 0″ in width shall comply with the requirements of Chapters 45 and 46. Maximum walkway surface height is 30″ above grade without guard rails.

** Walkway stair runs can be greater than 12′ without a landing.

APPENDIX N
BASIC LOAD ESTIMATING

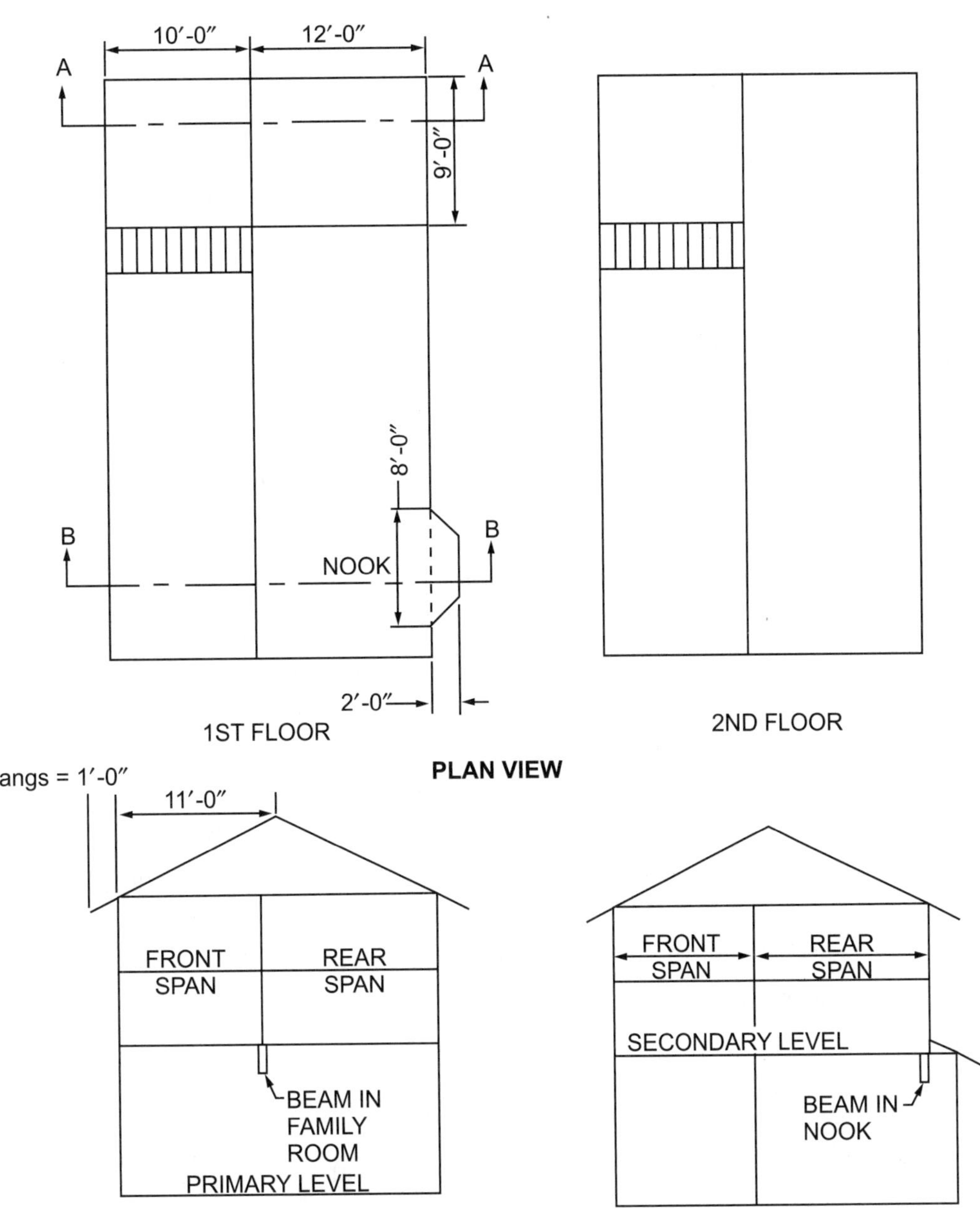

SECTION A-A

SECTION B-B

For SI: 1 inch = 25.4, 1 foot = 304.8 mm, 1 square foot = 0.0929 m^2.

ASSUMPTIONS (sleeping area live load; roof or stick frame rafters with no interior bearing):

Loads

Secondary floor level is 30# L.L. + 10# D.L.	= 40#/sq. ft.
Attic level is 20# live load + 10# dead load	= 30#/sq. ft.
Nook ceiling is 10# dead load (No attic storage)	= 10#/sq. ft.

Wall load

Studs @ 16", 1/2" gypsum	= 8#/sq. ft.

Roof load

20# live load + 10# dead load	= 30#/sq. ft.

EXAMPLE OF LOAD ESTIMATING LOAD ON BEAM IN FAMILY ROOM

Loads in Section A - A as follows: **Total Loads (in pounds/linear foot)**

2nd floor load $= \frac{(\text{front joist span } + \text{ rear joist span})}{2} \times \text{ 2nd floor } (\text{deadload} + \text{ load}) = \text{LOAD / linear foot}$

$= \frac{(10+12)}{2} \times (10+30) = \frac{(22)}{2} \times 40 = 11 \times 40 = 440 \text{ pounds / linear foot}$

Interior wall load = wall weight per square foot x wall height = LOAD/linear foot

8 pounds/sq. ft. × 8ft. = 64 pounds/linear foot (Wall weight can vary. Verify actual weight of materials used.)

Attic load $= \frac{(\text{front joist span } + \text{ rear joist span})}{2} \times \text{ attic } (\text{deadload} + \text{ live load}) = \text{LOAD / linear foot}$

$= \frac{(10+12)}{2} \times (10+20) = \frac{(22)}{2} \times (30) = 11 \times 30 = 330 \text{ pounds / linear foot}$

Roof load: No roof load is transmitted to the beam in the family room. Roof load = 0

Total Load on Beam in Family Room = 834 pounds/1 foot.

Beam span in family room is 9 feet and total estimated load is 834 pounds/linear foot:

By using Table No. N-1, the required beam is 4 @ 2 × 12 SYP or SPF

OR

By using Table No. N-2, the required minimum flitch beam is 2 @ 2 × 8 with $^1/_2''$ × 7″ steel plate bolted with $^1/_2''$ bolts spaced at 2′ o.c.

EXAMPLE OF LOAD ESTIMATING ON BEAM IN NOOK AREA

Loads in Section B - B as follows **Total Loads (in pounds/linear foot)**

2nd floor load $= \frac{(\text{front joist span } + \text{ rear joist span})}{2} \times \text{ 2nd floor } (\text{deadload} + \text{ live load}) = \text{LOAD / linear foot}$

$= \frac{(0+12)}{2} \times (10+30) = \frac{(12)}{2} \times (40) = 6 \times 40 = 240 \text{ pounds / linear foot}$

Exterior wall load = wall weight per square foot × wall height = LOAD/linear foot

= 8 pounds/sq. ft. × 8ft. = 64 pounds/linear foot (Wall weight can vary. Verify actual weight of materials used.)

Attic load $= \frac{(\text{front joist span } + \text{ rear joist span})}{2} \times \text{ attic } (\text{deadload} + \text{ live load}) = \text{LOAD / linear foot}$

$= \frac{(0+12)}{2} \times (10+20) = \frac{(12)}{2} \times (30) = 6 \times 30 = 180 \text{ pounds / linear foot}$

Roof load $= \frac{(\text{front rafter span } + \text{ rear rafter span})}{2} \times \text{ overhang } (\text{deadload} + \text{ live load}) = \text{LOAD / linear foot}$

$= \left[\frac{(11+11)}{2} + 1\right] \times (10+20) = \left[\frac{(22)}{2} + 1\right] \times (30) = 12 \times 30 = 360 \text{ pounds / linear foot}$

Nook ceiling load $= \frac{(\text{joist span } + \text{ joist span})}{2} \times \text{ ceiling } (\text{deadload} + \text{ live load}) = \text{LOAD / linear foot}$

$= \frac{(0+2)}{2} \times (10+0) = \frac{(2)}{2} \times (10) = 1 \times 10 = 10 \text{ pounds / linear foot}$

Nook roof load $= \frac{(\text{rafter span } + \text{ rafter span})}{2} \times \text{ roof } (\text{deadload} + \text{ live load}) = \text{LOAD / linear foot}$

$= \frac{(0+2)}{2} \times (10+20) = \frac{(2)}{2} \times (30) = 1 \times 30 = 30 \text{ pounds / linear foot}$

Total Load on Beam in Nook = 884 pounds/1 ft.

Beam span in nook is 8 feet and total estimated load is 884 pounds/linear foot.

By using Table No. N-1, the required beam is 3 @ 2 × 12 × Southern pine, or 4 @ 2 × 12 Spruce-pine-fir

OR

By using Table No. N-2, the required minimum flitch is 2 @ 2 × 8 with $^3/_8$" × 7" steel plate bolted with $^1/_2$" bolts spaced at 2' o.c.

TABLE N-1
WOOD BEAMS AND GIRDERS (19%) #2 GRADE, ALLOWABLE LOADS IN POUNDS PER LINEAR FOOT SIMPLE SPAN, DEFLECTION = L/360, LOAD DURATION FACTOR 1.0, ADEQUATE BEARING AND LATERAL SUPPORT MUST BE PROVIDED

2 × 8 ($1^1/_2 \times 7^1/_4$)						
SPECIES SPAN[2]	SPRUCE-PINE-FIR[1] NUMBER OF MEMBERS			SOUTHERN PINE NUMBER OF MEMBERS		
(feet)	2	3	4	2	3	4
3	1133	1700	2266	1457	2186	2914
4	727	1091	1454	935	1403	1870
5	535	803	1070	688	1032	1376
6	424	636	848	538	807	1076
7	350	525	700	400	600	800
8	270	405	540	309	464	618
9	215	323	430	246	369	492
10	175	263	350	200	300	400
12	107	161	214	123	185	246
14	68	102	136	78	117	156
2 × 10 ($1^1/_2 \times 9^1/_4$)						
SPECIES SPAN[2]	SPRUCE-PINE-FIR[1] NUMBER OF MEMBERS			SOUTHERN PINE NUMBER OF MEMBERS		
(feet)	2	3	4	2	3	4
3	1776	2664	3552	2283	3425	4566
4	1054	1581	2108	1355	2033	2710
5	749	1124	1498	963	1445	1926
6	581	872	1162	747	1121	1494
7	475	713	950	570	855	1140
8	401	602	802	440	660	880
9	321	482	642	350	525	700
10	261	392	522	285	428	570
12	183	275	366	200	300	400
14	135	203	270	147	221	294
2 × 12 ($1^1/_2 \times 11^1/_4$)						
SPECIES SPAN[2]	SPRUCE-PINE-FIR[1] NUMBER OF MEMBERS			SOUTHERN PINE NUMBER OF MEMBERS		
(feet)	2	3	4	2	3	4
3	2800	4200	5600	3600	5400	7200
4	1482	2223	2964	1906	2859	3812
5	1008	1512	2016	1296	1944	2592
6	764	1146	1528	982	1473	1964
7	615	923	1230	783	1175	1566
8	514	771	1028	604	906	1208
9	431	647	862	481	722	962
10	351	527	702	392	588	784
12	246	369	492	274	411	548
14	182	273	364	203	305	406

For SI: 1 foot = 304.8 mm.

1. Spruce-Pine-Fir not Spruce-pine-fir (Southern) is used in this table.
2. Span in clear span - effective span for bending and deflection is clear span plus 3 inch.

TABLE N-2
FLITCH PLATE BEAMS-DESIGN VALUES AND ASSUMPTIONS

Steel- Fb = 24000(psi) E = 29000000(psi)
Wood- Fb = 1200(psi) E = 2900000(psi)
Deflection- 1/360 of Span
(Top of Beam Laterally Supported)

2 - 2 x 6				ALLOWABLE LOAD (pounds/ft)					
1	PLATE	Bm Wgt (lbs/ft)		8	10	13	15	17	21
		Span (ft)	Plate	1/4 x 5	3/8 x 5	1/2 x 5	5/8 x 5	3/4 x 5	1 x 5
		6.00		756	965	1175	1385	1595	2014
		7.00		555	709	863	1018	1172	1480
		8.00		411*	520*	638*	739*	848*	1067*
		9.00		289*	365*	442*	519*	596*	749*
		10.00		210*	266*	322*	378*	434*	546*
		11.00		158*	200*	242*	284*	326*	410*
		12.00		122*	154*	187*	219*	251*	316*

*Denotes Load Controlled by Deflection

2 - 2 x 8				ALLOWABLE LOAD (pounds/ft)					
1	PLATE	Bm Wgt (lbs/ft)		11	14	17	20	23	29
		Span (ft)	Plate	1/4 x 7	3/8 x 7	1/2 x 7	5/8 x 7	3/4 x 7	1 x 7
		6.00		1406	1818	2229	2640	3051	3873
		7.00		1033	1335	1637	1939	2242	2846
		8.00		791	1022	1254	1485	1716	2179
		9.00		625	808	991	1173	1356	1722
		10.00		506	654	802	950	1098	1394
		11.00		400*	516*	631*	746*	862*	1092*
		12.00		308*	397*	486*	575*	664*	841*
		13.00		243*	312*	382*	452*	522*	662*
		14.00		194*	250*	306*	362*	418*	530*
		15.00		158*	203*	249*	294*	340*	431*
		16.00		130*	168*	205*	243*	280*	355*

*Denotes Load Controlled by Deflection

2 - 2 x 10				ALLOWABLE LOAD (pounds/ft)					
1	PLATE	Bm Wgt (lbs/ft)		14	18	22	26	30	37
		Span (ft)	Plate	1/4 x 9	3/8 x 9	1/2 x 9	5/8 x 9	3/4 x 9	1 x 9
		6.00		2310	2990	3669	4349	5029	6388
		7.00		1697	2197	2696	3195	3695	4693
		8.00		1299	1682	2064	2446	2829	3593
		9.00		1027	1329	1631	1933	2235	2839
		10.00		832	1076	1321	1566	1810	2300
		11.00		687	890	1092	1294	1496	1901
		12.00		576	747	917	1087	1257	1597
		13.00		492	637	782	926	1071	1361
		14.00		409*	528*	647*	765*	884*	1122*
		15.00		332*	429*	526*	622*	719*	912*
		16.00		274*	353*	433*	513*	592*	752*
		17.00		228*	295*	361*	427*	494*	627*
		18.00		192*	248*	304*	360*	416*	528*
		19.00		164*	211*	259*	306*	354*	449*
		20.00		140*	181*	222*	263*	301*	385*

*Denotes Load Controlled by Deflection

2 - 2 x 12				ALLOWABLE LOAD (pounds/ft)					
1	PLATE	Bm Wgt (lbs/ft)		18	22	27	32	36	46
		Span (ft)	Plate	1/4 x 11	3/8 x 11	1/2 x 11	5/8 x 11	3/4 x 11	1 x 11
		6.00		3437	4452	5468	6483	7498	9529
		7.00		2525	3271	4017	4763	5509	7001
		8.00		1933	2504	3076	3647	4218	5360
		9.00		1528	1979	2430	2881	3333	4235
		10.00		1237	1603	1968	2334	2699	3430
		11.00		1023	1325	1627	1929	2231	2835
		12.00		859	1113	1367	1621	1875	2382
		13.00		732	948	1165	1381	1597	2030
		14.00		631	818	1004	1191	1377	1750
		15.00		550	712	875	1037	1200	1525
		16.00		483	626	769	912	1054	1340
		17.00		414*	535*	657*	778*	899	1142*
		18.00		349*	451*	553*	655*	757	962*
		19.00		297*	384*	470*	557*	644	818*
		20.00		254*	329*	403*	478*	552	701*
		21.00		220*	284*	348*	413*	477	606*
		22.00		191*	247*	303*	359*	415	527*
		23.00		167*	216*	265*	314*	363*	461*
		24.00		147*	190*	233*	276*	320	406*

*Denotes Load Controlled by Deflection

APPENDIX O

FOAM PLASTIC DIAGRAMS

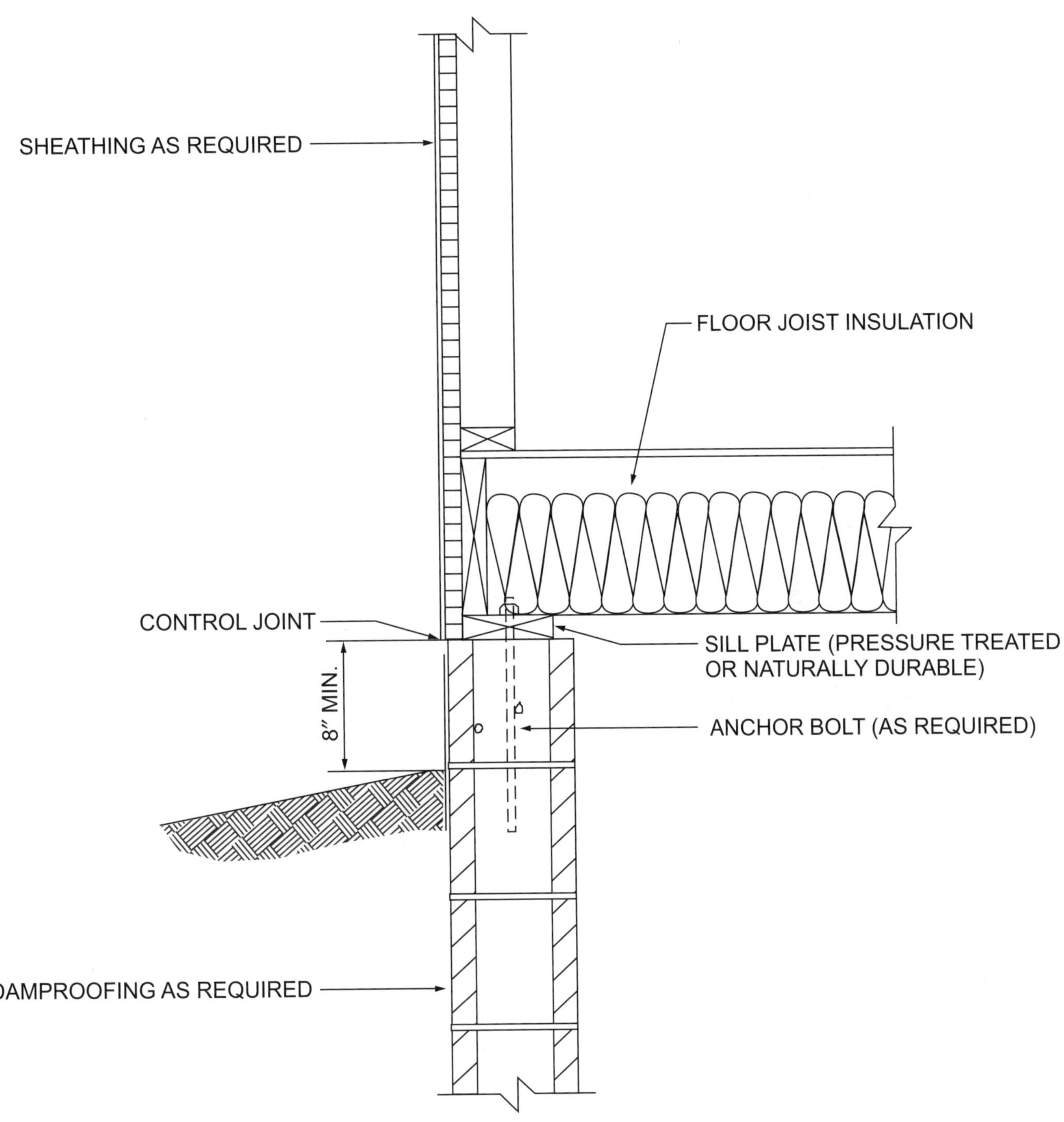

For SI: 1 inch = 25.4 mm.

FIGURE O-1
FOUNDATION WALL

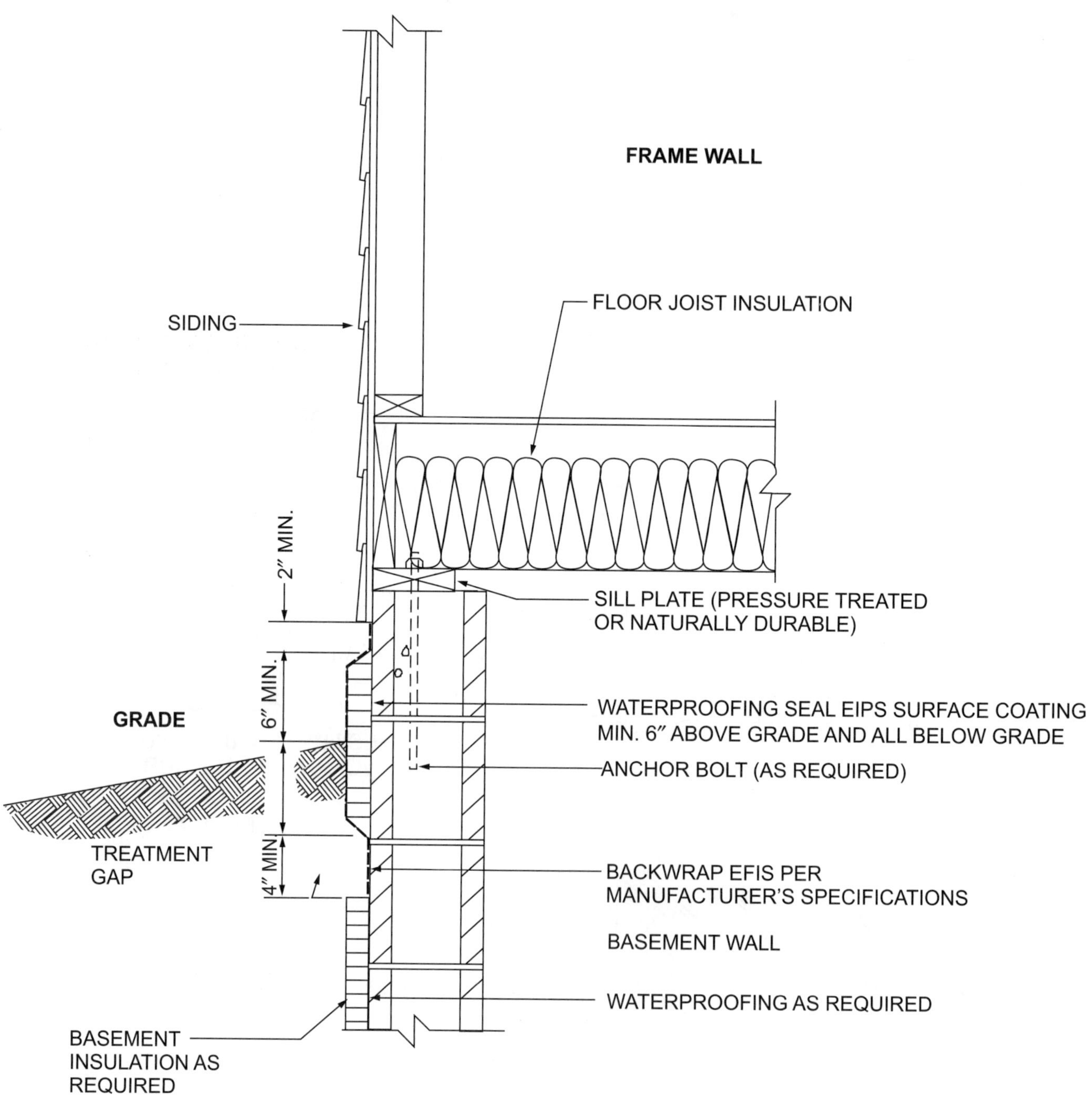

For SI: 1 inch = 25.4 mm.

FIGURE O-2
BASEMENT WALL

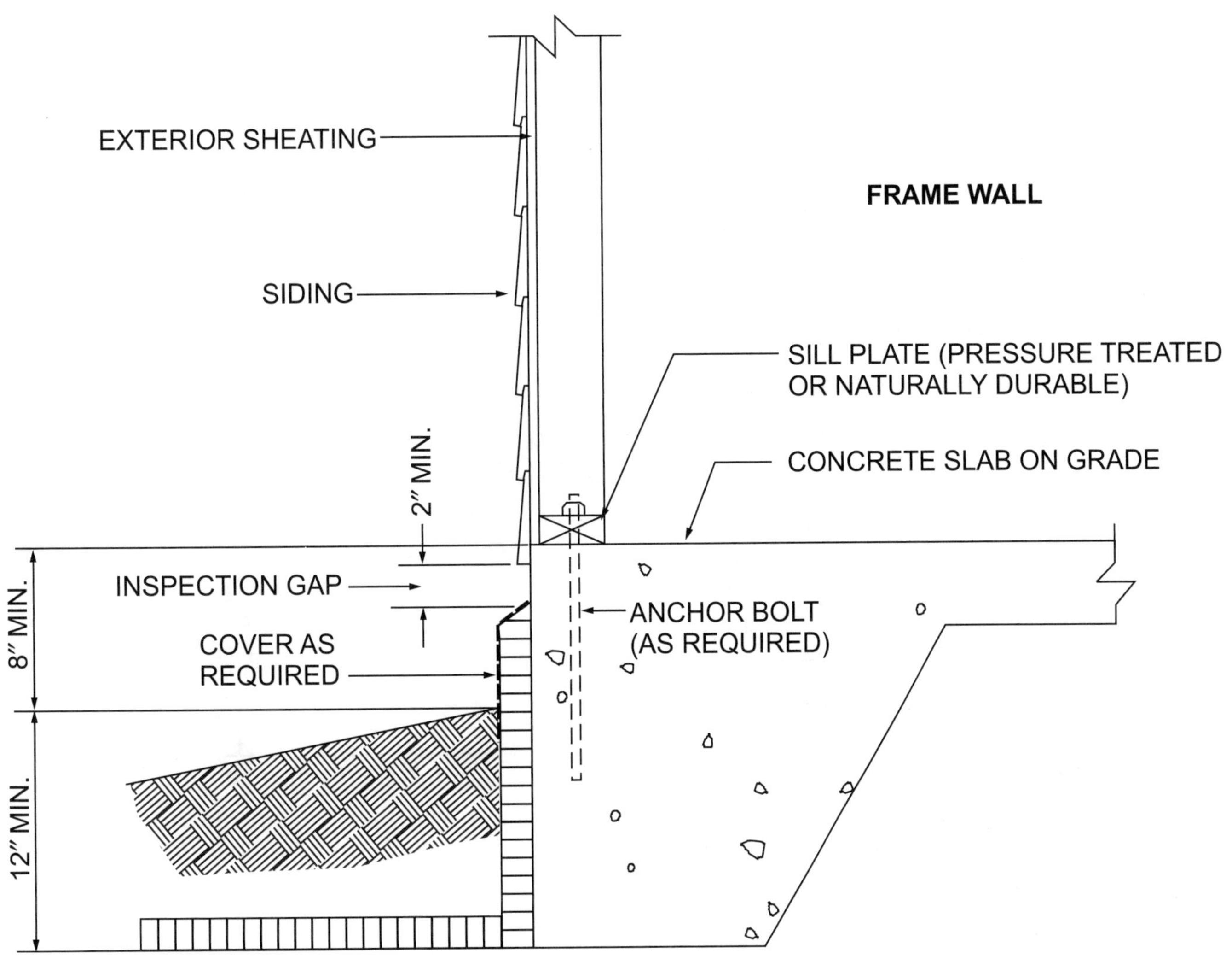

FOUNDATION INSULATION
24″ VERTICAL DEPTH OR A COMBINATION OF VERTICAL AND HORIZONTAL DIMENSION EQUAL TO 24″

For SI: 1 inch = 25.4 mm.

FIGURE O-3
FRAME WALL

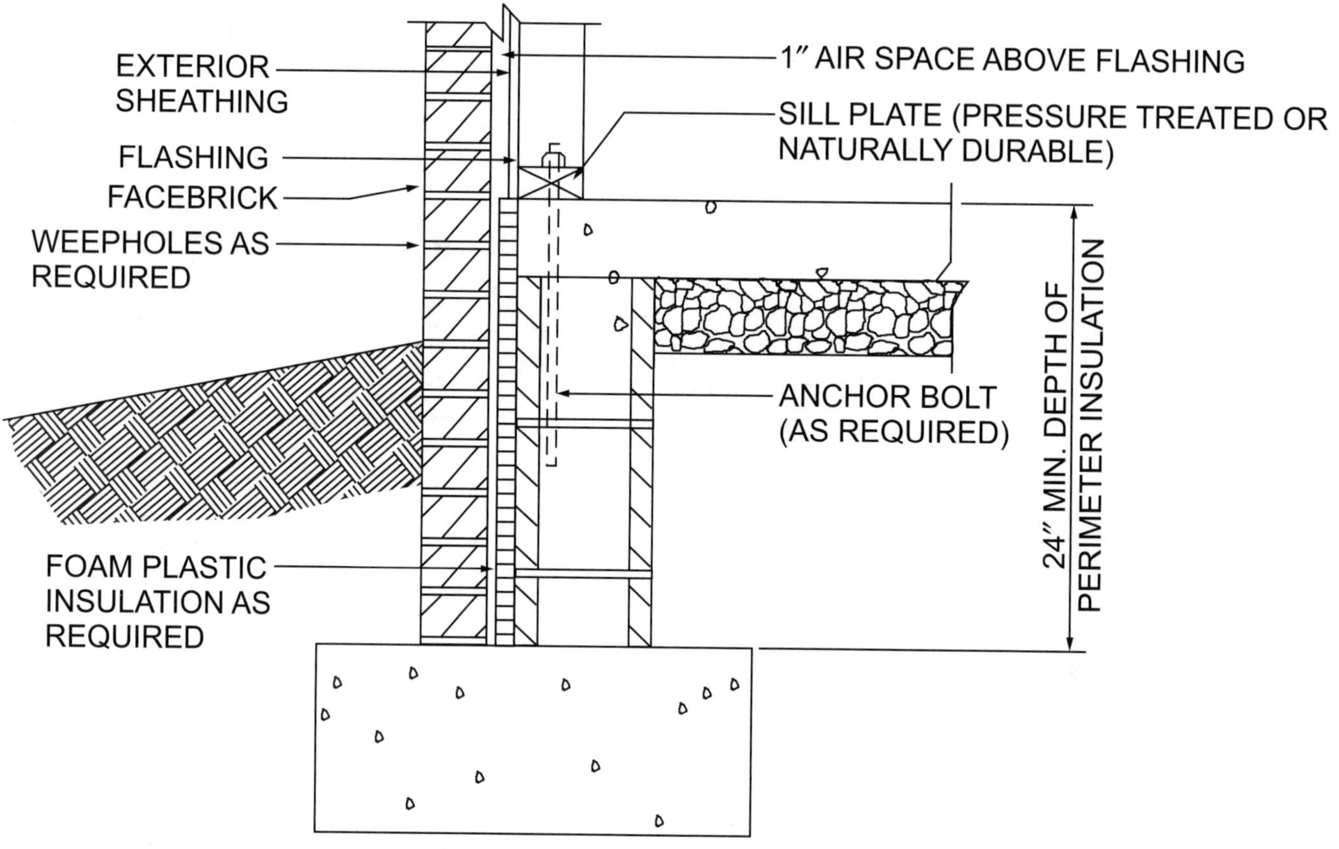

For SI: 1 inch = 25.4 mm.

FIGURE O-4
FRAME WALL

APPENDIX P

DWELLING UNIT FIRE SPRINKLER SYSTEMS

SECTION P2904 DWELLING UNIT FIRE SPRINKLER SYSTEMS

P2904.1 General. Where installed, residential fire sprinkler systems, or portions thereof, shall be in accordance with NFPA 13D or Section P2904, which shall be considered equivalent to NFPA 13D. Section P2904 shall apply to stand-alone and multipurpose wet-pipe sprinkler systems that do not include the use of antifreeze. A multipurpose fire sprinkler system shall supply domestic water to both fire sprinklers and plumbing fixtures. A stand-alone sprinkler system shall be separate and independent from the water distribution system. A backflow preventer shall not be required to separate a stand-alone sprinkler system from the water distribution system.

P2904.1.1 Required sprinkler locations. Sprinklers shall be installed to protect all areas of a *dwelling unit*.

Exceptions:

1. Attics, crawl spaces and normally unoccupied concealed spaces that do not contain fuel-fired appliances do not require sprinklers. In *attics*, crawl spaces and normally unoccupied concealed spaces that contain fuel-fired equipment, a sprinkler shall be installed above the equipment; however, sprinklers shall not be required in the remainder of the space.
2. Clothes closets, linen closets and pantries not exceeding 24 square feet (2.2 m^2) in area, with the smallest dimension not greater than 3 feet (915 mm) and having wall and ceiling surfaces of gypsum board.
3. Bathrooms not more than 55 square feet (5.1 m^2) in area.
4. Garages; carports; exterior porches; unheated entry areas, such as mud rooms, that are adjacent to an exterior door; and similar areas.

P2904.2 Sprinklers. Sprinklers shall be new listed residential sprinklers and shall be installed in accordance with the sprinkler manufacturer's installation instructions.

P2904.2.1 Temperature rating and separation from heat sources. Except as provided for in Section P2904.2.2, sprinklers shall have a temperature rating of not less than 135°F (57°C) and not more than 170°F (77°C). Sprinklers shall be separated from heat sources as required by the sprinkler manufacturer's installation instructions.

P2904.2.2 Intermediate temperature sprinklers. Sprinklers shall have an intermediate temperature rating not less than 175°F (79°C) and not more than 225°F (107°C) where installed in the following locations:

1. Directly under skylights, where the sprinkler is exposed to direct sunlight.
2. In *attics*.
3. In concealed spaces located directly beneath a roof.
4. Within the distance to a heat source as specified in Table P2904.2.2

TABLE P2904.2.2 LOCATIONS WHERE INTERMEDIATE TEMPERATURE SPRINKLERS ARE REQUIRED

HEAT SOURCE	RANGE OF DISTANCE FROM HEAT SOURCE WITHIN WHICH INTERMEDIATE TEMPERATURE SPRINKLERS ARE REQUIRED[a,b] (inches)
Fireplace, side of open or recessed fireplace	12 to 36
Fireplace, front of recessed fireplace	36 to 60
Coal and wood burning stove	12 to 42
Kitchen range top	9 to 18
Oven	9 to 18
Vent connector or chimney connector	9 to 18
Heating duct, not insulated	9 to 18
Hot water pipe, not insulated	6 to 12
Side of ceiling or wall warm air register	12 to 24
Front of wall mounted warm air register	18 to 36
Water heater, furnace or boiler	3 to 6
Luminaire up to 250 watts	3 to 6
Luminaire 250 watts up to 499 watts	6 to 12

For SI: 1 inch = 25.4 mm.

a. Sprinklers shall not be located at distances less than the minimum table distance unless the sprinkler listing allows a lesser distance.

b. Distances shall be measured in a straight line from the nearest edge of the heat source to the nearest edge of the sprinkler

P2904.2.3 Freezing areas. Piping shall be protected from freezing as required by Section P2603.6. Where sprinklers are required in areas that are subject to freezing, dry-side-wall or dry-pendent sprinklers extending from a nonfreezing area into a freezing area shall be installed.

P2904.2.4 Sprinkler coverage. Sprinkler coverage requirements and sprinkler obstruction requirements shall be in accordance with Sections P2904.2.4.1 and P2904.2.4.2.

P2904.2.4.1 Coverage area limit. The area of coverage of a single sprinkler shall not exceed 400 square feet (37 m^2) and shall be based on the sprinkler listing and the sprinkler manufacturer's installation instructions.

P2904.2.4.2 Obstructions to coverage. Sprinkler discharge shall not be blocked by obstructions unless additional sprinklers are installed to protect the obstructed area. Sprinkler separation from obstructions shall comply with the minimum distances specified in the sprinkler manufacturer's instructions.

P2904.2.4.2.1 Additional requirements for pendent sprinklers. Pendent sprinklers within 3 feet (915 mm) of the center of a ceiling fan, surface-mounted ceiling luminaire or similar object shall be considered to be obstructed, and additional sprinklers shall be installed.

P2904.2.4.2.2 Additional requirements for sidewall sprinklers. Sidewall sprinklers within 5 feet (1524 mm) of the center of a ceiling fan, surface-mounted ceiling luminaire or similar object shall be considered to be obstructed, and additional sprinklers shall be installed.

P2904.2.5 Sprinkler installation on systems assembled with solvent cement. The solvent cementing of threaded adapter fittings shall be completed and threaded adapters for sprinklers shall be verified as being clear of excess cement prior to the installation of sprinklers on systems assembled with solvent cement.

P2904.2.6 Sprinkler modifications prohibited. Painting, caulking or modifying of sprinklers shall be prohibited. Sprinklers that have been painted, caulked, modified or damaged shall be replaced with new sprinklers.

P2904.3 Sprinkler piping system. Sprinkler piping shall be supported in accordance with the requirements for cold water distribution piping. Sprinkler piping shall comply with all requirements for cold water distribution piping. For multipurpose piping systems, the sprinkler piping shall connect to and be a part of the cold water distribution piping system.

P2904.3.1 Nonmetallic pipe and tubing. Nonmetallic pipe and tubing, such as CPVC and PEX, shall be listed for use in residential fire sprinkler systems.

P2904.3.1.1 Nonmetallic pipe protection. Nonmetallic pipe and tubing systems shall be protected from exposure to the living space by a layer of not less than $^3/_8$ inch (9.5 mm) thick gypsum wallboard, $^1/_2$ inch thick plywood (13 mm), or other material having a 15 minute fire rating.

Exceptions:

1. Pipe protection shall not be required in areas that do not require protection with sprinklers as specified in Section P2904.1.1.
2. Pipe protection shall not be required where exposed piping is permitted by the pipe listing.

P2904.3.2 Shutoff valves prohibited. With the exception of shutoff valves for the entire water distribution system, valves shall not be installed in any location where the valve would isolate piping serving one or more sprinklers.

P2904.3.3 Single dwelling limit. Piping beyond the service valve located at the beginning of the water distribution system shall not serve more than one *dwelling*.

P2904.3.4 Drain. A means to drain the sprinkler system shall be provided on the system side of the water distribution shutoff valve.

P2904.4 Determining system design flow. The flow for sizing the sprinkler piping system shall be based on the flow rating of each sprinkler in accordance with Section P2904.4.1 and the calculation in accordance with Section P2904.4.2.

P2904.4.1 Determining required flow rate for each sprinkler. The minimum required flow for each sprinkler shall be determined using the sprinkler manufacturer's published data for the specific sprinkler model based on all of the following:

1. The area of coverage.
2. The ceiling configuration.
3. The temperature rating.
4. Any additional conditions specified by the sprinkler manufacturer.

P2904.4.2 System design flow rate. The design flow rate for the system shall be based on the following:

1. The design flow rate for a room having only one sprinkler shall be the flow rate required for that sprinkler, as determined by Section P2904.4.1.
2. The design flow rate for a room having two or more sprinklers a shall be determined by identifying the sprinkler in that room with the highest required flow rate, based on Section P2904.4.1, and multiplying that flow rate by 2.
3. Where the sprinkler manufacturer specifies different criteria for ceiling configurations that are not smooth, flat and horizontal, the required flow rate for that room shall comply with the sprinkler manufacturer's instructions.
4. The design flow rate for the sprinkler system shall be the flow required by the room with the largest flow rate, based on Items 1, 2 and 3.

5. For the purpose of this section, it shall be permissible to reduce the design flow rate for a room by subdividing the space into two or more rooms, where each room is evaluated separately with respect to the required design flow rate. Each room shall be bounded by walls and a ceiling. Openings in walls shall have a lintel not less than 8 inches (203 mm) in depth and each lintel shall form a solid barrier between the ceiling and the top of the opening.

P2904.5 Water supply. The water supply shall provide not less than the required design flow rate for sprinklers in accordance with Section P2904.4.2 at a pressure not less than that used to comply with Section P2904.6.

P2904.5.1 Water supply from individual sources. Where a *dwelling unit* water supply is from a tank system, a private well system or a combination of these, the available water supply shall be based on the minimum pressure control setting for the pump.

P2904.5.2 Required capacity. The water supply shall have the capacity to provide the required design flow rate for sprinklers for a period of time as follows:

1. 7 minutes for *dwelling units* one *story* in height and less than 2,000 square feet (186 m^2) in area.
2. 10 minutes for *dwelling units* two or more stories in height or equal to or greater than 2,000 square feet (186 m^2) in area.

Where a well system, a water supply tank system or a combination thereof is used, any combination of well capacity and tank storage shall be permitted to meet the capacity requirement.

P2904.6 Pipe sizing. The piping to sprinklers shall be sized for the flow required by Section P2904.4.2. The flow required to supply the plumbing fixtures shall not be required to be added to the sprinkler design flow.

P2904.6.1 Method of sizing pipe. Piping supplying sprinklers shall be sized using the prescriptive method in Section P2904.6.2 or by hydraulic calculation in accordance with NFPA 13D. The minimum pipe size from the water supply source to any sprinkler shall be $^3/_4$ inch (19 mm) nominal. Threaded adapter fittings at the point where sprinklers are attached to the piping shall be a minimum of $^1/_2$ inch (13 mm) nominal.

P2904.6.2 Prescriptive pipe sizing method. Pipe shall be sized by determining the available pressure to offset friction loss in piping and identifying a piping material, diameter and length using the equation in Section P2904.6.2.1 and the procedure in Section P2904.6.2.2.

P2904.6.2.1 Available pressure equation. The pressure available to offset friction loss in the interior piping system (P_t) shall be determined in accordance with the Equation 29-1.

$$P_t = P_{sup} - PL_{svc} - PL_m - PL_d - PL_e - P_{sp} \quad \textbf{(Equation 29-1)}$$

where:

P_t = Pressure used in applying Tables P2904.6.2(4) through P2904.6.2(9).

P_{sup} = Pressure available from the water supply source.

PL_{svc} = Pressure loss in the water-service pipe.

PL_m = Pressure loss in the water meter.

PL_d = Pressure loss from devices other than the water meter.

PL_e = Pressure loss associated with changes in elevation.

P_{sp} = Maximum pressure required by a sprinkler.

2904.6.2.2 Calculation procedure. Determination of the required size for water distribution piping shall be in accordance with the following procedure:

Step 1–Determine P_{sup}

Obtain the static supply pressure that will be available from the water main from the water purveyor, or for an individual source, the available supply pressure shall be in accordance with Section P2904.5.1.

Step 2–Determine PL_{svc}

Use Table P2904.6.2(1) to determine the pressure loss in the water service pipe based on the selected size of the water service.

Step 3–Determine PL_m

Use Table P2904.6.2(2) to determine the pressure loss from the water meter, based on the selected water meter size.

Step 4–Determine PL_d

Determine the pressure loss from devices other than the water meter installed in the piping system supplying sprinklers, such as pressure-reducing valves, backflow preventers, water softeners or water filters. Device pressure losses shall be based on the device manufacturer's specifications. The flow rate used to determine pressure loss shall be the rate from Section P2904.4.2, except that 5 gpm (0.3 L/S) shall be added where the device is installed in a water-service pipe that supplies more than one *dwelling*. As alternative to deducting pressure loss for a device, an automatic bypass valve shall be installed to divert flow around the device when a sprinkler activates.

Step 5–Determine PL_e

Use Table P2904.6.2(3) to determine the pressure loss associated with changes in elevation. The elevation used in applying the table shall be the difference between the elevation where the water source pressure was measured and the elevation of the highest sprinkler.

Step 6–Determine P_{sp}

Determine the maximum pressure required by any individual sprinkler based on the flow rate from Section P2904.4.1. The required pressure is provided in the sprinkler manufacturer's published data for the specific sprinkler model based on the selected flow rate.

Step 7–Calculate P_t

Using Equation 29-1, calculate the pressure available to offset friction loss in water-distribution piping between the service valve and the sprinklers.

Step 8–Determine the maximum allowable pipe length

Use Tables P2904.6.2(4) through P2904.6.2(9) to select a material and size for water distribution piping. The piping material and size shall be acceptable if the *developed length* of pipe between the service valve and the most remote sprinkler does not exceed the maximum allowable length specified by the applicable table. Interpolation of P_t between the tabular values shall be permitted.

The maximum allowable length of piping in Tables P2904.6.2(4) through P2904.6.2(9) incorporates an adjustment for pipe fittings, and no additional consideration of friction losses associated with pipe fittings shall be required.

P2904.7 Instructions and signs. An owner's manual for the fire sprinkler system shall be provided to the owner. A sign or valve tag shall be installed at the main shutoff valve to the water distribution system stating the following: "Warning, the water system for this home supplies fire sprinklers that require certain flows and pressures to fight a fire. Devices that restrict the flow or decrease the pressure or automatically shut off the water to the fire sprinkler system, such as water softeners, filtration systems and automatic shutoff valves, shall not be added to this system without a review of the fire sprinkler system by a fire protection specialist. Do not remove this sign."

P2904.8 Inspections. The water distribution system shall be inspected in accordance with Sections P2904.8.1 and P2904.8.2.

P2904.8.1 Preconcealment inspection. The following items shall be verified prior to the concealment of any sprinkler system piping:

1. Sprinklers are installed in all areas as required by Section P2904.1.1.
2. Where sprinkler water spray patterns are obstructed by construction features, luminaires or ceiling fans, additional sprinklers are installed as required by Section P2904.2.4.2.
3. Sprinklers are the correct temperature rating and are installed at or beyond the required separation distances from heat sources as required by Sections P2904.2.1 and P2904.2.2.
4. The pipe size equals or exceeds the size used in applying Tables P2904.6.2(4) through P2904.6.2(9) or, if the piping system was hydraulically calculated in accordance with Section P2904.6.1, the size used in the hydraulic calculation.
5. The pipe length does not exceed the length permitted by Tables P2904.6.2(4) through P2904.6.2(9) or, if the piping system was hydraulically calculated in accordance with Section P2904.6.1, pipe lengths and fittings do not exceed those used in the hydraulic calculation.
6. Nonmetallic piping that conveys water to sprinklers is listed for use with fire sprinklers.
7. Piping is supported in accordance with the pipe manufacturer's and sprinkler manufacturer's installation instructions.
8. The piping system is tested in accordance with Section P2503.7.

P2904.8.2 Final inspection. The following items shall be verified upon completion of the system:

1. Sprinkler are not painted, damaged or otherwise hindered from operation.
2. Where a pump is required to provide water to the system, the pump starts automatically upon system water demand.
3. Pressure-reducing valves, water softeners, water filters or other impairments to water flow that were not part of the original design have not been installed.
4. The sign or valve tag required by Section P2904.7 is installed and the owner's manual for the system is present.

TABLE P2904.6.2(1) WATER SERVICE PRESSURE LOSS (PL_{svc})[a,b]

FLOW RATE[c] (gpm)	$^{3}/_{4}$ INCH WATER SERVICE PRESSURE LOSS (psi)				1 INCH WATER SERVICE PRESSURE LOSS (psi)				$1^{1}/_{4}$ INCH WATER SERVICE PRESSURE LOSS (psi)			
	Length of water service pipe (feet)				Length of water service pipe (feet)				Length of water service pipe (feet)			
	40 or less	41 to 75	76 to 100	101 to 150	40 or less	41 to 75	76 to 100	101 to 150	40 or less	41 to 75	76 to 100	101 to 150
8	5.1	8.7	11.8	17.4	1.5	2.5	3.4	5.1	0.6	1.0	1.3	1.9
10	7.7	13.1	17.8	26.3	2.3	3.8	5.2	7.7	0.8	1.4	2.0	2.9
12	10.8	18.4	24.9	NP	3.2	5.4	7.3	10.7	1.2	2.0	2.7	4.0
14	14.4	24.5	NP	NP	4.2	7.1	9.6	14.3	1.6	2.7	3.6	5.4
16	18.4	NP	NP	NP	5.4	9.1	12.4	18.3	2.0	3.4	4.7	6.9
18	22.9	NP	NP	NP	6.7	11.4	15.4	22.7	2.5	4.3	5.8	8.6
20	27.8	NP	NP	NP	8.1	13.8	18.7	27.6	3.1	5.2	7.0	10.4
22	NP	NP	NP	NP	9.7	16.5	22.3	NP	3.7	6.2	8.4	12.4
24	NP	NP	NP	NP	11.4	19.3	26.2	NP	4.3	7.3	9.9	14.6
26	NP	NP	NP	NP	13.2	22.4	NP	NP	5.0	8.5	11.4	16.9
28	NP	NP	NP	NP	15.1	25.7	NP	NP	5.7	9.7	13.1	19.4
30	NP	NP	NP	NP	17.2	NP	NP	NP	6.5	11.0	14.9	22.0
32	NP	NP	NP	NP	19.4	NP	NP	NP	7.3	12.4	16.8	24.8
34	NP	NP	NP	NP	21.7	NP	NP	NP	8.2	13.9	18.8	NP
36	NP	NP	NP	NP	24.1	NP	NP	NP	9.1	15.4	20.9	NP

For SI: 1 inch = 25.4 mm, 1 foot = 304.8 mm, 1 gallon per minute = 0.063 L/s, 1 pound per square inch = 6.895 kPa.

NP - Not permitted. Pressure loss exceeds reasonable limits.

a. Values are applicable for underground piping materials listed in Table P2905.4 and are based on an SDR of 11 and a Hazen Williams C Factor of 150.

b. Values include the following length allowances for fittings: 25% length increase for actual lengths up to 100 feet and 15% length increase for actual lengths over 100 feet.

c. Flow rate from Section P2904.4.2. Add 5 gpm to the flow rate required by Section P2904.4.2 where the water-service pipe supplies more than one dwelling.

TABLE P2904.6.2(2)
MINIMUM WATER METER PRESSURE LOSS (PL_m)[a]

FLOW RATE (gallons per minute, gpm)[b]	$^5/_8$-INCH METER PRESSURE LOSS (pounds per square inch, psi)	$^3/_4$-INCH METER PRESSURE LESS (pounds per square inch, psi)	1-INCH METER PRESSURE LOSS (pounds per square inch, psi)
8	2	1	1
10	3	1	1
12	4	1	1
14	5	2	1
16	7	3	1
18	9	4	1
20	11	4	2
22	NP	5	2
24	NP	5	2
26	NP	6	2
28	NP	6	2
30	NP	7	2
32	NP	7	3
34	NP	8	3
36	NP	8	3

For SI: 1 inch = 25.4 mm, 1 pound per square inch = 6.895 kPa, 1 gallon per minute = 0.063 L/s.

NP - Not permitted unless the actual water meter pressure loss is known.

a. Table P2904.6.2(2) establishes conservative values for water meter pressure loss or installations where the water meter loss is unknown. Where the actual water meter pressure loss is known, P_m shall be the actual loss.

b. Flow rate from Section P2904.4.2. Add 5 gpm to the flow rate required by Section P2904.4.2 where the water-service pipe supplies more than one dwelling.

TABLE P2904.6.2(3)
ELEVATION LOSS (PL_e)

ELEVATION (feet)	PRESSURE LOSS (psi)
5	2.2
10	4.4
15	6.5
20	8.7
25	10.9
30	13
35	15.2
40	17.4

For SI: 1 foot = 304.8 mm, 1 pound per square inch = 6.895 kPa.

TABLE P2904.6.2(4)
ALLOWABLE PIPE LENGTH FOR $^{3}/_{4}$-INCH TYPE M COPPER WATER TUBING

SPRINKLER FLOW RATE[a] (gpm)	WATER DISTRIBUTION SIZE (inch)	AVAILABLE PRESSURE - P_t (psi)									
		15	20	25	30	35	40	45	50	55	60
		Allowable length of pipe from service valve to farthest sprinkler (feet)									
8	$^{3}/_{4}$	217	289	361	434	506	578	650	723	795	867
9	$^{3}/_{4}$	174	232	291	349	407	465	523	581	639	697
10	$^{3}/_{4}$	143	191	239	287	335	383	430	478	526	574
11	$^{3}/_{4}$	120	160	200	241	281	321	361	401	441	481
12	$^{3}/_{4}$	102	137	171	205	239	273	307	341	375	410
13	$^{3}/_{4}$	88	118	147	177	206	235	265	294	324	353
14	$^{3}/_{4}$	77	103	128	154	180	205	231	257	282	308
15	$^{3}/_{4}$	68	90	113	136	158	181	203	226	248	271
16	$^{3}/_{4}$	60	80	100	120	140	160	180	200	220	241
17	$^{3}/_{4}$	54	72	90	108	125	143	161	179	197	215
18	$^{3}/_{4}$	48	64	81	97	113	129	145	161	177	193
19	$^{3}/_{4}$	44	58	73	88	102	117	131	146	160	175
20	$^{3}/_{4}$	40	53	66	80	93	106	119	133	146	159
21	$^{3}/_{4}$	36	48	61	73	85	97	109	121	133	145
22	$^{3}/_{4}$	33	44	56	67	78	89	100	111	122	133
23	$^{3}/_{4}$	31	41	51	61	72	82	92	102	113	123
24	$^{3}/_{4}$	28	38	47	57	66	76	85	95	104	114
25	$^{3}/_{4}$	26	35	44	53	61	70	79	88	97	105
26	$^{3}/_{4}$	24	33	41	49	57	65	73	82	90	98
27	$^{3}/_{4}$	23	30	38	46	53	61	69	76	84	91
28	$^{3}/_{4}$	21	28	36	43	50	57	64	71	78	85
29	$^{3}/_{4}$	20	27	33	40	47	53	60	67	73	80
30	$^{3}/_{4}$	19	25	31	38	44	50	56	63	69	75
31	$^{3}/_{4}$	18	24	29	35	41	47	53	59	65	71
32	$^{3}/_{4}$	17	22	28	33	39	44	50	56	61	67
33	$^{3}/_{4}$	16	21	26	32	37	42	47	53	58	63
34	$^{3}/_{4}$	NP	20	25	30	35	40	45	50	55	60
35	$^{3}/_{4}$	NP	19	24	28	33	38	42	47	52	57
36	$^{3}/_{4}$	NP	18	22	27	31	36	40	45	49	54
37	$^{3}/_{4}$	NP	17	21	26	30	34	38	43	47	51
38	$^{3}/_{4}$	NP	16	20	24	28	32	36	40	45	49
39	$^{3}/_{4}$	NP	15	19	23	27	31	35	39	42	46
40	$^{3}/_{4}$	NP	NP	18	22	26	29	33	37	40	44

For SI: 1 inch = 25.4 mm, 1 foot = 304.8 mm, 1 pound per square inch = 6.895 kPa, 1 gallon per minute = 0.963 L/s.
NP - Not permitted
a. Flow rate from Section P2904.4.2.

TABLE P2904.6.2(5)
ALLOWABLE PIPE LENGTH FOR 1-INCH TYPE M COPPER WATER TUBING

SPRINKLER FLOW RATE[a] (gpm)	WATER DISTRIBUTION SIZE (inch)	AVAILABLE PRESSURE - P_t (psi)									
		15	20	25	30	35	40	45	50	55	60
		Allowable length of pipe from service valve to farthest sprinkler (feet)									
8	1	806	1075	1343	1612	1881	2149	2418	2687	2955	3224
9	1	648	864	1080	1296	1512	1728	1945	2161	2377	2593
10	1	533	711	889	1067	1245	1422	1600	1778	1956	2134
11	1	447	586	745	894	1043	1192	1341	1491	1640	1789
12	1	381	508	634	761	888	1015	1142	1269	1396	1523
13	1	328	438	547	657	766	875	985	1094	1204	1313
14	1	286	382	477	572	668	763	859	954	1049	1145
15	1	252	336	420	504	588	672	756	840	924	1008
16	1	224	298	373	447	522	596	671	745	820	894
17	1	200	266	333	400	466	533	600	666	733	799
18	1	180	240	300	360	420	479	539	599	659	719
19	1	163	217	271	325	380	434	488	542	597	651
20	1	148	197	247	296	345	395	444	493	543	592
21	1	135	180	225	270	315	360	406	451	496	541
22	1	124	165	207	248	289	331	372	413	455	496
23	1	114	152	190	228	267	305	343	381	419	457
24	1	106	141	176	211	246	282	317	352	387	422
25	1	98	131	163	196	228	261	294	326	359	392
26	1	91	121	152	182	212	243	273	304	334	364
27	1	85	113	142	170	198	226	255	283	311	340
28	1	79	106	132	159	185	212	238	265	291	318
29	1	74	99	124	149	174	198	223	248	273	298
30	1	70	93	116	140	163	186	210	233	256	280
31	1	66	88	110	132	153	175	197	219	241	263
32	1	62	83	103	124	145	165	186	207	227	248
33	1	59	78	98	117	137	156	176	195	215	234
34	1	55	74	92	111	129	148	166	185	203	222
35	1	53	70	88	105	123	140	158	175	193	210
36	1	50	66	83	100	116	133	150	166	183	199
37	1	47	63	79	95	111	126	142	158	174	190
38	1	45	60	75	90	105	120	135	150	165	181
39	1	43	57	72	86	100	115	129	143	158	172
40	1	41	55	68	82	96	109	123	137	150	164

For SI: 1 inch = 25.4 mm, 1 foot = 304.8 mm, 1 pound per square inch = 6.895 kPa, 1 gallon per minute = 0.963 L/s.
a. Flow rate from Section P2904.4.2.

TABLE P2904.6.2(6)
ALLOWABLE PIPE LENGTH FOR 3/4-INCH CPVC PIPE

SPRINKLER FLOW RATE[a] (gpm)	WATER DISTRIBUTION SIZE (inch)	AVAILABLE PRESSURE - P_t (psi)									
		15	20	25	30	35	40	45	50	55	60
		Allowable length of pipe from service valve to farthest sprinkler (feet)									
8	3/4	348	465	581	697	813	929	1045	1161	1278	1394
9	3/4	280	374	467	560	654	747	841	934	1027	1121
10	3/4	231	307	384	461	538	615	692	769	845	922
11	3/4	193	258	322	387	451	515	580	644	709	773
12	3/4	165	219	274	329	384	439	494	549	603	658
13	3/4	142	189	237	284	331	378	426	473	520	568
14	3/4	124	165	206	247	289	330	371	412	454	495
15	3/4	109	145	182	218	254	290	327	363	399	436
16	3/4	97	129	161	193	226	258	290	322	354	387
17	3/4	86	115	144	173	202	230	259	288	317	346
18	3/4	78	104	130	155	181	207	233	259	285	311
19	3/4	70	94	117	141	164	188	211	234	258	281
20	3/4	64	85	107	128	149	171	192	213	235	256
21	3/4	58	78	97	117	136	156	175	195	214	234
22	3/4	54	71	89	107	125	143	161	179	197	214
23	3/4	49	66	82	99	115	132	148	165	181	198
24	3/4	46	61	76	91	107	122	137	152	167	183
25	3/4	42	56	71	85	99	113	127	141	155	169
26	3/4	39	52	66	79	92	105	118	131	144	157
27	3/4	37	49	61	73	86	98	110	122	135	147
28	3/4	34	46	57	69	80	92	103	114	126	137
29	3/4	32	43	54	64	75	86	96	107	118	129
30	3/4	30	40	50	60	70	81	91	101	111	121
31	3/4	28	38	47	57	66	76	85	95	104	114
32	3/4	27	36	45	54	63	71	80	89	98	107
33	3/4	25	34	42	51	59	68	76	84	93	101
34	3/4	24	32	40	48	56	64	72	80	88	96
35	3/4	23	30	38	45	53	61	68	76	83	91
36	3/4	22	29	36	43	50	57	65	72	79	86
37	3/4	20	27	34	41	48	55	61	68	75	82
38	3/4	20	26	33	39	46	52	59	65	72	78
39	3/4	19	25	31	37	43	50	56	62	68	74
40	3/4	18	24	30	35	41	47	53	59	65	71

For SI: 1 inch = 25.4 mm, 1 foot = 304.8 mm, 1 pound per square inch = 6.895 kPa, 1 gallon per minute = 0.963 L/s.
a. Flow rate from Section P2904.4.2.

TABLE P2904.6.2(7)
ALLOWABLE PIPE LENGTH FOR 1-INCH CPVC PIPE

SPRINKLER FLOW RATE[a] (gpm)	WATER DISTRIBUTION SIZE (inch)	AVAILABLE PRESSURE - P_t (psi)									
		15	20	25	30	35	40	45	50	55	60
		Allowable length of pipe from service valve to farthest sprinkler (feet)									
8	1	1049	1398	1748	2098	2447	2797	3146	3496	3845	4195
9	1	843	1125	1406	1687	1968	2249	2530	2811	3093	3374
10	1	694	925	1157	1388	1619	1851	2082	2314	2545	2776
11	1	582	776	970	1164	1358	1552	1746	1940	2133	2327
12	1	495	660	826	991	1156	1321	1486	1651	1816	1981
13	1	427	570	712	854	997	1139	1281	1424	1566	1709
14	1	372	497	621	745	869	993	1117	1241	1366	1490
15	1	328	437	546	656	765	874	983	1093	1202	1311
16	1	291	388	485	582	679	776	873	970	1067	1164
17	1	260	347	433	520	607	693	780	867	954	1040
18	1	234	312	390	468	546	624	702	780	858	936
19	1	212	282	353	423	494	565	635	706	776	847
20	1	193	257	321	385	449	513	578	642	706	770
21	1	176	235	293	352	410	469	528	586	645	704
22	1	161	215	269	323	377	430	484	538	592	646
23	1	149	198	248	297	347	396	446	496	545	595
24	1	137	183	229	275	321	366	412	458	504	550
25	1	127	170	212	255	297	340	382	425	467	510
26	1	118	158	197	237	276	316	355	395	434	474
27	1	111	147	184	221	258	295	332	368	405	442
28	1	103	138	172	207	241	275	310	344	379	413
29	1	97	129	161	194	226	258	290	323	355	387
30	1	91	121	152	182	212	242	273	303	333	364
31	1	86	114	143	171	200	228	257	285	314	342
32	1	81	108	134	161	188	215	242	269	296	323
33	1	76	102	127	152	178	203	229	254	280	305
34	1	72	96	120	144	168	192	216	240	265	289
35	1	68	91	114	137	160	182	205	228	251	273
36	1	65	87	108	130	151	173	195	216	238	260
37	1	62	82	103	123	144	165	185	206	226	247
38	1	59	78	98	117	137	157	176	196	215	235
39	1	56	75	93	112	131	149	168	187	205	224
40	1	53	71	89	107	125	142	160	178	196	214

For SI: 1 inch = 25.4 mm, 1 foot = 304.8 mm, 1 pound per square inch = 6.895 kPa, 1 gallon per minute = 0.963 L/s.

a. Flow rate from Section P2904.4.2.

TABLE P2904.6.2(8)
ALLOWABLE PIPE LENGTH FOR $^3/_4$-INCH PEX TUBING

SPRINKLER FLOW RATE[a] (gpm)	WATER DISTRIBUTION SIZE (inch)	AVAILABLE PRESSURE - P_t (psi)									
		15	20	25	30	35	40	45	50	55	60
		Allowable length of pipe from service valve to farthest sprinkler (feet)									
8	$^3/_4$	93	123	154	185	216	247	278	309	339	370
9	$^3/_4$	74	99	124	149	174	199	223	248	273	298
10	$^3/_4$	61	82	102	123	143	163	184	204	225	245
11	$^3/_4$	51	68	86	103	120	137	154	171	188	205
12	$^3/_4$	44	58	73	87	102	117	131	146	160	175
13	$^3/_4$	38	50	63	75	88	101	113	126	138	151
14	$^3/_4$	33	44	55	66	77	88	99	110	121	132
15	$^3/_4$	29	39	48	58	68	77	87	96	106	116
16	$^3/_4$	26	34	43	51	60	68	77	86	94	103
17	$^3/_4$	23	31	38	46	54	61	69	77	84	92
18	$^3/_4$	21	28	34	41	48	55	62	69	76	83
19	$^3/_4$	19	25	31	37	44	50	56	62	69	75
20	$^3/_4$	17	23	28	34	40	45	51	57	62	68
21	$^3/_4$	16	21	26	31	36	41	47	52	57	62
22	$^3/_4$	NP	19	24	28	33	38	43	47	52	57
23	$^3/_4$	NP	17	22	26	31	35	39	44	48	52
24	$^3/_4$	NP	16	20	24	28	32	36	40	44	49
25	$^3/_4$	NP	NP	19	22	26	30	34	37	41	45
26	$^3/_4$	NP	NP	17	21	24	28	31	35	38	42
27	$^3/_4$	NP	NP	16	20	23	26	29	33	36	39
28	$^3/_4$	NP	NP	15	18	21	24	27	30	33	36
29	$^3/_4$	NP	NP	NP	17	20	23	26	28	31	34
30	$^3/_4$	NP	NP	NP	16	19	21	24	27	29	32
31	$^3/_4$	NP	NP	NP	15	18	20	23	25	28	30
32	$^3/_4$	NP	NP	NP	NP	17	19	21	24	26	28
33	$^3/_4$	NP	NP	NP	NP	16	18	20	22	25	27
34	$^3/_4$	NP	NP	NP	NP	NP	17	19	21	23	25
35	$^3/_4$	NP	NP	NP	NP	NP	16	18	20	22	24
36	$^3/_4$	NP	NP	NP	NP	NP	15	17	19	21	23
37	$^3/_4$	NP	NP	NP	NP	NP	NP	16	18	20	22
38	$^3/_4$	NP	NP	NP	NP	NP	NP	16	17	19	21
39	$^3/_4$	NP	NP	NP	NP	NP	NP	NP	16	18	20
40	$^3/_4$	NP	NP	NP	NP	NP	NP	NP	16	17	19

For SI: 1 inch = 25.4 mm, 1 foot = 304.8 mm, 1 pound per square inch = 6.895 kPa, 1 gallon per minute = 0.963 L/s.
NP - Not permitted.
a. Flow rate from Section P2904.4.2.

TABLE P2904.6.2(9)
ALLOWABLE PIPE LENGTH FOR 1-INCH PEX TUBING

SPRINKLER FLOW RATE[a] (gpm)	WATER DISTRIBUTION SIZE (inch)	AVAILABLE PRESSURE - P_t (psi)									
		15	20	25	30	35	40	45	50	55	60
		Allowable length of pipe from service valve to farthest sprinkler (feet)									
8	1	314	418	523	628	732	837	941	1046	1151	1255
9	1	252	336	421	505	589	673	757	841	925	1009
10	1	208	277	346	415	485	554	623	692	761	831
11	1	174	232	290	348	406	464	522	580	638	696
12	1	148	198	247	296	346	395	445	494	543	593
13	1	128	170	213	256	298	341	383	426	469	511
14	1	111	149	186	223	260	297	334	371	409	446
15	1	98	131	163	196	229	262	294	327	360	392
16	1	87	116	145	174	203	232	261	290	319	348
17	1	78	104	130	156	182	208	233	259	285	311
18	1	70	93	117	140	163	187	210	233	257	280
19	1	63	84	106	127	148	169	190	211	232	253
20	1	58	77	96	115	134	154	173	192	211	230
21	1	53	70	88	105	123	140	158	175	193	211
22	1	48	64	80	97	113	129	145	161	177	193
23	1	44	59	74	89	104	119	133	148	163	178
24	1	41	55	69	82	96	110	123	137	151	164
25	1	38	51	64	76	89	102	114	127	140	152
26	1	35	47	59	71	83	95	106	118	130	142
27	1	33	44	55	66	77	88	99	110	121	132
28	1	31	41	52	62	72	82	93	103	113	124
29	1	29	39	48	58	68	77	87	97	106	116
30	1	27	36	45	54	63	73	82	91	100	109
31	1	26	34	43	51	60	68	77	85	94	102
32	1	24	32	40	48	56	64	72	80	89	97
33	1	23	30	38	46	53	61	68	76	84	91
34	1	22	29	36	43	50	58	65	72	79	86
35	1	20	27	34	41	48	55	61	68	75	82
36	1	19	26	32	39	45	52	58	65	71	78
37	1	18	25	31	37	43	49	55	62	68	74
38	1	18	23	29	35	41	47	53	59	64	70
39	1	17	22	28	33	39	45	50	56	61	67
40	1	16	21	27	32	37	43	48	53	59	64

For SI: 1 inch = 25.4 mm, 1 foot = 304.8 mm, 1 pound per square inch = 6.895 kPa, 1 gallon per minute = 0.963 L/s.
a. Flow rate from Section P2904.4.2.

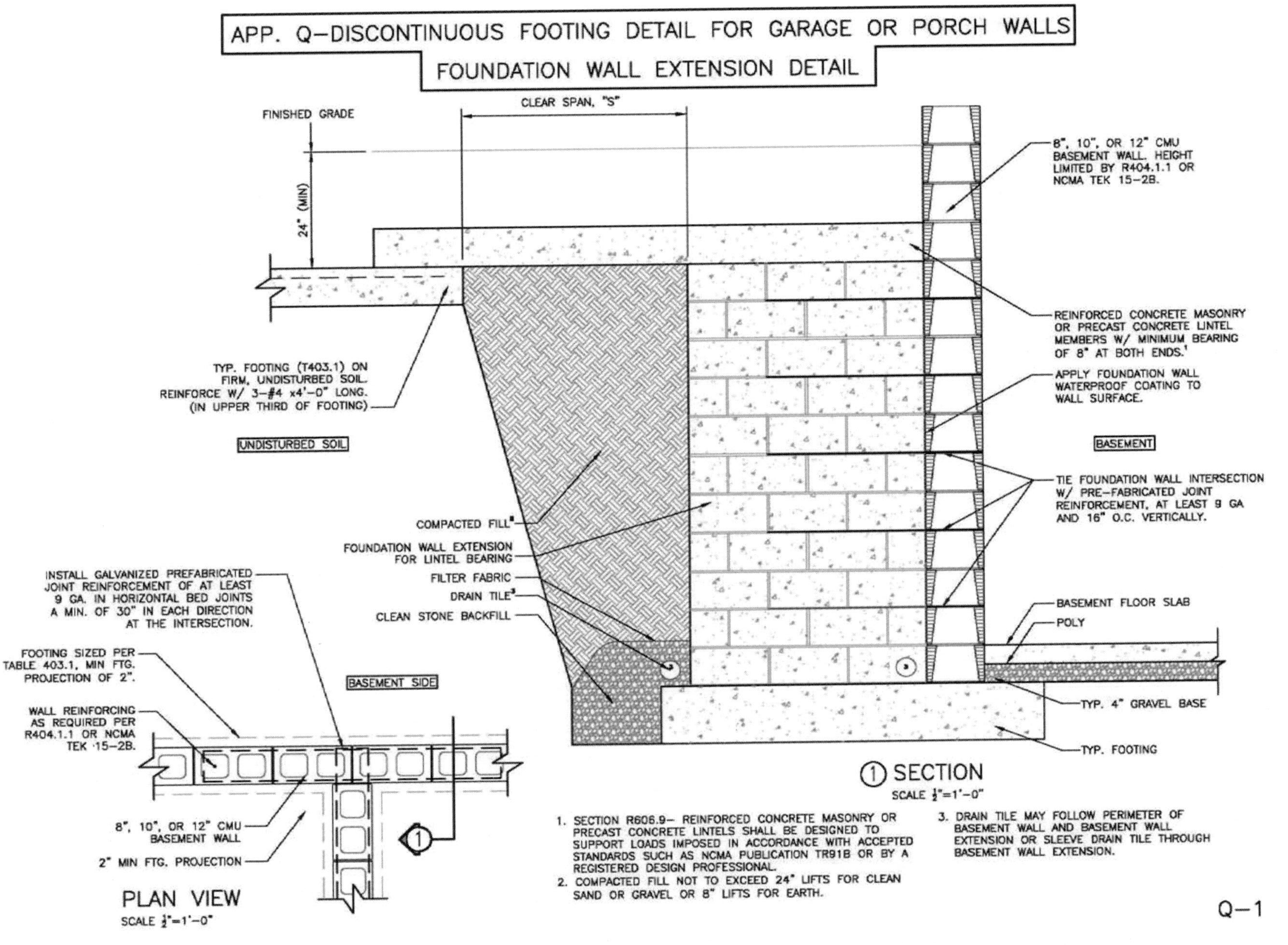

APP. Q–DISCONTINUOUS FOOTING DETAIL FOR GARAGE OR PORCH WALLS
FOUNDATION WALL EXTENSION DETAIL
CLEAR SPAN, "S"
FINISHED GRADE
24" (MIN)
8", 10", OR 12" CMU BASEMENT WALL. HEIGHT LIMITED BY R404.1.1 OR NCMA TEK 15–2B.
REINFORCED CONCRETE MASONRY OR PRECAST CONCRETE LINTEL MEMBERS W/ MINIMUM BEARING OF 8" AT BOTH ENDS.1
APPLY FOUNDATION WALL WATERPROOF COATING TO WALL SURFACE.
BASEMENT
TIE FOUNDATION WALL INTERSECTION W/ PRE-FABRICATED JOINT REINFORCEMENT, AT LEAST 9 GA AND 16" O.C. VERTICALLY.
TYP. FOOTING (T403.1) ON FIRM, UNDISTURBED SOIL. REINFORCE W/ 3–#4 x4'–0" LONG. (IN UPPER THIRD OF FOOTING)
UNDISTURBED SOIL
COMPACTED FILL2
FOUNDATION WALL EXTENSION FOR LINTEL BEARING
FILTER FABRIC
DRAIN TILE3
CLEAN STONE BACKFILL
BASEMENT FLOOR SLAB
POLY
TYP. 4" GRAVEL BASE
TYP. FOOTING
INSTALL GALVANIZED PREFABRICATED JOINT REINFORCEMENT OF AT LEAST 9 GA. IN HORIZONTAL BED JOINTS A MIN. OF 30" IN EACH DIRECTION AT THE INTERSECTION.
FOOTING SIZED PER TABLE 403.1, MIN FTG. PROJECTION OF 2".
WALL REINFORCING AS REQUIRED PER R404.1.1 OR NCMA TEK 15–2B.
BASEMENT SIDE
8", 10", OR 12" CMU BASEMENT WALL
2" MIN FTG. PROJECTION
PLAN VIEW
SCALE 1/2"=1'–0"
1 SECTION
SCALE 1/2"=1'–0"
1. SECTION R606.9– REINFORCED CONCRETE MASONRY OR PRECAST CONCRETE LINTELS SHALL BE DESIGNED TO SUPPORT LOADS IMPOSED IN ACCORDANCE WITH ACCEPTED STANDARDS SUCH AS NCMA PUBLICATION TR91B OR BY A REGISTERED DESIGN PROFESSIONAL.
2. COMPACTED FILL NOT TO EXCEED 24" LIFTS FOR CLEAN SAND OR GRAVEL OR 8" LIFTS FOR EARTH.
3. DRAIN TILE MAY FOLLOW PERIMETER OF BASEMENT WALL AND BASEMENT WALL EXTENSION OR SLEEVE DRAIN TILE THROUGH BASEMENT WALL EXTENSION.
Q–1

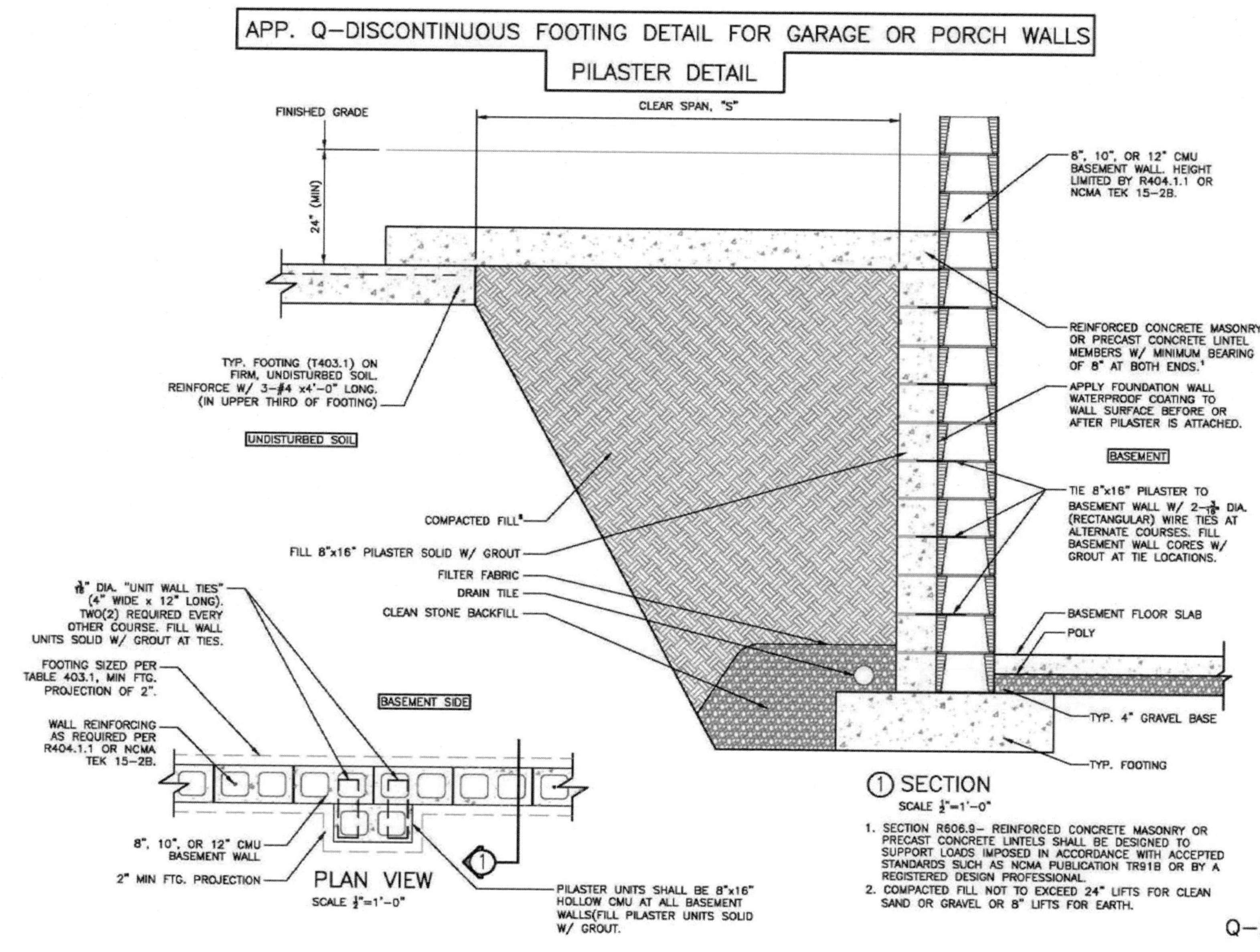
APP. Q–DISCONTINUOUS FOOTING DETAIL FOR GARAGE OR PORCH WALLS
PILASTER DETAIL
FINISHED GRADE
CLEAR SPAN, "S"
24" (MIN)
8", 10", OR 12" CMU BASEMENT WALL. HEIGHT LIMITED BY R404.1.1 OR NCMA TEK 15–2B.
REINFORCED CONCRETE MASONRY OR PRECAST CONCRETE LINTEL MEMBERS W/ MINIMUM BEARING OF 8" AT BOTH ENDS.1
APPLY FOUNDATION WALL WATERPROOF COATING TO WALL SURFACE BEFORE OR AFTER PILASTER IS ATTACHED.
BASEMENT
TIE 8"x16" PILASTER TO BASEMENT WALL W/ 2–3/16" DIA. (RECTANGULAR) WIRE TIES AT ALTERNATE COURSES. FILL BASEMENT WALL CORES W/ GROUT AT TIE LOCATIONS.
BASEMENT FLOOR SLAB
POLY
TYP. 4" GRAVEL BASE
TYP. FOOTING
TYP. FOOTING (T403.1) ON FIRM, UNDISTURBED SOIL. REINFORCE W/ 3–#4 x4'–0" LONG. (IN UPPER THIRD OF FOOTING)
UNDISTURBED SOIL
COMPACTED FILL2
FILL 8"x16" PILASTER SOLID W/ GROUT
FILTER FABRIC
DRAIN TILE
CLEAN STONE BACKFILL
3/16" DIA. "UNIT WALL TIES" (4" WIDE x 12" LONG). TWO(2) REQUIRED EVERY OTHER COURSE. FILL WALL UNITS SOLID W/ GROUT AT TIES.
FOOTING SIZED PER TABLE 403.1, MIN FTG. PROJECTION OF 2".
WALL REINFORCING AS REQUIRED PER R404.1.1 OR NCMA TEK 15–2B.
BASEMENT SIDE
8", 10", OR 12" CMU BASEMENT WALL
2" MIN FTG. PROJECTION
PLAN VIEW
SCALE 1/2"=1'–0"
PILASTER UNITS SHALL BE 8"x16" HOLLOW CMU AT ALL BASEMENT WALLS(FILL PILASTER UNITS SOLID W/ GROUT.
1 SECTION
SCALE 1/2"=1'–0"
1. SECTION R606.9– REINFORCED CONCRETE MASONRY OR PRECAST CONCRETE LINTELS SHALL BE DESIGNED TO SUPPORT LOADS IMPOSED IN ACCORDANCE WITH ACCEPTED STANDARDS SUCH AS NCMA PUBLICATION TR91B OR BY A REGISTERED DESIGN PROFESSIONAL.
2. COMPACTED FILL NOT TO EXCEED 24" LIFTS FOR CLEAN SAND OR GRAVEL OR 8" LIFTS FOR EARTH.
Q–2

INDEX

C

D

E

F

G

H

I

J

K

L

M

R

S

T

U

V